WOJCIECH LIPOŃSKI

WORLD SPORTS ENCYCLOPEDIA

With special contributions by:
Marc Farmer, Jean-Yves Guillain, Kevin Hagarty,
Guy Jouen, Kevin Meynell, Krzysztof Sawala,
Carlos López von Vriessen, Piotr Zięba

St. Paul  MBI    Poznań

World Sports Encyclopedia
Copyright © 2003 by Oficyna Wydawnicza Atena

This edition first published in 2003 by MBI, an imprint of MBI Publishing Company
Galtier Plaza, Suite 200, 380 Jackson Street, St. Paul, MN 55101-3885 USA

The information in this book is true and complete to the best of our knowledge. All recommendations are made without any guarantee
on the part of the author or publisher, who also disclaim any liability incurred in connection with the use of this data or specific details.

We recognize that some words, model names and designations, for example, mentioned herein are the property of the trademark holder.
We use them for identification purposes only. This is not an official publication.

This publication has been made possible thanks to a generous grant from UNESCO's Department of Education.
Oficyna Wydawnicza Atena wishes to express its deep gratitude to Mr. Hamid Oussedik and Mr. Marcelin Dally for their help in coordinating the project.

Some materials used in this publication have been collected as part of research project 6P05D 0621, conducted under the auspices
of the Polish Committee of Scientific Research (Komitet Badań Naukowych) and aimed at revitalizing Polish traditional sports.

Editor
Kevin Hagarty

Editorial staff
Graham Crawford, Colin Phillips, Ben Paflin, Patrick Tracy

Portions of this book have been translated from *Encyklopedia sportów świata*, published by Oficyna Wydawnicza Atena in the Polish language in 2001.

Translators
Dorota Brach, Graham Crawford, Agnieszka Ekert, Marcin Feder, Magdalena Jarmołowicz, Wojciech Krawczyk, Radosław Krynicki,
Zbigniew Nadstoga, Joanna Sałaciak, Krzysztof Sawala, Tomasz Skirecki, Maciej Tumasz, Jarosław Weckwerth

Internet research
Tomasz Kopyciński, Krzysztof Sawala

Graphic design
Krzysztof Sawala

Layout and typesetting
Atena Typesetting

Cover design
Dariusz Krupa

Illustrations
Błażej Tomczak, Przemysław Tomczak, Urszula Kurzawa

Photographs
Associated Press, Corel Professional Photos, EPA, Gazeta Wyborcza, Getty Images, International Tchoukball Federation (www.tchoukball.org),
JUMP Photo, Kriselu Editorial, Olympic Museum Losanne, Polish Press Agency PAP, Pospress, Singapore Sports Council, Tiger Mountain,
Third Light Photography, www.bouletfermat.com/backgrounds
(for names of individual photographers see p. 600)

ISBN 0-7603-1682-1

MBI titles are also available at discounts in bulk quantity for industrial or sales-promotional use.
For details write to Special Sales Manager at:
Motorbooks International Wholesalers & Distributors
Galtier Plaza, Suite 200, 380 Jackson Street, St. Paul, MN 55101-3885 USA.

For distribution outside the USA, Canada, and the UK contact
Oficyna Wydawnicza Atena
Wawrzyniaka 39, 60-502 Poznań, POLAND
phone/fax: (48) (61) 843-0800   e-mail: atena@mtl.pl
www.owatena.com.pl
www.sportencyclopedia.com

Printing and binding
Ozgraf, Olsztyn, Poland

In order to form a just estimation of the character of any particular people, it is absolutely necessary to investigate the sports and pastimes most generally prevalent among them. War, policy, and other contingent circumstances, may effactually place men, at different times, in different point of view; but, when we follow them into their retirements, where no disguise is necessary, we are most likely to see them in their true state, and may best judge of their national dispositions.

Joseph Strutt
Sports and Pastimes of the People of England
1810

The celebration of indigenous and traditional forms of sports and games, which derive from the roots of many different communities, is a growing feature of contemporary culture. In 1999, ministers and senior officials responsible for physical education and sport, meeting at Punta del Este, Uruguay, pledged their support to a policy of preserving and enhancing traditional and indigenous sports based on the cultural heritage of regions and nations the world over, including a list of the world's traditional games and sports. This matter has considerable significance in the modern world, which – in its search for spiritual strength turns with increasing frequency not only towards universal values but also towards regional values and the historic roots of particular communities. The fact that sports and physical education draw on rich local traditions by no means diminishes the role of major sports and games or universal systems of physical education. On the contrary, learning from ancient practices and the traditions of sometimes seemingly remote cultures enriches the means with which sports and physical education can influence communities and become more effective in reaching their individual members, as well as underscoring how much the peoples of the world actually have in common.

For a number of reasons, many traditional sports and games have been neglected, sometimes completely forgotten, in many countries. It is our duty to revive them. The *Encyclopedia of World Sports* is exactly such an effort. Based on wide-ranging research, this admirable publication compiles information on more than 3,000 sports and games from dozens of the world's cultures. We value it as an essential work of reference that will contribute greatly towards creating and developing the international community's awareness of the immense richness and diversity of indigenous sports. It is also a thorough response to the call put forth at the Punta del Este Conference for the preparation of a list of the world's traditional sports and games.

UNESCO has been closely involved in the progress of this project and is pleased to publish this work under its auspices. This involvement is in keeping with several articles of the International Charter of Physical Education and Sport, which speaks of sports programs that should respect 'the institutional, cultural, socio-economic and climatic conditions of each country' (Art. 3) and that 'the collection, provision and dissemination of information and documentation on physical education and sport constitute a major necessity' (Art. 8).

The encyclopedia does not as yet contain data on the native sports and games of every single country in the world, as many nations have either no publications or institutions to deal with their native sports and games, or are faced with economic or political difficulties that leave the issue to be resolved in the future. However, with the surging interest in traditional sports, it is a certainty that subsequent editions will be expanded to include even more information, including areas of indigenous sports and games that may be missing from this first edition. Knowledge begets knowledge; therefore it is our intention that this publication will stimulate new research and a continued exchange of information.

UNESCO wishes to congratulate the author and the publisher, who embarked upon a challenging path when seeking to bring this ambitious project to such successful fruition. We are proud to have offered our support for this publication, which we anticipate will enjoy a truly international circulation.

Koichiro Matsuura
Director-General
UNESCO

OLYMPIC MUSEUM
INTERNATIONAL OLYMPIC COMMITTEE

C'est toujours un grand plaisir pour le Musée Olympique de saluer la parution d'une nouvelle encyclopédie consacrée au monde des sports, laquelle a choisi de faire une place importante aux Jeux et au Mouvement olympique.

Un tel ouvrage montre toute la détermination de l'auteur, qui poursuit la son excellent travail de recherche sur les sports les plus divers. Wojciech Liponski n'est pas un inconnu pour les chercheurs du Musée et le Centre d'etudes Olympiques de Lausanne, puisque notre bibliotheque possede déja un certain nombres des ses écrits référencés.

Tous les sports qui nous sont présentés ici sont l'expression du génie national des peuples qui depuis toujours n'ont cessé d'inventer des formes de compétitions, pour se mesurer et faire valoir leurs habiletés propres, et des types de jeux par équipes pour mettre en valeur leurs capacités a s'entendre sur un terrain pour le plaisir de relever des défis.

On trouvera également dans ce livre tout ce qui fait la richesse du patrimoine sportif de chaque pays ainsi que les particularités des sports traditionnels. Grâce a cette somme tres bien documentée, le lecteur ne manquera pas de se passionner, a la découverte des richesses et des traditions sportives de toutes les nations.

Nous souhaitons bonne chance a la jeune maison d'édition polonaise qui a décidé de relever le défi de la publication d'un tel livre spécialisé qui, nous en sommes convaincus, rencontrera un large public en Pologne avant peut-etre, d'etre proposé aux lecteurs enthousiastes d'autres pays.

Françoise ZWEIFEL
Director

It is always a great pleasure for the Olympic Museum to welcome the publication of a new encyclopedia of sports promoting the Olympic games and movement.

This work indicates the author's determination to continue his excellent research in the area of world sports. At the Olympic Museum and Research Center in Losanne, Prof. Wojciech Lipoński is not a newcomer: our library already boasts a good number of his publications.

All sports presented in this book demonstrate the national genius of numerous communities, which – for thousands of years – have been inventing new forms of competition testing their abilities and new forms of team sports reflecting their ability to communicate on the playing area for the joy of accepting new challenges.

Here, the reader may find everything which forms the sports heritage of every country, as well as the characteristic features of traditional sports. This well documented volume offers a rich presentation of the sporting traditions of world nations.

We wish great success to the young Polish publishing house that decided to tackle the tremendous challenge of publishing such a special book, which we are convinced will be universally accepted both by Polish readers and readers around the globe.

Françoise ZWEIFEL
Director

MINISTRY
OF NATIONAL EDUCATION AND SPORT
OF THE REPUBLIC OF POLAND

In recent years we have witnessed a rapidly growing trend to revive indigenous and traditional sports. Often ignored on the level of professional competition, they are, however, strongly supported by various nations which – recognizing sport as an unquestionably special manifestation of human cultural activity – value them as a means of presenting their cultural heritage.

Compiling in one volume over 3,000 sports and sporting games from all over the world goes a long way toward realizing the richness of human culture in an area that goes well beyond the limited scope of the several dozen sports that dominate the media. It now appears that there are many smaller nations and communities, among which the number of locally practiced sporting games amaze us.

The sporting heritage of these communities and indigenous peoples has until now gone unrecognized in international sports encyclopedias.

The *Encyclopedia of World Sports*, an exhaustive work of research by a Polish scholar, published by a Polish publishing house under the auspices of UNESCO, and brimming with little-known sports of various nations, offers a fascinating survey of their unique cultural heritage as displayed through sports. As a result, it will not only be sport that will benefit from this effort, but also the diversified international culture. We are proud that this project, which originated in Poland, has been realized in cooperation with internationally recognized centers of sports research, sports museums, centers of sports ethnography, and renowned experts the world over.

Krystyna Łybacka
MINISTER
OF NATIONAL EDUCATION AND SPORT
OF THE REPUBLIC OF POLAND

POLISH POST

The relationship between postal stamps and sports originated with the Greek Post, which – as commissioned by the Greek Parliament and the King – issued on 25 March 1896 a series of 12 stamps depicting motifs of ancient mythology and the Acropolis. Half of the proceeds from selling these stamps was spent on reconstructing the Olympic stadium in Athens.

Soon, other functions of postal publications were acknowledged, mainly the great educational and promotional opportunity which they provided. Stamps placed on letters and cards reach millions of people around the world, presenting them with outstanding sports achievements and events, commemorating the names of sports champions, and spreading the idea of noble and fascinating competition.

I am convinced that many a young boy or girl have selected their favorite sports discipline by browsing through collections of sports stamps. I also strongly believe that the presentation of sports stamps in this encyclopedia greatly enriches its esthetic value.

In the traditional relationship between sports and the world's postal services, now over a century old, numerous countries have issued hundreds of thousands of stamps, cards, and postmarks featuring sports and Olympic motifs.

Designers of postal publications have spared no effort to present the beauty and unique nature of various forms of sport in miniature graphic form. Those which adorn the following pages are a precious complement to the individual entries.

The Polish Post, like the postal services of many other countries, has always been a strong supporter of sports and has frequently demonstrated its intention to promote all forms of sporting activities. Since 1933 it has issued several hundred stamps with sports motifs. The first series depicted the Polish aviators Żwirko and Wigura, the winners of the 1932 Berlin Aviation Challenge. The Polish Post was also the first in the world to commemorate an Olympic gold medallist: the stamp celebrating the long jump victory of Elżbieta Duńska-Krzesińska in Melbourne in 1956 appeared within days of her achievement. Recent issues present the beauty of ski jumping and depict the success enjoyed by Adam Małysz at the Salt Lake City Winter Olympics. A special series of stamps prepared for the 28th Olympic Games in Athens in 2004 bridges old and modern times by combining the ancient motifs with contemporary elements. The designer places color figures of various athletes against the background of the Acropolis, the statue of Nike of Samothrace, and ancient reliefs depicting competition between Greek Olympians. Although the series itself will not be issued before 2004, we have decided to present it in this splendid publication.

Proud of its on-going relationship with sports, the Polish Post heartily endorses the publication of the *Encyclopedia of World Sports*, which it considers an invaluable resource and a splendid instrument for the promotion of the sports of various nations. The stamps for this publication were selected by leading Polish philatelists, to whom we are grateful for their wonderful contribution.

Leszek Kwiatek

Leszek Kwiatek
DIRECTOR GENERAL
POLISH POST

ABBREVIATIONS OF FREQUENTLY QUOTED WORKS

ARL – John Arlott, *The Oxford Companion to Sports & Games*, Oxford University Press, London–New York–Toronto, 1975.

CDOS – Parke Cummings, ed., *The Dictionary of Sports*, A., Barnes & Co., New York, 1949.

CHB – *C'hoariou Breizh. Guide annuaire des princinpaux jeux traditionnels de Bretagne*, Skol-Uhel ar Vro – Institut Culturel de Bretagne.

CHUR – Winston S. Churchill, *My Early Life, A Roving Commission*, The Reprint Society, London, by arrangement with Macmillan and Co., London, 1944.

CONS – Tim Considine, *The Language of Sport*, Facts on File, Inc., New York, 1982.

DRV – Rafael Aguirre Franco, *Deporte rural vasco*, segunda edicion, Editorial Txertoa, 1983.

EAI – *The Encyclopedia Americana.* International Edition, Americana Corporation, Danbury, Connecticut, 1979.

EDS – *Enciclopedia dello Sport*, Edizioni Sportive Italiane, Roma-Firenze, 1964.

EJ – *Enciklopedija Jugoslavije*, Izdanj i naklada Leksikografskog Zavoda, Zagreb, MCMLV.

EOS – *Encyclopedia of Sport*, vol. 1-2, London, 1908.

EP – *Etnografia Polska*, a scientific periodical published by the Institute of History of Material Culture, Polish Academy of Sciences.

EWS – *Encyclopedia of World Sport*, David Levinson & Karen Christensen, eds, ABC-Clio, Santa Barbara, California–Denver, Colorado–Oxford–England, 1996.

FISME – *Fizkultura i sport. Małaja encyklopedija*, Raduga, Moskwa, 1982.

GADOMP – Alan Armstrong, *Games and Dances of the Maori People*, Viking Sevenseas, Paraparaumu, 1992.

GHJD – Rafael Aguirre, *Gure Herria. Juegos y Deportes del Pais Vasco*, Kriselu Editorial, San Sebastian, vol. 1-3, 1989.

GID – Jørn Møller, *Gamle idrætslege i Danmark*, vol. 1-4, Idratshistorisk Varksted, Slagelse, 1997.

GIZ – I.N. Chkhannikov, *500 gier i zabaw*, 2nd ed., Sport i Turystyka, Warsaw, 1953.

GOMS – Iwona Kabzinska-Stawarz, *Games of Mongolian Shepherds*, the Institute of History of Material Culture, Polish Academy of Sciences, Warsaw , 1991.

HEDSGDC – *The History, the Evolution and Diffusion of Sports and Games in Different Cultures*, ed. P.P. De Nayer & R. Renson, HISPA – Katholieke Universiteit, Leuven, 1975.

HGVB – Erik De Vroede, *Het Grote Volkssporten Boek*, Leuven, 1996.

IJHS – *The International Journal of the History of Sport*, London.

IOA – *The International Olympic Academy*, Yearly Reports of the International Olympic Academy.

JDTE – Rafael Garcia Serrano, *Juegos y deportes tradicionales en Espana*, Madrid, 1974.

JTP – Maria da Graça Sousa Guedes, *Jogos Tradicionais Portugueses*, Instituto Nacional dos Desportos, Lisboa, 1979.

JYDLCH – Oreste Plath, *Juegos y Diversiones de los Chilenos*, Instituto de Educación Fisica de la Universidad de Chile, Santiago de Chile, 1946.

JYDV – Rafael Aguirre Franco, *Juegos y deportes vascos. Cuerpa Anexo Enciclopedia Sistematica*, segunda edicion, Aunamendi San Sebastian, 1978.

JYTE – Cristóbal Moreno Palos, *Juegos y deportes tradicionales en Espana*, Alianza Editorial Consejo Superior de Deportes, Madrid, 1992.

LJP – *Les jeux populaires. Eclipse et renaisssance. Des traditions aux régions de l'Europe de demain*, Jean Jacques Barreau i Guy Jaouen, eds., Confederation FALSAB, Morlaix, 1998.

MEN– Frank G. Menke, *The Encycylopedia of Sports*, 4th rev. ed. by Roger Treat, A. S. Barnes and Company – South Brunswick & New York; Thomas Yoseloff Ltd, London, 1969.

OCAS – *The Oxford Companion to Australian Sport*, 2nd ed., Wray Vamplew, Katharine Moore, John O'Hara, Richard Cashman, Ian Jobling, eds., Oxford University Press, Melbourne–Oxford–Auckland–New York, 1994.

OES – John Lowell Pratt & Jim Benagh, *The Official Encyclopedia of Sports*, Franklin Watts, New York, 1964.

OGIAG – *The Olympic Games in Ancient Greece*, ed. N. Yalouris, Edothike Athenon, 1982.

OM – *Olympic Message*, The International Olympic Committee, Lausanne.

OR – *Olympic Review*, The International Olympic Committe, Lausanne.

OXEN – Joseph B. Oxendine, *American Indian Sports Heritage*, Human Kinetics Books, Champaign, Illinois, 1988.

PISHPES – Proceedings of the International Society of History of Physical Education and Sport.

PS – *Przegląd Sportowy*, a Polish sport daily.

RAD– Benjamin G. Rader, *American Sports: From the Age of Folk Games to the Age of Spectators*, Prentice-Hall, Englewood Cliffs, New Jersey, 1983.

RIG – *Rig*. Tidskrift utgiven av föreningen för Svensk Kulturhistoria i Samardete med Nordiska Museet och Foklivsarkivet i Lund.

STRUTT – Joseph Strutt, *Glig Gamena Angel Deoth, or the Sports and Pastimes of the People of England*, White and Co, Longman etc., London, 1810.

SESS – *1o Seminario Europeo di storia dello Sport. La Comuna Eredita dello Sport in Europa*, Scuola dello Sport – CONI, Rome, 1996.

SIN – *Sports International*. The Journal and Newsletter of the Centre for International Sports Exchange, London.

SP – *Sport*. A Monthly Publication of Sports Media Corporation, New York.

SSC – *Sports*. A Publication of the Singapore Sports Council.

SSSS – *Sport as Symbol, Symbols in Sport*. Proceedings of the 3rd ISHPES Congress, ed. Floris van der Merwe, Proceedings of the 3rd ISHPES Congress, Cape Town, 1995 (1996).

ST – *Stadion*. Internationale Zeitschrift für Geschichte des Sports.

TAPL – William Taplin, *The Sporting Dictionary and Rural Repository of General Information upon Every Subject Appertaining to the Sports of the Field, Inscribed to the Right Honourable, The Earl of Sandwich, Master of His Majesty's Stag Hounds*, by ..., in two volumes, for Vernor and Hood, Longman and Rees, J. Scatherd, J. Walker and J. Harris, London, 1803.

TFKU – C.W. Krilienko et al., *Tradicij Fizicznoj Kulturi w Ukrajini*, Institut Zmistu i Metodiw Nawraczannia, Kiyev, 1977.

TGDWAN – Alyce Taylor Cheska, ed., *Traditional Games and Dances in West African Nations*, International Council of Sport, Science and Physical Education, Verlag Karl Hofmann, Schorndorf, 1987.

TGESI – Alice Bertha Gomme, *The Traditional Games of England, Scotland and Ireland, With Tunes, Singing-rhymes, and Methods of Playing According to the Variants Extant and Recorded in Different Parts of the Kingdom, Collected and Annotated by ...*, vol. 1-2, vol. I, 1894; vol. II, 1898.

TRAMCHIN – Mu Fushan, Wu Yazhu, Li Xingxiang, Weu Baoliang, *Traditional Sports and Games of National Minorities in China*, transl. into English Song Xianchun, Tourism education Press, Beijing, 1988.

TSKAG – H. Murat Şahín, *Türk Spor Kültüründe Aba Güreşi*, Gazientep Üniversitesi, Ankara, 1999.

TSNJ – *Tradicionális Sportok Népi Játékok – Traditional Sport, Folk Games*, Szerkesztette – ed. Siklódi Csilla, a Sportmúzeum Kincsei Sorozat, Budapest, 1996.

YOSICH – *5,000 Years of Sport in China. Art and Tradition*, Musée Olympique Lausanne – Musée National du Sport, Beijing – Musée National des Arts Asiatiques Guimet, Lausanne, 1999.

ABBREVIATIONS

NATIONALITIES & REGIONS

Afg. = Afghan, Afghani
Afr. = African
Alb. = Albanian
Amer. = America, American
Amerind. = Amerindian
Ang.-Sax. = Anglo-Saxon
Aus. = Austrian
Austrl. = Australian
Azt. = Aztec
Basq. = Basque
Beij. = Beijing
Bret. = Breton
Brit. = British
Bulg. = Bulgarian
C.Amer. = Central American
Can. = Canadian
Ceyl. = Ceylon
Chin. = Chinese
Dan. = Danish
Du. = Dutch
Eg. = Egyptian
Eng. = England, English
Esk. = Eskimo
Est. = Estonian
Eur. = European
Fil. = Filipino

Fin. = Finnish
Flem. = Flemish
Fr. = French
Georg. = Georgian
Ger. = German
Gk. = Greek
Hisp. = Hispanic
Icel. = Icelandic
Ind. = Indian
Indo-Eur. = Indo-European
Indon. = Indonesian
Ir. = Irish
Ital. = Italian
Jap. = Japanese
Kaz. = Kazakh
Kir. = Kirghiz
Kor. = Korean
Lat. = Latin
Lith. = Lithuanian
Lond. = London
Manch. = Manchurian
Mold. = Moldavian
Mong. = Mongolian
N.Amer. = North American
N.Zeal. = New Zealand
Nig. = Nigerian

Norw. = Norwegian
O.Fr. = Old French
O.Gk. = Old Greek
O.Icel. = Old Icelandic
Pak. = Pakistani
Pol. = Polish
Port. = Portuguese
Poz. = Poznanian
Rom. = Romany
Rum. = Rumanian
Rus. = Russian
S.Amer. = South American
Scand. = Scandinavian
Scot. = Scottish
Serb. = Serbian
Sloven. = Slovenian
Span. = Spanish
Swed. = Swedish
Taj. = Tajik
Turk. = Turkish
Uzb. = Uzbek, Uzbeki
Vik. = Viking
War. = Warsawian
Wel. = Welsh
Yug. = Yugoslav

OTHER SHORTCUTS

abbr. = abbreviation
approx. = approximately
assn. = association
b. = born, born in
c. = about (*circa*)
cent. = century
cf. = compare (*confer*)
d. = died, died in
def. = defined, definition
dept. = department
dial. = dialect
DIY = do-it-yourself
e.g. = for example (*exempli gratia*)
ed. = edited, edition, editor(s)
esp. = especially
est. = estimated
estab. = established
et al. and others (*et alii*)
etc. = et cetera, and so forth
etym. = etymology, etymological
hist. = history, historical

hp = horsepower
i.e. = that is (*id est*)
ibid. = in the same place (*ibidem*)
illus. = illustration
incl. = included, including
Is. = Island
km/h = kilometers per hour
kW = kilowatts
lit. = literally
max. = maximum
min. = minimum (and also: minute)
mod. = modern
m/s = meters per second
mph = miles per hour
Mt. = Mount
num. = number
obs. = obsolete
par. = paragraph
plur. = plural
prob. = probably
pron. = pronunciation, pronounced

quot. = quoted, quotation
ref. = reference
sb. = somebody
sing. = singular
sp. = spelled, spelling
stand. = standard
sth. = something
trad. = traditional
trans. = translation, translated
U-21 = under 21 (years of age)
ult. = ultimately
usu. = usually
var. = variety, variant (of)
vol. = volume(s)
vs. = versus
wt. = weight
WWI = World War I
WWII = World War II

WEIGHTS & MEASURES

in. = inch(es)
ft. = foot, feet
yd. = yard
yds. = yards
mi. = mile(s)
sq ft. = square feet
cu. ft. = cubic feet
sq. mi. = square mile(s)
gr. = English gram(s)
oz. = ounce(s)
fl. oz. = fluid ounce(s)
lb. = pound
lbs. = pounds
mm = millimeter(s)

cm = centimeter(s)
m = meter(s)
km = kilometer(s)
sq. km = square km
m^2, m^3 = square meters, cubic meters
g = metric gram(s)
kg = kilogram(s)
sec. = second(s)
min. = minute(s)
hr. = hour
hrs. = hour(s)
yr. = year
yrs. = years

COMPETITIONS

Ol.G. = Olympic Games
E.Ch. = European Championships
Pol.Ch. = Polish Championships
W.Ch. = World Championships
W.Ol.G. = Winter Olympic Games

INTRODUCTION

<u>HOW MANY SPORTS ARE THERE IN THE WORLD?</u>

After years of research, we have to admit that we still do not know, that is, we do not know exactly. So far we have accumulated information regarding as many as 8,000 indigenous sports and sporting games, of which more than 3,000 have been included in the present publication. These come from various regions and cultures, sometimes very distant from one another, such as Great Britain, Nigeria, Mongolia, Korea, Japan, China, Arab countries, the Maori cultures, India, the Innuits, and numerous others. This is an on-going project and new entries are being added to our swelling database almost daily as a result of correspondence with ethnographic institutes, museums of sport, and individual scholars around the world.

Precisely defining what is and what is not a sport is no easy task. In this book we consider sport as a form of human activity (sometimes combined with the effort of animals or using vehicles or various devices), the outcome of which is determined by the physical, more than intellectual, effort. This distinction rules out competitiveness as the sole or even principal element defining sport and thus such activities as board games (e.g. chess) or card games (e.g. bridge or poker) are not included here, even though they have enjoyed the status of sport for a long time. After all, we have chess Olympiads and bridge world championships, the participants of which compete against one another in order to determine the winner. Although their physical, and especially psychophysical abilities allow them to keep in shape during play, they are not a direct competitive factor and do not immediately determine a win or loss. An immense number of such games, as well as their 'intellectual' (as opposed to 'physical') nature calls for further research and a separate publication. This also holds for games of chance.

This encyclopedia is quite a departure from all international encyclopedias thus far published, which focused mainly on well known, major or international sports, barely noticing or completely neglecting the incredible cultural richness and great multitude of indigenous, traditional, historical, regional, and folk sports and games of various nations and ethnic minorities, many of which are fascinating not only for their differences, but as often as not, their similarities, showing features common to all peoples the world over.

There are a number of handy specialized guides and dictionaries, which present the tradition of individual countries, regions or ethnic groups. None of them, however, are intercultural. Spanish, Danish, Estonian, Basque, or Arab publications present the richness of their own sports tradition and leave it at that. British sport dictionaries and encyclopedias offer information on numerous English, Scottish, or Welsh sports and pastimes, but leave out Celtic and Breton sports, which must be searched for elsewhere. There is no single publication discussing the many fascinating sports of the Slavic, Arab, African, and South American nations. No publication so far has brought together such sports as Indian *chungkee*, Japanese *hagoita*, Polish *czoromaj*, African *zuar*, Basque *aizkolaris*, Afgan *buzkashi*, Mayan *pokyah*, Danish *langbold fra anholt*, Maori *poi waka*, Chinese *cricket fights*, Mexican *pelota purhepecha encendida*, Greek Orthodox *cross diving*, English *Eton wall game*, Flemish *krulbol*, Turkish *yagli güreş*, Germanic *agnon toss*, Taiwanese *woodball*, Hindu *kabaddi*, Scottish *tossing the caber*, Portuguese *jogo do pau*, French *decapitation de l'oie*, Italian *gioco del ponte*, Irish *iomáint*, Pakistani *gulli dunda*, Korean *ssirŭm*, Swedish *pärk*, Breton *gouren* and Spanish *castells*, just to name a few. And what about the extinct sports of ancient Egypt, Greece, Rome, China or the pre-Columbian cultures of the Americas? Medieval and chivalric sports such as *quintain*, *running at the ring* and its Croatian equivalent *alka*? The multitude of animal sports like *bear baiting*, and the less cruel though equally dramatic *quagga*, *goat* and *pigeon races*? Most of us associate *high jump* with a horizontal bar, though in many cultures participants improvise a bar, while in the Scottish *hitch and kick* the object is to touch a suspended tambourine or bell with one's foot.

This encyclopedia is bursting with breath-taking stories which present the limitless richness of human cultures and sporting activities from pre-historic to modern times, including such relatively recent sporting extravaganzas as *B.A.S.E jumping*, *underwater football*, *sandboarding*, *kite skiing*, *zorbing* and *horseball*, among many others.

Including every last sport in the world has proved impossible, but those herein discussed disclose endless human ingenuity. Though there do exist certain sports that can be practiced solo, the vast majority of athletic games require shared participation. Humankind is indeed a social animal and sports are intrinsically human. We hold out the hope that with this book readers will begin to appreciate the vast number of sporting pastimes that are common for people around the world.

Wojciech Liposński
March 2003

CONTRIBUTORS

This publication would not have been possible without the splendid contribution from a great number of persons and institutions, all of whom deserve special attention and our deep gratitude. Below, listed alphabetically, are those who were so generous in answering our endless queries, provided fascinating information, materials, and photos, devoted their precious time to patiently explain complicated matters regarding the origin, etymology, and the finer points of rules of various sports, consulted individual entries or whole groups of entries, or gave their kind permission to use their publications, including those on numerous web pages.

Soliman   A L J A B H A N, former Secretary General of the Saudi Arabian Olympic Committee, provided many valuable materials, including a unique dictionary of Arab sports and games *Min Al 'Ābina Ash-Sha 'Biyya* (*Our Sports and Games*, 1983). The dictionary was translated from Arabic by Dr. Michael Abdalla, a lecturer of the Arabic language at the Institute of Linguistics, Adam Mickiewicz University, Poznań, Poland;

Michele A N D O L I N A of NET MEDIA, USA, provided photos of oyster shucking;

Arantxa   A R Z A M E N D I from the Central Municipal Library of San Sebastian, Spain (Udal Liburutegi Nagussia, Donostia) conducted library research of high scholarly value regarding Basque sports;

Peter B A R N E S, Secretary of the British Cycle Speedway Council, provided materials on the history and current status of *cycle speedway*;

Willy B A X T E R, President of the Celtic Wrestling Federation, provided numerous materials on different varieties of wrestling and verified all wrestling entries;

Maria Lluïsa B E R A S A T E G U I i D O L C E T, Head Librarian at the Department of Culture the Self-Government of Catalonia, Spain (Generalitat de Catalunya), sent us rare collections regarding Catalan sports;

Ricardo Navarrete B E T A N Z O, President of the Chilean Olympic Committee, provided the *Encyclopedia of Chilean Sports* and other materials;

Profesor Alida Zurita B O C A N E G R A, President of the Mexican Federation of Traditional and Indigeneous Sports and Games (Federacion Mexicana de Juegos Y Deportes Autoctonos Y Tradicionales), provided precious materials and unique photos of Mesoamerican sports and games;

Rudy B O N D U E of Koninklijke Wielerclub in Gent, Belgium, provided materials regarding *cycloball*;

Janos   B R E N D E L, a scholar in Hungarian culture and lecturer at Adam Mickiewicz University in Poznań, Poland, patiently explained difficult matters regarding the traditional sports of Hungary;

Chris B R O O M E, President of the Human-Powered Vehicle Association, provided information and photos for the entry on *unrestricted bicycles*;

John B U R N E T T, Curator of the Department of Ethnology of the Scottish National Museum, provided materials regarding traditional Scottish sports and games;

Daniel B U S C H B E C K, Marketing Director of the International Tchoukball Federation, provided valuable materials regarding *tchoukball*, including the official rulebook and photos of the game;

Julio C A L E G A R I, President of the International Tchoukball Federation, provided materials for *tchoukball*;

Professor Pierre   C H A R R E T O N of Jean Monet University in Saint-Étienne, France, successfully lobbied among various French institutions which provided materials regarding French sport-related literature;

Carsten C L A S O H M provided photos for the entry on *quintaine*;

Roberto C U B E D D U offered his kind permission to use information and photos of *gymkhana* from his web page www.horseclub.co.uk;

Světoslava D A N E Š O V A, Secretary at the Czech Republic Embassy in Warsaw, Poland, provided numerous materials regarding Czech sports;

Pierre D E R N I E R, provided materials on *underwater hockey*;

Professor Jan D Z I E D Z I C of the Poznań Academy of Physical Education provided materials regarding sports for the disabled, including his book *Kultura fizyczna osób niepełnosprawnych* (*Physical Culture of the Disabled*, 1996);

Henning E I C H B E R G of the Danish Academy of Physical Education and Sport (Gerlev Idraetshojskole) permitted us to use his co-authored book *Les jeux Populaires. Eclipse et renaissance*, edited by Jean Jaques Barreau and Guy Jaouen (1998) and provided numerous other materials;

Alexander   F E N T O N of the European Ethnological Research Centre in Edinburgh sent us a number of issues of *Review of Scottish Culture* with plenty of papers on Scottish traditional sports and games. Professor Fenton did not spare efforts to meet our every request regarding rare articles unavailable outside Scotland;

Dr. Nikos F I L A R E T O S, President of the International Olympic Academy at Ancient Olympia, offered great support during my frequent visits to the Academy and granted his kind permission to reproduce various materials;

Julián Gomez F U E R T E S, Director of the Sports Program of the Department of Basque Culture, Youth and Sport in Spain (Departamento de Cultura Euskera, Juventud y Deportes);

Doktor Iwona G R Y S, Director of the Museum of Sport and Tourism in Warsaw, Poland;

Jerzy G R Z E S I A K and Krzysztof   P I E C H offered materials regarding korfball;

Jean-Yves G U I L L A I N, sport historian from the University of Lyon, France, offered invaluable help in verifying entries regarding traditional French sports, as well as contributing a number of new entries;

Professor Ulf H A N N E R Z of the Department of Cultural Anthropology has contacted me with various specialists in the history of sport and ethnography of Scandinavian countries;

Mike H A S L A M, President of the International Dragon Boat Federation, provided materials regarding dragon boat races;

Professor Mats H E L L S P O N G of the Institute of Ethnology at Stockholm University offered a large number of his publications regarding dozens of traditional sports including his splendid *Den folkliga idrotten*;

Trevor H I L L verified some wrestling entries and provided a number of excellent wrestling photos;

Marco I M P I G L I A, an Italian sports historian, provided valuable materials regarding *volata*;

The I N T E R N A T I O N A L   K O R F B A L L   F E D E R A T I O N in Bunnik, the Netherlands, provided korfball photos;

Jón M. Í V A R S S O N, President of the Icelandic Glíma Association (Glímusamband Íslands), provided precious materials regarding the history and current status of various traditional and national sports of Iceland;

Guy J A O U E N, President of the Breton Confederation and President of the European Traditional Sports and Games Association, offered invaluable help in verifying Breton sports, provided information and photo materials on various traditional Breton games, and contributed a number of new entries;

Profesor Ian J O B L I N G, Director of the Department of Human Movement Studies at the University of Queensland, provided various materials on Australian sports, including the *Oxford Companion to Australian Sport* (2nd ed. 1994), which he authored and edited together with such specialists as Wray Vamplev, Katharine Moore, John O'Hara and Richard Cashman;

Iwona K A B Z I Ń S K A - S T A W A R Z, a scholar at the Institute of Archeology and Polish Ethnology of the Polish Academy of Science provided her research works regarding the traditional sports and games of Mongolia, including a book entitled *Games of Mongolian Shepherds*;

Pekka K Ä R K K Ä I N E N, a sports historian and scholar at the University of Jyväskylä, Finland, provided materials regarding Finnish traditional and national sports;

Antoni K A R W A C K I, former President of the Polish Federation of Field Hockey, verified the hockey entries;

Professor Hasan K A S A P of the University of Istambul provided materials regarding the history and cultural richness of various types of Turkish wrestling;

Milan K A Š K A, Marketing Director at the Velke Popovice Brewery in the Czech Republic, provided information and photos of *barrel rolling;*

John S. K E N N E D Y, Director of Operations at the United States Bicycle Polo Association, provided photos for *bicycle polo*;

Gerry K E R K H O F offered materials regarding *bull running*;

Professor Bruce K I D D, a former long distance runner, whom I met at the Olympic Games in Tokyo, now the Director of Faculty of Physical Education and Health of the University of Toronto, provided numerous books and other sources regarding dozens of sports, as well as verifying some entries;

Maria-Zoi K O N T O U of the Aristotle University in Thessaloniki, Greece, provided materials regarding traditional sports of modern Greece;

Małgorzata K R A M of the Polish Federation of Horse Riding, a juror in *carriage driving*, acted as a consultant regarding the rules of that sport;

Michael L A C H A P E L L E, General Manager of the Canadian Olympic Committee, provided materials on Canadian sports, especially *lacrosse*, as well as contacting me with various federations of Canadian Indian sports;

Pere L A V E G A of Instituto National de Edecatione Fisica in Cataluna offered invaluable help in verifying entries on Basque sports;

Nadia L E K A R S K A of the Bulgarian National Olympic Committee spent a lot of time answering my questions regarding the sports and games of Bulgaria and provided a publication entitled *Physical Culture and Sport in Bulgaria Through the Centuries*;

Professor Manfred L Ä M M E R from Deutsche Sporthochschule in Cologne, Germany, the largest and most outstanding Sports Academy in Europe, and Secretary General of the European Committee of Fair Play, provided dozens of rare books regarding the history of German, European and Asian sports;

Milda L A U R U T E N A I T E, Director of the Department of Physical Education of the Lithuanian State Department of Sport and Physical Education (Ku-no Kultu-ros ir Sporto Departamentas prie Lietuvos Respublikos), provided materials regarding Lithuanian traditional sports;

Professor Tony M A N G A N, Editor-in-Chief of *The International Journal of the History of Sport* (London), offered many contacts which proved very valuable for obtaining information on many rare, historical and traditional sports and pastimes;

Cornel M A R C U L E S C U, Director of the International Swimming Federation (FINA), provided materials regarding the swimming sports;

António Teixeira M A R Q U E S of Universidade do Porto, Faculdade de Ciencias do Desporto e de Educação Física, provided the encyclopedia of Portuguese sports and games entitled *Jogos Tradicionais Portugueses*;

Kevin M E Y N E L L and Marc F A R M E R contributed entries on *longtrack* and *grasstrack*;

Jean-Paul M A Z O T, Secretary General of Association des Ecrivains Sportifs in Paris, provided various sources regarding the French sport literature;

Bill M E L L E N, the Chairman of the Great Chesapeake Bay Schooner Race, gave his permission to use the web materials for *schooner race*;

Dr. Jørn M Ø L L E R of the Danish Higher School of Physical Education and Sport (Gerlev Idratshojskole) provided numerous materials regarding Danish sports and traditional games, including a splendid 4-volume encyclopedia of Danish sports and games entitled *Gamle idratslege i Danmark* (1997). I would not have beeen able to thoroughly research this book, however, without the help prof. Eugeniusz Rajnik, Director of the Institute of Scandinavian Studies, Adam Mickiewicz University, and his devoted students, who helped me translate the most most difficult passages (the group included K. Bartkowiak, K. Glazik, M. Kłusek, W. Grabek). Jørn Møller also provided original photographs of various Danish sports and games;

Profesor Ioannis M O U R A T I D I S of the Departament of Physical Education and Sport at the University of Thessaloniki offered invaluable help in obtaining materials on ancient Greek sports. During our frequent encounters at the International Olympic Academy in Olympia, Greece, as well as during various international conferences, he patiently answered all my complicated queries;

Emilia M U C H L A, a graduate of the Asian studies at Adam Mickiewicz University in Poznań, Poland, and a translator from Tartar and Turkish, skillfully translated all materials regarding Turkish wrestling;

Edward N I E M C Z Y K, a pioneer of sports for the disabled in Poland, provided materials regarding the history and status of various sports practiced by such remarkable people;

Javier N I E T O from the library of the Catalonian National Institute of Physical Culture in Barcelona, Spain (Institut Nacional d'Educacio Fisica de Catalunya), provided many precious materials;

Padraig O'D A L A I G H (Patrick D a l l y) provided numerous materials on the history and tradition of Irish sports;

Miquel O R T I N, General Director of the International Baseball Association, offered a variety of materials, which explained the intricate differences between American and international baseball;

Clea Constantinou H A D J I K E S T E P H A N O U P A P A E L L I N A, a scholar from the University of Cyprus, provided materials on ancient Greek sports practiced on the Island of Cyprus, including *Athletics in Ancient Cyprus and the Greek Tradition from 15th/14th century BC – AD 330*;

Jan P A T E R S O N, Director of the Educational Sector of the British Olympic Association and the British Olympic Foundation, offered valuable materials regarding sports and pastimes in Great Britain, including a copy of Joseph Strutt's *Sports and Pastimes of the People of England*;

Charles P I G E A S S O U from Faculté des Sciences du Sport et de l'Education Physique at the University of Montpellier provided materials regarding traditional French sports, especially *joutes languedociennes*, and a valuable publication on folk sports entitled *Entre tradition et modernité le sport*;

John P R O U G H of the Japanese Swordmanship Society provided information and photos of *naginata*;

Profesor Dietrich Q U A N T Z from Deutsche Sporthochschule, my research colleague of many years, offered a number of books and other materials regarding the history of European sports;

Jan R A T A J C Z A K of the Voltige Section of the Polish Horseriding Federation offered materials on equestrian acrobatics;

Russell R E I D of Feather River College provided *broom polo* photos;

Elżbieta R O S T K O W S K A and Małgorzata H A B I E R A of the Academy of Physical Education in Poznań, Poland, provided materials for *swimming* entries, especially *synchronized swimming*;

Richard R E I S N E R consulted the entry on *Australian football*;

J. P. S A B E N - C L A R E, Director of the historical College of Winchester, provided materials on sports practiced in Winchester College and other English public schools;

Tina N. S C H U H, Secretary and Race Coordinator of Swamp Buggy Inc. in Naples, Florida, provided splendid materials and photos regarding *swamp buggy races*;

Graem S H A W from the National Library of New Zealand provided materials regarding Maori sports and pastimes;

Martti S I L V E N N O I N E N from the Departament of Physical Education of the University of Jyväskylä offered materials regarding traditional Finnish sports;

Doug S M I T H of Pickle-Ball, Inc. in Seattle, Washington, provided materials and photos of *pickleball*;

Mercedes S O C O R R O - L A M A R, lecturer of Spanish at the Adam Mickiewicz University in Poznań, Poland, together with Judyta Wachowska, Magdalena Małecka, and Katarzyna Mądra, patiently translated materials from Spanish and prepared poetry selections regarding the traditional Basque sports;

Sigitas S T A S I U L I S from the International Orienteering Federation provided materials regarding various orienteering sports;

Dr Katalin S Z I K O R A from Magyar Testnevelesi Foiskola in Budapest offered materials regarding Hungarian sports, as well as a dictionary of Finnish and Estonian sports edited by Dr. Sklodi Csilla;

David T E R R Y from the British Society of Sports History answered my queries regarding rare sports in Great Britain in long and detailed letters;

Philippe T H I E B A U T, Technical Director of Fédération Française d'Equitation, provided materials on *horseball*, including a manual of this dynamically developing and fascinating sport;

Mike T H O M S O N, Secretary General of the World Curling Federation, patiently answered my queries and provided splendid photographs;

Kadri T U G L U from Ankara, Turkey, President of the Öludeniz International Games, provided splendid materials regarding *paragliding*, especially the photos from Öludeniz;

Krzysztof T Y S Z K I E W I C Z, my friend of many years, offered invaluable help in translating German sources;

Profesor Carlos Lopez von V R I E S S E N from Universidad Católica de Valparaiso, Chile, provided a set of his publications on Chilean sports, consulted various entries and contributed several new ones, which he wrote especially for this publication;

Douglas van W O L D E provided photos of town criers;

Erik De V R O E D E, Curator of Sportmuseum Vlaanderen in Leuven, provided his articles from international journals and a copy of his impressive encyclopedia of Flemish sports *Het Grote Volkssporten Boek* (1996), as well as a set of illustrations of traditional Flemish sports;

Sepp W A G N E R gave us his kind permission to use his web page information and photos regarding *schwingen;*

Mian Abdul W A J I D, General Director of the Pakistani Olympic Museum, offered explanations of Pakistani national sports, in particular an elaborate study of *gulli dunda* prepared for this publication;

Andrzej W A S I E L E W S K I, head of the Goverment of Osieczna, Poland, provided information and illustrations of various regional sports;

Michael W E L L S of Third Light Photography Ltd. provided splendid *punting* photos from Scudmore Punting Company in Cambridge, England;

Chris W H Y A T T verified the entry on *cricket;*

Roedy W I R A N A T A K U S U M A H of Vancouver, Canada provided photos of *pencak silat;*

Piotr Z I Ę B A offered invaluable help in verifying entries regarding martial arts, as well as contributed a number of new entries;

Leszek Z I Ę T K I E W I C Z of the Cultural Center at Krotoszyn, provided materials on *beret throwing;*

Françoise Z W E I F E L, Director of the Olympic Museum in Losanne, Switzerland, and Martinne Fekete-Forrer from the same museum provided a whole range of materials, including photographs of artefacts from the museum's permanent collection and special exhibitions;

Anonymous rangers and employees from New South Wales' National Parks and Wildlife Service provided precious materials on various Australian outdoor sports and sporting activities, especially *bushwalking;*

Librarians at the International Olympic Academy at Olympia and the Academy's Deans: the late Otton S Y M I T S E K and Kostas G E O R G I A D I S offered great support in my research on the history of ancient and Olympic sports;

All perons and institutions mentioned above testify to the splendid international scholarly and intellectual solidarity, which I have experienced and without which the *Encyclopedia of World Sports* would have appeared in a much more modest form, if at all. I thank them all cordially.

A

WORLD SPORTS ENCYCLOPEDIA

A bracciuta wrestlers.

A BRACCIUTA, also known as *e vince*, a Corsican var. of trad. wrestling [Ital. *a* – by + *braccio* – arm]. A sport practiced on Corsica until WWII. After the end of the war it lost its popularity. Competitors wrestled in the standing position, and never on the ground, with their arms wrapped around each other. During the past few years a bracciuta supporters have been trying to revive this sport following a more general tendency to preserve local traditions.

A BRAZZOS, also known as *a francas*, a trad. form of wrestling practiced until c.1970 on Sardinia. A competitor would grab his opponent by the collar, if they fought in jackets, or otherwise by the forearms and try to force him to the ground by applying appropriate collar grips and trying to trip him up.

A LA BADDI, see >BOLD I HUL.

AARI TALKA, also *ahari talka*, a Basq. animal sport where 2 rams butt or ram one another until one wins; see >RAM FIGHTS.

AASTASE LEIVAKOTI TOSTMINE, Est. for 'lifting of a sack full of food enough for one year'. A competitor kneels on the right knee, places a 2m-long rope on the ground and presses the rope to the

Abseiling in natural surrounding.

Abseiling has been successfully used for industrial purposes. Here a team of abseiling glaziers clean and repair one of the faces of 'Big Ben', the clock tower of the Palace of Westminster in London.

Acrobatics.

ground by putting the toes of his right foot in the middle. Then he grabs the rope ends with one hand pulling them across his left shoulder, lifts the right foot up and tries to stand on the left foot. He cannot support his body with his free hand.
M. Värv et al., 'Traditional Sports and Games in Estonia', TSNJ, 1996, 32.

ABA GÜRESI, a form of Turk. wrestling popular mostly in the Gaziantep and Hatay regions and also, to a limited extent, elsewhere in Turkey. Still practiced by the Turks in a form virtually unchanged throughout the centuries. *Güresi* means hand-to--hand combat incl. wrestling. Competitors fight standing and the holds they apply are somewhat similar to those typical of >JUDO. Aba güresi is popular mainly in rural areas although matches are also held in towns and cities. *Aba* stands for the thick woolen cover sported by the wrestlers. The cover is worn like a small jacket or an ancient tunic or, sometimes, even like a ceremonial robe fastened with bands tied under the armpits. It is usu. made into a waist-length garment and is never tucked in, but worn hanging loosely. Some *abas* are longer and reach down to the knees. There are also sleeveless *abas*, some elbow-length and some covering the whole arm. The abas worn in the Gaziantep and Hatay regions are particularly varied as far as their shape, texture and colors are concerned. Most popular is the red aba – *kirmizi aba* which looks like a sleeveless ceremonial robe and both its front and back are mostly red with white vertical stripes. There are 2 thick stripes and 2 thinner ones running parallel to them. Furthermore, the thick white stripes have a red, mottled pattern embroidered on them. According to H. Murat Sahin, a Turk. historian of wrestling, this type of aba is usu. worn by wrestlers from poorer villages, where people make their living from land farming. Another type of aba is the grey aba – *boz aba* – usu. worn by people living in valleys and by

small rivers. The black *aba* – *siyah aba* – is, in turn, typical of land farmers from villages located on the bigger Turk. rivers. Both the grey and black aba are woven in the same way as the red aba. An *Urfa aba* – i.e. the aba from the town of Urfa – is usu. sported by farmhands and shepherds. A *çuha aba* – i.e. a cloth aba – is much richer as it is adorned with borders embroidered with gold or silver thread. It usu. consists of 2 pieces, one reaching down to the waist and the other, outer piece hanging down to the knees. They are sewn together. Such abas are only worn by outstanding wrestlers who can afford to parade their status or nobler descent.
H. Murat Sahin, 'Salvar güresi', *Turk Sport Kulturunde Aba Güresi*, 1999, 39.

ABAOGO, a racket and palm-leaf shuttlecock game played in Côte d'Ivoire in Africa. A form of the Nigerian game of >EGEDE.

ABSEILING, an adventure sport of descending of a steep face by means of a double rope fixed above the climber. It has always been part of the climbing experience and was also used for industrial or commercial purposes, but only in recent decades has abseiling become a separate tourist activity. Abseiling off overhanging cliff faces is a safe and very exciting outdoor adventure, offering breathtaking views and a fascinating experience. No special level of fitness or previous experience is required. Unlike bungy jumping, the speed of descent is in the hands of the climber, who can go fast, slow, or even halt in the middle of the rock face to admire the view. The main principle is to descend on the rope, while controlling the friction of the rope with the use of various methods: 1) no other equipment except for the rope is used. Thus, it is necessary to wear leather gloves and shoulder cloth to avoid skin burns; 2) a doubly looped tape sling is placed around the waist, with one part brought up between the legs from back to front and connected to the other part using carabines. The rope is then run through the carabines and over the shoulder; 3) abseiling with various types of descenders; 4) abseiling with the use of a belay plate.

ABUM BIBUM, a ball game, most likely based on the old games played at cloister schools and hence, most likely, the Latin-based name [Lat. *ab* – from + *bibo* – drink]. It was practiced in a number of C Eur. countries including Germany and Denmark and was also called *abricos* – apricot. The Danish used to play a similar game called >STANTO. In stanto, however, the ball was thrown into the air instead of being bounced off a wall or fence. A game of abum bibum involved 5-12 players. A number of letters (starting from 'a' corresponding to the number of players was then written on a wall or fence with a piece of chalk. One of the players threw a ball against the wall and shouted a word starting with a letter that was among the letters written on the wall. So, if there were 5 players, he would have to come up with a word starting with a, b, c, d, or e. Those players whose names did not start with a, b, c, d, e, etc. (depending on the number of players) and which,

therefore, did not correspond to the word shouted by the player at the wall started running away. A player whose name did start with the letter corresponding to the initial letter of the word shouted by the first player had to catch the ball. After catching the ball he would shout, 'Stanto!' and all the players had to stop. The one with the ball would aim and throw the ball at one of his colleagues. If he managed to hit someone, he himself started running away with the others, whereas the one that was hit shouted, 'Stanto!' again to make the others stop and tried to hit one of them. If he did not manage to hit anyone, he had to pick the ball up off the ground. In the meantime, the others were running away even farther and only stopped when they heard 'Stanto!' once more. Moreover, some of them might have already reached the so-called safe zone where they could not be aimed at and hit anymore. Sometimes all the players reached the safe zone before being hit. When a player earned as many as 10 penalty points (lines or marks) – one awarded for each lost game – he had to run to a distant point. This penalty was called running the gauntlet (*løbe spidsrod*), which might have involved being given a beating with a cap (*slag med Huen*) or so-called swimming across the Red Sea (*sejle over det røde Hav*), which meant being tossed in the air on the arms and hands of the other participants.
J. Møller, 'Abum-bibum Aabricos', GID, 1997, 1, 31.

ACCROSHAY, see >LEAP FROG.

ACQUAKART, also known as *aquakart*, [Ital. *acqua* or Lat. and international *aqua* – water + *kart* or Eng. *cart* – a vehicle]; a type of flat, light motorboat weighing up to 50kg, designed to enable convenient transport, e.g. on top of a car, and also a name for the sport of acquakarting. The boat is usu. propelled by a 5-15hp engine and can go as fast as 40km/h. It replaced the hydrocart.

ACROBATIC FEAT(S), 1) any exercise or series of bodily exercises of a high degree of difficulty and deliberately pushing the limitation of the human body in artificially created, often extreme situations requiring a high degree agility, suppleness and sense of balance; 2) any instance of such exercises being performed, usu. for show, e.g. at circuses, during street performances, sports competitions, etc. For the etymology see >ACROBATICS.

ACROBATICS, the ability to perform bodily or >ACROBATIC FEATS significantly exceeding ordinary, average human abilities [Gk. *akrobateo* – walk on the edge, climb; *akra* – the farthest, the highest + *bateo*, also *pateo* – cover, stack, put sth on sth, e.g. a foot on the ground, walk]. Acrobatics by itself does not constitute a sport in its own right, but is an umbrella term for a family of sports based on performing acrobatic feats and in this sense it is the starting point for activity aimed at attaining physical perfection, physical control, and mental clarity. Acrobatics, interpreted as above, has given rise to a range of autonomous sports such as >AERIALS, >EQUESTRIAN ACROBATICS, >BICYCLE STUNTS, and >SPORTS ACROBATICS, or to a number of competitive forms whereby bodily feats have been replaced by special apparatus, e.g. >AIRPLANE SPORTS, >BICYCLE STUNT RIDING, >FREE-STYLE PARACHUTING, >SKY SURFING. Different var. of acrobatics have been present in almost all cultures throughout the world. See, for example, >LIAN ACROBATICS, >ACROBATICS ON A POLE, >BAXI, >C'HOARI CHOUK-LAMM-PENN, >GLE GBEE, >KAO GLE, >KYSSE DØRKÆLLINGEN, >LAVE GRISE, >MALLAKHAMB, >POTETEKE, >TUMI, >VOLADEROS LOS, >ZASHUA.

History. Based on the etymology of the word one might guess that the oldest forms of acrobatics were known as early as in ancient Egypt, where they constituted a part of burial ceremonies. A very unique form of bull-back acrobatics (>TAURO-MACHY) was practiced in the 2nd cent. BC on Crete. The Gk. and Roman cultures often associated acrobatics with ritual dances that intentionally introduced an element of danger in order to excite the dancers and send them into a trance. The Greeks called such acrobatic feats *thaumata* – feats exciting wonder (also *thaumato-poija* – great achievement, pursuit of wonderfulness). So while acrobatics had never been a part of sports or public life, it greatly contributed to their development. Plato felt that doing difficult exercises was useful in building character and personality. The Roman physician, Claudius Galenus (129-199 AD) held that certain elements of acrobatics had prophylactic and therapeutic properties and recommended tiptoeing along a line drawn on the ground. In the Middle Ages, similar to the earlier Eg. custom, acrobatic feats often, albeit unofficially, accompanied burial ceremonies in some W and S Eur. countries. An acrobat playing with the Grim Reaper was an embodiment of the symbolic victory of life over death and at the same time reinforced belief in life after death. Because the Church disapproved of acrobatics, it was regarded as common entertainment. This also resulted from the fact that acrobatics evolved towards theatrical performance, losing its metaphysical symbolism and simply becoming a source of income for the performers. Eur. rationalism also played a role here, regarding acrobatic feats as unproductive, pointless and contemptible. Towards the end of the Middle Ages, Italy was considered the country where acrobatics was most popular. A. Tuccaro (c.1535-c.1610) was the most famous acrobat at the turn of the 16th cent. He started his career at the court of the Aus. emperor Maximilian II and in 1570 became the official *saltarin du roi* (king's acrobat) to Charles IX of France. In 1599 he published the most impor-

The Mongolian Jagaantsetseg acrobatic group.

tant work of his life *Trois dialogues de sauter et voltiger en l'air* (*Three dialogues on jumping and vaulting*). In his book Tucarro gave detailed descriptions of 54 types of jumps and explained, using 88 woodcut illustrations, how they should be performed. Unfortunately, his attempts to elevate the status of acrobatics in the Aus. and Fr. courts proved futile. His book had, however, some influence on the development of Eur. gymnastics, as some of the feats he performed, including the horse jump as well as rings and horizontal bar exercises, were adopted by such theoreticians as the Ital. G. Borasatti, who included them in his book *Il Ginnasta in Practica, ed in teoria* (*The Gymnast in Practice and Theory*, 1753). By the same token, a Ger. educator, J.F. Guts Muths based his work *Gymnastik für die Jugend* (*Gymnastics for Youth*, 1793) on Tucarro's teachings. The development and spread of gymnastics significantly limited the importance of acrobatics as the art of perfecting the body and turned it into a discipline whose sole aim was to push the human body to its limits. Soon after, in the second half of the 18th cent., acrobatics was incorporated as one of the major circus arts. The trapeze was introduced in 1859. However, given the fact that acrobatics was often linked to juggling and conjuring, it was looked down on by polite society. Such attitudes were further supported by the fact that acrobats were ready to go to extremes to attract attention. In the 1850s and '60s a Fr. acrobat, C. Blondin (J.F. Gravelet, 1824-97), did several tightrope walks over the Niagara Falls in front of large audiences. His first walk took place on 30 June 1859; his tightrope was about 335m-long (1,100ft.) and stretched 49m (160ft.) above the falls. In subsequent attempts he used stilts and was blindfolded. He also performed his breathtaking stunts at the Crystal Palace in London. Acrobatics was revived in the 20th cent. along 2 parallel lines: 1) through the appearance and development of >SPORTS ACROBATICS and by introducing elements of acrobatics to established sports such as figure skating; and 2) thanks to the renaissance of the circus arts enriched with new, e.g. oriental or theatrical, elements. The introduction of some elements of Chin. acrobatics, less athletic but more gentle, has proved especially popular. At the same time, Can. Cirque de Soleil, established in the 1980s, developed a new type of circus show based on a dramatic plot similar to old commedia dell'arte routines.

H. Burgess, *Circus Techniques. Juggling, Equilibristics*, 1976; W. Deonna, *Le symbolisme de l'acrobatie antique*, 1953; G. Strehly, *L'acrobatie et les acrobates, texte et dessins*, 1892; R. Toole-Scott, *Circus and Allied Arts. A World Bibliography*, vols. 1-2, 1960.

ACROBATICS ON A POLE, ancient Chin. acrobatic feats performed on a pole with a small platform on the top. It constituted an event during trad. folk games and *baxi* festivals (>BAXI).

ACROSKI, also *ski ballet* or *figure skating on skis*, one of the 4 main events of >FREESTYLE SKIING. According to FIS rules, it 'consists of jumps, spins, somersaults and steps linked together in a well-balanced program performed, in harmony, to the skiers' choice of music'. The technical merit score includes the degree of difficulty and execu-

Clad in luminescent suits, a pair of acroskiers practice their routine against the setting sun.

tion, judged by 2 judges, accounting for 50% of the total score. The artistic impression, accounting for the remaining 50%, is judged by 3-5 referees, taking into consideration the musical interpretation, variety and ingenuity, and the esthetic quality of the skier's movements, incl. their smoothness, dynamics, body balance and control.

One basic factor influencing the execution of an acroski program is the length of the poles and skis. The poles, used in somersaults and jumps, may not be longer than the skier's height. The minimum length of the skis is determined by multiplying the skier's height by 0.81, so that, e.g. a skier with a height of 175cm must not use skis shorter than 141.75cm. Skis longer than 160cm are banned.

Acroski has been featured in the programs of FIS competitions since 1979 but, in contrast to 2 other freestyle events (>MOGULS; >AERIALS), it is not on the official Olympic program, even though it was a demonstration sport in Calgary in 1988 and Albertville in 1992.

AD-DAYRA, Arab. for 'a wheel', also called *aš-šahd* – meaning unknown. A game described in the dictionary of Arab sports and games by M. Ibrahim al--Majman called *Min al'abina ash-sha 'biyya* (*Our folk games*, 1983, 61-2):

A circular field of about 2m in diameter is prepared. Each player places two or more pits inside the circle. The pits are arranged so that they form a circle. Each player has two pits he then uses to 'shoot' with (by flicking). The players take their turns shooting. If any of the players manages to hit any of the pits placed inside the circle, that pit is removed from the circle. If he misses, the player standing on the far side of the circle starts shooting. The first pit is called a šqah. The next player to take his turn shooting (i.e. after the player on the far side of the circle has missed) is the one standing closest to the šqah. He should hit any pit which will then be removed from the circle. He may also attempt to hit one of the pits so that it skips over and hits the šqah. The player who hits any of the pits from the farthest distance is declared the winner and takes all the pits used to play the game.

AD-DNANA, an Arab boys' game of rolling a wheel. Described by M. Ibrahim al-Majman in his dictionary of Arab sports and games:

It is a boys' game without any time limits or specific rules. In pre-bicycle times, instead of the rim of a bike wheel, the boys used a piece of metal wire bent so that it resembled a wheel. Today those who want to stand out paint the rim with colored paint [...]. The wheel or rim is called a dnana [plural dnanat] or a gant' [plural gunut]. The wheel has to be light, easy to push and roll

Acrobatics on a pole. A bronze mirror, Ming Dynasty (1368-1644). The design on the back shows an acrobat performing on a pole. On the left is a 2-story pavilion with a person in it and a vase on the rail. On the right is a heavenly palace, with a wheel in flames and a fairy riding on a crane – the symbol of longevity. The performance is accompanied by 3 artists.

A

WORLD SPORTS ENCYCLOPEDIA

on the ground. It can also be a metal band from a barrel. The wheel is rolled with a rod or stick. A can is attached to the end of the stick, e.g. a palm tree stem, so that the stick makes a noise when touching the wheel. Sometimes colorful feathers are attached to the other end of the stick (i.e. to the grip). The rules, number of players and the field are determined each time by the children themselves who also invent various obstacles and additional elements of the game. Sometimes they roll their wheels uphill, sometimes on the muddy bed of a pond and quite often they look for special obstacles such as, for example, sand dunes. The winner, in recognition of his skill, often gets pieces of cake from his rivals. In the past children from rich families would attach a flashlight or other trinkets to their sticks which made the others feel envy and admiration – for such flashlights could only be purchased during foreign travel.

[Min al'abina ash-sha 'biyya, 1983, 26-8].

ADI MURAI, an old Hindu martial art related to >KALARI-PAYAT. It consists of exercises and martial arts based on the following 5 techniques: the defensive >OTTA, the offensive >KUTTACUVAT, bare-handed combat >KAIPOR, short-stick combat >KURUVATIPPAYATTU, long-stick combat >NETUVATIPPATATTU and also >KATTIVELA, which entails bare-handed combat against an opponent wielding a knife.

ADUU KHUMIKH, Mong. for 'herding of horses', a type of agility game popular in Mongolia. It employs the talus bones of small animals. These are shaped like a number of small joined balls so they are deemed handy for the purposes of the game. They stand for herds of animals and are called the *aduu* – horses. A game is played with 3-5 such bones depending on the players' skill level. An unlimited number of players can be involved in a game. The bones are thrown up in the air and have to be caught in a specific, pre-defined way. Depending on the way in which the bones are caught one can differentiate between 2 principal types of the game: the *uul* (Mong. for 'a mountain'), whereby the bones should fall onto the back of the hand and the *tal* (steppe, rangeland), whereby the bones are supposed to be caught with the palm. The players take their turns one after another until the first round is completed. The next round follows. If one of the players drops even one of the bones he is eliminated from the game. The one who manages to catch all the bones for the greatest number of rounds wins.

Aerials are judged for air, form, and landings.

ADUU SHURGUULAKH, Mong. for 'breaking a horse'. A trad. type of competition popular among Mong. shepherds. A few unbroken horses are selected and then driven by a mounted competitor. His task is to catch one of the horses with a lariat. If he misses he is replaced by another competitor. The fastest and most skilled in catching horses wins. Cf. >RODEO.

ÆGBOLD, see >BOLD I HUL.

AERIALS, one of the 4 events of >FREESTYLE SKIING, featured, along with >MOGULS, on the Olympic program. The discipline has been on the official FIS program since 1979. It was introduced as a demonstration sport during the 1992 W.Ol.G. in Albertville, and became a full-fledged Olympic sport in Lillehammer in 1994. The task is to ski down a relatively short course with small ramps enabling short jumps combined with acrobatic maneuvers. The skis used are usually shorter than the skier's height. The suits are similar to those used in downhill skiing, with an obligatory helmet and arm and leg protectors.

An aerial ramp or 'kicker' looks much like a small ski jumping hill, differing in the angle of the approach (55-65°) which makes swift take-off possible. It is 1.5m wide, with an in-run at an angle of 20-25° and

a max. length of 55-65m (up to 55m in the Olympic version; the skier does not have to use its full length). Towards the end of the in-run, the course ascends over the ramp, forming a 'table', and leading to the kicker itself, propelling the skier into the air. A little further, there is the 'knoll' leading to the landing area, similar to those in regular ski jumping hills but smaller, inclined at an angle of 34-39°, about 30m long, and leading towards the finish line. The height of the ramp depends on the skier's choice but is always directly related to the angle at which the ramp is inclined:

large ramp: 3.5m – 65°± 1°
medium ramp: 3.2m – 63°± 1°
small ramp: 2.1m – 55°± 1°

The skier selects, at his own discretion, the size of the ramp that is most suitable for the planned maneuver. The smallest ramps are mainly used in practice or during less important events, with less experienced participants. During a maneuver, the skier may reach heights of up to 3m. To absorb the shock at landing, the snow is made less packed in some parts of the landing hill. The jumps are judged by 5-7 judges, positioned on a special stand near the ramp. The score includes 3 elements: 1) the air, including the take-off, height and distance, 2) the form, or the esthetic quality of the maneuver, and 3) the landing. Between 3 and 5 judges judge the first 2 components, with 2 judges marking the landing. The score consists of 20% for the air, 50% for the form and 30% for the landing. The individual components are added and multiplied by the so-called degree--of-difficulty factor (DD). The participants must execute different maneuvers in different rounds of the event (the FIS rules require at least 2 different types of landing). The most frequent maneuvers include the somersault (a natural result of skiing up the in-run), the double and triple somersaults, and the (single, double, triple or even quadruple) twist.

AEROBATICS, flying an airplane or a group of planes through a number of acrobatic maneuvers, unusual in comparison with regular flying techniques, the difference being the position of the plane, its speed, and the suddenness of its twists and turns. According to the Federal Aviation Administration (FAA) definition an acrobatic flight is 'an intentional maneuver involving an abrupt change in an aircraft's attitude, an abnormal attitude, or abnormal acceleration, not necessary for normal flight' (Section 91.71). Depending on the direction of the forces affecting the plane at a given moment the aerobatic figures are called upright or inverted and depending on the way the rudder is handled they are either quick, also known as autorotational, or slow (controlled). The range of figures presented determines whether the competition is deemed to be held at a primary or advanced level. As an organized sport aerobatics is practiced in front of an audience, whereas more practical applications of aerobatics include testing new plane types, military training or actual air combat. Aerobatics contests are held in a zone called an aerobatics zone, usu. an area 100m^2, as marked on the airfield surface. The most popular aerobatics figures include:

ROLL – a figure involving a single, complete rotation of an airplane (or glider) about the axis of the

Aerial acrobatic pilot Frank Ryder practices his acrobatic performance over Narragansett Bay, USA.

fuselage. It might be performed during a horizontal flight, vertical ascent, nose-down descent or turn. One might differentiate between autorotational rolls, consisting of a dynamic, self-induced rotation of the plane, and controlled rolls, performed during slow self-induced rotations, often at a specific angle;
SPIN – the descent of the aircraft, nose-down, along a spiral path of relatively small diameter. A full spinning rotation is called in pilots' jargon a 'turn of spin'. Such turns of spin are self-induced and result from autorotation. Depending on the tilt of an aircraft fuselage against its axis one might differentiate between steep spins (at 20-30°), sloping spins (at 30-50°) and flat spins (at more than 50°). Finally, depending on the aircraft position with regard to its helical path, one can speak of normal spins and inverted spins;
FALLING LEAF – involves the loss of altitude by a plane (or glider) by means of deep glides from the right side to the left side alternately without any marked translation;
LOOP – a maneuver executed by an airplane in such a manner that the aircraft describes a closed curve (a circle) in a vertical plane whereby the transverse axis of the aircraft is parallel to the lifting surface and constantly moves in a horizontal plane. If, during the execution of a loop, the pilot is inside the circle being described the loop is called normal (regular). If the pilot is outside the circle the loop is called inverted;
HALF LOOP – a half of a loop (see above), a figure that consists of moving from descending (nose-down) flight to inverted flight;
WINGOVER – a maneuver involving a steep, climbing turn to a near stall, then a sharp drop of the nose, a removal of bank and a final leveling off in the opposite direction;
SPIRAL GLIDE – a prolonged, deep gliding turn combined with an accelerated loss of altitude along a helical path at a sustained 90° angle;

Championship events include women's and men's individual events, pairs, mixed pairs and trios.

BUNT – a maneuver involving a half roll, whether quick or controlled, to put an aircraft into an inverted flight followed by a half loop going down to put the plane into a horizontal flight which enables the pilot to make a U-turn by means of a vertical maneuver accompanied by an accelerated loss of altitude; IMMELMANN – a maneuver in which an airplane makes a half loop upwards followed by a half roll that puts the plane into a horizontal flight enabling the pilot to make a U-turn by means of a vertical maneuver accompanied by a gain of altitude.

The figures executed during aerobatics competitions are described in Aresti's *Catalog* and classified according to Aresti's aerobatic diagram system.

History. Aerobatics began as an international competition in the 1960s. World competition and the development of the sport is supervised by the International Aerobatics Committee. See also >AEROPLANE SPORTS.

AEROBICS, a system of physical exercise aimed at increasing the oxygen level in the blood and hence the name [Gk. *aerobes* – full of air]. In aerobics there are 2 principal styles and, at the same time, 2 major development stages. The first is called *high impact* as it employs exercise types where both feet lose contact with the ground (as in running or running and standing jumps). This can lead to tendon and joint injuries, esp. in overweight people. Therefore, a new style, called *low impact*, was developed in the second half of the 1970s. In low impact aerobics one has to lift only one foot while the second foot acts as a shock absorber. Low impact exercises include brisk marching in place, forward-, back-, and side-steps, stepping up onto a low platform, etc. Apart from the 2 main styles a number of aerobics var. have emerged. Some examples include: DANCE AEROBICS, a system of rhythmic exercises done (as if danced) to music. This var. appeared during the second low impact stage of aerobics development. The aim of dance aerobics is not only to burn excess calories but also to develop a sense of rhythm and feeling for the beauty of movement in those who practice it.

WATER AEROBICS, also called *aqua aerobics*. A type of aerobics where the exercises are done in a swimming pool. It was introduced in the 1970s to eliminate 'hard' contact with the ground and, at the same time, required greater effort on the part of the participants in overcoming water resistance. As time passed water aerobics developed its own exercise types with no equivalents in regular aerobics. It is most widespread in countries with an abundance of swimming pools or appropriate climatic conditions where it can be practiced in the open air, esp. the US, Canada and Australia.

STEP AEROBICS, a type of aerobics employing a low platform that is 90cm long, 30cm wide and 15-25cm high. This var. of aerobics was developed in the second half of the 1970s by G. Miller who suffered a knee injury and started looking for an appropriate exercise type that would allow bending the knee joint and applying mild and controlled strain to it. Initially introduced as an exercise type within trad. aerobics, it quickly attracted many people and evolved into a semi-autonomous var. with new ex-

ercise types being constantly added to it. There are a number of step aerobics var. including the *step base*, i.e. a series of simple exercises for beginners, and the *step pump* where the step exercises are done with light weights or barbells.

AFROBICS, aerobics exercises employing Afr. music. The exercises are typically very dynamic and imitate trad. Afr. dance movements.

KANGOOROBICS, aerobics-like jumping exercises done in thick-soled shoes of high shock elasticity [Eng. *kangaroo* + *bics* – an ending borrowed from *aerobics* pointing to certain similarities between the 2 sports].

SLIDE AEROBICS, exercises done on a very rough mat. It involves sliding shoe-soles on such a surface to overcome its resistance.

History. The term was coined by K. Cooper, a USAF physician. In his 1968 book *Aerobics* he presented the results of his research into coronary disease, which in the 1960s accounted for 55% of deaths in the US. The book was also meant as a manual on what exercises one should do to avoid a heart attack. In the same year the Congress of International Military Sports agreed for Cooper's program to be implemented in the US, Sweden, Austria, Finland, South Korea, and Brazil. Through the military, but esp. thanks to the families of servicemen who also participated in the exercise programs, aerobics gradually gained in popularity. The popularity of this new sport was further enhanced after the publication of

the subsequent books by Cooper: *The New Aerobic*, 1970, *Aerobics for Women*, 1972, and *The Aerobics Way*, 1977. Cooper found a valuable ally in J. Sheppard Missett who in 1968 started propagating a special program of exercises done to jazz music (>JAZZ GYMNASTICS). Finally, J. Sorenson combined these 2 programs into dance aerobics (see above) where elements of dance were intertwined with exercises selected in such a way so as to improve the efficiency of the circulatory system in participants, mainly women. Since women are less prone to coronary diseases and disorders, aerobics started quickly evolving into a training program aimed at giving one's figure a better shape and at preventing obesity. To attract men, coeducational aerobics classes were organized. As a result aerobics boomed in the 1980s. Its popularity was boosted further by the famous actress J. Fonda who, like R. Simmons, made a series of special TV shows, tapes and records (*Jane Fonda's Workout Record* of 1982 being the most popular one). As a result aerobics became popular all over the world and aerobics classes were held not only in special clubs but also at schools or by religious organizations. The number of participants in aerobics programs in the US was estimated at 6 million in 1978, 19 million in 1982 and 22 million in 1987. Later the number of participants grew more slowly and it reached a steady level of 25 million in 1995. Initially, the term stood for any type of exercise done in the open air whether pursued individually or in small groups and extended into running, swimming and gymnastics. In the 1980s the name referred more precisely to exercise done to music and, contrary to the original meaning of the term, indoors more often than outdoors.

In the early 1980s aerobics became a professional sport. In 1983 K. and H. Schwartz organized the first US aerobics championships under the auspices of a newly estab. institution called the National Aerobics Championships. In 1989 H. Schwartz greatly contributed to the founding of the International Competitive Aerobics Association. The first W.Ch. was held in 1990 with 16 national teams participating and the competition was broadcast to 30 countries around the world. The 1994 W.Ch. attracted participants from 35 countries and in 1995 the competition was broadcast to 175 countries. The first professional aerobics W.Ch. was held in 1997. Championship events include women's and men's individual events, pairs, mixed pairs and trios.

J.G. Bishop, *Fitness through Aerobic Dance*, 1992; Ż. Barańska, *Aerobic*, 1983; C. Casten, P. Jordan *Aerobics Today*, 1990; M. Charell, *Aerobic Gymnastik für Alle*, 1983; K.H. Cooper, *Aerobics*, 1968; K.H. Cooper, *The New Aerobics*, 1970; M. Cooper and K.H. Cooper, *Aerobics for Women*, 1972; H. Fidusiewicz,

Jane Fonda's Workout Record *greatly contributed to popularizing aerobics.*

Step aerobics.

Low impact dance aerobics – the beauty of movement.

A WORLD SPORTS ENCYCLOPEDIA

Aerobic, 1984; L. Francis, *Aerobic Dance for Health and Fitness*, 1983; O. Kuźmińska, *Aerobic – taniec i gimnastyka*, 1984; K.S. Mazeo and L.M. Mangili, *Fitness through Aerobics and Step Training*, 1993; S. Rome, *Bewegung das Spass mach*, 1983; E. Grodzka-Kubiak – personal communication.

AEROPLANE SPORTS, sports disciplines in which different aeroplanes are used. As such, aeroplane sports are also called *aviation sports* or *aviation*.

The resistance of water aerobics provides ultra-low impact.

Airplane sports on postage stamps.

They take the form of various rallies and challenges, with aircraft exhibitions and displays of flying technique as well as different navigational tasks. The best results in individual contests and aircraft types are recorded. Additionally, the best results of test planes, passenger planes and military planes are recorded, a departure from pure sports competition. Other factors contributing to this include the development of aviation technology, which reduces the role of man in flying and increases plane speeds to such an extent that it is hardly a spectator sport. Purely sporting var. of aeroplane sports are still practiced using trad. propeller planes, which fly at relatively low speeds.

History. The history of aeroplane sports is, of course, closely intertwined with the history of the aeroplane itself. Although the first designs of a heavier-than-air powered flying machine appeared at the end of the 18th century, aeroplanes could not yet be built for the lack of an appropriate engine. The invention of the modern aeroplane is attributed to an Englishman, G. Cayley (1773-1857), the author of engine aviation theory. In 1792 he designed and built a model of a propeller plane, which he never launched. From 1800 to 1810 he studied the theory of aerodynamics and discovered the lifting surface principle and gave the theoretical foundations for both propeller and gliding aviation. In 1840 he designed a ship which had the features of a helicopter and an aeroplane. In 1853 Cayley built a prototype of an aeroplane, which managed to take off for several seconds but was unable to remain aloft. The

first plane similar to the modern aeroplane was designed and patented in 1842 by another Englishman: W.S. Henson (1812-88). Supposedly, his plane had a steam engine. In 1843 Henson described his invention in a book *Aerial Steam Carriage*. Work on the theory and practice of engineless flights continued at the same time and contributed enormously to the discovery and application of flight principles and many structural elements common for gliders and later also aeroplanes. In 1896-1903 the American S.P. Langley (1834-1906) determined the law of dependence between aerodynamic lift and the speed of the aerofoil, and also designed the first aeroplane with a petrol engine. Unfortunately, owing to faulty take-offs using a catapult, he crashed the plane twice and eventually discontinued the tests. However, soon after Langley's death in 1906 his aeroplane, rebuilt and properly launched, managed to take off and fly over a distance of about 1km. An aeroplane built by the Wright brothers, Wilbur (1867-1912) and Orvill (1871-1948) played the decisive role in the development of powered flight, building on the experience of another designer of gliders, O. Chanute (1832-1910). On 17 Dec. 1903 in Kitty Hawk (South Carolina, USA), in a homemade plane with a petrol engine, the Wright brothers made the first, historic aeroplane flight, 53m long, remaining airborne for 12sec. On the same day they made a few more flights, the longest of which was about 260m and lasted 59sec. In the following years they perfected their aeroplane and their flights were longer – up to about 100km. In 1908 they made their first flight with passengers on board and in 1909 they opened the first school for pilots and an aeroplane factory in the USA. In Europe the first successful flights were made by the Brazilian A.S. Dumont in 1906, C. Voisin (1907), H. Farman (1908), F. Ferber (1908), and E. de Nieuport (1909) – all from France. In 1907 the Frenchman P. Cornu made the first hanging flight on a prototype helicopter. After a period of pioneer take offs and flights came a period during which pilots covered increasing distances and cleared natural obstacles, e.g. stretches of water or mountain ranges. In 1908 L. Blériot (1872-1936) from France flew over the Eng. Channel; in 1911 P. Pierr, also from France, flew from London to Paris and J. Vedrines flew from Paris to Madrid (landing en route). In 1913 the Peruvian Belovucic flew over the Alps and M.B. des Moulinas from France covered a distance of 5,000km in 46hrs: Paris-Belgrade-Warsaw-St. Petersburg-Stockholm-Copenhagen-Paris. Also in 1913 another Frenchman, R. Garros, flew over the Mediterranean Sea and the *Daily Mail* put up a prize of £10,000 for a flight across the Atlantic without landing. The prize waited several years to be collected. The first pilot to make a transatlantic crossing, with 3 landings en route, was the American A.C. Reid, who took off from Rockway in New York state and reached Plymouth in England on 31 May 1919. The first to fly across the Atlantic without landing was Sir J.W. Alcock (1892-1919) with navigator A.W. Brown (4 June 1919) in a Vickers Vimy aeroplane. They took off in St. John in New Foundland and reached Clifden in Ireland (Alcock was killed the same year in a crash over France). In 1924 the Americans L. Smith, E. Nelson and L. Wade flew round the globe (with landings en route). In the same year a Fr. entrepreneur, R. Orteig, offered a prize for a solo flight across the Atlantic. This was won by C. Lindbergh (1902-76) in a plane called The Spirit of St. Louis. Lindbergh took off on 20 May 1927 from New York and landed 33hrs. and 30min. later at Le Bourget airport in Paris. Lind-

bergh described his experience in 3 books: *We* (1927), *Of Flight and Life* (1948) and his autobiography *The Spirit of St. Louis* (1955), which won the Pullitzer prize. The awards and cups presented by private persons and editors of large magazines were vital to the development of aviation as they stimulated technical progress. An organization of aeroplane sports developed in 1905 when the Fédération Aéronautique Internationale, FAI) was established. The Federation set rules for recognizing records and organizing competitions. The 1st International Challenge of Tourist Aeroplanes was held in 1928 and then every 2yrs. until 1934. The challenge was well known on the international arena. The first 2 challenges were won by a German, F. Morzik, the next 2 by the Poles F. Żwirko and S. Wigura (1932) and J. Bajan with navigator G. Pokrzywka (1934). The start to the 1934 Challenge was in Warsaw, following the principle that each subsequent challenge would be held in the country of the contestant who had won the previous challenge. Thus, the 1936 Challenge was also to be organized by Poland; however, because of the high costs, Poland had to decline. During the last years before WWII the novelty of aeroplane sports began to wear off and the pioneer period drew to a close. But the flights of those early days had a truly sporting character as they were attempts to tame airspace, and man, engaging all his intellectual and physical potential and his will, battled with nature; the struggle itself was like an epic adventure. From this point of view aeroplane sports of the pioneer period can be regarded as sports practiced singly, similar to >SOLO SAILING and >MOUNTAIN CLIMBING. This situation prevailed until flying technique reached a level where the role of human effort was significantly reduced and any point on the globe could be reached relatively easily. The process was accelerated by the development of military aviation, first during WWI and then, to a much greater extent, during WWII, particularly once jet engines came into use. After 1945 the development of aeroplane sports, devoid of the value of the initial conquests, focused on competitions organized along standard routes. Today the main forms of aeroplane sports include tourist rallies, combined with navigation tasks and aeroplane tests and aviation acrobatics, >AEROBATICS. The best known sports events include: the Ralph Pullitzer Cup held in the USA since 1920, FAI flights, and a rally around Sicily. W.Ch. in aviation have been held since 1977 under the auspices of the FAI. Compared to the early days, modern aeroplane sports are characterized by their low rate of development, typical of events in which there is little left to prove. A revival, perhaps, might be brought about if some of the technological advances, esp. the electronic ones, could be abandoned and the old combat between man and nature could be restored, as in the case of solo sailing.

The Internet: www.iac.org; B. Arct, *Poczet wielkich lotników*, 1966; Z. Brodzki, S. Górski, *Lotnictwo*, 1970; K. Chorzewski, *Z dawnych lotów*, 1975.

AFGHAN ARCHERY, an Asian type of archery displaying all of the characteristics of >ORIENTAL ARCHERY but having distinct ceremonial applications, e.g. practiced esp. during trad. weddings. Shortly before a wedding ceremony the groom's best men competed in an archery contest set by the bride's family, shooting arrows at a piece of glass. The bride and the groom could only meet if one of the contenders hit the target and broke the glass. Afghan wedding shooting was initially organized using bows

Airshows draw thousands of spectators annually.

Afghan archery.

and arrows, and later using firearms, which in the 19th cent. gradually displaced the former.

AFRICAN BALL TOSS, also *coconut golf*, a game played in W Africa, esp. in Guinea and on the Ivory Coast. Each player has one coconut in his hand. In the middle of a field of unrestricted dimensions a fist-sized hole is dug. One by one the players roll their coconuts towards the hole. The first player to roll his coconut into the hole – or, if no holes are scored, the player whose coconut came closest to the hole – starts the game. He receives a point if his coconut hits the hole in the next end, and then takes it out of the hole and takes a place nearby. Now other players try to score holes, but he strikes at their coconuts with his own in an attempt to prevent them from scoring. If, nevertheless, any player manages to hit the target then he also gains a point. The game lasts until all players have scored 1pt.
A. Taylor Cheska, 'Ball Toss', TGDWAN, 1987, 22; C. Lombard, *Les jouets des enfants bauole,* 1978.

AGBÂRIN, also known as >ARIN, a boys' game played in Yorubaland in Nigeria. An agbârin field, called an *ojuşä,* is 12ft. (3.65m) long, 4ft. (1.22m) wide and is divided with a transverse line into 2 equal parts called homes – the *Iles*. An agbârin game is played by 2 individual players or 2 teams. The game employs large, brown, elliptical pits (or seeds, stones). 21 pits are spaced evenly so that they form a square of 7 rows with 3 stones each on each half of the field. Near the halfway line there is a pit called the devil on the path – *esu ona*. Each player has 2 additional pits and from behind the end line of his half throws them toward his opponent's half so as to displace the pits arranged there. If he hits the devil on the path, he loses all the points scored so far. The throw technique is similar to that of skipping stones over water. Each displaced pit is then collected by the player who displaced it and used in subsequent throws. The one who collects all the pits belonging to his opponent wins the round. If a game consists of more rounds, the players or teams change sides after each round. Agbârin is usu. played by small boys aged 5-10 but also by adolescents or even adults. It is usu. played from August until March when the weather is slightly cooler. According to the elders of Ekiti, if you persist in playing agbârin after the domesticated birds have gone to sleep you will gradually go blind.
Jeux et jouets de l'ouest africain, 1995, I; A. Taylor Cheska, 'Agbârin or Arin', TGDWAN, 1987, 18; E. Vermand, *Jeux africains. Notes Africaines,* 1944, 21.

AGNON TOSS, the practice of tossing a javelin similar to a harpoon [see >HARPOON TOSS]. Agnon was a battle weapon of Germanic peoples, esp. Frankish tribes, and had a spearshaft with a javelin tipped with a barbed head, which made it difficult to snatch from its target. A thick rope, fastened to the bottom of the spearshaft, unfolded during the toss, which allowed for snatching the enemy's shield. Young Germanic warriors practicing agnon tossing in peace time had all the elements of a spontaneous competition.

AGON, Gk. pl. *agones,* 1) in ancient Greece – competition, contest or struggle in any field including sports, literature, art, etc.; 2) a deity embodying competition; see >AGONISTIKE.

AGONISTIKE, Gk., in ancient Greece – a struggle or competition, most frequently held as sports games but also as artistic or literary contests. Named after Agon, a deity personifying competition and struggle, including sports events. According to Pausanias the Agon statue in Olympia depicted a man with long jump weights (*Hellados Periegesis,* V, 20,3; V, 26,3). Hermes Enagonios is also deemed to have been a patron deity of agonistike.

AHEL KARR, in full *an ahel karr*, Bret. for 'cart axle lifting', *le lever de l'essieu* being its Fr. counterpart. It consists of adding increasingly heavier weights to

Aikido channels one's vital energy to purify body and mind.

a cart axle (usu. with the original wheels taken off), in a manner similar to adding weights to the bar in weightlifting. A competitor, depending on the local custom, lifts the axle with 1 or both hands. The object of the contest is to hold the axle in the air for a specified period of time, usu. 3mins. After all the competitors have made successful attempts at a given weight, more weights are added. The one who lifts the heaviest axle-weight the greatest number of times in the last round wins.
F. Peru, 'La tradition populaire de jeux de plein air en Bretagne', LJP, 1998.

AHIMÉ, see >FA KOR.

AIKIDO, a Jap. martial art involving hand-to-hand combat and weapon combat, e.g. knife combat [Jap. *ai* – harmony, union + *ki* – spirit, universal power + *do* – rule, principle, way, method]. It draws upon the samurai tradition generally known as *budo*. It is similar to >JU JUTSU and >JUDO but relies to a greater extent on turning an attacker's strength and momentum against himself. It also makes use of pressing nerve points or centers to bring down an adversary but forbids any offensive holds, throws and locks since it is only a defensive martial art and can only be used in response to an attack. Aikido also focuses on mastering control over one's body and mind in difficult situations. Its origins date back to the 14th century AD. In 1925 a Jap. martial arts expert Ueshiba Morihei (1883-1969) decided to systematize the rules of aikido and turn them into official sports regulations. He followed the approach adopted when >JU JUTSU had been made into an official sport. According to Ueshiba Morihei, aikido is based on *ki*, a mystical, quasi-religious and almost cosmic concept of 'vital energy'. The major aims of aikido are to use this energy 1) to purify oneself and improve the quality of one's spiritual life and bodily health and 2) against an adversary to gain full control over him. Students of aikido strive to focus and control the ki that is centered in the abdominal region just below the navel. The purpose of this exercise is to make the ki flow out of the body and to control that flow. Failure to do so temporarily deprives a student of

his ki. Prolonged ki brings poor health and its permanent loss results in death. According to the aikido philosophy, systematic practice and hard work aimed at controlling the ki followed by mastering appropriate martial art techniques leads to understanding the forces of nature, makes a person resistant to any outside aggression and fatigue and endows him with a 'sixth sense' that makes it possible for him to anticipate events about to happen. It brings order into one's life and frees one of existential concerns. In the case of immediate danger and during a fight it enables one to control an adversary and subject them to one's will.
Techniques. Aikido is based on bends and twists, applied esp. to the wrist, elbow and shoulder regions (*kansetsu-waza*) and on sudden pushes and hits (*atemi-waza*). The aikido repertoire also includes certain hits or blows that may lead to an opponent's death or grievous bodily harm. These are, of course, not employed during aikido competitions. The person under attack is called *nage* and the assailant – *uke*. A very special form of defense is the exaggerated reaction to an assault consisting of a series of falls turned into somersaults and jumps which are aimed at making it impossible for the assailant to take full advantage of the suddenness of his attack. Another objective is to fall in such a way as to avoid injury. Aikido movements are jointly called the *kata*. When practicing aikido, students form pairs to perform the kata, alternating the positions of the uke and the nage.
Outfit and equipment. Aikido fights are held in a room called a *dojo* (practice hall). The fighters wear thick, cotton, kimono-style tops with a wide ankle--length skirt or trousers. This outfit is called a *haka-ma*. To represent proficiency in various kata forms aikido employs a system of colored belts. Usu. a novice wears a white belt, more proficient students sport orange, green, blue and brown belts. An expert wears a black belt. It is extremely difficult to attain all the consecutive levels of proficiency and it takes years to go from one level to another.
History. Before developing his own system, Ueshiba Morihei, the father of modern aikido, studied several forms of Asian martial arts and self-defense. He drew extensively from >JU JUTSU created by Sokaku

Ahel karr – cart axle lifting.

Ueshiba Morihei – the founder of Aikido.

A

**WORLD SPORTS
ENCYCLOPEDIA**

Koichi Tohei (b. 1920, 10th Dan).

Steven Seagal (b. 1951, 7th Dan).

Kanetsuka Minoru Sensei (b. 1939, 7th Dan).

Takeda who taught him self-defense (1915-19). Takeda's ju-jutsu school was then known as >DAI-TO RYU AIKI JU JUTSU. In 1919 M. Ueshiba started his spiritual studies with Onisaburo Deguchi, a master of the neo-Shintoist school of *omoto-kyo*, as his teacher. The philosophical foundations of omoto-kyo became the spiritual basis of aikido. M. Ueshiba founded his own school in Ayabe and perfected it to such an extent that Takeda himself decided to visit him to see some of the elements newly introduced into the system. After the visit he added some of the new elements to his *daito-ryu* and called it daito ryu aiki ju jutsu. Takeda authorized M. Ueshiba to use this name as a representative of his style. In 1935 M. Ueshiba became fully independent and declared his preferred martial art fully autonomous. Later he changed the name of his style a few times into *Aioi-ryu Aiki Bujutsu*, *Aiki-Budo* and *Ko-Budo*. The term *aikido* has been in use since 1942.

Aikido became popular after admiral Isamu Takeshit (1869-1949) became familiar with M. Ueshiba's school and recommended him to the Emperor's courtiers, the military, and businessmen. This enabled him to move the school to Tokyo, organize aikido shows and finally to obtain accredita-

the purposes of Takeda's daito-ryu. Takeda, not unlike many other masters, kept his knowledge only to himself and died without leaving a written account of the principles of his art. His disciple, Negokitchi Sagawa, says in his manual *Practice Aiki* (1913) that students of daito-ryu (ju jutsu) employed the concept of aikido in a way similar to that in which M. Ueshiba incorporated it later into his teachings. This, however, does not alter the fact that because Takeda did not give a precise definition of his ju jutsu style and left many technical details unexplained it was much easier for M. Ueshiba to fill in the missing bits and develop his own aikido style. Shortly after WWII M. Ueshiba established his own organization called Aikai-kai whose aim was to propagate aikido. His work was continued by his son Kisshomaru (b.1921). According to his father's beliefs, which he fully accepted, he opposed any competitive form of aikido. The Aikai-kai school remained faithful to the principle that the sole aim of aikido is to develop aikido students' physical, volitional and moral qualities. A large number of M. Ueshiba's and his son's disciples did not share these views and began to establish their own aikido schools and associations.

school of >KORIN-DO; K. Shinizu organized the school of >TENDO-RYU.

Such great variation among aikido schools and styles makes it impossible for it to function on the international arena as a uniform sport. Nevertheless, aikido in general is gaining popularity, esp. in the US, France, Germany and Great Britain. The largest number of schools and clubs is located in France. In 1993 there were about 2,500 of them in France alone. In this way France surpasses even of Japan itself where there are only 1,600 schools or clubs. The US comes third with 1,200-1,300 schools or clubs. There have been attempts at unifying the respective styles and ensuring their uniform global representation. In 1976 the *aiki-kai*-style schools formed the International Aikido Federation, which in 1995 had member clubs from 29 countries. *Yoshin-kan* schools set up the International Federation of Yoshin-kan Aikido (1990). In 1993 the Tomiki Aikido International Network (TAIN) with affiliated clubs and schools from 9 countries came into being. Since 1989, every 2yrs., TAIN has held an international championship for its members. All the remaining styles have been trying to form a federation. If one managed to bring all the

One step faster than the opponent.

tion from the Dai-Nippon Butoku-Kai, i.e. an association of all officially recognized Jap. martial arts and self-defense schools.

After the basic aikido system had been developed, a number of var., including e.g. >TOMIKI incorporating knife combat, appeared. The Féderation Internationale d'Aikido (International Aikido Federation) was estab. in 1974 and Tokyo was made its official seat. Apart from Japan aikido is esp. popular in the US, Germany, Switzerland and Austria. The popularity of aikido, alongside other Oriental martial arts, is on the rise.

Philosophy. The concept of *aiki*, dating back to the Edo era, i.e. to the rule of the Tokugawa Dynasty, is the key to understanding aikido. In 1764 one of the masters of an early ju jutsu school known as >KITO (also *kito-ryu*) wrote the famous *Toka mondo* (*A Debate by Candlelight*). It defines aikido as the moment of examining an assailant by observing his breath. Another Jap. work *Budo-hiketsu aiki no jutsu* (*Secret Methods in martial art techniques*, 1892) explains that the concept of aiki means 'one step faster than the opponent'. It also says that to be faster than the opponent according to aiki principles means to be able to immediately see through his intentions and be faster in uttering a battle cry. We do not know how aiki was practiced or what kind of martial art techniques had been developed to implement the aiki principles prior to the emergence of aikido proper, e.g. for

In 1977 K. Tomiki (1900-79) estab. the Japan Aikido Association. Tomiki had been M. Ueshiba's disciple since 1926 and enjoyed his full support when he received the 8th dan from him. Tomiki wanted to develop the foundations for *randori* – a training match, similar to those typical of other Far Eastern martial arts such as judo or >KENDO. The fact that he introduced a number of controversial novelties such as knife combat and exercises resulted in a long and heated debate on to what extent aikido can still be deemed to conform to its original principles and when it ceased to be what it was meant to be. Another disciple of M. Ueshiba, Koichi Tohei (b.1920) had studied in Kobu-kan since 1940 and later he became chief instructor in Aikai-kai. After Ueshiba's death he was to take the school over but resigned in favor of M. Ueshiba's son, Kisshomaru. What followed was a period of internal disagreements on the issue of leadership and as a consequence Tohei decided to leave and founded his own Ki Association (Ki no Kenkyu-kai).

Independent martial arts systems constituting aikido var. or semi-autonomous styles were also created by the followers of Ueshiba: M. Mochizuki (b.1907) who after the death of his master developed an autonomous style called >YOSEI-KAN; N. Inoue (1902-94) developed >SHINEI-TAIDO; K. Sunadomari (b.1923) founded the school of >MANSEI-KAN; M. Hiraio (b.1930) co-operated with Ueshiba until the end of WWII and then opened his own

different aikido styles together under the umbrella of one organization, the result would probably be the largest Far Eastern martial arts association in the world and, moreover, one of the largest sports organizations in the world in general.

There is a special, Eng.-language aikido magazine called *Aiki Journal* estab. by S. Pranin which enjoys world-wide renown.

G. Bennett, *Aikido Techniques and Tactics*, 1998; S. Pranin, *The Aiki News Encyclopedia of Aikido*, 1991; S. Pranin, *Takeda Sokaku and Daito-ryu Aiki Jujutsu*, 1992; S. Pranin, *Aikido Masters: Prewar Students of Morihei Ueshiba*, 1993; F. Shishida and T. Nariyama, *Aikido Kyoshitsu* (in Japanese), 1985; K. Sunadomari, *Aikido kaiso Ueshiba Morihei*, M. Ueshiba's biography in Japanese, 1969; K. Ueshiba, *Aikido no kokoro (Dutch Aikido)*, 1981.

AIPOLAMPAS, see >TORCH RELAYS.

AIR CHAIR, a piece of water sports equipment and a sport, the object of which is to glide on water behind a motor boat. The air chair consists of a seat fixed on a large runner, to which a long keel with a float is attached. The construction enables 2-phase gliding. At low speeds both the rider and the equipment is supported by the runner. At higher speeds the resistance of the water causes the runner to emerge above the surface. Its function is gradually overtaken by the rising float, situated at the lower end of the keel. The rider sits on the seat, supported by a special bail, with his feet resting against the runner. At top speed he seems to be sitting on a jib rising from the water, the runner levitating almost 1m above the surface. The float resembles an airplane in construction: it has 2 wings and ailerons at the tail. The low resistance of the water makes it possible to glide behind a >JET SKI. The gliding technique is easier than in >WATER SKIING or >WAKEBOARDING. The equipment makes it possible to perform aerial evolutions of medium difficulty, ensuring a mild and fairly safe landing.

History. The idea of the air chair originated among water sports enthusiasts practicing >KNEEBOARDING on the Colorado river. The initiator of the air chair was M. Murphy and the first equipment constructor – B. Wooley. In 1989 the Air Chair Company, which manufactures equipment, came into being. This brought the sport a degree of popularity.

AIROLO-CHIASSO, an unusual relay race walking competition held in Switzerland each mid-October since 1962 between the Airolo and Chiasso relay teams composed of 5 competitors each. The race distance is 115km divided into a few stages. The race starts at 6:30 a.m. The first stage ends in Giornico. It is 27km long and runs down along a winding mountainous road. The second stage to Bellinzona is 30km long and is mostly flat. Then, there is another flat, 8-km stage followed by a steep ascent of 6km leading up to Monte Ceneri. The next stage ending in Lugano is 19km long and is hilly, whereas the last stage is initially flat but becomes hilly in the second half (and is particularly difficult and dangerous due to heavy vehicle traffic).

AIRPLANE, an Eng. name given to the exercises done by Native Alaskans and other Native Amer. Indians and constituting one of the competitive events during Native Amer. Indian folk games. A competitor lays face down on the ground, his legs straight and held together, arms extended out at right angles to the body, so that he resembles an airplane. Three assistants take him by the hands and legs, lift him up, hold him some 3ft. (about 90cm) above the ground and carry him around. The object of the game is to remain in this stiff, unnatural position as long as possible. A competitor whose body sags below the shoulders or whose buttocks rise above the arms is eliminated. The one who endures the longest and is carried the longest distance is declared the winner. According to local sports terminology airplane is one of the so-called arctic sports. It is a separate event during the North Amer. Indigenous Games.
The Arctic Sports, the Internet: http://www.first-nations.com/naig97/arctic-sports/as-airplane.htm

AIRPLANE SPORTS, see >AEROPLANE SPORTS.

AIZKOLARIS, a Basq. lumberjack competition consisting of chopping large logs with an ax [Basq. *aizkora* – ax, also Span. *corte de troncos* – cutting through trunks]. The most popular event is a time trial in chopping through short pieces of trunk placed in a transverse (horizontal) position on the ground whereby a competitor stands astride the trunk section and chops down the middle. The trunks used in aizkolaris are thicker than in the Ang.-Sax. >TIMBER SPORTS. Chopping through a vertically placed piece of trunk (Span. *corte vertical*) or individual and pairs sawing events (*tronzadora – una persona* and *tronzadora – parejas*, respectively) are less common. The national championship is held in 3 categories according to trunk diameters, i.e. 60, 54, and 45in. respectively (*pulgadas*). The min. diameter in the horizontal trunk chopping event is 36in. (about 91cm) and the max. diameter is not limited but is usu. 72in. (about 182cm), sometimes 80in. and over 100in. in exceptional cases. The number of trunks is agreed upon by the competitors beforehand usually from 6 to 20 (less frequently 2-4) logs per competitor. Sometimes trunks of different diameters are selected. For example, during the Basq. Country championship in 1981 each participant had to chop 6 trunks of 60in. and 6 of 72in.; in 1983 – 4 trunks of 72in., 4 of 60in. and 4 of 52in. The competitors usu. chop more thinner and fewer thicker trunks. 72in. and thicker trunks are not so easily obtainable these days so very often competitors have to chop through 2 or 4 trunks instead of just 1. In 1968 a competition was held in Tolosa which involved chopping through 4 trunks of 108in. (about 274cm) each. In 1924 J.A. 'Keixete' chopped through 20 54-in. trunks in the following (accumulated) times (in min. and sec.):

1 – 2'27", 2 – 5'06", 3 – 8'01", 4 – 11'12", 5 – 13'38", 6 – 17'20", 7 – 20'10", 8 – 23'25", 9 – 26'10", 10 – 29'34", 11 – 33'05", 12 – 37'07", 13 – 40'50", 14 – 44'32", 15 – 48'17", 16 – 52'14", 17 – 55'55", 18 – 60'25", 19 – 65'07", 20 – 69'32" (final result).
Aizkolaris competitions are held in main town squares or *corrida* arenas (San Sebastian, Bilbao in Spain, etc.) and outside cities and towns at pic-

Aizkolaris competitors go at it in a series of 20 logs each; it will require well over an hour's sustained chopping to dispatch them all.

nic grounds and often attract as many as 20-30,000 spectators and are broadcast on TV and on the radio. Large groups of contestants can be seen competing simultaneously. At the national Basq. Country championship, there are, e.g., 40 short trunks and 40 competitors.
The ax used in aizkolaris competitions is called an *aizkora* in Basque and there are 3 basic types: 1) an *illargi-aizkora* (literally a moon-shaped ax) whose blade gets symmetrically wider towards the cutting edge of the blade which is crescent-shaped; 2) a *bizkaya aizkora* – a Vizcaya ax with a blade wider by the handle and with the relatively straight cutting edge slanting down towards the handle; 3) a *napar aizkora* – a Navarre ax with a blade of equal width but slightly slanting towards the handle. There is a wide variety of local competition types and in 1970 the Federación Navarra de Atletismo (Athletic Federation of Navarre) adopted a uniform set of aizkolaris rules. These rules are adhered to during the Basq. Country and Navarre lumberjacks' championship (Reglamento del Campeonato Vasco-Navarro de Aizkolaris).
History. The oldest mention of aizkolaris dates back to the 16th century. The Basq. Country and especially the Vizcaya and Guipúzcoa regions were then the main source of material for the shipbuilding industry. Other regions of the country did not have such thick forests and this prevented aizkolaris from spreading to these parts. The Basq. Country was also famous for burning charcoal, which was essential in gunpowder-making, and therefore competitive wood chopping was rather popular among charcoal burners. The leather tanning industry was also one of the driving forces behind aizkolaris since it created a steady demand for bark. On the whole, the timber industry was booming which is best exemplified by the 1787 figures concerning the

Qyarzun valley where 7,425 oaks, 19,600 beeches and 19,655 chestnut trees were felled in just one year. Locally held competitions became regular and widespread at the beginning of the 20th century. In 1903 the corrida arenas in Tolosa, Azpeitia and San Sebastian were used for the first time as aizkolaris competition venues and the first outstanding aizkolaris competitors such as J.M. Goenaga Odriozola, nicknamed 'Achumberia', and P.M. Otaño Eceiza (1870-1956), nicknamed 'Santa Agueda', became widely known. A duel held on the 27th Dec. 1903 at the corrida arena in Azpeitia is considered the greatest aizkolaris contest of all time. The competitors chopped through 4 almost 2m-thick trunks (in a 4-log event called *kanako egurrak* in Basque and *cuatro de vara* in Spanish). The odds on 'Achumberia' were 5/1 against. The duel attracted about as many as 5,000 spectators. After chopping through the first log 'Santa Agueda' was 1min. 35sec. ahead of his rival, after the second log his lead extended to 7min. 32sec. but after the third 'Achumberia' was in the lead 58sec. ahead of 'Santa Agueda'. After 76mins. 'Achumberia's' lead was so substantial that 'Santa Agueda' conceded defeat 2mins. before the competition officially ended. Two more outstanding wood choppers at the turn of the 19th century were J. Soraluce Arrizabalaga 'Korta' (1868-1954) and J. Aramburu 'Keixete' (1881-1962). Between the world wars, I. Elorza 'Kortaberri' and Arrizabalaga 'Ondárroa' were considered the most famous competitors and I. Orbegozo Juaristi 'Arriya', J. Iturbe 'Aguiñeta' and J.J. Narvaiza 'Luxia' were widely admired during the first 2 decades after 1945. In 1970s and '80s there was a number of renowned lumberjacks including: J. Orbegozo, F. Astibia, M. Irazustra, J.J. Nervaiza, J. Aierbe and J. Aguite. The Span. championship is held in the Basq. Country and it is traditionally dominated by Basq. competitors. There is a tendency to establish contacts with competitors from countries where timber sports are also popular. In 1976 a W.Ch. in Basq. Events was held in San Sebastian that attracted wood choppers from Australia, the US and Canada. The championship events included 1) individual chopping of 2 horizontal and 2 vertical 45in. logs (winner: Jackson of Australia, time: 1min. 58sec.); 2) 3-person team chopping of

WORLD SPORTS ENCYCLOPEDIA

A

The day of the ax duel has come – that great, old tradition.

6 vertical 45in. logs, 6 vertical 54in. logs, 3 vertical 45in. logs and 3 vertical 54in. logs followed by 3 horizontal 60in. logs and 3 horizontal 54in. logs (winners: Australia, time: 58min. 31sec.); 3) individual chopping of 45in., 54in., 60in. and 45in. horizontal and vertical logs (winner: a competitor nicknamed 'Arriya II', time: 14min. 41sec.); 4) the same combination for teams of 3 (winners: the Basq. Country, time: 45min. 49sec.).

The best Basq. choppers are praised by local poets (who are rarely translated into other languages). Their poetry is devoted to wood and expresses emotions related to wood, wood felling and woodworking as in the following song of Basq. lumberjacks:

Of all the trees the most admirable is
the beech in forest dark.
Sweet words you have for me,
but your heart belongs to another,
May the Lord of Heaven make you
Love me.

Another anonymous song of Basq. charcoal burners and lumberjacks is included in an anthology of Basq. poetry published in 1956 by A. Zaval:

On this day in Bazan-Garaya
There was a message from Lorenzo that he concluded a contract
with Amorraya for tree felling;
[...]
Our whole team went there
To help him ...
The team paraded solemnly
through Bazan-Garaya
But hardly had the tree felling started
When many people got carried away:
And they made a ten duro bet
That Bordabi would not manage to win,
And he won easily:
Such was the pleasure he took in his work.
In the trunk of a tree
Fire sparked instantly

And the bark was soon covered
With a delicate veil of smoke.
And Bordabi was very eager
To climb there at any cost,
And although he won the bet easily,
He came down terribly dirty.
When the tree was just about to fall,
there gathered, as was said,
Droves of people looking:
'Will it fall in the right place?'
There are many in Oyarzun,
Who do not know much about trees.

A great Basq. poet N. Ormaechea 'Orixe' called *el grand bardo guipuzcoano* (the great bard of Guipúzcoa) depicts the legendary axmen in his *Euskaldunak*. This 40-stanza poem talks about an ax bet where the 2 best chopping teams, of Leiza and Huici, enter a competition to settle long-standing animosities:

The day of the ax duel has come
That great, old tradition
Leiza and Huici shall compete [...]
On the hill the snow is almost half-thigh-deep,
No one, who can move, shall stay in
Leiza. Black spots appear on the white background,
Like flies on milk; or, to be precise, like
Cranes, one after another.
Leiza has a long-standing case against
the Larraun Valley. And while they try very hard
They cannot have it resolved in their favor; but this time
Leiza hopes that they will win.
The duel is very dramatic:
In the first half of the eleventh, it still
turns his face to the one from Leiza, but soon after to
The one from Huici. He works more slowly, he chopped through
the log with a six-hit advantage and
So he climbs the next one ...

Leiza wins beating Huici by 30 logs and the opponents agree on a return match. The tradition has it that you always have to give your opponent a chance and the prize is a herd of rams.

20 minutes into the event and a quarter way through their logs.

Competitors themselves also write about their feats. In 1965 an improvising poet, M. Machin, nicknamed 'Errekalde', wrote an eulogy for M. Irazusta. See also >DRWALI ZAWODY, >TIMBER SPORTS.

R.A. Franco, 'Aizkolaris', DRV, 1983, 32-56; R.A. Franco, 'Aizkolaris', JYDV, 1978, 107-196; *Herri Kirolak, Aizkolariak*, 13-20.

AJAQAQ, a Native Amer. Indian throw-and-catch game played by the Greenland Inuit and resembling the Dan. >BÆGERBOLD, and the Fr. >BILBOQUET. It involves throwing a piece of bone (*knogle*) or a seal's tooth (*tandstykke*) up in the air and trying to put a stick through a hole (*hul*) bored in the bone. The hole's diameter is only slightly larger than the stick's cross-section. The piece of bone thrown up in the air is tied to the stick with a piece of string that is 30-40cm long so that the bone is never out of the thrower's range.

J. Møller, 'Ajaqaq', GID, 1997, I, 125.

AKONTISMA, [Gk. *akontisma*], in ancient Greece a javelin throw event employing a spear called *akontion*, heavier than >APOTOMEUS used in >PENTATHLON (ANCIENT). Initially an *akontion* had a bronze head and later an iron one. The legend, later confirmed in one of Pindar's odes, had it that javelin throwing was introduced as one of the Ol.G. events by one Frastor who had participated in the mythical games held by Heracles. The first mention of putting a spear to a sporting use comes from Book XXIII of Homer's *Iliad*:

Finally the son of Peleus brought into the ring a long-shadowed spear and an unused cauldron with a floral pattern, worth an ox. He put these down, and the javelin-throwers rose to compete. The two men that stood up were imperial Agamemnon, Atreus's son, and Meriones, Idomeneus' worthy squire. But the swift and admirable Achilles interposed, saying: 'My lord Atreides, we know by how much you excel the rest of us and that in throwing the spear no one can compete with your prowess. Accept this prize and take it with you to the hollow ships. But if you are agreeable, let us give the spear to my lord Meriones. That is what I at all events suggest.

To this decision, Agamemnon King of Men made no demur. So Achilles gave the bronze spear to Meriones, and the King handed his own beautiful prize to his herald Talthybius.

[Homer, *The Iliad*, Penguin Books Ltd., Harmondsworth, 1976, p. 436]

In *The Iliad* and *The Odyssey* there are, however, numerous mentions of soldiers 'taking pleasure in discus, javelin throw and archery' in between battles. As a competitive event javelin throwing had 2 varieties, namely distance and target. The javelins used during games had no spearheads. To give a javelin a better balance and to shift its center of gravity forward a tiny piece of wood was tied to its front. A competitor would take a short run-up and throw the javelin. Akontisma constituted a separate event during smaller, local games held, for example, in Kea. The target throw event was usu. held for mounted competitors. It was one of the most important exercises done at the Athens gymnasium. It was recommended by both Plato and Xenophon. It also constituted one of the events at the Panathenaea and Theseia (also in Athens). According to various vase paintings, the mark used in the competition was a round target similar to those used in modern shooting targets with a well-marked central point and 2 large concentric circles. Upon hitting the area between the smaller circle, located closer to the center, and the center, a competitor scored fewer points than if he had hit the bull's eye. The third target area, between the smaller and bigger circle had an even lower point value. The second circle was also the target borderline and any hit outside this line was declared invalid. The target was attached to a pole at the height of a horse's neck. Akontisma was not, however, one of the most highly valued and appreciated events since the prizes for winners were the smallest of all those awarded during the Panathenaea and Theseia. An akontisma prize was only 5 oil amphorae (whereas a winner of the 1 stadion race received 50 amphorae and a winner of the two-horse team chariot race received as many as 140 amphorae). The horseback javelin throw was considered the most important event at the Argos games held in honor of Hera, the patron goddess of the city. The javelin throw event held there was called an *agon chalkeos* – a bronze shield competition – since a shield was the main prize. This prize was held in high esteem which is best exemplified by such ancient Gk. proverbs as 'worth the Argos shield' (used of somebody who surpasses everybody else, not necessarily in a competition) or 'as proud as if he had won the Argos shield'. Contrary to the Hera games held at Olympia, the Hera games of Argos were for men only.

K. Paleologos, 'Javelin', OGIAG (1982, 196-201).

AKROCHEIRIA, in ancient Greece – arm wrestling exercises done by athletes, esp. by wrestlers, pancratium contestants and fist fighters. Most likely, they also constituted a popular pastime among ordinary people. The term also used to denote >AKROCHEIRISMOS. See also >ARM WRESTLING.

AKROCHEIRISMOS, also known as *akrochirismos* or *akrocheiria* [Gk. *akrocheiriso* – wrestle at arm's length]; an ancient form of Gk. wrestling similar to >PANKRATION and also one of the pancratium techniques. It allowed finger and arm twisting. A contest ended when one of the fighters conceded defeat. A Sicilian wrestler famous for fighting in such a manner was nicknamed Akrocheirismos. Pausanias claims in his *Hellados Periegesis* that 'he could not defeat his opponents by bringing them down but always won by twisting their fingers' (VI, 4,2). A similar nickname – Akrochersites (Digital) – was given by the Greeks to Sostratus of Sicyon who according to Pausanias 'grabbed his opponents by their fingers and twisted them and would not let go until he noticed that the opponent refused to fight any longer' (VI, 4,1).

AKROTERI PUNCHING, the oldest known form of >BOXING, practiced according to fixed rules on the ancient island of Thera in the town of Akroteri. Located in the vicinity of Crete (approx. 60mi. away), the island remained within the Crete-Mycenaean culture. Around 1500 BC part of Thera was submerged as a result of a volcano erruption and an earthquake, sometimes associated with tectonic movements which around the same time caused the biblical deluge. The part of the island which survived is now called Santorini. No written text was preserved that would explain the local art of punching. Yet, while conducting lava excavations in Santorini in 1967-74, Gk. archeologist Spiridion Marinatos found a partly destroyed fresco portraying a punching fight between two boys wearing gloves similar to modern boxing gloves, except that they wore them on their right hands only. The role each hand played could have been different: one hand punching, while the other executed movements unknown today or was simply used to repel the opponent. The only elements of uniform are girdles and beads on the shoulder and neck of one of the fighters, which could have denoted his rank. The neatly cut hair is fixed into a tress and short locks at the front, around which the scalp is shaved and painted blue. The scene shows a graceful fight, lacking any clear signs of violence. This type of fight must have been quite significant for the local culture. The fresco entitled 'Boxing children' belonged to a residence that archeologists call the West House. Until the island was destroyed, Acroteri witnessed many forms of sport games and festivals, which is indicated by other paintings. The fight depicted in 'Boxing children' was surely part of their program. The fresco can be seen at the National Archeological Museum in Athens. See also >ANCIENT PUGILISM.

AK-SUNG, Turkmen for 'white bone'. A Turkmen folk team competition. Each team is composed of 10 players who select a field allowing for unrestricted movement. An elderly villager, acting in the capacity of a referee, throws a white bone (usu. from a camel or a horse) up in the air and the players have to intercept and then convey it, by means of short passes or throws, to a particular player standing at a certain distance from the others. If they achieve this, the team gets a point or wins the match.

AL SAWALJAH, Arab. for 'sticks for beating or attacking' [Arab. plur. of *al sawlajan* – crooked stick]. The number of players given in the oldest sources is not precise and according to some of them there were as many as 17 players. It seems, however, that usu. there were only 7. There are numerous mentions of al sawaljah in Persian literature. Some old stories of the Persian Sasanian Dynasty refer to Shapur, the son of Ardashir I (who ruled in the 3rd cent. BC), whose legitimacy was widely questioned. Ardashir, however, decided to recognize him as his successor when he saw Shapur play al sawaljah. This description does not mention horses and that is why many historians like to think of al sawaljah as one of the oldest forms of >FIELD HOCKEY. The great Persian poet of the Middle Ages, Al-Firdousi (932-1020, also known as Al-Ferdowsi), describes in his epic *Shah-nameh (Book of Kings)* the feats of prince Guschtaaba who mastered al sawaljah and defeated another ruler who had abducted his daughter and thus forced him to return her.

Al sawaljah was also known in Egypt, esp. during the reign of the Mamluk Dynasty when a special pitch known as Bab Alloq and later as Al-Quala was built in Cairo. In 1435 a Span. traveler P. Tafur described a game of al sawaljah he saw played at the court of the Eg. sultan Barsbay Malik al-Ashraf.

The Turks who conquered Persia borrowed amply from Persian culture. In this way they contributed to popularizing al sawaljah throughout the territories they occupied. After the Turks captured Constantinople in 1453, Sultan Mehmed II had an al sawaljah field built near Hagia Sophia. During the rule of Abbas I (1588-1629), around the time when Persia regained its independence after Arab and Turk. rule, the largest al sawaljah field in the world which also included spectators' stands was built between his royal palace and a mosque in Esfahan, then capital of Persia.

The cultural significance of al sawaljah was so great that many poets used it as a symbolic element in their religious metaphors. A Persian poet Abu Al-Majd Sana'i (d.1141) wrote about al sawaljah in his great poem *The Garden of Truth and the Law of the Path (Hadîqat al-haqîqa):*

He who acquired and understood faith
He mastered the ball and hammer of eternity.

In another poem he wrote:

You belong to Allah, wherever you go
For you are the ball sometimes,
And sometimes the hammer striking it.

Women were also allowed to play the game. One of the Persian stories mentions Princess Hemma-i who played al sawaljah to help her recover after the loss of her son. In his epic *Khassro-Shirina* a poet named Nidrami describes 17 girls playing al sawaljah on horses.

AL SAWLAJAN, an Arab. name for a crooked stick used in the original var. of the game that later evolved into >POLO. The name of the stick is in some places also the name of the game itself although most frequently the plural form of >AL SAWALJAH was used.

ALASKAN HIGH KICK, a folk jump-and-kick event popular among Native Alaskans. A player starts by grasping his foot by the sole with the opposite hand. The player jumps and tries to kick a small piece of fur hung on a wooden stand with the free foot while maintaining his hold on the other foot. After each series of attempts by all the players the target is raised by 2in. (about 5cm). The players have 3 attempts at each height. The player who kicks the target at the highest height will be declared the winner. In the event of a tie, the target will be lowered 1in. (about 2.5cm) and the competitors have 3 attempts. The one who kicks the target at this height the most times wins. If there is still no winner, the winner will be determined by counting the total number of kicks at all the previous heights, with the lowest number of successful attempts prevailing.

According to the local sports terminology Alaskan high kick is one of the so-called arctic sports. It is a separate event during the North Amer. Indigenous Games. Cf. >HITCH AND KICK, >ONE FOOT HIGH KICK, >TWO FOOT HIGH KICK.

The Arctic Sports, the Internet: http://www.firstnations.com/naig97/arctic-sports/as-alaskanhighkick.htm

AL-BA' 'A, an Arab game from the Qsim region resembling the Pol. >KLIPA, >SZTEKIEL, and other Eur. and Asian games such as the Pak. >GULLI DUNDA and involving driving a peg sharpened at both ends into the ground. The game has been described in M. Ibrahim al-Majman's dictionary of Arab sports and games as:

An interesting folk game that requires good light. That is why, most frequently, it is played in the summertime in the day or at night when the sun or moon shine. I do not have a clue where the name of the game comes from. In the Sdir and Najd area, it is called a miqra'a w bir (a stick and a well), and in the south of the kingdom [of Saudi Arabia] they call it a mqzara w bir. The number of players ranges from 2 to 11. A ba' 'a is a hard peg 10cm long and half an inch thick (about 1.27cm). The peg is well-polished and both ends are sharpened. The players also need a mi'm,l, i.e. a wooden stick 70cm long which is as flat as a ruler and 5cm wide, as well as a rectangular pit 15cm long, 3cm wide and 10cm deep. The pit is dug in the middle of a circle whose diameter is 10m. The ba' 'a is placed over the pit in a transverse position. The players form two teams. After it has been decided by lots which team is to start (team A), the starting team take their positions inside the circle and the other team (team B) stays outside the circle. One of the team A players stands in front of the pit holding a stick in his hand. One end of the stick is placed under the small peg placed over the pit. When he shouts, 'Algensau!', team B players shout 'Nad'wa bikom!' – this is the signal to start the game. The first player flicks the peg up and tries to hit it out of the circle. If he fails to do so and the peg lands within the circle or it is intercepted by team B, team A loses this round and team B takes over. When the peg lands outside the circle it remains in the possession of team A who try to drive it towards a stick put into the pit and belonging to one of the team B players. If they manage to hit the stick or if the peg lands within a stick's length of the pit, team A retains the possession of the peg. If they fail to do so, team B takes the peg over. Then the player who stood by the pit hits one of the ends of the peg with his stick to send it flying up in the air and then he hits the peg once again to send it out of the circle. If he does not succeed in doing so and the peg lands within the circle his team loses the round and team A takes over and starts the game anew. A hit which sends the peg flying up in the air is called a hedel. If the peg lands outside the circle, the player who sent it out continues to play giving consecutive numbers to each successful hit: hedlen [<hedel – second], *yittit (third), etc. The eleventh hit is called 'aša el-gadde (lit. grandmother's supper). At this stage the team A player is accompanied by the team B player who did not put the peg into the pit. As 'the guilty one' he has to run from the place where he made his last throw to the pit. He has to run very fast and keep repeating the words el-qed'd' qad'd'a. If he manages to reach the pit, he is saved. If not, he has to suffer another penalty, he will have to carry the player with the stick on his shoulders until they reach the pit. He cannot be assisted in this task by anyone. The player who hits the peg is allowed to run after the peg so that he may hit the peg once again when it is still in the air. This is still treated as one hit. However, the number of hits may never exceed eleven. The game is a lot of fun. It is slightly dangerous, however, especially that in the past it was played in densely populated places. How many a time was a passer-by hit on his head by the flying peg! That is why the game has to be played in an open and spacious area.*

[*Min al'abina ash-sha 'biyya* (*Our folk games*), 1983, 35-7]

Boxing children, *a fresco from Santorini portraying Akroteri punching.*

ALPINE SKIING OLYMPIC CHAMPIONS

MEN'S DOWNHILL

1948 Henri Oreiller, FRA 2:55.0
1952 Zeno Colo, ITA 2:30.8
1956 Toni Sailer, AUT 2:52.2
1960 Jean Vuarnet, FRA 2:06.0
1964 Egon Zimmermann, AUT 2:18.16
1968 Jean-Claude Killy, FRA 1:59.85
1972 Bernhard Russi, SWI 1:51.43
1976 Franz Klammer AUT 1:45.73
1980 Leonhard Stock, AUT 1:45.50
1984 Bill Johnson, USA 1:45.59
1988 Pirmin Zurbriggen, SWI 1:59.63
1992 Patrick Ortlieb, AUT 1:50.37
1994 Tommy Moe, USA 1:45.75
1998 Jean-Luc Cretier, FRA 1:50.11
2002 Fritz Strobl, AUT 1:39.13

continued on next page...

26

A WORLD SPORTS ENCYCLOPEDIA

ALPINE SKIING OLYMPIC CHAMPIONS

... continued from previous page

MEN'S SLALOM
1948 Edi Reinalter, SWI 2:10.3
1952 Othmar Schneider, AUT 2:00.0
1956 Toni Sailer, AUT 3:14.7
1960 Ernst Hinterseer, AUT 2:08.9
1964 Pepi Stiegler, AUT 2:11.13
1968 Jean-Claude Killy, FRA 1:39.73
1972 Francisco Ochoa, SPA 1:49.27
1976 Piero Gros, ITA 2:03.29
1980 Ingemar Stenmark, SWE 1:44.26
1984 Phil Mahre, USA 1:39.41
1988 Alberto Tomba, ITA 1:39.47
1992 Finn Christian Jagge, NOR 1:44.39
1994 Thomas Stangassinger, AUT 2:02.02
1998 Hans-Petter Buraas, NOR 1:49.31
2002 Jean-Pierre Vidal, FRA 1:41.06

MEN'S GIANT SLALOM
1952 Stein Eriksen, NOR 2:25.0
1956 Toni Sailer, AUT 3:00.1
1960 Roger Staub, SWI 1:48.3
1964 Francois Bonlieu, FRA 1:46.71
1968 Jean-Claude Killy, FRA 3:29.28
1972 Gustav Thöni, ITA 3:09.62
1976 Heini Hemmi, SWI 3:26.97
1980 Ingemar Stenmark, SWE 2:40.74
1984 Max Julen, SWI 2:41.18
1988 Alberto Tomba, ITA 2:06.37
1992 Alberto Tomba, ITA 2:06.98
1994 Markus Wasmeier, GER 2:52.46
1998 Hermann Maier, AUT 2:38.51
2002 Stephan Eberharter, AUT 2:23.28

MEN'S SUPER G
1988 Frank Piccard, FRA 1:39.66
1992 Kjetil Andre Aamodt, NOR 1:13.04
1994 Markus Wasmeier, GER 1:32.53
1998 Hermann Maier, AUT 1:34.82
2002 Kjetil André Aamodt, NOR 1:21.58

WOMEN'S DOWNHILL
1948 Hedy Schlunegger, SWI 2:28.3
1952 Trude Jochum-Beiser, AUT 1:47.1
1956 Madeleine Berthod, SWI 1:40.7
1960 Heidi Biebl, GER 1:37.6
1964 Christl Haas, AUT 1:55.39
1968 Olga Pall, AUT 1:40.87
1972 Marie-Theres Nadig, SWI 1:36.68
1976 Rosi Mittermaier, W. Ger 1:46.16
1980 Annemarie Moser-Pröll, AUT 1:37.52
1984 Michela Figini, SWI 1:13.36
1988 Marina Kiehl, FRG 1:25.86
1992 Kerrin Lee-Gartner, CAN 1:52.55
1994 Katja Seizinger, GER 1:35.93
1998 Katja Seizinger, GER 1:28.89
2002 Carole Montillet, FRA 1:39.56

WOMEN'S SLALOM
1948 Gretchen Fraser, USA 1:57.2
1952 Andrea Mead Lawrence, USA 2:10.6
1956 Renée Colliard, SWI 1:52.3
1960 Anne Heggtveit, CAN 1:49.6
1964 Christine Goitschel, FRA 1:29.86
1968 Marielle Goitschel, FRA 1:25.86
1972 Barbara Cochran, USA 1:31.24
1976 Rosi Mittermaier, W. Ger 1:30.54
1980 Hanni Wenzel, LIE 1:25.09
1984 Paoletta Magoni, ITA 1:36.47
1988 Vreni Schneider, SWI 1:36.69
1992 Petra Kronberger, AUT 1:32.68
1994 Vreni Schneider, SWI 1:56.01
1998 Hilde Gerg, GER 1:32.40
2002 Janica Kostelic, CRO 1:46.10

WOMEN'S GIANT SLALOM
1952 Andrea Mead Lawrence, USA 2:06.8
1956 Ossi Reichert, GER 1:56.5
1960 Yvonne Rügg, SWI 1:39.9
1964 Marielle Goitschel, FRA 1:52.24
1968 Nancy Greene, CAN 1:51.97
1972 Marie-Theres Nadig, SWI 1:29.90
1976 Kathy Kreiner, CAN 1:29.13
1980 Hanni Wenzel, LIE 2:41.66
1984 Debbie Armstrong, USA 2:20.98
1988 Vreni Schneider, SWI 2:06.49
1992 Pernilla Wiberg, SWE 2:12.74
1994 Deborah Compagnoni, ITA 2:30.97
1998 Deborah Compagnoni, ITA 2:50.59
2002 Janica Kostelic, CRO 2:30.01

WOMEN'S SUPER G
1988 Sigrid Wolf, AUT 1:19.03
1992 Deborah Compagnoni, ITA 1:21.22
1994 Diann Roffe-Steinrotter, USA 1:22.15
1998 Picabo Street, USA 1:18.02
2002 Daniela Ceccarelli, ITA 1:13.59

At the end of his description Ibrahim al-Majman, apparently unfamiliar with the Eur. counterparts of this sport, likens it to >GOLF.

ALFAMOS, Gk. *alphamos* [Gk. *affalomai* – bounce, jump down]; a type of long jump practiced in ancient Greece whereby a competitor would thrust his legs forward in a scissors-like manner; practiced mainly as an exercise by >HALMA athletes.

AL-GAFZ FAWGA AL-AYDI W AL-AQDAM, an Arab jump over the hands and legs of sitting people [Arab. *al-gaf* – jump + *fawga* – seat, sitting, *all-aydi* – hands + *al-aqdam* – legs], a type of competition popular among Assyrians living in Syria. During a contest 2 competitors act as the height scale and bar, not unlike the equipment used in high jump. To do this they sit on the ground in an L-seat position facing each other, their feet touching, and one of them raises one of his feet above the other so that the heel of the raised foot touches the big toe of the foot resting on the ground. The other competitors, who are not sitting, take a running jump over the feet of the competitors sitting on the ground. Next, the second sitting competitor adds to the height of his partner's feet the height of one of his own feet by raising his straight leg over the feet of his partner, heel to toe. This is followed by a series of jumps at this new height. Subsequently, the same sitting competitor places his leg above the 3 feet, thus putting the straight-leg 'bar' at the height of 4 'feet'. A series of jumps at the height marked by the uppermost foot follows. After the possibilities of raising the 'bar' by this method have been exhausted, the 2 sitting competitors raise their bodies to the last height achieved and add the palms of their hands one by one. The position of their arms at each subsequent height is marked by placing the splayed fingers of their hands on top of one another vertically so that the little finger of the lowermost hand is placed at the height of the big toe of the uppermost foot whereas the little finger of each subsequent hand touches the thumb of the hand directly above. After each limb has been added to mark a given height, all the competitors make their attempts. The competitor who clears the highest level wins. Given the fact that the length of each foot is usually 25--30cm and that the width of spread fingers is usually 15-20cm, the total height may reach up to 180--190cm. However, most of the time the competitors are unable to clear such heights.
Source: M. Abdalla. See >KHAZZA-LAVIZZA.

AL-HAGLA, an Arab game equivalent to >KLASY and >HOP-SCOTCH, and resembling >AL-HUD'D'A and >BERBER but played on a different field. Also known as a *'teba* in the town of Najid and its vicinity, al-hagla consists of hopping on one leg around a diagram drawn on the ground. The game has been described in the dictionary of Arab sports and games by M. Ibrahim al-Majman:

It is played by both boys and girls. There have to be at least two players. The players draw 10 fields on the ground and give each field a unique name: 'il-wahed [one]; 'il-tann [second]; 'il-talt [third]; 'iskin [knife]; 'id-dibb [bear]; al-mistrah [rest]; ag-ganne [paradise]; an-nar [fire]; mdaqq el-bzar [seeder]; al-mid'la' [germination].
The so-called qahf (a flat stone or a palm-sized wooden die) is placed in the first field. The rules of the game are similar to those observed in al-hud'd'a [...]. The ritual accompanying the game is, however, different. The winner holds the loser by the ear and they stand together on the al-mid'la' field. Here the winner says twayyis mba' (lit. the mule has been sold) and the loser replies mba' (has been sold). The winner goes on to say ummak bissuq tbi' sluqq (your mother sells young beet leaves at the market) and the loser replies mba' (has been sold), etc.
[*Min al'abina ash-sha 'biyya* (*Our folk games*), 1983, 54-6].

AL-HOL, a game popular in the Gulf countries. The object of the game is to get through the defenses of an opposing team and reach a certain spot on the field. A team usu. consists of 10-14 players. A player (*saari*) has to reach a place called a *mahba* after passing the tackling players from the defending team.
There are several types of players: a *saari* (a running player), a *haris* (the defender of *mahba*) and a *tba'* who accompanies the *saari* and protects him against the defenders' tackles or, should such a need arise, replaces him in trying to reach the *mahba*.
The game has been described in the dictionary of Arab sports and games by M. Ibrahim al-Majman:

Croatian knights stand in line before they start to run the Alka competition at the 287th traditional Alka Festival in Sinj, Croatia.

First they decide where the mahba is going to be, then they select a saari and then the direction in which the attacking team is going to run, i.e. the so-called sarwa. When the saari is touched by a defending team's player the defending team becomes the attacking team and vice versa unless the tba' manages to immediately touch the player who touched the saari. Then the attacking team may continue their attempt to reach the mahba. When the saari manages to pass all the defending team's players including the haris and touches the mahba, his team scores a hol, i.e. a goal. The game becomes interesting when both teams are on a par and one team has only a tiny lead over the other.
[*Min al'abina ash-sha 'biyya* (*Our folk games*), 1983, 50-2]

There is no time limit, a game ends when the players decide so. It is often played in the evenings on summer days after supper. No special outfit is required.

AL-HUD'D'A, an Arab game similar to such Eur. games as the Pol. >KLASY, Eng. >HOP SCOTCH, and another Arab game known as >BERBER. Al-hud'd'a stands for a surface with lines or a chessboard and refers to a figure drawn on the ground. Competitors hop around this diagram. It has been described in the dictionary of Arab sports and games by M. Ibrahim al-Majman as:

An individual game played both during the day and at night since it does not require particularly good light [...]. There have to be at least two players. To play the game they need a flat bone or a small wooden block. The field, preferably sandy, is divided into four 250x70cm boxes. The first box is called an al-mal'aba, the second a malina, the third an umm hd'ud' and the fourth an umm el-qbis. The third box is divided by two parallel lines. At the beginning of the game the players stand at the starting line. One of them throws the bone into the first box and then hops on one leg so as to touch the bone which he kicks only once to send it out of the box. He continues on the same leg to touch the bone lying outside the box. When outside of the field the player can rest for a while standing on both legs. In this way he passes the first box. Now, he throws the bone into the second box and hops on one leg from the 1st box into the 2nd box where he can rest standing on both legs. Then the player lifts one foot and with the toes of the other foot he pushes the bone away to remove it from the box. Hopping on one leg he has to go through the 1st box to leave the field. The leg on which the competitor hops cannot touch the dividing line between the boxes. In this way the competitor completes the 2nd box. In order to score the 3rd box he does the same, however, the bone cannot land between the two parallel lines dividing box 3. The player cannot touch the ground between these lines with his foot, either. While hopping towards the 3rd box he can rest on both legs while in box 2. When driving the bone out of the filed the player can do it in a number of stages: first he can kick it into box 2, where he can rest on both legs, and then to box 1 and only then outside the whole field. Hopping on one leg from box to box the player has to touch the bone each time. After completing the 3rd box the competitor rests outside the field and from there he has to throw the bone into the 4th box. Then he hops on one leg into box 1, then box 2 (where he can rest on both legs), and through box 3 into box 4 where he stops on one leg and touches the bone with the foot. He hits it with the toes and moves it into box 3, then into box 2 (where he can rest on both legs) and then to box 1 and finally out of the field altogether. The last jump has to be planned in such a way that the player's foot touches the bone lying outside the field. In this way he completes the 4th box and scores one point.
In the next round it is the other competitor's turn to play. The game ends when one of the competitors makes a mistake. The number of rounds is determined before the start of the game. Moves that are disallowed are: touching the ground with the other foot (unless in box 2); touching any of the lines with the foot; placing the bone between the dividing lines in box 3 or touching this area with the foot; driving the bone out of the field on its sides; failure to touch the bone (whether lying in the next box or outside the field) with the foot. When any of the above infringements occur, the player is eliminated and the second one takes over. If the second player also makes a mistake, the first player resumes his turn from the box where he made the mistake. Within one given box the player can move on one leg in all directions. This is important because it makes it possible for him to assume a good position before making a jump.
[*Min al'abina ash-sha 'biyya* (*Our folk games*), 1983, 40-3]

AL-HUFRA, Arab. for 'hole in the ground'. The game consists of throwing pits into a hole called a *buh* (lit. a sea shell; perhaps a sea shell was placed on the bottom of a hole to facilitate taking the pits out of the hole; *buh* also describes the way in which the pits are arranged). The game of al-hufra has been described by M. Ibrahim al-Majman in *Min al'abina ash-sha 'biyya* (*Our folk games*). The game is played according to exactly the same rules as those observed in >AD-DAYRA and >LU'BAT AL-BUH:

A player moves 5m away from the place called buh. After the order in which the players will take their turns has been determined by lots, all the respective players shoot by flicking their fingers. If one of them hits the seeds already in the hole they all are handed over to him. When he misses, the player standing on the other side of the hole at the greatest distance from the buh starts shooting. A player takes possession of all the seeds in the hole only when the pit used for shooting stays in there.

ALINDISSIS, also *alindesis*, a var. of Gk. wrestling where fighters initially competed in the standing position but with fighting on the ground also allowed [Gk. *alindeomai* – wallow]. Alindissis stood in direct opposition to the standing-position wrestling called >ORTHOPÁLE. The wrestlers fought until one of them decided to give up. See also >PALE.
K. Paleologos, 'Wrestling', N. Yalouris, ed., *The Olympic Games in Ancient Greece*, 1976; W. Baxter, 'Les luttes traditionnelles a traverse le monde', J.J. Barreau and G. Jaouen, eds., *Les jeux populaires*, 1998.

ALKA, a type of Dalmatian lance-and-ring horse race [Croatian *alka* – ring, Turk. *halka* – ring, hoop, rim]. Widespread in the past, alka had many local varieties. In the version preserved in Sinj the object of the game is to put a lance through a target of 2 metal rings of about 5 fingers in diameter (i.e. approx. 15.8cm, for according to the trad. Croatian system of weights and measurements 1 finger equals 2.634cm). The rings are hung on a specially braided hemp rope stretched across a road and attached to poles placed on either side of the road. The rings are concentric, i.e. the smaller one is inside the larger and is attached to it by 3 cords which makes them look similar to the Mercedes trademark. The cords divide the target area into 3 unequal scoring zones between the 2 rings. The number of points scored depends on the zone hit by the lance. A hit in the middle of the smaller ring gives 3pts., a hit in one of the 2 smaller zones between the rings is worth 2pts.

and a hit in the remaining, larger zone scores 1pt. If a competitor picks the rings up with the lance then throws them up in the air and catches them again with the lance his score is doubled. The lance is 2.8m long and the run-up distance is up to 170m. Each competitor has 3 attempts. In the event of a tie, the number of attempts is increased until a winner emerges.

History and tradition. Alka is a relic of the old knights' tournaments. Alka contests were held since the Middle Ages in many Dalmatian cities such as Zadar (until 1820), Makarska (until 1832) and Imotskom (until about 1840). It also had an on-foot var., popular in Split, Šibenik, and Skradina which is now extinct. Alka is best preserved in Sinj, hence its full name: *sinjska alka*. Sinjska alka contests are held on the Sinj-Split highway to commemorate a battle of 1715 when the Sinj inhabitants, led by I. Filipović Gréić and P. Vucković, repelled an attack by a Bosnian pasha Mehmed. Subsequently Filipović issued an edict establishing knightly horse races 'so that posterity should not forget about the brave feats of their ancestors'. The competition is held on the Sunday closest to the battle's anniversary, 9 August.

Alka contests are preceded by elaborate rituals. Traditionally, only contestants from Sinj and Centinska Krajina are allowed to take part. The contestants dubbed 'alkars' (*alkari*) prepare appropriate weapons and ornate clothing, often worn only on this occasion. The Sinj Museum has a large collection of weapons and clothing that can be rented by those wishing to participate in the contest or in the procession that accompanies it. Alkar clothing may also be purchased at the local market. The parade of the alkars that precedes the contest proper is the highlight of the whole celebration. Each member of such a procession has his place determined by local custom. The column is led by pages (*alkarski momci*) and their master (*harambaša*). They are followed by a *štinoša*, i.e. a shield bearer, and mace bearers (*buzdovanari*). Then, there are 2 boys from Centinska Krajina leading a horse named Edek to remind everyone of the horse taken in 1715 from the Turk. pasha. The horse wears the original ornate caparison captured from the Turks. Edek is followed by 2 rows of the alkars themselves. Each alkar is accompanied by an associate (*kum*) and a page (*momak*). Both the *kum* and *momak* wear regional folk costumes. In the middle of the train there is the headman and the chief referee of the contest (called *nadzornik natjecanja* in Croatian and *alaj-cauš* in Turkish). After the alkars have paraded in front of the guests of honor, the trumpeters proclaim the start of the competition. An alka tournament always attracts many spectators from all over Dalmatia. Older burghers, who in their youth used to be alkars themselves, act as tournament referees. Cf. >QUINTAIN, >RUNNING AT THE RING.

Alka, EJ, 1955, 1, 67-8; J. Boko, *Sinjska alka*, Jardan, 1927, 131-6; Š. Milinovic, *Hrvatske uspomene iz Dalmacije. Sinjska alka*, Vienac, 1895, 16, 257-60; L. Žunic-Baš, *Folk Traditions in Yugoslavia. Ten Tours*, 1965.

ALL-AROUND, an Ang.-Sax. var. of >DECATHLON, popular esp. in the USA, which includes: 100yd. >SPRINT, >SHOT-PUT, >HIGH JUMP, 880yd. >RACE WALK, >HAMMER THROW, >POLE VAULT, 120yd. >HURDLES, 56lb. >WEIGHT THROW, broad jump and 1mi. run. It has been played since 1884 during all-Amer. championships (excl. 1915, 1922-1941, 1943-1949). In 1914, 1916 and 1918 the Amer. all-around champion was Avery Brundage, later president of the IOC.

AL-LAQSA, Arab. for '(small) stones', a game played in most, if not all, Arab countries and particularly popular in Syria and Saudi Arabia, esp. in the town of Al-Ihsa and in the neighboring areas.

In the Najd area the game is called an as-saqla [plur. masaqil]. The name comes, most likely, from the fact that it employs small stones that are called masaqil except one stone dubbed a hal [Arab. for 'uncle'] or a milqas. [...] The number of players varies from 2 to 6. However, the more there are, the more interesting and fascinating the game becomes. Both sexes are allowed to play. There is no time limit. A game of al-laqsa may last until the players tire of it or until it gets dark or until they lose their patience. A game consists of the following stages:
Stage one (a kamš). A player takes all the stones with his hand, mixes them and then tosses them up so that they fall onto the back of his hand. If even one of the stones falls to the ground the player is eliminated from the game for one round unless the players decide otherwise.

Stage two. The stones are scattered on the ground and then each stone is picked up individually. It may be difficult to pick up those stones that are touching one another since it is not allowed to move any stone other than the one being lifted (each time a stone moves a player is eliminated). The player cannot separate touching stones by blowing or moving them apart with a stick. Here, he has to determine exactly how the stones are lying so that he can decide which of the stones may be picked up safely. Of the five stones lying on the ground, the player selects one which is then called a milqas. He tosses the milqas up and while it is in the air he picks up one of the four stones lying on the ground. The player has to coordinate his movements in such a way that he catches the falling milqas while holding the stone picked from the ground on his palm. In this way the player collects all the stones from the ground. Each stone that was picked up earlier has to remain in the player's fist. Each time the player wants to pick up the next stone from the ground, he has to toss the milqas up first. Once he has picked up all the stones, he keeps them in his clenched fist.

Stage three. All the stones are on the ground. After tossing the milqas up, the player picks up two selected stones without moving any of the stones.

Stage four. All the stones are on the ground. After tossing the milqas up, the player picks up three selected stones. Only then does he pick up the fourth one. While collecting the first three stones the fourth stone must not move.

Stage five. All the stones lay on the ground. After tossing the milqas up, the player picks up all the stones at one go [...].

Stage six (a tazaqzoq). All the stones lay on the ground. The player picks up the milqas, selects one stone and picks it up and only then does he toss the milqas up while holding the other stone. Then he places the first stone on the ground. The player repeats this action four times until he picks up and puts back all four stones. The remaining part of this stage is similar to stage three but the player throws the milqas up in the air only after he has picked up two stones from the ground. So he repeats this action twice.

Stage seven (a talhus). With all the stones in the clenched fist, the player tosses the milqas up and immediately drops all the stones on the ground. Before the milqas falls to the ground, the player tries to draw a line on the ground with his index finger, then collect all the stones and while holding them catch the milqas with the same hand.

Stage eight (a daqqa). The player tosses the milqas up and places his right open palm on the ground and then tries to collect all the stones and catch the falling milqas with the same hand.

Stage nine (a mabhar – a censer). The competitor bends his left palm into a tent-like shape so that the stones can be placed between the fingers. Then he tosses the milqas up and has to put one stone (starting from the one placed between the little and ring finger) in the tent (i.e. put it in the space between the palm and the ground) and catch the milqas before it falls to the ground. After all four stones have been put in the tent, the left hand is freed and with his right hand the player has to pick the stones up from the ground and catch the milqas before it falls to the ground. The game may be made more difficult as, after the first milqas throw, an opponent may demand that the player put two, three or all the stones into the tent in one attempt.

Stage ten (a fawqiyye – catching from above). The player places his open left palm on the left thigh. After scattering the stones on the ground he asks his opponent which of the stones should be the milqas. Then, the player throws the selected stone up in the air and repeats the sequence of actions performed during stage two but does not place the individual stones on the ground but holds them in his hand until the end. So when he makes the last throw he should have three stones in his fist.

Stage eleven (a tahtiyye – catching from below). The player places his open left palm on the ground, to the left of the left thigh. Then, he repeats all the actions as performed during stage ten with one exception. Each time after the player has tossed the milqas up, he covers the stones with the left hand. If, during this or any of the preceding stages, any of the stones falls to the ground the player is eliminated for one round.

Stage twelve (a dzwara). The player splays the thumb and index finger of the left hand and touches the ground with their tips so that they make a bridge-like or crescent-shaped structure. After the stones have been scattered on the ground the opponent determines which of them should be the milqas. Now, the player has to toss the milqas up with his right hand to such a height that he has enough time to push one of the stones lying on the ground under the bridge and catch the falling milqas. After all four stones have been pushed under the bridge the player collects them with the right hand and then tosses the milqas up still holding the stones. When the milqas is still in the air, the player drops the stones to the ground and then catches the milqas before it falls on the ground. The most important rule of the game is that the milqas should always be caught with the right hand. A game starts with the words hilli biha to which the opponent replies tani biha. Each instance of cheating is called a zonaqš; la tzoneq means 'don't cheat'. The players may introduce modifications to the rules of the game at will.

[Min al'abina ash-sha 'biyya (Our folk games), 1983, 44-5]

AL-LIBIDA, an Arab game of hide-and-seek.

It is popular among both boys and girls. It can be played anywhere (there are 2 teams of 2 or more players), even in apartments. It is also known as a tahfiyye, glimd'a and gmi'a. After finding a good place to hide all the members of the hiding team shout, 'Ša'rur!' (find me). When the players of one team are looking for their places to hide, the players from the other team should

WORLD SPORTS ENCYCLOPEDIA

A

ALPINE SKIING EVENTS

Downhill

Slalom

Giant slalom

Super-G

Hansruedi Gertsch, Ralf Djmovits, Eveline Binsack and Stefan Sigrist (the order of the climbers could not be identified by source) on their way to the top of the Eiger mountain in the Swiss Alps, Friday, September 10, 1999. It was the first climb of the Eiger via the tricky north face.

19th cent. alpinism.

Modern alpinism.

keep their eyes closed. When the members of the searching team find a player from the hiding team they score 1pt. and it is their turn to hide. When the hiding team manages to reach and touch a pre-determined spot, it scores a point.

[*Min al'abina ash-sha 'biyya (Our folk games)*, 1983, 53-4]

AL-MUTABARA, see >LU'BAT AL-BUH.

ALPINE COMBINATION, see >ALPINE SKIING.

ALPINE SKIING, a type of >SNOW SKIING incl. events in which the objective is, generally, to ski downhill along a set route as fast as possible. The 2 main events are >DOWNHILL SKIING and >SKI SLALOM. There are also combined events: downhill plus slalom or downhill plus slalom plus giant slalom. Even though there are many similarities between alpine skiing and freestyle skiing, such as racing downhill, >FREESTYLE SKIING has not been traditionally considered a discipline of alpine skiing. **History.** As the name implies, alpine skiing was born in the Alps, with Brit. sportsmen actively involved in the process. In the 19th cent., Brit. people played an important part in many winter sports, including >ALPINISM. However, the alpine nations (Italy, Austria, Germany, Switzerland, and France) came to dominate the discipline early on. In the 2nd half of the 19th cent., the main centers of alpine skiing were located in those countries, including Cortina D'Ampezzo, Chamonix, Davos, Garmisch-Partenkirchen, Innsbruck and St. Moritz. Most of W.Ol.G. and major international events, such as World Cup competitions, were organized at those locations.

At the beginning of the expansion of alpine skiing, the British could not overcome the resistance of the Scandinavians, who held that alpine skiing 'contradicted the principles of skiing'. In 1926, the Brit. members of the Alpine Club issued a memorandum with a draft of alpine skiing rules and sent it out to all national ski associations, asking them to include alpine skiing in the program of the W.Ch. As there was no reply, they organized in 1931 the first independent alpine skiing W.Ch. at Mürren, Switzerland. After a period of discussions on the alleged superiority of Nordic skiing over alpine skiing, which culminated in the 1930s, the Scand. countries gradually began to take part in alpine events, and the role of Canada and the US grew after 1930, with more and more skiing centers being set up, esp. in the Rocky Mts. The Scandinavians, Canadians, and Americans later proved capable organizers of alpine events, hosting Winter Ol.G. and taking top places in the competitions. Among Asian nations, Japan was the first to achieve a high level of alpine skiing, organizing many prestigious events, incl. two

W.Ol.G. (Sapporo 1972 and Nagano 1998). Leisure alpine skiing has also developed in N India, with 2 important centers in Gulmang (Kashmir) and Kufri (Himachal Pradesh). Among the most famous competitors in the history of alpine skiing are multiple W.Ol.G. and W.Ch. medallists such as the Austrians A. 'Tony' Sailer (b. 1935), K. Schranz (b. 1938) and F. Klammer (b. 1953); the Frenchman J.C. Killy (b. 1943); the Italian G. Thoeni (b. 1951, 4-time winner of the World Cup, among other prizes); the Swede I. Stenmark (b. 1958); the Luxembourger M. Girardelli (5-time World Cup winner); and among women, the Austrians M. Moser-Proell (b. 1953, 5-time World Cup winner 1971-75), and P. Kronberger, V. Schneider (Switzerland), and M. Walliser (France), who dominated ladies' alpine events of the 1980s and 1990s.

ALPINISM, mountain climbing in the Alps. In the 19th cent. the Alps, due to their favorable location in the heart of Europe, became the first mountain range to be explored by Eur. climbers. This followed from a number of factors, the most important being 1) the fact that 19th-cent. Europe was the place where the idea of modern sport was developed and that extended into >MOUNTAIN CLIMBING; 2) the Alps, located in the center of the Eur. continent, attracted climbers from neighboring countries where there were no mountain ranges suitable for climbing; 3) the fact that there were many trading and communication routes connecting the south and north of Europe that led through the Alps which resulted in a well-developed network of hotels and inns as well as chalets and that mountain guides were widely available. This greatly facilitated the exploration of the Alps for tourist and recreational purposes. The absence of such favorable conditions resulted in the fact that the Pol. Tatra Mountains were only made accessible to tourists and mountaineers well over 100yrs. later than the Alps and almost a century later than the Himalayas and the Andes. It was Brit. climbers who shaped alpinism as a sport. The fact that the unique philosophy, ethics and social standards of alpinism were shaped by the representatives of the Brit. Isles, which themselves lack any major mountain ranges, is among the greatest paradoxes in the history of world sport.

History. The origins of alpinism date back to 1336 when the renowned Ital. poet Petrarch climbed Mt. Ventoux (at 1,920m). Twelve of the most important Alpine peaks had been climbed by 1600. In 1786 a Fr. climber M.G. Paccard with his guide J. Belmont were the first to reach the summit of Mont Blanc, at 4,810m. The most significant events in the history

of alpinism are the ascent of the Wetterhorn by Sir A. Wills (in 1854) and the climbing of Mont Blanc without the assistance of guides by 4 Englishmen – Hudson, Kennedy and Christopher and Grenville Smith (1855). Within the next decade the English climbed all the highest and most difficult peaks in the Alps. In 1865 E. Whymper climbed the most daunting of all Alpine peaks – the Matterhorn (at 4,478m). The Alpine Club based in London was estab. in 1857. A number of local Alpine clubs such as the Österreichischer Alpenverein (1862) and the Schweizer Alpen Club (1863) were estab. soon afterwards. In 1863 the London club started publishing *The Alpine Journal*. The local clubs were set up to match the British in their accomplishments which is best exemplified by the famous address by R.T. Simler entitled *To the Swiss climbers and friends of the Alps*. Soon after a number of national Alpine associations were estab. in France, Italy and the US. The period between 1890-1914 is known as the silver age in the history of alpinism. After all the major Alpine summits had been climbed, discovering new ascent routes became the priority of climbers. A.F. Mummery was undoubtedly the most outstanding climber of that period. After a quiet period during WWI and the worldwide crisis in the 1920s and '30s alpinism developed into so-called 'extreme climbing' based on looking for the most difficult routes at the most difficult times of year. In 1931 T. and F. Schmidt climbed the north face of the Matterhorn and in 1936 the infamous (due to the large number of fatal accidents there) north face of the Eiger was finally conquered. These events mark the end of the explorative period in the history of alpinism. Already at the turn of the 19th cent., mountain climbers shifted their interest onto the more difficult and less accessible mountain ranges of the Himalayas, the Andes, and the mountains of Africa. By the end of the 1930s the Alps had ceased to be the center of mountain climbing, although they did remain an attractive training ground for climbers. Moreover, as a way of approaching nature, the philosophy of the human struggle against the forces of nature and space, the metaphysics of solitude, and the escape from the bustle of industrialized civilization, all originating from the period of the exploration of the Alps, remained a truly humanistic appeal unmatched by other sports. That is why alpinism ceased to be merely the art of mountain climbing and became a way of life for those seeking an alternative lifestyle to that offered by 20th-cent. civilization. And although various mountain ranges higher than the Alps pose greater challenges for mountain climbers, it was the Alps and Alpine climbers that created this coherent

system of intellectual principles. All subsequent systems of thought are still based on the mountain philosophy as shaped in the Alps in the 19th century. Although alpinism in the original meaning of the term stands for mountain climbing in the Alps, it is often extended to mean any mountain climbing activities. It was used in this sense in the name of the Polish Alpine Association (Polski Związek Alpinizmu), although the activities pursued by its members are not restricted only to climbing in the Alps.

ALTER BÄR, Ger. for 'an old bear', a type of a running game; see >PLINIE.

AMERICAN BOWLING, in the US a game usu. associated with *ten pin bowling*, also referred to as *ten pins*, as 10 pins are placed in an equilateral triangle with 1 corner pointing toward the players. In the first row there is 1 pin, in the second 2, in the third 3 and in the fourth 4. The following var. of the game can be distinguished according to the type of pins.
Big-pin bowling, with pins 15in. (38.1cm) high that weigh 3lbs. 10oz. (roughly 1.5kg); the ball weighs 10-16lbs. (about 4.5-7kg), and it is informally accepted that women use lighter balls than men; the diameter of the ball is 8in. (21.6cm), the circumference is 27in. (68.58cm); each ball has 3 apertures in it for the index and middle fingers and the thumb.
Small-pin bowling, or **duckpins**; pins are $9^3/_8$in. (23.81cm) high, $4^1/_8$in. (10.5cm) in diameter and weigh 1lb. 8oz. A standard small-pin bowling ball has no fingers holes and it is smaller and lighter than in ten-pin bowling; it is 5in. (12.7cm) in diameter and weighs 3lbs. 12oz. (1.5876kg).
Rubberband duckpin, in this var. each pin in its thickest place is belted with rubber, making the game more dynamic when the ball hits the pins. The game has the same playing rules and technical standards as small pin bowling, above. Pins of a similar shape and also with bands of rubber but of a slightly different size are used in the Canadian var. of bowling known as >FIVEPINS.
Candlepins, the name derives from the characteristic slender shape of the pins, each 15in. tall (about 38cm). The pin has a symmetrical shape and can be placed on the ground on either tapered end. The ball is smaller than in other var. of bowling and has a diameter of 4½in. (approx. 11.5cm). Rather than the trad. black, the ball is red. The automatic device setting up the pins is also different due to the unique shape of the pins. Each pin slides down a special gutter into a trough in a conveyor belt, which moves crosswise. The belt passes the pins one by one on to the upper part of the feed, where they are put upright. Then, a frame grips the pins in the desired configuration and sets them up back on the track. The rules for candlepins do not differ from those in standard big-pin bowling. The popularity of candlepins in the USA and other Eng.-speaking countries is slipping. It is, however, practiced as the main var. of bowling in New England, esp. Massachusetts, the seat of the Massachusetts Bowling Association. Some historians argue that candlepins is the oldest var. of bowling, pointing out the similarities between candlepins and the pins painted on the walls of some Eg. pharaohs.
For all the above var. the same track standards are used, 60ft. (18.3m) length and 104cm width; the game is played individually or in teams of 2-5 players. One round consists of 10 turns, 2 throws per turn (except for candlepins and duckpins, in which there are 3 throws per each turn). The weight of each ball is tested on a special scale, and its size is inspected with a simple metal or plastic frame with a round hole, through which the ball should pass without resistance. Each pin that is knocked over scores 1pt.; if a player knocks over all the pins with one bowl, he receives the bonus of 2 additional throws and the points he scores during these throws. Any sports outfit is accepted; players usually wear multi-colored, soft-soled, lace-up sports shoes with heels of hard gum.
Technique and tactics. The ball is obligatorily thrown underhand, usu. after 4 steps. Neither during nor after the throw, until the ball reaches the pins, can one touch or transgress the foul line, i.e. the end line of the approach.
History. The tradition of this game does not differ from that of other bowling games. Various Eur. var. were brought over to N.America by emigrants, esp. Ger. and Du.; other forms began to emerge from these games and an attempt was made at standardizing them in 1895 by the Amer. Bowling

Congress, ABC. In 1901, under ABC auspices, the first men's championship was organized. ABC's official publishing house is *Bowling Magazine*. In 1916 the Women's International Bowling Congress, WIBC was founded, while in 1935 the Amer. Junior Bowling Congress, AJBC was estab. as an organization for youths under 18 yrs. of age. The next stage of the development of Amer. bowling was the creation of the Professional Bowlers' Association (PBA) in 1958. As a quickly developing discipline, the sport soon emerged as a profitable branch of the sports and entertainment industry. The owners of bowling facilities founded the Bowling Proprietors' Association of America, BPAA, which sponsors annual All-Star Match Game Championships in the USA. Since 1987 the Amer. Machine and Foundry Company, a producer of bowling facilities and other sports equipment, has risen to the fore among bowling-alley proprietors and operators. In 1994 it became the biggest bowling proprietors' association, with 413 bowling-alleys. Outside the US, AMF owns 120 alleys.
The most remarkable player ever is D. Carter from St. Louis, 6-time Bowler of the Year, fourfold winner of the All-Star Championship PBA, fivefold Champion at the World Invitational and at many other events. Some outstanding players after WWII

Bowling legend Dick Webber bowls on an AMF regulation wooden lane in the middle of Broad Street in front of the New York Stock Exchange.

The world's No. 1 ranked bowler and PBA player of the year in 1999, Parker Bohn III, bowls in the Japan Cup Tournament in Tokyo.

are D. Webber and T. Hennessey, and among women M. Ladewig. In the 1960s the number of ABC members in the United States reached 5 million, with over 3 million women in WIBC. The number of bowling alleys exceeded 11,000 with 160,000 tracks approved by ABC.
Outside the USA Amer. bowling did not gain much immediate popularity due to the existence of other bowling games already well-rooted in local tradition. In Canada, however, Amer. bowling was most readily adopted, though duckpin was given preference there, unlike in the USA. In 1928, the Can. National Duckpin Bowling Congress (NDBC) was estab., and began to exert influence back onto the USA, where the Amer. Rubberband Duckpin Congress was set up in affiliation with the Can. organization. In the 1950s and 1960s intense advertising campaigns resulted in a gradual development of Amer. bowling in such countries as Canada, the UK, Germany, Denmark, Norway, Sweden, Finland, and Australia. Consequently, in affiliation with Fédération Internationale des Quilleurs, FIQ, the World Tenpin Bowling Association (WTBA) was founded as an autonomous wing of FIQ. Under the auspices of FIQ-WTBA the World Tenpin Team Cup is organized. Also the World Ninepin Bowling Association co-

operates closely with FIQ. The champions include not only Amer. players, such as L. Zikes (1963) and M. Soudt (1975), or R. Steelsmith (1987), but also, with increasing frequency, representatives of other nations: e.g. Swedes G. Algeskog (1954), N. Backström (1955) and M. Karlsson (1983), Finns K. Asukas (1958) and M. Koivuniemi (1991), Britons D. Pond (1967), or Austrl. E. Thompson (1979). Amer. bowling is also rapidly developing in Asian countries, esp. Japan and Malaysia, and in Arab countries, esp. United Arab Emirates, whose representatives have even held the chairs of FIQ Vice-president and Secretary General. P.S. Nathar from Malaysia has been the President of WTBA since 1999. Among women, players from Eng.-speaking countries dominate, esp. those from the USA and Canada, e.g. Amer. H. Shablis (world champion in 1963 and 1967), S. Jo Shiery (1987), Can. C. Willis (1991) and the player from the Commonwealth of Puerto Rico, A. Gonsales. Also representatives of other countries have been awarded championship titles, e.g. Ger. A.D. Hafker (1975), and Filipino B. Coo (1979 and 1983).
H. Harrison, *Play the Game. Ten Pin Bowling* (1988); J. Lowerson, 'Bowls and Bowling', EWS (1996, I, 139-147); P.J. McDonough, Bowling, EAI, 1979, 4, 367-370); J.L. Martin, R.E. Tandy i C. Agne-Traub, *Bowling* (1994); Consultant: G. Cwojdziński.

American 10-pin bowling equipment.

American postage stamps honoring legendary football coaches.

Bear Bryant
USA 32
Vince Lombardi
USA 32
Pop Warner
USA 32
George Halas
USA 32

AMERICAN FOOTBALL, a pop. Amer. game played between 2 teams with the use of an oval-shaped leather-covered ball. Each team consists of up to 45 players, including substitutes, only 11 of which may be on the field during play, usu. as separate teams for offense and defense.
Rules of the game. The object of the game is to score more points than the opponent. To achieve that, each team must, while in possession of the ball, force its way as far as possible into the opponent's half and thereby reach the end zone. When advancing on the field, a team has to carry the ball at least 10yds. (about 9m) forward in a max. of 4 attempts, called 'downs'. If they succeed, another series of 4 downs is granted in order to cover another span of 10yds., etc. If they fail, possession of the ball goes to the other team. A common 4th-down play, conceding the unlikelihood of completing a 10-yd. gain is the punt, when the ball is kicked deep into the defenders' field in anticipation of a turn-over. Unlike in >RUGBY, from which modern Amer. football evolved, the ball can be passed forward, but only from behind the line of scrimmage. The best way to score points, achieving the greatest amount of them at one attempt (6), is the 'touchdown', i.e. carrying or catching the ball beyond the goal line. A successful touchdown grants the right for a so-called

A WORLD SPORTS ENCYCLOPEDIA

The San Francisco '49ers are a day late and a dollar short as the Washington Redskins lay it on the line.

'conversion', i.e. an attempt to score 1 or 2 extra points from a line set between the inbound lines at the minimal distance of 3yds. (2.74m) from the goal line (in college football the distance is 2yds. – 1.83m). Those extra points can be scored in 3 ways: 1pt. for placing the kicked ball over the 10-ft. high crossbar and between the goalposts; in professional games – 1pt. for another touchdown beyond the rear goal line, in the college version – 2pts. Extra points can also be scored within a team's own goal, if the defending team plays the so-called 'safety', i.e. passes the ball beyond the end line, or when the defenders intercept the ball or seize a dropped (fumbled) ball, e.g. when preventing the attackers from scoring a point. Scoring points from deep in the field, by kicking the ball above the crossbar and in between the goalposts, can be attempted at any time during the match, though it is generally resorted to only during a 4th down when the completion of a 10-yd. gain seems unlikely. Called a 'field goal', a successful kick of this kind scores 3pts. Before 1909 a field goal scored 5pts. Records of the longest field goal are registered and the current record of 67yds. was estab. in 1977 by Russell Exleben. The same distance was achieved by Sten Little, also in 1977, and by Joe Williams in 1978.

Professionals and university teams play 60min., whereas college teams play 48min. Thus a match is divided into 15- or 12-min. quarters. A break after the 1st quarter is 15min., after the 2nd – 30min., but after the 3rd it takes only as long as is necessary to

cerning any matter related to the match are final; the umpire – taking a position behind the defending team's half, supervises the uniforms, gear, and players' behavior; the head linesman – always positioned at the constantly fluctuating line at which the ball is being competed for ('the line of scrimmage'), sees that the rules of the game are observed; the line judge – assists the head linesman; the field judge – keeps the time and controls the scoring board; and the back judge – supervises the back part of the field where no major actions are being carried out at a given moment.

Playing field and equipment. The playing field is 120yds. long by 53yds. 1ft. wide, with 2 end zones 10yds. deep. It is within these end zones that 6-pt. touchdowns can be scored. The playing field is covered with perpendicular stripes or yard lines that are marked every 5yds. (4.57m). Viewed from above the lines resemble a grill, hence their name – the gridiron. The line crossing the field in the middle, 50yds. (45.72m) from each end, is referred to as the 50-yd. line, while the incremental lines approaching either end are called the 45-yd. line, 40-yd. line, 35-yd. line, etc. Portable vertical markers easily visible to both players and spectators are manned at the sideline to indicate the distance remaining to achieve a 10-yd. gain within the allotted 4 downs. The field is also divided in 3 parts by 2 longitudinal inbound lines, also known as inbound marks or hash marks, that delimit the space for each restart of play. After each tackle, out, or dropping of the ball outside the in-

of the crossbar have remained the same. The height of the posts, measured from the lower crossbar, is 20ft. (6.10m). The width of the professional goal is 18ft. 6in. (564cm), in college football it is 23ft. 4in. (711.2cm).

The oval ball is filled with compressed air and is covered with fair-brown leather. The longitudinal axis of the ball is 11-11½in. (about 28-29cm), the circumference along the longitudinal axis is 28-28½in. (roughly 71-72cm), along the lateral axis – 21¼-21½in. (about 54-54.5cm); weight: 14oz. (around 397g).

The uniform has a number of protective elements securing the player against the opponent's abuse. The basic components of the uniform are shoulder, wrist, thigh, and knee pads. The head is protected with a helmet equipped with a face mask forming a kind of grate shielding the player's face.

History. The actual beginning of American football is thought to have taken place in 1869 when some Amer. universities took up Brit. football. The game was immediately supplemented with elements originating from other var. of football and, thus mutated, its own deviant evolution was well under way. In the academic year 1873-74, sports activists and coaches from Columbia, Princeton, Rutgers, and Yale Universities made a decision that the rules of the game should be unified as the growing number of local var. made any match between 2 different schools nearly impracticable. As a result, in 1873 during the intercollegiate conference in New York, unified rules were introduced, still heavily dependent on Eur. football. In addition, the Intercollegiate Football Association (IFA) was established. Meanwhile, in the spring of 1874 the pioneers of Brit. rugby appeared in the USA. Its rules started to infiltrate into Amer. football, which in 1874-80 contributed to dissecting Amer. football into a var. closer to Eur. football and a var. remaining under the heavy influence of rugby. In 1876, after Harvard University joined IFA, a new organization was established: the American Intercollegiate Football Association, which issued a new set of rules that tipped the scales in favor of rugby. In 1877, the number of players in a team was set at 15, though the playing time remained the same as in Eur. football, i.e. 90min. In 1876, the prototype of the modern outfit was presented for the first time: knee breeches and padded shirts protecting collarbones, as well as pads covering thighs. Later on, the pads were separated from shirts and pants, forming therefore an independent element. In 1888, it was decided that Amer. football would henceforth be dependent neither on rugby nor Eur. football and its development would be autonomous. Nevertheless, elements of both predecessors are visible in the game even today. For instance, the gridiron is

A Stanford football game at California Memorial Stadium, 20 May, 1926.

change halves. The halves are changed after each quarter. Can. football more closely resembles the US game than it does either soccer (>ASSOCIATION FOOTBALL) or rugby.

Before the game starts, the captains accompanied by the referee toss a coin. The winner has the right to select a half for his team or the right to start a game (the so-called 'kick-off'). Professional matches are administered by 6 arbiters, university ones – by 4-6. The arbiters are as follows: the referee – responsible for the entire game, his decisions con-

bound lines, play is restarted from a point on such a line. In the center of each goal line is a U-shaped goal supported by cantilever jibs 10ft. (3.05m) tall. At that same height the lower crossbar is located. There is no upper crossbar. Formerly, instead of cantilever jibs, the goals had posts that were stuck in the ground and joined by a crossbar forming an H-shaped goal. The cantilever jibs are intended to improve safety by removing posts which players might otherwise crash into. Yet, despite the change of its shape the inside area of the goal and the height

similar in size to the rugby field and the rules for scoring points resemble those employed in rugby. In 1880, the number of players was reduced to 11. The brutal character of the game and growing number of crippling injuries and even deaths provoked severe public criticism, which resulted in prohibiting the game for 1 year at Harvard University in 1885. In 1894, the AIFA underwent a crisis precipitated by the withdrawal of Harvard University and Pennsylvania State University from the organization as a result of pressure exerted by other member-universities. That same year the New York University Athletic Club invited both schools excluded from the AIFA to a joint debate aimed at establishing new rules of American football. Modifications included, among other things, reduction of playing time to 70min. In 1895, the AIFA was dissolved and the following year the Intercollegiate Football Conference was constituted. Up to that time, American football was growing mostly under the auspices of universities. The first attempts to organize professional teams were made in the 1890s and historically the first professional match was played in 1895 between the teams of Latrobe and Jeanette in Pennsylvania. Most of the players were amateurs but the Latrobe team invited John Brallier, a famous football player, offering him a fee of $10, which he accepted. Thus, Brallier became the first professional player in the history of Amer. football. In 1895-97 the first permanent professional teams were established, the oldest among them being Duquesnes from Pittsburgh and The Olympics from McKeesport. The formation of professional teams led to a conflict between the collegiate and professional football systems, a conflict that – though resolved for some time – in fact continues to this day, as the recruitment emissaries of professional football clubs constantly troll college teams in an effort to lure away fresh, young talent with lucrative contracts.

In 1905 there were 18 fatalities in football matches and 159 serious injuries, such as basal skull, spinal column and limb fractures. The public campaign against Amer. football reached its peak in 1906; US president T. Roosevelt warned the football organizations that he would have no other option but to propose a law prohibiting the game unless some effective action were taken in order to reduce the game's violent nature. An emergency conference of representatives of 62 universities was convened, resulting in the banning of mass formation and other hazardous practices. The conference also resulted in the founding of the Intercollegiate Athletic Association of the United States, which in 1910, changed its name to the National Collegiate Athletic Association (NCAA). In 1905-10 the association introduced

First down or fumble?

a number of restrictions into the rules of the game, the obligation to wear a helmet among others. In order to supervise the game and to prevent brutal actions better, it was decreed the parties organizing a match must provide not only a referee but also 2 umpires and a linesman. One of the tasks of the linesman is to be the first to intervene in a case of any violation occurring on the most important front of the game, i.e. the line of scrimmage. Despite continued criticism and the rather dangerous character of the game (or, perhaps owing to it), the popularity of football grew rapidly and already in 1926, in Soldier Field stadium in Chicago, the number of spectators watching a match reached 100,000 for the first time in history. In 1939, the first televised transmission was broadcast (Fordham-Waynesburg, 34:7). Currently, the major college football organization is still the NCAA. University teams are involved in a highly complex system of league and prestige matches. The list of teams classified according to the NCAA criteria as College Division I contains nearly 200 names. Such a large number of teams would seem excessive until we take into account the fact that in the USA there are more than 3,700 colleges, many of which have their own football team. Since 1976, the best teams are qualified in 11 territorial groups, formed by local College Football Conferences: Atlantic Coast, Ivy League, Big Eight, Big Ten, Mid-America, Southern, Southeastern, Southwestern, Pacific Ten, Western Atlantic, and Big West. Unofficially, the NCAA recognizes as the best national team the one selected in the plebiscites carried out by journalists of the Associated Press (AP) since 1936, and by coaches voting under the auspices of United Press International (UPI) since 1950. If the 2 plebiscites select different teams, the NCAA recognizes both as champions. Particular prestige is attached to competitions held in the strongest centers of college football. In order to take part in such a competition a team has to go through a system of qualifications. The trophies obtained by the winners of such competitions are named after the local stadiums. The most prestigious are: the Rosebowl, played in Pasadena since 1902; the Orange Bowl (Miami, 1935); the Sugar Bowl (New Orleans, 1935); the John Hancock Bowl (El Paso, 1936, but since 1989 called the Sun Bowl); the Cotton Bowl (Dallas, 1937); the Gator Bowl (Jacksonville, 1946); the Citrus Bowl (Orlando, 1947); the Liberty Bowl (Memphis, 1959); the Peach Bowl (Atlanta, 1968); the Fiesta Bowl (Tempe, 1971); the All American Bowl (Birmingham, 1977); the Holiday Bowl (San Diego, 1978); the California Bowl (Fresno, 1981); the Aloha Bowl (Honolulu, 1982); the Freedom Bowl (Anaheim, 1984); and the Indepen-

dence Bowl (Shreveport, 1984). In addition, since 1986 the Hall of Fame Bowl in Tampa and the Freedom Bowl in Tucson have been held. The most recent of the important football events is the Blockbuster Bowl which has been held in Miami, Florida, since 1990. Theoretically, the college var. does not have a professional character, in practice however, as a result of considerable stipends and benefits, it has become a reservoir of talent for professional football. Therefore, college football players are usu. younger than their professional colleagues.

Professional American football's history is shorter than that of its college counterpart. In 1920, the American Professional Football Association was estab., which in 1922 was renamed the National Football League (NFL), a name still in use today. Although the Great Depression of the 1930s and WWII frustrated the NFL's progress, postwar television broadcasts saw a burgeoning in the sport's popularity. In 1945-46 a competing All American Football Conference (AAFC) was formed, which in

A 19th century game of American football.

1950 was united with the NFL. In 1959, in Texas the American Football League was constituted. For a few years the existing organizations competed with each other, then in 1966 they started to cooperate, and in 1970 they united to operate simultaneously as the National Football Conference and the American Football Conference. Each of them is in charge of 3 regions: Eastern, Western, and Central. The winners from both conferences play the final match for the title of the best professional team, known as the Superbowl, which has been played every January since 1967. The hegemony of the 2 conferences was challenged in 1974 by the new World Football League, which played summer games. No match for NFL/AFL domination, however, the WFL was dissolved after just 2 seasons. Similarly, the ill-fated United States Football League (USFL) was formed in 1983 in an effort to fill the spring/summer gap. Though, on average, games enjoyed upwards of 24,000 spectators per game and were broadcast on ABC and ESPN, nearly every club suffered crippling financial losses, mostly due to the exorbitant salaries required to recruit the best college and 1st-string NFL players. Former Heisman Trophy winners (see below) such as H. Walker, M. Rozier, and D. Flutie were drafted, along with such names in the game as J. Kelly, R. White, and S. Young. As a last-ditch

AFL CHAMPIONS
1960 Houston Oilers
1961 Houston Oilers
1962 Dallas Texans
1963 San Diego Chargers
1964 Buffalo Bills
1965 Buffalo Bills
1966 Kansas City Chiefs
1967 Oakland Raiders
1968 New York Jets
1969 Kansas City Chiefs
AFC CHAMPIONS
1970 Baltimore Colts
1971 Miami Dolphins

1972 Miami Dolphins
1973 Miami Dolphins
1974 Pittsburgh Steelers
1975 Pittsburgh Steelers
1976 Oakland Raiders
1977 Denver Broncos
1978 Pittsburgh Steelers
1979 Pittsburgh Steelers
1980 Oakland Raiders
1981 Cincinnati Bengals
1982 Miami Dolphins
1983 Los Angeles Raiders
1984 Miami Dolphins
1985 New England Patriots
1986 Denver Broncos
1987 Denver Broncos
1988 Cincinnati Bengals
1989 Denver Broncos
1990 Buffalo Bills
1991 Buffalo Bills
1992 Buffalo Bills
1993 Buffalo Bills
1994 San Diego Chargers
1995 Pittsburgh Steelers
1996 New England Patriots
1997 Denver Broncos
1998 Denver Broncos
1999 Tennessee Titans
2000 Baltimore Ravens
2001 New England Patriots
2002 Oakland Raiders

Underlined teams are Superbowl Champions

Amsterdam Admirals Quarterback (#7) Will Furrerr holds on to the ball before being sacked by London Monarchs Line Backer (#97) Horace Morris and Defence End (#99) Jerry Drake in London during a World League American Football match.

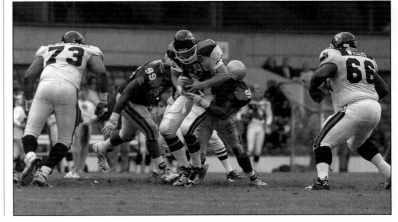

effort to salvage the league, plans were laid to switch to a fall season and there was significant chaos as teams merged or pulled up stakes to cut their financial losses. However, direct competition with the NFL was never to be tested. Though the USFL won an anti-trust suit against the NFL in 1986, the award amounted to just $3.00, not even enough for a ticket to a game, and the league folded under the burden of a $160 million debt.

Every year, both college and professional football organizations grant titles to the best players and coaches, and special awards for memorable achievements. The best college players in the USA are determined by a poll of sports writers and are granted the Heisman Trophy. Since 1935, the best college coach has been elected by the American Football Coaches Association and since 1957 a simultaneous plebiscite for the best coach has been carried out by the Football Writers Association of America. In most of the cases, however, the winner of both plebiscites is the same person. J. Paterno is considered the most outstanding college coach, as he was unanimously selected in both plebiscites in 1978, 1982, and 1986. A classification 'coach of all times' continues; this title is granted to the coach who leads his team to the greatest

by D. Butkus (1972). One of the most engrossing diaries recorded by a coach is a sports autobiography written by G. 'Bo' Schembechler and M. Albom (1989). The dehumanizing character of the game was revealed by an ex-player, D. Meggyesy, in his book, *Out of Their League* (1971). Among the most severe indictments against Amer. football, is *They Call It a Game* by B. Parrish (1971). Although the quantity of Amer. movies centering on football does not approach that of boxing or baseball motion pictures, there are several worthwhile films touching on social problems, such as *The Longest Yard* (1974) directed by R. Aldrich. Other movies dealing

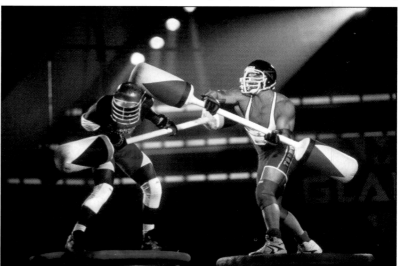

American gladiators go at it in the Q-tip quarterstaff 'tug war' and other events.

number of victories. At the moment, the coach of all times is P. 'Bear' Bryant with 323 victories, followed by an outstanding coach of the '40s, A. Alonzo Stagg with 314 victories.

Among professional football players the most important trophy is the Jim Thorpe Trophy, granted to the most valuable player selected since 1955 by the NFL Players' Association under the auspices of the World Almanac. There are also classifications for sportsmen playing in particular positions. Such plebiscites are held for the best player of both a given year and of all times. The most celebrated coaches, activists, and players are honored with a place in the Hall of Fame, located in Canton, Ohio. The number of individuals commemorated in the Hall of Fame is currently reaching 200, among them there are such names as J. Thorpe, R. Grange (who, upon retirement, became one of the most eminent sports journalists and writers), W. Lanier, B. Nagurski, and O.J. Simpson (now more famous for having been acquitted of the murders of his wife, N. Brown, and her companion, R. Goldman, than for his sports achievements and subsequent acting career). Among coaches one of the more conspicuous characters was the legendary V. Lombardi, often cast as the author of many a ruthless tactic whose sole object was winning and credited with turning the old adage, 'It's not whether you win or lose that counts, but how you play the game,' on its ear. Though immortalized as having pronounced the famous maxim: 'Winning isn't everything, it's the only thing,' what Lombardi actually said was, 'Winning isn't everything, but wanting to win is,' an axiom also attributed to the so-called 'Babe Ruth of Golf', A. Palmer, among others. This all-or-nothing mentality was perhaps more aptly phrased, 'Show me a good loser and I'll show you a loser.' This challenge has been var. attributed to Lombardi, S. Spurrier, L. Durocher, G. Steinbrenner, and even P. Newman. Actually, this nice-guys-finish-last sentiment was the work of K. Rockne, who declaimed back in the '20s: 'Show me a good and gracious loser, and I'll give you a failure.' Lombardi's philosophy might be better served by words he actually did utter: 'Some of us will do our jobs well, and some will not, but we will be judged by only one thing – the result.'

American football in literature and movies. Among a number of diaries and biographies of celebrated players the ones that seem most stimulating are: *Better Scramble Than Lose* by F. Tarkenton and J. Olsen (1969); *Joe Namath's Sportin' Life* by M. Allen (1969) and by the player himself *I Can't Wait Until Tomorrow* with R. Schaap (1969); and *Stop-Action*

with problems related to Amer. football include *Against All Odds*, a story of a player who was excluded from a club after an injury (starring J. Bridges and R. Ward), and *Everybody's All-American* (1988) directed by T. Hackford and starring J. Lange, D. Quaid, and T. Hutton.

F. Bisher, et al., *The College Game* (1974); *Official National Football League Record Book* (annual edition); G. Plimpton, *Paper Lion* (1964); G. Plimpton, *Mad Ducks and Bears. Football Revisited* (1973); O. Rowe, *American Football. The Records* (1988); R. Smith, *Big Time Football at Harvard* (1994).

AMERICAN GLADIATORS, a type of combat sport introduced in the 1990s. The sport uses modern technologies and symbols as a background for fights between specially trained competitors. There are many events, with new ideas constantly being added, and various names: 'sky track' – triple races on mountaineering clamps fastened to the ceiling; 'tower' – climbing a 'skyscraper' with concrete walls and difficult artificial elements; 'tug war' – where the fighters use Q-tip shaped lances to knock the opponents off rocking, unstable platforms suspended at a height of about 2m, several meters from each other, over thick mats meant to cushion the fall; 'swing shot' – where the participants, suspended on rubber ropes from the ceiling, attempt to attach balls to a flexible column; 'crunch time' – where 5 participants try to snatch balls from one another and place them into cone-like cylinders. There are time limits in all the events, and exceeding them is punished with the so-called 'penalty pits'. Television has made Amer. gladiators popular but it is difficult to characterize the current events due to the continual changes introduced to maintain viewer interest. Outside the USA, the sport is also popular in Germany.

AMODO, a shuttlecock and racket game practiced by the Chin. Miao minority, similar to >INDIACA and >BADMINTON. The shuttlecock has a base made from bamboo creepers 3cm in length, into which feathers plucked from a live cock are secured. The racket is wooden and elliptical in shape, 30cm long and 3cm thick, with a rectangular handle carved from wood, traditionally cut from remote mountain forests. The considerable effort involved in acquiring this special wood is believed to help the player obtain success. The game is played by both men and women, mainly during the Chin. spring festival. In the past it was used as an element of competition between wooers.

Mu Fushan et al., 'Shuttlecock (Amodo)', TRAMCHIN, 110.

AMPE, a rhythmic Afr. game, played by girls in Ghana and Nigeria. The game is played by 6-12 girls who form a semicircle, with the leader standing in the middle. The object of the game is to react properly to the actions performed by the leader. Usually, the players have to clap their hands, make 3 jumps up in the air, followed by a 4th jump accompanied by moving one leg forward. Nobody knows which leg the leader will put forward. If the first girl in the semicircle puts forward the same leg as the leader, the leader starts playing against the next girl in the semicircle and so on. If the leader and the girl she is playing against fail to put the same leg forward in 3 attempts, the leader is eliminated and she has to go to the end of the semicircle. Her position is filled in by the girl who was the last to be successful in her attempts against the leader. A leader who plays successfully against all the girls in the semicircle stands first in the semicircle.
O. Blum, *African Dances and Games. Manual of African dances and games for Children and Teenagers,* 1969; A. Taylor Cheska, 'Ampe', TGDWAN, 1987, 20; S.E. Hunt, *Games and Sports the World Around,* 1964.

ANATROCHASMOS, in ancient Greece – running backwards, a competitive form of foot exercise [Gk. *ana, anusis* – end, back, rear + *trochazos* – run, running]. Cf. >PLETHRIZEIN.

ANCIENT PUGILISM, 'no-holds-barred' fist-fighting. Fist-fights were known in Sumeria c.2600-1900 BC and in ancient Egypt. Eg. pugilism is reflected in the Meri Re painting in Tell-El Amarna which depicts a fight being a combination of boxing and wrestling. Similar fighting scenes are encrusted on the tomb of Kheruef in Thebes (c.1365 BC) and on a relief of unknown origin from the Ny Carlsberg Glypothek collection in Copenhagen. As for the majority of those monuments it is uncertain whether they depict sporting fights or combat scenes. Sporting fights are presented on Cretan paintings from the Middle Minoan period (2000-1500 BC). In 1966, Prof. S. Marinatos, conducting an archeological excavation on the island of Santorini near Crete, found a fresco at the site of ancient Akroteri. The fresco portrays a punching fight between 2 boys. The fighters have girdles and hair-cuts fixed into tresses and wear boxing gloves on their right hands (>ACROTERI PUNCHING). After the Achaean conquest, c.1400 BC, Minoan pugilism spread all over Greece. The earliest literary description referring to ancient pugilism is a fight between Epeus and Euryalus included in Book XXIII of *The Iliad*. The duel took place during the funeral games held in honor of Patroclus and the prizes sponsored by Achilles were given both to the victor and the loser:

Thereon the son of Peleus, when he had listened to all the thanks of Nestor, went about among the concourse of the Achaeans, and presently offered prizes for skill in the painful art of boxing. He brought out a strong mule, and made it fast in the middle of the crowd – a she-mule never yet broken, but six years old – when it is hardest of all to break them: this was for the victor, and for the vanquished he offered a double cup. Then he stood up and said among the Argives, 'Son of Atreus, and all other Achaeans, I invite our two champion boxers to lay about them lustily and compete for these prizes. He to whom Apollo vouchsafes the greater endurance, and whom the Achaeans acknowledge as victor, shall take the mule back with him to his own tent, while he that is vanquished shall have the double cup.' As he spoke there stood up a champion both brave and of great stature, a skilful boxer, Epeus, son of Panopeus. He laid his hand on the mule and said, 'Let the man who is to have the cup come hither, for none but myself will take the mule. I am the best boxer of all here present, and none can beat me. Is it not enough that I should fall short of you in actual fighting? Still, no man can be good at everything. I tell you plainly, and it shall come true; if any man will box with me I will bruise his body and break his bones; therefore let his friends stay here in a body and be at hand to take him away when I have done with him.' They all held their peace, and no man rose save Euryalus son of Mecisteus, who was son of Talaus. Mecisteus went once to Thebes after the fall of Oedipus, to attend his funeral, and he beat all the people of Cadmus. The son of Tydeus was Euryalus's second, cheering him on and hoping heartily that he would win. First he put a waistband round him and then he gave him some well-cut thongs of ox-hide; the two men being now girt went into the middle of the ring, and immediately fell to; heavily indeed did they punish one another and lay about them with their brawny fists. One could hear the horrid crashing of their jaws, and they sweated from every pore of their skin. Presently Epeus came on and gave Euryalus a blow on the jaw as he was looking round; Euryalus could not keep his legs; they gave way under him in a moment and he sprang up with a bound, as a fish leaps into the air near some shore that is all bestrewn with sea-wrack, when Boreas furs the top of the waves, and then falls back into deep water. But noble Epeus caught hold of him and raised him up; his comrades also came round him and led him from the ring, unsteady in his gait, his head hanging on one side, and spitting great clots of gore. They set him down in a swoon and then went to fetch the double cup.

[trans. by S. Butler]

Another ancient description of a pugilism bout is included in Book V of Virgil's *The Aeneid*:

The race thus ended, and rewards bestow'd,
Once more the prince bespeaks th' attentive crowd:
'If there he here whose dauntless courage dare
In gauntlet-fight, with limbs and body bare,
His opposite sustain in open view,
Stand forth the champion, and the games renew.
Two prizes I propose, and thus divide:
A bull with gilded horns, and fillets tied,
Shall be the portion of the conqu'ring chief;
A sword and helm shall cheer the loser's grief.'
Then haughty Dares in the lists appears;
Stalking he strides, his head erected bears:
His nervous arms the weighty gauntlet wield,
And loud applauses echo thro' the field.
Dares alone in combat us'd to stand
The match of mighty Paris, hand to hand;
The same, at Hector's fun'rals, undertook
Gigantic Butes, of th' Amycian stock,
And, by the stroke of his resistless hand,
Stretch'd the vast bulk upon the yellow sand.
Such Dares was; and such he strode along,
And drew the wonder of the gazing throng.
His brawny back and ample breast he shows,
His lifted arms around his head he throws,
And deals in whistling air his empty blows.
His match is sought; but, thro' the trembling band,
Not one dares answer to the proud demand.
Presuming of his force, with sparkling eyes
Already he devours the promis'd prize.
He claims the bull with awless insolence,
And having seiz'd his horns, accosts the prince:
'If none my matchless valor dares oppose,
How long shall Dares wait his dastard foes?
Permit me, chief, permit without delay,
To lead this uncontended gift away.'
The crowd assents, and with redoubled cries
For the proud challenger demands the prize.
Acestes, fir'd with just disdain, to see
The palm usurp'd without a victory,
Reproach'd Entellus thus, who sate beside,
And heard and saw, unmov'd, the Trojan's pride:
'Once, but in vain, a champion of renown,
So tamely can you bear the ravish'd crown,
A prize in triumph borne before your sight,
And shun, for fear, the danger of the fight?
Where is our Eryx now, the boasted name,
The god who taught your thund'ring arm the game?
Where now your baffled honor? Where the spoil
That fill'd your house, and fame that fill'd our isle?'
Entellus, thus: 'My soul is still the same,
Unmov'd with fear, and mov'd with martial fame;
But my chill blood is curdled in my veins,
And scarce the shadow of a man remains.
O could I turn to that fair prime again,
That prime of which this boaster is so vain,
The brave, who this decrepid age defies,
Should feel my force, without the promis'd prize.'
He said; and, rising at the word, he threw
Two pond'rous gauntlets down in open view;
Gauntlets which Eryx wont in fight to wield,
And sheathe his hands with in the listed field.
With fear and wonder seiz'd, the crowd beholds
The gloves of death, with sev'n distinguish'd folds
Of tough bull hides; the space within is spread
With iron, or with loads of heavy lead:
Dares himself was daunted at the sight,
Renounc'd his challenge, and refus'd to fight.
Astonish'd at their weight, the hero stands,
And pois'd the pond'rous engines in his hands.
'What had your wonder,' said Entellus, 'been,
Had you the gauntlets of Alcides seen,
Or view'd the stern debate on this unhappy green!
These which I bear your brother Eryx bore,
Still mark'd with batter'd brains and mingled gore.
With these he long sustain'd th' Herculean arm;
And these I wielded while my blood was warm,
This languish'd frame while better spirits fed,
Ere age unstrung my nerves, or time o'ersnow'd my head.
But if the challenger these arms refuse,
And cannot wield their weight, or dare not use;
If great Aeneas and Acestes join
In his request, these gauntlets I resign;
Let us with equal arms perform the fight,
And let him leave to fear, since I resign my right.'
This said, Entellus for the strife prepares;
Stripp'd of his quilted coat, his body bares;
Compos'd of mighty bones and brawn he stands,
A goodly tow'ring object on the sands.
Then just Aeneas equal arms supplied,
Which round their shoulders to their wrists they tied.
Both on the tiptoe stand, at full extent,
Their arms aloft, their bodies inly bent;
Their heads from aiming blows they bear afar;
With clashing gauntlets then provoke the war.
One on his youth and pliant limbs relies;
One on his sinews and his giant size.
The last is stiff with age, his motion slow;
He heaves for breath, he staggers to and fro,
And clouds of issuing smoke his nostrils loudly blow.
Yet equal in success, they ward, they strike;
Their ways are diff'rent, but their art alike.
Before, behind, the blows are dealt; around
Their hollow sides the rattling thumps resound.
A storm of strokes, well meant, with fury flies,
And errs about their temples, ears, and eyes.
Nor always errs; for oft the gauntlet draws
A sweeping stroke along the crackling jaws.
Heavy with age, Entellus stands his ground,
But with his warping body wards the wound.
His hand and watchful eye keep even pace;
While Dares traverses and shifts his place,
And, like a captain who beleaguers round
Some strong-built castle on a rising ground,

Ancient pugilism.

Boxing children – *a Minoan fresco from Acroteri on the Thera Island c.1550 BC (National Archeological Museum, Athens).*

Views all th' approaches with observing eyes:
This and that other part in vain he tries,
And more on industry than force relies.
With hands on high, Entellus threats the foe;
But Dares watch'd the motion from below,
And slipp'd aside, and shunn'd the long descending blow.
Entellus wastes his forces on the wind,
And, thus deluded of the stroke design'd,
Headlong and heavy fell; his ample breast
And weighty limbs his ancient mother press'd.
So falls a hollow pine, that long had stood
On Ida's height, or Erymanthus' wood,
Torn from the roots. The diff'ring nations rise,
And shouts and mingled murmurs rend the skies,
Acestus runs with eager haste, to raise
The fall'n companion of his youthful days.
Dauntless he rose, and to the fight return'd;
With shame his glowing cheeks, his eyes with fury burn'd.
Disdain and conscious virtue fir'd his breast,
And with redoubled force his foe he press'd.
He lays on load with either hand, amain,
And headlong drives the Trojan o'er the plain;
Nor stops, nor stays; nor rest nor breath allows;
But storms of strokes descend about his brows,
A rattling tempest, and a hail of blows.
But now the prince, who saw the wild increase
Of wounds, commands the combatants to cease,
And bounds Entellus' wrath, and bids the peace.
First to the Trojan, spent with toil, he came,
And sooth'd his sorrow for the suffer'd shame.
'What fury seiz'd my friend? The gods,' said he,
'To him propitious, and averse to thee,
Have giv'n his arm superior force to thine.
'T is madness to contend with strength divine.'

A

WORLD SPORTS ENCYCLOPEDIA

The gauntlet fight thus ended, from the shore
His faithful friends unhappy Dares bore:
His mouth and nostrils pour'd a purple flood,
And pounded teeth came rushing with his blood.
Faintly he stagger'd thro' the hissing throng,
And hung his head, and trail'd his legs along.
The sword and casque are carried by his train;
But with his foe the palm and ox remain.

[trans. by J. Dryden]

In spite of the long traditions going back to Cretan culture and the times of Homer, the Greeks included pugilism only in the XXIII Ol.G. in 688 BC (>PYGME). The bouts were conducted in honor of Apollo the Pyctes (the Pugilist) who was regarded as the mythic codifier of ancient pugilism. Apollo drafted the rules of pugilism after a victory over Phorbas, a strong-man from Phocis. The latter had stood in the way of pilgrims heading to the Delphic oracle and only agreed to let the pilgrims pass through on condition one of them defeated him in fist-fighting. Phorbas had killed all pilgrims with his bare knuckles until he was challenged by Apollo who was upset by the absence of the faithful in his shrine. The god killed Phorbas in a bare-knuckle duel. In other Gk. Myths, the originators of ancient pugilism were Theseus and Heracles. A similar story of pugilism's origin is included in the myth about the Argonauts who after having passed into the Black Sea came to the land of the Bebryces, a Bithynian tribe. Their king, Amy-cus, compelled strangers to box with him in order to pass through. As an invincible puncher, Amycus had killed all opponents until he was defeated by Poly-deuces of the Argonaut party. Polydeuces did not kill the king in the fight but forced him to promise he would never again harass travelers. The ancient fist-fighters were not limited to mythological characters. Philostratus demonstrates not only the divine but typically human characteristics of a good boxer: long and strong arms, broad shoulders, long neck and hard, tough fists. The mental features of a good boxer, according to Philostratus, include endurance and the will to fight and win. Numerous winners' names and descriptions of victories have survived. Most interesting are those punchers who fought not to kill their opponents but treated pugilism as a feat

Pugilists. A terra cota from the Euphrates region, 2000 BC.

Pugilists. An image from a Greek vase.

of strength and technique. Dio Chrysostom records the feats of Melankomas of Caria in Asia Minor, who won countless bouts without receiving a blow. Pausanias mentions Melancomas of Elis who de-feated 3 opponents without being hit even once during the Ol.G.
One of the most famous ancient Gk. punchers was Glaukos of Caristos, who won once in the Ol.G., twice in the Pythean Games, and 8 times in the Isth-mian and Nemean Games. The only puncher to win in all 4 great Hellenic games, i.e. Olympic, Nem-ean, Pythian and Isthmian, was Moschos of Colo-phon. Other famous punchers were Agesidamos of Locris, Alcainetos of Lepron and his son Hellanicos, Daipos of Croton, Eucles of Rodos, Eythymos of Locris, Cleitomachos of Thebes, Theagenes of Tha-sos, and Tisandros of Sicily.
The rules of ancient Gk. pugilism were probably fixed by Onamastos of Smyrna, the first Olympic punch-ing champion. These rules remained in force until the 3rd cent. BC and differed substantially from mod-ern boxing. Although the detailed regulations have not survived, the rules were known to exclude all wrestling-like holds and hitting the opponent's gen-itals, hitherto common in non-Hellenic cultures where 'all-in' methods of fighting were practiced. Despite the fact that protective boxing gloves were already known in Cretan culture, they were not used at the major ancient games. Instead, the punchers wrapped their fists with straps of leather. Homer mentions the protective leather straps in the Iliad. The straps were called *meilichai* or *strofiai* and re-mained in use until the 5th cent. BC. In Plato's times the straps were padded with layers of wool called the *sphariai*. Around the 4th cent. BC, proper box-ing gloves wrapped with hard cowhide straps (*oxeis himantes*) were introduced. The new gloves not only protected the puncher's fists, but also made hits more effective. Punches executed with those gloves were solid enough to deform parts of an opponent's body, particularly the head. This is corroborated by references in the literature of ancient Greece and by the nickname of one of the punchers – Otothladi-as – Cauliflower Ears. The punchers then began to wear ear protectors called *amphotides* or *epotides*. They comprised two thick leather straps wrapped around the head and covering both ears. No pro-tectors, however, were perfect. In the 1st cent. AD, Lucilius ridiculed the boxer Stratophon, whose face became so deformed after numerous bouts that the citizens of his hometown were not able to recognize the boxer on his return. The Romans introduced im-proved fist straps. At the ancient Roman games, special iron or lead knuckles called *caesti* were used to hurt the opponent (cf. Fr. *casse-tête* used for street fights). One of the characters of *The Aeneid*, Entel-lus used '...the gloves of death, with sev'n distin-guish'd folds of tough bull hides; [...] spread with iron, or with loads of heavy lead' (trans. by J. Dry-den). This form of hand protection was most likely unknown in the times of *The Aeneid* (after the Tro-jan War) but it was used in the book by Virgil, who was acquainted with Roman pugilism of the 1st cent. BC. In Virgil's times, pugilism was gradually becom-ing a spectacle. It was no longer a feat of strength and skill but a fulfillment of the cathartic bloodlust of the mob. Ancient pugilism disappeared together with the ancient games for a few centuries from the Eur.

sports scene. The last known Olympic pugilism champion was a certain Barasdates. Pugilism was revived a few centuries later in various parts of the Eur. continent; see >BOXING, >FRENCH BOXING, >OLD RUSSIAN BOXING, >SAVATE.

ANDARINES, a trad. long-distance walking race practiced chiefly in Navarre in the Basq. Country and also in the Fr. part of the Basq. Country [Span. *an-dar* – walk]. >RUNNING is also allowed but accord-ing to C.M. Palos >RACE WALKING is 'the primary form of movement'. An andarines competition in-volves covering a specified distance (usu. between two distinct geographical features such as towns) in the shortest possible time. It is either an individu-al time trial or a 2-competitor race. The best anda-rines competitors were held in high esteem by Iberi-an societies. One of the most celebrated events in the history of andarines is the 1903 5-day walk from Burdeos to Paris by a Fr. Basque nicknamed Mar-questan (real name unknown), along with a race held in 1908 between an andarines competitor nick-named Naparzar and 2 famous Juanagorri runners, Domingo and Antonio Igarabide (father and son). When the second race was held D. Igarabide was 79. The competition took place along the Tolosa-Pamplona-Tolosa route which is 124km long (Na-parzar won). This route is one of the most popular and is famous for other important duels and indi-vidual feats. In 1915 N. Azpeitia, nicknamed El Abuelo (The Grandfather), was the first to walk this distance in under 20hrs. (17hrs. 53mins.). The first Span. andarines championship was held in 1909 and F. Echarri was the first champion. One of the most famous andarines athletes was A. Uria who used to hold the records for many famous routes (e.g. Barcelona-Bilbao and Santander-Bilbao). He was also one of the people who used andarines to revive Basq. patriotism by staging walks to famous Basq. historical monuments (e.g. to the 4 most fa-mous Basq. cathedrals).
C. Moreno Palos, 'Andarines', JYTE, 1992, 36.

ANDARTZA, a Basq. var. of folk weightlifting. The weight used in andartza resembles that used in ordinary weightlifting but it is usu. smaller; its length never exceeds 2m. It is lifted with one or both hands. Metal discs are attached (and added) to both ends of the bar. In 1901 Hernani (nicknamed Eltzekondo) was the first man in history to lift a weight of more than 100kg with one hand. He also lifted a weight of 132kg with both hands.
C.M. Palos, 'Andartza', JYTE, 1992.

ANDAS, full name *jogo das Andas*, a Port. var. of stilts feats [Port. *jogo* – play, game + *andas* – stilts]. One of the most characteristic features of andas is that it consists not only of very attractive stilts feats, but also of hand-to-hand stilts bouts; see >WALK-ING ON STILTS.
M. da Graça Sousa Guedes, 'Jogo das andas', JTP, 1979, 61.

ANELZINHO, Port. for 'ring' or 'wedding ring'; in full *jogo do anelzhinho* [Port. diminutive of *anel* – ring]. The game uses a long rope with a wooden or metal ring threaded on it. The ends of the rope are tied together so that it forms a circle held by the players who also form a circle around it. The number of play-ers depends on the length of the rope. The ring is moved along the rope by the players who try to conceal it with their hands. All the players pretend to be passing the ring to the next player, although only one of them holds the ring and indeed does so. Another player standing in the middle of the circle is to guess where the ring really is. If he suc-ceeds, he replaces the player with the ring who, in turn, moves to the middle of the circle.
M. da Graça Sousa Guedes, 'Jogo do anelzhinho', JTP, 1979, 20.

ANIMAL BAITING, a cruel game known and prac-ticed in the past in many Eur. countries. Its origins date back to the Middle Ages. Animal baiting flour-ished in the 16th-18th century. It was banned in England in the 19th cent. following the protests of animal rights activists. Major animal baiting var. in-clude >COCK FIGHTS, bullbaiting and bearbaiting, described below. Other animal fights were also staged, e.g. involving dogs set on a wild boar tied to a pole and horse or donkey 'bouts'. The latter were, however, not that popular since horses and donkeys were not aggressive enough. Animal baiting shows often involved animals blinded on purpose (esp. bulls, bears and wild boars). Dogs were blinded only rarely and cocks never. The fights were controlled by animal masters known in England as bear-wards. Animal baiting was so popular that Henry VIII estab. a special office of the Master of Royal Bear and Dog Games. This testifies to the extreme social importance of the sport. In 1561, during the reign of Elizabeth I, Sir S. Duncombe was licensed to stage such fights. His license gave him the right to derive 'sole profit of the fighting and combating of wild and domestic beasts in England for the space of fourteen years'.

Most of the spectators took extreme pleasure in watching such fights. This is best exemplified by the preserved documents. R. Laneham (or Langham) described dog and bear fights at the Earl of Leicester's court in one of his letters written in 1575 in the following way: 'it is a sport very pleasant to see the bear, with his eyes leering after his enemies approach; the nimbleness and wait of the dog to take his advantage; and the force and experience of the bear again to avoid his assaults: if he were bitten in one place, how he would pinch in another to get free; that if he were taken once, then by what shift with biting, with clawing, with roaring, with tossing, and tumbling, he would work and wind himself from them; and, when he was loose, to shake his ears twice or thrice with the blood and the slaver hanging about his physiognomy'.

Not everybody shared these feelings of brute satisfaction. J. Stubbs wrote in 1579 with disgust: 'What Christian heart can take pleasure to see one poor beast rend, tear and kill another and all this for his foolish pleasure'. In 1666 S. Pepys wrote in his famous diary that animal fights were 'a very rude and

BEARBAITING was known in almost all Eur. countries but seems to have been most popular in England where, since the 16th cent., a special royal official known as the Master of the Royal Game of Bears and Mastiff Dogs was responsible for staging bear and dog fights. For this he received a salary of 16 pence a day. There used to be special bear gardens in London. The most famous of them was located near the Globe theater. It was built in 1526 on the bank of the Thames in the district of

Bear baiting – 'blood and slather'.

Southwark. Two bear arenas were situated in the London parish of the Most Holy Redeemer in the so-called Paris Garden. They both had special scaffolds for the spectators. A London antiquary J. Stow (1525-1605) described these places and warned the prospective spectators that they 'won't see anything pleasant until they pay one pence to enter, one pence to get a seat and one pence to remain calm'. A bear garden existed also by the royal palace. Bearbaiting was esp. popular among the Tudors. After the coronation ceremony in 1553, Mary I treated the Fr. delegation to a sumptuous dinner accompanied by bull and bearbaiting shows. Reportedly, the Queen took extreme pleasure in

injuries). The bear was chained to a stake by the neck or leg. His teeth were often made blunt. On special occasions several bear fights were staged consecutively. The bravest animals were rarely killed since they usu. attracted large crowds of spectators. Bets were accepted during each show. Bullbaiting was often provided as a companion diversion. Asian and Siberian peoples held similar but bloodless bear fights; see >YI WRESTLING.

DOG FIGHTS constituted a separate diversion. Dogs were set at one another individually or in pairs. A description of such a 'dog doubles duel' that took place during Queen Anne's reign (1702-14) has been preserved: 'At the Bear Garden in Hockley in the Hole, neat Clerkenwell Green, this present Monday, there is a great match to be fought by two dogs of Smithfield Bars against two dogs of Hampstead … for one guinea to be spent'. Dog fights, that – second to bull and bearbaiting in the past – were, however, much easier to stage, have survived to our times and continue to be organized either legally or illegally.

ANIMAL SHOULDER-BLADE THROW, a trad. contest encountered in the Altai Mountains and described by the Rus. ethnographer G.N. Potanin *(Ocherki severno-zapadnoy Mongolii*, 1881). A bovine shoulder-blade was thrown over a river. Another event involved breaking a shoulder-blade with one strike of the hand. See >SEER SHAAKH.

ANTHIPASSIA, [Gk. *anthipassia* – a mutual charge of 2 cavalry units]; a type of military exercise in ancient Greece whereby 2 cavalry units faked a mutual charge. When they made contact the riders passed each other, moved towards their rear, made a turn and faked another charge. At the end

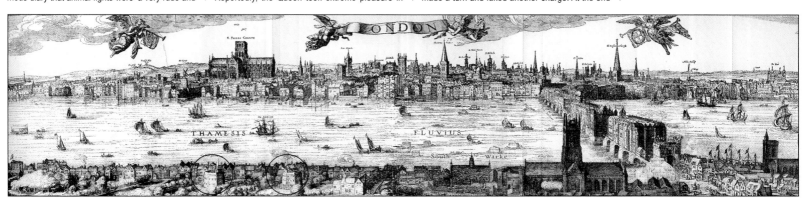

Visscher's view of London, 1616, with The Globe Theater (right circle) and the Bear Garden (left circle), where bear-baiting shows were held.

nasty pleasure'. J. Evelyn, thought to be the first Eur. ecologist, who started his campaign against excessive emissions to air in London as early as in the 17th cent., also opposed, in his memoirs, animal fights held in London's Bankside: 'there was cock-fights, dog-fights and bull and bear baiting. It being a famous day for all these butcherly sports or rather barbarous cruelties … all ended and I must heartily weary of the rude and dirty pastime'. Such opinions were, unfortunately, extremely rare.

Animal fights took place on specially prepared fields, often surrounded by spectator stands. A Ger. traveler, one Hentzner, who visited England towards the end of the 16th cent., described such an arena in his Latin *Diary* (p. 42) of 1598: 'it is a place similar to a theater, where bulls and bears are baited. The animals are chained to stakes by the neck or leg and then large Eng. bulldogs are set on them. Naturally, the dogs themselves are at risk of being horned or bitten by the bulls or the bears. It also often happens that the dogs are killed instantly but they are immediately replaced by new ones who are not so injured or tired'.

The most popular animal baiting var. included:
BULLBAITING, which, similar to bearbaiting (see below), dated back to the Middle Ages and flourished in the 15th-18th century. A bull was usu. attacked by 4 to 6 dogs. The spectators got esp. excited when the 'dogs caught the bull by the snout'. A successful dog was said to have pinned the bull. Despite the fact that bullbaiting is no longer practiced, the English still breed a special type of bullbaiting dogs known as bullmastiffs. Similar to other animal fights, bullbaiting was banned in England during Cromwell's Protectorate (1649-61). It was revived after 1661 but was permanently outlawed in the middle of the 19th cent. (1835).

watching these. The French liked the fights so much that they went to the Paris Garden the next morning to watch more of them. In 1580 Elizabeth I received the Dan. Ambassador in Greenwich and treated him to a bull and bearbaiting show. According to R. Holinshed's *Chronicles of England, Scotlande, and Irelande* the Dane and his retinue 'expressed inward-conceived joy and delight with shrill shouts and variety of gestures'.

Desiderius Erasmus visited England several times in the 15th and 16th cent. and observed that 'there are many bear farms in this country where bears are bred to fight' (*Adagia*, 1508, 361).

Similar to other animal fights, bearbaiting was banned in England during Cromwell's Protectorate but was immediately revived in 1661 after the Restoration. In 1802 the Brit. Parliament tried to outlaw bearbaiting following a motion initiated by W. Wilberforce supported by R.B. Sheridan, a playwright. The motion was, however, defeated by traditionalists supported by one of the most famous public speakers of that time – W. Windham, who accused the proponents of the ban of attempting to destroy the Eng. tradition. He also suggested that the motion was initiated by the Jacobins who wanted to overthrow the rule of democracy in England. Only in 1835 did the Brit. Parliament officially outlaw bearbaiting shows. Despite this, bearbaiting shows continued to be staged in certain towns such as Wirkworth (until 1840), Eccles (until 1842) and West Derby (until 1853).

Dogs used in bearbaiting shows received special training. Usu. 4 dogs were loosed on one bear. Tired dogs were replaced with fresh ones and the fight continued until the bear was bitten to death or unfit to fight (bears were often spared to be used in subsequent fights after they had recuperated from their

of the exercise they formed a close phalanx. Anthipassia formed part of the Panathenaea from about the 4th cent. BC but was held independently of other horse-riding events.

N.B. Crowther, 'Team Sports in Ancient Greece', IJHS, 1995, 1; N. Yalouris, ed., *The Olympic Games in Ancient Greece*, 1982.

ANTONIUS, a ball game known in many Eur. countries under the same name pronounced differently in various countries. In Denmark it is also known under different regional names. For example, in Vallekilde in W Zealand it was called an *over* – lit. 'above, over'. In Krøjerup it was referred to as a *husbold* – lit. 'a game over a house', and in Herfølge it was known as a *bedstemor over taget* – lit. 'a grandmother's throw over'. The players formed 2 teams standing on opposite sides of a detached, relatively low building. A player from one team threw the ball over the roof and the players of the other team had to catch it. If successful, the catcher's team would sneak around the corner of the building, appear briefly, and shout 'Antonius!'. The player who caught the ball would then try to hit one from the throwing team, who would remain on the roof, waiting for the ball to be returned. If somebody was hit with the ball, he would become a member of the opposing team. If not, the players could carry on in two ways: either as a kind of sting ball or the teams would continue to throw the ball over the roof. In either case the team that eliminated all the players from the other team was declared the winner.

J. Møller, 'Antonius', GID, 1997, 1, 16.

APARAR O PIÃO, a Port. variety of tops whereby a humming top picked from the ground spins on the palm of a hand, see >PIÃO.

The illustration from a printed handkerchief (c.1850) below depicts a scene of rat-catching, a cruel animal baiting sport once popular in London. Tiny the Wonder was the champion rat-catching terrier at the Blue Anchor Tavern in Finsbury. Although he weighed only 5½ lbs., he could kill up to 200 barn rats within an hour.

A

WORLD SPORTS ENCYCLOPEDIA

Aquaplaning.

APENE, in ancient Greece – races of mule-driven carts introduced in 500 BC during the 70th Ol.G. [Gk. *apene* – a team of mules]. The first winner of an apene contest was Tersios of Thessaly. The event was discontinued after the 84th Ol.G. (held in 444 BC). Pausanias explained in his *Hellados Periegesis* why this happened: 'Apene has neither an ancient origin nor is especially pleasant to watch and besides the Eleans faced an eternal curse if they started breeding these animals in their country. For apene is a chariot driven not by horses but by mules' (V, IX, 2); see also >CHARIOT RACING.

APORRHAXIS, [old Gk. *apporeo* – e.g. fall + *axon* – axis], a type of an ancient Gk. ball game. Information on the sport is incomplete but from preserved sources it seems that the object of the game was to bounce the ball up and down against the ground. There had to be at least 2 players. The one who managed to intercept the flying ball more times was declared the winner. Later, the players started bouncing the ball against walls. Aporrhaxis was then probably adopted by the Romans and the legionnaires popularized it throughout the Roman Empire. Thus, most likely, it produced many local varieties such as the Span. >PELOTA, the Fr. >JEU DE PAUME, and the oldest forms of >HANDBALL known on the Brit. Isles.

APOTOMEUS, an ancient Gk. name for a javelin type and an event forming a part of the >PENTATHLON. Apotomeus was different from a spear. It was made of a single piece of wood sharpened at one end. It was also lighter than the spears used in combat. It did not have a metal head, either, which is reflected in its name [Gk. *apotomas* – splinter, chip, strip of wood]. In the middle of the javelin there was a leather loop, called *ankyle*, which the thrower held with his thumb and index finger. The loop was used to apply spin to the javelin – after throwing it the competitor held the loop for a short while. The loop unwound and made the javelin spin. A throw was declared valid when the javelin landed within an area marked by 2 lines running parallel to the throw direction and the starting line (see >AKONTISMA).

APPLE FEAT, an ancient Ir. sport involving throwing a stone the size of an apple for distance. Stone throwing was part of military training, but at the same time was treated as a competitive event. For practice sessions the Irish used apples in order to avoid

The resistance provided by the water makes aqua-jogging an ideal low-impact exercise.

injuring onlookers. Stones or apples were sometimes placed in a small hollow on the inside of a shield (so that they were at hand during combat) and called heroes' stones. In some old Ir. documents there are references to apple feats which read that after iron had been introduced (c.9th-8th cent. BC) some of the *re*, i.e. Ir. rulers, started using iron balls for their practice throws. During religious and ritual ceremonies some Celtic tribes threw the specially prepared ... brains of their foes to demonstrate the supremacy of one tribe over another. A brain was

extracted from a smashed skull and then hardened in a special lime mixture. It was then used not only for apple feat but also in some other ball games, e.g. >BRAIN BALL.

AQUABOBBING, an aquatic sport consisting of planing over the water surface on an aquabob while being towed by a motorboat. An aquabob resembles a tricycle with ski-like runners instead of wheels. The pivoting front runner is attached to the handlebars and the 2 remaining runners are permanently fixed to the frame under the saddle. The bob is usu. approx. 180cm long, 60cm wide and its height measured at the saddle is usu. 50cm. Initially, in the 1960s and the early 1970s, the runners were made of wood but today they are made of various plastics. No special outfit is required in aquabobbing; in the summertime the competitors usu. wear swimsuits and an inflatable life vest. When the weather is colder, wet suits are worn.
Riding technique. Aquabobbing resembles >WATER SKIING, although it is easier since a competitor does not have to hold the towing line in the hands as it is attached to the front of the bob. An aquabobber does not have to tense his leg muscles to keep his balance, either. He sits astride the saddle while his feet rest on the side runners. The towing motorboat usu. moves at speeds around 40km/h, keeping the bob and the bobber afloat.
Aquabobbing is usu. practiced on lakes or along the seashore and the distance to be traveled is from 3 to 5km. It is made more attractive and demanding by adding evolutions such as slalom or varied slalom, which involves riding against the waves, greatly facilitated by the rigid frame of the bob. It is best to compete in slalom while being towed by a powerful motorboat at speeds up to 60km/h. A competitor can start riding in two ways: 1) the aquabob is placed in shallow water, near to the shore, the front, pivoting runner set in the anticipated riding direction; the bobber stands astride the bob but does not sit down until the bob starts moving; or 2) the bob floats in the water and the rider lies face down on the saddle with his legs spread and his hands on the handlebars; by keeping his trunk afloat he significantly reduces the weight of the bob, so it can accelerate faster. In case of a fall the towing line is released automatically. A ride ends near the shore; when the bob slows down and submerges under its own weight, the rider jumps off into the shallow water.
Events. Aquabobbing is usu. practiced for recreational purposes, but special competitions include the following events: 1) time trials, where national and international records are maintained; 2) time trial buoy slalom; 3) slalom and tricks; 4) slalom across the waves.
History. Aquabobbing appeared in Switzerland in 1967 on Lake Neuchâtel near Lausanne. It was invented by a Swiss, L. Guggi (b.1945) and first dem-

onstrated also by a Swiss, B. Gaille (b.1942). In 1968 he set the first world record in a non-stop 10mi. (about 16km) ride reaching a speed of 72km/h. In the 1968-69 period Lake Neuchâtel remained the sole aquabobbing center in the world, followed by the establishment of another center on Lake Morat in 1970. In the same year aquabobbing was demonstrated at the Brussels exhibition of inventions where it won a gold medal in the sports category which greatly contributed to its becoming more popular, especially in Belgium and Holland and later in

The joys of aquaplaning.

the Mediterranean and Black Sea countries, including Yugoslavia.

AQUA-JOGGING, a running-like exercise resembling >JOGGING but practiced in water and consisting of running over a lake, sea or river bed. The level of difficulty may be controlled by running in gradually deeper water [Lat. *aqua* – water + Eng. *jogging*]. It also is practiced in swimming pools as a form of rehabilitation exercise combined with other exercises done to music and called *aqua-fitness*. A special var. of aqua-jogging practiced by persons recovering from coronary disorders is called *cardio-aquajogging*. Aqua-jogging is especially popular in N.Zealand (at the Active Christchurch center in Christchurch), Germany (Stadtbad in Charlottenburg), and the Netherlands (Zwembaden in Zaanstad), where special aqua-jogging classes are organized. For those who like more structure and instruction or cannot fit into scheduled class exercises, low impact exercises can usu. be done individually at general pool times. Aqua-jogging is also employed by professional athletes during endurance training.

AQUAPLANING, a water sport of moving behind a motorboat on a large wooden or plastic raft-like plane called an aquaplane, which is 5½ft. long, 2½ft. wide and weighs 20-70lbs. The runner stands at the back of the plane, with both feet locked in special grips and holding 2 ropes ended with handles or knotted at the ends to ensure stability during the ride. The towing rope (approx. 50-75ft. long) is attached to the bottom of the aquaplane at its front, causing it to rise during the ride. The min. speed required for a smooth ride is 10-14mph. The max. speed is around 60mph, but the average speed rarely exceeds 20mph.
History. Aquaplaning was invented in the USA in the 1950s and reached the peak of its popularity in the 1960s and 1970s, when it was gradually replaced by other similar water sports like >WATER SKIING and, later, >WAKEBOARDING, which offer a similar effect, but require much lighter, and thus more portable, equipment.

AQUATIC BASKETBALL, a swimming pool game, in which the ball is thrown to a basket similar to that used in >BASKETBALL; the game has been popularized since 1952, mainly among women in Germany and Italy, where it has been called *pallacanestro aquatica*.

AR BAZH A BENN, also spelled *ar vazh a benn*, see >VAZH A BENN.

AR BAZH YOD, also spelled *ar vazh yod*, see >VAZH YOD.

AR C'HOARI MELLAD, see >C'HOARI MELLAD.

AR C'HRAVAZH, see >C'HRAVAZH.

AR GOUREN, see >GOUREN.

Aquatic basketball.

AR MAEN POUEZ, see >MAEN POUEZ.

AR SARC'H, see >GWINTRAN AR SARC'H.

AR VAZH A BENN, also spelled *ar bazh a benn*, see >VAZH A BENN.

AR VAZH YOD, also spelled *ar bazh yod*, see >VAZH YOD.

AR VELL, see >VELL.

AR VOUTELENN, a Breton var. of >SHEAF TOSS-ING, with a sheaf of about 8kg. Using a pitch fork, the best players can throw the sheaf nearly 10m.

AR WERN, see >WERN.

ARAB ROWING, a var. of rowing practiced in long boats with up to 200 oarsmen in 2 or 4 rows. In the 1970s the tradition of arab rowing was revived in the United Arab Emirates on the initiative of sheik Zayed Bin Sultan Al Nahyan. The first regattas took place in 1974 and since that time they have been part of the National Holiday celebrations.

ARAB SAILING, a var. of oar-sail sailing based on the tradition of Arab sailboats used in the region of the Persian Gulf. In the 1970s attempts were initiated by Sheik Zayed Bin Sultan Al Nahy-an to reconstruct the old forms of Arab sailing in the United Arab Emirates. Regattas are held in wooden sailboats, 43ft. (approx. 13m) long. The sails are made only of natural materials, usually cotton. The first regattas were held in 1974. The regattas are held to mark the celebrations of National Day in the United Arab Emirates.
Internet: http://www.ecssr.ac.ae.land.boatr.htm

ARADO CANARIO, a trad. Span. plow lifting contest, popular esp. in the Canary Islands [Span. *arado* – plow + *canario* – Canarian]. The competition employs a Canarian plow which is some 4.25 to 4.75m long (incl. the legplow beam) and weighs about 100kg. A contestant has to grab it by the beam (*timon*) and lift it through 90°, plowshare up. He may support the beam with his hip. Lifting techniques are different in different parts of the Canary Islands. F. Rodrigues Franco (nicknamed Farro de Mespalomas) of the Canary Islands was one of the best arado canario competitors in history.
C. Moreno Palos, 'Arado canario', JYTE, 1992, 227-8.

ARBA RACING, a trad. sport of the Kazakhs, consisting of a horse race, accompanied by a contest in gearing up a horse and harnessing it to a cart.

ARBALESTRA, Ital. longbow archery contests held annually in the towns of Gubbio (C Italy) and Sansepolcro (Tuscany).

ARCATHLON, [Lat. *arcus* – arch, bow + Gk. *athlon* – contest], a type of >BIATHLON. The name was initially used when referring to any type of event combining archery with cross country skiing, skating or roller skating. At present, the term arcathlon is used to describe a summer event that is a combination of target archery shooting and running, whereas the event combining archery with cross country skiing is referred to as >SKI-ARCHERY (also ski-arcathlon or ski-arc). In arcathlon the typical course is between 5 and 10km. Athletes make 3 shooting stops, shooting 4 arrows at each. Targets are 16cm in diameter and are positioned 18m from the shooter. After the first leg the runners shoot from a standing position, after the second – from the kneeling position, after the third – from the lying position. Bows are normally stored at the shooting range, but competitors have the option of carrying them. Then, the bows must be large enough to be carried on the shoulder. The arrows are kept in a quiver. In the Eng.-speaking countries a typical event

consists of three 1mi. runs, each followed by 4 arrow shots. The sport is officially supervised by the International Archery Federation (Fédération International de Tir a l'Arc, FITA). It is also popular among biathletes who often practice it for training purposes during the summer season. That is why the sport is also supported by the International Biathlon Union (IBU). Arcathlon is also officially supported by the United States Olympic Committee and so might be included in the Olympic program in the future.
The Internet: the United States Olympic Committee Online – http://www.usoc.org/sports_az/ar/az_rules.html

ARCHERY, a sport involving shooting arrows with a bow at a target or distance; or, as in one of the Jap. var. of archery, to improve one's concentration and mental condition. At present, several var. of sports archery can be distinguished: >OUTDOOR TARGET ARCHERY, >FIELD ARCHERY, >ROVING ARCHERY, >FREESTYLE ARCHERY and >FLIGHT SHOOTING; see also >ARCHERY FOR THE DISABLED. In ancient times archers also competed in shooting arrows for depth into targets made of wood or soft metal. In numerous cultures equestrian archery was also very popular (cf. >UMA YUMI, >IN-UOMONO, >KASA-GAKE, >YABUSAME), esp. among Native Americans who had mastered this skill to a level of excellence. Due to the rapid introduction of firearms and gradual disappearance of in-

Arcathlon.

digenous Amer. cultures, little information on the original Native Amer. art of archery has survived. In some Amer. tribes the ancient art has been revived in various folk sports e.g. >TE'XWETS SA'KWELA'X practiced by the Stóólo tribe. Self-improvement is the purpose of an indigenous Jap. var. of archery called >KYUDO; other numerous var. of archery practiced in Japan include >RYO, ibahajime, >JYA-RAI, kojumi, >NORIJUMI, >TANGONO KISHA, >KUSAJISI, >BUSHA, >JUMIHAJIME, >MARU-MONO and >MOMOTE. In C Asia 2 types of archery, i.e. >WINESKIN SHOOT and >SUR KHARVAKH (the latter known in Poland as >STRZELANIE DO CZAPKI) enjoyed great popularity. Archery has been common in a variety of forms and styles among individual nations of Asia; see >AFGHAN ARCHERY, >BURIAT ARCHERY, >CHINESE ARCHERY, >CHUKCHEE AND KORIAK ARCHERY, >KALMUCK ARCHERY, >MONGOLIAN ARCHERY, >TIBETAN ARCHERY and >PARTHIAN ARCHERY. Archery contests were also held on occasions of weddings or funerals; cf. >BURIAL ARCHERY. Eur. archery traditions were represented by >ENGLISH ARCHERY, >CROSSBOW SHOOTING, and sports competitions of >ARCHERY GOLF, and >CLOUT SHOOTING.
History. The bow was probably invented between 15000 and 5000 BC; it was certainly used in Assyria from 4000 to 3000 BC. The weapon was refined in ancient Egypt, where its use was depicted in many drawings. From the period of the Middle Kingdom (2200-1700 BC) comes a description of Prince Sinuhe preparing his bow for battle: 'I spent the whole night testing my bow and preparing arrows.' Archery was at that time a crucial element of royal and aristocratic education. A relief from the temple in Karnak depicts the son of Pharaoh Tuthmosis III – the later Tuthmosis IV (1412-03 BC) – practicing archery under the supervision of the God Seth who is instructing the young ruler how to place his hands on the bow. A scene from a Min tomb presents another heir apparent to the Eg. throne – the future Pharaoh Amenhotep II (1438-12 BC) – practicing archery with his instructor. The ancient, partly illegible inscription underneath reads: 'Draw the bow to the ear, make it a powerful...' Above the relief another inscription reads: 'The royal son is playing with the bow and arrows in the courtyard of the Thinis

Palace.' Amenhotep II, according to an inscription on his tomb, could not find anyone who was able to draw his bow. Sports archery was already practiced in the times of Tuthmosis III (1490-36 BC), the most warring pharaoh in Eg. history, who truly appreciated proper military training, incl. archery. An inscription on the stela of the Month Temple in Erment informs the visitors that '...when he shot an arrow into the target, the wood cracked like papyrus.' Amenhotep II practiced target archery while riding a chariot. In that particular type of archery, shooting accuracy was not as important as the depth to which the arrow entered the target. A great deal of information on the archery practice of an Eg. ruler was discovered in the tomb of Tutankhamen by a Brit. archeologist, H. Carter, who found numerous wall drawings and a well-preserved collection of the pharaoh's bows and arrows; see >TUTANKHAMEN'S ARCHERY. Archery contests were later held by Tutankhamen's successors Ay (1339-35 BC) and Ramses II (1290-23 BC). Archers were the most important troops of the Eg. army. In the writing system of ancient Egypt, the hieroglyph depicting an archer meant 'the army'. Archery training is mentioned in the Book of Psalms of the Bible. In Psalm 18:34, David, while praising goods provided by the Lord, says:

He trains my hands for battle;
My arms can bend a bow of bronze.

Two archery metaphors are also used in Psalm 144:1-6, in which David asks God to 'train his fingers for battle' and then to 'send forth lightning and scatter the enemies; shoot your arrows and rout them.'
The ancient Greeks knew the bow (*toxon*) since the onset of their civilization. In the early centuries the best archers were the Cretans. The bow and arrow became a primary military weapon in the Myceaean period. The earliest description of an archery contest can be found in Homer's *Iliad*.
In Homer's *Odyssey*, upon his return home to Ithaca, Odysseus proves his identity by drawing a bow that no one else was able to draw and then shooting all Penelope's suitors. In later centuries the bow was used more as a hunting than military weapon, becoming the main attribute of Artemis, the Gk. goddess of the hunt, identified with Diana by the Romans. It was only in the 5th cent. BC in Athens that

Ancient archery, Mesopotamian art.

Ar voutelen.

Dhow sailboats compete in the Maulidi festival, an annual celebration marking the birth of Mohammed, the founder of Islam, in the coastal island town of Lamu.

A

WORLD SPORTS ENCYCLOPEDIA

Archery for the disabled on a postage stamp.

F.L. Bilson's archery for the disabled.

the bow and arrow was revived as a weapon of war. During the battle of Salamis (480 BC) each Athenian ship carried 4 archers on board. 300 Attic archers took part in the battle of Plataea (479 BC). In the Hellenic period (336-30 BC) archery became part of the training program of the ephebes; various archery training systems were taught in Gk. gymnasions. The Romans began to use the bow as a military weapon after the second Punic war (218-201 BC). Muhammad (c.570-632), the originator of Islam, perceived archery training in the Koran as a religious duty. In the north of Europe archery was an important element of Scand. cultures. Numerous references to archery can be found in the Old-Icel. *Edda* and in S. Sturlasonn's sagas about ancient Norw. kings, known as *Heimskringla*. One of the Norw. chiefs, Einar Tambarskjaelve could shoot a blunt arrow through a thick cowhide. The bow became the primary military weapon in the medieval Brit. Isles and contributed to the development of the sport of archery as a form of defensive training. In England and other Eur. countries archery was regularly practiced by town guilds (>KÖNIGSSCHIEßEN,

Archers at the ready.

>COCK SHOOTING), originated in the 11th cent. Shooting tournaments, with the use of the longbow, crossbow, and later firearms, gained wide popularity by the end of the Middle Ages. Shooting with crossbows and rifles at birds (>FREISCHIEßEN) became common in many countries. Especially popular was parrot shooting, known as >POPINJAY or >PAPINGO SHOOTING, in which a living bird was replaced with a figure or target representing a parrot. From the 12th untill 14th cent. several royal decrees were issued which obligated Eng. knights to practice archery on a regular basis. In the mid-16th cent., long before firearms were invented, R. Ascham wrote *Toxophilus* (*The Lover of the Bow*), one of the most significant treatises on the art of archery. Initially, in archery contests at >CHIVALRIC TOURNAMENTS, various types of bows were used. Later, they were replaced with the crossbow, invented by the end of the 11th cent. and popularized between the 12th and 14th cent. In Poland, a popular competition was shooting at a wooden figure of the rooster and smashing it into pieces (cf. >COCK SHOOTING). Shooting at caps and targets with concentric scoring rings became popular during chivalric tournaments in the 13th cent.

The emergence of firearms altered the nature of archery from a military skill to a sheer sporting event. The process of replacing bows and arrows with firearms was long and gradual. The range and accuracy of early harquebuses, blunderbusses, and muskets was far behind those of the longbow and crossbow. In 1644, during the Eng. Civil War, the royalists were still using archers in battles with Cromwell's troops. Most likely, the last recorded use of the military bow in Europe took place during a skirmish between the Scot. clans of MacIntoshes and MacDonalds in 1788. The bow and ar-

Long out-moded by firearms, both bow and arrow continue to undergo technological modifications.

row remained in use on other continents for much longer. In 1860 the Chinese were still using bows and arrows at the battle of Ta-ku; bows were also used by Native Americans as a weapon of war in the mid-19th cent. Along with the foundation of archery societies and federations, various forms of sports archery were popularized, most notably >OUTDOOR TARGET ARCHERY.

D. Barrington, *Observations on the Practice of Archery in England*, 1785; A. De Berties, *Le Tir d'Arc*, 1900; E.H. Burke, *The History of Archery*, 1957; K. Celsch, *Bogenschiessen*, 1975; K.M. Haywood & C.F. Lewis, *Archery*, 1997; F. Lake and H. Wrought, *A Bibliography of Archery*, 1974; M. Loades, *Archery. Its History and Forms*, 1995; Z. Łotocki, *Łucznictwo*, 1934; W.F. Paterson, *Encyclopedia of Archery*, 1984; D. Roberts, *Archery for All*, 1971; F.W. Schwarzlose, *Die Waffen der Alten Araber aus ihren Dichtern dargestellt*, 1886; R. Stein, *Archers d'autrefois – archers d'aujourd'hui*, 1925; R. Zawiślański, *Łucznictwo*, 1952.

ARCHERY DARTS, a game combining archery and darts. The target is similar to a dartboard but slightly larger. Archers shoot at it from a distance of 10yds. (9.144m), while darts players continue throwing their darts standing at the usual distance. The dartboard is divided into numbered sectors with central inner and outer bull's-eyes as in a regular game of darts.

ARCHERY FOR THE DISABLED, a var. of archery practiced by the disabled on wheelchairs. It was originated by F.L. Bilson who devised it as a form of physical rehabilitation in the National Center for Spine Injuries in Stoke Mandeville, England. The sport has been part of many international competitions, including the Paralympic Games. The first archery contest took place in 1948 in Stoke Mandeville; see also >SPORTS FOR THE DISABLED.

ARCHERY GOLF, a hybrid between >GOLF and >ARCHERY, played on a standard 18-hole golf course (optionally, 2 rounds can be played on a 9-hole golf course). Contestants shoot arrows at 'holes', which are tennis balls resting on a wire hoop 10cm above the ground and placed level with the hole on the right side of the green, away from the putting surface. Instead of tennis balls white cardboard discs 4in. in diameter may be used. Archers begin by shooting their first arrow from the 'tee' position and continue to shoot successive arrows from the spot where the preceding one landed. To complete a hole the archer must dislodge or hit the tennis ball (cardboard disc). The par for each hole is the number of arrows shot plus any penalties incurred for an arrow landing in a bunker or within 1m of the target (1 penalty stroke), or a lost arrow (2 penalty strokes). Archers usu. shoot in groups of 4 and no archer is allowed to 'tee off' until the preceding group is on the next tee. The archer furthest from the hole shoots first, but for safety reasons (the angle of the shot) the sequence may be changed. The archer who won the previous 'hole' shoots first at the next tee. The archer with the lowest number of strokes wins the competition. If there is a tie, the last 'hole' is played again to decide the winner.

Equipment. Archers may use arrows of any type, except broadheads, and with a max. diameter of 10mm). A standard set of arrows is similar to that of

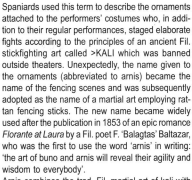

golf clubs: carbon arrows are used for max. distance, aluminum arrows – for shorter fairway shots, 'judo point' arrows – for getting close to a 'hole', and 'blunt point' arrows – to hit the target. There are also special 'flu-flu' arrows with extra large feathers for short distance shots. There are no restrictions as to the type of bow, except that no bow sights can be used. The use of arrows and bows presents a danger to fellow contestants and so extra caution must be taken at all times throughout the competition, esp. as regards the elevation of shots. Archery golfers may also compete with regular golfers, in which case they are usu. given a handicap to compensate for the greater accuracy of shooting an arrow as compared to hitting a golf ball.

Archery, EAI, 1979, II, 212; http://www.centenary-archers.gil.com.au/archery.htm

ARGOLLA, a Span. game in which wooden balls are hit with a stick through a small metal ring that is dug or driven into the ground [Span. *argolla* – ring]. The game was most popular in Spain at the turn of the 16th cent. Very little precise information is preserved, but some terms connected with the game appear in various dictionaries. *Cabe* meant the distance between 2 balls that was shorter than the length of a bat; *choclon* described sending the ball through the ring; *choclar* was used when the ball passed through the ring. The word *argolla* is used in modern Span. for >CROQUET, which is roughly similar to historical argolla.

C. Moreno Palos, 'Argolla', JYTE, 1992; R. Garcia Serrano, 'Argolla', JDTE, 1974, 185.

ARIN, see >AGBÂRIN.

ARKAN THROWING, a Turk. roping technique similar to Amer. >LASSOING, using a piece of thick, stiff rope (*arkan*) with a tightening loop at the end. Cf. Mong. >URGA, >TYNZJAN, >LASSO, LE, >LAZU.

ARM PULL, the Eng. name of a competition held by Native Alaskans and Native Amer. Indians of N Canada, in which 2 contestants pull arms locked at the bent elbow. The contestants face each other sitting on the floor. The left leg of each of them is straight and the right leg is bent over the opponent's straightened leg. They lock right or left arms (then the position is reversed) at the bent elbow and try to pull the opponent over, touch his head to their chest or straighten out his locked arm. The competition consists of the best of three pulls. According to the local sports terminology arm pull is one of the so-called arctic sports. It is a separate event during the N.Amer. Indigenous Games.

The Arctic Sports, via the Internet: http://www.first-nations.com/naig97/arctic-sports/as-armpull.htm

ARM WRESTLING, a competition between 2 players sitting at a table. The players rest their elbows on the table top, interlocking their right (or left) hands with their opponents subsequently trying to force the back of the opponent's hand to touch the table's surface. The one who succeeds wins the bout. The competition is known in many countries, e.g. Denmark – *lage arm* [Dan. *lage* – to put + *arm* – a hand], Poland – *walka na ręce* [*walka* – *fight* + *ręce* – hands], Russia – *ruchnaya barba* [Rus. *ruchnaya* – hand (adj.) + *barba* – fight, wrestling], Spain – *pulsolaris* [Span. *pulso* – wrist + *laris* – noun ending], Germany – *Armdrücken* [Ger. – *Arm* – hand + *drücken* – to press], etc. Another Ger. var. of the game is called *Bankdrücken*, in which the rivals face each other sitting astride a bench, on which they rest their arms [Ger. *Bank* – a bench + *drücken* – to press]. In another variety of arm wrestling the opponents stand with their legs astride to keep their balance, raise their arms parallel to the ground and their forearms perpendicular to it. The hands are either interwoven or simply touch one another with flat backhands, which eliminates the tendency to pull the opponent's hand downwards. The other hand should be kept on the hip. In this variety it is more difficult to determine the winner, as there is no clear surface which the loser's hand must touch.

In the USA, arm wrestling contests are organized under the auspices of several organizations, the largest of which – the World Armsport Federation (WAF) – consists of over 50 national associations, incl. the prestigious Amer. Arm-wrestling Association (AAA). The main international events are world and continental championships. A spectacular development of arm wrestling took place under the sponsorship of the Heublein Co., which – together with WAF – organizes the most renowned contests, e.g. the international Yukon Jack Tournament. Events are held in different weight categories: up to 75kg (165lb.), 90kg (198lb.) and above 90kg. In international events tables usu. have elbow supports. Among the leading arm wrestlers are: M. Maker, J. Brezek, C. Dean, D. Jones, and D. Patten. The sport was showcased in the movie *Over the Top*, dir. by M. Golan, starring S. Stallone, 1987.

J. Möller, 'Lage arm', GID, 1997, 4, 39; C. Moreno Palos, 'Pulsolaris', JYTE, 1992; J. Townes, 'Arm Wrestling', EWS, 1996, I, 47-50.

Arm wrestling is a sport popular in many world regions and cultures.

Arm wrestling. A relief from Mereruk of Saqqara's tomb, c.2400 BC.

ARMBALL, an unspecified type of ball game differentiated in old Eng. sources from >HANDBALL. Referred to in R. Mulcaster's (c.1530-1611) work entitled *Positions* (1581); perhaps similar to >BALLOON-BALL.

ARMESLOENGJA, see >SLENGJETAK.

ARMKAST, a Swed. var. of folk wrestling whereby the opponents grab each other by the collar while standing face to face. Esp. popular in Lapland [Swed. *arm* – arm + *kast* – throw]. Armkast is a wrestling var. classified by the Swed. sports ethnologist M. Hellspong as a sub-type of the more widely known >KRATAG; similar forms of wrestling in various parts of Sweden are called >ARMTAG, >KRAGTAG, >KRAVETAG, >SLÄNGTAJ, >TA RÖCK.

ARMTAG, a Swed. variety of folk wrestling with various holds and grips on the opponent's clothing [Swed. *arm* – arm + *tag* – grasp, grip, hold]. Armtag is most popular in the Dalarna region in Sweden and a sub-type of the more widely known >KRAGTAG. There are also other varieties confined to certain regions of Sweden such as >ARMKAST, >KRAVETAG, >SLÄNGTAJ, >TA RÖCK. According to W. Baxter, its Fin. counterpart is called *soulipaini*.

W. Baxter, 'Les luttes traditionnelles a traverse le monde', LJP, 1998, 83.

ARNIS, also known as *arnes,* a Fil. martial art. The name was derived from the Span. term *arnes de mano*, lit. a masterly show, hand equilibristics. The Spaniards used this term to describe the ornaments attached to the performers' costumes who, in addition to their regular performances, staged elaborate fights according to the principles of an ancient Fil. stickfighting art called >KALI which was banned outside theaters. Unexpectedly, the name given to the ornaments (abbreviated to arnis) became the name of the fencing scenes and was subsequently adopted as the name of a martial art employing rattan fencing sticks. The new name became widely used after the publication in 1853 of an epic romance *Florante at Laura* by a Fil. poet F. 'Balagtas' Baltazar, who was the first to use the word 'arnis' in writing: 'the art of buno and arnis will reveal their agility and wisdom to everybody'.

Arnis combines the trad. Fil. martial art of kali with elements of a Fil. stick-fencing art known as >SOLO BASTON, >DOBLE BASTON, and >ESPADA Y DAGA (>ESKRIMA), to which certain elements of Euro-Amer. boxing were added after the Span.--Amer. war (1896-98) and the Fil.-Amer. war (1898--1942) and which later incorporated some features of Jap. martial arts after the Jap. occupation of the islands (1942-45). Apart from a whole array of evolutions and acrobatic feats, arnis also borrowed certain elements of clothing and the system of proficiency-level marking with colored belts from various Jap. and Kor. martial arts. The first arnis competitions were held in the 1920s. The competitions consisted of full-contact fights without specific regulations and were staged without any protective equipment. P. Yambao was one of the most renowned arnis fighters in the 1920s and '30s. Arnis competitions were extremely popular, but arnis became the national Fil. sport only as late as in the 1970s. In 1966, A. Roces, the then Secretary of State in the Philippine Ministry of Education, made a very emotional speech on the subject of arnis:

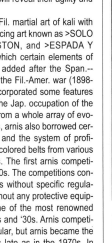

> *Arnis is a neglected aspect of our culture that is as old as the Philippines themselves. It is the core of the Philippines, their culture and temperament. In pre-historic times it was treated as a form of recreation. The inhabitants of the Philippines learned arnis in the same way as they learned religion, singing and Sanskrit. At that time it was not only a fencing art as we like to think of it today. It had two distinct dancing and martial art varieties known as sayaw and sinulog, respectively, which had both an artistic and entertaining nature.*

The Samahan sa Arnis ng Pilipnas (Association of Arnis of the Philippines, abbreviated to National Arnis Philippines or NARAPHIL) was estab. in 1975. In the same year it organized the first ever all-national arnis competition in Manila. The competition was then organized every few years and has been held annually since 1986. NARAPHIL is a member of the Philippine Olympic Committee. Arnis was a demonstration sport during the South-East Asian Games in 1991. NARAPHIL has been lobbying for the inclusion of arnis as a demonstration sport during the Ol.G.

C. Cañete has become one of the most outstanding arnis fighters of present times. Arnis is popular in the US, where the first full-contact competition was held in New York sponsored by the Philippine-born A.P. Mariñas. The World Eskrima-Arnis Federation (WEKAF) was estab. in 1987 in Los Angeles. The fist US Championship was held in 1988 in San Jose in California. WEKAF was also one of the co-organizers of the first W.Ch. which took place in Cebu, the Philippines in 1989. The participants came from the Philippines, the US, Australia and a few Eur. countries.

Fundamentals. The rules of the sport that are in force at present were largely developed by NARAPHIL in 1991. In the competitive variety of arnis two competitors fight on a mat of about 8m² or 9½ sq. yds. They are divided into weight categories similar to wrestling or boxing. The competitors fight with cane sticks 30in. (76.2cm) long and 1in. (2.54cm) thick. Points are awarded for clear hits on specified areas of the body or for knocking the weapon out of an opponent's hands. A fighter who scores 5pts. more than his opponent or manages to knock the stick out of his opponent's hands twice is declared the winner. If a competitor commits 3 fouls by hitting his opponent on prohibited areas, he loses the fight. The match consists of three 2min. rounds. The match is supervised by a main referee and 2 assistant referees. To reduce the likelihood of injury, fighters wear helmets and steel-plated hand, chest and thigh guards.

C. Cañete, D. Cañete, *Arnis Eskrima. Philippine Stick-*

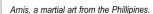

Arnis, a martial art from the Phillipines.

WORLD SPORTS ENCYCLOPEDIA

Arrisulatzalleak.

One of many varieties of arrijasoketa.

fighting Art, 1976; R.A. Presas, *Modern Arnis. Philippine Martial Art*, 1993; M. Wiley, *Martial Arts, Philippines*, in: *Encyclopedia of World Sport*, 1996, III; P. Yambao, *Mga Karunungan sa Larong Arnis (Knowledge of the martial art of arnis)*, 1957.

ARPANA, a sport of Basq. lumberjacks involving sawing long logs into small stump-like pieces with a handsaw. See >TRONZOLARIS.

ARRIJASOKETA, also known as *harrijasotzaileak* or *harrijasoketa*, a Basq. var. of weightlifting and a celebrated ancient Basq. sport. Its Span. counterpart is called *levantamiento de piedra* or boulder lifting. Over time boulders originally used in the competition have been replaced with special granite or other hard rock weights in which special holes are drilled and filled with lead to a specific weight. The lifter, called a *harrijasotzaile*, makes his own decision as to what an appropriate weight is at a given moment. The weights are ordered from local stoneworkers and are usually 1kg heavier than the previous record set by a given (the same) *harrijasotzaile*. I. Perurena of Leiza is considered one of the greatest boulder lifters of all time. He started his career when he was 17 and lifted a weight of 170kg. At 31 (in 1987) he was lifting more than 300kg and his record reached 318kg. The current arrijasoketa world record is 320kg and was set by Perurena's disciple – M. Saralega of Navarre in 1995.
R. Aguirre, 'Harrijasotzaileak', GHJD, 1989, I, 217-35; C. Moreno Palos, 'Arrijasoketa', JYTE, 1992, 217-20.

ARRISULATZALLEAK, also spelled *arrisulat zalleak* [Basq. for 'rock drilling', Span. equivalent *barrenadores*, lit. 'borers' or 'piercers'], a folk competition consisting in boring a hole through a large rock or boulder, usu. a granite one, with a tool resembling a pointed crowbar or drill called an *arri*. An *arri* is usually 180-200cm long and weighs, depending on the local custom and type of event, from 10 to 30kg. Competitors have to bore a hole through a rock which is 30-80cm thick. Though the total area of such a rock remains unspecified, it has to be large enough for a competitor to easily stand on it and for the bored hole to be far enough from the edge of the rock so that no part of the rock breaks off. In order to prevent rocks from breaking apart during a competition, they are often buried in the ground so that their upper surface is at ground level. This sport is practiced in the province of Navarre and in the Basq. Country, especially in Guipúzcoa in places such as Berriatúa, Berrio, Bérriz, Deva, Eibar, Ellorio,

Elgóibar, Ermua, Garagarza, Mallavia, Málzaga, Marquina, Mendaro as well as in the province of Azpeitia (Azcoitia, Cestona, Landeta, Nuarbe, Oñaz, Régil, Urrestilla, Vidania). It originates from the tradition of boring holes in quarries for explosives to be put in. The competitive variety of arrisulatzalleak developed rapidly after mechanical equipment, and especially pneumatic drills, had been introduced to quarries. While the old skill of boring holes in rock manually had become obsolete, it remained a highly valued craft among stoneworkers who preserved it as a form of sport. Although arrisulatzalleak competitions were held as early as in the 19th cent., the official beginning of this sport was marked by the first public contest held in 1906 in Régil among F. Achúcarro, A. Achúcarro, and an unknown stoneworker from Iciar nicknamed Etxaiz. The greatest 20th cent. rock borers were L. Maria Arrasate from Motrico, J. Arrilaga from Igueldo and P. Irusta from Deva. A duel held in December 1920 between P. de Artzabal and Iñashio (first name unknown; both from Deva) is considered the greatest rock-boring contest of all times. The duel consisted in boring two holes through a 28cm-thick boulder with Artzabal winning and completing the task in 8min. 55secs. Completing the same task took his rival 9mins.
R. Aguirre Franco, 'Barrenadores o Arrisulatzalleak', JYDV, 1978, 453- 45; C.M. Palos, 'Barrenadores', JYTE, 1992.

ARTAZAKU GARREIZTZAILEEN LASTERKETA, Basq. for 'races with sacks full of grain', Span. *carrera con sacos de maiz*. A folk competition which involves running with a sack full of grain carried on one's shoulders and supported with both hands resting on the neck. Non-competitors are allowed to help a competitor put the sack on his shoulders. The race distance is 40m and has to be covered twice in one go. The first leg is deemed completed when the runner touches the ground behind the 40m line with his foot and then runs back to the start.
R. Aguirre, 'Artazaku Garreiztzaileen Lasterketa', GHJD, 1989, vol. III, 105.

ARTISTIC CYCLING, a competitive sport of figure bicycle riding employing special bicycles with a reinforced frame, the center of gravity pushed significantly lower, the saddle moved towards the back and placed over the rear wheel as well as a fixed gear allowing for pedaling both forwards and backwards. All the respective events are held among both individual competitors and teams of 2 (pairs), 4, and 6. It is worth stressing that artistic cycling is a separate sport from its newer var. called >BICYCLE STUNT RIDING. All cyclists select the figures they want to perform from a list of 150-200 recommended figures so that in individual attempts they perform 28 figures, 22 figures in pair events and 25 figures in team performances (each team consisting of 4 or 6 members). The performances are accompanied by music selected by the competitors. According to the official rules 'each figure has a points value depending on the level of difficulty. Adding up the value points of each figure leads to the total difficulty points. The performance starts with the lowest and finishes with the highest level of difficulty. The judges subtract points depending on the number and kind of mistakes they see during the performance. The judging is divided into performance and difficulty'.
History. Artistic cycling dates back to a point in time when the advancement of bicycle technologies allowed for bikes to be used to execute complex evolutions. The origins of artistic cycling can be linked to circus arts and reach back to the 1880s. The first sports artistic cycling organizations were established in Germany, Austria and Switzerland at the beginning of the 1890s. The first unofficial Artistic Cycling W.Ch. were held in the US in 1888 and N.E. Kaufmann, an American of Ger. origin, became the first world champion. This championship was, however, not recognized in Europe. The first E.Ch. took place in 1895. The first official W.Ch. took place in 1956 to commemorate the 60th anniversary of the sport's existence. Artistic cycling is supervised by the International Cycling Union (Union Cycliste Internationale, founded in 1900) and is practiced mainly in the Czech Republic, Germany, Austria and Switzerland. The 2000 W.Ch., involving artistic cycling and cycle ball events, attracted as many as 21 national teams with a total of 172 competitors, 102 journalists and 22 TV crews from all around the world, which points to the growing popularity of this attractive sport.

Muhammad Atik of Malaysia in action during the Junior Bicycle Stunt Flatland Competition at the Asian X-Games in Kuala Lumpur, Malaysia.

ARTISTIC GYMNASTICS, see >RHYTHMIC GYMNASTICS.

ASCETICISM IN SPORT, the voluntary exercise of will and the denial of desires followed by an athlete to eliminate factors hindering maximal sporting performance. Being a professional athlete in modern times requires abstaining from certain normal pleasures of everyday life and that is why many athletes are said to practice voluntary asceticism. Setting rigid principles not only with regard to bodily control or food consumed but also moral standards seems to be one of the fundamental principles of asceticism in sport. It consists in observing these principles not only during competitions but also, first and foremost, in training and in other, non-sports, activities. However, due to the fact that sports competitions are turning into shows and becoming more media events than sports events, more and more athletes are finding it increasingly difficult to withstand the pressures and temptations, and while they still observe the rigorous standards of bodily exercise, they fail to observe the long-standing moral standards in sports. Asceticism in sport dwells upon ages of different var. of asceticism as practiced for religious purposes, especially in Hinduism, Islam, and Christianity. These religions treated asceticism as the practice of the denial of physical or psychological desires offered as a sacrifice to God.
The term asceticism comes from the Gk. *askeo* – exercise, training. Homer used the verb *askein* to express the concept of 'practicing an art or agility'. That is why the title ascetic was originally given to those people who managed to achieve high proficiency in the skills of warfare and in sports by practicing rigorous self-control. Later, some philosophical schools, particularly the Pythagoreans, Stoics and Cynics, applied the term to a system of exercise and moral denial aimed at spiritual improvement. Since following a certain physical regimen was the most efficient way to test one's willpower, it soon turned out that this element dominated the way in which certain schools drawing upon the principles of asceticism formulated their ideas. This way of thinking was particularly typical of Pythagoras of Samos who is said to have coined the *soma-sema* ('the body as the prison of the soul') formula. This approach was also adopted in Christianity, esp. by St. Augustine, and further strengthened by the teachings of the Gospels and the words of Jesus as reported by Saint Mark: 'If anyone wants to come with me, he must forget self, carry his cross, and follow me' (8, 34). In the first ages of Christianity, due to the fact that Christians were widely persecuted, the practice of asceticism was treated as a method of preparing oneself for martyrdom. Then it evolved into a method of displaying one's devotion to God

WORLD SPORTS ENCYCLOPEDIA

A

by means of self-denial. 'Let us not love the world – wrote St. Augustine – for all that is worldly is a desire for the flesh, a desire for the eye and the vainglory of life' (*Of True Religion,* LIV, 104). The most widely-known ascetics of the Middle Ages were, among many others, St. Alexis and Duke Peter of Luxembourg who died at the age of 18. It was widely assumed that mortification was the best way to secure God's forgiveness or to express one's gratitude for salvation, recovery from an illness, etc. Irrespective of the religious and spiritual results of such undertakings, they required exceptional physical fitness and often resembled professional sports feats. C. de Blois, to thank God for freeing him from Eng. captivity, ran barefoot on snow from La Roche Derrien, where he was captured, to Treguier, where St. Ivo's relics were kept. >FLAGPOLE SITTING, whose most famous representative was St. Simeon Stylites, was a unique form of ascetic demonstration. Flagpole sitting required immense physical strength and psychological endurance.

Non-Eur. religions, such as Hinduism, considered harsh treatment of one's body as one of the distinct characteristics of persons considered saints. Asceticism never, however, consisted in inflicting pain on oneself, its sole aim was to master self-control and to attain higher forms of being. In Chapter XVIII of the religious poem *Bhagavadgita* Krishna says: 'He who tortures his body, tortures me, for I live in him'. The aim of Hindu asceticism was to find a moderate path, a compromise, between yielding to one's desires fully and extreme bodily and moral discipline. A modern athlete in his attempt to excel at sports resembles the old ascetics. The very activity of practicing a given sport requires making significant sacrifices. There is a number of sports that especially favor asceticism. They include those sports or events that are characterized by prolonged and monotonous effort such as cycling or long-distance running, and especially marathon running. A Pol. sociologist of sport, A. Ziemilski, wrote that 'the faces and the bodies of those completing a long-distance race resemble the medieval Passion pictures rather than depict complete satisfaction; oxygen deficiency invokes agonal expressions on the faces of the competing and finishing rivals' (*Sport stadionów a rzeczywistość społeczna*, 'Kultura i Społeczeństwo', 1964, 4). Putting a lot of effort into competition is not the only element of asceticism in sport. Equally difficult is trying to eliminate all these elements of normal life that might negatively influence the proper, proscribed course of training or the actual performance during a competition. This concerns, first and foremost, those activities that negatively influence a given type of sports activity (e.g. a long-distance runner should not take long bicycle rides, as bicycle riding involves muscles in a different way than running and this may reduce the effectiveness of one's running exercises). Furthermore, one has to give up all stimulants and addictive substances such as cigarettes, alcohol, or coffee in larger amounts.

One of the most widely discussed and controversial issues is pre-competition sexual abstinence. Many coaches advise their athletes to abstain from sexual intercourse 2-3 weeks before an important competition, which, given the fact that modern athletes compete almost every week, amounts to complete sexual abstinence during a given sports season. Sometimes this leads to major disagreements between athletes and their coaches.
D. Gelpi, *Functional Asceticism*, 1966; A. Tyszka, 'Filozofia pogardy ciała', *Olimpia i Akademia. Szkice o humanistycznej treści sportu*, 1970.

ASH WEDNESDAY FOOTBALL, a folk and ritual ball game of medieval tradition, once played in many areas of Europe, usually as a return match the day after >SHROVE TUESDAY FOOTBALL. The game was also played by younger boys, therefore Ash Wednesday was locally called the Boys' Day. Some forms of Ash Wednesday football have been preserved today in Asbourne and Derby in England.

ASIAN BOAT RACING, a sporting event popular in many cultures, esp. of the Far East. Typical Asian boat races are rowing or, sometimes, sailing events held in Bengal, in South China, and on the Jap. island of Riukiu. A unique variety is >DRAGON BOAT RACING. Asian boat races, often religious in nature, are connected with burial ceremonies and the symbol of a boat as a carrier to the underworld, similar to certain Eur. traditions (e.g. Charon, ferrying the souls of the deceased across the river Acheron; cf.

also the symbolic elements in >SIBERIAN SLEDGE RACING). In certain beliefs in S China there is also the reverse possibility of conveying the departed back to the world of the living during important holidays so that they can be reunited with their relatives. In Chin. mythology the departed also cross a symbolic river. They begin their journey at the spot where the sun rises and return at night to the living world. Races of this kind used to be held on the 5th day of the 5th lunar month, which marks the beginning of the rainy season and has a tremendous influence upon the crops (rice seedlings are moved from their incubators to the water fields). This is also a time when, according to Chin. philosophy, the transformation of *yin* into *yan* is completed.The relation between the boat races and the symbolic crossing of the border between life and death is reflected in the Chin. name of the event: *king tu* – to fight and to cross. The ideas of cycles in nature and crossing the border between life and death are also symbolically reflected in Laotian boat races held in August and October. According to local beliefs, the August races provoke the departed to compete with the living and so the spirits dwelling over water extents descend to the rice fields. For that reason each boat manouvers from the main water bed of the river towards its estuaries, while the route of the October races is reversed so that the spirits can return from the rice fields to their abode. In this way 'the participants of boat races symbolically cross the border between 1) the dwelling places of spirits and humans, 2) the elements of water and earth, 3) the environment in its natural form (river) and one which is man-made (rice fields). Boat races not only symbolize the change, but also take part in establishing a new desired order'.
I. Kabzińska-Stawarz, 'Competitions in Liminal Situations. Comparative Study of Asian Cultures', ETHP, 1994, 18; S. Kang, 'Toward a New Understanding of the Culture of the East Asians: Cinese, Korean, and Japanese', EWS, 1974, III, 1.

ASIAN INDIAN WRESTLING, a generic name of a number of wrestling varieties including >INBUAN, >KIRIP, >MALL-STAMBHA, >MIZO INCHAI, >MUKNA, >MUSHTI, >SALDU and >NAGA WRESTLING. Hand-to-hand combat has been popular in India since prehistoric times. The legend has it that the mythical Pandava brothers – Arjuna and Bhima – were outstanding archers and wrestlers. A Port. envoy who visited the town of Krishnanagar, the capital of the Nabadwip maharajahs, noticed that Rajah Krishnadev, the then ruler of the province, was an excellent wrestler and rider.
Today, the most popular type of Asian Ind. wrestling is the most static, i.e. involves long periods of waiting for the most opportune moment to attack. Match time is not limited. Limb and finger breaking is allowed. The fighters have to go through 2 stages of initiation. The first stage involves novices who, after mastering the required number of holds, grasps, and grips (*penčas*), are promoted to the second 'grade' – called a *pulvan* to describe a perfect wrestler. Upon receiving the title of *pulvan,* the novices become professional wrestlers.

ASOL AAP, an Ind. canoe-type boat race. The number of participants is generally from 40 to 90 depending on the size of the canoe. The canoeists use a simple, one-blade oar held in both hands. Asol Aap is indigenous to the Nicobar Islands in India, a group of islands in the Bay of Bengal. The canoe's

length is approx. 100ft. (30m). The race takes place at sea and only 2 teams participate at a time. The competition is organized and controlled by the Nicobar Athletic Association.

ASOL-TALE AAP, an Ind. canoe race for 1 or 2 competitors on sand. A folk competition held on the Nicobar Islands in India, a group of islands in the Bay of Bengal. The hull of the 'boat' is built from the trunk of a coconut tree. The participants sit in their canoes keeping one leg in the canoe and the other one on the ground. They move their canoe forward with an 'oar' (one oar per competitor) which is a stick driven into the ground with both hands around a spot near a given competitor's hip. The crew uses these sticks and the force of their limbs to drive the canoe through the sand. Usu. there are ab. 15 to 20 competitors. There are no hard rules concerning the size of the 'boat', but it is generally assumed that the canoes used in the same competition should be roughly the same size.
The Internet: http://w3.meadev.gov.in/sports/tr_games/asol.htm

ASSOCIATION FOOTBALL, also *soccer*, a team game played between two 11-player teams. The object is to put the ball in motion with the feet and other parts of the body (other than arms and hands) and to score goals. The goalkeeper is the only player who has the right to play with his hands. The team scoring a greater number of goals dur-

Above: Wrestlers practice a move at Guru Hanuman Akhara, a place where they learn and practice wrestling, in New Delhi, India. Wrestling, which dates back to 3000 BC, was once a favorite pastime of kings and princes. Thousands of years later, the discipline still holds the same techniques. The ancient master-disciple relationship still persists as students learn to wrestle on mat and mud. Only the arena has changed and students compete for international wrestling.

Below: Dharmender, a young wrestler of Chandiram Akhara, a place where they learn, live and practice wrestling, makes a bridge during their morning practice in New Delhi, India.

WORLD SPORTS ENCYCLOPEDIA

Above: a postage stamp commemorating the 100th anniversary of Wembley Stadium in London; below: a football motif on a postage stamp issued for the 1972 Munich Olympics.

Gabriele Bella, after Franco (c.1610), Football at Sant' Alvise, *c.1779-1792, oil on canvas.*

Poland in World Cups (below), and a stamp issued for the World Cup in Spain (bottom).

ing a predetermined time wins. See also >FOOTBALL FOR THE DISABLED.

The playing field, also referred to as a pitch, is rectangular, usu. 100-110m (110-120yds.) by 64-73m (70-80yds.). Less important matches can be played on a field as small as 90x45m. The pitch is a level grass lawn. In the middle of the end lines, called goal lines, there are goals, 7.32m (8yds.) wide and 2.44m (8ft.) high; the width being measured between the inside edges of the posts, and the height – between the ground and the lower edge of the crossbar. The width of the posts should not exceed 12.7cm (5in.). The space behind the goal is protected with a net, usually laced, which prevents the ball from going out and makes it easy to determine whether it went in between or past the posts. In front of each goal there is a goal area, marked with a parallel line, 5.5m in front of the goal line, and 2 perpendicular lines placed 5.5m to the right and left of the posts. A penalty area is marked in a similar way, with a parallel line at a distance of 16.5m in front of the goal line, and 2 perpendicular lines 16.5m from the posts. **Equipment.** The ball weighs 396-453g, with a circumference of 68-71cm.

Players. Each team consists of 11 players, including the goalkeeper. The number of defense, midfield and forward players varies, and depends on a team's tactics. A max. of 3 players can be substituted in the course of a single match. The goalkeeper can be replaced by any player, if necessary.

The object and course of the game. The object of the game is to score a goal by placing the ball in the opponent's goal. A goal is scored if the entire ball crosses the goal line between the posts and under the crossbar, provided it was not struck with a player's arms or from an offside position. Goals accidentally scored against one's own team are also counted, including ones struck with the arm (e.g.

during a clumsy defense of one's own goal). According to the rules a player is in an offside position if he/she is near to his/her opponent's goal line than both the ball and the second last opponent. Offside does not apply if a player receives the ball while still in his own half of the field. An offside position is not penalized by a referee, unless the offside player touches the ball, challenges an opponent, or is directly involved in an exchange in which the ball is passed. There is no offside if a player intercepts the ball from an opponent, goalkeeper's kickoff, referee's throw, a corner kick or a throw-in. The playing time is 2x45min. for seniors, 2x40min. for juniors (15-18yrs. old), and 2x30min. for juveniles (below 15). The duration of the game can be adjusted for veterans, depending on their age. Halftime must not exceed 15min. The referee can prolong the game with the time needed to execute free kicks, substitute players, remove seriously injured players, etc. The team which won the toss of a coin has the right either to choose their half or to begin the game. During the kickoff, executed after the referee's signal, all players of each team must remain in their half. The player starting the game must not touch the ball a second time before another player has touched it.

Teams change halves after halftime and the kickoff is executed by the team that selected their half at the beginning of the match.

Fouls are committed when the rules of the game are violated by: a) kicking or attempting to kick an opponent; b) tripping an opponent; c) jumping on an opponent; d) holding an opponent with one's hands; e) hitting or attempting to hit an opponent with one's hands; f) pushing an opponent; g) tackling an opponent without a ball; h) spitting on an opponent; i) deliberately touching or handling the ball during the game (not applicable in the case of a goalkeeper). These fouls are penalized with a direct free kick, taken from the place where the foul occurred, directly at the goal. In the case of an indirect free kick, awarded to penalize minor offences, the ball can be directed at the goal only after a pass. During a free kick other players must be at least 9.15m (10yds.) away from the ball. A foul committed in the penalty area is penalized with a penalty kick, i.e. a direct kick at the goal from a point 11m (12yds.) in front of the goal. During a penalty kick, all players, excluding the kicker and the goalkeeper, must remain outside the penalty area, and at least 9.15m (10yds.) away from the ball.

When the ball leaves the field by crossing the goal line after having been touched by a member of the defending team, a corner kick is awarded, taken from the place marked with a flag, located at the intersection of the goal and touch lines. A goal may be scored directly from a corner kick or from an attempt made in the vicinity of the goal. Players must be at least 9.15m (10yds.) away from the ball when a corner kick is being executed. A foul also includes dangerous play, challenging an opponent possessing no ball, blocking a running opponent, playing for time. A yellow card is used to caution a player for: entering or leaving the field during the game without the referee's signal, expressing dissatisfaction with the referee's decision, violating rules in a manner impeding the game or committing a dangerous foul, thus violating the rules of fair play. A player is given a red card, after which he has to leave the field of play, for a violent foul or for a play that endangers an opponent's health, or for committing another offence after having already been cautioned. **Officials.** A team of officials consists of a referee, whose task is to supervise the current situation on the field and stay close to the ball, although far enough so as not to disturb the game, and linesmen moving along the touchlines. In recent years a fourth official was introduced, responsible e.g. for assisting with substitution procedures during the match. He also supervises the replacement of footballs and may officiate if any of the three referees is unable to continue.

The uniform consists of shorts, a shirt with a number on it, long socks under which players wear shin guards, and special shoes. The shoes' uppers are made of leather, the soles are now made of plastic but formerly they were made of thick leather. Soles are equipped with a number of threads holding studs made of leather, rubber or aluminum, called cleats.

History. The origin of football is connected with the overall development of >BALL. Several Eur. countries, mainly England, France, and Italy, claim to be

An association football English Premiership game.

the cradle of modern football. History has proven that many a ball game originated in the Middle Ages in France and Italy, some of which were similar to modern football. Nonetheless, modern football's rules developed in England. The earliest information recorded by folklore researchers concerns a ball game, played since the 4th cent. in Britain occupied by the Romans, in which the ball was moved by kicking, but was also carried in the hands, which may be traced to Mediterranean cultures and a var. of football popular in that region, such as >FAININDA, >FOLLIS, or >HARPASTON. These ancient ball games had nothing in common with the football that developed later, but they stimulated Britons' interest in such games as they had not previously known. Historians' opinions vary. F. Peabody Magoun is convinced there is no proof for the existence of a game which may be treated as the predecessor of football: 'There is no evidence of football among Celts of pre-Roman Britain (before 43 AD), nor can we assume that the Celts learned it from their conquerors since, as far as is known, football was not played by the Romans'. Another historian, W. Andrews, maintains that the ante-predecessor of football was introduced to Britain by Romans and 'is our oldest sport'. S. Glover records in the *History and Gazetteer of Derbyshire* (1831-32), that in Derby parties of people during which various city quarters fought for a ball were popular from 217 AD until the beginning of the 19th cent. According to Glover, the custom of playing football was to develop after the victory of British warriors over a Roman cohort in the vicinity of Derby. Captured Roman soldiers are said to have been rushed through the town gate and to commemorate this event, city dwellers every year ran through the town gate, rolling a ball symbolizing their defeated enemies. Such theses cannot be corroborated at the current stage of research but such a genesis of football is deeply rooted in the Brit. consciousness. Ashbourne, Derby also has its own legend commemorating victory over the Romans (cf. >SHROVE TUESDAY FOOTBALL). Another famous folk tale says that the local ball game was first played after a victory over Vikings rather than Romans. Later, a football match became a part of the Lent tradition and has been played on each Shrove Tuesday up to modern times. The game is played along the main street of the town. The goals are approx. 3mi. apart (almost 5km). The game was repeatedly prohibited in the past due to its brutal character, but public opinion always pressed for its reinstatement. Finally, it was recognized as a folkloric attraction and since 1928 it has been played every year and sponsored interchangeably by the Prince of Wales and the Duke of Windsor. In the past, matches were played between St. Peter's and All Saints parishes, whereas nowadays every city dweller can take part in the game as the number of players is unlimited.

The earliest testimony to the existence of a football game in Britain dates back to the post-Roman period and was found in Nennius's Latin chronicle *Historia Brittonum* (*The History of the Brits*). King Guorthigirn (later referred to as Vortigern) had his aides

dispatched to search for a fatherless boy, in order to sacrifice him in a bloody ceremony. The king's aides found a boy named Ambrosius Guletic (often associated with the legendary Merlin, king Arthur's spiritual protector), engaged in a ball game (pilae ludum faciebat pueri) with a group of other boys. Nennius does not explain what kind of game it was, that is why it should not necessarily be associated with the origins of football. William Stephen's work, *The Life of St Thomas* (*Vita Sancti Thomae*, 1175), contains a description of games and pastimes of London citizens:

After the midday meal the entire youth of the City goes to the fields for the famous game of ball (Post prandium, exit in campos omnis iuventus urbis ad iusum pilaa celebrem). The students of the several branches of study have their ball; the followers of the several trades of the City have a ball in their hands. The elders, the fathers, and men of wealth come on horseback to view the contests of their juniors, and in their fashion sport with the young men; and there seems to be aroused in these elders a stirring of natural heat by viewing so much activity and by participation in the joys of unrestrained youth.

[trans. F. Peabody Magoun]

sequently by Henry IV (1401) and Henry VI (1424). In Scotland Jacob II instructed that: 'The King forbids any man to play at football on pain of 4 d. to be paid to the lord of the land as often as he is convicted, or to the sheriff of the land or to his agents, if the lords are unwilling to punish such trespassers' (1457). A similar prohibition was issued by Jacob IV in 1491. The prohibitions applied to common people but not to the rulers, as the treasurer of the very same Jacob IV spent 2 shillings in 1497 to purchase a number of *fut-balles* for a game which the king himself participated in. The game was again banned by Henry VIII, reigning 1509-1547, and in 1572 it was likewise banned by his daughter Elizabeth. Even in 1779, J. Wonkell of Durham was sentenced to a week in custody and rigorous penance in church for 'shameless practicing of fute ball.' The cruelty and low social status of the game are confirmed by numerous literary works. Shakespeare's references to the game reveal how infamous it was among the aristocracy. In the *Comedy of Errors* (around 1590), Dromio asks Adriana: 'That like a football you do spurn me thus.' In *King Lear* (1604-05, I, 4) we find the following dialogue:

pus Act in Great Britain, the fundamental Brit. legal instrument providing for human rights (1679). Thanks to the regulations and rigors exercised in Brit. public schools, the game which originated in the Middle Ages among commoners, gradually evolved into modern football. In 1855, the first football club was established – the Sheffield Club. In 1860, the London Football Association was established, converted in 1863 into the Football Association (FA). Since then, football practiced within the association became known as association football, and then as soccer, in order to differentiate it from other, similar games which also incorporated the word football in their names. The title 'plain football' was also used, however it was subsequently abandoned. Since 1866, when the offside rule was introduced, the Football Association embarked on constant improvement of the rules standardizing the game throughout England. By 1903, all of the principal rules had been created, and although modified repeatedly, they form the core of the rules applied to this day. Football clubs were established outside the Brit. Isles as well, as in 1880-88 in Denmark, the Netherlands, and Germany. The game was

A new soccer (association football) ball introduced during the 2002 World Cup.

Brad Friedel of the USA saves a penalty from Eul Yong Lee of South Korea during the FIFA World Cup Finals 2002 Group D match played at the Daegu World Cup Stadium, in Daegu, South Korea.

No details of the character of the game have survived. We do know, however, it was very brutal and condemned by the Church and royal authorities. In 1324, Edward II issued a Latin proclamation prohibiting the game:

Whereas there is great uproar in the City, through certain tumults arising from great footballs in the fields of the public, from which many evils perchance may arise – which may God forbid – we do command and do forbid, on King's behalf upon pain of imprisonment, that such game shall be practiced henceforth within the city.

[trans. F. Peabody-Magoun]

In 1349, the game was described in Edward III's statute accurately enough to identify it as a predecessor of modern football. In 1365, it was prohibited as a game 'of no value' which simply drew young men away from their military exercises. The ban proved ineffective, because in a similar document written in French, Richard II prohibited 'all playing at ball.' Richard II's prohibition was confirmed sub-

STEWARD OSWALD
I'll not be struck, my lord
LORD KENT
Nor tripped neither, you base foot-ball player!

The infiltration of people from a lower class into the upper one, so characteristic of Eng. society, contributed in the 18th cent. to the gradual popularization of the game in elite public schools, where numerous local var. of football developed when the game mixed with the Scot. dribbling game. At the turn of the 18th and 19th cent., such new varieties formed the foundations of the future football. The status of local ball games in schools such as Eton, Harrow, Winchester and Rugby was so strong, that when in 1823, W. Webb Ellis violated the rules, initiating what later turned out to be >RUGBY, he was severely rebuked by school authorities for acting against tradition. T. Hughes (1822-96), author of the famous autobiographical novel *Tom Brown's School Days* (1857), compares the Brit. football of the 1830s and '40s to an instrument such as the Habeas Cor-

popularized, without much success though, after 1885 by Ir. emigrants in the USA, where it began to enjoy minor but constant popularity only after 1910. The first national associations appeared in the following order: England – 1863, Scotland – 1872, Wales – 1876, Ireland, Denmark – 1889, Argentina – 1893, Switzerland – 1895, Belgium – 1895, Chile – 1895, Italy – 1898, the Netherlands – 1899, Germany – 1900, the Czech Republic – 1901, Hungary – 1901, Norway – 1902, Austria – 1904, Sweden – 1904, Paraguay – 1906, Romania – 1908, Spain – 1913, the USA – 1913, Brazil – 1914, Portugal – 1914, France – 1918, Yugoslavia – 1919, and Poland – 1919. The national Ir. association was established under Brit. rule and its traditions are currently continued in Northern Ireland. The association of Ireland, as an independent country, was established after Ireland gained its independence in 1921. In 1882, on the Eng. FA's initiative, the first International Football Association Board (IFAB) was established, incorporating the countries of the Brit. Empire. In view of the Brit. origin of the game, its by-

Brazil's Pele – the 'king of football'.

WORLD SPORTS ENCYCLOPEDIA

SOCCER WORLD CUP FINALS

MEN

1930 Uruguay 4-2 Argentina
1934 Italy 2-1 Czechoslovakia
1938 Italy 4-2 Hungary
1950 Uruguay (def. Brazil, Sweden, and
      Spain in a group format)
1954 West Germany 3-2 Hungary
1958 Brazil 5-2 Sweden
1962 Brazil 3-1 Czechoslovakia
1966 England 4-2 West Germany
1970 Brazil 4-1 Italy
1974 West Germany 2-1 Holland
1978 Argentina 3-1 Holland
1982 Italy 3-1 West Germany
1986 Argentina 3-2 West Germany
1990 West Germany 1-0 Argentina
1994 Brazil (3-2 on penalties) Italy
1998 France 3-0 Brazil
2002 Brazil 2-0 Germany

WOMEN

1991 USA 2-1 Norway
1995 Norway 2-1 Germany
1999 USA 0-0 China
      USA won, 5-4, on penalty kicks

CONCACAF GOLD CUP

MEN

1963 Costa Rica
1965 Mexico
1967 Guatemala
1969 Costa Rica
1971 Mexico
1973 Haiti
1977 Mexico
1981 Honduras
1991 United States
1993 Mexico
1996 Mexico
1998 Mexico
2000 Canada
2002 United States

EUROPEAN CHAMPIONS

MEN

1960 Soviet Union
1964 Spain
1968 Italy
1972 West Germany
1976 Czechoslovakia
1980 West Germany
1984 France
1988 Holland
1992 Denmark
1996 Germany
2000 France

laws reserved the right to authorize all and any rules concerning football. Some countries, such as Belgium or the Netherlands, were interested in close cooperation with the Brit. IFAB and suggested spreading its activities over countries outside the Brit. influence. Their applications concerning admission to the IFAB were examined for a long time and consulted with all IFAB members, though no final decision was forthcoming. In 1903, a similar application was submitted by France but it was rejected by the IFAB, as a result of which France, accompanied by the representatives of Belgium, Denmark, Spain and the Netherlands, estab. in Paris in 1904 the International Federation of Football Association – Fédération Internationale de Football Association (FIFA). The British-zone countries did not join the association at first, although they declared they would cooperate. Finally, they joined FIFA in 1906. Two years later, the Amateur Football Association (AFA) broke off from the Eng. FA and intended to join FIFA as a separate entity. Its application was turned down on the grounds that only an organization which controlled football activities as a whole in a given country might be a member of FIFA. After WWI, FIFA was reactivated and attempted to return to the status it had built up before the war, while taking into consideration the new map of Europe. In the meantime, the British sought to dominate FIFA by convening a conference in Brussels, in 1919, attended by Brit., Fr., Belgian, and Luxembourg delegations. The participating countries decided not to maintain any sporting relations with federations from Austria, Germany and Hungary, i.e. countries which belonged, during the war, to the Central Alliance. The position was opposed by Denmark, Finland, Norway and Sweden, which convened a separate conference in Göteborg and voted for maintaining relationships with all countries, regardless of political configurations. This position was soon backed by the influential Ital. association which had not taken part in the Göteborg conference. The 'Brussels group', in turn, established a temporary organization called the Federation of National Football Associations, FNFA. France and Belgium gradually withdrew, fearing that the disputes might disturb the football tournament at the 1920 Ol.G. in Antwerp. Up to that moment, i.e. until football was incorporated into the Olympic program, the British had played the leading role, winning gold medals twice (1908 and 1912). In 1920, the Brit. team participated in the Ol.G. under the Brit. flag for the last time. Neither the joint representation of Great Britain nor any of its national representations would participate in Ol.G. again until 1939, a conspicuous absence which obscured the real picture of international football. In the meantime, the group of countries that had gathered in Göteborg in 1919, decided to continue their membership of FIFA, which left British-controlled countries alone. In 1920, these countries withdrew from FIFA altogether and expelled it from the International Football Board controlled by the British, which was responsible, as agreed with FIFA, for the rules of international football. After having won its independence, Ireland abandoned the British and formed, in 1921, the Football Association of Ireland (FAI) which was independent from the association set up under British reign. The new association was admitted as a FIFA member in 1923. The remaining Brit. associations were still at odds with FIFA despite repeated attempts at

conciliation. The dispute concerned the acceptance of both Irish associations which was objected to by the British who opted for a single association they could control. The problem of recognizing both Irish associations, settled temporarily for major events, was not settled finally and positively until as late as 1954. In 1923, FIFA sent a conciliatory letter to the Brit. FA. Great Britain returned to FIFA for a short time under 4 conditions: 1) FIFA rules would not violate the legal status between associations of Brit. countries; 2) rules concerning the income from international matches collected by

a result of which the British decided not to send a team to the 1928 Ol.G. in Amsterdam and to re-sign from FIFA. Only after tedious negotiations in 1946-47 did the British return to FIFA. Below is J. Arlott's evaluation of the more than 20yr. absence of the British in international football:

During the period from 1928 until the outbreak of the Second World War the standard of play in British football failed to advance to the extent that it did in many countries in Europe and in South America, and the disassociation from FIFA was the main reason for what amounted to stagnation – the conse-

A British Premiership game between Manchester United and Arsenal.

FIFA would not apply to matches between national teams of individual Brit. countries; 3) any amendments made by FIFA must be initially accepted by the International Association Football Board, which would also be represented in FIFA's management; 4) FIFA would not interfere with the management of football within the area under Brit. influence. The parties did reach agreement on the fifth point: the relationship between Brit. amateur and professional football. These questions, presented during the FIFA congress in Rome in 1926 were not supported by national associations. Pressed by continental associations, the congress passed a resolution that was in clear opposition to the Brit. expectations: 'We acknowledge FIFA as the highest authority on all matters concerning football, and that it must not allow anyone else's management or influence in the said matters.' The dispute became even more bitter with the Comité International Olimpique's (CIO) position on amateur sports, as

quences of which were not appreciated until competitive international football was resumed after the war. At the same time, although there was a considerable growth in membership and the world cup was successfully inaugurated, FIFA suffered from contact with the British Associations that was limited to meetings of the International (Football) Association Board and to the exchange of opinions.

In the 1920s and '30s, strong sports individuals appeared, attracting considerable admiration on the part of spectators, which was intensified by the development of radio and mass sports press. Among the first heroes were Span. goalkeeper R. Zamorra (1901-78) and Brazilian forward L. da Silva (b. 1913). Europe's strongest national teams before 1939 were: Germany, Italy, France and Spain. Football was first played at the Ol.G. in 1900 and since then has always been present in the Olympic program, with the exception of the 1932 Ol.G. in Los Angeles. At the 1904 Ol.G. the only players were the Canadian team

Zinedine Zidane (in white) of Real Madrid – among the best teams in Europe.

and 2 local Los Angeles teams. In 1919-39, football became the most popular sport in Europe and South America. After WWII, it returned to the international arena stronger then ever. The development of mass media, especially TV, contributed to the rapid increase in the game's popularity, which resulted in a greater number of international events. Since 1955, the Eur. Cup has been played; since 1960 – Cup Winners' Cup, discontinued in 1999. The Eur. National Champions' Cup has been played since 1955--56. Its name was changed in the 1991-92 season to the Champions' Cup, also known as the Cham-

Since 1992, on Saudi Arabia's prince Faisal bin Fahd bin Abdulaziz Al-Said's initiative, the (continental) Confederation Cup is played, in which champions of 6 continental confederations play, accompanied by a number of runners-up. The Confederation Cup events were ignored by Europe at the beginning. The W.Ch. of national teams has been played since 1930, when Uruguay won the trophy in Montevideo. The W.Ch. of club teams was inaugurated in 2000 and the first event took place in Brazil, with the São Paulo Corinthians as the winners.
Each country where football enjoys popularity has

finals, they lost the final to West Germany 3:2 (after having led 2:0). Apart from Hungary, also the USSR and Yugoslavia qualified for the finals of the World Cup, reaching the quarter-finals, as well as Czechoslovakia (1962 runner-up) and Poland (3rd place in 1974). Before 1939, Great Britain won 3 Olympic gold medals and then withdrew from Olympic tournaments. After 1945, Ol.G. were dominated by 'state professionals' from socialist countries. From 1952-80, all Olympic gold medals and the majority of silver and bronze medals were awarded to national teams from socialist countries. The opening of the Ol.G. for professionals, gradually introduced in the '80s during J.A. Samaranch's term of office, increased the competitiveness of the Ol.G. in relation to the World Cup, which was opposed by FIFA. The dispute was settled with an agreement, according to which only players up to age 23 could compete in the Ol.G. In this way, the Ol.G. football tournament actually turned into a youth tournament. Since the 1996 Atlanta Ol.G., this limitation has been lifted and 3 players above the age limit were allowed to play in each team. The following are the most remarkable players of the first years of the post-WWII era: Brazilian Pele (E.A. do Pele, b. 1940), Ger. F. Beckenbauer (b. 1945), Eng. R. Charlton (b. 1937), Dutch J. Cruyff (b. 1947), Span. A. di Stefano (b. 1926), Port. E. da Silva Ferreira (b. 1942), Fr. of Pol. origin R. Kopaczewski-Kopa (b. 1931), Eng. S. Matthews (b. 1915), and Hungarians S. Kocsis (1929-1979) and F. Puskas (b. 1927).
Currently, there are almost 200 national associations incorporated in FIFA whose headquarters are located in Zurich, Switzerland. FIFA's highest authority is the congress, convened every 4 years. The organization also supervises the activity of continental football associations in Europe, Africa, Asia, S.America, N.America, and Latin America.
Women's football has enjoyed worldwide popularity since the late 1970s. The Women's World Cup has been played since 1991. At the 1999 World Cup, 16 national teams participated and the US team, coached by T. DiCicco, won the Cup after defeating the Chinese on penalties (there was a draw in regular time). The final match, played in the Los Angeles Rose Bowl stadium, attracted 90,000 spectators, a testimony to the popularity of women's football. M. Hamm, often referred to as the 'Ronaldo of women's football', was the top player of the 1999 World Cup. The event's top scorer was S. Wen, with 7 goals. Similarly to the men's World Cup, the main trophy was designed by W. Sawaya, a Milanese jeweler. The Olympic tournament of women's football was first held at the 1996 Atlanta Ol.G. In the final match, the USA beat China 2:1. The bronze medal was awarded to Norway. The Sydney Ol.G. tournament was won by the Norwegian national team, with the USA as runners-up and the German team coming in 3rd. The tournament's top players were Norwegian Marianne Pettersen and German Doris Titschen. Ever growing, women's football is often treated as a sport of the future. Speaking of the role of women's football during the 2nd World Cup in 1995, FIFA president, J. Blatter, said that women show us how the game should be played – with elegance, the game's object in mind and fair-play. After the 1999 World Cup, the President added that football's future belongs to women. The final proof of that will have to wait for the election of a female as FIFA president.

WORLD SPORTS ENCYCLOPEDIA

A

pions' League. The Fair Cities' Cup, played since 1955, changed its name to the UEFA Cup during the 1971-72 season. The E.Ch. have been played since 1958. The Super Cup (since 1972) was played between the winners of Cup Winners' Cup and the Champions' Cup. Since 2000, Europe's Super Cup has been played between the winners of the UEFA Cup and the Champion's Cup. In Africa, the following championships are played: 1) the Africa Champion's Cup, 2) the Africa Cup Winners' Cup, 3) the African Football Confederation Cup. S.America's most important events comprise: the Copa Libertadores for national champions and runners-up; the Copa Conmebol (formerly the Spercopa, equivalent of the Eur. UEFA Cup), the Copa Mercosur for 5 teams chosen by the associations of Argentina, Brazil, Chile, Paraguay and Uruguay. The Copa Interamericana is a cup played by league champions of both Americas. Events staged in Asia include the Asian Champion's Cup and the Cup Winners' Cup.

a well developed system of league, cup and other types of games. The income generated by these events became the subject of serious disputes between FIFA and CIO. Until CIO began to observe the amateur formula, there was a specific division between the roles of Ol.G. which gathered the best non-professional teams, and the World Cup open for anyone, which meant for professionals mainly. This division has long been blurred, however. Since 1945, national teams of the USSR and so-called socialist countries which did not officially recognize professional sportsmen but their players enjoyed social benefits and fictitious jobs unrelated with their sports activities provided by the country. As a result, 'officially' amateur national teams, actually consisting of 'state professionals', were able to compete with Western professionals. A team from a socialist country, Hungary, won the Ol.G. for the first time in 1952, and placed second in the 1953 World Cup when, having defeated England in the semi-

Michael Owen of Liverpool scores his second goal during a match against Manchester City.

A

WORLD SPORTS ENCYCLOPEDIA

Football in literature, film, and the arts. The earliest pictures and descriptions of football games which preceded the modern game date back to the Middle Ages (cf. >BALL). Modern football was taken up by literature and art only recently, because before the sport was considered to be of a rather plebeian nature and it lacked the artistic sponsorship that was enjoyed by horse riding and tennis. Italy's initial reluctance, after WWI, toward football, inspired by the Fascist government and connected with attempts to replace the game with >VOLATA, died away once Italy was entrusted with the organization of the 1934 World Cup. The Fascists' inclination to oversize their activities was demonstrated by the construction of the monumental Foro Mussolini sports center (now the Foro Italico). Numerous marble sculptures of sportsmen were placed there, including C. De Veroli's *A Footballer in Repose* (*Calciatore in riposo*) near the Marble Stadium (the *Stadio Marmi*) and O. Taddeini's *A Footballer* (*Calciatore*). The era's most famous work is a large statue by G. Tomini *Footballers* (*Calciatori*, 1938) which adorns St. Francis's Plaza in Rome. During the 1932 Ol.G. in Los Angeles, the Italian E. Drei was distinguished for his sculpture entitled *Football Player* (*Giocatore di calcio*). Nazi Germany boasted a colossal football-themed sculpture by E. Encke (*Fussballer*, 1936). B. Sintenis's *Fussballer*, which took a bronze medal in the Olympic literature and art con-

Darmstadt in 1926. The play presents the adventures of a forward bought by a club's chairman. After years of sporting successes, the player becomes handicapped and is abandoned by his club. He decides to find an ordinary job and emigrates to America, where he is employed as a steam engine stoker. He spends his leisure time playing football with his co-workers. One day, the ball is kicked so high that it lands among the elders of an Indian tribe dwelling near the railroad. One thing leads to another and the story concludes with the chief's son leaving for the town to try to become a footballer and the main character marrying the witch-doctor's daughter and then becoming the chief himself.

After WWII, F. Krivet's play titled *Wearing Red and White* (*Stimmung Rot-Weiss*, 1971) became a reflection on the contemporary phenomenon of mass sports events. It was based on the everyday life of the Ger. Rot-Weiss club from Essen. The play analyzed the mass hysteria element in football and was an attempt at relieving social aggression related to it. It was staged as a multimedia show, color slides and sound recordings were employed. Football's nationalistic character was criticized in H. Pillau's play *War of States* (*Länderkampf*, 1971). Ger. and Ital. mountaineers meet in a mountain refuge in Austria and become friends. During a radio broadcast of a Germany vs. Italy match the friends become enemies. R. Wolf is the author of *A Goal is a*

Eve (*Im Sache Adam und Eva*, 1971) is a comedy, written by R.O. Strahl. The play's plot is an official East German marriage test, during which the fiancé turns out to be an enthusiastic footballer, while his fiancée cannot stand football. Consequently, a test committee concludes that it is not recommended for them to get married. Football also appeared in Ger. radio programs and plays, e.g. L. Harig's *Fussball* (1966; recorded at the RS radio station in 1967) and *Das Fussballspiel* (1966, recorded in Wiesbaden and Stuttgart radio stations in 1967 and 1969). In the first play, a man talks to a woman among a cheering crowd at a football match. The conversation's fragments are interlaced with sport reports. The second play shows how a football match can be depreciated and become a sort of a military duel, similar to battles fought between ancient Roman gladiator teams. F. Kriwet's radio plays also dealt with football: *Perfect Luck* (Modell Fortuna, 1971), *The Ball* (1974) and *Radioball* (1975). *Perfect Luck's* main character is the fan lingo, separated from the crowd's voices recorded during a real game. *The Ball* represents the system of values in the football milieu. It is a collage of statements of fans and passers-by, with emphasis on aggression. *Radioball* concentrates on football jargon broadcast directly to apartments and public places. R. Wolf is author of 2 radio-plays: *Hot Atmosphere of the Match* (Die heisse Luft der Spiele, 1973) and a stereo-collage *The Hour of Truth*, based on the book of the same title (*Die Stunde der Wahrheit*, 1980). Another of Wolf's radio plays, *Cordoba*, was based on reports of the Germany vs. Austria match played at the 1978 World Cup in Argentina. A. Behrens wrote a malicious Bundesliga radio play satire *Der syntetische Seler*, 1973. The play's leitmotif is that the football league is in fact a TV league and the team guaranteeing the highest ratings is the champion. The idea of this radio play came from the same author's utopian novel *The TV League* (Die Fernsehliga). The radio play titled *Teamwork*, based on K.E. Ewerwyn's novel with the same title, critically depicted West German professional football (recorded in 1971). It reveals how the sporting reality is distorted when unfair economic rules are applied to it. In the author's opinion, football is artificially glorified by employing Jahn's idea. The most remarkable Pol. fine arts work with football as the subject is J. Klukowski's relief *The Football Players* (*Piłkarze*), awarded the golden medal at the 1932 Los Angeles Ol.G. J. Ślusarczyk's bronze sculpture titled *The Footballers* (*Futboliści*) was presented during the 1948 London Ol.G. In the '20s, V. Hofman painted several portraits of Wisła Kraków football club players. R. Malczewski repeatedly exploited football in his paintings, the most famous of which was *Sport on the Outskirts* (*Sport na przedmieściach*), representing a spontaneous match against the background panorama of a city and factory chimneys. In 1937, W. Podoski made a beautiful and dynamic drawing titled *Football* (*Futbol*). A. Pietsch's aqua-fortis etching with aquatint titled *The Goalkeeper* (*Bramkarz*) was awarded a bronze medal at the Polish exhibition *Sports in the Arts* in 1959. In 1948, J. Żuławski made a ceramic mosaic titled *The Football Match* (*Mecz futbolowy*). *The Big Game* (*Wielka gra*), a novel by A. Reksza and M. Strzelecki, printed in parts in *Przegląd Sportowy* newspaper (1935-36), enjoyed vast popularity. It was reprinted several times. In 1939, the same writers also published a novel titled *Boys Kick the Ball* (*Chłopcy kopią piłkę*, 1939). E. Wilk's short story *The Big Match* (*Wielki Mecz* 1939), which depicted the tragedy of a Pol. immigrant in Germany, induced much reflection among the readers of *Ilustracja Polska*. T. Boy Żeleński mocked football anomalies and ridiculous situations in his *Footballer's Couplets* (*Kuplety futbolisty*, 1918), while K. Wierzyński paid tribute to football in a tome of poems *Olympic Laurels* (*Laur olimpijski*), which was awarded a golden medal at the Olympic Art and Literature Competition during the 1928 Amsterdam Ol.G.:

Here is the great Coliseum of the world
Here beats the heart of all life and desire
Here an enigma unites, enthusiasm makes kinsmen
Of one million people spread through the arena

[trans. Clark Mills]

After WWII, hooliganism reared its ugly head at football stadiums, culminating with tragedies at Heysel and Bradford stadiums, which involved loss of life, the new phenomenon was reflected in the poetry of the Pole K. Zuchora and the Briton D. Masterson

Thomas Linke of FC Bayern Munich tackles Rivaldo of AC Milan during The Champions League match at The Olympic Stadium, Munich, Germany.

Top and below: fans displaying their colors.

test in Amsterdam in 1928, was created even earlier. Football themes were present in the painting of German H. Spiegel (*Fussballspiel*, 1936), Belgian A. Osta (*The Football Player*, a bronze medal in the Olympic literature and art contest in Antwerp, 1920), Frenchman A. Virot (*Football Scene*, a silver medal in a similar contest in Amsterdam, 1928). After WWII, football motifs were taken up by a Dan. sculptor, K. Nellemose, Ital. painters G. Capogrossi, V. Piscopo, R. Guttoso, Englishman C. Hall, Belgian P. Daxhelet, Austrian W. Kaufman, and A.W. Diggelman of Switzerland. Pen-drawn football scenes were created by Ital. artist M. Riccobaldi del Bava.

Many works of Fr. literature have been devoted to football, most famous of which became the second part of H. de Montherlant's *Les Olympiques*, titled *Les onze devant la porte d'orée* (1924). In Czechoslovakia, football became the subject of K. Čapek's satirical novel *The club of Eleven*. In Ger. literature, the subject was reflected by M. Vischer's play *The Footballer and the Indian* (*Fussballspieler und Indianer*, 1924), a grotesque burlesque staged in

Goal (*Punkt ist Punkt*, 1972), a parody of the behavior of spectators, activists, sport commentators, and football players at a stadium. The play was staged in Aachen's Werkstattheater in the form of a literary collage with cabaret lyrics and dialogues. U.K. Koch's play *Grabi! Grabi! – or a satirical football play* (*Grabi! Grabi! – ein satirische Fussballstück*; Grabi is a diminutive of footballer J. Grabowski's name) coupled cabaret and comedy elements and was staged in Theater am Turn in Frankfurt. The play consisted of 32 short acts and an epilogue. It is the story of 3 young and talented Eintracht Frankfurt juniors who consider Grabowski a hero. Two of them decide to become licensed footballers. The third of them, not a very intelligent sort, becomes a professional. At least 2 plays devoted to football were written in the former East Germany. One of them is J. Gross's *The Match* (1978) whose subject is a match followed by riots caused by football fans during which a man is knifed to death. Young football fans are arrested but all they do is discuss the match and its result. Another play *Concerning Adam and*

(cf. >METAPHORIC FOOTBALL). Children's literature forms a separate genre, with Poland's most famous example by A. Bahdaj *0:1 'Till Halftime* (*Do przerwy 0:1*). The novel served as the basis of a TV series. Social anomalies appearing in football, especially corruption scandals and league intrigues were the subject of movies: J. Dziedzina's *The Holy War* (*Święta wojna*) and J. Zaorski's *The Football Poker* (*Piłkarski poker*). Football was also a frequent theme in a number of songs.

J. Bangsbo, B. Peitersen, *Soccer: Systems and Strategies*, 2000; B. Beswick, *Focused For Soccer*, 2001; M. Dean, *Spotlight on Football*, 1981; E. Dunning, P. Murphy and J. Williams, *The Roots of Football Hooliganism. An Historical and Sociological Study*, 1988; R. Glavin, *How to Play Soccer*, 1988; A. Gowarzewski, *Encyklopedia Piłkarska*, vol. 1-22, 1988-1998; F.P. Magoun, *History of Football. From the Beginning to 1871*, 1938; B. Murray, *Football. A History of World Game*, 1994; E. Piasecki, *Piłka nożna polska*, 1906; *The Sunday Times' Illustrated History of Football*, ed. D. Heslam et al., 1994; J. Walvin, *The People's Game. The History of Football Revisited*, 1994; N. Whitehead & M. Cook, *Soccer Training. Games, Drills and Fitness Practices*, 1988; P Young, *A History of British Football*, 1968.

AT GLIMAST, a general term for a type of wrestling as practiced in the Faroe Islands. The word *glíma* is an ancient word used in the Faroese language, esp. in the verb form *glímast*. A distinction was made between *berjast* (to fight) and *glímast* (to wrestle), the former referring to a type of violent combat, while the latter – to wrestling for entertainment. Two contestants coming together to *glímast* would first select a field on which the bout would take place. The winner would decide on the limits of the field at his own pleasure.
Three types of grips are known in the Faroe Islands: >AXLATÖK (shoulder grip), >BROERATÖK (brother grip), and BRÓKATÖK (trouser grip). Which of these forms was proper >GLÍMA, or whether any of them was a form of glíma, is unknown. Glíma is no longer practiced on the Faroe Islands. It became extinct at the end of the 19th cent. or the beginning of the 20th cent. Neither is it possible to say whether these forms of wrestling are identical to glíma wrestling in Iceland, although they are clearly forms practiced for enterntainment. The verb *at glímkast* refers to a friendly sport activity.

T. Einarsson, 'Faroe Islands', *Traditional wrestling in the Northern Countries*, 1988. Cons. by M. Ívarsson.

AT HINKE, a Dan. var. of >KLASY, usu. played on a pavement. It has a number of sub-types and further variations. Similar to other hopscotch-like games at hinke consists in jumping from box to box on one leg while moving a stone with one foot according to certain rules. Major *hinke* varieties include:
AT HINKE RUDER, Dan. for 'hopscotch in diamonds', e.g. king of diamonds, (>KLASY, >HOP-SCOTCH), involving hopping clockwise around a square diagram divided into 9 smaller boxes, numbered from 1 to 9, starting with the left bottom box. A player starts his journey from field no. 1 and then gradually, as in many other games of the same kind (>KLASY, >HOP-SCOTCH), moves a stone on the ground and completes the respective, consecutively numbered boxes going from 1 to 9, then from 9 to 1 and once again.
FLYVER, Dan. for 'a flier', a counterpart of the Pol. *samolot* (an airplane, >KLASY) and Port. >JOGO DO AVIAO. The diagram resembles an airplane as it is composed of 2 rectangles joined lengthwise – they form the 'tail' of the plane (with the 2 shorter sides being the starting line). Then, there are 2 long rectangles joined at the shorter sides form the 'fuselage'. 4 rectangles perpendicular to the 'fuselage' form the 'wings' of the plane and the rectangle above them is the 'cockpit'.
HINKE SNEGL, Dan. *snegl* – a snail, a counterpart of the Pol. game with the same name (>KLASY) and of the Port. >JOGO DO CARACOL. Here, the number of boxes is greater than usual (16 instead of 11) and there is no special 'heaven' box (the middle box is the box no. 16). When a player reaches the middle of the 'snail' he can rest, i.e. stand on both legs. Each of the players can write their name in one of the boxes to mark their own rest area and the other players cannot put their foot on it. When a player puts his foot on somebody else's box or on a line he is eliminated. The one who completes the greatest number of fields is declared the winner.
HOPSKOK, a game similar to the Ang.-Sax. >HOP-SCOTCH, but employing a diagram with differently numbered and named boxes. The first box is a rectangle whose shorter side forms a part of the starting line and whose longer side runs alongside the whole length of the field. This box is called a *himmerige* – the kingdom of heaven, heaven. The next box is identical in shape and is dubbed *Danmark* – Denmark (or *Norge* in Norway). Above both rectangles there is a square divided with by 2 diagonals into 4 triangles. The lowermost of them is called a *timeglas*; the right-hand side one is a *sideglas 1*; the left-hand side one is called a *sideglas 2* and the uppermost triangle is named a *sidste timeglas*. The rectangle above the square is dubbed *lille China* – little China and it is narrow and thus easy to hop through but difficult to put the stone in. It is followed by another rectangle that is 3 times bigger than the little China. The whole diagram is topped with a semicircle called *helvede* – hell.
MAND, Dan. for 'man', a game employing a diagram with boxes similar to that used in the Pol. *chłop* ('peasant', >KLASY). The starting line is adjoined by 3 rectangles or squares arranged vertically. The 2 rectangles that are joined at the shorter sides form the arms of the man. They are followed by yet another rectangle or square that is the 'neck'. Above the neck there is the 'head', i.e. a semicircle divided into 2 equal fields. The 'head' and the 'neck' are joined so that the uppermost side of the rectangle or square is, in fact, the diameter of the semicircle.
PARADIS, Dan. for 'paradise', a game employing the same rules as those characteristic of the Ang.-Sax. >HOP-SCOTCH and the Pol. >KLASY. A player throws a stone into a given box and jumps on one leg into the next box. While jumping back he kicks the stone out of the diagram sending it behind the starting line. This is repeated with the subsequent, consecutively numbered boxes and after the player has reached the *hat*, he goes back. The diagram consists of 2 pairs of rectangles, the lowermost pair is numbered 1 and 2, followed by rectangles nos. 3 and 4 above them. Above the 4 rectangles there is a square divided by 2 diagonals into 4 triangles. The lowermost triangle is box no. 5, the left-hand side one has no. 6, the right-hand side one is box no. 7 and the uppermost triangle is box no. 8. The square is followed by 2 pairs of rectangles (identical to those numbered 1 to 4) which are boxes 9 to 12. The rectangles are followed by a semicircle whose diameter equals the width of the whole diagram. This box is called a *hat*.
PIGE IN LABYRINT, Dan. for 'a girl in a labyrinth', a game employing a complex diagram resembling a long, winding and intertwining line which forms a labyrinth. The object of the game is to reach the exit of the labyrinth and drive a stone out of it while avoiding any dead ends. Compare the Ang.-Sax. >HOP-SCOTCH, Arab >AL-HUD'D'A, >AL-HAGLA, >BERBER, >LU 'BAT UMM AL-HUTUT, Ger. >FUßSCHEIBENSPIEL, Pol. >KLASY and Port. >JOGO DO AVIÃO.

J. Møller, 'At hinke', GID, 1997, 3, 22.

AT HYTTE, Dan. dial. for 'to throw', a simple folk ball game whereby two partners throw a ball to each other. The players score points for successful catches. The size of the ball and the material from which it is made are not specified and depend on the local custom and availability of materials. Often it is a home-made fabric ball sometimes richly embroidered with folk patterns.

J. Møller, 'At hytte', GID, 1997, 1, 9.

AT KLAVES, Dan. for 'in chains', a type of struggle similar to wrestling. Two competitors stand arm to arm and competitor A puts his right arm around his opponent's neck whereas competitor B puts his left arm around his opponent's neck. Competitor B grabs his left hand with his right hand and competitor A puts his left arm under B's left knee and joins his hands. A's task is then to lift B whereas B will try to free himself from A's hold by arching his body.

J. Møller, 'At klaves', GID, 1997, 4.

AT RYKKE EN FINGER UD, Dan. for 'to pull out a finger' [Dan. *at* – to + *rykke* – pull + *en* – one + *finger* – finger + *ud* – out]. A Dan. type of struggle whereby one of the competitors bends his elbow, puts his middle finger in the space between the forearm and the upper arm so formed and places his hand on his neck. The task of the second competitor is to pull the finger out of the hold by tugging at this arm of his opponent to which the locked finger belongs.

J. Møller, 'At rykke en finger ud', GID, 1997, 4, 17.

AT VENDE EN MAND, Dan. for 'to turn a man'. A trad. Dan. form of wrestling whereby one of the competitors lays face down on the ground with his limbs spread wide so that he resembles the letter 'X'. The second competitor stands astride over him grabs him around the waist and tries to turn him onto his back. The attacker may move freely.

J. Møller, 'At vende en mand', GID, 1997, 4, 41.

ATA SO, a game of imitating animal movements played in Nigeria, especially by boys of up to 10 years of age. The participants sit in a row with their legs stretched forward. The 'king' of all the animals and birds sits some 15yds. (13.5m) in front of them. He calls out 1 or 2 boys from the line to serve him. After some deliberations he sends them back. Each messenger is given the name of an animal. They cannot say the name but try to imitate this given animal's actions and movements. Then they touch all the players asking, 'What do you eat?'. The boy to whom this question is addressed says the name of the animal he thinks his colleague was imitating. If he is right he scores a point and the messenger returns to the 'king of animals'. If none of the players guesses the name of the animal, the messenger says 'I am going away with my ...' and gives the name of the animal in question and also returns to the 'king of animals'. The king thinks up a new name and the messenger again imitates this animal and then asks the same question starting at the other end of the line. The player who scores most points in a number of such rounds is declared the winner.

P.G. Brewster, 'Some Nigerian Games with their Parallels and Analogues', *Journal de la Société des Africanistes*, 1954, 24; A. Taylor Cheska, 'Ata so', TGD-WAN, 1987, 21.

ATEMI JUTSU, [Jap. *atemi* – hits, blows + *jutsu* – skill, action]. Atemi jutsu is not a sport in its own right but a set of special skills which is part of the Jap. forms of hand-to-hand combat where it specifies the admissible types of hand blows (with a fist, heel of hand, elbow or fingers) and leg kicks (with a knee, heel, side of foot and also sole). Atemi jutsu (or atemi, for short) is taught in >JUDO within one of the so-called self-defense kata (*goshin jutsu no kata*). The aim of employing atemi jutsu is to temporarily disable an opponent by making him faint or inducing local paralysis. The ancient samurai used atemi jutsu to kill an opponent.

ATHABASCAN WRESTLING, a wrestling variety popular among the Athabascan living in Alaska and NW Canada. The winner could even win a few women whereas the loser was disgraced but could regain his esteem if he won his subsequent matches.

ATHLESIS, Gk. *athlesis*, in ancient Greece – a form of combat between strongmen, especially wrestlers; see >ATHLETICS.

ATHLETIC DECATHLON, [Gk. *deca* – ten + *athlon* – competition] a series of 10 track and field contests for men, which is a wide-ranging test of not only sports skills but also a test of stamina throughout sustained and versatile effort. The athletic decathlon includes: (day 1) 100m dash, long jump, shot put, high jump, 400m dash; and (day 2) 110m hurdles, discus throw, pole vault, javelin throw, 1500m run. The results of each contest are converted according to scoring tables adopted by the IAAF. The participant amassing the highest total score in all the contests is the winner. In Eng.-speaking countries, esp. in the USA, another var. of athletic decathlon is practiced, known as >ALL-AROUND, whose arrangement is different and which is usu. held on a single day. The athletic decathlon is the most demanding TF event. However, due to the abundant number of contests and lack of intermediate results to be compared, the event is taxing for spectators as well. For that reason, to avoid disorganization during TF meetings, the decathlon is sometimes held as a separate competition.
History. The idea of an all-around test of a human's fitness originates from the ancient Gk. >PENTATHLON. *The Song of the Nibelung* shows that Germanic tribes engaged in a 3-contest competition which included the javelin throw, throwing a large stone, and a long jump. In the Middle Ages, at some courts, multi-contest events were held among knights, which in different periods and in different countries con-

Postage stamps from a post block depicting various stages of development of association football.

DECATHLON OLYMPIC CHAMPIONS

1904	*Thomas Kiely, IRE (6036)*
1906-08	*Not held*
1912	*Jim Thorpe, USA (8412)*
1920	*Helge Lövland, NOR (6803)*
1924	*Harold Osborn, USA (7711)*
1928	*Paavo Yrjölä, FIN (8053)*
1932	*Jim Bausch, USA (8462)*
1936	*Glenn Morris, USA (7900)*
1948	*Bob Mathias, USA (7139)*
1952	*Bob Mathias, USA (7887)*
1956	*Milt Campbell, USA (7937)*
1960	*Rafer Johnson, USA (8392)*
1964	*Willi Holdorf, GER (7887)*
1968	*Bill Toomey, USA (8193)*
1972	*Nikolai Avilov, USSR (8454)*
1976	*Bruce Jenner, USA (8617)*
1980	*Daley Thompson, GBR (8495)*
1984	*Daley Thompson, GBR (8798)*
1988	*Christian Schenk, E. Ger (8488)*
1992	*Robert Zmelik, CZE (8611)*
1996	*Dan O'Brien, USA (8824)*
2000	*Erki Nool, EST (8641)*

A

WORLD SPORTS ENCYCLOPEDIA

sisted of various events, the most frequent being: jumps, throws, horse riding, and wrestling. The abovementioned var. of multi-contest competitions did not have a direct influence on the athletic decathlon which, in the form of the all-around referred to above, was held for the first time during the US Championships in 1884. The Eur. var. modeled after it, developed c.1900 in Denmark where the first substantiated athletic decathlon competition took place in 1902, after which it became popular throughout Eur. and was also adopted in the USA. The first to become an Ol.G. event was the Amer. all-around, in the 1904 Ol.G. in St. Louis. It was not present in the 1908 Ol.G., only to be reinstated in its contem-

porary form during the 1912 Ol.G. in Stockholm. The most outstanding competitor of the pioneering period was an American of Native Indian descent, Jim Thorpe (1888-1953), who, in Stockholm, won both the decathlon and the pentathlon held at that time as well. Thorpe was later stripped of his medals for having allegedly accepted bribes during baseball and Amer. football games. The title of the Ol.G. winner was then granted to a Swede, H. Wieslander. Thorpe's medals were restored posthumously by the International Olympic Committee in 1982 he is now listed as a joint winner together with Wieslander. Up to the 1928 Ol.G., the decathlon was dominated by Scandinavians and Americans. In the 1932-52 Ol.G.,

medals for all three winning positions were acquired by US athletes. The most eminent US decathlete of that time was 'Big' B. Watson who won during the Amateur Athletic Union (AAU) Championships in 1940, achieving a score 400 points higher than the one achieved by the second best competitor. WWII robbed from Watson an opportunity to win the desired Olympic medal, as the Ol.G. of 1940 and 1944 were cancelled. As a result, Watson fell into depression. Immediately after WWII, the leading decathlete was considered Estonian H. Lipp, who achieved in 1948 a result that beat the world record and surpassed by 445 points the score of B. Mathias – an Olympic winner in 1948 and 1952. Lipp, however,

Some events of athletic decathlon:
1. 1500-m flat run: Tomas Dvorak (Czech Republic) i Erki Nool (Estonia)
2. 110-m hurdles: Dean Macey (USA)
3. discus throw: Dan O'Brien (USA)
4. long jump: Mike Maczey (Germany)
5. javelin throw: Tomas Dvorak (Czech Republic)

could not compete in the 1948 Ol.G. because the USSR, of which Estonia formed a part, did not participate in those Ol.G. Although in the 1948 Ol.G. Mathias was the winner, the *Track and Field News* selected Lipp as the best decathlete of the year. In 1952, Lipp, considering himself a representative of Estonia and not of the USSR, declined the offer to take part in the Ol.G.. A symbolic compensation for Lipp's moral sacrifice was granted to him during the 1992 Ol.G. in Barcelona where he was accorded the honour carrying the Est. flag. Nevertheless, the role of the USSR's athletes was growing in the 50s and its crowning achievement was the series of duels between W. Kusnietsov and the best US decathlete, R. Johnson, during international competitions in which both the USSR and the USA participated. These two sportsmen were joined during the 1964 Ol.G. by Chinese Yang Chuan Kwang. The decathletes could only meet during Ol.G., for the USSR did not recognize Taiwan and the authorities did not agree to have the USSR team compete with teams of countries they did not recognize (e.g. during international TF meetings). The most eminent decathletes of modern times are: double gold medallist D. Thompson from Great Britain, B. Jenner from the USA, and Czech, R. Zmelik. The popularity of the decathlon can be proved by the IAAF's data that indicates about 5,000. decathletes worldwide – of which about 1,100 from the USA – have taken part in the competition at least 2 times.
The current key athletes can be defined on the basis of the number of medals granted to national teams in the course of the 1992 and 1996 Ol.G.: the USA – 4, Czech Republic – 3, Germany and Uzbekistan – 2, and Belarus, Estonia, Spain, Hungary and France – 1 each.
S. Rosin, *Daley Thompson, The Subject Is Winning*, 1983; B. Jenner and P. Finch, *Decathlon Challenge. Bruce Jenner's Story*, 1977; F. Zarnowski, *Track and Field, Decathlon*, 1996, Ill.

ATHLETIC PENTATHLON, a 5-event track and field contest intended to display the participants' sporting ability. The composition of events has been different at various stages of development of the athletic pentathlon and depended on the participants' age and sex. The once-popular women's pentathlon, held over two consecutive days, included the 100m >HURDLES (formerly 80m), >SHOT PUT, and >HIGH JUMP on the first day; and the >LONG JUMP and 800m run (formerly 200m) on the second day. The men's pentathlon is held in one day and includes the long jump, javelin throw, 200m run, discus throw and 1,500m run. Scoring is on a points basis, following the pentathlon point tables; the winners are determined by total scores from the 5 events. Both women's and men's events are not currently held during international competitions.
History. As in the case of other >MULTI-TRIALS, the model for the athletic pentathlon was the ancient >PENTATHLON, consisting, however, of different events. The athletic pentathlon appeared first in modern times during the Much Wenlock Games in England in 1868. The events differed from the ancient original. This pentathlon was considered the most prestigious of all competitions in the Much Wenlock Games. Another form of the athletic pentathlon based on the ancient competition was a men's event held at the 1906 Mesolympic Games in Athens. It included the long jump, discus throw, javelin throw, a race the length of one stadium (192m) and wrestling, the latter being an extension beyond the modern pentathlon idea understood as a track and field event. The winner was the Greek M. Dorizas. The present composition of the athletic pentathlon, i.e. the long jump, javelin throw, 200m run, discus throw, and 1,500m run, appeared first at the 1912 Ol.G. in Stockholm. In the early varieties of athletic pentathlon, scoring was not the sum of points won in all events but the sum of penalties. The athlete with the lowest penalty score became the winner. The pentathlon with penalty scoring was part of the Ol.G. in 1920 and 1924. The most outstanding pentathletes were F. Bie (Norway) in 1912 and E. Lehtonen (Finland) in 1920 and 1924. Exclusion of the men's pentathlon from the Olympic program decreased the interest in the sport as a TF event. The athletic pentathlon has been part of the program of the US Championships since 1920. It is still widely practiced at many US universities.
The women's pentathlon event was first held in the USSR in 1923. Initially, the women's pentathlon comprised the 100m run, 800m run, long jump, high jump, and javelin. In 1947, the composition was altered and it included the shot put, long jump, 100m run, high jump, and javelin. In 1949, the present-day pentathlon composition was estab. in the USSR and then, after IAAF approval, included in the Olympic Games in 1964. In 1972, the hurdles distance was changed to 100m, and the records were reset. The last women's pentathlon was held at the Moscow Ol.G. in 1980. In the 1984 Ol.G. in Los Angeles the women's pentathlon was replaced with the >HEPTATHLON. The most outstanding women pentathletes were I. Press, USSR (Olympic champion 1964); M. Rand, UK (Olympic vice-champion 1964); I. Becker, West Germany (Olympic champion 1968); M. Peters, UK (Olympic champion 1972); S. Siegl, East Germany (Olympic champion 1976).

ATHLETIC RUNNING, a group of ancient and modern track and field running events. According to modern criteria athletic running is divided into >FLAT RACES, >HURDLING, >STEEPLE CHASE and >CROSS-COUNTRY RUNNING. To comply with IAAF regulations athletic running events should take place at a stadium with an oval running track of 400m whereby the track should not be narrower than 7.32m, i.e. it should have at least 6 lanes of 122cm each. International competitions should be held at 8-lane tracks, and if possible the track should be delimited with a curb that is 5cm high and at least 5cm wide. During all races over distances of up to 400m runners must remain within their lanes for the entire race. In races over distances over 100m the starts are staggered so that each runner will cover an equal distance. During the 800m races and 4x400m relays the runners must remain within their lanes for the first 100 and 500m, respectively. In >RELAYS there are special zones within which the baton must be passed.
History. Track and field athletics developed in ancient Greece, where, however, the whole body of competitive running events was not treated as a separate sport in its own right. Athletic running events gained this status as late as in the 19th cent. in England where modern track and field athletics emerged as a conglomerate of various events. Athletic running first developed at Eng. public schools and later at the first sports clubs and associations. Further, track and field running events acquired their present shape and status during the so-called 'olympic games' held in the town of Munch Wenlock since 1850 when they were initiated by W.P. Brookes. The Eng. Athletic Association greatly contributed to developing and codifying the present repertoire of athletic running events. After Pierre de Coubertin had revived the modern Ol.G. in 1896, the athletic running events began developing in a way that incorporated the traditions and expectations of various nations. Finally, the International Amateur Athletic Federation (IAAF), estab. in 1912, took over full responsibility for organizing officially recognized international athletic running competitions, esp. at the Ol.G. or continent championship levels. For detailed history of the respective athletic running events see >TEAM RUNNING, >LONG DISTANCE RUNNING, >CROSS-COUNTRY RUNNING, >HURDLES, >RELAYS, >MIDDLE-DISTANCE RUNNING, >STEEPLE CHASE, >MARATHON, >ATHLETIC SPRINT. See also >RUNNING.
D.E. Martin & P. Coe, *Better Training for Distance Runners*, 1997; S. Petkiewicz, *Biegi lekkoatletyczne*, 1936.

ATHLETIC SPRINT, also *short runs*, a group of athletic competitions in which the object is to race against the clock in runs shorter than 500m or 600yds. With respect to distance, different tactics and physiological conditions, athletic sprint is usu. divided into 1) short athletic sprint run over distances of 50-200m or 50-220yds. and 2) extended sprint, 300-500m and 300-600yds., respectively. Most typically athletic sprints are run over distances of 100, 200 and 400m, which are featured in the program of continental championships, W.Ch. and Ol.G., and in Eng.-speaking countries – 100yds, rarely 110yds., 220yds., and 440yds. The distances of 50yds., 50m, 60yds., and 60m are most often run indoors, although a 60m race was included in the program of the 1900 and 1904 Ol.G. and is still often featured in the summer competitions organized for children and school students. Athletic sprint also includes >TRACK AND FIELD RELAY.
History. The tradition of short races belongs to the oldest forms of human competition and goes back as far as prehistoric times. Then, however, they were occasional and not yet a permanent fixture. Athletic sprints were first featured in the old Gk. games, where they were run over distances of 1 and 2 stadiums >STADIODROMOS, >DIAULOS). These early races correspond to present-day 200- and 400-m runs. When the ancient games declined, organized forms of short runs were hardly practiced. Historical sources describing races in Eur. and Amer. civilizations usu. referred to >LONG DISTANCE RUNNING. In Renaissance Rome races over a distance of 200-300m were held. Organization of modern short distance races, presently called athletic sprints, started at the beginning of the 19th cent. at English universities. Initially the distance was about 400-500yds. (about 365.76-457.2m) and were included in >MIDDLE-DISTANCE RUNNING. In 1843 sprints (over varying distances) were included in the program of school competitions. Sprints over distances of 100 and 330yds. were started in 1850 at Exeter College in Oxford, followed by sprints over the distance of 440yds. Until the end of the 19th cent. trad. sprints at Brit. and Amer. universities included runs over distances of 100 and 440yds. However, 220yd. sprints were also held since the 1870s, having been

Athletic running.

part of the US championships since 1876. Yard distances were replaced with metric distances at the Ol.G. in 1896, although Great Britain retained yard sprints. The United States adopted a rule according to which metric sprints were held in Olympic years and pre-Olympic years (although less consistently) and yard distances in other years. In the 1840-70s yard sprints were run at times, which, converted to metric sprints, were 11.5sec. (100m) and 54.0sec. (400m). Progress was attributed to improved training, start technique and equipment. In 1884 C.H. Sherill, a student of Yale University (USA), adopted a start from a crouching position with one hand resting on the track. This technique, called hand-spring start, was improved by T.L. Nicholas from Monmouth (Great Britain) – from a crouching position the sprinter leapt into full stride. During the 1896 Ol.G. T. Burke, an Amer. sprinter, popularized the hand-spring start, winning the 100- and 400-m sprints. Although starting blocks had been known in the USA since 1929, they could not be used until 1934. In 1929 G. Simpson's world record (9.5sec./100yds.) was not recognized because of his use of starting blocks. Starting blocks at the Ol.G. were first allowed in 1948. Tracks were initially built on compacted soil or on grass. In 1968 the New York Athletic Club built the first cinder track. A clay track had been built in 1911, with the top surface made of ground brick. In the middle of the 1960s synthetic-compound tracks appeared. Very often track design determined the results. Many years before synthetic-compound tracks the clay track in the Letzigrund stadium in Zurich was considered the fastest in the world, thanks to specific, resilient, carrier features. Many

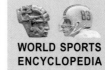

100-M DASH OLYMPIC CHAMPIONS

MEN
1896 Tom Burke, USA 12.0
1900 Frank Jarvis, USA 11.0
1904 Archie Hahn, USA 11.0
1906 Archie Hahn, USA 11.2
1908 Reggie Walker, S. AFR. 10.8
1912 Ralph Craig, USA 10.8
1920 Charley Paddock, USA 10.8
1924 Harold Abrahams, GBR 10.6
1928 Percy Williams, CAN 10.8
1932 Eddie Tolan, USA 10.3
1936 Jesse Owens, USA 10.3
1948 Harrison Dillard, USA 10.3
1952 Lindy Remigino, USA 10.4
1956 Bobby Morrow, USA 10.5
1960 Armin Hary, GER 10.2
1964 Bob Hayes, USA 10.0
1968 Jim Hines, USA 9.95
1972 Valery Borzov, USSR 10.14
1976 Hasely Crawford, TRI 10.06
1980 Allan Wells, GBR 10.25
1984 Carl Lewis, USA 9.99
1988 Carl Lewis, USA 9.92
1992 Linford Christie, GBR 9.96
1996 Donovan Bailey, CAN 9.84
2000 Maurice Greene, USA 9.87
WOMEN
1928 Betty Robinson, USA 12.2
1932 Stella Walsh, POL 11.9
1936 Helen Stephens, USA 11.5
1948 Fanny Blankers-Koen, NED 11.9
1952 Marjorie Jackson, AUSTRL 11.5
1956 Betty Cuthbert, AUSTRL 11.5
1960 Wilma Rudolph, USA 11.0
1964 Wyomia Tyus, USA 11.4
1968 Wyomia Tyus, USA 11.08
1972 Renate Stecher, E. GER 11.07
1976 Annegret Richter, W. GER 11.08
1980 Lyudmila Kondratyeva, USSR 11.06
1984 Evelyn Ashford, USA 10.97
1988 Florence Griffith Joyner, USA 10.54
1992 Gail Devers, USA 10.82
1996 Gail Devers, USA 10.94
2000 Marion Jones, USA 10.75

200-M DASH OLYMPIC CHAMPIONS

MEN

1900 Walter Tewksbury, USA 22.2
1904 Archie Hahn, USA 21.6
1908 Bobby Kerr, CAN 22.6
1912 Ralph Craig, USA 21.7
1920 Allen Woodring, USA 22.0
1924 Jackson Scholz, USA 21.6
1928 Percy Williams, CAN 21.8
1932 Eddie Tolan, USA 21.2
1936 Jesse Owens, USA 20.7
1948 Mel Patton, USA 21.1
1952 Andy Stanfield, USA 20.7
1956 Bobby Morrow, USA 20.6
1960 Livio Berruti, ITA 20.5
1964 Henry Carr, USA 20.3
1968 Tommie Smith, USA 19.83
1972 Valery Borzov, USSR 20.00
1976 Donald Quarrie, JAM 20.23
1980 Pietro Mennea, ITA 20.19
1984 Carl Lewis, USA 19.80
1988 Joe DeLoach, USA 19.75
1992 Mike Marsh, USA 20.01
1996 Michael Johnson, USA 19.32
2000 Konstantinos Kenteris, GRE 20.09

WOMEN

1948 Fanny Blankers-Koen, NED 24.4
1952 Marjorie Jackson, AUSTRAL 23.7
1956 Betty Cuthbert, AUSTRAL 23.4
1960 Wilma Rudolph, USA 24.0
1964 Edith McGuire, USA 23.0
1968 Irena Szewinska, POL 22.5
1972 Renate Stecher, E. GER 22.40
1976 Bärbel Eckert, E. GER 22.37
1980 Bärbel Eckert Wockel, E. GER 22.03
1984 Valerie Brisco-Hooks, USA 21.81
1988 Florence Griffith Joyner, USA 21.34
1992 Gwen Torrence, USA 21.81
1996 Marie-Jose Perec, FRA 22.12
2000 Marion Jones, USA 21.84

R. Tait McKenzie's Sprinter *on a postage stamp issued for the 1976 Ol.G. in Montreal.*

world records were achieved there, including in 1959 the first official world record of 10.0sec. in a 100m sprint made by German A. Hary (b. 1937). The first to use shoes with spikes was W.B. Curtis in 1868. By 1904 all the psychological barriers of individual sprints had been overcome. A result below 10sec. in the 100-yds. sprint was first achieved by J.H. Owen, USA (9.8sec. – 1880); below 11sec. in the 100m sprint – F. Jarvis, USA (10.8sec. – 1900); below 22sec. in the 220yds. sprint – G.G. Wood, Great Britain (21.8 – 1886); below 22sec. in the 200-m sprint on a straight track – A. Hahn, USA (21.6 – 1904); below 50sec. in the 440-yd. sprint – L. Myers, USA (49.2 – 1979); below 50sec. in the 400-m sprint – M. Lond, USA (49.4 – 1900).

Until 1968 records in sprints were taken with the accuracy to 0.1sec., later – 0.01sec. At the Ol.G. time was first measured to the accuracy of 0.01sec. in Munich (1972).

50-YD. SPRINT. Usually not featured in outdoor events, except for lower rank competitions, e.g. school competitions for younger children or recreational events for the elderly, it is a frequent feature in the indoor events, particularly women's competitions. For example, it was part of the program of the US women's indoor championships from 1927 through 1964, when the 50yds. sprint was replaced with the 60yds sprint. The best 50yds sprint runners were M.L. Carew, a 4-time US champion (1929-32); I. Daniels – a 3-time US champion (1956-58); and W. White, also a 3-time US champion (1961-63). W. Rudolph won the 50-yd. sprint twice and S. Walasiewicz (Poland) – once (1934).

60-YD. SPRINT. Sometimes featured in the summer events in Eng.-speaking countries, particularly in the USA, more often it was an indoor event. The 60-yd. sprint has been a permanent feature of the US women's indoor championships since 1965. Among the winners was W. Tyus (1965-67).

60-M SPRINT. This sprint was featured in the 1900 and 1905 Ol.G.. Though it has always been a typical event of indoor men's and women's competitions, it has never been a permanent feature of the major international summer events. At the 1900 Ol.G. the 60m sprint was won by an American A. Kraenzlein; at the 1904 Ol.G. the winner was A. Hahn (USA).

110-YD. SPRINT. In the first decades of the 20th cent. it was a substitute for the 100-m sprint. The best 100m sprinter of the 1920s was American C. Paddock, who in 1921 won it in 10.2sec. Although this result was achieved on a distance longer than 100m by 58cm, it was not recognized as a world record as it did not correspond to the distance set in the rules.

100-M SPRINT. Ever since the beginning of this event the best sprinters came from English-speaking countries. Before 1914, apart from J. Jarvis, the best sprinter was D. Lippincott, who established one of the most surprising world records at the time during the eliminations to the 1912 Ol.G. – 10.6sec. In the late 1920s and the early 1920s the event was dominated by Americans: E. Tolan and R. Metcalf (their personal best results were 10.3sec.); and later Jesse Owens (1913-80), whose personal best was 10.2sec. In the history of the Ol.G., out of 23 100-m sprint finals, only 2 were won by contestants from outside Eng.-speaking countries: in 1960 as mentioned, Hary from Germany and in 1972 a representative of the USSR – W. Borzow. US sprinters won 14 times; representatives of Great Britain – 3 times; Canadians – twice; and representatives of Trinidad and South Africa – once each.

In the semi-finals at the 1964 Ol.G. an American R. Hayes won the 100-m sprint in less than 10sec. – 9.9sec., which was not recognized as the wind speed was slightly higher than permitted. The first sprinter who had the same result officially recognized was an American J. Hines (1968). J. Hines also got an officially recognized time of less than 10sec. measured electronically (9.95sec. – 1968).

Women's sprint developed to some extent from the second half of the 19th cent. under the auspices of the YMCA. From 1921 women's competitions in athletic sprints, initially over the distance of 60m, were featured in the program of the games organized by the International Federation of Women's Sport. The 100-m sprint was featured for the first time in the Ol.G. in 1928. The best sprinters in 1928-39 were H. Stephens (USA) and S. Walasiewicz-Olson (Poland), who in 1934 set a world record (11.6sec.), beaten by F. Blankers-Koen from Holland, the 1948 Ol.G. champion in 100-m, 200-m, 4x100-m sprints and 80-m hurdles. In the 1950s the best women sprinters in the world came from Australia: S. de la Hunty-Strickland, M. Jackson and E. 'Betty' Cuthbert. W. Rudolph, the heroine of the 1960 Ol.G., won gold medals in the 100-m and 200-m sprints and 4x100-m relay sprint. Rudolph was the first woman to make 11.0sec.; the result, however, was not recognized. The only women who won the Olympic gold in the 100m sprint twice were W. Tyus (1964, 1968) and G. Devers (1992 and 1996). The first woman to run the 100-m sprint in less than 11sec. was R. Stecher-Meissner from the GDR (10.8sec. – 1973). A result below 10.8sec. measured electronically was made by E. Ashford (USA, 10.76sec. – 1984). At the 1988 Ol.G. in Seoul F. Griffith-Joyner not only won the Olympic gold but also set a fantastic world record, one which still stands – 10.45sec. Unlike B. Johnson, who was disqualified during the Ol.G., Griffith-Joyner was never proved to have taken any doping; however, her sudden death in 1998 seems to be the price she paid for setting the record in the 100-m sprint at a time which was rarely attained by men.

200-M AND 220-YD. SPRINTS. Both sprints are usu. run on a track with a circumference of 400m or 440yds., with half of the sprint run alongside the curve, and the other along a straight track. Very popular, particularly in the USA, are both sprints run on a straight track, with separately recorded world records. The first sprinter to run the 'straight track' sprint in less than 20sec. was T. Smith (19.5sec. in the 220-yd. sprint – 1966). When synthetic-compound tracks appeared, in some countries of Western Europe the 200-m sprints were run on a track with a circumference of 500m (with a less sharp and shorter curve), which helped get better results, however not officially recognized by the IAAF.

220-YD. later 200-M SPRINTS were run in Great Britain and the USA from the turn of the 1860s. This sprint was included for the first time in the US championships in 1877, and in the Ol.G. in 1900. From then on, until the 1960 Ol.G., when the winner was L. Berutti from Italy, only Amer. and Can. contestants won the 220-yd. and 200-m sprints. At the Ol.G. in 1904, 1932, 1952 and 1984 all the medals in sprint were taken by Americans; at many other Olympics – by representatives from Eng.-speaking countries: USA, Great Britain, Australia, Canada, Trinidad, Jamaica and India (1900, 1908, 1912, 1920, 1924, 1964, 1968, 1976). Between 1964 and 1968 US sprinters dominated again. The 200-m sprint at the 1972 Ol.G. was won by W. Borzow (USSR), at the 1976 Olympics by D. Quarrie (a Jamaican training in the USA). The 1980 Ol.G. were not attended by Amer. sprinters and the 200-m sprint was won by an Italian P. Mennea. From 1984 to 1996 all gold medals were again won by Americans (see below). At the Ol.G. in 1992 and 1996 the 200-m sprint finals featured 5 US sprinters, 2 sprinters from Great Britain, 2 representatives of Namibia, 2 from Nigeria, and 1 each from Trinidad, Barbados, Cuba, Belgium and Brazil.

Women's 200-m sprints were included in the Ol.G. in 1948. The first winner was F. Blankers-Koen (Holland). Until the end of the 1960s the best in the 200m sprint were sprinters from Holland, Great Britain, USA and Australia, and later also Poland (I. Szewińska-Kirszenstein). In the 1970s the lead was taken by sprinters from the GDR. Supremacy in the 200-m sprint was regained by Amer. sprinters at the 1984 Olympics, to be broken by M.-J. Perec of France at the 1996 Olympics in Atlanta. The first sprinter to achieve a time under 25sec. was K. Hitomi from Japan (24.7sec. – 1929); in less than 24sec. – M. Koch (21.56sec. – 1988). The 200-m sprint, in the past rarely featured in the indoor championships, became the standard event of E.Ch. and W.Ch. when synthetic-compound tracks were introduced.

400-M AND 440-YD. SPRINTS are run on a track 400m and 440yds. long. Until the 1912 Olympics this sprint was part of medium distance races, run on tracks without lanes, later on tracks with the handicap. Until 1960 a start from a straight adjacent to the entry into the first turn was allowed. Until the introduction of the synthetic-compound track sprints started on 500-m tracks. The 440-yd. sprints were first introduced in about 1834. Official world records have been taken since 1864. The first official 400-yd. sprint world record holder was B.S. Darbyshire from Great Britain (56.0sec. – 1864). The first result below 50sec. was made by L. Myers, USA (49.2sec. – 1879); below 49sec. – also L. Myers (48.6sec. – 1881); below 48sec. – M. Long, USA (47.8sec. – 1900); below 47sec. – B. Eastman, USA (46.4sec. – 1932); below 46sec. – J. Lea, USA (45.8sec. – 1956); below 45sec. – A. Plummer, USA (44.9sec. – 1963); below 44sec. – L. Evans (43.8sec., measured electronically – 43.86sec. – 1968). Because of the initial dominance of sprinters from Eng.-speaking countries, 400-m sprints were run relatively rarely, practically since their introduction in the Ol.G. in 1896 and hence the world record in the 400-m is later than that in the 440-yd. distance. The first official world record in the 400-m sprint was set by T. Burke, the winner of the 400-m sprint at the first modern Ol.G. in 1896 (54.2 – 1896). The existence of parallel tables of unofficial and official W.Ch. is an obstacle to determining the holders of particular records even today. Moreover, Eng.-speakers more often ran the yard sprints than metric sprints and because of this a greater frequency of good results in the 440-yd. sprints was obtained. Some tables feature conversion of these results into the 400-m sprints, others do not, featuring records in only the 400-m sprints, much worse than the former. According to the tables, which comprise all the results, the first result below 50sec. was made by an Englishman, L. Tindall, as early as 1899 (48.5sec.); the tables, which do not feature sprints run over non-metric distances, have M. Long, USA (49.4sec. – 1900) and C. Reidpath, USA, with the result below 49sec. (48.2sec. – 1912); a result below 48.0sec. according to 'complete' tables was first made by an American M. Long (47.8sec. – 1900), and according to the 'strict' tables by E. Lidell, Great

Jon Drummond of the USA gets ready to run in the Men's 100-m dash at the Olympic Stadium for the 2000 Olympic Games in Sydney, Australia.

Britain (47.6sec. – 1924). Both tables started to feature one result when sprinters beat 46sec. – the first sprinter to have done this was H. McKinley from Jamaica (45.9sec. – 1948). The first sprinters to have run in less than 45sec. were the finalists of the 1960 Ol.G.: O. Davis, USA (winner) and K. Kauffmann, FRG (44.9sec. – 1960); in less than 44sec. – L. Evans, USA (43.8sec. – 1968). Evens has also run in less than 44sec. measured electronically (43.86sec. – 1968). The first result below 43.5sec. was made by H.B. Reynolds (43.29sec. – 1988). M. Johnson got close to finishing the sprint in 43.0sec. – his best result at the 1999 W.Ch. was 43.18sec. At all the earlier Olympics (until the 1976 Ol.G., where the 400-m sprint was won by A. Juantorena), all the winners came exclusively from Eng.-speaking countries, among them Jamaicans studying in the USA. At the 1980 Olympics in Moscow, in which the Amer. team did not participate, victory went to W. Markin, USSR; since 1984 Amer. sprinters have again been dominating the 400-m sprint.

WOMEN'S 400-M SPRINT was featured in the program of the E.Ch. in 1958, and in the Olympic program in 1964; earlier considered to be too 'strenuous' an event for women. However, 400-m sprints were run by women at lower rank competitions. The first historical Eur. champion, a representative of the USSR, J. Parluk, ran the sprint in 54.8sec. Until the mid 1960s the best sprinters came from the USSR and Eng.-speaking countries. At the 1964 Olympics in Tokyo all the medals were won by representatives of the Eng. Commonwealth countries. The best sprinter at the time was E. 'Betty' Cuthbert, Australia, at the same time the only woman in history, who in her Olympic career won medals in all the sprints, i.e. 100-m, 200-m, 400-m and the 4x100-m relay sprint. Between 1968-76, after a short dominance of Fr. sprinters, the lead was taken by sprinters from the GDR, USA and I. Szewińska from Poland, the first woman to have run the 400-m sprint in less than 50sec. (49.9sec. – 1974). Szewińska improved this result twice; in 1976, in the Olympics finals, she ran in 49.29sec. (measured electronically). After Szewińska the best 400-m sprinters were J. Kratochvilova and M. Koch. The only sprinter in history who won the Olympic gold twice was M.-J. Perec of France (1992 and 1996).

The first historical world record was set by B. Hjulhammar, Sweden (1,12,5sec. – 1914). The first result below 1min. was made by K. Hitomi from Japan (59sec. –1928), below 59sec. – N. Halstead, Great Britain (58.8sec. – 1931); below 58sec. N. Halstead (56.8sec. – 1932); below 57sec. – Z. Pietrova, USSR (56.7sec. – 1950); below 56sec. – U. Jurevitz, GDR (56.7sec. – 1953); below 55sec. – Z. Safronova, USSR (54.8sec. – 1955); below 54sec. – J. Grieveson, Great Britain (53.9sec. – 1962); below 52sec. – N. Duclos, France (51.7sec. – 1969); 51sec. – M. Neufville, Jamaica (1970). The first result below 50sec. measured with a stopwatch was made by I. Szewińska, Poland (49.9sec. – 1974); the first result below 49sec. measured electronically – Ch. Brehmer (49.77sec. – 1976); below 49sec. M. Koch (48.94sec. – 1978); below 48sec. – also M. Koch (47.16sec. – 1982).

ATHLETICS, [lat. *athleticus* – athletic, see also >ATHLESIS]. Originally the term *athlesis* meant any type of ancient Gk. sports struggle with special reference to combat sports. The term was later adopted in various phonetic forms in a number of Eur. and non-Eur. languages where it underwent various shifts of meaning. English itself gives it various meanings especially across the Brit. and Amer. varieties. In the US *athletics* stands for all sports requiring physical fitness (excluding mind games) whereas in Great Britain the same term is only equivalent to track and field athletics. In Germany the noun *Athletik* stands for power struggle sports, especially wrestling. In the Pol. language the term athletics is usually combined with adjectives such as 'ciężki' ('heavy' whereby the phrase stands for sports such as weightlifting and wrestling) and 'lekki' ('light' whereby the phrase stands for track and field sports although it used to include gymnastics).

ATHLON, a Gk. term for a prize in a competition and later the name of the competition itself. A similar concept was first used in Homer's *The Iliad* where the games held in honor of Patroclus (Book XXIII) were described as *athla epi Patroklo*. Together with >ATHLESIS and >ATHLOS, the word ath-

lon is, in the majority of the Eur. languages, the root of the names of sports such as >ATHLETICS, >TRACK AND FIELD ATHLETICS and terms such as athletic, athlete, etc.

ATHLOS, Gk. for 'a prize contest' or 'military combat'. One of the words which, in the majority of Eur. languages, constitute the root of the names of sports such as >ATHLETICS, >TRACK AND FIELD ATHLETICS and terms such as athletic, athlete, etc.

ATT KASTAS, one of the numerous Swed. var. of folk wrestling whereby the 2 competitors stand facing each other and put their arms around each other [Swed. *att* – to + *kast* – throw].

ATT TAKES, a Swed. var. of wrestling practiced for fun [Swed. *att* – to + *take* a dialectal form of *tag* – grasp, grip, hold]. Mentioned by a Swed. ethnographer P.A. Säve in *Gotländska lekar* (*Gotland's games*, 1948).

AUDARYSPAK, see >SAIS.

AUSTRALIAN FOOTBALL, called 'footy' in informal Austrl. sports lingo. A var. of a ball game played with an oval ball on an oval field. Some elements of the game make it similar to >RUGBY and >AMERI-

the goal posts, 6pts., called goals, are scored, but the ball must not touch the posts, otherwise only 1pt. is awarded. A single point is also scored if on its way into the goal the ball touches any of the players. If the ball goes between a goal post and a behind post, 1 behind point is scored. A single point is scored irrespective of whether the ball, after being kicked towards the goal, touches any player or not. If the ball directed towards touches any of the posts, no point is scored and the ball is out. The ball may go between the posts at any altitude, however, the points are scored only if there is no dispute as to the ball's going between the imaginary elongations of the posts. The playing field is marked with a white line to define the playing area. A square, called the Center Square (45mx45m), is located in the center. A center circle (3m) is located in the center square. Defensive and offensive areas are line marked with a 50m arc from each goal face. The team's back half line is the opponent's forward half line, and vice versa.

The ball is oval and its circumference in longitudinal axis is 29.5in. (73cm), and the longest circumference on the cross-section is 22¾in. (55cm). It weighs 16-17oz. (452-483g) inflated between 62-76 Kpa.

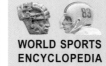

400-M DASH OLYMPIC CHAMPIONS
MEN
1896 Thomas Burke, USA 54.2
1900 Maxey Long, USA 49.4
1904 Harry Hillman, USA 49.2
1906 Paul Pilgrim, USA 53.2
1908 Wyndham Halswelle, GBR 50.0
1912 Charles Reidpath, USA 48.2
1920 Bevil Rudd, SAF 49.6
1924 Eric Liddell, GBR 47.6
1928 Ray Barbuti, USA 47.8
1932 Bill Carr, USA 46.28
1936 Archie Williams, USA 46.66
1948 Arthur Wint, JAM 46.2
1952 George Rhoden, JAM 46.09
1956 Charles Jenkins, USA 46.85
1960 Otis Davis, USA 45.07

James Gallagher (#12) for the Crows kicks under pressure during the round 15 AFL match between the Adelaide Crows and the St. Kilda Saints played at Football Park in Adelaide, Australia.

CAN FOOTBALL. A match is divided into four 20-min. quarters. The playing time does not include so-called 'waste time', i.e. the time during which the ball is out of bounds or the periods between scoring a goal and the subsequent restarting of the game. Teams change halves after each quarter. The first interval (the quarter time) takes place after the first quarter and lasts 3min., the half-time is held after the second quarter and lasts 25min., the 3-quarter time, takes 6min. The time collected for stoppages in each quarter ('time on') is added when 20mins. has elapsed to complete each quarter. Overall, a match may last up to 150mins.

The field is oval and is generally referred to as 'an oval'. It is 150-200yds. (135-185m) long and max. 120-170yds. (110-155) wide. The goals have a very original shape. They are constructed of 4 vertical posts without crossbars, placed in a straight line at the elongated ends of the oval. The middle goal posts (6m high) are 7yds. (6.40m) apart. At the same distance 2 behind posts (3m high) are positioned each side of the goal posts. If the ball goes between

Teams and positioning. The game is played by 2 teams, each consisting of 18 players and 2 substitutes. No player is designated as goalkeeper. At the beginning of the game, players take positions which suit their team best, including positions on the opponent's half. Each team is divided into 4 divisions: attackers, defenders, wings and a following division. The attackers division includes a full forward player, positioned near the opponent's goal. A forward line, standing near the opponent's goal, includes a so-called left forward pocket and a right forward pocket. Left forward flank, right forward flank and center half forward players are positioned on the halfway line. The center player is located near the center circle; the left and right wing players take their positions close to the halfway line. Ruckmen play near the center. The 1st ruck, usually the tallest player, occupies the center and his task is to compete for the ball when the game is initiated at the center of the field. Two 2nd rucks assist him from the right. Left of the 1st ruck there is a rover. The center half back, the left back flank and the right back flank play on

1964 Mike Larrabee, USA 45.15
1968 Lee Evans, USA 43.86
1972 Vince Matthews, USA 44.66
1976 Alberto Juantorena, CUB 44.26
1980 Viktor Markin, URS 44.60
1984 Alonzo Babers, USA 44.27
1988 Steve Lewis, USA 43.87
1992 Quincy Watts, USA 43.50
1996 Michael Johnson, USA 43.49
2000 Michael Johnson, USA 43.84
WOMEN
1964 Betty Cuthbert, AUSTRAL 52.01
1968 Colette Besson, FRA 52.03
1972 Monika Zehrt, E. GER 51.08
1976 Irena Szewinska, POL 49.28
1980 Marita Koch, E. GER 48.88
1984 Valerie Brisco-Hooks, USA 48.83
1988 Olga Bryzgina, URS 48.65
1992 Marie-José Pérec, FRA 48.83
1996 Marie-José Pérec, FRA 48.25
2000 Cathy Freeman, AUSTRAL 49.11

A WORLD SPORTS ENCYCLOPEDIA
52

Important Australian football terminology:

backing up – supporting a player possessing the ball by following him and staying ready to intercept the ball if the player finds himself in any danger;
blind turn – a feint intended to mislead an opponent;
crumb – a ball dropped by a player;
drop kicking – a ball is kicked the moment it touches the ground;
finger-tip mark – the interception of a ball pitched so high that it cannot be grabbed with the hands but only stopped with the fingertips, and then pulled down and held before the game is continued;
fly – a high jump to reach the ball;
full-back line – an imaginary line along the goals, lateral to the oval, whose midpoint is occupied by a full back. The full-back line marks the so-called left forward pocket and the right forward pocket;
goal-to-goal line – an imaginary line connecting the centers of both goals;
key position – a term applying to any player along the goal-to-goal line; the key position can be taken by a full forward, a center half forward, a center half back and a full back;
kick-off area – similar to the European goal area, although it only comprises the area between central goal posts; the ball is kicked from this area after a behind point has been scored or the ball has crossed the side line along the goal;
pack – a group of players fighting to intercept the ball from the ground or from the air;
punt kicking – kicking the ball some 18in. (around 46cm) above the ground after it has been dropped vertically on the foot;
ride – a player supports himself on the opponent's shoulder when jumping high to reach for the ball;
screamer – a spectacular interception of an airborne ball, a mark;
shirtfront – challenging an opponent by hitting him in the chest with one's shoulder.

An AFL match between the Adelaide Crows and the St. Kilda Saints played in Adelaide, Australia.

the center half back line. The field's left pocket near the goal is defended by a left back pocket, whereas the right one is defended by a right back pocket, and a full back is positioned near the team's goal.
Umpires. The umpire team consists of 5 persons. The whole game is controlled by a field or central umpire. Two boundary empires control side lines; 2 goal umpires, one for each team's goal, control the correctness of points scored. A 6pt. goal is signaled by raising 2 flags, and one flag is raised for a 1pt. goal. Additionally, 2 timekeepers, one for each team, supervise the duration of the match.
Course of the game. Team captains toss a coin to select halves. The game begins when the umpire bounces the ball high in the air into the center circle. Usually the tallest players, who are over 1.80m tall, are selected to compete for the ball. The game is restarted in the same way after each 6pt. goal. The ball is then delivered to the field umpire by goal umpires, who run continually so as not to delay the game. After a single point is scored, the game is not restarted in the center but is kicked from the goal area by an opposing defender. If the kicker crosses the goal area line before the kick is taken, the umpire stops the game and restarts it from the center of the goal area line. If the ball leaves the field of play, a throw-in is executed by the umpire. The throw-in is usually 15yds. (about 14m) long. Every player has the right to challenge a thrown-in ball, however, it is usu. the ruckmen who do this. The object of the game is to score more points than the opponent. A goal can only be scored if a bouncing ball is kicked. Neither the offside rule as in >FOOTBALL nor knock-on rule as in >RUGBY applies, and the ball can be kicked toward the goal from any place within the field. Long kicks are a characteristic feature of Australian football and they are used both to pass the ball to another player and to attempt to score a goal. Goals are scored from any direction and from any distance, often exceeding 60yds. (55m).
A player can run holding the ball but it must be bounced at least once in 15m. The ball can be passed to other players by kicking or punching it but not by throwing. A penalty free kick is awarded to the opponent if the ball is passed with the use of the hands employing any technique other than punching. A player who intercepts the ball after it has been punched, must continue to play in accordance with the general rules, i.e. bouncing the ball at least once every 15m and must not hold it even for a very short moment.
If a ball kicked has travelled unhindered at least 15m without touching the ground, it can be intercepted, which is referred to as a mark. A chest mark is the capture of the ball with one's chest and hands. A mark awards a player with an unhindered kick or disposal. An opposing player will stand the mark and challenge the kicker by jumping or waving his arms. If, however, he approaches too close to the opposing player, the kicker is awarded a bonus of being moved 50m closer to goal. The kicker can also determine to play on by fisting the ball to a teammate, but in so doing makes the ball live again.
Penalty free kicks are awarded by the umpire in the following situations: 1) a ball is thrown, instead of being fisted; 2) the opponent is seized by the neck, arms or legs; 3) the ball is kept too long while a player is intercepting it or trying to attack (both situations require a player to get rid off the ball immediately by passing it to one of the teammates unless a player lost his balance); 4) the ball is dropped by a player grabbed by an opponent, with the exception of a player who loses his balance; 5) the ball is trapped by a player who has fallen over and is lying on the ball; 6) an opponent is pushed on the back or the face; 7) an opponent is hit with the hand; 8) an opponent with no ball in possession is challenged; 9) an opponent with no ball in possession is grabbed; 10) deliberate playing for time; 11) running with a ball over more than 15m without dribbling it. Furthermore, penalties include awarding the opponent a shorter distance from the goal, e.g. if a player who was penalized continues the game rather than give the ball to the opponent, a bonus consisting of restarting the game 50m closer to the goal is granted. A player challenging his opponent may seize him by the waist as well as push him away with hips or shoulders. Each player may guard his teammate against the challenging opponent. This activity, known as shepherding, is allowed if a 'shepherd' remains at least 5m away from the ball and does not commit any breach. A player committing a breach of the rules cannot be sent off during the game. Nevertheless, those who do commit offence are cautioned and their names are recorded by the umpires and are officially reported to the club representative immediately after the match. If the offence is serious, the player is judged by a court consisting of independent sports officials and administrators, headed by a professional stipendiary magistrate. The tribunal can acquit a player after interrogating involved parties, including the player himself. A player can only be penalized by being fined or suspended for a determined period of time or number of matches, proportional to the offence.
History. The first match in Australia was played in 1829 by Ir. soldiers serving in the Brit. military forces. Although little is known of the rules followed during the match, it is assumed the soldiers played >GAELIC FOOTBALL, one of the 2 most popular sports in Ireland. More recent theory, however, suggests a game based on Eng. or Ir. football in its early stage of development typical of the beginning of the 19th cent. Similar matches were played over the next 20 yrs. by Brit. and Ir. immigrants, mainly gold miners in the state of Victoria. According to I. Jobling, an Austrl. sports historian, they did not contribute much to the beginnings of Austrl. football (OCAS, 36). In 1850-60, students of Scotch College in Melbourne played a game incorporating elements of both Eng. >ASSOCIATION FOOTBALL and >RUGBY. In August 1858, in Melbourne, a match whose rules are somewhat vague was played between Scotch College and Melbourne Grammar School teams. Teams consisted of approx. 40 players and the goals were about 1mi. (1.6093km) apart. After about 5hrs., Scotch College scored a goal. For a long time, the match was thought to have been the first club and intercollegiate match in the history of Austrl. sport. It is commemorated with a plaque in Yarra Park, near Melbourne Cricket Ground (MCG). Meanwhile, historians discovered that another match, between Melbourne Grammar School and St. Kilda Grammar School, had been played 2 months earlier. Both matches were based on the var. of football known in Eng. public schools. In 1858, Thomas Wentworth Wills (1835-80), a graduate of Rugby, who had been active mostly in >CRICKET to that point, wrote a letter to *Bell's Life in Victoria*, in which he suggested that football clubs should be estab. in Australia. In 1859, Wills along with 6 other members of MCG, all graduates of Eng. public schools, 2 of whom were also graduates of Cambridge University (J.B Thompson and W.J. Hammersley), drew the first outline of principles applied in what later developed into Austrl. football. The rules were a combination of elements borrowed from games trad. to Harrow and Winchester, mostly rugby. One important and easily recognizable tendency in establishing these rules was an effort to reduce the brutality of rugby rules. The rules prohibited, among other things, challenging players with no ball in possession. The ball could be passed anytime, a kick should be taken no later than after a 3-yd. run and the ball could not be thrown. There was no offside rule, which led to the creation of unique rules, maintained in Austrl. football to this day, allowing the ball to be passed to a teammate by punching it with one hand while the other hand supports it. In 1860, running with ball was excluded, which almost annihilated the dynamics of the game. In 1866, Will's cousin, H.C. Antill Harrison (1836-1929), was entrusted with the modification of the rules. From then on, a player was allowed to run with the ball, provided he bounced it every 5-6yds. The length of the field was reduced to 200yds. and its width to 150yds. Since 1869, only an oval ball has been in use, which had not been a rule before. A rule according to which the team which scores 2 goals wins, whether it happens after 1hr. or 2 days, was in force until 1869. The playing time was gradually shortened after 1869 and instead it was the final score that determined the winner at the end of the match. Before 1872, not all matches were administered by an umpire. Instead, the course of the game was controlled to a large extent by the team captains. In that time, the game developed mostly in Victoria state and the rules established there are known in the history of Austrl. sport as the Victorian Rules or the Melbourne Rules. In 1874, a rule saying that a goal may only be scored by kicking the ball rather than by carrying it across the goal line – which had been the case so far – was instituted. One of the most significant achievements of Austr. football is the fact that the brutality, so characteristic of similar Ang.-Sax. games such as rugby or >AMERICAN FOOTBALL, was eschewed and effectively prevented. 'Rabbiting', i.e. a challenge similar to tackling, was banned in 1859 and 'slinging', i.e. bringing an opponent down on the ground was prohibited around 1875. The fact that early Austrl. football was a complimentary sport for cricket players, who often came from the middle and upper classes, contributed to the sport's character, since one could not socialize with a black eye. Football's elitist status was suppressed by social tendencies, typical of 19th-cent. Australia, which appeared in the ever-developing tradition of the weekend, and reduced working time on Saturdays, which made Austrl. football an increasingly popu-

Lleyton Hewitt, a renowned tennis player, takes part in a Charity Australian football match between The Adelaide Legends and Port Adelaide held at the Adelaide Oval in Adelaide, Australia.

lar entertainment among workers, shop owners, office and bank clerks. By the early years of the 20th cent. it was widespread, played in parks without admission tickets. I. Jobling, Austrl. sports historian, believes that the fact Austrl. football was first played in parks, as well as many of the features characteristic of its early stages of development, were responsible for its popularity (OCAS, 28). As a result of organizing the game in parks, the early shape of the field was a rectangle. The oval shape was adopted when the game's popularity made it move to cricket fields (the 1880s and '90s).
In 1877, seven clubs from Victoria established the Victorian Football Association, VFA. In the same year, 4 clubs from Adelaide, estab. the South Austrl. Football Association, SAFA. In 1885, the Western Austrl. Football Association, WAFA, was founded. These organizations competed not only in sport but also in the influence they had on the evolution of the rules of the game, e.g. originally Austrl. features of the game started to prevail in the province of Victoria, while in Sydney and Queensland the game shifted in the direction of Eur. football and rugby, rejecting the Victorian Style. Clubs and associations which had not made their final choice began to lean towards the rugby style. Consequently, a division line was drawn, separating interests in different var. of football that predominated within a given area. Australians professionally connected with sport call this line the Barassi Line (Barassi was a famous Austrl. football player). One sports historian commented: 'Australia is divided by a deep cultural rift between the north and the south known as the Barassi line. It runs between Canberra, Broken Hill, Birdsville and Manangrita and it divides Australia between Rugby and Rules,' (OCAS, 263). Austrl. football was particularly threatened by the economic recession of 1893-95, during which a number of weaker Victorian clubs went belly up. The well-established and already verified Brit. standards, prevailing on the other side of the Barassi Line, proved more successful during this struggle for survival. As a result, in 1897, the first Austrl. league called the Victorian Football League (VFL) was established. It comprised 8 clubs and guaranteed regular income from tickets, which facilitated the clubs' existence. At the same time, rules were changed in order to make the game more attractive. In order to reduce chances of a draw and to make scoring easier, additional side posts were added in 1897. A player had the right to intercept the ball if it was airborne for at least 10yds., which prevented players from practicing short, unspectacular passes. Furthermore, the number of players was reduced from 20 to 18 (in 1930 one substitute was allowed, a second was introduced in 1946; however, until 1978, substitutes could only substitute injured players; only after 1978 could they be introduced to the game for tactical reasons). Such modifications led Austrl. associations and clubs to gradually adopt the system developed in the VFL. In 1906, the Australasian Football Council was formed. NAFC. Austrl. championships were played from 1908; initially every 3yrs. every 5yrs. from 1961. These, however, were overtaken from 1977 by the establishment of State of Origin football matches. The players receive substantial remuneration but there are only a few full-time professionals in Austrl. football. Each Austrl. state, and separately the city of Canberra, have their own leagues that are coordinated by AFL. The Victoria state league evolved nationwide from 1987 by admitting teams from other states and by increasing the total number of teams from 12 to 14. In 1990, it was renamed the Austrl. Football League, which now numbers 16 clubs. Indeed, 4 of the 6 most recent premierships have been won by interstate clubs, Adelaide in 1997-98 and Brisbane 2001-02. The strongest and most renowned clubs include: Melbourne Football Club estab. in 1858; Geelong FC – 1859; Carlton FC – 1864; South Melbourne FC – 1874; Port Adelaide FC – 1870; St. Kilda FC – 1873; Essendon FC – 1873; North Melbourne FC – 1877; Norwood FC – 1878; Fitzroy FC – 1884; Richmond FC – 1885; Collingwood FC – 1892; and East Fremantle FC – 1898.
Among the most celebrated players of all time are: K. Bartlett (b. 1947, played 403 matches 1965-83 and kicked 778 goals), H. Bunton (1911-55, a 3-time Brownlow Medallist); P. Burns (1866-1951, nicknamed 'Peter the Great of Austrl. football', considered the best player of the early years of football); B. Cable (b. 1943, one of the best rovers in history); R. Cazaly (1893-1963; a legend among football players; 'Up there Cazaly!' became a popular song in the 1970s and subsequently the title of an AFL anthem, composed by M. Brady); J. Dunstall (b. 1964, one of only 4 players to kick more than 1,000 goals in the VFL-AFL, he kicked 1,254 between 1985 and 1998); J. Dyer (b. 1913, nicknamed 'Captain Blood'; one of the best ruckmen ever); G. Farmer (b. 1935, nicknamed 'Polly', a remarkable ruckman; his achievements were outstanding); K. Farmer (1910-82; in the period 1929-41 he scored 1,419 goals in South Austrl. football), P. Hudson (b. 1946; one of the best goal kickers, in 1967-74 he scored 617 goals, an average of 5.8 per match, in 1971 he kicked a record-equalling 150 goals); T. Lockett (b. 1966), in his 281 career matches (1983-2002) he kicked 1,360 goals, the greatest number of goals scored by an individual in VFL-AFL competition; D. McNamara (1887-1967; first to kick the ball over a distance exceeding 100yds.); Sir D. Nicholls (1906-88; the first big indigenous star of Austrl. football, at the same time an athlete and sprinter; an Aborigine who became a preacher and subsequently was knighted by Queen Elizabeth in 1972); L. Matthews (b. 1952, played 332 matches in 4 premierships with Hawthorn FC 1969-85, universally noted as the greatest player of all time; premiership coach Collingwood 1990 and Brisbane 2001-02); L. Nash (1910-86), a truly gifted footballer and Australian Test cricketer; B. Pratt (1912-2001, scored 681 goals in his career, VFL record holder with 150 goals in 1934, R. Reynolds (1915-2002, a 3-time Brownlow Medallist), B. Skilton (b. 1939, a 3-time Brownlow Medallist; one of the greatest of any era, a roving wizard with amazing skills; A. Thurgood, (1874-1927; nicknamed 'Albert the Great', one of the first big football stars), M. Tuck (b. 1953, VFL-AFL games record holder, 426 between 1972-91; E.J. Whitten (1935-1995), a prodigious kick, a flawless mark and unequalled hand skills, he cultivated the use of the 'flick pass' – the ball is hit with the palm of the hand while the elbow is straightened, which produces a very accurate and fast flight – the keepers of the rules outlawed its use; J. Coleman (1928-73), although his football career was cut short by injury, his exploits as a full-forward is perpetuated in the Coleman Medal for player kicking the most pre-finals goals each year.
The most acclaimed coaches include: J.F. McHale, nicknamed Jock (1882-1953), set a unique record by coaching one of the top teams – Collingwood FC – in 714 matches across 37 seasons; K. Sheedy (b. 1947), coach of Essendon FC in more than 500 matches in 22 seasons since 1981; R. Barassi (b. 1937), first a remarkable player of Melbourne FC, then a player with Carlton FC; coached North Melbourne FC and then Sydney FC; the inventor of a dynamic running game style as opposed to the traditional, defensive mark-prop-kick game style; J. Kennedy, nicknamed Kanga (b. 1928), a remarkable player and coach of several clubs; created a training system based on universal exercises and aggressive intercepts. D.N. Kerley (b. 1934), specialized in leading average clubs to the top, admired by fans who sometimes even followed him changing their club favorites.
The following are among the officials and activists who contributed substantially to the game's successes and development: Dr. A.J. Aylett, OBE, (b. 1934), first a player of the North Melbourne FC, then the VFL's chairman (1977-84); C. Brownlow (1861-1924), a remarkable player in the early stages of Austrl. football, one of creators of the VFL and a co-author of a number of the rules; the prestigious Brownlow Medal is awarded for great skill and fair-play during league matches. K. Luke (1898-1971), the advocate of the commercialization of Austrl. football, an official at the 1956 Melbourne Ol.G. P. Pembroke Page (1889-1986), introduced a modern administration of Austrl. football, an official at the 1956 Ol.G. Many ex-players became successful sports journalists, e.g. P.J. Beames 'Age' (b. 1911); L.C. Richards (b. 1925), radio and TV commentator, contributing to the prestigious *Sun* daily, author of numerous books on sport (see below); J. Worrall (1863-1937), an outstanding football coach and cricket player, a journalist working for *The Australasian* magazine.
Women. Austrl. football has always been perceived as a male sport. Recently, Australia has seen a debate whether to allow women to play the game or

BROWNLOW MEDALLISTS

YEAR	MEDALLIST	CLUB
1924	E. 'Carji' Greeves	Geelong
1925	Colin Watson	St. Kilda
1926	Ivor Warne Smith	Melbourne
1927	Syd Coventry	Collingwood
1928	Ivor Warne Smith	Melbourne
1929	Albert Collier	Collingwood
1930	Stan Judkins	Richmond
	Allan Hopkins	Footscray
	Henry Collier	Collingwood
1931	Haydn Bunton	Fitzroy
1932	Haydn Bunton	Fitzroy
1933	Chicken Smallhorn	Fitzroy
1934	Dick Reynolds	Essendon
1935	Haydn Bunton	Fitzroy
1936	Dinny Ryan	Fitzroy
1937	Dick Reynolds	Essendon
1938	Dick Reynolds	Essendon
1939	Marcus Whelan	Collingwood
1940	Des Fothergill	Collingwood
	Herbie Matthews	Sth. Melbourne
1941	Norman Ware	Footscray
	--------SUSPENDED DURING WWII --------	
1946	Don Cordner	Melbourne
1947	Bert Deacon	Carlton
1948	Bill Morris	Richmond
1949	Ron Clegg	Sth. Melbourne
	Col Austen	Hawthorn
1950	Alan Ruthven	Fitzroy
1951	Bernie Smith	Geelong
1952	Roy Wright	Richmond
	Bill Hutchison	Essendon
1953	Bill Hutchison	Essendon
1954	Roy Wright	Richmond
1955	Fred Goldsmith	Sth. Melbourne
1956	Peter Box	Footscray
1957	Brian Gleeson	St. Kilda
1958	Neil Roberts	St. Kilda
1959	Bob Skilton	Sth. Melbourne
	Verdun Howell	St. Kilda
1960	John Schultz	Footscray
1961	John James	Carlton
1962	Alistair Lord	Geelong
1963	Bob Skilton	Sth. Melbourne
1964	Gordon Collis	Carlton
1965	Ian Stewart	St. Kilda
	Noel Teasdale	Nth. Melbourne
1966	Ian Stewart	St. Kilda
1967	Ross Smith	St. Kilda
1968	Bob Skilton	Sth. Melbourne
1969	Kevin Murray	Fitzroy
1970	Peter Bedford	Sth. Melbourne
1971	Ian Stewart	Richmond
1972	Len Thompson	Collingwood
1973	Keith Greig	Nth. Melbourne
1974	Keith Greig	Nth. Melbourne
1975	Gary Dempsey	Footscray
1976	Graham Moss	Essendon
1977	Graham Teasdale	Sth. Melbourne
1978	Malcolm Blight	Nth. Melbourne
1979	Peter Moore	Collingwood
1980	Kelvin Templeton	Footscray
1981	Bernie Quinlan	Fitzroy
	Barry Round	Sth. Melbourne
1982	Brian Wilson	Melbourne
1983	Ross Glendenning	Nth. Melbourne
1984	Peter Moore	Melbourne
1985	Brad Hardie	Footscray
1986	Robert DiPierdomenico	Hawthorn
	Greg Williams	Sydney
1987	Tony Lockett	St. Kilda
	John Platten	Hawthorn
1988	Gerard Healy	Geelong
1989	Paul Couch	Geelong
1990	Tony Liberatore	Footscray
1991	Jim Stynes	Melbourne
1992	Scott Wynd	Footscray
1993	Gavin Wanganeen	Essendon
1994	Greg Williams	Carlton
1995	Paul Kelly	Sydney
1996	Michael Voss	Brisbane
	James Hird	Essendon
1997	Robert Harvey	St Kilda
1998	Robert Harvey	St Kilda
1999	Shane Crawford	Hawthorn
2000	Shane Woewodin	Melbourne
2001	Jason Akermanis	Brisbane
2002	Simon Black	Brisbane

A WORLD SPORTS ENCYCLOPEDIA

Auto street racing – the early days.

Jackie Stewart's test, also called 'auto-tennis'.

Alain Prost takes the lead in his McLaren during the 1986 Monte Carlo Grand Prix.

To boldly go – autocross.

not – the conclusion is as yet unknown. Women have been keen spectators of the sport from its very beginning. The Austrl. *Herald* reported in 1895 that, 'a large contingent of the fair sex were in a crowd of two thousand people who had gathered on a Saturday afternoon to watch a match of the fledgling code.' The way women participated in football performances made the historian R. Hess conclude that, 'Sport, and particularly football, during the sexually repressive reign of Queen Victoria, enabled women to admire male bodies in a socially acceptable way.' However, female fans did not always behave properly. In 1897, the *Argus* magazine reported:

The woman 'barracker', indeed, has become one of the most objectionable of football surroundings. On some grounds they actually spit in the faces of players as they come to the dressing rooms, or wreak their spite much more maliciously with long hat pins. In the heights of this melee some of the women screamed with fear. Others screamed 'Kill him'. One of these gentle maidens at the close of the struggle remarked regretfully that it was pity they 'let off' the umpire in the geelong match, as they should have killed him. Yet these women consider themselves respectable, and they 'support' football, which is consequently in a serious decline.

Nevertheless, unsporting behavior on the part of women was infrequent. At the beginning of the 20th cent., the authorities of individual Austrl. football organizations were prob. the first, on an international scale, to notice different psychological needs of female sports fans frequenting stadiums. F. Garlick of the Melbourne *Punch* observed that women needed a calm place at the stadium, without any men, where they could comment on the game and 'talk to their heart's content,' whereas, 'the mere male prefers to be where he can smoke his clay, and emphasize his ideas about the umpire, and generally, to talk in strain that the gentle Annies wouldn't approve of.'

Some Austrl. stadiums, e.g. Victoria Park in Melbourne, developed a tradition of reserving some sections for women and children. Seats located nearest the field were usually reserved for women with children, and some sections of the central grandstands were reserved for those women who wanted to exchange their opinions concerning the game away from the company of men. Having other expectations than men, women often reacted in a different way, often disapproving of violent actions and cheering handsome players rather than the best performing ones. Once, one of the ladies watching an Essendon vs. Carlton match, after the umpire had made a wrong decision, approached the board and in the midst of the silence that ensued the erroneous arbitration bawled towards the umpire: 'You are getting money under false pretences! You don't know the game any more than a baby in arms!' On the following day, the newspapers reported that, 'the umpire palpably winced.' Women also encouraged participation in matches as a way of drawing the men away from pubs and alcohol. The first groups declaring such opinions were established alongside the Collingwood and Essendon clubs. Usually such groups were dominated by elderly women. The most famous of such organizations is the *Dolly Greys* which still operates alongside the FC Collingwood up to this very day. Women played an important role in the development of Austrl. rules football being a 'behind-the-scenes' factor working on their potent husbands or establishing their own associations which in turn supported a club's activities. In 1989, Footscray FC, which was about to go bankrupt, was rescued by a protest organized by club boosters, including a very active and influential women's lobby. Women's first attempt at playing Austrl. football took place in 1876, when one of the female students of the Presbyterian Ladies' College applied to the school authorities to establish a football club. She justified her plea saying that she noticed, 'how much fun, enjoyment and excitement boys seem to have in that fun.' Females' attempts to play football, initiated in 1899, were scarce and often mocked by the press. No records of women's games have survived, since such games were generally ignored by schools, clubs and mass media. Such was the product of the Victorian moral censorship which did not allow women to participate in male sports (such an approach was even more blatant in the case of Eng. football).

Australian football in literature. In the course of its 150yrs. of development, Austrl. football has become an element of the Austrl. cultural consciousness to the same degree as Eur. football in Europe. It is reflected in literary works devoted to this unique discipline. In 1876, an anonymous poet wrote:

A splendid picture do they make,
These heroes of the red and blue
As ranged in order now they stand
And twice ten thousand eyes upon them fixed
With full ten thousand forms around them
A glorious setting for a noble theme.

Already in the early years of Austrl. football – when the dispute about including >RUGBY standards was being resolved – the first literary works appeared, taking an unequivocal stance in the discussion, rebuking the game's brutality. In 1875, T. Jones described in *The Footballer* a rugby ruck as the last barbarian relic. W.T. Goodge wrote in 1899 in a poem titled *What's It Coming To*, depicting preparations for a match:

And don't forget the ambulance
And surgeon three or four,
And wools and lints and lots of splints
And bandages galore;
And let the players make their wills
And fix the fray that comes to

In a book titled *Town Life in Australia* (1883), R. Twopenny described Australian football as a sport, 'by far the most scientific [...] altogether the best.' The Barassi Line, dividing Austrl. fans, seems to divide sports writers as well. It has even been researched in sociology theses and comparative analyses, e.g. prof. Bradley's treatise *Barassi and Hamlet: A Comparative Study in the Tragic Hero*. A. Summers, an open supporter of the game, observed in her novel *Damned Whores and God's Police* (1975) that, 'the disdain many intellectuals feel for the activities of the masses does not so often extend to [Austrl. rules] football, which secures often

fanatical support.' The most famous Austrl. poem on sport, *Life Cycle* by B. Dawe, starts with the following words:

When children are born in Victoria
they are wrapped in the club-colours,
laid in beribboned cots,

Austrl. drama writer, L. Esson referred to Austrl. football in 1927, in his letter to V. Palmer, as 'the most serious matter in the State.' As a Carlton FC fan, he became a part of the sport's history by pronouncing his statement, first printed in the *Age*, and then repeated by many, that to see one's favorite team win is 'to see my love come to me.' In the book titled *The Australians*, G. Johnston quotes a Sydney citizen saying that 'Melbourne has no summer, only a period of hibernation between football seasons.' The most acclaimed literary works praising Austrl. football include L. Sandercock's collection of short stories *Up Where Cazaly? The Great Australian Game* (1981) and a collection of essays by G. Hutchinson titled *From the Outer. Watching Football In the 80s* (1984). Both books favor the conviction that Austrl. football is a cultural phenomenon, important for its egalitarianism, esthetic quality, and positive influence, free from any major social controversies. However, literary critics of Austrl. football differ in these matters.

The most serious literary works touching on the theme of the game include 2 collections of short stories – A. Hopgoods's *And the Big Men Fly* (1969) and B. Oakley's *A Salute to the Great McCarthy* (1970), as well as a popular theater play by D. Williamson *The Club* (1978). These works concentrate on the ins and outs of the Austrl. football world, the officials' murky businesses, mass media hypocrisy, footballers' dramas, rather than on the game as such. At some point in time, protagonists of all stories withdraw from sport and return to their pre-sport surroundings for 'therapy' because, as one of them – J. McCarthy – puts it: 'I went too close to the bright lights and copped a fast burn on the behind.' In Williamson's theater play *Club*, Geoff Hayward says: 'If you really want to know, what's going on is that I'm sick to death of football [...] It's all a lot of macho-competitive bullshit.' In his 2 short stories from the collection *Going Home* (1986), Aborigine writer A. Weller, takes up the illusory civilization of Austrl. natives based on football. The character attempts to decipher the world of white values and live up to them, hoping that their high social status would help him with the task. Billy Woodward, a character from the collection's title story, learns that sacrificing oneself for football means nothing among white people and does not change the player's racial situation. The main protagonist of the second short story, Reg Cooley, tries to imitate his brother, a successful football player, and dies hit by a stray police bullet. The narrator concludes the story with the following words: 'Here lies not only a Polly farmer, Lionel Rose or Namatjira; only a small-town halfcaste who tried to raise himself out of the dirt and was kicked back down again ... Only a halfcaste who had lived in a world of football and dreams.' Native Australians were not the only ones to be disappointed with the game. Nevertheless, the power of its influence has not diminished over time and, as the abovementioned George Johnston affirms in *The Australians*, 'No other sporting event in Australia draws a crowd as big or committed as this. For a time men become gods and heroes.'

J. Harms and I. Jobling, 'Australian Rules Football. Saturday Afternoon Poetry', *Journal of Australian Studies*, September 1996; R. Hess, *Women and Australian Rules Football in Colonial Melbourne*, IJHS, 13, 3, 1996; T.D. Jacques, *Australian Football. Steps to Success*, 1994; R. Stremski, *Kill for Collingwood*, 1986; W. Vamplev, B. Stoddart, *Sport in Australia. A Social History*, 1994; *The Oxford Companion to Australian Sport*, ed. W. Vamplev, K. Moore, J. O'Hara, R. Cashman, I. Jobling, 1994; Consultants:: Kevin Taylor, Footystats, Australia, Richard Reisner.

AUTO STREET RACING, automobile races within city limits, very popular at the beginning of the 20th cent., now in decline, mostly because of the high speed and danger to both drivers and spectators, but also due to the rapid development of race tracks. One of the relics of that form of automobile racing is the Monte Carlo Rally, held annually despite growing concerns regarding safety conditions. An informal and illegal var. of automobile street racing is >DRAG

Juha Kankkunen and co-driver Juha Repo (both from Finland) leave a cloud of water in their Hyundai Accent WRC, Car #19, during the world's toughest rally, The Safari Rally Kenya 2002, second leg near Ngema Control 4.

CAR RACING, arranged spontaneously in Amer. cities in violation of a strict police ban and practiced with the use of amateur cars.

AUTO-TENNIS, a sport whose aim is to compete in precision vehicle driving so as not to spill a ball placed on a special flat 'platter', usu. made of a motorcycle tire covered with plastic film and mounted to a car's hood in such a way that the driver can easily see the ball. The object of the game is to reach the finish line without spilling the ball. For training purposes the ball is usu. attached to the 'platter' with a piece of fishing line so that the driver does not have to stop to pick up the ball each time he spills it. Auto-tennis was developed by the Scot. Formula 1 driver J. Stewart.

AUTOCROSS, a timed, cross-country race. Since 1984, according to the Fédération Internationale de l'Automobile regulations, autocross races have been held over rugged, sandy, muddy or grassy courses of 600 to 2,000m. The straight legs of a given course must not be longer than 180m and the first turn must not occur less than 45m away from the starting line. For safety reasons spectator stands must be located at least 23m away from the curves and at least 18m away from the straightaways. Trees and railings must be at least 18m away from the edge of a course. There are numerous autocross classes and categories. In England, for example, there as many as 30 such categories. E.Ch. for A, B and special 3,500cc categories have been held since 1982. The cars usually do not have windscreens and windows, their chassis are reinforced and extra, anti-capsizing protective devices are added. One of the autocross var. is called *cross-country* rally cross.

History. Autocross developed in England where the first hill-climbing and timed cross-country vehicle races were held soon after WWI. In 1925, after a tragic accident involving spectators, public road races were banned and, therefore, races were only held over private roads. The Southport and Saltburn events became the most prestigious of all. In 1926 a new type of race, called the freak hill-climb, was introduced. Freak hill climbing became immensely popular all over England in the 1930s. The races had to be suspended during WWII but were revived in 1946. The first 'modern' autocross race was organized in 1947 by the Hagley and District Light Car Club near Stourbridge-Bridgnorth, Shropshire. The club experimented with various course and race types which contributed greatly to the standardization of the rules of the sport. The new events that were developed in this way included the two-at-a-time circuit race and the knock-out hill-climb. The sport began developing rapidly as it was extremely exciting to watch and attracted huge crowds even during local events

held far away from major towns and cities. A breakthrough came in 1954 when W. Cawsey, the President of the Taunton Motoring Club organized the first Bank Holiday autocross show. In 1959 Taunton Motoring Club obtained the first official license to organize autocross competitions. At the same time the Royal Automobile Club used the Taunton Motoring Club rules to develop a nationwide set of regulations. This resulted in the fact that more and more local motoring clubs, although with smaller budgets than the leading clubs, could organize major competitions by setting more attractive and difficult courses than those offered during even the most prestigious events. This coincided with car manufacturers and individual inventors developing special autocross equipment including engines, car bodies and tires. In the 1960s autocross races were dominated by Ford. However, they soon had to face fierce competition from the Mini-Cooper and VW Beetle. Separate winter competitions have been held since 1963. The competitions became even more attractive after tobacco companies and car lubricant manufacturers started sponsoring such events in 1966. British TV began broadcasting autocross shows in 1967. Today, autocross events receive extensive satellite and cable TV coverage.

In the US, the term autocross is used to refer to a completely different sport. Amer. autocross, also known as Solo II, stands for car contests held in large parking lots, runways or kart courses. Drivers compete in individual time trials along a special, bollard-marked course. They drive regular cars at speeds of up to 70mph. For knocking over 1 bollard drivers are awarded 1 or 2 penalty seconds that are deducted from their final time. The drivers, in order to be allowed to compete in local and state competitions, must be members of the SCCA (Sports Car Club of America), which is an organization that has supervised motor sports in the US since the 1950s.

AUTOGRASS, a form of >CAR RACING, in which specially prepared saloon cars compete on an oval 440yd. track laid out on a natural surface, which may be grass, dirt or mud. The object is to beat the opponents in the race to the finish line in a set of 4-8 laps, with up to 10 cars participating in a race. Cars race in 10 different classes. Most major meetings are staged over 2 days. The sport is popular in Great Britain, where it is administered by the National Autograss Sport Association.

AUTOMOBILE RALLIES, also *auto rallies* or *car rallies*, long distance >AUTO RACING events in which competitors cover a set course – on a public road or an offroad, usu. rough terrain – in one or more legs (some of them being special stages), within a set time limit. Rally distances vary from several dozen to several thousand kilometers. A crew con-

sists of 2 people: a driver and a co-driver or pilot. While the driver drives the vehicle, the pilot's task is to read the course map and provide the driver with information regarding the nature and surface of the course, the type and curvature of bends, the nature of obstacles, etc. This information allows the driver to take appropriate action such as selecting the right gear, taking the bends at an appropiate angle, selecting the right speed, etc. The above data is collected and written down by the pilot during training sessions which allow the crew to study the course prior to the rally. Each crew receives a road book (or maps) and a time card which lists the distance of each leg and the time limit in which the crew must reach subsequent control zones.

History. Auto rallies are the oldest form of auto races held on public roads. The Paris-Rouen race (approx. 130km) organized by a Fr. newspaper, *Le Petit Journal*, on the initiative of its Editor-in-chief M.P. Giffard, is considered the first such race. The development of auto racing, incl. rallies, was significantly influenced by automobile associations, esp. national associations such as the oldest of all Automobile Club de France (estab. 1894), and similar organizations in Belgium (1896), Great Britain (1897), Holland, Switzerland and Italy (1898), etc. Auto rallies have also been gaining popularity in Asia. In 1898 the International Association of Automobile Tourism (AIT) was estab., and in 1904 the Association Internationale de Automobiles Clubs (AIACR) was formed, the latter transformed in 1946 into the International Automobile Federation (Fédération Internationale de l'Automobile,

Automobilism – an offroad rally, literally.

A 1914 photo of manufacturer Henry Ford with inventor Thomas Edison in one of Ford's automobiles in Florida.

FIA), which controls the sport today. The division of automobile events into racing and rallying began in the early decades of the 20th cent., when the first close-circuit tracks for car racing were built. In the early history of auto rallies the outcome was primarily dependent upon the automobile construction rather than the ability of drivers. Technological progress has eliminated the former factor in favor of the latter. Auto rallies enjoyed great popularity mostly in Europe, while various forms of auto racing dominated in the USA. On other continents, where automobile production was less developed, auto rallying remained marginal, with the most famous multi-country rallies including the 16,000km Paris-Peking rally (initiated by Europe in 1907 and won by Ital. S. Borghese) and the 20,000km world rally (initiated by the USA in 1908). In 1911 the first Monte Carlo rally (RMC) was organized on the initiative of the local Automobile And Cycling Club, with only 23 drivers participating. RMC has been held annually until this day, with several intervals caused by wars and the 1974 fuel crisis.

Until WWII auto rallies had been exclusive events attracting mainly the upper social classes. With time the sport became more diversified and included various national events organized by national automobile clubs, as well as regional, local, and specialized rallies, such as >ENDURANCE RALLY, >VINTAGE AUTO RACING, etc. After WWII many new auto rallies came into being incl. the famous Safari Rally held in the wilderness of Africa (for both cars and motorcycles), the Paris-Dakar rally, or the irregularly held London-Sydney rally (since 1968), London-Mexico rally (since 1970), etc. In Eastern Europe the most popular event was the Peace and Friendship Cup rally held until the collapse of communism. A new development was the initiation of auto rallying in Asia – e.g. the Indian Monsoon Rally, Cahrminar Rally, or the most difficult, 4-leg Himalayan Car Rally from Himachel Pradesh to Uttar Pradesh. Since 1973 automobile rallies have included the classification of W.Ch. for car manufacturers and later also E.Ch. for drivers and pilots. In 1994 the FIA introduced the classification of World Rally Championship for drivers and co-drivers, which since 1997 has included 14 rallies held in Europe, Africa, Asia, S.America, Australia, and N.Zealand. The development of cheaper production technologies and the sponsorship of auto industry giants made the auto rallying sport much more accessible. The same sponsorship, however, renders the involvement of independent, unaffiliated drivers virtually impossible. Among the most famous rally drivers are R. Altonen, J.

Kankkunen, T. Makinen (Finland), S. Blomquist (Sweden), V. Elford, C. McRae, R. Burns (Great Britain), S. Zasada (Poland), C. Sainz (Spain).

AUTOMOBILISM, an activity and a way of living involving the use of motor vehicles for everyday, recreational and sports purposes.
Etymology. The name originates from the term 'automobile' which, mainly in the Eur. languages as derived from the Gk. and Latin sources, is used to describe a self-propelled vehicle [Gk. *autos* – self, alone + Lat. *mobilis* – mobile]. In French the term is *automobile*, in Spanish *automóvil*, we also have the Ital. *automobile*, Ger. *Automobil*, etc. The Pol. term '*samochód*' is an imprecise loan translation of the original appellation. At the same time, Polish does have the original term 'automobil', which today has an archaic or ironic meaning, and is often abbreviated to 'auto'. As a result, most Eur. languages developed similar or almost identical names for the sport (compare the Pol. *automobilizm*, Fr. *automobilisme*, Span. *automovilismo*, Ital. *automobilismo*, and Ger. *Automobilwesen*).
Initially, similarly to aviation, auto racing was reserved for the elite and was an important stage in man's conquest of the surrounding natural world. At present, auto racing is almost devoid of any such connotations since nature and space are being conquered by other types of terrestrial and space vehicles. At the same time, auto racing became regarded as one of the human pursuits that have greatly contributed to destroying the environment. This results chiefly from the unchecked development of roads that destroys fragile ecosystems and contributes to polluting the environment, and especially the air (despite improved engines, unleaded petrol and catalytic converters). Auto racing has, however, maintained or even developed its immediate utility to humans by providing comfortable means of transportation. Its sports forms still serve as a testing ground for new car manufacturing technologies. >CAR RACING and its numerous subvarieties such as >DRAG CAR RACING, that are held in artificial conditions, focus chiefly on technical developments, whereas car rallies and >AUTOCROSS competitions are aimed at enhancing certain human skills such as the ability to drive a vehicle in naturally or artificially difficult conditions (e.g. during indoor auto- and motocross events or

Automobilism – a winter rally.

A photo of the 1906 Model K, the first six-cylinder Ford automobile.

Awarkuden, a colored design after Bramati, c.1840, Museum of History, Santiago de Chile.

tional life in 11 centuries, 2001, an unpublished manuscript. Consulted by Jón Ívarsson.

AYATORI, a Jap. variety of a game aimed at performing various movements with a piece of thread held with splayed fingers known in Europe as >CAT'S CRADLE. A game of ayatori is usu. played by two persons who wind the thread into complex figures changing hands from time to time and passing the thread to the partner.

>DEMOLITION DERBY races consisting in destroying an opponent's vehicle, etc.). There is more and more interest in other varieties of extreme auto racing varieties such as >TRUCK RACING or tractor pulling contests.

History. The beginnings of auto racing date back to the invention of the car. The first vehicle propelled with a steam engine that moved along the ground (and not railway tracks) was constructed in 1769 by a Frenchman, J. Cugnot. In the 19th cent. Eur. and Amer. inventors developed a number of steam engine vehicles. Auto racing took off when the Ger. inventors, S. Marcus (1831-98), C.F. Benz (1844-1929) and G.W. Daimler (1834-1900) developed their first internal combustion engines. In 1870 Marcus constructed the first vehicle propelled by an internal combustion engine. He improved his design further in 1875. In 1888 he developed a 4-stroke engine with electric ignition. Benz demonstrated his first car in 1885 and Daimler in 1886. In 1889 Daimler patented the V-type engine and in 1890 he estab. the first car factory in history. There, he built the first Mercedes car, named after his daughter who died in 1900. The earliest automobile competitions were organized in Europe and the US in 1894-1900. The first of those took place in 1894 in France along the 127km Paris-Rouen route. It was organized by M.P. Giffard, the Editor-in-chief of *Le Petit Journal*. The race attracted as many as 21 drivers with cars powered by both internal-combustion and steam engines. Prince de Dion won the race reaching an average speed of 18.6km/h in his steam-engine vehicle. The Automobile Club de France, the first organization of this kind in the world, was set up in the same year. Similar associations were then estab. in Belgium, England (the Royal Automobile Association, 1897), Holland, Switzerland, Italy (1898), and Germany (1899). The International Association of Automobile Tourism (AIT) was estab. in 1898 and the Association Internationale des Automobile Clubs (AIACR) in 1904. The AIACR was renamed in 1946 the International Automobile Federation (Fédération Internationale de l' Automobile, FIA).

In the US auto racing developed independently of Europe. The first car race took place in Chicago in 1895 under the auspices of *The Chicago Times Herald*. The first prize went to J.F. Durea who was, at the same time, one of the first Amer. car manufacturers and whose car reached an average speed of 7.5mi/h, i.e. slightly more than 12km/h. This points to the fact that initially the Amer. cars did worse than their Eur. counterparts. The oldest automobile organization in the US is the United States Auto Club (USAC). There is no single national Amer. automobile organization although the majority of the Amer. associations are represented in the FIA by the Automobile Competition Committee of the United States (ACCUS). The most renowned ACCUS members are the United States Auto Club, the National Association for Stock Car Auto Racing (NASCAR, estab. 1947), the Sports Car Club of America (SCCA, estab. 1945) and the National Hot Rod Association (NHRA, est. 1951; see >DRAG RACING). See also >GYMKHANA.

P. Frere, *Sports Car and Competition Driving*, 1963; A. Gregoire, *L'aventure automobile*, 1953; J. A. Litwin, *Współczesny sport samochodowy* (*Contemporary automobile sport*), 1976; M. Latco, *Histoire mondiale de l'automobile*, 1958.

AUX BARES, a Fr. game with rules similar to those observed in the Dan. >BARLØB and the Eng. >PRISONER'S BASE.

AVIATION SPORTS, see >AEROPLANE SPORTS.

AWARKUDEN, an aboriginal game of chance played by the Mapuche Indians (Araucanians) in Chile employing beans as dice, popular up until the middle of the 20th century, and originally known variously as ligue, llighen, lleghcan and lüq. The eventual name, awarkuden, deriving from the words awa (kidney beans) and kuden (to play), dates back to the 16th century when this legume was brought from Europe. Two or 4 players would sit opposite with crossed legs. A referee then gave a signal to start. By turns, each player threw a handful of beans, colored black on one side, over a cloth on the ground. Before the beans hit the ground they had first to pass through a hoop (chudughue) placed horizontally on a 60-cm rod attached to a woolen blanket (manta). A player earned points for beans that landed black side up. Large bets were once placed on the outcome, and songs, prayers, invocations, and magical manipulations accompanied matches. Awarkuden was an equal-opportunity pastime and was enjoyed alike by men, women, children and seniors. From the 17th century on, awarkuden began also to be enjoyed by non-Mapuche. The earliest mention of awarkuden dates back to Alonso de Ovalle's *Histórica Relación del Reyno de Chile*, published in Rome in 1646. Though the game is no longer practiced, lonkos (chiefs) and machis (shamans) chant kidney bean songs to this day. See also >KECHUKAWE.

M. Manquilef, 'Comentarios del Pueblo Araucano II. La Gimnasia Nacional', Revista de Folklore Chileno, 1914, vol. 4, no. 3-5, p. 75-219; L. Matus Zapata, 'Juegos y ejercicios físicos de los antiguos araucanos', BMNCH, 1920, vol. 11, p. 162-197; O. Plath, *Juegos y Diversiones de los Chilenos*, 1946; C. López von Vriessen, the Internet: www.deportesmapuches.cl; www. galeon. com/indiansports, 2002.

AXE BENDING, Pol. *zwijanie tasaka*, an old Pol. display of physical strength, in which the contestant would bend the blade of an axe or halberd using only his hands. One athlete known to have been able to do this was a hero of the Battle of Grunwald (Tannenberg, 1410) between Poland and the Teutonic Knights, Powała of Taczew. His feat was described by H. Sienkiewicz in his novel *Krzyżacy* (*The Teutonic Knights*). The Grand Master, Konrad von Jungingen, praises the quality of the Order's iron and is challenged by the Polish knight:

Powała of Taczew reached with his hand and picked up an ell-long axe used for cutting meat, which he bended effortlessly like paper into a tube. Then he raised it up so that everyone could see it and handed it over to the Grand Master.

– If your swords are made of this iron – he said – there is not much you can do with them [...]

– Holy Liborius! – cried the Grand Master – your hands are of true iron!

AXLATÖK, an old Icelandic form of wrestling (shoulder grips). Arms are laid alternately and grips are taken on shoulders sleeves or the collar. Similar to >GLÍMA various hip- and foot tricks are used.

T. Einarsson, *The developing of glíma in Iceland's na-*

German Chancellor Gerhard Schroeder, left, holds the steering handle of the 'Benz Motorwagen', the world's first automobile, as he and Juergen E. Schrempp, right, CEO of DaimlerChrysler, perch upon this antique during Schroeder's visit to the DaimlerChrysler headquarters in Stuttgart, Germany.

Bending various metal objects, such as axes or rods, has long been popular entertainment. Here Freddie Steele, middleweight champ, strikes a familiar strong-man pose.

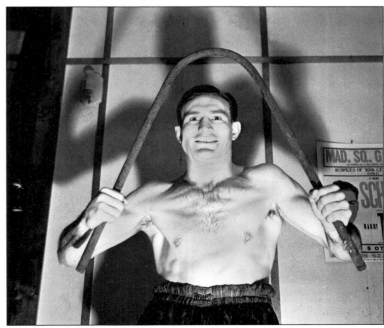

B

B.A.S.E. JUMPING, a var. of >COMPETITIVE PARACHUTING, in which jumps are made from tall structures or rocks. The acronym B.A.S.E. is decoded as Buildings, Antenna, Span, Earth – the type of locations, all of which must be tried in order to qualify as a B.A.S.E. jumper. The inventor of the sport was a Slovak constructor S. Banič (1870-1941), who in 1913 constructed a prototype parachute with which he jumped from a 41-floor building in Washington in front of the US Patent Office and military representatives, followed by a jump from an airplane in 1914. His patented parachute became standard equipment for US pilots during WWI. In 1975 Don Boyles became the first person to B.A.S.E. jump the Royal George Bridge, while in 1976 Owen J.Quinn parachuted from the World Trade Center. Modern B.A.S.E. jumping began in 1980, when a group of 4 friends – Phil Smith, Phil Mayfield, Jean and Carl Boenish – jumped from the El Capitan rock in Yosemite National Park (California) using modified skydiving gear. C. Boenish, considered to be the father of modern B.A.S.E. jumping, died in 1984 during a leap from a Norw. cliff.

The number of deaths and accidents resulting from B.A.S.E. jumps has led to the sport being banned in many countries. For that reason designing the jump, getting to the jump area and preparing escape routes to avoid arrest often require more time and determination than the jump itself.

The parachutes used in B.A.S.E. jumping are specially designed to open at a dangerously low height. Reserve chutes are dispensed with, as opening them would be impossible anyway. A leap from a height of 1,000m lasts approx. 4sec., 2sec. of free falling and 2sec. after the opening of the parachute.

Favorite B.A.S.E. jumping locations are: the Perrine bridge (476ft. or 150m), located on the Snake River outside Twin Falls, Idaho; Great Trango (6,200ft. or 2,100m), a cliff in Pakistan; the Statue of Jesus in Rio de Janeiro; Twin Towers in Kuala Lumpur (294m); the Salto del Angel falls in Venezuela (420m); the Troll Wall cliff in Norway (1,800m). One of the most exciting locations for B.A.S.E. jumpers is also the Santo de las Golondrinas cave in central Mexico (420m).

There are several BASE jumping federations, e.g. Cliff Jumpers Association of America and Austrl. B.A.S.E. Association. The cradle of Eur. B.A.S.E. jumping is Norway, whose unique nature and landscape has made it the Mecca of jumpers from all over the world.

BABELSTÅRNET, Dan. for 'the Tower of Babel'. A simple game requiring strength and agility. Five players stand on the ground holding their hands. Their knees are bent and slightly forward so that they touch one another. Next, four players climb onto them, then three, then two and finally one so that they form a tower. On a signal the base players straighten their knees and the whole tower falls apart; compare the Spanish >CASTELLS.
J. Møller, 'Babelstårnet', GID, 1997, 3, 95.

BACKHOLD, a Scot. var. of folk wrestling that, together with the Icel. >GLÍMA and the Bret. >GOUREN, is one of the events supervised by the International Federation of Celtic Wrestling (estab. 1985). Backhold was made popular in the US in the 19th cent. by Scot. immigrants. Some sources claim that A. Lincoln (1809-1965), the US President, himself practiced backhold. Backhold is largely similar to >CUMBERLAND AND WESTMORELAND, a wrestling var. popular in N England. Backhold wrestling is one of the oldest and, at the same time, simplest combat sports and various depictions of backhold matches may be found on crosses and stones dating back to as early as the 7th and 8th cent. Backhold rules are very simple – the competitors stand facing each other, put their right hand under the opponent's left arm and their left hand on the opponent's right arm. Then, they rest their chin on the opponent's right shoulder. When an umpire decides that this initial hold has been applied properly, he shouts, 'Hold!' or 'Wrestle!'. The first fighter to touch the ground with any part of his body (with the obvious exception of the soles of his feet) or to break his hold loses. There is no par terre fighting and the bout lasts until one of the wrestlers has been floored five times. Backhold wrestling was made esp. popular by D. Dinnie and Rob Roy MacGregor. In 1853 the former became a backhold champion defeating, at the age of 16, D. Forbes, the then heavyweight wrestling champion. In addition to the champion title, Dinnie received £1 in prize money.
The Internet: www.scotwrestle.co.uk/i.html

BAD, a simple folk var. of >CRICKET esp. popular in the countryside and on the outskirts of towns. Instead of a bat and a ball the players use a stick and a stone. The name of the sport – bad – is probably a regional, dialectal variant of bat and does not have anything to do with bad as in 'evil'. In some areas the game was also called świnka (see >CZOROMAJ). TGESI, 1894, I, 11.

BADDI, A LA, an Ital. type of ball game, esp. popular in Sicily, wherein the players have to put a ball into a number of holes dug in the ground. Its rules are very similar to those observed in the Dan. >BOLD I HUL.

BADDIN, a folk variety of ball game in which the ball is put in motion with a crooked stick, similar to >SHINNY and, possibly, to >FIELD HOCKEY. Popular in Cheshire, England in the 19th century. TGESI, 1894, I, 12.

BADMINTON, one of the many varieties of a game employing a shuttlecock and lightweight rackets often described as the world's fastest racket sport. It was named for the English town of Badminton; compare >INDIACA, >VOLANT, >HAGOITA.

Field and equipment. A badminton court is 13.4m-long and 5.18m-wide for singles and 6.1m-wide for doubles. A net, which is 152cm high in the middle and 155cm at the poles, stretches across the width of the court at its center. In the past the shuttlecock was made of 14 to 16 natural feathers inserted into a small, cork hemisphere. A nylon shuttlecock with a rubber base is used more frequently nowadays. The shuttlecock is 6.4-7cm-high and weighs 4.7-5.5g. The frame of the racket including the handle may not exceed 680mm in length, while the strung surface may be a max. of 280mm in overall length and 200mm in overall width.

Fundamentals. Badminton events include men's and women's singles, men's and women's doubles and mixed doubles. The shuttlecock is served across the court diagonally from the right and left side of the court alternately. When the score is 0 or the total combined score is an even number the shuttlecock is served from the right-service court and when the total combined score is an odd number from the left-service court. In doubles the first service is always made from the right-service court irrespective of the score. When a game starts, and especially when the racket touches the shuttlecock, the players have to stand within the confines of their side of the court. When serving, a player may only hit the shuttlecock after it has fallen below his or her waist. A service is not repeated if the shuttlecock touches the net. A point is awarded to a player or pair when the receiving player makes a mistake, i.e. fails to hit the shuttlecock or returns it so that it falls outside of the court. If the serving player makes a mistake the score does not change but the shuttlecock goes to the other player. One set of a badminton match lasts until 11 (in women's singles) or 15 (in men's singles) points have been scored by one of the players. In the case of a 9:9 or 10:10 tie in women's singles or a 13:13 tie in men's singles, the player who was the first to score a given number of points has the right to set 12 (women) or 16 (men) as the winning number of points to be scored. By the same token, in the case of a 14:14 tie in a men's match the winning score may be set at 17 points (a tie-breaker). The basic badminton strokes, similarly to tennis, are called forehand, backhand and smash.

History. Some Ang.-Sax. badminton experts say that it originated from an ancient game from the Far East which consists in flicking up a ball of animal hair, a bunch of oakum or wool or a weight with feathers attached to it. In the Anglo-Saxon tradition the same game is known as >SHUTTLECOCK, the Koreans call it >CHEGI CHAGI, the Chinese >TEBEG and the Mongols >TEBEG ÖSHIGLÖÖKH. The origins of badminton in England date back to the times when a special racket called a battledore was added to the original game employing just a weight with wisps of wool. This new game was aptly called >BATTLE-DORE SHUTTLECOCK. Irrespective of the fact whether such or similar games existed, badminton started in India with a local trad. game called >POONA which was brought to England by the returning colonial officers around 1871-2 and was first demonstrated in England in 1873 during a garden party at the duke of Beaufort's country estate in Badminton, Gloucestershire. The original Indian rules of the game were observed in England until around 1877, when a group of badminton enthusiasts from the Bath Badminton Club sought to make the rules of the game more uniform. Their standardized rules remained in force until the establishment of the Badminton Association of England in 1893

30-year-old Austrian parachutist Felix Baumgartner jumps from the arm of the colossal Jesus statue above the Brazilian metropolis Rio de Janeiro, the first to tackle one of the greatest challenges in the extreme sport of B.A.S.E.-jumping.

Scottish backhold wrestling.

Competitive badminton.

(or 1895 according to some sources) which introduced its own set of rules that have remained largely unchanged to the present day. The first unofficial All-England championships for men were held in 1899 and the first official ones took place a year later in 1900. In 1910 there were around 300 badminton clubs in England, in 1930 there were as many as 500 and in 1960 more than 9,000 clubs operated in England which points to the fact that the sport has been developing dynamically over the past few decades. Badminton appeared in Canada around 1890, it was brought to the US around 1900 and the Germans officially recognized it as a sport in 1902. A several-time Ol.G. medallist in tennis and a two-time Wimbledon champion, K. MacKane-Godfree made badminton extremely popular in the 1920's. The International Badminton Federation (IBF), world governing body of the sport, was formed in 1934. Today, the IBF has about 80 national federation members. Badminton began developing rapidly after the Thomas Cup (donated in 1939 by George Thomas the first and one of the most celebrated IBF presidents) tournament was held for the first time. The Thomas Cup is considered the men's team world championship. A women's tournament enjoying a similar status is the Uber Cup which started in

Badminton – a doubles game.

1956. Until 1976 the All-England Championships were deemed to be the unofficial singles world championship. However, in 1977, the first official world championship was held. Initially, it took place every 3 years but has been organized every 2 years since 1983. The most distinguished players in the world include women's world champions L. Koppen (1977) of Denmark, H. Aiping (1985, 1987) and L. Lingwei (1983, 1989), both from China; and men's world champions F. Delfs (1977) of Denmark, I. Sugiarto (1983) of Indonesia, H. Jian (1985) and Y. Yang (1987, 1989), both from China. The best professional badminton players come from Indonesia, South Korea, Malaysia, the US, Canada, Mexico, Denmark, Sweden, Great Britain and Germany. At the 1992 Ol.G. in Barcelona it became a full-medal Olympic sport. A Korean badminton player, C. So-Young became the first Olympic champion among women and A. Budi Kushma was the first Olympic

gold medallist among men. Badminton has also developed rapidly as a popular recreational and family sport and today it is commonly played in holiday resorts, at schools and during weekend trips.

BÆGERBOLD, a simple Dan. game requiring agility [Dan. *bæger* – cup, bail, chalice + *bold* – ball, sphere]. It employs a device consisting of a 30cm wooden handle with an open goblet-like container resembling the bowl of a cup or chalice attached to it. A 50cm piece of string with a wooden ball attached to one of its ends is fastened to the handle in its mid-length. A player puts the ball in the bowl and throws it up in the air. The object of the game is to catch the falling ball again in the bowl. Bægerbold resembles the French >BILBOQUET and the Greenland Inuit >AJAQAQ.
J. Møller, 'Bægerbold', GID, 1997, I, 17 and 125-7.

BÆLTAG, Dan. for 'a grip by a belt'. A simple type of wrestling. The opponents grab each other anywhere by their trouser belts. See also >CLOTHES HOLD (BELT HOLD) WRESTLING.
J. Møller, 'Bæltag', GID, 1997, 4, 43.

BÆLTETRÆKNING, Dan. for 'belt tugging'. An old type of Scand. athletic contest described in sagas. The game employed a loop of about 1m in circumference made of twined leather straps, thin wicker or rope. When both players fought in a standing position the object of the game was to pull the loop out of the opponent's hands. When one of the players was sitting and the other standing, the one who forced his opponent to move from his original position was declared the winner. It was also possible to set several opponents on to one.
J. Møller, 'Bæltetrækning', GID, 1997, 4.

BÆNDAGLÍMA, an Icel. type of glíma competition popular among Icelandic fishermen and farmers. A bændaglíma competition was held among a number of teams traditionally representing different fishermen's cabins from temporary camps set up near fishing grounds. A similar form of competition was held among the farmers. In an 1840 bænda-glíma competition held on Grund in Eyjafjördur in N Iceland approx. 120 farmers and farm labourers is said to have participated. A bændaglíma competition held in Laugarvant in S Iceland in 2000 gathered 90 competitors. The teams usu. stood opposite each other. The leader of each team was called *bóndi* (pl. *bændur*), which means a 'farmer'. The oldest mentions of bændaglíma contests date back to the early Commonwealth times (930-1262). Bændaglíma fights usu. accompanied various holidays, esp. religious ones, and were also associated with weddings and other festivities.

BÆNKEMAD, Dan. for 'eating from a bench'. A bully game involving 3 participants. One of them is pressed against a bench, the second player holds him by twisting his arms around the back of the bench, and the third one tickles and pricks the 'victim', who must try to prove how tough he is.
J. Møller, 'Bænkemad', GID, 1997, 3.

BÆRE EN MAND PÅ VRISTERNE, Dan. for 'to carry somebody on the instep of a foot'. One of the players sits on a chair and places his hands behind the back of the chair. The second player stands behind the chair to support it so that it does

not fall over during the exercise. The sitting player raises his legs and a third player stands on the insteps of his feet.
J. Møller, 'Bære en mand på vristerne', GID, 1997, 3, 83.

BÆRE I GULDSTOL, a Dan. counterpart of >KING'S CHAIR.

BAGATAWAY, an ancient game played by N.Amer. Indians, particularly by the Algonquian (Algonkian) and Iroquoians, it is also called *baggataway* or *bag-atonay*, depending on the Amer. Indian language from which the name was borrowed or the spelling adopted by the colonists in their accounts and means *war's little brother*. It consisted of fighting for control over a small ball of unspecified dimensions with a crooked stick similar to a simple pastoral staff with leather-strap or string net or racquet attached to the crooked end and used to catch the ball. The ball was then passed to a player from the same team with a sudden catapultic movement (and not hit as with a modern racquet). It was also possible to carry the ball in the small hollow of the net. The aim of the game was to take the ball to a distinct topographic feature in a given area or past a marked line. The field was not limited, it often extended over an area 5-15km long. In 1763 the Chippewa used the game as a stratagem before capturing Michilimackinac, a fort established by Eur. settlers (now known as the town of Mackinac). Some time after laying siege to the fort the Indians started playing the game pretending to have lifted the siege. The settlers took keen interest in the game and left the fort to watch it closer. At the same time a second group of Chippewa, who had hidden earlier, seized the open fort and slaughtered both the fort defenders as well as the onlookers who had nowhere to escape. Bagat-away was widespread throughout the Amer. continent. In 1834 the famous Amer. artist G. Catlin (1796-1872) saw and painted a batagaway game played by the Choctaw in Oklahoma. In Canada, batagaway and a similar game played by the Mohawk called >TEWAARATHON gave rise to the Can. summer national sport called >LACROSSE. Similar sports were also practised by numerous tribes living in what is now the SE part of the US such as Creek, Cherokee and in the Mississippi area by the Choctaw, who called their var. of the game >TOLI. Up to date, ethnographers have identified 48 N.Amer. Indian tribes which practice games similar to bagataway.

BAGWATCH, an old game practiced in India consisting of a stone-throwing competition held between 2 teams representing, e.g., 2 different villages.

BAJ, also known as *baj haran*, a Mong. archery contest consisting in shooting at the baj – i.e. a special construction described below. Baj was particularly popular among the Buriats, a people living in Cent. Asia, whose traditions and customs are based on the Uighur culture (which, in turn, is a mixture of the Mong. and Turk. cultures). The baj consisted of 3 masts dug into the ground at a distance of 1-2 bows from one another in such a way that they formed a triangular base. The tops of the masts were tied together with a piece of string and the empty space among the masts was filled with turf. Small pegs topped with triangular pieces of turf (called 'camel's humps') were attached to the tops of the masts. The upper part of the construction formed in this way constituted the target at which the competitors shot. During breaks the competitors greased the 'humps' which has been interpreted by various ethnologists as an offering and imploring gesture addressed to the deities carrying their arrows. The symbolic meaning of such a gesture was not only restricted to the contest period but also extended onto any real-life combat where hitting an opponent was definitely more important but there was no time to make such offerings. Certain Buriat groups included archery in the so-called *taylagan*, i.e. a feast to celebrate certain important dates during a calendar year such as the New Year, the beginning of summer or the harvest offering to Mother Earth, etc. On such occasions archery contests were often accompanied by other events and especially by horse races (>BURIAT HORSE RACING).

BAJDAKI, a large, wide boat used for different purposes, including competitions, on the rivers of Russia and Ukraine. Bajdaki appear frequently in H. Sienkiewicz's *Ogniem i mieczem* (*With Fire and Sword*) including the most famous scene of a battle between the Cossacks and the Pol. mercenary in-

WORLD SPORTS ENCYCLOPEDIA B

Badminton on a postage stamp.

Bagataway players in two works by George Catlin.

B
WORLD SPORTS ENCYCLOPEDIA

Ball, unearthed in Dangyangyu, Henan Province, Tang Dynasty (618-907), terracotta.

Standing Ball Player, a South American terracotta figure, c.300-1000 B.C.

Women Playing Ball, a mosaic from Sicily, c. 300 BC.

fantry led by Captain J. Werner who prefers death over breaking his contract and defecting to B. Khmelnytsky (vol. 1, Chapter XIV).

BAJGA, an equestrian competition popular among the Kazakhs and also a long-distance – up to 30km – horse race typical of the Kirghiz.

BAJING BOXING, a style of >GONGFU popular and practiced in the village of Bajing in the Chin. province of Fucien. The fighter's clenched fists move similar to the hand movements observed in horse-riding. Bajing boxing consists of a series of movements with exotic names such as 'half-tiger, half-dragon', 'tiger's imitation', 'five tigers', 'seven stars', 'seventeen Buddha's disciples', etc. Basic forms of Bajing boxing involve 12 exercises which are mastered by each fighter in three respective grades (of difficulty). Each of the forms has an offensive and defensive var. depending on the situation in which a student of Bajing boxing may find himself. All the respective moves are performed in their basic forms or in combinations thereof. The moves are rhythmic but rapid. Great emphasis is placed on acquiring self-confidence in action.
Mu Fushan et al., 'Bajing Boxing', TRAMCHIN, 74.

BAKBOLLING, the Flem. name of a Belgian folk game more widely known under its Fr. name of >TROU-MADAME.

BALANEIA, in ancient Greece, huge complexes of baths and sports facilities located within gymnasiums and private houses or operating as an independent system of public buildings. The name was also used to denote various hygienic and recreational activities pursued therein, including taking baths and massages and being involved in the social and intellectual life of the community who gathered there [Gk. *balanejon* and Lat. *balneae* – baths]; see >BATHS.

BALD KIRGHIZ COMPETITION is considered by many ethnologists a symbolic attempt to invoke the forces of Nature (in this particular case to induce growth of hair which, among many peoples of Central Asia, was a symbol of masculine strength). It involved 2 brave men who butted each other. Depending on local custom they fought until the first blood was shed or until one of the competitors fell to the ground or fled.
I. Kabzińska-Stawarz, 'Competition in Liminal Situations', EP, 1994.

BALIBALIGUN, see >MPEEWA.

BALL, the name of any of various rudimentary games involving a spherical or oval body of the same name. A ball is either solid or hollow, it is made of various flexible materials and it is filled with air or liquid or stuffed with some other material. Depending on the type of the game the ball is either thrown, kicked or hit with any part of the body, a stick, a bat or a special racket.
Etymology. Since ball games were first played in Southern and Western Europe, it is in the languages of these countries where the name ball and other phonetically similar expressions – based on the same Proto-Indo-Eur. source – appeared. It is possible to assume that the term was first developed in the Mediterranean and later in the Germanic languages. That is how the Proto-Indo-Eur. *bhel* or *bholn* (meaning 'swell, turn into a spherical surface') evolved into the Gk. *phallus* – a penis with a rounded head and round testicles and the Latin *follis* (a leather sack, bellows or bag) and *pila*. In Proto-Germanic the term was *bholn* and later it turned into the modern Ger. *Ball*, English *ball*, Swed. *boll*, Dan. *bold*, Du. and Flem. *bal*, etc. The Romance languages have the Ital. *palla*, Fr. *balle*, Span. *bola*, which might have been derived from the Lat. *palla* – covering, casing, coating made from leather or other material. The Lat. *pila* might have evolved from the Indo-Eur. *bhel*. *Bhel* also gave rise to the O.Eng. *boll* – a sphere. The Modern Eng. *ball* developed as early as during the Middle Ages (i.e. between the 11th and 15th cent.). In 1205 the term appeared in plural in the *Lay Folk's Mass Book* 'sume heo driven balles wide zeond ba feldes' (they sometimes kicked balls across fields). In the 13th and 14th centuries balls, the word pronounced or spelled in ways very similar to contemporary ones, were already popularly used in many sports in the majority of West Eur. countries. In English the object was most frequently called a *bal*, in Fr. *balle* gradually replaced the earlier *paumeilasoule* after it was first used by

F. Rabelais in his *Gargantua and Pantagruel* (1534). The term ball was later incorporated into various compounds coined to refer to different ball game varieties such as football, basketball, volleyball, handball, etc. The Pol. name of the object and the game comes from the Lat. *pila* (compare also the Span. *pelota*). Its original form '*piła*' was almost identical to the Latin source – but this was later, around the end of the 15th or beginning of the 16th century, replaced by the diminutive *piłka*. The term was used by Ł. Górnicki in his *Dworzanin Polski* (*The Polish Courtier*, 1566) and J. Kitowicz (1728-1804) described the 18th century ball in the following way:

A ball is a sphere of wool or oakum bound together with thread, then covered with leather or colored cloth; some put a fish or calf bone inside so that the ball was more flexible.
[A description of everyday customs during the reign of Augustus III, recorded after 1781 and published in 1840]

H.D. Richardson described a ball in his *Holiday Sports and Pastimes for Boys* (1848): 'the ball is made of a blown bladder, cased in leather, formed of a portion of the offal of the slaughter-house, which can be readily obtained from any butcher. The bladder is not blown until after it has been placed in the case, the orifice of which is duly furnished with leathern thongs with which to close it'.
History. It is impossible to establish when the ball came first into use. Many historians claim that some peoples treated it as a symbol of the Sun – the life-giving deity. Others maintain that ball games have their origin in a pre-historic game of trying to seize an object, e.g. a rock or fruit, carried by another player. Irrespective of the above hypotheses, it has

A marble relief from the Archeological Museum in Athens shows a Greek athlete kneeing a ball in a practice session, evidence that the Greeks enjoyed some form of football.

been established beyond any doubt that ball games were developed separately and in parallel by many ancient cultures. A ball game that became later known as >TSU-CHU appeared in China around 2700 BC. Later, during the Heian period (784-1185 AD), the game was 'exported' to Japan where it was further modified and where it became popular as *mari koju* or >KEMARI. Ball games were also popular in Africa, Australia, Indonesia and in both Americas (esp. among the Eskimo, see >ESKIMO BALL) where numerous rock murals or pottery depictions of such sports were found. These games, however, did not contribute to the development of modern ball games. The true predecessors of our contemporary ball sports were developed in the Middle East from where they spread to the Mediterranean. First ball games, such as >HATHOR'S BALL, must have

Lord Frederick Leighton, Greek Girls Playing Ball, oil on canvas, 1889.

appeared in ancient Egypt. Hathor's ball was a ritual game that was depicted in the wall painting next to Hathor's altar room in the Deir-er-Bahari temple. The mural depicts Thutmose III carrying an orange-sized ball in his left hand. He is about to hit the ball with a curly stick. In the background there are 2 priests holding balls in a way similar to contemporary basketball players before making a free throw. The rules of the game are, unfortunately, unknown. R.W. Henderson proved in his *Ball, Bat and Bishop* (1947) that most of the contemporary ball games originated from the ancient Eg. religious rites and only then were adopted into secular folk tradition. H.J. Massingham claims that before human beings started the symbolic fight for a ball, there appeared the 2 opposing sides resembling natural opposites such as winter vs. summer (represented in ancient Eg. myths by Horus and Seth). From the Papremis temple records we know of such symbolic fights between the followers of Osiris and the priests defending the temple. Similar symbolic fights where the two sides represented major opposites are also known to have existed in other cultures. Massingham writes:

No sooner are we back in antiquity than we find it was the teams that made the game. Wherever it was played among peoples who retain or retained traces of the archaic culture which once overspread the world, we are made aware that it was a formal and sacred rite, conducted between two sections of the community whose political existence depended upon the division. ... Out of this dualism arose the ball game which, in the Pacific and Morocco ... was a ritualistic, spectacular exhibition of this dual grouping in action.
[H.J. Massingham, 'Origins of Ball Games', The Heritage of Man, 1929]

Later, ball games spread into the countries that had some contact with the Eg. culture, i.e. Assyria, Mesopotamia, Babylonia, Phoenicia and finally Greece where more new varieties of ball games such as >FAININDA, >EPISKYROS or >HARPASTON were developed. Modern Eur. ball games were influenced by the Arab (Saracen) invasions of southern Europe in the early Middle Ages. In the 8th cent. the Saracen reached what is now central France and that is why they are credited with introducing Oriental ball games involving crooked sticks such as the Fr. *chicane* that allegedly originated from the old Persian *czigan* (see >CHUGAN). This hypothesis is somewhat questionable since similar games were known earlier across the Roman Empire. Therefore, according to some scholars such games were indeed borrowed from Eastern countries but via the Roman Empire which would explain the extreme popularity enjoyed by stick-and-ball games in Gaul (France), Spain and Portugal. Due to the lack of historical evidence it is impossible to prove or disprove either of the two hypotheses. Ball games involving the use of crooked sticks were also popular in the Celtic countries of the Brit. Isles (see the Ir. >CAMÁNACHT, Welsh >KNAPPAN and Scot. >SHINTY). At least a few ball games were developed after some pagan elements had been incorporated into the Christian tradition – compare for example >SHROVE TUESDAY FOOTBALL or >EASTER BALL. The first advanced ball sport in Europe was LA >SOULE practiced in France since at least the 12th century. La soule had a number of varieties which all involved 2 teams fighting for a ball with their hands, legs or thick sticks. La soule is popularly thought to have given rise to many ball games of today. It is, however, highly questionable whether la soule was later developed into >ASSOCIATION FOOTBALL. Even if it gave rise to games such as the Italian >CALCIO, it could not have shaped modern soccer since the latter unquestionably evolved from the ball sports practiced in the Brit. public schools from where it spread throughout the rest of Europe in the 19th century. Due to the fact that la soule was a very brutal game, state and church authorities tried to stop people from playing it by imposing various restrictions or even bans (royal edicts, bans imposed by town mayors, etc.). Charles V of France officially banned the sport in 1369. In 1440 the Bishop of Trier threatened to put a curse on all those who dared to play the game in his diocese. The bans resulted in la soule evolving into the milder >JEU DE PAUME that was developed principally by the upper classes that also feared the Church the most. The brutality of the game was replaced by the precision of the strokes and the skill of sending the ball to a specified part of a playing field. A number of elements that required conceptual and tactical thinking which, coupled with the fact that the size of the field was reduced, contributed to eliminating the spontaneity and uncontrolled dynamics of the game (la soule matches were often held between 2 towns or 2 parishes within the same city and the teams, often composed of several hundred members, wreaked havoc and destruction as they moved along the course set for a particular match). In order to attain yet greater stroke precision the players used bats with a head growing flatter and wider (this is how rackets were developed) or, in other game varieties, hammer-like bats. The game was further standardized when an open field was replaced with a field laid down within the confines of a monastery or castle walls.

There is no point in enumerating all the ball games that developed in the 19th and 20th cent., but to hint at the multitude of such sports, it is enough to name just a few major ball games involving a basket such as >BASKETBALL, >NETBALL, >KORBBALL, >KORFBALL, >KURVBOLD, equestrian basketball known as >HORSEBALL, and several others. In modern times ball games, freed from their religious functions and associations, became a universal symbol of fun and entertainment. In some respects certain ball games, such as association football, became so popular that they, again, involve elements of idolatry and ritual, although based on different tenets, which today involve media- and social engineering-based crowd manipulation techniques. At the same time there are numerous ball games practiced in many non-Eur. countries that are still relatively unknown. A lot of research has been done recently into C Amer. ball games (see >MESOAMERICAN INDIAN BALL GAMES). New N Amer. Indian ball games are being constantly discovered, e.g. >TOLI played by the Stóólo tribe. See also other ethnic ball games such as >AMERICAN FOOTBALL, >ASSOCIATION FOOTBALL, >AUSTRALIAN RULES FOOTBAL, >BADMINTON, >BALLON FRANÇAISE, >BATINTON, >BASEBALL, >BASKETBALL, >BEUGHELBAL, >BRIDEBALL, >CANADIAN FOOTBALL, >FAININDA, >GAELIC FOOTBALL, >HANDBALL, >HARPASTUM, >HATHOR'S BALL, >KNAPPAN, >KNATTLEIKR, >MESOAMERICAN INDIAN BALL GAMES, >MOTORCYCLE BALL, >PASSAGE BALL, >PÄRK, >PELOTA TARASCA, >PELOTA VASCA, >PESÄPALLO, >POKYAH, >TABLE TENNIS, >TLACHTLI, >ULAMA, >VOLLEYBALL.

R.W. Henderson, *Ball, Bat and Bishop*, 1947; H.J. Massingham, 'Origins of Ball Games', *The Heritage of Man*, 1929.

BALL AND BONNETS, an old Eng. game popular in the countryside and on the outskirts of towns. Any number of players arranged their hats, caps or berets in a row and one of the boys tried to put a ball in one of them. If he succeeded, the boys ran in different directions except the one into whose bonnet the ball was put. He had to take the ball out and shout: 'Stop!'. When the players stopped the boy with the ball tried to hit any of them with it. If he missed a stone was put in his cap. If the boy who was trying to put a ball in one of the caps missed, a stone was also put into his cap and then he had to try to put the ball into the caps again. The play continued until there were 6 stones in one of the caps. The one who was the first to collect 6 stones had to stand against a wall and spread his hands on it. Then, he was hit on his hands several times with the ball. The hits were called 'buns'. The game usu. lasted until every player got his share of buns.

TGESI, I, 14-5.

BALL CHASING, a simple swimming game described by Rus. author, I.N. Chkhannikov: 'Two competitors stand on the shore of a lake, each holding a ball. On the first signal, they throw their balls as far as possible to the water. On the second signal, they jump into the water and swim towards the balls trying to catch the opponent's ball. Whoever returns with the opponent's ball to the shore wins the race. The balls must be marked differently'.

I.N. Chkhannikov, 'Ball chasing', GIZ, 1953, 81.

BALL DIVINATION, a type of fortune telling popular in England in the past, in which the span of a given person's life was predicted on the basis of how many times they managed to catch a ball thrown up in the air. This game accompanied the pagan May Day festival celebrations during which the ball was thrown over a leaf-and-branch garland stretched between two homes or trees (>MAYPOLE); see also >KEPPY BALL.

BALL HOCKEY, a sport similar to >ICE HOCKEY but played in summer at regular-size outdoor rinks where, since the ice has long been melted, the surface is concrete. Players wear running shoes instead of skates, and uniforms much less elaborate than those used in ice hockey. They must, however, wear regular helmets and use regular ice hockey sticks (no plastic blades are allowed). It is recommended that they use knee and elbow pads as well as face masks. The goalkeepers must wear full protective gear. The Can. Ball Hockey Association was established in 1978 and the first Can. men's championships were held in the same year. Can. women's championships have been held since 1987. Ball hockey is also played in other countries, e.g. the USA, the Czech Republic, Slovakia, Switzerland, Germany, Austria, Bermuda. E.Ch. have been held since 1995 and W.Ch. since 1996. The sport is administered by the International Street and Ball Hockey Federation.

BALL IN THE DECKER, a simple ball throwing game popular among Eng. boys in the 19th cent. The players would place their caps alongside a wall and one of them would try to put a ball in one of the caps. If he did, the owner of the cap into which the ball was put would take the ball out and start running while the others would chase him. When they caught him he took over as the one trying to put the ball into one of the caps.

TGESI, 1894, I, 15.

BALL OF SCONE, a local var. of >SHROVE TUESDAY FOOTBALL played in the Scot. town of Scone, and hence the name. It was different from the Eng. var. in the playing techniques and in the way the players were selected and divided into teams. It was also more similar to modern handball and the ball itself could not be kicked. The game was played by teams consisting of bachelors and married men respectively and not representing two districts of a given town as in many other Brit. varieties of Shrove Tuesday football. The following description of the game dates back to the 18th century:

Every year on Shrove Tuesday, the bachelors and married men drew themselves up at the cross of Scone on opposite sides. A ball was then thrown up, and they played from 2 o'clock till sun set. The game was this. He who, at any time got the ball into his hands, ran with it till overtaken by the opposite party, and then, if he could shake himself loose from those on the opposite side, who seized him, he ran on: if not, he threw the ball from him unless it was wrestled from him by the other party, but no person was allowed to kick it. The object of the married men was to hang it, i.e. to put it three times into a small hole in the moor, the dool or limit on the one hand; that of the bachelors was to drown it, i.e. to dip it three times into a deep place in the river (Tay), the limit on the other. The party who could effect either of these objects, won the game. But if neither party won, the ball was cut into two equal parts at sun-set. In the course of the play one might always see some scene of violence between the parties; but as the proverb of this part of the country expresses it, all was fair at the ball of Scone.

[*The Statistical Account of Scotland*, XVIII, Edinburgh, 1796]

The custom is supposed to have had its origin in the days of chivalry. An Italian, it is said, came to this part of the country, challenging all parishes, under a certain penalty in case of declining his challenge. All the parishes declined the challenge excepting Scone, which beat the foreigner; and in commemoration of this gallant action the game was instituted. Whilst the custom continued, every man in the parish, the gentry not excepted, was obliged to turn out and support the side to which he belonged; and any person who neglected to do his part on that occasion was fined; but the custom was abolished a few years ago.

BALL OFF BOARD, Rus. *myatch ot borta*, a Rus. ice hockey game played by 2 teams of 5 players each. The rink's dimensions are not specified; they depend on local conditions. The goals are 2 boards 3-4m long and 25cm wide, mounted on ice. According to I.N. Chkhannikow, 'The game consists of striking the ball or puck against the team's own board so it bounces into the opponent's playing area. The opposing team must return the ball in the same manner. The ball can be passed among the striking players only three times before it is shot into the opponent's area. The striking team earns a penalty if: 1) the ball enters the opponent's field after having been hit directly with the stick; 2) after bouncing off the board the ball fails to cross the centerline and enter the opponent's field of play; 3) the ball goes out of bounds; 4) the striking players have played the ball more than 3 times before shooting it into the opponent's half'. The match consists of two 15-min. periods. The team with the fewest penalty points wins. The game is controlled by a referee.

I.N. Chkhannikov, 'Myatch ot borta', GIZ, 1953, 88-89.

BALL OFF WALL, Rus. *myatch ot styeny*, a Rus. street game. The field is 20m long and 15m wide and is adjacent to a wall on its longer side. It is divided in half with a string hung on 2 posts, 1m above the ground. On each half of the field there is a circle, 1.5m in diameter, marked on the ground. A rectangular area 20m wide and 3m high is marked on the wall. The rectangle is divided into two parts corresponding to the two playing areas of the field. The game is played by 2 teams of 5 players. The teams stand on both sides of the dividing string. No player may stand in either circle. According to the Rus. author, I.N. Chkhannikow, the passage of play is as follows: 'A player of the serving team throws the ball against the wall. After bouncing off the wall the ball must enter the opposing team's half. The opposing team's players must return the ball the same way. They may catch and throw the ball or hit it with head, hands or legs. The ball can be passed among the striking players only 3 times before it is shot into the opponent's area. The serving team earns a penalty point if: 1) the ball enters the opponent's area without having bounced off the wall; 2) after bouncing off the wall the ball hits the ground on the serving team's area; 3) the ball bounces off the wall outside the marked rectangular area; 4) the ball is out of bounds after having bounced off the wall; 5) the ball has been played more than 3 times by the serving players before hitting the wall. The receiving team earns one penalty point if the ball bounces off the wall and hits the ground on its area. The receiving team earns 3 penalty points if the ball falls within the circle on the ground or any receiving player steps into the circle'. A match consists of 3 rounds. A round is 15 penalty points. After each round the teams change sides. The team with the fewest penalty points wins the game.

I.N. Chkhannikov, 'Myatch ot styeny', GIZ, 1953, 45-46.

BALL RACE, see >BALL RACING.

BALL RACING, also known as *kick-ball race*, a type of a racing competition combining running and kicking a ball popular among the Native Indians of N America and especially in the SW part of America. The game involved pursuing a ball that was kicked with the instep. The size of the ball depended on the tribe but it was usu. 2.5in. in diameter (a little bit less than 6.5cm). The ball was carved out of wood or a round stone was used. The Mandans of the Great Plains used a ball of stuffed billy-goat leather. F. Densmore obtained such a Mandan ball in 1912. At present the ball is at the Smithsonian Institution in Washington, D.C. Sometimes, instead of a ball, the Native Amer. Indians kicked a short round peg of 1in. in diameter (2.54cm). It was usu. made of wood but sometimes also bone pegs were used. Ethnographers who observed the game played by various tribes at different points in time from the end of the 18th cent. until the beginning of the 20th cent.

Ball hockey.

BALL HOCKEY MEDALLISTS

EUROPEAN CHAMPIONSHIP

1995 –	*Slovakia*
	Czech Republic
	Slovakia 'B'
1996 –	*Czech Republic*
	Slovakia
	Germany
1997 –	*Slovakia*
	Czech Republic
	Austria
2000 –	*Czech Republic*
	Slovakia
	Switzerland

WORLD CHAMPIONSHIP

1996 –	*Canada*
	Czech Republic
	Slovakia
1998 –	*Czech Republic*
	Slovakia
	Canada
1999 –	*Slovakia*
	Canada
	Czech Republic
2001 –	*Canada*
	Czech Republic
	Slovakia

64
B WORLD SPORTS ENCYCLOPEDIA

A postage stamp commemorating B. Abruzzo's, M. Anderson's, and L. Newman's transatlantic balloon flight in 1978, for which the US President presented them with a special Congressional Gold Medal in 1979.

found out that the most popular distance over which a ball race was held was 25mi. (about 40.2km). The distance was laid out over a circuit with distinctly marked starting and finish lines. The circuit was marked with crossed branches, mounds of stones and other similar objects. Older members of a given tribe who did not participate in a race were stationed alongside the route and acted as referees. Ball races were held among pairs or teams of 4 to 6. The races were usu. men's events but there were also women's ones. Women did not kick the ball but instead pushed it with a forked stick. Sometimes, instead of a ball, women used small rings that were also pushed with a stick. Both men and women were prohibited from touching the ball with their hands. In the case of team races, the respective members of the team took turns in kicking the ball. The contestants were virtually naked. Men only wore a narrow band around their hips. Some tribes allowed sandals to protect the feet if a race course ran through a rocky terrain or an area with prickly vegetation. The insteps, with which the ball was kicked, were never protected and many observers reported that they became injured or seriously bruised towards the end of the race. The naked parts of the body, esp. the chest, arms and face were covered with colorful paintings. Contestants hair was braided or arranged in a bun sitting on top of their heads so that it did not get in the way. A starting line was drawn on the ground. The race began with a signal, usu. a long cry. They tried to kick the ball as far forward as possible which was a major factor, apart from speed and endurance, in ensuring final success. Another crucial skill was the ability to keep the ball on the race track. Sending the ball into bushes or rock crevices slowed teams down or even lost them the race. To facilitate extracting the ball from such places competitors from tribes that only allowed kicking the ball often carried special sticks used for such circumstances. It was, however, forbidden to use the hands at any time. Ethnographers who observed ball races in the 19th cent. estimated that on average the runners used to send the ball some 30ft. (about 9.14m) up in the air and some 100ft. away (about 30.48m). The best kick ever recorded sent a ball some 100yds. away (about 91.44m). In the team variety of ball races the members of the team who did not have to kick the ball at a given moment ran forward as fast as they could to reach the kicked ball as quickly as possible to send it further on. The runner who came closest to the ball or peg was the next to kick or push it. Sometimes the spectators accompanying the players were on horseback. F.W. Hodge (1864-1956), an Amer. archeologist and ethnographer, who researched the Zuni culture saw a ball race observed by some 200-300 mounted spectators 'those, who more than any others, are interested in the outcome of the race by reason of the extent of their prospective gains or losses. When one side follows closely in the track of its opponents, the horsemen all ride together; but when by reason of accident or inferiority in speed, a party falls considerably in the rear, the horsemen separate to accompany their prospective favorites. If the season is dry, the dust made by galloping horses is blinding; but the racers continue, apparently as unmindful of the mud-coating that accumulates on their almost nude, perspiring bodies as if they were within but a few steps of victory' ('A Zuni Foot Race', AA, 1890, 3).

Julius Caesar Ibbetson, The Ascent of Lunardi's Balloon from St. George's Fields, *1785, oil on canvas.*

A postage stamp issued for the Gordon Bennett Challenge in 1934.

Ball races were usu. held in spring. The racing season started in early spring with practice races and minor competitions. Major, ritual races were held in late spring or early summer. Farming tribes held the race after the major crops had been planted. The races took place as the tribe awaited maize and other crops to mature. The Pima Indians thought that the ball, endowed with magical powers, made the competitors run faster. By the same token, the Hopi thought that the pegs they used in their variety of the game contributed to improving their speed. An Amer. ethnographer C. Lumholz who observed the Tarahumara ball races noticed that

a race is never won by natural means. The losers always say that they were influenced by some herb and became sleepy on the race-course, so that they had to lose. The help of the medicine man is needed in preparing the runner for the race. He assists the manager to wash the feet of the runners with warm water and different herbs, and he strengthens their nerves by making passes over them. He also guards them against sorcery. Before they run he performs a ceremony to 'cure' them.

Celebrations that accompanied a ball race started in the evening. The runners spent the night in contemplation and underwent various rituals. Great emphasis was laid upon the occurrence of certain natural phenomena during the night preceding a race. A thunderstorm or shooting stars were deemed a good sign. If the players heard an owl's cry they thought it to be a particularly inauspicious sign and usu. postponed the race until another day. Ball races were most popular among the Zuni, Pima, Papago and Tarahumara.

W.C. Bennett, R.M. Zingg, *The Tarahumara. An Indian Tribe of Northern Mexico,* 1935; J.B. Oxendine, *American Indian Sports Heritage,* 1988; M.C. Stevenson, 'Zuni Games', AA, 1903, 5.

BALL TO NEIGHBOR, a Rus. ball game played in school gyms and common rooms. The players stand in a circle at shoulder-distance from one anther. A selected player called the 'picker' stands outside the circle. The circle players throw the ball to one another and the picker runs outside the circle trying to pick the ball by touching it. The ball can only be passed to the nearest player on the right or the left side. A player who violates this rule becomes the picker. If the picker manages to touch the ball in the air he joins the circle and is replaced by the last player who threw the ball. If the picker touches the ball in a player's hands this player takes his place.

I.N. Chkhannikov, 'Ball to neighbour', GIZ, 1953, 15-16.

BALL TO ONE'S OWN, Rus. *myatch svoyemu*, a Rus. ball game played by 3 teams. The players of one team stand in a circle facing the outside, at shoulder distance from one another. The players of the other 2 teams form an outer circle, 4 steps from and facing the inner circle players. A player drawn by lot from the outer circle teams steps inside the inner circle. The outer circle players start the game and throw the ball to their own player in the middle over the heads of the inner circle players. The inner circle team tries to intercept the ball in the air. If the player in the middle catches the ball a penalty is scored by the inner circle team. The game consists of three 10-min. rounds. In each round a different team takes its position on the inner circle. The team with the fewest penalties wins.

I.N. Chkhannikov, 'Myatch svoyemu', GIZ, 1953, 15-16.

BALLE AU CAMP, a Fr. folk game dating back to the Middle Ages. The game was played by two teams with an unspecified number of players. A line was drawn towards the end of each team's field. The object of the game was to throw a ball behind the end line of the opposing team [Fr. *balle* – ball + *au* – on, onto, to + *camp* – field].

W. Endrei and L. Zolnay, *Fun Games in Old Europe,* 1986, 89.

BALLE AU POT, LA, a Fr. type of ball game in which the players have to put a ball into a number of holes dug in the ground. Its rules are very similar to those observed in the Dan. >BOLD I HUL.

BALL-GAME AT ULGHAM, THE, Lat. *ludens ad pilum as Ulkham,* a medieval game described in the Eng. *Calendar of Inquisition* (1280, published in 1916) in association with a very tragic accident:

Henry, son of William de Ellington, while playing at ball (ludens ad pilum) at Ulkham on Trinity Sunday with David de Keu and many others ran against David and received an accidental wound from David's knife of which he died on the following Friday. They were both running to the ball, and aran against each other, and the knife hanging from David's belt stuck out so that the point though in the sheath struck against Henry's belly, and the handle against David's belly. Henry was wounded right through the sheath and died by misadventure.

BALLON AU POING, Like >JEU DE LONGUE PAUME, ballon au poing (Fr. for 'ball played with the fist') belongs to the great family of games played with hands. Invented by the Greeks, it was codified under Louis XIV before gaining widespread popularity in the 19th cent. More alive than ever, it remains today one of the sports most practiced in Picardy. The playground has a rectangular form and is framed at the ends by posts (5m high) called *rapports*. The leather ball used is similar to that of the handball game, and has a weight oscillating between 450gr. and 480gr. (seniors). The ball is struck with the assistance of the wrist protected by a band of canvas. A team engages the match shooting from its side and must send the ball beyond the line of cord placed in the middle of the ground. The 2 teams directly return the ball on the volley or after one rebound. As in every game of gain-ground, the players try to launch the ball as far as possible in the adversary camp or to make it rebound beyond the line between the two rapports.

BALLON FRANÇAISE, Fr. *French ball*, a var. of >JEU DE PAUME. The ball used for the game is of football size. The rectangular field is 70m long and 13-14m wide. It has rounded corners. A centerline divides the field in half. On one half of the field, 24--26m from the centerline, a service line is marked. The serving team must throw the ball from the zone between the centerline and the service line. The passage of play is similar to >JEU DE LONGUE PAUME with two exceptions: 1) two throw lines are drawn from the spot on the ground the served ball has hit; the ball must cross the throw lines after each subsequent service; 2) the ball can be played with any part of the body, mainly with the hands or feet. The players wrap their hands with linen tape for protection. The ball can only be caught with two hands. A game consists of six rounds. Each round is sixty points; fifteen points are awarded for each successful play. A thirty-point advantage is necessary to win a round, e.g. 60:30, 75:45. The game is played by two teams of six players each.

BALLOON-BALL, also known as *ballon-ball play*, an unspecified type of ball game mentioned by J. Strutt in *Glig Gamena Angel Deoth, or the Sports and Pastimes of the People of England*: 'The balloon-ball seems certainly to have originated from the hand-ball, and was, I apprehend, first played in England without the assistance of the bracer' [STRUTT, 89]. Balloon-ball is, most likely, just another name of >BALOON BALL referred to by numerous Eng. writers and described by A.B. Gomme.

TGESI, 1894, I, 16.

BALLOONING, Fr. *acension(s) en ballon*, Ger. *Ballonfahrt*, unpowered balloon flight in precision, distance or altitude competition. A sports balloon is an aircraft consisting of 1) a fabric bag filled with a lighter-than-air gas or hot air and 2) a basket or gondola for the crew. Additionally, a modern balloon would have navigational instruments, a radio, meteorological equipment and, perhaps, some amenities. In the case of long-distance flights a balloon would also carry appropriate supplies of food. Modern hot-air balloons are made of nylon or polyester with a polyurethane or silicone coating to improve their aerodynamic performance by reducing their porosity. The baskets or gondolas are made of wicker or rattan with ballast sand bags hung alongside their rims. The ballast bags are dropped to increase a balloon's altitude. A gas balloon will go down if the gas contained in the balloon bag is released by opening the so-called navigation valve. In case of danger the gas may be released quickly via an emergency valve. In the case of hot-air balloons the cruising altitude is changed by controlling the temperature inside the balloon bag. Alongside the lower part of the bag there is the so-called rain gutter which prevents rainwater from getting into the gondola. Balloons usu. take off in the morning or in the afternoon since the weather and atmospheric conditions are most stable and the best forecasts are made at these times. Take-offs are scheduled for afternoon only on special occasions.

During the majority of international competitions balloon pilots score points for reaching certain destinations or targets. When a target has been reached the pilots drop special markers which are often small bags with 66-in. (ab. 168cm) ribbons attached to them. The bags are filled with flour, weigh between 70 and 100g and are called baggies in the international balloonists' jargon. When a balloon has to fly over a number of targets, a number of differently marked baggies is dropped. When the wrong baggie is dropped over the wrong target the pilot receives penalty points.

The fact that it is still impossible to achieve accuracy in controlling a balloon and returning to the departure point has prevented it from becoming a popular means of transport. However, the fact that the flight path is largely unpredictable lends excitement, making ballooning more attractive as a sport. Motor-propelled balloons that are steerable are called >DIRRIGIBLE BALLOONS (AIRSHIPS).

History. Balloons were used in the first successful human attempts at flying. Archytas of Tarentum (c.400 BC) is said to have been the first balloon constructor in the history of mankind. R. Bacon (c.1214-c.1294), an Eng. scholar and mathematician, was the first to form a theory of balloons and ballooning. He contemplated the possibility of flying with a ball of thin copper film with a hole at the bottom to let hot air in. In 1650 a Span. Jesuit F. Lano de Brescia carried out an unsuccessful experiment of flying with empty metal balls. In 1709 in Lisbon, B. de Gusmão, a Port. inventor, managed to launch a balloon of an unknown design and fly several meters up in the air. Unfortunately, his balloon crashed and he was killed. In 1782 the Montgolfier brothers, Jacques Étienne (1745-99) and Joseph Michel (1740-1810), built a paper balloon filled with air heated with burning straw. On 5 June 1783 at Annoay, France they demonstrated a similar balloon to the general public thus confirming that such a ballon would indeed rise. This date is considered the official date of the first unmanned balloon flight. At Versailles, they repeated the experiment with a larger balloon on 19 Sept. 1783 before the King's court with which they sent a sheep, rooster and duck aloft. On 21 Nov. 1783, the first manned flight took place when J.F. de Pilâtre de Rozier (1756-85) and François Laurent, Marquis d'Arlandes (1742-1809) took off from Bois de Boulogne and sailed over Paris in a Montgolfier balloon whose bag was made of fabric coated with natural rubber. J.M. Montgolfier made another manned flight in Marseilles on 19 Jan. 1784 carrying 6 thrill seekers. The Montgolfier brothers wrote their *Ballons Aerostatique* (*Air Balloons*) in 1784. Their work paved the way for further development of ballooning. Soon after the first flight by the Montgolfier brothers, a Fr. physicist, chemist and inventor J.A.C. Charles (1746-1823) employed the law of combining volumes (developed earlier by L.J. Gay-Lussac) and together with B.F. de Saint Fond he flew a balloon filled with hydrogen. Their balloon was also the first to use a rubber coating for the bag. This resulted in the rapid development of gas balloons and a gradual decline in the popularity of hot-air balloons. Two years later, on 7 Dec. 1795, J.P.F. Blanchard (1753-1809), a Fr. balloonist, and the Amer. physician J. Jeffries made the first crossing of the Eng. Channel with an 'air craft' (*vaisseau volant*). The flight was very dramatic with the balloonists almost falling into the sea. They ascended over Dover but later the two aviators were compelled to heave all cargo, including their trousers, overboard. They managed to land safely in Guines near Calais. Following these successful flights balloonists in Europe and the US developed a taste for various ballooning displays and shows which resulted in several significant inventions and technical developments being made. They also contributed to shaping the rules and principles of competitive ballooning. Blanchard himself made about 60 balloon ascents, including some in the US, but died during his last flight over the Hague on the 7th Mar. 1809. Military uses for balloons were soon developed. Balloons were first used by Napoleon III in 1859 during his Italian campaign and later by both sides in the Amer. Civil War (1861-65). In 1897 a Swed. engineer and polar explorer S.A. Andrée took off together with N. Strindberg and K. Fränkel from Spitsbergen in the direction of the North Pole. On their way there the aviators dropped a number of messages and reports some of which were later recovered. After a 65-hour flight the balloon descended to the ground some 800km from the North Pole and the crew were forced to try to walk back. They died of hunger and exhaustion on Ostrov Belyy (White Island). Sport ballooning began in earnest in 1906 when the Amer. publisher James Gordon Bennett (1841-1918) offered an international trophy for annual long-distance flights. The competition was indeed held annually 1903-16, 1920-31 and 1933-38 but was discontinued in 1939. It was revived in 1983 and has been held since at irregular intervals. In 1910 E. Schweizer made the first aerial crossing over the Alps. To commemorate this event a transalpine competition (International Ballooning Week) is held annually in Mürren. In 1913 a Ger. aviator G. Kaulen set the first world record for the longest balloon flight. His flight lasted 87hrs. during which he covered a distance of 3,527km. After World War II an increase in the use of airplanes for transportation and military purposes resulted in waning interest in balloons. However, as a result of the introduction of appropriate legislation, especially in the USA, Western Europe and Australia, balloon-

ing was gradually restored to its previous status. E.Ch. have been held since 1972. In 1960 an Amer. P.E. Yost (b. 1919) revived hot-air ballooning using a burner placed over a propane container. This event marks the beginning of a new chapter in sport ballooning. Hot-air ballooning W.Ch. have been held since 1974 and classic gas ballooning W.Ch. have been taking place since 1976. The introduction of synthetic materials, adopted from the aerospace industries, and the development of in-flight electronics also brought about a ballooning revival and resulted in the aviators making attempts that were previously unthinkable. There were 17 failed attempts to make an aerial crossing over the Atlantic before 1978. In 1978 an Amer. crew with B. Abruzzo, M. Anderson and L. Newman finally made a successful flight over the Atlantic in their balloon called Double Eagle II. The route they followed was 5,150km-long; they took off from the small island of Presque in Maine and landed safely near Miserey in France. The flight took 137hrs. and 18min. In 1984 J. Kittinger was the first person to make a solo crossing of the Atlantic. A number of round-the-world flight attempts failed in the 1995-98 period. A Brit. balloonist B. Jones with his Swiss partner B. Piccard were the first ones to succeed in doing so in March 1999. They cruised around the world in 19 days and 22hrs. They were able to achieve this by flying a hybrid balloon. A hybrid balloon combines some features of a trad. gas balloon located in the upper part of the balloon bag with an additional helium heater placed in the lower, separate part of the balloon bag. This solution has been proven to greatly improve balloon control. Such hybrid balloons are called Rosier balloons after one of the pioneers of ballooning, the Fr. aviator J.F. de Pilâtre de Rozier.

World ballooning competition and the development of the sport is largely supervised by the International Aeronautical Federation (Fédération Aéronautique Internationale, FAI) based in Paris. In the US, which currently is the country where ballooning is developing most dynamically, the most important supervisory body is the Federal Aviation Agency. The FAA is also responsible for balloon pilot certification. Ballooning as a competitive sport is overseen in the US by the Balloon Federation of America, BFA which is a part of the National Aeronautic Association, NAA. Ballooning and its development is further influenced, not only in the US but also world-wide, by the Hot Air Balloon Club of America and the Balloon Club of America. Given significant differences in construction and running costs most of the balloons used in international and local competition are hot-air balloons. Whereas the amount of butane needed for one hot-air balloon flight costs about $30, it takes about $3,500 to fill a gas balloon with hydrogen (most popular in Europe) or helium (widespread in

Preparations of brothers Montgolfier for a ballon flight in 1783.

BALLOONING WORLD RECORDS

record altitude:
34km 668m (M.D. Ross and V.A. Prather, USA, 1961)

record distance:
40,814km (25,361mi) (B. Piccard, SWI and B. Jones, GBR, 1999)

record distance solo: 20,413km (12,687mi) (S. Fossett, 2002)

record duration: 477hrs. 47min. (B. Piccard and B. Jones, 1999)

shortest time around the world:
320hrs. 33min.: S. Fossett; Northam, W AUSTRAL to Queensland, AUSTRAL 3 July, 2002

record speed by manned balloon:
200.24mph (322.25 km/h) (S. Fossett, July 1, 2002)

20,000 hot-air balloonists can't be wrong.

Ballooning.

American adventurer Steve Fossett lands his balloon at Darhum Downs, 1,200 kilometers (750 miles) from Brisbane, Australia, Thursday, July 4, 2002 after making his record-breaking solo around-the-world balloon flight.

Bältesspänning.

the US). Thus, there are about 20,000 hot-air balloonists worldwide and fewer than 30 gas aviators (1999). The US, Germany, Great Britain and Australia are considered to be the ballooning superpowers. The annual Albuquerque International Balloon Fiesta taking place in Albuquerque, New Mexico, USA is considered the largest ballooning event in the world.

The development of ballooning in Europe and the US is hindered by the fact that there exist very dense air traffic networks and there are huge, densely populated areas unlike in Australia. Australia, however, due to the fact that is located far away from the other ballooning superpowers, finds it difficult to attract and host major international events over its territory. The most important Austrl. events include the Easter competition in Canowindra, New South Wales and the Seppeltsfield Meeting in Barossa Valley. An Austrl. aviator P. Vizzard won the World Champion title in 1983. The sport of ballooning is managed in Australia by the Austrl. Ballooning Federation. Ballooning has also been gradually developing in Asian countries, especially in India where ballooning activities are coordinated by the Balloon Club of India (with its seat in New Delhi). Apart from distance flights, world records are also maintained for altitude ascents. Altitude ascents developed in the 20th cent. thanks to the pioneers of stratospheric flights, the Swiss-born twins Auguste (1884-1963) and Jean-Felix Piccard (1884-1963). Auguste, who was a physicist, ascended in 1932 to 16,940m. Jean-Felix became an Amer. citizen in 1931 and lectured in aeronautical engineering at the University of Minnesota. On the 23rd Oct. 1934, with his wife Jeanette, he made the first successful stratosphere flight through clouds, ascending to a height of 17,672m. Later he acted in the capacity of a flight consultant during the ascent of Skyhook whereby M.D. Ross became the first man to exceed a height of 30km or 100 thousand feet (34,668m or 113,740 feet). In 1956 the Strato-Lab project, with the aim of investigating the stratosphere, was launched in the US. Within the framework of this project, on 4 May 1961, M.D. Ross climbed to 34,050m.

Women's ballooning. Madame Thible, who made her balloon flight in Lyon in June 1784, was the first woman-balloonist in history. However, ballooning was not popular among women until the beginning of the 20th cent. After WWII women started taking part in hot-air balloon competitions. One of the most outstanding women balloonists is currently a Pole, J. Matejczuk, who won the World Cup 3 times in the 1990s.

Ballooning in literature. Illustrations and engravings depicting ascending balloons appeared quite often in newspapers and special publications at the end of the 18th and in the 19th century when ballooning feats were often the highlight of the day in larger towns and cities. The number of such illustrations and engravings is extremely large and there must have been several thousand of them published in Europe and the US. One of the earliest and most beautiful prints is the Lunardi's Ballo Ascent of 1784 by J.J. Brewer depicting Lunardi's flight over London. Rarely did a balloon flight constitute the main motif of a literary work, rather it formed a part of a larger whole. Nevertheless, some authors made a balloon the main hero of their writings. In his short story, 'The Unparalleled Adventure of One Hans Pfall', E.A. Poe (1809-49) wrote that after 5 years of the disappearance of his hero, an inhabitant of Rotterdam, a strange balloon with a lunarian appeared over the city to drop a letter saying that Pfall had made it to the Moon. J. Verne wrote his *Five Weeks in a Balloon* in 1863. A balloon escape from a besieged city during the Amer. Civil War is the starting point for another of his novels The *Mysterious Island* (1874). A number of ballooning pioneers' memoirs have also appeared in print. One of the most dramatic accounts of balloon journeys is the diary of the Swed. polar explorer S.A. Andrée (1854-97). The diary was found in 1930 by a Norwegian expedition led by G. Horn by the bodies of Andrée and his associates who died in of hunger after their balloon crashed near Ostrov Belyy. The balloon was also used as an element of metaphor in poetry, for example, by the Amer. poet S. Plath (1932-63) where 'the clear vowels rise like balloons' (*Morning song*). E.E. Cummings wrote that 'it's spring when the world is puddle-wonderful the queer old baloonman whistles far and wee' (*Chansons Innocentes*). A Pol. writer S. Zieliński published his column entitled *Wycieczki balonem* (*Balloon Excursions*) in the Warsaw *Kultura* (*Culture*) weekly 1962-78. The aim of his column, which later appeared as a 6-volume book with the same title, was to portray reality from a certain distance and altitude.

Z. Burzyński, F. Janik, M. Pietraszek, *Balony*, 1958; L. Ruth, *Balloon Digest*, 1995; S. Sarnowski, *Żegluga powietrzna*, 1922; D. Wirth, *Ballooning. The Complete Guide to Riding the Winds*, 1982.

BALLS IN THE CIRCLE RACE, a school game popular in many countries of Eastern Europe played by an even number of contestants (16-22). Contestants form a circle and count to 2, thus dividing themselves into two teams: 'ones' and 'twos'. The master of the game gives each team a ball, placing the balls at a distance of half a circle from one another. At a signal both teams begin to pass their balls amongst themselves, avoiding the players of the opposite team. The team that passes the ball around the circle faster wins the game. Transporting the ball faster to a pre-selected spot scores 1 pt. The total number of points scored in 5 rounds determines the winner. In another variety the ball is passed without omitting the players of the opposite team, who try to slow down the process.

I.N. Chkhannikov, 'Balls in the Circle Race', GIZ, 1953, 7.

BALLS ON PODIUM, a sport in which five cement balls 50cm in diameter are lifted and placed on a 5-step podium. On each step there is circular piece of rope, which prevents the ball from falling off. The competition is held in pairs: two players try to lift their cement balls and place them on the podium. The highest steps are next to each other on the same level, while the lower steps go outwards. The record time in completing the task is 38sec. The best competitors after 1994 were M. ver Magnusson from Iceland and M. Hoeber from Austria.

BALOO, see >BALOON BALL.

BALOOME, see >BALOON BALL.

BALOON BALL, also known as *baloon* or, according to some old sources, *baloo* or *baloome*. A type of ball game dating back to the 14th century. The ball was made of an inflated animal bladder contained in a leather casing. A game of baloon ball consisted in hitting the ball with the hand. On their hand and part of the forearm the players wore a special wooden guard called a bracer. The player standing at the opposite end of a field tried to return the ball by hitting it with his bracer. Little is known about the game and the way in which the players scored their points but it is assumed that baloon ball matches were held for pleasure rather than as a form of competition. Ben Johnson (c.1572-1637), the English playwright, referred to this game as baloo and T. Randolph (1605-35) called it baloome in his *Poems*. It was also mentioned by T. Middleton (1580-1627) and J. Donne (1572-1631) in his *Poems* as baloun. One of the keenest baloon ball players was Prince Henry, the son of James I, the King of England. Baloon ball was also described by J. Strutt in *Sports and Pastimes of the People of England* (1810, II, 3) and by A.B. Gomme (TGESI, I, 16).

BAL-PLEOUWE, a ball game mentioned in a manual for the guidance of women recluses outside the regular orders called *Ancrene Wisse* or *Ancrene Riwle* (*Guide for Anchoresses* or *Rule for Anchoresses*) written in prose by an anonymous priest for his 3 sisters around 1230. The original manuscript is in the Corpus Christi library in Cambridge and was translated into English by M.B. Salu (1956); see E.J. Dobson's study *The Origins of Ancrene Wisse* (1976).

BALSER, a Cockney name of >MARBLES.

BÄLTESSPÄNNING, a Scand. folk sport especially popular in the south of Sweden and in Norway. Two competitors stood back-to-back. They were tied up in such a way that they could only move their arms from the elbow down. In their hands they held knives the blades of which were sheathed in straps of leather so that only the tip of the blade remained bare. The opponents then tried to injure each other. Usually, the players agreed before the match on how big a part of their knife blade should remain exposed. The players fought until one of them decided to give up. In some cases the competitors fought until one of them was killed which resulted in suits filed by the family of the slain fighter. Bältesspänning matches, similarly to other folk competitions, were usu. held in a special, fenced square called a *vall*. The first mentionings of the vall date back to some of the oldest Norse sagas. The term persists in modern Swedish to denote a sports field in such names as Arosvallen, Slottskogvallen and Tingvalla.

History. Bältesspänning dates back to the Middle Ages when it was considered to be a type of duel rather than a form of sports competition. Duels that could result in the death of one of the participants were banned in Sweden in the 17th cent. and this ban certainly covered bältesspänning fights. Until this date the blades of the knives used in such duels were probably not sheathed at all. By introducing such a form of protection the advocates of the game were, most likely, trying to convince the authorities that wounds inflicted with such a weapon could not be fatal. Bältesspänning was described in greater detail only as late as the 18th cent. by P. Rudebeck (*Småländska Antiquiteter*, manuscript in the Royal Library, Ch 32) and S. Krok (*Urshults Pastorats inbyggares seder*, published in 1922 by N. Werner in *Småländska Hembygdsböcker*, 1922). An in-depth ethnographic study of bältesspänning was carried out by a Swed. ethnographer G.O. Hylten-Cavallius in the 1863-68 period. Bältesspänning was also one of the major themes of B. Nordenberg's (1822-1902) paintings. The best known of all the bältesspänning paintings is called 'Swed. Peasants' Wrestling'.

M. Hellspong, 'A Timeless Excitement. Swedish Agrarian Society and Sport in the Pre-Industrial Era', IJHS, Dec. 1997.

BAMBOO-STICK RELAY RACING, a game of the Chin. She minority of the Ningde province. The game is conducted with the use of a small bamboo stick the length of 1 chi (1 chi = approx. 30cm) and app. 1.5cm in diameter, which is batted out of a circle of app. 5 chi (1.5m) in diameter with a bat, twice as long, i.e. the length of 2 chi (app. 60cm). After the batter has struck the stick out of his circle, his opponent (or the opposing team) tries to catch it on the fly. The player who catches the stick uses the bat to measure the distance from the spot where he caught the stick to the circle from which it was batted. For each length of the bat he scores one point. If the stick falls to the ground, it is picked up and thrown back to the circle. The batter may then either bat it back into the field again or catch it first. If he catches the stick, he gets to measure, using his bat, the distance from the circle to the spot from which it was thrown and scores an appropriate number of points. If he bats it back, however, the opponents may not catch it, but the batter automatically measures the distance from the circle to the spot where the stick landed. If the batter fails to catch the stick thrown back at him or to bat it back into the field, the distance between the circle and the spot where the stick landed is measured by the player in the field, who not only scores the points, but also becomes the next batter and the entire procedure is repeated. The game resembles another Chin. game called >FLYING CUDGELS, the main difference between the two being in the fact that in *flying cudgels* the small stick is placed on the ground before it is batted into the field. The remaining elements make the game similar not only to *flying cudgels*, but also Arabic >AL-BA' 'A, Eng. >TIP-CAT, Indon. >TAK KADAL, Pakist. and Ind. >GULLI DUNDA, Pol. >KLIPA, >SZTEKIEL, >KICZKA, Fr. *pilouette*, Bret. *mouilh*.

Mu Fushan et al., 'Bamboo-Stick Relay Racing', TRAMCHIN, 72.

BANDO, Burmese for 'a way of a warrior' [Burmese *ban* – warrior + *do* – way]. A Burmese martial art, which – being originally a type of hand-to-hand combat – was part of the trad. Burmese style called Thaing, which included Bando, Lewhay (boxing), Naban (wrestling), Banshay (fighting with weapons). Being primarily a system of training the military, Thaing was modernized in the 1930s. Currently the term *bando* is used to denominate all Burmese martial arts. Bando emphasizes initial withdrawal followed by an attack outside the opponent's reach with the employment of all parts of the body. Once the initial technique is delivered, grappling and locking techniques are used. The sporting variety of bando resembles >THAI BOXING, althought the rules are more liberal.

BANDY, a sport similar to >ICE HOCKEY played, however, on a much larger rink, the size almost that of an >ASSOCIATION FOOTBALL pitch, which, therefore, makes it difficult to hold bandy matches indoors. The sport is particularly popular in Russia and the Scand. countries where the rinks are built in winter by flooding a football pitch or some other, similar field.

Rink, equipment and fundamentals. Players wear skates and use curved sticks, some 1.2m long, to hit a small ball. In the past, instead of a ball, the game employed a rounded wooden block. In 1904 it was replaced by a wooden ball covered in leather. At present the ball is filled with cork and is 2in. (c. 6cm) in diameter and weighs 2.1-2.2oz. (58-62g). Its color is bright, usu. red, which makes it easier for the players to follow it. The object of the game is to put the ball into the opposing team's goal. The goals are situated at the opposite ends of the rink and are 2.1m high and 3.5m wide. The goalie does not use a stick but, alone among the players, can touch the ball with his hands or any part of his body or use his wide shin pads to deflect the ball. Outside of the penalty area he may only kick the ball. The rink is divided into two halves and play commences at the center circle which is 10m wide. At the 'stroke-off' there can be only 2 players, representing the opposing teams, inside the circle. A semicircular penalty area, which is 17m in diameter, is marked with a line in front of a goal. Penalty strokes are taken from a spot located 12m away from the end line. The rink is 90-110m long and 45-65m wide. There are 2 halves of 45min. each for men and boys aged 16-18, of 35min. for women, girls aged 16-18 and boys aged 14-16 and of 30min. for boys aged 13-14. In the case of a draw there is overtime of 2 halves of 15min. If the overtime still ends in a draw the sudden death principle is applied. A team is composed of up to 11 players – 10 outfield players and a goalie. In countries where bandy matches cannot be held outdoors they are played on regular ice hockey rinks by smaller, 7-player teams.

Etymology. The term bandy was not initially related to the game in question. Instead, it was probably used for any type of a ball passed with a stick. The first evidence of its verbal use comes from W. Shakespeare's *Romeo and Juliet*. In act II, scene 5, l. 12-15 Julia, waiting for her nurse to come back with news from Romeo, utters the following words:

Had she affections, and warm youthful blood,
She'd be as swift in motion as a ball;
My words would bandy her to my sweet love,
And his to me ...

The name of the game in question might have been derived from the old Eng. game of bandy ball that involved striking a ball with a curved stick. The game was played on the ground and not on ice. A similar game was known in East Anglia as >BANDY-CAD and as >CAMBUCA elsewhere.

History. Bandy originated, most probably, in the Netherlands where a similar game was played as early as in the Middle Ages. Then, it was 'borrowed' by the English, most likely by the courtiers of William III, king of England (1689-1702). This is, however, questionable since we also know that the English played a game, borrowed from the Celts, involving a ball and crooked sticks much earlier. There were also the Welsh >KNAPPAN, Scottish >SHINTY and Irish >HURLING, which were, however, not played on ice. Therefore, it is also possible that the two traditions merged over time. Bandy became esp. popular in the NE part of England where there were numerous bogs that froze easily during winter. That is where the first official rules of the game were developed and the first official bandy competition was held (in 1882). The National Bandy Association was estab. in England in 1891. In the same year it organized the first official international match between England, represented by the English Bury Fen club, and Holland, represented by the Haarlem team. The captain of the Bury Fen team, C.G. Tebbutt, brought the game to Sweden, provided the Stockholm Gymnastic Society with equipment and offered his services as an instructor (1894). Bandy became enormously popular and the Swed. Bandy Society was established in 1925. By 1926 there were almost 200 bandy clubs in Sweden and as many as 455 in 1990. The first Ger. clubs were established in Leipzig and Berlin in 1898. The Anglo-Dutch bandy was called in Germany 'hockey with the ball' (*Eishockey mit dem Ball*). The first Norwegian bandy club opened in 1903 and the first Finnish one in 1908. Towards the end of the 19th cent. the game was brought to Russia where the first bandy match was held in 1898. Here, bandy was called 'Russian hockey' (*russkij hokiej*). The International Bandy Federation (IBF, formerly Internationale Federation für Eishockey mit dem Ball, IFEB) was estab. in 1955. The sport is most popular in Germany, Russia (in 1922-91 the USSR), Sweden, Norway and Finland. Compare >BROOMBALL.

S. Almkvist, *Bandy*, 1919; 'Bandy', *Kleine Enzyklopädie – Körperkultur und Sport*, 1965; M.P. Juchno, *Igrajtie w russkij hokiej*, 1952; A. Tebbut, 'Bandy', *Encyclopaedia of Sport*, vol. 1, 1897.

Barefoot waterskiing.

BANDY BALL, an old. Eng. game in which a crooked stick was employed to hit a ball the size of 2 fists. The rules of the game have not been preserved. Bandy ball is thought to have influenced the development of the game of >BANDY, which is played on ice, as it is known today. The term bandy was also used to denote the stick used in the game. Forby's 19th-cent. work *Vocabulary of East Anglia* reads that 'a bandy stick was made of hard wood or worn-out shoe reinforced with metal or of an animal horn or hoof. A ball was made of a tree outgrowth or knot which was then carefully rounded'.

TGESI, I, 16.

BANDY HOSHOE, an old Eng. folk ball game involving pushing a ball with a crooked stick, esp. popular in Norfolk and Suffolk. The etymology of the name is complex and partially obscure. Its first and simplest constituent part, i.e. 'bandy', meant to throw a ball from side to side and finally it was adopted as the name of the whole game. 'Ho' is probably an abbreviation of horse or horselike and might have also been derived from such interjections as, 'Ho!' or 'Hoe!' used to denote a destination or pace. Shoe stood for a hoof or boot. 'Hoshoe' derived from 'horseshoe' would then stand for something made of a horse hoof, which was often used to produce the end, lower, and crooked part of the stick. The ho! + shoe interpretation is also a plausible one since parts of the bandy stick were often made of worn-out shoes which were reinforced with metal and into which a stick was inserted as a handle. The whole stick resembled a modern golf club, with a much larger head. In the western part of Sussex the same game was called >HAWKY. Bandy hoshoe is often associated with >BANDY BALL and perhaps it was one of its varieties. The rules of the game have not been preserved.

BANDY WICKET, a simple folk var. of >CRICKET played with a crooked stick, esp. popular in the former county of Norfolk and now in Cambridgeshire and on the Isle of Ely (Moor). The wicket was often replaced with bricks put on one another or with sticks forming a trestle.

TGESI, I, 17.

BANDY-CAD, also known as *gad*, a game popular in England in the past whereby a ball of an unspecified size was hit with a stick which was most likely crooked. The rules of the game have not been preserved. Bandy-cad is thought to have influenced the development of a number of English games such as >GOLF and >BANDY, which is played on ice. Sometimes it is associated with >BANDY HOSHOE, >SHINTY and >TIP-CAT.

BANGEUNG, an ancient Kor. var. of >FALCON HUNTING. Historical sources clearly indicate that it was the most popular of aristocratic sport activities in Korea throughout the Middle Ages. King Jin-Pueong (579-632) is said to have been so keen on bangeung that he often neglected state affairs.

BANGLADESHI ROWING, a variety of rowing practised in long boats with up to 20 oarsemen and a helmsman. The most popular events are the regattas held on the river Burgiganga.

BANKE PLØKKER I, Dan. for 'to drive pegs in'. A simple arm wrestling game. Two competitors face each other and they put forward their fists so that one of the players places his fist on top of his opponent's fist. The one whose fist is on top tries to hit his opponent's fist and at the same time avoid hitting his own. To do so he suddenly pulls it away just before hitting his opponent's fist. The other player tries to avoid being hit by also withdrawing his fist.

J. Møller, 'Banke pløkker', GID, 1997, 3, 78.

BANKE UD, Dan. for 'to strike out, striking out'; a Dan. children's game. The players form a circle except one who goes around the outside of the circle and strikes one of the players by pushing his or her back. The player struck has to catch the one who pushed him or her during one circuit of the circle. If the chased player is caught or does not manage to take the place of the one who was struck, he or she has to try again.

J. Møller, 'Banke ud', GID, 1997, 2, 26.

BAQUET RUSSE, a humorous Bret. agility test and a folk parody of the medieval >QUINTAIN. A water receptacle, often a washtub, is hung on special stands some 2.5-3m above the ground. A plank with a hole in it is placed under the container. The object of the game is to put a spear or a stick through the hole while riding a cart that is drawn or pushed by another player. The plank is devised in such a way that if the 'knight' misses the hole the contents of the water receptacle are emptied onto his head.

F. Peru, 'La tradition populaire de jeux de plein air en Bretagne', LJP, 1998.

BAR, a trad. Scot. game, in England known as *bars*. Most likely it is identical to >PRISONER'S BASE. Banned in Scotland by King James IV's edict of 1491 saying 'there shall not be any duels in towns [...] nor any bar games'.

TGESI, I, 18.

BAREBACK RIDING, one of the >RODEO events.

BAREFOOT WATERSKIING, popularly called *barefooting*, a type of water skiing possible only at high speed, which counterbalances the relatively small area of the contestant's feet (compared to the area of water skis). Apart from riding in a straight line the technique includes numerous evolutions. Some examples of tricks are: tumbleturns, toe holds, toe turns, line steps, 180 and 360° turns and for the top skiers, 540 and even 720° combinations are possible. Initially, foot-to-foot riding was most common, doubling the area of 1 foot and making jumps possible. Jumping was soon perfected with the buttock technique, where the participant approached the take-off on his buttocks and landed on his feet. This technique enabled longer jumps, but considerably limited the number of successful landings. In 1989 another technique was evolved, which made it pos-

Bandy ball.

A bandy ball stick.

BANDY WORLD CHAMPIONS:

1957 USSR
1959 USSR
1961 USSR
1963 USSR
1965 USSR
1967 USSR
1971 USSR
1973 USSR
1975 USSR
1977 USSR
1979 USSR
1981 Sweden
1983 Sweden
1985 USSR
1987 Sweden
1989 USSR
1991 Russia
1993 Sweden
1995 Sweden
1997 Sweden
1999 Russia
2001 Russia

B

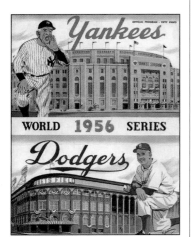

The official program of the 1956 World Series.

sible to jump over 20m: at the top of the take-off the rider pushes the lower part of his body forward and lowers the stick, taking a position parallel to the surface of the water. He keeps this position for most of the jump and then lowers his legs, landing simultaneously on his feet and buttocks.

History. The forerunner of the sport was C. Sligh, who in 1947 in Winter Haven, Florida, reached the conclusion that the area of the feet will suffice to ride behind a motor boat, provided the speed is high enough. Using this idea the 17-year-old A.G. Hancock conducted an appropriate experiment, becoming the first barefoot waterskiier. Because neither of the two sought publicity, it was D. Pope Jr. – in whose father Hancock confided his experiment – who became known as the initiator of the sport, which was quick to gain popularity. The first major event was held in 1961 in the USA. In the 1960s the sport became known to Australians, who in 1967 were the first to try jumping. In the '70s the jumping technique was already substantially elaborated. It was presented to Americans during the 1973 international championships in Cypress Gardens. Jumping was included in the official program as late as 1978. The first world record was set up by the Australian G. Rees, who jumped 13.41m. In 1989, thanks to M. Seipel's (USA) new technique, he improved this record to 22.1m. The new technique made barefoot waterskiing a cult sport. The 1996 world record was 27.7m (set by the Australian J. Sears). Top contestants of the '90s were also B. Brzoza, M. Seipel, R. Scarpa, L. Bower and J. Kretchman.

BARETTE, a Fr. game resembling >RUGBY; popularized among women after 1919.

BARLEY-BREAK, an old Eng. run-and-catch game. Its name originates from the fact that a game of barley-break was played among heaps or stacks of barley. Also called *last couple in hell*. The field of unspecified dimensions was divided into 3 parts with the middle one called hell. A pair of players, usu. a boy and a girl, stood in hell. Couples from the other 2 parts of the field tried to overcome the couple in hell by compromising their territory by suddenly running in and out of hell. The couple in hell tried to catch those making incursions over the borders of hell, and if they succeeded those caught remained in hell until the end of the round. The last couple to be caught in hell remained there to catch the other couples in the next round; compare >PRISONER'S BASE.

BARLØB, a Dan. complex running game. The origin of the name is unknown. The game is played by 2 teams on a trapezoid-shaped field. The players from the opposing teams stand behind the two non-parallel sides of the figure. There are two 4 sq. m 'prisons' located in diagonally opposite corners of the field. Team A sends a 'skirmisher' whose task is to tease team B. Team B sends 2 or 3 players whose task is to catch the 'skirmisher'. He cannot catch the team B players but team A can send more players to catch them. Each field player may leave

The main event of the Beer Festival in Burton includes rolling wooden barrels over a ¾-mile course.

the field and return at any time and is then deemed to be a new player. If somebody catches a player from the opposing team he shouts 'stop' to stop the game. Then, everybody returns to their original places (behind the line) and the person caught is put in 'prison'. Now, it is team B's turn to start play. The team whose player is in 'prison' has to reach and free him by touching him. The prisoner has to have at least one leg in 'prison'. If there are more players in prison only one of them has to have his foot in 'prison' (whereas they all may hold one another by the hand and can stretch out into the field, then it is enough to touch only one of them to free them all). After a prisoner has been freed the teams return to their original places and the game starts anew. When a given team captures 3 prisoners it scores a specified number of points. If a pursued player runs out of bounds he goes to prison but if he leaves the field across the opposing team's line he can go around the field to his team's side and the play is not stopped. The teams either score points or there is a specified time limit – in which case the total number of captured prisoners counts. Barløb resembles the Eng. >PRISONER'S BASE and the Fr. >AUX BARES.

J. Møller, 'Barløb', GID, 1997, 2.

BARRA WRESTLING, see >CARACHD BHARRAIDH.

BARRA, an ancient folk game of India resembling >TUG-OF-WAR. A barra competition was usu. held during local religious holidays among teams from various villages.

BARREL LIFTING, an old Celtic sport consisting of lifting and carrying stave wooden barrels. Historians claim the barrels used for the sport were of two kinds: 1) 60cm in height and diameter; 2) 45cm in height and 30cm in diameter. The barrels weighted from 30 to 175kg, depending on the load. Cf. >DŹWIGANIE BECZEK.

D. Terry, 'Sport and Health of the Ancient Celts', T. Terret, ed., *Sport et sauté dans l'historie*, 1999.

BARREL ROLLING, a Fin. annual event in which teams of two compete by rolling 160-liter beer barrels along a 250-m course with the help of wooden sticks. The event is part of the Sonkajärvi County Fair and the winning pair receives the title of Finnish Barrel Rolling Champions.

A similar event has been held since 1933 in Burton upon Trent (Great Britain). Its tradition dates back to the 1920s, when Eng. breweries were using 36-gallon barrels, each weighing approx. 40kg. They had to be rolled over a ¾-mile course with the use of bobbing sticks. When wooden barrels were replaced with aluminum kegs, the tradition was interrupted. In 1996 it was revived as an international event, now part of the Burton Beer Festival. Teams compete for the Silver Trophy of Burton over a 130m course. In 2000 the women's race was won by the Czech Champions from Velke Popovice Brewery in a record time of 40.43sec.

Similar events are also held in other beer producing countries, e.g. in the Czech Republic, where teams compete in the so-called 'Beer Mile' over a 593.95m course.

Consultant: M. Kaska, Velke Popovice Brewery.

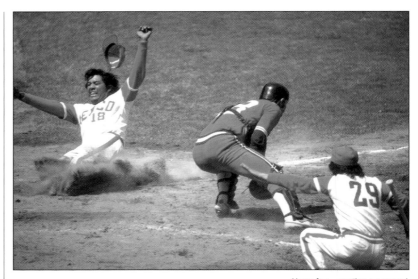

Home free – another run scored.

BARREL TOURNAMENT, Rus. *turnir na botchkakh* a form of competition in which 2 contestants sit astride 2 barrels floating on water, with bungs on one side. The contestants have long poles ending in rope loops, with which they try to snatch the bungs on the opponent's barrel and move the barrel so that the opponent falls into the water. The game is described by I.N. Chkhannikov (GIZ, 1953, 82).

BARRENADORES, see >ARRISULATZALLEAK.

BASEBALL, the Amer. national sport whose international popularity is on the rise. It involves striking a hard, leather-coated cork-and-rubber ball with a rounded club called a bat. The object of the game is to hit a ball pitched by a fielding team's player out of reach of the fielding team and score points by running a complete, counter-clockwise circuit around the 4 bases laid out in a square.

Fundamentals. A game of baseball is played between 2 competing teams of 9 players each. The 2 teams alternate positions as fielders and batters (they are 'at bat'). The first pitch is thrown by a *pitcher* standing on a 'mound' in the middle of the diamond field towards home plate. There are 2 players at home plate: *a batter* and a catcher who kneels down behind him. The task of the batter is to hit a flying ball with the bat and send it out of reach of the fielding team and run a complete circuit around all the bases for a run. A run may be completed in stages whereby the runner stops at the respective bases. A runner may be put out by the fielding team's players. They can do it when they intercept the ball before it touches the ground or hit the runner or the base which he has just left or is approaching with the ball. A player standing within the confines of a base is safe and cannot be put out. The task of the catcher is to catch the ball when the batter fails to hit it. To do that he wears a large glove or mitt which significantly increases the area of his palm. A similar mitt is worn by the first baseman who acts as an infielder, whereby the remaining players of the fielding team wear smaller gloves. A team remains at bat until 3 players of that team have been put out. Then, the teams alternate their positions and the fielding team becomes the batting team and vice versa. A game of baseball consists of 9 innings during each of which, each team has a turn at bat. If the score is tied after 9 full innings the game is continued until one of the teams wins. A baseball game is refereed by up to 4 umpires. Less important games may be refereed by only one umpire who mainly ensures that both the pitcher and the batter play in accordance with the rules. During more important games there are additional umpires who make sure that all the respective base players also play fair. Each team consists of players specializing in certain tasks. Apart from a pitcher and a catcher each team consists of the following players: the 1st baseman, the 2nd baseman, the 3rd baseman, a shortstop (positioned between 2nd and 3rd base), a right fielder, a center fielder and a left fielder. All the players of the batting team take their turns as batters. Any player can be substituted at any time but once he has been taken off the field he cannot return.

A baseball field is fan-shaped and consists of an infield and an outfield. The infield is a 90-ft. (about 27.45m) square. The 3 bases are located in the re-

The official program of the 1987 World Series.

Baseball, *anonymous.*

Thomas Eakins, Baseball players practicing.

Abner Crossman, Baseball in England, *19th cent.*

Grand Championship Match, *a lithograph from the workshop of Currier and Ives.*

spective corners of the square. An imaginary line that connects home plate and 2nd base constitutes an axis along which the ball should be batted within 45° on either side. All the bases, except home plate, are numbered consecutively anti-clockwise. Home plate is the base at which a batter stands. Directly opposite it, on the square's diagonal, 60ft. and 6in. away there is the so-called pitcher's mound from where the pitcher pitches the ball to the batter.

Equipment and uniform. Baseball players use a bat that is a smooth, round stick not more than 2¾ in. in diameter at the thickest part and not more than 42in. in length. The bat is one piece of solid, usu. ash, wood or light metal. Towards the handle end the bat tapers off to a knob that prevents the batter's hands from slipping off the bat. The baseball itself is usu. a fair-beige sphere formed by yarn wound around a small core of cork, rubber or similar elastic material, covered with 2 stripes of white horse- or cow-hide, tightly stitched together (usu. with red thread). It shall weigh not less than 5 but not more than 5¼ oz. avoirdupois (142g) nor measure less than 9 or more than 9¼ in. in circumference (23cm).

Traditionally, all players on an Amer. league team wear uniforms that consist of three-quarter knickers, knee stockings and leather shoes. The players wear a long-sleeved jersey undershirt and a half-length-sleeved flannel overshirt. The overshirt includes a number that is displayed on the back some 15cm above the waistline. The players also wear long, tight-fitting trousers and a protective helmet. The players wear caps and, in the case of the team at bat, also colored helmets similar in shape to such a cap but offering protection to the sides and back of the head. The catcher wears a protective helmet with a face mask, a chest protector and a large leather mitt not more than 38in. in circumference (96.5cm) and not more than 15½in. from top to bottom (39.4cm). The first baseman also wears a mitt measuring about 30cm from top to bottom.

Today, the players are less willing to wear trad. uniforms. This is largely due to the fact that new types of fabrics have been introduced. In the past the baggy and loose-fitting three-quarter knickers were to ensure unrestricted movement. Today they are often replaced with tight-fitting ankle- or half-shin-length trousers, similar to leggings, which are elastic and thus do not restrict movement. The uniforms became more attractive and richly adorned. In the South the players wear undershirts more similar to a T-shirt in shape. Departures from the trad. baseball uniform are most visible during games organized by the International Baseball Federation and less during professional league matches.

Social importance. Baseball, similarly to Brit. >CRICKET, includes many elements forcing cooperation among players from opposing teams, as in the case of a batter and a pitcher. Although the pitcher wants to throw the ball in such a way as to make it as difficult as possible for the batter to hit it, the rules of the game and the fact that each pitch is closely supervised by an umpire force him to adhere to certain regulations concerning the area at which the throw should be aimed (i.e. above the batter's waist and within the reach of his arms). It is also worth remembering that the ball may only be hit out of reach of the fielding team, which enables the players of the batting team to start running around the bases to score their points, after a pitch made by a member of the fielding team itself. So it transpires that one of the main ideas of the sport, apart from competition, is cooperation between opponents. This seeming paradox reflects one of the most basic principles underlying social interaction in Eng.-speaking culture whereby close cooperation is often required of individuals or groups whose particular interests may be conflicting ones.

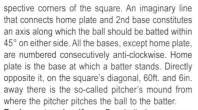

A catcher in full gear.

WORLD SERIES (MAJOR LEAGUE BASEBALL)

1903 Boston Red Sox 5-3 Pittsburgh Pirates
1904 no series
1905 New York Giants 4-1 Philadelphia Athletics
1906 Chicago White Sox 4-2 Chicago Cubs
1907 Chicago Cubs 4-0 Detroit Tigers
1908 Chicago Cubs 4-1 Detroit Tigers
1909 Pittsburgh Pirates 4-3 Detroit Tigers
1910 Philadelphia Athletics 4-1 Chicago Cubs
1911 Philadelphia Athletics 4-2 New York Giants
1912 Boston Red Sox 4-3 New York Giants
1913 Philadelphia Athletics 4-1 New York Giants
1914 Boston Braves 4-0 Philadelphia Athletics
1915 Boston Red Sox 4-1 Philadelphia Phillies
1916 Boston Red Sox 4-1 Brooklyn Dodgers
1917 Chicago White Sox 4-2 New York Giants
1918 Boston Red Sox 4-2 Chicago Cubs
1919 Cincinnati Reds 5-3 Chicago White Sox
1920 Cleveland Indians 5-2 Brooklyn Dodgers
1921 New York Giants 5-3 New York Yankees
1922 New York Giants 4-0 New York Yankees
1923 New York Yankees 4-2 New York Giants
1924 Washington Senators 4-3 New York Giants
1925 Pittsburgh Pirates 4-3 Washington Senators
1926 Saint Louis Cardinals 4-3 New York Yankees
1927 New York Yankees 4-0 Pittsburgh Pirates
1928 New York Yankees 4-0 Saint Louis Cardinals
1929 Philadelphia Athletics 4-1 Chicago Cubs
1930 Philadelphia Athletics 4-2 Saint Louis Cardinals
1931 Saint Louis Cardinals 4-3 Philadelphia Athletics
1932 New York Yankees 4-0 Chicago Cubs
1933 New York Giants 4-1 Washington Senators
1934 Saint Louis Cardinals 4-3 Detroit Tigers
1935 Detroit Tigers 4-2 Chicago Cubs
1936 New York Yankees 4-2 New York Giants
1937 New York Yankees 4-1 New York Giants
1938 New York Yankees 4-0 Chicago Cubs
1939 New York Yankees 4-0 Cincinnati Reds
1940 Cincinnati Reds 4-3 Detroit Tigers
1941 New York Yankees 4-1 Brooklyn Dodgers
1942 Saint Louis Cardinals 4-1 New York Yankees
1943 New York Yankees 4-1 Saint Louis Cardinals
1944 Saint Louis Cardinals 4-2 Saint Louis Browns
1945 Detroit Tigers 4-3 Chicago Cubs
1946 Saint Louis Cardinals 4-3 Boston Red Sox
1947 New York Yankees 4-3 Brooklyn Dodgers
1948 Cleveland Indians 4-2 Boston Braves
1949 New York Yankees 4-1 Brooklyn Dodgers
1950 New York Yankees 4-0 Philadelphia Phillies
1951 New York Yankees 4-2 New York Giants
1952 New York Yankees 4-3 Brooklyn Dodgers
1953 New York Yankees 4-2 Brooklyn Dodgers
1954 New York Giants 4-0 Cleveland Indians
1955 Brooklyn Dodgers 4-3 New York Yankees
1956 New York Yankees 4-3 Brooklyn Dodgers
1957 Milwaukee Braves 4-3 New York Yankees
1958 New York Yankees 4-3 Milwaukee Braves
1959 Los Angeles Dodgers 4-2 Chicago White Sox
1960 Pittsburgh Pirates 4-3 New York Yankees
1961 New York Yankees 4-1 Cincinnati Reds
1962 New York Yankees 4-3 San Francisco Giants
1963 Los Angeles Dodgers 4-0 New York Yankees
1964 Saint Louis Cardinals 4-3 New York Yankees
1965 Los Angeles Dodgers 4-3 Minnesota Twins
1966 Baltimore Orioles 4-0 Los Angeles Dodgers
1967 Saint Louis Cardinals 4-3 Boston Red Sox
1968 Detroit Tigers 4-3 Saint Louis Cardinals
1969 New York Mets 4-1 Baltimore Orioles
1970 Baltimore Orioles 4-1 Cincinnati Reds
1971 Pittsburgh Pirates 4-3 Baltimore Orioles
1972 Oakland Athletics 4-3 Cincinnati Reds
1973 Oakland Athletics 4-3 New York Mets
1974 Oakland Athletics 4-1 Los Angeles Dodgers
1975 Cincinnati Reds 4-3 Boston Red Sox
1976 Cincinnati Reds 4-0 New York Yankees
1977 New York Yankees 4-2 Los Angeles Dodgers
1978 New York Yankees 4-2 Los Angeles Dodgers
1979 Pittsburgh Pirates 4-3 Baltimore Orioles
1980 Philadelphia Phillies 4-2 Kansas City Royals
1981 Los Angeles Dodgers 4-2 New York Yankees
1982 Saint Louis Cardinals 4-3 Milwaukee Brewers
1983 Baltimore Orioles 4-1 Philadelphia Phillies
1984 Detroit Tigers 4-1 San Diego Padres
1985 Kansas City Royals 4-3 Saint Louis Cardinals
1986 New York Mets 4-3 Boston Red Sox
1987 Minnesota Twins 4-3 Saint Louis Cardinals
1988 Los ANgeles Dodgers 4-1 Oakland Athletics
1989 Oakland Athletics 4-0 San Francisco Giants
1990 Cincinnati Reds 4-0 Oakland Athletics
1991 Monnesota Twins 4-3 Atlanta Braves
1992 Toronto Blue Jays 4-2 Atlanta Braves
1993 Toronto Blue Jays 4-2 Philadelphia Phillies
1994 no series
1995 Atlanta Braves 4-2 Cleveland Indians
1996 New York Yankees 4-2 Atlanta Braves
1997 Florida Marlins 4-3 Cleveland Indians
1998 New York Yankees 4-0 San Diego Padres
1999 New York Yankees 4-0 Atlanta Braves
2000 New York Yankees 4-1 New York Mets
2001 Arizona Diamondbacks 4-3 New York Yankees
2002 Anaheim Angels 4–3 San Francisco Giants

History. Baseball is based on a number of folk games, including >CRICKET and >ROUNDERS, brought to America by the Eng. settlers in the 16th to 18th cent. period. Before the emergence of baseball proper there was a number of similar games such as >BASTE-BALL, >GOALBALL, >NEW-YORK-BALL, >ONE-OLD-CAT, >ROUND BALL, >TOWN-BALL and >TWO-OLD-CAT played in the Eng. colonies and later in the US. In the 2nd half of the 18th cent. Bostonians used to play a 1-base game of one-old-cat that was later turned into a two-base two-old-cat and finally, towards the end of the century, into a 4-base town-hall. Apart from >CRICKET the colonists also enjoyed a game called *New-York-ball* or *New-York-game*. Both games mingled and intertwined at the turn of the 18th cent. and evolved into a number of locally played bat-and-ball games. Around 1820 a game employing 4 bases, marked with poles, became widely popular in the New York area. This game was more intricate than the Bostonian town-hall. In 1833 members of the Boston Olympic Club played a 4-base game combining elements of town-hall and New-York-ball. The term baseball first appeared in written sources, newspapers and literature during the 1835-41 period when flagpoles, to which players ran, were replaced with specially marked fields called, from then on, bases. During that period teams usu. consisted of 11-15 players or, sometimes, even 20 players. In 1842 the exact dimensions of the field were standardized, the number of players was limited to 12 and an official referee (umpire) was introduced. In 1845 the first ever Amer. baseball club, called the Knickerbocker Baseball Club (KBC), was established in New York. In 1846 KBC appointed a committee on rules that developed baseball rules which have remained largely unchanged to the present day. The first official game to be held according to these rules took places during a picnic in Hoboken on 19 Apr. 1846 (KBC played the New York Nine Club, estab. in 1846). In 1849, for the first time ever, players wore official club uniforms, setting the standard for all subsequent baseball uniforms: loose-fitting, three-quarter knickers, a shirt with short or rolled-up sleeves. Initially, players wore a small hat with a narrow brim. Later, they switched to a cap with a sun-visor that gradually grew longer. The cap remained a standard part of the baseball uniform and also became widely popular in other sports and yet later as a part of everyday, casual attire where it is known as the baseball cap. Several dozen clubs that recognized KBC rules were estab. in the US in the 1846-56 period. In 1857 the first Amer. federation of amateur clubs called the National Association of Baseball Players (NABP) was established. After having become popular in East Coast cities baseball reached the West Coast around 1860. The first Californian baseball club to be set up was the San Francisco Base-Ball Club (1860). In 1868 the Cincinnati Red Stockings introduced a new type of baseball trousers. In 1869 it became the first club to go entirely professional. This date marks the beginning of professional baseball. In 1871 the first professional baseball federation, known as the National Association of Professional Base-Ball Players (NAPBBP), was established. NAPBBP developed a system of national leagues. Around the same time NABP ceased to exist. In 1876 yet another professional league – the National League, or NL – came into being. The NL-approved league rules proved to be highly-selective as they excluded cities with a population of less than 75,000 since, according to the rules, adequate income from ticket sales could not be guaranteed at such places. In 1879 one more league system – called the Northwestern League – was set up. In 1882 the Amer. Association of Baseball Players (AABP) came into existence as a rival organization of the NL. A huge number of various leagues and game systems, largely ephemeral in their character, was estab. by the end of the 19th cent. Of these, only the National League, whose revenue exceeded $1 million in 1891, survived. In 1900, the Old Western League, which started out as a small, regional association, became a pan-state organization and was renamed the Amer. League (AL). Since that time the NL and AL have remained the main driving forces behind baseball's development and although they have been at odds as rivals, their cooperation has been maintained by and through the National Baseball Commission (since 1903) and the Advisory Council (1921-present). The best teams from each league have met since 1903 in an annual, Fall series of games called the World Series. Since 1933 All-Stars Games have been held between the 2 leagues' teams of their best players. In the 1933-47 period it was the fans who selected (by vote) the players to participate in an All-Stars Game. Since 1947 the All-Stars players have been selected by a council of players, coaches and managers from both leagues. In 1948 the revenue from an All-Stars Game exceeded, for the first time in history, $10 million. As much as 75% of the money from All-Stars ticket sales went to the players themselves. When television became more responsible for generating profit on all baseball games, not only the All-Stars Games but also regular league season games, tension mounted; there were player strikes within both leagues due to the fact that the players wanted to secure increasingly higher incomes for themselves.

Baseball, along with boxing and track and field athletics, played a very important role in the fight against racism. In 1947 the AL allowed Afr.-Amer. players to participate in regular league games. And although Afr.-Americans played every now and then in minor leagues and less important games the breakthrough came in 1947 when Jackie Robinson (1919-72) became a regular team member of the Brooklyn Dodgers, which was then one of the leading teams in the league.

The most outstanding figures in baseball history are honored with plaques in the Baseball Hall of Fame at Cooperstown, N.Y. and they include: Ty Cobb (1886-1961), Babe Ruth (1895-1948), Cy Young (1867-1955), S. Kourfax (b.1935), S. Musial (b.1920, of Pol. origin) and J. Rice (b.1935).

The most famous baseball club in history was the Brooklyn Dodgers, of the National League, which was moved to Los Angeles in 1958 after encountering numerous problems with obtaining land to develop its new sports facilities, and became the Los Angeles Dodgers. Other major NL clubs include the Atlanta Braves, Chicago Cubs, Cincinnati Reds, Philadelphia Phillies, Pittsburgh Pirates, St. Louis Cardinals and San Francisco Giants. The most outstanding clubs of the AL in recent years have been the Baltimore Orioles, Boston Red Sox, California Angels, Chicago White Sox, Cleveland Indians, Detroit Tigers, New York Yankees and Texas Rangers. In addition to the major leagues, a number of smaller, local leagues operate independently of the NL and AL. In 1947 there were as many as 52 Amer. league systems, in 1967 there were 19 leagues, though by 1975 that number was down to just 11. At present many local, minor leagues cooperate closely with the 2 major ones and sell their best players to them. Apart from the professional leagues, the National Baseball Congress of America has operated in the US since 1934 as an association of amateur, including school, teams and organizations.

WORLD SPORTS ENCYCLOPEDIA

B

Ready for action: the batter awaits the ball which the pitcher is about to release.

Baseball in Cuba. Baseball was brought to Cuba in 1866 when N. Guillot returned home after having graduated from an Amer. university and started popularizing it. Soon he was joined by E. Bellán who used to be a baseball player in the US. The first baseball club in Cuba – the Habana Baseball Club – was estab. in 1872. The Matanzas Club was set up in 1873 and the Almandares Club in 1878. The first baseball game was held in 1874 between Habana and Matanzas. Some 200 baseball clubs appeared in Cuba before 1900. In 1877 the Cubans played their first international game against a team of the US fleet that came to Cuba. After WWII, the Havana Cerro stadium became the most important baseball arena in the whole of Cuba. The 1959 Revolution has greatly contributed to the development of baseball in Cuba as it made it widely accessible to the poorer classes for whom access to sport and the possibilities of social advancement related thereto had been barred up to that point. Despite political terror, sport in general and baseball in particular has been specially promoted by the authorities which quickly made the Cuban team one of the best in the world. The Cuban national team can be called the best amateur team in the world as by 1995 it had won 21 out of 24 world championships. It is also a 9-time winner of the 12 Pan-Amer. Games held to date. It was also the first Olympic gold medal winner in 1992 in Barcelona. The Cuban team also won the gold medal 4 years later in Atlanta.

Baseball in other Latin American countries. Baseball was introduced in the Dominican Republic in 1868 by Cuban emigrants who fled Cuba after the outbreak of the civil war in that year. Baseball reached Mexico in 1877 where it was played by Amer. sailors in the port of Guayamas and by railway workers in Nuevo Laredo. A number of baseball clubs sprang up in Mexico in the 1880s. It was brought to Panama, which was under Amer. administration, in 1882. An Amer. citizen visiting Nicaragua presented baseball in 1889 to D. Arellano who then started promoting it among the natives. Venezuelans were introduced to baseball by a Cuban E. Cramer in 1895. In 1947 the New York Yankees toured Venezuela. In Puerto Rico baseball became known after a Spanish officer described it in 1896 after having seen it in Cuba. Baseball is still one of the most popular sports in the above countries despite the widespread poverty and political instability in the region. Many outstanding players from Latin America come to play in the major US clubs as they came earlier to play in the so-called 'black clubs'.

Baseball has been known **in Japan** since the 1870s when it was introduced to some Jap. schools in the aftermath of Japan's opening up to the outside world and becoming gradually westernized. The first schools that introduced baseball were the Ichiko College in Tokyo, Meiji Gakuin and the famous Waseda University. The Ichiko College was the main baseball center in the 1880-1900 period. In 1896 the Ichiko team beat the team of Americans living in Japan representing the Yokohama Country Athletic Club which was a major media event not only in Japan but also in the US. Soon after 1900 it was Waseda and Keio Universities that became the lead-

Baseball is gaining popularity outside the USA. Above: players of the Spanish national team.

A postage stamp commemorating the 100th anniversary of baseball in the USA.

A Cuban baseball postage stamp.

Some of the amateur players belong to the Amateur Athletic Union (AAU), which has a membership extending over a number of various sports. For some years now the AAU has held annual championships for schools and universities. >SOFTBALL is a milder baseball variety especially popular among school pupils and students as well as women, and community groups.

International baseball outside of the USA. Early attempts to popularize baseball in Great Britain and Ireland at the turn of the 19th cent. failed. In 1931 a former Amer. baseball player L. Mann together with A. Brundage, who later became the President of the IOC, organized in the US the National Baseball Congress, or NBC, whose aim was to make baseball into an international sport by, among other things, securing a place for it at the Ol.G. Baseball was presented as a demonstration sport at the 1936 Olympics in Berlin, the 1952 Ol.G. in Melbourne, in 1984 in Los Angeles and in 1988 in Seoul. It became a full-medal sport in 1992 in Barcelona. In 1935 Mann, Brundage and a Jap. professor Takiso Matsumoto started promoting baseball in Japan (see below). In 1938 the International Baseball Federation was estab. in the US. The organization changed its name several times before becoming the International Baseball Association, IBA in 1993 (Span. Associatión Internacional de Béisbol). However, due to the fact that the IBA has applied its former names inconsistently, most frequently calling itself a 'feder-

ation', one might get the impression that several organizations existed in parallel. During the first few years of its existence, the IBA had a membership of 21 national organizations and in 1998 there were as many as 107 national federation members with more (Uzbekistan and Cyprus) waiting to be accepted. Since 1938 the IBA has organized the World Cup series which was, at the same time, deemed to be the W.Ch. Since 1958 the Global World Series has been held regularly and the youth W.Ch. known as the World Youth Series since 1957. Until 1996 the IBA was an amateur-only association. In 1996 it decided to accept professional teams into the Series as well. The IBA is now recognized by the IOC as the only representative of baseball as an Olympic sport. It also publishes the *World Baseball Magazine* (in Eng. and Span.). The Eur. Union of Baseball was set up in 1953. Since 1963 it has held the Eur. Cup series.

Outside of the US baseball was most popular in Latin Amer. countries such as Cuba and Mexico and, after WWII, in countries occupied by Amer. military forces, i.e. Japan and West Germany. In other countries baseball was initially developing on its own basing on the Amer. rules. This situation changed when the International Baseball Federation was estab. in 1938. The IBF was independent of all the Amer. organizations and its aim was to popularize baseball worldwide and to make it an Olympic sport, which proved to be a success (see below).

Warming up.

John Updike, the author of Hub Fans Bid Kid Adieu.

ing centers of Jap. baseball. Their annual games became a major event in Japan which often led to street riots instigated by the opposing teams' fans which resulted in the tournament being banned (it was not revived until 1925). In 1915 the first all-Jap. tournament for schools (the Summer National Baseball Tournament of Secondary Schools) began to be held on a regular basis. A similar tournament has also been held in spring since 1924. In 1925 a 6-team league of Tokyo schools with teams from secondary schools of Keio, Waseda, Meiji, Hosei, Rikyo and an all-Tokyo university team came into being. Semi-professional clubs and such outstanding personalities as B. Ruth, J. Fox and L. Gehring started coming to Japan to participate in demonstration games. In 1935 following an invitation extended by Takiso Matsumoto, a professor of Meiji University, an all-Amer. national team selected by National Baseball Congress activists and managed by L. Mann and A. Brundage came to Japan for a series of demonstration games. Until WWII the major forms of baseball in Japan were the school, university and semi-professional baseball partly sponsored by the Jap. National Railways. Semi-professional games and tournaments began in 1927. In 1936 the Jap. Professional Baseball Association was established. The association was, however, ignored by Jap. traditionalists and major dailies such as Yomiuri. This situation changed after 1945 when baseball was employed as one of the elements of the reconstruction programs implemented after WWII. An amateur University League was launched in 1946 and trad. school tournaments were revived in the same year. In 1949 Jap. professional teams split into two leagues – the so-called Central and Pacific Leagues. Each league having 6 teams. The Yomiuri daily, which used to look down upon baseball, is today the official sponsor of the Yomiuri Giants. Other leading Jap. teams include the Hanshin Tigers and Kintetsu Buffaloes. The most outstanding players of the 1960s and 70s were Sadaharu Oh (b.1940) and Shigeo Nagashima (b.1936).

The most important baseball center in Japan is the Koshi-en training center and stadium in Osaka. There is a total of about 4,000 amateur school and university baseball teams. Following a very complex system of qualifying games, a total of 50 teams is selected to participate in a final series that is held 2 times a year. An annual Japan vs. the US national teams series similar to World Series has been taking place since 1972. It is estimated that Jap. baseball games are watched by some 20 million spectators a year. The rules of the game are identical to the Amer. ones but the cultural context is totally different. Despite the fact that Japan opened up to the outside world in 1867, the Japanese had only had a superficial knowledge and understanding of Eur. and Amer. culture. Baseball, not unlike other sports that were being popularized in Japan, was not treated as a source of team-work and the values of competition, which were dominant in the US, but rather as an inspiration for further development of individual qualities, esp. those related to the samurai tradition. Mental training has incorporated from the very beginning of the history of baseball in Japan some elements of Zen meditation which is well-reflected in game rituals. The social structure of teams and clubs is also different, being based on a vertical hierarchy called a *Bu*. The younger and less experienced play-

A bseball field is fan shaped, with an infield and outfield. Below: Fenway Park Stadium in Boston.

Montreal Expos' Orlando Cabrera slides safely into home plate as Philadelphia Phillies' catcher Mike Lieberthal tries to tag him out under the watchful eye of umpire Sam Holbrook during 8th-inning NLB action in Montreal.

ers are required to display an almost feudal subordination to the older players, the coach and the club management. These unique traits developed in the initial period of Jap. baseball in Ichiko and when the graduates of this school took managerial and coaching positions elsewhere they became popular throughout the country. This stark contrast between Amer. and Jap. baseball was depicted in *Mr. Baseball* directed by M. Schepisi (1992). The movie tells the story of an Amer. baseball player J. Elliott (played by T. Selleck) whose professional career is coming to an end and who signs his last contract with the Chinichi Dragons of Nagoya where his Amer. baseball customs and traditions clash with the Jap. ones, which are, quite naturally, totally different.

After an initial period of dependency on the Amer. baseball tradition, Jap. baseball began to develop rapidly on its own and even started influencing other countries including the US. The breakthrough came when the supreme skill of Jap. players was recognized in the US and when Amer. professional clubs started recruiting Jap. players. One Japanese who played in the US was the best Jap. pitcher ever – Hideo Nomo – who became a Los Angeles Dodgers player in 1955.

Apart from Japan, baseball also gained popularity in Korea and Taiwan and in some other Asian countries to a lesser extent. In 1979 the authorities of the People's Republic of China allowed for baseball to be practiced in their country. Its popularity has been on the increase in Australia, where it was pioneered by N. Pratt, and Oceania since the 1950s.

Canada has participated in the World Cup since 1967. In 1998 the number of baseball players there was estimated at 1 million (including school teams). **In Europe**, where there has been a large number of indigenous sports that were much more popular, baseball remained largely unnoticed. Shortly after the end of WWII baseball was introduced to West Germany by the Amer. soldiers who occupied the country. In 1953 an Amer.-Ger. organization called Amateur Baseball Federation Deutschland was estab. in Mannheim. Later on, baseball became moderately popular in Belgium and the Netherlands and also in Italy and Spain. Most Eur. countries had estab. their national baseball associations or federations by 1999.

Women and baseball. The role of women in the history of baseball has still not been investigated fully. Baseball used to be treated as a men-only sport and only when softball, i.e. a baseball variety with simplified rules, became more popular did the role of women become more significant. However, as early as in the 19th cent. there were at least a few attempts to build women's teams at some Amer. colleges. Towards the end of the 19th cent. there were women's teams at private baseball clubs. Around 1900 there were at least 6 women who participated in men's minor leagues. They were there to make the games a little bit more attractive. L. Arlington used to sometimes play a round in one of the minor leagues. A. Wess played regularly for 16 years in one of the private men's leagues run by her father. Local beauty queens often participated in various games and tourna-

ments, irrespective of their often inadequate skills, merely to attract more spectators. Such players included L. Murphy, J. Caruso and A. Clement who took part in 50 games over a period of 7 years. Women also owned baseball clubs, for example, after inheriting them from their fathers. One of the most famous baseball clubs in history – St. Louis Cardinals – belonged for 7 years to H. Britton who proved to be an excellent manager. In the 1930s and 40s and all-Black baseball club called Newark Eagles was owned by E. Manley. B. Dirkinson, who was a professional track and field and golf athlete, participated in a number of demonstration games held in the period between the world wars. One of the most celebrated woman-players before WWII was M. Gisolo who in 1928 became a member of the men's Amer. Legion team. The All Amer. Girls' Professional Baseball League (AAGPB) existed for a short period of time soon after the end of WWII. This event was later depicted (with additional fictitious motifs) in a movie called *A League of Their Own* directed by P. Marshall (1992). After the AAGPB was disbanded one of its coaches – B. Allington – organized a traveling women's team which played demonstration games against men's teams (1954-57). Games played by this team involved the exchange of pitchers between the women's and men's teams. The team was eventually disbanded because the enterprise turned out to be unprofitable. At the same time there was an overall tendency to admit more and more girls to league and school teams. In 1973 a court issued an unprecedented decision that girls had the right to participate in their school baseball teams. See also women in >AUSTRALIAN RULES FOOTBALL and >ASSOCIATION FOOTBALL.

Baseball in mass media and literature. Baseball was the first sport in the US to owe its popularity to organized commercial and publicity campaigns pursued in the press and later in other media, i.e. radio, film and TV. In 1853 a New York daily, *Mercury*, published the first modern account of a baseball game with a certain literary flavor to it. The report was written by W. Cauldwell, the owner and editor-in-chief of the paper. In 1861 H. Chadwick, the editor of the first regular sports column in Amer. history published in the *New Clipper*, organized the New Clipper Cup tournament. In 1890 the NL started publishing its *Sporting Times* which played a significant role in popularizing baseball in the US. At present there are several dozen magazines devoted exclusively to baseball, the biggest of which is called *Baseball Digest* (estab. 1942) with a circulation of 240,000 copies in the 1970s (and 225,000 copies in the mid-1980s). At the same time most of the major dailies such as *The Washington Post*, *The New York Times* and *USA Today* feature extensive baseball supplements. Since the end of the 19th cent. Amer. newspapers have often discussed major sports events, incl. baseball games, on their front pages. Many talented journalists such as G. Rice, P. Gallico and R. Lardner often wrote about baseball. Few magazines and newspapers have neglected to devote space to baseball or sport in general. The invention of the radio and its rapid spread in the 1920s and the period of its peak popularity in the 1930s and 40s attracted millions of new baseball fans. As early as in 1926 the World Series was broadcast by as many as 26 radio stations. The most outstanding radio sports commentator of that time was G. McNamee (a former crooner who also specialized in boxing and Amer. football). Due to the fact that many managers expressed their concern that radio broadcasts would drive people away from the stadiums, baseball's popularity on the radio was initially artificially checked. However, this resistance was finally overcome with the help of L. McPhall, the manager of the Cincinnati Reds, who initiated a new type of mass media cooperation with baseball clubs based on contracts that guaranteed certain income for the clubs to compensate for the potential decrease in the number of live spectators at stadiums. As radio became more and more popular these contracts brought much more revenue than ticket sales. When television was introduced the character of the game was further modified by the need to introduce artificial lighting. In 1935 the Cincinnati vs. Philadelphia game was the first event in world sports history to be held at night by electric lighting. In the same year the game between the Jap. national and the National Baseball Congress teams was, for the first time in history, broadcast intercontinentally. Since 1946 almost all clubs have played their games in the evening or at night which not only contributed to increasing their attractiveness

Ten thousand eyes were on him as he rubbed his hands with dirt
Five thousand tongues applauded when he wiped them on his shirt.

Then while the writhing pitcher ground the ball into his hip,
Defiance gleamed in Casey's eye, a sneer curled Casey's lip.
And now the leather-covered sphere came hurling through the air,
And Casey stood a-watching it in haughty grandeur there.
Close by the sturdy batsman the ball unheeded sped –
'That ain't my style', said Casey. 'Strike one', the umpire said.
From the benches, black with people, there went up a muddled roar,
Like the beating of the storm waves on a stern and distant shore.
'Kill him! Kill the umpire!' shouted some one on the stand;
And it's likely they'd have killed him had not Casey raised his hand.

With a smile of Christian charity great Casey's visage shone;
He stilled the rising tumult; he bade the game go on;
he signalled to the pitcher, and once more the spheroid flew;
But Casey still ignored it, and the umpire said, 'Strike two'.
'Fraud!' cried the maddened thousands, and the echo answered 'fraud!'
But one scornful look from Casey and the audience was awed [...].

The sneer is gone from Casey's lip, his teeth are clenched in hate;
he pounds with cruel violence his bat upon the plate.
And now the pitcher holds the ball, and now he lets it go,
And now the air is shattered by the force of Case's blow.

Oh! Somewhere in this favored land the sun is shining bright;
The band is playing somewhere, and somewhere hearts are light.

publicized corruption and game fixing scandals involving the 1919 Chicago White Sox which ended with harsh sentences and expulsion of players. Other movies devoted to baseball include *The Court-Martial of Jackie Robinson* (1990) by L. Peerce – a story of overcoming the race barrier by the main hero, *Bad News Bears* (1976) – a tale of hopeless, lovable little-league underdogs beating the odds, and many more.

E. Allen, *Baseball. Play and strategy*, 1982; *The Baseball Encyclopaedia,* Macmillan (published annually); G.I. Berlage, *Women in Baseball. The Forgotten History,* 1994; R.F. Burk, *Never Just a Game. Players, Owners, and American Baseball,* 1994; L. Koppett, *A Thinking Man's Guide to Baseball,* 1967; H. Turkin & S.C. Thompson, *The Official Encyclopaedia of Baseball,* (over 10 editions) 1970-80; D.Q. Voigt, *Baseball. An Illustrated History,* 1987; R. Whiting, *You Gotta Wa,* 1989, J. Kindall, J. Winkin, eds. *The Baseball Coaching Bible,* 2000; P. McMahon, M. Johnson, J. Leggett, *Baseball: Skills and Drills,* 2001.

BASE-BALL, an old Eng. game popular in Suffolk linked to the Eng. >ROUNDERS, which, in turn, gave rise to >BASEBALL.

BASKET ENDBALL, according to P. Cummings, a game somewhat similar to basketball, the court being divided into 3 zones, and as many as 21 players on a team. Each zone is divided in half, each half being occupied by an equal number of opposing players. Dribbling is forbidden, and players must stay within their assigned zones. The object

A baseball bat and ball.

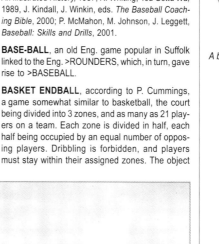

Designer balls.

A baseball game between Princeton and Yale University teams.

but also allowed certain games to be held on working days in addition to weekends. During the initial stage of TV development the broadcasts were dominated by radio commentators who were flexible enough to adapt to the needs of the new medium. One of them was J.H. 'Dizzy' Dean, formerly an outstanding St. Louis Cardinals pitcher and who finally, together with another baseball player – B. Blattner, created the famous CBS show called *Game of the Week.* The most famous Amer. commentator – H. Cosel – who hosted ABC's *The Wide World of Sport,* created by an outstanding reformer of sports television R. Arledge, also began his career as a radio newscaster. According to statistics, 80 million Americans watch the World Series games every year which is the best testimony of the appeal and influence exerted by this sport in America. Baseball has also featured as the central theme of many Amer. literary works. In the 19th cent. the famous poem *Casey at the Bat* (1877) by E. Thayer was made so popular by actor De Wolfe Hopper that it was recited in public some 3,000 times including by the spectators before the start of many games:

The outlook wasn't brilliant for the Mudville nine that day;
The score stood four to two with but one inning more to play.
And then when Cooney died at first, and Barrows did the same,
A sickly silence fell upon the patrons of the game [...].

A straggling few got up to go in deep despair. The rest
Clung to that hope which springs eternal in the human breast;
They thought if only Casey could get a whack at that –
We'd put up even money now with Casey at the bat [...].

Then from five thousand throats and more there rose a lusty yell;
It rambled through the valley, it rattled in the dell;
It knocked upon the mountain and recoiled upon the flat,
For Casey, mighty Casey, was advancing to the bat [...].

And somewhere men are laughing, and somewhere children shout;
But there is no joy in Mudville -mighty Casey has struck out.

One of the best known literary works on baseball is D. Wallop's novel *The Year the Yankees Lost the Pennant* (1954). There are also numerous well-known short stories devoted to baseball including O. Johnson's *The Hummingbird* (1910), J. Thurber's *You Could Look It Up* and many other references to baseball as in J. Updike's *Hub Fans Bid Kid Adieu* (1960). R.W. Henderson's scientific and cultural treatise *The Doubleday-Cooperstown Myth* published as a chapter in a book on the genesis of many ball games *Ball, Bat and Bishop* (1947) proved esp. significant as it refuted certain preconceptions of baseball. There have also been numerous true accounts, memoirs, collections of reportages, biographies and essays such as T. Meany's *Baseball's Greatest Players* (1953), G. Holland's *Baseball and Mr. Rickey* (1955), J. Brosnan's *The Pennant Race Begins* (1962), T. Boswell's *How Life Imitates the World Series* (1982) and many more. Of the players' memoirs the most interesting are T. Williams's *My Turn at Bat* (1969) and also D. Strawberry's *Darryl* written together with journalist A. Rust (1992). Of all the biographies and autobiographies of coaches and managers (earlier players, most frequently) the most interesting are *White Rat. A Life in Baseball* – an autobiography by W. Herzog written together with journalist K. Horrigan (1987) and *Stengel. His Life and Times* by R.W. Creamer (1984). One of the most engrossing autobiographies of a baseball umpire is *The Umpire Strikes Back* (1982) by R. Luciano written together with journalist D. Fisher. True stories were also used to prepare many excellent screenplays as in *Eight Men Out* (1988) directed by J. Sales and based on E. Assinof's book. The movie tells the story of one of the most widely

is to pass the ball to teammates from zone to zone, and thence into the basket. 1pt is awarded for passing the ball to a teammate in the attacking zone, 1 for a sucessful free throw, 2 for a goal from the field. Three periods of equal length are played, and in each the players change zones in rotation so that each player successively occupies all 3 during a game'. The game also bears a striking similarity to >NETBALL and some other Eur. forms of basketball games, such as Dan. >KURVBOLD, Dutch >KORFBALL, and Ger. >KORBBALL. Cf. also >BASKETBALL GAMES.

P. Cummings, 'Basket Endball', CDOS, 1949, 27.

BASKETBALL, an indoor court game, in which 2 competing teams have 5 players at any time during the play. The aim of the game is winning points by throwing the ball into the opponents' basket. The court is 26m long and 14m wide. In the middle of both end lines are backboards on hanging or standing jibs, with baskets 45cm in diameter, mounted in the middle, hanging 3.5m high. The ball is dribbled and thrown. A successful shot within the 3pt. line is worth 2pts., while a basket made from beyond it is worth 3pts.

History. Similar games were known in various countries long before our modern basketball came into being. Inhabitants of C America, esp. the Maya, the Olmecs, and later on also the Aztecs knew several varieties of rubber ball games, in which the aim was to put it through a stone rim mounted vertically (not horizontally like in mod. basketball) at a certain height (>MESOAMERICAN INDIAN BALL GAMES, >POKYAH, >TLACHTLI). The games, described in diaries and geographical treatises, became known in Eur., esp. the Netherlands, and then in Germany. One such description, contained in the work *Wahrhaftigen Abkonterfeyung der Wilden im Amerika,* 1603 (*The real description of the Wild in America*),

Troy Eash of the District 8 Virginia Beach Little League Challengers hits the ball during the first game between teams in the Little League Challenger division for mentally and physically disabled children on the South Lawn of the White House.

Basketball motifs on a stamp issued for the World Games of Salesian Youth in 2001.

B

James Naismith, the inventor of basketball.

BASKETBALL OLYMPIC CHAMPIONS

MEN
1936 United States
1948 United States
1952 United States
1956 United States
1960 United States
1964 United States
1968 United States
1972 Soviet Union
1976 United States
1980 Yugoslavia
1984 United States
1988 Soviet Union
1992 United States
1996 United States
2000 United States
WOMEN
1976 Soviet Union
1980 Soviet Union
1984 United States
1988 United States
1992 Unified Team
1996 United States
2000 United States

spurred the development of similar games in Germany, in several mutually independent forms. Probably it was one of these examples that gave O.H. Kluge, a Ger. teacher, in 1875 the idea of a game in which the ball is thrown into a rim mounted on a post without a backboard. The game, initially called *ballkorb*, was later renamed >KORBBALL [Ger. *Korb* – basket] owing to the elastic basket attached to the rim. A game of a similar name >KORFBALL and meaning the same [Du. korf- basket] was invented in the Netherlands in c.1900 and is nowadays developing independently from basketball. The list of basketball games was completed with Dan. >KURVBOLD, and temporarily in the US – >BASKET ENDBALL (see also >BASKETBALL GAMES). Modern basketball reaches back to 1891, when the teachers' board of the Training School in Springfield, run by the YMCA (now Springfield College, Massachusetts, USA) commissioned J.A. Naismith (1861-1939), a sports teacher, to create an attractive sports game of interest to young people in winter, when outdoor games could not be played. Naismith rose to the board's challenge, mounting 2 fruit baskets on the balconies in the gym and dividing students into 2 teams of 9, who competed in throwing a football ball into the baskets. The baskets had bottoms; this disadvantage and the difficulty of taking the balls out after every score lead to the removal of the bottoms and replacing the wicker walls with string nets, hanging from steel rims (1906). More or less at the same time special backboards behind the baskets appeared, which facilitated hitting the target. The backboards and new baskets drastically changed the initial playing technique. In 1894-96 the YMCA was busy popularizing basketball. In 1896 the sports activities of the YMCA began to be subordinated to the Amateur Athletic Union (AAU). In 1908, the majority of school and university teams, dissatisfied with the membership of the AAU joined the National Collegiate Athletic Association (NCAA). In 1915 both organizations formed the Joint Committee of Basketball Rules, which was the leading body in the development of basketball and its rules until 1932, when the Federation of International Basketball (Fédération International de Basketball Association, FIBA) was created. Basketball was included in the Ol.G. in 1936 for the first time, even though it had been a presentation game in St. Louis at the 1904 Ol.G. Starting from 1936 the Ol.G. have been won by US teams, with the exceptions of 1972

One of the best players in NBA history – Michael Jordan.

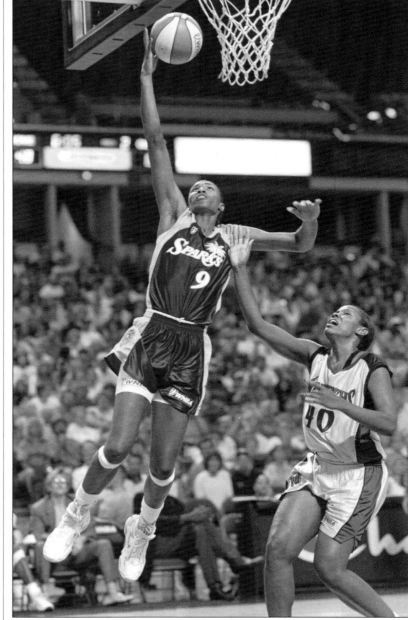

The popularity of women's basketball is on the rise.

and 1988 Ol.G., when Soviet teams won, and 1980, with Yugoslavia winning in the US's absence when they boycotted the Moscow Ol.G. Until 1988 professionals were not allowed to take part in Olympic basketball, a formal ban waived for the first time in 1992 at the Ol.G. in Barcelona, where the Amer. Dream Team was allowed to play on special conditions, incl. a suspension of drug screening.

Professional Basketball began to develop almost parallel to amateur basketball. In 1898 the National Basketball League was created in the US, which encompassed a number of eastern states, but lasted for just 2 years. Also in 1898 the New England League was founded. Since c.1920, professional basketball started to develop ever more dynamically. This led to the crystallization of several strong teams, attracting increasing numbers of fans; 23,000 spectators witnessed the 1922 match between the Original Boston Celtics and a Cleveland team. The Amer. Basketball League (ABL) created in 1925, soon stole the show, and remained at the top until the 1932-33 season. In 1937 another National Basketball League was set up, one having nothing in common with the one founded in 1898. In 1946 the competitive Amer. Basketball Association (ABA) was created. In 1949 the ABA and NBL merged, creating the National Basketball Association. The Harlem Globetrotters were a separate phenomenon in professional basketball. Founded in 1927 by A. Saperstein (1903-66) and consisting of black players only, the team's impeccable playing techniques and showmanship made basketball a spectacle tinged with humor and circus acrobatics. The team's theme music *Sweet Georgia Brown*, resounding before every match, became later on irrevocably associated with basketball. Even before

1939 the Harlem Globetrotters had visited 75 countries, popularizing the game on an international scale. Saperstein's death shook the team's structure, but it continues its mission to this very day.
A. Alaczaczjan, *Nie tol'co o baskietbolie*. 1970: R.J. Antonacci, J. Barr, *Basket-ball*, 1963; S. Goldpaper, *Great Moments in Pro Basketball*, 1977; C. Gommendy, *Le basket-ball*, 1955; M. Hansenne, *Le basket-ball*, 1964; Z. Hollander, ed., *The Modem Encyclopaedia of Basketball*, 1979; T. Huciński, I. Wilejto-Lekner, F. Makurat, *Vademecum koszykówki*, 1996; J.S. Hult & M. Trekel, eds., *A Century of Women's Basketball. From a Frailty to Final Four*, 1991; P. Jackson, *Maverick. More than a Game*, 1975; J. Mikułowski, H. Oszast, *Koszykówka*, 1973; W.G. Mokray, ed., *Encyclopaedia of Basketball*, 1963; Ch. Mullin, B. Coleman. *Młody koszykarz*, 1996; J. Naismith, *Basketball. Its Origin and Development*, 1941; G. Nelson, *E!evating the Game. Black Men and Basketball*, 1992.

BASKETBALL GAMES, a group of ball events, whose common trait is throwing a ball into a basket, usu. mounted upon a jib or a post. The games are thought to have originated with the pre-Columbian C Amer. >TLACHTLI and >POKYAH. Influenced by C Amer. games, a Ger. teacher O.H. Kluge created the basics of >KORBBALL in 1875. Independently, but under the same influence, at least 3 other basketball games were invented: Du. > KORFBALLL, created 1902 by a Du. teacher N. Broekhuysen, Brit. >NETBALL, and Dan. KURVBOLD invented prob. in 1899 but popularized on a wider scale early in the 20th cent. With the exception of Ger. Korbball, the first mod. basketball game, the development of all basketball games was governed by the mechanism of adapting Amer. basketball, which is evinced

WORLD SPORTS ENCYCLOPEDIA

B

Basketball is also a popular street game.

by numerous borrowings and the initial, pioneering rules of play, which, once removed from the main stream of development of Amer. Basketball, became the characteristics of other games. This phenomenon can be observed in other sports disciplines: isolated institutions, esp. schools adapted the newly created game to their particular needs, heedless of fidelity to the original game. This usu. pertained to the initial stages in a given sport, when no organizations forcing standardization of rules were yet present. Thus, when organizations unifying a given sport type were finally set up, the diversification as far as the rules of play and group identity was so advanced that it was not possible to include those varieties in the mainstream development of this sport, in this case basketball. However, a reverse process of basketball upon other varieties can also be observed. Netball gained considerable popularity in the US as 'female basketball'. We do not know to what extent independently or under Eur. influence, in first half of the 20th cent. in the US games competing with the game created by J. Naismith developed, like the Eur. varieties of basketball games mentioned above and brought by immigrants, and also >BASKET ENDBALL, played on a court divided into 6 zones, which the players were not allowed to leave. Games such as >BASKET ENDBALL referred to the main var. of Amer. basketball with the word *basket* or even the whole name >BASKET-BALL. Despite various other words appended to this name, the confusion was great. Until 1970, the Austrl. and N.Zeal. var. of netball were called women's basketball despite glaring differences; they displayed temporary approximations to each other or to the Amer. var. before they were finally made uniform in the 1960s under the influence of Brit. netball, the name of which they accepted and finally gave up the name basketball. Esp. in new environments one game would be taken for another, as was the case with netball being confused with Amer. basketball. In the initial stages of basketball games, when knowledge of particular varieties of the games was not widespread, the representatives of Amer. basketball would visit Amer. and Eur. schools, clubs and other organizations where basketball games were played, hoping to win them over for the mainstream variety, i.e. Amer. basketball. As they demonstrated the rules of play and training - sometimes even managing to succeed - new borrowings from Amer. basketball resulted, without the slightest intention of adopting its rules. Of all these games, the form of basketball created in 1891 by J. Naismith, developed in the US and popularized by Amer. soldiers in Eur. towards the end of WWI and the Young Men's Christian Association (YMCA), gained the most widespread international recognition. All the same, netball is also characterized by steady development; in some countries of the Commonwealth it has gained the status of the most frequently practiced or even national women's game (Austrl. and N.Zeal.). Also Du. >KORFBALL is developing rapidly. Dan. >KURVBALL was the first to disappear in the 1930s, and basket endball followed suit due to the emergence of Amer. basketball. The influence of Ger. >KORBBALL started to diminish after WWII, the game had been kept up in Austrian schools until the 1960s and in East Germany, where it disappeared soon after the unification and

nothing has been heard of it after 1990. In the late 1970s another game which can also be classified as a basketball game was invented, played on horseback, called >HORSEBALL.

BASTE-BALL, one of the many bat-and-ball games popular in the British colonies in America in the 17th and 18th cent. Baste-ball, together with >GOAL-BALL, >CRICKET, >NEW-YORK-BALL, >ONE-OLD-CAT, >ROUND-BALL, >ROUNDERS, >TOWN-BALL and >TWO-OLD-CAT, contributed to the development of the Amer. >BASEBALL.

BAT FOWLING, according to *The Sporting Dictionary* by W. Taplin (1803) it was a 'favourite sport with farmer's servants on a winter's evening ... The party should not consist of less than four; two of whom are provided with long flimsey hazel sticks, or hurdle rods; the third carries and manages the flap (or folding net) and the fourth a candle and lanthorn, suspended to the end of a pole seven or eight feet long. Upon the net being spread, by separating the side rods to their utmost extent, before the cornrick, out-houses, eaves of stable thatch yew hedge, or whatever spot it is intended to try, the candle and lanthorn is then to be held up as nearly the centre of the net as possible, but at about three or four feet distance, just before the assistants begin to beat the rick thatch, or hedge, with their poles; when the birds being thus suddenly alarmed from their resting place, make instantly for the light, when the net being directly closed if by a skillful proctitwier. The success is beyond description; it being not uncommon thing in large remote farms and in severe winters to take twenty or thirty dozens of sparrows and other small birds in one evening's diversion'.
TAPL, 53-4.

BATE, also known as *quinet*, a type of a Fr. game similar to the Pol. >KLIPA and >SZTEKIEL, the Eng. >TIP-CAT, and the Pakistani >GULLI DUN-DA; esp. popular in rural areas. >PILAOUET (Fr. pillouet) and mouilh are its Bret. counterparts.

BAT-FIVES, a ball game wherein a small ball is hit with a bat against a wall of the court by an individual player or by a pair of players alternately. It developed in 19th-cent. England from >FIVES, where the players used their bare hands.

BATHS, facilities designed for bodily cleanliness and relaxation in the form of bathing, showers, massage, physical exercises, etc. Public baths were known in ancient Egypt where they served three basic purposes: ritual ablution for maintaining religious purity, healing with holy water, and providing comfort and pleasure. According to some Eg. hieroglyphic inscriptions decoded in modern times, Eg. priests were obliged to wash their bodies four times a day. Fragments of ancient Eg. baths from c.1350 BC survived in Akhenaton. Baths and swimming pools were also built by the Sumerians in the town of Kish, near the site of ancient Babylon. It was the Sumerians who first used vertical conduits to carry water onto upper floors of buildings. Ablution has been an important part of Jewish culture and religion, often referred to in the Bible. The Jewish tradition of ritual cleansing called the *mikhvah*, established during the exodus of Jews from Egypt, is practiced up to the present day. The laws concerning ritual bathing and

the water of cleansing are discussed in the books of Leviticus and Numbers of the Old Testament. In Biblical times the Jews would anoint their bodies with fragrant oil after bathing. The custom of body oiling was also popular among ancient Greeks and Romans. The first permanent baths were constructed by the Jews during the reigns of David and Solomon. During his reign over Israel, David seduced Bathsheba, wife of Uriah the Hittite, and sinned with her after he had seen her bathing from the roof of his palace. In the Temple of Solomon water was kept in ten voluminous vats, made by Hiram of Tyre. Washing with water is frequently mentioned in the New Testament, so is baptism with water initiated by St. John the Baptist in the Jordan River.
Ritual bathing is also an important element of the Hindu religion. According to Hindu mythology, the goddess Ganga – daughter of the God Himalaya – was brought to Earth by King Bhagiratha in the form of the Ganges River (Hindu *Ganga*) to free the souls of sixty-thousand sons of King Sagara, burnt to ashes by the angry Vishnu. The practice of washing away the ashes is still a Hindu symbol of liberation. According to the Hindu tradition, the bodies of the deceased are to be washed in the Ganges before cremation and then the ashes are cast upon the river. The banks of the Ganges feature some of the oldest bathing facilities in the history of human civilization, built c.3000 BC in Mohenjo-doro. Their central part was a pool 7.3x12.2m. Private houses around that area were later equipped with bathrooms and efficient water-supply systems. Today, ritual baths take place along the entire river, whose banks have special steps called *ghats,* allowing Hindu pilgrims to go down and immerse themselves in the water, at least one time in a lifetime. The most significant immersion holy places are Hardwar and Varanasi. Hardwar in the state of Uttar Pradesh, about 175km north-west of Delhi, is the site of the headworks of the Ganges Canal system. It is famous for the temple of the Goddess Ganga (*Gangadwara*) and a huge bathing ghat featuring the alleged footprint of the God Vishnu on a stone. Annually, the place is visited by about 2mln pilgrims. Every twelve years, Hardwar becomes the site of a great bathing pilgrimage called the *Kumbh-Mela*. In 1998, about ten million pilgrims participated in the ceremony. During the Kumbh-Mela pilgrims must abstain from eating meat and drinking alcohol. The other site of religious bathing – Veranasi (Benares), situated about 640km north-west of Calcutta – is believed to be the site of the first preaching of Buddha and one of India's oldest cities. Veranasi features about 1,500 temples, incl. mosques, which attract crowds of pilgrims every year. Modernized river frontage and special beds and basins fulfill the religious need of the Hindu pilgrims and secure the constant flow of the 'holy water'.
The earliest bathing facilities within Gk. civilization were built in ancient Crete c.2000-1800 BC. The remains of bathing rooms have been found in the palace of Knossos. The Cretans had very efficient water-supply systems and were able to carry water onto the upper floors of buildings. A few stone bathtubs from c.1700-1400 BC survived in Knossos as well. In *The Odyssey*, Odysseus takes a bath while staying in the palace of Circe. During the Persian Wars (499-479 BC) Gk. young men were toughened in gymnasions by showering with cold water. The

River baths in renaissance Paris. A lithograph by Marlet (1771-1847).

B WORLD SPORTS ENCYCLOPEDIA
76

most common form of baths in ancient Greece were >BALANEIA (O.Gk. *balaneion*, Lat. *balaneae* – baths), complex hygienic and exercise facilities were built within private houses, gymnasions, or as separate public buildings, designed for public bathing, relaxation and social and cultural entertainment. Men and women bathed separately. Far more advanced in design and organization than the Gk. facilities, although modeled on them, were the Roman baths called *thermae*. Initially, they were private or gymnasion rooms; in the Hellenic period the thermae were built as public complexes of rooms. Around four thousand baths were estimated to have

Hans Bock the Elder, The Bath at Leuk, *1597, tempera on canvas.*

Sir Lawrence Alma-Tadema, The Baths of Caracalla, *1899, oil on canvas.*

Roman baths at Bath, England.

functioned in Rome by the end of the 4th cent. BC. Thermae were also built in other great cities of the Roman Empire. The most renowned baths were in Stabiae near Pompeii (destroyed by the eruption of Vesuvius in 79 AD) and Agua Sulis in Roman Britannia (present-day Bath). Remains of ancient Roman baths were also discovered around London. A well-preserved bath was discovered at the site of a Roman villa in Chedworth, Gloucestershire. The greatest imperial thermae were constructed after 31 BC and were named after the emperors who founded them: the Baths of Agrippa, the Thermae of Diocletian, the Baths of Domitian, the Baths of Caracalla, the Baths of Constantine, Trajan's Baths, and the Baths of Titus.
Roman thermae functioned as municipal facilities charging entry fees (*vectigalia*), being important sources of income for the city; or as private enterprises charging fees both for admission and services. Roman emperors maintained the social prestige of public baths by awarding the right to free bathing services only to the most respectable citizens, esp. soldiers and politicians. In all periods of their historical development Roman baths consisted of the following parts: dressing room (Gk. *apodyterion*); oiling room (Gk. *alejptérion*, Lat. *unctorium*); cold room (Gk. *psychrolusion*, Lat. *frigidarium*); warm room (Lat. *tepidarium*); and steam room (Gk. *pyriatérion*, Lat. *laconicum* or *sudatio*). This last one was a semi-circular room with a shallow pool with hot bathing water (Lat. *labrum*); it had a round opening in the ceiling used for ventilation. In smaller thermae the tepidarium and laconicum were located in a single room called the caldarium. Roman baths also had club and social rooms, swimming pools, playing courts, libraries, dining halls and wine cellars. They were richly decorated with marble reliefs and mosaics. The tepidarium of the Baths of Caracalla was later reconstructed by Michelangelo as part of the interior design of the church Santa Maria degli Angeli; the Baths of Caracalla served as a design model for the building of the Pennsylvania Station in New York.
The Gk. as well as Roman baths served as important centers of cultural and social life. The Baths of Caracalla housed a theater and were a place of numerous philosophical and literary debates. Their area covered eleven hectares and could accommodate up to 1,600 bathers. The Baths of Diocletian were twice as large and housed an 88.4m-long swimming pool (larger than modern Olympic pools). Like in Gk. *balaneia*, men and women bathed separately. Mixed bathing was practiced in the last centuries of the Roman Empire, although it was severely condemned by Emperor Hadrian, Marcus Aurelius, and Justinian. The sumptuous Roman baths were fed by aqueducts carrying water from nearby reservoirs, incl. Lake Albano, 294m above sea level, around which luxurious bathing resorts were built in ancient times. In later centuries, the papal palace of Castel Gandolfo was built in the area. Many Roman thermae have survived until present times. In parts of the Baths of Caracalla modern opera performances are staged.
The tradition of steam baths, according to the Gk. historian Herodotus, is derived from the Scythians – an ancient people inhabiting the territory of present-day Ukraine. The Scythian bath was a tent pitched over a large cauldron containing heated stones, on which the bathers threw water and hempseed to create an intoxicating steam. According to modern historians, the Scythian bath gave rise to contemporary Russian baths and Finnish sauna.
Baths were known also in the Middle Ages, often as places of social prestige, similar to those of ancient Rome. Roman-like baths were common in Gaul of the Merovingian and Carolingian age. Charlemagne used to enjoy bathing in special facilities built around a Roman spa near his residence in Aquisgranum. Roman steam bath systems were enormously popular in Byzantium and were later incorporated into the Turkish baths. In the east and north-east of Europe bathing facilities were based on the ethnic traditions of ancient Avars and Slavs, who arrived in the period of great peoples' migrations from the 7th to 10th cent. Slav baths impressed the Arabian traveler and merchant Al Bekri, who visited the territory of present-day Poland:

They build a wooden bathing house and seal it with tree resin [...]. A fire is kindled in one corner of the house. In the ceiling there is a hole for smoke to escape freely. Once the fire is burning the bathers close the windows and doors very tight. They have special water vessels and pour water on the fire to make steam. They are also holding dried twigs and wave them in the air to direct steam. Sweating heavily, the bathers heal themselves so that no sign of spots or abscesses is left on the skin.

In the early Christian ages, the pagan traditions of ancient Rome were often despised and condemned. In particular, bathing naked was frowned upon by the early Church Fathers. Many Roman aqueducts and public baths were destroyed in the course of invasions by Vandals, Huns, and Goths. The medieval ascetic discipline gave birth to traditions of mortification of the flesh, fasting, flagellation, and openly demonstrated disregard for bodily hygiene. In the 11th cent., Adalbert, the Bishop of Hamburg, abstained from washing all his life, among other practiced forms of mortification of the flesh. Despite numerous 'exemplary' decisions of this kind, many people, especially in monasteries and convents, realized the necessity of practicing good hygiene. Queen Etheldreda of East Anglia, as described by Bede the Venerable in his chronicle, decided to practice personal hygiene after she had chosen to live a convent life: 'It is reported of her, that from the time of her entering into the monastery, she never wore any linen but only woolen garments, and would rarely wash in a hot bath, unless just before any of the great festivals, as Easter, Whitsuntide, and the Epiphany, and then she did it last of all, after having, with the assistance of those about her, first washed the other servants of God there present' (*Historia ecclesiastica gentis Anglorum*, IV, 19, trans. L.C. Jane). Medieval towns with narrow streets and houses devoid of basic sanitary facilities, sewage system or water supply were often plague ridden. The largest pandemic of the Black Death ravaged Europe in the 14th cent. Chroniclers estimate that the mortality rate due to the plague reached up to three fourths of the population in some regions. In Florence alone, one hundred thousand people died from the disease, i.e. 2/3 of its population, within three years. Outbreaks of the plague were not associated with lack of sanitary facilities but they were often blamed on witchcraft and the ill intentions of the Jews, which led to increased persecution of the latter. In the Middle Ages baths were found at royal courts, mansions and in some monasteries. The rulers of many countries treated baths as places for official audiences or even government meetings. Bathing with the king equaled placing trust in the invited guest, an award or reprimand. The English Order of the Bath established in 1399 is derived from royal bathing tradition. Similar bathing customs were observed in Poland. The Polish medieval chronicler Gallus Anonymous noted that King Boleslaw the Brave (992-1025) rewarded and reprimanded his knights in a bath:

When those sent for finally arrived [...] they were led to the king's bath. There, King Boleslaw flogged them severely while bathing together, and reminded them of their noble ancestors by saying 'You, you descendants of such noble families, you should not have committed the fault!'

Gallus' imprecise description makes, however, no reference to the kind of baths used by the Polish king. Most likely, the old Polish baths were modeled on some Scandinavian patterns brought to the country thanks to the king's sister, Świętosława, who was the wife of the Viking king Sweyn Forkbeard. Viking bathing consisted of pouring water over the body and flogging it with twigs.
In 1376, Duke Janusz of Mazovia built a sumptuous bath in his castle. The Polish king Wladislaw Jagiello (1351-1434) and Grand Duke of Lithuania Vytautas (1350-1430) took a bath every day except Sundays as it was strictly forbidden by the Church. Duke Svitrigaila appealed to the Pope for dispensation and special permission to take a bath on Sunday as well. Another Polish king, Sigismund the Old (1467-1548) would bathe once a week.
In the 15th cent. the public awareness of health and hygiene increased. In Renaissance Italy new types of baths were constructed on the basis of ancient patterns, featuring public swimming pools, music and consumption of wine. Similar baths, although far more modest appeared in other Eur. countries. With the Renaissance came hydrotherapy. In the 13th cent. a Welsh physician, Rhiwallon of Myddwai, recommended medical therapy using cold water. In Poland, the royal medic and professor of the University of Padua, J. Struś regarded hydrotherapy and hygiene as crucial elements of medicine; a monument erected in his honor in Poznań, Poland features the Greek Goddess Hygiea sitting on a pedestal. In the 16th cent. the city of Krakow had eleven public bathing facilities and numerous private baths owned by the wealthy bourgeoisie. Men and women bathed separately in Poland; mixed bathing was practiced in other western countries; e.g. in Finnish saunas. M. Kromer in his chronicle *O sprawach, dziejach i wszystkich innych potocznościach koronnych polskich* (On the Issues, History and All Other Events in the Polish Kingdom) noted the immense popularity of baths in Poland: 'The Poles care for bodily improvement in summer and winter, visiting baths and thermal spas'. Numerous royal, municipal and private baths were founded in 16th-

Roman baths at Bath, England.

cent. Lvov. Every school student in Lvov could use the public baths three times a week free of charge. In various cities the right to a free bath was given to priests and their assistants who administered last rites. There were special craft guilds of bath workers performing a variety of functions, e.g. floggers and wine bearers. The ownership rights to municipal baths were often the subject of litigation between the craft guilds of barbers and bath workers. Public baths in Poland became so common that hygiene in them was often very difficult to maintain. Ł. Górnicki complained in the 16th cent.: 'When one finds himself in a public bath he will suffer all kinds of inconveniences. Some smear their bodies with vodka and soap, others with medical ointments. Somebody blows up bubbles, another drinks wine [...]'. The most famous Pol. bath was founded by the Wielopolski family in Pińczów and it featured shower stalls, swimming pools, an elaborate water-supply system, etc. It was even described in an anonymous poem:

Suddenly water rains down on you
From the ceiling, the walls, the floor
From all sides and water instruments around
From amazing stone statues.

Contrary to some common beliefs and later Ger. propaganda, portraying Poland as an underdeveloped country – also in the field of public hygiene – Pol. towns and aristocratic residences were among the cleanest in Europe, being far ahead of France, for example. In the 17th cent., according to some historical sources, the hygienic ritual of Fr. kings consisted of wiping the face with a wet towel. Queen Elizabeth I, as well as the Pol. kings Sigismund III Vasa and Wladyslaw IV, would take a bath once a month in a special tin tub. In the Kazanowski Palace a special conduit was installed carrying in cold and hot water separately. By the end of the 17th cent. all Pol. towns had public baths. The bathing tradition began to decline in Poland with the ascension of the House of Saxons to the Polish throne. In the 16th and 17th cent. the city of Poznań had 11-17 public baths, none of which survived the Saxon era. The pioneer of public baths in the United States was B. Franklin. British colonization of India and the necessity of frequent bathing in the tropical climate accounted for the popularity of private baths in many houses in Britain. Due to extensive contacts between Britain, France and Turkey, Turk. baths became popular as well. The first Turk. bath in England was founded by D. Urquhart in London in 1862. In the years to follow, Turk. baths became immensely popular in other western countries, particularly in the USA, where they became a kind of social institution. Bathing scenes in Turk. baths are frequent motifs in English language films and literature. As a result of industrial and urban development and increasing microbiological research, most advanced countries began to conduct preventive measures against the unsanitary conditions of public baths. In 1846, a special act of law regulating the organization of public baths and laundries was passed in Great Britain. Together with the development of modern plumbing and sewage systems as well as waterworks and sanitary engineering, a number of houses and apartments were equipped with private bathrooms. In 1851 a bathroom with a bathtub was installed in the White House in Washington DC. In the first decades of the 20th cent. the private bathroom became a symbol of luxury unavailable to the majority of people. This situation began to change in the 1930s. Today, various kinds of public baths are still in demand, resulting from modern cultural trends, fads and modern ways of bodily maintenance. A revival of Russian and Turk. baths as well as Finnish saunas can be observed in many western countries; numerous municipal recreational centers encompass swimming pools, saunas, fitness and massage clubs. Modern civilization has rediscovered well-known ancient inventions.

G. Ashe, *Tale of a Tub*, 1950; A.T.A & A.M. Learmonth, *Ganges River*, EAI, 1979, 12; C.F. Mullett, *Public Baths and Health in England in 16th-18th Centuries*, 1946; R. Reynolds, *Cleanliness and Godliness*, 1946; G.R. Scott, *The Story of Baths and Bathing*, 1939; H.J. Viherjuuri, *Sauna, the Finnish Bath*, 1960.

BATINTON, adaptation of >BADMINTON with >TABLE TENNIS scoring. It can be played in the singles system or in pairs, both indoors and outdoors. The court size is 10.97x3.66m, though the width can vary from 3.05 to 3.96m. The breadth of side lines is 1.27cm, and the top of the net is at 1.52m above ground. The bat resembles a table tennis bat, but it is longer. Its total length incl. handle is 41cm.

Rules. A game begins with a service from the right-hand corner towards the right-hand corner of the opponent's half. The objective is to hit the shuttle-cock onto the opponent's field before he manages to receive it, or to force him to net the shuttlecock or hit it outside the field, unable to receive it properly. The game ends when one of the players scores 21pts., on condition that the other player scores at least 2pts. less. If the score is 20:20 (20-all), one can only win 22:20, or 23:21, and so on. Each player can service as many times as is needed to score 5pts. by either player, after which the other player starts serving. The players serve in turns from the right- and left-hand sides of their own fields, but each service is directed at the right-hand side of the opponent's field. Only underhand services are allowed, but later during the game the shuttle can be received in any types of shots, as long as it is kept up in the air and within the field. The touchline marks the field area and a point is scored whenever the shuttle hits the ground within this line.

Technique. 3 types of shots are used in batinton: 1) drop shot, performed quickly and steadily, in order to hit the shuttlecock clearly above the net; 2) high-back court drive, performed high in mid-air and difficult for the opponent to receive when he is standing close to the net the idea being to score a point by hitting the shuttle on the back side of the opponent's field when he is near the net; 3) smash, i.e. a rapid shot on the opponent's field at a maximum acute angle.

History. Batinton was invented by the N.Zealand bombing officer P. Hanna, in charge of leisure and entertainment in his unit stationed in Cologne, Germany, at the close of WWI. He was ordered by his superior general to 'organize entertainment, lay on laughter unlimited and rollicking recreation: games galore, games that every man can play.'

Hanna delineated 4 parallel fields within each tennis court available, so as to allow the maximum number of soldiers to play simultaneously. After the war the game began to lose its popularity and significance. At the beginning of WWII the game was reborn in Australia, also due to numerous technical improvements, e.g. the introduction of plastic bats with reinforced plywood (1952), or plastic-skirted rubber-nosed shuttles around 1956, which preceded the same improvement in badminton. In 1962 batinton was displayed in a series of demonstrative matches in London. The game then spread over several countries but waned in competition with the game of badminton after 1970.

BATON TWIRLING, the art of twirling a baton popular in many countries. In the US, baton twirling also involves dance movements and marching formations adopted from the Deep South musical tradition, especially steps and moves performed during the parades of Afr. Amer. jazz bands. Baton twirling, usu. set to dance music, displays agility and grace. As time passed the choreography of baton twirling shows became more and more elaborate so that it developed into a kind of artistic sport. Naturally, the key piece of equipment employed during a show is the baton. Traditionally, it was a wooden rod with a weighted metal bulb at each end. Nowadays, it has been replaced with a light metal pipe with rubber bulbs on its ends. The fact that light metals have been employed in baton design resulted in broadening the range of evolutions to be performed. Numerous baton twirling contests and competitions are held in the US.

History. The origins of baton twirling in the US are not clear. One of the theories says that baton twirling shows were held in Pennsylvania as early as the 18th cent. where they were introduced by Dutch settlers. The most dubious part of this account is that the baton evolutions were allegedly performed with a Swiss flag. Another source claims that baton twirling displays have been held regularly at Millsaps College in Mississippi since after the Amer. Civil War (1861-65).

Initially it was mostly men who were the drum majors. Since the 1930s there were more and more women drum majorettes, and baton twirling gradually became more of an aesthetic show rather than strictly the action of conducting an orchestra. The growing importance of the entertainment aspect of the show, especially given the requirements of TV broadcasts, resulted in the need to introduce further modifications. In response to that the conductors employed additional 'assistants', usu. male but later female ones as well. Initially there was usu. only one female assistant, then two and finally a whole troop of specially trained girls performing various exercises and evolutions. Soon a special type of uniform, combining in a rather eclectic way diverse elements of various military uniforms, was introduced. That is why one often sees a hussar jacket together with a ulan high, four-cornered cap, white ladies' boots and miniskirts, etc.

In the US there are a number of baton twirling associations of which the biggest are the United Stated Twirling Association (USTA) and the National Baton Twirling Association (NBTA). They were both established in the mid-1950s and they both hold annual all-Amer. championships. They also support and assist in organizing locally held shows and competitions. Finally, they cooperate closely towards introducing baton twirling as an Olympic event. Similarly to many other athletes representing various sports, outstanding baton twirling performers are eligible for the Presidential Sports Award sponsored by the Amateur Athletic Union (AAU).

Baton twirling is especially popular among Amer. military and school bands but given their official status they are frequently prohibited from sporting too gaudy uniforms. Baton twirling is esp. common and popular during various sports events. However, after a period when baton twirling enjoyed extreme popularity, there has been a clearly observable decline, perhaps due to limited financial resources available to schools and the fact that students are seeking part-time employment and thus have less time to engage in extracurricular activities.

C. Atwater, *The Fundamentals of an Art and a Skill*, 1964; F.W. Miller, G. Smith and P. Ardman, *The Complete Book of Baton Twirling*, 1980.

BATTLE OF THE BRIDGES, see >GIOCO DEL PONTE.

BATTLE ROYAL, an Amer. type of boxing whereby there is a number of fighters, at least 3, in the ring. They fight for survival; the one who is the last left standing is declared the winner. It is banned in the majority of states, compare >WRESTLE ROYAL. P. Cummings, CDOS, 1949, 30.

BATTLEDORE SHUTTLECOCK, also known as *battledore and shuttlecock,* a simple game of flicking up a weighted tuft of wool, feathers or animal hair with a simple wooden racket called a battledore. In the Brit. colonies where cork-producing trees were widespread the shuttlecock was usu. made of a tuft of feathers stuck into a head of cork, and was also called *shuttlefeather.* The object of the game was to send the shuttlecock up in the air and hit it with the racket as many times as possible.

History. Many historians and ethnographers trace the origins of the game down to an ancient Oriental game which is now called >TEBEG in China, >TEBEG OSHIGLOOKH in Mongolia, >CHEGI CHA-GI in Korea and >ZOŚKA in Poland. The game was brought to Europe in antiquity or in the early Middle

Sir Lawrence Alma-Tadema, The Baths (An Antique Custom), *1876, oil on canvas.*

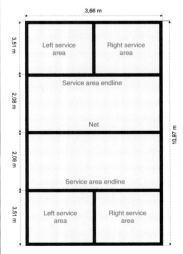

A batinton court.

A Florida State Seminoles baton twirler heats things up on the field at Doake Campbell Stadium in Tallahassee, Florida.

WORLD SPORTS ENCYCLOPEDIA

Ages via various routes including the Middle East and Greece. It has been known in England since at least the 14th cent. One of the keenest battledore shuttlecock players was Prince Henry, the son of James I. In R. Hartley's collection of manuscripts in the British Museum there is a manuscript no. MS 6391 which reads 'His Highness playing at shittle-cocke with one farr taller than himself, and hittyng him by chance with the shittle-cock upon the fore-head' (GOME, II, 1930). The Earl of Northumber-land one of the co-conspirators in the Gunpowder Plot (1605), the conspiracy to blow up the English Parliament and King James I, spent his time in the Tower of London playing battledore shuttlecock. This is confirmed by some receipts for battledore shut-tlecock equipment found among his documents.

The game was also popular among commoners. In West Ridings in Yorkshire the game was played in many villages during local festivals on the 2nd Sunday of May. In Leicester battledore shuttlecock games were always a part of Shrove Tuesday celebrations, also known as Shuttlecock Day. The game was often accompanied by special songs sung while flicking up the shuttlecock. Often it was thought that the number of successful hits equaled the number of years until one's marriage or death:

Shuttlecock, shuttlecock, tell me true,
How many years have I to go through.

Certain fortune-telling elements were also present in the Wakefield and Deptford areas. The number of successful hits was used to foretell the number of years to be spent at school, the number of future children, the name of a future husband or wife, etc.:

How old am I?
How long am I going to live?
How many children shall I have?

Black currant,
Red currant.
Raspberry tart,
Tell me the name
Of my sweetheart.

Similar songs were composed in the streets of Lon-don. They were not always directly connected with play but their rhythm matched that of the game:

One, two, three, four
Mary at the cottage door,
Eating cherries off the plate,
Five, six, seven, eight.

Up the ladder, down the wall,
A twopenny loaf to serve us all;
You buy milk and I'll buy flour,
And we'll have pudding in half an hour.

Probably in the 17th and the 18th centuries battle-dore shuttlecock and its varieties known in other Eur. countries became mixed with two other racket games, i.e. >INDIACA, brought to Europe from the Amer. colonies, and >VOLANT. Some historians of sport claim that >BADMINTON originated from bat-tledore shuttlecock. Such claims are questionable but it is, however, certain that badminton did indeed supersede the majority of all other racket-and-shut-tlecock games.
A.B. Gomme, 'Shuttlefeather', TGESI, 1898, II, 192-6.

BATTLES BETWEEN CITY DISTRICTS. This tra-dition is as old as the history of the division of cit-ies into districts or – as in Christian Europe – par-ishes (cf. >SHROVE TUESDAY FOOTBALL). The tradition of battles between city districts also evolved in the Middle Ages in the large cities of Central Asia, such as Buchara, Samarkand, or Tashkent. A popular form involved fist fighting, head bouncing and kicking between groups of men, women and even children. Another popular vari-ety was a pick-a-back fight, in which one of the partners functioned as a 'horse' and the other – as a 'rider'. At an early stage it was only the 'riders' who carried out the fight, but once the atmosphere got hotter, the 'horses' joined in, as it was discov-ered by an ethnographer O.A. Sucharieva. In the 10th cent. during the muslim holiday of *kurban bajram* a violent form of competition in the Turk-men cities of Central Asia involved fighting for a camel's head between city districts, esp. if the city was separated by a river. A Russian ethnographer S.P. Tolstov derives this tradition from the dualist nature of socio-territorial and ritual divisions, which led to the formation of urban phratries and an in-evitable competition between them.
I. Kabzińska-Stawarz, 'Competition in liminal situations', p. II-III, EP, 1993, XXXVI,1; 1994, XXXVIII, 1-2; O.A. Sucharieva, *Tradicyonniye sopernichestva mezdu chastyami gorodov w Uzbekhistane*, 1958.

BATTLES BETWEEN VILLAGES, events that de-rive from ancient times. In the Celtic tradition a typ-ical example is that of a violent football game called >KNAPPAN. In Russia there used to be a trad. of boxing fights between villages (see >OLD RUS-SIAN BOXING). In Korea, villages separated by a creek or river held stone fights on the 16th day of the New Year. The fighting continued until one of the participants fell dead or injured to the point that he could not get up. A Rus. scholar M.I. Nikitina believes such fights were held in Korea as early as 2000 years ago. She also claims that local rul-ers participated in the fights in an effort to raise the morale of their community for the coming year. In larger rural areas fights were held between par-ticular communities (similar to >BATTLES BE-TWEEN CITY DISTRICTS). An example is the Hin-du people of Naga, who held fights regularly once or twice a year. Among the Mong. peoples there was a long trad. of wrestling bouts between representa-tives of settlements divided according to whether they lived to the east or west of a ritual heap of stones called an *owoo*. See also >STONE FIGHTING.

BAXI, Chin. for 'agile feats'. A type of athletic, ac-robatic and juggling show popular in ancient Chi-na during the Yuan Dynasty (1271-1368). The shows drew upon the ancient tradition of baixi, i.e. 'the feasts of one hundred pleasures'. Baxi shows date back to the twilight period of the Han Dynasty (202 BC- AD 220). Baxi was a very particular kind of agility exhibition involving ropedancers, acrobats and jugglers performing various stunts. Such games had different names depending on the ep-och. For example, during the T'ang Dynasty they were called *zaxi* – lit. one hundred miscellanea – whereas during the Yuan Dynasty (1271-1368) they were referred to as baxi – agile feats, finally dur-ing the reign of the Manchu Ch'ing (1644-1911) they were named *zashua* – various amusements.

History. The oldest mentioning of similar games – referred to as the Chiyou games – dates back to the reign of the so-called Western Han Dynasty (25-220). According to a Chinese chronicler, Sim Qian (135-93), such games were held regularly in Jizhou to commemorate a great Chinese hero known as the Yellow Emperor and his struggle with a bull-headed, 4-eyed and 6-handed dragon named Chiyou. Baxi games featured various displays of physical strength such as hand-to-hand combat, rock lifting as well as ball, furniture and knife juggling called *dulu*, etc. Such displays were accompanied by musical and theatrical performances, especially pantomime shows in which dressed-up actors pre-sented the adventures of the Yellow Emperor and Chiyou the Dragon. Emperor Han Wu Ti (141-87 BC, lit. the Military Ruler) sought to establish contacts with countries west of China. While his diplomats were returning from their foreign travel they were joined by various artists, musicians and acrobats who contributed greatly to enlivening the games that Han Wu Ti held in 108 BC for his subjects and for-eign delegations. The fights and shows were held on an enormous stage surrounded by special box-es for officials and less elaborate stands for the com-moners. According to some preserved accounts the spectators sometimes traveled several hundred ki-lometers to see the games. The games were dubbed 'the feasts of one hundred pleasures' and they or similar events were held until the end of the reign of the Han Dynasty. The games usu. consisted of 3 parts: a parade of wild and exotic animals from the Emperor's gardens, followed by displays of 'mag-nificent illusions' including singing, dancing, visual and sound performances and finally of athletic and acrobatic feats (rock- and weightlifting, hand-to-hand combat, hand walking, pole vault, ropedancing, fire-and knife-eating shows, snake charming, etc.). Sim-ilar festivals were also attended by foreign guests including athletes from the Mediterranean. A Chi-nese chronicler, Fan ye, reported that in 120 a num-ber of artists and athletes from Syria, which was then a part of the Roman Empire, came to one of the games. Some paintings found on the walls of the Yangzishan tomb located near Cheng-du in the Si-chuan province depict scenes from such 'feasts of one hundred pleasures'. Baxi games were often copied or imitated during smaller festivals and feasts which are often referred to in numerous old Chinese texts and must have been the inspiration for many Chinese artists who had been fond of depicting var-ious artistic performances and acrobatic shows for large audiences in their paintings, sculptures, etc. Such scenes are presented in the paintings found in the Yinan and Wuyingshan tombs in the Shan-dong province. The most popular acrobatic feats performed during such games included handstands on wall edges, masts, etc. (>ACROBATICS).
J.-P. Descroches, 'The Human Body and its Metamor-phoses. Acrobatics', YOSICH, 1999, 20-3.

BAYONET FENCING. The target area is the op-ponent's body from the knees upwards, except for the forearms and the back of the head. Touches on the inside of the elbow are valid, whereas those on the kneecap are not. The first fencer to score 3 touches wins. A competitor who during a bout drops his rifle with fixed bayonet, loses a point to his op-ponent. A movement of the bayonet designed to block an attack is called a parry. The attacker can lunge again, if the other competitor does not ri-poste immediately. Simultaneous attacks and ri-postes by both competitors earn them points. If, however, the end result is 2 all, the competitors continue until one of them scores the winning point.
Equipment. The weapon used in bayonet fencing is a rifle or its imitation, shaped like a military rifle; a sports bayonet on a spring is attached to the ri-fle. On its end is a leather knob to prevent injury. The length of the rifle with the bayonet cannot be longer than 136cm, and the min. weight is 2.500g. In training wooden bats are used. The competi-tor's head is protected with a wire mask and the hands with thick gloves. The torso is covered with a plastron (chest protection) with sleeves attached.
History. The oldest form of fighting similar to bayo-net fencing is probably fighting with a knife which resembles the Eur. bayonet attached to a long stick. It is an element of the national Indonesian and Ma-lay sport >PENCAK SILAT. This, however, did not influence the development of military and later com-petitive bayonet fencing in Europe. Competitive bay-

Battledore shuttlecock.

Bayonet fencing.

each (3 court players and a goalkeeper), consists of 2 halves of 10min. each, with a 5-min. half-time break. Each half is scored separately and if both are won by the same team, the score is 2:0. If the score is tied in any of the halves, the winner of the half is decided by a 'golden goal'. If each team wins a half, the 1:1 match score is broken by a 'one player against the goalkeeper' tiebreaker, in which each team nominates 5 players (of the total of 8) who take throws alternatively with the opposing team.

Bazhig kamm, a 16th cent. relief.

onet fencing derives from military fighting using a bayonet attached to the rifle, used to take enemy positions. The bayonet is believed to have been developed in Bayonne, France, about 1640, by M. de Puységur. It was first used in military action in 1647, when troops under the command of de Puységur attacked Ypres. Early bayonets consisted of a spike or dagger equipped with a handle that fitted into the muzzle of a musket. This first type, the plug bayonet, had several drawbacks as a weapon. No shot could be fired until the bayonet was removed; if pushed in too tightly, it was difficult to remove; if not tight enough, it might fall out or remain in the body of an enemy. About 1700 the attachment was modified to fit around the barrel of the musket, allowing the gun to be fired with the bayonet in place. This type of attachment, the socket bayonet, was used by the British, Ger. and Fr. armies. At the beginning of the 19th cent. Napoleon's army used a spring protection to prevent the bayonet from sliding off the barrel. The bayonet was used for military purposes throughout the 19th cent. A particularly great number of soldiers were killed with the bayonet during WWI. During WWII the importance of the bayonet declined as other methods of fighting became more dominant. However, it was not eliminated completely and was used as a supplementary weapon, attached to machine guns. The bayonet is still in use, particularly by the marines. As in the 18th-20th cent. the bayonet was very useful in battle, armies developed different training methods. Fixed or mobile mannequins, on wheels or runners, made of bundles of sticks or cane or straw fixed in a special frame, pierced with bayonets by the soldiers during training, became an everyday feature of the barracks in every army. A popular form of exercise was also fencing with a live partner; in this exercise the bayonet's tip was covered with a bundle of compacted cane or little sticks, braced with metal rings, or with a leather knob. There were attempts to make bayonet fencing a competitive event. A sporting variety of the rifle with the bayonet attached to it on a telescoping device that allowed the bayonet to slide back during the hit, and a leather tip, filled with compacted oakum or rubber to protect against injury, were designed. Around 1952 a rifle with an electronic bayonet was designed; it signaled the accuracy of hits in a manner similar to that employed during fencing competitions. Bayonet fencing has never become a competitive fencing sport. An attempt to make bayonet fencing part of competitive fencing was made by Poland in 1949. However, the International Fencing Federation didn't show much interest in the proposal. Bayonet fencing was practiced in Pol. clubs, particularly military ones, and in the clubs of the Soldiers' Friends' League (Liga Przyjaciół Żołnierza, LPŻ) between 1949 and 1954. At around the same time bayonet fencing was introduced into the program of the Polish Fencing Championships and was part of the education program in the *Służba Polsce* (Service for Poland, SP) organization. In Poland bayonet fencing was popularized by M. Paliga, champion of Poland 1950-53, and A. Przeżdziecki. Fencers using other fencing weapons sporadically tried their hand at bayonet fencing, e.g. H. Nielaba, the 2nd runner up in the Pol. championships. in 1952. The Pol. championships as a separate event were held in 1950, and from 1951 to 1953 jointly with other fencing events. Team championships were organized very sporadically. In 1952 the title was won by a team repre-

senting Silesia (south of Poland), followed by those representing Warsaw and Wrocław. Bayonet fighting never had the same kind of romance attached to it as to other duels with side arms, but was more associated with a lethal attack by an anonymous mass of soldiers. Other factors for its low popularity include the pain inflicted during the competitive fight, felt despite the protection, including a chest protector that was thicker than that used in trad. fencing. The latter reason was frequently given by bayonet fencers who took part in competitions.
A. Brzezicki, ed. *Szermierka na bagnety. Regulamin zawodów*, 1950; K. Laskowski, *Sportowa szermierka na bagnety*, 1951; Z. Czajkowski, 'Bagnet', *Nowa szermierka*, 2nd ed. 1954; 'Bayonet', EAI 1979, vol. 3; Consultant: M. Łuczak, AWF Poznań.

BAZH A BENN, see >VAZH A BENN.

BAZH DODU (DOTU), see >BAZHIG KAMM.

BAZH YOD, see >VAZH YOD.

BAZHIG KAMM, Bret. for 'crooked stick', also *bazh dotu*, a Bret. game of pushing a ball with crooked sticks, belonging to the >JEU DE CROSSE family. At the start of a game, the ball, or rather a hard sphere made of solid wood or round rock or specially prepared bone, is placed in the center of the field. After it has been decided by lots which team is to start the game, each team tries to put the ball in one of the two holes (*poullig*) dug at each end of the field. In the past, one team tried to put the ball in the hole at its own end of the field, whereas the other tried to interfere with their play. In the 20th cent., when the rules of the sport were updated, this principle was changed. At present the attacking team's task is to put the ball in the hole at the end of the defending team's half, which makes bazhig kamm more similar to modern team sports such as >FIELD HOCKEY or >HURLING. Originally, the number of players on each team was not specified. A match would last many hours depending on the players' stamina. The players usu. suffered numerous injuries after being hit with an opponent's stick or by the hard ball.
History. Some researchers claim that bazhig kamm is the oldest Eur. form of soccer. Such claims have been put forward after examining indistinct rock carvings on dolmens, prehistoric ritual structures found in Brittany. The carvings depict people with crooked sticks in their hands. Unfortunately, this hypothesis can be neither fully proved nor invalidated. In *The Life of Saint Barbe* (*Vie de Sainte Barbe*) two shepherds play ball with crooked staffs called *cammel* to make themselves warm. A bas-relief in the portico over the entrance to the Saint Martyrs' Church in Finistere is thought to be the oldest representation of the game.
F. Peru, 'La tradition populaire de jeux de plein air en Bretagne', LJP, 1998.

BEACH HANDBALL, a game which – similar to >BEACH SOCCER and >BEACH VOLLEYBALL – is modelled after its popular and well-established Olympic counterpart, >HANDBALL. It is played with a nonslip, rubber ball approx. 17.5cm in diameter (16.5cm for women) and weighing 360g (290g for women), on a rectangular sandy beach court 27m long and 12m wide, with the layer of sand at least 40cm deep and a free area of at least 3m outside the court. The sidelines and outer goal lines are marked by an elastic marker tape of around 8cm width. The game, played by 2 teams of 4 players

The team that scores more goals after 5 throws wins the match. At the beginning of the tiebreaker action, each of the nominated court players has to stand with one foot on the right or left point where the goal line and the side line cross. When the referee blows the whistle, the player plays the ball back to his goalkeeper. During this pass the ball is not allowed to touch the ground. Once the ball has left the thrower's hand, both goalkeepers may move forwards. The goalkeeper with the ball must remain in the goal area. Within 3sec. he must either take a shot at the opposing goal or pass the ball to his team-mate who is running towards the goal of the opponents, without the ball touching the ground. The latter must receive the ball and try and score a regular goal. Any violation of rules by the attacking players ends the attack. If the defending goalkeeper violates the rules

Beach handball.

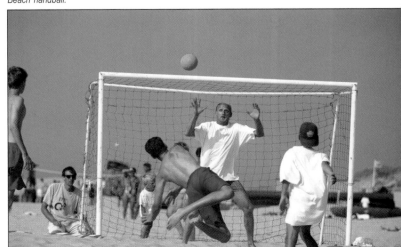

B **WORLD SPORTS ENCYCLOPEDIA**

of defence, a 6m throw is awarded to the attacking team and if they score a goal, they win an extra point. During the regular time, 1pt. is won by scoring a goal, and an additional point is awarded for 1) a goal scored whilst "in flight", 2) a goal scored by the goal-keeper from the playing area, 3) a goal scored by a 6m throw. Each half of the game begins with a ref-eree throw and after a goal is scored the game is restarted with a goalkeeper throw from the goal area. If the ball touches the ground and remains there for more than 3sec., it may not be picked up by the player who last touched it. Running more than three steps with the ball and double dribbling are illegal. All players play barefoot, but the use of socks and bandages is permitted. The game is fast and many goals are usu. scored. The sport is governed by the International Handball Federation (IHF).

BEACH SOCCER, a var. of >ASSOCIATION FOOT-BALL played on sand beaches. It has been a popu-lar recreational game for years, but became a for-mally organized sport in 1993, when the Interna-tional Beach Soccer Federation (IBSA) and Beach Soccer Worldwide came up with the official Laws of the Game. The first professional beach soccer event took place in July 1993 in Miami Beach, Florida, and included teams representing the USA, Brazil, Argen-tina, and Italy. The first Pro Beach Soccer W.Ch. was held in 1995 in Rio de Janeiro, with 8 teams participating (Brazil took the gold medal, the USA – silver, and England – bronze). In 1996-97 the Beach Soccer Company organized a Pro Beach Soccer Tour – a series of 60 games held worldwide with the participation of several top soccer players (Michel, E. Cantona, Romario, Zico, and Junior). In 1998 the Eur. Pro Beach Soccer League was initiated and has been continued until this day.
The playing area. Beach soccer is played on a rect-angular sand court the size of 28x37m, delimited by four lines: 2 sidelines and 2 base lines, with 4 red flag poles marking the corners and 2 additional red flag poles placed in the perimeter zone at 1m from the point of each sideline equidistant from the cor-ners to form an imaginary line dividng the court into 2 equal halves. The lines, belonging to the playing area, are formed by a 10cm wide tape, made of a resistant material in contrasting color with the sand. The court is surrounded by a 2m wide perimeter zone. The penalty areas are defined by 2 imaginary lines, parallel to the baselines, which unify 4 yellow flag poles placed toward the exterior of the perimeter zone at 1m from the point on the sidelines mea-sured at 9m from each corner. The penalty spot is

Ex-Manchester United star Eric Cantona (left) in action during the Kronenbourg Beach Soccer Cup played at Hyde Park, London.

the center of each of these imaginary lines. The goals, placed in the center of the base lines, are 5,50m wide and 2,20m high. The ball measures 68-71cm, weighs 396-440g, and should have a pres-sure of 7lb. It is made of leather or a synthetic material.
Attire. Players uniforms consist of shorts and shirts. Players may also wear socks, light footware, elastic ankle and foot wraps, and plastic goggles for eye protection.
Rules of the game. The game is played by 2 teams of 5 players, of whom one is a goalkeeper and may touch the ball with his hands within the goalkeep-er's area. 3-5 substitute players are allowed and must remain in the designated bench area through-out the game. There are no limits for substitutions. The min. number of players on the court is 3 for each team. If a team remains with less than 3 play-ers due to disciplinary expulsions, it is declared the loser with a result of 10:0 for the winning team. Games are directed by: one 1st referee, one 2nd referee, a timekeeper, and a 3rd official. The dura-tion of the game is 3 periods of 12min. each, with 3min. breaks between periods for changing sides. The winner is the team that: 1) scored the most goals in regular time; 2) scored the 'golden goal' in extra time played for 3min.; 3) scored one more goal in a penalty shoot-out. Various fouls and misbehaviour are punished with a yellow, blue, or red card. The latter two inflict a penalty of exclusion from the game for 2 min., during which time the given team plays without a replacement. Other rules are similar to reg-ular football, except that restarting the game after the ball had left the court within the sidelines may be done with the hands and feet.
The Internet http://www.beachsoccer.com/index2. asp?main=rules.htm

BEACH VOLLEYBALL, a var. of >VOLLEYBALL, with only 2 players on each side, played on a sandy court, typical of beaches (hence the name), and with a different scoring system. As in classical volleyball the object is to send the ball repeatedly over the net to ground it on the opponent's court, and to prevent the ball from being grounded on its own court. If the ball drops on the court of the serving team, the op-ponents score a point or take over the service. A point can be scored only by the serving team (ex-cept for the third decisive set, when the score is tied to 1 all; see below). If a service is won by the op-posing team, they win the right to serve and if their return is not saved they score a point. The ball is put into play by a player who serves the ball by hit-ting it over the net to the opponent's court. The serv-ing player is changed after each service. A team is allowed to hit the ball three times but a player is not allowed to hit the ball twice consecutively. A beach volleyball match is played in 2 so-called formats. Format A means a single set match, in which the first team to score 15 points with a 2-point advan-tage (i.e. min. 15:13) wins. If the match is tied 14 all, the game is continued until one team gains a 2 point advantage (e.g. 16:14 or 17:15). The 17th point is a border point, which means that if the match is tied 16 all, the first team to score 17 points wins. In for-mat B there are 3 sets and the winner is the first team to win 2 sets. In the first two sets 12 points are needed to win the set (with a 2 point advantage, e.g. 12:10); in case of a tie 11 all, the game is con-

A beach soccer court at Hyde Park, London.

tinued until one team scores a 2 point advantage (e.g. 13:11, 14:12 or 15:13). 15 points is the border, i.e. a 14 all tie is broken by the first team to score the 15th point. In the third decisive set, if each team has earlier won one set each and the third set de-cides the winner, a win with a 2-point advantage is needed (there is no border point, which means that the final score can be 18:16, 25:23 etc.). Further-more, the third set is played according to tie-break rules, i.e. points are scored after each service irre-spective of whether it is won by the serving or re-turning team. Before the game the side and the right to play are decided by lots. The team winning the toss can choose between the side or the right to play. If any player leaves the pitch during the game, a walkover is called. No substitutions are allowed during the game. In the course of the game players can take any position on the court.
The court is a 18m x 9m rectangle. The proper court is surrounded by a free zone of min. 3m in width and min. 7m in height. In international matches the free zone is larger, i.e. 5 and 12.5m. The court is marked with ropes or bands of a contrasting color (dark blue is recommended). The sand surface must be even and free from pebbles and shells, which could lead to injury. In international matches the sand layer must be min. 30cm thick. Side lines must be 5-8cm wide. There is no central line under the net. The serving spot is behind the end line and is limit-ed by an extension of the side line (i.e. the serving player can move back between the extensions of the side lines and is restricted only the free space available there; serving from on top of any object is not allowed). During night international matches il-lumination must be min. 1,000-1,500 lux. The net is 1m wide and 9.5m long and is hung above the cen-tral axis of the court. The mesh must be 10cm square. In men's matches the net is hung at a height of 2.43m and in women's matches – 2.15m. The edges are made of 5-8cm wide dark blue or bright bands. Under the top band there is a line, which is used to tighten the net when it is tied to the posts. The posts must be round and smooth, 2.55m high, and 0.5-1.0m from the side line. At the height of the side lines 5-8cm wide dark blue bands are sewed on the net. Their surface is considered an integral part of the net. The side bands above the net are extended by the so-called antennas, which restrict the ball on the sides. The antennas are flexible rods, 1.8m long and 10mm in diameter. Up to the height of 1m they are fixed along the side bands and ex-tend over the net by 80cm. The top part of the an-tenna is painted in stripes of 10cm wide, with con-trasting colors. Black and white are recommended.
The ball is round, with a circumference of 65-67cm, and weighing 260-280g. The top layer is made of soft leather, yellow, orange or pink, and protected against water absorption. Inside the leather surface there is an inflated tube. The pressure inside the ball must be 171-221 bar (0.175-0.225 kg/cm^2).
Team and clothes. The team consists of 2 players, of which one acts as captain. The players wear shorts or swimming trunks. They either don't wear any shirts or wear tank tops, with numbers '1' or '2'. In games played without the shirts the numbers are fixed to the shorts or trunks. The game is played barefoot, unless the referee decides otherwise.
History. First matches on a beach rather than on

an indoor court were played in the 1820s. This was in Santa Monica in California. Over a short time the sport became very popular as a family game with families of 6 players competing. Beach volleyball became a flag discipline of nudists in 1927 when it was played in Francoville, a nudist camp near Paris. The game in which two players competed against two opponents was first played in the 1930s. In the 1950s its popularity was at a peak. In 1965 the California Beach Volleyball Association (CBVA) was founded. In 1983 another organization was founded – the Association of Volleyball Professionals (AVP), which defends the players' rights and sees to the integrity of beach volleyball. In 1986 women established their own federation: the Women's Professional Volleyball Association. The year 1993 was a turning point for players and fans of the discipline – beach volleyball was included in the program of

caught. The game is played over a certain area (usu. a town square) or in a number of streets of a given city. When the opposing team players think they are at a safe distance from the chasers they shout, 'Relievo!'. That is when the pursuit begins. A player who is caught is brought to the den. He can escape from the den when the tenter, after getting carried away, puts both feet inside or outside of the den. A prisoner may be also freed if a member of his team runs through the den without being caught.
A.B. Gomme, 'Bedlams or Relievo', TGESI, 1894, I, 25.

BEDSTEMOR OVER TAGET, see >ANTONIUS.

BEER KEG CARRY, see >DŹWIGANIE BECZEK.

BEGGAR RACES, held in Estonia on St. Martin's Day (10 Nov.) for male and on St. Catherine's Day (25 Nov.) for female beggars. The competitors wore

throwing bones at one of the guests but he returned them with such force that one of the bones turned the head of one of the giants so that it was facing the wrong way. The anonymous *Anglo-Saxon Chronicle* reports that when the Danes began their sack of England in 1012 they seized Aelfheah, the Archbishop of Canterbury. He was held for several months without ransom, which he refused to pay with money that the poor would have had to supply as taxes. Aelfheah was then 'pelted with ox bones and heads' remaining from the Viking feast held in the Cathedral. Aelfheah braved these insults until one of the Vikings aggravated by the Archbishop's tenacity instead of a bone 'threw an ax at him hitting his skull so that he immediately fell and his pious blood spilt on the ground and his soul started its journey to Lord's Kingdom'.
J. Møller, 'Benkast', GID, 1997, 1, 134.

WORLD SPORTS ENCYCLOPEDIA

B

Brazil's Sandra Pires (center), leaps in the air to spike the ball against Portugal's Maria Jose Schuller, left, as her partner Adriana Samuel (right) looks on during the Olympics women's beach volleyball quarterfinals in Sydney.

the 1996 Olympic games in Atlanta. The men's game was won by Americans K. Kiraly and K. Steffes, the women's game by J. Silva and S. Pires from Brazil. In 2000 at the Olympic Games in Sydney the men's match was won by D. Blanton and E. Fonoimoana from the United States and the women's match by Australians N. Cook and K.A. Pottlarst.
The Internet: www.bvbinfo.com and www.volleyball.org; www.fivb.ch/EN/BeachVolleyball/Rules/rules.htm

BEARBAITING, see >ANIMAL BAITING; see also >BLOOD SPORTS.

BEDLAMS, lit. 'a scene or state of wild uproar or confusion'. A name of an Eng. running street game involving the catching of players from one team by the players of the other. The name of the game comes from a London dialectal word for wild uproar or commotion. *Bedlam* stands in fact for Bethlehem and was also a familiar name for the Hospital of St. Mary of Bethlehem in London, a lunatic asylum from where such wild uproar was often heard. It was also called *relievo* [from Eng. *relieve*]. In some varieties of the game the word *relievo* was replaced with some other word – e.g. *delievo* [from Eng. *deliver*].
A game of bedlams is played by 2 teams of 2-5 players. A square whose side is 4-6 steps called a *den* is drawn on the ground, usu. with chalk, at one end of a bedlams field. The first of the teams stands at the front line of the den and is led by a *tenter*. The tenter guards the den and keeps at least one of his feet inside of the den at all times. The task of his team is to catch one of the opposing team's players and to put him in the den. The players run away and try to avoid being

masks and sheepskin coats turned inside out. After the race the competitors were invited to homes where they were offered food.

BELLIE-MANTIE, a Scot. var. of >BLIND MAN'S BUFF.

BELLY-BLIND, a Scot. var. of >BLIND MAN'S BUFF.

BEND-LEATHER, a term for skating or sliding on ice so thin that it almost gives way under a skater's or slider's weight. Boys, to demonstrate their courage, skated or slid on 'bend-leather' ice crying, 'Bend-leather, bend-leather, puff, puff, puff!'
TGESI, I, 28.

BENIN WRESTLING, an old and extinct wrestling variety that was popular in the African state of Benin. The main prize was a woman whom the winner later married.

BENKAST, Dan. for 'a bone throw' [Dan. *ben* – bone + *kast* – throw], an old game played by the Vikings. During a game a person who misbehaved 3 times during a feast was seated on the farthest chair from the *sjoekonga* – the king of the fleet – and became a target for the remaining participants of the feast who threw bones at him. If he was good at dodging the bones he could return to his original seat. One of the first mentionings of benkast appears in the Lat. chronicle by S. Aggesen *Historia Regum Danicae compendiosa* (*Short History of the Danish Kings*, 1185). A Dan. chronicler S. Grammaticus wrote in *Gesta Danorum* (*Story of the Danes*, 1185-1222) that during a mythical wedding two giants started

BERBER, an Arab var. of a hopping game known as >KLASY played by individual competitors on a soft, stoneless field so as to prevent foot scratching or injury. The number of players is unlimited but usu. there are 2-7 of them. First, the participants determine by lot the order in which they are going to compete. Then, they delimit the field composed of rectangular, 2x1m boxes. Each box has a unique name: a *hadi* (first), a *tani* (second), a *bajt an-nar* (house of fire). In the Qsim area the house of fire is called a *umm al-qabis*. The remaining fields are called a *bajt ar-raha* (house of rest) or *an-nasam* (breath of air, i.e. a place where one may cool down) or *al-mulajjina* (place of soothing) and a *berber* or *berber 'agam* (Persian for 'hiding place'). Sometimes the 4th and 5th boxes are bigger. The 3rd box is usu. full of lines drawn on the ground for it is the 'house of fire', i.e. a place where the player may neither rest nor put a stone used in the game. The stone is cylindrical in shape, it is polished and some 7cm-long and 2cm in diameter. Sometimes the stone is made of burnt clay. In the past it was also made of wood. In any case, the stone has to be smooth, light and must roll easily when kicked.
The game is started by placing the stone in the first box about 1m away from the starting line. Then, a player jumps to hit the stone with one foot while holding the other up. If the stone lands on a line or the player touches a line or lowers the raised foot to the ground he is eliminated. Then, someone says, 'Majjit.' (dead) and the next player takes his turn. When a player has completed the first box, he returns to the starting line hopping on one leg. How-

Beach volleyball

B
WORLD SPORTS ENCYCLOPEDIA

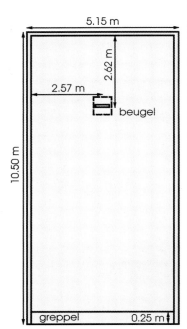

From the Middle Ages to teenagers – beugelen.

Beugelen lane.

(diagram labels: 5.15 m, 2.62 m, 2.57 m, beugel, 10.50 m, greppel, 0.25 m)

ever, first he sends the stone there pushing it with the foot. While in the first box, the player picks the stone up and throws it into the middle of the second box, then hops from the starting line and into the 1st box and finally from the first box into the 2nd. While in the 2nd box, he tries to kick the stone so that it passes the 3rd box and lands in the 4th. Next, the player jumps on one leg over the house of fire where he cannot stop as it is 'on fire'. This means that from the 2nd box he has to jump into the 4th one – the house of rest. Here, he can rest by standing on both legs or even sit down. Then, the player should send the stone back into the 1st rectangle with one kick. After resting some more, he should once again jump over the 3rd box, i.e. the house of fire, and stop in the 2nd box on standing one leg and subsequently hop into the first box. From here, he should kick the stone with one foot and send it into the 5th box, then jump from the 1st box into the 2nd, then into the 4th, have some rest there, and finally jump into the 5th box, where the stone should be. After making the final jump he should land in such as way as to touch the stone. After that the stone should be hit out of bounds (across the starting line) and the player should return to the 1st box (of course, following the pattern described above). Upon reaching the 1st box, he must make one, final jump to reach and touch the stone. Once a player succeeds in doing so, he has completed the 1st round and scored 1pt. While jumping the player must not touch any of the lines with his foot, the stone must not land on any line or in the house of fire, one must not stop in the house of fire under any circumstances, one foot has to be up at all times except in the house of rest where it may touch the ground, the stone must not be lifted with the toes but must be flicked up with one kick and only then may a competitor start hopping. Moreover, the last time the stone is kicked it must not be sent in the direction opposite of the starting line.

The rules of the game do not require a competitor to hop on the same leg all the time, he may switch legs. It is, however, vital that one foot remains raised at all times. The legs may be changed only when making a turn at the starting line before a new stage in one round or at the house or rest. When within a given box, the player may move on the right or left hand side of the box to keep his balance. Meccans play berber both during the day and at night. During the day they play it in the afternoons and at night at half-moon.

M. Ibrahim al-Majman, *Min al'abina ash-sha 'biyya* (*Our folk games*), 1983, 13-5.

BERET TOSSING, an unusual sport begun in 1996 by the Krotoszyn Culture Center in Krotoszyn, Poland, when World Beret Tossing Championships

Adrien Pietersz van de Venne, Summer Landscape With A Ball Game (Beugelen), c.1617.

best ten participants go on to the final round, where they have three attempts each. Each throw in which the contestant has not stepped over the throwing line, and the beret has landed between the lines demarcating the landing sector is valid. The distance from the throwing line to the *antenka* in middle of the beret, measured along a straight line, is deemed the final, official result. The income from the entrance fees (which were set in 1999 to 10 Polish zloties per contestant) is divided in two, of which one half goes to the winner, and the other – to the local animal shelter. The record distance thrown by the first winner of 1996, A. Pieńkowski – 28.16m – was entered in *The Guinness Book of Records*. So far, the following throwers have been world masters: 1996 – A. Pieńkowski – 28.16m; 1997 – P. Bukowski – 23.43m; 1998 – A. Kuszczyński – 33.23m; 1999 – Ł. Piewa – 27.57m, 2000 – E. Szczur – 40.98m (current world record), 2002 – M. Cierniewski – 27.53m *Oficjalny regulamin Mistrzostw Świata w Rzucie Beretem*, 1999; Consultant: L. Ziętkiewicz, Director of the Krotoszyn Culture Center.

BESTIARIA, also used as a plural noun – *bestia*, fights of humans against wild animals held in circuses, especially in ancient Rome [Lat. *bestia* – a wild animal]. Bestiaria have been classified mistakenly as gladiator-type feats despite the fact that the competitors were called *bestiarii* [Lat. sing. – *bestiarius*] and they constituted a separate class with a separate social hierarchy. There were 2 *bestiarii* categories among the fighters: convicts who fought lions and tigers with their bare hands were called the *trinqui*, and *bestiarii* proper, i.e. slaves

wheeled combat or travel cart] or by archers – the *sagittarii*, sing. *sagittarius* [Lat. *sagitta* – arrow]. M. Grant, *Gladiators*, 1967.

BEUGELEN, older names – *boghelen, bogelslaen*; a Flem. folk sport whose Fr. counterpart is called a *jeu de passé*; its Eng. equivalent being >CLOSH. It is currently popular in the border region where Belgium, the Netherlands and Germany meet and especially in the Belgian Limbourg and Du. Limburg as well as the Ger. Grefrath and Mönchengladbach. **Fundamentals.** A beugelen team consists of 2-4 players. Each team has balls in a different color so as to easily differentiate among them. A game of beugelen is played on a flat, rectangular lane which is 10.5m long and 5.15m wide and usu. surrounded with a wooden board or fence. The surface of the lane is made from a special clay mortar that is 10cm thick and is covered with a layer of finely sifted sand. It is important to keep the lane moist at all times so as to prevent a dry lane from facilitating the movement of balls used in the game. At one end of the lane there is the so-called starting groove (*grep*) running across the full width of the field. A ring of 28cm in diameter is put in the middle of the lane some 2.5m from the end line with the bottom part of the rim pressed tightly against the ground. Balls used in the game are usu. 15-18cm in diameter and weigh 4-4.5kg. In the past they were made of ironwood, while today they are made of polyester. The balls are not hurled by hand, but with a wooden, wedge-shaped pallet which resembles a dibble. The task of a player is to put his own ball through the ring to score a point. A player may also score a point by hitting an opponent's ball in such a way that it passes through the ring. When a ball passes the *grep* line coming from the direction opposite to the play direction a given team loses a point. The game is played until one of the teams scores 30pts.

History. Beugelen was developed in the Middle Ages. The oldest mentioning of the game dates back to the 14th cent. At that time beugelen was widespread throughout Europe. It has been known in Bruges, Belgium since c.1461. First reports of beugelen being played in major Flem. and Du. towns date back to 1508 (Amsterdam), 1533 (Turnhout), 1562 (Nijmegen), 1550 (Venlo), 1569 (Nieuwpoort), 1598 (Mechelen), 1624 (Ghent) and 1659 (Roermond). Outside of Flanders and the Netherlands beugelen was also known in Germany and Switzerland, esp. in Basel (since 1438) and in Coburg (since 1616). It was also popular at different times and in different areas of Italy, Spain and Portugal, and even in Great Britain, although it was much less popular there than in the area of its origin. Its Ital. var., called >PALLAPORTA, still existed in 1967 on the Eolie Is. near Sicily and its Port. form, named >JOGO DO ARCO, was still practiced in 1979. One of the most famous beugelen enthusiasts was Desiderius Erasmus (1469-1536) who included a rather detailed description of the game in his *Dialogii familiares*. P. Breughel (c.1520/30-1569) and many other Du. painters sometimes painted games of beugelen. Since the turn of the 16th cent. beugelen had been an event at folk markets, feasts and religious holidays. Various Du. sources, including poetry, contain numerous descriptions of the game of varying quality and degree of detail. One of the most fa-

Bestiaria on a Roman mosaic.

A beret tosser attempting to beat the 40.98m official world record.

accompanied the local Folk-Fest events. As the official rules of the tournament state, 'any person may take part, irrespective of their age, gender and outlook on life, the only prerequisite being a sense of humor. The competition is held without divisions into categories, age groups etc. A black men's beret is used whose edge is reinforced on the inside with a length of wire to ensure rigidity during flight. In the middle of the top surface of the beret, the trad. *antenka* [short rigid tassel] must be added'. Each player is allowed two throws in the qualifying round. The

or sometimes free people were those equipped with various weapons. During the period when Christians were persecuted in the Roman Empire the *trinqui* were often followers of Jesus Christ. One of the largest shows at which Christians were eaten alive by wild animals was held by Caesar Marcus Aurelius (121-180 AD), the author of the 177th edict in which he denounced Christianity as a religion threatening the interests of the Roman state. Wild animals were also confronted by the *essedarri* on chariots [Lat. *essedum* – a Celtic 2-

mous accounts of the game is included in an anthology entitled *Minneplicht ende Kusheits-kamp, als mede Verscheyden Aardighe en Geestige Nieuwe Liedekens en Sonnetten. Kinderwerck, ofte Sinnebeelden van de soelen der kinderen* (published in Amsterdam in 1626). There is also a 1657 description of the game included in a Lat. textbook *Dialogii familiares litterarum tironibus in pietatis, scholae, ludorum exertationibus utiles* by A. Van Toren. After a period of extreme popularity from the 16th until the 19th cent. the game had become almost extinct by the end of the first half of the 20th cent. It died out in Flanders soon after the end of WWII. By the end of the 1970s the only areas where it was still played were the Belgian Limbourg and Dutch Limburg. The Dutch Beugelen Association (Nederlandse Beugelbond) was established in 1933. A similar Belgian Beugelen Association (Belgische Beugelbond) was estab. in 1985. In Germany there are 2 beugelen clubs in Grefrath and Mönchengladbach. Recently the game has been revived in line with the general policy of cultivating old regional traditions. There are some 200 active beugelen players in Flanders and Holland, according to the Nederlandse Beugelbond, the total number of players is 1,050 with some 600 playing the game regularly. See also >TAFELBEUGELEN.

H. Smeets, *Beugelen: een geliefd spel in vroeger tijden*, 'Jaarboek Heemkundige Vereniging Maas- en Swalmdal', 1987, 7; E. De Vroede, *Het eeuwenoude beugelspel*, NVVC, 1989, 9; E. De Vroede, *Het grote Volkssporten Boek*, 1996; E. De Vroede, 'Ball and Bowl Games in the Low Countries: Past and Present', *Homo Ludens – Der Spielende Mensch*, 1996, vol. VI.

BEUGHELBAL, a Du. var. of >BOWLING dating back to at least the 15th cent. and played indoors or on ice. The object of the game is to put a ball through a vertically placed ring whose lower part is driven into the ground or ice. Thus, the ring positioned in this way resembles a stirrup [hence the name – old Du. *beughel* – stirrup + *bal* – ball, sphere]. The ball is hit with a bat similar to a battledore or a small oar. At present the game is only played locally and in 1970 the Nederlandse Beugelbalbond based in Roermond had a membership of around 250.

BHRAMANSHRAM, an old Ind. type of race walking described by Someshwar in *Manas Olhas* (1135 AD) together with weightlifting (>BHRASHRAM) and wrestling (>MALL-STAMBHA) events.

BHRASHRAM, an old Ind. type of weightlifting described by Someshwar in *Manas Olhas* (1135 A.D.) together with race walking (>BHRAMANSHRAM) and wrestling (>MALL-STAMBHA) events.

BIATHLON, [Gk. *bi* – double + *athlon* – competition, contest], a name used to describe sports combining 2 skills, most frequently cross country skiing or cross country running (in summer) with shooting – usu. involving a rifle but also a bow (>SUMMER BIATHLON; >WINTER BIATHLON; >ARCATHLON; >SKI-ARCHERY).

BICYCLE STUNT RIDING, also *freestyle bicycle stunts*, a sport performed on modified BMX bicycles, originated by a bicycle producer Hoffman Bikes from Oklahoma (USA). Its main idea is to execute a number of acrobatic evolutions while riding a bicycle on

Ryan Nyquist rides his bike on a ramp in the Bicycle Stunt Park during the X-Games at First Union Square in Philadelphia, Pennsylvania.

a track resembling a rollerskating half-pipe, though much bigger. The riders move towards the upper edge, gain momentum and perform various evolutions. The bikes have a special construction which makes it possible to use them inside the half-pipe, which is transported to the event's location on trucks. The most common evolutions include:

– *double peg grind* (a *50/50 grind*) – both pegs grind across the edge of the pipe
– *back flip* – a flip to the back while flying above the edge of the half-pipe
– *fakie bar spin* – turning the handle bar around the axis while in the air
– *fakie grind* – similar to peg grind but done backwards
– *feeble peg grind* – one peg grinds across the edge
– *lean air* – the bike and the body remain horizontal while flying over the edge
– *nac nac* – one leg is thrust forward above the handle bar while flying over the edge
– *540 degree turn* while flying over the edge of the half-pipe
– *900 degree turn* while flying over the edge of the half-pipe
– *stool on the back peg* – the rider stands on the edge of the back peg near the wheel's axis on the edge of the half-pipe
– *stunt on the back peg* – evolutions performed on the the half-pipe edge while standing on the back peg
– *superman air* – the rider spreads his legs and separates the body from the bicycle except for the hands, which hold the handle bar
– *tail whip* – a 360 degree turn while all parts of the body are off the bike except the hands which hold the handle bar
When performing the stunts riders wear helmets and other protective clothing.

History. The sport is a var. of cycling practiced on BMX bicycles (cf. >CROSS BMX, >BMX RACING). It was invented and codified by M. Hoffman (nicknamed Condor), who worked out the style of acrobatic evolutions executed in a half-pipe, which he modelled after a similar skateboarding event and adjusted to the requirements of cycling. Having suffered injuries in a dangerous accident, he began producing freestyle stunt bicycles. In 1955 Hoffman Bikes exported 7,000 bikes to more than 40 countries. The evaluation of the riders depends on the quality of the stunt (*point scoring tricks*). Bicycle stunt riding events include: Vert, Street/Stunt Park, Dirt, Flatland, Downhill.

BIDDY BASKETBALL, an Amer. var. of children's basketball, see >MINI BASKETBALL.

BIDDY-BASE, one of the names of >PRISONER'S BASE used in Lincolnshire, England.

BIDE TIL BOLLE, Dan. for 'to bite a bun' [Dan. *bid* – bite + *till* – by + *bolle* – bun, roll]. A game whereby two players have to eat buns hung on a piece of string. To make it more difficult for them they must not use their hands and the strings are held by two other players who try to jerk the bun up so that the other player cannot bite into it.

J. Møller, 'Bide til bolle', GID, 1997, 4.

BIEG ROZSTAWNY, 1) an alternative Pol. name for >RELAYS, 2) an old Pol. game which aimed at 'imitating our forefathers' favorite method of sending

messages using dispatch riders who changed horses at special stations along the route.' E. Piasecki differentiated between 2 major forms of *bieg rozstawny* depending on the place where it was held: a) Its proper, original form requires a vast open space and takes place on a (remote but passable) highway. If there are to be two teams of 10 competing over a distance of 1km, the whites shall be positioned on the left and the reds on the right side of

A bicycle stunt rider goes into orbit at the Planet X Summer Xtreme Games in Melbourne, Australia.

the road. The first two competitors of each team stand at the starting line and the remaining players are positioned at 100m intervals along the road so that the last ones stand 100m away from the finish line. Both first runners receive a 'message' (a letter in a cardboard tube, a band or a flag) and start running to pass it to the 2nd member of their respective teams. The 2nd runner passes it to the 3rd and so on. The team whose message reaches the finish line first is declared the winner.
b) The game may be played in a school sports field. The 'whites' and 'reds' stand along the longer sides of the field (e.g. the whites on the left and the reds on the right side). Members of each team stand facing each other at specified intervals. On a signal runners no. 1 (white and red alike) start running towards their respective runners no. 2 and pass white and red bands or flags to them. Then, runners no. 2 start running towards runners no. 3, they then run towards runners no. 4 and so on. The team who manages to reach the finish line is declared the winner. (E. Piasecki, 'Bieg rozstawny', in: *Zabawy i gry ruchowe dzieci i młodzieży*, 1916).

BIEGANIE DO METY, Pol. for 'running to the finish line', an old Pol. running game constituting a part of an international family of running games known as >PLINIE.

BIERKI, an old peasants' game of agility especially popular in the Polish countryside. It has been described as follows: 'out of bark cut into thin pieces they make various figures they call the King, Steward, Master, Village Head, farmer, farmhand, etc. Each of the figures has a specific value and a number of boys standing close together put these figures on the backs of their hands and toss them up in the air and then catch them with the palms and the one who catches the most valuable figure wins'. Ł. Gołębiowski, *Gry i zabawy różnych stanów* (*Games and pastimes of various social classes*), 1831, 64-5.

BIGE, a Hung. var. of a game similar to the Pol. >SZTEKIEL or the Eng. >TIP-CAT and some other related games. It had different names such as, for example, *pilincka* or *dólé* in different parts of Hungary. A game of bige involved flicking up a short, pointed stick and hitting it with a longer stick to send it flying as far as possible. While the short stick was in the air the hitter tried to reach a specific destination to score a point.

W. Endrei & L. Zolnay, *Fun Games in Old Europe*, 1986.

BIGGLY, see >BLIND MAN'S BUFF.

BIG-PIN BOWLING, a variety of bowling, see >BOWLING.

Bicycle stunt riding motif on a postage stamp.

B
WORLD SPORTS ENCYCLOPEDIA

Bilboquet, also known as bilbocatch and 'cup and ball' – the 'easy' method.

Billiard trick and fancy shots.

Filipino Francesco Bustamente during a pool billiard World League competition.

BILBOCATCH, a game of coordination involving throwing up in the air and catching a ball on a string [Fr. *bille* – ball + *bouquer* – hurl, throw]. It probably originated from its Fr. prototype known as >BILBOQUET. It has also been known in Eng.-speaking countries as *cup and ball*. The ball may be caught in two ways, easier and more difficult. The easier way is to catch the ball in the large cup at one end of the handle. The more difficult way involves turning the handle upside-down and trying to catch the ball on the narrow end. The Eng. writer J. Austen is reported to have been a keen bilbocatch player.

BILBOQUET, a Fr. game of coordination in which a ball on a string is thrown into the air and must be caught [Fr. *bille* – ball + *bouquer* – hurl, throw].

The ball may be caught in two ways, easier and more difficult. The handle to which the string with the ball is attached has two endings – one is a cup and the other (on the other end of the handle) is a point. In the easier method the ball is caught with the cup and in the more difficult the ball (with a special hole bored in it) has to be caught with the pointed end of the handle.

Bilboquet has been known in France since at least the 16th cent., and King Henry III is known to have enjoyed playing it. Later it became popular in many Eur. countries including England where it was called >BILBOCATCH and Poland (where it was known under its Fr. name). The Pol. var. was described by Ł. Gołębiowski:

In bilboquet a ball on a string attached to a wooden or bone cup is thrown up in the air and has to be caught into the said vessel. The ball has additionally a hole bored in it and more skillful players turn the cup upside down and try to land the ball on the rod attached to the bottom of the cup.

[*Gry i zabawy różnych stanów*, 1831, 29]

BILLET, a local name of >TIP-CAT used in Derbyshire, England.

BILLIARD TRICK AND FANCY SHOTS, also *artistic pool*, a competition for billiard players who execute various stunts with billiard balls, incl. sending a ball through the triangle, landing a ball in a basket held above the table, crashing various figures constructed of several triangles placed on the balls, etc. The sport is developing dynamically, with various types of championship competitions held annually. A trad. artistic pool event is held without the judges and the final result is decided by the applause of the spectators. The top players in recent years included: H. Friedemann, B. Wołkowski, C. Darling, N. Mannino, T. Rossman, M. Massey, S. Pelinga.

BILLIARDS, any of various games involving hitting a designated number of small balls with a long stick called a cue. A game of billiards is played on a special, usu. rectangular table surrounded by a cushioned rail bordering. The table and cushions are topped with a feltlike tight-fitting cloth that is usu. green, sometimes blue and very rarely of a different color. The name of the game comes from an old Fr. word *billert* – a long stick. There are 3 major types of billiards games played on tables of different sizes and shapes: 1) a group of games called >CAROM BILLIARDS played with 3 balls on a table that has no pockets; 2) >POOL BILLIARDS whereby points are scored by striking balls into 6 pockets arranged along the table's side cushions with one of its most popular varieties being >SNOOKER, which is often

considered a separate game, and 3) >ENGLISH POCKET BILLIARDS which is played on a table with pockets but where points may be scored in 2 ways, namely by striking them into the pockets or by playing cannons where the cue ball hits 2 other balls in succession, similarly to carom billiards. Additionally there are billiards varieties that do not form a part of any of the 3 above-mentioned main types, e.g. Mississippi, Rocks of Scilly, etc. (see below).

MISSISSIPPI, a var. of billiards played on a parallelogram table. Instead of regular pockets, it has a widening recess located along one of the sides. In it there are 15 perforations or small arch-shaped gates into which balls are struck. Each hole or gate has a numeric value (from 1 to 15) assigned to it which corresponds to the number of points scored by a player for striking a ball into or through it. A player scores 15pts. for striking the ball through or into a gate or pocket located centrally in the recess. According to a description presented by J. Strutt in his *The Sports and Pastimes of the People of England* (1810, 266) the players, depending on the type of the game, had from 4 to 6 balls that were sent individually towards the recess. The balls could bounce off the side cushions. The player who was the first to score 120pts. was declared the winner.

THE ROCKS OF SCILLY, a billiards-like game described by J. Strutt in *The Sports and Pastimes of the People of England* (1810, 266-7). It was played on a rectangular table curved at the top which was more elevated than the bottom. A wooden hollow trunk, open at both ends, ran along the longitudinal axis of the table. A ball was placed in the trunk and then driven with a round baton of wood towards the far end so that it climbed the elevated surface, bounced off the rounded top side and returned to the main table area. The main table area contained some arch-like gates usu. numbered from 1 to 5. The numbers equaled the points value of each gate. If a player failed to put the ball through any of the 5 gates he had to relinquish his run at the table.

There are as many as 110 billiards varieties of all types. They were developed largely in the 19th cent. breeding numerous variants that remained more or less similar to their original counterparts. The fact that there are more and more unified international and televised tournaments has resulted in the fact that these numerous varieties have become more and more similar again (e.g. carom billiards games employ a standardized Amer. table irrespective of where the games are held or of whether there exist some national or regional varieties).

History. Nothing is really known about the origin of billiards. It is assumed that the game was devel-

Louis Leopold Billy, A Game of Billiards, *oil on canvas, 1807.*

oped towards the end of the Middle Ages when certain outdoor ball games were adapted so that they could be played indoors at noblemen's houses. Such a hypothesis was put forward by J. Strutt in his *The Sports and Pastimes of the People of England* (1810): 'The invention of this diversion is attributed to the French, and probably with justice; but at the same time I cannot help thinking it originated from an ancient game played with small bowls upon the ground; or indeed that it was, when first instituted, the same game transferred from the ground to the table.' (p. 265). The earliest reference to such an adaptation is made in the Middle-English romance entitled *Ipomedon* written around 1440. The romance seems to be an imitation of an earlier Fr. poem *Huon de Rotelande.* The Fr. poem mentions a game involving stone balls played on a floor in a castle. When such a game was played the balls tended to bounce off pillars and walls and therefore the game evolved and became played on a platform initially made of solid stone. And although some sources claim that the first billiards table was installed at the court of Louis XI of France in 1429, the first confirmed reference to billiards comes only from around 1574. The then Fr. monarch Henry III (who was also the King of Poland from 1573 to 1574) ordered that one of his courtiers, H. de Vigne, design a billiards table made of a polished stone slab with wooden housing and legs. The table was to be brought to the Château de Blois castle. By the end of the 16th cent. table billiards had already been introduced to the majority of royal courts throughout Western Europe. In 1576 the imprisoned Mary Stuart complained in one of her letters that on Elizabeth I's orders she was deprived of her billiards table. Billiards was already widely popular at that time which is best exemplified by the numerous literary references to it such as those in E. Spenser's *Mother Huderd's Tale* (1591). W. Shakespeare mentions billiards in his *Anthony and Cleopatra* when in Act II Cleopatra says to one of her ladies-in-waiting, 'Let it alone; let's to billiards: come, Charmian'. Since Shakespeare obtained lot of information for his plays from authentic historical sources, many billiards historians assumed that the Eng. playwright had also some information on billiards having been played in ancient Egypt, at least during Cleopatra's rule. This led to a long and heated debate on the ancient origins of the game. Billiards, or rather its numerous varieties, was initially played with 2 balls on a table with different obstacles such as gates, spires, certain figures borrowed from chess (especially queens and kings) and various arrangements of pins. The hypothesis on the ancient origin of billiards was fi-

nally disproved only as late as in the second half of the 20th cent. The game was popularized throughout Eur. courts by Louis XIV the Sun King of France. An old print made by a Fr. artist G. Trouvaine depicts the King engrossed in a game of billiards. The first detailed description of the game was recorded by C. Cotton in his *Compleat Gamester* (1674). One of the prints included in this book pictures players using cues slightly crooked at their ends. The cues had a rectangular cross-section and the balls were not struck with the thin but the thick end of the stick. Moreover, the balls were not hit directly with the tip of the cue but from the side, similarly to contemporary golf. Straight cues were introduced as late as in the 17th cent. They were, however, still rectangular in their cross-section. The modern cue with a round cross-section and a leather tip is thought to have been developed by a Fr. captain of the Royal Guards, one Mingaud, who is said to have improved the design while serving time (1798-1806) for being in opposition to the Fr. Revolution. The legend has it that he was saved from being guillotined by a judge who was a keen billiards player. Until the second half of the 19th cent. billiard balls were made of ivory. Basic billiards equipment also evolved over time. A description of the game included in an anonymous work entitled *The School of Recreation* (1710) reads that the game was played on a rectangular table with only 3 pockets, all placed along only one side. In the middle of the table there was an iron, arch-shaped gate and a likeness of a king. Both figures could be placed anywhere on the table. The object of the game was to put a ball through the gate so that it went round the king. Only then could a player attempt at putting it in one of the 3 pockets. In England this billiards var. was called the *French Game.* A similar game borrowed, most likely, from Italy was called a *Truck* or *Trucks* [Lat. *trochus* – a playing ring; see >TROCHUS].

Billiards was so popular that it was often banned from public places. During George II's reign (1727-60) the Eng. Parliament introduced a ban on installing billiards tables at public houses. Anyone who violated the ban was subject to a very high fine of £10. Despite that, billiards was gaining in popularity. In 1799 an Eng. entrepreneur J. Thurston estab. the first ever billiard table factory. In this way he contributed to standardizing billiards table dimensions and, indirectly, the rules of the game. In 1835 he was the first to install rubber cushions and in 1842 he replaced those with cured rubber ones. In 1868 J. Hyatt, an Amer. inventor, made the first plastic balls – in this case of a substance being a mix of nitrocellulose, camphor and alcohol. In the 1920s

the balls began to be made of artificial phenol resins. Such plastic balls were much cheaper than those made of ivory and they contributed to making billiards accessible to poorer players.

Until the end of the 18th cent. billiards was an elitist sport. The first open tournaments were held in England at the beginning of the 19th cent. The most outstanding player of that time was E.J. Kentfield who remained the English champion for 24 consecutive years (1825-49). In 1849 he was finally beaten by J. Roberts. Billiards became popular internationally in the second half of the 19th cent. after it had become established as a sport in its own right in the US. It became so popular there that one of the Amer. Presidents – J.Q. Adams (1825-29) wanted to have a billiard table installed at the White House. However, the more conservative part of the general public opposed this move, calling it the introduction of gambling at the top echelons of state authorities, and the purchase became an item of congressional debate. However, the case was dropped since many Congressmen were keen billiards players themselves. In this situation the advocates of conservatism decided to strike directly against the President and sued an owner of one of the private billiards parlors. Had they won their case, they would have established a precedent that would have been also binding upon the President. Meanwhile, the parlor owner pointed to the fact that the President of the US himself played billiards and thus every rank and file citizen should also have the right to play the game if the Amer. Constitution were to be preserved. The case was finally dismissed. The most famous Amer. billiards champions include A. de Oro (1887-1919), R. Greenleaf (1919-37), W. Mosconi (1941-55) as well as A. Cranfield and L. Lassiter in the 1960s and 70s. The main US billiards organization is the Billiard Congress of America (BCA) established in 1948. The BCA organizes the annual Open Pocket Billiards Championships, thought to be the professional W.Ch. The BCA also holds tournaments for amateur players, including all-university and women's championships. In Great Britain and in the majority of the Commonwealth countries billiards competitions are overseen by the Billiards Association and Control Council (BACC) established in 1919 after the merger of the English Billiard Association (est. 1885) and Billiard Control Club (est. 1908).

Carom billiards gained international popularity later than English billiards. However, the first three cushion W.Ch. was held in the US as early as in 1878. The first balk line W.Ch. was held in 1918. The most outstanding carom billiards player of all time was

A billiards tournament.

A disabled billiards player.

WORLD SPORTS ENCYCLOPEDIA

B

W. Hoppe of the US who remained the world champion for 49 consecutive years (1906-55)! Since 1959 the Union Mondiale de Billard (UMB) has been the largest carom billiards organization in the world. The World Confederation of Billiards Sports (WCBS) was established in 1992 and became recognized by the International Olympic Committee soon after. Before that date there were a number of world-wide and continental organizations for the respective billiards varieties such as the World Pool-Billiard Association (WPA) or various Eur. carom or pool billiards and snooker federations. In 1998 these numerous Eur. federations were disbanded and they formed the much stronger Eur. Confederation of Billiards Sports (ECBS) which is the Eur. branch of WCBS. In 1998 the State University of Physical Education and Sports in Kiev, Ukraine, established the first ever department of billiards. To stress the importance of this development the then President of WCBS, J. Sandman, moved the headquarters of the organization to Kiev where it remained until the expiry of his term of office (1999).

BILLY BLYNDE, a regional var. of >BLIND MAN'S BUFF.

BILLY-BASE, one of the locally used Eng. names of >PRISONER'S BASE.

BING-SHANG QIUXI, an old Chin. variety of football played in winter on ice.

BIRINIC, a Bret. var. of the table game of >SKITTLES.

BIRLING, also *burling* or *logrolling* (the latter is also a separate event), a sport of Amer. and Canadian woodcutters, who compete in performing various evolutions while standing on floating logs. The sport was initiated around 1840 by woodcutters, who cleared the Amer. forests to accomodate westward expansion. In its present form birling includes the following events:
LOG RACING, also known as *polling*, which is a race between competitors standing on floating logs and pushing off the bottom with long poles;
LOGROLLING – 2 contestants standing on the same log try to force one another off the log by rotating it with their feet and causing the rival to lose balance and fall into the water. Each fall brings the opponent a point. The match is played until the maximum of 3pts are scored by both players. However, if one player scores 2 consecutive points, he wins the match;
TRICK RIDING – a competition in demonstrating

Trick riding – performing acrobatic stunts on a floating log.

A logrolling competition.

various acrobatic evolutions while standing on a floating log.
Birling has resulted from the efforts to improve the woodcutters' skills of rafting the logs down the river, avoiding 'traffic jams' during rafting, speeding up the transportation of rafts to the sawmill, etc. It was encouraged by the sawmills which funded awards for winners. During birling events betting is common. The first historically documented birling events were organized in a Can. woodcutters camp in 1840. From Canada it spread to New England and gained tremendous popularity in Maine. In 1888 the first birling competition was held for the public. Ten years later the first all-Amer. championship, called the Burling W.Ch., was held on the initiative of the Lumbersmen's Association of America in Omaha, Nebraska during the Trans-Mississippi Exhibition. Preparations for this event included codifying the regulations, which have survived almost unchanged until this day. This championship has been held irregularly ever since. Birling shows are often staged during various sport events, e.g. boating or canoeing competitions.

BISUL, an old name for >HAPKIDO.

BITTLE-BATTLE, a name for >STOOL-BALL used in Sussex.

BJERGTROLD, Dan. for 'mountain troll' [*bjerg* – mountain + *trold* – troll]. A Dan. game often played during physical education classes at kindergartens and early school grades. The player selected to be the troll is tied to a pole around which the remaining contestants deposit their valuables. The players have to outsmart the troll and get their possessions back. A player who is touched by the troll changes places with him.
J. Møller, 'Bjergtrold', GID, 1997, 2, 46.

BJOLKE, a Dan. dial. word for 'a beam' [*bjælke* – beam, wooden peg]. An old Dan. game employing a wooden peg driven into the ground at which players threw flat stones or metal rings. Before doing this a number of buttons or coins were placed on top of the peg. The number of coins placed by a given player on the peg equaled the number of throws he subsequently had. The action of throwing stones or rings at the peg was called *at bjolke*. Nowadays the term is no longer used but the game is still played in Denmark. The player who managed to knock the peg over was declared the winner. The player whose coin finished closest to the peg began the next round.
J. Møller, GID, 1997, 1, 97.

BLACK MAN'S TIG, a game employing a rope tied to a pole or a gate. One of the players holds one end of the rope and tries to use it to catch another player passing near the pole or through the gate. A player who gets caught starts helping the first player catch all the other players and so on until all players have been caught.
TGESI, I, 34.

BLIND BELL, a regional var. of >BLIND MAN'S BUFF.

BLIND MAN'S BUFF, the most popular name for a game in which a blindfolded person tries to catch

Logrolling events are also held for children.

and identify the other players, often teasing him, or special objects. Sometimes the rules of the game are quite opposite – all the players are blindfolded except one whom they have to catch or follow. The game is known in practically all Eur. countries. In the past it was not only a children's game but also a pastime popular at royal courts and among middle classes. It comes in different varieties as described below and is often accompanied by rhymed songs, recitations or dialogs such as:

How many horses has your father got in his stables?
Three.
What colour are they?
Red, white and grey.
Then turn about, and twist about,
And catch whom you may.

[TGESI, 37]

Come, shepherd,
Come, shepherd,
And count your sheep.
I cannot come now,
For I'm fast asleep.
If you don't come now,
They'll all be gone.
What's in my way?
A bottle of hay.
Am I over it?

[TGESI, 37]

The number of similar games and rhymes is simply enormous. The most popular varieties played in the Eng.-speaking countries are:
Belie-mantie, a Scot. var. of blind man's buff played in the Clyde valley. Its most characteristic feature was that 'he who was the chief actor was not only hoodwinked, but enveloped in the skin of an animal' [TGESI, I, 27].
Belly-blind, a Scot. var. known in Cladesdale, Roxburgh and the neighboring areas.
Biggly, an Eng. var. from Cumberland.
Billy Blind, a Scot. var., also known as Billy Blynde.
Cock-stride, a game in which 'one boy is chosen as Cock. He is blindfolded, and stands alone, with his legs as far apart as possible. The other boys then throw their caps as far as they are able between the extended legs of the Cock. After the boys have thrown their caps, and each boy has taken his stand beside the cap, the Cock, still blindfolded, stoops down and crawls in search of the caps. The boy whose cap he first finds has to run about twenty yards under the buffeting of the other boys, the blows being directed chiefly to the head. He becomes Cock at the next turn of the game' [TGESI, I, 74].
Fr. blind man's buff, a variety in which 'the children kneel in a circle, one standing blindfolded in the middle. The kneeling children shout, *Come point to me with your pointer*' [TGESI, I, 145].
Giddy, a girls' var. of blind man's buff played to the following song:

Giddy, giddy, gander,
Who stands yonder,
Little Bessy Baker,
Pick her up and shake her;
Give her a bit of bread and cheese,
And throw her over the water.

In the game there is 'a girl blindfolded, her companions join hands and form a ring around her. At the word *Yonder* the blindfolded girl points in any direction she pleases, and at line three names one of the girls. If the one pointed at and the one named be the same, the one named is the next to be blinded; but, curiously enough, if they be not the same, the one named is the one. Meanwhile, at line four, she is not *picked up*, but is shaken by the shoulders by the still blindfolded girl; and at line five she is given by the same *bread and cheese*, i.e. the buds or young leaves of what later is called *May* (Cratoegus oxyacantha); and at line six she is taken up under the blinded girl's arm and swung round' [TGESI, I, 150]. This variety is reported to have been popular in Warwick.

Glim-glam, a var. known and practiced in the Scot. counties of Aberdeen and Banff.

In addition there are numerous other Eng., Scot., Ir. and Amer. blind man's buff var. such as: *Blind Bucky Davy; Blind Harie; Blind Hob; Blind Nerry Mopsey; Blind Sim; Buck Hid; Chacke Blind Man; Hoodle-Cum-Blind; Hoddman Blind; Hooper's Hide; Jockie Blind Man; Pointing Out a Point* and *Willy Blindy.*

In a special variety of the game called the *Blind Bell* the roles are reversed: 'a game formerly common in Berwickshire, in which all the players were hoodwinked except the person who was called the Bell. He carried a bell which he rung, still endeavouring to keep out of the way of his hoodwinked partners in the game. When he was taken, the person who seized him was released from the bandage, and got possession of the bell, the bandage being transferred to him who was laid hold of' [TGESI, I, 36]. Elsewhere in England a similar game was called *jingling.* It was one of the events during the Chipping Campden folk games, also known as the Cotswold Olympic Games. In Scotland jingling was 'a rougher game played at country feasts and fairs in which a pig takes the place of the boy with the bell' [TGESI, I, 36].

In *blind man's stan* the players had to find and break bird eggs taken from the nests. 'The eggs are placed on the ground, and the player who is blindfolded takes a certain number of steps in the direction of the eggs; he then slaps the ground with a stick thrice in the hope of breaking the eggs; then the next player, and so on' [TGESI, I, 40]. *Pillie-winkie*, a game played in Fife, was equally brutal. 'An egg, an unfledged bird or a whole nest is placed on a convenient spot. He who has what is called the first pill, retires a few paces, and being provided with a cowt or rung, is blindfolded, or gives the promise to wink hard (whence he is called *Winkie*), and moves forward in the direction of the object, as he supposes, striking the ground with the stick all the way. He must not shuffle the stick along the ground, but always strike perpendicularly. If he touches the nest without destroying it, or the egg without breaking it, he loses his vice or turn. The same mode is observed by those who succeed him. When one of the party breaks an egg he is entitled to all the rest as his property, or to some other reward that has been previously agreed on. Every art is employed, without removing the nest or egg, to mislead the blindfolded player, who is also called the Pinkie' [TGESI, I, 41].

Games similar to blind man's buff are known practically throughout the world. The following are just a few selected examples:

In Poland, according to 19th-cent. ethnographer Ł. Gołębiowski, the game was called a *ślepa babka* (lit. 'little blind grandmother') or *zmrużek* (which translates roughly as 'squinting eyes') and consisted in blindfolding one player whose task was then to catch the remaining persons. 'In this game one is blindfolded and the others run away. The blind one continues his pursuit until he catches someone. Then, the caught one is blindfolded. The blindfolded player has to be warned of any danger to his life and limb so that he does not hurt himself. The game is also popular among country people in the Podlasie region where the scarf used to blindfold players is replaced with a cap pulled over one's eyes' (*Gry i Zabawy różnych stanów – Games and Plays of Different Classes,* 1831, 68-9).

The game in which the situation was reversed, i.e. where everybody was blindfolded except the pursued player is called *ciuciubabka* ('pish-pish' or 'little grandmother'). In one of its varieties, according to Gołębiowski, 'the players are not blindfolded but their hands are tied behind their backs and that is how they have to catch the one who runs away. Jumps to the side and supple twists are needed here to catch anyone' (ibid.: 69).

In yet another Pol. var. called a *derkacz* ('corn crake' or 'landrail') 'only two play the game while the others remain spectators. They are both blindfolded, one has two pieces of wood one smooth and the other with a number of grooves. He runs the smooth one against the grooved one to imitate a corn crake cry and that is how the other one finds and hits him. The game is very amusing for the spectators to watch since when there is no need the players run away from each other, walk at a certain distance from each other and look scared but when they get near each other they suddenly become calm and attentive' (ibid.).

In Portugal the 2 most important var. have always been:

Cabra-cega, full name – *jogo da cabra-cega*, lit. a blind goat [Port. *cabra* – goat + *cega* – blind]. One person is blindfolded and starts a dialogue with the remaining players:

Where do you come from, blind goat?
From Vizela.
What do you carry in your basket?
Cinnamon.
Will you give me some?
It's not for me, it's for my old one.

The players try to steal a pinch of 'cinnamon' from the 'blind goat' – i.e. they pinch 'her'. The one who is caught swaps places with the 'goat'. In one of its sub-varieties the 'goat' does not try to catch the others but guesses who pinched 'her'.

Ronda que ronda, full name *jogo da ronda que ronda* – 'what goes around, goes around'. The player in charge of the game points to other players and says:

Daddy, daddy,
Little duck, little tiny duck.

This is followed by a counting-out rhyme in which one child is selected to be blindfolded. The other players hide and the one in charge of the game asks the child where the others have gone. If the child guesses right, the one in hiding is asked to come out, if not – the blindfolded child starts looking for the others. A player who is seized has to be given a piggyback ride (or lit. a horseback ride – *á cavalitas*) back to the one in charge of the game. The game has different names in different parts of Portugal, e.g. *carrachucho, á carrachucha, ás carracholas.*

A wide variety of blind man's buff-like games developed in Denmark:

Blindebuk, lit. a blind billy-goat [Dan. *blinde* – blind + *buk* – billy-goat, buck]. One of the players is blindfolded and turned around to make it harder for him to find the other players. Often various poems or rhymes are recited at the start of the game.

Blindebuk med stok, lit. a blind billy-goat with a stick. The blindfolded player is led by another player with a stick in his hand. The remaining players go around them singing a song. At some point the player who is leading the blindfolded one passes the stick to one of the other players who has to whistle and make other sounds so that the blindfolded player might guess who it is.

Blind jagt, lit. a blind pursuit or hunt. A blind man's buff variety in which 2 blindfolded players grab the ends of 2 ropes tied to a pole. One of them additionally holds a scarf tied into a knot and the other a bunch of keys which he shakes from time to time. The task of the 'scarf-bearer' is to catch the 'key-keeper' and to hit him with the knot.

Blind kat, lit. a blind cat. A game very similar to blind man's buff in which the blindfolded person has to recognize a person by touching him or her. The other players go around the blindfolded player singing a song. At some point they stop and the blindfolded player has to guess who is in front of him by touching the person with his hands.

Føle med skeer, lit. feel with spoons [Dan. *føle* – feel + *med* – with + *skee* – spoon]. In this game a player sits blindfolded and he is given spoons. His task is to touch one of the players with the spoons and identify him. To do so, he has 3 attempts.

Hans og Grethe, Hans and Grethe, a game involving 2 players sitting on chairs inside a circle. One of them is named Hans and the other Grethe. Hans is then blindfolded and his task is to catch Grethe who does everything 'she' can to escape him. When Hans decides that it is impossible for him to catch Grethe without any help he calls 'Grethe' to which she answers 'Hans', to let him know where she is, and flees.

Katten after musene, lit. a cat after mice. A game involving a larger number of players that are divided into the teams of 'cats' and 'mice'. The cats hold a sneaker in their hands and the mice have sticks with which they scratch the floor. A cat has to hit a mouse with the shoe.

Markus og Lukas, Mark and Luke, a game involving 2 players – Mark and Luke – standing at a round table with one hand on the edge of the tabletop. In the second hand they hold a scarf tied into a knot. They are both blindfolded and walk around the table. When one of them thinks the moment is most opportune he says his name and then the second player has to hit him with the scarf. The players may try to dodge the 'blows' but must not let go of the table.

Posten går, lit. the mail is coming. A game similar to blind man's buff in which the players sit on chairs around their blindfolded friend. Each player is assigned a number. The 'blind' player says 2 numbers and the named players have to swap places. While they do so, the blindfolded player tries to catch one of them and identify him. If he fails to identify the person, he must set him free and the game continues. If he succeeds, they swap places.

In the Arab world, the most popular blind man's buff counterpart is the game of *'ish*. One of the players is blindfolded and the remaining players throw a rag folded into a kind of ball between the extended legs of the blindfolded player and return to their places. Then, the blindfolded player is prompted – by a clap of the hands or some other sound – to start searching. The player who is caught swaps places with him.

In Italy a similar game is called a 'blind fly' (*musca cieca*), in Germany and Austria – a 'blind cow' (*Blindekuh*) and in Russia – a *zhmurka.* Games resembling blind man's buff to a greater or lesser extent were also known outside Europe, for example in Mongolia *zorkhoo iamaa* (lit. 'a wolf and a goat').

History. The oldest mention of a game similar to contemporary blind man's buff comes from *Onomastikon* written in the 2nd cent. by a Gk. rhetor and lexicographer Julius Pollux. He dedicated *Onomastikon* to his former pupil, the Roman emperor Commodus. The work mentions a game called *chalke muia* [Gk. for 'copper' or 'biting fly']. In the game the head of one of the players was covered with a hood or a scarf was put around his eyes. He then announced that 'he was going to catch every biting fly' whereas the other players shouted back that he would not be able to do it and made various sounds to tell him where they were. Additionally, they often came near to him and hit him with whips made of papyrus. The game was introduced to Europe by Roman legionnaires. A similar game played in France in the Middle Ages was called a *collinmaillard* after a soldier who was blinded during the battle of Liège in 999 but continued to fight with his enemies before he was killed. After his death he was made a knight and to commemorate his extraordinary feats Robert II (Robert the Pious) of France introduced a special event into his >CHIVALRIC TOURNAMENTS. The event involved a group of blindfolded knights who fought (with blunt swords) with 'seeing' knights.

A.B. Gomme, TGESI, 1984, I, 36-40, 145, 152, 223, 285; 1898, II, 41, 46; M. da Graça Sousa Guedes, 'Jogo da 'cabra-cega', JTP, 1979, 19-20; 56-7; J. Møller, 'Blindebuk and other entries', GID, 1997, 2, 95-101; TGESI, I, 73-4; TGESI, I, 150; TGESI, I, 152; TGESI, II, 41.

Francisco de Goya, Blind Man's Buff, *1789, oil on canvas, detail.*

BLIND MAN'S STAN, see >BLIND MAN'S BUFF.

BLINDEKUH, Ger. for 'a blind cow', a Ger. var. of >BLIND MAN'S BUFF.

BLOKMAND OG JORDMAND, a Dan. run-and-catch game. Its name specifies two contestant types or states, i.e. a player who stands on a rock and a player who stands on the ground [Dan. *blok* – rock, stone, solid material + *mand* – man, human being + *og* – and + *jord* – earth + *mand*]. The name of the game signifies the fact that the players who are being chased may only be caught when they are the *jordmand* (i.e. earth people), i.e. they run or stand on the ground. When they take refuge on specially arranged rocks they become the *blokmand* (i.e. rock people) and cannot be caught. A player who gets caught becomes the catcher.

J. Møller, 'Blokmand og jordmand', GID, 1997, 2.

B

BLOOD SPORTS, a group of sports with the object of killing an animal for sport; entertainment referred to also as *field sports* in Eng.-speaking countries comprises traditionally >HUNTING; >COURSING, >COCK FIGHTING, >ANIMAL BAITING; Apart from the Ang.-Sax. sports the generic name blood sports includes also >CORRIDA, and Afg. >BUZKASHI.

BLOW POINT, an old Eng. game involving throwing small darts at a wooden block, similar to >DARTS.

BMX RACING, see >CROSS BMX.

BOAR FIGHTING, an event that was usu. held before young Spartan men's fights during games known as >PLATANISTAS. According to Pausanias, 'At the sacrifice the youths set trained boars to fight; the company whose boar happens to win generally gains the victory in Plane-tree Grove' (*Description of Greece*, III, 14, 10, transl. W. Jones, H. Ormerod).

BOARDING, see >SNOWBOARDING.

BOAT JOUSTING, a type of rowing event combined with a jousting tournament. Competitions of this type have been organized in many countries across many periods. An ancient Eg. bas-relief dating to 2980 BC shows the crews of two boats fighting with long poles. In western Europe, knightly

Entourage in tow, Oxford pulls away to victory over Cambridge during 2002's University Boat Race held on the Thames in London.

Bobsleighing in the early 20th cent. (above) and during the Olympic Games in Utah (below).

jousting tournaments gave rise to some 'plebeian' jousting forms, including boat jousting. In Germany, boat jousting is called *Fischerstechen*. Until the end of the Middle Ages, boat jousting events were organized in many Dan. seaside towns located on major rivers, such as Keterminde, Svendborg, Fåborg, Nyborg, Nakskov or Korsår, under many names, the most common being >DYSTLØB. In France, boat jousting competitions were organized in the northern cities on the shores of the English Channel, the Bay of Biscay, on the Mediterranean shores in the south, as well as on rivers in inland cities. The most famous boat jousting events included those organized in some Languedoc towns,

such as Sète (formerly Cette), Agde and Frotignan, as well as those held on the Bay of Biscay shores (where they were called >JOUTES GIRONDINES). The oldest such event, dating back to 1550 and organized to this day, is held in Lyon (>JOUTES LYONNAISES). The Agde competition was initiated in 1601, the Frontignan games – in 1629, and the Paris tournament – in 1704. There is a trend today in many Eur. towns, e.g. Coudekerque (1956), to revive the tradition. Similar events have also been organized in Italy. Cf. >TILTING ON SKATES, >WATER QUINTAIN.
J. Møller, 'Dystløb', GID, 1997, 4, 77; C. Pegeassou, 'Les joutes languedociennes. Le prix de la tradition dans les enjeux de la modernité', *Entre tradition et modernité – le sport*, 1995, 24-31.

BOAT RACE, THE, a name used when referring to the Oxford-Cambridge boat race. The first Boat Race was held in 1829 on the Thames near Henley (which today lies within the Greater London limits). Initially, The Boat Race was not held regularly and the second competition did not take place until 1836. It became an annual event in 1839. In 1845 the course was moved from Henley to the Putney-Mortlake leg of the Thames (today also in the Greater London area). The length of the course is 4.25mi. (6.8km). The Race was undecided only once when one of the rowers broke his oar soon before the finish line. The Cambridge team won by 6ft. but J. Phelps, the then race umpire, called a 'dead-heat to Oxford by six feet'. The rowers usu. cover the distance in about 20min. but the record time was set at 16min. 19sec. in 1998 by the Cambridge team. The Oxford team won the 148th Boat Race in 2002, as of which, the aggregate score is 77 to 70 for Cambridge.
The Boat Race attracts millions of people in front of TV screens every year and some 1 million spectators along the banks of the Thames.

A licensed bobrun skater heading down the track.

BOB CHERRY, an trad. Eng. game involving catching cherries in one's mouth while jumping and without using one's hands. Artificial fruit was hung on a rope during all seasons except summer. An old print that belongs to the British Museum and a picture in J. Strutt's *Glig Gamena Angel Deoth or the Sports and Pastimes of the People of England* (1803) depict not only cherries but also bigger fruit and perhaps also meats. The print depicts 4 friars jumping up to reach a ball hung slightly above their mouths – the ball may be a big fruit or a piece of ham.

BOBRUN-BIKING, a unique and spectacular sport in which bikers compete for time riding down an ice-covered, half-pipe-shaped track, which is primarily used for >BOBSLEIGHING and >TOBOGGANING. The bikes are equiped with spikes attached to the tube for a better grip. The most famous event is held in February on the famous St. Moritz bobsleigh track. Cf. >BOBRUN-SKATING.

BOBRUN-SKATING, a unique and spectacular sport in which skaters compete for time skating down an ice covered half-pipe-shaped track, identical to that used for >BOBSLEIGHING and >TOBOGGANING. Competitons are held between individual skaters or teams of 3, with the time being stopped after the 3rd racer passes the finish line. Among the best known events is the International Swiss Championship in Bobrun-Skating held on the famous St. Moritz bobsleigh track. Participants must have a license from an active hockey club and wear a hockey player's uniform.

BOBSLEIGHING, also called *bobsledding*. A winter sport of timed sliding down an ice-covered run on a sled called a bobsled, bobsleigh or bob.
Equipment and run. A bobsled is a type of a sleigh equipped with 2 pairs of runners whereby the front pair may be turned with a wheel similar to that of a car's steering wheel (more typical of Amer. bobs) or a control stick used to pull a series of ropes that make the runners turn (more popular in Europe). A bobsleigh is also equipped with a brake that is a toothed bar pressed against the ice between the rear runners. The brake may only be used in case of danger and must not be used in any other situation as it makes deep grooves in the ice covering the run which might pose a danger for other competing teams. If a team applies a brake (even in an emergency), it is disqualified. The rear of a bob is equipped with handles used in pushing the sled at the start to attain maximum starting velocity. There are two types of sleigh – 2-man bobs and 4-man bobsleighs. Until 1931 there were also 5-man sleighs. The Eng. language used to differentiate between the terms *bobsled* – first made in 1888 and meaning any type of a bob and *bobsleigh* – first made in 1895 and meaning a bob with additional ballast to attain higher speeds. Rules limit a 2-man sled weight to 165kg and the combined team-and-sled weight to 390kg. In the case of 4-man bobs the figures are 230 and 630kg, respectively. The max. length of a 2-man sled is 2.7m and of a 4-man bob – 3.8m. Bobs attain speeds of up to 160km/h. 4-man sleds are driven by the captain of a team. The brakeman is the last team member to board the bob.

The bobrun used at official competitions must be at least 1,500m long (it is usu. 1,600m long) with an average slope of 9% (up to 15%). The turns must not exceed 18m in radius and their slope must be from 2 to 7m. The best runs in the world are the Mount van Hoevenberg run in Lake Placid including the famous Shandy Curve turn, the Cortina d'Ampezzo run in Italy, the Garmish-Partenkirchen, Hahnenklee-Bockwiese, Onberhof and Friedrichsrode runs in Germany, the Engleberg run in St. Morritz in Switzerland, the L'Alpe d'Huez run in Grenoble in France and the Solleftea run in Sweden. **History.** The first bobsled was designed by one Mr. Townsend of the US in 1886. Other sources claim that the first bobsled was conceived by W. Smith from England in 1888 and actually made by a Swiss blacksmith C. Mathys. Bobsleighing became immediately popular in the Alpine countries and later in the US. The first organized competition, called the Bobsledding Festival, was held in 1898 on the Cresta Run in St. Morritz, Switzerland. A permanent, artificial bob run was constructed in St. Morritz in 1903. The second permanent run was built in 1907 in Davos. The first national championship was held in 1907 in Germany and a similar competition was begun a year later in Austria. The first E.Ch. took place in 1914. In 1923 bobsledding became an internationally recognized sport following the establishment of the International Federation of Bobsledding and Tobogganing (Fédération Internationale de Bobsleigh et de Tobogganing, FIBT). Bobsledding was included in the first Olympic Winter Games at Chamonix, France in 1924 and has been a part of it ever since with the exception of the 1960 W.Ol.G. World Championships, initially only for 5-man teams, have been held regularly since 1927. The best teams before 1939 were the US, Germany, Austria and Switzerland. After 1945 they were joined by Canada and Italy and the GDR (in the 1972-90 period). Today the best teams are Austria, Germany, Switzerland and Italy. Their greatest rivals are the British, Russians, Ukrainians, French and Czechs.
A. O'Brien and M. O'Brien, *Bobsled and Luge*, 1976.

BOCCIA [Ital. *boccia* – a ball], in Eng. tradition also *bocce*, a ball game played one-on-one or by teams, similar to Fr. >BOULES and Eng. >LAWN BOWLS. In the one-on-one variety each competitor has 4 balls, while team boccia is played by 2 teams of 2-4 players, each having 2 balls. Once made of wood or metal, the balls are now plastic except for trad.

Professional bodyboarder Tara Higgins rides a wave during the women's competition at the Schlitterbahn water park in New Braunfels.

local matches. The aim of the game is to throw one's balls as close as possible to the target ball called *palino* or *boccino*, which is smaller. The player whose balls are closest to the target ball wins the game. The number of points scored in a game is equal to the number of balls positioned closer to the *pallino* than any of the opponent's balls. The game is made up of 9 rounds played on a specially marked court with walls. The court's length is 24-28m, its width – 3-6m. There are many varieties of the game, some of them including carom elements similar to >BILLIARDS, except that no sticks are used (*giocata a punto, giocata a raffa, bocciata di volo*). A common feature of all varieties is that the ball is thrown from one's hand. The balls are 9-13cm in diameter, while the *pallino* is 4-6cm in diameter. See also >BOCCIA FOR THE DISABLED.
History. Legend has it that boccia was invented by a Spartan named Timokrates around 500 BC. When Greece was subdued by Rome, the legionaries took it with them to the Pennine Peninsula. In the Middle Ages it spread over southern France and Switzerland, where local varieties of boccia came into being. In 1898 the 1st regional boccia organization called Bocciofila Piemontese was formed, followed in 1919 by an all-Italian Unione Bocciofila Italia, re-organized in 1956 as Unione Boccia Internazionale (UBI), which affilitates the national boccia unions of Italy, France, Switzerland, Belgium, Spain, and Yugoslavia. Two other important federations, Federazione Italiano Sport Bocce and Federazione Italiana Gioco Bocce, at first operated independently, but in 1978 joined the UBI. A separate, though smaller, federation, called Federazione Internationale Giocata Boccia (FIGB), operates in Switzerland, Germany, and Italy and, because of the similarities between boccia and >BOULE, has joined the Confèdèration Mondiale des Sport Boules (FMSB) founded in 1985. The number of boccia players is estimated at approx. 165,000 in more than 4,000 clubs (excluding the masses of recreational boccia players enjoying the game in city parks and country squares, estimated at 12-15 million people).
Outside of Europe boccia has been developing dynamically in Australia, where it was brought by Italian emigrants in the early years of the 20th cent. to be played at first on a local and recreational level. A new wave of emigrants in the 1950s led to the formation of ethnic federations and in the 1960s boccia became a professional sport in Australia. In 1967 The Victorian Bocce Federation was formed, fol-

lowed by a similar organization in Western Australia. In 1970 the 1st Austrl. championship was held and in 1971 The Bocce Federation of Australia was established, which decided to join not the UBI, but the Fr. Fèdèration de Boules, which in 1985 was reorganized into the FMSB.

BOCCIA FOR THE DISABLED, a var. of >BOCCIA adapted for persons with various physical disabilities, esp. those on wheelchairs. Basic rules are identical, but disabled players are less restricted as to the way of setting the balls in motion, e.g. they may

WORLD SPORTS ENCYCLOPEDIA

B

Cuno Amiet, The Blue Landscape (A Boccia Rail), *oil on canvass.*

use additional devices such as special boccia sets and ramps. The throwing balls are additionally covered with leather, while the target *pallino* ball is white. There is an individual and team variety and competition events are held mainly indoors. In 1992 the game was included in the program of Paralympic Games in Barcelona, with the participation of 42 players from 11 countries. The sport is governed by the International Paralympic Committee, IPC). Cf. also >SPORTS FOR THE DISABLED.
The Internet: http://info.lut.ac.uk.research/paad/ipc/boccia/boccia.htm

BOCK, Ger. for buck, billy-goat or ram. A type of a game which is called monk (>MUNK) in Denmark and involves trying to knock down a three-legged 'pin' by hurling wooden sticks or blocks at it.

BODYBOARDING, a var. of >SURFING, originated in 1971 in Hawaii by a surfing legend Tom Morey. From its early days bodyboarding has grown into an international sport. The first major professional competition, held at the Banzai Pipeline with a $5,000 award budget, was won by J. Patterson. Over the years the pipeline competition evolved into what has become known as the World Bodyboarding Championships. It took several years before a uniform set of rules, first formulated by the Honolulu Bodysurfing Club, was adopted by all the major bodyboarding organizations, one of the most important being the Global Bodyboarder Organization.

A bobsleghing stamp issued for the 1966 W.Ch. in bobsleighing in Cortina D'Ampezzo.

Drugs-free bodybuilding – the next Olympic discipline?

Bodybuilding: an equal-opportunity sport.

BODY BUILDING, a sport, the object of which is to shape one's body with exercises from various disciplines. At first, strength exercises and static muscle flexing were practiced; as the sport developed, exercises became more dynamic and variable. Now international championships are held in 3 basic categories:

1) evaluation of the figure, evaluation of the musculature and a freestyle routine accompanied by music (in the amateur version of the sport all three elements are judged separately and are added up to give a single score; in the professional version the first two elements are judged jointly). In professional events there are no weight categories; in amateur events the categories are as follows: up to 52, up to 57 and above 57kg (women) and up to 65, 70, 75, 80, 90 and above 90kg (men).

2) pairs, evaluated as above. In mixed pairs an extra criterion is the match of the contestants.

3) fitness, a strictly feminine competition (although its introduction among men is being considered). It consists of figure evaluation and a freestyle routine with elements of acrobatics and strength exercises, the object of which is to present the beauty of the body in motion. Height categories are applied.

History. Body building stems from the natural human aspiration to improve one's body. The technical means of achieving this have their origins in the training of ancient athletes in different cultures and periods, esp. the late 1800s and early 1900s. After WWII beauty and figure contests were very popular (esp. the Mister USA contest). The body building movement owes a lot to Steve Reeves, the 1947 Mister USA. In 1946 B. and J. Weider initiated the International Federation of Body Builders, IFBB). Other organizations included the International Federation of Weightlifting and Body Building (Fédération Internationale d'Haltérophile et Culturiste, FIHC) and the National Amateur Body-Building Association, NABBA (founded in England, but active also in other countries). Since the late '70s hormones and anabolic steroids have been used to facilitate muscle growth. Unlike Olympic sports, body building went unsupervised in this aspect. This led to the abuse of various substances. In spite of this in 1998 the IFBB received temporary acknowledgement from the IOC. Permanent acknowledgement and affiliation was conditioned by a fundamental change of rules regarding forbidden medicines. The process was commenced by IFBB president B. Weider and supervised by E. H. Rose, a Brazilian professor of medicine and the president of the International Federation of Sports Medicine, FIMS. New, strict rules were introduced during the 1998 IFBB congress. Their effectiveness remains to be seen. Body building may be introduced in the 2004 Olympic Games

in Athens, as a show discipline. The IFBB associates 74 national federations. There are also continental federations – the Asian Body-Building Federation was the first among them. However, there is still no Eur. federation. There are many body building magazines worldwide. The most prestigious ones are *Muscle Magazine* and *Muscle and Fitness*.
A. Klein, *Little Big Man. Gender Construction and Bodybuilding Culture*, 1993; S. Zakrzewski, *Siła – sprawność – piękno*, 1974; the same, *Jak stać się silnym i sprawnym*, 1976; B. and J. Weider, *The Weider Book of Bodybuilding for Women*, 1981; Consultant: P. Filleborn.

BOGELSLAEN, see >BEUGELEN.

BOGHELEN, see >BEUGELEN.

BOK, also known as *mongol bok* or *mongul bok*. An international name used sometimes to denote a Mong. var. of wrestling whose full name is >BÖKHIIN BARILDAAN.

BÖKHIIN BARILDAAN, often *buh* in international sport terminology, Mong. wrestling, a combat sport practiced by the Mong. peoples and forming a part of the trad. 3-event warriors' contest called >ERIIN GURVAN NAADAM. The importance of this sport in the everyday life of Mongols is best demonstrated by a saying, 'There is no Mongol who cannot wrestle.' Experts in Mong. culture say that trad. wrestling is the Mong. national sport, enjoying a status similar to that of soccer in Brazil, ice hockey in Canada or bullfights in Spain (I. Kabzińska-Stawarz, *Games of Mongolian Shepherds*, 1991, 86). Depending on the region and customs of a given people, the aim of a fight is to make an opponent touch the ground. Various traditions differ, however, in their definition of a take-down or pin. According to the Mongolian Tuvas and also Buryats and Turkmens, a fighter loses his fight if he so much as touches the ground with his hand. The Chukchis and Kalmyks say that a fighter is defeated when one or both of his shoulder blades touch the ground. The Kazakhs also consider it a defeat when one of the fighters touches the ground with his side. In the Hui and Yakut traditions a fighter is declared defeated when he touches the ground with three points of his body, especially with a leg or legs above the knees, arms, etc. Both wrestlers are accompanied by their seconds who can advise them during a match or try to encourage a cowardly competitor to fight harder by hitting him lightly with a stick or patting his hip. Unlike in the Mediterranean tradition common to the peoples of Syria, Turkey and ancient Greece – and also shared indirectly by many Asian nations (in India and Tibet) – bökhiin barildaan wrestlers do not cover their bodies with oil. What is more, there was

a strict ban in Mongolia on a wrestler greasing his body. A wrestling match is preceded by a ritual dance resembling a bird's flight. One of the characteristic features of bökhiin barildaan matches is that they are held between wrestlers from a settlement divided into two parts, usu. living east and west of a ritual mound of stones called an *owoo*, or into the left and right wing. When wrestlers from other settlements are taking part in a competition, the opponents are said to represent different territories. Sometimes they represent two different social groups. The competitors are thus dubbed 'our' (home) and 'their' (visiting) wrestlers – *nilag* and *dalag*. During the *megdzemiń czonchor* festival matches are held between lamas and shepherds. The shepherds are called 'the black' – *char* and the lamas are named 'the yellow' – *szar*. Of all the ritual procedures preceding a wrestling match, the touching of the ground with the hands seems to be of particular interest. A competitor touches the ground as it is considered the source of all vital forces. Legend has it that even Genghis Khan (c.1155-1227), the great Mongol conqueror, used to touch the ground with his hands asking for strength. Loose earth from a wrestling arena is sewn into a wrestler's everyday clothes, especially into the collar of his outer jacket or coat. A winner also touches the ground with his hands after the match. Touching the ground with one's hands during play, however, forfeits the match. Different peoples of Central Asia treat contact with the ground in different ways. The Mongols manifest it, for example, by rubbing sand into the palms of their hands, by washing their hands with moist sand, by throwing sand up in the air or even by wrestlers' throwing sand at each other. Kabzińska-Stawarz writes that:

the behavior of the competitors, who took a long time to make circles round the place of the fight, who rubbed their hands with sand and threw it in the air, resembles the behavior of enraged bulls before a fight. A reference to this animal is also found in Kirghiz wrestling competitions, when the herald riding round the audience and calling the volunteers for the fight invites 'those who attack like a bull' to enter the arena.

As a part of the pre-match ritual a wrestler takes a short, slow run during which he imitates a bird's flight, arms spread like wings.

The wrestler imitating a bird wanted to resemble an eagle or the mythical bird called Khan Gard (whose prototype is the Indian Garuda), or he wanted to show that he was as strong as the bird. Mongol' beliefs (as well as the beliefs from Southern Siberia) associate the eagle and the Khan Gard with the Sun, the eagle being aditionally considered the ancestor of the first shaman, who is also regarded as the first smith.

[ibid.]

Winners have always received prizes in Mongolia. In 1863 Russian ethnographer Y. Shishmariev reported that during a contest which he observed, after the first victory a wrestler would receive various articles of everyday use, after the second victory he got a ram, after his third victory – two rams, after he defeated his fourth opponent – a horse, etc. The two best wrestlers of each tournament would win a camel, a horse, a cow, a ram and a bolt of silk. According to some accounts, in the 19th cent. a winner would receive several cattle. In 1906 first prize in one of the tournaments was 63 livestock including some horses, second prize was 45 cattle and third – 27 cattle. One of Kabzińska-Stawarz's sources reported that in modern times first prize often amounts to 100 tugrik, second was 70 tugrik, third – 40, fourth – 30 and fifth – 20 (at the beginning of the 1990s 1 US dollar would buy 3.5 tugrik). Prizes such as clothing or tea have also been popular. Tsevel, a Mong. author, records in *Mongolyn bökhün tüükhaim* (1951, after Kabzińska-Stawarz) that, in the past, articles of wrestling clothing or weapons (most frequently bows and arrows, sabres, chain mail and spears) were also awarded as prizes.

A bökhiin barildaan wrestling bout at the National Wrestling Hall, Ulaanbaatar, Mongolia.

A wrestler, called *bökh* (*buh*), who won 5 or 6 matches was given the name of falcon (Mong. *nachin*) or hawk (*khartsaga*), depending on the area he came from. After 6-8 victories a wrestler was titled elephant (*zaan*) and after 9 victories he could call himself lion (*arslan*). A wrestler who won all the qualifying matches starting at the lowermost, local level of *naadam* and all the way up to the national level of *ikh naadam* had the right to call himself 'the great champion' – *avarga*. An undefeated champion was dubbed a 'giant' – *daian varga* or 'sacred giant' – *darkhan avarga*. In Mongolia a bökhiin barildaan champion who remains unbeaten for some time is also considered one of the *mergen* – champions or masters of agility. This name is not, however, reserved only for wrestling champions and is also applied to, for instance, >MONGOLIAN ARCHERY champions. The *mergen* tradition dates back to ancient times and ancient heroes also known as *mergen*. Their feats have been described in the Mong. epic entitled *Gesar* (also called *Gesariad*).

Clothes worn by Mong. wrestlers, varied and richly adorned in the past, are at present almost uniform and are based on old Khalkha clothing. A wrestling suit consists of short, tight-fitting leather pants. The oldest mentioning of similar pants dates back to the Middle Ages. Such pants were then worn by Middle Eastern wrestlers. Khalkha wrestlers also wore short, frontless and long-sleeved coats covering only their shoulders and arms. This coat was fastened at the front with a cord knotted on the naked abdomen near the navel. Apart from such scanty cladding, a wrestler wore no other clothes to cover his torso. In some areas, however, a wrestler would wear a broad belt or even three belts combining into a kind of an apron during those wrestling matches held on the occasion of the spring offering made on the ritual stone mound, or *owoo*. A wrestler's coat fastened with leather straps or narrow strips attached across the chest was also popular. A Dan. ethnologist, H. H. Hansen, wrote that in Inner Mongolia, the wrestlers would compete in coats with red, square badges adorned with representations of tigers or green embroidery. Wrestlers' coats were sometimes adorned with a representation of ram horns called *Özlii* (in many cultures of Central Asia ram horns are considered the symbol of masculinity or strength derived from the Sun). The fact that such embellishments were added to a wrestler's uniform stresses the importance and role of wrestling and it is a testimony of the vital link maintained by humans with forces which determine their fate. A wrestler would also wear *mongol gutal*, i.e. leather shoes, somewhat similar to cowboy boots, with toecaps curved upwards. At ankle height the leather gave way to lengths of cloth swathed around the shins all the way up to the knees. This type of a wrestler's suit was particularly popular in Western Mongolia. A cap was considered a crucial element of a wrestler's uniform. Kabzińska-Stawarz writes that in the past:

> *a competitor's cap [...] was seen as a symbolic equivalent of the whole costume and at the same time as the equivalent of the competitor himself. The cap was highly valued by the Mongols. If a wrestler wore a cap, he was considered to be fully dressed. Before a fight, the competitor handed his cap to the second, which indicated that he was ready to fight, or that he had undressed. The dropping of the cap by the second signified the competitor's defeat. Seconds took a firm hold of caps and they took geat care so that the cap did not fall. Competitors wore caps as a sign of respect.*

Colors also played a very important role. Reds and blues were the most popular.

> *For the Turko-Mongol peoples the red color and the blue color have a symbolic meaning; the red color being generally considered the color of and the symbol of blood, life, and fire, while the blue color – the symbol of the sky. At the same time, both colors symbolize the beginnings, or the sources of life.*

Koumiss forms an essential part of a Mong. wrestler's diet (unlike in >KIRGHIZ WRESTLING where it was eliminated from the menu). After a match the wrestlers receive a few handfuls of dry cheese, called 'white food' – *tsagaan idee*, from the referee. The cheese was crumbled or cut into small pieces. The winner would eat some of it, distributed some cheese among the spectators and would throw the rest to the cardinal points, the spectators, the *owoo* stone mound, where the spirits of his ancestors lived, the mountains and the sky representing the forces of Nature, thus thanking them for the victory and expecting the energy contained in the food to return to him during his next matches. The Myanghats, an ethnic minority in Mongolia, used to scatter the 'white food' before a match. Before they started wrestling, the Myanghats would walk around the *owoo* three times throwing the cheese up in the air. According to some 19th cent. ethnographers, after the match the wrestlers would eat beef or sheep bone marrow in front of the spectators. To do that they had to break the bones first. Such bone-breaking to reach the marrow was chiefly meant to demonstrate a wrestler's strength. At present this custom is no longer observed. Mongol shepherds used to believe that the wrestlers were the embodiment of ancient heroes and that they could help other people improve their lives by sharing the 'white food' with them.

In some settlements wrestling matches were also held by 10-12-year-old boys who would fight at the foot of the *oboo*. One of Kabzińska-Stawarz's sources explained that

> *There was an 'oboo', which just needed children's wrestling to be organized. It was very happy then. Every year on a Takhilt Mountain, Uvs aimag, 'oboo takhikh', and children's wrestling were organized. It took place in autumn. The children's contests were similar to those of the adults. Winners were also given 'tsagaan idee', though they did not share it with the spectators.*

I. Kabzińska-Stawarz, *Games of Mongolian Shepherds*, 1991; I. Kabzińska-Stawarz, 'Competitions in Liminal Situations: Comparative Study of Asian Cultures', p. I, *Ethnologia Polona*, 18, 1994.

BOKSE, pressing with a fist or table boxing. A Dan. game requiring physical strength. In bokse 2 fighters sitting on opposite sides of a table, put one hand with fist clenched on a line drawn in the middle of the table and press them against each other. The object of the game is to push the opponent's fist back onto his half of the table.
J. Møller, 'Bokse', GID, 1997, 4, 51-2.

BOLD FOR EN STEN, a Dan. folk game played at Homsland Klind with a bat and a ball according to rules similar to those observed in a game called >DRAMMERT. Similar to drammert it involves two 5 to 8-member teams. The teams draw lots to determine which team is going to field (outer) and which bat (inner). The difference between drammert and bold for en sten is that in bold for en sten the outer (fielding) team are equipped with bats with which they try to hit the ball sent flying by the inner team who are batting (in drammert the outer team do not have bats). At the start of the game a player from the inner team tries to send the ball as far away into the field as possible. The outer team try to hit the ball sending it back towards the batter or at least stop it with their bats before its stops by itself. If they manage to hit the ball with their bats the batter is struck out. If they fail to do so, the batter places his bat on a stone demarcating the batting area (also batting box, base or plate) and a member of the outer team tries to hit the bat left in this position by striking the ball with his bat from the spot at which the ball stopped. Hence the name of the game [Dan. *bold* – ball + *for* – for + *en* – indefinite article + *sten* – stone, rock]. In the first round of the game it was enough to hit the bat but in the second round the outer team had to actually hit the stone on which the bat was placed. If the ball hit the bat so that it fell off the stone the batter was struck out, if a field player missed the bat, the batter advanced to the second round of the game where he had to send the ball flying after a so-called double arm swing (*vippes*). During the second round, the fielding team had the right to try to hit the flying ball again (i.e. they had a second attempt) and if they failed to do so the inner team players counted the number of steps from the outer team player who stood closest to the spot at which the ball stopped and multiplied the number they obtained by five (in *drammert* the number of points scored was the actual number of steps without any additional multiplication). The product became the number of points scored by the batting team. Then, the batter continued to play the game by starting the first round anew.
J. Møller, 'Bold for en sten', GID, 1997, 1, 69.

BOLD I HUE, a var. of the Dan. game of >BOLD I HUL.

BOLD I HUL, Dan. for 'ball in the hole'. In this game the player who holds the ball rolls it towards a row of holes dug in the ground along the line of throw. The number of holes is equal to that of players; behind each hole a large stone is placed and to the left of each hole, 5 small stones. Then, the draw begins: the players line up with their backs facing the holes, they cover their faces with caps, and one of them, pointing to one of the holes, asks: 'Is that your hole?' After the draw, each thrower steps onto a line marked beforehand. The player whose hole is the closest commences the game; he rolls a ball – if the ball misses and no hole is filled in, it is the next player's turn. If he hits, the tender of the hole takes the ball over, whereas the rest of the players run to the safety zone. If one of those fleeing is hit with the ball, he moves one of the stones beside his hole from the left to the right. Now, the game is taken over by the tender of the second hole (counted from the throwing line), etc. The player who is hit 5 times (all his stones are placed on the right side of the hole) is out of game as *udsjid-ing* – the one who

A bökhiin barildaan wrestler.

B

WORLD SPORTS ENCYCLOPEDIA

is down. The game continues until only one player remains in the field – the winner. The large stones are used for stopping the holes whose tenders have been eliminated from the game, to prevent stray balls from falling into them. In the northern part of Bornholm no large stones were used, with only 3 small ones in the game. The loser was struck with an open palm into 'stewed beef' (*bankekød*). In the south of the Falster Island (Sydfalster) the game was known as *standerale* (all stops). No predeter-

Bold i hul.

mined safety zone was used here; the players fled until the player holding the ball commanded, 'Stanto!' which was an order to stop. In the locality of Fuur, the game was called *trille i hul* (to roll towards a hole); a ball was rolled not from one side but from both sides – alternately. In Diernisse a similar game was played without any holes and was dubbed, rather amusingly, *træd an til flæsk og pølse* (fall in for fat pork and sausage); the players would line up and the one beside whom the ball stopped grabbed it, whereas the rest would flee until they heard, 'Stanto!' at which point they stopped as in other versions of the game. The one who missed was eliminated and must be 'stoned' (*stenet*); he held the ball in his left hand, turned around so as to face the wall, and threw the ball over his right shoulder. When the ball touched the ground, the players took it and threw it at the standing 'sinner' (*synder*) three times. In the neighborhood of Odense the game was called *nummer stanto* (numbered stanto). A ball was thrown against the wall across specially marked places that were numbered from left to right (1 place per player). The player on the right side, whose number was the highest, was supposed to roll the ball towards the remaining stands. The player at whose stand the ball stopped was to catch it, shout, 'Stop!' and hit one of the other players. In Hasseris, another variety of bold i hul was named *bold i hue* (ball in cap), since the stands were marked not with holes but players' caps instead. In the town of Fredericia the game of *staabold* used to be played, in Ulkebøl – *ægbold* (lit. egg ball). In Germany, similar games were named *Stehallee*, *Lochball*, *Trenselen* or *Trudeln*; in Sweden *gropboll* or *bollsta*; in France *la balle au pot*; in Italy *la pietruzza*, whereas similar games were called *budella* in Modena, *fosetta* in Calabria, and *a la baddi* in Sicily.
J. Møller, 'Bold i hul', GID, 1997, 1, 33.

BOLDSPIL FRA LUNDE, Dan. for 'a ball game from Lunde', a game similar to the Eng. >CRICKET but played on a field with just one wicket [Dan. *bold* – ball + *spil* – game, play + *fra* – from + *Lunde* – a name of a Dan. town]. Boldspil fra Lunde employs a standard air-filled rubber ball (*gasbold*) of 6-7cm in diameter and a flat, wooden bat (*boldtræ*) which is usu. 10-15cm wide. The gate used in the game is similar to a regular cricket wicket (*cricket gærde*) and consists of three poles driven into the ground and a small bar placed on top of them. The attacking team's task is to knock the wicket over.
A game of boldspil fra Lunde involves two teams of 4 to 10 members. They draw lots and one team becomes the fielding team called the outer or ball-catching team and the second team becomes the batting or wicket-defending team. A wicket defender (*spilleren ved gærde* or *gærdespilleren*) stands close to the wicket with his face turned towards it and with his back to the fielders. He throws the ball over his head towards the fielders who try to catch it. If they manage to do so the wicket defender is eliminated from the game without scoring. He is replaced by another player from the same team who throws the ball in the same manner. If none of the field players catches the ball, one of them picks it up later from the spot it landed at and throws it at the wicket. The wicket defender cannot do anything to stop the ball. If the ball hits the wicket he is eliminated and replaced by another player from the same team. If the thrower misses the wicket, the wicket defender picks the ball up, throws it up in the air with his left hand and hits it with the bat while it is still in the air. Similar to the first stage of the game the field players try to catch it. If the flying ball is caught by one of the fielders the wicket defender is eliminated, if not – the first fielder to reach it throws at the wicket but this time the wicket defender may defend the wicket by trying to hit the ball with his bat. The wicket defender scores 1pt. for each successful hit. The aggregate number of points scored by all wicket defenders from one team becomes the inner (defending) team's total score. Then, the teams change places and the game starts anew. The winner is determined on the basis of the two teams' total scores.
J. Møller, 'Boldspil fra Lunde', GID, 1997, 1, 70.

BOLICHE, a popular Chilean var. of bowling that developed in the colonial period after the arrival of the Spanish [Span. *boliche* – bowling alley]; also known as *emboque* [Span. for 'passing through a hole'].
O. Plath, 'Boliche', JYDLCH, 47-48.

BOLILLOS, DE, a Span. folk var. of bowling popular in the Soria province in NE Spain. De bolillos is a male counterpart of a female bowling game known as *bolos sorianos*, see >JUEGO DE BOLOS.

BOLLEBANEN, see >PLATTE BOL.

BOLLEN, see >PLATTE BOL.

BOLLSTA, see >BOLD I HUL.

BOLOS ARAGONESES, different var. of bowling typical of Aragon in Spain and esp. in the Aragonese province of Huesca, where bowling was banned in 1879 for distracting people from their work.
BOLOS BENASQUESES (*Quilles Benasque*), played by women in Benasque (Huesca), involves trying to knock down 9 pins usu. 40-50cm high, weighing some 400g and spaced at 40cm intervals. The ball used to knock them down weighs 5 to 6kg.
JUEGO DE BIRLLAS DE 'MULLÉS'. The game dates back to the period preceding the Roman occupation of the area. The object of the game is to knock down 9 pins called *birllas* (*bitlla* in Catalonia and *birla* in Valencia). The 3 var. of the game employ different types of pins but they are usu. 36-40cm-high and weigh up to 1.1kg. The ball used to knock them down is made of wood, is 70cm in circumference and weighs up to 4kg.
Other, Aragon var. of the game are called *palitrocs* and *palistroques* and are popular in Peralta de la Sal and Binéfar, respectively. See also >JUEGO DE BOLOS.
C. Moreno Palos, 'Bolos benasqueses; Juego de birlas de 'mullés'', JYTE, 1992, 124-7.

BOLOS ASTURIANOS, different var. of Span. bowling games popular in Asturias, a former province and kingdom in Spain which is characterized by its distinct culture, quite different from the rest of Spain. For this reason local sports, although considered Span., are often discussed in encyclopedias and

ethnographic studies as separate from the Span. ones. The major bolos asturianos var. include:
JUEGO DE BATIENTE, a game employing a rectangular lane (*bolera*) which is usu. 34-51m long and whose width is unspecified (usu. 3-4m). The lane is divided into 3 major zones: the approach (or throw zone – *zona de impulso*) which is 14-15m long; the ball lane which is 16-32m long; and the pin zone (*losera*) which is 4m long. The number of pins varies but irrespective of their number there are always two in a row at the front with the rest arranged into 3 rows behind them (3 rows of 3 pins in a game of 11 pins and 3 rows of 4 pins in a game of 14 pins). The ball (*bolada*) rolls along a wooden trough (*rodao*) with a rounded bottom which is 16-32m long and which ends just in front of the first 2 pins. The pins are separated from the trough by a bar which the ball has to jump over and a transverse beam (*losera*) onto which the ball has to roll to reach them. The ball is 14-18cm in diameter and weighs from 3 to 5kg. Each pin that has been knocked down but remained within the *losera* is worth 1pt. A pin that has been knocked down and rolled out of the *losera* and stopped before the end wall of the lane (which is 1.8m-high and is called a *ciebo*) is worth 10 points. If a pin is knocked down and flies past the *ciebo*, the player scores 50pts.
BOLOS DE TINEO, employs a rectangular *bolera* which is 30-35m-long and 10m-wide. There are 20-22 cylindrical pins. The pins are 16-18cm-high, are 3cm in diameter, are made of beech or apple wood and placed in a line crosswise to the ball's path. The ball is 9cm in diameter, weighs from 0.6 to 1kg and is made of wood filled with metal. The object of the game is not only to knock down the largest possible number of pins but also to place the ball as far away from the throw line as possible and as close to a thick beam (called *viga*), located at the other end of the lane, as possible. The minimum scoring distance is marked with a 10pt. line called *raya del diez* which is drawn 4m in front of the beam. If the ball passes this line, the player scores 10pts. for each pin knocked down. If the ball knocks a number of pins down but does not pass the 10pt. line, the players scores only 1pt. for each pin knocked down. If the ball knocks down at least one pin and flies over the lane-end beam, the player scores 50pts. and automatically wins the game. Throws are made from an area called a *poyo* (bench) which is a slightly raised platform with a small hollow (called a *cueva*) in front of it. The *cueva* serves to prevent a thrower from stepping over the throw (foul) line. The *poyo* is trapezoid in shape. The side adjoining the *cueva* is straight and the remaining 3 sides are slightly curved.
JUEGO DE CUATREADA, [Span. *juego* – play, game + *cuatreada* – fourfold, quadruple]. The lane (*bolera*) is circular in shape. The circle's radius is 225cm and one side of the circle is as if cut off by the throw line. The lane is divided into 3 main parts, the throw zone (approach), a square zone called a *castro* with a *caja* (box, chest) inside where the pins are placed. There are 9 bigger pins arranged in 3 rows of 3 and 1 smaller pin (called a *biche*) which is placed behind the last row of the bigger pins. The bigger pins are 52cm-high, 7.5cm in diameter at their base, grow slightly thicker to 7.8cm in diameter in the middle of their height and then taper to 4cm at the head. They are topped with a head that is 5.9cm in diameter. The *biche* is 28cm-high, 6.8cm in diameter at its base, 7.0cm in diameter in mid-height and its head is 4.4cm in diameter. Both types of pins have a stabilizing base made of metal. Balls of 10-11.5cm in diameter are made of special variety of oak (*encina*). The object of the game is not only to knock the pins down but also to knock them out of the *castro*. The balls are thrown in such a way so as to land them within the *castro* and make them hit the pins. Each ball that bounces in the *castro* and rolls out of it is worth 3pts. even if it does not knock any pins down. If it stops inside the *castro* it is worth 6pts. Each pin that is knocked down but stays within the *castro* is worth 1 additional point. If a pin rolls out of the *castro* it is worth 4pts. If the only pin to be knocked down is the *biche*, the player scores 4pts. If the *biche* is knocked down but the ball rolls out of the *castro*, the score is 0. A player scores 5pts. if he knocks down the pin in the center. The players compete individually, in pairs and in teams. During a one-to-one match each player has 6 balls, in pair-to-pair contests each of the 4 players has 3 balls and in a contest involving 5-member teams each of the 10 players has 2 balls. A round is completed when all

the players have thrown all their balls. A game of juego de cuatreada consists of 4 to 20 rounds, depending on prior arrangements.
C. Moreno Palos, 'Juego de bolos: Juego de cuatreada; Asturias', JYTE, 1992, 84-7; 91-5; 331-5.

BOLOS BURGALÉS, a folk var. of bowling popular mainly in the province of Burgos [Span. *bolos* – bowling + *burgalés* – of Burgos, pertaining to Burgos]. It has been developing under the supervision of the local branch of the Federación Española de Bolos. The game is played on a rectangular lane called a *bolera*, which is 30-35m long and 8-11.5m wide. Players are divided into 2 teams with an equal number of members. The players compete individually, in pairs, threes, fours or even teams of 8. In championship games each team must have a specific number of substitute players. There are a number of bolo burgalés var., the most popular being *pasabolo*. Pasabolo involves knocking down 3 pins marked 1, 2 and 3 placed in a special area called a *castro*. The approach, called *el pato*, is a raised platform, made of stones in the past and of concrete nowadays, with a small ledge protruding in the direction of the pins. The ledge ends with a plank that rises to 30-40cm above the platform level to prevent a contestant from falling down after making a throw. Then, *el pato* turns into a rock slab which is at least 1.4m long and 1m wide. The first pin is placed some 3.4 to 3.6m away from *el pato*. The middle pin (or pin no. 2) is deemed to have been knocked down only when at least one more pin is knocked down along with it. A ball thrown by a player has to bounce off the ground in front of the castro and then hit the pins. If the ball comes to rest within the castro it is called a 'bald' ball (*calva*) and no points are scored irrespective of the number of pins knocked down. If the ball hits the line marking the beginning of the castro the throw is called a 'bite' (*muerde*) but is deemed valid. There are three lines behind the castro. The first one is called the *real* and it is located 7-8m from the end of the castro and has a value of 10pts. The second line is called the *medio* and its point value is 20. The third, last line is called the *aacabado* and its point value is 40. These points are scored by the player as bonus points, depending on the distance traveled by the ball and pins after a successful hit. Behind the 3rd line there is a small fence of up to 80cm in height used to stop the rolling ball and pins. The scoring system is unusually complex and depends largely on the playing method and the local rules of the respective bolo burgalés var. such as *dibla con minche, mano natural, mano con minche*, etc. See also >JUEGO DE BOLOS.
C. Moreno Palos, 'Bolos burgalés', JYTE, 1992, 90.

BOLOS CÁNTABROS, different var. of Span. bowling games that originated in the former historic province of Cantabria in the NW Spain (now the provinces of Burgos and Cantabria). A very distinct and unique culture has developed in Cantabria and as a result its bowling games are quite exceptional and very different from the Span. and Basq. bowling sports. The major bolos cantabricos var. include:

high, 4cm-wide at the base and 2.5cm-wide at the conical upper end. The pins are arranged in a rectangle of 3 rows of 3 pins located towards the end of the *zona de bolos*. The pins are spaced 2.25m apart from one another. An additional, smaller and brightly painted pin is placed some 2.25m behind the last row of the bigger pins. The smaller pin is only 25-30cm-high, 3cm-thick at the base and 2cm-thick at

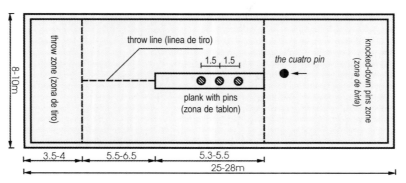

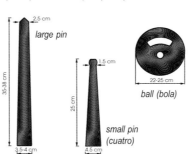

Bolos cantabricos: a bolos de San Pedro de Romeral lane (above) and ball and pins (below).

the top and has a head of 3-3.5cm in diameter. Bolo pasiego balls are rather large – 32-35cm in diameter – and weigh some 5 to 7kg. The throw (foul) line (*raya de tiro*) is located some 10m away from the first row of pins. The game consists of two stages. The object of the game is to knock down as many pins as possible. The role of the smaller pin is not explained in the preserved rules (most likely its point value is higher than that of the remaining pins).
BOLOS DE SAN PEDRO DE ROMERAL, a type of a bowling game popular in the village of San Pedro de Romeral (lit. a village of St. Peter of Chamomile) and in the neighboring areas in the north of Spain. The *bolera* is a rectangular lane which is 25-28m long and 8-10m wide comprising the throw, pin and ball-rolling zones. Each player usu. has 2 balls which are made of nut or beech wood. The balls are 22-25cm in diameter and weigh some 5 to 7 kg. A game of bolos de San Pedro de Romeral involves 3 pins shaped like narrow cones which are 38cm high and are placed in a row one after the other on a plank located in the middle of the lane. There is also a fourth, additional pin (called a *quatro*). The *quatro* is 25cm-high and is put on the ground, behind the plank, slightly to one side of the lane. If the ball hits the plank and knocks some of the pins down, the thrower scores 1pt. for each. The player scores 4pts. if he knocks the *quatro* down. A game consists of a number of rounds called a *chico* or *partida*. A round is completed when one of the players or teams has scored a total of 25pts.
PASABOLO DE LOSA, also known as *pasabolo de ruedabrazo* [Span. *pasa* – passage + *bolo* – pin + *losa* – board, surface; *ruedabrazo* – a circular swing of an arm]. Pasabolo de losa is esp. popular in the Transmiera area in the north of Cantabria, Spain. The lane, called the *bolera*, is a rectangle that is at

least 29m long and 20m wide. The *bolera* is divided into 2 parts. The first part comprises 3 zones, i.e. the throw zone, a board (*losa*) on which pins are placed and which is 100-130cm wide and 150-190cm long, and, finally, the so-called knocked-down pins zone (*lugar de birle*). The second part of the lane is another rectangle with a semi-circle of a 12m radius inscribed into it. A large part of the semi-circle's diameter adjoins the rectangle. The pins are not knocked down with a ball but with grindstone-shaped objects similar to small cheese rounds. The diameter of the grindstone-like block measured from its center to the beginning of the rounded edge is 10-14cm whereas its total diameter is 13-16cm. The block usu. weighs from 1.3 to 2.5kg. The pins (cylindrical in shape) are 30-34cm high and 2cm thick. 9 such pins are arranged on the *losa* into a square of 3 rows of 3 pins. The first row of the pins is placed 7.5m from the throw line and the throw zone which is a shallow, 30cm-deep hollow that is 2m long and 8-10m wide. The width of the throw zone is, however, not specified in the official rules. Each pin that is knocked down is worth 1pt. If a player knocks down the middle pin without sending it to either side of the lane, he scores 2pts. If a pin is knocked down and pushed into the semi-circle, the player scores 10pts. If the pin is pushed behind the semicircle, the player scores 11pts. A round (*chico*) is deemed completed when one of the players or teams has scored 50pts. A game of pasabolo de losa usu. consists of 4 rounds and involves individual players or teams of 2 to 6.
A game of *bolos de tres tablones* (>JUEGO DE BOLOS) is also popular in Cantabria and other, neighboring provinces.
C. Moreno Palos, 'Juego de bolos. Cantabria', JYTE, 1992, 95-101.

BOLOS CARTAGENEROS, is a var. of Span. folk bowling practiced in the vicinity of Cartagena and La Unión in south-eastern Spain. The game is played on a rectangular lane which is 80-90m long and 8-11m wide. At each end of the lane there is a wooden beam (called a *tronco de palmera*) marking the limits of the lane. The game may be played along both directions (i.e. start at either end of the lane) but the direction must not be changed in the course of a single round. Balls are made of hard wood and are 10-12cm in diameter and weigh from 725 to 1050g. Pins are extremely slender and are 30-35cm high and 1-2cm wide at the base and 1cm-wide at the top. Each pin is divided into 3 sections marked with different colors. The bottom-most section is painted red, the middle one – white or yellow – and the top section is red again. Given the fact that the pins are very thin, they are placed in wet clay to prevent them from falling down. A game of bolos cartageneros employs 9 such pins arranged in 3 rows (*andanás*) of 3. The rows are set 20m apart so that the first row is as much as 40m away from the

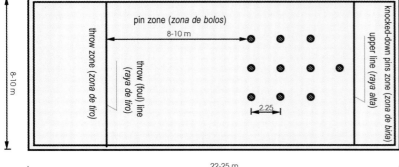

Bolos cantabricos – pasabolo de losa (pasabolo de rudebrazo): a cross-section of the knocking block.

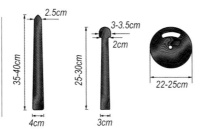

Bolos cantabricos: a bolo pasiego lane (above) and ball and pins (below).

BOLO PASIEGO is popular in the Pas Valley (*Valle de Pas* – hence the name), esp. in the village of San Pedro de Romeral and in former Cantabria (i.e. the NW part of Spain). A bolo pasiego lane (*bolera*) is a rectangle which is 25-30m-long and 8-10m-wide and is composed of 3 major parts: the throw zone (*zona de tiro*), the pin zone (*zona de bolos*) and the knocked-down pins zone (*zona de birla*). There are 9 candle-shaped wooden pins which are 35-40cm-

last row. The pins forming one row are spaced 90cm from each other. The distance from the throw line to the first row of pins is 20m. The game is played by 2 teams of 7 players. Each player has one ball to throw in one round. A team is headed by a captain called *manilla* (lit. a small hand). The *manilla* is always the second to make his throw. A proper game of bolos cartageneros consists of 2 rounds with a 19min. break between the rounds (the sources consulted did not provide an explanation of the unusual duration of this break). Each round consists of 11 'services' or 'serves' (the odd number is to rule out the possibility of a draw). Each successful attempt (i.e. a service) is worth 1pt. When one team has scored 6pts. the round comes to an end since it is no longer possible for the other team to win this particular round. A service is deemed won by the team that managed to send more knocked down pins behind the so-called fluke line (*linea de chamba*). The fluke line is drawn 20m behind the last row of pins. Behind the fluke line there is the so-called knocked-down pins zone (*birlaera*) which is 10m long and extends over the full width of the lane. This zone ends with a palm-tree beam (*tronco de palmera*) used to stop the balls and pins. If the teams score the same number of points within one service play the one who was the first to achieve the score is declared the winner.

C. Moreno Palos, 'Bolos cartageneros', JYTE, 1992, 130-2.

BOLOS DE CUENCA, a Span. ball throwing game similar to bowling practiced solely in the town of Cuenca and the neighboring areas in the central-eastern part of Spain. The objects to be knocked down are not regular pins but poplar rods called *palos*. They are some ½in. in diameter (approx. 1.2cm), 95-110cm high, and are driven into the ground in 3 rows of 3 so that they form a 6.2x6.2m square. The distance between any 2 rods is slightly more than 3m which makes hitting them with a ball extremely difficult. The game is played on a rectangular lane (called a *bolera*), which is 28m long and 8m wide. The lane surface is made of pressed and smoothened earth. Balls are 25-30cm in diameter and are made of pine or poplar wood and are surrounded with metal bands. Each contestant has one ball. The distance from the throw line (*mano*) to the first row of rods is 17m. The distance from the hindmost row of rods to the lane end is 6m. The end of the lane is marked with a beam that stops the balls (*viga de revatida*). The object of the game is to knock the rods down with the ball. This is extremely difficult because of the thinness of the rods and the relatively large distance between any two rods; see also >JUEGO DE BOLOS.

C. Moreno Palos, 'Bolos de Cuenca', JYTE, 1992.

BOLOS GALLEGOS, a folk var. of bowling characteristic of the Span. Galicia [Span. *bolos* – pins, bowling + *gallegos* – Galician]. There are 2 main types of bolos gallegos:
BOLOS CELTAS, lit. Celtic pins, a game played on a lane which is 35m long and 10m wide. At one end of the lane there is a throwing zone which is a 3x3m square. 6.5m from the edge of the throwing zone, which is at the same time a throw line, there is a granite slab [Span. dialectal *pedra bolleira*; Span. *piedra bolera*], which is 110cm long and 70cm wide. The slab is placed in a longitudinal position (i.e. its shorter side faces the oncoming balls). 9 small pins are arranged on the slab in 3 rows of 3. The arrangement is, however, quite unusual as the figure formed by the pins is not a square but a trapezium. Additionally, each row of pins is arranged at an angle with respect to the throwing direction. The pins are made of wood and are barrel-shaped. They are 8-9cm high, the base and top are 2.5cm in diameter whereas the thickest part of a pin is 6cm in diameter. A pin weighs 225g. Balls are made of wood, are 13cm in diameter and weigh 2kg. The object of the game is to throw a ball in such a way that it, together with the largest number of knocked down pins possible, should reach the lane endline which is drawn 28.5m away from the hind edge of the granite slab.
CANTEIRO is a game that usu. involves teams of 4 players. The lane used in the game is 25-27m long. Some 3-4m away from the throw line there is a transversely placed, rectangular board on which 10-14 (depending on the local custom) pins are arranged in one row, also situated transversely to the throwing direction. The pins are 7-10cm high and come in 2 varieties: 1) they are either shaped like two

A set of pins and a block for playing bolos riojano de mujeres.

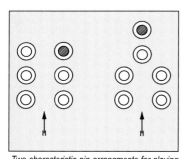

Two characteristic pin arrangments for playing bolos riojano de mujeres (the minca pin is marked)

The pin, block, and pin arrangement in juego manillas.

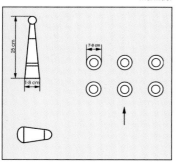

Bolos vascos.

cones joined at their bases or 2) they are cylindrical in shape with a light bulb-shaped top. The balls are made of wood, are 15cm in diameter and weigh some 2kg. The object of the game is to throw a ball in such a way that, together with the largest number of knocked down pins possible, travels as far away as possible. To facilitate subsequent measurements there are 2 crescent-shaped lines drawn within the lane. They are located some 10 and 20m away from the nearest end of the board. Some 2-3m behind the 20m-line there is a net (called *red*) to stop the balls and pins. A player may score 10pts. when the ball passes the 10m-line without knocking down any pins or for each pin that stops behind the 10m-line. He scores 20pts. when the ball has passed the 20m-line or for each pin that lands behind this line. See >JUEGO DE BOLOS.

C. Moreno Palos, 'Bolos celtas', JYTE, 1992, 129; same author, 'Bolos o canteiro', JYTE, 1992, 127-8.

BOLOS MARAGATO, is a folk bowling game popular in the town of Astorga and in its vicinity (in the Span. province of León). Due to the fact that this small area of some 400 sq. km. has always been isolated from the rest of the country, the local people have managed to preserve their customs, traditions and sports, including bolos maragato, in a largely unchanged form. The game is played on a rectangular lane (*bolera*) which is some 50m long and 20m wide. The object of the game is to knock down and send as far away towards the end of the lane as possible 11 pins placed on a special rock (*piedra*) in specially carved hollows. To make the pins even more stable they are driven into wet clay put into the hollows. There are 9 large, cylindrical pins that are 15cm high and 3cm in diameter and 2 smaller pins, called *cuatras*, which are 8cm high and 3cm wide at the base. The *cuatras* are topped with a sphere that is 4cm in diameter. The pins are arranged into a square – the larger ones form 3 rows of 3 pins and the 2 smaller ones are placed halfway between each pair of the 3 pins forming the first row of the square so that there are actually 5 pins in this row. Three crescent-shaped lines are drawn within the lane. Their radius is as if anchored at the spot where the middle-of-the-square pin stands. The first line is drawn 10, the second 20 and the third 30m behind this spot.

Throws are made from 4 spots called *pozas* or puddles. Three of them are located alongside one straight line which extends transversely with respect to the longitudinal axis of the lane, 4m away from the *piedra* and at 2.5m intervals from one another. The middle puddle is called the first puddle (*primera poza*) and the two side ones are called *cruzada izquierda* (left diagonal) and *cruzada derecha* (right diagonal), respectively. Behind them there is the last puddle or *ultima poza*. Instead of a ball the game employs wooden cuboids with a 15x12cm rectangular base. The cuboids are 20cm high. The game is usu. played by 2 teams of 3. The game proceeds along the following rules: first, the so-called royal throw (*a la real*) is made. The contestant to make it stands in the first puddle. The contestants continue to make their throws from this puddle until 52pts. have been scored. The team who loses has the right to select a new puddle in the next round. The following scoring system is observed: 1) pins that are knocked down from the rock but do not cross a 15m-line are worth 1pt. each – the 2 smaller pins are worth 4pts. each here; 2) pins that are knocked down and stop behind the 15m-line are worth 15pts. each; 3) pins that are knocked down and stop behind the 20m-line are worth 20pts. each; and 4) pins that are knocked down and stop behind the 30m-line are worth 30pts. each, irrespective of whether these are the larger or the smaller pins. The team which put more pins behind the 15m-line has the right to start the next round of the game. A proper game of bolos maragato usu. consists of 8 rounds (*juegos*). If the game ends in a draw, there is an extra round played until one of the teams has scored 52pts.

C. Moreno Palos, 'Juego de bolos maragato', JYTE, 1992.

BOLOS RIOJANO, a simple bowling game especially popular in the province of Rioja. It has two major varieties – one for men (*bolos riojano de hombres*) and one for women (*bolos riojano de mujeres*). BOLOS RIOJANO DE HOMBRES, a game played with simple wooden blocks on any flat surface without the need to delimit a specific lane. Instead of a ball the game employs a cone which is some 10cm long, 4cm wide at the base and 2cm wide at the top, which is thrown towards a set of conical pins which are 16cm high, 4cm wide at the base and 2cm wide at the top. The blocks (pins) are arranged in one row, only 3cm away from each other. The throw line is only 2m away from the pins. The game is played by individual contestants or teams of up to 6 members. Usually, however, it is 3 or 4 member teams that compete against each other. The contestants bet for money or material objects which are put on the ground before the game begins. Each team (or individual player) has 3 cones to make their throws. The object of the game is to knock down all the pins except one which must be left standing. If a player or a team succeed in doing so in their first attempt they stop playing and the other player or team takes over. A round (*juego*) is deemed over after two such plays have been completed (one play consisting of 3 attempts by each competitor or team). In the case of a draw, the players or teams play another round and so on until a winner has been determined. Knocking down all the pins equals defeat. The winner or winning team takes all the objects or money deposited on the ground. The Basque Country which is situated next to Rioja has developed its own variety of bolos riojano de hombres called *juego de manillas riojano*. In this var. throws are made with cone-like blocks with their tops as if cut off. The blocks are called *manillas*. Each player has 3 *manillas*. They are thrown at 6 conical pins which are 25cm high and 7-8cm wide at the base. They are arranged into 2 rows of 3. There are no strict rules as far as the dimensions of the lane are concerned but usu. it is 10m long and the first row of pins is some 5m away from the throw line. The object of the game is to knock down all the pins except one. If a player succeeds in doing so in his first attempt he scores 15pts., if he needs two attempts he scores 10pts. and if he does it only after his third attempt the score is 5pts.

BOLOS RIOJANO DE MUJERES, a game similar to its male counterpart. It does not require a special lane and is played on a flat, smooth surface from which any obstacles have been removed. Throws are made with cylindrical blocks that are 20cm long, 3.5cm thick and are made of pine or beech wood. There are 6 smaller and 1 bigger pin. The smaller ones are conical, 36cm high and have a small sphere attached to their tops. They are spaced at 10-15cm from each other and arranged into 3 rows of 2. The larger pin called a *minca* is placed sideways to the smaller pins. Similarly to the men's variety the players make bets before a game begins. A player or team scores 2pts. when one of the smaller pins is knocked down. The bigger pin is worth 10pts. A play in which a player knocks down all the pins including the *minca* is called *hacer el veinte* (making/scoring twenty) since it is worth 20pts. There is another game in Rioja called *juego de bolas de matute* which is played, chiefly by women, in the town of Matute and its vicinity. The object of the game is to knock down 7 pins with a ball thrown from only 2m away. The pins are some 30cm high, consist of as if 3 sections and are topped with a 2cm-sphere.

C. Moreno Palos, 'Juego de bolos riojano de hombres. Juego de bolos riojano de mujeres', JYTE, 1992, 114-5; same author, 'Juego de manillas riojano', JYTE, 1992, 109; R. Garcia Serrano, JDTE, 1974, 164-6.

BOLOS SERRANOS, also known as *bolos andaluces*. A Span. folk bowling game popular in Andalusia [Span. *bolos* – pins, bowling + *serrano* – mountainous, mountaineer's; *andaluces* – Andalusian]. There are 2 major types of bolos serranos, namely the high mountains variety (*modalidad alta montana*) and the valley variety (*modalidad del valle*).

MODALIDAD ALTA MONTANA is popular in towns such as Arroyo, Cazas de Carrasco, Cazorla, Coto Rios, El Cerezo, Frio, Hornos, La Iruela, La Matea, La Toba, Los Anchos, Miller, Pontones, Rio Madera, Santiago de la Espada, Torre del Vinagre, Vadillo and Villacarrillo. There is a throw line (*linea de tiro*) which is a crescent which is a few meters long. Behind the line there is a throwing zone which is a 1.5x5m rectangle including a short run-up track. The main part of the lane is some 67m long and it becomes gradually narrower towards its end where a small, 50cm-high wooden wall (*tablon*) is installed. The pins are not knocked down with a ball but with a flat grindstone-like blocks which are 17-20cm in diameter, weigh some 3kg and are made of oak or sometimes of other types of wood. There are two 7cm-deep holes drilled in the block. The smaller one is meant for the thumb to be placed in and all the remaining fingers are put into the larger one. The block is used to hit a smaller single block that is called a *mingo*. The *mingo* is 15-17cm in diameter and weighs some 800g. It is made of olive or pine wood and placed not far away from the thrower on a short plank or board arranged along the longitudinal axis of the lane. The object of the game is to hit the round block with the grindstone-like block so that both objects travel as far towards the end of the lane as possible. There are 10 to 130pt. scoring zones marked every 3.5 to 4.5m on the side lines of the lane. The number of points scored by a player corresponds to the points value assigned to the zone in which the two blocks stop. Each team is usu. composed of 5 players but there as many as 10 players on a team in championship competitions. Each player makes 1 throw during one round. If one of the players sends the *mingo* behind the *tablon* his team wins a given round.

MODALIDAD DEL VALLE is popular in towns such as Arroyo del Ojanco, Benetae, Cañada Catena, Cortijos Nuevos, El Ojuelo, El Robledo, Segura de la Sierra, Orcera, Puente Cénave, Siles, Torres de Albanenez, Valdemarin and Valle Trujala. The game employs 20cm-balls made of oak. Each player has 2 balls. A round consists of 1 throw with each ball. The number of rounds is agreed upon before a game. In the final round each player has only one attempt (as opposed to the usual 2). The object of the game is to knock down as many of the 3 pins as possible. The pins are called *mingos* and are cylindrical in shape with a rounded top. They come in different sizes – the first one is 20cm high and 5cm thick, the second and third are 15cm high and 4cm thick. They are arranged in one row along the longitudinal axis of the lane, the larger pin being the first in the row. The first of the smaller pins is placed several centimeters behind it and the second several centimeters behind the first smaller one. The first pin is worth 4pts., the second – 2 and the third 1pt. Additional points may be scored if the first (larger) pin is knocked down and out behind a border line (called a *linea de borre*) – such a play is worth 10pts. if all the pins are sent behind this line or 2pts. for each pin that crosses it. If the ball crosses the border line the player scores 5pts., even if he did not manage to knock down any pins. The lane (*bolera*) is usu. situated in a ravine and that is why it has different shapes and lengths depending on the particular location.

C. Moreno Palos, 'Bolos serrano', JYTE, 1992.

BOLOS VASCOS, a number of various folk bowling games popular in the Basq. Country [Span. *bolos* – pins, bowling + *vascos* – Basque]. Sometimes mistakenly treated as a sub-type of the Span. >JUEGO DE BOLOS. There are, naturally, close connections between the two groups of bowling sports manifested, for example, in the fact that some bolos vascos varieties are also popular outside of the Basq. Country – e.g. *bolo murciano*. On the other hand some non-Basq. varieties have been imported to the Basq. Country from the neighboring regions, e.g. *juego de manillas riojano* (>BOLOS RIOJANO). The most popular *bolos vascos* varieties are:

ESCUTXULO, also known as *eskuzulo*. A game popular throughout the whole Bay of Biscay area. The lane, called a *bolatoki*, is a rectangle which is 22-25m long and 1.5-5m wide. 20m away from a throw line there is a stone slab (*losa*) dug into the ground. Its area has to be sufficient to arrange the pins into a 1.4x1.4m square. Modern lanes have a concrete slab. 9 pins, called *brillas*, are arranged on the slab. They are 42cm high and conical in shape with a rounded head. In the middle of the lane there is a plank or board placed along its longitudinal axis. The plank is 5-6m long and 20-24cm wide. The task of a player is to throw a ball so that it lands on the plank and rolls along it towards the *losa*. To the left, some 6.5m away from the leftmost pin there is another, smaller pin called *pequeña*. The *pequeña* is 28cm high. The game employs 22-24cm-balls which weigh some 7-8kg and are made of a special var. of oak (*encina*).

The object of the game is to throw the ball in such a way so as to put it on the plank along which it should roll towards the pins so as to knock as many of them down as possible. Additionally, the ball should not turn aside from the plank and hit the *pequeña*. After making the throw the player must not cross the lane line (*peralte*) until the ball has stopped or has passed the *losa* front edge. If the player does step over the lane line, e.g. after a too forceful throw, the play is declared invalid and the player is dubbed *chaparro* (a midget, dwarf).

When the player knocks 1 pin down he scores 1pt. The game is played by individual players or teams. The most outstanding escutxulo players were: in the pre-1914 period – Aristizábal of San Sebastian and his long-time rival M. de Santiago of Aya; in the 1920s – F. Altube, J.M. Errasti 'Txertudi' and B. Arruti 'Largo'; in the 1930s – R. Badiola; during WWII – J. Aldanondo, R. Olloquiegui and A. Ugarteburu; and after 1945 – J. Ugaldo, J. Marco, and E. Zabalegubi. The main escutxulo competitions are the All-Spain Championship, a series of annual qualifying tournaments (*torneo regularidad*), the Legazpia tournament and the Guipúzcoa Province Championship. The most prestigious escutxulo venue is Plaza de la Trinidad in San Sebastian.

IRUTXULO, a game played in the Guipúzcoa and Alava provinces and on the coast of the Bay of Biscay. The lane (*bolatoki*) is a rectangle that is 24m long and 2.5m wide. It is divided into 4 zones: an approach (*pista de lanzamiento*), ball-slide zone (*pista de deslizamiento*) and pin zone (*zona de birlas*) towards which a ball rolls or slides along a long plank, and a ball-stopping zone (*amortiguador de bola*), which immediately follows the former, pin, zone Balls are 16-18cm in diameter and weigh from 3 to 5kg. Three conical, 22cm-high pins, called *birlas*, are arranged in a row along the longitudinal axis of the lane and are spaced at 1m intervals. The object of the game is to knock down the pins with a ball that initially rolls along the plank and then on the ground. A player (*bolari*) may throw the ball from where he stands or take a short run before doing it. A throw involves a twist of the player's body followed by a swing of the arm and a thrusting of the hand that holds the ball forward. The ball has to land on the lead-up plank. If the ball misses the plank the throw is declared invalid (*ol-uts*).

GOBIATARRA, also known under its full name of *juego de bolos gobiatarra*. A bowling game played in the Gobea Valley area [hence the name: *juego* – game, play + *bolos* – pins, bowling + *gobiatarra* – Gobean, of Gobea]. Also known in Alto de la Tereja, Murga de la Horca, Osma and Fontecha. There are minor technical differences among gobiatarra varieties as played in different places but the object of the game is always to knock down a number of pins arranged on 3 planks. There is a row of 3 pins on each of the 3 planks placed along the longitudinal axis of the gobiatarra lane. All the pins together form a square or a trapezoid. The planks are sometimes placed parallel to one another and sometimes radially so that they form two letters 'V' abutting on each other. The pins are usu. arranged symmetrically, i.e. the first pin is placed at one end of the plank, the second in the middle and the third at the other end. In the case of the 'double-V' arrangement the pins are farther away from the thrower – the first pin being put in the middle of a plank. Pins differ depending on the region but usu. are conical with a sphere-like top. They are some 50-60cm high and 6-7cm

Handling the ball in bolos vascos.

Throwing the ball in bolos vascos.

Bolos vascos: varieties of gobiatarra.

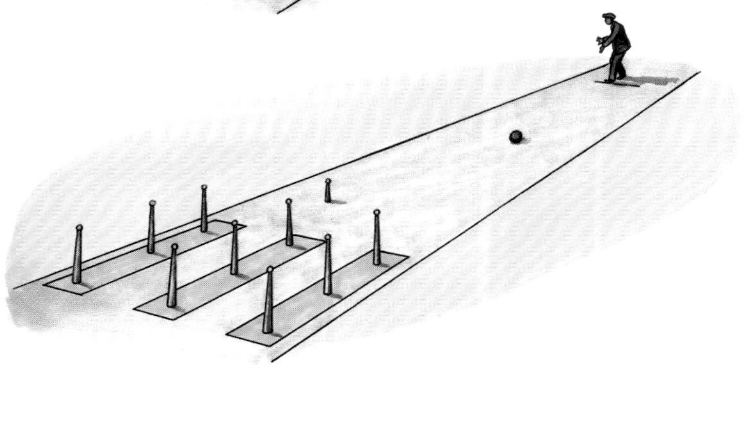

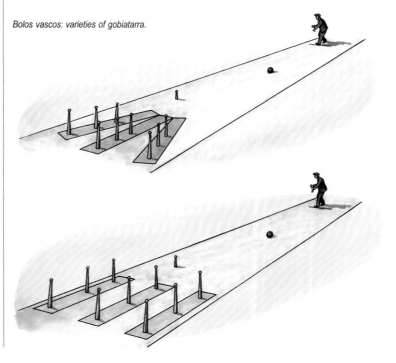

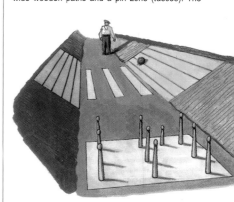

B

WORLD SPORTS ENCYCLOPEDIA

wide at the base. Apart from the regular pins there is an additional one placed by one of the planks. This pin is called a *miquis* or *mico* and it is also conical but two times smaller than the other pins. When it is knocked down a player scores additional points. Each player has 3 balls, the size of which depends on the local custom. Each throw is made in 2 stages. First, a player makes his throw from a spot called *pato*. Then he moves to the spot where the 1st ball has stopped. By the same token, he subsequently

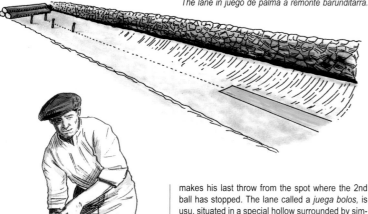

The lane in juego de palma a remonte barunditarra.

Ball handling in juego de palma a remonte barunditarra.

makes his last throw from the spot where the 2nd ball has stopped. The lane called a *juega bolos,* is usu. situated in a special hollow surrounded by simple spectator stands with an amphitheatrical layout. If a player knocks down the middle pin in any of the rows he scores 2pts. (*doseo*). All the remaining pins are worth 1pt. If the smaller pin is knocked down in the first attempt together with some other pins the player scores 4 additional points (*cuatreo*). If he knocks down only the small pin, he scores 5pts. In the 2nd attempt (or 2nd throw) the player should not aim at the smaller pin as he will not score any points if it is knocked down. If a player knocks down all the middle and rear pins without knocking any of the 1st row pins he is said to have made a 'bald' (*calva*) throw. If the ball does not reach the rear pins the throw is called 'dead' (*morra*) even if the pins forming the 2 first rows have been knocked down. If the ball does not knock any of the pins down a throw is declared invalid (*blanca*).

NUEVE AYALÉS, also known under its full name of *juego nueve de Ayalés*. The name comes from the name of the town of Ayala where the game is most popular. It is, however, also practiced in places such as Urcabustais, Arrastaria, Llodio, Lezana, Oquendo and Arceniaga. The rectangular lane used to play the game is called a *corridor* (*carrejo*) and it is usu. located in a natural or artificial hollow in the ground. It does not have clearly specified dimensions but it usu. is some 20m long, 2m wide and is located in a hollow that is some 1.5m deep. The sides of the hollow are sloping and are provided with wooden planking at those spots where the balls usu. divert from their course so that they can bounce off the sides of the lane. Along the upper edges of the hollow there are benches for spectators. Pins (called *birlos* or *txirlos*) are arranged into 3 rows of 3 and are placed on a rock slab (*losa*) located at the far end of the lane. A slope behind the *losa* is going up over a distance of some 2m to slow the rolling balls down. Additionally, the

The lane in juego de palma de tres berantevilles.

Ball handling in juego de palma de tres berantevilles.

lane ends in a special beam construction to stop the fastest-moving balls. The pins are conical, 50-60cm high and 7-8cm wide at the base. They are spaced at 60cm intervals. Between the middle and leftmost pin of the first row there is an additional, smaller pin called *chiquito* or *cuatris* (little boy or fourth grader). There are 3 planks along which the balls roll, placed between the throwers and the pins. They are 2.5 to 3m long. The planks come in different sizes depending on the local custom. Their width varies from 30 to 50cm. Balls used in the game are the largest employed in Span. bowling games as they are 25 to 30cm in diameter and weigh up to 12kg. The object of the game is to knock down as many pins as possible. Each pin knocked down is worth 1pt. If a player knocks down the middle pin of the second row he scores 2pts. The small pin is worth 4 points if some other pins are knocked down along with it. If it is the only pin to be knocked down, its point value goes up to 5. Throws are made from a spot called *pato*. Each player makes only one throw in each round. A round consists of a series of throws made by all competitors. A game usu. comprises 2 rounds. In the case of a draw a third, extra round follows.

NUEVE LOSINO, also known under its full name of *juego nueve losino*. A bowling game popular in the Valderejo valley. The name stands for 'a new game variety' (as opposed to older ones) [Span. *nueve* – new + *losino* – a flat slab]. It is played on a rectangular lane which is 50m long and 4-6m wide. Throws are made from a spot called a *pato*. Pins are conical, some 50cm high and are arranged into 3 rows of 3 placed on 3 parallel planks. The planks are 3m long, 1m wide and are spaced at 1.15m intervals. Balls whose size depends on the local custom weigh from 3 to 12kg. Beside the larger pins there is also a smaller one called a *mico* which is worth more points than the larger ones when knocked down. The object of the game is to score as many points as possible by knocking down as many pins as possible in 3 throws via a ball which should land on one of the 3 planks.

JUEGO DE PALMA A REMONTE BARRUNDITARRA, also known as *barrunditiarra*. A game popular in the Barundia valley (also spelled Baruntia and hence the name) and especially in the towns of Villa de Salvatierra and Araya. The game is played on a rectangular lane (a *bolatoki*) which is 15m long and some 2.5m wide. The right side of the lane is a wall made of stones or rocks which is 60-80cm high. The wall is shaped like an arch which makes it possible to apply trick throws. In the first stage of a throw the ball has to land on a plank which is 3 to 4m long. At this point the ball cannot change direction. Some 4m away from the far end of the plank there are 4 cylindrical pins which are 30cm high and have knoblike tops whose diameter is not specified but usu. varies from 4 to 7cm. The pins form a triangle. Two of them are placed at a distance of 1.5m from each other along the throw line which runs, in turn, along the right hand side of the lane. The 3rd pin is placed opposite the 2nd (i.e. the hindmost) to the left. The last, the 4th one, on the side of the triangle that connects the 1st and the 3rd pin. In some local var. of the game the pins form an irregular trapezoid whose shorter side faces the thrower. Behind the pins there is an obstacle made of 3 thick logs whose respective sizes are similar to that of a railroad tie. Two of them are placed immediately on the ground and the third on top of them so that they form a 2-tier pile. Their task is to stop the balls and pins.

JUEGO DE PALMA DE CUATRO DE LA LLANADA, a bowling game practiced in the towns of Arana, Araya, Campezo, Cigoita, Villareal and Zuya, all situated in the Llanada de Alava region, and hence the name. The lane ends with an obstacle made of a number of thick logs placed one on top of another and supported with vertical poles. Initially the ball rolls along a plank which is some 3m-long and 35cm-wide. The lane is divided into 3 parts, namely a *pato*, also called a *parro*, which is the place from where throws are made, a path-like part made of 20cm-wide and 15m-long planks along which the balls roll and, finally, a *loma* – i.e. the area where the pins are arranged. The sides of the lane are often stone walls. The object of the game is to knock down 4 pins which are 35cm high and 8cm in diameter. They are arranged so that together with the lead-up plank they form an irregular letter 'Y'. The first pin (*canton*) is placed on the plank towards its far end. The remaining pins are placed

so that they form the diagonal arms of the letter 'Y' extending towards the end of the lane. The one placed closer to the canton is called *medio* (middle one) and stands some 2m away from the end of the lead-up plank. The third pin is called *carraca* (a piece of junk) and is placed in the left-end corner of the lane. Finally, the fourth one, called *guarda* (guard) is placed in the right-end corner of the lane. The balls are made of oak or nut wood, are 15cm in diameter and weigh some 2kg. The number of points scored equals the number of pins knocked down. To score any points, however, it is necessary to always knock the canton down. If a player fails to do so, even if he knocks all the remaining pins down, he scores no points.

JUEGO DE PALMA DE TRES BERANTEVILLES, a game played in the Ayuda River valley, the Berantevilla district and especially popular in the towns of Armiñon and Estabillo. The game is played on rectangular lane, which is called a *juega bolos*. The lane is some 20m long, 3m wide at the thrower's end and 2m wide at the pins' end. It is divided into 3 parts – a throwing zone (*pato*), 18m-long and 25cm-wide wooden paths and a pin zone (*tascos*). The

Bolos vascos: juego de nueve ayalès.

pin zone consists of a number of pegs driven into the lane so that their tops are level with the lane surface. The tops of the pegs are used as bases for pins. The 3 pins employed in the game are called the first foremost (*cantón*), middle (*medio*) and last (*ultimo*) and are similar to those employed in *juego de palma de cuatro della llanada* described above. Balls are 15cm in diameter.

JUEGO DE PALMA DE TRES RIBEREÑOS, a game popular in the Alava province in the towns of Salinillas de Budadón, Sammaniego, Santa Cruz de Fierro and Zambrana. A lane (called a *bolatoki*) is composed of a 20x4m rectangle. Pins are conical, 30cm high and 7-8cm wide at their base and made of oak or nut wood. 3 pins, called a *cantón*, a *medio* (middle one) and *ultimo* (last one) are arranged in a row. They are spaced at 1m intervals. The balls are made of oak or nut wood. They are rolled towards the pins along a long plank. The object of the game is to knock down as many pins as possible in one attempt. A round in which a player manages to knock down all 3 pins is called *tresada*; and a round in which he knocks down 2 pins – *dosada*. Each part (a *partida*) of the game consists of 2 rounds (*dos juegos*). Each player makes 2 throws in each round.

JUEGO DE PALMA SALINERO, a game played in the Añana district. A lane, called a *juega bolos,* is a 30x3-4m rectangle. A throw is made from a square approach called a *pato*. The *pato* is immediately followed by a *traviesa* – a wooden path laid along the longitudinal axis of the lane along which balls are rolled. The *traviesa* is 20m long and 35cm wide. The lane is usu. surrounded with boulder walls which are some 70-80cm high. The lane ends with a wooden fence made of planks or logs.

The game employs 3 pins called a *canton* (extreme one), *medio* (middle one) and *ultimo* (last one). They are 38cm high and 8cm wide in mid-height. There is a fourth pin called a *chiquito* (little boy, tot) which is significantly smaller than the remaining ones although there are no exact specifications as to its size. The 3 larger pins are arranged into a row along the longitudinal axis of the lane; the *canton* is placed on the plank towards its far end, the *medio* is 3.15m away from the plank end and the *ultimo* 2.5m behind the *medio*. The smallest one, *chiquito*, forms a gate-like structure together with the *canton* as it is placed beside it, on the ground, some 15-20cm to the side.

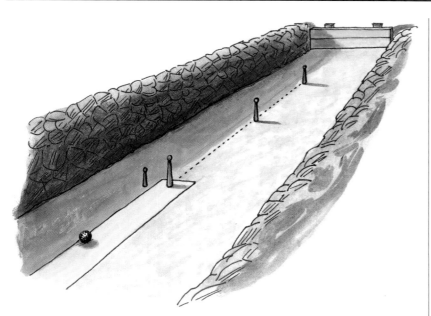

Bolos vascos: juego de palma salinero.

A ball thrown by a player should 'slide' along the plank and not fall off it at any point. A throw is deemed valid if the ball passes between the *canton* and *chiquito*. Subsequently, any of the remaining pins which are knocked down bring 1pt. A throw is also valid if the ball knocks the *canton* down without touching the *chiquito*. If a player fails to do it, even if he knocks all the remaining pins down, the throw is deemed invalid. The *medio* and *ultimo* cannot be knocked down by a returning ball that has bounced off the lane-end fence, either.

JUEGO DE TRES ARAMAISOTARRA, the name of the game comes from the Aramaisotarra valley. The game is popular in Guipúzcoa and Vizcaya. It is played on rectangular lane called a *bolalekua* which is 18m long and 3-4m wide. Its surface is full of bumps introduced deliberately. On the right hand side the lane abuts a boulder wall and on the left hand side a 30-cm-wide ditch. In the first stage of a throw, the ball is rolled along a 1.5m-long and 30-35cm-wide plank. Balls are made of a special var. of oak and their surface is rough. They are 22-25cm in diameter and weigh up to 8kg. Given the fact that both the lane and ball surfaces are rough the game may be played only by the most experienced bowlers. 3 pins called *birlos* or *txirlos* are conical, 35cm high and are arranged into a row along the longitudinal axis of the lane. They are spaced at 50cm intervals. The number of points scored equals the number of pins knocked down.

R. Aguirre, 'Bolos', GHJD, 1989, II, 63-96; R. Aguirre, JYDV, 1978, 420-52.

BOLSTÅ, also known as *gropboll*. A Swed. variety of a game consisting of rolling balls into holes in the ground with rules similar to the Dan. >BOLD I HUL and esp. popular in Åkermark.

BOLTEKAST, Swed. name of a Fin. wrestling var. in which opponents grab each other by their trousers. The Swed. name was used in Finland during the Swed. occupation [Swed. dialectal *bolt* or *bult* – drive a pin or wedge in or coll. thrash somebody + *kast* – throw]. Currently, the sport is better known under its original, Fin. name of >VYÖPAINI.

BÖMBÖG NAMNAKH, Mong. for 'shooting at balls from horseback'. One of the trad. Mong. games in which riders shoot arrows at 3 balls, filled with soft material (usu. pressed grass) and covered with leather, while riding a horse at full speed.

BONGHI, an old Kor. game similar to the Eur. game of >GOLF. The name comes from the words *bong* meaning stick and *hi* – game, play. The descriptions of the game that have survived to present times quite clearly indicate bonghi's similarity to golf defining it as a game employing a stick and a ball and involving driving the ball into a hole in the ground in as few strokes as possible. A court record dating back to 1456, i.e. the period of King Secho's rule, contains a very detailed description of the game: 'The king together with his courtiers watched a game of *bonghi* played at his court [...]. The ball has to be driven with various sticks into holes surrounded with different obstacles. The game can

be played by individual players or teams composed of up to 10 members. The players use various sticks and a ball. The ball is made of wood or nephrite and its size corresponds to that of an egg. A bamboo stick consists of 3 elements: a handle, stem and head. The stem is made of 2 pieces of bamboo wrapped in cow leather. If the leather layer is thin the ball may be sent high up in the air, if the layer is thick the ball flies low. There might also be sticks with soft padding – such sticks are used to only roll the ball. So depending on the purpose or place the game employs various sticks which are named after their shapes. A bonghi course is full of holes located up on a series of steps or among small castle models which constitute obstacles to be overcome by players. The ball reaches the target, i.e. falls into a hole, depending on a player's technique – either flying, spinning or rolling along a slope or other part of the course. The rules say that if the ball falls into a hole after only one stroke the player scores 2 points. In all other cases the player scores only 1 point. A ball may be hit two or more times to move it from the spot at which it rests until the final destination has been reached. Each player has his own ball and during one game his ball may hit an opponent's ball only once. If this happens for the second time he is automatically disqualified. Depending on the spot at which the players stand they may either remain standing up or stoop (there are more positions and further rules of the game)'.

History. According to the above mentioned court record of 1456, King Secho together with his courtiers and family watched bonghi games played by his friends and relatives. Due to the fact that bonghi was mentioned in Korean sources a year earlier than golf in the famous edict by the King of Scotland (1457) some Kor. historians (e.g. Koo-Chul Jung) try to suggest that golf actually originated in Korea. This proposition is inadmissible for at least 2 reasons: 1) the Kor. variety did not have any influence on the shape of golf as we know it today and constituted a similar game which, nevertheless, developed in isolation from golf; 2) a game similar to golf, although named differently, was played in Scot. hamlets situated near Hadrian's Wall as early as around 1100, which further supports the hypothesis on the Ang.-Sax. origins of golf. Moreover, a Chin. historian Gunson Ho mentioned (1926) that a game called >CHÚI WAN was introduced to China during the reign of the Sung Dynasty (960-1279).

Koo-Chul Jung, *Erziehung und Sport in Korea im Kreuzpunkt fremden Kulturen und Mächte*, 1996.

BONNETY, a trad. game played by Eng. boys who held one another by the hands and formed a circle inside of which they placed their caps. Then, still holding one another by the hand, they tried to move in such a way as to make one of the players touch or kick one of the caps lying on the ground. If this happened the boy was declared the loser and as a punishment all the remaining boys threw their caps (or *bonnets* – hence the name) at him.

BONSOR, see >MARBLES.

BOOMERANG THROW, a throwing event using a hyperbolically curved wooden object with a length of 30-35cm and a width of up to 3cm, originally a throwing weapon ['boomerang', from the language of New South Wales Austrl. natives, *voomera*]. The arms of a boomerang are not always of equal dimensions, and are often flattened in the central part. The angle between the arms depends on the construction, and may be between 90 and just under 180 degrees. One of the types used in sport has 3 rather than 2 arms, looking much like older airplane propellers. (Such boomerangs usu. have larger dimensions, between 38 and 91cm from end to end.) The thickness of a sport boomerang is usu. about 4-6mm. Boomerangs are made of various kinds of wood, e.g. maple, mahogany, ash, Fin. birch or even pine for lack of other types of wood. Sport boomerangs may also be made of synthetic materials, such as carbon fiber, polypropylene, polystyrene etc. The boomerang is thrown in a rotational motion but, contrary to popular belief, it does not always return to the thrower if he misses the target. The phenomenon of 'return' was only present in certain types of boomerangs used for ritual purposes and in games. The boomerang is usu. thrown at a target, but there are also trick events, and 'doubling' (throwing 2 boomerangs simultaneously). The so-called 'Australian round' combines distance, accuracy and catching.

History. Boomerangs were used by indigenous Australians until the early 20th cent. but the principles of boomerang throwing were known not only in Australia. Ancient mural paintings provide evidence that boomerangs were familiar as early as prehistoric times. The oldest known boomerang was excavated in Obłazowa Cave in Poland in 1998. It was made of polished mammoth tusk about 20,000 years ago. Boomerangs were also used in ancient Egypt. A number of extremely valuable Eg. boomerangs were discovered in 1922 by the Brit. archeologist Howard Carter in the tomb of Tutankhamen (they are currently held at the Eg. National Museum in Cairo and at the Metropolitan Museum of Art in New

The boomerang – it seems to have a mind of its own.

York). Ancient Eg. boomerangs were used in small game and bird hunting. Scenes depicting boomerang throws can be found in numerous Eg. paintings. However, Eg. boomerangs were constructed so that they did not return to the thrower in the event of missing the target. Boomerangs were also used by some Amer. Indian nations, and among Germanic tribes in Europe. The old Germanic god Wotan (Woden) owned a special hammer which, according to legend, after being set into rotational motion, returned to the god if he missed the target.

After the boomerang lost its importance as a weapon, the first attempts were made at using it in sport. The popularity of boomerang throwing in Australia arose in the 1960s. In 1969, the Boomerang Association of Australia was established, and the first Austrl. championships were organized in 1971. The main objective of the Association was to develop boomerang throwing as a sporting event, establish rules and facilitate contacts between boomerang fans. Since that time, national and state championships have been organized in Australia. The first larger international event was begun in 1988 at Barooga, New South Wales, under the name of the International World Boomerang Throwing Cup. To-

B

Boull-ten.

Boule Nantaise.

Boule Morlaisienne

A game of boules.

day, the event is attended not only by Australians but also by competitors from such countries as the USA, France, Germany, Switzerland, the Netherlands and Japan. Boomerang throwing has seen rapid growth in the USA, where the United States Boomerang Association has many clubs in most states. There are also specialized boomerang manufacturers and shops in Australia, USA, Canada, UK and Germany. There are also boomerang magazines, such as the Amer. *Boomerang News*.
'The Art and Sport of Boomeranging', *Smithsonian*, August 1970; 'The Boomerang Boom', OR, Dec. 1995-Jan. 1996; J. Gibney, 'Boomerang-throwing', *The Oxford Companion to Australian Sport* (1994); H. Hess, 'The Aerodynamic of Boomerangs', *Scientific American*, Nov. 1968, CCXIX; Internet: http://www. usba.org/ boomerangfaq.html.

BORD AND CORD, a name of an Eng. football game popular in the 16th cent. of which not much is known. It was mentioned by an Eng. antiquary, draftsman and writer J. Nichols in his *The Progress and Public Processions of Queen Elizabeth* while describing a party held in her honor by the Earl of Hertford at his mansion in Elvetham, Hampshire: 'after dinner about three o'clock, ten of his lordship's servants, all Somersetshire men, in a square greene court before her majesties windowe, did hang up lines, squaring out the forme of a tennis-court and making a crosse line in the middle; in this square they played five to five

with hand-ball at board and cord as they tearme it, to the great liking of her highness'. Given the fact that the number of players on each team was specified at 5, many sport historians regard the above excerpt to be the oldest known mentioning of a sport called >FIVES, and fives itself is often thought to have originated from bord and cord.

BOSNIAN WRESTLING, a folk var. of wrestling popular in Bosnia and similar (or identical) to >PEHLIVAN WRESTLING, widespread in the former countries of the Ottoman Empire. Bosnian wrestling rules were standardized around 1950. The matches are accompanied by musical performances and are usu. held to celebrate various family occasions.

BOSSELN, a Dan. variety of the Ger. >BOSSELSPIEL. A game of bosseln usu. involves from 10 to 20 people. They use wooden balls filled with lead weighing approx. 0.5kg. In the past the 2 teams playing the game represented 2 opposing villages. The object of the game is to cover the specified distance, often of 10 to 20km, with the smallest possible number of throws. The teams take turns and after each subsequent throw the place where a given team's ball has landed is marked and the throw number is recorded. Depending on prior arrangements the next thrower stands at the spot where the ball first touched the ground after it was thrown by his teammate or at the spot where the ball has actually landed. J. Møller, 'Bosseln/Klootschießen', GID, 1997, 1.

BOSSELSPIEL, [Ger. *Bossel* – playing ball + *Spiel* – game, play]. A ball throwing game, esp. popular in E Friesland, employing wooden or metal balls which were thrown along a road. Contestants throw balls of approx. 10cm in diameter, usu. painted black and red to distinguish between the contestants, along a road. The object of the game is to cover the specified distance with the smallest possible number of throws whereby a specified number of points is scored by the player whose throw is longer or the longest. It often happens that the balls fall into roadside ditches or bogs from where they have to be fished out with special scoops on long poles. The scoops consist of metal loops, slightly larger in diameter than the balls themselves, and small metal arches attached to the loop to support the ball. Bosselspiel dates back to the Middle Ages. Today, given the heavy traffic on the roads, the players have to put up special signs saying *Bosselspiel* to warn drivers against 'flying balls'. Compare >BOSSELN, >KLOOTSCHIEN and >KLOOTSCHIEßEN.

BOSS-OUT, see >MARBLES.

BOTE LUZEA, one of the oldest and simplest var. of >PELOTA VASCA.

BOTHOAN, a Fil. warrior-training school dating back to the times of the Eur. Middle Ages. It involved physical exercise and hand-to-hand combat training. Around 1250 chief (*datu*) Sumakwel wrote an epic

poem describing how 10 chiefs from S Borneo had to run away from their oppressors and settle on the island of Panay. To avoid being driven away from their new homes in the future they decided to train their youth in martial arts. The style or school they developed became known as bothoan. It involved a number of subjects including astrology, physical exercise and martial arts. Later, bothoan was influenced by other sports and martial arts such as the Chin. kun tao, the Indon. >PENCAK SILAT and the Malay langka silat. The principles of bothoan spread from Panay onto the neighboring islands so that when F. Magellan invaded the isle of Mactan located in the vicinity of Panay in 1521 the natives offered fierce resistance. They turned out to be particularly good at spear throwing and killed, among others, Magellan himself. Later, the inhabitants of the Philippines also developed other hand-to-hand combat styles such as >ARNIS, >ESKRIMA and >KALI when they had to oppose Span. and Jap. aggressors.

BOULE À UN PLOMB, a var. of >BOULLOÙ, originally played with wooden bowls in the counties of Leon, Tregor, and Cournouaille. The rules are quite similar to the ordnary >BOULE BRETONNE. Consultant: G. Jaouen, FALSAB.

BOULE BRETONNE, the most popular game in Brittany, along with *palet sur planche*, enjoyed by thousands in the Morbihan and the Côte d'Armor. Nearly every parish has its own playing alleys (some-

times as many as 30, as in the case of Quimperlé). Major tournaments are organized by 3 federations, while hundreds of competitions are held during such local festivals as >PARDON, LE. Consultant: G. Jaouen, FALSAB.

BOULE LYONNAISE, a var. of the Fr. >BOULES developed and practiced in Lyons.

BOULE MORLAISIENNE, a Fr. name of a local, Bret. var. of bowls [Fr. *boule* – ball + *morlaisienne* – of Morlaix]. The bowl has a diameter of 13.5cm and has 5 lead weights, one of which is used to deviate the bowl's course. It is forbidden to throw the bowl. Consultant: G. Jaouen, FALSAB.

BOULE NANTAISE, a bowling game played on a curved area 15mx5 m, located often beside pubs. The excellent rolling surface accounts for why the player does not need any power to push (not throw) the bowl which is 14 cm in diameter.

BOULE PENDANTE, LA, lit. 'a hanging ball'. The Fr. name of a local Bret. bowl game [Fr. *boule* – ball + *pendtante* – hanging, hung].

BOULES FLAMANDES, see >PLATTE BOL.

BOULES, a Fr. ball game also called *boule* (singular) [Fr. *boule* – ball]. The name is a generic one and refers to a group of similar games popular throughout France and differing in minor details

Boules.

depending on local custom. The object of these games is to throw balls in such a way so as to place them as close as possible to a specially marked target, usu. a smaller ball of a different color. The contestant whose balls land closest to the target is declared the winner. The most popular boules varieties are >JEU PROVENÇAL and >PÉTANQUE.

BOULL-TEN, also known as *boullten*. A local Bret. var. of an indigenous ball game [Bret. *boull* – ball]. It is practiced only in the SW of Brittany. Each contestant throws 3 balls towards a target located some 8.5m away. The target consists of a wooden platform with 3 other balls arranged on it. The object of the game is to knock the platform balls off. When the middle ball is knocked off, the player scores 2pts. Each of the side balls is worth 1pt. The game continues until the player has scored 21pts. or more. Consultant: G. Jaoen, FALSAB.

BOULLOÙ, a family of bowls known since medieval times, many var. of which are popular in Brittany. Generally, the object of the game is to throw bowls as close as possible to a small target bowl, referred to as *mestr bihan* – little master. The winning player or team is the one whose bowls rest closest to the mestr bihan – the total of each thrown bowl's distance from the target is taken into account. A similar rule is followed in a number of other Eur. var. of the game, such as Ital. >BOCCIA, Fr. >BOULE, and Eng. >LAWN BOWLS.

Bolloù, however, has its own characteristics which make the game different from all the others: bowls not only can be thrown and rolled towards the target, but also they can be thrown against the lane's side boards or even lobbed at the bowls surrounding the mestr bihan to knock them away. The game is played on a number of occasions such as religious holidays, the beginning or end of a school year, family celebrations, etc.

The oldest forms of the game were practiced in casual alleys or village and town squares. The size of such 'lanes' used to be diverse. Nowadays they are more uniform usu. 15-18m long and 4m wide. The lane is fenced in with wooden boards. Formerly, depending on local traditions, players used cannonballs, bowls carved of stone, or made of wood. Around 1900, following the example of Eng. lawn bowls, they started to make bolloù bowls of guaiacum wood. In some regions of Brittany the bowls are weighted down with pieces of lead. Those regions even developed a tradition of applying a different number of leaden weights inside a bowl. In the Tregor region 1 weight is used, in Léon – 3, in the neighborhood of Morlaix – as many as 5. Currently, bowls made of plastic, manufactured in Italy for playing *bocci*, are becoming increasingly popular.
F. Peru, 'La tradition populaire de jeux de plein air en Bretage', LJP, 1998; Consultant: G. Jaouen, FALSAB.

BOULOÙ-POK DE GUERLESQUIN, a ball throwing game practiced solely in Brittany in the town of Guerlesquin. Contestants throw wooden balls with lead inside, called *boulù-pok* and resembling quoits, towards a previously specified target. The most important bolwhere-pok de Guerlesquin event is a contest called the 'world championship' held on one of the days immediately preceding Lent.
F. Peru, 'La tradition populaire de jeux de plein air en Bretagne', LJP, 1998; consultant: G. Jaouen, FALSAB.

BOUNCER, see >MARBLES.

BOWL SPOT-BOWL, an Ang.-Sax. game similar to >LAWN BOWLING and played according to similar rules. The object of the game is to put one's balls as close to a smaller, white-painted ball (called a 'spotball') as possible. The main difference between bowl spot-bowl and lawn bowling is that the former may employ any balls, e.g. >CROQUET ones.
P. Cummings, 'Bowl spot-bowls', CDOS, 1949, 46.

BOWLINE STRETCHING, see >DECK GAMES.

BOWLING, a catch-all name for any of various games in which a heavy ball or other object is rolled down a long and usu. narrow lane to knock down an object or a group of objects. The targets to be knocked down or otherwise moved are either 1) pins – i.e. wooden objects in various shapes set in various groups and knocked down by a rolling ball – pin games include various bowling varieties such as >AMERICAN BOWLING, >EUROPEAN BOWLING, and others such as >DUCKPINS, as well as the Can. >FIVEPINS; there are also numerous folk bowling types such as the Brit. >SKITTLES, Span. *bolos*; Basq. >BOLOS VASCOS; Ger. *Kegeln*; Pol. >GRELE; Du. >GAAIBOL, etc., which have never

Apollonius, A professional boxer resting, a bronze statue, 1st cent. BC.

Apollonius, A professional boxer resting, detail of the boxer's wrapped hand.

become popular internationally; or 2) other balls (also called target balls, target bowls) which are usu. smaller and of different colors than the bowls that are rolled. The object of such games is usu. to put one's own bowls near the target ball/bowl and to displace the opponent's bowls so that they are as far from the target ball as possible.

BOX LACROSSE, an indoor var. of >LACROSSE, often referred to by the players themselves as *boxla* or *indoor lacrosse* and played on a regular >ICE HOCKEY rink without the ice. Box lacrosse is played mainly in the summer months. It is more dynamic than regular lacrosse. The teams consist of 6 players each (5 field players and a goalkeeper). Box lacrosse is a contact sport. The playing time is 4 quarters of 15min. or, similar to ice hockey, 3 periods of 20min. The number of substitutions is unlimited. Players are subject to 2min. penalties for infringing the rules of the game. Box lacrosse distinguishes among as many as 8 age categories from children below 12 years of age to senior players of 21 years and over and to veterans of 35 years and more. Adults play the game professionally. At present, there are some 25,000 box lacrosse players in Canada as compared to a total of 28,000 all lacrosse varieties players. Its origins date back to the 1930s where it was introduced to revive the waning interest in outdoor lacrosse.

BOXE FRANÇAIS, see >FRENCH BOXING.

BOXING, direct fighting with the fists. Boxing is one of the oldest forms of combat and of combat sports despite the fact that its rules and social importance have changed throughout the ages. The oldest forms of boxing date back to ancient times where they were first known in the Euphrates area, later flourished as a constituent of the Hellenic games and were then turned into a popular entertainment to satisfy the low instincts of the general public in Greece, after it had become a part of the Roman Empire, and in Rome itself (>ANCIENT PUGILISM). In the Middle Ages boxing was also popular in Eastern Europe, especially in Russia and on the Pol.-Rus. border (>OLD RUSSIAN BOXING). Despite its ancient origins boxing as we know it today chiefly developed in the Ang.-Sax. countries – initially in England and later in the US. Therefore, when speaking of the older, non-Ang.-Sax. forms of boxing we should use the term pugilism to stress the historic and cultural differences, whereas the term boxing should be used solely when referring to the sport of fist fighting as developed later in Britain.

Fundamentals. The object of the fight is to deal as many blows with one's fists on one's opponent as possible and, at the same time, avoid his punches. The fighter who scores the greatest number of points or makes his opponent unable to continue fighting in any other legal way is declared the winner. The only legal blows are those dealt with a closed glove on the front of the opponent's torso above his waist or on his face. Hitting below the belt and hitting the opponent's neck or back, especially around the kidneys is considered foul play. It is also forbidden to hit an opponent with an open glove as well as deal blows with the head, shoulder, forearm and elbow. Furthermore, the boxers must not hold each other with one or two arms or, in other words, clinch. Blows

may be exchanged only after a signal marking the beginning of a round and during a round, when the fight has been stopped by the referee, it may be resumed only on his clear signal. When one of the fighters touches the floor with any part of his body other than his feet or when he falls to the floor or stands stupefied or hangs on the ropes or, in other words, is knocked out, the referee starts counting aloud from 1 to 10 with intervals of a second between the numbers. If the fighter fails to resume fighting on the count of 10, he is deemed to have been knocked out. After each knock-out, the fighter has to undergo a detailed medical examination. If a boxer is knocked out 3 times within one year, his boxing license is revoked. Boxing matches take place in a ring which is a raised square platform enclosed with ropes. The name 'ring' as used today has little to do with the original boxing arena which, as the name rightly suggests, was circular in shape and was simply delimited by a circle of spectators following a given fight. The first 'artificial' boxing rings were also circular in shape. Later the shape changed into a square whereas the name remained. The fight is controlled by a referee, who officiates in the ring, and is marked by judges. At smaller contests and during less important matches there are usu. 3 judges whereas a panel of 5 judges must be present at major international competitions. The outcome of the match may be determined in several ways: 1) a win on points – at the end of a contest, the boxer who has been awarded the decision by a majority of the judges is declared the winner; 2) a win by a knock-out – if a boxer is down and fails to resume boxing within 10 seconds, his opponent is declared the winner; 3) a win by a giving in by a second – a second may give in for a competitor; 4) a win by the Referee Stopping the Contest (RSC) – the referee may decide to discontinue the fight when one of the boxers is outclassed, injured so that in the opinion of the referee a boxer is unfit to continue, etc.; 5) a win by a disqualification – a boxer may be disqualified by the referee for not observing the rules and fair play principles; 6) a win by a walk-over – declared in favor of the appearing fighter after one of the boxers has presented himself in the ring fully attired for boxing and his opponent has failed to appear; 7) a no contest win – due to one of the boxers being overweight; 8) a no contest win – due to one of the boxers being banned from fighting upon medical examination by a doctor; and 9) a draw – when the majority of the judges scored the competition equally, especially at major competitions such as national championships, international competitions, Ol.G. as well as world and continental championships.

A statue of a boxer, 1st cent. BC, bronze.

The statue of Apollonius on a postage stamp issued for the 17th Ol.G. in Rome.

A boxing match depicted on a clay amphora, Greece, 5th cent. BC.

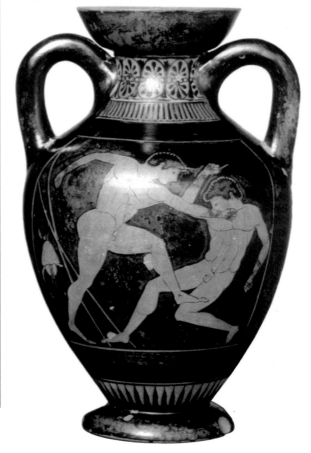

WORLD SPORTS ENCYCLOPEDIA

B

At present, matches are held between boxers of the same weight category. In ancient times and in many folk varieties of boxing there were no clear weight classification systems although most of the matches were held between boxers of similar weight, strength or size. For example, during the ancient Ol.G. in Greece bouts between men and young boys were not allowed and separate contests were held for both age categories. The number of weight categories has tended to vary even in modern times

George Bellows, Two Members Of Our Club, *oil on canvass, 1909.*

George Bellows, Stag At Sharkeys, *oil on canvass, 1907.*

Young, Fighting boxers, *a bronze sculpture.*

Rudolph Belling, A Boxer, *bronze statue, 1929.*

and the overall tendency has been to increase the number of categories. During the first half of the 20th cent. there were 7, 8, 9 and finally 10 weight categories, respectively. At present there are as many as 12 weight categories that have to be observed during Ol.G., W.Ch. and continental championships organized under the auspices of the Association Internationale de Boxe Amateur, AIBA (International Amateur Boxing Association). These are: light fly (up to 48kg), fly (up to 51kg), bantam (up to 54kg), feather (up to 57kg), light (up to 60kg), light welter (up to 63.5kg), welter (up to 67kg), light middle (up to 71kg), middle (up to 75kg), light heavy (up to 81kg), heavy (up to 91kg) and super heavy (over 91kg). As far as professional boxing, chiefly supervised by the 3 largest federations or associations – i.e. WBC, WBA and IBF, is concerned there are as many as 17 weight categories. A title won in the heaviest category equals the title of all weight categories. Twelve out of the 17 professional boxing weight categories correspond to the 12 Olympic boxing categories (although not always directly), whereas the remaining 5 do not have such counterparts. In addition, certain federations or associations apply different names to the same weight categories, for example: the light fly weight (up to 48kg) is sometimes called *mini-flyweight, straw-weight* or *minimum weight.* There is often an additional up-to-49kg category named *light-flyweight* or *junior-flyweight.* The up-to-51kg (112lbs.) category is called *flyweight,* the up-to-52kg category (115lbs.) is known as *super-flyweight* or *junior-bantamweight,* the up-to-54kg category (118lbs.) is dubbed *bantamweight,* the up-to-55kg category (122lbs.) is referred to as *super-bantamweight* or *junior-featherweight,* the up-to-57kg category (126lbs.) is called *featherweight,* the up-to-59kg category (130lbs.) is known as *super-featherweight* or *junior-lightweight,* the up-to-61kg category (135lbs.) is named *lightweight,* the up-to-64kg category (140lbs.) is referred to as *light-welterweight* or *junior-welterweight,* the up-to-67kg category (147lbs.) is called *welterweight,* the up-to-70kg category (154lbs.) is dubbed *light-middleweight* or *junior-middleweight,* the up-to-73kg category (160lbs.) is known as *middleweight,* the up-to-77kg category (170lbs.) is called *super-middleweight,* the up-to-79kg category (175lbs.) is referred to as *light-heavyweight,* the up-to-88kg category (195lbs.) is dubbed *cruiserweight* or *junior-heavyweight,* and finally the over-88kg category (195lbs.) is called *heavyweight.*
Etymology. The word 'boxing' comes from the English verb 'to box' meaning to strike with the hand or fist and from the noun 'box' that, among its numerous meanings, also stands for a blow with the hand or first, especially on the head. In old England the name was used to refer to a sport of bare fist fight-

ing. The origins of the English term are, however, unclear. There are 3 main theories on the origins of the word *box.* The first and the simplest one claims that the word is an onomatopoeic representation of the sound made upon dealing a blow similarly to the old Greek word *pyks* used to refer to the same type of sound. The second theory says that the word is an all-Germanic expression taken over into English from old Ger. similarly to the Low Ger. word *baksen* or Modern Ger. *baksen, boxen,* or Dan. *baxe* or Swed. *baxas, boxas.* The third theory also dwells upon an old Germanic prototype which is, however, said to have been derived from a different word, namely an appellation corresponding to the Old Teutonic *boki,* Early Dutch *beuk,* Middle Dutch *boke, böke* and Middle High Ger. *bochen.* Irrespective of all the above hypotheses, the word box or boxing acquired its present meaning in 16th- or 17th-cent. England. This is best exemplified by the oldest usages of the word box in the English language as in the work by W. Horman *Vulgaria* (1519) which reads at one point 'He was boxed out of the place'. The 1589 work of R. Harvey *Plaine Perceval the Pacemaker of England* includes the following line: 'To boxe a shadow and beate their knuckels against a bare wall'. The oldest purely sports-related meaning of the word box has been discovered in the 1657 translation of Seneca's *Hippolytus* by J. Studley: 'The naked fist found out to scratch and cuffe, to boxe and bum'. The 1765 work of Tucker entitled *The Light of Nature Pursued* reads 'Two men boxing together in the next street'. The English translation of Homer's *Odyssey* prepared by an English poet W. Cowper includes the following fragment: 'To leap, to box, to wrestle'. In the 19th cent. the original meaning of the term was expanded further to include 'to hit with a gloved fist' and this sense was subsequently propagated throughout Europe and later loaned into almost all the languages in whose cultures boxing began to be practiced.
History. Street or folk fist fights that gave rise to modern Eng. boxing that later spread throughout the world were never related to other similar Eur. traditions. Modern boxing developed rapidly in Great Britain thanks to very favorable cultural and social conditions that also led to the development of the proper rules of modern sport in general. The natural inclination of human beings to fight was turned into a standardized system by the English aristocracy who, when staging boxing matches, attempted to turn them into organizationally and aesthetically coherent shows whereby the fighters' chances had to be equal. The first written mention of this process comes from the 'London Protestant Mercury' of January 1681: 'Yesterday a match of boxing was performed before his Grace, the Duke of Albermale, between his butler and his butcher. The latter won

English capital until 1729. In 1741 after the death of one of the boxers called G. Stevenson, J. Broughton (1704-89) developed a new set of rules that made boxing less violent. They banned hits under the belt, introduced 30sec. breaks after knock downs and, finally, introduced a square ring enclosed with ropes. His rules appeared in print in 1743. They were yet again significantly amended in 1838 by the London Prize Ring – the largest London company promoting boxing matches. The new rules remained in force till around 1865 when A. Chambers – a boxer – the Marquess of Queensberry and J. Chamberlain – a journalist – prepared yet another set of rules that became widely accepted in Great Britain and in 1872 were adopted in the US. The rules introduced 3-minute rounds, special protective gloves and 3 weight categories. They also prohibited hair pulling and kicking which, although not explicitly recommended, had been 2 techniques often previously employed during matches. The division into amateur and professional boxing also became more apparent since the date this set of rules was introduced.
Amateur boxing. Amateur boxing developed from professional boxing in the second half of the 19th cent. Initially it appeared in England as a sort of fashion and applied art, one of the subjects taught to young boys reared to become gentlemen. It was included in the Olympic program only as late as in 1904 in St. Louis where the contest was held in 7 different weight categories. The Fédération International de Boxe Amateur (International Federation of Amateur Boxing) was established in 1920. In 1946 it was renamed the Association Internationale de Boxe Amateur, AIBA (International Amateur Boxing Association). Initially, it was the Eur. countries that dominated in the AIBA, whereas amateur boxing in the US was still governed and controlled by professional associations and was treated as a training ground for the most talented young fighters before introducing them to the professional ring. In the 1920s amateur boxing strengthened its position significantly thanks to the fact that boxing contests were included on the Olympic program and the fact E.Ch. were held regularly. Olympic competition was initially dominated by the Eng.-speaking fighters from Great Britain, Canada and the US who won all the gold medals in 1920 in Antwerp (except one that went to a Frenchman). During the next Ol.G. in 1924 in Paris the Eng.-speaking fighters continued to dominate the boxing scene but they had to resist fierce competition from Scandinavian boxers. Unfortunately, the very strong Ger. team did not compete at either of the above mentioned Olympics although boxing's popularity had virtually exploded in Germany at that time. The first E.Ch. was held in 1925 in Stockholm. This competition was dominated by the Swedes who won the Nations Cup for 3 individual gold medals

Three-boxer teams engage in a bare-knuckle fight in the painting by George A. Hayes.

the prize, as he hath done many times before, being accounted, though but a little man, the best at that exercise in England'. Basic rules and terminology, including the name 'ring', were also developed at that time. In 1719 J. Figg, considered the father of modern boxing, challenged other fighters to compete with him for the title of all-England champion. A series of regular championship matches followed during which J. Figg managed to retain his title until 1730. In 1719 he also established the first ever boxing school which became a model for at least 12 other famous boxing schools that operated in the

(O. Andren – feather weight, S. Johansson – light weight and B. Persson – heavy weight). Additionally, 2 more gold medals went to the Danes – H. Nielsen (welter) and T. Peterssen (light heavy) and Scand. domination became a fact. The remaining gold medals went to E. Pladner of France (fly), A. Rule of England (bantam) and F. Crawley of England (middle). The second E.Ch. took place in 1927 in Berlin and the Germans won 4 gold medals and the Nations Cup. The next two championships (1930 and 1934) were held in Budapest and the next in 1937 in Milan where Poland won 2 gold medals, 2 silver ones and the Nations Cup. The Poles defended the Cup during the next E.Ch. in 1939 in Dublin where they won 1 gold, 3 silver and 1 bronze medal. At the same time the major international competition remained the Ol.G. where the Europeans competed with Amer. fighters. During the 1932 Ol.G. in Los Angeles only one European, I. Eneker of Hungary, managed to win a gold medal. 4 golds went to Eng.-speaking boxers (2 to the US, 1 to Canada and 1 to RSA) and the 2 remaining ones were awarded to

the US won 2 golds each and the remaining golds went to Algeria, Bulgaria, Ireland, Kazakhstan, the Democratic People's Republic of Korea, Russia, Thailand, Ukraine and Hungary.
Professional boxing. Boxing has always been a professional sport in England and the US. Irregular and poorly paid boxing matches were turned in the 19th cent. into a highly commercialized and well-organized entertainment industry. Professional W.Ch. date back to Amer.-British matches held in

er's victory over his white opponent was shown to the general public played a very important role in breaking the racial barrier in the sport. The movies, however, lacked the live aspect offered by direct broadcasts from boxing matches. The gap was initially (in the 1920s) filled by radio which, obviously, fell short of the visual part of a broadcast. The two complimentary media, i.e. picture and sound, finally put an end to the so-called *Age of the Player* and marked the beginning of the *Age of the Spectator*.

Marvin Johnson, a bronze medalist at the 1972 Olympics in Munich, Germany, won the light-heavyweight title three times and compiled a 43-6 record, 35 KOs, while boxing as a pro from 1973 to 1987. He retired after losing a rematch to Stewart in Trinidad in 1987, at the age of 33. His two losses to Matthew Saad Muhammad are classics in the 175-pound division.

Lenox Lewis trounces Mike Tyson to regain the title of World Heavyweight Champion.

Bernie Briscoe, one of the best fighters to never win a world title. Back in the days when there was only one world title, this dangerous puncher policed the middleweight division during a career which began in 1962 and ended in 1981. He scored 53 knockouts and compiled a record of 66-24-6.

Argentines. However, during the 1936 Ol.G. in Berlin the Americans won only 1 silver and 1 bronze medal. 2 gold medals went to France and Germany respectively and Hungary, Argentina, Italy and Finland won in the remaining categories.
After WWII the number of countries whose athletes aspired for boxing fame grew dramatically. The E.Ch. in 1947 in Dublin and in Oslo in 1949 as well as the 1948 Ol.G. in London were dominated by competitors from those countries that suffered relatively minor damage during WWII, i.e. Ireland, France, Hungary, Italy, Sweden, Holland, Czechoslovakia, Argentina and South Africa. In 1952 when the Soviet boxers entered international competition the situation changed dramatically. During the 1952 Olympics 5 gold medals went to the US but as many as 3 went to the USSR. During the 1953 E.Ch. in Warsaw Poland won as many as 5 golds which turned Poland into a boxing superpower for a brief period of time. And although Poland maintained its strong position until the 1970s, the amateur boxing scene in the 1954-74 period was dominated by Soviet boxers. This trend was reversed in 1974 when during the 1st amateur W.Ch. in Havana it was the Cuban team that took 5 golds. They repeated this extraordinary feat during the 2nd W.Ch. in Belgrade (1978) and during the 3rd W.Ch. in Munich (1982). During the 1980 Ol.G. the Cubans took as many as 6 golds. T. Stevenson, who won 3 consecutive Olympic golds (in 1972, 1976 and 1980), was the most outstanding Cuban fighter of the 1972-80 period. Due to the fact that socialist countries did not compete during the 1984 Olympics and the fact that Cuba also boycotted the 1988 Seoul Olympics, Cuban fighters disappeared from the Olympic scene although they continued to dominate other international competitions. After they returned to the Olympic family they took 11 golds during 2 consecutive Games (7 in 1992 in Barcelona and 4 in 1996 in Atlanta). Germany and

the 1810-70 period. The first unofficial W.Ch. match was held between T. Cribb (1781-1848) of England and an African-Amer. T. Molineaux (Cribb won). Subsequent W.Ch. fights took place often although irregularly. They were often accompanied by disputes among various boxing managers, promoters and boxers themselves over the rights of a particular to country to stage such a fight and the very right to award the title of World Champion to the winner. Until 1834 the matches were held exclusively in Great Britain but dating from the 1835 visit of J. Burke to the US the two countries alternated in organizing W.Ch. fights. The matches were usu. held according to the London Prize Ring rules which were replaced in 1885 by the Marquess of Queensberry rules. The first W.Ch. match held to Marquess of Queensberry rules took place between J.L. Sullivan (1858-1918) and D.F. McCaffery, although many sources wrongly maintain that it happened only in 1892 during the match between Sullivan and J.J. Corbett. Development of professional boxing was hampered by the fact that in many countries public fist fights were illegal. In the US the ban was first lifted by the state of New York in 1896. Since that date Boxing W.Ch. matches have become one of the most popular international displays open to the general public. Boxing bouts have always been deemed epic shows – the spectators following the adventures of an individual hero with whom they can identify. That is why boxing has often been more influential than many other sports. This trend was further enhanced by the development of various visual media, initially the cinema but later the television as well. In fact, the cinema proved to be much more effective in popularizing boxing than TV. The first movie depicting a boxing match was the filmed report from a fight between an African-Amer. boxer J. Johnson (1878-1946) with J. Jeffries (1875-1953) that took place in 1910. The fact that a black fight-

As a result many boxers, including J. Dempsey (1895-1983, real name W. Harrison) – the World Champion of all weight categories in the 1919-26 period after defeating G. Carpentier of France, J.J. 'Gene' Tunney (1897-1978) – world champion in the 1926-28 period or J. Barrow 'Joe' Louis (1914-81) – world champion in the 1937-49 period, were elevated to the status of celebrities. With the advent of television, boxing became even more popular than ever, but at the same time TV broadcasts, in which the fighters were shown from a very close distance, contributed to the demythologization of the boxing hero and introduced more and more elements characteristic of show business. The very first fighter to achieve fame and renown thanks to TV was R. Marciano (a pseudonym of R.F. Marchegiano, 1923-69) who won the W.Ch. title after defeating J. Walcott (1925-56). Muhammad Ali (the name taken by Cassius Clay after his conversion to Islam), a several-time world champion (see below), was one of the few fighters who single-handedly tried to take advantage of the media.
Until the end of the 19th cent. boxing matches were organized and promoted by numerous, often short-lived, companies established especially for such purposes and only rarely by strong, professional clubs. In the second half of the 19th cent. the largest US boxing fights organizer was the New Orleans Olympic Club. In parallel, there appeared a significant number of individual boxing entrepreneur-managers, e.g. J.W. Coffroth (active from 1898 until around 1910, especially in California; he later switched to horse racing). The most famous promoter of boxing matches was G. 'Tex' Rickard (1871-1929), the first entrepreneur in history to earn over 1 million dollars on a single match (Dempsey vs. Carpentier in 1919). During his career Rickard organized 4 more matches that earned him in excess of 1 million dollars. After his death, his assistant – M. Jacobs – took over his

Joltin' Jeff Chandler was the WBA bantamweight champion from 1980 to 1984. Chandler boxed from 1976 to 1984 and had a 33-2-2 record, 18 KOs.

B

WORLD SPORTS ENCYCLOPEDIA

business and became equally as prominent a promoter as his master. He established a company called Twentieth Century S.C. that won a monopoly on organizing the most important matches in the US. The company, under Jacobs's management, organized as many as 550 professional matches and was later sold to J.N. Norris who changed its name into the International Boxing Club with branch offices in New York, Detroit, Chicago and St. Louis. After TV had become widely popular and accessible, the era of the great promoters and mangers came to an end. W.Ch. matches began to be organized by large associations such as the World Boxing Council, one of the major boxing federations, established in 1963. Soon its supremacy in the world of professional boxing was challenged by the World Boxing Association, WBA, which replaced the Amer. National Boxing Association (est. 1926). Naturally, there are a few more international associations such as the International Boxing Federation (IBF, est. 1983) and the World Boxing Organization (WBO, est. 1988). In addition, there are a number of US-based organizations aspiring to organize major international matches, e.g. the United States Boxing Association, North Amer. Boxing Federation, National Boxing Association (NBA), New York State Athletic Commission as well as the Europe-based Eur. Boxing Union. The 4 first organizations mentioned above, i.e. the WBC, WBA and IBF, are the largest in the world and they compete fiercely with one another to attract more celebrity boxers, more media attention and to extend their 'market' share. Only very infrequently do they co-operate and jointly award Championship titles. Until 1978 the 3 organizations jointly awarded Super Champion titles. After that date they failed to reach agreement and, for example, in 1986 the 3 major boxing federations had their own heavyweight champions which was further complicated by the fact that there were 2 championship bouts a year and each time the championship was won by a different fighter which resulted in there being a total of 6 world heavyweight champions in one year! After 1990 the 3 organizations agreed on mutual recognition of their heavyweight champions (with J. Buster' Douglas becoming the first Super Champion followed by E. Holyfield). Such agreements, if concluded at all, usu. refer only to the heaviest categories whereas the lighter categories remain as unregulated as ever. For example, in 1991 out of all the 14 weight categories in which W.Ch. fights were held by the 3 federations, they only recognized a joint Super Champion in the cruiserweight (E. Holyfield) and lightweight (P. Whitaker). Additionally, the WBC and IBF agreed to mutually recognize their champions in 2 more categories, namely welterweight (S.

Brown of the US) and junior-welterweight (J.Ch. Caesar of Mexico). In all the remaining weight categories the 3 organizations maintained their own classification. The most popular champions of the 1980s and 90s were M. Tyson (the WBA Champion in 1986 and 1988) and R. Bowe (the WBC Champion in 1992). In 1991 E. Holyfield became both the WBA and WBC Champion.

Professional E.Ch. have been held since 1913. Their winners often became world champions later, e.g. I. Johansson of Sweden (the 1956 Eur. and 1959 world champion) or L. Lewis of Great Britain (the 1991 Eur. and 1992 world champion).

Given the changes introduced to the Olympic Charter in 1991 that ruled out the possibility of attaining a high level of boxing competence by truly amateur fighters, the differences between professional boxing as represented by the organizations named above and amateur boxing governed by the AIBA became virtually theoretical. And although OI.G. participants must not receive any remuneration for their Olympic achievements they, and the winners in particular, are entitled to receive money from other sources. As a result the WBC, WBA and IBF organize as if 'ad hoc' individual W.Ch. matches whereas the AIBA maintains its complex system of W.Ch. tournaments with their qualifying rounds, quarterfinals, semifinals and finals. The AIBA W.Ch. take place every 4 years. Therefore, the boxing scene is unusually fragmented and the respective World Champion titles awarded by the numerous organizations are never fully 'genuine' since not all the federations recognize the same boxers as their champions in the same weight categories. On top of that, such champions only rarely participate in the AIBA-sponsored W.Ch. Spectators only very infrequently know which of the boxing organizations has organized the fight they are watching and they usu. tend to only support those boxing celebrities whose sporting and non-sporting achievements (e.g. fights, rapes, trials, financial scandals etc. in which they were involved) have been publicized by the media.

Women's boxing. The first recorded women's boxing fight took place in London in 1720. Another famous fight took place between Nell Saunders and Rose Harland in New York's Hills Theater in 1876. However, many countries in which men's boxing enjoyed great popularity maintained legal restrictions which prohibited women to fight. Some of these restrictions were not lifted until the end of the 20th cent. In 1904 a display women's boxing fight was held during the OI.G. in St. Louis. Nevertheless, occasional events did not put women boxers at par with men until 1975, when Eva Shain became a licensed judge of men's boxing fights organized by

the New York State Athletic Commission. Also in 1975 Caroline Svendsen became a licensed boxer and had her first fight with Pat Pineda a year later. 1977 saw the appearance of the first outstanding indivduality of women's boxing – Cathy 'Cat' Davis, who fought a widely promoted fight with Margie Dunson in Fayetville, North Carlina. The USA Boxing Board of Governor did not recognize women's boxing until 1993, when Dallas Malloy won her sex discrimination suit. In 1996 a fight between Christy Martin and Deirdre Gogarty was held. That same year the British Amateur Boxing Association lifted the 116-year-old ban on women's boxing in England. In 1999 the first boxing fight was held between a woman and a man (Margaret Mc Gregor vs Loi Clow in Seattle, Washington). Women's boxing began to gain rapid popularity after Laila 'She-Bee-Stingin',

Laila Ali, (right) daughter of Muhammad Ali, during her bout against Suzy Taylor at Aladdin Casino in Las Vegas, Nevada.

daughter of Muhammad Ali, fought Jacqui Frazier, daughter of Joe Frazier, in 2001.

Boxing in literature and art. The dramatic and symbolic character of a boxing match has always been a source of inspiration to artists. The very first London street bouts were depicted in various engravings. A special type of boxing portrait showing a person as if ready to fight was also developed. The famous English Romantic poet, Lord Byron was a keen boxer and W. Scott enjoyed watching boxing matches. Unfortunately, their interest in boxing was not reflected in their works. A typical street fist fight was portrayed by C. Dickens in his novel *David Copperfield* (1849). G.B. Shaw devoted a whole book to boxing (*Cashel Byron Profession*, 1886). Outside of the British Isles the first famous boxing episode appeared in V. Hugo's *L'Homme qui rit* (*The Man Who Laughs*, 1868). A special variety of popular literature devoted to boxing was developed in 19th-cent. England by the first sports journalists, e.g. P. Egan, the founder and editor of 'Pierce Egan's Life in London and Sporting Guide' weekly. He later collected the boxing stories and essays published in his weekly into a book entitled *Boxian or Sketches of Ancient and Modern Pugilism from the days of the Renowned Broughton and Slack to the Championship of Cribb* (1818). One of the most renowned written texts devoted to boxing is *The Fight* (1822) by W. Hazlitt, a social philosopher, writer and literary critic. In the US boxing was a major theme of so-called 'street, bar and ring' literature. This type of literature usu. portrayed the vicissitudes of down-and-outs and, although most of the works of this 'genre' were of mediocre quality, it also included such outstanding creations as the whole series of boxing short stories by J. London with the most famous entitled *The Mexican*. Boxing was a recurrent motif in E. Hemingway's works (e.g. *Fifty Grand*). It was also a popular theme among Amer. painters, e.g. G.W. Bellows (1882-1925) and his series of paintings and engravings including *Stag at Sharkey's* (1907), *Both Members of this Club* (1909) and *Dempsey through the Ropes* (1924). The popularity enjoyed by boxing resulted in the popular literature devoted to the subject being virtually produced on a mass scale. It was usu. published in sports periodicals as was the case with H.C. Witwer's novel *The Leather Pushers* (1929) and the novel episodes as well as short stories published in the Polish 'Przegląd Sportowy' ('Sports Review') including J. Ball's *Pięścią zdobędę świat* (*I'll Conquer the World with My Fists*), M. Konarski's *Ostatni mecz* (*The Last Match*), A. Len's *Ostatni mecz* (*The Last Match*) and E. Wilk's *Mało Serca* (*Small of Heart*). Their most overused motif is a boxing match in which one of the fighters stands a chance, apart from winning, of solving some 'real-life' problem. This paradigm was perfected by J. London and E. Hemingway. However, as mentioned earlier it was generally overused and thus the plot was usu. rather banal which was ridiculed as early as in 1934 by B. Fink in *Przegląd Sportowy*:

What naive rubbish our authors write about boxing! They always think about New York, 23rd Avenue, a 'boxing room', an old manager named Joe, two boxers, one of whom once stole the other's wife, shot his cow or robbed him of his inheritance. And finally fate sets them once again against each other and for 10 rounds the good one takes uppercuts, hooks and straights, etc. In the eleventh, when he is close to giving in, he sees a sad smile on his former wife's face or suddenly remembers his cow [...]. This excites him so much that he immediately knocks his opponent down. That is how justice is done and then the story ends (1934, 93).

This often criticized model was followed by the majority of popular literary works of that period. This is best exemplified in W. Preiss's short story *She* when the hero becomes a boxer only to avenge his wife who was murdered by one of his boxing opponents when they were both gold miners. Popular boxing literature, as opposed to such distinguished works as those by J. London or E. Hemingway who tried to employ boxing as a metaphor of human fate, was usu. primitive and always had a happy ending as in the anonymous short story *Boxer and Diessy* where a boxer, D. Browning, immediately after winning his match, is pulled into a beautiful millionaire's car and 'somebody's warm hands took his hands and D. Browning, the Champion of 3 southern states, did not know himself when his lips surrendered to the sweet torture of Diessy's hot lips' (1934). Such 'works', irrespective of the country in which they were produced, usu. dwelt upon Amer. motifs. At the same time, original Amer. works were translated into the majority of Eur. languages. The 'American model' was so popular that non-Amer. authors often assumed Amer.-sounding pseudonyms to sell better. L. Carry, an author whose name is nowhere to be found in Amer. literature encyclopedias, was one of such authors. He was particularly popular in Poland for his novels whose episodes appeared regularly in 'Ilustracja Polska' ('Polish Illustration') and were later published as separate novels including *Droga na ring* (*The Road to the Ring*, 1936), *Ring wolny* (*Box!*, 1937) and *Hrabia wraca na ring* (*The Count Returns to the Ring*) published after 1945. The motif of an immigrant who tries to improve his status in the US by becoming a successful boxer was another popular and abused theme. It was used in many novels and short stories including S. Gajos's *Czternasta runda* (*The Fourteenth Round*, 1935). Only very rarely do we encounter works that devoted some thought to the sport and attempted a deeper sociological analysis of the phenomenon.

There are also numerous real-life accounts, reports, descriptions, biographies and memoirs devoted to the theme of boxing. The best and most well-known works of that category include J.J. Corbett's *The Roar of the Crowd* (1926) including the description of his fight with J.L. Sullivan (1885), the literary accounts of J. Lardner's fights published in the 'New Yorker' and later as novels, e.g. *The White Hope and Other Tigers* (1946), the former world champion, G. Tunney's, memoirs *The Aspirin Age* (1946, including an account of his fight with J. Dempsey) and such socially-aware boxing reports as those by H. Cosel including the most famous one called 'His Name is Muhammad Ali' in *Cosel by Cosel* (1973).

Boxing has always been a popular movie theme. The first major boxing film was, in fact, a documentary of the J. Johnson vs. J. Jeffries match where a black boxer defeated, for the first time in history, a white one. Boxing match reportages remained the main 'genre' until the appearance of TV broadcasts. All major World Champion title matches were filmed, especially in the 1920s and 30s, to be later shown in movie theaters across the world. The most popular 'movies' made in this way were those showing J. Dempsey and G. Tunney's fights. At the same time, there appeared the first feature films. The 'Kino' ('Cinema') weekly reported that boxing was by far the most popular movie theme in the 1919-39 period, a fact which it ridiculed in the following satire:

During the last-but-one show
They are playing the usual sort of movie -
Chases, boxing, motorcycles,
Some gang of muggers
And cowboys, the brave cowboys.

Nevertheless, boxing still remains one of the major sources of inspiration for moviemakers. It is particularly popular among Amer. and Fr. directors. Usually, however, Eur. filmmakers try to paint a more in-depth picture of the sport, the people involved and the social problems it creates as in A. Esway's *L'Idole* (1947, starring Y. Montand) and the Polish movie *Bokser* (*A boxer*) by J. Dziedzina and starring D. Olbrychski (1967). P. Solan, a Czech director, made a movie based upon a novel by a Polish writer J. Hen *Bokser i śmierć* (*The Boxer and Death*, Czech title – *Boxer a smrt*, 1963). Its plot revolves around a boxing match between a Ger. commander of a concentration camp and a Polish boxer, one of his prisoners. The Ger. officer intends to continue his boxing career after the end of the war and he employs the Pole as his sparring partner. The prisoner, on the other hand, sees their training sessions and the upcoming match as an opportunity to defeat his sworn enemy.

The biggest box office hit of the last few decades was *Rocky* directed by J. Avildsen (1976, starring S. Stallone). The movie was partially based on the story of R. Marciano who was a media star who went from rags to riches because by becoming a famous boxer. The movie had 3 sequels, namely *Rocky II*, *Rocky III* and *Rocky IV* which also became very successful pictures thanks to the fact that they followed the principle of offering 'simple emotions and clear-cut philosophy' (*American Film Now*, 1979).

D. Brailsford, *Bareknuckles. A Social History of Prize-Fighting*, 1988; H. Cosel, 'His Name is Muhammad Ali', *Cosel by Cosel*, 1973; E. Gorn, *The Manly Art. Bareknuckle Prize Fighting in America*, 1896; F. Stamm, *Pamiętniki*, vols. 1 & 2, 1955.

BOYIKKUO, a trad. sport similar to >FIELD HOCKEY popular among the Daur, an ethnic minority in China. At present it is played on field hockey or football pitches. In the past the goal was marked by two poles driven vertically into the ground, nowadays regular field hockey goals are used. The game is played by two teams of 11 players (10 outfield players and a goalkeeper). The 'L'-shaped boyikkuo sticks are 80cm long and are more similar to >ICE HOCKEY rather than field hockey sticks. The ball is made of hard wood, usu. of an apricot tree root. There is also a boyikkuo variety employing a burning ball. The ball has a hole bored into it where some flammable material, e.g. oakum soaked in oil, is put. (In the past the whole ball was saturated with oil). Then, fire is set to such a ball. The children's variety of the game employs soft balls made of animal hair.

Mu Fushan et al., 'Daur Boyikkuo', TRAMCHIN, 52.

BRAGWA, Arab. for 'kneeling down'. A game whose rules are not clearly specified. It is mentioned by M. Ibrahim al-Majman in his dictionary of Arab games and sports *Min al'abina ash-sha 'biyya* (*Our folk games*, 1983). It might be related to >ŠRIH EŠŠARH which also involves kneeling.

BRAIN BALL, an Eng. name for a football game popular in ancient Ireland. The ball was made of a brain extracted from a foe's skull and hardened with lime. Brain ball matches had a ritual character, they were religious ceremonies and, at the same time, constituted an instance of a public display of superiority of one tribe over another. Since Celtic priests and sages, i.e. the Druids, who acted as referees during such matches thought that the brain was the center of a person's will, brain ball matches must have constituted a religious form of acknowledging that an enemy's will and soul had been subjected to the players, with the ball serving as a magic symbol of supremacy and strength.

BRÅTAS, one of a number of dialectal names of a Swed. folk wrestling of the 'one hold' variety popular in the Medelpad region; see >BRYGGAS.

BRAUTBALL, DER, Ger., see >BRIDEBALL.

BREAKING HORSESHOES, an old soldiers' pastime; one of the trad. feats of strength, once performed by Pol. knights. See also >AXE BENDING. A short description of a horseshoe breaking contest is found in *The Deluge*, a novel by H. Sienkiewicz:

The soldiers showed off, each with what he could do: the Keyemliches, Kosma and Damian, immense and awkward figures, amused the king by breaking horseshoes, which they broke like canes; he paid them a thaler apiece, though his wallet was empty enough [...]

[vol. 2, chapter. XXIII]

BRETON WRESTLING, see >GOUREN.

BRICHE, a medieval Fr. var. of >BLIND-MAN'S BUFF. A blindfolded player touched with a stick the other players who then had to recite a piece of text or sing a song. While doing that a player changed his voice and swapped places with somebody else to make it more difficult for the blindfolded player to identify him. When a player was identified, he replaced the blind man. One of the documents written at the Fr. king's court in 1277 reported that the game 'had been played in the streets among neighbors'. Another document dating back to 1408 reads that contestants 'sat on the ground'.

W. Endrei and L. Zolnay, *Fun and Games in Old Europe*, 1986, 89.

BRIDEBALL, Ger. *der Brautball*, Pol. *piłka narzeczonych*, also known as *bride's ball*. A folk game known in Europe in the past, sometimes played along with >EASTER BALL. Brideball dates back to the early Middle Ages when pagan and Christian rites clashed in many Eur. countries. Brideball comes in 2 main var. i.e. *fiancée ball* (*bride's ball*) or *fiancé ball* (*groom's ball*). Around Easter, girls from Tragemünde who wanted to get married asked young married women who had got married during the past year for a special ball made of cloth filled with oakum. Then, they played with the ball in a pine forest until the ball was torn. Near Schwedel, young people gathered in a soon-to-be-married couple's house and passed a ball among themselves while singing a special ball song. In Camwern near Sandow on the Elbe there was a similar custom involving singing the following song:

Green leaf, green leaf,
This summer, this summer,
All girls are full of life.
We want to have the bride's ball
And if she does not give the ball to us
We'll take away her man.

A Ger. ethnographer, W. Mannhardt, described in his *Wald- und Feldkulte* (*Forest and Field Cults*, 1875) how the pagan symbolism of green leaves was incorporated into the Christian symbolism of Resurrection and rebirth of all life: 'Brideball is closely related to green leaves and new life [...]. This seems to be of particular importance for the newly wed couple [...]. The importance of the brideball ritual becomes apparent thanks to certain circumstances in which the Church decided to sanctify or even Christianize [certain pagan rites] and endow them with a new interpretation by using them in liturgy to symbolize Christ himself'.

In many areas brideball was played on the occasion of the >MAIBAUM festival when it was combined with *mailehen* – a particular kind of a 'beauty contest' culminating in crowning the 'Queen of May'. Elsewhere in Germany, girls would play similar games with local rules. A similar tradition involving young men developed in Vieux-Pont in Normandy. There, young married men who wedded before a given Palm Sunday would drop a ball with small coins inside from the church tower. The ball was then used by young bachelors who would play with it until it got torn. The first one to tear it apart so as to reach the coins hidden inside would be the first to get married and get a substantial dowry. Elsewhere in Normandy, a soon-to-be-married man would throw a ball over a church roof. Two teams – of bachelors and married men – gathered on the other side of

A poster for the Johnson-Jeffries fight.

A movie poster for Vainqueur par amour 1933.

Boxing motif on a stamp issued for the 9th Ol.G. in Amsterdam in 1928 (above) and the 1953 E.Ch. in boxing in Warsaw (below).

Broomball game at Bear Trap Ranch in Colorado Springs.

Broom polo.

the building would fight for the ball to prove their superiority. In Chatelain de Mareuil in the historical province of Berri each newly wed man was obliged to present his master with a LA >SOULE stick and 2 new balls after the second night spent together with his wife. Until at least 1554 in Rochefort, Pluherlin there was a custom according to which a man who was the last to get married in a given year had to present a ball to his master. Then, the master would order him to start a brideball game by throwing the ball over a public bread oven. The thrower was, however, tied by his leg to the wall around the yard of the local Nôtre Dame de la Trouchaye church. If he missed, he had to pay a fine. In the Ger. town of Ellichsleben a young couple who did not conceive a child within one year of their marriage would throw a spiked ball to young boys.

The tradition was also popular in England where matches were often held during the carnival period (>SHROVE TUESDAY FOOTBALL). In G. Chapman's (c.1559-1634) comedy *Sir Gyles Goosecap, Knight* (written c. 1601-06) the main hero explains his intentions in the following way:

GOOSECAP
Why, Madam, we have a great match at football towards, married men against bachelors, and the married men be all my friends, so I would fain marry to take the married men's part, in truth.
HIPPOLYTA
The best reason for marriage that I ever heard, Sir Giles.
[V.1, line 78ff]

In many brideball var. the ball was thrown or passed by hand. An unusual brideball game, somewhat similar to LA >SOULE, was played every Christmas until at least 1857 in St. Cybardeaux in the Charente Maritime department on the Bay of Biscay. All the men who got married during a given year chipped in to buy a new ball. The game was played along the banks of the Charente River by young, unmarried men. The one who succeeded in delivering the ball to a given destination received a prize offered by all participants. Quite often players drowned during a match. That is why a similar game was banned in the Morbihan department (along the Atlantic coast above the mouth of the Loire River). Balls were of different sizes and made of leather, wool, cloth filled with sawdust, etc. Sometimes they were full of needles, which made the game more difficult.
H. Gillmeister, *Die mittelalterlichen Ballspiele: eine Chronologie ihrer Entwicklung,* Stadion, 1984, X; H. Teichler, ed., *Sportliche Festkultur geschichtlicher Perspektive,* 1990.

BRIDGEBOARD, an Eng. game employing small metal balls rolled towards a portable one-foot (0.3048m) plank or board which could be placed virtually anywhere. On one side the board had 9 square notches separated with narrow projections. During the game the board was placed horizontally with the 'teeth' turned towards the ground and thus it looked like a bridge with 10 spans. J. Strutt (STRUTT, 1810, 242) claims that it was precisely this image that gave the game its name. The notches were numbered 1 to 9 but not consecutively. The numbers were assigned to the neighboring notches in the following order: 6, 2, 3, 1, 5, 8, 7, 9, 4. The notches were usu. 1in.-wide (2.54cm). J. Strutt reports that the balls were rolled from 5-6 feet away from the board (some 1.52 to 1.82m). A player who scored the largest number of points by driving the balls through the notches (or under the 'spans') was declared the winner. A ball that hit a 'support' was given to the owner of the board (TGESI, I, 45). Cf. >NINE HOLES and >TRUNKS.

BROAD JUMP, see >LONG JUMP.

BROERATOK, Scand. for 'a brotherly hold'. Opponents, while standing, grab each other by the arms at shoulder height. The object of a match is to floor an opponent so that he touches the ground with any part of his body above the feet. Some scholars, incl. W. Baxter, claim that broeratok is identical to >AXLATÖK and similar to the Icelandic wrestling var. known as >HRYGGSPENNA. Broeratok is one of the 3 types of folk wrestling popular in the Faroe Islands whose indigenous culture is a mixture of original Norwegian culture as introduced by the first settlers and of Dan. culture introduced later. The Faroese call all three varieties jointly >AT GLIMAST.
W. Baxter, 'Faroe Islands, in: Les luttes traditionnelles a traverse le monde', LJP, 1998, 82-3.

BRÖGGAS, one of a number of dialectal names of a Swed. folk wrestling of the 'one hold' var. popular in the Halland region; see >BRYGGAS.

BRÓKATÖK, a Nordic wrestling term denominating a hold by the trousers. In the Faroe Islands – BRÓKATÖK; in Norway >BUKSETAK, in Sweden – >BYXKAST, >BYXTAG; in Iceland – >BUXNATÖK, >BRÓKATÖK – all of the above are techniques of glíma and had been practiced before the invention of the glíma belt in 1907.
T. Einarsson, *Traditional wrestling in the Northern Countries,* 1988.

BRÖKKAS, one of a number of dialectal names of a Swed. folk wrestling of the 'one hold' var. popular on the island of Västergötland; see >BRYGGAS.

BROOM POLO, a var. of >POLO adapted for the needs of beginners or less advanced players. A larger and softer ball is used (often a basketball ball) and, instead of mallets, players use broom-shaped sticks or regular brooms.

BROOMBALL, 1) a team sport in which a ball is moved towards the opponents' goal with the use of sticks with a rubber, oar-shaped ending. The game is played on an ice rink the size of 61x26m, surrounded by walls. A team is comprised of 6 players including a goalie. Instead of skates, players wear soft, thermo-insulated shoes and various body protectors incl. helmets. The duration of a game is 40min., divided into two 20-min. periods. It was invented in Canada, from where it spread to several countries, including the USA and Australia, where several teams competed in a league in Canberra, which later expanded over 4 provinces. In 1988 the best Austrl. team, the ACT Animals, made a tour of Canada. In 1991 the World Broomball Tournament was inaugurated at Victoria, Canada; 2) an Eng. name of a Rus. game similar to >ICE HOCKEY, but played with birch tree brooms instead of hockey sticks.

BRÖTAS, one of a number of dialectal names of a Swed. folk wrestling of the 'one hold' var. popular in the Södermanland region; see >BRYGGAS.

BROWAR, also known as >CZOROMAJ, or *świnka*. A kind of ball game popular in Poland from the end of the 17th cent. throughout the 18th and 19th cent. Its aim was to shoot a ball or sphere into holes in the ground using a stick. The court, often grass, of unspecified size, had in the middle of it a hole 30cm in diameter, just slightly bigger than the ball itself. This hole was called *browar* (brewery) or *chlew* (pig-sty) and around it was a circle, 5-15m in diameter, of smaller holes, the number of which was smaller by one from the number of players. Each hole was 'guarded' by one player. At the beginning of the game the ball, called *beczka* (barrel) or *świnka* (piggy), 10-20cm in diameter, was placed outside the circle. The player not guarding a hole tried to direct the ball into the centerfield with a stick and place it inside the center hole. Other players used their sticks to prevent this and steal the ball into 'their' holes. As soon as the ball was inside the *browar* (or *chlew*), each player would change his position and signal it by placing his stick in a new hole. The player without a hole, standing outside the circle, also had the right to win a hole and his position was taken by the player who failed to secure a hole for himself; and a new round followed. The number of rounds varied in different regions of Poland. A similar game was also known in France under the name of LA >TRUIE.

BRYDEKAMPE, a Dan. group of wrestling and combat sports (lit. breaking fights) including: >AT KLAVES, >KRUMME ET BEN, >AT VENDE EN MAND, >BÆLTAG, >BRYDES MED TOMMELFINGRENE, >BUKSETAG, >FRIDBRYDNING, >KRAVETAG, >LIVTAG, >NAKKEDRAG, >LÆGGE ARM, >SPÆNDE FINGRE, >VÆDDER PÅ FINGRENE and >VRIDE KAPUL.

BRYDES MED TOMMELFINGRENE, Dan. for 'thumb wrestling'. Opponents put their right arms forward so that their thumbs touch. The wrestler who manages to press his opponent's thumb so hard that he has to kneel down or give up is declared the winner.
J. Møller, 'Brydes med tommelfingrene', GID, 1997.

BRYGGAS, one of the numerous Swed. var. of 'one hold' wrestling popular esp. in Scania. Opponents stand slightly stooped, face-to-face and put their arms around each other, similarly to >LIVTAG. A wrestler is declared to have won the match when he manages to 'break' his opponent at the hips (i.e. if he manages to tilt his opponent's torso to the side) or when he quickly pulls his opponent to his body and knocks him down by 'breaking' his back by tilting it in the direction away from his own body. The name of the sport, similarly to other names of local varieties of bryggas such as *bröggas* (used in Halland), *brökkas* (in the west of Gotland), *brötas* (Södermanland) and *bråtas* (Medelpad), is a dialectal version of the Swed. verb *bryta* – to break.

BRYTA RYGG, Swed. for 'catching by the back'. A form of folk wrestling popular in the Swed. Delsbo and Hälsingland regions [Swed. *bryta* – catch + *rygg* – back] similar to >KNÄPPA RYGG. The Swed. sports ethnologist M. Hellspong classified it in his *Brottning som folklig lek* as a var. of >LIVTAG (cf. the paragraph on >LIVTAG, RIG, 1991, 4).

BUCKERELS, a type of Eng. street game known as early as during the reign of Henry VIII. Later the game fell into oblivion and no details have been preserved.

BUCKSTICK, see >NORTHERN SPELL.

BUCKSTICK, SPELL AND ORE, one of the many games involving striking small balls out into a field. The game employs a small ball (*ore*) which is placed on a lever (*spell*) and launched into the air. While in the air the ball is hit with a bat resembling a butt of a rifle (*buckstick*). The rules of the game are similar to other games of the same family, e.g. >NORTHERN SPELL and *knur and spell.*

BUDELLA, an Ital. var. of a game involving rolling balls into holes dug in the ground. It is popular in Modena, while the neighboring areas follow rules similar to those of the Dan. >BOLD I HUL.

BUFFALO FIGHTS, a sport popular in some regions of Central Asia, e.g. in Vietnam or among the Miao People (Cent. and S China), known in Thailand as Meo; it is often part of a Harvest Festival. In Vietnam, the Do Son Buffalo Fighting Festival, held on the 9th or 8th lunar month in Hai Phong, is one of the most popular of 60 trad. festivals held annually and the preparations for it take several months. The competition is usu. between two villages, whose inhabitants encourage the buffalo to fight by cheering and using sticks. Before the fights villagers visit their ancestors' graves. The fighting itself is accompanied by expressive music played on bone pipes, drums and gongs. According to a Rus. writer R.F. Its, 'the louder the drums, the better the crops'. Two buffalos are led into the arena and fight until one of them gives up and runs away. The winner remains in the arena and goes on to fight another buffalo until the final winner is determined.
R.F. Its, 'Miao. Istoriko-etnograficheskiye ocherki', *Trudy Instituta Etnografiji,* 1960, 60.

BUFFALO RACES, see >WATER BUFFALO RACES.

BUGEI, an ancient Jap. martial art involving the use of various weapons for military purposes. It flourished during the Tokugawa shogunate period (1615-1868). As far as its spiritual aspect is concerned, bugei was based on the principles of Shintoism, mikkyo (Esoteric Buddhism) and some other elements of Buddhism. Most of the bugei styles have been long forgotten. This has resulted from the fact that masters dying without any disciples did not pass their skills and knowledge to anyone. Bugei made use of various weapons including bows and arrows, swords, spears (known as *yari*), halberds, chains and sickles. Modern followers of bugei mainly focus on their spiritual development and avoid competitions which may lead to serious injuries.

BUGÓCSIGA, a Hungarian var. of >TOPS.

BUH, a simplified and incorrect name of Mong. wrestling often used in international literature; see >BÖKHIN BARILDAAN.

BUJUTSU, a Jap. martial art which almost fell into oblivion after swords were banned in Japan in 1876. It was revived as >BUDO which, in turn, gave rise to many combat sports based on ancient traditions. This process is best exemplified by the turning of >JU JUTSU into >JUDO.
D.F. Draeger, *Modern Bujutsu and Budo,* 1974; L. Frederic, *A Dictionary of the Martial Arts,* 1991; D. Mitchell, *The New Official Martial Arts Handbook,* 1989.

A referee watches traditional South Korean farm bulls lock horns during a bull fighting festival in Chongdo.

Bull fights in the Bosnian village of Stricici, 30km from Bania Luka, have been part of a traditional annual festival for almost 40 years.

BUKSETAG, a Dan. folk wrestling var. which involves grabbing an opponent by his trousers [Dan. *bukser* – trousers + *tag* – holding, throwing]. The fighters stand face-to-face and grab their opponent by the belt so that one hand is placed in the front and the second in the back. The object of the game is to lift the opponent from the ground and above one's shoulders. Other folk varieties of hand-to-hand combat also employ holds by other parts of an opponent's clothing; see >CLOTHES HOLD (BELT HOLD) WRESTLING.
J. Møller, 'Buksetag', GID, 1997, 4, 44.

BUKSETAK, also known as *broktak,* a Norw. var. of folk wrestling which involves grabbing an opponent by the trousers and flooring him. The oldest depiction of the Norwegian buksetak is a statuette that was probably made in the 12th cent. and was later found in Lom in the Godbrandsdal region. It is now on display at the De Samndvikske Samlinger in Lillehammer and it depicts 2 hooded wrestlers slightly stooped towards each other and holding each other by the trousers at the hips. Buksetak was most likely one of the most popular wrestling varieties in Norway and the traveling buksetak wrestlers known as *famntakarar* appeared as early as in the Middle Ages. They made their living by staging fights during fairs, weddings and local holidays. Compare the Dan. >BUKSETAG and the Swed. >BYXTAG; see also >WRESTLING WITH CLOTHES PULLING.

BULANG BALL, a Chin. game using balls made of bamboo fibers, 8-10cm in diameter. Bulang ball has 2 var. The first one is similar to a school game once played in schools in Poland and other Eur. countries, called >RZUCANKA. An unspecified number of players stand in a circle. One player tosses a ball high up in the air. The player standing nearest to the falling ball must catch it and toss it up again. The players who fail to return the ball must sing a song or perform a dance as a penalty. The other var. of Bulang ball is played by 2 teams of players, also standing in a circle. The player who tosses the ball tries to make it fall near one of his or her team mates who then is allowed to catch it. If the ball falls near an opponent, the tossing player is 'penalized' in the same way as in the first var. of the game.
Mu. Fushan, et al., 'Bulang Ball', TRAMCHIN, 162.

BULKYO MU SOOL, a Kor. martial and self-defense art practiced in the Kor. Buddhist monasteries. It combined elements of old non-Buddhist Kor. tradition with elements of Buddhism [Korean *bulkyo* – Buddhist + *mu sool* – martial art]; compare also >KOONG YOONG MU SOOL.

BULL FIGHTS, a form of fighting between animals, different from >CORRIDA, where a bull fights a man. Man's role in these bull fights is limited to training the animals and – during the fight – stimulating and agitating them. Among the most popular varieties of bull fights are:
DONG, MIAO AND YI BULL FIGHTS. Among the Dong people bull fights are held during the Hai Festival, which is organized twice a year (in the winter and spring) and lasts 12 days. The bulls wear bronze bells on their necks, while on their backs is a special yoke with a flag that bears a Chin. inscription: 'two dragons fighting for a treasure'. One of the bulls is usu. called a water dragon, while the other – a tiger. Three more flags – red, yellow and green – are placed in a special stand. Bull owners challenge one another ceremoniously, after which the fight begins. The bulls are led towards one another by men from two opposite directions. The fight begins with a gun shot, the sounding of an instrument called *lusheng*, and the striking of a bronze bottomed kettle-drum. The bulls gore one another until one of them becomes weak. Then fight administrators separate the bulls. The sounding of a gong announces victory. The winning bull is decorated with color ribbons and walked around the arena. Among the Miao people (in Thailand known as Meo), inhabiting central and southern China, bull fights were arranged on the harvest holiday in the 9th or 10th lunar month. The fights were usu. between 2 villages, the inhabitants of which agitated their animals with sticks and cries. Prior to the fights villagers visited the graves of their ancestors. The fights were accompanied by music played on bone pipes, drums and gongs.
Mu Fushan et al., *Bullfight*, TRAMCHIN, 120.
BOSNIAN BULL FIGHTS were organized by the shepherds near Bosanska Kraina and several other regions of Bosnia after the summer haymaking as a form of competition between 2 villages. Villagers select their best bulls, which undergo many trials. The winning bull is paraded towards the village and keeps his title until the next season.
CH'EDONGO SO SSA-EUM, a Korean var. of bull fighting. Bulls charge one another with their heads and the one which makes its opponent withdraw, wins the fight.
CHON WUA, a Thai var. of bull fighting prob. introduced by the Portuguese during the colonial times, esp. in the kingdom of Ayutthaya in the 16th and 17th cent.

BULL RACING, or *bullock racing* (Indonesian *kerapan sapi*), a form of competition between teams of bulls, each pulling a rider and sled. After a series of heats held at different parts of the island, the finals take place in Pamekasan, the capital of Madura, an island located NE of Java. The races provide the biggest tourist attraction on Madura and are held regularly several times a month, while the national championships take place annually after the harvest in September and October.

BULL RUNNING, Span. *encierros de torros*, a form of entertainment that originated in the Middle Ages and involving the running of bulls along city streets. In Great Britain the oldest such event was held in Stamford and its earliest records date back to the times of King John Lackland (1198-1216). A bull was let out into the city streets on 13 November and was accompanied by the town inhabitants who ran along teasing the animal with sticks and spiked cudgels.

A poster advertising the Pamplona fiestas.

Muscles strain at the start of the bullock race in March 1992, the high point of the so-called Rural Olympics, in the Punjab town of Kila Raipur.

B

WORLD SPORTS ENCYCLOPEDIA

By the end of the day the exhausted animal would fall down and was killed on the spot, roasted and eaten. In 1788 the mayor of Stamford, backed by Lord Exeter, tried to put an end to this barbaric form of entertainment but – having no legal support – had to yield to the centuries-old tradition. In 1836 The Society for the Prevention of Cruelty to Animals sent its officials to Stamford to stop the event, but their mission met with hostility and brought about riots in defence of the tradition. In 1838 another unsuccessful attempt to ban bull running in Stamford and other English towns was made by the Ministry of the Interior, which set out constables, soldiers and the police to preclude the event. In 1840 the townspeople of Stamford themselves decided to break the tradi-

Santo Domingo. The song goes like this: 'We ask San Fermín, as our Patron, to guide us through the Bull Run and give us his blessing.'
At eight o'clock sharp the 1st rocket is launched announcing the opening of the gates of the small corrals of Santo Domingo, while the firing of the 2nd indicates that all the bulls have left. From then on the animals run along the following course: they go up the Santo Domingo rise and cross the Town Hall Square in order to run in line down the Calle Mercaderes. A closed curve leads into the Calle Estafeta, the longest part of the route which is followed by a small part of the Calle Duque de Ahumada, also known as the Telefónica stretch, which gives access to the dead end street which leads to the Bull Ring.

bout the bull is teased by a Chin. 'torrero'. In the past, bull wrestling competitions were held in natural conditions, on pastures at the foot of the hill serving as the grand stand for spectators. Currently, bull wrestling is part of various folk games held in stadiums, supported by the government of the People's Republic of China.
Bull wrestlers wear garish, red costumes consisting of ankle-long pants and one-sleeved, velvet or brocade shirts. The pants have stripes of different color and trad. Chin. ornaments. The top edge of the shirt is hemmed around with a broad belt of fabric in different colors. The wrestlers also wear cone-shaped caps with pompons, similar to the Turk. kepi. 'Le renversement du buffle', *Les sports traditionnels en Chine. Chine – Aperçu général*, Beijing, 1991.

BULL-RIDING, one of the >RODEO events.

BUMMERS, a Scot. game involving swinging a peg on a long piece of rope to make a loud whistling sound. According to a Scot. lexicographer, J. Jamieson, who recorded the name in his *Etymological Dictionary of the Scottish Language* (1808), it comes from the English word *booming*.
TGESI, I, 51.

BUMPING RACE, a form of a processional rowing race originally held on rivers too narrow for more than 2 boats to move side by side. The boats are started one after another from a rope held by the coxswain, the other end of the rope being fastened to a post on the towpath. The objective is to bump the boat in front (hence the name) and, by doing so, exchange places in the starting order during the next race. A bump is deemed to have taken place when a boat touches any part of the boat in front of it (including the rudder or crew), the coxswain of the leading boat acknowledges, by raising his hand, that the bump has occurred, or when one boat rows clean by another. Crews are grouped into divisions (depending on the results from the previous year), with each division racing several times in one day and the worst division going first. The regattas usu. last 3-4 days and crews are released in different sequences according to a specially prepared schedule. A consistently successful crew will rise up the starting order until it reaches the top, earning the title of 'Head of the River', while any crew that successfully catches – or bumps – the boat ahead of them on all four racing days wins a set of miniature blades.
The best known bumping races are those held on the Isis, which is the name of the river Thames at Oxford, and the so called Summer Eights. The Oxford races were established in 1889 and continued annually until 1968 (interrupted only during war times). In 2000 the City of Oxford Rowing Club revived the tradition. Similar events held in Cambridge on the river Cam are called The May Races and The Lent Races.

BUNG THE BUCKET, an acrobatic game involving two teams of contestants. Members of the first group called the 'buckets' stoop and form a row of players standing one behind another with their hands placed on the hips of their teammate immediately in front of them. The angle between their torso and legs is straight and the first player in the row places his hands against a wall or fence to keep the balance of the whole row. Boys from the second group called the 'bungs' jump onto their backs and move towards the wall shouting: 'Bung the Bucket, one, two, three. Off, off, off'. If one of the 'buckets' gives way under a 'bung's' weight, the teams change places. If the 'buckets' hold out, the game contin-

A bumping race.

As revelers pack the surrounding balconies, bulls race past runners, some falling, others climbing to safety, at the entrance of Estafeta street, leading to the bull ring during the 5th bull run of the San Fermin festival in Pamplona.

Runners dash along the 1/3-mile route through Rawhide Wild West Town in Scottsdale, Arizona, as they participate in Rawhide's Running of the Bulls.

tion in order to avoid further conflict with the government. Soon other English towns followed the ban.
A bull running tradition, dating back to the 13th cent. or earlier, is still very much alive in the Basq. city of Pamplona, where it is part of the Sanfermines, a fiesta to commemorate San Fermín, once held on 10 Oct., but later moved to 7 July. The Sanfermines arose out of the conjunction of 3 separate fiestas: that of a religious nature in honor of San Fermín which has taken place since time immemorial, the commercial fiesta held since the 14th cent., and the taurine festival centered around the bullfights, also held since the 14th cent. The Sanfermines reached the peak of their popularity in the 20th cent. The novel *The Sun Also Rises* (also known as *Fiesta*), written by E. Hemingway in 1926, encouraged people from all over the world to come and take part in the fiesta of Pamplona and esp. the dangerous bull run, which is held every morning at 8 o'clock, 7-14 July. A few minutes before the race is due to begin the youths who will make the run entrust themselves to San Fermín and sing 3 times before a niche of the Saint decorated with the scarves of the peñas, or social groups, which is located on the Cuesta de

Once all the bulls have entered the taurine enclosure a 3rd rocket goes up while the 4th indicates that the beasts have entered the bullpens and the Bull Run is over.
The run lasts for 3min. on average, but is prolonged if any of the bulls should get separated from its brothers. Although all the stretches are dangerous, the curve of the Calle Mercaderes and the stretch between the Calle Estafeta and the Bull Ring are those which hold the most risk.
At present overcrowding is one of the main problems of the Bull Run and increases the danger of the run; only fool-hearty youths attempt to hold out for more than 50m before the bulls.
Althoguh squadrons of security guards and first aid assistants attend to all sections of the route, the danger of the run has resulted, between 1924 and 1997, in 14 deaths and more than 200 injured by the bulls.
http://www.spanish-fiestas.com/spanish-festivals/pamplona-bull-running-san-fermin.htm

BULL WRESTLING, a folk competition popular in the Chin. regions of Xiangsi and Shenyang, consisting of wrestling bulls with bare hands. Before a

A bumping race.

ues until one or more of them finally gives in. The team who manages to force the 'buckets' to give in more times is declared the winner.
TGESI, I, 52-3.

BUNGEE JUMPING, jumps made from heights with the feet tied to an elasticated rope. The name derives from thick rubber ropes made of multilooped lengths of natural rubber bound together by the same material (a bungee), used to fasten loads in cargo planes. There are 2 main bungee jumping systems. In the system created by A.J. Hacket from N.Zealand, a single rubber rope made of one material is used. Its length is adjusted to the jumper's weight. The rope is fixed at the ankles by a nylon loop, under which a towel is placed to protect the jumper against bruises. This system allows for a gentle deceleration. The rope extension ratio is 4:1. In the Amer. system, developed by John and Peter Kockelman, a nylon rope is used, identical to that used on aircraft carriers to stop landing planes. The rope is fixed to the participant's ankles, arms or waist by means of a harness, similar to that used in alpine climbing. Instead of adjusting the rope's length to the jumper's height, individual cords are added or taken away from the rope. It is assumed that a single cord corresponds to 23kg of weight. The volumetric resistance of the cords is about 680kg. Compared to the N.Zealand system, the jumper in the Amer. system decelerates more sharply and less pleasantly. The rope extension ratio is only 2:1.
History. The oldest form of head down jumping, using some flexible material, was recorded by ethnographers among the inhabitants of Easter Island. Local legend has it that the first jump from a tall tree, using plant sprouts, was made by a woman, who was running away from her evil husband. Having tied the sprouts to her feet, she jumped and saved her life, while the husband, jumping after her, killed himself and in this way was punished for his bad character. A religious ritual of jumping was observed in 1955 by journalists of the 'National Geographic'. In 1971 K. Müller, also working for the 'National Geographic' was the first white man to make this type of jump. The description of the Easter Island ritual provided by Müller encouraged members of the Dangerous Sportsman's Club, Oxford University, to make similar jumps, using bungee ropes, from the Clifton Suspension Bridge in Bristol (75m high), in 1979. Later they made similar jumps from the Golden Gate Bridge in San Francisco and the Colorado's Royal George bridge. In 1987 A. J. Hacket from New Zealand made the first jump from the Eiffel Tower in Paris. Also in 1987 the first paid jumps were organized in New Zealand by Hacket and J. and P. Kockelman in USA.
Soon attempts were made to make the jumps more attractive, e.g. jumps were made with an approx. 30-kg sack full of sand held in the hands and released when the rope was most extended. The rope, without the weight of the sack, returned to its original height with higher energy and speed. It turned out, however, that jumping with additional weight results in excessive strain of the eyes and the circulatory system, which, in case of poorer health, can lead to permanent damage of the eyes and the circulatory system. Experiments in pair jumping using one rope led to a number of lethal accidents or severe injuries. Presently jumps are made not only from high buildings, towers and bridges, but also from balloons and helicopters. The longest jumps are approx 500m. Original competitions are organized, e.g. picking different objects from the ground or fishing them out of the water. A jump must be so accurate that when the rope is most extended the jumper is close to the ground or water surface, without hitting the ground or water. Jumps with acrobatics during the flight are also attempted.
J. Tomilson, 'Bungy jumping', *Encyclopedia of Extreme Sports*, 1996; the Internet: http://www.bungee.com

BUN-HOLE, see >MARBLES.

BUNO, one of the folk var. of Filipino wrestling; see also >DAMA.

BUNTING, one of the var. of the Eng. >TIP-CAT.

BURIAL ARCHERY, a form of archery competition held on occasions of funerals, common in ancient Greece. During the siege of Troy and funeral games in honor of the fallen Patroclus, the Achaeans staged an archery contest involving shooting at a pigeon (Homer's *Iliad*, Book XXIII). Burial archery is still practiced among some peoples of Cent. Asia, such as the Chukchee, Koriak, and a few Mong. tribes; see >CHUKCHEE AND KORIAK ARCHERY; >MONGOLIAN ARCHERY.

BURIAT ARCHERY, a type of archery similar to >MONGOLIAN ARCHERY. The differences between the two types are fairly insignificant. In the 19th cent, Buriat archery consisted of shooting arrows at small leather bags filled with camel wool; unlike the Mong. var., which involved shooting at large sacks (*sur*) made of camel hides. An ingenious form of Buriat archery is >BAJ. In the early 19th cent. the Buriats awarded prizes in stock to victorious archers, in a similar way to other Mong. peoples. The prizes included horses, camels, sheep, bales of silk, bags of tea, etc. Since the mid-19th cent., due to extensive contacts with Rus. culture, the Buriats have preferred money prizes.

BURIAT BALL, an obsolete ball game of the Buriat, a people commonly associated with the Mongol culture. The Mongols do not play any ball games in modern times; only some remarks referring to the ancient games have survived (>MONGOLIAN POLO, >MONGOLIAN FOOTBALL). Like >KALMUCK BALL, the Buriat ball was made of different materials in different Buriat territories. It resembled a small leather pillow or a bundle of rags tied up with leather straps or strings. The game was also played with a bundle of leather straps or bristles. Buriat ball was mainly played in summer and fall.

BURIAT HORSE RACING, a form of >HORSE RACING popular among the Mong. Buriats, who derive their traditions from the Uigurean (a mixture of Mong. and Turk.) culture. Together with other forms of physical competition, such as archery (>BURIAT ARCHERY), horse races formed the sporting program of so called *taiuagans*, celebrations of annual landmarks such as New Year, the beginning of summer, the fall offering of the harvest to Mother Earth, etc. The manes of horses participating in the race were decorated with red or white sashes (according to Buriat beliefs, red and white have the same symbolic value). The owner of the winning horse received a bowl of koumiss (fermented mare's milk liquor), which he sprinkled over the horse's head and back. Then he passed the bowl over to the elder of his family, who took a sip, delivered a eulogy to the horse and the rider, and finally finished the drink.

BURIAT LAMA RACES were held in monastery gardens shortly before a ceremony of summoning guardian spirits. They were held, similarly to the summoning ceremony, at the beginning of the 5th lunar month.
G. Cybikow, *Buddyjski pielgrzym w świątyniach Tybetu*, Pol. edition 1975.

BURIAT SPEAR THROW, a Buriat folk style of spear throwing using a special target with holes. The objective is to drive the spear through the holes without hitting the target.

BURLY WHUSH, also known as *burly whoosh*. A popular Eng. ball game in which one of the players bounces a ball off a wall and shouts the name of the player who is to catch it before it falls to the ground. All the remaining players run away. If the player fails to catch the ball, he shouts 'Burly whush!', which means that the other players have to stop. Then, he picks up the ball and throws it at another player. If hit, he now takes the ball and shouts the same words while aiming at another player. Those players who have managed to hide round the corner of a building or behind a fence or wall have to stick one hand out so that the thrower may hit them. The game continues until one of the players misses. Then, the game is started anew. The game continues until all the players have been the thrower.
TGESI, I, 53-4.

BUSHA, an ancient Jap. type of archery which involved shooting arrows while walking. It was not as popular as many various types of horseback archery. Busha flourished towards the end of the Heian epoch (the 12th cent.) and at the beginning of the Hōjō epoch. See also other types of foot archery such as >JUMIHAJIME, >KUSAJISI and >MARUMONO.

BUSHWALKING, a sport developed in Australia in the second half of the 19th cent. It is closely connected with the heroic attempts to walk across the Australian continent. The first such attempt was made by the R. O'Hara Burke (1821-61) expedition. In 1860 Burke, together with 3 companions – C. Gray, J. King and W.W. Wills, tried to walk across the continent departing from the south and arriving at the north coast. They reached the Gulf of Carpentaria marshland but being extremely exhausted decided to turn back not knowing that they were only a few hundred meters from the coast. All members of the expedition, except King who was rescued by Aborigines, died of exhaustion and hunger. The first successful walk across Australia was completed a year later by a Scottish traveler J.D. Stuart (1815-66). After the end of the so-called 'heroic era', walkers started covering particular routes, usu. laid down between two distinct geographical features. These walks were timed. The Melbourne Amateur Walking and Touring Club, an organization whose activities also involved bushwalking, was established in 1894. Timed walking died out at the beginning of the 20th cent. However, a number of clubs specializing in bushwalking as a new form of active tourism began to spring up. One of the driving factors behind the development of bushwalking was the idea of >SCOUTING. The term *bushwalking* began to be used in the 1930s as a name of an activity combining tourism and sight-seeing, and soon after also environmental protection. It was to distinguish random outings from systematic and purposeful activity involving physical effort and communing with nature. The most dynamic of the aforementioned clubs was the Smile-Away Club with a membership of several thousand. In the 1960s various bushwalking clubs played a key role in introducing >ORIENTEERING to Australia. They also made rock climbing more popular than ever. In the 1970s some clubs specialized in 24-hour endurance bush walks which soon evolved into a sport in its own right known today as >ROGAINING. However, trad. bushwalking, downplaying the competitive aspect and focusing more on developing physical stamina and the love of nature, remained popular.
Bushwalking is particularly popular in the Austrl. states of Victoria, New South Wales and also in Queensland. Due to varied climatic conditions in these states, the bushwalking varieties practiced there are slightly different from one another. In New South Wales and Victoria it is possible to engage in bushwalking all year round. However, due to the fact that Queensland, the Northern Territory and Western Australia are located in a subtropical zone, it is possible to practice bushwalking there only during the Austrl. fall, winter and spring as the summer months are far too hot and bushwalking may turn out to be too dangerous even for the most experienced and best-trained walkers.
The basic equipment used in bushwalking includes a compass, first aid kit, water-proof matches, rain gear, the map of a given area, comfortable hiking shoes, warm clothing (esp. useful during the night), tent and a portable cooker. The sport is so popular in Australia that there is even a special bushwalking supplies chain of stores there. The most popular bushwalking grounds include the vicinity of Stirling Range and Kimberley in Western Australia; Kakadu National Park and Arnhem Land Plateau in the Northern Territory; Sydney Harbour National Park, Royal National Park and the Blue Mountains area in New South Wales as well as Tasmania.

Bungee jumping on a bicycle.

Bungee jumping's point of no return.

Bushwalking.

Buzkashi in Afghan art

Buzkashi in the snow, *A. Shokour Khesrawi*

E.H. Smith, 'Bushwalking', *The Oxford Companion to Australian Sport,* 2nd ed., 1994; author unknown, *Bushwalking in Australia,* SS March, 1993.

BUSK, Dan. for 'a bush'. A simple or even primitive school game mentioned by J. Møller in his lexicon of Dan. sports *Gamle idrætslege i Danmark* (*Sports games in Denmark*, 1997, 3, 70). Four players grab an unsuspecting fifth one by his hands and legs, swing his body and throw him into the bushes.

BUTIK, Dan. for 'a shop, boutique'. A Dan. game involving throwing and driving pegs into the ground so as to knock down one's opponent's pegs. The first contestant takes a swing and drives his peg into the ground. The remaining competitors also drive their pegs into the ground trying to knock down the peg of their immediate predecessors. After all the players have driven their pegs into the ground, the first one takes his peg out and drives it into the ground again trying to knock down as many standing pegs as possible. If he fails, he is replaced by the next competitor. The player whose peg is the last to remain standing is declared the winner, compare >KONGEPIND, >PATØK.
J. Møller, 'Butik', GID, 1997, 4.

BUXNATÖK, one of the oldest hand-to-hand combat arts that later developed into the Icelandic >GLIMA. The name of the sport comes from the word *bux* – meaning trousers combined with the verb to grab – *tök;* compare also other forms of folk wrestling involving trouser holds and clothes pulling.

BUXUS, a var. of >TOPS practiced in ancient Rome and similar to the Gk. >STROBILOS. Due to the fact that, despite numerous references to the game in literature, no detailed descriptions were preserved it is difficult to account for the technicalities and determine the differences or similarities between buxus and another toy named after a wheel- or ring-pushing game called >TROCHUS. An obscure description of the game is found in Ovid's *Tristia* (*Sorrows*):

We now have some free time and the foul-mouthed
crowd's squabbles give way to new entertainments;
Now the talker takes to a lighter occupation,
Now he likes a ball, a trochus spinning fast.

[*Tristia*, I, III, 12]

The *Memoirs of Martinus Scriblerus* attributed to J. Arbuthnot (1667-1735) raise similar doubts. Martinus's father, Cornelius, also ponders the similarities between the two games as he does not want his son Martinus to play the game without determining first whether trochus corresponds to the well-known game of tops or whether it is the game where boys propel a wheel with a stick. Buxus was also mentioned by a Roman writer Levinus Lemnius and by Persius, a Roman poet, in his *Satire III*.
In Virgil's *Aeneid* there is a section devoted to buxus which is employed as a metaphor to depict the rage felt by one of the Furies, namely Alecto of Amata upon hearing that Latinus wanted to marry off their daughter Lavinia to a foreigner. Thus, Alecto undertook to put other women against Latinus:

then indeed, stung by infinite horrors, hapless and frenzied, she rages wildly through the endless city. As whilom a top flying under the twisted whipcord, which boys busy at their play drive circling wide round an empty hall, runs before the lash and spins in wide gyrations; with witless ungrown band hang wondering over it admire the whirling boxwood; the strokes lend it life: with pace no slacker is she borne midway through towns and valiant nations.

[VII, 376-384; *Virgil's Works*, Random House, 1950, trans. by J.W. Mackail]

BUYI THROWING OF PRINT BAGS, a form of competition among the Chin. Buyi people in which a player targets his opponent (boy or girl) with bags hand-sewn from colorful cloth strips and filled with peas, rice or date plum stones. Players standing in rows and maintaining a 10m distance between the rows, face one another and start the game by throwing their bags high into the air. Later they begin to target selected opponents, who may either dodge or catch the bag. It is the method of tossing that counts: the bag tossed over the shoulder may be rejected. The player who fails to catch any bag tossed at him or her must offer a prize (e.g. a silver hairpin, necklace, bracelet or ring). Refusal to accept the prize is tantamount to a rejection of the opponent.
The game follows an ancient tradition, according to which a girl called Kangmei decided to find a brave and honest husband by selecting him from among various competitors with a symbolic bag toss. It is played during the Chin. New Year festivities, as well as during various other festivals, family and public gatherings. Participants wear splendid trad. costumes and are accompanied by music played on a 4-string instrument called *yueqin*, as well as whistling produced by placing tree leaves in the mouth.
Mu Fushan et al., 'Buyi Throwing Print Bags', TRAMCHIN, 126.

BUZKASHI, sometimes spelled *buskaši.* A brutal Asian game involving a fight among mounted warriors competing for a billy-goat's, calf's, lamb's or, in the past, a wolf's carcass. Buzkashi is the national game in Afghanistan. Outside Afghanistan it is most popular in Mongolia and in the territories incorporated into the Rus. empire and later the USSR, i.e. Kazakhstan, Tadzhikistan, Uzbekistan and Kirghizstan. It is also practiced in outer China, esp. in the Xinjiang province.
Buzkashi is not a single sport, but constitutes a family of horse sports referred to in many C Asian and Middle Eastern cultures and languages as either blue wolf, i.e. buzkashi proper, or as the fight for a billy-goat.
BLUE WOLF, or gray wolf, i.e. buzkashi proper. The name points to the very origin of the game when riders competed for a wolf's carcass. In ancient C Asia the wolf symbolized evil that had to be not only defeated but also discouraged from returning. The fact that the wolf was blue or gray is a reference to the sky which was deemed to be the abode of deities, good and evil ones alike, and the gray or blue color was to signify that the wolf was an embodiment of evil. The Turkmen stressed the fact that the evil animal had come from above by throwing the carcass down from the roof of a *yurt* (tent) and onto a square where the game started. By the same token, the Kirghiz living in the Tien Shan range on the Chin. border would throw the carcass up before starting the game to symbolize the fact that the wolf had descended from the sky.
FIGHT FOR A BILLY-GOAT. Wolves' carcasses were later replaced by billy-goats' ones due to the fact that it became increasingly difficult to hunt down a wolf. The wolf population had been decimated and had to be replaced by a domesticated animal that was always 'at hand' should the men wish to play the game on the spur of the moment. The peoples who borrowed the game into their tradition later, after wolves' carcasses were no longer used, called it the fight for a billy-goat. In some cases, the origin of the name was different. The Kazakhs, for example, treat goats as the root of all evil, not wolves. They called goats 'devil's beasts' and thus found replacing wolves with goats even easier than others. According to many peoples' beliefs the person who offered a billy-goat found favor with their deities. A Rus. ethnologist G.N. Simakov reported that some Kirghiz tribes living in the Pamirs used to fight not for a billy-goat but a human being. The victims were usu. selected from among prisoners of war. It is not known when this 'tradition' was discontinued.
A game of buzkashi, and esp. the ritual accompanying it, is different among various peoples. The overall aim of the game was to spectacularly kill an animal symbolizing evil and death. The game was full of cruel ceremonies. To prevent evil from spreading among the people the legs of an animal were first cut off below the knees. Some peoples tied the animal to a horseman's saddle and then ripped its legs and head off while it was still alive. The game (with a few exceptions described below) was played by individual riders who fought for the carcass alone. In a sense the game was very 'democratic' – virtually anyone could participate. A Rus. ethnographer A. Khoroshchin researching the Turkmen var. of buzkashi observed in 1874 that in the course of the game 'the rich and famous become equal to the ragamuffins'. Kabzińska-Stawarz adds that the game 'temporarily and indirectly removed class barriers which points to the fact that it was equally popular among all social classes'.
There are also team var. of buzkashi, e.g. the Kazakh *koh-par.* According to old sources 'it is a team sport, very old and popular in Kazakhstan [...] there are two teams of riders (the number of riders is not fixed and is agreed upon before a game) which stand facing each other on a field. A regular billy-goat is placed half-way between the two teams. The game starts on a referee's signal. Each team attempts to seize the goat and carry it to a specified spot. The team who does so first is declared the winner. Usu. one of the best riders picks the billy-goat up and rides very fast to a specified spot while the members of the other team chase and attack him while his teammates try to protect him, employing special holds and grips. The game is very complicated and requires superior horse-riding skill since a rider has only his body and knees to direct the horse. When one of the opposing team members snatches the billy-goat from the carrier, the teams switch their roles. The game is played during folk holidays and festivals and attracts many spectators' ('Sport regionalny', in: *Sport w ZSRR*, author(s) unknown, trans. from Russian, 1948, 215).
Players prepare for the competition by killing the goat to be later used during the pursuit. Before actually killing the goat they say a prayer which the Kirghiz call *bata*. The same prayer is also said just before the game proper starts. Depending on the local custom the carcass is thrown to the ground, towards the spectators feet or onto a house's threshold. Finally, at the end of the game the battered carcass is presented to the local chief.
If the game is played to accompany a wedding, the carcass is thrown before the bride's father or onto the threshold of his yurt. Sometimes the carcass is also thrown before the groom and only very rarely before the bride herself. In some Turkmen tribes it is the bride who takes the carcass and the groom has to pursue her. Apart from weddings buzkashi games are held to celebrate a birth of a son (sometimes also of a daughter if a given couple had to wait for a baby for a long time) or the first step made by a baby. In the south of Kirghizia buzkashi games always accompany the annual ghost-summoning festival. In the north, however, such conduct is deemed unbecoming. After the game there is usu. a sumptuous feast during which the winner receives his prize. Among the Kirghiz the prize is usu. a gaudy and richly ornamented gaberdine. The winner will immediately put it on to show it to his friends and relatives asking them to carry the news of his victory across the steppe.
G.N. Simakov observed that after the game the carcass, irrespective of its condition, was always washed, put into a large pot and cooked. Neighbors and relatives were then invited to eat the meat. The participants of the feast would say that the 'meat was touched by the hands of our people and therefore it has medicinal properties'. If the carcass had been torn apart during the game, the head and legs went to the one who killed it before the game commenced. The remaining players collected the pieces of flesh scattered throughout the field, divided them among themselves and took them to their yurts. There they cooked the meat and treated their neighbors and relatives to it.
A very special buzkashi var. was the Tadzhiki fight for a billy-goat in water. This var. was also known to the semi-nomadic Uzbek living on the Kashkadarya steppe. The competition involved killing a few goats (during a ritual ceremony) which were then thrown into water (usu. a river). Then, mounted riders fought for the carcasses. After the game local farmers cleared the water (or rather the river banks) of their weed and rush. This ritual was called 'opening up the eyes of springs'. Nevertheless, until the 1940s or '50s, the Tadzhik also fought for the carcasses on the ground. The 'ground' buzkashi was discontinued in the Soviet Tadzhikistan in the late 1940s as a result of an accident in which one of the players fell off his horse and lost his eye. In 1965 an Amer. ethnologist L. Dupree observed a 'water' buzkashi in the Tadzhiki village of Aq Kupruk. The game was also played by the Uzbek when large reservoirs were constructed on the Zeravshan River. The construction crews respected the local custom and before filling the reservoirs with water they allowed the local tribes to drive their horses through the soon-to-be-flooded areas. These horse drives constituted an excellent opportunity to hold 'water' buzkashi competitions.
Afghan buzkashi. A fight for an animal carcass is still practiced in Afghanistan, where – for certain historical reasons (see below) – the game is still almost identical to the original buzkashi. It is still very brutal there despite the fact that it has become gradually 'milder' among other peoples. Afghan buzkashi usu. accompanies important clan holidays. On the first day, the clan members and their guests simply feast. On the second day, they travel onto a steppe

or meadow where a goat or calf carcass lies prepared. The number of players is not specified. Usu. a game of Afghan buzkashi involves from about a dozen to several hundred riders. The object of the game is to pick up the carcass without dismounting and run away. It is a very dangerous task given that one is surrounded by a number of other riders and their pushing horses. The players compete individually. The longer the game lasts, the higher the prize. In the past it was rifles, horses or cattle that were awarded as prizes, recently money has become the main type of prize. The fact that the prize amount is growing is heralded by a specially appointed

A game of buzkashi

'shouter' – a *jorchi*. Finally, there emerges a player who manages to snatch the carcass and escape the crowd. The *jorchi* celebrates this moment with special rhymed words of praise:

Oh Hadji Ali's horse,
Ridden by Ahmad Gul,
Jumps like a doe
But sees like a leopard.

How he snatched,
How he showed them who he was,
How Hadji Ali's name became revered,
How we all hear about him,
How complete is his fame.

A game of buzkashi usu. consists of many rounds, depending on the wealth of the *khan* who sponsors it. No combined scores are maintained. All disputes arising in the course of the game are settled by the *khan* himself.
History. Buzkashi has been always played by the Turkmen cast of the *khans*, especially strong in Afghanistan. Sponsoring buzkashi competitions contributed to elevating their social status (*tooi-wala*). The competitions were usu. held in winter on the occasion of clan holidays called *toois*. The *khans* usu. raised special buzkashi horses and hired skilled buzkashi riders called *chapandazan*.
The Afghan buzkashi, despite the tortuous history of the country has been preserved in the form closest to the original buzkashi. Nevertheless, the incorporation of many areas in Asia into the USSR in the 1920s proved to be rather destructive for the game as a whole. Although the official Soviet policy was to promote local folk sports and games, the authorities tried to eradicate those which seemed to be out of line with the principles of the new system. Buzkashi was declared too connected to the old social system and too brutal. Despite that buzkashi has never been totally rooted out in the Asian Soviet Republics and has survived to the present day. In many cases buzkashi competitions were supported to varying degrees by the local authorities. It is, however, difficult to speak of the game as flourishing as there were no adequate social structures to restore the game to its former status. Buzkashi has been best preserved in Afghanistan which has never been under direct Soviet rule.
In 1955 Mohammad Zahir Shah, the king of Afghanistan, organized the first buzkashi tournament in his attempt to turn the game into a sport. The aim of this competition was also to elevate the status of the Afghan monarchy and attract tourists to the country. The competition was held on the king's birthday. The task of organizing the competition was entrust-

ed to the Afghan Olympic Committee. As a result two forms of buzkashi emerged. The first, trad. var. was called a *tudabarai* and the second, sports one, was called a *garajai*.
In *garajai* a winner was determined on the basis of the total number of points scored in a number of events. When a competitor committed a 'foul' a certain number of points was deducted from his total score. Instead of a typical flight with his loot (i.e. an animal carcass), a competitor had to ride around a pole with a flag and drop the carcass into a special circle called a *daiwra* drawn on the ground. The king became the supreme referee and host of the competition and after each competition he organized a sumptuous feast for all the participants. Until the Soviet invasion in 1979 the competition was held on a regular basis in Kabul. After the collapse of the monarchy in 1973 the competition continued to be held under the auspices of the then Afghan President Mohammad Daoud (1973-77) as a part of the UN Day celebrations. After the Afghan communists seized power they moved the competition date to that of the anniversary of the October Revolution anniversary. The political chaos that swept through the country after the Soviet invasion in 1979 resulted in the gradual eradication of the game which was finally dropped from the official sports events calendar in 1983. Since that time, although still practiced, buzkashi competitions have been held only sporadically as trad. folk events called *tudabarai*. Today, the competitions organized by the Afghan refugees living near Chitral and Peshawar, Pakistan, are deemed those most similar to the original buzkashi contests.
Buzkashi was an exotic source of inspiration for Western literature and film. This is best exemplified by J. Kessel's novel *The Horsemen* (1967) which was later turned into a movie likewise called *The Horsemen* (1971) starring O. Shariff and J. Palance. J. Bronowski wrote an anthropological

and historical monograph of buzkashi entitled *The Ascent of Man* (1974) which was later filmed into a popular science series.
G.W. Azoy, *Buzkashi. Game and Power in Afghanistan*, 1982; R. Michaud and S. Michaud, *Horsemen of Afghanistan*, 1988; I. Kabzińska-Stawarz, 'Competitions in Liminal Situations: Comparative Study of Asian Cultures', p. I, *Ethnologia Polona*, 18, 1994; 1-2; G.N. Simakov, *Obszczestwiennyje funkcji kirgiskich narodnych razwleczenij w konce XIX – naczale XX w.*, 1984.

BUZZ AND BANDY, a local var. of >FIELD HOCKEY played in the Eng. towns of Shrewsbury, Munch Wenlock and in neighboring areas.

BYGGE LAD, Dan. for 'to build a platform'. A simple acrobatic exercise involving two gymnasts who stand facing each other. A third one lies chest-down resting on their shoulders. A fourth acrobat stands or sits on his back.
J. Møller, 'Bygge lad', GID, 1997, 3, 90.

BYXKAST, a Swed. name of a Fin. wrestling var. in which opponents grab each other by their trousers [Swed. *byxor* – trousers + *kast* – throw], >BYXTAG being its proper Swed. counterpart. The Swed. name became popular in Finland during the Swed. occupation. Currently, the sport is better known under its original, Finnish name of >VYÖPAINI. See also >CLOTHES HOLD (BELT HOLD) WRESTLING.

BYXTAG, a Swed. var. of folk wrestling whose most important element is pulling an opponent by his trousers [Swed. *byxor* – trousers + *tag* – hold, grasp]. A Swed. ethnologist M. Hellspong claims that byxtag is a generic name for a family of wrestling sports also including >DRA BÄLTE (pulling by a belt) popular in Småland (also known as >DRA REM – pulling by a leather strap). The var. of wrestling popular in Bjuråker in Helsingoland was rather unusual as it involved grabbing an opponent's collar, similarly to >KRAGTAG, only then followed by trousers pulling. In Kråksmåla in Småland the opponents pounced on each other and then grabbed each other's belt with one or two hands depending on the prior arrangement. After they wrestled for a while in the standing position, they usu. fell to the ground and the one who managed to press his opponent to the ground first was declared the winner. A belt was an indispensable accessory in this type of wrestling but it sometimes happened that wrestlers wanted to make a fight more difficult for their opponents and they took their belts off on purpose. The differences among grabbing one's opponent by the collar, lapels or trousers were not defined precisely in many areas but wrestlers' clothing evolved in time until a special belt greatly facilitating applying holds and grasps was developed. The large number of different byxtag varieties testifies to its great cultural importance in the Scand. countries similarly to other wrestling var. involving clothes pulling so popular among other nations. See >CLOTHES HOLD (BELT HOLD) WRESTLING.
M. Hellspong, 'Byxtag', 'Brottning som folklig leg', RIG, 1991; M. Hellspong, 'Byxtag', *Den folkliga idrotten*, 2000.

WORLD SPORTS ENCYCLOPEDIA

B

Mounted Afghans enjoy a traditional game of buzkashi in Golbahar, north of Kabul.

C

C'HOARI BOULLOÙ, see >BOULLOÙ-POK DE GUERLESQUIN.

C'HOARI CHOUK-LAMM-PENN, Bret. for 'head over feet', a local game with acrobatic elements.

C'HOARI GALÔJ, a Bret. game in which metal rings are thrown at a pole stuck into the ground.

C'HOARI MELLAD, Bret. in full *ar c'hoari mellad*. In lower Brittany an equivalent of >VELL, and the Fr. >SOULE, LA. Cf. >MELAT.

C'HOARI PATATI, a Bret. children's game called in Fr. *cheval fondu*, in Eng. >LEAP-FROG, and in Pol. *żabie skoki*.

C'HOARI STOUV, a var. of a Bret. game in which metal disks are thrown at a target. Cf. >QUOITS.

C'HRAVAZH, a complete Bret. name is *ar c'hravazh*, in Fr. – *la civière*. A popular form of competition in which contestants lift weight loaded onto a wheelbarrow without a wheel. A lifter crouches, grabs the wheelbarrow's handles and attempts to stand up, tilting the wheelbarrow forward to prop it on its nose. The best competitors are able to lift 500-600kg in one quick snatch. The competition is popular in a few parishes around Lanion and Tréguier. However, it is considered a harmful activity that leads to serious spinal injuries.
F. Peru, 'La tradition populaire de jeux de plein air en Bretagne', LJP, 1998.

CABER TOSSING, see >TOSSING THE CABER.

Calcio on a postage stamp.

CABINET BALL, a type of a game played on a standard volleyball court but using a small medicine ball – 12in. (30.48cm) in diameter, 6lbs. (2.75kg); the net at the height of 8ft. (2.43m). Because of its weight the ball cannot be returned the same way as in volleyball, therefore any manner of throwing and catching it is acceptable, other than bouncing. There are 9 players in each team.

CABRA-CEGA, Port. type of >BLINDMAN'S BUFF; full name is *jogo da cabra-cega*.

Franco, Football at Sant Alvise, c.1610, print.

Giuoco del Calzo che si fa nel Brissaglio de' Aluse la Quaresima nel quale non giuocane se non li Gentili huomini.
Giacomo Franco Forma con Privilegio.

CAICHE, old Scot. var. of >HANDBALL.

CAID, Ir. Gaelic, the original name for >GAELIC FOOTBALL.

CALCIO, an old Ital. name for any ball game. Currently, this name is often applied to the most popular of the ball games, i.e. >ASSOCIATION FOOTBALL. The rules of calcio developed in 14-16th cent. in Florence, from where the game spread throughout Italy. A. Scaino wrote about it in 1555, and in 1580 calcio was described by G. di Bardi in his *Discorso sopra il giuoco del calcio fiorentino*, which was dedicated to F. de Medici, a member of the famous Ital. family, who played calcio as a young man and then became known as the game's protector. He was so celebrated in W Europe that his fame echoes in J. Webster's comedy *The White Devil*, 1612 (see also >EASTER TUESDAY GAME). In 1611 in Venice, a Gk. poet G. Koressios published a work exalting calcio and titled *Diegesis tou kleinou agonos tou Florentinon, dia stichon*. The first descriptions reveal the game was played twice a year, on the first Sun. of May and on 24 June, at the *Piazza della Signora* in Florence by 2 teams of 20-40 players. The objective of the game was to place the ball, throwing or kicking it, in the opponent's field. Depending on the local arrangement, the target was the center of the square, a gate or the city gateway. Out of those three, the city gateway became the most popular, and when a playing field was moved outside the city walls, an imitation of such a gateway was constructed (a prototype of the modern goal). Teams playing calcio are the first example in the history of sport where different colors of outfit were deliberately employed to identify 2 teams.

CALCIO FIORENTINO, Ital. for 'Florence football'. A trad. game resembling football that was played in Florence [Ital. *calcio* – ball game + *fiorentino* – Florentine]. It is the most representative var. of >CALCIO IN COSTUME; practiced from the twilight of Middle Ages and developed in Renaissance in Florence. The game was played at the *Santa Croce* [Holy Cross] square around New Year's Eve and during the carnival.

CALCIO IN COSTUME, a family of trad. Ital. ball games that were practiced in a number of cities around the country with players wearing colorful outfits either hist. or mod. One of its most popular var. is >CALCIO FIORENTINO.

CALF-ROPING, one of the >RODEO events.

CALISTHENICS, a term originating from O.Gk. *kallas* – beauty and *sthenos* – strength, employed mostly in Anglo-Saxon countries to refer to: 1) any athletic exercise; 2) an equivalent to >GYMNASTICS; 3) art of achieving strength and beauty of the physical body at the same time; 4) an obsolete equivalent to the term 'exercises for females'.
When calisthenics was first introduced into the Eng. system of female exercise, it encountered strong resistance because its rigorous character clashed with the liberal quality of Eng. sports. In his *Dictionary of*

Sports (1835), H. Harewood offered the following opinion on the subject: 'though we think that they should never be omitted, yet we consider those exercises which were taught as founded on erroneous principles. A system of healthy and graceful exercises for females may be established, but those which are now generally practised in English boarding-schools are wrong in principle.'
The principles of calisthenics originate from traditions of Eur. gymnastics, mostly from the principles developed by J.B. Basedow and applied in his

With their instructor on the platform, officer candidates of the Women's Army Auxiliary Corps, WAACS, start off their day with a calisthenics drill wearing fatigue uniforms at Fort DesMoines, Iowa, on Aug. 8, 1942 as part of the war effort.

school in Dessau, named Philantropinum (1774). In the USA, the canons of Eur. gymnastics were first employed in 1823 at Round Hill School where, soon after, K. Beck – a Ger. teacher of gymnastics and a translator of F.L. Jahn's works into Eng. (see >GYMNASTICS) – started his Amer. teaching career. In 1825, PE classes based on the Ger. model were introduced in a number of New York schools and a year later such classes were inaugurated at Harvard University. The first originally Amer. work devoted to PE classes, *The Importance of Physical Education* by J.C. Warren, appeared in 1831. Until then, the term calisthenics was not used in reference to physical exercise. It was popularized in the USA by C.E. Beecher (1800-1878), the author of the first Amer. program of physical exercises for women, adopting certain principles of early Swed. gymnastics, esp. its therapeutic role. First, she introduced it at the Hartford Female Seminary (1824) and then, on a larger scale, at the Western Female Institute in Cincinnati (1837). The term was also made widely known thanks to 2 books by Beecher: *Course of Calisthenics for Young Ladies* (1832), and *A Manual for Physiology and Calisthenics for Schools and Families* (1856). Based on the calisthenics principles developed by C. Beecher, who associated exercises with light equipment such as beanbags, clubs, and dumbbells, Amer. pedagogue, D. Lewis, proposed his system of >LIGHT GYMNASTICS.

CALLING OUT, a school and backyard ball game, in which one player throws the ball into the air and calls the name of the person to catch it. The person called must run and catch the ball before it falls to the ground, after which he may throw it into the air and call the name of the next person to catch it, etc. In a more advanced form the game is played in a circle 4-5m in diameter and the player throwing the ball up from the center of the circle must reach the place of the player whose name he called. In this form it is practiced e.g. in Denmark as *lyrebold*. In one var. of lyrebold players stand in a row along a straight line, separated by a distance of 3m from one another, while the player throwing the ball stands at the left side of the row. The player called must catch the ball and replace the thrower, who runs towards the opposite end of the row. The remaining players close the gap left by the player called.
J. Møller, 'Lyrebold', GID, 1997, 1, 15.

CAMÁNACHT, also *camán*, an old Ir. game in which a ball was pushed with sticks. The object

Two camels trip one another with their heads during Turkey's largest camel wrestling festival in Selcuk.

match the wrestling camels as to their specific style of fighting, which is meant to prevent injuries and, thus, reducing the stock.

CAMEL RACES (MOUNTED), a trad. form of racing popular in many Arab and some Afr. countries, deriving from a several-thousand-year-old tradition of camel breeding and their use as a means of transportation. Camel races are a tourist attraction in Kenya and are divided into amateur and professional categories. The leading jockey of the 1990s was Laverani. Probably the largest camel racing event is held in Saudi Arabia, with 3,000 jockeys participating. In almost all Arab countries local races are held with 25-30 jockeys competing during a season that lasts from September to the 9th month after the ramadan, ending with the coming of spring. Camel races are also held in India, Pakistan and the Republic of Chad, which still maintains camel troops as part of its armed forces. Systematic research on camel racing was initiated in the United Arab Emirates, which also established an antidoping center. Unlike many other countries, the UAE banned child jockeys from the sport and prohibited the use of young camels as the sport could hinder their development. In 1989 sheikh Khalifa bin Zayed Al Nayhan established the Embryo Transfer Research Center, which functions under the auspices of prince Abu Dhabi. Its goal is to increase the fertility of top-class animals, which normally produce offspring once every 2 years. The first animal was born in the center in 1990.

Although camel racing originated in Arab countries, it is also a popular entertainment sport in Australia and the USA. When discovering the Austrl. mainland, the early pioneers considered camels an important means of desert transportation. In 1840 the first herd was imported from India. In 1866 approx. 260 camels escaped and scattered around Australia, making the country the only one in the world where wild camels still survive. Camel breeding in Australia has progressed so much that today the country exports the animals to Arab nations. A natural consequence of this development was the initiation of camel races. The most prestigious event in Australia is the Camel Cup Race in Alice Springs, which – contrary to the events in Arab, Asian, and Afr. countries – is open also to women. Among

Crazy Camel and The Light wrestle in front of female camel, Emine, right.

was to defeat the opposing team by pushing the ball across the goal line of the playing field, and in later versions – into the goal. The game was practiced mostly in northern parts of Ireland and together with >IOMÁINT it was a predecessor of >HURLING, which is one of the 2 national sports of Ireland (see also >GAELIC FOOTBALL). In Camánacht the ball was mostly rolled on the ground, unlike in iomáint where upper passes dominated. In 1830 the game was practiced in Trinity College at Dublin University, where later on its rules were formalized and applied in the winter season of 1870/71. At the end of the 1870s Catholic student teams played matches with Protestants. At that time, however, camánacht became influenced by Eng. forms of >FIELD HOCKEY, which discouraged Ir. patriots from playing. Since then, the game's further evolution was affected mostly by iomáint, which was not 'contaminated' by Eng. influence.
A. Ó'Maolfabhail, *Camán. Two Thousand Years of Hurling in Ireland*, 1975.

CAMBUCA, also *cambuc*, a game known in old England. It consisted of striking a ball of indeterminate size with a club. The game derived from a medieval game known in W Eur. as >CAMBUTA. No rules have survived to this day. Cambuca is believed to have influenced the development of other ball games in Eng. that were played with the use of a curved stick, such as >GOLF and >BANDY. In his work titled *Glig Gamena Angel Deoth, or the Sports and Pastimes of the People of England* (1810), J. Strutt claims that cambuca is responsible for the evolution of earlier forms of golf, which was originally known as >GOFF: 'In the reign of Edward the Third, the Latin name Cambuca was applied to this pastime (goff), and it derived the denomination, no doubt, from the crooked club or bat with which it was played,' (STRUTT, 94).

CAMBUTA, a medieval game that consisted of striking a ball with a curved stick. No rules have survived. In Eng. a game deriving from cambuta was known as >CAMBUCA [medieval Lat. *cambuta* – a curved shepherd's stick, pastoral]. The similarity of names implies a relationship between these games.

CAMEL FIGHTS, an event popular among the Torgut people of W Mongolia. In Iran and among the Turkmen living on the Amur river camel fights were part of celebrating various muslim holidays. A white scarf was tied around the animal's forehead to nominate it as a competitor. Today camel fights are a popular tourist attraction in various countries, e.g. in Turkey, where they are referred to as camel wrestling (deve güreşi) and have enjoyed a long tradition dating back to nomadic times. They are held in Aydin, the Aegean region (Izmir, Manisa, Mugla, Denizli), the Marmara region (Balikesir, Çanakkale), the Mediterranean region (Burdur Isparta) and some other provinces. The wrestling period comes in the winter months (Dec.-March). Camels used for wrestling are a special crossbreed being the result of the mating of a female, dromedary camel called a *yoz* and a male, Bactrian camel called a *buhur*. On the day preceding the actual event camels are paraded by their owners to the accompaniment of music played on trad. instruments. The fights usu. begin in the morning and last throughout the day. They are held in 4 categories: ayak, Orta, Başalti and baş. Winners are determined by the rival's escape (the winner successfully wrestles its rival out of the field), cry (the rival cannot stand the force of the winner and gives out a cry), or fall (the winner knocks its rival down and sits on it). The bout may also end in a tie or in the owner's acknowledging his camel's defeat by throwing a rope into the field and surrendering his animal in order to prevent its sustaining injuries. Each camel wrestles only once a day and the bout lasts 10-15min. Special care is taken to

the best jockeys of the 1990s were: E. Hall, N. Young, D. Holliday and G. Jackson. Another country in which camel racing developed rapidly was the USA, where camels had been brought by the army to be used as a means of desert transportation after the Mexican War of the 1840s. In the long run the army gave up the use of camels, although the animals remained in the postal service. Currently camel racing enjoys the biggest popularity in California, Nevada and Arizona. The most prestigious events are the Benicia Camel Race in Pine Lake, the races during the annual Riverside County Date Festival at Indio, California, the Virginia City Camel Races and Governors Cup in Virginia City, Nevada. The leading organization is the International Order of Camel Jockeys estab. in 1970 in Nevada. According to its

C WORLD SPORTS ENCYCLOPEDIA

statute, it is a non-profit organization, the goal of which is to provide entertainment and promote camel racing as a major sport. Among the best jockeys are D. Hyn and K. Bond.

CAMMOCK, also *comocke*, an old Eng. game resembling today's >FIELD HOCKEY. The etymology of its name reveals that the Eng. borrowed the game from the Celtic *camanachd*, i.e. contemporary >SHINTY.

Camels named Modheia, left, Sandy and Will Show Ya, right, charge for the finish line in the third race in Sydney's first camel race meet at Royal Randwick race course.

CAMOGIE, a national Irish sport for women being the modified version of men's >HURLING [Ir. gaelic *camog*, diminutive of *caman* or *camanan* – a curved stick). The aim is to score a goal with a small ball hit by curved sticks. The basic difference between camogie and hurling is that in the former no bodily contact is allowed.

Rules. The game is played by 2 teams of 12 players each. A team consists of a goalkeeper, fullback, centre back, left back, right back, mid-field, left-wing, right-wing, full forward, centre forward, left forward, and right forward. The game lasts over two 25-min. periods and is arbitrated by the main referee and two goal umpires. Each team is allowed to replace 3 players during a game.

Pitch, equipment. The pitch has the size of 100-120x60-75yds. (91-110 x 55-68m). The stick is curved, has a flat surface, and is lighter than the one used for hurling and is 3ft. (91 cm) long. The ball is 9-10in. (23-25cm) in perimeter. The goal is 15ft. (4,6m) wide and has two bars: one 20ft. (6.1m.) and the other – 7ft. (2.1m) above the ground. A goal scored between bars scores 1pt., while a goal scored below the lower bar scores 3pts.

Attire. Players wear blazers over short, sleeveless dresses, black stockings with footbal-like leggins and light shoes with small lifts. Similar to men's hurling, players often use helmets to protect themselves against being hit in the head with the stick or ball.

History. The origin of the game is connected both with the Irish national independence movement and women's liberation movement on the turn of the 19th century. Women associated in the Gaelic League, aimed at preserving the Irish tradition, denationalized and subdued by the political dominance of England, decided to expand their activity by means of including sports hitherto reserved for men. At first they played straightforward hurling games and later began to adapt the rules to their specific abilities and needs. Pitch size was reduced, a lighter stick was introduced and bodily contact was banned. The first game played according to the modernized regulations was held in 1904 in Navan (35km NW of Dublin). Also in 1904 The Camogie Association of Ireland (CAI) was formed (called in gaelic Cumann Camogaiochta na Gael). At first camogie was restricted mainly to Dublin and Co. Louth. The spread of the game took place after the first academic competition called Asbourne Cup in 1915, which introduced camogie to other academic centers besides Dublin, i.e. Cork, Belfast and Galway. In the 1920s Ireland's strive for independence hindered the development of the sport. In 1932 CAI obtained the status of a national Ir. organization and began to organize the country's championships. The city and county of Antrim joined the traditionally strongest camogie centers led by Dublin, which won most championship titles after 1932. In independent Ire-

land, from approx. 1950 camogie began to emerge in counties, where it had been practically unknown before. Special instructor's courses and training camps for players enabled the spread of the game to the regions of Wexford, Kilkenny and Tipperary, which became the leading camogie centres. CAI now incorporates 27 local associations and more than 400 clubs with a total number of players exceeding 100,000. County championships are played both in the pro and junior category, along with various other championships and school events.

CAMP, an Eng. game that used to be popular in Suffolk County, esp. in the area between the Orwell and Alde Rivers and around the Hollesley Bay, and in Norfolk County. Goals, 10-15yds. (approx. 9-13m) wide, were located at a distance of approx. 150-200yds. (approx. 137-183m). The ball resembled the one used in cricket. There were 10-15 'sidesmen' (players) in each team which lined up in 2 rows, facing their own goals – the rows standing at a distance of about 10yds. (9m) from each other. The referee tossed the ball up so that it fell in the middle of the area between the rows. The moment the ball touched the ground, teams started competing for it. The ball could be both caught and kicked but for the most part it was kicked. It could be thrown to a partner but not passed hand to hand. To score a goal, named a 'notch' or a 'snotch', a player had to carry the ball across the goal line. No goal was scored if a player threw the ball between the poles instead of carrying it. A goal was not scored if a player carrying the ball towards the line was grabbed and stopped even for a moment by an opponent. After a goal was scored there was a break. The match was not usu. played within any predetermined time but rather up to the agreed score, generally 7-9. If a larger ball was used, e.g. a football one, the game was called a 'kicking-camp'. In the countryside boys usually played barefoot, whereas in the vicinity of urban areas they wore shoes – this var. of camp was rebelliously dubbed a savage camp.

History. Most prob. camp is a derivative from soldiers' ball games that were practiced in army camps. In King Henry VI's edict dated 1486, the game is mentioned as camping pightel (camp enclosure, meadow), possibly after the place outside the tent area where the matches were arranged. T. Tusser (1524?-80), the author of an agricultural treatise *Hundreth Good Pointes of Husbandrie* (1557), recommended camping pightel as a method for improving grass growth:

In meadow or pasture (to grow the more fine)
Let campers be camping in any of thine;
Which if ye do suffer when low is the spring,
You gain to yourself a commoding thing.[...]
Get campers a ball,
To camp therewithall.

In documents made by a municipal government in the 15th cent. we find records describing suburban fields for playing camp. The presence of old varieties of the game in a number of Eng. towns is corroborated by the names of quarters or streets, e.g. in Sheffield the street named Capo Field could be

found on a city map dated 1736 as the Camper Lane which led to a nearby school where a camp playing field was located. In Norton Woodseats the places known as Upper Campfield and Lower Campfield are frequently referred to as Camping Fields. According to A.B. Gomme, they may be a place where football and other village games were practiced.
A.B. Gomme, 'Camp', TGESI, 1894, I, 56-58.

CAMP-BALL, one of the old Eng. ball games that served as a prototype for >FOOTBALL. In the play *The Blind Beggar of Bethnal Green* (1659) by J. Day appears a camp-ball player whose name is Tom Stroud. He brags 'I'll play a gole at camp-ball.' In the work titled *Sports and Pastimes of the People of England* (1810) J. Strutt maintains that the primary difference between football and camp-ball was the fact that the latter was played with no spatial limitations, so that players could enjoy it more: 'Campball [...] is only another denomination of football, and is so called, because it was played to the greatest advantage in an open country.' (p. 94).

CAMPDRAFTING, a folk sport practiced in Australia and counted among events linked to the >RODEO tradition. Competitors ride on horseback into a herd of cattle gathered in a specially prepared area [Austr. Eng. slang *camp* – a pasture] and they select an animal and drive it from the herd, following the rules of the game, in the shortest possible time, along a staked lane [Austr. Eng. slang *pasterskidrafting* – cattle selection]. Up to 1994 there was no separate organization that would administer campdrafting. At the beginning of the '90s, the Bushman's Carnival Association (Austr. *bushmen* should not be confused with Afr. ones) made an attempt at introducing standard rules. The largest competitions are Warwick Gold Cup and Risdon Cup – both held in Warwick in the state of Queensland. See also >COUNTRY SHOW SPORTS.

CANADIAN FOOTBALL, a game similar to >AMERICAN FOOTBALL, though not quite identical. The fundamental differences include: 1) The number of players. There are 12 rather than 11 as in Amer. football. The extra team member is called the backfield player. 2) The size of the playing field is different: 110yds. by 65yds. compared to 100yds. by 53yds. in the Amer. variety. 3) The end zone is 25yds. instead of 30ft. 4) A team has to cover a 10-yd. distance using only 3 downs rather then 4 as is the rule in Amer. football. 5) The scoring system is different. The conversion scores either 1pt., if the ball is placed between the goal posts, or 2pts. in the case of a successful touchdown within the end zone.

History. The basis for Can. football appeared in 1881-90 when Canada saw the first appearances of Brit. >RUGBY. In the early days of Can. football the game was dominated by rugby elements and overseen by the Can. Rugby Association (CRA). However, in the course of time features of Amer. football infiltrated the game, which gradually departed from rugby. But it was only in 1950 that the Can. Professional Football Association was established. In 1959, the Can. Football League was formed, consisting of a Western Football league

Adapted from hurling 100 years ago, camogie is played by over 100,000 girls and young women.

Canoe polo has been around since the 1930s, but the international rules were fixed only some 15 years ago.

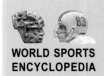

and an Eastern one. The substantial similarities between Can. and Amer. football have allowed players from both countries to play alternatively in the leagues of one or the other variety. For example, in 1950, upon the dissolution of the Amer. Conference Professional League, most of its players flocked to joined Can. teams. The sport is mostly popular with university and high school students where rugby used to be practiced before. A soft version of rugby is also employed in schools as a preparatory exercise for Can. football games. The Can. Rugby Association has not, however, been dissolved and it still operates as an autonomic organization.

F.G. Menke, 'Canadian (Rugby) Football', MEN (1969, 446-448); F. Consetino, 'Football, Canadian', EWS (I, 346-351); F. Consentino, *The Passing Game. A History of CFL* (1995).

CANDLEPINS, the name originates from the slender and rather rare shape of skittles that resemble candles. Candlepins is a var. of >TEN-PIN BOWLING. See also >BOWLING; >EUROPEAN BOWLING.

CANLIE, a game played in Scotland (Aberdeen). A selected player, called a 'canlie', defends a limited area of the playing field across which other players rush at short intervals. The canlie's objective is to catch one of the running players to make him a new canlie. A similar game was denominated 'tig' in Lanark and Renfrew Counties and in Mearns County it was called 'tick'.
TGESI, I, 58.

CANNE, a Fr. fight with the use of sticks that resembles Eng. >QUARTERSTAFF and Pol. >PALCATY. It developed from medieval folk and knights' traditions, according to which a young boy was trained before he fenced using a genuine weapon. Canne includes the skill of rotational movements, parrying, and lunging. The weapon is a cane with identical tips, referred to as *canne é épée* or *canne armée*. The tradition of canne was partially rejuvenated with the growth of >SAVATE.

CANOE POI, see >POI WAKA.

CANOE POLO, a competitive open-air or indoor ball game between two teams of players paddling polo kayaks. The aim of the game is to score goals either by playing the ball with a paddle or by throwing it with the hands into one of the goals fitted with nets and suspended above the surface of water on both ends of the playing area.
The rules. The playing area should have a length of about 40m and a width of about 25m. The water throughout the playing area must be at least 90cm deep. The goals consist of open frames 1m high by 1.5m wide hung vertically with the lower inside edge 2m above the surface of water. The frameworks of the goals are rigid. In an indoor facility for playing canoe polo, there must be a height of at least 3m without obstacles, and a min. ceiling height of 5m, above the playing area. Each team consists of 5 players on the playing area (including the goalkeeper) and 3 substitutes at any one time. Players may be substituted at any moment of the game. All players of a given team must have kayaks and helmets of the same color to facilitate identification. Body protection must also be worn

by the players throughout the game. Playing time consists of 2 periods each of 7-10min. with 1-3min. half-time interval. The teams change ends after each period of play. The winning team is the one which scores more goals within the set time limit. Two extra 3min. play periods with a 1-min. break is awarded by the referee if the game ends in a tie. If the extra playing-time yields no result, a series of tiebreaker shots is ordered with players from each team alternating shots at the same goal.
The referee tosses a coin to determine turns. Tiebreaker shots are to be performed by all 5 participants from both teams. If, after each team has had 5 tiebreaker shots, the score is still equal then the teams take another series of shots, 5 each, until, with an equal number of tiebreaker shots, one team has scored more goals. The game is controlled by 2 referees in kayaks. They are dressed in black to facilitate identification. The referees are accompanied by 2 linesmen and a timekeeper. To commence the game the players must take their positions in a row on the back goal line. One of the referees throws the ball towards the central part of the playing area. Two chosen players, one from each team, try to reach the ball and pass it over to other players from their team. The aim is to score a goal by passing the ball through the plane of the front of the goal frame of the opponents' goal. The ball must not be prevented from entering the goal by a defender's paddle entering the goal from behind. Touching an opponent's kayak or person with a paddle, attempting to play the ball with a paddle within 1m of a player, and blocking an opponent not in possession of the ball are illegal. Like in soccer, unfair play and infringements are penalized by distribution of yellow and red cards. A yellow card stands for 2min. out of play, whereas a red card rules the player out until the end of the game. The infringement may be penalized also by rewarding a goal penalty-shot, taken from the 6m line. All other players must be in the other half of the playing area until play restarts. The shot is taken when the referee blows the whistle. The player taking the shot must not play the ball again until it has touched another player or another player's equipment or the goal frame.
Equipment. The ball is identical to that used in >WATER POLO for games played by men, the circumference 68.5-71cm and 400-500g of weight. The kayak may not be longer than 3m and not less than 2m, not wider than 60cm but not less than 50cm. The weight of a dry kayak may not be less than 7kg. The front and rear impact zones must be rounded. The radius of curvature of the front impact zone: 3-5cm, of the rear impact zone: not less than10cm. The paddle must have a max. length of 220cm, the blades are to be positioned at an angle of 90° to each other. The blades are not to be more than 50x25cm, curvature radius: 3cm. The paddle may not have sharp projections or edges or other dangerous features, e.g. metal tips. The cockpit is protected from water by a special skirt, which is especially important when the boat capsizes. The players wear 15mm-thick life jackets and helmets with face protectors guarding them against injuries.
History. The first attempts at organizing canoe polo took place in 1930s. After WWII it became popular first in Germany and England where the annual national cup has been organized since

1969. Unified international rules were introduced no sooner than 1987. The discipline is subject to the rules and regulations of the International Canoe Federation (ICF).
The first W.Ch. in Sheffield, England, were held in 1994. The championships have been held biannually ever since. Austrl. men proved to be the leading competitors: they swept the board until 1998. Austrl. women dominated (championship in 1994 and 1998) together with female representatives of England (gold in 1996). The first E.Ch. were held in Rome in 1995 and have been continued in 2-yr cycles ever since.

CANOEING, or *flat water canoeing*, a term for a sports discipline in which 2 types of boats and 2 manners of advancing on water are employed: >KAYAKING, in which a kayak originating from Native Alaskan traditions is used; and proper canoeing which uses boats that originate from traditional canoes developed by Native Amer. Indians of N.America, propelled with a single-blade paddle by a paddler kneeling on one knee. An original canoe was made from sheets of leather or bark stretched on wooden or bone ribbing and was propelled with short single-blade paddles. Despite significant technical and structural differences between them, kayaking and canoeing are supported by the same national and international federations and are treated together. The fact the two sports were combined under the same name (canoeing) prob. stems from a series of general similarities between them, such as the narrow boats made from leather sheets spread on the ribbing, which makes them very responsive to paddler's maneuvers. Eur. cultures were not familiar with similar solutions, other than Wel. >CORACLES which were built from sheets of leather spread on the ribbing but their shape differed largely, as they were oval or circular. Both canoe and kayak arrived from N.America in Europe in a similar way, which is why they were both associated as a single product of local Amer. tribes. The original word derives from the name used in Arawakan, first recorded by Columbus according to Span. spelling rules as *canoa*, which then was adopted in Span. with no further modifications and soon after was borrowed by other Eur. languages (Fr. *canoe*, Du. *kano*, Ger. *Kanu*, Ital. *canoa*, Pol. *kanu*). As a result, in the majority of Eur. languages sports races in Indian boats acquired names based on this word, e.g. Eng. canoeing, Ger. *Kanusport*, Du. *kanosport*, Swed. *kanotidrott*, etc.
Boat structure and paddling technique. A canoe resembles a dug-out. Original canoes had a rounded bow and stern that protruded above the boards. The canoe's shape is symmetrical, and instead of a rudder it has a straight keel, protruding 30cm below the bottom. A single boat is 5.2m long, 75cm wide, and weighs 16kg; a double one, 6.5m – 75cm – 20kg, respectively; and a multiple canoe, usu. for 7 people, 11.1m – 85cm – 50kg. The paddles are single-bladed and the paddlers kneel in the boat facing the direction of movement.
Events. Races are held for singles (C1), doubles (C2), and 7-member teams (C7), over a distance of 200-1,000m, separately for men and women; C1 and C2 can also take part in a mountain slalom (see >WHITE WATER KAYAKING AND CANOEING).
History. The tradition of canoe building originated among the tribes of Native Amer. Indians in N.America, particularly in today's Canada and the N USA. Two basic types of Indian canoes were known: 1) constructed on a wooden, sometimes bone, ribbing covered in animal skins or bark (the

A foul is committed while vying for possession.

A canoe polo player sizes up his target.

C

region of the Great Lakes and NE coast of N.America, esp. among Algonquians and Iroquois); 2) constructed from a burned or bored tree trunk, referred to as dug-outs by colonists, mostly used on the W coast of Canada, esp. by the Kwakiutl, Haida, Tlingit, and Tsimszian people. The largest boats used in that area could seat 40 persons. A characteristic feature of canoes is the lack of a rudder and good responsiveness achieved by means of shifting pad-

Canoeing by a waterfall.

Portaging a shallow stretch.

Winslow Homer, Canoe in Rapids , 1887, oil on canvas.

Canoeing motifs on postage stamps issued for the Olympics in Sydney (below) and Seoul (bottom).

dles from one board to the other and by the streamlined shape of the double-bow hull. Modern canoes maintain the trad. shape but they are made of different materials. Until recently, the basic ones were waterproofed plywood, fiberglass, and aluminum, whereas today it is mostly plastic, which – thanks to mass production – has facilitated the popularization of the discipline by reducing the costs of equipment. The earliest description of a canoe, without using the name, dates back to the beginning of the 11th cent. and appears in a Scand. saga about Leiff Ericson, relating the adventures of Norsemen (Vikings) who were the first Europeans to reach N.America. It can be deduced from the saga that Norsemen prob. got as far as the Gulf of St. Lawrence where they encountered Native Amer. Indians for the first time.

On one sunny day,
while beholding the river,
they saw a multitude of
boats covered in leather.
They were propelled with paddles
that swung in the air
and then splashed against water
like flails against the threshing floor.
The boats headed towards the sun
and the people sitting in them were swarthy [...]
with their hair pinned up in disorderly manner.
They stood still for a while,
looking bewilderingly at the newcomers.
Then, suddenly turned the boats back
and disappeared behind a riverbend.

But Norse discoveries did not contribute to the knowledge of Europeans about the Amer. continent. Only after Columbus's discovery did Europeans learn about Native Amer. Indian culture. European culture adopted then a number of agricultural achievements revealed by Native Americans (potatoes, corn, tomatoes, tobacco), as well as artisanship in wood and leather. At that time, Eur. settlers learned about suede, moccasins, wigwams and tee-pees, and of course about boats. In 16-19th cent., various types of canoe were used for transportation and communication along the rivers of N America. They were employed esp. by trappers who often transported skins over a distance of hundreds of kilometers in order to supply trading factories. As motor vehicles were not available at that time, canoes were often the best means of transportation also for settlers heading west, through regions where woods made it impossible to go in a wagon and rivers and lakes formed natural routes. The canoe's advantage over wooden boats, besides easy maneuvering on difficult rivers, was its light weight which made it easy to carry whenever travelers wanted to change streams or to go around waterfalls, which acquired its own name: 'haulover' or 'portage'. M. Lewis (1774-1809) and W. Clark (1770-1838) made a sub-

stantial part of their 4,800-km journey (1804-06), during which they prepared the earliest maps of N America (see also >GEOGRAPHICAL EXPLORATION), in canoes. After it had become popular with Ang.-Sax. settlers in America, the canoe started to be used for sports competition. In the 1850s, first local canoe races were organized, which at the end of the 19th cent. turned into a sports discipline, mostly thanks to the activities of the Can. Canoeing Association, founded in 1881. The association was the starting point for the first eminent canoeists. Canoeing, along with kayaking, was incorporated in the 1936 Ol.G. in Berlin. The most memorable canoeist of the 1930s is Canadian F. Amyo – the winner of singles at the 1936 Ol.G.; after WWII it was a Czech, J. Holeček – a double Ol.G. winner in C1 – 1,000m, in 1948 and 1952, and the world champion of 1950 in the same event. Rumanian, L. Rotman (b. 1934), turned out to be an exceptionally versatile sportsman, winning two Ol.G. gold medals at the same 1956 games, in different categories, C1 – 1,000m and C1 – 10,000m. Hungarian, J. Parti (b. 1932), was an Olympic winner in 1960 and a double world champion in C1 – 1,000m, as well as a double Ol.G. silver medallist in 1,000m (1952) and 10,000m (1956), not counting a few E.Ch. titles. In 1970-82, Hungarian T. Wichmann (b. 1948) was a 7-time world champion in C1 – 1,000m and 10,000m, and a winner of 2 silver and 1 bronze Ol.G. medals. At the same time, he was a several-times world and Eur. champion in kayaking, therefore he should be recognized as the most outstanding figure of the two disciplines in history (in total he won 17 W.Ch. medals, 3 Ol.G. medals and 4 E.Ch. ones). In the late 80s and in the course of the 90s, the most interesting seem to be the achievements of Bulgarian M. Buchalov (among others, an Ol.G. winner in C1 – 1,000m, in 1992) and of a Rumanian pair, I. Patzaichin and T. Simionov, double Ol.G. winners in C2 – 1,000m (in 1980 and 1984). In recent years among the most outstanding canoeists were: M. Doktor (Czech Rep.), Olympic champion from Atlanta (500m

and 1,000m), G. Kolonics (Hungary), Olympic champion from Sydney (500m), and A. Dittmer (Germany), Olympic champion from Sydney (1,000m).
R.R. Camp, *Young Sportsman's Guide to Canoeing*, 1962; C.W. Handel, *Canoeing*, 1956; R.H. Perry, *Canoeing for Beginners*, 1967; B.A. Roth, *The Complete Beginner's Guide into Canoeing*, 1977; K.G. Roberts & P. Shackelton, *The Canoe, A History of the Craft from Panama to the Arctic*, 1983; R. Slim, *The Canoe Handbook*, 1992.

CANYONING, also known as *canyoneering*, a sport that combines rock climbing, hiking, plunging into mountain pools, rappelling to the river canyon floors, swimming in narrow canyon passages, abseiling waterfalls, and cascading chutes. For safety reasons the sport is rarely practiced without guides, who are familiar with every pool, slide, and waterfall in the particular canyon. Although canyoning was largely unknown until the 1990s, its history goes back to the 1930s. It is not certain whether aboriginals were exploring canyons, but there are signs of their presence near the Blue Mountains sandstone canyons, like the cave close to the Bell Road near Mt. Bell, or the aboriginal rock art/sculptures on the Tessellate

Pavements north of Mt. Wilson. The first canyons visited by Eur. explorers are said to have been The Grand Canyon at Blackheath and Empress Creek at Wentworth Falls. In the 1930s members of the Sydney Bushwalkers (SBW) made an unsuccessful attempt to penetrate Arethusa Canyon from below. In the 1940s they were followed by K. Iredale, and in 1945 by the YMCA Ramblers and Sydney University Bushwalkers. In the 1950s members of the Catholic Bushwalking Club (CBC) explored Mt. Hay Canyon and climbed up the cliffs near Butterbox Point but did not descend the canyon. It was descended later by the Sydney Technical College Bushwalking Club (STCBWC). Several years later members of CBC did explore the canyon trusting they were the first to do so. That is why 2 names are used with reference to it, namely 'Butterbox Canyon' (by CBC) and 'Mt. Hay Canyon' (by STCBWC). STCBWC were also the first to descend the main canyons at Kanangra Walls. Another important figure connected with canyoning was C. Oloman, who was the first to look for canyons systematically. Together with other members of SUBW he explored Thunder Canyon (1960), the Carmarthen Canyons, and canyons in Wollangambe Wilderness, Dumbano, and Bungleboori Creeks.
In order to make this sport as safe as possible, several safety requirements have been established. The most important ones state that: all members must have their own set of abseiling gear so as to get on and off the ropes quickly; an experienced person should set up the ropes (making sure there are no tangles or knots) and lead any abseil; the group must be extremely careful descending a canyon whenever there is a risk of thunderstorm; and the first person to do a water jump should check the pool for rocks and submerged logs.
There is also a code of ethics that anyone practicing this sport must obey. According to the rules one should abstain from using bolts or pitons unless there is no other belay point. In seldom visited canyons natural ropes (e.g. manilla rope) should be

Olympic canoeing.

used, due to their decomposing properties. Finally, it is forbidden to mark out the route in and out of the canyon.
The most prominent associations connected with canyoning are the Amer. Canyoneering Association, the Commission Europeene de Canyon (Germany) and the Ital. Canyoning Association which in April 2000 estab. the National Canyoning School.

CAPIE-HOLE, an old Eng. folk game in which a ball is thrown into a hole in the ground ['capie' means more or less covered]. The game was also known as 'the Hole'. A spot from which balls were thrown was identified as the 'strand'. The distance between the strand and the hole was not fixed, it depended on the size of the ball and the player's skills. In Scotland a similar game was practiced with 3 holes. The winner was the player who managed to place the ball in the hole the greatest number of times within an agreed number of throws.
TGESI, I, 58.

CAPOEIRA, a Brazilian trad. sport being a fusion of wrestling, music, dance, rhythm, acrobatics and ritual. It is particularly popular around Bahia. Players are referred to as *capoirista* and the dance/fight is

WORLD SPORTS ENCYCLOPEDIA

C

Back to nature on a canyoning expedition.

performed within a circle called *roda*. Capoeira first spread as a form of rural and street fight, often between rival gangs, the main goal of which was to use deceptive techniques such as mock escape or mock fall in order to deal an unexpected blow. The richness of ducking and attacking movements, combined with the natural agility of the practitioner, produced dramatic visual effects, developed esthetically when capoeira became a regular sporting activity. The turning point in the development of the sport was the addition of rhythmical drumming and later dance during Brazilian folk holidays. The basic sound effect is that of an *atabaque* (a trad. oval--shaped African drum) and also *berimbau* (a one--string, bow-shaped instrument, with an empty, dry gourd attached to one end to give resonance). Other instruments include: *pandeiro* – a kind of tambourine; *reco-reco* – a piece of dry and hollow bamboo, which produces a sound by having its surface scratched with a stick; *agogo* – bells. A capoeira show begins with a solo played on *berimbau*, during which two opponents begin a bodily display. Gradually, other instruments join in, the effect of which is a heavily syncopated rhythm. The players wear white uniforms – baggy pants and loose T-shirts, often decorated with color strings (usually gold) and embroidered. The fight proper begins with the sign of the cross made by both opponents. In rhythmical, circular movements they approach one another and deliver blows by both their hands and legs, at the same time trying to avoid the blows of the opponent. A characteristic kick is called *rabo de arraia* – stingray's tail; it is delivered when the player turns his back on his oppoent to mock his escape and at the same time thrusts his leg backwards to kick the deceived opponent.

The introduction of music turned capoeira from a street fight into a skill bordering on a martial art and dance. It is now possible to see people in parks and streets practising capoeira in a way resembling certain Asian practices.

Etymology and linguistic heritage. The name capoeira is a Port. form of a word borrowed from the language of Brazilian Indians, in which it described a small partridge, whose male is very jealous and engages in fierce fights with his rivals. The movements it makes are like those of fighting slaves, which could have been first observed during the times, when escaped slaves formed independent mountain and jungle territories called *quilombos*, where they met the Indians. The oldest record of the word capoeira to describe a fight is from 1770.

History. Capoeira derives from a hand-to-hand combat and games imported to Brazil by Afr. slaves in the 17th cent. The main areas of slave trade were the harbors of Bahia, Recife, and Rio de Janeiro. In its earliest form capoeira was known here as >CAPOEIRA ANGOLA, even though different varieties were brought not only from Angola, but also other regions of W Africa, even Bantu. The oldest froms of capoeira developed in *senzalas* or slave settlements located near sugar cane and tobacco plantations. Within a century the number of slaves in Brazil grew to approx. 1 million. A growing number of escapes led to the establishment of many *mocambos* – communities of escaped slaves living in *quilombos*, settlements concealed in the mountains or in the jungle, where methods of hand-to-hand combat

were practiced. The largest of them was Palmares, established by 40 slaves who escaped from Recife and with the help of the Indians reached an otherwise inaccessible mountain region, from where they conducted guerilla warfare (called jungle wars) against the white slave owners. At the peak of its development Palmares had 20,000 inhabitants, including an Indian minority, as well as white outcasts. Neither slave hunters nor punitive expeditions could eliminate such independent territories. In 1630 the Dutch troops which defeated the Portuguese unsuccessfully tried to pacify Palmares. Hand-to-hand combat was used in ambushes and in a difficult terrain. At the same time a folk culture including music and dance developed dynamically in the region. The overlap of these activities produced the rapid development of capoeira. Festivities following a successful raid over the white slave owners brought about constantly richer musical and dance forms connected with capoeira. After a series of slave revolts and the abolition of slavery in 1868 the escaped slaves mingled into the slum areas of Brazilian towns. As those areas grew, capoeira became a method of street fight used extensively by slum gangs. At the end of the 19th cent. capoeira was regarded as dangerous and was banned by the Brazilian criminal code. Another law was soon introduced allowing the authorities to pursue those practicing capoeira and, in extreme cases, banish them from the country. The official ban and preventive measures led by a famous officer of the Brazilian police, Sampaio, drastically limited the public scope of capoeira during the 1920s. A musical trace of police actions against the capoeiristas can be found in the elements of rhythm played on the drums: the accelerated *aviso* warned against an approaching policeman, while *cavalaria* signalled a police squad approaching to eliminate capoeira in the region. In order to carry out their actions effectively, the police learned capoeira techniques. Despite police actions and the ban on capoeira in Salvador, the first schools of capoeira

Capoeira.

were established by the now legendary masters – Mestre Pastinha and Bimba. Bimba formed a new style called Capoeira Regional, in contrast to the trad. Capoeira Angola. He was also successful in convincing the local authorities of the significance of capoeira to Brazilian culture. In 1937 Bimba was invited by the Brazilian President to conduct a public demonstration of capoeira. Having gained official support, Bimba estab. a school of capoeira, which initiated a new stage in its development, marked by the spread of capoeira clubs and the introduction of capoeira into schools and universities. The sport is now a strongly supported element of Brazilian folk tradition.

CAPOEIRA ANGOLA, the most ancient name for the Brazilian folk sport >CAPOEIRA and the original but also more primitive form of the same sport. The Capoeira Angola player is called 'angoleiro' to differentiate him from a player who practices a more modern version of that martial art.

CAPTIVUS, see >PLINIE.

CAR LIFTING, a sport consisting of lifting a car by a single competitor. Car lifting has numerous varieties. The so-called car walk is one of the constituent events of the World's Strongest Man Competition – a car with the roof and floor removed is carried with harnesses as far as possible.

CAR RACING, a group of sporting disciplines in which the competition is between various classes of automobiles, both passenger cars and trucks, factory made or specially constructed for racing purposes. The competition is for speed, i.e. the goal is to cover a given distance in the shortest time. Races are held on specially built circular courses, usu. 3-5km in length, as well as on roads or speedways, in 3 basic categories of cars: tourist, sports, and race cars, each category subdivided into classes according to the type of car and engine size. There are 6 basic groups in 2 categories. Category I includes production models and is subdivided into class N – stock cars with at least 4 seats and produced at a level of at least 5,000 per year; class A – tourist cars with at least 4 seats and produced at a level of at least 5,000 per year and approved by the International Automobile Federation (FIA); class B – GT (grand tourisme) production models with at least 2 seats and produced at the level of at least 200 per year. Category II includes: class C – sport cars with at least 2 seats; class D – racing formula cars, incl. F-1, F-3000 and F-3; and class E – racing cars of an open formula, with no constructional limitations. Internationally, the biggest popularity is enjoyed by Formula 1 races, while in the USA that status is reserved for indy cars (see below). Most auto giants, such as Ford, Fiat, etc. sponsor their own racing formula events. Constantly growing sports are also >VINTAGE AUTO RACING and >TRUCK RACING.

The most famous race courses in Europe are Le Mans (with the legendary 24-hour race) in France, Italy's Monza, and Germany's Nürburgringen. The largest and most prestigious race cources in the USA are Indianapolis Motor Speedway (Indiana) and Laguna Seca in Monterey (California). The India-

Capoeira.

C

**WORLD SPORTS
ENCYCLOPEDIA**

*Ferrari race cars on a Hungarian
postage stamp.*

FORMULA 1 WORLD CHAMPIONS
1950 N. Farina, ITA
1951 Juan Manuel Fangio, ARG
1952 Alberto Ascari, ITA
1953 Alberto Ascari, ITA
1954 Juan Manuel Fangio, ARG
1955 Juan Manuel Fangio, ARG
1956 Juan Manuel Fangio, ARG
1957 Juan Manuel Fangio, ARG
1958 Mike Hawthorne, GBR
1959 Jack Brabham, AUSTRAL
1960 Jack Brabham, AUSTRAL
1961 Phil Hill, USA
1962 Graham Hill, GBR
1963 Jim Clark, GBR
1964 John Surtees, GBR
1965 Jim Clark, GBR
1966 Jack Brabham, AUSTRAL
1967 Denis Hulme, NZL
1968 Graham Hill, GBR
1969 Jackie Stewart, GBR
1970 Jochen Rindt, AUT
1971 Jackie Stewart, GBR
1972 Emerson Fittipaldi, BRA
1973 Jackie Stewart, GBR
1974 Emerson Fittipaldi, BRA
1975 Niki Lauda, AUT
1976 James Hunt, GBR
1977 Niki Lauda, AUT
1978 Mario Andretti, USA
1979 Jody Scheckter, RSA
1980 Alan Jones, AUSTRAL
1981 Nelson Piquet, BRA
1982 Keke Rosberg, FIN
1983 Nelson Piquet, BRA
1984 Niki Lauda, AUT
1985 Alain Prost, FRA
1986 Alain Prost, FRA
1987 Nelson Piquet, BRA
1988 Ayrton Senna, BRA
1989 Alain Prost, FRA
1990 Ayrton Senna, BRA
1991 Ayrton Senna, BRA
1992 Nigel Mansell, GBR
1993 Alain Prost, FRA
1994 Michael Schumacher, GER
1995 Michael Schumacher, GER
1996 Damon Hill, GBR
1997 Jacques Villeneuve, CAN
1998 Mika Hakkinen, FIN
1999 Mika Hakkinen, FIN
2000 Michael Schumacher, GER
2001 Michael Schumacher, GER
2002 Michael Schumacher, GER

Formula 1 car racing.

napolis course is, in fact, a racing town with state of the art technical facilities and a tourist center serving up to 400,000 spectators coming from all over the USA and abroad.

History. The oldest forms of car racing date back to the times when the first automobiles were constructed and at first were identical with >AUTOMOBILE RALLIES. They were held on public roads, most often between cities, with the race distance forming a loop. The first modern races were organized by an American living in Europe J. Gordon Bennett. Since 1903 they were held on looping tracks. See also >AUTO RACING.

FORMULA 1. Grand Prix races are held in spec. constructed cars during a season that lasts from March to October. The history of F-1 derives from the tradition of national Grand Prix (GP) races in various countries, initiated on the Le Mans course in France in 1906. The first GP winner was F. Szisz in a Renault, whose average speed was 101,17km/h. In the 1930s the national GPs led to an international competition, esp. between It. and Fr. car producers. This competition soon became nationalist in nature, particularly when the government in Germany was taken over by Hitler (1933), which began a period of domination by Mercedes and DKW. The requirements of international competition has led to standard regulations of GP races, which in 1934 limited the weight of cars to 750kg. Before 1939 the most famous drivers were: Italians C.G. Campari (1892--1933), T. Nuvolari (1892-1953), A. Vrazi (1904-48); Germans R. Caraciolla (1901-59), H. Stuck von Villiez (1900-77), B. Rosemeyer (1909-38), Americans L. Meyer (b. 1904-95), W. Shaw (1903-54). The leading car makes before 1939 incl. Alfa Romeo, Bugatti, Mercedes-Benz, Auto Union, Maserati, and Ford. After WWII GP races were resumed in 1948 in 2 categories according to engine size: F1 with engines without supercharging were up to 4500ccm, supercharged engines up to 1500ccm, and F2 for engines of lower capacity. GP championships for drivers began in 1950, for car producers – in 1958. In 1954-60 swept capacity of engines was limited to 2500ccm without supercharging and 750ccm with supercharging. In 1961-66 engines with supercharging were banned, while swept capacity was limited to 1500ccm due to the high mortality rate of race drivers. The weight of cars was limited to 450kg without fuel. In 1966-88 engines without supercharging were limited to 3000ccm and those

with supercharging to 1500ccm. In 1977 Renault introduced engines with turbo-compressors, which significantly improved the cars' performance. In 1986 engines without supercharging were withdrawn from the races for one year, while in 1988 engines with turbo-compressors were banned and replaced with engines without supercharging, but with swept capacity up to 3500ccm. In 1995 the swept capacity of engines was limited to 3000ccm. Regulations introduced in 1996 limit F-1 to 4-stroke engines without supercharging and with no more than 12 cylinders of a total swept capacity up to 3000ccm. Four-wheel drive, ABS, active suspension, four-wheel steering are all banned (having been individually allowed for some time). The development of F-1 was marked by the increase in the number of race teams: from 6 in 1961 to 12 in 1972 and 18 in 1975, and soon the number of cars had to be limited. There are currently up to 16 races (minimum 8) held in different regions with 26 cars participating. According to the original scoring system, the first six cars on the finish line score in the following way: 1st position – 9 pts, 2nd position – 6 pts, all subsequent positions from 3rd to 6th – 1 pnt less. Until 1959 an additional point was scored for the fastest lap time. In recent years the rules were modified and the winner gets 10 pts, while the next five score the same as before.

Cars represent their producers, such as BRM (Brit. Racing Motors), Honda, Ferrari, Porsche, Maserati, etc. After 1945 the companies raced independently or in various combinations, e.g. Brabham-BMW, Williams-Ford, Lotus-Ford, Tyler-Ford, Cooper-Climax, Lotus-Climax, McLaren-Honda, McLaren-Porsche, Williams-Renault, etc.

Among the best drivers in the history of F-1 were: N. Farina (Italy), who won the 1st F-1 race in 1950 in an Alfa Romeo; M. Fangio, who won 5 times – in 1951 and 1954-57 in various cars; A. Ascari (Italy) – 1952-53, Ferrari; J. Brabham (Australia) – 1959, 1960, 1966); J. Stewart (Scotland) – 1969, 1971, 1973; N. Piquet (Brazil) – 1981, 1983, 1987; N. Lauda (Austria) – 1975, 1977, 1984; A. Prost (France) – 1985, 1986, 1989. In the 1990's the leading drivers were: A. Senna (Brazil) – 1988, 1990, 1991; M. Schumacher (Germany) – 1996, 1997, 2000, 2001; M. Hakkinen (Finland) – 1998, 1999.

OPEN FORTUNA. In winter the F-1 W.Ch. are extended over a series of races called Open Fortuna sponsored by Nissan. The races are held mainly in Japan, but also in Europe, e.g. in Valencia. There

are 13 teams and 20 drivers, with the leading drivers excluded. All drivers have the same Nissan cars with up to 2.0 litre engines and Michelin tires, reaching speeds up to 300km/h.

FORMULA 2. After limiting the engines of F-1 to 1,500ccm in 1961, it seemed that F-2 would disappear, as the difference in capacity was only 500ccm. Yet, in 1964 new regulations for F-2 admitted production engines engines up to 1,000ccm. In 1967, when the limit in F-1 was raised to 3,000ccm, F-2 production engine capacity limit was raised to 1,600ccm and in 1972 – to 2,000ccm.

FORMULA 3 was introduced in 1964 and replaced the earlier junior formula. It was originally limited to single seat cars with engines up to 1,000ccm. In 1971 the capacity limit was raised 1,600ccm and in 1974 – to 2,000ccm for production engines with limited air intake (a choke channel in the feeding system). International championships have been held since 1973.

NASCAR (National Association for Stock Car Auto Racing) seems to be the most popular and best financed form of car racing in the USA. The formula includes 50 qualifying races held annually on oval courses, esp. in southern states. The best known courses are located in Daytona Beach and Talladega. Only one race is held on a road course at Riverside. The average race distance is 100-500mi. Courses have different lengths, e.g. the Atlanta loop is 1.522mi. with the record loop speed 169.9mph. In 1998 J. Gordon became the champion.

INDY 500 races, held on the largest course in the world in Indianapolis (USA), have the status of All-American Championships and are almost as popular as NASCAR. They were originated in 1909 by J.A. Allison and C.G. Fisher over a 2.5-mile course. Currently races are held in single seat cars over a 500-mi. course. Approx. 20 qualifying races held on oval loops in northern US states lead to the finals at Indianapolis. The Indianapolis 500 together with the two most important qualifiers – the Ontario 500 and the Pacono 500 – form the so called Triple Crown.

>VINTAGE AUTO RACING is a form of car racing in which the competition is between old models of cars. The history of car racing has known numerous other formulas, the discussion of which exceeds the scope of this publication. The most spectacular development of various national, regional and brand formulas took place in the 1960s and included, among others:

FORMULA V, popular esp. in the USA, with competition between primitive cars built on the chassis of the Volkswagen 'Beetle';
FORMULA 5000, introduced in Great Britain in 1970, intended as a competition between Europe and the USA;
FORMULA ATLANTIC, a continuation of the previous Formula 3 with engine capacity up to 1,600ccm;
Formula F – Ford, a Brit. formula including British-made Ford cars, with various national varieties such as French F Renault or F Italia (Fiat cars). Its equivalent in the former socialist block countries was F-Easter, with engines up to 1,300ccm.
D. Nye, The Autocourse History of the Grand Prix Car 1966-91, 1992; J.A. Litwin, Współczesny sport samochodowy (Modern auto sport), 1976; J.A. Litwin, Zarys historii sportu samochodowego (An Outline of History of Auto Sport), 1980.

CARACHD BHARRAIDH, a folk var. of Scot. wrestling practiced on the island of Barra that belongs to Outer Hebrides [Scot.-Gaelic carachd – wrestling + Bharraidh – name of the island in Gaelic], also known under its Eng. name >BARRA WRESTLING. The fight starts in a standing position but is continued in the on-the-ground position as well. The winner is the contestant who pushes the opponent outside the limited area, which makes this discipline similar to Jap. >SUMO. See also >CORAIOCHT.

CARACHD UIBHIST, Eng. Uist wrestling, a folk var. of Scot. wrestling practiced on 2 islands belonging to Outer Hebrides, whose Eng. names are the N Uist and the S Uist and whose original Scot.-Gaelic name is the Uibhist [Scot.-Gaelic carachd – wrestling + Uibhist – joint name for the Uist islands]. The discipline was also practiced on a small island of Benbecula. The winner has to strike the opponent down 3 times. Hip throws are accepted but no leg hooks are allowed. Before the actual fight starts, a coin is tossed to determine which arm and in what way bars the other in the starting grip. See also >CORAIOCHT.

CARDBOATS, an event of humorous character held in Singapore during the Singapore River Regatta with boats of unconventional shapes made of impregnated cardboard. During the show the public enjoy such spectacles as lotus-shaped sailboats (1989), a single chimney steamboat (1990), etc. The initiators of the event were the students of the National University of Singapore. In a somewhat similar event, called cardboard races, various types of cardboard-made vehicles are sledded downhill. Cf. >FLOATING ON ANYTHING.

CAROM BILLIARDS, a billiards game that originated in France. Carom gave rise to the majority of the contemporary carom billiards games [Fr. < Span. carambola or carrambola – a name of a fruit whose shape is similar to that of billiards balls – also a fluke or a chance]. The term carambol was extended over time from the balls themselves onto the instance of them striking one another, which characterized the game better. Hence, in the majority of Eur. languages, including Polish, the name also means any kind of a crash, e.g. a car crash or accident. All carom billiards games, irrespective of the variant being played, are based on one common principle, namely that points are scored only after the cue ball has touched, irrespective of whether it bounces off the cushions or not, all the remaining balls on the table. The type of strikes and their sequence has been specifically defined for all the respective carom billiards varieties. All carom billiards games are played on a table with no pockets. Usu. the table is a 5x10ft. (c.152x304cm) rectangle. There are also 4.5x9ft. (137x274cm) and 4x8ft. (122x244cm) tables. A table is divided into various zones with lines drawn on its surface. This is done to facilitate placing of the balls at required spots. The cue ball is always white. 3 balls are used – one red, one white without spots (white ball) and one white ball with a red spot (spot white ball). The red ball always functions as an object ball and it is never used to shoot the break shot or to strike another ball. The white balls are used by both players as their cue balls whereby one of the balls is used by one player (e.g. the white one) and the other by the second player (e.g. the spot white one). The other white ball not used by a given player as his cue ball is treated as an object ball on a par with the red one. When the second player takes over the white balls as if change places – the cue ball of

the first player becomes the second player's object ball and vice versa. For the opening break the white ball which is currently the cue ball is placed on the head string within 6in. of the center spot. The opponent's cue ball is on the head spot and the red ball on the foot spot. The object of the game is to shoot the cue ball in such a way so that it touches the 2 remaining balls. Such a play is worth one point. For the opening break to be legal, the cue ball must hit the red ball first. In some carom billiards games the number of cushion touches is unspecified whereas others require a specific number of off-the-cushion bounces. Although shooting the break shot is a relatively easy part of the game, the remaining shots

and plays are much more difficult. The most difficult shots are those aimed at object balls that have stopped in one of the table's corners. The corner is usu. a 4.5x4.5in. (11x11cm) square at the intersection of 2 cushions. A skillful play at such a ball configuration is called a crotch and it is worth 3pts. If a player misses his shot he loses 1pt. and his opponent takes over. The player who takes over must not move the balls but play them as they are.
The game is supervised by a referee who may be assisted by a scorekeeper. The most popular carom billiards varieties are:
THREEBALL, also known as straight rail, which is played, as the name suggests, with 3 balls. For the opening break to be legal the cue ball must touch the 2 remaining object balls, one of which is placed directly opposite the cue ball towards the foot cushion and the second is placed next to the cue ball. The number of off-the-cushion bounces is not specified and sometimes it is possible to make your play in such a way that the cue ball does not touch the cushions but hits the object balls directly. Since this variety is relatively simple it is now usu. played only by novices. It was dropped from the world championship program in the 1960s because the best players could shoot up to 3,000 shots without making any mistakes. This resulted in long matches which could proceed for hours. This, in turn, deprived the game of the aspect of direct competition. In consequence, threeball was eventually called the no contest game and replaced by a more difficult variety called three cushion (see below).
THREE CUSHION is, similarly to threeball, played with 3 balls. The general rule is the same as in threeball, i.e. the cue ball must always strike the 2 remaining object balls. Additionally, a three-cushion billiard is valid and is a count of one in any of the following cases: 1) the cue ball strikes the first object ball and then strikes three or more cushions before striking the second object ball; 2) the cue ball strikes three or more cushions and then strikes

the two object balls; 3) the cue ball strikes a cushion, then strikes the first object ball, and then strikes two or more cushions before striking the second object ball; 4) the cue ball strikes two cushions, then strikes the first object ball, and then strikes one or more cushions before striking the second object ball.
BALK LINE, derives its name from 4 additional dividing lines called balk lines which break the billiards table up into 8 rectangular side fields and 1 rectangular central field. The 8 side fields that abut on the cushions are the balks proper. When 2 balls stop in one of the balks the regular carom billiards rules change. Depending on the various sub-types of balk line billiards the object of the game is then to drive

Petty Enterprises Dodge Intrepid R\T (#45) during the MBNA America 400 NASCAR Winston Cup Series 2002 at Dover Downs in Dover, DE.

A cardboard train full of passengers speeds downhill during the annual Cardboard Races at Loon Mountain Ski Resort in Lincoln, New Hampshire.

the balls out of a given balk. When 2 balls stop in the central field there are no additional rules other than those typical of regular carom games. The main balk line billiards sub-types are assigned special numbers depending on the distance (measured in inches) at which a balk line is drawn from the cushion. This number also specifies the sizes of the respective balks and, at the same time, is a good indicator of the level of difficulty. The most popular sub-types are 14, 18 and, in the case of bigger tables, even 28in. games (34, 44 and 68.5cm, respectively).

Car park or cross golf.

The inch number is then further supplemented by another number, either 1 or 2, which indicates the type of rule to be applied during a game when 2 balls stop within one balk. So when the players choose to follow the 14.1, 18.1 or 28.1 rules this means that they have to put the 2 balls out of a given balk with one stroke whereby they score 1 point for each such successful shot. In 14.2, 18.2 or 28.2 a player has two shots to do the same. Here, however, he may only drive one ball out at a time (i.e. the second ball has to remain within the original balk after the first shot). If, after being hit out of the original balk, the first ball returns to it, the player has to start the whole play anew but he does not have to relinquish his visit to the table. If a ball or 2 balls stop on one of the balk lines, the player himself decides to which balk they should belong. Then, he tries to strike the balls into the balk he chose. If 2 balls stop at the same line they may be both assigned to the same balk. This is of great importance when 2 balls that stopped at the same dividing line touch each other or are *frozen*. In this situation, whenever one of the balls is hit, the second will move. Then, the object of the game is to force the ball that is not hit directly but only bounces off the one that is hit directly into the balk that was earlier named as the destination for both balls. If the ball that is not hit directly stops in a different balk than the named one, the player must relinquish his run at the table. When the 2 balls are being driven out of the respective balks it is usu. not possible to shoot a regular carom (i.e. to score a shot whereby all 3 balls hit one another in succession). Here, it is enough to hit one of the object balls with the cue ball. However, when the 2 object balls are in different balks the regular carom billiards rules re-apply.

Carriage driving on postage stamps.

Running a four-in-hand team through the obstacle course.

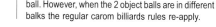

Another difficulty introduced to all balk line billiards subtypes is the so-called *anchors*. The anchors are 7x7in. (17x17cm) squares drawn at the intersection of the balk lines with the cushions. When 2 balls are 'anchored' within the same anchor box they have to be driven out as in the case of 2 balls stopping within the same balk. However, given the size of the anchor this task is much more difficult to complete. Therefore, each balk line billiards game has as if 3 levels of difficulty: 1) regular carom billiards play in the central part of the table and when the 2 balls are in different balks; 2) a more difficult level involving driving 2 balls out of one balk; and 3) the most difficult play aimed at driving 2 balls out of one anchor.

In addition to the above balk line sub-types there are 2 more major varieties:

BANK BALK LINE. When 2 balls stop within one balk or anchor they have to be driven out in a way similar to the one described above with one additional difficulty. The cue ball has to hit a cushion (or a *bank*) before hitting a given object ball.

RED-BALL BALK LINE. The additional rule here is that the first ball to be driven out of a balk or an anchor is to be the red ball.

CARPARK GOLF, also *cross golf*, an unofficial rouge var, of >GOLF, not endorsed by the PDGA or WFDF, in which the game is played in junk yards or multi-level car parks, where cars function as holes and tee. One internet source offers the following description:

Find nearest multi-level carpark. Players take turns selecting holes and tees. Examples include: 1) that pole in the opposite corner of this level; 2) the white Mazda on the floor below; 3) into the first shoping trolley we see on the top level, tee off from the ground floor. The ultimate hole, however, is always from the top level of the carpark to a pole 2 or 3 levels down (but still well

above the ground). The ballsy play is to launch the disc off the roof in the vain hope that it will float back in 3 levels down. Carpark golf is best played at night to avoid too many angry car owners mobbing you as they see their pride and joy being selected as hole no. 5.

http://www.afda.com/discsports/other_disc_sports.htm

CARREIRA DE LA FOGAZA, Span. var. of a folk race similar to LA >ROSCA. In the Gallic dialect the name signifies a race for a loaf of bread [Gallic *carreira*, Span. *carrera* – race + *fogaza*, Span. *hogaza* – loaf of bread]. The race is usually held in summer with adolescent boys as competitors. It is connected with crop harvests and the celebration of chamomile (*celebración de la romeria*). Competitors run along a predetermined route, which is different in different localities, and the winner is awarded a loaf of bread, baked especially for this occasion.
C. Moreno Palos, 'Carreira de la fogaza', JYTE, 1992, 37.

CARRERA CON SACOS DE MAIZ, see >ARTAZAKU GARREIZTZAILEEN LASTERKETA.

CARRIAGE DRIVING, a competitive sport involving driving horse-drawn vehicles. Driving competitions are held for teams of four-in-hand horses, four-in-hand ponies, pony pairs, horse pairs, and horse and pony singles. There are 3 types of competitions, which can be combined: Competition A

– Dressage, Competition B – Marathon, Competition C – Obstacle racing. In the years 1973-74 special 'marathon' vehicles were introduced into the A and C competitions. They are more maneuverable and have a more 'compact' design. Vehicles for competition B have disk brakes, torsion bars, and dampers. A marathon vehicle should weigh no more than 350kg for horse pairs, and no more than 600kg for four-in-hand teams.

COMPETITION A – DRESSAGE. In the dressage test the following aspects are judged: the freedom and regularity of paces, harmony, lightness and ease of movement, and impulsion and correct positioning of the horses on the move. The dressage competition is held in an arena 100x40m. Each team is required to perform a series of movements with a number of changes of pace, walk, collected trot, working and extended trot. Before 1987 Competition A consisted of 2 tests: presentation and dressage. The former part was withdrawn from international competition due to the incomparability of various teams and wide discrepancies in judges' assessments. Presentation test (general impression of the horses, harness and vehicle) is currently an extra exhibition event, which underlines the traditional character of the sport. The drivers and grooms must be dressed accordingly to the style of the vehicle and harness. The drivers must wear driving aprons, hats and gloves. The driver must also carry a whip of a suitable style and the lash must be long enough to reach all the horses.

COMPETITION B – MARATHON is to test the fitness and stamina of the horses and the judgement of pace and horse control by the driver. The total distance of the marathon must not exceed 27km and consists of 5 sections, covered at different paces: section A – 10km at any pace, section B – 1.2km at

Turning on a dime in carriage driving.

walk, section C – 5km at trot, section D – 1.2 at walk, section E – at trot. The last section includes up to 8 obstacles built around natural features.

COMPETITION C – OBSTACLE DRIVING, usu. held on the last day of a driving event, is to test the driving accuracy as well as fitness and suppleness of the horses. It takes place in an enclosed arena, on a course including a max. of 20 obstacles (cones). The drivers wear the same outfit and use the same vehicles as in competition A.

History. The tradition of carriage driving can be traced back to Eng. >COACHING, however much lighter vehicles are used. One of the oldest driving competitions is the international contest held in Aachen since the mid-1930s. In 1969, on Poland's initiative carriage driving was included in the sports program of the Fédération Equestre Internationale (FEI). The first international competition under the auspices of the federation was held in Lucerne, Switzerland in 1970. The E.Ch. in carriage driving have been held every two years since 1971; the W.Ch. every 2 years since 1972. Initially, only four--in-hand teams participated in the championships; pairs were included in 1985. The best national teams at the W.Ch. and E.Ch. have been those of Poland, Hungary, Germany, the UK, the Netherlands, Sweden, Belgium, Switzerland, France, USA and the Czech Republic. The most outstanding carriage

drivers in history are multi-time world and European medallists: S. Fulop, G. Bardos, I. Abonyi from Hungary, and T. Velstra from the Netherlands.
One of the greatest contributors to the development of the sport was Poland, where carriage driving enjoyed huge popularity for many centuries. The first carriage in Poland was that of Queen Jadwiga brought from Hungary in 1384. Similarly as in W Europe carriages were at first treated with disdain by knights and nobles, used primarily as a means of transportation for women, children and the elderly. In the 16th cent., richly decorated carriages began to be used by monarchs and the aristocracy. Carriages became common means of transportation at the turn of the 18th and 19th cent. The development of railways in the 19th cent., replaced horse-drawn carriages on longer routes. The latter remained in use locally until the 20th cent.
The origins of the sports variety of carriage driving date back to races organized by the Polish nobility on the occasion of weddings or family reunions. The actual beginnings of the sport go back to exhibition contests organized in local stud farms in the 1950s and the impact of larger international events, e.g. driving contests in Aachen and Leipzig. Since the 1960s Pol. drivers have been world leaders. The team of Z. Szymoniak represented Poland in Leipzig 1962; in Aachen in 1967, Z. Waliszewski took the first place in pairs. Poland's proposal to establish a Carriage Driving section within the FEI was approved at a meeting of the federation in Brussels in 1968, after which the sport of carriage driving gained significant international recognition. The international fixed rules of competition were drafted after consultation with C. Matławski, the director of the State Stud Farm in Gniezno, Poland. A great propagator of international carriage driving was J. Grabowski, the director of the State Stud Farm in Kwidzyn, who organized the first promotional competition after the inclusion of the sport in the FEI.

E.B. Jung, *Combined Driving*, 1980; K. Lincoln, 'Carriage driving', EWS, 1996, I, 174-177; D. Nowicka, *ABC powożenia*, 2000.

CARRICK, one of the old names for the Scot. game of >SHINTY, used in Fife County.

CARROUSEL, traditionally a name for an amusement or competition with the element of revolving. From this word derived the term 'carousel', or merry-go-round, a machine with seats which rotates around its axis. The name, however, comes from a medieval equestrian Ital. tournament (Ital. *carosello*, Fr. *carrousel*) – *torneo cavalleresco mediovale*. Knights rode in circles, performing the prescribed moves. This originated probably from the medieval Naples folk game, *carusello*. Initially the word meant a clay ball. Players would run around in a circle and try to hit the opponent in the circle with the *carusello*. This origin is confirmed by later equestrian tournaments where riders would eliminate each other by throwing clay balls. Such events were held in castle yards and town squares, also in N Europe. They were usu. accompanied by a tilting competition, where contestants aimed at a ring. Chivalric carrousel can be found in many old illustrations, though no major work of art seems to depict it. The theme of folk carrousel, however, is present in the play of Hung. author F. Molnar *Liliom* (1909), which in 1945 was made into a musical by R. Rodgers and O. Hammerstein entitled *Carousel* (the setting was changed from Hungary to New England).

CASHORNIE, a trad. Scot. game in which 2 teams equipped with sticks compete in placing a ball in holes in the ground that serve as goals [Eng. *cash* + *hornie*].

TGESI, I, 59-60.

CASTELLS, also *castillos humanos*, *torres humanas*, popularly *castellers*. A trad. var. of acrobatics practiced in Catalonia. The name prob. derives from Span. a *castello* – a castle, as the structures formed by acrobats resemble multi-story castle donjons. The place of each acrobat (a *castellero*) in a given structure is determined by the head of the group (the *cap de la colla* or the *jefe de la colla*) selected from among the participants. There are 3 basic structures, referred to as a *pilarso* (a large pole) or an *espadate* (stick out like an epee), formed by the acrobats: 1) formed by one acrobat at each 'story' (a *torre* – a tower); 2) formed by two participants at each story; 3) the most complex (a *castillo* – a castle) where the fundament is formed of the 'saucepan' (the *casuela* or *cassola*). When the pedestal is formed of 4 players and the upper 'thinner' part resembles a needle stuck into a pin cushion, the entire structure is referred to as the needle inside (*aguja al medio* or *agulla al mig*). The most popular structure is the one with lower stories formed by 3 acrobats, holding each other by the arms, who are named after the numerals indicating the consecutive stories on which acrobats are placed, starting from the 1st story – *baixos* (3 acrobats) proceeding upwards to the 2nd – *segons* (3 acrobats), the 3rd – *tergos* (3 acrobats), the 4th – *cuarts* (3 acrobats), the 5th – *quints* (3 acrobats), the 6th – *sisens* (3 acrobats), the 7th – *dosos* (2 acrobats), the 8th – *axecador* (1 acrobat), the 9th – *enexeneta* (1 acrobat). There are also structures formed of 4 acrobats up to the 4th story that carries a pair holding another one or 2 acrobats who form another story.
The castells competition uses a complex system of scoring according to tables that evaluate each structure and its quality in the scale ranging from 75 to 3,480pts. The scoring depends on the number of stories in the structure, whether the planned finial (*arriba*) was achieved and whether such elements as the foundation support of the *agulla al mig* type, stabilizing support *forro* or *manilla*, etc., were employed. The combination where acrobats outside the core construction use their hands to prop up the second-story acrobats' buttocks is called *piña* – pineapple, as the construction looks like a pineapple turned upside down with the hand props as leaves. The act of construction is referred to as *cargar* or *carregar*; collapse of the construction is called *derrumbe del castell* or *llenya o cayguda*; emergency jump of the acrobat at the top – *aleta*; planned disassembly – *desmontar el castillo* or *descargar* or *decarregar*.
History. The origins of the event go back to a pagan ritual imitating the growth of crops. The imitation can be exemplified by the *pilarso* or *espadate* construction where each story is formed by a single acrobat and the entire figure sways lightly in the wind, thus resembling a stalk. The oldest report on castells – in the form of an engraving preserved in the hermitage of Virgen de la Puente Santa in Zorita, in the Province of Cáceres – dates back to the 7th cent. Castells were originally celebrated only in Spain, but in the course of colonial conquests they became popular in other Spanish-speaking countries, particularly in Mexico. In Spain, the region where they are most keenly practiced is Catalonia with its capital in Barcelona. Castells are a culmination of a regional dance originating from the locality of Sena in the Huesca Province where it is called a *dance*. A spectacle named *Els Xiquets de Valls* stemming from ancient times and incl. the display of castells, is held annually in Tarragona, NE Spain. The tradition is also cultivated in the Provinces of Segovia, Valladolid and some regions of Aragon.

C. Moreno Palos, 'Castells', JYTE, 1992, 43-45; R. Garcia Serrano, 'Torres humanas', JDTE, 1974, 112-114.

CAT, a trad. Eng. game resembling games known in Poland as >SZTEKIEL or >KLIPA, a Pak. game of >GULLI DUNDA, or a Bret. one named >PILAOUET (*mouilh*). The game is also known under a different name, i.e. >TIP-CAT (see the rules there).

CAT AND DOG, a trad. Eng. game practiced in Scot. Counties of Angus and Lothian. A.B. Gomme describes the game as follows:

Three play, and they are provided with clubs. These clubs are called 'dogs'. The players cut out two holes, each about a foot in diameter, and seven inches in depth. The distance between them is about twenty-six feet. One stands at each hole with a club. A piece of wood about four inches long and one inch in diameter, called a Cat, is thrown from the one hole towards the other by a third person. The object is to prevent the Cat from getting into the hole. Every time that it enters the hole, he who has the club at the hole loses the club, and he who threw the cat gets possession both of the club and of the hole, while the former possessor is obliged to take charge of the Cat. If the Cat be struck, he who strikes it changes places with the person who hold the other club; and as often as these positions are changed one is counted in the game by the two who hold the club, and who are viewed as partners.

[TGESI, I, 60]

CAT AND DOG HOLE, a game similar to >CAT I' THE HOLE. One of the 'dogs' (players) holding a 'catch-brod' (a stick or a bat) propped against the ground, stands about 1½ft. (approx. 45cm) away from a 'dog-hole' (a hole in the ground), bent forward and guarding it. The other player stands several yards off and tries to throw a ball into the dog-hole whereas the dog guarding the hole attempts to prevent a successful throw by clearing the ball. If the dog succeeds, the players change positions and the one who cleared the ball scores a point. Otherwise, the throwing player scores a point and the game continues with the players in the same positions. In another version of cat and dog hole, the ball is thrown at a stone instead of a hole. In a version with 3 players further elements are added: to score a point after clearing the ball, the dog has to run to the throwing point and make it back to the stone (or dog-hole). If the third player manages to catch the ball in the meantime, he throws it at the stone (or dog-hole) thus depriving the dog of the right to hit the ball in following turns and replacing him. Cf. >CAT AND DOG.

CAT I' THE HOLE, the full name is cat in the hole, also sp. cat-in-the-hole. A ball and running game with the use of clubs, practiced mostly in Scotland, esp. in Fife and neighboring counties. The number of players on the playing field varied from place to place but it was always equal to the number of holes plus 1. According to A.B. Gomme, the course of the game was as follows:

Three play, and they are provided with clubs. Theses clubs are called 'dogs'. The players cut out two holes, each about a foot in diameter, and seven inches in depth. The distance between them is about twenty-six feet. One stands at each hole with a club. A piece of wood about four inches long and one inch in diameter, called a Cat, is thrown from the one hole towards the other by a third person. The object is to prevent the Cat from getting into the hole. Every time that it enters the hole, he who has the club at that hole loses the club, and he who threw the cat gets possession both of the club and of the hole, while the former possessor is obliged to take charge of the Cat. If the Cat be struck, he who strikes it changes places with the person who hold the other club; and as often as these positions are changed one is counted in the game by the two who hold the clubs, and who are viewed as partners, [TGESI, I, 60].

Participants form a human tower called castell *in the village of Arbo del Penedes in eastern Spain during summer festivities.*

Castells.

C

WORLD SPORTS ENCYCLOPEDIA

CATAMARAN, [Tamil *katta* – to tie + *maram* – tree trunk], a type of sports equipment and the name of the water sport originating in Polynesian tradition. The catamaran consists of two hulls and is powered with oars, sails or a motor engine. Originally a wooden log was attached to the hulls for balance. Cf. >TRIMARAN, >TRIFOILING.

CAT-BEDS, a game played using a knife. As A.B. Gomme relates: in secrecy from others, one of the players cuts as many pieces of turf, with their sides at various angles, as there are players. The pieces are cut only along the sides and they are of different

A Polish catamaran during The Race regattas.

sizes. Each player selects one piece by throwing a knife at it, aiming at the smallest one that will be easiest to pick up. After selecting a piece of turf, participants have to explore with their fingers its outline and then cut it from below and pick it up. The piece can be cut from below only as deep as was indicated by the knife after the first throw. The last player to pick his piece up, usually the largest one as the smaller ones have already been picked up, is supposed to carry it in his hands at a certain

In the days before pedals there was the celeryfer.

distance, moving on his elbows and knees. The distance is determined by a player from the neighboring piece who throws a knife from under his leg. If, while carrying the piece of turf, the player drops even the tiniest piece, the remaining participants can throw earth balls and other materials found on the pasture at the unlucky one, as the game was mostly popular while grazing cattle.
A.B. Gomme, 'Cat-Beds', TGESI, 1894, I, 61.

CATCH BALL, a conventional name of men's and women's ball game practiced in Oceania. The game consists of throwing the ball between 2 teams. The opposing team tries to catch the ball on the fly. The most original form of catch ball is >KANGAROO BALL.

CATCH THE SALMON, a simple run-and-catch game. 2 players hold a piece of rope or a jump rope and run about attempting to catch other players into their 'net.'
TGESI, 410.

CATCH-AS-CAN-CATCH, a Scot. var. of wrestling whose name is nearly identical with the style developed in England and then in the USA (see >CATCH-AS-CATCH-CAN). Its rules, however, were different, e.g. an opponent had to be held down on the ground for 3sec. after a fall, the so-called pin fall. The Scot. variety formed a separate event in Highland Games and Gatherings until the turn of the 1960s. The peak popularity of catch-as-can-catch fell at the beginning of the 20th cent. In 1905, a fight between G. Hackenschmidt and A. Monro attracted 20,000 spectators at an outdoor stadium. The press reported that the only reason why the number was not double that, was the weather. The fight lasted 33min. 50sec. with Hackenschmidt the victor.

CATCH-AS-CATCH-CAN, an Eng. predecessor of an Olympic style known as >FREESTYLE WRESTLING. Historically, the name originates from the term referring to an Eng. wrestling style popular since the Middle Ages. The earliest representation revealing the character of the style is a bas-relief on a pew in a church in Halsall. The style evolved in the 14th cent. and was also known as the 'Lancaster style'. It was also characterized as the most brutal among the three Eng. wrestling styles (*Encyclopedia of Sport*, vol. 2, 1898). In the *History of Wigan* (1882), Brit. specialist, D. Sinclair, maintains that c.1570 the Lancashire style was practiced in special tight jackets. Wrestlers from lower strata who could not afford such jackets often fought wearing briefs only. In the 19th cent., catch-as-catch-can became the starting point, if not the foundation, of the development of freestyle that we know today. A number of holds and techniques that later infiltrated into other styles were invented then, e.g. full nelson, half nelson, double nelson, Lancashire lock, etc. The name 'nelson' was introduced after the famous victory of Brit. naval commander, H. Nelson, at Trafalgar (1805). If this is true, the reason could be the similarity between the hold, from which it is difficult to break free, and Nelson's tactics, according to which once the French were 'embraced' by the admiral's fleet, all possible escape routes were cut off. After the undisputed influence of catch-as-catch-can on freestyle, the latter started to absorb other styles, such as Turk. >YAGLI GÜRES, which in turn affected catch-as-catch-can. An important step in that process was the incorporation of freestyle into the Ol.G. program and its popularization by Ital. E. Porro. The retroactive influence of a new, eclectic freestyle, reaching much further than traditional Lancashire style, contributed substantially to the eradication of many traditional and original elements of catch-as-catch-can. According to W. Baxter, these new freestyle elements had a 'devastating effect and took the sport from its British/American roots' (LJP, 72). Historians question the origin of some of the freestyle elements. One such disputable feature is defeat by being pressed against the floor, introduced in 1921 by FILA, on the initiative of Fr. representatives. At the same time, Brit. author, P. Longhurst, in his *Wrestling* (1917) claims that the rule stems from catch-as-catch-can and not from other forms of Eur. wrestling. The original elements of the sport were best preserved in the Amer. variety where the name catch-as-catch-can expanded later over both freestyle, derived from >LOOSE HOLD and forming an Ol.G. event, and a var. of public wrestling in which any hold is allowed. At the beginning of the 20th cent., catch-as-catch-can wrestling meetings referred to as W.Ch. were held in the USA (in 1914

and 1917 the winner was the Pole W. Cyganiewicz and in 1921 and 1922 his brother W.Z. Cyganiewicz). Because of the dynamic development of boxing and other show disciplines, catch-as-catch-can began losing on popularity in the '20s and '30s, which resulted in extensive liberalization of the rules, intentional brutalization of fights with simultaneous inclusion of farce elements and clearly prearranged results – all of which was supposed to attract spectators. In the '50s, the idea of catch-as-catch-can as a style in which anything goes was used by the communist propaganda as a symbol of the Amer. political system. The rapid popularization of television led to the inclusion of a number of theatrical elements into fights that verged on parody, which was however quite popular in the '80s and '90s, in the so-called 'all-in shows'. Today, such activities are more often referred to as American wrestling.

CATCHERS, a bat and ball game. One of the 2 players bats a ball and the other player catches it and asks: 'How many?' referring to a distance from the batter, measured in bat-lengths. The batter responds in a rhyme:

Two a good scat
Try for the bat.

If the distance to the ball is longer than 2 bat-lengths, the ball is batted again, this time, however, the distance grows to 3:

Three a good scat
Try for the bat.

Finally, the distance quoted is long enough so that even a player of limited skills will fit in.
TGESI, I, 64.

CATCHHOLD, a var. of trad. Eng. wrestling similar to Greco-Roman wrestling – any holds below the waist were forbidden. The fight started with the 'referee's hold' where the opponents put one arm on the other's head and the other arm on the opponent's shoulder. This style disappeared at the beginning of the 20th cent.

CATCHING THE GREASED PIG, also *chasing the greased pig, greased pig, greasy pig*; an Eng. folk sport consisting of chasing and catching a running pig covered with grease. The winner was usually given the pig as the prize. The sport was the humorous concluding event of the Much Wenlock Olympic Games held in 1850 (a local attempt to revive the ancient Olympic Games in England). During a chase after a greasy pig in Shrewsbury, in 1858, the running pig managed to skillfully dodge the pursuing contenders. As it was humorously described by a local newspaper: 'The pig led its pursuers over hedge and ditch right into the town where it took ground in the cellar of Mr. Blakeway's house; and where it was captured by a man called William Hill' (*Shrewsbury Chronicle*, 9 Oct. 1858).
A similar sports event, called *catching a greased pig*, is part of Amer. >RODEO. In some Eur. countries the sport is part of the maypole celebrations; see Ger. >MAIBAUM, Eng. >MAYPOLE, or Span. >PALO DE MAYO.

CAT-GALLOWS, an old Eng. folk form of high jump practiced mostly among children. It consisted of jumping above a horizontal bar supported by 2 poles stuck in the ground. According to A.B. Gomme the name derives from the fact that the bar was high enough to hang a cat on it (TGESI, I, 63). The game was also known as *cat-gallas*.

CAT'S CRADLE, a pop. folk game for usu. 2 persons, widely known throughout Eur. and N.America. The players create between splayed fingers patterns of a string or cord loop, which are passed from hand to hand or player to player. In Jap. tradition a similar game is called >AYATORI, and among the Maori – >WHAI.

CAVING, see >SPELEOLOGY.

CELERYFER [Fr. *célérifère*, Lat. *celer* – fast + *ferro* – carry], a type of a 2-wheeled vehicle with no pedals, which is moved by pushing the feet against the ground. It was used to practice a historical var. of >CYCLISM which was a predecessor of modern >CYCLING.

CELTIC CHARIOT RACING, Chariots were used by ancient Celts mainly in combat but also in exercises during   time. Celtic charioteers perfected their driving skills by driving in an artificial crowd, imitating a battle crowd, and negotiating specially dug pits and ditches. An ancient Celtic written source claims that, on one occasion, 17 chariots were damaged in a single exercise, which attests to the scale of the phenomenon. Chariot bottom boards were usu. made of spruce, while the side walls – of wicker. A chariot was drawn by 2 horses, with 2 people aboard – a charioteer and a fighter. A 1902 sculpture by T. Thornycroft at the head of London's Westminster Bridge shows the likely structure of a Celtic chariot (the statue depicts Boudicca, the legendary Celtic woman-leader who led an uprising against the Romans in 61 AD). During his 2 unsuccessful attempts at conquering Great Britain in 55 and 54 BC, Julius Caesar encountered Celtic charioteers and admitted that their skills in using

Boudicca (Boadicea) riding a chariot. A monument by Thomas Thornycroft in London, England.

the chariots, as well as their tactics (previously unknown to him), caused much confusion among his soldiers. He devoted considerable space to a description of the Celtic carts and the acrobatic fighting techniques in his *Gallic Wars*:

Their mode of fighting with their chariots is this: firstly, they drive about in all directions and throw their weapons and generally break the ranks of the enemy with the very dread of their horses and the noise of their wheels; and when they have worked themselves in between the troops of horse, leap from their chariots and engage on foot. The charioteers in the mean time withdraw some little distance from the battle, and so place themselves with the chariots that, if their masters are overpowered by the number of the enemy, they may have a ready retreat to their own troops. Thus they display in battle the speed of horse, [together with] the firmness of infantry; and by daily practice and exercise attain to such expertness that they are accustomed, even on a declining and steep place, to check their horses at full speed, and manage and turn them in an instant and run along the pole, and stand on the yoke, and thence betake themselves with the greatest celerity to their chariots again.

(trans. W.A. McDevitte and W.S Bohn)

The driving skills of Celtic charioteers and the construction of the chariot itself impressed the Romans so much that they borrowed some elements and used them in their own circus chariot races. Additionally, a cart used in combat or racing also came to be called *essedum* in Latin, the word being a borrowing from Celtic languages. See also >CHARIOT RACING.

CERUVADI, a type of a trad. Ind. fight with the use of short sticks. It forms one of the elemental skills practiced as a part of >KALARI-PAYAT. Cf. fight with the use of long sticks >KETTUKARI.

CH'AJON-NORI, a folk Kor. game in which 2 *dongch'ae* (long 'vessels' made of wood and old rice stalks), each borne by several strong men with a captain, repeatedly ram into each other. If the captain falls or if the *dongch'ae* is allowed to touch the ground, the opposing team wins.

CH'EONGDO SO SSA-EUM, Kor. bull fighting in which 2 bulls butt their heads and push each other backwards. The first bull to back off loses. See also >BULL FIGHTS.

CHACKE BLYNDMAN, one of a number of Scot. names for >BLIND MAN'S BUFF.

CHACO INDIAN HOCKEY, a game featuring a ball made of wood or rope, similar to >FIELD HOCKEY. Played by the S.American Chaco tribes, sometimes instead of a war, as a way of proving superiority over a neighboring tribe.

CHAIN CHASE, or *the net*, a Rus. school sports game. 'Two players are the «catchers», the remaining players spread out on the playing field. The catchers hold each other by the hand and, running together try to catch any other players. A player is caught if he or she is embraced with both hands by the catchers. Each player caught joins the catchers and forms a chain which grows longer as more players are caught. The game is over when all the players are caught in the «chain».'
I.N. Chkhannikov, 'Chain chase', GIZ, 1953, 11.

CHAIR LIFTING, a feat of skill consisting of lifting up a chair by holding one of its legs. The arm movement must be sharp enough to lift the chair in one continuous motion. Chair lifting is known in many countries, e.g. *løfte stol* in Denmark.
J. Møller, 'Løfte stol', GID, 1997, 3, 104.

CHAKRA, an old Ind. var. of a discus found in excavations of Harappa and Mohenjodaro from the period known as the Civilization of the Indus River Valley (2500-1550 BC). According to the Ind. mythology, Krishna was to have thrown a huge discus named *sudarshan chakra*.
The Internet: http://w3.meadev.gov.in/sports.htm.

CHALITA, a tournament game in which a ball is struck with a bat, similar to >PALANT.

CHALKE MUIA, see >BLIND MAN'S BUFF.

CHANDIMU, a folk var. of >ASSOCIATION FOOTBALL played in Tanzania. The number of players usu. ranges from 2 to 15 in each team. Playing time, also undefined, quite often extends to many hours. The goals are marked by posts, frequently with no crossbar, or stones. The ball is made of whatever can be found, usu. rags or various African fruit.

CHARIOT RACING, races using chariots drawn by horses or other animals. Double or quadruple teams used in ancient times were usu. made up of horses or foals, but also of mules or even donkeys. In the Gk. tradition, quadruple-team races were called >TETRIPPON, while the Romans called them quadrigas (>QUADRIGA RACES). Double-team races were called >SYNORIS, and were divided into adult horse races (>HIPPON), foal races (>POLON SYNORIS), and mule races (>APENE, also, officially, *synoris hemionon*). However, chariot races were known not only in Greece and Rome. Two-wheeled combat chariots were also used by ancient Egyptians and Assyrians, as testified by numerous records, murals, bas-reliefs and sculptures. It seems a fair guess that spontaneous races used as military exercise were also known in those cultures. Another type of combat cart developed among the

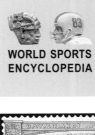

Chariot motif on a postage stamp issued for the 1896 Olympics in Athens.

Chariot racing on a Greek amphora (left) and on a silver coin (below).

Brit. Celts. However, the information we have on Celtic chariots is only fragmentary; see >CELTIC CHARIOT RACING. Julius Caesar is one writer who mentions Celtic combat carts, stressing the exceptional agility the Celts showed, which means they could not have practiced chariot driving exclusively during battles. Caesar liked the chariots so much that he ordered them to be brought to Rome. They were used in >GLADIATORIAL FIGHTS by the so-called *essedarii* (gladiators of a kind, introduced by Caesar and called so from the Latin word for Celtic chariots, *essedum*).

Charlton Heston drives a chariot toward the finish line in a scene from the 1960 Metro-Goldwyn-Mayer classic Ben-Hur (above). Teams of horses bolt from the starting gates pulling their chariot drivers in Ogden, Utah (below).

Chilean rodeo.

Cheese rolling.

Goya, A Chicken Fight, *oil on canvas.*

CHASING A GIRL, a type of horse race after a running girl, once popular among numerous peoples of central Asia, including the Kirghiz and Kazakhs. The horse races were often held during religious holidays, e.g. on the eve of Ramadan, among the Muslim Kirghiz. A few grooms-to-be could participate in the chasing; the winner had the right to marry the girl. The girl ran from a starting point to a marking post, then she had to touch the post or go around it and return to the starting point. The chasers were to catch the girl before she reached the post but she could defy 'kidnapping' by lashing the contender with a whip, esp. the one she did not intend to marry. Whip bruises on the contenders' faces were quite frequent. Among the Kirghiz, the girl could free herself if she took the cap off the chaser's head. If a man failed to catch the girl, his parents were often obliged to pay a ransom in cattle, or in modern times, in money, to the girl's parents. Chasing-a-girl races were held among different peoples on different occasions. In some areas, a few officially approved fiancés started the chase right after the matchmakers had performed their ceremonies. In other areas the chase was held as a confirmation of marriage. The groom had to confirm his right to the bride by racing and winning against other contenders. In the Kazakh tradition, the chasers were supposed to snatch a shawl tied to the girl's left shoulder (>HORSE RACING FOR A SHAWL). In the Georgian >MARUA, the shawl belonging to the bride was to be snatched from the mouth of a fleeing mounted rider. In modern times chasing a girl has become a form of popular entertainment, without any marital consequences for the participants. A similar type of horse racing competition was known among some Mongolian tribes. After receiving the gifts (*kalym*) from the groom's parents by the bride's parents, the bride went around the groom's yurt several times, imitating the movement of the sun. In the last round, the groom was to pull the bride off the saddle and place a velvet scarf called a *chadag* on the horse. If he failed to do that he brought shame on his house and family and might have lost his right to the girl; cf. >FIGHT FOR A BRIDE, >BRIDEBALL.

CHASING GIRLS, a trad. sports game played by the Kazakh minority in China. Boys and girls on horseback get in pairs and take positions about 800m before a starting line marked on the ground. While riding slowly toward the start line the boy tries to court the girl with words and gestures. The girl must not ride faster than the boy or ride away from him. Once they both reach the start line, the boy turns back and gallops away from the girl who chases him and lashes him with a whip – in present times, only symbolically. Many skillful boy riders manage to escape. Once whipped, the boy must continue his escape but he is not allowed to overtake the chasing girl or defend himself in any way. The girl stops whipping the boy once they reach a designated end line. The game is usually watched by a huge audience heartily applauding the escapee or the chasing girl.

Mu Fushan, et al., 'Chasing Girls', TRAMCHIN, 9.

CHATIÈRE, LA, Fr. name for a Bret. game of >TOUL AR C'HAZH.

CHAUSSON, an old Fr. fight in which kicks played a decisive role [Fr. *chausson* – a soft shoe, slipper]. Chausson was particularly popular in the 18th cent. among Fr. sailors and longshoremen, esp. in Marseille. Therefore, an alternative name of the activity was *jeux de Marseille*. At the beginning, the game developed independently from similar forms of fighting. Soon, however, it began to blend with >SAVATE. Both disciplines influenced each other heavily throughout the 19th cent., especially after 1820 when chausson began to be practiced in Paris. Its peak popularity was during the reign of Louise Philippe (1830-48), after which it was overwhelmed by >FRENCH BOXING, which was a merge of savate and Eng. >BOXING.

CHECKSTONES, see >MARBLES.

CHEESE ROLLING, a form of competition in which the participants engage in chasing chunks of cheese weighing several pounds down hill. The competition is usu. a part of food festivals held in various places in Great Britain (also in other countries). Probably the best known is the Cooper's Hill event held annually on the last weekend in May between Gloucester, Stroud, and Cheltenham in the Cotswolds. It has a tradition which is over 100 years old, the origins of which are obscure. In 1998 the competition was banned due to a high number of injuries – both to the participants and the spectators – which had occurred the previous year. In 1999, however, the competition was restarted. There are 4 races held on the day, incl. a ladies event. A different var. of cheese rolling is held in the old Roman town of Chester (Great Britain), where major dairy firms compete in running rolls of cheese down one of the town's historic straight streets.

CHEGI CHAGI, a Kor. equivalent of the Eng. >SHUTTLECOCK, Pol. *Zośka*, Chin. >TEBEG, and Mong. >TEBEG ÖSHIGLÖÖKH.

CHEIBI GAD-GA, one of the most ancient folk martial arts practiced in the state of Manipu in India. Two opponents fight using a shield covered with leather and a special bat *cheibi* resembling a thin club about 2-2½ft. (approx. 60-76cm) long. The club is covered with oakum and leather on its thicker, striking end to minimize the blow. The fighting ring is a circle of around 7m in diameter, inside of which the fighters' starting positions are marked by 2 lines 1m apart.

CHEIRONOMIA [Gk. *cheir* – hand + *nemein* – to deal, or *nomeus* – the one who deals; dealing blows with hands], in ancient Greece a var. of practice or sportive fight resembling shadow boxing or sparring. At that time the term had 4 basic meanings: 1) training before a fist fight, also known as >SKIAMACHIA; 2) the method of fighting or training in which one makes the opponent hit the air by dodging their blows; 3) hand exercise practiced at the end of classes in the bar to the accompaniment of a wind instrument called *aulos*; 4) making gestures that accompany dancing parades.

CHECH FUN, a Bret. var. of >TUG-OF-WAR.

CHENCO, a game played by Native Amer. Indians inhabiting SE parts of today's USA. The objective is to win a bet and the game itself consists of shooting the slingshot at a predetermined target. The first Eng. settlers dubbed the game *chunkey* and both names were applied simultaneously to another, much more popular game, mostly known as >CHUNGKE. See also >SLING SHOOTING.

CHERRY PITS, a game in which fruit pits were used, which in the course of time prob. evolved into a game with leaden counters. Concurrently there existed a game *cherry-pit* where the 'pit' in singular referred to a hole in the ground. Preserved descriptions of the game are contradictory and unclear, e.g. A.B. Gomme provides one under the entry *cherry pit* (TGESI, I, 66), and another one while comparing the game with a different one known as *pits* (TGESI, II, 45; see also >MARBLES, subentry PITS). In the first description Gomme relates that the cherry pits were thrown into a small hole in the ground and the same rules were applied while playing with leaden counters, labeling the game as *dumps*, though under a separate entry about dumps, Gomme does not mention leaden counters and unambiguously interprets the game as *marbles* (see >MARBLES, subentry DUMPS). In the second description found under *pits*, Gomme, referring to a separate entry, *cherry pit*, in the same work, in 2 different places employs 2 different names, with a slight difference in spelling; which is, however, crucial for interpreting the game's fundamentals: first she quotes *cherry-pit* with the word *pit* in the singular (TGESI, I, 66) adding the information that the pits were thrown into a hole in the ground. Then, under the entry concerning a different game, *pits*, she makes a reference to *cherry pits*, this time using the plural, accompanied by information excluding holes in the ground but still unclear as to the rules of the game: 'The pits are thrown over the palm; they must fall so far apart that the fingers can be passed between them. Then with a flip of the thumb the player makes his pit strike the enemy's and wins both' (TGESI, II, 45). There could not be two mutually independent games with a similar name, i.e. *cherry-pit* and *cherry-pits*, as, while describing one game, Gomme validates its identity with the other one, confirming that by a reference to a relevant page.

TGESI, II, 45; TGESI, I, 66.

CHEUCA, an old game practiced by the Aracuaño Native Argentinean Indians resembling today's >FIELD HOCKEY. The name of the game also signifies a curved stick. The first Eur. descriptions dating back to the 16th cent. tell us the Aracuaño used a ball either made of wood or sheathed with leather, whereas the size of the playing field depended on the number of players which was not fixed. The Eur. witnesses most frequently saw teams of 4, 6 or 8 players and fields measuring around 100x10 steps, sometimes 300-500m long. Points were scored by crossing the opponent's goal line. The Aracuaño treated the game as both physical and military exercise. The game reveals evident resemblance and relationship with the Chilean game of >CHUECA.

W. Krämer-Mandeau, *Tradition, Transformation and Taboo. European Games and Festivals in Latin America, 1500-1900*, IJHS 1992, 1.

CHICKEN FIGHTS, a simple game for 2 pairs of players, described by I.N. Chkhannikov. The pair consists of a 'horse' and a 'rider' sitting on his back. The fight takes place in water which reaches the 'horse's' chest. The pair which knocks the rival's 'rider' down into the water, wins the game. A land var. of the game was painted by Goya.

I.N. Chkhannikov, 'Mounted water fight', GIZ, 1953, 79.

CHIDAOBA, one of the international spellings of the name for Georg. wrestling. See also >KARTULI CHIDAOBA.

CHILEAN RODEO, Span. *el rodeo chileno*, a variety of >RODEO as practiced in Chile. It is quite different from the N.Amer. version, as it excludes, in its trad. form, tying horses and breaking them in. The main skill of Chilean rodeo riders (*huasos*) is herding cattle into a crescent-shaped corral. *Huasos* wear characteristic ponchos and woolen caps or hats. The most outstanding *huasos* of the 1990s included M. Valenzuela and J.M. Reyes. The oldest records of competitions that with time turned into Chilean rodeo date back to 1556, when the Span. captain G. de Orense ordered a roundup of cattle in the town of Cabildo (province of Aconcagua). While forming herds, the participating soldiers spontaneously competed and tried driving their horses into the sides of bulls. Today, the sport is controlled by the Chilean Rodeo Federation.

O. Plath, 'El rodeo', JYDLCH, 54-56; The Internet: http://www.cnn.com/WORLD/9604/14_chile.rodeo

CHINESE ARCHERY, the earliest traces of archery in China come from the Paleolithic Period, c.26000 BC. They were stone arrowheads found in the village of Shiy-kun in the Shang-xi province. The shape of arrows from the Neolithic Period, c.3000-4000BC

found in China suggests knowledge of the early features of the oriental bow – a type of weapon developed later in the area. The reign of the Shang dynasty (17th-11th cent. BC) marks the emergence of a refined composite bow with limbs made of various kinds of wood. The ancient Chinese exercised great care about their bows. This has been confirmed by archeological finds in the form of special bronze pads, called *bi*, incrusted with turquoises, placed on the bow to prevent it from warping. One such pad was found in Anyang, in the present-day Hunan province. First Chin. arrowheads made of bronze come from the periods of the Shang (c.1523-1028 BC) and Chou (c.1027-256 BC) dynasties. From the period of the so-called Warring States (c.403-222 BC) come metal arrowheads with artistic harpoon-like edges. That type of arrowheads, judging from their painstaking construction, must have been used for exhibition and sports contests rather than for military purposes.

Archery was a crucial element of aristocratic and civic education in ancient China. Confucius (Chin. *Kung Fu Cy*, 551-479 BC) considered archery an important exercise, which trained precision, patience and self-control. During the reigns of the Chin (221--206 BC) and Han (206 BC-220 AD) dynasties the first rules of Chin. archery were formed and later included in the two earliest archery manuals in world history: *Fengmen Shefa* (*The Thresholds of Archery*) and *Li Jiangjun Shefa* (*The Methods of Li Archery*). The results of good archery education proved useful in combat or during archery contests or shows. Testing archery skills of candidates for state officials was a regular custom practiced at many Chin. royal courts as the state officials had to prove their usefulness during wartime as well. Archery contests were integral parts of various courtly celebrations. Competitions varied but it is possible to reconstruct the general course of a court archery tournament of the classic period of Chin. civilization, based on numerous works of art and literature. The tournaments were usually held outside the royal palace, on a terrain adjacent to swampy areas to prevent injuries to the public from stray arrows. The visual and musical setting of the tournaments was sumptuous and diverse. Each contestant came onto the range brandishing his clan colors. The tournament was commenced by a courtier – chosen by the emperor to supervise the competition – who shot four arrows in four different directions. The archers shot arrows standing on a wooden podium. First, each contender shot 2 arrows in complete silence. The following rounds were accompanied by music and shouts of the audience if the target was hit. After the tournament the archers formed two rows – the winners and the losers. The winners were invited to make a toast from a horn; and the losers from a bronze vase. Most arrows had angular metal heads with a long rod stuck into the wooden shaft.

The flights and wooden shafts of Chin. arrows have not survived. One of the inventions of medieval China was the so-called 'singing arrow', which made a characteristic sound in flight intended to scare the enemy. Chin. archers used special nocked bracers to draw the bowstring. The bracers allowed for better drawing and shooting accuracy and protected the fingers against the released bowstring. Wealthy archers wore bracers made of precious stones such as turquoise, jade, or nephrites; or had them decorated with miniature patterns and ornaments.

In the so-called Spring and Autumn Period (770-476 BC) the Chinese invented the crossbow – 1,500 years before the weapon appeared in Europe (CROSSBOW SHOOTING). The crossbow was then refined during the reigns of the Chin (221-206 BC) and Han (202 BC – 220 AD) dynasties, gradually replacing the bow and arrow as an infantry weapon. The invention of gunpowder in China in the 10th cent. had no influence on the use of the bow and the crossbow. Only after the introduction of firearms did Chin. archery begin to decline. The bows gave superior velocity of the arrow in comparison to crossbows, and were irreplaceable weapons of mounted troops. Equestrian archery was enormously refined in China under the Mongolian dynasty of Yuan (1271-1368). Apart from military archery also courtly or 'sports' archery competitions were popular. The contests were held in royal residences, parks and gardens as part of theatrical reenactments of battles and hunts. In the 11th cent., a particular form of entertainment appeared called >TOUHU, a sport consisting of throwing arrows at a mark with bare

Archer's ring, China, Han dynasty, 3rd cent. BC-3rd cent. AD, turquoise, Musée national des Arts asiatiques-Guimet, Paris.

hands.

Outside the imperial court archery contests were held also among less affluent Chin. aristocracy and wealthy townsfolk, even after the introduction of firearms. Those competitions were, however, far more modest. Each commenced with a feast and consisted of 3 shooting rounds.

In the beginning of the reign of the Ming dynasty (1368-1644), Emperor Zhu Youngzhang ordered inclusion of archery in school curricula and organization of school archery championships. By the end of the Ming reign the bow and the crossbow began to decline as military weapons. Archery as a military skill disappeared during the reign of the Manchu dynasty of Ch'ing (1644-1911), although Emperors K'ang-hsi (1662-1722) and Ch'ien-lung (1736-95) were known as fine archers. In the 19th cent. archery lost the official support of the imperial court due to the spread of firearms. Archery was retained in various local folk forms, as sports activity, esp. among the Yi people, one of the Chin. ethnic minorities living in the southern provinces of Kwangsi, Kweichow, Sichuan and Yunnan. The tradition of archery tournaments plays a very important role in Yi mythology. The most worshipped Yi mythical hero, Zhigealong, was supposed to have shot down five moons and six suns and save the earth from burning to ashes. Yi archers use bows made of mulberry wood, famous for increased resistance to stretching. The bowstring is made of cow intestines. Yi archery contests are held in two basic events: target shooting and distance shooting. The archers can shoot arrows while standing on the ground or riding on horseback. The Yi organize archery competitions on occasion of weddings or funerals.

G. André, 'Arrow Games. Hunting, Contests and War', YOSICH, 1999, 38-41; anon., *Les sports traditionenels en Chine*, 1991; Y. Hong, *Weapons in Ancient China*, 1992; R. Roth, *Histoire de l'archerie. Arc et arbalète*, 1992.

Arrowhead, China, warring states era, 5th-3rd cent., bronze, jade stand, Musée national des Arts asiatique-Guimet, Paris.

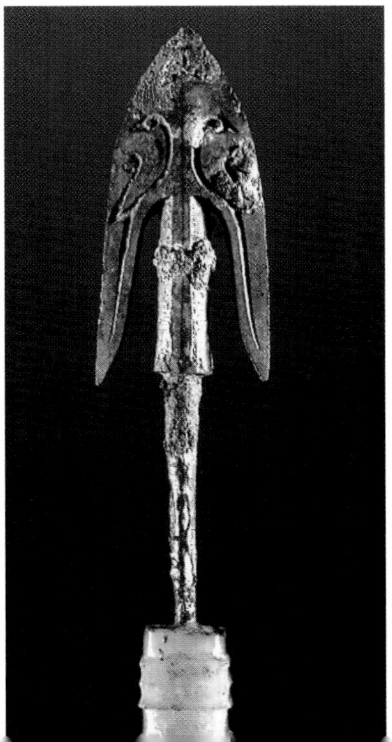

CHINESE CROSSBOW SHOOTING. For a long time crossbow shooting with arrows was considered an invention of medieval Europe (>CROSSBOW SHOOTING). In fact, it appeared much earlier in ancient China, although whether it had any impact on the development of similar weapons in Europe is doubtful since there are considerable differences in the construction of the drawing mechanism, whose complex metallurgical processing would not be easy to emulate even taking advantage of modern machinery. Other preserved elements of the mechanism (the oldest dating from the 3rd and 4th cent. BC) prove the exquisite artistry of Chin. inventors and designers.

History. The crossbow was invented in ancient China during the so-called period of Spring and Fall (770-476 BC) It was greatly improved under the dynasty of Qin (written also as Ch'in, 221-206 BC) and Han (202 BC-220 AD). The invention of gunpowder in the 10th cent. decreased the importance of neither Chin. archery nor crossbow shooting until firearms were developed. It was used in the military until the beginning of the 10th cent. It was used not only for the military purposes, but also in training young warriors. It can be assumed that the crossbow was used in sports competitions together with the old >CHINESE ARCHERY.

5000 Years of Sport in China. Art and Tradition, Olympic Museum, Lausanne 1999.

CHINNA ADI, a Tamil school of marshal arts based on the Chin. marshal arts. Popular in the Ind. province of Tamil Nadu.

CHINNA ADI, an Ind. var. of marshal arts, closely related to >ADI MURAI. Known and practiced in the region of Travancore in SW India. It reveals a certain influence of the Chin. schools of marshal arts, thus the name of *chinna*.

CHIVALRIC TOURNAMENTS, or 'tourneys', in Medieval Europe, public contest between armed knights, practiced, with rich ceremonial, during public events and court holidays. According to the first ethnographer of Eng. sport, J. Strutt, a tournament should be understood as 'every kind of military combat made in conformity to certain rules, and praticed by the knights and their esquires for diversion or gallantry'. Strutt divides chivalric tournaments into the following types: 'tilting and combating at the quintain, tilting at the ring, tournaments, and justs' (Strutt, 103). However, chivalric tournaments included more than just the above-mentioned events, e.g. blunted sword fencing. >RUNNING AT THE RING became the most popular event, often organized on its own, and is held in many Eur. towns even today. Knightly >QUINTAIN developed into a folk variant, still practiced in many regions of western Europe, and known as >WATER QUINTAIN.

Chivalric tournaments were organized in castle yards or open fields. In both cases, the knights' movements were limited by barriers known as the 'lines', made of wooden posts and logs. For foot combat, these formed special partitions, while for quintain, a barrier known as the 'tilt' was usually built within the lines, reaching more or less the horses' underbellies. The two knights charged at each other along opposite sides of the tilt. The object was to unseat the opponent with one's lance. To moderate the force of the blow, the tips of the lances were blunted in various ways, depending on the period and region, e.g. by using a knob covered with leather.

Etymology. It is not completely clear what the origin of the words 'tournament' and 'tourney' was. The opinion prevails that it derives from the Vulgar Lat. verb *tornidiare*, 'to turn'. Vulgar Lat. formed the basis for Romance languages at the turn of the ancient times and Middle Ages. So, the name could refer to turning one's horse during combat, making circles around one's opponents etc. In this meaning, the word is believed to have passed into Old Fr. *torneie* or *torneier*, and then into other Eur. languages, incl. Middle English *tournement* (cf. modern Ger. *Turnier*). Sometimes, the word is derived from the name of the town of Tournai or Torunay, in modern Belgium, where some of the first tournaments in history were held. The Lat. prototype of the name was Turnacum, perhaps stemming from a regional transformation of the name of the turmae riders who were stationed there, or the adjective turmalis applied to Roman riders (*equites*). J. Strutt derives the word 'tournament' from Old Fr. *tournoy*, which was in turn a transformation of the name of Troy, and the games

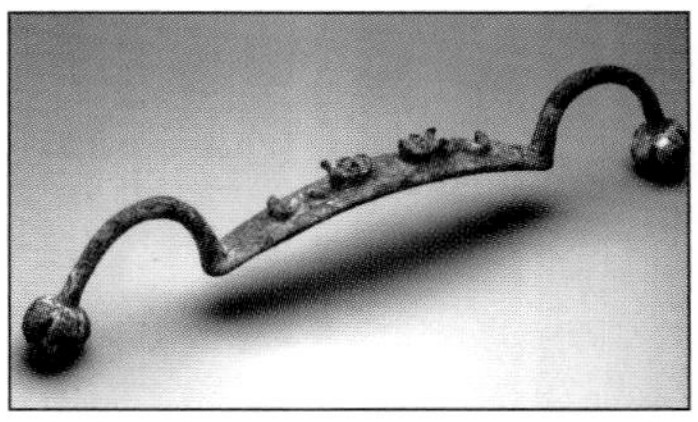

Bow strengthener, northern China, end of the Shang dynasty, 12th cent., bronze, turquoise inlays, Musée national des Arts asiatiques-Guimet, Paris.

Pot for arrow throwing, China, Ming dynasty (1368-1644), bronze, China Sport's Museum, Beijing.

Archer's ring, China, Han dynasty, 3rd cent. BC-3rd cent. AD, jade, Musée national des Arts asiatiques-Guimet, Paris.

WORLD SPORTS ENCYCLOPEDIA

A chivalric tournament on a book illustration.

Albrecht Dürer, Swordfighting, 1512, drawing.

Lucas Cranach the Elder, Tournament with Lances, detail, 1509, woodcut.

Giacopo Bellini, Tournament, lead point.

organized in the Roman Empire on the Trojan model – *ludus Troiae*. There were many descriptions of such games in ancient Gk. and Roman epics, and these were taken to Rome, according to legend, by Trojans led by Askanius, the son of Aenaeas (Strutt, 114-117). The theory is supported by the fact that many medieval knightly literature sources, especially poetry (see below) refer to ancient Trojan legends, including references to the games.

History. The first record of tournaments dates back to 882 or 884, when Ludwig the German, the ruler of the East Frankish kingdom, and emperor Charles the Bald, organized a knightly show in Strasbourg. The Frankish historian Nithard writes that many mounted knights charged at each other with great impetus, as if they were opposing armies, and acted out a battle. A report has been preserved that the show included tilting using blunted lances but these were not used to hit people. One can assume that the blunting was a precaution against accidentally injuring somebody when showing off one's equestrian skills. In 1066, on the occasion of the death of Baron Geoffroi de Previlly (or Preully or Previlli, according to some other old sources), a record was entered in the Chronique de Tours to the effect that he had been the inventor of tournaments (*inventor tournamentorum*). One could suppose that he was the codifier of the custom that must have existed in non-codified forms before. Original forms of tournaments lacked the subsequent sophistication, and the fights between knights or groups of knights looked much like actual combat, including taking hostages. The anonymous *Vie de Guillaume de Marechal* describes a tournament fight in the following way:

Each one helps his comrades to hit accurately and take hostages, at the same time defending each other and fighting back [...]. They separated at the nones, but did not leave as there were still things to be done. Some looked for their friends who had been taken in the battle. Some looked for their harnesses. Still others asked those who had taken part in the battle whether they knew anything about their relatives, or who took them hostage. And those who had been taken hostage asked their friends for ransom or deposit.

A satirical poem showing how knights were obliged to participate in tournaments dates back to the 13th cent.:

If wealth, Sir Knight, perchance be thine,
In tournaments you're bound to shine;
Refuse – and all the world will swear
You are not worth a rotten spear.

[Strutt, 1810, V]

King Edward I of England was among the most famous participants of tournaments, delaying his return to England from his expedition to the Holy Land by several months to take part in a number of tournaments in Italy and France (1273-74). The growth of tournaments was inseparably connected with the literature and art that documented them. Poets always accompanied tournaments, e.g. bards exalting the feats of King Arthur (however, tournament scenes were rare in their work). In France, the most famous eulogist of chivalry was Chretien de Trois, while Heinrich von Veldecke was the precursor of chivalric epics, the author of the *Eneit*, a poem based on a Fr. reworking of Virgil's *Aeneid*. Von Veldecke modeled the central plot of the poem, the description of Aeneas' wedding, on festivals and tournaments organized in Mainz in 1184 on the occasion of the knighting of the sons of Emperor Frederick Barbarossa. Other outstanding poets exalting knightly endeavors included H. von Aue and W. von Eschenbach, living at the turn of the 13th cent. Within Eng. literature, one of the most valuable descriptions of a tournament is to be found in the *Ipomedon* (or *Ipomadon*), an Eng. reworking of a Fr. poem by Huon de Rotelande dating to the late 12th cent. An extensive description of a field of combat, lines, and the bouts themselves is included in the poem:

The kyng his sonne a knyght gan make,
And many another for his sake;
Justes were cryed ladyes to see,
Thedyr came lordes grete plente.
Tournementis atyred in the felde,
A thousand armed with spere and sshelde;
Knyghtis began togedre to ryde,
Some were unhorsyd on every side,
Ipomydon that daye was victorious,
And there he gaff many a cours;
For there was none that he mette,

But he hys spere on hym woulde sette:
Then after within a lytell stounde,
Horse and man both went to the grounde.
The Heraudes gaff the child the gree,
A thousand pound he had to fee;
Mynstrellys had giftes of golde,
And fourty dayes this fest was holde.

[Strutt, 118-119]

Greg Oatley, 28, of Oxford, Michigan (USA), left, jousts with Sam Brafford, 35, of Jackson at the 18th annual Renaissa

Poland was the first East Eur. country where chivalric tournaments were to catch on. Gall Anonymous describes in his *Chronicle* how young Bolesław Krzywousty (later king of Poland) was knighted in 1100. Another Pol. medieval chronicler, J. Długosz, attributes in his *Dzieje Polski* (History of Poland) the first Pol. tournaments to Bolesław Chrobry, who allegedly organized a tournament on the occasion of his wedding with Judith in 984, and then to celebrate the visit by Emperor Otton III in 1000. According to the later chronicle of M. Bielski, one could conclude that the first Pol. tournament actually took place in 1142. At this date, Bielski records the following information, probably borrowed from an unknown hand-written source:

It so happened then, that when Peter the Dane married his girl off to Jaksa [...], a Serbian prince called Windisch by the Germans, he also invited Dobiesz to the wedding for races, as he was an extraordinary racer; and there went Dobiesz, having prepared well [...].

Large chivalric tournaments, dazzling with splendor and attracting knights from foreign countries, could only be organized at powerful court centers. The Hohenstauff court in Germany, the Eng. royal court, and – in E Europe – the court of the outstanding 14th-cent. King of Poland Kazimierz the Great could ensure such conditions. During his coronation in 1333, and then during the famous 1363 convention of kings and emperors in Cracow, whole days were, as Długosz writes, 'spent in great joy

and happiness on dances, chivalric tournaments and feasts' (IX, 2). During the reign of Władysław Jagiełło, tournaments abounded, with the most impressive during a visit by Sigismund of Luxembourg in Cracow (1398) and the king's wedding to Sophia (1424). At the same time, Pol. knights travelling around Europe impressed foreign courts with their military skills and prowess. The most famous of their achievements was the victory at a tournament in Buda (1412) by a team led by Dobko of Oleśnica, and the defeat of the supposedly unbeaten John of Aragon by Zawisza Czarny in the presence of the Span. court (1417).

With time, more and more descriptions of chivalric tournaments appeared in Eur. literature. The Pol. book *Dzieje w Koronie* (History of the Polish Kingdom) by Łukasz Górnicki includes descriptions of tournaments organized on the occasion of the wedding of Prince E. Ostrogski and B. Kościelecka (1539). The young King Sigismund August joined the tournament, fighting against the groom. However, the description of the tournament held during the King's wedding with Catherine of Mantoa is much richer, giving an excellent portrayal of the Eur. chivalric customs of the times:

Anyone was allowed (as long as he behaved according to the articles nailed to the castle's doors) to come and compete against whoever appeared in the square, so that the second had to fight two or three, time after time, before he made it to the other side. And as they fought in closed helmets, each one had some sign on it. And the King and the Queen with all their guests beheld from a high gallery specially made for that purpose. Having with him those gems that were presented to the fighters. Among all the fighters, the greatest thank was achieved and the first gem was taken by the equerry of the Prussian Prince [...], who carried a lady's shoe on his helmet.

It was in medieval times that chivalric culture produced unique ethics, respected during serious military combat and demonstrated during the tournaments. On the basis of such principles the term of 'fair play' was coined. It appeared twice in W. Shakespeare's play *King John*, and although it did not concern tournaments or sport directly, it has entered the language and later began to be associated with sport. This happened when chivalry lost its importance and some chivalric forms of compe-

After many vicissitudes, the furious Zborowski pounced on Tęczyński with his weapons in the King's presence. Wapowski stepped between the two, to stop a bloody duel that would spoil the atmosphere of the celebration. Zborowski hit Wapowski with his czekan (see >CZEKAN THROWING), and injured him so that Wapowski died some time later. Zborowski was sent into exile, returned illegally, was arrested and executed after a famous trial.

mous Three hundred novels. In Novel 153, he writes that in Ital. cities 'it was the order of the day for craftsmen, down to bakers or even carders, usurers and petty criminals, to knight themselves'. In Novel 64, he depicts an elderly burgher who travels to the town of Peterola, where one could pretend to be a knight for a low price by borrowing a horse and taking part in chivalric tournaments. However, some teases tie a thistle to the tail of his horse, and the frightened animal bolts towards the 'knight's' home, where his spouse uses a ladle to express her views about the endeavor.

Nearly 60 years after Sacchetti (c.1450), J. Coeur, the finance minister of King Charles VIII of France, commissioned a sculpture depicting a tournament fought on donkeys and ostentatiously mounted it on the frontage of his palace. Some time later, L. Ariosto (1474-1533), recalling in his epic *Orlando Furioso* (1532) a tournament allegedly organized during the reign of Charlemagne, mockingly pointed out that in those time, kings and princes took part in tournaments rather than cooks and courtiers.

An important element of the critique of tournaments was satire directed at the fall of the knightly spirit among effeminate courtiers or even soldiers. For instance, during the reign of the Vasa dynasty in Poland, tournaments started losing their former splendor, which was assisted by the general downfall of the knightly spirit among the nobility. The aristocracy, lazed away by the prosperity of the 'golden age', became more and more settled and lazy. The Pol. poet J. Kochanowski pointed that out in his song *Zgoda (Concord)*:

And the knightly craft, of which Poland used to be so proud,
So that she never feared her enemies,
Has cheapened among the people: the armors have rusted,
The spear shafts have dusted over, the shields have grown mouldy.

The moralist S. Starowolski soon stroke a similar note in his *Reformacyja obyczajów polskich* (Reformation of Polish Habits): 'And thus, from the once famous noble cavalry, that gave us the name of equites, we have become cart riders and cushion sitters now, dragging beds and stools with us [on war expeditions]. An armed and mounted soldier has disappeared, and the comforts have killed the virile strength in us' (c.1650).

At the same time, the new advances in military technology, especially the development of firearms, and the downfall of hand-to-hand combat in favor of manipulating nameless masses of soldiers, expunged the former ethics and techniques. The processes undermined the meaning of tournaments as events serving the practice of combat skills and glorifying knighthood. Knights wearing iron armor, wielding two-handed swords and heavy lances became anachronistic in the battlefield towards the end of the 15th cent. M. Cervantes's (1547-1616) satirical reflection on Don Quixote's fate as a symbol of knightly nobleness and bravery, impossible to implement in the new reality, marks the end of the spiritual strength of knighthood and their tournaments.

The history of tournaments was evidenced in many works of art and literature. The most famous among them come from western Europe but it is worth noting that eastern Europe had some achievements in the field as well. There are paintings, like the huge four-part fresco at Wawel Castle in Cracow, Poland, depicting tournament scenes. In more modern times, the famous watercolor *A chivalric tournament at Wawel Castle* was painted by S. Noakowski in 1928. Tournament scenes associated with the legend of King Arthur are to be found in the historic Knights' Tower at Siedleniec Castle in Lower Silesia, Poland. There are historic Arthurian Courts, associated with medieval knightly tradition, in Toruń and Gdańsk. Literary sources include chiefly historiographic works, diaries and heraldic books. There are also fragments devoted to tournaments in the poetry of S. Twardowski and A. Zbylitowski, a charming element of historical literature.

R. Barber, J. Baker, *Tournaments, Jousts, Chivalry and Pageantry in the Middle Ages*, 1989; J.M. Carter, *Medieval Games. Sports and Recreations in Feudal Society*, 1992; S.K. Kuczyński, *Turnieje rycerskie w średniowiecznej Polsce*, 1992; W. Lipoński, 'Piewcy i krytycy chwały rycerskiej', *Sport, literatura, sztuka*, 1974, 43-51; V. Olivova, 'Rytiřské turnaje', *Teorie a Praxe Télesne Výchovy*, 1989, 1; L. Zecević, 'Tournaments and Chivalry in Bosnia and Herzegovina', PISHPRES, 1991.

tition, esp. fencing and horse events, became the basis for modern sporting events, while maintaining their ethical values.

Shakespeare was also the inventor of the term 'foul play'. Tournaments were regularly accompanied by shocking displays of ungentlemanly conduct. A Pol. chronicler, S. Orzelski, gives a report of one such event that occurred during a tournament organized to celebrate the coronation of King Henry Valois of France, who had briefly ruled Poland before being elected the King of France. During the tournament, the lance of the magnate Samuel Zborowski was chosen by an insignificant nobleman of a lesser rank, a servant of another nobleman:

Among [...] the lances, there was, however, one displayed by Samuel Zborowski, with a card attached in which Zborowski challenged anybody who equaled him in birth and prowess to crumble his lance with him to the King's health. Many read the card but no one took on the challenge. In the end, one Janusz of Croatia, a servant of Count Jan Tęczyński, the Castellan of Wojnice [...], took out Samuel Zborowski's lance [...]. Samuel, thinking [...] that Tęczyński sent a foreigner of base birth on purpose, to insult him, sent one Mościński to fight the Croatian, a nobleman servant of his, while he himself challenged the castellan through couriers. Tęczyński, guessing that the challenge was made with a hostile intention, justified himself to the couriers that he had not issued any order to the Croatian, and had not meant to insult Zborowski. Zborowski, in anger [...], sent the challenge again through his servants to Tęczyński [...].

Apart from examples of such behavior, the dangers of tournaments provided an argument against them, leading to many bans, especially by the church. Initially, the effects were meager. Soon after King Henry II of England issued a ban, his successor Richard the Lionheart founded a special order for tournament winners. However, when in 1559 King Henry II of France was killed after a lance struck him in the eye, and another Fr. King, Charles IX, was seriously injured in a duel against Duke de Guisse, tournaments were given up in France. Soon, Louis XIII issued an official ban on tournaments, and ordered the safer >CARROUSEL to be organized instead. With the demise of tournaments in France, their popularity dwindled in the whole of Western Europe. Soon, they disappeared completely and were only reinvented in the Romantic times of the 19th cent. as a way of reviving the glory of the Middle Ages. In 1858, a tilting tournament was included in the program of the Much Wenlock Ol.G., one of the attempts at reviving the Olympic tradition made by W.P. Brookes. The riders, wearing medieval attire, competed in tilting at the ring. The event was modeled on the description in J. Strutt's *The Sports and Pastimes of the People of England* (1801).

Tournaments have been the object of much criticism and satire since the Middle Ages. The Italian writer Franco Sacchetti wrote a series of parodies about knighthood, included in the series of his fa-

...stival in Holly, Michigan.

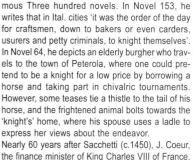

WORLD SPORTS ENCYCLOPEDIA

C

Chivalric tournaments on postage stamps.

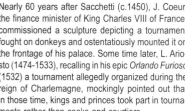
A modern re-enactment of a chivalric tournament at the Castle of Golub-Dobrzyń in Poland.

CHIWA-GORISHI, a folk var. of Turkm. wrestling.

CHŁOPIEC, Pol. for 'boy', also known as *chłopiec game*. A Pol. peasants' game played in the 16th cent, the rules of which did not survive.
Ł. Gołębiowski, *Games and pastimes of various social states*, 1831, 63.

CHOCA, also in old texts *joch de la choca*, a Span. game dating back to the Middle Ages, in which a wooden ball, referred to as choca, was struck with a shepherd's crook called *gayardo* [Span. dial. *cayado*]. Choca is prob. a predecessor of >CHUECA. The game used to be practiced around Navia de Eo in Asturias. It was also known under the same name in some regions of Portugal.
R.G. Serrano, 'Choca', JDTE, 1974, 186.

CHODYLI, a Rus. equivalent of >WALKING ON STILTS.

CHON WUA, a Thai var. of >BULL FIGHS, probably brought by the Portuguese during their first colonial explorations in Thailand's predecessor – the kingdom of Ayutthaya in the 16th and 17th cent.

CHONO TARVAGATSAKH, Mong. the wolf and the marmots, a children's recreational game. The biggest child plays a 'bad wolf' whereas others act the part of 'marmots'. The wolf is supposed to catch marmots when, at a given sign, they leave their 'burrows' (circles marked on the ground with a line or stones) in order to change them with others. A marmot touched by the wolf leaves the game crying, 'I've been eaten!' The activity stops when all the marmots have been devoured. In some other versions of the game, one of the children acts as the king of wolves to whom hunting wolves bring their prey. The game starts with one of a series of special dialogs in which the marmots ask the wolf about different things such as a wagon – *tereg*, arrows, bow, and fire. When it turns out the marmots need those things to shoot the wolf in the head, the latter gets angry and attacks the terrified marmots.

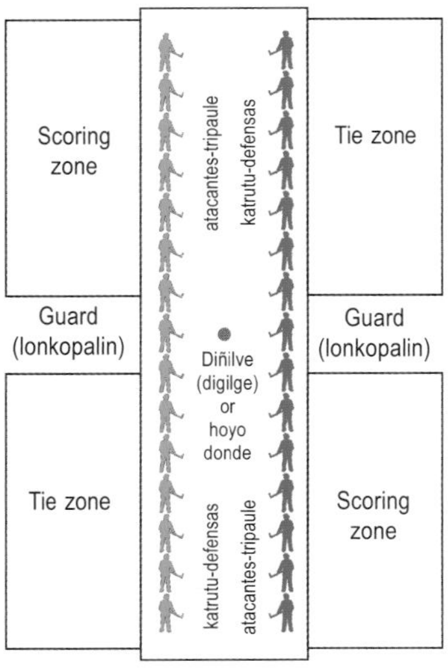

A chueca field and player set-up.

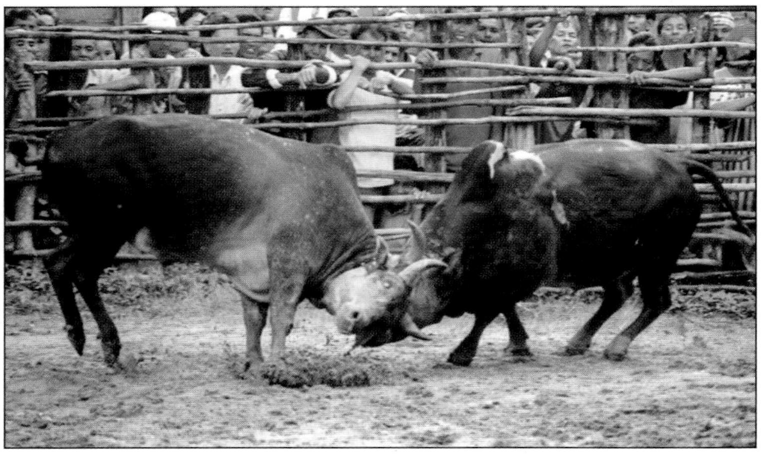

Bull fights in Thailand (chon wua).

While the symbolic image of the wolf as a representative of evil and aggression is obvious, the marmot in old Mong. legends represents a hunter upon whom a spell was cast changing him into an animal the moment his arrow missed the intended target when the fate of others was at stake. Before the metamorphosis, he cuts off his thumbs and feet, which in Mong. symbolism stand for strength and skill at archery. The way a marmot walks resembles a human walking on stiff feet and the marmot's paws do not have visible fingers that would be equivalent to thumbs. According to one of the legends the archer's transformation into a marmot occurred after he failed to shoot down one of the redundant suns in the sky that caused drought on Earth; according to another legend, it occurred when he shot at a constellation of stars that caused excessive chill during winter.

CHOULE, one of the former names for >SOULE, LA.

CHOULE, a medieval game popular throughout Europe, in which a wooden ball was struck with a club. There were a number of var. of the game, the most widespread one being *chouler à la crosse*. When brought to Flanders and the Netherlands in the 16th and 17th cent., it became the ancestor of >KOLVEN and if we agree that kolven contributed to the development of >GOLF, choule had an indirect share in its evolution.

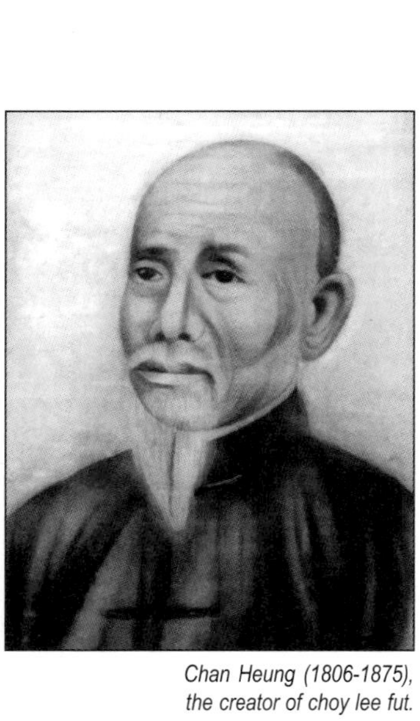

Chan Heung (1806-1875), the creator of choy lee fut.

CHOW, a Scot. var. of a game in which a ball was struck with curved sticks. Goals are scored in a series of shots taken alternatively by 2 teams standing in front of each other. The objective of the game is to launch the ball across the opponent's goal line. The pitch is short enough for the players to send the ball from one end to the other with a single strike. One team lined up along the goal line pitches the ball towards the opposing team – lined up the same way – who attempts to prevent the ball from crossing their line and strike it back. The starting team launches the ball from a platform to give it enough momentum, such a shot is referred to as a 'deli-chap', probably a clipped form of 'devil chap'. A successful shot that scores a goal is called in Scot. Eng. a 'dule-chap' – a stupid strike.
TGESI, I, 68.

CHOY LEE FUT, also *Tsai Li Fut* or *Choi Li Fut*. A southern style of >GONGFU, belonging to the group of external waijia styles of buddhist origin. While the styles of N China were used in open spaces, over large steppes, those of S China were confined to the narrow streets of congested cities, numerous rice fields, and boats. Therefore, southern styles involve a large number of hand techniques applied in one single stance. Choy Lee Fut was developed at the beginning of the 19th cent. by Chan Heung (1806-1875) and forms a very offensive style with a multitude of techniques. An adequate Choy Lee Fut technique requires fast, deceptive footwork and a powerful and flexible waiste.The turning waiste accelerates the movement of flexible hands, which make use of the centrifugal force and execute a series of sweeping blows combined with leg techniques. Circular blows are delivered in almost all directions – top to bootm and bottom to top, horizontally, and at a 45 degree angle. Hand techniques include: Chap Choi (a straight, stabbing or thrusting, punch with the hand position made by folding the fingers at the first joint past the knuckles and bracing them on the side by laying the thumb parallel to the hand to create a flat fist); Gwa Choi (a backfist or back knuckle strike); Pow Choi (an uppercut being an up-lifting or cannon strike); Kup Choi (stamping fist – an over head straight-arm downward strike mainly targeting the head); Sow Choi (a sweeping strike). Although Chin. kung fu is often nicknamed 'sothern hands, northern legs', Choy Lee Fut also involves a number of leg techniques, such as: Chan Gerk (a very powerful side kick targeting the head or the torso); Dung Gerk (a powerful straight front kick targeting the torso and head region); Ngow Sow Gerk (a back turning kick, hitting with the heel; it can be both offensive and defensive); Deng Gerk (a circular kick utilising the turn of the hip); Jahp Gerk (a deceptive, straight, strong, and sharp kick); Chow Gerk (a short sweeping kick directed at the lower legs); Dung Charn Gerk (a backward turning thrusting kick that utilises both the turning energy of the deng gerk, and the thrusting power of the charm gerk); Yerng Gerk (a deceptive, fast knee strike coming from the back foot), Sow Gerk (a long and low kick aimed at the opponents lower legs). Advanced drill makes use of a wooden dummy for practicing both hand-to-hand combat and the use of as many as 17 different weapons. There are 47 forms of hand-to-hand combat (incl. 4 internal Qigong forms), 45 forms of armed combat, 18 forms of dummy drill, 13 forms of set sparring (incl. bear arms against weapons), 55 forms of set sparring with weapons (some against a greater number of opponents), and 10 forms of lion dance.
History. The founder of the system, Chan Heung (1805-1881), was born in the village of Ging Mui (the district of Ngai Sai in the area of Sun Wui) in the province of Guangdong and began his martial arts training at the age of 7 under his uncle Chan Yuen Woo, a Shaolin disciple. Then he became a student of master Lee Yau San and later met a Shaolin monk Choy Fook under whom he studied kung fu for 10 years, before he finally developed his own style named after his masters Choy Lee Fut (*Fut* in Cantonese means buddha and points to the buddhist origin of this art). He taught the system to his son Chan Koon Pak, who taught it to his son Chan Yiu Chi, who in turn passed it to his son Chan Wan Hon, who taught it to Chan Yong Fa. Choy Lee Fut is very popular in Hong Kong, Malaysia, Australia, and the USA.

CHUCKS, an Eng. game mostly popular among girls. Originally it was played with the use of 5 shells. When played with small pebbles it was also known as *checkstones* or *fivestones*. Cf. >JACKS.

CHUECA, the Span. name of a unique type of aboriginal >FIELD HOCKEY developed by the Mapuche Indians (Araucanians) of Chile – who continue to use its original names: *palin* and *palitun* – and still played with enthusiasm in many rural Mapuche towns and cities from the Bio-Bio River to the Province of Osorno. In 1558, Gerónimo de Bibar recorded that the conquistadors, the first Europeans to encounter the game palin, dubbed it 'chueca' (in full: *juego de chueca*) after a similar game then practiced in Spain (see >CHUECA below). In the 21st century, Mapuche organizations, with the support of the Chilean government, are taking an active interest in promoting palin (chueca) matches across the country: in villages, in towns, in the South of Chile, and even in Santiago and Valparaiso (2003). Chueca has become one of the major symbols of indigenous Chilean tradition. During the Scout Movement's 1999 World Jamboree in Chile, chueca was selected a representative element of the national culture. Although today basic written rules do exist, for centuries they have been transmitted orally from generation to generation, and vary from place to place. Prior to beginning a game, the 2 'center players' with their teams lined up and ready, agree to which version of the rules they will adhere to, and negotiate the finer points of handling special situations that might arise. Though a referee (*rannieve*) and linesman are on hand to arbitrate important matches, players themselves observe an honor code and can generally be counted upon to assure fair play. The organization of chueca matches takes 2 forms. The so-called 'encounters' (*encuentros* or *winkapalin*), becoming increasingly popular, feature as many as 15-20 participant communities. The 'great palin festivities' (*füchapalin* or *palinkawiñ*) involve just 2 communities and are extremely popular among the Mapuche because they offer an excellent opportunity for friends and relatives to meet. One community invites another for a palinkawiń on a certain date. Full of good will, the participants of each team pair off with their counterparts from the opposite team to form a dyad (*kon*) in a friendly gesture of commitment.
Equipment and field. The sticks (*weño*), grasped with both hands, are curved and vary in length (105-122cm) and weight (.4-1.05kg). Thicker, heavier sticks used by the centers are called *lonkoweño*. *Lonko* (guardian) is among the many names used for the center players who function as both coaches and captains. The ball is 3-5cm in diameter, weighs 45-60g, and goes by various names such as *fogvl* and *füngül*, according to the area, but is usu. called *pali*, a native term deriving from Span. >PELOTA. It is usu. either an oak or hazel knot or a tightly wound coil of llama wool, very tight and stitched into an encasement of fresh cowhide. The barefoot players tie their pant legs at the ankles or roll them up to the knees, and sport a bandana as a headband (*trarilonko*). During a game they do not wear masks, feathers, or face paint. The field is a roughly 12x200-m strip of grass or earth, marked with slight grooves. The arrangement of players on the field before the match begins is distinctive. The 2 teams are arrayed in 2 long rows, face to face, just 1.5m apart. The players are spaced along the length of the field so as to occupy an extension of every 50m in a field of 200m. This placement changes as soon as the match begins since players located at the ends of these rows are already in motion as the ball approaches them. The unique positioning of the players during the game is essential, as action is confined to whichever sector of the field the ball is in. Players in the other sectors maintain their positions and wait for the ball to enter their territory to be shuttled along until it is lined up for a shot (*malkotun*). Opposing teams have the same odd number of players. A 200-m field requires 15 players per team. For smaller fields this diminishes to 13, 11, 9, etc. At the beginning of a game the centers flip a coin to determine which side each team will play. When one scores a total of 2 *tripai* (goals) the teams change sides; when matches are divided in 2, there is also a change of sides at the beginning of the 2nd period.
The object and course of the game. Before taking their positions on the field, each team forms a circle around its center and challenges the opposing team

by screaming the *avavan*: '*Ay ayayayayay mari chi hueun!*' ('We will win ten times!') from the opposite end of the field. These exclamations are accompanied by the clacking of their sticks over their heads (*maloweñon*). The game then commences in a way similar to field hockey's 'bully' system – eliminated from regulation play some years ago – with a face-off (*llintun*) in the middle of the field with the ball placed in a little hole or small depression (*diñilwe*). Each team tries to play the ball to its left toward the scoring zone and hit it across the goal line (*tripalwe*) to score a point (*raya*). Once the ball is set in the diñilwe, both centers bend down to cup the ball with the curve of their lonkoweño and, upon a signal from the referee, perform a quick *topaiweño*, clacking the distal ends of their sticks above the ball one or more times depending on the region, before immediately commencing to struggle for possession of the ball (*hollan la bola*). Once the ball is scooped out of the diñilwe, it is passed to the left to the quicker center's waiting teammates. The receiving 'attackers' try to lead the ball, running and hitting it (*witrulon*) along the ground or through the air, to the tripalwe, which, depending on the field, is a distance of 60, 80, or 100m, i.e. half the total length of the field. Since the playing field is so narrow, tactics are relatively limited. The primary defensive action (*kachi*) consists of charging at great speed in an effort to prevent a goal by intercepting the ball and knocking it out of bounds, at which point the llintun face-off is repeated and play resumes. An alternate name for the kachi maneuver (*katrü*) comes from the fact that the 'stoppers' (*katrütufe*) who flank the center on the right hit the ball across the long *katrülwe* (sideline). This relentless pattern of swift attack and determined defense quickly escalates into a frenzied scramble; leaving some players knocked to the ground. However, in chueca, unlike such extremely rough traditional Mapuche sports as >LINAO, meting out undue physical abuse on one's opponents is frowned upon. Obviously, in the course of play, players do collide and controlled chest charges (*pechadas*) are permitted. But tripping, pushing, hooking, premeditated blows with one's weño, and grappling with an opponent so as to prevent him from playing, are not tolerated. Other fouls include touching the ball with the hand, kicking the ball, and throwing one's weño at the ball. The players equate fairness and good sportsmanship with honor and dignity, and even assume the objectivity of a referee when verifying the legitimacy of a point scored against them. Before a match begins, they shake hands with their counterparts across from them on the other team and promise each other a fair game. All players commit themselves to playing as chivalrous gentlemen and vow to invite each other whenever future matches are organized. After a match, the gracious winners always challenge the losing team to a rematch the following year. Lavish banquets with abundant meat, bread, vegetables and drinks follow the more important matches. In order to score a goal, the ball must cross the tripalwe. There is no goalkeeper. A linesman for each goal line, along with nearby players from both teams, certifies the legitimacy of each tripai. The matches take place in 2 sets of 20-30min., each one with an intermediate break of 5-7min. Since a draw is not possible, a series of midfield free shots, adopted from the penalty shots of >ASSOCIATION FOOTBALL, and involving 3 players from each team, is used as a tie-breaker.

The players. Adult males representing Mapuche communities and ranging from 15 to 65 years of age are all referred to as *palife* (Span. *chuequero*). Almost all players receive a name according to the position they take in the field and the function they perform. In modern chueca, only some of these names continue to be used and in some cases there are several names for one position. For example, in addition to lonko, the central player of each formation can be referred to as the *diñilfe, dünülfe, dünüllkamañ, lonko, ñidol*, or *hollador*, and even *elkonafe* (coach). The ideal center is a hefty man of great experience, one who commands respect; it is he who assigns his teammates to their positions and distributes them on the field. Centers maintain their positions throughout an entire match. The players positioned next to the centers are called *tako* and serve as support. As soon as they receive the ball they pass it along to their teammates. The players at the ends of the formation are called *wechuntufe* or 'punteros' (forwards). These are either attacking players (*atacantes* or *sacadores*) called *wechuntotripalfe*, who convert the points, or *wechuntokatrütufe*: defenders or stoppers (*defensores* or *atajadores*). The forwards (both scorers and defenders) must be fleet of foot and have perfected techniques of receiving passes and hurling the ball great distances with speed and precision. Another technique, called *malkokantun*, is to 'carry' the ball several meters without letting it fall to the ground by bouncing it repeatedly off one's stick. The player to the right of the scoring player is called *inapetcha* ('second scoring player') and assists the scorer. Living memory bears witness to the possibility for the long-distance shooter (*chañatufe* or *chañato*), positioned behind the center, to whack the ball the full 80-100m diagonally to the goal. Though it has been several decades now since the last such play was witnessed in the Malleco Province, such an astonishing hit, referred to as a 'crack', was greeted with deafening cheers from the players and spectators of both teams.

History and tradition. Originally played by Mapuche men, women and children, the game dates back at least several hundred years (see >PRE-COLUMBIAN GAMES OF THE AMERICAS). Both the field and the number of players on it were once much larger. Games were played in a series, the winners taking 2 out of 3 sets. A team had to win 4 to 0. Each point scored by the losing team annulled one of the winning team's points, as a result of which games often lasted several days. It is probable that chueca has its origin in funeral rites and other mystical practices, though even in the early days, face paint, feathers and masks were seldom used. During the 8 days prior to a match, players were subjected to a strict regimen that included sleeping on the field in the open air, abstaining from eating salt and meat, and remaining chaste (*ülwentun*). They also began taking ice-cold waterfall baths (*traitraiko*) each morning. They engaged in secret rites under the guidance of a shaman woman (*machi*), injecting themselves with a powder of ground puma bones and stone dust to increase their vigor. In order to insure good luck on the turf, they would take the skull of a famous player from the past to the match, and secrete it in the branches of a nearby canelo tree (Drimys winteri). It was believed the opponents, too, cast spells to secure victory with magical powers. Pregnant women could not approach players prior to or during a game, but they participated in counteracting the opponent's spell by preparing a powder made of the talons of a 'traro' or 'pueco' bird to make their men more skillful. The powder was rubbed over lightly cut skin or under fingernails to confer the grip and grace of these birds of prey upon the players. In addition, on the day preceding the event, weño to be used during the match were placed on the tomb of a late, great player whose spirit and skills then passed on to the team, aiding them by fending off the opponents' spells.

In some regions the game still features religious ceremonies (*dagun*) and players, sticks, ball, and field are all submitted to ritual charming by machi assisted by lonko. On the eve of an important match a rite (*nguillatun*) is performed involving the participation of the whole community. Machi, lonko and other players of each reservation join a throng of fans behind the goal lines and petition the god *Nguenechen* to look kindly on the team's endeavor. Following the prayer and after midnight, the players perform a 'palin dance' ceremony (*perulpalin* or *kallfülikan*). The next day, the players themselves sing trad. songs (*paliwe-ül*), inviting the spectators to the game. They bring to the match a bunch of canelo branches known as *weñufoige* and place it near the goal line to induce a raya. Throughout the entire game, the teams are encouraged from the sidelines with music, special 'chueca songs', and dances, all performed by the spectators to the rhythm of a magic drum (*kultrun*), and contrived to entice the ball towards where they are located in order to obtain a raya for their team. In modern times, it is not uncommon to see fans brandishing the Chilean flag (*weñufoige*). In some cases the movement of the pali functions as an oracle that gives answer to the problems of the community. Throughout the game the spectators (100-500) surround the field, right on the outer edge of the boundaries, including the goal area. They are, therefore, in constant danger of being struck by a stray ball, stick, or hurtling player. With the Span. invasion the contest became part of the warrior's discipline. Despite Eur. cultural patterns imposed later, the game was preserved in remote settlements beyond the reach of Span. control, in particular eluding the oppression of their clergy who considered chueca a remnant of pagan times. In response to such adversity, the ideal of the Mapuche youth was to become a bold warrior and skilled palin player. The sport later evolved into a competitive diversion. Large bets were placed. In the 19th century there were professional players who won substantial sums of money, animals, textiles, weapons, or other prizes (*palicatun*). From the 17th to the 19th century, the church and state conspired to prohibit the game and systematically persecuted organizers, players, and even spectators, yet clandestine matches continued unabated. Chueca passed from Chile to Argentina and Great Chaco at the beginning of the 18th century, and eventually emerged as the social, recreational game that it is today, complete with communal festivities (*kawiñ*) conducive to group unity.

The game has developed its own system of coded signals and gestures made with the eyes, head, and hands that players use to indicate where the ball should be directed in order to surprise the opponent. When verbal communication is necessary, players resort to cryptic phrases agreed upon beforehand and unintelligible to the opponents, such as: 'I am as strong as an oak!' (lit. 'I am an oak's trunk' – Span. *yo soy cuerpo de roble*), 'I am a dog's head!' (*yo soy la cabeza de perro*), or 'I am a lion's leg!' (*yo soy pierna de leon*) – in the local trad. a 'lion' stands for 'puma'.

The first illustrations of chuecan iconography appear in Ovalle's *Histórica relación del Reyno de Chile* (A Historic Account of the Kingdom of Chile, published in Rome in 1646). Other specimens include: Frezier (1732), Molina (1776), Gómez de Vidaurre (1789), Famin (1839), Bramati (c.1840) and Gay (1854). A 1.53-m bronze figure, *The Chueca Player*, by sculptor Nicanor Plaza (1844-1917), was acquired in 1880 by the National Museum of Fine Arts of Santiago, where it can still be seen. Chueca and other sporting games of the Mapuche (see >PILLMATUN) were included in the program of the First National Olympic Games of Santiago, Chile, in 1909.

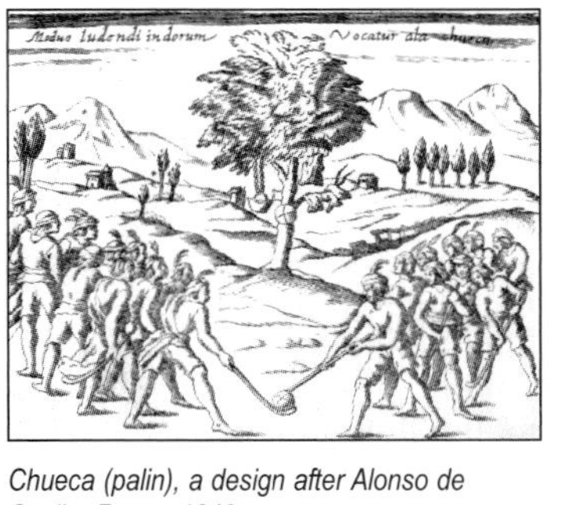

Chueca (palin), a design after Alonso de Ovalle, Rome, 1646.

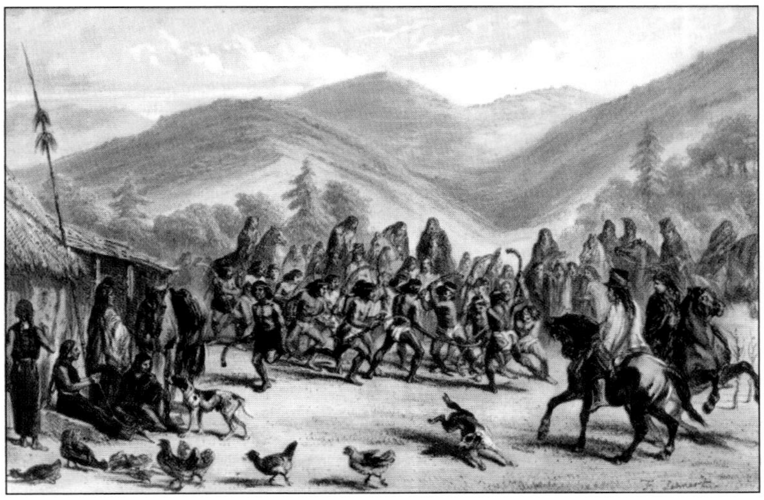
Chueca (palin), a colored design after Claudio Gay, Paris, 1854.

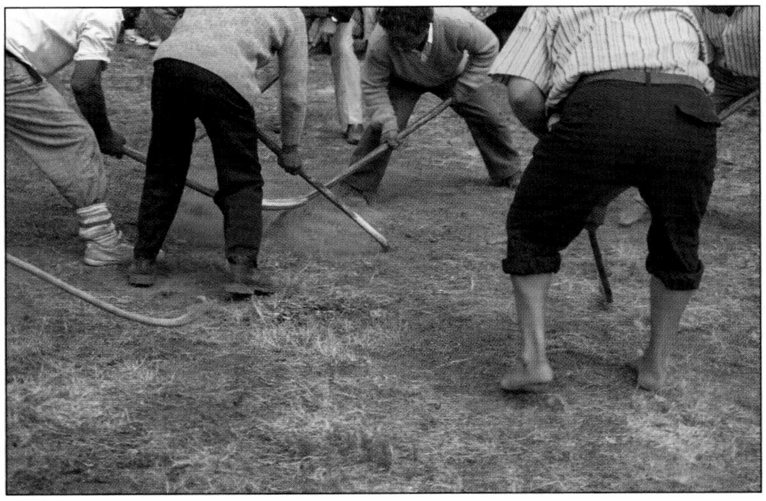
A modern game of chueca (palin).

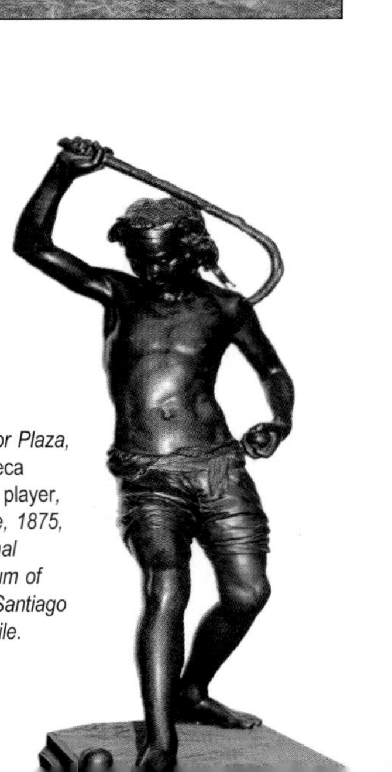
Nicanor Plaza, A chueca (palin) player, bronze, 1875, National Museum of Arts, Santiago de Chile.

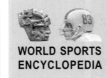

C WORLD SPORTS ENCYCLOPEDIA
130

Over the centuries, the ancient playing fields were lost, but palin-related place names indicating where great fields were once located persist, testifying to the importance of this aboriginal, Chilean game. Over the course of time the ancient game of palin has undergone considerable modification. The number of players has dwindled from hordes numbering in the hundreds to a max. of 15 per team. The size of the field, once more than 1km long is now 200m or less. The duration of a match, too, has shortened from the *fuchapalin* of old, which routinely lasted several days, to contests of 1 hour or less. Not even

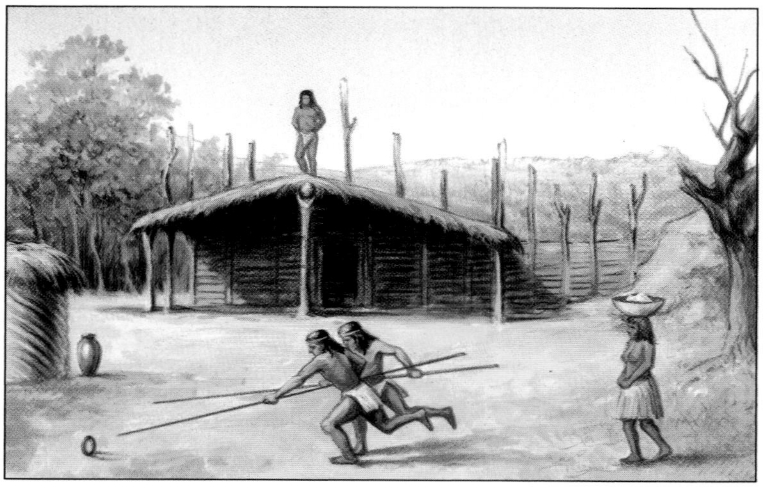

North American Indians playing chungke.

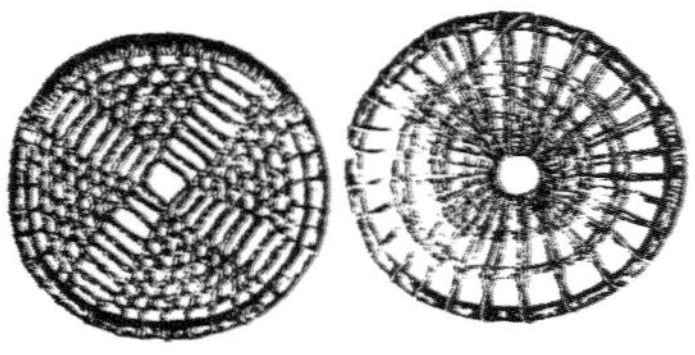

Woven circles for playing chungke.

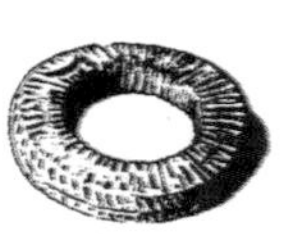

A stone ring for playing chungke.

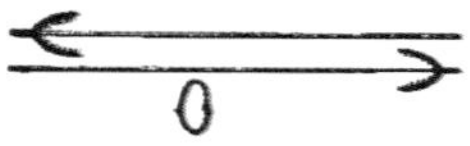

Chungke sticks and wicker ring.

Indians playing chungke on a painting by George Catlin.

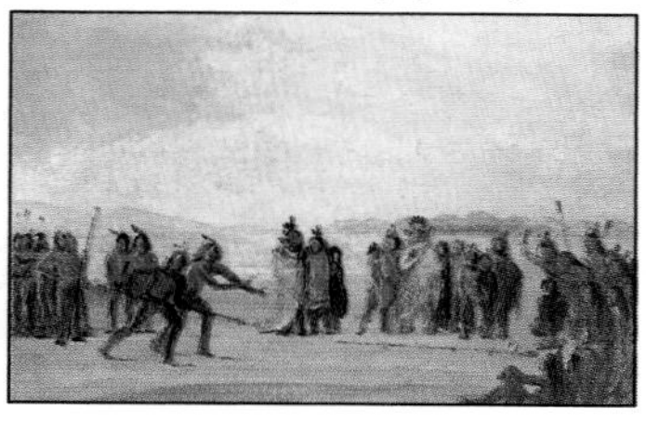

girls play these days, whereas women were at one time active participants. Glorious games starring extraordinary players have all but vanished, as has the extravagant wagering that once drove the game's frantic pace. The countless ritual ceremonies once held to honor and favor the players have been reduced to but a handful. The once sacred, martial, competitive, often violent game of multiple motives has metamorphosed into the sporting, peaceable, recreational pastime that is modern chueca. See also >AWARKUDEN and >KETCHUKAWE.

T. Guevara, 1898-1927; L. M. Zapata, 1909-1920; M. Manquilef, 1914; E. Robles, 1914; O. Plath, 'Palin o palitun – Juego de chueca', JYDLCH, 1946, 12-15; C.L. von Vriessen, 'El palin o chueca de los Mapuche en Chile', *Educación física*, Chile, 1992, 228, 5-10; C.L. von Vriessen, 1984-2002; the Internet: www.deportesmapuches.cl, www.galeon.com/indiansports

CHUGAN, a Persian name for a game in which a ball is struck with a curved stick. Chugan historically contributed to the development of >POLO; in some areas of the Middle East it was also known as >DARAB-NAMAH. The term chugan was adopted in Eur. languages during the period of the Crusades, Fr. being the first to incorporate it as *chicane*. Some researchers claim the word *jockey* originates from the name of the game, as it originally indicated a horse rider, but not all etymologists agree. It is possible the term is related to the concept of a Gypsy as a traveling horse rider, which later became identified only with the itinerant ethnic group. As the game had no Eur. equivalent, its name evolved into terms connoting sth. unusual or confusing both in the negative sense (an element of pressure) and the positive one (amazement at sth.). This meaning became a vehicle for the word to make its way into Eur. languages, e.g. Ger. *Schikane*, Gk. *tzykanion*, Pol. *szykana*, and, of course, Eng. *chicanery*.

CHÚI WAN, also sp. *chúiwan*. Chin. for 'striking a ball with a stick.' An old Chin. game resembling mod. >GOLF. It was played during the reign of the Sung dynasty (960-1279). According to a Chin. historian, Gunson Ho, the size of the course differed depending on the number of partakers which was unlimited. Starting points, usu. a max. of 1ft. wide, were located in various points directing the game east towards holes marked with colored flags. The distance between the starting point and the hole was agreed before the game, depending on the skills and strength of the players. The balls, whose weight was proportionate to the clubs, were made of mahogany or other hard wood. The clubs' heads were also made of hard wood, their handles – of bamboo, both parts tied together with animal intestine and glue. The club's length was adjusted to the player's height and weight. If the number of players was 10 or more, 2 equal teams were established and the game was referred to as a large assembly; if it ranged from 6 to 8 it was called a middle assembly, and below 6 – a small assembly. Immediately before a match, the participants gathered together and agreed on the order of players to strike the ball. Then, a representative of each team commenced the game. There were many different types of strokes, the most popular being 'a stepping forward stroke', 'a standing still stroke', 'a squatting stroke', and 'a far stroke'. Points were scored for each hole and there were also special prizes. Finally, the rules of the game that have survived to be described by Gunson Ho mention 21 different penalties that were imposed on offending players.

Gunson Ho, *Physical education in China*, 1926, 27-28.

CHUKCHEE AND KORIAK ARCHERY, folk archery practiced on numerous religious and social occasions such as childbirth, weddings and funerals by the Chukchee and Koriak peoples. It served as a deterrent against evil ghosts and was held together with football, running and wrestling competitions, commencing the hunting season. The Chukchee believed that winning in sports games indicated success in hunting; see also >CHUKCHEE RACES, >CHUKCHEE BALL, >CHUKCHEE WRESTLING. Due to cultural closeness between the Chukchee and the Koriak most sports traditions are shared by the two nations.

CHUKCHEE BALL, a ball game practiced along with archery contests, wrestling bouts and annual hunting by the Chukchee people. Winning the ball game, according to the Chukchee, was to signify successful hunting.

CHUKCHEE CIRCLE RUN, an unspecified type of competition popular among the Chukchees. Such circle runs constituted a part of religious offering celebrations.

I.S. Wdowin, *Oczerki istorii i etnografii Czukczej*, 1975.

CHUKCHEE RACES, were held together with ball games, archery contests and wrestling matches before major annual hunts. The Chukchees believed that if one was successful in competition, he would also be successful in 'competition with animals'. The competitions marked the beginning of many Chukchee holidays and festivals and were held at the seaside. The tradition of marking the beginning of a religious holiday with a running competition died out probably in the mid-19th cent. Sometimes a running contest was held after reindeer races and a wrestling competition. In some areas Chukchee competitors ran with sticks in their hands. The races were long-distance team events which were so exhausting that many runners dropped out along the way. The settlement with most runners completing the race was declared the winner. See also >CHUKCHEE AND KORIAK ARCHERY, >CHUKCHEE BALL and >CHUKCHEE WRESTLING.

CHUKCHEE WRESTLING, practiced alongside running, Chukchee ball sports, and archery before major annual hunts. See also other Chukchee sports such as >CHUKCHEE RACES, >CHUKCHEE AND KORIAK ARCHERY and >CHUKCHEE BALL.

CHUKGUK, a football game practiced in old Korea, dating back to the Middle Ages. Its rules resembled to some extent old var. of Eur. football. A characteristic element of the game were the goals which instead of a crossbar, as old pictures demonstrate, were equipped with a net or cloth spread between the two goalposts across the upper part. Points were scored aiming not in between the posts but at the net. The ball was about the size of a cannoball, made of leather stuffed with fur. A match was played either by single players or teams. Chukguk appears in *Samguk Sagi* (Chronicles of the Three Kingdoms) written by sage Dae-mun Kima who lived during the Songdok times (702-737). One of the episodes describes an incident when Kim Yousin, the ruler of the Shilla kingdom, while playing with Chun-chu, caught his foot on a leather strap holding up the opponent's pants which, as a result, fell down.

CHUNGKE, also spelled *tchung-kee*, *chunkey*, or *chunky*, a variety of an Indian game once played by the Choctaw tribes in the Mississippi Delta and the Arapaho and the Cheyennes in what is now Oklahoma (USA). The essence of the game was to throw a pole approx. 3m long into a stone cirle 11-13cm in diameter (cf. present day >HOOP-AND-POLE). The majority of descriptions written by Eur. travellers and colonists come from the 17th and 18th cent., which suggests that this period was the peak of the game's popularity. Chungke is part of a large family of Indian sports, differently desrcibed by dozens of tribal languages, but occuring in the diaries of white travellers and colonists in America as hoop-and-pole. The essential difference between chungke and the hoop-and-pole games was that the circle in the latter was made of wood or wicker rather than stone. Also, some varieties of hoop-and-pole were played on ice as winter games, while chungke is exclusively a summer sport. Besides the games using a circle with a hole, there were probably varieties using a round stone without a hole, which may be an older variety. This is suggested by *The History of American Indians* written in 1775 by an Amer. traveller and trader J. Adaire (approx. 1709-1783), who claims that the Mississippi Choctaw 'have near their statehouse a square piece of ground well cleaned, and fine sand is carefully strewn over it, when requisite, to promote a swifter motion to what they throw along the surface. Only one, or two on a side, play at this ancient game. They have a stone about 2 fingers broad at the edge, and 2 spands round; each party has a pole of about 8ft. long, smooth, and tapering at each end, the points flat. They set off abreast of each other at 6yds. from the end of the playground; then one of them hurls the stone on its edge, in as direct a line as he can, a considerable distance toward the middle of the other end of the square: when they have ran a few yards, each darts his pole anointed with bear's oil, with a proper force, as near as he can guess in proportion to the motion of the stone, that the end may lie close to the stone – when this is the case, the person counts two of the game, and, in proportion of the nearness of the poles to the mark, one is counted, unless by measuring, both are found to be at equal distance from the stone. In this manner, the players will keep running most part of the day, at half speed, under the violent heat of the sun' (1775, ed. 1968, p.401).

CHURCH AND MICE, an old Scot. game known and practiced in Fife County. Its course and objectives were identical to those of >SOW-IN-THE-KIRK.

TGESI, I, 69.

CHUTE, a Rus. ball game, in which the ball is batted into the field, similar to the Eng. family of games using a trap or spell, such as >TRAP, BAT AND BALL, >NORTHERN SPELL, etc. The game is usu. played by 2 teams of 2-5 players, but it may also be played by 2 single players. Two parallel lines are marked on the playing area at a distance of approx. 30 paces from one another. Between them, approx. 12 steps from the dike and 18 steps from the finish line, a simple ball launching device is constructed in the form of a wooden slat placed with one end on the ground, while the center is supported by a C-shaped beam. The player of the team that goes first hits the raised end of the slat with a bat, sending the ball (placed on the other end) into the air, after which he begins to run to the finish line and back to the dike line, where he picks up his bat and returns to the launcher. The players of the other team must pick up or catch the ball and carry it to the launcher before the batter gets there. If the batter is quicker, he scores a point, otherwise he is eliminated, the ball is placed on the launcher, and the opponents get their turn to bat. The batter loses his turn if the ball fails to reach the finish line or the bat is not thrown behind the dike line.

I.N. Chkhannikov, 'Chute', GIZ, 1953, 41-42.

CHWYTKA, an old Pol. term for any game in which a ball is caught with the hands. In his work *Games and pastimes of various social states* (1831), Ł. Gołębiowski informs the Pol. king Zygmunt III Waza played chwytka. The author enumerates the following varieties of the game: >EKSTRAMETA, >KASZA, >ŁAPA, >META, >PALANT, >PODBIJANKA, and >ŻYDEK. Chwytka is mentioned, among others, by the writer Klementyna z Tańskich Hoffmanowa in her description of Jan Kochanowski's childhood: 'The boys threw a chwytka up, and then caught it skillfully' (*Jan Kochanowski in Czarnolas. Pictures from the Turn of the 16th Century*, 1842, 186).

CIP, also *szewc* (Pol. for 'shoemaker'), *knyp* or *gnyp*, a Pol. game in which one is supposed to plunge a knife into the ground, throwing it from various positions, usu. squatting. The technique of the game consists of a series of knife 'shots' in various positions of the body, hand, and the knife, driving its blade into the ground without it falling over under its own weight. The game starts with the so-called 'turnover' – throwing a knife from an open palm with the knife's handle directed towards the thrower and the blade along his fingers. The knife is to be spun with a flick of the wrist so that it turns and lands with its blade in the ground. The second combination consists of identical movements but the starting position of the knife is not in the open palm but on the back of the hand, which is far more difficult as the blade cannot thus be grasped with the fingers. Then, there is a series of 'fingershots'. In each fingershot the knife's tip is placed on each fingertip with the other hand supporting the tip of the handle to maintain the knife in balance and then throw it with a 360° turn in the air and finally have it dive into the ground. Next figure is the 'hand' which starts with the knife's tip resting on the palm, and then on the back of the hand. Afterwards, the knife's tip is placed on the elbow, shoulder, chin, nose, and forehead. The last combination completing the round is the 'cabbage' – the blade is held between two knuckles of the index and middle fingers, clenched into a fist. The idea is to throw the knife hard enough from between clenched fingers so that it gathers enough momentum to drive the blade into the ground. If the knife is standing, the player takes it out holding it by the blade between the middle and ring fingers (also clenched), and so on – 4 times in total. Cip is played either 'on one hand' – the round includes all the aforementioned combinations played along one hand and arm; or 'on two hands' – the round including the same combination but along both hands. There are a number of var. of the game, e.g. the whole series along one hand and then along the other, or one combination along each hand alternatively – i.e. turnover from the left hand and then from the right, fingershots from the left hand and then from the right, etc.

History. The beginnings of the game are obscure. Probably it developed about 200-300 yrs. ago in Ger. towns where it became popular with boys and young men of the lower social strata, during the times when mass entertainment was not yet known. Emergence of clubs for young people, television, and much later, discos, led to the decline of many simple games, including cip which is not so popular any more.

CIRCUS ACROBATICS, different var. of >ACRO-BATICS employed in circus shows, incl. demonstrations of suppleness, exercises with gymnastic apparatus such as the trapeze and various suspended rings and bars, including the so-called *salto mortale* (i.e. the somersault of death) where a flying acrobat has to be caught by another acrobat, ropedancing, rope cycling, the 'Wall of Death' (performed on bicycles and motorcycles), etc. Circus acrobatics constitutes an important development path within acrobatics in general. Although circus acrobatics is a bodily exercise, it is not treated as a sport since it lacks the competitive element. Historically speaking, however, circus acrobatics has had a significant influence on modern >SPORTS ACROBATICS. By the same token, lots of elements borrowed from sports acrobatics – especially the scientific principles of training, fitness etc. – are employed at present in circuses. See also >ACROBATICS ON A POLE, >BICYCLE STUNT RIDING, >BAXI, >CASTELLS, >C'HOARI CHOUK-LAMM-PENN, >EQUESTRIAN ACRO-BATICS, >GLE GBEE, >KAO GLE, >KYSSE DØRKÆLLINGEN, >LAVE GRISE, >LIAN ACRO-BATICS, >MALLAKHAMB, >POTETEKE, >TUMI, LOS >VOLADEROS, >ZASHUA.

CIRIT, a Turk. horseback riding competition combined with a javelin throw. The riders gallop on horseback and throw short javelins at one another. The game's objective is to catch one's opponent's javelin while it is airborne. Cirit is particularly popular in E Turkey in the Konya Province.

CIUECA, see >CHUECA.

CIVIÈRE, LA, Fr. for 'stretcher' or 'wheelbarrow'. A Fr. name for a Bret. form of a folk competition >C'HRAVAZH.

CLEAN-AND-PRESS, a weightlifting event performed in a standing position, which was once part of the >OLYMPIC WEIGHTLIFTING TRIATHLON, discontinued in 1973. It is still practiced in a lying position as part of >POWERLIFTING.

CLIMBING, see >INDOOR CLIMBING, >MOUNTAIN CLIMBING.

CLIMBING MOUNTAINS OF SWORDS AND PLUNGING INTO SEAS OF FLAMES, a type of two-part competition held in the third lunar month by the Lisu people in the Chin. province of Yunnan, esp. in the area of Tenchgong and Yinkgijang. The event begins with jumps and other evolutions performed in the 'sea of flames' provided by some burning branches of a walnut tree scattered around a field. When the fire begins to die out, groups of daredevils run into the field of still glowing branches and compete in performing dangerous stunts like jumps, races, or rolling over the glowing branches. To avoid burns evolutions must be executed quickly, which makes the display very dynamic, similar to >JUMP-ING OVER FIRE. In the second stage competitors climb a 15-20m ladder, in which the rungs are replaced with swords, the number of which averages 36. Most of the swords are placed horizontally, with their edges pointed upwards, so that barefooted climbers must step on their edge. Several spokes, however, are made of 2 swords crossed at right angles. The climbing technique requires a compromise between speed, which carries the risk of injury, and precision. Climbers wear trad. red uniforms and immediately prior to the event drink a cup of wine. The competition is accompanied by fireworks and the sounding of drums. Conquering the 'mountain of swords' is celebrated by standing on one's hands on the topmost spoke.
Mu Fushan et al., 'Climbing Mountains of Swords and Plunging Into Seas of Flames', TRAMCHIN, 166.

CLOCK GOLF, a miniature version of >GOLF, in which only putters are used and the only method of striking the ball is putting. The course is a circle, 20-25ft. (approx. 6-7.5m) in diameter, with numbers 1-12 along its circumference as if on a clock dial, hence the name. Inside the circle, but not in the center, there is a hole whose distance from each number is different. The game consists of putting the ball into the hole from each numbered spot in turn. The scoring may follow the 'match play' system, i.e. on the basis of total points scored for each spot (there is only one putt for each spot, if the ball does not reach the hole no point is scored); or the 'medal play' system, i.e. the number of puts should be minimal, but if the hole is missed the ball is putted until it falls in.

CLODDY, a Brit. var. and regional name for >SKIT-TLES. The name prob. derives from the heavy and cigar-like shape of skittles used in the game. See also >CLOSH, >DUTCH BOWLS, >HALF-BALL.

CLOSH, an Eng. var. of Flem. and Du. >BEUGELEN, Ital. >U TRUCCU, >PALLA MAGLIO, Port. >JOGO DO ARCO. The name closh is of unknown etymology, its other meanings include various types of games in which a bowl is struck, usu. with a special rod with a flattened, spade-like ending or a hammer, towards a protruding object. In some parts of Eng. the same name is used with reference to >SKIT-TLES. In the 16th and 17th cent. the family of closh games was quite fashionable in W Eur., as can be seen in paintings of that age, e.g. P. Brueghl Older (1525-69). It is said closh was Erasmus Desiderius's favorite pastime.

CLOTHES HOLD (BELT HOLD) WRESTLING, popular throughout the world and esp. in Europe. The main distinguishing feature of this wrestling var. is that the competitors apply holds to various parts of their opponent's clothing, usu. trousers, sometimes jackets, shirts, ties, etc. The object of the game is invariably to floor one's opponent or raise him up in the air. The elements of clothing to which the holds were applied evolved over time, becoming better suited for the purposes of wrestling (e.g. they were reinforced, made stiffer or were equipped with special handles facilitating the grip). This is best exemplified in the case of the Icel. >GLÍMA where holds were initially applied to the upper part of a wrestler's trousers which was later turned into a type of harness made of leather straps. Apart from glima the most popular var. of wrestling with clothes pulling are the Icel. >SVIPTINGAR, Dan. >BUKSETAG, Swed. >BYXTAG, Aus. and Ger. >HOSENLUPF,

Aus. >JUPPENRINGEN and >KÄRNTENRINGEN, Aus. and Ger. >RANGELN, Swed. >KRAGTAG, Swiss >SCHWINGEN and >KRAGENRINGEN as well as Kor. >SSIRŮM.

CLOUT SHOOTING, a var. of archery in which a shooter aims much higher than usual so that an arrow arcs down into a special target made of a piece of cloth or a flag spread on the ground placed at a great distance from the archer. The distance is measured in scores of yards (sets of 20yds.): usu. 8-10 score yards (approx. 146-182m) for men and 6-8 score yards (110-146m) for women. Traditionally, the target used to be made of a relatively small piece of cloth ('clout' is an O.Eng. word for 'cloth') with a black spot in the center. Today, a flag with a circular target, 24ft. (7.32m) in diameter, drawn on it is used. The target is made of 5 concentric scoring circles of the following sizes: the 1st circle, referred to as the 'foot', is 18in. (0.457m) in diameter; the 2nd, 'half a bow' – 3ft. (0.914m); the 3rd, 'a bow' – 6ft. (1.829m); the 4th, 'a bow and a half' – 9ft. (2.743m); and the 5th, 'two bows' – 12ft. (3.658m). The greatest number of points (5) can be scored by hitting the smallest circle and the following circles score as follows: 4, 3, 2, and 1 respectively.

CLUB BALL, an old Eng. ball game in which a ball is struck with a straight stick, as opposed to games where a curved stick was used, such as O.Eng. >CAMMOCK, O.Fr. >JEU DE MAIL, O.Du. >HET KOLVEN, or Scot. >GOLF. Club ball and >TRAP, BAT AND BALL influenced the development of at least 2 Eng. games: >STOOL-BALL and >CRICKET. The earliest references and descriptions of the game date back to the mid 12th cent. Many a time it was forbidden, like other ball games, because it 'drew the strong and healthy men from practicing the commendable art of archery' that was believed to be of far greater service to town dwellers in the event of war. King Edward III's edict prohibiting ball games clearly singles out club ball. During the Tudor's reign it was very popular with urban inhabitants. Henry VIII was the first ruler to approve of the game, if played within the confines of a household yard and not in public – a condition that was seldom observed.

Circus acrobatics.

C

Etymology. The name club ball probably derives from middle Eng. *clubbe*. The term was apparently acquired by Eng. during its intense contacts with Scand. languages, which took place after the Viking invasion of England and during the existence of Danelaw – an independent Skand. territory – and finally during the reign of Canute the Great and his 2 sons (11th cent.) when Ang.-Dan. kingdom existed. Consequently the Eng. word *club* derives from O.Norse *klubba, klumba* which originally referred to sth. hard, compact, and then to a thick stick or a

and coachmen struggled for the title of the best. Simultaneously, an aristocratic genre developed in coaching, in which snobbish gentlemen from elite families competed as coachmen. Races were often accompanied by numerous and high-stake bets.

The history of coaching records starts with Sir J. Palmer who, in 1784, covered a distance of 107mi. (around 172km), from Bath in Somerset County to London, achieving an average speed of 7mph (11.3kmph). Until then, coaches were pulled by 3 horses; from 1784, four horses were used, as they

profile of a road, depending on the traffic that it was intended to carry. The earliest such roads were constructed by the Bristol Turnpike Trust financed by a toll charged on the London-Bristol turnpike (149mi., i.e. about 240km). The new, significantly better, standard of traveling set by the turnpike increased the traffic on it, which saved the Trust from impending bankruptcy. By 1823, McAdam standards had been adopted by 71 turnpike companies, whose roads totaled approx. 1,800mi. (2,900km). So rapid an expansion of comfortable roads incited further growth of coaching whose popularity peaked during the years 1825-38. The development of railroads that commenced around 1824, on the one hand reduced the number of regular stagecoach lines but on the other, encouraged coaching's growth as a sports discipline. The stagecoach races of old occurred with much less frequency; instead, coaching was dominated by aristocratic phaetons and landaus that raced for the honor of their stable, often merely to settle a bet between 2 gentlemen. In the 1860s, prince Beaufort organized famous races challenging various opponents on the Brighton-London rout, 53mi. (approx. 85km). The best result of the route was achieved by J. Selby in 1886, who covered the distance in 7hrs. 50min, changing an 8-horse set 14 times.

In 1807, the first coaching club, the Benson Driving Club, was established (it closed in 1853). In 1808, its major competitor, the Whip Club, appeared (it lasted only 30yrs.). The most influential, however, was the Four-in-Hand Club which operated from 1850 to 1926. Tandem driving – i.e. 2 horses harnessed one in front of the other, instead of one beside the other, pulling a cart – evolved into a separate sports discipline, whereas coaching disappeared the moment motor vehicles appeared on the roads, as the growing traffic impeded sports activities on public roads. The definitive finale of coaching began in 1896 with the repeal of a law according to which each motor car was supposed to be preceded by a servant carrying a red flag warning pedestrians about a dangerous vehicle, accompanied by the cancellation of a speed limit for motor cars, which up to that moment was 2mph (around 3km/h). Before, such limits had thwarted the automobile's competitive character and retained deference for horse-drawn carriages. The fact that the first motor car races, e.g. Brighton Car Rally, were organized on the traditional coaching London-Brighton route, acquired a certain symbolic meaning. Long-distance coaching transportation became even less attractive when the use of other means of mass transportation, such as railroads, buses, and then planes, became widespread. Therefore, coaching began its evolution towards a purely sporting discipline, where the technique of driving is graded and tracks are closed circuits, instead of intercity routes. In 1958, on the initiative of the Coaching Club, founded in 1870, the Brit. Driving Society was established which soon after played an important role in the popularization of coaching as a sports discipline on an international scale (cf. >CARRIAGE DRIVING).

T. Bradley, *The Old Coaching Days in Yorkshire*, 1889; T. Cross, *The Autobiography of a Stage Coachman*, vol. 1-3, 1861; H.E. Malet, *Annals of the Road or Notes of Mail and Stage Coaching*, 1876; S. Skoczylas, *O zaprzęganiu koni i powożeniu*, 1935; W. Wilson, *Coaching Past and Present*, 1885.

Coaching.

club. In his work titled *Sports and Pastimes of the People of England* (1810), J. Strutt suggested a different etym. of the name, deriving it from the Wel. *cwlpa* and Skand. *bol* – sth. round, a sphere, a ball. For etym. of *ball* see >BALL.

CLUBBY, Eng. folk game similar to >FIELD HOCK-EY. See also >DODDART.

CLUBS, one of the pieces of apparatus used in women's floor gymnastics; and the name of an individual floor gymnastic event in which the contenders perform exercises using a pair of clubs. A club is 40-50cm long and consists of a shaft and an oval head. In the past clubs were used as weapons of war in many cultures. Traditional war clubs are also used as sport apparatuses by some Chilean natives; see >LONCOQUILQUIL.

COACHING, driving carriages, mostly mail stagecoaches. The sports form of coaching began developing in England at the end of the 17th cent. and continued throughout the following century. Its popularity peaked toward the end of the 18th and the 1st half of the 19th cent. when the construction of coaches and the quality of roads were substantially improved. Coachers' emulation in the rapidity of public transportation augmented the dynamic development of Eng. sport at that time. As a result, individual coach lines embarked on a peculiar competition in covering given routes in the shortest possible time

were easier to manage and kept the rhythm better. In June 1807, as the first sports magazine – *The Sporting Magazine* – informs, a record on the London-Stamford route was established on the North Road where the distance of 90mi. (approx. 145km) was covered in 9hrs. 4min., i.e. at an average speed of 16kmph.

From the very beginning of their history, coaching races were associated with fatal accidents. As early as 1709, a parliamentary act imposed a fine of 5 pounds, a substantial sum at that time, on any coachman who caused a a carriage accident in which passengers were involved. In 1808, a drunken coachman attempting to break a record on the Portsmouth-London route, caused an accident in Putney as a result of which one of the passengers died. In July 1815, a coach going from Hinckley to Leicester killed as many as 5 fares. The *St. James Chronicle* launched a campaign to stop racing on regular passenger lines, as a result of which a law against 'wanton or furious driving' was passed in 1820. On some occasions accidents were caused by horses left unattended. Animals trained in racing sometimes started to compete with a passing coach when a driver was absent. Similar cases were so frequent that in 1806 a special law was issued according to which a fine could be imposed for leaving a coach and horses unattended.

In time, coaching races attracted increasing numbers of spectators. To better enable viewers, and then magazine readers, to tell one stagecoach easily from another the vehicles were given individual names. In 1808, a race between coaches named *Patriot* and *Defiance* going from Leicester to Nottingham was observed by thousands of spectators. The fierceness of the competition and emotions it stirred can well be imagined when one considers that *Patriot* finished only 2min. ahead of *Defiance* on a route of 26mi. (42km), which it covered in 2hrs. 10min. with 12 passengers on board and changing horses only once, in Loughborough.

A breakthrough was made in the year 1818 when extensive rebuilding of Eng. roads started with the use of macadamization. The term originates from the name of the initiator of the reform, Scot. engineer, J. Loudon McAdam (1756-1836). Macadamization of roads consisted mostly of hardening the pavement by means of any available materials, including broken stone, bricks, and crushed metal, mixed with clay and sand and then rolled. McAdam also introduced standards defining the width and

COARSING, a form of hunting game, generally regarded as one of >BLOOD SPORTS. A pair of hunting dogs are let off to track an animal and fetch it to the hunter. The most famous event has been held in Altcar near Fornby in England since 1836. It is known as Waterloo Cup, from the name of the local Waterloo Hotel, where the contestants are accomodated.

COBBIN-MATCH, a cruel Eng. school game [prob. *cobby* – resistant, hard, hard-headed + *match*]. Two participants seize a 3rd by the hands and legs and swinging, crash his body against a tree trunk. The winner is the party who endures the largest number of crashes.

TGESI, I, 71.

COCARDE, Fr. for 'a bow'. A name for one of the numerous Bret. var. of bowling games that were locally popular. Cf. >BOULOU-POK DE GUERLESQUIN.

COCHONNET, Fr. for 'a piglet'; also *jeu de cochonnet*. A bowling game from the >BOULES family,

Spectators watch a cock fight in San Juan, Puerto Rico.

whose tradition stems from the Middle Ages. The object is to pitch the bowls so they come to rest as close as possible to the smallest one, referred to as the cochonnet, and at the same time to push the opponents' bowls as far as possible from the piglet. Although today the cochonnet is a ball smaller than all the others, in the past it used to be a small metal figurine used in ancient Rome for telling the future. The figurine was a legacy left in France after the Roman conquest. In the course of time it was exchanged for a modern smaller ball.

W. Endrei and L. Zolnay, *Fun and Games in Old Europe*, 1986, 112.

COCK BOXING, a type of boxing practiced in China by the Dai people. It consists of copying the cock's movements – throwing one's arms like wings, rapid head movements, quick jumps to and fro, and so on. Naturally, the fight includes elements of dancing.
'Peacock Boxing', TRAMCHIN, 150.

COCK FIGHTING, 1) Span. *juego de gallos*, a type of animal competition, one of the oldest forms of entertainment, known in the countries of the Orient since ancient times. Around the 5th cent. it gained popularity in Mediterranean countries. Its introduction to Greece is attributed to an Athenian politician Themistocles. After the incorporation of Greece into the Roman Empire, it became a favourite pastime of Roman legionaries, e.g. in Roman Britain, where it was adopted by the Anglosaxons. Eng. king Henry the VIII raised its status to a royal sport. Eng. colonial expansion from the 16th cent. onwards spread the popularity of the sport to N.America and the Carribean region, and later also to Australia. At the same time the sport was made popular in S.America by the Spanish. By the end of the 17th cent. the interest in cock fighting diminished among the upper social classes, who considered it a barbarian sport, while its popularity grew among the lower classes. In 1697 the cock fighting pit at London's Whitehall was closed down. In 1849 cock fighting was banned altogether in Great Britain, followed by Canada and most Amer. states. Cock fights are still held, legally or half-legally, in the West Indies and Asia, in such countries as: Bali, China, the Philipines, Iran (with a tradition reaching back to Persian times) and Japan. In some regions cock fights are a remnant of funeral feasts, which were accompanied by various forms of games. In some countries, e.g. in Sumatra, they were held on the Circumcision Day, but – with the gradual disappearance of old religious beliefs and rituals – they began to accompany such commonplace events as local fairs. The cocks used in the bouts, similar to race horses, come from multi-generational breeding farms. The basic breeding history is thousands of years old, during which a special breed, different from the domestic breed, was formed. Cocks selected for fighting weigh 1.5-4 kg and are teamed in pairs of similar weight. The birds admitted to fight must be at least 1yr. old. They are specially trained to develop the desired groups of muscles. To harden their skin, so that it is less vulnerable to injuries, a special form of massage is used. The cocks also have their combs cut off, so that these may not be attacked. To compensate for varying spur sizes, the ones with smaller spurs have metal gaffs added, 4.5--7.5 cm long. When sharp edge spurs are used, only one (called a *slasher*) is put on. In some Asian countries, e.g. in India, gaffs and slashers are banned. The birds have a trainer called a *pitter* or *handler*. The fighting arena, called a pit, is a sandy rink with walls around it. The fight is conducted by a referee, whose decisions are final. A series of bouts which determines the winner is called a main.

A. Dundes, *The Cockfight. A Casebook*, 1994; J. Gajek, *The cock in traditional beliefs*, ATN, 1934; T. Pridge, *The Story of Modern Cock-fighting*, 1938; M.J. Sarabia Viejo, *El Juego de Gallos en Nueva España*, 1972.

2) a fight in which 2 players in a knee-bended position push each other. Both players, with sticks tied under their knees, try to force the opponent out of a circle 2.5-3m in diameter drawn on the deck. The game is often used as a school exercise and is one of a var. of >DECK GAMES.

COCK FIGHTS, a form of hand-to-hand combat practised among the people of Nagaland (India), esp. the Sema people. Competitors take positions and begin to execute kicks similar to >TAE-KWON-DO. It is allowed to target any part of the oppo-

nent's body except for the crotch. Use of the hands is banned. The fight continues until one of the rivals surrenders.

COCK SHOOTING, a sport known in the Middle Ages, in the old towns, practiced to perfect the defense skills of town inhabitants. The objective was to shoot at a target – a wooden or clay figurine of a cock or hen. The contest was won by the contestant who shot off the last piece of the figurine. According to a Pol. author, Ł. Gołębiowski, the 'target was a little hen or a little wooden cock; he who shot it last, was appointed the cock king for the entire year, given many prizes, exempted from customs duty when importing wine or any other merchandise, and he made use of his privilege. Apart from the above mentioned benefits, he also had some other small income adequate to his crown [...] in particular a fee from bowling games [...]. He, who shot last before the king, i.e. before the one who shot off the cock, was appointed court marshal and carried the marshal's truncheon, i.e. a mace, before him' (*Gry i zabawy różnych stanów*, 1831, 113).
In many countries other birds were the target; a parrot was particularly popular (Eng. >POPINJAY, Scot. >PAPINGO SHOOTING, Fr. >PAPEGAUT, LE). With time, however, a round target with a clearly marked bull's eye and 2-4 larger circles scoring fewer points became most popular in many countries. Initially, contestants used bows and hence the Latin name (*Fraternitates Sagitariourum*) of townsmen's associations which practiced this sport. In the 12th cent. the bow was replaced with the crossbow and in the middle of the 15th cent. – by firearms. The first shooting associations affiliated with merchant and craftsmen guilds were established in the Netherlands in the 11th cent. In Germany annual shooting competitions for the king's title were called >KÖNIGSSCHIEßEN. The first towns with similar organizations on Pol. soil were Świdnica (1253) and Poznań (1256). In Lvov, which was frequently besieged by the Tartars and Turks, there was a tradition of cannon shooting. Targets were replaced with figures representing the enemy: a horse rider in the Turk. dress, a vizier's tent etc.
The most deep-seated tradition of cock shooting is connected with Cracow. It was described by Ł. Gołębiowski in *Gry i zabawy różnych stanów* (1831):

When the religious sacrifice was made, the entire group, with music and drums, accompanied by the roar of cannons and mortars, went to the firing range. In the front there were roisterers dressed in Turkish, Persian and Tartars clothes, who shouted in different voices, jumped and sang. They were followed by the gilds, in order of seniority, and behind them there were shooters right in front of the king, on whose chest, on a

large silver chain there was a cock in a golden crown, which the king would give to his successor today. As soon as the roisterers, with the 'aimer', in the Turkish dress richly decorated with gold, silver and corals, approached the firing range, cannons and mortars were fired and a sort of 'interregnum' was announced. When the cock, having withstood thousands of shots, was finally killed, the cannons were fired for the third time and the trumpeter announced the name of the new king.

The old song of the roisterers, who participated in the event, has also been preserved:

Go to it, roisterers
strike sparks out of the harquebus
he who shoots the cock
He will hear a grateful note
And he who knocks the cock out
Vivat king! Long live!
[...]
Go to it, roisterers
learn to use the harquebus.
And when the time comes to scuffle with the Turk,
The dog will remember the cock
May God grant! ...these beasts
The cock king will kill.

The contest lasted several days. In Poland it was usually organized on St. John's day (24 June). Contests were also organized during harvest festivals. Cock brotherhoods, since the 19th cent. also called shooting societies, were in a sense the first sports clubs. Cock brethren built firing ranges, club

Cock shooting in Cracow, Poland.

A man urges his rooster on during a cock fighting tournament in Kabul, Afghanistan.

rooms, and later opened libraries which became centers of cultural and social activities. During partition times shooting societies opposed the oppressors and attempts were made to disband them. Shortly after the last partition of Poland in 1795 the patriotic activity of shooting societies was banned in the areas annexed by Russia and Austria. The last cock king before the fall of Poland in 1795 was S. Piątkowski. Shooting societies were given their rights back in Galicia after 1846, during the liberalized policy of Emperor Franz Josef. In areas annexed by Prussia shooting societies were never disbanded but since 1852 they were gradually Germanized. Many societies existing in the towns of Wielkopolska were completely Germanized. Reborn after 1918, they existed until 1939, maintaining and upholding the old traditions and the practical shooting skills, only to be disbanded once more after 1945 as 'bourgeois organizations', although the authorities permitted their symbolic, folkloric activity. In many towns the societies were revived after 1989.
Initially women did not take part in cock shooting. They were first permitted to take part in the contest in Śmigiel, and later in a few other towns, i.e. in Bytom, where for the first time in the history of cock societies a woman, B. Wiśniewska, won the title of cock queen in 1999.

J.M. Carter, *Medieval Games, Sports and Recreations in Feudal Society*, 1992; T.A. Jakubiak, *Kurkowe bractwa strzeleckie w Wielkopolsce*, 1986; H.-T. Michaelis, *Schuetzengiden*, 1985; R. Renson, 'The Flemish Archery Gilds: From Defense Mechanism to Sports Institutions', *The History, the Evolution and Diffusion of Sports and Games in Different Cultures*, ed. P.P. de Nayer, M. Ostyn and R. Renson, 1976, 135-159; T. Schnitzler, 'Quantification on Results in Late Medieval Crossbow and Rifle Shooting', IJHS, 10,2, 1993.

COCKLY-JOCK, a simple Eng. throwing game in which one builds a pile of stones and then throws other stones at it. Similar to *castles* and Pol. >SER.

COCK-STEDDING, an Eng. game mentioned in *Portsmouth Telegraph*, 27 Sept. 1873, as a very popular one in the city, but no description provided.

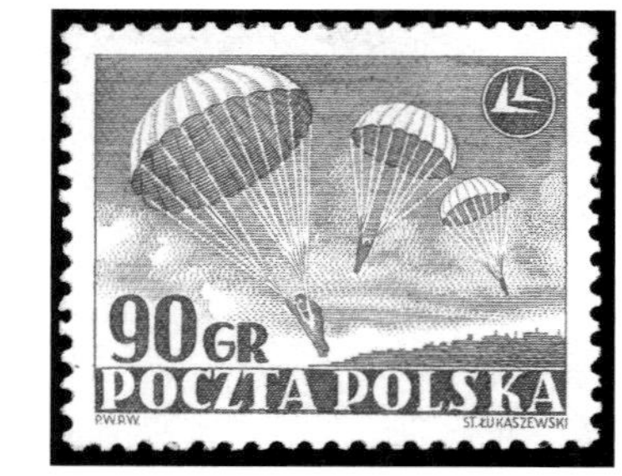

Competitive parachuting on a postage stamp.

COCK-STRIDE, an Eng. school game. A boy selected at random to play the cock stands blindfolded with his feet wide apart. Other participants throw their caps between the cock's legs as far as possible. The cock attempts to catch the caps and if he manages the owner of a cap has to run a distance of about 20yds. down a gauntlet of other players who punish him with slaps, usu. on the head. After being punished, he becomes the next blindfolded cock. See also >BLIND MAN'S BUFF.
TGESI, I, 73-74.

COCK-THROWING, a var. of Eng. folk competition in throwing sticks at a rooster tied to a pole. It accompanied the celebrations of Shrove Tuesday. Cf. >HEN-THRASHING. See also other forms of competitions that accompanied these celebrations, such as >SHROVE TUESDAY FOOTBALL.

In competitive parachuting the sky's the limit.
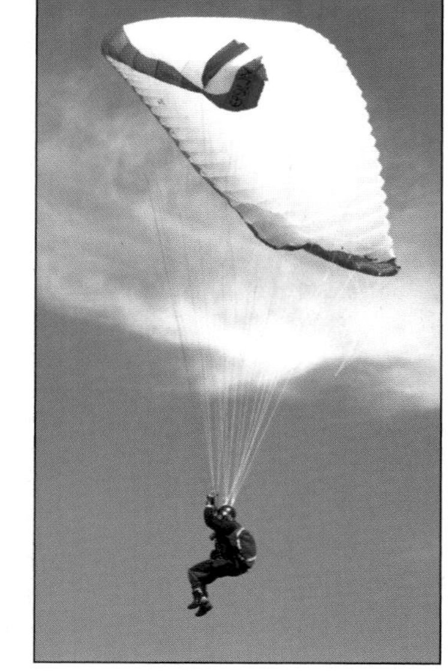

CODEBALL, two var. of ball games, developed in 1927 based on the idea of US sports activist and coach W.E. Code. In 1929 codeball was incorporated into the program of the US Amateur Athletic Union, gaining the status of an independent sports discipline. Both var. use a rubber ball of 15.24cm in diameter, which can be touched only with the legs and feet.
The first type, referred to as *codeball-in-the-court*, is played indoors on a court identical to a >HANDBALL court, between singles or doubles. The partners take turns to kick the ball against the wall, attempting not to let it touch the ground or allowing it to bounce once and prevent the opponent from doing the same. The game is continued until one team or player has scored 21pts.
The second type, known as *codeball-on-the-green*, is played in the open air. Its rules are similar to those employed in >GOLF. The course is a lawn with 14 holes whose openings are encased in metal (usu. aluminum) cones with their tops cut off, resembling little volcano craters. The cone has a base of 40-41in. (101.6-104.1cm) in diameter, and it is 7in. (17.78cm) tall with the crater's diameter of 18in. (45.72cm). The craters are located at a distance of about 50-300yds. (45.72-274.32m). The ball can be placed at the top of a crater only by kicking, without using the hands or any part of the body other than legs and feet. The winner is the player who manages to place the ball in all the craters in the fewest number of kicks.

CODLINGS, a simple game resembling >CRICKET, but instead of a ball it is played with a stick. It used to be popular with those social strata that could not afford a ball. Other similar games were known as >TIP-CAT, *tip and go* and *tip and slash*. In some respects they were close to the family of games referred to in different countries as >KLIPA, >AL BA' 'A, >GULLI DUNDA, *mouilh*, or >PILAOUET.
TGESI, I, 76.

COGS, a simple Eng. game in which stones are cast at other stones piled up in a heap. Cf. >COCKLY-JOCK or Pol. >SER.
TGESI, I, 77.

COITS, Cornish var. of >QUOITS, including one which is an equivalent of >HORSESHOE PITCHING.

COLLAR AND ELBOW WRESTLING, an Ir. var. of folk wrestling. Wrestlers fight holding each other by the collar with one hand and by the arm, close to the elbow, with the other. This form of wrestling is also known as *square hold wrestling* – after the 4 points of the body by which participants can grab the opponent during the match. The history of the discipline goes back to ancient Ireland – a similar technique was supposed to be employed by Cuchulain, the main character in the Ir. national epos *Tain Bó Cualinge*. However, in the epos, wrestling appears in the context of a competition whose objective is to rip the clothing off the opponent, which to some extent can also be related to collar and elbow wrestling.
In 632 BC, during an equivalent of the Ol.G. in ancient Ireland, the discipline formed a separate event, but no precise information as to its character has survived – early sources indicate here and there that the victory could be achieved in different ways during different periods and in different areas. One could win after knocking an opponent down on the ground or when the opponent touched the floor with two or three points of his body. Brought to the USA by Ir. immigrants, this type of wrestling became quite popular in the 18th and 19th cent. It is believed it was George Washington's favorite form of wrestling when he was young. At the end of the 19th cent. collar and elbow wrestling was replaced in the USA and Great Britain by >CATCH-AS-CATCH-CAN. The same name was used for Wel. wrestling practiced in special jackets, therefore sometimes referred to as jacket wrestling. It disappeared during WWII, replaced by >BACKHOLD.

COMMENIUS' BALL AND BOWL GAMES, varieties of ball and bowl games mentioned by Commenius after his stay in England in 1640-41. Information about them is included in *Orbis sensualium pictus* (*The World through the senses*) (1658) chapter CXXXIII *Ludus pilae* (ball games) and CXXXVI *Ludi peuriles* (boys' games). The book is a catalogue of things that a child learning about the world should know. Among these things Commenius mentions manifold games including bowl games, incl. a game in which a mysterious bowl is thrown upwards into a ring with a stick. 'Boys would play either at clay bowls (*globis fictilibus*), or at throwing a bowl towards pins (*jactantas globum at conos*), or at throwing a bowl upwards through a ring with a stick (*spherulam clava mittentes per annulum*).' Commenius, however, neglected to mention the name of the game of throwing a bowl to a ring. Since the name has not been recorded in Anglophone sources either, it is lost and we do not know what game he meant. A game similar to the one described by Commenius is mentioned by J. Strutt in his *Glig Gamena Angel Deoth, or the Sports and Pastimes of the People of England* (1810).
Commenius describes a bowl which had to pass through a ring mounted high up, while Strutt talks about a ring positioned on the ground. The fact that the ring may have been up but on a rod or jib posted on the ground may account for this seeming contradiction. Apart from the mysterious bowl game, in another chapter Commenius also mentions a game, which in a parallel Fr. text he describes as >JEU DE PAUME, and in Ger. simply as *das Ballspiel* (a ball game). In his account the ball is large and filled with air and is prob. an animal bladder, which runs contrary to the sizes and construction of the ball in *jeu de paume*. The ball is struck with the fist. So, either Commenius lacked a detailed description of *jeu de paume*, or he encountered a different game, which he mistakenly called *jeu de paume*. 'A ball is thrown by one and caught by another and then played back with a racket; it is a game of the nobility for the exercise of the body. A balloon, an enormous air-filled ball, is thrown into the air and hit forcefully with a racket with a flap.'

V. Olivova, *Jan Ámos Komenský (1592-1670) a pohybove hry, Teorie a Praxe Telesne Výchovy*, 1980, 28,9; Joh(annes) Amos Comenii, *Orbis sensualium pictus quadrilinguis hoc est omnium fundamentalium in mundo rerum et in vita actionum pictura et nomenclatura Latina, Polonica, Gallica, et Germanica editio nova... to jest Jana Amosza Kommeniusza świat malowany rzeczy widocznych pod zmysły podpadających w cztererch językach czyli wszelkich rzeczy na świecie i działań ludzkich wyobrażenie i wyjaśnienie po łacinie, po polsku, po francuzku i po niemiecku edycja nowa zupełnie przeyrzana i poprawna*, 1818, 'Ludus pilae – Granie w piłkę', p. 400-406; 'Ludi pueriles – Gry dziecinne', p. 408-410.

COMMON, also in various Eng. dial. *comun*, and Ir. *kamman* (perh. under the influence of Celtic >CAMÁNACHT and *camán*). One of the local var. of the game in which a ball is struck with a curved stick, similar to >SHINNY or >FIELD HOCKEY.
TGESI, I, 77.

COMOCKE, see >CAMMOCK.

COMPETING FOR A BRIDE, various events testing the ability to win a bride, popular in many cultures and assuming different forms depending on local tradition and conditions. A scholar in ludic culture J. Huizinga wrote in his book *Homo Ludens* (1938) that 'it is not a coincidence that competition performs a very significant role in selecting a bride or a groom. [...] It is not important whether such activities have been passed on in a legend or myth, or whether they can be traced in real life behaviour. What is of essence is that the concept of competing for a bride can be imagined.' I. Kabzińska-Stawarz believes that 'in the efforts to win a bride competition functions as a peculiar sacrament, which gives birth to a new social arrangement'.

J. Huizinga, *Homo Ludens*, 1938; I. Kabzińska-Stawarz, 'Competition in Liminal Situations. Comparative Study of Asian Cultures', ETHP, 1994, 18.

COMPETITIVE PARACHUTING, a discipline of aeroplane sports in which aeronauts compete in jumping from an airplane, a balloon or a special parachute tower using a parachute. A system of special openings in the canopy and its different shapes allow for relatively precise control of the parachute. Competitive parachuting comprises a number of competitions, recently on the increase, of which the most frequent include: precise landing jumps, jumps with delayed parachute opening, group jumps, flights on a board similar to a snowboard. Competitive parachuting is practiced individually and as a team sport, separately by women and men and, in group competitions, by both women and men. According to the data of the American Parachuting Association, one in 80,000 jumps is lethal.
History. The use of the parachute was first suggested in drawings and sketches by Leonardo da Vinci. However, the first practical parachute was invented in about 1605 by F. Verantius, who dropped animals equipped with a parachute. He explained the design of his structure in *Machinae novae* (New machines). The first man who used 2 specially designed large and reinforced umbrellas to jump from a 5m post was the Frenchman S. Lenormand (1783). The French aeronaut Jean Pierre Blanchard dropped a dog equipped with a parachute from a balloon in 1785, and in 1793 claimed to have made the first successful human parachute descent (although he broke his leg). A few months later his compatriot A.J. Garnerin made a similar jump, thus starting a period of regular parachute shows. In 1908 the American L. Stevens designed a folded parachute, manually opened during the fall. Until that time parachutes were attached to a frame and suspended under balloons. Once the folded parachute had been invented, it could be taken on board the plane and used as a lifesaving device. In 1912, in St. Louis, an American called Berry made the first jump from a plane (so far jumps had been made from balloons). Dur-

ing WWI parachutes were used for military purposes – from 1918 onwards German pilots used parachutes to save their lives when their planes were shot down. In 1919 L. Irvin designed a parachute which has not changed for decades: a mushroom-shaped canopy with shroud lines, to which belts fastened on the parachutist's body are fastened. During WWII, armies made extensive use of paratroops, or parachute troops, who were often flown behind the enemy lines in transport planes; they were usu. landed from low altitudes and their parachutes were arranged to open automatically, as the soldiers jumped, by means of long straps attached to the carrying plane. All these developments helped improve parachute design and jumping technique. Although the first parachute competitions were held in the USA as early as 1918, and the first international competitions were organized there in 1919, uniform rules were made in the USSR, where parachute competitions were organized to train military paratroopers. Competitive parachuting developed rapidly after 1945. In 1948 a Frenchman, L. Valentin, discovered the technique of slow and stable descent, which helped to control the flight of the parachute and contributed to the development of accuracy jumps. The first world championships were organized in 1951 in Yugoslavia; they have been held every two years since then. Competitive parachuting is governed by the International Aeronautic Federation (Fédération Aéronautique Internationale, FAI, established in 1905).

The routine character of competitive parachuting led to the development of more dangerous varieties such as >FREESTYLE PARACHUTING, SKY SURFING, >B.A.S.E. JUMPING.

COMPETITIVE ROWING, a form of competition between boats propelled by single-handed oars fastened in rowlocks and fulcrums protruding beyond the boat's sides. All crew members except for the coxswain sit inside the boat facing the stern. Regattas are held on courses 2km long for men, 1km for women, and shorter for junior categories. Olympic regattas are held in the following boat classes: for women – single scull (*skiff*), double scull (since 1996), double lightweight scull, quadruple scull, coxless pair, and eight; for men – single scull, double scull, double lightweight scull, quadruple scull (since 1996), coxless pair, coxless four, coxless lightweight four, and eight. The W.Ch. include 24 events: men – single scull, single lightweight scull, double scull, double lightweight scull, quadruple scull, quadruple lightweight scull, coxless pair, coxless lightweight

pair, coxed pair, coxless four, coxless lightweight four, coxed four, eight, and lighweight eight; women – single scull, single lightweight scull, double scull, double lightweight scull, quadruple scull, quadruple lightweight scull, coxless pair, coxless lightweight pair, coxless four, and eight. In the years 1900-88 the Olympic programme included a coxed four.

History. Although the Venetian regattas (>REGATA STORICA) were historically the earliest rowing event, it was the British who formed the basis for the development of modern competitive rowing, which owed much to the splendid system of rivers and canals inherited from the times of the Roman occupation of Britain (43-410). The use of rowing boats for transport in Britain has also been greatly influenced by the Vikings, who conquered much of Britain and established a political structure called Danelaw. At first five and later seven cities forming the skeleton of Danelaw – both harbours and inland cities – created probably the oldest modern federation of commercial cities in Europe. The communication between them occurred mostly along numerous waterways, which led to the development of rowing transport. The regulation of the river Thames during the reign of Henry VIII (1509-47) made river transport even more popular, and suddenly the number of transport boats and ships increased significantly. One of the drawbacks was the great number of accidents, which the king wanted to eliminate by issuing an edict requiring the transport companies to obtain a royal license. In Henry's lifetime the number of master's licenses reached 3,200, while the number of journeyman's licenses, allowing one to steer rowing boats and galleys, exceeded 5,000. License exams were accompanied by demonstrations of rowing skills, which directly resulted in the development of competitive rowing in Britain. In 1715 an Eng. actor T. Doggett established a prize for the crew winning the London-Chelsea rowing race, which was held for the new rowing licensees. The race has survived until today and is still financed by the interest earned on Doggett's contribution. The number of all kinds of rowing races held in Britain in the 2nd half of the 18th cent. kept growing, although for a long time they were participated in only by the lower classes. It was not until 1829 during a meeting between the students of Oxford and Cambridge that rowing competition was recognized as a sport 'becoming a gentleman'. Since that time the race between the crews representing both universities, each comprised of 8 oarsmen, has become an annual event held on the river Thames on the Saturday preceding Palm Sunday. Another famous rowing event is that of the Henley Regatta, which first took place in

1839. They are held in 7 categories, but the best known of them is the single race for the prize of a Diamond Oar, considered the most prestigious individual rowing trophy in the world. The first rowing club was founded in the USA (The Castle Garden Boat Club in New York). The first continental Eur. club was the Rowing Club established in Hamburg (1836) by the Germans and the representatives of Eng. trading companies residing in the city. In 1852 the first Yale-Harvard rowing race took place, modelled after the famous Oxford-Cambridge event. The first rowing regatta in Russia was held in 1858. In 1892 the International Federation of Rowing Associations (Féderation Internationale des Societés d'Aviron, FISA) was formed. Since 1893 E.Ch. in rowing have been held, transformed in 1973 into W.Ch. In 1900 rowing became an Olympic sport and – in different class configurations – has remained such until today. Until 1939 competitive rowing had been dominated by the British, Germans and Americans. After WWII this domination was gradually broken by the countries of the Soviet bloc, esp. USSR and East Germany. Beginning with the W.Ch. of 1975 and Ol.G. of 1976 competitive rowing was almost totally dominated by East Germany. During the 1976 Ol.G. East German crews won 9 of the 14 gold medals. With the boycott of the Ol.G. in 1980 by the Western countries, this domination became even greater: East Germany won 11 of the 14 gold medals. During the 1988 Ol.G. in Seoul (Korea) East Germany won 8 gold medals. Competitive rowing was also popular in West Germany, where the first Academy of Rowing was formed in 1968. After the unification of Germany the strength of the new German representation has not been proportional to the earlier potential of its two former republics. During the 1992 Ol.G. Germany won only 4 gold medals and during the 1996 games in Atlanta – only 2. Among the greatest individual athletes in history are: J.B. Kelly senior (USA, 1889-1960), 3-times Olympic champion in the single skull and the double skull (1920, 1924); his son J.B. Kelly junior (b. 1927), two-times winner of the Diamond Oar in Henley; J. Beresford (Great Britain, 1899-1977), Olympic champion in the single scull 1928, coxless four 1932, double scull 1936, and winner of various other trophys; V. Ivanov (Russia, b. 1938), 3-times Olympic champion in the single scull 1956, 1960, and 1964, and world champion in the single scull 1962; P. Karpinnen (Finland, b. 1953), Olympic champion in the single scull 1976, 1980, 1984, and world champion 1979, 1985; S. Redgrave (Great Britain, b. 1962), 5-times Olympic champion (coxed four 1984; coxless four 1988, 1992, 1996, 2000).

WORLD SPORTS ENCYCLOPEDIA

C

Thomas Eakins, Max Schmitt In A Single Skull, *oil on canvas, 1871.*

Thomas Eakins, John Beaglin In A Skull, *oil on canvas.*

Alfred Sisley, Rowing Regatta At Hampton Court, *oil on canvas, 1874.*

Competitive rowing: a double skull race.

WORLD SPORTS ENCYCLOPEDIA

A poster advertizing the Harvard-Yale rowing race.

A postage stamp issued for the 1970 European championship in competitive rowing in Hungary.

Rifle shooting.

Competitive rowing: women's coxless pair.

Women's competitive rowing developed more slowly. Rowing was for a long time considered as too difficult a sport for women. It became an Olympic event in 1976, while the first W.Ch. with the participation of women took place in 1974. One of the most outstanding modern athletes is B. Peter of East Germany, 4-times world champion (incl. skiff 1990) and 2-times Olympic champion in the double scull (1988) and the quadruple scull (1992).

W.J. Bingham, T.H. Hunter, T.D. Bolles, F.Britain, *Rep Top Reminiscences of Harvard Rowing*, 1948; E. Halladay, *Rowing in England. A Social History. The Amateur*

Debate, 1990; H. Hänel, *Rudern*, 1963.

COMPETITIVE SHOOTING, indoor and outdoor sport in which contestants fire small arms at stationary targets. The oldest type of shooting, going back to prehistoric times, is >ARCHERY. In the Middle Ages archery was improved when the bow and the bowstring were reinforced and a lever was used to pull back the bowstring, which led to the invention of the >CROSSBOW. The invention of gunpowder, initially used mainly in cannons, led to the development of firearms, which became the basis of different varieties of rifle and pistol shooting and, in some case, even cannon shooting, as for example the competitions organized in many towns of Europe in the 16th and 17th cent. to train artillery men in accurate shooting (e.g. in Lvov in present-day Ukraine). In Europe all forms of shooting, from the bow to firearms, were developed in towns by shooting brotherhoods (>COCK SHOOTING, KÖNIGSSCHIEßEN). In the 19th cent. the trad. types of shooting were expanded by target shooting, trap shooting and skeet (see below) and at the end of the 1980s shooting using paint bullets (>PAINTBALL); see also >SHOOTING FOR THE DISABLED.

There are a dozen or so varieties of competitive shooting, incl. official Olympic events. The rules of the most popular forms of Olympic shooting were changed many times and they can hardly be discussed here in detail. At the 2000 Ol.G. in Sydney 16 shooting events were held, 9 for men and 7 for women. They included: men – air pistol – 10m; air rifle – 10m; rapid fire pistol – 25m; rifle three positions – 50m; pistol – 50m; rifle, prone – 50m; running target – 10m; shotgun – double trap; shotgun – trap. Women competed in: air pistol – 10m; air rifle – 10m; rapid fire pistol – 25m; rifle three positions – 50m; shotgun – trap; shotgun – double trap; shotgun – skeet.

Shooting can be divided into *rifle shooting* (presently not incl. in the Ol.G.), *small bore rifle, pistol, rapid pistol* and *shotgun* (skeet, trap and double trap) and *air shooting*, which comprises *air pistol* and *air rifle*.

In **air shooting** bullets are accelerated by compressed air, the targets are 10m from the shooters; both women and men compete in rifle and pistol.

AIR PISTOL was introduced at the 1988 Ol.G. in

Seoul. In the Olympic events women fire 40 shots within 75min. and men 60 shots during 45min.
AIR RIFLE was introduced at the 1984 Ol.G. Women fire 40 shots within 75min., men 60 shots within 105min. In the final round both women and men fire 10 shots within 75sec.

In **bullet weapons** Olympic shooting is divided into *small bore rifle* and *pistol*. In pistol shooting the targets are usually 25m from the shooters and in small bore rifle – 50m.

PISTOL (men) – in the first round the shooters take 60 shots which they must fire within 2hrs. In the final round they take 10 shots; each must be fired within 75sec.; the event was introduced into the Olympic program in 1896.

RAPID PISTOL (women) – in the first round competitors take 30 shots within 6min., 5 shots in each series. In the second round women take 30 shots, having 3sec. per shot. Men take 60 shots to revolving targets, which appear for 4-8sec. The finals consist of 2 series of 5 shots, which must be fired within 4sec. to each target.

Competitive rowing: a Harvard-Yale race.

Running target shooting gold medallist from the 2000 Sydney Olympic Games, Yang Ling (China).

RUNNING TARGET is one of the first events of Olympic shooting; removed from the Olympic program for 70 years, reintroduced in 1972. Only men compete. Targets are 10m from the shooting positions (formerly 50m). Competitors first fire 30 shots at a suspended target (they have only 5sec. to fire each shot) and in the second series they fire 30 shots, having only 2.5sec. per shot. In the finals 10 shots are fired, five to each of the 2 targets, within 2.5sec. per shot.

SMALL BORE RIFLE where competitors shoot from three positions: standing, lying and kneeling. Women take 20 shots in each position and men 40 shots to a target 50m away. Competitors take 60 shots in the standing position within 90min.

SMALL BORE RIFLE PRONE – shooting at a target 50m away, called the English Match; the name was coined at the 1908 Ol.G. in London, where the event was held for the first time).

Shotgun is a type of hunting and competitive shooting in which shot is used instead of bullets; there are two varieties – skeet and trap, and double trap.

SKEET – an early form of skeet was invented about 1915 by a group of Massachusetts hunting enthusiasts. To increase the variety of shooting angles possible in trap-shooting, the Massachusetts group began to fire at the clay targets from a series of 12 stations arranged in a circle 25yds. (22.86m) in diameter; the new sport was first known as round-the-clock shooting. About 1920 the shooting circle

became a semicircle, and a second trap was added to provide additional firing angles. The sport grew rapidly, and in 1926 a national magazine offered a prize for a suitable name. The winning name was skeet, an old Scandinavian word meaning 'shoot' (Nor. *skjotte* or *skyte*, or Swed. *skjuta*) and the prize went to G. Herburt, an American of Scand. origin who won the first skeet competitions organized by the 'National Sportsman' in 1910.

Skeet offers a greater var. of shooting angles than trap-shooting. In skeet, 2 traps, located 40yds. (36.58m) apart, release the clay targets alternately or simultaneously along fixed, intersecting flight paths. The traps are housed in brick or cement-block structures, which are connected by a semicircular footpath. A firing station is located next to each house, 5 others are located at regular intervals along the path, and an eighth station is at the center of the semicircle. During one round, which consists of 25 shots, a contestant fires from each station at 2 targets released consecutively by different traps, from 4 stations at 2 targets released simultaneously by the traps, and at a single target from a station determined according to certain rules.

Most skeet competitions are decided on the basis of total hits scored on 100 or more targets; champions often score 100 hits out of as many tries. Skeet tournaments are divided into classes based on the shooters' averages. The standard skeet events are 12-, 20-, and 28-gauge; .410-bore and doubles contests. W.Ch. matches are held yearly. Skeet shooting has been an Olympic event since 1968, and men and women compete on equal terms.

TRAP – was developed in England late in the 18th cent. The first targets were live pigeons, which were released from under old hats, and later from cages known as traps. The sport was first practiced in the United States early in the 19th cent. and was popular by midcentury in a number of areas, notably Cincinnati, Ohio, and around New York. In subsequent decades the scarcity of live pigeons prompted American trap-shooting enthusiasts to create ingenious artificial targets. Among the substitute targets first tried were glass balls filled with feathers and solid iron pigeons mounted on long metal rods. Platter-shaped clay pigeons were developed about 1880. The subsequent introduction of standardized traps facilitated nationwide competition.

Trap-Shooting competition takes 3 forms, namely, singles, handicap, and double-target shooting. In all three the targets are hurled from a single trap, and 12-gauge shotguns are used. In singles shooting, contestants fire from a series of 5 stations located 16yds. (14.63m) behind the trap. At a signal from the contestant, the clay target is hurled forwards into the air, away from the firing line. In order to simulate the unpredictable flight patterns of birds taking wing, the targets are sprung out of the trap at various angles and in various directions. The clay pigeons rise to a min. height of about 10ft. (3m) and, unless hit, fall to the ground about 150ft. (45m) from the trap. Champions often hit as many as 99 out of 100 targets.

Women's rifle shooting Olympic gold medallist at Sydney, Renata Mauer (Poland).

WORLD SPORTS ENCYCLOPEDIA

C

In HANDICAP TRAP-SHOOTING, contestants possessing superior records must shoot from stations located 17 to 27yds. (15.54 to 24.68m) behind the trap. The added distance, or handicap, enables trap-shooters of only average ability to compete on equal terms with experts. In double-target shooting, the trap springs two clay pigeons into the air simultaneously in different directions. Good trap-shooters are able to shatter both targets in mid flight.

Trap-shooting has been an Olympic event since 1900, and is competed in on equal terms by both men and women. There are 200 clay pigeons to shoot and the best trap-shooters will shoot more than 190. The Olympic program included other shooting events, using different military rifles and pistols, at various metric and yard distances (from 20m and 25yds. to 800m and 1,000yds.), at deer and boar; some events were divided based on the number of shots fired (single and double); shots were taken at live pigeons etc. In 1900 33 shooting events were held, at the 1936 Ol.G. only 2 events and at the 1928--32 Ol.G. no events were held. The program of the International Shooting Federation at E.Ch. and W.Ch. includes also standard pistol shooting, competitive pistol shooting and pistol with central ignition. Competitive shooting events are organized for the police, military, anti-terrorist groups, but the sport is also practiced in secret terrorist camps. A form of developing competitive shooting is practical shooting, where a competitor shoots at unknown places or targets, or reacts to them as if in danger.

History. The genesis of small arms is not known. Probably competitive shooting evolved as follows: around the 2nd-3rd cent. – black gunpowder was invented in ancient China; around the 10th cent. – gunpowder was used in China to launch fireworks; around 1300-1320 – the first cannons (a var. of firearms) were made in Europe; around 1381 – during the one hundred years' war the first specimens of personal firearms were made, in France called *bastons-à-feu* and *fire sticks* in England. In the first quarter of the 14th cent., the firelock was developed, a simple, smooth-bore tube of iron, closed at the breech end except for an opening called a touchhole, and set into a rounded piece of wood for holding under the arm. The tube was loaded with shot and powder and then fired by inserting a heated wire into the touchhole. Later models had a saucerlike depression, called a flashpan, in the barrel at the outer end of the touchhole; a small charge of powder was placed in the flashpan and fired by applying a so-called slow match. The slow match, consisting of a piece of cord soaked in a solution of potassium nitrate and then dried, smouldered without flaming or becoming extinguished. The charge of powder in the flashpan was difficult to ignite, was frequently affected by moisture in the atmosphere, and required repriming just before use to ensure against misfires. About the middle of the 15th cent. a type of musket called the matchlock was introduced. This weapon was essentially the same as the firelock, except that the slow match was clamped in the top of a device called a serpentine, an S-shaped piece of metal pivoted on the center. Pulling with one finger on the bottom of the serpentine, as on a trigger, moved the top with the attached slow match into the priming pan, which contained the firing charge of gunpowder. Because only one finger

was needed to fire the weapon, the matchlock left both hands free to hold and aim the firearm. A refinement in the shape of its stock to permit firing from the shoulder produced the harquebus.

An improvement in the firing mechanism of small arms, called the wheel lock, was invented around 1515. It consisted of a spring-driven wheel, which, when released by a trigger mechanism, rotated a hardened steel rim against a lump of iron pyrites, throwing a shower of sparks into the powder in the priming pan and thus firing the weapon. At approx. the same time as the wheel lock, gunsmiths introduced rifled barrels. About 1540 the first pistol was made by an Ital. gunsmith, C. Vitelli; the name *pistol* probably comes from the town of Pistoia, where the gunsmith lived and worked. The wheel lock was too complicated and expensive for general acceptance; early in the 17th cent., the snaphance was invented. This type of firing mechanism consisted of a hammer powered by a trigger spring and bearing a piece of flint; when the trigger was pulled, the hammer struck the flint against a serrated steel striker plate located above the priming pan and thus produced a shower of sparks.

The final development of the flint-ignition firearm was the flintlock (about 1600). It resembled the snaphance, except that the striker plate was L-shaped; the bottom limb of the 'L' was used as a cover for the priming pan, to protect the powder from moisture until the upper limb was struck by the flint of the hammer. This action produced a shower of sparks when the powder in the pan was uncovered. The flintlock was the prevailing type of small-arms weapon for both shoulder guns and handguns from the end of the 17th cent. to the middle of the 19th cent. Smoothbore flintlock muskets were the primary military weapon for infantry in the armies of the principal Eur. powers. In 1807 the Scot. clergyman and inventor A.J. Forsyth invented the percussion-ignition system, making possible the development of successful breech-loading firearms, that is, firearms loaded through the rear of the barrel rather than through the muzzle. In 1814 the Englishman J. Show designed the first bullet with a cartridge firing the missile when struck with a little hammer and later with a firing pin. In 1818 an Englishman called Eggs invented a primer with fulminating mercury and in 1827 a German, J.N. Dreyse, invented a breech-loading rifle. Many early 19th-cent. breech-loaders used a cartridge containing only powder and ball; the weapon was usually equipped with a nipple holding a percussion cap that was fired by the impact of the hammer, or striker, when released by the trigger. In the 1850s self-contained center-fire cartridges came into use. Their design, with one-piece case, is essentially identical to modern center-fire types. In 1836, the Amer. manufacturer S. Colt patented the so-called Colt revolver, which had a single barrel and a small, revolving cylinder with 6 chambers; a similar revolver was developed at about the same time by the Amer. gunsmith E. Wesson, but Colt won patent rights to the new pistol. The Colt revolver was loaded with a percussion cap, powder, and balls. The cylinder of the Colt was automatically turned when the hammer was drawn back for cocking, and the gun was then fired by pulling the trigger. In the 1850s the bullet replaced the percussion cap, powder, and ball, and in 1873 the so-called double-ac-

tion revolver was developed, making it possible to turn the cylinder, cock the hammer, and fire the gun with a single pull on the trigger. In 1866 an American, O.F. Winchester, built the first semi-automatic rifle. In the development of the small arms most important were the designs of an American, J.M. Browning, the inventor of a small revolver named after Browning, and the inventions of Germans P.O. and W. Mauser, inventors of firing pin small arms (1863) and magazines for automatic weapons.

In the 15th and 16th cent. members of shooting brotherhoods in England replaced bows and crossbows with fire arms. In the 17th cent. competitions of cock brotherhoods were held in different small arms categories, but also in cannons, mortars and falconets (>COCK SHOOTING, >FREISCHIEßEN, >KÖNIGSSCHIEßEN; cf. also >PARROT SHOOTING). The first shooting organization using small arms in sports competitions was the St. Sebastian Society in Cologne, Germany (1463). The target was known before small arms were invented, but the oldest targets in competitive shooting included wooden figures, most often resembling cocks. The first real targets were introduced at the beginning of the 19th cent. A quick development of this technique was observed esp. in the Ger. shooting societies after their reform in 1852. In 1861 the Allgemaine Deutsche Schützenbund was founded; it preferred bullet shooting as an element of military preparation.

In 1832 the High Hats hunting club was established in England. Its members shot at live pigeons released from under special high hats at a signal (>PIGEON SHOOTING). Due to criticism club members replaced the pigeons with a special device, the so-called trap. This gave rise to trap-shooting – glass balls filled with feathers were replaced with ceramic discs. In 1860 the trap was used to catapult clay pigeons – brittle platters made from a mixture of limestone and pitch; around 1865 these were in turn replaced with red balloons. A trap and discs made of a mixture of silt and tar (about 1880) was invented by McCaskey from Britain. An improved trap was patented in 1883 by C.J. Barrett and J.E.B. Bloom, which accelerated the development of trap shooting. In 1910 a form of trap shooting called *round the clock shooting* developed in the USA. The shooter stood between the catapults and turned clockwise during shooting, like the clock between 12.00 and 6.00 pm.; this event was eventually called skeet.

Modern forms of competitive shooting originated in Great Britain. The rapid development of >HUNTING in the 18th cent. led to the devastation of birds and game; hunting societies reintroduced the old charters and created new ones to protect fauna. Simulated hunting was organized; around 1830 hunters started to shoot at models imitating animals (roe deer, boar etc.) and also at birds specially bred for hunting purposes, particularly pigeons. The activity of the High Hats Club and the invention of disks and trap led to the development of trap shooting. Bullet shooting, developed by cock brotherhoods, quickly became very popular, esp. in Germany, as part of the military reorganization of the townspeople shooting societies in 1853, and later when the Allgemeine Deutscher Schützenbund was established.

Competitive shooting is also a form of military training, in which the moral contradiction of this

Olympic rapid fire pistol shooting.

Competitive shooting on a postage stamp issued for the 1988 Olympic Games in Seoul.

C

**WORLD SPORTS
ENCYCLOPEDIA**

sport was revealed, which, despite the bloodless forms of the competitions, aim at improving the art of killing. Similar trends can also be observed in other sports disciplines which derive from warfare, but their actual relationship with killing is weakened as they are no longer used in combat (archery, javelin throw, fencing). Shooting continues to be a military skill, which is a clear contradiction with the aims of sport, and particularly with the message of peace advocated by the Olympic idea. The presence of competitive shooting at the Ol.G. (1896) was a tactical move by P. de Coubertin; the then presidia and boards of national sports unions and international sports federations were dominated by military circles. In the following years attempts were made to eliminate competitive shooting from the Olympic program; it was not featured in the Olympic games in 1904 and 1928. Today, in the opinion of many advocates of the pacifistic role of the Ol.G., competitions involving the use of lethal weapons should not be part of the program, except perhaps of air guns. The first W.Ch. in sports shooting were held in 1897; the International Shooting Union (Union International de Tir, UIT) was estab. in 1907. Until 1939 the best competitors came from France, Germany, Sweden, the USA, Canada, Hungary, Italy and Great Britain, and in individual events, Poland. After WWII the group of countries competing for champion titles was expanded by Bulgaria, the USSR (after 1989 the Community of Independent States, and then Russia), Japan, China, Yugoslavia and South Korea. After 1990 many competitors, who earlier represented the USSR or the CIS, started to represent the new states, such as Kazakhstan (S. Beliaev, who won 2 silver medals at the 1996 Ol.G.) and W. Wokhmianin – bronze medal winner at the same Olympic games. Russians continued to win championships titles and medals, particularly in free pistol (B. Kokoriev, Olympic champion in 1996) and air pistol (A. Kadzibekov, Olympic champion in air rifle; M. Logvinienko – double gold medal winner in 1992 in sporting and air pistol, and silver medallist in 1996 in air pistol, and O. Kluczniewa, Olympic champion in air pistol). Some good competitors came from China (e.g. Ling Yang, Olympic champion in 1992, 1996 in shooting at a moving target, and Jun Xiao, who won the silver medal in the same event). Among the Koreans Olympic golds were won by En Chul Lee in the Eng. match and Kab Soon Yeo in air rifle. At the 1996 Ol.G. gold medals in trap shooting were won by the Australians M. Russel (double trap) and M. Diamond (trap) and D. Huddleston, also from Australia, won the bronze medal in double trap. The greatest individualities in the history of competitive shooting include O. and A. Swahn, father and son, who won a total of 15 Olympic medals, 6 gold. Oscar won the silver medal at the age of 73 in Antwerp in 1920 in shooting at a running deer.

J.A. Alieksandrovic, *Sportiwnaja strielba iz wintowki*, 1957; T. Burnand, *Chasse á tir*, 1963; P. Dubonnet, *Le tir de chasse*, 1958; *Handbuch für das Sportschiessen*, 1955; S. Mazur, *Strzelectwo sportowe*, 1988; G. Montagu, *Sportsman's Directory or Tractate on Gunpowder with Some Remarks on Fire Arms*, 1792; J. Ruffer, *The Big Shots. Edwardian Shooting Parties*, 1989.

CORACLES, [Wel. co*rwgl, corwg*, O.Wel. *corwc* – boat]; a regional var. of >ROWING practiced by Celts on the Brit. Isles since antiquity. In the Ir. and Scot.-Gaelic tradition a similar type of boat is called *curach*, in the local dialect in Uist in the Outer Hebrides, off the Scot. shore – *crannghal*. In the Gaelic languages of Scotland and Ireland *crannghal* means 'boat ribbing' which is covered with hide. Coracles is practiced on bowless, flat-bottomed boats of the same name. A wooden or wicker frame is covered with hide or large bark flakes, and is usu. about 8.5m long and 5.5m wide. The boat is propelled with single oars without locks. The oldest description of a boat of this type is to be found in a Gk. *periplus* (i.e. a voyage description) stemming from mid 6th cent. BC, which was partly preserved in its Lat. translation in a much later work of a Roman poet Rufus Festus Avenus entitled *Ora maritima* (*Voyage Along the Shore*). Avenus describes boats called *corioque* used for communication between Cornwall and the island of Ushant (Uxantis in ancient times): 'They cover their keels with neither pine nor fir, as is usual, but – surpris-

ingly – build their ships of sewn hides, and in this hide-ship they traverse the high seas'. Boats of this type, owing to their lightness and flat bottom were used for transit on inland reservoirs and marshland. Despite the seemingly fragile construction they served for sea voyages between the Brit. Isles and the Eur. continent. 'They may seem a very dangerous vehicle to the modern people, wrote a Scot. Folklorist E. Dwelly, but our forefathers trusted their lives to this craft, to carry them through the most adverse weather conditions'.

CORAIOCHT, Ir. folk wrestling similar to other Gaelic forms of wrestling, esp. to Scot.-Gaelic ones that were practiced on Outer Hebrides >CARACHD UIB-HIST and >CARACHD BHARRAIDH in the vicinity of Connemara, Galway and Donegal. A characteristic feature is the referee's command starting the fight and obliging the opponents to hold each other in a proper position: 'One hand above, the other below!' In the early days, it was wrestlers themselves who decided which one of them would hold his arms above those of the other. Nowadays there are specific rules defining it: the right arm of each wrestler is always below the left one. A trad. form of coraiocht was nearly completely forgotten at the beginning of the 20th cent. Currently the *Cumman Coraiocht Cheilteah h'Eirnann* is vigorously popularizing the discipline as an element of Ir. heritage.

CORNHUSKING, a form of competition in which the contestants try to husk the most ears of corn before loading husked cobs into a wagon, 62-66in. in height, with a 4th bang board above the bed. Contestants are grouped into classes depending on their age and the time limit.
History. Cornhusking was one of the first steps involved in preparing corn meal. Pioneer families used the ground meal to make mush and various kinds of corn bread. Corn was a basic food of the pioneers, and they ate it in some form at almost every meal. Although today the process is automated, farmers have competed in manual cornhusking for sporting purposes since 1980, when the National Rules Committee established the rules of the competition in Omaha, Nebraska. Nebraska's nickname is the Cornhusker state. The first National event took place that same year at Oakley, Kansas.

CORNISH HURLING, a game stemming from the same tradition as the Irish national game of >HURLING, but retaining some distinct characteristics. Old, locally preserved forms of hurling are played in St. Ives on the western tip of Cornwall, the old mining settlement of St. Agnes on the northern coast and St. Columb Major in central Cornwall.
R. Carew described two Cornish variants of the game in his 1602 *Survey of Cornwall*. The first variant, known as 'hurling to country', seems to be the older one, and is still practiced in the above-mentioned towns. The name derives from the objective of the game, which started in the town's square and continued to a designated point outside the town, 'in the country'. Each team may have had a different goal, e.g. a tree, that they had to reach with the ball (there were no regular goals as we

know them today). A 'return match' was usually played in the opposite direction a few days later. At St. Columb Major, one of the teams consisted of townspeople, while the other – of people of the same parish but living in the country. In that variant, two teams participated. The number of players in each team was not defined, and could even be different. The ball was about 10cm in diameter, made of apple wood and coated with silver, so hard that all the shutters in town were closed and all shop windows boarded up. Outside the town limits, the game was made more interesting by the changing landscape, with both teams using their knowledge of the terrain. Hurling to country was mainly played by farmers and farm workers, never by gentlemen.
The second variety mentioned by Carew was known as 'hurling to goal'. It is no longer played due to its complexity. Two, relatively small, teams, played on a pitch. The number of players and pitch dimensions were not pre-defined, and depended on local conditions, e.g. the size of a field just outside the town. The objective was to reach the goal line but the ball could only be passed backwards. The most interesting element was that, in the case of a conflict between players, the game was stopped and the players involved fought a wrestling match. After the game was resumed, the ball was awarded to the team whose player had won the fight. Matches were most often played after weddings. Hurling to goal was played by more affluent townspeople and farmers. With the 'refinement' of pastimes during the industrialization era, the game became anachronous, and declined.
R. Holmes, 'The Survival and Revival of Traditional Sports and Games in Cornwall', LJP, 1998, 139-140.

CORNISH LUGGERS' REGATTAS, regattas that have been organized in Cornwall for at least 200 years. Cornish fishermen race on sailing boats normally used to fish mackerel, oysters or prawns. Typical boats are 7-10m long single-mast boats with a lugsail (trapeze-shaped sail) and a staysail hoisted on a yard protruding from the bow. In 1912, motor boats were introduced, but the motor event has never achieved prestige comparable to that of the sailing event. In the past, the regattas were mainly used to improve the sailing and fishing skills at times free from actual fishing. In the more recent years, the purely sporting element has begun to prevail, even though sailing boat fishing has retained some importance. The regattas are supervised by the Cornish Lugger Association and the Falmouth Working Boat Association. Among other things, the associations maintain boats that have been decommissioned but are in working condition, so that they can be used for racing. One of the factors that has aided the growth of purely sporting regattas has been bonhamia, an oyster disease which has caused oyster fishing to be given up in certain waters. Specific sailing techniques have developed in Cornish luggers' regattas, e.g. moveable ballast, which makes it possible to position the boat more flexibly in relation to the wind. Cf. >SKÜTSJESILEN.

A convoy of cornhuskers.

Dancing with death – corrida.

CORNWALL AND DEVON, a trad. wrestling style popular with Celtic descendants in Cornwall and Devon Counties. A wrestling historian, W. Baxter, wrote that the Devon style was indistinguishable from Cornish wrestling except for a ruthless practice of putting on shoes, sometimes reinforced with a metal fitting, to kick the opponent in the shanks. About 1880, two styles were officially combined into a single one, since referred to as *Cornish wrestling*, also *Cornish style*, or more adequately but less frequently *cornwall and devon*. Nevertheless, up to the beginning of the 1960s in some regions of Devon, the local style had its own competitions, separate from the Cornish style. The match is fought in a standing position, wrestlers wearing special jackets that allow them to grab each other by the lapels. The wrestler who touches the floor with two shoulder blades and one hip, or two hips and one shoulder blade at the same time, loses.

History. The tradition of Cornish wrestling goes back to the Middle Ages. In the battle of Agincourt in 1415, the Cornish soldiers held a flag with an embroidered picture of 2 wrestlers in a trad. hold, known in Cornwall as a 'hitch'. When meeting with the Fr. king Francis I in Calais, Henry VII took some Cornish wrestlers with him to have them fight with Fr. wrestlers. Some historians derive Cornwall and Devon from Eng. wrestling in which opponents grabbed a special girdle instead of a jacket. R. Carew wrote about it in his *Survey of Cornwall* in 1602. Up to the middle of the 18th cent. Cornish wrestlers enjoyed great social prestige in their country. New customs, esp. those established in the 2nd half of the 18th cent., substantially reduced the status of trad. wrestling in that region. Yet, Cornwall and Devon survived through the difficult 19th cent. in miners' towns where it was still very popular. While the Cornish mines were running out of tin, emigrants were spreading the idea of the discipline throughout the entire Brit. Empire. Around 1870, the final exhaustion of tin resources in the area, led to the largest unemployment in the history of Cornwall and mass migrations of young people, and consequently another crisis in the history of Cornish wrestling. After WWI, the Cornish Wrestling Association was founded in order to modernize the rules. Timed rounds and scoring were introduced. Some wrestlers and activists from the old school did not accept the modifications and they established their own association. Only after WWII did the two factions join as one in the face of the invasion of new sports, which was gradually impairing the public interest in old types of wrestling. Cornwall and Devon continues to develop in a number of communities as a part of their efforts to preserve cultural and ethnic traditions, the leader being the Celtic part of Brittany in today's France. There is a number of local tournaments and competitions. Cornwall is a member of the *Fédération Internationale des Luttes Celtiques*.

CORRIDA, bullfighting which ends in the death of the bull, nowadays confined to Spain, Portugal, SW France, Mexico, Ecuador, Columbia, Peru and Venezuela. Even though it is best known in the Iberian tradition, an independent tradition of bullfighting has been in existence in Nepal since 1940, where bloody bullfights have been conducted to honor the goddess Kumari.

Etymology. The full Span. name of the corrida is *corrida de toros*. – fighting the bulls [*corrida* – running, race, competition *toro* – bull], also *juego de toros* (contest against the bulls).

Architecture of arena. The central part of the building, *plaza de toros*, is a round arena proper. Its *medios*, or the middle, is the field of combat. The arena, usu. 45-50m in diameter, is surrounded by a wooden platform, about 1.2m high. All larger Span. towns have several arenas, many smaller ones also have one, if less spacious. The largest arena, however, is to be found not in Spain but in the capital of Mexico (*Plaza México*).

Calling a corrida. A corrida is traditionally advertised on posters (*carteles*), even though the local press, and for some years also electronic media, are also involved. Seats in the shade (*sombra*) are more expensive than those over which shade passes gradually (*sol y sombre*), and seats that are in full sunshine all the time (*sol*) are even cheaper. Seats located furthest from the arena, the upper rows of the gallery (*andanada sol*) are the cheapest. The most prestigious are boxes not far from the local dignitary, often the town mayor, who officially supervises the corrida, usu. assisted by a technical advisor and assessor, as well as a former matador.

Gear. Matadors still sport the trad. *traje de luces* (suit of lights), close-fitting and richly embroidered silk costume. The clothes consist of a *casaquilla* (a jacket) and a *taleguilla* (pants reaching below the knee). The matador wears a *camisa de torear*, (a loose lace shirt) under the jacket. *Medias* (Silk stockings), *zapatillas* (black shoes) and a *montera* (a bicorned hat) complete the outfit. A novice matador, a *novilliero*, that is about to fight a bull for the first time and gain *alternativa*, i.e. pass a sort of public exam-

Francisco Goya, Corrida, *oil on canvas, 1812-15.*

ination to become a full matador, does not wear his hat on his head but carries it in his hand. On entering the arena, the matador has a *capote de paseillo*, a heavily ornamented parade cape on one shoulder, which he takes off for the fight; the *banderilleros* also wear a similar cape. The jackets of the banderilleros and the *picadores* are similar but less ornate. Moreover, the picadors do not wear hats but *castoreños* (beaver-pelt cylinders); they also wear *calzonas* (leather pants), *botas* (heavy leather shoes) and *monas* (steel leg armor).

Persons accompanying the fight. According to an unwritten but closely observed custom, every matador has his own team, *cuadrilla*, which consists, first of all, of 3 footmen, *banderilleros*, and two riders with lances – *picadores*. The team is completed with 2 back-up picadors and a *puntillero*, who deals the deadly blow, should the bull not be killed by the matador's *estoque* (sword). The task of a *monasibio*, dressed in a red shirt, is to draw the attention of the bull away from e.g. a picador who was knocked down from his horse. An *aranero* evens out the sand-covered arena, and a special carpenter – a carpintero – fixes any damage to the boards. A *mulilero* removes the carcass of the bull with a mule cart. Novice matadors are dubbed *novilleros*, the apprentices *becerristas* – lit. young bulls.

The spectacle. The corrida traditionally starts in the afternoon, often called *tarde de toro* – an afternoon with a bull. The show usu. begins at 5 o'clock. The traditional corrida consists of 6 fights, in which 3 matadors kill 6 'fighting bulls' – *toros de lidia*. The spectacle commences upon a signal from the *presidente*, generally the mayor or another important official, who is lodged in the major, richly ornamented box in the shade (*sombra*) and whose task is to supervise the proceedings. The signals are given with scarves of different colors. The beginning is marked with a white scarf. Accompanied by loud *paso doble*, *alguaciles* (constables), dressed in black costumes from the era of King Philip II, enter the arena. Matadors and their cuadrillas, with other accessory persons, immediately follow the alguaciles. They greet the officials in the main tribune, and move on to the part of the arena at the *callejon*, or the board. 2 alguaciles, moving in a semicircle meet in front of the main tribune, where the host of the spectacle hands over the key to the bullpen, known as the *toril*. At less important shows the key is dropped into the hat of one of the alguaciles, at more important ones a special messenger brings it down. After the gate of the toril has been opened, the matador assumes his stance in the middle of the arena and awaits the first bull.

The matadors' intermediaries, usu. senior banderilleros, conduct the *sorteo*, or drawing lots for the bulls. The lots, pieces of paper, contain the names of bulls. Just before the bullfight begins, a breeder's representative sinks a small spear into the bull's

Corrida, a 19th cent. lithograph.

Roberto Domingo y Fallola, In The Bullring, *1913, oil on canvas.*

Jose Jiménez y Aranda, The Bullring, *1870, oil on canvas.*

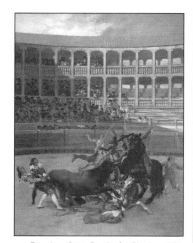

Francisco Goya, Death of a Picador, 1794.

Francisco Goya, A scene from Corrida, 1824-25.

Francisco Goya, Corrida, 1824-25, oil on canvas.

Francisco Goya, Village Bullfight, 181-19, oil on wood.

Francisco Goya, A Bullfight, oil on canvas.

Francisco Goya, The Courage and Agility of Juanito Apiñani, 1815-16, etching and aquatint.

loin which is embroidered with ribbons the colors of which symbolize particular breeders. Now the gates of the toril are opened and the first bull charges the arena, taunted by the banderilleros, who run out from and hide behind the pre-boards, which are lower than the boards proper. If the charge of a bull is exceptionally promising, the matador may decide to confront him without the banderilleros' preparation. In this case he greets the bull by passing at him with his cape in a kneeling position (*cambiada de rodillas*), laying the cape directly on the sand and flicking its edge to make the bull go past him. In other cases, before the matador starts the fight, the bull is taunted by one of the banderilleros, who makes a number of passes (*lances*) with his cape. Since they imitate the matador's role, the passes in this case are described as *doblando*, or doubling. *Largas*, or passes performed with one hand, in which the edge of the cape is drawn on the ground, right in front of the bull's head, serve the purpose of identifying his predilection for charging with one horn, his types of turns or sudden stopping during a charge, etc.

After the banderilleros have finished their show of courage, the picadors enter the arena on horses protected against injury with special padding (*peto*). Every picador has a lance (*pica*) about 2.5m long. The lance has to target the muscles in the area of the animal's wither, so that it hangs down his head, without which the matador would not be able to kill the bull with his sword. After 3 lancings, in which the horse clashes with the bull, the 3 matadors take the floor. 3 pairs of small, adorned spears or arrows have to be driven into the vicinity of the shoulder blades, each hit being announced with a flourish. The highlight of the spectacle is the display of work with the *muleta – la feana de la muleta*. Here the matador has to show his control of the bull's movements in a chosen direction and an ability to avoid his charges. There is a wide array of various techniques of muleta passes, like *derechazo* and *manoletina*, in which the matador often directly collides with the bull. After this display is over, 'the moment of truth' arrives; the matador provokes the animal with the muleta to hang its head towards the left and, at the same time, drives his sword between the bull's spades above his right horn. A successful blow is greeted with a loud 'Olé!' from the public. Upon the wish of the president the matador may cut off the bull's ear or tail as a keepsake.

History. Even though nowadays the corrida is practiced mainly in Span.-speaking countries, its history, evolving out of the buffalo cult, reaches back to the prehistory of development of humankind. Cave paintings indicate that buffaloes and bulls were of paramount interest to hunters and, with time, became objects of religious beliefs and cults. The bull as a symbol of fertility can be traced back to as early as 12,000 yrs. ago, a fact which was not connected with the reproductive potential of the animals *sensu stricto*, but with an observation that wild pastures, once trampled by the animals' hooves, raked with their horns and fertilized with their feces were more fertile. Connected with this attitude was the invention of agricultural implements, as the edges of the oldest hoes and ploughs were armed with animal horn. Killing a buffalo was tantamount to sapping its mythical power, and horns were the symbol of it. It was this that the buffalo cult in oldest human cultures came from. The oldest known legend in the hist. of man, the Babylonian-Assyrian legend of Gilgamesh, includes a plot of killing the Bull of Heaven. In the Hindu Rig-Veda sacrificing bulls was routine. From the eastern cultures the ritual passed on to Mediterranean countries, incl. Egypt. In 3,000-1,500 BC in Crete, enormous buffalo horns carved in stone were one of the major religious symbols, which is borne out by relics discovered by archaeologists, esp. in the vicinity of the Palace at Knossos. The first varieties of games connected with the cult of the buffalo can also be observed in Crete (>TAUROMACHY). In continental ancient Greece the cult and symbol of the bull or ox played an important role and is present in many myths and legends. A bull or a buffalo was slaughtered to honor Zeus (*bouphonia*), a ritual connected with a symbolic judgment over a bloodied knife, which was thrown into the sea to cleanse murderers of blood-guilt; the power to do so was one of the godly prerogatives of Zeus. In the cult of Dionysus, after imbibing large quantities of sacrificial wine, vital organs were cut out of the live animal and eaten raw. Migrating

Matador Manuel Ruiz Valdivia is pinned to the ground by a bull during a corrida in Madrid's Las Ventas arena. Surprisingly, he was not hurt in the incident.

Greeks and Etruscans transplanted the cult of the bull onto the Italian Peninsula (in its original form the word *Italia* meant 'the land of cattle'). After the Italian Peninsula had been brought under Roman control, the cult of the bull continued, but gradually moved, in a vulgarized form, onto circus arenas. Here evolved forms of bullfighting that can be considered to be the beginning of the corrida – they consisted of a duel between a single gladiator, equipped with a small shield and a sword and an intentionally riled bull. In Ovid's *Fasti* (*Calendar*) one learns that in order to enrage the bull Romans availed themselves of a red cloth. In 206 BC the Romans brought under their rule the territory of today's Spain, where at the same time a strong Mitraic religion developed, i.e. belief in Mitra, a deity of mixed Indo-Iranian origin. One of the bases of this cult was the belief that the creator god Ahura Mazda ordered Mitra to kill a bull, out of whose blood and body grew wheat, sprang wine and other goods useful to the race of men. To commemorate this event, bull sacrifices were carried out, which in the course of centuries received a framework that, in tandem with the Roman circus experiences, gave rise to today's corrida. When Christianity took over in the Roman empire, animal sacrifices were prohibited by Theodosius the Great towards the end of the 4th cent. However, bullfighting did not quite disappear, due to the distance from Rome, and soon invasions of the barbarian Visigoths in the 5th cent. were responsible for a rebirth of the games, in which, however, the religious aspect gave way to the spectacle. The Saracens (Arabs, Moors), who invaded the Iberian Peninsula in the 8th cent., did not know bullfights but soon took to them. A motif of offering a bull to the ruler and his court is frequent in Moor ballads, it was there that the corrida acquired the character of a spectacle which added splendor to court celebrations. In 1080 the first spectacle described as a corrida took place. It accompanied Sancho de Estrada's, infante's of Aville, wedding ceremony. In 1090, Rodrigo Diaz se Bivar, a Span.

hero known as El Cid, organized bullfighting spectacles. Another famous event of this type was staged in 1107 on the occasion of Blasco Muñoza's wedding. In 1133 a large corrida took place in Varea on the occasion of Alfons' II coronation; the same ruler ordered that a festive corrida be organized in Leon on his daughter's wedding. Spanish rulers took immense interest in corrida in the 16th and 17th cent. Charles V visited bullfights in Valladolid in 1527, as did Philip IV, despite the pope's interdicts. Pius V issued the most categorical ban in 1567, censuring all Christians partaking in the fights and those who watched as well. The interdict, like on many other occasions remained on paper only.

Royal and aristocratic support exacted the splendor and glamour of the corrida, which remains so characteristic of it to this day. The rich setting began to be an end in itself, even though Philip V, worried by the numerous deaths and maimings of his young knights, forced upon the aristocracy and nobility to give up such tests of masculinity. The corrida started to gain independence from the protectorate of the nobility and developed forms of a spectacle; professional matadors began to appear and the role of the horse diminished. Picadors gained an accessory status in the show after 1726, in the times of Francisco Romero (1700-40). The role of the matador as the main actor of the play was on the increase. J.R. Costillares (1729-1800) perfected the role of the muleta, which became now an important decorative element, adding beauty to the fight, out of the mere piece of cloth that it had once been. Pedro, F. Romero's grandson (1754-1839) became the best known family member, killing 6,000 bulls in 28 years. He set up the first school of toreadors in Seville, in 1830. The spectacle of the corrida was becoming richer gradually in the 19th cent. In 1913, J. Belmonte (1892-1962) introduced passes with a red muleta: before him the matador simply leapt aside from a charging bull; now he started to perform a sort of dance, full of emotion and danger, whose highlight was making the animal run around the matador while almost brushing against him. Belmonte tried to avoid leaping from the bull and redirect the charge to his side with an appropriate pass with the muleta. The new style received the name *de frente* or daring. Thanks to this, the *matador de toros*, which means the killer of the bull, started to evolve into a toreador – *toreo*, where the act of killing the bull remained the final point of the show, but the aesthetic and emotional aspect of the fight was brought to the forefront. Around 1922, Belmonte went a step further, by introducing a style of *toreo des tres cuartes*, in which not only did he not leap away from the bull, but took one step forward with the right leg, which made the impression of his colliding with the animal. Belmonte's ill-fated rival in this golden era of the corrida, J.G. Joselito (1895-1920), prematurely paid with his life at the horns of the bull Bailador. D. Ortega perfected the toreo del tres cuartes style in the 1920s and 1930s. Shortly before WWII a new style, *toreo de perfil* appeared, a fight from the profile, which consisted of directing the bull with the muleta in such a way that at some point in time the toreador and the bull face the same direction, and stand profile to profile. This gives the impression of the toreador having full control of the animal. 1963, which was when M.B. El Cordobesa (b. 1937) appeared on the arena, marked the advent of a style depicted as *tremendismo* – alarming – and striving for a spectacular effect. El Cordobes would kneel in front of a charging bull, only to pass him to his side with the muleta at the very last moment, or would jump onto his back, etc. Mexican matadors who rose to fame were C. Arruza, R. Gaona, S. Perez, L. Garza and M. Espinosa (nicknamed Armilita).

Corrida in literature. Obviously innumerable Span. literary works have been dedicated to the corrida. A. Ganivet identifies it as an important part of Span. heritage in *Idearium española* (*An image of Spain*, 1896). Bullfighting constitutes the leitmotif of V. Blasco Ibáñeza's novel *Sangre y arena* (*The blood and the arena*, 1908), E. Quirogi's *La ultima corrida* (*the Last Corrida*, 1958), L. Alasa's short stories *Adios cordera* and numerous verses, including the famous work of F.G.Lorka, mourning the death of a matador who was a friend of the poet *Llanto por Ignacio Sácheza Mejiasa*, 1935). The motif of the corrida is also present in another of Lorka's works, *El toro la muerte y el aua* (*The bull, death and water*). Many poets have chosen the bull as a subject of their poetry, like M.J. De Larra in the 19th cent. (*Los toros*), J.M. Cossio, who in his beautiful ode mourned over the death of matador Pedro Romero (*La fiesta de toros en Madrid*, 1926); a whole volume of poetry was dedicated to the corrida by R. Morales (*Poemas de toro*, 1943). Verse on this topic is a subject of a number of anthologies and studies, of which the largest consists of 7 volumes (*Relaciones poéticas sobre las fiestas de toros*, 1972-73), but smaller ones abound: J.M. de Dossío, *Los toros en la poesia castellana*, 1931; R. Montesinos, *Poesia taurina contemporaneos* (1961), M. Roldán and M. Escelicer *Poesia hispanica del toro* (1971). The subject of the corrida is so frequent in Fr. literature that anthologies and studies of the kind of A. Luboc's *Les 'Toros' dans la literature francaise* (1946) were written. One famous Fr. writer who took up the subject is H. De Montherlant, who had tried bullfighting himself and had even been gored by a bull in 1925; his experiences and observations are included in the novel *Les bestiaires* (*Animal Tamers*, 1926). Literature is enriched with matadors' and toreadors' diaries, of which the most frequently translated into foreign languages were the C. Arruza's reminiscences entitled *My life as a Matador* (1956). R. Cambria, with a collection of essays *Los toros. Tema polemico en el ensayo del singlo XX* (1974) initiated the polemic current in literature, which is on the increase now. For representatives of other literatures, the corrida was usu. an attractive, exotic, but minor topic. In E. Hemingway's *The Sun also Rises* (1926), lady Brett Ashley embarks on a journey to Spain while awaiting a divorce. Here, among other adventures, she experiences a love affair with toreador Pedro Romero. J. Mitchener discusses issues of the corrida in his reportage *Iberia* (1968). The corrida is also the subject of R. Daley's book *The Swords of Spain* (1966) and K. Tynan's *Bull Fever* (1967). See >ANIMAL BAITING, >BULL RUNNING.

G.A. Becquer, *Tipos y constumbres la corrida de tore en Aragon*, no year given 19th cent..; B. Conrad, *The*

Encyclopedia of Bull Fighting, 1961; G. Marvin, *Bullfight*, 1994; J. Maldonado, *Tarde de toros* 1992.

CORWG, CORWGL, CORWC, see >CORACLES.

COTSWOLD WRESTLING, the name derives from the Cotswold Hills on the Welsh-Eng. border. A style similar to >CORNWALL AND DEVON, often identified with >NORFOLK STYLE.

COUNTRY SHOW SPORTS, in Anglo-Saxon tradition the name refers to a group of sports accompanying local agricultural exhibitions or athletic shows of itinerant showmen. It includes a number of events originating from Eur. traditions, such as *chasing the greased pig*, >TIMBER SPORTS, >HAY TOSSING, >SHEEP SHEARING, and >PLOWING MATCHES. One of the typical country show events was an open boxing challenge against an itinerant boxer, held in special boxing tents. The challengers were local people who fought with the boxer. Such itinerant boxers were an equivalent of Eur. itinerant athletes, weightlifters, and wrestlers. An itinerant career was many a time a way to retreat from professional boxing. Many such show sports acquired local features. There were also certain events popular only within a given locality, such as *rolling-pin throws* or *rabbit-skinning contests*. Nowadays, new elements appear in country show sports, such as *tractor ballet*, incorporated into the show in the USA in the 1920s.

COURSE O' PARK, an old Eng., probably children's game the rules of which have not survived. It is mentioned in a 19th-cent. poem *The Slighted Maid*:

Buff's a fine sport,
And so's course of park.

COURSING, a hunting event rated among >BLOOD SPORTS, in which hounds or other dogs are released in couples in order to chase their quarry and bring it to their owner. The most renowned international coursing competition has been held in England since 1836 in Altcar, near Formby, as the Waterloo Cup – from the local Waterloo Hotel where participants and hosts are installed during the event. See also >FALCONRY and >FOX HUNTING.

COURT TENNIS, see >ROYAL TENNIS.

COURTE PAUME, an abbr. name for >JEU DE COURTE PAUME.

CRAB-SOWL, also *crab-sow*. An old Eng. street game practiced in the neighborhood of Barnes Common in the Lincolnshire County [*sowl* is a dial. form of *sool*]. The game consisted of striking a beer-barrel bung with a stick into the goal or across the opponent's goal line. In time, instead of a bung, players used a small ball, which made the game similar to >FIELD HOCKEY.

CRATES, an Eng. var. of >NINE HOLES.

CREW, see >COMPETITIVE ROWING.

CRICKET FIGHTS, an original form of competition in old China, continued until the present time during local festivals and fairs. They have the character of simple entertainment, usu. held after lunch. 2 crickets are put on a special 'arena', i.e. in a flat bowl, covered with a transparent net so that the fight can be observed. As the cricket does not live long, about 8-10 months, it must be skillfully prepared for the fight. Cricket catching has become a special skill, as when a good specimen is found, its owner can win many times. The innate aggression of male crickets against other male crickets is used. The 'contestants' try to pluck the opponent's legs or feelers. Crickets are trained not only how to attack but also other formats of combat. Cricket fights are often compared to >GONGFU. It is estimated that a well trained cricket can apply about 20 methods of attack.

Cricket boxes, in which they were brought to matches organized by royal courts, made of china, were genuine masterpieces of art. The most original porcelain boxes include ball-shaped ones from the Kangxi period (1662-1722). Most of them, however, were rectangular, as those from the Qianlong period (1736-95). Today ordinary boxes are made of bamboo. Training boxes are differently designed. The basic equipment for catching and training crickets includes: a wide variety of nets – from nets mounted on a long pole, resembling traditional butterfly nets, to small sieves, used to select and quickly cover breeder crickets; different transport cases and containers, 'arenas' and train-

ing boxes, the design of which triggers the cricket's natural defensive instincts and permits the trainer's intervention through the holes, containers which protect crickets against the light so as to arouse them by rapid illumination just before the fight etc. As the fight is preceded by a 'concert' given by crickets, the sounds they produce are made more resonant when special metal vibrators (long brass rods coiled at one end) are put into the boxes. The coil intensifies the sound and gives it a musical character. Before the fight the crickets are kept in the boxes at high temperature, the walls are covered with knitted wool, thick felt or thick cloth. During the fight the crickets are stroked with special brushes, made of mouse hair. When the owner has more crickets fighting, multi-storey boxes are built. A fight usu. lasts about 15min. Defeated crickets, without legs and feelers, are simply thrown away. Exceptionally brave crickets are buried with full honors, the funeral resembling

WORLD SPORTS ENCYCLOPEDIA

C

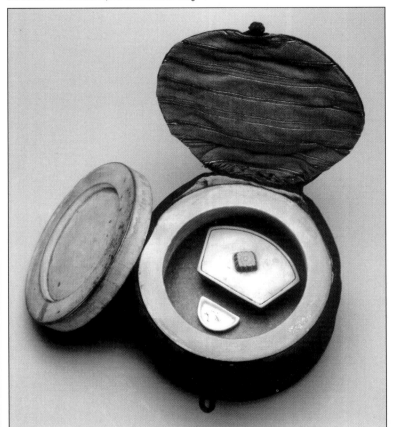

A cricket box, terracotta house and furnishing in a fleecy cover, Beijing.

Arena for cricket fights, enamelled porcelain set in bamboo cane, plaited white cover, late 18th cent., Jingdezhen.

C **WORLD SPORTS ENCYCLOPEDIA**

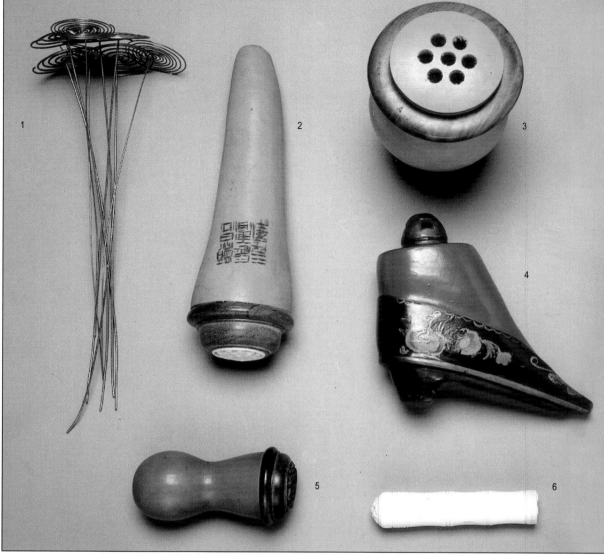

1) Copper song vibrator attached to the inside of cricket cages, Beijing region; 2) Calabash cricket cage, detachable bone and bamboo cover, Beijing region; 3) Calabash cricket cage, detachable cover, Beijing region; 4) Cricket cage styled after a ladies' shoe for bound feet, in wood and lacquer, 19th cent., Fujian; 5) Painted calabash cricket cage, 19th cent.; 6) A small cylindrical bone cage with perforated cover for carrying crickets in the pocket, 19th cent.

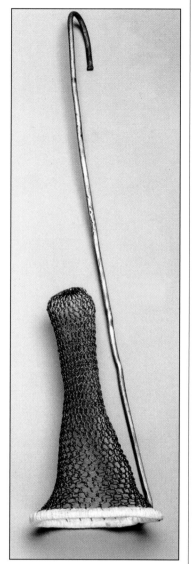

Rigid hoop net in copper mesh for catching the cricket as it leaves the hole, Beijing.

Bamboo cricket cage with 2 compartments to separate the 2 rivals before combat, Shanghai.

Two spherical cricket cages, China, Jiangxi, Qing dynasty, Kangxi period, with porcelain enamel.

Cylindrical cricket cage, China, Jiangxi, Qing dynasty, Qianlong period, with porcelain enamel.

Brush cases in mouse whiskers and bamboo with bone tip, Canton.

funerals of dogs and cats in Great Britain. In many cases, following the court tradition, crickets are buried in special small caskets, which today can be found in many Chinese museums and which were displayed, together with many other implements used during cricket fights, at the exhibition

5,000 years of Sports in China. Art and Tradition (Lausanne 1999).

History. The oldest information about crickets kept by scholars as pets comes from the Tang dynasty (618-906). Cricket fights were organized for the first time in 1000 AD. They became particularly popular during the rule of emperor Xuande (or Ksuang-zong, 1426-35). The emperor's personal porcelain box for the crickets, decorated with dragons, the symbol of the emperor's family, has been preserved. Cricket fights were also very popular among the lower strata of the population, simply because this was a sport in which everybody could take part. In the 18th and 19th cent. cricket fights became universal entertainment in China. After WWII the government of the People's Republic of China put a ban, not so much on cricket fights, as on the bets that were placed. Despite this, even today cricket fights are very common, particularly in the suburbs and in smaller towns. F. Dautresme, 'The Cricket Champion of the Ring', YOSICH, 1999, 118-121.

CRICKET SPITTING, a competition consisting of spitting live crickets for distance. The event has been organized annually by the Southwestern University in Lafayette, Louisiana since 1999. The event is watched by fifteen thousand spectators every year. In the opinion of the organizers the aim of the com-

petition is to raise the contenders' awareness of nature. This is somehow contradicted by the accompanying events during which cookies with fried crickets and other fried insect dishes are served.

CRICKET, Eng. national sport played on a grass-covered field. Only in areas characterized by a long dry season, where the maintenance of grass is difficult, is cricket played on hard-packed earth or concrete grounds. Each team has 11 players. The game consists of playing the ball by delivering, batting it with a special bat and catching it in the field.

Field and Equipment. While the cricket field has no firmly fixed shape or size, cricket is most often played on a flat field varying 100-160yds. (90-150m) across and often bounded by a fence. A meticulously prepared rectangular area of close-cropped grass in the center of the ellipse constitutes the 10-ft.-wide, 22-yd.-long (approx. 3x20.12m) pitch. Around each wicket at each end of the pitch are the playing areas, shaped like a flat-roofed H with wings, each consisting of a bowling crease (the line from which the bowler throws the ball with his hand) and a popping crease, where the batsman (the player who defends the wicket and bats the ball into the field) stands. In the middle of each bowling crease a wicket is set up. Both pairs of creases run crosswise to the longitudinal axis of the field and are 12ft. (3.66m)

Queensland vs. England three-day-tour match at the Allan Border Field cricket ground, Brisbane, Australia.

long, the distance between them being 4ft. (1.22m). The sidelines, which connect the creases, reach 4ft. (1.22m) back as well, forming some space open from the back, within which the bowler delivering the ball towards the opposite wicket gathers momentum. A wicket consists of 3 stumps, 28in. (about 71.12cm) high, of round cross section, which are hammered into the ground at opposite ends of the middle field. The stumps are just close enough together that a cricket ball cannot pass between them. Two wooden crosspieces (bails) sit atop the adjacent pairs of stumps in wooden grooves. Each bail connects the outermost and the middle stump. The whole wicket is 9in. (22.86cm) wide. Each bail is 4³/₈in. (11.11cm) wide, including the outer edges. The diameter of the bail is not specified, however, the bail cannot stick out beyond the stumps more than ½in. (1.27cm) because of its thickness. The construction of a bail is not homogenous: it is thinner at the ends overlapping with the vertical stumps, and it is thicker in the segments between the stumps, where it is often ornamentally creased. The bails are not permanently fixed to the stumps and hit with a ball; the construction may be easily toppled, thus, breaking the wicket. The wicket has featured different shapes and sizes throughout the history of the game. In 1744, the wicket consisted of only 2, instead of 3 stumps, i.e., it used to be narrower than it is today (6in., i.e. 15.24cm). The oldest recorded (1744) dimensions of the stumps forming the wicket amount to 22in. (55.88cm). Current dimensions have been in force since 1931. **The oldest balls,** as indicated in the records, 'were made of anything that could be sewn or joined in a circular shape'. In the mid-18ᵗʰ cent., the ball, covered with leather and dyed red, weighed 5-6oz. (142-170g). Nowadays, balls are made of handmade twine wound around a cork core and enclosed in leather, traditionally dyed red. The circumference is between 8¹³/₁₆ and 9in. (22.38-22.86cm). The ball weighs between 5½ and 5¾oz. (156-163g). The leather covering consists of 2 appropriately shaped hemispheres joined with a single equatorial seam, used to facilitate gripping the ball with the fingers and 'curling' the ball while throwing. Since the hardness of the ball may pose a threat of injury, wicket keepers wear characteristic white protective pads covering the shins and the lower part of the stomach, similar to the protective equipment worn by >HOCKEY goaltenders and >BASEBALL catchers. **The Bat** has a shape similar to a short paddle with a small rounded handle in the upper part. The oldest surviving sticks, constructed in the 18ᵗʰ cent.,

were not all straight, but bent in the shape of a vertically stretched letter 'S'. The present design was introduced about 1775. Despite a few slight proportional modifications since then, it has remained characterized by straight edges of the main part, with which the ball is hit, i.e. the blade, and soon after it first appeared, the blade acquired a hump sloping both from the handle and the toe side of the bat. The peak of the hump falls at about ¹/₃ of the bat's length from the toe, and at about ²/₃, from the handle end. The central part of the bat overlapping with the hump is called the *meat* in players' jargon. The handle is coated with rubber, overlapping with the blade in a wedge-shaped manner, and often wrapped around with a cord. There is no limit on the weight of the bat, but the average weight of this piece of equipment varies within 1oz. of 2lb. 5oz. (approx. 1.020-1.077kg). A regulation bat should not exceed 38in. (96.52cm) in length or be wider than 4¼in. (about 10.8cm). **Rules of Play.** A coin toss determines the order in which teams bat. The captain of the side winning the toss may elect to bat or field first. The fielding side disperses around the field, to positions designed to stop or catch the ball during the play. The captain of the batting side determines the order of defending the wicket and batting by his players. The player who defends the wicket and bats is called the *batsman*. At the same time, the captain of the opposite, fielding team appoints the first player, who is referred to as the *bowler*, to deliver the ball, and a player who stands bending or squats behind the batsman – the *wicket-keeper*. His task is to help his team to get the batsman out by, among other tactics, catching any balls the batsman has missed and passing them quickly to the fielders. The strategic task of the wicket-keeper is to observe the weaknesses of the batsman and pass that information on to the captain, who may regroup his team based on this intelligence. However, any change in the lineup first set may occur only if the captain of the opposite team agrees. The two first batsmen stand at the opposite wickets, but only one of them is called the *striker* – the one who receives the ball delivered by the bowler and attempts to bat it in the field. In the meantime, the other batsman, the *non-striker*, bides his time. The bowler, who represents the fielding team, tries to bowl the ball in such a way as to break the opponent's wicket. He delivers the ball from the area near the opposite wicket to the wicket defended by the batsman. From the point of view of the bowler's throw, the field is conventionally split; the *on* and *off* sides are determined by whether the

striker is right- or left-handed. The on side is also called the *leg side* because it is the side the batsman's legs are on. The ball can theoretically be bowled over-arm, under-arm, or round-arm, but once committed, the manner of delivery must be adhered to. If the bowler intends to change his method of delivery, he must first inform the umpire, who passes it on to the batsman, so that the bowler cannot

Philip Hermogenes Calderon, Captain of the Eleven, *1898, oil on canvas.*

C

WORLD SPORTS ENCYCLOPEDIA

use shock tactics. The majority of deliveries in cricket are bowled over-arm, which is most effective. The main task of the bowler is to put the batsman out, which may occur in situations specified as: 1) bowled – consists of breaking the wicket completely, i.e. when both of the bails have been dislodged and have fallen to the ground; 2) caught – if a fielder catches the ball on the full after the batsman has hit it with his bat or touched it with his hand or glove, but before it has touched the field; 3) leg-before wicket (abbr. LBW) occurs if the batsman misses the ball with his bat, but intercepts it with part of his body when it would otherwise, according to the umpire, have hit the wicket. The batsman is allowed to stop the ball only with the bat or the hand holding the bat; if the batsman stops the ball with any other part of his body, he is out. The LBW law has undergone many modifications over the years and a strict range of criteria must be met for it to apply; the law's complexity often gives rise to heated debate and even accusations of dishonesty; 4) stumped – this occurs if the batsman defending the wicket steps outside the popping crease and the wicket-keeper gathers the ball and breaks the wicket with it; 5) hit wicket – if the batsman touches and breaks the wicket with the bat, any part of his body or dislodged articles of his uniform, including protective equipment; 6) run out – if the fielder breaks that batsman's wicket with the ball, when: a) the batsman is taking a run to change places with the thus far inactive non-striker; it is the wicket to which the batsman is running that has to be broken, b) when the batsman has left his position, but, for some reason, the run was aborted, then it is the wicket that has been left that has to be hit; 7) the batsman defending the wicket catches the ball with his hands. He can do so without being out only if asked to do it by a member of the opposite team; 8) if having properly stopped the ball with the bat or the hand with the bat, e.g. after unsuccessful batting, he 'corrects' the bat with another strike to start the run; 9) if knowingly and actively he disturbs the players of the opposite team. The fielder who puts out the batsman asks the umpire a traditional question, 'How's that?' In response, the umpire says either: 'Out!' which

means that the batsman is eliminated, or 'Not out!' when the conditions for elimination have not been fulfilled and he plays on. The moment the batsman has been removed, he is immediately replaced by the next player appointed by the captain, until there are no more players left, which means the round (*inning*) comes to a close.

If the batsman (striker) succeeds in batting the ball into the field, both he and the, thus far, inactive batsman (non-striker) run to change places at the wickets as many times as they can manage during the flight of the ball. The moment the ball is caught by the fielding side, the run must stopped. It is a crucial moment in the game because the number of completed runs adds points to the total score in the match, thus determining the victory.

The roles of the teams then swap. The team that scores the most runs wins, the final tally being the difference in score. Thus, if the winning team earned 200 runs during the match, and the defeated one 180, the victorious score amounts to 20.

Etymology. There are a number of hypotheses concerning the origin of the name 'cricket'. One suggest a stem from the old English *crice* or *cryce*, which referred to a stick or bar marking the target in ancient ball games. Another hypothesis speculates that the name stems from the Old French *cricquet*, meaning a kind of a pole. Yet another version has it that the name of cricket comes from the Flem. saying *met de krik ketsan* – which means 'to hit the ball with a bent stick' [*krik,* also in dialectical variants *krek,* and Du. *kruk* – a bent stick]. One tempting theory asserts an onomatopoeic etymology of the word: hitting the ball with the bat gives a short, sharp sound, 'Krrik!' which has an English counterpart, the noun and the verb *creak*. But whatever the origin, the earliest surviving written record of the term 'cricket' is attributed to J. Derrick (1598), in *The Guild Merchant Book*. The earliest known dictionary entry mentioning the game is that of the term *crosse* found in the 1611 French-English Dictionary of J. Cotgrave.

History. The history of cricket dates back to the 12th cent. A list of the personal belongings of Edward I from 1300 includes entries that can be treat-

ed as cricket equipment. A drawing from 1344 depicts players, one of whom is throwing the ball while another is waiting to hit it with a stick. In 1477 Edward IV banned cricket as the game disturbed the archery exercises on the fields near London. In his edict, the game is called *hands in – hands out*. In the 16th cent the game developed in the counties of Surrey and Hampshire, and was becoming increasingly popular also among the students of public schools in Guildford and Winchester. At the beginning of the 17th cent., a puritan outcry denounced cricket as a threat to mores, morals, and religion itself. In 1620, young Oliver Cromwell, future leader of the Puritans, was accused of taking part in the "dishonorable game of cricket", and the city of Maidstone was castigated as 'shameless', because its citizens played the game. The citizens of Eltham, in Kent in 1654 and Boxgrave, in Sussex County in 1662, too, found themselves stigmatized by church authorities for enjoying the odd game of cricket. After a number of religious disputes, including those concerning the relations between cricket and gambling and the playing of cricket on Sundays, in 1748, the Royal Jury Court held forth a verdict concerning the lawfulness of cricket in England, declaring cricket a masculine game which, in and of itself, was not sinful. However, the court lamented the evil abuse of the sport at the hands of gambling ne'er-do-wells when any purse in excess of 10 pounds was at stake, ruling that such betting represented the only real legal infraction.

The first match between the teams of Kent and Surrey counties was played in 1728. The London Cricket Club, the first such organization, was established around 1744. The Half-Penny-Down Club, founded in 1750, operated for over 40 years. Until 1700 the game had been played without wickets; instead holes in the earth had been used. The London Cricket Club specified the current shape of the wickets in 1777. In 1788 the club drafted regulations, which continue to be the basis for current cricket development. In 1784 a group of Eton College graduates popularized the game among Englishmen in India, where the Calcutta Cricket Club, comprised

A cricket match.

Shane Warne of Victoria attempts a catch off of the bowling of Cameron White during the ING Cup match between the Victorian Bushrangers and Tasmanian Tigers at the Melbourne Cricket Ground in Melbourne.

mainly of white colonists, was created (1792). The first Hindu club was not created until 1883. In 1800 cricket spread to Western India, in 1803 to Australia, in 1808 to Cape Town in S.Africa, and, finally, to N.Zealand. The first match between England and Australia was played in 1861. This gave rise to the tradition of similar meetings between Eng.-speaking countries, esp. former possessions of the Brit. Empire and those that nowadays form the Commonwealth. W.G. Grace (1848-1915) is considered the most outstanding cricket player in the history of the sport. He introduced a new dynamic style of play, set a number of world records and actively practiced the sport, in combination with some other sports, for the impressive span of over half a century (from 1857 to 1909). In 1895, an Englishman, A.C. McLaren (1871-1944) set the first world record of over 400 runs in one match, scoring 424 runs This record was not broken until 1930 when an Australian, D.G. Bradman (b. 1908), achieved 452 runs, a record which survived a further 29 years. Bradman was the first Austrl. cricket player to receive a noble title for his sporting achievements; J.B. Hobbs (1882-1963) followed in 1953. In addition to the International Cricket Board (ICB), the Eng.-speaking countries where cricket is most intensely played form the Cricket Conference consisting of representatives of England, Australia, India, N.Zealand, Pakistan, W India and S.Africa (which was excluded from the association for some time in protest of its apartheid policies). In many countries there are central cricket organizations, however, in the homeland of the game, England, this role has been traditionally performed by the Marylebone Cricket Club, responsible also for the development of cricket and its regulations on the international level. Moreover, there are school organizations, such as the Eng. Schools and Welsh Secondary Schools Cricket Associations. Since 1873 league matches have been played in England at the county level. In Australia such matches are played at the state level, while in N.Zealand they are played at the district level. Among the international competitions, test matches, played between the Commonwealth countries are considered the most prestigious.

The development of television, along with increased competition with other sports, esp. >FOOTBALL, contributed to a decline in interest in cricket in the 1980s among both participants and spectators. One reason for this was the lengthiness of cricket matches, which frequently lasted up to 5 days. Therefore, suitable initiatives, which aimed at shortening matches to a single day (so-called *one-day-cricket*), appeared. In 1997 Lord MacLaurin proposed a cricket reform with the aim of simplifying the game system to adapt it to the needs of the sports entertainment industry and the specific requirements of televised transmission. One of the basic organizational changes was a departure from the traditional system of county games in favor of league systems similar to Amer. >BASKETBALL, organized in regular conferences with annual play-offs between the best teams. The matches were duly shortened to just 2-3 hours. Mass media dubbed this new formula *quick cricket, quicker cricket* and, in the US,

kwikker cricket. MacLaurin's propositions also took aim at promoting greater accessibility and popularity of cricket among the youth, esp. in schools, where the sport's development has stagnated of late. This feat is to be implemented by introducing a considerably shortened variation of the game along with providing schools with cheap, mass produced plastic equipment; see also >PUDDEX. Cricket together with >BASTE-BALL, >GOALBALL, >NEW-YORK-BALL, >ONE-OLD-CAT, >ROUND BALL, >ROUNDERS, >TOWN-BALL, >TWO-OLD-CAT.

H.S. Altham & E.W. Swanton, *A History of Cricket,* 1962; *Can 'Kwikker Cricket' Match Up?* NW, 18.08.1997; J. Nyren, *Cricketers of My Time,* 1836; W.J. Lewis, *The Language of Cricket,* 1934; R.S. Rait Kerr, *The Laws of Cricket. Their History and Growth,* 1950; P. Rice, *How to Play Cricket,* 1988; E. Roberts, *Cricket in England 1894-1939,* 1946; M. Rundel, *The Dictionary of Cricket,* 1996; E.W. Swanton, *The World of Cricket,* 1966.

CRICKO, an Austrl. sport which is a combination of >CRICKET and >VIGORO. Invented about 1940 by J. Turner and P. Mullins from Kangaroo Point in Brisbane. That same year, the New South Wales Cricko Association was established. By 1950, in Sydney and Newcastle 53 cricko clubs were opened. In 1941, a similar association, incorporating 8 clubs, was established in Queensland with a head office in Brisbane. The game became particularly popular with women. In 1941, the first competition between teams from Sydney and Brisbane took place, where the prize was a Silver Helmet containing the ashes left from the wickets used during the first cricko matches. The Sydney-Brisbane matches were played up to 1966. In the 1960s, the game's popularity declined and, after 1966, in Sydney it disappeared completely. However, it was still popular in Brisbane, where in 1990 there were still 5 A-class teams and 4 reserve teams of the same class.

Rules. Identical with those applied in cricket expanded by an element borrowed from vigoro – an obligatory round, encircling the goals after pitching a ball beyond the 'crease'.

CROOKY, an old Eng. game practiced in County Clare, Ireland. Apparently it was brought there by Fr. immigrants. Up to the middle of the 19th cent., it resembled >FIELD HOCKEY because of a small ball and curved sticks that were used in it. According to A.B. Gomme, around the 1850s, in Kilkee, the game was played with the use of wooden mallets, evolving thus into a var. of >CROQUET.

CROQUET, a sport involving rolling balls by means of wooden mallets. The name of the game comes from Fr. *croquet* – a small, bent, hook-shaped stick. The object of the game is to deliver the balls through hoops positioned on the playing field and forming var. configurations depending on the kind of game. Though mallets (Fr. *maillets*) may be of different shapes and sizes in different var. of croquet, they are often comprised of a head which is square or round in cross section mounted on a handle whose length equals the distance from ground to the player's wrist. Traditional wickets were made of round

wicker twigs; these have gradually been replaced by metal and plastic. Croquet balls, traditionally made of wood, have in recent decades come also to be made of plastic, gum, or pressed cork, and are colored blue, red, black and yellow to identify the players. Different var. of the game have separate requirements concerning size and weight of the balls as well as the court. Major var. of croquet are now believed to be the British var. (also known as association croquet), the American var., and >ROQUE, a derivative of croquet.

The British version (association croquet) is played on a grass or earth court the size of which is given in ft. in Brit. and Commonwealth nomenclature and in yd. in the USA. Hence the standard court is a rectangle measuring 35yds. or 105ft. (about 32m) by 28yds. or 84ft. (about 25.6m). There are 6 hoops on the court: 4 in the corners and 2 in the center of the court, along its diameter. Each hoop is made of solid metal and consists of two uprights connected by a crown. A hoop must be 12in. in height above the ground measured to the top of the crown and must be vertical and firmly fixed. The uprights and the crown must have a uniform diameter of $^5/_8$in. (1.59cm) above the ground. The inner surfaces of the uprights must be approximately parallel and not less than 3¾in. (about 9.53cm) apart. The balls are 3$^5/_8$in. (9.21cm) in diameter and must weigh 16oz., so the diameter of each ball is only 3.22mm fewer than that of a hoop. In the center of the court there is 1 peg, or in the so-called Willis setting there are 2 pegs at opposite sides of the court, which makes the game more difficult. The peg is a rigid cylinder with a height and uniform diameter above the ground of 18in. (45.72cm) and 1½in. (3.81cm) respectively. A mallet consists of a head with a shaft firmly connected to its mid-point at right angles to it so that they function as one unit during play. The head must be rigid and may be made of any suitable materials, provided that they give no significant playing characteristics regardless which end is used to strike the ball. Its end faces must be parallel, essentially identical and flat The mallet must weigh between 2¾ to 3¾lb. (about 1.25-1.70kg). The head is made of guyak wood in heavier categories and of boxwood in lighter categories. It may have a square or round diameter of 2¾ to 2½in. (5.71-6.35cm). The face of the head is equipped with a brass buckle to prevent the wood from splitting. The shaft is usu. made of

Winslow Homer, A Game of Croquet, 1866; oil on canvas.

Winslow Homer (1836-1910), Croquet Scene, oil on canvas, 1866.

A game of croquet.

Leon Wyczółkowski, A Game of Croquet, oil on canvas.

hickory, ash-wood or malacca. Mallets for recreational purposes are often plastic.
When the first Eng. Championships took place in 1867, the court was 66 by 48ft. (20.12 by 14.63m). There were 9 hoops of 8 ins. (20.32cm) each, and the ball was 3½in. (8.89cm) in diameter. In 1870 the size of the court was extended to 150 by 105ft. (32 by 45.72m), whereas the width of the hoops was decreased to 4in. (10.16cm). In 1871 the number of hoops was reduced from 9 to 6. Such a setting came to be known as the Halle Setting and it was binding in England in 1871-1992. Until 1914 the sequence of strikes was fixed so that blue, red, black and yellow balls had to be struck consecutively. After 1914, around the time this rule was abandoned, balls of $3\frac{5}{8}$in. (9.21cm) and hoops of 3¾in. in width (about 9.53cm) were brought into play; these sizes persist today. In 1922 the Willis setting was introduced, and in 1928 the lift shot which reduces the starting shot from 30 to 13-19m became binding. The lift shot stands for shooting the ball not directly with a mallet but with some other ball which begins the game indirectly by being set in motion from under the player's foot.

Ryan Simpson of St. John's College displays his form during the 17th Annual Annapolis Cup Croquet Match against the Naval Academy at Annapolis, Maryland.

Oxford students enjoying a game of croquet.

General rules of play. At the start of a game, the player entitled to play first places one of his balls on any point of the baulk-line (starting line) and plays the first stroke of his turn. At the end of that turn the adversary plays one of his balls into the game from any unoccupied point on the baulk-line. The court is symmetrical, therefore the players may equally well start the game from either baulk-line: front or back. The object is for each side to make its balls score 12 hoop points and a peg point before the other side, which means 26pts. when there are 2 balls per player, 13pts. for each ball. A ball scores a hoop point by passing through the correct hoop in the order 1, 2 (left side of the court), 3, 4 (right side of the court), 5, 6 (in the center of the court), and then 1-back, 2-back, 3-back, 4-back, penultimate and rover in the reverse direction. A ball that has scored all 12 hoop points is known as a rover. It may then score a peg point and is removed from the game. If the ball hits a peg before passing through all hoops the given player loses points scored up to that moment in the round. A round is completed on passing all hoops in due order with one's balls. The winner is the player who achieves this in the fewest shots. In Great Britain the final score is arrived at by deducting the losing team's scores from the winner's scores. If, then, the winner got a full 26pts. whereas his opponent scored for e.g. 19, the total winning points equal 7. In Australia and N.Zeland the sum of the winner's scores is given without the necessity of detracting the loser's points from it, which would be 26:19 in our exemplary case. The sides take turns. Each turn may be played with either of the side's balls. The striker is initially entitled to play one stroke, after which the turn ends unless in that stroke the striker's ball scores a hoop point for itself or hits another ball. If the striker's ball scores a hoop point for itself, the striker becomes entitled to play one extra stroke known as a continuation stroke. If the striker's ball hits another ball, it is said to roquet that other ball and the striker becomes entitled to play a croquet stroke. After playing a croquet stroke the striker becomes entitled to play a continuation stroke. A system in which each player is to perform one shot at a turn irrespective of the resulting passing or failing to pass the hoop is also an acceptable option. In the team game each player may shoot at any ball of his team's balls on condition that he does not shoot at the same ball twice in a row after all of the balls of two teams are in play. Any ball in hand that has left the court must be replaced on the yard-line at the point nearest to where it left the court, and any ball in hand in the yard-line area must be replaced on the yard-line area at the point nearest to where it came to rest. The yard line is not marked on the court, it is an imaginary line of an inner rectangle of the court, whose sides are parallel to and 30in. (76.2cm) from the boundary. When the game is played individually between 2 players each of them has 2 balls at his disposal; when doubles are played, each pair has 2 balls at their disposal. Traditionally blue and black balls play against red and yellow ones.
The American version is played on grass courts without boundary lines, usu. the central playing area is 60ft. (about 18.3m) long and 30ft. (9.14m) wide. The hoops are positioned as follows: 2 at each longer side of the court and 1 in the center. Right at the starting line there is also a home stake in the vicinity of which the game must be started but which the ball must not touch. Straight behind the home stake there is a double hoop, i.e. 2 neighboring hoops 0.5m apart. At the other side of the court a turning stake accompanies an identical double hoop. Behind these double hoops the inserted stakes make it difficult for the ball to leave the hoop. Moreover, there are 7 hoops in the center of the court, including 2 doubles and two stakes. Scoring the hoops takes place usu. in the direction from the first double hoop, then the first left, center, second left, the opposite double, turning stake (by touching or by-passing according to the agreed rules), second right, the center again, the first right, the first double again, and the final touching of the home stake. It is not allowed to end the game by passing the last hoop and touching the home stake in one stroke. Passing a ball through a single hoop entitles a player to one extra stroke while delivering the ball through a double hoop with one stroke entitles him to 2 more strokes. Making the game more difficult for one's opponent by striking his balls "accidentally" into disadvantageous terrain while striking one's balls is allowed.
History. Croquet's ancestry can be traced at least to the 14th cent. One of the hypotheses is that it developed as an indoor form of lawn bowling to be played during the winter, with added hoops and mallets to make the game more challenging on the much smaller playing area. This indoor version of lawn bowling then moved back outdoors and became known in France as *paille-maille* (Ital. >PALLA-MAGLIO) and Engl. >PALL-MALL. The Stuarts are credited with popularizing the game in England, as Charles II played it while in exile in France. Later, during the 17th cent., it was played by Charles II and his courtiers also at St. James's Park in London. The anglicized name of the game: Pall Mall became the name of a nearby street. "Mall" then turned into a generic word for any street used for public strolls. At the end of the 17th cent. this form of entertainment died out for reasons unknown only to regain popularity in the late 1850s and the early 1860s when it appeared under the new name croquet (from a Fr. word of a hooked stick), which has been used ever since. It was probably J. Jaques who reintroduced croquet in 1852. About 1857 the game seems to have been taken up by the Irish. From Ireland it was brought back to England, where Whitmore introduced it around 1860. Routlege's *Handbook of Croquet*, which was among the first written set of croquet rules, was published in England in 1861 and inspired a wave of popularity that swept across the Atlantic. Whitmore was the initiator of the first English Championships held unofficially in Moreton-in-the Marsh, Gloucestershire in 1867. Whitmore issued a handbook the following year entitled *Croquet tactics,* the first book describing the techniques of the game. Also in 1868 or, according to other sources in 1870, the All England Croquet Club was founded and organized the English Championships the same year. Between 1896--97 the first national federation, the United All England Croquet Association, was established. The resulting wide popularity croquet enjoyed in England was abundantly commented on in the Eur. press, which popularized the game even further in many countries on the continent. Between 1875-1900 croquet began losing the fans to tennis, golf, and badminton. In 1880 the All England Croquet Club added "and Lawn Tennis" to its name as a result of the rising popularity of tennis, and in 1980 became the All England Lawn Tennis Club, with the omission of the name croquet altogether. Croquet was saved from oblivion to a great extent to thanks its staunch proponents and the early croquet associations, which introduced several var. of the game best, suited to var. categories of players as far as age and levels of performance are concerned. Among the different var. of croquet there is a highly sophisticated 9-wicket game as well as an easier, recreational version. Just when croquet was fading out in Europe, i.e. in the 1890s, the game was adopted in the USA and was very quick to gain popularity. In 1882 National Croquet Association (NCA) was founded in America. Out of S. Crosby's initiative the Association carried out a reform of the game and introduced an additional var. called *roque* (by omission of the first and last letter in the word croquet). It enjoys esteem in clubs in England, at Cambridge and Oxford Universities, which have their own students' clubs. In the USA Harvard, Yale and Virginia Universities may boast the longest academic tradition of playing croquet. The game is most widely played on the East Coast, esp. in suburban clubs of Philadelphia, Washington, and New York. The MacRobertson International Shield is acclaimed the most important trophy. The United States Croquet Association with headquarters at the Hurlingham club is the major organization organizing most of the championships at various levels in the USA. It acknowledges 6 types of membership: private, country and sports, resorts and hotels, real estate, college teams, and retirement communities. In England championships of an open form are organized for singles and pairs, with additional divisions into men, women and mixed team categories. The most prestigious trophy is the President's Cup. Apart from England and America croquet has enjoyed wide popularity in Australia, where the first club was founded in1866 in Kyneton, Victoria, and the next appeared in Kapunda, South Australia. The first organizations outside of the club structure were created in Tasmania in 1908, then in Victoria (1914), South Australia (1916), New South Wales (1918), Queensland (1922), and Western Australia (1928). The Victoria Association proved to be the most vibrant and it was there that the first matches against England were held (since 1925). The Australian Croquet Council was created only as late as in 1950. It has since changed its name to the Australian Croquet Association. At present Australia constitutes the largest croquet center. In 1994 the number of registered players performing the game on a professional basis amounted to about 6,000. The most prestigious croquet contest in the world, the MacRobertson Shield, originated in Australia. The name comes from the name of the sponsor, Austrl. businessman Sir Macpherson Robertson. Initially only contestants from England and Australia could take part in it, then N.Zeland was also allowed. The tournament is held every 3 to 4 years, alternately in one of the 3 countries. Although the Australians initiated the event, they have not managed to win since 1937.
J. Arlott, 'Croquet Association', ARL, 1975, 215-224; D. Miller and J. Thorpe, *Croquet and How to Play It,* 1966; M. B. Reckitt, *Croquet Today,* 1956; J. W. Solomon, *Crocquet,* 1966.

CROSS BMX, a var. of cycling in which special small bicycles are used whose wheels are 20in. (50.8cm) in diameter, which are not equipped with gears [*B* stands for 'bicycle' + *MX* for 'motorcross'], also sp. *bmx*. A race is held on a short natural track, 300-400m long, with mounds and sharp bends with bales of pressed straw at the sides. The racers are equipped with protective garments and helmets. No age limits apply. A field var. of cross bmx is carried out in the form of 'observed trials', where the bikes are equipped with a special low gear for steep hills, jumping over stumps, trunks, and rocks, etc. The pedals are permanently coupled with the rear wheel, which makes balancing on the bike in a difficult area easier, e.g. on the verge of a rock a cyclist can move both forward and backward. The bike's frame is reinforced to make it withstand whatever humps, holes, and mounds it may encounter. The objective of observed trials is not only to achieve the best time but to cover the entire track without touching the ground, so-called 'dabbing'. The discipline was developed with the intention of improving cycling skills and the ability to ride a bike in difficult conditions for children aged 10-12. However, soon it became quite popular among older cyclists and nowadays it is mostly 20-to-30-year-olds who practice this discipline. International championships are held in a senior category (above 19 years old) and under-21's one (17-18) both for women and men.

History. Cross bmx first took root in Santa Monica, California, in 1969. In the '70s, the discipline spread across the USA and in the '80s it achieved international status. Today, national championships are held in about 30 countries. In Eur. the first cross bmx competition took place in 1978 and in 1981 the International BMX Federation was established which has organized W.Ch. and World Cups since 1982. Since 1993, the event has been incorporated into the *Union Cycliste Internationale*. In addition, it has continued to develop in a number of independent organizations. In the USA, there are approx. 60,000 cyclists associated with an organization integrated with the Union Cycliste Interna-

tionale, with another 40,000 united under the auspices of the independent American Bicycle Association. Until the turn of the '70s and '80s, bmx cycling was mostly practiced in the form of races on 300-400m-long tracks (a form which is still popular). In the '80s, other forms evolved, such as bmx acrobatics either on a flat surface or in half-pipes that are also used for >SKATEBOARDING. Originally, during acrobatic shows in half-pipes standard bmx were used, later new constructions made inroads which led to establishing a new discipline >BICYCLE STUNT RIDING.

CROSS DIVING, a trad. event that is part of the Greek Orthodox Church's celebrations of the Epiphany celebrated in January throughout the world. After water is blessed, the bishop pours it into the bay, where it can be symbolically spread over the entire sea. Then a crucifix is thrown into the freezing water and young men dive for it. After the cross is retrieved, the priests and the fortunate diver return to the church for a ceremony and blessings. The entire ritual is accompanied by prayers and chants. The event takes place in many countries, such as Greece, Russia, Bulgaria, USA etc. In Bulgaria it is called *wadene na krysta* and has a long tradition reaching back to the Middle Ages.

CROSSBOW SHOOTING, i.e. shooting with the use of a device similar to a bow, whose arms, however, are shorter and require a special mechanism to pull the string. The arms, whose span varies from 20 to 50cm, were originally made of wood strengthened with horns and animal tendons. Between them, there is a special groove for bolts – a shorter version of an arrow – propelled with a string which can be released with a trigger. The string was originally pulled with the use of a simple lever that made it possible to use the weapon even for relatively weak persons, as it did not require such strength as was needed in traditional archery where longbows were used. In the 15th cent., the so-called arbalest appeared, equipped with a steel bow and a crank mechanism that used much more leverage than a conventional

one and, as a result, increased the weapon's power and lengthened the arrow's trajectory to over 100m. Light crossbows with a traditional lever were still used for smaller game hunting. At the end of the Middle Ages, a crossbow using metal bolts was introduced. The bow's advantage over a longbow consisted of the ability to wait for a shot with the weapon fully prepared without straining oneself by keeping the bowstring pulled. In addition, a crossbow facilitated easier aiming at the target thanks to limit-

A Greek Orthodox worshipper from Thessaloniki braves freezing winter weather to dive into Istanbul's Bosphorus and retrieve a wooden cross in a ceremony commemorating the baptism of Jesus Christ.

ing the strain put on shooters' arms and stabilizing the entire device by pressing its butt against the shoulder. A bolt is released after pulling the trigger and activating the releasing mechanism.

History. The crossbow was invented in ancient China [>CHINESE CROSSBOW SHOOTING]. The mechanical parts that have survived after ancient Chin. crossbows caused a sensation during the exposition *5,000 Years of Sport in China, Art and Tradition*, organized in 1999 by the Olympic Museum, in Lausanne, because until then it had been believed the crossbow was a Eur. invention. Although the hordes of Huns and Avars that were repeatedly plundering Europe did leave some of their military inventions (e.g. the stirrup), somehow the crossbow was never one of them. Probably the reason for that was the fact that Europe was only visited by mounted cavalry able to cover great distances, whereas the Asian infantry, that actually used crossbows, never made it to the Eur. continent. Mounted warriors preferred a short, heavily bent bow instead of a crossbow because the process of pulling the string in the latter was rather complex and time consuming. If and when the introduction of the crossbow into Eur. military tradition related to oriental influences, is rather difficult to say. Although there is no doubt the crossbow was known in ancient China, its role as a sports discipline was established in Europe during the Middle Ages thanks to the activities of shooting associations (see >FREISCHIEßEN, >KÖNIGSSCHIEßEN, >COCK SHOOTING). Significant differences between mechanisms used in Eur. and oriental crossbows suggest these two have in fact little in common. However, it is possible that the general idea of a string pull was borrowed from Asian cultures and then improved upon with the military mechanics developed up to Roman times and employed in Europe, such as in catapults used during sieges. Traditionally, it is believed French knights were the first to use crossbows in Europe around the 10th cent. Originally, the instrument was used only for hunting but from about the 11th cent. it was used for military purposes as well. Its use as a weapon of war was so shocking to the Christian world that the Church regarded the crossbow as an immoral device. In the 12th and 13th cent., the crossbow was a standard accoutrement of special infantry units, whereas municipal associations began to popularize sports crossbow shooting. The use of the crossbow as a sports weapon was accelerated substantially by the invention of firearms. At the end of the Middle Ages, crossbow shooting tournaments transformed – esp. in Flem., Ital, and Ger. cities –

Contestants fly over a jump at the 2002 Summer X Games Downhill BMX race at Woodward Camp Inc. in Woodward, Pennsylvania.

Women's Biker-X during the ESPN X- Games at Crested Butte Mountain in Crested Butte, Colorado.

into special, almost ritual, events, held during festivals and resembling knights' tournaments. The most famous of such tournaments began to acquire an international character as early as in the 15th cent., attracting the best shooters from abroad. The most prestigious among them were the tournaments organized in the 16th cent. in Heidelberg, Passau, Ulm, Rottweil, Stuttgart, Vienna, Regensburg, Worms, and Munich. Most Eur. cities admitted contestants only if they could present a special invitation, known in Germany as a *Ladebrief*, they had received beforehand. The earliest surviving specimen of such a letter of invitation dates back to 1398 and was sent by the city of Cronberg, it is the so-called *Cronberger Handschrift*. The German scientist, E. Feys, collected 33 similar documents, dating 1477-1500, from all over Germany and Flanders. Analyzing them in chronological order, one can observe the evolution of rules and customs related to crossbow shooting concerning, for example entrance fees, technical specifications of allowable weapons, variations in the size of shooting galleries, characteristics of targets, number of attempts per contestant, type of prize, etc. In one case, a whole paragraph is dedicated to specifying the actual size of a foot (a *Werkschuh*, or an old form *werckschu*) used in a given city. An invitation was usu. accompanied by a picture or a leather cut-out of a werckschu, such as was the case with the following invitation sent in 1493 by the city of Worms:

And the 'seat' (Sitz), from where to shoot will be at a distance of 280 'werckschu' from the target. It is the same 'werckschu' you will find enclosed. One will shoot in a ring of a diameter also specified in this letter... And he whose bolt hits the circle scores. And you will have 40 shots in this competition... and he whose shot hits the target and does not miss it scores.

[trans. by T. Schnitzler]

In the period when crossbow shooting developed during tournaments organized by merchants' and

Traditional, annual crossbow shooting tournaments take place in many European towns.

craftsmen's guilds, the scoring system distinguished only a hit or a miss. However, if a bolt hit the very center of a target, esp. if it split a bolt previously fired, special scoring was applied, e.g. the score might have been doubled. The surviving prints indicate that the target circle was usu. painted black and its edge was white or vice versa. In the course of the 15th cent. the number of circles grew, thus making the scoring system more complex. In 1493, in Caster near Bergheim, the participants of the local *Schiess Spiel* were already using a 5-circle target. In the 16th cent. the most popular was a 4-circle target but even 7-circle targets could be encountered in some places. The scoring was held by a target referee, known, depending on local traditions, as a *zieler* or *zeiger*. Beside a target there was a

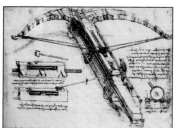
Leonardo da Vinci, A Crossbow.

small stand for target referees where they retreated for the moment when shots were executed after which they approached the target and took down the result. A successful shot was usu. marked as a circle, the most frequent symbol used in medieval cities throughout Europe. Though a multi-circle target must have required a more complex scoring system, researchers are still puzzling over what it may have consisted of. In Trier, 4 different symbols were used to mark hits but the meaning of the symbols has not yet been deciphered. We do not know, for example, what the symbol for a miss was (a

gellen – a whistler, prob. from a whistling sound of a bolt missing the target). All we know with certainty is that the bolts placed in the dead center were marked as circles with little crosses above them. If there were differences in opinion or doubts, a target was taken down and presented before a larger group for inspection. At times a participant missed the target spectacularly, as was the case in Trier, where the local referees recorded that on the Tuesday following Easter, Jakub Preess from Oppenheim placed his 4th bolt in a roof of one of the houses. From the surviving records it can be deduced that the average crossbow shooting tournament lasted 5 days. At the end of the 15th cent. regulations employed during such competitions were standardized. A target was usu. a circle 12-18cm in diameter, about 80-95m from the shooter (targets used for the first models of firearms were up to 1.5m in diameter, which, in terms of accuracy, proves the substantial advantage of crossbows over the earliest rifles). Each shooter could execute around 40 shots. The number of contestants depended on the size of the city hosting the tournament and varied from several dozen to several hundred. In 1470, in Augsburg, 460 crossbow shooters participated in the same competition. Because some of the competitors made attempts to cheat by using mechanical hand-props concealed beneath their sleeves, a rule was introduced according to which shooters had to execute their shots with their arms bare. Prizes, referred to as 'adventures' (*Abentheuer*, cf. modern *Abenteuer*), depended on the affluence of the host city. Historians believe the highest of them were equivalent to approx. 3,000 EURO. The prizes were awarded not only for the shooters coming in the first place but also for those coming less. In Nuremberg, in 1458, the prizes were given to 27 competitors who achieved from 7 to 11 hits.

Some of the more affluent cities used to send rhymed invitations that included a description of a tournament so that the invitee could prepare himself better. Among the most effective advertisements for a crossbow shooting tournament was a description of the preceding competition held in the same place. In this way a rhymed chronicle was written; a number of such poetic invitations have survived. These soon evolved into a literary genre referred to as *Reimspruch* (in old form *Reimspruh*, lit. rhymed predicate). The precursor of the genre was Prichenmeister, a jester and troubadour who praised shooting tournaments held in various cities. The most famous poet writing this kind of rhymes was L. Flexel (16th cent.), author of 9 pieces. He was the one to establish the Reimsprüche canon, which the author described in the following way:

It is part of the event to write letters of invitation. Everything was described precisely so that nothing is left out of which is part of the tradition of marksmen's tournaments.

[tras. by T. Schnitzler]

From the rhymes it can be deduced that a competition was supervised by a special 9-member committee whose responsibility was to maintain a record of the results achieved in the course of the event and then rank the marksmen from best to worst.

And there should be officials who should act as record keepers to list the marksmen.

Nine should be elected, five of those who represent the visitors and four from home

[trans. by Thomas Schnitzler]

Each Reimspruch contained a list of winners from the preceding tournament that had been held in a given city. The winner of a given event earned special mention from the poet:

Finally one must mention the best: the noble yeoman Johann Falker of Frankfurt who has won the ox

[trans. by T. Schnitzler]

A popular activity was a match between 2 rival cities. In 1419-31, the citizens of Goslar challenged the inhabitants of Helmstedt a number of times. Many such crossbow shooting tournaments did not stand the test of time and could not compete with modern forms of shooting. In the majority of municipalities crossbow shooting was abandoned in the 18th cent. In some of them, however, it survived right through to the 1950s when a renaissance of the discipline began. In 1956, the International Crossbow Shooting Union was established and 2 years later annual E.Ch. were inaugurated and since 1979 regular W.Ch. are held as well. The most complete and grand continuation of traditional, annual crossbow shooting tournaments can be presently observed in Italy, in the town of Gubbio. Crossbow shooters (*balestrieri*) compete for a colored flag (*palio*). In Belgian crossbow shooting, still practiced today, instead of bolts special bullets are used.

G. André, '(Chinese) Arrow Games. Hunting, Contests and War', YOSICH, 1999, 38-41; J.M. Carter, *Medieval Games. Sports and Recreations in Feudal Society*, 1992; P. Dubay, *Arc et Arbalète*, 1978; E. Freys, *Gedruckte Schützenbriefe des 15. Jahrhunderts*, 1912; R. Payne-Gallwey, *The Cross-Bow*, 1903; R. Roth, *Historie de l'archeire. Arc et arbalète*, 1992; T. Schnitzler, 'Quantification on Results in Late Medieval Crossbow and Rifle Schooting', IJHS, 10, 2, 1993; K. Wassmannsdorff, *Das Prieschenmeister Lienhard Flexel's Reimspruch über das Heidelberger Armbrustschießen des Jahres 1554*, 1886; K. Zieschang, *Vom Schützenfest zum Turnfest*, 1977.

CROSS-COUNTRY RUNNING, a type of a track and field long-distance running event over open country usu. held over a non-typical distance (IAAF recommends distances of 4-12km for men and 2km for women). Cross-country races are held as individual, team and relay events. Younger competitors run over distances between 2 and 4km. During local competitions organizers rarely adhere to IAAF-recommended distances.

History. The tradition of cross-country running is related to hunting activities pursued in the past and the need to communicate. Elements of cross-country running are found in various cultures across the world, i.e. *tarahumara races*, the Inca running envoys carrying messages across the forests and mountains of S America, the Hawaiian >KUKINI RACES or the New Guinean >CUMNGO RACES. In ancient Ireland running across woods constituted one of the trials which determined whether a boy was fit to become a Fenian warrior (>FENIAN RUNNING). A runner had to avoid being caught by his pursuers and at the same time prevent his specially braided hair from coming undone and should not break even a single branch. Cross-country run-

The crossbow provides increased stability and allows the archer to release the bolt at his leisure.

Over the river and through the woods cross-country runners take the scenic route.

ning was also known in the Balkans (>MONTENE-GRO RACES). The sport started developing in its modern form at the beginning of the 19th cent. in England when it was treated as a method for reviving natural forms of movement that had become distorted or were lost or forgotten in an industrialized urban environment. Initially, cross-country running was a mix of cross-country running as we know it today and a cross-country >STEEPLE CHASE. A significant event in the history of cross-country running was the founding of the Crick Run at Rugby School in 1837. A similar run was held in 1838 by students of medicine in Birmingham. Since that time cross-country running had been gaining popularity at Eng. secondary schools and universities. In 1867 it was introduced to the Eng. track and field championships. The races were held over open country or through woods and courses were usu. marked with red ribbons tied to tree trunks or specially prepared poles. Hence the Eng. name of the sport – *paper chase*. The ribbons had to be found so that a runner knew whether he was following a correct route. To this extent, the paper chase resembled modern >ORIENTEERING. Paper chasing began to die out in the 1890s, lamented by the author of the *Encyclopaedia of Sports* 'it is with sorrow that we have to record the fact that every year the paper chase finds a smaller place in the fixture card of leading clubs, and that it is being displaced by the ever-increasing number of races with their attendant prizes [...] so often as to become quite monotonous' (1897, vol. 1). In the US the sport became a part of the national track and field championships in 1890 and cross-country races have been held ever since except the 1893-96 and 1899-1900 periods as well as 1902 and 1904. Irrespective of the type of cross-country events held, both England and the US were some 50 years ahead of the rest of the world and particularly Europe where until 1939 street races were far more popular than cross-country ones. Only after WWII could continental Eur. events, such the famous *cross* organized by the Fr. paper *L'Humanite*, match the Brit. events as far as their popularity and the number of participants was concerned. Cross-country was introduced to the USSR in 1922 and became popular in Soviet bloc countries, where it was used for propaganda purposes after 1945.

Cross-country running was included on the Olympic program in 1904, 1912, 1920 and 1924. Most of the gold medals went to Finns – H. Kolemainen (1912) and P. Nurmi (1920 and 1924) – and to the Finnish team (in 1912, 1920 and 1924). Americans won only once (in 1904).

CROSS-COUNTRY SKIING, see >SKI RUNNING COMPETITIONS.

CROSSE, LE JEU DE, see >LACROSSE.

CROSSERIE, a Fr. game in which a ball is moved with a curved rod ending in a net like in >LACROSSE. The game developed in certain parts of France, the model being >SOULE, LA. Its richest forms grew shortly before the Fr. revolution in Avranches, dept. of Manche. Every year, on Shrove Tuesday (*Mardi Gras*), the local bishop and his canons, holding the playing rods, marched in a proces-

sion of lower clergy and local people towards a nearby beach in the vicinity of Pont-Gilbert. There, a match was played and each successful action was saluted by the cathedral bells. An identical custom was practiced in the beaches of the neighboring isle of Mont Saint Michel, where crosserie was played as early as 1840, as well as in the town of Genets.

CROWN GREEN BOWLS, also *crown green bowling*. An Eng. var. of >LAWN BOWLS. The fundamental difference consists of the playing surface which instead of being even, is raised 8-18in. (20.3--45.7cm) towards the center, forming a so-called crown. Therefore, in order to differentiate between crown green bowls and a game held on a flat surface, the latter is often referred to as flat green bowls. The green is a square whose sides are 30-60yds. (27.4-54.9m), the most frequent dimensions being about 40yds. (36.6m). The surface is marked at 3 most important points: the central top of the green, referred to as the crown; central entrance that must be located more or less in the middle of one of the sides; a distance of 4yds. (3.66m) from the green's edge, indicated by special poles in its 4 corners. Similarly to flat green bowling, in crown green bowling the object is to throw one's bowls as close as possible to the 'jack' or the 'target bowl'. At the same time, players attempt to push the opponent's bowls away from the jack. Each bowl closer to the jack than the opponent's one scores a point. The winner is the party who scores 21 or 41pts. first. The latter scoring is applied mostly by the local Brit. Lancashire Professional Bowling Association. Unlike in flat green bowls, the crown green var. does not have regulations determining the size of bowls. The liberty was so great here that finally in 1968 a regulation prohibiting the use of bowls of the size of the jack was issued. Nevertheless, some informal standards are observed, according to which most bowls weigh between 2½-3lbs. (1.1-1.5kg). Usually crown green bowls are a little smaller than those used in the flat green version, although in both games the bowls' center of gravity is shifted by means of a bias. Unlike in flat green, the bias is not standardized; most often it reaches the level that would be an equivalent of 2¼ size in a 5-pt. flat green scale. In addition, the bias in crown green bowls is incomparably more important than in the other game, because the curvature of a bowl's trajectory can be added to or leveled with the course's slope. Some players, esp. professionals, use more than one set of bowls, whose bias is different, to be applied depending on the type of course and tactical assumptions during a match. The jack also has different sizes from organization to organization. However, according to the rules of the British Crown Green Amateur Bowling Association and the British Parks and Recreation Amateur Bowling Association, its diameter should be min. 3¾in. (9.53cm) and max. 3⁷/₈in. (9.84cm). The jack's average weight is 21oz. (595g).

While throwing a bowl, the player stands with one foot on a mat referred to as a 'footer' (in flat green bowls, the foot may lose contact with the footer but it must not cross the mat's limits). If throwing with the left hand, the left foot is on the footer, and if the right hand is used, the right foot occupies the mat. Should this rule be violated, a throw is deemed in-

valid. The mat used in crown green bowls is smaller than in the flat green counterpart and it is round, 4in. (10.2cm) in diameter.

A referee in the crown green version has more powers than in flat green bowls. He interprets any doubts not covered by the rules and settles any disputes among players. The referee's decision is final.
ARL, sub-entry 'Crown Green Bowls', 1975; J. Lowerson, 'Bowls and Bowling', EWS, I, 1996.

CRUOL, a lawn game from the >CROQUET family which originated in Croatia at the time of the First Crusades. Legend has it that Prester John and his followers camped for the night in the hills near what is now Smiljan on their way back to the Adriatic Sea. When fires lit the night sky, a strange hoard of domestic cats approached the camp. Familiar with these creatures, the soldiers fed them with scraps of half-rotted meat. However, one knight, Alfons DeCruol, became most agitated and began kicking the cats, all the while raving of imps and servants of Baphomet. His comrades thought him to be mad and tried to restrain him, but Alfons grabbed a war hammer, knocked many heads, and charged into the woods. His fellow knights rushed after him and found him crying, 'Baphomet! I see the enemy!', after which he plunged into a small clearing and vanished into thin air. A moment later, a loud blast knocked the remaining soldiers back from the clearing and when they came round again, there was a large pentagon with raised edges formed in the earth with a large head of reddish stone in the center. The head was vaguely human, with long thick 'tails' growing where the hair and beard should be.

A crown green bowling match (below) and a set of bowls (above right).

Outside the pentagon, Alfons lay dead with his war hammer shattered. Having returned to the camp with Alfons' body, the knights discovered the cats had become the same reddish stone and appeared as devilish imps with feline features. Prester John deduced that the head belonged to an unholy underworld lord whom Alfons called Baphomet and who was in the process of entering our world. Baphomet sent the cat-imps out as spies to see if our world was hospitable and used the pentagon as a magical blind. Not fooled by the illusions, Alfons whacked the unholy lord on the skull, broke his

Crown green bowls.

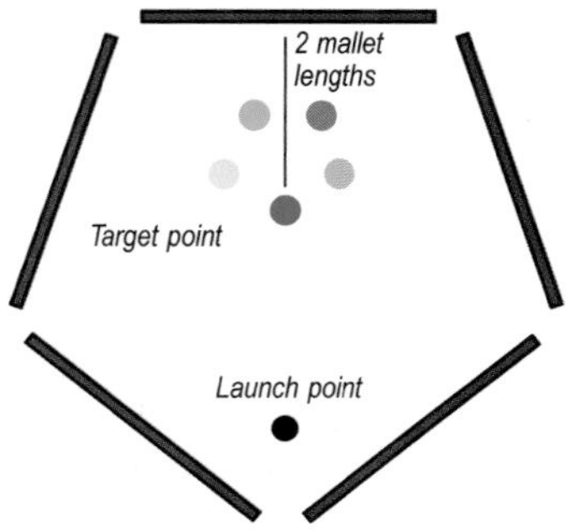

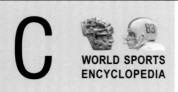

An arena for playing cruol.

concentration, and interrupted the spell. The petrified head and cat-imps returned home as souvenirs, but later disappeared together with the Knights Templar. Storytellers who retold the legend often demonstrated the head-whacking with war hammers and iron balls and it soon developed into a sport, which – by the 16th cent. – went into oblivion, overshadowed by a more popular croquet. At the end of the 20th cent. the game was revived in North Carolina by the Independent Society of Faith, a small religious community.

The arena is a small pentagon with rails along each side and open pockets at the corners. Each side rail is 10ft. long and each pocket is 7in. wide. Rails are flat on the inside and approx. the same height as the balls.

Rules. The object of the game is to send all the opponent's balls through the pockets and have only one's own balls remain in the arena. Each player has 3 balls (2-player game), 2 balls (3-player game), or 1 ball (4-6-player game) plus a cue ball the color of his mallet. The first player places his cue ball on the launch point and knocks it toward the other balls. With each swing, a player tries to knock his cue ball into an opponent's ball, which becomes the target ball (the so-called 'roak'). The player continues his turn as long as he successfully roaks the target ball or 'croaks' it through a pocket, after which he selects a new target ball. Croaking means aligning one's cue ball against the target ball, placing a foot on top of the cue ball, and knocking the target ball in any direction, which ends the turn (unless the target ball is pocketed). Knocking one's own non-cue ball or an opponent's ball other than the target ball through a pocket is considered a 'banzai' and ends the turn. Balls that are knocked out of the arena are returned to the launch point (cue ball) or target point (the opponent balls).

CRUSHED STONE LIFT, a var. of weightlifting consisting of lifting a bar to which 2 Plexiglas boxes are attached at each end. The boxes, measuring 60x60x60cm each, are filled with crushed stone. Crushed stone lift is one of the constituent events of the World's Strongest Man Competition.

CSIGA, a Hung. var. of >TOPS.

CUCAÑA, LA, a Span. var. of >GREASED POLE.

CUDDY AND THE POWKS, a Brit. wrestling game. One of the participants gets down on all fours and two other players sit on his back, facing each other and holding each other's hands. The cuddy is supposed to carry the 'passengers' over a predetermined distance. If he succeeds, one of the passengers [a *powk* = a *pouch* or a *blister*] becomes the cuddy. The game's starting position is similar to the one used in Dan. >REJSE SIG MED MAND PÅ RYGGEN, in which the 'donkey's' objective is to throw the others off his back by standing up, instead of carrying them as in cuddy and the powks.

A.B. Gomme, 'Cuddy and the Powks', TGESI, 1994, I, 84.

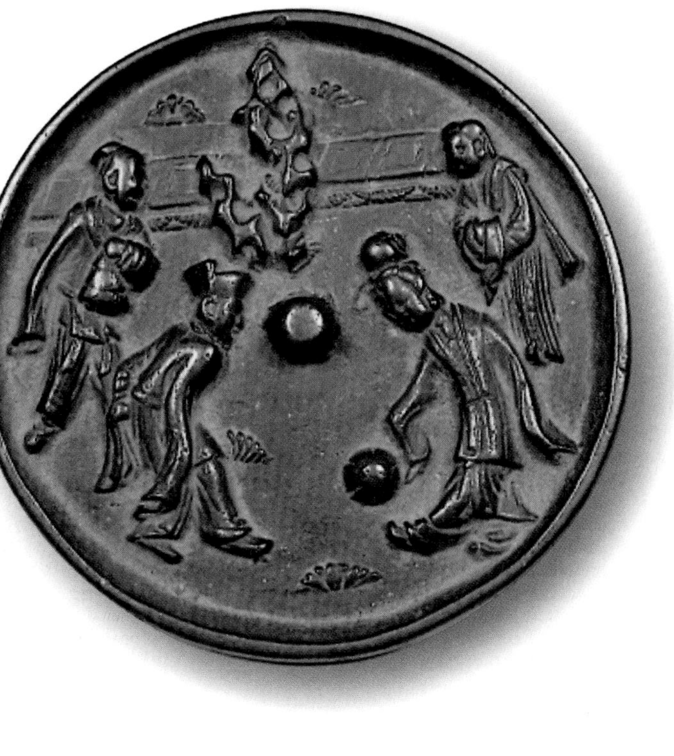

The Chinese football game of cuju. A bronze mirror, China, Song dynasty (960-1279).

CUDGEL, an Eng. folk game whose rules are similar to those of >CRICKET, but instead of a ball a small wooden pin is used, referred to as a 'cat' and instead of goals there are 2 holes in the ground located within a few steps of each other, each surrounded by a circle around 1ft. (30cm) in diameter. There are 2 teams of several players, out of which 2 players, known as 'batsmen', defend the holes using a long stick placed in the hole to prevent the cat from falling in. A player who wins the toss throws the cat, attempting to place it inside the circle surrounding the opposing team's hole. If the cat rests in the hole, the batsman defending it leaves the game and is replaced by another player from the same team. If the 'bowler' (the throwing player) misses the hole but manages to place the cat inside the circle, both bowlers leave the playing field and either agree or toss a coin to decide which of them is going to hold the cat during the next phase of the game. They come back onto the field, hiding the cat so that the batsmen are not able to tell who is holding it. Both bowlers kneel in front of their holes and the batsmen are supposed to guess which of the two kneeling players is holding the cat. One of the batsmen runs up to the kneeling bowler and puts his stick into the hole behind him, while the other batsman runs towards the other hole. If the first guessed correctly and pointed to the bowler holding the cat, the bowler, before the other batsman makes it to his hole, throws the cat into that hole, which eliminates the running batsman and scores a point. If a batsman points to the wrong bowler, the one kneeling in front of the other hole throws the cat at the hole behind the 'wrong' bowler. If the cat lands in the hole, both kneeling players become batsmen, and the one who threw the cat into the hole starts the game again.

A.B. Gomme, 'Cudgel', TGESI, 1994, I, 84-5.

CUEPAS, a Span. game practiced by Native Latin Amer. Indians according to rules similar to those employed in Fr. >BOULE, however the bowls used are much smaller and are made of wax.

CUJU, a term used in ancient China for football which is sometimes commonly referred to as Chin. football (>TSU-CHU). A probable var. of the name is >TSU-KIH. Numerous sources agree on the fact that the number of players in a team was not fixed. There could be 2-10 footballers in each team. Sometimes a match was played singles. Different var. of the game had different names, such as a 'rolling ball' – a game in singles, or a 'double game' – a game in pairs. The more members were in each team, the more poetic was the name of the game. Starting thus with a 3-player team upwards, the names were as follows: 'dodging a blooming branch', 'meteors chasing the Moon', 'little buds', 'flowers falling on water', 'the immortal eight crossing the sea', 'umbrella fanning', and 'hitting a flower's heart'. In his *Dongjing Menghualu*, ancient the Chin. writer Yuan-lao described a match held at the Huizonga court. From the description it can be gathered the object of the game was to score a goal by placing the ball between 2 poles adorned with colored bands. The match was played by 10-player teams. The team to start the game was determined by way of drawing. Teammates could pass the ball one to another only on their own half and when the border of the half was reached a player had to execute a long kick towards the opponent's goal. If the opponents intercepted the ball before it reached the goal, the game was continued, this time, however, in the opposite direction. We do not know what happened when a goal was scored; whether the ball was returned to the scoring team to allow them to repeat their attempts until the opponents stole the ball back, or whether it was the opposing team who then took possession of the ball, in turn. No scoring rules have survived either. We do not know if there was a time limit or a match was played until a predetermined number of goals. In different times the game was organized in a different way. During the Tang dynasty (608-906 AD) the ball was hard and heavy, made of unidentified materials, perhaps of wood. In the course of the Song dynasty it was substantially improved, as it was made of an animal's bladder or leather prob. stuffed with pressed bristle. Yang Shigu (581-645), the author of *Comments on the Book of Han*, described a cuju ball as made of leather and stuffed with hair and pieces of fur. Similar balls were still present in the 20th cent. In the Middle Ages, a sophisticated method of producing light balls filled with compressed air was developed. First, pieces of smooth and soft leather were stitched tightly together. Then, a ball was inflated and immediately cooled by submerging it in cold water, which made the material even more airtight. Until balls with rubber bladders were developed in the 19th cent., a Chin. leather ball filled with compressed air reigned supreme as the best construction known to man.

History. The earliest records of football games date back to the reign on the Shang dynasty, i.e. the 16th--13th cent. BC A game, of which little is known today, was played by soldiers. One of the oldest Chin. written records *Zhanguo ce* mentions an affluent region of Linzi where people played ball of an indeterminate type during the Warring States Period (approx. 403-222 BC). The first reference to a ball propelled with the legs dates to the Han dynasty period (206 BC-220 AD). The text containing 25 rules of cuju is considered the earliest written record in the history of Chin. sport. Emperor Han Wu Ti (which means Warlord) made football an element of military training. Responsible for the execution of the Emperor's order was a military commander, Huo Qubing (d. 117 BC), also known from a military campaign against a tribe referred to in Chin. historiography as Hsiung-nu (also sp. Xiongnu). Later, Emperor Taizu (960-975) played football as a young man with his brothers: Zhao Kangyi, Zhao Pu, Zheng En, Chu Zhaofu, and Shi Shouksin. Emperor Hizong, reigning from 1101-25, was an avid supporter of cuju. There are even anecdotes revealing his predilection for football. According to one of them, Huizong offered a court post to a certain messenger only because he turned out to be a skilled footballer. The former messenger became a supervisor and organizer of football matches and earned himself the nickname Gao Qiu – Great Ball.

In the Middle Ages, cuqiu competed for popularity with a Chin. predecessor of polo, >JIQIU. In the course of time, jiqiu began to fall out of favor because it required large horse farms and extensive meadows, both of which were on the wane. Although horse breeding did not disappear completely, it ceased to play an important role in an economy based on rice cultivation, in which manual work and oxen were mostly employed. At the same time, different var. of football were making inroads among inhabitants of rapidly growing cities. In many places early forms of football games survived until the beginning of the 20th cent. when new Western types of games were introduced in China, esp. through schools sponsored by the YMCA. Thus, Eur. football introduced at St. John's College in Shanghai in 1900, by Professor Walker (first name unknown), an Englisman, marked the end of Chin. football.

J.P. Desroches, '(Chinese) Ball Games: Polo and Football', YOSICH, 1999; Shao Quinlong, *The History of Sport In China Since Antiquity*, 15-19.

CULECHE, a folk var. of Azerbaijan wrestling. According to W. Baxter the rules and technique are similar to those exercised in >TURKISH WRESTLING (see >KUŞAK GÜREŞI). Wrestlers wear special pants, like in >PEHLIVAN WRESTLING. The contest is accompanied by sounds of pipes and drums.

'Culeche, Les luttes traditionnelles a traverse le monde'. LJP, 1998, 78

CUMBERLAND AND WESTMORELAND, a var. of wrestling practiced in England and known under the same name in Cumberland, Westmoreland, and some other counties bordering Scotland, where its rules developed and where the style was popular, also under the name of 'backhold'. According to William Baxter: 'this style [...] consists of standing work only with a fixed hold taken by placing the right hand under opponent's left hand and joining the hands. Victory is gained if any part of an opponent's body touches the ground or if he breaks his hold, the area is unlimited when practiced outdoors' [LJP, 72]. Baxter also asserts that 'Cumberland Style is the oldest continually organised combat sport in England and records have been kept of competition winner since 1824.' The first Cumberland and Westmoreland association was established in approx. 1727, operating in London where the first fights of such a type in the entire history of wrestling were organized. The major contest was held annually on Shrove Tuesday. The conservative approach of managers prevented the infiltration of various elements from modern sports disciplines which preserved the original character of the sport. Until 1865, the asso-

Cumberland and Westmoreland wrestling.

ciation was the only such type in London but the numerous amateur wrestling clubs established up to that time posed serious competition, which led to conflicts within the association where conservative and progressive tendencies clashed. Consequently, the association was dissolved in 1895. In the NW part of England, a tradition developed according to which a winner was granted a special belt that he could wear on the first Sun. after a fight. Today, the custom of granting a belt to a winner is popular in many other var. of wrestling throughout the world. In the 19th cent., a cumberland and westmoreland wrestler, W. Richardson, won around 240 belts in various tournaments and was nicknamed Belted Wull. In 1870, the first championship belt was granted in wrestling championships of the USA, held in Ir. >COLLAR AND ELBOW WRESTLING style, and its winner was J.H. McLaughlin. In 1861, the first wrestling fights were organized in Australia. In the 1870s, popular France vs. Great Britain fights were held alternately in French and Cumberland and Westmoreland styles. The most famous among them were the duels Le Beoeufe vs. Wright and Dubois vs. Jamieson from Ciberlnad (wrestlers' first names are unknown), which were witnessed by around 10,000 spectators.

CUMNGO RACES, races held among young boys popular in Cumngo in central New Guinea. The most characteristic feature of a Cumngo race is that each contestant has to reach the same finish line (a specifically marked topographic feature) located in a wooded or bushy area by following a path that is different from any other competitor's. Thus, he is unable to follow the performance of his rivals. Only at the finish line do the runners find out who won.

CURLING, a winter sport in which special stone weights equipped with handles are slid on ice. The official Eng. name for the weight (Eng. is an official lang. of the World Curling Federation) is the 'stone'. The object of the game is to slide stones as close as possible to a circular target, referred to as the 'house', that is marked with concentric colored circles on the ice. The length of the lane that incorporates houses on both ends is 146ft. (44.50m), and its width is 15ft. 7in. (4.75m). The diameter of the house's outer ring is 6ft. (1.83m), and the inner rings are 4ft. (1.22m) and 2ft. (0.61m) in diameter. The target's center, known as a 'tee', is 6in. (15cm) in diameter. Each lane has 2 houses, located symmetrically on both ends of the run-up, so that the game can be played in two directions, although each round is continued only in one direction. The diameter of stones is about 30cm and their height varies from 10-13cm. Their wt. is also different, depending on local rules, usu. up to 27kg. In official international matches that are recognized by the WCF stones weigh 44lbs. (19.96kg); the upper limit on their circumference is 36in. (91.44cm) and the min. height is 4½in. (11.43cm). A stone can be slid on either top – one being larger than the other – depending on the type of ice. Stones are slid starting from the 'foot line' marked with two rubber curbs referred to as 'hacks' which serve as a support for players' feet when starting the slide. The inner edge of each hack has to be 3in. (7.62cm) away from the central line

and their length must not surpass 8in. (20.32cm). The hacks are fixed to a wooden beam frozen into ice at the depth of 2in. (5.04cm). There are two 4-player teams; sometimes 5-player teams are accepted where one of the players is a 'skip' (head of the team) who selects the 4 who are to play at a given moment. The skip can occupy any position on the rink, whereas other team members can only take the positions indicated by the skip. No footwear that damages the ice can be used; spikes are forbidden. One shoe has a smooth sole to facilitate sliding and the other has it rough to enable pushing on the ice. Team members are obliged to wear uniform suits with player's surname on the back. If there is more than one player with the same surname, these should be preceded by the first name initial. Slides are executed between the teams alternatively and each player can execute 2 slides in each round. In order to achieve better precision players make the stones rotate during the slide, i.e. they curl them, hence the name – curling. If a handle slips from the stone during a slide, a player has the right to take the turn over again. A characteristic element of curling is warming the ice up in front of the stone, using

ing the opponent's stone is referred to as a 'wick'. The distance between the house's center and the closest point on a stone is measured with a special tool. The time limit for 10 ends is 75min. In the course of the game no electronic communication gear, such as cellular phones or walkie-talkies, is allowed. **History**. The origins of the game prob. date back to the Middle Ages. The first descriptions of similar folk games come from Flanders, where they formed an element of *kluyten* tradition, as well as from Scot-

A 19th cent. curling match from London Illustrated News.

land. The development of curling is prob. related to the travels of Flem. craftsmen who moved to Scotland at the turn of the Middle Ages and the Renaissance. The oldest Scot. stone preserved comes from Stirling and the date carved on it reads 1511. A stone from Dunblane is only a little younger (1551). In some pictures of Du. masters, e.g. P. Breughel 'The Elder' (*Winter Landscape*), we can see curling players in the background. Nevertheless, it was not Flanders but Scotland that exerted the major influence on the modern form of the game. About 400

Sir George Harvey, The Curlers, *before 1835, oil on canvas.*

special brooms, to improve its progress. Touching the stone during the slide, after the run-up, is prohibited. A player who touches the stone after it has been released by a throwing team member is disqualified, which implies lesser chances of the team as a whole as the disqualified member cannot score points any more. The game is performed in 10-14 rounds, known as 'ends'. A point is scored when a stone either touches or enters the house and comes to a standstill closer to the house's center than the opponent's stone. A configuration of a team's stones protecting one another from the opponent's strikes is referred to as 'building a house'. A stone that protects another fellow stone is dubbed a 'guard'. A fast-sliding stone is called a 'runner' and one that is barely touching the house is labeled 'bitter'. Finally, strik-

ballads and songs related to curling have survived, which proves the abundance of the local tradition. The best stones were made of stone mined in the Aisla Craig quarry in the Firth of Clyde. The most famous stone manufacture opened in the 19th cent. in Mauchline in Ayr County. Although small, informal curling associations have been present in Scotland from the 18th cent., the oldest best-known one that performed a significant role in curling's development was the Dudington Curling Society, established in Edinburgh in 1795. In 1834, the Amateur Curling Club of Scotland developed the first, relatively uniform, set of rules. In 1838, the Grand Caledonian Curling Club was founded and soon after it had absorbed the Amateur Curling Club of Scotland it became an organization recognized as the first

Curling.

C

The Japanese curling team coax their stone along the ice.

WORLD SPORTS ENCYCLOPEDIA

international authority on the game's rules. In 1842, the club changed its name to the Royal Caledonian Curling Club (RCCC). Around the 1750s, the game made its way into the N Amer. continent, starting from the area of today's Canada. It was popularized by Scot. soldiers in Quebec City during the 17-year war, esp. by the troops of Gen. J. Wolfe, c.1756-63. The players used the frozen St.

Curling on a Canadian postage stamp.

Lawrence River as their rink and cannonballs as stones. In 1807, Scot. immigrants established the Royal Montreal Curling Club; other Can. curling associations were founded, also out of Scottish initiative, in Kingston (1820), Quebec (1821), and Halifax (1824). From c.1820, in circumstances similar to Can. ones, curling made inroads in the USA, esp. in the area of the Great Lakes where natural climatic and topographic conditions were favorable. As early as 1819, a group of Scots popularized curling in the state of New York. The first important club in that area was the Orchard Pontiac Club founded in 1839 in Michigan. Soon curling was expanding throughout the USA as dynamically as in Scotland itself. A Can. historian, G. Bryce, emphasized in his work *The Scotsman in Canada* that:

Perhaps the crowning success of Scottish nationality in Western Canada is the spread of the great Scottish game of curling [...]. Almost every railway town in Western Canada early in its history erects a commodious building, which is flooded on the interior ground floor and forms an ice sheet which lasts [...] for three or four months.

Curling performed a momentous role in effacing differences among the states and fostering democracy. In 1840, the newspaper *Toronto Examiner* underlined that 32 players participating in the tournament organized in the city represented all classes of citizen, irrespective of their social or financial status. In 1855, the *Montreal Gazette* proudly declared:

Amongst the players we noticed the Merchant and the Mechanic, the Soldier and the Civilian, the Pastor and his Flock, all on equal footing for the game of curling levels all ranks.

Critics of the game claimed, however, that the major reason for its popularity was not sport as such

Cycle polo ball and mallets.

Cycle polo boasts 12 decades of tradition.

but rather a pretext for a special warm-up. A Can. historian, G. Redmont, reports 'consumption of copious quantities of whiskey during the matches.' In Canada, a tradition has evolved according to which top dignitaries of the country – governors general, and other eminent politicians, take part in popular curling competitions. The first to have the courage to play with ordinary citizens was a Brit. governor of Canada, Earl of Dalhousie who became a member of the Quebec City Curling Club (1828). In his book *Early Life in Upper Canada* (1933), a Can. historian E.C. Guillet stresses that 'The Governors of Canada have usually taken an active interest in the game,' among them such names can be cited Governor General, Lord Sydenham, and Governor of Upper Canada, Sir George Arthur. The keenest fan of curling was Governor General, Lord Dufferin (1872-78), who used to watch public matches and had a curling rink constructed as an official element of the governor's residence, Rideau Hall. The Governor of Canada founded a Governor General's Prize that has become the most precious curling trophy in Canada. At the moment, curling is recognized in Canada among its national sports and since 1972 it has been incorporated in official government programs promoting Canada abroad. The largest curling center in Canada is the state of Manitoba, and the largest club is the Flin Flon Club with its 54 curling lanes, including 40 for women.

A popular poem by E. Shepherd described the democratic character of the game in the following way:

Here Peer and friendly peasant meet,
Aukld etiquette has lost her seat,
The social broom has swept her neat,
Beyond the pale o'Curling.

The first international match was played between Canada and the USA on Lake Erie, in Buffalo, in 1865. In the second half of the 19th cent., curling was popularized in Scand. countries, esp. in Sweden, and in the 1930s, even in N.Zealand and Australia, where matches have been organized since 1933 on artificial ice rinks located in 2 urban centers – Melbourne and Brisbane. In 1991, the Pacific zone countries established the Pacific Curling Federation whose founding members are Australia, N.Zealand, and Japan. In 1966, out of the Royal Caledonian Curling Club's initiative, the International Curling Federation was founded, which soon after was renamed as the World Curling Federation seated in Edinburgh. The first WCF W.Ch. was a competition held in 1959 between 2 champion teams of Scotland and Canada who competed in a tournament consisting of a series of 5 games. In 1959-67, the tournament's sponsor was the Scotch Whisky Association. In that period participation in the championships grew from 2 to 8 national representations: the USA joined in 1961, Sweden in 1962, Switzerland and Norway in 1964, France in 1966, and FRG in 1967. A condition for a national federation to become a member of the WCF is to organize at least a 3-month period of competitions on either natural or artificial rinks. In 1968, the championship's sponsor, Air Canada, began awarding the Air Canada Silver Broom to winning teams. In 1973, the number of national teams represented at W.Ch. reached 10 for the first time. As a result of Air Canada's eventual withdrawal from sponsorship in 1985, the major participants in the W.Ch., i.e. World Curling Federation, The Royal Caledonian Curling Club, and Hexagon Curling International Corporation, Toronto, signed in Broomhall, Fife County, Scotland, a contract under which the Hexagon Curling International Corporation became responsible for the organization of the following W.Ch. Since 1989, W.Ch. are held both in men's and women's categories. The most frequent winner in the curling W.Ch. has been Canada (25 times), while the second place is occupied by the USA (4 titles). Since 1995, the W.Ch. have been sponsored by Ford. Under-21's W.Ch., originally only boys, have been continued since 1975. Their initiator was the East York Curling Club from Toronto, where the first under-21's curling W.Ch. were held.

Women's curling. In 1977, the first women's curling championships were held, but the World Curling Federation (at that time the International Curling Federation) have admitted women only since 1978. The first women's championships under WCF's auspices took place in 1979 in Perth, Scotland, where the following 11 national teams competed: Canada, Denmark, England, France, FRG, Italy, Norway,

Scotland, Sweden, Switzerland, and the USA. The winning team is awarded the World Women's Curling Championship Trophy. The trophy is a challenge prize and it remains the federation's property. In the women's W.Ch. history the best team is Canada that has been victorious 10 times and the second best is Sweden with its 4 victories.

The first under-21's women's W.Ch. were held in Chamonix (France). Since 1989, women's and men's under-21's have been organized together. The winning team is awarded the World Junior Women's Curling Championship Trophy.

W.Ch. are organized annually. Since 1975, also E.Ch. have been held, in which up to 1997, in men's competition, Scots won 8 times, Swiss – 6 times, and Germans – 4 times; in women's events, during the same period, Sweden was victorious 10 times, FRG – 6 times, and Switzerland – 4 times.

Curling at the Ol.G. The sport was included into the Olympic program in 1924, in Chamonix as a men's demonstration sport. The winning team was Great Britain, and then, in the 1932 Ol.G. in Lake Placid, it was Canada. In the 1988 Calgary Ol.G. curling was still a demonstration sport, although this time in both men's (Switzerland achieved the first place) and women's (Sweden was the winner) categories. In 1992, in Albertville, the women's demonstration competition was won by Germany, and the men's event by Switzerland.

The first full-medal Ol.G. tournament in Nagano (1998) featured 8 teams, selected in the course of qualifications that consisted of scoring points for places achieved by each team during the 3 consecutive W.Ch. preceding the year when the Ol.G. were held. In the women's category the winner was Canada and among men it was Switzerland. In the 2002 Ol.G., the 9 best teams were admitted.

Games resembling curling were also developed in other countries. Cf. Ger. >EISSCHIEßEN, Icelandic >KNATTLEIKR and Mong. games incorporating an element of sliding stones in ice, such as >MÖSÖN SHAGAI KHARVAKH.

World Curling Federation, Official Handbook, rev. ed. 1996; W.A. Creelman, *Curling Past and Present*, 1950; E. Richardson, J McKee, D. Maxwell, *Curling*, 1962; G. Redmont, 'An Analysis of the Evolution and Diffusion of the Sport of Curling in North America', HEDS-GDC, HISPA, 1975; E.A. Sautter-Hewitt, 'Curling From Pastime to Olympic Sport', OR, 1994, 316; R. Wels, *Beginner's Guide to Curling*, 1969.

CYCLE POLO, also *bike polo, polo on wheels*, a variation of >POLO with bicycles being substituted for the ponies; cf. >CYCLOBALL. The game is played by 2 teams of 4 players. For recreational matches regular tourist bicycles can be used. The ball is a tennis ball; a bike polo mallet is 75-85cm long. Players wear T-shirts and tennis shoes. A game is made up of four 7½-min. chukkas, with three 3-min. breaks in between. According to US rules, the chukkas last 10min. each and there is a 2-min. break between the first and second chukka, and third and fourth chukka and a 10-min. half-time. The playing field is a grassy area 100x60yds.

History. The game was invented in 1891 by an Ir. cyclist, R.J. Mecredy, a member of the Ohnehest Cycling Club in Dublin, and the editor of the sports magazine 'Irish Cyclist.' The inaugurational cycle polo match was played on 10 Oct. 1891, with the participation of about forty cyclists. Soon after the Sheen Horse Club was founded in England, and by 1914 there were about 100 cycle polo clubs with 1,000 players in the British Isles. The first international match was played between England and Ireland in London's Crystal Palace. Both World Wars contributed to the fall in game's popularity in Britain, however cycle polo was revived in former Brit. colonies, particularly in India and Australia, thanks to Brit. troops who used bicycles to hone their equestrian polo skills. The sport was also introduced to Belgium, France, and the Philippines. In the USA the game was first practiced in 1897; the first American cycle polo club was founded in Milton, Massachusetts. After 1903 a huge number of clubs appeared, some of which exist to the present day. Cycle polo is a popular weekend recreational sport practiced in the Central Park in New York City. Its governing body in the USA is the United States Bicycle Polo Association; in Asia it is the Asian Cycle Polo Federation, which comprises 6 national federations, including the largest Cycle Polo Federation of India with 10,000 members. Cycle polo was included in

Cycle polo.

the program of the 1908 Ol.G. in London as an exhibition sport. It was also one of the events of the Asian Games in 1982 (later replaced by the Malaysian >SEPAK TAKRAW).

J. Arlott, *Bicycle Polo*, ARL, 1975; P. Bhandari, *Polo on Wheels, a Popular Sport*, OR Dec. 1995 – Jan. 1996; http://www.bikepolo.com/about.html

CYCLE SPEEDWAY. Races are held on tracks similar to those in speedway, but shorter (45-100m). The rules are similar to those applied in speedway. In a single race 4 riders race against each other over 4 laps, starting, like in speedway, when the start net is jerked up.

History. Cycle speedway originated in England, where it developed after WWII. The Cycle Speedway Council has its seat in Poole in England. Individual and team W.Ch. and E.Ch. have been held since 1958, usually every 2 years, in the senior and junior (up to 18 years of age) categories. Every year the Grand Prix Europe and Team Europe Cup are held. Cycle speedway is best developed in England, Australia, the Czech Republic, Denmark, Holland, Ireland, Scotland, Sweden and Wales. M. Newey, world champion in 1996-97 and S. Harris, world champion in 1999 have been the best riders in recent years. Recently cycle speedway has been exported to the former communist countries in Europe, mainly Poland, where it started to develop at the beginning of the 1990s. In 1994 the first organization was established, the Rawicki Klub Sportowy Pavart. In 1995, also in Rawicz, the Polish Cycle Speedway Association, affiliating 10 clubs, was established. From Apr. to Oct. teams compete in a series of meets; the best teams compete in play-off races. In 1996 Rawicz was the venue of the Cycle Speedway E.Ch. and in 1997 of the Team Cycle Speedway Europe Cup. Polish riders have ranked among the best riders in the world ever since they began taking part and have been winning medals since 1995. In 1999 K. Włodarczyk was Eur. senior champion and the Pol. team won the silver medal.

During the W.Ch. held in Rawicz between 2-4 July 1999, with 170 riders and 7 national teams participating, Poland won the world champion team title. R. Witham (Ed.), *50 Years of Cycle Speedway*, British Cycle Speedway Council, 1957.

CYCLING, a group of sporting events in which the contestants, or teams of contestants, move on bicycles, or on vehicles which historically preceded the creation of the bicycle, such as the *célérifère*, *velocifère* and velocipede. The basic types of cycling are >MOUNTAIN BIKING, >CYCLO-CROSS, >ROAD CYCLING, >TRACK CYCLING, including >MOTOR-PACED CYCLING, >CROSS BMX, >CYCLING MARATHON, and >CYCLISM. Bicycle based activities include >CYCLOBALL, >CYCLE POLO, >BICYCLE STUNT RIDING; a cycling race forms part of the >TRIATHLON. See also >UNRESTRICTED BICYCLES.

History. Cycling as a sports discipline was preceded by numerous attempts to construct man-powered vehicles. In 1649, a J. Hautsch from Nuremberg built a 4-wheeled vehicle, allegedly powered with a spring mechanism, but in reality run by 2 men hidden inside the vehicle who turned a crank connected to the wheels. Also in Nuremberg, in 1685, a paralyzed watchmaker, S. Farfler constructed a tricycle powered with the arms by means of a crank and a toothed gear on the front wheel. Around 1750, an Englishman, J. Vevers built a 4-wheeler powered with leg-cranks, which was steered with reins attached to the rolling mechanism of the front wheels. In 1789, *Journal de Paris* brought news of a tricycle constructed by J.P. Blanchard, a famous balloon designer, constructor and pilot (1753-1809), and his assistant

Bottom left and below: cycle speedway.

Maguriere (see >BALLOONING). The real beginning of the evolution of a vehicle which was to become today's bicycle is marked by the *célérifère* [Fr. *célérifère* from Lat. *celer* – fast + *ferro* – carry], a vehicle designed and built by an anonymous constructor for one count De Sivrac and demonstrated on the grounds of the Palace Royale in Paris in 1791. The vehicle had no handlebars, consisted of 2 wooden wheels with spokes, and a wooden frame on which the cyclist would sit astride as if on a horse, pushing his legs against the ground. The subsequent versions, known as the *velocifère*, became increasingly lighter and more comfortable. A mechanism allowing for steering the front wheel was used for the first time by baron K. Friedrich von Drais (1795-1851) in his eponymous 'draisine' [Ger. *Draisine*; the name was later applied to a self-propelled rail-vehicle also invented by Drais]. In 1818, a Fr. store belonging to M. Garcin by way of experiment purchased 2 draisins, and in order to popularize them on April 5th organized a race in the Luxembourg Garden. This was the first documented cycling race. Following a report in the *Journal de Paris* the next day, 'the race itself was splendid, but its finale was obscured by a throng that rallied round the participants to such an extent that it successfully prevented them from completing the set 600-m distance'. Such intense interest in races encouraged the organization of new ones in the sub-Parisian locations of Monceaux, Sceaux, Belleville and Monfermeil (1818). A few months later, H.O. Duncan, an Eng. eyewitness to the Parisian races, published *The World on Wheels*, a work that greatly contributed to the popularization of the 2-wheeled vehicles called in England by this time bicycles [Fr. *bicyclette*, Sp. *bicicleta*, Ita. *bici-*

cletta, Lat. prefix *bi-* meaning double + *cyclus*, Gr. *kyklos* – wheel = lit. 'two-wheeler'] in England. Already in 1819 an Eng. craftsman, D. Johnson, built the first iron bicycle called a *hobby-horse*; all told he produced some 700 of these. The same constructor also built the first bicycle with a ladies' frame. 1819-20 marked the first wave of popularity of bicycles in England. In 1821, an Englishman L. Gompertz endeavored to apply a rope-crank drive, whose mechanism was similar to today's chain, but abandoned this idea in the face of technical difficulties and a slumping demand for such vehicles. As a consequence of bad press and disenchantment with poor roads, the bicycle fad had been on the wane since 1821. Then M. Lagrange came along, constructed bicycles between 1824-28. His greatest feat was the completion of the 30km from Beaune to Paris in less than 2hrs. on a bicycle of his own devise. This achievement was so widely commented upon in the press that this nearly forgotten invention was suddenly thrust back into the limelight. A Scot. smith, K. Macmillan (1810-78), added pedals to the bicycle in 1834. His were, however, not coaxial like mod. pedals, but were fixed on levers hinged to the frame near the handlebars which in turn were joined to the

WORLD SPORTS ENCYCLOPEDIA

C

A postage stamp issued for the 100th anniversary of the Warsaw Cycling Society.

Henri de Toulouse-Lautrec, a cycling poster for the Simpson bicycle chain, 1896.

C WORLD SPORTS ENCYCLOPEDIA

MEN'S ROAD CYCLING WORLD CHAMPIONS

1927 Alfredo Binda, ITA
1928 Georges Ronsse, BEL
1929 Georges Ronsse, BEL
1930 Alfredo Binda, ITA
1931 Learco Guerra, ITA
1932 Alfredo Binda, ITA
1933 Georges Speicher, FRA
1934 Karel Kaers, BEL
1935 Jean Aerts, BEL
1936 Antonin Magne, FRA
1937 Eloi Meulenberg, BEL
1938 Marcel Kint, BEL
1946 Hans Knecht, SWI
1947 Theodore Middelkamp, NED
1948 Briek Schotte, BEL
1949 R. Van Steenbergen, BEL
1950 Briek Schotte, BEL
1951 Ferdi Kubler, SWI
1952 Heinz Muller, RFA
1953 Fausto Coppi, ITA
1954 Louison Bobet, FRA
1955 Stan Ockers, BEL
1956 R. Van Steenbergen, BEL
1957 R. Van Steenbergen, BEL
1958 Ercole Baldini, ITA
1959 André Darrigade, FRA
1960 Rik Van Looy, BEL
1961 Rik Van Looy, BEL
1962 Jean Stablinski, FRA
1963 Benoni Beheyt, BEL
1964 Jan Janssen, NED
1965 Tom Simpson,, GBR
1966 Rudi Altig, RFA
1967 Eddy Merckx, BEL
1968 Vittorio Adorni, ITA
1969 Harm Ottenbros, NED
1970 J-P Monsere, BEL
1971 Eddy Merckx, BEL
1972 Marino Basso, ITA
1973 Felice Gimondi, ITA
1974 Eddy Merckx, BEL
1975 Hennie Kuiper, NED
1976 Freddy Maertens, BEL
1977 Francesco Moser, ITA
1978 Gerrie Knetemann, NED
1979 Jan Raas, NED
1980 Bernard Hinault, FRA
1981 Freddy Maertens, BEL
1982 Giuseppe Saronni, ITA
1983 Greg Lemond, USA
1984 Claude Criquielion, BEL
1985 Joop Zoetemelk, NED
1986 Moreno Argentin, ITA
1987 Stephen Roche, IRL
1988 Maurizio Fondriest, ITA
1989 Greg Lemond, USA
1990 Rudy Dhaenens, BEL
1991 Gianni Bugno, ITA
1992 Gianni Bugno, ITA
1993 Lance Armstrong, USA
1994 Luc Leblanc, FRA
1995 Abraham Olano Manzano, SPA
1996 Johan Museeuw, BEL
1997 Laurent Brochard, FRA
1998 Oscar Camenzind, SWI
1999 Oscar Freire Gomez, ESP
2000 Romans Vainsteins, LAT
2001 Oscar Freire Gomez, SPA
2002 Mario Cipollini, ITA

rear wheel by connecting rods. The rear wheel was larger than the front one to increase speed. Coaxial pedals, driving the front wheel directly (without transmission), were first employed by a Frenchman, P. Michaux, in 1861. In order to increase the speed, the front wheel was made larger, which resulted in the characteristic silhouette now so well known from sketches and early photographs. At the time of its introduction, however, it was both an oddity and a sensation. The advent of pedals was accompanied by a new name: vélocipede [Fr. vélo – wheel + pèd, abbr. of pèdale – pedal]. The front wheel of the largest-ever velocipede, constructed by J. Renard, was 2.92m in diameter, and the cyclist needed special stilts to reach the pedals. In other constructions a chain transmission was used – not in order to increase the speed of the velocipede due to the transmission, but to enable the velocypedist to reach the pedals by locating them above the hub of the front wheel. The velocipedes of the 1860s usu. consisted of a steel frame and wooden wheels with spokes; the tires were of steel tape. When P. Lallement, a Frenchman, brought over such a construction to the US, the vehicle was mockingly derided as the 'bone-shaker' by the local press. Solid rubber tires, and later pneumatic tires were a major improvement. Although rubber vulcanization had been used in shoe making since 1839 by Amer. captain of industry C. Goodyear, the process was applied to the bicycle tire as late as 1868, initially in solid tires. That same year ball bearings were introduced, and in 1869, metal wheel rims with steel spokes, which considerably reduced the weight of the velocipede. 1870-90 saw the gradual approximation of the construction of the velocipede to today's bicycle owing to technical improvements devised by J.K. Starley, an Englishman, in 1885, which allowed for a smaller front wheel, and the pneumatic tire used in 1888 by J.B. Dunlop (1840-1921), which although known since 1845, had not been used in bicycles due to technical difficulties. Track cyclists rejected pneumatic tires until 1893 because of the frequency with which they would fall off the rim and leak air. A. Stock, an American, was the first to trade in his old velocipede and in 1893 turned up sporting a bicycle with wheels of similar diameter. This mod. bicycle would gain increasing importance for utility transportation, in tourism as well as professional sports. Since that time frame and wheel proportions have been improved, the shape of the handlebars has fluctuated, more effective brakes,

a variable gear system and tires that could be replaced simultaneously with the inner tube have been introduced. But no breakthrough inventions have been made to radically alter the general construction assumptions worked out in the second half of the 19th cent. Instead, the greatest advances have been made in the types of materials used (duralumin, compounds), which reduced the weight and increased the durability of the bicycle. City bicycles or bicycles for car transport now come equipped with a foldable frame. Bicycles designed to suit such new cycling sports as mountain biking and bicycle stunts are highly specialized and are made of materials used in space technology. Even so, none of these improvements, impressive as they may be, have departed from the general concept of the vehicle that evolved towards the end of the 19th cent.

Just as important is the development of cycling societies. As early as 1838, the Cyclists' Touring Club, the first known club of its kind was, established in England. In 1861-67 numerous races were organized in France, inspired by the growing number of manufacturers and stores, the likes of P.E. Micheaux, the Oliver brothers, and Peugeot. In 1865, a large race was held for the prize of Amiens. The first international competition, organized by the bicycle manufacturing Oliver brothers, was held on 31 May 1868 in Saint Claude Park, Paris. J. Moore, an Englishman, won the 1,200-m race. In 1869 Véloce Club de Paris was established, which organized the first road race, from Paris to Rouen, a distance of some 123km. Probably the oldest cycling federation was founded in England in 1878, subsequently in France and Denmark (1881), Belgium and Canada (1882), Switzerland and Bohemia (1883). Events called 'world championships' had been organized in France since 1874. The official amateur track W.Ch. had been organized annually since 1893, and road W.Ch. since 1921. Initially events of this type were supervised by Association Cycliste Internationale (set up in 1892), which was not recognized in France, and since 1900 by the International Cycling Union (Union Cycliste Internationale, UCI), the only cycling federation recognized by the IOC. The UCI is responsible for cycling at the Ol.G., included since 1896. The annual W.Ch. of professionals had been held since 1895, road W.Ch. since 1927. In 1967, escalating conflicts between amateur and professional cycling caused a division and creation of 2 separate federations: the International

Amateur Cycling Federation (Fédération Internationale Amateur de Cyclisme, FIAC) and the Professional Cycling Federation (Fédération Internationale du Cyclisme Professionel, FICP). With the downfall of communism in Eastern Europe, however, the cornerstone of amateur cycling as represented by the national cycling federations of the so-called socialist countries, which for ideological reasons officially promoted amateur cycling and rejected 'capitalist professionalism', crumbled. In response, the 2 federations merged again in 1993 into the UCI, which has been indivisible ever since. Apart from the UCI, there are also the International Association of Cycling Races Organizers (Association Internationale des Organisateurs des Courses Cyclistes) and the European Velodrome Cycling Union (Union Européenne des Velodrômes d'Hiver, UEVH).

Time-trials. Almost since the very dawn of cycling, attempts at covering the longest possible distance within a set time of 1hr. or 24hrs. and tackling records over a given distance have been the obsession.

Bicycle, health and social mobility. In its initial stages, cycling considerably increased mobility in society. The bicycle became one of the major means of individual transport, facilitated contact with nature, intensified man's activity, and made many aspects of life easier. Mass production of cars in highly industrialized countries, in the US before 1939, in others after 1945, stymied the growth of cycling as a means of individual transportation. The car may have increased the individual's mobility in the social sense, but definitely had a detrimental effect upon the physical fitness of the public at large. Bicycles returned in the 1960s as a means of short-distance individual transportation, partly owing to the congestion of towns and cities, and partly as a means towards an end, this being health matters: the bicycle calls for physical exercise in a civilizationally unwelcoming environment, in an era of automatization and mechanization of all activities, elevators, escalators and food processors, where all human needs can easily be met. In many countries the bicycle is favored by commuters not due to shortcomings of the mass transit infrastructure but because of the health bonus it offers to say nothing of ecological matters; in the Netherlands and Denmark e.g. at certain times all city transportation comes to a standstill in order to allow waves of cyclists to pass through. In the 1970s bike racks began to appear on cars with increasing frequency. Now a bicycle could easily be hung and transported, enabling

The peleton during the largest cycling event of the Eastern Bloc – The Peace Tour.

Unai Etxebarria of Venezula and Team Euskaltel-Fuskadi leads the peloton during stage 10 of the 2002 Tour De France from Bazas to Pau, France.

A postage stamp issued for the 25th Peace Tour.

combined commuting from greater distances to satellite parking lots and then riding to work or to school.

Cycling and social development. Cycling is the first discipline in the hist. of world sport to be practiced with a complicated, mass-produced mechanical device. This has had far-reaching consequences for society, esp. during the early, pioneering period when the bicycle grew into an increasingly familiar part of human life, but still present nowadays, with the bicycle coming back as a healthy, ecologically sound transportation alternative.

The influence of cycling upon social customs and relationships can be divided into two major periods: 1) an élitism period lasting up to c.1914 and 2) a period of popularization of the bicycle. Cycling played a major role in the women's liberation movement, which will be discussed in detail below.

In the élitism period, the velocipede and bicycle were exclusive products purchased at a premium, and standing out as conspicuous novelties among utility products. This brought about a specific evolution in the cycling milieu, the symptoms of which were an exclusively of individual cycling organizations and the subsequent conscious development of a sense of élitism among their members, usu. not class-bound (even though the price of the vehicle and club dues effectively prevented poorer enthusiasts from joining). Owning and using a bicycle, which from an extravagant means of transport turned in the 1880s into a group identity symbol, was tantamount to being included in the 'cycling elite', a high society distinction and sometimes even isolation from society. The bicycle was the only affordable vehicle, before the advent of cars and motorcycles, that facilitated city dwellers' contact with nature without having to resort to means of mass communication, e.g. railway, and it gave an advantage over those who were not lucky enough to possess one. It was for this reason that e.g. Fr. cyclists called their annual celebration 'the ball of the non-exhausted' (Bal des Inrevables). The hermetic character of cyclists' societies reached its climax in 1890s. In 1896, The Vienna Cyclists' Club agreed on a design of a *pancyclicon*, a spacious building, or a center equipped with facilities, club rooms, guest rooms for traveling cyclists from other locations, restaurants, a printing works, and editorial offices of the club's bulletin. According to excerpts from contemporary press, 'this endeavor is not meant to be profitable, but springs from love of the pneumatic rim and drinking in of the spirit of this sport [...]. We, the people of body – the Vienna cyclists say – are one, belong to one another and want to be on our own in our own place, we are a rolling commune, a state within a state, a state on wheels [...]. Here we perceive this magical bond

between man and object. What man has created, an inert object, breathes a new spirit into him' (TI, 1896). The customs and attitudes of cycling societies in other Eur. countries were similar. Numerous club mansions, resembling the Vienna pancyclicon, if smaller, were built. Their architecture had an eclectic character which would, all the same, provide for social and sports needs of the users. Journals dedicated to cycling, like the Fr. *Vélo,* Pol. *Koło* or *Cyklista* [*Wheel* and *Cyclist* respectively], stressed the distinct character of the cyclists' environment in terms of the sport and customs, but tried to popularize the very aspects that constituted this distinct character. The moment they succeeded marked the end of the era of élitism. Apart from the centripetal, elitist and isolationist tendencies, which had an interim character, there were also centrifugal tendencies, whose results were decidedly farther-reaching in the already-mentioned women's liberation movement, and in a more general battle for a new concept of hygiene and health in the industrial era, of special importance in large cities. Cyclists embarking on lengthy routes contributed to the development of road networks and posted the first road signs. However, the most spectacular element in the melting away of cycling isolationism was the development of cycling spectacles, i.e. track cycling, and giant road races, soon in many stages, which were now observed by the general public and reported upon not by cyclists' journals, but by popular daily press with growing sports sections and modern, specialist sports magazines which had appeared in Germany and France shortly before WWI. This press addressed the public, not the cycling idealist. Multistage cycling races, like Tour de France and Giro d'Italia, which reached the remotest parts of countries, had an enormous effect on the development of the sport in village and small-town communities in the pre-radio and pre-television era, for they presented a stunning exhibition of the joys of cycling in places where it would otherwise have remained unknown. The advent of mass communication changed the status of cycling. On the one hand, cycling has managed to retain the character of a spectacle, even though its poetics changed, but on the other, it has become an accepted alternative to a lack of daily physical exercise. This was no easy assumption, however, and occurred only after much heated debate on the influence of cycling upon health.

Cycling and health matters. In the initial stages of its development, cycling, along with boxing, was targeted for its alleged injurious detrimental effect on human health – medicine was oblivious to the benefits of intensive exercise. Even authorities in

Starting a time trial.

C

medicine believed that effort is only then beneficial to body development 'when muscular movements are made slowly and without too much strain' (A. Jarnatowski, *Higiena czyli nauka o zdrowiu*, 1878). According to these beliefs, cycling several dozen kilometers seemed 'a severe threat to health'. All the same, the recklessness and barbarity with which the first cyclists treated their bodies, completing tours and races of hundreds or even thousands of kilometers to a large extent served only to justify the concerns of the doubting doctors. Since 1873 long-distance large-wheel velocipede races had been held over routes exceeding 1,000km, which with the vehicles clumsiness and heaviness, resulted in frequent accidents and fatigue. In 1886, T. Stevens attempted to go round the globe on a bicycle. In 1901 K. Kocięcka, a Pole, covered a distance of 1,500km from Petersburg to Warsaw within 12 days. Alarm over supposed health risks quieted down fastest in Britain, where already in 1897 *The Encyclopedia of Sport* presented a medical point of view on intensive cycling, but not carried to the extreme, treating it as an effective measure against 'all forms of hysteria, headaches, anaemias neuroses and psychic disorders'. It is record cycling, esp. road cycling, which raises justified doubts in medical circles. Multi-stage races belong to the most strenuous unilateral loads on the organism. One of the social grounds for the existence of sport, incl. cycling, is reaching beyond the average abilities of the human body, indispensable for practical and cognitive reasons, in physical and physiological betterment and for technological improvement of objects that serve humankind. If the limit to a non-professional without special training is cycling 35-50km a day, one is hard pressed to find a reason why a cycling race should exceed 100-150km. Longer routes cater merely to the emotional aspects of titillation and have no rational justification. To test health and recreational advantages of cycling one does not need experiments involving 24-hr races of 300-500km, as in the traditional Fr. race Paris-Bordeaux, or in Poland Poznań-Warsaw. The problem is actually appreciated by international sports organizations, which recently have shortened the then mammoth routes of road races, and also races held at the Ol.G. and W.Ch. Just the same, this endurance-type of cycling is developing, with the distances of several thousand km

Aristidis Konstantinidis of Greece won the gold medal in the 87-km Marathon Cycling event at the 1896 Olympic Games in Athens, Greece.

covered with only the briefest breaks for sleep, as in the Race Across America, held since 1982 (>CYCLING MARATHON). Cycling treated as an experiment laboratory enjoys the pride of place in the less hazardous to health >BICYCLE STUNTS, or in >MOUNTAIN BIKING, where the technical worthiness of vehicles is put to the test, and as a consequence improved, in difficult conditions but less hazardous to the cyclist.

Cycling and the women's liberation movement. Women have been cycling almost since the dawn of the sport. D. Johnson, already mentioned, differentiated as early as 1819 the construction of men's and ladies' *célérifčres*. Women took part in the first in hist. long-distance road race from Paris to Rouen (about 123km) in 1869, with an unnamed English lady coming in 29th out of 300 – mostly male – cyclists. More popular and frequent at the turn of the 20th century were ladies' long-distance tours. At that time cycling became a form of demonstrating the equality of women, thus constituting one of the major elements of the general social changes brought on by sports. Women's cycling during its initial decades was severely criticized by opponents of the liberation movement in the conservative press. But here women's cycling was aided by cyclists' societies' journals. It was in these magazines that satires and pamphlets against conservative circles were published. Since the end of the 19th cent. women's track cycling races have been held; much interest was stirred by the 1908 race on Dynasy in Warsaw, which was reported by the press along with precious photographs (*Świat*). Women's ambitions were reinforced by progressive intellectuals and writers, like E. Zola (1840-1902) in France or B. Prus (1845-1912) and A. Oppman (1867-1931) in Poland, authors of verses supporting the liberation movement through sports. Cycling ceased to be associated with the women's liberation movement once it became popular and ceased to be provocative, esp. after WWI, when other women's sports appeared and the general achievements of the women's liberation movement became apparent in sports; women were taking part in the Ol.G. Nowadays feminist tendencies have found other venues for their activities, these being sports like >WEIGHTLIFTING, and >BOXING, which still allow for contesting the traditional division of roles in women's and men's sports.

F. Alderson, *Bicycling. A History*, 1972; L. Baundry de Saunier, *Le Cyclisme*, 1892; same author, *Histoire generale de la vèlocipèdè*, 1891; E. Bertz, *Philosophie des Fahrrads*, 1900; A. Blondin, *Le Tour de France*, 1972; R. Böhm et al. (eds.), *Cycling*, 1954; V. Breyer, R. Coquelle, *Les rois du cycle*, 1898; E.R. Burke, *Serious Cycling*, 1995; J. Friel, *Cycling Past 50*, 1998; N. Henderson, *European Cycling. The 20 Classic Races*, 1989; J.M. Lelièvre, *La passionante histoire de la bicyclette*, 1971; P. Liggett, *The Complete Book of Performance Cycling*, 1992; P. Nye, *Hearts of Lions. The History of American Bicycle Racing*, 1988; R. Watson, M. Gray, *The Penguin Book of the Bicycle*, 1978; H.G. Wells, *The Wheels of Chance*, 1896; L. Woodland, *Fit For Cycling*, 1988.

CYCLING FOR THE DISABLED, a form of cycling adapted to the needs of the handicapped. People with a severe vision impairment and the blind compete on tandems in 2-man teams with a seeing rider in the front saddle. For competition among the physically disabled, people with multiple sclerosis and other conditions standard cycling bicycles are used, provided the handicap is not advanced and does not prevent the participant from maintaining balance. If, however, balance is frequently lost, tricycles with the standard wheel size are used to increase stability. There are also special bicycles adapted for specific kinds of handicap, enabling the rider to e.g. pedal with one leg only. International championships include individual and 3-man-team events. See also >SPORTS FOR THE DISABLED. The Internet: http://www.paralympic.org

CYCLING MARATHON, a cycling, point-to-point endurance race, over a distance a few times longer than the average cycling road race stage, i.e. 120-150km (formerly 250km). The longest and hardest contemporary cycling marathon is the Race Across America, RAAM, held annually since 1982 from California to the East Coast, over a distance of about 3000 miles (4700-4800km). This 'ultra-marathon' is a one stage event just with a few sleeping breaks.

The RAAM participants qualify for the race on the basis of their performance in a series of shorter preliminary races. Usually, from twenty to forty percent of cyclists qualify, and not many of them are able to finish the race. Both men and women can participate in the RAAM.

History. The cycling marathon originated from long cycling road races held usually on difficult routes. The pioneer of the cycling marathon was an Englishman, T. Stevens, who rode his bike around the world in 1886. The Tour de France was also a marathon-like race in its early years, as the six constituent stages were covered day and night. Later on the stages of the race were shortened and night stages were abandoned. For many years the Paris-Bordeaux one-stage race over the distance of 500km was referred to as a cycling marathon. In the 1960s a long Poznań-Warsaw (300km) cycling race was occasionally held in Poland.

The predecessors of the world's longest and most difficult world's cycling marathon, i.e. the Race Across America were individual north-south and east-west crossings of the continent. In 1978, J. Marino covered the distance from Santa Monica, California to New York City in 13 days, 1hr. and 20min. In 1982, Marino with other famous Amer. cyclists such as M. Shermer and L. Haldeman organized a mass event known as the Great American Bike Race from Santa Monica to the Empire State Building in Manhattan. The race, widely covered by television, was won by L. Heldeman. After the huge success of the event, J. Marino founded Ultra-Marathon Cycling, Inc., which became the RAAM's governing body. The RAAM always commences in California and finishes in one of the cities east of the Mississippi, e.g. Atlanta, Georgia or Atlantic City, New Jersey. Women took part in the RAAM for the first time in 1984, when after a dramatic race, two cyclists S. Hayden Clifton and P. Hines took first place in 12 days 20hrs. and 57 min. Since 1989 the RAAM has also been a four-person relay event. In 1995 the winner of the individual RAAM was R. Kish (8 days, 19hrs, 59min.), while the relay event was won by the Kern-Wheelman team in 5 days, 17hrs. and 5min.

Ron Shepherd, *Cycling. Race Across America*, EWS, 1996, I; M. Shermer, *Race across America. The Agonies and Glories of the World's Longest and Cruelest Bicycle Race*, 1993.

CYCLISM, an old name for cycling and, at the same time, a cultural trend influencing its early development. In those days it was identified with tricycles and then, as the technology advanced, with bicycles. Cyclism's peak popularity falls on the period 1885-1900. It brought a number of cultural phenomena that are reflected in a distinct vocabulary, customs, outfit, and even in a characteristic philosophy of life of cyclists as a consciously detached social group. An informal Eur. center of cyclism was Vienna where local cycling organizations raised a monumental building named *Pancyclicon* (Germ. *Panzyklikon*) that housed parlors, publishing house, magazine editor's office, etc. Outside Austria, cyclism was extremely popular in all Eur. countries and the USA. Before cars and motorcycles became so widespread, it was cyclism that heavily influenced the expansion of the road network and the introduction of the first road signs. As an independent socio-sports movement, it disappeared at the beginning of the 20th cent. giving way to >CYCLING, both its recreational and professional var. [Fr. *Cyclisme*; Ger. *Zyklismus*; Ital. *ciclismo*; Lat. *cyclus*; Gk. *kyklos* – a wheel].

CYCLOBALL, a team ball game played by two teams on bicycles. The aim of the game is to shoot a ball into the opposing team's goal, using the wheels of bicycles. Players cannot touch the ball with their hands or feet. Cycloball has 2 varieties: 1) indoor cycloball, played on a wooden or plastic surface. The field is 12-15m long and 9-12m wide; the goal is 2x2m; the ball is 16-18cm in diameter. A game consists of two 7-min periods (men) or two 5-min. periods (women and juniors). After the break the teams change ends. Teams consists of two players each; 2) outdoor cycleball, played on a grass field. The field is 60m long and 40m wide; the goal is 4m wide and 2.25m high. A game consists of two 20-min. periods. Teams consist of six players each. A bicycle weighs no more than 13kg. If a player in the field touches the ball with any part of his body he or she must resume play from his own goal area. Free

Cycling for the disabled

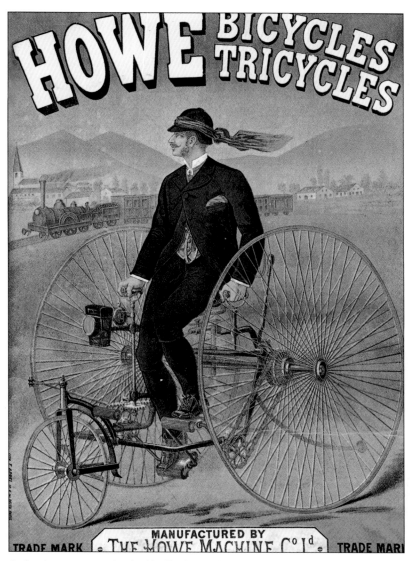

Cyclism. An anonymous poster advertising bicycles and tricycles, c. 1880.

before the game. In the course of the game each hole was guarded by one player who signaled his presence by putting a club into a hole. The bowl, known as a 'barrel' or a 'piggy' – in some areas a wooden ring – was 10-20cm in diameter. A player who was not guarding any hole, called a 'shepherd', attempted to place the bowl (ring) in the central hole by means of striking it with a club. Other players, equipped with identical clubs and acting within the zone of their own holes, attempted to stop the bowl and put it into their own little holes. The moment the bowl rested inside the brewery, each player was supposed to change position, again signaling the change by placing their club in a new hole. The shepherd, who did not have his own hole before, had the opportunity to win one now, when one of the other players left his hole unattended. The player dispossessed of a hole became a new shepherd and a new round started. The number of rounds in each region of Poland was different. A similar game was also known in France as >TRUIE, LA.

CZYŻ, also *krypa*. One of the names for a Pol. folk game also known as >KLIPA, which was a local var. of the game referred to in other regions as >KICZKA.

Cycloball.

Cyclo-cross.

shots are used, similar to soccer; cf. >CYCLE POLO.
History. The origins of the sport date back to the 1890s. The game became widespread after WWI. Formerly, cycloball was played on regular bicycles; at present cycloball bikes have a special construction involving a shorter crossbar and elevated handlebar stem. The bikes have no brakes and can be pedaled back and forth. Cycloball enjoys great popularity in the Netherlands, Belgium, Germany and the Czech Republic. In each of these countries national championships are held. In the former East Germany the sport used to be part of PE classes in some schools. The Cycloball W.Ch. have been held since 1929.

CYCLO-CROSS, a variety of off-road cycling on routes of about 25km, with courses of about 3km. Because of unnegotiable terrain, about 1/3 of a race involves walking and carrying the bicycle. Even though the development of cyclo-cross goes back at least to the 1920s, the official W.Ch. have been taking place since 1967. The first world champion in cyclo-cross was R. Vermeire (Belgium), a 1970,'71, '74, '75 and '77 world champion. Apart from Belgium, the country to be reckoned with was Czechoslovakia, esp. since the 1980s, with its riders scooping 6 individual world champion titles (M. Fisera in 1981-82; R. Simunek in 1983-4; K. Camrda in 1988 and O. Glajza in 1989). The development of >MOUNTAIN BIKING and >CROSS BMX visibly diminished the popularity of cyclo-cross.

CYKANION, an ancient game practiced in Byzantium in which a ball is struck with crooked sticks by players on horseback. Similar to >POLO and prob. deriving from Persian >CHUGAN. There are many indications that in the Middle Ages, cykanion gave birth to some Eur. games, e.g. Ger. >SCHAGGUN.

CZADZ, a simple old Pol. game in which children competed for little gifts, candies, nuts, and sometimes money, thrown by adults.

CZAJKI, a type of a narrow Cossack boat propelled with a number of oars and equipped with 2 rud-

ders, which Cossacks used in the 16th-18th cent. for their warfare on large rivers, esp. the Dnieper, and in the Black Sea. Like Vikings they made long sea crossings to plunder various lands getting as far as Turkey. The oarsmen, who worked in 3 shifts round-the-clock for a number of days in a row, had to be exceptionally strong both mentally and physically, which was achieved by means of a special training for young Cossacks. One of the tests that determined who deserved the name of a 'real Cossack' consisted of crossing the Dniester terraces in such boats (>PODOLANIJE DNIPROWSKICH POROGIW).

CZEKAN THROWING, a form of exercise and competition in the old Pol. army. The *czekan* used in the throws was a long war hammer with an axe head, employed in combat to shatter opponents' armor. Another type of Pol. war hammer was the *obuch* (diminutive *obuszek*), equipped in the lower part of the handle with a long spike used to pull enemies off their horses. The *husaria* (Pol. heavy cavalry, the 'winged horsemen') often organized czekan throwing competitions where the objective was to throw the hammer as high up as possible and grab it by the handle on its way down. A description of the game is given by H. Sienkiewicz in his novel *Potop* (*The Deluge*). Cf. >MIETANNIE KELIEPU, >MOUNTAIN AXE THROWING.

CZOROMAJ, also *browar* [brewery] or *świnka* [piggy]. A var. of a ball game played formerly in Poland, esp. from the end of the 17th to the beginning of the 19th cent. The object was to strike a ball or a bowl with a club into holes in the ground. The course, usu. a lawn of indeterminate size, had a hole in the center, whose diameter was about 30cm – a little more than the bowl's diameter. In some areas instead of a bowl a little wooden ring was used. Depending on local traditions, the hole was referred to as the 'brewery', 'kettle' or 'pigpen'. It was encircled by a 5-15m ring of smaller holes whose number was equal to the number of players minus 1. Usually it was players themselves who dug the holes right

D
WORLD SPORTS ENCYCLOPEDIA

DA', a game whose rules remain rather vague. Practiced in Mecca, it is mentioned by M. Ibrahim al-Majman, with no further description, in his dictionary of Arab games and sports, titled *Min al'abina ash-sha 'biyya* (*Our Folk Games*, 1983).

DAB AND STICK, a Brit. representative of a family of games in which a wooden bowl (in this case a 'dab') is tossed into the air and then struck with a stick onto the course. Major representatives of the same family are *knur and spell* (see >NORTHERN SPELL) and >TRAP, BAT AND BALL.

DAB-AND-TRICKER, also *dab-an-tricker*. A Brit. var. of a game in which a wooden bowl (a 'dab') is pitched into the air by means of a lever [*tricker*, prob. from Eng. *trigger*] and then struck out onto the course. It belongs to a larger family of games whose major representatives are >TRAP, BAT AND BALL and *knur and spell* (see >NORTHERN SPELL). In dab-and-tricker a bowl was a little larger than usual (a bit smaller than a billiard ball) and it was struck with a bat resembling a bottle stuck at the end of a long, thin rod.

DAB-AT-THE-HOLE, see >MARBLES.

DÆK, Dan. for 'to guard', a ball game partially resembling >PALANT and partially >CRICKET. In S Jutland the game is played by 2 teams – one playing outside (*ude*) and the other inside (*inde*). The wicket is made of a large stone or a 1m-long plank stuck on its end in the ground. A player, standing at a distance of 5-6m from the wicket, attempts to hit it with a ball thrown in an underhand style. Another player is a 'cover' (*dækker*), an equivalent of a batsman, and his task is to clear as far as possible, using a special bat, the ball thrown at the target, and then to score points. The points are scored as follows: after clearing the ball the batsman has to run to the base and return to the wicket. There are 3 types of wickets at various distances; the closest one scores 5pts., a farther one – 15, and the farthest one – 25pts. If a pitcher succeeds in hitting the stone (or a plank), the batsman is out of the game and he is replaced by another player. The game continues until all players from one team are defeated, after which teams change places and the batsmen become pitchers and vice versa.
J. Møller, 'Dæk', GID, 1997, 1, 71.

DAITO RYU AIKI JU JUTSU, one of the best known styles of >JU JUTSU, developed by T. Sokaku (1860--1943), who lived in Shirataki on the island of Hokkaido. M. Ueshiba, the inventor of >AIKIDO, was under the substantial influence of this style. Around 1922 Takeda extended the original name of *daito ryu* into *daito ryu aiki ju jutsu*. As Ueshiba was Takeda's student at that time; before the former became an independent master, his style was also referred to as daito ryu aiki ju jutsu. Later on his school was named *aikido*. A characteristic feature of daito ryu aiki ju jutsu is a combination of features originating in a number of >BUDO schools, esp. *ono-ha Itto-ryu*. Its objectives reach far beyond mere self-defense; by creating a balance between the body and spirit, it strives for the development of valuable social features in the practitioner who can therefore achieve harmony with the surrounding universe. S.S.M. Yoshimitsu (1045-1127), a *sho* instrument virtuoso, is considered the distant founder of this martial art. One story relates that while accompanying the shirabyoshi dancers on his instrument, he observed that despite the dancers' elegant, fluent, and ever-changing movement, they admitted no openings (*suki*). From this he perceived the principle of a non-form (*mukei*), which belongs to the realm of humans, but reaches beyond the material form, and he mastered the deepest essence of *aiki*. Yoshimitsu lived in the town of Daito, hence the presence of this element in the name of the sport. The thinker passed his knowledge on to descendants of the Takeda family from the Kai Province (today's Yamanashi Prefecture). The family had been losing power since 1537 and with the death of their most outstanding representative – T. Shingen, a distant relative – Kunitsugu taught the art to the Hidetada shogun's family. The shogun's son, A.H. Masayuki combined Yoshimitsu's achievements with court etiquette (*oshikiuchi*) which resulted in the art of self-defense that he employed for schooling his own guards. Independently, the Takeda family safeguarded Yoshimitsu's art and they passed their heritage down to S. Takeda who developed daito ryu aiki ju jutsu.

Dakyu on a Japanese drawing.

Dakyu.

DAKYU, a Jap. game akin to >POLO and >FIELD HOCKEY. It has been played since approx. 700 AD, when the emperor's edict banned equestrian sports, which became so popular in Japan that horse fodder became scarce. By the emperor's order dakyu, a pedestrian sport, was to replace all equestrian events. In its oldest form the game consisted of hitting a round stone or ball with long-handled mallets. The oldest surviving written documentation of the game comes from 727 AD and describes a competition held in Kasugano in the province of Nara. During the Heian dynasty (781--1180) the game spread rapidly and incorporated elements of games similar to present day field hockey, such as >MARI UCZI, or *indi uczi*. At first the game was played on pitches not limited to any size. The aim was to send the ball to the opponent's zone. In the 15th cent. the size of the pitch was limited. In the 16th cent. the game started to be played on horseback, which made it similar to >POLO and later to >LACROSSE, because the mallet was replaced with a cane that had a protruding metal net into which the ball was caught and with which it was set in motion. The aim of dakyu played on horseback is to throw a ball into the opponent's circle (approx. 60cm in diameter). The game usu. ends, when one team scores 12pts.

DALIANGXIAO, a game popular with the Bai people who live in the city of Dali, in the Jünnan province. Other names are also applied such as: *bawang whips, silver-good whips, heroes' whips*, and *flower sticks*. Daliangxiao is a mixture of dancing and rhythmical gymnastic exercise. The basic equipment is a thumb-thick bamboo stick about 1m long, referred to as a 'whip'. It has 9 square-shaped holes with small crossbars, each strung with 3-4 copper coins. Both ends are decorated with pompoms and the handle is covered in silk string. Shaking the stick produces the characteristic sound of clinking coins. The game's objective is to perform complex acrobatic movements while rhythmically knocking the stick against one's legs, hands, chest, and the floor. The movements are organized in a dance during which a dancer jumps up, crouches, runs, and makes various gestures.
Mu Fushan, et al., 'Daliangxiao', TRAMCHIN, 142.

DALIES, [from Eng. *dally*] a children's game in which small bones or wooden chips are thrown. Its rules are similar to those applied in >HUCKLEBONES. A special var. of the game is known as *fivestones*. Cf. >JACKS.

DALLERBAKKER, Dan. slang for 'a beard that hurts'. A school exercise aimed at improving students' resistance to pain. Students squeezed another student's head, rubbing his ears at the same time. The drill was reported as a bully exercise in a lexicon by J. Møller, *Gamle idrætslege i Denmark* (*Sports Games in Denmark*), 1997, 3, 69.

DAMA, a folk martial art practiced in the Philippines. So far, its rules have not been elaborated methodologically to make it a professional discipline, which is likewise the case with some other martial arts from the same region (>BUNO). Therefore, this sport remains a local and spontaneous phenomenon.

DANCE MARATHON, a dancing competition in which those who continue to dance longest win. Although the idea as such originated in Europe, its final form was developed in the USA in the 1920s. Its popularity peaked during the Great Depression of the '30s. Competition rules differed from place to place. At the beginning, however, generally the winner was a single dancer who was free to change partners during a contest and whose total dancing time was longest. Usually, contestants were individual persons rather than couples. Another general rule concerned timing: 45min. of dancing plus a 15-min. break. This cycle repeated until exhausted competitors withdrew and only 1 pair remained on the dance floor. In later periods, instead of the total time of a single dancer, the total time of a pair, which could not change during the entire event, was counted. The center of a ballroom or a gym was converted into a circular dancefloor, surrounded with seats for spectators. There was also a special place for orchestra and a first-aid point that was open to the view of spectators to augment the spectacle with dramatic scenes of fainted competitors being revived. During different periods, dance marathons were known under various names, such as endurance dance, nonstop dance, long-distance dance, jitterathon, speed derby, and walkshow.

History. The first attempts at setting dance records, undertaken in various countries shortly after WWI, stem from the ever-present craze for breaking all kinds of records started around 1914. People were fascinated with treks to the North and South Poles, pioneering flights, swimmers crossing sea straits, and any other events pushing human limits further and further. The possibility of breaking a record in even a far less heroic sphere of life created an illusion of participating in the general race after fame. Such an atmosphere was conductive to various contests, such as those in eating (e.g. eggs or pancakes), drinking (e.g. beer or milk), kissing, chewing gum, etc. One of the most celebrated records of the beginning of the '20s was that established by S. Kelly in >FLAGPOLE SITTING. Dance marathons were also supposed to prove that anybody could become famous. As C. Martin – a dance marathon researcher – maintains: 'One did not have to be Lindbergh, or Ederle, even an average person could win fame.'

At the beginning, dance marathons formed an additional element to public parties or those held in dancing schools. In the course of time, however, they appeared in many clubs that wanted to attract clientele. On 18 Feb. 1923, two Brit. dance instructors – O. Finerty and E. van Ollefin from Sutherland – established a record, dancing continuously for 7hrs. The result was published by the press which incited a series of similar attempts made in Edinburgh, where a new record of 14hrs. 26min. was set, in Marseille (24:04), and in Paris (24:20). In response to Eur. records, G.G. Grundy – owner of the Audubon Ballroom in New York, on 168 Street – invited New Yorkers to take up the challenge. A. Cummings started her marathon on 30 March 1923, at 6:47p.m. and stopped dancing on 31 March at 9:57p.m., establishing thus a record of 27hrs., dancing foxtrot, one-step, and waltz unceasingly. She changed her dancing partners 6 times. An orchestra and 2 record players played music interchangeably. The main referee was the owner of the club. Before the end of 1923, the record was bettered a number of times, reaching a result of 90hrs. 10min. nonstop (J. Curry, April 19, Cleveland). After the combination of breaks and dancing intervals was introduced in 1923, the record grew to 217hrs. (B. Brand, June 10, St. Louis). In 1924-28, dance marathon acquired features of a commercial show

for which entrance tickets had to be purchased. During the Great Depression, it became even more dramatic because a number of impoverished participants saw the prize as an opportunity to substantially improve their standing. C. Martin referred to such marathons as 'part of a culture of poverty.' Competitors dropping out due to exhaustion, not necessarily a result of prolonged dancing but perhaps malnutrition, became an everyday phenomenon, esp. during small local marathons where the elimination system was more lax, admitting people from all social strata. The first dance marathon culmination was a show organized in 1928 in Madison Square Garden in New York by M. Crandall under the name *Dance Derby of the Century*. Sensing that the competition itself would not secure sufficient public interest, Crandall combined the show with sports and dramatized theatrical elements, and priced seats not only in accordance with their location but also based on the time of day. The most expensive tickets covered the afternoon and evening hours, as well as the forecasted culmination of the event, whereas the cheapest ones covered late night and morning hours. Prices also differed depending on whether it was one of the first days of the event or one of the last. For example, during one of Crandall's marathons, tickets that had been $1.50 during the first week, shot up to $3.30 during the second. After New York, Crandall organized the same event in Dayton and Hollywood, and finally opened a permanent ballroom in Pittsburgh. Shortly after that, he went even further in promoting his show by organizing the International Endurance Dancing Championships. The prize was $5,000 (quite a substantial amount at that time). The contest was held in pairs and disqualification or dropping out of one of the partners prevented the other from continuation. The first championships were contested by 91 pairs, the second – by more than a 100, finally reaching 132 the same year. Crandall made every possible effort to have famous actors and sportsmen participate in the event, which served to heighten public excitement. Among the actors participating in Crandall's marathon was J. Scott from the New York Apollo Theater. In addition, rest periods were introduced during which dancers could take a massage or shave. Those who fainted were attended to at first-aid points open to the public's fascinated eyes. Various competitions in specific dances enriched a marathon. An official set of regulations established by Crandall required that:

All of the entrants competing have been pronounced physically fit by the Official Medical Board who will be in attendance at all times throughout the contest. Teams may be backed by a City, Chamber of Commerce, Ballroom or business enterprise. Changes of wearing apparel will be allowed during the rest periods only. Contestants who do not keep fully dressed in accordance with the regulation are subject to disqualification. No changes of partners will be permitted. When one member of a team withdraws, the entry is withdrawn. Rules and regulations will be strictly enforced by a referee. Expert masseurs, masseuses, hairdressers, tonsorial artists, manicurists, chiropodists, and other attendants for the comfort of the dancers will be in attendance at all times. Contestants are required to dance one hour and rest fifteen minutes [...]. The rest period must be taken simultaneously by all dancers desiring to take advantage of the rest period, but teams are permitted to dance on without taking rest if they so desire; but if the entrants do not take the rest period this does not permit them to add the elapsed time to their new rest period. Waltz, fox-trot, two-step and smile five-minute sprints for cash prizes will be staged throughout the contest. Entrants, however, are not compelled to enter these sprints unless they so wish. The rules do not require entrants to be dancing, as long as they are in the dance position and moving. Should partners separate while on the floor, the floor manager is instructed to give them a ten-minute warning. Failure to then be in position will result in the team being eliminated.

The rules, however, were often modified depending on the circumstances and city where a marathon was taking place, esp. if sponsors using a marathon for advertisement required such changes. A representative of the Amateur Athletic Union assessed that each team of dancers coved around 40mi. (65km) daily. After a few days of dancing, most of the contestants suffered hallucinations, being convinced they had found themselves in a situation completely disconnected from reality. A number of pairs who received prizes for supporting dance competitions or smile five-minute sprints were not even aware they had won such

prizes or what they had won them for. During a record dance marathon in Pittsburgh, after a lapse of 303hrs., there were still 3 couples dancing. After an examination, a doctor who was on duty, D.E. Sable, concluded that none of the 6 dancers was capable of continuing the competition. Journalists from serious periodicals, who had a chance to observe dance marathons, did not conceal their contempt:

Reading about the stirring incidents aroused our editorial curiosity and we decided to have a look. We did. What a cruel disappointment. Nothing exhilarating happened for our benefit. It was as dull as a six-day bicycle race. The couples did not even dance – except occasionally. Mostly they walked around the floor. And often they stopped to take a drink, to chat with friends among the spectators, to have a facial massage or shampoo. At such times they merely shifted their weight from one foot to another so as not to be declared out of the contest. Evidently the reporters for the daily newspapers had better luck or better imaginations then we had.

[*Nation*, 23 June, 1928]

The character of an event depended also on the inventiveness of the main sponsor. Crandall was the forefather of an entire group of managers and directors specializing in dance marathons, the most

Modern dance marathon.

notable of whom was H.J. Ross (b. 1893). Besides organizing various marathons in the USA he was the first to tour in Europe (1931-32) with a series of events he designed. Every now and then the managers introduced innovations. In 1933, a dance marathon in Tulsy included a race of 105 laps around a dance floor referred to as the 'grind'. Supplementary contests of symptomatic names were held, such as zombie treadmill, back-to-back struggle, hurdles, circle hotshot, heel-and-toe race, dynamist sprint, duck waddles, bombshell, etc. Their objective was to eliminate the weakest. In 1928, showbiz coordinators discovered that the public was absorbed in speculating a possible love affair between the teammates, so the next step was to select such couples that would even get married on the dance floor, which in the '30s turned into a routine. Many of such marriages were prearranged and they disintegrated after a short time. More imaginative managers even organized imitations of marriage ceremonies that were presented to the public as real, but actually did not meet certain official requirements, so that teammates could go their own ways after a competition. In the later period of dance marathon's development, parodies of marriage ceremonies were freely presented without any pretence of being genuine. Such ceremonies were particularly numerous during

marathons hosted by H. Ross in Corpus Christi, Pensacola, and Galveston. The most celebrated of these 'cellophane weddings', as they were called, were the ones 'contracted' by M. McGee with W.D. Rogers from Galveston and J. Yohstock with A. Ehlinga from Cincinnati.

Public resistance. In many places, authorities frowned upon 'dancing demoralization' and sought to prevent dance marathons under a number of pretexts, the most popular of which was a protestant tradition, dating back to the 17th cent., prohibiting any public entertainment on Sundays. This ban was evaded by organizing dance marathons as private parties. Prohibition was also used as a tool to combat dance marathons. In 1923, in Huston, 7 dancers were accused of being intoxicated during a marathon organized by McMillan's Dancing Academy. The only reason the suspects were not arrested was the reaction of spectators who defended the dancers against the police. A reverse situation took place in Cedar Love, Louisiana, where a dance marathon was disrupted by the hostile attitude of the local Methodists and Presbyterians who jointly forced dancers and managers to leave town. In New York, dance marathons were obstructed on the basis of a paragraph from the local regulations concerning any sports and public forms of competition, according to which: 'It shall be unlawful for any contestant to continue in such a race or contest for a longer time than twelve hours during any twenty-four hours.' The regulation was eluded by taking dancers on a bus shortly before midnight and transporting them to a different ballroom where, officially, a completely unrelated party was being held, so that the time limit could be counted again. Such a solution, however, led to conflicts because record holders from other states did not want to recognize New York records, asserting that contests were not continuous. The rule established in 1928, allowing short breaks or rest periods during a dance marathon put an end to such frictions. In a number of states, special commissions were set up in order to analyze the hazards related to dance marathons. In 1931, Texas authorities issued the first law directly concerning dance marathons and any other similar events, according to which such activities could not last more than 24hrs. In 1935, the law was moderated allowing dance marathons of up to 7 days, but still limiting the participation of each single dancer to 24hrs. max. In 1933, several legal regulations limiting or prohibiting dance marathons were introduced in the states of New York, Maine, and New Hampshire. In the last of these, however, the law

Contestants compete in a 1928 dance marathon contest in Culver City, Calif. Dance marathons became entertainment fixtures during the Depression era years in the 1920s and '30s.

WORLD SPORTS ENCYCLOPEDIA

D

applied only to women, whereas in Maine there was a provision for lifting the ban in a given locality 'after a vote [...] by the legal voters of said city or town.' In 1935, the states of Connecticut, Georgia, Indiana, Iowa, Kansas, South, and North Dakota published local laws that univocally prohibited dance marathons. They were soon after joined by Florida, Michigan, Minnesota, North Carolina, Ohio, Rhode Island, and Wisconsin where such laws are still applicable to this day. In total, dance marathons were substantially limited or prohibited altogether in 17 states. On top of that, some municipalities established their own local limitations and bans. The fines for organizing a dance marathon in Texas were 'not less than $100 nor more than $1,000.' In Connecticut, the same offense could result in a min. of 6 and a max. of 12 months of imprisonment and/or a fine amounting to $1,000. Doctors and owners of schools of dancing got involved in the anti-dance-marathon campaign as well. L.H. Chalif, Vice President of the Amer. Society of Teachers of Dancing, declared in 1923 that dance marathons are 'dangerous to health, useless as entertainment and a disgrace to the art and profession of dancing.' A referee of trad. dancing competitions held in Terrace Garden Dance Palace, E. Hubbel, affirmed once in the *New York Times* that dancing marathons corrupt dancing because after a few hours of continuous exercise no dancer is able to preserve the beauty of movement. Public criticism was considerably stimulated by sporadic reports of the death of an exhausted dancer.

The sponsors of dance marathons attempted to reduce public aversion by softening the forms of competition and renaming them; e.g. walkathon was proposed at the beginning of the '30s. C. Martin described this new dance marathon formula as 'an amalgamation of social dance, popular music, theater, and sport.' The events included a number of supplementary social interactions and contests. The professional character of dance marathons also led to substantial decreases in ticket prices, down to 25-40 cents. In 1935, a group of businessmen sponsoring dance marathons established the National Endurance Amusement Association (NEAA). The goal of the organization was to lend the marathons higher entertainment, formal, and social standards. A group of professional endurance dancers, such as Billie and Mac McGreevy (prob. a fictitious name of a fictitiously married couple), crystallized from a group of marathoners. On 9 Feb. 1931, the couple set the record of nonstop dancing amounting to 1,264hrs. A specialized category of referees and floor managers, such as R. Long, appeared and there were even specialized coaches, e.g. E.M. Bernard. Splendor to the most important events was added by the presence of famous singers, e.g. J. Shannon, and orchestras, e.g. the Rio Grande Orchestra. A special category of dance marathon hosts developed. Certain radio repor-

ters, such as J. Negley, became widely celebrated thanks to their coverage of dance marathons. Among newspaper publishers L. Wall, the publisher of the *Galveston Daily News* and the *Galveston Tribune*, was one of the few who treated dance marathons seriously. *Miami Sports* also dedicated a good deal of attention to dance events.

The development of dance marathons ceased with the outbreak of WWII. Once the USA joined the conflict in Dec. 1941, dance marathons came to be seen as rather frivolous. Immediately after WWI, dance marathons had been a form of escape from frustration, unemployment and poverty. The year 1941 revived the national economy. As C. Martin put it: 'Industry had revived, and people were going back to work. Who had the time to sit around for hours watching people in a circle on a dance floor? Life had a purpose once again.' Both during the war and shortly after it, there were attempts to bring dance marathons back, but they never regained their former splendor. The last classic dance marathon in the USA took place in 1952, but before its influence disappeared completely from Amer. public life, it gave birth to new phenomena. The idea of endurance competitions before the eyes of spectators found new forms in running and roller-skating marathons. And although spin-off varieties of marathon, e.g. the jump-rope-a-thon for heart, have become regular charity fund-raising events, these new forms have never achieved the status that dance marathons enjoyed during their peak popularity period.

Dance marathon was immortalized in an acclaimed novel *They Shoot Horses, Don't They?* (1935) by H. McCoy (1897-1955). The novel invokes the reality of dance marathons organized by H. Ross in the Park Ballroom in Crystal Beach. The book is an allegory and existential reflection on the destiny of man, symbolized in a dancing competition. The novel was the basis for S. Pollack's movie under the same title, starring J. Fonda. Similar symbolism can be found in a play by J. Havoc, *Marathon '33* (1969).

F.M. Calabria, 'The Dance Marathon Craze', JPC, 1976, 10. G. Eells, 'Some 20,000 Were in «Marathon Dance» Biz at Zenith of Craze', *Variety*, 7 Jan. 1970; C. Martin, *Dance Marathons. Performing American Culture of the 1920s and 1930s*, 1994; P. Sann, *Fads, Follies and Delusions of the American People*, 1967; J. Scott, 'We Danced All Night and All Day!', *Ballroom Dance Magazine*, July 1961.

DANDI, a type of fencing with the use of sticks, practiced in India.

DANGER BALL, a Rus. game using a croquet ball which is rolled towards a target. The target is marked with 3 concentric circles in the middle of the field. The smallest circle is 1m in diameter, the middle one – 1.75m, and the outer one – 2.5m. A brightly-colored (usu. orange or red) croquet ball is placed in the middle of the inner circle. Two pa-

rallel lines are drawn on both sides of the target, at a distance of about 6 steps from the outer circle. Players with croquet balls stand on the lines. The game may be an individual or team game. If the team version is selected, the players stand alternately with players of the opposing team, so that 2 players of the same team facing each other may co-operate. Placing the ball in the outer circle scores 1pt., in the middle circle – 3pts., and the inner one – 5pts. Players may agree to aim for rolling balls, too. If two balls collide, both players score double the amount of points. If they do not, they lose 2pts. each. The brightly-colored ball is an obstacle. Hitting the bright ball loses points: if the ball is not knocked outside the inner circle, the player loses 1pt., if the ball leaves the inner circle – 3pts. are subtracted, and if it reaches the outer circle, the player loses 5pts. If the bright ball is knocked out of the hole target area, the responsible player loses all the points. The first player to score 20pts. is declared the winner.
I.N. Chkannikov, 'Danger Ball', GIZ, 1953, 42-44.

DANSKERE OG TYSKERE, Dan. for 'Danes and Germans'. A Dan. game in which the 19th-cent. wars between Denmark and Germany are imitated. Two teams of 'soldiers' stand at some distance from each other in 2 marked circles that symbolize states. The object of the game is to catch the enemy and drag him into one's own circle, or to knock an opponent over in his own area grabbing his waist. The game terminates when all the soldiers from the same team are either 'dead' or 'imprisoned'.
J. Møller, 'Danskere og tyskere', 1997, 4, 54.

DARDOS, see >JUEGO DE DARDOS.

DARI-BAPKI, Kor. for 'crossing the bridge'. A lovers' favorite demonstration consisting of repeated crossing of one or a number of bridges. Dari-bapki was a best-preferred pastime of Kor. girls and boys until the end of the 19th cent. The word *dari* has 3 meanings: a leg, the moon, and a bridge – all of those attributes represent the essence of the romantic formula of the game whose established rules said that boys and girls should cross a bridge and if possible – many bridges, at night. It was believed that those who managed to cross 12 bridges (or 1 bridge 12 times) before dawn would remain in good health for another year. Throughout Korea bridges were crossed during a Jan. full moon. A group of young participants was supposed to cross a bridge or to walk around towers of a Buddhist temple singing and dancing. It was, perhaps, an opportunity to meet new people. This custom gave birth to the religious ritual game of >TAPDORI.
Koo-Chul Jung, *Erziehung und Sport in Korea im Kreuzpunkt fremder Kulturen und Mächte*, 1996, 62.

DARTS, a throwing game involving throwing darts with metal spikes at a target. The darts are between 5 and 6½in. (12.7-16.51cm) long, usually 6in. (15.3cm). The main part is called a 'barrel', made of a hard material, usually wood, plastic or brass. A metal spike is attached to the front part of the barrel, and 4 feather or plastic fins to the rear. Indoor competitions involve throwing from a distance of 8, 8½ and 9ft. (2.43, 2.59 and 2.74m, respectively), while the much rarer outdoor competitions may use distances of up to 20-30ft. (about 6.10-9.14m). The throws are made from the so-called 'toe line' or 'hockey'. Indoor events use targets smaller than those used outdoors (18in. or about 45.7cm in diameter, with targets measuring 6ft. or 183cm in outdoor events). Various types of targets are used, but two are the most popular. The first is called the 'target face', with 5 scoring rings, 5, 10, 25, 50 and 75pts., counting from the outside, and a central ring scoring 100pts. The other type, known as 'round the clock', is more complex. A 'bull's eye' is located in the middle, and is worth 50pts. A narrow ring (about ¹/₅in. or 8mm wide), worth 25pts., surrounds it, with the 'single-score ring' further away from the center, where points are scored in irregularly marked radial zones: 1, 18, 4, 13, 6, 10, 15, 2, 17, 3, 19, 7, 16, 8, 11, 14, 9, 12, 5, 20. The next narrow ring is known as the 'treble ring', and the number of points scored is triple the amount marked for the radial fields. The next, broader ring scores single amounts of points. The last, narrow ring, closest to the edge of the target, is known as 'doubles', and scores double amounts of points. On the edge of the target, there

A self-scoring dart board.

AZUCA GRAEZ NR 1

An estimated 6 million people play darts on a regular basis in British pubs and clubs.

is a ring where the points are actually marked but hitting it does not score any points. The target is placed on a wall so that the bull's eye is at a height of 5ft. 8in. (about 172cm).

Playing with a target with normal rings involves the simple scoring of points. The most popular of such games is known as 'high score': the first player to reach 1,000pts. wins. The second var., 'round the clock', usually involves scoring points in the correct order from 1 to 20 (even though these are not marked on the target in the same order). After scoring on the single score ring, the player is supposed to score on the double and treble rings, and finally hit the bull's eye. Individual varieties of the game, differing in the techniques and order of scoring, are called by the same names as in darts baseball, and the scoring systems are also similar: all fives – only points divisible by five are valid; halve it; closing; scram; and Shanghai.

History. The earliest records of dart-like games date back to Korea, where the game was known as >TUHO. A similar game, called >TEKA, was played by the Maoris before Europeans arrived in New Zealand (today, it has been revived as one of many trad. sports). A similar Ger. game, dating back to the Middle Ages, was known as >PFEILWURFSPIEL. However, the Eng. variant has had the strongest influence on modern darts. The earliest records date back to the 15th cent. Darts were the favorite pastime of Anne Boleyn, a wife of Henry VIII, who gave the king a darts set as a present. In the 19th cent., the game developed a variant known as >PUFF-DARTS, puffed from pipes by blowing into them. The trad. var. of darts became one of the most popular pastimes in Brit. pubs at the turn of the 19th and 20th cent. In 1908, the magistrate of the city of Leeds sought to determine whether the game was gambling or recreation. The local court was asked for advice. If the game was considered gambling, it would be banned. However, the ruling was that it was not, after all, gambling, making possible its further growth. In the 1930s, the first larger national events started in the UK. Among them, the Lord Lonsdale Trophy, organized since 1938, has reached the highest prestige. In 1953, the National Darts Association of Great Britain (NDA) was established. In 1966-67 as many as 40,000 pubs and clubs with about 1 million players took part in qualifications for the Lord's Taverners Seven Darts Tourney. Media interest, especially on the part of TV, led to a further, rapid growth of darts. The game proved perfectly suited to the needs of TV, and has been frequently televised. Darts scenes have made it into Brit. TV series such as *Coronation Street* and *East Enders*. However, the popularity led to some organizational splits. After WWII, the Brit. Darts Organization (BDO) with 25,000 players in 64 countries worldwide was considered to be the strongest association. However, it was soon overtaken by the World Darts Federation (WDF), with over half a million players in more than 50 countries. Recently, some officials and players broke away from it, forming

the World Darts Council (WDC). Each of the federations organizes large international events, competing for prestige, and some of them are considered continental or world championships. The BDO Embassy World Professional Darts Championships and Winmau World Masters as well as the Skol W.Ch. under the auspices of the WDC are thought to be the most important tournaments. There are national federations in several Commonwealth countries, e.g. the Darts Federation of Australia. New Zealand organizes the Pacific Cup, which is the most important event in the Pacific region. Brit. players have always been considered the best, with J. Pike (1903-60), B. Duddy in the 1970s, and R. Harrington more recently. Record durations of accurate target hitting are recorded. The current record, set in 1986, is 100,101pts. in 3,732 throws, made by the Scotsman A. Downie. Prizes in international professional events usually reach $15,000-$30,000, and up to $100,000 in the most important events. An estimated 6 million people play darts on a regular basis in Brit. pubs and clubs. The game is also popular in the USA, where the Amer. Darts Association has about 100,000 members.

DASHI NĚ TREG, Albanian for 'a ram at the marketplace, or a ram for sale, a team game for children [Alb. *dashi* – ram + *ně* – on, in + *treg* – marketplace]. Two teams consisting of an unspecified num. of players, usu. 10-12, compete on a rectangular field, divided into halves by a middle line. Each team forms a circle, within which one player – *the ram* – is placed. The aim is to transport *the ram* into the opponent's half beyond the line by the circle's pressing against the other team, while preventing the opponents from doing likewise. The succeeding team wins the game.

Source: Arben Kaçurri, Albanian Olympic Committee; also by the same: *Heritage* – 'System of values and device of education', a paper delivered at XI Seminar for Postgraduate Students, International Olympic Academy, Ancient Olympia, 2001.

DATIM LUDERE, a Vulgar Lat. term for what should be *dadatim ludere* [Lat. adverb *dadatim* – giving to each other, returning to each other + *ludo, ludere* – play]. A term for a group of old >ROMAN BALL games that, according to Pol. ethnographer Z. Dowgird, 'included the simplest and most primitive games in which basically only 2 elements occurred: pitching and catching a ball. All the parties present in the playing field cooperated with one another.' (Z. Dowgird, *Forms of Palant in the Area of Poland,* unpublished doctoral dissertation, 1966, 72). Cf. >EXPULSIM LUDERE, >RAPTIM LUDERE.

DAVSAND IAVAKH, Mong. for 'a journey for salt'. A trad. Mong. game in which players form a caravan of female camels and merchants. One of the participants acts as a male camel that attacks the caravan attempting to run away with the female camel carrying salt. The merchants defend their caravan, but if the attacking camel succeeds in kidnapping

one of the female camels, he is the winner. The merchants score a point when they successfully defend their camels. The presence of salt in the game is related to the immense importance of this substance in the process of food preservation, indispensable for people living on the steppes. The game actually symbolizes the struggle to survive.

DAWAZHI, Uighur for 'tight-rope walking', a form of acrobatic stunt popular among the Chin. Uighur minority. A rope, 80m in length, is stretched between the tip of a pole, 30m high, and a metal hook fastened into the ground, forming an incline supported at several points by trestles or jacks made from pairs of shorter poles. The walker, without the aid of any safety devices and with his eyes blindfolded, moves up the rope with a balancing rod in his hands. During the performance the walker frequently slides down the rope performing numerous acrobatic stunts. After reaching the top the performer slides down the rope to the great applause of the spectators.

History. According to Uighur sources dawazhi has a 1,400-year-old tradition. The oldest source speaks of three female monsters, who appeared in the mountainous southern part of Xinjiang province and caused mischief to the local countrymen by flying in the air and provoking devastating hurricanes, storms and locust attacks. In an effort to defeat the monsters a young villager called Wubuli found a tall tree and stretched a rope from its top to the ground. By climbing the rope he managed to gain the height required to kill the flying monsters. His brave deed is now commemorated through the practice of davazhi.

Mu Fushan and others, 'Davazhi', TRAMCHIN, 2.

DÉCAISSER LA GRENOUILLE, also *écaisser la grenouille.* In Bret. dial. of the Rennes area (Bret. name is Roazon) roughly 'tearing frogs' legs' [Fr. *dé* – tearing, depriving of sth. or degrading and *é* – change of state + Bret. dial. *caisse,* Fr. *cuisse* – leg + *la* – feminine article + Bret. dial. *guernouille,* Fr. *grenouille* – frog]. According to a Fr. researcher

Datim ludere – a variety of Roman ball, a Roman fresco.

of children's games, L. Esquieu, this cruel game consisted of tearing a live frog by two 3-player teams. 2 boys held each other by the hands and the third one lay across his partners' arms. The boys carried by their teammates attempted to snatch a frog from each other's hands, finally tearing it in two. The winning party was the one who managed to tear off a fragment of the frog, usu. its larger limb. Some time later, a similar game, named >TOUSEG, was continued in Brittany with the use of an imitation frog made of wooden plank.

164

D WORLD SPORTS ENCYCLOPEDIA

In this var. of decapitation du coq, the cock is suspended on a rope some 3m above the ground and is targeted by men on bicycles.

DECAPITATION DE L'OIE, a folk game played in France and Brittany, formerly a frequent event during pardons and festivals (see >PARDON, LE), in which a live goose is partially buried in the ground and players compete in tearing off its head. Cf. Swed. >DRA HUVUDET AV GÅSEN. In another var., called *decapitation du coq*, a live rooster was used.

DECATHLON, [Gk. *deca* – ten + *athlon* – competition] any multi-discipline sports competition consisting of 10 contests. In modern sport the most popular var. are >ATHLETIC DECATHLON and its Amer. version >ALL-AROUND. See also >WEIGHT-LIFTING DECATHLON.

DECK GAMES, sports and games played aboard ships in special allocated spaces so that objects used for the game would not slide or go overboard. Many deck games have been adaptations of regular 'land' games or sports to deck conditions. Deck games are organized as a means of recreation for sailors and passengers on board ships. Due to their isolated and recreational nature the deck competitions have never been organized into leagues or professional events.

History. The origin of the majority of deck games remains unknown. They underwent a rapid development in the steamship era, in which the new types of ships guaranteed better board stability, necessary for practicing various games aboard. The games served as diversions during long and tedious ship voyages. Initially, some trad. sailor games were played, later shore sports were adopted, particularly ball and bowling games in which balls were replaced with various types of disks. At the turn of the 19th and 20th cent. the following deck sports and games were played as part of the program of many Brit. shipping lines: high jump, long jump, triple jump, sack race, wheelbarrow race, jumping over rolling barrels, and even potato races consisting of picking up potatoes scattered along the deck and carrying them, one at a time, to a bucket positioned on the other end of deck. The most popular deck games include:

A shuffleboard diagram on the deck of a cruise ship.

DECK BILLIARDS, also *skittle-board*, a game similar to >BILLIARDS but played on a larger area marked on deck. The game is played with wooden disks pushed with long-handled drivers fitted with a semi-circular shoe, which fits the disk, increasing shot precision.

BULL, also *bull's head*, a game consisting of tossing disks or rings made of various materials. The playing pieces are most often rubber disks, canvas bags filled with sand or, sometimes, coin-size lead rings cased in leather. Each player has 6 disks or bags and throws them onto a scoring diagram. There are two most common kinds of scoring diagrams: 1) a diagram having 12 squares, made up of 2 columns of 6 squares. Ten squares have different numerical values. The 2 top squares contain either a capital letter B or a bull's head symbol. If a player throws a B, anything he or she has scored in the column of squares below the bull square is cancelled; 2) a scoring diagram consisting of 12 squares, made up of 4 rows of 3 squares each with the furthest row showing the right-hand bull, the number 10, and the left-hand bull. The remaining numbers (1 to 9) are allocated to the three lower rows such that the aggregate number in each line is 15 with the usual sequence of numbers 3-5-7; 4-9-2; and 8-1-6. The winner is the player who first completes the full sequence of the board by covering the numbers 1 to 10 consecutively, followed by the right--hand and left-hand bulls, and then returning in reverse order to number 1. When a player has thrown his or her 6 disks (or sandbags), the last square he or she covered in correct sequence is noted, and the next player takes his or her 6 throws. All throws must be taken clearly and disks must rest within a square without touching the lines. A disk, however, may be driven completely into a square by another one and, if in the correct sequence, count. Throwing a disk (or a sandbag) into an out--of-sequence square results in penalty points. The penalty rules vary on different ships and different shipping lines. The most frequent penalty is starting the entire sequence over from the beginning, while a player whose disk or bag falls off the board is penalized by dropping back one number. The throwing distance is arbitrary.

DO-DO, also *spiropole* or *tether-ball*, a game invented by B.B. Cowe, played for the first time on the *Dunvegay Castle*, a Brit. ship owned by D. Curry, in 1897. Do-do is played by doubles with partners facing each other at the 4 corners of a square marked on the deck. The game is played using a tennis-size ball made of natural rubber or oakum covered with leather. The ball hangs on a cord from the top of a 2-m-high post, positioned in the middle of the square field. The cord is long enough so the ball could be suspended slightly above the deck. The players use small wooden rackets to strike the ball alternately. One team strikes to wind the string with the ball from their right to left, and the opposing team attempts the reverse. The team which manages to wind the string with the ball completely round the post wins. In another version the cord is attached to a spiral and teams attempt to wind it up or down. One form of the game, commonly played 1-on-1, uses no rackets and a volleyball.

MARINE GOLF, a game played according to the rules of >GOLF. Instead of balls, round disks are used, pushed with clubs along the deck. The holes are circles marked on the deck, slightly larger in diameter than the disks. Detailed rules and play of the game depend on the size of decks and playing areas.

DECK CROCQUET, a game similar to >CROCQUET. Disks substitute for balls and they are pushed with special mallets resembling >GOLF and >POLO clubs.

DECK CRICKET, a game similar to regular >CRICKET, played on a smaller area marked on shipboard. Initially, the game was played with a tethered ball, to avoid losing too many cricket balls in the sea. Few players, however, found that satisfactory. Later, nets rigged from awning spars to the deck enclosed a playing area 30ft. (9.14m) wide and 60ft. (18.3m) long, to prevent the balls from falling into the water and passengers from possible injury. An area, extending the width of the playing space and reaching 8ft. (2.4m) from a line drawn about 15ft. (4.6m) from the wicket, was worth one run; the next area extending for a further 8ft. was worth 2 runs; a slightly bigger area, extending for a further 9ft. 6in. (2.9m) was worth 3 runs; and beyond that was the boundary and 4 runs. Deck cricket enjoyed its greatest popularity in the era of big ocean liners, which could allocate a large area of deck space for the game. Development of air passenger traffic and the substitution of big passenger liners with smaller and more economical vessels after 1945, caused the game to fade away almost entirely. Sporadically, however, deck cricket matches are still played on the initiative of groups of Brit. passengers or tourists.

SLINGING THE MONKEY, also *bowline stretching*, a contest in which competitors are hung up by the legs with ropes, swinging head-downwards, with their hands just able to reach the deck. In other versions of the game, the players were hung by the legs and one arm. In order to win the contest the players were required to perform a var. of chores. In the simplest sailor's version of bowline stretching, a single contender held a packed wad of canvas and tried to throw it at the passers-by who teased him by tapping, ear-snapping, etc. If a passer-by was hit with the canvas wad, he took the hanging player's place. In another version, several contenders were hung at the same time, each holding a piece of chalk. At the fancy of the spectators, the contenders were to draw figures on the deck. The winner was the contender who, in the opinion of the spectators, managed to draw the best series of figures. Each consecutive figure had to be drawn further from the last spot, which resulted in contenders performing humorous, monkey-like movements, applauded by the audience. On some ocean liners and cruise ships the contenders were required to write love letters, instead of drawing figures, which then were evaluated according to their 'literary' quality. Slinging the monkey was primarily a sailor's game practiced also on small liners carrying Eur. immigrants to America and Australia. When immigrants were replaced by tourists, such bowline stretching contests gradually began to decline.

DECK QUOITS, a game consisting of tossing quoits (rope rings) at various targets. The quoits can be tossed at a peg, over which they must fall to score; to a target of circles of different values chalked on the deck; or into a bucket. Typical deck quoits is played on a field with two circular targets, each on one end, similar to a >CURLING rink. The playing area is 36ft. (10.98m) long and 6-8ft. (183-244cm) wide. The target is 4ft. (122cm) in diameter and consists of three concentric circles, each worth a different number of points. The center, smallest circle is 3pts., the middle circle is 2pts., and the outer circle is 1pt. The game can be played by singles or doubles. In the women's var. the quoits are tossed at a target from behind the ladies' line, marked 29ft. (8.9m) from the target. Women must stand with their feet behind the marked line, and not outside the ends. The gentlemen's line is 34.5ft. (10.52) from the target. Men must stand with the foremost foot inside the small circle of the opposite target. Each player has either 3 or 4 quoits. The object of the game is to place one's quoits as near as possible to the center mark of the target. Quoits falling short of the dead line (or ladies' line) do not count and must be removed promptly; rolling quoits do not count either. A quoit touching a circle will score the number of the outer ring. Bumping one's own or an opponents' quoits to further one's own interests is permitted; scoring, therefore, is done only once a match is over. The game is won by the first player (or pair of players in a doubles match) to score 21pts. A match is won by the player or pair winning the most of 3 games. Opponents stand together at the ends of the pitch in the singles game, and play from each end alternately. In doubles, partners stand at opposite ends, each against an opponent. Quoits must be thrown only backhand and over the center line.

SHUFFLEBOARD, also *shovelboard*, a game consisting of shoving wooden disks on a plain surface at a mark. Shuffleboard has several varieties; the original Brit. var. was first played on shore in the 15th cent., only later to become one of the most popular deck games. The rules and dimensions of the playing area vary. Most frequently, shuffleboard is played with disks about 1in. thick and 6in. (152mm) in diameter, which are pushed along the deck with long-handled drivers fitted with a semi-circular shoe that fits the disk. The game may be played by singles or doubles. Each player or pair is provided with 4 disks of different colors. The court is 46ft. (14.02m) long and usually 6ft. (1.83m) wide. Identical scoring diagrams are marked on each end of the field. Placing a disk on a particular square of the diagram scores a specific number of points. The scoreboard is oval shaped and contains a 3ft.-wide square divided into 9 equal sections, numbered from 1 to 9, in a sequence 6, 7, 2, 9, 4, 3, 8, 1, 5 clockwise from the upper right corner. Each numbered section is 1ft. wide. On the inside and the outside of the square are 2 adjacent half-circular areas. The outer area is marked +10pts. and the inner is marked -10pts. In the men's version the players shove the disks from behind the gentlemen's line, 33ft. from the edge of the scoreboard, which serves both as a throwing line and the outer boundary of the court. The ladies' line is 30ft. from the edge of the scoreboard. If a disk stops short of the ladies' line in the men's game it is removed from play. The object of the game is to shove the disks into the highest numbered sections. The players shove their disks alternately with their opponents; they may also knock their own or another's disks into or out of any square. The player's score is indicated by the squares in which the disks rest when all the disks have been played. A match is usually played to either 50 or

100 up. In each consecutive game of the match, the player or pair who shoved first in the former game play second in the next one, as there is clearly an advantage for the player or pair who shove second. A disk touching any line on the court does not score. The game may be played in singles matches or in doubles. In singles, opponents play from the same ends; in doubles, partners stand at opposite ends so that two players, one of each side, are at each end.

The original 19th-cent. Brit. deck shuffleboard was first adopted as a recreational game in Amer. hotels and resorts and then, after modification, it made a successful comeback as a deck game. The court is 52ft. (15.85m) long and 6ft. (1.83m) wide. The bases of the triangular scoring diagrams are parallel to and 8ft. (2.44m) from the court's end lines. Each diagram is 9ft. (2.74m) long and 6ft. (1.83m) wide at the base. Lines parallel to the base divide each diagram into two 7-, two 8-, and one 10-pt. sections. Extending 1.5ft. (45cm) below the base is a penalty area costing 10pts. The scoring diagrams are 12ft. (5.49m) apart. In the area between the diagrams, 2 parallel lines, 3.66m apart, mark the dead zone. Any disk that stops within the dead zone is removed from play. As in the Brit. var., the game is played with disks about 1in. thick and 6in. (152mm) in diameter, which are pushed along the deck with long-handled cue sticks fitted with a semi-circular shoe that fits the disk. The cue stick is usu. 5-6ft. 3in. (153-188cm) long. Players push the disks from behind the penalty area toward the opposite scoring diagram. A player's score is indicated by the sum of the numbers on sections in which his disks rest when all the disks have been played. A disk touching any court line does not score. Each player or pair is provided with one set of disks (4 black or 4 red) and pushes them alternately with his or her opponent. Apart from placing the disks on the sections of the scoring diagrams, the players can also knock the opponent's disks out, preferably into the penalty area, in which case the opponent's score is reduced by 10pts. The knock-out play is known as *caroming*; its name borrowed from the terminology of >CAROM BILLIARDS. Other game tactics include skillful guarding of one's own disks or blocking the opponent's disks. A winning point total is usually set at 50, 75, or 100pts. The game is played by singles and doubles, in men's and women's categories.

The earliest references to shuffleboard come from the 18th-cent. The development of shuffleboard rules could have been influenced by some earlier Eng. games such as >LAWN BOWLING, Scot. >CURLING, shove-ha'penny, and other bowling games. From c.1870 the game was played on passenger ships cruising between Britain and Australia. In 1913, the Amer. hotel proprietor, R. Ball from Daytona Beach, Florida introduced shuffleboard as a recreational game on land for his hotel guests. The game became so popular that it spread rapidly throughout the United States. In 1931, the National Shuffleboard Association was founded in St. Petersburg, Florida and devised uniform rules for the sport. By 1969, shuffleboard had been played by six million people in the USA; 455 towns had 5,000 courts altogether, in municipal parks and recreational areas. The sport is most popular in Florida, in which it is played in over 200 shuffleboard clubs, by 40,000 regular players, on about 2,500 courts. The greatest shuffleboard center is St. Petersburg, Florida, which boasts the top shuffleboard club in the country – the Mirror Lake Club –comprising a few thousand members and owning over 100 courts. The US shuffleboard national championships have been held since 1931. The two most prestigious tournaments are held either in Traverse City, Michigan (in summer) or in Florida (in winter). Owing to the modest physical effort required for the game, shuffleboard is a favorite of the elderly and retired. Shuffleboard is also popular in Canada, Mexico and on cruise ships worldwide.

DECK TENNIS, a combination of trad. >LAWN TENNIS and >QUOITS. The game is played using a quoit, or rubber ring, 1.5in. thick (1.27cm) and 6in. in diameter. The players throw the ring to one another across a net suspended over the center of the court. The ring must be returned by the receiver from the position in the court in which he or she catches it. Players must not hold on to

the ring unnecessarily. If a player's hand touches but drops the ring, it counts against him. Should the ring touch a boundary line and pass out of bounds, it is considered to have fallen within bounds. Even if the ring is already out of bounds, any player attempting to catch it and failing to do so will lose the point. If a foul serve is falling out of bounds and an opponent does not attempt to catch it the server loses a point. Players must not use both hands while catching or serving the ring. They are not allowed to serve or return the ring with both feet off the deck. Scoring, according to J. Arlott, is like that of tennis and advances 15, 30, 40, advantage, game; according to F.K. Perkins, like that of volleyball, i.e. a game is won by the player or pair that first scores 15pts., provided the winning player or pair is ahead by 2 or more points; there are 2 games to a set. A match consists of 3 or 5 sets. Deck tennis can be played by singles or doubles. The size of the court varies, depending on the deck space available. Generally, singles courts, according to J. Arlott, are between 30 and 40ft. (9.1-12.2m) long and from 10 to 15ft. (3-4.6m), or, according to F.K. Perkins, 12 to 18ft. (3.66-5.49m) wide. In the faster doubles game, the length may be less, 28-34ft. (8.5-10.4m), but the width should not exceed 15ft. (4.57m). There is a neutral space extending 3ft. (0.9m) on either side of the net across the width of the court. Players standing over the neutral line are faulted; they may stretch their hands over the neutral line but not over the net. If the ring falls within the neutral space the point is lost. Parallel to the neutral line and 6-8ft. (1.8-2.4m) from each end of the court there are other lines known as back lines. The center line, making 4 divisions, extends from the middle of the back line to the middle of the neutral line on each side of the net. The object of play is to deliver the ring over the net to the opponent's half. Forehand and backhand deliveries must be given but not overhand ones or deliveries from a height above the shoulder. If the ring touches the net in service it must be played again. The rules of deck tennis are similar to those of Pol. >RINGO.

Apart from the above, deck games include also >COCK FIGHTING, understood as a wrestling competition between 2 squatting contenders, who push each other off using their arms.

DEFENDING THE CITY, also *ball out of town*, a Rus. school game played with a croquet ball and hockey sticks. The pitch is 30 steps long. Its width depends on the number of players. It is divided by 2 straight lines, parallel to the finish lines and about 5 steps from them. There are therefore 3 zones: the field and 2 cities. Each of the 2 teams has 5-15 players. Captains stand in the middle of the pitch and the rest of the team on the inner line of the cities, 2 steps away from one another. A draw determines which team goes first. On a signal from the referee the captain of the starting team places a croquet or rag ball on the ground and hits it with his stick in the direction of the opposing city. The other team defends the city without going beyond the line and tries to attack the other city. Every time the ball crosses the outer line of the city the attacking team scores a point. When the ball does not reach the inner line, however, the team loses a point. One or more players may stop the ball, but only one may hit it. In order to stop or hit the ball any player may leave his place and move around the whole city. The first team to score 10pts. wins. When the game is repeated, teams change cities. In the case of a draw, the game is played a third time.

I.N. Chkhannikov, 'Defending the city', GIZ, 1953, 100-101.

DEHVADA, in Hindu tradition 'a way of the body', treated as one of the ways to complete the realization of human life. Dehavada assumes that a human being can achieve salvation by way of physical perfection – *kaya sadhana*, i.e. by understanding and controlling the body and its functions. The postulates of dehvada can often be found in the works of ancient Ind. literature, such as the songs of *Rigveda*, *Ramayana*, and *Mahabharata*. The major protagonists of those works possessed a skill of controlling their bodies trained in archery, horse riding, swimming, wrestling, ancient forms of weightlifting, hunting, and charioteering.

DELFINSPRING, Dan. for 'dolphin's leap'. An old mountebank's stunt and today a fitness exercise practiced during PE classes. The players get down on all fours beside each other and the one in the middle starts the competition by rolling under a neighbor who is supposed to roll over the middle player and the following one, who then is to roll under. The game continues until one of the players makes a wrong move.

J. Møller, 'Delfinspring', GID, 1997, 3, 48.

DEMOLITION DERBY, a gladiatorial automobile event in which the object is to eliminate the oppo-

The dog-eat-dog world of the demolition derby arena.

nent by running into his car and disabling it so that he cannot continue the race. Races are held on specially prepared arenas. There are no classes or categories. Drivers must not run into opponents' doors, nor may they hit a car that has already been knocked over. A car that is immobile for more than 2min. is disqualified. The winner is the driver whose car is still operational after all opponents have been eliminated. Drivers use sedans with a hard and permanent roof. The sport is particularly popular in the USA. In Europe, it is called 'bangers racing', but it is not very common.

Demolition derby.

DERBY, the name originates from the name of the city and, at the same time, the seat of an Eng. aristocratic family, a member of which initiated in 1780 a flat race of 3-yr.-old horses at a distance of 1.5mi. (2,414.016m) which has been held annually on the first Wed. in June, on the horserace course in Epsom in England. The name derby also applies to races of 3-yr.-old horses outside Epsom, on the Eur. continent, at a distance that was rounded down to 2,400m. Another, still broader, meaning of derby

Thèodore Gericault, Derby at Epsom, *oil on canvas, 1821.*

WORLD SPORTS ENCYCLOPEDIA

Johnny Murtagh on Sinndar during the Epsom Derby.

is a competition accessible for all. In some Eur. countries derby means any sports competition between partners or teams from the same locality.

DET MÆRKELIGE DYR, Dan. for 'strange animal'. A Dan. form of 1-on-1 competition. One participant holds the other, who is standing upright, by the neck and wraps his legs around the other's waist, then releases his hands and lowers his body to touch the floor. After that, he puts his head, arms, and shoulders in between the other's legs and grabs his ankles. At the same time, the standing participant bends forward propping his hands on the floor. In such a position the competitor bent forward attempts to move ahead on all fours, whereas the other one makes every possible effort to stop his opponent from walking, pulling him by the ankles while pressing his legs against opponent's back. The winning competitor is the one who succeeds in walking farthest despite his opponent's efforts. Another way of achieving one's victory is by dropping the 'upper' partner to the floor, which is no easy task, if his legs hold firmly on the back of the strange animal's 'lower' part and his hands hold the other's ankles firmly.
J. Møller, 'Det mærkelige dyr', GID, 1997, 3, 17.

DEUTSCHE BALLSPIEL, DAS, the 18th-cent. name for >SCHLAGBALL – a Ger. bat and ball game. This name was suggested by PE pioneer J.C.F. Guts-Muths (1759-1839). See also >PALANT.

Det mærkelige dyr – a 'strange animal' indeed.

DEVIL AMONG THE TAILORS, a var. of >SKITTLES.

DEVON AND CORNWALL, also *devonstyle*, see >CORNWALL AND DEVON.

DHANUR VEDA, lit. 'bow and arrow'. In the Sanscrit tradition it meant not only the ability to use a bow and arrows, but was also a symbol of using other hand weapons with skill. The knowledge of dhanur veda is contained in 2 great epic poems of India – the *Mahabharata* and *Ramayana*. Certain passages describe how noble heroes, usually princes, guided by their guru, acquire extraordinary fighting skills and how they implement them to defeat their enemies. The most famous guru teaching his disciples self-control and psychologically refined fighting skills was Drona. The clash between subtle and brutal skills takes place during the fight between arrogant and undefeated Bhima and Arjuna, who is strong through meditation and physical skills shaped through persistent self-development. Chapters 249-252 of the surviving text in the tradition of dhanur veda, known as *Agni Purana*, written as late as the 8th cent. AD, function as a manual of fighting technigues, which contains the subtle 'holy knowledge' of mantra (mental exercises) and the fighting methods, as opposed to the purely physical, primitive 'profane knowledge'. It lists exercises for 5 categories of fighters (fighting on combat wagons, on elephants, on horseback, on foot, as well as wrestling). Participants must master 5 types of weapons: launchers (such as slings or bows and arrows), projectiles (e.g. spear), launching weapons that remain in the fighter's hands (e.g. lariat), hand weapons (all kinds of side-arms) and empty-handed, hand-to-hand combat. These skills were required of the highest Hindu classes i.e. the *brahmins* and *kshatriya*, whose obligation is to pass this knowledge on to the lowers classes in order to maintain the social order.

DHOPKHEL, the most popular folk sport in the state of Assam in India. The matches are held mostly during the *Rangoli Bihu* festival of spring. There are two var. of the game – for men and for women. The game is played by 11 players using a rubber ball, in a pitch about 125m long and 80m wide. In the middle between the goal lines, on the right side, there is a central point. Every 12ft. (about 3.66m) in 2 directions from the central point, 4 lines, referred to as *kai*, parallel to the goal lines, are marked. At the point where these kai lines touch the sides of the pitch there are flags. Flags are also placed in the corners. On each side of the pitch there is a

point located in line with the central point, at a distance of 13ft. 6in. (about 4.12m) from the center. Each of those 2 points forms the center of a circle referred to as a *gher*. Inside each of the circles there is a player called a *katoni* who is the goal for the attacking team that attempts to hit the opponent's katoni with the ball in order to eliminate that team member from the game and therefore decrease the number of players in the opposing team. A player who has not been eliminated from the game is labeled a *ghai*.

The match starts with throwing the ball up – a *dhop*. A player from the team that has won, by way of drawing, the right to start the game has to throw the ball so that it rests on the opposing team's half. Should the ball come to rest elsewhere, the throw must be repeated. The dhop should be received by the opposing team and if they fail to do so, the ball goes to the team whose player performed the dhop. A player who caught the ball after the dhop heads for the gher – the circle – located in the opponent's half attempting to hit the katoni standing there. If the ball misses the katoni, the throwing player's team must not repeat the attempt and the player who missed lobs the ball towards the opposing team, in a throw resembling the dhop. As a result, the opponent gains the opportunity to hit the katoni standing on the other half. If either katoni is hit below the waist, the so-called *kota*, they lose their ghai status and become *hoia* or *bondha* and are supposed to move to the opposite half where they attempt to catch the ball to regain their right to play on their own half. Moving to the opposite half is referred to as *aulia* and the return to one's own half, after catching the ball – *hora*. The return, however, is conditioned by certain additional requirements: the ball must not be caught within the zone bordered by the kai lines, after catching the ball the player has to cross 2 kai lines without crossing any of the pitch's borderlines. When a given team loses 10 players who had occupied hoia and bondha positions, the last remaining ghai becomes the ghai katoni. If that player receives a kota, such a situation is referred to as the *piriutha*, which gives the victory to the team achieving that stage. If two teams lose the same number of ghais, the game ends in a draw.

DIAULOS, a foot race practiced in ancient Greece, also during Ol.G., at a distance of 2 stadiums [Gk. *dia* – double + *aulos* – among others a synonym for a stadium]. Like in other foot races, the runner started from the *balbis* – a stone beam with transverse grooves on it, for the feet. He crossed 1 stadium, reached the turn-around point (*kampter*), ran around the pole called *terma* and raced back along the same course as before but in the opposite direction. The diaulos was incorporated into the Ol.G. during the 14th ancient Ol.G. in 724 BC. The first historical winner was Hypenos from Pisa; the last one, in 153 AD – Demetrios from Chios. The distance varied from one ancient Ol.G. to other, as it depended on the length of the stadium. The longest one was the Olympic stadium – 192.27m, in Delphi – 165m, during the Panathenean games – 177.55m, and in Epidaurus – 181.08m. Therefore, the distance in each case was twice a given stadium's length, i.e. 384.54m, about 330m, 355.1m, and 362.16m accordingly.

DINNIE STYLE, an old var. of Scot. wrestling developed by a famous strongman, D. Dinnie, c.1870 when, after his failures in the >CUMBERLAND AND WESTMORELAND style, where the match was held in a standing position, he introduced an on-the-ground position which had previously been unknown in Scotland. Some elements of the Dinnie style were perfected in 1930 by W. Carmichael, although up to WWII these rules gained little popularity. The fight starts in the classical standing position, but after either of the wrestlers falls to the mat it is continued as in freestyle wrestling. The winner has to make the opponent touch the mat with both shoulder blades.

DIP O' THE KIT, an Eng. village game whose rules have not survived, but possibly related to >KIT-CAT.

DIRIGIBLE BALLOONS (AIRSHIPS), (Lat. *dirigere* – to direct, to steer), a var. of lighter-than-air crafts equipped with a bag containing a gas to lift the ship, a means of propulsion, means for adjusting buoyancy, and one or more gondolas for the crew, passengers, and power units. The first successful airship was that of the Fr. engineer and inventor H. Giffard, who in 1852 constructed a cigar-shaped, non-rigid gas bag 44m (143ft.) long, driven by a screw propeller powered by a 2.2-kW (3-hp) steam engine. Giffard's airship could be steered only in calm or nearly calm weather. Count Ferdinand

von Zeppelin (1838-1917), the Ger. inventor, completed his first airship in 1900; this ship had a rigid frame and served as the prototype of many subsequent models, called zeppelins. Airships were used during WWI for military purposes. Able to fly over long distances and reach speeds of 125km/h, they were used to cross the Atlantic as early as 1924; some flights were part of competitions consisting in trans-Atlantic flights, typical of the 1920s (see >SOLO YACHTING and >AEROPLANE SPORTS). The international competition in reaching the poles was particularly spectacular. In 1926 the Ital. airship *Norge*, a semi-rigid craft of about 18.4 million liters (650,000cu.ft.) capacity, with R. Amundsen (1872-1928) on board, flew from Spitsbergen, Norway, over the North Pole to Teller, Alaska, where

the ship was dismantled. Another polar flight was tried 2 years later in a similar ship, the *Italia*, by Ital. general U. Nobile (1885-1978), but after passing over the Pole it crashed on the return flight, with the loss of 8 lives. The rescue expedition took the life of R. Amundsen. Nobile's crew was rescued by the Russian icebreaker *Krassin*. Numerous crashes of passenger crafts based on Zeppelin's idea resulted in the discontinuance of airship construction. The crash of the *Graf Zeppelin*, which burnt after a flight over the Atlantic in 1937, was particularly dramatic. It took the lives of most of about 160 passengers on board. Presently attempts are being made to revive airships filled with non-flammable gas and using the latest technological advances of aviation technology.

The German zeppelin Hindenburg bursts into flames on May 6, 1937, killing 36 people.

An airship on a German postage stamp.

A bronze discus thrown by Exoidas during a contest in Kerphallenia, 6th cent. BC.

Ancient discus throwers.

A modern dirigible balloon, the famous 'Goodyear Blimp' over Warsaw, Poland.

DISC GOLF, see >FLYING DISC.

DISCATHON, see >FLYING DISC.

DISCOBOLIA, a var. of >DISCUS popular in ancient Greece was, during the first few centuries, a separate type of sport practiced at a number of local competitions. However, at the most important ancient games, including Olympic ones, it was not a separate event but formed a part of the ancient >PENTATHLON.

Equipment. The oldest discus found within the circle of ancient Gk. culture is a clay discus from Crete, whose origin dates back to approx. 1750-1600 BC. It is covered with inscriptions that have yet to be deciphered. Discuses depicted in *The Iliad* and *The Odyssey* are made of stone and iron; a discus brought by Achilles to his companions during the games in honor of Patroclus (Book XXIII of *The Iliad*) is an 'iron quoit.' Whereas in vol. 8 of *The Odyssey* Odysseus defeats his rival Euryale in a stone discus throw. The largest stone discus found during excavations carried out in Olympia is 32.5cm in

Discus motif on a postage stamp issued for the 1920 Olympic Games in Antwerp.

D

WORLD SPORTS ENCYCLOPEDIA

The discus throw on postage stamps issued for the Olympic Games in Athens.

A Roman copy of Myron's The Discus Thrower, marble, 1st cent. AD.

diameter and weighs 6.63kg. Dimensions of preserved discuses that were used during ancient games vary from 17 to 30cm, they are 1.5cm thick in the center and their weight is between 1.35 and 4.75kg. As Pausanias wrote in his *Description of Greece* – in Olympia, the so-called Sicyonian People's Treasury, 3 identical bronze quoits were kept 'for the contest of the pentathlum' in order to ensure the same conditions of competition to all competitors taking part in it (VI, 19, 4).

Technique of throw. In the depictions provided by Philostratos and Papinius Statius we read that the discus was thrown from a starting line marked in a stadium by a stone slab referred to as the *balbis*, approx. 48cm wide. From vase paintings and My-

ron's sculpture *Discobolus* it can be deduced that later on a turn also developed, however it was most probably not as full as today's spinning pivot. According to a Pol. historian of ancient sports, R. Gostkowski, a discobolus 'stood at his post with his left foot put forward, holding the discus in his left hand. Then, he swung his left arm raising the discus, after which he stretched his arms forward, grasped the discus with his right hand and raised it to the level of his head. Next, he swung his arms with increasing strength, lowering them along the right and left sides, all the while gripping the discus with his right hand only. He stepped forward with his right foot, shifting all his weight onto it. Finally he spun his body clockwise, swung his arm with all his strength and let fly the discus. Most probably, before releasing the discus he swiveled with all his might along the axis of his body in order to be able to throw the discus with optimum force. An instant before the throw, the discobolus tilted forward and squatted, while his left knee drew near the right one. All this took but a split second so that the discus could be thrown as far as possible' (*Sport in Antiquity*, 1959). According to Papinius Statius, the pentathlete Flegias could throw the discus over the Alpheus River from one bank to another, which would be approx. 50m (this seems rather improbable, even taking into account the weight of the lightest Gk. discuses). It is believed the best verifiable record ever set in the discus in ancient times was that of Faillos from Crotone, who achieved a distance of 95 Delphic feet (28.31m). During the games, the distance achieved was marked with stones, lines or wooden pegs. The number of throws required in pentathlon is unknown. Possibly it varied from one type of game to another.

History. The oldest verbal reports about discobolia can be found in Gk. myths. The mythological inventor of the discus was apparently Perseus who, during a demonstration contest, accidentally hit his grandfather Acrysios. In Pausanias' report, 'Perseus, in the full bloom of his youth and filled with joyous pride for having invented the discus, appeared publicly, demonstrating his skill. Akrysios,

unintentionally, but in accordance with the will of the gods, found himself on the trajectory of the hurled discus and fell down upon receiving its blow' (*Description of Greece*, VI). According to another myth, the god Apollo, while practicing the discus, fatally injured a boy named Hyacinthus, from where blood bloomed the flower called hyacinth. The discus is mentioned in both Homer's eposes (protagonists throw stone and iron discuses). In the *The Iliad* discobolia is played in honor of Patroclus, who died during the siege of Troy:

Achilles next offered the massive iron quoit which mighty Eetion had erewhile been used to hurl, until Achilles had slain him and carried it off in his ships along with other spoils. He stood up and said among the Argives, 'Stand forward, you who would essay this contest. He who wins it will have a store of iron that will last him five years as they go rolling round, and if his fair fields lie far from a town his shepherd or ploughman will not have to make a journey to buy iron, for he will have a stock of it on his own premises.' Then uprose the two mighty men Polypoetes and Leonteus, with Ajax son of Telamon and noble Epeus. They stood up one after the other and Epeus took the quoit, whirled it, and flung it from him, which set all the Achaeans laughing. After him threw Leonteus of the race of Mars. Ajax son of Telamon threw third, and sent the quoit beyond any mark that had been made yet, but when mighty Polypoetes took the quoit he hurled it as though it had been a stockman's stick which he sends flying about among his cattle when he is driving them, so far did his throw out-distance those of the others. All who saw it roared applause, and his comrades carried the prize for him and set it on board his ship.

[Trans. by Samuel Butler]

Discobolia was incorporated in the Ol.G. together with the >PENTATHLON in 708 BC (XVIII Ol.G.). Thus, discobolia (as a component of the pentathlon) underwent similar transformations as other Gk. sports and continued until the last ancient Olympic Games in 392 AD; the pentathlon was practiced a little longer at local games, e.g. in Antioch until 510 AD. The history of discobolia is preserved in numerous monuments of literature and art. There are, among others, vase paintings and sculptures. Discobolia, which died as a sports event, was reborn as a symbol of classical sport and its modern Olympic equivalent the moment Olympia was discovered by modern archeologists.

A number of literary works devoted to the modern var. of >DISCUS employ metaphors that invoke the ancient discobolia.

DISCUS, 1) (preceded by *the*) the event or sport of throwing the discus; 2) a circular and flat object, used by athletes in throwing competitions during ancient games. Cf. >DISCOBOLIA and modern >DISCUS THROW.

DISCUS THROW 1) an event of the ancient Gk. pentathlon; see also >DISCOBOLIA; 2) a modern

athletic field event. In both cases, the idea is to throw a round, flat object (the discus, Gk. *discos*) as far as possible.

Equipment and throwing circle. A modern discus consists of the body, usually made of wood, surrounded by a metal rim, with an adjustable weight in the center. The overall mass of the discus is 2kg for men (at a diameter of 219-221mm and thickness of 44-46mm), and a minimum of 1kg for women (180-182mm and 37-39mm, respectively). The throwing circle has a concrete surface and a diameter of 245-250mm. The circle is demarcated by a metal rim, 6mm wide, painted white. The edge of the rim must be flush with the surrounding surface, while the surface of the actual throwing circle is 14-

Janus Robberts takes his final turn in the championship flight of the men's discus at the NCAA outdoor track and field championships in Baton Rouge, La.

26mm below that level. The circle is protected by a U-shaped safety cage, 4m high. The 'mouth' of the cage, opening onto the landing sector, is 6m wide. The landing sector is marked with two lines at an angle of 40°. Throws landing outside the landing sector are invalid. Measurements are made between the closest mark the discus makes on the ground and the inner side of the metal rim surrounding the throwing circle. The tolerance of measurements is 1cm.

Throwing techniques. The classical discus throw involved positioning oneself at a right angle with respect to the direction of the throw, and whirling with the discus a number of times and finally releasing it. That was also how the discus was thrown in the early days of the modern event. With time, more efficient techniques were developed, with a starting position facing away from the direction of the throw, and a quick twist adding speed to the motion of the discus in the athlete's hand.

Organization of the event. If there are fewer than 8 athletes in the competition, each contestant has 6 attempts. If there are more participants, each has 3 qualifying attempts, after which 8-12 finalists are allowed a further 3 attempts. An attempt is deemed valid if the contestant has not touched the upper surface of the metal rim with any part of his body, has not stepped outside of the throwing circle, and has left it via the back part only after the discus has landed within the landing sector.

History. In ancient Greece, the discus throw was not a separate event, being included in the >PENTATHLON. Renaissance educators promoted the discus throw as a valuable type of bodily exercise. In Poland, for example, the introduction of the discus was advocated by Renaissance writer A. Frycz Modrzewski in his treatise *O naprawie Rzeczypospolitej*. About 1800, the Ger. pioneer of gymnastics J.C. Guts Muths introduced into his system of exercise throws using metal discs. The revival of the discus in the Olympic tradition occurred after Greece was liberated from Turkish occupation in 1829, and was associated with the Pan-Hellenic Olympic Games in 1859, 1870, 1875 and 1889. At the same time, the discus was included in the program of the Ol.G. organized by W.P. Brookes at Much Wenlock, England, from 1849. The inclusion of the discus into the modern Olympics, revived by P. de Coubertain in 1896, was instrumental to the growth of the event. During the 1908 Ol.G., a Gk.-style discus event was organized in addition to the modern discus throw, using a reconstruction based on Myron's discus thrower sculpture and vase paintings. An American, M. Sheridan, won the tournament (37.99m).

During the 1912 Ol.G., a both-hands contest was organized, where aggregate results were recorded. A Finn, A. Taipale, was the winner with 82.86m (44.68+38.12). Among men, the next distance barriers were: 40m – M. Sheridan (40.72m – 1902); 50m – E. Krenz (51.03m – 1930); 60m – J. Silvester (60.56m – 1961); 70m – M. Wilkins (70.24m – 1976), all of them Americans.

Amer. throwers have dominated the history of the discus, both as far as Ol.G. contests and world records are concerned. In the 1930s, Finns took over for a short time, thanks to a new stzle they had developed (known as the 'Finnish' technique). Just after WWII, an Italian, A. Consolini, played an important part in the development of the discipline. A. Oerter (USA) – Olympic champion of 1956, 1960, 1964 and 1968 – was the greatest discus thrower of all time.

Women's discus was first recognized on an international level in 1922, and was included in the Women's World Games in 1926, 1930 and 1934. It made its first Olympic appearance during the 1928 Ol.G. in Amsterdam, where Pole H. Konopacka (1900-1989) was the winner. Konopacka also broke 3 official world records (and a further 4 unofficial ones) between 1925 and 1928. Her successor J. Wajsówna broke 6 officially recognized world records, won the event during the Women's World Games of 1934, as well as 2 Olympic medals (bronze in 1932 and silver in 1936). Another great personality of the 1930s, and Wajsówna's greatest competitor, was German G. Mauermayer, the 1936 Olympic champion and 8-time world record holder. After 1945, Soviet contestants became the main power (they had achieved results better than world records even before WWII but were not recognized due to the political isolation of the country). Soviet world record holders and Olympic medallists included N. Dumbadze, N. Romashkova-Ponomaryova and T. Press. F. Melnik-Veleva was a leading thrower of the 1970s. In the late 1970s, the East Ger. throwers E. Schlaak-Jahl and M. Hellmann managed to beat their Soviet competitors quite often. Since the reunification of Germany, the discus tradition has been upheld by W. Ilke, the Olympic champion of 1996.

The history of breaking distance barriers in women's discus is as follows: 30m – V. Gourard (France; 30.10m – 1924); 40m – J. Wajsówna (Poland; 40.34m – 1932); 50m – N. Dumbadze (USSR; 50.5m – 1946); 60m – L. Westermann (FRG; 61.26 – 1967); 70m – F. Melnik-Veleva (USSR; 70.70m – 1975).
The Book of Rules, Athletics. Discus Throw, 1998; Polish Athletic Federation, *Przepisy zawodów w lekkoatletyce. Rzut dyskiem*, 1996.

DISH-A-LOOF, [Eng. *dish* + *a* – on + Scot. *loof* - a hand] a game of Brit. boys in which players all piled their hands on a table and then snatched their own hand from under the 'heap' of others' hands. The first participant placed a hand on the table and the remaining, one after another, each put a hand on top of it. This was then repeated with the other hand. The first player was supposed to pull his hand out and put it on the top of the rest. The winner was the one who succeeded in pulling his hand out the largest number of times. In various areas of England the game was practiced in different versions under different names. In *dump* and *hard knuckles* instead of open palms the heap was constructed of clenched fists.
A.B. Gomme, 'Dish-a-loof', TGESI, 1894, I, 97-8.

DISKAR TI AR C'HURE, Bret. for 'the ruins of the curate's house', a Fr. equivalent is *abattre la maison du vicaire*. A Bret. children's game.
F. Peru, 'La tradition populaire de jeux de plein air en Bretagne', LJP, 1998.

DISTANCE FLYING DISC, see >FLYING DISC.

DISZNÓZÁS, Hung. for 'grazing the pigs', also *kanásziáték* – 'piggy game'. An old Hung. folk game close

A diver executing a pike.

to Fr. >TRUIE, LA and Pol. >CZOROMAJ. The object was to strike a ball or a bowl with a stick so that it would come to rest in a hole in the ground.
W. Endrei and L. Zolnay, *Fun and Games in Old Europe*, 1986, 112.

DIVING, a competitive sport in which the contestants make twists and dive into the water from a diving highboard (5 or 10m high) or a springboard (1 and 3m high). There are 6 dive types: forward dives, reverse dives, backward dives, inward dives, twist dives and armstand dives. Springboard and highboard dives are classified into 3 types: the layout, in which the body must not be bent and the arms are kept straight and the feet together; the pike, in which the body is bent at the hips and straight at the knees; and the tuck, in which the body is compactly bunched, while the diver clasps his or her ankles. At competitions men make 11 dives from the springboard and 10 from the highboard; women make, respectively, 8 and 10 dives. In the first part of the diving program obligatory dives are made (men – 6 dives, women – 5); in the second part free dives are made (5 and 4). The final score depends on 2 factors: subjective evaluation of style and the degree of difficulty of each dive. The 2000 Ol.G. in Sydney introduced another diving event: synchronized diving with 2 events for men and 2 for women (3m and 10m).

History. Diving is an ancient sport. In the Gk. colony of Poseidonia (Lat. Paestum, today Pesto) in S Italy, there was a water jump, 2.6m high, made of dressed stones, with a beam facing the water, located by the swimming pool. A drawing of the jump has been preserved on an ancient fresco (presently in the local museum in Pesto). Practiced for recreation, diving was not included in the ancient Ol.G. The modern history of diving was started by the Ger. club Tychyschen Frösche in 1840. In 1886 Deutsche Schwimmverband organized the first national championships. E.Ch. (springboard) have been held since 1889 (highboard since 1926). From Germany the sport was taken to Scand. countries and the USA, where diving from the highboard was more popular than diving from the springboard. For this reason only highboard diving was included in the Ol.G. held in St. Louis (1904). The first historical diving competition was won by G. Sheldon from America. Springboard diving was introduced during the 1912 Ol.G. held in

Stockholm (highboard) and during the 1920 Ol.G. held in Antwerp (springboard). W.Ch. have been held since 1973.

Apart from the basic Olympic competitions, in the past, so called 'fantasy diving' was also part of the program (1912-1924) and, once, during the 1908 Ol.G. in St. Louis, so called 'long diving' (long jumps into water). As soon as the sport left the borders of Germany, it became dominated by contestants from the United States. At times they were contested by representatives of Germany and Sweden, and since the 1960s, particularly among women, by representatives of the GDR and USSR. Periodically, other countries, e.g. Italy, Mexico, Great Britain and FRG and since the 1984 Olympics, also China have had their short-lived stars.

The best divers in the early history of diving were Germans, who had a decisive influence on the establishment of style criteria: G. Hax (Eur. champion in 1894, highboard), O. Hoof (Eur. champion from 1898 through 1906, highboard), Luber, Eur. champion in 1926 and 1927 and second in the 1912 Ol.G. (played an important role in the development of diving style). Other Olympic champions included: K. Dibiasi from Italy (1968, 1972 and 1976, highboard), American S. Lee (1948, 1952, highboard). G. Louganis won both diving competitions (springboard and highboard) during both the 1984 and 1988 Ol.G. He was also a silver medal winner at the 1976 Ol.G. (highboard). During the 1988 Games he won despite an accident in which he caught his head on the springboard's edge – similar accidents have, in the past, been fatal. Since the middle of the 1980s an increasingly important role in diving, both in men's and women's competitions, has been played by the Chinese. The first Chinese to win the Ol.G. was Z. Jihong (1984, highboard) and the W.Ch. – M. Gao (1986, springboard). Among men S. Sun won the gold medal at the W.Ch. in 1991 and the Ol.G. in 1992. During the 1996 Ol.G., of the total number of 12 medals in both competitions, including men and women, divers from China won 5, of which 3 were gold (among women: F. Mingxia, 2 gold; among men: X. Ni, gold, springboard, Y. Zhuocheng, silver, springboard, and X. Hailiang, highboard).

Diving is a spectacular sport, dynamically developing. Traditionally included in >SWIMMING, today it is more and more often treated as a separate discipline. Despite this, it does not have its own

...continued on next page

D WORLD SPORTS ENCYCLOPEDIA

federation but is affiliated with the International Federation of Amateur Swimming (Fédération International de Natation Amateur, FINA).

G. Eaves, *Diving. The Mechanics of Springboard and Firmboard Techniques*, 1969; F. Froboess, *Fell's Official Guide to Diving*, 1956; D. Smith and J. H. Bender, *Inside Diving*, 1973.

DIVING FOR PEARLS, a Chin. game practiced by the Manchurian people since the Middle Ages. It imitates on land the action of diving for pearls and throwing them into a basket by one team, which is interfered with by another team. To some extent the game resembles such Euro-Amer. sports involving throwing a ball into a basket as >BASKETBALL or >NETBALL, and esp. >BASKET ENDBALL. The

Synchronized pikes.

...continued from previous page

WOMEN'S PLATFORM
1912 Greta Johansson, SWE 39.9
1920 Stefani Fryland-Clausen, DEN 34.6
1924 Caroline Smith, USA 33.2
1928 Elizabeth Becker Pinkston, USA 31.6
1932 Dorothy Poynton, USA 40.26
1936 Dorothy Poynton Hill, USA 33.93
1948 Vicki Draves, USA 68.87
1952 Pat McCormick, USA 79.37
1956 Pat McCormick, USA 84.85
1960 Ingrid Krämer, GER 91.28
1964 Lesley Bush, USA 99.80
1968 Milena Duchková, CZE 109.59
1972 Ulrika Knape, SWE 390.00
1976 Elena Vaytsekhovskaya, USSR 406.59
1980 Martina Jäschke, E. GER 596.25
1984 Zhou Jihong, CHN 435.51
1988 Xu Yanmei, CHN 445.20
1992 Fu Mingxia, CHN 461.43
1996 Fu Mingxia, CHN 521.58
2000 Laura Wilkinson, USA 543.75

WOMEN'S 3-M SYNCHRO
2000 Vera Ilina/Ioulia Pakhalina, RUS 332.64

WOMEN'S 10-M SYNCHRO
2000 Na Li/Xue Sang, CHN 345.12

'pearl' is a ball of undetermined size. The playing area is 28m long and 15m wide, divided into a 'diving' zone with a basket, a blocking zone and a 'water' zone. The game is played by 2 teams of 6 players each. The diving zone is occupied by one player of a given team (diver), whose task is to finish the team's action and throw the pearl into a basket located on the ground. The blocking zone

Cliff diving – an extreme form of diving.

is occupied by 2 players of a given team, who try to intercept the pearl being passed to the opposing team's diver. The remaining 3 players stay in the water zone, passing the pearl between themselves to deceive the opponents and drive the pearl to the blocking zone, from where it can be passed on to the diver. The team with the highest number of pearls in the basket wins the game.

Mu Fushan et al., 'Diving for Pearls', TRAMCHIN, 56.

DJIGHIT-ZARHYS, a horse-riding show practiced by Kazakhs.

DJIRIITI, a horseback riding game similar to *jousting*, involving throwing a javelin with a blunt tip. Two riders attempt to hit each other with the javelin in a series of brisk attacks and escapes on horseback.

DLHA META, Slovak for 'a long finish'. A game in which a ball is struck with a stick, similar to >PALANT.

DOBLE BASTON, a Fil. var. of fencing with the use of 2 sticks simultaneously. It is a combination of the trad. Fil. fight of >KALI and a Eur. technique brought in the 19th cent. by Filipinos who studied in Spain [Span. *doble* – double + *bastón* – a stick, a cane]. Cf. >SOLO BASTON.

DODDART, [from Eng. *dodder*] an Eng. folk game resembling >FIELD HOCKEY and Scot. >SHINTY, but played without goals. A match is played by 2 teams of any number of players, depending on the circumstances and availability of participants. The teams are selected by two captains who take turns choosing team members from the group of those interested in playing. The objective is to lead a wooden bowl, referred to as an 'orr' or a 'coit', depending on local traditions, across the opponent's goal line, dubbed an 'ally', a 'hail-goal' or a 'boundary', striking it with crooked clubs. In some regions of England the game was known as *clubby* [from Eng. *club*]. Sometimes it was mistaken for >SHINNY whose objective was to lead a bowl up to a predetermined point rather than have it cross a goal line.

DODGEBALL, a game played between 2 teams of an agreed number of players, whose objective is to eliminate participants by hitting each of them with a ball. One team forms a circle and the other is located inside. The encircling team attempts to hit the inside players with a ball (volleyball, basketball, handball, etc.). In the single var. the winner is the last player to be hit with the ball; in the team var. the winner is the team that succeeds in removing the entire opponent's team in the shortest time, in

Multi-ball dodgeball.

the course of 2 rounds with each team holding a different position, alternatively inside the circle and forming the circle. There is also a var. of dodgeball in which pairs of players from the encircling team attempt to reach a base located at a distance of 60ft. (18.3m) from the circle's edge – the team holding the ball tries to eliminate the running pair. Another var., called *prison dodgeball*, involves 2 teams, each possessing half of a basketball court with 'prisons' on the other side of the opponents' half at the end of the court. This version follows the basic rules described above except that once struck, a player goes to the prison but can still play and he can even liberate himself by hitting an opponent with a ball from there. If a player who is targeted manages to catch the ball, the thrower goes to prison. Sometimes several balls are used at once to make the game more dynamic.

DØDNING, Dan. for 'a dead body's ghost'. A Dan. game from the family of running games with 2 bases. A participant has to run from one protective zone to another, keeping away from 2 catchers.

The first runner is caught by either catcher who pats him on the back and shouts: 'Puf!' After that, the runners have to be caught by at least 2 opponents, as one catcher can only grab the runner to prevent his escape and yell: '*Dødning, dødning, dødning!*' until one of the remaining catchers encircles the victim and shouts, 'Puf!' Cf. >GÅ OVER ELVEN, >KÆDETIK, >KLIM-KLEM, >TAMANJ, >TULLEHUT, >TYRHOLDE. See also >KREDSTROLD for similar races across a single protective zone.

J. Møller, 'Dødning', GID, 1997, 2, 54-55.

DO-DO, see >DECK GAMES.

DOLICHOS, a long-distance run that formed an event during Ol.G. in ancient Greece. It was introduced at the 15th Ol.G. in 720 BC. The distance covered in dolichos remains a subject of dispute among sport historians. Hypotheses vary, suggesting from 7 to 24 laps around a stadium track. The prevailing theory, however, claims it was 23 laps, which would mean that in Olympia it was 23x192.27m, i.e. 4,422.21m, whereas for the games held in Delphi a stadium of about 165m would be 3,795m, during the Panathenean Ol.G. (a stadium of 177.55m) – 4,037.65m, and in Epidaurus (a stadium of 181.08m) – 4,164.84m. In modern times, dolichos was present during the neo-Hellenic Ol.G., organized in Greece before 1896.

DOŁKI, Pol. for 'holes', an old school game known before 1914 in the Kingdom of Poland. It was popularized by E. Piasecki in whose work *Zabawy i gry ruchowe dzieci i młodzieży* (*Games and Pastimes of Schoolchildren*, 1916) we read that the game started with children digging as many holes in the ground (each hole half a step from the other) as there were players. The holes, large enough to hold a ball, were dug along a straight line. Then, each player selected one hole and took a position beside it – the best players ('mothers') located at the 2 extremes of the line. One of the mothers started the game rolling the ball along the line towards the other mother. If the ball made it to the other end without falling into any of the holes on its way, the receiving mother took it and rolled it back. When the ball fell into one of the holes, the 'owner' took it out and attempted to hit any of the players who were fleeing in all directions. When the throwing party missed, their hole was filled in with a little stone, a chip, etc. referred to as an 'egg' or a 'child'. If the thrower hit one of those fleeing, the hit player grabbed the ball and attempted to hit someone else, and such throwing continued until one of the players missed. At that point, one of the mothers started the game again. The match continued until one of the participants accumulated a predetermined number of eggs (e.g. 10), after which an 'execution' took place. The player whose hole was full of eggs first received as many hits with the ball from each participant as the number of eggs in their holes fell short of the predetermined quantity.

Thanks to Piasecki's description, the game became popular in Pol. schools, where it was practiced in 1918-39 and then for a few years more after WWII.

DON'T GO UP THE HILL, a Rus. winter game, popular especially in the countryside, and sometimes played during PE lessons at school. The main accessory is a snow ball, 1.2-1.5m in diameter. According to the Rus. author I.N. Chkannikov, the game is played in the following manner: 'The players, holding one another's hands, form a circle around a large snow ball, the 'hill'. At a signal, the circle starts turning left (or right), and the players try to use sudden movements to push one another onto the 'hill'. Those who are shoved onto the ball, are excluded'. Usually, 4 players participate. The dimensions of the ball should allow 2 players to embrace it in the upper part. The last person on the field, not shoved onto the ball, is declared the winner.

I.N. Chkannikov, 'Don't go up the hill', GIZ, 1953, 98.

DONGBATIAO, a trad. activity popular among the Chinese minority of Naxi, related to the >WU SHU tradition and practiced at family gatherings, weddings and religious festivals. It consists of a dance that imitates work activities or the movements of animals and birds, e.g. knife sharpening, or dancing with swords, cocks, or swans etc. Characteristic moves include jumping over a solid, round, 4-legged table while holding a sword, fencing, pole vaulting etc. All this is accompanied by the sound of silver bells and the hanging of colorful ribbons. Mu Fushan et al., 'Naxi Dongbatiao', TRAMCHIN, 140.

DONKEY RACES (MOUNTED), a type of race popular in some Afr. and Asian cultures; also known in certain Eur. countries, where they are considered a lower form of entertainment to horse racing. Around 1450 J. Coeur, minister of finance at the court of the Fr. King Charles VII, ordered a sculpture depicting a jousting tournament on donkeys and placed it on the pediment of his palace as an expression of his derisive attitude towards >CHIVALRIC TOURNAMENTS. Donkey races were part of the Brit. Cotswold Games, also known as Robert Dover's Ol.G., where they were held for the first time in 1808 over a distance of 1 Eng. mile (1,609.3m). The rider who scored the most points in 3 consecutive races won the competition and an award of 1 guinea. In Kenya, donkey races are part of the Maulidi Festival, which marks the birth of Mohammed, the founder of Islam.

DONKEY RACES, races included in the program of the Cotswold Games – folk games that were held in Chipping Camden, England (at the foot of the Cotswolds hills – hence the name), between 1612 and 1852. Donkey races were first held in 1808 along a one-mile course. The competitor who won the largest number of points in 3 races was declared the winner. One guinea was the prize.

DOOR DEN UIL BOLLEN, a Flem. name for a Belgian folk game, currently known under the Fr. name of >TROU-MADAME.

DOPPELPASS, a var. of a quick football game played by 2 teams consisting of 2 players in the field and a goalkeeper [Ger. *Doppel* – double + *pass* – pass].

DORGOTSOKH, Mong. for 'a badger'. A trad. Mong. running game, esp. popular with children from the Khalkhasa tribe. It is played only by boys aged 10-13. One team remains seated in a circle surrounding a boy called a *dorgotsokh*. The other team, deployed outside the circle, attempts to touch the badger. They must not, however, cross the encircling line of the sitting team blocking the attacks. A boy acting as the badger has a symbolic tail pinned to his back. In modern times it is a rat's tail, but it used to be the tail of a genuine badger hunted down by adults. In the Elet tribe a similar game is referred to as *the wolf and the geese*. The geese are surrounded by a circle of sitting children while the wolf sneaks around trying to catch one of them. In order to do that, it is enough to touch a goose, after which it is considered dead. The wolf checks to see if a goose is really dead by tickling it, and the goose must not laugh. The game continues until all the geese are dead.

DOSTAVANYE KOLODOK, Rus. for 'reaching for logs', a Rus. sport, basically a 2-man tug-of-war in which the goal is to reach a log standing a certain distance away; 2 contestants hold with one hand the opposite ends of a thick rope, about 2m long; to help hold the rope, short poles have been tied to its ends so that the knot is on the inside or the rope has been passed through a hole drilled in the pole, behind which a thick knot is tied; another way of fixing the rope to the poles is with a loop at the rope ends into which a pole with a small notch in the middle is put; the contestants hold the rope with one hand and pull it taut; about 1m away from the extended free hands of the contestants a log or a bottle is put; at a signal the contestants start to pull the rope, each towards himself, so as to pull the opponent to their side and reach the log or bottle. I.N. Chkhannikov, 'Dostavanye covodok', GIZ, 1953, 24.

DOUBLE BALL, South Amer. Ind. game, also referred to as *twinball* by Amer. colonists and ethnographers, sometimes called maiden's ball or women's ball because it was mostly played by females. Single cases of the game played by males were observed among a few Ind. tribes in California and among the Stóólo people living on the western coast of Canada and the USA, e.g. on Vancouver Island, in the Fraser Valley, and in Washington. Two games, whose names are a challenge to pronounce (>TS'IITS'QWEL'Ó'ÓL), are popular among the tribe members, one of which is a typical double ball. In 1851, G. Copway – a traveler and ethnographer – wrote about the Missusauga tribe:

The most interesting of all games is the Maiden's Ball Play [...] The majority of those who take part in this play are young damsels, although married women are not excluded.
[*The Traditional History and Characteristic Sketching of the Ojibway Nation, 1851; quotation after J.B. Oxendine, American Indian Sports Heritage, 1988*]

The game was rich in traditions and appears in Ind. mythology. In one myth popular among the Wichita people, 'About Seven Brothers and One Woman', the main character could escape the dangers she was confronted with, thanks to 7 men who threw a double ball and ran after it. Ethnographers have found another 5 stories in the traditions of the Wichita tribe where the double ball appears. The game was supposed to attract men. In 1851, G. Copway, remarked on the role of the double ball in women's advances towards men:

Young women of the village decorate themselves for the day by painting their cheeks with vermilion and disrobe themselves of as much unnecessary clothing as possible, braiding their hair with colored feathers, which hang profusely down to the feet. At the same time the whole village assembles, and the young men, whose beloved are seen in the crowd, twist and turn to send shy glances at them, and they receive their bright smiles in return.
[ibid]

Equipment. Players used two oval balls joined with a leather belt or 2 sacs of a pear shape, made of a single piece of leather that narrowed down at the point the sacs were joined, forming thus a kind of a dumbbell. The balls were about 7-8cm in diameter, the length of the leather strap was approx. twice the balls' diameter, i.e. 12-15cm. The dimensions of a pair of sacs were similar. Some tribes, instead of balls or sacs, used wooden pegs tied with a leather strap or rope. The pegs resembled track and field relay batons, 15-25cm long, 2.5-7.5cm in diameter, made of solid wood. The leather joint between the balls was used for picking the object up and throwing it with the use of a stick (approx. 4ft. long, i.e. 1.2m), made of a flexible willow branch, crooked at the far end. The balls were caught on the crooked tip and held there by centrifugal force. Sticks for beginners had special cuts on the crooked end so as to facilitate catching. Sticks were often elaborately decorated with painted or burned patterns and reliefs. The balls, sacs, and pegs were also embellished.

Playing field. A playing field did not have the same size in all places. Its length varied from 250 to 350m. According to the testimonies of a number of Eur. observers, a playing field used by the Cree people was about a mile long, i.e. more than 1,600m. Common natural landmarks such as boulders or trees served as goals, lacking these, goals were made

of poles, or mounds of sand or stones. Usually a goal was about 12-15ft. (3.6-4.5m) wide.
Course of the game. The number of players varied from tribe to tribe. According to information provided by observers at the end of the 19th cent. and the beginning of the 20th cent. a team could have 6-100 players. The object of the game was to intercept the double ball with one's stick and carry it to one's own goal. Therefore, a team's goal was actually defended by the opponent, a reverse situation compared to Eur. games using goals. Amer. painter G. Catlin, who watched the game in the 1830s played by tribes from the Mississippi basin, commented that:

Don't go up the hill.

They have two balls attached to the ends of the strings, each about a foot and a half long; and each woman has a short stick in each hand on which she catches the string with the two balls and throws them, endeavoring to force them over the goals of her own party.
[quoted after Oxendine]

The goal was called in Ind. languages goal, home or base. Unfortunately, no detailed description of the rules or tactics of the game has survived.
S. Culin, *Games of the North American Indians*, 1907; J.B. Oxendine, *American Indian Sports Heritage*, 1988.

DOUBLE ROW BALL RACE, a Pol. school game described by E. Piasecki in his *Zabawy i gry ruchowe dzieci i młodzieży* (*Games and Pastimes of School Children*):

The children are divided into 2 teams, standing next to one another and forming a double row. The first players of both rows (called 'whites' and 'reds') are given a football. At a signal both pass the balls backwards over their heads. The balls are

Jockeys on their mounts during the donkey races in the coastal island town of Lamu in Kenya.

D
WORLD SPORTS ENCYCLOPEDIA

received in the same manner and passed on backwards. When the ball reaches the end of the row (if it is dropped, the player must step out, pick it up and return to his row), the last player steps to the outside of his row, runs forward, steps in as the first player of his row and begins to pass the ball backwards. This is repeated until all players have had a chance to run. Whichever row does it first, wins the game.

DOWLING, an Eng. var. of a ball game similar to >RUGBY, practiced from the 19th cent. in the Shrewsbury Public School. In the 1886-87 school year it was discontinued and replaced with >FOOTBALL. The pitch's dimensions and the manner of passing the ball resembled rugby. A player who received an airborne ball within 10yds. of the goal, had the right to take a shot at the goal. In the case of the player's offside position, the same right was granted to the opposing team. The difference between dowling and rugby can be seen in the scoring system – in the former only goals actually achieved were scored. No points could be scored for placing the ball behind the opponent's goal line. The winner was the first team to score 5pts. In the event that 5pts. could not be

king downhill skiing and >SKI SLALOM modern sports. In 1905, on the initiative of M. Zdarsky, the first downhill course was marked out in Müchenhole. The growth of downhill skiing, similar to the whole of Alpine skiing, was for a long time burdened by conflict with the Scandinavian-dominated ski organizations. The FIS, founded in 1924, allowed downhill skiing as a demonstration event during the 1924 World Championships. The event was also unofficial during the 1929 FIS W.Ch. at Zakopane, Poland. A Pole, B. Czech, won the competition. Downhill skiing was finally included in the official Olympic program during the 1936 games in Garmisch-Partenkirchen. World Championships have been held since 1931, and annual World Cup events since 1967. The skier with the largest number of points after a series of events organized at many locations, initially in Europe but today on all continents, is declared the winner of the World Cup. The most famous personalities in the history of downhill skiing include multiple World Cup winners: Frenchman J.C. Killy (1967, 1968, also 1968 Olympic champion and 1966 world champion), the Austrian K.

are also allowed, however, the boy is handicapped in that he can pull the rope with one hand only. M. Hellspong, 'Organized, Traditional Sports on the Island of Gotland in the Eighteenth and Nineteenth Centuries', SSSS, 1996.

DRA HUVUDET AV GÅSEN, Swed. for 'tearing off a goose's head'. A cruel folk competition popular in ancient Sweden. It consisted of tearing a goose's head off with one's bare hands [Swed. *dra* – to pull + *huvud* – a head + *av* – from + *gås* – a goose]. Cf. Fr. and Bret. >DECAPITATION DE L'OIE, >DÉCAISSER LA GRENOUILLE, and other folk games that involve tormenting animals, such as >ANIMAL BAITING or >SLÅ KATTEN UR TUNNAN.

DRA REM, a Swed. var. of folk wrestling in which the opponents start the match by pulling each other's belt [Swed. *dra* – to pull + *rem* – a leather strap]. Practiced on the Småland uplands. According to a Swed. ethnologists M. Hellspong, dra rem belongs to a family of wrestling in which various forms of pulling the opponent's pants were employed. The principal representative of the family is >BYXTAG. See also >DRA BÄLTE.

Norway's Kjetil Andre Aamodt speeds down the course during the downhill portion of the men's combined alpine skiing event in Snowbasin, Utah at the Salt Lake City Olympics.

scored within the maximum playing time, i.e. 3x60mins., the winner was the team which had scored the greater number of points.

DOWNHILL SKIING, one of the events of >ALPINE SKIING, involving racing downhill along a course about 3-6km long, with altitude differences of 500--800m for women and 800-1,000m for men. The courses are marked out so that the times are about 1min. 50sec. for women and about 2 mins. for men. According to FIS rules, the course must be marked with red flags on the left-hand side, and green ones on the right. Especially dangerous places are marked with yellow flags. At bends, organizers must place control gates at least 8m wide, with red banners on high poles set into the ground. The surface of the course must be smooth and at least 30m wide. Before a competition, there must be 3 (previously 2) days of practice, aimed at familiarizing the participants with the course and thus preventing accidents. Since the 1992 Olympic Winter Games, participants set out at 2-min. intervals (previously, 1min.). The time decides the results. Falling or supporting oneself during the race does not cause disqualification.
History. Non-codified forms of downhill skiing have been practiced in Alpine countries since about the middle of the 19th cent., with folk forms going back at least several hundred years. Members of the Brit. Ski Club, who visited the Alps annually at the turn of the 19th and 20th cent. contributed to ma-

Schranz (1969-70, 1962 world champion), the Italian G. Thoeni (1971-73), the Swede I. Stenmark (1976-78), the Swiss P. Zurbriggen (1984, 1987, 1988 and 1990; 1985 world champion); and among women – the Austrian A.-M. Proell-Moser (1971-75 and 1979; 1980 Olympic champion and 1974 and 1978 world champion) and the Swiss Maria Walliser (1987 and 1989 world champion, 1986 and 1987 World Cup winner). J. Bisaga, K. Chojnacki, *Narciarstwo zjazdowe*, 1997; M. Zastoń, *Podstawy narciarstwa zjazdowego*, 1996; J. Zielonacki, *Narciarstwo zjazdowe*, 1979.

DRA BÄLTE, a Swed. var. of folk wrestling. In the starting hold the opponents are pulling each other's belts [Swed. *dra* – to pull + *bälte* – a belt]. Practiced in the Småland uplands and in Jät where it is also known as >DRA REM (pulling a leather strap). In Jät, wrestlers would lend their belts to those who did not have their own or whose belts were not resilient enough. According to a Swed. ethnologist of sport M. Hellspong, dra bälte belongs to the family of wrestling in which various techniques of pulling the opponent's pants were applied, the major representative of which is >BYXTAG.

DRA HANK, a tug-of-war between 2 opponents. A Swed. folk sport incorporated into >STÅNGASPELEN, as well as in a competition named >VÅG – a team tournament in which individual scores of 5-9 competitors are added up to calculate the total score for a given team. Matches between boys and girls

DRAB AND NORR, a Brit. var. of a game in which a wooden bowl, a *norr*, is tossed up with the use of a special launcher [*drab* is a regional var. of *trap*] and then struck onto the field to score a point. The game belongs to a larger family whose principal representatives are >TRAP, BAT AND BALL and >NORTHERN SPELL.

DRAG CAR RACING, also in short *drag racing*. A special form of car racing in which the object is to achieve the greatest speed in the minimal elapsed time (ET) on a short distance, usu. employing experimental fuels. It is held on a track of ¼mi. (402m) or ⅛mi., min. 50ft. (about 15m) wide, with a shut down area, i.e. the track behind the finish line for braking, of at least 200m. Drag car racing vehicles are mounted on an elongated chassis, referred to as a rail or slingshot. Rear driving wheels are nearly as large as those on a tractor and are called slick tires. Front wheels are much smaller, about the size of bicycle or motorcycle wheels. The driver's cockpit is located in the main body between the wheels. In some crafts, the engine is placed in front obstructing the driver's view. The most modern constructions have the engine installed at the back. The capacity of engines used in the USA – where drag racing is most developed – is limited to 800cu.in. (13 liters). The most powerful engines reach 1,500hp. Numerous classes are organized on the basis of the fuel used and the type of structure. Fuel groups include vehicles propelled with gas and methanol or nitromethane, also called 'topfuel' or, simply, fuel. Some vehicles are also equipped with a parachute extended after crossing the finish line in order to shorten the braking distance. Competitions are held in 6 major classes (also organized according to whether the gearbox is automatic or stick-shift): Top Fuel Eliminator; Funny Car Eliminator; Pro Stock Eliminator; Pro Comp Eliminator; Modified Eliminator; Super Stock Eliminator. In total, there are no fewer than 75 classes in drag car racing. A vehicle starts when the lights change. The lights resemble standard streetlights but there are more of them, hence the slang term for them 'Christmas tree'. The lamps go from top to bottom in the following order: 1 red; 5 amber, lighting up from top to bottom informing the driver he should prepare to start; 1 green, signaling start; and the last, bottom one, red which lights up in the case of a false start. The lamps light up at half-a-second intervals and are located 20ft. (6m) in front of the starting line. Timing is carried out electronically.

Drivers compete in pairs. The one who wins can proceed to the next round. The score achieved in each competition accumulates. The best drivers meet at the annual Winston Finals. The most widely known and highly valued tracks are located in Gainesville, Florida, and Reading, Pennsylvania (the Keystone Nationals). Among the most celebrated competitions are the Winter Nationals in Los Angeles, the Spring Nationals in Bristol, Tennessee, and the National Meet in Indianapolis. An annual contest referred to as the W.Ch. (though in fact, mostly drivers from 7 US regions take part in it, whereas drivers from abroad are few and far between), is held in Toulouse, Oklahoma. Before each race, cars go through a strict technical check-up to reveal any possible inconsistencies with the parameters required during a given race. Drivers receive a special license from the major drag car racing organization, the National Hot Rod Association (NHRA). Besides professional drivers there are also amateurs who drive their own, specially tuned vehicles. After acquiring a sufficient level of skill, some of them go pro.

History. The sport was initiated in the 1930s in California. The idea of such competitions, as B. Dyer-Bennet explains, was psychologically driven. According to Bennet, S California was the place where westward migration, or Manifest Destiny, came to its end, forcing those who still sought for its continuation to try to cross other borders. A trial and error process led to the construction of a vehicle tuned to achieve max. speed over a short distance. At the beginning racers drove mostly Model-T and Model-A Fords, as well as some Chevrolets. Drag racing was officially recognized in 1937, when the Southern California Timing Association (SCTA) incorporated the results achieved by drag racers into its official lists. There was, however, one condition: races could not be held on public roads. The first important drag racing site was the bed of Muroc Dry Lake. Still, races organized on public roads were common, a trend against which Amer. police would try to combat for the next few dozen of years. After WWII, demobilized army mechanics looking for a vent to their motorization aspirations and expertise grew interested in the new sport. In 1946-48, the drag racing vehicle acquired its trademark shape. In the same period, its current name 'hot rod' (probably from its elongated shape) appeared in the USA and was finally accepted about 1950 by the press both in the USA and worldwide. At the beginning there was also another name, originating from Canada, 'jet job', but it failed to catch on. The racing movement related to the new discipline was also called, unofficially, the Hot Rod Movement. In 1951, Hot Rod magazine proposed the establishment of an association and soon after the Amer. National Hot Rod Association was set up. International recognition of drag car racing took place in 1965 when it was officially acknowledged by the Fédération Internationale de l'Automobile. In the course of the '60s and '70s, the sport was popularized in other Eng.-speaking countries, as well as in Japan, Germany, Italy, and Sweden. Nevertheless, in none of them has it achieved the popularity it enjoys in the USA. The most eminent representatives of drag car racing are: D. 'Big Daddy' Garlits, (b. 1932), who was the first to exceed the limit of 200mph (322km/h), and Kenny Bernstein, who was the first to exceed

the limit of 300mph, achieving the speed of 301.7mph (485.53km/h) in 1992. Seven years later, Tony Schumacher surpassed the limit of 330mph. The fact of achieving great speed does not necessarily mean that a vehicle has covered a distance in the shortest time. Here, the record belongs to Kenny Bernstein with 4.477sec. (2001).

Women have become interested in drag car racing only quite recently. However, the number of female race drivers is growing rapidly. One of the most acclaimed female racers is S. 'Cha Cha' Muldowny (b. 1940), a world champion whose record 4.974sec. was established during Keystone Nationals in Reading, Pennsylvania in 1989. Cf. >DRAG MOTORCYCLE RACING and >DRAG RACING.

J. Arlott, Motor Racing: Drag Racing, 1975; B. Dyer Bennet, Drag Racing, 1996, I; L.K. Engel, The Complete Book of

Drag racing: Del Worsham and his Pontiac Firebird Funny Car won the 18th annual NHRA Checker Schucks Kragen Nationals at Firebird International Raceway in Chandler, Arizona. Worsham, from Chino Hills, California, ran the quarter mile in 4.946 seconds at 312.86mph to defeat John Force in the final.

Auto Racing, 1969; W. Parks, D. Racing, Yesterday and Today, 1966; The Internet: www.nhra.com

DRAG MOTORCYCLE RACING, a special form of motorcycle racing in which the object is to achieve the greatest speed in the minimal elapsed time (ET) over a short distance, usu. using experimental fuels. Cf. >DRAG CAR RACING and >DRAG RACING.

DRAG RACING, a specialized form of car or motorcycle racing based on reaching great speeds over relatively short distances, usu. thanks to the use of experimental fuels. Cf. >DRAG CAR RACING, >DRAG MOTORCYCLE RACING.

DRAGON-BOAT RACING, also dragon racing or dragon boats, a competition between dragon-shaped boats, with the bow shaped like a dragon's open mouth, the sides forming the body and the stern fashioned after the tail. According to the regulations, a standard boat is manned by an average of 22 paddlers, who paddle at the pace set by the beating of a drum placed inside the boat. In some races the competition is between larger boats of 40-50 crew members.

History. The tradition of dragon boat racing derives from ancient China. Legend has it that the first race took place in 400 BC to commemorate the death of the poet Chu Yuan (or Qu Yuan), who had been banished by corrupt judges, whose greed for money and immorality he branded in his writings. He wandered around China, writing poetry which praised the beauty of his homeland and expressed his affection for it. Upon hearing

the news of the outbreak of another war, he rushed to offer his help to the Emperor but, rejected, lost faith in the moral rebirth of his country. On the 5th day of the 5th lunar month of the Chin. calendar he jumped into the Mi Lo river in the province of Hunan and committed suicide. According to old Chin. texts, several fishermen attempted to rescue him by 'beating the water with oars to chase off dangerous fish and dragons and throwing rice into the river to calm its current', but their efforts were fruitless. Later one of the rescuers supposedly encountered the ghost of the departed poet, who told him that the God of Dragons had kidnapped him and was awaiting a sacrifice of rice rolled in bamboo leaves and silk cloth. The fishermen complied with this request during a race held to commemorate Chu Yuan and the event

became part of Chin. tradition. An important element of the races is eating rice dumplings stuffed in bamboo leaves (tzung-tzu). According to other hypotheses, the sport is connected with the holiday of the summer solstice and the sacrifice of gifts and endeavors offered to the deities to stop the shortening of days. There is indirect evidence that in the early history of the holiday the Dragon God was offered human sacrifices in boats sunk

Dragon boat racing – neck and neck.

in the river. The origins of the sport may also be connected with the tradition of the dragon as a life-giving god of water and rain. This would explain the offering of rice dumplings as a symbol of the harvest. Irrespective of myths and legends, dragon boat racing has become a permanent element of Chin. culture, although the isolation of China hindered its spread to other countries. In 1655 a number of Chin. sailors were shipwrecked in Nagasaki (Japan) and originated the Jap.

tional crews of such countries as: Sweden, Thailand, Brunei, Bangladesh etc. The toughest race is held in the class originally called The International Dragon Boat Championships, later renamed The World Invitational Dragon Boat Race (WIDBR), with the strongest crews representing Australia, Indonesia, the Amer. club Hanohano from San Diego, and the Davina Sports and Fitness Club from Singapore. Other high ranking crews include New Zealand, Hongkong and Thai-

Asian event is the Penang International Boat Festival in Malaysia held since 1978. Other important dragon boat races are held in San Diego (California), Hamburg (Germany), China, Taiwan, India, Australia, Macao, Japan, New Zealand, Great Britain and Sweden. Training centers for dragon boat paddlers are located e.g. at Jatiluhur lake in Indonesia and in Singapore (Kallang Water Sports Centre). The center in Wellington, N.Zealand affiliates 3,500 active paddlers incl. 1,000 school children. The most important regatta in New Zealand is held during the Lambton Harbour Festival. Large regattas take place in Melbourne and Sydney (Australia). The largest regatta in Europe takes place in Malmö (Sweden) and is the high point of a series of events held throughout the year and gathering more than 90,000 paddlers.

In the 1980s the first non-Asian national championships were held and first national dragon boat associations were established. The first dragon boat race in Great Britain took place in 1987 in Shadwell Basin (London), witnessed by the Prince of Wales. A year later the United Kingdom championships were held and the Brit. Dragon Boat Racing Association was established. Its membership increased from 700 in 1988 to 14,850 in 1998. The Brit. royal family maintains their interest in the sport, Prince Charles himself participating in one of the races as a member of the Eton College crew. In 1990 the Eur. Dragon Boat Federation (EDBF) was formed and in 1991 – the International Dragon Boat Federation (IDBF). Both preceded the formation in 1992 of the Asian Dragon Boat Association (ADBA). The year 1996 saw another Brit. initiative in the form of the Commonwealth Dragon Boat Federation.

The 1st W.Ch. were held in 1995 in Yue Yang in China, followed by events in Hongkong (1997), Great Britain (1999) and the USA (2001). Separate W.Ch. for club crews were initiated in 1996 in Vancouver (Canada), also held bi-annually.

The old traditions of the sport prevail in the symbolic blessing of the boats before the start. Some crews also include a bowman, who watches the water surface, reenacting the search for the drowning poet Chu Yuan. Yet another way of preserving the tradition is throwing rice seeds (chang) into the water, as well as eating rice dumplings (*bak chang* or *zong-zi*), popular both among the oarsmen and the spectators. The dumplings, stuffed with finely chopped pork, are served with mushrooms or shrimp.

Boat construction. The early boats were dugouts made by hollowing out the trunk of a tree. Later the hull was put together from wooden staves, in modern times replaced by Fiberglas. A standard boat is up to 12m long, approx. 1.2m wide and 0.6m high counting from the keel to the top of the side (excluding the dragon's open mouth). The weight must not exceed 500kg. The boat is manned by 24 oarsmen and a drum beater, who sits on the bow facing the crew (sometimes that function is reserved for the trainer).

Character of the race. Races are usu. held over distances of 500-900m at the mouth of a river or in a bay. Boats navigate along a straight line, propelled by single-bladed paddles. The rowing technique is optional. The boat whose dragon head crosses the finish line first wins the race. There are two types of race: a speed and obstacle race. In the latter, 5 buoys with colored flags float on the left-hand side of each course. The drum beater must pick up all the flags from the side of the boat and present them to the judges at the finish. If he misses a flag, the boat must maneuver back. The most popular flag race is the Friendly Merlion held in honor of a mythical creature, half lion half fish, a statue of which stands in the entrance to Singapore harbour. Trad. dragon boat races were a male event, but under the influence of feminist organizations women have been admitted. At first boats for women were the same as for men, but in 1992 the dragon's head and tail were replaced with the head and tail of the mythical bird of Egypt – the Phoenix, and the name of the sport was modified accordingly to >PHOENIX-BOAT RACING.

Dragon boat racing – a 2,400-year-old tradition.

trad. of the sport. The tradition of dragon boats has also developed in India and Bangladesh under the name 'peacock boats', and in Thailand, where they are called 'swan boats'. Modern forms of dragon boat racing spread internationally, owing to the event held at Hongkong since 1976, organized by the Hongkong Tourist Association, at first irregularly, but then annually, in June or July, as part of the Dragon Boat Festival (*Tuen Ng*). Since 1982 the competition has been joined by Europeans, pioneered by Brit. crews. This spectacular event is witnessed by approx. 250,000 people every year. Another prestigious event is the annual Singapore International Dragon Boat Races (SIDBR) held at Marina Bay since 1978. It was initiated by Tan I Tong, the President of the Singapore Tourist Promotion Board (STPB). Both events commemorate the death of Chu Yuan on the 5th day of the 5th lunar month (June) and include various races, such as the competition between crews representing trade enterprises (Inter Business Houses), hotel management (Inter Hotels), administration and government (Inter Constituency), schools (Inter School), unions (Inter Union), National Championships (separately for men and women, incl. crews from such countries as Canada and Great Britain). The International Plate races usu. gather lower ranking na-

land. The number of crews competing for a place in the finals exceeds 70 (in 1991 the WIDBR in Singapore gathered 71 crews and 1,800 paddlers). Singapore also hosts another event, the Singapore River Regatta, held in August in the Kallang Basin at the mouth of the river. The regatta is part of the National Day Carnival celebrating the anniversary of Singapore's independence and their program includes other rowing and kayaking events, humorous competitions of couples rowing in tubs (>TUB RACES), races of trad. Chin. boats (>SAMPAN), races of unconventional boats constructed of impregnated cardboard (>CARD-BOATS), a display of lotus-shaped boats, races of boats built from beer cans, and water skiing events. Dragon boat races are usu. a 2-day event. On the 1st day all crews compete to qualify for the 6 places in the 2nd day finals. The governing body for the sport is the Singapore Dragon Boat Association (SDBA, est. 1987) and the strongest clubs in Singapore are: People's Association Adventure Club, Singapore Technical Institute, Bedok Vocational Institute Nanyang Junior Club, Singapore Armed Forces Reservists Association (for men) and Police Sports Association, Punggol Point Canoe Club, National University of Singapore, Sembawang Canoe Club (for women). Outside of Hongkong and Singapore the most prestigious

'Singapore Dragon Boat Association Formed', SS, Nov./Dec. 1987; 'Dragons in Marina Bay', SS, July 1987; 'Singapore Regattas: The Dragon's Share', OR, Dec. 1995-Jan. 1996; XXV, 6; 'The Dragon Boat Legend', SS, July 1991.

DRAMMERT, a Dan. game from the baseball family, prob. related with a Bornholm var. of >PIND known as >GROSS. The game is played by 2 teams of 5-8 players. The match starts with an opening serve during which teams contend for their place on the field. One of the players in the middle serves towards the back part of the field (*bagmål*), marked by a single line on the ground. The serve is carried out in 2 phases. First, the server launches the ball as far into the field as possible. The team playing on the outside attempts to catch the ball or at least block it before it comes to rest. If they succeed, the server loses the serve; if the ball is neither intercepted nor blocked, the server sticks a pole in the ground on the bagmål line, and the outside team tries to hit the pole with the ball, rolling it on the ground from the point where it came to rest. If the ball comes to rest only a few meters from the serving point, for instance as the result of a poor serve, the pole has to be hit by a blindfolded player. If it stops rolling far in the field, the outside team stands single file with their legs wide apart, forming a line directed towards the pole. If the ball hits the target, the server loses the right to serve; if it misses – the server proceeds to the second phase that starts with a double stroke (*et vip*) in which the ball is first tossed up in the air and then smashed. Again, the outside team attempts to seize the ball and if they fail, the distance between the ball and the nearest player is counted in steps. The number of steps automatically becomes the number of points scored by the serving team (or the number of points subtracted from the score of the receiving team). After that, the server starts the first phase again.
J. Møller, 'Drammert', GID, 1997, 1, 68.

DRÄNGALÖFTEN, a Swed. var. of *lifting stones* [Swed. also Dan. *dräng* – a boy or a farm-hand + *löfte* – a promise]. The name refers to both the stones that are lifted and the folk competitions related to them. The curious name originates from a test of maturity administered to young men who wanted to be accepted as grown-ups among other males, as well as a practice of testing a farm-hand's strength when considering him for a job (cf. <DRÄNGASTENAR). See also >LYFTESTEN, >LYFTESTEN, >KAMPASTEN. Cf. Basq. >ARRISJASOKETA, Dan. >STENLÖFTNING, also >GGET, >KÖLNÅKERN, >KUNGSSTEN, >KUNGSSTENARNA, >STORA OCH LILLA DAGSVERKARN, >TYFTEHÖNAN.
M. Hellspong, 'Lifting Stones. The Existence of Lifting Stones in Sweden', ST, 1993/94, XIX/XX.

DRÄNGASTENAR, Swed. for 'swashbuckler's lifting stones' [Swed. also Dan. *dräng* – a boy or a farm-hand + *sten*, pl. *stenar* – a stone, pl. stones]. One of the Swed. names for both the stones themselves and the competitions related to them. In the past competition was used for testing the masculinity among young men who wanted to be accepted as grown-ups, as well as a potential worker's strength (cf. <DRÄNGALÖFTEN). The most famous drängastenar used for testing hired hands are the 2 stones from the court of Kägelholm, known as >STORA OCH LILLA DAGSVERKARN. See also >LYFTESTEN, >KAMPASTEN, >KUNGSSTEN, >KUNGSSTENARNA, >LYFTESTEN. Cf. Dan. >STENLÖFTNING, Basq. >ARRISJASOKETA, also >GGET, >KÖLNÅKERN, >TYFTEHÖNAN.
M. Hellspong, 'Lifting Stones. The Existence of Lifting Stones in Sweden', ST, 1993/94, XIX/XX.

DRIJTFOL, a Du. var. of >TOPS.

DREIDEL GAME, a Jewish game deriving from Biblical times, played on the 8th day of Hannukkah, the Feast of Dedication, which comes on the 25th day of the month of Kislev (immediately preceeding the Christian Christmas). The holiday commemorates the recapturing of the Jerusalem Temple by Judas Maccabaeus from the Syrian Greeks in 164 BC. The game is played with the use of a hexagonal top, with a round handle in the upper part to allow spinning, and a conically-shaped lower part. Each of the other 4 walls of the top carry one Hebrew letter: *nun*, *gimel*, *heh*, and *shin*, which stand for *Nes Gadol Hayah Sham*, meaning 'A great miracle happened there'. The words refer to an oil lamp, which – according to a legend – was found in the temple with an amount of oil sufficient for it to burn for 1 whole day and which, nevertheless, kept burning for 8 days until the Jews found more oil. The tradition of the feast is described in the Talmud and mentioned in the first Maccabean Book of the Old Testament (IV, 52-59). To play the game, each player must have a number of markers (candy, pennies, marbles, or other small objects), which he puts on the table. Then each player spins the top and waits for it to land and show the result on the wall which stays up: *nun* means the player gets nothing, *gimel* – the player takes the whole pot, *heh* – the player takes half the pot, and *shin* – the player gets nothing and must add one marker to the pot. The game ends when one of the players has collected all markers.
L. Barbarash, 'Dreidel Game', *Multicultural Games*, 1997, p. 24-25; A.W. Miller, 'Hanukkah', *Encyclopedia Americana International*, 1979, vol. 13, p. 780.

A dreidel.

DRIKKE AF GLAS MED OMVENDT HÅND, Dan. for 'to drink from a glass with an upturned hand'. A Dan. demonstration of one's dexterity. A performer holding a glass between the index and middle fingers, with the palm facing up, is supposed to drink the contents, reaching below the bent elbow of the other arm, without spilling a drop.
J. Møller, 'Drikke af glas med omvendt hånd', GID, 1997.

DRIVE SO GENNEM BYEN, old Dan. for 'to lead a sow through the village'. A game that used to be practiced in the Kolding region, similar to >SO I HUL. On the field there are holes in the ground, located every 12-15m and referred to as cities (*byer*). The number of cities is equal to that of players minus 1. The ball is called a sow (*so*). The party holding the ball, i.e. the swineherd (*sodriveren*), using a crooked stick, is supposed to lead the sow through the cities to the central hole, known as a 'butter hole' (*smørhullet*). The other players must each guard their own small hole (*hul*), and at the same time prevent the swineherd from leading the sow through their city by beating the sow out of town. Like in *so i hul*, if the swineherd manages to place his stick in the hole guarded by any other player, they change places. If, however, the swineherd succeeds in leading the sow to the butter hole, he can select any smaller hole he wishes and the player deprived of his place becomes the swineherd. If the swineherd manages to lead the sow to the butter hole 3 times, all the players lose their places and have to compete for them again in a race. The one who fails in finding a hole becomes the swineherd and the game continues.
J. Møller, 'Drive so gennem byen', GID, 1997, 1, 79.

DRIVING A WHEEL, or *driving a hoop*, a simple children's game known in ancient Greece as >TROCHOS and in Rome as >TROCHUS, the idea of which is to drive or roll a wheel in front of oneself. In its oldest forms the wheels were made from withe or wicker. Later, mainly in the cities, children began to use various round objects such as kitchen braziers, barrel rims, bicycle wheels, etc. The wheel may be driven by striking it with a hand or a stick, or pushing it with a piece of wire with a hook at one end. At the beginning of the 19th cent. in some Eur. cities young players joined clubs of wheel drivers, the largest of which was formed in Paris in the 1920s and had several hundred members. The game could not compete, however, with other, more attractive sports. Encyclopedias or dictionaries usu. ignore the game as trivial. Yet, its description can be found in e.g. J. Møller's *Gamle idrætslege i Danmark* (1997, see >TØNDEBÅND), M. da Graça Sousa Guedes' *Jogos tradicionais portugueses* (1979, see >JOGO DO ARCO), or M. Ibrahim al-Majman's *Min al'abina ash-sha 'biyya*, (1983, see >AD-DNANA).

DROMOS, a generic name for foot races used in ancient Greece. The following types were known: a short run of 1-stadium length, a 2-stadium length run – referred to as >DIAULOS, a long-distance run >DOLICHOS, and >HOPLITODROMO – a run of hoplites in full suits of armor.

DROP HANDKERCHIEF, a children's game not unlike >BANKE UD or *duck, duck, goose*, played mostly by girls; a number of its varieties existed throughout England, Wales, and Scotland. According to A.B. Gomme, the Eng. var. was most frequently played as follows:

The children stand in a ring. One runs with a handkerchief and drops it; the child behind whom it is dropped chases the dropper, the one who gets home first takes the vacant place, the other drops the handkerchief again.
[TGESI, I, 109].

During the game various songs were sung, whose lyrics differed from region to region. Often, instead of a handkerchief a glove was used. In the Dorsetshire version of the game girls sang as follows:

I wrote a letter to my love;
I carried water in my glove;
And by the way I dropped it –
I dropped it, I dropped it, I dropped it.

The song continued until the handkerchief (or glove) was 'stealthily dropped immediately behind one of the players, who should be on the alert to follow as quickly as possible the one who has dropped it, who at once increases her speed and endeavors to take the place left vacant by her pursuer. Should she be caught before she can succeed in doing this she is compelled to take the handkerchief a second time. But if, as it more usually happens, she is successful in accomplishing this, the pursuer in turn takes the handkerchief, and the game proceeds as before,' [TGESI, I, 110-111]. In Fochabers, NE Scotland, the following song was used:

I dropt it, I dropt it,
A king's copper next,
I sent a letter to my love,
And on the way I dropt it.

During the game played when the above lyrics are sung, 'the players forming the ring are forbidden to look around. The one having the handkerchief endeavors to drop it at someone's back without his or her knowledge, and then to get three times round the ring without being struck by the handkerchief. If the player does not manage this she has to sit in the centre of the ring as *old maid*; the object in this version evidently is not to let the player upon whom the handkerchief is dropped be aware of it' [TGESI, II, 418].
Another var. of the game was *black doggie*: The players join hands, form a circle and stretch out as far as each one's arm will allow. One player is outside the ring. When she sees they can stretch no further she cries out, 'Break!' at which point they all loose hands and stand as far apart as possible. The player outside then goes round the ring singing: *I have a black doggie, but it winna' bite you, nor you, nor you*, until she comes to one whom she chooses; she then throws the handkerchief down on the ground behind this one quietly. If this player does not notice the handkerchief, no-one in the circle may tell her, or they are 'out'. The player who dropped the handkerchief walks round until she comes again to the one behind whom she dropped it. She picks it up and tells her she is 'burnt'. Then this player has to stoop down on her knees and is out of the game. Should the selected player notice the handkerchief, she picks it up and pursues the other round and through the ring, following wherever the first one leads until she catches her; they then change places; should she not follow the exact way the first player went, she too is out and must go down on her knees.
In Fraseburgh in Aberdeen county, Scotland, a similar game was played in which all the players were kneeling, with the exception of the party running around the circle and singing: 'Black Doggie winna tack you, nor you.'
In Beddgelert, Wales, an analogous game was referred to as *Tartan Boeth*. It was close to the Eng. var. but the song had mixed Eng. and Welsh lyrics:

Tartan Boeth, oh ma'en llosgi, Boeth iown
Hot Tart. Oh it burns! Very hot!

The handkerchief was dropped when the words 'Very hot!' were pronounced.
A.B. Gomme, 'Drop Handkerchief', TGESI, I, 109-112; II, 418.

Drwali zawody

Underhand chop

Hot sawing

DRWALI ZAWODY, Pol. for 'lumbermen's competition', a Pol. var. of >TIMBER SPORTS, in which various sports events are based on activities related to the logging, processing, and floating of timber. Certain forms of lumbermen's competition were practiced in Poland already in the 19th cent., although at that time they did not have any permanent organizational pattern. In the 1970s, *Lasy Państwowe* (the company responsible for the management of state-owned woodlands) took over the sponsorship of drwali zawody which became esp. popular in the region around Poznań and Toruń. For a number of years the discipline was popularized by such enthusiasts as J. Flisykowski,

D

J. Kapral, and R. Kukliński. The forms adopted in Poland acquired a number of original features that are not be encountered in other countries. The following events were the most frequent ones: precise tree cutting, so that the tree falls exactly on a predetermined point; tree lopping measured in time and exactness; fast assembly and disassembly of a chainsaw; the so-called *przerzynka*, i.e. cutting through a log placed on a plank, without touching the plank; precise cutting through a log; tests of theoretical knowledge. The event fell out of favor at the beginning of the '90s as a result of social and economic changes, not least of which the fact that most lumbermen were dismissed from state-owned companies and had to start their own priva-

ancient Latin literature makes reference to shell, rather than stone, throwing. In ancient Greece, a similar game was known as >EPOSTRAKISMOS and in ancient Rome as >TESTULAM MARINAM IACERE. Ducks and drakes have been known in all Eur. cultures, which is corroborated by the fact that each language has its own term for the game. In Eng., in addition to ducks and drakes and skipping stones, there was also an alternative name 'pay-swad'. In Ger. the game is known as *Hüpfsteine werfen* (to throw a jumping stone); in Dan. *storske smut* (cod's run) or *slå smut* (hit and run); in Ital. *sparare frottole* (to shoot ducks). In Poland, the game is referred to as *puszczanie kaczek* (Pol. *puszczanie* – letting off + *kaczki* – ducks). In Corn-

stanów (*Games and Pastimes of Schoolchildren*, 1831), Ł. Gołębiowski reports that a match started with sticking a pole into the ground, after which each player holding a club and standing at a distance equal to the length of 10 clubs from the pole, pitched their club at the target attempting to knock it over or at least hit it. Those who did not miss the pole had the right to reduce their distance by a length of 1 club and throw again. The players who had missed had to increase their distance from the target by the length equal to the distance between the point where their club came to rest and the pole. The winner was the player who finally succeeded in knocking the pole over.

DUJIANZI, hitting a small shuttlecock with one's hand [Chin. *dujianzi* – throwing a shuttlecock], a game played by the Chinese minority of Dong during the Spring festivals that accompany the planting of rice, as well as during the Fall harvest-home festivals. It originated from the tradition of rice planting, when field workers passed to one another small bunches of rice seedlings by tossing them from hand to hand. As the tradition developed, participants started to use leaves of ripe rice straw, which they tied to small wooden rings or balls for greater efficiency. The game is also used as a form of courtship and is called 'flying flowers of love'. It can be played by pairs, but may also be a team sport, when a selected player of one team, called *zhaigong*, stands between the 2 teams and tries to intercept the tossed shuttlecock. When successful, he returns to his team, while a selected player from the other team takes over the role of *zhaigong*.
Mu Fushan et al., 'Kicking the Shuttlecock', TRAMCHIN.

DUKAWA WRESTLING, used to be practiced in Nigeria and was connected to the ritual in which young women chose their prospective husbands.

Among the Dukawa of Nigeria, it is an accepted custom for girls to select their husbands at wrestling matches. Girls in search of a husband attended the public exhibitions of athletic skill armed with a small bag of flour. The choice was signified by the girl sprinkling the flour on the head of her chosen one, whereupon the athlete's father immediately entered into negotiations with the parents of the girl.
[R. Briffault, *The Mothers*, 1927]

DULU, in ancient China – the Han dynasty, 202 BC--220 AD and the following periods – a demonstration of skills performed by jugglers and athletes. Cf. >BAXI.

DUND KHURUU OLOKH, see >KHOMKHOI KHURUU BARIKH.

DUNDAKH KHURUU, see >KHOMKHOI KHURUU BARIKH.

DUTCH BOWLS, another name for >SKITTLES, prob. coined after a var. of skittles was introduced in England during the reign of the Du. dynasty of Orange in the 2nd half of the 17th cent. See also >CLOSH, >CLODDY, >HALF-BALL.

DVA SHTCHITY, Rus. for 'two mountain tops', a Rus. street game. According to I.N. Chkhannikov the game starts with marking 2 circles, 1.5m in diameter each, at a distance of 1.5m from each other, either on a wall or a fence at the level of 1.25m above the ground. Between the circles – the targets – a goalkeeper is located and at a distance of 10 steps from the wall, behind a line, the remaining players are positioned. Their object is to hit either of the targets with a ball, throwing or kicking it from behind the line. The goalkeeper can shield the circles with his body, catch the ball or kick it back, but loses 1pt. for each successful hit. After losing 3pts., the defeated goalkeeper is replaced by the player whose hit subtracted the last point from the keeper's pool.
I.N. Chkhannikov, 'Dva Shtchity', GIZ, 1953, 44-45.

DYREKAMPE, Dan. for 'animal fights' [Dan. *dyr* – an animal + *kamp* – a fight]. A var. of >ANIMAL BAITING. In Denmark the most common form was setting dogs upon a bear.
J. Møller, 'Dyrekampe', GID, 1997, 4, 90.

DYSTLØB, a Dan. var. of >BOAT JOUSTING [Dan. *dystløb* – tournament; *dyst* – fight, duel + *løb* – course, progress]. Two teams fight against each other, each boat's stern equipped with an additional, protruding deck where a competitor holding a long lance with a blunt tip is perched. At the outset the boats pass each other in peace, most often twice,

Drwali zawody, national woodcutting championships in Olsztyn, Poland.

te businesses, which scattered them all around the country, therefore any group initiative was seriously undermined. In 2001, the Lasy Państwowe made new attempts at organizing a competition and getting in touch with international federations that are involved in similar activities. See also >AIZKOLARIS.
Consultants: J. Flisykowski and R. Kukliński; *Lumbermen's competition regulations*, Dyrekcja Generalna Lasów Państwowych, 1993.

DRZEWKO MAJOWE, a Pol. equivalent of >MAYPOLE and >MAIBAUM. Cf. >GAIK MAJOWY.

DUATHLON, 1) a name which is a hybrid of Lat. and Gk., referring to a combination of 2 events or a fight between 2 opponents [Lat. *duo* – two + *athlon* – competition, fight]. As a combination of 2 sports or events it is equivalent to the term >BIATHLON; 2) a sport competition consisting of 3 successive attempts in 2 events: a 5-km run, a 40-km cycling race, and a 5-km run again [Eng. Gk. *duo* – two, double + Gk. *athlon* – competition]. In international competitions the distances are 5, 40, and 10km respectively, whereas in long-distance competition they are 10, 60, and 10km. Duathlon is a derivative of >TRIATHLON and it is administered by an independent commission of the International Triathlon Union (ITU, 19891). The major international meeting is the W.Ch. and Duathlon Grand Prix.

DUCK, DUCK, GOOSE, see >DROP HANDKERCHIEF.

DUCKPINS, a var. of >TEN-PIN BOWLING in which both the bowl and the pins are half the standard size. The name originates from the stocky shape of pins. For technical details concerning the equipment and the game see >BOWLING.

DUCKS AND DRAKES, a competition in throwing stones which are supposed to bounce across the surface of water as many times as possible, often called *skipping stones*. Probably this form of competition was already known in antiquity, though

wall, the game is called *scutter* (sth. that scampers away) or *tic tac mollard* (swish swish mill). Ducks and drakes has not been treated as a serious competition and has been neglected by ethnographical lexicons and sports encyclopedias; it did appear in some general dictionaries, though. An exception to that rule being an entry 'Ducks and Drakes' in a monumental work by A.B. Gomme, *The Traditional Games of England, Scotland, and Ireland* (1894, vol. II, 114-116). Another exception is the entry *Slå smut* in a 4-volume encyclopedia *Gamle idrætslege i Danmark* (*Sports games in Denmark*, 1997, 1, 125) by J. Møller. The game consists of curling a small flat stone in the index finger, resting it on the middle finger and steadying it with the thumb, and tossing it sidearm, low and level to the surface of the water, which allows the stone to bounce or skip across it a number of times. The winner is the thrower whose stone bounces the greatest number of times. In Ang.-Sax. tradition, a single bounce is called a duck, a double – duck and drake, a triple – halfpenny cake, and so on up to 6:

A duck and a drake
And halfpenny cake,
And a penny to pay the old baker,
A hop and scotch in another notch,
Slitherum, slatherum, take her.

A satirist, S. Butler (1613-1680), refers to ducks and drakes in his famous *Hudybras* (1663):

What figur'd slates are best to make
On wat'ry surface duck and drake.

Some attempt has been made to actually manufacture and market ideal, i.e. artificial, ceramic skipping stones out of terra-cotta or clay, but naturally fashioned stones found at the water's edge are preferred.
A.B. Gomme, 'Ducks and Drakes', TGESI, I, 114-116.

DUCZA, a game popular with Pol. boys, mostly from noble families living in the area of the Podlasie Province. In his work *Gry i zabawy różnych*

Dźwiganie beczek – a barrel lifting and carrying event at a Polish brewery

dates back to 1658 and dzhilitanie was still popular in Balkan countries up to the beginning of WWII. According to V. Vrcevitch, the author of *Srbska Narodne Igre* (1859), the 19th-cent. match started with 2 boys mounting their horses and looking intensely into each other's eyes, challenginglz. They agreed who was going to be chased based on whose horse was faster. That rider set off at full tilt shouting, 'Strike me, Omerago! Don't spare me, as I'm not going to spare you, either!' Before the challenged rider managed to turn around towards the running opponent, the latter was at least 20m away. Then, the attacker threw his javelin at the runaway and immediately after that, whether he hit or missed, he himself started running away as the roles were reversed. When the first pair had finished, another took their positions and the game started again. When some clumsy player threw a javelin and missed all the others had a good laugh at him. See also >JAVELIN THROW.

DŹWIGANIE BECZEK, Pol. for 'beer keg carry'. A folk sport practiced in Pol. Upper Silesia at least from the end of the 18th cent. A heavy barrel is lifted with 2 hands and carried over an unspecified distance. Barrels were usu. filled with sand or water. Dźwiganie beczek was a test for candidates who applied in breweries for the job of coachman. In the 18-19th cent. it was one of the events during folk games initiated by count J. Górzycki in Kamień, near Brzozowice. A similar present-day event is part of the Strongmen's Contest. Yet another similar event is held annually in Boników (Poland), where contestants compete in throwing empty beer kegs for distance.

Kazimierz Fajkielt setting a new world record of 14.18m in throwing empty beer kegs.

in order for opposing teams to size each other up. At the third passing, each lancer attempts to knock his rival into water. Depending on local traditions, boat crews number 3-8 oarsmen. Since the 13th--14th cent. regattas accompanied by lance fights have been organized in many Dan. cities. In *A Description of Norse Countries* by O. Magnus (1490--1557) there is a print representing dystløb played on boats with two oarsmen and one lancer. Behind the contenders there is an unusual barge that serves as a floating grand stand complete with roofing. Both fighting boats and floating stands testify to the popularity and significance of dystløb where vessels were constructed for such a singular purpose. Various local and religious holidays served as opportunities for playing dystløb, as did – like in Kerteminde – anniversaries of local skippers. Such contests had diverse names: in Nyborg on Fyn Island they were denominated *at skydes i strande*, in Svendborg on the same island *at støde i havet* or *at skyde i søen*, in Fåborg, also on Fyn Island – *at skyde i vandet*, in Nakskov on Lolland Island – *at være i stranden*, in Korsør on Sjælland Island – *at springe i stranden*. See also Fr. >JOUTES GIRONDINES, >JOUTES LANGUEDOCIENNES.
J. Møller, 'Dystløb', GID, 1997, 4, 77.

DZHIGITOVKA, a var. of dynamic acrobatic stunts performed on a galloping horse. The tradition originates from Caucasia and in the course of the 19th cent. it spread among Cossack regiments. A number of elements were later adopted by circus acrobats. The most frequent individual stunts are jumping off and on a galloping horse, picking up various objects from the floor during the ride, riding under the horse's belly, and passing from one side of the horse to another under its throatlatch at full gallop. Among team stunts the most popular are pyramids formed on the backs of galloping, yoked horses.

DZHILITANIE, Serb. for 'a javelin throw' [Tur. *dzhilit* or *dzhirit*, Serb. *dzhilit* – a javelin]. In former times a sport practiced in Serbia and Bosnia in which one horseman throws a javelin at another. The object is to take the rider down from the horse with the fewest throws possible. Thus, the best score is gained when the opponent falls on the ground after a single throw. The riders make 1 attempt after each turning of the horse. The sport deriving from knightly traditions was enhanced with tournament elements and was originally practiced at court festivals, weddings, etc. The first complete description

Dystløb – Danish boat jousting.

E

WORLD SPORTS ENCYCLOPEDIA

E PAPA WAIARI, see >TI RAKAU.

E ROPI, a var. of a Maori hand game. See >MAHI RINGARINA.

E VINCE, see >A BRACCIUTA.

E'DEM LAH, Arab. for 'a thrown bone'. A game popular in Saudi Arabia, esp. in the area of Qsim. From a dictionary of Arab games and sports by M. Ibrahim al-Majman we learn it is a team game played by 4, 6, 8, or 10 participants. It is played at night, sometimes by the dim light of a waning or recently new moon. The necessary object is a bone, or a piece of wood, or stone and as many *gatra* as there are players (a *gatra* is most probably a dialectal name for an object made of a thick rope or leather strap, as it can be bundled, and it is used for striking). The players are divided into 2 teams and all of them stand at the starting point, one beside the other, to be able to see the piece of bone and remember it well. One of the team A players says: 'E'dem lah', and the team B players respond: 'Wen rah?' (Where is it?), after which an A player strikes with all his might at the object using his gatra. Once the bone (or wooden chip) has been pitched, the opposing team disperses in search of the object. The player who finds it shouts: 'Sara!', and starts running towards the starting point while his partners do their best to protect him. If he reaches the place, team B scores a point. If, however, the object is taken from him on the way and then pitched again, the opposing team wins.
Min al'abina ash-sha 'biyya, 1983, 38.

EASTER TUESDAY GAME, a trad. ball game played on Easter Tuesday in the town of Workington in England. According to local beliefs, the players who perform badly during the game will become ill during the upcoming harvest season.

EASTER BALL, Lat. *pila paschalis*, Dan. *påskebold*, a folk pastime from the early Christian Middle Ages, combining pagan, Muslim and Christian elements. The precise origin of Easter ball remains unknown.

A two-year-old boy, assisted by his dad, takes part in the annual White House Easter Egg Roll in Washington. The race, usually presided over by the President and First Lady, involves pushing an egg with a spoon towards the finish line on the South Lawn.

Most likely, in many areas of medieval Europe, the Church dioceses combined Easter celebration with some common local pagan observances of the coming of spring. At least in some of those places the pagan traditions must have included various ball games as they later became part of Christian celebration. This is confirmed in Lat. sources in which the team games played at Easter are referred to as the *Pila Paschalis*. Once a pagan ball game had been adopted in one diocese it was later borrowed by and practiced in other dioceses and parishes. Local forms of Easter ball were popular in medieval Scandinavia (esp. Denmark), England and Germany. In Germany and Normandy, the game commenced with a kick-off outside the church building. The ball had to pass over the church roof to the awaiting crowd of players. In the north of England the kick-off was traditionally performed by a local coalheaver. In Tangermünde, Easter ball was a game played by brides (>BRIDEBALL). In Denmark, the game was played in churchyards, e.g. in Mors, or even graveyards, e.g. in Ljørslev. Easter ball games in Denmark were mostly of the bat-and-ball variety, whereas in England and Germany they were football and handball games. A 14th-cent. frieze in a church in Ørslev depicts a number of characters playing ball and dancing. This may have been proof of an existing link between Easter ball games and church services. In the winter of 1923-24, a few old moldering balls were discovered in the cathedral in Arhus, under the tombstone of H.M. Storm, who died in 1659. There are several theories referring to those unusual finds. Some historians claim the balls were hidden there by pupils of the church school who played with them in the church building. Ball games were probably played in Arhus during official church holidays and the balls might have got lost in some places in the church. Perhaps Strom had been an exceptional Easter baller, or perhaps an opponent of the tradition had sabotaged the game by hiding the balls. Maybe that was just a convenient storage place.
Easter ball varieties were also known in parts of France, esp. in those in close vicinity to the Saracen occupied territories. The Arabs had occupied the Iberian Peninsula for a few centuries and in the period of their greatest expansion some elements of Arab culture, such as folk games, might have penetrated into the territory of France. This may explain the link between old Persian game of >CHUGAN or *czigan* and the Fr. *chicane*. One of the earliest mentions of Easter ball comes from the 12th cent. and refers to a local custom observed in Auxerre. The dean of the collegiate church in full liturgical outfit would receive a ball from a young novice and then lead a procession along the church. The congregation sang the liturgical song *Victimae Paschali Laudes* and clapped their hands and the dean would dance to it with the ball in his left hand. At a certain point of his performance the dean handed the ball over to the person next to him and then the congregation began passing the ball along. After the ball reached the entrance door it was thrown out in front of the church and the crowd commenced a rough ball game consisting of snatching the ball from one to another. The records of the Auxerre province include information that 'The ball game was common in other churches. The events of the Auxerre church had a more decent form in the bishops' palace in Vienne.' The expression 'a more decent form' referred to the fact that the ball in Vienne was not played inside the church but in front of the bishops' palace. The game was held on Easter Monday to the accompaniment of church bells. First, the crowds of players feasted by long tables with meat, beer and wine set around the church. After the feast was over, the archbishop threw the ball among the congregation and the game commenced. Both the faithful and the clergy took part. Similar games were played in Rheims. In the St. Stephen Church in Vitré, in the department of Ille-de-Vilaine, another ceremony took place. During the Elevation the local tenant-in-chief placed a ball underneath the altar. Jean Beleth, a Parisian theologian, vehemently opposed church ball games in 1165. His most particular criticism was directed towards bishops who participated in the games: 'There are churches in which it is customary for bishops and archbishops to stoop to playing ball with the lower clergy'. G. Durandus, the Bishop of Mende (near Avignon) complained in 1286 that 'On Easter, in some areas of our country the prelates play games with common clergymen in monasteries or bishops' residences, stooping to football, singing and dancing.' The balls used for the game were made of various materials including oakum, sawdust, or hay covered with leather or fabric. Sometimes wooden balls were used. Often before a game the ball was submerged in scalding water so that no one could hold it for too long during play. For the same purpose, the balls were also studded with needles or pins; cf. >GOOD FRIDAY FOOTBALL, >EASTER TUESDAY GAME.
J. Møller, 'So i hul – og 99 andre gamle boldspil og kstelege', GID, 1997, vol. 1; R.W. Henderson, *Bat, Ball and Bishop. The Origins of Ball Games* (1947); F. Peabody Magoun, *History of Football from the Beginning to 1871* (1938).

ÉCHASSES, Fr. for >WALKING ON STILTS.

ÉCAISSER LA GRENOUILLE, see >DÉCAISSER LA GRENOUILLE.

EDUO, a game originating from the Tibetan traditions in which stones are launched by means of a braid referred to as an *eduo*, resembling >WIUCHA or a sling. The eduo is a special braid of 2 strings of yak's hair, one dyed white, the other black, about 3cm thick. In the middle of the braid an elliptically-shaped piece of leather is fixed, into which a stone is placed. Then the eduo is folded in two and a player grabs one end in his hand and the other – ending with a loop – is fixed to his finger. When the eduo is spinning fast enough above the thrower's head, he lets loose one end of the braid releasing the stone in the desired direction. Throwing the stone in the right direction is the essence of the game. The trick is to release one end of the braid when it is directed towards the predefined aim. Nowadays, competitions are held in 2 categories: throwing the longest distance and throwing at a target, one usu. made of circular shooting targets. The best shooters are able to score an exact hit or one within several cm from a distance of about 200m. Originally, eduo was used for self-defense or for shepherding cattle: a stone shuttling above the cattle's heads produced a sharp swish which scared the animals as if it were a whip. Only in extreme situations was the device used for actually hitting an animal.
Mu Fushan, et al., 'Eduo', TRAMCHIN.

EFEININDA, see >FAININDA.

EGEDE, also *oyo*. An Afr. team game practiced in the vicinity of Ekoi and Ibibio in Nigeria. The equipment used in the game includes a racket and shuttlecock, therefore egede is on the one hand similar to >LACROSSE in its manner of returning the shuttlecock, and on the other hand, to >INDICA, >VOLANT, >BADMINTON, or >BATINTON owing to the shuttlecock itself. The racket (*ikpo-oyo*), about 18in. (45cm) long, is made of a branch crooked into a loop with a shallow basket fixed to it and made from the piassava tree lianas. The size of the racket's striking surface is not predetermined and varies from player to player. A shuttlecock (*oyo*) is made of palm tree leaves fastened with the piassava tree lianas. Because of its substantial size it is not served with the use of a racket but rather thrown at the opponent who attempts to catch it with his racket. The court, about 12yds. (11m) long, without side lines, is divided into 2 halves by a perpendicular line in the middle.
Rules of the game. The players are arranged into 2 equal teams, usu. up to 9 in each. Each player holds his own racket. The right to start a match is decided by means of tossing a coin. The teams line up on their sides of the court and the first players in the row throws an *oyo* at the opponent's half. If the *oyo* is not caught, neither team scores a point; if it is caught in the basket a point is scored by the catching team. The first catching does not account for a point, but only gives the right to score; only after the shuttlecock is caught for the second time, a player scores a point for his team.
At the second capture, the player who has succeeded in catching the oyo has the right to take 'prisoner' the player who threw it. The prisoner stays on the opponent's half until he manages to capture the shuttlecock thrown by the team he originally belonged to. After returning to the home half the prisoner then has the right to throw first. The throws are executed alternatively by each team, one player after another. The shuttlecock must not be thrown above the players' reach. If a caught oyo falls on the ground, the thrower scores. If a throw is so strong

that the catcher breaks his racket while attempting to catch the object, one of the prisoners is set free. If the *oyo* is captured by more than one player (e.g. after having been caught it falls off the basket but is caught by another player before hitting the ground) neither of them has the right to a prisoner as Nig. tradition says no prisoner can have 2 masters. In the course of the game the teams can exchange prisoners on the initiative of the team that has lost the greater number of players. The winner is the team which scores a predetermined number of points and takes an agreed number of prisoners. Then, another set is played. The competition is, however, so fierce that a match usu. does not exceed a single set.

In the province of Ashanti, in Ghana, a somewhat different var. of the game is practiced. From the A.W. Cardinall's description we learn that the shuttlecock was traditionally made of an old corncob wrapped up in leaves and tied with a string. Each player holds a racket similar to that used in Nigeria. The object of the game is to throw the shuttlecock above a string made of climbers and hung across the road at the height of 8ft. (2.44m) to have the opposing team catch it before it touches the ground. The winner is the team which first succeeds in catching the shuttlecock 7 times.

P.G. Brewster, 'Some Nigerian Games With Their Parallels and Analogues,' *Journal de la Société des Africanistes*, 1954, 24; A. Taylor Cheska, 'Edege or Oyo (Noose Catch)', TGDWAN, 1987, 24-26; O.F. Raum, 'The Rolling Target (Hoop and Pole) Game in Africa,' *African Studies*, 1953, 12.

EGG AND SPOON RACE, a trad. competition known in a majority of Eur. countries but apparently most popular in Denmark where it is called *æggeløb* [Dan. *æg* – egg + *løb* – run, race]. Each contestant receives a spoon on which he places an egg. Then, the runner has to cover a specified distance making sure that he does not drop the egg. If the egg drops and breaks the competitor is disqualified. There are also egg race relays in which a team has only one spoon and egg. A var. of the game is popular in the US, where the most famous event of this kind is the White House Easter Egg Roll.

J. Møller, 'Æggeløb', GID, 1997, 4, 99.

EGNE FINGRE, see >SJIPPE OVER EGET BEN.

EGYPTIAN BOXING, a var. of fist fighting known in ancient Egypt. According to ancient prints blows were dealt with arms spread wide apart, the arm movement resembling the movement of a windmill. The oldest prints depicting Eg. boxing come from the Mery Ra tomb in the Minia province and from the Ptah Hotep tomb located in the town of Saqqarah in Lower Egypt.

EGYPTIAN HANDBALL, a game of catch practiced by girls in ancient Egypt 5,000 years ago. In the game 2 girls, each sitting on the back of another girl bent forward, threw a ball back an forth. The girls bent forward could not, however, support themselves with their hands propped against the floor. The essence of the game was to catch the ball without losing one's balance. The ball was made of leather or papyrus stuffed with rammed hay or leaves. If made of papyrus, the ball was a disposable one. The game is represented on wall paintings found in the tombs of Eg. rulers near the locality of Saqqarah.

EGYPTIAN WEIGHTLIFTING, a competition, known in ancient Egypt, in which competitors lifted a sack of an elongated shape full of sand, with one hand. A weightlifter grabbed a sack by its neck and snatched it upwards so that the centrifugal force would make the sack 'stand' upside down in the air. If the soft sack collapsed while being snatched, because of insufficient centrifugal force, the attempt was considered unsuccessful.

EGYPTIAN WRESTLING, a var. of wrestling popular in ancient Egypt. All the preserved records point to the fact that in this type of wrestling the fighters competed in a standing position while holding each other above the waist. This means that Eg. wrestling was rather similar to the modern Greco-Roman style. One of the oldest depictions of the sport is a mural found in the tomb of Ptahhotep – a 5th Dynasty (2470-2320 BC) ruler. The mural shows 6 pairs of wrestlers competing simultaneously during a court ceremony. Numerous drawings and statuettes depicting Eg. wrestlers were made in Aswan, Deir El Bersheh, Meine and Beni Hassan during the so-

called Middle Kingdom period (22nd-17th cent. BC). The number of wrestling pairs fighting simultaneously was a direct reflection of a given ruler's or ceremony's status. The Amenemhet tomb mural shows 59 fighting pairs while the Baqti III tomb painting depicts as many as 219 pairs. The paintings found in the Neher tomb in Deir El Bersheh are the first to depict umpires. A tomb mural discovered in Medinet Habu shows an umpire giving a warning to a fighter failing to observe the rules of fair play. The best wrestling pictures as far as their artistic quality is concerned have been found in Ramses III's (1190-1158 BC) tomb which may indicate that during his reign Egyptian wrestling was at the peak of its popularity. After the end of the so-called New Kingdom (17th-11th cent. BC), wrestling murals were no longer painted in tombs, which may suggest that the sport died out around that time.

EISKEGELN, Ger. for 'ice skittles' [Ger. *Eis* – ice + *kegel* – a skittle]. A var. of skittles in which the skit-

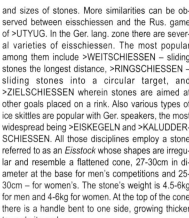
Egyptian boxing.

tles are knocked over with a special stone slid on ice. The skittles are fixed on a special frame, with their bottoms hanging above the surface of the rink, and the stone is supposed to catch on them with its handle and thus knock them out of the frame. The stone is a typical one employed in other games played in the Ger. lang. area, with the only difference in its height, usu. 38cm, that allows knocking the skittles over with the handle. Similarly to other var. of *Eisschießen*, the stone (*Eisstock*) has the shape of an irregular flattened cone with a base 27-30cm in diameter. It is made of wood padded with metal [*Fuss*, in Ger. lit. a foot; also *Laufsole*, *Sole* – a sole] and weighs 4-6kg. Cf. >KALLUDER-SCHIEßEN, >RINGSCHIEßEN, >WEITSCHIEßEN, >ZIELSCHIEßEN.

'Eischessen', *Kleine Enzyklopädie Körperkultur und Sport*, 1965, 283-285.

EISSCHIEßEN, Ger. for 'sliding on ice', lit. 'ice shooting', also *Eisstockschiessen*. A group of sports events in which stones are slid on ice either to reach the farthest distance or to hit a target, in a manner similar to >CURLING but employing different shapes

and sizes of stones. More similarities can be observed between eisschiessen and the Rus. game of >UTYUG. In the Ger. lang. zone there are several varieties of eisschiessen. The most popular among them include >WEITSCHIESSEN – sliding stones the longest distance, >RINGSCHIESSEN – sliding stones into a circular target, and >ZIELSCHIESSEN wherein stones are aimed at other goals placed on a rink. Also various types of ice skittles are popular with Ger. speakers, the most widespread being >EISKEGELN and >KALUDDER-SCHIESSEN. All those disciplines employ a stone referred to as an *Eisstock* whose shapes are irregular and resemble a flattened cone, 27-30cm in diameter at the base for men's competitions and 25-30cm – for women's. The stone's weight is 4.5-6kg for men and 4-6kg for women. At the top of the cone there is a handle bent to one side, growing thicker towards its end.

History. The traditions of the game among Ger. speakers date back to the Middle Ages. More ad-

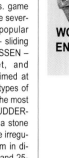

Egyptian weightlifting.

Egyptian handball.

vanced var. appeared in the Alps around the 17th cent. Until quite recently, the game had a purely folk character. The first official Ger. championships were organized in 1926. Eisschiessen also developed in Austria and was a demonstration sport during the winter Ol.G. in 1936 and 1964. After 1945 it was favored by the GDR authorities. In 1950 the International Eisschiessen Association (International Eischiess-Verband, IEV) was established – its current name is the Föderation für Eisstockschiesse, IFE. The federation is comprised of nearly 20 national organizations, e.g. from Germany, Austria, Switzerland, Italy, the USA, and Canada, as well as about 250,000 players. In 1951 the first E.Ch. were held, after which W.Ch., held every 4 years, began. 'Eisschiessen', *Kleine Enzyklopädie Körperkultur und Sport*, 1965, 283-285. W. Neumbromer, *Der Eisschiess Sport*, 1961.

EKAK, an Afr. folk game practiced in Nigeria which consists of throwing a small ring onto a 3-in. (7.5cm) tall pin stuck in the ground. The ring was made of string or thin wire and its diameter reached around 2in. (5cm). A.W. Cardinall observed a var. of the game shortly before 1927. He did not, however, mention any specific name:

Another game played in the village street requires merely a noose of fine twine (a strand of piassave will do), and some sand. This latter is heaped up and one of the players buries the noose under the heaped-up sand. Then each player in turn takes a small stick – a thorn from a lime tree is usual – and sticks it into the heap of sand where he expects the noose to be, the hider being the last to play. The end of the string is then uncovered and pulled. and if a thorn is inside the noose, that thorn's player wins.
[*In Ashanti and Beyond*, 1927, 251-252]

P.G. Brewster, 'Some Nigerian Games With Their Parallels and Analogues', *Journal de la Société de Africanistes*, 1954, 24; A. Taylor Cheska, 'Ekak (Ring and Pin)', TGDWAN, 1987, 27.

EKSTRAMETA, a var. of a ball game practiced in Poland prob. from around the 17th cent., mostly in towns and monastic schools and peaking in popularity in the 18th cent. It belongs to the family of ball games referred to in old Pol. as >CHWYTKA. A very general and somewhat incomplete description of the rules of the game can be found in Ł. Gołębiowski's *Gry i zabawy różnych stanów* (*Games and Pastimes of Various Social Classes*) (1831). Four players take positions marked with stones surrounding the 'finish' (*meta*) and another four stand in the center of the finish. The 'outside' players pass a ball one to another and at the third throw a player has the right to make an attempt at hitting one of the 'inside' players with the ball. If the thrower misses, he steps aside and is out of the game; if he hits one, the hit party is excluded from the match. The game continues until all the players but one are out. At the end, the winner, chased by the others, is supposed to run around the finish, encircling it once.

ELEPHANT POLO, a var. of >POLO played on elephants. There are no restrictions as to the height, weight or sex of the elephants. The game is officiated by a senior umpire together with an assistant umpire mounted on the referee elephant and the official referee who can be on the referee elephant or be positioned on the sideline near the center of the field. There are also two goal judges, one at either goal, who declare the goals scored. The game is played by four mounted players on each team. The pitch is 120m long and 70m wide, marked with a center line, a circle with a radius of 10m in the center of the field. A semi-circle, in front of the goals, with a radius of 20m, measured from the center of the goal line at either end of the pitch forms a semicircle called the D. The game consists of two 10-minute *chukkas* of playing time, with an interval of 15 min. Elephants and ends of the pitch are changed at half time. Elephant polo is played with a standard size polo ball made of willow root or plastic, about 3-3½in. in diameter, weighing about 4oz. The ball is hit with mallets with long shafts, proportional to the height of the elephants. No team may have more than three elephants playing in one half of the pitch at any given time. The play starts when the umpire throws the ball between 2 opposing elephants inside the ring, from outside the center circle. The end of a chukka is signaled with a bell or a bugle. A goal is scored if the ball travels over and across the goal line. No more than one elephant from each side is allowed in the D. When a player from one team commits a foul, the opposing team is allowed a free hit from the spot the foul occurred (spot hit). If a foul is committed within the D, the opposing team is given a spot hit from a point on the 20m semi-circle line opposite the middle of the goal. The ball may only be hit once, i.e. should a player miss the ball, additional swings at the ball may not be taken. Fouls include hooking the opponent's stick; standing 'on' the ball; intentionally hitting another player or umpire with a stick; and deliberately crossing in front of an elephant when the opponent is moving with a ball. An example of dangerous play can be the so-called 'round house' swings. Such swings are allowed only if there are no other players, or elephants, at risk of being hit. If the elephants get too close to each other the umpire can stop the play and separate them. The use of the *ankush* (a riding crop) is generally forbidden during the game; the ankush may be carried on elephants considered dangerous by the mahouts. If there is any failure in the elephant's harness, the play is stopped to repair it. Should a stick be broken, when play is in the D, the game is not stopped until the ball leaves the D. For a broken stick when play is outside of the D, the game is stopped while the player changes his stick. The players must wear polo helmets or trad. sola

topis. Should a player's hat fall off outside the D, the game is stopped while the hat is recovered; should the hat fall inside the D, the game continues and will only stop when the ball is outside the D. At the end of each match the elephants are given sugar cane or rice balls with vitamins, while the players can have cold beer or soft drinks, and not vice versa, as is humorously stated in the official elephant polo rules. In case of a draw, a penalty shoot-out is used. The penalties are taken from the center of the D line with no elephant defending the goal. Should it still be a draw after all four players from each team have made their hit then a sudden-death penalty shoot-out is used to determine the winner.

History. The origins of elephant polo played without fixed rules go back to the 1960s. The game was initially practiced on the international level by rich amateurs of exotic sports. Elephant polo is ardently supported by the Nepalese government as an important part of the national heritage. The Elephant Polo World Championships have been held since 1981. The top teams from two international elephant polo leagues play the final game. In 1982, the World Elephant Polo Association, WEPA was formed in Chitwan, Nepal. Every December, the Nepal Open Tournament is held in Megauly under WEPA auspices. The sport is primarily practiced in Nepal, but it is also known in India, Sri Lanka, Burma, and in South Africa, Namibia, Tanzania and Mozambique. In African countries elephant polo is a popular tourist attraction. The world leading teams, both national and international, include: National Parks Nepal, Swissair, Brit. Gurkha Gladiators, Chivas Regal (India), Eldorado (USA), Screwy Tuskers (USA), Harry Winston Rough Cuts (Japan), Cresta Poonanhis (South Africa), International Mercenaries, and Ladies International Team.
World Elephant Polo Association, The Internet: http:// www.elephantpolo.com

ELEPHANT RACES (MOUNTED), a form of competition on specially harnessed elephants practiced in the countries of SE Asia, part. in India and Pakistan. See also >ELEPHANT POLO.

ELUOSI CUDGEL STRIKING, a throwing game practiced by a Chin. national minority of Rus. origin, also popular with the Kirghiz and Uygurs. It originates from the Rus. tradition of >GORODKI with which the game shares the general rule of throwing a stick at little structures made of pins. For the most part the game is played in teams of 5 players, but there are also singles and doubles versions. Each team has at least 10 cudgels, 80cm long and about 5cm thick. The course has a rectangular shape, though its size differs from place to place. In the center of the rectangle there is a 3x3m square referred to as the castle. In the middle of the castle 5 wooden pins are placed on their ends – each pin is

Elephant races.

ELEPHANT POLO IN NEPAL

about 18cm long and 6.5cm thick. The object of the game is to knock the pins over and out of the castle's area by throwing cudgels at them. Each player is entitled to 2 throws per round. During competitions held as military training time limits apply. The player who succeeds in knocking 1 or more pins out of the castle's area has the right to halve the distance from the target, which gives him an advantage when striking other pins. A round ends when all the pins are knocked out of the castle's area. The winner is that team, or player, who manages to knock out a greater number of pins in a predetermined series of rounds.
Mu Fushan, et al., 'Cudgel-Striking. Eluosi (Russian)', TRAMCHIN, 14.

ENDURANCE DANCE, see >DANCE MARATHON.

ENDURANCE HORSE RIDING, one of the horse riding events recognized by the Fédération Equestre Internationale (FEI, International Equestrian Federation), and supervised by the Endurance and Long Distance Riding International Conference (ELDRIC), which is an autonomous organization co-operating with and recognized by FEI. The objective is to ride along a course 40-160km long (or sometimes longer). In the international arena, endurance horse riding is divided into 2 categories – 'A' events are held on courses 141-160km long, while 'B' events – on courses 80-140km long. The age of the horse is not strictly defined, but it may be inferred from associated rules that it cannot be younger than 5 years, with horses aged 9-15 considered the most suitable. The longest distances (160km and more) take between 15-20hrs. to complete, depending on local terrain conditions. In the lower categories, participants set out individually every 3-5mins. In the higher categories, all participants start simultaneously but the referee may order individual starts under special circumstances. A team consists of 4 riders, with the 3 best ones classified. Men and women are classified together. There is no junior category but a separate category for 'younger' riders (aged 18-21) does exist. Participants are equipped with maps. The courses are marked using tapes, flags, or paint or chalk symbols. Every 40km, there are veterinary gates, where the horses undergo detailed examination, and are allowed to continue only if the results are acceptable. Depending on the creativity of the organizers, an event may be organized along a loop about 40km long, with the vet stand always in the same place, or along a single loop covering the whole distance (e.g. 160km), with several stands at different locations. The time that the rider and horse are allowed to spend at the vet stand is not fixed, and may vary between 15 and 40mins.; however, it must be the same for all participants. One characteristic feature of long distance endurance riding is the use of the so-called 'easyboots' in place of lost horse shoes. Recently, horse-and-rider teams have been accompanied by service cars with increasing frequency, and service intervention is allowed in specially designated areas. It seems, though, that help from the service cars has gone overboard, and is distorting the idea of endurance riding as a 'natural' sport.
History. The first endurance riding events were organized at the turn of the 19th and 20th cent. These included two parallel races between Berlin and Vienna, and Vienna and Berlin (about 600km). After a number of decades of moderate popularity, the 1980s saw a rapid growth of endurance riding, especially in France. In 1997, an ELDRIC meeting in Arles separated endurance riding from 'horse riding marathons' that are longer than 160km. There are W.Ch., as well as continental championships. The W.Ch. are held every 2 years, and the continental events – in the years between the W.Ch. The top endurance horse riding countries include France, the USA, New Zealand and the United Arab Emirates.
L.E. Hollander, *Endurance Riding from Beginning to Winning*, date unknown; M. Kram, personal contact; E. Szarska, *Vademecum rajdowca konnych rajdów długodystansowych*, 1998.

ENDURANCE RALLY, a type of motorcycle rally organized partially along public roads and partially along courses set in difficult terrain, aimed at testing the vehicle's endurance (hence the name).
History. Although the first rallies testing the endurance of motorcycles were organized as early as towards the end of the 19th cent., the 1,000-Mile Reliability Trial, held in England in 1900, is usually con-

WORLD SPORTS ENCYCLOPEDIA

E

sidered to have been the first real endurance rally. Since WWII, increased traffic along public roads has forced organizers to look for less frequented courses in the countryside.

ENGLISH ARCHERY, a type of archery developed in medieval England; it became one of the foundations of modern sports archery. The most distinctive feature of Eng. archery was the use of the longbow, often as tall as the archer himself. An average longbow weighed about 100lbs. and shot arrows with an effective range of about 220yds. A well-trained archer could hit a target from a distance of 140yds. The longbow had two main varieties: the strung bow, permanently braced with a relaxed bowstring; and the unstrung bow, braced only when in use. Eng. bows were made of yew, imported from Italy or Spain, or of ash or elm wood. The bowstring was made of tightly plaited hemp strings. Mainly wooden arrows were used, but more effective were steel arrows. Two main kinds of arrows were used. The longer, more accurate *flight arrow* was 37in. long and was mainly used for shooting at longer distances. It had a shuttlecock-like elongated head with four edges, and rounded aerodynamic feathering. The *sheaf arrow* was used at shorter distances to penetrate the opponent's shield or armor, rather than for accurate shooting. It was heavier, shorter and had a sheaf-like head. Rectangular feathering with sharp edges gave the sheaf arrow its characteristic loud sound exerting a psychological impact on the enemy. The Eng. longbow was 5 to 6 times more effective in range and accuracy than the continental crossbow (>CROSSBOW SHOOTING).
History. The appearance of the Eng. longbow derived probably from 2 archery traditions: Welsh archery featuring long bows; and Norman battle archery brought to England after 1066. The latter was a battle skill consisting of eliminating the enemy troops before the cavalry charge, used effectively during the battle of Hastings. The Normans used short bows. The proper longbow, ultimately of Welsh origin, was adopted by the Eng. army later and allowed the archers to shoot more accurately and at a more effective range. The new weapons were employed by the army of Edward I (1237-1307) in 1277 during his Welsh campaign. Initially, within the Eng. army there were only 100 longbowmen. In 1282, 1,000 Eng. archers were sent against the Welsh ruler, Llewellyn ap Gruffodd, and vastly contributed to the final subjugation of Wales. The longbows continued to be used in the Eng. army under Edward II. Thanks to the longbow troops, the commander-in-chief of the royal army defeated the defiant Earl of Lancaster at the battle of Boroughbridge in 1322. The Eng. longbowmen, however, became most renowned during the reign of Edward III (1327-1377). The Eng. longbow made its famous contribution to the victories over the French at the battles of the Hundred Years' War (1337-1453). At the battle of Crécy (1346), the Eng. archers utterly defeated the Fr. cavalry, leaving 1,500 Fr. knights dead, while losing about 50 men. At Agincourt (1415), the Eng. troops, counting only 1,000 men-

Top and above: endurance rally – testing both rider and vehicle.

at-arms and 5,000 longbowmen, defeated a Fr. army twice as large, which lost about 7,000 men, with Eng. casualties of 450. Indeed, one hypothesis accounting for the popular 2-fingered, reverse peace/victory gesture – meaning essentially the same thing as a raised middle finger – has it that at this time the French took to cutting off the fingers of captured Eng. archers and that the now old familiar suggestion was originally intended to defiantly show one's fingers intact.
The medieval tradition of Eng. archery is closely connected with the legend of Robin Hood. His tomb near the Nottingham Castle features the following inscription:

Here underneath this laitl stean
Lais Robert Earl of Huntingtun,
Near arcir ver as hei sa gud
An pipl kauld mim Robin Heud
Sick outlaws as hi an is men
Wil England nivr si agen.

Robin Hood's archery skills are part of numerous tales and stories about his life and adventures. He would shoot an arrow through a rope of the hangman's noose and free the convicted or participate in an archery contest in disguise and win the silver arrow of the Sheriff of Nottingham in an archery contest. The winner of another Nottingham archery contest was Little John, a close friend and companion of Robin Hood. The dying Robin Hood was supposed to have indicated his burial site by shooting out an arrow in an unknown direction.
Archery contests were frequently organized in various Eng. towns. At present, many Eng. streets and squares bear names reminiscent of the old archery tradition, e.g. Archery Row, Butt Field, Butts, etc. The contests were aimed at improvement of shooting accuracy among soldiers and townsfolk in preparation for wars and sieges. In London, a huge archery range was located in Moorfields (present-day

Moor Gate). Other archery training grounds included Islington and Finsbury to the north of the Thames, where contests with qualifying rounds, finals and awards were held. The contests were often accompanied by music and later by wagering. H. Machyn mentioned in his diary an archery contest between a few nobles and a group of London barbers held in 1562, with the accompaniment of a band consisting of six drummers and one flutist. The winners were awarded with a sumptuous supper. Several weeks later a similar contest was held between 2 groups of believers – one dressed in yellow, one in red – from St. George's parish, accompanied by a band consisting of 4 flutists and 6 drummers. The prize for victory was also a sumptuous feast with barrels of beer and wine provided by the losers.

The statue of Robin Hood at Nottingham, England.

The invention of firearms did not immediately eliminate the bow and arrow from the equipment of the Eng. army. Owing to tremendously effective range and accuracy, the longbows remained weapons of the Eng. army for much longer than bows and crossbows in other Eur. armed forces. A huge influence on the long-lasting prestige of the Eng. bow was exerted by *Toxophilus* (The Lover of the Bow, 1545), a philosophical treatise on archery written by the Eng. pedagogue, R. Ascham. A sermon devoted to archery, addressed to Edward VI (1537-53) was delivered by Bishop H. Latimer. Longbow troops were excluded from the army in 1595, during the reign of Elizabeth I. The queen's decision aroused huge opposition among army officers and a wide public debate about the merits of longbows vs firearms. Further development of firearms excluded the bow and arrow as a military weapon but popularized archery as a sport. An important archery event in England is the Ancient Scorton Arrow contest, held annually in Yorkshire since 1673. The contest's originators were lovers of the medieval art of archery who wanted to maintain the old tradition. In 1676, Charles II Stuart commissioned the Royal Company of Archers, which became the honorary royal guard and commenced organization of annual archery competitions. In 1781 (1782 or 1790 in different sources) the Toxophilite Society was established in England, becoming the Royal Toxophilite Society in 1847 (Gk. *toxon* – bow + *philein* – to love). In 1844 the first of the Grand National Archery Meetings – the Brit. championships – was held in York, and the Grand National Archery Society became the governing body of the sport in the UK, incorporating international archery rules and regulations and marking the beginning of modern sports archery; see >OUTDOOR TARGET ARCHERY.

E. Burke, *The History of Archery*, 1958; S. Knight, *Robin Hood. A Complete Study of the English Outlaw*, 1994; E.K. Milliken, *Archery in the Middle Ages*, 1967.

ENGLISH POCKET BILLIARDS, a type of >BILLIARDS with a large number of varieties (see below). It is played on a table with 6 pockets whose sizes depend on the size of the table. The trad. Eng. pocket billiards table is 6ft. and 1½in. wide (about 183-184cm) and 12ft. long (about 366cm). Eng. pocket billiards is a compromise between >CAROM BILLIARDS and the numerous >POOL BILLIARDS varieties. From carom billiards it borrowed the 3 balls and the principle of employing carom shots to move the balls around the table and from pool billiards the principle that points are finally scored by putting the balls into the pockets.
Fundamentals. At the start of the game there are 3 balls on the table. They are identical to the balls employed in carom billiards games and are called the white ball, the spot white ball and the red ball, respectively. The white ball and spot white ball may both function as cue balls. But the red ball may never be used as a cue ball. Since there are 2 players playing a game one selects the white ball as his cue ball. The second player uses the spot white ball as his cue ball. So if the player who selected the white ball as his cue ball is at the table he uses both the spot white ball and the red ball as object balls. When the player who selected the spot white ball as his cue ball is playing, he aims his carom shots at the white and red balls. Points are scored when: 1) a player puts any of the balls into a pocket. When the white ball (or the spot white ball in the case of the second player) is pocketed, a player scores 2pts. When he pockets the red ball he scores 3pts. This scoring method is called a *winning hazard* or simply a *hazard* or, sometimes, a *pot*; 2) a player shoots a carom, i.e. when his cue ball hits the two object balls in succession. Here, he scores 2pts. irrespective of whether the cue ball hit the 2 balls one after another or simultaneously (e.g. when the 2 balls touch each other). Points scored in this way are called a *cannon* or *carom*; 3) a player puts the cue ball in one of the pockets after it touched one of the object balls. Points scored in this way are called a *losing hazard* or a *loser*. He scores 2pts. if the cue ball touched the second white ball and 3pts. if the cue ball touched the red one. When the red ball is put into the same pocket or different pockets 2 times in a row it is returned onto the table and placed on the so-called *center spot* (i.e. a spot at the intersection of the longitudinal and transverse axes of the table). If it is put into a pocket one time or many times but not in a row (i.e. white balls are put into the pockets in between), the red ball is returned onto the table and placed on the so-called *billiard spot* (i.e. a spot at the intersection of the table's longitudinal axis and an imaginary transverse axis drawn at $^{1}/_{8}$ of the table length from the foot cushion).
A player continues playing until he makes a shot after which he does not score any points. Then, the second player takes over. A game of Eng. pocket billiards is played by 2 individual players or 2 pairs. Sometimes a different number of players is allowed. To avoid a situation whereby one of the players plays on end without making any mistakes, various additional restrictions are introduced, especially at the championship level. For example *losing hazard* points may only be scored until a player has won 15pts. in a row (during less important games the upper limit here is 25pts.). The upper limit for *cannons* is usu. 35pts. After each series of points scored by the same type of shot a player has to switch to a different scoring method. For example, after scoring 15 consecutive *losing hazard* points the next point has to be scored by a *winning hazard* or *cannon* (*carom*), etc. A special point-winning rule called an *indirect cannon* is introduced during the most important championship games. *Indirect cannon* means that after touching the first playing ball the cue ball must bounce off a cushion at least once before touching the second playing ball. A game of Eng. pocket billiards is supervised by a *referee* whose decisions are final. He may be accompanied by an auxiliary referee, the so-called *marker*, who keeps the score.

ÉPÉE, see >FENCING.

EPHEBIA, (Gk. *ephebos* from *hebe* – young manhood), in ancient Greece an obligatory military service of youths aged 18-20. It was enforced in Athens from around the 5th cent. BC. It included both physical exercise and the study of poetry, music, and singing. It applied only to free citizens of the Athenian city-state (*polis*). In the Hellenic period (336--30 BC) it spread throughout Greece at a time when military and sports exercise was decreasing in favor of intellectual education. Ephebe training continued for 1 year and was carried out in a *gymnasion*. A gymnasion was a building complex that developed from simple training grounds and wooden barracks into a complicated set of constructions resembling a park full of stone buildings with refined columns, where rooms for training, massages, strolls, and studying were located. Those buildings included first of all the *palaistra* – originally a place for wrestling exercises (Gk. *pale* – wrestling), later on also used for other disciplines; then the *ephebeion* – a building for certain exercises and studying, including a library, and rooms for discussions and lectures in philosophy; next there was the *ksystos* – a kind of portico or hall under a roof supported on columns. The ksystos had a length of 1 stadium (which was a Gk. measure of length; depending on local measurements it was roughly 160-190m) and was located along the wall of the principal building of the gymnasion. It was used for physical exercise in bad weather, esp. for running races in winter. The last major building was a stadium where various competitions were organized. The ephebes' teachers were the *sophronistai*.

EPISKYROS, also in full form *sphaira episkyros* [Gk. *sphaira* – a ball + *skyros, skyrotos* – stone, cobble-stoned]. A team ball game practiced in ancient Greece. The number of players varied in different times and places. The size of the playing field is unknown but likely differed substantially from place to place depending on local traditions. There is no doubt, however, that the pitch was divided into 2 halves by a line marked with chalk or a string of stones onto which a ball was placed. Behind each team a goal line was marked to delimit the playing field. The object of the game was to snatch the ball sitting on the halfway line and to throw it across the opposing team's line, prob. above the opponents' heads. The opponents were forced, therefore, to move away from the halfway line as they were supposed to catch the ball before it crossed their goal line. After catching the ball, the team holding it attempted to throw it in the same way across the other team's goal line. The team first to succeed in pitching the ball across their opponent's goal line was the winner.
History. Episkyros was described in the work entitled *Onomasticon*, written by Gk. lexicographer Julius Pollux (Gk. Polideukes), who lived in the 2nd cent. AD in Egypt. The game is also pictured in a relief from around the 4th cent. BC sculpted on the foundation of one of the 3 so called Kouros statues, placed on the Themistocles wall in Kertameikos. Though the relief portrays two 3-player teams, this should not necessary be taken as proof that the number of players in an episkyros team was 3, since the artist might have presented only a selected incident of the game. Another game that was similar to episkyros was practiced in Sparta, as described by Pausanias in his *Description of Greece* (III, 14, 6). It was organized annually with teams of up to 15 players competing for a prize. The game was played in the nude, as in the Gk. Ol.G., though it never became an Olympic discipline. Most prob. it formed an element of the ephebes' – youths aged 18-20 – training called *agoge* and practiced in gymnasiums. Lukian describes the game as brutal, for players assaulted one another and hit their opponents with all their might. It can be concluded from one of the ancient inscriptions that an award in episkyros matches was a sickle. The prizes given in that Spartan var. of the game seem to have had more of a symbolic and prestigious value than any material worth.

N.B. Crowther, *Team Sports in Ancient Greece*, IJHS, 1995; L. Gründel, in *Archäologischer Anzeiger*, 1925, I-II; K. Schneider, *Sphaeristerium* in *Paulys Real Encyclopädie*, ed. G. Wissow, 1929.

EPOSTRAKISMOS, Gk. for 'throwing shells'. An equivalent of >DUCKS AND DRAKES [Gk. *ep, epi* – on, over + *ostrakon* – a shell + *-ismos* – nominal ending]. In ancient Rome the same game was referred to as >TESTULAM MARINAM IACERE.

Equestrian acrobatics.

EPWORTH HOOD, a trad. Brit. ball game, at least several hundred yrs. old, practiced in Epworth in North Lincolnshire. Two spontaneously organized teams compete for a ball. The goals are 2 selected inns located in 2 neighboring villages. The winning team is the one who succeeds in carrying the ball to their inn, where not only fame but also appropriate food and drinks are awaiting the victors. A similar game, albeit one richer in traditions and better preserved, is practiced in the nearby town of Haxey. See >HAXEY HOOD.

EQUESTRIAN ACROBATICS, extreme bodily exercises performed while riding a horse. Acrobatics on horse certainly dates back to ancient times and most likely people started practicing it as soon as the horse began to be domesticated and used for riding. Acrobatics on horse were used in many cultures and in many epochs for military training purposes and also evolved into a type of artistic show. According to H. Sienkiewicz's *Great Trilogy*, it was the Tartars who were the masters of horse acrobatics and some Poles – including colonel Michał Wołodyjowski, who surprised his Swed. opponents with his horseback tricks in *The Deluge* – took lessons from them. Acrobatics on horse developed in the 18th and 19th cent. in circuses. The breakthrough came when P. Astley (1742-1814), an Englishman, introduced horseback feats as a part of a circus show. In 1768 he established a riding school in London where he trained horseback acrobats. Since that time acrobatics on horse have been an indispensable element of all circus shows throughout the world. They involve jumps off and onto the back of a moving horse, riding a horse in the standing position (facing forewards or backwards, individually or in pyramids made of a number of acrobats) and rolling round the horse's girth or its neck, etc. See also >DZHIGITOVKA, >PUSZTA ÖTÖS, >EQUESTRIAN STUNT RIDING.

EQUESTRIAN ARCHERY, a form of archery consisting of shooting arrows while riding a horse. Equestrian archery was virtually unknown in antiquity as the Mediterranean cultures did not know the stirrup which guaranteed the stability of the rider necessary for precise shooting. The breakthrough in the development of equestrian archery seems to be credited to the ancient Parthians who originated the so-called 'Parthian shot', consisting of shooting arrows to the rear while riding at full speed with the rider's body half-turned (Cf. >PARTHIAN ARCHERY). The stirrup introduced first by the Huns

and then Mongols provided a huge impetus to the development of equestrian archery among the peoples of Asia. Equestrian archery was not popular in medieval Europe, as knightly military training gave preference to heavy cavalry rather than light mounted archers. The invention of firearms displaced equestrian archery as a weapon skill. The art of equestrian archery was mastered by the Amer. Natives after they had assimilated the horse brought to the New World by the Spanish in the 16th cent. (>INDIAN HORSEBACK RIDING). Amerindian horseback archery vanished together with the extermination of Native Amer. tribes in the second half of the 19th cent., although it was the subject of numerous paintings by Amer. and Eur. artists. The most famous paintings and drawings representing

mounted Amer. Natives while hunting buffalo with bow and arrows were made by C. Russell (1864-1926); the Ital. artist, C. Linati, who visited the US-Mexican frontier in 1828; and the German H. Möllhausen who toured the USA in the years 1853-54. Equestrian archery was immensely popular in Japan, where it was known as >UMA YUMI and had a few varieties such as >KASA-GAKE and >YABU-SAME. A form of Jap. equestrian hunting archery called >INUOMONO gave rise to sports archery.

EQUESTRIAN EVENTS, competitions in horse riding which aim at showing the mastery of perfect riding technique and control over the animal, esp. in jumping, dressage and Three-Day Event.
JUMPING (fr. *Sauts d'obstacles*) is performed in a special field – *parcours*. It covers 7 kinds of competitions: 1) normal, won by the rider who completes the course in the shortest time and getting the smallest number of penalty points; 2) fault and out; 3) six bars; 4) the puissance, with obstacles gradually raised but no time limit; 5) baton relay, passing the whip; 6) accumulator, with each participant adding the results of completing the course on 2 different horses; 7) The Nations' Cup, which involves 4-rider teams, with the best 3 scores summed up.
Sportswear consists of a hard hat, red jacket (or club colors), white breeches and long boots. Ladies wear the same but their jackets are black, rather than red. Military staff are allowed to wear their uniforms.
DRESSAGE covers a show of riding skills, ability to control the horse's pace, precision of its movements and submission to the rider's will. There are 3 levels of increasing difficulty: 1) *Prix St. George*, 2) *intermediare*, 3) *Grand Prix*. Crops are not used.
Men and women wear the same clothing: a black top-hat, red or navy dress coat, white shirt and tie, white gloves, white breeches and long boots.
THREE-DAY EVENT (*concours complet*) includes: 1) dressage; 2) endurance tests incl. cross-country run on roads or natural paths with a set speed of 12-20km/h; *steeplechase* on a 3-4km course with a set speed; a 5-8km *cross* with a set speed; 3) *showjumping*, testing the horse's condition after previous competitions. The dress for the Three-Day Event depends on the kind of test. For the *dressage* part it is the same as the dressage uniform, the showjumping suit is worn for the showjumping part and the cross-country test requires a helmet, a polo shirt, breeches and boots.
History. Domestication of the wild horse was in itself a prototype for equestrian events. In the beginning, it was purely practical. Ancient Egypt was the scene of the first attempts to associate the horse's movements with some aesthetic value, and it was

Anonymous, Balance, *1647, copperplate.*

Equestrian events: dressage and jumping on two 1967 Polish postage stamps.

Equestrian events – the horse as an extension of the rider's will.

Equestrian events.

Up and over during the sauts d'obstacles.

also where the first training rules were created. On the stele of Amenophis the 2nd in Giza, there is an inscription: '[...] when he was young he loved his horses and took pleasure in them. He was patient in breaking them in, training them and discovering their nature.' A treatise by Kikkulis, the stableman of the king of Mittania, Suppliuliumas, written around 1350 BC, was the first known manual of horse training and constituted a great step forward in the development of the field. The ancient Greeks consolidated a horse riding methodology which in many respects is still valid. It was most comprehensively expressed in 2 treatises by Xenphon of Athens (c.450-355 BC) – *The Cavalry Officer (Hipparchikos)* and *The Art. of Horsmanship (Peri hippikes)*. Since the times of Solon (7th-6th cent. BC), owning a horse and the ability to ride it were considered in ancient Greece a sign of membership in the privileged class of riders (*hippeis*). Some equestrian events became part of the ancient Olympic games, but did not include those that were based on demonstration of control over the horse and its abilities. However, the ancient Romans watched horse shows, during which troops demonstrated their skills in maneuvers and group riding. Roman patricians' houses used to have miniature hippodromes for practicing in. The theory of horse riding as a branch of knowledge disappeared together with the Roman Empire but the migration of nations did not stop its practical development. An important step forward was the Asian invention of the stirrup, which revolutionized horse riding. The Huns popularized it in Europe, and it allowed more efficient steering of the horse, together with a more stable position of the rider in the saddle. In the Middle Ages, treatises on horse riding began to be written again, esp. in France and Germany, and during the renaissance in Italy. Its development was centered around royal and aristocratic courts. There, it was meant to satisfy mili-

tary needs, as well as add splendor to court celebrations. In the 18th cent., the circus started to have its share in the development of horse riding, esp. after the changes that were introduced by the 'father of modern circus' P. Astley. He considered horse riding and acrobatics the main domain of circus art. In 1768, he founded a *Riding School* where he introduced the principles of riding displays. In 1782, he built a circus amphitheater. At the same time, his former collaborator, C. Hughes also developed riding techniques by opening a riding school. In the US, similar activities were initiated by J.B. Ricketts. In the 19th cent, there was further development of court and military riding schools, with the most influential and famous ones in Vienna, Paris, Madrid and Berlin. The father of modern horse riding is considered to be an Ital. officer and instructor, F. Caprilli (1868-1907). He wrote a textbook called *The Rules of Riding* (1901). The best riders in history are considered: A. Podhajsky (1898-1973) an Austrian officer, for many years a director of the Spanish Riding School in Vienna, R. D'Inzeo from Italy and H.G. Winkler from Germany.

On the international arena, equestrian events take place under the supervision of the Fédération Equestre Internationale FEI, est. 1921. The prototype for modern competitions were military horse championships, started in France in 1900 and organized as a way of testing horses' bravery in battle. After 1902, similar competitions took place in Italy. They were included in the program of the Ol.G. in 1912. World Cup competitions have been organized since 1966, also every 4 years but in the gap between the Ol.G. The final rules for the Three-Day Event were established after the WWII, and it is performed as an individual and team competition. Riders to win the Olympic gold twice are: Dutchman C. Pahud de Mortanges (1928, 1932) and New Zealander M. Todd (1984, 1988). In team competitions, a limited number of countries have won throughout the years: first, Sweden and the Netherlands, then the USA, Germany, Great Britain, Austria and Italy. Showjumping is also practiced as a single and team competition, and was included in the Ol.G. in 1900. The most prominent riders in its history are: German H.G. Winkler (Olympic champion in 1956, W.Ch. champion in 1954 and 1955), Italian R. D'Inzeo (Ol.G. champion 1960, Ol.G. silver medallist 1956, W.Ch. champion 1956). The World Cup finals started in 1953, and were then organized annually, later to be held every 4 years (in non-Olympic years). Dressage became part of the Ol.G. in 1912, and the W.Ch. has been held every 4 years since 1966. The following are considered the best participants in the history of the sport: H. Saint Cyr from Sweden (Ol.G. champion 1952 and 1956), C. Stückelberger from Switzerland (Ol.G. champion 1976 and W.Ch. champion 1978, silver W.Ch. medallist 1975 and 1977), R. Klimke from Germany (Ol.G. champion 1984, W.Ch. champion 1982, W.Ch. silver medallist 1985), N. Uphof from Germany (Ol.G. champion 1988 and 1992, W.Ch. champion 1990, W.Ch. silver medallist 1989). In team competitions, the world champions have traditionally been riders from France, Germany, Switzerland and, periodically, the USSR. There are also professional equestrian events organized under the auspices of commercial bodies, such as The British Show Jumping Association and Amer. Horse Show Association. The biggest permanent equestrian arenas are located in Aachen, Dublin, Geneva, Lisbon, Madrid, New York, Niece, Ostende, Paris, Rome, Toronto and Vienna.

S. Breza, *O sztuce jazdy i o koniu w służbie sportsmena*, 1926; K. Drawler & H. Franke, *Turnierreiter und Reitturniere*, 1976; M.E. Ensminger, *Horsmanship*, 1959; B. Oettingen, *Über die Geschichte und die verschiedenen Formen der Reitkunst*, 1885; L. Kon, *Jazda konna*, 1953; J.F.M.D. Saint-Phaller, *Equitation, vol. 1-2*, 1907.

EQUESTRIAN STUNT RIDING, an event in which various acrobatic stunts are performed by a rider while galloping on a horse in a circle. The horse is kept on a lunging-rein (a form of tether) by an assisting trainer.

Competitions are held individually or in teams. Teams consist of 8 riders, both boys and girls, under 18 years of age. The performance includes a mandatory program of 7 exercises executed in segments 4+3 within a time limit of 8½ min. and a freestyle program executed within a time limit of 5min., which does not specify the nature of stunts (jumps,

Equestrian stunt riding.

pyramids, flips etc.). If the mandatory program extends beyond the time limit, the extra time is subtracted from the freestyle program limit. Each team is allowed one substitute rider and one lunging assistant. The individual mandatory program includes 7 exercises and has no time limit, while a freestyle program includes also 7 exercises and lasts 1min. Both team and individual events have a carefully designed aesthetic and choreographic setting and are executed to the accompaniment of music, which is also evaluated by the judges in the freestyle program.

History. The sport derives from man's earliest attempts to master horseriding. The art of executing complex evolutions on horseback was viewed by many peoples and cultures as a skill defining the prestige of a mounted warrior. Such was its status in e.g. Oriental, esp. Mong., horseriding, as well as among the North Amer. Indians after the horse had been introduced there by the Spanish in the 16th cent. The development of equestrian stunt riding owes much to the horseriding displays popular within the Byzantine Empire. A Fr. writer M. Montagne wrote about 2 riders seen in Constantinople, who displayed their riding skills in such a way that each of them rode 2 horses standing with one leg on one horse and with the other leg on the second horse and who – while galloping – also stood on their heads in the saddles and executed a number of stunts, e.g. one climbed on the back of the other, etc. In the mid-18th cent. two Eng. horseriders Price and Johnson displayed stunts while simultaneously riding 2 horses. They switched from horse to horse, stood on one leg or on their heads in the saddle, formed a bridge with their hands on one horse and their legs on the other, etc. Such displays gained a great popularity in the following decades in many Eur. countries, where they were brought by Eng. stunt horseriders, whom we frequently know only by their last names: Balp, Bates, J. Hyam, Potts, Sampson, and Wear. Hyam was accompanied by a Fr. girl-rider named Masson, who displayed her skill in riding with one leg in the saddle and the other on the horse's head. In 1772 Englishman P. Astley revolutionized the circus by introducing stunt horseriding as the main event. He continued his successful series of Eng. circus perfomances in Paris and Vienna. The leading acrobats in Astley's equestrian circus were: Englishman C. Masson, Genoan L. Chiarini, and Frenchman P. Mahyeu. In 1790 Mayheu published a richly illustrated book of horseriding stunts, many of which were later adopted by the sport of equestrian stunts. In the 19th and 20th cent. acrobatic horseriding became routine in all circus performances, of which one of the most outstanding was the Franconi Olympic Circus, famous for its women-riders and 'horse ballerinas', such as C. Loyo, P. Cuzent, A. Lejars, C. Lerous, P. and M. Annato, L. Bassin, and E. Krenzow; and men-riders, such as P. Cuzent, J. Lejars, and G. Ciniselli (later a circus owner himself). Famous riders in other circuses included the female acrobats A. Fillis (Great Britain), A. Drouin, D. Dupont (France), E. Guerra, and T. Renz, and male acrobats F. Baucher or the brothers J. and F. Clarke from A. Rancy's circus. However, the circus origin of equestrian stunt riding delayed the recognition of the event as a sport. It was included as a one-time event called 'figure riding' in the program of the 1920 Ol.G., but – derided as being a mere circus art – it was given up as an Olympic event. The winners of the 1920 individual event were T. Bonckaert (Belgium), S.S. Field (France), and T. Tinet (Belgium), while the team event was dominated by Belgium (gold), France (silver), and Sweden (bronze). The development of equestrian stunt riding after WWII eventually led to its full recognition as a sport, though not until 1983, when an appropriate branch division was established within the International Horseriding Federation. E.Ch. have been held since 1984, followed by W.Ch. The leading riders include 3-time world champion C. Lensing (Germany) and the winner of many W.Ch. and E.Ch. medals D. Otto (Germany). The most outstanding teams include Germany, Switzerland, the USA, Sweden, and Poland.

B. Danowicz, *An Olymic Circus* (1984), personal information from J. Ratajczak and S. Kęszycki, Polish Horseriding Federation.

ERHIM-BUHUDBUR, wrestling practiced by Buryat – a community of Mong. origin. The discipline is similar to Mong. wrestling >BÖKHIIN BARILDAAN (BUH). The two differ, however, in some elements of the technique and outfit employed during matches. The fight is lost by a wrestler who touches the floor with any part of his body other than his feet and legs up to the knees. While the wrestlers from Mong. tribes fight wearing tight leather shorts, Buryat wrestlers wear long leather pants made specially for the occasion. They often roll up their pant legs for the fight. Similarly to other types of Mong. wrestling, erhim-buhudbur wrestlers are bare-chested. Directly before the fight the opponents make various ritual gestures, among which the most characteristic is rubbing lumps of earth between the palms. The gesture is not only supposed to make the fighter's hands less slippery (which, to some extent is not unlike modern weight lifters, wrestlers and gymnasts rubbing their hands with talc) but also to symbolize the wrestler's unity with the soil. Many Mong. tribes believed that a man's contact with the soil increases his reserves of vital energy. Among other Mong. tribes, a similar contact with the soil was established by touching the ground, by washing one's hands with wet sand, or by pelting sand at the opponent, which was esp. popular among shepherds. The rules governing wrestling matches among the peoples of Central Asia forbade the use of oil for rubbing into the wrestler's body before the fight, which was a rule in Gk. wrestling. After the match, the winner is rewarded with a bowl of alcohol, part of which he spills around as an offering for defending spirits. Then the bowl is handed to the family patriarch. The old man takes a small mouthful of the liquid and returns the bowl to the winner, who drinks it up. A special var. of erhim-buhudbur is a match among the representatives of the same village, divided into eastern and western parts whose borders are drawn from a ritual heap of stones known as an *owoo*.

I. Iwona Kabzińska-Stawarz, *Games of Mongolian Shepherds*, 1991; by the same author, 'Competition in liminal situations', p. II, EP, 1993, XXXVII, 1.

ERIIN GURVAN NAADAM, in Mong. 3 games of warriors or men; 3 major Mong. sports identified as a test of manhood and played in the form of a triathlon. The series includes horseracing (>KHURDAAN MOR'), wrestling (>BÖKHIIN BARILDAAN), and archery (>SUR KHARVAKH) contests. A trad. competition was held among 512 contestants who gathered during New Year's Eve referred to as the *Naadam*. After the 1921 revolution, which left Mongolia under the heavy influence of the USSR, a new ideology made the eriin gurvan naadam a part of the New Year's games, eradicating, however, a number of trad. rituals. During the contest participants are divided into the 'left' and the 'right' competing in pairs according to a system similar to the Eur. cup system. The 2 contestants who make it to the end, defeating all other competitors, fight for the title of the *Naadam* winner. In a horserace 2- to 6-year-old horses are used and the distance covered depends on the horse's age: for 2-year-olds it is 15km; for 3-year-olds about 20km; for 4-year-olds about 25km; for 5-year-olds about 28km; and for 6-year-olds and older about 35km. The competition was a form of physical training for warriors of ancient Mongolia. The most prestigious holiday during which the eriin gurvan naadam is held, is *Ikh Naadam*. In *Games of Mongolian Shepherds* Kabzińska-Stawarz reports that every year in the middle of July, great games, referred to as *Ikh Naadam*, are organized in the capital of Mongolia. This occasion brings together the strongest wrestlers, the best archers, and the fastest horses with their riders. Prizes, titles, and fame await the winners. Their names make it to the front pages of newspapers, their photographs adorn magazine covers, and they are interviewed by TV journalists. Within a few minutes the entire country learns about the results of their competition. Even in the pre-mass-media era the news about the best competitors and the fastest horses spread swiftly, only by the word of mouth, and *naadam* winners enjoy respect among the people.

Similar events are also organized locally on a relatively smaller scale. After the 1921 shift and then during Mongolia's membership in the socialist block, the competition acquired a strong trait of ideological propaganda. While keeping the form of old sports events intact, attempts were made to isolate them from an ancient feudal tradition, attaching symbolism to 'the revolution defeating the anachronic past'. Hence the competitions were accompanied by marches in which people held large banners portraying communist leaders and presenting appropriate slogans. The new ideology eradicated a number of old customs, esp. those related to religion. Initially, appearances were feigned in order to maintain some of the religious customs. During the ceremonies the lamas were allowed to pray for rain and a good harvest and to participate in the *Ikh Naadam* marches. However, in the course of time, the policy of secularization of the eriin gurvan naadam deprived the event of any religious content. The *Ikh Naadam* became not only a celebration of sports events but also an occasion during which the economic achievements of the country were summed up. During the ceremonies the most excelling workers and the most successful superintendents of Mong. kolkhozes (in Mong. *somons*) were recognized and rewarded for their work. Permits for smaller, local events of that type were issued on the basis of the economic output of a given area and its ideological involvement. A positive result of that period was the implementation of certain overall standards that made the competition more of a modern sports event. In addition, ironically enough, the eriin gurvan naadam became more democratic at that time because everybody meeting appropriate physical conditions – irrespective of their social origin and position – was admitted. The modernization was also apparent in the types of weapons selected for shooting contests; old bows and arrows were exchanged for firearms. The program was expanded with other modern sports disciplines such as football and weightlifting. Despite the ideological pressure and the advent of modern sports, trad. forms of the eriin gurvan naadam survived in Mongolia thanks to small, private celebrations such as a wedding or the birth of a child. The political reforms introduced after 1990 have done much to revive old traditions but modern civilization's tendencies will undoubtedly forestall a complete resuscitation. The new-era rationalism implanted here by means of Marxism precludes a return to old religious beliefs. In addition to a rather shallow traditionalism, Mong. youths are less interested in trad. sports in favor of more attractive, modern and televised forms that are making inroads from the West. Prob. only after it has satisfied its hunger for the culture of the outside world, from which it was isolated for so long, will Mongolia look back with greater appreciation for its heritage and attempt to return to its earlier traditions, of which the eriin gurvan naadam is an integral part.

EROBRE FLAGET, Dan. for 'capture the flag'. A Dan. running game practiced during PE classes. The playing field is divided into 2 zones, each belonging to a team. Each player places a piece of their personal belongings on the ground within their team's home zone. Then players attempt to invade the opponent's area, snatch one of the personal things placed there, and return to the base without being caught. If a player is caught, he goes to 'prison' from which he has to be freed before his team can continue the game. The player is set free when touched by a teammate and when both the prisoner and the teammate make it back to their base. The winning team is the one who first captures all the items left in the opposing team's base. In the past the object to be captured used to be a flag. In the modern var. of the game a flag as such is seldom used. Older sources do not mention that the flag was supposed to be captured as the last object, either. Perhaps, seizing all the items from the opponent's base was automatically considered as winning his zone, therefore capturing the flag.

EROBRE LAND, Dan. for 'conquering a country'. A Dan. game played with the use of a knife. A square of land, min. 2x2m, is divided into halves and one of the players starts a match by throwing a knife so that its blade plunges into the opponent's half. The place where the knife comes to rest serves as the starting point of a new line, drawn in accordance with the direction indicated by the blade's edges, that divides the opponent's 'country' into 2 parts. The opponent has the right to select the part he wants to keep, the remaining lot becoming the thrower's property. The next throw reduces the rival's country again and the game continues until the lot forming a country is so small that its owner is unable to occupy i.e. stand on it. Each party continues throwing until the knife misses the target or hits the ground with only a part of the blade, or a different part altogether, and is thus unable to stand on its end. The players can also agree the game is lost by the party whose country becomes a triangle that was hit by the opponent 3 times in a row.

J. Møller, 'Erobre land', GID, 1997, 4, 63.

ESKIMO BALL, an indigenous ball game practiced by the natives of Greenland. The game was observed by J. Davis in 1586. Another var. of Eskimo ball was practiced until the 1850s around Point Hope in western Alaska as part of whale-hunting celebrations. The game was played on a 10mi.-long field and usu. lasted a few days. Eskimo ball was also played by women.

H. Kamphausen, 'Traditionelle Leibesübungen bei autochtonen Völkern', H. Ueberhorst, ed., *Geschichte der Leibesübungen*, 1980, vol. 1.

ESKIMO GYMNASTICS, term for acrobatic exercises performed by certain N.Amer. Eskimo tribes on a suspended rope made of braided seal hide.

ESKRIMA, a Fil. school of marshal arts which consists of fencing with 2 types of weapons used at the same time: an épée held in one hand and a dagger in the other [Fil. Span. *eskrima*, Span. *esgrima* – fencing]. An alternative name is >ESPADA Y DAGA.

ESNE ONTZI GARRITZEA, a Basq. var. of a milkmen's race; its Span. equivalent is *portadores de bidones de leche* [in Span. lit. milk-can carriers]. The competitors carry 2 cans filled with milk or water at a predetermined distance. The winner is the contestant who succeeds in covering the distance, which differs from one neighborhood to another, in the shortest time.

R. Aguirre, 'Esne ontzi garritzea', GHJD, 1989, III, 101.

ESPADA Y DAGA, an alternative name for a Fil. var. of fencing called >ESKRIMA. A fencer uses simultaneously an épée (or its wooden imitation), held in one hand, and a dagger (or a type of a bayonet) in the other [Span. *espada* – an epee + *daga* – a dagger].

ESPALDA NEGRA, Span. for 'a black backside'. A type of duel with the use of fencing weapons, usu. épées with blunt tips. Espalda negra was particularly popular in Span. colonies, where it was treated as both military and sports training that kept soldiers in good shape. Observed by South Amer. Indians, it became an element of the trad. Ind. game of >JUEGO DE DARDOS.

W. Krämer-Mandeau, 'Tradition, Transformation and Taboo, European Games and Festivals in Latin America, 1500-1900', IJHS, 1992, 1.

ETON FIELD GAME, one of the ball games practiced in Eng. public schools. At the turn of the 18th cent. and in the first half of the 19th cent. those ball games evolved into the modern >FOOTBALL. The rules of the Eton field game (Eton is a town in England where one of the oldest public schools is located) crystallized in the 18th cent. The matches were, and still are, played on pitches of different sizes, depending on the size of the recreational space available, but for the most part the game is played on a standard school playground, referred to as 'the Field', 130x90yds. (118.87x82.29m). At the beginning the field's size varied within the following ranges:

EQUESTRIAN OLYMPIC CHAMPIONS

THREE DAY EVENT
1912 Axel Norlander, SWE, Lady Artist
1920 Helmer Mörner, SWE, Germania
1924 Adolph van der Noort van Zijp, NED, Silver Piece
1928 Charles Pahud de Mortanges, NED, Marcroix
1932 Charles Pahud de Mortanges, NED, Marcroix
1936 Ludwig Stubbendorff, GER, Nurmi
1948 Bernard Chevallier, FRA, Aiglonne
1952 Hans von Blixen-Finecke II, SWE, Jubal
1956 Petrus Kastenman, SWE, Iluster
1960 Lawrence Morgan, AUS, Salad Days
1964 Mauro Checcoli, ITA, Surbean
1968 Jean-Jacques Guyon, FRA, Pitou
1972 Richard Meade, GBR, Laurieston
1976 Edmund 'Tad' Coffin, USA, Bally-Cor
1980 Euro Frederico Roman, ITA, Rossinan
1984 Mark Todd, NZL, Charisma
1988 Mark Todd, NZL, Charisma
1992 Matthew Ryan, AUS, Kibah Tic Toc
1996 Blyth Tait, NZL, Ready Teddy
2000 David O'Connor, USA, Custom Made
SHOW JUMPING
1900 Aimé Haageman, BEL, Benton II
1904-08 Not held
1912 Jean Cariou, FRA, Mignon
1920 Tommaso Lequio di Assaba, ITA, Trebecco
1924 Alphonse Gemuseus, SWI, Lucette
1928 František Ventura, CZE, Eliot
1932 Takeichi Nishi, JPN, Uranus
1936 Kurt Hasse, GER, Tora
1948 Humberto Mariles, MEX, Arete
1952 Pierre Jonqueres d'Oriola, FRA, Ali Baba
1956 Hans Günter Winkler, GER, Haila
1960 Raimondo D'Inzeo, ITA, Posillipo
1964 Pierre Jonqueres d'Oriola, FRA, Lutteur
1968 William Steinkraus, USA, Snowbound
1972 Graziano Mancinelli, ITA, Ambassador
1976 Alwin Schockemöhle, FRG, Warwick Rex
1980 Jan Kowalczyk, POL, Artemor
1984 Joe Fargis, USA, Touch of Class
1988 Pierre Durand, FRA, Jappeloup
1992 Ludger Beerbaum, GER, Classic Touch
1996 Ulrich Kirchhoff, GER, Jus de Pommes
2000 Joroen Dubbeldam, NED, Sjiem
DRESSAGE
1912 Carl Bonde, SWE, Emperor
1920 Janne Lundblad, SWE, Uno
1924 Ernst Linder, SWE, Piccolomini
1928 Carl-Friedrich von Langen-Parow, GER, Draufgänger
1932 Xavier Lesage, FRA, Tame
1936 Heinz Pollay, GER, Kronos
1948 Hans Moser, SWI, Hummer
1952 Henri St. Cyr, FRA, Master Rufus
1956 Henri St. Cyr, FRA, Juli
1960 Sergey Filatov, URS, Absent
1964 Henri Chammartin, SWI, Wörmann
1968 Ivan Kizimov, URS, Ikhor
1972 Liselott Linsenhoff, FRG, Piaff
1976 Christine Stückelberger, SUI, Granat
1980 Elisabeth Theurer, AUT, Mon Cherie
1984 Reiner Klimke, W GER, Ahlerich
1988 Nicole Uphoff, W GER, Rembrandt
1992 Nicole Uphoff, GER, Rembrandt
1996 Isabell Werth, GER, Gigolo
2000 Anky van Grunsven, NED, Bonfire

125-142yds. (115-130m) by 90-97yds. (82.29-88.7m). The goals, however, irrespective of the field's size are always the same: 12ft. (366cm) wide and 7ft. (213.4cm) high. 3yds. (2.74m) from the goal line there is a parallel penalty line, also known as a 3-yd. line. At a distance of 15yds. from the goal line, also parallel to it, there is the so-called 15-yd. line. The ball is 2 times smaller than today's football. Playing time is 2x50min. In the official matches the number of players was 11, including goalkeepers, whereas in recreational meetings it can be higher than 20. The game starts with a bully formed by 4 players from each team (in the past it used to be 2). The ball can be kicked and carried in the hands. It must not, however, be passed to players outside the bully. A bully consists of playing in direct contact with other players joined in a tight formation, as if the ball were not operated by a number of players but by one only (the rule of 'play as one man'). The bully's object is 'to make ground forward' and to shift with the ball towards the opponent's goal. Such a formation is referred to as a 'bully rush'. A typical position of a player forming a bully is bending forward, with the ball at his feet. The bully is formed by the following players: 1 post, 2 side-posts, 1 back up post, 3 corners, and 1 flying man who stays at the back of the bully. The fly's function is to inform the bully, either by shouting or gesturing, about the current situation, but also – should a need arise – to seize the ball if it slips from the formation, but only if it happens as a result of an opponent kicking the ball. The ball must not be received from a teammate. The player who falls out of the bully must not touch the ball before he returns to the bully. A player possessing the ball, when he sees he will fall out of the bully, passes it to the nearest teammate. The opponents attempt to seize the ball, moving in the opposite direction. Placing the ball in the opponent's goal scores 4pts. 3pts. can be scored as a result of a 'rouge' – a tangle in front of the goal that leads to a goal as a result of rather the opponent's error than a clear kick. A rouge goal is scored when the ball lands between the goalposts after bumping against one of the defending team's players, or after a careless kick towards one's own goal. The condition for scoring a goal thus achieved is touching the ball by one of the attacking team's players when the ball is still within the goal area. The players who do not form a part of a bully are referred to as the 'behinds' and their role is to make an additional obstacle for the opponents' bully advancing towards their goal. The behinds have the following names and functions: 'goals' (an equivalent of a goalkeeper), 'long behind' – closer to the goal, and 'short behind' – closer to the bully. The match is run by 2 umpires. In the course of the 19th cent. a rule was introduced according to which a foul committed in the opponent's penalty area resulted in an umpire's decision to start a new bully at a distance of 1m from the goal of the team whose representative committed the offence. 3 fouls equal 1 goal.

History. The earliest mention referring to a ball game in Eton is a note made by W. Horman, a principal of the school in 1502-35, included in the list of Lat. maxims for the students (1519), where we can read: 'We will pley a ball full of wynde.' Eton was the cradle of a number of ball games, 2 of which, other than Eton field game, have survived to this day. Up to about the middle of the 19th cent. there were many student sports clubs, usu. grouping students from the same dormitory or the same year. Each group cherished their own traditions. In the 1st half of the 19th cent. there were at least 3 different traditions in Eton. The first, called *lower college* (the name of the college behind which the playing field was located), was a game in which the primary feature was throwing a ball at the target-goal. The second, was throwing a ball against the wall, which was the origin of >ETON FIVES and >ETON WALL GAME. The third, was a game that gave birth to the modern Eton field game. In the course of the 19th cent. those originally spontaneous games underwent certain formalization, establishing thus a tradition of a sports school. This tradition was also influenced by the general development of Eng. sport, esp. ball games. A lot of these games disappeared the moment the rules of football were systematized. The last reference to a match at the lower college is dated 1863, when the standardized rules of football were introduced in England. However, Eton field game somehow survived that regularization and from c.1830 a rather fierce competition could be observed between the ball teams and >FIELD HOCKEY ones, which also produced a number of borrowings from one discipline into another.

A heavily modified version of Eton field game is still continued at the Eton Public School – it is an obligatory subject for the freshmen. The principal competition, referred to as *House Ties*, is held every year during Lent, i.e. in the 2nd half of Feb. and the 1st half of March, with 26 teams, representing the same number of student dormitories, competing according to a cup system.

J. Arlott, *Eton Field Game*, 1975; H.C. Maxwell Lyte, *A History of Eton College1440-1910*, 4th ed., 1911; J.J. Pawson, *The Eton Field Game*, 1935.

ETON FIVES, one of the 3 major var. of >FIVES, played at Eton Public School (also Eton College) as a double game in a court surrounded by 3 walls against which a ball is bounced with a fist enveloped in a special leather glove. The ball is hit either with the hand or wrist. Except for some sporadic and officially unrecognized cases, there is no single var. of the game, the major reason being an uneven surface of the wall, which makes a single game impracticable. Whereas, having 2 players – one located at the 'upper' and the other at the 'lower' part of the court – solves the problem to a satisfying degree.

Outfit and equipment. The player's kit consists of a white shirt and shorts. The ball is made of cork and rubber, painted white. Its size is not fixed but for the most part balls similar in size to >GOLF balls are used. From 1852 to the outbreak of WWII the major supplier of Eton fives balls was Jefferies Malings Ltd., which also produced balls for other Eng. games such as >RACQUETS, >ROUNDERS, and >STOOL-BALL. In 1941, Ger. bombings over London destroyed the factory; it was never reestablished. Those balls were hand made of heavily packed felt or wool covered in leather patches. After 1945, the dominating position among ball producers was taken by the Baden Fuller (1960). The ball they produce was officially certified in 1963 by the EFA [Eton Fives Association]. However, that ball was thought to be too fast for certain courts, therefore from 1964 it has been made in another 'slower' version as well. The ball is made of a mix of cork and rubber covered in a special white mass that forms, depending on the model, 3-5 layers.

Rules of the game. A court, surrounded by the walls of the Eton chapel, or any similar construction with 3 walls, consists of the upper court – defended by one player of each team, and the lower court – defended by the other player of each team. The match starts with a serve, usu. the serving team is selected by means of a draw or a coin toss. The serve is correct only if the ball hits the wall at the height of players' shoulders without any spin or trick so that the blocker is able to receive it. The blocker has the right to accept the serve or not. Should the serve be dismissed by the blocker, the server is obliged to keep repeating it until the opponent accepts it. Usu. players do not abuse that right as they are fully aware of the fact that in the next part of the match a blocker becomes a server and the tables can turn. After a correct and accepted serve, the teams continue hitting the ball alternatively against the wall until one of them is unable to return it. The match continues until one of the teams scores 12pts., usu. in a series of 5 games whose results are added up. The winning team has to achieve at least 2pts. of advantage, similarly to table tennis or volleyball, i.e. when one team scores 12 and the other has achieved 11, the final result must not be 12:11 and the match has to continue until a result of 13:11, 14:12, 15:13, etc. is achieved. A point is won after each rally. When a rally is won by the double who is not a serving party at the moment, they are granted the right to a single serve without scoring a point. If the serving team wins such a rally, they are granted the right to serve until it changes again in a series of 2 rallies lost in a row. If a one-time serving team loses their serve, the right to serve comes back to the other team. The server, in addition to the rule of having his serve accepted by the blocker, has to follow another rule according to which he is obliged to set one foot on the lower court and to keep it there until the ball hits a wall. The playing technique includes 2 major ways of returning the ball: the first consists of hitting it against the right-hand wall so that the ball ricochets towards the front wall above the ledge located at the height of 4½ft. (1.37m) – the second ledge being located at the level of 2ft.

(roughly 60cm); and the other technique consists of directing the ball towards the front wall above the ledge, but from a distance of max. 3ft. 8in. (1.12m). Such a distance is marked by the so-called 'blackguard' – a horizontal line running from the court floor up to the ledge. The principal function of the serving player, located 'on the top step' – a position closest to the front wall, is to make the match more dynamic and to control its tempo. This requires not only precise movements but also technical versatility from the player. During the game both partners have to cooperate closely, for many returns that cannot be received in the upper court are relatively easy to take care of in the lower one. Sometimes the front player withdraws from receiving the ball in a quite unexpected manner, which requires an instantaneous reaction on the part of the back player. Although during the match the players have to be able to return the ball with either hand, the structure of the original Eton court, beside the chapel, gives preference to the skill of playing with the left hand, which puts south-paws at a decided advantage.

After each return of the ball a player is supposed to step aside to make way for the opponent to facilitate his return. However, the dynamics of the game are so intense that very often players get caught up and inadvertently block their way. That is why the match is accompanied by frequent loud commands 'let', although the general rule is to make way even before the opponent's call. Good sportsmanship reigns supreme and the players behave in so fair a manner that school matches are held without any referees. High-ranking matches, esp. among various schools, are run by the so-called marker who makes a decision in the case of any questionable situation.

History. Eton fives, similarly to other var. of >FIVES, originates from the Fr. Medieval game of >JEU DE PAUME. The oldest form of fives, other than the Eton one, was described as a game arranged by the jarl of Hertford in 1591 to entertain Queen Elizabeth while she was visiting the jarl's manor. The first occurrence of fives in Eton was documented in 1825. The court's prototype is a nook in the wall of the Eton chapel where students waiting for the morning service before their classes played with a ball. The limitation of the number of players in each team to 2 is conditioned by the size of the nook that served as court. The game became so popular with the students that in 1840, the then principal, Dr. E.C. Hawtrey, decided to construct a court which would reflect the basic features of the chapel nook with some modifications that would make the game more dynamic and less restricted. By 1847 the students' interest in the game grew to such an extent that a further 8 courts were built. Today, in Eton there are as many as 40 Eton fives courts. It is the largest concentration of such courts in the world. Up to 1877 when an Eton graduate, A.C. Ainger, codified and published the rules of the game, they were passed down orally from year to year. Then, Eton fives was adopted in other schools. In 1870, Harrow College – the first after Eton – incorporated the game into its curriculum. The first match between Eton and Harrow, won hands down by the Eton team, was held in 1885. A year later, Harrow was followed by other schools: Charterhouse, Highgate, and Westminster. By 1914, England had developed an extensive inter-school Eton fives competition system. Between 1890 and 1900 twelve Eton fives courts were constructed on the Cambridge campus. A number of courts were also built in private country halls. However, the private owners pay scant attention to the dimensions of the original court, which led to a substantial departure of a country var. of Eton fives from its original form. Eton graduates who assumed directorial positions in schools throughout England introduced the game all around the country. Between WWI and II a major Eton fives center was set up in London with the Queen's Club as the leader. The growing popularity of the game resulted in the proliferation of various interpretations of the original rules described by Ainger. That is why, the Eton Fives Association established later on, issued a more precise set of regulations that became official as of 1931. After WWII, the game was introduced in some 30 Eng. schools. Currently, Eton fives is practiced in close to 50 schools, recreation centers and clubs throughout England. The game is also played in some schools in Malaysia, Nigeria, and in some Eur. countries where the principles of Eng. upbringing by means of sports activities were popularized – not infrequently by Eton graduates. Within the Common-

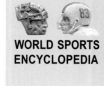

wealth it can be observed that the countries that adopted *fives* sooner also cherished other games from the group, such as >RUGBY FIVES or >WINCHESTER FIVES. A country where Eton fives gained clear advantage is Australia, where the beginnings of other var. of *fives* were rather unpromising. A sudden change in favor of Eton fives came in 1954 when the Church Grammar School in Geelong popularized the game after a series of student exchanges with a school in Shrewsbury. The first Eton fives court in Malaysia was constructed in 1905 in Perak. In Nigeria the game was implanted by one of the teachers of the Birnin Kebbi Provincial School, Mr. Hobgen, who constructed 2 courts on the school playground in 1922. In 1963 the game was so popular in Nigeria that the Eton team visited the country giving a series of international demonstration matches. In 1965 the Nigeria national representation played a run of matches with a representation of the Eton Fives Association, and in the following year Nigerian players visited England. One of the intentions behind those international contacts was the standardization of the rules on an international scale, for up to that time Nigerians played without gloves using a tennis ball. Eton fives is also practiced elsewhere in Europe. In 1924, the principal of Zuoz High School (Switzerland), Mr. Spencer, had 3 Eton fives courts constructed within the school's premises and in 1930 the Eton College team played a series of matches there. Since then, the Zuoz school maintains regular contacts with a number of Eng. schools. More courts were raised in Switzerland in the *Institut Montana* in Zugerberg bei Zug, near Zurich, and then in the Arvey bei Villars school – both toward the end of the '20s. Friendly matches between Swiss and Eng. teams are still held regularly. In Germany at least 2 courts were constructed in the '50s – in Düsseldorf and in Wallenburg. In Austria an Eton fives court forms a part of a hotel's recreational infrastructure in Mönchstein. Despite numerous imitators, both national and foreign, Eton has maintained its position as the largest Eton fives center. The college also organizes the Eton fives Eng. national championships.

ETON WALL GAME, the oldest form of football played in Eton College in England. The game has no direct relationship with another old form of football played in Eton, known as >ETON FIELD GAME. The name Eton wall game originates from the location of a unique playing field at the edge of school premises, in a narrow belt along the Slough Road. The shape of the pitch corresponds to the wall's configuration, its architectonic elements, and natural surroundings, including neighboring trees; its dimensions are as follows: length 118yds. (107.90m), width – depending on the point of measurement – only 4--5yds. (3.66-4.57m), the wall is 11ft. (3.35m) tall. This wall is traditionally used as the stand for students and other spectators watching the match who, according to an early tradition, used to dress formally, wearing top hats. The wall that continues along the Slough Road is joined from the left, at a right angle, by another wall in which, at a distance of 19yds. (17.37m) from the walls' junction, there is a gate marking the width of the zone where *shies* (small points) can be scored, which is also a small goal that facilitates more points if, after scoring a small point, the ball is placed in the goal. The width of the opposite end of the pitch is marked by an elm, a tree standing at a distance of 31yds. (28.35m) from the wall. As on that far end of the playing field, where the elm is standing, there is no gate, its outline is painted in white on the tree's trunk. The width of scoring zones, marked by the gate on the one end and by the elm on the other, is therefore different at each end of the pitch, although their depth at each end is the same – 30½ft. (9.30m). The scoring zone at the gate's side is traditionally called *good calx* – lit. good lime, meaning the line marked with lime, or possibly a good hoof or fist [Lat. *calx* – lime, line marked with lime, but also fist, hoof]. At the elm's end, the scoring zone is named *bad calx* – bad lime, hoof, etc. A goal is scored by carrying the ball into the opponent's scoring zone. During the first days of the season the field is covered with grass, but after numerous matches it is soon worn out, whereas on rainy days the playing field becomes a bog. A characteristic feature of an Eton wall game match is its resemblance to Amer. mud wrestling. Playing in such conditions often concludes in a draw with no points scored, as neither of the teams is able to break

through to the opponent's scoring zone. In addition, the narrowness of the field makes the game rather static, where the players wrestle one with another to get hold of the ball and they elbow their way towards the opponent's zone, instead of developing dynamic tactical actions. The players' assignments are varied and depend on the place each player is allotted. The moment the game commences, starting from the center, in each team there are 3 players called the *walls*, a little farther from the wall, at the level of the walls, there are 2 second-line players, known as the *seconds*, the next 2 are the *thirds*, and then 2 *fourths* and 2 *fifths*. While struggling for the ball, all players are involved mostly in forming a *bully* (colloquial Eton equivalent of *scrimmage*). At some distance towards each team's own field, there are 2 players who form the *behinds*, the one closer to the center circle is a *flying man* or a *fly* and right beside the scoring zone there is the *long*. In the past the 11th player, known as the *goals*, supported defenders. That position, however, was eliminated because of the player's scant participation and subsequent ennui.

Course of the game. The match consists of 2 halves, 30min. each, with a 5-min. break. More important matches are run by a referee and 2 umpires; matches of lesser importance are run by 1 referee. The ball is close in size to a volleyball. Moving forward with the ball is possible only in a bully, maintaining physical contact with other players, or by pressing the side of one's body against the wall. Passing the ball forward or backward is forbidden. Only lateral passes, along a line perpendicular to the wall, are permitted. Leaving the bully of players with the ball is considered an offside position. Players in a bully can shove and push away, and even box, the players of the opposing team but only with an *inside hand* and not the hand which is directed outside the bully – an *outside hand*. A player who is squashed to a degree where a lesion is possible cries, 'Air!', at which the bully has to dissolve, in order to enable the injured party to get out of the crowd. When the ball crosses the touch line parallel to the wall, it is considered dead the moment it loses speed itself or touches any player or a spectator. The game is resumed by forming a bully at the point where the ball was judged to be dead. There are 3 major tactics employed during the game: 1) a tight formation of players along the wall, which consists of squeezing through, with the ball held at the side of the wall used as a protective flank that blocks attacks; other players form a bully around the one who possesses the ball, moving along the wall with him (*bully play along the wall*) and they struggle not to let any opponents through to the one who holds the ball; the game looks like a waving crowd of players trying to squash one another against the wall; 2) a bully rush; the bully moves towards the scoring zone without touching the wall in a so-called loose bully; this tactics is most often applied as a transitional one, generally it does not achieve the final target of carrying the ball to the scoring zone; it is, however, useful when the ball is driven away from the wall and the team wants to keep it and bring it back to the wall at the first possible opportunity; if loose bully tactics are exercised for too long, however, it usu. leads to a turn-over or the ball being *dead* outside the pitch; 3) kicking the ball towards the scoring zone; this element is employed at the final phase of the game, when the bully holding the ball manages to approach the opponent's *calx*; theoretically it can be used at any time during the game but from too great a distance it is obviously ineffective and, moreover, can result in a disadvantageous situation if one of the opponent's behinds manages to steal the ball and kick it back to his own team's bully, which means a loss of the ball for the first team. Kicking the ball in such a situation is the only permitted way of passing the ball forward.

Penalties are administered rather rarely, usually after a cry produced by a flying man whose function is to direct his team's play by calling out. The most frequent penalty, resulting in a turn-over, is starting the game with a bully after a referee's timeout. More serious fouls are penalized with an additional 10yds. granted to the opponents.

The moment the players of the team that holds the ball reach the opponent's *calx*, there can be 2-phase scoring. Within the *calx* the ball can be passed backwards (*furking*) and the attackers' objective is to complete the first phase of scoring a 'small point'

known as a *shy*. Efforts to score a shy start on the *calx* with a bully into the center of which the referee throws the ball. Touching the ball before it hits the ground and throwing it against the wall achieves a shy. When a team scores a shy, it has the right to a free kick towards the goal, i.e. at one end – towards the gate in the wall, and at the other – towards the frame painted on the elm's trunk. Hitting such a small target is so difficult that it only happens every couple of years. The final score, therefore, is usually determined by means of 'small points', i.e. shies. Eton wall game is played only in Eton, along the wall on Slough Road and, unlike other football games originated in Eton, it does not have counterparts in other Eng. schools or outside England (see also >ETON FIVES, >ETON FIELD GAME). At first, probably at the end of the 18th cent., the game was played by two 11-player teams, after WWII teams

Above: View of Eton College (1685) and British Prince Harry demonstrating his skills at Eton wall game.

The Wall Game, *a painting by William Evans, the teacher of drawing at Eton in the years 1823-53.*

E WORLD SPORTS ENCYCLOPEDIA

The Fédération Internationale des Quilleurs, estab. 1952, is comprised of 54 national federations and associations, boasting upwards of 15 million bowlers.

A postage stamp marking the 100th anniversary of German bowling.

A bowling ball.

consisted of 10 players, the goals having been dispensed with.

History. The first games could not have been played before 1717, as this was the year the wall along Slough Road was constructed. If there had been an older version of Eton wall game played on those premises, it would have had both a different character and name. There are some references reporting that before 1850 a similar game was practiced along another wall on the Eton school playground. History of the school (founded in 1440) influenced the establishment of the tradition. Initially, the school was a foundation for 70 boys who were later christened *Collegers*. In time, the school started to admit students who did not avail themselves of foundation's support and who were designated *Oppidans* [Lat. *oppidum* – town]. The major Eton wall game match is still played on St. Andrew's Day – 30 Nov., between the teams of *Collegers* and *Oppidans*. It is the only match open to the public during the year, and due to its long tradition is mentioned in the British press. It is preceded by a series of training matches, played from Sept. by student teams against teams made up of senior students and teachers, the objective being to check the players' physical condition and select team members. Selection does not follow any uniform rules: the *Colleger's* 10 are selected from 70 college members, whereas the 'town' team – from an incomparably larger group of 1,100 *Oppidans*.

For the first hundred years or so, Eton wall game was played unsystematically. The tradition of regular matches started to stabilize at the beginning of the 19th cent. The oldest yet incomplete description of the game dates back to 1820. Descriptions that provide a complete historical picture of the game begin to appear after 1845. Originally the game was

European bowling.

played according to trad. principles that were passed down orally from one generation of students to the next. The first codification of the rules was done in 1849, remaining practically unmodified to these days – except for some minor adjustments and the reduction in the number of players from 11 to 10 (after 1945). In 1852 the colors of teams playing the major, annual match on St. Andrew's day were determined: to this day *Collegers* play in fair scarlet shirts with white stripes, while *Oppidans* wear dark scarlet ones with orange stripes. Since 1845 to the present day, the number of matches won and lost is more or less the same for each team, however a large portion of the matches end in a draw. The most outstanding player in the history of Eton wall game was *Colleger* J.K. Stephen in 1876-77. To his honor, during a ceremonial dinner after each annual match, a toast in Latin is proposed: *In piam memoriam J.K.S.*

EUANDRIA, [Gk. *euandria* – physical fitness, physical fullness of perfect people]. In ancient Greece a beauty contest, esp. popular in towns, held only among males.
N.B. Crowther, 'Male Beauty', *L'Antique Classique*, LIV 1985.

EUROPEAN BOWLING, a family of >BOWLING games in which a heavy ball is rolled down a long, narrow lane to knock down a group of objects known as pins. The pins are arranged at the far end of the lane near the pit. There are at least several dozen var. of Eur. bowling the most popular of which are ninepins played on asphalt, bohle and schere lanes and tenpins (referred to in the present book as >AMERICAN BOWLING) that in the 19th cent. supplanted the game of ninepins brought to America by early Du. colonists.

In ninepins the pins are set up in a 3 pins x 3 rows square formation with one corner toward the bowler. In the game of tenpins the pins are placed a foot apart in a triangular arrangement so that there are 1, 2 , 3 and 4 pins in the four rows, respectively.

Asphalt lanes are popular in Europe since they are the cheapest to construct and easiest to maintain as opposed to wooden (bohle) lanes. The lane is 1.5m wide and 25m long (incl. 19.5m of the lane proper and 5.5m of the approach). The lane is flat along its entire length. The name asphalt is now used for historical reasons since modern lanes are covered with a synthetic surface.

Bohle lanes have a wooden, slightly concave plank which is 35cm wide. The lane is 29m long (including 23.5m of the lane proper and 5.5m of the approach). The concavity varies along the plank and it is 4.5mm in the middle of the lane, then grows gradually shallower until the plank is completely level at 12.5cm before the first pin.

Schere lanes are similar to bohle ones, they are 24m long (incl. 18.5m of the lane proper and 5.5m of the approach). Their width varies. The first half of the

lane is 35 or 42cm wide and then it grows gradually wider until it reaches 1.25m near the pit. The lane concavity is the deepest at 35mm some 75cm from the start of the lane and it continues until 75cm before the first pin from where it grows gradually shallower until the plank is completely level at 12.5cm before the first pin.

The balls were trad. made of wood, usu. of lignum vitae. Recently they have been replaced by synthetic balls. The diameter and weight of a ball varies across different bowling games.

History. Archaeologists have discovered bowling balls, pins and other equipment in an Eg. child's grave dating back to 5200 BC. In Europe bowling was known among Germanic tribes as early as in the 2nd cent. AD. In Germany a simple bowling game (called *Steinzielstossen*) involving 3, 7 or 9 stone pins (*Keilen*) was practiced as early as in the Middle Ages. According to Germanic beliefs bowling was a magical game and after the introduction of Christianity bowling games were played during folk festivals which incorporated some elements of pagan rites. The oldest mention of bowling in Germany comes from the Rothenburg Chronicle (1157). In the Cologne city archives there is an old resolution by the Town Council of 1325 prohibiting bowling games winners from demanding too much prize money from the defeated. In 1463 the Frankfurt am Main Town Council organized a festival for all burghers involving a bowling competition. M. Luther is reported to have been a keen bowler. In the 18th and 19th cent. Eur. bowling was adopted by the Ger. middle classes as their favorite pastime supported by various merchant and other lodges. Bowling alleys were also constructed as public buildings near inns, restaurants and taverns. The Deutscher Kugelnverband was established in Dresden in the 1885/86 winter season but no uniform rules were developed until the early 20th cent. A pamphlet on bowling written by W. Pehle, the secretary of the Dresden association, was brought to the US around 1890 which helped popularize the sport there. The Amer. Bowling Congress, which was organized in 1895, established standard playing rules and regulations. This resulted in there appearing a number of distinctly different Amer. bowling var. They all use a flat lane and 10 pins (instead of the Eur. nine). Hence the name – tenpin bowling or tenpins. In 1926, Finland, Germany, the Netherlands, Sweden, and the USA chartered the International Bowling Association (IBA). The Fédération Internationale des Quilleurs (FIQ – International Federation of Bowlers) was established in 1952 to incorporate and replace the IBA. The FIQ is divided into 4 sections – tenpins, asphalt, bohle and schere. World and continental championships have been held since 1953. At present the FIQ has a membership of 54 national federations and associations and over 15 million players.

A direct hit – one evighedsstikbold player pegs another.

M.F. Collins & C.S. Logue, *Indoor Bowls*, 1976; G. Cwojdziński, *Techniczne i technologiczne aspekty rozwoju kręglarstwa w ujęciu historycznym (Technical and Technological Aspects in the Development of Bowling in Historical Perspective)*, in: *Z najnowszej historii kultury fizycznej w Polsce (Of the Newest History of Physical Culture in Poland)*, edited by B. Woltman, 2000, vol. IV, 187-198.

EUTAXIA, [Gk. *eutaxia* – symmetry, regular location, discipline]. Horse shows in ancient Greece.

EVIGHEDSSTIKBOLD, Dan. for 'continuously hitting a ball'. An entertaining group game in which everybody is attempting to hit everybody else with a ball that must not be dribbled. If a player has been hit, he has to sit on the ground immediately. The only way to 'get free' is to catch the ball as it passes, but the player must not move from the place where he was hit. After catching the ball, the sitting player must first pass the ball to an incarcerated comrade. If the other sitting player receives the ball, the throwing party can stand up and join the free players. The participant who caught the ball can then be set free and so on until all the players are free. If the ball touches the floor while being passed, neither party can take advantage of such a pass, but the game continues and nobody is excluded.
J. Møller, 'Evighedsstikbold', GID, 1997, 1, 26.

EWENKI ROPING HORSES, a trad. Chin. game practiced by a national minority known as Ewenki (also Owenki). The game forms a part of a regional Mikuole holiday. The competition consists of catching an unbroken horse by means of a characteristic loop made of rope fixed at the end of a long pole. The object of the game is to knock the horse down and to cut a tuft of its mane as a sign of victory over the animal.
Mu Fushan, 'Ewenki (Owenki) Roping Horses', TRAMCHIN, 54.

EXEBITI, a Dan. game involving a long square-shaped die whose ends are sharpened like a pen-

An extreme cycler on top of the world.

cil's. On the sides of the die there are numbers 1, 2, 10, and 12. This 'exebiti' is placed on a board propped aslant against a wall. The board is surrounded by a circle. Players are grouped into 2 teams – hosts and guests. The hosts strike the exebiti with a stick so that it spins in the air, pronouncing at the same time distorted Lat. words, *'Exebite, exaksebiti'* [Lat. *excipite, ecceaccipite* – strike it, look, accept]. The guest team responds: *'Roti,'* which refers to the circle [Lat. *roto* – a circle]. Then, a serve is executed by striking the exebiti with a stick and guests try to catch the die while it is airborne, in order to throw it into the circle. If they fail, they throw the exebiti from the place where it came to rest. Should the die land in the circle, points are scored and the server is exchanged for another player from the same team. If the die falls onto the line marking the edge of the circle, the throw is repeated. The game continues until 50pts. are scored by adding up the numbers revealed by the exebiti on its topside after each throw.
J. Møller, 'Exebiti', GID, 1997, 1, 124.

EXPULSIM LUDERE, Lat. for 'playing while pitching', bouncing (a ball). The phrase is not the actual name of a game, as it only describes the way a ball is returned. However, as the original name did not survive, this phrase describing the game, used in a number of original ancient texts, was adopted as its name. Expulsim ludere was one of many Roman ball games and its object was to bounce a ball against the wall. Although the rules were not preserved, it is believed the game did not differ much from the contemporary Eng. >ONE-WALL HANDBALL or Pol. >ŚCIANA. The size of the ball was not fixed, but it had to be small enough to hold the ball in one hand. Some sports historians claim the game was played up to 21pts. and the same system was adopted in some present-day games such as >TABLE TENNIS. The size of the pitch is also unknown but in the case of street games the playing field was most prob. marked by the walls of surrounding build-

ings, city walls, etc. The game was also practiced on the public pitches known, according to Gk. tradition, as *sphaerista*, as well as in gymnasiums. Theories maintaining that in some areas, in later phases of its development, the game was played with the use of rackets, seem rather far-fetched; there is no convincing proof that ancient Greeks or Romans knew or used rackets in any ball game. They knew, however, a type of leather glove which could have been used in expulsim ludere. The glove was referred to as *follis pugilatorius* – lit. 'a bag for boxing', which might suggest the ball was struck with a fist. In such a context, the glove is mentioned by Plautus – a Roman comic dramatist, and Lucan – a Roman poet. The game was popular with different social strata and it was practiced in various conditions and places, from streets to comfortable private playing fields. Cf. >DATIM LUDERE, >RAPTIM LUDERE.

EXTREME CLIMBING, sometimes also called *nontechnical climbing*, as opposed to trad. >MOUNTAIN CLIMBING for which a lot of equipment is used. Extreme climbing is practiced with almost no equipment at all, except for specialized shoes resistent to wear, and no protective gear. Extreme climbers also use a bag with talcum powder, fastened to a belt, for rubbing their hands. The sport is usu. practiced in lower rock formations, though the most experienced climbers try their luck 'free-soloing' on higher and more dangerous mountain faces. When practiced alone, without assistance or rope protection, extreme climbing involves a tremendous risk. Among well-known specialists in extreme climbing are the Frenchmen I. Patissier and P. Edlinger, who climbed the Sugar Head Mountain in Rio de Janeiro (Brazil) without assistance. In the trad. classification of difficulty levels, mountain slopes that can be climbed without equipment are marked as level III (which are slopes to be climbed with the help of hands and legs; additional equipment being used only if absolutely necessary), though extreme climbers often try for level IV slopes (where the use of ropes and other equipment is necessary), and even level V slopes (where the use of hooks is necessary). In many cases extreme climbers use only ropes and hooks, even though a slope's level of difficulty requires direct assistance. Cf. >SCALING.

EXTREME CYCLING, cycling in conditions of paramount difficulty, including such life-threatening conditions as a hill-climb and a down-hill on an active volcano, a feat achieved in January 1998 in Hawaii. >CYCLING MARATHON and more difficult varieties of >MOUNTAIN BIKING, esp. down-hills, can also be regarded as examples of extreme cycling.

Because it's there – extreme climbing.

F

Wallerant Vaillant (Flemish, 1623-1677), Portrait of a Boy with a Falcon, oil on canvas.

Limbourg brothers, Les tres riches heures du Duc de Berry: Aout (August), 1412-16, illumination on vellum, Musée Condé, Chantilly.

FA KOR, a Ghanaian lottery game whose other var., differing in certain minor details, are also known in other countries of W Africa. In Benin it is called *l'odjo, ahimé* or in Fr. *le paradis* or *le marché*. In Togo, it is known as *le pardis*; in Guinea – as *kékéréba*; and in Mauritania – as *le sig*.
The game is played by an even number of participants, each equipped with a pawn (e.g. a small stone). There is also a prize, e.g. a small stone different from the pawns. The prize needs to be small enough to fit into a clenched fist. The playing field takes the form of 7 concentric circles whose radii decrease by 1in. (2.54cm). The circles are marked on the ground with a stick or with chalk on a hard surface. The smallest circle forms the center of the field. The object of the game is to move one's pawn towards the center. The pairs of players sit outside the field of play, opposite one another. They place their pawns outside the largest circle and they draw straws to decide who has the right to make the first movement. Player A hides the prize in one fist, so that nobody can see which, stretches his arms forward, fists clenched, and asks player B which hand is holding the prize. If the guess is correct, player B takes the prize and the roles change. If, however, player B guesses wrong, A moves his pawn one circle in towards the center (after the starting round – onto the outermost circle). The player whose pawn reaches the center first is the winner.
A. Taylor Cheska, 'Fa kor', TGDWAN, 1987, 28-29.

FÆNGSEL, Dan. for 'a prison'. A Dan. running game in which teams A and B occupy halves of a playing field where they mark, usu. with stones, the so-called prison. Team B lines up along the central line that divides the field, but still standing within their home half. Team A is organized into 2 subgroups, each of which lines up along one sideline. At the sound of the starting signal, one of the B players starts running, attempting to circle the A team prison, while at the same time one of the A players tries to catch the intruder. Should the B player be caught, he is tapped on the head by the opponent who says, 'Kodla!' as a result of which the apprehended player has to move into the A team prison. However, if the B player succeeds in encircling the opponent's prison and manages to return to the B team half, the teams change their arrangement and now it is team A who tries their luck with the opponents waiting at the sides to imprison them.
J. Møller, 'Fængsel', GID, 1997, 2, 73.

FAININDA, [<O.Gk. *faininda paidzein* – to play faininda], a var. of a ball game played in ancient Greece. Detailed rules did not survive. Rudimentary mentions of faininda are found in the writings of king Jobas of Mauritania, together with the name of an expert and trainer of faininda named Fenestius. The name of faininda was equivalent to the O.Gk. verb meaning 'to show' and most probably came from a deceptive movement used in the game of first showing the ball to the opponent and then quickly hiding it or passing to a partner in an unpredictable direction. Surviving mentions of faininda in ancient literature indicate that the game was extremely popular in the 4th and 3rd cent. BC. We also know some name of faininda players, e.g. Atenajos or Autifanes. According to some ancient authors and certain modern-day historians, faininda was identical to another game called >HARPASTON.

FALCONRY, also *hawking*, the sport of employing falcons, hawks, and sometimes other birds of prey in hunting small game. The falconers, usually mounted, fly their falcons at smaller birds or animals. Although the name of the sport clearly refers to falcons, many other birds of prey have been used by the falconers. As Ł. Gołębiowski mentions in *Gry i zabawy różnych stanów* (Games and Pastimes of Various Social Classes, 1831):

The birds of prey trained for falconry [...] include golden eagles, goshawks, mountain hawk eagles, saker falcons, sparrowhawks, merlins, northern hobbies, gyrfalcons, kestrels, peregrine falcons, and other accipiters. All of them are popularly called 'falcons'. The most valued foreign prey species include Caucasian eagles, small Tartar eagles, as well as Danish, Icelandic, and Maltese falcons. Pol. falcons from the Podole region are famous all over Europe as well as hawk species such as the Lithuanian saker falcons and gyrfalcons [...].

The equipment used for training hawks included a leather hood for covering the bird's eyes called a rufter; leather thongs, called a 'jesses', attached to

A Gentleman with a Falcon, an engraving.

the bird's legs; and a cord on which the lure was whirled. The hawk was carried to the training place on a long pole (288cm), pointed on its lower end to easily stick it in the ground. On its upper end the pole had a short crossbeam, plate or crossed goose wings for the hawk to perch on.
Hawk training, according to Ł. Gołębiowski, had the following course:

Thomas Couture, The Falconer, 1855, oil on canvas, Toledo Museum of Art.

The falconers carry the hooded birds on the poles for several nights and days to be broken in to people and the life of falconry. Their legs are tied with leather thongs. Then, they are taught to fly on a cord and return to the pole where they are fed. The birds have small bells tied to their legs to facilitate tracing them if they are lost.

In old falconry manuals the hawks were divided into those used in open country, swamps, woods, and waters. The birds were trained respectively, depending on the owner's needs.

The hawk with a rufter is carried to hunting on the heavily gloved fist. Once game is spotted, the rufter is taken off and the bird flies to it, kills it, and returns to the glove where it is fed. When hunting with the saker falcon, greyhounds beat the cover; when flying hawks pointers are used to retrieve the kill. Each kind of hawk is fit to fly at different game. Eagles and true falcons are flown at heron and crane. As Mikołaj Rej puts it in his 'Life of an Honest Man', when a hawk is tamed and hooded, it follows you wherever you roam, serving you well. Saker falcons are the cruelest, as they tend to tear game apart; that is why Opaliński, the tutor of Sigismund II Augustus, the king of Poland, would not have allowed his royal student to fly saker falcons [...]. In partridge hunting, once game is trailed by the hounds, it is approached by the falconers from two sides. One flies the hawk and it flushes the game, returning to the other falconer who is holding the pole. The flushed game is then caught in the net. Hawking partridge is best in the harvest season. Sparrowhawks are most effective when flying at pigeons, sparrows and larks. The choice of the season of the year is crucial when it comes to falconry. Saker falcons are most often used for hunting from summer till late fall. Falconry hunting using the sparrowhawk commences around St. Bartholomew's [...]. In snowy weather,

saker falcons are best flown at hare and in rainy weather at partridge. On windy days, only goshawks should be used for hunting quail. The saker falcon flies swiftly in the morning, the goshawks are better in the afternoon.

History. Falconry was already practiced in the Far East in the early Middle Ages. In Korea, the art of falconry was known as >BANGEUNG during the period of the Three Kingdoms (37 BC – 935 AD). The earliest reference to Jap. hawking *hoyo* comes from 1076 AD. Falconry traditions have been maintained among the Tajik and the Kirghiz. Asian falconry traditions were brought to Europe by the Huns in the last decades of Roman Empire. The first legal regulations concerning falconry in Europe come from the Frankish state. Hawking arrived in Europe from the south, via the Iberian Peninsula, along with the invading Saracens. One of the greatest falconry lovers of the Middle Ages was Emperor Frederick II (1194-1250) who wrote the first treatise on the sport. Falconry was extremely popular in Europe between the 10th and 17th cent. After enclosures of open land and gradual deforestation of W Eur. falconry began to fade away but it never died out. A gradual but moderate revival of the sport took place after WWI. In 1923, the Order for Achievements in Falconry was established in Germany. An ardent supporter of falconry in Germany was the Nazi leader, H. Goering. The sport was also revived in France and Great Britain, where the British Falconers' Club was founded in 1927. A similar organization was formed in the USA by Luff Meredith in 1942. Falconry has been a trad. pastime of Ind. maharajas. The sport has gradually declined among the higher classes of Ind. society since the country gained independence in 1947. Hawks are still widely trained for hunting in Punjab.
M. Mazaraki, *Z sokołami na łowy*, 1977; E.B. Michell, *The Art and Practice of Hawking*, 1900; M. Woodford, *A Manual of Falconry*, 1960.

FALSE LION, the full Eng. name is *game of the false lion*, a Senegalese game, esp. popular in Saint Louis. The game is played by a group of women, a man dressed up as a woman, a man dressed up as a lion, 2 medicine men and *griots* (folk story-tellers). The player acting as lion is nearly naked, painted white with chalk. His back is covered with a lion's skin, and his head and shoulders with rags. The game is based on the Walo (also sp. Walof) legend about a man who was kidnapped and mauled by a lion, under whose power he afterwards remained. The game is usu. organized by women. It starts with the scene in which a roaring lion leaps over a group of people. In the past, the role of lion was played by a person who was actually attacked by the animal, however today, when such accidents are rather rare, the lion part is given (for a certain charge) to a robust and strong man; hence the name of the game. The false lion is accompanied by 2 false medicine men who fulfill the animal's wishes when it chants spells. The lion scours the town to the rhythm of a water tom-tom beaten out by the women, who are at a certain moment replaced by the griots. The group of females is led by the man dressed up as a woman. They sing and clap their hands rhythmically for the lion who advances with dance-like movements. Suddenly, one of the medicine men stops the dance and the lion leaps over the crowd who

A splendid display of falconry can be seen at Rosenborg Castle, Austria.

195

WORLD SPORTS ENCYCLOPEDIA

F

run away in mock panic. The lion pretends to be attacking women but finally he lets them go as he is actually looking for a man or a young male. Should he fail in his search the dance starts again and finally the lion decides to kidnap a woman. From this point onwards the ritual may take the following directions: 1) if the victim has a talisman – *fassi*, that was purchased at least one day or night before (its genuineness is checked by one of the medicine men supporting the lion), and if the fassi is approved, the lion lets the kidnapped party go; 2) if the victim has no talisman, she has to recite from memory a magic incantation starting with the following words: 'Spare me in the name of Mahomet', and if the text is recited correctly, the lion lets the prey go; 3) if the victim has no fassi and does not know the incantation by heart, the lion kidnaps and pulls her about, tearing her clothes into rags until one of the medicine men saves her. The role of the man dressed up as a woman remains rather unclear. According to some ethnologists, the game is a secularized form of an ancient religious ceremony held by Afr. hunters' associations. Other ritual forms practiced in Africa, which involve animals, do not have the element of competition between a human and an animal, as in false lion, but are rather forms of ritual dance with a fixed scenario. Depending on local traditions, the part of the lion can be taken by a leopard or a panther, as is the case with dances of the Wobe tribe in the Côte d'Ivoire.

C. Béart, 'D'une sociologie de peuples africans a partir deleursjeux', *Bulletin l'Institut Français d'Afrique Noire*, 1959, 3-4; A. Taylor Cheska, 'Game of the False Lion', TGDWAN, 1987, 31-32.

FAMNKAST, a Swed. var. of folk wrestling [Swed. *famn* – an embrace, a grip + *kast* – a cast]. Its Fin. equivalent is >RINTAPAINI.

FANG, an Icel. type of wrestling (see also >FANGBRÖTH). A more gentle variety of fang played for fun and entertainment was >LEIKFANG, which contrasted with >ILLSKUFANG – a fight with the aim of causing pain or doing physical harm to the opponent, even provoking his death. The word *fang* is the Icel. word for the space in the front of a person´s torso between his arms. Therefore, a wrestler in the fang zone is the one who is held by the opponent in between his arms. In ancient Iceland the word *fang* referred to any fight, both real and feigned, that was conducted without weapons. In this respect the term *fang*, with no additional modifiers, had 3 basic meanings: 1) a fight to death during a real battle or a duel, esp. when a warrior who had lost his weapon resorted to hand-to-hand fighting techniques practiced in the course of military training, esp. at a young age. Thus, fang was a type of a martial art employed both for attack and defense, quite often in the case of neighborly disputes or during feasts. During a real fight all kinds of tricks – some lethal – were allowed, including twisting an opponent's limbs, spine, and neck; 2) a fight provoked in order to stay in good shape or just to kill time during the winter season, when the Vikings did not put out to sea or went on horseback for their plundering raids. Fang was also practiced in order to warm oneself up in winter and, after the introduction of Christianity, before entering a cold church; 3) a fight for pleasure derived from physical effort and competition during feasts, among shepherds while grazing their herds, and in Christian times after mass, as well as in first monastic and then public schools. The forms of fang that did not involve real fighting were also referred to as *leikfang* [old Icel. *leikur* – entertainment, competition for fun + *fang*, = wrestling]. It consisted of a duel between 2 partners facing each other unarmed, with their hands uncovered, sometimes naked or wearing a special outfit, which later on was supplemented with special straps for improved grip. Spontaneous and folk forms of fang were frequently much the same as >GLÍMA, but the fight was more loosely controlled and more moves were allowed. The name of this kind of wrestling was *lausatök* (see >LAUSAGLÍMA, loose-grips). All kinds of grips were allowed, such as knocking the opponent over with a strong kick to the ankle – the so-called *bolabragd* (bull's trick); neck hold – *hálsbragd*; swing pass – *draugasveifla* (lit. 'appearing like a ghost'); side throw – *skessutak*; side turn – *skessubragd*; lifting throw – *veltibragd*; foot lift – *músarbragd*; stepping on the opponent's toes – *tábragd*; bending sidewards – *sveifla*; knee pass – *knébragd*; two-hand pliers – *grikkur*; backward side throw – *magabragd*; back throw with lifting – *backbragd*; pulling an opponent's arm or shoulder – *hnykkurinn*, and 27 other holds and ways of pulling the opponent's arms or shoulders, all of which were aimed at dragging the opponent off the balance and knocking him down. The winner was the wrestler who managed to maintain his balance while knocking the opponent down. If both participants fell down and touched the ground with their bodies, the wrestler who succeeded in standing up first was the winner. This type of wrestling (*lausatök*), with its less strict rules compared to those applied in glima, was, according to a historian of wrestling, T. Einarsson, even more popular than glima in some areas. Sometimes, because of the adverse weather conditions so characteristic of northern countries, gripping the opponent's pants during a glima match held in the open air in winter was difficult because the clothing was stiff with frost, while in the fall it was slippery with moisture.

Indoor matches were possible thanks to the convenient arrangement of a typical village house or residence. The central part of the main hall was at a lower level than the surrounding space which was used for sleeping or sitting, and during a fight it served as a natural small auditorium. In pagan times fang competitions were accompanied by a number of symbols and rituals. The fighters wore shoes marked with runic symbols, most often a *ginfaxi* – a circle with a cross the arms of which ended in additional arms, perpendicular to the principal ones, in a way resembling a swastika, and with an arrow in each of the main arms. Another runic symbol was the *gapaldur*. According to an old legend, the wrestlers should have a *ginfaxi* under their toe and a *gapaldur* under their heel. In the Icel. book of laws – the *Jónsbók* – dating back to c.1281, there is a phrase considered the first legal regulation concerning sport: 'Whoever takes part in a friendly hand-to-hand competition (*leikfang*) or in tug-of-war with fur (*skinndráttur*), does so at their own responsibility and may withdraw from it at any time'. *Skinndráttur* was a var. of genuine hand-to-hand fight. Two men sat opposite each other on the floor with a fur between them. Each pushed his feet against the other's and tried to snatch the fur from the opponent. The most noble sporting var. of fang was >GLÍMA, the name of which did not at first refer to wrestling, but rather to any action taken for the purpose of amusing oneself [O.Icel. *glegamena*, then *glimae* – joyful game; O.Icel. *gle* – joy + *gamena* – game]. In ancient Icel. culture, fang also formed a part of a general set of exercises and games with physical education elements, which were referred to as >ÍTHRÓTTIR. In Thingvellir, the place where in the 11th cent. the *Thing* – the first modern Icel. parliament – gathered, there is a place called Fangbrekka, lit. the Wrestling Slope, located at the foot of the Efrivellir hill, where a natural, large auditorium was situated, and wrestling matches were held in a circle with a specially leveled surface. The idea of fang as a wrestling fight penetrated very deeply into the Icel. culture, which can be seen in the language: the word *fang* was adopted in many fixed expressions and phrases that refer not only to fighting but to a number of other situations. Hence, the word *vidfangsefni* – wrestle, fight also means 'to have problems', and *ad ljá fangstad á ser* – lit. use that hold, refers to a situation in which one person defers to another.

Source: correspondence with Jón M. Ívarsson.

FANGBRÖTH, the complete Icel. sp. of *fangbröd*. A general term for Icel. wrestling, basically equivalent to >FANG [Icel. *fang* – a fight + *bröd* – catch, hold].

FANGE I RÆVESAKS, Dan. for 'catching in a trap'. A Dan. var. of wrestling in which one wrestler gets down on all fours with his legs and hands tied. His opponent sits beside him and puts one leg in between the tied hands and the other in between the tied legs. The opponent's task is to bend far enough under the hog-tied wrestler's belly to reach with his head to the other side. But the tied one will fall on his side, preventing the opponent from pulling his legs and hands, as a result of which the opponent is caught in a trap. There is, however, a way to avoid this: the legs have to be pulled out quickly just before putting one's head under the hog-tied wrestler's belly.

J. Møller, 'Fange i rævesaks', GID, 1997, 4, 51.

FANGE SPILLEKORT, Dan. for 'catching playing cards'. A game of skill in which one player holds a playing card on the upper edge in between his thumb and index finger and the other player keeps his thumb and index finger at a distance of 1cm from the lower edge of the card. The player holding the card releases it and the other one is supposed to catch it without moving his arm from the spot.

J. Møller, 'Fange spillekort', GID, 1997, 3, 79.

FANGEDANS GRØNLANDSK FANGELEG, Dan. for 'chasing dance', a Greenland chasing game. Participants line up in 2 rows (girls in one, boys in the other) facing each other at a distance of 1m. When the music starts, 1 dancer from the left end of each row leaves their team and starts to run. The boy is supposed to catch the girl, but they can only run sideways. The dancers can run between and around the rows. If the boy touches the girl, they both go to the right-hand ends of their rows, and another pair continues the game. Then, the roles change and the girls chase the boys.

J. Møller, 'Fangedans grønlandsk fangelang', GID, 1997, 2, 21.

FÅNGKAST, see >FÅNGTAG.

FÅNGTAG, a var. of folk wrestling practiced in the N of Sweden; starting from the Värmland region towards the south, an identical, game is known as *fångkast* [Swed. *fång* or *fånga* – catch + *tag* – catch; *kast* – cast]. In the area of Vilhelminy and Lapland a similar form of wrestling is referred to as *kastfang*. The event has been incorporated by the Swed. sports ethnologist, M. Hellspong, into a larger group of folk wrestling called >LIVTAG.

FAST DRAW, a form of competition based on the traditions of the Amer. West. It consists of drawing a revolver and shooting with accuracy in the shortest possible time. The competition is held both in women's and men's categories. The caliber of the revolvers used does not exceed 45. The most popular is an old type of *ruger blackhawk* caliber 0.357 with a barrel reamed to caliber 45. Other types in use include *colt* and *ruger vaqueros* caliber 45. All of them are adapted for fast shooting, e.g. instead of steel cartridge chambers they are equipped with aluminum ones that are lighter and therefore can revolve a split second faster. The use of live cartridges is strictly forbidden. The events are divided into those where blank cartridges are used and those with wax cartridges. The targets in blanks are balloons, 4in. (about 10cm) in diameter, that blow up after being hit by the gunpowder dust. Therefore, to improve their efficiency cartridges are filled in with an additional layer of coarse-grained powder, the so-called 'kicker', which does not burn completely during shooting. Wax bullets are placed at the tips of blank cartridges, usu. right before shooting. There are 2 types of holsters in use: an open one, which is loose enough to make drawing the gun easier, and a traditional one which fits tightly around the weapon. Shooting time is counted from the moment a referee switches on a flashing light that is located, depending on the type of competition, either above or within the target. A stopper is switched off automatically by means of a system of sensors and mechanical latches that are coupled with the target and activated in the case of a hit.

BLANK EVENTS. 'Standing blanks' (referred to in regulations as SB): 5 shots are fired at 4 or 9 balloons from distances of 8, 10, and 12ft. (249, 305, and 366cm respectively). Shots at 9 balloons are always taken from a distance of 12ft.

'Walking blanks' (WB): a series of 5 shots fired at 4 balloons while the shooter is walking. Depending on the decision made by the hosts of a given competition, the target can be either stationary or it can be located on a walking cart controlled so as to move at a fixed distance of 8ft from the walking shooter. The shooter must maintain a constant forward motion at all times.

'Double blanks' (DB): 2 rows of 4 balloons are placed in front of the shooter who is standing at the tip of the angle made by the rows of balloons. The competitor first fires at 4 balloons holding the weapon in his left hand, then passes the revolver to his right hand and the remaining balloons are shot at. There are 6 shots total and the balloons are placed every 6ft. (about 183cm). There is also a var. of DB with 9 balloons that are situated 8ft. (about 249cm) apart with the first balloon at a distance of 12ft. (about 366cm) from the contestant.

'Blank targets' (BT): the target is a round metal plate with a hole of 4-9in. (1016-2286mm) in diameter. Right behind the hole there is a balloon that can be

A fast draw competition.

FAST DRAW RECORDS IN OPEN AND TRADITIONAL COMPETITIONS (2001)

SB 4-in. balloons at 8ft. (Index):		
MEN		
open	*E. Hill*	*0.219sec.*
traditional	*H. Darby*	*0.252sec.*
WOMEN		
open	*L. Mastro*	*0.255sec.*
traditional	*P. Franks*	*0.294sec.*
SB 4-in. balloons at 8ft. (Elimination):		
MEN		
open	*E. Hill*	*0.208sec.*
traditional	*E. Thielke*	*0.236sec.*
WOMEN		
open	*L. Mastro*	*0.246sec.*
traditional	*J. Tryon*	*0.273sec.*
SW at 15ft. (Index):		
MEN		
open	*J. Nelson*	*0.240sec.*
traditional	*R. Parmentier*	*0.280sec.*
WOMEN		
open	*L. Fair*	*0.319sec.*
traditional	*J. Barry*	*0.357sec.*
DB 4-in. balloons at 8ft. (Index):		
MEN		
open	*B. Mernickle*	*0.377sec.*
traditional	*R. Parmentier*	*0.404sec.*
WOMEN		
open	*D. Wiwchar*	*0.494sec.*
traditional	*L. Faughn*	*0.577sec.*

F
WORLD SPORTS ENCYCLOPEDIA

FAUSTBALL

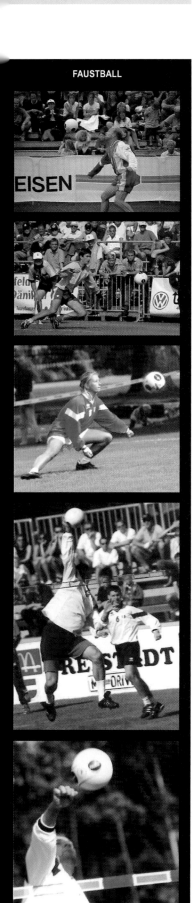

hit only if a 'bullet' goes through the hole.

WAX EVENTS. 'Standing wax' (SW): 5 shots fired from distances of 5, 8, 10, 12, and 15ft. (153, 244, 305, 366, and 457cm respectively). The target is a steel wall, several cm wide and about 2m tall, in the center of which, at the height of the shooter's hips, there is a flashing light signaling the beginning of a shooting series.

'Step-back wax' (SBW): stepping backwards, a contestant takes 5 shots, each from a different distance: 5, 8, 10, 12, and 15ft. (153, 244, 305, 366, and 457cm respectively).

'Step-up wax' (SUW): the same combination as in SBW in the reverse order.

'Walking wax' (WW): identical to walking blanks, but instead of blanks, wax cartridges are used.

'Double wax' (DW): identical to double blanks, but instead of blanks, wax cartridges are used.

'Wax targets' (WT): 2 series of shots at 2 different steel plates. The first plate is 14½x30½in. (3,683x7,747mm) and 6ft. (180cm) tall, and the second is 20x40in. (51x102cm) with its top edge at a height of 64in. (about 163cm) above ground level. The third target is a concave, round metal plate 18in. (4,572mm) in diameter. A shot is acknowledged as a hit when the bullet hits any part of a metal plate.

History. Fast draw was known in the Wild West since the beginning of the settlement process. The skill was employed both in real and pastime competitions. Between 1900-50 the entertainment forms evolved into more and more uniform sporting events. In the '50s, when a tradition of national US championships was established, the rules were standardized. Dee Wolem from Knott's Berry, who was able to fire 3 shots at a silver dollar tossed into the air, is considered to be the pioneer of this sports discipline. At the beginning there were 2 organizations promoting fast draw: the Midwestern Fast Draw Association and the Western Fast Draw Association, which were united in 1976 as the World Fast Draw Association (WFDA). Fast draw is gradually being popularized in other countries, esp. in Great Britain and Japan, where local types of weapons and different targets are used.

What Is Fast Draw?, The Internet: World Fast Draw Association: http://www.fastdraw.org

FASTELAVNSLØB, Dan. for 'carnival run'. A trad. folk form of contest between a boy, who runs alone, and 12 girls who run in a relay. The distance was usu. about 3-4km. In one of the run's varieties the boy covered the distance on horseback, but at each station where a new relay of girls started, he was supposed to dismount and then get on the horse again.

J. Møller, 'Fastelavnsløb', GID, 1997, 4, 105.

FAT TUESDAY SPORTS, see >SHROVE TUESDAY FOOTBALL, >WÄDELÖB.

FAUSTBALL, a sports discipline in which a ball is supposed to be returned, by hitting it with a clenched fist [Ger. *Faust* – a fist + *ball* – a ball], over a tape. It is a Ger. equivalent of Eng. >FISTBALL (1). The game is also similar to Dan. >NARREBOLD and Pol. >PIĘSTÓWKA. The ball can be touched only with either the fist or the shoulder. When serving, a player must be in contact with the court, touching it with at least one foot. The serve is valid if the ball touches either one of the opponents or their half of the court. When serving, a player may touch the ball only once. After entering either half, the ball can be struck 3 times, similarly to >VOLLEYBALL, plus it can be bounced once against the floor. When the ball is struck simultaneously by 2 players, it is considered to have been struck 2 times. The tape and the poles supporting it must not be touched by the players or the ball. The leather faustball has a circumference of 65-71cm, and it weighs 300-350g. The court is 50m long and 20m wide (in the indoor version it is 40x20m) and it is divided in half by the center line. At a distance of 3m from the center line, on both sides, there are 2 perpendicular base lines. The end lines (up to 5cm wide) belong to the playing area, i.e. if the ball bounces against it a serve or a return is considered valid. A color tape, which in the past used to be a hemp rope, is stretched at a height of 2m between 2 poles. Both teams are to keep returning the ball over the tape until one of them makes a mistake, which terminates a point. A team scores a point after each successful breakaway or the opponent's error. The match continues up to a time limit of 2x15min. as opposed to a score

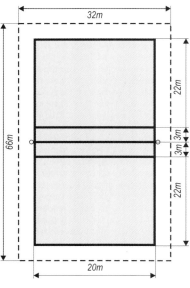

A faustball court.

limit with the highest score winning. Each half of the match is prolonged by the length of time outs called for within its duration. In the case of a draw, the match is prolonged by 2 periods of overtime, 5min. each, which are accompanied by a new draw to select a half and first serve. If overtime does not bring a conclusion, the referee calls for another 2x5min. overtime and should this one end in a draw, the match is pronounced unconcluded and a new match is organized at a later time. Each team consists of 5 players. The game starts with a serve performed with a clenched fist across the center line towards the opposing team's half. The right to choose end is carried out by means of drawing lots, if one team chooses ends, the other has the first serve. Subsequent serves are performed by the team who lost the point. The match is run by a referee and 2 linesmen equipped with signaling flags. The referee moves between the center and the base lines along the sides of the court facing away from the sun. Each team designates a scorer, both of which are responsible for keeping the scores during the match.

History. The traditions of faustball prob. date back to ancient times. The prototype could have been a game known as >EPISKYROS, continued later on in the Middle Ages in Italy as a var. of >PALLONE AL BRACCIALE. In the course of the 17th cent. it spread across Germany where its modern history began. In 1880, a principal of the Physical Education Teachers School in Munich, H.G. Weber, introduced faustball as an element of PE classes. In 1896 (according to some other sources in 1893) the first systematically organized set of rules was published. In 1921, the first Ger. championships in faustball took place and after 1945 the game was concurrently practiced in both Ger. states, where 2 separate organizations operated under the same name Deutschen Faustball-Verband (German Faustball Association). In 1960, the International Faustball Association (Internationaler Faustball-Verband) was established, which, as the number of members from out-

side of the German-speaking zone was growing, started to use its Eng. name: the International Fistball Association (IFA). In 1965, the first E.Ch. were held, and in 1969 – the first W.Ch. In international meetings Germany is accompanied by such countries as Argentina, Austria, Brazil, the Czech Republic, Chile, Namibia, Switzerland, Uruguay, the USA, and Italy. Since 1994, women's W.Ch. have also been held. Furthermore, both women and men's teams participate in the World Cup. The leading teams are Germany, Austria, and Switzerland. Faustball is becoming popular also in Asia, esp. in Japan, as well as in Southern Africa.

W. Braungardt, 'Faustball', *Turnspiele*, 1949, 8-17; 'Fistball. A 2,300 Year-Old Game', SS, Sept. 1983.

FELL RUNNING, a var. of >SLOPE RUNNING practiced in England and Wales. According to Brit. journalist and encyclopedist of sport, J. Arlott, it is a test of stamina for both long-distance runners and mountain climbers, and its name was coined in the hills of N England where it is practiced. The courses are either out-and-back ones, usu. upwards and then back downwards along the same track, or circuits, i.e. in the shape of a loop, where the runner follows different paths when climbing and descending the hill. The distances vary from 2 to 40mi. (3.2-64km) depending on local traditions. The rules concerning the race, outfit, and security are identical with those applied in >HILL RUNNING. The main difference is that it is more frequent in England than in Scotland, to collect credits for the largest number of summits visited by a runner.

History. Fell running competitions originate from the folk traditions of running races held in the Lake District since the Middle Ages. Some of the disappearing forms acquired the features of a modern sports discipline in 1868 when in Grasmere the first race of professional mountain guides was organized. In 1970, the Fell Runners Association (FRA) was established, incorporating also a similar discipline popular in Scotland and known as >HILL RUNNING. Since 1972, the Great Britain Championships have been held, and the runner who achieved the highest score in a series of predetermined races has been awarded the title of Fell Runner of the Year. The formula and the name of the competition were modified in 1981 during the British Fell Racing Championship. As the championships incorporated mostly the races organized in England and because they were held under the name which was not used in Scotland, in 1983 a separate FRA subcommittee was established in Scotland and in the following year an independent organization was constituted under the name of the Scottish Hill Running Association

Liathah ridge, one of numerous mountain ranges in Ireland where fell running competitions are held.

(SHRA). Sportsmen from both countries take part in a number of competitions, the most popular being the race from Fort William to the highest summit of Great Britain, Ben Nevis, in Inverness. It is the longest course on the island, running up to an altitude of 4,406ft. (about 1,343m) at a distance of about 15mi. (about 24km).

The most eminent runners in the history of fell running are, among others: E. Beard from Yorkshire, who set records on the majority of courses in England and Wales; P. Hall, who in 1964 brought the Scot. hegemony in the Ben Nevis race to an end; and Mike Davis from Reading – a 4-time winner of one of the most prestigious Eng. races called the Three Peaks Race, that has been held in Yorkshire since 1954. Another very important race is the Three-thousander – a Welsh race inaugurated before WWII whose name originates from the fact that runners reach an altitude above 3,000ft. (914m) when racing along the group of Welsh summits in Caernarvonshire which includes the highest of them, the Rhydd – 3,560ft. (1,112m). After climbing that, the race continues along 13 other peaks of a compara-

first fencer to score 5 hits in 6min. wins the bout. If none of the fencers scores 5 hits in that time, the winner is the fencer with the greater number of hits. In sabre, hits, or points, may be scored by cutting in a slashing motion with the edge of the blade. Scoring is similar to that employed in foil – the first fencer to score 5 hits wins the bout and if neither fencer scores 5 hits in 5min., the winner is the one with the greater number of hits.

History. The history of fencing proper is divided into 2 periods: the first, in which side arms were an important element of warfare and exercises and training during times of peace were meant to improve the military skills; and the other, in which the skill of fencing was not required in the army as new fighting techniques were developed and fencing lost its military character. In warfare ancient fencing was a basic military skill. Probably the oldest artefact is the bronze sword of Saragon, ruler of the Kingdom of Ur in S Mesopotamia (from about 5000 BC). The Divine Sword (Rusandjino Tsurugi), presumably owned by the Jap. prince Yamoto Takeruno Mikoto, is about 2,000 years old. In the Mediterranean re-

the insoles of the shoes must not have armor plates but only legs of cloth and simple leather shoes and spurs. As regards the head, nape or neck – each should cover them with a tin hat or a fur cap; the best cover they can get. And the weapons: first they must have spears, a sword and an axe and no other weapon, small or large such as a knife, misericord or a battle axe. And each must have a horse with proper harness – a bridle, well fastened saddle without anything which could throw the rider or injure the opponent or his horse such as a blade sticking out from the side or any other implement of that kind, which must not be there. And the appointed time, that is the day and place for that duel we decide to be in our courtyard, from this Tuesday in two weeks, that is on the first Tuesday after St. Lucia at six in the afternoon when each of them must appear in the tilt yards with the objects mentioned, ready mounted as stated above.

At the time when a heavy sword was used in Europe, the light-armored Arab cavalry used a light sword with a curved blade, and damascened steel contributed to the development of the armorer's craft, characterized by rich and sophisticated ornamentation. This weapon came to Europe via the Iberian Peninsula. In the 15th-17th cent. it was brought to

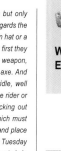

WORLD SPORTS ENCYCLOPEDIA

F

A fencing bout.

ble altitude, e.g. Gluder Fawr (3,279ft – 999.5m), Carned Llywelyn (3,427ft. – 1,044m).
J. Arlott, *Fell Running*, OCSG, 1975, 300-301; B. Smith, *Stud Marks on the Summit. A History of Amateur Fell Racing 1869-1983*, 1983; N. Matthews and D. Quinlan, *Fell and Hill Running*, 1996.

FENCING, a sporting competition using human experience in the use of side arms formerly for defense and military purposes. Thanks to the design of the weapons and protective clothing injuries or death are eliminated. A scoring system, different for each weapon, is used to decide the winner. Three weapons are used in modern fencing: the foil, the épée, and the sabre. In the past the rapier was a separate category, where the weapon was the traditional Fr. rapier – a sword with 2 cutting edges, which in the sports version was a sword with a cup-shaped hilt and a long slender blade with a blunt tip. In the past there were attempts at including >BAYONET FENCING in fencing, but the genesis of bayonet fencing is different and, moreover, the bayonet is still used for military purposes. Fencing bouts are conducted on a strip approximately 2m wide and 12m long in foil, and 24m in sabre, épée and bayonet fencing. Different rules apply to each weapon. In foil, points are scored for hits with the tip. Only hits on the torso are counted. The first fencer to score 5 hits wins the bout. If during 5 min. neither of the fencers scores 5 hits, the winner is the fencer with the greater number of hits. In épée, the entire body, head to foot is a valid target. The

gion side arms were first used in Egypt, where wooden staves were used in fencing exercises (>PALCATY). Short swords were also known to the Greeks and Romans, however, the most popular in the Roman army was a short sword borrowed from the Celtic peoples, consisting of a long, sharp-edged or pointed blade fixed in a hilt (unlike the traditional swords in which the blade was of equal width lengthwise). The Celtic sword was used by Roman gladiators (>GLADIATORIAL FIGHTS). In the Middle Ages the sword was heavy, often held in both hands. It was used in war and in the so-called wager of battle (a pledge to do battle to decide guilt or innocence by single combat). Before the fight the duellers or their seconds agreed what would be permitted in the fight and what would not. Some texts of such agreements have been preserved. In Poland, for example, the *Written contract for the wager of battle between Mikołaj Thurski and Mikołaj Smolikowski* from 1511, reads as follows:

Since Mikołaj Thurski of noble birth, party of the first part, and Mikołaj Smolikowski of noble birth, party of the second part, have come to us for reason of a conflict that they have come to, we, having heard the pleas of both of them, have allowed them to fight a duel in our courtyard. As regards the armor, weapons, horses, place and hour of this fight, all this has been clearly written in this contract engraved in this wood. And so when fighting on horseback the armor of both duelists should conform to the following: the breastplate must be made of metal sheet but it should not have metal sleeves but only sleeves of leather; likewise the wrist guards and knee-pads from the knees down to

Europe together with the armies of the Ottoman empire, via Hungary and Poland, two countries which knew a curved sword, the prototype of the later sabre, brought there in the late Middle Ages by Asiatic peoples – the Ottoman Turks and Mongols (Tartars). After gunpowder came into general use, heavy defensive armor became obsolete, and the sword became a defensive as well as offensive weapon. The basics of fencing were shaped in the second half of the 18th cent. and throughout the 19th cent. After WWI fencing proved useless in the army, but gained importance as a sport. WWII proved once and for all the uselessness of side arms, even in the cavalry, and this spelled the final end to the military character of fencing. However, the relation between bayonet fencing and the military continued until the mid 1950s. Marxbruder Gild in Lowenberg (Germany), estab. in 1383, is probably the oldest fencing association. Its members used heavy medieval swords. Lighter swords were used by the members of the Gessellschaft der Fechter, established in 1570, and the St. Michael's Brotherhood in Ghent. The latter is still active and organizes prestigious international fencing competitions.

During the Restoration, the art of fencing became one of the most important elements of a noble education. In the 16th cent. most fencing schools were located in Italy. The most famous was established by A. Marozzo. The skill of Ital. fencers was known and valued in all Europe. In 1599 the famous treaty on fencing was written by an Eng. fencer, G. Silver, *Paradoxes of Defence*, in which the author stressed

Victor Marie Picot, after C.F. Robineau, A Fencing Match between Mademoiselle La Chevaliére d'Eon de Beaumont and Monsieur de St. Georges, *1787, copperplate.*

parrying and immediate riposte; so far attack had been the basic fencing technique. Towards the end of the 16th cent. Fr. schools offered advanced level fencing training. In 1570 H. Saint-Didier increased interest in fencing terminology, naming individual movements and positions. Initial attempts to protect the fencers against injury were made at the beginning of the 16th cent. In 1515 a Spaniard by the name of G. de Cordova designed a hand guard. The foil, a long thin sword, came into being in Italy in the 17th cent. [Ital. *floretto* – a small flower, a decorative trinket]. The development of the foil as a sporting weapon resulted in a number of improvements, which contributed to the greater safety of the fencers (a leather tip on the blade's end and the first types of face masks). A prototype of the fencing face-mask was designed after 1750 by the Frenchman, La Boissiere. These improvements led to changes to the other weapons – sabre, épée and rapier, which had been very dangerous until that time. The Eng. fencer J. Godfrey used to say: 'all the knowledge I have I got from the wounds on my head' (1747). The 19th cent. brought further progress in the improvement of side arms; they became lighter and more flexible, and military features were eliminated. The basic types of protective clothing were designed in the second half of the 19th cent. Impartial refereeing was first employed at the épée competition in 1932, when the weapon was rigged to an electric device that registered the hits. Such an electric device was employed for the first time at the bayonet fencing competitions in 1952, and in 1957 at the foil competitions. The sabre was last in adopting this device (at the 1989 W.Ch.) because of problems with closing the electric circuit when the hit was made. Until the end of the 19th cent. the main fencing centers were in the army and townspeople's associations, and sports clubs in Great Britain. After 1848 continental Europe witnessed a rapid development of fencing in townspeople's associations, particularly in Germany, where the first fencing clubs were established in Hanover (1862), Offenbach (1864), Frankfurt and Cologne (1865). Sabre and foil were included in the Ol.G. in 1896 and épée in 1900. Women's foil became an Olympic event in

A fencer in full gear.

1924 and épée in 1996. A wooden stave event was featured in the Ol.G. only once, in 1904. A mixed tournament for professional fencers and amateurs was held at the Ol.G. in 1896-1900 in the foil and at the 1900 Ol.G. in the épée. An individual junior tournament in the foil was also held only once (1904). The International Fencing Federation (Fédération Internationale d'Escrime, FIE) was established in 1913. The FIE began organizing E.Ch. in 1921, in which only men's épée events were held, followed by sabre (1922) and foil (1926). Women's foil was added to the E.Ch. in 1929. In 1937, E.Ch. were replaced with W.Ch. (in Olympic years they were held as part of the Olympic tournament). Women's épée was added to the W.Ch. as late as 1989. Initially the French dominated all the men's events (E.-H. Gravelotte, G. Alibert), and the Greeks to a lesser extent (sabre – I. Georgiadis, foil – P. Pierrakos-Mavromichalis). Cuban R. Forst was twice Olympic champion in the épée (1900 and 1904). Representatives of France, Italy and Hungary dominated fencing until fencers from the USSR and Poland appeared in the 1950s and 1960s. Belgium, Germany, Sweden, Switzerland and Great Britain enjoyed occasional successes.

Sabre. The first Olympic sabre competitions were won by Greek I. Georgiadis (the 1896 Olympics and the so-called 'inter-Olympics' held in 1906); Frenchman G. de la Falaise (Olympic champion in 1900); and Cuban M. Diaz (1904). Hungary became an important player after the victories of J. Fuchs, Olympic champion in 1908 and 1912. The best Hungarian sabre fencers included, e.g. S. Posta (Olympic champion in 1924), A. Gerevich (Olympic champion in 1948 and world champion in 1951 and 1955), P. Kovacs (Olympic champion in 1952 and world champion in 1953), R. Karpati (world champion in 1954, 1959 and Olympic champion in 1956 and 1960); in more recent times P. Gerevich (world champion in 1977), G. Nebald (world champion in 1985, 1990), B. Szabo (Olympic champion in 1992). Italian sabre fencers also took a few medals: N. Nadi (Olympic champion in 1920, 1922-1923); A. Montano (world champion in 1938 and 1947); G. Dare (world champion in 1949); M. Maffei (world champion in 1971); M. Montano (world champion in 1973 and 1974). Champion titles were also won by J. Levasseur (world champion in 1950) and J. F. Lamour (world champion in 1987 and Olympic champion in 1988), both from France; J. Pawłowski (world champion in 1957, 1965, 1966 and Olympic champion in 1968) and D. Wódke (world champion in 1981), both from Poland; representatives of the USSR, among them J. Rylski (world champion in 1958 and 1963), M. Radita (world champion in 1967), W. Sidjak (world champion in 1969 and Olympic champion in 1972), W. Krovopuskov (Olympic champion in 1976, 1980 and world champion in 1982), W. Nasilimov (world champion in 1975 and 1979), G. Kierienko (world champion in 1989 and 1991) and a fencer representing the Community of Independent States, S. Pozdniakov (Olympic champion in 1996). Team

world and Olympic championships were most often won by Hungary, Italy and the USSR. Poland was team world champion in 1959, 1962, 1963 and 1969. The dominance of representatives of these countries was only sporadically broken by athletes from other countries, e.g. A. de Jong from Holland, twice the Eur. champion (at times when no W.Ch. were organized), and – after WWII – W. Etropolski from Bulgaria, world champion in 1983.

Foil. The first champions were French, among them E.H. Gravelotte, Olympic champion in 1896, and E. Coste, Olympic champion in 1900. R. Fonst from Cuba was Olympic champion in 1904. Until 1939 all Ol.G., W.Ch., and E.Ch. titles, both individual and team, were taken by the French and Italians. The best fencers among them were: N. Nadi (Olympic champion in 1912 and 1920), G. Gaudini (bronze medallist in 1928, Olympic champion in 1932 and 1936, champion of Europe in 1930 and 1934) – all from Italy, and R. Ducret (Olympic champion in 1924 and bronze medallist in 1920) and L. Gaudin (Olympic champion in 1928) from France. After 1945 foil was dominated by C. D'Oriola from France (Olympic champion in 1952 and 1956, silver medallist in 1948 and world champion in 1947, 1949, 1953, and 1954). His compatriots were world champions twice – J.-C. Magnan in 1963 and 1965 and C. Noel in 1973 and 1975; he also won the bronze medal at the 1972 Ol.G.). The Frenchman P. Omnes was the Olympic champion in 1992 and the world champion in 1990. Among Russians A. Romankov is considered the best foil fencer – a 5-time world champion (1974, 1977, 1979, 1982 and 1983), who, however, never won the Olympic gold (silver in 1976 and bronze in 1980). Among Germans the best foil fencer was F. Wessel, double world champion (1969 and 1970); among Italians – F. dal Zotto, Olympic champion in 1976 and A. Puccini, Olympic champion in 1996. In the 1960s and at the beginning of the 1970s a significant role was played by Poles – R. Parulski was the world champion and E. Franke (1964) and W. Woyda (1972) were Olympic champions. In 1972 Poles won the team Olympic gold and the W.Ch. in 1978. The Pol. team also won the Olympic silver in 1996 and 3 Olympic bronzes (1968, 1980 and 1992). Team Olympic and world championship titles were most often won by Italy, France, the USSR, and – sporadically – Cuban (1991). Hungary, a real power in other fencing weapons, has not had the same success in the foil: M. Fulop was world champion in 1957 and J. Kamuti won the Olympic silver in 1968 and 1972. The Hungarian team has won 4 Olympic bronzes (1924, 1952, 1956 and 1988).

Among women, E. Osijer from Denmark was the Olympic champion in foil in 1924. H. Mayer from Germany was the Olympic champion in 1928, world champion in 1937 and champion of Europe in 1929 and 1931; I. Elek from Hungary was world champion in 1934, 1935, and 1951 and Olympic champion in 1936 and 1948; E. Preiss from Austria was Olympic champion in 1932, and world champion in 1947 and 1949. In the 1950s the best fencers came from

199

WORLD SPORTS ENCYCLOPEDIA F

Italy: I. Camber, Olympic champion in 1952 and world champion in 1953; A. Ragno-Lonzi, Olympic champion in 1972; D. Vaccaroni, world champion in 1983; G. Trillini, world champion in 1991 and Olympic champion in 1992 (third at the 1996 Olympics); and from the USSR: A. Zabielina, world champion in 1965 and 1970; J. Novikova, Olympic champion in 1968 and world champion in 1969; W. Sidorova, world champion in 1977 and 1978; from Hungary: O. Szabo, world champion in 1962; I. Rejtö, world champion in 1963 and Olympic champion in 1964; and from Germany: H. Schmid, Olympic champion in 1960 and world champion in 1961; C. Hanisch, world champion in 1979, 1981 and 1985; A. Fichtel, Olympic champion in 1988 and world champion in 1986 and 1990. The dominance of the Italians, Hungarians, Russians and Germans was sporadically broken by the French, e.g. M.-Ch. Demaille, the world champion in 1971 and P. Trinquet, Olympic champion in 1980, and Romanians E. Stahl, world champion in 1975. Team classification was very similar to the individual.

In the épée Cuban R. Fonst was twice Olympic gold medallist, in 1900 and 1904. The Frenchman L. Gaudin was Olympic champion in 1928 and Eur. champion in 1921; at the same time he was very successful with the foil. The Ol.G. in 1932 and 1926 were won by Italians C. Cornaggia and F. Riccardi. The Italians were also team Olympic champions in 1920, 1928 and 1936 (in 1924 and 1932 the team Olympic champions title was won by the French). After WWII the best épée fencer was E. Magiarotti from Italy, many times individual and team Olympic champion and world champion with different weapons; individual Olympic champion in the épée in 1952, team Olympic champion in 1936, 1952, 1956; individual world champion in 1951 and 1954; team world champion in 1937, 1949, 1951, 1953, 1954 and 1955. In total he won 6 Olympic golds, 5 silvers and 2 bronzes, and 26 medals at W.Ch. In 1958 he was considered by the International Fencing Federation the best fencer of all times. His brother Dario won Olympic silver in 1952 and the W.Ch. in 1949. Other great épée fencers include: the USSR – G. Kriss, Olympic champion in 1964 and world champion in 1971, and Olympic silver medallist in 1968; A. Nilanchikov, world champion in 1966, 1967 and 1970; R. Edling from Sweden, world champion in 1973 and 1974; A. Pusch from Germany, Olympic champion in 1976, and world champion in 1975 and 1978; the Frenchman P. Boisse, Olympic champion in 1984 and world champion in 1985 and P. Riboud, world champion in 1979 and 1986, and winner of the Olympic silver in 1988 and bronze in 1980 and 1984. The best épée teams have come from Italy, France, the USSR and France, except for 1974-77, when the Swedes dominated the team championships. Among Poles only B. Andrzejewski was world champion in 1969. The Pol. épée team won 2 Olympic medals: bronze (1968) and silver (1980).

In women's épée, introduced into the world championships in 1989, the best fencer was M. Horvath, Olympic champion in 1992 and world champion in 1991. L. Flessel from France was Olympic champion in 1996. The best teams have come from France, Hungary, Russia and Italy.

G. Andrieu, 'L'Escrime et le duel a la fin du XIXème siecle', PISHPES 1991, 1993; M. Bettenfeld, *L'art de l'ecrime*, 1885; Z.Czajkowski, *Teoria I metodyka współczesnej szermierki*, 1968; ibid., A. Durski, *Szkoła szermierki siecznej*, 1879; J. Kevery, *Szermierka na szable*, 1952; A. Mahon, *The Art of Fencing*, 1734; J. Pawłowski, *Trud olimpijskiego złota*, 1973; J. Wężowski, *Szermierka*, 1976; consultant: M. Łuczak, AWF Poznań.

Fencing on water.

FENCING ON WATER, Ital. *la scherma nautical*, a type of rowing competition combined with stick fencing. The best known variety of fencing on water was the competition held in Cagliari in S Sardinia. The 19th cent. painting by G.M. Granieri *Cagliari marinaro* (presently at the Museo Civico in Turin) features boats with fencers. Each boat has 4 rowers; a special platform is attached to the stern on which there is a fighting fencer, the fifth member of the crew. The boats approach one another so that the fencers can begin the fight, the object of which is to knock the opponent into the water. Each fencer has a wooden stave and a shield. The competitions were started in the 18th cent. by nomadic mercenaries from the Val d'Aosta family living in Piedmont. Cf. >BOAT JOUSTING.

FENIAN RUNNING, constituted a part of the >FENIAN WARRIOR TRIAL in the pre-medieval Ireland. Runners had to go through a deep forest and all the young men undergoing the trial had to reach a specified destination and avoid being caught by a troop of warriors pursuing them. A runner's hair was braided in a special way and was not supposed to come undone while he was running through thick bushes. He was to avoid getting wounded and was to break no branch belonging to any bush or tree or even lying on the ground. His failure to observe the above rules resulted in his disqualification.

FENIAN TRIAL OF EARTH AND SPEAR, one of the tests, usu. the first one, in a series which formed the >FENIAN WARRIOR TRIAL. It consisted of burying a candidate in the ground up to this waist, after which he was equipped with a hazel stick and a shield in order to defend himself from 9 warriors who would then throw spears at him or would approach and try to stab him. The candidate was disqualified without a chance to retake the test if he showed any signs of fear.

W. Lipoński, *Narodziny cywilizacji Wysp Brytyjskich*, 1997; P. MacCana, *Celtic Mythology*, 1975.

FENIAN WARRIOR TRIAL, an all-encompassing test of a young candidate for a soldier in the troops of Fionn MacCumhail, the leader of Ireland (?-283 AD). Fionn organized a folk army of soldiers who followed rules of honor during combat and since then those rules have been referred to in the Celtic culture as *cothrom na feinne* (Fenian fair play). The army's achievements in defending the poor are the stuff of legend. Whether a candidate was admitted into the Fenian army or not, was not conditioned by noble ancestry but rather by moral and physical qualifications, which conformed to an O.Ir. principle: *is ferr fer a chiniud* (a man is better than his descent). A candidate for Fionn's crew, who were known as the Fianna or Fenians (from Ir. *féinnidh*), had to pass a series of tests arranged in a kind of a 'multiathlon' or a multi-discipline event. In the first of them a nominee was dug up to his waist in the ground and received a hazel stick and a shield with which to defend himself against spears thrown at him by 9 warriors (>FENIAN TRIAL OF EARTH AND SPEAR). He could show no sign of fear. The next trial was a run through woods, escaping from a group of soldiers who chased the candidate (>FENIAN RUNNING). Other tests included jumping over a bow, crawling under a partner's legs spread below the knees, accompanied by pulling a thorn from his foot while crawling all the while. Pulling the thorn was a symbol of sensitivity to any forms of suffering which the Fenians attempted to prevent.

W. Lipoński, *Narodziny cywilizacji Wysp Brytyjskich*, 1997, 68-69; P. MacCana, *Celtic Mythology*, 1975, 106-109.

FENLAND SKATING, a folk var. of Eng. long-distance skating that contributed significantly to the popularization of this discipline in Great Britain. The name originates from marshy areas, covered with shallow waters, in E Anglia, esp. in Lincolnshire as well as in Cambridgeshire, Norfolk, Suffolk, and Huntingdon, along the Great Ouse, Nene, Welland, and Witham Rivers' estuaries into the Wash inlet, and in the swamps surrounding the rivers far inland. In winter, the areas, which are also called the Fen Country or Fens, turn into huge ice rinks. The longest stretch of frozen Fenland that can be covered on skates without obstacle is 73mi. (about 117.5km).

History. The oldest historical testimonies concerning fenland skating date back to the 12th cent. Although skating employed in transportation, as well as in some spontaneous forms of competition, were already known in the Middle Ages, the first competition with fixed rules was held in 1814 and it was won by a skater named Young, from the village of Mepal in Cambridgeshire. In time, skating in the area of Fenland turned into public competitions that became very popular. The most famous was the contest in Chatteris in Cambridgeshire. In 1824, during one of those long-distance skating races, thousands of spectators gathered in their carriages along the riverbanks. In 1882, 'A Handbook of Fen Skating' by N. Goodman was published. From 1820, fenland skating was practiced by professional skaters who raced for prizes. In the Croyland race, where about 4,000 spectators watched the race along a track 2mi. long, Gittam from Nordelph, Norfolk, won 5 guineas. The runs were usu. organized in pairs, mostly over a distance of 2mi. To ensure a better spectacle, the racing track was limited to 0.5mi. (about 800m) and the contestants skated in 2 directions turning at barrels placed at each end. The winner of a given race qualified for the next round, and the winner of the final round was also the victor of the entire competition. In 1823, the winner of such a competition was J. Young from Nordelph, after defeating May from Upwell in the final round with a time of 5min. 33sec. The same year, Gittam, after a running start and skating with a tail wind, covered the distance of 1mi. (1.609km) in 2min. 29sec. In the 1850s and at the beginning of the 60s the leading skater was W. Smart from Welney. His achievements attracted the largest number of spectators in the history of fenland skating – more than 5,000. Smart covered the distance of 1mi. in 2min. 2sec. In 1875, the title of Fenland champion was taken by his nephew, G. Smart, who held it until 1889. Later on, the title was taken over by 2 other skaters from the Smart family. Besides the Smarts, top skaters include: Greenham (the champion in 1908 and 1912), Pearson (1929 and 1933), and N. Young (1952, 1954, 1956, and 1962). The amateur National Skating Association established in 1879, chose Fenland for their tournaments which were held mostly in Bury Fen and Lingay Fen. In 1894, the amateur Duddleston Cup 1-mi. race was established. Another well-known tournament is the Prince of Orange Bowl, held over a distance of 1.5mi. In the 19th cent. the growth of fenland skating was gradually hindered by the drainage process that decreased the watery surface. Up to the 1930s the area was the cradle of Brit. skating. When artificial rinks appeared, liberating this sports discipline from quirks of the weather, the situation changed significantly. Nevertheless, local and traditional competitions are still held, weather permitting. They are organized by the local agency of the Brit. NSA, the Fens Centre Committee.

A. Bloom, *The Skaters of the Fens*, 1957; J. Arlott, 'Fenland Skating', OCSG, 1975.

FER À CHEVAL, a Fr. var. of >HORSESHOE PITCHING, practiced in S regions of France, where in the local *occitan* language it is known as *jòc de ferradura*. The object of the game is to throw a horseshoe towards a peg (*piquet*) 20-30cm long, fastened in the ground. The throwing area is 15.25m long and 3.05m wide. The starting line is 12.2m from the peg. If the horseshoe hits the peg and lands around it, the thrower scores 3pts. If it additionally touches another horseshoe, the thrower scores 6pts. If the horseshoe hits the peg, but lands close to it, the thrower scores 2pts. 1pt. is scored if the horseshoe lands near the peg and close to the opponent's horseshoe.

Top to bottom: fencing on a postage stamp for the 1992 Olympics in Barcelona; a stamp issued for the Junior World Championships in fencing in Warsaw; a stamp issued for the Polish fencing championship; fencing motif on the stamp for the 1928 Olympics in Amsterdam; fencing motif on the stamp for the 1956 Olympics in Melbourne.

F

Field hockey on a Polish postage stamp.

The Australian goal keeper during a field hockey match at the Los Angeles Olympic Games in California.

FETTER-CUTTING RACE, a type of race popular among the peoples of C Asia, especially the Kazakh, Kirghiz and Turkmen peoples. The aim of the race was to encourage a child to learn to walk sooner and ensure his safe passage from infancy to childhood. Peoples of C Asia have always highly valued the ability of a child to become self-sufficient as soon as possible. A baby who was about to begin to walk was put on the finish line and its legs were bound together with colorful threads. The race was held among older, 7-12-year-old children. The task of the winner of the race was to cut through the fetter on the child's legs for which he received a prize. A fetter was cut with a knife provided by the family of the fettered child. Most frequently the actual knife used to cut through the fetter constituted the prize for the winner. In some areas the fetter was made of just black and white threads and the race involved not only children but also youths, adults and even the elderly.
I. Kabzińska-Stawarz, 'Competition in liminal situations', part II, EP, 1993, XXXVII, 1.

FIELD ARCHERY, known since 1935, when a group of enthusiasts organized the first field archery competition in Redlands, California, USA. It consists of shooting at targets resembling game animals with circular targets on them. The 'animals' are irregularly scattered in natural surroundings, among trees and bushes. Field archery is supposed to resemble the original primitive hunting with the use of a bow and arrows. It is practiced mainly in the USA, where around 10,000 archers are associated in more than 800 clubs. In 1939, the National Association of Field Archery was established in the USA and since 1946 annual W.Ch. have been held. The discipline is currently under the auspices of FITA, which also developed field archery regulations. A var. of field archery is >ROVING ARCHERY.

FIELD HOCKEY, a team game featuring a small ball moved about with the use of curved sticks along a rectangular grass field, either natural or artificial, or a wooden floor in a hall. Teams are composed of 11 players each. Because the ball is hard, the goalkeeper must wear protective guards and a helmet with a mask. He or she must also wear different clothes than the rest of the team with much more padding. The ball is made of cork and twine covered by either leather or plastic. It weighs 5½ to 5¾oz. The stick has a flat face on the left-hand side of the blade (or head, as it is usu. called) and the other side is curved. The head is made of wood and must have no metal fittings, sharp edges or splinters. It must be narrow enough to pass through a 2-in. ring. The max. weight of the stick is 28oz. for men and 23oz. for women. The recommended size of a field hockey pitch (playing field) is 50-60yds. wide and 100-110yds. long. At each end there is a goal, 12ft. wide and 7ft. high, which is surrounded by a striking circle which is 16yds. in radius. The sidelines and the goal line are part of the playing area; therefore, the ball is not out of play until it has completely crossed the line. The game is played in two 35-min. halves with an interval of 5-10min., at which time the teams change ends. In event of an injury the clock is stopped. There are 2 umpires and 1 or 2 timekeepers. Each umpire supervises half of the field divided by an imaginary line from one corner of the field to the other.

History. The game is one of the oldest sports in the world. Archeological excavations show primitive forms of the sport in China dating back as far as 4650 BC. A similar game was played in India from about 550 BC. The army of Alexander the Great encountered the game's Asian prototype in the years 334-331 BC and brought it to Europe. The game traveled from Greece to Rome, and, with the expansion of its empire, along the Iberian Peninsula and the British Isles, occupied from 43 to 410 AD. At the same time, another wave of borrowing from Asia came to the Mediterranean with peoples from Asia Minor, Persians and – later – Arabs. A Muslim historian Tabari (839-923) describes events from 230 AD, when an Arab ruler, Ardashi I, was supposed to legitimize his son by recognizing him among a hundred, 'or even a thousand other boys', similar in height, dress and behavior. Ardashi recognized his son without difficulty, 'and then he ordered him to lead everybody to the palace court. There, they were given curved sticks and played ball, while the king watched them with pleasure'. The game's development in the Middle Ages is uncertain. Probably, under the influence of Roman sports and partly influenced by the Arabs, the game known as >SOULE A LA CROSSE developed in France and in the Iberian Peninsula. Historians point to its associations with Span. >CHUECA, Port. >CHOCA, Basq. >TXOKO, >CHOULE, Wel. >KNAPPAN, Ir. HURLING, Scot. >SHINTY (see the list of other related sports under >HOCKEY). There were also numerous folk varieties of similar games, which are not sufficiently described to trace their origin unequivocally, such as >BADDIN, >BANDY BALL, and >BANDY-CAD (GAD). Another line of borrowing from India was started by the Brit. colonists. Modern Brit. field hockey developed on such a basis, regardless of the forms existing earlier in Europe. The first modern rules of field hockey were formulated in Great Britain in 1875. In 1886, the first field hockey federation, known as The Hockey Association, was created. In the same year, it was joined by Ireland, Scotland and Wales. The Europeanized form of field hockey was later popularized in India, which in colonial times included Pakistan. In Asia, Eur. rules superseded most of the old similar games. However, thanks to their long tradition the Asian nations have

A women's field hockey match between Korea and Spain during the 1992 Barcelona Olympic Games.

always been among the world leaders in the game. The game was included in the programme of the Ol.G. in London in 1908. Lack of interest among participating countries lead to its subsequent withdrawal from the Ol.G., until it returned in 1920. Both in 1908 and 1920, England won. In 1928, India participated in the Olympics for the first time, starting a long line of victories. They won in 1928-56, 1964, 1980, and in all other games they were either in the medals or in the finals. Other outstanding teams included Pakistan, Germany, N.Zealand, Great Britain, the Netherlands and Australia. In the 1950s the indoor var. started to develop (>INDOOR HOCKEY). In 1971, the first W.Ch. were held, won by Pakistan. Currently, there are over 60 organizations in the International Field Hockey Association (Fédération Internationale de Hockey sur Gazon, FIGH, est.1924). The most prominent players in the history of the sport have been: Ind. treble gold medallists D. Chand (1928-1936, played barefoot) and B. Singh (1948-56), later Dutchman F.J. Bovelander and Australian M. Hager. **Women's field hockey** developed independently of the men's variety. The first associations were founded in Great Britain and the USA from about 1887. In 1924, the International Federation of Women's Hockey Associations (IFWHA) was created. Also a co-educational variety (>MIXED HOCKEY), with teams consisting of 6 men and 5 women each, developed independently. Women's field hockey was included in the Ol.G. in 1980, won by Zimbabwe. Since then, the leading teams have come from Czechoslovakia (until divided in 1992), the Netherlands, Germany, Spain, Great Britain, the USA and South Korea.
A.L. Delano, *Field Hockey*, 1966; R.Y. Fison, R.L. Hollands, *Hockey*, 1951; V. Gros, *Inside Field Hockey for Women*, 1979.

FIELD TENNIS, one of the first names for >LAWN TENNIS, used c.1880-90.

FIELDBALL, a name referring in Ang.-Sax. culture to 2 field-ball games. 1) A game combining elements of handball and football, played on a pitch 180ft. long and 100ft. wide (54.86 and 40.48m respectively). Each team consists of 11 players and the object of the game is to score a goal. The game is intended for girls and it is practiced mostly in girls' schools. 2) An Amer. term for 11-player >TEAM HANDBALL. Despite its being removed from the program of international matches, it is still practiced in the USA, esp. in certain schools. It differs from its prototype in a number of details that developed on Amer. soil during WWII. From the *Encyclopedia Americana International* we learn that the Americans labeled the game fieldball in order to detach it from its Ger. roots.
The game is played by two 11-player teams. The pitch is 100-110yds. by 60-70yds. (91.44-100.58m by 54.86-64m). The goalposts are 10ft. (3.05m) wide and 8ft. (2.44m) high. The ball is 24in. (60.96cm) in circumference. The most popular distribution of players is 5-3-2 and the goalkeeper is the only player who has the right to kick the ball. The penalty area is 20x6yds. (18.23x5.49m). The halves and the right to start the game are decided by means of tossing a coin. A player cannot hold the ball longer than 3sec. and must not take more than 3 steps while holding it, after which the ball has to be passed on

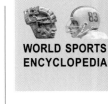

to another player. The ball can be knocked out of, but it cannot be wrenched from, the opponent's hands. The match consists of 2 halves, 30min. each; women and younger players' matches last 2x20min.

FIERLJEPPEN, complete name: *fierljeppen ou*, Eng. name *barrier broad jump*. Du. trad. var. of a long pole vault across a water hurdle, usu. a narrow stream or watercourse. A jump is made with the aid of a pole, 4.5-6m long, which a running jumper plunges into the bed of the hurdle to be overcome; the jumper leaps from one bank to the other, holding the pole as close to its top as possible. See also >LONG-POLE JUMPING.

FIGHT FOR A BALL, a Rus. school or party game for 2 teams consisting of 6-12 players each. Players stand in a large circle approx. 8m in diameter. Along its circumference several smaller circles (app. 1m in diameter) are drawn, the number of them being equal to the number of players of both teams minus 2. The large circle is broken into 2 halves by a middle line. One player of each team is a defender and stands in the center of his half circle. Defenders face one another, separated by the middle line, and hold one hand behind their backs. The referee starts the game by throwing a ball into the air and each of the defenders tries to hit it with his fist into his half. Players standing along the half circle, wearing numbers, try to pass the ball from one to another in the sequence corresponding to their numbers. They may not change their positions and must remain within their small circles. If the ball successfully passes through all team members and is then passed to the defender, the team scores a point. The defender of the opposite team meanwhile tries to intercept the ball and direct it to his teammates, who then start to pass it among themselves in the right sequence. After scoring a point, the defender changes places with the next player. The round lasts until all players of a team have functioned as defenders and is won by the team which completes that task the fastest. The game lasts 3 rounds. After each round the teams change sides.
I.N. Chkhannikov, 'Fight for a ball', GIZ, 1953, 28-29.

FIGHT FOR A BRIDE, a trial which candidates for a husband must undergo in many cultures. The development of industrial civilization has destroyed similar traditions, the traces of which can be found in modern Eur. culture only in legends and tales. In one Mong. legend, a hero, Buydar, in order to win his bride, must undergo a series of trials lasting over 3 months: he uses all his power to knock his opponent to the ground and then lifts him up with only his thumb; he shoots arrows at 60 carriages full of wood, leaving not one splinter on them. His accuracy is so great that the arrow goes through an opening in the hip bone, then passes through the eye of a needle and finally lights a faggot. A Bashkir wheedler, Alpamish, with a huge bow 360ft. tall, shoots an arrow 30ft. long, which passes through a large tree trunk. In versions told by the Turkmen Oguz the same hero shoots at a copper pot, a golden bottle-gourd or the jewelry of the girl he wants to marry. For a long time civilization did not interfere significantly with these traditions, although it occasionally introduced technical details. In an Uzbec epic a hero trying to win the hand of the beautiful Barchin uses just one bullet to knock down seven minaret towers, then wins a hand-to-hand combat with 70 rivals, rips a silk rope made from 4 poods of yarn, wins a horse race that lasts several days, and lifts up a large camel and carries him 3 times around the yurt. In one version of the epic about Alpamish the hero unsuccessfully attempts to take Barchin into his yurt. In return he has to solve 3 rhymed puzzles, after which Barchin is finally won and Alpamish, following the ancient tradition, is allowed to put his hand on her breast. A Hindu hero Arjuna from Book I of the Mahabharata reaches the target while shooting between the spokes of a turning wheel.
Various forms of tests for bridegrooms survived among many Siberian peoples until the end of the 19th cent. and required no supernatural abilities. This is not to say that passing these tests was easy. Among the Siberian Koriacs a candidate, having worked for a designated time for his future father-in-law, had to make his way through a close circle formed by the girl's family, who surrounded the girl and defended her by all means available, including beating and kicking. Having passed through, the man had to symbolically rip the girl's clothes, cut off the straps binding her hands and touch her private parts. If he failed, he had to go look somewhere else. Yet another trial awaited the candidate among the Nganasan people, who had to compete by trying to snatch the girl from other candidates and pull her to his side. The successful candidate would put the girl on a sled and try to escape with her, while his rivals brutally interfered by throwing a lasso on him in an attempt to pull him down. This fight was treated very seriously and sometimes ended in the candidate's death.
Yet another type of fighting for a bride was a competition in which the candidates would fight over certain objects that comprized the girl's dowry, such as skins or linen, which they had to snatch away from the girl's hands. A long and successful defence by the girl indicated her virtue and her longtime efforts to preserve it. In the Persian myth of Goshap Chahum the candidate for her hand, named Giv, must first win a race, then snatch a rug on which the girl sits, and finally rip it in half to demonstrate his strength. The myth clearly indicates that between the race and the trial of the rug Goshap Chahum becomes pregnant and so the trial eventually leads to marriage and sanctions the child's rights.

FIGHT FOR A CARPET, a form of competition that accompanies wedding ceremonies, popular esp. among the Mong. Bayats. It was the second event in the Mong. >WEDDING SPORT EVENTS.

FIGHT FOR A NEW YURT, a type of wedding competition among the peoples of C Asia. It was often the first in a series of events or demonstrations of skill that accompanied the wedding ceremony among the Mong. peoples. The object of competition was a new yurt prepared by the parents and relatives of the bridegroom. Here is an ethnographic description of the event:

The yurt was transported to the girl's camp, where part of the ceremony took place, and then back to the bridegroom's family camp, where the newlyweds were to live. The fight would occur between two groups. One was the attackers – young, strong men on brisk horses, who represented the girl. The yurt was defended by the other group of men, representing the bridegroom, armed with ropes, straps and sticks with which they tried to discourage the horses and the attackers, who attempted to break the ropes and tear off the covering of the roof and walls of the yurt. If they were successful, the marriage vows were broken.

I. Kabzińska-Stawarz, 'Competition in Liminal Situations', p. II, EP, 1993, XXXVII, 1.

FIGHT FOR A PUCK, a simple Rus. skating-hockey game played by 2 teams of 10-15 people each on a square rink of a size approx. 50x50 steps. Both teams assume the start off position (unspecified) and 2 players (one from each team) begin the game by a hockey-like face-off. The game continues in the way described by I.N. Chkhannikov:

Each team tries to maintain the possession of the puck by passing it among themselves, while the other team tries to snatch it away from them and keep possession etc. The game lasts 10 minutes. The team that gains possession more times, wins the game. Holding the puck with the stick is banned. Once this rule is violated, the referee blows his whistle and the puck must be passed immediately. When the puck leaves the rink, a player of the opposing team brings it back into the game at the same spot. Each player is allowed to strike the puck only three times in a row.

[I.N. Chkhannikov, 'Fight for a puck', GIZ, 1953, 92]

FIGHT ON A BEAM, a simple game of strength, once popular in the Soviet Union and other countries of the socialist block as a day room and holiday activity. The suggested equipment incl. wooden poles driven into the ground, on which a construction from wooden planks approx. 15cm in width was built to form a podium with a main level and 2 side steps. The main level was approx. 2m long and 75cm high, the side steps – 80cm long and 45cm high. The side steps were used only to climb up to the main level, on which the bout took place. Two opponents, standing astride and facing each other, extended their arms and with a sparring motion and hand blows tried to knock their opponent off balance. The level of difficulty could be increased by conducting the fight while standing on only one leg.
I.N. Chkhannikov, 'Fight on a Beam', GIZ, 1953, 62.

FIGHTING FOR A GOAT, see >BUZKASHI.

FIGHTING FOR BALANCE, a game recommended in the former Soviet Union and the countries of the socialist block as part of the so-called cultural education programs for holiday centers, day care institutions, etc. The main attribute was a balance beam made from a shaved, wooden beam 20-25cm in section and 6m in length, supported by poles 80cm in height. The basic variety was a beam set on 2 poles with a gangway at each end. The gangways had crossbars as foot supports. Another variety was the so-called flexible beam, which has supported only on one side by 2 poles located at a distance of 1m from one another. The beam was fastened to the end pole, while the other pole had a semicircular notch in which the beam rested. The section of the beam decreased from 25cm on one end to 15cm

Fierljeppen.

on the other. The beam was fastened to the poles by metal clamps. According to I.N. Chkhannikov, the competition had different forms:

Keeping balance, one should walk the beam from one end to the other and then turn back or walk backwards. It was also possible to walk sideways. On the flexible beam all exercises had to be done individually, while on the beam with both ends supported a pair competition was possible. The competitors walked towards each other from the opposite ends and either had to pass one another in the middle or try to knock the opponent off the beam. It was often a team sport, where knocking the opponent off the beam scored one point. The winner remained on the beam and fought the next opponent. The team with more points won the game.

[I.N. Chkhannikov, 'Fighting for balance', GIZ, 1953, 65-66]

FIGHTING IN A CHAIN, a game of strength incorporated into the school program in many countries.

Players are divided into 2 teams and face one another, standing in 2 rows on lines separated by 10 steps. The teams approach one another and stand on the center line in such a way that each member of one team stands between 2 members of the opposite team (with the exception of the players on both ends, who have an opponent on one side only). Players interlock hands and wait for a signal on which they try to push the players of the opposing team behind their starting line. If they are successful, they win the game. If the chain breaks during the fight, both 'culprits' are eliminated.

[I.N. Chkhannikov, GIZ, 1953, 5-6]

FIGURE ROLLER SKATING, a variety of >ROLLER SKATING in which the outcome is determined – similar to the >FIGURE SKATING var. of >ICE SKAT-

Johann Heinrich Lips, Barrier Broad Jump, *1793, copperplate.*

F

WORLD SPORTS ENCYCLOPEDIA

Joseph Farias and Tara Becker, the winners of the Junior Dance Team competition at the US roller skating championships in Lincoln, Neb.

ING – by the quality of evolutions executed while skating. The competition is held as individual events (mandatory figures, short program and freestyle), couple events and group events for women, where 4 skaters simultaneously perform a 3-min. program. An additional event is dancing. E.Ch. have been held since 1937 in individual and couple events, while the W.Ch. – since 1947. The most outstanding individuals among the men include K.H. Losch (Germany, world champion 1958-66), M. Obrecht (Germany, world champion 1970-72), T. Nieder (Germany, world champion 1976-78), M. Butzke (Germany, world champion 1979-82), M. Biserni (Italy, world champion 1984-86), and S. Guerra (Italy, world champion 1987-89, 1991-92). Among women the best skaters have trad. also come from Germany and Italy and included: A. Bader (Germany, 4-time world champion 1965-68), S. Müllenbach (Germany, world champion 1973-75), C. Bruppacher (Germany, world champion 1982-84), F. Rio (Italy, world champion 1949, 1951), Ch. Santori (Italy, world champion 1985-87), R. del Vinaccio (Italy, world champion 1988-91). The domination of Germans and Italians was interrupted by an American, N. Dunn, world champion in 1976-78.

Couple skating had been dominated until 1967 by Germans, then by Americans who won the W.Ch. 19 times in the years 1968-86. In 1987-88 the event was won by an Ital. couple Mezzardi-Trevisani, which was followed again by the domination of Amer. couples – first Armstrong-De Motte (1989), then Jerne-McGrew (1990-91).

A.V. Phillips, *The Complete Book of Roller Skating,* 1979.

FIGURE SKATING, a var. of >ICE SKATING in which skaters perform specified figures and ballet movements in a graceful manner. Figure skating has 3 divisions: single figure skating, pair figure skating, and ice dancing.

Rules of competition. The performance of individual skaters or skating pair is assessed by a team of judges. The number of judges is odd and ranges from 3 to 9 on a panel, depending on the type of competition. Nine judges assess the Ol.G. and W.Ch. competitions. The marks awarded by each judge range from 1 to 6.

Figure-skating figures and movements have evolved over a period of time. New figures introduced into the sport are usu. named after their first performers, e.g. the Salchow after the Swede U. Salchow (1877-1949); or the Ritteberger after the German W. Rittberger, who introduced the figure in 1910. Single figure skating jumps were replaced with double jumps in the 1920s, first among male skaters. In 1936, a Brit. female skater, C. Colledge performed the double Salchow for the first time, which became a huge sensation. The first double Axel was performed by the American R. Button in 1948. At the Winter Ol.G. in 1952 Button performed also the first ever triple Rittenberger and a spiral jump from a squat position, later named the Buttonsitz. The first skater to perform a triple Axel was the Canadian V. Taylor in 1978; the first female skater to do the same was M. Ito in 1990. At present triple Axels are complemented with other figures, i.e. combined with other double or triple jumps or another spin or movement.

History. The origins of figure skating are closely connected with the work of the Amer. ballet master J. Haines (1845-79), who migrated to Austria during the Amer. Civil War. In Europe, Haines adapted his techniques based on dance movements to ice-skating and began to popularize the new sport, becoming the father of modern figure skating. To commemorate the life of the great master Haines's portrait is displayed in the Vienna Ice-Skating Club (Wiener Eislauf Verein) and one of the streets in Prague has been named after him. His tombstone in Finland features the inscription: 'The Amer. Skating King'. E.Ch. in men's singles figure skating have been held since 1890 and the W.Ch. since 1896. For the first time, men's, women's and pair figure skating events were included in the Olympic program in 1908 and Antwerp (1920) as part of the Summer Olympics. Figure skating has constituted part of the Winter Ol.G. since they were inaugurated in 1924. The 1930s saw the rapid development of new skating movements, techniques and means of artistic expression. Since the 1950s figure skating has become a huge media spectacle of high technical standards. The emphasis on the spectacular aspect of the sport led by the end of the 1960s

to the departure of figure skating from its ballet and dance tradition towards elaborate acrobatic techniques, especially in the men's events.

Men's figure skating. The 1920s were mostly dominated by the Swede G. Grafström, Olympic champion in 1920, 1924, and 1928, and world champion in 1922-24 and 1929. In the 1930s the figure skating lead was taken by the Austrian K. Schäffer, Olympic champion in 1932 and 1936, and world champion in the years 1930-36. After WWII R. Button became a 2-time Olympic champion and 5-time world champion (1948-52). H.A. Jenkins, the 1956 Olympic champion, won the W.Ch. 4 times in the years 1953-56; D. Jenkins, the 1960 Olympic champion, was also a 3-time world champion in the years 1957-59. The 1960s did not see any other multi-champions although M. Schenelldorfer from West Germany managed to win Olympic gold and W.Ch. in 1964; the Austrian E. Danzer was a 3-time world champion in the years 1966-68, but never won Olympic gold, unlike O. Nepeli from Czechoslovakia (Olympic champion, 1972; and world champion 1971-73).

Figure skating: women's competition.

Two US skaters dominated the sport the 1980s: S. Hamilton (Olympic champion 1984; world champion 1981-84) and B. Boitano (Olympic champion 1988; world champion 1986 and 1988). K. Browning from Canada was the world champion in the years 1989-91 and 1993 but he never won the Olympic gold medal. At the 1992 Winter Ol.G. in Albertville the championship was won by W. Pietrenko from the CIS; in Lillehamer by A. Urmanow (Russia); and in Nagano by I. Kulik (Russia).

Women's figure skating. Organized events of women's figure skating date back to 19th-cent. Scandinavia. Before 1906 women's figure skaters did not participate in the world championships. During the 1906 W.Ch. Mrs. M. Syers who decided to compete together with the male skaters, took second place, just behind the famous Swede U. Salchow (1877-1949). After this remarkable feat the ISU set up separate Women's W.Ch. in 1908. Also, in 1908 women's events were included in the Ol.G. Until the early 1930s women's skating was far below the level of men's skating due to the mere imitation of men's skating techniques and training as well as to the limited body movements imposed by wearing long skirts. Skating outfits which exposed the female body above the ankles were regarded as immoral at that time – although in the 17th cent. the Fr. ambassador to the Netherlands wrote to King Louis XIV that the young Duchess of Orange skated wearing an unusually short skirt, reaching only down to her knees. The breakthrough was made by the Norwegian S. Henie (1912-69), who became a US resident in 1940. At the age of twelve, Henie started to skate wearing a short skirt, which did not hinder any of her skating movements, thus making way for her older colleagues. She also improved female skating techniques by introducing elements of ballet and combining them with the natural movement of a woman's body.

After WWII women's figure skating came to be dominated by representatives of the UK, USA, Holland and Germany, and later by skaters from the USSR and East Germany. The most famous women's skaters of the 1950s were J. Altwegg, UK (Olympic champion 1952, world champion 1951); T. Albright, USA (Olympic champion 1956, world champion 1953, 1955); and C. Heiss, USA (Olympic champion 1960, world champion 1956-60). The 1960s were dominated by: P. Flemming (Olympic champion 1968 and world champion 1966-68) and the Dutch S. Dijkstra (Olympic champion 1964 and world champion 1962-64). In the late 1960s the East Germans started to dominate women's figure skating competitions, in particular G. Seyfert, world champion in the years 1969-70. East Germany became a women's figure skating power again in the 1980s thanks to K. Witt, twice Olympic champion 1984 and 1988, and world champion 1984, 1985, 1987, and 1988. At the 1992 W.Ol.G. in Albertville the gold was won by K. Yamaguchi, who had also won the world championship a year earlier. The Olympic champion from Lillehammer was O. Baiul (Ukraine) and the winner of women's figure skating event from Nagano was T. Lipinski (USA).

Pair skating. Pair figure skating W.Ch. have been held since 1908. The breakthrough in pair skating technique and performance is credited to the 1939 world champions, M. Herber and E. Bayer. After 1950 the best figure skating pairs included the Canadians: B. Wagner and R. Paul (Olympic champions 1960, world champions 1957-60); and the Russians: L. Bielousova and O. Protopopov (Olympic champions 1964 and 1968, world champions 1965-68), I. Rodnina and A. Ulanov (Olympic champions 1972, world champions 1969-73), and I. Rodnina and A. Zajcev (Olympic champions 1976, 1980 and world champions 1974-78). The collapse of the USSR and emergence of the CIS sports team and then Rus. national team did not affect the performance level of Rus. skaters. Olympic gold and silver medals won by the Russian figure skating pair became a sort of tradition. J. Gordjejeva and S. Grinkow were Olympic champions in 1988 and 1994, and world champions in 1986, 1987, 1989 and 1990. At the 1992 W.Ol.G. in Albertville the gold was won by the Rus. pair N. Miszkutiono and A. Dmitriew (world champions 1991-92); in Nagano the gold medallists were O. Kozakova and A. Dmitriew.

Ice dancing. The first ice-dancing W.Ch. were held in 1951. During the 1972 Winter Ol.G. in Sapporo ice dancing was included as an exhibition event; it became a permanent Olympic event at Innsbruck Winter Ol.G. in 1976. The 1970s were dominated by the Rus. pair, L. Pachomova and A. Gorszkow, the first Olympic champions in 1976 and world champions in the years 1970-74 and 1976. At the 1984 W.Ol.G. in Sarajevo, the British pair J. Torvill and C. Dean combined their ice-dancing experience with a new kind of television esthetics. Ice dancing had hitherto developed within its own domain, while televised broadcasts had sought to influence the sport's presentation. Torvill and Dean gave ice dancing a new artistic dimension and, at the same time, a new quality of television appeal. Until the appearance of the Brit. pair, most ice dancers had performed to a regular, steady tempo, and despite the artistic quality of music and dance the sport gave the impres-

Figure skating: men's competition.

sion of a 'pleasant monotony'. Torvill and Dean's choice of M. Ravel's *Bolero* with a strongly marked ascending rhythm as their musical background made their performance an exhilarating epic. The falling of both dancers to the ground at the end of their performance was a natural consequence of the growing musical and artistic tension. The performance was enthusiastically received by the audience and the judges, who all unanimously gave it the highest 6-point marks. The Brit. pair indicated a new way of seeking esthetic patterns but their performance was also a blind alley in the development of ice-dancing. Their vivid departure from 'pure' ice skating and introduction of movements in which not only the skates remained in contact with the ice surface, contradicted the tenets of ice-skating as art. Paradoxically, the artistic impression made by Torvill and Dean turned out to be an esthetic astonishment which to a large extent determined their success. Falling onto the ice copied by some later ice-dancing pairs would soon become a routine and even irritating. At the 1988 winter Ol.G. in Calgary the gold was won by the Rus. pair J. Gordiejewa and S. Grinkov, who showed perfect mastery of the conservative Rus. ice skating school combining technical excellence with ballet traditions.

Many ice dancers, e.g. the Fr. pair I. and P. Duchessnay, regarded the case of Torvill-Dean as a form of search for new ways of artistic expression and technical perfection using any means, and often used shocking forms of their own expression lacking however any artistic creativity. In cases of numerous ice dancers 'innovation' began to dominate over true artistic expression. The Olympic champions from Albertville 1992 and Lillehammer 1994 – M. Klimova, S. Ponomarenko and O. Griszczuk, J. Platov – represented the school of 'joyful beauty' as well as technical and artistic perfection but they created no new solutions and imitated the achievements of their predecessors. At the same time ice-dancing forms began to affect pair figure skating, where emphasis was put on more 'poetic' expression, as in the cases of N. Miszketeniuk and A. Dmitriev (Olympic champions 1992), and J. Gordiejeva and S. Grinkov (Olympic champions 1994). In Nagano, the gold and silver were won the Russian pairs O. Griczuk and J. Platov and A. Krylova and O. Owsiannikov, and bronze went to the Fr. pair, M. Anisine and G. Peizerat.

Team figure skating began to develop in the 1930s in the USA, mainly in the form of ice shows, either as live or movie spectacles. The ice show gained popularity primarily as a live spectacle where the audience could admire its brilliant and gorgeous fea-

tures in a direct manner. Among the most famous ice shows are the *Holiday on Ice Shows*, which have become a huge success all over the world.

Apart from ice shows, certain forms of amateur team skating were developed around 1956 by school teachers from Ann Arbor, Michigan. Simple school skating exercises soon gave rise to an independent sport consisting of the collective performance of 12-24 skaters in various age categories. Team skating became an official sport under the auspices of the ISU in 1994. In the 1980s amateur team skating shows developed in France, soon gaining popularity in other Eur. countries. The first international team skating championships took place in 1996.

L. Copley-Graves, *Figure-Skating History. The Evolution of Dance on Ice*, 1992; J. Hennessy, *Torvill & Dean*, 1983; R.S. Ogilvie, *Competitive Figure Skating. A Parents' Guide*, 1985; B. Smith, *Figure Skating. A Celebration*, 1994; W. Starosta, *Łyżwiarstwo figurowe*, 1980; A. Szeluchin *Liedowaja simfonia*, 1967; J. Whedon, *The Fine Art Of Ice Skating*, 1988.

FIK-FAK, a var. of >PATØK.

FINGERLEG, Dan. for 'playing with fingers'. Two players touch hands with the tips of their index, ring, and little fingers. The middle fingers are crooked downwards forming a 'bridge'. Then, they try to draw away one finger at a time. The index and little fingers are easy to withdraw but the ring ones seem to have a mind of their own.

J. Møller, 'Fingerleg', GID, 1997, 3.

FION, an Afr. game known in Eng. as *leap frog*. A game played on the Cape Verde islands, esp. on Fogo. On Sao Antão it is called *gurdion*. Fion is a combination of a 'which hand' guessing game and leap frog. Three players take part in the game and the 4th one waits his turn. One of the players commands, 'Ando etrual', after which everybody puts their hands against their chests, with either the back of the hand or the palm facing out. The player whose hands are in a position different than the hands of the 2 remaining ones loses and is replaced by the waiting player. In the next round, the player who lost returns to the game and another round starts. This time the loser is that player whose hands are in the same position as the hands of the returning participant. The second loser is given the role of a 'frog' who stands on all fours with his back stretched out. Players who lose the following rounds have to jump over the frog 3 times. The first jump is called a *fion*, the second – a *tape*, and the third – a *marton*. Up to the third jump, the players must not touch the frog with any part of their body except their hands. Who-

ever fails to do so, becomes a frog. At the fourth jump, one may kick the frog on the bottom with the right foot, calling out, '*Purdab!*' (I'm blessing you with my pardon). Anyone who forgets to pronounce the words becomes a frog himself. After that, the players form a circle around the frog and they walk around it. When facing the frog, they say, '*Madam musu musoi!*' and when they go behind the frog's back, they kick it on its behind. A player who kicks any other part of the moving frog, replaces the participant in the center of the circle.

A. Taylor Cheska, 'Fion (Leap Frog)', TGDWAN, 1987, 30.

Members of Finland's synchronized skating team 'Step By Step' perform during the senior short program of the Snowflake International Synchronized Competition at the Civic Center in Providence, Rhode Island, USA. Seventeen teams from four countries competed in the annual 3-day event, each team consisting of 12-24 skaters.

FIRE, AIR, AND WATER, an Eng. ball game. Players form a circle in the center of which there is a player holding a ball attached to a long string that enables the player to pull the ball back after it has been thrown. When the central player throws the ball he calls out one of the 4 elements and the catching participant, before the others count to 10, is supposed to name one creature living in the element named by the thrower. Should he fail, he loses both the ball and a point. If fire is called out, the catching player has to remain silent. In Ireland, after the first time fire is called out, the catching party had to reply 'Salamander!', after the second time – 'Phoenix!', and only after the third call was silence the correct answer. A similar game was played for >MINERAL, ANIMAL, VEGETABLE.

A.B. Gomme, TGESI, I, 122.

FIREBALL, a Native Amer. ball game played until the 20th cent. The game was practiced among the Native Americans of the Iroquois League, which had been founded before the first Eur. settlers came to America and ceased to exist only in 1801. The League was originated by the legendary Chief Hiawatha and since pre-Columbian times it had consisted of 5 Iroquois nations: the Mohawk, Oneida, Seneca, Onandaga and Cayuga. In 1722, the Tuscarora joined the league. The origins of fireball remain unknown. Ethnographic research among tribal leaders has confirmed the view that the natives have played fireball since ancient times. The last fireball game was reported to have been played in July 1986 by the Tuscarora, in a reservation near Niagara Falls.

Course of play. A football-size rag ball or a bundle of leather straps plaited with wicker (or wire) was immersed into flammable fluid – traditionally melted fat – or in modern times in kerosene, crude oil or gasoline. The soaked ball was then set on fire in the middle of the playing field before the game started. The aim of the game was to throw, or more often, kick the ball towards the opponent's goal line or a simple goal cage. The game was played until the ball burned up, usu. about 20min. The team which scored more points won. The flaming ball made the game very dynamic as it could not be held or stopped for too long. The goalkeeper was entitled to wear a pair of special gloves. All players could use special protective shoes. The game was only played at night, the goal line marked with torch lights, which made the game a spectacular event. Once kicked or thrown the ball glowed more intensely increasing the game's attractiveness. The number of players

WORLD SPORTS ENCYCLOPEDIA

F

Figure skating: ice dancing competition.

*An illustration to Juliana de Berners' The
Treatyse of Fyssynge with an Angle.*

A fine specimen.

Fish hunting in ancient Egypt.

was unspecified. Ethnographic records show the number of fireball players ranging from a few to a few dozen per team. A folk var. of fireball known as >PELOTA PURHÉPECHA ENCENDIDA is still played today in C America. Cf. >INDIAN FOOTBALL and >MESOAMERICAN INDIAN BALL GAMES.
G.C. Baldwin, *Games of the American Indian*, 1969; W.M. Beauchamp, 'Iroquois Games', JAF, 1896, 9; W. Hough, 'Games of Seneca Indians', AA, 1888, 1; A.A. MacFarlan, *Book of American Indian Games*, 1958; J.B. Oxendine, *American Indian Sports Heritage*, 1988.

FIREOGTYVE KEGLER, also *24 kegler*. A Dan. game of 24 skittles, practiced mostly outdoors, on a lawn or the ground. The object being thrown is made of wood and resembles a large hammer. Nine wooden skittles are arranged in a square 3 by 3, one of whose angles is facing the thrower. In the middle of the square there is a skittle marked with a tuft of horse mane at the top. Knocking down this skittle scores 12pts. – hence its name: 'the duodecimal king' (*Tolvkongen*) – which is the greatest number of points that can be scored for a single skittle. The distance between the throwing line and the closest skittle, whose position is referred to as the front corner (*forhjørne*), is 10m. The skittle placed in the corner farthest from the throwing line (i.e. the rear corner – *baghjørne*) is a little smaller than the duodecimal king, but still taller than the remaining skittles, and is marked with a tuft of horse mane. Its name is 'the ninthly pot' (*nipotten*). The game continues until 24pts. are scored. If a player knocks down the duodecimal king and the ninthly pot with a single throw, he scores 21pts. Therefore, it is enough to knock down 3 other skittles in the following throw to score the maximum number of points. If a player knocks down the 8 skittles surrounding the king, he scores 24pts. If more points are scored than the 24 which is necessary, the game continues, the next throw counting backwards, etc.
J. Møller, 'Kegler', GID, 1997, 1, 100.

FIRTRÆK, Dan. for 'a four-pull', [Dan. *fire* – four + *træk* – a pull]. A Dan. form of tug-of-war in which a rope tied up in a loop about 1m in diameter is used. Four participants make a quadrangle whose sides are marked by the rope they are holding. Behind each player, at a distance of 1m (beyond the player's reach), there is an item, a stick for example. The object of the game is to pull the 3 opponents so that you can grab the item placed behind you.
J. Møller, 'Firtræk', GID, 1997, 4, 25.

FISH FIGHTING, a trad. sport of Thailand and some of the neighboring countries. Banned in Bangkok, it is now practiced only in the provinces. The fighting fish called *lukpah*, indigenous to the ponds, canals, and marshes of Thailand, are kept individually in

jars filled with pond water. Before the contest, the adversaries are placed alongside each other in their jars to work up animosity. This is also the time to place bets, based on the form and reaction shown by the fish. When fighting is agreed upon, the fish are scooped out of the jars and carefully placed in a larger container. Only males fight, as they develop natural animosity. The ordinary lupkah is frequently replaced by thoroughbreds called *lukmoh.*During the fight the rivals get at each other, biting fiercely and cruelly, flitting up and down the water, and maneuvering for positions. It is a mortal combat, with parts of gills, fins, tails, and scales being continually chewed off. According to the Tourism Authority of Thailand, 'the lukmoh is a tough customer that does not know the meaning of defeat'. See also other animal sports, such as >ANIMAL BAITING, >BULL FIGHTS, >CAMEL FIGHTS, >COCK FIGHTING.

FISHING, the rules and practice of competing in catching fish with a rod or events imitating it. Professional angling has a number of varieties:
FLOAT FISHING, practiced both on rivers and still waters with a min. of 1.0m and a max. of 8.0m depth. The equipment includes a rod, line, float, weights to balance the floats and one hook. The use of reels and supplementary equipment, such as landing net, platform, etc, is allowed. It is permitted to use plant and animal baits, while the use of artificials, spawn, dead or live fish is banned. A single tournament round lasts 3hrs. The winner is the angler who scores the most points calculated on the basis of the weight of fish caught (1pt. for each kilogram). The catch does not include fish which crossed the angler's sector boundaries while being landed or which came off the hook.
SPINNING, practiced in 2 forms: classical and catch-and-release. The classical competitions are held in two categories – shore spinning and boat spinning. Live fish may not be used as bait. A fishing round lasts 4-7hrs. The score is determined by the weight of fish caught in grams. In the catch-and-release category only barbless hooks can be used and each angler must have a landing net. The score reflects the length of the fish caught in centimeters multiplied by 10. In both varieties landing the fish with ores is banned.
FLY FISHING, practiced in 3 forms: classical fly fishing in running waters, catch-and-release, and fly fishing in still waters. All baits except for flies, including artificial flies, are banned. In all 3 varieties the score reflects the length of fish caught, although it is arrived at by applying a different calculation method than in catch-and-release spinning and depends on the type of fish: trout and grayling – 300pts., sea trout – 500pts., and bullhead – 700pts. for those fish reaching the minimum size, below which the fish is not classified. Every centimeter above the minimum size scores 30-70pts. Three additional points are scored for other types of fish (providing their min. size is reached) and 5pts. for every centimeter of fish without a min. size. Classical fly fishing competitions are held from the shore or while wading. A fly fishing rod is used with a mobile spool reel and a fly line with up to 2 flies. In catch-and-release events the angler must scoop the fish out with a landing net. After the judges measure the fish, it is released

A relaxing way to while away the time.

back into the water. In still water events the rules are similar to classical events, though the principles of catch-and-release fishing may also be applied.
ICE FISHING, practised on frozen water basins, where the ice cover is at least 15cm thick and the line length is min. a 10m. The rod's length is a min. 30cm. Fish are caught with the use of minnow immitation jigs, ice flies or a floater set. One round of competition lasts a min. of 1.5hrs. and a max. of 3hrs. The score equals the total weight of fish caught in grams. Dirty, snowy or icy fish decrease the score by 5 percent.
OPEN SEA FISHING, is subject to the Amateur Open Sea Fishing Regulations. Competitions are held from the natural shore, embankments, or vessels. The min. rod length is 1.5m. There are no limitations as to the type of hook or anchor. Both natural and artificial baits are allowed, such as pikers, shiners, rubber or plastic baits, etc. A round of fishing lasts up to 5hrs., while in poor weather conditions it lasts a min. of 2hrs. The fish caught is killed. The score equals the total weight of fish caught in grams.
CASTING, a group of events in which competitors use fishing rods with leaders and artificial flies to cast a line for accuracy and distance. The events include:
1) FLY ACCURACY. Competition rods are up to 3m in length, with a mobile spool reel, a line of 13.5m in length, and a tournament fly on a barbless hook. Casts are made from a platform 50cm high, 150cm long and 120cm wide to 5 target basins, each basin 60cm in diameter, made of plastic or metal, with a turned up edge 3cm high, filled with water. The targets are black, green, blue or brown and are positioned in the following way: No. 1 – 8m to the left of the competitor; No. 5 – 13m to the right; No. 2, 3 and 4 – on the line between No. 1 and No. 5. Target no. 3 is always directly in front of the casting platform. The competitor is allowed a number of false casts and he starts with a fly in his hand and a rod-length of fly line from the tip. Proper casts are conducted in the following sequence of targets: 3-1-4-2-5-3-1-4-2-5. After each false cast, there must be at least one proper attempt to reach the target basin. During proper casting the competitor concludes 2 rounds of casts in the following sequence: 1-2-3-4-5 and no false casts are allowed. The time limit to conclude the casting is 5min. 30sec. Each successful hit on the target is awarded 5pts.
2) FLY DISTANCE SINGLE-HANDED. The rod and casting platform are similar to (1), and the time limit is 6min. Casting is for distance only, with 1m scoring 1pt. The distance is measured with an accuracy of 1cm tolerance, from the spot where the fly landed to the center of the front edge of the platform. The longest cast wins the event, while 2 longest casts are added to the score in the combination.
3) SPINNING ACCURACY ARENBERG TARGET, 7.5g. Equipment: a rod min. length 137cm, max. 250cm, with at least 3 rod rings and a tip ring; open-faced spinning reel, standard spool; min. line length – 22m; and a plastic, drop-shaped plug 7.5g. The court: an Arenberg target of green coloured ground-cloth or plastic, with 5 concentric rings marked white, max. 2cm thick and of diameters, respectively, 0.75 – 1-35 – 1.95 – 2.55 – 3.15m. The center target is a flat disc of 0.75m in diameter, max. thickness

10mm, and black. There are 5 casting stations arranged round the target. The first and last station are on a straight line from the centre of the target over the target corner. The other 3 stations are placed between the first and last station, the farthest, if possible, with the wind from behind the caster. Each station is marked with a white starting board 1m long and 10cm high. Each caster makes two casts from each station, starting with the plug in his hand. The sequence and style of casting is as follows: station 1 – underhand pendulous cast, distance 10m; station 2 – right-hand side cast, distance 12m; station 3 – over-head cast, distance 18m; station 4 – left-hand cast, distance 14m; station 5 – optional style cast, distance 16m. The scoring for each cast is, respectively, 10, 8, 6, 4, and 2 pts. Dragging of the plug on the ground is not allowed and yields a 0 score.

4) SPINNING ACCURACY, 7.5g. The rod, reel, line and plug are the same as in (3). There are 5 targets, which are yellow discs 0.76m in diameter and a max. of 10mm thick placed perpendicular to the casting stations. There are two rounds of casts and in each of them the caster makes 2 casts to each target – a total of 20 casts. The time limit is 8mins and each hit brings 5pts.

5) SPINNING DISTANCE SINGLE HANDED, 7.5g. The rod, reel, and plug are the same as in (3). The line is 0.18mm in diameter throughout its entire length. The court is a triangle, the top of which is in the center of the white starting board 1.5m long and 10cm high. At a 100m distance from the starting board the court is 50m wide. The distance between the starting board and the nearest obstacle within the court must be a min. of 13m. Each caster has 3 casts, one in each round. The time limit is 1min for each cast. The style of casting is optional. The casting distance is measured with a tolerance of 1cm from the plug's landing spot to the center of the starting board. Only the longest cast determines a competitor's score (1m = 1pt.).

6) FLY DISTANCE DOUBLE HANDED. The equipment includes: any rod max. 5.2m in length, reel, line max. 120g in weight and min. 15m in length. The fly and platform are identical to (1) and the court identical to (5). The 2 longest casts produce a score, in which 1m = 1pt. The time limit is 7min.

7) SPINNING DISTANCE DOUBLE HANDED. The equipment includes: any rod, any reel, a line of a min. 0.25mm in diameter, a white plastic plug 18g in weight. The court is identical to (5). Each caster makes 3 casts in 3 rounds. The style of casting is optional. The longest cast in each round produces a score, in which 1m = 1pt. The time limit is 1min. The distance is measured from the plug's landing spot to the center of the starting board.

8) MULTIPLIER ACCURACY. The equipment includes: any single-handed rod, a multiplying reel with standard spool, any line min. 26m in length, plastic plug 18g in weight. The court is identical to (4), but the distance to the first target is 12m and to the last target – 20m. Casting style is optional and the time limit is 10min. Each caster makes 2 rounds of 2 casts to each target from 5 stations (a total of 20 casts). Each hit scores 5pts.

9) MULTIPLIER DISTANCE DOUBLE HANDED. The equipment includes: any rod, a multiplying reel with standard spool, a line of 0.25mm in diameter, and a plug of 18g in weight. The court is identical to 5) and the casting style is optional. Each caster has 3 casts, carried out in 3 rounds. The longest cast, measured from the plug's landing spot to the center of the starting board, produces a score (1m = 1 pt.)

Events for men may be individual competitions or combinations (pentathlon – events 1-5; distance duathlon – events 6-7 and multiplier duathlon – events 8-9). Events for women may be individual or combinations (pentathlon – events 1-5; multiplier duathlon – events 8-9). Additional pentathlon and triathlon events are held for children and juniors.

History. Fishing is one of man's oldest ways of acquiring food. Its origins date back to the stone age, when the use of bare hands or a spear turned out to be inefficient. Evidence found in caves and other primitive habitats of man indicates that at first a simple construction was used for fishing, made from stone or flint pieces tied to a thin line made of plant fiber or animal gut. The main concept of fishing has not changed much from ancient to modern times. Numerous drawings and paintings found in the art of ancient Egypt confirm the use of a short stick and a line for fishing purposes and indicate that in Egypt

fishing received for the first time in history a high social status and was considered an art form. It is also in Egypt that we find the first traces of fishing as a form of competition. Eur. fishing had to wait much longer to receive a similar status. The earliest evidence indicating that the contemporaries of Homer knew the technique of fishing with a hook and bait is a scene from the *Odyssey* (Book XII), in which Scylla captures Ulysses' 6 companions:

As a fisherman, seated, spear in hand, upon some jutting rock throws bait into the water to deceive the poor little fishes, and spears them with the ox's horn with which his spear is shod, throwing them gasping on to the land as he catches them one by one, even so did Scylla land these panting creatures on her rock and munch them up at the mouth of her den, while they screamed and stretched out their hands to me in their mortal agony.

[trans. Samuel Butler]

Another important literary description of rod fishing is found in *Idyllia* by Teocritus (3rd cent. B.C.). The hero, a fisherman named Aspahlion, describes his dream, in which he has caught a fish, giving many technical details regarding making a rod and methods of fishing. Among other Gk. authors who wrote about fishing were: Herodotus, Plato (*Laws*, VIII), and Aristotle (*The Natural History of Animals*). These examples apart, fishing is not a subject frequently found in pre-hellenic Gk. literature and there is no evidence – similar to Egypt – of any attempts to raise its status. Numerous traces of fishing can be found in ancient Rome, of which the most famous and most frequently quoted by writers and scholars, is the fishing duel between Anthony and Cleopatra, best described by Plutarch in his *Lives*, which was later used by W. Shakespeare in his play *Anthony and Cleopatra*. In 169 AD the Gk. poet Oppian wrote his *Halieutika (On Fishing)*, in which – besides technical details – he described the battles between anglers and fish and clearly stressed the sporting nature of these events. Fishing has also been described by Ovid in the surviving 130-verse fragment of his *Halienautika*, written during the poet's exile in Tomi. Plinius the Elder dealt with fishing in his *Historia Naturalis* (Book IX), and passages on fishing can also be found in the works of Cicero, Horace, Juvenalis, Plinius the Younger, and Plautus. Knowledgeable and technically detailed reports on fishing have been written by Marcus Terencius Warro in his *Res rusticae libri tres*, while a poem by Decimus Ausonius Magnus Mosel offers an extensive description of rod fishing during a river trip.

In modern times fishing has been written about very extensively. Early Christian communities viewed fishing not only from the utilitarian, but also religious and symbolic point of view. Evidence is ample – from the Scriptures to the medieval apocryphal texts describing fishing expeditions and the role of Jesus Christ. Furthermore, Christian art is full of symbolic representations of fish and fishing. The first printed treatise on fishing was the translation of Oppian's *Halieutika* published in Antwerp around 1492 by the printer M. van der Goes. In 1496 *The Treatyse of Fyssynge with an Angle* appeared in England, printed by W. de Worde in Westminster as the 2nd part of the *Book of St. Albans*. Its author was probably J. de Berners, living at the turn of the 14th cent., who was one of the first women in England to practice sport and write about hunting and fishing. The treatise is clearly a compilation of earlier, no longer surviving texts, which was discovered in 1882 by the Eng. scholar T. Satchell. The beginning of the 16th cent. saw a proliferation of texts on fishing. In Italy Sannazar wrote his *Piscatoria* (1526) and A. Calmo – *Rime piscatorie* (1557). In Germany numerous treatises on the household included chapters on fishing. In France C. de Gamon published his *Les pêcheries* in 1599, while C. Gauchet – *La plaisir des champs* in 1604. The most important Fr. work on the subject – *Les ruses* innocentes – was written in 1600 by F. Fortin and is often viewed as the greatest Fr. contribution to the development of fishing.

The modern sporting nature of fishing was ultimately shaped in England in the 17th and 18th cent. Sport fishing found its way not only into household treatises, but also scholarly works on sport, as well as separate works on the subject. Among the most important of these are: J. Dennys' *The Secrets of Angling* (1613), T. Barker's *Art of Angling* (1651), I. Walton's *The Complete Angler* (1653), R. Venables' *The Experienced Angler* (1662), N. Cox's *The Gentleman's Recreation* (1674), and Gilberts' *The An-*

gler's Delight (1676). In the 18th cent. the popularization of sport fishing coincided with the dynamic development of the publishing business. Among the best known publications of that period are: C.G.'s *The Secrets of Angling* (1705), R. Howlett's *The Angler's Sure Guide* (1706), by the same author *The Whole Art of Fishing* (1714), J. Sauders' *The Compleat Fisherman* (1724), and R. Brookes' *The Art of Angling* (1740). T. Fairfax's *The Complete Sportsman* (c. 1760) includes a chapter on sport fishing, which the author considers one of the most important of sports. The above list should also include such important works as T. Shirley's *The Angler's Museum* (1784) and T. Best's *A Concise Treatise on Art of Angling* (1787). 19th cent. Eng. literature on fishing grew in volume and was divided into subcategories on the professional and technical aspects of fishing and its literary, social, and cultural aspects. Among the latter, the most important works include: Daniels' *Rural Sports* (1801) and H.D. Salmon's treatise reviewed by W. Scott in the 'Quarterly'. In 1835 a series of T.T. Stoddard's books formed the first encyclopedia of fishing called *The Art of Angling as Practised in Scotland*. In 1839 the songs and poems published by the same author praised the many charms of the sport of fishing.

The advancement of fishing in Britain in the 1st half of the 19th cent. was much greater than the achievements of other Eur. countries and the USA. It was not until the 2nd half of the century that fishing was recognized as a sport in most countries of W and C

Boat fishing in the open sea.

Competitive fishing.

Fishing is a one of the most popular pastimes worldwide.

F

Europe. In Germany this development greatly owed to the publishing of M. von dem Borne's *Handbuch der Angelfischerei* (1875), while in France – A. Petite's *La truite de riviére* (1897).

Advanced sport fishing techniques brought about a decline in fish stocks in the most industrialized countries, and uncontrolled industrial development and systems of river regulation in the 2nd half of the 19th cent. caused an almost complete destruction of the plant and animal life in some parts. The counterreaction came from fishing associations, which began to include in their statutes provisions aimed at protecting the natural environment. The lowering of fish stocks also contributed to the development of a new sport fishing event – distance and accuracy casting, which – with the dramatic ecological situation around the globe – keeps growing in popularity. Sport fishing has been incorporated in the legal statutes of many countries as part of their system of instruments aimed at controlling natural resources and preserving the natural environment. By 1939 powerful fishing associations were formed in most Eur. and Eng.-speaking countries around the world. In 1952 the International Sport Fishing Federation (Confédération Internationale de le Péche Sportive, CIPS) was formed in Rome, with its headquarters in Vienna. It is the governing body for the sport of natural fishing. In 1956 the International Casting Federation (ICF) was established in Oakland (USA), which promotes the sport of distance and accuracy court casting. Both organizations joined forces in 1970, forming one organization, though keeping their respective names. The organization holds world championships and registers world records both within natural sport fishing and casting.

T. Nally, *The Complete Book of Fly Fishing*, 1993; Ch. Waterman, *A History of Angling*, 1981; W. Zeiske, *Angle Richtig*, 1974; see also works quoted above.

FISTBALL, an Eng. term for a number of disciplines: 1) An Eng. equivalent of Ger. >FAUSTBALL and Pol. >PIĘSTÓWKA. 2) A game similar to Ang.-Sax. >HANDBALL, where the ball is struck with a clenched fist instead of a racket; however this game differs from the majority of its counterparts because players can use both hands and in addition, the ball can be kicked. Players wear special gloves and they play in a typical >SQUASH court using a standard tennis ball. The match consists of 3 sets, up to 9pts. each. The winner, however, has to gain an advantage of at least 2pts. Nowadays, the players are also the only umpires. 3) A ball game practiced in the past in Brit. colonies in Amer., of which little is known today. 4) A name applied to some var. of >FIVES in which the ball is returned with a gloved fist.

St. Simon the Flagpole Sitter, a 16th cent. icon at the Historical Museum in Sanok, Poland.

FIST CUFFS, formerly *fistycuffs*. An Eng. term for boxing in the times before organized fights with bare fists existed. Currently, the term functions as a jocular reference to any spontaneous fight, including brawls.

FIVEPINS, an Eng. bowling game with the use of 5 pins. Also *Canadian fivepin*, a var. of bowling classified as *small pin bowling* (>BOWLING), in which figures made of 5 pins are used. The pins are 12in. (31.8cm) tall and fitted with a rubber band, located in the lower part, which makes each strike more dynamic. The bowling ball has no finger-holes, is made of hard rubber, and is 5in. (12.7cm) in diameter. The alley is a standard one with parquet flooring, 18.3m long and 104cm wide.

FIVES, a game in which a ball is returned with the palm against a wall, or walls surrounding a court. Probably it originated from Fr. >JEU DE LA PAUME. After the development of jeu de la paume led to the invention of a racket, the progress of games where a ball was struck directly with the palm changed its direction. In order to increase the surface of the palm and to make it more resistant to contact with the small, hard ball, players began to use gloves, which finally acquired a shape resembling a frog's webbed foot, with the web made of hardened leather. Such var. of paume were brought from France to England giving birth to Eng. handtennis, which acquired the name >HANDBALL in the second half of the 16th cent. Fives prob. is a descendant of team var. of paume. Most lexicographers view handball and fives as belonging to the same category of games in which a ball is returned with the palm. The entire category is sometimes also referred to as handball: 'A popular English form of handball is fives,' (CDOS, 196). The earliest historical reference to fives is prob. the description of the welcome that Jarl of Hertford gave to Elizabeth I in his residence in Elvetham, in Hampshire, in 1591. An Eng. antiquarian, painter, and writer, J. Nichols, described the event in *The Progress and Public Processions of Queen Elizabeth*:

[...] after dinner about three o'clock, ten of his lordship's servants, all Somersetshire men, in a square greene court before Her Majesties windowe, did hang up lines, squaring out the forme of a tennis-court and making a crosse line in the middle; in this square being stript of their dublets, they played five to five with hand-ball at board and cord as they tearme it, to the great liking of Her Highness.

[STRUTT, 88].

The name fives originates from the number of players that each team had in the earliest form of the game. The phrase 'five to five' clearly refers to Jarl of Hertford's 10 servants. However, a number of fives specialists claim that 'five to five' is actually the score rather than the number of players and the game mentioned in the above quotation is one of the varieties of jeu de paume. The *Oxford Companion to Sports & Games*, by J. Arlott (1975, p.291) and a number of other dictionaries and encyclopedias, such as *The Cambridge Encyclopedia* (1991, p.447), affirm the name fives stems from the number of fingers or from the scoring system rather than from the number of players. The name of the game also appears in the anonymous *Divine Tragedy* (1636, 8): 'He had a purpose [...] to goe in the Lords Day [...] to play at sport, called fiues.' In the 1726 *Terrae Philosophiae* by Amherst we can read about 'the old ball-court, where I have had many a game at fives.' In the famous 1755 *Dictionary of the English Language* by Samuel Johnson the definition of fives is rather scant in details: 'A kind of play with a bowl,' thus we can only speculate as to the actual number of players in a fives team during the 17th and 18th cent. To refute that there were 5 of them is equally legitimate as claiming that their number was exactly the same as in the earliest versions, i.e. 5. It is possible that the 5-player game simply lost gradually on popularity. When fives was adopted by Eng. public schools it was usu. played by 2- or 4-player teams. >WINCHESTER FIVES with its 4-player teams would therefore be a remnant of a period when it was decided that for some reason 5 players was too many. Doubles became the rule in >ETON FIVES and >RUGBY FIVES. Singles were the least popular game.

In general, the object of the game is to return the ball served by an opponent, before it touches the ground, so that it bounces against the wall. If the ball fails to hit the wall or if the return is incorrect a player loses a point. Details of the rules of the game, the ball's structure, and the number of walls fencing the court, vary from one version of the game to another. In certain Eng. schools, for example, a var. of fives evolved in which instead of the palm a bat is used to return the ball, see >BAT-FIVES.

J. Arlot, 'Eton Fives, Rugby Fives, Winchester Fives', OCSG, 1975.

FIVESTONES, see >JACKS.

FLAGPOLE SITTING, a type of competition in which contestants climb a pole and perch at the top the longest possible time. The tradition of this competition goes back to the times of Simon Stylites (c.390--459), a Syrian hermit and the first of the Pillar Saints (Lat. *sancti stylitae*), who in an act of religious devotion renounced earthly life and perched upon a pole which he himself erected for 37 or, according to other sources, just 26 years. Born in Cilicia, as a young man he moved to Antioch in Syria, where for 10 years he lived as a hermit. Probably in 433 he decided to build his pole. It was about 18m tall, with a platform atop which he prayed and preached to the pilgrims who came to listen to him. He ate simple food, delivered to him on a rope by his listeners. Canonized by the Church, his holiday is celebrated by the Catholic Church on 5 Jan. and the Orthodox Church on 1 Sept. He was followed by many other medieval ascetics. When pole sitting became more common, it was practiced by wandering strangers, who tried to earn their living and fame in this way. At the beginning of the 20th cent. pole sitting became an occasional form of record breaking, something that fascinated people at that time, inspired by the achievements of great individualities, who kept on breaking different barriers, including the explorers of poles, swimmers crossing difficult straits, airmen making pioneer flights etc. Record breaking in less heroic activities, but those available to great masses because of their everyday character, gave the illusion of participation in larger-than-life accomplishments. This is when competitions against the clock or eating (drinking) the greatest quantities of different foods (eggs, pancakes, beer etc.), or prolonged kissing, or gum chewing etc. appeared. The most spectacular attempts at record breaking at the beginning of the 1920s included >DANCE MARATHON. The most famous record holder in pole sitting was A. Kelly, best known as 'Shipwreck' Kelly, who became known in 1924 but claimed that he had inadvertently attempted to break a record in flagpole sitting in 1920 while watching one of J. Dempsey's boxing matches, when he was thrown down from the 3rd floor by the crowd. He claimed that in an effort to save his life he grabbed a flag pole, where he sought refuge for some time, waiting until his oppressors lost interest and went away. Convinced of his stamina and strength, he decided to make flagpole sitting his living, and started to take bets against his remaining on the pole, without a platform, with his legs and hands clasped around the pole. The story proved to be a hoax, repeated only to lend splendor to his stunts. Another story is that Kelly, who was employed as a professional stuntman in Hollywood, decided to attempt to sit on a flagpole in response to a dare from a Hollywood friend. He sat upon the pole for 13hrs. and 13min. and began a national spectacle. In 1927 he set a record in standing on the rounded (about 15-20cm in diameter) end of a flag pole atop a 13-storey building in St. Louis, fastened with special hoops. He stood there for 7 days, 13hrs. and 13min., and drank enormous quantities of coffee, shaved and manicured to please the photographers. This stunt earned him $100. After a few other stunts like this he died in poverty in 1952. The police found his body on the street, his pockets full of newspaper clippings with stories regaling his former achievements. He had a few rivals during his lifetime, the most famous of whom was A.O. Foreman, a 15-yr-old girl, who, in an attempt to break Kelly's record, sat atop a thick flagpole in Baltimore for 10 days, 10hrs., 10min., and 10sec. (the result was perhaps rounded). She was presented with a diploma recognizing 'the pioneer spirit of early America' by the mayor of Baltimore. The stunt was imitated by many Baltimore youth – to the extent that the city authorities began to check each time whether the pole was secure. Flagpole sitting died out around 1929 with the coming of the Depression, but during its heyday, it certainly caught the nation's fancy.

FLAT GREEN BOWLS, one of a number of names for a group of bowling games referred to jointly as >LAWN BOWLING, *lawn bowls*, or simply *bowls*. The name flat green bowls applies to those games that are held on a flat strip of grass called a 'rink' as opposed to those that are played on a square field whose surface ascends towards the center referred to as the 'crown'. Games held on such an ascending field are known as >CROWN GREEN BOWLS.

FLAT HORSE RACING, a form of >HORSE RACING in which mounted riders compete over different track lengths and in different horse age and breed categories. Races are held on circular tracks and often have Eng. names that reflect both the nature of the race and distance, which is usu. equivalent to a similar race in England. E.g. a derby indicates a race in the same category and over the same distance as the original Derby held at Epsom since 1779 (3-yr-olds, the distance – 1.5 Eng. mile, i.e. 2,414m). Other such events include Oaks, 2000 Guineas, St. Léger, etc. There are a few exceptions to this rule, e.g. in the Amer. Kentucky Derby riders compete over a distance of 1.25 Eng. mile (2,011m).
Customs connected with the races and the jockeys' attire also have an Eng. background. Jockeys wear a colored peaked cap, a colorful jacket, breeches

'horse-power' of that motor and let him run faster. Therefore, Sloan places his saddle close to the scapulae, mounts the horse close to its head and holds the crossed reins a foot from from its ears, placing his hands on both sides of the neck'.
[*The Principles of Sport Horseriding*, 53]

Sloan's technique was later improved by raising the stirrups, so that the jockey's knees are on a level with the horse's front short rump and during the gallop, when the horse's neck is extended forwards, the jockey's hips are an extension of the horse's neck.
History. Riding on horseback is in all likelihood a younger tradition than riding a horse-driven, 2-wheeled carriage. This apparently surprising sequence can be explained by the low height of early horses, which – through careful breeding and selection – by the turn of the 1st and 2nd millenium BC in the Middle East reached a size that made riding on horseback possible (>CHARIOT RACING). At the time when mounted horse races were part of the Gk. Ol.G., the horses of the Persian ruler Darius were approx. 132-142cm high and weighed 230-270kg., while modern race horses average 158-166cm in height and weigh up to 510kg. In the Egypt of the Pharaohs horses were still low and not much larger than donkeys. The exact time when riding on

horse on a military expedition. The games described by Homer in the *Iliad* (approx. 9th cent. BC) included no horseback riding, which was introduced into the olympic program during the 33rd Ol.G. in 648 BC, later than chariot racing (688 BC). The event was stud-horse racing (*keles*), as opposed to the races of mares (*kalpe*), introduced during the Ol.G. of 496 BC, and races of colts (*polon keles*), introduced in 268 BC. The remaining documents indicate that in ancient Greece jockeys rode bare-back, with reins, no bit, and with a short whip. Stirrups were not known until they were brought to Europe by the ancient Huns, so riders kept balance with their legs. Races started with a trumpet signal and, similar to chariot racing, victory was awarded to the horse owner rather than the jockey, although this often happened to be the same person. Flat horse racing caught on in Rome and with the Romans went to Britain, where horse breeding was raised to such a level that race horses (together with race dogs) began to be exported to the capital of the Empire. Horse breeding and the use of horses for transportation and sport became so popular among Romanized Britons that that it survived the fall of the Roman Empire. The horse played an important role in the clash between the Romanized celtic tribes and the new conquerors – the Angles, Saxons and Jutes

Edouard Manet, At the Races, *oil on canvas, c.1875.*

Edgar Degas, The Race Track. Amateur Jockeys, *oil on canvas, 1876-77.*

Edgar Degas, Before the Race, *oil on canvas, c.1882.*

Flat horse racing, with its high stirrups and the characteristic crouch of the jockeys.

and riding knee-boots, which originated at the end of the 18th cent. During many races in Great Britain, the USA and Australia there is also a dress code for the audience: e.g. in Ascot men must wear a dress coat and grey top-hat, while women – an elegant gown and broad-brimmed hat.
The modern riding technique has been developed by the jockeys themselves. In the mid-19th cent. F. Archer (1857-86) invented a riding technique of letting out the horse while galloping. In a Pol. horse riding textbook it was described as 'sitting in the saddle with one leg almost straight and the body leaning forward. This helps the rider feel the horse's movements better by allowing the rider to maintain close contact with the horse and letting it forward. The rider must be very sensitive, however, so as not to impede the horse's movements. Following Archer's style is very difficult and few riders are successful' (*The Principles of Sport Horseriding*, 1932, 53). The short-legged jockey T. Sloan (active 1889-1906) used his handicap to develop a 'monkey's crouch'.

Observing the horse's movements he came to believe that they are based on the operation of the scapulae and front legs, while the croup moves fluently upwards and forwards and is like a motor that thrusts the weight of the horse agaist the support provided by the scapulae and the front legs. He concluded that by taking the weight off the back of the horse will increase the

horseback appeared alongside chariot riding is unknown. It probably took place in Assyria and Egypt, though the chronology cannot be traced as the old Eg. word *htr* meant both a horse and a two-wheeled carriage. Ancient Eg. iconography favors depictions of chariots over those of horseback riders. Most surviving drawings and reliefs present donkey riders, for donkey riding preceded riding on horseback. Depictions of horseback riders appear later and are scarce, e.g. the image of the Assyrian goddess Astarte (also worshipped in Egypt) riding on horseback. Astarte's cult in Egypt culminated in the New State era (17th-11th cent. BC), which may indicate that riding on horseback originated in Assyria and together with the cult of Astarte moved on to Egypt. A hieroglyphic inscription concerning Pharaoh Tutmozis IV contains the phrase 'brave like Astarte on *htr*', which suggests that the Paraoh practiced riding on horseback. The practice of horseback riding is also confirmed by the remains of mummified horses found in the tomb of Queen Hatshepsut at Deir el Bakri. Bigger horses were a product of breeding measures and selection of the largest individuals carried out c.1350 BC in Mitanni (modern Cappadocia), which was integrated into the Assyrian-Babylonian Empire. Kikkulis, a horse trainer for king Suppliuliumas, wrote the first treatise on training horses for racing, in which he recommended 144 days of training, followed by a hunting test or taking the

– who arrived in Britain in the 5th cent. The legend of King Arthur, a celtic defender of Britain against the Anglosaxons, contains many descriptions of victories accomplished by his knights with the use of horses. The formation of the class of knights and the relation between its ethos and its military and jousting accomplishments raised the prestige of horseback riding as an attribute of nobility. The dynamics of horseback riding improved further after the conquest of Britain by the Vikings, whose riding accomplishments are much less known than their ships. However, in the 2nd stage of their operation in Britain their mobility on horseback was an important tactical element aimed at misleading the enemy. Having landed, the Vikings would pillage a given territory, then speedily ride to a pre-selected spot unknown to the English, at which they boarded their ships. The settling of the Vikings within the Eng. Danelaw led to the adaptation of their breeding techniques by the local communities. The arrival of William the Conqueror (1066) brought to England startwart continental horses, which perfectly suited the needs of cavalry units. In this way the Brit. horse breeding tradition absorbed elements of celtic-Roman, Scand. and Norman breeding culture. The Eur. art of horse riding was revolutionized as a result of Arabic expansion, which took place in the era of Mahomet (570-632 AD). The Arabs, then called Saracens, entered S Europe through the Iberian

Henri de Toulouse-Lautrec, The Jockey, *1899, color lithograph.*

Edward Degas, At the Races in the Country, *1870-73, oil on wood.*

F

WORLD SPORTS ENCYCLOPEDIA

Juliusz Kossak, Horse Races, *oil on canvas.*

Flat horse racing on a Polish postage stamp.

Gustave Doré, The Epsom Derby.

Peninsula and reached the center of modern day France, where they were stopped by Charles Martel in the battle of Tours (732). The Arabs introduced into Eur. horse riding such elements as the saddle and a new pure breed of horses ever since called Arabians, very fast though less resistant to fatigue. In 1100 the Eng. king bought the first Arabians, which he began to crossbreed with Eur. horses. Arabians appeared on the continent on a large scale after the crusades. Disputes between the owners of breeds in England led to betting and racing, the oldest mention of which comes from 1174, a date considered to be the origin of modern flat horse racing. In medieval England horse racing events were more frequent than jousting tournaments. In 1512 during the local event in Chester an annual symbolic award was established – a wooden ball decorated with flowers, replaced in 1540 with a silver one. The Chester race is now considered to be the first regular, annual cup event. During the reign of Queen Anne (1702-14) racing for prize money (irregularly taking place since the times of Richard I, 1189-99) became common. In the second half of the 17th cent. flat horse racing was introduced in N.America. After the English recaptured the Du. territories in N.America in 1664, the governor of New York, R. Nichols, initiated an annual horse racing event, at first held on farm horses. In 1730 the first race stud horse (Bay Bolton) was brought to America and in 1738 – the first full bred mare (Bully Rock). These two started the Amer. breed of race horses. The great open spaces of the Amer. continent created a great demand for saddle-horses. In Europe flat horse racing evolved towards luxury entertainment, while in N.America they remained connected with daily needs, transportation and administrative services (such as postal service, government messenger service etc.) much longer. This explains the surprising fact that the first riding club was formed not in Britain, but in the N.Amer. colonies (the Maryland Jockey Club, 1743). The first Eng. club was established in 1751 (the London Jockey Club, later renamed the Jockey Club of England). In 1799 the Earl of Derby started a racing event at Epsom, which became a model for all Eur. and Amer. race events. In most Eur. countries local flat horse racing events had been known since the early Middle Ages. A form of such races called >CARROUSEL was held during the Renaissance in France, while races around city squares were popular in Italy (incl. the most famous >PALIO held until today). As the Eng. race formula became internationally recognized, regional events lost much of their splendor and now maintain only a trad. value. The first Eng.-style Eur. race events took place in France (1776), Poland (1777), Russia (1803) and Germany (1822). Until the middle of the 19th cent. flat horse racing in Europe maintained the status of an exclusive social event, usu. combined with horse breed exhibitions. After 1848 the spectrum of the audience broadened, while racing was combined with gambling and soon became dominated by betting. In Europe betting was limited to the track, while in Britain and other Eng. speaking countries it spread into the city. At the same time gentlemen's races with stable owners as riders gradually disappeared.

The jockey became the pivotal figure, quickly turning into a professional athlete, hired by the stable owner. Prob. the most famous jockey in history was the American E. Arcaro (1916-97), 5-time winner of the Kentucky Derby and twice the winner of the Triple Crown awarded for coming first in Derby, Belmont Stakes and Peakness. His career total of prize money won exceeded 30 million dollars. Another high-ranking jockey was J. Longden (b. 1907), the first jockey in history who won over 5,000 races (6,032, to be specific), a record beaten in 1970 by W. 'Willie' or 'Bill' Shoemaker (a.k.a. 'The Shoe', b. 1931), who won almost 9,000 races until 1989. Shoemaker also set a record of a number of races won during one season (485 in 1953). The most prestigious races in Great Britain are: the St. Léger, held since 1776 in Doncaster, Yorkshire; the Derby, held since 1779 at Epsom, Surrey; the 2000 Guineas in Newmarket, Suffolk. Coming first in all 3 wins the jockey the Triple Crown, considered the most important horse racing award in the world. Among other important British races are those at Ascot, Berkshire, held since 1703 under the patronage of the royal family. The most important Amer. events are: The Washington International, a prestigious event, where participation is by invitation only; the Saratoga Springs Cup; the Kentucky Derby at Churchill Downs; the Preakness Stakes at Pimlico; and the Belmont Stakes at Belmont Park. The latter 3 combine into the Amer. Triple Crown. Besides these, there are 56 tracks in the US, which regularly hold international races, and several hundred tracks that hold local events. The most prestigious events in Ireland are the races at Curragh, Kildaire; in Australia – Melbourne Cup; in France – Prix de Diéne and Prix del'Arc de Triomphe at Longchamps in Paris; in Italy – Derby d'Italiano. There is no single international federation affiliating the various organizations and jockey clubs. Each country that organizes flat horse racing events has a multitude of local organizations of horse breeders and jockey unions. Periodical publications on flat horse racing include year-books with horse pedigrees, such as the *British General Stud Book* estab. in 1791, or with results of particular races, such as the Brit. 'Racing Calendar' estab. in 1727. The oldest stable is that in Newmarket, Suffolk (England), est. in 1660 by King Charles II and raised to the status of National Stud after World War II. Also in Newmarket is the headquarters of the Brit. Jockey Club. Being a predominantly professional sport flat horse racing is not included in the program of the Ol.G., although the changing attitude of the IOC towards the idea of amateur sport may result in following the path opened by basketball or tennis and acknowledging flat horse racing as an olympic sport.
Horse racing in literature and arts see >EQUESTRIAN EVENTS, The horse in literature and arts.
H. Aublet, L.N. Marcenac, *Encyclopédie du cheval*, 1964; R. Berenger, *The History and Art of Horsemanship*, vol. 1-2, 1771; J.B. Creamer, ed., *Twenty-Two Stories about Horses and Men*, 1953; M.E. Eusminger, *Horsemanship*, 1959; J.L. Hervey, R.F. Kelly, *Racing in America*, vol. 1-5, 1959; B. Oetinger, *Über die Geschichte und die verschiedenen Formen der Reitkunst*, 1885; W.H.P. Robertson, *The History of Thoroughbred Racing in America*, 1964.

FLAT RACES, a group of >ATHLETIC RUNNING races ranging from >SPRINT to >MARATHON and including >RELAYS and >TEAM RUNNING. The main distinguishing feature of flat races is that they do not involve any officially placed obstacles such as hurdles, fences or ditches. A flat race course consists of a starting line, a track of a length typical of a particular event and a finish line.

FLAT SKIING, a type of skiing almost identical with cross-country skiing. Cultivated in countries that have sufficient snowfall but few mountains, e.g. Kazakhstan, the homeland of many outstanding runners who were once members of the Soviet team.

FLAT WATER KAYAKING, var. of sports competition held in kayaks. The term kayak itself stems from Inuit kayak also spelled *kyak, kyack* or *kiak* - a canoe covered with animal skins. The name stood for a small rib-framed canoe covered with animal skins, completely enclosed except for an opening for each occupant, propelled by a single paddle with two blades without support. Nowadays kayaks are constructed in a similar way with plastics more and more often substituting the originally applied wood, and with new technological advances introduced in place of old solutions. The shape of paddles has been maintained. At sporting competitions 1-, 2-, and 4- man crews take part in events for women and men at varying distances of 200-1,000m and, depending on the num. of crew members and the distance particular events are abbr. as K-1 200, K-2 500, K-4 1000 etc.
History. Until the mid 19th cent. Kayaks were characteristic only for the Esk. culture [see >KAYAKING]. In 1851 in Leipzig, the kayak show by Native Alaskans included experimental rides for the spectators. Around 1860 Scotsman J. MacGregor constructed a kayak which he started using for tourism and excursion purposes on the rivers and on lakes of England, Scotland, Germany and Scand. countries. In 1865 MacGregor founded the Brit. Royal Canoeing Club. Three years later there were about 300 kayaks registered in several Brit. clubs. The boats, constructed along the same general assumption, differed in dimensions and in the particular solutions applied. This led, in turn, to the first attempts at standardization. The first similar Fr. club was estab. c.1869 and in 1871 the New York Canoe Club was founded. In 1874 N. Boshop made an excursion from Quebec to the Gulf of Mexico in a kayak constructed of impregnated paper. In 1880 the Amer. Canoe Federation was established and it started organizing a number of regattas. Between 1880-90 there were already 40 types of different kayak competitions held in the USA, 18 of which have survived to this day. On the Eur. continent kayaking gained popularity most rapidly, apart from England, in Germany where A. Heurich constructed the first foldable kayak in 1904. In 1907 the first kayak shipyard of J. Klepper, which has survived until today, was built in Rosenheim. In 1914 Deutscher Kanuverband was brought to life. After a period of stagnation caused by WWI kayaking became a popular form of entertainment and it flourished. Journalists, writers took excursions down the rivers and lakes and their press reviews or books

played an important role in even greater propagation of recreational kayaking. In 1928 a German named Römer set off to paddle a kayak across the Atlantic but the attempt failed and the adventurer drowned in the vicinity of the Virgin Is. after having left Sao Tome Is. In 1886 the first international regatta, still held, took place in the USA (since 1995 known as International Challenge Cup). In Göteborg (Sweden) the international kayaking regatta was organized in1923 and this event resulted in founding Internationella Representantskapet for Kanotidrott (in Ger. since 1924 Internationale Repräsentantschaft für Kanusport respectively) following the initiative of Austria, Denmark, Germany, Sweden and the USA. The overt cooperation with Nazi Germany of WWII blemished the good name of the organization. It operated until 1942 and was then substituted by a new body, Fédéra-

FLEMISH BOWLING GAMES, games that are to some extent similar to Brit. >SKITTLES, Ital. >BOCCIA, and Fr. >BOULES, however some substantial differences can be observed. First of all, in the case of Fr., Ital., and Brit. bowling games the target is a smaller bowl which changes its location as a result of being struck by larger bowls. In Flem. bowling games, the target is a wooden peg, stuck in the ground, or a hole in a square field called a 'box'. In >BEUGELEN it is a ring through which a bowl has to pass, in >TROU-MADAME – a small goal. A number of the Flem. bowling games instead of spherical bowls use ones resembling a loaf of bread or wheel of Swiss cheese. In Flanders, each region has its own var. of bowling games and none of them, with the exception of *trou-madame*, is popular outside its region of origin. The most favored among them are: >GAAIBOLLEN, >PLATTE

Indon. tribes in order to instill in them some sense of competition, which they lacked. The experimental group was formed by children from the Dani tribe. Attempts were made to teach them a technique of fighting with the use of a stick, which is characteristic of martial arts from the island of Java. However, the efforts failed as the children adopted the discipline depriving it of competitive elements. Similar reactions were observed on the part of other tribes when they were taught cricket.

FLOATING ON ANYTHING, a form of competition held annually on the Necko Lake in Augustów, Poland, in which competitors construct their own ingenious, often extravagant, floating vehicles and race them across the lake for the title of Poland's Floating-On-Anything Champions. Similar events are held in various other countries.

WORLD SPORTS
ENCYCLOPEDIA

F

Flat water kayaking.

tion Internationale de Canoë et Kayak (or International Canoe Federation respectively) in 1947. The first E.Ch. were held in 1933 in Prague. Since 1938, as a result of Ger. lobbying, kayaking has been included in the agenda of Olympic events. In 1938 the first W.Ch. were organized in Waxkohn, Sweden (no W.Ch. have been held since 1969). Until 1939 the most successful competitors were Germans, Austrians, Dutchmen, and Scandinavians, esp. Danes and Swedes. Representatives of Hungary (15 medals at the World Cup in 1954), the Soviet Union, Romania, Czechoslovakia, East Ger., West Ger., and Poland yielded similarly effective performances.
The most influential individuals in the history of kayaking are believed to be: the Olympic champion of 1948 and repeated world champion in K-1-for all distances, Swede G. Fredrikson (during 1948-54); the Rumanian A. Vernescu in K-1 500 1961-67; W. Parfenowicz (USSR) 1979-83, who won the title of Olympic champion 7 times in tandem with various partners in K-2 for 500 and 1,000m. R.Helm from East Ger. was the most frequent world and Olympic champion for 1,000m (1976-83). For the shorter distances: 500 and 1,000m the Romanian V. Diba was the most effective competitor 1974-78. The Italian, O. Perri swept the gold 3 times for long, 10,000m, distances (1974-77). In the case of 4-man crews, teams from both Ger. countries, Hungary, Romania and the USSR won the majority of medals. K. Bluhm (Germany) was the outstanding personality of the '90s. He claimed gold in the 1992 Ol.G. in K-1 500 and K-2 1,000, as well as in 1996 in K-2 500 and the silver in 1996 Ol.G. in K-2 1000 (all of the medals in tandem with T. Gutscche)
L. Kwiedosjuk-Pinejewa (USSR) is regarded the kayak genius among women athletes. She won the 1964 and 1968 Ol.G. in K-1 500 and the W.Ch. in 1966, 1970, and 1971. In the 2nd half of the 1980s and 1990s B. Schmidt from Germany was the most successful woman kayaker – she won the World Cup in 1987 and 1989, K-1 500 at the 1992 Ol.G., and K-2 (together with A. Nothnagel) and K-4 in 1988. K-2 and K-4 were generally the domain of representatives from Germany, the USSR, and to a lesser degree from Hungary and Sweden.
C. Chenu, *En Canoë*, 1928; S. Deicke, H.J. Lotsch *ABC des Wasserwanderns*, 1963; J. Drabik, *Kajakarstwo*, 1991; D. Harrison, *Sea Kayaking Basics*, 1993; J.M. Lipawski, *Sport kajakowy* (Kayak Sport), 1934.

BOL, >KRULBOL, and >SCHUIFTAFEL, whereas some other games, such as >PIERBOL and >VLOERBOL, that used to be widely practiced, are rapidly losing popularity.
E. de Vroede, 'Ball and Bowl Games in the Low Countries: Past and Present', *Homo Ludens – Der Spielende Mensch*, 1996, vol. VI; by the same author, *Het Grote Volkssporten Boek*, Leuven, 1996.

FLIGHT SHOOTING, its object is to shoot an arrow as far as possible. A var. is >FREESTYLE ARCHERY, also known as free-style shooting, in which archers use over-sized bows and, while shooting, lie down on their backs with their feet supporting the grip and pull the bow string with both hands.

FLIP THE STICK, an Eng. term for a sports discipline which was experimentally introduced among

FLOORBALL, also called *unihockey*, a game similar in nature to >INDOOR HOCKEY and >FIELD HOCKEY, but played according to different rules and governed by a separate federation. The name *unihockey* (or *unihoc*), used in some countries (e.g. Poland, Germany, Sweden etc.), derives from Latin *unus* – unique, the only one and *hoc* – <hockey. The Eng. name *floorball* originally meant a type of ball game played on a hard surface. The game underwent a rapid development in many countries; in Russia and Scandinavia it is known as *inne-bandy*, in Finland – as *salibandy* and in Japan – as *unihoc*. The playing area is usu. 40m long and 20m wide (min. 36x18m and max. 44x22m). It is surrounded by a board fence, 50cm in height, with rounded corners similar to that in >ICE HOCKEY. At the youngster level the game is played without the

Flat water kayaking.

The 1st Floating-On-Anything Championship at Augustów, Poland, lives up to its name.

F

goalkeeper, with smaller goals 60x90cm in size. At junior and senior levels the goal, the size of 105x140cm, is defended by a goalkeeper, who kneels in front of it. He wears special protective gear, 5-finger gloves and a mask with a face grid, but has no stick. Goals used for practice sessions are smaller (45x60cm). Goals are positioned in the center, 3.5m from the back board. In front of the goal is a marked area, called the crease, 5m wide and extending 4m into the rink. Teams consist of max. 20 players, of whom 5 are field players (at senior level the goalkeeper is an extra player), but the game can be played by teams consisting of 3 or 4 field players. Field players may be substituted every 2-3min. throughout the game, which is divided into three 20-min. periods with intervals of 10min. between each. At the youngster level games are usu. shorter: two 5-min. periods with an interval of 1-10min. The goalkeeper has no stick, but he

A floorball match.

A floorball goalkeeper's helmet and sticks.

wears wide leg guards and gloves that protect him from being hit by the sticks or the ball. He may catch the ball, but within 3sec. has to put it back into play within his own team's half. The players' sticks are 95cm max. in length (shorter at the youngster level), corked at the end of the shaft and with plastic, often open-work blades. They may not be used above the waist line. The ball is made of white plastic, 72mm in diameter, weighs 23g and has 26 holes each with a diameter of 10mm. At the youngsters level the game is often co-educational: teams consist of 3 boys and 2 girls. The game is controlled by 2 referees. At the professional level there is a separate team classification for men and women.

History. Floorball originated in the 1950s. in the US, at first as a game called *floor-hockey*. Players used hockey pucks, which wrecked the floor and were soon replaced with lighter balls. Regular hockey sticks were modified by replacing the solid blade with open-work ending. The first tournament was held in Michigan in 1962. In the 1970s the game was introduced in Sweden, where it quickly gained popularity in schools and amateur clubs under such names as *softbandy*, *floorbandy* etc. In 1981 the first national federation was formed – Svenska Innebandy Forbundet, and in 1990 there were approx. 1,500 clubs with approx. 70,000 players. In 1986 the International Floorball Federation (IFF) was formed in Huskvarna. Floorball is now played in more than 20 countries, incl. Scandinavia, Australia, Belgium, the Czeck Republic, Estonia, Japan, Lithuania, Germany, Poland, Russia, Singapore, the USA, Hungary and others. In 1994 the first European Championships were held in Helsinki, in 1995 – the first Men and Women's W.Ch. in Switzerland, in 1996 – the second Men's W.Ch. in Stockholm, and in 1997 – the Second Women's W.Ch. The first world champions among women were the teams of Sweden (1997) and Finland (1999) and among men – Sweden (1996 and 1998). In 1997 Eur. Cup Competition was introduced.

K.-H. Seiler-Sandviken, *The rules of unihoc*, 1995; the official IFF website: http://www.floorball.org/

FLY BALL, an Eng. sport similar to tennis played with the use of a racket made of solid wood. Instead of a trad. tennis ball, a badminton shuttlecock is used. The court is 23ft. (about 7m) long, and 10ft.

6in. (3.2m) wide for singles and 13ft. 9¹/₈in. (4.2m) – for doubles. The net is stretched at the level of 51in. (1.3m). The scoring system is the same as in >BADMINTON. The match consists of 3 sets, up to 30pts. each. The winner is that player, or couple, who has won 2 sets.

FLYING CUDGELS, a game popular among the Tujia people of the Chin. province of Hunan. Cf. also similar games of other nations, such as Arab >AL BA' 'A, Eng. >TIP-CAT, Indon. >TAK KADAL, Pak. and Ind. >GULI DUNDA, Pol. >KLIPA, >SZTEKIEL, >KICZKA, Fr. >PILAOUETTE, Breton *mouilh*. The game uses cudgels about 70cm long and 3-4cm in diameter, and smaller wooden pegs about 20cm long. The format of the game may be singles, doubles or team. A small peg is placed on the edge of a rhomboid-shaped hole in the ground, to be then flicked up with the larger cudgel. The opponent tries to intercept the peg in the air. If he succeeds, he becomes the 'hitter' himself. If he fails, the hitter puts his cudgel down across the hole in the ground, and the opponent picks the peg up from where it landed and tries to throw it so as to hit the cudgel. If he hits it, he may take over as the hitter, but if he misses, the game goes on to the next stage. The hitter throws the peg high up in the air, and if the other player succeeds in catching it before it lands, he may take over as the hitter. If he fails, he picks up the peg from where it landed and tries to throw it into the hole in the ground. However, the hitter now tries to hit the peg with his cudgel so as to prevent it from entering the hole. If the peg is hit, the catcher tries to catch it again. If he fails to catch it, the hitter uses his cudgel to measure the distance between the hole and the place where the peg has finally landed. The multiple of the cudgel length defines the number of points the hitter scores. The players then swap roles and the above stages are repeated.

Mu Fushan et al., 'Tujia Flying Cudgels', TRAMCHIN.

FLYING DISC, a family of games in which players throw a special disc whose edge is rolled in, enabling thus the disc to fly steadily. The following 3 techniques of throwing are most popular: 1) a throw resembling a backhand tennis return, the disc is held at the level of the thrower's chest and then released pushing the hand forward and rolling the disc clockwise, if thrown with the right hand, or counter-clockwise if thrown with the left; 2) an overhead toss, resembling a baseball pitcher's throw; 3) the disc is held below the waist with the palm facing the hip, after which the hand is raised and, just before the disc is released, it is rolled out in order to give it the right spin.

Flying disc is a generic term and it is very often used interchangeably with frisbee. Such a use can be explained by the common origin of the games and the similarity between the objects being thrown. However, in the course of time the 2 games evolved into different activities, the disks' parameters started to vary and separate organizations were established for each of them. On the other hand, today's categorizations into flying disc and Frisbee competitions are more a result of a convention than the actual difference between the two. The 4 basic types of flying disc games are as follows:

ACCURACY, 4 throws aimed at a 2-m tall net are executed from each of the 7 different stations. A

thrower scores 1pt. for each hit. Stations are located at different distances and various angles from the net, which varies the scale of difficulty.

DISTANCE (THROWING), whose object is to throw the disc over the longest possible distance. The 1999 world records were established by A. Bekken (130.09m) in the women's category, and S. Stokeley (200.01m) in the men's category.

MAXIMUM TIME ALOFT, the object being to maintain the disc airborne as long as possible. The 1999 world records belong to A. Bekken (11.81sec.) in the women's category, and D. Cain (16.72sec.) in the men's category.

THROW, RUN AND CATCH (TRC), the object is to throw a disc over the longest possible distance and catch it before it touches the ground. In 1999 world records were established by J. Horowitz (60.02m) in the women's category, and H. Oshima (92.64m) in the men's category.

International meetings, including W.Ch., are held in women's and men's categories as multiathlon events called the overall open, as well as in *ultimate*, *disc golf*, and *guts* events (see below). Other forms of flying disc events, although originating from the same activity, evolved into separate disciplines, often administered by separate organizations. Below is a list of such disciplines organized alphabetically, as the hierarchies employed by players are often incomprehensible for outsiders:

AEROBIE, a type of flying disc differing from the trad. disk by the fact that it has a hole in the middle which helps throw it farther [probably Eng. *aerobee* from Gk. *aero* – aerial, spatial + *bee*, a name given in the 1950s to the first Amer. rockets launched into outer space]. Used in distance throwing rather than in trad. catching games. On average an Aerobie can be thrown as far as 150-200m. *The Guinness Book of Records* reports that the farthest throw to-date was made (in 1999) by S. Zimmerman of San Francisco who sent the disk flying 419yds. (383.13m).

BUTT-GUTS, according to the official regulations of The World Butt-Guts Federation it is a game played between two singles or doubles whose object is to hit the opponent's buttocks (or butt) with a flying disc. The game starts with one team turning their backs on their opponents so that their buttocks are exposed as targets. Each player from the throwing team attempts to hit any of the opponents on the buttocks. A successful throw earns a thrower prestige among other players; otherwise he is booed by both opponents and teammates. After each of the throwing team members has executed a throw, the teams change roles. Any type of disc can be used, with the exception of disc-golf one. The teams are not obliged to wear any distinctive uniforms because they are far enough from each other to avoid any ambiguity. In general, the rules are so constructed that only minimal preparations of players and field are necessary to start the game. The field consists of 2 parallel lines some distance apart, which are referred to as butt lines and can be marked, for instance, with a bottle at each end of the line. The surface is undetermined, although a well-mowed lawn is suggested. Before the throwing team starts, they bark the command: 'Butt up!', after which the opponents are supposed to adopt the so-called butt stance that is to be maintained until the end of a throwing series. The butt stance can also be a moving pattern

A frisbee disc competition in Washington, D.C.

which, however, has to be regular and predictable. Otherwise, any irregular movement is treated as a flinch, in the case of singles, or an invalid butt stance, in the case of team play. On assuming the butt stance, the receiving team has to signal, either vocally or by raising an arm, their readiness to play. The teams alternate in throwing and receiving the discs and the number of exchanges has to be even. A successful throw is when a disc squarely whacks an opponent's posterior, however, the throws must not be too hard, or else they will be judged by other players as fouls. Should any of the players be injured, his team can take a substitute at any time. A substitute can be any player who is not a registered member of any other team for the given tournament. The player who was injured must not return to play during the same match. The game has a clearly humorous character.

CARPARK DISC GOLF, the game is held on a special course or a >GOLF course. Participants throw discs into baskets mounted on platforms surrounded by chains which make it easier to place the disc in the basket. The basket's diameter varies from 80 to 150cm. The disc is smaller and heavier than those used in other flying disc events. Other rules follow >GOLF standards, i.e. the winner is the player who succeeds in placing a disc with fewest throws over a given stretch of the course. In the USA, around 500 disc golf courses can currently be found.

DISCATHON, a var. of disc golf in which players attempt to go through a course in the shortest possible time from a predetermined direction. In order to make the game more dynamic, each player uses 2 discs.

Description of All the Official Disc Sports, Internet, http://www.afda.com; J. Townes, 'Flying Disc', *Encyclopedia of World Sport*, D. Levinson & K. Christensen, eds., 1996, vol. I.

DOUBLE DISC COURT (DDC), a game played in doubles with 2 discs at the same time. The object is to force the opponents to possess of both discs at the same time. The court is formed of 2 identical 13x13m squares, usu. about 17m apart, one for each team. The min. distance between the squares is 5m. Each corner of each court has to be marked with a conspicuously painted bollard. Each disc weighs roughly 110g. During the game the players must not touch or cross the lines indicating their squares. The match starts with simultaneous serves of opposing teams whose objective is to return the incoming disc fast enough to leave the opponents with 2 of them. Single points are scored when the opponents: 1) do not catch a properly thrown disc, or after catching it, let it fall down within their court's borders; 2) throw the disc incorrectly, i.e. so that it lands outside the receivers' square. Two points can be scored when the opponents are in possession of 2 discs or if they touch 2 discs at the same time (double touch). The disc falling onto the opponents' court can score a point only if it fell at a min. 30° angle. The game continues up to 15 or 21pts. The winner is required to gain at least a 2-pt. advantage over the opponent (cap score). In S California, the DDC league championships are held. Double disc court has its own Double Disc Court Players Association, although on the international scale the sport is under the auspices of The World Flying Disc Federation (WFDF).

Description of Double Disc Court, The Internet: www.wfdf.org

FIVE HUNDRED, a var. of flying disc played by 2 teams of any number of players. The teams line up in front of each other, 30-40m apart. A player of one team throws the disc at the opponents who attempt to catch it. The throws can be difficult but they have to be at least feasibly catchable. The winner is the team that scores a greater number of points, however, usu. the 2 extreme scores – i.e. those achieved by the best and the worst players – are not counted in the final score. Each catch is scored differently: 50pts. for receiving a properly executed throw; 100pts. for saving a dubious throw; -50pts. for an uncontestable throw intercepted by the opponents as a catchable swill; -100pts. for an uncatchable throw; 100pts. for a properly executed throw that was not caught by the opponents; 50pts. for a layout catch; -50pts. for not lying out for a catchable throw.

GUTS, independently from the name flying disc the name *Frisbee* or *frisbie* is in use. A number of ambiguities arose as a result of this fact. The prototype

of a Frisbee disc was a baking tin in which the US-based Frisbie Pie Co. sold their pies. Frisbee's and flying disc's origins are common, the equipment operates on the basis of the same laws of physics and the technique of throwing is similar but Frisbee's subsequent development, both in the character of the game and in the equipment used, was different. Finally, disputes between the enthusiasts and the establishment of separate organizations for Frisbee and flying disc resulted in a situation in which both disciplines are treated as independent and unrelated games that use similar equipment (a situation analogous to that of netball and basketball). The major types of Frisbee games are:

ULTIMATE FRISBEE, a combination of elements borrowed from other games, such as football and basketball. It is played without any referee and its rules are simple. Two teams of 7 players play on a 70x40-yd. (64x36m) court with 25-yd.-deep (23m) end zones. The object is to throw the disc into the opponent's end zone. Teammates can pass the disc one to another before the actual attacking throw that can be executed from any place and at any angle. The player in possession of the disc must not run with it and has to execute a throw within 10sec. after catching it. Any physical contact between players is considered a foul, which does not, however, imply a change in possession of the disc. If a player claims no foul was committed a given action is repeated. The game is characterized by a high level of fair play. In professional matches players usu. refrain from any acts of aggression and the idea of winning at all costs is socially discredited, so players routinely acknowledge their own fouls. If the disc touches a line, the throwing team loses its possession. The game was initiated by students of Maplewood High School in New Jersey, with the first matches played on a school parking lot. Within a few years the game was popularized in high schools and universities throughout the USA. In 1972, the first intercollegiate match between the teams of Rutgers and Princeton Universities was held in New Brunswick, New Jersey. Later, the game spread to 20 other countries and in the 90s there were around 15,000 players all over the world.

HOTBOX, a var. of ultimate frisbee played by smaller teams of 2-3 players. The playing field consists of a square, 1x1 or 2x2m, functioning as a throwing target, located in the center of a larger square whose side is 8-16m. The rules are similar to those employed in ultimate frisbee, though the time to execute a throw after catching the disc is shorter – 5sec. instead of 10 – and points are scored by throwing the disc into the central square instead of the opponent's end zone. In the case of a turnover, the team gaining possession of the disc has to throw it outside the large square before they attempt to score a point.

CANINE FRISBEE, a game in which discs thrown by people are intercepted and brought back by specially trained dogs. The local rules vary from place to place. Usually the result depends on a dog's skill in catching the disc and the time in which the disc is brought back to the place from which it was thrown.

History. The earliest games consisting of throwing a flying disc among players were known in the USA already in the 19th cent. Their appearance was, however, only local and rather episodic. The competition organized by Middlebury College, Vermont, where in 1939 the students used tin baking plates during a picnic is considered the actual beginning of the history of flying disc as a sports discipline. The event is commemorated with a monument on the school's campus of a dog catching an airborne disc in its mouth. The original name of a flying disc, i.e. frisbee, originates from the name of a baking company established in 1871 by W.R. Frisbie. There are 2 theories concerning the beginnings of the game, jocularly referred to as the Pie-Tin School and the Cookie-Tin School. Despite differences in the type of pastry products both schools admit that the beginning of frisbee is closely related to pie tins on which products and a conspicuous brand name were placed. Yale University students supposedly threw such tins (sometimes not quite empty) alerting those in the path of its trajectory with the loud call: 'Fris-

Juliana Korver of Iowa throws a putt at the 2001 Pro Disc Golf World Championships at Como Park in St. Paul, Minnesota (USA). Korver won the women's title.

bee!' Some historians report that it was actually the other way round: it was the baking company that used pie tins shaped after a flying disc known in the USA since the 1850s. In the 1940s and '50s similar inventions were noted in various towns and villages which sometimes argue their share in the origins and the development of the game. Independently from Frisbie pie tins, a similar flying disc was con-

WORLD SPORTS ENCYCLOPEDIA

F

Above: Sydney, a mixed breed, grabs the frisbee thrown to her by owner Scott Vanbeekom at the Southwest Regional Final held in Pasadena, Calif., one of seven qualifying events in the ALPO Canine Frisbee disc Championships.

F

structed in 1948 by a WWII veteran pilot and a building inspector from California, W.F. Morrison, who wanted to provide people with a pastime related to UFOs that were so timely a topic in those days. He constructed a disc made of a composite of butyl and stearate. His first disc was called the Flyin' Saucer and then came the Pluto Platter. He tried to popularize his invention during public performances on various holidays. Apart from that, in the '50s, E. Robes, an inventor from New Hampshire, started to produce flying discs that he called space saucers.

Freestyle frisbee.

In 1956, Morrison sold his patent to Wham-O, a toy factory in San Gabriel, California, which was set up and managed by R. Knerr and A.K. Melin, graduates from University of Southern California. The company is known for having introduced a number of very popular toys and recreational gear (for instance the >HULA-HOOP). After finalizing a deal with Morrison, they launched mass production of discs in 1957. Later, Knerr was to say that at the beginning the sales of flying discs were rather modest but both partners had a strong conviction that

the thing would catch on some day. During their marketing trips, when they advertised the new product to sports and toy stores, they arrived at university campuses on the E Coast where the original pie-tin was already relatively popular. Similarly, in Bridgeport, Connecticut, local community used Frisbie Pie Co. pie tins for playing. When the businessmen learned about it, they simply modified the spelling of the name calling their product Frisbee. In 1958, the Knerr and Melin Wham-O product started to catch on. In that same year, the first International Frisbee Tournament was held in Escanaba, Michigan. By 1964, Wham-O was launching a heavier, 'professional', model of the frisbee. In 1967, on the initiative of E. Headrick, one of the Wham-O managers, the International Frisbee Association was established. When Wham-O was acquired by one company after another the Frisbee patent changed owners a number of times and currently it is held by the Mattel Corp. The first Wham-O discs had the following inscription on them: 'Play Catch! Invent games!' This motto led to the invention of various games using the disc. All of these games can be categorized as flying disc ones, although sometimes they are purposefully claimed to be exclusively frisbee games. Nowadays, there is more than one federation overseeing such games. Some of the games, such as butt-guts or double disc court, developed their own associations.

The popularity of flying discs grew rapidly in the course of the '60s. From the moment the flying disc was launched to 1996 the number sold in the USA alone has exceeded 100 million and it is estimated that annual sales excel that of other sports equipment, including baseballs, basketballs, and (Amer.) footballs. Such rapid growth is attributed by psychologists to a number of factors, such as: 1) simplicity, which allows playing the game at little cost in virtually any place; 2) fascination with space travel which flying discs bring to mind; 3) general progress in the recreational attitude of Amer. society; 4) acceptance of the flying disc by youth subcultures; 5) introduction of the flying disc in schools as a PE tool. Outside the USA, the flying disc developed substantially in Scand. countries. In 1985, The First World Flying Disc Conference was held in Helsinborg, Sweden. It was attended by 19 countries forming the World Flying Disc Federation (WFDF), which in 1987 was admitted as a member of the General Association of International Sports Federations. The WDFD organizes annual W.Ch. in men's and women's categories. The leading male players of the late 90s were, among others, American C. Daman and Swede C. Sandröm, and among women, Norwegian S. Wentzel, Americans A. Bekken and B. Verish, and Swede R. Olnis. In the USA, in 1993, flying disc was admitted as one of the events for the Presidential Sports Award.

Flying fox.

FLYING FOX, an adventure activity in the form of a cable slide high above a gorge or precipice. Participants 'fly' across on a zip wire, attached to a special body harness, and are then pulled back to the gorge or pull themselves back, hand over hand, so there is no walkout. Sometimes compared to >BUNGY JUMPING, it offers the same adrenaline rush, but is much safer. Flying fox can also be practiced in specially built venues.

FLYING HANDKERCHIEF, a school game played in Rus. primary schools. One player is chosen to be the 'chaser'. He counts, '1, 2, 3' out loud, while all the other players scatter in all directions. The chaser is supposed to catch and touch the player who has in his hand a handkerchief with a knot tied in the middle. This is not easy, as the players circulate the handkerchief among themselves. If anyone drops the handkerchief, he must immediately pick it up, as the chaser may start chasing him only then. A caught player takes over from the chaser. It may so happen that the chaser becomes tired and cannot catch any of the players. He may then stop and call 'Make a circle'. The other players surround him in a circle and the rules change. The handkerchief is passed quickly from hand to hand or tossed about the circle. Now, it is easier for the chaser to intercept the handkerchief and swap places with the player who has failed to pass it on. Instead of a handkerchief, a ring made from the material used in the gird of riding tackle may be used. A little bell is attached to it. In this variation, the game is called the 'flying bell'. Cf. Eng. >DROP HANDKERCHIEF.
I.N. Chkannikov, 'Flying handkerchief', GIZ, 10-11.

FLYSURFING, see >KITEBOARDING.

FØDE EN BJØRN, Dan. for 'giving birth to a bear'. A folk game in which one of the 3 participants lies down on his belly with his head pointing north. The second player lies on the first one – head pointing east. The third one lies on top with his head pointing south. The bottom and the top players grab each other's legs and squeeze the middle player whose task is to free himself. This can be done if the middle player stands on all fours, raising the other two who, sooner or later will have to let go because of the strain.
J. Møller, 'Føde en bjørn', GID, 1997, 3, 19-20.

FOETH-BAL, an old name for Eng. >ASSOCIATION FOOTBALL, used in the 17th cent. by the Dutch traveling in England; prob. deriving the name from its Du. equivalent >VOETBAL. The name foeth-bal was recorded by D. Souter, a pastor from Haarlem, in his treatise *Tabula Lusoria. Alea, et variis Ludis Libri III* (1622). The name appears in a passage where var. of football are listed: 'The fourth variety of the ball game is *harpastum* (called foeth-bal by the English), which thanks to its circular roundness is pitched above the ground.' Cf. >HARPASTON.

FOIL, see >FENCING.

FOLLICULUS, a diminutive of Lat. >FOLLIS, whose primary meaning is a small leather sac, but it also means a ball covered in leather. The term refers not only to a ball but also to an ancient game. It is believed the game was played with the fists. From a brief remark in one of Plautus's plays it can be deduced that one of the objects of the game was preventing the ball from touching the ground and keeping it airborne as long as possible.

FOLLIS [Lat. *follis* – a small sac], a type of ball for playing with and the name of a game practiced in ancient Rome. Its Gk. equivalent was *kene*. Surviving information about the structure of the follis is contradictory. The game cannot be fully reconstructed either for lack of detailed enough descriptions. Some researchers hypothesize the game was played with the use of bats with flattened tips, which allowed the players not only to strike the ball but also catch it and carry it. Brit. historian, F.P. Magoun, believes that follis was similar to >BAGATAWAY – a game of Amer. Indians which was a predecessor of >LACROSSE (*History of Football. From the Beginnings to 1871*, a chapter about the origin of ball games, 1938). A Span. researcher, C.M. Palos, when writing about the influence of ancient sports on modern ones, claims that follis was a game for 'the children, the elderly and physically weaker people' (*Juegos y deportes tradicionales en España*, 1992, 165). We do not know if follis was in any way – and if so,

what way – related with >FOLLICULUS whose name is a diminutive of the same vocable, implying therefore that the ball used in that game was smaller.
'Follis', *Paulys Real Encyclopädie der Classischen Altertumwissenschaft*, ed. G. Wissow, 1909, vol. XIV, I.

FOOLISH BOWLING, an Eng. bowling game of which hardly anything is known. The bowl used in the game was semispherical. The game as such prob. originated from a similar one, known in Flanders as >PIERBOL, or from its var. called *zottebol*. Foolish bowling was particularly popular in Lancashire, where in the city of Littleborough there was the Foolish Bowling Association of Littleborough.

FOOT BRIDGE, a simple game of skill played in water. Two boats with their sterns facing one another at a distance of 2-3m are connected by a footbridge approx. 5-6m in length. The players must pass from one boat to the other without losing their balance and falling into the water.
I.N. Chkhannikov, 'Footbridge', GIZ, 1953, 81.

FOOTBAG, also known as *hacky sack*, a game of a number of variations played solely by kicking a ball known as a footbag. The main var. of footbag are: *footbag consecutive*, *footbag net*, *footbag golf* and *footbag freestyle*. There are various kinds of fields on which footbag is played, but the object kicked – a leather bag filled with a soft material, in the past; a miniature soccer-type bag, nowadays – is always the same and has the following dimensions: 1-2.½in. (2.54-6.35cm) in diameter and weight of 0.71-2.47oz. (20-70g). The footbag is round, covered with pliable covering and filled with a soft material (oakum or foam) in the form of loose pellets.
History. The game was initiated in the USA in the 1970s when M. Marshall observed a game of the Native Americans which consisted in flicking up with the foot and leg a leather bag filled with soft material. In 1972, having undergone knee surgery, J. Stalberger was in need of a good rehabilitation exercise and, after a meeting with Marshall, he came to the conclusion that the game, which they both called *hacking the sack*, was just what the doctor ordered. Soon afterwards, Marshall and Stalberger set up a company named Kenn Corp. to manufacture the necessary equipment for the game, which they then started to popularize. Despite Marshall's premature death, Stalberger was quite successful. He also laid the foundations for the National Hacky Sack Association. The popularity of the game grew even more after the *Hacky Sack* book was published by the Klutz Press. Kransco and Wham-O soon held rights to sell equipment for footbag. The most widespread variation of footbag is *footbag freestyle*.
Footbag is administered on the international scale by the International Footbag Advisory Board (IFAB) that publishes the official bulletin 'Rules of Footbag Sports.' The Board pays special attention to *fair play*, it being enforced not by the game's rules or regulations, but rather by a player's moral responsibility. Art. 102 of the IFAB by-laws reads as follows:

Footbag sports have traditionally relied upon a spirit of sportsmanship which places the responsibility of fair play on the players themselves. Highly competitive and committed play is encouraged, but never at the expense of the bond of mutual respect between players, adherence to the agreed upon rules of any event, nor the basic enjoyment of play. Protection of these vital elements serves to eliminate adverse conduct from the playing field. The responsibility for the maintenance of this spirit rests on each player's shoulders.

According to art. 107 of the by-laws, the tournament director has the right to disqualify any player who

exhibits violent, obscene, abusive, disruptive, destructive, or illegal behavior, is continually annoying to other players, cheats, or otherwise attempts to create an unfair advantage for himself or disadvantage for others through a circumvention of the rules, or otherwise causes substantial hardship, inconvenience, or annoyance to spectators, officials, or other players.

Regulations enforcing fair play are to be found throughout the by-laws, e.g. in the sections dealing with lodging protests, reinterpreting and suspending regulations, etc. Very few other sports incorporate fair play principles into their regulations to such a degree and so consistently. This is perhaps a reflection of the popular belief that the preservation of the values of noble competition in the present state of degradation of international sports is only possible within the lesser known sports which are less prone to mass media and market pressures.

Players are grouped not only according to the their sex and age, but also particular skills, since there is a tendency to avoid having players of different abilities compete, thus weaker players not only avoid humiliation, but are also encouraged to improve their skills. Behavior contrary to fair play principles may be grounds for suspending an entire tournament by the tournament director. A given player is also limited in the number of tournaments they participate in, which is meant to diminish the possibility of a few outstanding players dominating all others. For example, a participant of an individual freestyle tournament is not allowed to take part in a following team tournament.
FOOTBAG CONSECUTIVE, a variation of footbag played individually or in teams; the object is to keep the footbag airborne using only the feet and knees. The winner is the player who kicks the footbag the greatest number of times before a drop or a foul occurs (e.g. touching the footbag with any part of the player's body above the waist, leaning against the ground or a wall, etc.). In speed events there is a set time period in which to achieve the highest number of kicks.
Any smooth, hole-free surface can serve as a field. If indoors, it is recommended that there is overhead clearance of at least 6ft. (183cm). The footbag must satisfy general conditions applicable to all variations of footbag. There is also a preference for automatic or electronic devices used for counting kicks. Each rally starts with a hand serve. Every time the player kicks the footbag, he scores 1pt. Each player is allowed a number of rallies which is determined by the umpire, a rally being an uninterrupted series of kicks between the serve and the drop or the foul, e.g. touching the footbag with a part of the body above the waist (*upper body foul*). Novice players are usually granted 3-5 rallies, intermediate players 2-3, and advanced players 1-2.
In pair play, the players keep the footbag airborne in a series of kicks between each other and each is allowed to kick the footbag up to 25 times before passing it to the other player who is obliged to continue the game with the same number of kicks.
In team play, a group of 3 or more players aims at keeping the footbag airborne for as long as possible. Each player is allowed to kick the footbag up to 5 times before passing it to another player. Each kick scores 1pt. The rally ends when the footbag touches the ground or is touched with an upper body part 5 times by the same player.
In the 'one pass' system, the most dynamic one, the player is obliged to receive and return the footbag with a single kick. Each kick scores 1pt. The rally ends when the footbag touches the ground or is touched with an upper part of a player's body even a single time, or when a player kicks the footbag even once before executing a pass.
In the '1-up-5-down' system, 2 players attempt to keep the footbag up with a changing number of kicks. At the beginning of the round each player is allowed to kick the footbag once before passing it, and having received the footbag back must kick it twice before passing it back, and then 3, 4, 5 and back downwards 4, 3, 2, 1. The total of all the kicks or the number of successful rounds constitutes the score, where a round is a series of kicks 1-2-3-4-5-4-3-2-1 executed by each player. The rally ends when the footbag touches the ground, when a player fails to maintain the 1-2-3-4-5-4-3-2-1 series, or when the footbag touches a player's body above the waist.
TIMED SINGLES. One player attempts to kick the footbag as many times as possible within a pre-determined amount of time, usually 10min. The rally starts with a hand serve at the start of the timer. The situation in which the player starts the game before the timer's notice sign (*the early start foul*) does not disqualify the player, but instead 10pts. are subtracted from the future score as a penalty. Players must alternate feet between kicks, with penalties assigned for non-alternating kicks. Each kick counts for 1pt. and the rally ends when the footbag touches the ground, an upper body foul occurs, or the time limit elapses.
A TIMED SINGLES RALLY consists of alternating double kicks of the footbag. A triple kick with the same leg is considered a foul. The rally ends when the footbag touches the ground, an upper body foul occurs, the player kicks the footbag a particular number of times, or the time limit elapses.
DOUBLES DISTANCE ONE PASS. The field is marked by two parallel lines, one 10ft. (304.8cm) away from the other. Each line is at least 20ft. (610cm) long and 2in. (5.1cm) wide. Players are grouped along the 2 lines on the perimeter of the field, one team facing the other. The game starts with a hand serve of one player and the other kicks the footbag. They attempt to kick it as many times as possible and are given 1pt. for each kick. The best score of 3 rallies is accepted as the final score. Touching the line or the field between the lines is a

Footbag, also known as hacky sack, is a popular form of recreational sport.

foul. The rally ends when the footbag touches the ground, an upper body foul occurs, or a player touches the line.
In FOOTBAG CONSECUTIVE a record series of kicks are registered. In women's singles, the 1997 record of 24,713 kicks in 4hrs. 9min. 27sec., is held by C. Constable; in the singles open 63,326 kicks in 8hrs. 50min. 42sec., by T. Martin (1997); in the women's doubles, 34,543 in 5hrs. 38min. 22sec., by C Constable and T. George (1995); in the doubles open 132,011 in 20hrs. 34min., by T George and G. Lautt (1998). Additionally, A. Linder set the 1996 record of 1,019 kicks in the 5-min. open, and I. Fogle set the 1997 record of 804 kicks among women.
FOOTBAG FREESTYLE. The players attempt to kick the footbag in an artistic style. The performance is assessed on the basis of a number of esthetic criteria. The aspects of the performance taken into consideration are the following: 1) choreography and the choice of music, 2) degree of difficulty, 3) variety and originality, and 4) technique. During the game the player moves around a circle, approx. 40ft. (12.2m) in diameter, drawn in the field. The game may take place indoors, provided there is a clearance of at least 20ft. (6.2m) above the ground. The surface is optional (grass, wood), as long as it is free from obstructions or holes. The player may use more than 1 footbag in the game.
In footbag freestyle players can play individually, in twos or in threes. An individual performance time cannot exceed 2min., 3min. in the case of pairs or triples. The tournament director sets a time limit. A team performance is assessed in the same way as an individual one, with a separate score for cooperation and synchronicity. Performances are assessed by a panel of umpires, among whom there are players previously defeated in the tournament or those who have already presented their performances. A penalty point (*drop*) is given when the footbag is dropped on the ground.

COMPETITIVE FOOTBAG.

Competitive footbag.

A variety of footbags.

The popularity of this form of footbag can be seen in the tournaments at which records in simultaneous participation are broken. The greatest number of freestyle footbag players participated in the 1996 tournament performance in St. Patrick High School in Chicago, where 933 players performed simultaneously.

FOOTBAG GOLF. The object of the golf game is to traverse a course from beginning to end in the fewest number of kicks of the footbag. Before the game starts, the tournament director examines the footbag. Then the game is started with a hand serve followed by a footbag kick from the *tee* area, which is a square of 6 sq. ft. (5.57m^2). The place where the footbag comes to rest is marked with a marker and the footbag is then carried 12in. (30.5cm) farther. The objective is to kick the footbag into a hole, 18in. (45.7cm) in diameter, placed on a platform 18in. above the ground. If the footbag stays in the hole or on its edge, a point is scored; if the footbag falls out, no point is scored and the game continues from the place in which the footbag came to rest. If the footbag is lost in the rough, the player, compulsorily accompanied by the whole team, has 2min. to find it. If the footbag cannot be found, the game continues from the previous position of the footbag, or as close to it as possible. The size of a single course, measured from the tee area to the hole, should be 20-50ft. (6.1-15.24m). Kicks from the outside of the course are possible and a point is scored if the footbag rolls into the hole. To score a point when kicking from the inside of the course, the player must kick the footbag directly into a hole, without it rolling on the ground. The player whose footbag is farthest from the hole starts a particular round of kicks.

One of the advantages of this form of footbag is both its social and recreational nature accompanied by its smooth action and low costs of equipment.

History. The first official game was played in Delta Park, Portland, Oregon in 1982, and was organized by John Stalberger.

FOOTBAG NET. In this style, players kick the footbag with their feet or shanks over the net which is 5ft. (152.4cm) in height (measured in the center). In singles, one player can kick the footbag twice; in doubles players of one team is allowed to kick the footbag 3 times, where the third kick must be directed to the opponents' half. Any contact of the footbag with the upper part of the players' bodies constitutes a violation of the rules. The footbag is made of vinyl or is covered with leather. The players determine its kind and size before the game starts. If no compromise can be reached, the umpire is to decide. The teams toss a coin to choose the court sides. The court is 20x44ft. (6.09x13.41 m), divided by a longitudinal line, thus resembling a >BADMINTON court. The square on the right-hand side of a given half is called the *even side* and that on the left-hand side is the *odd side*. The same court is used for both singles and doubles. Its area can be individually decided, however the surface must be smooth and free from holes. The lines setting the perimeters of the court are 2in. (5.1cm) wide and belong to the playing area (*played in-bounds*), i.e. the footbag dropped on the line is not out. The footbag touching the net, or the lines supporting the poles, etc. is considered a foul. The serve consists in kicking the footbag across the court and over the net as in tennis. There are 3 sets of 11 or 15pts. each. Players change halves after 1 set. In the third set, or in a 1-set game, halves are changed after one of the players has scored 6pts. (in a game up to 11pts.), or 8pts. (in a game up to 15pts.). The set is won by an advantage of 2pts., which means that in certain situations when no 2-pt. advantage occurs the game continues indefinitely. For example, in a 15-pt. game the final score can be as high as 17:15, 20:18, etc. Only the serving player or team can win points; the other party must first be granted the right to serve by winning an 'empty' point which does not count in the final score (similar to volleyball before 1999). The 3-set game is the most common option. Here the victor must win 2 out of 3 sets.

The rules governing doubles follow those of >VOLLEYBALL: each team is allowed to kick the footbag 3 times on their side of the court, where the third kick must be delivered over the net to the opponents' side.

In the 1970s and 1980s, a Philippine sport >SEPAK TAKRAW influenced the development of footbag net; this could be seen in the manner of receiving the footbag with the foot above the net.

The leading players of the 1990s were Americans: K. Schults, A. Marcussen and C. 'Crass' Eddicott.

J. Townes, *Footbag*, EWS 1996, I; The Internet: http://www.footbag.org/faq

FOOTBALL, a name initially defining in Eng., and subsequently in many other languages, a family of team games whose object is to move a ball to a specific goal. It may be a goal or the back (goal) line of the field and sometimes both. In some cases, the name football accompanied by some other term refers to a ball game that uses a different goal, e.g. >LAWN FOOTBALL.

Etymology. The original Eng. name consists of 2 elements whose origin and meaning seem quite apparent [foot + ball]. Therefore, the popular interpretation was that the name meant, from the very beginning, a game in which a ball was put in motion with the foot. However, this is the case of only some games whose names are derived from football and it applies mainly to >ASSOCIATION FOOTBALL (i.e. soccer) and its historical predecessors, e.g. >WINCHESTER COLLEGE FOOTBALL, >HARROW FOOTBALL, >RADLEY GAME, and >ETON FIELD GAME. The 'foot' element seems unjustified in the names of many other games since the ball is put in motion with hands, the feet being used only sporadically, which puts in question the presence of this element instead of, for instance, the fist or the palm. This applies, among others, to aquatic football, a var. of >WATER POLO, where it is technically impossible to play with the feet; >GAELIC FOOTBALL, in which the players use their fists to put the ball in motion, although kicking is also acceptable. In >RUGBY, the actual full name of which is 'rugby football', both hands and feet are used but due to the origin of the game the name football is justifiable here. Many games originated in the 19th cent. acquired the name football almost automatically, although players used both feet and hands. They include such games as >AMERICAN FOOTBALL, >AUSTRALIAN FOOTBALL, >CANADIAN FOOTBALL. These names demonstrate unequivocally that the tendency to use the term to refer to a foot-sized ball, rather than only a ball kicked with the foot, persists. Another proof of the same tendency is >SKI FOOTBALL, in which the feet and the legs do not touch the ball which instead is only passed from hand to hand by skiers, and yet the word football forms a part of the game's name. This nomenclature, applying to both old and modern sports, demonstrates that football used to refer to a foot-sized ball, which in time also encompassed a ball kicked with the foot. The conviction that the meaning of football was different in the past could be easily corroborated with analysis of historical documents which reveal that the medieval var. of the game – which were predecessors of modern football – consisted mostly of carrying the ball in hands rather than only kicking it. The game in which a large ball was used was often quite brutal and therefore royal, church or municipal authorities prohibited it from time to time. Consequently, a foot-sized ball was distinguished from smaller balls that posed less threat to players and spectators (cf. >ROYAL TENNIS). Nevertheless, due to imperfect knowledge of Latin a term *pila pedalis* – a foot-sized ball, contained in a number of documents, was translated as a ball moved with the foot. The first Eng. writer dealing with sport, J. de Berners, in *The Book of St. Albans* attributed to her, when defining a ball incorrectly associated the term *pila pedalis* with football. Her description of a coat of arms contains details, given in Lat., of the meaning the term *pila* had in medieval England:

Sometimes, the Latin term pila *refers to 'a piece of wood' put under the bridge span... and sometimes it is understood as a round device for playing. The thing meant to be played with the hands is then described as a* pila manualis, *and when played with the feet, it is called a* pila pedalis.

D. Wedderburn's *Vocabula*, published around 1633, contains a monologue about a ball kicked with the foot, referred to by the author as a *pila pedalis*. In 1666, four Oxford students were suspended in their rights, due to their excessive fascination with football (*lusus pilae pedalis*), resulting in poor performance at school. Although the terms *pila pedalis* and *pila pedarius* were often used interchangeably, it should be assumed that both var. of the game played with a large ball existed in the Middle Ages and were apparently mistaken one for the other. As a result, the term football acquired the meaning referring primarily to a ball moved with the foot instead of a foot-sized ball.

The ordinances prohibiting the game were announced to the public by heralds or preachers. Therefore, it was necessary to translate the original Lat. text to native languages. The equivalent of the Lat. name was soon coined. In Middle English, it was spelled in several different ways, e.g. *footebale. fotebal, foteballe, fotebale, footte ball, fout baule, fut ball, fute ball, futballe, footballe, foote ball, futeballe playe, foot e ball* along with several other forms which evolved into the modern football. One of those Eng. prototypes of football makes its first appearance rather late, in 1424, in Henry VI's edict, where we can read: 'the king forbiddes bat na man play at be fut ball under the payne off.' The Eng. term coexisted throughout the 15th cent. with its Lat. prototype. In the 16th cent. the Eng. name became more widespread in vernacular Eng. as well as in literature. A. Barclay's 1515 *Eclogues* contain the following text: 'the sturdie plowmen driving the foote ball'. The foot-sized ball was severly criticized in, among others, T. Elyot's *Book Called the Governour*, large parts of which are devoted to football, e.g.: 'Foote balle wherin is nothinge but beastly furie and extreme violence, wherof procedeth hurte and consequently rancour and malice do remaine with them that be wounded.' Only after the rules of modern football developed in 19th-cent. England did the name football start to refer to mostly – but not only – a game consisting mainly of kicking the ball. When in the 2nd half of the 19th cent. Eng. football games became popular in Europe, the term spread throughout most of the Eur. languages. In Germanic languages, the

Matthäus Merian the Elder, The Lilies of the Valley Are Often Mistaken, *copperplate, c. 1615. Two men are inflating a ball with a metal pump against a background of a ball game going on in the meadow.*

similarity of individual elements of the name, such as the foot or the ball, made the assimilation even easier despite slight differences in spelling, as in Dan. *fodbol*, Du. *voetbal*, Swed. *fotbol*. In Romance languages, the Eng. name underwent local phonetic and spelling modifications, however, in Fr. it remained unchanged. In Span. the word is sp. *futbol*, and in Rum. – *fotbal*. The local tradition of football proved stronger in Ital., where even after the Eng. term has been assimilated, the old Ital. name *giocco di calcio*, or *calcio*, is still in use. Also Hungarian resisted the Eng. influence using its own word – *labdarúgas*. Slavic languages, despite slight spelling differences, retained similarity to the Eng. prototype: Rus., Ukr., and Byelorussian – *futbou*, Serbo-Croatian – *futbal*. In Pol., the name football appeared in the late 19th cent. and referred only to a game in which the ball is kicked. At the beginning, the original Eng. name was used, then it was modified into *futbal*, occasionally the Ger. *fussball* was employed, and finally the modern form *futbol* appeared. Around 1900-04 the Pol. translation – *piłka nożna* – appeared, fully accepted by the press in the '20s. From then on, both names, *futbol* and *piłka nożna*, have coexisted.

Assuming, as suggested by the historical documents discussed above, that the name football originally referred to a foot-sized ball, it is obvious that the name received a new meaning when football rules developed. The word 'foot' started to be associated with the part of the body that was applied to the ball in order to put it in motion. The Pol. name *piłka nożna* is not a faithful translation, since it replaced the original 'foot' with 'leg'. In Eng., however, the term does not apply only to games in which solely feet are employed but it is used to refer to other games, e.g. the abovementioned rugby-football. In the USA, Canada, Australia or Ireland, the term football is applied to games that have little in common with the Eur. football. Therefore, in order to make a precise differentiation between these games and football, the name 'association football' started to be employed. As it was too long it was soon replaced with a more manageable substitute, composed of the 'soc' element taken from the word as[soc]iation, double 'cc' and a suffix '-er', resulting thus in a new name – 'soccer'.

History. The earliest reference to football on the Brit. Isles may be found in the *Historia Brittonum* written by a Celtic chronicler, Nennius, who lived in the 9th cent., and it concerns the rule of a Celtic king Guorthigirn (later referred to as Vortigern) in the 5th cent. The king ordered his aides to look for a fatherless boy in order to sacrifice him in a bloody ritual. The king's aides found such a boy having an argument with other boys over a ball game called *pilae ludus* (a ball for playing). Unfortunately, there is no description of the game and it is hard to say whether it had anything in common with the later football. The first mention of a football game, identified by the historians to be actual football, is found in W. Fitzstephen's *Descriptio Nobilissimae Cavitatis Londoniae* (*A Description of the Noble City of London*, 1774). The work contains a chapter devoted to the games and amusements of London citizens (*De ludis*), with the following passage concerning football:

After the midday meal the entire youth of the City goes to the fields for the famous game of ball (Post prandium, exit in campos omnis iuventus urbis ad iusum pilaa celebrem). The students of the several branches of study have their ball; the followers of the several trades of the City have a ball in their hands. The elders, the fathers, and men of wealth come on horseback to view the contests of their juniors, and in their fashion sport with the young men; and there seems to be aroused in these elders a stirring of natural heat by viewing so much activity and by participation in the joys of unrestrained youth.

[trans. F. Peabody Magoun]

The name *goal*, referring to a goal, was first used in relation to football in 1577 in R. Stanyhurst's (1547-1618) *Description of Ireland*. The author arguing with A. Cope on the lack of snakes in Ireland, claims that he had known about it 'before e beare the ball to the goale.'

F. Peabody Magoun, *History of Football from the Beginning to 1871*, 1938; J. Marshall Carter, *Medieval Games. Sports and Recreation in Feudal Society*, 1992; J. Strutt, *Glig Gamena Angel Deoth. The Sports and Pastimes of the People of England*, 1810; R.W. Henderson, *Ball, Bat and Bishop. The Origins of Ball Games*, 1947; B. Schröder, *Der Sport in Altertum*, 1927.

FOOTBALL FOR THE DISABLED, a var. of soccer (>ASSOCIATION FOOTBALL) adapted for the disabled, particularly those suffering from multiple sclerosis. Generally, the games are conducted according to FIFA regulations, although many detailed rules have been amended, e.g. no off-sides, smaller field and goal size, depending on the players' needs. The game is played by 2 teams of 11 players, similar to >FOOTBALL. So far, i.e. 1999, the game has been played by men only. Football for the disabled is part of the Paralympic Games. See also >SPORTS FOR THE DISABLED.
The Internet: http://www.paralympic.org/sports/sections/soccer/general.htm

FOOTBALL WITH A SEVERED HEAD, a primitive sport using the severed head of a defeated enemy as a ball. Playing with a human head, dried skull or specially prepared, hardened brain has a long tradition among certain primitive cultures. Myths and stories about playing football using a human

Girls at a Ball Game, *a Roman mosaic from Villa Piazza Armerina, Sicily.*

head abound, for instance, in various traditions of the Brit. Isles. Somewhat enigmatic references to playing with a brain extracted from the enemy's head can be found in ancient Celtic stories. The peculiar game was described by the Brit. sports historian David Terry:

When an enemy champion had been defeated in battle the head was removed. The brain was extracted and mixed with lime to harden and made into balls. Such a ball was considered magical and supposedly more powerful than a stone. The brain-ball was occasionally used in games of hockey and kicked about as in a game of football; and here we may reflect on the similar myths around the world relating to the origin of football.

[D. Terry, *Sport and Health of the Ancient Celts*, in T. Terret, ed., *Sport et santé dans l'histoire*, 1999, 64]

The folklorist and historian of Derby County, S. Glover, traces back the tradition of the ball made of a human head to Roman Britain:

There exists a tradition, that a cohort of Roman soldiers, marching through the town of Derventio, or Little Chester, were thrust out by the unarmed populace, and this mode of celebrating the occurrence has been continued to the present day. It is even added that this conflict occurred in the year 217, and that the Roman troops at Little Chester were slain by the Britons.

[*The History Gazeteer, and Directory of the County of Derby*, 1829]

According to other legends, the game's tradition goes back to the time of the Viking invasions, when a Viking raiding party was defeated by the English

in Kingston-upon-Thames and the victorious English played football with the severed head of the Viking leader. Historians question those legends as actual evidence. The stories mentioned might have been combinations of Celtic traditions, actual military events, folk imagination, and wishful thinking. Playing with an enemy's head is recorded in much later Brit. documents. In 1321, the Oldynton brothers from Darnhall murdered John de Boddeworth, a servant to the abbot of the Vale Royal Monastery in Cheshire. The court records read that the murderers 'kicked John's head about like a ball with their feet' (as modum pilae cum pedibus suis conculcaverunt). Before modern historians began to call the tradition of playing with a severed head into question, the game was mentioned in quite a few literary works, which may suggest that some forms of this gruesome competition were real. The anonymous Arthurian romance from the 14th cent., *Sir Gawain and the Green Knight* includes a description of the beheading of the Green Knight and an ensuing ball game with his head played by King Arthur's knights: '...and many kicked it with their feet as it rolled away.' During a court trial in 1790 presided over by Baron Beoumount Hotham, concerning earlier violent events of the Shrove Tuesday ball game in Kingston-upon-Thames, the defendants invoked the ancient tradition of playing with a human head, dating back to the Viking times: 'The Captain of the Danish forces having been slain, and his head kicked about by the people in derision, the custom of kicking a Foot Ball on the anniversary of that day has been observed ever since.' A local historian W.D. Biden described the violent Shrove Tuesday game (see >SHROVE TUESDAY FOOTBALL):

Two rival companies of men collect about the Druid's Head Inn in the Market-place; and at eleven o'clock the foot Ball is started. The sport continues with much spirit during the day; one party endeavouring to kick the ball to the Great Bridge and the other party to Clattern Bridge; at five o'clock the game ceases and all parties adjourn to talk of their exertion, and to enter on the business of another year with a firm determination to renew their riotous sport on the next anniversary of their forefathers' prowess.

The custom of playing with an enemy's head was deeply imbedded in Brit. consciousness, which was reflected in various literary works, such as in *The White Devil* (1612, IV, 2; lines 134-5) by J. Webster (c.1578-1632). In this long poem, Francesco de Medici calls with contempt on his enemy Brachiano:

Football (soccer) for the disabled.

Like the wild Irish, I'le nere thinke the dead,
Till I can play at football with thy head.

In an 18th-cent. gothic play *The Castle Spectre* by M.G. Lewis (1775-1818), staged in the Drury Lane Theatre in London in 1797, a servant recalls that 'Lord Hildebrand who was condemned for treason some sixty years ago, may be seen in the Great Hall, regularly at midnight, playing foot-ball with his own head.'

The tradition of playing with the enemy's head was also known in other cultures; it was common, for instance, among 17th-cent. Cossack troops, as mentioned in the novel *With Fire and Sword* by H. Sienkiewicz. A Cossack colonel, Barabas, serving in the Pol. army is punished after having refused to join Khmelnytsky's party:

It seemed that no one wished to raise his hand first at the old man. But unfortunately the colonel slipped in blood and fell. Prone he did not rouse that respect or that fear, and immediately a number of lances were buried in his body. The old man was able only to cry: 'Jesus, Mary!' They began to cut the prostate body

Football tennis.

Fox hunting.

to pieces. The severed head was hurled from boat to boat, like a ball, until by an awkward throw it fell into the water.

[vol. II, chapter XIV]

W.D. Biden, *The History and the Antiquities of the Ancient and Royal Town of Kingston-upon-Thames*, 1852; F.P. Magoun, *History of Football from the Beginnings to 1871*, 1938.

FOOTBALLTENNIS, also *soccertennis, foottennis, foot volleyball, legball, footvolley, nohejbal* (Czech), *Fussballtennis* (Ger.), *tennis ballon* (Fr.). A hybrid between soccer, tennis, and volleyball, resembling >SEPAK TAKRAW, played by teams consisting of 1 (singles), 2 (doubles), or 3 (triples) players. The size of the playing court is 8.2x12.8m for singles and 8.2 (max. 9.0) x 18m for doubles and triples. The court, surrounded by lines, is split into 2 halves by a net, which is tensioned at both ends so that its top part extends 110cm over the surface. The ball, made of synthetic or natural leather, is 680-710mm in circumference and weighs 396-453g.

Fork throw.

Rules of play. The rules are similar to volleyball, except that the ball may not be touched with the hands. A service is executed by kicking the ball by foot from the zone behind the base-line, outside the playing court. If the ball touches the net and lands on the opponent's service zone, the service is repeated. The players of the opponent's team may not touch the ball until it has touched their own half of the playing court. After the ball has been served, it may drop once (singles) or twice (doubles and triples) before it is returned by the opponents. The opponents may play the ball amongst themselves twice (singles) or 3 times (doubles and triplets) before returning it over the net and within the playing court. In doubles and triples the same player is not allowed to touch the ball twice in succession. When a team has returned the ball successfully, the opponents play it according to the same principles, except that they do not have to let the ball drop down to the ground. The ball is played until one team (player) commits a fault, in which case the opponents score 1pt. Faults include: letting the ball touch the court twice in sequence without being touched by a player; letting the ball bounce off the court and return to the opponents' court without touching it first; volleying the served ball without letting it touch the ground; touching the net with any part of the body during play; touching the base line or side line with the ball or foot during the serve; landing the ball outside the opponents' service zone on the serve; touching the ball with the hand or arm; returning the ball outside the opponents' playing court; stepping into the opponents' court after having played the ball; holding or pushing the opponent with one's hands; playing the ball twice in sequence (except for singles). The match is played until one team has won 2 sets. To win a set a team must score 11pts. with a min. lead of 2pts. Otherwise a set is played until a lead of 2pts. is achieved.

History. The game was invented in Bohemia in the 1920s. and from there it spread across Europe. In 1975 the oldest US footballtennis team was formed Berkely, California. In 1987 the International Footballtennis Association (IFTA) was formed with its headquarters in Switzerland. W.Ch. for men have been played biannually since 1994 and E.Ch. – also biannually – since 1991. The first W.Ch. for women (in doubles and triplets) took place in 2000 in Kosice, Slovakia. The leading national teams are those from Slovakia, the Czech Republic, and Romania. The Internet: http://mujweb.cz/www/footballtennis/

FØRE KRIG, in Dan. to fight a war. A simple game in which stones, of the size of fist or a little larger, are placed in 2 ranks – like soldiers of 2 enemy armies (*Krigshærene*) – facing each other at a distance short enough for the players to be able to throw stones at the opponent's 'soldiers'. The combat is held either between 2 individuals or 2 teams who alternate in throwing stones. The enemy who hits the other party's stone incorporates the 'prisoner' into their own army. The game continues until all the stones become soldiers of the same army, whose leader automatically becomes the final victor.
J. Møller, 'Føre krig', GID, 1997, 96-98.

FORK THROW, an unusual event involving throwing a pitchfork at sheaves positioned at a defined distance. The pitchfork must be thrown so that it pops balloons attached to the sheaves.

FOSETTA, an Ital. game in which a ball is thrown into a series of holes in the ground. Similar to Dan. >BOLD I HUL; practiced in Calabria.

FOUR BY FOUR, also *4x4*, a var. of off-road car racing in which different vehicles are used: from light single passenger cars to heavy trucks. The common feature of all the vehicles is that they are equipped with four wheel drive, also 4WD.
The Internet: www.4x4now.com

FOX, see >MUNK.

FOX AND GEESE, see >MARBLES.

FOX HUNTING, one of the oldest chase hunting pastimes, derived from aristocratic hunting traditions. Modern fox hunting took shape by the end of the 18th cent. with the decline of big game in W Europe. It consists of the chase of a live fox, or a mounted rider playing the role of the quarry, by horsemen. The 'fox' rider sets off before the other participants, leaving trails to be followed by the pursuers. Fox

hunting is practiced today in exclusive riding clubs as a tourist attraction or a form of marketing for prospective horse buyers. The sport is also practiced using motorcycles or cars as a form of cross-country race. Traditional fox-hunting in Great Britain is currently the subject of heated controversy on anti-cruelty grounds.

FRÄMPÄRK, see >PÄRK.

FREE DIVING, a sport involving moving under water without using any surface or external equipment (hence the name). Depending on the type of gear used, there are 3 main var. of free diving: breath-holding diving, snorkel diving and diving with an aqualung (scuba diving). One of the greatest dangers in free diving is oxygen starvation, sometimes leading to so-called 'shallow water blackouts' (where the diver temporarily loses his eyesight), or even death in extreme cases. Many divers practice holding their breath using Eastern techniques borrowed from *yoga* or >TAIJIQUAN.

Depending on the weight used, there are 3 var. of free diving: fixed weight (or fixed volume) diving (the current world depth record is 73m, achieved by the Frenchman E. Charrier in 1995); diving with weight, which is removed at some depth to facilitate resurfacing; and absolute diving (unlimited weights are allowed; divers use special lifts or inflatable containers; descent speeds may reach 4.6m/sec. in this variant; the record depth is 162m, achieved by Cuban F. 'Pipin' Ferreras-Rodriguez).

In addition to those divisions, there are also 'deep diving' and 'shallow diving'. However, there is no agreed boundary between the 2 levels, and they are similar in many respects at 'border' depths, usu. about 60-90m.

Professional events include fast surface and underwater swimming, and orienteering below the surface. Underwater events are organized along zigzag courses with 5 (men's) or 3 (women's) buoys that one has to reach using a compass and a distance meter.

There is also an event involving breath-hold swimming, freestyle, with distances of 40m-50m. New sports related to free diving have been increasing in popularity, including >UNDERWATER HOCKEY and >UNDERWATER RUGBY. Some countries still allow underwater hunting.

One characteristic of free diving is the 'fight for survival' underwater, where man is, after all, a 'foreign body'. Technical devices help achieve this, such as aqualungs, whose reliability is essential not only for the effectiveness of a diver's actions, but also for his life, to a much more immediate extent than the equipment used in other sports. Diving to greater depths is usually done in pairs to facilitate a rescue operation, and to make it possible for 2 divers to share a single aqualung in an emergency, by sharing the mouthpiece. Underwater, divers use an international sing language to communicate.

History. Diving (used, for instance, to approach enemy ships and sink them) was known in ancient times. Aristotle, Thucydides and Herodotus mention the Greeks using reeds to breathe underwater when approaching enemy ships during the siege of Syracuse in the 5th cent. BC and during the Peloponesian War (431-404 BC). The Romans used special helmets equipped with reeds or, later, special breathing pipes, probably made of metal.

Deep sea diving was also known to the Vikings. The O.Eng. poem *Beowulf* contains a description of the feats of the Dan. hero Beouwulf, the son of Ecgtheow, who liberates people from persecution by the monster Grendel and his mother. After getting even with Grendel himself, Beowulf decided to take on his horrible mother on the bottom of an underwater cave:

Straightway plunged in the swirling pool,
Nigh unto a day he endured the depths
Ere he first had view of the vast sea-bottom.
Soon she found, who had haunted the flood,
A ravening hag, for a hundred half-years,
Greedy and grim, that a man was groping
In daring search through the sea-troll's home.

A dramatic fight follows, with Beowulf winning and cutting off the monster's head. With this trophy,

[...] he, who had compassed the fall of his foes
Came swimming up through the swirling surge.
Cleansed were the currents, the boundless abyss,
Where the evil monster had died the death
And looked her last on this fleeting world.
With sturdy strokes the lord of the seamen

Freestyle parachuting.

To land came swimming, rejoiced in his spoil,
Had joy of the burden he brought from the depths.
[trans. from O.Eng. by J.B. Trapp]

Breath-hold diving is used in fishing pearls, shell-fish and sponges from the ocean floor on the islands of the Pacific. The best divers may reach depths of up to 60m, and sporadically even 120m. In modern times, simple breathing apparatuses were first used for military purposes about 1682 in France and Germany. J. Skrzetuski, the main character of *With Fire and Sword* by the Pol. writer H. Sienkiewicz, used a reed in his underwater escape from Zbaraż, besieged by B. Chmielnicki's troops in 1649. Sienkiewicz based his description on the actual diving technique used by the Cossacks and known as >PIRNANNI U VODU. Free diving was first used for scientific and sporting purposes after the Fr. hydro-biologist J.Y. Cousteau started his goggle diving experiments. With the help of his co-worker and friend Y. Le Prieur, he improved a number of devices used in free diving, including the snorkel. The device allows for dives lasting up to 45sec. without breathing, and is often used for >UNDERWATER CROSSBOW SHOOTING. The introduction of foam wetsuits in the 1950s and 1960s made it possible to dive in colder waters.

The barrel-shaped diving suit introduced by the British J. Lethbridge in the early 18th cent. is considered to have been the beginning of diving with apparatuses supplying air. Lethbridge's idea was used for repairs of ship hulls. A diver wearing the suit could use the supply of air to dive to depths of up to 10ft. (about 3m). In 1819, the German A. Siebe made a brass helmet and a diving suit connected to a simple pump that supplied air through a pipe. The air, compressed by the pump, prevented water from entering the suit, and escaped through the trouser legs after being used. In 1830, Siebe improved his invention by introducing a closed suit, the prototype of modern suits used in underwater work. A break-through in the development of diving techniques came with the theoretical and empirical research on decompression during resurfacing by the Frenchman P. Bert (c.1880), and later by the Eng. physiologist J.S. Haldane (1907). This was first used for diving in shipyards. In the 1930s, the US Navy used a mixture of helium and oxygen for breathing for the first time. Amer. divers, wearing 'frogsuits', started reaching depths of up to 100ft. (about 30m). This technique was used in sabotage during WWII, both by the allies and the Third Reich. Another invention made by J.Y. Cousteau in 1942, that of the so-called reducer, proved important not only in military but also in civilian diving. Soon, Cousteau, together with his co-worker É. Gagnan, improved goggle diving techniques and made the first aqualung [Lat. *aqua* – water + lung] (1943), making it possible to take larger amounts of compressed breathing gas under the surface. The same year, Cousteau made the film *Eighteen Meters Deep* (*Par dix-huit mètres du fond*). In 1945, Cousteau shot another film, *Épaves*, and the most famous of the 3 – *The Silent World* (*Le monde du silence*) – was filmed in 1956. The films, together with a number of books and new developments in diving equipment, led to the rapid growth of scuba diving in the 1950s. Further improvements

were introduced by the Group for Underwater Research founded by Cousteau in Toulon. The center soon became the world's leader with respect to researching human capabilities of working underwater, not only with a breathing apparatus. In 1959, the World Confederation of Underwater Activities (Confédération Mondiale des Activités Subaquatiques, CMAS) was founded, under whose auspices the events of the W.Ch. are organized.
Consultant: Krzysztof Saracen.

FREESTYLE ARCHERY, also *freestyle shooting*. A var. of archery practiced mostly in Eng.-speaking countries. It differs from trad. archery in that the bow is larger and its string tighter, which makes the archers employ an unconventional shooting technique: they lie down on their backs and, supporting the grip with both feet, pull the string with both hands. Events are held both in men's women's categories. The world record in 1933 was 518yds. (473.66m), whereas in 1958 it was already 790yds. (722.38m). Although F.G. Menke's *Encyclopedia of Sports* states that in 1969 the world record was 575yds. 2ft. (525.83m), this falls far short of the 1958 record, which, according to the available information, has never been beaten.

FREESTYLE PARACHUTING, a var. of >COMPETITIVE PARACHUTING in which the jumper executes a number of prescribed figures before opening the parachute. These figures are far more complex than the incidental figures observable during an ordinary free fall. The elements that are judged during parachute acrobatics competitions are the duration and correctness of the figures. There are individual and team events. The most frequent individual figures include rolls, spins, loops and spiral glides; the most popular team figures are the diamond, the caterpillar, the arrowhead, the star, the Canadian Tee, the snowflake and the monopod.
History. Parachuting acrobatics developed, similar to other competitive parachuting varieties, after the Fr. jumper, L. Valentin, improved free fall techniques (1948). Individual parachuting acrobatics started in the 1950s and its team variety in the 1960s. Parachuting acrobatics became esp. popular around the world after J. Frankenheimer's *The Gypsy Moths* starring G. Hackman, B. Lancaster and D. Kerr. The first W.Ch. was held in 1975. Jumps involving the largest number of jumpers are noted as parachuting acrobatics records; the record jump so far – involving 200 jumpers – was made in 1997 over Myrtle Beach in S California. See also >B.A.S.E. JUMPING.
J. Tomlison, 'Parachuting', *Encyclopedia of Extreme Sports*, 1996.

FREESTYLE SKIING, a variety of skiing combining elements of downhill skiing and acrobatics but using shorter skis. It includes 4 basic events: >ACRO-SKI, >MOGULS, >AERIALS and a combination event (featuring all 3). Two freestyle events – aerials and moguls – are part of the Olympic program. They were introduced as demonstration sports during the 1992 games in Albertville, and as regular events, both for women and men, during the 1994 games in Lillehammer. Despite the similarities between freestyle skiing and >ALPINE SKIING, the former is not considered an alpine event.

History. The earliest displays of acrobatic skiing skills were associated with the Eur. beginnings of >SKIING, both alpine skiing and >NORDIC SKIING. Skiing has been practiced for several hundred years in the Norwegian region of Telemark, including displays of spins, jumps and downhill races, combined with acrobatics, depending on local traditions and the skiers' inventiveness. The feats were usually performed on so-called 'wild courses' (*ville lâmir*), where

World champion free diver Tanya Streeter holds onto the sled as she decends in her attempt to break the 'No Limits' world record in free diving Saturday, Aug. 17, 2002 off the coast of Providenciales, Turks and Caicos. Streeter reached a depth of 160m (525ft.) on one breath of air.

On a single breath of air, fashion model Mehgan Heaney-Grier of Little Torch Key, Florida, begins her plunge to a depth of 165 feet off the Florida Keys, to break her own American women's free-diving record by 10 feet.

WORLD SPORTS ENCYCLOPEDIA

F

FREE DIVING WORLD RECORDS

Female Constant Ballast, Sea – *Tanya Streeter (USA) – 67m*
Male Constant Ballast with Bi-Fins, Sea – *Umberto Pelizzari (ITA) – 80m*
Male Constant Ballast with Monofins, Sea – *Patrick Musimu (BEL) – 87m*
Female Constant Ballast, Fresh Water – *Tanya Streeter (USA) – 57m*
Male Constant Ballast, Fresh Water – *Benjamin Franz (GER) – 66m*
Female Variable Ballast, Sea – *Yasemin Dalkilic (TUR) – 105m*
Male Variable Ballast, Sea – *Umberto Pelizzari (ITA) – 131m*
Male Variable Ballast, Fresh Water – *Heimo Hanke (GER) – 110m*
Female No Limits, Sea – *Audrey Mestre (FRA) – 170m*
Male No Limits, Sea – *Pipin Ferreras (CUB) – 162m*
Male No Limits, Fresh Water – *Heimo Hanke (GER) – 112m*
Female Free Immersion, Sea – *Deborah Andollo (CUB) – 74m*
Male Free Immersion, Sea – *Pierre Frolla (MONACO) – 73m*
Female Free Immersion, Fresh Water – *Tanya Streeter (USA) – 55m*
Male Free Immersion, Fresh Water – *Patrick Musimu (BEL) – 65m*
Female No Limits Tandem, Sea (DEMONSTRATION) – *Karoline Dal Toé (BRA), Audrey Mestre (FRA) – 91m*
Mixed No Limits Tandem, Sea – *Audrey Mestre (FRA), Pipin Ferreras (CUB) – 103m*

F

WORLD SPORTS ENCYCLOPEDIA

the terrain actually enforced them. In the 1920s and '30s, the brothers Sigmund (1907-94) and Birger (b.1911) Ruud used various forms of acrobatics in their ski jumping practice. They also took part in ski jumping displays, where the participants would jump in pairs, in 'parallel' on the same hill. In the Alpine region, M. Zdarsky (1856-194), a skier and gymnast, used elements of both main skiing events in his practice. The Swiss F. Oguey practiced acrobatic skiing

serious spine injuries in the first stage of the development of freestyle skiing, which led to a series of court trials, resulting in a lack of support and even hostility on the part of the Amer. skiing community, and the banning of some especially dangerous maneuvers. In 1979, the FIS took control of freestyle skiing, which caused a drastic change in the discipline's status. The first official W.Ch. were held at Tignes, France, in 1986. All freestyle events were

In the case of stalling, the referee may stop the fight and to force the players to be more active he may order a so-called lock (the rules here are identical to Greco-Roman wrestling). Bouts are also held on a square mat whose side is at least 12m-long, whereas the central wrestling area, which is circular in shape, must be at least 7m in diameter and is surrounded by a 1m-wide passivity zone. The wrestlers must wear soft shoes with tall and rigid tops to prevent ankle injury. The wrestlers fight in a standing or par terre position.

The wrestlers are divided into weight categories, identical to those observed in Greco-Roman wrestling. Since 1997 there have been the following 8 categories: 48-54kg, up to 58kg, up to 63kg, up to 69kg, up to 76kg, up to 85kg, up to 97kg and 97-130kg. In the 20th century there were, however, different numbers of the respective categories which amounted to as many as 10 before the last change. The presentation of the most outstanding wrestlers that follows below is ordered according to the 10 weight categories observed before 1997.

History. Freestyle wrestling was derived from numerous Eur. wrestling var. (>WRESTLING) and developed rapidly after it was included in the world and continental championships as well as Olympic programs. Before 1939 the most outstanding freestyle wrestlers came from the US, Hungary, Finland, Estonia, Switzerland, Sweden and also France. After 1945, the Soviet Union (and later the Commonwealth of Independent States and finally Russia), Bulgaria, Hungary, Sweden, Japan, Iran, Turkey, the US, Korea and Cuba (since the mid-1980s) came to the fore. Usu. the bouts that attracted the most attention were those between super heavyweight fighters. The first renowned fighter in this category was B. Hansen of the US – the 1904 Olympic champion (after defeating F. Kungler also of the US). The first official world champion was B. Antonsson of Sweden (1951). I. Ivanitskiy of the USSR dominated in the 1962-67 period after winning all the world and Olympic champion titles in his category (6 in total). Another outstanding super heavyweight champion was A. Medvied – also of the USSR – who won 5 gold and 4 silver medals in the 1968-72 period. Before that he competed in the up-to-90kg category where he won 'only' 4 golds. S. Andiyev of the USSR won 5 super heavyweight W.Ch. and Ol.G. golds in the 1973-1980 period. S. Tshasimikov of the USSR won the World and Olympic titles in 1979 and 1981-83. Yet another distinguished super heavyweight champion was B. Baumgartner of the US, 4-time Olympic medallist (2 golds in 1984 and 1992, silver in 1988 and bronze in 1996) and the 1986 world champion.

In the light flyweight (up to 48kg) category the first Olympic champion was R. Curry of the US (1904). Later, this category was withdrawn from the international events program and it returned only in 1969 during the W.Ch. when the title went to I. Javadi of Iran (who won the next 2 consecutive world champion titles in 1970 and 1971). H. Isayev of Bulgaria became the world champion in 1974 and 1975 and the Olympic champion in 1976. The best ever competitor in this category was S. Kornilayev (world champion in 1978-79 and 1981-82);

In the flyweight (up to 52kg) category the most renowned wrestlers were Y. Takada of Japan (world champion in 1974, 1975, 1977, 1979 and the Olympic champion in 1976) and V. Yordanov (7-times world champion in the 1983-89 period and the Olympic champion in 1996);

In the bantamweight (up to 57kg) category the most outstanding wrestler was S. Byeloglazov – the winner of 8 W.Ch. and Olympic medals in the 1980-89 period (he also won the up-to-62kg world championship in 1982 and 5 additional E.Ch. titles);

In the featherweight (up to 62kg) category the best wrestler ever was J. Smith of the US – the winner of 6 gold medals during W.Ch. and Ol.G. in the 1987-92 period. Three W.Ch. and Olympic medals went to M. Dagistanii of Turkey (1957-60), O. Watanabe (1962-64), and M. Kaneko (1966-68) – both of Japan;

In the lightweight (up to 68kg) category the most outstanding wrestler in history was A. Tshadzhayev – world and Olympic champion in 1983, 1985-88, 1990-92. A. Mohaved of Iran won 6 golds (1965-70). P. Pinegin of the USSR won 4 golds (1962-64);

In the welterweight (up to 74kg) category the best wrestlers were E. Gabibi Gourdarzi of Iran (1959, 1961-62) and L. Kemp of the US – 3-times world champion (1978, 1979, 1982);

Freestyle skiing and snowboarding.

techniques and moguls in the 1920s and 1930s. In 1926, the Ger. physician F. Reul wrote a treatise about the acrobatic possibilities of skiing. However, attempts to combine acrobatics with skiing in Europe never went much further than programs complementing other, trad. skiing events. Freestyle skiing only started emerging as an independent discipline in the early 1950s, when S. Ericksen (b. 1927), slalom champion during the 1952 Ol.G. in Oslo, emigrated from Norway to the USA. The Swiss A. Furrer (b. 1937), a skier, writer and TV host, also contributed to the growth of freestyle skiing.

About the mid-1960s, the first events as we know them today appeared, and the first rules started taking shape. The first competition ever was organized in Waterville Valley, New Hampshire, USA (1966). The first professional competition took place in 1971, while the first World Cup event was held in 1978. In the 1970s, national championships were organized in a number of W Eur. countries. Despite all that, the sport evolved chaotically and irregularly, with much resistance from conservative skiing officials associated with both alpine and Nordic skiing. In addition, a number of Amer. freestyle skiers suffered

Freestyle skiing.

demonstration sports during the 1988 and 1992 games in Calgary and Albertville, respectively. Two freestyle events, moguls and aerials (but not acroski) were included in the official program during the 1994 games in Lillehammer. Top skiers (see the individual events) come from Scandinavia, W Europe and N.America. They are being slowly joined by Russian skiers as well as some skiers from the former Soviet republics. L. Cheryazova (Russia) won the aerials gold medal in Lillehammer. One negative factor is the growing specialization of skiers, who usually take part in just one event each, leading to a decrease in the importance of the combination event. For instance, there was no combination event during the 1991 Norw. championships due to a lack of candidates who could take part in all 3 of the events. *FIS Freestyle, General Rules for Scoring. Judging Manual,* 1993; 'Freestyle Skiing', OR Febr./March, 1998; S. Lolan, 'Skiing, Freestyle', EWS, 1996, III; T. Wiński, *Balet na szczycie śniegu. Free style,* 1983.

FREESTYLE WRESTLING, one of the wrestling styles used in international competition in which, similar to >GRECO-ROMAN WRESTLING, the object is to pin one's opponent. However, under international rules the grips and holds are not restricted to those applied above the waist and any fair hold, trip or throw is permitted. Any hold that endangers life or limb is illegal – strangleholds or figure-4 head scissors, for example, are forbidden. Similar to Greco-Roman wrestling, if nobody gets pinned, the winner is the wrestler who has scored the most points during the match. The bout is officiated by a referee who awards points or announces the result of a given match. His decision must be confirmed by the other 2 referees, i.e. the judge and the mat chairman. The decision may be accepted by a 2 to 1 majority. The bout consists of 2 rounds of 3min. each with a 1min. break in between. In the case of a draw, the match goes into overtime of 3min. without any break. So in total, the match may last up to 9min. Additionally, one of the wrestlers must score at least 3pts. for the match to end after 6min. In the mid-1990s the 2-round system was replaced with a 1-round system whereby the round lasted for 5min. and the overtime for 3min. This system was applied during the 1996 Atlanta Ol.G. but was later discontinued.

Freestyle wrestling

WORLD SPORTS ENCYCLOPEDIA

F

In the middleweight (up to 82kg) category the most frequent W.Ch. and Ol.G. winners were M. Mehdizadeh of Iran (1961-62, 1965), P. Gardev of Bulgaria (1963-64, 1966), and M. Schultz of the US (1984-85, 1987);

In the light heavyweight (up to 90kg) category the most outstanding wrestler was M. Hadartshev of the USSR (and later CIS) who won 7 gold medals during the major international events in the 1986-92 period. L. Tediashvili of the USSR won 4 Olympic and W.Ch. golds (1973-76). A. Medvied, who later became a super heavyweight wrestler, also won a number titles in this category (1962-64, 1966);

In the heavyweight (up to 100kg) category the most outstanding wrestler was L. Khabelov (world and Olympic champion in 1985, 1987, 1990-92; he also won a number of silver W.Ch. medals and E.Ch. golds – 1985, 1987-88, 1992).

After the new division into weight categories was introduced the following wrestlers became the 2000 Olympic champions: 48-54kg – N. Abdulayev of Azerbaijan; up to 58kg – A. Dabir of Iraq; up to 63kg – M. Dumakhanov of Russia; up to 69kg – D. Igali of Canada; up to 76kg –B. Slay of the US; up to 85kg –A. Saytyev of Russia; up to 97kg – S. Murtasaliyev of Russia and 97-130kg – D. Moussoulbes of Russia. P. Godlewski, *Olimpijskie turnieje zapaśnicze 1896-1996*, 1996; G. Kent, *A Pictorial History of Wrestling*, 1968; N.I. Myagtshenkov, *Klasiczeskaja i wolnaja barba*, 1984; P. Godlewski, *Sport zapaśniczy w Polsce w latach 1890-1939*, 1994; Z. Ratajczak, W. Stecyk – personal communications.

FREISCHIEßEN, a shooting competition held in Ger. cities since the Middle Ages, organized by mayors or city councils, open to everybody unlike annual competitions for a title of a local king in which only members of local merchant or craft guilds could participate (>KÖNIGSSCHIEßEN) that were hosted by shooting associations or guilds. Freischießen's main objectives were to improve defense skills of citizens and to strengthen good relationships with neighboring cities, esp. those with which the hosting city maintained close commercial relations. The event was also a demonstration of joint power of various municipalities, which in times of feudalism, when local wars and invasions were common, was a stabilizing element. Contests were usu. held at a city or guild rifle range – a wooden construction, often equipped with roofing that protected shooters either from sun or rain – during important folk festivals. At the beginning, contestants used bows, then they switched to crossbows, and from the end of the 15th cent. – rifles. In the transitional period between the 15th and 17th cent. both firearms and crossbows were used. The peak popularity of freischießen falls on the 16th cent. The event was accompanied by numerous rituals and songs, often composed especially for that occasion; L. Flexel – a jester and a poet – was a famous composer of freischießen songs. In order to take part in the contest, a partaker had to receive one of the special invitations that were sent to most eminent shooters from other cities. On one occasion, in 1467, the city of Munich paid 3 guilders to Lienhart Kletel, a scribe, for copying 200 letters of invitations that were sent to best shooters across Germany (which does not mean, however, that all 200 accepted the invitation). At the end of the 15th cent. the first printed letters appeared, which were easier and cheaper to copy. The oldest printed letter preserved to this day dates back to 1477 and was presented by the city of Nördlingen to the city of Strasbourg, inviting the latter's representation to participate in a shooting competition. From the invitations that survived it can be deduced that citizens of Strasbourg and Nördlingen had a reputation of having the best shooters, as the number of invitations they received substantially exceeds that of any other city, among which such names as Essen, Cologne, Augsburg, and Kitzingen can be enumerated. A freischießen contest could be participated by any free citizen; criminals, exiles, and residents of the towns recognized as hostile to the hosting town were excluded. The invitees were supposed to arrive at least one day before the contest and they were expected to pay a small entrance fee, the amount of which had been stated in the invitation. The shooting usu. started in the morning. In the case of bow and crossbow shooters, a city scribe marked each arrow with the owner's name in order to avoid any disputes as to whose arrow was closer to the target. The distance to tar-

gets differed from place to place and it was measured in different units, such as steps, strings, elbows, feet, etc. On average, however, the distance would range 70-90m. The arrow's diameter was specified in a letter of invitation either by a picture or a whole made in the paper – the partakers were supposed to check their arrows against that specification. In one of the letters quoted in a book edited by E. Freys we find the following instructions: 'no arrow can be thicker than the one that can go through the hole made in a larger circle attached to this letter' (*Gedruckte Schützenbriefe des Jahrhunderts*, 1912). Measurements of the 'model' holes in the preserved letters indicate that the accepted diameter of arrows ranged from 19mm, in Munich, to 28mm in Landshut. As the units of measurement were numerous and differed from place to place, the letters usu. contained a specimen of the measurement standard applied in the hosting city and information about the distance between the shooting platform and the target. There were 3 methods of defining that distance: 1) a letter contained information about the measurement standard used in a given area – e.g. foot (*Werksschuh* later *Fuß*), elbow (*Elle*), bar (*Gerte*), and less frequently fathom (*Klafter*) – and the distance was expressed in one of those units; 2) a letter contained a piece of string whose length was equivalent of one local measurement unit, and information was given how many such units would cover the distance from a shooter to the target: 'the target is going to be placed at a distance equal the length of the enclosed piece of string multiplied by 40.' That method was used, for instance, in Nördlingen. In both cases the invitee could examine himself whether the distance described in a letter was actually the one applied by the hosts; 3) the last method consisted of indicating the number of steps. In order to standardize the distance, it was measured by 2 selected shooters. This method was applied in Offenburg. A letter dated 1477 reveals further details: 'The shooting platform shall be at a distance of 115 steps from the target, and such distance will be measured by 2 shooters, one who arrived from the most distant city and the other who came from the closest one.' As we can see no representative of the hosting city of Offenburg was responsible for measurements, which makes the entire procedure more credible. In Nuremberg, however, the distance was measured by the representatives of the farthest city and the host.

The shooting procedure was governed by a set of regulations: the shooter had to be sitting on a special stool with his back in an upright position; arms could not be touching the trunk of the body; no belts or leather straps could support the arms or tie them to the weapon; shooting with 2 bullets or arrows at the same time, which contestants sometimes attempted to get away with in order to increase their chances, was prohibited. Another proof of participants' inventiveness is frequent bans on using bullets equipped with ailerons. The entire process was supervised by committees made up of an odd number of members to avoid draws in voting (usu. 5 or 7

people). The prizes, usu. referred to as 'adventures' (*Abenteür*), were for the most part pecuniary, e.g. in 1586 in Munich it was 102 Rhine guilders. Prizes around 100 guilders were most often granted in large cities only. Other forms of prizes included pots made of valuable ores, golden chains and goblets, silver plates, etc. In addition to the prize awarded for best results, sometimes there was also a prize for the best shooter who arrived from the most distant town. If 2 participants achieved the same results, an 'overtime' type of situation (*Stechen*) was administered in which each party had a right to a single shot. Shooting competitions were sometimes accompanied by other events, such as jumping contests or foot races in which shooters took part as well. Freischießen competitions started to collapse in the 17th cent. The thirty-year war (1618-48) contributed substantially to that process. The appearance of professional mercenaries that could be afforded by affluent city communities put the usefulness of military training for townspeople in question. This was reinforced by the changes in the military technique of defense; city walls were deprived of their role and the function of heavy artillery was growing. Competitions organized for members of shooting associations survived thanks to the organizational unity, but freischießen either disappeared completely or was absorbed by modern forms of sports shooting. A. Edelmann, *Schützenwesen und Schützenfeste der Deutsche Städte vom 13. bis zum 18. Jahrhundert*, 1890; K. Kosudo, 'Open Shooting Festivals (Freischießen) in German Cities', IJHS, March 1999, 16, 1.

FRENCH BOXING, Fr. *boxe française*. Different from 'classical' boxing in that kicking is allowed, which brings the sport close to >THAI BOXING and contemporary >KICKBOXING. Fr. boxers use gloves.

The origins of Fr. boxing derive from >SAVATE and partly >CHAUSSON lore. C. Lecour (1808-1894), a disciple of the savate creator and codifier M. Casseux, is considered to be the creator of Fr. boxing. Lecour opened his own savate school in 1830, attended mainly by rich middle-class representatives, industrialists, journalists, and even artists. In 1830, after he lost a boxing match against the British boxer O. Swift, Lecour began studies in England on the then developing sport of >BOXING. On his return, he continued his studies under the guidance of the Eng. trainer Adams (forename unknown), who was living in Paris at that time. After he gained enough experience, Lecour enriched savate with elements of Eng. boxing, naming the new discipline *French boxing* (boxe française). In 1932 he drew up a Fr. boxing honorary code of conduct. Soon Fr. boxing became the dominant Fr. combat sport. Due to its tradition it was referred to as savate Fr. boxing (savate boxe française). In 1860s J.P.Charlemont (1839-1914) developed Fr. boxing in the Fr. army during his service in Algeria. When he returned to France, he founded a Fr. boxing school. Using the new fighting methods, he challenged English-style boxers, fencers and stick-fighting champions. Fighting with his fists, feints, and kicks, he went unbeat-

F

WORLD SPORTS
ENCYCLOPEDIA

en for a number of years. In 1871 Charlemont as a fervent Paris Commune activist had to escape to Belgium, where he developed his system and published his first manual on Fr. boxing (1877). His methods gained so much popularity that they were recognized in France as useful for military training and Charlemont was granted political amnesty in 1879, one year before the universal amnesty for politicians connected with the Commune. On his return to Paris Charlemont estab. the famous Fr. Boxing Academy, which he headed until 1899, when his son Charles took over the academy after him. After 1899 Fr. boxing world championships were occasionally organized. The first champion was Charles Charlemont Jr., after he defeated Br. J. Driskoll, the trad. Eng. boxing middle-weight champion. Soon regional and national championships were also organized in France. In 1920s and 1930s there were about 500 Fr. boxers in a number of clubs in Paris, Lyon, Marseilles, Siouren, and Lille. French boxing was a demonstration sport at the Olympic Games of 1914. However, Eng. boxing gradually overshadowed it and in 1937 the last Fr. boxing championship was organized in France. In 1938 the Charlemont academy was closed down, and in 1940 there were only about 100 Fr. boxing fighters. During WWII Fr. boxing virtually disappeared despite the efforts of the activist P. Baruzi. Only in 1965 Baruzi managed to organize the National Fr. Boxing Committee in France, which soon comprised 30 clubs. In 1976 the Committee turned into the National Fr. Boxing Federation, and after it spread to other countries in 1985 it assumed the name of the International Federation of Savate and Fr. Boxing. Now women are also allowed to practice the sport. French Boxing, The Internet: http://cclib.nsu.ru/win/projects/satbi/satbi-e/martart/boxefr.html; consultant: Jean-Yves Guillain, University of Lyon.

FRENCH WRESTLING, Fr. *la lutte français*. A wrestling style similar to >GRECO-ROMAN WRESTLING with which it was unified at some point in time. It was popular in the 19th cent. and at the beginning of the 20th cent. in circuses. Any holds below the waist or the use of legs and feet were prohibited.
History. Legend has it that the inventor of la lutte français was a Napoleanic veteran nicknamed Exbrayat from Dent du Midi living on the French-Swiss border, an area renowned for ages for its wrestling activities; thus it is possible that Exbrayat only modified the existing forms. He called his style *mains plates* (open hands) in order to emphasize the fairness of this style of fight as opposed to the ruthless hand-to-hand fight >SAVATE in which hits

with clenched fists were accepted. The new style caught on in nearby Lyon and then in Touluse and Bordeaux. The final rules, developed by I. Truquettil, were officially approved in 1848 by delegates of wrestling associations from Arles, Bordeaux, Lyon, Mauhors, Nimes, and Toulouse. The supporters of such new rules were mislead to believe that in ancient times holds below the waist and tripping an opponent's feet were forbidden. Soon, as a reference to the Roman era, the style was also called *lutte romaine* and in Bordeaux and Lyon – the Greco-Roman style. Fr. wrestling's popularity grew after it started to be staged in wrestling circuses. Thus, an intellectually and esthetically idealized model of wrestling, invoking a non-existent ancient progenitor turned into the basis for a new style which spread quickly throughout France and then other Eur. countries, as well as the USA. An international exhibition held in Paris in 1889 presented this style of wrestling as a product of Fr. thought. The major place of Fr. wrestling events, referred to as W.Ch., was Parisian Cirque d'Hiver. It was here that various similar styles from Germany and Scandinavia began intermingling with one another. A significant moment in the development of the style combined E.Ch. and W.Ch. in Vienna in 1898, which were then continued until WWI, giving birth to a style known today as Greco-Roman wrestling, which was heavily influenced by Ol.G. tournaments (after its rather unsuccessful debut at the 1896 Ol.G., Greco-Roman wrestling was planted solidly only in 1980). Before that came to pass, however, while the style's name continued to be alternatively Fr. wrestling, Gk., or Greco-Roman wrestling, professional wrestlers made steady inroads. The most celebrated wrestler of that time is thought to have been Estonian G. Hackenschmidt, world champion in 1898, 1900, 1901. Other eminent wrestlers were P. Pons of France (world champion in 1899), and Dane J. Pedersen (world champion in 1903). The prestige of the style must have been quite high in those days, which can be deduced from the fact that the European champion in 1903, Czech G. Fristensky, was granted 320 acres of land by the 1st president of independent Czechoslovakia, J. Masaryk, for his achievements in promoting the country when it was still under foreign rule. Since the Olympic variety stabilized and official W.Ch. were estab. – independent from dictatorial inclinations of managers from Paris, Vienna, or Petersburg – already using the name Greco-Roman style, a new era in wrestling commenced in which circus wrestling slowly but steadily gave way to the Olympic one.

FRIBRYDNING, Dan. for 'freestyle wrestling'. A no-holds-barred form of trad. wrestling, in which the term 'freestyle' is taken literally. The only restriction imposed on the wrestlers is that their grips must not pose any danger to the opponent's health. Blocking with one's leg is allowed and the fight continues on the ground up to the moment in which one of the fighters touches the floor with a predetermined part of the body. Cf. >FREESTYLE WRESTLING, >CATCH-AS-CATCH-CAN.
J. Møller, 'Fribrydning', GID, 1997, 4.

FRISBEE, see >FLYING DISC.

FRÖBEL'S PLAYGROUNDS, kindergarten playgrounds designed to provide comprehensive development for the child, invented by the Ger. educator F. Fröbel (1782-1852). One of the objectives was to give children an opportunity to be in touch with nature, in line with the idea of the Fr. philosopher J.J. Rousseau. According to Fröbel himself, 'children should exercise and practice their skills in joyful play [...], and the playground should provide them with the appropriate tasks to exercise their bodies and stimulate their souls to learn about nature and the surrounding world'. Fröbel himself opened the first playground in Blankenburg, Thuringen. Initially, the idea developed well, and several playgrounds were set up across Germany but social and political radicalism caused the education ministry of the most important Ger. state of Prussia to impose a ban on playgrounds that was in force between 1851 and 1860. Fröbel died in 1852, without living to see the ban lifted. After it was finally abolished, the idea resurfaced, first in Germany (mainly thanks to Baroness B. von Marenholz-Bölow), and then in other Eur. countries. In France, Fröbel's playgrounds were organized in the so-called 'maternal schools' (*écoles maternelles*) but the Franco-Prussian war and the Fr. dislike towards all things Ger. that entailed soon broke the borrowing trend. In the US, E. Palmer Peabody was an advocate of the idea, opening the first playground in Boston in 1860, and establishing the 'playground movement'. Soon, the idea began to spread thanks to the commitment of S.E. Blow who set up the first playground in St. Louis in 1873. In Italy, the idea of Fröbel's playgrounds was mainly taken up by a propagator of similar initiatives M. Montessori, after whom a presschool method has been named. In England, Fröbel's playgrounds boosted the nursery school movement. Playgrounds began appearing throughout Europe. However, about 1890, the bringing up of children came to be dominated by new pedagogical and psychological trends. Especially criticized was the static character of play in Fröbel's playgrounds, the limitation of independent experience etc. New types of playgrounds began appearing, where physical activity, including sports, were accented, along with cognitive elements. Though Fröbel's playgrounds in their original form are a thing of the past today, they paved the way for newer upbringing methods, including physical education.
W.H. Kilpatrick, *Froebel's Kindergaten Principles*, 1916; E.M. Lawrence, *Froebel and English Education*, 1969.

FULDE, a Dan. game for 4 players divided into 2 teams and equipped with bats and a ball [Dan. *fuld* – full, complete]. Partners from the same team stand facing each other, at a distance short enough for the players to be able to pass the ball. The first of the 2 players stands in front and is referred to as the *formand*, the second, positioned at the back, is called the *bagmand*. Each player holds a thick bat, approx. 30in. (76cm) long, for striking a ball made of cork tightly covered in yarn, often with a pattern (*mønster*) made in colored wool. The right to serve is determined by tossing a coin. The formand of the serving team passes the ball to the bagmand who attempts to strike it, directing the ball towards the opposing team's bagmand whose task, in turn, is to return it from volley back to the serving base. In the course of such an exchange both formands try to strike the ball, too. Their intentions, however, are different: the serving team formand wants to prolong the ball's trajectory when it is heading towards the opponent, whereas the receiving team's formand tries to return the ball before it reaches the bagmand, forcing this way the serving team to withdraw. The object of the game is to drive the opposing team back by striking the ball as far behind the rival as possible. The team that succeeds in pushing the

A children's playground in England. 'London Illustrated News', 19th cent.

opponent farther back is the winner. Fulde was practiced by young males on the first days of summer, on the fields and roads.
J. Møller, 'Fulde', GID, 1997, 1, 69.

FULLE, a regional sp. of Dan. *helle* – a shelter. A folk game for 3-4 players that used to be practiced in S Jutland. Players walk around one of the participants attempting to hit him with a ball. The attacked party can defend himself with 2 sticks that he uses to strike the ball as far away as possible. The ball is to be thrown by the attackers from the place where it came to rest, therefore the farther it is returned, the more difficult the task to hit the defender, who can also dodge the strikes by jumping within a limited area bordered by lines that must not be crossed. The size of the area remains unknown, but it seems that it differed from one local var. of fulle to another. The attacking parties could pass the ball to one another to gain better striking position. If the ball missed the target and came to rest beside the defender, he could pick it up with the sticks (never touching the ball with his hands) and return it as far as possible to make another strike more difficult for the attackers. When the player equipped with sticks was hit, he picked the ball up with his hands and was replaced by the successful thrower, who would take the defending position. If the ex-defender succeeded in hitting the former attacker at the first attempt after being 'released', such a hit was recognized as 'revenge' and the 'avenger' would become the winner. Otherwise, the game continued on.
J. Møller, 'Fulle', GID, 1997, 1, 28.

FUßSCHEIBENSPIEL, a Ger. var. of a street game in which a stone or a small plate made of brick or metal is shifted, pushed by the player's foot, from one field onto another [Ger. *Fuß* – a foot + *Scheibe* – a little disk + *Spiel* – a game]. It belongs to a large international family of games such as Pol. >KLASY, Ang-Sax. >HOP-SCOTCH, Dan. >AT HINKE, etc. It exists in a number of varieties, the most popular of which are the following:
PARADIS, similar to a Dan. game of the same name (*at hinke*) and played according to different rules on various fields, 2 of which seem to be most frequent: 1) A playing field consisting of 3 rectangles, bordering one with the other with their longer sides, and numbered 1, 2, and 3. The longer upper side of the top rectangle borders with a square divided into 4 triangles by 2 diagonal lines. The bottom triangle (closest to the starting line) is numbered 4, the left one – 5, the right one – 6, and the top one – 7. Above the square, there is a semicircle – number 8 – whose straight line is bordering with the entire structure; 2) The starting line borders with 4 rectangles, arranged in pairs placed one beside the other, one rectangle above the other, which are numbered 1-2 and 3-4. The pairs border with a square divided into 4 triangles, with the bottom triangle (closest to the starting line) bearing number 5, left one – 6, right one – 7, and the top one – 8. Above the square, there is a combination similar to the one that borders with the starting line: 2 pairs of rectangles numbered 9-10 and 11-12. The rectangles are topped by a semicircle that borders with them with its straight line and is numbered 13.
HIMMEL UND HOLE, a group of games also referred to as *Fußscheibenspiel* with 3 most frequent playing fields: 1) three rectangles, bound one with another by their longer sides, and numbered 1, 2, and 3. The longer upper side of the top rectangle borders with a square divided into 4 triangles by 2 diagonal lines. The bottom triangle (closest to the starting line) is numbered 4, the left one – 5, the right one – 6, and the top one – 7. Above the square, there is another rectangle (number 8) that borders with a semicircle (number 9), whose straight line is bound to the entire structure; 2) similarly to the foregoing combination, the starting line is a base for 3 rectangles, bound one with another by their longer sides, and numbered 1, 2, and 3. The square with triangles is identical, but the top triangle borders with the bottom of another series of 3 rectangles numbered 8, 9, and 10; 3) the most original is the field starting with 3 squares, one placed on top of another, numbered (counting from the starting line) 1, 2, and 3. Above the third square there is an irregular area whose borders are formed by the extensions of the playing field's sides tangent with a circle whose diameter equals the width of the playing field. The half of the circle closer to the starting line forms the edge of the field. The circle itself is divided radially

into 6 equal parts, numbered clockwise 5-10, starting from the bottom. After reaching the circle, the player changes direction of movement and passes through each part of the circle. In other var. the direction of movement is changed in the air during the jump from the last square. Cf. Arabic >AL-HUD'D'A, >AL-HAGLA, >BERBER, >LU'BAT UMM AL-HUTUT, Pol. >KLASY, Port. >JOGO DO AVIÃO, >JOGO DO CARACOL.

FUTSAL, also *indoor soccer.*, a var. of >ASSOCIATION FOOTBALL played indoors according to modified rules. There are several var. of indoor soccer, differing mainly in the size of the court and the number of players (ranging from 5 to 11 a side). However, the only var. officially supported by the international football federation FIFA is called futsal, which is an international term derived from the Span. or Port. word for 'soccer' – *futbol* or *futebol* – and the Fr. or Span. word for 'indoor' – *salon* or *sala*. The game is also often referred to as *five-a-side*.
History. Futsal originated in 1930 in Montevideo, Uruguay and was devised by J.C. Ceriani as a version of association football (soccer) for youth competition in YMCAs. It gained rapid popularity in S.America, esp. in Brazil, from where it spread throughout the world. Brazil still remains the world center of futsal and many of its leading soccer players (incl. Pele, Zico, Socrates, Bebeto, etc.) began their careers playing five-a-side. This accounts for the world famous style of Brazilian soccer players displayed on a full-size field. The first international competition took place in 1965, when Paraguay won the 1st S.Amer. Cup. The next 6 S.Amer. Cups were won by Brazil, which also won the Pan Amer. Cup in 1980 and 1984. The 1st futsal W.Ch. was held in 1982 in Sao Paulo under the auspices of FIFUSA (Federación Internacional de Fútbol de Salón), before its members integrated into FIFA in 1989, and Brazil took the gold. The 2nd W.Ch. (Spain, 1985) was also won by Brazil, while the 3rd W.Ch. (Australia, 1988) was won by Paraguay. In 1989 the direct sponsorship of the event was taken over by FIFA and subsequent W.Ch. tournaments were held as follows: 1989 – Holland, winner: Brazil; 1992 – Hong Kong, winner: Brazil; 1996 – Spain, winner: Brazil; 2000 – Guatemala, winner: Spain.
Equipment and rules of play. The rules of futsal are modelled after association football (soccer) with some important differences. The game is played on a basketball-size court without the use of sidewalls. The pitch size for international events is a min. of 38m and a max. of 42m in length, and a min. of 18m and a max. of 22m in width. The penalty area is defined by a quarter circle with a 6m radius. One penalty mark is drawn 6m and the second penalty mark 10m from the midpoint between the goals. The goal is 3m wide and 2m high. The ball has a circumference of 62-64cm and weighs 400-440g. A match is played by 2 teams of up to 5 players each, of whom one is a goalkeeper. The max. number of substitute players is 7 and the number of substitutions during a match is unlimited. The match lasts 2 equal periods of 20min. (stopped clock) with the halftime interval not exceeding 15min. Each team is allowed 1 time-out of 1min. in each half. When the ball is knocked out of play (which incl. touching the ceiling), the game is restarted by a kick-in, which must be taken within 4sec. of taking possession of the ball. The goalkeeper restarts the game with the goal clearance, i.e. by throwing the ball from within the penalty area. There is no offside rule and no shoulder charges or sliding tackles are allowed. The goalkeeper may not touch by hand any ball played back and only one back pass to the goalkeeper is allowed. According to the 5-foul limit rule, beginning with the 6th accumulated foul recorded for either team in each half the defending team may not form a wall to defend a free kick, which must be taken directly at the goal. If the 6th foul is committed in the opposing team's half or in one own's half in front of an imaginary line parallel to the halfway line and passing through the 2nd penalty mark, the free kick is taken from the 2nd penalty mark. The team that has scored more goals within the time limit wins the match. If a match ends in a draw, the referee may order extra time or a penalty shoot-out, depending on competition rules. The game is controlled by 2 referees.
The governing body for the sport is FIFA's Committee for Futsal, which – among other efforts – is calling for including futsal in the 2008 Ol.G. in Peking.

FUTSU-TAISO, Jap. for 'normal gymnastics'. A general gymnastics system modeled on Western systems and introduced together with other Western borrowings with the intention of modernizing Japan in the 2nd half of the 19th cent. It was promoted by an Amer. pedagogue G.A. Leland who was invited to Japan in 1879. His knowledge was based on the experience of the Amer. physical education of the time. At the same period, the Japanese were developing the system of the so-called >LIGHT GYMNASTICS, created by D. Lewis.

WORLD SPORTS ENCYCLOPEDIA

F

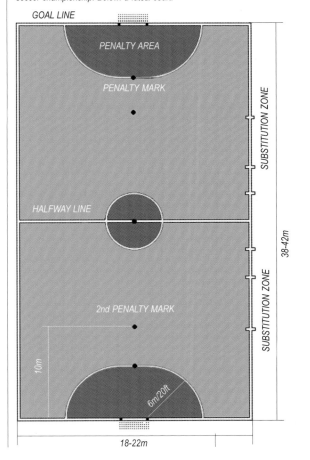

Above: Italy and Uruguay get their kicks on a glass-enclosed court in front of the Giza Pyramids near Cairo, in the opening match of Egypt's first International five-a-side indoor soccer championship. Below: a futsal court.

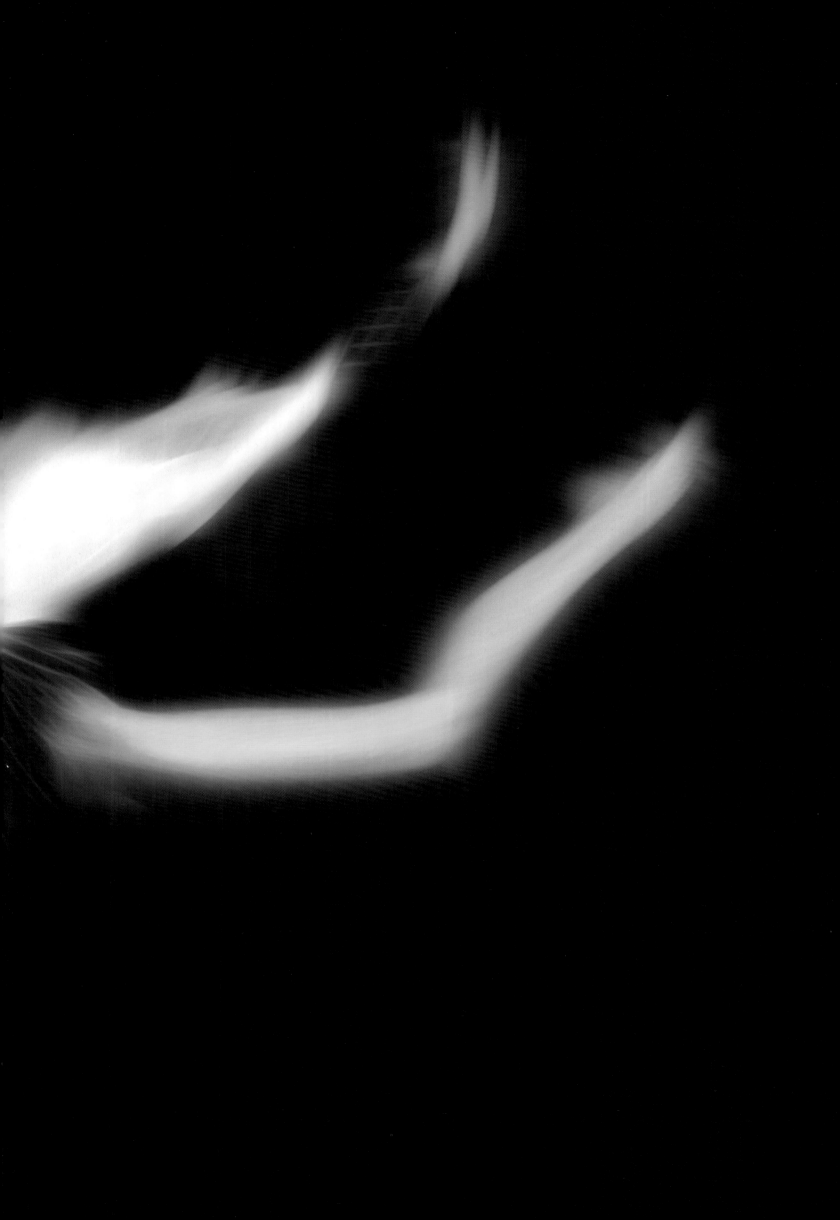

G

**WORLD SPORTS
ENCYCLOPEDIA**

GÅ KRABBEGANG, Dan. for 'crab walk'. A Dan. form of an acrobatic exercise in which the performer lies on his belly, with both feet against a wall, and attempts to walk backwards up the wall to the point where he is able to touch the wall with his lips. Known from Iceland around 1900.
J. Møller, 'Gå krabbegang', GID, 1997, 3, 20.

GÅ NÆVESKRIDT, Dan. for 'passing the fist'. A Dan. folk acrobatic demonstration in which the performer rests his fists on the floor and then, crouching, walks through the arch formed by his frame without touching the floor with any part of his body other than his fists and his feet. It originated in Iceland c.1900.
J. Møller, 'Gå næveskridt', GID, 1997, 3, 20.

GÅ OVER ELVEN, Dan. for 'crossing the river' [Dan. *gå* – to go + *over* – across, over + *elv* – a river, brook]. A game practiced during PE classes, whose object is to cover a distance from one protective zone to another without being caught. Across the middle of the gym there is a 'river' with ice floes in it (e.g. drawn on the floor with chalk). The banks of the river are demarcated by gymnastic benches. The participants are supposed to cross the river as frequently as possible jumping from one ice floe onto another. The ice floes, however, are patrolled by the catcher stalking for players who are crossing the river. A player is safe when on the banks but if captured in the river he becomes the catcher. Each new catcher starts from a floe located in the middle of the river. If he falls into the water, he has to start again from the central ice floe. Any player who slips into the water replaces the catcher. Cf. >DØDNING, >ISBJØRN OG LANDSBJØRN, >KÆDETIK, >KLIM-KLEM, >TAMANJ. See also similar games that involve crossing a certain zone, such as >KREDSTROLD.
J. Møller, 'Gå over elven', GID, 1997, 2, 54.

GÅ PÅ JAGT, Dan. for 'going hunting'. One of the players is appointed a 'hunter' whose task is to 'shoot' at other players, referred to as hares, with a ball. If a hare is shot down it becomes a greyhound

that assists the hunter by cornering the hares. The greyhound attempts to catch a running hare and hold it for a moment so that the hunter can shoot the prey down. The last hare to be shot replaces the hunter.
J. Møller, 'Gå på jagt', GID, 1997, 1, 24.

GÅ TIL ISLAND EFTER SILD, Dan. for 'going to Iceland to get some herring'. A folk form of demonstrating one's physical fitness. A performer stands with his back to a wall with his heels touching it. The goal of the demonstration is to reach an object placed on the floor at some distance from the wall. The performer 'walks' on his hands, which placed in clogs, towards the object, grabs it with his teeth (doing a push-up) and then withdraws towards the wall. Both feet have to be in contact with the wall at all times and the floor must not be touched with any part of the body other than the hands in the clogs.
J. Møller, 'Gå til Island efter sild', GID, 1997, 3, 98.

GÅ UNDER STOKKEN, Dan. for 'walking under a stick'. A game similar to >KUPJAKEPIPROOV. The performer, standing with his legs apart, holds one end of an 80cm-long stick, while the other end is propped against the floor or the wall behind him. Holding on to the stick, the performer tilts backwards trying to go as low as possible and then return to his original position.
J. Møller, 'Gå under stokken', GID, 1997, 3.

GAAIBOL, also *gaaibollen*, Flem. for. 'bird bowls'; a Flem. folk game. On an inclined ramp, referred to as the *bard*, 2.3m long with the rear part rising to a level of 24cm above the floor, there are 8 or 9 small wooden blocks called *gaaien* (singular *gaai*) that are fixed to the ramp with special catches to prevent their slipping down. The object of the game is to throw a circular wooden block, resembling a small roll of cheese, 8cm thick and 12cm in diameter, so that it knocks the greatest possible number of blocks off the ramp. The approach alley in front of the ramp is 15-20m long. One of gaaibol's var. is >SPRANG-GAAILBOLLEN.
History. The oldest reference to gaaibol (1800) speaks of a game practiced in the district of Courtrai (in Flem. Kortrijk). The game, however, must have existed earlier as can be deduced from the fully developed features it already possessed at the beginning of the 19th cent. Gaaibol reveals certain influences from Flem. crossbow and longbow shooting that can be noticed in the name's allusion to birds. It seems the game was a folk imitation of crossbow, longbow and rifle shooting (cf. >COCK SHOOTING), which was practiced in Eur. cities only by affluent merchants and craftsmen. Poorer citizens, who did not have access to weapons, had to make do with stones which they hurled at similar targets. This can be deduced from the present shape of the gaaibol alley (or the ramp) at the end of which wooden blocks (in the past these could have been 'birds') are placed in order to be knocked off with a disc that may have been a stone in days of old. In some Flem. villages the blocks are still adorned with feathers. Similarly to crossbow and longbow shooting, gaaibol winners are granted the title of king. The game developed mostly in the W and E parts of Belgian Flanders and in some villages of Du. Zeeland. In the neighborhood of Bruges there is an active gaaibol organization promoting an annual *Kriterium Brugsch Handelsblad* competition. In 1949, the organization developed regulations that unified some of the local var. of the game. The same set of rules is applied during the annual Belgian championships.
E. de Vroede, *Het Grote Volkssporten Boek*, Leuven, 1996; by the same author, *Ball and Bowl Games in the Low Countries: Past and Present*, in *Homo Ludens – Der Spielende Mensch*, 1996, vol. VI.

GAAIBOLLEN, see >GAAIBOL.

GAELIC FOOTBALL, a national game of Ireland, the second most popular after >HURLING. It is played by two 15-player teams, goalkeepers included. Until the turn of the 19th and the 20th cent. each team comprised 20 players. During games of lesser importance, a referee is entitled to reduce the number of players in a team, should any shortages in this respect occur. The playing field is 140-160yds. (129-147m) by 84-100yds. (75-92m). The ball is 27-29in. (68.5-73.5cm) in circumference and it weighs 13-15oz., i.e. 368-425g (after the metric system had been introduced the lower limit was rounded to 370g). The object of the game is to place the ball in

a goal. The ball can be passed by kicking or fisting. It can be caught only after it has bounced against the ground and flicked up with the foot, which is the fundamental skill necessary to play Gaelic football. The ball can then be carried over any distance, provided it is properly dribbled, i.e. bounced against the foot and caught every 4 steps. A player can also move dribbling the ball against the feet every 3 steps without catching it at all. However, the ball can be caught if intercepted directly from the air before it touches the ground. Then it can be carried in the hands over 4 steps, after which it must be dribbled once and passed by kicking or fisting it. The H-shaped goal is 21ft. (6.40m) wide, with the crossbar at the level of 8ft. (2.44m) and the poles 16ft. (4.88m) tall. When the ball is sent into the goal under the crossbar and in between the poles, the attacking team scores 3pts., if above the crossbar – 1pt. No offside position rule applies. A match is administered by 5 umpires: 1 referee and 4 goalsmen (2 at each goal line). The playing time used to be 2x40min. but today it is 3x30min. and the referee has the right to prolong a game if any waste time occurred during the match. The highest-ranking games played between counties or provinces last 3x35min. A break between each 2 parts of the match takes 10min. The game starts with the referee tossing the ball between 2 central players from the opposing teams. Each team can substitute 3 players during a match. The matches are held in 3 age categories that apply both to men and women: seniors (over 18), younger seniors (16-18), and juniors (up to 16).
History. The earliest references to a game which was prob. the predecessor of Gaelic football played by Celts date back to the 1st and 2nd cent. AD. After most Celtic traditions had been eradicated on the Eur. continent, the game developed in the Celtic countries on the British Isles. Gaelic football's antecedents evolved mostly during the Middle Ages. The Municipal Archives of Dublin are in possession of documents certifying the existence of a game whose rules were formalized around 1527. Depending on local traditions and the historical period, the number of players in a team varied, reaching even 100 players. In the course of time, it was reduced to 30, 25, 21, and today it is 15. For ages, Gaelic football was accompanied by a number of ceremonies related to annual festivals or various poetry and dancing competitions. In the 16th cent., a custom appeared according to which players wore hats with bands in the team colors. The modern form of Gaelic football developed from 2 var. of the game which used different names in the past.
The records concerning old forms of Gaelic football are unsystematic. We know that in 1731, in Dangan, Meath, an important match was played between the teams of married and single men. Ten years later, a match was held on the frozen surface of the Liffey river. Until 1884, the game had a rather brutal character, as one of its objectives was simply to eliminate as many opponents from the game as possible. English documents provide a series of names that were applied to Gaelic football in the course of its history, such as 'rough and tumble' or 'corner to corner'. In 1884, after an exceptionally barbarous meeting, Tiperary vs. Carrick, during which a number of players suffered serious injuries, M. Cusack (1847-1906) and D. and M. Davinow, the most celebrated Ir. sportsmen of that time, proposed regulations which formed the foundations of modern Gaelic football. That same year, on Cusack's initiative, the Gaelic Athletic Association (GAA, or Cumann Lúthchleas Gael) was established. The Association oversaw the development of both Gaelic football and >HURLING, as important elements of Ir. tradition and culture. It was also connected with the nationalistic movement for the independence of Ireland and the cultural movement aimed at reestablishing national traditions, known as the Celtic Renaissance. In 1887, the GAA prohibited games with Brit. teams and impeded participation of any Ir. players who tarnished their honor with any form of collaboration with the British, esp. if they served in the Brit. army or police, or if they informed against their compatriots. The prohibition was lifted only in 1971. However, the GAA still continues to support local culture threatened by Anglicization. Among the first and foremost recommendations the GAA dispenses to the clubs is the cultivation of Gaelic as the national language of Ireland:
1) Identify members who are interested or proficient in Irish.

For the past 30 years football contests have occurred between Australia and Ireland using a variety of 'hybrid' rules. In 1998 an 'International Rules' series was developed and a 4-year commitment made to play an annual series between the 2 different codes, Australian football and Gaelic football.

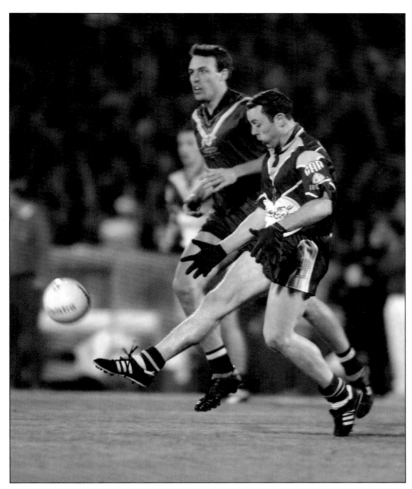

International rules football – a hybrid between Gaelic football and Australian football.

2) Communicate in Irish with above members.
3) Establish a sub-committee to promote Irish within the club.
4) If sufficient demand exists within the club, set up an Irish class in association with the Vocational Educational Committee/Adult Education Officer.
5) If there are not sufficient members in the club, consult with the County Irish Officer or other clubs about providing classes [...].
6) Develop continuity by providing these lessons on an annual basis. [*An t-Oifigeach Gaelige sa Chlub*]. The GAA sponsors the Gaelic football league and the Inter-Provincial Railway Cup. Teams from 4 historical provinces of Ireland, including Northern Ireland: Ulster, Munster, Leinster, and Connacht, participate in the All Ireland Championship whose finals are held on the 3rd Sunday of Sept. The winner is awarded the Sam Maguire Trophy. In summer National League meetings are held. The teams are categorized into the 1st and the 2nd Divisions. Each year the 2 worst 1st-Division teams drop to the 2nd, whereas the 2 best 2nd-Division teams advance to the 1st Division. Gaelic football is equally popular in Ireland as football in England or continental Europe. The statistics indicate that around 250,000 Irish citizens practice Gaelic football on different levels, from recreational to professional, out of a total of about 3.6 million inhabitants. The Croke Park Stadium in Dublin – the largest one in Ireland – seats close to 80,000 spectators. The game is also practiced, although on a much smaller scale and mostly among Ir. immigrants, in England, Scotland, the USA, Australia, New Zealand, and Canada. The best organized are the events in Australia and New Zealand, in which the best teams from both countries compete for the Australasian Cup in senior and junior categories. Similarly to the situation in Ireland, Gaelic football players worldwide often practice also >AUSTRALIAN FOOTBALL. In Canada, there are 2 different Gaelic football competitions, one in Ontario and the other in Brit. Columbia. An extra participant to the Ontario tournament is the team representing Quebec. As of today, there are no national Canadian championships, although teams from both competitions play friendly matches once in a while. In the USA, the major Gaelic football centers are Chicago, New York, and Boston. International matches are played in Ireland mostly between the US and Ir. teams. As

Eur. football is only a little less popular in Ireland than the Gaelic one, a number of players often practice both disciplines.
Women's Gaelic football is administered by the GAA Ladies' Gaelic Football (Cumman Peile na mBan) that has about 110,000 members.
Gaelic football in literature. Although Gaelic football's traditions are almost as long as those of >HURLING, the beginnings of the game were not reflected in early Ir. literature. It was prob. the result of its lower status compared to hurling which was practiced even by the nobility. Irish poet, M. Curt, described c.1600 a game he used to play as a young boy over the Boyne river. Another poet, Concanen, portrayed a match between the Lusk and Swords teams:

International rules football.

Ye champions of fais Lusks and ye of Swords,
View well this ball, the present of your lords,
To outward view, three folds of bullock's hide,
With leather thongs bound fast on every side,
A mass of finest hay concealed from sight.

Twenty years later, yet another poet, R. Murphy, depicted a Gaelic football match played by 12-player teams. The game was accompanied by activities that resembled wrestling.

M. de Búrca, *The G.A.A. A History of the Gaelic Athletic Association*, 1980; *GAA Coaching News*, P. Ó'Dálaigh, ed. 1990-98; *Cumann Lúthchleas Gael. Referees' Guide to the Playing Rules of Hurling and Football*, 1991; P. Ó'Dálaigh, ed., *An t-Oifigeach Gaelige sa Chlub*, 1992.

GAIK MAJOWY, Pol. for 'May bosket', an ancient pagan festival originating from fertility rites and the awaiting of summer crops. Despite its pagan origin the celebration has survived to this day in a number of Eur. countries, sometimes being celebrated as a religious festival (>MAIBAUM, >MAYPOLE, >PALO DE MAYO, >SOMMER I BY). In W and C Poland it was observed up until the middle of the 17th cent. Ł. Gołębiowski reports that gaik majowy was certainly known during the reign of the last Jagiełło rulers: 'Slavs used to welcome the spring by singing and dancing on green grass. During the reign of the last king from the Jagiełło dynasty, Zygmunt August, there were regions where married women still celebrated on green pastures, forming circles, swaying gently, and singing songs that praised the long-awaited spring' (*Gry i zabawy różnych stanów*, 1831, 185). Games and frolicking were accompanied by demonstrations of physical fitness and agility, such as jumping over a bonfire, simple foot races and throwing competitions. Throughout the 18th and 19th cent. the remnants of this tradition have blended in Poland partially with trad. Pentecost celebrations, partially with trad. recreational trips made in May, and with folk forms of competition such as climbing a pole covered with lard (cf. >MAJÓWKA). In the E of Poland, esp. in Lithuania and W Byelorussia (at that time referred to as Lithuania), which were united with Poland, gaik majowy traditions lived on much longer, at least until the beginning of the 19th cent. As Gołębiowski accounts: 'Around Pinsk and in other parts of Lithuania, as far as I can remember from the days of my own youth, people gathered on pastures where they put a green tree adorned with colored ribbons. Young girls, married women, boys, and men arrived at that place, led by a comely virgin who embodied the goddess Maya. A green wreath embellished her temples and from head to toe she was covered in birch sprigs. The word 'Maya! Maya!' was repeated frequently in various chants and participants danced around the adorned tree. Nowadays, the same celebration is held at Pentecost. A maid is dressed in a robe made of birch twigs and other girls walk and dance around her singing:

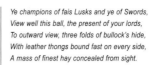

G

The old gailloche from western Brittany.

Around this green shrub
A circle of lentils has been sown
He who picks the lentil up
Shall make this girl his own'

The decline of old folklore transformed the former traditions into simple recreation, which resulted in the formation of the new custom of *majówka*.

GAILLOCHE, an E Bret. var. of *galôj* once played in W Brittany.

GAK AL-HAŠBA, Arabic for 'strike with wood'. A trad. game mentioned by M. Ibrahim al-Majman in his dictionary of Arab games and sports *Min al'abina ash-sha 'biyya* (*Our Folk Games*, 1983, 72-73). The participants, seated in a circle, pass amongst themselves a piece of wood, saying, 'Gak al-hašba'. A receiving player has to respond very quickly with, 'Hašba 'ala al-Éabaši'. If he fails to do so quickly enough or mispronounces the phrase, the remaining participants have fun spanking him.

GAKOM SLISEL, Arabic for 'here comes *Slisel*'. A game played in Saudi Arabia, esp. in the Qsim region. *Slisel* is one of the participants, selected for this role. From the description of the game found in the dictionary of Arab games and sports by M. Ibrahim al-Majman, *Our Folk Games*, we learn that the game is best played during the day or bright summer night. It is a running game played by about 10 participants, each one holding their own *gatra*, also referred to as *gâtra* or *šmag*. The term 'gatra' is unclear, as it does not appear in any of the available Arabic dictionaries; most prob. it refers to a thick rope. A literal translation of *šmag* or *gbala* is 'scarf'. After drawing lots, one of the players becomes Slisel and takes position at the starting point, accompanied by a referee, while other players walk approx. 10m away. The finish is located about 100m from the start. The referee grabs Slisel's leg with one hand and the end of his gatra – with the other, and calls out: 'Gakom Slisel!' (Here comes Slisel!). The others respond: 'Hudduh' (Let him in). The referee continues: 'Akal 'aš,kom' (He's eaten your dinner); 'Hudduh' – say the others. The referee advises: 'Sabah

Galoche bigoudène.

bilzakom' (He's having your delicacies); 'Hudduh' – respond the others, again. Finally, he says: 'Qad'a rašakom, trah gakom' (He's picked your cress, he's coming), after which Slisel is released and starts running towards the other players. A player who is hit with Slisel's gatra before reaching the finish becomes Slisel himself. The game used to be popular throughout the entire country and among the peoples living on the gulf coast.
Min al'abina ash-sha 'biyya, 1983, 93-40.

GAKVRA-BUKRTI, a Georg. folk game quite similar to the Eur. >PALANT.

GALASIN, an Indon. sport played on a court the size similar to that of a >BADMINTON court, therefore players quite often use existing badminton courts. The court is divided into 6 segments by 1 lateral line and 2 perpendicular ones. On each of the perpendicular lines (2 inside the court and 2 marking the ends of the court) there is 1 guard and the 5th guard is responsible for the lateral line in the center of the court. The guard on the 1st line is supposed to move to the 4th line and then to return to the 1st line without being touched by any of the guards on the remaining lines. The lateral-line guard is supposed to prevent the runner from changing sides. If, however, the 1st-line guard succeeds in changing sides without being touched by the lateral-line guard, the game continues. The running player can place only 1 foot outside the court at a time.

GALHOFA, a Port. trad. var. of wrestling practiced in some villages in the province of Braganca. The opponents, embraced in a standing position, attempt to throw one another to the ground. According to W. Baxter, nowadays it is practiced only in 3 localities. 'Les luttes traditionels a travers le monde' (Eng. version 'Wrestling'), LJP, 1998, 77.

GALOCHE BIGOUDÈNE, a trad. Bret. throwing game, particularly popular in the Bigoudène area, but also known in CW France. It consists of throwing an iron disc (cf. >QUOITS) towards a wooden cylinder-shaped block 11.5cm tall, known as a *galoche*. At the top of the cylinder there is a coin. The object of the game is to knock the coin down. The winner is the party whose disc rests closest to the coin after being thrown. The game is being codified in order to make it more attractive. For the most part it is played in 2-player teams. Cf. >GALOCHE SUR BILLOT.
F. Peru, 'La tradition populaire de jeux de plein air en Bretagne', LJP, 1998.

A galoche sur billot player.

GALOCHE SUR BILLOT, a Bret. throwing game in which a small rectangular wooden skittle, referred to as the *galoche*, 6-7cm tall, is placed on a thick platform, also made of wood. A player, standing about 9m from the platform, tries to knock the galoche off with the use of 6 large discs, 11cm in diameter and weighing 900g, per round. The game is played in 2 rounds and the winner is the player who succeeds in knocking the galoche off the platform the greatest number of times. The game is characteristic of the area around Petit Trégor and Trégor.
F. Peru, 'La tradition populaire de jeux de plein air en Bretagne', LJP, 1998. Consultant: G. Jaouen, FALSAB.

African wrestling.

GALONDEE JUMPING, a var. of ski jumping with the use of skis for downhill racing instead of typical ski-jumping equipment. The jumps are usu. much shorter compared to trad. ski jumping distances as the boots and feet are fixed to the skis. Sometimes galondee jumpers use standard ski jumps, but most often competitions and shows are held on naturally shaped hills and larger moguls.

GAMBIAN WRESTLING, a var. of wrestling the object of which is to throw one's opponent to the ground. The loser joins his teammates waiting for their turn to fight. If he thinks that he lost by chance, he may ask for the bout to be repeated. If his 'appeal' is admitted, he must report for the rematch immediately. If there are 2 wrestlers with an equal number of victories, the winner is determined by a match between them.

GAME OF HAILES, a ball game similar to such games as >FOOTBALL, >FIELD HOCKEY. Invented at the beginning of the 18th cent., it had disappeared by the end of the century but was reinvented at the beginning of the 19th cent. by students of the Edinburgh Academy. The size of the field was similar to that of a football pitch. In order to score a point, the players had to bounce the ball off either of the walls located on the goal lines. The rubber ball, slightly bigger than a tennis ball, was propelled by spoon-shaped sticks (*clacken*), to those used in hockey similar but not as curved. The ball could also be kicked or caught with the hands, the latter only if the ball had not come into contact with the ground. Picking the ball up off the ground was forbidden and running with the ball was allowed only when it was carried in the spoon of the stick, which made the game similar to >HURLING. The annual Silver Clacken competition was held from 1891.

GAOSHAN POLE BALL, a Chin. game consisting of striking a ball with long bamboo poles. The ball is 10cm in diameter and is made of cane covered with tree bark. Players stand in a circle, each holding a bamboo pole. One player without a pole takes his position in the middle of the circle and tosses the ball high up in the air, while the remaining players try to hit the ball with their poles. The game is over when each player has hit the ball at least once. Usually, by the end of the game the tossing player sends the ball out near the least experienced players in the circle. The player who hits the ball the most times during the game wins. In Gaoshan mythology, hitting the ball means freeing oneself from evil and danger, and the start of a happy life. In one of the myths, long ago, the Gaoshan people found a piece of ever-burning firewood in a forest, which allowed them to maintain fire in their homes. The firewood was guarded night and day by young villagers. One day a demon in the form of a tiger sneaked into the village to steal it. One of the young guardians noticed the tiger, grabbed a long pole and started poking the beast with it. To commemorate that legend, the Gaoshans estab. pole ball competitions in which the ball would symbolize the evil tiger.
Mu Fushan, et al., 'Gaoshan Pole Ball', TRAMCHIN, 76.

GARAJAI, see >BUZKASHI.

GASING, a Malayan var. of >TOPS, popular among the Malaki people. A place most famous for gasing is the area of Bansda Hilir. Large tops resemble discuses and each weighs about 5.5kg. At the top they have a pin around which a string is wound and then pulled to make the top spin. The string is attached to a stick, forming a kind of a whip whose lashes maintain the spinning. During competitions the winner is usu. that person who succeeds in keeping the top spinning for the longest time. The best players can keep the top spinning for more than 2hrs.

GATEBALL, a game similar to >CROQUET, developed as a recreational sport for children in Memuro, Hokkaido, in 1941 and spreading out very rapidly since its birth, especially among senior citizens, as a leisure activity, but also as an internationally recognized sport. Passing several stages of its improvement in rules, it has evolved into an intellectual field sport and is now popular not only in Japan, but also in China, Chinese Taipei, Korea, Australia, N.Zealand, the USA and several more countries in Asia and South America. The number of players worldwide is now estimated at over 10 million.

The court. There are no special ground requirements for a gateball court: either an earth court or a turf court can be used. The size is approx. 25x20m.

Equipment. The 4 types of equipment are: sticks (mallets), balls, gates, and a goalpole. The stick (once wooden, but now more often made of carbon, titanium, aluminum, stainless steel, etc.) has a shaft, which is at least 50cm in length, and a head, which is 18-24cm in length, with a face (where the player hits the ball) of 3.5-5cm in diameter. Balls, originally wooden, now made of synthetic resin, are 7.5cm in diameter.

Rules. A coin toss allows the captain of the winning team to select either red or white balls (red strike off first). Players strike a series of numbered balls, beginning with ball 1, and then proceeding in order to ball 10. The color of the balls alternates; the red balls bearing odd numbers, and the white balls – even numbers. The game is played between a red team and a white team, each with 5 members. The red team wears tags numbered with odd numbers, the white team – with even numbers. The playing order advances from player 1 to 10. The game continues for 30min. A time limit of 10sec. applies between strokes. Each player attempts to pass through the 3 gates in the correct order and direction and then hit the goal-pole. 1pt. is scored for each gate and 2pts. for the goal-pole, making it a total of 25pts. that one team can score. The team that scored more points within the time limit, wins the game.

After going through a gate the player has a continuation stroke. The first gate must be passed in a single stroke from the starting line and in doing so, must not leave the court. Any other ball considered to be obstructing the successful passage of a ball through that first gate may be temporarily removed. If a player fails to run the gate or goes off court after running that first gate, then the ball is retrieved and the player awaits his next turn at the starting area. A ball out of bounds is an out-ball, if the whole of the ball is outside the playing line. If a player hits his own ball out of bounds, it becomes an out-ball. If a ball goes out of bounds as a result of a 'spark' (see below), that ball becomes an out-ball. A fault made on the court by a striker in play will result in that player's ball being removed and becoming an out-ball and his turn ending. An out-ball is played in at a player's next turn, but may not touch another ball or the ball becomes an out-ball again.

Technique. The technique used for playing gateball is called touch and spark. Striking a ball so that it hits another ball (either from the striker's team or the opposite team) is called a touch. If both the striker's ball and the ball it touched are inside the court, the striker is entitled to a spark. In order to spark a ball, the striker should pick up the ball that his ball touched and step on his ball with 1 foot (his left foot if he is a right-handed player). Then he places the lifted ball against his ball, facing it in the direction he wishes to move it, and strikes it, as in croquet, so that the impact moves the ball. If the spark is successfull, the player is entitled to strike his ball again.

The governing body for gateball is the World Gateball Union (WGU) estab. in Sep. 1985 in Japan. It has 13 affiliated member countries.

The Internet: croquet.alphalink.com.au/gateball.htm; www.gateball.or.jp/English/letstry.htm

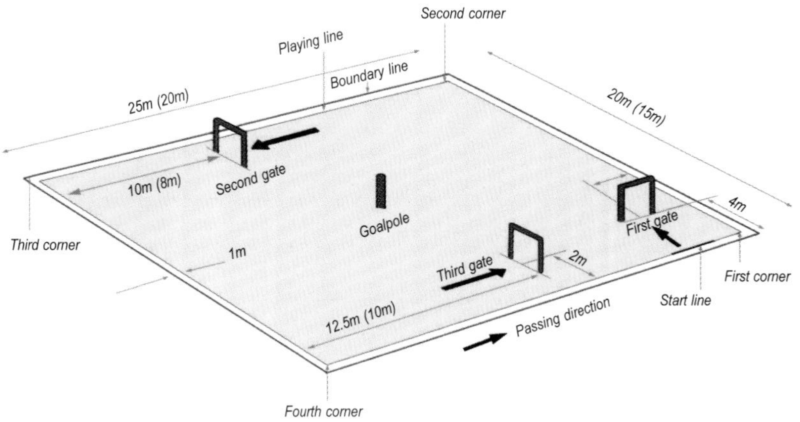

A gateball court.

GBANG, an Afr. game played by the Kpelle tribe in Liberia. It consists of throwing snail shells, referred to as *cowries*, onto the ground. The result is determined by the number of shells that come to rest with their hole facing the ground or the sky. The game is similar to Nig. >IGBA-ITA, >IGBA-EGO, and a game known in Côte d'Ivoire as >NIGBÉ.

GE INDIAN RELAY, a var. of a race in which contestants compete in carrying thick logs, about 1m long and about 90kg in weight, practiced during the annual holidays of the Ge Indians in S America. See also >LOG RUNNING.

GEGG, an Eng. game also known under its full name of *smuggle the Gegg* (a 'gegg' is any object used for the game, e.g. a penknife). Players are grouped in 2 teams referred to as the 'ins' and the 'outs'. The outs receive the gegg, hide themselves, and give the ins a starting signal by shouting, 'Smugglers!' The ins are supposed to locate and capture the smuggler holding the gegg. If they succeed, the teams swap roles.

GELLA-CHUT, Hindu for 'running king'. A folk sport practiced by the inhabitants of Tripura state in NE India. Two teams of 7-10 players each take part in the game. One of them is referred to as the outside team and the other as the inside team. The inside group chooses one of its members to be king who takes a position about 20-25m from his partners who, in turn, are supposed to stay within their field known as the *ghar* (the house). Members of the outside team are scattered around. The king's task is to get through to his subjects in the ghar and the outside team's objective is to capture the running king. If they succeed, the king is eliminated from the game and the outside team wins. At that point the teams change places and a new king is selected from among the former outside team. The king's subjects can help him by forming a corridor or a chain along which he can run. If an outside team member touches an opponent (other than the king), he is considered 'dead' and must not continue playing, which facilitates the king's escape. Cf. >KABADDI.

GEOGRAPHICAL EXPLORATION, an activity aimed at searching for unknown parts of the world, involving an element of risk, adventure, and mental and physical stamina and abilities. The most ancient geographical explorations are related to the migrations of the first primitive peoples who were looking for new hunting areas or places to gather fruit for food. The migrations of Mong. tribes from Asia towards the Americas (c.30,000-8,000 BC) and the expansion of Indo-Eur. groups within Europe are the earliest examples of geographical exploration stimulated by conditions of group subsistence. In the 3rd and 2nd cent. BC at the meeting point of the Mediterranean and Asia, a series of movements of various tribes took place, as a result of which the first politically organized structures were established. Those movements were the first in the history of mankind to possess features of intended and controlled expansion (Babylonia, Assyria, and ancient Egypt). The Biblical escape of the Israelites from Egypt and their search for the Promised Land have all the features of geographical exploration. In the 2nd cent. BC in Europe a number of migrations took place whose indirect result was the exploration of new lands. The oldest legendary records of such journeys are thought to be Gk. myths, such as the one about the discovery of Colchis in the course of the Argonauts' quest of the Golden Fleece, or the discoveries made by Odysseus on his way back from Troy to Ithaca. Both events have abundant literary documentation in the Hellenic culture: the earliest record of the Argonaut myth is to be found in Archilochus's writings and Odysseus's adventures as a discoverer of lands unknown to the Greeks are the major subject of Homer's *Odyssey*. For the Mediterranean cultures, the moment of paramount significance as far as geographical discoveries are concerned is breaking through the Pillars of Hercules, i.e. the Strait of Gibraltar, and the first explorations in the Atlantic Ocean. Those achievements were accomplished by anonymous sailors and tin merchants, prob. of Iberian origin, who founded Tartessus, the oldest Eur. city on the Atlantic coast. In their search for tin they got as far as the coasts of modern day France up to islands referred to in ancient Gk. sources as the *nessoi Oistrymnides*, and in Lat. as *insulae Oestrymnides*. The largest of the islands, Uxantis (today's Fr. Insle d'Ouessant; in Eng. Ushant), just like nearby Cornwall, possessed rich deposits of tin. Tartessian merchants did not sail that far however and the ore was brought by local sailors who – according to the Gk. *peryplus*, a description of sailing achievements dating from the 6th cent. BC – could also have reached the coasts of Ireland, which at that time was referred to as the Sacred Island (*Insula Sacra*). The *peryplus* survived only in the form of quotations provided in the much later geographical poem by the Roman poet R.F. Avienus, titled *Ora maritima* (*Coastal Navigation*). The 'tin route' from the Mediterranean Sea to the Ushant Isl. and British Isl., which were called by Herodotus Tin Islands (*nesoi Kasiterides*), was kept in secrecy by the Phoenicians and Carthaginians who controlled the narrow pass between the Pillars of Hercules up to the conquest of Tartessus. Their monopoly of Atlantic merchant shipping was broken by the Roman Empire in the 2nd cent. BC. Before that happened, however, a Gk. geographer and navigator Pytheas from Massala managed to confuse the Carthaginians and slipped through the Strait of Gibraltar and c.330 BC navigated around the British Isles and some parts of the N Eur. coast, reach-

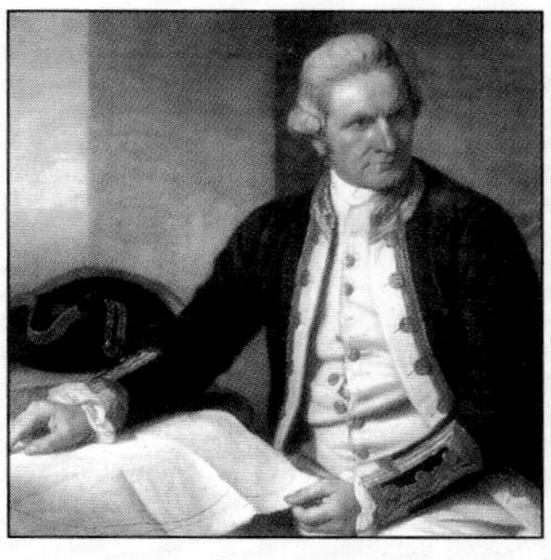

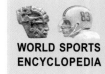

James Cook (1728-1779). Born in the Yorkshire village of Marton, Cook joined the Royal Navy and took part in a number of see voyages which brought him the fame of a most oustanding explorer. In 1769 he discovered New Zealand and 1770 he sighted the east coast of Australia, both of which he claimed as a British possession. He was the first to cross the Antarctic Circle. He discovered South Georgia Island, the Sandwich Islands, and the Hawaiian Islands. He died at Kealakekua Bay (Hawaii) in a battle with the natives.

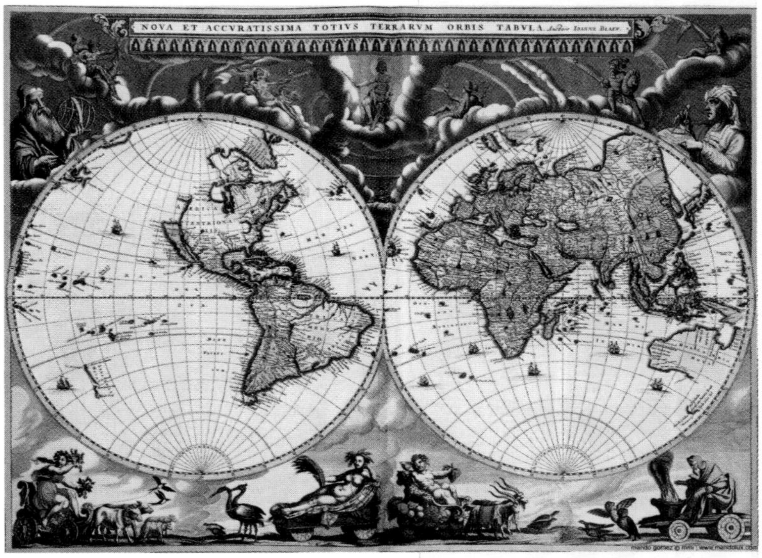

Copernican map of the world.

Vasco da Gama (c.1460-1524). Born at Sines, SW Portugal, he was selected by King Manuel I to discover the sea route to the distant spice lands. In 1498 his expedition rounded S Africa and reached Calicut, India. In 1502 he returned to Calicut and was made Portuguese viceroy of India, with the lofty title of Lord of the Conquest of Ethiopia, Arabia, Persia, and India. Having made Portugal the leading commercial nation of Europe, he died in India, and was buried in a monastery.

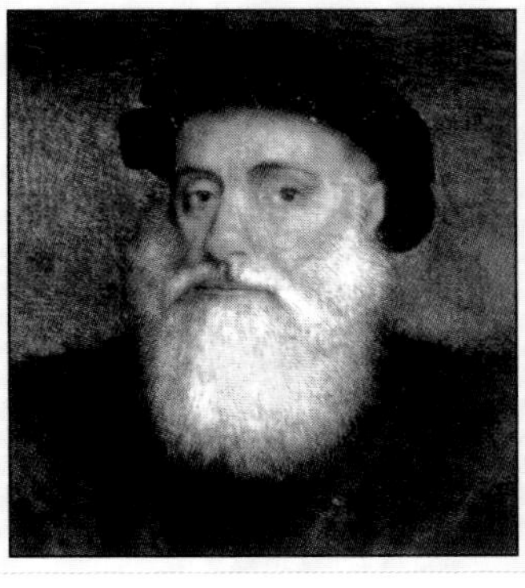

G
WORLD SPORTS ENCYCLOPEDIA

Thor Heyerdahl and his Kontiki raft.

Hernando Cortes (1482-1547).

Two stamps commemorating Polish paleontological (1963-71) and ethnological (1963-80) expeditions in Mongolia.

ing a mysterious land or an island that he called *Ultima Thule* in his report titled *Peri okeanu* (*About the Ocean*), which we know only from quotations found in other works of Gk. literature. Contemporary geographers are not positive if that land was the coast of today's Norway, Spits Bergen, or Greenland. The endeavors of Mediterranean sailors were not the only example of attempts to discover new lands in ancient times. In 1947, a Norw. scientist T. Heyerdahl (b. 1914) made a sea journey from the coast of Peru in S Amer. to the Polynesian archipelago of Tuamot on a reed raft called Kon-Tiki which was made according to ancient prototypes. Then in 1970, he navigated across the Atlantic on the *Ra II* – a boat made of papyrus reeds; and in 1977-9 – across the Indian Ocean on a boat made of cane and called *Tiger*, proving in this way that long transoceanic journeys were possible for explorers in the early stages of the human history. In a number of ancient cultures we can come across stories about conquests of distant lands. Such legends, for instance, can be found in the *Lebór geabhala Eireann* (*The Book of the Conquest of Ireland*). Some fragments of the book, which was written as late as the Middle Ages, describe events that took place c.1800 BC and narrate some phases of the conquest of Ireland by invaders arriving from the Eur. continent. It is a mythological record of 6 migrations and conquests of Ireland. The exact timing of those events is a matter debated by scientists today. After the fall of the Roman Empire, the barbarian invaders, such as the Goths, Vandals, and Huns who entered the empire's past domain, as well as the Slavs and Avars who 'only' reached C and E Europe, discovered new territories, thus extending their knowledge of the world. From the 6th cent. AD, Ger. tribes, initially known as Suyons, but later referred to as Vikings throughout Europe, began a period of sea and land conquests. Besides looting and pillaging the Vikings made a number of geographical discoveries. In the 10th cent. they colonized Iceland, arrived in Greenland and the E coasts of Labrador, and then they may well have moved along the E coasts of N America getting as far as Florida, as some historians claim. Their discoveries did not, however, enter the general awareness of Europeans. The development of commercial relationships with far-east Asia in the course of the Middle Ages resulted in numerous overland journeys during which various territories were discovered. The most celebrated figure of those journeys was M. Polo (1254-1323) from Venice. In 1271, accompanied by his father Niccolo and his uncle Matteo, he took the first step in a nearly 3-yr. long trip to China, where he stayed for about 17yrs. A part of his return journey to Venice was made by sea, through the Strait of Hormuz (1295). The fact that Eur. was isolated from the Far East because of the expansion of Islam and the conquest of the Holy Land instigated the first attempts to recapture it in a series of Crusades that were inaugurated by the speech of the Pope Urban II at the Council of Clermont (1095). In total, between 1096 and 1291 there were seven Crusades which, despite some partial victories, did not liberate the Holy Land, but which substantially increased the mobility of people in Europe, developed sea transportation that was used to deploy armies, all of which formed foundations for Eur. expansion onto other continents. In the 15th cent., Port. sailors discovered further parts of the Afr. coast from the W. The most eminent leader of such explorations was Henry the Navigator (in Port. Don Henrique Navigador, 1394-1460) whose traditions were then continued by B. Diaz (c.1450-1500) who circumnavigated the Cape of Good Hope in 1486. At that time the discovery of heliocentricity and the spherical shape of the Earth made by Copernicus (Mikołaj Kopernik) led to attempts aimed at reaching Asia by sea heading westwards. C. Columbus (Cristoforo Colombo, Cristóbal Colón; 1451-1506) who wanted to reach India from the W, reached instead the Amer. continent (1492) and a little later (1498), V. da Gama (c.1460-1524) sailed to India by circumnavigating Africa. Columbus's and da Gama's expeditions marked the beginning of an era of great geographical exploration that continued for another 200yrs. One of the most important events in the history of geographical explorations was F. Magellan's (Fernão de Magalhães, c.1480-1521) expedition during which he circumnavigated the globe. Another continent to be explored was Australia, originally named New Holland. The earliest documents containing

information about Australia, were recorded by Du. navigators. In 1770, an Eng. sailor J. Cook (1728-79), on behalf of Great Britain took possession of the E coast of Australia, giving it the name of New South Wales. The series of 3 trips Cook made circumnavigating the globe actually closed the era of geographical exploration at sea. Each grand discovery made by navigators usu. led to a phase of land exploration, often including the ruthless conquest of indigenous peoples. That phase was commenced in the history of America by the Span. conquistadors. In 1519-21, H. Cortez (Herman Cortés, 1482-1547) overthrew the ancient Aztec empire and conquered a territory that mostly covers the area of today's Mexico. In 1531-1533, F. Pizarro (c.1471-1541) vanquished the Inca empire in Peru, which opened the way to explore S America from the west. At the same time overland exploration continued in various regions of N America by Span., Fr., and Eng. colonizers. In 1804-6, M. Lewis (1774-1809) and W. Clark (1770-1838) organized an expedition that crossed the continent from E to W both overland and by boat (using Indian boats called *kanu*, see >CANOEING). In 1861, a Scot, J.D. Stuart (1815-66), crossed Australia from S to N. It should be noted, however, that R. O'Hara Burke (1821-61) was close to achieving it first, but gave up because of exhaustion not knowing that the coast which he was attempting to reach was only several hundred meters away from the point he ordered the retreat of his group, only to die of exhaustion a few days later.

North America as divided by European powers.

The first significant penetrations of the Afr. interior (1840-71) were carried out by a Scot, D. Livingstone (1813-73), who died during his last expedition, which was a pretext for H. Morton Stanley to start in 1871 a huge rescue operation. Having found Livingstone's body, Morton Stanley continued the former's explorations and finally reached the source of the Congo. As unexplored areas were becoming fewer and fewer, esp. after the 1850s, the character of geographical exploration altered. Expeditions became a kind of a race towards the last enclaves never seen by man. The best example of such competition was the rivalry among polar explorers whose efforts contained many features of a sporting competition where physical fitness, determination, and psychological strength were indispensable. Among those expeditions the most significant were those that on the one hand ended in failure but on the other, blazed a trail for others to follow: a balloon trip that ended in the deaths of S.A. Andrée (1854-97) – a Swed. explorer – and his companion; an expedition by Norw. explorers, N.A.E. Nordenskiöld (1832-1901) and F. Nansen (1861-1930). The latter crossed Greenland on skis (1888) and led the *Fram* expedition (1893), on a ship that drifted among icebergs up to 84°N. The South Pole was reached in 1911 by the Norw., R. Amundsen (1872-1928), who was only a little ahead of the Brit., R.F. Scott (1868-1912), who died of exhaustion and hunger on his way back. The North Pole was first reached by plane (1926) by R.E. Byrd, who got there 2 days ahead of Amundsen's flight on the airship *Norge*. The South and North Poles were the last 'unknown' places to be reached and the age of geographical exploration came to an end.

GGET, a boulder from Öland, Sweden. Its name is also used to refer to local folk competitions in stone lifting. The stone is oval and on its surface we find a carved inscription indicating its weight (95kg) and the year 1824, which most prob. is the year a series of competitions was inaugurated in which the stone was used. See also >LYFTESTEN, Dan. >STEN-LØFTNING, Basq. >ARRIJASOKETA. Cf. >DRÄN-GASTENAR, >DRÄNGALÖFTEN, >KAMPASTEN, >KÖLNÅKERN, >KUNGSSTEN, >KUNGSSTENAR-NA, >STORA OCH LILLA DAGSVERKARN, >TY-FTEHÖNAN.
M. Hellspong, 'Lifting Stones. The Existence of Lifting Stones in Sweden', ST, 1993-94, XIX-XX.

GIALKI, a var. of Iranian wrestling practiced in the northern provinces of the country. Similar to >MA-ZANDERANI.

GIANTS' FIGHTING, a trad. Kor. sport popular esp. among wood-cutters. Each team constructs a gigantic figure made of wood and straw and by manipulating a long shaft with attached ropes fights the figure of the rival team. In the past up to several hundred men participated in such fights. The gigantic figures, later built only of wood, reflected mythical heroes of the past and their achievements. The trees chopped for the making of the figures were carried to the village in a festive procession. The wood-cutters dressed ceremonially and offered sacrifices to the spirit of the mountains, asking his permission to log in the forest. The fight was led by a commander who took up a position on a specially constructed platform.

GILSSAMNORI, also sp. *Gill-Ssam-No-Ri*, Kor. for 'a spinning competition'. A Kor. women's game related to rituals ensuring good harvest in the following year. According to the rules of the game, from July 16 to Aug. 15 of each lunar year, all the women from a given village were supposed to spin while singing, all day long from dawn to dusk. Entire villages participated in the competition. The winner was the village that succeeded in producing the largest amount of yarn. It was believed the harvest of the losing party would be far poorer in the following year than that of the winners. The defeated village was obliged to cover expenses related to food and drinks served during the game. Kor. ethnographers suggest that gilssamnori was a rite of initiation, a test of a woman's maturity.
Koo-Chul Jung, *Erziehung und Sport in Korea im Kreutzpunkt fremder Kulturen und Mächte*, 1996, 62.

GITCHO, see >MARI UCHI.

GIULES, also *gjules, gjuleš*. An Azerbaijani var. of folk wrestling influenced by >TURKISH WRESTLING, esp. >KUSAK GÜREŞI.

GIUOCO DA PUGNA, an Ital. game in which a ball is supposed to be returned to the opponent's half by striking it with the fist [Ital. *giuoco* – a game, competition + *da* – preposition + *pugna* – a fist]. The game was a var. of *giuoco della palla* (>PALLONE AL BRACIALLE) that, in turn, was a descendant of the ancient game of >FOLLICULUS or >EPISKY-ROS. The first description of giuoco da pugna can be found in A. Scaino's work titled *Trattato del Giuoco*

Battle of the bridge in Venice.

della Palla, published in Venice in 1555. A match was played by two 3-player teams. The ball was served only from one end of the playing field, about 90m long, whose right side was marked with a wall against which the ball was returned. The field was divided into 2 halves with a string hung across, along its shorter axis. When serving, a player jumped from a special platform (a springboard) which facilitated a higher jump and thus a longer serve. The ball weighed about 1kg and was about 36cm in diameter. The object of the game was to make the ball cross the farther end line of the opponent's half. The scoring was similar to the system employed in >JEU DE LA PAUME and in so-called *real tennis* (see >ROYAL TENNIS). In 1796, J.C.F. Guths-Muths referred to giuoco da pugna as a national game of Italy in which even distant cities competed one with the other and which used to attract a multitude of spectators and players from all over the country. In the course of the 16th and 17th cent. the game spread throughout Germany where the wall lining the field on one side was eliminated. Before its Ger. sequel was developed, i.e. >FAUSTBALL, the game was rather modestly popular in Germany. In Spain, giuoco da pugna influenced the evolution of >PELOTA that was also played on a field lined by a wall on one side (Cf. >ETON WALL GAME). In France, the features of the game could be noticed in the abovementioned *jeu de la paume*, and in England – in >FISTBALL. Each of those games grew in its own country and new elements were added here and there, which led to substantial differences among them, sometimes resulting in mutually exclusive features of a newer version compared to the former one.

GIOCO DEL PONTE, Ital. for 'game of the bridge', also spelled *giuoco del ponte*; a centuries-old trad. of mock battles still taking place in such cities as Pisa and Venice. Dating as far back as the Renaissance, the original events appear to have been put on as extravagant gladiatorial spectacles to impress visiting dignitaries, though they also served to boost the local economy and allowed citizens an opportunity to express pride not only in their quarter or guild but, later, Pisan autonomy from Florence, while blowing off considerable steam in the process. Early tournaments employed wooden sticks, lances, poles, fists, and formidable paddle-shaped *targoni*, narrow shields that could deal a blow as well as fend one off. Teams of as few as 20 or as many as 320 deployed at each end of a bridge and attempted to cross from opposite directions, forcing the opponents to give way. The combat was genuine and partakers were often seriously wounded or were knocked into the water. Because of its ruthless character, the fight was periodically prohibited in the 16th and 17th cent. A drawing by an anonymous artist representing giuoco del ponte can be found in the collection of the Biblioteca Marciana in Venice. Now held late in the afternoon and on into the evening of the last Sunday in June before crowds ranging from 70,000 to well over 100,000 spectators, il Gioco del Ponte is the culminating event of Pisa's *Giugno Pisano*, a

month-long festival including such events as the *Luminaria* and the *Regatta del San Ranieri*. Rival factions – from the *Mezzogiorno*, (comprised of teams from the old S quarters of San Antonio and San Martino, as well as the Delfini, Dragoni, Leoni, and San Marco neighborhoods), and the *Tramontana*, (teams representing the old N quarters of the San Maria and San Francesco, joined by teams from the districts of Calcesana (Calci), Mattaccini, San Michele, and Satiri) - promenade with full medieval pomp and pageantry along opposite banks of Pisa's Arno river, meeting at the Ponte di Mezzo, the bridge spanning the Arno at the Borghi-Corso Italia axis, upon which they battle. In days of old the battles were full-scale no-holds-barred melees with much splitting of heads, participants being tossed into the river and, not infrequently, audience participation in the form of projectiles hurled from balconies and rooftops, even the roofing tiles themselves. The modern version, a boon to kicking off summer tourism, takes the form of a sort of reverse >TUG-OF-WAR, more of a 'shove-of-war' wherein the opposing sides simultaneously attempt to claim the Ponte di Mezzo by pushing the massive *carrello*, a 7-ton cart on 50-m rails, off the bridge on the opposing team's side, and deposing the other side's banner. J.C. English of St. Bonaventure University and E.B. English of Jamestown Community College, 'Il Giuoco del Ponte of Pisa: The Sport of Battle and Pageantry from the Renaissance to the Napoleonic Era', 1983; K.M. Phillips, III, 'Il Gioco del Ponte'; The Internet: www.qsl.net/ik5ztt/Game.htm; www.comune.pisa.it/turismo/manifestazionistoeriche/giocoponte-gb.htm; www.pisaonline.it/Pisa/eventi/e-giocodelponte.htm

GIUOCO DELLA PALLA, see >PALLONE AL BRACIALLE.

GJUAJTJAE LEPURIT, Alb. for 'rabbit or hare hunting', an Alb. team game of searching for a small bag filled with straw or hay [Alb. *gjuajtjae* – hunting + *lepurit* – rabbit, hare]. The well hidden bag is searched for by two teams of an unspecified num. of players. The player who finds it scores a point for his team.
Source: personal inform. from Arben Kaçurri, Alb. Olympic Committee; also by the same: *Heritage* – 'System of values and device of education', a paper delivered at XI Seminar for Postgraduate Students, International Olympic Academy, Ancient Olympia, 2001.

GLADIATORIAL FIGHTS, duels to the death fought in the circus arenas and amphitheaters of ancient Rome and other cities of the Roman Empire. Mortal combat as an entertaining spectacle can be seen in >NAUMACHIA, an ancient imitation of sea battles. In the Roman Empire fights between humans and animals, which were referred to as >BESTIARIA, were also staged.
Etymology. The name *gladiator*, whose modern form is identical to its Lat. original (plural *gladiatores*), stems from the name of a double-edged short sword (0.6m) known as a *gladius*. Its blade was wide at the handle and tapered towards the tip. A gladius formed a part of the elementary equipment of the

Roman army. Both the sword itself and its name were borrowed from the Celtic culture of the Gauls. There is a whole family of Lat. words and terms related to it, such as for example: *digladior* – to fight to the death; and *gladiatura* – a gladiatorial fight. The noun *gladiatorium* had 2 meanings and could refer both to fights and to the payment earned by the winner.
Types of fights and gladiators. The fights were organized in a number of events that were grouped in 2 categories: heavily armored and lightly armored. Each category had a few varieties. The most popular type of heavily armored fight was the one between 2 gladiators equally equipped with a helmet adorned with feathers and furnished with a movable visor (*galea*), a pad made of leather and metal to cover the left leg (*ocrea*), a sword (*gladius*) or a spear (*hasta*), and a large circular shield (*scutum*). The arm fending off the blows, usu. the right one, and genitals were protected with a pad made of thick leather (*manicae*). Similar armor was originally used by the Samnites, an Ital. tribe who clashed repeatedly with Rome. In 310 BC, one of the Roman allies captured a large supply of Samnite armor and it was donated to schools of gladiators. The fighters who wore that type of armor, even after it was improved later on, were referred to as Samnites. There were also fights of heavily armored gladiators on horseback and in combat wagons. Gladiators were called according to the type of armor they wore. If the armor resembled the one used by the Gauls or Thracians, the gladiator wearing it – irrespective of whether he was a representative of a given nation or not – was referred to as a Gaul or a Thracian accordingly. Gladiators were adored by the public more or less the way football, baseball, or basketball players are idolized today. Sometimes this affinity was perverse. Caligula, a Roman Emperor, was a supporter of Thracians and at times he expressed his preference in rather cruel ways. When Columbus, a gladiator using a net as a weapon, defeated one of the Emperor's favorite Thracians, Caligula had the winner poisoned by pouring a special mixture over his wounds, and in memory of the event the poison was called 'columbina'. When a gladiator named Proculus overpowered a Thracian, Caligula had the victor tied and cut his throat. Another supporter of Thracians was Titus. When Docletian heard one of the free citizens of Rome denigrating Thracian gladiators, he had the offender captured and thrown to wild dogs.
Thracians were equipped with a curved sword (*sica*) and a square or round shield (*parma*). Unlike Samnites they wore 2 thigh pads instead of only one. Their legs were covered in leather bands (*fasciae*). The most famous Thracian gladiator was Priskus from Smyrna. The most popular event of lightly armored fighters was a fight between the one equipped with a net, called a *retiarius* and the one equipped with a sword, a trident, or a spear resembling a harpoon made from tuna bones (*fascina*), referred to as a *secutor*. In addition, he had a dagger or a small sword, *gladiolus*. A retiarius fought without any armor, his chest and head bare. Sometimes he wore a headband. His shoulder that was not protected by the net (usu. the left one), was covered with a leather or metal pad – *galerus*. Gladiators fighting as retiariuses were often called *myrmyllons*, after their fish insignia [*mormylos* – sea fish]. Retiariuses were considered gladiators of a lower order (see below Gladiators in literature and art), that is why some of them attempted to fight also as Samnits. A secutor was also sometimes referred to as a provocateur [Lat. *provocator*].
There were also horseback events called *andabatae*. The riders wore chain armor of a southern type, like Roman horseback soldiers known as *cataphracti*. A characteristic element of armor used during the andabatae was a helmet with visor that did not have any holes. Thus, the fighters were effectively blinded which evidently served to make such matches more exciting for the spectators. Julius Caesar introduced the *essedarii* who fought riding battle carts [Lat. *essedum* – a Celtic 2-wheel battle or traveling cart]. There were 2 gladiators on each cart: a coachman and a fighter.
The *sagitarii* (sing. *Sagittarius*), i.e. the archers, fought with wild animals or one another. There was also an infantry gladiator equipped with a spear that he hurled using a leather strap or belt (*hasta amentata*). Two small swords, referred to as daggers, were used by the *dimacheri* [Lat. *di* – affix denoting two or a double character + *machaera* – a knife, short

G

WORLD SPORTS ENCYCLOPEDIA

Gladiator's helmet.

The Colchester vase.

Fighting gladiators, a miniature sculpture.

sword]. We do not know yet what the gladiators referred to as *scissors* looked like nor what techniques they employed during combat. Another classification of gladiators grouped them into the ordinary ones – *gladiatores ordinarii* and those who fought in midday – *gladiatores meridiani*.

To amuse the public, there were also fights of dwarves referred to as *gladiatores nani*. Opulent dignitaries could also afford fights that were carried out in their residences during feasts. Gladiators fighting in such circumstances were referred to as room gladiators – *gladiatores cubicularii*. In the late Roman Empire, gladiators provided for by the state were called *gladiatores fiscals*, or *Ceasariani*. Fights were usu. one-on-one but battles between squads were organized from time to time as well.

Gladiators were mostly prisoners of war, slaves, and people sentenced to death who chose this 'lesser-evil' alternative in order to prolong their lives. The status of gladiator was not necessarily lifelong. Sometimes a sentence of hard labor for life was commuted into a 2-year stint in a school of gladiators and 3 years of fighting. If a gladiator managed to stay alive, his sentence was considered served out. An exceptionally interesting performance could even win a slave his freedom. It was not infrequent, however, that freemen opted for a gladiator's career, as it was an exceptional opportunity for climbing up the social ladder for outcasts and down-and-outs. When Septimius Severus decided to recruit Praetorian Guards of Germanic origin, nearly all of the dismissed Roman guards enrolled in gladiator schools. Sometimes people from an upper social stratum fought as gladiators, too. Lucian from Samosat, a Gk. writer, describes a case of an impoverished aristocrat who accepted to appear in the arena in order to finance a sumptuous funeral for his father. During the reign of Julius Caesar, 2 senators crossed swords on an arena wearing gladiator's outfits. Once, irritated with senators, Nero suggested they should stand up and fight in the arena to prove their manly vigor. Caligula was notorious for sadistically forcing his dignitaries to participate in fights.

The voluntary participation of Roman citizens from the upper strata became so widespread that in 69 AD Aulus Vitellius issued an edict according to which they were prohibited to, as Tacitus put it, 'tarnish their reputation with gladiatorial games.' The gladiators' popularity in the Roman Empire could be compared to that of sports stars today. Here and there the name of a winning fighter could be seen painted in red on a wall. Some of such graffiti, although mostly worn out, have survived on the Roman monuments, e.g. an inscription praising an edile, Maius, for hiring a famous gladiator, Paris.

Ceremonies and the course of a fight. On the eve of the day of games, a dignitary or patrician funding the event invited gladiators and most eminent spectators to a banquet. The day of the games started with a parade of chariots and gladiators wearing purple coats with golden embroidery. The fighters entering the arena recited a formula addressed to the major dignitary or founder hosting the games who was present; often it was the Emperor himself: *Ave Caesar, morituri te salutant* (Hail Caesar, those about to die salute thee!). The fights started with bloodless shows, often they were duels with the use of wooden weapons, performed by fencers – *paegniarii*. Once the spectators had warmed up, the real fights commenced. Those gladiators who revealed any fear were forced to come out to the arena and at the signal of their coaches they were flogged by slaves with special leather belts (*lorarii*). Each blow that either wounded or made the opponent fall down was welcomed with the cry, *'Habet hoc habet!'* (He's had it!). A gladiator who fell down wounded had the right to ask for mercy, raising his hand with the index finger pointing upwards. His opponent could either finish him off or spare him. The decision was to be made by the highest dignitary sitting on the grand stand, often the Emperor himself, whose decision usu. conformed to the expectations of the public. Traditionally it is believed that he either put his thumb down, which meant death for the wounded fighter, or put it up, which meant mercy. It is not, however, quite clear if the interpretation of the gesture was not the other way round, as the Lat. saying *vertere, premere policem* could also mean that a thumb up ordered the winner to strike the deadly blow, and a thumb down – to put the weapons down. After each series of fights a detailed list of profit and

loss was made out. Beside the name of each gladiator who fought on a given day the following abbreviations appeared: *P(erit)* – died, *V(icit)* – won, and *M(issus)* – lost but was spared. Those contenders who were spared did not leave the arena through the main gate but through the one referred to as the *Porta Sanivavaria* – the Gate of Sane and Alive.

Arenas. The character of the show influenced the architecture of amphitheaters. The earliest known arenas are not located in Rome but in Campania, Pompeii, and Capua. There was also an amphitheater in Puteola. On average they seated about 20,000 spectators. The first gladiatorial fights in Rome were held on market squares, and then on the main square Forum Romanum. The earliest Roman amphitheaters had wooden grand stands. But still, in 53 BC, when the first stone amphiteater was constructed, Gaius Scribonius – friend to Julius Caesar – had a large wooden amphiteater built. Even as late as in 29 BC, a rich executioner serving Augustus Caesar, Titus Statylius Taurus, built an amphitheater that was partially made of wood. The construction, which was located in the vicinity of a gladiator school run by the Taurus family, burned down in the great fire that destroyed a large part of Rome during Nero's reign. Although in Rome stone constructions were making inroads quite quickly, the provinces and small cities were dominated for a long time by wooden structures which collapsed once in a while. One of such devastations that happened in the city of Fidena in 29 AD has even been described by Tacitus.

In the year of the consulship of Marcus Licinius and Lucius Calputnius, the losses of a great war were matched by an unexpected disaster, no sooner begun than ended. One Atilius, of the freedman class, having undertaken to build an amphitheatre at Fidena for the exhibition of a show of gladiators, failed to lay a solid foundation and to frame the wooden superstructure with beams of sufficient strength; for he had neither an abundance of wealth, nor zeal for public popularity, but he had simply sought the work for sordid gain. Thither flocked all who loved such sights and who during the reign of Tiberius had been wholly debarred from such amusements; men and women of every age crowding to the place because it was near Rome. And so the calamity was

all the more fatal. The building was densely crowded; then came a violent shock, as it fell inwards or spread outwards, precipitating and burying an immense multitude which was intently gazing on the show or standing round. Those who were crushed to death in the first moment of the accident had at least under such dreadful circumstances the advantage of escaping torture. More to be pitied were they who with limbs torn from them still retained life, while they recongised their wives and children by seeing them during the day and by hearing in the night their screams and groans. Soon all the neighbours in their excitement at the report were bewailing brothers, kinsmen or parents. Even those whose friends or relatives were away from home for quite a different reason, still trembled for them, and as it was not yet known who had been destroyed by the crash, suspense made the alarm more widespread.

[Trans. by A.J. Church, W. Jackson-Brodribb]

In another collapse of an amphitheater, which took place during the reign of Antoninus Pius, 1,112 people died and several thousands were wounded.

The supreme model of an ancient amphitheater was the Roman Coliseum (Lat. *Colosseum*). Construction work started by Vespasian (69-79 AD) were completed by his son Titus in 80 AD. The building is 527m in circumference and about 50m tall. There were 5 stories, 80 aisles, and 45,000 seats. Its opening was celebrated with 100 days of games during which about 5,000 wild animals and some 3,000 gladiators died in fights. Comparably huge and sumptuous games were held in other metropolises of the Empire, such as Berytus (today's Beirut). Although it is true that from time to time Christians were indeed executed in this or some other way in the Coliseum, anti-Christian persecution during the reign of Nero (54-68 AD) seems highly unlikely as Christianity was barely developed. Such executions, however, were carried out in circuses, such as *Circus Neronianus*, which were numerous both in Rome and in other parts of the Empire.

History. The ancient Roman custom of a fight to the death originates from the Etruscan tradition of funeral fights, during which the offering formed of prisoners of war was supposed to commemorate the soldiers who died in combat and to persuade the gods to look upon the newcomers with a favorable

Two ancient Roman daggers used by gladiators for their fights in the Colosseum are seen on display during the unveiling of the 'Sangue e Arena' (Blood and Arena) exhibition in Rome.

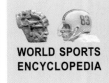

eye. Frequent contacts between Etruscan cities and Rome – which in the 6th cent. was even governed by Etruscan rulers – facilitated cultural borrowings whose number grew substantially later on, after Etruria was taken over by the Empire in the 3rd cent. BC. The connections between gladiatorial fights and Etruscan customs can be observed in some characteristic rituals that accompanied the fights, e.g. when a defeated gladiator could not stand up he

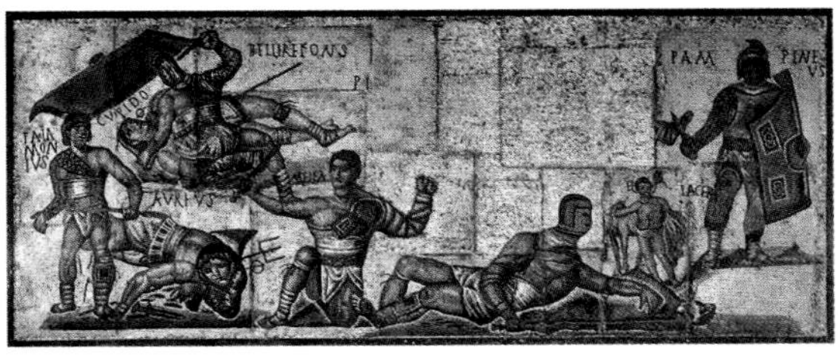

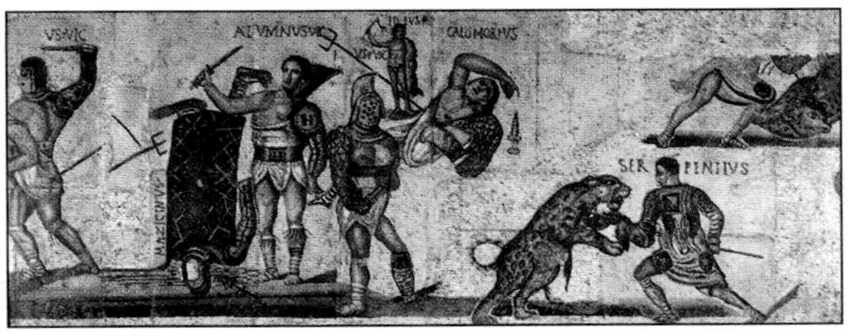

Roman mosaics depicting gladiatorial fights.

was dragged out of the arena by a slave wearing the costume of Charun, the Etruscan god of death. The term for a gladiators' teacher and the principal, a *lanista*, is of Etruscan origin. A gladiatorial duel itself was referred to as a *munus*, plur. *muenera*, which meant an obligation towards the dead. Gladiators were also known as the *bustuari* – funeral stake comrades. The growing power of the Empire and the Romans' demand for entertainment led to rapid evolution of fights that turned into a show which instead of being related to religious events became increasingly associated with pure entertainment, following the famous Roman maxim *panem et circenses* – bread and (circuses) games. A breakthrough was the gladiator games in 264 BC during the 1st Punic War. On the day Brutus Pera, who as the story goes was responsible for implanting the custom of gladiatorial fights in Rome, was buried, his sons organized 3 simultaneous fights on the market place. Two years later, a similar event was reported to have taken place in Carthage. In 174 BC, in Rome, during an event funded by Flaminius in order to commemorate the death of his father, 74 gladiators fought for 3 days. The spreading formula of gladiatorial fights made the spectators either forget or never learn the original purpose of such an event. A funeral was not the only nor even major pretext, other included a great victory of the Roman army, the election of a new ruler of Rome, and finally the games were organized with the express purpose of relieving the growing dissatisfaction of citizens. In this context, gladiatorial fights became an element helping to contain and manipulate public opinion. In addition, many emperors supported the games as a form of popularizing the ideal of masculine toughness lacking among the effeminate dwellers of Rome. Thus, the number of events grew rapidly and the increasing demand for gladiators gave birth to all kinds of supporting institutions, such as special schools that were organized in the form of barracks and were known as the *ludi*. The largest ludi were located in Rome, Capua, Ravenna, Pompeii, and Alexandria. The school community was referred to as a *familia gladiatora* – a gladiators' family. The golden age of gladiatorial fights fell on the reign of Trajan (98-117 AD). In 107, about 10,000 gladiators fought on arenas spread far and wide across the Empire.

The most eminent gladiator of all times is thought to have been Publius Ostorius, an emancipated slave, who won 51 fights. However, the historical reports available focus mostly on the story of Spartacus, a Thracian slave who led a revolt of gladiators (74-71 BC). The gladiators' skills and training allowed them to win a number of battles with the regular Roman army which finally managed to quash the revolt attacking the rebels with 10 legions at the same time. The growing entertainment business related to gladiatorial fights also led to numerous abuses. During Nero's reign the phenomenon became so notorious that the emperor issued an edict that prohibited such events in Roman provinces administered by some of the most corrupted governors. Before that happened – as Tacitus reported in his *Annals* – the office-holders haunted their subjects with plunders and games equally, hiding their crudity under the cloak of liberal government, (XIII, 32).

Gladiatorial fights often served as a tool for winning support of the people on one's way to a political career. Livineius Regulus, sentenced by Nero to exile from Rome for his crimes, found himself in Pompeii where he attempted to regain his political position by organizing gladiatorial games and bull fights for the citizens of Stabia, Sorento, and Noccera where no amphitheaters could be found. Therefore, the stadium in Pompeii was often filled to the brim, which finally led to a massacre and the first ever case of a stadium closing due to rioting spectators, as described by Tacitus:

About the same time a trifling beginning led to frightful bloodshed between the inhabitants of Nuceria and Pompeii, at a gladiatorial show exhibited by Livineius Regulus, who had been, as I have related, expelled from the Senate. With the unruly spirit of townsfolk, they began with abusive language of each other; then they took up stones and at last weapons, the advantage resting with the populace of Pompeii, where the show was being exhibited. And so there were brought to Rome a number of the people of Nuceria, with their bodies mutilated by wounds, and many lamented the deaths of children or of parents. The emperor entrusted the trail of the case to the Senate, and the Senate to the consuls, and then again the matter being referred back to the Senators, the inhabitants of Pompeii were forbidden to have any such public gathering for ten years, and all associations they had formed in defiance of the laws were dissolved. Livineius and the others who had excited the disturbance, were punished with exile.

[Annalia, XIV, 17, transl. by A.J. Church, W. Jackson-Brodribb]

The period of decline of gladiatorial fights started in the 4th cent. AD, mostly because of protests against their brutality voiced by supporters of the Christian doctrine, which had come to dominate Rome. Although Constantine the Great sponsored some gladiatorial events at the beginning of his reign, in 326, influenced by the voices from the first council of Nice, he issued an edict prohibiting them altogether. According to the edict, the offenders sentenced to gladiatorial fights were supposed to be sent to mines and quarries instead. The emperor's ordinance was not, however, fully observed and even Constantine himself negated his own orders, giving his consent to gladiatorial fights in the cities of Umbria. In an effort to eliminate of such entertainment from public life altogether, the Christian Church declared that gladiators, their teachers, and those who organized fights could not be baptized. Still, even after Christianity was recognized as the major religion in the Roman Empire, gladiatorial fights persisted. One after another, pressed by the Church, the emperors announced edicts prohibiting the games. In 399, Honorius ordered the closing of the last gladiator schools in Rome. We do not know the exact date of Saint Almachius' (in Gk. tradition Telemachos) act, in which he attempted to separate fighting gladiators, after which he was lynched by infuriated spectators. Some historians claim it could have taken place about 392 and others say it was 404. The fights went on in Rome until 339-340 while in other parts of the empire, despite official prohibition, they were tolerated much longer. Anastasjus I turned a blind eye to them and in 523, an Ostrogothic ruler of Rome, Theodoric, expressed his disapproval of such practices, which indicates they still existed. Finally, gladiatorial fights were abolished completely in 681.

Women also participated in gladiatorial fights, which is a fact consigned to oblivion today, perhaps because their share was incomparably smaller than that of men. One of the proofs of women's gladiatorial fights is a separate term for a female gladiator – *gladiatrix*. In the British Museum there is a bas-relief representing a female gladiators' fight in Halicarnassus that was also a birthplace of 2 gladiatrix known in history by the names Achilla and Amazonia. Petronius mentions a female gladiator of Bret. origin who made a name for herself as an *essedaaria* – a gladiatrix fighting in a combat cart.

When an Armenian king, Tridates, was visiting Rome, Patrobius, a slave freed by the emperor, organized a special performance in which mixed squads of Afr. gladiators fought against each other. At the times of Nero even mannered Roman aristocrat ladies fought as gladiators. Tacitus reports with horror that one them 'brought shame on her kind by standing in the arena.' Only in 200 AD, Septimus Severus, advised by his legal council, published an edict prohibiting women's fights.

Gladiators in literature and art. From time immemorial gladiatorial fights were either praised or severely criticized by ancient writers and philosophers. Already in Virgil's *Aeneid*, describing Rome's beginnings, we can find, in vol. XI, that during the funeral of prince Pallas:

Manacled captives there were consigned to be gifts to the dead – Victims whose blood would be sprinkled upon the altar flames.

The day the Coliseum was opened is eulogized by Martial who is flattering Titus in the 3rd epigram of his *Epigrammaton*:

Here where the glittering solar colossus views the stars more closely and where in the central road loft machines grow up, the hateful of the beastly king used to radiate its beams, at the time when a single house used to occupy the whole city. Here where the mass of the conspicuous and revered amphitheater rises up, the pools of Nero once stood. Here where we marvel at that swiftly built donation, the baths an arrogant field had deprived the poor of their homes. Where the Claudian portico spreads its shade afar, the farthest part of the palace came to an end. Rome is restored to herself, and under your direction, O Caesar, those delights now belong to the people which once belonged to the master.

[Martial, *De Spectaculis*, II]

The symbolic significance of the Coliseum was observed by Venerable Bede (c.673-735), who quoted a prophecy of Ang.-Sax. pilgrims:

While the Coliseum stands, Rome shall stand; when the Coliseum falls, Rome shall fall; when Rome falls, the world shall fall.

Gladiators and their fights are the subject of dozens of literary works, most of them critical, written by such classical authors as Lucian, Pliny the Younger, Plutarch, and Cicero. The fights were particularly bitterly attacked by philosophers, the fiercest among them being Seneca the Younger who referred to gladiatorial fights as plain homicide. When Athenians, in their rivalry with Corinth about whose city was more important, proposed gladiatorial fights as one of the tests, one of the philosophers addressed them with these words: 'Athenians, before you accept the proposal, do not forget to destroy the altars of deities of mercy.' An uncompromising approach against the fights was adopted by Christian philosophers. Tertullian, c.200 AD, rejected the rationalization that forcing death row convicts to fight as gladiators can be considered a just punishment as they would have been executed anyway. A similar critical attitude was adopted earlier by Seneca, who wrote:

By chance I arrived at a midday interval, expecting fun and jokes, some relief and relaxation after the sight of human blood. Quite the opposite! All previous fights were compassionate by comparison — no trifling now, just sheer murder! No protection for the fighters, their whole bodies exposed to every thrust, they themselves striking home with every thrust. And this the crowd enjoys more than the pairings of real gladiators, whether ordinary or even those by special request. Of course they do! Not a helmet or shield to parry the sword. What need of protection? What need of skill? They only delay death. In the morning, men are thrown to the lions and bears; at noon, to the spectators. They call for the killers to be thrown to other killers, the victor to be saved for new slaughter; for these fighters the end is always death. Fire and sword rule the day. So it goes on, till the arena is empty.! 'But', you say, 'he was a robber, wasn't he, he killed a man.' Well and good, he's a murderer and has got his deserts. But you, you miserable wretch, what gives you the right to enjoy

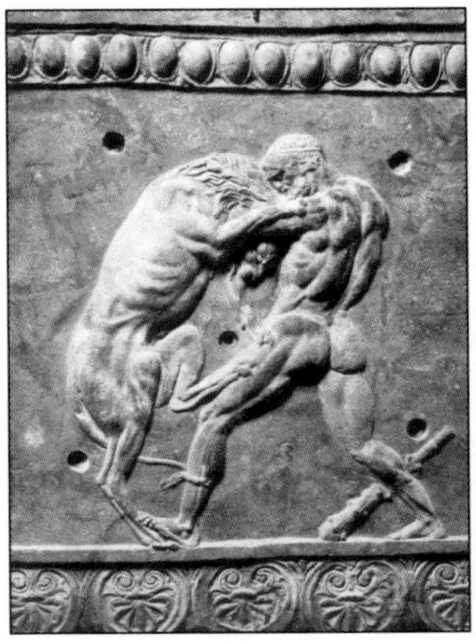

A gladiator wrestling a lion, a relief from the Vatican Musueum in Rome.

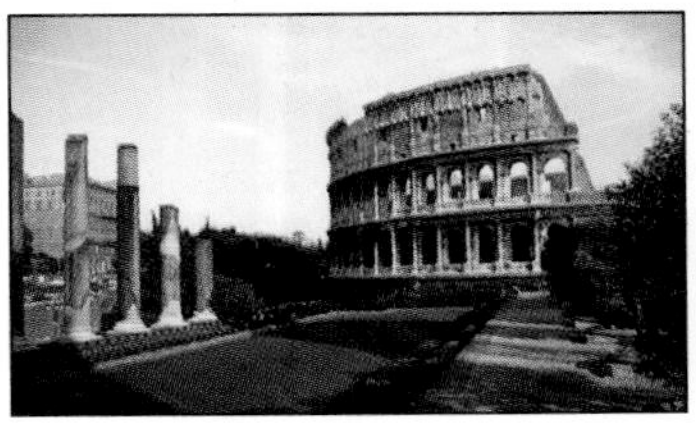

Rome's Colosseum.

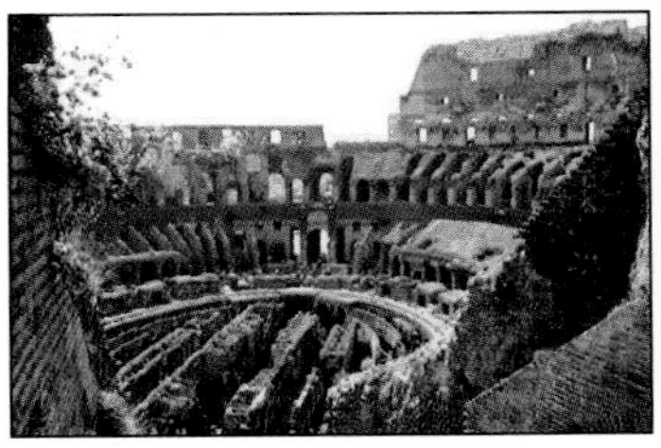

The arena at Rome's Colosseum.

The Dying Gaul.

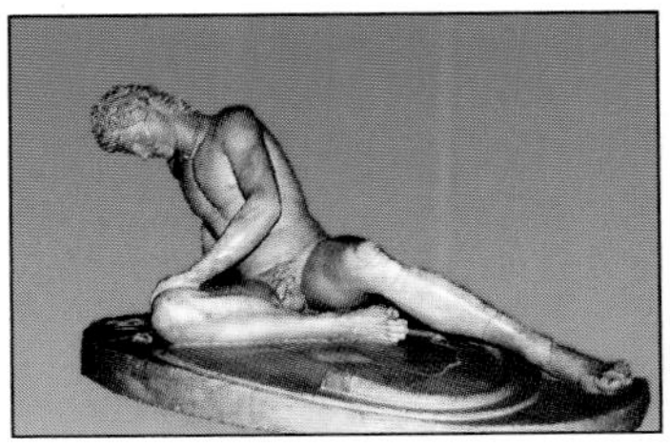

G

WORLD SPORTS ENCYCLOPEDIA

the spectacle? 'Kill him, beat him, burn him!' 'Why does he run on the sword so timidly?' 'Why doesn»t he hit back?' 'Why doesn»t he want to die?' 'Flog them into fighting!' 'Breast to naked breast, that»s how they should strike and meet the sword!' But it's an interval! Well, can't they cut a few throats then, just to pass the time?

[Seneca, *Letters to Lucilius*, VII, 3ff.]

The faction of censors was joined by one of the most eminent Fathers of the Church, St. Augustine, who describes in his *Confessions* a visit to an amphitheater that his companion Alipius had to pay, being forced by his own friends. There, Alipius yielded to the magnetism of the games:

When he saw the blood, the wild enjoyment took power of him and, instead of turning back, he fixed his eyes on the arena, unconsciously absorbing the madness, imbibing the murderous fight, delighting in the bloody ecstasy.

[Trans. by Krzysztof Sawala]

However, Libanios, a thinker contemporary to St. Augustine, known for his education and good manners, praised gladiators, calling them 'apprentices of heroes from Thermopylae.'
Gladiators have become a pretext for moral and esthetic polemics, a symbol of the cruel inclinations of human nature in modern literature. An ancient sculpture representing a wounded gladiator just before his death, known as the *Dying Gaul*, belongs to one of the most popular genres within the subject. Canto IV of the *Childe Harold's Pilgrimage* by

C.A. Barton, *The Sorrows of the Ancient Romans. The Gladiator and the Monster*, 1993; M. Grant, *Gladiators*, 1967; D. Martucci, *Roman Emperors and Their 'Sportsmen'*, OR, 1991, 287; by the same author, 'Pompeii, the First Stadium Disqualified', OR, 1990, 274.

GLE GBEE, lit. ' long spirit'. A combination of dance and acrobatics practiced by the people of the Dan tribe in Liberia. Performers use 10-ft. (3m) long stilts, whose upper end reaches their knees, and they wear white-and-blue costumes consisting of pants, a shirt, a belt with little bells, and animal fur worn on the back. They wear masks and their hair is bound with a leather strap, adorned with little shells, into a cone on the top of the head. They dance to the rhythm of drums, performing various and complicated acrobatic evolutions, such as feints, jumps, walking with a stilt put forward as far as possible, etc. At one point they may make 7 jumps backwards, or pretend to be falling onto the spectators, which is prevented by assisting dancers. If there are any hills around, the performers walk up to the top and then slide down; sometimes they perch on the roofs of the houses surrounding the place where the performance is staged. Although the gle gbee demonstrations were initially associated with water spirits, the religious element plays a rather minor role and their objective is mostly entertainment. White people first witnessed gle gbee in 1860 in the village of Butus.
A. Tylor Cheska, 'Gle Gbee', TGDWAN, 1987, 85.

GLIDING, a discipline of sports aviation. Flight depends on searching for thermals along mountain slopes or hillsides, under or near cumulus clouds, or over arid terrain. The quality of gliding craft is evaluated by the so-called glide ratio, which is the relation between the horizontal and vertical distance that the glider travels. A glide ratio of 40, for example, means that for every kilometer the glider loses in altitude, it travels a horizontal distance of 40 kilometers. High-performance gliders can have a glide ratio of 50 or more. Gliders used in competition are capable of maintaining air speeds of over 170 km/h. Gliding comprises the following competitions, in which national and international records are taken: 1) absolute altitude; 2) gain in height from the lowest 'free' flight altitude to the highest altitude; 3) open flight – the longest distance from start to any place of landing; 4) target flight, in which the allowed deviation from the designated landing place is contained within a circle of 2km in diameter; 5) target return flight, landing in the 2km diameter circle from which the start was made; 6) speed flight over a 100-200-300km triangle.
Glider pilots can have 4 skills categories: A, B, C and D. The last has 3 classes with silver, gold and

diamond badges.
Glider competitions are held in the open class, with a wing span of up to 15m and varying-wing structure and in the standard class, with the wing span up to 15m but with a fixed-wing structure.
History. Gliding preceded aviation in the times before engines were used to propel aircraft. The idea of using air to sail goes back to the beginnings of mankind – many legends from different cultures are sufficient evidence: the Gk. legend about Icarus and Daedalus, the Chinese legend about the flying chariot of prince Ki-Kung-Szi, the Persian legend about the flying carpet etc. In China about 500 BC Kung-Szu Tse designed kites. In ancient Greece Archtos of Tarent attempted to design a balloon and is said to have built a model of a flying pigeon around 400 BC. The first theoretical dissertation about man's ability to fly was written by R. Bacon (about 1214-94) and entitled *Epistola fratris Rogeri Baconis de secretis operibus artis naturae et de nullitate magiae (A letter of Brother Roger Bacon about the secrets of the forces of nature and the nonentity of secret arts*, around 1250). Attempts at the first gliding designs were made by L. da Vinci (1452-1519), the father of human aeronautics, painter, architect and designer. Attempts at flying were made by dozens of designers, among them the Englishmen A. Cayley (1773-1857), the inventor of the modern aeroplane and the lifting surface (airfoil), who was first to fly his aerial carriage in 1853, and J. Stringfellow. In 1856 a Frenchman J.-M. Le Bris (1812-72) built a glider model and made a few attempts at getting it airborne. The first to demonstrate the advantage of curved surfaces for aircraft wings was O. Lilienthal (1848-96), the author of *Der Vogelflug als Grundlage der Fliegekunst (Birdflight as the Basis of Aviation*, 1889) and the designer of many aerial carriages. In 1890-91, together with his brother Gustav, he built a glider with arched wings like a bird's in which he flew over a distance of 15m, and later 350m. After making more than 2,000 flights, he was killed when his glider crashed. Other pioneer aeronauts included the Amer. inventor Octave Chanute (1832-1910). In 1896-98 he built multiplane gliders on which his assistants made about 2,000 short flights without any crashes. Chanute was the first person in the history of aviation to design height and direction controls. Other inventors were working at the same time in the United States, among them the Wright brothers, who built the first engine plane, using Chanute's experience, and who made about 1,000 flights – the longest of which was 9min. 45sec. – on a self-designed glider. The chief impetus to the modern development of gliders, and the art of flying them, came from Germany. In the years following WWI, Germany, which was forbidden by the Treaty of Versailles to manufacture powered aeroplanes suitable for military use, turned to building gliders and to studying glider flight. German aeronautical engineers discovered the great efficiency of light craft with long, birdlike wings, and the meteorological conditions under which soaring flight could succeed. After 1920 a Gliding Center was established in Rhön-Wasserkuppe in Germany, which prior to 1939 exerted a decisive influence on the development of gliding in Europe. Competitive centers were opened in Combergrasse in France, Itford Hill (Great Britain), Planierskoe in the Crimea (USSR) and in Bezmiechowa (Poland). In 1922 a German A. Martens made a flight of 66min. and in 1922 a Frenchman L. Bossoutrot and a German W. Kleperer made the first successful attempt at using thermal currents. These became routinely used in gliding by W. Hirth (1930). In 1937 the first W.Ch. were held in Rhön-Wasserkuppe, won by H. Dittmar (Germany). WWII interrupted the development of gliding; however design work continued, although with a military bias – gliders started to be used for assault purposes, both by the Germans (the assault of Crete; the 'Otto' campaign aimed at freeing Mussolini) and by the allies (airborne assault at Arnhem).
Gliding is practiced under the auspices of national aeroclubs, which, in turn, are governed by the International Aviation Federation (FAI, est. 1905). World championships under the auspices of the FAI have been held since 1948, every 2 years, initially without division into classes, between 1952-56 in one- and 2-seater classes. In 1948 the International Scientific and Technical Gliding Organization was established. Gliding is not an Olympic sport.

Gliding.

G.G. Byron is devoted to the sculpture:

I see before me the Gladiator lie;
He leans upon his hand – his manly brow
Consents to death, but conquers agony,
And his droop'd head sinks gradually low –
And through his side the last drops, ebbing slow
From the red gash, fall heavy, one by one,
Like the first of a thunder-shower; and now
The arena swims around him – he is gone.
Ere ceased the inhuman shout which hail'd the wretch who won.

Another remnant left after gladiatorial fights are certain symbols often used to refer to harmful tendencies in modern sport, where the number of victims who permanently injure themselves or even lose their lives is growing. Although modern sport does not assume death as the final goal of a competition or a fight, the requirements that need to be satisfied in order to achieve victory are often so excessive that they result in the death or debilitation of sportsmen who may be considered modern gladiators.
The popularity of the 2000 Ridley Scott film *Gladiator*, starring R. Crowe and running over 2½hrs., testifies to our continued fascination with mortal combat.

Stamps commemorating the International Gliding Competition in Poland in 1954.

Glima wrestlers.

GLÍMA, Icel. *glima*, also plur. *glimur*, folk wrestling in Iceland, presently with the status of a national sport (*Thjotharithrott Íslendinga*, in the Icel. original *Tjóðarijtrótt Íslendinga*). In former versions of the game, the objective was to knock the opponent over, so that he touched the ground with his chest, or touched the ground, depending on local customs and the historical time, twice with one knee or both. One of the characteristic, although not exclusive, features of the oldest forms of the game was a grip in which one wrestler would grab his opponent's trousers. Ready-made clothes, however, proved too weak and many wrestlers could not afford special tailor-made trousers, so c.1905-08 a kind of girth (*glimubelti*) was introduced that consisted of a waist belt and two leather straps worn around the upper part of the thighs, connected with the waist belt by a type of garter. When fighting, wrestlers get hold of the opponent's waist belt or thigh straps. A wrestler's costume (*glimumenn*) is a kind of leotard (*glimuföt*), covering the legs entirely; in former times the feet were as well covered in stockings. Leggings go as far down as the upper rim of the boots and are tucked inside. The upper part of the leotard resembles a typical tank-top A-shirt with very narrow shoulder straps. Shorts are worn over the *glimuföt*. If the fight takes place indoors, the floor of the ring is usually made of wood.

Rules. Wrestlers fight in the upright position. After saluting by shaking hands, they stand opposite each other, so that their right arms are in line. When the fight starts, the wrestlers get hold of the opponent's waist belt with the right hand, and his right thigh strap with the left hand. During the fight they are not allowed to release the opponent's straps, nor can they look down, as the rule says the wrestlers fight rather feeling their way with their bodies than using their eyesight. Taking small steps, the wrestlers turn around clockwise. Apart from wrestling with their hands, all the time holding the other wrestler's straps, one of the basic ways to knock the opponent over is an attempt to lift his foot off the ground with the use of one's own foot. To achieve this, the wrestler can: 1) perform a special

hook where his foot presses against the opponent's ankle lifting the foot off the ground, which, if done properly, topples the opponent to the ground; 2) lift the opponent's leg either against the front or the back, tripping him up. Another way of winning the fight is to try to lift the opponent off the ground by simultaneous use of one's hands, feet and hips. The fight is won if any part of the opponent's trunk touches the ground. In 1913-88, glima was fought in 3 weight categories (light, middle, and heavy weight). A new 5-weight system was introduced in 1988: up to 68, 74, 81, 90, and over 90kg. In 1999, the up-to-68 weight category was abandoned, so now there are just 4 categories. There are about 50 varieties of glima which, according to a great many experts in the field, stem from 8 basic wrestling grips or, according to others, from 10 basic grips. The grips are called *bragd* and can be executed in many variations and applications whose number ranges from 2 to 16. This gives a total of 36 grips used during the fight, the most important among which are: the *outside stroke* or *leg trick* (leggjarbragd); *heel hook* (hælkrókur), existing in 3 versions, the *inside-click* (*innanfótar hælkrókur hægri á vinstri*), the *cross click* (*innanfótar hælkrókur hægri á hægri*), and the *back-heel* or *back-heel hook* (*hælkrókur fyrir bade*); the *twist over the knee* or *knee jerk* (hnéhnykkur); the *outside hip* (*hnéhnykkur á lofti*); the *hook* (krækja); *askew glima* (snidglima); the *crotch trick* (*klofbragd*); the *loose hip* (lausamjödm); the *full* or *half buttock*, *hip jerk* (mjadmarhnykkur).

History. Glima dates back to the oldest period of the Vikings' settlement in Iceland shortly before 1000. The name glima, *glegamena* in the oldest form, then *glimae*, in O.Icel. signified the festival of joy or gentleness, which stood in opposition to real fighting which was neither about joy, nor about gentleness, but rather brutal victory. The very term was known under an almost identical name, as *glee gamena*, in Danelaw, the part of England occupied by the Vikings from the end of the 9th cent. to the beginning of the 12th. Initially, the name apparently signified any activity done for fun and pleasure,

which can be testified by the Eng. equivalents of similar terms which, nevertheless, evolved in a slightly different direction: *gleeman*, O.Eng. *gleoman* – a poet who brought joy by reciting poetry or singing; *glee gamena* – all types of entertainment or festivals in Iceland, whose name was later reduced to signify only one type of gentle entertainment, namely wrestling done for pleasure, as opposed to other kinds of 'serious' wrestling, e.g. >FANG or >HRYGGSPENNA. Glima also appears in the 13th cent. O.Icel. texts denoting a sport which earlier, and for a period in contemporary times, was known as >BUXNATÖK. Glima was very often described in O.Icel. sagas, e.g. *Egils Saga Skallagrímssonar* and G*innboga saga ramma*. In one book titled *Crymogea*, written in Latin by A. Jónsson the Wise, we find praise of glima in the following words: 'men wrestled eagerly, since they were testing their manhood; they did it, however, without harm or offence.' In pagan times glima had also a magical aspect to it, which is testified by the placement of magical symbols on the wrestler's footwear. One of the best known such symbols is *ginfaxi* – a circle cut across by a cross on whose arms there were transverse lines (3 on each) and arrows (1 on each).

There are 3 main theories attempting to explain the appearance of glima in Iceland. According to one, glima developed at the time when Christianity was coming to the island as a substitute for abolished pagan customs. In this sense, glima was meant to prevent the neophytes from feeling alienated from the old tradition. The other theory advocates that some primitive forms of glima developed somewhat later in the monastic schools founded in Skálholt in 1056 and Hólar in 1107. There, pupils from rural areas would bring various competitive and entertaining games which, later on, were stripped of their brutal elements, so as to make them acceptable for teachers. The very name of glima was meant to underscore the game's gentleness and harmlessness, without which it might easily have fallen along the wayside. The 2 theories are not contradictory and probably they both explain some factors that led to the appearance of glima in Iceland. It is a historical fact that the schools in Skálholt and Hólar played a decisive role in the formation of the purely sportive rules of the game. The schools' significance grew when they became bishopric schools (in 1552 and 1556 respectively). Teachers approved of the game as a means of dealing with the youth's hyperactivity. What is more, cold dormitories were often a ring for boys who fought to warm up (Iceland had hardly any forests, thus there was no wood or other heating material available). Later on, another similar school was founded in Bessastadir, near Reykjavik (presently the seat of the President of Iceland). While other schools tolerated and, to a certain degree, supported glima as a form of recreation, in Bessastadir it became a legitimate and obligatory element of the curriculum. Graduates, holding clerical and government positions, propagated glima outside of school. In this way, the sport gradually gained national recognition, backed by prestigious figures who, since their school years, cherished the conviction that glima constituted an important element of national culture. 19th cent. Icel. literature testifies to the presence of glima in different communities, among which were shepherds and fishermen. Among the latter, a particularly interesting evolution of the game could be observed. There evolved a custom according to which the crew of a boat used to build their hut *búdir*, forming a very closely related community named the same way as the hut. Bad weather did not favor fishing, but was perfect for wrestling. As a result two var. of glima developed: the individual type, called *free glima*, or >LAUSAGLÍMA, which was fought between any 2 wrestlers; and a team variety, where one *búdir* would challenge another, >BÆNDAGLÍMA – crew or team glima. In trad. glima, whose modern professional varieties crystallized from the second half of the 19th cent. through the beginning of the 20th, some of the most outstanding wrestlers, who at the same time propagated a new formula of glima in which leather straps started to be used, were J. Jósefsson, the 1907-8 champion of Iceland and S. Pétursson, the 1920-23 champion. Exceptional wrestlers, often fighting in the classical style, represented Iceland at various Olympic Games, without much success, how-

J. Jósefsson – the glíma world champion 1907-08.

G

WORLD SPORTS ENCYCLOPEDIA

ever. Jósefsson took part in the London Olympic Games in 1908 as a classical style wrestler, but he dropped out in the qualifying round because of a minor injury. Pétursson reached the semi-finals at the Stockholm Olympic Games in 1912. Among modern wrestlers, G. Agustsson (b. 1918) was considered to be one of the best athletes in the '40s. In 1943-47 he held the title of the champion of Iceland in all weight categories. A. J. Larusson won in *Islandsgliman* as many as 15 times in the '50s and the '60s. J. Sveinbjörnsson was a victor of *Islandsgliman* in 1992-3 and 1995, and in 1994 as well as 1995-99 – I. Sigurdson, followed by the almost equally talented A. Frithriksson.

Regardless of professional achievements, the Icel. Glima Association stresses the sport's national heritage role and aims at popularizing it among young people, especially at schools. To achieve this, they organize a great number of tournaments in different age categories. The most prominent tournament is the Championships of Iceland in all weight categories, called *Islandsgliman*. A very characteristic feature of this tournament is the fact that all the wrestlers fight in one common category, regardless of weight. The winner is granted the title of the 'King of Klima' and, since 1900, is awarded the *Grettisbelti* or the Champion's Belt. Icel. championships are also held in particular weight categories during the event named *Landsflokkagliman*. Participants of all age categories are divided into groups: 9 groups for men and 5 for women. There are also *Sveitaglíma Íslands* – wrestling glima matches between 2 or more teams; in a junior and women's categories each team has to put up 4 wrestlers, whereas in the men's category a team is made up of 5 wrestlers. Each wrestler from a team fights each wrestler from other teams and the team with the greatest number of individual victories is the winner.

Among women, glima has gained acceptance and popularity relatively recently, i.e. in the 1970s, and particularly in the 1980s, but it was not before 1988 that women were officially allowed to participate in glima fights. The best wrestlers of the 1990s were K. Ólafsdóttir, I. G. Pétursdottir and S. Björnsdóttir. Glima is among the sports controlled by the International Federation of Celtic Wrestling, founded in 1985. The fact that the Vikings from Iceland enslaved a great number of Celtic inhabitants of the British Isles serves as an explanation of such a name. The descendants of the slaves constitute from 5 to 15% of the whole Icel. population, depending on the source. Apart from that, the Icelandic Glima Association has introduced in Iceland other wrestling styles, such as Scot. >BACKHOLD and Bret. >GOUREN that are characteristic of Celtic countries. Now international matches in these styles are organized in Iceland. See also >CLOTHES HOLD (BELT HOLD WRESTLING).

T. Einarsson, *Glima. The Icelandic Wrestling*, 1984; T. Einarsson, 'Sportive Wrestling in Iceland Sagas and Oldest Code of Icelandic Laws in the 12th century', PISH-

Goalball – a sport for the blind which is now played also by non-visually impaired athletes.

PES 1991, ed. R. Renson, T. Gonzalez Aja, et al 1993; G. Jonsson, ed., *Egils Saga Skallagrimssonar in Islendinga sögur*, Vol. VII, Reykjavik 1943; G. Jonsson, ed., *Ginnboga saga ramma in Islendinga sögur*, Vol. IX, Reykjavik 1943; *Skýrsla Glímusabands Íslands og Glímuáebók*, 1998; consultant: I. M. Ivarsson.

GLOES KAT, see >GRÆSSE KO.

GOALBALL, a type of ball game invented for the blind, which has become so popular that it is also practiced by players not visually impaired who blindfold themselves in order to compete on par with blind players. The court is 18x9m. The ball is 76cm in diameter, weighs 1.25kg, and has a perforated surface and metal strips inside that make noise while the ball is being rolled, which allows the blind players to locate it. Goalball is practiced both by females and males. The game is played by 2 teams of 3 players: 1 center and 2 wings. They are supposed to stay within their team area, also known as the defense area, which is delimited by a goal line and a line parallel to it at a distance of 3m. The players put on blanked out goggles that must not be touched during the game. This effectively blinds those whose sight is only partially impaired or who have unimpaired vision – such players being more and more frequently encountered in integrative matches. The match lasts 14min. and is played in two 7-min. halves, with a 3-min. break. Each team has the right to three 45-sec. intervals during the game. While playing, players kneel, propped up on their hands. The wings are situated at the sides within the zone marked by lines 1.5m long running crosswise. The middle players control their position thanks to a line 15cm wide, which can be felt and marks the middle of the playing field. Most often the lines are marked with a tape onto which another narrower tape is sealed, which produces a hump easily felt with the

Goalball.

palms. Another solution, employed in Poland, is sealing a string under the tape. Total thickness of tapes and hump must not exceed 3mm. The ball must not be kept by the same player for more than 8sec. The objective is to roll the ball to the opponent's goal, the width of which is equal to that of the court (9m), with a height of 1.3m. The opposing team is supposed to win the ball before it is rolled into their goal. Every player has the right to defend the goal with their hands. When the ball is won, it is thrown back towards the goal on the opponent's half. The game is continued by exchanging throws. When the ball is thrown, it must touch the floor before the overthrow line, also called the high ball line, and from there has to be rolled on the court's surface. If this condition is not met, the ball is considered high and a goal scored after such a high ball is not acknowledged. The halves are drawn by tossing a coin. The game is administered by a referee, goal umpires, timers and linesmen. Penalty kicks are taken from the team's own goal area. Time for a penalty kick is not counted as playing time.

History. The game was invented in 1946 by an Austrian, H. Lorencezen, and a German, S. Reindle, as an element of rehabilitation for the disabled after WWII. In its beginnings it differed substantially from the modern version: the goals had different dimensions, instead of a sound ball they used strings with bells that were hung at the level which allowed the ball to touch them giving away its position, etc. Today's rules evolved through a process of trial and error. In 1980, in a form similar to the modern one, goalball was incorporated in the Paralympic Games. The strongest women's teams on the international scale are Germany, Finland, and the USA (medallists at Paralympic Games in Atlanta 1996), and men's teams of Finland, Canada, and Spain (also medallists at Paralympic Games 1996).

GOAT RACES, a trad. sport practiced since 1925 in Tobago, esp. in the town of Buccoo, where the main event comes on Easter Tuesday. At first the venue was along a village road called Chance Street, but over the years it has moved to a plot of public land. The race takes place over a stretch of turf 100m in length. Prior to the race the jockeys walk the course in search for any irregularities and warm up by doing several sprint starts and stretching exercises. Then the jockeys and goats line up in the starting gates. The jockeys do not ride their steeds, but rather hold the animals with a sturdy rope and – when the gates open – run alongside.

The sport is modelled after horse racing, with stables, owners, trainers, jockeys, and the steeds, which are carefully selected and trained. The training of jockeys is equally important, because they must match the pace of their steeds during the race. Races are held in 2 classes (C1 or C2), determined by the age of the steeds. Many goat racing events have corporate sponsors. Each race is accompanied by a vivid commentary.

GOBS, see >HUCKLEBONES.

GOCZ, also sp. *goch, goč*. A var. of folk wrestling known and practiced in Armenia.

GOFF (also sp. *gouff*). One of the earliest, simple var. of >GOLF. The two differed firstly in the ball used during the game, the goff one was made of leather stuffed with feathers, and secondly in the number of

Jockeys race their goats at the Buccoo Goat Race Festival in Buccoo, Tobago. The winner of the race, which started in 1925 as a working class alternative to horse racing, is awarded 1,000 Trinidadian dollars (about $160), a bottle of rum, and a trophy with a golden goat perched on top.

holes on the course. The extent to which goff was a game related to today's golf is arguable. Perhaps the entire difference amounts to the distinctly spelled name. It is, however, possible that golf was concocted from a number of different games and goff was one of the major of them, but not the only one. This is corroborated by the assumption that the letter *l* appearing in golf was borrowed from Du. *kolven*, whereas the original Brit. games adding to the development of golf did not use *l* in their names, an

GOLF, a game in which a small ball is struck with a special curved club, on a characteristic field, the so-called golf course, whose topography is varied and interrupted with natural obstacles that are arranged there on purpose. The object of the game is to place a ball in a hole with the minimal number of strokes. A typical golf course consists of 9 or 18 playing fields, depending on the size, each containing a tee and a hole, also known as cup, dug in the ground and located on the so-called green – an area covered with

his or her way to score all the holes. The par total rarely exceeds 72. Golf courses usu. have fields of varied par scale. The most frequent combinations are: four 3-par holes, four 5-par holes, and ten 4-par holes. A score of 1 stroke under par on a hole is referred to as a 'birdie.' The invention of such a name is usu. attributed to one of 2 players who lived at the turn of the 19th cent. – A.H. Smith (nickname Ab) or A.W. Tilinghast. In both cases the anecdote reports on a particularly good stroke that was called a 'bird'

Putting on the green.

interpretation enriching the history of golf and allowing us to explain one of the stages of its development. In his famous work *Glig Gamena Angel Deoth, or the Sports and Pastimes of the People of England* (1810), J. Strutt reports:

Goff, according to the present modification of the game, is performed with a bat, not much unlike the bandy: the handle of this instrument is straight, and usually made of ash, about four feet and a half in length; the curvature is affixed to the bottom, faced with horn and backed with lead; the ball is a little one, but exceedingly hard, being made with leather, and [...] stuffed with feathers. There are generally two players, who have each of them his bat and ball. The game consists in driving the ball into certain holes made in the ground, which he who achieves the soonest, or in the fewest number of strokes, obtains the victory. The goff-lengths, or the spaces between the first and last holes, are sometimes extended to the distance of two or three miles; the number of intervening holes appears to be optional, but the balls must be struck into the holes, and not beyond them; when four persons play, two of them are sometimes partners, and have but one ball, which they strike alternately, but every man has his own bandy. It should seem that goff was a fashionable game among the nobility at the commencement of the seventeenth century, and it was one of the exercises with which prince Henry, eldest son of James the first occasionaly amused himself , as we learn from the following anecdote recorded by a person who was present: At another time playing at goff, a play not unlike to pale-maille, whilst his schoolmaster stood taking with another and marked not his highness warning him to stand further off, the prince thinking he had gone aside, lifted up his goff-club to strike the ball; mean tyme one standing by said to him, beware that you hit not master Newton, wherewith he drawing back his hand, said, 'Had I done so, I had but paid my debts'.

GOJUKKEN, a var. of an old Jap. art of archery >TOSIYA, addressed to young people. Similarly to tosija the object of gojukken was a proper shot executed by a kneeling archer so that the arrow would fly along the W veranda of Sanju-Sangen-Do temple, from S to N, without touching the temple's wall or low eaves. The difference, compared to tosija which was addressed to grown-ups, consisted of the distance, which was 90m instead of 120m. Another event within the tosija system was >HAN-DO, where the distance was approx. 60m.

special well-mowed grass. Each tee and each green is numbered and in the course of the game the player is supposed to go through them according to their numbers, following the rule: a ball shot from the 1st tee is to be placed in the hole within the 1st green, from the 2nd tee – in the hole within the 2nd green, etc. Each hole is marked with a flagpole, referred to as a pin, displaying its number. A pin is temporarily removed when a player makes the final putt attempting to place a ball in the hole. The distance between a tee and a hole is not regulated by any rules and usu. varies from 100 to 600yds. (90-550m). In most cases, each field within the course has 3 different spots to start the game from. Each spot is identified by 2 markers located 5yds. apart. A tee has to be placed on an imaginary line between the 2 markers. At the very edge of the course there are markers for champions (back markers); a player starting from such a spot has to cover the longest, i.e. the most demanding, distance to reach the hole. The markers located in the middle of the course (middle markers), situated much closer to the hole, are meant for average, recreational players. Front markers, designed for women, are closest to the hole. Each field has its par, i.e. an estimated standard number of strokes necessary to cover a distance between a tee and a hole. The par depends on the length of a given field. According to United States Golf Association (USGA) standards, the pars for given distances are as follows:

	Men	Women
Par 3	up to 250yds.	up to 210yds.
Par 4	251-470yds.	211-400yds.
Par 5	471yds. and more	401-575yds.
Par 6	575yds. and more	

The standards are treated only as guidelines and are adjusted to the level of difficulty of a given course, its undulation, etc. The result of a given player in a competition is determined on the basis of the ratio of the total par number for a given course and the actual number of strokes executed by the player on

which was then made into a diminutive. A score of 2 strokes under par on a hole is called an 'eagle' and a score of 1 stroke over par for a hole is referred to as a 'bogey.' The term applying to an evil or mischievous spirit was coined around 1890 in Great Britain at the United Service Club, where most of the members were serving in the military. An unfortunate player who exceeded a predetermined limit was first called 'colonel Bogey', which was shortened to bogey. The same term is also applied to a par increased by 1, intended at some courses for an average player as opposed to a professional one. A hole is usu. 4in. (about 11cm) in diameter and its size was determined somewhat by accident, when 2 players in St. Andrews criticized the naturally made holes because of their uneven edges, which makes them difficult to score. They decided to use a drain-pipe, which they found nearby, whose diameter was 4in. and after some time the size became an international standard. If a field has 9 holes, the players,

A game of golf in Scotland.

A game of golf in a 19th cent. lithograph.

236

G WORLD SPORTS ENCYCLOPEDIA

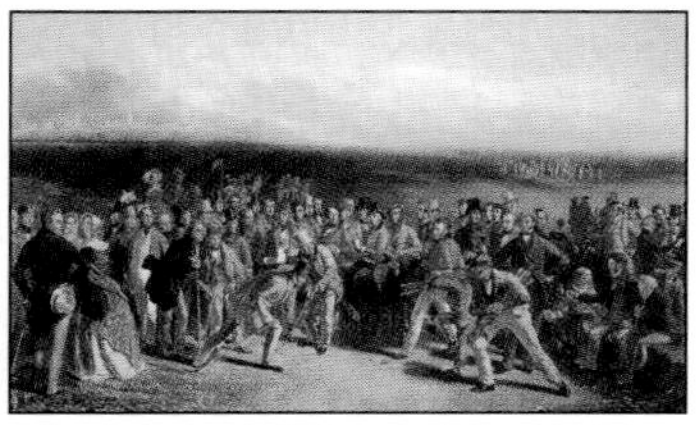

Charles Lees, Golf Players. A Great Match on St. Andrews Fields, *oil on canvas.*

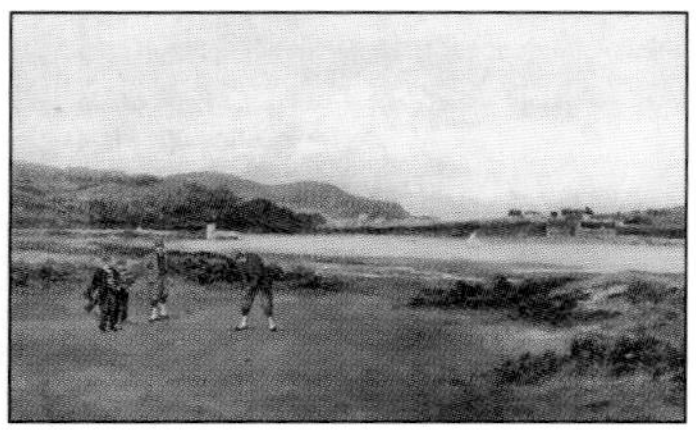

Douglas Adams, The Putting Green, *oil on canvas.*

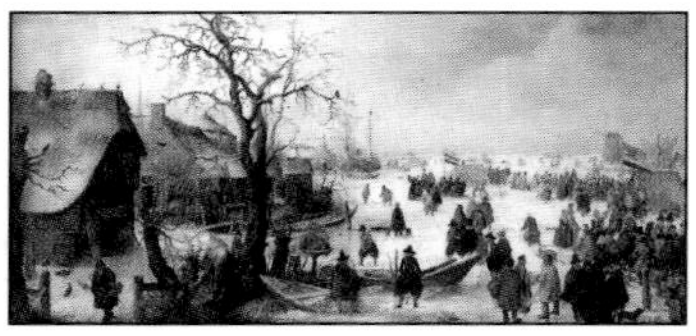

Hendrick Avercamp, Winter Scene On a Canal, oil on wood.

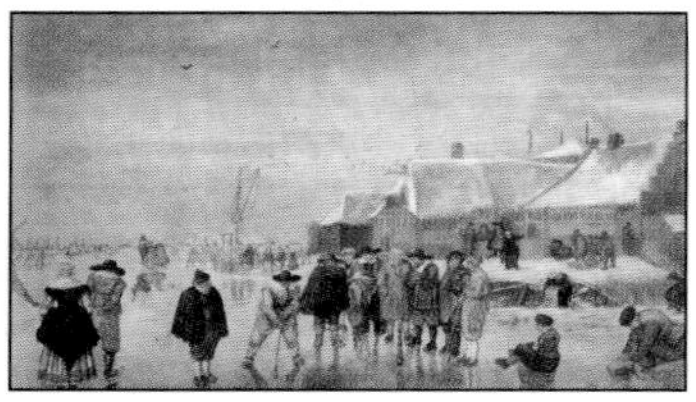

Putting On Ice.

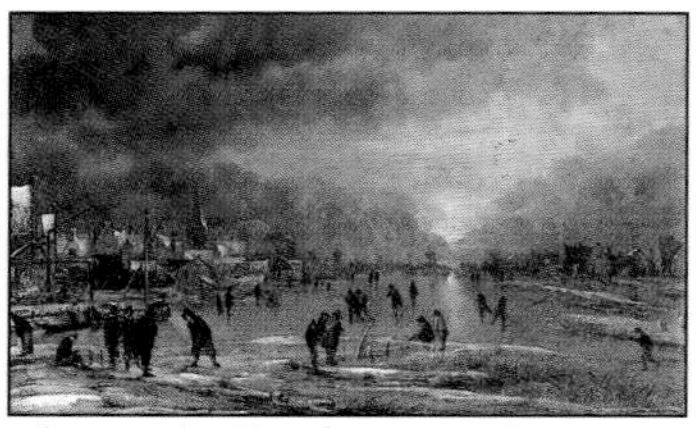

Aert van den Neer, Sports on a Frozen River, oil on wood.

in order to make an entire round, have to cover the total distance twice. A golf match, depending on the type of players and their mutual agreement, consists of 1-4 rounds. A golf course is usu. located on a lightly undulated field. The area varies from 50 to 300 acres, i.e. about 20-121 ha. The total length of an 18-hole field is usu. 3.5-6.5km. For example in Milton, Florida, USA, it is 6,691yds. (6,115m); in Hashimoto, Japan – 6,423yds. (5,870m); in Braselton, Georgia, USA – 6,967yds. (6,368m); whereas the historical course in St. Andrews had only 6 holes and was just a few hundred meters long.

The most popular obstacles are bushes along the main lane of the course, a small sand dune called a sand trap, a pond referred to as a water hazard, etc. A particular var. of sand trap is the bunker, quite similar to a standard trap but historically originating from a sand-filled hollow made by sheep hiding from strong wind. Other types of sand obstacles include: cat box, beach, Egyptian Bermuda, litter box, white face, etc. The courses constructed at the seaside or along riverbanks use natural elements to form obstacles, such as a larger than usual beach, or a river itself. Sizes of courses as well as distances between obstacles are not predetermined.

Basic equipment is composed of 14 clubs with different heads, used in different situations to execute various types of strokes. Usually they are 4 or 5 clubs whose heads used to be made solely of wood, hence their name – the woods. Nowadays, their heads are made both of wood and plastic or metal. The woods are numbered 1-5. The next category is formed by 8 clubs with iron heads – the irons, numbered 1-9. They are used for the longest starting shots as well as for striking the ball upwards, for instance when overcoming an obstacle. The irons are grouped into 3 categories: long irons (numbered 1-3), middle irons (4-6), and short irons (7-9). In addition, the so-called utility irons are employed to retrieve a ball from a difficult place. Examples of such utility irons are a sand wedge and a pitching wedge. The third category of clubs is putters, ended with a small metal bar and used for precise light strokes, referred to as putts. The clubs' length, conforming to USGA regulations, has to be 35-43in. (about 90-109cm). The head's length must exceed its thickness. As early as 1810, players started to cover golf clubs with varnish to protect them from the harmful effects of bad weather. Iron heads started to be used at the beginning of the 20th cent., and in 1926, despite the vehement protests of the St. Andrews club, they were introduced officially. Within the following decade they became a commonly accepted standard. Clubs are carried in a special sack, hung across the shoulder, invented in the 1870s by an anonymous designer, and popularized by the Royal North Devon Club. Today the sacks form a part of a characteristic 2-wheel trolley used by golfers and called a caddy. The name 'caddy' originates from Fr. *cadet* – younger or lower in rank, a term brought together with Fr. servants to Scotland during Mary Stuart's reign, later modified into *cahdie* and then adopted from Scot. in Eng. as caddy or caddie. The first caddy known in history by name was A. Dickson who carried clubs for a Prince of York and then for the King of England, James II in Edinburgh (1681-82). Originally, the caddy's job was to maintain a course and equipment in good condition, and before teepegs were introduced, to make small hillocks to place a ball on for the starting shot. Later on, when course services gradually grew into a specialized group, the caddy became a direct assistant to the golfer, carrying his equipment. In 1939, shortly before WWII broke out, in Great Britain alone there were 11,000 caddies working in various places. The caddy's position was in many cases the first step in a golfer's career and a number of leading players can serve as examples here, one of them being F. Ouimet (1893-1967) who defeated Brit. H. Vardon during the US Open in 1913 (terminating thus the era of absolute British domination in the history of golf). Later, Ouimet became one of the major reformers of golf regulations and the first foreigner who was made the captain the Scot. St. Andrews team. In some cases, experienced caddies held on to the profession, evolving into highly specialized assistants of players, providing not only technical but also psychological support, as was the case with the most famous of Scot. caddies, T. Anderson, who assisted players – A. Palmer among others – for 32 years. Frequently, however, the leading players hire professional psychologists to support them. One of the greatest golfers of the 1990s, B. Mayfair, hires for example R. Rottel, a professor of psychology of the University of Virginia, USA. Sometimes players, esp. elderly ones, instead of walking use battery-electric carts when covering longer distances on a course.

Balls have different sizes depending on specifications applied. According to Amer. ones a ball should be $1^{11}/_{16}$in. (42.67mm) in diameter, whereas according to those published by the St. Andrews Golf Club in Scotland it should be $1^{5}/_{8}$in. (41.15mm). Both systems determine the max. weight that should not exceed $1^{5}/_{8}$oz. (45.926g). Until the end of the 19th cent., the balls were made of leather stuffed with various materials, e.g. pressed goose feathers, hence their Eng. name used at that time: 'feathery'. In 1848, gutta-percha was applied for the first time as a raw material for balls and, as a result, in time a new jargon term for balls was coined – 'guttie', or 'gutta'. The invention is attributed to a pastor, Dr. Paterson, who is said to have received a little statue of Vishnu, a Hindu god, which was insulated with gutta-percha to protect it against damage. The pastor squeezed and kneaded the substance, making a ball of it. Then, he used the ball to play golf. However, gutta-percha balls did not catch on immediately, because their aerodynamics was far from satisfactory; after a speedy flight the ball abruptly fell down on the ground. Only after some time was it noticed that scratches left on the surface of the ball by a club improve the ball's aerodynamics, which led to a conclusion that if the ball is covered with small hollows, its trajectory will be prolonged. The longest distance covered by a smooth gutta-percha ball was 175yds. (about 160m) and the one covered by a ball with hollows exceeded 200yds. (180m), which allowed a player to reach the putting green with one shot. Players soon began experimenting with little pins stuck in the ball. This idea was dismissed, however, when it was observed that the pins actually reduced the ball's trajectory. Today's golf balls are covered with about 300 so-called dimples that trigger an aerodynamic phenomenon as a result of which it is easier for the player to hit the target. There were also other experiments in which a ball was filled with, for instance, water and oil. At some point the guttie's competitor was a ball called the putty or eclipse ball. The ingredients of which were kept confidential and, as no specimen of the ball has survived, it is hard to say with all certainty what it actually was. We can, however, be positive the filler contained cork chips mixed with India rubber. Although putty was more durable than guttie, its trajectory was incomparably shorter, which is what ultimately tipped the scales in favor of the latter. In 1898 or, according to some sources, in 1899, C. Haskell, a dentist from Cleveland, Ohio, constructed a ball filled with a hank of elastic threads placed in a caoutchouc cover. Nowadays, golf balls are made of either 2 parts: a core made of natural or synthetic caoutchouc covered with a hardened coat with dimples; or of 3 parts: a polymer core, a hank of elastic threads, and a coat made of balata (a type of natural or synthetic rubber). The level of hardness varies and it is scaled from 80 – best for beginners, to 100 – intended for professional players. There are also hollow training balls made of soft plastic whose surface is covered with dimples. Such balls allow a player to practice even in small rooms without causing damage.

The economic impact of golf concerns not only professional players. In 1935, in Great Britain alone 588,000 of golf clubs and approx. 11 million balls were produced. This was the beginning of a huge golf equipment market whose first large shareholder was the Eng. *Dunlop Rubber Company*. In 1994, Americans spent about $20 billion for golf gear and services related to the game. In the mid '80s, TV became an influential factor in determining the character of golf competitions. The PGA annual prize pool in 1954 was $23,108 and within 9 years shot up to $47,550. A. Palmer's income earned during one season surpassed $100,000 in 1962 – it was the first case in the history of golf when such money was earned within a single season. In 1995, income earned by each of the 3 following golfers in the course of a single season exceeded $1 million; they were: D. Stockton (b. 1941), with an income of $1,303,280; J. Colbert (b. 1941) – $1,167,352; and B. Murphy (b. 1943) – $1,146,591. The *Senior Tour*, a series of competitions for players above 50, incorporated in 1990 as many as 42 meetings whose total prize pool amounted to $25 million. S.A.G.M. Crawford, a historian and researcher of golf's cultural contexts, observes that no other sport comes even close to the level of golf in offering such fame and financial prosperity to players who are advanced in years (EOW, I, 386).

Major courses. The St. Andrews course is considered to be a model one. Other vintage courses are the Prestwick Course in Scotland and Hoylake course located in the vicinity of Liverpool. In the USA, the earliest and originally unofficial courses were constructed in Burlington, Iowa (1883), Oakhurst, West Virginia (1884), and Dorset Golf Links. The oldest courses that are still in use are: Dorset Field Club (originally named Dorset Golf Links) founded in 1886, and Foxburg Golf Club, Pennsylvania, founded in 1887 and later renamed Foxburg Country Club. In 1888, a Scot, J. Reid, aided by his Amer. neighbors constructed a course in Yonkers, New York, that was named St. Andrews Golf Club of Yonkers after of the oldest Scot. club. The first professional course in the USA was constructed near Southampton on Long Island, designed and constructed by, W. Dunn, a Scot, assisted by architect S. White, and financed by W. Vanderbilt and a company of his wealthy friends. That construction became a model for a number of courses and it contributed significantly to the further development of golf in the USA. Around 1900, there were 982 courses in the USA, including 90 complete ones, i.e. with 18 holes. At the beginning of the '70s, the number of golf courses in the USA surpassed 10,000. The most beautiful ones are considered the Augusta National Golf Course and the one located in Sotogrande, Spain.

The game can be played between 2 opponents, in pairs, and in teams. A match can be held in either of the 2 systems, selected by the players before they start. In the first system, referred to as match play,

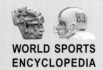

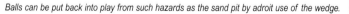

Balls can be put back into play from such hazards as the sand pit by adroit use of the wedge.

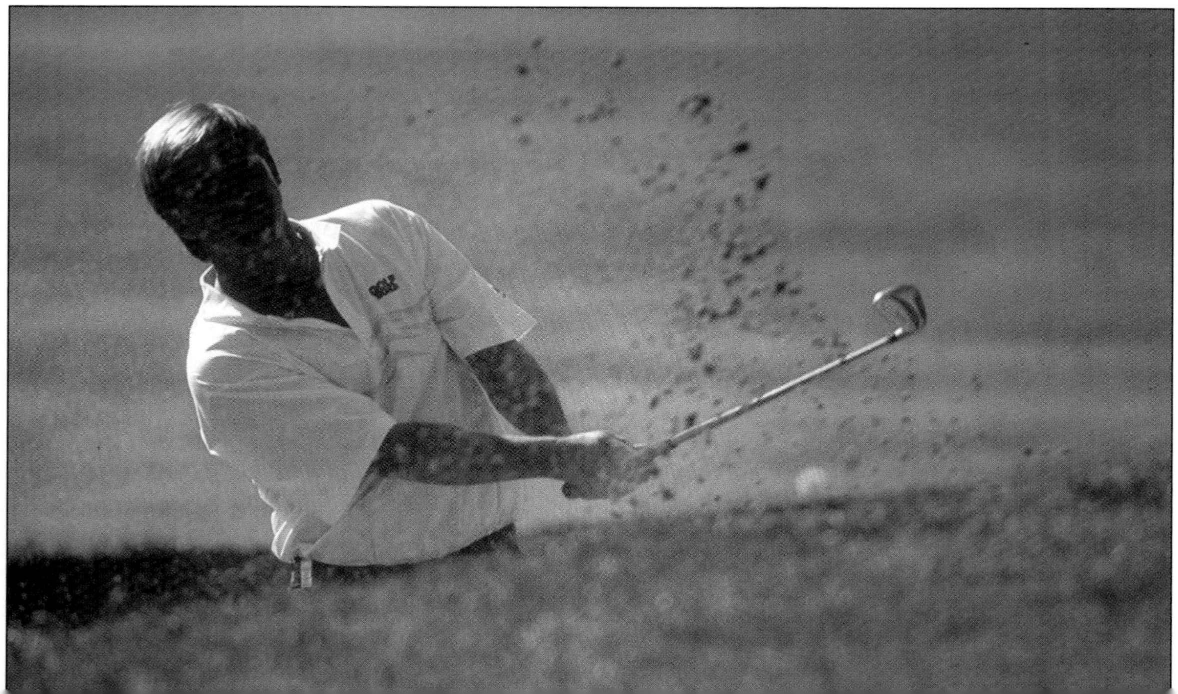

players are supposed to score the holes with as few strokes as possible. Each hole has its winner. The player who is the winner of the greatest number of holes wins the entire match. In the other system, stroke play, the winner is that golfer who executes the smallest number of strokes throughout the entire match, irrespective of the number of holes scored as first. Technically, a match starts from the teeing ground. The ball is placed on a small wooden or plastic peg, stuck in the ground. The peg is called a tee and it was invented by an Amer. dentist, W. Lowe, and then popularized in the '20s. Before it was introduced, the ball was placed on a small mound of earth. On some of the more trad. courses, players still use a box filled with dirt to make such mounds when necessary, because a stroke taken from a mound instead of a peg is still allowed by the applicable rules, although rather rare.

Etymology. The origins of the term *golf* are not clear. It is prob. related to the Du. and Flem. game >KOLVEN and the word for club – *kolf*. The Du. origin of the game is also discernible in some of the vocabulary characteristic of golf, such as 'stymie' (cf. Du. *stuit mij*) – a term describing a situation in which between a hole and a ball there is another player's ball obstructing the way. Similarly, Eng. 'tee' stems from a Du. term for a mound of ground from which the ball was started. The earliest example of a name resembling the modern one dates back to 1457, when the game was mentioned in one of the decrees prohibiting it. In the course of the following 200 years, golf's name evolved into a series of various spellings, such as *gouff* (1491), *goiff* (1538), *goft* (1615), and *gouf* (1711). Since the close of the 1750s the modern spelling 'golf' has been in use. However, in his work *The Sports and Pastimes of the People of England* (1801), J. Strutt is consistent in using the >GOFF spelling, perhaps referring to one of the var. of golf. In the 19th cent., the word 'golf' infiltrated into all the Eur. languages with no major modifications of spelling or pronunciation, and later, into most of the remaining languages.

Cultural context. Golf, although far more egalitarian than before, maintains its exclusive character in private clubs where membership fees range from several hundred dollars to over $100,000 annually. Some private clubs have been accused of supporting a policy of ethnic discrimination. In 1995, a former player at the Kansas City Country Club, T. Watson, told a journalist that he resigned his membership in the club because they voted against admitting a person of Jewish origin. In the USA, there are relatively few players of Afro-Amer. origin and it seems that as far as emancipation processes are concerned golf is several dozen years behind boxing, track and field, or basketball, where ethnic barriers and prejudices have been left far behind. Until the '70s, unofficial methods were employed in order to prevent Afro-Americans from entering the Augusta National Golf Club course. Leading golfers, such as Trevino or Nicklaus, not only declined to accept any role accelerating the integration process but even participated in racist tournaments in South Africa against the wish of the State Department. Supporters of racial integration among golfers were few and far between. At the beginning of the '90s, some light in the tunnel appeared in the form of the first outstanding Afro-Amer. talent, Tiger Woods, then a Stanford University student and later a great star of golf.

Golf in literature, movies, and the arts. The earliest attempts at literature devoted to golf can be found in the first sports magazine *The Sporting Magazine* and then in *The New Sporting Magazine*. The turn of the 19th cent. brought the first significant works of writers who touched upon the subject of golf. Some authors adopted the sport as the focal point of their literary endeavors. P.G. Wodehouse (1881-1975), author of several dozen golf stories, is considered the most eminent among them. In their famous anthology of the best works devoted to sport, *Great Stories from the World of Sport*, P. Schwed and H. Warren Wind report that, 'Of the many toprung humorists who have contributed short stories to golf's extensive literature, no one has quite approached P.G. Wodehouse in capturing the full personality of the game – above all, the sinister way it has of seizing the souls of otherwise sound citizens and turning their life into a Hell Bunker on earth'. The most acclaimed short stories of Wodehouse are *The Heart of a Goof* (1923), *The Clicking of Cuthbert*, and *Chester Forgets Himself*. Another outstanding writer dedicated to golf matters is B. Darwin (d.

1961, great grandson of C. Darwin). His feature articles and sketches published in *Times* and *Country Life* were collected and published together in a few books, e.g. *Playing the Like*, *Out of the Rough*, and *Green Memories*. He is also the author of a golf novel *The World That Fred Made* and a series of albums and historical studies, such as *Golf Courses of Great Britain* and *Golf Between Two Wars*. A classic of the golf genre is a humorous story by D. Jenkins, *The Dogged Victims of Inexorable Fate*. Various categories of golf literature, including memoirs and collections of reportages, were taken up by ex-golfers, and later sports journalists: R.T. Jones Jr. (b. 1902), G. Sarazen (b. 1902), F. Pennink, L. Crawley, S. McKinley, and P. Ward-Thomas. Among more celebrated writers who touched upon golf we can find J. Updike with his famous scene from the tetralogy about Harry 'Rabbit' Angstorm. A golf match also featured large in one of the James Bond stories.

Golf has often been the subject of feature films. In their 1987 *Sports Films. A Complete Reference*, H.M. Zucker and L.J. Babich list the titles of as many as 48 feature films dedicated to golf. The most acclaimed among them were *Follow the Sun* (1951), a story of the life of Ben Hogan, starring G. Ford; and a comedy *Caddyshack* (1980). In 1952, a movie titled *Pat and Mike* was released, in which K. Hepburn plays a character whose name is Pat Pemberton – an itinerant tennis and golf player. Her manger is Mike Conovan (S. Tracy), and her competitor was an actual athlete, B. Didrickson-Zaharias.

On TV. Golf became present on small screens at the end of the '50s with a weekly program *Wonderful World of Golf* hosted by G. Sarazen and J. Demaret. A series of golf tournaments was organized in the '60s, starring A. Palmer and his 'circus' called *Arnie's Army*. Such shows contributed significantly to the rapid popularization of the sport in the USA. Broadcasts in other countries soon followed suit. A poll carried out by the Television Bureau of Advertising in the early '90s indicated that the percentage of citizens voting in major elections is the largest among viewers interested in golf broadcasts. When it turned out that golf (and not, as might be expected, >BASEBALL or >AMERICAN FOOTBALL) attracts 35% more viewers voting in the elections than the second top group of TV watchers, the game's rank raised considerably in TV networks. The leaders in promoting golf on TV were ABC, NBC, and ESPN networks. In 1995, the first round-the-clock channel devoted exclusively to golf was established in the USA. According to television experts, golf makes one of the greatest technical challenges for broadcasters, as it implies difficulties unknown in any other discipline due to the substantial lengths of courses, movement of players, various types of surface where a falling ball, striking the ground, requires a separate microphone that is able to pick up characteristic details of a given situation, etc. In his radio and television broadcaster's manual *Sports Broadcasting* (1995), C. Cowdy calculates that a first-class broadcast of a high-ranking golf match requires no fewer than 14 cameras, 7 towers for cameramen, 11 VCRs, approx. 100,000ft. (33km) of sound cable, approx. 120,000ft. (39km) of video cable, and 35 separate microphones for the so-called spotters, i.e. persons who are to signal a move to be made to inform the sound and vision directors which part of the network needs to be activated. Spotters use either hard wire or walkie-talkie. Special microphones adjusted to the specific environment of a golf course (first employed by NBC) are planted at various points to pick up sounds coming from spectators, clacks of clubs against a ball, thumps of balls falling onto different surfaces (sand, water, a hole, etc.). In order to avoid any disorder in broadcasting, each technical division uses its own microphone system, e.g. the scorers use a wireless closed-circuit system that is not linked with any other microphone system present on the course. In order not to disturb players or spectators during the event, kilometers of wires are installed under ground by means of a special machine called a sod-cutter whose central part is a knife spinning at 45°. The wires are placed about 3in. (7-8cm) under a strip of turf that is delicately cut through and lifted by the machine, and then replaced to its original position. The entire process of installing necessary TV gear before an important competition can take 4-5 days. An effort to liven things up and tailor events to the particular needs of a televised broadcast resulted in the establishing of the so-called Skin Games (also

Skin Tournaments) in 1984. Their initiator was a TV producer, D. Ohlmeyer, and engineers, J. Comare and H. Ruiz. The idea of Skins Games was based on a rivalry among only 4 contracted golfers, which made the tournament more compact and dynamic. They compete for huge amounts of money at each hole, which makes the show even more exciting for viewers because instead of waiting long hours for the final score they can watch a series of matches, prized separately, in the course of a single tourna-

It all comes down to this...

ment. At the same time, Ohlmeyer's approach provides viewers with a more complete picture of a game by using wireless cameras and microphones, approaching the players close and broadcasting their comments, etc. Wireless cameras and microphones that were used during Skin Tournaments made the entire installation procedure much simpler and limited the number of cameras to an average of 8, including 4 cameras placed on stands. The number of links to audio line, however, increased from 70 to 150. The Skin Tournaments were first held only in between high-ranking 'real' competitions as a kind of filler to sports programs. Soon, however, they became popular enough to establish their own season. Numerous techniques employed originally during Skin Games were adopted in the broadcasting of trad. golf games. In Europe, TV golf was popularized by the *Eurosport* channel.

History. There are a few different hypotheses concerning the birth of golf. One of them claims that golf originates from ancient Eg. fertility rites in which a little ball was struck with a club. In Asia, there were games resembling golf, too, e.g. >CHÚI WAN. The most feasible theory asserts certain connections between today's golf and a game known in ancient Rome as >PAGANIKA. In the course of Roman expansion the game was popularized in W Europe and

G

WORLD SPORTS ENCYCLOPEDIA

then introduced in its primitive form in such places as Britain under Roman occupation. As early as 1100 AD, a game similar to golf was practiced in Scot. villages located north of Hadrian's Wall that once marked the border of the Roman Empire in Britain, which corroborates the assumption of Roman origins of the game. In 1457, golfers playing on the fields that surrounded Scot. cities disturbed training sessions of the king's archers, as a result of which James II prohibited playing the game within the city limits. The ban was lifted in 1491. After that, a rapid development of the game can be observed thanks to the rulers of Scotland, James IV and Mary Stuart, whose interest in the game was derived from their willingness to follow the Catholic Church's recommendations that rulers should attempt to satisfy believers' needs for entertainment after Sun. mass by means of various games. This had fatal consequences when the Stuarts ascended to the Eng. throne. Their positive attitude to the sport clashed

with puritan beliefs and there was much strife when James II issued the *Declaration of Sport* in 1618. The first match was, to some extent, international, and was held in 1682, when James II, accompanied by an Edinburgh shoemaker, J. Patersone, nicknamed Far and Sure, defeated 2 English noblemen. The first permanent golf course, founded by Mary Stuart in St. Andrews (c.1552) is still considered one of the best in the world. The first golf association, The Royal Burgess Golfing Society in Edinburgh, was prob. established in 1608. However, no document corroborating that fact has survived. The first documented association, the Honorable Company of Edinburgh Golfers, was established in 1744. A year later, the Company organized the Silver Club tournament and the 13-item regulations followed during the game became the basis for the rules employed in following matches but, moreover, in the regulations adopted by the Royal and Ancient Golf Club of St. Andrews (founded in 1754). The Club soon became a top golf administrative body in Britain and then worldwide. At the same time, until the beginning of the 19th cent., a game known as >GOFF developed in England whose features could be partially based on the sport evolving in Scotland and partially on Du. >KOLVEN that could have been brought to England by courtiers of William of Orange. Because of significant similarities between the games and their close relationship that developed in Great Britain throughout the 19th cent. they were finally unified. In 1919, the Royal and Ancient Golf Club of St. Andrews adopted a structure of an association of members, as a result of which, out of 1,750 permanent members of the club, 700 come from countries other than Great Britain, representing 50 different states in total. Since 1952, St. Andrews club has shared its responsibility for the international status of golf with the United States Golf Association. The original Du. var. of golf was first brought to America by colonists from the Netherlands (c.1650 in the area of New Amsterdam), but no information about the game has survived covering the period between the moment the colony was taken over by the English (1664) to the 1750s. It was the Scot. soldiers fighting for the Brit. army in the Amer. war for independence who popularized golf in America (1775-83). The cornerstone of the game's permanent presence in Amer. culture is thought to be the press announcement in *John Rivingstone's Gazette*:

To the golf players: The season for this pleasant and healthy exercise now advancing, gentlemen may be furnished with excellent clubs and the veritable Caledonian balls by enquiring at the printers.

At the beginning, the interest of Americans and Canadians in golf, although quite stable, was rather modest. Only after such clubs as the Foxburg Golf and Country Club in Pennsylvania (1887) and St. Andrews Club of Yonkers in New York (1888) were established, did golf popularization acquire substantial dynamics. In 1895, in the USA, J.P. Lee published a model manual *Golf in America. A Practical Manual* and in 1897, the first US intercollegiate competitions were held, in which L.B. Bayard from Princeton won the individual classification and Yale – the team classification. Golf became popular in other countries only in the 20th cent. Still, its highest prestige is maintained mostly in Anglo-Saxon countries. With the exception of a few private clubs, it no longer enjoys quite the elitist status it once held. In Great Britain there are around 2,000 golf associations and in the USA – nearly 2,500. The number of golfers in both countries amounts to about 4 million and 21.7 million respectively (1994). Recreational and friendly golf matches in Australia were initiated immediately after 1820 by Scot. A. Reid, on his farm near Hobart. In Canada, golf's popularization has become quite dynamic since the first historical recreational meeting on Priest's Farm, near Montreal (1824). The first regular golf association in Canada, Montreal G.C., was estab. by Scot. A. Dennistoun, in 1873. In N.Zealand, the *Otago Daily Times* announced the establishment of the Dunedin Golf Club in 1871. The club's initiator was a Scot, C.R. Howden. Other than in Eng.-speaking countries, golf is practiced in France (since c.1856), in Germany (since c.1890), and most recently, for the last few decades, in Japan, South Korea, and Singapore. At the beginning golf was treated solely as a pastime. In 1860, a match played on the Prestwick course was won by W. Park Senior who is considered the first professional golfer. Nowadays, golf is played

by both professionals and amateurs. An important role in the popularization of the game was played by country clubs, where golf acquired the status of a prestigious recreational activity. There is no worldwide golf federation. The most influential organizations are: The United States Golf Association (USGA, founded in 1894 or 1891) and the Royal Ancient Golf Club of St. Andrews (RAGC). In 1951, the two organizations signed an agreement unifying the fundamental rules of the game. Separate associations have been established for professional players, the most important of which are the Professional Golf Association of America (founded in 1916) and the Professional Golfers Association of Great Britain, which operate on the basis of bilateral agreements. Golf events are usu. held separately for amateurs and professionals, but there are tournaments open to both categories, too. The most important amateur events are the British Amateur, Canadian Amateur, Curtis Cup, and Walker Cup. In addition, E.Ch. are held annually. An unofficial equivalent of W.Ch. is the eponymous Eisenhower Cup, founded by the US president. Amateur golf was listed as an Olympic event twice (1900 and 1904) but it was rather modestly popular at that time. At the 1900 Ol.G. in Paris, representatives of only 3 countries participated in the men's and women's contests (both winners were Americans: C.E. Sands – men and M. Abbot – women). Nevertheless, as a result of the pressure exerted by Americans, esp. enthusiastic G. McGrew – the president of the Glen Echo Country Club in St. Louis, golf remained on the Ol.G.'s program in 1904 discrediting itself completely by putting up only representatives of the USA and one Can. player, G. Lyon, who actually won the entire competition. This determined golf's fate in the following Ol.G. in London without any question. In addition, the representatives of the strongest Brit. club, i.e. the Royal and Ancient Golf Club in St. Andrews, fearing another defeat, voiced their protest against introducing golf in the Ol.G. because, as they argued, the discipline was not present at ancient games, either.

A golfer who wants to become a professional player has to go through 5yrs. of so-called apprenticeship. Among the professionals, the most prestigious events are the Ryder Cup, a tournament held every 2 years and treated as an unofficial Eur.-Amer. contest, and the PGA Money Winning Champions. Professionals are also awarded the annual Vardon Trophy for playing with the fewest strokes. The most important opens, i.e. events in which both professionals and amateurs can participate, are the British Open and Canadian Open.

The first prominent golfer is thought to have been W. Hagen (1892-1969), a professional player who triumphed 4 times in the British Open, also famous for his cocky phrase pronounced at the beginning of a match: 'Who's going to be second?' American, R. 'Bobby' Tyre Jones (1902-71) is considered among the best golfers of all times on the international scale – an amateur coming up to professional standards, referred to by the press as a part-time professional. Thanks to his wavering between the status of amateur and professional, he could become the only golfer in history who achieved the Grand Slam, winning in the course of a single season (1930) the 4 greatest trophies of both categories, i.e. the British Amateur, British Open, USGA Open, and USGA Amateur. During 14yrs. of his career he was the best player of the year, based on the number of victorious tournaments, 13 times. Other leading golfers were: in the '40s, B. Nelson, B. Hogan, and S. Sned (all b. 1912); in the '50s, A. Palmer (b. 1929); and in the '60s, J. Nicklaus (b. 1940) who maintained his high position on the international arena exceptionally long, into his 50s. The greatest golfers of the '80s and '90s are considered: E. Es from S Africa (b. 1969); British J. Daly (b. 1966); Americans D. Stockton (b. 1941), J. Colbert (1941), and B. Murphy (b. 1943); and from non-English-speaking countries: Japanese M. 'Jumbo' Ozaki, his brother, T. 'Jet' Ozaki, and Argentinean R. de Vincenzo. The most outstanding players are commemorated in the PGA Hall of Fame, established in 1940.

The highest-ranking international events are thought to be the British Open (since 1865), British Women's Amateur (since 1883), British Men's Amateur (since 1885), Canadian Amateur (since 1895), U.S. Men's Amateur (since 1895), U.S. Women's Amateur (since 1895), U.S. Open for Men (since 1895),

Elliot Staples chips the ball onto the Astroturf green on the frozen Bering Sea during the Bering Sea Ice Golf Classic off Nome, Alaska. The annual event raises money for the Lions' Club.

Hendrick Avercamp, Ice Scene with Golfers, oil on panel.

Canadian Open (since 1904), Masters Tournament (since 1934), U.S. Open for Women (since 1946; since 1953 under the auspices of the USGA), U.S. Men's Professional (since 1916).

Women's golf. Until the beginning of the 19th cent. golf in Great Britain was accessible only to men (with the exception of the royal family). In 1810, the Musselburgh Club admitted sailor's widows to play. The majority of men's clubs did not admit women. Therefore, in the 1860s, the first exclusively women's clubs were established, e.g. the Westward Ho! Club (1868). The Brookline Country Club, founded by a group of Boston Brahmin, allowed mixed membership and games. In 1895, the Meadow Brook club in Hempstead, New York, organized the first Women's Amateur Championship in which 13 golfers participated. The winner was Mrs. C.S. Brown (according to the customs of that age, a woman was presented by the name of her husband). Around 1898, a group of women rebelled against the discrimination exercised in one of the oldest Amer. Clubs, the St. Andrews Golf Club of Yonkers, and established their own association, the Saegkil Golf Club, which possessed its own 6-hole course. Despite all these frictions, golf was one of the first sport events, if not the very first one, in which both sexes were involved in direct competition against each other. Women's golf owes a lot to G. Collett, and then to a versatile Amer. athlete, M. 'Babe' Didrickson-Zaharias (1914-56) who was one of the first women to earn substantial money playing golf, e.g. in 1948 she received $3,400. She was also the first female athlete to be commemorated by the US Postal Service, which issued a stamp with her portrait; a stamp representing R. Tyre 'Bobby' Jones was also issued at the same time. In 1944, together with P. Berg and L. Suggs, she initiated the Women's Professional Golfers Association, transformed in 1950 into the Ladies Professional Golfers' Association. The association operated as an independent entity until 1953 when emancipation processes allowed the USGA to take over women's golf. That same year, the USGA organized the Women's Open Championship. In the '60s, lower prestige attached to women's tournaments in such disciplines as tennis and golf, as well as smaller prizes, led to great protestations touching strongly on feminist philosophy, that are referred to as the Women's Sport Revolution. In 1976, the earnings of J. Rankin (b. 1945) exceeded a total of $100,000 (which was the first such case among female golfers), and in 1985, N. Lopez (b. 1957), earned more than $400,000. A.

Sorenstam (b. 1970), the 1995 world champion, gained that same year $660,224, surpassing thus the half-a-million barrier. Outstanding women golfers of the '90s also include: British L. Davies (b. 1963), and Swede H. Alfredson (b. 1965).

Currently, the most important women's tournaments are: the US Women's Open Championship, USGA Women's Amateur, Women's British Amateur, Women's PGA Money Winning Champions, and, held in Hashimoto, Japan, the Ladies Professional Golf Association Tournament.

P. Ballingall, *Learn Golf In a Weekend*, 1991; D. Chmiel, K. Morris, *Golf Past 50*, 2001; W. Glad, C. Beck, *Focused For Golf*, 1999; B. Hagan, *Power of Golf*, 1961; D. Hill & N. Seltz, *Teed Off*, 1977; A.E. Killeen, D. Owens & L.K. Bunker, *Golf. Steps to Success*, 1995; B. Madonna, *Coaching Golf Successfully*, 2001; A. Morrison, ed., *The Impossible Art of Golf: An Anthology of Golf Writing*, 1995; R. Moss, 'Sport and Social Status: Gold and the Making of the Country Club in the United States 1882-1920', IJHS, 1993, 1; E. Steart & H.E.B. Gunn, *Golf Begins at Forty*, 1977; H.W. Wind, *The Story of American Golf*, 1975.

GONGFU, also *kung fu*, a trad. Eng. rendering of the name for Chin. martial arts. In Chin. 'gongfu' means 'work, effort, or skill acquired by hard work. In the 1960s and '70s Western mass media used the term to refer to Chin. martial arts. The term used in China before WWII was *Kuo shu (Guoshu)* – the national art. After the war the People's Republic of China revived the old term >WUSHU (Chin. *Wu* – military + *shu* – art), which has a broad meaning and is currently associated with a sporting version of the Chin. martial arts. There is a great difference between the sporting forms (i.e. sequences of smoothly connected movements, practiced exclusively for esthetic purposes and physical fitness, on the one hand, and the old, trad., and dangerous skill. Many trad. techniques are lethal. Hand-to-hand combat is referred to as *Chanfa* or *Chuanshu*.

There are about 2,000 primary styles and thousands of lesser ones, a number of which are still unknown. Chinese gongfu gave birth to nearly all the martial arts of Korea, Japan, and SE Asian countries, such as >JU JUTSU, >KARATE, >TAE-KYON, etc. It also influenced the single combat techniques in Malaysia, Indonesia, and the Philippines. Nearly every trad. gongfu style includes 4 levels of fighting: *ti* – leg techniques, *da* – strikes, *shuei* – throws, wrestling techniques, and *na* – locking techniques and disabling holds (>QIN NA). Gongfu developed in 2

major genres: the Buddhist-origin styles (related with the Shaolin temple traditions) and the Taoist-origin styles (associated with Wu Dang and Emei centers). Another classification distinguishes between the Neijia 'internal' styles and the Weijia 'external' styles, as well as between the northern and southern styles. Neijia employs in-depth knowledge of biomechanics, breathing control, and the circulation of internal energy or *Qi*, which, after years of training, leads to proficiency in fighting, available even at an advanced age. The major internal styles include: >XINGYI-QUAN, >TAIJIQUAN, *baguazhan* and *luhe ba faquan*. The external styles start training by preparing the body in a series of exercises aimed at improving strength, speed, and flexibility, which allows a trainee to achieve combat skills at a relatively young age, provided the training starts soon enough. They include Shaolin Changquan, Dang Langquan, Yingquan, Hung Gar, >CHOY LEE FUT, etc. Typical northern styles are characterized by the use of many leg techniques, great mobility, and fighting at longer distances (e.g. Shaolin Changquan, Chaquan, Tan tui), while southern styles include more hand techniques and the so called qin na techniques, e.g. Hung Gar, Chou Gar, >HUNG KUEN, etc. All divisions, however, are quite arbitrary. Over hundreds of years kung fu styles influenced and crossbred with one another, the result being many styles which can hardly be classified. Each trad. style, except for the 4 levels of fighting, includes techniques of fighting with long weapons (e.g. a spear, stick, halberd, etc.), short weapons (e.g. a sword, saber, etc.), and various kinds of original weapons (e.g. brushes of death, hooked swords, steel fans, etc.)

History. In 2600 BC, Emperor Huang Di (the Yellow Emperor) had his advisors develop efficient methods of military training. From a record dated 2500 BC we learn about the *Go ti* technique according to which the opponent was pierced with horns installed on a helmet. The fighting was probably ritual in nature. In the 6th cent. BC, *shang pu, shuei go,* and *shou pu* techniques were known and in the 3rd cent. AD, a doctor, Hua Tuo, described the fundamentals of breathing exercises based on imitating 5 different animals: tiger, deer, bear, monkey, and bird. The system, known as the Wuqinxi (games of 5 animals), was supposed to bring back one's energy, improve one's physical condition, and whet one's appetite. Around 525 AD, Bodhidharma (Chin. Da Mo), an Indian Buddhist master coming from a duke's family, went to China to popularize Buddhism. After a rather chilly welcome from the emperor of the kingdom of Wei, he settled down in Henan province, in the Shaolin (young forest) monastery where he became the first patriarch of Chan Buddhism (Jap. Zen). Chan is a var. of Buddhism, which teaches meditation as a form of acquiring spiritual insight and enlightenment. After Bodhidharma had noticed that most of the monks were too weak physically to be able to follow the strict spiritual discipline, he developed a system of 18 exercises intended to improve their physical and mental resilience and wrote 2 books: *Shi Sui Ching* (*Cleaning the Brain and Bone Marrow*) and *Yi Gin Ching* (*Transformation of the Muscles and Tendons*). Bodhidharma is an exceptionally eminent figure both for Chin. Buddhism and martial arts. The monks needed such skills to be able to defend themselves against outlaws while they were traveling across the country. After Bodhidharma's death, the Shaolin monks discovered that the Yi Gin Ching exercises enabled them to multiply their strength. Such was the beginning of the most celebrated training center for martial art experts. The single combat skills taught in Shaolin are also referred to as the 18-weapon skills, after the number of weapons that a proficient fighter was able to master. The style also included exercises of competences possessed by 5 animals: the dragon – developing attention and cleverness with focus on light and quick moves, as well as stillness; the tiger – strengthening bones, focusing on jumps; the leopard – developing strength and focusing on combat; the snake – practicing internal breathing, the Qi energy, stretching the body, and developing sensitivity and activity; the crane – developing concentration, equability, precision, determination in combat, and deceptive steps.

Shaolin origin is claimed in the case of the majority of the external styles and some internal ones. The styles stemming from the Wu Dang and Emei centers are substantially different from those above.

Gongfu. Shaolin Chang Quan. Golden rooster stance. Broadsword technique.

Chinese weapons: a, c – long-handed claw (zhua), b – Buddha hand (fou shou).

A Chinese boy monk from the Shaolin Temple in China's Henan Province shows off his gongfu skills during a show in Beijing.

Gongfu. Shaolin Chang Quan.

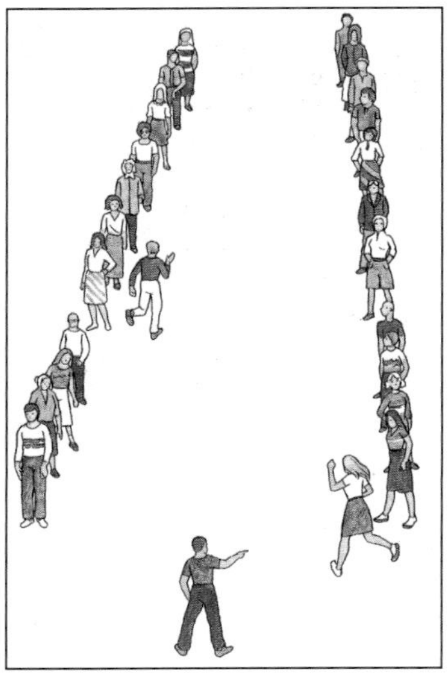

Gonka numyerov.

GORODKI BLOCK ARRANGEMENTS

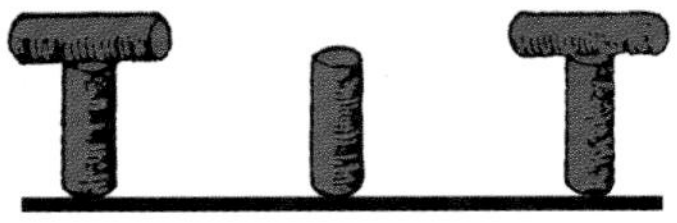

Sentries.

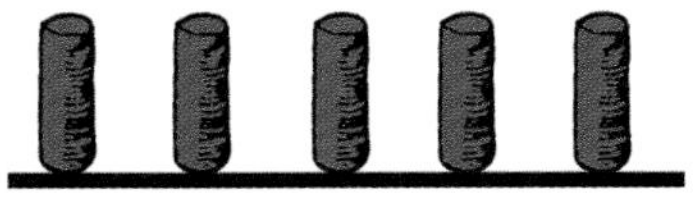

A fence.

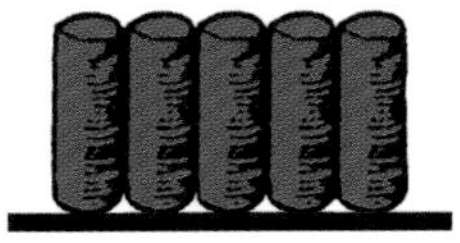

A wall.

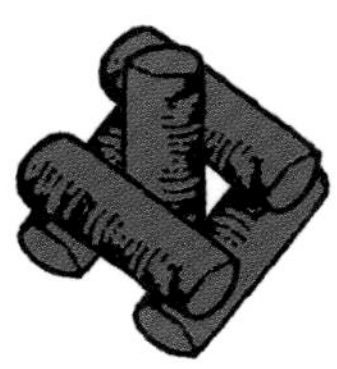

A well.

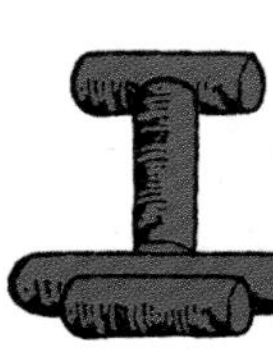

An airplane.

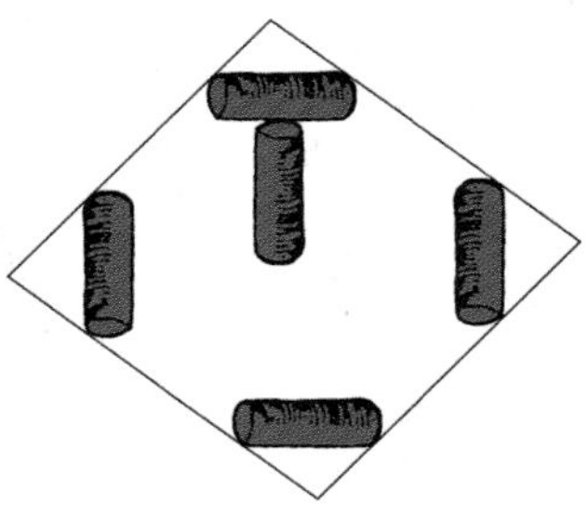

A letter.

gongfu was practiced by monks, laymen, entire families, and secret associations whose objective was the overthrow of any invading dynasty. The Mongolian Yuan dynasty and later the Manchurian Qing dynasty were their first targets. Such blatant insurrection resulted in an official ban against practicing the martial art under pain of death; those who continued in the discipline and were found out were duly executed. Even so, the gongfu masters who trained the insurgents managed to organize a number of uprisings. The last such anti-Manchurian rebellion in 1900 is famously known as the Boxer Rebellion (I Ho Quan) after the combat techniques employed by the rebels which lacked an exact equivalent in Western culture. After this ferocious and unsuccessful episode in Chin. history, gongfu's prestige as a military art that could stand up to Western firearms was severely eroded. In 1909, a renowned master, Huoyueunjiia, estab. the Chin Woo (Jing Wu) organization whose objective was to teach and popularize Chin. martial arts. Huoyueunjiia invited to collaboration such celebrated gongfu masters as Cen Zethin Zeng (the eagle's style), Lo Juan Yu (the north mantis's style), Wu Chien Chuwan (the Wu taijiquan style), Geen Cia Kuan (the xingioan style). After the Republic of China was formed in 1928, the Nan King Central Kuo Shu Institute in Nankin – then capital of China – was set up. Both organizations invited masters who shared their expertise and discussed the plans of gongfu's development in the new country, aiming at the preservation and cultivation of national heritage. Although the activity of such organizations was suspended during WWII, Chin Wo operates up to this day. After WWII, Chin. martial arts acquired a more sportive rather than military character. Simplified and modified versions of old styles were practiced as >WUSHU. More focus was placed on esthetics, often discarding the utilitarian character of martial arts. A coach was frequently accompanied by a choreographer subordinating the sequences of moves to the dramatic character of a sports event. Gymnastic fitness and acrobatic elements soon took on supreme importance, approximating thus martial arts to rhythmic gymnastics. Currently, trad. gongfu is much better appreciated in continetal China. The Kook Shun (Gush) organization is being developed in Taiwan and many other countries. It is predominantly sportive in nature, although it is also aimed at preserving the trad. martial art. Numerous gongfu masters operate in different parts of the world. One of the problems is finding the sense of purpose in trad. forms of training involving special skills, such as the 'iron hand', 'iron shirt', 'jumping skill', etc., because the realities of a modern combat field and even the needs of police forces are much different from trad. standards. The training of special squads able to utilize the old Chin. martial art skills must account for a short training period, which eliminates trad. systems requiring great effort. The aim of gongfu was to defeat the opponent by using all available means, incl. attacking the vital parts, which often ended in the opponent's death. Therefore, despite the advancement of gongfu science, the trad. form of this martial art is rarely practiced. Chin. martial arts are rich, versatile, extremely complicated, and difficult to master. They are also amazingly effective, although the mastering of an internal style requires up to 30 years of practice. Teaching of gongfu was limited to narrow groups of selected students and so combat sports, such as >JUDO or >TAEKWONDO, promoted by various Asian countries could find a mass audience, while trad. gongfu still remains partly veiled.

GONKA NUMYEROV (*number race*), a Rus. school running game, in which contestants line up in 2 rows separated by a distance of approx. 8m, facing forwards. A roll-call by each row designates a number to each contestant. The master of the game calls any number, at which point one contestant from each row steps out, runs around his row and returns to his place. Then another number is called and so on. The winner of each round scores a point and the total number of points determines the winning team.

I.N. Chkhannikov, 'Gonka numyerov', GIZ, 1953.

GOOD FRIDAY FOOTBALL, a rare trad. Eng. ball game connected with Easter. The game consisted of kicking the ball in the vicinity of fresh patches of potatoes. It was believed that playing the game would bring better crops in the future.

GORESH, a form of trad. wrestling in Turkestan, practiced in the standing position to musical accompaniment, usu. during family celebrations and holidays. The word goresz is also one of the generic terms for hand-to-hand fights practiced in Central Asia, such as >CULECHE in Azerbaijan, >GIULES in Kirghizia, >KOURECHE and >KURASZ in Kurdistan. Cf. Romanian and Kazak >KURESH, and Uzbek and Tatar >KÜREŞ, which have the same oriental etymology.

GORODKI, a trad. Rus. game in which sticks resembling baseball bats are thrown at cylindrical wooden blocks arranged in var. figures.

A playing field is rectangular, approx. 25-30m by 13-15m, however in spontaneous matches played on the squares and streets of Rus. cities, the size limits are not observed too rigorously. The field is divided into 2 parallel lanes, each for one player. At the end of each lane, about 2.5m before the end line, a 2x2m square is marked. On improvised playing fields, the squares are drawn on the ground, whereas on permanent ones they are made of concrete whose surface is equal to the surface of the field. Similarly, the edges of the field are either drawn on the ground or marked with lime or white tape. On each lane the so-called finish and the halfway point inform the players where the run-up starts and where a throw must be executed. The distance between the finish and the halfway point is not fixed as it depends on the player's age, sex, and skills. For boys, girls, and women, the halfway point is 5m, and the finish 10m, from the square. For men, the distances are 6.5 and 13m respectively. Throwing points at the halfway point and the finish are bordered on the sides by 2-m lines that must not be crossed during the game, which applies also to the lines marking the halfway point and the finish. A playing field is usu. situated so that behind the squares there is a wall, which makes the game easier, as the wooden blocks are not spread too far. If there is no wall, players build a small embankment made of ground, usu. 50cm tall. Permanent playing fields are situated in trenches whose walls prevent the wooden blocks from falling too far.

The throwing sticks (min. 2, usu. 3 or 4) are approx. 80-100cm long, have different diameters, and are made of wood. Each player can throw only his or her own sticks. The wooden blocks that form the target are 20cm long and 4-5cm in diameter.

In winter, the game is often played on ice, which makes it more dynamic as the hit blocks slide faster and farther than on the ground. The course's borders and playing positions are then marked with blue or red paint.

Rules of the game. Players throw wooden sticks, often reinforced with a wire or metal plates, at wooden blocks, arranged in certain figures according to predetermined order and patterns. The figures are constructed of 5 blocks and are thrown at in 2 games, a 'small game' and a 'large game'. The small game consists of the following figures: a fence made of blocks standing vertically at a distance of about 10cm one from another, a wall – the blocks are standing vertically close to one another; sentries – one block standing vertically flanked on the right and left by two pairs of blocks arranged in a T shape placed about 20cm from the central block; a well – 4 blocks placed horizontally forming a grate plus one standing vertically in the middle of the grate; a plane – 2 blocks form wings, 1 is the fuselage, 1 is the tail, and another one is the engine bordering with wings; a letter – 4 blocks placed horizontally, each in one corner of the square, plus 1 block standing upright in the center of the square. The large game consists of the following combinations: a letter – similar layout as in the small game but the central block lies horizontally instead of standing vertically; artillery – 1 standing block represents a commander at whose sides there are 2 cannons, each made of a block lying on the ground and another block, placed perpendicularly with one end propped against the ground and the other resting on the first block, aiming the 'barrel' upwards; an embankment – 3 blocks form a dashed line, the breaks equal to dashes, and behind the breaks the 2 remaining blocks form a similar line; a cannon – the barrel support and the wheels are made of 3 blocks, 1 block is the barrel resting on the front support and the rear support; a star – a standing block is surrounded by the remaining 4 blocks lying on the ground with their heads touching the central block; a crawfish – the blocks form two V letters, placed one beside the other, whose tips are linked with the 5th block; a fork – 4 blocks make two teeth of the fork and the last block is a short handle; a sickle – 1 block is the handle and the rest of them form a semicircle joined with the handle; an arrow – 3 blocks form the arrow's shaft and 2 blocks form its head.

In the last combination, a letter, the blocks have to be knocked out of the square 3 times in each game. The block standing in the middle of the letter is referred to as 'stamp' or 'seal'. To 'unseal' or to 'stamp' a letter means to knock the central block out of the square leaving the remaining blocks intact. If the letter is unsealed incorrectly, the seal is returned to its original position for the player to try again. However, each retrial implies a loss of one throwing stick. The first throw at each new figure is executed from the finish line and after knocking out even one wooden block, the thrower has the right to continue throwing standing before the halfway point line. A block is considered knocked out properly when it is moved outside the square and does not touch the square's border with any of its parts. If a block is knocked out towards the halfway point it is called a candle and a player places it vertically on the throwing line, which converts it, on the one hand, into an obstacle in knocking the remaining blocks out and, on the other, into a final target. The series of throws starts with a signal given by a referee. Two opposing teams compete on 2 parallel lanes. A throw is executed by swinging one's arm from behind the head or the trunk of the body. The scoring can follow 2 systems: 1) a number of throws necessary to knock out all the figures is counted and the team that executed fewer throws wins; 2) a number of rounds won by a team is counted instead of the number of executed throws. A match consists of 3 rounds and should one team win the first 2 of them, the third round is not held. Teams are composed of 5 players. Singles are also popular, esp. during less formal meetings.

Gouren (Breton wrestling), *a 19th -cent. engraving for* Le Lutteur *by Henri Rolland (1848).*

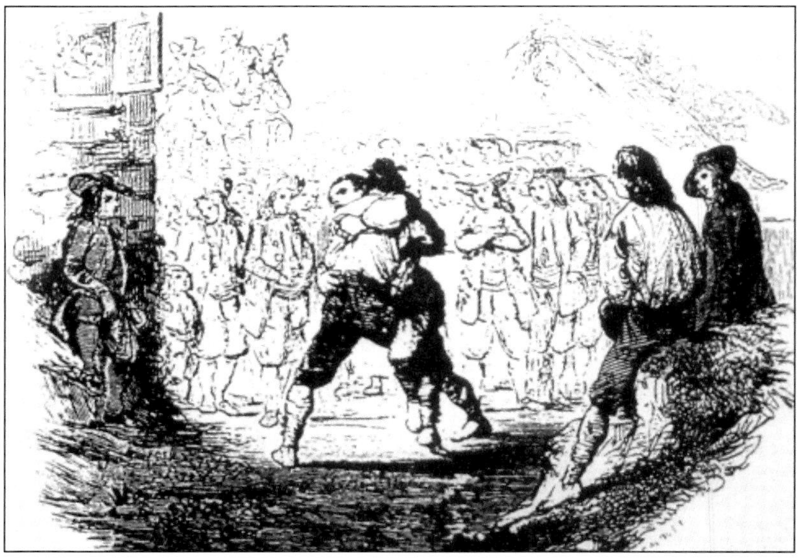

Gouren wrestling.

History. Gorodki has trad. folk origins and as an organized sports discipline it has been practiced in Russia (and the former USSR) since 1923. During the period of its peak popularity, in 1939, 100 teams competed in Moscow championships. Separate summer and winter, team and singles championships were held. In the 1950s, communist authorities attempted to impose the game on Poland but it never made inroads into the Pol. lifestyle and culture as Pol. society resisted the numerous Soviet patterns that were being thrust upon it at that time. Thus, unintentionally, gorodki's failure to catch on became an expression of Pol. political resistance, which was prohibited in other areas.

J. Riordan, 'Folk Games', *Stadion* 1986/87, 12/13; M. Skierczyński, *Wybijanka*, 1950; 'Wybijanka (Gorodki)', *Sport w ZSRR*, collective work, 1948, 153-4.

GOSHT, also *gošt* or *goughty*. A folk var. of wrestling in Tajikistan. Wrestlers fight in a standing position. The winner is the fighter who first forces the opponent to touch the ground with any part of the body other than the feet.

GOUREN, also *ar gouren* (Breton spelling *chouren*), a folk hand-to-hand combat sport popular in Brittany. It has a number of sub-var. of which *gouren* (also known as *ar gouren* or *chouren*) is the most popular. A fight is traditionally preceded by the challenge. A champion displays his trophy while walking inside a circle of spectators and potential opponents. The person who decides to fight him says: 'Chom't ho sao!' (Stay where you are!) and gives him a light pat on the shoulder to confirm that he has accepted the challenge. The opponents start the match with a mutual grip called an *accolade*. To win a bout, one has to floor one's opponent so that both his shoulder blades touch the ground. Then, the winner may challenge another opponent to fight with him. The one to win the last bout in a given tournament is declared the champion. The spectators are supervised by a special guard wielding a whip or a frying pan with a black bottom.

The wrestlers wear white shirts with short sleeves and three-quarter trousers. They fight on a sand-covered arena called a *tapis* which is usu. a 4-5m square. It is surrounded by the so-called protective zone (*bande de protection*) which is 1m-wide.

The wrestlers begin to compete in a standing position. They stand face-to-face, stooping slightly forwards. They put their arms around their opponent's neck with their fingers clenched tightly together so that a given player rests his chin on his opponent's right arm. He then places his left arm along his opponent's right arm and his right hand on the opponent's head. The players remain in this position until the umpire gives them a signal to fight (by saying *luttez* – wrestle). During the bout the players must not loosen their grip even when they twist their bodies or start fighting side-to-side (instead of face-to-face). The players must not hit or kick each other. While fighting the wrestlers must touch the ground at all times. When one of the players is lifted the bout is stopped. A player who wins 3 rounds is de-

clared the winner. He may also defeat his opponent by making him touch the ground with both shoulder blades, provided his buttocks are not touching the ground. If the opponent falls to the ground but touches it with his side or knee, etc., the attacking wrestler needs an additional throw in which he makes the opponent touch the ground with his hands. There are no separate weight categories but one of the fighters should not weigh more than 5kg more than his opponent. The umpires also make sure that the fighters' fingernails are not too long.

Before the fight the players take the following oath:

I do solemnly swear to fight loyally, without any trickery and brutality, to distinguish myself and my country and to testify to my honesty and my observance of the customs of my forefathers and I do hereby confirm this by raising my hand and by my cheek.

History. Breton wrestling dates back to King Arthur's times. King Arthur was the ruler who defended Celtic Brittany against the Ang.-Sax. invaders. Brittany, although a part of France today, was, in the 6th cent. AD, inhabited by people who had to flee Britain. They brought their customs along (this is best exemplified by the fact that the two names are very similar, also in French, compare *Bretagne* vs. *Grande-Bretagne*). According to some sources Breton wrestling was the favorite sport of King Arthur. The Arthurian tradition exerted a very strong influence on Eur. knighthood. Wrestling became one of the most basic military training exercises and, according to the Celtic tradition, was, at the same time, a magic ceremony. In pagan times wrestlers were thought to derive their strength from performing various magic rituals or from being protected by various deities. Later, they were said to be guarded by special patron saints. One of the most distinguished Breton

knights – B. de Guesclin (1320-80) was, at the same time, a very famous wrestler, rejected by his family due to his extreme ugliness. He gained fame when he arrived at one tournament dressed as a peasant and riding a draft horse. To compete he had to borrow a suit of armor. By winning the tournament he regained the esteem of his family but at the same he became a folk hero since the peasants thought he was one of them. Most likely, this led to the popularizing of the rural variety of Breton wrestling called *ar gouren*. Due to the fact that Breton wrestling bouts were deemed to involve occult practices, the sport was disapproved of by the Church. This led to its being banned in many areas in the 17th and 18th centuries. In the 19th cent. the sport was revived and became the national combat sport in Brittany. In 1927 Dr. C. Cotonnec established the Breton Wrestling Committee. Later, Cotonnec met M. Hooper of Cornwall, the then Chairman of the Cornish Folk Wrestling Association. Together, they organized a Celtic wrestling tournament in Quinperlé.

Today, Breton wrestling together with the Scot. >BACKHOLD and Icel. >GLÍMA, is one the major sports governed by the International Federation of Celtic Wrestling established in 1985.

R.Y. Creston, *La lutte bretonne a scaer*, 1957; G. Jaouen, *La lutte bretonne et ses origine celtiques*, 1986; Musee de Bretagne, *La lutte bretonne*, 1976; F. Peru, 'Ar Gouren, La tradition populaire de jeux de plein air en Bretagne', LJP, 1998, 54-5.

GOURET, LE, a Fr. trad. game, similar to Pol. >BROWAR.

GRÆNSEKAMP, Dan. for 'combat at the border', [Dan. *grænse* – border + *kamp* – combat]. A game played by 2 teams of any number of players, that stand facing each other on opposite sides of the central line, marked with a rope or a pole. The object of the game is to 'fish out' the players from the opposing team and drag them over the central line, which must not be crossed, holding them by the arms. The teams can line up, like in >TUG-OF-WAR, to increase the pull. The winner is the team which manages to pull a greater number of opponents over the central line, if the time is predetermined, or all of them – if there is no time limit.

J. Møller, 'Grænsekamp', GID, 1997, 4.

GRÆSRYTTER, Dan. for 'grass rider'. One of the participants gets down on all fours. On both sides 2 other players stand facing each other and place their hands on the back of the first one. Then, 2 more participants mount on the standing players' backs and attempt to knock each other down. The one who topples over first becomes a græsrytter, i.e. a grass rider.

J. Møller, 'Græsrytter', GID, 1997, 4, 48.

GRÆSSE KO, Dan. for 'grazing a cow', [Dan. *græsse* – to graze + *ko* – a cow]. A folk var. of wrestling that used to be popular in Denmark. Two wrestlers, tied with each other by their necks with a rope, stand facing each other, approx. 1m apart. The object is to pull the opponent to one's own side. The heads should be tilted backwards to avoid the rope's

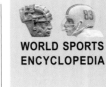
Grænsekamp.

G

WORLD SPORTS ENCYCLOPEDIA

sliding from the neck. Other var. of the game, only a little different, are known under such names as *gloes kat* (to stare at the wheels), *grinne ad ræven* (to grin at a fox), and *kattestrud* (cat fight). In these var. the wrestlers lie on their bellies, holding a stick in their teeth. The joining rope loops around their necks and then goes under the sticks.
J. Møller, 'Græsse ko', GID, 1997, 4, 19.

GRAND CHICHESTERA, also sp. *grand shistera* or *grand chistera*; see >PELOTA VASCA.

Grass skiing.

GRASS SKIING, the former name of >ROLLER SKIING, reflecting the practice of skiing on grassy slopes of mountains in the summer. The name lost currency once cross-country skiers took up skirollers and started using them on asphalt roads. The rollers have made it possible to ski on surfaces other than snow. Initially, the objective was to make it possible for 'traditional' skiers to practice during the summer. The first attempts were made in the alpine countries in the 1950s.

GRASSBOARD, also sp. in Ger. *Grasboard*. A racing competition on a 2-wheel vehicle resembling a large-wheeled scooter without handlebars. The front wheel is a typical mid-size bicycle one and the rear wheel is more similar to that of a car. The wheels are mounted to a frame with a small board in between them for the racer's foot. The front wheel is fixed to a special arching frame ending with a fork. It is turned by means of pressing on a mechanical device coupled with the frame. The size of the wheels, esp. the wide rear tire, makes the board go relatively smoothly even on rough terrain, usu. a grassy slope. One of the most popular events is a slalom between cubes made of pressed straw or hay.

Grass skis.

GRASSTRACK, a form of motorcycle track racing that takes place on grass circuits.
History. Motorcycle racing on grass took place in various countries during the early years of the twentieth century, but grasstrack did not become an organised discipline until the Auto-Cycle Union (ACU)

Grassboard.

in Britain banned racing on public roads in 1925. With public roads no longer available, motorcycle racers turned to privately-owned fields and in 1927, the Whitgift Club held the first recognised grasstrack meeting on an old golf course near Croydon. This meeting proved very successful and it was not long before the sport spread to other parts of Britain. There was, however, little uniformity amongst the tracks which ranged between 400 to 2,000m in length and often included steep climbs and descents akin to today's motocross courses.
By 1931, there were so many events that the ACU introduced rules for the sport and established separate capacity classes to ensure close racing. At the same time, the pre-war boom in >SPEEDWAY was attracting many grasstrack riders to a lucrative career on the shale (or cinders at that time), but they still rode in grasstrack events at the weekends using their speedway machines. These were much lighter and faster than conventional motorcycles, and despite attempts to restrict their use, they soon dominated the sport.
After WWII, the popularity of the speedway-style machines, which were more suited to flat oval tracks, hastened the demise of *hilly* courses, some of which were subsequently surfaced for road racing. From this point onwards, grasstrack started to become recognisable as the sport we know today.
Grass track racing was exceptionally popular in 1945-1960 in Poznań, Poland, where races were held on a steeplechase horse track. The leading cyclist, who specialized in this kind of racing, was Jerzy Mieloch – not only a talented cyclist but also a gifted constructor whose own modifications went far ahead of the technological development in motorcycle building of his times. Unfortunately, the political isolation of E Europe prevented him from testing his skill against that of Western motorcyclists.
Grasstrack is now raced in a number of Eur. countries, as well as Australia and N.Zealand. It is particularly popular in N Germany and the Netherlands where the flat terrain lends itself to the sport. Britain continues to hold a large number of events, although increasing urbanisation, and intolerance by the new generation of country dwellers, has caused problems finding suitable venues.
Traditionally, tracks are marked out in any suitable field that happens to be available, but it is becoming increasingly common for them to be based at permanent or semi-permanent venues. They generally range between 425 and 1,300m in length and usually (but not always) conform to an oval shape. The safety barrier consists of wooden boards or, as is common in Britain, four rows of ropes supported by stakes.
Unlike speedway, there are a number of different solo and sidecar classes in grasstrack racing. The solo bikes are similar to those used for speedway, but are slightly larger, have a more rigid frame, and rear suspension is necessary to cope with those bumpy fields. The premier class is for machines with an engine capacity of 500cc, but there are other classes for 350cc, 250cc and 125cc machines. Solos always race in an anti-clockwise direction.
Sidecars have always been part of grasstrack racing, but they present a particular problem. On the Eur. mainland, the sidecar is mounted on the right of the machine (a legacy of driving on the right) and they race in an anti-clockwise direction, while in Britain and Australasia, the sidecars are usually mounted on the left of the machine (a legacy of driving on the left) and they race in a clockwise direction. In addition, most Eur. federations restrict sidecars to an engine capacity of 500cc, while the clockwise countries permit an engine capacity of 1,000cc. Just to confuse matters further, some clubs in SE Britain hold events for right-handed sidecars as well. The Fédération Internationale de Motorcyclisme (FIM) is attempting to establish a universal sidecar class, but has not been successful to date.
Solo races usually consist of either 6 or 8 riders, while sidecar races usually consist of either 4 or 6 crews (rider and passenger). The system of scoring varies, but is usually similar to that found in other track racing disciplines. It should be noted that racing rules are often applied less strictly in grasstrack, and is not uncommon for a rider causing a stoppage to be allowed to participate in the re-run.
Many speedway riders learn their skills in grasstrack as it provides a relatively cheap and easy way to get started in track racing. It is still common for riders to participate in both disciplines, although

the demands of modern speedway make this more difficult than in the past. The top solo grasstrack riders usually also compete in >LONGTRACK, which is closely related.
K. Meynell, M. Farmer: http://www.meynell.com/speedway-faq/intro.html

GRAVELRAMA, a var. of racing up a hill on a surface covered in gravel, held annually in Obetz, Ohio, USA. All kinds of 4-wheel vehicles are allowed. The racetrack is 50m long and it ends with a sharp fault, which often makes the vehicles that have succeeded in covering the entire track catch on its edge. The leading racers of the 1990s were J. Wiggins and the Harneys (Richard – the father and Jeff and Greg – his 2 sons).

GREASED POLE, one of the most popular folk sports known in many countries. Its object is to climb a high pole, most often covered with a greasy substance – tallow, pork fat, oil or soap, to get the prize put on the pole's top. Depending on the local tradition, the prizes included: a demijohn of wine, sausages, sometimes animals such as a small pig, hen, goose, etc. In Span.-speaking countries a greased pole was often erected in the central yard of the village or town, whereas in the countries of C Europe it was erected occasionally, e.g. in parks or nearby forests, during picnics. The following types of greased pole are the most representative examples of the Eur. variety:
In Portugal greased pole is known as *mastro de cocanha* [Port. *mastro* – mast, pole + *cocanha* – abundance, wealth], also as *jog do mastro* [*jogo* – game, play + *mastro* – mast, pole]. The pole is greased with tallow; the prize on its top, on traverse beams, usually includes some delicacies, e.g. sausages.
In France greased pole is called *mât de cocagne* [*mât* – pole + *cocagne* – abundance], while in S France, dominated by a regional language called *occitan*, it is known as *l'abre de cocanha* and differs from other regions of France in many details, e.g. the length of pole (up to 15m).
In England greased pole is also known as *slippery*

Goya, The Greased pole, 1786-87, oil on canvas.

pole. The activity is better defined by the official name, used when greased pole is featured in the program of various folk events (although hardly in everyday conversation): *climbing of prize-draped tree*.
In Spain greased pole is mainly known as *palo lucio* (slippery pole) or *la cucaña* (abundance). Prizes are usually hung on a wheel fixed atop the pole. When the target was about to be reached, a folk ensemble consisting of trumpets and drums, started to play. Greased pole was often featured in the programs of the >PALO DE MAYO holiday. In varieties typical of Spain, associated with the holidays celebrated to commemorate the memory of various saints, greased pole was very popular in many Span. colonies in S.America, particularly in Nicaragua and

The head of a wrestler. Etruscan, 3rd cent. BC. The leather cap protected the wrestler against the opponent's trying to grip his hair.

In the Augur grave from 520-510 BC wrestlers battle over three precious metal vessels.

Mexico, among the Taos Indians from the Pueblo tribe. Greased pole was also known in Bolivia, where in about 1840 it earned the rank of a trad. pastime, enjoying the support of the Jesuits of Chiquita. Jesuits donated the prizes put atop the pole, such as shears, glasses and shawls.

In Brittany greased pole is called *ar wern*. The pole is greased with soap. The object is to reach the top and win the prizes put there, such as sausages, candy, toys and other small fancy goods. As the prizes are wrapped, a contestant must stay on the slippery pole for some time. Depending on the region, the prizes are hung on a single transverse beam, on 2 crossed beams, on a cart or bicycle wheel put atop the pole, etc.

The tradition of greased pole has nearly dyed out, parhaps for aesthetic reasons. Has modern man become so sensitive to dirt that a sport in which the contestant himself and his clothes become extremely filthy cannot withstand the competition of other, more hygienic forms of sport?

M. da Graça Sousa Guedes, 'Jogo do mastro o mastrode cocanha', JTP, 1979, 61-62; C. Moreno Palos, 'Cucañas', JYTE, 1992, 48; F. Peru, 'La tradition populaire de jeux de plein air en Bretagne', LJP, 1998, 48 and 60.

GRECO-ROMAN WRESTLING, one of the 2 most popular >WRESTLING styles in modern times included in the program of the Ol.G., W.Ch., and continental championships. In Greco-Roman wrestling the legs may not be used in any way to obtain a fall, and no holds may be taken below the waist. This makes modern Greco-Roman wrestling very similar to the wrestling style practiced in ancient Greece (and hence the name). Similar to >FREESTYLE WRESTLING, the object of the game is to pin one's opponent. If nobody gets pinned, the winner is the wrestler who has scored the most points during the match. The bout is officiated by a referee who awards points or announces the result of a given match. His decision must be confirmed by 2 other referees, i.e. the judge and the mat chairman. The decision may be accepted by a 2 to 1 majority. The bout consists of 2 rounds of 3min. each with a 1-min. break in between. In the case of a draw, the match goes into an overtime of 3min. So in total, the match may last up to 9min. Additionally, one of the wrestlers must score at least 3pts. for the match to end after 6min. In the mid-1990s the 2-round sys-

tem was replaced with a 1-round system whereby the round lasted for 5min. and the overtime for 3min. This system was applied during the 1996 Atlanta Ol.G., but was later discontinued.

In the case of stalling, the referee may stop the fight and to force the players to be more active he may order a so-called lock, in which the wrestlers stand face-to-face and place their hands around their opponent's shoulders (so that one hand is placed under the armpit and the other around the neck). The player who scored more points up to that moment has the right to apply the lock first, which gives him a certain advantage. If both players score no points or score an equal number of points the referee tosses a special blue and red token. When the token lands with the blue side up, the player wearing the blue uniform is the first to apply the lock. If it lands red side up, the other player does it. (To be clearly distinguished during a match, one of the wrestlers must wear blue and the other red). The player whose lock breaks first loses 1pt. If, within a period of 1min., neither of the players breaks his opponent's lock, the player who was first to apply it loses 1pt. and has to move to a par terre position, which, naturally, puts his opponent at an advantage. As some think this rule is unfair, it may be discarded in the near future. Bouts are held on a square mat whose side is at least 12m long, whereas the central wrestling area, which is circular in shape, must be at least 7m in diameter and is surrounded by a 1m-wide passivity zone. The wrestlers must wear soft shoes with tall and rigid tops to prevent ankle injury.

The wrestlers fight in a standing or par terre position. The standing position is defined as the position in which both players only touch the mat the soles of their shoes, whereas in the par terre position they both or one of them lies on the mat or touches it with any part of his body except the feet and both shoulder blades.

Technically speaking, the fight requires the application of various grips and holds such as suplexes, wrenches, gut wrenches and half-nelsons. Any hold that endangers life or limb, for example the full nelson, is forbidden.

The wrestlers are divided into weight categories. Since 1997 there have been the following 8 categories: 48-54kg, up to 58kg, up to 63kg, up to 69kg, up to 76kg, up to 85kg, up to 97kg and 97-130kg. These categories are observed in international competitions supervised by the Fédéracion Internation-

ale des Luttes Associees (FILA) that replaced the Fédéracion Internationale de Lutte Amateur (FILA – International Amateur Wrestling Federation). Before, however, the weight categories were different and they changed several times between 1896 and 1996.

History. Due to the fact that Greco-Roman wrestling drew heavily on the ancient Greek tradition it was initially referred to solely as Greek wrestling, especially in the 19th and at the beginning of the 20th century, despite the fact that it was not very similar to the Hellenic >PALE. Today, we also know that it was not the Greeks who invented the rule of admitting only above-the-waist holds and grips. In 1938 an Amer. scholar S.A. Speiser discovered an ancient statuette depicting two wrestlers holding each other above the hips in the Khafajah Temple near Baghdad. The statuette is said to be a typical example of Sumerian sculpture and its age is estimated at 5,000-7,000yrs. Additionally, all the preserved Eg. murals and statuettes depict wrestlers fighting in a standing position and applying their holds above their opponent's waist.

Classic Greco-Roman wrestling on a relief from the National Archeological Museum in Athens. One of the athletes is applzing the so-called 'ram's hold', while the other one is trying to push him off.

Modern Greco-Roman wrestling.

Women's olympic wrestling.

The modern history of Greco-Roman wrestling dates back to the first attempts to revive the Gk. Ol.G. Greco-Roman wrestling first formed a separate event during the 2nd of the so-called Hellenic Ol.G. with only one, unspecified weight category. K. Kardamylakis became the first Olympic Champion. Then, Greco-Roman wrestling was also included in the Hellenic Olympics program in 1875 and 1889. Greco-Roman wrestling was included in the program of the first modern Olympics in Athens in 1896. Just one weight class was contested – heavyweight – and Karl Schumann of Germany became the first Olympic wrestling gold medallist defeating G. Tsitas of Greece. W.Ch. have been held since 1921 under the auspices of the Fédéracion Internationale de Lutte Amateur (FILA – International Amateur Wrestling Federation) that was later renamed the Fédéracion Internationale des Luttes Associees (FILA). Initially, i.e. until 1939, the competition was dominated by Ger., Aus., Hung., and Scand. – esp. Swed. and Fin. – wrestlers. After 1945, the Soviet Union and other socialist countries such as Romania, Bulgaria and Poland came to the fore. They had to resist fierce competition from Ger., Eg. (especially immediately after 1945), Iranian, Jap., Kor., and Cuban (especially in the 1980s and '90s) wrestlers. Other countries where wrestling was practiced at a high international level included Finland, Hungary, Turkey and – until 1990 – Yugoslavia as well as the US (especially in the heaviest categories).

The most outstanding wrestlers in the 10 weight categories before 1997 include:

in the light flyweight (up to 48kg) category the first man to become a world-famous wrestler was G. Berceanu of Romania who won the W.Ch. in 1969, 1970 and the Olympic champion title in 1972. V. Zubkov of the USSR won the W.Ch. and the Olympic championship 4 times (1971, 1973-75) and M. Aletshverdiev and O. Kutsherenko – 3 times – 1985-87 and 1989, 1990, 1992, respectively;

in the flyweight (up to 52kg) category the most re-

A wrestling arena.

nowned wrestlers were B. Gurevich (Olympic and world champion in 1952, 1953 and 1958), V. Blagidzhe (1978, 1980-81) – both of the USSR and J. Rönningen of Norway (1985, 1990 and 1992);

in the bantamweight (up to 57kg) category the most outstanding wrestlers were O. Karavayev (World and Olympic champion in 1958, 1960 and 1961), R. Kozakov (1969, 1971 and 1972) and C. Serikov (1978, 1979 and 1980) – all of the USSR. Poland had 2 world champions in this category, namely J. Lipień (1973) and P. Michalik (1982);

in the featherweight (up to 62kg) category the best wrestler ever was the 4-time winner of W.Ch. and Ol.G. R. Rurua of the USSR (1966-69). The most distinguished Pol. wrestler in this category was K. Lipień (world champion in 1973 and 1974 and Olympic champion in 1976; he also won 4 silvers during W.Ch. and the bronze during the 1972 Ol.G.). Additionally, R. Świerad won the W.Ch. in 1982 and W. Zawadzki won the Olympic gold in 1992;

in the lightweight (up to 68kg) category the first official world champion was T. Schibilsky of Germany and the first Olympic champion – E. Porro of Italy (R. Watzl of Austria winning the so-called Intercalated Games in 1906). A. Supron of Poland won the W.Ch. in 1979 (he also won 3 silver and 1 bronze W.Ch. and Ol.G. medals). R. Wolny of Poland won the Olympic gold in 1996;

in the welterweight (up to 74kg) category the first officially recognized world champion was F. Altroggen of Germany (1910). The most outstanding wrestlers in this category were A. Kolesov (world and Olympic champion in the 1962-65 period) and V. Igoumenov (1966, 1967 and 1969-71) – both of the USSR;

in the middleweight (up to 82kg) category the first W.Ch. was won by S. Ahlquist of Denmark (1904) and the first Olympic champion was F. Martensson of Sweden (1908), although V. Weckmann of Finland, the winner of the 1906 Intercalated Games, is often deemed the first official Olympic champion. Other renowned wrestlers in this category include the following world and Olympic champions: A. Grönberg of Sweden (1948, 1950, 1952), G. Karthozya of the USSR (1953, 1955, 1956), B. Daras of Poland (world champion in 1985 and 1986) and P. Farkas of Hungary (1990-92);

in the light heavyweight (up to 90kg) category the first world champion was A. Hein of Germany (1905) and the first Olympic champion – V. Weckmann of Finland (1908). The most outstanding wrestler of all times in this category was V. Rezancev who won all the W.Ch. and Ol.G. golds in the 1970-76 period. Other distinguished wrestlers include M. Bullman of Germany (1989-92) and A. Malina of Poland (world champion in 1986);

in the heavyweight (up to 100kg) category, which was included in the international events program in 1969, the most outstanding wrestler was N. Balboshin – world and Olympic champion in the 1973-74 and 1976-79 periods. Other distinguished wrestlers in this category are A. Wroński (the 1988 and 1996 Olympic champion as well as the 1994 world

champion) and R. Wrocławski (the 1982 world champion);

in the super heavyweight (over 100kg) category, which has been included in the Olympic program since 1896, the first Olympic champion was K. Schumann of Germany and the first world champion – R. Arnold of Austria (1904). Other outstanding fighters in this category were the following world and Olympic champions: I. Kozma of Hungary (1962, 1964, 1966-68), A. Tomov of Bulgaria (1971, 1973-75), A Karelin of the USSR (later CIS) (1988-92).

After the new division into weight categories was introduced the following wrestlers became the 2000 Olympic champions: 48-54kg – Kwon Ho Sim of Korea; up to 58kg – A. Nazarian of Bulgaria; up to 63kg – V. Samurgachev of Russia; up to 69kg – F. Azcuy of Cuba; up to 76kg – M. Kardanov of Russia; up to 85kg – H. Yerlikaya of Turkey; up to 97kg – M. Ljundberg of Sweden and 97-130kg – R. Gardner of the US. P. Godlewski, *Olimpijskie turnieje zapaśnicze 1896-1996*, 1996; G. Kent, *A Pictorial History of Wrestling*, 1968; W.A. Martell, *Greco-Romano Wrestling*, 1993; W. Nowakowski & J. Grotkowski, *Zapasy klasyczne*, 1955; Consultants: Z. Ratajczak, W. Stecyk.

GRELE, also sp. *krele*. A Pol. trad. throwing game played on squares in front of inns. From the somewhat incomplete description provided by Ł. Gołębiowski in *Gry i zabawy różnych stanów* (1831) we learn that players, after a short run-up, threw wooden batons at wooden pins or poles ended with metal heads. The batons produced a characteristic clink while hitting against the metal surface and then were scattered in all directions. Gołębiowski also suggests that the game could have evolved into skittles, indicating a relationship between the name grele and Pol. term for skittles *kręgle*.

GREYHOUND RACING, a form of races, in which dogs follow a wild rabbit or hare, once real, then replaced with a mechanical device called a lure. In order to win, the dog must score more points than his competitors. Points are awarded according to various systems, e.g. 1) for getting ahead of other dogs by a distance measured in dog lengths (1-3pts.); 2) for being the first to reach the lure (1-3pts.); 3) for catching the lure in his teeth (1pt.). Dogs are categorized according to their weight and class (a 5-pt. scale – A, B, C, D, M). A dog usu. begins its career at class M, which includes novices (called maiden) or dogs that have never won a race (non-winners). Each time a dog wins a race, he climbs up in the hierarchy, until he reaches the highest possible rank – class AA. Three losses in a row cause the rank to be lowered by one class. That system has functioned in greyhound racing since 1948. A dog's racing career usu. begins at the age of 14-16 months and continues until the dog is approx. 3yrs. old. Before the start all dogs are placed in starting boxes. Race tracks are elliptical and have different lengths, depending on local tradition, but most frequently $^5/_{16}$ of a mile (503m), $^3/_8$ of a mile (604m) and $^7/_{16}$ of a mile (704m). The British Greyhound Derby is held on a 660yd. (604m) track, while Greyhound Cesarevitch is held on a 880yd. (805m) track. The longest track used for greyhound racing is 1,039yds. (950m). The dog's average speed is 60km/h. The race begins with the ringing of a bell, at which the starting boxes open automatically. Greyhound racing enjoys the greatest popularity in Eng.-speaking countries, where it is sometimes referred to as coursing or dog racing. It is always accompanied by betting.

Besides races with the use of a mechanical lure, there are also events in which dogs are tested chasing a live animal. Called open field coursing, this var. is popular in Great Britain, the USA and Australia, esp. in areas that suffer from overpopulation of wild rabbits. It is not accompanied by betting. The popularity of the sport has led to the development of a unique jargon. *Quiniela* – betting on 2 dogs of which either one may win, *perfecta* – betting on the winner and second best, or *trifecta* – betting on the first 3 dogs at finish line are just 3 examples of this.

History. Greyhound racing derives from the tradition of hunting with dogs. Originally, the basic form of verifying the dog's racing potential was testing its hunting abilities. During a hunt the dog had to catch fallow deer and later only a hare or wild rabbit. Some historians claim that greyhounds, the breed most often used for racing, developed as early as the 5th millenium BC, while according to others this did not take place until around 2000 BC. The earliest evi-

dence of greyhound breeding and their use for hunting purposes comes from the ancient Middle East. The sport was well established in Persia and Egypt, from where it was imported into Greece and Rome. During Julius Caesar's conquest of Gaul (55-54 BC) and later, during the Roman occupation of Britain (43-409), the Romans came into contact with the breeding achievements of the Celtic people and Britain became one of the major exporters of greyhounds used for racing within the Roman Empire. In the early days of his reign of Denmark and Britain (1014-1036) Kanute the Great issued an edict banning anybody below the rank of knight from greyhound racing. In medieval England, which suffered from a shortage of large animals, the use of dogs in hunting for small game developed as a popular form of competition. The democratization of greyhound racing took place against the royal will, as it was not until the reign of Elizabeth I (1558-1603) that lower social classes gained access to the sport. During the Elizabethan era Thomas Lord Norfolk provided the first written regulations of the sport. The length of track was fixed at 240yds. (219m) and the main objective was defined as the catching of the animal by the dog. Therefore, competitions could be won without the dog's biting the chased animal to death. The first events held according to new regulations took place at Kenilworth (Warwickshire) and Cowdray Park (Sussex).

In 1776 Lord Oxford established the first greyhound racing organization, Swaffham Club, which affiliated dog owners and organized races. Membership of the club was limited to 26 persons, which was to be equal to the number of letters in the Eng. alphabet. Soon other clubs followed, like the very well known Louth Coursing Society founded in 1806. An important stimulus to the popularization of greyhound breeding techniques was the book by a great admirer of the greyhound breed Rev. E.W. Barnard *The Courser's Companion and the Stud Book* (1828). In 1834 another breeder named Thacker wrote *Courser's Companion*, in which he put forward new regulations for greyhound racing, which soon became commonly adopted. In 1836 the first Eng. championships were held in Liverpool under the name of the Waterloo Cup (from the Waterloo Hotel in Liverpool, where the participants stayed for the event), which has remained the most prestigious greyhound race in Great Britain to this today. In 1858 the National Coursing Club was founded. The most famous team event was held on Salisbury plains near Stonehenge between Altcar Club and the All-World Team. The competition lasted 7 days and included several cup races in different categories.

Greyhounds were introduced into the USA at the beginning of the 19th cent. to help eradicate the rabbit pest. Along with the dogs, brought from England and Ireland, came the sport of racing.

The protests of animal rights organizations at the beginning of the 19th cent. led to efforts aimed at replacing a live rabbit with a mechanical device. The first such device was built in 1876 in Mendon, Massachusetts and consisted of a rail the length of the 450yd. (411m) track and a simulated rabbit hooked to a rope propelled along a straight track by a spinning wheel. The device was inconvenient for the spectators as it obscured the view and in 1907 O.P. Smith came up with an alternative device that moved around the circumference of the track. In the years 1909-12 the device was displayed during a series of exhibition races on temporary tracks in Tuscon, Houston, and Salt Lake City. Smith soon replaced the spinning wheel with an electric engine and the first modern lure track was opened in 1919 in Emeryville, California (some sources claim it was in Canada). Before his death in 1927 Smith founded the Greyhound Racing Association. The first elliptical track with an artificial lure was built in Great Britain in 1925 by an American, C. Munn. In 1926 the famous Belle Vue track was built in Manchester near a working class district, which contributed to the expansion of the sport's audience. By the beginning of the 1930s similar tracks were built in many Eng. and Scot. cities (in 1932 there were 187 tracks in Great Britain) and by 1939 greyhound racing became the second most popular sport in Scotland (after football). The most famous British track for greyhound racing was located on the outside of the athletic runway at the Olympic stadium in White City and was the home of the English Derby, the 2nd most prestigious event in Britain, after the Waterloo Cup. In 1927 the annual betting total of greyhound

racing in Britain exceeded £7 million. The largest tracks gathered 200-300 bookies and had an annual audience of approx. 20 million spectators. The popularity of greyhound racing in Great Britain was so great that a British MP J.H. Thomas challenged the sport in a parliamentary speech with corrupting the society and destroying the family. To meet this challenge, many tracks, beginning in 1934, estab. childcare centers, where parent-spectators could leave their off-spring for the duration of the races. Since 1925 races have also been held at night.

In the USA betting at greyhound races was illegal, which hindered the development of the sport. The first illegal betting track was opened in Hialeah in Florida (1922), then in St. Petersburg, Florida (1926), where the Gold Trophy and Derby, the leading American events, originated. The Florida tracks were legalized in 1932. Currently greyhound races are held legally in 18 American states on 51 tracks, of which 15 are in Florida and 6 in New England. The most prestigious event in the USA is the Flagler International in Miami, Florida. Other important events include the Wonderland Derby (Revere, Massachusetts), the International Derby (Raynham), and the American Derby (Taunton). In 1998 the net profit from greyhound racing in the USA was estimated at $225 million. Besides the USA and Great Britain, the sport also enjoys great popularity in Australia, particularly in New South Wales, where the first Australian track opened in 1927. The most prestigious Australian event is the Thousand, which takes

drew crowds of up to 17,000 at one event.

In the USA the governing bodies for the sport include the National Coursing Association (estab. 1906) and the American Greyhound Track Operators Association (estab. 1947), which not only organize the races, but also sponsor the Greyhound Hall of Fame, estab. in 1963 in Abilene, Kansas and modelled after other American sports. Each year the 8 best American greyhounds are selected, forming a sort of an All-American team. Another influential American organization is the Texas Greyhound Association. In Great Britain The National Greyhound Owners Club was initiated in 1998 by Mark and Martina Sullivan, dog owners from Sutton (Surrey). The growing popularity of the sport led to many greyhounds that ended their racing career being put to sleep or left without care due to the exorbitant cost of their upkeep. The situation became scandalous in the 1970s and 1980s. Cynological insitutions estimate that 20,000 greyhounds were killed in the USA in the 1990s. The media started showing dramatic footage of inhumane treatment of unwanted dogs. In the 1980s 143 cases of dogs being left tied to trees outside farms were reported, of which 70 ended in the dog's death. That figure includes only the recorded cases, which were presented in the media. Another form of inhumane treatment of retired dogs was the ritual killing with the use of electrical devices during social gatherings to commemorate the dog's successes. This led to the establishing of various animal rights institutions, such as Greyhound

Action from the Greyhound meeting at Brighton and Hove Dog Track in Hove, England.

place in Hobarth (Tasmania). Greyhound racing is winning over more and more fans in Canada, Columbia, Mexico and some Eur. countries, such as Spain, Portugal, Italy, and Finland.

One of the most famous greyhounds in history was Czarina, which belonged to Lord Oxford and which never lost any of the 47 races she ran. Her owner died as a result of excitement caused by her last race, in which she won against Maria. Among the leading greyhound breeders in 1890-1905 were G.F. and C.T. Fawcet from Saughall (Cheshire). T. Wright, who worked for the Fawcets as a trainer, led many dogs to victory at the Waterloo Cup, among them Fabulous Fortune (1896), Fearless Footsteps (1900, 1901), Farndon Ferry (1902), Father Flint (1903). After WWII the best breeder was P. Belgrave Lucas, whose dogs Lifeline and Latin Lover won the Waterloo Cup in 1949 and 1964, and on several occasions came 2nd or 3rd. The best known greyhound in the 1930s was the Irish-bred Mick the Miller, which won 46 of his 61 races. The most famous Austrl. greyhound was Chief Havoc, which won 26 of his 35 races and

Pets of America, a national voluntary organization which created a data bank of responsible homesteads for retired racing greyhounds. A similar organization was formed in Canada under the name Adopt-A-Greyhound. These organizations stand against the exclusively commercial use of dogs, particularly the mass killing of greyhounds whose racing career has ended.

Once the favorite pet of pharaohs and kings, in modern-day America the greyhound is merely the means to an end for an intrinsically cruel and unnecessary form of gambling. In dog racing, there is only one ultimate goal: profit. And when the graceful greyhounds don't meet that need, most are expendable. Some are placed as pets, but many must be killed – to the tune of up to an estimated 20,000 each year. The 'fortunate' ones are killed humanely. Other become documented horror stories. But thousands disappear to fates unknown.

Greyhound racing in literature and arts. The sport has been a popular subject in the arts for centuries. The Roman poet Ovid has compared Apollo's chasing of his beloved Daphne to a greyhound's chasing of a hare:

246
G WORLD SPORTS ENCYCLOPEDIA

Like a hound of Gaul starting a hare in an empty field, that heads for its prey, she for safety: he, seeming about to clutch her, thinks now, or now, he has her fast, grazing her heels with his outstretched jaws, while she uncertain whether she is already caught, escaping his bite, spurts from the muzzle touching her. So the virgin and the god: he driven by desire, she by fear. He ran faster, Amor giving him wings, and allowed her no rest, hung on her fleeing shoulders, breathed on the hair flying round her neck.

The oldest treaty on greyhounds is Flavius Arrianus' *Cynegeticus* (c.150 AD). The oldest Eng. hunting treaty by Juliana de Berners, included in the *Boke of St. Albans* (1486), has the following description of a greyhound:

A Grehound shold be heeded lyke a snake, And neckyd lyke a drake, Backed lyke a beam, Syded lyke a bream, Footed lyke a catte, Tayllyd lyke a ratte.

J. Chaucer also mentions greyhounds in his Canterbury Tales:

Greyhoundes he hadde, as swifte as fowels in flight; Of prikyng and of huntyng for the hare. Was al his lust, for no cost wolde he spare.

Examples of Eng. literary works which include references to hunting with dogs or dog races abound. Among the best known is R. Surtees' (1805-64) series of hunting and sport adventures of Mr. Jorrock, which was originally printed in *New Sporting Magazine* and later published as *Jorrock's Jaunts and Jollities* (1838). A 20th cent. example is R. Dahl's *Dog Race*, a short story originally printed in *The New Yorker* and later, under the title of 'Mr. Feasey', in a book *Like You* (1953).

Edward C. Ash, *The Book of the Greyhound* (1933); H. Edwards Clarke, *The Modern Greyhound* (1949), *A Complete Study of the Modern Greyhound* (1963), *The Greyhound* (1969); H. Dalziel, *The Greyhound* (1888); *Roots of the Greyhound* publ. by Greyhound Hall of Fame, Abilene (1990); Greyhound Protection League web page.

GRIBE TALLERKEN, Dan. for 'to catch a plate'. A game of skill in which a small plate is placed on a corner of a table, so that a part of it protrudes. A player attempts to pick the plate up with his palm, turn it upside down, and then place it back on the table. The moment the plate starts falling down after being turned, the player has to catch it with his thumb.

J. Møller, 'Gribe tallerken', GID, 1997, 3, 80.

GRIBERT, a Dan. ball game belonging to the baseball family [Dan. *gribe* – to catch]. The game can be played by any number of players, usu. there are anywhere from 2 to 10 of them. Gribert consists of actually only 1 phase of the baseball game, the one in which a ball struck out in the field is supposed to be caught. The ball, usu. a rubber or tennis one, is struck with a relatively short bat of a cane-like shape (*boldtræet*). The field's length is undetermined and its width ranges 20-30m. One of the players strikes the ball out into the field and the players on the field attempt to catch it. The right to strike is determined in the course of a preliminary contest in which each of the players throws a bat over a distance of around 15m and at the same time another player, standing about 3 steps from a thrower, tries to hit the airborne bat with a ball. Each player has the right to 3 attempts. The player who wins strikes the ball out into the field and continues to do so until one of the players on the field catches the ball before it hits the ground. Then the successful catcher becomes the batter and the game continues. If, before hitting the ground, the ball crosses either of the field's sidelines, the batter loses the right to bat. The game can be modified into an easier version by allowing the catchers to catch the ball after it bounces against the ground once.

J. Møller, 'Gribert', GID, 1997, 1, 68.

GRINNE AD RÆVEN, see >GRÆSSE KO.

GRØFTEKÆLLING, Dan. for 'witch in the ditch'. A running game that requires a ditch deep enough to cover the legs of a player standing in it. One of the players, referred to as the witch in the ditch, stands in the ditch and the remaining players line up along both sides of the ditch, far enough to prevent the witch from reaching them and then they jump from one side to the other while the witch's task is to touch a jumping player. The participant who has been touched becomes the witch in the ditch.

J. Møller, 'Grøftekælling', GID, 1997, 2, 60.

GROPBALL, see >PER I GROPEN.

GROPBOLL, also *bollstå*. A Swed. var. of a game in which a ball is thrown into a row of holes in the ground. The rules of the game are similar to those employed in Dan. >BOLD I HUL.

GROSS, also *pinje gross*. A Dan. game in which a wooden peg (a *gross*), 12-15cm long, whose tips are rounded, is struck with a bat, referred to as a *grossalen*. One of the 2 teams of 2-18 players digs a hole in the ground and places the peg in it. Then, one of the 3 possible serves is executed. The first type of serve consists of flicking the gross up from the hole with a bat while players of the opposing team attempt to catch it before it touches the ground. If they succeed, the serving player is eliminated from the game and replaced by another player from the same team. If the catching team fails in their attempt, they still have a second chance: they have to throw the peg at the bat placed across the hole. If they succeed in hitting the bat, the result is the same as if they had succeeded at their first attempt. A round continues until each player of a serving team has executed a serve and the last of them has been eliminated from the game. Then the teams change. The second type of serve consists of tossing the peg and striking it with the bat into the playing field. The distance reached by the gross is counted; if the server manages to flick the peg up 3 times with a bat before striking it into the field, the points are doubled. This time, the catchers are not supposed to catch the airborne peg; instead they pick it from the ground and throw it back towards the hole, defended by the server. If the peg lands in the hole or close to it (within a distance shorter than the length of the bat), the server is out of the game. In the third type of serve, the peg is placed on the edge of the hole, struck lightly so that the server can catch up with it while it is airborne and then strike it again into the field. The object of the defending team is to catch the airborne peg and then the game continues as in the first type of serve. The 3 types of serve are usu. employed gradually. The second type is used after a player has won the first one, and the third – after a successful serve of the second type. The game belongs to a larger family of similar games, such as Dan. >JEP, Pol. >KLIPA and >SZTEKIEL, Arab. >AL-BA' 'A, Pak. and Ind. >GULLI DUNDA, Bret. *mouilh*, Fr. >PILAOUET, and Eng. >TIP-CAT.

J. Møller, 'Gross (Pinje-Gross)', GID, 1997, 1.

GUDU, a Ceyl. var. of a game in which a stick with sharpened tips is struck out into the field. The rules are similar to those applied in Pak. and Ind. >GULLI DUNDA (*gulli danda, gilli danda, danda gulli*). Substantial similarities can be noticed in equipment and certain terminology. A longer stick, about 60-70cm, used for striking out a shorter one, is referred to, as in India and Pakistan, as a *danda*. The shorter stick, approx. 12cm, whose tips are sharpened, is called a *kuttiy'a* (in India and Pakistan – *gilli* or *gulli*). However, the games differ in some substantial respects. In Ceylon, the serving strike is executed after tossing the kuttiy'a from the hand, so that it can be hit with the danda. After a single game, the kuttiy'a is not returned to its original position; instead, players from the same team continue on the next game from the place where the kuttiy'a came to rest until all of them have had their chances. Only the opposing team starts the next round from the original serving area. If all the players from one team have executed their serves correctly in a given round, the opponents have to follow a certain procedure in order to gain the right to serve. One after another, they have to run from the place where they are standing to the hole marking the starting point of the game, without taking a breath. In order to prove they are not cheating, they have to repeat, 'Gudu-gudu-gudu…' all the way to the starting point. A player who chokes or stops repeating 'gudu' even for the briefest moment, loses and the team that had the right to serve so far, continues to do so but instead of renewing the game from the starting point, they begin from the point where the kuttiy'a came to rest after the last strike. This means that during the next attempt to win the right to serve, the catchers will have to cover a longer distance without taking a breath.

GUFA, also sp. *guffa, kufa* and in Eng. *goofa, goofah*, and *koofah* [Arabic *guffah* – a basket]. A large round or oval boat made of wicker, used since ancient times in Mesopotamia for transportation and sometimes for racing. It is propelled with a long paddle held with two hands by a paddler who stands at the bow dipping the paddle alternatingly on the left and right-hand side in order to keep the course.

GUGAHAWAT, also known in various Amerind. languages as *kakwasethi*, *ohonistuts*, and *oomatashia*; called >SHINNY by Eur. settlers and ethnographers as it reminded them of Ir. >SHINTY. Other sports bearing some similarity to this Native Amer. Indian sport include >FIELD HOCKEY and >ICE HOCKEY, esp. when gugahawat was practiced on ice in wintertime (though without skates). J.B. Oxendin, an Amer. sports historian, postulates that Amerind. games of the gugahawat type may well have influenced the development of today's >HOCKEY, although other specialists do not support this view. Games such as gugahawat had numerous varieties and were popular with tribes from the Atlantic coast to the Pacific, and from Canada to the southern borders of the Great Plains. The game was played mostly by children and youths, as well as by women, a fact that often escapes the awareness of historians used to dealing with Eur. women's sports. In his 19th cent. description, ethnographer E.T. Denig, claimed that in the Assiniboin tribe in Montana the game was practiced by all the members of the community. L.L. Meeker, when portraying games of Sioux Oglala in 1901, observed that 'shinny', as he referred to the game, was played by women and older boys and girls. One campsite challenged the other and although the game was not quite up to men's dignity, it was rarely limited to females only (*Bulletin of the Free Museum of Science and Art*, Philadelphia, 1901). However, Oglala males played much rougher matches compared to females' ones, which we learn from J.R. Walker's report dated 1905 in which the ethnographer depicts the male version of the game as 'more brutal but also more sportive'. He also observed that women's teams never play against men's. Another ethnographer, S. Culin, noted that the Makah tribe from the N-W Pacific coast played 'shinny' to celebrate a successful whale hunt.

Equipment. The sticks preserved in regional and ethnographic museums are usu. curved at the lower end, like the ones used in today's >SHINTY, and the curved blades widen and become flatter at the end, similarly to golf clubs, although gugahawat sticks are much larger. Old photographs indicate, however, that there were exceptions to such a shape. In a photo dated 1910, taken in Miller or Pierre in S. Dakota, sticks used by female players are nearly identical with the ones employed in today's field hockey, i.e. the end is not flattened. Average stick length was 36in. (approx. 91.5cm). Some sticks had a handle finished with a ball in order to facilitate player's control. Most of the preserved sticks are adorned with colored paintings or carvings representing animals, faces, landscapes, or geometric figures, esp. circles. Balls differed in size from one tribe to another and from one area to another. The smallest were about the size of a golf ball, whereas the largest exceeded modern basketballs in their dimensions. Also the building materials varied. In eastern N.America, as well as on the Great Plains, balls made from the skin of young goats were most popular. (Buffalo skin was never used, as it was too thick and too heavy.) The leather bag was filled with dried plants and then sewn with 1 or 2 central round seams running around in order to achieve a shape closest to that of a sphere. Some balls, e.g. used by the Penobscot, Sac, or Fox tribes, resembled leather sacs with ears made of leather straps sewn in between sheets. The ears were used to hang a ball on a peg after the game. A lot of effort was put into embroidering all kinds of decorations on the balls. According to one amateur ethnographer, at the end of the 19th cent. the Mohave tribe used to make the buckskin cover exactly the same way it was done when producing baseballs, although Indian balls were 'smaller and neater' and sticks 'trimmer and nicer'. In other regions balls were carved of solid wood or sometimes of bone. Like in traditional >LACROSSE, the wooden balls were made of knots, which made them exceptionally hard and resistant. There are also reports mentioning balls made of pumpkin, but these were likely decorative in character and were prob. only used during ceremonies preceding the actual match, rather than during the game itself.

The playing field was usu. a square whose sides measured about 200-300yds. (180-270m), but on some occasions the pitch was larger, e.g. the Mono

tribe, living in the area which is today's Modera County, played their matches on a field covering the space between 2 neighboring villages, around 7½mi. (12km) long. In winter, esp. in the Great Lakes region, matches were played on ice, though no skates were used. Such 'ice gugahawat' matches are still played by the Innu people from the Montagnais tribe in S Quebec. During such ice games players used sticks closely resembling modern hockey sticks. The goals were around 10-20ft. (3-6m) wide and were sometimes adorned like the sticks and balls. Some tribes did not use goals at all and the team that succeeded in placing the ball behind the line marking the end of the field scored a point. In yet other tribes, goals were marked with animal skins, or later with blankets, onto which the ball was supposed to be placed.

Course of the game. The game was played between 2 teams whose lineup ranged from 10 to over 100 players. The ball was placed in a deep whole in the ground in the middle of the field. At the command of an elder, who performed the role of referee, 2 representatives of opposing teams started to fight for the ball, picking it out of the hole and then passed it to their teammates. In some tribes, the referee used to start the match by throwing the ball up. Each team was usu. divided into defenders who guarded their goal and attackers, who were usu. more numerous. The ball could not be touched with the hands or arms. From the longest preserved description of the game, provided at the end of the 19th cent. by E.T. Denig and reporting a match played by the Assinboin people from the state of Montana, we learn that before the game each player had to ante up a shirt, arrows, shells, feathers, blankets, or any other tradable item to be placed in a kitty close to the middle of the playing field in care of 3 or 4 elders. After that, goals are constructed of poles and located at a distance of ¾ mile (about 1.2km) and the game consists of hitting the ball with sticks towards the poles which form the goal of the opposing team. Players strip down to their moccasins and hip sashes, paint their bodies, and line up along the lateral sides of the field, each player holding a 3½ft.-long stick curved at the end. The ball is cast in the air in the center of the course and struck by one of the players immediately upon touching the ground. Once the game commences, each party attempts to place the ball between the poles of the opponent's goal, and the winning team is the one succeeding in 2 out of 3 runs. If the players are well selected, the game can be quite amusing and, as the author put it, 'some splendid specimen of foot racing can be seen'. But should a player injure another with his stick, be it intentionally or inadvertently, a general brawl is embarked upon. Assuming, however, that the game is played with proper spirit and humor, the booty is finally handed by the elders over to the winning team.

G.C. Baldwin, *Games of the American Indian*, 1969; A. Taylor-Cheska, 'Ball Game Participation of North American Indian Women', *Her Story in Sport*, R. Howel, ed., 1982; M. Gridley, *American Indian Women*, 1974; J.B. Oxendine, *American Indian Sports Heritage*, 1988.

GUI KHEE, a Mong. game played by the tribe of Zakczyns with the use of a small piece of wood. Two teams sat in a yurt forming a circle, with their legs forward and knees bent, making thus a kind of corridor in which a chip of wood was passed. The team in possession of the wooden chip passed it from player to player under their knees in an inconspicuous manner. At some point the chip was stopped, although players kept on imitating movements as if it were still being passed in order to mislead to other team whose task was to guess who held the chip.

I. Kabzińska-Stawarz, *Games of Mongolian Shepherds*, 1991.

GUJ-BOZI, a trad. Taj. game played on horseback, resembling modern >POLO, although differing in the mallets, which are diagonal. A characteristic part of the players' outfit is embroidered leather pants. A regional var. of the game is >SOWORIGUJ. The goal is made of 2 poles stuck in the ground and the horses used by the players are small and nimble Pamir ones. As guj-bozi originates from the area close to the birthplace of polo – a point where the borders of Tibet, India, Pakistan, and Tajikistan converge, at the foot of the Himalayas and Tien Shan – its provenance is prob. the same as that of >PULU, which gave birth to polo.

GULLI DUNDA, also *gulli danda*, Pak. and Hindi for 'stick and bat'. Other var. of the name are also in use, such as *gilli danda, gulli danda, danda guli*. An Asian game, whose var. are practiced in India, Pakistan, and Sri Lanka, in which a small stick with sharp tips is struck out into the field with a larger bat. A Ceyl. variety of the game is >GUDU. A game can be competed in singles, between teams, as well as between a team and a single player. In a team-vs.-team game the number of members is not fixed but the teams have to be equal. The size and shape of the playing field is not determined either. The equipment used during the game consists of a *danda* (or *dunda*) – a bat whose length (12-18in., i.e. around 45-60cm) and diameter (1-1½in., i.e. about 2.5-4cm) vary depending on player's age and skill; and a *gulli* (or *gilli*) – a stick 4-6in. (10-15cm) long and about 1in. (2.5cm) thick. Both sticks are usu. made of the same type of wood. The gilli has both ends sharpened, whereas the danda – only one. An important element in the game is an elongated hole in the ground, referred to as a *khutti* (or *guchhi*), around 3-4in. (7.5-10cm) long, about 1½in. (less than 4cm) wide, and about 1in. (2.5cm) deep. Gulli dunda does not have a codified set of rules, therefore local versions are numerous.

Rules of the game. Before the actual match, each team determines the order of its players, by placing the gulli across the elongated hole in the ground and flicking it up with the use of a dunda. Those players who succeed in having the gulli make the greatest number of spins in the air win the first positions. When the order of players has been determined, the gulli is placed across the khuti again and the first player puts a bat underneath and strikes it as far as possible. When the gulli spins in the air and bounces against the ground (i.e. when it is still in motion), the opposing player (or players), standing at a certain distance facing the batter, attempt to catch it. If they succeed, the batter either gives up his position to the opponent – in singles, or is exchanged for a teammate – in team matches. If the gulli is not caught, the batter places his dunda across the hole in the ground and the opponents (or the opponent) have the right to throw the gulli, from the point where it came to rest, at the batter's dunda or into the khutti. If they succeed, i.e. if the gulli even brushes the batter's dunda or falls into the hole, the batter loses his position. If they fail, the batter places the gulli across the hole again, but this time he first strikes it lightly so that it only 'jumps' and then, when airborne, the gulli is batted again as far into the field as possible. The procedure is repeated until the batter loses his position. Each successful strike at the gulli into the field scores 1 point for the player or team at bat. In some var. of the game, if the batter is eliminated after the first strike, he has the right to 3 more bats. At the first attempt, the batter can touch the gulli and place it in a position most convenient for a strike; in 2 remaining attempts, he has to bat it to the position in which it was found. Should a batter miss when striking at the gulli, the attempt is considered as failed. In some local var., after 3 such attempts a batter is always exchanged for another player and the number of successful attempts is scored to his account. In other varieties, if all 3 attempts were successful, a batter can continue until he fails. Such a rule is usu. followed during a match of a single player against a team, in order to provide both parties with equal opportunities, which of course implies the opposing team does not have such a right. In all versions, however, a batter who fails all 3 attempts is out of the game. The scoring and the methods of measuring distances differ from place to place, too (the farthest bats carry the gulli at a distance of about 100m). If the gulli returned by catchers misses the batter's dunda and the khutti, the batter's team (or the batter alone) scores the so-called *annas*. One anna equals the length of a dunda. The winning team then demands a number of annas roughly equal to the number of dunda lengths covering the distance between the khutti and the place where the gulli came to rest after a bat. The opposing team can either accept the demand or not. In the latter case, the distance (in straight line) between the khutti and the gulli is measured with a dunda. If the measurement indicates the number that was demanded, points are scored and the game continues. If, however, there is a disparity, the batter is out of the game. The winner is the team (or player) which scores the greatest number of annas.

History. Based on the testimonies that have survived, such as drawings and references in the ancient literature of India, we can deduce that gulli dunda is around 5,000yrs. old. It cannot be disproved that it could have been brought to Europe by migrating Indo-Eur. tribes, giving birth to such games as Pol. >KLIPA and >SZTEKIEL, Eng. >NORTHERN SPELL and >TIP-CAT, Fr. >PILAOUET.

J. Arlott, 'Gulli Danda', OCSG, 1975, 412-414; M. Abdul Wajid, *Game of Gulli Dunda. Folk Game of Pakistan*.

GULLY, an Eng. var. of >TOPS in which at least 2 tops were used. The game was held within a zone referred to as a *gully*, which was usu. a street manhole cover or a flagstone. One of the players started to spin a top at a certain distance from the gully, attempting to direct the top towards the other player's top, in order to force it to enter the gully. If the attempt failed, the first player snatched the spinning top in one hand, using a special grip with 2 fingers, and threw it towards the opponent's top. This was repeated as long as the player was able to maintain the top spinning. If a top was spinning too slowly to snatch, it could be tipped with a finger, which was referred to in players' jargon as 'kissing'. This technique was forbidden among certain groups as making the competition too easy. If a player succeeded in driving his opponent's top into the gully, he had the right to attempt to destroy that top by taking out its peg. There were numerous ways to proceed, the most popular being an attempt at hitting the opponent's top from above while driving one's own top into its upper flattened part to destroy it as if using a wedge. If that did not bring the expected result, the winner had the right to throw the opponent's top against a wall 3 times. If the top was still in one piece, other players proceeded with further attempts. A player who succeeded in dismantling a losing opponent's top so that the peg fell out, could keep that part as a highly valued prize.

A.B. Gomme, 'Gully', TGESI, 1894, I, 186-7.

Afghan men play a variety of gulli dunda in Kandahar.

GUNGAWA WRESTLING, popular in Nigeria and famous for the elaborate ritual accompanying it:

> *A lone drummer comes to the center of the wrestling area to call the people to view the matches. After a few minutes he is joined by two other drummers. The drummers alternate rhythms in a joyful match of their own. [...] One wrestler begins the group dancing which follows. Slowly other dancers join the group. Eventually a few women join the dancing. They usually add a further element of sexual playfulness to the dance. The dancing increases in complexity as time passes. The drummers drink freely of millet beer and their rhythms become incredibly intricate. After one hour or so, the wrestling is ready to begin. The only person who dances for the entire period is the chief wrestler. During this period the priest may be conducting protective magic-making for his wrestler-patron.*

F.A. Salamone, 'Gungawa Wrestling as an Ethnic Boundary Marker', SSB, 1974, 3.

GUNG-DO, a Kor. var. of archery whose traditions date back to the early Middle Ages, when it formed one of the fundamental skills taught to the military elites [Kor. *gung* – a bow + *do* – ethical behavior, truth, and spirituality]. The art of gung-do was not

G

WORLD SPORTS ENCYCLOPEDIA

viewed solely as a physical skill, as it served also, if not first and foremost, to develop spiritual and leadership features. Owing to that, bowmen of the kingdom of Shilla (57 BC-935 AD), and then their Kor. successors, were head and shoulders above their neighbors not only in the technique they mastered but also in tactical competence and tenacity in combat. The unsurpassed skills of Kor. bowmen were duly noted by an ancient Chin. historian, Chi'en Shou (233-297 AD). Such an opinion was corroborated by the Shilla archers during the battle of

Gurdi altxatzea.

Hwant-san (660 AD) which was a decisive moment in the fall of the kingdom of Baeg-che and the process of unifying the Three Kingdoms. During the battle, the ruler of Shills, Kim Yu-sin – an outstanding bowman himself – defeated Baeg-che soldiers with his 50,000 Hwarangs (soldiers trained according to the rules of the Hwarang-do, an ancient Kor. school of martial arts). Their role in this battle could be compared to the one attributed to famous Eng. longbowmen in the battle of Agincourt under Henry V in 1415. Other famous bowmen were also Chu Mong – the founder of the kingdom of Koguryo; Wang-gon – the founder of the Koryo dynasty (the one that gave its name to Korea); and I Song-kye – the founder of the Chosun dynasty.

Box aerobics.

GUOGUIPO, a folk game resembling >FIELD HOCKEY, practiced among the Chin. Li minority. The basic equipment includes wooden L-shaped sticks and a ball of unspecified size made from coconut leaves. The ball must be spherical and hard enough to survive being hit by the sticks. A stubble field often functions as a playing area for 2 teams of 5 players each. Points are scored by driving the ball beyond the opposing team's back line. The team that scores more points within a designated time wins the game. A humorous tradition that accompanies the game is that the losing team must carry the winners from the field to the village. Mu Fushan et al., 'Guoguipo (Li Style Field Hockey)', TRAMCHIN, 86.

Stretching.

GURDI ALTXATZEA, also *orga jokua*. A Basq. folk sport in which a 2-wheel cart, or a set of 2 wheels and a shaft taken from a 4-wheel cart, is lifted and carried over a certain distance. Its Span. equivalent is *levantamiento de carreta* (cart lifting). While a cart is being turned, neither of the wheels can touch the ground. A lifter attempts to turn the cart along the circle whose center is marked by the shaft's far end, propped on the ground. In order for an attempt to be considered successful, the wheels have to be carried over a distance of at least 4m. The winner is the participant who manages to carry the wheels over the longest distance. R. Aguirre, 'Gurdi altxatzea', GHJD, 1986, III, 106.

GURDION, see >FION.

GUTS, a game in which a >FLYING DISC is used. A match can be played between singles and two 5-player teams. Players stand facing each other at a distance of about 14m and alternate throwing a flying disc with one hand as strongly as possible in order to make it difficult for the opponent to catch it, following, however, the rules of a proper throw at all times. A disc can be caught with either one or both hands. A point is scored when the opponent fails to intercept a well-thrown airborne disc. An incorrectly executed throw, e.g. when the disc's trajectory is out of the opponent's reach, scores a point in favor of the opposing team (or an opposing single player). A match is usu. played until either party scores 15pts. There are at least 2 var. of guts:

FLUTTER GUTS, in which a disc can be intercepted with only one hand and must not be trapped against the body. A distance between a pair of players is substantially shorter, only 2-3m. Only so-called soft throws are allowed. The preferred type of throws is a spinning throw which makes it more difficult for the rival to catch the disc. The scoring system is the same as in the main variety.

STUBBY GUTS, in which 2 teams stand facing each other at a distance of approx. 14m and each player has an empty, stubby beer bottle standing in front of him and a full one behind. Each thrower attempts to knock down the empty bottle standing in front of the opponent, like in skittles. If a throw is successful, a thrower has the right to take a mouthful of beer from the full bottle located behind him. Taking a mouthful of beer is also a player's reward when he succeeds in intercepting a particularly difficult throw, the so-called 'caught in the full', or when the defender disturbs an otherwise successful throw by, for example, shielding the target with his own body. The most spectacular type of throw is the 'hammer' after which a disc glides a few centimeters above the ground, almost touching it, which makes it more difficult to catch the disc and easier to hit the empty bottle. Another var. stemming from the original guts is butt-guts which, although organizationally independent, has not been officially recognized yet.

History. The beginnings of guts are unknown but some researchers (J. Townes) claim it is a soft version of circular saw blade throw – a hazardous activity performed some time ago by a group of Amer. college students with nothing better to do. The rules of the game were given a definite and formal shape in 1975, when the Guts Players Association was established in the USA.

Description of All the Official Discs Sports, Internet: http://www.afda.com; J. Townes, 'Flying Disc', *Encyclopedia of World Sport*, D. Levinson & K. Christensen, eds., 1996, vol. I.

GÜÜNII URS GARGAKH IOS, a Mong. holiday of milk mares. The holiday was held in summer and it was related to one of the most important elements of Mong. culture, i.e. the drinking of *kumys* – mare's milk. The ritual was accompanied by a kumys drinking competition, which turned into a separate competition event performed on various occasions, particularly during the kumys holiday >YSYECH.

GWINTRAN AR SARC'H, also *ar sarc'h*. A Bret. var. of weight lifting competition practiced in the neighborhood of Tréguier. Its Fr. equivalent is *le sac* or *l'arraché du sac* – sack snatching. It consists of lifting a sack filled with sand and putting it on one's back. Each contestant can make 3 attempts. F. Peru, 'La tradition populaire de jeux de plein air en Bretagne', LJP, 1998.

GYM-DANCE, a term proposed by a Pol. teacher of artistic gymnastics and sports dances, Olga Kuźmińska, to refer to a group of exercises and artistic forms of sport based on both gymnastic exercise and dancing [in Pol. *gim-taniec*]. According to Kuźmińska the beginning of gym-dance could be observed in the development of jazz gymnastics (see >JAZZ GYMNASTICS) and >AEROBICS. These forms gave birth to a large group of other similar activities that employed an attractive blend of physical exercise and dance. Kuźmińska groups such activities into primary forms that include conventional aerobics and its direct derivatives, break dance, and 2 other forms bordering on dance and recreational gymnastics:

CALLANETICS, a system of exercises improving one's figure, developed by Callan Pinkney, whose principle is to repeat a series of drills that focus on shaping particular groups of muscles that are re-

sponsible for the figure and esthetic appearance, esp. neglected ones.

STRETCHING, a set of stretching exercises used either as a separate activity or as an element introducing and closing an aerobics session.

The second group of gym-dances comprises a number of general exercising activities, practiced usu. without any equipment, such as:

ABDO FESS, a system of exercises aimed at strengthening and firming up the muscles of the abdomen and buttocks [*fess* – in Eng. slang is a jocular term for buttocks, borrowed from heraldic *fess point* – the central point of a heraldic shield].

BODY WORK, a term referring, among others, to general dancing exercises practiced to rhythmic music played during a session.

BODY SCULPT, a system of exercises aimed at 'sculpting one's body' in order to make it more attractive.

KIDS, a combination of aerobic exercises whose level of difficulty and attractiveness are intended to be appropriate for children. Cf. SENIOREN below.

POWER SCULPT, a system of exercises designed to improve the power of muscles by means of using various weights.

SENIOREN, a group of aerobic exercises whose level of ease and attractiveness are intended for persons advanced in years.

TONE, also *tone up*. A set of rhythmic exercises practiced in order to improve the attractiveness of one's body, esp. upper limbs, by means of light contractions of muscles with the use of 0.5-2kg dumbbells.

TOTAL BODY, a system of exercises that are selected and prepared in order to affect the entire body, viewed as a single unit, in a versatile way.

WALK, simple aerobic exercises, practiced while walking to the rhythm of music.

Another group of gym-dances comprises those activities that employ various gymnastic and sports equipment:

BODYBUILDING, a form whose name has been borrowed from >BODY BUILDING, although its traditions stem from aerobics. It employs various body-building exercises and equipment typically used during such activities.

BOX, a system of exercises based on the movements characteristic of >BOXING, i.e. jumping and swinging the arms in imitation of a fight, holding small dumbbells.

FIT BALL, a system in which a rubber ball is used to drill specific parts of body, esp. the buttocks, spine, and abdomen. Performers place a given part of their body on a ball and try to balance on it.

FUNKY, physical exercise dominated by elements of dance to the rhythm of funk music.

FUNKY STEP, a simple system of aerobic exercises practiced with the use of a step to the rhythm of funk music. See also >AEROBICS, subentry AEROBICS WITH A STEP.

PUMP, in which rhythmic movements against the resistance of a light weight are performed.

SPINNING, a var. of recreational exercise performed to rhythmic music on a special ergonometric bicycle equipped with gears that change the resistance of pedals, which allows a performer to modify the effort while keeping time with the beat.

A final group of particularly dynamic gym-dances comprises activities dominated by elements of dancing, such as:

AFROBICS, see >AEROBICS.

BRASILIAN, a system of exercises with the prevalence of elements borrowed from Brazilian dances and music.

EASY FUNK, a simple set of exercises with the use of funk rhythms as the background.

HIGH LOW, a combination of exercise with the prevailence of dancing to a changing rhythm, from slow to fast, up to 140 beats per min.

LATIN, a system of exercises employing a number of movements borrowed from Latin-Amer. dances.

LOW IMPACT, exercises dominated by dancing elements to the rhythm of approx. 124 beats per min.

The growing number of gym-dances comprises also such var. as: generally developing *becken-boden*, *casy-funk*, *gym-dos*, and *rucken*; exercises with the use of *in-line* equipment; and those dominated by dancing elements such as *hip-hop*, *hip-hop funk*, etc. As the number of combinations is growing, mutual interdependencies are becoming blurred and their product less prone to unanimous classification. O. Kuźmińska, 'Dynamiczny rozwój form tańca gimnastycznego', *Kultura Fizyczna*, 1998, 9-10..

GYMKHANA, 1) an equestrian festival combined with a display of horse riding skills; 2) a place where the festival is held; 3) a local sports holiday organized e.g. by schools, colleges, etc.; 4) a form of >AUTOCROSS or a series of events testing the driving skills, held on closed-circuit tracks which are sometimes set up on large parking areas or open fields. It is esp. popular in the USA. Contestants, who drive stock cars, must tackle a number of obstacles and stop the car in a designated area. The driver with the best time wins; 5) a similar event for motorcycle drivers. [Hindu *gendkhana* – a hall for playing esp. racket games, later also influenced by Gk. *gymnasion*].

GYMNASIA, in ancient Greece, all physical exercises perfecting the human body and performed naked; the word derives from the Gk. gymnos – naked, wherein all forms of exercise, gymnastic competitions and displays took place naked in Greece. The word gymnasia itself in Gk. meant exercising the body in general, and more particularly sporting competition, including that at games (where from time to time this word was used to refer to wrestling bouts) or training, or indeed practicing for any physical activity gymnasia were one of the basic forms of exercise used in sports and military training, which was accompanied by a range of related concepts, like *gymneteia* – the concept of nakedness as a form of demonstrating the culture of the body; *gymnasion* – the building in which exercising took place; *gymnasiarcha* – a teacher or instructor of gymnastics, etc. In Sparta a form of gymnastic display evolved, called *gymnopaidike*, which was reminiscent of a form of dancing, using movements associated with ancient sports, particularly wrestling, the pankration and also military training. The most important forms of gymnopaidike were the displays held during the *gymnopaidiai*, an annual festival celebrated in July for 6-10 days in memory of the victory of the Spartans over Argos in the so-called Battle of the 300 Heroes on the plains of Thyreatis (c.546 BC), later to honor the battles of Thermopylae (480 BC) and Leuctra (371 BC). During the course of the festival the highlight of the program was the display by the *ephebans*, which were composed of athletic and martial exercises as well as a variety of exercise of a musical-rhythmical nature performed for the Spartan elders as well as invited guests and foreigners.

GYMNASTIC ALL-AROUND, a combination of all events that are part of >GYMNASTICS, the outcome of which is determined by the scores in individual events during the same competition. In championship tournaments it includes the following events: for women – freestyle, balancing beam, asymetric bars, and vault; for men – freestyle, pommel, rings, parallel bars, high bar, and vault. During less important competitions some of these events are not included. Combination exercises are divided into mandatory and free. Until 1939 gymnastic multi-trials included also a 100m sprint, shot put, high jump or pole vault, and climbing a 7-9m rope.

GYMNASTICS, forms of exercise aiming at perfect bodily control developing out of the ancient traditions of >GYMNASIA – physical exercises and public displays performed naked in ancient Greece [Gk. *gymnos* – naked]. In modern language this name has two main meanings: 1) the group of competitive sports developed from or related to the traditions of gymnastics, such as >RHYTHMIC GYMNASTICS or Olympic gymnastics, >JAZZ GYMNASTICS; 2) physical exercises performed for purposes of health, recuperation or recreation discussed here, but also forming distinct gymnastic systems, such as >SWEDISH GYMNASTICS, >CALISTHENICS or the Japanese KEI-TAISO, later >FUTSU-TAISO.

History. The traditions of gymnastics reach back, as the name implies, to ancient Greece where a system of physical preparation developed among the ephebans – young men approaching the age of military service. They underwent a special regime, including training as part of the preparations for sporting games. The place where the young people gathered for the necessary lessons and exercises was called the *gimnasium*. The exercises carried out there were not gymnastics in the modern sense of the word, but were of a nature typical for ancient Gk. sport. More similar to today's gymnastics however were the public displays of the *ephebans* organized in many Gk. towns and termed >GYMNASIA, composed of rhythmic group displays to the accompaniment of music and song and also displays of horseriding and exercises of a military nature. In ancient Rome during military training pieces of equipment were used which are regarded as the prototypes for some of today's gymnastic disciplines, including an imitation of a horse. This exercise consisted of saddling and mounting a horse to a beat. However the Gk. and Roman traditions disappeared with the fall of the ancient Mediterranean world. It was only during the epoch of the Eur. Renaissance that certain educators, especially Ital. ones, attempted to revive the ancient traditions of bringing up young people based on the *gimnasium*. The best known undertaking of this type was the school created by V. da Feltre (1378-1446) known as the *Casa Giocosa* – the School of Joy, estab.1423. The tradition of the *gimnasium*, continued in Germany, led to the loss of the original sense of the word in the moment when J. Sturm (1507-1589) adopted the name *gymnasium* for the school he founded, which in many countries still denotes a kind of high school placing an emphasis on intellectual achievements, mainly studying Gk. and Lat., while at the same time ignoring gymnastics. As a result the modern Eur. *gymnasiums* for a long time lost their original link with physical education. The Renaissance, exploiting the experience of the ancients, introduced elements of modern didacticism to the development of gymnastics, which in relation to physical exercises was characterized by a thorough, calculated approach, which in turn formed the basis of a later conflict in gymnastic theory between those who saw it as purely a basis for physical culture with those propagating it as a sport. The development of gymnastics in Eur. schools really got underway in the second half of the 18th cent. and the early 19th cent. mainly due to the work of great teachers and physical education experts. In 1774 in Germany J. Basedow was the first to introduce gymnastics as a permanent teaching subject. The work *Gymnastics for Youth* (*Gymnastik für Jugend*, 1793) written by the Ger. J.C.F. Guts-Muths (1759-1839) is responsible for stabilizing the concept of gymnastics as an equivalent of physical education in schools. At the same time, a strong influence on the development of school gymnastics was exerted by, among others, U.A. Vieth (1763-1836), the author of *An approach to an encyclopedia of physical education* (*Versuch einer Enzyklopdie der Leibesbungen*, vol. 1-3, 1794-1818), and also the Swiss J.H. Pestalozzi (1746-1827), author of, among others, the work *On molding the body as an introduction to applying elementary gymnastics* (*ber Körperbildung als Einleitung auf den Versuch einer Elementargymnastik in einer Reihenfolge körperlicher bungen*, 1807). Of the remaining, great pioneers of modern Eur. gymnastics it is also important to mention the Swiss P.H. Clias (1782-1854), as well as F. Amorosa (1770-1848) operating in both France and Spain. All these educators, emerging from the Renaissance traditions (even though operating in their own times) based their systems on exploiting the natural movements of the human body, but aimed at separating individual movements into their component parts, so as to isolate them as a natural whole. The concept of Pestalozzi, who regarded every natural movement as a series of simple motions requiring isolating and separate training, went furthest. The research and exploits of the 19th cent. creators of Ger. and Scand. gymnastic systems went in this direction. The essence of the system created by F.L. Jahn (1778-1852) was the artificial separating out of natural human movements into individual mechanical elements, and then the creation and aesthetic elaboration of exercises perfecting individual elements of movement which did not appear in natural human movement. This artificial separation of movements into simple activities was at the same time a rationalist analysis in the spirit of the philosophy of the Renaissance as well as an equivalent of the then emerging theories of industrial technology and military ideas. These were characterized by a thought out, deliberate breaking down of activities into single elements in order to apply them more accurately whether at the behest of machines or the military. 'Industrial technology,' wrote capitalism's sternest critic of the time, Karl Marx, 'discovered [...] those few main forms of basic movement which compose all creative activity of the human body, regardless of the variety of equipment used' (*Das Kapital*). Jahn's system stipulated the carrying out of exercises with the aid of simple pieces of equipment, such as ladders, parallel bars, ropes, rings suspended from ropes, bars, and a wooden horse. All this equipment enabled the performing of movements similar to those occurring in real life, but at the same time standardized them and led to simplified imitations (e.g. the wooden horse and the related exercises as an imitation of a real saddle-horse). It was extremely impoverished, for example, in relation to the natural movements applied in, say, the middle ages, in knightly exercises or in the later English sports. Gymnastics in this understanding, nevertheless, encompassed many positive societal and philosophical values, important both for gymnastics as a future sport (which it would not develop into for over a hundred years), and also for the overall shape of the relationship of people to the surrounding reality. The logical system of exercises with equipment, in terms of physical culture, formed the first attempt on such a scale at going from exercises matching man to the demands of the environment, to adapting that environment to the needs and requirements of man. Many of the pieces of equipment used in Ger. gymnastic systems were carried over into gymnastics as a competitive sport. Another approach to gymnastics was practiced mainly in Scandinavia, disconnecting exercises from the human environment, giving up all equipment and adopting free exercises utilizing the body's 'pure' motor movements, which formed the basis for Swedish gymnastics. It was initiated by the Swede H. Pehr Ling (1776-1839), founder of the Royal Central Gymnastic Institute in Stockholm, as well as his son Hjalmar (1820-1886). A similar system was developed in Denmark by F. Nachtegall (1777-1847). The Scand. var. of gymnastics introduced logically calculated, unnatural movements into the exercises. They were needed, though, to compensate imbalances in muscle use (e.g. while at work) or conversely, to maintain the condition of those areas of the body which are underused as a result of the march of civilization and the disconnection of life from the natural movements necessitated by nature. In this way, on the one hand, gymnastics took human movement away from its natural form, while, on the other hand, it restored a civilizational imbalance. Over and above that, it enabled the cultivation of the body in all situations, and thus democratized access to physical culture through the almost total exclusion of expensive equipment, buildings and financial outlay. It also enriched bodily aesthetics and the possibilities of using new, previously unknown movement elements. The development of the institutions and therefore the organization of gymnastics took place at the turn of the 18th and 19th cent. The basis was the desire to organize healthy and moral counterbalances to the various threats of civilization. Following that it was discovered that organised gymnastic movement could be thoroughly exploited for political purposes, whether freedom fighters, nationalists or military. As early as 1805 in Denmark F. Nachtegall founded the first Military Gymnastic Institute in Eur. history. One effect of his actions was the general introduction of gymnastics to the Dan. school curriculum (1828). In such a way the Falcons gymnastic movement played an important role in integrating societies deprived of independence (Czechs, Poles, Serbs), similarly to the way the Turner movement, with a nationalistic ideology formulated by Jahn contributed to the spiritual

Kara-T-Robics.

Equestrian gymkhana.

Gymnastics.

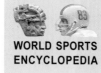

G

WORLD SPORTS ENCYCLOPEDIA

unification of scattered Ger. communities. In France the gymnastic movement played an important role in the biological and moral regeneration of the country following the defeat in the war of 1871. Gymnastics played a similar role in Austria, Switzerland, Belgium and Holland During the second half of the 19th cent. The development of organized gymnastics gathered pace. As early as 1832 the oldest Eur. society of gymnastics was created: *Eidgensische Turnverband* (ETV), which a year later organized the 1st Swiss Gymnastic Festival. In 1862 the *Falcon* (Czech *Sokol*) gymnastic movement was founded, which had a large influence on the development of similar organizations in Slavonic countries, including on Pol. soil (1867), as well as in the Balkan countries struggling for independence, especially Serbia (1882, the name *Sokol* was adopted there in 1892), and in Bulgaria where an identical organization, formed in 1878, took the name *Eagle* – Bulg. *Orel*, though slightly later there

self from sport in the Eng.-speaking understanding of the word. The longlasting isolation of gymnastics from sport also influenced its distinctly weaker growth in Ang.-Sax. countries in which sport dominated. In 1897 based on the VET the International Gymnastic Federation was created (Federation Internationale de Gymnastique, FIG), which quickly achieved a global range in terms of competitive sport (>OLYMPIC GYMNASTICS).

The existence of strong local, national and international organizations led to the enormous importance of gymnastics for the development of physical culture in the countries of continental Europe, and to a lesser, but observable degree in Eng.-speaking countries, including the USA, where gymnastics practiced for heath and aesthetic reasons is called >CALISTHENICS. This enabled parallel progress in medicine, physiology and hygiene, which in large measure found support in the gymnastic movement, initially to a degree greater than in other sports.

1859. As a division of home gymnastics is included *morning gymnastics*, and since the 1920s also radio gymnastics (see below).

Child gymnastics, dated, no longer applied term for those systems of physical education aiming at assisting in the physical and psychological development of children. The modern pioneer was the Ger. teacher J.C.F. Guts-Muths (1759-1839), author of *Gymnastics for Young People* (*Gymnastik für die Jugend*, 1793) and *Games for Strengthening the Body and Spirit for Young People* (*Spiele zur erholung der Körpers und geistes für die jugend*,1796). In Poland the first teacher concerned with training the bodies of children was J. Śniadecki (1768-1838), author of the work *On the Physical Upbringing of Children* (*O fizycznem wychowaniu dzieci*,1805). In the US, despite the dominance of sports, a strand of child gymnastics based on the Eur. systems could be detected, represented, among others, by the activities of D. Lewis, author of the work *New Gymnastics for Men, Women, and Children* (1862). As a distinct area of health activity, child gymnastics disappeared along with the development of all-encompassing adolescent physical education systems, where methods from beyond pure gymnastics are used, but from other areas founded on modern motor theory, physiology and also child psychology.

Gymnastics for hygiene, a var. of gymnastic exercises, usually systematized, popularized in the 19th cent. in order to improve the paticipants' physical condition and also to instil habits of good hygiene. The term is currently not in use. It was spread mainly by Pol. physicians like T. Jarnatowski (1832-1905), author of the manual *Hygiene, or the Science of Health* (*Higiena czyli nauka o zdrowiu*,1876) and S. Jerzykowski (1847-1927), who wrote *A treatise on the build, nourishment and care of the human body* (*Wykład popularny o budowie, pożywieniu i pielęgnowaniu ciała ludzkiego*,1874).

Infant gymnastics, a system of exercises created in the 19th cent. aimed at spreading the application of knowledge concerning the role of exercise in the child's development in the first years after birth. Taking into consideration the non-existence in those times of specialist centers, it was propagated mainly through advice manuals and popular handbooks.

Instructional gymnastics, any educational form of gymnastics that aims to physically train pupils, but also to influence their general upbringing, including moral aspects, hygienic awareness etc.

Gymnastics for health, a term coined in the 19th cent. encompassing the entirety of physical exercises whose guiding aim was improving health. In this regard, the majority of types of gymnastics, in their basic forms, constitute varieties of this. It includes gymnastics for hygiene, infant gymnastics, morning gymnastics, radio gymnastics and school gymnastics. However, certain var. of gymnastics, where health plays a role but is not one of the main aims, cannot be included, such as military, competitive or Olympic gymnastics.

Doctors in ancient times, such as Hippocrates and Gallen, already knew about the influence of physical exercise on health. The idea of influencing health through appropriately chosen exercises vanished in the Middle Ages, but was revived in the Renaissance thanks to doctors, like the Italian Girolamo Mercurialis (1530-1604 lub 1606), among others, who, in his work *De arte gimnastica* (*On the art of gymnastics*, 1601) dedicated much space to the health-giving and curative effects of physical exercise, which led to the belief that in caring for health, most effective is proper nourishment and practicing the appropriate exercises. In the course of the 18th and 19th cent. all the important Eur. gymnastic systems, such as those of J.C.F. Guts-Muths (1759--1839), J.H. Pestalozzi (1746-1827), G.U.A. Vieth (1763-1836), H. Pehr Ling (1776-1839), and in the USA, C. Beck (1798-1866), C. Esther Beecher (1800-1830), D. Lewis (1823-1888) as well as the Swedes working there, H. Nissen and N. Posse (1862-1895) and so on, contained extensive elements covering gymnastics for health. Of itself, though, gymnastics for health played a smaller role in Eng.-speaking countries, where more natural, less calculated forms of sport developed more quickly. These sports, in the course of the 20th cent., began to gradually replace the general health-giving function of gymnastics, particularly in schools, as a result of which gymnastics for health began to be limited to a curative role.

Moritz von Schwind, Gymnastics Ground, *1860, lead pencil.*

Albert Anker, The Gymnastics Hour, *1879, oil on canvas.*

also appeared a local organization calling itself the *Falcons*. The Bulg. *Falcons* competed for influence with the Gymnastic Society *Junak*, wherein the *Falcons* took on a more distinct sporting and military character, while *Junak* retained the nature of a typical gymnastic organisation. In Germany, where earlier gymnastic unions for individual regions existed, the national *Deutsche Turnerschaft* was created in 1868. Meanwhile, similar national unions arose suprisingly late in Scandinavia: in Norway (*Norges Turnforbund*, 1890), Sweden (*Svenska Gymnastikfrbundet*, 1891), and Denmark (*Dansk Turnforbund*, 1899). The dominant ideology in these societies, despite all the differences in historical circumstances and the actual political framework, was urban nationalist in all its possible varieties, from the liberationist ideology typical of the Slavic *Falcons* to the ethnic chauvinism of the *Deutsche Turnerschaft*. In the US gymnastics appeared around 1825 thanks to the Ger. emigres C. Follen, C. Beck, and F. Lieber. The first gymnastic society based on the Ger. *Turnvereinie* was founded in 1848 in Cincinatti, the first society based on the Czech *Falcons* in 1867 in St. Louis. The first teacher-training establishment providing instruction in gymnastics was the Normal College of the American Gymnastic Union (1866), currently affiliated with Indiana University. The body exercising the greatest influence on the development of gymnastics in the USA was the Amer. Amateur Union (AAU), under whose auspices the first championships were held in 1885. The foundation of the Physical Education department at Springfield College, run by the Young Mens' Christian Association (YMCA) had a large influence on the development of gymnastics in the USA (as with several other sports). The *Eur. Union of Gymnastic Societies* (*Vereinigung Europischer Turnverbnde*, VET) was created in 1881. It played a significant role in developing international gymnastic competition. Thanks to this internationally recognized rules and regulations began to gradually appear, enabling the crystallization of gymnastics as a sporting discipline, even though officially the VET distanced it-

In Asia the pioneer of gymnastics was Japan, where in the 19th cent., already under the influence of America, a Western style system was introduced called *kei-taiso*, later *futsu-taiso*. During the period of increasing militarization, gymnastics in Japan became subject to new military requirements. The relatively neutral, in this regard, 20th cent. system of school gymnastics >TAISO-KA, taught in Japan, which had developed, among others, under the influence of Amer. and Eur. teachers, was replaced in 1941 by the rigorous military system >TAIREN-KA. In China the beginnings of gymnastics are connected with the activities of PE teachers, particularly Guhwender (first name unkown) at the College of St. John in Shanghai. Over the course of several decades the power of Jap. and Chin. sporting gymnastics grew out of these traditions. A similar route, despite the ideological changes, was taken by gymnastics in Russia, later the USSR, from the fragile pioneering beginnings to later sporting dominance. In its historical development, gymnastics produced many varieties, for the most part weakly or not at all formalized, constituting a somewhat loose concept, often ephemeral or poorly defined, with many unformalized inter-dependencies between them. These varieties served widespread aims, such as health, education, hygiene, recreation, military etc. These were, in alphabetical (not chronological) order the following:

Astronaut gymnastics, or *cosmonaut gymnastics*, a var. of exercise used by astronauts during flights in order to maintain physical condition in the cramped and weightless conditions. The name was used mostly during the initial period of space flights; currently almost out of use.

Home gymnastics, a number of gymnastic exercises specially chosen to enable them to be practiced in the limited amount of space available in the home. From the very beginning of gymnastics, many of its propagators, particularly doctors, have put together popular compendiums serving the spread of home gymnastics. One of the first popularizers in Europe was a German doctor, M. Kloss, author of a handbook on the subject published in

School gymnastics, a term in some Eur. languages defining in a general way different gymnastic systems applied as part of schooling, synonymous with the concept of physical education.

Curative gymnastics, also *kinesotherapy* [<Gk. *kinesis* – movement + *therapeo* – to cure], a type of exercise aiming to restore the health of patients and convalescents, and also to prevent post-illness complications. Curative Gymnastics is mainly applied in injuries and illnesses of the motor and also respiratory system as well as in post-operative conditions where, through the appropriate amount of muscle activity, recuperative processes can be accelerated. It is also frequently applied in neurological diseases leading to muscular atrophy. The amount of exercise taken depends on the condition of the patient. The first phase consists of a series of breathing exercises followed by passive exercise, not requiring effort, then active exercising is gradually introduced and the degree of effort required slowly increased. The final phase often includes team games and movement aimed at improving both the physical and mental condition of the patients. The most frequently applied methods have been adapted from the Swed. and Ger. gymnastic systems. Currently curative gymnastics does not constitute a distinct, uniform gymnastic system, but rather draws on all var. of gymnastics and other sporting disciplines and rehabilitatory methods that can be applied in order to restore health depending on the particular type of illness or disability.

Radio gymnastics, a var. of *gymnastics for health* practiced following instructions given over the radio. Of necessity it must take into consideration the circumstances of the homes in which it was practiced. As a popular form of exercise, radio gymnastics began with the widespread ownership of radio sets in the late 1920s. Among the best known programs prior to 1939 was morning gymnastics (*Funkgymnastik*) broadcast in Germany which played a groundbreaking role in Europe (especially the LaMDo group of broadcasters from Langenberg Munster, Dortmund, and Cologne). The development of TV and the sports shown on it, the advent of >AEROBICS, as well as widely available videotapes led to the disappearance of this form of gymnastics.

Developmental gymnastics, any var. of gymnastics which aims at developing a child physically, shaping the desired physical and motor features.

Military gymnastics, a var. of gymnastics adapted to the needs of the army. As the Pol. historian of physical culture R. Wroczyński writes,

> *military gymnastics was intended to train recruits and encompassed a system of exercises which were to guarantee them the basic physical fitness necessary for combat training [...] it thus was connected, in the 19th cent., with specific changes in defence systems. This system was based on the general requirement of military service for young men and on the systematic training of reservists called to arms in times of danger. It constituted one of the elements of training, aimed at general physical fitness for coping with the rigors of military service as well as shaping particular conditioned skills [...] operating a weapon and carrying out tactical tasks. In time more and more weight became attached to disciplinary exercises, so-called drills, as directly shaping the ability to submit to the discipline so necessary during military service'*
>
> [*Powszechne dzieje wychowania fizycznego i sportu*, (*A general history of physical education and sport*, 1979), 169]

The term was coined by H.P. Ling (1776-1839), who also put together the relevant manual for the needs of the Swed. military. In 1805 in Denmark F. Nachtegall founded the first Military Gymnastic Institute in Europe. The concept was adopted by most Eur. countries, but particular emphasis was placed on it in the Prussian army, where A. Spiess (1810-1858) laid the foundations. In France the pioneer was an educator, exiled from Spain, F. Sotelo Amoros y Ondeana (1770-1848), Director of the Paris Military Academy after 1818. In E Europe it was most highly developed in Poland after 1918. One of the leading lights in this respect was Sikorski (1876-1940), founder of the Central Military Academy of Gymnastics and Sport in Poznań, the first of its kind in E Europe, which operated in Poznań between 1921-1926 and later became part of the State Institute of PE in Warsaw (presently the Warsaw Academy of Physical Education). The collapse of the major totalitarian systems, particularly the mainstay of military gymnastics that was the 'Prussian' element of the Ger. army up to the end of WWII, speeded up the decline of military gymnastics. The parallel changes in the requirements of modern armies gradually decreased the significance of military gymnastics particularly as more natural and attractive forms of sport, especially team sports, began to play a larger role in the physical preparation of soldiers, which the US army was heading towards prior to 1939. An ever increasing role in specialized sports training was played by martial arts, or – as in the case of the Israeli army – >KRAV MAGA. The remnants of military gymnastics survive only in more poorly developed armies more as a method of disciplining soldiers than as an actual factor in physical education.

GYÔGGU, also *gyeokgu*; and old Chin. game similar to >POLO, also popularized and developed in the Middle Ages in Korea under the same name. The Jap. equiv. is >DAKYU. The description of the game can be found in Sok-mo Hok's work *Dongkuksesigi* (1849). The playing field's size was rigorously determined. The earliest available information about the ball describes it as a wooden sphere covered with leather. According to the reconstructions made by Kor. historians of sport on the basis of available drawings, the sticks, up to 90cm long, were also made of wood and ended in a kind of curved spoon about 9cm long. Players used to ride small horses, resembling today's ponies (in Korea, normal horses were used). In China, horses' tails were either cut, or plaited and then rolled up. Players' costumes varied depending on the country and age. As far as the equipment is concerned, the differences were substantial between the ruling periods of each dynasty. In the course of the Koryo dynasty, players wore rather luxurious and decorative suits, whereas during the rules of the Chosons the apparel was rather modest by comparison.

History. The earliest available reference to gyôggu dates back to 918 AD. Kor. historians believe, however, the game's origins go even further back in time. Koo-Chul Jung maintains that the game was brought from the Chin. kingdom of Tang to Korea at the twilight of the Shilla state, i.e. around the 8th cent. AD. Though the first historical reference to Kor. polo is also dated 918 AD, we can assume that at that time the game was already quite popular throughout the country, which would suggest it had been introduced earlier, a hypothesis that is borne out by an analysis of the fragments of historical accounts available and the political background of the times. In September of 918 a reception for a Chin. general was held on polo grounds in Gekyung, a place which the king – himself a Gekyung citizen – established as the capital. Up until that moment, Gekyung had been but a small municipality. The historian muses as to whether the very first investment carried out in the newly declared capital could possibly have been a polo playing field. Consequently, he concludes that it is much more probable that the field had been constructed in Gekyung prior to 918 AD and that polo was a sport quite popular with the local aristocracy well before that date.

The game was among the favorite aristocratic pastimes during the Koryo reigns (918-1392). The sport's fortune was, however, rather capricious as it was opposed by Confucianists. Whenever they gained in influence, they sought to prohibit the game as socially noxious. Such efforts were then ignored when representatives of other intellectual orientations and who supported gyôggu rose to power.

In 982, chancellor king Tchoi, who was Confucianist, proposed to have the game prohibited unconditionally by law. He justified his proposal with the fact that during various Buddhist holidays thousands of monks slipped out to polo playing fields. Since monks did not keep horses, it is likely he did not mean the mounted gyôggu, but rather an offshoot closer to modern >FIELD HOCKEY, and known later as >TAGU. Particularly vehement attacks by Confucius's supporters against the sport in question took place at the final stage of the Koryo rule. A number of brief notices about the game have survived from that period. We learn, for example, that in 1149 the king had 18 players selected from among the cavalry to play the game, which he observed. According to the Confucianist elite, the *yangban* class, from among which many major officials and generals sprang, the landed gentry were so enamored with gyôggu during the Koryo rule that it led to the corruption of the knightly and upper classes who preferred to amuse themselves instead of taking an interest in the welfare of their country. In addition, it wrought havoc on the social hierarchy as skill in playing became more important in the court than the education one received. Taecho (T'aejo), a former general Yi Sông-gye who took over from the preceding king, sided with the yangban. Besides, the ruler's intention was to simultaneously reduce the influence of the noblemen, who often had their own cavalry units. On his order polo became subject to increasingly severe supervision and on a public scale it was actually banned altogether. It was continued in the king's

Military gymnastics.

own court but the event's splendor was reduced significantly. Taecho himself was an avid polo player. From a historical text known in the Kor. tradition as *Yongbiohtchonga* we learn about 2 techniques invented by the king (*tchini-magi* and *oht-magi*) as well as about how those who watched the king playing admired his skill and talent for the game.

It was only the 4th Choson dynasty king, Saechong the Great (Saechong Silrog or Saejong Silrog, 1418-50), who recognized in gyôggu a useful military drill. Against yangban pressure, Saechong not only lifted the ban on the game, but went on to make the discipline an obligatory element of the qualification exam for higher military officials. In the surviving records dating back to Saechong's reign we read that

> *during the gyôggu exam a candidate should be wearing an outfit as determined in the examination regulations. He is supposed to bring the ball close to the goal and shoot 3 times. If succeeding each time, a candidate can score 200 points; if 2 times – 100 points. If a candidate behaves properly during the practical exam and splendidly presents himself, he can score 150 points even though he fails all 3 times in executing proper shots with the ball.*

Saechong himself was an aficionado of gyôggu. During his time the most intensive growth of Choson dynasty culture took place and as a result, of gyôggu as well. His response to repeated yangban appeals was known far and wide: 'Gyôggu is not a mere game as thanks to its practice men can become superb warriors who are not only perfectly skilled horse riders but also experienced strategists.' The last surviving historical records of the game date back to the first half of the 16th cent., when Park Han-Ju, a subject of the despotic Yuhnsan-Gun king (1494-1506), pleaded with his master not to play polo so often. In response, the king exiled his vassal to a distant island. At that point the decline of the game's popularity commenced. After 2 wars (a Jap. invasion in 1592-98 and Manchurian invasion in 1627) the clamoring yangbans once again demanded the exclusion of the game from the state examination for military officials, claiming it never brought any benefits during the wartime. Despite all that, the game was every now and then included in the exams until as late as 1720 – a year dating the last available record of the sport. During the exam a candidate was supposed to place a wooden ball from a distance of 250 steps into a goal 5 steps wide. As an element of examinations the game never took the form of a match and was rather a demonstration of one's ability to execute certain technical skills.

Koo-Chul Jung, *Erziehung und Sport in Korea im Kreuzpunkt fremder Kulturen und Mächte*, 1996.

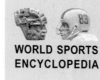

A Swedish postage stamp issued in honor of P.H. Ling (1776-1839), the founder of the Royal Central Gymnastic Institute in Stockholm.

A German postage stamp issued in honor of F.L. Jahn (1778-1852), an outstanding gymnastics scholar.

Gymnastic motif on a stamp issued for the 1956 Olympic Games in Melbourne.

H

WORLD SPORTS ENCYCLOPEDIA

HACHTLI, see >TLACHTLI.

HACKY SACK, also *hacking the sack, hackisac*, various old names for >FOOTBAG.

HÆNGE GRIS OP, Dan. for 'hanging a piglet'. A Dan. name for a fitness exercise also known in other countries and a common acrobatic stunt performed by a parent and child. Two athletes stand facing each other and hold hands. The smaller one climbs onto the bigger until upside down. Embracing the bigger participant's neck with his legs, the smaller one lets go of his partner's hands and hangs loosely. Finally, both participants hold hands again and the smaller one returns to the initial position with a back flip.
J. Møller, 'Hænge gris op', GID, 1997, 3, 57.

HAGOITA, also *yarihago, oibane*, a Jap. game using a feathered shuttlecock and wooden rackets, known since as early as the 14th cent.

HAIR CLIPPING RACES, a type of running competition popular among Mong. shepherds. The hair clipping ceremony is held for children of 3-5yrs., depending on local custom. The actual runners, 7-12yrs. old, have to reach the children whose hair is to be clipped and who are standing along the finish line. Their hair is cut by adults but the child runners connect, in a symbolic manner, the younger ones, whose hair is still unclipped, to the older children who have already undergone the ceremony. When questioned about this symbolic link, the shepherds were able to explain neither its significance nor the relationship between the races and hair clipping ceremonies. It seems that a full understanding of the ancient tradition has not survived to the present and today we witness only a hair clipping ceremony deprived of its original symbolic meaning.
I. Kabzińska-Stawarz, 'Współzawodnictwa w sytuacjach granicznych', part II, EP, 1993, XXXVII, 1.

HAKA, Maori term for a ritual dance closely related with the cult of physical fitness. Haka is performed before important events such as battles, hunting, religious or family festivals, etc. Although the word 'haka' is actually a general Maori term for dancing, today it is mostly applied to characteristic rhythmical moves referred to in Eng. as a posture dance, performed to the rhythm of choral chants. There are 5 principal forms of haka, each containing simple but spectacular movements that require great effort and physical resilience, bearing a certain resemblance to gymnastic, combative, and party-like movements combined. Therefore, the major var. of haka are also known as action dances.

HAKA PERUPERU is a dance with the use of weapons: a spear (*koi koi*), a club (*taiaha*), long sticks (*tewhatewha*), and short sticks (*patu*). The weapons are equipped with sophisticated handles and richly adorned. Before the actual dance starts, young dancers perform the *tutu ngarahu* (a test of physical readiness), during which they demonstrate to the elders, women, and even children, their skills, esp. their ability to jump high slapping their heels against their buttocks. Nihoniho – a Maori chief in the period of early colonization – provided the following explanation of such tests:

Before you go into battle, show your legs to the women, young folk and old men in a tutu ngaharu. Your women will not fail to notice the omens of the dance which lie in the correctness of posture or in the errors which you commit.

[After Alan Armstrong]

Among the most famous haka demonstrations there is the *Koia ano* dance developed by the Arawa and Taupo tribes:

Yes, indeed!
This is our battle dance!
We stormed the mighty palisades.
Behold the attack
Which laid low this formidable foe,
And the enemy dead
Who are strewn on our battlefield.

[Eng. trans. by A. Armstrong,
Games and Dances of the Maori People, 1986]

Jumps are accompanied by acrobatics and the brandishing of weapons. E.g. a spear is used in *ano te* or *ra te tai* – a movement similar to that made by weightlifters in which the spear is raised up to the chest and then above the head; *inahoki* – a spear is raised up the hips; *whakatiro* – a jump with the heels slapping against the buttocks and simultaneous sideward stretch of a hand holding a spear in a vertical position; *pare-rehwa* – the same type of jump with the hand stretched in front of the jumper; *wha* – both hands perform acrobatic movements holding a spear; *hei* – acrobatics in a kneeling position with the use of a spear.

HAKA POI is a dance combined with the demonstration of one's skills in using a wooden block, *poi*, tied to a string held by a dancer. Blocks are usu. in the shape of short cylinders or balls, 5-7cm in diameter, covered in flax fiber or *raupo* tree leaves, and adorned with trad. Maori *taaniko* patterns, feathers, or dog's fur. Poi are used in a dance of the same name, sometimes performed in boats, and in haka poi – a ritual dance. The principal haka poi figures are grouped into 3 types: figures performed with a single poi held in one hand (pendulum, rolling in and out, twisting the poi on the arm holding the string); with double poi – one in each hand (brandishing and swinging poi in different directions); and double poi held in one hand. Dancers can use either trad. poi or ones with shorter ropes.

HAKA POWHIRI, a welcome dance during which dancers perform with their hands movements resembling synchronic gymnastics, such as simultaneous stretching sidewards, lifting one hand bent at the elbow and lowering the other at the same time, and alternate raising of each shoulder. Haka powhiri can also be performed in pairs with partners executing various moves synchronically while sitting on the ground, standing, etc.

HAKA TAPARAHI, one of the var. performed without any weapon, led by a dance master, *kaeae*, who sets the rhythm. Dancers stand with their legs apart, straighten up, looking at one another or upwards. At the first command, 'Kia mau!' or 'Kia rite!' (Get ready!), they place their hands on their hips. After the second command, 'Ringa pakia!', they start clapping their hands against their thighs. In the course of a dance, the dance master signals different positions, such as *turi whatia* – bend your knees or *uma titaha* – stick your chest out. Each movement is coordinated with exaggerated grimaces that used to throw fear into the hearts of Eur. travelers: *whatero*

– sticking the tongue out, *pukana* – rolling of the eyes, *pikari* – goggling accompanied with a forward tilt of the head, *whakapi* – various grimaces of lips. A characteristic feature of haka taparahi is the lack of accompanying drums. The rhythm is set by short recitations and stamping of the feet. A visitor to Maoriland made the following comment about the dance: 'They frequently danced on our vessels and they danced so heavily that we were afraid they would break through the deck.' An example of a rhythmical recitation could be as follows:

Haka is a thing of word,
An expression of the heart to treasure,
An utterance of the mouth to listen to,
An outpouring of the body.

[Trans. A. Armstrong]

Haka taparahi has several var., each using different chants, the most popular of which is *Ka mate! Ka mate!* (It's death! It's death!), or the less dramatic *Poutini* (Star from the sky) and *Ringa pakia* (Clap your hands):

LEADER:
Slap your hands against your thighs!
Slap your hands, stomp your feet!
Look fierce!
ALL:
Indeed we are doing
just that!
LEADER:
Stretch forth your hands!
Hold them out to the
farthest horizons!
ALL:
We are!
LEADER:
Raise your voices in
the war cry!
ALL:
Yes!

[After A. Armstrong]

History. A Maori legend has it that haka was invented by Tanerore, son of Ra – the god of the sun – and Hine-raumati, goddess of the summertime. His dances can be felt on the earth by vibrations of hot air (*wiri*). People imitate such vibrations by swaying their hands in a characteristic way (*wiriwiri*). Legend has it that chief Tinirau had a favorite whale which was slain by a certain Kae – a member of a different tribe – of whom little was known but the fact that when smiling he exposed a crooked tooth that overlapped with his other teeth. Tinirau's envoys tried every trick they knew to try to make the sullen villagers laugh in order to identify Kae. All their efforts came to naught. Finally, one of them started to imitate the god Tanerore's haka dance. This quickly put everybody in stitches; Kae was given away by his crooked tooth, captured, and duly executed. Soon, haka became an expression of ethnic identity, a symbol of group unity both for males and females. The first Europeans arriving in N.Zealand observed with surprise that although haka is more often performed by men, women were not discriminated against among Maori people. In 1827, A. Earle commented: 'I was astonished to find that their women mixed in the dance indiscriminately with the men and went through all those horrid gestures with seemingly as much pleasure as the warriors themselves.' [After A. Armstrong]
Haka is a group dance, performed simultaneously by hundreds, sometimes thousands, of dancers. Males often danced naked or wearing only *maro* or *rapaka* – a piece of clothing covering hips and legs, made of wool dyed red and black. Today, both sexes wear *piupiu*, a skirt made of very colorful linen, which highlights choreographic and folkloric features of the dance. Males' pius are usu. knee-long, whereas females' ones are much longer. Women can also wear *korowai*, a patterned dress made of wide wedge-shaped pieces of fabric. Trad. Maori patterns, *taaniko*, also appear on headbands worn by women. Haka was adopted as a ceremony performed before matches in some sports disciplines popular in N.Zealand, esp. >RUGBY, where it is supposed to animate the players' combative spirit.
A. Armstrong, *Games and Dancing of the Maori People*, 1986, 40-57.

HAKKE KNIV MELLEM FINGRENE, Dan. for 'stab a knife between fingers'. A co-ordination game appearing in many other countries and cultures as well

A traditional New Zealand Maori welcoming party perform a Haka or wardance as Chinese President Jiang Zemin, center, looks on with New Zealand Prime Minister Jenny Shipley, and Governor General Sir Michael Hardy-Boys at Auckland airport.

and known in Eng. as *mumbletypeg* or *muble-the-peg*. A hand with spread fingers is placed on the table and the knife is thrust in the spaces between them. The point is to do it with maximum speed, while avoiding injuring oneself.
J. Møller, 'Hakke kniv mellem fingrene', GID, 1997, 3, 81.

HALF-BALL, a game similar to >BOWLING. The name comes from the fact that the pins are knocked down with a hard ball that is half the size of a cricket ball. Other names for the game include: *roly-poly*, *roley-poley* or *rollie-poly*, which are common names for various games that involve rolling a ball towards various targets. The target in the game consists of 9 conical pins, usually 15-20cm high. Eight of them form a circle just over 0.5m in diameter. The remaining pin, called the king, is located in the center of the circle. One of the 8 pins is clearly marked as the queen. Approx. 1ft. away, there is another pin, slightly bigger than the others, called the *jack*. Knocking down the king scores 3pts., the queen is worth 2pts., any other pin is 1pt. Knocking down the *jack* means deducting exactly the number of points the player would have got in the given throw, if he or she had not knocked the *jack* over. The game was particularly popular during local fairs and horse races in Scotland. Traditionally, the prize took the form of honey-cakes. According to some ethnographers, such as J. Strutt or A.B. Gomme, the game was initially identical with another bowling sport, known as >KAILS, which seems unlikely, considering the difference in the number of pins and the fact that in some versions of *kails* the ball is struck with a stick.
TGESI, II, 115-116.

HALF-HAMMER, a folk var. of >TRIPLE JUMP (STANDING), practiced in the Eng. county of Norfolk and the W part of Sussex. The starting position for the jump is standing on one foot. The landing is on the same foot, then followed by a jump on to the other foot. The origin of the name is unknown.

HALF-MARATHON, a footrace held over half the distance of the Olympic marathon race, i.e. 21,975m. Half-marathons are organized for those participants, who would not be able to cover a full-marathon distance otherwise. One of the most famous half-marathon events is the Souvenir Pierre de Coubertin held annually in France since 1980, in commemoration of the great originator of the modern Ol.G.

HALMA, an ancient Gk. form of >LONG JUMP, perhaps >MULTI-JUMPING, forming a part of >PENTATHLON. The real character of halma has not yet been convincingly resolved. Reconstructions of the length of the jump based on ancient descriptions suggest that it could have been twice as long as current jumps. The most famous ancient jumper, Phayllos of Kroton was alleged to have jumped the distance of 55 Olympic ft., which is approx. 18.2m. Chionis of Sparta's result was allegedly 52ft. or approx. 17.2m. These results equal the best achievements of present day >TRIPLE JUMP. Two contradicting hypotheses may be put forward: 1) it was really the long jump, and the ancient jumpers possessed secret abilities; 2) instead of the long jump it was the triple or even the quadruple jump. The latter hypothesis is supported by the fact that ancient sportsmen knew nothing of the recent discoveries in bio-mechanics and physiology and generally

A Greek halma jumper with weights.

achieved results lower than present ones, as shown by distances achieved in discus, javelin etc. It is unlikely that long jumpers were an exception in this matter. Perhaps the results given for halma were the sum of 3 separate jumps, instead of a single jump. Another mysterious element is the use of jumping-weights. These were similar to modern dumbbells and made of stone or metal. The oldest specimen, cast in lead, was found in Eleusis and is now at the National Museum in Athens. A desription of jumping-weights can be found in Pausanias's *Description of Greece*: 'They are half of a circle, not an

exact circle but elliptical, and made so that the fingers pass through as they do through the handle of a shield. Such are the fashion of them.' (5, 26, 3) The weights used during the Games at Olympia were 25-29cm in diameter, approx. 11.5cm long, 3.5cm wide, 2.5-4cm thick and weighed 2-4kg. They were supposed to lengthen the jump by increasing the weight of the jumper. As depicted in paintings on ancient vases, having gained greater momentum, the jumper threw away the weights in the second stage of the jump. It was thought that the decrease in weight during the descent would have an effect on the jump. Present experiments with jumping-weights have yet to confirm this.
C. Paleologos, 'Jumping', OGIAG, 1982, 176-179; S. Parnicki-Pudełko, 'Skok w dal', OIO, 1964, 48-49.

HALTE RÆV, Dan. for 'lame fox', a game often played during PE classes in kindergarten and early primary school. One participant becomes a fox, sleeping in its burrow, while the others run around. If any of them comes too close to the fox, he or she awakens and jumps out on one foot only and, pretending to be lame, tries to catch the person. The first one caught becomes the fox. However, if the fox puts the other foot on the ground, the players drive him or her back to the burrow.
J. Møller, 'Halte RÆV', GID, 1997, 2, 46.

HALTEROBOLIA, ancient weightlifting, a supplementary exercise rather than a competition in its own right. A sportsman lifted 2 large stones, each of them held from underneath by one hand. As can be seen in ancient vase paintings, the hands were alternated rather than lifting simultaneously. The famous Roman philosopher Seneca the Younger (c.4 BC-65 AD) complained about athletes practicing halterobolia: 'I live by the baths, which is the source of many a noise. Imagine all sorts of sounds that are obtrusive to the ears. Men with well-developed muscles are busy with their exercises and wave about

Two Greek vases depicting athletes in a weightlifting training session.

their arms heavily burdened with lead. I can hear them groaning as they strain and whistling when they let the air out afterwards'.
N.B. Crowther, 'Team Sports in Ancient Greece', IJHS, 1995,1.

HALVRAADDEN, Dan. for 'half-rotten'. A game from the baseball group, in which players play individually. The number of players ranges from 5 to 10 (usu. 7). One of the participants becomes 'half-rotten' – *halvraadden*, who occupies position 4 (see illustration), the rest are 'raw' – *fersk*. The division into 3 groups and assignment of positions in the field is performed by drawing lots, which takes the form of catching a stick. In the drawing ceremony – see >SPIL MED BOLDTRÆ – the participant who catches the stick closest to the ground becomes the *yderst raadden* – outside rotten, taking the most distant position 7, the 5th plays the *inderst raadden* – inside rotten. The players 1-3 form a separate group, aligned with player 4 but at a certain distance from him. From his position, player 4 serves the ball by hand in the direction of players 1-3. All 4 of them stand on the line which forms the inside base – *indermål*.

After the serve, the first of players 1-3 tries to bounce the ball into the field with the use of a wooden bat. He has 2 or 3 attempts at his disposal, as agreed in advance. After hitting the ball or having used all of his attempts, he can start running for the position called *ydermål*. A successful run scores a point, but on his way the batter may be got-out with the ball or caught by players 5-7, whose goal is to eliminate the runner. If they succeed, the batter becomes 7 and player 5 becomes 4, the half-rotten. Then the new 4 starts a new round by serving the ball at the

Sonia O'Sullivan (#239) of Ireland in action during the IAAF World Half Marathon Championships in Brussels, Belgium on May 5, 2002.

group standing on the indermål line. The player to hit the ball is now no. 2, which also occurs if no. 1 manages to reach the ydermål uncaught but decides to stay there because of lack of time or the risk of being got out on the way back to the base. Each of the players 5-7 who manages to catch the ball before it bounces (*Højninger*) automatically becomes no. 4. The players are allowed to catch the ball on the fly or after its first bounce off the ground.
There is a var. of halvraadden called *levende bold* [Dan. for 'live ball'], popular in and around Langa. It is different from halvraadden in the fact that only the serving player and the current batter play separately from the rest of participants in the field. The batter runs from the place called *formål*, to the base called *bagmål* and back. He gives up his position if he misses the ball an agreed number of times (1-3) or if he gets hit with the ball while running. The player can also be deprived of his position if he gets caught by any of the field players, but only if the ball is *levende* (live) – that is in motion.
Interestingly, the inhabitants of Silkeborge have a different name for a similar game – *at spille raaden*, the rotten game. Their groups of players are called

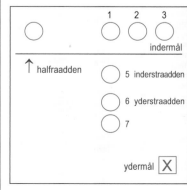
A table for playing halvraadden

H

**WORLD SPORTS
ENCYCLOPEDIA**

'ripe' – *moden* – and 'half-ripe' -*halvmoden*.
J. Møller, 'Halvraadden', GID, 1997, 1, 63.

HAMMER THROW, a trad. folk sport of Germanic and Celtic peoples, adapted to the needs of athletics as a separate field event in modern times. The objective was initially to throw for distance a real sledge hammer, which was then replaced by a metal ball ('head') weighing 7.257kg, attached to a steel wire 1.22m long. The throw is made from a throwing circle, 213.5m in diameter, surrounded by a metal rim, at least 6mm wide, whose top edge is flush with the surrounding ground, with the surface of the actual throwing circle 14-26mm below that. The throwing circle is surrounded on 3 sides by a U-shaped safety cage with the mouth at the front, 6m wide, opening onto the landing area. The cage consists of 7 segments, each 2.74m wide and at least 9m high. The maximum mesh size is 5cm for steel wire and 4.4cm for cord netting. The cage must be able to withstand the impact of a hammer moving at a velocity of up to 32m/s. Throwers may use protective gloves but wrapping 2 or more fingers together is prohibited (fingers may be wrapped individually). Wide belts protecting the lower back are allowed but no substances may be used to increase the friction of the throwing circle or footwear. If the hammer head detaches from the wire during a throw, the attempt may be repeated. The thrower may not step outside of the throwing circle before the hammer lands on the ground. The measurements are made between the inner edge of the metal rim around the throwing circle and the closest mark the hammer has left on the ground. The order of throws is decided by lots. Each thrower has the right to perform 2 trial throws. If there are more than 8 contestants in a tournament, a qualifying round is organized first, with 3 attempts for each thrower. Those who qualify for the final each have a further 3 attempts. If more than one participant achieves the 8th result, all contestants with this result are allowed into the final stage. The hammer throw used to be an exclusively male event but has recently gained some popularity among women.

History. The hammer throw was known in ancient times but was not practiced as a sporting event in Mediterranean cultures. The oldest records of hammer throwing are associated with the mythologies

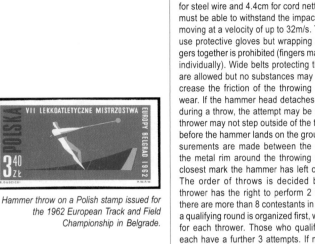

Hammer throw on a Polish stamp issued for the 1962 European Track and Field Championship in Belgrade.

Hammer throw is also an event of the Highland Games.

of ancient Germanic and Celtic peoples. The Norse god Thor, Odin's son, used a hammer for both combat and play. A whole book of the Icel. *Edda*, entitled *Thrymskvitha* (*The Lay of Thrym*), is devoted to Thor's endeavors aimed at regaining possession of his hammer, stolen by Thrym, the king of the giant Thurs ('Wild was Vingthor when he awoke, and when his mighty hammer he missed'). Thrym would only give back the hammer in return for the hand of the goddess Freyja. Trying to persuade Freyja to marry Thrym proved of no use. To be able to play and fight with the hammer again, Thor had to dress up as Freyja, and thus regain possession of his favorite weapon. Thrym was deceived:

*Then loud spake Thrym, the giants' leader:
Bring in the hammer to hallow the bride [...]'.
The heart in the breast of Hlorrithi laughed
When the hard-souled one his hammer beheld;
First Thrym, the king of the giants, he killed,
Then all the folk of the giants he felled. [...]
And so his hammer got Othin's son.*

[trans. H. Adams Bellows]

In Celtic mythology, there are 2 versions of the origin of the hammer throw. According to one of them, the wheel of the chariot of one of the heroes became seized up during chariot races. As the hero could not take it off to be repaired, he grabbed the whole axle and, by rotating it, caused the wheel to detach. According to the second version, the hero threw the whole axle with the wheel on it, so that it came in first at the finish line, and he thus became the winner. An event, held in Ireland to commemorate this legendary incident, involved throwing hammers made of stone discs with wooden handles. Similar implements were used to hammer in stockade poles in Celtic fortified towns known as *cranog*. The oldest records of throwing sledgehammers come from medieval Scotland, from where the sport spread to England. King Henry VIII used to participate in hammer throwing events, often winning them. Folk hammer throw styles are still to be seen in Scotland during the local Highland Games and Gatherings. In Ireland, the hammer throw became one of the main events of the Aonach tailtean Old-Ir. Games, reactivated in 1829. Finally, in the 19th cent., the hammer throw became one of the athletic field events. In 1866, it was included in the program of the Eng. Championships. The equipment and rules became increasingly standardized. However, even as late as 1897, the *Encyclopedia of Sport* (vol. 1) claimed that in spite of the standard hammer weight introduced in 1866, there was still considerable local variation in rules, and recommended using standards accepted by athletic organizations in the USA and UK. The first hammer throw record holder was Briton G.R. Thornton (27.70m – 1866). American J. Flanagan was the first to break the 50m barrier (50.01m – 1899). The barrier of 60m was passed by Hungarian J. Csérmák (60.34m – 1952), that of 70m – by American H. Conolly (70.34m – 1960), and 80m – by Russian B. Zaychuk (80.14m – 1978). Between 1866 and 1889, the best hammer throwers came from the Brit. Isles, especially Ireland. In 1889 (or 1890, according to some sources), J. Mitchell's world record of 130ft. 8in. (39.83m) opened the

Team handball.

'American era'. In 1892, Mitchell reached 140ft. 11in. (42.95m). Between 1896 and 1908, the Amer. J. Flanagan broke 8 world records, a feat which has not been surpassed since (his best result was 51.92m in 1908). After WWII, throwers from the USSR, USA and Hungary dominated, to later give way to Ger. competitors . The best throwers after 1945 included: I. Németh (Hungary), Olympic champion of 1948 and bronze medallist of 1952; M. Krivonosov (USSR), 4-time world record holder and Eur. champion of 1954; G. Zsivotzky (Hungary), Olympic champion of 1968 and Eur. champion of 1962; R. Klim (USSR), Olympic champion of 1964 and Eur. champion of 1966; J. Sedykh (USSR), twice Olympic champion (1976, 1980) and silver medallist of 1988. Top throwers of the 1990s included A. Abduvaliyev (Tajikistan), Olympic champion of 1992; and B. Kiss (Hungary), Olympic champion of 1996. K. Skolimowska (Poland) was the first to win the Olympic women's competition introduced in 2000. The Sydney Olympics men's competition was also won by a Pole, S. Ziółkowski. *The Book of Rules, Athletics. Hammer throw*, 1998; Polish Athletic Federation, *Przepisy zawodów w lekkoatletyce. Rzut młotem*, 1996.

HAN'-AND-HAIL, Scot. for 'catch and run for the goal'. A game known and played in the Dumfries region. Two goals, called *hails* or *dules* are set approx. 400yds. (365m) apart. Two teams occupy the area between the goals. The game is played with a soft ball similar in size to a grown man's fist, hit with an open hand as if with a racket. Initially the ball is served by a member of the team chosen by drawing lots. Then the players attempt to take possession of the ball on the fly. The one to catch it throws the ball in the direction of the opponents' goal. Alternatively, if the ball is caught after a single bounce, the player may still perform a throw but only with an additional obstacle, that is he must toss the ball between ground level and the level of his knees. The scoring team resumes the game.

HANDBALL, The name has 2 distinct meanings in the Eng. language: 1) a game for 2 teams of 11 or 7 players each, who move the ball with the hands, kicking it obviously not being allowed, and try to score goals. This var. is called >TEAM HANDBALL, or >OLYMPIC HANDBALL as it is known in Australia; 2) all other games that involve bouncing a ball without the use of a racket. In this meaning handball denotes, among others, several similar games where the ball is bounced off a wall rather than tossed over a net. Depending on the number of walls being used in the process, we speak of >ONE-WALL HANDBALL, >THREE-WALL HANDBALL or four-wall handball. Collectively, they are called *court handball*. In all these var. single and double matches are played. The aim of the game is the quickest scoring of a given number of points, usu. 21. Due to considerable input from the Ir. tradition, the game is frequently called >IRISH HANDBALL, and under this heading the game is described at greater length. The name used to refer to many games which involved bouncing the ball with the hand. It was also used for games that in later stages of development introduced rackets or their names. There are a number of such games that follow similar rules of bouncing the ball off the wall or a number of walls in a court. In the Eng. tradition, the most prominent example is a group of sports known as >FIVES. In the Fr. tradition these are some var. of >JEU DE PAUME, esp. >COURTE PAUME; in the Iberian Peninsula some kinds of >PELOTA, incl. Basq. >PASAKA.

HAN-DO, a var. of ancient Jap. archery >TOSIYA for adolescents. The aim was to shoot from a kneeling position so that the arrow would pass through the W veranda of the Sanju-Sangen-Do temple, going from S to N without hitting the walls or the low eaves. The factor differentiating it from tosija (for adults) was the distance, 60m instead of 120m. Another tosija-like competition for the young was >GO-JUKKEN with a distance of about 90m.

HANETSUKI, a Jap. game played with a feathered shuttlecock and wooden rackets, played mostly by girls, to celebrate Jap. New Year. After the racket, the game is also known as >HAGOITA.

HANG GLIDING, a sports discipline in which pilots soar in the air or ride on the ground, water, or ice by means of a hang glider. Traditionally, the most popular type of a hang glider has been one consisting of a light metal framework with a large sail stretched over it, useful for steering and maintaining altitude. Making use of currents and zones of warm air allows a pilot to hang glide for a considerable length of time. For training purposes, both

made about 2,000 flights but was killed on 10 Aug., 1896 during tests of a new construction. The consequent development of airplanes and gliders overshadowed hang gliding, which was then deemed archaic and futureless. At the beginning of the 1960s G. and F. Rogallo, Americans of Pol. origin, on a NASA order constructed a flexible wing allowing a spacecraft to maneuver and land smoothly on the earth. The wing was later named the 'Rogallo wing'. The aerodynamic experiments for the Rogallo wing construction proved also useful for individual flights. In 1969 the Austral. S. Moyes and Amer. B. Bennet, using the Rogallos' construction, made the first flights from Mt. Kosciusko in Australia on a parawing. In 1974 the first Europe Cup competition was organized in Switzerland. In the same year the International Hang Gliding Federation (Fédération Aéronautique Internationale, FAI) recognized hang gliding as a sports discipline and established the International Committee of Hang Gliding (CIVL). The first unofficial W.Ch. was organized in Austria in 1975, and an official one in 1976. Outside the USA after 1968 hang gliding developed most rapidly in Australia, however, due to a number of accidents and some local administrative problems the development of the sport was temporarily hampered. The change came in the mid-1970s, when the Austrl. association, ASSA, took over control of hang gliding development. In cooperation with the Austral. Transportation De-

punches. [Kor. *yu* –gentle + Chin. *Kwon* – fist + Kor. *sool* – fight + *hap* – coordination + *ki* – essence of power + *do* – way].

HAPKIDO, Kor. art of harmony and a sport. Its essence lies in linking co-ordination, strength and methods of defeating an opponent [Kor. *Hap* – co-ordination, *ki* – essence of strength, *do* – art, way]. Combat utilizes hand strikes, kicks, joint-locks, throws, restraints and chokes, mostly borrowed from a form of Jap. >JU JUTSU, known as aiki-ju-jutsu. The most important part of the preparations is the development of resources of the physical energy *tan-jon*. Hapkido advocates modesty, spiritual discipline, a humble attitude to the surrounding world and confidence in one's own abilities. The highest levels of initiation involve medical knowledge of the body and the art of healing. The history of hapkido goes as far back as the Shilla dynasty (also known as Silla, 1st-10th cent.). It was started among warriors called the Hwarang, famous for their courage and brutality. Some of their martial arts, associated with rules of Buddhist philosophy, became a basis for the development of hapkido during the Koryo period (10th-13th cent.). Then it was forbidden during the rule of the Yi dynasty, and survived only because Buddhist monks secretly practiced it in monasteries, taking it to higher levels of refinement. In its early periods, hapkido was also called other names, such as *soo bahk ki, bi sul, yu*

Hapkido.

Hang gliding tandem.

a novice and an instructor fly in a tandem glider.
Equipment. A hang glider is a light unpowered aircraft consisting of a delta-shaped cloth wing stretched over a framework made of light metals. The wings can be either soft, in which case the hang glider is a parawing, or they can be hard. The flier's body serves as the fuselage. He lands on his feet and starts off either by running down a slope or by being towed from the ground. The max. permissible weight of a hang glider is 50kg and the average length of a flight is several dozen km. High-performance flights on cutting-edge constructions routinely exceed 300km at altitudes of 3-4km. Cf. >PARAGLIDING.
History. Hang gliding traditions are as old as human attempts at flying. By the end of the 19th cent. hundreds of inventors had tried to design wings that, when attached to a man's shoulders or arms, would allow him to fly. Both Leonardo da Vinci and the mythological figure of Icarus pioneered in the field, but it is O. Lilienthal who is considered the real pioneer of hang gliding and >GLIDING, as he, after years of research and experimentation, managed in 1896 to fly over 30m. on silk wings stretched over a wooden framework. Lilienthal

partment a number of training courses were opened and pilot license degrees were defined. At the end of the 1970s ASSA became the Austrl. Hang Gliding Association, and then the Hang-Gliding Federation of Australia. The federation runs quality hang gliding training programs and controls legal issues. From the moment when S. Moyes won the W.Ch. in 1983 and 2 other Australians scored among the top ten pilots, Austral. pilots became dominant in the international competitions of the 1980s. Moyes won the W.Ch. gold medal once more in 1987, and 2 silver medals in 1985 and 1989. In 1985 the flight altitude exceeded 4km for the first time. L. Tudor broke this record with a 4,343.61-m flight over Horseshoe Meadow in California. The flight length record, also broken by L. Tudor in 1990 was 488km in a flight near the town of Hobbs, New Mexico, close to the Texan border. The area near this town is regarded as one of the best places for hang gliding.

HAP KI DO YU KWAN SOOL, also *yu kwan sool hapki do* – full versions of the old name of >HAP-KIDO. The name refers to mastering of the martial art by coordinating the essence of power with

sul (also spelled *yu sool*), *yuk wonsul* (*yu kwan sool*) as well as *yawala* and *tae kyun*.
Hapkido was banned during the Jap. occupation of Korea (1910-1945) and revived after WWII, although the Kor. War (1949-1953) was another obstacle in its development in Kor. society. It was also influenced by Jap. martial arts. Initially, masters of hapkido wanted to identify it with >JUDO. After the war, the Kor. government demanded the unification of all martial arts, thus forming the basis of >TAE-KWON-DO, but hapkido was excluded from the process. The tactics of hapkido are limited to self-defense, and forbid any attacks for one's own benefit, unless one is under attack. They cover punches, kicks and turns as well as the use of small objects such as a short stick or cane. As in judo, the levels of competence relate to 7 dans. As opposed to other Asian martial arts, hapkido does not form a unified official sport, so there are no strict rules to follow.
The father of modern-day hapkido is believed to be Yong Sul Choi. After his death, Suh Bok Sup, a former managing director of a winery producing the Korean wine Mak Ju, became the next grandmaster. He took up hapkido in 1948, after he met Yong Sul Choi, who was his employee. The details of their

Hang gliding.

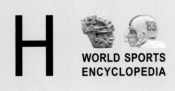

H

WORLD SPORTS ENCYCLOPEDIA

Harness racing.

POLSKA 2000 zł

ANDRZEJ MAŁKOWSKI 1889-1919

1911-1981

M. PIEKARSKI   PWPW 91

A stamp issued in honor of A. Małkowski (1899-1919), the founder of harcerstwo, the Polish scouting movement.

The world meeting of Polish harcerze near Gniezno, Poland.

Harness racing.

first meeting are significant. Suh Bok Sup who had been involved in judo, observed the elderly master handle a few much younger men during a brawl by the well at work. Then he asked the old man to demonstrate his skills and was defeated despite being much younger. Therefore, he decided to learn hapkido. After 3 years of training under the supervision of Yong Sul Choi, he supported the creation of the first *dojang* (Yu Kwan Sool Hap Ki Dojang). In 1958, the 2 masters named the sport Hap Ki Do. Soon arguments over leadership started, and a few different schools were created with alternative systems of exercises. The person to attempt their reconciliation was Jung Moon Kwan, who managed to unite schools in the Korean provinces of Kyung San and Chul Ra. The new organization was named Yu Kwan Sool Hap Ki Do.

One of the greatest supporters of hapkido is the Korean Kim Duck Soo. After a career as a competitor, he became a teacher of Amer. troops in Korea. Then he went on to train Kor. special police forces. Later, he trained military forces in the USA, where the state of Arkansas awarded him the title of Ambassador of Goodwill to the People of other States. In the middle of the '90s he announced work towards creation of stricter rules and organization of international competitions. The author of the first handbook of hapkido in the USA, He Young Kim.

K.S. Moorthy, 'Introduction to Martial Arts – Hapkido', SS, Jan. 1988; G. Punitha, 'Learn to Conquer Pain in Hapkido', SS, March 1991; M. Wollmershauser, *The True Origin of Hapkido. An Interveiw with Hap Ki Do MasterSuh Bok Sup*, Aug. 1994.

HARCERSTWO, Pol. young people's movement modeled upon Eng. >SCOUTING. Formed in 1910 by A. Małkowski (1899-1919). Since 1918, it has functioned within the framework of the Pol. Scouting and Guiding Association (ZHP – Związek Harcerstwa Polskiego). Between the years 1919-39, it played an important role in the patriotic and physical upbringing of the young. Among other things,

original educational methods were introduced. They were based on a close relationship with the natural environment, work for the benefit of others and individual independence. An important role in the development of these virtues was played by selected sports, esp. field games and winter games, as well as gliding, hiking and sailing. Gen. J. Heller (1873-1960) participated in ZHP activities between 1920-23. Led by Gen. M. Zaruski (1867-1941), harcerstwo contributed to the development of Pol. sailing, incl. marine sailing. In the 1930s, on the initiative of A. Kamiński, Cub Scouts and Brownie troops were formed for 6 to 11-year-olds. Between 1919-39 numerous scouting organizations were founded by Pol. emigrants abroad. The strongest of them was the Pol. Scouting and Guiding Association of Germany (ZHPwN) which operated unofficially from 1913 and officially from 1925 to 1939, with headquarters in Bytom. Because of their participation in the plebiscite and the Silesia uprisings, most of the leading scouting activists were later imprisoned and murdered in the concentration camps by the Nazis. Scouts and Guides took active part in the defense against Germans in 1939. One of the bravest episodes was the defense of the area of the parachuting tower in Katowice. During WWII (1939-45) the ZHP operated under the conspiracy code-name *Szare Szeregi* (the Grey Ranks) for boys and *Związek Koniczyn* (the Clover Association) for girls. Their leaders were, in succession: their creator, F. Marciniak (1939-43), S. Broniewski (1943-44) and L. Marszałek (1944-45). In 1944 the 2 organizations' memberships were respectively 10,000 and 8,000 boys and girls. They published several resistance movement magazines, such as *Brzask, Pismo Młodych* and *Źródło*. The activities of the *Szare Szeregi* were depicted in the novel *Kamienie na szaniec* (*Stones for the Rampant*, 1943). Members of the *Szare Szeregi* fought during the Warsaw Uprising (1944) forming the battalions *Zośka, Parasol* and *Wigry*. Guides took part as nurses and in communication services. In 1945, the ZHP was reactivated but only until 1950 when the Scouting Organization (OH, *Organizacja Harcerska*) was created. It was modeled upon the Rus. *Pionier* movement and operated within the structure of the Polish Youth Association (ZMP, *Związek Młodzieży Polskiej*). The trad. uniform was replaced with navy trousers/skirts, white shirts and red scarves. Despite the new enforced ideology some of the troops leaders managed to stick to the old values. The political changes of 1956 enabled the re-establishment of the ZHP. Over the next couple of years the organization gradually abandoned its old values and complied with the ideological requirements of the system. In 1974, the ZHP was forced to join the Federation of Socialist Youth Organizations. This move initiated the creation of unofficial forms of alternative harcerstwo. They operated illegally or semi-legally e.g. *Kręgi im. A. Małkowskiego, Związek Harcerstwa Rzeczpospolitej (ZHR)*, and the *Polska Organizacja Harcerska*. The National Committee for Restoration of the ZHP was created in 1989. The fall of communism and political changes of 1989 brought about a stark conflict between the leaders of the ZHP and a proportion of educators who opted for a radical return to the trad. forms of harcerstwo. The subject of the most heated debate was the Christian character of harcerst-

Sulky races.

wo. During this period, the radically trad. ZHR gained importance. Attempts to join the 2 organizations in 2000 were unsuccessful. The only compromise has been occasional co-operation required by the World Organization of the Scout Movements, necessary to participate in the annual jamborees.

During WWII, young people evacuated with Gen. Anders' army formed the basis for the Polish Scouting and Guiding Association Abroad (ZHP PGK – Pol. *Związek Harcerstwa Polskiego Poza Granicami Kraju*). Their leaders were among others: between 1967-88, R. Kaczorowski (the last President of the Polish Republic in Emigration), between 1988-94, S. Berkieta and from 1994 onwards E. Jaśnikowski. The main center of the organization is Great Britain but 7 regions (4 male and 3 female) totaling about 10,000 people are scattered around the globe and exist in Australia, New Zealand, the USA, Canada and France. In 1949, the organization succeeded in retaining its Pol. character despite attempts to incorporate it into the British Boy Scout and British Girl Scout Association.

J. Gaj, *Główne nurty ideowe w Związku Harcerstwa Polskiego w latach 1918-1939*, 1966; H. Kapiszewski, *Związek Harcerstwa Polskiego w Niemczech. Zarys historyczny ze szczególnym uwzględnieniem lat 1933-1939*, 1969; J. Kret, *Harcerze wierni do ostatka*, 1969; A. Małkowski, *Scouting in Poland*; T. Maszczak, *Wychowanie fizyczne w harcerstwie*, 1979; D. Protalińska, *Czerwone Harcerstwo Towarzystwa Uniwersytetów Robotniczych. Założenia wychowawcze i działalność*, 1965; J. Sosnowski, *Wychowanie polityczne w harcerstwie (Wychowanie do pokoju)*, 1946.

HARE AND HOUNDS, see >PAPER CHASE.

HARNESS RACING, or *sulky* (the name is also used to denominate a light, 2-wheeled carriage seated for one person, from old Eng. *solcen* – lazy, comfortable), a form of >HORSE RACING, originally held on horseback, but now held in 2-wheeled sulkys, driven by a single trotter, in 2 categories: trotting and pacing. Horse classes include 2, 3, and 4-year-olds, each class subdivided according to the horse's results in previous races. For trotting and pacing a different type of harness is used to achieve the desired gait. Races are held on a circular, outdoor track of unspecified length, the whole of which must be visible from the stand.

History. The origin of trotting as a type of gait is unknown. Trotting on horseback was introduced during the 71st Ol.G. in 496 BC (>KALPE). In the modern era horses were trained to trot on a mass scale beginning in 1778 in the racing stable of prince A. Grigorevich Orlov (1737-1807). Originally trotting races were held exclusively on horseback until c.1830 the sulky was introduced. Regular sulky races began in 1879 in the US. Among the advantages of that method of racing were: better efficiency in achieving the desired gait, unburdening the horse, better control of the horse by a sulky driver than a horseback rider, obtaining better results thanks to the introduction in 1806 of registering record runs over a 1-mi. distance. In 1892 in the USA wheels with spokes and pneumatic tires were used for the first time.

Harness racing enjoys the greatest popularity in Eng.-speaking countries. No international federation has been established yet. In the US the sport has been developing under the umbrella of the US Trotting Association, with dozens of tracks and various kinds of racing events – cups, championships (state, regional or federal) and league (Grand Circuit). Among the best known periodicals or annuals, presenting the trotters' pedigrees, race results, calendars of events, etc., are the Amer. *Trotting Register* and *Year Book*. One of the most prestigious events is the Roosevelt International.

The origins of harness racing in Australia date back to 1810, although a full-fledged development of the sport there was initiated in 1881 by an American, Dr. J. Weir. Among many organizations and clubs estab. in various Austrl. states the most important one is the Trotting Control Board formed after WWII. The sport is also very popular in Germany and France, where it is controlled by Societé du Cheval, estab. in 1864.

HARPASTON, Gk., also Lat. *harpastum* [Gk. *harpaston* – a game of stealing or snatching a ball; <old Gk. *arpazo*, *arpadzo* – to snatch, steal, kidnap]; a ball game played in ancient Greece, the rules of which did not survive, besides the information conveyed by the name of the game. Some ancient writers and modern-day historians claim harpaston to have been identical with another Gk. ball game called >FAININDA. Athenaios wrote in his *Peri boethematon*:

Harpaston, which is often also called faininda, is my favorite game of all. The effort and fatigue resulting from this ball game are extraordinary and involve sudden twists and turns of the shoulders.

The idea of phaininda was to deceive the opponent by various tricks with the ball, so that he would not know where the ball was and, consequently, could not intercept it. The words *harpaston* and *faininda* may have denominated 2 different actions, both complementary to the essence of the same game, in which one team strives to maintain the possession of the ball, while the other seeks to steal it. For that reason the game may have had 2 different names, originating at different times or in different regions, just as with many other sports (e.g. with >ROYAL TENNIS, which was alternatively called *real tennis* and *court tennis*). Another possibility is that one game evolved from the other and at some point the 2 existed independently. Ancient writers may have focused more on the similarities than the differences between the games and thus wrote about them as of one game, just like modern >FOOTBALL evolved from several earlier games that were developed independently, but later co-existed (cf. >HARROW FOOTBALL, >RADLEY GAME, >ETON FIELD GAME, etc.). Harpaston belongs to a group of games referred to as >SFAIROMACHIAI.

As the Roman Empire spread over Europe, so did harpaston, and in the process it underwent various transformations, which – in some cases – resulted in games that hardly resembled the original. Therefore, it is difficult to define the influence of harpaston on Eur. ball games. One of many var. of harpaston played around Europe reached Poland and was known as >POKUTA.

Harpaston was played with a small-size ball, which led the Ancients to call it 'little ball'. It was a team sport and the number of players of one team ranged from 5-12. It was played probably on a rectangular field of a size similar to that of a modern >HANDBALL court or >ICE HOCKEY rink. A coin toss decided the sides on which the teams would begin. One team tried to maintain possession of the ball on its side, while the other team struggled to steal it and carry it to their side of the field. It was probably only the player with the ball who could be charged. The ball dropped on one's own territory may have inflicted a loss of a point or an entire round. General remarks about the game can be found in the works of numerous ancient writers, but none of them quotes any detailed rules. Antiphanes is quoted by Athenaios to have remarked about one of the players that he 'caught the ball and passed it to his teammate, dodging the rival and laughing. That one grabbed the ball and dodged a charging opponent. The crowd accompanied the game with the cries of: 'Out of bounds!', 'Too far!', 'Behind him!', 'Over the head!', 'On the ground!', 'Up!', 'Too short!', or 'Pass it back!' In his treatise *On exercising with a small ball*, a famous ancient physician Claudius Galenus described harpaston to be a better exercise than wrestling and running because it involved all parts

of the body, took less time, and cost nothing. He also thought the game was an adequate tactical exercise for the soldiers and could be dosed with varied intensity. The 7th cent. writer Isidor of Sevilla indicated in his work *Originum sive etymologiarum libri XX* (*The Origins or 20 Books of Etymology*) that the main objective of the game was to keep the ball in the air as long as possible: 'When a player snatches the ball from another, he throws it in the air so as not to let it touch the ground'.

K. Schneider, 'Harpastum', *Paulys Real Encyclopädie der Classischen Altertumswissenschaft*, herausg. Wilhelm Kroll, 1912, vol. 14.

HARPASTUM, see >HARPASTON.

HARPOON TOSS, a hunting skill popular among the Eskimo and whalers consisting in aiming and throwing a device called a harpoon at the chased animal. A characteristic feature of a harpoon is a spearhead in the form of one or several barbed blades, which are driven into the animal's body and allow for tugging the hit animal towards the hunter with a rope attached to the bottom of the spearshaft.
Ethymology. The Eng. word *harpoon* derives directly from the Du. *harpoen* and once meant a type of hook. The Du. word, on the other hand, is directly related to its prototype, Lat. *harpagos*, which means a hook on a shaft, or a grapnel used for crushing the walls of besieged fortresses and comes from Gk. *harpagos* – a hook. Cf. Icel. *harpo* – to clip, to gird; Frank. *harper* – to catch with a harpoon.
History. The skill of throwing a harpoon was characteristic of the Eskimo, who used it when fishing or hunting from a kayak, but probably also of the Germanic tribes, which called it *agnon* – a type of javelin with rope used for snatching the enemy's shield (see >AGNON TOSS). The contemporary harpoon, however, derives from similar equipment used by the Eskimo, which had a blade tipped with a sharp bone that detached from the harpoon and remained in the hit animal's body. Around the 17th cent. non-Eskimo whale hunters adopted the general idea of the harpoon. A whaling harpoon of that time usu. had a spearhead with two hooked endings pemanently fastened to the shaft. In approx. 1848 L. Temple, a black American blacksmith living in a whaling settlement of New Bedford, introduced an Eskimo-type harpoon without the detaching blade. This was known as a *toggle harpoon*, which had a jagged edge called a *toggle* or *swivel head*, approx. 7in. in length, a steel head called an *iron shaft*, 3½ft. in length, and a long spearshaft called a *wooden pole* that ended in several shuttlecocks and the pulling rope. At the end of the 18th cent. a gun for launching harpoons was invented, but until the mid-19th cent. whalers preferred manual harpoons. Then, in 1865, Cpt. Eben Pierce perfected the gun which quickly superseded the manual harpoon and ended the Romantic era of harpoon whaling. Harpooning whales has ever after been purely a technical matter, deprived of the unique character of a competition between man and animal as part of nature and offering relatively equal chances. This process was completed at the end of the 1860s, when a Norw. Svend Foyn constructed a new spearhead with hinged hooks on the sides that spread open once the head pierced the animal's body, making it virtually impossible for the animal to escape. This deadly invention was further perfected by placing inside the spearhead a glass container with sulphuric acid, which exploded inside the animal's body and deployed the hooks.

Eduard A. Stackpole, 'Harpoon', EAI, 13, 809.

HARROW FOOTBALL, a var. of football game developed at Harrow College, England. The game is played with a special ball resembling a flattened sphere that is 11in. in diameter at the wider point and 10in. at the narrower. Historically, the ball was formed by sewing 3 pieces of leather together, so that the whole thing looked like a rounded wedge of a cake or a loaf of bread. Harrow is one of the oldest schools in England and one of the first to develop a sporting tradition. In the Middle Ages the school used to prepare poor boys for academia or a career as clergy. Sanctioned by Queen Elisabeth in 1571 and financially secured by J. Lyon. Among its graduates are, among others: the playwright R.B. Sheridan, Sir R. Peel, the great poet Lord G. Byron, Britain's prime minister Lord Palmerston, the writers A. Trollope and J. Galsworthy as well as W. Churchill. All pupils had contact with the game. The introduc-

tion of rugby in 1927 limited the scope of the game to the Easter period. The school team play against graduates (Old Harrovians) and younger teachers (Masters). The main matches are played at the school (House Matches). Another group of matches serves as a way of selecting the best players and training them before they play for the school team (mostly consisting of older pupils from the 6th form). In the 2nd half of the 19th cent. the number of players was set between 11 and 30. From the beginning of the 20th cent. the number of players had a tendency towards the lower end of the limit, finally being set at 11 in 1927. Historically, the game was played on the slope of a nearby hill, which formed the basis for calling the parts of the field 'top' and 'bottom'. If it rained the players became covered with thick mud. For practical reasons, from the 2nd half of the 19th cent. the games were played on a regular football ground, and from 1927 onwards, the games have been played on a rugby pitch with different goals. The goals or *bases* are like rugby posts

Henry Wood Elliott (1846-1930), Eskimo Man With Harpoon, *handpainted photographic enlargement, Smithsonian's National Anthropological Archives.*

In the waters off of Neah Bay, Washington, on a rainy day, Makah whaler, Donny Swan harpoons a float in preparation for the Makah Indians' first whale hunt in some 70 years. So much time has passed since the last Makah hunt in 1920, there is no one still alive who knows how to whale. And hunting whales, especially in small boats, especially in winter seas, especially gray whales, is fraught with peril.

WORLD SPORTS ENCYCLOPEDIA

without the crossbar and a base is scored if the ball passes between them at any height. The team with more bases scored wins. In cases when the ball goes over higher than the posts, the final say in determining whether it passed between the poles belongs to the referee. If the ball passes exactly over the post, it is called a *poler* and is not considered a score. There are no goalkeepers but, in the vicinity of his own base, any player can prevent the opponents from scoring by stopping the ball with his hands. Playing with the hands is otherwise forbidden except in the situation described below as 'taking yards'. A typical Harrow football team consists of 4 centres, 4 wings and 3 defenders: leftback, centre back and right back. The centres quite often play as a unit, forming a loose scrum. The wings can be either inside or outside.

A charcteristic feature of Harrow football is the offside rule. A player is caught offside if the ball being dribbled in front of him is touched by another player from his team. This rule practically bans passing the ball forward, as it would result in an offside each time the pass is successful. Therefore, the player must collaborate closely with other team members, who run on either side of him, remaining slightly behind. Another original feature is *taking yards*. It allows for the ball to be caught if taken on the full from a kick (with the exception of a basekick*)*, with a shout of 'Yards'. The catcher then has a free punt with a run-up of 3 paces. The free punt may result in shooting directly at the base, if within the player's reach. If not, he can gain some ground by kicking the ball up in the air while any of his team can take possession without the danger of being caught offside. The game is very dynamic and devoid of any breaks as the ball never leaves the pitch (as it does in football). Deliberately putting the ball out usually results in the attacking team being pushed back by 20-30yds. A player who tosses or rather rolls the ball back into play, using only one hand, is excluded from the rule of offside and can throw the ball into the opponents' field. Corners are allowed but seldom used. Bouncing the ball with the head is also allowed but rare due to the weight of the ball. Most balls are caught on the shoulder, which is called *fouling*.

Foul play used not to result in any direct penalty during the game – the referee would just stop the game shouting *'shame stop!'* The culprit would be punished off the field by the lowering of his social position among the students. Fouls were therefore uncommon. Nowadays, reaction to them is considerably more relaxed. The rules of the game gathered in the school code known as *Obiter Dicta* define the following situation: 'the rules ought to be followed in order to maintain their awareness, and all dubious cases should traditionally be resolved to the benefit of the opponent. If you break a rule inadvertently, stop the game yourself.' If the attacking team does not profit from the foul, the game is continued. Otherwise, the referee stops the game and bounces the ball on the ground. Any number of players from both teams may attempt to take such a ball over but they are not allowed to touch it until it makes first contact with the ground. The only situation when a referee can intervene and punish a player is when he fouls an opponent in the vicinity of the base. As there is no defined penalty area in Harrow football, the decision rests with the referee. He can order a *base-kick* or even remove a player from the field. Games of lesser importance are conducted without a referee, regular ones with 1 and more prestigious ones with 2, one for each half of the ground. They do not use whistles but have sticks in order to point to dubious situations or players making mistakes. The referee's decisions are final but the board of the school's *Philathletic Club* is available for appeal. Outside Harrow, the game is only played at Eton. The two schools play against each other.

P.H.M. Bryant, *Harrow*, 1937; E.D. Laborde, *Harrow School, Yesterday and Today*, 1948.

HASHING, non-competitive cross-county running of Brit.-Malaysian origin, especially popular in Brit. Commonwealth countries. Similar to >PODCHODY but performed at running pace. It dates back to 1938, when a group of young Brit. public school students and businessmen from Kuala Lumpur initiated the activity. It consisted of a 20-40 strong group of people running after 1 or 2 people known as *hares*, across the jungle and the swamp surrounding the city. The *hares* laid a trail in sawdust, chalk, flour or

Hashing. A drawing from Harper's Weekly.

bits of paper. This fact made hashing similar to the old Brit. >PAPER CHASE, except that it does not follow an easy, clearly laid trail but goes through deliberately chosen difficult areas, such as rifts, bushes, jungle, rocks, etc. The initiators of hashing in Kuala Lumpur are known only by their nicknames and surnames (their first names did not survive): 'G' Gispert, 'Horse' Thompson and 'Torch' Bennet. They were later joined by F. Woodward, P. Wickens, L. Davidson, J. Wyatt-Smith and M.C. Hay. During WWII, hashing disappeared, banned in Malaysia by the Jap. occupants (Gispert died during the siege of Singapore) but it was resurrected in the 1950s. In the '60s and '70s the sport expanded beyond Malaysia. It is now practiced in Singapore (the first club was set up in 1962), Australia (1967), New Zealand, Hong-Kong, the USA and Great Britain, among others. The official Internet bulletin of hashing mentions 1,470 clubs located in 184 countries, including Cyprus, Thailand, Indonesia, the Philippines and the Ukraine. Outside the Anglo-Saxon countries, the organizers were usu. Brit. expatriots rather than indigenous people. Their activities revolve around the so-called *Hash House Harrier Clubs*. The members gather once or twice a fortnight in order to go for a run, accompanied by a social gathering. In the official materials, there is no information about any international organization. Collaboration among clubs is based on trad. and social links without any formal dependency. The ultimate authority in establishing the rules of the game and resolving any possible disputes is the oldest of the clubs, the Kuala Lumpur Hash House Harriers Club. The rules, usually formulated in a playful manner, say the goal of the club's activities is 'promoting fitness among the members' but also 'curing weekend frustration, quenching thirst with good beer and convincing older members that they are not as old as they think'. Hence the ironic name for the gatherings: 'drinkers with a running problem'. On many occasions hashing is performed in public parks or even streets but the participants always strive to organize their runs in the countryside, esp. with varied topography. There are also new analogous forms of hashing using the bicycle (*bicycle hashing* or *bashing*) or on skis (*ski hashing*), as well as the swimming var. (*swim hashing*) or even *hashing on in-line skates*.

P. 'Flying Booger' Woodford, *Hash Primer*, 1995; The Internet: http://www.half-mind.com/

HAT TOSS, a sport event similar to >BERET TOSSING. The objective is to toss a hat so that it lands on a pole about 1-1.2m high. A pitchfork stuck in the ground serves nicely. There are 2 types of competition; to win, one has to either 1) hit the target the most times in an agreed number of attempts, or 2) hit the target from the greatest distance.

HATHOR'S BALL, a ritual ball game of ancient Egypt. The game is known from a wall painting in the temple of the Eg. god Hathor in Deir-er-Bahari. The painting portrays Pharaoh Thutmose III holding a corrugated bat made of olive wood in the right hand and an orange-size ball in the left hand. In the background, two priests are holding a ball in both hands as if performing a free throw in basketball. The rules of the game or its social significance remain unknown. The game was most likely more of a

Hat tossing.

ritual than sport. The inscription reveals a ceremony held in honor of Hathor and reads that 'all the foes shall perish'. According to researchers, the 'foes' refers to the unwanted winter to be driven or 'batted' out with the balls.

HATS IN HOLES, an old Eng. game popular with town and city boys. The name most probably derives from holes that were dug in the ground in order to plant hats in them, forming targets for tossing a ball. The game is played next to a wall and the throwing distance is approx. 25ft. The player whose hat gets the ball, has to pick it up and toss it towards the other players. If he misses, he takes his hat and leaves the game. The last remaining player tosses the ball at the other players' bottoms with full force.

A.B. Gomme, 'Hats in Holes', TGESI 1894, I, 199.

HATTIE, see >POP-THE-BONNET.

HAU KUEN, Chin. for 'monkey fist'. A var. of old Chin. martial art, dating back to the 7th-10th cent. and the T'ang dynasty. The name derives from a legend, in which it was used by a monkey to defend a Buddhist monk Tom Sang Chong in the course of his journey to Tibet, where he was to receive the writings of Buddha.

HAULING THE BEAM, a Rus. boating competition in which the contenders try to rope a floating beam and haul it to the shore. The sport was described by I.N. Chkhannikov: 'The beam with two iron hooks on its ends is weighted on the bottom side to prevent it from turning over. Once the beam is afloat, two boats start racing towards it. A boat crew consists of a coxswain, a rower and a roper. The crew which manages first to rope the beam and haul it ashore wins the race' (GIZ, 1953, 80).

HAWKEY, an Eng. trad. game in which a small ball is hit with sticks. The pitch is divided into 2 halves. The teams are located on their halves of the field and their members are not allowed to cross over at any point in the game. The objective of the game is to put the ball in the opponents' half so that it hits a net spread at the back, passing by the players who are trying to stop it. The game is usually won after scoring 9 goals. The number of players is not strictly limited, neither is the size of the field. The origin of the game's name is unclear. It resembles >HOCKEY, as does the activity of hitting the ball with the stick. However the word *hawk* might refer to the bird (as if the ball was falling onto a player like the bird) or a travelling salesman (whereas the ball circulates like a commodity). Traditionally, the British had many similar games; cf. >SHINNY, >SHINTY and >NOT.

A.B. Gomme, 'Hawkey', TGESI, 1894, I, 199.

HAWKY, an old Eng. folk game, played in western parts of Sussex. A small ball is pushed around with the use of curved sticks as in modern day >FIELD HOCKEY; the name is subject to a dispute whether it is a variation on hockey or refers to the curved stick, resembling the curved beak of the bird of prey; a similar game in Norfolk and Suffolk was called >BANDY HOSHOE.

HAXEY HOOD, a trad. Brit. ball game, played spontaneously since the Middle Ages in Haxey, Lincolnshire. A similar game is also known in Epworth (>EP-

WORTH HOOD). Haxey hood is played twice a year: on 6 Jan. and 6 July, during local festivals. The object is to carry a ball to one of the 3 inns that perform the role of goals. The winner is the team whose player manages to bring the ball to one of the inns, where a sumptuous treat awaits the victorious team. The ball must not be kicked or dribbled, but only snatched from opponents and thrown towards one of the inns. Any pass in a direction other than the one leading to an inn is prohibited.

Etymology. The name 'haxey hood' originates from the name of a town, Haxey, which in turn prob. stems from 'hox', a dial. form of the word 'hock'. The second element, 'hood', is associated with a local folk

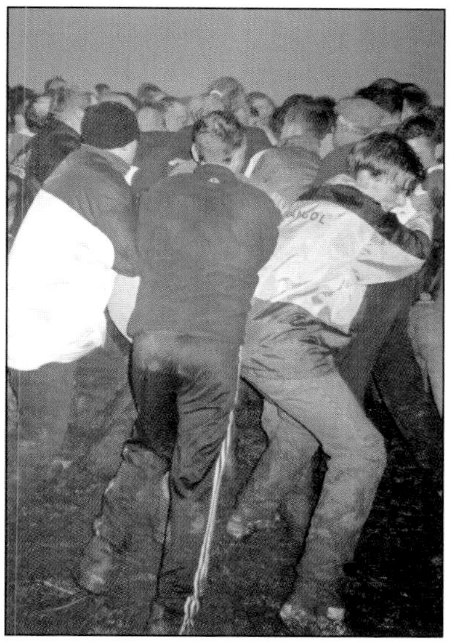

Haxey Hood Boggins forming a scrum.

tale according to which peasants caught the squire's wife's hood that was blown off her head by the wind. The players are referred to as Boggons (also Boggans), prob. from the bogs (or Scot.-Celtic *bogah*) that surround Haxey where the most heated parts of a match take place.

Course of the game. During the week preceding a haxey hood match, the players walk from door to door, collecting money in order to be able to organize the match and inviting everybody to the show. The gang is led by a Fool in a red costume wearing a hat adorned with feathers and red flowers. Similar hats are also worn by Boggons and, traditionally, each group member is wearing a scarlet flannel coat. On the match day the Fool's face is covered with a mixture of soot and ochre and he holds a whip that has, instead of a lash, a long stocking filled with bran. Anyone who comes too close, revealing thus lack of respect, is whipped with the stocking.

The match is preceded by a procession that starts early afternoon from the city and heads for the local parish church. The Fool has the right to kiss any woman he meets on his way. He is followed by 12 Boggons selected for the game. Today, Boggons are usu. players from a local football club. The team captain is referred to as the King Boggon, or Chief of the Boggons, or Lord of the Hood. While in a procession, he carries his team's emblem and a ball made of 13 willow twigs tied with 13 purple willow sprigs. The team challenging the Boggons is composed of citizens of Haxey, Westwood, and some other neighboring places.

When the procession reaches the churchyard, the Fool stands on a large stone, which was once the foot of a tall cross, and glorifies the player's skills inviting everybody to join the celebration. He also mentions mysteriously that two and a half oxen were slaughtered for the party and that the remaining half is still galloping across the playing field where, if necessary, it can be caught and placed on a spit. The speech is closed with a short summary of the rules recited in an old local dialect:

'Hoose agen hoose, tone agen tone,
If tho meets a man, knock 'im done
But don't ut him.

During the speech the Fool is put to a test, called Smoking the Fool. Ethnographer M. Peacock describes the ceremony as follows: 'He was suspended over the fire and swung backwards and forwards over it almost suffocated; then allowed to drop into the smoldering straw, which was well wetted, and to scramble out as he could.' Such literal smoking of the Fool was discontinued after the Fool actually once caught fire in 1956 because someone forgot to put it out. Although the fire was extinguished and the Fool saved, since that incident the smoking is only symbolic: a little pile of damp straw placed behind the Fool is lighted, producing a lot of smoke without any open fire.

After the speech and smoking ceremony, the Fool leads the crowd to a nearby hill. Boggons and their opponents stand in a circle and a preliminary game with the use of 'small hoods' commences. The hoods differ from the actual haxey hood ball as they are made of rags tied with ribbons. The Chief of the Boggons throws the hoods one after another and, as C. Hole described it:

As soon as the first Hood is thrown up, there is a fierce struggle for it, every man trying to seize it and carry it over the boundary of his own village. If any one manages to get it safely over the line and away, he can keep the Hood; but in order to do so he has to elude, not only the watchful Boggans, but all the other players who rush after him and try to wrest it from him. The function of the Boggans is to prevent the Hood from crossing the boundary. If one of them captures it, or even touches it, that Hood is 'dead', and is returned to the Lord to be thrown up again.

When the entire stock of hoods is used up and captured, the actual match, called the Sway gets under way. The principal ball is therefore referred to as the Sway Hood, and it is a symbol of the temporary power of those who hold it at a given moment. The game starts with the Sway Hood tossed by the Lord of the Hood or one of the local high-ranking officials invited as an honorary guest. The Boggons await standing in a circle and the moment the Hood is airborne they move on to form a kind of a scrum – larger than the one formed by rugby players – that goes down the hill and then in different directions, depending on who has the ball. The match usu. continues for 2-3hrs., until a representative of one of the teams finally makes it to one of the 3 inns where the winners' treat begins.

History. Like many other folk sports, haxey hood also has its legend explaining the beginnings of the game. In the 13th cent., while riding a horse on her way from Haxey to Westwoodside, Lady Mowbray lost her hood that was blown off by a sudden gust of wind. Twelve peasants working in the field nearby saw the flying hood and tried to catch it but the wind was so strong that it took them a while before they succeeded. As a reward for their efforts, Lady Mowbray donated 13 acres of land to the parish from which the peasants were coming and the profit made on that land was to be earmarked for an annual celebration commemorating this event, during which 12 men were to reconstruct the catching of the hood, which was shortly exchanged for a ball. The churchyard from which players set off bound for the playing field is believed to be a part of the legendary 13 acres. Contrary to the legend, the game actually dates even further back than the 13th cent. Ethnographers believe that the game and the festival accompanying it originated from a pre-Christian fertility rite related to offerings intended to secure a good harvest and to celebrate the end of winter. E.O. James claims the game is a relic of a ritual fight between the local communities and the hood was originally the half of an ox to which the Fool alludes in his speech, or even an ox's head offered to the deities to ensure a bountiful harvest.

J. Arlott, 'Haxey Hood', OCSG, 1975, 470; C. Hole, 'Haxey Hood', *Dictionary of British Customs*, 1995, 139-143; M. Peacock, 'The Hood-Game at Haxey, Lincolnshire', *Folklore*, 1896, VII; M. Robinson, 'The Haxey Hood Game', Folklore, 1956, 67.

HAY TOSSING, an event played according to variable local rules during folk festivals in many Eur. countries, esp. Ireland, from where emigrants took it to the USA, N.Zealand, Canada, and Australia. Outside of Ireland, it has gained the status of a prestige countryside sport in Australia. In both countries today, sacks filled with oat straws, weighing 3.6kg and 56-66cm long, are used instead of sheaves. Such 'sheaves' are tossed up over an elevated bar using two-prong pitchforks. The decisive factor is the height and time taken by a competitor to toss up a pre-defined number of 'sheaves'. The first sheaf tossing tournament was organized in 1914 during the S Austrl. Annual Show. S. Wait was the winner, tossing a sheaf over a bar at a height of 9.8m. In the 1940s, the Schwerdt brothers of S Australia dominated the event. In the 1980s and early 1990s, W. Schache was the best competitor, winning the Austrl. championships. The record height of 17.4m was attained by B. Mountrey of Tasmania in 1970. In France, a similar folk sport is known by the name of *lancer de la botte de paille* [Fr. *lancer* – to toss + *botte* – bundle + *paille* – straw] or *lance de la gerbe de paille* [Fr. *gerbe* – sheaf].

G. Crawford, 'Sheaf-tossing', OCAS, 1994, 378.

HAZENA, [Czech *haziti* – to toss], a ball game similar to modern handball. At the peak of its popularity, it was played almost exclusively by women. The field is 48mx38m and is divided into 3 parts: 'the white half-back area', 'the center area', and 'the red half-back area'. In the 'half-back areas' there are 'goal areas' 4x8m and the goals themselves, 2.35m high and 2m wide. The teams are 7 a side, including the goalkeeper. The players are only allowed to move within their assigned areas – the goalkeeper must remain within the goal area and the half-back areas; the defenders must stick to their own half-back area and the center area, whereas the attack can only occupy the center area and the half-back area of the opposite team. The player holding the ball can only take 3 steps. Corners are executed almost as in >FOOTBALL. Disputed situations are resolved by bouncing the ball off the ground between 2 players from opposing teams.

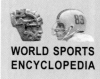

In various countries small sheaves in hay tossing competitions are replaced with large bales.

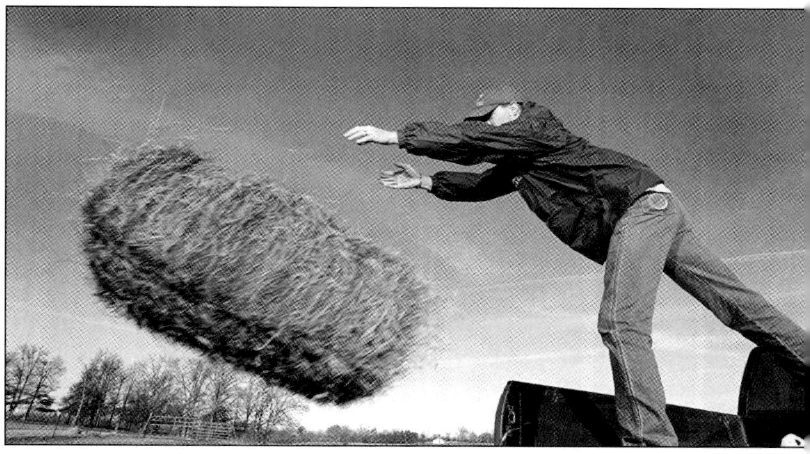

History. Hazena was created around 1905 by a Czech teacher A. Kristof. It quickly gained popularity in the country as well as in some other Eur. states. It was most popular between 1934 and 1938. The first world cup competition was held in 1934 in London, and won by a team from Slovenia, at the time representing Yugoslavia. The game declined in popularity during WWII, and its tradition has not been revived with the exception of limited presence in the Czech and Slovak Republics. The successor of the game is female >TEAM HANDBALL.

S. Jancalek, F. Taborsky, *Hazena*, 1973; S.Szmid-Berżyńska, W. Kwast, *Hazena-jordanka,* 1937; Z. Wyrobek, *Jordanka-hazena*, 1930; M. Bon, 'Historical Development of Hazena, Typically Women Game in Slovenia', SESS, 1996.

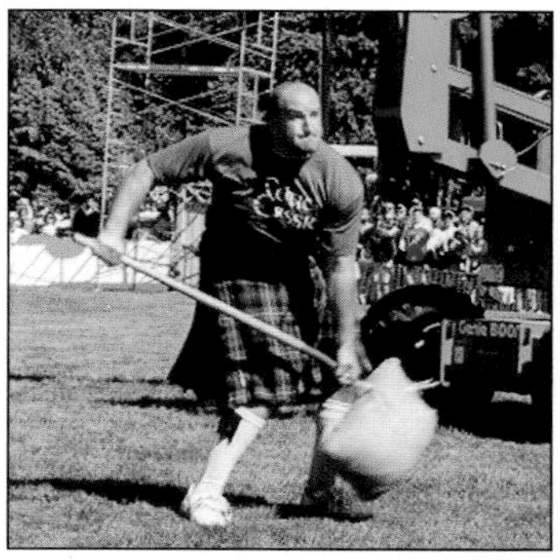

Top and above: hay tossing competitions.

HEAD PULL, Eng. name of a sport of Native Alaskans and Native North American Indians. Two competitors lie facing each other on the floor on their stomachs. A looped leather thong or belt, approx. 3ft. long and 1½in. wide, is placed over the backs of the players' heads just above the ears. Competitors rise to a push-up position with only hands and feet touching the floor, looking into each other's eyes. Then, at a signal, they pull with their heads, bracing with their hands and using their whole body strength to pull steadily backward. The pull must be directly back and parallel to the ground. There are 3 lines on the ground: a center line is drawn between the 2 competitors, and 2 additional parallel lines are drawn on either side of the center line. The object of the competition is to pull the opponent over the line parallel to the center line. The winner of a pull is declared if the opponent's hand crosses the parallel line, or if the opponent drops his head and allows the loop to be pulled off, or if any part of the body other than the hands and feet touches the floor. According to Amer. terminology, this is one of the so-called *arctic sports*, a separate competition among N.Amer. Indigenous Games.

The Arctic Sports, Internet: http://www.firstnations.com/naig97/arctic-sports/as-headpull.htm

H

WORLD SPORTS ENCYCLOPEDIA

HIGH JUMP OLYMPIC CHAMPIONS

MEN

1896 Ellery Clark, USA 1.81
1900 Irving Baxter, USA 1.90
1904 Samuel Jones, USA 1.80
1906 Con Leahy, GBR/IRL 1.775
1908 Harry Porter, USA 1.90
1912 Alma Richards, USA 1.93
1920 Richmond Landon, USA 1.935
1924 Harold Osborn, USA 1.98
1928 Robert King, USA 1.94
1932 Duncan McNaughton, CAN 1.97
1936 Cornelius Johnson, USA 2.03
1948 John Winter, AUS 1.98
1952 Walt Davis, USA 2.04
1956 Charles Dumas, USA 2.12
1960 Robert Shavlakadze, URS 2.16
1964 Valeriy Brumel, URS 2.18
1968 Dick Fosbury, USA 2.24
1972 Jüri Tarmak, URS 2.23
1976 Jacek Wszola, POL 2.25
1980 Gerd Wessig, GDR 2.36
1984 Dietmar Mögenburg, FRG 2.35
1988 Gennadiy Avdyeyenko, URS 2.38
1992 Javier Sotomayor, CUB 2.34
1996 Charles Austin, USA 2.39
2000 Sergey Klyugin, RUS 2.35

The high jump on a postage stamp issued for the 1966 European Track and Field Championship in Budapest.

HEADS OR TAILS, a game consisting in tossing a single coin and seeing which side is facing up when it lands. The player who has chosen the side that lands up wins. The coin toss (often simply 'the toss') is also used in many disciplines to draw the sides of the field, the right to serve, start the game etc. Gambling games using principles similar to heads or tails are also called *pitch and hustle* or *hustle cap*. In hustle cap, more coins are used, and the winner is the player who backs the prevailing side. Similar games, using many coins or other objects, such as cowry shells, are known in many cultures, cf. Nigerian >IGBA-EGO, >IGBA-ITA.

HEAP THE CAIRN, also locally *heap the cyarn*, simple endurance game, popular with students of old English schools, similar to >MORE SACKS TO THE MILL. One of the weaker participants is thrown onto the ground by his stronger colleagues. Then further participants are caught and thrown onto him, until the ones at the bottom of the heap cannot handle their weight. The game is accompanied by a rhyme.
A.B. Gomme, 'Heap the Cairn', TGESI, 1898, II, 428.

HEKS, Dan. for 'witch'. A Dan. var. of tag involving catching runaways. There may be a number of catchers, one of them being the witch, who 'freezes' (*forstene*) a participant with a pat (*slås*). The release of such a player requires a pat from another runaway accompanied by the word 'free' (*fri*). Alternatively, the player releasing another must jump over their back. In still another variant, the 'frozen' contestant spreads his/her legs and waits until another player goes through them to release him/her.
J. Møller, 'Heks', GID, 1997, 2, 69.

HEN THRASHING, an Eng. folk competition consisting of throwing sticks at a hen tied to a pole, associated with Brit. Shrove Tuesday celebrations (compare >COCK-THROWING). See also other games referring to this holiday, such as >SHROVE TUESDAY FOOTBALL.

HENGERLÉ, a Rum. bat and ball game similar to >PALANT, played in the Transylvania region. Compare Rum. >HOIMA.

HEPTATHLON, an athletic contest, an extension and Olympic continuation of >PENTATHLON. The men's heptathlon, one of the events of the Indoor W.Ch., comprises : 60m sprint, long jump, shot put, high jump, 60m hurdles, pole vault and a 1km run. A Pole, S. Chmara, won the gold medal at the E.Ch. in 1998 and in 1999 won the Indoor W.Ch. The women's heptathlon includes the following competitions, usu. held over 2 days: day 1 – 100m hurdles, shot put, high jump, 200m sprint; day 2 – long jump, javelin throw, 800m run. The first Olympic champion was N. Tykacenko, USSR. Later the best contestants came from the GDR, winning gold medals at the E.Ch. in 1982 and 1983 (R. Neubert). In their absence (as a result of the boycott of the 1984 Olym-

pics by East Eur. nations), the title of Olympic champion went to G. Nunn from Australia. J. Joyner-Kersee is considered the best heptathlon contestant ever, the world champion in 1987 and Olympic champion in 1998 and 1992. The Syrian S. Ghada was a surprise winner of the Ol.G. in 1996. The 2000 Ol.G. event was dominated by D. Lewis (Great Britain).

HERRE I RINGEN, Dan. for 'gentleman in the circle'. Two groups stand so that one is inside a circle drawn on the ground, preferably on a small mound, while the other remains outside. The goal is to take over the area inside the circle and maintain one's position there, king-of-the-hill style. Every man for himself, the winner is the last remaining competitor in the circle. Pushing and pulling are allowed but hitting and kicking are banned.
J. Møller, 'Herre I Ringen', GID, 1997, 4, 48.

HESTEVÆDDELØB, Dan. name for >HORSE RACING accompanied by betting [Dan. *hest* – horse, *vædde* – bet, *løb* – run]. Like in many other countries, the origin of this competition is in the Eng. tradition. The first race based on such a model took place in Denmark in 1689. It was a bet between the Eng. ambassador, R. Molsenworth, and the Dan. court's Master of the Horse, A.W. Haxthausen. The Dan. baron claimed that his horse would run 42km in 45min. The horse did it in 42min. but fell dead in the courtyard of the Frederiksborg castle.
J. Møller, 'Hestevæddeløb', GID, 1997, 4, 91.

HET KOLVEN, also >KOLVEN, old Du. game with a ball hit with the use of curved sticks. It is considered to be a predecessor of 2 separate modern sports: >GOLF and >FIELD HOCKEY.

HICK, STEP AND JUMP, an Eng. old folk var. of >TRIPLE JUMP, similar to >HALF-HAMMER.

HICKLING, a brutal form of folk wrestling formerly popular among mining communities in Derbyshire. At the end of the 19th cent., due to numerous cases of people becoming handicapped or even killed while practicing it, the sport was banned. It continued illegally, now in decline, although may still be found locally. The contestants fought, grabbing the opponent by the jacket. Kicking below knee-level was allowed and fighters wore reinforced boots to make it more painful. There were 3 ways to victory: by using a lever catch, causing great pain and making the opponent surrender; touching the ground with any body part above the knee; or a contestant's surrender due to exhaustion. A similar form of wrestling was known in Lancashire as *purring*.

HIGH JUMP (RUNNING), an athletic event in which a competitor has to jump over a high bar set between 2 vertical supports, taking off from 1 leg. The order in which the competitors jump is decided by draw. The judge announces the initial height and then the heights to which the bar will be raised. The last competitor in the contest has the right to set the height,

though it must be at least 2cm higher than the previous height. The run-up must be at least 15m long, at international competitions – 25m. A competitor can use markers to make the run-up easier and mark the take-off spot. Chalk or any other materials which leave a permanent mark are not allowed. The supports can be of any type, but must allow for free fall of the bar, when it is knocked off and must be at least 10cm higher than the greatest height of final jumps. The supports' ends cannot be covered in rubber or any other substance increasing friction or braking the fall of the bar. The distance between the supports cannot exceed 4m. The bar should be made of fiberglass or a similar material and should be round, except for the flattened ends resting on the supports. The bar is 30mm in diameter, slightly over 4m long and weighs up to 2kg. The landing area in the past was a sand heap, today foam-filled mats are used. The landing area should be 5x3m. Each contestant has 3 attempts to clear the bar at each height. When 2 or more contestants end with the same height jumped, a contestant who made fewer jumps in the course of the entire contest is awarded a higher position. Contestants can decide not to jump in a given round.

History. The high jump is a natural derivative of ordinary human activities, as natural and man-made obstacles have frequently needed to be overcome. In the folk variety it has been practiced in many cultures and civilizations. The trad. form, close to the modern one, of jumping over a wooden bar, has been practiced from time immemorial by the African tribe of Watusi in Rwanda, where the jumpers take off from springy termite mounds, reaching a height of about 2.5m. In ancient Egypt jumps over clasped hands were known; they persist in present-day Egypt and in Syria (>KHAZZA LAVIZZA). On the Indon. island of Nias the natives compete in jumps over stones or a wall, specially built for this purpose (>HIGH JUMP OVER A STONE). There is no evidence that the high jump was practiced in ancient Greece; this contest was not featured in the games organized there. In the Middle Ages, at the courts of some rulers, a >KING'S JUMP (also *royal jump*) was known; it was a combination of a high and long jump, across an increasing number of horses. Different var. of jumps in full armor over a horse or onto a horse were also practiced in the Middle Ages. There is a Scot. high jump without a bar, the object of which is to touch with a leg a bladder filled with air or a tambourine, raised at different heights (>HITCH AND KICK). Different var. of high jumps were recommended by J.C.F. Guts-Muths and F.L. Jahn in their gymnastic systems. The modern form of high jump comes from the Brit. Isles. The first rules of high jump were defined in 1834, e.g., the initial height which the contestant had to clear in the first jump to qualify to the next rounds. At that time it was 5½ft. (about 167.6cm). The high jump was included in the Eng. championship in 1866 and in the Amer. cham-

First unveiled at the 1968 Olympics in Mexico, the 'Fosbury Flop' revolutionized the running high jump.

pionship in 1876. Official records have been kept since 1864. The first record was set by a Brit, F.H. Gooch – 168cm (1864). The first contestant to have cleared 2m was an Amer., G. Horine (2.01m – 1912); 210cm was first attained by L. Steers (211cm – 1941); 220cm – J. Thomas (2.23m – 1960); 230cm – D. Stones (230cm – 1973), who later jumped 231cm (1976). Up to that height all the record-breaking sportsmen were American. This monopoly was broken by a representative of the USSR, R. Povarnicyn, who jumped 240cm (1985); he was beaten by I. Paklin, also from the USSR (241cm, 1985). The best high jumper in the second half of the 1980s and in the 1990s was a Cuban, J. Sotomayor, who regularly jumped 240cm. The best jumpers ever, also included J. Stiepanov and W. Brumel (USSR), who set 4 world records between 1961-63. In the 1970s representatives of GDR, FDR, China and Poland (J. Wszoła) were among the best performers. Better results were obtained when training techniques, and particularly the style, were improved. In the 19th cent. natural styles prevailed, e.g. Eastern cut-off (the jumper ran towards the bar and jumped with the legs drawn sideways), followed by the scissors style (in which the jumper's legs performed a scissor-like movement in clearing the bar). At the beginning of the 20th cent. the so-called roll style appeared, in which the jumper made a curved approach to the bar and cleared it with the hips thrust up, rolling the body over the bar. In the following years, particularly in the 1940s, '50s, and '60s the straddle jump dominated the contests, perfected by J. Thomas and W. Brumel. After the approach the right leg is straightened to provide full upward lift, then bends after becoming airborne while nearing the bar, straightening again at the bar. The body then rolls over the bar. During the 1968 Mexico Olympics, D. Fosbury used the 'flop' technique for the first time in which the jumper clears the bar headfirst and backwards. This style, although controversial, soon was commonly adopted and today is practically the only style seen during competitions. The other, much easier approaches, can still be seen at lower rank contests; they also continue to be used in physical education classes. During the Ol.G. in 1900-12, in addition to running high jump contests, contests in >HIGH JUMP (STANDING) were held.

Women's high jump, although sporadically practiced in the 19th cent., started to develop as an athletic contest in 1921, when it was introduced under the auspices of the International Federation of Women's Sports. In this pioneer period the best high jumpers were H. Hatt (Great Britain, 1922), H. Bonze (France, 1926), I. Braumüller (Germany, 1930) and S. Griene (Germany, 1934). Women's high jump was included in the Ol.G. in 1928. The first Olympic champion was E. Catherwood (Canada). World records have been kept since 1910. The first world record was set by C. Hale (USA, 141cm). The first female high jumper to have cleared 150cm was E. van Truyen (Belgium, 151cm, 1924); 160cm – M. Clark (South Africa, 160cm, 1928), who was beaten by J. Shiley (USA, 161cm, 1930). F. Blankers-Koen (the Netherlands) was the first to have jumped more than 170cm (171cm, 1943). After 1945 the best jumper was I. Balas (Romania), who was the first to have jumped 180cm (1958) and 181cm (1958). In 1961 Balas jumped 190cm. The first jumper to clear 2m was R. Ackerman from the German Democratic Republic (1977), only to be beaten the following year by a centimeter by Ital. jumper S. Simeoni.

HIGH JUMP (STANDING), a contest in which the contestant throws himself over a bar without a run-up, i.e. from a standing position; it was included in the 1900-12 Ol.G. As in the case of >LONG JUMP (STANDING), the best jumper was an American R. Ewry, who won all the Ol.G. between 1900-08 and set a few world records, the last in 1900 (165cm). After 1912 the contest was withdrawn from the Ol.G., and was only held for some time during local competitions organized in different countries, only to be abandoned completely in the 1930s. Cf. >TRIPLE JUMP (STANDING), >LONG JUMP (STANDING), >HIGH JUMP (RUNNING).

HIGH JUMP OVER A STONE, a form of folk high jump competition over a special stone or rock or specially built wall. It is practiced by some Asiatic peoples, including the Indon. tribe inhabiting the island of Nias, and also in some areas of India, e.g. by the Zemi tribe from N Cachar Hills. In the latter case the contestants were put to a test – first they had to jump onto a high stone, which eliminated those, who could not do this, and then they had to do a long jump from the stone. The contestant who jumped the farthest distance was the winner.

HILDEGARDA, an Eng. game similar to >CRICKET and >ROUNDERS; the field is identical with the one in cricket. In its center, a circle of approx. 30cm in diameter is the point from which the attacking team throw the ball; 10m away there are 3 targets on poles approx. 1.8m high, located so they form a regular triangle. The targets are elliptical and they resemble tennis rackets, as each consists of a frame with stringing. The target's pole divides it into 2 halves, which makes it harder to hit since hitting the pole does not count. The defending team stand by the targets. The thrower chooses one of the targets and tries to hit it unexpectedly so as to catch the defenders off guard. The ball is similar in size to a tennis ball. The defenders try to guard the targets using bats. The bat has a short handle, ending with a ball or a round plank. After a successful defensive bounce, while the ball is in the air, the defenders change their positions, which equals scoring 1pt. A player who has been through all 3 targets (in one or more throws) retires from the field, replaced by another player. While the ball is in the air, the attacking team tries to catch it and use it to hit any of the running defenders, in order to eliminate them from the game. The attackers score points if they hit the target or if they catch a ball that has bounced off a defender. They also score if any of the defenders touches the ball with anything else but his forearm or the bat. The number of players varies from 8 to 22.

HILL RUNNING, a form of >SLOPE RUNNING, a folk activity popular in Scotland, often with participants from other parts of Britain (>FELL RUNNING). The most prestigious run in Scotland, and in the whole of Britain, is the run from Fort William to the top of Ben Nevis in the Inverness county. The distance to the summit of Britain's highest peak (4,406ft.) is approx. 15mi., and it is also the longest ascending running track in Britain. In the runners' jargon both the mountain and the competition are called The Ben. The first modern competition on this distance took place in 1895 and was won by W. Swan, who ran it in 2hrs. and 41min. The record set in 1984 at 1hr. 25min. 34sec. by K. Stuart was not broken until 1998. The most famous Scottish runs are, among others, The Goat Fell Hill Race, started in 1953; Cairngorm Race (1957); Creagh Dubh Race

(1964) and, organized in the '60s, the Mamore Race, Achmony Race, Elidon Hill Race and Knockfarrel Hill Race. The rules of hill running, estab. by the Scot. Athletic Federation, stipulate that each runner be equipped with a compass, a whistle to signal danger or accident and a food supply of energy value equaling 20oz. of chocolate. During the run, the runners are dressed like athletes, but they must carry sacks containing extra clothing, esp. a waterproof suit or warm pants, a jacket, gloves and a hat in case they lose their way or are forced to wait for help. The most important part of the equipment is the footwear. Regular shoes were used until 1957, when spiked boots with leather tops were introduced. Currently, the runners use light man-made shoes with pyramid rubber studs, which improve running both uphill and downhill.

History: the oldest information on hill running comes from the Middle Ages, when it was part of various folk holidays as well as Highland Games and Gatherings. According to J. Beech, a researcher into the tradition of hill running, out of a few hundred folk holidays still celebrated, at least 25 include this competition. In the second half of the 19th cent. and in the early 20th cent. hill running was in crisis and competitions seldom took place. It was the Eng. >FELL RUNNING that helped to maintain the Scot. tradition. Under its influence old folk customs were enriched with modern organizational forms. In the 1950s and '60s Scot. hill running went through a period of dynamic growth, first in close collaboration with Eng. organizations, then with the Fell Runners Association (FRA), created in 1970. Under its guidance, the runners participated in an annual cycle of competitions enabling them to gather points that were eventually used to determine The Fell Runner of the Year. In 1981, the name of the cup was changed to the Brit. Fell Racing Championship, however it did not include a number of Scot. competitions. In 1983, this led to the separation of the Scot. FRA subcommittee, which developed a separate competition calendar under the old name of the Scot. Hill Running Championship. In 1984 the subcommittee was transformed into the independent Scot. Hill Running Association. The new Scot. calendar included 39 running events in the years 1983-85. Their number rose and 1996 saw 54 events; in 1998 there were as many as 79 competitions. In 1996 the number of amateur runners totaled 2,652. The rules of the Scot. Athletic Federation (SAF) are enforced, distancing the sport from professional acts, which dominate folk events such as Highland Games

WORLD SPORTS ENCYCLOPEDIA

H

Hill running: James Southam, left, and Darin Markwardt, close on his heels, race to the finish of the Wolverine Mountain Run in Anchorage, Alaska. A qualifying race for the World Mountain Running Trophy in Austria, the 5½-mile race climbs 3,600 feet to the summit of Wolverine Peak in the Chugach State Park just outside of Anchorage.

Esaias Van der Velde, The Joy of Ice on the Wallgraben, *1618, wood.*

and Gatherings. Currently, the SAF oversees hill running through the Scot. Hill Running Commission, estab. 1991-92. The most famous hill runner is E. 'Eddie' Campbell from Fort Williams, who participated in the Ben Nevis run 43 times, from 1951 until his death in 1995. He won 3 times, and several times was near victory. Other famous runners include J. 'Jamie' Thin and R. Morris.

Many hill runners are also fond of >ORIENTEERING. According to Beech, who is also an amateur, 'over the last 2 decades, hill running has become an important tendency in Scot. attempts at sport and leisure activities, and it has taken advantage of the country's topography'. The growing popularity of the sport has been manifested in the publication of a specialist magazine *Scottish Hill Runner*, and newsletters, which e.g. in 1998 were published by 11 hill running clubs. The sporting community is also supported by literature, the prime example of which is a 5-part poem by J. Jardine *Doon the Ben*. The poem depicts events of the 1971 run, when the fog and sudden changes of the weather caused confusion among the runners, some of whom managed to move from further positions to the top of the pack without passing any other hill runner in the process. J. Beech, 'Hill Running in Scotland', *Review of Scottish Culture*, 1998, 11, 135-148; H.D. MacLennan, *The Ben Race*, 1994.

HIMMELBOLD, Dan. for 'a heavenly ball', a game for 6 players, similar to Eng. >TRAP, BAT AND BALL. A thin long plank is placed across a thick log, forming a mini seesaw. The plank has a spoon-like cavity at one of its ends – this is where the ball is placed. Hitting the other end of the plank sends the ball into the air and the players try and catch it. The one who succeeds in doing so, gets the privilege of hitting the lever next. Himmelbold used to be played in Denmark – in Klitmøller and Thy, usually at the seaside. There was a similar game called *københavnsbold* – the Copenhagen ball, and also *københavnsnsklangbold* (lit. 'long Copenhagen ball'); contrary to what the name suggests, played in southern Jutland. J. Møller, 'Himmelbold', GID, 1997, 1, 18.

Hjørnekegler.

HINAM TURNAM, an Ind. game, imitating the struggle between life and death, reflected in the roles of the hunter and his prey, played by people – real animals are not involved.
The Internet: http://w3.meadev.gov.in/sports/tr_games/arun.htm

HINKE, also *hinke ruder, hinke paradis;* see >AT HINKE.

HIP-BALL GAME, Eng. name used internationally to relate to old and modern var. of games played in S.America. The games consist in bouncing the ball with the hip, esp. protected with a stone, wooden or leather shield. See also: >MESOAMERICAN INDIAN BALL GAMES; >POKYAH, >TLACHTLI, >ULAMA.

HIPPIOS, in ancient Greece, a medium distance run, 4 stadiums (>STADIODROMOS) long. The name came from a similar distance used in horse racing (Gr. *Hippos* – horse). Since ancient athletic stadiums lacked round running tracks, the runners completed the distance in 4 legs. As in other running competitions, the participants started from the *balbis*, a stone beam with footholds gouged into it. At the other end of the track there was a line called the *terma* or *gramme* (the terma indicated the finishing line in 1-stadium races; the gramme denoted the starting line at the end of balbis). The competitors turned round at the point that was 1 stadium away, called the *kampter*, marked with a wooden pole or a stone pillar. The start line doubled as the finish. It was marked with a straight line drawn on the sand, later replaced with wooden poles or stone pillars. It is likely that in hippios and in >DOLICHOS, the starting point was situated at the end of the track opposite to the starting point of the stadium-length runs so that in both competitions the finishing line was the same.

HIPPOLAMPAS, see >TORCH RELAYS.

HIPPON, Gk. name of cart races drawn by adult horses, as opposed to carts drawn by colts (>POLON SYNORIS) or mules (>APENE). There were 2 basic var. of hippon: 2-horse (>SYNORIS) and 4-horse races (>TETRIPPON, also see >QUADRIGA RACES). Races with 4-horse teams were introduced to the OI.G. in 680 BC; the first winner was Pagondas or Pagon of Thebes. The last information of such a competition is dated 241 AD, with a race won by a certain Titus Domitius Prometheus (also with 4 horses). Cf. >CHARIOT RACING.

HIPTOI, see >MAHI RINGARINGA.

HITCH AND KICK, an original form of high jump, practiced during Scot. Border Games. Instead of jumping over the crossbar, the contestants attempted to kick an inflated bladder suspended on a special hook or, even a tamborine, which rang when the attempt was successful. The effort was valid only if proceeded by a scissor-like crossing of the legs in the air. Those who were successful at one height were allowed to continue with the bladder or tamborine raised higher. The average height of such jumps was approx. 3m. Cf. >ALASKAN HIGH KICK, >ONE FOOT HIGH KICK, >TWO FOOT HIGH KICK.

HITY-HITY, a var. of seesaw, once popular in Somerset, England.

HIYANG TANNABA, the Manipur dialect for 'a boat race', a folk var. of rowing practiced in the Ind. state of Manipur as part of Lai Haraoba celebrations. There are only 2 boats (*he*) participating, each with rich and colorful decorations. Their length is not limited by the rules and they can hold an unlimited number of rowers, usually 20 or more. The rowers (*nou*) are dressed in colorful clothes. The boats' commanders sit in the prow. Judges situated at the start and the finish supervise the race. The spectators are divided into 2 groups *hiban chenba* and *khongban chenba*, who cheer the opposing teams.
The tradition of hiyang tannaba started in pre-historic times, during the race of the mythological heroes Lainingthou and Lairembi. Modern races are a re-enactment of that event, also called the *hikaba*. Hiyang tannaba crews are exclusively male.
The Internet: http://www.nic.in/manipur/games.htm

HJØRNEKEGLER, Dan. for 'corner pins', a game of bowling with 9 straight pins, or pegs, 7-8cm in diameter. In order to increase stability, the pins are inserted into the ground but not too deeply, so they can be knocked over. The players throw a T-shaped object resembling a wooden mallet with an elongat-

ed head. The players pair up and perform their throws from a distance of 4-5m from the opposite corners of the square formed by the pins. The team that knocks over the last pin wins.
J. Møller, 'Hjørnekegler', GID, 1997, 1, 101-102.

HJØRNESKINDLEG, a Dan. game of leather, [Dan. *hjørne* – corner + *skind* – leather + *leg* – game]. The object of the game is a piece of untanned leather, which is rolled tightly to make it easier to catch. The 4 players are located in the corners of the playing area, often a room or a school hall; a 5th player, situated in the middle, tries to take possession of the roll. No holds are barred including wrestling with the corner players.
History. The game dates back to Viking times and is well described in the old sagas. It is the only game whose rules have been relatively strictly maintained up to the present day; popular in the whole of Germanic Scandinavia.
J. Møller, 'Hjørneskindleg', GID, 1997, 1, 37.

Hendrick Avercamp, A Scene On the Ice, *watercolor.*

Hendrick Avercamp, Enjoying the Ice, *c.1630-34, oil on canvas.*

Hockey Players, *a Roman relief.*

HOCKEY, a family of team games consisting in hitting or pushing a small ball or puck, using sticks or rackets in order to score a goal. There are many historical and modern var. of hockey ranging from international to folk and local, e.g. >BADDIN, >BANDY, >BAZHIG KAMM, >CAMP-BALL, >CHEUCA, >CROSSERIE, >GAME OF HAILES, >UNICYCLE HOCKEY, >MIXED HOCKEY, >ICE HOCKEY, >FIELD HOCKEY, >ROLLER HOCKEY, >UNDERWATER HOCKEY, >HOLANI, >INJI UCHI, >JEU DE MAIL, >KERETIZEIN, >KHONG KANGJEI, >KNATTLEIKR, >KOORA, >MARI UCHI, >MELAT, >RINGETTE, >SHINTY, >SOLLEN, >SOULE Á LA CROSSE, >TCHOS AGADJI, >TS'IITS'QWEL'O'L. Also see: >CHACO INDIAN HOCKEY, >MECRANOTI INDIAN HOCKEY, >OCEANIAN PEOPLES' HOCKEY. There are games resembling hockey in terms of using the stick, with less emphasis on the curve of the stick and more on its widening, and also with a hollow used for catching the ball or carrying it as in >CAMÁNACHT, >CAMMOCK, >CAMOGIE, >HURLING, >KNAPPAN, >RINGETTE. Another group is formed by games utilizing sticks ending in a small racket for catching the ball and carrying it as in >LACROSSE and, preceding it, Native Amer. >BAGATAWAY, >TEWAARATHON, >TOLI. Some folk var. of polo resemble hockey when played on foot as in Chin. >JIQIU and Jap. >DAKYU. >BROOMBALL is similar to hockey played with special brooms to move the ball.
Etymology. The origin of the game's name is unclear. Specialists tend to associate the term with the O.-Fr. *Hoquet*, brought to England with the invasion of William the Conqueror (1066), where it

265
WORLD SPORTS ENCYCLOPEDIA H

gradually took its present form, spelling and pronunciation. The modern form was eventually adopted in France, although the original word also survived. In the first centuries following 1066, the spelling of the word varied greatly. One of the oldest examples is the inscription in the Statutes in Galway (1527), which mentions *hokie* – 'the hurling of a little ball with sticks or staves'. There were also other forms of the name, such as >HAWKY and >HAWKEY. In the 18th cent., the term clearly started to receive its present spelling, and become widely known. There is another possible origin of the name: in the eastern counties of England, there is a harvest home festival known locally as *hawkey, hawkie, horkey, hooky, hoacky, hoky, hoaky, hockay.* During such festivities, various games and competitions are organized. Among them, there were a few var. of a game played with a small ball pushed around with sticks, including curved ones. Perhaps some of them took the name from the whole festival, giving or strengthening the name of hockey. Both of these 2 derivations apply only to >FIELD HOCKEY. The name has been associated with >ICE HOCKEY since its development in the 19th cent.

HOEPELBOLLING, a var. of a folk game known in Belgium as >TROU-MADAME.

HOIMA, a Rom. game featuring a ball bounced into the playing area with the use of a bat, similar to >PALANT; also see Rumanian >HENGERLÉ.

HOI-POLLOI, a folk var. of hunting practiced in India regardless of caste membership and age – children also take part.

HOKKSA, a Siberian game similar to >POLO.
W. Endrei, L. Zolnay, *Fun and Games in Old Europe,* 1986.

HOLANI, a trad. Turk. game similar to early forms of >FIELD HOCKEY, practiced in certain rural parts of Turkey. The name refers to a round wooden puck or an object similar to a wedge, which is moved about with the use of sticks. The object is slightly bigger than a hockey puck. The sticks are rather primitive and the rules differ from region to region. The size of the field is not limited, and neither is the duration of the game nor the number of players. In some rural communities, during folk festivals the game is played all day long. The objective of the game is getting the puck to an agreed target, which is a point or a line.

HOLE TASO DUKANARAM, imitating the animal called *hole toso* from the cat family; a type of folk game in India. The animal is famous for running with one paw lifted up and beating the chest with the front paws while running round. In some parts of India, imitating these movements is considered an excellent exercise developing balance and co-ordination.

HOLLY TOP, see >KICK-BOARD, Cf. >SCOOTERS.

HOLUA, 1) a trad. Hawaiian sport of sliding down steep slopes using special sledges. The track may be as long as 3km. It is most popular on the Big Island of Hawaii. The runners are up to 3m long and bent round at the front. Many participants attempt to take a standing position during the ride, which is considered an achievement. However, the winner is the player who slides the greatest distance. The sport is included in the local festival of Makahiki. It is accompanied by betting. 2) a >SURFING term.

HOOD SKITTLES see >SKITTLES.

HOOP-AND-POLE, a trad. game of many Native Amer. tribes. There were also other Eng. names of this game: *wheel-and-pole* and *spear-and-ring.* The game had different original names in different tribes, which travelers who observed the game failed to note, hence it is known only by its Eng. equivalents. A similar game played by the Cheyenne was originally called >CHUNGKE. Hoop-and-pole is one of the oldest Native Amer. games described by colonists. It was played from the East Coast to the Mexican border. In N Canada, there is a winter var. (see >INDIAN WINTER GAME). It was presented in an artistic form by a Ger. H. Möllhausen, who traveled through the SW states of the USA with a federal research expedition. His painting shows a game played by the members of the Paiute tribe in the lower part of the Colorado River.
Equipment. The basic equipment consists of poles of varying lengths, ranging from 60cm to about 4m, 3-4cm in diameter, and wooden hoops or rings, made of bent cane or wicker. It is different from >CHUNGKE, which features rings made of stone but is considered by some researchers to belong the hoop-and-pole family.

HOP, STEP AND JUMP, see >TRIPLE JUMP.

HOPLITODROMO, also *hopliton dromos* or *hoplitodromia.* In ancient Greece, a race of hoplite warriors in full armor. Introduced to the Ol.G. in 520 BC. Philostratos, in his book *On Gymnastics*, says that this run was introduced to commemorate the Elean victory over the Dyme. Their struggle was supposedly so obstinate that they did not conform to the rule of suspending wars at the time of the Olympics *(ekecheiria),* and the decisive battle took place on the opening day of the games. The news was brought to the Olympic stadium by a armored soldier, which was later celebrated by introducing this competition. It was a part of Pythian Games from 498 BC. In Olympia it was carried out over a distance of 2 stadiums, in the Nemean Games – 4 stadiums, during the freedom celebrations (*Eleuteria*) at Plataeae perhaps as far as 15 stadiums. Plato, in his work *On State* suggested practicing for this competition at a distance of 60 stadiums in the case of heavy-armored soldiers and 100 for light-armored ones. That would be equal to approx. 19km in Olympic measures, 16.5km in Delphic measures, or 17.7km in Athenian measures. Initially the run was conducted in the full armor typical of the hoplites, consisting of a helmet *(kranos)*, a breast-plate and shin-guards *(knemides)*, and with the shield *(aspis).* Running with the spear was not practiced, probably for safety reasons but also possibly as an expression of the peaceful approach of the Greeks, who valued defense over attack. During the ensuing games, elements of armor gradually disappeared from the competition, eventually leaving the runners only with the shield. The shields were round, all of equal size and weight. The participants did not use their own shields. They were stored in the Zeus Sanctuary in Olympia. The winner of hoplitodromo, who at the same games also won races without armor at distances of 1 and 2 stadiums, received the title of triple victor – *triastes* (see: >STADIODROMOS, >DIAULOS).

HOPLOMACHIA, Gr. for 'armored fight'. A martial art with heavy weapons (javelin or sword), in the form of mock duels of armored opponents. Its aim was to prepare for combat. In its oldest forms, it was conducted untill first blood, as documented by the scene of Ajax's duel with Diomedes during the funeral games after the death of Patroclus. Achilles, while calling them to battle, says (Homer, *The Iliad*, book 23, trans. Ian Johnston, Malaspina University-College, Canada):

We're calling for two men,
two of the best, to fight for these prizes,
clothed in their armour, wielding their sharp bronze,
testing each other here before this crowd.
Whichever man hits the other's fair skin first,
under the armour, drawing his dark blood,
will get from me this silver-studded sword,
a lovely one from Thrace, which I seized from Asteropaeus.

The fight was so brutal and dangerous that it was later stopped and a prize was given to both contestants. The custom of fighting until first blood was later discontinued. The competition was at its prime when it was introduced to the program of certain Gk. games as *hoplomachikos agones*. This kind of exercise and competitions were not part of the upbringing of Athenian boys, which was regretted by Plato, who considered hoplomachia to be the most useful pastime for a citizen, next to horse-riding. It was later introduced as part of the systematic program of training for adolescent boys, known as *efebia*. A few var. of hoplomachia were included in the program of Spartan training, known as *agoge.* Masters of fencing and their students were called *hoplomachoi* (Gr. plural of *hoplomachos*).

HOPPE I REB, see >SJIPPE OVER EGET BEN.

HOP-SCOTCH, the Ang.-Sax. name for a family of games usu. played by girls, also known in Pol. as >KLASY, consisting in hopping across a grid drawn on the ground or pavement, together with moving a small flat stone from one square to the next (some var. do not conform to this description and feature other ways of moving across the grid; see a var. called *London*). The var. most popular in the Eng.-speaking countries are:
HOP-SCOTCH (proper), hops and passing of the stone are executed on a grid consisting of 9 squares arranged in the following manner: adjacent to the starting square 1, there are 2 squares – 2 and 3 – followed by a single square 4, which is again followed by a pair of squares – 5 and 6 – followed by a row of 3 consecutive squares 7-9. The objective of the game is to throw the stone on the squares according to their numbers, then hopping on one foot across the boxes, with the exception of the box with the stone, which has to be jumped over, then picking up the stone and returning to the starting box with identical jumps in reverse order. The clusters of boxes (squares 2-3 and 5-6) have to be passed in such a way that both feet land simultaneously, one in each of the 2 squares.
FINNISH HOP-SCOTCH, a var. of the game with the following 9-box grid: after 3 squares in a row, there is a cluster of boxes (4 and 5), followed by a single square (6) and another cluster (7 and 8). Adjacent to the latter pair, there is a semicircle with a diameter equal to the width of both squares (9). When the player reaches this box she must turn around in a hop.
HAP THE BEDS, a game consisting in jumping on one foot from one square to another in such a way that a flat stone is pushed across the grid. The grid is formed by 8 square boxes in a row, with the extreme 2 boxes called *kail-pots*. The player's task is to throw the stone into the box (first to box 1, then 2 and so on), hop along to the box containing the stone, and then push it while jumping through the remaining boxes and return to box 1.
HOP-CREASE, a local name for hop-scotch.
HOP-SCORE, in and around Sheffield, and in Yorkshire, *huckety* or *hickety-huckety* in west Somerset. The grids differ slightly across the varieties. The middle part remains the same – a square divided into triangles by 2 diagonals. The adjacent boxes all form a similar shape but they differ in the way they are divided. In the var. called hop-score, the bottom square is divided across into 3 equal rectangular boxes, and the top semicircle is divided into 2 halves by a perpendicular radius, while a rectangular box below the semicircle forms a whole. In another Brit. var., there are similar squares on both sides of the square with triangles, each quartered and numbered in pairs 1-2 and 3-4 (left to right). The triangles are numbered in the following way: 5 – bottom, 6 – left, 7 – right, 8 – top. The squares inside the top square are also numbered in pairs 9-10 and 11-12 (left to right). The semicircle has no number but contains a simplified drawing of a cat with whiskers. In yet another var., the square with triangles (numbered 2-5) is adjacent to a single rectangular starting box numbered 1. On top of the square, there are 2 rectangular boxes (numbered 6 and 7) in a row, each as wide as the square.

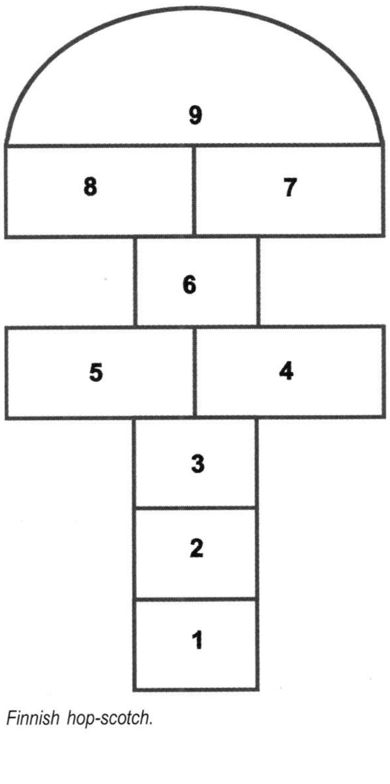

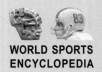

Finnish hop-scotch.

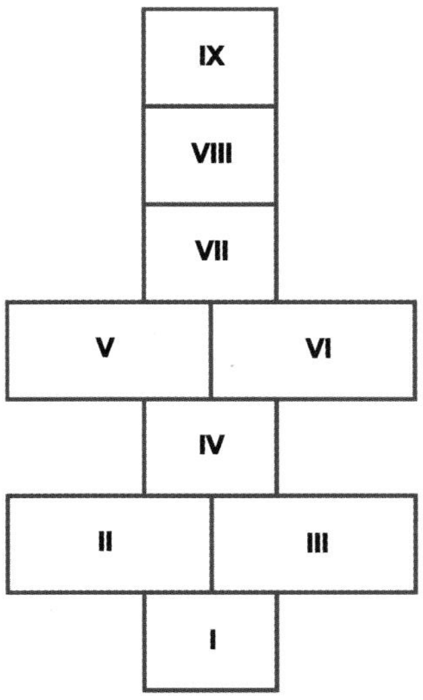

Hop-scotch proper.

Hoplidromo on a 1939 Greek postage stamp.
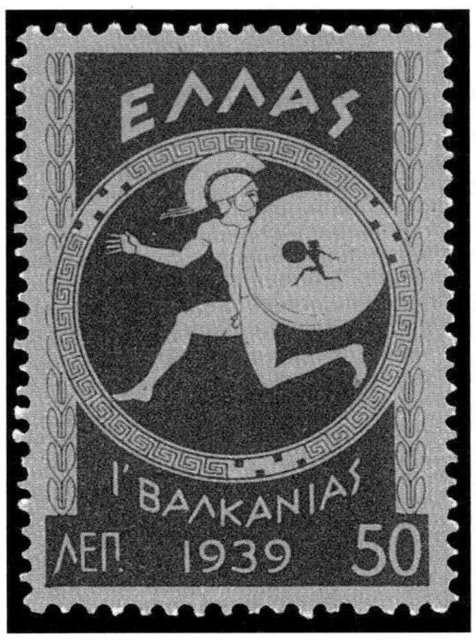

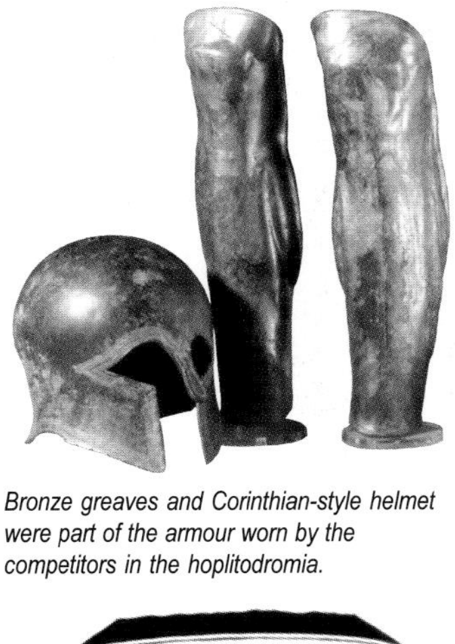
Bronze greaves and Corinthian-style helmet were part of the armour worn by the competitors in the hoplitodromia.

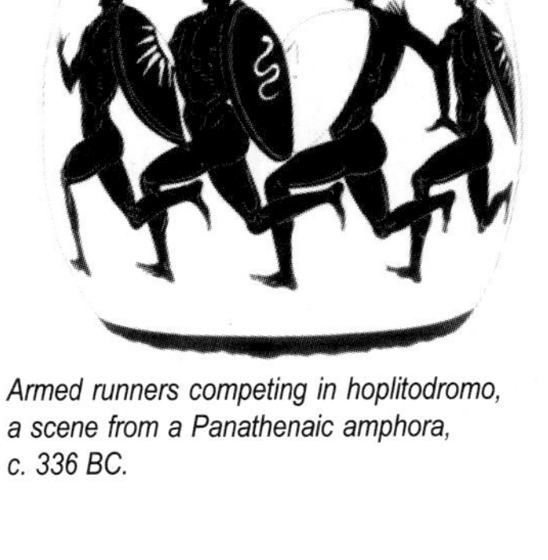
Armed runners competing in hoplitodromo, a scene from a Panathenaic amphora, c. 336 BC.

WORLD SPORTS ENCYCLOPEDIA

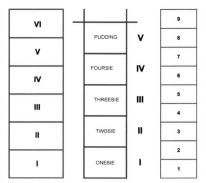

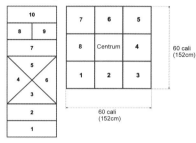

Ladder hop scotch with 6, 5, and 9 boxes.

LADDER HOP-SCOTCH, wherein the whole grid is 1m wide and 3-4 long, and divided by lines across into 5-9 rectangular boxes of equal size. They are numbered 1-9, starting at the bottom of the grid. The object of the game is to land the stone on box 1, then move it to box 2 with a light push with the side of the foot. The player jumps on one foot to box 2. The activity is repeated in box 3 and so on and then back to box 1. In the second round the whole activity is repeated jumping on the other foot. Another way of playing this game involves jumping over the box that contains the stone, picking it up and returning to the start in order to land the stone 1 box further. The whole activity is repeated until there is no further box to land the stone in. In some parts of England, there was a slightly different version of the game, with a grid consisting of 6 squares in a row. Above the top square, there were 'forks' created by prolonging the side lines of the figure. In southern England, this var. was called *beds*. The 5-square var. was called *hop-bed* in Stixwold (Lincoln county), *hop-score* in Yorkshire (this name also referred to other Eng. var. of hop-scotch) and *hitchibed* in Cleveland (Yorkshire). The original feature of this var. are names of boxes being diminutive forms of Eng. numerals: *onesie, twosie, threesie, foursie*. The top box was called *pudding*.

LONDON, with the boxes numbered in a zigzag manner, starting from 1-bottom left, 2-bottom right and so on. Adjacent to the top line, bordering with boxes 7 and 8, there is a semicircle called *London*. The player's task is to push the stone with the side of the foot, moving it from box to box, according to their numbers. The moves must be carried out in such a way that the stone goes through the crossing points of borderlines.

The word *London* is also featured in the semicircle of a grid used in another variety. The grid is of similar size but is divided with a dense net of 32 lines across it. The game is played by 2 people. The object is made of more 'precious' material – glass, china or sometimes paper – and called a *chipper*. Initially, it is located at the starting line. The game requires gentle moves to get the *chipper* from one box to the next. If it is made of paper, it is simply blown at. Wherever it stops, the player makes a small circle, which is called *making a man's head*. The chipper is returned to the starting point and the same player takes another turn, trying to place it in another box.

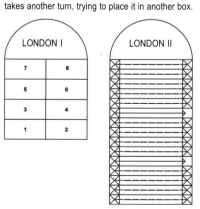

The game is continued until all the boxes are filled with *heads*. If the object is placed in a box that has been visited before, the player adds a torso, then arms, legs and so on. Once there are 3 complete human figures in a box, their arms are elongated across the whole width of the box, and it cannot be used anymore. The player who seizes all (or most, depending on agreement) boxes in this manner, wins the game. A player forfeits her turn if the object lands

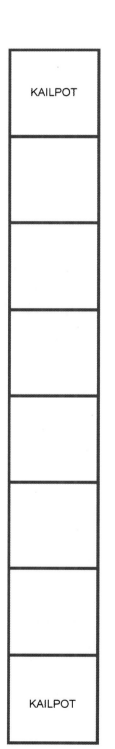

KAILPOT

KAILPOT

Hap the beds hop scotch.

on a line or outside the grid. Another player takes over and continues until a similar mistake is made. The players continue adding parts to the drawn figures. If the object lands on the *London* box, the player may take over any box, as if she had 3 complete figures there.

Playing with a piece of glass or china follows similar rules but the object is moved by hitting with the foot or by snapping the fingers.

PALLALL, also *pally-ully,* Scot. name for hop-scotch.

PICKIE, another Brit. var. of hop-scotch, is played on a grid 1.5m wide and 3-4m long, divided in the following way: the central square with triangles (numbered 3-6) is adjacent to 2 rectangular boxes (numbered 1 and 2) in a row, each as wide as the square. On top of the square, there is a rectangular box as wide as the square (numbered 7), followed by a pair of smaller squares, each occupying half the width of the square, numbered 8 and 9. Then there is another wide rectangular box numbered 10. The stone is called the 'pick'. The pick is first thrown into box 1

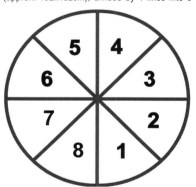

Pickie.   *Pick-up.*

and the player jumps to box 2. Then the player must kick the pick so that it goes across the starting line. In the next round the pick is thrown into box 2, then 3 and so on. From each of these boxes, the pick must return to the starting position, pushed by the feet in as many moves as the number of the box it was thrown into. After completing round 10, the game is continued in the reverse order starting with box 10.

PICK-UP HOPSCOTCH. Tossing the stone and hops are executed within a square grid 60x60in. (approx. 152x152cm), divided by 4 lines into 9

equal squares 20x20in. (approx. 50x50cm). The squares are numbered counterclockwise from 1 to 8, starting bottom right. The square in the middle is not numbered and is called the *center*. The game is started by tossing the stone into the center and hopping across the squares in order. After hopping onto a square, the player is supposed to toss the stone back to the center, then pick it up and carry on hopping to the next box.

TRAY-TRIP, also *pally-ully*. Descriptions of the var. of this game are contradictory. According to A.B. Gomme, the grid was round, divided into 8 equal wedges, numbered counterclockwise, starting bottom right. The pebble was first tossed into box 1, then picked up. The player would then hop around the whole grid on one foot. The pebble was then tossed into box 2, followed by a similar series of hopping, and so on. The 2nd round would consist in going across all boxes with the pebble placed on the toes, being careful not to touch any of the lines. The 3rd round would have the same objective with the pebble placed on the player's thumb. The 4th round would require bending forward, as the pebble was placed on the back. After the last box, the player was supposed to straighten up, catching the pebble with her hand. A dropped pebble made the whole round void. Around Whitby, pally-ully was

played pushing the object around with the foot. Some ethnographers claim that animal bones were used instead of stones. In Whitby, especially selected penny-sized stones were used.

SCOTCH-HOPPERS, a game mentioned in the *Poor Robin Almanac* for 1667, 1707 and 1740. The 1707 one contains an interesting note that 'doctors and lawyers will not have much to do this month, so if they will, they may play *scotch-hoppers*' (TGESI, 2, 182-3).

TOURNAMENT HOP-SCOTCH is an Amer. variety. The width of the whole grid is 60in. (approx. 152cm); the bottom segment is not square but rectangular, divided into 2 'wing' rectangular boxes numbered from right to left (1 and 2). The triangles in the middle square (also 60in. wide) are numbered: 3 – bottom, 4 – right, 5 – left, and 6 – top. Above the square, there is a rectangular box, as wide as the whole grid and 30in. long. On top of it, there is a semicircle with a smaller semicircle inside (numbered 8), with a diameter half that of the bigger one. The figure between the 2 semicircles is divided into 2 symmetrical halves, numbered 9 – right and 10 – left. The part of box 9 that is adjacent to box 7 is numbered 12 (there is no 11). The stone is pushed in order of numbers, ending with number 12. The jumps following the throw must be performed on one foot with the exception of boxes 1-2 and 4-5, where landing is on both feet simultaneously (see drawing).

See also Arab >AL-HUD'D'A, >AL-HAGLA, >BERBER, >LU'BAT UMM AL-HUTUT, Dan. >AT HINKE, Ger. >FUßSCHEIBENSPIEL, Pol. >KLASY, Port. >JOGO DO AVIÃO, >JOGO DO CARACOL.

C.A. Bucher, E.M. Reade, 'Hopscotch', *Physical Education and Health in the Elementary School,* 1969, 294-296; A.B. Gomme, 'Hop-Scotch', TGESI, 1894, 1, 223-227; *Pickie,* TGESI, 1898, 2, 451.

HORNIE HOLES, an old game of throwing animal horns (later also curved sticks or pegs) into holes in the ground, also called kitty-cat. The game is played by 2 pairs of contestants, each pair consisting of 'a principal' and 'an assistant'. The horn used for throwing is called 'a cat'. While playing the game the participants usu. chant a rhyming song:

Josk, Speak, and Sandy,
W' a' their lousy train
Round about by Edinborra,
We'll never meet again
Gae head 'im, gae hang 'im,
Gae lay 'im in the sea;
A' the birds o' the air
Will bear him companee.
With a nig-nag, widdy bag,
And an e'endown trail, trai;
Quoth he.

A.B. Gomme, 'Hornie Holes', TGESI 1894, I, 228.

HORNUS, a folk sport practiced in Switzerland, especially in the canton of Bern and, to a smaller extent, in other parts of the country. The idea of the game is put in flight a *hornus,* a small lens-shaped

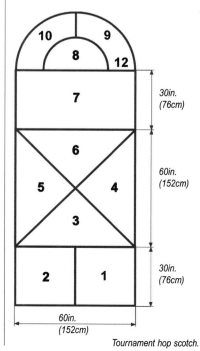

Tournament hop scotch.

Eugene Delacroix, Arab Horses Fighting in a Stable, *1860, oil on canvas.*

plate placed on a hollow rail that points upwards. Members of the throwing team hit the plate with an elastic wooden rod. Fielding players try and hit the hornus with a short-handled wooden shovel when it is in the air, or with a long-handled shovel when it is on the ground. They defend an area situated about 100m away from the point of tossing the hornus. Hitting the hornus or making it fall outside the defended area gives the attacking team minus points. Hitting the defended area gives them plus points. The teams are 16 strong. After each member of the attacking team has tossed the hornus, the points are summed up and the roles are reversed. A complete series of serves by both teams makes up a round. The team with more plus points wins. In the case of a draw the winners are decided by the number of minus points.

History. The oldest information about hornus comes from the 30-year-war period (1618-1648), but it is known that similar folk games were earlier played in France, Germany and the Aosta valley in Italy. J. Gotthelf (1757-1854), in his novel, *Uli der Knecht,* describes hornus as a ball game, played on fallow grounds in the spring and fall.

HORSE FIGHTS, a popular event in S Tajikistan accompanying ceremonies dedicated to cleansing water springs. The horses were teased and encouraged to fight by cries and sticks.

HORSE RACING FOR A SHAWL, a form of >HORSE RACING popular among the Tur. peoples of Central Asia. The winner of the race received a symbolic prize: a shawl or, in Mongolia, a belt of silk cloth called *chadag.* During the Tartar harvest holiday of spring crops called *sabantuy* men competed for shawls that belonged to young married women. Shawls or pieces of women's clothing symbolized the woman herself and her appreciation of the winner. Competitors, however, were limited to the members of the husband's family, which was prob. meant

Franz Roubaud, Horseman Riding in a Mountainous Landscape, *oil on panel.*

to protect the woman against being kidnapped, characteristic of >CHASING A GIRL.

HORSE RACING, a form of contest for riders on horseback, one of the oldest and most prestigious sports with numerous var. in different world regions. Among the best known historical and modern types of horse racing are: ancient Gk. >KALPE, >KELES, >POLON KELES; Mong. >KHURDAAN MOR'; modern Eur. >FLAT HORSE RACING, >STEEPLECHASE HORSE RACING; various trad. events: >UNMOUNTED HORSE RACING, >BURIAT HORSE RACING, >KHEVSUR HORSE RACING, >YAKUTE HORSE RACING, >KAZAKH HORSE RACING, >KIRGHIZ HORSE RACING, >YI HORSE RACING, >HORSE RACING FOR A SHAWL, >OSSETIAN HORSE RACING, >'RASKOLNITSY' HORSE RACING.

HORSE RIDING FOR THE DISABLED, a var. of >RIDING adapted for the needs of persons with various disabilities. The program of most international events and the Paralympic Games includes dressage. Riders use saddles adapted to various types of disabilities and are grouped according to the type and degree of disability. The sport develops under the auspices of the Horse Riding Committee of the Paralympic Games and also provides a recognized form of therapy, especially for children with MPD. Cf. also >SPORTS FOR THE DISABLED.

HORSE SPORTS, a group of sports practiced with the use of the horse, such as >RIDING, ancient and modern >FLAT HORSE RACING and >EQUESTRIAN EVENTS, >STEEPLECHASE HORSE RACING, as well as practiced in different countries >PALIO, >UNMOUNTED HORSE RACING, >BURIAT HORSE RACING, >KHEVSUR HORSE RACING, >YAKUTE HORSE RACING, >KAZAKH HORSE RACING, >KIRGHIZ HORSE RACING, >YI HORSE RACING, >HORSE RACING FOR A SHAWL, >OSSETIAN HORSE RACING, >'RASKOLNITSY' HORSE RACING, etc. The group includes also all kinds of races of vehicles pulled by horses, such as ancient >SYNORIS, >TETRIPPON, >CHARIOT RACING, and modern >COACHING or >CARRIAGE DRIVING. Other disciplines encompassed by horse sports include: >SKIJØRING, >YABUSAME, >PARTHIAN ARCHERY, >CHIVALRIC TOURNAMENTS, >ALKA, >RUNNING AT THE RING, >KIRGHIZ JOUSTING, >AL SAWALJAH, >GUJ-BOZI, >HORSEBALL, >JIQIU, >PATO, >POLO, >POLO-CROSSE, >SAGOL KANGJEI, and >SOWORIGUJ. See also different types of horse sports, competitions, and games, such as: >AUDARYSPAK, >BAJGA, >BUZKASHI, >DJIGHIT-ZARHYS, >DJIRIITI, >KYZ-KUU, >MARUA, >MOKNIEWA, >NIZA BAZI, >CHASING A GIRL, >TARCZIA, and >ZEGETEABA.

Horse sports in literature and art. The art of horseback riding has belonged among one of the most frequent topics of all major literatures of the world from the moment the horse was domesticated. In the ancient narrative literature of the Greeks, Romans, and Celts, heroes appear to be excep-

tionally adroit on horseback. Indeed, the horse itself is an inseparable part of many a hero's extraordinary achievements. The tradition of written works devoted to the horse commenced in Greece with Xenophon's *Hippike* (*The Art of Horsemanship*). The most celebrated Middle Ages characters, King Arthur and Roland, were always able horseback riders. The subject of horse sports, for a long time serving only as a background, evolved into an independent topic the moment modern horse riding developed in England in the 18th and 19th cent. Among the most acclaimed writers who exercised the subject of horse riding was C.J. Apperley writing pseudonymously as Nimrod for *The Sporting Magazine* and the *Quarterly Review*, but also publishing independent works, such as *The Chase, the Road and the Turf* (1833). Another outstanding representative of the genre was R.S. Surtees (1805-64), also cooperating with *The Sporting Magazine* and then *The New Sporting Magazine*. His comic short stories and essays devoted to sports – later published together in a single book titled *Jorrok's Jaunts and Jollities* (1838) – frequently touched upon horse sports. He also authored the novels *Handley Cross* (1843) and *Mr Sponge's Sporting Tour* (1853).

In the USA, the subject of horse sports appeared, for example, in the works of E.A. Poe (*Gordon Pym* and *Mezengerstein*), an equestrian aficionado. Among modern literatures, the Amer. one is prob. more frequently interested in horse sports than any other, with such names devoting their works to the subject as: N.S. Bond, C.E. Van Loan, R. Tooker, M. Thompson, J. McKenney, J.T. Foote, W. Brandon, and G.A. Chamberlain.

The tradition of sculptures dedicated to the horse is long and difficult to encompass in any single volume. Among the earliest such representations we can certainly include an Etruscan sculpture of cavalrymen, dating back to the 5th cent. BC and a dynamic bas-relief made by Phidias on the Pantheon's frieze representing a group of horsemen. Portraying mounted rulers and army commanders dates back at least to the times of Philip II, represented on coins, and his son Alexander the Great, pictured several times on his legendary Bucephalus. The Roman monument of Marcus Aurelius on horseback is among the most precious monuments of the antique

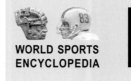

WORLD SPORTS ENCYCLOPEDIA

H

A poster for a horse racing event at Bézier, France, 1914.

Crosscountry horse racing.

Edouard Manet, Horse Race at Longchamp, *c. 1867, oil on canvas.*

Horseback riding is a popular, enen therapeutic recreational activity.

Horseball players battle over the ball.

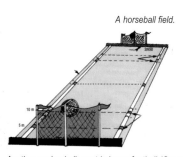

A horseball field.

Another equine ball sport is horse football (Ger. pferde fussball), in which – unlike in horseball – it is the horse, rather than the player, that kicks a huge soccer-like ball. One of the most popular breeds used for horse football is the Icelandic horse.

arts. In time, nearly every ruler was portrayed on horseback. The best masterpieces include the statue of Gattemelata in Padua, made by Florentine sculptor Donatello (1386-1466).

In the 16th and 17th cent., a tradition of Eur. horse-devoted painting was established. It developed in 2 directions: battle and portrait paintings. In the 18th cent., the subject of horse racing comes into view. Canaletto's (1721-80) *Brama del Popolo* belongs among the most renowned paintings that represent horse racing. In romanticism, horse scenes were painted by E. Delacroix, whereas purely sporting images were represented in the 19th cent. by T. Géricault, E. Dégas, and M. Liebermann. In England, the most outstanding horse painter is thought to be G. Stubbs (1724-1806) famous for his paintings of Lord Grosvenor's and the Duke of Richmond's stud farms. He was also author of a treatise *The Anatomy of the Horse* (1766) and was considered by the National Biography as, 'the first painter who mastered the anatomy of the horse.'

Z. Baranowski, *Koń i jeździectwo. Słownik hipologiczny*, 1989; J.B. Creamer, ed., *Twenty-Two Stories About Horses and Men*, 1953; S. Haw, *The New Book of the Horse*, 1993; L. Kon, *Jazda konna*, 1953; W. Lipoński, *Sport-literatura-sztuka*, 1974; H. Warren Wind, ed., 'Horses and Horse Racing' in *The Realm of Sport*, 1966.

HORSEBALL, a game being a combination of horseback riding, basketball and rugby. It is played by 2 teams of 4 riders each. The objective is to throw a ball, strapped in a harness of 6 strong leather handles, into a basket similar to that in basketball, but larger and mounted vertically. A special horse harness makes it possible to stand up in the saddle while riding and shooting and to dive deeply in order to pick up the ball from the ground.

Equipment. The ball is 65cm in circumference (60cm for junior players, 47cm for youngsters) and weighs, respectively, 600-700g, 500-600g and 400-500g, and resembles that of >ASSOCIATION FOOTBALL (a rubber bladder placed inside hexagonal, black and white leather pieces sewn together). It is placed inside a leather harness made of 6 straps protruding into a handle 41cm in length (39cm and

A basket used in horseball.

A harnessed ball for playing horseball.

A horseball game.

30cm for younger players), which makes it possible to throw the ball. The strap is 18-30mm wide (18-20 and 16-18 for younger players) and 6-8mm thick (respectively 4-8mm, 4-6mm). The horse harness is not precisely specified, except for the so-called martingale, which is allowed only in the form of a standing martingale in order to increase the rider's balancing movements and protect him against fatigue and back pain.

Rules. The game is conducted at full gallop and is, therefore, very dynamic. Before the player is allowed to take a shot, the ball must be exchanged at least 3 times between players. Contact between players is allowed, but must be under an angle of 45°, which is to eliminate heavier collisions and enable the player to push the opponent off the field.

History. The game originated in France in 1979. It is governed by the Fr. Equestrian Federation and is recognized by the International Equestrian Federation. In 1999 it incorporated 8 member countries. The best teams are from France, Portugal and Great Britain. New national organizations are being formed, e.g. the Brit. Horseball Association. The main event is currently the E.Ch., although a World Cup is soon to take place.

HORSESHOE PITCHING, 1) a family of games where the main objective is pitching a horseshoe onto a peg embedded in the ground at some distance. Well-known var. of horseshoe pitching include Dan. >SPILLE HESTESKO, Port. >JOGO DA FERRADURA, and Fr. >FER À CHEVAL; 2) the Amer. var., called *horseshoes*, involves throwing horseshoe-shaped metal 'shoes' onto stakes inserted in the ground about 15m away from the thrower. Usually, the game is played from 2 platforms at opposite ends of the field, called the 'pitchers' boxes', each 197x82cm. Each box has a wooden frame raised about 1in. (2.5cm) above the surface of the ground. The frame is the 'foul line' at the same time – the pitcher may not step over it when making the throw. The surface of the box is packed, leveled clay, sand or even sawdust. The target of the throw is the opposite box, with a stake in the middle, 1in. (2.5cm) thick and 12in. (30.48cm) high, inclined at an angle of 15° towards the pitcher. The distance between the stakes of opposite boxes is 40ft. (12.19m) for men and 30ft. (9.14m) for women. This can be reduced in leisure games, depending on the players' skills, and the stakes may be half the normal height (5--6in. or 12.7-15.2cm).

The 'shoe' has the typical shape of a horse shoe, but is equipped with special heel calks at the points, bent inside at a right angle. The calks may not be longer than ¾in. (about 1.9cm), and are designed to stabilize the shoe after landing. The whole shoe may not be longer than 7½in. (about 19.05cm) and wider than 7ins. (about 17.8cm). The max. weight is 2½lbs. (about 1.13kg).

The game may be played individually or in doubles. In a round, each player (or pair in doubles) makes one throw. In singles, the throws are made from the same box, in doubles – from opposite boxes.

Techniques. The pitch is rotational, with the shoe making a little more than one full rotation during

flight (depending on the grip: 1¼, 1½ or 1¾ rotations). A 1¼ turn pitch results from a grip on the left-hand shank (prong) with the fingers underneath and the thumb across the top of the shoe about halfway between the heel and toe calks. At release, the opening of the shoe is on the pitcher's left side. The 1¾ turn grip is similar but the pitcher holds on to the right-hand shank, and the opening is on the pitcher's right at release. In the 1½ turn grip, the thumb and index finger hold on to the left side of the shoe, near the prong, with the thumb along it, and the index finger underneath. The pitcher takes his position in the box, swings the shoe forwards and up. After locking onto the target, the pitcher swings the shoe back and forward again, and lets go in an arcing trajectory.

Scoring. Points are scored depending on the position of the shoe after landing. If the shoe lands so that it encircles the stake (this is called a 'ringer'), the pitcher scores 3pts. If the next pitch causes the shoe to be knocked off the stake, he loses the 3pts. for the ringer. Two ringers in one round score 6pts. (no bonus). If no pitcher succeeds in scoring a ringer, the shoe closest to the stake scores 1pt. If 2 shoes of the same pitcher land closer to the stake than those of the other pitcher, the former scores 2pts. If a player scores one ringer, and his second shoe lands closer to the stake than his opponent's, he scores 4pts. A shoe landing upright, against the stake but not encircling it does not score and is called a 'leaner'. In unofficial games, 2pts. may be scored for a leaner. The shoe must be within 6ins. (about 15cm) from the stake to score any points at all. If the shoes of both players land at exactly the same distance from the stake, they cancel each other out

Horseshoe pitching.

Above and right: A competitor tackles the course during the World Hovercraft Championships at Weston Park, Shropshire.

and no points are scored. In official games, the first side to score 50pts. wins, with 21pts. the usu. target in unofficial games.

History. The game was already known by Roman legionaires, shortly after the horse shoe was invented (c.150-100 BC). The Romans brought the game to Britain, and it developed there in Roman cities. It has been on the program of the Eng.Cotswold Games, initiated in the early 16th cent. However, some historians believe that the game did not descend from the Roman soldier game but from another game, known as >QUOITS. Horseshoe pitching started disappearing in Britain in the 19th cent. but grew in the USA, where it gained tremendous popularity that has survived to this day. The first American clubs specializing in horseshoe pitching were estab. in 1892 (Meadville, Pennsylvania; East Liverpool, Oklahoma). Today, apart from national championships, there are league matches in the USA. The game is controlled by the National Horseshoe Pitchers Association of America, estab. in 1915.
F.K. Perkins, 'Horshoe Pitching', in: *Encyclopedia Americana International*, 1979, vol. 14, p. 432; F.G. Menke, 'Horseshoe Pitching', in: *Encyclopedia of Sports*, 1969, 612-616.

HORUA, one of the names for sledding in the mud practiced by N.Zeal. Maoris, created by pouring water over sand; see >RETI; cf. >HOLUA.

HOSENLAUF, Aus. folk sport consisting of 2 people running in a pair of special large trousers [Ger. *Hosen* – trousers + *Lauf* – run].

HOSENLUPF, [Ger. *Hosen* – trousers + *lupfen* – to lift] a Swiss var. of folk wrestling that is known by the Eng. names of *breeches wrestling* or *boxershorts wrestling*. An essential but by no means the only feature of this competition is grabbing and knocking the opponent over, using specially prepared trousers: a wrestler puts a pair of linen shorts on, on top of a pair of loose, long trousers. The shorts are supported on the hip by a thick leather belt. The main part to be grabbed is the bottom edge of the shorts. This typically male competition has the status of a national sport in Switzerland. The oldest evidence of its being practiced is a 13th-cent. relief in the choir stalls of the cathedral in Lausanne. It shows 2 men playing hosenlupf. In 1805, hosenlupf became one of the main competitions at the folk festival in Unspunnen in the Bern area, organized according to the creed: 'Let the old customs revive, let the games of yesterday be celebrated'.
The fight takes place on a sandy surface. The participants must practice 4-5 times a week. The basic hold is the *kurz* – a short grab, in which grabbing the shorts is accompanied by a short grab by the neck, resulting in throwing the opponent onto his back. Another technique is a *cross jump*, consisting

of charging at the opponent with one's chest, at the same time placing the foot behind his heels and making him fall on his back. The prize in hosenlupf is usu. a young bull, which in Switzerland is called a *muneli*. The *muneli* has always been considered a symbol of maintaining links with the natural world. The sport currently enjoys great popularity. In Aug. 1995, 100,000 people participated in a festival celebrating the centenary of The Swiss Wrestling Federation. The leading wrestlers of the '90s were T. Sutter and E. Hasler. See >CORNWALL AND DEVON, >GLÍMA, >SWISS-STYLE WRESTLING.
U. Gfeller, 'Swiss Wrestling: A tradition that Transcends Fashion', OR, Dec. 1995 – Jan. 1996.

HOSONMU, a trad. Kor. sport practiced in the ancient kingdom of Koguryo (37 BC-668 AD). The idea was to dance on a large ball for as long as possible without losing one's balance. A similar feat can still be seen in the modern circus.
Koo-Chul Jung, *Erziehung und Sport in Korea im Kreuzpunkt fremder Kulturen und Mächte*, 1996, 62.

HOUSE-RUNNING, an eccentric and extreme form of sporting competition consisting of riding down the vertical walls of tall buildings, especially skyscrapers, on roller-blades. The participant is wrapped with a belt and linked to a line attached to the top of the building. The line is lowered together with the rider at the speed that is necessary for him/her to maintain contact between the blade and the surface of the wall. The slide is performed facing the ground, in a crouching position. The rider is equipped with a helmet and clothes of his choice, usually ¾-length trousers and a shirt.

HØVÆVEL, [Dan. *hø* – hay + *væve* – to weave]; a Dan. folk sport. A pole, 15cm in diameter, is stuck into the ground. An 18-20m rope is tied to the pole. One player grabs the other end of the rope and starts running around, winding the rope around the pole. The opponent also gets a piece of rope, 6-7m long with a heavy wooden block tied to each end. He grabs the rope in the middle and starts running to a set target. It is not easy as the blocks get in the way. Whoever gets to his target first, wins the game. Although the ropes are of different length, the balance is maintained by the fact that one player has the easier task but longer distance, while the other has it shorter but more difficult.
J. Møller, 'Høvævel', GID, 1997, 4, 96.

HOVERCRAFT RACES, a form of racing involving the use of relatively small, one man hovercrafts, which can top speeds of 70mph and can travel over land and water owing to the unique construction and the type of propulsion. A top mounted propeller forces air out of the back of the craft to create the forward motion. The air is channeled to the bottom of the craft and trapped by a flexible 'skirt', which

keeps the craft on top of the surface at all times. Steering the craft is possible by directing the air to the left or right side of the skirt with pilot-controlled rudders. The first proper hovercraft was made by Sir C. Cockerell in 1955.
Hovercraft races are held in several classes. The fastest class is Formula 1 with engine capacity over 500cc. The other classes include: Formula 2 (engine capacity between 250cc and 500cc), Formula 3

House running.

H

Hugge laks.

(engine capacity under 250cc), Formula Junior (engine capacity under 250cc), and Formula 25 (engine capacity max. 25hp). The races are held on tracks which are purposely challenging and include changes in terrain. The tracks must be wide enough to accomodate the gradual and delayed turning nature of the crafts.

The Internet: http://www.adrenaline-sports.net

HOYO, see >FALCONRY.

HRA NA SLEPOU BÁBU, see >BLIND MAN'S BUFF.

HRYGGSPENNA, an Icel. name of a simple Norse form of wrestling. Historically, it was a form of a duel, e.g. between antagonized neighbours, or a form of a competition for fun. Both forms differed slightly in the grabs but mostly in the level of brutality. In its oldest forms, hryggspenna was a means of solving arguments, incl. ones about land. A 'death stone' was used - it was a stone with a sharp edge situated at the level of the middle of the spine near the wrestling ground. The wrestlers tried to push their opponents to the stone and break their back with it, which usu. resulted in serious injury or even death. One original 'death stone' has been preserved in Hringsdalur in W Iceland. In the duel var. the wrestlers would initially stand, facing each other and bending forward. They grabbed each other's backs and tried to knock the opponent over by twisting their torso. In a serious fight, soft spots could be pressed with the chin, the back with the fist and so on. In the sporting var., grabs inducing pain were forbidden. The competitors would start as in the wrestling var. but holding each other by the waist, not the back, which made it difficult to twist the torso painfully. The objective was to knock the opponent over by swinging him until he lost his balance. The swinging would be from left to right and back and forth, accompa-

nied by characteristic movements by little steps. Throwing the opponent to the ground was forbidden as was tripping him up. The activist and the president of Icel. Glima Association, J.M. Ívarsson, mentioned that 'in the '60s, it was not uncommon for boys to test their strength with hryggspenna. I, born in 1948, did it too. Now it seems that this form of fighting disappeared completely'.

T. Einarsson, *Glima, The Icelandic Wrestling*, 1988; J.M. Ívarsson, Personal correspondence, 1999.

HUAPAO, a form of competing for a metal ring decorated with flowers that has been shot with a cannon (formerly with a catapult). The game is played by the Dong people in China during the Flower Festival on the third day of the lunar month. The competition is preceded with fireworks and banging on drums and gongs. A parade of the participants is lead by a jester who forces his way through the crowds. The flowered wreath is then shot and competed for, usually by representatives of a few neighboring villages. The game is executed in 3 stages, each starting with the shooting of a new wreath. The first signifies praying for wealth and the birth of new children, the second is dedicated to happiness and peace, the third is a good omen and fulfillment of wishes. The team who gets the wreath first, receives the gods' confirmation that the prayers of their village will be answered.

Mu Fushan, et al., 'Dong Huapao', TRAMCHIN, 118.

HUCKLEBONES, an Eng. game played with the use of the small knee bones of young sheep, popular especially in the eastern part of Sussex. In London it was called *gobs*. A similar game called *dibs* was popular in western Sussex. A game played with sheep bones was known in the ancient world and is mentioned by L. Lemnius. The following information included in a Dr Clarke's memoirs *Travels in Russia* (1810) indicates that the game was also known in other countries:

In all the villages and towns from Moscow to Woronetz, as in other parts of Russia, are seen boys, girls, and sometimes even old men, playing with the joint-bones of sheep. This games is called 'Dibbs' by the English. It is of very remote antiquity; for I have seen it very beautifully represented on Grecian vases; particularly on a vase in the collection of the late Sir William Hamilton, where a female figure appeared most gracefully delineated kneeling upon one knee, with her right arm extended, the palm of the hand downwards, and the bones ranged along the back of her hand and arm.

A similar game, played with the use of small shank bones, was popular in Mongolia and known as >ADUU KHUMIKH.

HUGGE BOLDEN, [Dan. *hugg* – to sever + *bold* – ball], a simple Dan. ball game. The playing area is agreed directly before the game, e.g. according to the conditions of the meadow or school playground. The game requires at least 4 participants but a greater number is preferred. They are divided into 2 teams: 1 draws the right to defend the ball while the other tries to capture it. A player under attack should pass the ball to another team-member or run away. The team who is in possession of the ball at a set moment in time, wins. Alternatively, the number of times that the ball is captured may be noted down and the game is decided in this way. In Denmark, this simple game without goals is considered a predecessor of >TEAM HANDBALL.

J. Møller, 'Hugge bolden', *Gamle idrætslege i Danmark*, 1997, 1.

HUGGE I AGER, [Dan. *hugg* – to sever + *ager* – land], a Dan. knife game. Two equal squares are drawn on the ground. The players take turns in thrusting the knife into the ground next to their squares; the depth of the thrust determines the length of the side of the square that is then cut off from the opponent's field. The player who is first to fill the opponent's field with his squares, wins.

J. Møller, 'Hugge i ager', GID, 1997, 4.

HUGGE LAKS, Dan. for 'cut the salmon'. A simple test of strength and dexterity. One of the participants gets down on all fours, the 2nd sits on his back, facing the feet, the 3rd sits on the shoulders of the 2nd putting his feet under his armpits. The top participant suddenly tries to stand up, dragging the one he is sitting on. The 2nd participant falls on the back of the 1st, and the 3rd falls on the ground. Apart

from the moment of showing off, the idea of the exercise is unclear.

J. Møller, 'Hugge laks', GID, 1997, 3, 94.

HUI BULL FIGHTS, a type of competition between humans and animals practiced among the Hui people in the Chin. province of Zheijang, esp. in the area of Jiaxin. The bull must be defeated in any style by the use of bare hands only. The fighter first provokes the animal by kicks and hand strikes, which is followed by a series of simulated attacks and escapes. When the bull gets tired, the fighter attempts to grab its horns and twist its head in order to breaks its neck. Various styles of fighting remain in different parts of the province: provoking the bull with one hand, both hands, arm strikes, etc. The winning quality depends upon the style of knocking the bull down. The highest acclaimed style is when the bull gets knocked down lying on its back with all 4 hooves in the air. A less respected victory involves knocking the bull down on to its side.

Mu Fushan et al., '(Hui) Bullfight', TRAMCHIN, 36.

HUKA KUKA, ritual wrestling accompanying the burial ceremony of Brazilian Kyukuro and Alahite Indians, as well as some other tribes of the Xingu river basin (a tributary of the Amazon). Warriors of the tribe that holds the ceremony take on those of all other tribes in pairs selected by the Elders. The purpose of the fight is to defend the tribe's honor. When the host tribe has selected its players, other tribes are invited to follow. Before the fight wrestlers kneel down to pray at a large sand pit. In that position they also begin the fight. Irrespective of the outcome, fights end with a friendly tap on the back, a sign that the art of wrestling has been offered to them by their deity in order to maintain peace and accord between tribes, rather than cause conflict.

HUL GUL, an Amer. game of chance where the objective is to guess if there is anything (like small balls, fruit pips or stones) in the opponent's clenched fist, and if so, how many objects there are. One of the players holds out a clenched fist and says the words, 'Hul gul', to ask the other player if the fist is full or empty. The other player, if he thinks there is something in the fist, says, 'Handful'. The next question follows: 'How many?' If the other player fails to guess, the first one takes away from him as many balls, pips or stones as he had held in his fist. If the other player succeeds in guessing the exact number, he is allowed to take the balls from the asker. Similar games are known across many cultures and nations, and include the Sanskrit *yui-eyui* and Nigerian *ibo* and *ipenpen*.

P.G. Brewster, 'Some Nigerian games with Their Parallels and Analogues', *Journal de la Société des Africanistes*, 1954, 24.

HULA-HOOP, a var. of a solo recreational dance, also an object of sports emulation. It consists of spinning a special rim – with the same name as the dance – around one's hips or other parts of the body. The object is to make the greatest number of spins or to keep spinning for the longest possible time. The hula-hoop has been used in various children's games since ancient times. The new idea, however, was to use it in order to spin it around one's body. R. Knerr and A.K. Melin from Wham-O, a company based in San Gabriel, California, USA, launched Hula-hoop fashion in 1957. They associated the hoop their company was producing with a Hawaiian dance called hula, or hula-hula, in which dancers accompanied ritual chants, old and improvised ones, by swinging their hips. The hula dance was supposed to bring rain or a good harvest. An old Hawaiian legend says the first hula performer was Hiyaka, a sister of Pele, the volcano goddess. Originally, only selected local dancers who went through special training in a tribal schoolhouse, called a *haalau*, and whose spiritual patron was a deity of the dance, Laka, could perform hula. After a few weeks' training, a student could be granted the status of *unika*, which allowed him or her to perform hula in public places. The principal figures of the hula dance comprise a standing position, referred to as *olapa*, and a number of figures in kneeling, sitting, and half-lying positions, known under the single term *ho-opa-a*. Different var. of the dance have several names originating from the names of percussion instruments or the lyrics of certain chants. Knerr and Melin employed their hoop to stimulate moves characteristic of the hula dance. Their idea was first popularized in the USA and then spread worldwide and with-

Hula-hoop.

Hunting art on Polish postage stamps.

Lucas Cranach, The Hunt.

J.B.J. Pater, Chinese hunting.

Hunting has traditionally been among the favored aristocratic pastimes in Great Britain.

in a span of only 3yrs., the hula-hoop was not only a popular dance and a recreational exercise, recommended esp. to women who wanted to keep slim, but also the object of numerous sports competitions. J.W. Kealiinohomoku, 'Hula', EAI, 1979, 14; J. Rutkowski, *Hula-hoop w 12 lekcjach*, 1959.

HULAJNOGI STREET RACING, see >SCOOTERS, >RADKI.

HULAMA, see >ULAMA.

HUMMIE, an Eng. folk game similar to >SHINTY but using a sheep vertebra instead of a ball. A curved stick was used to hit the vertebra. The origin of the name is unclear; in colloquial 19th cent. English the word 'hummie' could signify an inflammation caused by a blister on one's hand. It could, therefore, refer to abrasions on the players' hands, and, contemptuously, to opponents whose hands were too delicate to play the game. One confirmation of this might be a call, recorded in ethnographic sources, and uttered when a player mixed with those of the other team: 'Hummie, keep to your team'.
TGESI, I, 240.

HUND EFTER HARER, Dan. for 'a dog after hares', a Dan. game usually played by small children. One of the players is the 'dog', six other players are 'hares', while the rest, holding each other by the hands, try to keep the dog away from the hares. However, after there is only one hare left for the dog to catch, the other players raise their arms to grant him free access to that last hare.
J. Møller, 'Hund efter harer', GID, 1997, 2, 27.

HUND I LÆNKE, Dan. for 'dog on a chain', [Dan. *hund* – dog + *i* – in + *lænke* – chain]. A game played by Dan. children in kindergartens and during physical education lessons. One player uses one hand to grab a piece of rope attached to a peg inserted in the ground. The others place handkerchiefs on the peg, with knots tied on them. The object is to retrieve the handkerchiefs without being caught by the 'dog' who may try to do so using his free 'paw'. If all the players succeed, the dog has to make 3 runs between 2 rows of players who are allowed to slap him with their handkerchiefs.
J. Møller, 'Hund i lænke', GID, 1997, 2.

HUNG KUEN, Chin. for 'red fist', an old Chin. school of martial art, derived from the style known as >SIUM LAM PAI.

HUNTING, a sport involving stalking and killing wild animals, small game and game birds. Hunting can be practiced on land or under water, using a var. of weapons, implements and domestic animals, e.g. hounds, horses. In numerous countries hunt-

ing is practiced as a way of maintaining control over the population of wild animals, or as part of economic planning in accordance with cultural traditions and principles of ecology.

Hunting codes. 'Hunting for amusement, heedless of the laws of nature, is immoral and undeserving of the hunter' (M. Kolasiński). Modern sports hunting is strictly regulated by a set of universal and international, ethical and ecological norms and principles formulated over the centuries. According to M. Kolasiński, an instructor of the Pol. Hunting Association, hunters must abide by the codes of sportsmanlike behavior and, therefore, they must not: 1) introduce changes into the natural environment without any justified and reasonable cause; 2) kill or wound an animal when there is no possibility of retrieving it; 3) shoot from a distance which does not ensure shooting accuracy; 4) leave a wounded animal without killing it; 5) shoot when the game has no fair chance to escape; 6) shoot at game outside of hunting seasons; 7) shoot at endangered species; 8) use poaching methods in killing game; 9) argue about game during hunting; 10) hunt game pointed on purpose, e.g. released from cages before hunting.

The main controversy concerning modern sports hunting is the rapid development of hunting weapons and implements, which tips the balance in any confrontation in favor of the hunter. With the encroachment of civilization, pristine habitats are diminishing rapidly and wild animals have far poorer chances of surviving than ever before. Game has now become more of a victim than an 'adversary' in hunting, as a specific type of natural competition. After the 18th cent. some new forms of hunting began to appear, in which wild game – endangered due to land development, deforestation and the destruction of natural ecosystems – was substituted for with artificial targets for hunters; and trad. kinds of hunting were replaced with 'bloodless' hunting imitation games; see Eng. >FOX HUNTING, >FIELD ARCHERY or hunting versions of >PAINTBALL. Some modern sports events consisting of shooting at inanimate objects, such as trapshooting or skeet shooting, are derived from ancient hunting traditions (>SHOOTING). Bloodless 'hunting' trips into the wild, especially among underwater fauna, with a photo or video camera, enjoy increasing popularity.

History. Hunting for food was known to man in prehistoric times. Before the development of agriculture hunting often served as man's sole life support. The earliest forms of hunting for sport can be traced back to the earliest states and civilizations, when the needs of the ruling classes made them look upon hunting as pleasure and amusement rather than as a means of survival. Still, however, in some

cultures hunting out of necessity and hunting for pleasure co-exist in the present day. The rulers of ancient Egypt used to hunt wild animals while riding chariots. For Eg. nobles hunting served as a demonstration of courage and fulfillment of their craving for adventure. The development of pastoralism in ancient Greece and Rome furnished cities and settlements with most food and hides, and contributed to the development of hunting for pleasure. Hunting scenes were frequent subjects of classical mythology, customs, art and literature. Artemis, the Gk. goddess of the hunt and wild animals, bore the titles of Potnia Theron (Mistress of Animals) and Hekatebolos (The One Shooting from Distance). She was the patron of hunters who often erected wayside shrines for her, or hung her portrait on trees to win the Goddess's favors. After a successful hunt worshippers of Artemis made offerings of the head and hide of the killed animal. Artemis's Roman counterpart Diana enjoyed a similar cult as well. The first authors of serious treatises on hunting were the ancient Greeks. The most renowned was Oppian of Apamea, living in the 3rd cent. BC, who wrote a four-volume work *Kynegetika* (*On Hunting*), and an epic poem *Ikseutika* (*On Wildfowling*). Contests between men and wild animals such as lions, elephants, boars and bears were popular forms of public entertainment. In the times of Pompeius the Great (106-46 BC) 600 lions were killed during one public show. In the Middle Ages, hunting became a favor-

Hunting in ancient Egypt.

H

WORLD SPORTS ENCYCLOPEDIA

Frederic Remington, The Moose Hunt, c. 1890, gouache.

Deer Hunting, *watercolor.*

ite royal and noble pastime in England. The English were bowhunting masters and developed effective methods of hunting with hounds. Falconry, as a form of fowl hunting, was brought to the Eur. continent by the Arabs, who occupied the Iberian Peninsula for several centuries. In the 16th cent. extensive hunting in England was regulated by a number of limitations on hunting on public lands. The right to hunt was to a large extent attached to the ownership of land. Big game animals and many bird species became virtually extinct in England in the 18th cent. The ensuing, growing opposition to extensive hunting practices was expressed in anonymous treatises, such as *A Treatise on the Laws for Preservation of the Games* (1764), and numerous press articles. A series of special parliamentary acts followed, which focused on hunting regulations. At that time, hunting imitations began to be practiced as a sport using inanimate targets. The problem of game overexploitation and extinction of individual species also affected other Eur. countries. The auroch became extinct in the 16th cent.; the sable in the 18th cent. In N America, the clash of abundant game with highly advanced Eur. hunting methods resulted in the extinction of many species. As early as 1706, the colonial authorities of New York were forced to pass laws prohibiting hunting particular animal and bird species. Constant westward movement led to discoveries of new and richer hunting grounds, often taken by force from Amer. Natives. The transcontinental railway made it possible for a great number of hunters to explore the interior of N.America, particularly the profuse hunting grounds of the Great Prairies and Rocky Mountains, full of buffalo and bear; or Canada abounding in beaver.

In 1854 G. Gore began organizing the first buffalo 'hunting trains' that were followed later by huge buffalo hunting expeditions launched by dozens of Amer. entrepreneurs. Unlimited hunting virtually exterminated the buffalo population of N.America; in 1850 there were about 15,000,000 buffalo in the Plains, by the 1880s only a few hundred specimens survived. During a single hunting expedition to Wyoming and Montana several thousand buffalo were killed within a few weeks; in one valley near the Yellowstone River about 6,000 dead animals were found. The hunters took only the animal tongues and some parts of the meat leaving the carcasses to rot on the prairie. Extermination of the buffalo within a few dozen years vastly contributed to the decline of the cultures of Prairie Indians, which were based almost exclusively on buffalo hunting. 'Pseudo-hunting' practices in the USA and partly in Canada also led to the extinction of many other animal and bird species, such as the passenger pigeon, massively used for sports shooting by the end of

the 19th cent. In 1914, the last known representative of the species died in the Cincinnati Zoo. The disastrous situation of many species endangered with extinction led to the foundation of numerous preservation and game conservation schemes, such as Duck Unlimited (1938), a private organization studying bird populations and advising on what seasons and bag limits are appropriate to assure a continuous supply of birds. Uncontrolled hunting, especially big game hunting, survived longest in former African colonies. In the 1960s and 1970s African countries introduced legislation regulating hunting practices and game protection. Since the publication of a dramatic report on the endangered natural environment by the UN Secretary General U-Thant there have been no free, open hunting grounds in the world. In many areas of the world, however, governmental conservation schemes are fictitious and weak administration fails to exert effective control on illegal hunting and poaching. The practices of the former Soviet and E Eur. governments, consisting of the extensive sale of hunting licenses, opened large state-owned areas for licensed hunting but also led to the near extermination of the Siberian tiger. Strict protective laws have been introduced concerning trade in rare live wild animals and products from endangered species, e.g. ivory or rhinoceros horns, however their implementation is not always effective.

Women have also practiced hunting since ancient times, although to a lesser extent, as their participation in the hunt was often limited by religious

A hurdling sprint.

laws and cultural traditions. In classical mythology it was female divinities who were patrons of the hunt and wild animals, e.g. the Gk. Artemis and Roman Diana. Two medieval Eng. treatises on hunting, i.e. *On Hunting* and *On Hawking* (included in *The Book of St. Albans*), were written by a woman, J. Barnes, the wife of a landlord from Barnes near St. Albans. Queen Elizabeth I was also very fond of hunting and hawking.

P. Beckford, *Thoughts on Hunting*, 1781; K. Biały, *Podstawy łowiectwa*, 1994; I. Bobiatyński, *Nauka łowiectwa w dwóch tomach*, (1823-25); P. Brown, *Guns and Hunting*, 1955; A. Brzezicki, W. Mazurek, S. Mierzyński, eds., *W krainie łowów*, 1966; N. Cox, *The Gentleman's Recreation in Four Parts: Hunting – Hawking – Fowling – Fishing*, 1674; J.S. Gardiner, *The Art and the Pleasure of Hare Hunting*, 1750; A.H. Higginson, *An Old Sportsman's Memories*, 1951; W. Sarnowska, J. Fabiański, *Łowiectwo na ziemiach polskich*, 1976; personal info: M. Kolasiński, an instructor of the Polish Hunting Association, Poznań.

HUNTING OF THE MAN TRIBE, a sports game being an imitation of hunting, practiced by the Man people of China. The game is played by 2 teams of 3 players each. Each player has a wicker basket and a number of small bags filled with sand or balls made of packed animal fur. The aim of the game is to throw the balls or bags into the baskets carried on the backs of the opposing players. Before taking shots the players can pass the balls among themselves. The balls cannot be removed from the baskets. The team which manages to place more balls in the opponents' baskets wins. A match consists of two 10-min. periods. The size of the playing field varies, depending on local tradition. The number of balls or bags used in a single game is not specified. Mu Fushan, et al., '(Man) Hunting', TRAMCHIN, 62.

HURDLING, track-and-field event of running sprint races over distances ranging 50-400m (or up to 440yds. in Eng.-speaking countries) over a series of obstacles set a fixed distance apart which makes it possible for a runner to maintain a rhythm once set. International competitions, including the Ol.G. and W.Ch., involve a 10-hurdle 110-m race (with hurdles of 106.7cm) and a 10-hurdle 400-m race (with hurdles of 91.4cm) for men and 100-m (with hurdles of 84.0cm) and 400-m (with hurdles of 76.2cm) races for women. The hurdles shall not be more than 120cm wide and may be narrower depending on the width of a running lane. Their base-leg must not be longer than 70cm and must point toward the approaching hurdler. Runners must remain in assigned lanes throughout a whole race and in the 200-m and 400-m races the starts are staggered. Base-legs must be equipped with sliding weights to maintain a hurdle's balance. The force necessary to knock a hurdle down must not be less than 3.6 and not more than 4.0kg. A hurdle bar should be 7cm tall and painted with black and white stripes. The total weight of a hurdle must be at least 10kg. The height of the bar must be adjustable so that the same hurdle may be used during races over various distances. The number of hurdles that a competitor could knock down varied in the past and now a runner may knock as many hurdles as he likes provided that he does not do it

In the absence of natural predators, such as wolves, that would cull the weaker, sicker, older animals from a herd, controlled hunting by humans can reduce the danger of damage to both herd and habitat wrought by unchecked population.

with a hand and that he stays within the assigned lane for the entire race.

In the 100-m women's race hurdles are spaced in the following way: the first hurdle is set 13m from the starting line, then the hurdles are spaced 8.15m apart and the last hurdle is placed 10.5m before the finish line. In the 110-m men's race hurdles are spaced in the following way: the first hurdle is set 13.72m from the starting line, then the hurdles are spaced 9.14m apart and the last hurdle is placed 14.02m before the finish line. In the 400-m men's and women's races hurdles are spaced in the following way: the first hurdle is set 45m from the starting line, then the hurdles are spaced 35m apart and the last hurdle is placed 40m before the finish line. The 200-m race is held at many international competitions and although it has been officially recognized by the IAAF it has yet to be introduced to the Ol.G. or W.Ch. In the 200-m race hurdles are 76.2cm-high and are spaced in the following way: the first hurdle is set 18.29m from the starting line, then the hurdles are spaced 18.29m apart and the last hurdle is placed 17.10m before the finish line. During indoor competitions the most popular distances, in addition to the above, are 50 and 60m and, less frequently, 70 and 80m. The 60-m women's hurdle race was introduced in 1927 followed by the 80-m race which in 1972 was replaced by the 100-m race with 8 hurdles of 76cm. In addition, hurdle races constitute constituent parts of many other multi-event sports – e.g. the 110-m race is a part of the men's >DECATHLON and the 100-m race is a part of the women's >HEPTATHLON. The Amer. var. of decathlon known as >ALL-AROUND involves a 120-yd. hurdle race.

60M HURDLES used to be a major women's event at international competitions during the 1921-27 period. Later it was replaced by the 80-m race. As far as men's events are concerned, the 60-m race is held almost exclusively indoors where there are no 110-m running tracks.

80M HURDLES. A women's event held during the 1927-72 period. It was included on the Olympic program 1932-68. The best hurdler before 1939 was M. Didrickson of the US who won the 1932 hurdles gold (she also won javelin throw and came second in high jump; in the 1940s she became a golf world champion). In the 1945-56 period the two best hurdlers were F. Blankers Koen and S. De la Hunty-Strickland. After 1970 the race was dominated by Soviet and E Ger. hurdlers (later they also dominated the 100-m race) with serious competition from Austrl. racers such as M. Caird and P. Ryan-Kilborn.

100M HURDLES replaced the 80-m race and was first officially introduced to the Ol.G. in Munich in 1972. The fact that the distance was extended and that it required a longer step resulted in the fact that short, stocky female runners found it increasingly difficult to compete over this distance. Ger. hurdlers such as K. Balzer (the first woman to run the distance in under 13sec. – 12.9sec. in 1969), A. Ehrhardt-Jahns (1972 Olympic champion) and J. Schaller (1976 Olympic champion) of GDR are deemed to have been the best runners soon after the new distance had been introduced. In the 1990s the most outstanding 100-m hurdlers were J. Donkova of Bulgaria (1988 Olympic champion) and L. Narozhylenko of Russia later known as L. Enquist of Sweden (1991 world champion for the USSR and the 1996 Olympic as well as the 1997 World Champion for Sweden). Pol. hurdlers, especially T. Sukniewicz – a 3-time world record holder in 1970 (with her best result at 12.7sec.), T. Nowak, D. Straszyńska, G. Rabsztyn and L. Kałek-Langer, were also among the best in the world.

110-M HURDLES and its Ang.-Sax. equivalent of 100- or 120-yd. race is a men's event that has been held in England since 1864, in the US since 1876 and in Germany since 1903. The 110m hurdle race was introduced to the Ol.G. in 1896 and has been included on the Olympic program ever since. It is also a part of W.Ch. and all continental championships, the Eur. Cup and all the most important international competitions. During the 1864-86 period the race was almost an exclusively Brit. sport and was virtually unknown throughout continental Europe. Amer. runners first appeared as rivals around 1886. During the 1896-1912 period Amer. hurdlers won all the Olympic medals except silver in 1896. In the period between the two world wars the 110-m scene was dominated by Eng.-speaking runners who won all the Olympic medals during the 1920-1936 period

except bronze in 1924. After WWII it was the Americans who dominated the scene with the exception of M. Lauer who set a phenomenal world record at 13.2sec in 1959 that was only equaled in 1960 by L. Calhoun of the US who was one of the 2 hurdlers to win an Olympic gold twice (1956, 1960; the second one being R. Kingdom also of the US who won at the 1984 and 1988 Olympics). The first runner to cover the distance in under 17sec. was S. Palmer of Great Britain (16.2sec. in 1878), in under 15sec. – E. Thompson of Canada (14.4sec. in 1920), in under 14sec. – F. Towns of the US (13.7sec. in 1936). In 1971 R. Milburn covered the distance in exactly 13sec. and in 1979 R. Neremiah of the US ran 110-m in 12.8sec. (this time was taken manually). In 1981 he became the first man to have officially run the distance in less then 13sec. (12.93sec.; at electronic time measurement).

200-M HURDLES and its Ang.-Sax. equivalent of 220-yd. race are both men's and women's events. It is, however, more frequent at men's competitions. It was included on the Olympic program in 1900 and 1904 but despite being extremely spectacular it was later dropped. Its specific character is manifested by the fact that the race has low hurdles which makes it possible for the competitors to cover the distance in exceptionally fast times. The first person to run the distance in under 23sec. was J. Owens (22.6 in 1936) and later D. Styron of the US was the first man to run it in under 22sec. (21.9sec. in 1960). The event held alternately over the metric and yard distance constituted a part of the US championship, where the best results were achieved, during the 1887-1962 period.

400-M HURDLES, whose Ang.-Sax. equivalent is the 440-yd. race, is the only hurdling event that did not originate in the Eng.-speaking world since a 400-m hurdle race was first held in 1888 in France. Despite this, no Frenchman has ever become an official world record holder. A race over approx. the same distance measured in yds. has been held in Great Britain since 1867 where the first reliable result (of 67sec.) was recorded. However, because the race over this distance is taxing, it has always been far less popular than the 300-yd. hurdles. The 400-m hurdle race first became an official event during an All-German track-and-field championship in 1897. Later, it became popular in neighboring countries. It was introduced to the US, as a 440-yd. hurdle race, in 1914. Until 1927 the Americans competed only over the yard distance and since 1928 they have alternated the yard and metric distances during subsequent championships. The event was introduced to the Ol.G. in 1900 and has remained a part thereof ever since except the 1912 Ol.G. Since the time the race was introduced to the Ol.G. it has been dominated by Amer. runners who won most of the Olympic golds except 1928, 1932, 1968, 1979 and 1980 (in Moscow – where the Amer. team did not compete). The history of the event is full of dramatic events.

A 400-m hurdling race.

During the 1904 St. Louis Games the referees refused to recognize the phenomenal result of H. Hillman as a world record because the hurdles were too low. Due to the fact that at the time there was a rule that banned results that were achieved by hurdlers who knocked hurdles down, the results attained by F.M. Taylor of the US at the 1924 Ol.G. in Paris and R. Tisdall of Ireland at the 1932 Ol.G. in Los Angeles were disallowed as world and Olympic records. This led to a paradoxical situation whereby G. Hardin, who came second after Tisdall, was declared a world record holder. The most elegant hurdler of the 1920s was Lord Burghley (1901-81, later Earl of Exeter), who later became an Olympic movement activist and supporter. After winning the 1928 Ol.G. gold medal he was a prime candidate for the 1932 Olympic gold. Before the race, however, he learned that his greatest rival G. Hardin of the US who bore the Amer. flag during the opening ceremony had spent 2hrs. in the scorching Los Angeles sun, possibly diminishing his chances of winning the race. Burghley who had not participated in the ceremony decided to also spend 2hrs. in the sun in order to equal their chances and as a result he finished the race only fourth. His deed, however, became a classic example of the Olympic *fair play*. The first official world record holder was G. Shaw of Great Britain (at 57.2sec. in 1891). The first man to run the distance in less than 57sec. was G. Anderson of Great Britain (56.8sec. in 1910), in less than 55sec. – J. Norton of the US (54.2sec. in 1920), in less than 53sec. – J. Gibson of the US (52.3sec. in 1927), in less than 52sec. – A. Filipuy of Italy (51.9sec. in 1950), in less than 51sec. – G.C. Potgieter of RSA (50.7sec. in 1957), in less than 50sec. – G. Davis of the US (49.9sec. in 1958), in less than 49sec. – D. Hemery of Great Britain (48.1sec. in 1968). Hemery's result was declared 'unbeatable in the 20th century'. However, the assumption twice proved false since 4 years later J. Akii-Bua of Uganda became the first man to go under 48sec. – 47.8sec. according to a manual measurement and 47.82sec. according to an electronic measurement. K. Young of the US was the first to run the distance in under 47sec. (46.78 in 1992).

400-M WOMEN'S HURDLES. Women have competed over this distance sporadically since the turn of the 1960s. The first official world record was set by M. Sykora of Austria (at 57.3sec. in 1973). The first woman to run the distance in under 55sec. was T. Zelentsova of the USSR (54.89sec. in 1978), in under 54sec. – M. Ponomariova also of the USSR (53.58 in 1984) and in under 53sec. – M. Stiepanova (52.94sec. in 1986). K. Kacperczyk-Hryniewiecka of Poland was a 2-time world record holder in the 1970s (at 56.51sec. in 1974 and 55.44sec. in 1978). She was, however, unable to compete at the Ol.G. since the race became an Olympic event only as late as 1984.

H. Gralka, *Biegi przez płotki*, 1964.

Hurdling on a poster for the Olympic Games in Mexico 1968.

D.H. Diparus, 110 meters hurdler, Calamine, c. 1920.

H

HURLEY, the stick used in >HURLING. The name was also used to refer to a late-19th-cent. game which was an important stage in the growth of hurling. In 1884, the Irish Hurley Union was founded, where the game slowly absorbed influences from Eng. >HOCKEY. Soon, the Union's largest club, Dublin University Hurley Club, was transformed into Dublin University Hockey Club. Irish patriots saw that as a betrayal of the ideals of the Irish sport, and the name of 'hurley' acquired a negative overtone, failing to catch on. Eventually, the game came to be known as 'hurling'.

HURLING, also >HURLEY, a game similar to >HOCKEY but derived from the local Irish tradition. Two teams with 15 players each (including goalkeepers) participate. The pitch is 140-160yds. (127-146m) long and 90-100yds. (77-91m) wide. The ball, called *sliotar* or *sliothar*, has a cork core covered with horse leather, and is 23-25cm in circumference.

History. Hurling derives from old Celtic games, which also contributed to the growth of Scot. >SHINTY. There are some mentions of such ancient games in old Irish, pre-Christian literature, transcribed from oral stories by Irish monks in the 7-8th cent. The oldest of the sources is *Cath Maige Tuired*, which tells the story of the battle of Moytirra, allegedly reporting the events of 1272 BC. There is a scene in the tale where Tuatha de Danan, after invading Ireland, defeats the local *Fomori* people by first beat-

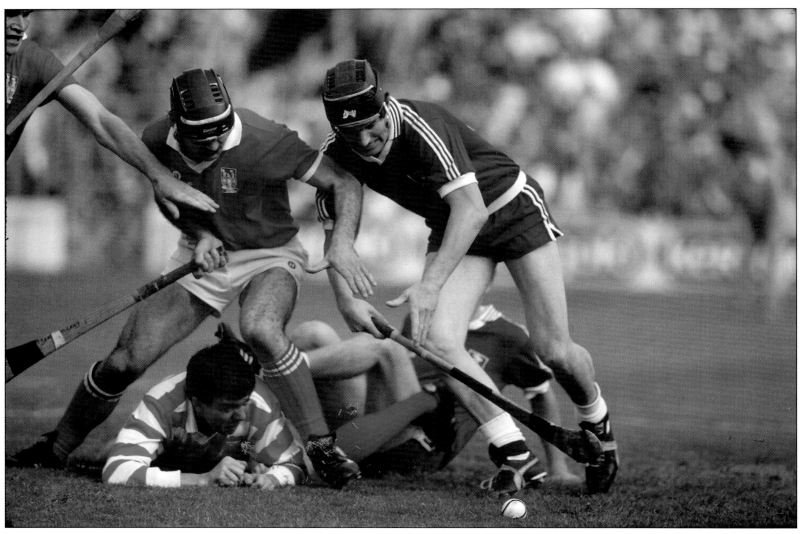

Tearing up the turf during the all Ireland hurling final.

Bill Hennessy of Kilkenny and Nicky English of Tipperary in action during the Tipperary vs. Kilkenny All Ireland Hurling Final at Croke Park, Dublin.

The sticks are 3ft. 6in. (107cm) long, and are equipped with slightly curved blades. The goals are H-shaped, 21ft. (6.4m) wide, with poles 15ft. (4.88m) high and a crossbar 8ft. (2.44m) high. Shooting the ball under the bar and between the posts scores 3pts., while shooting it over the bar scores 1pt. The ball can be balanced on the stick blade, which is one of the most difficult and spectacular elements of the game. However, this may not be done in the opponents' half of the pitch, where the ball must be hit, adding to the speed of the game. Protective helmets are recommended but not obligatory. If the ball goes over the side line, a side line ball is awarded against the team who committed the error. Tackling opponents is allowed, but pushing, pulling and charging from the front or behind is banned, and free balls are awarded for such offences. An official match usually consists of two 30-min. halves, or two 40-min. halves in more important games. The number of players used to be 21 in the 1870s and 1880s but was cut to 17 in 1892, and 15 in 1923. Original hurling is played exclusively by men; the var. played by women, with slightly different rules, is known as >CAMOGIE. Measurements have shown that hurling is the fastest ball game played on grass, and only somewhat slower-paced then >ICE HOCKEY.
Etymology. The original, Celtic name of the game appeared in a number of variants. >IOMÁINT was the old var. of hurling played in S Ireland, while >CAMÁNACHT was the most popular variant. However, the variants were slightly different, which made it difficult to refer to them by one name. The increasing dominance of English in Ireland led to the introduction of the modern name.

ing them at hurling and then winning a regular battle. Hurling is also mentioned in the old Irish book of *The Brehon Laws*, and the main character of the Irish national epic, Cuchulain, is portrayed as a hurling expert. His skills proved useful during a fight with his enemies, the sons of Conchobar:

Then they threw all their balls at him and he caught them, every single ball, against his breast. Then they threw their thrice fifty hurling-clubs at him. He warded them off so that they did not touch him, and he took a load of them on his back.

Cuchulain also demonstrated his abilities in the game itself:

Another time he was playing ball in the playing-field east of Emain, he alone on one side against the thrice fifty boys. He kept defeating them in every game in that way all the time.

Between 1527 and 1760, the brutal character of hurling led to the game being banned a number of times. In the 19th cent., hurling started acquiring the status of a modern sport, with 2 var. developing side by side in Ireland. The first one, known as *iomáint*, was especially popular in S Ireland. It was mainly played in the summertime, and the characteristic technique was lobbing the ball. The second variant, *camánacht*, was mostly played across the ground. *Camánacht* was introduced into Trinity College at the University of Dublin in 1830. That was where the rules of the game became codified, forming the basis for a game initially known as *hurley*, as records from 1870-71 attest. In the late 1870s, Catholic student teams played against Protestant teams. In 1897, the Irish Hurley Union was founded. However, when the sport started absorbing influences from

Chip Hanauer, driving the Miss Pico hydroplane, leads the field during the finals of the Madison Regatta in Madison, Indiana.

Eng. >HOCKEY, Irish patriot circles were discouraged from playing the game. As a symbol of the division, Dublin Hurley Club was renamed Dublin Hockey Club. From that time on, *iomáint* became the main source of influence within hurling. This was intensified by the downfall of many trad. forms of *camánacht*, which used to be played in Ulster, after the area was incorporated into the Brit. Empire by the Act of Union of 1801. The character of the Brit. occupation had a profound influence on the decline of many trad. Irish sports, along with the artificially triggered famine of the 1840s and the massive emigration of Irish people, mainly to the USA. However, all these factors also inspired a search for a remedy in the Celtic tradition. Organizations such as the Fenian Movement, Irish Republic Brotherhood and Land League were particularly active in the field. Sport, including hurling, was an important element of the movement. A breakthrough came with the foundation in 1884 of the Gaelic Athletic Association (Irish *Cumann Lúthchleas Gael*). The initiator of the GAA was the Irish patriot M. Cusack (1847-1906), who called hurling the 'bouquet of the Irish land'. He was assisted by C. Parnell (1846-91), the leader of the Land League, M. Davitt (1846-1906), and T.W. Croke (1824-1902), the archbishop of Cashel. To commemorate Croke's support for Irish sport, the GAA's seat was named Croke Park in his honor. The nation's largest stadium is situated at Croke Park, hosting the most interesting hurling and >GAELIC FOOTBALL events. After the GAA took over the control over these two sports, they both quickly attained the status of national sports, at the same time becoming important elements of the Irish independence movement. In 1887, the GAA imposed a ban on hurling and Gaelic football matches against Brit. teams, and banned not only foreign-

Hydrospeed.

ers from Irish teams, but especially those Irishmen who tarnished their reputation by collaborating with the Brit. government in any way, e.g. by serving in the Brit. army or police forces, or by informing them against their compatriots (the ban was only lifted in 1971). The attitude to Brit. sports was gradually mitigated with time. In 1910, the promoter of hurling and headmaster of St. Enda's school of Irish (Scoil Éanna), P. Pearse, voiced the following opinion: 'There is no need to condemn Eng. games; one simply has to play Irish ones'. After the Republic of Ireland was granted autonomy in 1922, the political role of sport, including hurling, was maintained. Ireland was one of the first Eur. nations where politicians demonstrated their connections with sport, frequenting important events accompanied by outstanding sportsmen. Among the latter, top hurling players included L. Meagher of Kilkenny and M. Mackey of Limerick in the 1930s; C. Ring and J. Doyle in the 1950s and 1960s; and K. Hogan in the 1980s and 1990s. There is also a category of so-called 'dual players', playing both hurling and Gaelic football, for example an outstanding player of the 1980s, D. Walsh.
Nowadays, annual Irish hurling championships are organized, leading to a final match at Dublin's Croke Park. The strongest teams originate from regions with the longest-standing traditions, such as Co. Clare, Cork, Kilkenny, Limerick, Tipperary and Wexford. Irish immigrants have attempted to popularize hurling in the USA, Canada and Australia but the game has not caught on outside Irish communities. However, the GAA's periodical *Coaching News* reported in the autumn of 1989 that the first Ger. hurling team was established in the town of Gosheim. The television era has enhanced hurling's appeal both in Ireland and among Irish expatriates.
Various old forms of hurling have been preserved in

other Celtic countries, such as Cornwall (>CORNISH HURLING) and Scotland (>SHINTY).
M. de Búrca, *The G.A.A. A History of the Gaelic Athletic Association*, 1980; N. Carroll, *Sport in Ireland*, 1979; Cumann Lúthchleas Gael, *Referee's Guide to the Playing Rules of Hurling and Football*, 1991; D. O'Connor, 'Hurling in Dublin', *GAA Coaching News*, Winter 1989-Spring 1990; R. Smith, *The Hurling Immortals*, 1969; A. Watson and J. Grisewood, 'The Coaching of Basic Hurling Skills', *GAA Coaching News*, Winter 1989-Spring 1990.

HUYTRUHUETUN, a type of slingshot made of a long, woven leather strap, (Span. *tirado con la honda*) one of the oldest weapons of the Chilean Araucanian (Mapuche) Indians. Araucana men known as *honderos* used to carry the huytruhuetun belted across their chests, with a substantial supply of stones in special large bags. During peace time, they practiced shooting stones for distance and at targets, which resembled Eur. sporting contests. One of the Span. chronicles of the Span. conquest of America reports how Caballero García Hurtado de Mendoza was knocked off his horse by a hondero using a huytruhuetun in 1557. Cf. Span. >TIRO CON HONDA. Today still practiced for chasing birds and hares, as well as a form of defense.
O. Plath, *Huytruhuetun*, 1946, 30.

HYDROPLANE RACING, a var. of >MOTORBOATING with the participation of hydroplanes – motor boats designed to skim the surface of the water by means of a bottom that consists in part of one or more flat surfaces sloping upwards towards the bow. Race hydroplanes are min. 20ft. in length excluding projections. The min. weight of the hull, without the driver, is 2,000lb. or 2,500lb., depending a class. The engines are 4-cycle, internal combustion engines, with max. 2 valves per cylinder and the toal capacity not exceeding 468 or 511 cubic in. In the USA, hydroplane races are organized by the American Power-Boat Association estab. in 1903, the most popular series being the Gold Cup Races held since 1904, the President's Cup, Harmsworth Trophy Races. W.Ch. are held under the auspices of UIM (Union Internationale Motonautique).

HYDROSPEED, an extreme sport, which – along with >CANYONING and >RAFTING – has been gaining great popularity in recent years. Having originated in France, it consists of swimming down wild, mountain rivers with the help of a small, 1m long, polyurethane board with special handles that provide the swimmer with a good grip and allow him to maneuver in dangerous waters. The board holds only the upper part of the swimmer's body, while his legs remain in the water. Other important ces of equipment include a 2-part suit and shoes, both made of Neopren, which protects the body against low temperatures, and a protective helmet. Practicing hydrospeed involves frequent injuries, mainly bruises caused by rocks or debri encountered by the swimmer along the way.

WORLD WATER SPEED RECORDS

YEAR — SPEED (MPH) — BOAT
1874 — 24.61 — Sir Arthur Cotton
1885 — 26.2 — Stiletto
1887 — 30.0 — Ariete
1895 — 33.75 — Boxer
1897 — 37.71 — Turbinia
1897 — 39.1 — Turbinia
1897 — 9.73 — Elaine
1900 — 42.73 — Viper
1902 — 22.36 — Mercedes
1903 — 45.06 — Arrow
1903 — 24.9 — Napier
1904 — 25.1 — Trèfle-à-Quatre-Feuilles
1904 — 26.65 — Trèfle-à-Quatre-Feuilles
1904 — 28.36 — Onontio
1905 — 29.3 — Challenger
1905 — 29.93 — Napier II
1905 — 32.45 — Dubonnet
1905 — 33.80 — Dubonnet
1906 — 34.17 — Legru-Hotchkiss
1908 — 36.6 — Dixie II
1910 — 43.6 — Ursula
1911 — 45.21 — Dixie IV
1912 — 46.51 — Maple Leaf IV
1912 — 58.26 — Tech Jr.
1914 — 59.964 — Santos-Despujols
1915 — 66.66 — Miss Minneapolis
1919 — 70.86 — Hydrodome IV
1920 — 74.97 — Miss America
1920 — 77.85 — Miss America
1921 — 80.57 — Miss America II
1924 — 87.392 — Farman Hydroglider
1928 — 92.83 — Miss America VII
1929 — 93.12 — Miss America VII
1930 — 98.76 — Miss England II
1931 — 102.16 — Miss America IX
1931 — 103.069 — Miss America IX
1931 — 103.49 — Miss England II
1931 — 110.22 — Miss England II
1932 — 111.71 — Miss America IX
1932 — 117.43 — Miss England III (K1)
1932 — 119.812 — Miss England III (K1)
1932 — 120.5 — Miss England III (K1)
1932 — 124.91 — Miss America X
1937 — 126.32 — Bluebird K3
1937 — 129.5 — Bluebird K3
1938 — 130.86 — Bluebird K3
1939 — 141.74 — Bluebird K4
1950 — 160.32 — Slo-Mo-Shun IV
1952 — 178.49 — Slo-Mo-Shun IV
1955 — 202.32 — Bluebird K7
1955 — 216.2 — Bluebird K7
1956 — 225.63 — Bluebird K7
1957 — 184.49 — Miss Supertest II
1957 — 239.07 — Bluebird K7
1958 — 248.62 — Bluebird K7
1957 — 195.331 — Hawaii Kai III
1957 — 187.627 — Hawaii Kai III
1959 — 260.35 — Bluebird K7
1960 — 192.001 — Miss Thriftway
1962 — 200.419 — Miss U.S. I
1964 — 276.30 — Bluebird K7
1967 — 285.21 — Hustler
1977 — 288.60 — Spirit of Australia
1978 — 317.60 — Spirit of Australia
2000 — 205.494 — Miss Freei

WORLD SPORTS ENCYCLOPEDIA

IBAHAJIME, an old Jap. form of archery, which was part of courtly etiquette. Cf. >JYRAI, >NORIYUMI, >TANGONO KISHA. See also Jap. forms of equestrian archery >KADAGAKE, >INUOMONO, >YABUSAME; cf. forms of foot archery >BUSHA, >JUMIHAJIME, KUSAJISI, >MARUMONO, >MOMOTE.

ICE BOATING, also ice-yachting, a var. of sailing on ice or hard snow in vehicles referred to as iceboats.
Equipment. An iceboat is a sailing vehicle comprising a hull, mast, sail, steering runner, and outrigged runners. The outrigged runners are fixed at a certain distance from each other to a pole, perpendicular to the hull, improving the vehicle's lateral stability. The runners can be made of steel, phosphor bronze, wood banded with a steel rail, or plastic. There are several types of iceboats, currently the most popular are: monotype double XV with a rear steering runner and a sail of 15m² and a single DN with a 6.5m² sail. The letters stand for *Detroit News*, a newspaper that announced in 1937 a contest for the best iceboat design; the winning design was produced and dubbed DN. In the USA and Canada E-Skeeters are quite popular with 75 sq.ft. (around 7m²) of sail and Renegades – a smaller version of a Skeeter – with a 67-sq.ft. (about 5.5m²) sail. There are also Amer. versions of recreational iceboats the most popular of which are double Arrows and Yankees.

issues, is selected by the Race Committee and regattas are overseen by race judges whose decisions are final. In 1966, the regulations applied in Europe were made compatible with those employed in the USA by the National Iceboat Authority.
History. The earliest attempts to use a sail in order to move a craft on ice date back to the 12th cent. when a sail made of skins was used to propel a sleigh in Lapland. However, the tradition of modern iceboats originates from the Netherlands where they were first used in the 16th cent. Their development accelerated considerably in the 17th-cent. Du. colony of the New Netherlands (today's New York state) where a unique climatic zone covering the area between Buffalo and Newburgh caused freezing and hardening of snow in winter which made it difficult to travel in wheeled vehicles but easier in sleighs. Such were the circumstances in which sailing sleighs found practical use in transportation. In the 18th cent., such sleighs started to be used on the Great Lakes and the Hudson River. Around 1790, O. Booth used iceboats to transport skins along the Hudson River in the vicinity of Poughkeepsie. In the 18th-19th cent., transportation iceboats made inroads in the area of Long Island, New York, on Lake Ontario, and on the Jersey River. Red Bank, near New York, became – in the middle of the 19th cent. – a leading ice boating center worldwide, which it still is today. In 1879, H. Relye constructed a double 3-runner iceboat called *Robert Scott*. It was the first

titions were established in the USA, among which the most celebrated were the Stuart International Trophy and the Hearst International Challenge Trophy. Until the turn of the '50s, Eur. ice boating developed independently from the Amer. one. In the first half of the 20th cent., the major centers were in the Netherlands, Germany, Austria, Sweden, Estonia, and Latvia. In the '60s, organizations from the 2 continents started to collaborate. Nevertheless, no single international organization has yet come into existence to unite the disparate factions. In the USA, ice boating is overseen by the Northwestern Ice Yachting Association (1912) and the Eastern Ice Yachting Association (1937).
In 1923 or 1928, the Europäischen Eissegelnunion (EEU) was formed in Riga by representatives of Austria, Estonia, Germany, Latvia, Lithuania, and Sweden. In 1934, prob. the first ice boating manual written in Polish, *Ice Sailing* by B. Czarkowski and J. Kuczyński, was published. In 1939, in Chicago, the International Skeeter Association was founded. An association that has international credit is the International DN Ice Yacht Racing Association (IDNIYRA) seated in Detroit and operating within the International Yacht Racing Union, IYRU. The DN class was recognized in Europe in 1964, and since 1966 and 1973 E.Ch. and W.Ch. respectively have been held in DN. The IDNIYRA has become the most representative organization in the world of ice boating. Leading boaters and world champions include: Americans T. Woodhouse (1974), I. Gougeon (1975 and 1982), and H. Bosett (1983), and Poles R. Knasiecki (1976) and B. Kramer (1978). The development of sports ice boating was partly responsible for the growing tendency to beat speed records. In 1885, J. Weaver reached 172km/h on the Navesink River and the barrier of 200km/h was overcome in 1907 by E. Price who achieved a speed of 231.7km/h in *Claret* on the Shrewsbury River in the vicinity of Long Branch, New Jersey. The speed record set in 1907 in Kalamazoo, Michigan, in *Wolverine* which covered a distance of 30mi. (around 48km) in 39min. 50sec. was broken only in 1953 by Perrigo who covered the same distance in 29min. 4sec. in *Thunderjet*. For some time, before motor vehicles acquired better capacities, iceboats were the fastest vehicles known to man. Until 1914, enlarging the sails was the main tactic for increasing speed. The largest of them were up to 50m². A sequence of serious accidents resulting from the loss of a boat's stability led to the reduction of sail sizes and the standardization of the iceboat.
L. Roberts, W.S. Clair, *Think Ice! The DN Ice Boating Book*, (1989); J. Townes, 'Ice Boating', EWS, II, 499-501.

John Stanton of Stamford, Connecticut, USA, sails across Great Pond in the morning fog during the New England Spring Classic ice boat regatta.

ICE BOWLING, a family of sports comprising mainly sliding or curling heavy objects called stones (because of the original material they were made of) on ice rinks. The goal is to place a stone of one's team closest to the center of the house, called the 'tee'. This is accomplished by sending one's stone to rest in a scoring position, by knocking opponents' stones out of the scoring position, and by guarding one's own stones with others. The team with the closest stone, inside the house, scores a point, or more if they also have the second closest stone etc. >CURLING, a Scot. sport nowadays practiced on an international and Olympic scale is the best known var. of ice bowling. Other, less renowned, varieties include Ger. >EISSCHIEßEN; >EISKEGELN and their var. >KALUDDERSCHIEßEN. The term ice bowling itself does not reflect the true character of the game as 'pins' stand for objects to knock down and >BOWLING or >EUROPEAN BOWLING denotes games in which knocking down pins is the object of competition. The correspondence of terms referring to these games stems perhaps from the fact that in most western languages sports involving sliding, hurling and curling bowls, discs and discuses on ice are submitted to similar rules and regulations as bowling sports.

ICE DANCING, see >FIGURE SKATING.

ICE HOCKEY. A game played by 2 teams moving on skates in an ice rink and aiming to score goals. A team is composed of 6 players, including a goalkeeper. The game is played with a puck, made of vulcanized rubber, or other approved material, 1in. thick and 3in. in diameter and weighing 5½-6oz. It is moved about the ice with the use of special sticks. The best players can move the puck as quickly as

An iceboating regatta.

Rules. The principal form of competition is a regatta comprising a series of races. The courses' length varies from 1 to 3km. A course is marked with 2 buoys: the upper one windward and the lower one leeward, which the boats encircle facing the port and starboard respectively, covering thus a figure-8 route. During a single race, boats usu. cover such a route 3 times. The starting line is placed at least 50yds. (about 46m) below the leeward buoy and its center should be marked by the line joining the 2 buoys. The starting iceboats are lined up along the start line, right of its center on odd-numbered positions and left of its center on even-numbered positions. In the case of the first race in a given regatta the positions are drawn in lots, in following races they are allotted depending on the places achieved in preceding races. The finish line is located at the level of the leeward buoy, perpendicular to the line joining the buoys; a line between the lower buoy and a special sign, or the buoy and a group of referees marks it. Each race has a time limit depending on current weather conditions and the class of starting boats. The course is so marked that its first stretch is covered against the wind, then the boats turn around the upper buoy counterclockwise and move with the wind towards the lower buoy. The course's location, esp. from the point of view of safety

model with front runners on a wide base – which secured better stability of the vessel – and a rear steering runner. Known as the Hudson River Type, it was the prototype for most of the iceboats built in America until the 1930s. In 1931, S. Meyer from Milwaukee built the first iceboat with front steering runners. The Joys Brothers manufacture launched the production of a smaller version of this boat, contributing thus to the further popularization of the sport. Meyer's model served as an inspiration for W. Beauvais whose *Beau Skeeter* became later a prototype of the E-Skeeter class which was the m ost frequent model employed during the Ice Yacht Challenge Pennant of America in 1951. In 1947, C. Bernard and F. Tatzlaff constructed their *Mary B*, which was the first iceboat to employ the advantage of light metals and plastics.
The first ice boating clubs and systematic competitions appeared at the end of the 19th cent. In 1881, the Ice Yacht Club in New Hamburgh, New York, organized the Ice Yacht Challenge Pennant of America, a highly prestigious trophy held up to this day (but for a break in 1902-22), and since 1951 under the auspices of the Eastern Ice Yachting Association, on the Greenwood Lake in New Jersey. Among the first winners were A. Frost in *Jack Frost* and J.E. Roosevelt in *Icicle*. Soon after, many other compe-

160km/h. The sticks are made of wood and end with a blade forming an obtuse angle with the handle. The official size of the rink is 200ft. (in Europe 56-61m) long and 85ft. (in Europe 26-31m) wide. The corners are rounded in the arc of a circle with a radius of 28ft. The goal posts extend vertically 4ft. (1.22m) above the surface of the ice and are set 6ft. (1.83m) apart, measured from the inside of the posts with a crossbar over the top. Match duration is 3x20min of actual play. One of the main attractions of the game is its speed. The best players can skate up to 40-50km/h.

History. Towards the end of the Middle Ages a game similar to the modern ice hockey was played in the Netherlands but it had no influence on what ice hockey is today. Its origin is unclear. Most probably it is an amalgamation of various Eur. games brought to N. America by the colonists mixed with similar native Amer. games. There are a few hypotheses. The most credible of them says that in the first half of the 19th cent. Brit. soldiers of Scot. and Irish origin, stationed in Canada joined the rules of summer varieties of hockey, known in Britain as >SHINTY and >HURLING, with a violent game that Native Americans played on ice. Another hypothesis talks about applying the rules of Can. >LACROSSE to games played on the frozen Lake Ontario, especially those popular among the Huron and Cherokee tribes. The first players most probably did not use skates, and the moment of their introduction remains unknown. As for their construction, it is also unknown whether they were native Amer. bone skates or the Eur. construction of metal and wood, later replaced by metal ones. However the Eur. style of skating was known in the area as early as the middle of the 18th cent. The earliest recognized ice hockey match was played by Royal Can. Rifles in 1855, in Kingston, Ontario, in a bay near the Tete du Pont barracks. Twenty years later 2 student teams at Montreal University played a match on the initiative of I.G.A. Creighton (1850-1930). The match was preceded by the formulation of rules that later became the basis for the present rules of ice hockey. For some time the number of players on the rink at any one time was 9, to be reduced to 7 at the end of the 19th cent. The first matches were played with a full rubber ball, later replaced by a wooden puck and eventually a rubber one. The first match to be played in front of a fee-paying audience took place on 3 March, 1875. In 1885, an ice hockey league was started in Kingston. In 1892, Lord Stanley of Preston (1841-1908), the Governor General of Canada, purchased a small gold-plated silver bowl from a London silversmith. The bowl was awarded to the best hockey team in Canada. Today, the original trophy is a museum exhibit, but every year its replica, known as the Stanley Cup is awarded to the best professional team in the league. This most prestigious award was the single most important element in the development of the game in Canada. Also in 1893, the first US ice hockey clubs were founded at Yale and Johns Hopkins' universities.

Professional ice-hockey. In 1909, the National Hockey Association (NHA) was founded in Canada and played the leading role in the development of professional forms of the game throughout the Amer. continent. For a time, there was a rival Pacific Coast Hockey League (PCHL), founded by L. Patrick (1883-1960) and his brother Frank (1885-1960). This league had great achievements in the development of artificial rinks as their clubs were located in the part of Canada that experienced relatively mild winters, not always guaranteeing natural freezing of the ice. A technology developed in the US was used, consisting of a layer of asphalt, with cooling pipes underneath. The asphalt rink was then covered with water, forming a surface of ice. The first artificial ice rink was built in Toronto in 1917 (earlier rinks in the US were used only for figure skating). In 1917, the NHA was reorganized and changed its name to the one it still holds today: the National Hockey League (NHL). In the beginning, the league was in competition not only with the PCHL, but also with the Western Canada Hockey League (WCHL, 1921-24). Towards the end of 1924, the PCHL together with the WCHL formed one Western Hockey League (WHL). Under their influence, a number of changes were introduced to the rules of the game, such as the goalkeeper's right to lose contact between the ice and his skates while defending the goal. Also passing the puck forward in the neutral area was allowed and the number of players was reduced from 7 to 6. The WHL survived only until 1925, because of the higher economic development of eastern and central Can. cities, offering larger audiences and higher salaries to the players. Starting with the 1926- 27 season, the NHL became the main ice hockey league, although in the beginning it consisted of only 5 Can. teams. After a short period of competing with various US leagues, the latter recognized their weakness and submitted to the NHL. The first US club to play in the NHL was the Boston Bruins. Other NHL clubs were formed in Boston, Chicago, New York, Pittsburgh, and Detroit. Dedicated ice hockey stadiums have been built since 1917. The NHL also incorporated the Stanley Cup, which in 1926 became the main trophy of the professional league. The best players annually receive a nest of special awards. Since 1917, the Art Ross Trophy has been awarded to 'the player who leads the league in scoring points at the end of the regular season.' The Hart Memorial Trophy (since 1923-24) is awarded to 'the player adjudged to be most valuable to his team.' Winners are selected in a poll among sportswriters and broadcasters in each of the 26 NHL cities. The Lady Byng Memorial Trophy (since 1924-25) is awarded to 'the player adjudged to have exhibited the best type of sportsmanship and gentlemanly conduct combined

WORLD SPORTS ENCYCLOPEDIA

Ice hockey on a stamp issued for the 1964 Olympic Games in Innsbruck.

Adame Deadmarsh (#28) of the USA and Joe Sakic (#91) of Canada vie for the puck during the men's ice hockey gold medal game of the Salt Lake City Winter Olympic Games at the E Center in Salt Lake City, Utah.

John Leclair (#10) of the USA looks on as his deflected shot is put past goalie Martin Brodeur (#30) of Canada by Brian Rafalski (#3) of the USA during the second period of the men's ice hockey gold medal game of the Salt Lake City Winter Olympic Games at the E Center in Salt Lake City, Utah.

ICE HOCKEY WORLD CHAMPIONS

MEN
1920 Canada
1924 Canada
1928 Canada
1930 Canada
1931 Canada
1932 Canada
1933 United States
1934 Canada
1935 Canada
1936 Great Britain
1937 Canada
1938 Canada
1939 Canada
1947 Czechoslovakia
1948 Canada
1949 Czechoslovakia
1950 Canada
1951 Canada
1952 Canada
1953 Sweden
1954 Soviet Union
1955 Canada
1956 Soviet Union
1957 Sweden
1958 Canada
1959 Canada
1960 United States
1961 Canada
1962 Sweden
1963 Soviet Union
1964 Soviet Union
1965 Soviet Union
1966 Soviet Union
1967 Soviet Union
1968 Soviet Union
1969 Soviet Union
1970 Soviet Union
1971 Soviet Union
1972 Czechoslovakia
1973 Soviet Union
1974 Soviet Union
1975 Soviet Union
1976 Czechoslovakia
1977 Czechoslovakia
1978 Soviet Union
1979 Soviet Union
1981 Soviet Union
1982 Soviet Union
1983 Soviet Union
1985 Czechoslovakia
1986 Soviet Union
1987 Sweden
1989 Soviet Union
1990 Soviet Union
1991 Sweden
1992 Sweden
1993 Russia
1994 Canada
1995 Finland
1996 Czech Republic
1997 Canada
1998 Sweden
1999 Czech Republic
2000 Czech Republic
2001 Czech Republic
2002 Slovakia

WOMEN
1990 Canada
1992 Canada
1994 Canada
1997 Canada
1999 Canada
2000 Canada
2001 Canada

Goalkeeper Mike Richter (#35) of the USA bows his head during the men's ice hockey gold medal game against Canada in Salt Lake City, Utah's E Center at the Winter Olympic Games.

with a high standard of playing ability.' The Vezina Trophy (since 1926-27) is awarded to 'the goalkeeper having played a minimum 25 games for the team with the fewest goals scored against it.' The Calder Memorial Trophy (since 1932-33) is awarded to 'the player selected as the most proficient in his first year of competition in the National Hockey League.' The winner is selected in a poll among sportswriters and broadcasters in each of the 26 NHL cities. The James Norris Memorial Trophy (since 1953-54) is awarded to 'the defense player who demonstrates throughout the season the greatest all-around ability in that position.' The Conn Smythe Award (since 1964-65) is awarded to 'the most valuable player for his team in the entire playoffs.' The winner is selected by the League Governors at the conclusion of the final game in the Stanley Cup Finals. The Lester B. Pearson Award is awarded to the player voted 'outstanding player' by the NHL players themselves. In addition to these, since 1930-31 a committee of NHL activists, sportswriters, TV and radio broadcasters picks the best players to form 2 All-Star Teams. Eleven professional leagues from the US and Canada are associated to the NHL. They work regionally and supply the best players to the NHL. The leading NHL clubs are the Toronto Maple Leaves, Edmonton Oilers and Montreal Canadians. An independent World Hockey Association has been operating in the US and Canada since 1972, trying to compete with the NHL.

Amateur hockey. While professional ice hockey dominated in the US and Canada, Europe has become the center of its amateur variety. The game reached the continent around 1900, initially as >BANDY. In the years 1904-05, proper ice hockey started to develop in France, Belgium, Switzerland, Germany, and the Czech Republic. In 1908, these countries formed the International Ice Hockey League (Ligue Internationale de Hockey sur Glace, LIGH). In 1978, the organization changed its name to International Ice Hockey Federation (IIHF). The IIHF does not cover professional ice hockey in N.America. The first amateur W.Ch. took place in Switzerland in 1911, but they were not recognized by the LIGH. It was won by the Can. amateur team. The WWI contributed to the increase of the popularity of ice hockey in Europe as it was one of the sports popularized by Amer. and Can. soldiers who came there after 1917. The second W.Ch., also not recognized by the LIGH, took place during the Summer (!) Ol.G. in Antwerp in 1920. Canada, represented by the Winnipeg Falcons, claimed victory again. The first W.Ch. recognized by the LIGH took place during the W.OI.G. in Chamonix in 1924. Until 1928, W.Ch. and E.Ch. were held every 4 years during Ol.G. Since Canada was the winner, it held the Olympic and W.Ch. titles and the best Eur. team had the E.Ch. title. Between the years 1930-71, W.Ch. and E.Ch. took place annually with the exception of Olympic years when they were included in the games. In 1972 LIGH decided to hold the events separately. In the 21 W.Ch. organized until 1953, Canada won 16 times, Czechoslovakia won twice and the US, G. Britain and Sweden each won once. In 1954 the USSR participated in the championship for the first time and it dramatically changed

the picture, breaking the long line of Can. supremacy. After 1954, the USSR won in 1954, 1956, 1963-71, 1973-5, 1978-79, 1981-84, 1986 and 1988-90. Canada won in 1955, 1958-59 and 1961. Czechoslovakia won in 1972, 1976-77 and 1985. Sweden won in 1957, 1962, 1987, 1991, and 1992. The USA won in 1960 and 1980. Since 1970, Canada has not taken part in the W.Ch. as a result of a conflict within the LIGH, concerned with the participation of professional players. Seemingly, the conflict was based on the strict adherence to the amateurism rule in Europe and breaches of the rule by players forming the Can. national team. The main reason was that the NHL feared a loss of prestige to the rival LIGH (and after 1978, IIHF, its successor). Actually, W.Ch. organized by the IIHF were gradually losing their appeal without N. Amer. players. Reconciliation among the world's leading ice hockey organizations became a necessity. It was achieved in 1977, when Canada returned to the championships. After 1975, the Conference on Security and

Co-operation in Europe and the resulting improvement of relationships between the East and the West allowed a gradual increase in sporting co-operation, incl. ice hockey. Although this process was slowed down in the wake of the Afghan conflict, the 1980s brought the political weakening of the USSR and Gorbatchev's *perestroika*. As a result, the first players from the USSR and other communist countries became involved in international ice hockey. After 1992, the Rus. representation, the main successor of the Soviet tradition, as well as that of the short-lived CIS, continued to play an important role in the international arenas but without their former supremacy. Despite the dismantling of Czechoslovakia, the Czech team maintained its leading role, becoming W.Ch. in 2000. Other successful teams in the last decade of the 20th cent. were Canada (World Champion 1997), Slovakia and Finland.

Women's ice hockey was played in Canada as early as the 1960s and '70s. In the 1980s and '90s it developed rapidly, first in the USA and Scand. countries, and later even in countries like China. It was introduced in the programme of the Ol.G. in Nagano in 1998. W.Ch. were held at irregular intervals (1-3 years) from 1990 onwards. Canada was consistently the best (1990, 1992, 1994, 1997, 1999 and 2000). Other medal positions were occupied by the USA, Finland, Norway and Denmark. Other leading women's teams are Russia and China.

N. Aaseng, *Hockey: You Are the Coach,* 1984; D. Beddoes, S. Fischler, J. Gilter, *Hockey – the Story of the World's Fastest Sport,* 1969; S. Cady, V. Stenlund, *High-Performance Skating For Hockey,* 1998; P.W. Twist, *Complete Conditioning for Ice Hockey,* 1997.

ICE SKATE SAILING, a sport in which the contestants move on skates using a sail that looks like a large kite, most often with a surface area of 35-95 sq. ft. (about 3.3-8.8m^2). In stable structures, which do not lend themselves to turn leeward or windward, additional triangular sails, resembling staysails, are used. What is important is to strike a balance between the sail and the skater's height. Most often it is assumed that half the length of the vertical sail's mast should reach up to the skater's shoulders. A great many manufacturers of yacht sails also manufacture ice skate sails. However, many ice skaters

Ice skate sailing.

prefer to make their own sails to suit their own expectations. The skates are elongated to provide for a greater stability of skating and limiting feet vibrations, but they do not prevent the skater's being bowled over by a wind-filled sail. In the 19th cent. in Norway, skate blades were lengthened to about 100cm. Presently, skates with blades 15-24in. (38--60cm) long are considered optimal, but since skates with lengthened blades must be specially ordered from the manufacturers, ice skaters very often use standard speed skates, which allow skating along a radius of 62-82ft. (19-25m). However, speed skates usually do not come with specially rigid shoes and do not protect against the loss of heat.

The basic challenge in ice skate sailing lies in maintaining the right posture. Typically, skaters' legs are slightly bent to absorb the uneven ice and the sail is held so that the ice skater is on the leeward side, before the sail, and the transverse rib supporting the sail rests on his shoulder on the windward side. Both hands hold the sail's vertical rib, below the transverse rib. Skates must be 10-15cm (4-6in.) apart; the leg on the leeward side is slightly advanced. Maneuvering, changing direction or skate sailing, deceleration and braking requires considerable skill and long training. This is particularly true of the upwind turn: the skater lowers the boom so that it rests on his shoulders on the back side. This increases the windage, resulting in the skater turning round his axis. A 180-degree downwind turn requires the skater to move the boom backward. The sail is luffed, which results in deceleration. Then the boom must be raised over the head, using both hands, so that each hand holds the boom on its side. The sail assumes a horizontal position, parallel to the ice surface and the wind does not blow against its surface, which results in the deceleration of the sail's driving force. The skater ends the turn using only the skates and, having turned, positions the sail at an angle necessary to continue sailing in a new direction.

Braking is possible by changing the direction of sailing, so as to lose wind strength by raising the sail and turning it so that it does not 'catch' the wind. Partial deceleration is possible through heeling – the sail is positioned at an angle which reduces the wind strength and the body is heeled to one side. Braking with skates is possible only when the sail is in the horizontal position with respect to the ice surface and does not catch the wind. Otherwise, when the sail surface is positioned with the wind, braking is either ineffective or can overturn the skater.

History. The beginnings of ice skate sailing are obscure. The oldest information is from 17th-cent. Holland where skates with metal blades were used for the first time, which considerably helped to dig the skates into the ice and maintain the desired direction and maneuver using the wind (bone skates used till then did not lend themselves to this operation, particularly against a side wind). In the 18th cent. a Swed. botanist, C. Linnaeus (1707-78) saw skaters 'with sails like wings' during his expeditions. In the mid 19th cent. ice skate sailing flourished on the winter frozen straits separating Denmark and Sweden. In Germany ice skate sailing was more recreational than competitive and at the end of the 19th cent. many ice skate sailors could be seen on Lake Muggelsee near Berlin, with two or even three persons holding one sail. First competitive contests were organized in 1887 on Lake Lilla Värtan, with sails about 45 sq. ft. (about 4.2m²). At the beginning of the 1890s, US ambassador to Sweden, W.W. Thomas, Jr., saw ice skate sailing being practiced between the isles of Stockholm, which he described in his book *Sweden and the Swedes* (1893). In 1896, an Eng. skater by the name of Adams (first name unknown) reached a speed of 30mph (about 48km/h) on the Whittlesey Mere Lagoon, Cambridgeshire, using a trapezoid sail. At the end of the 19th cent. and at the beginning of the 20th cent. weekly competitions in ice skate sailing were organized on the frozen Cove Pond in Stamford, Connecticut, USA, during which the skate sailors reached speeds of about 45mph (72km/h). According to the *New York Times* from 1915, the speed 'could have been greater were it not for the limitations of human stamina.' However, in the 1930s speeds of about 70mph (about 110km/h) were made on George Lake. Until the 1970s ice skate sailing was practiced with a sail on a cross structure resembling a kite, most often the shape of a trapezium. A classical sail was designed in 1917 by W. van B. Claussen (1888-1966), the founder of the Skate-Sailing Association of Amer-

ica. He called his sail Hopatcong, after the largest lake in upstate New Jersey, USA and the town on its shore. Shortly after 1970 a Swed. inventor, A. Ansar (b. 1942) built an aerodynamic sail, which surrounds the sailor and resembles the tucked wing of a plane. This helped reach speeds 4 times greater than the wind speed (with traditional sail speeds 2½ times greater than wind could be reached). In the 1980s a Swed. sail design, known as Dragon, became dominant (95 sq. ft.; 8.8m²). At the beginning of Jan. 1994 freezing rains along the mid Atlantic coast of the US covered large stretches of land with ice. In New Jersey a new form of ice skate sailing was observed – sailors climbed a hill in North Branch Park. When snowfall made this sailing impossible, one of the enthusiasts of this sport, R.H. Pace, very disillusioned, wrote this about sailing on 'ordinary' ice on the Navesink river near Redbank: 'When I sailed on this ice, I came to the conclusion that it is too flat; previously I experienced what paradise is' (quote after EWS, III, 858). Cf. >ICE BOATING; >ROLLER SKATE SAILING.

R. Friary, *Skate Sailing* (1996); ibid, *Sailing, Ice Skate*, in: EWS (1996, III); A. Sahlin, *Skridskosegling: Tekinik och Prylar* (distributed by the Ice Skate Sailing Sectioin of the Skate-Sailing Association of Sweden; the English language version available from the Skate-Sailing Association of America, 1989).

ICE SKATING, a sport consisting of gliding across an ice surface on skates. The following types of ice skating can be distinguished: >FIGURE SKATING, >SPEED SKATING, >SHORT TRACK SPEED SKATING, >SKATE MARATHON, and >ICE SKATE SAILING. Sports games based on ice skating include >BANDY, >ICE HOCKEY, and the winter var. of >KOLVEN. Ice skating was first developed in and confined to northern countries with colder climates. With the development of mass media, artificial ice rinks, manufacturing of cheap skates, ice skating became a major public sport and spectacle.

History. Skates are one of the earliest means of individual transportation known in N Europe. The Schweizerische Turn-und-Sportmuseum in Basel, Switzerland features specimens of bone skates from c.4000 BC. The first ice skates were blades made of bone fixed to shoe soles with leather straps. Later, their construction was refined along with the development of craftsmanship. The earliest written reference to ice skating can be found in the Old Icelandic *Edda*, which mentions the god of winter Ullr, the son of the goddess Syw, running on 'animal bones' – which could have meant either ice skates or skis. Ice skating as a means of transportation became very common in the Netherlands alongside the construction of the famous, numerous canals in the 12th cent. At the same time in England, ice skating was practiced on frozen peatbogs near London (present-day Moorfields) in the form of a violent competition called >TILTING ON SKATES. Skates made of metal blades fixed on wooden frames were first manufactured in Frisia c.1250 (in Du. sources) and in Scotland in 1572 (in Eng. sources). In Europe, the areas in which ice skating enjoyed great popularity included the Scot. Highlands, the Netherlands, and Scandinavia. The development of roads and horse transportation gradually displaced skates as a means of individual winter transportation. By the end of the Middle Ages ice skating became a typical winter, middle-class pastime in many W Eur. countries, as documented in numerous paintings from the 15th-19th cent. (see below: Ice skating in literature and art). In some northern countries, where rivers and lakes remained frozen for the whole winter ice skating was a significant means of winter transportation until the development of railway systems in the mid-19th cent.; or in remote rural areas, even till the beginning of the 20th cent.

As a sport, skating was practiced in Scotland in the 17th cent. In 1642, the Skating Club of Edinburgh was founded, soon followed by many others. In the second half of the 17th cent. recreational skating spread to England, based on Du. ice-skating brought to the country in 1660 by Charles II Stuart. In 1662, S. Pepys recorded in his *Diary* under the date of 15 Dec. that the Duke of Monmouth, son of Charles II skated on a frozen pond in St. James's Park: '...though the ice was broken and dangerous, yet he would go slide upon his skates [...] but he slides very well'. In 1772, R. Jones published *A Treatise on Skating* in London. In the 17th cent. Du. settlers brought the concept of ice skating across the Atlan-

tic to the New Netherlands. After capturing the colony's capital and renaming it New York, the English maintained the Du. ice skating traditions. The city and the state would soon become the main Amer. ice-skating center, having 27 frost days annually on average. Ice skating was brought to New England and Canada by Scot. settlers in the 18th cent. The first skating manual entitled *Über das Schlichtschuhlaufen* (On Ice Running) was published in Germany by G.U.A. Vieth (1763-1836). In the 19th cent. ice skating became the most popular winter sport in N and W Europe. Around 1830 an exclusive skating club called Les Gilets Rouges was founded in Par-

Gilbert Stuart, The Skater (Portrait of William Grant), *1782, oil on canvas.*

is. In order to distinguish themselves from others, club members wore characteristic red coats. The president of the club, J. Garcin, wrote a skating manual entitled *Real Ice Skating* in 1830, in which he indicated the need to combine technique and beauty in ice skating. In 1849, the Philadelphia Skating Club and Human Society was established with the aim of propagating ice skating but also to save the lives of unfortunate skaters who fell into the water after the ice broke. The members of the club always carried coils of rope. The first all-iron ice skate that clipped onto the boot was invented by American E.W. Bushnell, marking the beginning of mass ice skating. New York's Central Park, designed by C. Vaux and F.L. Olmstead and built in the years 1853-58, with its numerous ponds became a seasonal winter ice-skating center. In 1862, around 1,000-1,500 visitors from Boston came purposely to New York to skate in a local ice-skating center called Jamaica Pond. By that time New York ponds were visited by about 200,000 skaters a year (F.R. Dulles, *A History of Recreation*, 1940). In the years 1850-80, a number of skating clubs were founded in Europe and N.America which then began to merge into larger

Pieter Brueghel the Elder, Census at Bethlehem, *oil on canvas, 1566, Museum van Schone Kunsten, Brussels, Belgium.*

Charles Lees, Skaters on Duddingston Loch, Edinburgh.

Charles Leickert, A Scene On Ice near a Town.

A Skater, *a sculpture in marble.*

Goethe On Ice, *an engraving by L. Raab.*

skating societies and national associations. The first artificial rink was built in Nuremberg in 1864 (Ger. sources) or London in 1876 (Eng. sources). In 1892, representatives of the Netherlands, Sweden, Hungary, Great Britain, Austria and Germany founded the International Skating Union (ISU; first known under its Ger. name Internationale Eislauf Vereinigung). The introduction of Bushnell's steel skates influenced also the development of figure skating. After the combination of skating and ballet in 1864 and the construction of a longer speed skate by the Englishman C.G. Tebbutt the sport of ice-skating became divided into >FIGURE SKATING and >SPEED SKATING.

Skating in literature and art. The sport of ice-skating is clearly a Eur. cultural product conceived in N Eur. countries. Thanks to its cultural significance skating became a winter symbol and part of Eur. recreational heritage. The cultural impact of skating can be seen in The Census of Bethlehem (1556), a painting by P. Breughel the Elder, featuring some of the characters on skates. Skaters were frequent subjects of Flem. art. Beside P. Brueghel the Elder, skaters were painted by I. Breughel (1568-1625), P. Brueuhel the Younger (1564-1637), J. Van Goyen (1596-1656), Rembrandt H. Van Rijn (1606-69), F. Bol (1616-80), J. Van Ruisdael (c.1628-82) and R. de Hooghe (1645-1708). Skating themes were frequent in the paintings of H. Avercamp (1585-1634) and Scot. art. In Amer. art, the skating motif appears in The Skater by G. Stuart (1782, National Gallery of Art, Washington, DC), a famous portrait of William Grant. J.D. Prown, an Amer. art historian described Stuart's picture as a balance between stillness and motion, a subtle representation of the skating concept (American Painting. From Its Beginnings to the Armory Show, 1975).

Skating was often referred to in the Diaries of S. Pepys. On 1 December 1662 Pepys recalled walking across a park and '... where I first in my life, it being a great frost, did see people sliding with their skates, which is a very pretty art.' In 1683, during the heaviest winter of the century, the half-blind Pepys, who had stopped writing his diary (the last entry dated May 1669 ends with the following statement: 'And so I betake myself to that course, which is almost as much as to see myself go into my grave: for which, and all the discomforts that will accompany my being blind, the good God prepare me!') was able to skate on ice with N. Gwynn, mistress of Charles II. The Ger. poet, F.G. Klopstock (1724-1803), fascinated with ice-skating, wrote the remarkable Ode to Skating. Another great Ger. poet, J.W. Goethe (1749-1832) practiced ice-skating by night and admitted in one of his letters that skating was an inspiration for many of his poetic ideas. A skating Goethe was portrayed by W. Von Kaulbach, and his portrait became the later inspiration for the copperplate engraving by L. Raab (currently in Goethe-Nationalmuseum in Weimar, Germany). In The Pickwick Papers by C. Dickens, one of the characters, B. Sawyer, shows off his skating skills:

Mr. Bob Sawyer adjusted his skates with a dexterity which to Mr. Winkle was perfectly marvellous, and described circles with his left leg, and cut figures of eight, and inscribed upon the ice, without once stopping for breath, a great many other pleasant and astonishing devices, to the excessive satisfaction of Mr. Pickwick, Mr. Tupman, and the ladies; which reached a pitch of positive enthusiasm, when old Wardle and Benjamin Allen, assisted by the aforesaid Bob Sawyer, performed some mystic evolutions, which they called a reel.

Other characters, Pickwick's servant Sam Weller and a certain fat boy follow Bob Sawyer as well:

Mr. Weller and the fat boy, having by their joint endeavours cut out a slide, were exercising themselves thereupon, in a very masterly and brilliant manner. Sam Weller, in particular, was displaying that beautiful feat of fancy-sliding which is currently denominated «knocking at the cobbler»s door,' and which is achieved by skimming over the ice on one foot, and occasionally giving a postman's knock upon it with the other.

Finally, all gathered join the party and skate in single file:

'Keep the pot a-bilin', Sir!, said Sam; and down went Wardle again, and then Mr. Pickwick, and then Sam, and then Mr. Winkle, and then Mr. Bob Sawyer, and then the fat boy, and then Mr. Snodgrass, following closely upon each other's heels, and running after each other with as much eagerness as if their future prospects in life depended on their expedition [...] The sport was at its height, the sliding was at the quickest, the laughter was at

the loudest, when a sharp smart crack was heard. There was a quick rush towards the bank, a wild scream from the ladies, and a shout from Mr. Tupman. A large mass of ice disappeared; the water bubbled up over it; Mr. Pickwick's hat, gloves, and handkerchief were floating on the surface; and this was all of Mr. Pickwick that anybody could see.

Luckily, Mr. Pickwick was saved and, lying in bed in front of the fireplace and having drunk three bowls of punch, he was unanimously elected president of the club.

Skating is the theme of a children's classic Hans Brinker: or, the Silver Skates by the Amer. author M.E. Mapes Dodge (1931-1905). She never visited Holland but her thorough research of Du. culture and life, including Du. skating, earned her a great deal of respect among Du. critics.

The Amer. painter and illustrator, W. Homer, sketched a series of drawings devoted to ice skating for Harper's Magazine. Eur. 19th-cent. illustrations and engravings abounded in skating themes. They were widely published in newspapers and magazines before the development of photography. An ice-skating scene can also be found in Anna Karenina (1877) by L. Tolstoy.

Skating ceased to be a leading theme of Eur. paintings when it began losing its position as a prestigious social entertainment and art came to be dominated by abstractionism. In the early 20th cent. ice skating was occasionally depicted in all non-abstractionist art movements, e.g. Skaters by the Ger. expressionist, E.L. Kirchner (1880-1938) (currently in Hessiches Landesmuseum, Darmstadt). Skating

Elias van de Velde, Amusements on the Frozen Moat, *oil on wood, 1618.*

and sledding children are the subjects of Joy of Winter in Jungfernbruckestrasse (1911), a water-color painting by H. Zille (1858-1929). The remarkable final performance of the Brit. ice-dancing pair J. Torvill and C. Dean at the 1984 Winter Ol.G. in Sarajevo was portrayed by the official painter of the UK National Olympic Committee, K. Whitney. A speedskater was the main theme of the official poster of the Sarajevo Games, designed by C. Kostovic and K. Hadzic. Figure skating has been a favorite subject for hundreds of renowned photographers, e.g. B. Martin, P. Rondeau, E. Hartwig, P. Mystkowski and E. Warmiński. Finally, skating as a literary theme made its appearance in diaries of former skaters, e.g. Dick Button on Skates (1955), by D. Button, 1948 and 1952 Olympic champion.

N. Brown, Ice Skating, 1959; K. Kunzle-Watson, Ice Skating, 1996; K. Kunzle-Watson, S.J. DeArmond, Ice Skating: Steps To Success, 1996; Z. Nawrocki, Jeździmy na łyżwach, 1949; R. Nazarko, E. Szydłowska and W. Radwański, Łyżwiarstwo, 1987.

ICE SPEEDWAY, a spectacular motorcycle sport, in which contestants race their motorcycles around an oval ice track approx. 260-425m in length. Each race (or heat) is between 4 riders, who make 4 laps around the track counterclockwise. They score 3pts. for 1st place, 2pts. for 2nd place, and 1pt. for 3rd place. Riders reach speeds of up to 80mph (130km/h) on the straightaways and up to 60mph (100km/h) on the curves. The first officially recorded event took place in Eibsee, Germany in 1925. In the 1930s the sport was regularly practiced on frozen lakes in

54-year-old Per-Olov Serenius of Sweden, front, rides ahead of Germany's Guenther Bauer and Antonin Klatovsky of the Czech Republic on his way to becoming World Champion at the ice racing World Championship finals in Inzell, southern Germany.

Bavaria and at about the same time it spread to Scandinavia and Canada. After 1945 it gained recognition in Czechoslovakia and the USSR. Since the 1950s, the Russians have dominated the sport. E.Ch. have been held since 1963 and W.Ch. – since 1966. The majority of team and individual events are held in Russia, Sweden, and Finland, though events are also held in the Czech Republic, Germany, and the Netherlands. The motorcycles are similar to those used in regular >SPEEDWAY, with a longer wheelbase and a more rigid frame. The main difference lies in the tires. Those used in ice racing have inch-long spikes (90 in the front and 200 in the back), which are screwed into treadless tires to provide the traction. The spiked tires necessitate protective guards over the wheels, extending almost to the ice surface. The bikes have no brakes and, because of the tremendous amount of traction, are equipped with two-speed gearboxes. Instead of the wall surrounding a regular speedway track, there is a safety barrier consisting of straw bales or banked-up snow around the outer edge of the track. The unique riding style includes leaning the bike into the bends at an angle where the handlebars almost touch the surface of ice. Among the leading riders in the 1990s were Swedes: P.O. Cerenius and H. Simon, and Russians: J. Polikarpov, A. Balashov, W. Lumpov, and K. Dragalin.
K. Meynell: http://www.meynell.com/speedway-faq/intro.html

IDO, an Afr. game played in the Yoruba region in Nigeria. The name comes from *ido,* a plant whose stones are used for the game. A small hole, about the size of a boy's fist, is dug in the ground. Into it leads a gutter or an inclined board. Each player tosses one stone into the hole, then, when his turn comes, places two stones ('horses') at any point of the gutter and lets them slide down. After they have started sliding, the player may not influence their movement in any way. The 'horse' should land on top of the other stones. The player whose horse is the last on top takes all the stones from the hole. Other players' 'horses' are included in the winner's score but are used again in the next round. A similar game >ZULLI is known among the Yaur tribe.
A. Taylor Cheska, 'Ido', TGDWAN, 1987, 35-36.

IGBA-EGO, a game of chance originally played in Nigeria as >IGBA-ITA. Traditionally, players used 12 cowrie shells, which were later replaced with small coins. The rules are similar to >HEADS OR TAILS.
A. Taylor Cheska, 'Nigbé', TGDWAN, 1987, 50.

IGBA-ITA, 'toss and throw', a Nigerian game of chance played with cowrie shells. The first player tosses a handful of 12 shells. The score depends on the number of shells which fall hole up and hole down. The winning combinations are 6 of each or 11 hole up and 1 hole down. A combination of 4 hole up and 8 hole down means loss of turn. From 2-12 players take part in the game. Shells are increasingly replaced with coins, changing the name of the game to >IGBA-EGO (*ego* means 'money').
A. Taylor Cheska, 'Nigbé', TGDWAN, 1987, 50.

IGĘ, a game practiced in Yoruba, Nigeria, particularly popular with boys of about 10yrs. of age. It is played with 7 fruit pits, corn kernels, animal bones, little wooden chips, pebbles, etc. The object is to toss one of the objects and quickly pick up the ones scattered on the ground in order to be able to catch the falling object before it touches the ground. In the first phase, the objects are picked up one by one; in the second phase – 2 by 2; in the third – 3 by 3. Then, they are gathered in the following combinations 4+2 and 5+1. Finally, all 6 stones have to be picked up in a single attempt. While executing the series of tosses and pick-ups, all the objects that were picked up before have to be held in the same hand that tosses and picks up. If a player fails to do so, he loses his turn. On regaining his turn, the player starts at the point he lost it. In Africa, there are several var. of the game. In Congo, 2-4 participants usu. play it; Berbers play in teams of 4-6 and use 8 objects. The players from the Dogon tribe employ as many as 12-20 objects. In most of the cases, the tossed object is usu. larger than the remaining ones.

ILLSKUFANG, an O.Icel. type of >FANG wrestling, the object of which was to injure or even kill the opponent. [Icel. *illsku* – something bad, injury; *fang* – fighting at close quarters]. The opposite is >LEIK-FANG.

INBUAN, a trad. folk var. of hand-to-hand combat similar to wrestling practiced in Mizoram, India. The contenders fight standing in a circle 15-18ft. in diameter. The fighter who manages to lift his opponent off the ground and up into the air with a sharp movement using a special belt or rope is the winner. A bout lasts 3 rounds, 30-60sec. each, or ends once one of the fighters is lifted off the ground. During the fight the opponents must not bend their knees. The circle line cannot be crossed by the fighters. The fighting sport of inbuan was brought to the Lushai hills by the Mizos people from Burma. The first fights were said to be held in the village of Dungtland around 1750.

INDIACA, a game played with rackets and bird, similar to >BADMINTON and obsolete games like >VOLANT, the Jap. >HAGOITA and >HANETSUKI. The bird is cone-shaped, 6-8cm in diameter, about 8cm high and weighs 40-50g. A tuft of feathers 15-16cm long is attached to the top. The pitch (13m long and 5.5m wide) is divided in half with a net 1.85m high and 0.5m wide. The posts are 2.45m high. The game is played 1-on-1 or in teams of 2-6 persons. The awarding of points is like in >VOLLEYBALL. In team games the ball may be hit 3 times in one court.
History. The game originated among native S Amer. Indians. The name was imposed by Eur. colonists, who in the 1930s also added Eur. rules. Similar games were played by N. Amer. Indians, e.g. >TS'ÉQWELA, a game of the Stóólo tribe.

INDIAN COURIER RACES, practiced by specially trained runners from various Indian tribes in both Americas. The runners formed fraternities that may be called 'running societies' to which access was restricted or which were sometimes even secret. Their role was to carry important messages or small but precious objects. They served local communities, rulers and chiefs. The most famous of these 'running societies' were the *chasqui* (which meant 'to exchange' in the language of the Inca). *Chasqui* societies were first established around the 15th cent. and used a specially built system of roads of some 4,000km in total length. The roads connected N Ecuador with S Chile. Early Span. conquistadors observed that the *chasqui* system was far more efficient than their own horse mail. The Aztec had similar running societies. Thanks to them the news of H. Cortez's arrival reached Indian cities located some 400km away from the coast within 24hrs.
In 1680 the Indians living in the area that now constitutes the territory of New Mexico and Arizona rebelled against the Spanish who persecuted their medicine men and burned their ritual masks. According to the preserved reports, the initial success of the uprising was based on the fact that Indian couriers were able to carry messages concerning the preparations for the uprising and the exact date on which the operation was to commence over large distances (and more precisely over the 600-km route connecting the town of Taos in New Mexico with Second Mesa in Arizona) in relatively short periods of time. The Spanish were taken aback by this effective method of communication. The 'D-day' was determined on the basis of messages encoded in the form of knots tied on a length of rope that were untied one by one on each consecutive day, first by the runners and then by the recipients (i.e. all runners and then villages received ropes with the same number of knots and after the last of them was untied the Indians were to attack the Spanish). Unfortunately, the Spanish discovered the plot soon before the uprising was to start which forced the Indian couriers to do a third round of running during which they informed their forces to start the uprising sooner. This proved to be a successful strategy and the Indians overthrew the Span. rule for a period of more than 10yrs., after which the Spanish were never able to regain full control over the area.
Ethnological research confirms that these 'running societies', sometimes also referred to as 'Courier Corps', were somewhat similar to religious orders and that their members had a sense of their own uniqueness, leading lives full of sacrifice, following special diets and never marrying. These societies existed solely to serve their communities and runners derived no personal financial gain for the invaluable service they provided. However, when the white colonists started taking control of Indian land, the couriers were often hired to carry messages or small packages. One of the Span. commanders – L. de Ayala is thought to have said that Indian couriers should receive remuneration similar to that of town mayors for their excellent services. In 1903 an Amer. scholar, G. James, hired a young Indian runner who carried an important message from Arabia to the Kalama canyon which are some 72mi. (c.116km) apart. The runner returned after 36hrs. There are numerous accounts of such stories from the late 19th cent. including one about J. Bourke who paid the Ind. runners $2 for covering a difficult,

Indiaca.

sandy course of 21mi. (c.34km). Later, Bourke paid a Mohave runner to run from Fort Mohave to his reservation and back – some 200mi. (c.320km) in total. According to Bourke himself, it took the young Mohave only 24hrs. to cover this distance. So it appears that the runner had to cover a distance roughly equal to 8 marathon runs, completing each of the 8 'legs' in around 3hrs. Some fort commanders offered prizes for Indian winners of the races they organized. These races were held over various distances, depending on the local conditions. Most frequently such events attracted chiefly Apache and Navaho athletes.
P. Nabokov, *Indian Running,* 1981; J.B. Oxendine, *American Indian Sports Heritage,* 1988.

A shuttlecock used in indiaca.

INDIAN CHARIOT RACING, an event prob. adopted from the Roman tradition during the times of Alexander the Great. It became assimilated with Hindu beliefs, in which the horse is a symbol of brightness, sun, fertility, as well as power, struggle and even war. Indian chariot races were a means to battle evil spirits and as such formed the setting of certain religious holidays. Traces of their influence can even be found in China. A Rus. scholar of Chin. culture, S.G. Leskova, claims that a ceremony of driving away evil spirits took place in some regions of China at the end of the year and at the close of the spring season. Besides making rounds from village to village with burning lanterns to the accompaniment of cries and drum beating, races of 2-wheeled, horse-driven sulkies were frequently held. Such races are mentioned in a Chin. song *Mighty Horses*, in which 'the evil has been driven away by the chariots, all evil spirits have been defeated, there is no more squalor left' [quoted after I. Kabzińska-Stawarz].

A type of Indian football.

INDIAN FOOTBALL, a family of trad. games popular among native N.Amer. Indians, and, curiously, not unlike Eur. football, particularly on the eastern seaboard. Up-country the use of hands was allowed. In what is now New England the game was tranquil, but on the W coast, esp. among the Nishinam tribe – quite brutal. The ball was of various sizes, though usu. about 1ft. (just over 30cm) in diameter. Native Alaskans used richly embroidered balls made of hide, with a leather grip. The game is first mentioned by W. Wood in his description of an Eng. colony. He had no esteem for their ability to jinx the opponent: 'no cunning at all in that kind, one English being able to beat ten Indians at football' (*New England's Prospects*, 1634, 73). A decade later R. Williams, a Puritan pastor wrote that the Narranganset of Rhode Island 'have great meetings of foot-ball playing, only

Indians playing football on a drawing by Christopher Weiditz, 1529.

WORLD SPORTS ENCYCLOPEDIA

INDIAN SPORTS AND GAMES IN PAINTINGS BY GEORGE CATLIN

Women playing football, *1835-36.*

Choctaw Football Game, *1834-35.*

Chungke, *1832-33.*

Archery, *1835-37.*

Canoe Races in Sault St. Marie.

Charles Russell, Attacking.

in summer, town against town, upon some broad sandy shore' (*Key into the Language of America,* 1643, 73). In the late 18th cent. R. Bartram, an Amer. naturalist describing Cherokees and Choctaws wrote: 'the football is likewise a favorite, manly diversion with them. Feasting and dancing in the square at evenings, aids in their games' (*Travel through North and South Carolina, Georgia, East and West Florida,* 1791).

K. Blanchard, *The Mississippi Choctaws at Play. The Serious Side of Leisure,* 1981; A.A. MacFarlan, *Book of American Indian Games,* 1958; J. Mooney, *The Cherokee Ball Play,* AA 1890, 3; J.B. Oxendine, *American Indian Sports Heritage,* 1988.

INDIAN HORSEBACK RIDING, an art which developed only after the invasion of the Europeans. The horse, although it lived on the continents of North and South America in prehistoric times, became extinct probably c.10,000 BC. The first horses were brought to the New World by the Span. conquistador H. Cortez in 1516. Many tribes, lacking a word for 'horse', called it 'big dog'. Although peoples of the Yucatan Peninsula had earlier managed to withstand the Spaniards' attacks, despite the latter's fleet and fire arms, the sight of horsemen took them by surprise. With time, Native Amer. Indians created their own riding tradition. The first information of Indians adapting horses for their use comes from the period after 1598, when the Span. colonists began invading inland from the Gulf of Mexico in the direction of the Rocky Mountains and California. Initially the Spanish strove to hinder the Indians learning to ride, lest they should use the newly acquired skill against the aggressors. Yet the shortage of labor on new farms forced the Spanish to hire Indians after all. Among other tasks, they tended livestock – and thus came into close contact with the art of horseback riding. The other factor was a large number of runaway horses roaming the prairies in herds. Their redomestication by the Indians was a matter of only a few years. The first tribes to acquire the skill of horseback riding were the Apache and the Shoshone. The horse trade developed with its center in Santa Fe. The first mention of major mounted campaigns against the Europeans comes from the late 17th cent. By the early 17th cent., horses had come into the possession of most Indian tribes by way of trade, domestication and spoils. Some tribes of the Great Basin, however, regarded mustangs as game and, thus, a source of nourishment. Most tribes of S. and C.America were not as proficient in the art of horseback riding as their N.Amer. counterparts due to unfavorable mountain terrain. It was the peoples of the Great Plains who had the best achievements in developing their own methods of riding and breeding horses. Soon the Chicksaw and the Coctaw managed to produce their own breeds. The horse revolutionized the Indian way of life, enabling them to move faster, thus making bison hunting more efficient and thoroughly changing fighting tactics. Horse ownership became a sign of social prestige. The Comanche were reputed to be the best riders, while the Cayuse – the best breeders and tradesmen. The latter's share in the horse market was so substantial in the 18th and 19th cent. that the word *cayuse* became the word for *horse* in the local dialect of the settlers. Horses were also used for sports, i.e. racing and acrobatics, esp. in times of peace. Such races, held by young Sioux not far

Charles Russell, Buffalo Hunt.

from Fort Pierre, were witnessed and depicted by Swiss artist C. Bodmer (1809-93), who accompanied the Ger. prince Alexander Philip Maximilian on his voyage. With the exception of a few tribes (e.g. the Cherokee) Indians did not adapt horse-drawn carriages. They developed, however, their own method of transportation of passengers (such as the injured or elderly) and possessions: 3 long poles were taken from a wigwam, joined together with twine or leather straps and attached to each side of the horse, forming a kind of stretcher, which was dragged on the ground. The exceptional mobility of the Indians and their superior riding skill influenced also the immigrants' riding methods, forming >WESTERN HORSEBACK RIDING. Against common belief, it was not only the tribes of N.America who learned to use the horse. S.Amer. tribes, such as the Goajiro, the Mybaia and the Mocovialso also acquired the use of horses. Indian horseback riding traditions came to a virtual end with the downfall of the whole Native Amer. Indian culture, brutally looted and exterminated by Eur. aggressors and the US government. A.M Josephy, ed. *The American Heritage Book of Indians,* 1961; R.M. Utley and W.E. Washburn, *Indian Wars,* 1985.

INDIAN SPORTS AND GAMES, since ancient times the Indians of N. and S.America have practiced various sports and games which can be divided into 3 groups: 1) children's sports and games; 2) exercises and forms of competition enhancing physical skills of warriors, often connected with religious rituals; 3) forms of competition of religious nature only. Nothing is known about children's sports and games of the oldest and most highly developed Indian civilizations of S. and C.America. Some incomplete records of Span. colonists, Indian wall paintings, and archeological excavations of ancient playing fields provide evidence of various forms of sports competition closely connected to religious beliefs present among the indigenous peoples of C. America, first the Toltecs and then the Olmecas, Mayas, Zapotecs, and Aztecs. The native sports included original ball games in which the ball symbolizing the sun was subject to sports competition symbolizing the duel between the sun and the stars or between one of the mythical heroes and the sun (see >PRE-COLUMBIAN GAMES OF THE AMERICAS). According to archeological finds, the influences of C.Amer.

cultures reached far North, incl. the territory of present-day Arizona. The sports games were similar to the Maya >POKYAH or Aztec >TLACHTLI and nearly, as depicted in surviving iconography, culminated in human sacrifices. The only ritual game involving no human sacrifice seems to have been the ball game of the Miztec people. The sports and games of Amer. Indian tribes of the Great Plains, the E Coast and present-day Canada were very diverse. The most popular was the family of games referred to as >CHUNGKE, also known as *chung-kee, tchung-kee* or under the Eng. name of >HOOP-AND-POLE, the latter, however, included a wider number of games. Despite existing differences, the *chungke* games consisted of tossing poles into rolling wooden, wicker, or even stone rings.

The Indian tossing game was not only confined to boys and men as Indian girls, too, participated in that sport since the earliest times. Indian women took part in some sports as well. The most popular sport practiced – mainly by Indian women and children – was a game similar to the present-day field hockey, played among various Indian tribes and known by such names as >GUGAHAWAT, Ohonistus, Kakwasethi or Oomatashia, the latter called *Indian Shinny* by the ethnographers (cf. >SHINNY). The name is also applied to >TS'IITS'QWEL'O'OL, a trad. game of the Stóólo Indians.

Amer. Indians also practiced a game called >INDIAN FOOTBALL by the Eur. setlers. The original form of the Indian ball games was >FIREBALL. Three Can. Indian games i.e. >BAGATAWAY, >TEWAARTHON and >TOLI became international sports, later developing into the game called >LACROSSE by the Fr. Canadians. Today, lacrosse is a national sport of Canada, and also practiced as a school sport in many other Eng.-speaking countries. It remains unknown whether and how Amer. Indians used their dugouts and canoes covered with leather or bark for sports competition. The Ind. boats, however, gave rise to contemporary >CANOEING and the Eskimo kayaks became one of major forms of international sports competition and physical recreation (>KAYAKING). The Indians had not known horses before the arrival of Europeans. After the animals had become assimilated into the native cultures of the New World the Indians developed a genuine horse riding art visible in numerous horseback sports and games (>INDIAN HORSEBACK RIDING).

One contribution of Amer. Indians to contemporary

sport has been their rules of ethics. Amer. and Can. sports have widely drawn from Indian stoicism and spiritual self-control, characteristic of the ethical rules of numerous Indian tribes.

Out of a number of genuine, traditional Amer. Ind. sports some have become part of modern international competitions (>LACROSSE, >CANOEING, >KAYAKING).

K. Blanchard, *Play and Adaptation. Sports and Games in Native America*, 1984; R. Blasiz, 'The Practice of Sports Among the Indians of America', MAB, Dec, Jan 1933/34, 40; R. Hoffsinde, *Indian Games and Crafts*, 1957; A. A. MacFarlan, *Book of American Indian Games*, 1958; J. C. McCaskill, 'Indian Sports', IAW, 1936, 3; A. Whitney, *Sports and Games the Indians Gave Us*, 1977.

INDIAN WINTER GAME, a name given by Ang.-Sax. colonists to a N.Amer. Indian game in which contestants aimed long poles at rings rolled on ice or frozen snow. It is a winter variant of similar games of the >HOOP-AND-POLE family, which are played on the ground. The game was depicted by Swiss artist, C. Bodmer (1809-93). This took place in the settlement of Minnetaree, belonging to the Mandan Indians, about 45mi. up the Missouri river from Fort Clark (now the city Bismarck). Bodmer accompanied the Ger. prince Alexander Philip Maximilian in his voyage. In his memoirs from this journey (*Travels in the Interior of North America*) he writes that Mandans like to practice the sport esp. on Sundays. This roused the indignation of Ang.-Sax. protestants who considered it a day for prayer and Bible reading and failed to appreciate cultural diversity. Bodmer's often reproduced picture shows a group of youths, bare-chested in spite of the cold, practicing the sport on frozen snow or ice. Adults, dressed in warm furs, attend the match. Some spectators use rooftops as stands.

INDOOR BOWLS, a sport originating from >LAWN BOWLING and keeping its basic rules but played indoors. The chief differences are artificial grass and a bigger pitch. In professional indoor bowls the pitch is a square of 50yds. (45.75m). There are however pitches of smaller size, so that the game can also be played in village or small town sports centers. The >SHORT MAT GAME, originating in Ireland and assimilated in other parts of the Brit. Isles, is played indoors on lanes 40-50ft. (12.2-15.2m) long.

History. A form of indoor bowls was first played in the halls of aristocratic residences. The first conscious attempt to adapt the outdoor game for the indoors was made in 1888 by the Scotsman W. McRae. The sport was first practiced on specially prepared mats used by cricket players for winter training. Since at first it was regarded as an alternative to the summer game, it was termed *winter bowling*. Although it never lost the resemblance to its predecessor, indoor bowls soon caught on and became a sport in its own right. In 1905 the Edinburgh Winter Bowling Association came into being. The events were held in the Synod Hall, by one of the wings of the Castle. Around this time winter games were first held in London's Crystal Palace. This was initiated by W.G. Grace (1848-1915), a famous cricket player and an Eng. Bowling Association president of long standing. Winter events were also held in Alexandra Palace in London. In the early 1930s a special hall was built near Crystal Palace, meant exclusively for winter bowling. It survived the fire which destroyed Crystal Palace in 1936. The Crystal Palace and Alexandra Palace clubs were followed by many others in the early 1930s. Many existing sports clubs formed indoor bowls sections. Among them were: Crouch Hill, SE London, E London, W London, South End and (outside London) Bognor Regis, Bournemouth, Lyons, Margate and Newport. These clubs pressured the EBA to form an indoor bowling section, which it did in 1933. In 1935 in the London district of Maida Vale the Paddington Club was opened and it soon proved to be the best club in England. In Scotland, games were held regularly in the Glasgow Kelvin Hall; a hall specially meant for this sport was built in Ayr (1935) and in Shawbridge, incorporating as many as 12 courts. After the interim of WWII indoor bowls flourished. Its popularity was prompted in the '60s with the invention of artificial grass. The first full-size hall was built in 1961 in Cardiff, another in the winter of 1966-67 in Belfast. In 1967 the first Brit. Championships were held. The first champion and the best contestant of this time was D.J. Bryant (b. 1931), also a fine player of lawn bowling. In 1973 there were 125 indoor

bowling clubs in Britain. In 1970 the EBA agreed to transform its indoor bowling section into a separate association, known as the Eng. Indoor Bowling Association. However, as early as 1964 (1965 according to some sources), prompted by the competition from 2 women's federations as well as Scot. and Ir. organizations, the National Indoor Bowls Council (NIBS) was established. In the '70s the sport became popular in Australia, Switzerland and Canada. Its popularity was due not least to the flexibility

with which the size of the pitch can be adapted to local sports halls. On the international level the NIBS works along with the IBB, which since 1970 has been organizing international championships. The great interest that television has been taking in the sport (which can be played all year round) caused a boom in its popularity in the late '80s.

Women's indoor bowls was developing even before WWII, but a real breakthrough was the creation of the Eng. Women's Indoor Bowling Association (EWIBA). Similar organizations soon appeared in Scotland, Wales and Ireland.

Important events. The oldest women's event is the Yetton Trophy initiated in the 1953-54 season. The Aird Trophy, dedicated to H. Aird, one of the most excellent indoor bowls activists began in the 1968-69 season. The most important men's events are the Denny Cup (since 1935) and the international Hilton Cup (since the winter of 1935-36).

INDOOR CLIMBING, also called *sport climbing*, a form of climbing that imitates >MOUNTAIN CLIMBING, practiced on artificial walls, usu. indoors. The idea is to make climbing possible for people living in lowland or urban areas, etc. Indoor climbing was originally a form of practice for natural rock climbing, though it soon acquired the status of an autonomous sport regulated separately from other forms of climbing. Its main piece of equipment is a wall, with various irregularities, bends, curves, and – esp. at the top – overhangs. Climbers are protected by harnesses and ropes and falling off the wall poses no great risk to their health. They are equipped with a talcum powder bag fastened to a belt, which is used to make their hands less slippery. The beginnings of indoor climbing are connected with competitions in contest climbing in the former Soviet Union. The first W.Ch. took place in Frankfurt, Germany. The level of difficulty depends on the height which the competitors must reach within a given time limit. There are usu. no practice sessions and climbers compete in pairs. Two losses eliminate a climber from the event.

INDOOR HOCKEY, in Ger. *Hallenhockey*, a var. of >FIELD HOCKEY adapted to be played indoors. The number of players was initially limited to 7, currently to 6. The total number of team members participating in a single match is 12 with no limit on the number of replacements. Players are substituted without notifying the referee but only during intervals, after a score or in the case of an injury. The game lasts 2x20min. with a 5-min. break. Juniors and women play 2x10min. and 2x15min.

Above: Katie Brown of Lafayette, Georgia, works her way up the overhanging climbing wall during the finals of the Women's Climbing Difficulty competition at the X-Games in San Diego, California. Below: a sport climbing competitor.

WORLD SPORTS ENCYCLOPEDIA

Indoor tennis at the beginning of the 19th cent.

In-line roller skating motif on a Polish postage stamp issued in 1999.

In-line marathon.

respectively. The field is 40-50yds. (36.6-45.7m) long and 20-25yds. (18.3-22.7m) wide. The goals are 3yds. (2.74m) wide. The penalty spot is 8yds. (7.3m) away from the goal, and the penalty area is a semi-circle 10yds. (9.1m) in diameter. The ball weighs 156-163g and is 22.4-23.5cm in circumference, white or any other color that the teams agree to. The uniforms and other equipment is the same as in field hockey but the sticks often have an additional plastic cover to cope with the contact with the hard floor surface instead of natural or artificial grass. Because of the size of the court, the ball must not be hit hard and can only be pushed. When the game commences, all players must be in their own half. When a penalty is taken, the goalkeeper is the only member of the defending team allowed in the penalty area. There is no offside.

History. The game originated in West Germany in the 1950s and quickly spread to Belgium, Denmark, France, Holland, Spain, and Switzerland as valuable addition to the summer season and a form of winter training. It later developed as a separate discipline – the first national championships took place in 1961 in Poland and in 1962 in Germany. In the 1960s a leading Ger. player was C. Keller (b. 1939) who also excelled in the summer variety. Despite its independent development, indoor hockey is still supervised by the International Hockey Federation and the Eur. Hockey Federation. The most important international championships are the Indoor Nations Cup, held since 1974 for both men and women and having the status of E.Ch., and Inter Club Champions, held since 1990. The leading national teams besides Germany are: Austria,

In-line roller hockey.

the Czech Republic, Denmark, Spain, Poland, Russia, and Switzerland.

INDOOR LACROSSE, see >BOX LACROSSE.

INDOOR POLO, a variety of >POLO played indoors by 2 teams of 3 players. The field is 100yds. long and 50yds. wide, with wooden boards 4-4½ft. high to keep the ball in play. For safety reasons and due to the smaller playing area, indoor polo is played using an inflatable, leather-covered ball, similar to that used in >TEAM HANDBALL.

INDOOR SOCCER, see >FUTSAL.

INDOOR TENNIS, a game identical to >LAWN TENNIS, but played indoors in the winter, wherever a harsh climate makes it impossible to play outdoors year round. The most important winter indoor tournament is the US Open.

INJI UCHI, a 12th cent. Jap. game similar to modern >FIELD HOCKEY. Two teams strove to move a small, round stone into the opposing team's zone by using sticks.

IN-LINE FOOTBALL, also *rollersoccer*, a game similar to >ASSOCIATION FOOTBALL played on a roller-skating rink. The players use in-line skates, although box skates are permitted as well. The ball is kicked with the blade or the side of the foot. The ball is a round, leather-covered, inflated rubber bladder of the size of a regular football, i.e. 68-71cm in perimeter and 396-453g in weight. The game is played by 2 teams of 5 players. The playing surface is made of asphalt, concrete, or wood (indoor games). The field dimensions depend on existing conditions. The game can be played on regular roller-skating rinks, parking lots, indoor halls, etc. The goal is 3ft. high and 8ft. wide. The match consists of two 25-min. periods, with a 5-min. halftime break. Teams are allowed unlimited substitutions. Teams earn 1pt. for each goal scored; 2pts. are scored only if the ball passes between the legs of the goalkeeper on its path into the goal. Play does not stop after a goal is scored, similar to >BASKETBALL. If a match ends in a draw, the referee may order a 2-min. overtime, in which only 2 players from each team can play. For safety reasons the players are required to wear protective helmets, similar to those in ice-hockey. Fouls such as handball, dangerous play, etc. result in a penalty kick and a 2-min. time penalty.

History. The game's originator was Z. Philips, the main founder of the Rollersoccer International Federation, and the game was initially known as *zack-ball*. In 1995, the pioneers of in-line football, P. Marcus and A. Blumenthal, organized the first matches in Golden Gate Park in San Francisco. In 1996, the game was played in 5 US cities; in 1997, 9 US teams formed the Rollersoccer International Federation. The Internet: http://www.rlrscr.com

IN-LINE MARATHON, a long-distance racing competition on in-line skates. International in-line marathon events are held over distances ranging from the trad. Olympic marathon distance, i.e. 42km 195m, to 200km. During many in-line marathon events, half-marathons and short-distance races for children and elderly participants are organized as well. The most popular in-line marathons in Europe include the Hannover Inline Marathon, Rhein-Ruhr Marathon, Kölner Inline Marathon (since 1997), and Bayerischen Rollsport und Inlineverband Marathon in Munich. Famous US events include the Long Beach Inline Marathon, Big Grante Inline Marathon in Marengo, Wisconsin, and the Northshore Inline Marathon. Cf. >IN-LINE ROLLER SKATING.

IN-LINE RINGETTE, a variant of >RINGETTE played on in-line skates, rules as for ringette.

IN-LINE ROLLER HOCKEY, a game similar to >ICE HOCKEY, but played on the cement floor of a hockey arena or the plastic floor that is sometimes smaller than the rink, with the players moving on in-line roller skates (cf. >IN-LINE ROLLER SKATING). The teams are comprised of 5 players: a goalie, 2 defenders and 2 offensive players. The goals and sticks are identical to those in ice hockey, while the puck is hard and made of plastic. W.Ch. have been played annually since 1995 (both men and women) under the auspices of Fédération Internationale de Roller Sports, FIRS, and its International Committee of Roller Inline Hockey (CIRILH).

IN-LINE ROLLER SKATING, a var. of roller skating on skates in which the wheels are not placed in pairs but are aligned in a single row of highly flexible wheels made of polyurethane, which ensures good tractive adhesion and allows for skating on slightly rough ground, e.g. with small pebbles and sticks lying on the road. Standard in-line roller skates have 4 wheels, children's skates have 3, and for speed skating 5-wheeled skates are used. The wheel diameter for long distance skating is usu. 68-72mm, for speed skating 78-82mm. The rolling resistance

Tim Henman of Great Britain takes on Danai Udomchoke of Thailand during the BNP Paribas Davis Cup tie at the National Indoor Arena, Birmingham, England.

Fabiola de Silva of Brazil competes during the final round of the women's aggressive vertical in-line skating at the X-Games in San Diego, California.

WORLD SPORTS
ENCYCLOPEDIA

An in-line roller skate.

is reduced due to ball bearings installed inside the wheels. If more wheels are fixed on a skate, they are often positioned in the *rocker* style, i.e. not all the wheels touch the ground. In this way the skates are more agile, though less stabile. Because of the high risk of injury in the sport, skaters pad their knees, elbows, and wrists and wear protective helmets.

The sport is not yet fully fledged and many of its varieties are not yet formalized. In-line roller skating pioneers and the authors of the first manual are M. Powell, a figure ice skater and the founder of one of the first in-line roller skating clubs in Seattle and J. Svensson, the manager and captain of the Ultra Wheels team. The In-Line Skating Association, ILSA has existed since the beginnings of the 1990s. Currently, the most popular are the following types of in-line skating:

DISTANCE SKATING, (standard distance – 10km) or marathon distance competitions; marathons at distances of over 100km are also organized, the most popular marathon of this type is organized from Athens, Georgia, to the state capital, Atlanta, at a distance of 136km, which is covered by the competitors within about 4½hrs. See also:>IN-LINE SKATING MARATHON.

SPEED SKATING, organized usu. in indoor rinks at distances of 300m-2km; the distance of 500m is the most popular. The competitions are usu. organized on a 100m rink and the average time on this distance is 50sec.

HOCKEY, see: ROLLER HOCKEY.

ARTISTIC SKATING, modeled on figure ice skating; the most characteristic type of this still-developing sport type is street dance, but no rigid rules have yet been defined and much still depends on the skaters' creativity. This discipline is developing more slowly than long distance skating or roller hockey due to increased organization difficulties.

ROLLER DERBY, rugged jumping and figure skating on a banked track.

History. Probably the first in-line skates were designed on the initiative of L. Legrange to imitate ice-skating in the La Prophete opera house. The invention did not catch on because of the technical imperfections of the prototype, in which cotton spools were used. Throughout the following decades in-line skates were overshadowed by roller skates with wheels installed in pairs. It was only in the 1980s that for the purposes of training ice hockey players of the Amer. team in Minnesota a construction was built that is regarded as the first real prototype of contemporary in-line roller skates.

In 1997 the first film on in-line skating was made, called *Rolling*, directed by P. Entell.

F.J. Fedel, *In-Line Skating*, 1997; M. Powell and J. Svensson, In-Line Skating, 1998.

INSUKNAWR, a folk sport practiced in the state of Mizoram in India. Two contestants take the ends of a long bamboo stick, so that about 4in. (10cm) stick out from under their armpits. They try to push their opponent out of a circle 16-18ft. (5-5.5m) in diameter within 60sec. (This makes the game the opposite of >TUG-OF-WAR) Contestants may not kneel or lie down. The stick is about 8ft. (2.5m) long and 3-4in. (7.5-10cm) in diameter. There are 3 or 5 rounds. The contestant who has won most of them wins the match. If neither of the wrestlers gets pushed out of the circle within 60sec. the round is considered a draw. If three subsequent rounds end with a draw there follows a play-off with no time limit. Contestants are divided into 5 weight categories: below 50kg, 51-58kg, 59-66kg, 67-74kg and above 74kg. The Internet: http://w3.meadev.gov.in/sports/tr_games/insuk.htm

INTERLACROSSE, also *intercrosse*, a type of >LACROSSE, a mixed indoor game. Despite the unification of rules, elements may vary from region to region. Though the size of the pitch depends on the size of the building, a pitch of 40x20m is preferred, with the ceiling at least 5m high. The goal is square, in some countries (e.g. Belgium) 4x4ft. (122x 122cm), in others (e.g. Great Britain) 3x3ft. (91.4x91.4cm). A light metal stick about 1m long is used. Its head is made of plastic and resembles a small basket, like that in traditional lacrosse. The basket makes it possible to intercept a thrown ball, to transport and to pass it. The ball is soft and usu. a little bigger than a tennis ball. Each team consists of 5 players (including 1 goalkeeper). Contestants playing in the field wear protective goggles. The goalkeepers have protective pads on their chests, arms and legs and a helmet with a visor on their heads.

History. The Canadian Pierre Filion from Quebec initiated the game in 1979. In 1982 the Fédération Quebecoise de Crosse and the Fédération Internationale d'Inter-Crosse (FIIC), which associates 45 member countries came into being. During W.Ch. teams are randomly composed with the help of a computer. They are therefore mixed not only as regards the sex of the players, but also their nationality. As a result, no national team ever wins the W.Ch. In Canada the sport is practiced by 250,000 people, mainly in schools and under the auspices of the Young Women's Christian Association (YWCA) and the Young Men's Christian Association (YMCA). These organizations have helped to popularize the game worldwide. Nowadays it is increasingly popular in the USA, the UK, Belgium, Sweden and the Czech Republic. In 1999 the World Cup came into existence, satisfying the need for an international event with national representation.

INUOMONO, also *inuyo mono*, an old Jap. type of mounted archery. The arrows (*kaburaya*) flying through the air made a whistle-like sound. The in-uomono tradition dates back at least to the 14th cent. The rules were set in the 16th cent. Two concentric circles were drawn on the ground, the larger about 20m in diameter. Thirty-six mounted archers took part, each had 4 arrows. They galloped around the bigger circle, shooting at 10 dogs placed in the smaller ring. Whoever achieved the most well-aimed shots, won. See also other forms of ancient Jap. archery >YABUSAME, >KADAGAKE. Cf. forms of Jap. archery on foot, >BUSHA, >JUMIHAJIME, >KUSAJISI, >MARUMONO, >MOMOTE, and archery as court ceremonial >JYARAI, >NORIYUMI, >TANGONO KISHA.

IOMÁINT, also *iomáin*, an old Ir. ball game played with sticks, along with >CAMÁNACH a predecessor of >HURLING (which is now 1 of 2 national Ir. games – the other being >GAELIC FOOTBALL). Before the creation of hurling, iomáint enjoyed greatest popularity in S Ireland. It was played during the summer, with relatively thick sticks. The object of the game was to get the ball beyond the rear line of the pitch or into the goal. Unlike in camánach, over-hand passes were preferred. At first iomáint was insignificant in the creation of hurling, which, at the time was based chiefly on camánach. Only in the 1870s, after hurling began to be influenced by the Eng. >FIELD HOCKEY, did Ir. patriots turn to the 'pure' forms of iomáint.

In-line roller skating.

ROLLER SKATE HOCKEY (IN-LINE HOCKEY) WORLD CHAMPIONS
1936 England
1939 England
1947 Portugal
1948 Portugal
1949 Portugal
1950 Portugal
1951 Spain
1952 Portugal
1953 Italy
1954 Spain
1955 Spain
1956 Portugal
1958 Portugal
1960 Portugal
1962 Portugal
1964 Spain
1966 Spain
1968 Portugal
1970 Spain
1972 Spain
1974 Portugal
1976 Spain
1978 Argentina
1980 Spain
1982 Portugal
1984 Argentina
1986 Italy
1988 Italy
1989 Spain
1991 Portugal
1993 Portugal
1995 Argentina
1997 Italy
1999 Argentina
2001 Spain

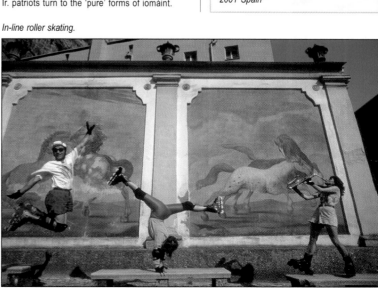

WORLD SPORTS ENCYCLOPEDIA

Iranian wrestling.

IOMÁINT GHALLDA, Ir. for 'strangers' hurling', a name given to forms of cricket popularized by the British in occupied Ireland before 1916. It suggested that cricket playing (as opposed to >HURLING) was unpatriotic.

IRANIAN WRESTLING, a catch-all name for trad. Iranian wrestling types whose origins date back to Persian times. They come in two major varieties, namely >VARZESH-E PEHLIVANI, most popular in the Khorasan province, and >KOSHTI CHOUKHEH.
History. One of the oldest and most beautiful descriptions of Iranian wrestling comes from the *Book of Kings* (*Shah-nameh*) written in 1010 by the Persian epic poet Ferdowsi (d. around 1020-26). *Shah-nameh* is a history of the kings of Persia from mythical times down to the 7th cent. The poem describes the adventures of Sohrab (also spelled Soohrab or Suhrab) and his father Rustum (or Rostam). Rustum had to leave Sohrab's mother, Tahmineh when he was overthrown by Shah Kavoos. Sohrab was so strong and agile by the age of 14 that he decided to look for his father to reinstate him to the throne. The treacherous Afrasiab, the ruler of Turan, then staged a fight between the father, whom he wanted to see killed, and the son, knowing that Sohrab had never seen his father before. Sohrab set out with his father's brassard, given to him by his mother. On his way to Persia Sohrab fought in a number of battles to free his country from Kavoos's rule. Finally, he met his father whom Kavoos ordered to fight him. The fight consisted of sword, spear, archery and horseback contests. The score was, however, tied since both fighters' skills were on a par. So the result was to be determined during a wrestling bout. Sohrab floored his father and was about to kill him with a knife. Then, Rustum told him that in the country where he came from there was an ancient custom that when an old champion was finally defeated, the new champion spared his life and gave him a second chance. In the second bout Rustum floored

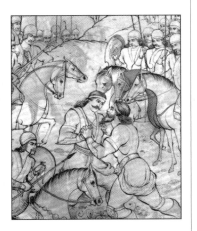

Above and below: the fight between Sohrab and Rustum. An illustration from the Book of Rulers.

and killed Sohrab thus winning the title of *jahan pehlivan* which translates roughly as 'the world champion'. This tradition is reflected in the modern Iranian wrestling rules which provide for the so-called 'second chance round'.
A. Behmanesh, 'Wrestling and Myth in Iran', in: *Olympic Review,* May 1993; N.H. Dole & B.M. Walker, *Flowers from Persian Poetry,* 1901; E.G. Browne, ed., *A Persian Anthology,* 1927.

IRISH HANDBALL, another name for an individual game known as >HANDBALL, whose rules (based on the Brit. >FIVES) originated in 19th cent. Ireland.
Court. The number of walls the ball is bounced against can vary (>ONE-WALL HANDBALL, >THREE-WALL HANDBALL, four-wall handball). The court sizes differed, depending on the time period and local tradition. The smallest one-wall courts in England are 10-14m long and 7-9m wide, with walls 4-7m high and 3-9m wide. The oldest Ir. courts, dating back to the mid-19th cent., were about 80x40ft. (24.4x12.2m). In the USA the first court was built in 1886 by P. Casey and measured 65x25ft. (19.8x7.6m), with the front wall 30ft. (9.14m) and the side walls 25ft. (7.62m) high. Nowadays most one-wall courts in the USA are 34ft. (10.36m) long and as wide as the wall, which is 16ft. (4.9m) high and 20ft. (6.1m) wide. Four-wall courts in the USA are 40ft. (12.2m) long and as wide as the front wall, which is 20x20ft. The side walls are also 20ft. high. The front wall in a traditional four-wall court in Ireland is 30ft. (9.14m) high and 28-30ft. (8.53-9.14m) wide, as is the court itself. At the highest point the side walls are as high as the front wall and get lower towards the back wall, which is 9ft. (2.74m) high. The court is divided into 3 zones: the front zone, the service zone in the middle and the receiving zone at the back. The front zone is 16ft. (4.88m) wide in a one-wall court and 15ft. (4.58m) wide in the American four-wall court. The service zone is 9ft. (2.74m) wide in a one-wall court and 5ft. (1.52m) in a four-wall court. The receiving zone, divided from the service zone by a so-called short line, is 18ft. (5.49m) wide in a one-wall court; in the Amer. four-wall court it is up to 20ft. (6.1m) wide and in the Ir. four-wall court – up to 30ft. (9.14m) wide. Three-wall courts are not standardized, so their arrangement depends on local tradition. Audiences used to prefer one-wall courts, since the stands could then be built on 3 sides. Three-wall courts allowed the stands to be built only at the back. Four-wall courts admitted only a few spectators above the walls. A major change came about with the introduction of see-through Plexiglas walls, which enable unlimited viewing.
The Ball. There are 2 types of ball, which offer different styles of play. In school and recreation games the soft ball is used. It is 1⅞ in. (4.76cm) in diameter, made of soft black rubber and hollow inside; it weighs about 2.3oz. (65.2g). The hard ball is smaller and used to be made of cork (now – hard rubber sewn up in goat skin or rubber inflated with gas). It weighs 1½-1¾ oz. (43-50g). It bounces more dynamically and hits harder, making the game much faster, hence the slang name 'alley-cracker'. It is usu. used in international events.

Rules. The object of the game is to score 21pts. Ir. handball is played individually or in doubles. The ball is hit with one hand, as if the hand were a small racket. The contestants may wear hard leather gloves. They may only hit the ball with one hand. Hitting with both hands or any part of the body other than the hand is not allowed, though kicking used to be accepted in old versions of the sport. The game starts anywhere in the service zone. The server bounces the ball on the ground and then hits it horizontally in the direction of the wall. (In a double game either contestant may serve. If he fails, the serve goes to his partner. Should his partner also fault, the serve goes to the opposing team.) On the rebound, the ball should be hit by the opponent. If it hits one of the players, it is considered 'dead' and the serve is repeated. In the four-wall version the ball, after being served, must reach the receiving zone past the short line, whether bouncing directly off the front wall or hitting other walls along the way. The situation when the ball does not reach the receiving zone is called a *short ball* and causes a loss of points. In the one-wall version points are lost when the ball goes beyond the back line of the court, the so-called *long line*. A correct ball which the opponent cannot hit is called a *placement*. When the ball bounces too low to be hit, it is called a *kill*; when it bounces too fast or too far off, it is called an *ace*. The basic hits are the *underhand* (used in serving – the arm does not go above shoulder level), the *overhand* (the arm swings from the back, above shoulder level) and the *sidearm* (similar to the *underhand* but accompanied by a pivoting of the torso – often used to take on and send *kills*).
History. Most sources claim that the oldest versions of the sport date back to ancient Rome, where it was practiced in the *thermae* (public baths). It was later introduced in countries conquered by the Romans, e.g. in France (where it became the source of >JEU DE LA PAUME) and Spain (a probable source of >PELOTA). *Jeu de la paume* was introduced in England after the Norman Conquest and popularized through dynastic and aristocratic connections, giving source to many similar games, e.g. >FIVES. Fives in turn was transported to Ireland by invading Eng. forces and originated what is now known as Ir. handball. There is a contrary hypothesis, according to which Ir. traditions of the game can be traced back to the 10th cent. The English would then have used it to develop fives. Fives may also have been influenced by both Ir. and Fr. tradition, esp. >JEU DE LONGUE PAUME. The first mention of a game identified by historians as a predecessor of Ir. handball dates back almost a thousand years. In the oldest Gaelic texts the term 'handball' appears at first as a name for the ball rather than the sport. That is the case with an anonymous romance about Alexander the Great, written c.1400-1450. In a document from 1483 the term appears with an extra Lat. explanation: 'An hand balle, pila manualis'. In 1581 R. Mulcaster mentioned the ball in *Positions,* a work dedicated to Elizabeth I. The sport's popularity greatly increased in 18th cent. Ireland. In the early 19th cent. the first matches between towns and villages as well as championships of the shires

took place. Ir. emigrants took the game to the USA, where they practiced on larger walls of existing buildings. The first permanent court meant especially for Ir. handball was built in 1886 in Brooklyn, NY, by P. Casey. The first international game was played by the Ir. champion J. Lawler and the Amer. champion P. Casey. The game consisted of a series of matches begun on 4 Aug. 1887 in Cork, Ireland. The return matches took place on 29 Nov. on the Brooklyn court. Casey won 11 matches, Lawler only 4. Casey remained international champion until his retirement from sports in 1900. From 1890 the USA witnessed the development of a var. of the sport which used a soft rubber ball with no leather covering. This ball was used esp. in the four-wall version in New York. Many centers did not accept the soft ball and strove to improve the hard ball. The result was a small rubber ball filled with gas – this guaranteed speed and hard hits. In Ireland the sport developed under the auspices of the Gaelic Athletic Association, GAA, founded in 1884. In 1924 the GAA initiated the creation of the Irish Amateur Handball Association (IAHA), whose rules eliminated the professional character of the movement. The first Ir. championships were held in 1925. The IAHA soon encountered serious difficulties in maintaining its independent status and became the Handball Council of the GAA. In the early 20th cent. the game was modified, e.g. the court became smaller. In the USA the one-wall version dominated, on account of lower construction costs or the possible use of walls built for purposes other than sport. Soon the game became very common on beaches, where it was played e.g. against changing room doors or walls dividing private property. It was popularized by many organizations: the Amateur Athletic Union (AAU), the Young Men's Christian Association (YMCA), the National Jewish Welfare Board, et al. In 1919 the AAU started presiding over US championships. This task was soon overtaken by the US Handball Association (USHA), which has its own magazine, *Ace*. In the 20th cent. Ir. handball spread internationally, e.g. to Argentina, Canada, Mexico. To Australia and N.Zealand the game was brought by Ir. immigrants c.1860. The first court was built in Melbourne, on Little Bourke Street. The first interstate championships were held in 1870 between New South Wales and Victoria. The first Austrl. championships were held in 1920. In Australia the three- and four-wall versions are most popular. The Austrl. Handball Council presides over the sport. The best Austrl. player of all time was P. Fallon, the winner of 11 singles and 8 doubles championships (1950-73). In 1964 the World Handball Council came into existence in the USA. Under its auspices W.Ch. are held every 3 years. Five countries participated in the first event (1964): the USA, Canada, Australia, Ireland and Mexico. These countries have been dominating the sport ever since. Despite efforts from organizations patronizing it, the game does not seem to involve more countries. One of the reasons for this is the lack of symbols finding social acclaim with which enthusiasts could demonstrate their group identity. Compared to modern sports, which involve all sorts of equipment, the simplicity of Ir. handball pales. In the USA the game's popularity has been declining since the 1940s, esp. in favor of >PADDLEBALL, a very similar game played with small rackets.

H.T. Friermood, ed., *Handball Official Unified Playing Rules*; by the same, 'Handball', *Encyclopedia Americana International*, 1973, vol. 13; J. Arlott, 'Handball, Irish', *The Oxford Companion to Games and Sports,* 1975; R. Doherty, *Handball*, 1971.

IRISH TRIPLE JUMP, an Ir. var. of >TRIPLE JUMP, which differs from it in that jumpers take off on the same leg for all 3 jumps. It was practiced until approx. 1914.

IRISH WRESTLING, a wrestling var. popular in Ireland similar to >CUMBERLAND AND WESTMORELAND. The only difference between the two varieties is the way in which a match starts. In Ir. wrestling competitors place one hand on their opponent's neck and the other on his elbow.

IS GORODA V GOROD, a Rus. baseball-like game played on a field with 4 bases (called 'cities'). The game is played by 2 teams of any number of members (usu. 5-8) with a softball-like ball and a wooden bat similar to that used in cricket. The playing field is a 60x20-step rectangle with an additional line drawn 3m from one end of the field. The line delimits a smaller box called a 'home'. The bases are circles that are 2 steps in diameter. They are placed along the longer sides of the field, with 2 bases at each side. On the right-hand side of the field there is the 1st base which is some 10 steps away from 'home'. The 3rd base is 20 steps away from the 1st one. Bases 2 and 4 are located on the left-hand side of the field, base 2 – 20 steps away from 'home' and base 4 – 20 steps away from the 2nd base. The object of the game is to hit a ball, thrown up in the air by the batter himself, into the field. A runner has to zigzag a complete circuit around all the bases for a run while the ball is in the air. However, it does not have to be the batter who does the zigzag run; it may be any of his teammates named by the team captain. The runner does not have to complete the whole run at once. If several players are waiting at the same base, they must all run towards the next base while the ball is airborne. When a run is completed successfully the team continues at bat. When a ball is hit out of bounds all the runs completed during such a play are cancelled and the runners have to return to the bases from which they started. A player running from the last (4th) base towards 'home' must not be struck out. The fielding team players try to intercept the ball and strike runners out by hitting them with the ball before they reach the next 'city'. If they manage to do so, they become the batting team. A game of Is goroda v gorod consists of 3 rounds.

I.N. Tchkannikov, 'Is goroda v gorod', GIZ, 1953, 47-9.

ISBJØRN OG LANDBJØRN, Dan. for 'polar bear and brown bear', one of a family of games where players run between 2 safety zones, trying not to get caught. Here 2 players (the 'polar bear' and the 'brown bear') try to catch the others. Both have their 'hunting grounds' that they may not go beyond. When they catch somebody, they shout, 'Stop!'. The 'victim' has to stand still until rescued by one of the other runners, who touches them and shouts, 'Free!'. Cf. similar games: >DØDNING, >GÅ OVER ELVEN, >KÆDETIK, >KLIM-KLEM, >TAMANJ, >TULLEHUT, >TYRHOLDE, and with a single safety zone, >KREDSTROLD.

J. Møller, 'Isbjørn og landsbjørn', GID, 1997, 2.

ISHITEKI-TAIIKU, a Jap. method of achieving physical and mental fitness (in the militarized Jap. system of education known as >TAIREN-KA) with the help of physical exercises testing esp. strong will. Cf. >TAIIKU-DO, >SPORTS-DO.

Irish wrestling.

ISKPA, a part of the *kowte*, a male rite of passage of the Nawdeba tribe in Togo, Africa. The boys are divided into 2 groups, the Éfalu and the Singaru. A group of young men, the Iskpa, also take part. The Éfalu have castanets and cudgels with metal ferrules. They wear metal collars, their arms and legs are attired in sheep fleece and their bodies greased with oil. The Singaru wear necklaces, bracelets, and colorful headbands tied at the nape of the neck. They carry a stick and a knife with a copper blade in their left hand, and a hatchet with a metal helve in their right. Their hips are covered with kuyagregu. Around their waists they have strings of beans which they have received from girls. The Iskpa wear white leather spats; they have a bell, a boar's tusk and strings of beans around their necks and bells at their hips. They are wrapped in the hide of any wild animal except monkey. They have a narrow, vertical shield in their left hand and a flat bell tied to their right thumb. Their hair, modeled in a concentric way and adorned with shells and feathers, resembles a crown. During the dance they take the boar tusk in their mouths and wrap the hide around their shoulders. The ceremony is accompanied by 2 big drums, a small one, a double bell, pipes and a poet's recitation (which may be replaced with an extra drum). Before the initiated stand casually dressed members of the Iskpa, whose task is to monitor the dance; if the dancers make mistakes, they have the right to scold or even whip them. The Éfalu begin their dance using castanets, their heads humbly hung low. One of the Singaru dances erect, waving a flag. The others move on all fours in single file, dragging their sticks and hatchets on the ground. They move to the beat of the drums, first forwards, then backwards. After a while they get up and do a vigorous, acrobatic dance to the rhythm of the recitation or the extra drum. When the iskpa drum sounds again, the Singaru resume their position on all fours. Meanwhile the Iskpa walk with verve, raising their feet high and twisting their trunk right and left, energetically enough to lose the feathers stuck in their hair and sound their bells. Cheered by the women and encouraged by the music, the Iskpa drop their mantle and begin a series of jumps. From time to time they throw their shields in front of a fellow dancer. If he is provoked to hit the shield with the bell on his right thumb, his movements are mimicked and mocked. Sometimes he hits the opponent rather than the shield, provoking a brief fight to settle accounts. The cortege passes through the whole village, stopping in front of the homes of the elders of the tribe. The more important a chief is, the longer the dance. The next day all the Iskpa dance with the adults. As a sign of equality, both groups assume places in the center of the village. Suddenly the dance transforms into an imitation of battle between the groups. Although no harm is intended, there may even be casualties. As an element of the rite, the newly initiated men chase the women. When a woman is caught, she must recite or sing praises of the man who caught her.

A. Taylor Cheska, 'Iskpa Dance', TGDWAN, 1987, 86-87; P. Wassungu, 'Classes d'âge et einitiation chez les Nawdeba', D. Paulme, ed., *Classes et associations d'âge en Afrique de l'Ouest*, 1969, 63-90.

ISMYENYENYE NOMYEROV, a Rus. school running game played by 2 teams with an even number of members. Each team is divided into 2 groups – the first one is called the 'ones' and the second the 'twos'. Two parallel lines are drawn on the ground at a distance of some 20 paces from each other. They are the starting lines. One line is the starting line for the 'ones' and the other for the 'twos'. The 'ones' and the 'twos' stand in 2 rows (1 row for each team). The distance between the 2 rows standing at the same starting line must be some 4 steps so that there is no interference between the runners. The first 'ones' start running towards the 'twos' to pass a flag to the first player in the 'twos' row. Then, the first 'two' runs back towards the 'ones' to pass the flag to the second player in the row and so on. A runner who has completed his run goes to the end of his team's row. The first team to complete the whole run is declared the winner.

I.N. Chkhannikov, GIZ, 1953, I, 23.

ISTLIAH TABAN, a folk type of hand-to-hand wrestling practiced in Lebanon.

ÍTHRÓTTIR, an O.Icel. term for physical activity among Vikings. It was supposed to increase fitness and bring enjoyment. The best known forms of Norse athletics are >FANG (a type of wrestling, practiced for over a thousand years), >GLÍMA (a variant of *fang*), >KNATTLEIKR (a game similar to grass hockey) and *Laugardagur* – bath day (Saturday).

J

JACKS, a game appearing in various countries in different cultural settings under diverse names. It has been known since antiquity and was still extremely popular in Europe right up until the dawning of the electronic era. Rather than the occasions now institutionalized by mass organizations, individual players once initiated casual games. The game was usu. played with 5 small (about 1cm in diameter) pebbles, although there were var. using 7 stones. Jacks was mostly a recreational social pastime exercised during picnics, on the beach, in military barracks, etc. A player starting the game threw all the stones into the air and tried to catch them on the back of his hand. From among the stones that rested on the back of his hand, the player selected the one judged most suitable for tossing first. The object of the game was to pick up one of the stones from the ground while the first stone was still airborne and then catch the tossed stone so that it did not touch the ground. The procedure was then repeated with all the remaining stones lying on the ground, clutching in the hand all the stones that had already been picked up. The player continued until all the stones had been picked up from the ground. The stones could be picked up 1 by 1 or, at further stages of the game, 2 by 2, 3 by 3, etc. up to 5, and back down, i.e. 5 by 5, 4 by 4, 3 by 3, etc. The player who failed to catch the tossed stone, or to pick the correct number of stones up from the ground, or to retain in his hand the stones picked up before, lost his turn. In days of old, bits of bone were used instead of stones. Modern jacks, however, are usu. metal or plastic, while a rubber ball is bounced and caught in place of tossing a stone in the air. The var. of jacks most popular in Eng.-speaking countries include:

CHECKSTONES, a number of small pebbles are scattered on a larger stone and while one of the pebbles is thrown into the air all the remaining ones have to be picked up and the thrown one caught before it touches the ground.

FIVESTONES, 5 stones are tossed in order to be caught on the back of the hand. After that, 4 stones are scattered on the ground and one is thrown into the air. In the first round the stones are picked up 1 by 1; then in combinations 2+2, 3+1, and finally all 4 at once. The round is closed in the same way it was started: all the stones are tossed and caught on the back of the hand. The 2nd round starts with tossing 1 stone and picking up only one of the 4, then picking up the stones strewn on the ground in the following combinations: 3, 2+2, 1+3, and 4. The round is completed with throwing all 5 stones into the air, catching them in the palm, tossing once again and catching them this time on the back of the hand like at the game's outset. Any error in the predetermined order of combinations implies the loss of one's turn. A similar game comprising 9 combinations and practiced in the S of Nottingham was called 'snobs'. In

A jaï alaï player

London, around Westminster, 4 pebbles were used, whereas a marble or glass ball fulfilled the role of the 5th stone.

JACKYSTEAUNS, or *jack*. A game popular esp. with girls, played according to standard rules of a 5-stone game but often with the use of plum or cherry stones instead of pebbles [TGESI, I, 259].

CHUCKS, played with the use of 5 shells. When played with pebbles, it was referred to as 'checkstones' or 'fivestones'.

In cultures other than Ang.-Sax., the best known var. of the game include: Arab >AL-LAQSA; Jap. *tedama*; Nig. >IGĘ; Port. >PEDRINHAS; Kenyan >KODI; Maori *koruru*; Pol. >KAMYCZKI. See also other games similar to jacks but played with the use of small wooden blocks or animal bones, such as >DALIES or >HUCKLEBONES.

Alice B. Gomme, 'Fivestones; Checkstones; Jacks', TGESI, I, 66; 122-129; 'Jogo das pedrinhas', JTP, 1979, 13-15.

JAGTBOLD, see >KRYDSBOLD.

JAÏ ALAÏ, also spelled *jai alai*, Basq. for 'the joyous feast'. A ball game played during this feast was so strictly associated with it that the name was soon used to refer to the game itself, in countries where other names for sports of the >PELOTA family were not based on old tradition. This concerns S. and C. America, the Caribbean, the USA, and the Philippines. On the Iberian Peninsula the term jaï alaï refers to large buildings housing >PELOTA VASCA matches (e.g. the indoor court Ezkurdi Jaï Alaï in Durango), usu. modern, concrete ones. No Span. or Basq. sports encyclopedia refers to pelota as jaï

Jaï alaï.

alaï. Amer. sources, however, often use the term regarding not only the Amer., but also Iberian var. of the game. Jaï alaï as a var. of pelota practiced beyond the Iberian Peninsula usu. played in a 3-wall court. For hitting the ball players use the *cesta* – a cross between a racket and a narrow, elongated, crescent-shaped basket. It is usu. made of wicker or, increasingly, rattan withes on a chestnut frame. At the end of the cesta there is a special glove, into which the player puts his hand. The length of the cesta is not determined officially, but adjusted to the needs of the contestant – 2ft. (60cm) on average. Nearly every player has his *cesta* custom made by an artisan called *cestero*. Courts are usu. 176ft. (53.65m) long and 95ft. (28.95m) wide. The one side which is not walled in has a metal net, about 44ft. (13.4m) high, behind which the audience is seated. The ball, made of kid leather with a rubber core tightly wrapped with string, is usu. 2in. (5.08cm) in diameter and weighs 4½oz. (127.5g). Its speed surpasses 200km/h. The game begins with one of the contestants throwing the ball against a wall with his hand. He must then catch the ball on the rebound with his cesta and then, using the cesta, throw it back against the wall. Now it is the opponent's turn to catch the ball with his cesta. This exchange goes on until one of the players makes a mistake, hitting the ball outside the permitted field or failing to catch a correctly thrown ball. This brings the opponent 1pt. In a match, 2 of all the contestants start playing. The game is played to 1pt. The winner stays in the court and the next player challenges him. Again, the game is played to 1pt. and so on. Each winner takes away the points of the previous winner, whom he defeated, so the whole tournament is over when the ultimate winner has the number of points amounting to the overall number of players not counting himself. Therefore if 8 contestants take part, the game is played to 7pts. The same rules apply to doubles. After WWII a so-called Amer. Qualifying and Finals Elimination System was introduced in Miami, Florida, in which groups of 8 contestants play to 5pts. The first 3 players to get 3pts. stop playing and earn the right to participate in the finals. The ultimate winner has to defeat his partners (2x2pts.=4pts.). The 5th point is given for the last game. If none of the contestants can win this way, the top 2 do a play-off. Beginning the play-off, each has 4pts. (3 scored in the eliminating round and 1 in the final round). The one who wins the play-off gets the 5th point, becoming the ultimate winner.

History. Jaï alaï originated at medieval Basq. folk feasts, first mentioned in the 13th cent. The game played during the feast soon spread all over the Iberian Peninsula and thanks to the Basques living on the Fr. side of the border adopted some elements of >JEU DE LA PAUME. Brought to S. and C. America, it originated numerous var. of *pelota*, in this part of the world referred to as jaï alaï and differing slightly from its Iberian predecessor. Some sports historians are of the opinion that the element of bouncing the ball against a wall was introduced into the game after its appearance in the New World. According to this theory it was the soldiers of the Span. conquistador H. Cortez (1485--1547), who took this element from the Aztecs and introduced it into games played in Spain, esp. in Andalusia. From there it spread all

Spectators watch and wager on a game of Jaï alaï in Milford, Connecticut, USA. The sport was eclipsed years ago as a gambling favorite by the slot machines and blackjack tables of the Foxwoods Resort Casino and Mohegan Sun.

over the country, esp. to the Basq. Province, where it was most prominent. In the 19th cent. the game became very popular in many countries of Lat. America, esp. in Mexico and Cuba. In the USA the sport became widely known during the 1904 Ol.G. in St. Louis. It was played as a show discipline by 40 contestants from Spain. Soon afterwards people started playing jaï alaï in Chicago and New Orleans. In 1924 it was introduced as a tourist attraction in Miami. Bets were legalized in 1936 and the first television broadcast took place in 1959. In the same year F. Castro came to power in Cuba, which caused a major wave of emigration. Cuban refugees reinforced the jaï alaï centers in Florida, esp. in Miami. Highly developed league systems can be found, apart from Cuba and Miami, in Mexico. The oldest form of betting is called *quiniela*, where the persons placing bets spot the first 2 places and win, no matter which of the 2 contestants took 1st place and which 2nd. In a more recent system, called *quiniela exacta*, gamblers specify, who will take 1st and 2nd place. Despite substantial differences, Amer. and Eur. var. of jaï alaï still have enough in common for Amer. league players to be recruited in the Basq. Province.

T.B. McNeil, 'Jaï Alaï', EWS, 1996, II, 519-521; F.G. Menke, 'Jaï-Alaï', EOS, 1969, 662-664; G.M. Ronberg, 'Jaï Alaï', EAI, 1979, 15, 667.

JAMB, an Uzbek folk sport, where mounted contestants shot at a silver coin attached to a high mast. The winner took the coin.

JAPANESE FISHERMEN'S REGGATAS, a trad. event held annually as part of the New Year celebrations and during the July music festival.

JAVELIN THROW, an athletic field event, deriving from a traditional combat and hunting skill, and involving throwing a javelin at a target or for distance. Throwing the javelin attained sporting status in various cultures and epochs. The modern javelin is 260-270cm long for men and 220-230cm long for women. The distance between the tip of the head to the center of gravity is, respectively, 90-106cm (formerly 90-110cm) and 80-95cm. The moving forward of the center of gravity in men's javelins was caused by the need to shorten the distances thrown, as they began reaching more than 100m and became dangerous for the spectators. The minimum weight, including the cord grip, is 800g for men and 600g for women. The length of the metal head is 25-33cm for both men and women. The diameter at the thickest point is, respectively 25-30mm and 20-25mm. Finally, the length of the cord grip is, respectively, 15-16cm and 14-15cm. According to IAAF rules, 'the javelin shall have no mobile parts or other apparatus, which during the throw could change its center of gravity or throwing characteristics'. Smaller javelins are used in junior and children's events.

The runway may not be shorter than 30m or longer than 36.5m (33.5m is considered to be the optimum length). The runway leads to the scratch line, which is an arc drawn with a radius of 8m. The arc consists of a band of wood or metal, 7cm wide, painted white. The landing sector is marked with two lines drawn radially at an angle of 29-30° from the center of the circle the throwing arc is part of. Gloves are prohibited but applying grip-improving substances to the hands is allowed. Each contestant may also make marks on the runway by placing sticks along it or applying adhesive tape (using chalk or making permanent marks is not allowed). Competitors may not step over the throwing arc or leave the runway before the javelin touches the surface of the landing sector. Measurements are made from the point of impact of the javelin head to the inside edge of the throwing arc. The order of throws is decided by lots. If there are more than 8 competitors, a qualifying round is organized first, with each thrower allowed 3 attempts. The best 8 competitors go on into the final round, where they each have a further 3 attempts. If more than one contestant achieves the 8th result, all the competitors with this result are allowed to go on to the final round. Each contestant is entitled to 3 trial attempts before the actual competition starts. The longest distance in the whole competition wins, irrespective of whether it is thrown at the 1st, 2nd, or 3rd attempt.

History. The tradition of the javelin dates back to prehistoric times when the ancients improved their throwing skills between military or hunting expeditions. At some point in history, such exercises must

have developed into sporting competitions. The rules of javelin throwing were first standardized by the Greeks, long before the first ancient Ol.G. The javelin is mentioned numerous times in both the *Iliad* and *Odyssey*. As an Olympic sport, the javelin throw was introduced during the 18th Olympiad in 708 BC (see also >AKONTISMA). In the Middle Ages, javelin techniques (not only throwing) formed the basis of knights' exercises. An improved version of the javelin, the lance, was not thrown but came to be used in >RUNNING AT THE RING, and for hitting targets in equestrian >QUINTAIN. The pioneers of modern gymnastics introduced various types of the javelin throw. F.L Jahn recommended throwing the javelin as an exercise developing overall agility and strength. The javelin Jahn used had a length of 6-8 Ger. feet (about 180-240cm), thickness of 1-1.5 Ger. inches (about 2.3-4cm), and a sharp metal head. Javelins modeled on the ancient tradition, with a loop to facilitate the throw, were introduced during the first Gk. Olympics in 1859. The winners of the javelin throw during the Pan-Hellenic Games were: N. Marcopoulos (1859), S. Ioannou of Gallipoli (1870) and M. Tzabaras (1875).

A javelin throw competition was also held (but just once) during the Much Wenlock Games in England in 1859 organized by W.P. Brookes on the model of the ancient Olympiads. During the first modern Ol.G. of 1896, a freestyle javelin throw competition was held but the event was later given up. The modern javelin was introduced during the so-called Intercalated Ol.G. of 1906. Prior to this, it had mainly been used in Scand. countries, especially Sweden and Finland, being called the 'Finnish javelin' for that reason. The Fin. javelin was introduced into the Olympic program in 1908. The javelins used were made of wood and had metal heads but without the military rims and notches. The shape of the head was an extension of the spar. A permanent cord grip to facilitate throwing was placed at the center of the spar, and the loop was abolished. Later, javelins made entirely of metal were developed. During the 1912 Ol.G., a both-hands contest was organized where the final result was an aggregate of the best throws from the left and right hands. A Finn, J. Saaristo, was the winner with a world record result of 109.42m (61.00m+48.42m).

Sweden was the first country to hold national championships (1904), and the USA was next (1909). One reason for the delay in the introduction of the javelin into the Olympic program was the fact that for some time it was considered a gymnastic event. The conflict between the gymnastic and Olympic movements

in the 19th cent. meant that gymnastics was considered separate from sport, and the free flow of ideas and experience between the two movements was hampered. This partly explains the dominance in the javelin throw of top gymnastic countries, such as Finland and Sweden. Until 1953, all the world records (which had been recorded since 1904) were held by Scand. sportsmen. The Swede H. Andersson was the first official world record holder (36.58 – 1904). His compatriot E. Lemming was a 4-time world record holder (1906-12), won the Intercalated Olympic competition at Athens (1906), won the Olympic gold twice (1908 and 1912), and was the first thrower to pass the 60m barrier (60.64m – 1912). The Finn M. Järvinen is considered to have been the javelin thrower of all time, with 12 world records between 1930 and 1936. The Finn E. Pentilla was the first to throw the javelin over 70m (70.01m – 1927). The introduction of an aerodynamically shaped javelin by F. Held (b. 1927) made it possible for him to break the 80m barrier (80.41m – 1953) but the Pole J. Sidło was actually the first man to throw a conventional javelin over 80m (80.15m – 1953). The javelin invented by Held was called by his name, while the classical javelin was called 'Finnish'. In 1959, American A. Cantello tried to revolutionize javelin throw by using a rotational technique (with a turnaround just before the throwing arc) but the style was soon banned by IAAF rules. Norwe-

Mick Hill of Great Britain in action in the Men's Javelin Qualifying at the Olympic Stadium of the Sydney 2000 Olympic Games in Sydney, Australia.

gian T. Pedersen was the first man to pass the 90m mark (91.40m – 1964), while the E. German H. Hoh – that of 100m (104.80m – 1984).

Women's javelin throw competitions were held as early as before 1914, but the event only gained popularity in the 1920s. It was included in the program of the Women's World Games in 1922 (until 1934). The pioneers included the winners of the first women's games: A. Pianzola (Switzerland, 1922), L. Adelshold (Sweden, 1926), and L. Schumann (Germany, 1930). Women's javelin became part of the Olympic program in 1932; the versatile American, M. Didrickson (1914-56), was the first winner. Before that, Didrickson was the first woman to break the 40m barrier (40.62m – 1930). The Czech D. Zátopková is considered the best thrower of all time – she was the first to pass the 50m mark (50.47m – 1952). After 1952, when A. Chudina (USSR) came second behind Zatopková, Soviet throwers increased in importance, winning most medals between 1952 and 1964. In that period, most major athletics events were won by the Olympic champions I. Jaunzeme (1956) and E. Ozolina (1960), closely followed by the silver and bronze medallists J. Gorchakova

JAVELIN OLYMPIC CHAMPIONS

MEN
1908 Eric Lemming, SWE 54.825
1912 Eric Lemming, SWE 60.64
1920 Jonni Myyrä, FIN 65.78
1924 Jonni Myyrä, FIN 62.96
1928 Erik Lundqvist, SWE 66.60
1932 Matti Järvinen, FIN 72.71
1936 Gerhard Stöck, GER 71.84
1948 Tapio Rautavaara, FIN 69.77
1952 Cyrus Young, USA 73.78
1956 Egil Danielsen, NOR 85.71
1960 Viktor Tsybulenko, URS 84.64
1964 Pauli Nevala, FIN 82.66
1968 Jânis Lusis, URS 90.10
1972 Klaus Wolfermann, FRG 90.48
1976 Miklós Németh, HUN 94.58
1980 Dainis Kula, URS 91.20
1984 Arto Härkönen, FIN 86.76
1988 Tapio Korjus, FIN 84.28
1992 Jan Zelezný, TCH 89.66
1996 Jan Zelezný, CZE 88.16
2000 Jan Zelezný, CZE 90.17

WOMEN
1932 Mildred Didriksen, USA 43.68
1936 Tilly Fleischer, GER 45.18
1948 Hermine Bauma, AUT 45.57
1952 Dana Zátopková, TCH 50.47
1956 Inese Jaunzeme, URS 53.86
1960 Elvîra Ozolina, URS 55.98
1964 Mihaela Penes, ROM 60.54
1968 Angela Németh, HUN 60.36
1972 Ruth Fuchs, GDR 63.88
1976 Ruth Fuchs, GDR 65.94
1980 Maria Caridad Colón, CUB 68.40
1984 Tessa Sanderson, GBR 69.56
1988 Petra Felke, GDR 74.68
1992 Silke Renk, GER 68.34
1996 Heli Rantanen, FIN 67.94
2000 Trine Hattestad, NOR 68.91

J

Javelin throw on stamps issued for the Olympic Games in Melbourne (1956, top), Mexico (1968, middle), and the European Track and Field Championships in Budapest (1966, bottom).

(bronze in 1952), N. Konyayeva (bronze in 1956) and B. Kaledene (bronze in 1960). In 1964, Ozolina passed the 60m mark as the first woman in history (61.38m). The victory of M. Penes (Rumania) in 1964 meant a shift in power; top contestants also included Hungarian A. Németh (Olympic champion of 1968) but GDR throwers dominated the event. E. German R. Fuchs was the Olympic champion of 1972 and 1976, while another thrower from that country, P. Felke, won the competition of 1988. M. Colon, winning the 1980 Ol.G., was the first of a host of Cubans who gained a strong position. T. Biryulina (USSR) was the first woman to break the 70m barrier (70.08m – 1980), while P. Felke – the first to reach 80m (80.00m – 1988).
The Book of Rules, Athletics. Javelin throw, 1998; Polish Athletic Federation, *Przepisy zawodów w lekkoatletyce. Rzut oszczepem*, 1996.

JAVELOT, a Flem. var. of javelin throw. The javelin was exceptionally large.

JAZZ GYMNASTICS, a musical-sporting discipline exploiting rhythmic body movements to a jazz musical accompaniment. It began as a sports-dance discipline in 1960 in Sweden and was popularized shortly afterwards in W. Germany. It was pioneered by the Swede Monika Bechman. She also formulated the first rules in the book *Jazz gymnastics in the home and at school* (*Jazzgymnastik i hem och shola*, 1966). In Germany, where it was initially dominated almost exclusively by dance forms, it was enriched by sporting-gymnastic movements. A precursor of the stronger location of Jazz Gymnastis as a sport was Hanna Preiss. Independently J. Sheppard Missett in 1968 began to popularize a programme of recreational exercises to a jazz beat which she called jazz exercise. A Pole, O. Kuimińska, pioneered Jazz gymnastics in E Europe, authoring many books which popularized this form of exercise at a time when Western forms of sport and music were not supported by the authorities in the region. Following 1971 various ways of joining jazz music and movement appeared in a range of eclectic forms of dance-gymnastics. Beat music also began to be taken into consideration. In the mid 1970s Uta Fischer-Munstermann carried out a successful synthesis of these developing tendencies, creating four main principles linking jazz gymnastics with Afro-American music and jazz dance: 1) polycentrism and isolation of movement, i.e. separating individual centers of bodily movement, which move as if isolated from one another; this is complete opposition to classical dance, where the body creates an integrated unit and its uniform tension does not allow for such 'isolation'; 2) 'internal movement', or the internal tensing and relaxation of individual centers of movement, carried out in a position of 'collapse', i.e. while leaning forward at the same time bending the knees; 3) multiplication, or repetition of a movement while enriching it with additional elements, 'accompaniments', more frequently and usually larger than a given basic movement; e.g. between 2 steps are performed additional sequences of hip or arm movements not involving the legs; 4) polyrhythms and multirhythms, that is, movements performed in

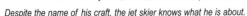

Despite the name of his craft, the jet skier knows what he is about.

time to varying rhythms and metres of individual musical instruments. An ecstatic-emotional element is also often encountered in jazz gymnastics, beyond the control of the participant. There are tendencies to eliminate these features of jazz gymnastics as being outside the perfect control necessary to achieve the desired aesthetic effect.
M. Bechman, *Jazzgymnastik i hem och shola* (1966); F. Hatchett, *Jazz Dance*, 2000; O. Kuźmińska, 'Muzyka w gimnastyce', *Kultura Fizyczna*, 1980, 2.

JEET KUNE DO, Chin. for 'the art of the intercepting fist', a martial art created by the actor Bruce Lee, based on the Chin. >GONGFU, with elements of Eur. boxing. After Lee's death his family and students founded a corporation to protect and develop his legacy >JUN FAN JEET KUNE DO.

JEG MELDER KRIG MOD, see >STANTO.

JEP, a Dan. folk game, where players hit a stick with a bat to send it as far into the field as possible. The same family of games includes: the Pol. >KLIPA and >SZTEKIEL, the Arab >AL-BA' 'A , the Indian-Pakistani >GULLI DUNDA, the Bret. >*mouilh*, the Fr. >PILAOUET and the Eng. >TIP-CAT. The term 'jep' is a diminutive of the name 'Jacob'. The game is usu. played by 2 (usu. female) contestants in a field of any size. The necessary elements are an 8-12cm long stick sharpened at both ends, a flat bat 40-50cm long and a hole in the ground. Two kinds of serves are used. In the first, the player places the *jep* horizontally over the hole and hits it from below with the bat, trying to get it as far out into the field as she can. Her opponent tries to catch it in her apron (when boys play they catch the stick with their hands). If she succeeds, she must throw it at the bat, which the batter now places over the hole. If the stick hits the bat, the players change places. In the second type of serve the batter puts the *jep* on the bat, tosses it into the air and then hits it into the field. If the catcher fails to intercept the stick, she tries to throw it back into the hole, which the batter now defends. If the batter saves, she keeps her position; if not, the players change places.
J. Møller, 'Jep', GID, 1997, 1.

JERNBANE, Dan. for 'the train game', a children's game. Players are divided into 2 teams, the 'hosts' and the 'guests'. There is a long line on the ground with crosswise lines for as many 'cars' as there are players (every 3m). Each guest gets into his car. The lines have to be so far apart that the guests cannot touch the hosts, who stand between the cars. The hosts have to run along the long line, from one end to the other. The guests, who try to catch them, can move only on the lines (hosts standing in between the lines are safe). The hosts get a point for every crosswise line their player gets past.
J. Møller, 'Jernbane', GID, 1997, 4, 101.

JET BOOT, see >RAFTING.

JET SKI, a name denoting equipment and sport practiced on motor mobiles, looking like water scooters, but having floaters instead of wheels and a combustion drive. Presently a water-jet engine is used to drive the mobile. It sucks water inside and ejects it as steam, which eliminates the danger of injury

650-ccm engines allow for speeds of 80km/h.

with the rotating propeller used in earlier versions. The steering block extends from the front to the back. The handles resemble motorcycle handlebars. Engines (300 and 650ccm) help reach 80hp and speeds of 80km/h. The name *jet ski*, although theoretically a trade name of the Kawasaki company, is generally used to describe all such mobiles. All jet skis are divided into 3 classes: *Sport Division* – comprising top class professional mobiles with lights permitting night rides, *Ski Division* – for one person riding in the standing position, and *Runabout* – mobiles for a driver and one passenger or a few passengers. Sports competitions are held in each class. There are 2 basic forms of competition: races along a course designated by buoys with various evolutions and *free style*. In the *free style* competition contestants must do, within 2min., a number of complicated maneuvers, such as: submerging the mobile in water and jerking it up, jumps in the air, twists made at full speed etc. At international competitions contestants are evaluated by 7 judges, who award from 1-10pts., the contestant with the most points winning the competition. As the ski jets can easily capsize, designers came up with a number of safety features, such as an automatic control mechanism in case the rider falls off and a rope connecting the rider with the engine ignition mechanism. When the rider falls off, the rope jerks and cuts the engine. The jet ski automatically recovers its balance and stalls until the rider boards it again.
History. Ski jets were invented in 1965 by C. Jacobson, who earlier had sponsored and organized motorcycle races, where the frequency of accidents and severity of injuries resulted in designing a soft, water base for a mobile with maneuverability similar to that of a motorcycle. In 1969 Jacobson registered the first water mobile of this type, called >SKIDOO – a pigeon on runners [*doo* – Scot. dial. pigeon]. The 'Bombardier' ski jet was modeled on the first *ski-doo* design. Plagued by countless problems, Jacobson discontinued production in 1971, when the design was taken over by the Jap. company Kawasaki, a motorcycle manufacturer. In 1973 Kawasaki produced the first model defined as Jet Ski, which quickly became the generic Eng. name for all mobiles of this type. In the first model the rider had to stand. In later models a seat was added, which decreased the resistance of air and considerably increased the mobile's stability and consequently the stability of the rider. Production of the former seatless class continues, although 95% of presently made jet skis are equipped with seats.
Jet ski enthusiasts tend to wax poetic, claiming that they feel truly free and experience untold satisfaction from the contact with water and air, which jet skis afford. Growing interest in jet skis has led to the organization of various international competitions. The most prestigious ones are held on the Hawaiian island of Maui.
J. Tomlinson, 'Jet ski', *The Ultimate Encyclopedia of Extreme Sports*, 1996.

JEU DE CHÔLE, a game born in Flanders in early Middle Ages, which also existed in N France under the name of >SOULE (*à la crosse*, with the stick). The club was made up of a long wooden stick (called *fût* in French) ended with a piece of iron. This metal head had 2 shares: the *plat,* which strikes the *soulette* (the ball) when this one was well placed on the ground, and the *pic,* which by its arched form allowed to leave the soulette from the ruts or to raise it higher. A *poignée* (handle) was at the other side of the stick. The play consisted in reaching a target with a ball with this club of the shape of a spoon. The target could be with several miles. Built in the past with cord of hemp, the ball is today made of leather or rubber pieces. With given rise to the golf, the game of chôle is always played in north of France and in Belgium.

JEU DE COURTE PAUME, [Fr. *jeu* – game + *courte* – short + *paume* – palm of the hand] a game dating back to the Middle Ages, yet played to this day, in a wider context referred to as >JEU DE LA PAUME. A small ball is hit between 2 players (or 2 pairs of players). Initially the game was played across a line drawn on the ground, then over a rope (later decorated with fringes) and since the early 17th cent. a net has been used for this purpose (though not exclusively). In the earlier stages of the sport's development players used their bare hands, but the 16th cent. witnessed the increasing use of rackets; the noun '*paume*' has been preserved in the name due to strong linguistic traditions. The '*courte*' element helps distinguish the game from similar ones with '*paume*' in the name. This regards local var. of *jeu de la paume,* as well as the team game >JEU DE LONGUE PAUME, whose court was longer than in jeu de courte paume (*longue* – long). The rules of jeu de courte paume are almost identical to those of >ROYAL TENNIS, its direct descendant, so that it is possible for players of both games to participate in common matches.

History. Jeu de courte paume dates back at least to the 13th cent. The most famous court of the game's early period was built at the beginning of the 15th cent. in Paris, on rue Grenier Saint Lazare, and called 'the little temple' (*Le Petit Temple*). A woman by the name of Margot (from Hainault) was reputed to have beaten all the men at the game in 1427. In the 16th cent., from the reign of François I (1515-47), a great lover of sports, the game began to gain social status and transformed from a folk pastime to a court amusement. Henri II (1547-59) played jeu de courte paume whole-heartedly, sanctioning the game's prestige. Around 1750, an event referred to at the time as W.Ch. was won by le Clergé de France (the Fr. clergyman). The sport was most popular in big cities, however local var. were developed in the country (in Picardie and Provence >JO DE PAUMO) and even influenced other nationalities: the Basques (>PELOTA VASCA, subentry ESKUZKA), the Spanish (on the Lanzarote Island >PELOTA MANO). The Basques and the Spanish took it to S. and C. America (>JUEGO DE LA CHAZA in Ecuador and Columbia). Nowadays in France the sport is supervised by the Fr. Jeu de Courte Paume Committee (*Comité Française de Jeu de Courte Paume*), a part of the Fr. Tennis Federation (*Fédération Française de Tennis*). Today in France there are only 3 clubs and 3 courts (in Paris, Fointainbleau, and Bordeaux). In Great Britain however there are 11 royal tennis clubs and 9 courts, in the USA 9 clubs and 7 courts, in Australia 3 clubs and 2 courts (1993 data). The most important Fr. events are the Silver Racket (*Raquette d'Argent* – held since 1899, hosted alternately by Paris and Bordeaux), the Paris Cup (*Coupe de Paris* – since 1910), the Bordeaux Cup (*Coupe de Bordeaux* – since 1919) and the French Open. In 1922 the first Burthurst Cup was held, since then held alternately in London and Paris. International cooperation consists of improvised agreements between Fr. and Ang.-Sax. organizations (other countries, such as Belgium and the Netherlands, participate to a lesser extent). W.Ch. are held irregularly. The greatest competitor of the 20th cent. was the Frenchman Pierre de Etschebaster, who won every championship between 1928 and 1955.

JEU DE FER, a game much resembling the Flem. >SCHUIFTAFEL, played by the Fr.-speaking population of Flanders, also known as >JEU DE TOQUE. The name comes from the iron discs used in the game [Fr. *jeu* – game + *fer* – iron], which are moved with sticks on a smooth table to knock down figures. The sticks are similar to billiard cues. The table is narrower and longer than a billiard table. The discs are about 1cm thick and 4cm in diame-

ter. The figures (5-7, depending on local tradition) are made of wood and resemble the chess king but are much larger, even as tall as 25cm. The discs must not fall into the grooves running along the back and side lines of the table.

JEU DE LA BOULE, a Fr. casino game played on a table in the shape of a large wooden bowl divided into sections, into which red and black balls are dropped. The complicated system of points is similar to that of *roulette,* and takes into account the oddness or evenness of the scored points, the color of the ball etc. The main difference between jeu de la boule and roulette is that here the bowl is bigger and does not move.

JEU DE LA PAUME, a medieval Fr. game in which players pass a ball over a piece of rope dividing the court into 2 halves (later a net suspended on 2 posts, with height decreasing in the middle). The game is generally the same as its Eng. var. known as royal tennis (for rules, court dimensions etc., see >ROYAL TENNIS). At the beginning, hands were used to hit the ball, and that is where the name of the game derives from [Fr. *jeu* – game + *paume* – palm]. Later on, bats and rackets were used but the original name stayed as a linguistic relic. The name 'jeu de la paume' is also used in France to refer to the original var. of the game, including >JEU DE LONGUE PAUME, which was a team game played without a net or rackets. An additional terminological problem is that all the diverse var. of the game were known by the abbreviated name *paume,* and the incorrect version *jeu de paume* has also been used (in the Fr. tradition, *jeu de paume* refers to the court rather than the game itself). In order to clarify the situation, the jeu de la paume committee (part of the Fr. Tennis Federation – Fédération Française de Tennis) decided to convert to the name >JEU DE COURTE PAUME, and changed its own name to Comité Française du Jeu de Courte Paume. Before this happened, though, the game made an episodic appearance at the Olympics in London (1908) under the then prevailing name of *jeu de la paume.* See also >JEU QUARRÉ, >JO DE PAUMO, >JUEGO DE LA CHAZA.

JEU DE LONGUE PAUME, a Fr. ball game of medieval origin, played outdoors in teams. The ball was hit with the bare hands [Fr. *jeu* – game + *longue* – long + *paume* – palm of the hand] and later with long rackets. Different sources give contradictory information regarding the rules of the game. The ball was probably bigger than in >JEU DE LA PAUME. The object of the game was to hit the ball so far that the opposing team would have to back off, in order to prevent the ball touching the ground. Sometimes teams would get pushed back beyond the end line of the court. Jeu de longue paume might have been the predecessor of other games of this sort, e.g. the Du. >KAATSEN, the Frisian >KEATSEN and var. of >PELOTA VASCA (subentries MAHAI JOKOA, JUEGO LARGO, BOTA LUZEA).

JEU DE MAIL, also *pall-mall,* an old Fr. ball game played with sticks. Already practiced in France in the 16th cent., it had rules and attitudes of play which very strongly resembled modern golf. The first rules on this game where printed in 1717 in France by Lauthier. There existed in fact 4 manners of practicing the play: *Rouët, Partie, Chicane* and *Grand Coup.* In the rouët version, the matches where played with 3 or 4 balls. The partie required teams with an equal number of players. Chicane resembled the current match-play disputed in golf between 2 players. It was practiced in open country and the players were to strike the ball at the precise place where it had fallen. The winner was the one which added up less blows to reach a given point. The grand coup simply consisted of a very long course where 2 or several players were struggling. Jeu de mail can be considered as the predecessor of many sports played with a cross, like >FIELD HOCKEY, >HURLING, >SHINTY and >LACROSSE.

JEU DE PAUME, a name erroneously used in many historical and encyclopedic works of reference to describe a game of medieval origin, where players stood facing each other and hit or threw a ball with their bare hands [Fr. *jeu* – game + *paume* – palm of the hand]. However 'jeu de paume' signifies only the court for this game and not the game itself, whose proper name is >JEU DE LA PAUME or >JEU

DE COURTE PAUME. Cf. >JEU DE LONGUE PAUME, >PAUME, >JO DE PAUMO.

JEU DE TAMBOURINE, see >TAMBURINO.

JEU DE TAMIS, see >TAMIS.

JEU DE TOQUE, a game played by the Fr.-speaking population of Flanders, also known as >JEU DE FER, similar to the Flem. >SCHUIFTAFEL.

JEU PROVENÇAL, a Fr. ball game of the >BOULES family. The name comes from the region of Provence, where the game is more popular than any other game of this sort. Another term for the sport is *le longue,* distinguishing it from >PÉTANQUE [Fr. *longue* – long; throws in jeu provençal are longer than in *pétanque*]. Jeu provençal rules allow the player to jump up while throwing the ball (pétanque rules do not allow that). The object of the game (as in most others of the boules family) is to throw the ball so that it lands as close to the target as possible.
Equipment. The throwing balls, measuring 7.05-8cm in diameter, are made of metal, usu. steel, and weigh 600-800g. Nowadays they are manufactured by specialized producers, who do not mark their weight or the degree of balancing (decentering the ball, by making it heavier at one side, is a common practice, serving to curve the ball's track). The target ball, in Provence referred to as *lé* or *gari* (in other regions *cochonnet* – piglet), is smaller than the others (25-35mm in diameter), made of wood and often painted white.
Pitch. In popular matches the pitch may be any flat area with a hardened surface, such as a town square, a park alley or a sidewalk. In official events the lane is 25m long and 3-4m wide.
Rules. The game is played individually or in teams, 2 on 2 or 3 on 3. Individual players have 3 or 4 balls, doubles players 3 balls and triples players 2 balls. The object of the game is to throw the ball in such a way that it stops closer to the target than the opponent's balls. The points are counted after all the players have thrown their balls (in one round, referred to as *mène*). 1pt. is awarded for every ball closer to the target than the opponent's ball. Depending on local tradition, a round is played to 11, 13, 15, 18 or even 21pts. One match consists of 3 rounds: *la partie* – the game, *la revanche* – the return match and *la belle* – the beautiful.

WORLD SPORTS ENCYCLOPEDIA

J

Adriaen van de Venne, Summer (A Jeu de Paume Before A Country Palace), *oil on canvas.*

Jeu de la paume. A 19th cent. lithograph.

J WORLD SPORTS ENCYCLOPEDIA

Course of the game. Coin tosses determine who chooses the starting spot, tosses the target ball and begins the first round. The winner of the toss draws a circle 35-50cm in diameter, which must be at least 1m from the nearest obstacle, such as a tree, a wall etc. He then throws the gari (lé), which should stop 15-21m from the perimeter of the circle, 3m from any obstacle along the line of throwing and 1m from any side obstacle. It must also be clearly visible from the throwing circle. The player throwing the ball has 3 chances to achieve this according to the rules. If he fails, the ball goes to his opponent or the other team. After one round the starting point is moved to a circle drawn around the gari – the lane is used in both directions. Players throw with one foot inside the circle. They may take 1 step while aiming and then 3 steps during the throw, but not before they release the ball. An exception is made for people with disabilities or over 65yrs. of age: they may bring the foot from the circle next to the one outside it. Each player's goal is to get the ball as close to the target as possible. Success achieved in the first throws may be short-lived, as the target ball is apt to change its position, being hit by other balls. After all the balls have been thrown the ball nearest to the target brings 1pt. If more than one ball is closer to the target than any of the opponent's balls, this brings accordingly 2, 3, 4 and in team games even 5 or 6pts. Players use 4 basic techniques: 1) *plomber* (beating down the ground) – a high throw guaranteeing relative precision – the ball hits the ground almost vertically and therefore stops in place. It does not roll a hard to predict distance; 2) *rouler* (rolling) – the ball is rolled from a low underhand; 3) *pointer* (pinpointing) – the ball is thrown at the ball of the opponent; 4) *tir* or *tirer* (shooting) – the ball is aimed at the ball of the opponent closest to the target. Thus the opponent's ball is thrown aside and the new ball occupies its position. A precise completion of this (called *carreau*) is the most spectacular element of the game. If the throw is too hard, i.e. the opponent's ball gets thrown aside more than 4m, it is considered void and all the balls are put back where they were before the throw. In team games it is common for each player on a team to specialize in a given type of throw (plomber, rouler, pointer, tirer).
History. Jeu provençal can be traced back to ancient ball games played when Provence was a part of the Roman Empire. For centuries it was a regional folk game. In the 19th cent. it evolved into a team game under the influence typical for the shaping of modern sport. The chief governing bodies of jeu provençal (and pétanque) are the Fédération Internationale de Pétanque et Jeu Provençal on international level and Fédération Française de Pétanque et Jeu Provençal (seated in Marseille) in France.

JEU QUARRÉ, a var. of >JEU DE LA PAUME, and>JEU DE COURTE PAUME, played on a court surrounded by a gallery of slightly different construction than its original [Fr. *jeu* – game + quarré – perhaps an old form of the modern *querre* – to seek – or a form of *quarrer* – to make a square or a figure of 4]. The most prominent feature of this sport is a lack of the architectural elements *dedan* and *tambour* (a pillar used to confuse the opponent by giving the ball an unexpected trajectory – for a closer description see >ROYAL TENNIS). The jeu quarré court had, however, 4 holes in its back wall, the purpose of which is unclear. They may have been aimed at and their number, as well as the square they were arranged in, gave the sport its name. The most famous court can be found in Falkland Castle, Scotland, where James V had it built in 1539. In the Basque Province a similar game called *pasaka en arkupe* developed (see >PELOTA VASCA).

JEUX DIRECTS, a Fr. counterpart of the Span. >JUEGOS DIRECTOS.

JEUX INDIRECTS, A Fr. counterpart of the Span. >JUEGOS INDIRECTOS.

JIKISHIN-KAGERYU, a var. of the Jap. sport >NAGINATA JUTSU.

JING POLE PROPPING, a sports competition popular among several tribes of China. In a var. practiced by the Jing, Tujia and Yao a 1.5m-long pole is used. Two contenders hold the pole on both ends at the height of their shoulders, placing both arms along the pole. They stand firmly on the ground with their left legs straight; the right legs are foremost and slightly bent. At the umpire's signal they

Jiqiu

start propping the pole, trying to push each other off. In the mid-distance between the contenders there is a cross line marked on the ground. The contender who first steps on the line while pushing the opponent wins.

Another var. of pole propping, without the mid-line, is practiced by the Jinuo people. The 2 contenders stand opposite each other holding a 2m-long bamboo pole between them. Behind each contender there is a line marked on the ground. Leaning slightly forward, at the umpire's signal, they start pressing on the pole with their bellies. The aim of the competition is to push the opponent across his back line. Pole propping can be also practiced by doubles.

Mu Fushan, et al., 'Jing Pole Propping', TRAMCHIN, 102.

JINGLING, see >BLIND MAN'S BUFF.

JINGPO BROADSWORD PLAY, a dancing game of the Chin. minority of Jingpo. Its object is to make displays with 1 or 2 broadswords held in the hands. The movement technique is borrowed from marital arts and comprises cuts, thrusts, head blows and parries. Special swords are used, approx. 80cm long, widening at the tip and relatively narrow at the hilt, with a delicately ornamented handle. Jingpo broadsword play is practiced by boys of 12 and up. The ability to spin the swords is considered a test of manhood. The rhythmical displays of Jingpo broadsword play are accompanied by music played with Chin. flutes, gongs and drums. In some regions inhabited by the Jingpo people girls and women take direct part in broadsword play, whereas in others they only accompany the boys and men by dancing and waving colorful shawls.

Mu Fushan et al., 'Broadsword Play', TRAMCHIN, 164.

JINUO CATAPULT SHOOTING, a competition of the Jinuo people of the Chin. province Yunan. The catapult, *nu,* resembles a bamboo bow with the bowstring made of animal tendons. In the middle of the string there is a container for the balls, which are made of specially hardened mud. The container, resembling a flat box, is open in the direction of shooting. Contestants shoot from about 50m off. The bow is 4 *chi* (just over 1m) long and 0.1 *chi* (2.53cm) thick.

Mu Fushan et al., 'Jinuo Catapult Shooting', TRAMCHIN, 154.

JIQIU, a var. of >POLO played in ancient China. Historians argue as to its country of origin. The game might have reached China from ancient Persia through other Asian countries or possibly it developed in China affecting the neighboring countries, including Persia, commonly regarded as the most probable origin country of polo. Another theory locates the birth of jiqiu in Tibet. One thing is sure, jiqiu has certainly enjoyed a long and celebrated tradition. The first mention about jiqiu included in a short anonymous poem comes from the age of the Three Kingdoms (220-265 AD):

A lonely ball,
A few riders after it,
Led by their strength and agility
To the promise of success.

The first rules of jiqiu were put down during the reign of the T'ang dynasty (618-906). They were included in the famous Rules of the Game – *Daquiu Yishu.* The jiqiu balls were made of stone, tempered clay, leather stuffed with wool or feathers, or tightly sewn leather straps, depending on local traditions and periods of game development. The ball was hit with a wooden stick with a flat blade resembling the modern field hockey stick. The size of the playing field was not specified. Hitherto, only one ancient playing field, dating back to 831, has been found at the site of the palace complex of Daminggong located in the suburbs of modern Chang'an (or Changa, Singan). The location of the field and the precise rules of the game are inscribed on a stone stela. A jiqiu team was called a *peng* and the number of players varied. The wall paintings from the tomb of Prince Zhanghuai (653-684 AD) depict 20 jiqiu players. In *Jiu Tangshu*, Liu Xu explains that a stronger team typically allowed a weaker team to have a larger number of players. The work includes a description of a match played in 709 AD between the Chin. team of 4 players led by Li Longji, the future Emperor Xuanzong (712-756) and the team of the Kingdom of Tibet numbering 10 players. The match was held on the occasion of the wedding of the king of Tibet and a princess from the Han dynasty. Each player wore a tunic with legs tucked in leather boots. The horse saddles were lavishly decorated. Surviving ceramic figurines frequently represent both male and female players with various artistic hairstyle buns. The horse manes were mostly plaited into 3 angular buns called *sanhua* – 3 flowers. The number of hair buns indicated the player's social position. The figurines found in tombs indicated the sports achievements of the deceased, which gives evidence of the game's prestige. In the Samarkand region bordering the ancient Chin. Empire the Sogdian people played jiqiu in characteristic tunics with legs, referred to as *hufu* – the barbarian garment. The players also wore headdresses resembling the more contemporary Siberian garrison caps worn by the Red Army, although slightly taller. The teams were identified by different colors or patterns embroidered on the tunics or, in later periods, capes put on top. An 8th-cent. figurine presents a female jiqiu player wearing a thick soft loincloth, which in the opinion of many Chin. sports historians could have been an indication of team membership. Such loincloths were, however, rare and probably were part of a local custom. The matches were accompanied by military bands. The aim of the game was to put the ball in a small net spread out between two goalposts placed in the ground 40cm apart. The match was officiated by a court elder exercising the function of a judge. Apart from the adult horse games also children's games on horses and mules were played in ancient China. In trad. Chin. art many depictions of polo players have survived.

History. The traditions of jiqiu go back to the Han dynasty. The game enjoyed high prestige at the court of Emperor Xuanzong (see above) who ordered, in a special edict, that the game be practiced throughout the land. Jiqiu was extremely popular among the military. The impact of the imperial edict was considerable enough for the game to be played even in those regions of the country where natural conditions were unfavorable. At that time jiqiu was played by women as well. This is evidenced by ceramic figurines clearly showing female players. The number of such figurines may account for a kind of women's equality of rights in that sport. By the end of the 8th and into the 9th cent., the game was often criticized by Chin. clerics and philosophers particularly for its immorality, rising violence, cruelty and lack of noble spirit. Players that would fall off their horses were sometimes trampled. The criticism became more intense after the death of young Emperor Muzong (reigning briefly between 821 and 824) of wounds sustained during a match. Following heavy criticism of cruelty involved in jiqiu, Emperor Wuzong (841-846) ordered his army to surround jiqiu players on a field in 844 and sentenced a few of them to death as an example. The game's popularity, however, would not be quashed so easily. In the so-called Period of Five Dynasties (907-960) jiqiu continued to be played in N China where it gained enormous prestige. Emperor Shengzeng was commonly known as a great lover of the sport (983-1031). During his reign, characteristic attire was developed for the players including an elaborately embroidered cape. The emperor ordered the construction of numerous playing fields including one at present-day Beijing. In the N part of the country, which enjoyed a brief independence, a professional caste of players developed. During the reign of the N Emperor Taizong (976-997), the matches were played using horses from the emperor's great stud farms where the animals had been trained for the game. The emperor would arrive at the field with his entourage and be presented with a symbolic scarlet ball in a gold casket. Toasts by the courtiers and emperor's guard officers would follow in honor of the emperor as well as an exchange of gifts and then the game began. Emperor Huiziong (1101-25) eshewed jiqiu in preference of other ball games, esp. >CUJU. Imprisoned by his political opponents who favored jiqiu the emperor was forced to watch the abhorred sport and even write a poem in appraisal of the game. Since then a division of ball games in China has been observed. In the N, jiqiu was still popular until the 18th cent. but gradually lost its courtly character. More often jiqiu was played by peripheral nomadic tribes that bred horses and had easy access to the animals. At the same time, mainly in S China where agriculture and urbanization prevailed, the common folk and emperor's courts took more interest in local var. of football such as *cuju*, a sport popular among the Chinese during the reign of the Ming (1368) and Manchurian Cing (also spelled Ch'ing or Quing, 1644-1911) dynasties.

JITTERATHON, see >DANCE MARATHON.

JO DE PAUMO, a regional var. of the medieval game of >JEU DE LA PAUME (also >JEU DE COURTE PAUME). It originated in Picardie and Provence (France). [Provençal *jo* – game + *paumo* – palm of the hand] Cf. >JEU QUARRÉ, >JUEGO DE LA CHAZA. Cf. also >PAUME, >JEU DE LA PAUME.

JOCH DE LA CHOCA, see >CHOCA.

JÒC DE FERRADURA, see >FER À CHEVAL.

JOCKIE BLIND MAN, see >BLINDMAN'S BUFF.

JOGGING, a light run practiced for recreation or health, without the element of competition. The runner burns about 70-80 calories per kilometer. Jogging is beneficial to the respiratory and circulatory systems. The distance most often recommended by physicians is about 3km. An aquatic var. of the sport is known as >AQUA-JOGGING.

History. For decades jogging has been practiced as an introduction to an athlete's warm-up or a form of cooling off after a major effort, esp. after a competition or training session. In the late 1960s alarming statistics were published concerning the increase in circulatory and respiratory diseases among urban populations. The reason for this growth was a sedentary way of life, due mainly to the development of motor transport. Jogging was therefore recommended as a preventive measure. The pioneers of the sport were the Amer. physician Thaddeus Kostrubala and the creator of >AEROBICS, Kenneth H. Cooper. Jogging was quick to gain popularity. A 1978 study of the Gallup Institute showed that

A quick 5K to start off the day.

11% of Americans jogged, which amounted to 15 million runners. Jogging should be practiced in a natural environment, e.g. in forests or parks. For the lack of such places it is often pursued in the streets of large cities, where it may not bring the desired effects, on account of considerable air pollution.

J. Henderson, *Jogging*, EAI (1979, 16); T. Kostrubala, *The Joy of Running* (1976); W. Lipoński *Jak biegać po zdrowie* (1985); B. Mitchell, *Running to Keep Fit* (1980).

JOGGLING RACE, a running race combined with juggling 3 balls held over various distances and in a form of a relay. Attempts to make the event more versatile incl. increasing the number of juggled balls.

JOGO DA FERRADURA, a Port. horseshoe throwing game, played chiefly by men [Port. *jogo* – game + *ferradura* – horseshoe, *ferreoa* – iron]; (Cf. also >HORSESHOE PITCHING). The pitch is about 15m long and usu. 2-3m wide. 1 or 2 pegs (*paulitos*), 20cm high and about 3cm in diameter, are driven into the ground. Throws are made from 10-12m away. Each participant has 5 objects shaped like a horseshoe (in the past real horseshoes were used). The horseshoe must be thrown in such a way as to hit the peg (or pegs) and rotate around it before touching the ground. Such a throw brings 5pts. If none of the horseshoes rotates around the peg, then at the end of a round the player whose horseshoe is closest to the target gets 3pts. There are 2 possible ways to organize the game: either 1 player throws

all his horseshoes one after another, followed by his opponents' doing the same, or players take turns at throwing. In either case, the first to score 30pts. wins. Throws can be made in a variety of ways. The player can, for example, hold the horseshoe by its middle, arching part and send it flying ends forward, without spinning in mid-air. It is also possible to hold the horseshoe by one of its ends. In that case the horseshoe makes either a half-turn or a whole turn before hitting the peg and rotating around it.
M. da Graça Sousa Guedes, 'Jogo da Ferradura', JTP, 1979, 64-5.

JOGO DA LARANJINHA, a Port. game played in the Minho region [Port. *jogo* – game + *laranjinha* – orange]. Players throw a large wooden ball (20-30cm in diameter, with holes for a better grip) at a smaller one, the so-called 'orange' (*laranjinha*). The lane (20mx1m) is divided into 3 zones: 1) the throwing zone, which the thrower may not go beyond, 2) the zone over which the ball must fly; its length depends on the skill of the players, usu. 4-6m; if the ball lands in this zone, the throw is cancelled and the thrower loses his turn, 3) the zone in which the ball rolls, preferably in the direction of the laranjinha, 14-16m long. For every time his ball hits the laranjinha, the player gets 1pt., or *risco* [*risco* – a notch; the points used to be recorded with notches cut in a stick or drawn on the ground]. The first to score 10 riscos wins. A thrown ball is not removed from the lane until the other players' balls have been thrown. One of the var. of the game known in Alto Minha is called *jogo da pela* or *jogo da bola* [*pela, bola* – ball]. The lane is usu. bigger, about 30mx2m. There used to be a custom of playing the game on Sundays, after mass. In many Port. cities there are antique jogo da laranjinha courts, walled in with columns from 2 sides. The most beautiful, the *patio do jogo da pela*, can be found in Coimbra, in the Park of the Holy Cross (*Jardim de Santa Cruz*). Recently in some regions the game is being modified. The orange is replaced with 3 skittles, sometimes arranged in the shape of a triangle. The ball should knock the skittles down. This var. is called 'American orange' (see >LARANJINHA AMERICANA), although the ball that gave the game its name has been eliminated.
M. da Graça Sousa Guedes, 'Jogo da laranjinha', JTP, 1979, 65-7.

Jogo do avião.

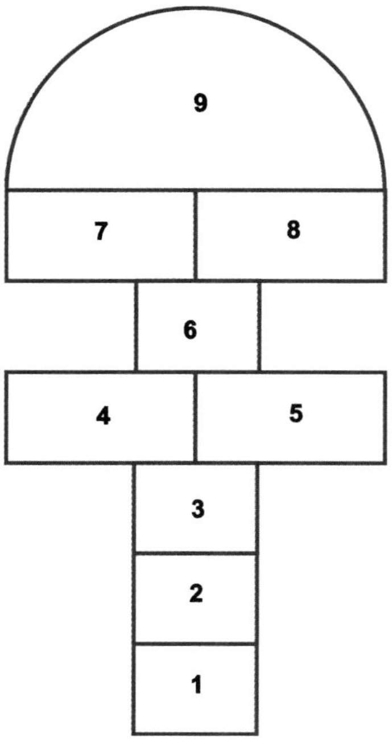

JOGO DA PÉL'A COVA, Port. for 'ball into the cove'. Players try to throw a ball into holes dug in the ground (the number holes corresponds to the number of players). Behind the row of holes there is a low wall. From one side the holes are blocked with a larger obstacle and from 2 sides – with bolsters made of sand or earth. Around all of this a large circular playing zone is marked. Players take care to get the ball into their own holes (they may use the back wall for this purpose). If the ball lands in another player's hole, all the players run away, except for the 'owner' of the hole, who chases after them and tries to hit someone with the ball. If he succeeds, he puts a stone (called *filho* – son) in the hole of the player he hit. If he misses, the *filho* is put in his hole. When someone gets 3-5 'sons' (depending on the agreement), he is out of the game. Whoever has the fewest 'sons' wins.
M. da Graça Sousa Guedes, 'Jogo da pél'a', JTP, 1979, 49-50.

JOGO DA PELOTA, a Port. folk version of >PELOTA VASCA, practiced in the region of Trás-so-Montes in NE Portugal, near the Span. border. It stems from more complex versions of similar games played in the Basq. regions of Spain and France. Two players bounce a ball against a high wall with their hands. There is a line on the wall 10m from the ground. Each time the ball is hit it must hit the wall above the line and then bounce on the ground. Players hit alternately. The serve is over when one player fails to hit the ball or if it hits the wall below the 10m line. This player loses a point and starts the next serve. Contestants may use either arm, and the overhand as well as the underhand, standing or jumping. The first to get 15pts. wins.
M. da Graça Sousa Guedes, 'Jogo da pelota', JTP, 1979, 67-8.

Jogo do pau.

JOGO DA PIPA, a Port. folk game involving a barrel [Port. *jogo* – game + *pipa* – barrel]. Players try to throw coins, bottle caps or small metal discs into a barrel with holes in the lid to score points. Sometimes particular scores may be attributed to certain discs or holes. The throwing distance is not officially determined.
M. da Graça Sousa Guedes, 'Jogo da pipa', JTP, 1979.

JOGO DA RAIOLA, a Port. folk game [Port. *jogo* – game + *raio* – ray], played mainly in the old province of Beira, now divided into 5 districts: Aveiro, Castelo Branco, Coimbra, Guarda and Viseu. Each player has a metal disc about 4-5cm in diameter or a large coin. They stand 8m (or in the case of lighter coins – 4m) away from a square divided by 2 central lines (known as 'rays') into 4 smaller squares. The player beginning the game declares which square he is aiming at. If he succeeds, he gets 5pts.; if all the players fail, 3pts. are awarded to the one whose coin was closest to the ray of the declared square. The game is played to 30pts. When one of the players gets 15pts. (and is in the lead), then the player with the lowest score has the right to change the position from which he throws (always keeping the distance of 4 or 8m from the square he is aiming at). Any player may suggest that the points for a toss be doubled (*dobragem*). If he misses, this score goes to his opponent.
M. da Graça Sousa Guedes, 'Jogo da raiola', JTP, 1979.

JOGO DA ROSA, see >JOGOS HÍPICOS.

JOGO DAS ANDAS, see >ANDAS.

JOGO DO ARCO, a Port. var. of >DRIVING A WHEEL [Port. *jogo* – game + *arco* – hoop]. Girls usu. trundled wooden hoops and boys metal ones, e.g. taken off a barrel or a bicycle. Races involving 7-8 people were very common. The hoop was pushed below half its height with a stick or metal rod with a u-shaped end. A thus trundled hoop was called *arco e gancheta* – a hoop with a hooked handle. Cf. the Arab >AD-DNANA
M. da Graça Sousa Guedes, 'Jogo do arco', JTP, 1979.

JOGO DO AVIÃO, Port. for 'the airplane game', similar to the Eng. >HOP-SCOTCH, Pol. KLASY, Dan. >AT HINKE, and Ger. >FUßSCHEIBENSPIEL. Children jump in a figure drawn on the ground. Here the figure is supposed to represent an airplane. It consists of 9 sub-figures. The game is begun from the 'tail', consisting of 3 squares. The 'first wing' consists of 2 crosswise rectangles (num. 4 and 5). Then there is one more square (num. 6), another 'wing' (7,8) and the cockpit (a semicircle, 9). Jumping on the 'wings', children must land with one foot in each of the two rectangles it consists of. See also the Port. >JOGO DO CARACOL and Arab >AL-HUD'D'A, >AL-HAGLA, >BERBER, >LU'BAT UMM AL-HUTUT, Pol. >KLASY.
M. da Graça Sousa Guedes, 'Jogo do avião', JTP, 1979.

JOGO DO CARACOL, a Port. children's game. Players hop on one leg on figures drawn on the ground. Here the figure is spiral-shaped like a snail's shell [Port. *jogo* – game + *caracol* – snail]. There are 11 sub-figures, 10 of them numbered and the middle one, called *ceu* – sky. The closer to the center, the smaller the figures get. The player tosses a small stone into each of the 'snail's' sub-figures and moves it with his foot. He must always hop one figure further than the one the stone is in, jumping over it. Having reached the center, the player goes back, each time tossing the stone one figure nearer. He loses his turn if he lands beyond the lines of the 'snail' or kicks the stone too hard. See also the Port. >JOGO DO AVIÃO, Eng. >HOP-SCOTCH, Arab >AL-HUD'D'A, >AL-HAGLA, >BERBER, >LU'BAT UMM AL-HUTUT, Dan. >AT HINKE, Ger. >FUß-SCHEIBENSPIEL, Pol. >KLASY.
M. da Graça Sousa Guedes, 'Jogo do caracol', JTP, 1979, 28-29.

JOGO DO ESPETO, Port. for 'the poker game' [Port. *jogo* – game + *espeto* – poker], a pastime popular in the province of Duoro Litoral. Four concentric circles, resembling those of a shooting target, are drawn on the ground. Players thrust a bar 40-50cm long, sharpened at one end, so that it lands as near to the center as possible. The smallest circle is worth 10pts., the following – 8, 6 and 4pts.; 2pts. are awarded if the poker lands in the area surrounding the largest circle. Participants aim from a few meters off (depending on skill) and to a previously agreed upon score.
M. da Graça Sousa Guedes, 'Jogos do espeto', JTP, 1979.

JOGO DO GALO, see >JOGOS HÍPICOS.

JOGO DO MALHO, a Port. folk game involving a sledgehammer (*malho de ferreiro*) and an iron ball (*bola de ferro*). Two exclusively male teams take part. A zigzagging lane is drawn on the ground. Wooden pegs are driven into the ground along it. The first player on a team puts the iron ball at the beginning of the lane and hits it with the sledgehammer. When the ball stops, another player hits it. This goes on until the ball gets to the end of the lane. The players hit the ball in such a way as to send it along the irregularities of the lane, but not beyond it. The team which completes the whole route with fewer hits, wins. Old descriptions of the sport remain vague as to the number and function of the pegs along the way. Perhaps they were supposed to be hit with the ball, or perhaps, on the contrary, avoided. Thus, some pegs may have meant a bonus score, while others a loss of points. Existing sources do not give the size or the weight of the ball, so those may have differed from region to region, or may simply have been taken for granted.
M. da Graça Sousa Guedes, 'Jogo do Malho', JTP, 1979.

JOGO DO PAU, a Port. var. of stick-fighting [Port. *jogo* – 'game, fun' + *pau* – 'stick']; considered the most typical of Portuguese folk sports; a kind of folk fencing practiced since the earliest times. The fight is conducted using long sticks whose length depends on the height of the players. A player stands holding the stick above his mouth. The sticks are made of wood without gnarls called *lodao*; the sticks were used by shepherds to drive away wild animals e.g. wolves and travelers used them for defense. Jogo do pau enjoyed enormous popularity in the Minhos region of N-W Portugal and Tras-os-Montes in the NE of the country, later being introduced to Lisbon. Jogo do pau is a subject of a considerable body of literature in Portugal. The best hitherto is the work by F. Hopfer *O jogo do pau* (On the Stick Fight) discussing the history, basic techniques and jogo do pau training. The first set of rules defining the conduct of fight and exercises was compiled by J.M. Saloio, an instructor of many disciples. In Portugal there are 3 schools of jogo do pau: 1) the Galician school (*escola galega*) popular in the Minhos and Tras-os-Montes regions, which promotes the thrust technique with the stick held in one hand, where, before making the thrust, the fighter rotates the stick above his head; 2) the Ribatejo school (*escola ribatejana*), also known as the *pateleira* school (*escola de pateleira*), characterized by short and accurate blows at close range and parrying the attacking opponent; and 3) the Lisbon school (*escola de Lisboa*), a defensive school with most sports features consisting of parrying the opponent's blows with similar blows but in reverse direction.
M. da Graca Sousa Guedes, 'Jogo do pau', JTP, 1979.

JOGO DO PAU-FERRO, Port. for 'the iron bar game', a folk pastime the object of which is throwing an iron bar sharpened at one end (a quarryman's crowbar – *pau ferro* – is often used). A line is drawn on the ground, marking the point throwers may not go beyond. Whoever makes the longest throw, wins, provided that the bar hits the ground with the sharpened end. In the regions of Minho, Trás-os-Montes and Douro e Beira Alta the bar does not have to dig into the ground, it is enough if it leaves a mark. However, a var. of the sport practiced in the region of Alentejo under the name of >BARRA requires that the bar be dug into the ground. The choice of throw-

ing technique is up to the competitors, who also determine the number of throws.

M. da Graça Sousa Guedes, 'Jogos do pau-ferro', JTP, 1979, 63.

JOGO DO PIÃO AS NICAS, a Port. var. of >PIÃO. See also >TOPS.

JOGO DO REBOLO, a Port. folk game played in the region of Beira Alta [Port. *jogo* – game + *rebolo* – a round whetstone. 2-4 players take part. There are 20 wooden skittles (*paulitos*) 30cm high and 1 wooden ball (*bola de buxo*) to each player. The pitch is 20x5m, with 20-30cm high pickets in the corners. Inside the pitch, about 3m from its shorter sides, there are 2 square (1x1m) slabs, usu. made of stone. Each of them holds 9 skittles, arranged in 3 rows of 3. One more skittle is placed 1.5m from the slab. This arrangement can be reversed (to face the opposite side of the pitch). There are 2 basic ways of playing the game: 1) *bota abaixo* [Port. knock, throw down] – consists simply of knocking down the opponent's skittles; whoever does it with fewer throws, wins; 2) after each player's turn the knocked over skittles are counted and then put back for the next round. The first to score 200pts. wins. A player scores 15pts. for knocking down the solitary skittle, 10pts. for each of the 3 middle skittles and 5 for any other. The etymology of the name is unclear. Perhaps in the past round whetstones were used instead of balls.

M. da Graça Sousa Guedes, 'Jogo do rebolo', JTP, 1979, 65.

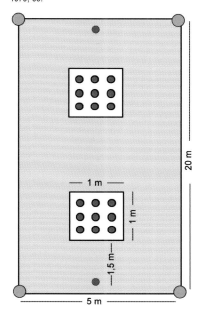

The pitch for jogo do rebolo.

JOGOS HÍPICOS, a Port. family of equestrian sports and games [Port. *jogos* – games + *hípicos* – equestrian]. Riders overcome various obstacles, ride over moving gangways, throw sticks, break clay balls, or snatch up objects from the ground at full gallop. In *jogo do galo* galloping contestants must catch a rooster and, without stopping, throw it into a cage a few meters away. In *jogo da rosa* participants must tear off a rose attached to the opponent's chest.

M. da Graça Sousa Guedes, 'Jogos Hípicos', JTP, 1979.

JOG/WALK, a recreational sport in which jogging is alternated with walking, depending on the fitness of the competitor. The idea was first presented in 1983 by the Singapore Sports Council and other organizations. That year 2 existing events, the National Walk (1971) and the National Jog (1975) were merged into one. In 1983 11,612 contestants took part; in 1990 this number increased to 29,152. To avoid overcrowding, starting points are set in many places: the MacRitchie Reservoir, Queenstown Stadium, Bedok South Secondary School, Toa Payoh Stadium, Delta Stadium, Hougang Stadium and Marina Park. The finish line is in the National Stadium. The distance, depending on the starting point, is 8-10km. All social groups take part, e.g. students, police officers, clerks, pensioners and even state officials. Often whole families participate – this makes it possible to classify jog/walk as a family sport. Every contestant, regardless of their time, receives a jog/walk completion badge. The event is held under the auspices of the Singapore Sports

A modern playground.

Council. Cf. >SMOKE-FREE WALK, >JOGGING, >RACE WALKING.

'Record 29,152 Participants at National Jog/Walk', SS, Aug. 1990; 'Jog/Walk Towards a Healthy Lifestyle', SS, Oct. 1991.

JOHNNY ON A BARREL, a water skill game with the use of a barrel and, fastened inside it, a pole which the player must climb. Described by a Russian scholar I.N. Chkhannikov, it was designed for holiday centers and water spas. 'Cross-bars are fastened to the bottom of the barrel and to the lid. Through the holes in the cross-bars a pole 3.5-4m in length is driven into the barrel, which is filled with sand up to 1/3 of its volume. Climb the pole to its top, before the pole leans down to the point when one must jump into the water'.

I.N. Chkhannikov, *GIZ*, 1953, 83.

JOKKE UGLER, Dan. for 'kicking owls', a demonstration of agility and strength. Hanging on the tie beam in the hayloft head down on one's calves, one must try to curl one's knees, thus bumping one's bottom against the beam.

J. Møller, 'Jokke ugler', GID, 1997, 3, 100.

JORDAN'S PLAYGROUNDS, the name applied to children's recreational centers in Poland, and the movement associated with them, modeled on similar initiatives in W Europe. The name derives from the name of the originator, H. Jordan (1842-1907), a physician and Ph.D. at the Jagiellonian University in Cracow, Poland. Jordan was also an activist and pioneer of modern recreation and sport for children and teenagers. In 1888, with the authorization of Cracow's Municipal Council (of which he was a member), he began building a playground at his own cost. The playground was partially modeled on >FRÖBEL'S PLAYGROUNDS and the achievements of the Eng. and Amer. playground movement, with some ideas of Jordan's own. The first playground was opened in 1889. Jordan's tried to put into effect the idea of making sports and games more democratic so as to include the lower classes. At the same time, the movement aimed at awakening and supporting a Pol. national consciousness at a time when an independent Pol. state was lacking. After 1890, Jordan's playgrounds started spreading, first to the other cities and towns of the (then Austrian) province of Galizien, and then throughout Poland, competing with other similar ideas, such as those of Fröbel's playgrounds and >RAU'S PLAYGROUNDS. The playground movement was an important factor contributing to the overcoming of the conservatism and conventionality of physical education teaching which in those times was mainly based on hackneyed gymnastic routines unappealing to the children's imagination. As opposed to Fröbel's playgrounds, which were quite static educationally, Jordan's playgrounds introduced sports in the Eng. and Amer. way – through natural movements such as those used in athletic events and various ball games, including elements of football and tennis for older children, where it was ahead of physical education at schools by about 60 years.

JORDEN ER GIFTIG, Dan. for 'the ground is poisonous', [Dan. *jorde* – ground + *er* – is + *giftig* – poisonous], a folk game in which catchers and runners may not touch the ground, but must use anything else in the area to get around. If a runner

touches the ground, he becomes the catcher or is eliminated from the game.

J. Møller, 'Jorden er giftig', GID, 1997, 2, 14.

JOUTES GIRONDINES, a Fr. folk sport where contestants, standing in boats, fight with long poles resembling knights' spears. Popular in the department of Gironde, at the mouth of 2 rivers, Garonne and Dordogne, which flow into the Bay of Biscay. This estuary is also called Gironde, hence the name of the sport [Fr. *joute* – duel, fight + *girondine* – of Gironde]. The joutes girondines originated in the late Middle Ages and flourished in the 16th-17th cent. See also >BOAT JOUSTING, >JOUTES LANGUEDOCIENNES.

JOUTES LANGUEDOCIENNES, boat jousting practiced in towns of the Fr. province of Languedoc: Agde, Aigues Mortes, Maguelone, Port St. Louis du Rhône, Sète and Frontignan (see >BOAT JOUSTING). The most colorful event is held in Sète, a port in the Hérault department, situated on a lagoon between the lake Etang de Berre and the Mediterranean Sea. The tradition dates back to 1666, when the port was founded. Boats from Sète and Frontignan compete, painted respectively red and blue, for easier distinction. Each boat, about the size of a fishing boat, has 20 oarsmen. There is an extra wooden deck attached to the stern. On the deck there

Jog/walk with hard weights.

Johnny on a barrel.

J

WORLD SPORTS ENCYCLOPEDIA

continued on next page...

stands a spearman with a spear about 2.5m long and a shield. In order not to hurt his opponent, the spearman may tilt only at the shield, which has a few concavities and a protective rim to prevent the spear slipping off it. Two opposing boats come from opposite directions and pass each other as close as possible. At this moment the spearmen try to knock each other into the water with their spears. The audience is assembled in riverside cafès and provisory stands. See also >JOUTES GIRONDINES, >JOUTES LYONNAISES.

J. Møller, 'Dystløb', GID, 1997, 4, 77; C. Pegeassou, 'Les joutes languedociennes. Le Prix de la tradition dans les enjeux de la modernité', *Entre tradition et modernité – le sport*, 1995, 24-31.

JOUTES LYONNAISES, a Fr. folk sport practiced in Lyon, imitating chivalric tournaments [Fr. *joute* – duel, fight + *lyonnais* – of the city Lyon]. Contestants fight in boats rather than on horseback. Popular at least since the mid-16th cent., probably even since the close of the Middle Ages, on the river Rhône. See also >BOAT JOUSTING, >JOUTES LANGUEDOCIENNES, >JOUTES GIRONDINES.

JOWLS, a trad. Eng. game resembling >FIELD HOCKEY and >SHINTY, played chiefly in the 18th and 19th cent. in Yorkshire, esp. near Whitby.

A ju jutsu fight.

JU JUTSU, also *ju-jitsu* [Jap. in Eng. transliteration *ju* – subtle + *jutsu* – skill, art], a Jap. method or school (*ryu*), or rather a family of schools and methods of defence and defeating the opponent by means of using and directing the opponent's energy and strength against him. Contrary to >JUDO (a sport deriving from ju jutsu), it involves holds that are dangerous to health and even life threatening, employed for the purpose of self-defence. After 1945 ju jutsu began to evolve as an independent sport, in which the most dangerous holds are barred. There are currently 2 main var. of ju jutsu:

The duo-system – aimed at displaying defence holds. Competition takes place between 2 pairs, of which one wears a red and the other a white belt. A bout is administered by 5 judges, each of whom may award marks on a 1-10pt. scale. The 2 extreme marks are discarded. The evaluation includes the attack and preparation for defence, as well as general effectiveness, attitude, self-control, and the efficiency of application of various techniques. The methods of attack are divided into 4 groups and the selection of appropriate defence is at the contestant's discretion.

The fighting system – the bout is fought in full contact by 2 contestants, according to precisely defined strikes and kicks targeted above the waist, throws, and holds on the ground. It is administered by a mat referee and 2 side referees. Decisions are made according to a principle of simple majority and are considered ultimate. The referees announce a *wazari* or *ippon* by raising a white- or red-sleeved hand; they also award points for a successful application of various techniques and announce penalties. Since 1998 W.Ch. are held in the following weight categories: women – up to 55, 62, 70, and above 70kg; men – up to 61, 69, 77, 85, 94, and above 94kg.

History. Although in modern times ju jutsu is closely connected with the samurai tradition, its oldest forms originated in India probably in the 10th cent. Later it spread to China, which adopted a more general approach to fighting, modelled after the idea of 'in yielding is strength', put forward by a Chin. strategist Hwang Shihkon. Japan became the last link in the chain of ju jutsu tradition, but it attributed it with the highest social significance and splendor. According to a Jap. document entitled *Kokushoji* ju jutsu was introduced to Japan by a Chin. monk Chen Yuan-Ping in 1627, although there is ample evidence that various Jap. ju jutsu masters, such as Hitotsubashi-Joken or Sekigushi-Jushin, operated years before the above date, while descriptions of ju jutsu can be found in such documents as *Yukisenjo Monogatari*, *Kuyamigusa*, or *Densho*, which predate 1627. This indicates that ju jutsu entered Japan in different varieties and at different times. More extensive research indicates that Chen Yuan-Ping has, in fact, introduced >KENPO, a var. of Chin. boxing, from which ju jutsu adopted certain striking techniques. No single historical model of ju jutsu exists, but rather there are various elements, identified in different regions and at different times, which evolved into separate varieties. One such prototype was the style of fighting called *yoroi kumi-uchi*. An old Jap. work *Bujutsu-Ryusoroku* (*Biographies of the Founders of Various Martial Exercise Schools*) mentions some 20 *ryu*, or schools of ju jutsu, including >DAITO RYU AIKI JU JUTSU, >KITO, >KYUSHIN, >TAKENOUCHI, >TENCHIN SHIN'YO. The split into a multitude of various schools took place in the Edo era, when the number of different *ryus* allegedly reached 700. In fact, various records name only 179 *ryus*, without offering any further details, except that they taught both the techniques of hand-to-hand combat and those involving the use of weapons. One of the first masters of the hand-to-hand ju jutsu technique was Takenouchi Hisamori (1502-1595), who founded the Takenouchi-ryu. The tradition of his technique was continued by various schools, which began to form the proper history of ju jutsu. They included the schools of Sekiguchi, founded by Sekiguchi Uijmune (1597-1670); Kito, founded by master Terada Massahige (1618-1674); Shibukawa, founded by Shibukawa Yoshikata (1652-1704); or Tenshin Shin'yo, founded by Iso Masatari (1786-1863). In the 17th and 18th cent. the styles of ju jutsu began to form one of the skills of *budo*, a martial art that allowed the samurai to dominate over the common people. The development of civilization and processes of democratization rendered ju jutsu useless in its traditional application. The emperor's order of 1871 banned certain samurai traditions, including the public display of weapons, which further lowered the significance of ju jutsu as a supplementary form of fighting with side-arms. In the middle of the 1880s dr. Jigoro Kano used the elements of ju jutsu, especially those deriving from the Kito and Tenchin Shin'yo schools, to form the concept of judo. That started a period of rivalry between judo and ju jutsu in Japan, with the former centered

around the famous Kodokan school of judo and the latter – around the Totsula school of ju jutsu. In 1886 the Police Council of Tokyo decided to test the usefulness and effectivess of both schools in action and held a tournament in which 15 students of each school participated. Out of 15 bouts 13 were won by the students of the school of judo, while 2 ended in a tie. The popularity of ju jutsu began to decrease until it was discovered that in life-threatening situations, which required not only to gain advantage, but to permanently immobilize the opponent, ju jutsu had a great advantage over judo. And so, especially in the 1920s and later, ju jutsu became part of the training routine of special police and military squads. In present times it is used along with various other martial arts and the Izraeli >KRAV MAGA to train the anti-terrorist squads.

The development of ju jutsu as a sport began after WWII on the initiative of Eur. countries, first under the auspices of the Eur. Ju Jutsu Union (EJJU) and the International Ju Jutsu Federation (IJJF). The similarity of the acronyms of IJJF and IJF (International Judo Federation) led the former in 1997 to change its name into Ju Jutsu International Federation (JJIF). The organization promotes the development of ju jutsu among men and women. The leading athletes come from the Netherlands and Germany. Japan at first tried to ignore the sporting var. of ju jutsu and did not enter the international competition until 1998. The most prominent official in the development of sporting ju jutsu is the former President of JJIF, Rinaldo Orlandi.

L. Frederic, *A Dictionary of the Martial Arts*, 1991; G. Kirby, *Jujitsu: Basic Techniques of the Gentle Art*, 1983; D. Mitchell, *The New Official Martial Arts Handbook*, 1989; D. Musser, T.A. Lang, *Jujitsu Techniques and Tactics*, 1999; K. Nakae, C. Yeager, *Jiu Jitsu Complete*, 1974; H. Reuter, *Jiu Jitsu. Ein Lehrbuch fuer Selbstverteidigung*, 1924.

JUDO, [Jap. *ju* – gentle + *do* – art, way], a method of self defense without weapons, using psychology and hidden motorial qualities of the human body, based on the old Jap. martial art of >JU JUTSU, but differing from it by the elimination of life-threatening holds and throws. It strongly stresses the philosophy, as well as the ethical dimension of sports fighting. In a moment of real danger it allows one to overpower the opponent without hurting him. A characteristic feature of judo is that contestants fall in such a way that the largest possible area of the body touches the ground, which minimizes the consequences of the fall.

Rules. In Jap. the fight is called *shiai* and the contestants *judoka*. The fight length used to be 3-20min. Now in major international events, such as the Ol.G., it is 3-7min. Victory can be achieved in a number of ways. The first and most highly prized is the *ippon* – the winner throws his opponent so that he falls on his back or his side; the winner does not lose his balance and has to hold the opponent down for 30sec. or force him to surrender with a chokehold or nelson. Surrendering can be communicated by

Men's judo.

Women's judo.

hitting the mat twice with the hand or by saying *maitta* – 'I surrender'. Winning is also possible by way of a double *wazari* (an 80-90% correct throw or holding the opponent down for 25-29sec.). Two *wazari* are treated as a single *ippon*. For a less effective throw or holding the opponent down for 20-24sec. the judoka is awarded a *yuko* (a 'near-wazari'). For a rather ineffective throw or holding the opponent down for 10-15sec. the contestant gets a *koka* (a 'near-yuko'). The fighting technique consists of throws (*nagewaza*), to be completed by using arms, legs, hips and holds known as *katamewaza*. The katamewaza can be classified into holds (*osaekomiwaza*), nelsons (*kansetsuwaza*) and chokeholds (*shimewaza*). Sometimes the contestant falls down in such a way as to make the opponent lose his balance. Prearranged show fights, known as *naganokata,* are fought using holds described as *katame-nokata*. Kicking and hitting with the hands is not allowed. Penalties are given for fouls, feinting, making the fight dangerous (esp. actions placing the spine and neck at risk) and avoiding fighting. The lowest penalty is the reprimand *shido*, the next – a warning *chui* and admonition *keikoku*. The highest is disqualification – *hansokumake*, which ends the fight. Each penalty is of advantage to the wronged party. A *shido* means a *koka*, a *chui* means a *yuko* and a *keikoku* – a *wazari*. The winner is called *tori* and the loser *uke*. The fight is supervised by one chief referee, 2 assistant judges sitting in the opposite corners of the mat, 2 time judges and a recorder. If, during the time provided for, neither of the contestants wins by *ippon* and the other elements point to a draw, another 5-min. round is ordered by the referee, during which the fight continues until the first point is scored (the 'golden point' rule). The referee gives commands in Japanese, e.g.:

Hajime – begin
Matte – separate
Sono-mama – do not move further (when the contestants are at the end of the mat)
Yoshi – go on, do not stop fighting
Jikan – the end
Hantei – decision (awaited from the assistant judges)
Sore-made – that is all, the end
Osaekomi – holding down
Toketa – interruption (when the contestant being held down manages to pull free).

Attire and gear. Contestants wear white or off-white suits called *judogi*. The *judogi* consists of a jacket, a pair of trousers and a belt. The trousers are wide (10-15cm from the contestant's leg to the trouser leg) and reach 5cm above the ankle. The jacket must be long and wide enough to cover the hips even when girded. Loose sleeves reach halfway down the forearm. Women must wear a T-shirt under the jacket. The belt is girded twice and tied in a flat knot, with the ends 20-30cm. To distinguish among contestants the belts come in 2 colors: red and white. In the '80s and '90s there was great pressure to introduce color suits in order to make it easier for TV-viewers to tell the contestants apart. A great supporter of this idea was a Dutch IOC member A. Gessink, who in the '60s was the first non-Japanese

contestant to achieve great success in the discipline. The attempt to introduce color suits, however, was unsuccessful, on account of strong judo traditions and their wide support. The color of the belt corresponds to the contestant's level of skill. The beginner's degrees are called *kyu*, which means 'student'. The beginner starts with the lowest, 6th degree, the *rokkyu*. The highest degree is the brown belt, *ikkyu*. The 10 master's degrees are called *dan*. The highest dan is *shodan*, indicated with a black belt. In sports, contestants rarely ever go beyond the 5th dan – *godan*. Judoka competing in international events usu. have the 4th or 5th dan. Higher degrees, awarded for exceptional ethical virtues or services to the sport, are of honorary character and reach the 12th dan, as yet never awarded. The institution awarding the highest dan is the Kodokan, a Jap. school and judo center, founded by Dr. Kano. There have also been cases of demoting a contestant for unethical behavior. In trad. fights the contestants are matched according to their degrees. In international competitions the decisive factor is victory in the qualifying rounds. The fighting takes place on the *tatami*, a mat 16x16m. It is allowed only in the center (10x10m). In 1972 a 1m wide belt was introduced called the 'danger area', thus limiting the 'safety area' to 9x9m.
Etiquette. In the oldest form of Jap. judo the etiquette was very complex. There were strict rules of bowing to the opponent, to the public and to the gods. This was respected even during training sessions. On coming into the training room (*dojo*) the judoka knelt on the mat, bowing to his teacher, the symbol of his organization (in competition – to a flag) and, depending on his religion, to a Buddha statue or a Shinto altar. After the training session (or the fight) was over, he gave the same series of bows, only in reverse order. In modern judo this procedure has been much simplified. Before the fight the contestants approach each other, stopping about 4m away and bowing low. After the fight they go back to their places and bow after the outcome has been announced by the judges. The bow is compulsory each time the judoka enters the dojo or leaves it.
Weight categories. Judo has 7 male and 7 female weight categories. The female categories are: up to 48kg, 52kg, 57kg, 63kg, 70kg, 78kg and above 78kg. The male categories are: up to 60kg, 66kg, 73kg, 81kg, 90kg, 100kg, and above 100kg. Until the 1984 Ol.G. in Los Angeles (inclusive) there was an 8th, all-weight category. There are also 5 team categories: up to 52kg, 57kg, 63kg, 70kg, and above 70kg (women) and up to 66kg, 73kg, 81kg, 90kg, and above 90kg (men).
History. The creator of judo was Jigoro or Jigarno Kano (1860-1938), a professor of Jap. philology. During his studies at the Tokyo University he came into contact with H. Wilson, a popularizer of Amer. sports in Japan. Initially Kano grew very interested in baseball, but then decided to use elements of his native culture to popularize sports in Japan. His determination grew stronger after his journey to England, where sports enjoyed high social prestige. On his return to Japan he created the discipline that would evolve to become judo, based on the >JU

JUTSU tradition. In this context ju jutsu was treated as a higher level of initiation, accessible to those who mastered judo. Outside Japan during the first decades the 2 names were used alternately. In 1882 Kano founded Kodokan, a sports school in which he taught judo. His goal was to teach his followers not only a new sports technique, but also certain ethical principles. The position of the teacher and master (*sensei*) is similar to that of the philosopher in an ancient Gk. gymnasium. Judo rules were finally set in 1888. In 1889 Kano made a journey across Europe, trying to popularize the sport. This effort was only partly successful. In 1911 Kano founded the Jap. Judo Federation. Judo was pronounced a national Jap. sport already during his lifetime (and the sport started being taught in schools). Outside Japan the first judo club came into being in 1895 in Great Britain, but it existed only for a short time. The first permanent club (Budokai) was founded in 1918 in Great Britain. In France and Germany the first clubs appeared in the '20s and '30s. In 1932 the Eur. Judo Union, EJU, was founded, and in 1951 – the International Judo Federation, IJF, was established. W.Ch. have been held since 1956. Jigoro Kano, and later his son Risei, tried in vain to introduce judo into the Olympic program. The first Ol.G. hosting judo were the 1964 Tokyo games (4 male categories). The 1968 Ol.G. in Mexico City did not include the sport. In 1972 and 1976 judo was held in 6 weight categories; in 1980 and 1984 in eight. Since the 1988 Ol.G. in Seoul there have been 7 judo categories. Female judo was first held in Seoul, but only as a show discipline. It was not until 1992 (Barcelona) that female judo was held as a regular discipline (and in 7 categories). In the first decades of the sport's existence it was naturally dominated by the Japanese, but in the 1961 W.Ch. it was a Dutchman, A. Geesink, who won the gold medal in the all-weight category (he repeated his success 3 years later and became Olympic champion during the 1964 Ol.G. in Tokyo).
L. Frederic, *A Dictionary of the Martial Arts*, 1991; D. Mitchell, *The New Official Martial Arts Handbook*, 1989; J. Pedro, *Judo: Techniques and Tactics*, 2001; J. Sławski, *Judo – pierwszy krok*, 1997; B. Tenger, *Bruce Tegner's Complete Book of Judo*, 1975.

JUDO FOR THE DISABLED, a var. of >JUDO adapted for the needs of persons with various disabilities. The regulations are based on those of the International Judo Federation (IJF) with regard to the type of disability. Bouts are held on mats with varied textures indicating competition area and zones, thus allowing athletes who are blind or have a visual impairment to compete. The sport was included in the program of the Paralympic Games in Seoul in 1988. Cf. also >SPORTS FOR THE DISABLED.

JUEGO DE FRONTON, a general Span. term for ball games (>PELOTA) played against a wall, rather than between partners, as in tennis.

JUEGO DE BOLOS, a general Span. term for skittles [Span. *juego* – game + *bolo* – skittle or ball], to be distinguished from the similar *juego de bolas*, which means >LAWN BOWLING. The term juego de bolos comprises various international kinds of >EUROPEAN BOWLING, as well as numerous folk var. of skittles. The games differ in rules and technical aspects depending on region and local tradition, e.g. > BOLO BURGALÉS, >BOLOS ARAGONESES, >BOLOS ASTURIANOS, >BOLOS CÁNTABROS, >BOLOS GALLEGOS, >BOLOS RIOJANO, >BOLOS SERRANOS and *bolos andaluces*. Some regional var., however, have become popular beyond their provinces of origin:
BOLOS DE TRES TABLONES, or 'three-board skittles', takes its name from 3 boards, or rather beams, at least 3.8m long, 35cm wide and 20cm thick. Three skittles are placed on each beam (9 in all). The beams are dug horizontally into the ground so that they stick out about 3-4cm above ground level. The distance dividing the nearest skittles is 110cm, so that all of them form a square (220x220cm). The boards are parallel to the direction of throwing. The board on the right is called *calle de pulgar* (alley of the thumb) or *calle de la derecha* (alley on the right). The board on the left – *calle de la mano* (alley of the hand) or *calle de la izquierda* (alley on the left). The middle board is simply called *calle de medio* (alley in the middle). The lane in which the boards are placed is 26m long and 6m wide and divided into 3 crosswise zones: 1) the throwing zone (*zona de tiro*),

Juego de bolos.

J

9.6m long; 2) the board zone, 4.8m long; and 3) the end zone (*zona de birle*), where the balls come to rest. The conical skittles are made of wood and reinforced at the base with iron rings. Walnut balls are preferred, but in some regions balls made of elm, beech or poplar are used. The diameter varies greatly from region to region, the weight being anywhere from 2.5 to 4kg. The object of the game is to throw the ball in such a way that it rolls on the board, knocking down the skittles. Each player (or team) has 4 throws in one turn, i.e. one throw for every board plus one extra, reserved for the board where the skittles were not knocked down. The game may be played individually or in teams of 2, 3 or 4. In individual games each player has 2 balls, in team games – one. The lanes (*bolera*) are flat, usu. made of a mixture of sand and well-hardened clay. The game is played chiefly in the province of Burgos, but also in Asturias, Cantabria and the Basque Region (Alava).

BOLOS LEONÉS, Span. for 'lion's eggs'. The game consists in knocking down 10 skittles with a hemisphere. The hemisphere is made of holm oak wood and its weight and size depends on the age category. For children the diameter is 10-13cm and the weight – 0.6kg; for seniors correspondingly 13-16cm and 0.8-1kg; for juniors and veterans 12-15cm and 0.8kg. The skittles are slender, truncated cones. Rules set up by the Span. Bowling Federation (Federación Española de Bolos) recommend 55cm high skittles with the base 10cm in diameter and the top 4cm in diameter for seniors and for lower age categories – correspondingly 50, 8 and 3.5cm. The lane is 25-30m long and 9-10m wide. about 0.5m from one end there is a square (1.3x1.3m), where the thrower stands. At the opposite side of the lane there is a circle 2.25m in diameter (until 1990 – 2.5-3.0m). Its circumference is called *raya de parada*, which the hemisphere should not go beyond. In this circle there is a square in which 9 skittles are placed in 3 rows. For seniors the side of the square is 1.4m and for younger contestants – 1.24m. The distance dividing the nearest skittles is 55cm for seniors and 50cm for younger players. Besides the 9 skittles there is another, known as *miche*, 30cm high, with the base diameter 7cm and the top diameter 3cm (for younger categories correspondingly 28, 6.5 and 3cm). The miche is placed on the player's right hand side, 70cm from the second row of skittles (62cm for younger contestants). The object of the game is to knock down as many skittles as possible (1pt. is awarded for each skittle). If any of the skittles knocks down the miche, the contestant is awarded 4pts. (hence the alternative name for the miche – *cuatro* – four). Bolos leonés is probably a derivative of the Flem. game of >PIERBOL, possibly brought to Spain by soldiers occupying the Netherlands from 1566-1609. It may also have originated from the French *jeu de siam*, one of the more important bowling games in W Europe. Bolos leonés is now played mainly in the area of Zaragoza, Madrid, Barcelona, and Bilbao. It is presided over by the Span. Bowling Federation. See also >FOOLISH BOWLING.

BOLO MURCIANO, a game played in the region of Murcia and Huerta, as well as Barcelona, Madrid and Valencia. The lane (*bolera*) is 36-40m long and 4-5m wide. The throwing area (*zona de tiro*) is 12m long, the lane is 20m long and the skittle zone (*zona de bolos*) – 8m long. The lane ends with a palm tree fence, which stops balls that are thrown over zeal-

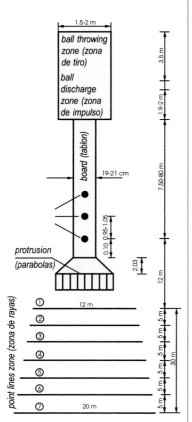

The pitch for playing pasabolo-tablón

Bolos leonés.

Juego de bolos.

ously. The balls are made of teakwood (*teca*), measure 10-11.5cm in diameter and weigh (depending on local tradition) 800-1,050g. The skittles are made of teakwood, guaiacum or olivewood. They are slender truncated cones 75cm in height, with a base diameter of 7cm, tapering to 3cm at the top. There are 2-3 players per team, each of whom has one throw per round (*mano*). The game is usu. played to 30 *manos*. It is known in numerous var., depending on the number and shape of the figures the skittles are arranged in as well as throwing techniques. It is therefore preceded by a draw determining which of the teams has the right to pick the skittle arrangement (the other decides on the throwing technique). The skittles are usu. placed 15-30cm from one another and formed into rectangles with various positioning in relation to the line of throwing.

BOLO PALMA, 'palm bowling', played on a flat surface, usu. a public square. The pitch is about 35m long and 8m wide, surrounded with a board. Within the pitch there is a lane 14-20m long. The throws are made from a distance of 14, 16, 18 or 20m, depending on the skill of the players. The 9 skittles, placed 65cm from one another, are arranged into a square. Each stands on an iron peg, at least as big as the base of the skittle. The pegs are fixed to a special wooden crate which is embedded into the ground so that the tops of the pegs are level with the ground. Behind the skittles there is the *campo de birle* that the balls roll into after hitting the skittles. The balls are 18cm in diameter and weigh 1.8-2.0kg. The skittles are traditionally made of wood with metal reinforcement at the base and measure 42cm in height, though it is becoming increasingly popular to use skittles which are only 28cm high. Players get 1pt. for every skittle they knock down. Individual games are played to 20pts., doubles to 35pts., triples to 50pts. and quadruples to 40pts. The game originated from local traditions of Cantabria and Asturias. In the 13th cent. it spread to the provinces of Burgos, Alava, Castille, Andalusia, Aragon, Navarra and the Basque Province, and is now known throughout Spain.

BOLOS DEL BIERZO, a kind of bowling which originated in the town of Bierzo (in the León Province), but known also in the region of Asturias and the province of Lugo. It comes in many var., all of which have a number of common features: 1) the balls are placed on a slab of stone; 2) players throw from a distance of 4-6m; 3) the skittles are conical and all of the same size, usu. 15-20cm high (as opposed to many other Iberian bowling games, where the skittles are of different sizes); 4) the skittles are placed 10-20cm from one another; 5) the object of the game is twofold: to knock down skittles and to get them beyond a line located some 20m from the throwing point; 6) throws are made with elongated oval balls of different sizes. The only exception is *juego del cuadro* ('game of four'), played in Oencia and Barjas, a mixture of games popular in Nierzo and Maragateria. 9 wooden skittles are arranged in the form of a square. The lane is 20-40m long. Other features of juego del cuadro correspond to the bolos del bierzo description (conical skittles of uniform size).

BOLOS SORIANOS, a bowling game played in the town of Soria, in NE Spain, as well as in Castilla and León. It is played exclusively by women. Its masculine counterpart is *juego de bolillos* (see be-

low). The object of bolos sorianos is to knock down 10 conical skittles (40-50cm high). One of them is larger than the others and, depending on local tradition, called *minga, pinca* or *cinca*. The skittles are usu. arranged into a circle with the minga in the middle. 1pt. is given for every knocked down skittle. The game is usu. played to 50-60pts.

JUEGO DE BOLILLOS [*bolillo* – bobbin] there are 6 conical skittles with round heads (15cm high). They are arranged in 2 rows of 3. Instead of a ball, a 15cm long wooden block (shaped like 2 cones joined by the bases) is used for throwing. There are 3 throws per round. The player to knock down the most skittles wins.

PASABOLO-TABLÓN, 'ball on the board' [*pasa* – passage + *bolo* – skittle + *tablón* – board], bowling game played on a very complicated lane known (just as in other Span. games of this sort) as *bolera* – bowling alley, or *carrejo* – corridor. The game is a less complex derivative of *pasabolo de tres tablones* (*bolos de tres tablones* – vide supra). It is played chiefly in Cantabria, Castille, León and the Madrid area. The bolera is 55m long. It begins with the 5m long throwing zone (*zona de tiro*). The board zone (*zona de tablón*) is next, 8m long and 19-21cm wide. Near the end of it 3 skittles are placed one after another (95-105cm away from each other). The last is 10cm from the end of the board. The 33-35cm high skittles are made of holly or holm oak. They weigh 200g, measuring 3cm in diameter in the middle and 1.5cm at the top and at the base. The ball is made of walnut or beech, measures 22-25cm in diameter and has 2 finger holes. The player must knock down the skittles. Points are awarded depending on how far the ball goes (which zone it reaches) after knocking the skittles down. The zones are marked with 7 crosswise lines – *rajas* – drawn 5m apart. The 1st raja is 12m from the end of the board. Each raja is longer than the previous one (the first is 12m and the last is 20m), so that the further away a zone is the bigger it is. This is in answer to the ball's tendency to drift off course as it rolls along. The 1st raja is worth 10pts., the 2nd – 20pts., the 3rd – 30pts., the 4th – 40pts., the 5th – 50pts., the 6th – 60pts., and the 7th – 70pts. If, however, the ball fails to knock down all the skittles, the 1st raja brings only 1pt.

History. According to Span. sports historians, juego de bolos can be traced back to Roman times (201 BC-409 AD), with Roman troops bringing the sport to the Iberian Peninsula. The first mention of juego de bolos after ancient times dates from the 11th cent. Initially most games of this family were referred to as *juego de birlas* or *juego de birlos*. Nowadays these terms are used to describe only some var. of the sport, esp. those played in Aragon. In the 16th cent., during the reign of Carlos I (1516-56) and Felipe II (1556-98), juego de bolos was already fully developed, compared to similar games in other countries, which even imported some of its features. References to the sport can be found in many literary works, often in the form of sharp criticism, e.g. in the moral treatise of F.L. Faxardo *Bitter Yet True Arguments Against Idleness and Games (Fie desengaño contra la ociosidad y los juegos*, 1603*)*. In 1627 the Santander city council banned juego de bolos under penalty of 200 maravedos (small coins in circulation from 1474-1848). In 1632

the sport was banned on all holidays in the province of Alava. This restraint was in force until 1829. Despite severe criticism and restrictions juego de bolos survived and in the 19th cent. flourished like never before. The competition of modern bowling weakened its position in Span. cities, but failed to eliminate it from the countryside. Nowadays trad. Span. bowling games are among the best preserved sports of this type in Europe. According to data supplied in the early 1990s by C.M. Palos juego de bolos is practiced in 62 small towns and villages in the province of Leon, 51 in Santander, 43 in Burgos, 26 in Cuenca, 23 Palencia and 21 in Asturias. Out of 50 modern-day provinces of Spain trad. folk bowling is still practiced in 41. The total number of villages keeping trad. bowling alive is 407. Juego de bolos is least popular in great urban areas, such as those of Madrid and Toledo, each having just one village where old bowling traditions are cultivated. Nearly every local community playing juego de bolos has developed its own specific form of playing. The sport is practiced under the auspices of the General Assembly of the Span. Bowling Federation (Asamblea General de Federación Española de Bolos) and numerous regional sports councils. Sometimes bowling games of the Basques are mistakenly included in the Span. traditions of juego de bolos. This is an oversight when one considers that Basques are ethnically distinct from the Spanish. Therefore Basq. games are described under a separate entry >BOLOS VASCOS.
C.M. Palos, 'Juego de bolos', JYTE (1992, 72-136); R.G. Serrano, 'Bolos', JDTE (1974, 127-184).

JUEGO DEL COROZO, a S.Amer. individual or team sport practiced on a flat rectangualr playing area approx. 30x15m in size. The object of the game is to strike the ball with a chistera-like bat into the basket located at each end of the playing area. Cf. >PELOTA VASCA, >JAÏ ALAÏ.

JUEGO DE DARDOS, a folk sport practiced in Nicaragua, where it developed under the influence of invading Span. forces [Span. juego – game + dardos – blades, spearheads]. Juego de dardos unites the traditions of >ESPALDA NEGRA (a schooling fight with blunt swords) and a trial or punishment popular among Native Amer. Indians, in which the condemned had to run through a gauntlet of warriors beating him. In juego de dardos real weapons were replaced with long, slightly curved wooden withes. Contestants were divided into pairs. The object was to fight despite the threat of being hit. Judges supervising the fighting wore capes and masks fashioned after a bull's head (the mask was fixed on a frame worn around the hips). Their task was to prevent contestants who were getting carried away from going too far. The oldest form of juego de dardos was observed by G.F. de Oviedo (1478-1557) in the early 16th cent. in Tecoatega, in present-day Nicaragua. It was a game resembling espalda negra. The boys taking part had painted skin and were adorned with feathers. They were accompanied by 20 musicians or so and singers and 10-20 dancers. A boy danced while the chieftain of the tribe threw a long wooden rod with a waxed end. After this performance the chieftain would attack the boy, stabbing him with the rod as if with a sword (over the entire body except for the head). After receiving 10-12 blows the boy was allowed to back out. The same happened to the other 3 boys. The rods, repeatedly striking the boys with great force, did not last long and had to be replaced frequently – the chieftain would wear out as many as 30 rods to whip 4 boys. This was clearly a rite intended to train young men to endure pain in battle. In later stages of development juego de dardos was enriched with elements of the battle itself. In the Diriomo village boys fought standing in 2 lines opposite each other. After the fight was over, a procession took place, parading the statue of the village's patron saint. Those carrying the statue collected gifts of food and drink, which they consumed until becoming intoxicated. W. Krämer-Mandeau, a historian of S. Amer. sports and games, writes: 'An inversion of a symbol grew out of these mystic Indian happenings at Diriomo; the Indians took an instrument of military oppression, deactivated it by replacing real swords with wooden weapons, and incorporated the new form into its festival tradition'. In Acobamba (Peru) a similar custom (taken from Span. invaders) was associated with a feast of fertility. Men flogged themselves until blood was drawn

and women collected the drops of blood into dishes to sprinkle over the fields, ensuring good crops. In this case an extra element was the Native Amer. Ind. tradition of spilling sacrificial blood on the ground. This custom was known among many tribes, e.g. the Ayamara, where it was free of Span. accretion. Young men were laid on the ground and lashed until blood was drawn. A similar ritual, called tinku, was known in Bolivia.
R. Fabian, Das blutige Fest, Der Stern, 1988, 5; W. Krämer-Mandeau, 'Tradition, Transformation and Taboo. European Games and Festivals in Latin America, 1500-1900', IJHS, 1992, 1.

JUEGO DE LA CHAZA, a regional var. of a game known since the Middle Ages as > JEU DE LA PAUME and >JEU DE COURTE PAUME. It originated in France and was transported by the Spanish and the Basques to S. and C.America [Span. juego – game + chaza – intercepting the ball]. Made esp. popular in Columbia and Mexico. The chaza is an equivalent of chase, a transverse line used in the Eng. and Fr. var. of the game. To score, a contestant should intercept the ball beyond this line. See also >ROYAL TENNIS.

JUEGO DE LAS OLLAS, a trad. Span. game, where players throw pots to each other [Span. juego – game + ollas – pots]. Usually those taking part form

der) and some are considered very prestigious. Juegos directos include: rebote (>PELOTA, subentry PELOTA VALENCIANA), pasaka, bote luzea a mano, laxoa and mahai-jokoa (>PELOTA VASCA).

JUEGOS INDIRECTOS, a Span. name for forms of >PELOTA which are played against a wall, so that the players do not have direct contact through the ball [Span. juegos – games + indirectos – indirect], as opposed to >JUEGOS DIRECTOS, where players face each other, separated only by a line or net. The corresponding Fr. name is jeux indirects. Juegos indirectos (dating back to the 18th cent.) are popular off-shoots of juegos directos but have never fully supplanted them. Juegos indirectos include: cesta punta, grand chistera, pala corta, pala larga, yoko garbi, sare (>PELOTA VASCA).

JUKENDO, a Jap. form of fencing. In the martial art long bayonets are used, but in the sports competition opponents fight with long sticks which have leather caps at the ends for protection. The contestant's outfit is similar to that worn in >JUDO, but often includes a black protective vest. Fighters wear helmets similar to those used in >KENDO. In 1955 the All-Japanese Jukendo Federation was founded. Outside Japan jukendo is practiced in some Asian countries, e.g. Singapore.
L. Frederic, A Dictionary of the Martial Arts, 1991; D.

WORLD SPORTS ENCYCLOPEDIA

J

Juego del corozo.

a circle and toss a clay pot to one another so that it does not fall and break. The game is especially popular in Galicia during the carnival.
C.M. Palos, 'Juego de las ollas', JYTE, 1992, 69.

JUEGO DE PELOTA, Span. for 'ball game', a name referring chiefly to a form involving bouncing the ball against a wall (deriving from Fr. and Basq. tradition). Often shortened to >PELOTA.

JUEGOS DIRECTOS, a Span. name for those forms of >PELOTA in which players face each other. Among the Fr. Basques this family of games is referred to as jeux directs. Players are divided only by a line or net [juegos – games + directos – direct], as opposed to >JUEGOS INDIRECTOS, where the ball is hit against a wall. Since the 18th cent. juegos directos have become less popular in favor of juegos indirectos. The games were initially played with a bare hand, later gloved. The gloves evolved, becoming bigger and bigger, until they became small rackets, which, depending on shape and size, were referred to as chesta punta or chistera. (In Lat. America, however, the terms cesta and chistera are synonymous.) Old forms of juegos directos played with bare hands are locally practiced to this day (in Basq. villages on both sides of the Fr.-Span. bor-

Mitchell, The New Official Martial Arts Handbook, 1989; K.S. Moorthy, 'Jukendo', SS, Sept. 1988.

JUMIHAJIME, a type of old Jap. archery, practiced near the end of the Heian (12th cent.) and in the Hōjō period. Contestants would be on foot rather than on horseback, as was the case in the popular >INUOMONO, >YABUSAME or >KADAGAKE. See other types of Jap. archery on foot: >BUSHA, >KUSAJISI, >MARUMONO and >MOMOTE. Cf. other forms of Jap. archery: > JYARAJ, >IBAHAJIME, >NORIYUMI and >TANGONO KISHA.

JUMP FOR A SHAWL, a type of folk competition popular among some peoples of C. Asia, particularly Turkmen. Young men jumped over the threshold of the yurt (or tent) and tried to get a shawl hanging up in the ceiling. The shawls were prizes for a successful jump. These contests were one of the attractions at Turkmen wedding ceremonies, witnessed by the Rus. ethnographer, A.N. Samoilovich (1906). Similar forms of competition were also known among Kazakhs. The Rus. ethnographer, N.L. Bernsztam, wrote that young Kazakh men competed for shawls of different size and value. The shawls were suspended from the ceiling or on the outside of the groom's yurt. The most valuable

J WORLD SPORTS ENCYCLOPEDIA

shawls were suspended from the highest points. The shawls suspended near the smoke hole in the yurt's roof were the most precious. The shawls were gifts given by the relatives of the bride and groom; cf. >TURKMEN HIGH JUMP.

N.L. Bernsztam, *Socjalno-ekonomiczeskij stroj orchono-enisjejskich tjuro w VI-VIII w.*, 1964; I. Kabzińska-Stawarz, 'Competition in liminal situations', part II, EP, 1993, XXXVII, 1; A.N. Samojlovich, *Turkmeńskie razwleczenija*, 1909.

JUMPING ON SKIN, a game practiced by Siberian peoples of Chukcha and Korjaks. A contestant stood on 2 sewn animals skins, most often reindeer or walrus, often strengthened with rope bindings. A few other participants held the skin by its edges or the rope binding and, once the contest was in position, jerked the skin up and down. The task of the participant on the skin was to keep upright and then to use the skin like a trampoline and attempt to jump as high as possible. The participant who made the largest number and the highest jumps was the winner.

JUMPING OVER BABIES, see >SALTO DEL COLACHO.

JUMPING OVER FIRE, a type of folk competition, known in many Asiatic and Eur. cultures, e.g. India, Azerbaijan, C. Asia, Carpathian cultures etc. In C. Asia jumping over bonfires was widely practiced by Turkmen, being part of religious celebrations connected with different phases of the Muslim lunar year. Turkmen believed that jumping over fire protected against illnesses and misfortunes. Similar forms of competition between young men can be found in the traditions of Azerbaijan. In India young men jumped over a bonfire during the Holi holiday in honor of Krishna and female shepherds, among whom the god was said to have lived in his youth. In Estonia jumping over fire was connected with divinations related to good health. The bigger the fire a participant jumped over, the longer he could expect to live.

In the Pol. and Slovak Tatras jumping over fire was often a form of competition among young shepherds

Jumping over fire.

Jumping over fire.

(Pol. *juhas*), who grazed their sheep on the meadows in the Tatra mountains, and earlier among the highwaymen who robbed the rich to give to the poor. Jumping over fire was often a frequent motif of Pol. art, often drawing on the highlanders' tradition. (Z. Stryjeńska, 1894-1976; W. Skoczylas, 1883-1934).

JUMPING OVER SLEDGES, a form of competition popular among the peoples inhabiting S Siberia, particularly the Chukczas, Ewenks and Yakuts. These are jumps over sledges about 0.5m wide, parked alongside one another so that there is a gap between them into which the jumper could land on both feet. Most often 24 sledges were parked in this way. The contestants jump, taking off from both feet and landing in the gap between the sledges on both feet. In each round there are more sledges to jump over. When they have jumped over all the sledges, they turn round and jump back. The winner is the contestant who makes the greatest number of jumps without losing his balance or stopping.

G. Absalyamov, M. Govorkov, V. Sinyawkiy, 'Ancient and Modern', *National Sports in the USSR*, 1980; I. Kabzińska-Stawarz, 'Competition in liminal situations', part II, EP, 1993, XXXVII, 1.

JUMP ROPE, also called *rope skipping* or *jumping rope*, an individual game or form of competition where the object is to jump over a piece of rope, swung by the jumper or by 2 others. This seemingly simple exercise is enjoyed by both schoolgirls and heavy-weight boxers, and has many var. aimed at practicing co-ordination, precision of movements, sense of rhythm, and balance. There are the following basic var. of rope skipping:

Both-feet jumps, where the skipping rope is swung in both hands over one's head and under one's feet. The more difficult version of this involves jumping a little higher up and swinging the rope twice under one's feet.

One-foot jumps with the other foot raised forward, where the rope is swung over the head and under the foot, with one spin per jump.

Trotting or jogging while skipping rope.

Swinging the rope (folded in 2) in 1 hand, and getting the rope under the feet during the jump, with 1 or 2 jumps for every revolution of the rope.

The 'matador' skip, involving regular trotting and swinging the rope from side to side rather than front to back.

Alternate jumps first on one foot and then the other, with the rope passing under one's crossed legs.

Swinging the rope under one's feet while high stepping in place.

Jumping over the rope swung when alternately crossing the arms in front of oneself and sticking

them out to the side. This is usu. referred to as the Maltese Cross (Port. *Cruz da Malta*).

Jumps on joined feet from one side to the other, with simulated twists of the legs and body, much like in a slalom.

The 19th-cent. folk sport and children's games researcher A.B. Gomme mentions the following types of rope skipping that were known in the UK in those days:

Pepper, salt, mustard, cider, vinegar – 2 girls turn the rope slowly at first, repeating the above words, then they turn it as quickly as possible until the skipper is tired out, or trips.

Rock the cradle – the holders of the rope do not swing it completely over, but rather from side to side with an even motion like a pendulum.

Chase the fox – 1 girl is chosen as a leader, or fox. The first runs through the rope, as it is turned towards her, without skipping; the others all follow her; then she runs through from the other side as the rope is turned from her, and the others follow. Next she runs in and jumps or skips once, and the other follow suit, after which she skips twice and runs out, then 3 times, the others all following until 1 trips or fails. The first one to do this takes the place of one of the turners, the turner taking her place as one of the skippers.

Visiting – 1 girl swings the rope for herself, and another jumps in and faces her, while skipping in time with the girl she is visiting. She then runs out again without stopping the rope, and another girl runs in.

Begging – 2 girls turn, and 2 others run and skip together side by side. While still skipping they change places; one says, as she passes, 'Give me some bread and butter', the other answering, 'Try my next-door neighbor'. This is continued until 1 trips.

Winding the clock – 2 turn the rope, and the skipper counts 1, 2, 3, up to 12, turning round each time she jumps or skips.

Baking bread – 2 girls turn, and another runs in with a stone in her hand, which she puts down on the ground, and picks up again while skipping. This type of skipping was usu. done to the rhythm of the following rhyme (which is chanted or sung):

Pass the baker,
Cook the tater.

The ladder – the girls run in to skip, first on one foot and then the other, with a stepping motion. This var. was often accompanied by the song:

Up and down the ladder wall,
Ha'penny loaf to feed us all;
A bit for you, and a bit for me,
And a bit for punch and Judy.

Jump rope.

Double Dutch, French Dutch – 2 ropes are turned alternately by 2 girls; the skipper has to jump or skip over each in turn. When the rope is turned inwards, it is called 'double Dutch', when turned outwards, 'French Dutch'.

History. The modern forms of rope skipping derive from folk games attested in various cultures. The oldest types seem to have originated in C and N Asia (e.g. Arab cultures call the game *qešto*). Rope skipping has always been very popular among Siberian peoples. The Maoris called rope skipping *piu*.

Among the Siberian peoples, the simplest form of rope skipping involved a long piece of rope being turned by 2 participants, with the other(s) jumping over it in the middle. The jumpers were supposed to make as many jumps as possible without being hit with the rope on any part of their bodies. Stepping on the rope or catching one's foot on it put one out of play. Among the Nanai and Ulch people, the line was spun like a 'fast clock hand' by one participant positioned in the middle, with the remaining ones running around him, trying to avoid being hit by the rope. The participant who came in for the lowest number of hits on any part of his body won. A similar game involved jumping over the rope while staying in one spot, and waiting for the rope to approach. The jumps were made on 1 foot or both feet, or, sometimes, on all fours. Among the Ulch, similar jumping was done when lying on one's belly or back. Amer. ethnologist C. Bell reports that in Tibet the captain of a rope skipping team would make additional movements while jumping – waving his arms and legs about in the air between the jumps until he got caught in the rope. The Tibetans skipped rope on the occasion of their New Year. People of any age, gender and social class would participate, even the monks. Most of the jumping was performed in one spot. Pol. researcher of Asian games and sport, I. Kabzińska-Stawarz writes:

The girls were the only ones that took a new year's walk combined with jumps over the rope during which they exchanged specific questions and answers. The questions and answers referred to the place the jumper was going to, the purpose of the journey, etc. The question about the purpose of the jumps was usually answered 'I'm intending to celebrate the new year'. [...] The association between the rope and a journey or road seems to be quite straightforward. This meaning of the rope is found in the beliefs and customs of many Asian (and non-Asian) peoples. The rope can also function as an intermediary between different worlds, as it is the case in Tibetan beliefs in which it assumes the function of a ladder used by spirits to reach successive strata of Heaven.

In Europe, rope skipping is known in most countries but it seems to have enjoyed greatest popularity in the Netherlands (*springtouw*), Germany (*Springtau* or *Sprungseil*), Portugal (*jogo da corda*), Denmark (*sjippe* or *hoppe i reb*) and Poland (*skakanka*). Eng. writer J. Strutt writes the following in his monumental *Sports and Pastimes of the People of England* (1803): 'this amusement is probably very ancient. It is performed by a rope held by both ends, that is, one end in each hand, and thrown forwards or backwards over the head and under the feet alternately. In the hop season, a hop-stem stripped of its leaves is used instead of a rope, and in my opinion it is preferable'. A.B. Gomme reports the extraordinary growth of rope-skipping in the Brit. Isles:

Apart from the ordinary, and probably later way of playing by one child holding a rope in both hands, turning it over the head, and either stepping over it while running, or standing still and jumping until the feet catch the rope and a trip is made, skipping appears to be performed in two ways, jumping or stepping across with 1) more or less complicated movements of the rope and feet, and 2) the ordinary jumping over a turned rope while chanting rhymes, for the purpose of deciding whether the players are to be married or single, occupation of future husband, etc.'

Gomme also describes var. of rope-skipping using simple, rhyming songs, often nonsensical, or connected with one of the above-mentioned themes:

Ipsey, Pipsey, tell me true,
Who shall I be married to?

Or another example taken from among the many Gomme gives:

Cups and saucers,
Plates and dishes,
My old man wears
Calico breeches.

The growth of rope skipping in the USA was greatly aided by the activities of B. Hinds in the 1970s. He was born into a disfunctional family in Kenosha, Wisconsin, and began his career as a criminal at the ripe age of 9. It was his boxing coach M. Simonsen who steered him off that path at 13. Hinds got to know rope skipping during boxing practice, and even though he then went on to become 4-time Wisconsin boxing champion, he decided to switch to rope skipping when he put on weight after finishing his boxing career and broke his leg when skiing. He returned to good health thanks to rope skipping, and then sought to popularize the exercises he developed. He used the observations by L. Garret, M. Sabie and R. Pangle of Peabody College, where a number of physical tests were introduced in 1964, including rope skipping, leading to a considerable improvement of the students' physical fitness. At the same time, Hinds used scientific publications by rehabilitation specialists of the Lankenau Hospital (D. Marrit Jones, C. Squires, K. Rodahi) and the research of J.A. Baker of Murray State University, an educational specialist at the state of Arizona. The latter proved in his studies that the effects of 10min. of intensive rope-skipping are equivalent to 30min. of jogging. He developed systemic principles of rope-skipping exercise under the name of 'Lifeline Rope', including intensity tables for various age groups for men, women and children. Hinds's appearance on J. Carson's popular talk-show added to the popularity of rope-skipping in the USA. Soon, Hinds became not only a popular jump rope coach and promoter but also the manufacturer of special equipment. He promoted rope-skipping as a method of fighting obesity, warning Americans that their prosperity and excess were making them 'a nation of fat men'. The popularity of rope-skipping as a means of fighting obesity was only offset after the appearance of >AEROBICS. In Singapore, rope skipping was introduced, on the initiative of the local Physical Education Association, into primary school curricula in 1989. This initiative was preceded by training programs for teachers under the guidance of the famous professional skipper, Austrl. K. Brooks. A national School Rope-Skipping Championship has been organized since 1989. The event is divided into the open championship, pairs and groups categories. The methodology of rope skipping and results at Jaya Primary School have been most impressive. Among the coaches who have improved rope-skipping techniques are the Singaporean Goh Choi Sim of Hong Wen School and S.H. Tay of the Fairfield Methodist Primary School in Taiwan. They supplemented the purely technical component with elements of choreography and gymnastics, e.g. exercises with hoops, thus introducing an artistic element into rope skipping. The first performer in the new program was the 11-year-old Lim Tin Yee, a schoolgirl of Singapore. This is how S.H. Tay justified the development of rope-skipping as an element of organized sport in schools:

Rope-skipping is a healthy sport. It is not advisable for young children to go jogging or swimming alone. They have to be accompanied by adults, so most children do not get as much exercise as they should. With rope-skipping, it is different, they can stay at home or even at the corridor and do as much skipping as they like. It keeps them fit and away from mischief as well.

Anon., 'Rope Skipping for Health and Fitness', *Singapore Sports*, Jan. 1988; 'Rope Skipping to Improve Fitness', *Singapore Sports*, Feb. 1988; A.B. Gomme, 'Skipping', TGESI, 1898, II, 200-204; B. Hinds, *The Lifeline Rope. The Proven Exciting New and Fun Way to Good Health*, 1975; I. Kabzińska-Stawarz, 'Współzawodnictwa w sytuacjach granicznych', cz. II. *Etnografia Polska*, 1993, XXXVII, 1.

JUMPING, see >B.A.S.E. JUMPING.

JUN FAN JEET KUNE DO, the name of the school continuing the martial art and philosophy of Bruce Lee, as well as the name of the corporation guarding his legacy. The name is a result of confusion regarding Lee's spiritual heritage and the creation of new clubs alternately called *jun fan* and *jeet kune do*. The former name is associated with the martial art and the latter – with its philosophical basis. In January 1996 Lee's widow, Linda Lee Cadwell, invited his daughter and students to discuss the future of the school of fighting conceived by her husband. A corporation was created which took the name (as was suggested by Lee's daughter, Shannon Lee Keasler) Jun Fan Jeet Kune Do, uniting the philosophical and technical aspects of Lee's work. The board of the corporation (described as the Nucleus) includes 13 of Lee's students, 5 students of the 2nd generation (i.e. the students of Lee's students) and Lee's wife and daughter. Former clubs, however, are still in existence. Shortly after the creation of Jun Fan Jeet Kune, Do Dan Inosanto, one of the Nucleus members, formed his own Jeet Kune Do association. It seems that the growing popularity of Lee's work (promoted by his films) may lead to further controversies as to which of his students and followers is entitled to continue his work.

As a corporation, Jun Fan Jeet Kune Do strives to preserve the memory of Bruce Lee as well as the creative development and educational dissemination of his ideas. The corporation's ethical code demands: 1) to always honor and protect the good name and memory of Bruce Lee and the art that he created; 2) to respect other members of the corporation and never speak ill of them; any conflicts should be solved privately or during board meetings, never in public; 3) to freely share one's philosophical observations and technical knowledge, in order to improve the individual qualifications; 4) to be fully responsible for the actions of one's companions, assistants, instructors, subordinates and other staff [...]; 5) to respect representatives of other martial arts.

Jun Fan Jeet Kune Do does not issue martial arts certificates, but does honor them.

JUNTA, also *ghjustra*, an old folk sport combining wrestling with fist fighting, similar to the ancient >PANKRATION, popular in Corsica. It died out during WWII. Recent years have witnessed attempts to restore it, not as a competition, but a technique of self-defense.

W. Baxter, *Les luttes traditionelles ō travers le monde*, in: J.J. Barreau and G. Jaouen, ed., *Les jeux populaires. Eclipse et renaissance*, 1998, 72.

JUPPENRINGEN, a trad. var. of Aus. wrestling in which the most frequently employed technique consists of grabbing the opponent by the lower parts of his clothing [Ger. *juppen* – pants + *ringen* – hand-to-hand fight, wrestling]. A match is held within a marked ring with wrestlers in a standing position. The one who first touches the floor with any part of his body above the knees loses the fight. Cf. >HOSENLUPF, >KÄRNTENRINGEN.

JYARAI, one of ancient Jap. forms of archery as part of court ceremonial. Cf. >IBAHAJIME, >NORIYUMI, >TANGONO KISHA; See also forms of Jap. mounted archery: >KADAGAKE, >INUOMONO, >YABUSAME. See also forms of Jap. archery on foot: >BUSHA, >JUMIHAJIME, >KUSAJISI, >MARUMONO and >MOMOTE.

A variety of jump rope.

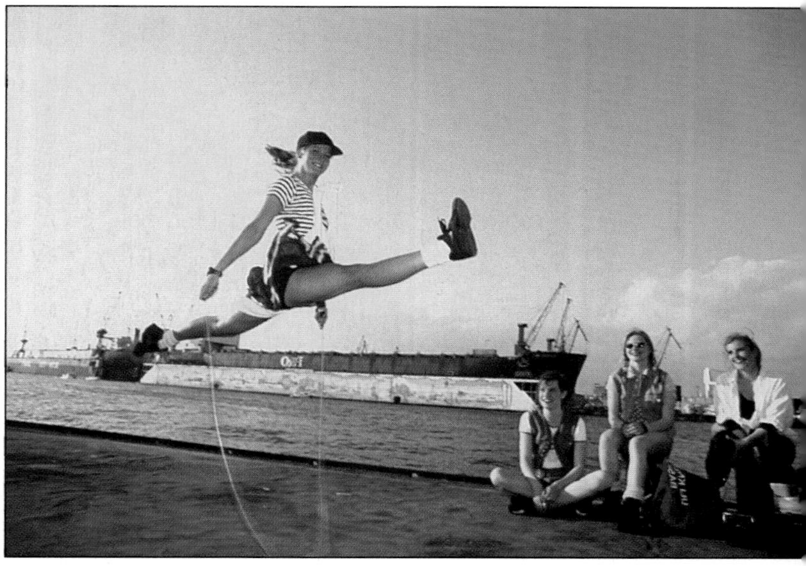

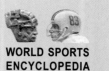

K

**WORLD SPORTS
ENCYCLOPEDIA**

KAATSEN, a Du. ball game played in the early Middle Ages known as *kaetspel*. In Friesland an almost identical game is called >KEATSEN. Similar games are played in Flanders as well. The significant differences between kaatsen and keatsen are as follows: 1) in Flem. kaatsen a team is composed of 5 players, in Frisian keatsen – 3; 2) scoring: 15-30-40 and 2-4-6; 3) circumference of Frisian ball 4cm, Du. 5cm; 4) playing are in kaatsen 73x19m, in keatsen 60x32m. General rules are almost identical in many var. also in Flanders. In both types of games 2 teams play a match, each having its side of the field. The game commences with a service from the side of the serving team towards the field of the opposing team. The ball must fall on the opposing side or – in the course of play – pass the line of contact with the ground from the previous serve. The receiving player must also pass the ball into the opponents' half or beyond the line of contact with the ground from the previous serve. When he succeeds in throwing the ball further than it fell in the previous serve, his team scores.

If the ball is thrown out of bounds or not received properly *kaats* is marked at the side line where the ball passed the line or at the extension between the bouncing point and the point where it stopped. After 2 *kaatsen*, teams change sides and the dividing line which had, until then, marked the equal halves, is substituted by the lines running parallel to the center line but dividing the field into unequal sides. This creates varying conditions for each of the teams. Except for this inequality of playing fields the game is run identically until further 2 kaatsen are marked.
History. The first record of kaatsen is from the allegorical medieval poem *Datt Kaetspel Ghemoralizeert* (1431) and from the Lat.-Du. dictionary *Tyrocinium language latinae* written in 1545 by P. van Afferden from Harderwijk. Kaatsen is one of multiple Eur. games derived indirectly from Rom. Traditions which led also to the development of, among others, Fr.>JEU DE LONGUE PAUME, Brit. >FIVES. Other Germanic games including Gotland's >PÄRK show the trace of having been influenced by kaatsen; several features that both games have in common speak in favor of such an assumption. Kaatsen and pärk are played with a stitched ball made of 8 strips of leather, the tradition of reading out a letter challenging the other party to a duel and betting on the winner has survived. Names suggest common origin, too. Conquering the enemy's land is called *casse* in W Wallonia, the Fr. speaking part of Belgium, and *kas* in the Swed. spoken in Gotland. It was also referred to as *datperck* in van Afferden's poem – similar to Swed. *park* – explained in Lat. As *scopus ludi*, that is the aim arrived at in the course of play. In 1902 the Royal National Kaatsen Federation was founded (Koninklijke Nationale Kaatsbond). It is the largest organization of its type but there are dozens of independent associations of this discipline in Wallonia and Flanders.

D. De Borger, 'De kaatssport in Vlaanderen', in: *Vlaamse Volkssport Dossiers*, 2, 1981; E. De Vroede: 'Past and Present, Ball and Bowl Games in the Low Countries in Homo Ludens'. *Der Spielende Mensch*, 1996, VI, E. De Vroede, *Het Grote Volkssporten Boek*, 1996; H. Gillmeister, 'Medieval Sport: Modern

Kabaddi.

Methods Research – Recent Results and Perspectives', IJHS 1988, vol. 5, no. 1; J.Kalma, *Kaatsen in Friesland; het spel met de kleine bal door de eeuwen heen*, 1972; J.A. Roetert Frederikse, ed., *Dat Kaetspel Ghemoralizeert*, Bibliotheek van Middelnederlandsche Letterkunde, 1915; R. Van Passen, *Kaatsspelen te Antwerpen in de 15de-18de eeuw*, Naamkunde, 1988-1989, 20-21.

K'ABA, Arab game of skill in which participants were to throw an animal bone, usu. a pastern bone. The result of the game depended on the position of the bone after it stopped on the ground: whether the player managed to position it vertically or, if not, what side it fell on: the convex or concave, wider or narrower, colored or unmarked part to the ground etc. No detailed rules, esp. concerning scoring, have survived. A general description of the game may be found in M. Ibrahim al-Majman's dictionary of Arab sports and games:

It is a very old game, exceedingly popular in the days of our fathers and forefathers. Unfortunately it fell into oblivion and today's youth recognizes it, if at all, only by name. [...] The game is called after the Arabic term ka'b. Such a requisite had specific shape, diameters and a characteristic groove. Often the players prepared it themselves, decorating the surface with watercolors, poured lead into the groove in order to increase its weight and called it saul. [...] Sometimes much smaller bones from calves and young goats were used but these were referred to as 'else. People enjoyed playing this game in yards and trade venues in the springtime and summer but not during rainy seasons. The ground appropriate for k'aba should consist of clay or hard, well-packed soil and should not be sandy or rocky. A circle or square is to be marked on the ground. Approx. 3m from this a straight line must be made and the players take varying positions in reference to the this line, measured in units called bau'. The players could remain seated or assume a standing position. A good player would say: 'He who wishes to compete with me has 1 bau' to the line'. It happened that before the game someone shouted: 'Alwan!' (colors) which meant that if the thrown saul stopped on the line colored side up this player would have the right to resume the game from this spot. Often such particular rules were agreed on in advance. The advanced player, however, treated his opponents always leniently and gave them many opportunities for winning, e.g. by allowing them to play from positions closer to the line, allowing them to sit or lay while throwing whereas he remained standing.

[Min al'abina ash-sha 'biyya, 1983, 20-22]

K'aba was known in several var., the most interesting of which was >KUBBA, played similarly but with 2 bones simultaneously.

KABACHI, also spelled *kabaci*, a Georg. var. of >WINESKIN SHOOT. The tournament was organized between competitors who aimed at shooting through a wine skin or a horse tail ensign and in modern times a rubber ball impaled on a 3-4m mast. The sport was first described by Ital. missionary A. Lombardi in the 17th cent. The description was accompanied by a drawing by another missionary Kastelio. cf. >JAMB.

Kabaddi.

KABADDI, a trad. sport of India with different regional nominal var.: *chedugudu* or *hu-tu-tu* (S India), *hadudu* (a male var.), and *chu-kit-kit* (a female var. in Eastern India). The all-popular name of kabaddi is typical of N India, though is more and more frequently used in the rest of the region. The game is played between 2 teams of 10-12 players each, of whom 7 are active at a time, while the remaining players are substitutes. In the N Ind. states of Punjab, Haryana, and Uttar Pradesh the game is played in a ring court 75-80ft. in diameter (22.86-24.38m) and that var. is called *amar kabaddi*. Two other var. are played on a rectangular court 12.5mx10m for men and 11mx8m for women. Yet another var., called *goongi kabaddi*, is played on an area of unspecified size, with only 2 players competing. The surface of the court is usu. clay with a thin layer of sand. The object of the game, which lasts 2 periods of 20min. each, is for one player of the attacking team to force his way through the circle formed by the defenders. The attacker or 'radar', called *sahi*, holds his breath and keeps crying 'Kabaddi!' throughout the offensive. Having entered the opponents' court the radar must touch at least 1 of the defenders (*japhi*) within 20sec. (or, in a trad. var., within the length of one breath), after which he must return to his team's court. The touched players are eliminated, which makes it easier for the next *sahi* to enter the opponents' court. The defenders try to stop the *sahi* for more than 20sec. (or until he has to take another breath) and if they succeed, he is eliminated. Teams take turns sending their subsequent *sahis*. A player that touches the court outside the marked lines is also eliminated. Players use no equipment and the game is controlled by 2 judges. The winning team scores 2pts. called *lona*. Cf. sports and games of other nations involving holding one's breath: >TATAU MANAWA, >KANKA BILO, >TIANG-KAI-SII.
There are 3 separate types of kabaddi played under different auspices. *Surjeevani kabaddi*, governed by the Kabaddi Federation of India, allows for the return of the eliminated players as soon as 1 of the opponents is eliminated. There is also a time limit and points are scored by the team which eliminates more opponents within that time limit. In *gaminee kabaddi* the eliminated players may not return to the game and the elimination of all the players of 1 team ends the game. In *amar kabaddi* the players touched by the *sahi* remain on the court, while the attackers are awarded 2pts. The team that scores more points within a time limit, wins the game.
Kabaddi is a national sport of India, esp. in the state of Punjab and among the Sikhs. It is played mostly by men and boys, usu. below 35yrs. of age. It is also known in other Asian countries, e.g. in Nepal, Bangladesh, Sri Lanka, Pakistan, and even Japan. In recent years the game has also become popular in Singapore, where the best known team is the Singapore Kabaddi Team of the Singapore Khalsa Association. Kabaddi is included in the program of Asian Games.

History. The origins of kabaddi date back to pre-historic times, when man learned to defend in groups against animals or attack weaker animals individually or in groups for survival and food. Concrete evidence indicates that the game existed 4,000 ago. Its several var. evolved spontaneously until the Kabaddi Federation of India (KFI) was established in 1950, followed by the Amateur Kabaddi Federation of India (AKFI) in 1973. The game became internationally recognized during the Asian Games in 1982, which led to the formation of Asian Kabaddi Federation (AKF), initiated by by S. Pawar, a kabaddi promotor from the state of Maharashtra. Teams representing India, Pakistan, Canada, Great Britain, and the USA participated in the first W.Ch. See also >RED ROVER.

Take My Breath Away, SS, Apr. 1993; R. Bhatia, 'Kabaddi and Sepak Takraw', in: *Sangam Book of Asian Games*, 1982; J. Arlott, 'Kabaddi', in: *The Oxford Companion to Sports and Games*, 1975.

KABAT, an Arab team sport. Two teams – the attackers and defenders (selected by drawing) – compete on a field formed by 2 rectangles 20x10m, separated by an area called *hatt en-nar* ('the line of fire'), which must be jumped over when attacking the opponents and in which players must not stop. The surface of the field should be relatively soft to prevent injuries in case of collisions or falls resulting from the violent nature of the game, which resembles karate and often leads to serious injury. The players are further protected by special uniforms made from materials resistant to easy wear.

The object of the game is to eliminate the opponents by kicking any part of their body, as well as hitting with the hands well defined body parts: both arms and the back. The attackers begin by jumping over the 'line of fire' into the opponents' side of the field and try to eliminate the defenders. The player who has been kicked or hit is called a *maijit* ('dead') and must leave the playing area. The defenders avoid being hit by chasing away around the field and dodging the attackers. If they are successful over a certain period of time, they are allowed to become the attackers. The team that eliminates all of the opponents and has at least one player left wins the game. The referee may be neutral, but is often a member of the attacking team. Because of weather conditions the game is usu. played in the morning or at the end of the day, often at night. The rules of kabat were developed by the people of Mecca, where the game has been known since ancient times. Similar games are played in Al-Ihsa' (*hol*), Nedjed (*shaqq el-qan*) and Jidda (*sari*).

M. Ibrahim al-Majman, *Min al'abina ash-sha 'biyya*, 1983, 13-15.

KADAGAKE, an old Jap. var. of >EQUESTRIAN ARCHERY. Other var. include >INUOMONO and >YABUSAME.

KÆDETIK, Dan. for 'touching with the chain', [*Kæde* – chain + *tik* – touch], a children's game. Players run between 2 safety zones, trying to escape the 'chain', which initially consists of 2 persons and grows longer as more children get caught. Only the 2 players at the ends of the 'chain' can do the catching. The runners may try to break the chain, which makes it harmless until it is joined back together. Cf. other games of this type: >DØDNING, >GÅ OVER ELVEN, >ISBJØRN OG LANDSBJØRN, >KLIM-KLEM, >TAMANJ, >TULLEHUT, >TYRHOLDE, >KREDSTROLD.

J. Møller, 'Kædetik', GID, 1997, 2.

KAENG RUER, Thai var. of >DRAGON BOAT RACING. Its origins can be traced back to the Middle Ages when Thailand was known as Aytthaya. Contests were held in the 10th and 11th cent. and were connected with the ceremonial display of new robes for the Buddhist monks. Crews were relatively small, 8-10 paddlers and a steersman, although crews of 21-50 were possible. Most often the distance covered amounted to 650m. Thai boats had the characteristic feature of being hollowed out teak trees. Kaeng ruer regattas are organized by the majority of Thai provinces, esp. Phichit, Narathiwat, Nakhon Ratchasima, Nan, Phitsanulok, Ayutthaya, and in the capital – Bangkok. The Phichib regatta which has been held annually for 85yrs. on the Nan river is considered to be the most spectacular and is viewed by thousands of tourists.

The Internet: http://www.columbia.edu/cu/thai/html/tea_sport.html

KAETSPEL, see >KAATSEN.

KAGE, game and endemic custom imbued with local color practiced among Li people in China. The players are to jump over bamboo poles arranged before the performance. At the beginning 2 thicker poles are lain on the ground, parallel to each other at a distance of 6-7m. Above them several shorter poles are positioned across, so that the whole construction looks like railroad tracks. Then the competitors take hold of the ends of the thinner poles, so that about 4-6 pairs stand face-to-face with lifted bamboo poles in their hands. The remaining players then try to jump over the bamboo poles put in motion by others, along the line marked by the long bamboo poles. Jumping proves difficult as the poles are moved up, and down, and across, their movement accompanied by the rhythmically uttered, 'Ge-da-da, ge-da-da.' Moreover the assistants in control of the poles try to clip the 'dancers'. Those who are not nimble enough and are clipped by the bamboo poles are eliminated from competition. Jumping is performed on 3 different heights in cycles: jumping over the poles held by seated, crouching or standing assistants. The winners are those who manage to jump over all of the poles in all of the 3 stages of the game. Contests are traditionally held separately for boys' and girls' teams. Customary awards are betel nuts (*pinang*) for girls and a bag of *shanlan* wine for men.

Mu Fushan, et al., 'Bamboo-Pole Jump', TRAMCHIN.

KAILS, spelled differently in various Eur. languages: *kayles, keiles, cayles*. One of the oldest bowling games which, most probably, gave rise to the >SKITTLES family and the Fr. name for bowling in general:

KAJAKVENDING, Dan. kayak flip. A line (6m long) is folded in two and hung, stretched taut, 2m above the ground. The contestant sits astride on the lines, straightens slightly his legs and crosses his feet; so as not to fall between the lines, he grasps at the lines in front and behind. The task consists in turning round the axis of the line and returning to the sitting position. The name stems from the underwater kayak turn performed to right a capsized craft while wild-water >KAYAKING.

J. Møller, 'Kajakvending', GID, 1997, 3, 55.

KAKJUE, a type of early medieval Kor. wrestling , a predecessor of the modern >SSIRÚM.

KALARI-PAYAT, the art of combat and self-defense stemming from India and popular in some other Asian countries, esp. in Malaysia; written also as *kalaripayit*. In the language of *Mallayam* in the state of Kerala it is extremely popular as *kalari payatt*. It is based on forces and skills acquired through meditation and persistent exercises together with religious ritual. Nowadays, there are 2 types of kalari-payat: the original, N type, practiced in the N and C part of Keral and S practiced by the Tamil living in the S part of the state. The sport is practiced solo and in pairs. The name kalari-payat means, literally, exercises in a special ground hollow called *kalari*. The spiritual element plays an important role in preparing students, because it allows them to keep their distance from the temporary world and to believe in their own skills. Therefore, it is essential to acquire the power and skill necessary in combat through meditation and persistent exercises together with religious ritual. The technique of kalari-payat learning consists of a number of elements similar to or

In Bombay to promote Kalari-payat, the ancient physical, cultural and martial art of the state of Kerala in southern India, Satish Kumar, left, and Shri Ajit perform a dagger fight.

quills. The earliest records of kails regard the game practiced as early as the first few cent. of the modern era by the tribes of Francs who transferred the game further to today's France. The detailed rules are unclear. J. Strutt believes that it was the oldest form of 9-set bowling, although the pins were set not to form a square but in a row and the number of pins in a game was not fixed (6-8). Moreover the pins had no identical dimensions like the average 9-set bowling pins – a pin known as the king was visibly higher (STRUTT, III, VI, 238-239). One of the game var. called club kayles in Eng. allowed for hitting the pins by throwing poles instead of bowls at them.

KAIPOR, Hindu fighting technique without resorting to weapons; belongs to one of 5 techniques applied in the >ADI MURAI fighting school.

borrowed from *yoga*. The practice starts at the age of 7, with getting to know one's own body and fathoming the knowledge about oneself. An acquaintance with kalari-payat once indicated that one belonged to a higher social caste in Kerala (*Nayars*) and the subcaste of Brahmans known as *Yatra*, also some lower castes like *chekavars*. The aim of the exercise was to reach the state of perceiving life as 'a flowing river'. Both boys and girls practiced the exercise. It was supplemented with special massage techniques, diet and restraint of certain bodily functions to achieve a perfect psychophysical state. Kalari-payat bodily exercises encompass, among others, a combination of a yoga posture (*asana*), special movement of legs (*cuvat*), kicks (*kal etupp*), various jumps and twists, coordinated movements of the arms and legs, repeated more and more

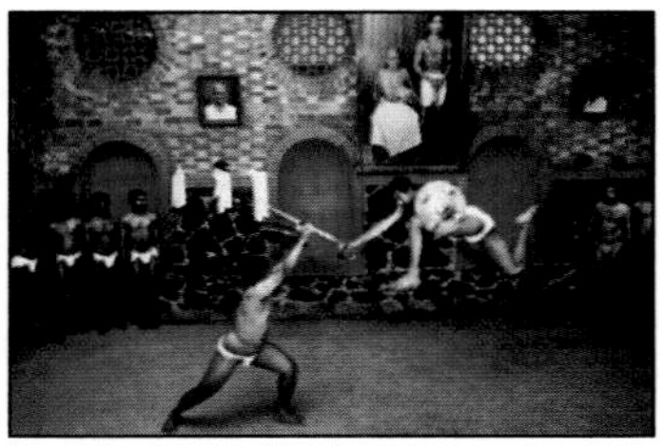

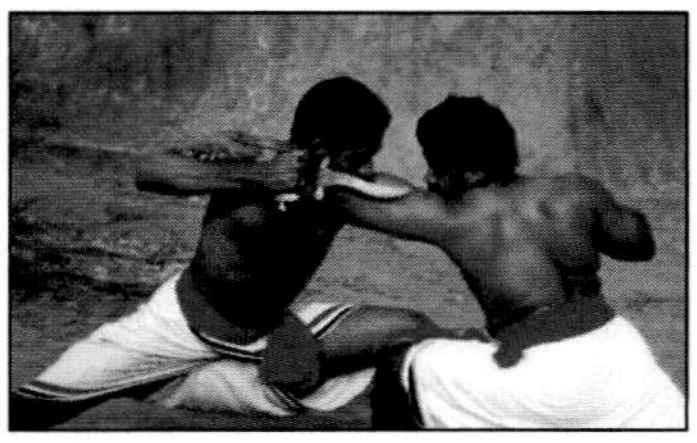

Top and above: kalari-payat.

quickly in increasingly difficult postures.

From the purely technical point of view, kalari-payat consists of dodging the attack of the opponent and then adding one's own destructive force so that the sum of both forces is applied against the attacker. Thanks to this tactic and skill the weaker party of the combat can still achieve the victory. Kalari-payat encompasses 18 basic training methods and about 400 combat techniques, such as, fallen-down techniques and steps, locks, chops, blows and punches, kicks, throws, pressure-point tactics and vital-point attacks. Hand weapons of all types – esp. sticks – are allowed. The technique of exercises and fighting with a stick is known as *kolthari*, fighting with a long stick is called *kettukari*, and with a short one – *kuruvadi*. In real-life combats, a sharp S–shaped, 60-70cm long stick (*otta*) made of tamarind wood is used for attacking the nervous system of the opponent. Metal objects used in the combat: daggers, various types of knives, swords and spears constitute the so-called *anga thari*. This group incorporates, among others, *puliyankam*, a type of sword, the mastery of which is one of the most important kalari-payat skills. Puliyankam fighting takes advantage of motions similar to a tiger's movements. For close-range fighting, *kattaren*, a type of dagger, is used. The *urumi* is a blade midway between a light sword and a saber. It is the deadliest weapon used in kalari-payat and can slice an opponent in half. Urumi fighting allows using a small shield. Kalari-payat accounts for combat with mixed weapon e.g. a warrior armed with a spear against a sword-armed opponent. The sword holder has to overcome the adversity of the length of the sword and make use of all the weak points of the spear-armed opponent. The technique of *verumkai* encompasses methods of bare-hand fighting using various grips, a piece of cloth or rope. There is a link between kalari-payat and the old Hindu combat school called >ADI MURAI. As a type of sport, kalari-payat is used only for self-defense. As in other Asian combat schools, belts denote the rank of the practitioner, a black one signifying the highest degree of mastery. The sport is also available to women. The combat takes place in silence. The grand kalari-payat master (*Maha Guru*) is acquainted not only with combat techniques, but also with methods of swift treatment of injuries. *Uzhichil*, a special massage of the nervous system using medicated oils (*gingli*) of a complex recipe, plays a crucial role in such treatment. The technique of *maipayatt* encompasses bodily exercises such as, twists, feints and jumps. It aims at maximizing control over one's body. For psychological preparation the technique of yoga is applied.

History. A number of ethnographers consider kalari-payat as older than >WUSHU, >KARATE and other Asian arts of self-defense. The oldest sources indicate that it appeared in the 12th cent., at the latest. It combines elements of 2 trad. Tamil martial arts and the Vedic tradition (>DHANUR VEDA). The present day kalari-payat has been shaped mainly by forms stemming from the region of today's Kerala state in the S of India. The myths describe a cruel hero Parasuram (lit. Rama with a Battle-Ax) who was born to liberate the Brahmans from the pride and willfulness of the warriors. He was endowed with a mystical force gained through arduous exercises and meditation, characteristic later for kalari-payat. There is evidence that the beginnings of kalari-payat date back to the 4th cent. AD and the framework of the sport was already rather well known about 1,000 years ago. Women participated in kalari-payat exercises from the very beginning, which is substantiated by the story of Unniyarchia, a mythological heroine who, thanks to the exercises, won numerous duels and battles. The first peak of kalari-payat's popularity occurred in the 14th, 15th, and esp. 16th cent., when it was a significant element of the social position among aristocracy, monks and soldiers from the region of Malabar. The greatest kalari-payat master was Thacholi Othenan in the 16th cent. Buddhist monks spread the rules of the art to other countries of the Far East, among others, to China and Japan. Both Chin. and Jap. researchers of martial art traditions agree that their development was at one time stimulated by kalari-payat techniques and principles, which were introduced in the Chin. monastery Shaolin by a Buddhist monk Bodidharma. Under the Brit. colonial government kalari-payat was banned. As the Brit. Empire was officially transformed into the Brit. Commonwealth of Nations (1931), the former bans were relaxed and in the '30s the first, after a long break, kalari-payat associations in India were created, the strongest being the Karari Payat Club, founded in 1938. After India regained independence in 1947, some attempts at restoring a number of folk sports, including kalari-payat, were made, but the process was very slow, due to the lack of specialists; only a few kalari-payat masters survived in the remote villages of India and Malaysia. In 1958, under the auspices of the Kerala Sports Council in India, the Kerala Kalarippayattu Association was created. At the same time 17 local clubs called *kalari* (named after the ground hollow) were founded. In 1995 the state of Kerala totaled already over 200 kalari. The Kerala authorities hold various forms of competitions with kalari-payat masters as referees. State Championships are held and the contestants receive various skill certificates and prizes.

After the All India Kalari Payat Federation was created in 1976, kalari-payat enjoyed mass appeal in Great Britain, Japan, Malaysia, China, Singapore and Indonesia. In Malaysia it was popularized by Mahaguru Ustaz Haji Mazha Haji Abu, who was also the initiator of a system called the International Self Defense Kalari Payat, FIDSK).

J.S. Alter, *The Wrestler's Body. Identity and Ideology in North India*, 1992; P. Balakrishnan, *Kalarippayatu. The Ancient Martial Art of Kerala*, 1995; *Kalari Payat* (basic information); K.S. Moorthy, 'Kalari-Payat: The Ancient Indian Martial Art of Self-Defence', SS, Nov./Dec. 1987; D.C. Mujumdur, *Encyclopedia of Indian Physical Culture*, 1950; P.B. Zarrilli, 'From Martial Art to Performance. Kalarippayattu and Performance in Karala', *Sangeet Natak*, 1986, 81-83; idem, 'Actualizing Power(s) and Crafting a Self in Kalarippayattu, a South Indian Martial Art and the Yoga and Ayurvedic Paradihms', *Journal of Asian Martial Arts*, 1994, 3, 3.

KALI, Fil. school of combat and self-defense stemming from the tradition of warrior education >BOTHOAN. It combines the elements of Chin. *kun-tao*, Indon. >PENCAK SILAT and Malaysian *langka silat*. It is based on 2 types of fighting methods and a medical skill. It is a hand-to-hand combat with or without weapons. For *panandata*, fighting with weapons, 5 types of weapons are used: a cut and thrust weapon: a type of machete, knife; a thrown weapon, like spears; a shooting weapon, like bow arrows; an elastic weapon, such as rope lasso; and a protective weapon, first and foremost, a shield. Each weapon can be used in 6 different ways: exercise or combat may be practiced solo or together with the opponent, with weapons which may be short or long, heavy or light, curved or straight, single or double-bladed, held with one or both hands. Hand-to-hand combat can be divided into 4 categories: blows, kicks, locks and vital pressure-point tactics. Blows can be divided into blows dealt straight ahead with an open palm or clenched fist, chops, jerking the opponent, pushing and scratching. Kicks encompass hits with one's foot, knees, feinting actions and swings. Locks include blocking the opponent's joint movement, breaking limbs, strangling, and squeezing different parts of the body. Pressing sensitive points and aiming blows at nerves paralyzes the opponent's movements. The art of kali was banned in the Philippines under Span. rule (1565-1898). Nevertheless, it survived thanks to the Eur. theater, used by the Spaniards in their missionary propaganda while converting the Filipinos to Catholicism. The Filipinos made use of a number of duel scenes, typical for theater plays. They extended the scenes so as they turned into pantomime interludes. The Spaniards tolerated it, if instead of regular weapons, their wooden imitations were used, because they knew that those moments attracted the Philippine audience to plays propagating the message of Christianity. At this time, among others, rattan stick fencing was developed. In the 19th cent., the first Filipinos went to study at Span. universities, bringing back to the Philippines the technique of modern fencing, which, combined with the art of kali, led to the emergence of new combat methods, such as >SOLO BASTON, >DOBLE BASTON and >ESKRIMA. Nowadays, kali is gaining popularity in the US, where it is practiced under the guidance of, among others, R. Faye of the Minnesota Kali Group.

KALMUCK ARCHERY, a var. of archery practiced by the Mong. Kalmuck, or Oyrat people, inhabiting the Stavropol region on the N flank of the Greater Caucasus. Kalmuck archery is very similar to >MONGOLIAN ARCHERY and displays all the basic features of >ORIENTAL ARCHERY. One of characteristic features of Kalmuck archery, noted by ethnographers already in the 19th cent., has been the symbolic – rather than material – role of the prizes awarded for victory in archery contests, e.g. hats, scarves or shawls. However, the Buriats, as opposed to the Kalmucks, introduced money prizes already in the 19th cent. Archery traditions are described in Kalmuck mythology. One of the heroes of the Kalmuck epic *Jangariada* could draw a bow in such a manner that the released arrow flew in the air for a few days and reached the end of the steppe. If he shot an arrow into the ground a horse could be tied to it and the arrow would resist the animal's pull.

KALMUCK BALL, a ball game practiced among the Kalmuck people. Like >BURIAT BALL this ball game was not played by all Kalmuck tribes. The ball resembled a small leather pillow or a bundle of rags tied up with leather straps or strings. The game was also played with a bundle of leather straps or rolled bristles. Kalmuck ball games were mainly played in summer and fall.

KALMUCK RACES were held to celebrate various religious holidays and family occasions such as weddings, the birth of a child or the symbolic cutting of a fetter placed on a child's feet to make him learn to walk sooner (>FETTER-CUTTING RACE). In contrast to many other peoples of C Asia, among which the winner of the race actually cuts the fetter on a child's feet, the Kalmucks have dropped that tradition and only imitate the action with appropriate gestures and movements of their hands.

KALMUCK WRESTLING, a trad. var. of wrestling popular among the Mong. Kalmuck, or, rather, Oyrat as the people prefer to call themselves. The Oyrat live in the Stavropol Kray in central Caucasus. The object of the game is to floor one's opponent so that at least one of his shoulder blades touches the ground. In the past the bouts were accompanied by elaborate rituals. Before appearing in the arena, the fighters received a new belt which they put around their hips. They were divided into 2 groups and they left the yurt together so that they did not know who would fight whom. W. Sieroszewski thought that the names of opponents were kept secret to prevent cheating and spell-casting. The fighters entered the arena wearing cloaks covering their whole bodies as well as their heads. After taking the cloaks off, the wrestlers shook hands, moved from the center and started marching around the arena briskly as if they were pursuing one another. At the same time they rubbed sand into their hands and threw it up in the air. Kabzińska-Stawarz offers the following explanation of this ritual:

> *One can distinguish [...] the following stages symbolized by the fighters' behavior: 1) the fetal stage (symbolized by the players entering the arena with their heads covered); 2) the birth (taking off the cloak); 3) unity, absence of any conflicts and the emergence of the two opposing elements (fighters' preparations for the bout); 4) creation of the Earth (sand throwing and rubbing sand into one's hands is similar to various mythical descriptions of how Earth was created and seem to be an imitation of the process).*

I. Kabzińska-Stawarz, 'Competition in Liminal Situations', II, EP, 1993, XXXVII, 1.

KALPE, Gk. for 'trot', mare trot racing for an unspecified distance, held in ancient Greece. It was introduced to the 71st Ol.G. in 496 BC, withdrawn together with mule-drawn carts (>APENE). Pausanias, in his *Wandering across Hellas* recalls that *kalpe* was finished in an extraordinary way: 'during the last lap the riders would get off the mares and run next to them, grasping the bridle' (V, 9,2). Pataikos from Dyme was the winner of the first *kalpe* competition, his name was the only one preserved on the winner lists in this sport category. While describing the statues of the Olympian winners, Pausanias (VI, 9, 2) mentions that: 'immediately behind the statue of Teognet there is a statue of a man who was not listed together with other Olympians, because he won the race called kalpe', which indicates that there was little prestige attached to *kalpe* racing.

KALUDDERSCHIEßEN, also dial. Ger. *Kaludderschißen*, a Ger. var. of ice shooting. In the Ger. tradition, a var. of a group of winter games commonly described as >EISSCHIEßEN. A large puck is pushed by the players across ice in an effort to hit slabs hung on a special frame at the end of the track.

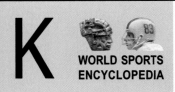

The slabs are numbered 1-9, the puck, called an iron (Eisstock), resembles those used in other var. of Schießen; it must be 38cm high to reach to the slabs, which are struck by the iron's wooden handle. The handle is tilted and tapered, getting thicker towards the end. The iron has the form of an irregular, flattened disc. Irons for men weigh 4.5-6kg and are 27-30cm in diameter at the base, while women's irons are 25-30cm and 4-6kg. The body of an iron (Stock-körper) used to be wooden, but today it is usu. made of plastic, with a metal sliding sole to reduce friction on the ice (Ger. Fuss for 'foot' or also Sole – 'sole'). Cf. >RINGSCHIEßEN, >WEITSCHIEßEN, >ZIELSCHIEßEN, and similar disciplines outside Ger. tradition., e.g.: >CURLING and >UTYUG.

KAMAYANARIAN WRESTLING, popular among the Kamayanara tribe living in Amazonia. The fighters would wrap their ankles and knees with pieces of cloth so as not to get hurt when kicked or falling to the ground.

KAMPASTEN, with a dial. var. kampsten, Swed. for 'combat stone', a boulder used in competitions, esp. for proving manliness. Afterwards, boys were considered men – herkarlar. Such tests were performed in the village of Fröreda in the parish of Järeda, in the parishes of Lönneberga i Högsby in Småland, and in the county of Västmanland and Närke in the region of Svealand. The name is also one of the terms referring to the Swed. folk competition in stone lifting. See also >LYFTESTEN, >DRÄNGASTENAR, >DRÄNGALÖFTEN, >LYFTESTEN; cf. Dan. >STENLÖFTNING, Basq. >ARRIJASOKETA; see also >GGET, >KÖLNÅKERN, >KUNGSSTEN, >KUNGSSTENARNA, >STORA OCH LILLA DAGS-VERKARN, >TYFTEHÖNAN.
S. Erixon, Svenskt folkliv, 1938; M. Hellspong, Lifting Stones. The Existence of Lifting-Stones in Sweden, ST, 1993-94, XIX-XX.

KAMPSTEN, see >KAMPASTEN.

KAMYCZKI, a Pol. var. of >JACKS. Usu. in the game 5 polished stones were used, although there were var. of this game with more stones, e.g. 7. The stones are usu. up to 1cm in diameter. The game was usu. played on a blanket, on the beach, or in holiday club rooms. Before the game started, each player scattered the stones in front of him/her by a movement similar to sowing grain within the range of roughly 0.5m. The game began by tossing all the stones into the air and then trying to catch them on the back of one's hand. The stone that fell on the ground was later used for tossing. If the player managed to keep all the stones on his hand, he had the right to choose the stone that was most convenient for tossing (usu. the smallest). If then 1 stone rolled off his hand, the rule was sometimes applied that the player had to perform penalty tosses, i.e. if 2 stones fell, the player had to take 2 turns instead of 1, etc. The player tossed the stone that had been chosen at will or selected as described above. He tried to catch it before it fell on the ground while simultaneously seizing the stones lying on the blanket. Stones had to be seized until the previously scattered stones found their way into the player's hand. Stones were caught 1 by 1, or, later during the game, by 2, 3, 4; in growing numbers: 1+2+3, decreasing: 3+2+1, or in combined numbers: 2+5, 5+1. At the end of the game the player usu. attempted to seize all the stones lying on the ground in one move. Any player who did not manage to seize the specific num. of stones from the ground before his tossed stone fell missed a turn. Additionally, if a player did not manage to hold the stones in his hand, he would miss the turn.

KANÁSZJÁTÉK, see >DISZNÓZÁS.

KANG SHANABA, Ind. folk sport known in the area of Manipur, traditionally practiced the day between the Manipuri New Year (Cheiraoba) and the holiday of Ratha Jatra. The beginnings of kang shanaba are recorded in the ancient myths. The game is played by 2 teams called kanghut. Each kanghut consists of 7 players symbolizing the days of the week. The most principal elements of the game are oval objects (called kang), which are thrown or rolled. They used to be made of climbing plants, however, at present, they are more and more often made of wax or lead and have an ivory core. There are 2 types of kangs: those used as targets (kangkhil) and the ones for rolling (kangkap). The side that should be aimed at is clearly marked on the kanghils. It is not allowed

to use the opponent's kangkaps, except for cases specified by the rules and if permitted by the referee. The playing course, 'the life field', is rectangular, about 36-42ft. (approx. 9.75-12.8m) long and 16½ft. wide. It is divided into 4 sectors with half-way lines along and across the course. On the lines marking the edges of the course, there are 30 kanghils, 15 for each team. They represent 30 days of a month. Along each of the 2 external lines of the course (lamtha kanghuls), there are 7 kanghils, the targets during the game. Along each of the 2 end lines (chekpheei kangkhuls) there are 8 kanghils. In this way, each team has 15 kanghils to aim at. The game consists in shooting at kangkhils with kangkapas in a way specified by the rules. Auxiliary lines leading towards kangkhil are called kangkhinpham liri, transverse lines facilitating the throw distance estimation – liri. To score a point, one has to make 3 accurate shots in a row: 2 from the standing position (chekphei) and 1 from the sitting position (lamtha). The first chekphei shot is called 'day' and the second 'night'. They are made alternately from the left and right side of the course (with the longitudinal halfway line as a point of reference). During shooting from the standing position, the free hand has to be held between the thighs. Successful completion of the shot from the seated, lamtha position is a complicated task, in which counts not only the fact of hitting the target, but also the kangkap's position after it has stopped. The kangkap's falling beyond the external lines results in the elimination of the player and his 'death' – shiba. If the kangkap stays within the borders of the course, the shot is called nandaba, and gives the right to make a traverse shot at kanghils, located along the sideline of the course. This traverse shot is decisive for scoring a point and is referred to as marak changba. Each player has only 1 chance to make the set of 4 shots, i.e. 2 chekphei, 1 lamtha, and 1 marak changba. The total number of points, accurate and missed shots of a team, determine the winners and losers. The game lasts for 4½hrs. and is played in 2 parts, with a break of 5min. After the break the teams change sides.

KANGAROO BALL, a ball game practiced by Austrl. Aborigines, esp.the Kalkadoon tribe of the Pacific Islands, a var. of >CATCH BALL. The game is played by 2 teams. The players of one team pass the ball to one another; the opposing players try to catch the ball in the air, performing characteristic kangaroo leaps. This keep-away type game is also known as kangaroo play; see also >OCEANIAN BALL GAMES.

KANGJEI SHANABA, see >KHONG KANGJEI.

KANGOO JUMPING, a form of jumping exercise with the use of Kangoo Jumps, safe, low impact rebound sport shoes, providing many health benefits, designed for people at any age. Producers of the equipment claim that the shoes can be used for: · jogging and running, home fitness, weight loss (trimming and toning), group fitness (Kangoo'Robic), athletic training (srength and conditioning), rehabilitation and injury prevention, children's education and games, correction and prevention of various health problems, global health, games, dance or just for pure fun. They can be used indoors, or outdoors on paved roads, dirt paths, grass, sidewalks, at the beach or even on snow.

KANKA BILO, Afr. game played in Ghana, esp. among children up to the age of 10 or so. There is no limit on the number of players. Play consists of counting consecutive objects, while holding one's breath. There are usu. 10-25 objects of similar shape and size; e.g. seeds, fruit, coins, pebbles etc. The player who manages to count most of them wins. The game starts with placing the markers in a row. Players take turns holding their breath and walking along the markers, touching each of them with their hand and repeating the word 'bilo'. They continue as long as they have enough air to say 'bilo' audibly. The player who reaches, in this way, the farthest marker in the row wins. In a different type of the game, instead of saying 'bilo,' the player says: 'la loo lu loo laloo lu'. If the player manages to count all of the markers, they start returning along the line. The Liberian >TIANG-KAI-SII is a var. of kanka bilo. See other games involving holding one's breath, such as >KABADDI, >TATAU MANAWA.
J.K. Adjaye, Teaching/Learning about African Society Games, 1983; A. Taylor Cheska, 'Kanka-bilo (Millipede)', TGDWAN,1987, 38.

KAO GLE, lit. 'ghost with a hook', or 'hook ghost', a ritual dance with masks resembling an acrobatic show, practiced by the people of Dan and its Yacuba sections on the Ivory Coast and in Gio, in Liberia. The main ceremony takes place every 6 years, on the occasion of a ghost holiday, which is to secure the abundance of cattle; lesser ceremonies are held on the occasion of other holidays. Kao Gle (a disguised person wearing a mask) and his assistants hold sharp-ended metal hooks. The masked person is wearing an outfit made of raffia creepers hanging to the ground. On his shoulders there are 2 covers of different length. There are some rags attached to the mask. A group of strongmen playing buffalo

Kangoo jumping.

horns, gongs and rattles made of bamboo or hollowed-out pumpkins participate in the ceremony. One of the bamboo rattles is used for indicating particular phases of the ritual.
The strongmen with the instruments surround the dancing Kao Gle, who is making ritual symbolic gestures. In this way they reach the center of the village. Kao Gle moves in reverse to the spectators: if they squat, he jumps and the other way round. Kao Gle throws the hook at the sky and wards off the evil spirits of witches, making violent gestures resembling blowing away cobwebs, which is a symbol of breaking off any relations with the witches leaving the village. The largest bamboo rattle gives the signal to stop and to start special asymmetrical Kao Gle dancing gestures. Kao Gle begins the dance of destruction, tearing off the roofing, treading on the linen taken down from fences and clothes lines, etc. When he returns after the symbolic act of destruction to normal dance, he throws the hooks under the feet of the musicians, who jump to avoid injury. The whole, through the return from the dangers and destruction to normality symbolizes the durability of the social order maintained against temporary threats.
A.Taylor Cheska, 'Kao Gle', TGDWAN, 1987, 88; R.F. Thompson, African Ary in Motion. Icon and Act, 1974, 160-166.

K

**WORLD SPORTS
ENCYCLOPEDIA**

KAPELA, also *kapele*, a folk sport once popular in the Kociewie region of Poland. It survived in the villages of Osówek and Szlachta in the first years after WWII. It consisted in throwing stones and hitting a stack of stones placed one upon another, usu. 5 in number, with the largest one on the ground and the smallest on top. The shape of the stack most probably gave the game its name as the target stack resembles a small chapel (Medieval Latin *capella* – 'chapel'). For the game's purpose flat roundstones of various sizes were used, found in great quantity in the areas of the villages of Osówek and Szlachta. Kapela players were usu. shepherds grazing cows and geese. The game was revived in the 1990s on the initiative of the local authorities of Osieczno. In a description provided by the area administrator, A. Wasilewski, the trad. game was played in the following way:

Top and above: kapela.

The size of the field is not specified. The game is usually played on a forest clearing, in the middle of which a stack of pebbles is positioned. The stack is guarded by the kapela master who is holding a cap or hat. At a certain distance from the stack stand the players whose aim is to knock the stack over by throwing stones at it. After toppling the stack the thrower runs for his stone while the master tries to put the stack back up. If the master rebuilds the stack before the thrower recovers the stone he can throw his cap at the player. If hit, the thrower becomes the new master. If, however, the recovering player squats near the stone he may not be thrown at by the master. The squatter may return with his stone only if the stack is toppled by another player. The player who was the kapela master for the longest time during the game is the loser. The kapela master can move around the field as he wishes. One of the dangerous moments of the game is the situation in which the stone lands near the stack as the recovering player may be hit by another player aiming at the stack.

The revived version of the game has been modified. The pitch is a circle 6m in diameter with the pebble stack in the center. The kapela master stands on the circle line to the right of the stack (as seen by the thrower). The outfield outside the pitch should be a square with at least 14m side length. The number of players is unlimited, however, 4-7 players is optimal. The course of the game differs from that of trad. kapela:

The kapela master is selected by lot at the beginning of the game. If a player throws the stone outside the square failing to hit the stack, he becomes the kapela master. The master can throw his cap at a recovering player only if the latter is close to his stone. The runner can dodge the master as he wishes. The following player cannot throw at the stack before the return of the recovering player.

In the revived version of kapela there is no squatting by the stone. The winner is the player who has managed to remain in the kapela master's position for the shortest time.
A. Wasilewski, *Rules for kapela*, unpublished typescript.

KAPLØB, Dan. for 'race running', [Dan. *kap* – race + *løb*-run]. Trad. races in Denmark were divided into timed and target runs. A target run was usu. held in a park or large garden grounds where a circular route was marked. The runners started off from opposite directions and ran towards the same finishing line, the faster runner winning. Timed races became popular with the invention of stop-watches. Even though Denmark had not been influenced by Brit. athletics, the run was similar to the Brit. model in that runners gathered at a starting point and on signal started to race towards a marked finish.

KAPUCHA TOLI, see >TOLI.

KAPUŚ, a Croatian folk game, similar to Pol. >PALANT.

KARAKUCAK GÜREŞI, in Turkey a major national var. of wrestling, in which the wrestlers do not first smear themselves with oil [Turk. *kara* – black + *kucak* – hold, grasp + *güreş* – fighting, including wrestling] unlike in the commonly known wrestling of the >YAGLI GÜREŞ type. In Turkey and the areas under its influence, where karakucak güreşi is popular, wrestling that involves body oiling is not practiced; the 2 traditions are mutually exclusive. Another feature of karakucak güreşi is the fact that wrestling competitors are chosen in a way that disregards the opponents' height, and instead are matched on the basis of their age and a subjective evaluation of their strength and fitness. Karakucak-güreşi wrestling types stem from Central Asia, and their character, rules and ritual have hardly changed since time immemorial. The wresting styles that resemble karakucak güreşi are also called free fighting (*serbest güreş*) and are known and cultivated among the Manchurian, Yakut, Crimean Tatar, Kazakh, Mongolian and Azer peoples and by the inhabitants of E and W Turkistan. Karakucak güreşi fights are held on holidays and family celebrations, e.g. weddings, accompanied by trad. Turk. music, *duval-zurna*, performed on a wooden pipe and a drum [Turk. *duval* – drum + *zurna* – pipe]. The pipe has finger holes and resembles a thick Eur. recorder or flute made from natural-colored wood, but it has a conical end, like a trumpet. The end may be made of wood or of metal. A zurna is embellished with a number of metal chains, often silver, with beads. While the zurna comes in only one shape in all Turk. regions, the drums do not: some are large drums, fastened to a belt in a similar fashion to a drum major, others are small and hand-held. However, one feature is common to all drums: the rhythm is struck with a single curved stick. The wrestlers put on special black trousers, called *pirpit*, for the fight, which is how the name of this wrestling style originated. Adherents of karakucak güreşi, which resembles >FREESTYLE WRESTLING, successfully compete in this style on the international level, including the Ol.G., W.Ch. and E.Ch.
In the Crimean-Tatar language the name *karakucak güreşi* is >KÜREŞ; in other cultures exhibiting Turkish influences it is >KURASZ (Uzbeki); >KURESH (Kirgiz) or in another dialect >GIULES.
H. Murat Şahin, 'Salvar güreşi', *Turk Spor Kulturund Aba Güreşi*, 1999, p. 34-35.

KARATE, in full *karate-do* [Jap. *kara* – empty + *te* – hand + *do* – rule or art = the art of the empty hand],

1) a self-defense and fighting method consisting of hitting the opponent's vulnerable body areas with the hand, elbow, knee, foot or head without using any weapons. The striking parts of the body are toughened and their striking force strengthened by means of special training, which fosters the skills necessary for hand-to-hand combat; 2) a sport based on this method, featuring a number of styles, non-hazardous to life and health owing to consciously stripping the blows of their ultimate striking force. Blows, strikes and kicks which result in the opponent being knocked to the ground are permitted, provided their force is reasonable. There are 2 basic fighting methods in karate: blocks and counterattack, which are on some occasions supplemented with throws and a technique of twisting the opponents' arms or legs. Hands and feet are used in the fight for blocking the opponent (blocks with the arms – *uke*) and dealing the following kinds of blows: pushes (*tsuki*), strikes (*uchi*) and kicks (*geri*). Karate trainees and fighters are known as *karateka*. Training and fighting sessions take place on a mat, in a room called a *dojo*. Present day karate is divided into modern and trad. karate. Average karate fans, and, regrettably, sports journalists, fail to distinguish the philosophical and technical differences between the two, which are best described by an expert from the Pol. periodical *Świat Karate* (*World of Karate*):

The cornerstone of traditional, or original, karate [...] is the 'final blow'. The final blow is defined as a technique that suffices to overpower the opponent. With the auxiliary techniques, the final blow focuses in itself the power of the entire body. Competition in traditional karate employs self-defense from start to finish, with the exception of the final blow which counts as a point. Moreover, in accordance with the rule saying that the final blow is the last blow dealt in a fight, the fight in traditional karate ends with a fighter scoring one point. Owing to a consistent application of this rule, the number of shifts and inaccuracies in the technique has been brought to a minimum. As in any other art of self-defense, the opponent's height and weight are not determined, and of no importance. What is more, many a time the attacker is of a sturdier build than the attacked. As a sports discipline, traditional karate treats competition as a further training session and a means toward general perfecting of human development through gaining emotional composure and internal discipline, and following etiquette. These ends combined make up the sporting rules of traditional karate.

Other, modern karate schools draw on traditional karate in their evolution. Their techniques and stances are based on strikes and kicks stemming from Japanese karate. They have introduced fundamental modifications despite preserving a surface resemblance, the central one being an alteration of the philosophical attitude and shifting the stress from the art of combat and self-defense to a scored sports competition, consisting of dealing blows and kicks. [...] Points in a sports fight can be scored for maximum speed and precision in hitting the object with a fist or foot. In this situation, the concept of the final blow becomes redundant, and, as a result, focusing the power generated by the movement of the entire body in one blow is no longer necessary, the stress being placed upon the economy of movements. In this crucial respect the body dynamics in modern schools is the opposite of that in trad. karate. The new schools compensated for the relinquishment of the concept of the final blow by way of introducing a multipoint scoring system. In modern karate we usu. have systems awarding three or six half-points. Traditional karate is about self-defense – as a consequence there are no weight divisions. Modern karate, however, sees fighting as a sports event, not an art. As a result, one of the modern schools has as many as seven weight divisions.

[Oct. 1998, p. 10-11]

There are 3 basic self-perfection elements in every karate school: *kata* – simulated fight with an imaginary opponent; *kumite* – fight with a real opponent; *kihon* – technique improvement.
Sports karate competitions consist of kumite or kata events, individual and team. Each team is made up of an uneven number of fighters. In sports karate the contestants are grouped in weight divisions, which is a criterion for opponent pairing. In trad. karate the fights are in the open category, where the karateka fight, in line with the philosophical rules of the sport, up to 1pt. (2 *wazarris* – 2 indecisive victories, or 1 *ippon* – a decisive victory). There are 3 var. of open category fights in trad. karate: a *shobu ippon*, i.e. fight up to 1pt. in an effective time of 90sec., a *sanbon shobu*, i.e. fight consisting of 3 *shobu ippons*, and a *jogai*, i.e. literally going outside the mat (going outside the mat twice means a *wazari* for the opponent). According to the rules of trad. karate, 'to score a point for a particular technique a contestant must retain an appropriate

Karate.

stance, stability and *zanshin*, the fighting spirit. While performing a given technique bodily contact is prohibited. In case of a contact blow, the assessment of its effects is left to the judge. And so, a) harmless contact, well and precisely controlled is 1pt.; b) contact causing visible injury to the opponent may result in the contestant's disqualification (*hansoku*); c) contact with negligible effect earns the contestant a warning (*chui*)'. Individual and team kata in trad. karate are 'scored with points. The judges in their assessment look for technical correctness of kata movements, their ordering, techniques sequencing and continuation, a kata-specific speed, and include an interpretation of the application of specific kata techniques. In team kata the additional element is synchronization of the movements of a team of three'.

Additionally, in trad. karate the following events are held:

fuku-go, or a karate biathlon, where alternately kata and kumite fights are held within one competition. The contestants simultaneously show combined kata called *kitei*. The contests in the qualifying round are arranged in such a way that kumite is fought in the final.

en-bu – a choreographed exhibition of the attack-defence technique lasting for 55-60sec., it is fought in all-male and mixed pairs and is scored with points, similarly to kata.

A number of fighting styles have developed, some of the most important being *shotokan*, *wado ryu*, *shito ryu*, *goju ryu*. International federations develop their own styles, for example in the World Karate Federation the valid styles are the 'WKF style' (named after the federation), *shotokan*, and *kyokushin*. Like the other far-eastern arts of combat, karate has a rich terminology (in addition to the terms explained above):

hajime – the start of the fight;
jogai – outside the mat;
kyu – trainee grades;
makiwara – a device for training the strength of the strikes;
monotochi – an order to return to initial positions;
obi – the belt;
sempai – a senior karateka;
sensei-ni-rei – a bow to the teacher;
otaga-ni-rei – a bow to fellow trainees;
tameshiwari – a strength test;
hikiwake – a draw;
atoshibaraku – 30sec. to the end of a contest;
fukushin-shugo – the judges' deliberation;
ketteisein – an additional contest in case of a draw.

The clothing called *gi* is a 2-part suit resembling loose pajamas made of thick white cotton. The trousers reach just above the ankle and are secured with a string or thin tape at the waist. The jacket is tied twice with a belt, the color of which indicates the grade of the karateka, from novice's white to the much vaunted *sensei*'s black. The intermediate colors in ascending order are red, yellow, orange, green, purple and brown. The fight is conducted barefoot.

History. The basic principles of karate have developed since at least the 17th cent. on Okinawa (cf. >OKINAWA-TE), where a number of southern styles of >GONGFU mingled with the local styles of com-

bat. Until the 1920s all names of karate techniques were descriptive. In the spirit of nationalist preparations for an imperial conquest, 'kara – Chinese + *te* – a hand' was changed into '*kara* – empty + *te* – a hand'. However, all experienced karate masters are well aware of the Chin. origins of the sport. All of the great 19th cent. Okinawa experts studied Chin. *gongfu* for many years, while karate – similar to most 'external' Chin. martial arts – was developed at the Shaolin temple. The genesis of karate reaches back to the old Chin. unarmed combat methods of antiquity and the Middle Ages. As far as the techniques are concerned, it evolved into a combination of the older Chin. forms of gongfu and Okinawan dancing style. An Ind. monk called Bodhidharma, who supposedly lived in the 6th cent. in the legendary Shaolin temple, is the legendary founding father of Chin. martial arts and combat prior to karate. The brutality of the ritual was softened by Buddhism, transforming it into an intellectually calculated method of self-defense. Modern karate schools bear a striking resemblance to the historical evidence concerning the 17th-cent. karate practiced on Okinawa and the Ryukyu Archipelago (located at the point where the Pacific and the E China Sea meet). Apart from Buddhism, karate was influenced by the Chin. occupation of the island in the 15th cent. The karate forms that developed out of the Okinawan traditions were thought to have originated from *chuan-fa*, a form that came to Okinawa from the Chin. territory of Fujian; it is from these forms that the *nan-pei-chun* style stems. An important factor in the development of the art of self-defense on Okinawa was a ban on carrying arms imposed upon the populace introduced in the 15th cent. – only nobly born fighters were allowed to use weapons. The subjects reacted to this state of affairs by developing karate, as situations requiring effective self-defense were commonplace. Since the inhabitants of Okinawa practiced their art in secret, they developed clandestine levels of introduction to karate, which are still observable in some elements of the ritual of this sport. They are sometimes described as Okinawan styles or schools – *Okinawa-de* (also *Okinawa-te* or *to-de*). From these later came the *shuri-te* style (named after the Shuri District, which encompasses also the *tomari-te* school) and naha-te (from the city of Naha) in the second half of the 19th cent., on which modern trad. karate is based.

In the initial decades of the 20th cent., as a result of a successful experiment with >JUDO, the karate tradition evoked interest and gave rise to attempts at reinvigorating old culture forms so that they could be juxtaposed with powerful Western influences. The 1930s saw the birth of a concept which turned karate into a method of upbringing suited for imperial politics. The outbreak of WWII and the military circles falling into disrepute hindered the process of using karate in upbringing. However, Amer. servicemen occupying Japan, after their return home, generated the first wave of interest in karate. At the same time Amer. occupational authorities encouraged the Japanese to develop such elements of their culture as would balance Jap. nationalism and militarism. Sports played a key role in these plans, which influenced the development of karate in the 1950s. Karate quickly spread throughout the world once Jap.

authorities recognized it as a national sports discipline. It soon transpired though, that the limited number of Jap. experts would not be able to provide for the increasingly numerous karate centers that began to sprout and grow dynamically in W Europe, the USA, and other countries. Many regions began independent work on their own var. of the sport. This resulted in school diversification and, indirectly, their severance from some original traditions. In 1959, in what was then W Germany, the first national karate association was founded. To halt further segmentation of karate schools, the World Union of Karate-do Organizations (WUKO) was founded in 1970. The effort to unite all karate organizations soon turned out to be mere wishful thinking, though. Nowadays a line is drawn between sports or modern karate, practiced under the auspices of the World Karate Federation (WKF), and trad. karate, which is supervised by the International Traditional Karate Federation (ITKF). For the time being, the IOC recognizes the WKF, which stands therefore a greater chance of introducing its karate version into the Olympics. Nevertheless, the IOC in its 101st Session in 1993 also defined trad. karate as 'practiced within the ITKF and subject to its regulations'.

The controversy of karate. Inappropriate ways of practicing this sport and its miscomprehension have lead to a multitude of accidents. Bodily harm is especially frequent. Ill-prepared instructors and trainees have been hurt and even maimed while inexpertly demonstrating a blow. Additionally, the pressure of popular films presenting Eastern fighting sports devoid of their deep spiritual foundations leads to misinterpretations which run clearly against the philosophy of karate, which favors restraint and composure, and not defeating the opponent out of blood-lust. Today this problem is raised in almost every karate handbook. The following quotation from the Pol. magazine *Świat Karate* underscores the scale of the problem:

Unfortunately, despite the lengths to which karate instructors have gone prove that a karate fight is not an ordinary brawl and is not meant as a coercive or belligerent measure, negative karate connotations have taken root in society. Even today, karate is misunderstood by some people as severe all-out fighting or mere board-breaking stunts. Naturally, karate is just a tool, it resembles a razor that can be used or abused depending on the intentions. A fight with someone who is first of all a dojo-mate and only then an opponent is a challenge that serves to raise the spirit but does not lead to a confrontation whose only aim is to show one's superiority. Strength and stamina, separated from the ultimate goal that they are to serve, became worthless artifacts.

[Oct. 1998,13]

L. Frederic, *A Dictionary of the Martial Arts*, 1991; G. Funakoshi, *Karate-Do Kyohan*, 1976; P. Hickey, *Karate Techniques and Tactics*, 1997; O. Masutatsu, *Karate kyokushinkai*, 1990; J. Miłkowski, *Karate. Wiadomości podstawowe*, 1985; T. Morris, *Karate. The Complete Course*. 1987; R. Murat, *Historia karate-do*, 1994; M. Nakayama, *Dynamic Karate*, 1967; M. Oyama, *Advanced Karate*, 1970; T. Suzuki, *Karate-do*, 1967; J. Świerczynski, *Karate*, 1983; personal interviews with A. Ładzińska, A. Suligowska and W. Kwieciński.

Leticia Montoya of Mexico competes against Elisa Au in karate during the Titan Games at San Jose State University in San Jose, California.

K

KARATEO, also *karari*, a Maori game, where a large wooden dummy is moved. The dummy is usu. 15-18in. (38-45cm), but sometimes even 1m high, or even as tall as a person. Its arms and legs are attached to the trunk with strings. Traditionally the person holding the dummy sings and imitates dancing movements.

KARAYA WRESTLING, a trad. var. of wrestling popular among the Karaya Indians living in central Brazil. Karaya wrestling matches were held when new settlers were challenged by the aboriginal inhabitants of a given area who wanted to test the newcomers. If a larger group, e.g. a tribe, settled close to the Karaya, they usu. invited their chief to compete.

KÄRNTENRINGEN, one of 3 trad. Aus. folk wrestling types, whose common feature is that fighters grasp each other's trousers. This var. is practiced in the land of Kärnten, hence the name [Ger. *Ringen* – wrestling]. Two contestants wrestle in a circle, in a standing position. The first to touch the ground with any part of his body except for the legs loses the match. Similar forms of wrestling are called, depending on the region, >JUPPENRINGEN and >HOSENLUPF.

KARPLE, the name of the equipment and the way of moving on snow, halfway between skis and >SNOW SHOES. Karple were used in times of old by the people of the Beskids mountain range (Poland). The chief difference between Pol. karple and Amer. snowshoes was that the former were made of solid wood, while the latter – of strips of leather stretched over a wooden frame. In 1851 L. Delvaux wrote: 'The runners hurry with their poles and wooden karple, which they fasten to their feet when in the woods to keep themselves from falling into the snow'.

KARTING, also go-karting and go-karts (go-carts), a sport practiced in small, 4-wheel vehicles with no doors or roof, powered by 2- or 4-stroke internal combustion engines. The length of a go-kart ranges from 5 to 8ft. (roughly 1.5-1.8m), the height must not exceed 25in. (63cm), and width 40in. (about 1m). Rims are typically 5in. in diameter (12cm); wheels with tires 9-17in. (23-43cm) in diameter. The whole body of a go-kart is surrounded by a protective bumper. Power is transmitted either by a chain or a drive shaft and a gearbox, which determines the primary division into classes. The engine is usu. fitted at the back, although there are models with the engine at the side or with 2 engines. Engine capacity ranges from 50 to 260ccm. The driver sits with his knees bent in front. Specialized classes of high-speed go-karts (sprint class) and long-distance go-karts (enduro class) can be distinguished. The most important formulas of international races are: 'formula A', 'intercontinental A', 'super A' (all with 100ccm engines with different tech. characteristics), and 'formula C'. The formulas are often additionally divided into junior categories in different age groups. There are also many regional and national formulas (e.g.: resa sport, junior piston sport, junior clubman), and company's formulas sponsored by the producers: formula Honda or formula Yamaha. They are often additionally subdivided according to the racers' age or the cubic capacity of the engine (yamaha light, yamaha heavy, yamaha junior). Just in Australia, there are as many as 4 national categories (national light, senior national light, junior national light, junior national heavy). In many countries, e.g. Germany, there are non-typical categories of 200-250ccm. Karts in those categories are called superkarts and races are usu. organized on car racing tracks instead of small karting tracks.

Go-kart races in Poland are organized in international formulas 'intercontinental A', (including the junior category), 'C' and 'intercontinental C'. Races in formulas 'A' and 'super A' do not take place. Races are also organized in regional categories: youngsters 50ccm, youngsters 60ccm, juniors 125ccm (12-19yrs. old), the racing class 125ccm, cadets (60ccm, usu. with lawn mower engines), and popular class which allows all kinds of 125ccm engines. Differences in design include go-karts with or without a gearbox, go-karts with different engine or gearbox types, etc.

History. The first carts were supposedly built by technical personnel at Amer. airfields towards the end of WWII. While waiting for crews returning from action, they would build and race in small carts fitted with pump or compressor engines. At the beginning of the 1950s the first races were organized with the use of go-karts resembling miniature models of racing cars. However, the concept of the discipline was shaped around 1956 in California thanks to A. Ingels, a serviceman at car races, who built the first vehicle resembling modern racing go-karts. He adopted a simple pipe frame structure and a lawn mower engine. Later, together with his friend L. Borrelli, Ingels founded the go-kart factory Caretta. Their

product quickly caught on as a leisure purpose vehicle. Soon other companies started producing go-karts, and at the turn of the 1950s and '60s there were already some 150 manufacturers of carting equipment in the USA. This result was the popularization of carting as a professional discipline, also outside the USA. The first races were organized at a parking lot next to the Rose Bowl sports complex in Passadena, California. The Go Kart Club of America, the first organization gathering racers and fans of karting was founded in 1957. In the following years many more associations were established, including the world's biggest organizations such as the World Karting Association and the World Karting Federation. Countries with the strongest interest in karting are: Australia, Denmark, Holland, Canada, Germany, Italy and the USA. The most important events are the W.Ch. in individual categories, continental championships incl. Eur., Oceania and N.Amer. championships, the A. Senna World Cup, and numerous international races, such as the Monaco Kart Grand Prix Invitational, the Italian Winter Cup, the Margutti Trophy, the Toshiba Max Championship, the Honda Challenge, etc.

As a rule, most karting racers switch to car racing after they have gained experience in karting. Only a few remain in the discipline in a more advanced age to reaffirm their position. Regardless of this changeability, in the 1990s the following racers acquired an international position: K. Herder (USA); T. Hunt, A. Gurr, A. Graham (Australia); B. Vroomen (Belgium); A. Dos Santos (Brasil); D. Fose, S. Harris (Great Britain); T. Vilander and H. Kovalainen (Finnland); J. Poncelet (France); N. Van der Pol (Holland), Y. Shibata, S. Imada, T. Sugiyama (Japan); S. Sodeberg (Sweden); M. Ardigo, D. Rossi, E. Gandoliffi, M. Rugolo, S. Cessetti, R. Quintarelli (Italy). In 1983 a team of Can. racers from Ontario: O. Nimmo, G. Ruddock, J. Timmons and D. Upshaw set an unmatched long-distance record, covering 1,108mi. (1,787km) within 24h. The record was set on a 1.6km track. The fastest karts in the world can go at more than 200km/h.

Z. Perzyński, S. Szeligowski, J. Wasiak, *Karting w szkole*, 1982; T. Rychter, *Karting*; L. Smith, *Karting* 1982; Personal communication: K. Kalicki, H. Śródecki.

KARTULI CHIDAOBA, also spelled *tchidaoba, tchdaobe* or *čidaobe*, a type of Georg. wrestling, usu. held to celebrate important family occasions or holidays and accompanied by music. Contestants try to floor their opponent on his back.

Wrestlers fight on dug ground, usu. barefoot or wearing light slippers. They are dressed in special wrestling jackets, girded with a strong sash. This outfit, called czochi, is very unique. Contestants fight tightly holding each other's sashes and make complicated movements, usu. with their legs. The fight is extremely fast. Seventy-six of the best contestants in 7 weight categories [...] participated in the 1939 Georg. Championships [...]. This event was preceded by regional championships, which attracted a few hundred competitors. This kind of wrestling is extremely popular in Georgia; nearly every village has its wrestlers and the fights are witnessed by hundreds of thousands of spectators.

[*Sport in the USSR*, 1948]

KAS AN TOUSEG D'AR MORE, a Bret. counterpart of the Fr. children's game *jeter le crapaud à la mer* – tossing the toad into the sea.

F. Peru, *La tradition populaire de jeux de plein air en Bretagne*, LJP, 1998.

KASA-GAKE, Jap. for 'the aimed-at helmet', an old Jap. form of archery, deriving from the >YABUSAME tradition. After the game was over, the participants threw their helmets into the air and shot at them with a bow. With time, the helmet was replaced with a round target (approx. 55cm in diameter) covered with leather, which the contestants aimed at from galloping horses. See also >INUOMONO.

W.R.B. Acker, *Japanese Archery*, 1965; E. Herrigel, *Zen in der Kunst des Bogenschiessen*, 1948; A. Sollier and Z. Gyobiro, *Japanese Archery, Zen in Action*, 1969.

KÄSIKAPULAN, a competition of Fin. lumberjacks consisting of pulling felled tree trunks on the ground, esp. popular in N Finalnd [*käsi* – manual + *kapula* – tree trunk].

KASTE KNIV, a Dan. game, where players throw a knife at a tree or a simple wooden target [*kaste* – throwing + *kniv* – knife].

J. Møller, 'Kaste Kniv', GID, 1997, 4, 68.

Karting – a sport for all seasons.

KASTE LÆSSETRÆ OVER HUS, Dan. for 'throwing the log over the house', [Dan. *kaste* – throwing + *læssetræ* – log + *over* – over + *hus* – house]. The contestant, in a standing position, takes a large wooden log, holds it vertically, bends his knees and heaves the log over the house, with the log landing on the other side of the building. This is a risky competition in view of possible damage to the roof, not to mention the possibility of the log rolling back down upon the thrower, therefore contestants take great care in preparing themselves for the task and measuring their strength.
J. Møller, 'Kaste læssetræ over hus', GID, 1997, 1, 133.

KASTE MED KØLLE, Dan. for 'throwing the mallet', a game played mostly esp. Sundays and holidays. The object of the game was to throw the mallet in a straight line (a curved throw did not count). Sometimes 2 towns or villages competed and their authorities funded special prizes.
J. Møller, 'Kaste med kølle', GID, 1997, 1.

KASTE MED LÆSSETRÆ, Dan. for 'throwing the log' [*kaste* – throwing + *læssetræ* – log], an old Dan. folk sport, where players throw a log used to weigh down hay on a cart. The participant balances the log vertically, then quickly bends his knees and throws it. The log should make a semi-turn and land as far away as possible. Whoever manages to throw the greatest distance, wins.
J. Møller, 'Kaste med læssetræ', GID, 1997, 1, 132.

KASTE STRYGE, also *spån*, an old Dan. game played near the end of the harvest [*kaste* – throw + *stryge* – to smooth; *spån* – cut with a scythe or sickle]. A rake was dug into the ground near the last sheaf. Harvesters approached it in turn and stood with their back to it. Holding their left ear with their right hand and looking over the left shoulder, they threw the straw-rope from the last swath backward. The person whose rope fell furthest from the rake got the title of 'farting mama' (*fismor*) or 'farting papa' (*fisfar*) [*fis* – fart; probably concerning the effort the participant had to make].
J. Møller, 'Kaste stryge (Spån)', GID, 1997, 1, 133.

KASTE TIL HIMMERIG, Dan. for 'throwing to heaven', an old game where players threw a knife into the ground. A figure is drawn on the ground, consisting of a circle representing hell (*helvede*), a rectangle or ellipse representing purgatory (*skærsilden*) and a cross, or a circle with a cross in it, representing heaven (*himmerig*). Between the figures 2 or 4 mouse holes are drawn (*musehuller*). Players each put a straw in 'hell' and then take turns to throw the knife so that it makes a turn and gets stuck in the ground. For every successful throw a contestant has the right to move his straw closer to 'heaven'. It takes 3 successful throws to get out of 'purgatory' (hence 3 fields in the ellipse) and 5 to get into 'heaven' (there are 5 fields in 'heaven').
J. Møller, 'Kaste til himmerig', GID, 1997, 1, 130.

KASTFANG, see >FÅNGTAG.

KASZA, Pol. for 'the buckwheat game', an old Pol. game played in schools in the 18th cent., a member of the >CHWYTKA family – a type of ball game where the ball had to be caught in various ways. Ł. Gołębiowski described kasza in *Gry i zabawy różnych stanów* (*Games and Pastimes of Various Social Classes* – 1831).

KAT MET TO HOVEDER, Dan. for 'the cat with two heads', [Dan. *kat* – cat + *met* – with + *to* – two + *hoveder* – heads]. Two contestants get down on all fours with their backsides to each other. One of them puts his legs under the other's abdomen and crosses them on his back. The opponent intertwines his own legs, crossing them under the other's abdomen. This way both pairs of legs are crossed, one on top of the other. In this position the players try to crawl in opposite directions to pull the opponent to their side. The tangle of legs forces the weaker of the participants to crawl backwards.
J. Møller, 'Kaste met to hoveder', GID, 1997, 4, 20.

KATO PALE, [Gr. *kata* – downward], a type of ancient wrestling par terre. See >PALE.

KATTESTRUD, see >GRÆSSE KO.

KATTIVELA, Hindi for 'knife against empty hand', a martial art and self-defense technique, one of the 5 basic Hindi fighting techniques of >ADI MURAI.

KAU WHAKATAETAE, a Maori art of swimming.

KAUKWALULE KWALULE, a Nigerian children's game, played esp. in the regions of Yao and Makonde [*kaukwelule* – cover his eyes]. Participants stand in a circle and chant, rubbing their hands against those of their neighbors: '*Kaukwalule kwalule*' – cover his eyes. In the next verse the text changes to '*Kajave, kajave*' – let's clap our hands. A child, clapping his hands, goes into the circle and kneels down. Another child stands behind him and covers his eyes with her hands. Someone from the circle pats the kneeling child on the forehead and asks, '*Vanyamputile?*' – who hit you? The child's eyes are now uncovered and he answers, '*Anomo amputile*' – he hit me, pointing his hand. If his guess is correct, he changes places with the person who hit him. If not, he stays in the circle and the game goes on until he guesses correctly. The children chant, '*Mkosele, tampute soni!*' – he didn't guess, let's hit him again.
P.G. Brewster, 'Two Games from Africa', *American Anthropologist*, 1944, 46; A Taylor Cheska, 'Blind Man's Buff', TDGWAN, 1987, 23.

KAV, also *kuk, kaud*; see >MUNK.

KAYAK RODEO, a var. of wildwater canoeing. Its most important element is evolutions performed in wildwater, e.g: overflip (turning the kayak in water) or vertical flip (setting the kayak in a vertical position and turning it around the v. axis). The time on the course does not matter, points are assigned for the number and technical correctness of evolutions. The kayak design differs from trad. kayaks and those used in mountain kayaking: the body is wider at the cockpit and flat at the ends, the front of the kayak is much shorter as compared to trad. models in order to make evolutions easier. Kayak rodeo started in the USA. The best sportsmen include: M. Lyle, B. Knapp, D. Gavere. The most important centers of kayak rodeo are located in Idaho, USA, an area with perfect conditions for kayak rodeo owing to its abundance of rapids.

KAYAKING, a var. of water sports practiced in kayaks and comprising both competitions held in kayaks as well as kayak traveling. The term kayak itself stems from Inuit kayak spelled also *kyak, kyack* or *kiak* – a boat covered with animal skins. The name stood for a small rib-framed canoe covered with animal skins, completely enclosed except for an opening for each occupant, propelled by a single paddle with 2 blades without support. Nowadays kayaks are constructed in a similar way with plastics more and more often substituting the originally applied wood, and with new technological advances introduced in place of old solutions. The shape of paddles has been maintained.
History. Kayaking originated in the Inuit culture where it was known as early as c.4000 BC. It enabled survival, was used for transportation and fish and water mammal hunting. The first encounter of the Europeans and Eskimos paddling in their kayaks recognized in the earliest sources as >UMIAK, dates back to the end of the 15th cent. *Umiak*, in

Kayak rodeo.

Eskimo language 'a canoe for women', was for the first time described by the Eng. sailor, M. Forbischer, (c.1535-1594) when he met Inuits using such kayaks in the area of today's Baffin Bay (possibly Davis Strait). Kayaking as practiced by the Eskimos was art in itself, which did not change the fact that the sea claimed the lives of many of them. The Eskimo word *pivoq* ('a sea voyage') also means 'they lost their life in a kayak'. An Amer. anthropologist P. Radin pointed to the Eng. translation of the hunters' poem of the Eskimos which described, among others, the role of the kayak:

I call to mind
And think of the early coming of spring
As I knew it
In my younger days.
Was I ever such a hunter!
Was it myself indeed?
For I see
And recall in memory a man in a kayak;
slowly he toils along in toward the shores of the lake,
With many spear-slain caribou in tow.
Happiest am I
In my memories of hunting in a kayak.
On land, I was never of great renown
Among the herds of caribou.
And an old man, seeking strength in his youth,
Loves most to think of the deeds
Whereby he gained renown
[After P. Radin, *The Method and Theory of Ethnology*, 1966, 96]

Intensified relationships between the Europeans and the inhabitants of Greenland and N.Amer. paved the way for many borrowings, including the kayak's construction. The first Eur. kayak is said to have been publicly displayed by a Saxon to king Augustus II, Elector of Saxony and King of Poland, on the Elbe river in 1723. In 1761 an Englishman named W. Hickey took his neighbour's kayak for a trip along the Thames and later described this experience in his memoirs:

Mr. Hindley [...] had a small canoe, which was kept in a narrow channel, or creek of the Thames, opposite his house, merely as a pretty object for the eye. [...] I prevailed on the gardener not only to let me have the use of it, but to make me a double-feathered paddle to work it with, which, when ready I began my manoeuvers, taking special care until I became used to my ticklish vessel, not to venture into deep water. This canoe was just my own length, only fifteen inches wide, and of so tottering a nature that bending my body to the right or to the left would endanger the upsetting it. During my practice I got many a ducking; but in a few weeks I became so expert in the management of it that I with confidence ventured into deep water. Both ends were exactly of the same form, so that I could go either way without turning; it had no seat, I therefore placed myself as nearly in the centre as I could, and working the feathers of the paddles alternately, went on at a quick rate. Having thus accomplished the perfect management of my little vessel, the next object I had in view was unexpectedly to exhibit myself in it, and thereby dreadfully to alarm my fond mother for the safety of her darling boy; to effect which cruel and ungrateful purpose, I fixed upon a day

Top to bottom: stamps issued for the kayaking championships in Poland (1961), Romania (1962), Czechoslovakia (1967), Finland (1973).

316

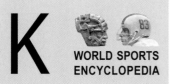

K WORLD SPORTS ENCYCLOPEDIA

when company were to dine at our house, who being assembled and walking upon the lawn previous to dinner, I embarked at Lord Radnor's and going round an island suddenly made my appearance in the middle of the Thames, opposite my father's, to the infinite terror and alarm of my dear mother.

[*Memoirs of William Hickey*, ed. 1960, p. 32]

In the 1st half of 19th cent. entertainment entrepreneurs toured throughout Europe with groups of Eskimos and Samoyeds. Some of the 'exotic shows' included the display of such kayaking skills as remaining in a capsized kayak head-under-water. In 1851 in Leipzig the kayak show by the Eskimos included experimental rides for the spectators. Around 1860 the Scot. constructor J. MacGregor constructed a kayak-later commonly imitated. MacGregor held many exemplary rides and voyages in his kayak on the rivers and lakes of England, Scotland, Germany, Sweden, and Finland. He also undertook a voyage to the Holy Land via the Mediterranean Sea, an event abundantly commented on by the Eur. press which considerably contributed to the propagation of kayaking. MacGregor founded the Royal Canoeing Club in 1865.

The development of a modern sports kayak may be considered from then on. For further development of kayaks in history see >FLAT WATER KAYAKING, >WHITE WATER KAYAKING AND CANOEING; also >CANOE POLO and >KAYAK RODEO.

C. Chenu, *En Cano*, 1928; S. Deicke, H.J. Lotsch, *ABC des Wasserwanderns*, 1963; J. Drabik, *Kajakarstwo-teoria i praktyka-sport, turystyka-rekreacja*, 1991; I. Granek, *Kanusport* 1970; D. Harrison, *Sea Kayaking Basics* 1993; B. Hoff, *The Tao of Pooh*, London 1982; R.R. Kowalski, *Kajakarstwo-wioślarstwo*, 1976; J.M. Lipawski, *Sport kajakowy*, 1934; B. Mason, *The Path of the Paddle*, 1980; J. Starzyński, *Tao kajaka*, 1997; J.T. Urban, ed., *White Water Handbook for Canoe and Kayak*, Boston.

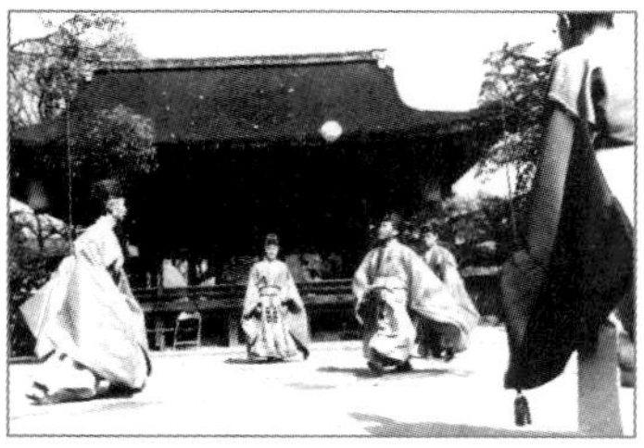

Modern kemari.

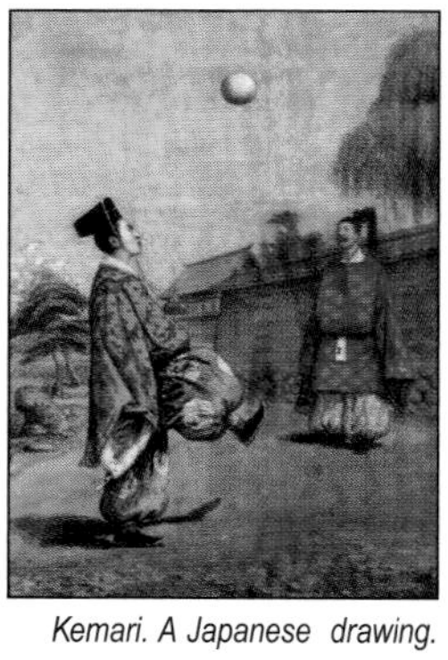

Kemari. A Japanese drawing.

KAZAKH HORSE RACING, a form of >HORSE RACING practiced not only in Kazakhstan, but also among the Kazakhs of other regions, incl. Mongolia. Races were held on religious holidays marking annual landmarks, such as the end of winter, the arrival of the warm season, the fall offerings to the deities, as well as weddings, burials, etc. In *kodboski aymak*, a Mong. district, the ethnographer I. Kabzińska-Stawarz observed a unique kazakh tradition connected with the races in honor of Kurman, the highest deity, who symbolized goodness. The races lasted 2 days and were accompanied by another event – wrestling. The competition was held between neighboring, but rival camps called *aile*. The owner of the winning horse received a prize in the form of another horse, selected by the family elder. The person donating the horse would receive a compensation in the form of another animal – a ram or goat, while the owner of the winning horse would return to his *yurt* or tent for a feast of freshly slain ram, attended by all the participants and spectators, who would also be fed with dairy products. Unlike the Mongols, the Kazakhs would also race mares (>KHURDAAN MOR').

Together with other forms of trad. competition, Kazakh horse races were part of a food holiday called *aš*, celebrating the contact with the spirits of the ancestors (the less wealthy Kazakhs celebrated *kickine aš* – lit. a small feast). The ritual feasts and forms of physical competition associated with them provided a link between the living and the spirits of the deceased, as well as god's providence.

KAZAKH WRESTLING, popular among Asian peoples living in Kazakhstan, essentially identical to the Mongolian >BÖKHIIN BARILDAAN, >BUH. A player was deemed defeated when one or both of his shoulder blades touched the ground or when he touched the ground with his side. The victory was only complete when the winner pressed his opponent to the ground with the whole weight of his body. A match was preceded by an elaborate ritual, somewhat different from the original Mong. one, during which the fighters first shook their right hands, then took 2 steps away from each other and finally turned around their left shoulder. The jacket worn by the competitors was also slightly different from the typical bökhiin barildaan outfit as it lacked the right sleeve. Kazakh wrestling competitions were held alongside >KAZAKH HORSE RACING contests. It was not uncommon that the 2 events were merged into one that started with equestrian wrestling continued on the ground after one of the players managed to dismount his opponent.

A kemari painting on a 6-part screen.

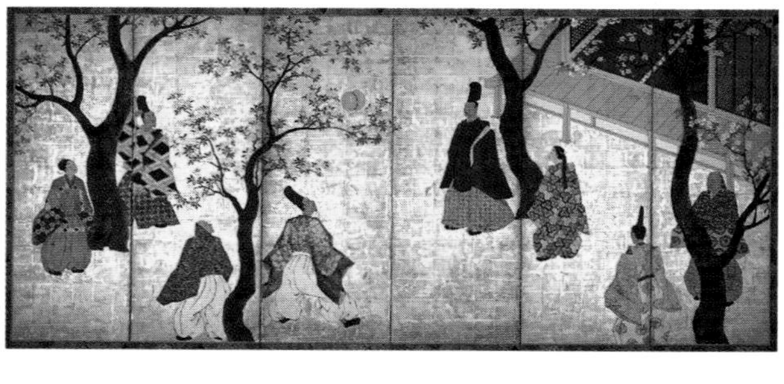

KE NANG HAUN, a fight between men and pigs, practiced in the Nicobar Islands, an archipelago belonging to India and situated in the Bay of Bengal. The fights are held during local folk feasts and are entered into only by men. Domesticated as well as wild pigs are used for the sport. The game starts with the pig in a bamboo cage. A string is tied to one of its legs and held by 2-3 people, who do not participate in the actual fight, which begins when one of the walls of the cage is smashed with an ax. One or 2 contestants – depending on the size and strength of the pig – await it 5-6m off. They try to grab the pig by its ears and hold it in place.

KEATSEN, a Frisian game almost identical to the Du. >KAATSEN. Also known in Flanders. It has the same medieval tradition as *kaatsen* although the two games originated in different geographical regions. The chief differences are: 1) the number of players – 3 on each team in keatsen and 5 in *kaatsen*; 2) the scoring system – 15-30-40 in keatsen and 2-4-6 in *kaatsen*; 3) the diameter of the ball – 4cm and 5cm; 4) the size of the pitch – 60x32m and 73x19m. The rules are almost identical. Among numerous keatsen var., *lolkama* seems to be the most popular. The development of modern keatsen began in 1853 with the founding of the Annual Keatsen Competition Coordinating Committee (*Directie van de Jaarlijkse Groote Kaatspartij te Franeker*).

KECHUKAWE, a popular game of chance of the Mapuche Indians (Araucanians) in Chile, played with 5-sided dice carved of wood, stone or bone. Its name derives from *kechu* (five). The pyramid-shaped die, approx. 2cm wide at the base and 2cm tall, was marked on the sides with painted symbols indicating the values 1-5. Two unique specimens of such dice (found in 1891 and 1895) are on display at the National Museum of Natural History of Santiago de Chile and two more, also dating from the late 19th century, are kept in Neuquén, Argentina. Two players sat in front of each other on the ground in a semicircle divided in 2 and used the same die to determine who went first. In each player's quarter-circle, 12 holes were marked, five at the lines of each sector. Before a die hit the ground it had first to pass through a hoop (*chudughue*) placed horizontally on a 60-cm rod at one side of the semi-circle. According to the indicated points, little stones were put in the marked holes. If the die fell on the side with fewer points – which was rather difficult – the player won instantly. More often the winner was the player who first filled the holes with little stones in his sector. Large bets were once placed on the outcome, and songs, prayers, invocations, and magical manipulations accompanied matches. Kechukawe was an equal-opportunity pastime and was enjoyed alike by men, women, children and seniors. The earliest references to kechukawe date back to Luis de Valdivia's *Arte y Gramática General de la Lengua que corre en todo el Reyno de Chile,* published in Lima in 1606, and Alonso de Ovalle's *Histórica Relación del Reyno de Chile*, published in Rome in 1646. From the 17th century on, kechukawe was well known and enjoyed by non-Mapuche and spread to Argentina in the 18th century. See also >AWARKUDEN.

L. Matus Zapata, 'Juegos y ejercicios físicos de los antiguos araucanos', BMNCH, vol. 11, p.162-1970; O. Plath, 1946; C. López von Vriessen, 'Juegos Aborígenes de Chile, contribución a una alternativa didáctica en la Educación Física latinoamericana', *Perspectiva Educacional,* 1995, p.35-44; the Internet: www.deportesmapuches.cl, www.galeon.com/indiansports

KEGLER MED OPHÆNGT KUGLE, Dan. For 'hanging ball bowling', a var. of bowling where the ball is suspended on a string from the arm of a pole. It is used as a pendulum to knock down the skittles. In folk tradition the string was tied to the branch of a tree or to a roof beam etc. There are 9 skittles, arranged in a square (3x3 rows). The ball hangs on the right side of the square. The length of the string makes the ball hit the skittles just below their thickest part. The skittle in the furthermost corner of the square (from the hanging ball) is smaller than the others and the one standing in the middle – the 'king' – larger than the rest. The ball must not be swung into the middle of the block of skittles. It should pass between the back corner skittle and the skittle next to it.

J. Møller, 'Kegler med ophængt kugle', GID, 1997.

KEIBA, a type of old Jap. horse racing practiced until 700 AD, when the emperor banned it. The reason for this was a shortage of fodder for an increasing number of horses. Details of the races are unknown.

KEIRIN, a Jap. track cycling event where cyclists follow a motorbike, which gradually accelerates. It began in 1948. Nine contestants ride simultaneously, starting from boxes similar to those used in horse racing. About 1.5 laps before the end of the race the motorbike pulls off the track, leaving it free for the finishing cyclists. Keirin is considered an extremely dangerous discipline with a high rate of accidents. In spite of this, it is exceptionally popular in Japan and is beginning to catch on in some W Eur. countries.

KEI-TAISO, a Jap. counterpart of the Amer. >LIGHT GYMNASTICS, introduced in Japan in the late 19th cent. on a wave of Western influence. The promoter of kei-taiso was Amer. educator G.A. Leland, who visited Japan in 1879. He built his idea on the experience of contemporary Amer. physical education specialists, esp. D. Lewis, the creator of light gymnastics. See also >FUTSU-TAISO, an eclectic system combining many traditions.

KÉKÉKÉREBA, see >FA KOR.

KELES, an ancient Gk. term for mounted horse racing (the word also meant a saddle-horse). Keles without further attributes was used to refer to gallop races of mares or stallions, esp. as opposed to trot races of mares (>KALPE). The term >POLON KELES meant colt races. Keles was introduced into the Ol.G. in 648 BC, being part of 33 games in all. The first keles winner was Krauksidas of Krannon. However, the horse's victory was acknowledged even if the horse lost its jockey on the way. (Cf. KHURDAAN MOR'). This is confirmed by an event which took place during the Games in 512 BC and has been described by Pausanias in his *Journeys through Hellada.* The mare Aura (owned by Feidolas of Corinth) 'accidentally threw the rider off her back at the beginning of the race, but continued to run correctly. When the trumpets sounded she ran even faster and came first. She stopped in front of the judges, assuming she had won. The Eleians declared Feidolas the winner' (VI, 13,9). Four years later one of Feidolas's sons won the keles, while the other was victor in another horse race. We know neither the name of the other race, nor the names of Feidolas's sons.

KEMARI also known as *mari koju*, a Jap. game consisting of flicking up a ball with the legs and keeping it in the air as long as possible. The ball can be flicked up or passed to other players. The leg kicking the ball should be stuck out forward, straightened at the knee with the foot lifted up slightly so the spectators are not able to see the shoe sole. The aim of the players is to coordinate harmonious movements of the body and the ball in order to achieve the highest artistic performance. Victory is not important as much as pure esthetic satisfaction and, as old Jap. documents put it, the 'joy for the eyes'. The game is played by 6 or 8 individual players and there are no time limits as to its duration. In modern times the game may be stopped by one of the players selected as the game leader and resumed after a break. Each game usu. lasts 10 to 15min. and is played by men as well as women. As a form of physical recreation kemari, regarded in Japan as a national sport, is often played by whole families and a game involving 3 generations is not a rare sight.

We are not certain about the appearance of players' attire in the earliest stages of the game's development but modern kemari's presentations involve colorful and lavishly embroidered outfits with a richness of ornaments unusual for other sports. The

players wear baggy, ankle-length trousers and tunics with broad sleeves covered with loose capes reaching below the knees. Sometimes the upper part of the garment has a different color than the trousers, sometimes the whole outfit is in one color. Light shoes and headdresses resembling Siberian garrison caps – although more colorful and richly embroidered – complete the players' attire. The pitch is 14x14m and occasionally divided in half by a wooden crossbar called a *shiboku*.

History. The game of kemari originated in China. It was most probably based on the Chin. ball game of >CUJU. Kemari was introduced to Japan twice: first, around 611 BC without any permanent follow-up and then in the Hejan era (781-1180 AD) when it gained the status of a court game. During the reign of Emperor Daigo (approx. 905 AD), kemari players managed once to keep the ball in the air flicking it up 206 times. The average amounted, however, to 50 times. The first peak of popularity was observed during the Kamakura era (1192-1333). In the eras of Muromachi (1392-1573) and Edo (1603-1867) the game was becoming more popular and was practiced by the common folk. Shogun Minamuto Leyori is said to have indulged in the game so much that he neglected the governing duties in his province bringing it to an economic depression. Since the 17th cent., the popularity of kemari began to fade away. In 1647 Shogun Tokugawa Lemitsu unsuccessfully encouraged people to practice kemari. The game must have maintained its popularity in some regions of the country however, as in 1683 one team was said to keep the ball in the air flicking it up 5,188 times without a drop. Despite decreasing popularity the game survived in a few regions of Japan until the beginning of the 20th cent. In 1905, by emperor's order, the Kamari Revival Society was founded, thanks to which the game survived until present time and together with the increasing interest in history and cultural heritage of various nations developed under new circumstances. The Kamari Revival Society based in the former imperial capital city of Kyoto sponsors 6 official events in full trad. splendor annually. Popular, less formal and colorful versions of kemari are practiced as well being useful healthy forms of social recreation.

'Kemari', *Traditional Sports in Japan*, catalog First International Festival of Traditional Sports and Games of the World, Bonn, 1992.

KEMPO, see >KENPO.

KENDO, a Jap. fighting sport practiced with a special sword [Jap. *ken* – sword, *do* – way, art; also Kor. *kumbo*]; a type of fencing stemming from the tradition of samurai fighting, *bu jutsu*. Kendo developed on the basis of fighting with metal swords called *ken jutsu*. Its popularity peaked in the 15th and 16th cent. Gradual elimination of the sword as a military weapon led to different sport var. of fighting . Mijamoto Mussahi, a wandering samurai is considered as the most outstanding fencer in Japan's history. As a 13-year-old boy he, supposedly, defeated the 12 best fighters, and later, on the basis of his experience, created a few types of kendo fighting. He based kendo on Zen and introduced meditation as an element of training. In the 18th cent., the metal sword was replaced with a wooden one, called *shinai*. Modern sport rules were formed in the second half of the 19th cent. The match, called *shiayi*, lasts 5min. and begins with the referees's command of 'Hajime!' The first contestant to score 2pts. (*ippon*) within the regular time wins the match. Scoring a point results from a symultaneous body, sword, and voice attack. A blow with the sword is valid only if executed with the end part (within approx. 1/3 of its length) and at one of the following valid target areas: 1) *men* (head): the forehead and the left and right areas above the temple; 2) *kote* (hand): the area on the forearm covered by the round patterned covering; 3) *do* (torso): the left and right sides of the 'do'; 4) *tsuki* (throat): the *tsuki-tare* (throat flap on the 'men') and the breast section of the 'do'. If only 1pt. is scored in the regular time, the scorer wins the match. If both contestants score 1pt. each, the match is extended over 3min. and the first contestant to score a point wins the match. If still no points are scored the referees may: 1) order another extra time; 2) award victory to the contestant whom they consider a superior one; 3) proclaim the bout as tied.

The equipment and attire include: *kendogu* or *bogu* – a grilled head gear, *tenugui* – a cotton cloth worn under the kendogu, *shinai* – a sword made of 4 split pieces of bamboo or a synthetic material, *kote* – gloves, *do* – body protection, *tare* – waiste protection, *hakama* – ankle-long skirt (dark for men and white for women), *keikogi* – jacket.

The basic technical elements include: *men-uchi* – a vertical strike against the opponent's forehead, *kote-uchi* – striking the opponent's right forearm, *douchi* – a slanted strike against the opponent's right side above the waiste, *tsuki-uchi* – a throat thrust.

In 1928 the All-Japan Kendo Federation was created. After WWII, Kendo was considered a military sport and was banned. After 1950 it was reinstated and it's popularity began to spread well beyond Japan. The first W.Ch., which are held every 3 years, took place in 1970 in Tokyo. Women were admitted to compete in the W.Ch. in 2000 during the tournament in Santa Clara, California. The sport is controlled by the International Kendo Federation (IKF). In Japan, about 5million enthusiasts practice kendo.

T. Otsuka, *Nihon Kendo no Shiso* (1995); Y. Sakaue, 'Kendo', EWS, 1996, II, 547-550.

KENNEDY GAME, see >SKI FOOTBALL.

KENPO, also *kempo*, a modern Jap. system of martial arts modelled on an old Chin. >GONGFU. In the 6th cent. it became an element of physical training of the followers of the legendary Buddhist monk Bhodidharma, who, on arriving at the later famous monastery Shaolin-ssu, discovered that full Buddhist discipline was beyond the abilities of his students. Bhodidharma created a system of exercises made up of elements of >QIGONG, *yoga* and a local Chin. fighting techniques. In a later period kenpo, combined with the principles of Chin. medicine, helped discover numerous points in the human body which could be used for healing, as well as aiming more effective blows in battle. Thus kenpo became a starting point for many oriental martial arts, e.g. >KARATE, >OKINAWA-TE, >TAEKWON-DO. Some of the styles of kenpo include: *kosho ryu kenpo*, *kosho shorei ryu kenpo*, *Chin. kara-ho kenpo karate*, *Shaolin kenpo karate*, *Amer. kenpo karate*, *white tiger kenpo karate*, *kajukenbo*.

W. Durbin, *Mastering Kempo: Philosophy, Techniques, Tactics, Training*, 2001; W. 'The Bam' Johnson, *The Complete Martial Artist*, 2001; L. Frederic, *A Dictionary of the Martial Arts*, 1991.

KENYAN GOAT RACES, a popular trad. sport in Kenya with a ceremony modeled on the Royal Ascot Horse Races. Each race is preceded by the introduction of goat contestants. While the goats (clad in covering coats with numbers embroidered on them) parade around the course, the announcer presents their past achievements. During the race proper, the goats are encouraged to run by a wooden construction on wheels, that stretches the entire width of the track. The animals run 2 laps, and then the winner is decided (often by chance).

The sport itself derives from a pig race held in Zimbabwe in 1991. A close friend of the organizer of the race decided to transplant the idea in Uganda. Since pigs and horses were too rare to be used for this purpose they had to be replaced with goats. A special committee formed to adjust the rules decided to model the event on the Royal Ascot Horse Race. Later it was adopted by Kenya.

KEPPY BALL, in a local dialect of Newcastle *keppy ba*, a ball to be caught. An old type of an Ang.-Sax. game esp. for women and girls. It consisted simply of throwing the ball into the air to be caught by another participant standing in a group or in a circle. The game was characterized by specific terminology, e.g. throwing the ball was described as 'cooking' it.

History. The name of the game, stemming directly from old Eng. (*cepan* – 'grasp', 'catch'), indicates that the game originates at least in the early Middle Ages. Its traditions have been preserved best in Newcastle, where it was played every year during Easter and Pentecost in a part of the city called Forth. The game was accompanied by trad. songs, connected to a characteristic fortune telling by means of the ball, called >BALL DIVINATION. A.B. Gomme has recorded one of the texts:

Keppy ball, keppy ball, Coban tree,
Come down the long loanin' and tell to me,
The form and the features, the speech and degree
Of the man that is tru love to be.

Keppy ball, keppy ball, Coban tree,
Come down the loanin' and tell to me,
How many years old I am to be.

J.O. Halliwell, a Brit. historian of literature and ethnographer, recorded in *English Nursery Rhymes*, 1842-46, another text:

Cook a ball, cherry tree;
Good ball, tell me
How many years I shall be
Before my true love I do see?
One and two, and that makes three;
Thankee, good ball, for telling of me.

A.B. Gomme, 'Keppy Ball', TGESI, 1894, I, 297-8.

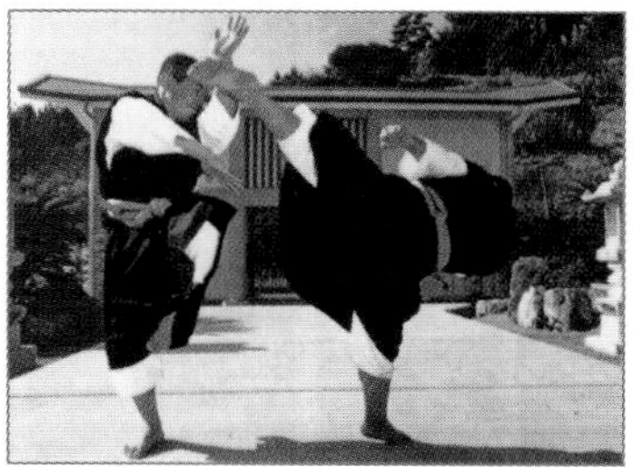

KERETIZEIN, also *keretizon* [Gk. *keratizo* – to hit with horns], an ancient Gk. ball game not unlike modern >FIELD HOCKEY and esp. Celtic sports like the Ir. >HURLING, Scot. >CAMÁNACHT and Welsh >KNAPPAN. The game was played with crooked sticks, probably one on one, as depicted in a relief from the 6th cent. BC, which can be found on the base of 3 *kouros* statues standing on the Wall of Temistocles in Kertameikos. Two contestants lean towards each other fighting for a ball which lies between their sticks – the resemblance to modern field hockey is striking. This struggle is witnessed by another 2 pairs of players holding their sticks (but without the ball), who are clearly awaiting their turn. It is also possible that keretizein was a team sport and

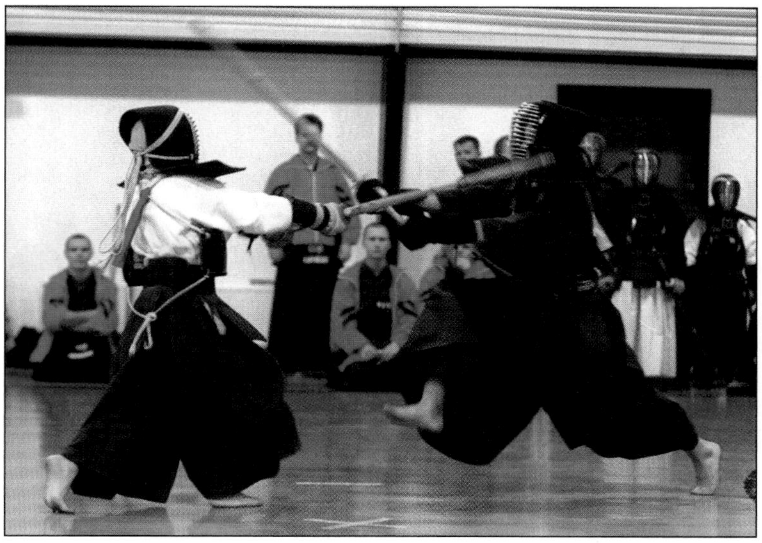

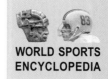

the relief depicts only a part of the game. Another sculpture worth mentioning is the statue of the famous orator Isokrates holding a playing stick; it can be found on the Acropolis.

KERYKON AGON, also *kerygma*, a competition of heralds, since 396 BC held on the first day of ancient Gk. Ol.G. [*keryks* – herald], along with a trumpeters' contest (see >SALPINGTON AGON). The winner – loudest and most eloquent of all – got the honor of announcing the beginnings and endings of Olympic events, esp. introducing competitors before the contest and proclaiming the winners thereof. Every herald had a special staff, the *kerykeion* – a sign of his dignity. The staff was made of laurel or olive wood and adorned with a garland of olive leaves. The *keryks* was a public post, found also outside Olympia and other games cities, but then the *kerykeion* would have an imitation of 2 serpents instead of olive leaves (the patron of the *keryks* was Hermes). The *keryks* enjoyed immunity, in Olympia as well as elsewhere. The name comes from Keryks, son of Eumolpos, the mythical initiator of the Eleusinian mysteries and a line of priests. Keryks took over the role of presiding over the cult of Demeter from his father. Information about kerykon agon winners is scarce. The oldest event took place during the 96th Ol.G. in 396 BC and was won by Krates of Elida. The Sicilian Archias of Hyblaia won the contest 3 times (104th Ol.G. in 364 BC, 105th Ol.G. in 360 BC and 106th Ol.G. in 356 BC). The winner of the 236th Ol.G. in 165 AD was Titus Aelius Aurelius Apolonius of Tarsus; of the 239th Ol.G. in 177 AD – Gaius Julius Bassus of Milet. Valerius Eclectus of Synopa won 4 times: 256th Ol.G. in 245 AD, 258th Ol.G. in 253 AD, 259th Ol.G. in 257 AD and 260th Ol.G. in 261 AD. The Roman emperor Nero was winner of the 211th Ol.G. in 65 AD, but since he also won the best tragedy competition, the lyre playing tournament and 3 different chariot races one might entertain the possibility that the titles were awarded out of courtesy and not, indeed, for actual merit.

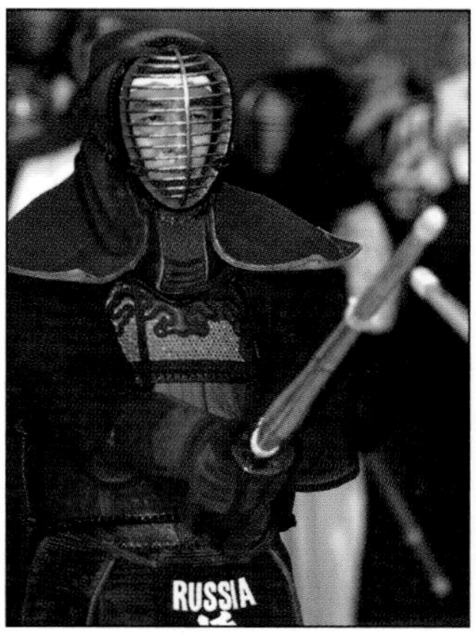

From top to bottom: Kenpo; a Kendo bout; a Kendo fighter in full gear.

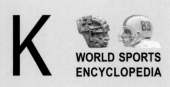

KESANIAN, a mild var. of >PENCAK SILAT. It resembles a highly esthetic dance, combining rhythmic movements to a drum or gong background with a show of skill and grace. It achieved its highest artistic form in the Minangkabau region on Sumatra.

KETTLE-PINS, see >KITTLE-PINS.

KETTUKARI, a trad. Ind. fighting technique with the use of long poles, a part of the martial art >KALARIPAYAT. Cf. >CERUVADI, which uses short sticks.

KHAZZA LAVIZZA, a high jump competition known in many countries of the Middle East since ancient times (e.g. in ancient Egypt). In the tombs of Ptahotep (2470-2320 BC) and Mereruk (2320-2160 BC), situated near Memphis, a total of 3 scenes depicting the khazza lavizza have been preserved. A boy jumped over the outstretched hands of 2 other boys sitting opposite each other. A similar pastime has been observed in the 20th cent. by Amer. archeologist E.S. Eaton in Jordan. Cf. >AL-GAFZ FAWGA AL-AYDI WAL-AQDAM.

KHEVSUR HORSE RACING, a form of >HORSE RACING popular among the Khevsurs of Georgia. Races are held on various occasions, e.g. funerals – 2-3 days after death, or as part of celebrations honoring the ancestors – 6 or 18 months after death. The most characteristic feature is the early stage of the race, which has no element of competition and is a type of parade of riders. During the parade the riders occasionally stop to rest and have a meal which is a continuation of the funeral feast. At the end of the parade riders, still on horseback, drink a horn of alcohol and begin the proper competition. One of the racing horses is the one that belonged to the deceased and is called 'the horse of his soul'. It is ridden by a relative of the deceased or a rider selected by his family, who organize the race. The horse carries on his back a sack with barley, which is to protect the animal against hunger in 'the other world'. According to I. Kabzińska-Stawarz, it is also richly equipped and decorated:

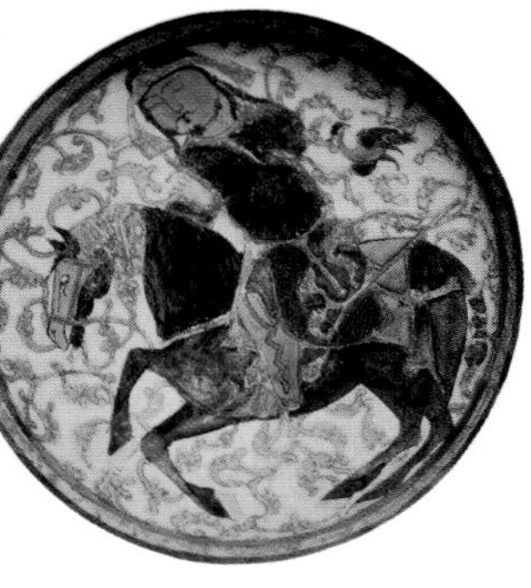

A Mongolian nomad on a late 12th-early 13th century bowl decorated with gilding and an overglaze.

Clothes belonging to the dead person and a bag containing a bottle of vodka were tied to the horse's saddle. The mane was plaited and adorned with colored ribbons and a narrow strip of dark red (or, less often, black) fringed material was tied round the animal's body. the belt rested on the horse's back and was tied under his belly. Sometimes, a woman' s belt was used. Another element of woman' s clothing in the rider's costume was a woman' s kerchief or a scarf tied round his head [...].

Scholars disagree as to the role of the belt and neck-cloth. W.I. Eliashvili claims the belt was used to help the rider keep his balance when riding on hill slopes, while the neck-cloth maintained the body temperature and protected the rider from getting a cold. I. Kabzińska-Stawarz, on the other hand, claims that Eliashvili:

offers a purely pragmatic explanation of the use of these accessories. According to him, the belt enabled the rider to keep his balance while riding on steep slopes, thus ensuring his safety. Tying a kerchief or a scarf round his head was supposed to prevent colds or injuries. Elashvili does not recognize any symbolic meaning in the belt or in the act of tying it round the horse. Considering the context of the funeral ceremony, I think that the act symbolizes change and at the same time serves the function of isolating the dead person from the community of the living. Additionally, the fact of using woman's clothes by a man, as well as their peculiar combination with the horse indicates the reversal of the existing order and accepted values, or a state of chaos, as a result of death. A peculiar exchange of clothes takes place, which is considered [...] to be a sign of confusion and a sign of the distruption of the social and cosmic order. Women themselves appear in the final sequence of the race organized by the Khevsur to collect the 'dead person's horse' on the finish line and to take care of it until it has rested. The special role of women in a funeral ceremony as well as the use of their clothes can be explained with reference to the symbolic relationship commonly believed to exist between a woman and death, death which contains the seeds of life. I believe more attention should be paid to the fact that the belt was tied on the belly of the 'horse of the dead person's soul.' I think it indicates the downward direction of the horse (which in a ritual represents the dead person), or the direction toward the underworld. It additionally indicated the reversal of the usual, everyday order (similarly to the knot of kerchief or the scarf tied on the back of the rider's head).

A detail of Grooms and Horses, *a handscroll in 3 sections in ink and color on paper, c.1296-1369.*

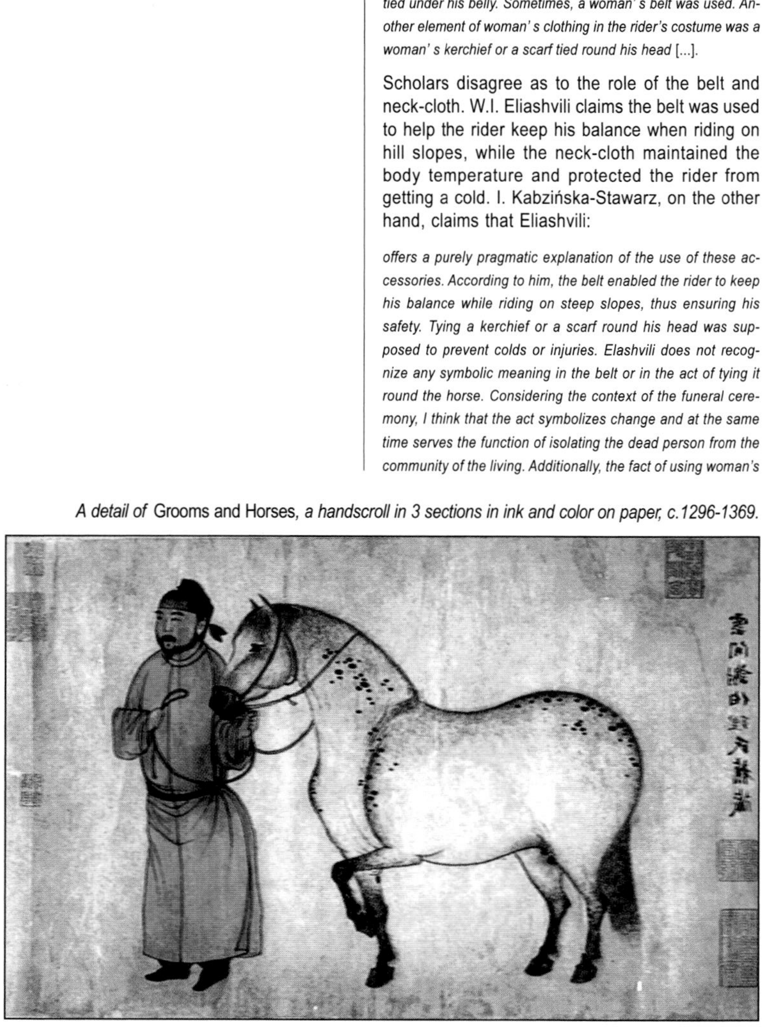

W.I. Elashvili, 'Iz istorii konnogo sporta v Gruzii. Chevsurke skacki cchen w prošlom i nastojašcem', *Sovetskaya Etnografia*, 1968; I. Kabzińska-Stawarz, 'Competition in Liminal Situations. Comparative Study of Asian Cultures', ETHP, 1994, 18.

KHO-KHO, one of the most popular trad. sports in India. The origin of kho-kho is difficult to trace, but many historians believe that it is a modified form of 'Run Chase', which in its simplest form involves chasing and touching a person. With its origins in Maharashtra, kho-kho in ancient times, was played on 'raths' or chariots, and was known as *rathera*. Like all Ind. games, it is simple, inexpensive and enjoyable. It does, however, demand physical fitness, strength, speed and stamina, and a certain amount of ability. Dodging, feinting and bursts of controlled speed make this game quite thrilling. To catch by pursuit – to chase, rather than just run – is the capstone of kho-kho. The game develops qualities such as obedience, discipline, sportsmanship, and loyalty between team members. The rules of the game were framed at Gymkhana Poona, when a Committee was formed in 1914. The first ever rules on kho-kho were published from Gymkhana Baroda, in 1924. In 1959-60, the first national kho-kho championship was organized in Vijayawada (Andhra Pradesh). The Government has initiated the following awards for the game: the Arjuna Award, the Eklavya Award for men, the Rani Laxmi Bai award for women, the Veer Abhimanyu award for boys under 18, and the Janaki award for girls under 16.

Rules. Each team consists of 12 players, but only 9 players take the field at a time. A match consists of 2 innings. An inning consists of chasing and running turns of 7min. each. Eight members of the chasing team sit in their 8 squares on the central lane, alternately facing the opposite direction, while the 9th member is an active chaser, and stands at either of the posts, ready to begin the pursuit. Members of the chasing team have to put their opponents out, touching them with their palms, but without committing a foul. All the action in kho-kho is provided by the defenders, who try to play out the 7min. limit, and the chasers who try to keep them at bay. A defender can be dismissed in 3 ways: 1) if he is touched by the palm of an active chaser who avoids committing a foul, 2) if he goes out of the limits on his own, 3) if he enters the limit late. Defenders enter the limit, in batches of 3. After the 3rd and last defender batch is out, the next batch must enter the limits, before a 'kho' is given by the successful active chaser. Defenders have full freedom of movement on both sides of the central lane, but the active chaser cannot change the direction to which he is committed. He cannot cross the central lane. An active chaser can change position with a seated chaser, by palming him from behind, and uttering the word 'kho' loudly, and simultaneously, chase or attack is build up through a series of 'khos' as the chase continues with a relay of chasers. At the end of the innings there is an interval of 5min. and an interval of 2min., in between the turns. Each side alternates between chasing and defense. Kho-kho can be played by men, women, and children of all ages. The game requires a modest piece of evenly surfaced ground, rectangular in shape (27x15m). The only equipment required are the 2 poles. The game lasts no more than 37min. The following championships are organized for this game: National, Junior National, Sub Junior National, School, Mini School, Primary Mini School Championship, National Women's, All India Inter University Championship as well as the Federation Cup. The primary sports body for this game is called the Kho-Kho Federation of India (KKFI). It has its branches in all the states and it has been conducting Mini, Junior and Open National Championships for both sexes, in many parts of India. A number of players have bagged the Arjuna Award. Some of these players are: Shri Shekhar Dharwadkar, Shri Shrirang Inamdar, Usha Nagarkar, Nilima Sarolkar, Achala Devare.

The Internet: http://w3.meadev.gov.in/sports/tr_games/kho1.htm

KHOMKHOI KHURUU BARIKH, Mong. for 'hold the index finger', a Mongolian dexterity game. One participant holds the other's index finger with both hands. The other player tries to release his finger from the hands of the opponent. A similar game, called *khomkhoi khuruu olokh* ('find the index finger'), is known among the Kalkhas people of Mongolia and among the Zakchins people (also Mong.), who call it *neg yo be* ('what does it mean?'). One player conceals his index finger in a tangle of his other fingers, while the other tries to guess where it is. Riddles are also a part of the game. If the middle finger rather than the index finger is involved, the pastime is called *dund khuruu olokh* ('find the middle finger') or *dundakh khuruu* ('middle finger'). The game is thus described by Pol. scientist specializing in Mong. studies, I. Kabzińska-Stawarz:

One of the participants looks for the middle finger of the opponent, which is hidden in a complicated arrangement of the opponent's interwoven hands. Pointing at particular fingers, the spaces between them, and the consecutive fragments of a twig which is held in the center of the whole construction, the player asks: 'what is it?' The opponent answers and then asks questions about the purpose of the first player's coming and about the progress in his journey. In the end, he catches the other by the forefinger, a series of riddles follows together with the above mentioned test of strength or the middle finger is pointed out.

[*Games of Mongolian Shepherds*, 1991, 79-80]

KHONG KANGJEI, also known as *Manipuri hockey* or *wrestling hockey*. This version of hockey is distinctively Manipuri in character, and as wrestling forms an integral part of the game, it is sometimes called Mukna – Kangjei or wrestling hockey. The origin of the game is traced back thousands of years to the prehistoric Hayichak era. According to one tale attached to the game's genesis, a young boy of the royal household was spotted playing with a curved club and a round object. He was immediately named 'Kangba' and eventually, when he ascended the throne of Manipur, he became a staunch supporter of the game, not unlike hockey, which the local people termed 'Kangjei Shanaba'. Another version has it that King Kangba began the games – Kangjei (hockey on foot) as well as Sagol Kangjei (polo). Manipuri hockey is as popular as the Manipuri game of polo. It is a 7-a-side game and each player plays with a cane stick, about 4-4½ft. in length, shaped very much like the present day hockey stick. The game starts when the ball is lobbed into play in center field (*hantre huba*). A player is permitted to carry the ball (made of bamboo root) and kick it, but a goal can only be scored when the ball is struck by the stick over the goal line. The ball, white in color, with a diameter of about 3-3½in. is called *kangdrum*. There are no goal posts. The game can turn into a trial of strength between opposing players. A player holding the ball and on his way to scoring a goal can be tackled by a player of the opposing side and made to submit to a trial of strength, locally known as *Mukna*, which is Manipuri wrestling. The game ends when one side or the other scores the agreed number of goals, and the duration is generally 90min. The strokes are usu. restricted to the nearside. This lends protection to the legs from an opponent's swinging stick. No player is permitted to tackle another player, obstruct him or hold him, if either is without a stick. The 7 players assume the following positions: 1) *pun – ngakpa* (full back), 2) *pun – ngakchun* (half back), 3) *punlluk* (left wing), 4) *langjei* (centre), 5) *pulluk* (right wing), 6) *pun – jen* (in), 7) *pun – jenchun* (in). The opposing team takes up positions in the reverse order.

Internet: http://w3.meadev.gov.in/sports/tr_games/khong.htm

KHURDAAN MOR', Mong. horse racing connected with religious ceremonies, cf. >KIRGHIZ HORSE RACING. The horse has always been of special significance to the Mong. people, whose swift cavalry

Mongolian horse riders.

made it possible for Genghis Khan (c.1155-1227) and his successors to create a great empire. This importance of the horse was reflected in the language, in which the word *chijmor* or *chiimortoi* ('horse swift as the wind') had many meanings, among others 'success', 'good fate', 'luck', 'good mood' and 'joy'. It was also used to signify a lucky or successful person, one 'riding a horse swift as the wind to happiness'. (In modern Mong. the word is *khii mor'*.) The Mong. symbolic representation of the horse was taken from Tibet, where the animal was depicted on prayer banners, with verses of a prayer for happiness in life accompanying the image. Similar banners were placed on Mong. yurts. Horse races were held during religious festivities, esp. the annual sacrificial ceremony owoo tachich, the New Year's celebrations and funeral ritual. The owoo tachich took place at the beginning of autumn. The *owoo* were sacred cairns, initially the tombs of prominent Moguls, later places of worship, where oblations of food were laid. Before the race the riders would circle the owoo three times. Another feast connected with horse racing was >GÜÜNII URS GARGAKH IOS, the 'milch mare holiday'. Pol. expert in Mong. studies I. Kabzińska-Stawarz interviewed an inhabitant of E Gobi, who described the event in the following way:

The races were held on owoo tachich to please nature. If nature is satisfied, the shepherds will enjoy a good life. They will have a lot of cattle and many riches. There is a close relatiion between man and nature.

Ethnographers estimate that in times of old as many as 3,000 horses took part in one khurdaan mor' event. In the 19th cent. this number dropped to 80-300, in the 20th cent. increasing to 1,300-1,600 (the *naadam* horse races). In the first half of the 20th cent. a horse had to be at least 4 years old (in western Mongolia at least 5 and among the Miangad people – at least 6). In the 18th and 19th cent., however, younger animals were allowed to compete. Nowadays in many regions the minimum age is set at 2-3 years. For a long time mares were excluded from competition.

A mare cannot be raced, just as a woman cannot wrestle. Women are considered inferior to men in that they are not strong enough. That is why mares are valued less than studs.

The horse's mane, believed to be instrumental in giving the animal divine support, was braided and often adorned with a red ribbon, as was the tail, which was also bent in half and tied up with straps of leather (usu. roe-deer). The harness and saddle were often decorated with silver – an element associated with the New Year and the future in general (though usu. riders used sheets of felt rather than saddles). The rider's outfit included a characteristic pointed hat and a tight colorful shirt. Traditionally, yellow was avoided as a color reserved for the lamas. However, during communist secularization the color was used ostentatiously and until the early 1990s yellow uniforms could be seen on exhibition

in the Ulan Bator Central Museum. Riders are often as young as 5-7 or 12-14 years. The shout to drive the horse – 'Gingoo!' – is used exclusively in races. Jockeys use a short whip, *tashuur*, but may not whip the horse too hard. The penalty for doing so is having one's prize made smaller. As the race finishes, the first 5 horses are taken by the bridle and led before a jury. They are called *airgiin tav*, 'the kumiss five', since their manes are sprinkled with the drink and the jockeys that rode them are treated to large quantities of kumiss and cheese. The first horse has to beat the others by trunk-length. It is praised with a song and a special speech, *ieröl*, which poetically extol its superior qualities, esp. speed and bravery. South of the Yellow River, in the Ordos region, during New Year's celebrations the horse was covered with a colorful cloth and an embroidered band was tied around its head – with the knot on the forehead. The horse winning the *khosuun nadaam* had the right to be given a special name. Usu. a special song was composed for the occasion. Pol. traveler S. Tymkowski observes in his diary *Travels to China via Mongolia 1820-1821*, published in 1828, that during one race, in which some 1,100 horses took part, at least 100 were given names. Rus. researcher Y. Shishmarev describes a race after which 160 of 480 horses were given names. Sometimes also the horse who came last was awarded and given a name, at times the same name as the winner. A young horse coming last received a boiled bone from a ram's neck and got the name *Khözöö* – Neck, *Khökh Bökhny Mor'* – Blue Horse or *Baiaan Khodood* – Rich Stomach. These names, allowing for future development, were supposed to encourage horse and rider to train harder for the next season. The gift of ram's bone is explained by a Mong. shepherds' proverb 'Better to break a bone than break the spirit'. Another explanation is that a ram's neck is very strong and this strength should pass on to the horse. The name 'Rich Stomach' refers to proper nourishment with which the horse ought to be provided to gain stamina. An 18th cent. Mong. statute, *Khalkha Jirum* declares that a jockey may win even if his horse did not make it to the finish line, provided that the rider himself manages to get up and pass the finish line before the others (a similar rule is applied in >KIRGHIZ HORSE RACING). Likewise, the rider's falling off did not disqualify the horse, who therefore had equal rights as its rider. Cf. >BÖKHLIN BARILDAAN, >KELES.

KHUSHGA KHARVAKH, Mong. for 'throwing at nuts', a trad. Mong. game with any number of participants. 50-60 nuts are put in a circle. Contestants throw a sheepskin ball or a round stone, trying to move as many nuts as possible outside the circle. To win, the contestant has to move all the nuts out of the circle with the smallest number of throws, or – when all contestants have the same number of throws – to move the most nuts.

KIBEL AND NERSPEL, the name to be understood as a bat and ball on a trap (Eng. Dialect of Stixwold

region: *kibel* – a bat, *ner* – a ball or rather a maple wood sphere, *spel* – kind of lever, trap, ejector). The game has many features in common with the whole family of games such as: >TRAP, BAT AND BALL, >NORTHERN SPELL, and other derivatives. The player places the ball on a special trap made of flexible board or branches, straining it and then slacking so that the ball is propelled vertically. The ball should them be struck with the bat. He who hits the ball the longest distance becomes the winner.
A.B. Gomme, 'Kibel and Nerspel', TGESI, 1984, I, 298-9.

KICKBALL, an Eng. name for a Native Amer. Ind. competition of kicking a ball. The most spectacular performances could be witnessed among the Tarahumara tribe, who could kick the ball as far as 300km.

KICK-BOARD, also *kick-board-scooter*, a type of kick scooter taking advantage of modern technology so that it may even be used during rush-hour commutes as an alternative to bicycling, as well as for recreation. Kick-board stands out from the other types of kick scooters because it is extremely handy, easy to fold, and carry, and makes use of materials and design solutions which have never been used in similar vehicles before. The frame is made of duralumin, the wheels of polyurethane. It weighs altogether 3.5kg. The most popular dimensions: footboard length: 65cm, width: 10cm, adjustable steering rod height: 68-95cm, handlebar width: 32cm; wheel diameter: 10cm. Dimensions of a folded kickboard: 68x20x10cm. Other names include: *scate scooter* and *holly top*.
History. The kick-board was created at the end of the 1990s and has become increasingly popular these past few years. The advertising campaign of a network of Amer. Warehouses K2 has done much to popularize kick-board. Apart from the USA, it has been most popular in Germany, France and Japan. In Wuppertal, nurses in the public hospital have been equipped with kick-boards. The vehicle is also used to get around airports and in hotels, where valets use kick-boards to return quickly to the hotel entrance after they have driven a car to the parking lot. Extreme sport implementing the use of the kick-board is developing quickly. Figures skating on half-rolls and other tracks and speed skating have been attempted. Undoubtedly, new events based on kick-boarding and similar to skateboarding or BMX cycling will be developed within the next few years.

KICKBOXING, also called *freestyle karate*, a sport combining elements of boxing and some oriental martial arts, esp. >THAI BOXING and Jap. >KARATE. Blows can be made with arms as well as legs. There are 3 fighting categories: semi-contact, light-contact and full-contact. Professionals fight only full-contact. In amateur fighting only blows above the belt are allowed, while professional fighting permits low-kicks (on the thighs). In semi-contact fights, held on an 8x8m floor, blows are feigned. In light-contact fights, held either on floors as in semi-contact or in boxing rings, blows must not be made with such force as to knock the opponent out. Full-contact fighting takes place only on boxing rings and allows full force blows as well as knock-out. Amateur and pro-

A local woman rides a kick-board in Shanghai.

Women's kickboxing.

K

WORLD SPORTS ENCYCLOPEDIA

fessional versions have different weight categories. Amateur fights have 3 rounds and professional matches – 12 rounds, 2min. each. All contestants wear special shoes and gloves. Amateurs also wear helmets.

History. The idea of kickboxing originated in the USA in the late 1960s, fully developing in the 1970s. As in boxing, there are many international federations

all of whom strive for supremacy in organizing national and international events. One of the most influential bodies is the World Association of Kickboxing Organization (WAKO), estab. in 1976. The World Karate Association (WKA, estab. 1978) and the International Sport Karate Association (ISKA, estab. 1986) both have important kickboxing departments. After a period of considerable popularity, the

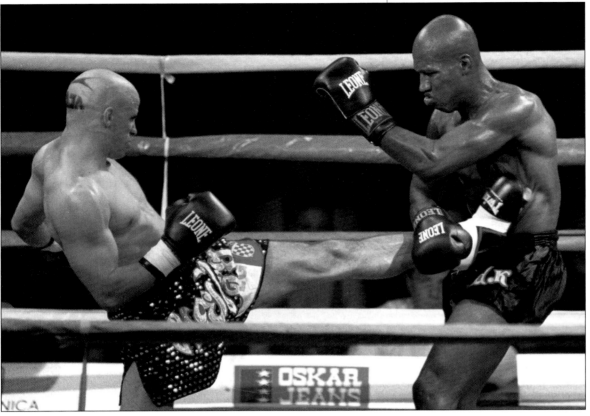

Men's kickboxing.

The slope variety of kilhoù bro leon.

sport had fallen out of fashion in the late 1990s. Many kickboxers went over to trad. professional boxing. International encyclopedias often neglect to list kickboxing as an important discipline.

L. Ufel, *The World of Kickboxing*, 1991.

KICKING CAMP, see >CAMP.

KICZKA, a Pol. family of batting games similar to >KLIPA and its var. Kiczka shows numerous similarities with other games, such as: >SZTEKIEL, >GULLI DUNDA, >PILAOUET, >POPICE, >TIP-CAT. Among many var. that were played in Poland, the most popular were:

KICZKA PROSTA, a game similar to *klipa* (in fact, sometimes considered to be its var.), in the region of Pol. Central Galicia known as *kot* (cat) or *pliszka* (robin), in the area of Cracow – as *cyrka*, in the region of Kashubia – as *pchła* (flea), and in Central Poland – as *czyż, krypa,* or *klipa*. There are 2 main var.:

Kiczka bez met was played in the area of Cracow and in Central Poland. It was identical to *kiczka z metami* up to the moment of releasing the kiczka. The subsequent stages of the game were described by E. Piasecki:

The difference [...] is that the released kiczka [a peg of soft wood 20cm in length and 2cm in diameter] which missed the palant [bat] is batted from the spot where it landed. Since there is no hole at this spot, the kiczka is either conically sharpened at both ends and is hit at the base or the players skilfully manouver it on the ground with the palant and – while it rolls – they place the palant under it, send it into the air, and bat it. If it then falls on the ground without being caught, the batter measures the distance between the spot where it landed and the hole in bat lengths and is awarded the equivalent number of points.

Kiczka z metami was played in central Galicia in the following way:

The selected player takes a position at the oblong hole and places a kiczka across it. This spot is called 'wygrana' [a winning area], 'dom' [a home], or 'królestwo' [a kingdom]. The rest of the players stand on 'the losing area', i.e. at the distance of 10, 15, 10 and 50 steps from the hole and mark their bases with stones.

[...] The player on the winning spot begins the game placing his

palant under the kiczka and batting it towards the other players. If one of them catches the kiczka, he goes to the winning spot. If the kiczka is not caught, the batter places his bat across the hole and one of the field players putts the kiczka on the ground towards the hole. If he succeeds, the batter is eliminated and is replaced by the putter. Otherwise the batter continues the game. He places the kiczka inside the hole so that one end extends slightly above the hole and leans towards the opponents. Then the batter hits that end sending the kiczka straight into the air and he bats it. If the batted kiczka is caught, the catcher gets 100pts and becomes a batter. If the kiczka is not caught, the batter scores the number of points equal to the distance in steps between the spot where the kiczka landed and the hole. The batter is also out when he fails to bat the kiczka 3 times in succession or he bats it closer than the 1st base (10 steps). The game continues until one of the players scores an agreed number of points (e.g. 1,000 or 3,000).

KICZKA RZYMSKA, a game known in Central Poland, which is played in a similar manner to *kiczka bez met.*

KICZKA Z MATKAMI, a team var. of *kiczka prosta,* played in both variants – as *kiczka z metami* and *kiczka bez met,* according to the rules discussed above, but with the following differences:

[...] having made appropriate measurements with the bat [...] one team stands on the winning spot and begins the play by batting the kiczka 3 times in a pre-defined sequence (the poorest batters go first). Teams change places if: 1) the batted kiczka is caught by one of the players of the rival team; 2) all batters are eliminated (having missed 3 times or if the kiczka hit the bat). Points scored by individual players are awarded to the team.

E. Piasecki, *Zabawy i gry ruchowe dzieci i młodzieży* (1916).

KIEKONLYÖNTI, Fin. for 'hitting discs', a Fin. folk game also called the 'game of the seven brothers'. Contestants hit discs with a stick as far as they can. Whoever hits the furthest, wins. The game originated in the Fin. province of Häme (once Swed. Tavastehus).

KIISA PÜÜDMINE, Est. for 'grasping the sheaf of straw', a folk game where players race using only their hands. There are many var. of the sport. In the most popular version the contestant moves, using only his hands, in the direction of a small sheaf, which he takes in his mouth and goes back to the starting point.

M. Värv et al., 'Traditional Sports and Games in Estonia', TSNJ, 1996, 31.

KIKOGO, a Kenyan game where players throw stones into holes dug in the ground.

KILHOÙ, in Fr. *le jeu de quilles,* a Bret. game of >SKITTLES, many distinct var. of which are still alive, such as the 9-pin, 7-pin, and 3-pin game.

Consultant: G. Jaouen, FALSAB.

KILHOÙ BIHAN, also called *birinig.* A Bret. equivalent of Eng. table >SKITTLES, played with 9 wooden skittles.

KILHOÙ BRO LEON, a Bret. form of >SKITTLES in which a player attempts to knock down 9 wooden skittles in 1 or 3 shots, using a bowl 18cm in diameter. In the *direct* var. players bowl from a distance of 7m, while in the *slope* var. the distance is 4m and the bowl must first climb a slope before coming back down on the pins.

KILHOÙ-KOZH, a Bret. form of >SKITTLES. 9 skittles are knocked down with various objects, e.g. wooden bowls (11.5cm in diameter), hammer heads or discs resembling small millstones. The game, until recently almost forgotten, is now being revived. In the province of Léon figures may be knocked down by balls on the rebound from the side of the lane. The center skittle is worth 9pts., the corner skittles – 5pts., and the others – 1pt. each. To get the highest score, all the remaining skittles must stand intact. The goal is to score as many points as possible with 5 shots. Cf. >QUILLES DU CAP.

F. Peru, 'La tradition populaire de jeux de plein air en Bretagne', LJP, 1998. Consultant: G. Jaouen, FALSAB.

KING'S CHAIR, a var. of a simple exercise done to different purposes during sport training, physical education classes and in rescue operations. Each participant grasps their right wrist with their left hand (or the other way round), and with the other hand they grasp the wrist of the other person so that a square, the chair's 'seat', is formed. The third participant sits on the hands thus braided. In Denmark, this exercise is described as being carried on a golden chair, in Poland as a little chair (krzesełko). The carrying of the 'king' was accompanied by nonsense rhymes, such as:

King, King Cairy
London lairy
Milk and Bread
In the King's Chairie

In the neighborhood of Keith, kings chair was played without any accompanying songs.
A.B. Gomme, 'King's Chair', TGESI, 1894, I, 304-5; J. Møller, 'Bære i guldstol', GID, 1997, 3, 95.

KING'S JUMP, also royal jump, a var. of high and long jump, practiced in the Middle Ages at the courts of some Ger. rulers. The object of king's jump was to jump over the backs of horses stood alongside one another, the number of which was gradually increased. Any jumping technique could be employed. Jumps were probably made from a specially made springboard. Legends have it that some knights jumped over 7 horses. However, the usual number was more likely 3-4. In Denmark the same name was applied to a game called *springe konge* [Dan. for 'royal jump' or 'king's jump']. Contestants were divided into 2 teams and formed 2 rows about 12m apart. The contestants in both rows held hands. One of the contestants was named the king, who in turn chose a contestant to run to the opposite team and attempt to break the chain they formed. If he managed, the players beyond the break point joined the opponents' team. If he did not manage to break the chain, he had to run back very quickly as the opponents started trting to encircle him. If the king lost all his players in this way, he had to break the opponents' chain himself in a max. of 3 attempts. Failing to do this, he was captured and the game ended. A player attempting to break the chain could not use the knees or the hands. A similar chain-breaking game played by children is called 'red rover'.
J. Möller, 'Springe konge', GID, 1997, 4.

KINGSEPAMANG, a trad. Est. shoemaker's game, described as follows:

Three trusses are made of straw and tied up at one end. This is called 'the shoemaker'. The shoemaker stands on the floor. One of the players is next to it, the other comes riding on a broom-stick and asks:
– Is the shoemaker at home?
– Yes, he is.
– What is he doing?
– Making shoes for his neighbours.
– Will he make a pair for me, too?
– No, he won't.
– Then I'll stab his eye.
– Go ahead, if you can, but the brow protects it.
Both players straddle on a stick with their back touching. One of them tries to knock the shoemaker down, the other facing it tries to lead the stick astray.
[Marge Värv et al., 'Traditional Sports and Games in Estonia', in: Siklódi CSILLA, ed., *Tradicionális Sportok, Népi Játékok – Traditional Sports, Folk Games*, 1996, 31]

KI-NI-HO-LO, a Hawaiian folk game, not unlike >PALANT.

KIRGHIZ HORSE RACING, a form of >HORSE RACING held during funerals or on annual holidays in honor of the spirits of the ancestors. The tradition of holding sport events, incl. horse races, after the death of prominent members of the community has been known in various cultures, e.g. in ancient Greece, where horse races were held after the death of Patroclus during the siege of Troy. Among Asian peoples it also manifested the role of the horse as an animal which carried the deceased to another world (sometimes this role was performed by another animal, e.g. a camel). The horse was also viewed as a link between the world of the dead and the living.

The unique role of the horse in a burial ceremony is manifested through its participation in the symbolic act of isolating the deceased, excluding him from the community of the living by riding around his corpse, his grave, his family or his belongings. The meaning of this ritual helps us understand the idea of such horse races.

In the final stage of the race the winner crossing the finish line rode to the yurt of the deceased, next to which a flag symbolizing his soul had been driven into the ground. The rider would break the shaft into

pieces and throw them into the fire, while the spectators cried: 'he broke the funeral flag'. A similar act prob. accompanied ancient >KIRGHIZ JOUSTING.

Destroying the flag indicated the end of the mourning period for the widow and the relatives of the deceased. It also ended the period of activity of his spirit, so dangerous for the living [...] Breaking of the flag or spear also marked the end of a stage in the life of the community, to which the deceased belonged. The deceased was excluded from the world of the living and his family members were received back into the community, of which they formed a part. Thus their period of mourning ended. Therefore, the rider who broke and burnt the funeral flag (or spear) performed an act which was fundamental for the further existence of his community. He restored its state of balance, violated by the death of a community member, and established a new order.

The racing horses were richly decorated in a way similar to *kirghiz jousting*. Their manes were plaited with ribbons and their tales tied in knots, a tradition which once indicated the readiness for a military expedition or battle, but which is also connected with the belief in the magical power of horse's hair, so characteristic of many Asian peoples. If the exhausted horse fell before the end line, the rider was allowed to finish the race on foot and even win the race, providing he carried with him the bridle or the head of his horse (cf. a similar tradition in >MONGOLIAN HORSE RACING).
I. Kabzińska-Stawarz, 'Competition in Liminal Situations. Comparative Study of Asian Cultures', ETHP, 1994, 18.

KIRGHIZ JOUSTING, a type of mounted combat using spears with sharp, metal heads. The bouts were conducted as part of All Souls' Day ceremonies and at the end of a period of mourning, which is indicated by an exclamation of, 'He broke the mourning flag' given by the spectators and the judges at the end of the fight, even though the actual breaking of the flag-staff does not take place. (The flag-staff continues to be broken in >KIRGHIZ HORSE RACING.) The bout began by challenging every man to fight, proclaimed by a herald, whose accompaniment of various instruments drew the attention of spectators.

If there is among you a hero as sinister as Almambet and as strong as Koshoi-khan, who will wear his arms and manages to catch up and defeat his enemy by forcing him out of his saddle and in the blinking of an eye can knock the enemy to the ground in one brisk blow – just as was done by Manas during the prayers to honor Keketei – if such a hero is among you, let him step forward on the arena and take the prize for victory.
After volunteers registered to fight and after the necessary preparations, the herald blew his pipe to start the competition. The bout was accompanied by music played on pipes, horns, drums called barabans, and – in modern times – also accordions. In the jousting bouts, similar to racing events, the horses' manes were decorated with ribbons and their tails bound in a knot. The event was controlled by judges. The fight usu. ended with the death of one of the participants, but the winner was exempt from punishment, unless he had violated the rules, in which case he had to give the family of his killed rival a number of horses proportional to his victim's social status. The lowest prizes noted by ethnographers amounted to 9 horses, the highest – 100. In modern times, beginning with the mid-19th cent., punishment was discontinued. G.N. Simakov derives the tradition of jousting from the Kirghiz military past and believes the bouts were a form of strict military training, rather than a sport. That, he says, is indicated by the fighting techniques, such as picking up the weapon from the ground at full gallop, avoiding the enemy's blows by hiding under the horse, etc. The violent form of jousting was eventually discontinued.
I. Kabzińska-Stawarz, 'Competition in liminal situations', p.II, EP, 1994, 1-2; G.N. Simakov, Obshchestvenniye funktsyi norodnih razviechenyi v kontse XIX – nachale XX w., 1984.

KIRGHIZ RACES, like >KALMUCK RACES, were held to celebrate various religious holidays and family occasions such as weddings, the birth of a child or the symbolic cutting of a fetter placed on a child's feet to make him learn to walk sooner (>FETTER-CUTTING RACE).

KIRGHIZ WRESTLING, popular among the peoples of C Asia and similar to the Mong. >BÖKHIIN BARILDAAN and >BUH. There were, however, numerous minor differences distinguishing the 2 var. According to Rus. ethnologist G.N. Simakov Kirghiz wrestlers did not drink much water and their staple food was wheat cooked in oil. As opposed to Mong. wrestlers, the Kirghiz thought that drinking koumiss before a match took away some of

the strength they accumulated. They also abstained from beer unlike Tibetan fighters.
G.N. Simakov, *Obshchestwyennye funktsy kirghiskich narodnych razwlechenyi w kontse XIX – nachale XXw.*, 1984.

KIRIP, a folk wrestling sport practiced in the Nicobar Islands belonging to India and situated in the Bay of Bengal. The fight begins with the contestants in a standing position, leaning forward slightly. They put their arms around each other in such a way that the hands are placed on the opponent's lower back. This hold may not be broken until the end of the fight. Contestants try to floor the opponent so that he falls on his back. One match has 3-5 rounds. The one to win the most rounds, wins the whole fight.

KIT-CAT, an Eng. game in which a wooden peg is batted into the field with a stick. The game is played by 2 teams of 3 players (although matches of 2- or 4-player teams have also been recorded), of whom only the members of one team have batting sticks approx. 2ft. (61cm) long. The field has 3 holes arranged in triangle, separated by a distance of approx. 20ft (approx. 6.1m) from one another. The players without the batting sticks throw the peg, called a kit-cat, which – according to an old description of the game – is 'not much thicker than a thumb'. The batters' task is to hit the peg into the air and begin to run along the triangle, placing their batting sticks into the holes and counting to 31. Scoring 31pts. by any of the players wins a game. If the kit-cat, after it had been batted, is caught by the other team, the batter loses his turn and is replaced by the next one, etc. When all the batters of one team have been eliminated, the round ends irrespective of the score, and teams change places. Teams usu. agree on the number of misses that one batter is allowed without being eliminated.
A.B. Gomme, 'Kit-Cat', TGESI, 1894, I, 310-311.

KITE BUGGY RIDING, one of various types of >KITE SPORTS, in which participants sit in small buggies, while holding and steering a kite, used as a driving force.

Kite buggy.

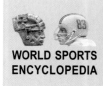

Riding a kite buggy is a year-round sport.

K **WORLD SPORTS ENCYCLOPEDIA**

KITE FIGHTING, an ancient Thai sport, a form of aerial battle, the goal of which is to eliminate rivals by means of entangling the kite's string with that of a rival kite in order to bring it down and capture it into one's own territory. Competitions are fought with 2 types of kites: *chula*, the male kite, which is 1.5m or more in length and shaped as a 5-pointed star, with up to 20 men required to manouver it, and *pakpao*, the female kite, 0.76m in length, diamond shaped with a long tail, flown by one person. The tournament rules provide for a min. of 2 chulas and 4 pakpaos to compete in a match. A chula team consists of the captain, 1 or 2 handlers to fly the kites, and a team of youngsters to run the string. The battle equipment includes 3-5 *champahs* - strips of split bamboo formed into grappling hooks and spaced along the string at intervals specified by the rules. The chula air space is divided into channels marked by red flags. There are over 50 rules governing the contest. If a chula successfully entangles a pakpao, it wins the battle. The same happens if it is caught in a pakpao loop, but can still land in its own territory. The pakpao scores only if the *chula* comes down in the pakpao territory. The favorite site for kite fighting is Sanam Luang – the Phramane Ground near the Grand palace in Bangkok. The tournaments are held in the summer, usu. between March and May. Kite fighting is popular throughout Indonesia and in other countries of SE Asia, mostly Singapore, where the sport has been practised since approx. 1969 and where a Kite Festival has been taking place since 1989 under the sponsorship of Mercedes and BMW. A var. of kite fighting is also popular among the Maori in New Zealand. See also: >KITE SPORTS.

'Kite Fighting over Marina South', SS, March 1989; H. Bennett, 'Games of the Old Maori', *Te Ao Hou*, Apr. 1958.

KITE FLYING, all types of sports where the main propelling force is provided by a kite. A kite is any heavier-than-air apparatus using the principle of aerodynamic lift to fly. From the technical point of view, there are 2 main types of kites. The first type has a rigid frame, onto which the lifting surface is stretched, while the second is flexible, and uses the phenomenon of filling the lifting surface by the air, much like in the hang-glider (which was actually developed as an extension of kite constructions). Trad. kites are equipped with so-called tails which stabilize the structure in the air. The structure described below, using a curved cross stick, does not need a tail. In the second half of the 20th cent., new, lighter materials led to the construction of kites whose shapes are not constrained in any way. The most popular form of kite flying is flying kites for height or time. There are also competitions where the uniqueness of construction or shape is the main factor. A new, spectacular discipline, known as >KITE FIGHTING, has been developing rapidly. In recent years, new forms of kites have appeared, not much different from hang-gliders, and they are used as the propelling force both over land and water in >KITEBOARDING, >KITE SKATEBOARDING, >KITE SNOWBOARDING, kite buggy riding, and >KITE JUMPING.

History. The art of kite flying originated, most probably, in the Far East. The first kites may have been constructed in China around 1000 BC. From China, kites 'migrated' gradually in 2 directions: to the islands of the Pacific, and to the Middle East. From there, the art of building kites arrived in Europe towards the end of the Middle Ages. The oldest Eur. record of kites was given by M. Polo (1254-1323), the author of the *Description of the World*, a report of his voyage to China between 1271 and 1295. The first Eur. picture of a kite was published in Holland in 1618. The kite was a simple one, with 2 sticks crossing in the middle and a paper supporting surface stretched onto them. In 1749, the Britons A. Wilson and T. Melville were the first to use a kite for scientific purposes: they built a chain of kites to measure temperatures at various altitudes. In 1752, B. Franklin used a kite to prove that lightning is an electrical charge. In the 19th cent., the number of scientific experiments using kites rose – among other things, the first attempts were made to lift a man into the air in an apparatus heavier than air. In 1825, the Englishman G. Pocock conducted an experiment in which his daughter Martha was lifted by a kite to about 300ft. (90m). Pocock also experimented with kites drawing carriages, reaching speeds of up to 20mph (32km/h) on a beach. In 1853, the Englishman G. Cayley conducted an experiment in which his pilot made the first gliding flight over a small valley using a specially adapted large kite. Caylay had known it was possible since 1804, when he made a similar experiment, without a human pilot but with a load attached to the kite. About 1890, the New Jersey photographer W. Eddy made a kite that used the Far Eastern experience. Up to that time, Eur. kites needed tails to add stability during flight. The Oriental idea of curving the cross stick of a kite made stable flight without a tail possible. In 1893, the Austrl. L. Hargrave made the first box kite.

Simultaneously, for many centuries kites were used in play. In the Far East, they added splendor to festivals and religious rituals. In Europe, they were mostly used as children's toys. Organized kite flying as a sport first appeared in the USA in the 1940s. In 1948, the Rogallo brothers built a kite shaped like a cubicoid, without ribbing, close to modern paragliders, which flew much better. In 1950 W. Allison used an independent bar structure, which looked like a half-barrel. The next invention came with D. Jalbert's 1953 box structure looking much like an airplane wing, with a bulge in the middle. R. Miller's Bamboo Butterfly kite was later used as the prototype of the hang-glider. The Amer. experience, combined with the Far Eastern tradition, led to the quick development of kite flying in Asian countries. Kites increasingly unusual shapes started appearing: flying dragons, snakes, birds and other animals. On the technical side, the new kites started including e.g. disc chains, air-filling 3-dimensional figures with rotating elements, and so on. The most famous annual kite shows include the display and contest organized in the Jap. town of Hamamatsu in early May, and the one in Shirone the next month. The festivals are attended by thousands of participants flying kites with dimensions reaching several meters. Similar events are also organized in Korea and Thailand, where, in addition to the sporting element, they function as tourist attractions. The Jap. *wan-wan* kite, first built at Naruto in the early 20th cent., is considered to be the world's largest ever kite. It was oval in shape, about 19.5m in diameter, and weighed approx. 4 tons. Today, the Jap. *o-dako*, approx. 14.6x11m in size, are considered the largest. They are flown at Hoshubana during Jap. Boys' Day in early May each year. Fifty boys have to hold the bridle line of an *o-dako*. The *takegoe* is another type of Jap. kite, made of a bamboo frame and paper covered with Jap. calligraphy and paintings depicting famous samurais or *kabuki* actors. These kites are flown during Jap. New Year celebrations, and are used to tell children's fortunes. A *takaoke* may be 10m in diameter. In Korea, kite festivals are organized in early spring, or the first month of the local lunar calendar. Such festivals are often associated with the ritual of driving away winter. Kites symbolizing the spring fight against those representing winter, while the participants shout, 'Let the evil go away, and let the blessed good come!' At the end of the ceremony, the kites are set free so that the evil powers of winter may go away. Kites known as *barroletas* are flown on All Saints' Day in the Guatemalan town of Santiago Sacatepéquez. The longer axis of these may be up to 6m long.

Unique forms of kite flying have developed among the Maoris of New Zealand, who call the sport *pakaukau* or *whakahorotaratahi*. The kites themselves, *manu tukutuku*, are made of the leaves of the *raupo* tree and plant stems. The most popular form of Maori kite is the triangular *taratahi*, made of empty plant stems, cut lengthways into halves and tied together tightly like in a raft. The bunches of leaves on the edges serve as ailerons. Twigs of the *manuka* bush are entwined into the structure to add flexibility. The largest structures may reach 15ft. (about 4.5m) in length, and are controlled by 2 men as 1 person could not do so in higher winds. Sometimes, they take the shape of crosses, human or animal faces (*manu*). Kites shaped like birds with spread wings are called *manu aute* [Maori *manu* – bird + *aute* – a kind of tree]. The most popular of these is the hawk-shaped one called *kahu*, and the single-winged *pakau*. Kites shaped like heads or faces are adorned on the edges with the hairs of the *kuri* dog and tufts of feather. To add sound to the spectacle, tails made of *kakahi* or *kuku* shellfish or *tuangi* snail shells are attached to the kites. In the old Maori tradition, now dead, the bridle lines were made using the *miro* process: they were woven of 3 kinds of plant fibers, including a special var. of flax, which produced lightweight and durable ropes. Maori kites were sometimes used for fortune-telling. A kite flying sharply up was seen as a good omen, while a spiral flight with poor climb was supposed to foretell bad luck for the kite's owner. The warlord of a village may have flown a kite in the direction of a hostile village; if an inhabitant of that village risked catching the rope dragged by the kite, it foretold bad luck for him. Free-flying kites were used to help find wrongdoers – they were supposed to fly over their homes or land near them. A trad. Maori story mentions a jealous husband who kept his wife, against the will of her family, on a deserted islet. The woman made a kite, to which she attached the emblem of her family. The kite, flying high over the sea, allowed the family to find and free her. Apart from being a pastime and sport, kites have also been used for military purposes, e.g. during both

It takes about a dozen people to get the 'Eagle Kite' of Indonesia aloft at National Monument park in Jakarta.

Kite flying.

323

WORLD SPORTS ENCYCLOPEDIA **K**

Dave Broome of Aptos, California, enjoying the best of both worlds during the kiteboarding competition of the Gorge Games in Hood River, Oregon.

World Wars. At the beginning of the 1940s, the American H.C. Sauls built huge kites which were tied to Amer. warships, making bombing from Ger. and Jap. airplanes more difficult. Another Amer. commander, P. Garber, used kites as training targets for anti-aircraft artillery.

Modern kites are more and more often built from new materials making it possible to give them more fanciful shapes as well as fly under the most demanding weather conditions. Kite flying competitions are organized in many countries, becoming increasingly popular. Record altitudes have been kept since 1919, when a chain of kites reached 32,000ft. (about 9755m). In 1967, an individual kite reached the height of 28,000ft. (approx. 8,535m). As far as record flight durations are concerned, a team led by W. Yolen kept a self-made kite in the air for 169hrs. (one full week plus 1hr.).

KITE JUMPING, one of the latest creative sports to have developed over the past decade; maximally long jumps are performed from the ground with a large kite, whose construction resembles a hang glider. Kite jumping differs from hang gliding in that it does not consist of making a long flight with a run-up down the hill or down the mountain, and the kite is not towed aloft by powered airplanes, but it is launched directly from the ground without any additional take-off assist, taking advantage of the aerodynamic lift of the kite and the wind.

KITE SKATEBOARDING, one of the newest extravagant sports taking advantage of a kite to move on a skateboard; the kite is a construction resembling a hang glider, with long lines enabling it to catch the wind in the upper atmosphere.

KITE SKIING, a combination of sports, in which a skier moves by taking advantage of a kite with long lines that enable it to catch the wind in the upper atmosphere.

KITE SNOWBOARDING, among the more eccentric sports disciplines invented in the 1990s consisting of surfing on a snowboard pulled by a large kite resembling a hang-glider.

KITE SPORTS, see >KITE FLYING.

KITEBOARDING, also *kitesailing, kitesurfing, fly-surfing,* a sport of surfing on water skis or a surfing board behind a large kite resembling a hang-glider. Most kite designs looking like hang-gliders, surfing boards are still experimental, although specialist sports companies have already started to manufacture kitesurfing equipment. The optimal, tested designs of surfing boards used in kitesurfing include the skimkiteboard and the kitesurfer. Speed depends on the speed of the wind, with respect to its direction, and is from 4 to 10 nautical miles/h (about 7.4-18.2km/h). Reservoirs with little traffic lend themselves excellently to this sport as kitesurfing requires a lot of space for each contestant. Ho'kipa Beach Park on the Hawaiian island of Maui is a favorite kitesurfing spot.

The following contests are held: down-wind long distance, wave riding and slalom. Unofficially, airborne tricks are also held. The contests are held separately for women and men.
History. Kitesurfing developed in the 1980s and soon gained the status of an independent sport in the USA, N.Zealand and in Europe. In France, Switzerland, the USA, Italy, Australia and on the Caribbean Islands there are kitesurfing schools. W.Ch. are organized. The pioneers of the discipline and at the same time the best kitesurfers include the Americans C. Roeseler (world champion in the multi-discipline event 1997), M. Flash (world champion in 1998), Brazilian M. Abreau, M. Waltz, D. Dorn, and among women T. Okazaki from Japan (world champion in the multi-discipline event 1998) and the American T. Roeseler.

KITO, also *kito-ryu,* one of the Jap. self-defense techniques belonging to the >JU JUTSU family.

KITSE LAUTAAJAMINE, Est. for 'herding goats into the shed', an Est. folk game. A large hole was dug in the ground (the 'shed'), and 4-7m off several smaller holes were made, one for each player (except for one, the 'goatherd', who did not have his own hole). Every player had a long stick for driving a wooden ball (the 'goat'). The 'goatherd' tried to get the 'goat' into the 'shed', with the others hindering him with their sticks. If he succeeded, all the players changed holes. In the confusion the 'goatherd' had a chance to find a hole for himself and have somebody else take his place. Another way of achieving this was to throw the stick into one of the small holes occupied by the other players. The person to whom the hole belonged tried to defend it. If he failed, he changed places with the 'goatherd'.
M. Värv et al., 'Traditional Sports and Games in Estonia', TSNJ, 1996, 31.

KITTLE-PINS, also *kettle-pins,* an old Eng. bowling game.

KIVGIQ, a physical activity involving dancing to drums and giving presents to friends and neighbors, practiced once by Inupiat Native Alaskans. The ceremony was accompanied by several sports competitions, such as jumping over oars, wrestling etc. The aim of kivgiq was to add color to the long winters and to fend off the cold during the most bitter frost. A similar ceremonial, *sayak,* was known among the Chukchi before Soviet rule. In the late 1980 the ritual of kivgiq was revived in Alaska thanks to G. Ahmaogak, mayor of North Slope Borough. The new version forbids, however, the consumption of alcohol, once an essential ingredient of the celebrations.
G. Ahmaogak, 'Remembering the Big Dances of Winter', Uiniq, May 1990, EWS, 1996, III, 1141.

KIWI NETBALL, a var. of >NETBALL created in New Zealand for the sake of kindergarten and early elementary school children. As opposed to its 'adult' counterpart, played chiefly by women, kiwi netball is enjoyed by children in mixed teams (though that

is not a rule). The baskets are hung lower, the ball is smaller and the scoring of points is much easier – all this to encourage children to play. Less strict rules include those regarding action after receiving the ball. Detailed rules can be found in the *Kiwi Sport Activities Manual,* published by the Hillary Commission for Recreation and Sport, 1988.

KLADASK, a simple Dan. ball game where the player tries to bounce the ball off the ground as long as possible, much like dribbling in many ball games. Various balls are used, usu. smaller ones. The player usu. recites the following little poem:

Daddy, Mummy, can I get married,
Can I get married, like so many young people do.
Daddy says no, Mummy says yes,
So we'll surely get married, we two.

J. Møller, 'Kladask', GID, 1997, 1, 9.

KLAPPE ØRE, Dan. for 'ear slap'. One participant sits on a chair and stretches out his hands, palms facing each other. Another contestant kneels before him, puts his hands on the other's knees and places his head between the other's hands. He now has to quickly withdraw his head, before the person sitting down claps his hands on the kneeling player's ears.
J. Møller, 'Klappe øre', GID, 1997, 3, 71.

KLASY, Pol. equivalent of >HOP-SCOTCH [*hop* – to jump + *scotch* – a line, scratch]; a family of children's games in which each player tosses a stone, a metal slug, a bit of brick or tile, sometimes a shard of glass or porcelain, a wad of paper, a bottle-cap, etc. into one of several compartments of a geometric figure drawn on the ground and then hops from one compartment to another, picking the stone up or kicking it, but always taking care to omit landing on whichever compartment contains the stone. *Klasy* is the plur. form of Pol. *klasa,* meaning 'class', the 'classes' here referring to the individual levels or 'grades' one progresses through, hopping from box to box. There are countless varieties of the game but their common feature is passing from one point to another in a series, hopping on one or both legs, accompanied by shifting one of the above-mentioned objects from field to field, according to specific patterns that vary from game to game. Differences concern such elements as the shape of the figures, the number of compartments, the sequence of passing through a given pattern, and the manner in which such patterns are passed through. Despite such variables, the games of different nations are in fact strikingly similar. One var. in Portugal is >JOGO DO AVIÃO, while in Germany they play >FUBSCHEIBENSPIEL and *Himmel und Hölle.* Arab culture is rich with games resembling klasy, among them >AL-HAGLA, >AL-HUD'D'A, >BERBER, and >LU'BAT UMM AL-HUTUT. In Poland, klasy games were known under an array of varieties including such colorful names as *bałwan* (snowman), *posuwanka-nóżka* (leg-shuffle), *posuwanka włoska* (Italian shuffle), *samolot* (airplane), and *ślimak* (snail). In his extensive work, *Gry i zabawy różnych stanów* (1839), Ł. Gołębiowski makes no mention of klasy or any other similar game for that matter. This conspicuous absence suggests that klasy games became popular in Poland only in the mid-19th cent.

Kite skiing.

VARIETIES OF KLASY

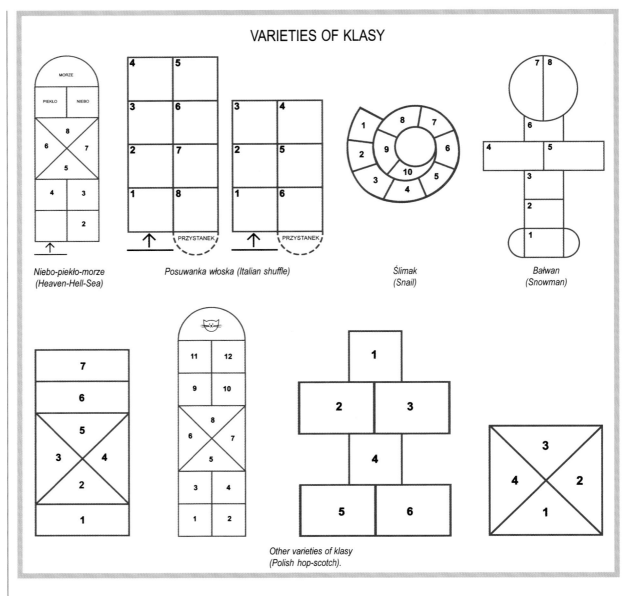

*Niebo-piekło-morze
(Heaven-Hell-Sea)*

Posuwanka włoska (Italian shuffle)

*Ślimak
(Snail)*

*Bałwan
(Snowman)*

*Other varieties of klasy
(Polish hop-scotch).*

or perhaps as late as the beginning of the 20th cent. Still, the game developed into a number of regional varieties.

BAŁWAN, the name of the game originates from a characteristic pattern of fields resembling a figure with its arms outstretched, i.e. a 'snowman' (see illustration). The lower part of the figure consists of 3 rectangles placed horizontally, one above the other. The lowest of them, marked as number 1, is embraced on each side by a semicircle, the diameter of which equals the length of the side. These semicircles do not generate any score. Fields 2 and 3 follow, supporting two 50% larger fields, 4 and 5. These overhang, forming the snowman's armspan, so positioned that the boundary between them is located on the vertical axis of the snowman in the middle of the top of field 3 and the bottom of field 6, which serves as the neck. The upper part of the neck is concave to support the circular head along its perimeter. The head is vertically halved, the left half comprising field 7, and the right – field 8. The game consists of tossing a small object, such as a pebble or woodchip, onto each field, one after another, over which a player must hop in the course of the game, starting with field 1. Fields 2 and 3 are supposed to be overcome with single hops on either leg (player's choice), whereas fields 4 and 5 have to be jumped upon simultaneously with one leg on each field. Then, a player hops onto field 6 (on one leg again), finally reaching the head with the left foot on field 7 and the right on field 8, after which the jumper is supposed to pivot back with a single jump in order to place the right foot on field 7 and the left on field 8. The return to the starting position follows the same pattern in a reverse order. After hopping onto field 2, the player picks up the pebble by bending at the waist (not the knees) and usu. projecting one leg out behind, and then finishes the round by jumping onto field 1 holding the pebble in one hand. In the following rounds, the pebble is thrown onto com-

partments at increasing distances, and is to be hopped over without pause. On their way back players pick up the stone and return with it to the starting field. After that, the same series of rounds is executed on the other leg. Any error in completing a given round eliminates a player from that round.

NIEBO-PIEKŁO-MORZE, Pol. for 'heaven-hell-sea', a game played on a complex playing ground (see illustration), approx. 8m long and 2m wide. The ground is divided into smaller areas, the lower part formed by a large, quartered square, resulting in 4 small squares numbered 2, 3, and 4 counterclockwise starting from the lower right-hand one. The lower left-hand square, from which the game begins, is left unnumbered. The large square borders along its topside with a square of equal size but this time quartered diagonally into 4 small triangles. The triangle located at the bottom bears the number 5, the left-hand one – 6, the right-hand one – 7, and the topmost triangle – 8. Upon these sit 2 squares the same size as the first smaller squares, set side by side, of which the left-hand one is referred to as 'hell' and the right-hand one as 'heaven'. Their topsides border with the bottom of a semicircle known as 'sea'. The object of the game is to reach the sea by tossing a stone onto each field, one after another, over which a player must hop in sequence. R. Trześniowski recounts the procedure as follows:

They enter the 2nd grade by putting the left foot on the 1st grade (the one that has no number on it) and the right foot on the 2nd. Players jump out of it at a half-turn backwards and then with both feet forwards. Similarly, they enter the 4th grade placing the right foot on it and leaving the left foot on the 3rd grade. In the same manner they jump onto grade 7, putting the right foot on it and the left foot on grade 6. After covering grade 8, they hop on 'hell' on either leg, then on 'heaven' with both feet, and finally onto 'see' again on one leg. The return way follows the same pattern. The winner is the player who reaches the see soonest without making a single error on the way. When a player misses a field while tossing a stone or touches

a line with either foot, the attempt is deemed a failure and needs to be repeated after the rest of the players have had a chance. When all the players have succeeded in the first round, they continue on to rounds 2, 3, 4 up to 8.

There are regional, and even national, varieties of this game. In England, a similar game, a var. of hopscotch, is known as *hop-score*.

POSUWANKA WŁOSKA, Pol. for 'Ital. shuffle', a game played on a rectangular field (see illustration) 3-4m long and 1.5-2m wide, depending on the number of rectangular fields inside and participants' skills. The playing ground consists of 2 rows of 3-4 rectangles. Each field is scored differently, e.g. if there are 6 fields in total (2 rows of 3 rectangles), the fields on the left are numbered 1, 2, 3 from bottom to top and those on the right 4, 5, 6 from top to bottom. Another scoring system, mostly popular in English-speaking countries, starts with 1 on the right-hand bottom field and continues on to 2, 3, and 4 upwards and then 5, 6, 7, 8 downwards in the left-hand row. The object of the game is to toss a stone so that it lands as close as possible to the center of field 1, while the player is standing in front of field 1. After that, a player hops on either leg onto field 1 and kicks the stone in order to move it onto field 2, then onto fields 3, 4, 5, and so on, depending on the number of fields. If the stone does not reach the neighboring field or misses it, the player loses his turn. In a different var. that employs the same playing ground, players toss a stone onto field 1 which they then must hop over on either leg, landing on field 2 and than continue hopping through all the fields, still on one leg only. Next, they pick the stone up and repeat the same procedure, now tossing the stone onto field 2, which has to be skipped. After the round skipping field 2 is completed, a series of rounds commences during which fields 3, 4, 5 and so on, are passed over one after another. Similarly to the first var., players lose their turn on making any error in the jumping series or in positioning the stone correctly. In both var. a throw after which the stone lands on a line is deemed incorrect and the thrower loses his turn. While hopping, players must not stop, nor may they touch a line with their foot.

ŚLIMAK, Pol. for 'snail', consists of hopping on either leg through steps that curl into a spiral figure resembling a snail's shell (see illustration). Players have to toss a stone onto a field and then move it forward with one foot while hopping. The snail usu. contains 11 fields, of which 10 are numbered and the central one, referred to as 'heaven', is not. The fields are of diminishing sizes, i.e. the longest are located on the outer-most coil and the shortest are closer to the snail's center. As with other var., if the player loses balance while hopping, or if the stone comes to rest on a line or misses the neighboring field, that player loses a turn. Nearly identical games are known in Port. as >JOGO DO CARACOL and in Dan. as hinke snegl (>AT HINKE).
R. Trześniowski, 'Posuwanka-nóżka' and 'Niebopiekło-morze' in Zabawy i gry ruchowe, 1995.

KLIM-KLEM, a Dan. children's game (the name is a nonsense word), often used during physical education classes in elementary school. Players run between 2 safety zones. Between them stands a contestant who catches the runners as they move from one zone to another (on the command 'Klimklem!'). A player who is caught becomes the klimklem. Cf. other games of this type: >DØDNING, >GÅ OVER ELVEN, >ISBJØRN OG LANDSBJØRN, >KÆDETIK, >TAMANJ, >TULLEHUT, >TYRHOLDE, >KREDSTROLD.
J. Møller, 'Klim-klem', GID, 1997, 2, 52.

KLIPA, [Ger. Klippe, Swed. klippa – sharp rock], a children's game popular in Pol. Silesia and E regions of Germany. The object of the game was to bat a peg conically sharpened at both ends (almost identical to >SZTEKIEL). Klipa was most popular in Upper Silesia in the 19th cent. A.O. Klaussmann writes:

The game of klipa was exceptionally popular. The klipa was a round stick about 10cm long, sharpened at both ends. It was hit with a bat at one end and flipped up. When it was in the air, the player tried to hit it once again, to send it as far away as he could. The klipa could be hit 3 times. Then it was estimated how many lengths of the bat a player had. If he did not find the number satisfactory, he measured the distance from the starting point with the bat. The game was played in 2 teams. If the party standing outside managed to catch the klipa, they won. After using the bat, the player placed it over the hole which the klipa was knocked from. The other party tried to throw the klipa back so that it would hit the bat. After making the throw, the player was out of the game. Without any doubt the game required much skill and sharpened one's ability to estimate distance.

The scoring system of klipa varied from region to region. Often for intercepting the peg in mid-air the team would be given 100pts. In the case mentioned by Klaussmann, when the klipa was not caught in mid-air, the team would throw it from the spot where it fell back towards the bat, now placed over the hole, where the klipa was first placed. If this attempt was successful, the team gained points and the serve; if not – it played in the field for another 3 rounds. The game could be played in teams as well as individually. Nowadays the word 'klipa' is often used ironically, as a term for a less than serious action. In the past, however, the game was important as part of physical education in areas and social strata where the practicing of sports was impeded by economic hardship. This was the case in many small towns and villages, with a shortage of playing fields, sports instructors and equipment. Klipa could be played in any conditions. Its significance decreased with the introduction of regular physical education classes for schoolchildren, the availability of sports gear and the development of new disciplines. Now the game is almost forgotten. Cf. similar games of other nations: >AL-BA' 'A, >GULLI DUNDA, >PILAUET.
A.O. Klaussmann, Oberschlesien vor 55 Jahren, (Górny Śląsk przed laty), Pol. translation by Antoni Halor, Muzeum Historii Katowic, 1997.

KLIS, a Bulg. game where players hit a stick with a bat to send it as far into the field as possible. The same family of games includes: the Pol. >KLIPA, >KICZKA, and >SZTEKIEL, Arab >AL BA' 'A, Indon. TAK KADAL, Lankan >GUDU, Fr. >PILAUET, and Eng. >TIP-CAT, >NORTHERN SPELL, and >TROUNCE-HOLE.

KLODSMAJOR, Dan. for 'clumsy person', an old Dan. game, where players aimed small wooden

blocks at another, cylindrical block, 45cm high and 10cm in diameter. On it each player placed a coin as forfeit. Whoever knocked this block down took all the coins which fell heads or tails (Dan. kløver or krone), depending on previous arrangement.
J. Møller, 'Klodsmajor', GID, 1997, 3, 70.

KLOOTSCHIEN, also >KLOOTSCHIETEN, a bowling game played on public roads in Holland and in some Ger. regions close to the Du. border. The game is a competition between 2 players who roll wooden or lead bowls along a public road. The winner is the player who covers a given distance with a smaller number of throws made from under the arm. The game is extremely popular in the area of Twente, where local clubs have a membership of 3,000 or more. A similar game is known in Ireland as >ROAD BOWLING, in Germany as >KLOOTSCHIEßEN, >BOßELSPIEL, or >BOßELN.

KLOOTSCHIEßEN, also BOßELN, a bowling game played on roads, originating from the same tradition as the Du. >KLOOTSCHIEN. It is played on the Frisian Islands, belonging to Germany, where some of its var. are referred to as >BOßELSPIEL.

KLOOTSCHIETEN, an alternative name for the Du. bowling game of >KLOOTSCHIEN.

KNÆKKE TØRV, Dan. for 'breaking the turf', a brutal schoolboy's game, practiced not only in Denmark. One person puts his knee to another's back and, grabbing his arms and shoulders, bends him backward, which can be injurious.
J. Møller, 'Knække tørv', GID, 1997, 3, 70.

KNÄPPA RYGG, a Swed. type of folk wrestling [knäppa – to embrace + rygg – back], practiced in the regions of Boda and Dalarna, similar to >BRYTTA RYGG. Swed. sports ethnologist M. Hellspong classified it as part of a general wrestling type >LIVTAG.
M. Hellspong, 'Brottning som folklig lek, Livtag', RIG, 1991, 4.

KNAPPAN, Wel. and Cornish [Celtic knap – to hit, strike], a game similar to the Gaelic >CAMÁNACHT, one of the predecessors of the modern >HURLING. P. Roberts, a Welsh amateur ethnographer from the 19th cent., unambiguously identifies the game as hurling ('the selfe same exercise'), he adds, though, that 'they call hurling, whereby it seemeth that this exercise is more ancient than formerly observed ... descended to us Welshmen from our first progenitors, the Trojans.' According to the oldest Brit. legends, it was the Trojan newcomers and their leader Brutus, who were the forefathers of the Brit. Isles' inhabitants, however, from a scientific point of view, this can be treated as merely a fairy tale. Many historians claim that knappan is a Brit. type of a game known in medieval France as la >SOULE, esp. its var. >SOULE À LA CROSSE. Roberts describes the game from before the codification of sports rules, which was far from the principles of fair play, as it is understood today:

The two companies, being come together about one or two of the clock in the afternoone, beginneth the play in this sort. After a crye made, both parties draw together into some plaine, all first stripped bare, saving a light paire of breeches, bare headed, bare bodied, bare legges and feete, their cloathes layd together in great heapes ... for if he leave but his shirt on his backe, in the furie of the game it is most commonly torne to pieces ... There is a round bowle prepared of a reasonable quantitie, soe as a man may hold it in his hand, and noe more ... boyled in tallowe to make it slippery ... This bowle is called knappan, and is by one of the company hurled bolt upright to the ayere, and at the falle, he that catcheth it hurleth it towards the countey he playeth for, (for gole or appointed place there is none, neither needeth any) for the play is not given over until the knappan be so far carried that there is no hope to returne it backe that night ... The knappan being cast forth you shall see the same tossed backward and forwarde, by hurling throwes in straunge sorte; for in three or four throwes, you shall see the whole body of the game removed half a mile or more, and in this sort it is a strange sight to see 1000 or 1500 naked men to come neere together in a cluster followinge the knappan ... There are, besides the corps or mayne body of the play, certaine scoutes or forerunners, whose charge is alwaies to keepe before the knappan which way soever it passes; these alwaies be of the adverse partie, between the other partie and home, least by surreption the knappan should be snatched by a borderer of the game, and so carried away by foote or by horse ... In this sorte you shall in an open field see 2000 naked people follow the bowle backward and forwarde, East, West, South and North, so that a straunger that casuallie

should see such a multitude soe ranging naked, would think them distracted ... In the furie of the chase they respect neither hedge, ditch, pale or walle, hille, dale, bushes, river or rocke, or any other passable impediment ... the horsemen have monstruous codgells ... as big as the party is able to weld, and he that thinketh himself well horsed means to his friends of the footmen to have the knappan delivered to him, which being gotten, he putteth spurres, and away as fast as the legges will carry. After him runneth the rest of the horsemen; and if they can overtake him, he summoneth a delivery of the knappan. If he hold the knappan it is lawful for the assailant to beat him with the codgell till he deliver it. Now at this play privat grudges are revenged, soe that for every small occasion they fall by the eares, which being once kindled between two, all persons of both sides become parties ... You shall see gamesters returne home from the playe, with broaken heads, black faces, brused bodies, and lame legges, yet laughing and jesting at their harmes.
[P. Roberts, The Cambrian Popular Antiquities, 1815, p. 110-111]

KNATTLEIKR, ancient Icel. name, also knattleikar, modern form: knattleikur, a var. of a game where a wooden ball was struck with a stick. It was played in Scandinavia at the time of the Vikings. As Norsemen settled in Iceland, the game spread throughout the island, and was played there for a few centuries, but did not survive to the present time. The fragmented var. of preserved descriptions does not allow the game to be fully reconstructed. Nevertheless, it seems to have been characterized mainly by: 1) the division of an unspecified number of players into 2 teams, 2) setting the wooden ball in motion with flat-ended sticks resembling paddles, slightly curved and maybe hollowed, so as to enable catching and carrying the ball to the target. The latter characteristic led the historian, E. Hertzberg, to compare it with Can. >LACROSSE and one of its predecessors >BAGATAWAY. J. Idorn, in turn, maintains that the ball was played not only with a stick, but was kicked and passed with a single hand as well:

[...] a solid wooden ball was thrown, kicked or batted down the field to be caught by one hand. It was played by two equal teams

Klipa and sztekiel are two almost identical Polish batting games.

326

K WORLD SPORTS ENCYCLOPEDIA

on a frozen lake or other level surface and the spectators watched from the surrounding mounds. The referee was usually the man upon whose fields the tournament was played. A tournament like this could last from one to 14 days.

B. Bjarnson, *Nordboernes Legemlige Uddannelse i Oldtiden*, 1905; E. Hertzberg, 'Norboernes gamle Boldspil,' *Historiske Skrifter tilegnede og overleverede* Professor Ludwig Daae, 1904; J. Idorn, 'History', *Sport in Denmark*, ed. Det Danske Selskab, 1978; M.W. Williams, *Social Scandinavia in the Viking Age*, 1920.

KNEEBOARDING, riding on water behind a motorboat, which is practiced kneeling down (because of the special construction of the kneeboard). Kneeboarding was popular in the 1970s, but was later superseded by the >AIR CHAIR, developed by M. Murphy and other kneeboarding enthusiasts. Kneeboarding is practiced on 2 types of boards: trick boards and slalom boards. The rope should be at least 45ft. long.

KNEEL JUMP, a trad. Inuit game. The contestant kneels on the ground before the starting line, touching his buttocks to his feet and holding his hands on his knees. He rocks his body forwards and backwards and then jumps forwards. The distance of the jump is measured from the starting line to the contestant's foot. Every participant has 3 chances. The best score is used for classification. The starting order is determined by a draw. If 2 contestants have the same results, they jump once again. The kneel jump is one of the so-called arctic sports. It is part of the program of N.Amer. Indigenous Games.

The Head Pull. The Arctic Sports, the Internet: http://www.firstnations.com/naig97/arctic-sports/as-kneel-jump.htm

KNIBE KAT, Dan. for 'pressing or pinching the cat'. A simple strength-testing competition, which used to be popular among Dan. peasants. One of them lay on the ground and another put him in a half-nelson. The former's task was to get up.

J. Møller, 'Knibe kat', GID, 1997, 3, 86.

KNIGHTS, see >RIDE PICK-A-BACK.

KNOR AND SPELL, see >NORTHERN SPELL.

KNUCKLE HOP, a kind of push-up competition in which the competitors rest on the knuckles of hands clenched into fists. Lifting the body off the floor, a competitor pushes off on his or her knuckles and toes, and hops forward, landing again on both knuckles and toes simultaneously. Rather than the number of push-ups, it is the distance the competitor can hop before quitting or lowering his or her body to the floor that is important. The competitor who covers the longest distance, measured from the starting point of the knuckles to the position of the knuckles at completion, is the winner. Knuckle hop is a trad. game of Alaskan and Can. Natives. As one of the so-called Arctic sports it has been included in the program of the North Amer. Indigenous Games.

The Arctic Sports: http://www.firstnations.com/naig97/arctic-sports/as-knuckle-hop.html

KNUR AND SPEL, see >NORTHERN SPELL.

KNUR, SPEL AND KIBBLE, see >NORTHERN SPELL.

KNURR AND SPELL, see >NORTHERN SPELL.

KØBENSHAVNBOLD, Dan. for 'Kopenhagen ball', also *københavsnsk langbold*, lit. 'Kopenhagen long ball', contrary to its name, a game played in S Jutland, similar to >HIMMELBOLD.

KOBUJUTSU, Jap. old combat techniques, a fighting school originating in Okinawa, an island between China and Japan that draws from the traditions of both countries owing to its location. Kobujutsu employs simple implements such as poles, rods, rice flails, and even rakes.

KOCH, an Armenian type of trad. hand-to-hand combat.

KOCZAŁKA, also *krążka*, a game played in the E regions of former Poland known as Polesie, the territory of today's Belorus. The name stems from the old Pol. word *kocz* or *kosz*, a Turk. borrowing meaning troops or a military camp. Oskar Kolberg, a Pol. ethnographer, observed koczałka in the village of Łysica before 1890:

As we were passing through the village, we stayed for a while to give our horses a rest, and we could see a strange folk game played on the flat area in front of the inn during a holiday, called koczałka or krążka. The youth of the village were divided in two groups, which were standing 40 sążeń apart (sążeń – ancient Polish unit of measure equal to 190cm). Each player was armed with a club. After each group formed itself into a line, a 3in. wide and 1in. thick wooden disk was thrown in front of one party. They pushed it with their clubs, and the other party was to throw it back in the opposite direction using their clubs. The disc was hit in different directions, similarly to cannon shots, that is, horizontally, in a ricochet and following a curved trajectory, according to the law of rebound. Thus, the disk was hurtling through the air and if it was not returned, it often dealt the players terrible blows in various parts of their bodies.

The moment one of the parties failed to return the disk thrown at one of its players by the opposite team standing in a line, the round was finished. The number of returned and not returned shots indicated the losers and the winners of the round. It was, most probably, the flight direction of the disk that determined which player should return the disk: the player in the most convenient position ran up to it and tried to throw it back. The considerable distance between the teams made it rather difficult to aim precisely at one, specific player to surprise him, for example, and this would have been especially challenging considering the long flight of the disk. The very distance between the teams facing each other was, probably, to protect against the heavy blows the disk dealt to the players if they missed it. Thanks to a distance of about 76m, the disk was already falling and the flight force was decreasing. If the distance had been shorter, the danger of injuring the body would have been greater.

Oskar Kolberg, 'Koczałka', *Dzieła wszystkie* (*Collected Works*), vol. 52, 19**.

KODI, also *kora*, a Kenyan game with rules similar to Eng. >JACKS.

KOGE FISK, Dan. for 'to cook a fish'. A Dan. game for 2 testing the players' stamina and strength, in which one player lies on the ground face down and the other stands and then walks on him until he believes his fish to be cooked. Whether the player is well done is tested by jerking his arms - should they be stiff the cooking has to be repeated until the fish is ready.

J. Møller, 'Koge fisk'. GID, 1997, 3, 67.

KÕIEVÉDU, an Est. competition similar to the well known >TUG-OF-WAR. In many regions of Estonia the teams pull the rope over a stream or ditch instead of a mere line drawn on the ground, with the losers ending up in water.

M. Värv et al., 'Traditional Sports and Games in Estonia', TSNJ, 1996, 33).

KOKH, also *koch*, a type of Armenian folk wrestling fought in a standing position. The competitors wear special belts and fight to the accompaniment of music at festivities and during holidays.

W. Baxter, 'Kokh', in: 'Les luttes traditionnelles a traverse le monde', LJP, 1998, 78.

KOK-PAR, see >BUZKASHI.

KOLF, also *colf*, an old Flem. and Du. game, from the Fr. *chouler á la crosse*, consisting of rolling and hitting a small ball with a rod over spacious grounds, frequently several km in length, to a special hole. In the manifold local var. the requirement of the game was to hit the ball into the holes faster than other players, but soon the rule to use as few strokes as possible prevailed. Kolf became so popular in the 16th and 17th cent. that it was frequently banned, which, all the same, failed to hinder its development. The game was illustrated on a number of Flem. and Du. paintings. Kolf played on larger grounds began to disappear, a fact attributed to a lack of open spaces in the increasingly more populous Flanders and the Netherlands. It was gradually replaced with a game of a similar character, but needing a smaller course, which gave rise to the mod. >KOLVEN. Cf. >GOLF.

E. De Vroede, *Het Grote Volkssporten Boek,* Leuven 1996; E. De Vroede, 'Ball and Bowl Games in the Low Countries: Past and Present', *Homo Ludens – Der Spielende Mensch,* 1996, vol. VI.

KÖLNÅKERN, the name of a boulder from Framgården in Sweden. It was discovered while clearing a field of stones, is described in the Swed. tradition as *brytöl*, and confirms a frequent custom in this country of using boulders as a gauge of strength. See also >LYFTESTEN, Dan. >STENLØFTNING, Basq. >ARRIJASOKETA; >DRÄNGASTENAR, >DRÄNGALÖFTEN, >GGET, >KAMPASTEN, >KUNGSSTEN, >KUNGSSTENARNA, >STORA OCH LILLA DAGSVERKARN, >TYFTEHÖNAN.

S. Erixon, *Svenskt folkliv,* 1938; M. Hellspong, 'Lifting Stones. The Existence of Lifting-Stones in Sweden', ST, 1993-94, XIX-XX.

KOŁO, Pol. for 'circle', a school game in which a leader is chosen and the rest of the players are divided into 5-6 groups and a circle, 3-4 steps in diameter is drawn. The players, one out of each group, stand on the circumference of the circle at regular intervals, facing its inside; behind them stand other members of their groups so that the whole figure resembles an armed star. The leader goes around the star and suddenly pats a player of a group of his choosing on the back while standing behind him. The remaining group members have to pass the pat on, one by one, to the person in front. The moment the last group member standing in the same arm of the star has been patted on the back, the whole group begins to race around the star and returns to the spot they started from. However, one place has already been taken up by the leader, so the person that comes last becomes the new leader and begins the next round.

I.N. Chkhannikov, 'Koło', GIZ, 10-11.

KOLONG; Afr. game of the Kpelle tribe in the town of Gbargasaukwelle and its neighborhood in Liberia. The game is played almost exclusively at night. The goal of the game is winning a mnemonic duel by completing an adage. The word *kolong* means its first part, the complete adage being *seeng*, which at the same time means the correct solution of a task. The game is played in teams; the first team offers a kolong, and the other discusses how to complete the adage. If the second team fails, the first team has still to give the correct answer to gain a point. If the team that is supposed to complete the seeng does it correctly, it is their turn to recite a chosen kolong. The game is very popular among the Kpelle because of the richness in adages of their language, maxims containing tribal rules of conduct in specific circumstances, esp. in solving conflicts. In this way the game ensures that the youth inherit (and the adults observe) tribal mores and morals, societal rules for solving real problems.

A. Taylor Cheska, 'Kolong', TGDWAN, 1987, 42-43.

KOLVEN, a Flem.-Du. game probably stemming from a Fr. var. of the Middle Ages game of >CHOULE, known as *chouler á la crosse*, in which a bowl or a ball was propelled with a curved stick towards a target, located sometimes even several km from the starting point. In Flanders and the Netherlands it evolved into a game initially called *colf* or >KOLF. It was characterized by a lack of direct bodily contact with partners in the game, and by individual striving towards the target, usu. a hole into which a ball had to be struck faster or with fewer strokes than other players. In a var. of kolven played on ice, the target was a metal rod driven into the ice in the closest vicinity of which a ball had to be brought. The game gained immense popularity in the 16th and 17th cent., to the extent of being prohibited by authorities in some locations. Its development is well documented on numerous Flem. and Du. paintings. Kolf began to vanish from c.1700, because of lack of open spaces in the increasingly more populous Netherlands and Flanders. It was frequently replaced with a similar game, which did not require a large course, and which gave rise to modern kolven. After a period of intensive growth throughout almost the whole of the Netherlands at the beginning of the 19th cent., interest in the game was on the wane in the second half of the century. To support the tradition, the Royal Kolven Union of Holland (Koninklijke Nederlandse Kolfbond) was set up, but after a short-lived revival the game ceased to be played in the first half of the 20th cent. Nowadays kolven is played almost exclusively in the N Netherlands in 35 clubs, which together have 18 courses, and in Utrecht and Sevenum. See also >HET KOLVEN.

Rules of play. Modern kolven is played on flat courses 17.52m long and 5m wide, surrounded by a wooden board. A wooden column 1m high and 15cm in diameter at each end of the course is situated about 1m from the end line. The course is divided into 12 zones with a rising number of points from 1 to 12 each. During the game each player is

Korfball.

entitled to 3 strokes in a row with a curved stick. The diameter of the balls is 10-12cm. With the first stroke of the ball from the back line, it must land as near as possible to the column on the other end of the course, at its end. The aim of the second stroke is to bounce the ball off this column so that it returns to the vicinity of the column near which the game took off. Now it has to be struck so that it bounces off the first column and flies as far as possible winning points.

S. Van Hengel, *Colf, Kolf, Golf, van middeleeuws volksspel tot moderne sport*, 1982; J. Temmerman, *Golf en kolf: zeven eeuwen geschiedenis*, 1993; E. De Vroede, *Het Grote Volkssporten Boek*. Leuven 1996; E. De Vroede, 'Ball and Bowl Games in the Low Countries: Past and Present', *Homo Ludens – Der Spielende Mensch*, 1996, vol. VI.

KOM HJEM ALLE MIN FUGL, Dan. for 'come home, my bird', [Dan. *kom* – come *hjem* – home *alle* – all *min* – my *fugl* – bird], a game played in Dan. kindergartens and in elementary schools at physical education classes. One of the players is a bird seller, another one is a merchant, the rest of the children are birds. The merchant steps back and gives names to the birds, i.e. an owl, eagle, etc. After a while the merchant returns and says he wants to buy e.g. an eagle. The player that is an eagle runs a few steps away when he is being paid for (the merchant strikes the seller's hand 10 times). Next the seller calls on his bird to come back to him. The player that is the bird attempts to run back to his place trying to dodge the merchant. J. Møller, 'Kom hjem alle min fugl', GID 1997, 50-51.

KOMA, Jap. var. of >TOPS. A koma is a disc made of wood, stone or shell that spins on a sharpened peg, and depending on type, is moved by hitting it with a rope or other komas. Some discs have openings that produce a characteristic sound while spinning. The name *koma* comes from the Koma area on the Kor. Peninsula, where the Japanese first encountered a game of this type at the beginning of Edo era (1603-1867).

KONGEBOLD, Dan. for 'royal ball'. A Scand. ball game. In the Dan. var. there are 5-20 players. The game starts with drawing lots at who is to be the king. The rest of the players stand in a semicircle at the same, 2-3-step distance from the king. The king throws a ball to each player in a row, and they have to return it according to certain rules. The king can throw the ball in any way, but the others must catch the ball in a prescribed way, each of them differently. Depending on the terrain, the throws are performed in 8, 10 or 14 ways. In the 8-way version the game looks as follows: the 1st player has to catch the ball with 2 open hands, the 2nd – with his right hand, from the bottom, the 3rd – with his left hand, from the bottom, the 4th – with the right hand from above, the 5th – with a left-hand upper-grip, the 6th – with both hands with the wrists crossed, the 7th – with crossed wrists, but the ball has to be caught with one hand only, then passed into the other hand and with this hand returned to the king, the 8th – has to catch the ball with 2 rolled fists. After the se-

ries of throws is finished, the king moves 5-6 steps back and starts the same round of throws, but this time only to one player, who has to catch the ball in all 8 ways. If he succeeds in doing so, he becomes the next king, if not, then the king repeats the series with the 2nd, 3rd, 4th and so on player until the next king is elected.
J. Møller, 'Kongebold', GID, 1997, 1, 13.

KONGEPIND, Dan. for 'royal peg'. A Dan. folk game consisting of throwing and driving pegs into the ground in such a way as to knock down the opponents' pegs. Each player has got a peg 50-60cm long and 2-3cm in diameter. A circle of a 50-60cm radius is drawn on soft ground. The players draw lots to see who goes first, and the 1st player throws his peg so that it sticks into the ground. The 2nd player throws his to drive it into the ground and knock down the opponent's peg. If his peg falls over he loses a point, if it does not, and levers and knocks down the opponent's peg he gets a point. Now the 3rd player drives in his peg, at the same time trying to knock down the 2 former ones. If during this attempt the peg falls over, the player loses 2pts. Next the 4th player takes his chance with the same aim. The player that is the first to win 10pts. is the king (*Konge*). Sometimes the game is carried on to 25pts., and then the person that wins 10 is the king, 20 – the emperor (*Kejser*), and 25 – the pope (*Pave*). Cf. >PATØK.
J. Møller, 'Kongepind', 1997, 4.

KONGERIGER, Dan. for 'game of kingdoms', [Dan. *kongerige* - kingdom]; a ball game involving throws towards a target. The players stand in a large circle, each drawing a smaller circle (roughly 1m in diameter) around himself. In the center of the large circle, in his own concentric circle, stands the king. To initiate the game, the king tries to hit one of the other rulers in their lesser kingdoms (i.e. circles) with a ball; if hit, the player becomes his captive, and his kingdom becomes his territory. If he misses, then the player who got hit instead of the player aimed at, or the player off whose circle the ball bounces gets the ball. He has now the right to throw the ball and regain some of the land won by the king from the middle. The aim of the game is for one king to win all kingdoms.
J. Møller, 'Kongeriger', GID, 1997, 1, 23.

KÖNIGSSCHIEßEN, a type of a shooting contest in Ger. towns under the auspices of merchant and craftsmen guilds for the title of shooting king, which is awarded for 1 year until the next contest [Ger. *König* – king, *Schießen* – shooting], a Pol. counterpart of Königsschießen is >COCK SHOOTING.

KOONG YOONG MU SOOL, a Kor. martial art and self-defense understood as both a courtly and knightly art. [Kor. *Koongyoong* – the royal court; *musool* – martial art]; see also >BULKYO MU SOOL.

KOORA, Arab ball, a type of game resembling modern >FIELD HOCKEY. Played in Algeria, in the vicinity of Menea. According to early 20th cent. travelers played only in spring.

KORA, see >KODI.

KORBBALL, a ball game classified as one of the >BASKETBALL GAMES, also those less popular, like >KORFBALLL, >KURVBOLD, >NETBALL; the name comes from the Ger. *Korb* – basket and *Ball* - ball. The game involves 2 teams of 7 players. The court (*Korfballlspielfeld*) is 60m long and 25m wide, and there are posts on either end of the court, without backboards, 7m from the end lines, on which baskets are mounted 2.5m above the ground on a short jib, 45cm in diameter. The circumference of the ball is 58-60cm, its weight 400-500g. Around each post with a basket a circle of 3m in circumference is marked, described as the basket zone (*Korbraum*). Players are not allowed to play within this circle, directly in front of the basket, with the exception of the defender, the sentry of the basket (*Korbwächter*). The court is divided by a midcourt line into 2 zones. 4m from the post with the basket there is a free throw point (*Freiwurfmarke*). A basket or a soccer ball may be used. The aim of the game is to throw the ball into the opposing team's basket. The play-time is 2×5min., a player can take only 3 steps with the ball, and the ball can be held no more than 3sec. in a player's hands.

History. Ger. teacher O.H. Kluge (1813-82) invented the game and published the rules in *Deutsche Turnzeitung* magazine It was initially called *Ballkorb*, and was played mainly in Ger. schools. Basketball players perfecting their shooting accuracy without the help of a backboard also took it up. The game continued after 1945 in E Germany (no data concerning it after 1990). It had been used in Austria in school physical education curricula but gradually disappeared in the 1960s displaced by more attractive ball games.
W. Braungardt. 'Korbball', *Turnspiele*, 1949, 50-59; interview with H. Andrecs from the Aus. Sports Ministry, 1999.

KORFBALL, Du. korfbal [*korf* – basket, *bal* – ball], a ball game included in the >BASKETBALL GAMES family, along with the major group member >BASKETBALL, and the less popular >KORBBALL, >KURVBOLD and >NETBALL, in some countries known as *corfball*.

The aim of the game is to throw the ball into the opposing team's basket. The basket is made of 2 rims 39-41cm in diameter joined with an elastic sleeve and located on a 3.5-m post. The function of the sleeve is to slow down the ball while it passes the rims, so that the correctness of each throw can be observed, similar to the net under the basket in basketball. The sleeve is 25cm deep, and the upper rim 2-3cm thick. The sleeve used to be made of rattan twigs. In 1999 the IKF congress approved synthetic sleeves, previously used only in experiments. The baskets face the middle of the court and have no backboards.

The ball is 68-71cm in diameter and weighs 425-475g. The passing of a ball through the basket is worth 1pt. The posts with baskets stand 10m from the end lines in the outdoor var. and 6.7m in the indoor var. (in the initial period of the game 3.3-4.4m) Outdoor korfball is played on grass courts 60m long and 30m wide (initially up to 90m long and up to 40m wide), indoor korfball on courts 40m long and 20m wide. Play-time in outdoor korfball is 2×35min.

A korfball player.

Korfball.

K

WORLD SPORTS ENCYCLOPEDIA

and 2×30min. indoors. A 3-zone var. of the game used to be played, nowadays 2-zone korfball is played, in which the court is divided into 2 equal parts, on which half of one team and half of the opposing team play, i.e. half of the team play in the offense zone, and the other half in the defense zone. Korfball is played by teams of 8. A team consists of 2 subteams, 2 men and 2 women each. 1 female and 1 male pair play in the offense, and the rest in the defense zone. Once a player is allocated a zone, they must not leave it until positions in the whole team rotate, which occurs in both teams simultaneously every second point gained, and the defense players go into the offense zone and the other way round (regardless of the fact who gained the points). These frequent changes are intended to form a universal player, able to play in any position. The players are allowed to go round the posts but must not use them for rapid changes of direction, for example by holding to it. The players cannot run or dribble the ball, hit the ball with the fist; kicking the ball, playing in the lying position, passing the ball to the partner without throwing it are likewise disallowed. Snatching the ball away from the opponent and double-teaming are also not permitted. Korfball is a non-contact game. A male player must not block a female opponent and vice versa. Pairs of same-sex opponents cover each other; the rationale for this in the officially approved rules is 'conscious promoting of a double rule of co-education and co-operation'. A throw towards the basket is allowed only when a player defending the basket is further from it than the attacker; if he is closer to it, then it is considered effective defense and a throw in this case is void, even if the ball passes through the basket rims. This rule enables a smaller player to defend his basket from a taller person (which is practically impossible in Amer. basketball), since in order to prevent the other team from scoring it is enough for him to stand between the attacker and the basket. The ball is thrown from a max. distance of 15m. This exacts quick passing, for the player in possession of the ball can neither dribble nor run to approach the basket, while a defense player can at any moment and for any length of time, stand between him and his target.

History. Korfball was created by a Du. teacher, N. Broekhuysen. In 1902 he took part in a course in playing >RINGBOL in Sweden; he changed the rules of the game turning it gradually into korfball. In late fall 1902 he organized a course, which attracted around 100 participants and whose consequence was a creation of the first 2 clubs: Openluchtspel Amsterdam and Wit en Schotsch, and shortly afterwards De Eerste Amsterdam Korfball Club. In 1903, on his initiative, the Du. Korfbal Association was

founded. The game quickly took off in the Du. colonies, esp. in Indonesia, Du. Guyana (Suriname), and the Netherlands Antilles, where interest in the game persisted after the fall of colonialism. The first historic match of korfball outside Europe was played in 1919 in Indonesia. The game gained popularity in Belgium, where its national association was founded in 1921. Korfball was presented to a wider public during the 1920 (Antwerp) and 1928 (Amsterdam) Ol.G. In 1924 the International Korfball Bureau was created, which was transformed into the International Korfball Federation (Federation International de Korfballl, FIK) in 1933. In 1935 a national federation in Surinam was founded, but it took no part in the Eur. games until the mid-1970s because of the distance from Europe. In 1946 the Netherlands and Belgium were joined by great Britain, where the Brit. Korfball Association was set up. Until the 1960s, little happened in korfball, despite regular games between the 3 international association members. In 1963-74, of Brit. initiative, the Triangular Trophy was held, the first in London. W Ger. membership gave FIK a boost in 1964, as did Spanish in 1973. In 1967 FIK organized the Eur. Cup, but the out-of-proportion name was soon dropped, and the games turned into the International Youth Tournament, IYT), since 1973 played by 5 states, with the reservation that the Netherlands put up 2 teams, as the Netherlands and E Netherlands. In the Netherlands and Belgium a 3-zone var. of korfball was played, whereas in Spain and Germany a 2-zone system was beginning to develop. In 1975, during the 2nd IYT in Marbella the members tried to arrive at a compromise by playing an outdoor tournament according to indoor rules. All the same, storm clouds were gathering; teams playing in accordance with different rules were 'incompatible'. Federation authorities attempted, in 1976, to impose that the tournament be played according to the 3-zone rules, which lead to a protest and a withdrawal from the tournament by Spain. In 1976-79 international tournaments were played according to 3-zone rules. Luxembourg joined the federation in 1976, but since 1978 Spain and W Germany refused to participate in a tournament played according to rules they could not abide by. In 1981 the federation decided that the 2-zone system would form the basis for the games. The last 3-zone tournament was held in 1986. Since the 1981 death of FIK president Herman Duns, an annual 2-zone Challenge Cup, named in his honor, has been held. In 1987 the first E.Ch. were held with 12 national teams as participants. There were also non-Eur. members in the federation, which did not participate actively in Eur. Games; Papua joined the federation in 1973, Australia in 1977. The development of korfball in Australia was directed by R. Kirk-

by, a Briton, whose actions won him so much support from state authorities that the game won the status of a school game and subsidies along with it. In 1978, after a series of presentation matches, the US joined the federation, France in 1982, Portugal in 1987, Denmark and Poland in 1988. In 1995 the state and national federations membership rose to 32. Bearing in mind the growing numbers of Eur. members, a separate E.Ch. Committee was set up in 1995. The first W.Ch. were organized in 1978 for 8 participants. The next W.Ch. were held in 1984, 1987, 1991, 1995 and 1999. Since 1995, the world winner has received the Nico Broekhuysen World Cup. In 1982, FIK changed its Fr. name to the International Korfball Federation, which left its mark upon the abbreviation, now the IFK. It was as the IFK that the federation joined the General Association of International Sports Federations (GAISF) and then the International World Games Association (IWGA). As a consequence, korfball was put on the agenda of the non-Olympic International Sports Federation of the General Assembly of International Sports (1985, 1989, 1993, 1997) organized by the IWGA. Since 1994 the IFK has held W.Ch. of Youth Teams. Since 1990, separate Championships of Asia and Oceania have been organized, and since 1998 joint Asian-African Championships.

The Netherlands and Belgium have traditionally been leaders in korfball, with France, Germany and Great Britain following close. Until 1999 all W.Ch. titles had been won by the Netherlands. The sport's recent dynamic development can be seen not only in the IKF's expansion, but also by growing numbers of international games on various continents. Korfball for the educationally challenged is developing equally fast – it was included as a presentation discipline in the program of the Special Ol.G. held in Groningen (the Netherlands) in 2000. 12 teams took part. The IOC provisionally approves the IKF, but korfball is not an Olympic event. Exceptionally festive W.Ch. are planned for 2003, on the 100th anniversary of the discipline. In their publications, the IKF describes itself as 'the only mixed-team sport', which is overstating things since for around 20 years similar rules have pertained to Can. >INTERLACROSSE.

K. Piech, *Korfball. Technika – metodyka – trening.* parts I-2, 1996; International Korfball Federation. *The History of the IKF and the World and European Youth Championships,* 1997; The International Korfball Federation, *Korfballl,* 1992.

KORIAK ARCHERY, see >CHUKCHEE AND KORIAK ARCHERY.

KORIN-DO, Jap. martial art belonging to the >AIKIDO tradition, created by Minoru Hiraio (b. 1930), a student of Morihei Ueshiba, who was the inventor of aikido. He cooperated with Ueshiba until the end of WWII, and subsequently created his own style and the school of korin-do.

KORRIKOLARIS, also *korrikalaris,* a var. of trad. Basq. runs at various distances, ranging from several to over 100km. At longer distances the run is broken up by fast walking. Classified as trad. Iberian folk runs (*carreras populares*). In the korrikolaris tradition, the 17-km long route from Lazunza to Casa Forestal, connecting Villabona and Aya, is the most recognized. The race held on the route Tolosa-Pamplona-Toloza is a korrikolaris classic, with a distance of 124km. Of the shorter distance runs, the 18-km route from the market square Llodio to Plaza de España in Bilbao is considered very difficult – it goes uphill almost all the time until passing over the summit of Pagassari. Another short but excruciating route is between Elgoibar and located high up in the mountains Azcárate. Bets are usu. placed on the competitors, with the number of spectators at large events topping several thousand.

History. Korrikolaris was mentioned in late medieval writings, the oldest known formula, frequent in the 19th cent., being a bet between 2 herdsmen, who were to get to a finishing line 5-20km away in the open field. The rules of the mod. var. began to take shape in the early 20th cent., when trad. runs would finish on a square or a local corrida arena in larger towns. The first competitions with the finishing line located in the corrida arena were held in 1903. Often runners from other countries are invited, most frequently from neighboring France. The earliest famous competitions were those between S. Laza from Algeria and J. Bacho from France. In 1922 a

Korrikolaris.

well-known competition was staged, between J. Etxenagusi'a, a Basque, and De Nyse, a Belgian on the Zaruz-Aya course, 13km long; the run finished with a tragedy because while the leader, De Nyse achieved the finish in 54min. 5sec., J. Etxenagusi'a fainted without ending the race and died the following day in the hospital. The 17-km race from Villabona to Aya in 1936 between J. Aldasoro and P. Ugalde, both coming from Andoian, is considered the most famous race ever. Ugalde gave his opponent a 10-min. handicap, and then managed a narrow victory of a mere 26sec. in 1hr. 18min. In 1954 the public imagination was captured by a race between herdsmen A. Medilueta from Huarte and M. Iriarte from Buztinza proceeding along a 9-km course between Casa Foresta and San Miguel; Iriarte won. Spaniards J. Epelde, F. Landa, J. Echevarria and P.I. de Azpeita are considered the best korrikolaris competitors of the 1950s. In the 19th and 20th cent. korrikolaris had a mixed and amateur character, but many runners enjoyed their fees, collected esp. from bets and local prizes in kind. M. Aldaz from Oria and P. Irizar from Andoain were the first to become professionals in 1953. In the late 1960s and '70s the most popular were races between U. Zinkunequi from Aguinaga, Albeniz Iruntxibwerri and J.M. Irazu from Asteasu, and in the '80s J.M. Azpiroza and Chiquito de Aya (Basq. Txikito de Huici).

There are also record-breaking attempts made on the natural Basq. routes, and exceeding certain time barriers has the same importance for local communities as the great achievements of modern sports professionals, i.e. the breaking of the 4min. barrier in a 1mi. race by R. Bannister. In korrikolaris, nobody had been able to negotiate one of the most famous routes, from Durango to Bilbao, 6,040m long and very difficult, in less than 20min., even J. Sucunza's record of 20min. 32sec. seemed unbreakable. When C. de Arruis set a new record of 18min. 57sec., the event was widely publicized in the local press.

Routes leading over mountain tops, like Pagassari, Archanda, Monte San Sebastian (Valmaseda), Ganecogorta, Kolitza, Serantes, etc., are a separate category.

In the 1970s and early '80s, korrikolaris was going through a period of intense development, which slowed its pace as Spain became more democratic and opened to the world. However, its position is bound to remain strong, as from the end of the 1980s it was reinforced with tendencies of saving and cherishing the tradition of folk sports in the EU, of which Spain has been a member since 1986.
R. Aguirre Franco, 'Korrikolaris', DRV, 1983, 81-86; R.A. Franco, 'Korrikolaris', JYDV, 1978, 301-333; *Herri Kirolak, Korrikolaris*, 30-31.

KORUKU a Maori game similar to Eng. >JACKS. The game is played on hardened soil with 5 stones, 4 of which are placed at the corners of the game field. Players start the game with the 5th stone they hold in their hand.

KORURU, a Maori var. of >MARBLES.

KOSHTI CHOUKHEH, also *kushti choukheh,* a local var. of Iranian wrestling practiced in the Khorasan province. The competition is held on a grass rink. Similar to >VARZESH-E PEHLIVANI wrestling, the competitors are dressed in pants skin-tight below the knee, richly embroidered, and having ornamented knee-shields. The fighters smear their bodies with oil before they start. Victory is won by throwing the opponent on his back. In events with a large number of competitors the victories in respective fights are added.

KOSSAUM, Kor. folk game with a rope placed on the shoulders of opposite team members. The aim is to pull at the rope in such a way that the opposing team is pressed to the ground.

KOT, (Pol. for 'a cat'), one of many names for a Pol. folk game, used formerly in C Galicia to describe a game known in other places as >KICZKA or >KLIPA. A game similar to Eng. >KIT-CAT, along with many others in this family of games.

KOTODWE BO NKATE, see >MPEEWA.

KOTSIA, a modern Gk. folk game played with painted bones from animal legs, played shortly after Easter. Each bone is painted in 4 colors, the aim of the game is to throw a random bone on the ground and then throw another one into the air and catch it so

that the hand which catches the bone exposes the same color which can be seen on the top of the bone which is on the ground.

KOURECHE, a var. of folk wrestling practiced in Kurdistan. According to an expert of this sport, Briton W. Baxter, koureche wrestling resembles Turkish >KARAKUCAK GÜREŞI.
W. Baxter, 'Les lutes tarditionnelles a traverse le monde', LJP, 1998, 78.

KOWAL, see >ŻYDEK.

KRABI-KRABONG, lit. the art of sword fighting, a Thai var. of fencing, often combined with a kind of dancing to background music. Tourism has been the major factor in propagating krabi-krabong as a form of performance. Display of the fighters' skills for tourists takes place mainly at Sanam Luang, a square in Bangkok. Most significant presentations of not only krabi-krabong but also other trad. Thai sports take place annually, on the 4th of April. The weapons include side-arms as well as various kinds of staffs. One of the characteristic features of krabi-krabong is the possibility of contending with 2 pieces of identical weapons simultaneously, one in each hand. Inflicting injury on the opponent does not end the fight. Krabi-krabong tradition may be traced back to the 15th cent when it started to be practiced in Siam (ancient Thailand) in the circles of the ruler Narusen's Guards.

KRĄG, a Rus. form of competition once popular among Pol. peasant children. Łukasz Gołębiowski called it 'a local but very amusing game' and went on to observe: 'The boys holding sticks in their hands divide themselves into 2 groups, one of which chooses a place, marks it and within its borders rolls a wooden disc with their sticks; the other group strives at having the disc pushed beyond the marked finishing line as their victory depends on this. When they achieve their aim they become masters of the field until their opponents drive them off their 'realm' (*Games and Pastimes of Various Social Classes*, 1831, 64). The game has been described even more precisely by E. Piasecki in his work *Sports and Games Involving Movement for Children and the Youth*: 'Game of boys and young rustics of various regions of Poland':

The boys divide themselves into two teams separated by 40-50m of an even field (possibly some not too busy street). Each of the boys has a 'club' or 'pusher', i.e. a heavy stick. A player of the randomly selected beginning team serves by rolling the wooden disc (most often a ring 30cm in diameter hauled out of a thick beech board) so that it gets as far as possible in the direction of the opposing team. When one of the latter manages to bounce the disc with his club so that it returns again to the serving team, only the one 'bounce' counts.
When the disc is struck squarely and with such force that it jumps up and then comes down exactly in the same place, the situation is called 'a mountain'; a mountain is a counterpart of 3 bounces. After the first strike there is another one (of the team that has been serving) etc., until the disc reaches the finishing line or until it is recaptured. In such cases it is taken over and rolled by the adversaries of the team that had committed a fault.

Cf. >PÄRK.
Ł. Gołębiowski, *Games and Pastimes of Various Social Classes*, 1831; E. Piasecki, *Games and Pastimes of Children*, 1916.

KRAGENRINGEN, Swiss folk wrestling the object of which is to floor an adversary by grasping them by the collar [from Ger. *Kragen* – collar *Ringen* – wrestling, hand-to-hand fighting]. The adversaries fight in a standing position; victory can be achieved by a sudden twist and pulling one's opponent by the collar so that he loses his balance and falls to the ground; see also >CLOTHES HOLD (BELT HOLD) WRESTLING.

KRAGTAG, also *krawataj* in a dial. var., Swed. folk wrestling the object of which is grasping the opponent's clothing while standing face-to-face [Swed. *krag* – collar *tag* – grasp, grip]; holds are regulated: the contestants should grab each other crosswise, i.e. with one hand by the collar at the nape, and the other by the lower lapel; the grasp may not disregard certain local regulations; if it is too high, it is considered unfair and called 'thievish' – *tjyvtag* (a term that appeared in the Regna region and in the E part of Gottland Island. The objective of the fight is to retain one's balance despite being tagged by one's opponent and to knock this rival down. In some var. helping oneself with one's legs is allowed. One

of the major tricks is to press one's breast to the opponent's breast and then pull one's body back suddenly so that the rival follows the attacker. At this moment an instantaneous twist of the body may result in throwing one's competitor against the floor and locking his body with one's own. This trick is called *lappkast* – a Lapponian grasp; considered to be very dangerous, in some var. of kragtag it is treated as a transgression of the rules. If, however, an attacked fighter manages to neutralize or fight off such a strike, he may utilize the opponent's force to

Juan Manuel Azpiroz 'Txikito de Aia' during a korikolaris race at Plaza de Toros de Azpeitia, 1942.

his own advantage so that the attacker falls down first, finds himself blocked in a turnabout by the body of the attacked and is thus forced to lose the game. This grip is also referred to as *lapptaj, finntaj, finntakast* (Fin. for 'throw' or 'grip') or *rysskast* – Rus. throw. An interesting phenomenon from the cultural point of view was that a dangerous and often barred throw is associated with and named after a particular foreign nationality, i.e. Rus. or Fin. Not surprisingly, thus, in a Du. var. of this kind of fighting a similar grip is known either as Rus. – *ryssänkasti* or as Rum. wrestling – *mustalaspaini*. In Iceland the same grip is called *Trollkvinnoknepet* – troll's hag trick. Some of the grips in kragtag were incorporated from >MUSTLASEMAADLUS, called also Rum. wrestling, a var. of hand-to-hand fighting propagated by the Swed. settlers in Estonia. This kind of fighting enjoys widespread popularity almost throughout the whole of Sweden; the least hist. evidence of its presence is found in the region of Mälarlanddskapen. In other parts of Sweden similar types of wrestling are practiced as >ARMKAST, >ARMTAG, >KRAVATAG, >KRAVETAG, >SLÄNGTAJ, >TA RÖCK.
M. Hellspong, 'Kragtag, Brottning som folklig lek', RIG, 1991, 4; M. Hellspong, 'Kragtag', *Den folkliga idrotten*, 2000, 21-24.

K

WORLD SPORTS ENCYCLOPEDIA

KRAV MAGA, the art of combat and self-defense mastered in the Israeli army in the early 1950s. The objective was to teach self-defense effectively to a max. number of people in the shortest period of time possible. Officer I. Lichenfield, a sports instructor at the Wingate Institute, introduced an appropriate set of exercises and fighting methods into the basic training of Israeli Defense Forces. He has also become the first chairman of the Krav Maga Association, a position that he still holds. Over time krav maga has also been adopted by the Israeli police, the interior armed forces and in Mosad.

The basic difference between krav maga and other self-defense systems is a lack of rules and regulations. There are also no fixed sets of movements or strikes like in Asian combat sports. The emphasis is placed on fast response, impromptu composition of movements. Krav maga is a total method making use of any element that may destroy the attacker. Krav maga practitioners learn to identify the human body's weakest points and how to attack those points

pline has been introduced in the USA by R. Mizrachi. The rising popularity of krav maga will most probably lead to the eventual establishment of a sports version of this art of defense.

KRAVETAG, Dan. var. of Scan. wrestling involving wrestlers gripping each other by the collar; its Swed. counterpart is >KRAGTAG (also kravatag); in other parts of Sweden similar var. of wrestling are known as >ARMKAST, >ARMTAG, >SLÄNGTAJ, >TA RÖCK.

KRĄŻKA, a feminine form of 'krążek' (Pol. 'disc'), see >KOCZAŁKA.

KREDSTROLD, Dan. for 'troll's ring', [Dan. *kreds* – a circle, ring *trold* – a troll]; a fitness game included in the program of children's physical education classes. A ring in which the troll is positioned is marked in the middle of the playing field. The object of the game is for the other players to run through the ring without being caught by the troll. The one who is caught

days while the rest of the youth entertain themselves. No wonder that a great emphasis is put on appropriate preparation before the event starts, including the earliest possible rising and a great deal of accompanying excitement: after all, the whole day is to be devoted to fun and feasting, with the prospect of further festivities to come. Everybody is allowed to milk the cows entrusted to them for the time being and use as much of their milk as the contestants fancy. Everyone contributes to the feast, too. The feast used to be held on a fixed date, the 1st of May, in ancient, pre-Christian times so it seems even more jolly when it happens to take place on this date now. Boys and girls take their Sunday's best with them and dress themselves up after they complete the race. If two or more contestants reach the finishing line together the problem arises whom to call the king or queen. In order to dispel any doubts, the vying herdsmen have to compete at another distance, marked this time with bolts at the starting line, and with the 'royal couple' from the previous year waiting at the finishing line with wreaths and flowers for the winners along with the judges and the observers. The contestants stand at opposite sides of the road so that they do not commit any fault and do not disturb one another. When the final winners are acclaimed the gifts are distributed among them: flowers and feathers for the king, ribbons and jewelry for the queen. The monarch offers some of his flowers to the queen but they are then intercepted by the public. Out of these flowers wreathes for the queen and king as well as for the spectators are made. Some of the flowers are arranged at the village monument of a Saint, or the village cult post. This is performed by the girls, whereas the king, with the queen at his side, appoints his officials and courtiers: the major-domo, the cook, those who will have to collect wood, bring water, and those who will be employed in preparing the feast. Everyone brings eagerly whatever they can offer out of their stock. Some accompany the king and the queen, observe the progress of preparations, poke fun at the lazy or slower workers, and enjoy chatting, joking or singing with the royal couple. In this way morning passes into noon and as mid-day approaches the cook and his apprentices bring in food and drinking water or milk, as no other drinks are allowed then, arranged on elegant tablecloths. When the steaming-hot bowls are distributed in line, the sound of a kind of trumpet or pipe (Bazoka) beckons all the herdsmen to approach their seats. The king and queen take the best seats with their officials round them as they wish. Others soon fill the remaining places, while the worst seats are left to the latecomers who will, at least not experience hunger at such a lavish feast, although they will be the objects of jokes. Everyone has a separate spoon at their disposal but they use often one bowl from time to time treating bread as plates and sharing knives. Groats with milk, potatoes, noodles, and geese or other meat is what they indulge in. When everyone has finally eaten his fill, the cook and his assistants cart away the leftovers and sweep the place clean.

At the approach of evening, everyone dresses in their Sunday attire; new wreathes and fresh bouquets are prepared in place of those used earlier and by now withered. An orchestra employing the talents of any musicians on hand is quickly assembled and villagers playing pipes, trumpets and other instruments join in. From the cattle, which have remained in the meadow grazing, an exceptionally shapely and fine-looking ox is selected and then wrapped up in white cloth so that no part of its body can be seen except for the horns which are, anyway, decorated with flowers. If the owner of the animal fails to recognize his ox, he will have to buy it back. Later on the crowd sets off for a triumphant procession.

The major-domo opens the procession with a pistol in one hand and a whip in the other, followed by 12 herdsmen equipped also with whips; after them comes the first singing girl accompanied with another 12 supporting voices, every girl holding baskets full of petals. The ox is led alongside the public; the queen has 2 assistant girls at her disposal. The village's 2 eldest herdsmen, along with 12 more herdsmen brandishing whips, accompany the king. The major-domo may fire his rifle once the procession gets out of the village. The joy and fun and excitement reaches its peak when the villagers come to greet their village administrator, as the girls come forward with gifts for him and the supposed owner of the ox identifies himself. Then bets are placed, and finally the ox is assisted to its owner who is so generous with his money that they can all go together to the nearest inn and continue the festivities for 3 consecutive days. The villagers dance, drink, and entertain themselves whereas the unlucky herdsman duty-bound to guard the cattle all alone but for a pack of faithful dogs, may join the others no sooner than after sunrise.

[Games and Pastimes of Various Social Classes, 1831, 120-122]

KRULBOL, a Flem. folk game played by 2 teams; the object of the game is to roll bowls resembling a quern-stone or round Swiss cheese in such a way that they get as close as possible to the peg. Victory is ascribed to the team that positions more bowls closer to the peg, which is 25-30cm high, and 5-8cm thick. Various strategies may be employed to achieve this: 1) to roll the bowls as close as possi-

Richard Douieb, President of the European Krav Maga Federation, demonstrating krav maga techniques in Poznań, Poland.

in case of an assault. The technique of kicking and hitting in the vulnerable body zones is strongly emphasized and mastered. In more advanced phases of fighting, staffs, rifles and bayonets are used. Blows inflicted with bare hands are taught to the apprentices according to the Eur. boxing school. At present no sport stemming from krav maga is being practiced. There exists, however, a system of stages marked by the color of a belt: white for the beginners, yellow, orange, blue, and brown for the intermediate stages of initiation, and black as the highest possible stage. The Krav Maga Association in Israel issues appropriate certificates.

Sports tracksuits are most often used for exercising, white vests and soft footwear are, however, preferred. When it comes to more advanced training, protective clothing such as ankle pads, protective cups, and face masks, are introduced. Boxing gloves, too, are used for parts of the training.

Krav maga is steadily spreading around the world, mainly across the USA. The biggest centers outside Israel are in New York and California (Los Angeles, Reseda, La Jolla and Ashwood). The disci-

by the troll becomes a troll himself. Cf. games in which the object is to run between 2 zones, i.e. >DØDNING, >GÅ OVER ELVEN, >KÆDETIK, >KLIM-KLEM, >TAMANJ, >TULLEHUT, >TYRHOLDE. J. Møller, 'Kredstrold', GID, 1997, 2, 53.

KREISEL, Ger. var. of >TOPS.

KRELE, see >GRELE.

KRÓL PASTERZY, Pol. for 'shepherd king', a kind of contest involving cattle driving by herdsmen in former Poland, in the Kujawy region. If herds of 2 contestants reached the finish line simultaneously, a running field was prepared by marking the starting and finishing lines with wooden bolts for the additional, deciding stretch of the race. Łukasz Gołębiowski described the race as follows:

In the Kujawy region there is a tradition of driving cattle to an agreed point on the first day of Whitsuntide. The herdsman who arrives at the finishing point first is bestowed with the title of king. If the winner is a maiden, she becomes queen. The contestant who reaches the finishing line last is awarded the dubious honor of taking care of all the cattle him- or herself for 3

ble to the peg; in this tactic, pushing back the opponent's bowls is of secondary importance; 2) to push the opponent's bowls back as far as possible. Each bowl closest to the peg scores points. The general object of the game, despite obvious differences (no icy surface, rolling bowls instead of curling stones) resembles the rules of the Scot. >CURLING. In both curling and krulbol the playing field is used first forward, and then, when the first round is over, the direction changes to backward without displacing the bowls (stones). The word *krul* itself indicates similarities between the sports because in Flem. it means exactly the same as *curl* in Eng. The interesting thing is, however, that in curling, contrary to what the name suggests, there is no curling movement of the stones involved, which may suggest that the idea of placing the stones in the center of the field was borrowed from krulbol. It is a possible result of Eng.-Du. co-influences (e.g. in the times when the ruling Eng. dynasty of Orange was of Du. descent). In such a form the game reached Scotland. The hypothesis is, however, not supported by anything but the similarity of the game's name and its meaning.

Playing lane and equipment. An oval or rectangular playing lane of no specified size. Its longitudinal axis amounts to about 7-8.5m, width to about 2.2-4.2m. A kind of peg or stake is mounted vertically on the ground at a 1-1.5m distance from each side of the lane. The bowls are about 20cm in diameter and weigh 2-3.5kg; they are made of a synthetic material known as wartex. Formerly the wooden bowls, still used in another var. of the game, used to be slightly smaller, up to 1.2kg. The bowls have rounded edges resembling car tires; it enables curling them by means of appropriate inclination towards one side at the moment they achieve momentum. This technique makes it possible for the contestant to approach the peg or the opponent's rings from one side or another and strike the opponent's bowls back from the peg. The task is, nevertheless very difficult, and requires the application of much strength because the bowls tend to fall over once they stop moving, making it extremely hard to push them with other bowls in motion. Every player has 2 bowls at their disposal.

History. The oldest existing trace of krulbol in Flem. culture is a small picture representing this game, which decorates the framework of a harp made c.1650. The authorship of the picture is ascribed to J. Couchet (c.1611-55). The oldest written records come from the second half of the 17th cent. These are the only descriptions that allow for the recognition of this sport. Krulbol became the name of the game in the 19th cent. Its popularity peaked in the second half of the 19th cent and the first decades of the 20th cent. It was then that Flem. and Du. emigrants had a hand in propagating the game in the USA and Canada. Soon the tradition of holding championships in emigrant circles arose. The event takes place on the 21st of July on annual basis. In Belgium krulbol is supervised by the Vlaamse Krulbolbond association and the Belgische Krulbolbond federation.

E. de Vroede, *Het Grote Volkssporten Boek*, 1996; idem, 'Ball and Bowl Games in the Low Countries: Past and Present', *in Homo Ludens – Der Spielende Mensch*, 1996, vol. VI.

KRUMME ET BEN, in full: *at krumme et ben,* Dan. for 'bending a leg' or 'in order to bend a leg'. An old form of Dan. wrestling. One of the contestants lays himself on the table, takes hold of the table top, and then lifts one leg straight upwards. The other player aims at bending his enemy's leg at the knee. To achieve this he puts his arm in his opponent's knee bend and the other hand under the opponent's shin. If he succeeds in bending the other man's leg, he wins the test. Then the players switch roles. Depending on detailed rules agreed on by the parties the winner is the player who succeeded in bending his opponent's leg or avoided bending his own knee more times.

J. Møller, 'At krumme et ben', GID, 1997, 4, 39.

KRYDSBOLD, Dan. for 'cross ball', called also *jagtbold* – lit. 'hunting ball'; the number of players has to be divisible by 4; the players form 2 concentric circles with an equal number of players. The players comprising the inner circle turn their backs to the center, and the players in the outside circle face them; the distance between the circles has to be at least 1m. The lineup of both circles alternates players from each team; every other player belongs to the same team. They stand in such a way that members of opposite teams face each other, every player standing between 2 opponents, whereas his allies are the 2 players standing on either side of the opponent directly across from him. At least 2 balls are used; balls of different colors are best suited for the game. In each team, a player from the outer circle – chosen by drawing lots – starts the game; he has to pass the ball to one of his partners in the inner circle. The game can be played in different ways, e.g. it can be agreed that both balls should zigzag in the same direction, a round lasting as long as it takes for the balls to return to the player who started the game or the balls may be passed in opposite directions. In each case, the team whose ball returns to the initial position first wins. The number of rounds can also be agreed on. As a penalty, the player who has dropped the ball has to count to an agreed number before he is allowed to continue the game, which slows the play down and hampers the chances of winning. When 4 or 8 balls are used, the teams receive an equal number of them and begin the play from an appropriate number of places. Similarly to the previous variant, it can also be agreed on whether the balls should move in the same or in opposite directions. The most popular form of krydsbold, with a greater number of balls, is the 'perseverance' play, which lasts until all the balls have been fumbled, the team that has played longest winning.

J. Møller, 'Krydsbold', GID, 1997, 1.

KRYSA, (also Pol. *szczur* – 'rat'), a Pol. sporting game. Players stand in a circle, 5-7m in diameter. One player squats in the middle holding a 3-4m-long rope with a ball or sandbag attached to one end. He or she then starts spinning the rope around, gradually increasing the speed, while the players in the circle try to skip it. Whoever touches the rope is out. The game can be played by individuals or teams; the team with the fewest errors wins. In another var. the players in the circle try to jump onto the rope and stop it from spinning rather than skip it. A player who manages to spin the rope around the circle without being stopped qualifies for the next round.

I.N. Chkhannikov, 'Podcinanka', GIZ, 1953, 17-18.

KTO SYILNYEYE, Rus. for 'who's strongest?', a strength-testing game similar to tug-of-war. 2 players holding a rope stand on opposite blocks and try to pull the opponent off his podium. This is usu. repeated 3 times. The surface of a block is 80x80cm, slanting; the front side is 40cm high, the back – 25cm. The blocks are placed about 3m from each other.

I. N. Chkhannikov, 'Kto syilnyeye', GIZ, 1953, 67.

KUBB, pron. *kib*, an outdoor game played chiefly in Gotland [Swed. *kub* – cube], on a rectangular pitch 5x8m, with 21 blocks of various shapes all made of Gotland pine. The 4 thinnest (2x2x30cm) are placed in the corners of the pitch to outline it. The biggest (9x9x30cm) – called the 'king' (*konung*) – is placed in the center. Its upper part is usu. narrowed, making it look like a square-based bowling pin with the head also 9x9cm. There are 5 blocks 7x7x15cm (*kubbs*) on each of the 2 boundary lines (parallel with the corner blocks). The kubbs and the konung are painted with bright colors: red or yellow, often with a white stripe or white flecks like that of a toadstool. The corner blocks and the blocks used for throwing (sticks 30cm long, 44mm in diameter) are usu. the color of unseasoned wood. The object of the game is to knock down the kubbs by throwing the sticks. The team standing on one side of the pitch tries to knock down the kubbs at the opposing team's end. Teams throw alternately. The winner is the team who is first to knock down all the opponents' kubbs and the 'king' (which may only be knocked down at the very end – if it gets knocked down during the game, it is set back up and the team who did it loses all the points they have scored up to this moment). The number of members on a team varies from 2 to 20. Championship teams consist of 6 members of both sexes.

History. The game originated in Gotland. In the last couple of years it has gained considerable popularity in many countries other than Sweden, e.g. In the USA and Australia. The biggest championships are held in Rone (in Gotland) and are regarded as W.Ch. In 1997 76 teams took part in the W.Ch. The youngest contestant was 8 years old, the oldest 85. Until 1999 all W.Ch. were won by Sweden. In 2000 the US team won for the first time.

Katarzyna Tubylewicz, *Harce Wikingów*, *Gazeta Wyborcza* (*Wysokie Obcasy*), 10 Nov. 2000; *What is kubb?* http://www.vmkubb.com

KUBBA, an Arab game played with 2 specially prepared goat or calf instep bones, similar to >K'ABA (played with only one bone). The player throws the bones into a circle or square from about 3m away, first having said which side the bone will land on, e.g. longer or shorter, convex or concave, colored or uncolored.

Remy Cogghe, *A Game of Bowls in the Village Square*, 1899, oil on canvas.

KUCIE, an obs. Pol. game of country boys, played with a rag ball in the Rzeszów region until around 1939. E. Piasecki, a pioneer of Pol. physical culture, writes:

Two small stones are dug into the ground of an oblong pitch, 10-12 steps from each other, in order to mark the standing points. Children are divided into two groups facing each other. A draw determines which team has the first throw. The other team has the right to choose their side of the pitch. One contestant from each team stands facing his opponent, with his right foot on the stone. The others try to catch the ball and pass it to him. The player whose team goes first tries to hit his opponent with the ball. Teams throw alternately. When a player is hit, he makes room for another from his team. The team who hits the most players, wins. The thrower is allowed to fake a throw. The opponent may not take his right foot off the stone, but is free to move with the rest of his body.

[*Zabawy i gry ruchowe dzieci i młodzieży*, 1916]

KUKINI RACES, a type of endurance race held on the Hawaiian Islands among professional runners called *kukini*. The runners practice regularly. The winner receives a prize. The kukini are popular and admired, especially by young boys who try to imitate their feats by organizing mock, mini-races. Kukini races, together with other forms of folk competition, games and bets, are based on a very special form of philosophy of competition known as *ho o papa*.

KUKSUN-DO, one of medieval Kor. martial arts, along with >PUNGWAL-DO and >PUNGRYO-DO a part of *hwarang-do*, a system of knightly education.

KULANIE KULOTKA, Pol. for 'ring rolling', [Pol. *kulać* – to roll + *kulotko* – a dialectal name of a round rolling device], a Pol. trad. game practiced in the village of Bukówiec Górny in the region of Wielkopolska. The object of the game, the *kulotko*, was a wooden ring 10cm in diameter and 2-4cm thick. It was usu. obtained by cutting a ring from a round wooden stump, while more lasting ones were cut out of a wooden plank. The most advanced types of kulotko were made by local carpenters on turning lathes. The essence of the game was to roll the ring between 2 teams with the use of a rectangular wooden stick 12-15cm wide, with a handle for both hands on one end and a slant on the other end. The slant made it possible to hit the ring close to the ground, using the entire width of the stick. The length of the stick was unspecified and varied to accomodate the height of each player. In the simplest forms of the game, practiced by younger children, sticks were not used. Older kids used them, as they made it possible to hit the ring harder, let it roll farther and made it more difficult to be intercepted by the oppo-

The peg and rings for playing krulbol.

K
WORLD SPORTS
ENCYCLOPEDIA

nents. That var. was called *kulanie kulotka na zagony* (rolling the ring to the field), for often the stronger team pressed so hard that the ring would leave the playing area and fall into the adjacent fields. A local ethnographer, A. Kowol-Marcinek offers the following description:

The game would start by one team rolling the ring towards the other. Each roll was to be efficient, i.e. properly directed and strong enough to let the ring go as far as possible. The task of the opponents was to either try to stop the rolling ring or to hit it back with a stick. If they failed to do so, they had to move back to the place where the ring stopped. If they succeeded in stopping the ring, both teams maintained their positions, while hitting the ring back allowed them to gain area. Such a hit they would call a winner. The other team would then have to move back and assume positions to avoid being surprised by the next rolling of the ring.

No players lived to see the ethnographic description of the game, which made Kowol-Marcinek express his frustration at not knowing the way the outcome of the game was determined: 'How they finally decided which team was the winner, I have no way of knowing'. However, taking into account similar ball games played in W Europe, it is highly probable that the team which managed to gain more area won the game. It must have been possible to use the entire playing area, beginning with the initial positioning of players on both sides of the middle line. For every area gain the team would score a point and after a number of points scored, teams would return to the original position (see >JEU DE LONGUE PAUME; >KAATSEN; >KEATSEN). According to Kowol-Marcinek:

For ring rolling, particularly the field variety, kids would gather very anxiously – it was a serious matter. Every player's or team's ambition was to defend their position and not let the opponents gain area. Sometimes the game would remain in one place for a long time, which indicated that nobody could gain advantage. The most fierce competition took place when older kids joined in. The main village road would then become totally congested by the ring rollers. In the general noise and turmoil one could only distinguish cries of encouragement, accompanied by dull sounds of the ring hit so hard that it would occasionally break into pieces. If the ring survived, the sticks would sometimes break. Everything, however, could be remedied and the ruthless

A kulig in the Polish mountains.

Kulig.

game went on. Often one could see one team forcing the other to draw back by at least half a kilometer. Such was the distance over which they often had to play: teams losing and gaining back the area, while victory passed from hand to hand.

Antoni Kowol-Marcinek, 'Kulanie kulotka', *Dawne gry i zabawy dziecięce w Bukówcu Górnym*, Wojewódzki Dom Kultury, Leszno 1999, p. 28-29.

KULI, a Bulg. folk game resembling >PALANT.

KULIG, also *kulik* in trad. Pol. spelling, a winter horse sleigh ride similar but not identical to >SZLICHTA-DA, a var. of >SANNA, mainly practiced by the nobility. The name kulig derives possibly from the Ger. adjective *kugelig* – 'rolling'. Ł. Gołębiowski provides another etymology: 'A pole with a ball on top was sent from household to household in call for a kulik (Pol. *kula* – ball). The ball gave the name to the game' (*Gry i zabawy różnych stanów*, 1831). The tradition of kulig comes from the Courland-Lithuanian border, the N regions notorious for much heavier winters than in C Poland. During the few hundred years of the Pol.-Lith. Union the tradition of kulig became widespread all over the country. Sleigh riders would visit local villages and manors. The rides were organized together with ceremonial parties, dances, singing and rifle shooting. A permanent element of kulig was a race of horse-drawn carts on forest roads or in open areas. Specially made kulig sleighs were lavishly ornamented with various carvings and lined out with soft pillows and pelts. The most complete kulig description was made by Ł. Gołębiowski:

The joyful pastime of kulig was close to the heart of the people of the north in wintertime. During heavy frosts, between Christmas and Lent, many have enjoyed winter games in the city and the countryside for a long time. Participants gathered from the entire province awaiting impatiently the snow and proper weather for sleigh riding. They set up the order of sleighs and planned the route, time, and extra activities on the way.

When the weather was good enough participants got dressed up properly and took to their sleighs. With musical accompaniment and flaming torches the kulig started at dawn and went from house to house. The participants greeted villagers or invited them to join the ride. The peasants often half-awake ran out to the front of their houses and gazed at this beautiful sight. The kulig went through an open gate and arrived in front of a farmer's house. The farmer welcomed the guests who joined in dances with his wife and other girls dressed up beautifully. Children who had run after the kulig watched the dancers with awe. The latter stopped ever and anon to drink a toast to the host, his family, his health and all the guests gathered. This way the participants continued until a sumptuous supper, after which they danced and sang songs until the break of dawn. After breakfast the kulig went on joined by the host farmer or his family, and it grew longer as it collected more and more participants from other households. In some wealthy houses the whole party would stop even up to a few days. And again the kulig celebrations were full of joyful laughter, talking, jokes, pranks and parlor

games. Sometimes a hunting or fishing trip was organized. Women joined in or helped out with meal preparation and took care of the guests. The kulig hosts boasted of their livestock, horses, and collections of weapons just to make the stay of the guests more pleasurable and memorable.

Occasionally, the kulig participants arrived at a birthday party. The host houses were full of stock and the riders were treated generously and their satisfaction was always shown openly. A great friendly atmosphere was equally shared by all. A spirit of utmost gratitude abounded as well. No one ever gave insult, no one felt disregarded. All past discords were quenched down; all the good things were given priority. Today, it is hard to imagine that kind of omnipresent kindness and wholeheartedness. The joy was shared by priest, knight, and commoner alike. Some hosts knew the kulig was coming, some were utterly surprised at the sight of the riders wearing colorful outfits and facemasks. If the party knew beforehand that the host lacked food or beverages, the supplies were provided on sleighs. Sometimes accomodations were difficult as a kulig host might not have enough rooms to put everybody. In such a case, people slept in a local inn, manor, presbytery or other premises, or spent the night dancing. While playing, participants made business contacts or marital relationships. A lad would sit next to a beautiful lass, care for her, wrap her in blankets and close rapport was established. Accidents happened, but if someone fell down he was immediately helped up. Friendship ruled among the riders and misunderstandings were immediately sunk in good wine.
On narrow forest paths short sleds were used that were drawn by 1, 2, 3, or 4 ponies in tandem. The sled was decorated with an emblem of eagle, pelican, bear, Negro, Turk, mermaid or virgin.

Whoever still remembers anything of that past fun would definitely recall the hospitality, good nature and warmth of those people living like one big family joined by fun. The kulig was a great opportunity to multiply good spirits using the goods of nature and to maintain the ancient tradition. With the first days of Lent the kuligs subsided; participants returned home fixing sleds and horseshoes and calmed down in prayer before the coming of Easter.

[*Games and Pastimes of Various Social Classes*, 1831, 122-130]

Sometimes winter conditions thwarted sleigh-riding plans: 'A shortage of snow or changing weather conditions were sometimes a hindrance to kulig.' A sleigh ride, under the pretext of cold served often as a convenient rationalization for the consumption of alcohol, as was observed in a poem by an anonymous author in the Pol. newspaper *Monitor*:

The aim of the kulig
Since the Popiel King
Has always been a good-time drink.

333

The cultural heritage of kulig was indeed very rich and kulig themes were often present in art and literature. An example of trad. Pol. kulig was described in the memoirs of L. Clermont, secretary to Marysieńka, the wife of Pol. King Jan III Sobieski in 1695. The same kulig was depicted by Ł. Gołębiowski:

A number of noble persons came on invitation to the Palace of the Daniłowicz family – the later site of the great Załuski Library. The ride commenced at 3 p.m. on a trumpet signal. First, rode twenty four mounted Tartars from the guard of Prince James. Then, ten big sleds with different music bands, each drawn by four horses in hand. The musicians included Jews with dulcimers, Ukrainians with pipes, Yannisaries with trumpets, and many others coming from different manors. Next rode sleighs covered with Persian carpets, or leopard or sable furs. Elder nobility rode in sleighs; young courtiers on horseback. The horses wore lavish ornaments of all sorts. The number of all those sleighs was one hundred and seven. The last in the ride was a sleigh in the shape of Pegasus in which eight lads were sitting and reciting poems. The Royal Guards closed the procession. The party went first to the Sapieżyński Court, then to the Royal Princess, Voivod Potocki, and to the town of Ujazdów. Wherever they came the host opened his wine cellars and his wife the pantries. The guests feasted as much as they could. The music was played, the party danced and after a while all moved on. The last stop of the ride was the Royal Palace in Wilanów, where the royal couple welcomed everyone wholeheartedly. The entire procession was lit by over 800 torches [...].

The best known literary works devoted to kulig are *Kulig* (1783), a comedy in 5 acts by J. Wybicki and a famous description of sleigh ride of Andrzej Kmicic and Oleńka Billewiczówna, characters of *The Deluge*, a novel by H. Sienkiewicz. A famous artistic painting of kulig is *Kulig litewski* (Lithuanian Kulig) by A. Wierusz-Kowalski (1884).
The tradition of kulig (lacking, however, its former splendor) survived until the first decades of the 20th cent. It faded away in 1945 after communist rule was introduced in Poland and Pol. nobles were deprived of their property. Suppression of the old tradition was connected with an intentional destruction of surviving relics of Pol. noble culture. Despite this unfavorable situation kulig was maintained on a few stud farms, where special sleigh rides were organized for state dignitaries and foreign visitors. After 1989 some traditions of kulig were partially revived, alas a mere shadow of their former splendor and ritual. At present the name *kulig* is used to denote a ride of a few sleds tied to a horse-drawn cart, or drawn by a horse or vehicle, e.g. tractor or car.

KULKI, Pol. equivalent of >MARBLES.

KUM-HWAN, an old. Kor. ball game, played in the Shilla kingdom (57 BC-935 AD). The game was begun by a religious ceremony and a procession carrying a gold-coated ball. The exact rules are unknown. Tchoi Tchi-Won, a Shilla poet, writes:

I move with the ball, I swirl right, then left. Everything appears before my eyes reflected in the ball as if in a mirror. This mysterious image gives me more joy than a good friend. Now I could believe the world is full of peace.

Koo-Chuk Jung, 'Erziehung und Sport in Korea', *Kreuzpunkt fremder Kulturen und Mächte*, 1960, 60.

KUMOTERKI, also *kumoterska gońba* (Pol. for 'Godfather's chase'), Pol. races of one-horse sleighs, typical for the Podhale region. The most popular events are held annually in Szaflary in the Podhale region during the Mountain Carnival, initiated in 1973 by J. Koszarek, the director of the local community center. In 2003 the Association of Tatra Highlanders initiated a cup system of Godfather's chases, with events in Zakopane, Bukowina Tatrzańska, Ludźmierz, Biały Dunajec and Kościelisko.

KUNG FU, see >GONGFU, >WUSHU.

KUNGSBOLL, a Swed. game resembling >PALANT [Swed. *kung.* – king, *boll* – ball]. Cf. Fin. >KUNIGAS PÄLLO.

KUNGSSTEN, Swed. for 'King's Stone', the biggest of 3 stones which could be found in the Öja parish in W Södermanland on the Hjälmaren lake. Kungssten also meant a test of strength, which a candidate for the leader of a local band of thieves, *Öjabussar*, had to pass to get the title of 'king' (*kung*). The test would take place on a characteristic rock shelf known as the Öja bricka. Candidates for gang members had to undergo the test of lifting the 2 lighter stones. The rock shelf and the stones disappeared around 1847-49; they were probably used for the reconstruc-

tion of a local church. See also: >LYFTESTEN; Dan. >STENLØFTNING; Basq. >ARRIJASOKETA. Cf. >GGET, >DRÄNGASTENAR, >DRÄNGALÖFTEN, >KAMPASTEN, >KÖLNÅKERN, >KUNGSSTENARNA, >LYFTESTEN, >STORA OCH LILLA DAGSVERKARN, >TYFTEHÖNAN.
M. Hellspong, 'Lifting Stones. The Existence of Lifting-Stones in Sweden', ST, 1993-94, XIX-XX; R. Dybeck, *Runa. En skrift för Nordens fornvänner*, 1865.

KUNGSSTENARNA, Swed. for 'King's Stones', a local var. of stone-lifting. The stones lay in Brömsboro, on the one-time Swed.-Dan. borderland, between Södra and Blekinge in SW Sweden. They may have been used by farm-hands for strength-testing competitions, perhaps also by landowners hiring wage-earners. The stones were described by N. Wessman, a judge travelling the area in 1756. In the 19th cent. the competitions were relinquished. In 1876 A. Södermark, saw the stones thrown into the local river Brömsbäcken. See also: >LYFTESTEN; Dan. >STENLØFTNING; Basq. >ARRIJASOKETA. Cf. >GGET, >DRÄNGASTENAR, >DRÄNGALÖFTEN, >KAMPASTEN, >KÖLNÅKERN, >KUNGSSTEN, >LYFTESTEN, >STORA OCH LILLA DAGSVERKARN, >TYFTEHÖNAN.

M. Hellspong, *Lifting Stones. The Existence of Lifting-Stones in Sweden*, ST, 1993/94, XIX/XX

KUNINGAS PALLO, Fin. for 'royal ball', a game resembling the Eng. *longball* and the Pol. >PALANT, influenced by the Swed. >KUNGSBOLL; played in various forms in the past, it lost popularity after the introduction of >PESÄPALLO (created in 1922, partially based on kuningas pallo) to schools and the army.
Rules. The pitch is 22-33m long and 20-30m wide, the ball approx. the size of a man's fist, the bat a little smaller than in >BASEBALL. There can be 8, 9, 17, or 22 players on a team, each of them may bat 3 times. The pitcher may bat 4 times, once he has finished pitching. The best batter is awarded the title of 'king' (*kuningas*) and may bat 6 times in the next round. The balls are lobbed. The batter may bat, but does not have to. In either case he may try to run to score a point on the finish line, which is about 40-50m away, or wait in the 'hiding place' for a better chance to bat. A better batting gives him more time to reach the finish line and score a point. A running batter is in no way protected and may therefore be eliminated from the game, if hit by the ball or touched by a member of the opposing team. In that case the ball goes to the opposing team and the batter's team plays in the field. The batter can avoid this by instantly catching the ball that hit him and throwing it at any member of the opposing team – or by touching a

member of the opposing team with his hand (if previously touched). If he succeeds, his team not only keeps the ball but also has the right to score points by running to the finish line.
Source: P. Kärkkäinen, Jyväskylä University, Finland.

KUPJAKEPIPROOV, an Est. Folk game. A stick of about 1-1.5m is rested against the wall. The contestant grasps the stick with both hands (one at each end) and tries to pass under it without altering its position.
M. Värv et al., 'Traditional Sports and Games in Estonia', TNSJ, 1996, 31.

KURASZ, also in international spelling *kourache*, an Uzb. form of folk wrestling, related to Tartar > KÜREŞ and Turk >KUSAK GÜREŞI. The wrestlers wear colorful gaberdines girded with sashes similar to the Turk. *kusak*, which may be seized by the opponent during the fight. When Uzbekistan was a Soviet republic kurasz was used to popularize sports in this region. Regional and republican competitions were held. In modernized kurasz contestants were divided into 6 weight categories. The best kurasz contestant is believed to have been A. Atabayev, the 1946 all-weight champion.

WORLD SPORTS ENCYCLOPEDIA

K

Kumoterki races in the Polish Tatra Mountains resort – Zakopane.

Wrestling competitions are held on holidays in so-called chaikhans (a kind of eastern restaurant), where the audience sit cross-legged on carpets and drink chai (tea) from special cups, piaua. The wrestlers fight in the middle and the eldest spectator is the judge. This is an old custom, respected for centuries. Enormous chaikhans seat hundreds of people. In the capital of the Uzbek Republic, Tashkent, open wrestling events are held regularly in the largest chaikhans of the city. Sometimes they last as long as 12 weeks, 15 pairs or wrestlers fighting every day. During 2 weeks in July 1947 the matches were attended by 15,000 spectators. The public's interest in the event is availed by sports organizations, which set up extra boxing fights, gymnastic shows and Greco-Roman wrestling in the chaikhans.
[Sport w ZSRR (Sport in the USSR)]

Cf.: >CULECHE, >GIULES, >GORESZ, >KOURECHE, >KURESH, >KÜREŞ.

KÜREŞ, a trad. type of wrestling practiced by the Crimean Tartars, closely linked to the Turk. >KUSAK GÜREŞI. The matches take place usu. on 6 May, on the first day of summer – the colorfully celebrated Hidirelles feast. As in similar competitions of this type, the wrestlers do not take off their clothing, except for shoes and overcoat (or jacket, as is usu. the case in modern times). When the names of the competitors are called they shake hands, stand opposite each other and grasp each other's trouser belts (in the past colorful sashes, *kusak*, were used, similar to those in kusak güreşi). They try to throw the opponent to the ground so that he touches a

K
WORLD SPORTS ENCYCLOPEDIA

marked area on the ground (şalka) with his back. When this happens a second time the match is over. Grasping the legs is strictly forbidden. If neither of the wrestlers succeeds in throwing the opponent to the ground, they may win by points awarded for being active in the fight. The spectacle is accompanied by drum and fife music (similar to the Turk. *davul-zurna*) of strongly punctuated rhythm in keeping with the tempo of the fight (>TURKISH WRESTLING). Küreş is a part of a family of Middle East wrestling sports under etym. and phon. similar names: >CULECHE, >GIULESZ, >GORESZ, >KOURECHE, >KURESH, >KURASZ. See also >TURKISH WRESTLING. This kind of wrestling also influenced some Eur. border countries, e.g. Rumania.
H. Murat Şahin, *Türk Spor Kulturunde Aba Güreşi*, 1999.

KURESH, a Kir. type of hand-to-hand fighting. Cf. other sports of the same oriental origin: Tartar >KÜREŞ, Rum. and Kaz. *kures*, Kir. >GIULES, >GORESH. See also > TURKISH WRESTLING.

KURNIMANG, a folk form of skittles which used to be practiced in Estonia, esp. by children herding cattle. The object of the game was to knock down 6 vertical pickets with a stick.
M. Värv et al., 'Traditional Sports and Games in Estonia', TNSJ, 1996, 35.

KURUVATIPPAYATTU, an old Hindi fighting technique involving long sticks, one of the 5 basic techniques of the Hindi martial art. >ADI MURAI.

KURVBOLD, a Dan. ball game resembling the Ger. >KORBBALL and the Du. >KORFBALL but differing from them by the sizes of pitch and equipment and a greater number of zones which may not be entered by particular players. The ball, about the size of a basketball, must be thrown into one of 2 baskets on either sides of the pitch. The baskets, 50cm in diameter, are installed on 3m high poles without backboards. The pitch is a rectangle of 36x18m, divided into 9 zones. There are 9 players on a team – one of each team in every zone. Players may not go beyond their zones. When schoolchildren play the pitch and ball are smaller. In unofficial matches there may also be fewer players on a team (though no fewer than 5); in this case some of the zones are left unoccupied. The players bounce and throw the ball but may not hit it with their fists. A player holding the ball may take no more than 2 steps. A player sending the ball into the basket can do it standing still and may not be attacked. In the case of a foul the ball goes to the opposing team (a turnover of possession is the basic penalty). When 3 fouls are made the referee orders a free throw. One match lasts 2x20min.
History. In June 1897 F. Knudsen, a subsequent popularizer of sport and exercise, took part in a course of ball games in Nääs, near Göteborg, along with Finns, Norwegians and 3 Americans. Later Knudsen wrote 'We played every day from 9-11a.m., from 1-4p.m. and from 8-10p.m. We practiced especially langbold, cricket, football, slyng-

Küreş.

bold and a new kind of Amer. basketball, which is perfectly suited for girls'. Thus the Danish took up the idea of Amer. >BASKETBALL, possibly not knowing the details and adapting it freely to their own tastes. The Brit. >NETBALL came into being in a similar way. Kurvbold may have been more influenced by other Eur. games of basketball type (such as korbball and korfball, created in the late 19th cent.). According to *Gymnastikhåndbogen*, a handbook of physical exercise:

Basketball is a completely new game which originated in America, where it is played no less willingly by women. Like our >LANGBOLD, it is played in different ways, but lately some specified rules have been introduced, like in football or cricket, which are gradually adopted in many schools and educational institutions throughout America. Girls and boys can play together, the game can be played where neither cricket nor football can be played for lack of space. It does not require much training and can be played indoors as well as outdoors.

[ed. II, 1901]

Some rules adopted by kurvbold from early basketball (such as the number of players – 9) have been kept, although they have become obsolete in basketball itself. After 1901 kurvbold gained great popularity among women as a surrogate for football, the introduction of which by J. Skrumsager of Totftlundgård at the turn of the century ended in failure. In 1905 during a conference in Sønderborg the S Jutland Sports Association (Sønderjusk Idråtsforenings Årsmode) included kurvball in their program. In 1907 the game brought on a debate on the decency or indecency of girls practicing sports. In the '20s kurvbold was at the height of its popularity. By 1939, however, the S Jutland Sports Association included as few as 26 kurvbold players, compared to 897 in 1934. The late '30s and esp. the post-war period brought about serious competition from international ball games, which, offering chances of participating in international events, gradually diminished the popularity of kurvbold.
J. Møller, 'Kurvbold', GID, 1997, 1, 41.

KUSAJISI, a type of old Jap. archery, practiced near the end of the Heian (12th cent.) and in the Hōjō period. Contestants would be on foot rather than on horseback, as was the case in the popular >INUOMONO, >JYBUSAME or >KADAGAKE. See other types of Jap. archery on foot: >BUSHA, >JUMIHAJIME, >MARUMONO, and >MOMOTE. Cf. other forms of Jap. archery: >UMA YUMI, > JYARAI, >IBAHAJIME, >NORIYUMI and >TANGONO KISHA.

KUŞAK GÜREŞI, a type of Turk. wrestling of the Pehlivan tradition (>VARZESH-E PEHLIVAN). The basic technique is lifting the opponent by his sash and throwing him to the ground [Turk. *kusak* – sash + *güreşi* – grabbing, fighting]. The tradition of the sash dates back to the Middle Ages or perhaps even to the times when the Turks were nomads roaming the steppes of Asia. The sashes, decorated with colorful woven patterns, are in themselves true works of art – the most famous ones are manufactured in the Antep region. They appear throughout Antalya under different names, depending on the pattern, origin and fabric. The contestants fight on 3 levels: standing up (15min.), leaning over (20min.) and low to the floor (25min.). If during this time neither of the players throws the opponent to the ground (*şalk*) or wins through counting, the match is prolonged 10min. The winner of all 3 levels is awarded the title of 'pehlivan', the chief wrestler (*pehlivan havasi*). A form of kusak güreşi is also practiced in Uzbekistan and countries with Uzbek minorities (esp. in the former USSR), usu. during holidays or weddings. Children also practice the sport: boys gather round and sit in a circle; the tallest is appointed the leader (*anabaşi*). According to H. Murat Şahin, a Turk. wrestling historian, the game looks like this: the leader asks the children, 'Who is the pehlivan?' and one of the others replies, 'I am the pehlivan'. The leader then takes the boy's hand and asks, 'Who will fight this boy?' and one of the children replies, 'I will'. The leader takes his hand too and announces the beginning of the fight, pronouncing the boys' names. The children, girding themselves with sashes, take the ends with their hands. The boy who lifts the other up and throws him to the ground, wins. Tripping is allowed, but if a boy wins by tripping the leader walks him around the circle of spectators and asks, 'Winner or loser?' If even one says, 'Loser', the boy is knocked down. If all the children

agree that a given contestant won, the leader then asks them, 'Is everything all right?' If they answer, 'Yes', the leader, holding the winner's hand, inquires 3 times, 'Is there a rival for this contestant?' If none can be found, the winner gets presents and the title of *pehlivan*, but if there is a volunteer, the series of matches goes on until no-one wants to challenge the ultimate winner.
H. Murat Şahin, 'Kuşak güreşi', *Türk Spor Kulturunde Aba Güreşi* (1999, 35-6).

KUSHIYA, also spelled *koušija;* also called *warene* or *domle*. A type of folk bare-back horse racing, organized annually in Bulgaria 33 days before Easter, on the eve of St. Theodore's Day (*Todorov Den*), thus also referred to as *todorica* or *tudorica*. The contestants are young men, esp. those about to get married, who wish to prove their masculinity. The horses' manes are artistically braided and the route is decorated with garlands; the races are accompanied by song and dance. The riders have to go around the town or village, starting from its center and covering a distance of 300-1,000m. The prizes are objects voluntarily offered by the spectators, usu. clothing, pottery or tapestries.
W. Tsonkov, 'The Bulgarian People and the Popular Forms of Physical Education', A. Solakov, ed., *Physical Culture and Sport in Bulgaria Through the Centuries*, 1983, 30.

KUSHTI CHOUKHEH, an alternative spelling of the local form of Iranian wrestling >KOSHTI CHOUKHEH.

KUTTACUVAT, a Hindi technique of self-defense emphasizing the offensive, one of the 5 basic techniques of the Hindi martial art >ADI MURAI. Alternated with the defensive technique *ottacuvat*.

KWADRANT, a Pol. sport partially based on Amer. >BASEBALL. Its rules were elaborated in 1930 by T. Chrapowicki, H. Olszewska, S. Połomski, W. Sikorski and Z. Wyrobek. It was popularized as a school sport also in the first years after WWII. It resembled baseball in that there were 9 players per team and the pitch was 40x40m. The direction of the game was determined by the diagonal at the beginning of which the batting took place. If a player batted the ball successfully he would run around the square, thus scoring a point. The chief differences between kwadrant and baseball were that the player batted the ball from his own hand (not from the throw of the opposing team's pitcher) and that it was played for time (2x15 min.) and not for rounds.
Z. Wyrobek, *Kwadrant*, 1930; T. Gradowska, *Palant i kwadrant*, 1951.

KWÍKWELTÓÓL (in the spelling of the Native Amer. Ind. tribe Stolóó: *kwíkweltó:l*), a type of wrestling practiced by the Stolóó tribe, which inhabits areas on the W coast of N.America, on the US-Canada borderland, on Vancouver Island, in the Fraser Valley and on the borders of the State of Washington. A competitor fights standing up and tries to throw his rival to the ground. At all times must he keep his right hand on his opponent's left shoulder and his left hand on his opponent's right arm. If for any reason this grip is broken the game is interrupted and resumed after the rivals have returned to this position. The technique of knocking the opponent down includes lifting him off the ground and throwing him over one's hip. Tripping is strictly forbidden.

KYLISIS , Gk. for 'rolling in the dirt'. An ancient kind of wrestling in which opponents were allowed to fight even if knocked to the ground (as opposed to >ORTHOPÁLE, where contestants fought standing up). Throttling the opponent was also allowed. The fight ended when a contestant surrendered or became unfit to fight. See also >PALE.

KYPRIA PALE, Gk. for 'Cypriot wrestling'. A sport known in antiquity, mentioned by Hesychius (3rd cent. BC): 'by some called fighting by any means, by others plebeian and clumsy on account of the fact that Cypriots fight with no respect for rules'.

KYRKBÅTAR, Swed. for 'church boats'. A custom which existed in regions of Sweden abounding in lakes and waterways and consisted of going to Sunday service in boats referred to as 'church boats'. Returning from church, people often practiced various folk sports.

KYS KATCHAR, also *kys tashar*, a form of folk Kir. mounted wrestling. The object of the sport, in which

horses are mounted barefoot is to push the opponent and his horse out of a circle 25-30m in diameter, so that at least 2 of the horse's feet are outside the ring. The chief difference between kys katchar and its Kaz. var. >SAIS is that here contestants may fight with only 1 hand; also, the horse's movements are used to a greater extent. Traditionally, contestants wore leather trousers with 1-1.5m wide legs, which were turned up to the knees for the duration of the fight, and leather vests, usu. made of chamois or deer hide. An important element of the outfit was a wide leather belt, usu. made of deer hide and tightly buckled at the waist; on top of it the contestant would wear yet another belt, made of leather or cloth. G.N. Simakow, a Rus. ethnologist, writes that a similar set of clothes was worn by Manas – a hero of the Kir. national epos of the same title – and his squad.

G.N. Simakow, *Obshcherstvyennye funktsyi kirghizkikh norodnich rozwletchenyi w kontse XIX – nachale XX w.*, 1984.

KYSSE DEN STORE FORHAMMER, Dan. for 'kissing the sledge-hammer'. A folk Dan. pastime. The player grasps a sledge-hammer standing on its head, thumb up with his right hand. Turning his arm he lifts the hammer so that the head is at his mouth level. Holding a heavy sledge-hammer in this position is very difficult, esp. that the player's hand is twisted downwards. He must maintain this position for a moment and then kiss the head of the hammer to complete the exercise.

J. Møller, 'Kysse den store forhammer', GID, 1997, 3, 105.

KYSSE DEN STORE TÅ, Dan. for 'kissing the big toe'. An old Dan. folk pastime. The player sits down, takes his foot in his hands and tries to bring it close enough to his lips to kiss it. A harder version of the exercise is done standing up.

J. Møller, 'Kysse den store tå', GID, 1997, 3.

KYSSE DØRKÆLLINGEN, Dan. for 'kissing the door'. A Dan. competition in which the player stands abdomen upwards on his hands and feet, with his head hanging down. He gradually nears the door with his hands. The object of the game is to be close enough to the door to kiss it. If the player is successful, he tries again, this time starting from further away. Whoever accomplishes the feat starting from the greatest distance, wins.

J. Møller, 'Kysse dørkællingen', GID, 1997, 3.

KYSSE KNIV, Dan. for 'kissing the knife'. A Dan. game of dexterity. The player squats before a half-open penknife stuck in the ground. He puts his hands on the ground so that the tips of his middle fingers touch the knife. He then tries to reach his thumbs as far out from the knife as possible. He turns his hands around his thumbs and puts his feet in the space between hands and knife. In this position he must take the knife out of the ground with his mouth and get up. He must not lose his balance or take his hands off the ground.

J. Møller, 'Kysse kniv', GID, 1997, 3.

KYUDO, also *kyu-jutsu*, a trad. form of Jap. archery, closely linked with the Buddhist philosophy Zen. The idea of kyudo is described as 'aspiring to truth through the bow'. The object of kyudo is not to shoot the best score but to attain the state of highest concentration by taking aim and to experience it as aspiring to perfection (which, in the Zen philosophy, is identical with aspiring to truth – *shin*, good – *zen*, and beauty – *bin*). When the contestant decides they have achieved the desired state of concentration, they release their inner energy by shooting. They should, but do not have to hit the target, which has no punctual value. The targets are made of paper or mat spread over a wooden ring about 36-40cm in diameter. White paper is used for practice, while during festive events the targets are covered with golden foil or drawings depicting historical scenes. Sometimes the targets are covered with patterns similar to those used in modern Eur. sports targets. The arrows are blunt, ending with round knobs. The feathering is traditionally made of actual feathers, rather than a synthetic substitute. The length of the arrow is fitted to the physical qualities of the contestant, i.e. one *yazuka* – the span from the neck to the tip of the index finger plus the width of the hand. In one practice session the archer shoots 20-40 arrows. They are made according to different standards, traditionally of bamboo, more recently of aluminum (esp. outside Japan), which prolongs their life. The shooting distance is 25-28m. The test shots, however, are made from just a few steps away from a target made of tufts of grass or hay (*makiwara*). There are 2 styles of stringing the bow: *shamen uchiokoshi* (the bow is strung before being leveled, diagonally to the body) and *shomen uchiokoshi* (the bow is strung above the head and then lowered). The bows are exceptionally large – up to 3m long, 1/3 of the length below the handgrip and 2/3 above. The weight of the bow is not predetermined and spans from 13-40kg, the average being about 18kg. The rules say it must be adjusted to the weight and height of the contestant. The bows are made of hard plywood and covered with bamboo. The top layer is often coated with lacquer, partly for aesthetic reasons, partly for protection against moisture. An important element of kyudo is the ceremonial accompanying it. Usu. 6 competitors take part in one kyudo session, one standing half a step behind the next. They must have enough space to be able to move about freely. Women wear trad. colorful kimonos, men – loose dark trousers and white shirts. All archers wear special gloves. As K. Shibata, a Jap. kyudo master, writes: 'kyudo is not about hitting the target. What is important, is the precision and inner discipline, the connection between the archer's consciousness, his bow, the arrow and the mind. Kyudo is a kind of meditation practiced standing up. When the arrow is released, it reflects the state of the mind as if in a mirror. The target becomes the mirror. By shooting the arrow you discipline your ego, you perceive your own state of consciousness'.

History. The kyudo tradition stems from the *kyudjutsu* – an ancient Jap. art of shooting to kill, cultivated in the Heki school and using the tradition of ceremonial archery of the Ogasawa school. The beginnings of kyudo date back to the 4th-5th cent., when Confucianism reached Japan. Confucius claimed that archery best shapes a person's character, enabling them to achieve the state of perfection by focusing on the goal, practicing perseverance and precision of action. Both Jap. warriors, to whom the bow was an instrument of war, and courtiers, focusing more on the ceremonial, enriched their art through the ages with influences of Shintoism and *Zen*. A legend from the Heike dynasty mentions an archer who with one arrow from a kyudjutsu bow could sink two ships by piercing their sides. In those days the loudness and striking force of a bow was described by the number of men required to string it well. (The best archers could do it alone.) The bow, with which the 2 ships were allegedly sunk, had the force of 7 men. A medieval archer practicing kyudjutsu had to shoot a couple of hundred arrows a day. Archery lost significance after the introduction of firearms. In the 19th-20th cent. it almost fell into oblivion but never vanished completely. It was practiced at the Imperial University in Tokyo, where professor H. Toshizane combined the kyudjutsu martial art with elements of ceremonial archery. That was the beginning of a shooting style named after him, which enjoyed great popularity. After WWII the US authorities in occupation banned all Jap. martial arts, incl. kyudjutsu. Kyudo, however, as non-aggressive and focusing on inner self-improvement, was not only allowed but even widely encouraged as an element of re-educating the society. In 1953 the All-Jap. Kyudo Federation (Zen Nihon Kyudo Renmei) was founded. Soon afterwards the first kyudo handbook, *Kyohon*, was published. The Kyudo Federation has 80,000 active members in Japan. Many more people practice the sport without formal membership in any organization or as members of spiritual congregations – e.g. Heki Ryu Bishu Chikurin-ha, whose traditions go back to medieval times and which stresses the philosophical aspect of kyudo more than any other school. The Choozen-ji temple school takes Zen as its philosophy. The many kyudo schools favor different elements of the sport and are in constant dispute over their superiority. During the late '80s and early '90s the Eur. Kyudo Federation, which organizes annual sessions, was founded. In the USA the first session took place in 1993 in San Jose, California.

W.R.B. Acker, *Japanese Archery*, 1965; E. Herrigel, *Zen in der Kunst des Bogenschiessen*, 1948; K. Makiwara, *The Art of Japanese Archery*, The Internet: http://www.negia.net/~pdarden; A. Sollier and Z. Gyobiro, *Japanese Archery. Zen in Action*, 1969.

KYU-JUTSU, see >KYUDO.

KYUSHIN, one of the Jap. schools of self-defense of the >JU JUTSU family.

KYYKKÄ, a Fin. game similar to the Rus. >WYBIJANKA (>GORODKI). To score, a contestant throws a stick at a row of 20 wooden figures and tries to knock one down. In double and team matches there are 40 figures. The game originated and is most popular in Karelia.

Equipment. The wooden throwing sticks (*sauva*) are rounded and resemble >PALANT sticks. Each player has 4 sticks, in double matches a team has 8. They are 85cm long, 70cm of the stick is 8cm in diameter, the remaining 15cm taper down to about 4-5cm and serve as a handle. The figures to be knocked over consist of 2 pickets, one on top of the other. A single picket, also rounded wood, is 10m high and 7-7.5cm in diameter. The surface with which one picket touches the other is slightly leveled.

Pitch. The pitch is symmetrical and may be used in 2 directions, but only one side at a time is used when one player or team throws. The pitch is 20m long and 5m wide, divided into 3 segments along its longitudinal axis. The 5m long segments at each end serve alternately as a zone from which (*heittoneliö*) or into which (*pelineliö*) the players throw. The 10m long segment dividing the two is in turn divided into five 2m long segments. The wooden figures are placed regularly or randomly on the lines dividing *heittoneliö* and *pelineliö* from the middle segment.

Course of the game. The game begins by a drawing (*hutun keitto*), which determines, which team gets a given side of the pitch. The contestant beginning the game throws from the *takaraja* – the back line of the *heittoneliö*. The next 3 throws are made from any part of the *heittoneliö*. After a certain number of figures have been knocked down the stick must land outside the pitch. When the player has used all 4 sticks his opponent takes his turn at throwing (in the opposite direction). Players throw alternately until one of them knocks down all his figures, placing them outside the *pelineliö*. Points are summed up after each turn of 4 throws: 1pt. for every figure outside the *pelineliö*, minus 1pt. for every figure in the *pelineliö* (knocked down or not), minus 1pt. for every stick in the pitch. If all the figures are knocked down in fewer than 4 throws, 1pt. is awarded for every unmade throw. The best ever score for one series is 30pts. (the Fin. record). Kyykkä theoreticians assume that the best players may in the future score 34 (out of 40) points. In express matches the number of rounds is limited to 3 or 4.

KYZ-KUU, a kind of horse-riding competition of the Kaz. people.

Above and top:the practice of kyudo.

Below: Yoshiyuki Kobayashi, right, from Japan, offers students guidance during the annual National Japanese Archery Seminar at San Jose State University in San Jose, California.

WORLD SPORTS ENCYCLOPEDIA

L

A goal action during the Major League Lacrosse game between the Long Island Lizards and the Rochester Rattlers at Hofstra Stadium in Hempstead, New York.

Kevin Finneran (#33) of the Long Island Lizards carries the ball while Cory Kahoun (#19) of the Rochester Rattlers defends in a Major League Lacrosse game at Frontier Field in Rochester, New York.

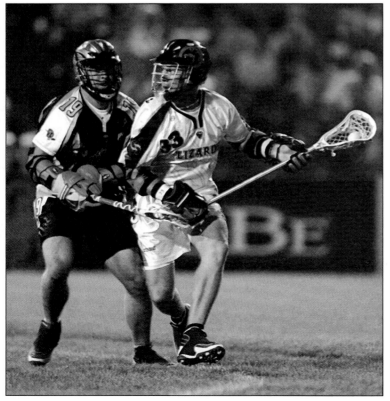

LA BALLE AU POT, see >BOLD I HUL.

LACHOA, a var. of >PELOTA.

LACROSSE, [Fr. *lacrosse* – crooked stick, crosier], Can. national summer team sport consisting of putting a ball in motion using a racket spread at the crooked end of the stick. The ball is not bounced as in tennis but caught in the net of the racket-shaped stick. The aim of the game is to shoot the ball into the opponent's goal. A var. known as >BOX LA-CROSSE is played indoors at smaller playing fields and halls as a school and recreational game. Co-ed games are also played >INTERLACROSSE.

Pitch and Equipment. The grass field trad. measured in yards, currently more uniformed in meters, is 100m x 55m. The square goal with posts and crossbar is 1.83m long. The goals are located at opposite ends of the field. They are within the field, not on the endlines, which makes it possible to play the ball from behind the goals, as in >FIELD HOCK-EY. The rubber ball is approx. 19.7-20.3cm in perimeter and weighs 14.2-14.88dg. A men's team numbers 10 players; a women's team 12. In women's matches bodily contact is forbidden, allowed otherwise in men's matches. A match duration is 4x15min. for friendly and club matches, 4x25min. for international matches, and 2x25min. for women's matches regardless of types of competition.

Rules. The aim of the game is to play the ball into the opponent's goal. Each goal counts 1pt. The goalkeeper defends the goal and carries a crosse with a wider net than those of other players. A goalkeeper is the only player who can catch the ball with his hands. Like in hockey the ball may be played from behind the goal which is placed 13.7m from the endline. The speed of a slung ball can reach 160km/h.

History. Games similar to lacrosse were played by various native Amer. tribes: Iroquois, Algonquian, Creek, Choctaw and Cherokee before the arrival of Europeans in America. In the Algonquian language the game was known as >BAGATAWAY. The Mohawks called it >TEWAARATHON and the Choctaws >TOLI. The first Fr. settlers of present-day Canada dubbed the Indian games lacrosse, due to the crooked rackets. Lacrosse matches were connected with religious rituals. The participating teams would count a few hundred players, far greater than contemporary teams of 10-12. The size of the playing field was not defined and sometimes extended several kilometers in length. Around 1842, together with foundation of the Montreal Olympic Club, lacrosse was ultimately adopted by the Canadians. On the initiative of the club 2 matches were played on 28 and 29 Sep. 1844. The first match was performed by 2 Ind. teams consisting of 6 players each; the second was played between a Can. team and an Indian team and ended in a blow-out for the latter. The surviving descriptions of the matches provide evidence on application of rules characteristic for today's lacrosse. Similar games were played in the Olympic Club in following years. In 1851 the Canadians scored a victory for the first time. In the years 1856-61 other lacrosse clubs were founded. In the 1860s a Montreal dentist, G. Beers, established uniform rules of play influenced by the rules of teewarathon known to him. In 1867, on the initiative of Beers, the National Lacrosse Association was founded, the predecessor of the present Can. Lacrosse Association (Association Canadienne de Crosse). In 1874 the game was brought to Australia and in 1877 to England. In the USA the beginnings of lacrosse go back to the 1870s although the first Amer. club was founded in 1881 and one year later the first Amer. league was set by the universities of Harvard, Princeton and Columbia. Attempts to make lacrosse a professional sport failed in the 1920s. During the OI.G. of 1904 and 1908 lacrosse was part of the Olympic program. In 1978 and 1994 lacrosse exhibition matches were played during the Commonwealth Games. Although lacrosse was declared by the government as the national sport of Canada in 1959 it was not officially confirmed by the National Sport Act until 1994. In 1967 the Lacrosse Hall of Fame was opened in New Westminster, Brit. Columbia. It displays the achievements and memorabilia of the most famous teams and players. In Canada the number of active professional players of all lacrosse var. increased from 14,106 in 1984 to 27,047 in 1998, counting amateur players the number amounts to 100,000. The primary share in this increase is held by indoor box lacrosse, whereas the outdoor version is clearly losing popularity. During the men's World Cup held every 4 years since 1967 Canada has usually had problems with putting up the national team of satisfactory level and recruits mainly from among the box lacrosse players. For many years the leading national team has been the USA. Canada won the title for the first and only time in 1978 and usually has taken the 2nd or 3rd position since then. Canada has never won the World Cup in women's lacrosse (held also every 4 years since 1982) or Junior Lacrosse World Cup (held since 1995). The sport of lacrosse enjoys the greatest popularity in school clubs and universities, in which the number of players is hard to define but most likely reaches a few hundred thousand. Outside Canada and the US lacrosse is practiced in Australia, Great Britain, Japan, Belgium, Singapore, the Czech Republic, Denmark, France, Italy, and Sweden. On the international level the governing body for men's indoor and outdoor competitions is the International Lacrosse Federation, ILF, which in 1998 comprised 11 member countries. For women's lacrosse the international governing body is the International Federation of Women's Lacrosse Associations (IFWLA). The third international lacrosse organization is the Federation Internationale d'Inter-Crosse (FIIC) managing the development of the co-ed interlacrosse.

W. G. Beers, *Lacrosse. The National Game of Canada*, 1869; Canadian Lacrosse Association, *Lacrosse. Canada's National Summer Sport*, 1995; *Coaching Youth Lacrosse. American Sport Eduacation Program*, 1997; P.E. Hartman, *Lacrosse: Fundamentals*, 1968; W.K. Morill, *Lacrosse*, 1966; B. Richey, ed., *Selected Field and Lacrosse Articles*, 1963; B. Scott, *Lacrosse. Technique and Tradition*, 1976.

LADDERBOLLING, the Flem. name of a Belgian folk game now known under the Fr. name of >TROU-MADAME.

WORLD SPORTS ENCYCLOPEDIA

L

LÆGGE ARM, a Dan. var. of >ARM WRESTLING [Dan. *lægge* – lay, put down + *arm* – arm].

LAJKONIK, a var. of folk show performed in Kraków, Poland, esp. during Christmas octave. *Lajkonik* is a figure of a rider specially fastened to a horse dummy as to create an impression of a mounted rider. Ł. Gołębiowski depicts a lajkonik from the turn of the 18th and 19th cent. in the following way:

The rider is in Tartar attire, wearing yellow boots and holding a great scepter in his hand. He walks and swings to the music played on drums and trumpet. Occasionally, the lajkonik jumps up or charges sideways chasing away the on-lookers. Many a spectator climbs trees or roofs just to take a look at him.
[*Gry i zabawy różnych stanów*, 1831, 98]

The lajkonik shows were traditionally performed and currently imitated as follows:

After the Corpus Christi procession comes to an end, spectators of all sex, class and age rush to the plains outside the bishop's palace along Bracka, Wiślana and Franciszkańska Streets and gather to await the coming of the Raftsmen's Guild and the lajkonik who, after the service, stride easily to the point of meeting. The entire party arrives under the Bishop of Cracow's window and greets him brandishing a flag. After the greeting the lajkonik starts running among the crowd chasing people away. The crowd must give him right of way, those who do not are treated with the scepter. After the show the lajkonik rejoins the guild and leads them back, marching up front like a great chief. Finally, the procession arrives in the district of Zwierzyniec for a modest but joyful feast. (ibid., 98-99)

History. The tradition of lajkonik is linked to a historical event during the reign of Pol. Prince Leszek Czarny. In 1281 a raiding party of Tartars threatened Kraków. The following event was described by Ł. Gołębiowski:

The news reached those observing Corpus Christi that the Tartar raiding party was approaching, raping and pillaging in the district of Zwierzyniec. The town folk were terrified [...] many thought they should surrender to the bloodthirsty assailants and hope for mercy. All of a sudden one of the guilders jumped out up front and, brandishing the flag with a white eagle, began to encourage the others to fight bravely against the foes, yelling, 'Follow me Brethren! Charge at these robbers! We shall not let them pillage our land!' Having gathered quite a crowd of armed followers he attacked the Tartars in Zwierzyniec. In a few hours the banks of the Vistula River were littered with enemy corpses and the water turned red from Tartar blood. The courageous leader put on the outfit of the dead Tartar chief and was triumphantly led into the city. The crowds welcomed him with joy at a place near the Vistula Gate, where today the Raftsmen's Guild is rejoined by the returning lajkonik.
[ibid., 100]

This legend cannot be satisfactorily verified due to a lack of precise sources. An event of this sort, however, could well have taken place and the tradition later maintained by the Kraków guilds, esp. the aforementioned raftsmen's guild. The historical records of lajkonik include the names of the most famous performers. As Ł. Gołębiowski wrote: 'In 1824 the lajkonik rider was a 60-year-old,

Kulisiewicz, one of the leading raftsmen displaying great youthful stamina and enthusiasm.'
The Turk. wars, esp. the victory of Vienna (1683) brought the popularity of Turk. artifacts to Poland and influenced the trad. outlook of lajkonik in the second half of the 17th cent. and the first half of the 18th. In the 19th cent. during the Pol. national revival under the liberal Austrian rule the lajkonik tradition was revived. In 1904 Pol. painter and playwright S. Wyspiański designed the lajkonik attire and equipment still used today. Lajkonik is currently included in numerous cultural events in Kraków and is a tourist attraction of the city.

LAMJEI, the trad. tax-collector's (*pannas*) race popular in the Indian state of Manipur. Various distances are run in various areas, usu. about half a mile (800m). The qualifying round is organized in pairs, in a cup system, with the winner of each heat continuing on to the next stage, and the loser dropping out. The winner of the final heat is declared the best runner of the year but only after symbolically touching *kanglasha*, the statue of a dragon. Each year's winner may participate in the next year's final heat without taking part in the qualifying round. All winners are also granted periodical or lifelong tax exemptions (depending on the class of the runner, his results, and the style of his victories).
The Internet: http://w3.meadev.gov.in/sports/tr_games/arch.htm

LAMPADEDROMIA, also *lampadephoria*, Gk. for 'the torch race', a type of ancient Gk. relay race run in teams or individually, depending on the type of ritual it accompanied and the local conditions. Torch races never came to be an independent Olympic event in ancient Greece; rather, they accompanied religious ceremonies or festivals. As the historian of ancient physical culture B. Kunicki writes,

it is believed that the origins of the lampadodromia were associated with the religious ceremony of carrying the fire needed for ablutions, lighting sacrificial or funeral pyres, and especially with the cult of Prometheus, and the ritual of periodically replacing the old fire burning at the prythaneion and private homes with new fire, ignited at a god's altar; the carriers of the fire ran so that the fire would not be contaminated by the environment but at the same time so that it would not inauspiciously fizzle out and would instead augur good fortune. With time, though, the cult aspect diminished until the race took on a character of almost purely sportive competition.

The races were run on foot, or, as Plato states in *The Republic* (book I, 1), also on horse back, under the name of *apipolampas* or *hippolampas* (see below). Horseback lampadedromia is depicted on a bowl (or *krater* in Gk.), dating back to c.410 BC, and today held at the Brit. Museum. The tradition of horseback lampadedromia originated in Thrace (as confirmed in Plato's work), and was associated with the lighting of the fire on the altar of the goddess Bendis, the Thracian counterpart of Artemis. In the period of co-operation between the Thracians and Athenians (due to the Thracian rulers Sitalkes (429

BC) and Kotys (380 BC)), the tradition was transferred to Piraeus. The torch was passed from one rider to the next at full gallop. The distances covered by each horse and rider are not known.
A bas-relief is held at the Brit. Museum, depicting Artemis picking up the torch from a runner. Right behind the runner, there are 2 gymnasiarchs standing, and 2 teams of 4 runners each, which suggests that the lampadedromia was often run as a relay race. After his victory at Troy, Agamemnon alleged-

Lajkonik.

ly ordered a relay race with torches along a course from Troy to Argos. Torch races were also part of the funeral ceremonies of important citizens. They were also an inseparable part of the nightly mystery plays, that is secret rituals in honor of certain gods. In Athens, the lampadedromia was organized only on moonless nights, which made it even more mysterious. Two main types of lampadedromia were recognized: the *panatheneas*, run in honor of the goddess Pallas Athene, and the *teseidas*, during the festival of Theseus. The race in honor of Athene started at the city walls, on the road from Athens to the Academy Gardens, leading to the altar of Prometheus. Five teams of 40 people took part, with participants running in lines next to each other, handing the torch on approx. every 25m. The prize was awarded to the team which was the first to hand over their torch to the priests on the steps of the altar. The race in honor of Theseus followed a different pattern: at the start, the torch was carried by children, while the following changes made no distinction between the ages of the runners. As was usual for Gk. athletes, the runners were naked. The teseidas was organized until the 2nd cent. BC. The lampadedromia was supervised by a representative of the city called the *archon basileus*, accompanied by other officials known as the *hieropoioi* and *agonothetai*. One function the basileus performed was picking up the torch from the hands of the last runner and lighting the fire on the altar, or passing the fire on to a priest who did so. The coaches who trained the runners were called *lampadarchai* and also performed the functions of referees. The citizens of a Gk. city who were supposed to finance the lampadedromia were called *lampadarchaj*. Outside Athens, the races involved teams of 48, 40 or 10 runners, depending on the size of the city and the local tradition. Lampadedromia was also organized in Olympia from the first Olympiad of 776 BC, as attested by Philostratos in his *Peri gymnastikos*. However, the Olympic torch race was not an event of the games themselves. It was run over a distance of 1 stadion by the youngest pilgrims coming to the games. The winner had the right to light the fire on Zeus's altar, which symbolized the beginning of the games. However, other sources claim that the race was run without torches, and that the winner received the torch from the priest on the steps leading to the altar to light the fire on it. Similar races were run during the Delphic games, where young runners ran a distance of about 1.5km from the gymnasion to the altar of Apollo. In Epidaurus, the distance was about 800m from the altar of Asklepios to the altar of Apollo Maleatas.
A lampadedromia was also organized in Cyprus, among other places. Records have been preserved describing annual games held at Chytri. One of the most solemn lampadedromias was held in 170 BC

Lajkonik on a Polish postage stamp.

Lampadedromia on ancient Greek vases.

Thalia Prokopiou, right, in the role of high priestess offers a clay pot to Anna Skoulikidou containing the flame used to light the Olympic torch during a practice ceremony for the Salt Lake City Winter Games amid the ruins of temples of Hera and Zeus in Ancient Olympia, Greece.

L

*Lanzamiento de barra aragonesa:
the Aragonese barra.*

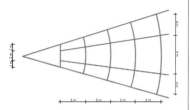

*Lanzamiento de barra aragonesa:
the V-shaped landing sector.*

on the occasion of the birthday of the ruler Ptolemy VI Philometor, and the next – at his enthronement in 146 BC.
C. Constantinou-Hadjistephanou, *Athletics*, 1991; C.D. Corral, *The Olympic Flame*, 1988; *Leksykon antycznego sportu*, L-M, 1996.

LANCASHIRE STYLE, see >CATCH-AS-CATCH--CAN.

LANCER DE LA BOTTE DE PAILLE, LE, see >HAY TOSSING.

LANCER DE LA GERBE DE PAILLE, LE, see >HAY TOSSING.

LANGBOLD, [Dan. *lang* – long + *bold* – ball] the most popular Dan. bat-and-ball game. Some var. of langbold do not use a bat – the small ball is struck with the hand. In those areas where langbold has been played using a bat (since the Middle Ages), various types can be encountered, from small ones, held in one hand only, up to large 2-handed ones. In the past, textile balls were used, with the core made of one or more used bottle corks. The corks were wrapped in paper or canvas, and then densely wrapped with string so that the ball had a total diameter of about 2½in. (6.3cm). The ball was divided horizontally or vertically into 8 parts, each of which was then covered with a different pattern of chain embroidery in various colors. The embroidery, apart from its decorative function, was supposed to secure the string wrap in place, protecting it against unwinding or slippage. The ball could also be covered with leather or strong fabric. In another method, the corks were wrapped in a number of layers of wool or yarn unraveled from old clothes or socks. Then the ball was moistened with saliva and coated with long cow hairs. The layer of cow hair was about ¼-½in. (0.6-1.2cm) thick. In some areas, the core of the ball was made of roof moss, pieces of thick rope etc. A layer of unraveled wool or yarn was then wrapped around the core, and embroidered as in the first type. The artistic qualities of the ball were one unique feature that differentiated langbold from all other Eur. bat-and-ball games. Today however, such artistic balls are rare, and wherever langbold

Langbold fra Anholt.

is still played, factory-made rubber balls are used. A long street or driveway was often used as the pitch. The sides or ditches formed the natural borders of the pitch, along which 2 base lines (*målene*) were designated, about 60 steps apart. The bases were known by various names, depending on the region; the most widespread name was *slågmål*, distinguishing it from the back line – *baglinje*. Other names included the *formål* ('front line') and *bagmål* ('back line'), or the *springet* and *maalet* used in Humlebæk, *indermaal* and *raadengrav* in Bjerregrav, *howdedskytte* and *biskytte* in Zealand, and *hovedbo* and *tilflugstbo* in Smollerup. About 1837 in Århus, the back line became known as the *knæller* ('kneeler'), perhaps because one had to kneel on it to pass over it. The bases were not always represented by lines drawn across the pitch – sometimes, as in Anholt, they were marked with stones or piles of stones, or by a nearby tree, as in Bramdrup. The fixed points of reference in the shape of the 2 base lines make langbold different from >SLÅGTRILLE. Cf. >SLÅ TRILLA.

Two teams with 4-25 players each participate. The match starts with drawing to decide ends. One team take positions in the 'infield' (*inde*), while the other – in the 'outfield' (*i marken*, literally 'in the field'). The infield team take their positions behind the front base line, while the opposing outfield players position themselves anywhere they like between the 2 base lines. The game is started by the pitcher (*opgiveren*), who throws the ball from a position about 3m in front of the base line. Then the batter (*slåeren*) has to hit the ball with his hand or bat; the ball is not allowed to land beyond the side lines. A point is scored if the batter manages to run to the front base line and back to his own base line. The slåeren might refuse the ball and start running once the ball thrown towards him has passed the base line; however, he is not allowed to run with the ball in his hand. In some var. of the game, an additional goal was used (*råddengrav* or *skidten* in LØng and KrØjerup, *skytten* in Herlufsholm; *havnen* in NeksØ; *springfuren* in Bramdrup; *springerren* in Århus; *springskidtet* and *råjmol* in other areas and at other stages in the history of the game). In Fyn, standing in the goal was known as 'standing on the root' (*stå på roden*), while in Hundstup – as 'standing to courage' (*stå til moks*). Those players who have hit the ball but not started their run yet can 'hide' in such an additional goal. If the batter succeeds in completing the run, the next player of his team takes over as the batter. In most var. of the game, the last player of a team is entitled to 3 hits. In some areas (Alsted near SØro), the whole team had to make the run. The teams change sides 1) after one of the players of the infield team, when running to the opposite base line, or returning to his own base line, is struck with the ball; 2) when one of the outfield players catches the ball in the air and hits it against the ground catching a ball in the air scores half a point, and the teams change sides after 1pt. is scored; 3) when the batter hits the ball so that it lands outside the side lines, or beyond his own goal; 4) when a running player returns to the goal he has just left to avoid being hit with the ball. This is how Nielsen recalled in 1905 how langbold was played in Dan. villages and towns:

The Sunday afternoon game of langbold, in the company of dressed-up girls and boys from the town, the runs after the ball and the throwing of it at the back of a running opponent, the shrieks of the girlfriends and laughter of the boys, was all superb fun that I will never forget. Langbold was usually played in Denmark in the spring, most often in the late afternoon, just before sunset. The falling darkness created a special atmosphere which appears in many diaries and descriptions of the game.

J. MØller, 'Langbold', GID, 1997, 1, 53.

LANGBOLD FRA ANHOLT, (Dan. *lang* – long, far + *bold* – ball + *fra* – from + *Anholt* – a Dan. island in the Kattegat Strait). The ball used for the game has a lead core and is layered with yarn and leather. The hardness of the ball may constitute a hazard of injury. A Dan. researcher of trad. sports, J. MØller quotes an opinion of one of the players: 'We, small boys were afraid of being hit by the ball batted by one of the older players.' Due to this fact the trad. ball was replaced by a rubber one.
The ball is hit with a heavy 2-hand bat. In the children's var. a lighter bat is used. The game is played by at least 4 players, usu. 2 per team, sometimes more. The pitch is 60-100m long with a centerline dividing it in 2 parts called the *midterbrand* – 'mid-

dle fire'. At the head of the pitch a home base is located called the *inderbrand* – 'inside fire'. Within the base in the middle of the endline, the *opgiversted*, or batter's plate, is located. Right next to the plate there is an on-deck circle – *raaddenfod*. The outside base the player runs to and from is marked with a stone stack at the opposite end of the pitch. The outside base is called *udebrand* or known locally as *yderbrand* – lit. 'outside fire'. The rules of play are similar to most bat and ball games. Two teams of players compete: the inside team (*indehold*) and the outside team (*udehold*). The drawing of positions is made by placing players' hands one upon another on the bat. The inside team players take turns at bat from the opgiversted. While the ball is in the air they try to run to the midterbrand and then udebrand avoiding being off-side (*svedet*), i.e. being hit or caught by a player from the opposite team. The outside base is taken if a player manages to stop for a short time 1 step from the stone stack. After a player is hit or caught another player bats the ball. After the last player of the batting team is hit or caught the teams exchange positions. The player on the midterbrand or the home base must not be hit or caught. The player who gets to the home base without being hit or caught is entitled to another bat. As the bat is held in both hands the batter cannot pitch the ball himself, the ball is therefore pitched by an opposite team player. The batting sequence of players of each team is not regulated. Each player is entitled to 1 bat only. A player may earn another bat by running to the middle base and successfully returning to the home base. A player is not under obligation to run after batting the ball. The last batting player is more privileged and entitled to 4 bats. Langbold fra Anholt used to be played traditionally around Easter and, occasionally, in other seasons. The game is gradually fading away due to the tiny population of Anholt, an island of only about 300 people.

J. MØller, 'Langbold fra Anholt', GID, 1997, 1, 58.

LÅNGBOLL, also *längboll*, a Norw. bat-and-ball game.

LANZAMIENTO DE BARRA, Span. name for a metal rod or short crowbar throw (Span. *lanzamiento* – throwing + *barra* – rod, bar, pole). It has many var. depending on the size of rods and the material they are made of as well as throwing techniques. In the Iberian Peninsula the following main var. may be distinguished: >LANZAMIENTO DE BARRA ARAGONESA, >LANZAMIENTO DE BARRA CASTELLANA, >LANZAMIENTO DE BARRA ESPAÑOLA, >PALANKARIS (LANZAMIENTO DE BARRA VASCA); cf. also >TIRO DE BARROT.

LANZAMIENTO DE BARRA ARAGONESA, a Span. game where a metal rod or tube is thrown for distance [Span. *lanzamiento* – throw + *barra* – rod, crowbar + *aragonesa* – Aragonese]. The senior event uses a metal rod, shaped much like a crowbar, 81cm long and 3cm in diameter, with a weight of 7.257kg. At one end, the barra has a flat part, 10cm long and 4cm wide. Apart from the senior event, there are 4 other age groups. Children aged 8-11 (the *infantil A* class) and 12-14 (*infantil B*) use a *barra* weighing 3kg; those between 15 and 17 years (*juvenil*) use a 5-kg rod; and those in the junior category (18-20 years) use a full-weight barra. Only males participate. There are also excellence categories throwers are assigned to: category III is awarded for distances under 13m; category II – 13-15m; category I – for distances over 15m.
The landing sector is V-shaped, with the side lines at a 45° angle. The throwing area is in the corner where the lines join. A thick wooden beam, square in cross-section, 2m long, separates the throwing area from the landing sector. Every 5m within the landing sector, arcs are drawn on the ground to facilitate the measurement of the distances.
The thrower takes a grip on the barra more or less at its mid-point and twists his body backwards holding the barra in his outstretched hand, much like in the first stage of a discus throw. Then he makes a quick swing, turning his body in the direction of the throw. When the hand with the barra reaches its extreme position at the front, the thrower releases the rod.
There are 2 stages in a competition – the qualifying round and the final, with 6 throwers participating in the latter. Each contestant is allowed 4 attempts in each round.

341

The participants wear white trousers or shorts, sports shirt and white sweatshirts (this is obligatory for official contests). Today, the event is regulated by the rules of the Aragonese Sports Federation.

History. Just like in other regions of Spain, throws using various kinds of metal rods, collectively known as barras (despite structural differences) have had a tradition in Aragon dating back to at least the 16th cent. They have enjoyed special popularity in the areas of Huesca (Also de Sobremonte, Biscarrués, Blesa), Zaragoza (Aldehuela de Liestos, Alfamein, Boquiñeni, Ricla) and Teruel (Alba del Campo, Anadón, Ariño, Monreal del Campo). In the first decades of the 20th cent., the original Aragonese tradition started dying out in the face of competition from modern sports, also partly due to the popularization, starting in the mid-1920s, of the all-Span. barra throw (>LANZAMIENTO DE BARRA ESPAÑOLA). The Span. Civil War (1936-37) was another element that contributed to the downfall of lanzamiento de barra aragonesa. In 1942, an association was estab. in the village of Miralbueno near Zaragoza under the name of the Friends of the Barra (Amigos de Barra), which tried to revive the tradition of the Aragonese barra. In 1956, the association was integrated with the Aragonese Federation of Athletics (Federación Aragonesa de Atletismo), while M. Bazán developed uniform rules of lanzamiento de barra aragonesa. Official regional competitions were started in 1968. In 1983, the rules were improved by the Aragonese Federation of Traditional Sports (Federación Aragonesa de Deportes Tradicionales).

C.M. Palos, 'Lanzamiento de barra aragonesa', JYTE, 1992; 58-9; 299-300; Federación Aragonesa de Deportes Tradicionales, Reglamento de barra aragonesa, 1983.

LANZAMIENTO DE BARRA CASTELLANA, a Castilian sport where a metal rod or crowbar is thrown for distance [Span. *lanzamiento* – throw + *barra* – rod, crowbar + *castellana* – Castilian; older sources also use the name of *desta* for the *barra*]. It is one of a family of similar Span. sports using rods called *barras* but is different from the others in using different equipment and throwing techniques. The rod, made of pure iron (*hierro homogéneo*) is 75cm long, with a circumference of 12cm, and a min. weight of 5kg. At one end, the rod has a point similar in shape to a sharpened pencil. The length of this conical part is 12cm. The other end has a cork or screw plug (*tornillo*).

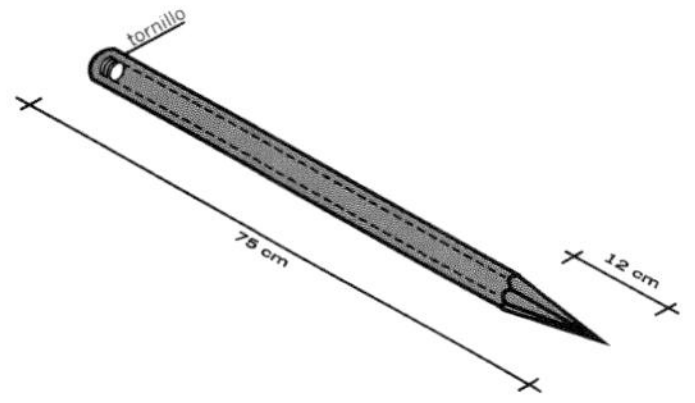

Lanzamiento de barra castellana: barra.

The throw is made from the so-called *pate de lanzamiento*, trapezoid in shape, placed at a right angle to to the direction of the throw. The longest side of this throwing area, 100cm long, connects the lines, drawn at an angle of 90°, that demarcate the V-shaped landing sector (*sector de caida*). The lines intersect on the shorter side (80cm long) of the throwing area. Both of the shorter sides of the trapezoid are 50cm long, converging in the same direction as the landing sector lines but not parallel to them.

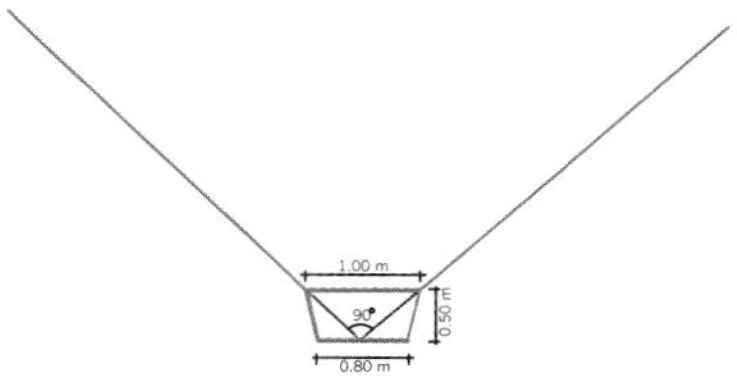

Lanzamiento de barra castellana: throwing area.

History. The oldest records of lanzamiento de barra castellana date back to the 16th cent. The game was mentioned by such authors as C. Méndez (1553), F. de Luque Fajardo (1603) and M. de Jovellanos (1812). Outside Spain, the game was mentioned by the Italian Mercurialis (1569). In 1611, S. Covarrubias described a contest organized by Castilian and Aragonese millers and involving throwing rods that were normally used to put millstones onto axles, which may explain the strange shape of the Castilian barra, sharpened at one end. The Span. *Diccionario de autoridades* (1729) described lanzamiento de barra castellana as a 'kind of pastime that improves the strength and agility of youngsters'. Various forms of the game were standardized in 1985 for the purposes of official competitions by the Council for Education and Culture of Castille and León. The sport today is cultivated under the auspices of the Federación Castellana de Atletismo (FCA) who organize local competitions and register record distances.

C.M. Palos, 'Lanzamiento de barra castellana', JYTE, 1992.

LANZAMIENTO DE BARRA ESPAÑOLA, a Span. sport of throwing a metal rod. In the folk tradition, contestants used rods of varying (albeit similar) dimensions, but limited by the rules of the Span. Royal Athletics Federation (Real Federación Española de Atletismo). Today, official competitions use a rod with a length of 1.50m, and a min. weight of 3.5kg. There is a thicker part at one end of the rod (the *cono* – [fir] cone) with a total length of 38cm (the root ring 1.5cm long and 1.55cm in diameter; the length of the part next to the root is 27.5cm, the diameter increasing from 2.25cm to 3.1cm; and the top part of the 'cone', known as the 'head' (*cabeza*), is 9cm long, 3.1cm in diameter). The longer part, adjacent to the root, called the 'tail' (cola), is 1.5cm in diameter and has a min. length of 109cm. The throw is performed from a runway (*terreno de impulso*), 4m wide and 20m long, similar to the javelin throw. The throwing line is an arc, like in athletic throwing events. The main throwing techniques include:

The torso throw (*a pecho or bularrez*), where the rod is held by the thinner part, at some distance from the end, more or less in the middle, with a straight arm, swung backwards below the shoulders. The left foot should touch the throw line, while the right one should be kept behind. The thrower makes a half-turn, and then releases the barra, cone up. The right foot may cross the line but the left foot should not be moved.

The half-turn throw (*a media vuelta or biraka*), where the barra is held as above but the thrower starts about 10m from the line, and runs up to it with a number of rapid turnarounds (*giros rapidismos*) adding momentum to the throw.

The throw 'from under one's legs' (*bajo piernas* or *ankape* or *lanzamiento entre piernas*), where the thrower starts about 1m from the throwing line, holding the barra by the upper part, slightly below the cone. He spreads his feet and swings back and forth, with the barra between his legs. After he straightens up, he makes a jump to add momentum to the throw and simultaneously releases the barra. He may touch the line after the jump.

Before each throw, the contestants lubricate the rod with soap or olive oil to add to the skid during the throw.

Special stands, called the *enterezadores*, are used to measure the distance thrown. Each such stand is made of a tapered tree trunk, pyramidal in shape, cut and rounded at the top, 55cm high, with a square base 35x35cm (25x25cm at the top).

History. The all-Span. tradition of lanzamiento de barra española was derived to a large extent from the Basq. game of >PALANKARIS even though the equipment and techniques used by the Basques are different. All the same, Basq. throwers have played an important, sometimes dominant, role in the modern lanzamiento de barra española. As many other var. of Basq. rod throws, the game originated in the work of stonemasons. The Span. historian N. Azcona reports that Basq. stonemasons working at the Escorial (the Royal Palace in Madrid) under King Philip II entertained themselves by organizing crowbar throwing competitions. In the following centuries, rod throws developed spontaneously among Span. people, with a vast range of equipment and throwing techniques. After WWI, folk sports started gradually disappearing in Spain (like in other countries) as a result of urbanization and competition from modern sports. Rod throws survived mainly in the Basq. country. However, under the influence of the Castilian Athletic Federation, who in 1925 included the local var. of the barra throw (>LANZAMIENTO DE BARRA CASTELLANA) in the program of their championships, the Royal Span. Athletic Federation started considering introducing a similar event into their nationwide competitions. This initiative resulted in the organization of an exhibition of Basq. metal rod throwing equipment at Tolosa (Basq. Berazuri) in 1926. One of the rods was selected as the nationwide model to be later called the barra española. J. Iguaran, Professor at the Escuela Central de Gimnasia at Toledo, and a member of the Span. Olympic Committee, was the initiator of the adaptation, and the pioneer of the movement aimed at converting barra into a modern sport. During the International Congress on Physical Education at Burdeos, an exhibition was organized to present the tradition and technical aspects of lanzamiento de barra española. An exhibition was also staged in Prague during the rally of the Czech Sokol sport organizations. F. Loriente, a member of the Span. delegation, presented the game there. At the initiative of the Central School of Physical Education in Toledo and the Span. Olympic Committee, the game was a demonstration sport on the program of the 1936 Ol.G. in Berlin (however, the demonstration was cancelled due to the Span. Civil War). Between 1930 and 1958, Span. Championships were organized (suspended in 1936-43 and 1956). In 1944, the Span. Athletic Federation recommended regular championships which led to an increase in barra's popularity. As soon as barra was included in the general sport development program, the results improved quickly. During the first Span. Championships in 1930, Capo, a Catalan, was the winner with a distance of 18.45m. Two years later, Diminchin came first with 32.62m, while Aguirre of Guipúzcoa reached 40.75m in 1944. In 1958, M. Clavero became the first thrower to break the 50m barrier, reaching 51.57m. The Basque F. Errazquin, Span. champion of 1933, 1945, 1949-52, 1954 and 1957, is considered to have been the best thrower of all time (he enjoyed a similarly successful career in the Basq. var. of the barra throw). There were attempts in the 1950s to incorporate barra throwing techniques into the javelin throw. Using his barra experience, Errauzquin threw 74.32m with the lighter athletic javelin without any preparation, beating the then current record of Spain by more than 10m at the age of 49. Some elements of barra techniques were imported into athletic field events by outstanding javelin throwers such as the Norwegian E. Danielsen (including the jump to the other foot, adding momentum to the throw at release). The elements imperceptibly permeated general javelin technique. However, the turnaround technique (*biraka*), used in Spain by, among others, Errauzquin and M. de la Quadra Salcedo, and later developed by an American, A. Cantello, was resisted by the International Amateur Athletics Federation (IAAF). Since then, IAAF rules state that 'non-orthodox styles are not permitted'.

C. Moreno Palos, 'Lanzamiento de barra española', JYTE, 1992, 51-55 and 294-298.

LANZAMIENTO DE BARRA VASCA, see >PALANKARIS.

LANZAMIENTO DE MAKILLA, Span. for 'the makilla throw' [Span. *lanzamiento* – throw + *makilla* – a type of a wooden walking stick]. An old Basq. sport probably derived from using the makilla for self-defence, for instance throwing it at attackers. As far as the technique is concerned, lanzamiento de makilla is similar to barra throws (>LANZAMIENTO DE BARRA). The longest distances win in the occasional competitions. The makilla is also used in acrobatic shows.

C. Moreno Palos, 'Lanzamiento de makilla', JYTE, 1992.

LANZAMIENTO DE PIEDRA, see >STONE THROW.

LANZAMIENTO DE PIÉRTAGA, a Span. and Basq. throwing event using a lance with a spar approx. 4m long, made of hazel wood, and equipped with a metal head [Span. *lanzamiento* – throw + *piértaga* – lance].

History. Lanzamiento de piértaga originated in the Basq. country, where the oldest records concerning the *piértaga* date back to the Middle Ages. In the 13th cent., the *piértaga* was a typical weapon of Basq. warriors. It is mentioned in the 15th-cent. Fuero de Navarra. A shorter var. of the lance, about 2-3m long, was also used in the Canary Islands, where it was known under the names of *astia*, *regatón* or *lanza*. The *piértaga* was also used in competition during

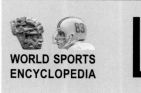

WORLD SPORTS ENCYCLOPEDIA
L

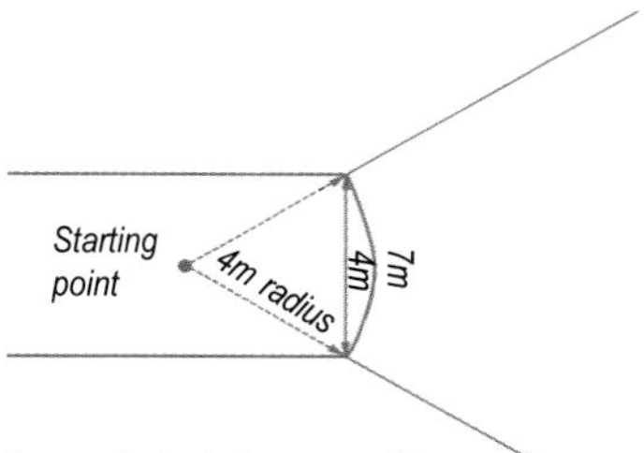

Lanzamiento de barra española: throwing area.

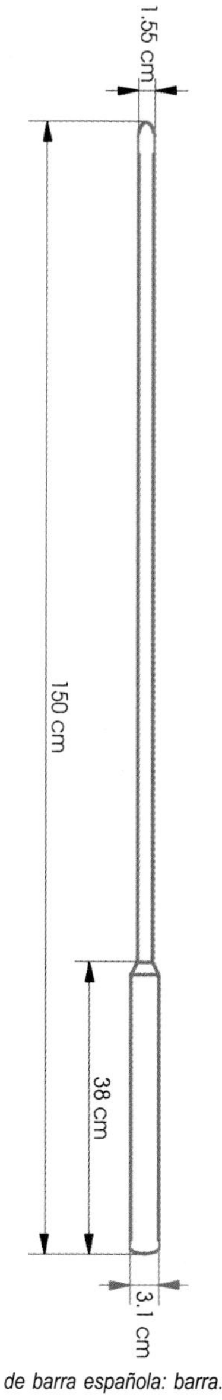

Lanzamiento de barra española: barra.

exercise – both by foot soldiers and horsemen. As newer combat techniques developed, the *piértaga* became a trad. sport. Shorter and more manageable lances (*lanzas*) came to be used by soldiers, while a stick called the *cana*, devoid of any military functions, was used in sport. Records have been preserved suggesting that sporting throws using the *cana* were something of a fashion in the 17th and 18th cent.

C.M. Palos, 'Lanzamiento de piértaga', JYTE, 1992, 69.

ŁAPA, (Pol. for 'hand'), also *ściana* (Pol. for 'wall'), an old Pol. school game, popular in the 18th and the first half of the 19th cent. The game was played by 2 persons. One of them, called the target player, placed his hand on the wall, and the other – the serving player – would throw a ball, 5-7cm in diameter, at it to score a point. The server had to catch the ball after it bounced off the wall, whether it hit

leather straps (*huascas*) about 1m long; in some var., 2 of the balls were covered with leather. The laqui was used in hunting and combat. Before the laqui was thrown, the thrower spun it above his head so that the balls would cause the leather straps to wrap around the victim. Some throwers could reach distances of up to 70m. The Araucanas always carried the laqui attached to their saddles as a favorite weapon and an element of their apparel. The laqui was also used by peasants in S Chile. In their spare time, the Mapuche would practice throwing the laqui at targets and organize spontaneous competitions. Today it is scarcely used, but is still sold in shops.

O. Plath, 'Laqui', JYDLCH, 1946, 28-9.

LARANJINHA AMERICANA, Port. for 'Amer. orange', a Port. var. of >SKITTLES. The game uses a large ball (*bola*) and 3 skittles (*paulitos*) arranged in a triangle. The name derives from that of another

cultivated in the Americas, esp. the USA and Argentina, on its own or within >RODEO, where it is an important element of some events, such as >CALF-ROPING. There is also a tradition of roping among the S.Amer. Araucana Indians (>LAZU), as well as in some Middle East and Asian countries, esp. Turkey and Mongolia; cf. Turk. >ARKAN THROWING and Mong. >URGA.

LASTO FARDO JASOTZEA, Basq. for 'lifting hay pallets' (*levantamiento de ardos de heno* is the Span. equivalent). A folk sport where large wooden pallets loaded with packed hay (about 0.75m³ in volume) are pulled up on a piece of rope. The rope passes through a compound pulley suspended at a height of about 8.5-9m on a special structure or beam in a large barn. The pallet with the hay is at one end of the rope (which is also wrapped around the hay to prevent it from falling off the pallet), while the competitor, at the other end, may use any techniques he likes to pull it up – for instance by pulling from the ground, or by jumping up, hanging on to the rope, and riding it down.

R. Aguirre, 'Lasto fardo jasotzea – Levatamiento de fardos de heno', GHJD, 1989, III, 101-102.

LATERAL RUNNING, a type of running in which the speed of movement is as important as a runner's suppleness and coordination of movements. Running styles differ depending on the length of lateral steps and arm swings. The competitors must not step over the lines delimiting their respective tracks but their face may be turned to either direction. They can also change sides while running. Lateral running distances are 100, 200, 400 and 800m.

LAUSAGLÍMA, Icel. for 'free glíma', also *lausatok* – 'free hold', a form of wrestling closely associated with the tradition of >GLÍMA. It was usu. practiced in fishing villages and settlements, and did not match the high requirements of its prototype. There was also a team var. of glíma, called >BÆNDAGLÍMA.

W. Baxter, 'Les lutes traditionnelles a traverse le monde', LJP, 1998, 84; T. Einarsson, *Glíma. The Icelandic Wrestling*, 1988.

LAUSATOK, see > LAUSAGLÍMA.

LAVE GRISE, Dan. for 'doing piglets', a Dan. game. One participant gets down on all fours, while the other sits on his back, facing backwards. He then makes a forward somersault and gets into a bridge, holding the first participant by the waist, and then returns to the starting position.

J. Møller, 'Lave grise', GID, 1997, 3, 54.

LAVE SMEDJE, Dan. for 'doing the blacksmith'. Six players form 2 rows facing each other. A further 6 get onto their shoulders. The 'mounted' players hold each other firmly by the shoulders. The 13th player gets in between them and tries to separate them. The connection between this and the name of the game is unclear.

J. Møller, 'Lave smedje', GID, 1997, 4, 52-53.

LAWN BOWLING, also *bowling on the green* or *lawn bowls* sometimes abbr. to *bowls* – by all these names lawn bowling has been around for several thousand years. Some rules have changed over time but the fundamentals are consistent, certainly since the game's historic record was started in the 14th cent. It was then that the game was threatened by global politics. Lawn bowling was banned for commoners in France and England because archery, essential for defense, was losing popularity. In Scotland the game continued uninterrupted, a favorite among even such legendary notables as Sir Walter Scott and Robert Burns. Today's rules, the flat lawn, and even a dress code seem to derive from the Scottish. Over time, waves of Scot. emigrants took their game with them and estab. clubs in many countries. New Jersey can be credited for lawn bowling's resurrection in the US, when a small private club was started in 1879.

Lawn bowling is distinguished by the use of a biased ball. It is deliberately lop-sided so that it always curves toward the flat side as it slows down. The object of the game is to obtain points by getting one's ball(s) closest to a small white ball, the 'jack', which may be anywhere between 75 and 108ft. away. The skill is to gauge the curve to achieve this even when an opponent may have guard balls blocking the jack. The balls, or bowls as they are known, vary in size, weight, and degree of bias. Local conditions are factors in selecting bowls. Bowls are

Carlos Mendez, 13, practices his pigeon-toed lasso stance at the San Antonio Charro Ranch in San Antonio, Texas.

Alfred Jacob Miller, Lassoing Wild Horses, watercolor with gouache.

Frederic Remington, It Was To Be A Lasso Duel To The Death, 1901, pen and ink.

the hand or not, and kept on throwing. If the ball failed to hit the opponent's hand and the server failed to catch it, he became the 'łapa', and placed his hand on the wall. The players also changed sides if the ball hit any part of the target player's body but the hand on the wall. The game was described by Ł. Gołębiowski in his *Gry i zabawy różnych stanów* (Games and Pastimes of Various Social Classes, 1831).

LAPTA, a folk bat-and-ball game, mentioned in many Rus. literary works. The game is played by 2 teams of 5-15 players each. The pitch is 70-80m long and 30-40m wide. The ball is 8-10cm in diameter, the bat (lapta) is 70-80cm long. The batting team hits the ball out from behind one end line of the pitch serving as a 'home line'. After hitting the ball the batter or a few players of the batting team start to run to the other end line, and then return to the home line. A successful homerun scores 1pt. for the batting team. The fielding team tries to catch the ball on the fly or pick it up off the ground and then get one of the runners out by throwing the ball at him. After a runner is out the fielding team scores a point and the teams change sides on the pitch. The team which scores more points within a specified number of changes wins the game. Cf. >GORODKI.

'Lapta', *Bolshoya Sovietskaya Encyklopedija*, ed. B.D. Viedenskij, 1953, vol. 24, 296; J. Riordan, 'Folk Games and Fake Games in Soviet Times. The Case of Gorodki and Lapta', *Stadion*, 1989, 15.

LAQUI, also *laque*, Span. *boleadoras*, a form of entertainment and competition among the Araucanian (Mapuche-Pehuenche) Indians in Chile. The laqui consisted of 3 stone balls tied together with

Port. game, >JOGO DA LARANJINHA, where the ball was aimed not at skittles but at another, smaller ball, called the 'small orange' (*laranjinha*). Most probably, under the influence of Amer. >BOWLING, the small ball was in time replaced with the skittles but the old name was retained (with the addition of the word *americana*). The ball is made of wood, has a diameter of 20-30cm and weighs 5kg. It has a number of fingerholes. Similar to the older *laranjinha*, the course is a rectangular alley, usually 30m long and 2-3m wide, divided into 3 zones by transverse lines: 1) the throwing zone, which the player cannot leave when making his throw; 2) the flight zone – the player must throw the ball so that it does not touch the ground within this zone; if it does so, the throw is not valid, and the player loses his turn; the length of this zone is not fixed and depends on the skills of the players (usu. 3-6m); 3) the roll zone, where the ball may land and roll towards the 3 skittles. A player scores a point (*risco*, literally 'scratch' or 'incision', probably from scratches made on the ground or a piece of wood to keep track of the current state of the game) for each skittle he hits. The first player to reach the agreed number of riscos is declared the winner.

M. da Graça Sousa Guedes, 'Jogo do laranjinha', JTP, 1979, 65-67.

LASSO, LE, the Fr. name of a racket-and-shuttlecock game using a palm leaf shuttlecock and played in Côte d'Ivoire, W Africa. It is a var. of the game known as >EGEDE in Nigeria.

LASSOING, a type of sport where the object is to throw a piece rigid rope (the lasso) so as to catch the target in the loop at the end. Lassoing is mainly

343

delivered either forehand or backhand, and never aimed straight at the jack. Which a bowler selects is dependent on the position of other bowls already in play. Similar games: >BOULES and >BOCCIA are not held on grassy ground.

LAWN BOWLS, also *lawn bowling, bowling on the green,* or – informally – *bowls.* One of the oldest Brit. bowling games. It consists of rolling a bowl (in some local var. also discusses) on a flat lawn. Regardless of the local var., the major goal of the game is to roll the bowl towards an object, be it another, smaller bowl of a different color called a 'jack', or a peg driven into the soil. In this respect lawn bowls belong to the same games family as Ital. >BOCCIA, Fr. >BOULES and >PÉTANQUE. >CROWN GREEN BOWLS, a specific type of lawn bowls, is played on a green rising in the middle and according to slightly different rules (thus the original lawn bowls is described as >FLAT GREEN BOWLS in contrast to *crown green bowls,* the 'crown' being the elevated middle of the green). Indoor lawn bowling (>INDOOR BOWLS) is yet another type of lawn bowls.

The green and equipment. The game is played on a square green, made of carefully evened grass which is grown on esp. arranged layers of breakstone, sand and soil. The size of the green, once free and varying with local conditions and tradition, is now regulated by the rules of the International Bowling Board (IBB), which set out the min. size of 120ft. (36.58m) and the max. size of 132ft. (40.23m) for the sides of the green. In local, less important games, greens of 99ft. (30.17m) are allowed. The permitted size is bigger for indoor bowls, owing to greater elasticity of the indoor green. The green is divided into 6 rectangular rinks, the size of which should be between 18ft. (5.48m) and 19ft. (5.79m). Rinks a min. of 14ft. (4.27m) are allowed in less official games. The green should be surrounded by a ditch 8-15in. (20.3-38.1cm) wide and 2-8in. (5.1-20.3cm) deep below the green level and enclosed by a bank a min. of 22.9cm high and sloping at up to 35°, so that it is not an obstacle. The bowls used to be made of wood, frequently of guaiacum, renowned for its hardness, but today they are made of hardened rubber or synthetic compositions. The bowls are black or brown, while the jack is always white. The diameter of the bowls should be between 4⅝in. (about 11.75cm) and 5⅛in. (about 13cm), and their weight should not exceed 2lbs. 8oz. (1.59kg). The bowls are slightly flattened on one side to intentionally shift their center of gravity (this imbalance being termed 'bias') and achieve a curved path once thrown. Each bowling association must have at least 1 master bowl against which to measure the bias and size of its bowls before every competition. The correctness of the bias of the master bowl has to be supervised by the IBB, which stamps the bowl to this effect. Additionally, each bowl used in official competitions has to be tested at least once a year and be stamped by the IBB or a national lawn bowling association. The shape and weight of the bowls is inspected by licensed testers. The diameter of the jack should be 2¹⁵/₃₂-2¹⁷/₃₂in. (6.27-6.43cm) and its weight 8-10oz. (226.79-283.49g). The size of the mat from which the bowls are delivered is 24in. (60.96cm) by 14in. (25.56cm). The front edge of the mat is to be positioned at a distance of not less than 6ft. (1.84cm) from the rear ditch (behind the player) and not less than 76ft. (23.16m) from the front ditch (in front of the player).

Rules of play. Lawn bowls can be played individually, in doubles or in teams of 3 or 4. In individual contests players have 4 bowls each, in doubles each pair has 4 bowls, a triple has 3 bowls at their disposal, and a quartet 4. The bowls are thrown, and after a short flight cover the rest of their path by rolling on the green. A toss of a coin decides who is to deliver first. Every end is started by the player of the team that won the previous one and played on the green in the reverse direction. The player that wins the right to deliver first throws the jack and then throws the first bowl. The players alternate in delivering the bowls, so that each individual player, or a team member, throws only one bowl, then the opponent or a member of the opposing group delivers. The procedure continues until there are no more bowls left. The object of the game is to position the bowls as close as possible to the jack, while trying to cannon the opponent's bowls away from it. The throws can be performed from any side of the green. The bias of the bowl allows for a curved path lead-

ing to the most advantageous positions, esp. when removing the opposition's bowls from the side positions. The end finishes when all bowls have been delivered onto the green. The score of an end is determined with a tape measure, with which the distance between the bowls and the jack are measured. Each bowl that is nearer to the jack than that of the opposition is worth 1pt. If the bowls are at the same distance, the end is said to be tied. It is usual to play up to 18 or 21pts. The distance between the jack and a given bowl is normally taken with special compasses with a tape measure. If a bowl falls outside the green, the distance is recorded with an ordinary tape measure, since the regulations state that compasses are to be used for bowls on one plane only. The jack and the bowls are delivered from a mat put on the green. According to par. 27 of the IBB rules, players should stand on a mat when delivering the jack and bowls with at least 1 foot on or over the mat. Flouting this rule is termed 'foot-faulting', and a bowl rolled in such conditions is 'dead'. If such a bowl disturbs the arrangement of bowls (called the head) near the jack, the judge may ask for the head to be restored to its previous pattern, rule that its influence was negligible and the game can be continued, or consider the whole end dead and rule that it is to start anew.

History. The game has been known in England since at least the beginning of the 13th cent. – the period that the manuscript in the Royal Library at Windsor comes from. The Eng. Southampton Club, founded in 1299, is recognized as the oldest bowlers' association. The game has been subject to bans issued by the king, bishops and town authorities. The last royal order was formally binding until 1845, and it banned bowls being played by craftsmen, journeymen and servants on the grounds of their superiors, with the exception of Christmas. Bowls was allowed in one's own house and garden, and that is why the game acquired a private status over the centuries. Between 1541-55 the proprietors of large grounds could purchase licenses for public games. Biased bowls were introduced in the 16th cent., and technical methods of achieving an appropriate curvature of the path were described by R. Recorde, the Eng. mathematician, in *The Castle of Knowledge* in 1556. The game has earned a number of mentions in Eng. literature, e.g. in Shakespeare's *King Richard II*:

QUEEN:
What sport shall we devise here in this garden,
To drive away the heavy thought of care?
FIRST LADY:
Madam, we'll play at bowls.
QUEEN:

'T will make me think the world is full of rubs,
And that my fortune runs against the bias.

[III, 4]

Expecting a message that the Span. Armada had been sighted off the Eng. coast, Sir Francis Drake is said to have played bowls in order to calm down and collect his thoughts. He is reported to have been in the midst of a game with his captains at the Pelican Inn on Plymouth Hoe in S England when a messenger came with the news. Drake replied: 'We have time enough to finish the game and beat the Spaniards, too', which he did in 1588. The game was also mentioned in *Declarations of Sports* published by King James II in 1618, in a fragment that immediately follows the list of games that the king recommended his subjects play after Sunday Mass, but is an enumeration of games toward which the king felt less benevolent:

We do here account still as prohibited all unlawful Games to be used upon Sunday only; as Bear and Bull-baiting, and at all times in the meaner sort of People by Law prohibited, Bowling.

The game, against which the meaner folks were advised, was indulgently played by the upper class, including the Stuart court. It is also frequently mentioned by S. Pepys in his diary written between 1660 and 1669. T. Paine, the famous Eng. radical, and later a revolutionary journalist in the New World and an advocate of independence for the colonies, before leaving England used to play lawn bowls in Lewes, Sussex, where he founded a club which exists to this day, despite manifold alterations. In the mid 1700s enthusiasm for the game began to wane in England, but its popularity was on the rise in Scotland. Already in 1740 T. Bicket founded a public lawn bowling green in Kilmarnock (Gaelic – *Cill-mhefrnag*). The first attempts to standardize the game along the lines of modern sports took place in 1849 thanks to W.W. Mitchell. From Scotland it returned to England and around 1900s flourished in the South Counties. In the 19th cent. Scot. emigrants brought the game to Australia, N.Zealand, S.Africa, India and Canada. It even became popular in Japan, where it is still played today. The first players' federations were set up in New South Wales and Victoria, Australia (1880). In 1886 the first large bowling association was founded. The earliest organization on the national level was created in Australia in 1911 (the Austrl. Bowling Council). Great Britain, despite the existence of local federations, waited quite some time to see large federations founded (1892 in Scotland, 1903 in England, 1904 in Wales and Ireland). In 1904 a similar federation was founded in S.Africa. The Eng. Bowling Association (EBA) proved the most influential. It was able to attract lo-

Once banned by kings and bishops, the 700-year-old tradition of lawn bowling is still going strong.

Adriaen ven de Venne, Tennis Game, gouache.

George Bellows, Tennis at Newport, 1920, oil on canvas.

John Lavery, A Game of Tennis, 1885, water color.

Tennis Party, *a 19th cent. engraving.*

cal organizations and federations – 35 out of 38 Eng. counties. Because of a disagreement on the rules of standardizing the game between the EBA and some local organizations, a new organization was set up in 1926: the Eng. Bowling Federation (EBF). At the same time the Brit. Crown Green Association, set up in 1903, was actively promoting only 1 var. of lawn bowls known as crown green bowls. In 1932 it changed its name to the Brit. Crown Green Bowling Association. All 3 organizations soon started to hold separate national championships. The Brit. Isles Bowls Council (BIBC), set up in 1962, enabled co-operation between competing federations and started to co-ordinate women's lawn bowling federations. On the international level all federations now co-operate within the International Bowling Board (IBB), set up in 1905. The seasonal limits on lawn bowling have encouraged a Scotsman, W. McRae, to devise an indoor variety of lawn bowls, which had been known before, but had not been treated as a separate game. Typical of the Eng. lawn bowling federations was their keenness to court affluent members. Sea resorts, a favorite with the Eng. establishment, were targeted for high-profile competitions. Also, lawn bowling clubs were founded with Eng. tourists in mind in such places as Spain and Portugal. Regardless of the federation type, the amateur character of the game was underscored. The old puritan rule prohibiting the game on Sundays was observed until 1962. The game was brought to the New World by English colonists in the 18th cent. Even G. Washington played lawn bowls on his own private green. The first Amer. Club was founded in 1879 (the Dunellen Bowling Club), and in 1915 the Amer. Lawn Bowls Association was created, in Buffalo. The sport is co-ordinated by the IBB on the international level. The first W.Ch. were held in Sydney in 1966. Both lawn bowls and indoor lawn bowls are played.

Women have played lawn bowls almost from its very inception, which is confirmed by the excerpt from Shakespeare quoted above, but this fact was restricted to the upper class only. The surge to popularity of women's lawn bowls was spurred by the advancing emancipation of women shortly before and after WWI. In 1931 the Eng. Women's Bowling Association and soon afterwards the Eng. Women's Bowling Federation were set up. These 2 organizations compete with each other until this day and hold separate national championships. And, similarly to men's organizations, co-ordination between the 2 is ensured by the BIBC.

R.D.C. Evans, *Bowling Greens. Their History, Construction and Maintenance*, 1992; *International Bowling Board. Laws of the Game*, 1990; Scottish Bowling Association, *Bowls for the Beginner*, 1992.

LAWN FOOTBALL, a game combining elements of tennis and football. Two players or 2 pairs take part, and the game is played on a court 15-25m long and 6m wide. The court is divided into halves by a crossbar rather than a net. In the middle of each half, a circle with a diameter of 1.52m is marked, equidistant from the side lines, and 2.44m from the crossbar. The game begins in a kick-serve from the middle of the circle; the ball must land in the serve circle on the opposite side. An unsuccessful serve loses not only the right to serve but a point as well. The rules of the game are similar to those of tennis and volleyball, but the set is won after one side scores only 5pts. There are 4 sets to a match, and the sides change ends after 2 of these. The side who scores more points in the total of 4 sets wins the match (the number of sets won or lost does not count). In the event of a tie, a deciding 5th set is played. The ball may bounce any number of times before it is passed onto the opponent's side of the court.

History. The game was invented c.1885 by A. Tebbutt and G.A. Du-Soulay of Winchester, England. It was played at Winchester College. In 1895, W. Pickford and J.A. Nethercote formulated stricter rules of lawn football and established the Eng. Lawn Football Association. There are some organized matches in England. The sport is quite popular as a form of football training.

LAWN TENNIS, a form of tennis played on grass, clay or synthetic surfaces. The name is reminiscent of the time when the game was played exclusively on grass courts. The introduction of clay and synthetic surfaces has resulted in the name being obsolete and more and more frequently replaced with >TENNIS. See also >ROYAL TENNIS.

Lawn tennis.

The idea of the game is to hit a ball with a racket over a net to the opponent's half of the court in such a way as to make it difficult for the opponent to return the ball. Failing to return the ball or hitting it out of the court results in points being scored by the opponent. The court is a rectangle 23.77m (78ft) in length and 8.23m (27ft) or 10.97m (36ft) in width (respectively for a single or double game). The net, dividing the court into 2 equal halves, is 91.5cm (3ft) high in the middle. Each half of the court is divided into the service court and the back court by a service line running across the court between the single court sidelines at a distance of 6.4m (21ft) from the net. The service court is further divided into 2 equal parts separated by a center service line running down the middle of the court from the net to the service line. Its imaginary continuation ends with the center mark drawn inside the court, which bisects the base-line. The base-lines and center mark are white and 10cm (4in) in width, while all the other lines are white and 5cm (2in) in width. The rubber ball is filled with air and covered with a thin layer of yellow or white fabric. It is between 6.35-6.668cm ($2^1/_4$-$2^5/_8$in) in diameter and weighs between 56.7-58.5g (2-$2^1/_{16}$oz). The frame of the racket with the grip may not exceed 81.28cm (32in) in length, and the strung area must not exceed 39.37cm ($15^1/_2$in) in length and 29.21cm ($11^1/_2$in) in width. Winning the match depends on the number of sets won. In order to win the set, a player must win 6 games, with the opponent winning not more than 4. When both players have won 5 games in a set, play continues until one player gains a 2-game advantage. To win a game a player must score points irregularly counted from 0 ('love', prob. from Fr. *l'oeuf* – an egg, or the shape meaning '0' or Du./Flem. *lof* – honor from *omme lof spelen* – playing for honor, having scored no points): 15-30-40-game (the Fr. maintain that the original scoring was derived from their early currency which came in these same increments). A score of 40-40 is called a deuce (from Fr. *deux* – 2 or together) and to win a game a player must gain an advantage of 2pts. The first one is called an advantage and if a player fails to win the next point, the score returns to deuce. The scoring system resulted in many excessively long matches. The longest singles match was played in 1966 in the King's Cup in Warsaw between W. Gąsiorek (Poland) and R. Taylor (Great Britain) and lasted 126 games (27:29; 31:29; 6:4). The longest doubles match was played by R. Leach/R. Dell who defeated L. Schloss/T. Mozur 3:6; 49:47; 22:20; 22:20, having played a total of 147 games!

In order to avoid such marathons a tie-breaker was introduced in 1970 and is played when both players have won 6 games in a set. To win the tie-breaker (and the set) a player must score 7 pts. provided he leads by a margin of 2 pts. If the score reaches 6pts. all, the game is extended until this margin can be achieved.

In 1958 an American, J. Van Allen, suggested another system of scoring called the Van Allen Streamlined Scoring System (VASSS). Players continue

until one of them scores 31pts., alternating the service every 5pts. A 2-pt. advantage is necessary to win.

Attire. In the past men wore white suits, ties and hats, while women – long white dresses or skirts and white blouses, which resulted in tennis being called a 'white sport'. That style of dress is no longer practiced; neither has the trad. white color survived, much to the regret of tennis conservatives. Modern players wear shorts or skirts, and T-shirts. Light shoes made of rubber and linen were replaced by specialized shoes made of leather or synthetic materials.

History. The game was invented in 1873 by an Englishman W.C. Wingfield, who developed and simplified the rules of royal tennis. At first, Wingfield called the new game *sphairistike* [Gr. *sphaira* and Lat. *spaera* – a spherical object] and intended it to serve as an amusing diversion during popular social gatherings called garden parties. His game differed from modern tennis in many details, such as the shape of the court (2 trapezoids narrowing towards the net) or an arched net lowering towards the center like in royal tennis. The scoring system was similar, however: 15-30-40-game. In the years 1873-75 *sphairistike* was inconsistently adopted in various social centers and clubs and split into many var. similar in the general idea, but differing in detail. In 1875 representatives of London clubs agreed on uniform regulations concerning e.g. the height of net poles (1.52m or 5ft. at the sides and 1.22m or 4ft. at the center). Following the suggestion of J.M. Heathcote, expressed in a letter to *Field* magazine, the rubber ball was covered with white flannel. In the following years *Field's* shares became a major impulse for the development of the game, leading to such modifications as the lowering and straightening of the net (1880). In 1880-90 the game began to be called *field tennis*, a name that soon gave way to lawn tennis. In 1877 S.W. Gore was the first to return the ball directly from the air and, in fact, played the first volley, which was formally introduced into the regulations only after a dispute lasting several years. In 1878 the winner of the 2nd Wimbledon Tournament (see below) played the first ever lob. In 1881-85 brothers William and Ernest Renshaw began to use a new tactic of approaching the net and playing a powerful shot known as a smash. Some sources attribute this innovation to an Englishman O.E. Woodhouse, who supposedly played it during the Staten Island Cricket and Baseball Club Tournament in 1880. The first open tennis tournament was organized by H. Jones at the All-England Croquet Club at Wimbledon and it began the history of the world-famous Wimbledon Tournaments formally played under that name since 1877, when *Field* magazine founded a cup. In 1874 an American, M. Ewing Outerbridge, saw the English play tennis in the Bermudas and started the game in the USA. In 1881 the United States Lawn Tennis Association was established, which in the following years played an important role in the standardization of international regulations. In Germany tennis became known

An early 20th cent. lawn tennis game.

Andre Agassi

Serena Williams

Venus Williams

Martina Hingis

Pete Sampras

Boris Becker

John McEnroe

Jimmy Connors

Stefan Edberg

thanks to some Eng. tourists vacationing at Bad Homburg and later in Baden--Baden, where the first important Eur. tournament was played in 1884. In England in the years 1875-86 the All-England Croquet Club remained the dominant organization. The year 1884 saw the failure of an attempt to form a national organization, which came into being only in 1888 as the Lawn Tennis Association. In 1900 an American, D.F. Davis, founded a cup for the winner of an annual team match between the USA and Great Britain. The event soon obtained international recognition, although during the first few decades it was totally dominated by the national teams of Great Britain, the USA, and Australia, with the exception of 1927-32, when the famous Fr. musketeers (see below) won the Davis cup for France. That domination was again broken only in 1982, when the cup was won by Czechoslovakia. Efforts to make tennis a world-wide sport were intensified by the the International Lawn Tennis Federation (ILTF) estab. in 1913 and later renamed the International Tennis Federation (ITF; Fr. Fédération Internationale de Tenis, FIT). Besides Wimbledon and the Davis Cup, the tournaments that enjoy the greatest prestige are: the French Open held since 1952 on R. Garros courts, the Australian Open (since 1905) and the US Open (since 1881). These tournaments, together with Wimbledon, form what is known as the Grand Slam held as 4 events for men since 1925 and for women since 1922. Among women who won the Grand Slam were M. Connolly (USA, 1953), M. Court-Smith (Australia, 1970), S. Graf (Germany, 1988), while among men – D. Budhe (USA, 1938) and R. Laver (Australia, 1969). Other important tournaments include: King of Sweden Gustav V Cup, Volvo Grand Prix, and Hazel Hotschkiss Wightman Cup for women, once held bi-annually and now annually as a team match between the USA and Great Britain.

Tennis players are grouped in 3 categories: 1) full professionals, 2) semi-professionals eligible for financial awards, 3) amateurs. Most contemporary events are held in an open formula, with all categories of players allowed to participate.

The level of tennis in various countries has always depended on outstanding individuals, such as W.T. 'Big Bill' Tilden (1898-1953), the winner at Wimbledon in 1920, 1922, 1930 and in the doubles in 1927 with T. Hunter. From 1920-26 Tilden did not lose a single match. In 1931 he formed a professional group called 'Tilden's Circus'. Other legendary players include the famous Fr. musketeers: J. Borotra, the 'Flying Basque' (1898-1994), H. Cochet (1901-87), J. Brugnon (1895-1978), R. Lacoste (1905-96). The American champion of Wimbledon J. Kramer (b. 1921) became famous after 1947, when he

formed 'Kramer's Circus', a group of professional players similar to that of Tilden. Among leading world tennis players have always been those from Great Britain (until 1945), the USA, Australia, and France (since the 1920s), with other nations represented by such names as J. Drobny and I. Lendl (Checho-slovakia), M. Santana (Spain), A. Metreweli (USSR), G. Villas (Argentina), B. Borg (Sweden), I. Nastase (Romania), T. Ocker (Holland), R. Ramirez (Mexico), B. Becker (Germany) and others.

Lawn tennis was played at the Ol.G. in 1896-1924, was later discontinued as a result of a disagreement between the ILTF and IOC on the issue of amateurship, and returned to the Ol.G. in 1988 in Seoul.

Women's lawn tennis has always been equally popular, although it entered the Ol.G. in 1900, 4 years later than men's. Similar to men's tennis it was excluded from the Ol.G. between 1924 and 1988. The most outstanding player in history was S. Lenglen (France, 1899-1938), a 15-time winner at Wimbledon incl. 6 singles titles, who lost only one game in her entire career (US championships in 1921 with M. Mallory). She introduced the men's style of hitting the ball into women's tennis and became the first woman to play tennis professionally. She was equalled by the American H. Wills Moody (b. 1905), a 12-time winner at Wimbledon, incl. 9 singles titles in the years 1924-38. At the beginning of the 1970s the American B.J. King launched a feminist action called the 'Battle of the Sexes'. She claimed that while women's tennis was in no way inferior to men's, the mass media discriminated against women and devoted much more attention to the men. Challenged by a 57-yr.-old B. Riggs, who claimed that even at his age he would not let a younger woman win a match, she defeated him in full view of a crowd of 30,472 at the stadium and 50 million TV viewers. This had a direct impact on raising the status of women's professional tennis, which has ever since been recognized by the media, owing much to other great individuals of women's tennis, incl. American C. Evert, Czech-born Americans M. Navratilova and M. Hingis, Argentina's G. Sabatini, Germany's S. Graf, American J. Capriatti or the Williams sisters.

P. Albaran, H. Cochet, *Histoire du tennis*, 1960; W. Baddeley, *Lawn Tennis*, 1895; J. Brown, *Tennis. Steps to Success*, 1995; E. Gologor, *Psychodynamic Tennis. You, Your Opponent and Other Obstacles to Perfection*, 1979; R. Lardner, *The Underhanded Serve, or How To Play Dirty Tennis*, 1968; S. Mead, *How To Succeed In Tennis Without Really Trying*, 1977; E.B. Noel, J.O.M. Clark, *A History of Tennis*, vol. 1-2, 1902; P. Metzler, *Advanced Tennis*, 1972; S. Palfrey, *Tennis For Anyone!*, 1971; S. Ramo, *Extraordinaery Tennis For Ordinary Player*, 1970; W.F. Talbert, B.S. Old, *The Game of Singles in Tennis*, 1962; W.T. Tilden, B. Destremeau, *Tout le tennis*, 1955.

L

WORLD SPORTS ENCYCLOPEDIA

LAXOA, a var. of >PELOTA VASCA.

LAYADORES, a Span. and Basq. form of competition in digging in the ground using *layas* – characteristic 2-pronged pitchforks. A *laya* looks much like the small letter 'h', where the 2 tines are driven into the ground by pressing on the crosspiece while holding on to the handle above. The tines of a laya, before being buried in the ground, may reach up to the participant's knees. There are several construction types: the tines may be straight and the handle bent forwards at a gentle angle; or the tines themselves may be slightly curved, much like in a regular pitchfork. The handle usu. has a knob at the end for better grip. The whole laya is about 75-80cm long. Each competitor has 2 layas, one under each foot. He buries them in the ground alternately, stepping hard on them to loosen the ground, and moving forward as if on stilts by the length of the ground he has thus loosened. For the best diggers, one step means loosening the ground along a stretch of about 25cm. In the past, layadores was an important element of peasant culture, at the same time improving the quality of fieldwork through play. The introduction of machines has turned layadores into a folk sport devoid of its former practical application.
R. Aguirre, 'Layadores', GHJD, 1989, II, 37-9; C. Moreno Palos, 'Layadores', JYTE, 1992, 287.

LAZU, also *ladu*, Span. *lazo*, a var. of lasso used by the Araucanian (Mapuche) Indians of Chile: a length of rope with a loop at the end used for throwing at a victim and hog-tying it from a distance. The earliest known Araucana lazus were finger thick and made of climbers; later, old men wove them out of horse hair and thin straps of leather. According to observations made by Eng.-speaking ethnographers visiting Chile, lazus were 13-18m long. They were also used for all kinds of displays, like spinning them above one's head at great speed. The Araucanas started learning how to use the lazu as boys. An important stage in the development of the lazu came after the Spanish brought horses to S.America, as the lazu could be used on horseback (which, incidentally, proved quite troublesome for the Araucana's Eur. enemies). Span. chronicles of the conquista period include reports of how Span. soldiers were 'hog-tied' with lazus. Lazus were also used to catch animals during pasturage. See also >LASSOING.
O. Plath, 'Lazu', JYDLCH, 1946, 27-8.

LE LONGUE, see >JEU PROVENÇAL.

LEAP THE BULLOCKS, also called *loup the bullocks* and *leap the long mare*, see >LEAPFROG.

LEAPFROG, a type of competition which, according to R. Trześniewski's description, involves a number of 5- to 6-member teams. 7-10 steps in front of each team there is the so-called 'frog' (or sometimes 'ram'), i.e. a player who bends over and rests his hands on his knees. The first jumper of each team takes a running start and leaps over the 'frog' springing from the ground and resting his hands on the frog's shoulder blades, so that he straddles the frog as he goes over. All the players of a team leap over one another successively in the same manner. The team whose players are the first to complete their round of jumps are declared the winners. In order to prolong a leapfrog competition the teams may be stationed alongside a circle so that the leaps may be continued without any limitation in their number but within a limited field. The teams decide on the number of circumferences to be covered to constitute a full round of the game. Almost identical types of leapfrog competitions are known in all Eur. educational systems, the differences usu. being the depth of the incline, the place where the frog's or the jumper's hands are put (e.g. on the buttocks instead of the shoulder blades; in some versions the frog is squatting with his head bowed). In Denmark leapfrog is called *springe buk* – jumping over the buck. Similarly to the Pol. *baranie skoki* (rams' jumps), here one of the players acts as the 'buck' (or 'ram'), i.e. he bends over at the waist. The second player takes a running start and jumps over the buck resting his hands on the buck's back, runs a further 3m and then assumes the buck's position himself. If the player who is to act as buck is tall he may rest his hands on his ankles. In the Eng.-speaking world the game is usu. called leapfrog. If there are additional, more difficult elements introduced into the game, it is called differently to reflect the type of jumping techniques or of competition rules. A leap-

frog var. in which one foot is added to the short run distance before each leap is called *foot and over* (meaning one foot more). A.B. Gomme describes leapfrog and *loup the bullocks* in the following way:

> One boy stoops down sideways, with his head bent towards his body, as low as possible. This is called 'Tucking in your Tuppeny'. Another boy takes a flying leap over the 'frog', placing his hands on his back to help himself over. He then proceeds to a distance of some four or five yards, and, in his turn, stoops in the same manner as the first boy, as another frog. A third boy then leaps first over frog no. 1, and then over frog no. 2, taking his place as frog no. 3, at about the same distance onwards. Any number of boys may play in the game. After the last player has taken his leap over all the frogs successively, frog no. 1 has his turn and leaps over his companions, taking his place as the last in the line of frogs. Then no. 2 follows suit, and so on, the whole line of players in course of time covering a good distance.
> [GOMME, I, 327-8]

In 19th-cent. London boys knew a type of leapfrog whereby the 'frog' stood with his side rather than his back towards the jumpers. After the first series of jumps someone would cry, 'Foot it!' meaning simply 'stop'. The frog would then turn his outside foot 90° from the direction from which the jumpers came. In this way he would mark a distance of 1ft., where he moved his feet, and thus was 1ft. farther away from the original starting line. The last jumper would once again shout, 'Foot it!' and the players would go on like that until only one remained (the other ones being eliminated after unsuccessful attempts). Another form of leapfrog consists not in all players leaping over one 'frog' but in all players jumping over one another. Here the rule is that the players stop and bend over at a distance of 2-4 steps between players. The only one who does not have to bend is the last player who then takes a short run and jumps over all the bending players until he reaches the last one in the row. Then he bends over and the first of the 'frogs' does the same. In this way the row of players 'travels' forward. In the Eng.-speaking world this type of leapfrog is called *leap the bullocks* or *loup the bullocks* in Scotland or leap the long mare in Cornwall. Different types of leapfrog games with different numbers of steps before a jump or different ways of springing from the ground are called on the Brit. Isles *kicking the brogue, scuddieloof, catskip, hitch steppin'*, Otho and *lang-spang*, depending on the area. In Ireland, a similar game ad-

ditionally employing a stool placed on the frog's back is called *Riding Father Doud*. A very specific type of leapfrog known as *accroshay* (an apparently meaningless name, though possibly Pig Latin for 'across') was developed in Cornwall. One of the players bends over as in regular leapfrog and the remaining players place small objects such as pens, boxes, caps, etc. on his back. Therefore, each consecutive jumper finds it increasingly difficult to jump over such a laden frog. A jumper who makes any of the objects fall is eliminated. The one who is the most delicate and does not knock any of the objects down is declared the winner.
A.B. Gomme, 'Loup the Bullocks', TGESI, 1894, I, 351; J. Møller, 'Springe buk', GID, 1997, 3, 14; R. Trześniewski, 'Barani skok', ZIGR, 1995, 342-3.

LÈCHE-POÊLE, a trad. Fr. game where the participants use their mouths or noses to detach coins 'glued' with fat to frying pans suspended above their heads so that they have to jump up to reach them. A similar game is known as 'lick the pan' in England, and >LIPAT AR GLEURC'H in Brittany.

LEFKAWELLUN, Span. *carreras a caballo*, a var. of horse racing of Araucanian (Mapuche, Pehuenche, Huilliches) Chilean Indians. The sport developed after Europeans introduced horses into S.America. S.Amer. Indians quickly proved excellent riders (just like their N.Amer. counterparts), often surpassing their Eur. teachers. One outstanding lefkawellun rider was chief Lautaro. The Indians showed off their skills not only in combat but also during family or religious festivals. Initially, lefkawellun races may have been run with or without saddles. Later, the first primitive Indian saddles were made by the Mapuchos of blankets covered with sheep skins (*pellones*). Leather straps connected the saddle to the rest of the harness, but without the buckles and pins found in Eur. saddles. The saddle was permanently connected to the bridle, and only rarely removed from the horse's back, which meant that one did not need to prepare before riding (this was important in the period of guerilla fighting against the Europeans). The reins were made of untanned leather. The triangular stirrups were made of flexible twigs, usu. wild linden (*colihue* – Chusquea culeu).
A lefkawellun race was preceded by a magical ritual which was supposed to bring good luck: the horse was rubbed with pieces of leather of other animals,

Layadores.

or feathers of fast-flying birds to fill its body with their skills. At the starting line, earth dug from cemeteries or the fat of predators was placed (usu. of 'lions' – that was the name the Spanish applied to all the great cats they encountered in S.America) so that cemetery or animal spirits would disturb the opponents' horses. Pregnant women were not allowed to observe this ritual so that those evil spirits would not pass into their offspring. As opposed to the main var. of lefkawellun, run along a circular course, races along straight courses were known as *lefun*. Today it is practiced without harness on straight tracks of 150-500m as part of national and rural feasts.
O. Plath, 'Lefkawellun', JYDLCH, 1946, 26-7.

LEFTING, see >LYFTESTEN.

LEIBRINGEN, [Ger. *Leib* – belly + *Ringen* – wrestling], a simple Swiss wrestling style where the main technique is to push one's stomach against the opponent.

LEIKFANG, a trad. var. of hand-to-hand combat in Iceland [Icel. *leika* – play with something + *fang* – wrestling]. The tradition dates back to the times of the Viking migration to Iceland in the Middle Ages. Leikfang was different from the major, rather brutal var. of Icel. wrestling, esp. >ILLSKUFANG, in being more 'gentle' and in the more amicable approach of the participants to each other. The Heiöarviga saga (c.1200) describes how the techniques were constrained – e.g. using weapons was not allowed. Even so, fatalities and injuries were quite common, which is attested by the Jónsbók book of laws (1281), where a separate article was devoted to leifkang, saying that 'whoever participates in a friendly fight of leikfang, does so at his own responsibility'.
The rules, reconstructed on the basis of the Heiöarviga saga, were as follows: 1) each wrestler could take a hold on any part of the opponent's body; 2) all holds were legal; 3) in the most common hold, the wrestler took a hold with his arms on the upper part of the opponent's body – the saga calls this hold *axlatök*, or 'axe hold'; the idea was to knock the opponent over to his back (which was, in turn, called *hryggspena* – 'reaching the ground with one's back'); 4) it was also legal to knock the opponent over with a twist of the body, usu. accompanied by a trip or a barge. Touching the ground with any part of one's body other than the feet was tantamount to losing the fight. Violent movements aimed at overturning the opponent were known as brögó (Sing. *bragó*). A var. of leikfang where holds on the opponent's trousers were allowed was called >BUXNATÖK, which was the predecessor of >GLÍMA, a wrestling style popular since the end of the Middle Ages.
T. Einarsson, 'Sportive Wrestling in Iceland Sagas and Oldest Code of Icelandic Laws in the XIIth Century', PISHPES, 1991, ed. R. Renson, T. Gonzalez Aja et al., 1993; Consultant: Jón M. Ivarsson.

LEISURE SKIING, different var. of >SKIING, where the objective is not achieving professional-level results, but active recreation, psycho-physical regeneration, contact with nature, or simply achieving satisfaction stemming from one's own fitness. Cross-country leisure skiing is practically equivalent to ski tourism and ski hiking. Wintertime leisure skiing, both cross-country and alpine, is extremely popular in the northern and western countries. Its popularity soared after F. Nansen's (1861-1930) ski crossing of Greenland described in his book *På ski over Grønland*. This is how he advocated the need to ski in general:

Can you imagine anything more charming than racing down tree-lined slopes when the winter air and fir twigs brush past your face, and the sight, mind and muscles are set to avoid every danger [...]. At such times, man is as if united with the skis and nature.

As professional skiing developed, so did leisure skiing. Skiers would make solo or group trips. Between 1890 and 1914, esp. popular was ski mountain climbing along easier slopes. With time, the trips of leisure skiers lost their intimate character as leisure skiing, esp. downhill, grew more and more popular when equipment began to be manufactured on an industrial scale. The gear was constantly improved, and so were skiing techniques. When cable railways and ski-lifts appeared, Alpine leisure skiing became a pastime devoid of much physical effort, because the skiers did not have to climb the mountain any more before racing downhill. The first ski-lift, powered by a horse gear, was built in Pilnitz, Germany, in 1900. In 1952, a year considered to have been the turning point in the history of winter leisure skiing, there were 152 ski-lifts and 16 chair-lifts in Austria alone. Today, there are several thousand ski-lifts of various types in the Alps. Downhill skiing has become the most popular form of winter leisure skiing. The growing demand for equipment has led to the growth of a whole industry, which in turn has boosted the interest in leisure skiing through its many advertising campaigns. Frequently, names of famous professional skiers are used in such campaigns, so that the growth of leisure skiing depends closely on the development of professional skiing. To make leisure skiing independent of weather conditions, and possible in areas other than mountains, more and more artificial PVC slopes are being built around the world.
Leisure skiing is growing in Europe, N.America, and some Asian countries, such as Korea and Japan. The main centers are located in the Alps (Innsbruck, Cortina d'Ampezzo, Albertville), the Rockies (Denver, Colorado in the US, and Calgary in Canada), and elsewhere.

LEON WOW, a Thai var. of kite flying. The first records of leon wow date back to the 13th cent., the period of the Sukhotai kingdom. Leon wow gained popularity in the 19th cent., during the reign of King Rama IV (1851-68) who issued a special edict allowing leon wow shows near the royal palace in Bangkok. The main type of kites used in leon wow are those used for displays and >KITE FIGHTING, known as *pak-pao* and *chula*, respectively. The pakpao kites represent the male gender, while the chula – the female. Today, displays and fights are held on many occasions, esp. in March and April, in Sanam Luang square near the Temple of the Emerald Buddha in Bangkok.
The Internet: http://amazingthailand.siamu.ac.th/specialinterest/traditionalthaisports.htm

LET HUND, Dan. for 'light dog'. A Dan. touch-chasing game where one can avoid being caught by dropping to the ground. If a player is patted by the chaser before touching the ground with a part of his body other than the feet, he then helps the chaser. However, the chaser must first pick him up of the ground. The game is used in physical education classes for younger children.
J. Møller, 'Let hund', GID, 1997, 2.

LEUO, a trad. ball game formerly popular in Georgia. It involved snatching the ball from the opponent's hands using one's hands or feet. In the past, leuo matches were played between whole villages.

LEVANTAMIENTO DEL ARADO, Span. for 'lifting the plough', a folk strength contest in the Canary Islands. A heavy plough with a long wooden shaft is placed on the ground, and a strongman takes a hold on it to lift the plough into a vertical position. During the operation, the end of the shaft may be stuck into the ground, making it easier to achieve the feat.

LEVANTAMIENTO DE PIEDRA, also *levantador de piedra*, see >ARRIJASOKETA.

LEVENDE BOLD, see >HALVRAADDEN.

LEVER DE LA BANNIÈRE, the Fr. name for a Bret. contest of strength, where the objective was to raise or lower a long pole with a church banner or, sometimes, a cross on it. In the past, the game was esp. popular in the Léon district of Brittany. To win, one had to take a hold on the pole as close to the end as possible, and hold it so as to counteract the leverage. To hold a heavy banner or cross by the end and keep it horizontal, as close to the ground as possible, was considered to be the greatest achievement. Lever de la bannière shows often took place during services, which led to opposition from clergy. This is how the rector of Commana described lever de la bannière, and the resulting conflicts in the parish in 1777:

Already when the banners and crosses are still in front of the church, at the very beginning of the procession, young boys swarm around them and each one wants to carry something. They quarrel and push, or even fight, and all this in the face of the Sacred Sacrament carried in the procession. To gain more freedom in what they are planning to do, the youths move as far away as possible from the ministers, and these often lose them from sight. Then the youths debate, grinning from ear to ear, and getting ready for the crosses and banners; they incline them, or even allow them to fall to the ground, causing shouts of disrespect. The priests are forced to leave their places to prevent the din. That is what processions look like in the parishes of Commana and Saint-Sauveur, and if one knows nothing of the custom, he may think them folk festivals. The glory of those who carry the banners and crosses is added to by their weight when they are inclined in the agreed manner. That is why there are no poles for crosses or banners heavy and large enough to match the fun of those who carry them. Somebody has even noticed [...] that they put stones between the linens of the banners to make them heavier [...]. Respected citizens deplore this, and the local authorities have forbidden those practices in their decisions of the 26th of May and 17th of August of last year. They have appointed and obliged one of the members of the parish committee to appeal even to the authority of the Parliament, should this prove necessary, to stop all this.

[Quotation after: H. Eichberg, 'Rising Cross in Brittany', 'Revolution of Body Culture? Traditional Games on the Way from Modernization to «Postmodernity»', LJP, 1998, 202-3]

LEVER DE LA PERCHE, the Fr. name for a Bret. contest of strength where a heavy, long pole was lifted and lowered. The contestant who was able to manipulate the pole in the proscribed way was declared the winner. He was supposed to take a hold on the pole as close to the end as possible, counteracting the leverage; see >SEVEL AR BERCHENN.

LIAN ACROBATICS, ancient Chin. acrobatic feats performed on the brim of a large pot called a lian, a vessel holding large quantities of alcohol prepared for huge feasts attended by many guests. Most preserved Chin. sculptures depict 2 performing acrobats. However, a sculpture found in Qilibe in the Luoyang region depicts 3 such acrobats. The acrobats performed handstands on the brim of a lian and moved along the brim combining into various configurations with their partner.
J.-P. Desroches, 'The Human Body and its Metamorphoses. Acrobatics'. YOSICH, 1999, 32.

LIGHT GYMNASTICS, a system developed by an Amer. pedagogue, D. Lewis (1823-88), and introduced in elementary schools in Boston in 1853. In 1861, Lewis opened the Normal Institute for Physical Education that popularized light gymnastics. The system as such has not stood the test of time, but its influence is visible in a number of other systems, exercises, and games employed in Amer. schools. It was also imitated in PE classes in Japan (>KEI-TAISO).

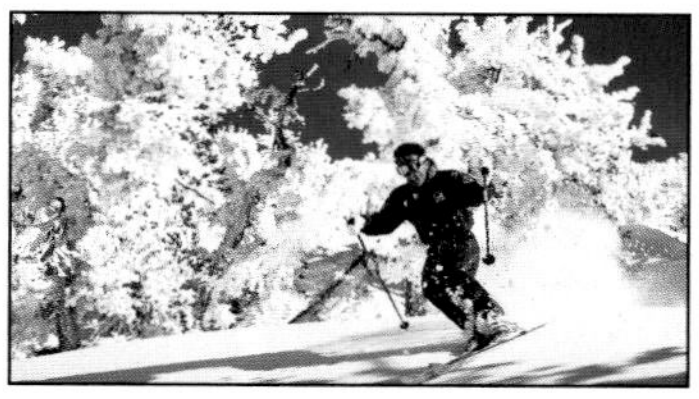

Leisure skiing.

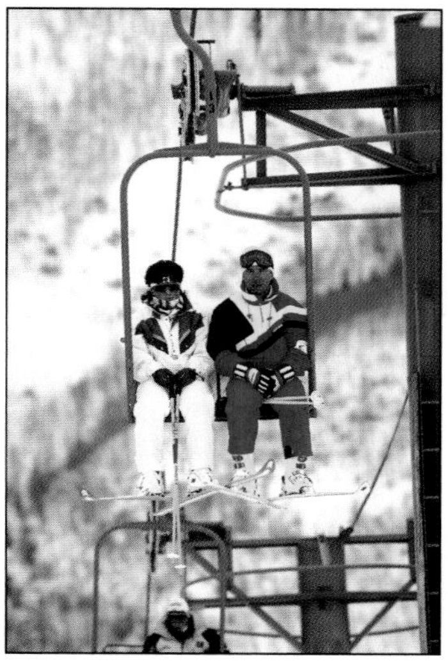

A double chair lift takes skiers to the top of the slope. The first lift, built over 100 years ago, was powered by a horse gear.

Lian acrobatics.

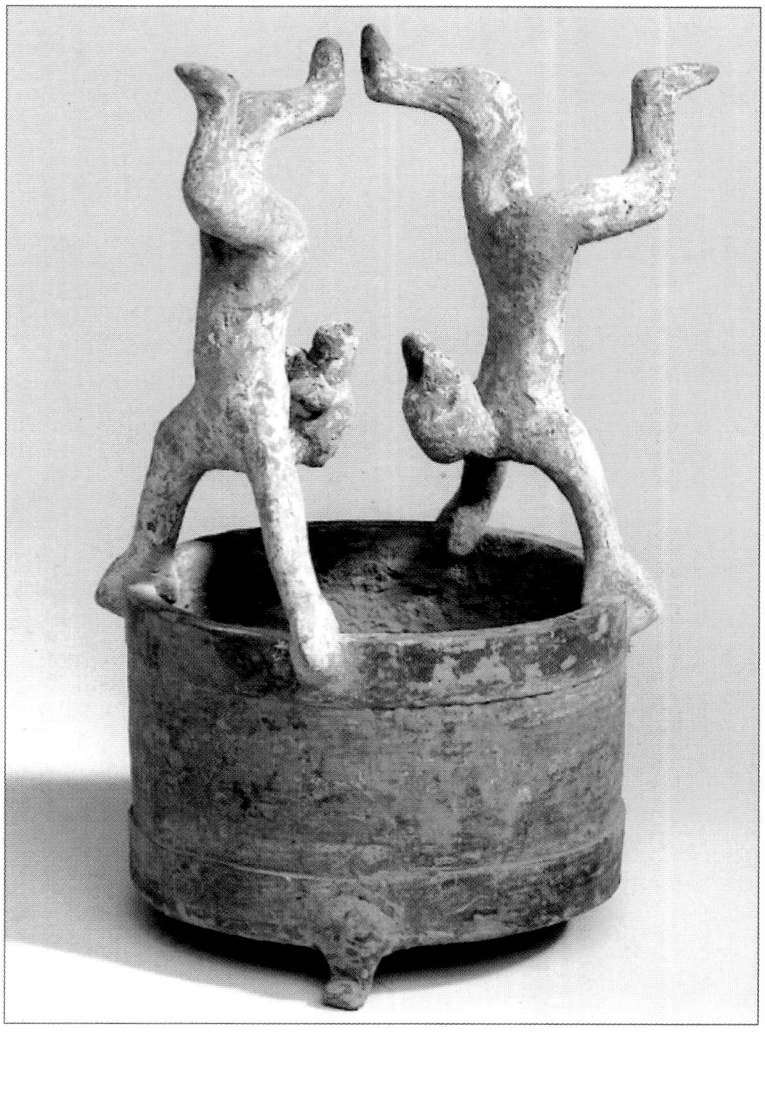

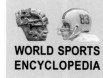

L

WORLD SPORTS ENCYCLOPEDIA

Lokotx edo sokor apostua.

LIJFVAT, a wrestling style practiced among the Boers in S.Africa. In some regions, also known as *neergooi*.

LIMBO, a trad. S.Amer. sport similar to Hindu >KA-BADDI. Bouts are carried out to the accompaniment of music.

LIMPOTTER, Dan. for 'tentacles', a game where the participants are caught by a 'witch' (cf. >HEKS). Several areas are drawn on the ground where the witch may catch the players, each with enough space for one person. A player, once caught, may be rescued by another by running up to him and touching him. However, there is a risk that the 'rescuer' will be caught himself by stepping on the 'tentacles' (the catching area) and being trapped.
J. Møller, 'Limpotter', GID, 1997, 2, 70.

LIMPY COLEY, a game formerly played in County Antrim, N.Ireland. The rules have not been preserved. Perhaps it may have been associated with >HURLING, the tradition of which is derived from the old Ir. hero Cuchulain, the main character of the Irish national epic *Tain bó Cuailnge* – the Eng. rendering of Cuchulain is Coley or Cooley.

LINAO, also *inao*, a no-holds-barred aboriginal ball game played by the Mapuche-Huilliche in Chile involving 2 teams (see >AMERICAN FOOTBALL and >RUGBY). The names mean 'to fight with a ball' and 'to persue someone running', respectively [*lingh* (to fight); *nahl* (ball); *inar* (to follow)]. Due to the game's inherent all-out violence – probably inspired by the not inconsiderable sums once wagered – it was considered good preparation for battle. In order to make the grade, players had to be skilled at avoiding altogether or minimizing the damage wrought by flying fists, head butts, and general pushing and shoving. The ball, 15cm in diameter, was made of such edible types of algae as *cochayuyo* (Durvillea utilissima) and *luche* (Ulva lactuca) or of seaweed, covered with woolen cloth or leather, or of wood or rags of minor size. The traditional field was usu. a level rectangular spread of grass, approx. 60x120m, in the middle of which was situated a central, neutral field, 5m wide and parallel to the short lines of the field, within which goal-lines of 2-6m were placed, delimited by 2 slight twigs, tightly fastened. In order to limit injuries resulting from collisions with them, these twigs were padded with grass. The teams'

capitanes threw lots (see >AWARKUDEN and >KE-CHUKAWE) to determine which directions each team would play; once this matter was settled, each team played its side of the field without changing direction midway through a game, as is common in many sports. There were 11 players per side, the swiftest in front, the nimblest in the center and the most stalwart taking up the rear to assist and defend the others. A thrower from one of the teams, elected by a referee (*rannieve*), stood at centerfield and began the game by throwing the ball up with all his might. As it came down, within the neutral area, the other players, from both teams, starting from their respective positions on the field, would rush toward the center to try to catch the ball before it hit the ground. Whoever got there first and managed to wrest possession of the ball from the others, would then tuck it under his left armpit and bolt toward the goal, trying to avoid all opponents who hampered his progress and sought, through various means, to relieve him of the ball. Knee-gutting, tripping, the dealing ferocious blows to incapacitate the opponent, and full-contact grappling was all standard procedure. If the ball carrier felt he was about to be overwhelmed by defenders, he could seek momentary refuge in the neutral area in the middle of the field, where his opponents were not allowed to touch him and he could pass the ball to a teammate. The aim of the ball carrier was to reach and pass through his team's goal line with ball and body, on top of which he would have to separate himself from and throw down the goalkeeper (*tekuto*), who was usu. one of the most formidable players in terms of size, strength and skill. When the ball carrier attempted to hit the ball toward the goal line, several opponents positioned behind the goalkeeper would try to obstruct the entrance of the ball. If they caught the ball in midair, the point was annulled; even though it had passed between the goal posts, it had not touched the ground. Normally only a few *entui* or *rayas* (points) were scored due to the great capacity of the defenders. The game often lasted for as long as 6 hours of agitated and quick running in all directions of the field until participants were utterly spent (Cf. >PILLMATUN). An exhibition match held in Castro (Insel Chiloé) in 1983 lasted only 8 minutes each side; apparently latter-day practitioners are no match for the extraordinary physical resistance of their progenitors. In the past there were as many as 100 barefoot players covered only with leggings (*chiripas*). The game was extremely rough. Many spectators were on hand at important matches to lay bets and encourage the players with enthusiasm. During their physical preparation they practiced running with feints and sudden changes of direction. A good 2 weeks prior to a match, players were subjected to a strict regimen of fasting and chastity, and began taking ice-cold waterfalls baths (*traitraiko*) each morning. They engaged in secret rites under the guidance of a shaman woman (*machi*) to bewitch the ball and fortify the players. They rubbed their bodies with ointment (*fletar*) of sea-wolf oil (*lame* = lobo marino; Otaria marina), and with blood and marrow of an enchanted calf (*kamahueto*). Thus the bodies of the players remained anesthetized against violent blows and fatigue (see >YA-NOMAMO DUELS). The sea-wolf oil also shielded them from the cold and allowed them to slip out of an opponent's grip. Calves' horns were buried in the field near the goal line to stop the ball of the adversary. Before a match a team's shaman would chant *romanceo* songs to cast a spell on the ball and poured purified water over the players to increase their vigor. Normally the teams represented neighboring communities or small villages. One village, located in the South-East of Ancud on the Great Island of Chiloé, still bears the name Linao. The earliest mention of linao dates back to 1870. Along with other sporting games of the Mapuche, it was incl. in the program of the First National Olympic Games of Santiago, Chile in 1909. See also >CHUECA.
L. Matus Zapata, 'Juegos y ejercisios fisicos de los antiquos araucanos', BMNCH, 1920; C. López von Vriessen, 'Juegos Aborigenes de Chile, contribución a una alternativa didáctica en la Educación Fisica latinoamericana', Perspectiva Educacional, 1920.

LIPAT AR BILIG, see >LIPAT AR GLEURC'H.

LIPAT AR GLEURC'H, also *lipar ar bilig*, Fr. >LÈCHE POÊLE. A trad. Bret. game where a frying pan, smeared with fat, is suspended above the heads of the participants so that they can only reach it by

jumping up. Coins are 'glued' to the thick layer of the fat. The objective of the game is to jump up to the pan and remove a coin with one's mouth or nose (the participants' hands are tied behind their backs). In England, a similar game is known as 'lick the pan'.
L. Peru, 'La tradition populaire de jeux de plein air en Bretagne', LJP, 1998.

LISHYNYI MIATCH, a game involving 2 balls and played by 2 teams of 5. The playing field is a 40x20 step rectangle which is further divided into 3 zones. The 2 end zones are 15 steps deep and the middle zone is 10 steps long. The end zones are called 'houses' and the middle one the 'field'. The game starts with 2 players (1 from each team) sending a football towards the opposing team's home. The ball may be returned with any part of the body both when flying, rolling or bouncing off the ground. The object of the game is to skillfully manipulate the balls so that both of them end up on the opposing team's side at the same time, which is worth 1pt. The game continues until one of the teams has scored 20pts.
I.N. Tchkhannikov, 'Lishynyi miatch', GIZ, 1953, 54-5.

LITHOBOLIA, [Gk. *lithos* – stone + *bolia* – throwing; analogous to >DYSCOBOLIA]. Ancient Gk. stone throwing. A natural form of rivalry practiced outside of Ol.G. It was also used as physical exercise in Gk. gymnasions.

LIVTAG, [Swed. *liv* – life, meaning the vital part of one's body, where the spine is + *tag* – hold], a folk wrestling style formerly known in the whole of Sweden but today practiced only in Scania, Småland, Dalarna and Jämtland; the first region from which livtag disappeared was the area of Lake Mälaren. There are also regional names applied to livtag, deriving from the characteristic holds: >RYGGTAG ('back hold'), *ryggkast* ('back throw'), also *röggtaj* and *röggtag* in dialectal variations. The fight starts in an upright position, with the wrestlers taking a characteristic hold on each other: the right arm is placed on the opponent's shoulder so that one's elbow is at his neck height, with the hand in the middle of his back, while the left arm is placed under his armpit, and the hands are clasped on the rival's back. In some areas, the wrestlers bent their knees slightly, which was called *tjuvben* ('thief legs') or *krokben* ('crooked legs'). There is some controversy regarding this in Swed. ethnology, but it cannot be resolved due to the disappearance of many forms of livtag. Some researchers believe that bending one's knees was only allowed after special agreement between the wrestlers, and was considered a less 'honorable' form, treated as a 'witch trick' (*käringknep*). Å. Einarsson, a researcher of Scandinavian wrestling styles, thinks that any forms of tricks were banned from this form of wrestling.
After taking hold on each other, the wrestlers made a number of swings back and forth. The result was decided by the strength of the hold, and resisting the pull forward. Livtag was different from other forms of wrestling in that it did not allow releasing the hold, while, for instance, classical wrestling, seemingly similar, used the position only as the starting position, after which the fighters were allowed to use other holds. Some older descriptions say that the fight could only start after it was ascertained that the wrestlers had taken a strong enough hold on each other, which they had to let each other know. So, livtag was, like many other types of Swed. wrestling, 'one-hold' wrestling. The hold itself, along with the style, were called by various dialectal names, such as >BRYGGAS, >BRÖGGAS, >BRÖKKAS >BRÖTAS or >BRÅTAS. All of the above words are dialectal var. of the word *bryta* – 'to break'. On the other hand, none of them uses the Swed. word for wrestling – *brottning*. The Dan. equivalent of livtag is called by the same name, while the Fin. one is known as >RINTAPAINI.
M. Hellspong, 'Brottning som folklig lek, paragraph Livtag', RIG, 1991, 4; M. Hellspong, 'Livtag', Den folkliga idrotten, 2000, 17-20.

LOBBER, an old Eng. game using a peg about 3in. (7.6cm) long, or, in more modern times, a small hard ball. Two holes were made in the surface of the pitch, about 15-20 steps apart (2 stones could also be used), serving as targets. Two teams participated, each with 3-4 players, plus the 'lobber' himself. The lobber threw the peg or ball, aiming at 1 of the holes or stones. In front of it, a batsman was positioned, who was supposed to hit the peg or ball with his bat (or hand, in more primitive versions of the game). A round went on until all players were eliminated as a result of their unsuccessful efforts (or successful efforts of the opponents). So, if the lobber hit the hole or stone, the batsman was put out of play, and replaced by the next player in his team, and so on. One of the requirements of the game was for 2 defenders to swap positions during the throw but it is not clear whether this applied to 2 specifically designated players or to the batsman as well. If the throw was performed at the moment of the swap, a player was eliminated but it is not known which one and in favor of which team – was this considered to be an error of the defending team (e.g. 'premature run') or the lobber (e.g. an excessively delayed throw after a feint, which misled the runners)? It is not clear, either, who intercepted the ball in the air to eliminate the batsman, and how the lobber was put out of play. The preserving rules suggest that the outfield team designated 1 permanent lobber who was allowed to continue throwing even if he failed to perform good throws, so that a round went on until the defending team were all out. Or perhaps the lobber was eliminated, ending the round for the fielding team. There was also a var. of the game where the lobbers of the opposite teams threw alternately at targets located at opposite ends of the pitch.

A.B. Gomme, 'Lobber', TGESI, 1984, I, 331.

LOCHBALL, [Ger. *Loch* – hole + *Ball* – ball], also *Steht Allee*, a Ger. ball game where the ball was thrown into a row of holes dug in the ground. The rules followed those of Dan. >BOLD I HUL. A similar Pol. game is known as *świnka* or >CZOROMAJ.

LOCTA, [Span. dialectal *locta*, Span. *lucha* – hand--to-hand combat, incl. wrestling], a Span. type of hand-to-hand combat practiced in the province of Galicia by young peasant women. There are no details in the available sources.

C. Moreno Palos, 'Otras luchas rituales', JYTE, 1992.

L'ODJO, see >FA KOR.

LØFT STEN, see >STENLØFTING.

LÖFTESTEN, see >LYFTESTEN.

LOG RACING, one of the events of >BIRLING, the sport of Amer. and Can. lumberjacks.

LOG ROLLING, one of the events of >BIRLING, the sport of Amer. and Can. lumberjacks.

LOG RUNNING, also *log racing*. A trad. form of competition popular among S.Amer. Indians, esp. the Timbira and Krahow tribes of central Brazil. During the rainy season men and women compete in carrying tree trunks over a distance of 5-12km. The weight of the trunks depends on the age and sex, e.g. adult men usu. carry trunks up to 100kg. The races are held annually as a relay event: teams carrying the trunks change every 100-150m with new carriers replacing the exhausted ones. The sport is also treated as a ritual of initiation for youngsters aspiring to adulthood. Membership of a relay team is for life. The ultimate goal of the event is not the victory itself, but developing team spirit. The Timbir culture focuses not on the success of an individual, but rather on the idea of collective action and the competition between teams. An orig. var. of log running has developed among the Ge tribe, where all the participants form a relay team and pass trunks weighing up to 90kg among themselves.

LOGGATS, an old Eng. game involving rolling or throwing short, round tree stumps ('loggats'). In some regions of England, they were used to shake trees when the fruit was impossible to reach from a ladder. In the sporting var., the stumps were thrown at a stick dug into the ground. The player whose stump landed closest to the stick or overturned it was declared the winner. In the times of Henry VIII, the game was placed on the list of banned sports.

TGESI, I, 332; STRUTT, VII, 239.

LOITA, LA, plur. *loitas*, a Span. folk style of wrestling, with rules similar to those of Port. >GALHOFA, formerly practiced in Galicia. The word 'loita' is a dialectal var. of Span. *lucha* – wrestling. Loita games usu. took place in Aug., as a form of entertainment accompanying the flax harvest. The owners of larger farms were natural sponsors of the fights, funding small prizes. Loita fights are not practiced any more.

W. Baxter, 'Les luttes traditionnelles a traverse de monde', LJP, 1998, 85; R. Garcia Serrano, 'Loita', JDTE, 1974, 89-90.

LOKOTX EDO SOKOR APOSTUA, Basq. for 'collecting maize into a basket'. The Span. equivalent of this Basq. game is known as *lokotxas* or *recogida de mazorcas* [Span. *recogida* – collection + *mazorca* – cob]. The participants are supposed to collect as many maize cobs as they can while running. The cobs, whose number depends on the local tradition, are placed in a row, 1.25m apart. There may be 25 cobs in 1 row, 50 cobs in 2 rows, or 75 in three. A participant may only pick up one cob, and has to return with it to the starting line, place it in the basket and only then return for the next one, further away. The participant who succeeds in collecting all the cobs within the shortest time wins. The baskets look much like hot-air balloon baskets but they are smaller, 50-60cm across and high. The shapes depend on local tradition – sometimes the baskets are shaped like simple cylinders, but they may also look like upside-down bells.

R. Aguirre, 'Lokotx edo sokor apostua. Lokotxas', GHJD, 1989, III, 96-97; C. Moreno Palos, 'Recogida de mazorcas', JYTE, 1992, 39.

LOLKAMA, see >KEATSEN.

LONCOQUILQUIL, Span. *porra*, *macana*, or *maza*, a type of club used by S.Amer. Indians, esp. in modern Chile; also, a type of exercise and style of fighting. The loncoquilquil was a weapon used in combat and hunting, with many local var. It was improved by adding some Span. elements after the arrival of Europeans. The 16th-cent. Span. writer Alonso de Góngora Marmolejo claimed that the loncoquilquil was 'as long as a cavalry lance but where the head should be, it is bent like an elbow. The Indians can hit very hard with them'. One type of loncoquilquil was the *macana* club, wooden, with a stone at the end; the *porra* was a shorter type; while the *maza* was made of *duro enebro* (juniper tree). One of Chile's first Span. governors, Pedro de Valdivia, was captured by Indian forces during a skirmish and killed with a loncoquilquil at Tucapel. Today it is no longer in use.

M. Manquilef, 'Comentarios del Pueblo AraucanoII. La Gimnasia Nacional', *Revista de Folklore Chileno*, 1914, vol. 4; O. Plath, 'Loncoquilquil', JYDLCH, 1946, 30-31.

LONCOTUN, Span. *forcejeo* (or *forejear*) *cogiendose de los cabellos*, a wrestling style formerly cultivated by Chilean Indians. The object was to throw the opponent to the ground by pulling his hair. This was made easier by special hair styles – they shaved the tops of their heads but left long hair on both sides. Short hair was a dishonor for the Indians in that area, and saying that someone had short hair meant he was weak. The fighters started by facing each other, took their ponchos off and grabbed each other by the hair. The fight went on until one of the participants surrendered. Sometimes the fights took on a more serious turn – they were used, e.g., to solve neighborly disputes. Both men and women could participate. During the fight, the contestants hurled abuse at each other, the worst of which included 'miser' (ruin), 'scrooge' (picaro) and 'thief' (ladronazo). The fights were also fought to regain lost honor – one's own or that of one's relatives, esp. father or wife. In the period of wars against the conquistadores, the Indians shaved their hair short to avoid being grabbed by it in combat, as Spaniards would often do this off the backs of their horses. As a result, the game died out during the conquista, and was partially revived only after the area was pacified by the invaders.

LONKOTUN IN THE CHUECA GAME. Formerly, when a >CHUECA player committed a serious foul against his opponent, the latter took justice in his own hands. He grabbed the opponent strongly by the hair and forced him violently to lie down on his knees and to touch the floor with his forehead. The offender would have to accept the punishment without uttering a word or face being expelled from the game by the referee and losing the bet that he had agreed on with his opponent. Once the problem was settled, the offended player felt satisfied and the offender recognized his fault, the game continued as if nothing had ever happened. This action of immediately avenging the offence was called *lonkotun* ('hair fight'). It was a moment awaited for not only by the spectators but also by the players. This type of fight was very common, but only practiced during the games of chueca, and nowadays not used any more.

C. López von Vriessen 1990, 1991; O. Plath, 'Loncotun', JYDLCH, 1946, 22-24.

LONG DISTANCE KAYAKING, a sport involving kayak racing over a distance several times longer than the trad. regatta distance. The most famous long distance kayaking event is the Durban Marathon in Pietermaritzburg, S.Africa. See also >KAYAKING.

LONG DISTANCE RUNNING, in track and field athletics, races ranging from 2,000m up. In Eng.-speaking parts of the world a long-distance race is, according to the *Encyclopaedia of Sport*, 1898, vol. 2, 57, any face ranging from 1 statute mile (1609.3m) up. In most countries the distances are measured according to the metric system; in Eng.-speaking countries, however, the distances have traditionally been expressed exclusively in miles which is still very often the case. Long-distance races are held outdoors on running tracks, and also as >CROSS-COUNTRY RUNNING events, as well as indoors. >STEEPLE CHASE is a very particular var. of long-distance races. Major track and field events such as the Ol.G., as well as world and continental championships, etc. usu. include 5,000- and 10,000-m races (and their mile counterparts, i.e. 3- and 7- or 5- and 10-mi. races, in Eng.-speaking countries, though the 10-km race, called the '10K', has been popular in the US for decades) and the >MARATHON. The first few Ol.G. of the modern era abounded in long-distance running events. Later, many of these events, such as the team 5,000-m race (1900) or the team 3-mi. race (1908) (>TEAM RUNNING), were discontinued. Individual 5-mile events were held during the 1906 and 1908 Ol.G. 2-, 3-, 15-, 20-, 30- and 100-km races as well as 2-, 3-, 6-, 10-, 15-, 20-, 30- and 100-mi. races are also held during various track and field competitions and records set at these distances are officially maintained. Another category of officially maintained records extends onto timed events such as the 1- or 10-hr. runs.

History. Distance running competitions date back to prehistoric times and were popular among many different cultures. The oldest known forms of long-distance running that may be classified as competitive appeared in ancient Greece. A long-distance race over an unspecified distance constituted a separate event during the games held in honor of Patroclus as described in Book XXIII of Homer's *Iliad*. A long-distance race called the >DOLICHOS was introduced at the 15th Ol.G. in 720 BC. Long-distance running was popular among various, independently developing civilizations and was most often related to the need to carry messages over long distances. In pre-Columbus S.America, and esp. in the Inca state, permanent long-distance relays were maintained by runners called *chasqui* whose task was to ensure that messages were passed from the capital to remote provinces. By the same token the Tarahumara and Seri S.Amer. Indians developed a form of running competition whereby the runners sought to enhance their stamina. Public running competitions over distances of up to 3.5km were held in medieval and Renaissance Italy, esp. in Rome. Traveling long-distance runners entering into bets that they would cover a specified distance within a specified period of time appeared in 17th cent. England and later throughout the rest of Europe, e.g. in Germany. Such runners continued to pursue their profession until the second half of the 19th cent. and the earliest mentioning of such a run dates back to, most likely, 1653 when an unknown runner ran a distance of 32km from London to St. Albans. This form of long-distance running flourished in Great Britain at the end of the 18th and at the beginning of the 19th cent. when prizes often amounted to as much as £1,000. In 1801 a runner known as Barclay covered a distance of 110mi. (approx. 177km) in 19hrs. 27min. In Germany the leading bet runner was J. Geringer who also toured Poland. In 1825 he took part in a race in Warsaw where he covered a distance of 1.5 Pol. mile (about 11.2km) in 35.5min., a result which is similar to those of modern 10km runners. In 1826 a Polish runner, H. Pawłowski, ran from Warsaw to Raszyn and back (the time has not been preserved). A Ger. runner named Itau was particularly popular in Poland in the second half of the 19th century and in 1866 and 1872 he toured the cities of the Grand Duchy of Poznań: 'One Mr. Itau of Hamburg presented on Sunday afternoon his skills of fast running. He covered the distance from Brama Dębińska (Dębina Gate) to Dębina and back in just 50 minutes and the show attracted a large enough crowd of spectators' (*Dziennik Poznański* – Poznań Daily, 5 Sep.

10,000-M RACE OLYMPIC CHAMPIONS

MEN

1912 Hannes Kolehmainen, FIN 31:20.8
1920 Paavo Nurmi, FIN 31:45.8
1924 Ville Ritola, FIN 30:23.2
1928 Paavo Nurmi, FIN 30:18.8
1932 Janusz Kusocinski, POL 30:11.4
1936 Ilmari Salminen, FIN 30:15.4
1948 Emil Zátopek, CZE 29:59.6
1952 Emil Zátopek, CZE 29:17.0
1956 Vladimir Kuts, USSR 28:45.6
1960 Pyotr Bolotnikov, USSR 28:32.2
1964 Billy Mills, USA 28:24.4
1968 Naftali Temu, KEN 29:27.4
1972 Lasse Viren, FIN 27:38.4
1976 Lasse Viren, FIN 27:40.38
1980 Miruts Yifter, ETH 27:42.7
1984 Alberto Cova, ITA 27:47.54
1988 Brahim Boutaib, MOR 27:21.46
1992 Khalid Skah, MOR 27:46.70
1996 Haile Gebrselassie, ETH 27:07.34
2000 Haile Gebrselassie, ETH 27:18.20

WOMEN

1988 Olga Bondarenko, URS 31:05.21
1992 Derartu Tulu, ETH 31:06.02
1996 Fernanda Ribeiro, POR 31:01.63
2000 Derartu Tulu, ETH 30:17.49

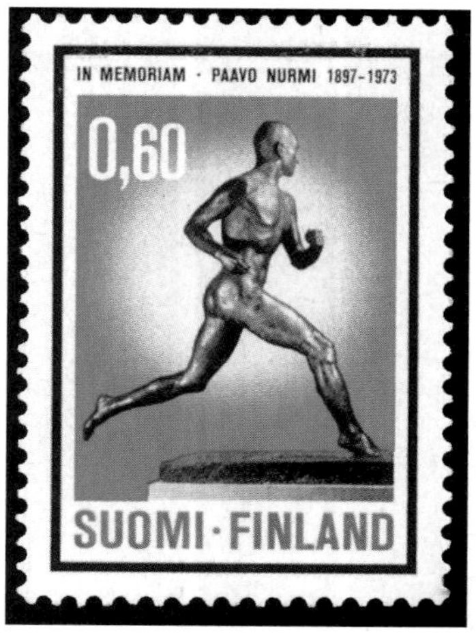

A Finnish stamp in honor of Paavo Nurmi.

Paavo Nurmi, the 'Flying Finn', one of history's most stupendous long distance runners. He was the first to win 5 gold medals during a single Olympic Games. Among other events, he won 1,500- and 5,000-m races, with but a half-hour's break between events.

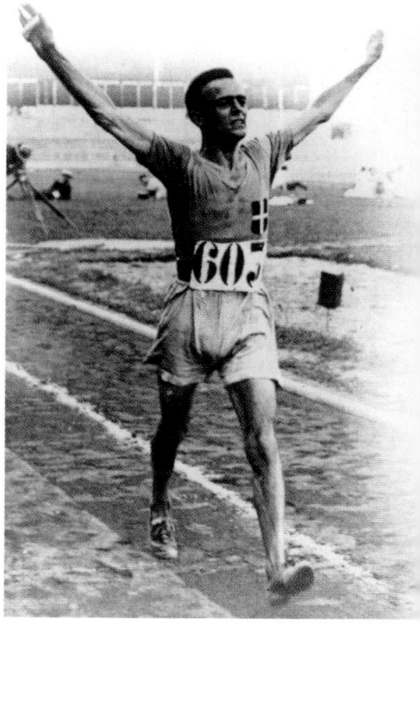

1866). The fact that professional runners observed a strict training regimen is best exemplified by comparisons of their results along the same routes achieved at different points in time: 'On Sunday, Itau, a runner, covered the distance from Brama Dębińska (Dębina Gate) to Dębina and back in 40 min. [...] and later he displayed his skill running in the direction of Szeląg' (*Kurier Poznański* – Poznań Herald, 18 June 1872). It is difficult to say when, precisely, long-distance running became part and parcel of modern, amateur track and field athletics. The be-

Lapped runner Hannou Boutayeh of Morocco, left, prepares to block Kenya's Richard Chelimo, center, and allow teammate Khalid Skah right, to pass during the 10,000-m race in Barcelona's Olympic Stadium. Skah crossed the finish line first, but was disqualified under Rule 143 for receiving assistance.

ginning of modern long-distance running may be marked by the cross-country race held during a students' competition in Birmingham in 1838. The oldest officially recognized and codified long-distance running event was the 2mi. race for which world records were maintained by the Eng. Amateur Athletic Association since 1865. These records were then recognized by the International Amateur Athletic Federation (estab. 1912). The first officially recognized world record holder was Brit. runner R. Webster who in 1865 ran 2mi. in 10min. 5sec. 3-, 4-, 5- and 10-mi. races had been introduced by 1889. After the Brit. model of competitive and amateur sport had become widespread throughout continental Europe, metric distances gained more recognition and at the beginning of the 20th cent. the most popular metric distances included the 3,000-, 5,000- and 10,000-m races, which are still most popular today. The 5,000- and 10,000-m races became permanent Olympic events at the 1912 Games in Stockholm. At the same time international competitions have been held and world records have been maintained for 15,000- and 20,000-m races (since 1913), 25,000-m races (since 1920) and for 30,000-m races (since 1915). Despite the fact that competitions over the above distances have been held rather infrequently, the 15-, 20-, 25- and 30-km race world records are still maintained. World records for 1-hr runs have been maintained since 1884.

The 2,000-m race is not held during international competitions. It typically constitutes a part of smaller, local competitions and is often held for U-21s or for training purposes.

The 3,000-m race has been a part of international competitions since the beginning of the 20th century. The first official world record was set by a Fin. runner H. Kolemainen at 8:36.8 in 1912. A Belgian runner G. Reiff was the first man in history to run the distance in under 8min. (7:58.8 in 1949).

Three long-distance runners on a Panathenaic amphora from c. 333 BC

The 3,000-m race often constitutes a part of international track and field competitions but is never held during the Ol.G., W.Ch. or E.Ch. A 3,000-m team race was held during the 1912, 1920 and 1924 Games and it has been one of the major women's long-distance races since 1970.

The 3,000-m women's race was officially introduced to the Ol.G. in 1984 and served as an experiment paving the way for other long-distance women's races to be held during Ol.G. The 3,000-m women's race was held during the 1984 and 1988 games and was later replaced by the 5,000-m race. M. Puica of Rumania (the 1984 Ol.G. gold medallist), W. Sly of Great Britain as well as T. Samolienko (the 1988 Ol.G. gold medallist) and J. Romanova (the 1992 Ol.G. gold medallist), both of Russia, are deemed to be the best 3,000m women runners. The first woman to run the distance in under 9min. was L. Bragina of the USSR (8:53.0 in 1972). She was also the first to cover the distance in under 8min. 30sec. (8:27.12 in 1976).

The 5,000-m race was introduced to the Ol.G. in 1912. World records have been maintained since the same year. The first official world record holder was Fin. runner H. Kolemainen. Initially, Fin. runners dominated during 5,000-m races and they won all the gold Olympic medals before WWII apart from the 1920 Ol.G. in Antwerp. After 1945 a number of outstanding runners from various countries, incl. a Czech E. Zatopek who was equally good over all long distances, managed to overcome the Fin. hegemony but they never came from just one country. The best 5,000-m runners came from the USSR, Great Britain and, since the second half of the 1960s, from Africa, esp. Kenya, Ethiopia and Morocco, and also from other European countries such as Italy and Spain. The versatile L. Vire, who managed to win 2 consecutive victories in the 5,000- and 10,000-m races at the Ol.G. revived, to a certain extent, the Fin. long-distance running tradition. A one-off victory of B. Schul at the 1964 Ol.G. did not make the US a 5,000-m superpower.

The first runner to cover 5,000m in under 14min. was Swed. athlete G. Hägg (13:58.2 in 1941), in under 13min. 30sec. – a Kenyan K. Keino (13:24.2 in 1965) and in under 13min. – S. Aouita of Morocco (12:58.39 in 1987).

The 5,000-m women's race was first held at the Ol.G. in 1996 in Atlanta where it replaced the 3,000-m race. The competition was, similarly to other women's long distances, dominated by runners from China, Japan and Kenya with Eng., Ital., Rum., and Rus. runners also noticeable. The first Olympic gold medal in the 5,000-m race went to Xia Wang of the People's Republic of China with P. Konga of Kenya and R. Brunet of Italy coming 2nd and 3rd.

The 10,000-m race has been a part of the Ol.G. since 1912, but official world records have been maintained since 1911. A Fr. runner J. Bouin became the first world record holder finishing his race in 30:58.8 in 1911. The first one to run the distance in under 30min. was a Finn T. Mäki (29:52.6 in 1939) and the first to cover 10,000m in less than 29min. was E. Zatopek (28:54.2 in 1954). An Australian R. Clarke was the first to run 10km in under 28min. (27:38.4 in 1965).

In the 1911-39 period, similarly to other long-distance races, 10-km competitions were dominated by the Finns. They won all the Olympic golds in that period except 1932 where J. Kusociński of Poland interrupted the Fin. monopoly. In the 1947-54 period the most outstanding runner was E. Zatopek who was a world record holder and the winner of the 10-km race during the 1948 Ol.G. in London and the winner of not only the 5,000- and 10,000-m races, but also the marathon at the 1952 Ol.G. in Helsinki. The latter achievement not to be repeated. After the end of the 'Zatopek era', Soviet runners such as V. Kuc and P. Bolotnikov dominated the 10-km scene for a few years. After 1960 no single country has managed to dominate 10-km races to the extent Finns had done before WWII. A number of runners coached by N.Zealander A. Lydiard and a few Americans, incl. a Native Amer. Indian, W. Mills, who won the gold medal at the 1964 Olympics, became famous during various periods in 10-km race history. In the '70s the old Fin. tradition was revived by various Suomi runners including L. Vire who won the 10,000- and 5,000-m gold medals at 2 consecutive Ol.G. in 1972 and 1976. Afr. runners had started to quickly gain international renown since the second half of the '60s. They began to dominate the 10-km race scene at the 1968 Ol.G. with the victory of B. Temu of Kenya. Towards the end of the '70s Ethiopian (H. Gebreelasie, winner of the 10-km race at the 1996 Ol.G.), Moroccan (B. Boutaib, 1988 and K. Skah, 1992), Kenyan (M. Yifter, the winner of the Olympic gold in 1980), and Italian (A. Cova, 1984) runners followed in his footsteps.

The 10,000m women's race was introduced to the Ol.G. in 1988 in Seoul. Initially the races were dominated by the USSR, GDR and later Asian runners – esp. of the People's Republic of China and Japan; subsequently Kenyan, Ethiopian, Port. and, to a lesser extent, Brit. and other competitors took over. O. Bondarenko of the USSR won the first 10km women's race in Seoul with E. McColgan of Great Britain and J. Zhupieva of the USSR coming 2nd and 3rd. The 1992 Barcelona Ol.G. gold medal went to D. Tulu of Ethiopia and the 1996 Ol.G. 10-km race winner was F. Ribeiro of Portugal. During the E.Ch. the 10,000-m race was held for the first time in 1986 and the first W.Ch. 10-km women's race took place in 1987 (with I. Kristiansen of Norway winning both races).

H. Higdon, *Run Fast. How to Train for a 5-K or 10-K Race*, 1992.

LONG DISTANCE SWIMMING, a type of >SWIMMING (see the adventure of Odysseus), over long distances. The sport was already known in ancient times. In one ancient story, a young man by the name of Leander from Abydos, situated on the east side of Hellespont (present-day Dardanelles), would swim at night across the strait to Sestos to meet Hero, a priestess of Aphrodite, with whom he fell in love. Hero guided him through the darkness with the light of a torch. One night the light was extinguished in a storm and Leander drowned. When the following day Hero saw her lover's body cast ashore she threw herself off a cliff to her death. This love story with numerous references to the art of swim-

Long distance swimming.

ming was mentioned in Ovid's *Heroides*, a collection of fictional poetic letters. In one of the letters Leander confides in Hero as follows:

Night was falling [...] when, a lover, I slipped from my father's door. Without delay, shedding my clothes, and with them my fear, I calmly slid my arms into the flowing water. I spoke these words or ones not unlike them, the waters I shouldered parting before me, of themselves. The waves shone with the image of the reflected moon and it was bright as day in the silent night. There was no voice anywhere: nothing came to my ears, except the murmur of the waters, parted by my body [...] Then, both my arms growing weary, at the shoulder, I raised myself strongly, high above the waves. Seeing a distant light, I said: 'My fire is in that fire: that is the shore that holds my light. And sudden strength returned to my weary arms [...] Another light's more certain for me: my love, that guides me, doesn't wander in the darkness. While I gaze on it, I might swim to Colchis, [...] and I might outdo young Palaemon [...] Exhausted, I can scarcely drag myself through the vast waters, and often my arms are wearied by the endless motion. When I tell them: 'The reward for your labours will not be small, soon it will be granted you to embrace your lady's neck, they gain strength right away, and strain for the prize, like swift horses of Elis, released from the starting gate.

[Trans. A.S. Kilne]

In response, Hero warns Leander against taking excessive risks.

In this way, o youth, conqueror of the swollen waters, you scorn what the straits may do, though you fear them. Ships built with skill can be sunk by the waters: do you think your arms are more capable than oars?

[Trans. A.S. Kilne]

The theme of Hero and Leander was later adapted by such authors as C. Marlowe (1564-93) in the play *Hero and Leander* (1598), finished by another Eng. playwright G. Chapman (1599-1634); T. Hood (1799--1845) in the poem *The Bridge of Sighs*; T. Nashe (1567-1601) in the burlesque *Lenten Stuffe* (1599); and by F. Shiller (1759-1805). The feat of Leander was repeated by G. Byron who traveled to the Middle East in 1810. He made the crossing from Sestos to Abydos together with his friend Lieutenant Ekenhead, in 70min. In 1821, an Eng. politician W. Turner attempted to cross the Hellespont the other way, but he failed. Later on, Turner belittled Byron's feat, as the latter supposedly swam with the tide and reached the other shore quite easily. According to Turner 'Whatever is thrown into the stream on this part of the Eur. bank must arrive at the Asiatic shore'. Byron replied sharply in London press that: '...with regard to the difference of the current, I perceived none; it is favourable to the swimmer on neither side.' Concluding the argument Byron asked his adversary the question 'Why did he not try the Eur. side? If he had succeeded there, after failing the Asiatic, his pleas would have been more graceful and gracious.' After crossing the Hellespont, Byron, swam over long distances in other places, e.g. in Venice, from the isle of Lido to the Rialto Bridge. He recalled that:

In 1818, the Chevalier Mengaldo (a gentleman of Bassano), a good swimmer, wished to swim with my friend Mr. Alexander Scott and myself [...]. We all three started from the Island of the Lido and swam to Venice. At the entrance of the Grand Canal Scott and I were a good way ahead, and we saw no more of our foreign friend, which, however, was of no consequence, as there was a gondola to hold his clothes and pick him up. Scott swam on till past the Rialto, where he got out, less from fatigue than from chill, having been four hours in the water, without rest or stay, except what is to be obtained by floating on one's back – this being the condition of our performance. I continued my course on to Santa Chiara, comprising the whole of the Grand Canal (besides the distance from the Lido), and got out where the Laguna once more opens to Fusina. I had been in the water, by my watch, without help or rest, and never touching ground or boat, four hours and twenty minutes. To this match and during the greater part of its performance, Mr. Hoppner, the Consul-general, was witness.

In 1875 the Englishman M. Webb swam across the Eng. Channel, a distance of 33.5km from Calais to Dover, without any assistance (earlier, American P. Boynton covered the same route using a life belt for rest stops). The first female swimmer to make the Eng. Channel crossing was the Amer. G. Ederle in 1926. The Channel Swims gave rise to a series of long-distance crossings organized in other places of the world. In 1947, the Englishman T. Blower swam across the Irish Sea at its narrowest point from Ireland to Britain (45km). In 1948, the Peruvian swimmer D. Carpio crossed the Strait of Gibraltar (13km). Various swimmers also swam over long distances down rivers. In 1935, P.A. Candiotti from Argentina covered a distance of 452km down the Parana River, in 84hrs. Four years later, American C. Giles swam down the Yellowstone River covering a distance of about 463 km in 77hrs. and 31min. In 1940 J.V. Sigmund swam 470km down the Mississippi in 89hrs. and 42min. In 2000 a Slovenian swimmer M. Strel swam the Danube River (2,860km) and had achieved the world's long distance swimming record (3,004km) in 58 days. In 2001 he achieved one more world record – 504km of nonstop swimming in the Danube within 84hrs. and 10 min. In 2002, he swam the Mississippi River (3,885 km) in 68 days. Among women swimmers, M. Huddlesoton from the USA set the first time record of continuous swimming in a pool (87hrs. 27min.) in 1931. The current record holder is the American A. Streeter (212hrs. 30min.). In June 1998, an Austrl. marathon swimmer S. Maroney swam a record-breaking distance of 120mi. (192km) from Mexico to Cuba. Apart from individual crossings, numerous long distance races are organized as well. The most significant event is the Wrigley Swim, estab. in 1927 between Catalina and Los Angeles, California; later held on Lake Ontario over a distance of 10mi. Since 1929 a separate Wrigley Swim women's event has been held. Also on Lake Ontario, a 10-mi. swimming race has been held since 1952 as part of the annual Canadian Water Carnival. One famous Eur. event is a swimming race down the Danube River over a distance of 130km.

LONG JUMP (RUNNING), also *broad jump*, an athletic contest, in which competitors try to cover the farthest distance possible with a running jump from a fixed board or mark. Presently jumpers take off from a wooden board and land in a specially designed landing area filled with sand. In an athletic contest the order of jumpers is decided by lots. If there are more than 8 contestants, there is a qualifying round, in which each jumper makes 3 qualification jumps followed by 3 final jumps. When more than 1 contestant achieves the 8th qualification result, all of them have the right to continue in the final round. Jumps are made into the landing area filled with sand. Its length is not defined by the rules, but it should be sufficient to allow safe landing at a distance from the end edge. The min. width is 2.75m and the max. is 3.0m. The sand should be slightly wet. After each jump the sand is leveled. The run up should be at least 40m long and, conditions permitting, preferably 45m long and 122-125cm wide. Jumps are measured from the board edge, perpendicular to the take off line or its extension to the nearest mark left in the sand by any part of the contestant's body. In order to accurately measure the run up and correctly hit the board, the contestants can use markers nailed into the track or colored self-adhesive tapes attached to the side of the run up. Use of chalk or any other substances that leave a permanent mark is not allowed. Contestants take off from a board embedded in the track so that it is level with the run up and the landing area. The board should be rectangular, made of wood or another material of similar mechanical properties, 121-122cm long, 20cm wide and 10cm thick. On the board's edge, in a shallow depression, there should be a plasticine slat, 10cm wide and 121-122cm long, which indicates a foul jump – stepping over the board is equivalent with touching the plasticine slat, on which a clear mark is left.

History. The need to jump over obstacles and cracks in the ground was the primary reason for which man perfected long jumping. The oldest known sporting form of long jump was practiced in ancient Greece (>HALMA). However, the contest was not practiced singly, but formed part of the >PENTATHLON. In the Middle Ages long jump was considered a valued skill of knights. During tournaments, contestants in full armor jumped over a water ditch. Different var. of long jump are known in many folk cultures, particularly in N Europe. The Ger. *Niebelungen Lieds* contains a description of a contest incl. elements of both high and long jumps. A jump over a gill or canyon during the escape of a folk hero from the oppressors chasing him is a frequent element of old legends, e.g. Robin Hood. In Poland and Slovakia a similar element is featured in the legends of the villain Janosik, who is said to have jumped the gorge of the Dunajec river between 2 rocks. Long jump as an exercise of skills useful in life was promoted by the Ger. educator J.C.F. Guts-Muths (1759-1839) in a chapter entitled *Der Sprung in die Weite in Gymnastik für die Jugend* (1804, 213-217). The modern long jump derives from England. In 1851 long jump was included in the athletic contest held at Exeter College in Oxford. Since 1864 it has been part of the athletic championships of England, and since 1876 – of the USA. Better and better results were achieved as the technique was perfected and as the >SPRINT developed since the speed of the run up is one of the most important elements of the running long jump. E.Ch. in long jump have been held since 1938, W.Ch. since 1983. Indoor W.Ch. and championships of some continents, incl. Europe, are also held. The long jump is part of most athletic contests held all over the world, such as national, continental, or Commonwealth championships, the Eur. Cup, held since 1965 and, since 1998, Golden League meetings. In 1896 the long jump was included in the Ol.G. During the Ol.G. held in 1900-12 apart from the running long jump >LONG JUMP (STANDING) was also held (later abandoned).

Initially contestants jumped using a natural style, with the legs thrust forward immediately after take off. In 1901 an Irish P. O'Connor was the first to use the hitch-kick technique, in which the running movement of the legs and arms is continued during the flight phase. The first athlete to jump 7m was I. Lane from Ireland (7.04m – 1894), 8m – J.C. 'Jesse' Owens (8.13m – 1935). Owens' record was beaten 25 years later by R. Boston (8.21m – 1960). During the 1968 Ol.G. R. 'Bob' Beamon set a world record with a nearly 9-m long jump, later referred to as the 'jump of the 21st cent.' (8.90m). However, the result did not last until the 21st cent., as it was beaten twice during the 1991 W.Ch. in Tokyo by the Americans M. 'Mike' Powell (8.95m) and C. Lewis (8.91m), who took 2nd place in the contest. Up to the present contestants from Eng.-speaking countries have dominated in running long jump, initially from Britain and Ireland, then from the USA. Tables of world record holders include only a few names of contestants from outside this group, e.g. S. Cator, Haiti (1928), who trained in and represented the USA, C. Nambu, Japan (1931) and I. Ter-Owanesjan, USSR (1962 and 1967).

Women's long jump started to develop after 1921, under the auspices of the International Federation of Women's Sports (Fédération du Sport Feminin International). The contest was included in the US championships in 1923, in the E.Ch. in 1938 and in the Ol.G. as late as 1948. The first female long jumper to jump 7m was W. Bradauskiene (USSR, 7.09m – 1978). The world record is currently held by G. Czistiakova (7.52m – 1988).

Women's long jump.

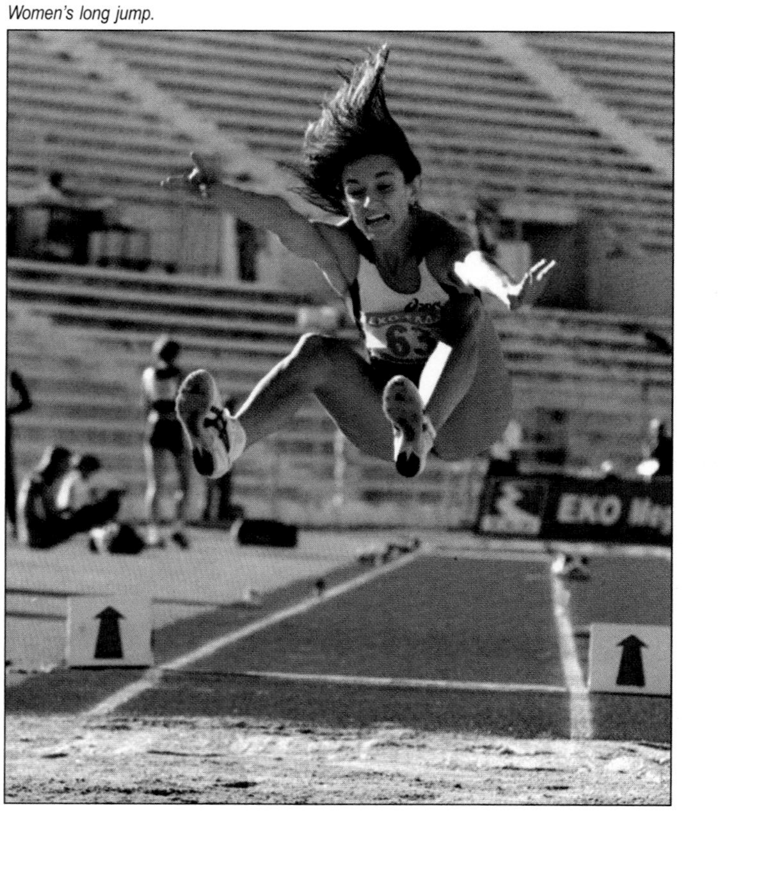

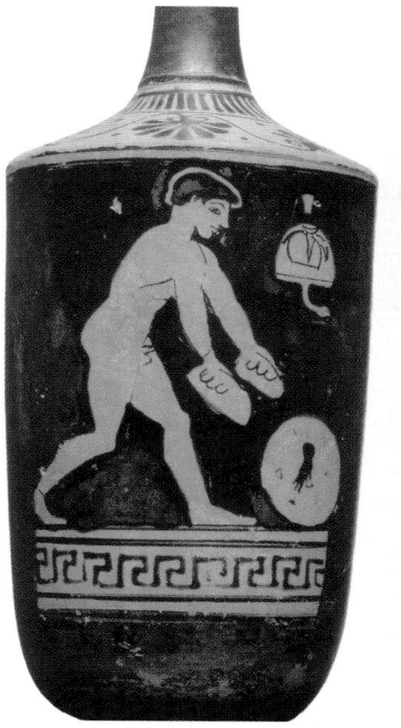

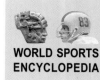

A Greek athlete performing a long jump with halters on a clay amphora, c.475-470 BC.

Bob Beamon of El Paso, Texas digs his feet into the sand pit after a record-shattering long jump of 8.90m on his first attempt in the Summer Olympic Games in Mexico City, Friday, Oct. 18, 1968.

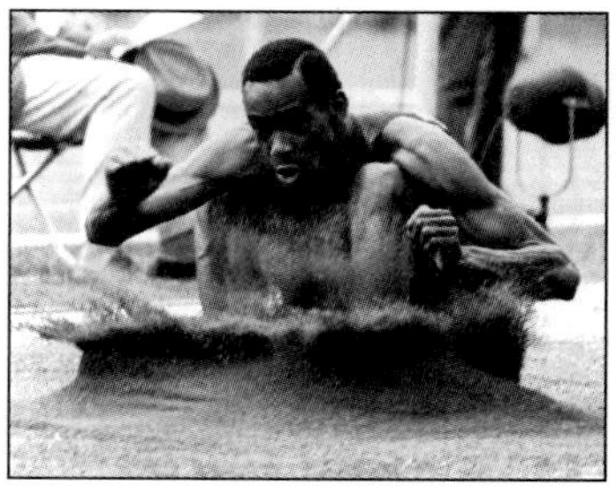

352

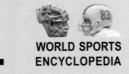

L WORLD SPORTS ENCYCLOPEDIA

LONG JUMP (STANDING), a sports competition in which a contestant takes off and makes a leap forward from a standing position, having set his shoulders and body swinging; it was included in the Ol.G. in 1900-12. The best standing long jumper was American R. Ewry, who won the event at the Ol.G. in 1900, 1904 and 1908. His best jump, made at the 1904 Games, was 346.6cm.
Long jump (standing), abandoned after the 1912 Ol.G., was continued in some countries, and is still among the events practiced in PE classes in the US, but gradually disappeared as an event of athletic contests. However, it remained as a contest in women's championships until 1964. The best female standing long jumper was K. Mearls, 5-time US champion (1927-31), whose best result was 8ft. 3¾in. (252.5cm). The last US champion in standing long jump was B. Beckwith (269.5cm – 1994). Cf. >TRIPLE JUMP (STANDING), >HIGH JUMP (STANDING), >LONG JUMP (RUNNING).

LONG JUMP OLYMPIC CHAMPIONS

MEN
1896 Ellery Clark, USA 6.35
1900 Alvin Kraenzlein, USA 7.185
1904 Myer Prinstein, USA 7.34
1906 Myer Prinstein, USA 7.20
1908 Frank Irons, USA 7.48
1912 Albert Gutterson, USA 7.60
1920 William Pettersson, SWE 7.15
1924 DeHart Hubbard, USA 7.44
1928 Ed Hamm, USA 7.73
1932 Ed Gordon, USA 7.64
1936 Jesse Owens, USA 8.06
1948 Willie Steele, USA 7.82
1952 Jerome Biffle, USA 7.57
1956 Greg Bell, USA 7.83
1960 Ralph Boston, USA 8.12
1964 Lynn Davies, GBR 8.07
1968 Bob Beamon, USA 8.90
1972 Randy Williams, USA 8.24
1976 Arnie Robinson, USA 8.35
1980 Lutz Dombrowski, GDR 8.54
1984 Carl Lewis, USA 8.54
1988 Carl Lewis, USA 8.72
1992 Carl Lewis, USA 8.67
1996 Carl Lewis, USA 8.50
2000 Iván Pedroso, CUB 8.55

WOMEN
1948 Olga Gyarmati, HUN 5.695
1952 Yvette Williams, NZL 6.24
1956 Elzbieta Krzesinska, POL 6.35
1960 Vera Krepkina, URS 6.37
1964 Mary Rand, GBR 6.76
1968 Viorica Viscopoleanu, ROM 6.82
1972 Heide Rosendahl, FRG 6.78
1976 Angela Voigt, GDR 6.72
1980 Tatyana Kolpakova, URS 7.06
1984 Anisoara Stanciu, ROM 6.96
1988 Jackie Joyner-Kersee, USA 7.40
1992 Heike Drechsler, GER 7.14
1996 Chioma Ajunwa, NGR 7.12
2000 Heike Drechsler, GER 6.99

LONG JUMPING (INTO WATER), held only once during the 1908 Ol.G. in St. Louis. The first three places were taken by Amer. sportsmen: 1) W.E. Dickey (19.5m); 2) E.H. Adams (17.53m); 3). B. Goodwin (17.37m).

LONGA META, a Hung. bat-and-ball game, similar to Pol. >PALANT. See also Hungarian >METTEN.

LONG-DISTANCE DANCING, see >DANCE MARATHON.

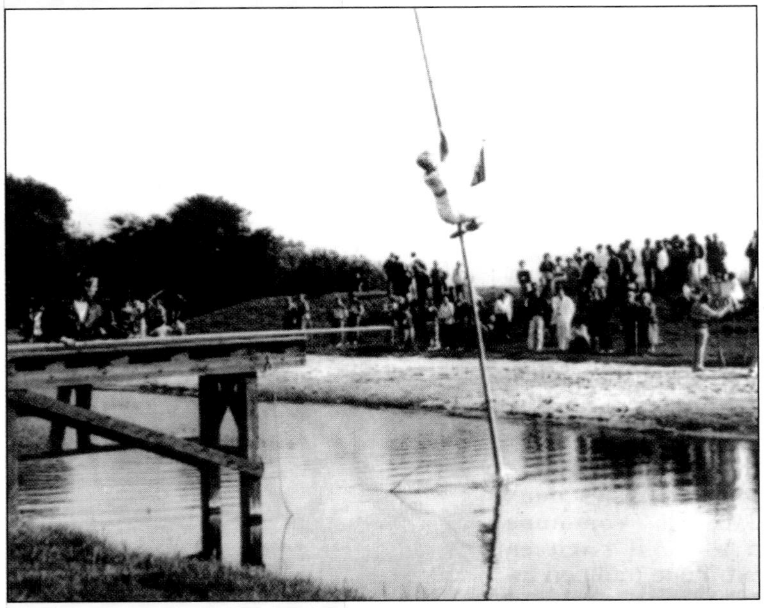

Long-pole jumping.

LONG-POLE JUMPING, also *long-pole vaulting*, a jump in which the contestants cover spaces using a pole. Practiced in many Eur. cultures during the times when lack of roads and bridges forced people to cross rivers, marshes and crevasses. Inasmuch as crossing a wide river in this way was not possible, smaller brooks could be crossed in this way by people equipped with an appropriate pole. Long-pole jumping was practiced in ancient times. However, it was not a separate event at the ancient games in Greece and Rome, but only a skill, useful, for example, in the army. It was also practiced by the shepherds from northern Greece to cross mountain crevasses. Perhaps with colonists from Greece it migrated to Georgia, where it was practiced until the 20th cent. as a folk sport.
The skill of long-pole jumping was used by the Vikings – having left their ships they covered long distances of the countries they conquered, e.g. in southern France or England. Long-pole jumping was advocated by a Ger. educator J.C.F. Guts-Muths (1759-1839) as a physical education exercise. Long-pole jumping became particularly popular in the Netherlands, where a dense network of canals made direct contact between people more difficult. An original form of long-pole jumping over the canals, >FIERLJEPPEN, developed there. In the neighboring Belgium it was known under its Fr. name *saut du canal à la perche*.
J.C.F. 'Guts-Muths, Der Sprung mit dem Stabe', *Gymnastik für die Jugend*, 1804, 241-156.

LONGTRACK, see >SPEEDWAY.

LONGUE, LE, see >JEU PROVENÇAL.

LOOP AND BALL, an Ir. ball game, the predecessor of >CAID, the original form of >GAELIC FOOTBALL.

LOOSE HOLD, the name applied to 4 similar Brit. wrestling styles. There were small differences between the 4 var. but the common trait was that fighting was allowed on the ground. About 1900, under the influence of the Lancashire styles and >CATCH-AS-CATCH-CAN, all the styles were 'united' into one but the name was preserved. Cracking the opponent's knuckles was allowed until 1921. After 1921, the amateur var. started using rules similar to those of FILA freestyle wrestling. At the same time, professional loose hold started degenerating and merging with similar Amer. styles, which made it a kind of farce, with arranged results and quasi-dangerous brutal shows.
The name 'loose hold' was also applied to a style of wrestling practiced in Central Scotland, which started merging with the free style typical for Lancashire (catch-as-catch-can) in the 19th cent. Independently from freestyle, loose hold survived a little longer in athlete troupes travelling around Scotland as late as c.1980 (or perhaps even to this day).

LOPTA, a Serb bat-and-ball game similar to Pol. >PALANT.

LOUP THE BULLOKS, see >LEAPFROG.

LU'BAT AL-BUH, 'the game of buh', an Arab game where the object is to throw fruit pips at targets. The word buh itself stands for sea shells, so perhaps the game used shells in the past, or a shell may have been used to collect and arrange the pips. The game is also known as *al-mutabara*, literally 'survival' or 'continuation'. M. Ibrahim al-Mayman gives an unclear description in his dictionary of Arab sports and games:

The game requires strong, agile fingers and an ability to hit targets. At least two people participate [...]. On the surface of the playing field, as many 30-centimeter lines are drawn as there are players. Two pips are placed on each line, and each player holds another two in his hand. He places one of them in the hollow formed by the index and middle fingers and the thumb of his left hand. [The pip is placed on the thumb facing up, while the index and middle fingers are crooked behind the pip; when the player releases them, the pip is propelled forward.] The player stands about 5m from the buh. It is good to hit a pip on any line but if the attacking pip does not reach the last line, the player repeats the shot. If he hits the target, he becomes the owner of all the pips in the line. If there are no pips on the hit line, shooting is started from the other side by that player whose pip is furthest away from the buh. He shoots his first pip, called the šqah, and then the next player takes over. If he hits any pip on any line, he becomes the owner of all the pips in that line. If he hits the šqah, he gets all the pips in all the lines. If he does not hit any pip, all the pips go to the player who is furthest away in his shooting.
[*Min al'abina ash-sha 'biyya*, 1983, 61]

LU'BAT AR-RAMIA, Arab. for 'the throwing game', also *sab' hgarat* – 'seven stones'. A game described in M. Ibrahim al-Mayman:

A folk game used to practice hitting targets and making feints so that the opponent cannot hit the target. Seven small stones and a small ball are used. A small circle is drawn on the playing field, and the stones are placed in it, in a heap. Each team should have at least 3 players. A player of the first team throws the ball at the heap. If he misses, he is replaced by another player of the same team. This goes on until the heap disintegrates. Then, the players of one team run away, while the other team chase them, trying to hit them with the ball. This goes on until all the players are hit. Each player who has been hit is put out of play in that round of the game. However, the players try not only to avoid being hit but also to build a new heap of the stones before the last player is put out of play. If they succeed in doing so, they win the round. [There are the following additional rules:] A player may avoid being hit by heading the ball away as far as he can, which results in the opponents needing more time to reach it. He can use the time to put the stones back into the heap [obviously heading the ball away does not count as being hit]. A player who has been hit and put out of play may rejoin the game if his team succees in rebuilding the heap.
[*Min al'abina ash-sha 'biyya*, 1983, 70-71]

LU'BAT AT-TAGRIR, [Arab. *lu'bat* – game + *tagrir* – incentive], a trad. Arab game whose objective is to develop a sense of direction in the desert.

This is a very old game, developing shrewdness and sense of direction. The playing field, ideally with a sandy surface, is 50x20m. Two teams, A and B, participate, each with 3-6 players. They start by positioning themselves in a circle in the middle of the field. One of team A's players says: We're going eastwards. However, the objective is to mislead the opponents, so team A proceed in a direction different to that which they have announced. The players of team B do the same: they announce they will go north but actually go south. They come back after some time, to rejoin at the same place, but only after marking [their path] with straight and curved lines, each about 4m long, which they draw on the ground using their hands. Then the teams swap places, and one team tries to reconstruct the path of the other team, following the lines and arrows, trying to discover and obliterate as many of them as possible. After that, they come back to the circle and use a 1-meter stick to measure all the lines they have not spotted and erased. This is performed by the players of both teams [one monitoring the other]. The team that has more undiscovered and unerased lines remaining wins.
[M. Ibrahim al-Mayman, *Min al'abina ash-sha 'biyya*, 1983, 66]

LU'BAT AZ ZAGWA, Arab. for 'the basket game', also *hami aš-šah* ('the shah's defender'), a game described in M. Ibrahim al-Mayman's dictionary of Arab sports and games:

Each team consists of 3-6 players led by a šeh (sheikh). One team starts the game by positioning themselves in the middle of the playing field (they will defend access to their shah), while the other – on the perimeter. The sheikh of the first team, positioned on the start line, shouts: 'ilayk az-zaqwa' ('take the basket'). The sheikh of the other team asks then, 'ma fiha' ('what's in it?'). The first sheikh responds, 'fiha zbib 'ahdar' ('there are green raisins inside'). On hearing that, the second calls: 'hatiha' ('hand it over'). Upon that, the sheikh of the first team sends one of his players in the direction of the first sheikh, and so does the second, sending one of his players to meet him and overwhelm him. If the attacker fights his way through and reaches the back line of the opponents' part of the field, his team scores a point. However, if he is stopped or gives up on the attack and returns to his original position, the point goes to the defending team. The game goes on [until all players have gone]. Then, the teams change ends. In the past, the sheikh had a stick which he used to hit the oncoming attacker but today the stick has been replaced with a rag ball [which is thrown at the attacker to put him out of play].
[*Min al'abina ash-sha 'biyya*, 1983, 59-60]

LU'BAT EL MARQA', [Arab. *lu'bat* – game + *marqua'* – passing over], an Arab game using a ball made of a rolled-up piece of cloth about 1m long. The course of the game as described by Arab sources is difficult to understand. M. Ibrahim al-Mayman's dictionary of Arab sports and games presents the game in the following way:

Two teams participate, with 2-4 players each. One of the players of the team starting the game hides a small stone in his hand. All the players on his team hold out their clenched fists. The opposing team has three ball throws to determine which of them contains the stone. If they do not guess after the first three throws, they throw the ball to each of the players in turn, asking 'hat etdan' ('give us the stone'). If they finally find the stone, each player of that team hits a chosen player of the opposite team as many times as the predefined stake of ransom was [it is not clear from the text what the ransom consists of]. *However, each time they fail in finding the stone, the players of the team with the stone hit a player of the guessing team as many times as the ransom was defined to be* [it is not clear whether the hitting is done with the hand or the ball, and how many times the player is hit – probably as many as the guessing team missed the hand with the stone earlier, which would mean that the number of the 'penalty hits' rises until the guessing team find the hand with the stone].
[*Min al'abina ash-sha 'biyya*, 1983, 65-66]

LU'BAT KASIR 'UDA, Arab. for 'breaking a stick', [Arab *lu'bat* – game + *kasir* – breaking + *'uda* – stick], an Arab sport where the object is to throw shepherd's crooks at a target, described by M. Ibrahim al-Mayman in his dictionary of Arab sports and games:

A straight line, about 2m long, is drawn on a level playing field. At least three players must participate. All of them take positions behind the line. One player, selected by drawing lots, drives his stick in the ground about 10m away from the line. The stick becomes the target for the other players who try to hit it with their own sticks. If one of them succeeds in doing so, his stick becomes a new target. After the lying stick is hit, its owner, together with the owner of the first target stick, runs towards them, picks them up and races to his original positions. Whoever loses the race, hands his stick over to serve as a new target, driven in the ground at the original place. If no player succeeds in hitting the stick, all of them run towards the sticks lying on the ground, pick them up and race back to the throwing line. Whoever comes in last, hands over his stick as the new target.

[Min al'abina ash-sha 'biyya, 1983, 64-65]

The second round of the game is played in a similar way but there are new elements in the final stage, not quite clear in the Arab sources. The course of the second stage may be as follows: If the stick is hit by only one player in the second stage, and his stick is not hit by any others, he makes another attempt and is given a chance to 'secure' his victory. He should jump on one foot to the place where all the sticks are lying, pick them up following the succession of throws, and hold them in his hands so that they do not touch each other. He continues on one foot to the first stick, driven in the ground at the beginning, and stops there. If he touches the ground with his other leg while jumping, or if the sticks touch each other, he loses. However, if he succeeds in picking up the sticks on one foot, he puts them down on the ground in one place. All the other players then run up to him, put him on a 'chair' made of one stick or a number of them (depending on his weight), and carry him triumphantly to the throwing line, where he may start the next round.

LU'BAT SAB'EL-HAGAR, Arab. for 'the seven stones game', described by M. Ibrahim al-Mayman in his dictionary of Arab sports and games:

This old game is usually encountered in the area of Sdir. The main skill is accurate throwing, which all boys like, irrespective of age. Seven flat hand-sized stones are used, formerly called farš, arranged in a heap. The attacking team hit the heap with a small rag ball. In some villages, the game is called sab' d'obat [alternative spelling tobat].

The players form two teams: one team attacks the heap, the other defends it. If the attackers break the heap up, the defenders put it back up but lose one player. If the attackers fail to break up the heap, the ball is taken over by the defenders who try to hit one of the attackers with it. A player who is hit is put out of play. Then, all players of both teams try to catch or pick up the ball. If the attackers take the ball over, they may try hitting the heap again but if the defenders catch the ball they try to hit one of the attackers. Again, a player who is hit is put out of play. The game goes on until only one player is left in either team. The referee then declares the victory of that team. The referee may be one of the players, or a person from outside if he is accepted by everybody. During the game, the teams swap roles: the attacking team become the defenders and vice versa. The game is similar to >HOL played in the eastern regions of the kingdom [of Saudi Arabia]. It also recalls some modern games, such as volleyball or handball. The area of the playing field is agreed at the beginning. A player aiming at the heap is about 10m away from it. That is where the start line is drawn. However, a player aiming at an opponent must be at a long distance from it. Some

players of the defending teams are allowed to interfere with the attacking players to intercept the ball and then put attackers out of play by hitting them with it. It must be remembered, though, that some defenders defend the target – the pile of stones – by blocking it with their bodies.

[Min al'abina ash-sha 'biyya, 1983, 29-30]

LU'BAT UMM AL-HUTUT, Arab. for 'chessboard game'. An Arab game similar to street >HOP-SCOTCH, played not only by children but also by adult women. M. Ibrahim al-Mayman gives a description in his dictionary of Arab sports and games:

The game is played especially by children but also by young girls, and sometimes, albeit rarely, by older women. It has some charm to it in the summer, when the players are not wearing heavy clothes, and city squares are dry, well treaded. It is known by many names: 'adem (a 'small bone' – from a bone used in the game, 5x4cm, which can be replaced by a small, light, flat stone called farš), hutta (lit. 'line'), 'atba (lit. 'threshold', on which the players stand on one foot), and in Mecca – berber ('Berber') or berber 'agam ('Berber-Persian'). It is not a team game but two or more players may participate. It may be played in various ways.

The players draw boxes on the ground, as in the picture, and decide the order of jumps. After the bone or stone are thrown into the first box, the first player jumps on one foot over it into the second field, and from there – into the third. He can rest on both feet in the fourth and fifth boxes, called mustarah ('rest'). Then, he continues on one foot into the sixth box, and then into the seventh and eighth, which are again a rest zone. Then he puts his right foot in the seventh box, and the left one – in the eighth. He turns around and goes back all the way. When he reaches the second box, he must bend down and pick up the bone or stone, and jump over the first field outside of the pitch. In the second round, the bone or stone is thrown into the second field, which the player must avoid when jumping over all the fields of the chessboard. If he completes all the boxes, throwing the bone or stone into each successive one, he stands with his back to the first box and throws the bone or stone behind, outside of the chessboard. Now, after jumping on one foot through all the boxes, he stops in the eighth and from there he must jump so as to land by the bone and touch it with his feet. Then, he goes back to the start line, stops with his back to it, and sings the stanza: 'ahed w 'illa mahed?' ('take it or not?'). After one of the opponents answers 'All,h a'lam' ('God knows best'), he throws the bone again, this time so that it lands within the chessboard. The box where the bone lands will now be marked as his box. The opponents are banned from that box, and cannot stop in it. Only those players are put out of play who commit some error. Finally, the player who has brought under his control the most boxes, wins. Additionally, there are the following rules: a player who touches the ground with both feet at a prohibited place loses a round; if the bone lands on any of the lines demarcating the boxes, or in the wrong box, the player loses a round; if a player loses a round in the

second or third box, he continues from the next field rather than from the beginning in the next round; if a player's foot touches the box with the bone, or any other prohibited box (owned by an opponent), the player loses a round.

[Min al'abina ash-sha 'biyya, 1983, 30-34]

LUCHA DE BANDERA, LA, also *lucha de la cruz* [Span. *lucha* – wrestling + *bandera* – banner + *cruz* – cross], a Span. trad. style of wrestling known in the area of Zamorra in the province of Salamanca. To win, a wrestler had to knock his opponent down onto his back. Lucha de bandera was esp. popular during family meetings and folk festivals. The original name, implying a connection with banners, derives from a custom of the local shepherds who put up high masts with banners or crosses in their pastures or camps, challenging shepherds from other villages or pastures. There are some simi-

Traditional luge races.

larities between lucha de bandera and Scot. >BACKHOLD, explained by an old story, according to which a type of wrestling was made popular in the area by Scot. soldiers who were stationed there during the Napoleonic wars. It then started developing independently. However, most wrestling historians think that the actual prototype of lucha de bandera was the Span. wrestling style of *lucha leonesa*. Lucha de bandera started disappearing as a result of the repression during the Span. Civil War, and finally disappeared c.1940.

LUCHA DE RONCAL, a Span. trad. wrestling style similar to >LUCHA DE BANDERA, LA, but differing in some technical details and customs. It was practiced in a different area, that of Roncal in the Pyrenees. W. Baxter, 'Les luttes traditionnelles a traverse le monde: Lucha de roncal', LJP, 1998, 85-86.

LUCTA ERECTA, a var. of ancient Roman wrestling, fought in an upright position and modeled on Gk. >ORTHOPALE wrestling [Lat. *lucta* – wrestling, lit. fight + *erecta* – erect], as was opposed to >LUCTA VOLUCTATORIA.

LUCTA VOLUCTATORIA, a variant of ancient Roman wrestling, modeled on Gk. >KATO PALE or >KYLISIS wrestling [Lat. *lucta* – wrestling, lit. fight + *volutatoria* – wallowing; cf. Gk. kylisis – wallowing in dust], as opposed to >LUCTA ERECTA.

LUDENS AD PILUSM AD ULKHAM, see >BALL GAME AT ULGHAM, THE.

LUG AND BITE, also *luggery-bite*, an old Eng. primitive form of rivalry, practiced esp. by boys in Lincolnshire and Lancashire. One of the participants threw an apple, while the rest raced to catch it. Whoever caught the apple tried to eat it as fast as possible, while the others pulled him by the ears to make him give it up.
TGESI, I, 361.

LUGE, 1) riding on a luge; 2) winter sports discipline in which contestants ride a luge in a specially prepared course (although artificial courses are available, where competitions can be held in summer without snow or ice). Contestants ride singly against the clock. The total result is the combined

Women's singles luge.

Luge on postage stamps issued to commemorate the Winter Olympic Games in Innsbruck in 1964 (below) and 1978 (bottom).

LUGE OLYMPIC CHAMPIONS

MEN'S SINGLES
1964 Thomas Köhler, GER 3:26.77
1968 Manfred Schmid, AUT 2:52.48
1972 Wolfgang Scheidel, E. Ger 3:27.58
1976 Dettlef Günther, E. Ger 3:27.688
1980 Bernhard Glass, E. Ger 2:54.796
1984 Paul Hildgartner, ITA 3:04.258
1988 Jens Müller, E. Ger 3:05.548
1992 Georg Hackl, GER 3:02.363
1994 Georg Hackl, GER 3:21.571
1998 Georg Hackl, GER 3:18.436
2002 Armin Zoeggeler, GER 2:57.941

MEN'S DOUBLES
1964 Josef Feistmantl, Manfred Stengl, AUS 1:41.62
1968 Klaus Bonsack, Thomas Kohler, E GER 1:35.85
1972 Horst Hornlein, Reinhard Bredow, E GER 1:28.35
Paul Hildgartner, Walter Plaikner, E GER 1:28.35
1976 Hans Rinn, Norbert Hahn, E GER 1:25.604
1980 Hans Rinn, Norbert Hahn, E GER 1:19.331
1984 Hans Stanggassinger, Franz Wembacher, FRG 1:23.620
1988 Jorg Hoffmann, Jochen Pietzsch, E GER 1:31.940
1992 Stefan Krausse, Jan Behrendt, GER 1:32.053
1994 Kurt Brugger, Wilfried Huber, ITA 1:36.720
1998 Stefan Krausse, Jan Behrendt, GER 1:41.105
2002 Leitner, Patric-Fritz, Resch, Alexander, GER 1:26.082

WOMEN'S SINGLES
1964 Ortrun Enderlein, GER 3:24.67
1968 Erica Lechner, ITA 2:28.66
1972 Anna-Maria Müller, E. Ger 2:59.18
1976 Margit Schumann, E. Ger 2:50.621
1980 Vera Zozulya, USSR 2:36.537
1984 Steffi Martin, E. Ger 2:46.570
1988 Steffi Martin Walter, E. Ger 3:03.973
1992 Doris Neuner, AUT 3:06.696
1994 Gerda Weissensteiner, ITA 3:15.517
1998 Silke Kraushaar, GER 3:23.779
2002 Sylke Otto, GER 2:52.464

time of 4 runs. The min. length of the race course between start and finish lines must be at least 1,000m for men's singles and at least 800m for women's singles and men's doubles. International events are held over the distances of 1,500m (men's singles) and 1,050-1,200m (doubles and women's singles) The course must include curves, left and right, a 180° curve, the so-called labyrinth (a series of small curves that alternate in direction), and one S-curve, i.e. a sequence of 2 connected curves that alternate in direction. The course slope must be 8-11% of its length. Luge is also connected to some folk sports, such as Siberian >JUMPING OVER SLEDGES.

History. The oldest sleds having 2 runners were probably known 15,000-10,000 BC in S Asia and later in Scandinavia. Archaeological excavations confirmed the presence of simple sleds in the Alps, at approx. 1000 BC Probably at the same time N.Amer. Indians used sleds – a prototype of the toboggan, later 'inherited' from the Eur. colonists. Similar vehicles were in use in S-E Siberia, which is most likely connected with the common origin of the Mongoloid peoples, who inhabited Asia and America, when both continents were joined by an ice bridge near the Bering Strait. If this were true, the genesis of the toboggan must have been much older than the oldest excavations suggest and go back to the time of the land bridge, dated at approx. 28,000-26,000 BC. The first period of sled development, of any design and in any territory, is connected with a structure, first towed by man, then by domesticated animals, mainly reindeer and dogs. Sleds of this design, although improved technically, continue to be used for transportation purposes in Siberia, Alaska, Canada and Greenland. Sleds were also used in ancient China, on frozen lakes and rivers. >SIBERIAN SLEDGE RACING derives from the old tradition of sled use in Siberia. >SLED DOG RACING, modeled on the way in which N.Amer. trappers traveled, has become very popular in recent years.

A different sled design was popular in the Alps, where in earlier times they were used to transport timber. Sleds had thick wooden runners, with high circular curves in the front. The oldest descriptions of Alpine sleds come from the Middle Ages. Horse-drawn sleds were very popular in the Middle Ages in C and E Europe, particularly in Germany, Poland and Russia. Initially they were transport carriages in which in winter the wheels were replaced with runners. In the 15th and 16th cent. passenger sleds developed, mainly among the nobility. Development of sleds had its peak at the turn of the 17th cent. They were upholstered with furs and damask, their front was sculpted in mythological figures or animals and decorated with wood-carvings or metal elements (e.g. silver fixtures) and they were used by aristocrats and nobility and later also by burghers for amusement (>SZLICHTADA, >KULIG). Smaller sleds, used for recreation, started to develop in parallel with the development of towns, when their inhabitants looked for new forms of recreation. This was the case in the mountain areas, e.g. in the Alps, Sudety Mountains and Carpathians as well as on flat areas, where severe winter conditions prevailed. In Russian towns, on the plains, structures referred to as 'icebergs' developed. These were wooden structures resembling modern ski jumps, but without the end ramp, with a gentle slope ending at the foot of the 'iceberg'. Often 2 towers were built, opposite each other, so that the riders having finished their run from one tower immediately started to climb the other tower, in this way increasing the total number of runs. The largest structures of this type were built as late as the 18th cent. in Moscow and Petersburg. However, it was the Alps that had the greatest influence on the development of the luge. This is where the basic structure of the luge was developed – with curved runners in the front and the rider's seat fastened on carrier poles, mounted perpendicularly to the runners. This structure, despite many modifications and improvements, is still in use today (disregarding some modern types of recreation sleds made of plastic in which the rider's seat is fastened to a thick plastic board that changes in its bottom part into runners and without carrier poles).

A sled design by M. Tietze (1935) was a breakthrough in the development of sports sleds. The center of gravity was lowered, particularly in the back part, runners were made wider, wooden and steel elements were replaced with lighter and stronger plastic ones. There was no front bar, which made them more flexible. The back was lowered and the front raised. This helped to better manouver the sleds and improved their traction properties. Beginning at the turn of the 1950s, the percentage of plastics in sled design started to increase. Some companies, e.g. Grasser from Austria, manufactured sleds completely made of plastics (except for steel bridges). Attempts to use fishplates on the runners (depending on the weather), and runner heating, have been banned since 1972.

It is difficult to say when sleds started to be used in spontaneous sports competitions. The first records of luge competitions in Europe are from 1520-1552 and describe Alpine woodcutters sliding down the mountain slopes. Interest in the Alps by Brit. tourists in the last 20yrs. of the 19th cent. helped to make the luge a modern sport. At the initiative of the British, on 12 Mar. 1883, the first luge competitions were held in Klosters-Davos (Switzerland) along a distance of 4km. The winners were Minsch from Austria and Robertson from Australia. Attempts to unify the different rules of luge competitions and sled designs were made by the Internationaler Schlittensportverband, estab. in 1913, which also initiated the first E.Ch. in 1914, which were won by R. Kauška (a Czech). WWI interrupted the union's activity. Its place was taken in 1923 by the Fédération Internationale de Bobsleigh et de Toboganning, FIBT). Its dominant event initially was <BOBSLEIGHING and >SKELETON. In 1935 a luge section was established as part of FIBT and R. Loteczko (?-1944) from Poland was elected its president. In the same year a German, M. Tietze, designed a sports sled, which started the evolution of sleds, the basic piece of equipment used in the luge. Tietze was also the most outstanding luge rider before 1939 – he won 5 gold medals at E.Ch., then the largest luge event. In 1949 the luge section of FIBT was revived; in 1951 it started to organize E.Ch. and in 1955 W.Ch. At the W.Ch. in 1958 in Krynica (Poland) the Fédération Internationale de Luge de Course, FIL) was formally estab. (in fact, it existed since 1957). In 1964 luge became an Olympic event. After 1949 the best riders came from Austria, the GDR, FRG, Italy, and, sporadically, Poland.

Women's luge started to develop dynamically when the luge became part of the E.Ch. in 1928. The first Eur. women's champion was H. Raupach from Germany. The Women's W.Ch. have been held since 1955 (the first champion was K. Kienzl from Austria). Later the most outstanding women riders included M. Schumann from the GDR, a 4-time world champion (1973-77) and the Ol.G. champion of 1976, as well as S. Martin-Walter, a 4-time world champion (1983-87) and the Ol.G. champion of 1984. After 1990 the best riders were G. Weissensteiner, who represented Italy, S. Erdman (the GDR), who won the W.Ch. in 1989 and 1991 and a few silver medals at the W.Ch. and the Ol.G. in Nagano. See also >POTKUKELKKAILU.

Luge – a doubles race.

LUK HOOP PAT FAAT, a Chin. school of physical exercise and psychophysical perfection; a so-called 'gentle' var. of martial arts.

LUKING, an Eng. game where a small ball is batted out into the playing field using a long bat or a short lever. The details of the rules have not been preserved but according to J. Arlott they were similar to those used in the other games of the same family, such as >TIP-CAT, >TRIBET, >DRAB AND NORR etc. The origin of the name is not clear, perhaps it derives from a dialectal var. of the word 'lugging', from 'lug' in the meaning of 'stick'.
OSCG, 1052.

LURETIK, [Dan. *lure* – lie in wait for something + *tik* – a short pat] a Dan. game where one of the participants stands with his back to the others, who run under his outstretched arms. His task is to pat them on their backs. A player, once caught, stands beside the one caught previously.
J. Møller, 'Luretik', GID, 1997, 2, 39.

LUSUS PILAE CUM PALMA, [Lat. *lusus* – game + *pila* – ball + *cum* – with + *palma* – palm] a ball game played in ancient Rome. The details of the rules are not known but they may have involved bouncing the ball off a wall using one's hand, or perhaps passing it between partners standing at some distance from each other. The game may have been associated with ball games that developed in countries that had been parts of the Roman Empire. There were probably some connections between it and such Brit. games as >HANDBALL and >FIVES, Fr. >JEU DE PAUME, as well as some var. of Span. >PELOTA. It has not been ascertained whether lusus pilae cum palma was in any way related to the game referred to as *palmaria* in old Latinate literature. One hint may be the etymology of both names, associated with the word 'palma'. However, the word 'palmaria' may have also been used to refer to folk festivals held after military triumphs, deriving from the word for palm twig (palma) which was a symbol of victory in ancient Rome (>PALMARIS).

LUURI VEDAMINE, an Est. var. of > TUG-OF-WAR. Two participants, connected by a rope tied around their necks, try to pull each other past a specific point, e.g. a threshold. It has different forms, e.g. the players may stand face to face or back to back. In the latter case they pull the rope while remaining on their hands and knees.
M. Värv et al., 'Traditional Sports and Games in Estonia', TSNJ 1996, 33.

LYFTESTEN, Swed. for 'stone lifting'. The name occurs in a number of dial. var.: *lyftsten*, *löftsten*, *lefting*. The places where the stone lifting competitions took place were known, depending on the region, as *lyftestenar*, >DRÄNGASTENAR or >KAMPASTEN (with the dial. var. *kampsten*). However, lyftsten, as opposed to all the regional names, is an all-Swed. term. The names often derive from the features, characteristics or functions of the stone, e.g. after lifting the >KUNGSSTEN, or 'king stone' one was awarded the title of the 'king of the youngsters' in the parish of Öja. The oldest records mentioning stone lifting in Sweden date back to the Middle Ages, with more precise descriptions going back to the 16th cent. In 1544, the Protestant Parliament (*Riksdag*), during its session at Västerås, passed a number of bills condemning indecent customs, including games in city squares where stones were lifted (*llyftieval* or *lyfteval* in modern spelling): 'whoever runs a house of games or lefftieval shall pay a fine of three öre to the king'. In his *History of Nordic Peoples* (1555), O. Magnus wrote: 'They throw stones or boulders, or lift heavy objects like they lift injured during the battle'. The first mention of using the same name – *lyftesten* – for both the stone and the actual action of lifting dates back to the late 17th cent. In the area of the old Dan.-Swed. borderland, between Södra Möre and Blekinge, the so-called 'royal stones' or >KUNGSSTENARNA were situated, used by the local people in strongman shows until the mid-19th century.

In the early 20th cent., the Swed. ethnographer E. Elgqvist made an inventory of stones used in lifting contests in S Sweden, esp. in the province of Kronoberg. One conclusion from the inventory is that lyftesten was tremendously popular in the area, esp. as a form of competition that accompanied midsummer night celebrations, which is testified by the names of the places where such stones were found – they also served as venues of midsummer night festivals, e.g. Midsommarbaken in Karryd, Sjösås parish. Stone lifting was also done at crossroads and inns whose owners kept stones and reaped additional profits from gambling among their guests. Stones famous locally as difficult to lift were also found within private estates, where guests to weddings, baptism parties etc. competed in lifting them. Two such stones have been preserved near Hårestorps farm in Norregård, Kalvsviks parish. There were also cases of stone stealing. The Swedish researcher G. Drouge, who studied place names in the county of Bularen in 1938, described how a stone traditionally known as Tyftehönan, and formerly lying within the boundaries of Tyft farm, Naverstad parish, Bohuslän, was appropriated, 'in such a dishonest way', by the neighboring farm of Stengrimseröd. In some villages, stones were placed in public squares used for meetings and games, e.g. Majängen ('May meadow') in Skärtyrad, Dädesjö parish. At Nöbelle, Vederslöv parish, whoever managed to lift the local stone and carry it to the manor could on that day drink at the inn at the landlord's expense. During a *brytöl* – a neighborly self-help operation when stones were cleared from fields – the largest stones were often used in throwing and lifting competitions. One of the most famous stones, dug up during a brytöl at Framgården, Råvmarken c.1850, was known as >KÖLNÅKERN, and was used in local stone lifting competitions.

Depending on the forms of competition, lyftesten served various purposes. The most important of these were:

1) Testing the manhood of young people (including male initiation). This use was first described by S. Erixon in his *Ynglingalaget* (1921). The author describes how village youth communities developed, imitating relations between the adults (*byalag*). Demonstrations of physical strength, including lyftesten, played the role of one – but not the only one – of adulthood tests in village communities. Below is Erixon's description:

We have examples there of some strength tests one must undergo before going on to the adult community. Among them is the so-called fight stone (kampasten) that boys are supposed to lift at the village of Fröreda, Järeda parish, Aspelandhundred, Smland. If they can do so, they are no longer considered half-adults, but helkarlar – full men.

G. Eeg-Olofsson, a Swed. researcher specializing in customs associated with stones, estimated that out of the 192 examples of stone lifting in various regions of Sweden that she had studied, 88 were various forms of initiation tests, enabling one to achieve the status of a man, or to participate in a selected group of the male community, or even to exercise the right to marry. Even elements of admitting to sexual initiation were found in such tests. This was visible e.g. in the custom recorded at Älvkarleby, northern Uppland, described to G. Eeg-Olofsson by one of the locals (who, all the same, did not know the custom from his own experience but only recounted what he had heard from his father):

At the half way point (on the route to a mountain pasture), there was a lifting stone and every boy had to lift it to be allowed to

approach the girls in the pasture. If a boy did not succeed in doing so, he was held in contempt as a weakling, and was sent back home.

In the 18th-cent. diary of C.G. Tessin, there is a mention to the effect that a strongman who was able to lift stones that other men in the locality could not raise was given such respect that nobody would dare to fight with him until somebody finally succeeded in lifting the same stone:

In Göthala [...], there are two large stones but there was a Pole at that estate who beat the boys and slipped into the stable to steal hairs from horse tails (to prove his courage). None of the pupils dared to hit back because the Pole could lift the Göthala stones on his own. Finally, the pupils gave up on stealing horse tail hairs and started practicing on those stones, with poor results at the beginning. They moved them a bit, turned them over a bit, and then lifted them a bit, and finally managed them after two or three months. Only then did they gather into a pack and returned the Pole all the insults they had suffered. That was how they measured and weighed their abilities, and since then they were less timid when stealing horse tail hairs in Göthala.

[Dagbok, manuscript at the Royal Library in Stockholm, p. 127, quoted after M. Hellspong]

2) Testing suitability for work. In the past, Swed. landowners sometimes tested the strength of farm workers by making them to lift stones before offering them employment:

Toftaholm used to have a huge manor in the old days, and many day farm workers had to work there to pay back their land or farmsteads. The best workers were not always sent to the manor [...] so it was no wonder that the managers tested their fitness. The Toftaholm lifting stone, was useful and provided an enjoyable show for the managers and many workers that gathered there.

[The Archive of Folk Customs of Lund University, manuscript, M6516, 1-104]

According to a report E. Elgqvist obtained from P.G. Vejde, the cantor of the local church, 'no man was given employment at Toftaholm manor unless he managed to lift the stone'. A similar custom was recorded at Kägelholm manor on Lake Väringen, Närke, where 2 stones known in the local tradition as the >STORA OCH LILLA DAGSVERKARN ('Big and Small Day Workers') were used to test farm workers' strength.

Testing suitability for work also functioned in fishing communities. In 1754, C. von Linne wrote in his *Diary*:

Here, on the lake side, 50km from the village, they have their fishing net [...]. Many people have their shares in the seine, and for that reason they send their representatives to assist during fishing with the seine. No one will be accepted as a worthy representative unless they lift a round stone over their head. The stone weighs about 112 pounds and lies by a path, a little way above the mountain pastures, after one crosses the river.

[Dalaresa, Iter delacrlicum, jämte Utlandsresan, Iter ad exteros, och Bergslagsresan, iter ad fodinas, 1953]

The tests described above were typical of rural communities who singled out their fittest members in that way. At the same time, for those who could not pass the tests, they were incentives to invest more effort in matching one's partners. In this way, through strength tests, the rural community controlled the quality of their work, and, as a consequence, the quality of their lives that depended on intense daily effort.

However, testing suitability for work through stone lifting was not a widespread procedure. G. Eeg-Olofsson classified only 4 out of her 192 examples of stone lifting as suitability for work tests.

3) Forms of entertainment which also added to one's prestige in a community. Out of her 192 examples, Eeg-Olofsson classified 63 as 'pleasure' and 80 as 'sport', the distinction between the two apparently in the lifting of stones just for the fun of it versus serious competition with other lifters.

A typical Swed. stone for lifting was egg-shaped. Sometimes, smooth surfaces were preferred but stones with rough edges, making the hold more difficult, were also used. At times, lifting stones were specially polished. The oval stone known on the island of Öland as the ägget was famous for its being particularly difficult to take a firm hold on (and lift). It was used by local strongmen from 1824. In turn, the stone of Vedåsa, Agunnaryd parish, was difficult to lift due to its sharp edges. Only exceptionally were some of the stones equipped with special handles to facilitate the lift (the handles were also used

to tether horses). Lifting stones from various regions of Sweden weighed between 70 and 200kg. The heaviest ones were not lifted by one man but by a whole team, not infrequently causing injuries. E. Elgqvist describes how a man by the name of Agga-Johan of Nottebäck parish suffered permanent injuries due to his attempts at lifting the stone of Skeda. In most cases, candidates were allowed to rest the stone on their knees before actually lifting them. In the public areas of many villages, there were many stones of varying weights which were used for practicing and checking stone lifting skills. At a crossroads near Frösjöhult, Urshult parish, Oxahall, the ethnographer E. Elgqvist found 8 stones of gradually increasing weights. The commonest technology used for weight grading was making flat, round stones of varying sizes, as the usual, oval stones, could not be placed on top of one another. By contrast, graded millstone-shaped stones enabled this: after the largest stone was lifted, the next, smaller ones were put on top of it, to make a pyramid. This may be confirmed to some extent by a record in the archives of the parish of Gräsmark, district Värmland: 'when a stone was lifted, a strong man could put a smaller one on it to add to the weight' [quotation after M. Hellspong]. Irrespective of the shapes of the stones (which have not been preserved), and the techniques used for placing them on top of each other, it was doubtlessly a folk var. of graded >WEIGHTLIFTING. Cf. >ARRIJASOKETA, >STENLØFTNING, >TYFTEHÖNAN, >GGET.

There was also some humor in the tradition of stone lifting. There is an inscription on the stone of Västra Älmhult, Urshult parish, Småland, reading:

Turn me over
and you will see amazing things.
Once someone succeeded in accomplishing this difficult task,
they could read the inscription on the other side of the stone:
Turn me back over,
for I have cheated many in this way.

M. Hellspong, 'Lifting Stones. The existence of Lifting-Stones in Sweden', ST, 1993-94, XIX-XX; M. Hellspong, 'Lyfta sten', *Den folkliga idrotten*, 2000, 43-64; G.O. Hyltén-Cavallius, *Wärend och widarne* (1863-8); E. Elgqvist, 'Något om lyftestenar', *Nordiskt folkminne. Studier tillägnade C.W. von Sydow* (1928).

Lyftesten.

Stone lifting is a popular traditional sport of many nations. Below is a Basque endañeta contest at the Plaza de Constitucion.

MAADLEMINE, a popular, collective name of 3 var. of Est. wrestling, each using different types of holds. The aim of the bout is to topple the opponent.
SULITSIMAADLEMINE, 'waist hold', the wrestlers clasp each other with one hand over the arm and with the other from under the arm and join their fingers on the other's back.
RINNUTSIMAADLUS, 'lapel grappling', the wrestlers seize each other by the lapels of their jackets.
PUKSIVARVLIMAADLEMINE, 'waistband wrestling', the wrestlers hold each other by the waistband. The rules are agreed on before the bout and the contestants act as referees themselves.
M. Värv, et al., 'Traditional Sports and Games in Estonia', TSNJ, 1996, 33.

MADERA RACES, trad. ox races practiced on the Port. island of Madera, popular among boys up to the age of 16. Each contender drives a pair of oxen joined at the heads with a yoke to which 2 long poles are attached. The driver stands behind the oxen on a crossbar which joins the 2 poles.

Ar maen pouez Breton championship competition.

MAEN POUEZ, in full, *ar maen pouez*, a Bret. var. of weight throwing, known in France as *le lancer du poids*. The competitors take a run-up and then throw weights, usu. round stones of about 20kg., from behind a throwing line, which cannot be crossed. The length of the run-up is not specified, but is usu. 3 steps. Maen pouez is practiced under the auspices of the Breton National Federation of Athletic Sports.
F. Peru, 'La tradition populaire de jeux de plein air en Bretagne', LJP, 1998. Consultant: G. Jaouen, FALSAB.

MAG, a Brit. game consisting of throwing stones at and knocking down stacks of pebbles; cf. >SER.

MAHAI JOKOA, also *mahi jokoa*, Span. *juego dela mesa*, a Basq. var. of >PELOTA VASCA.

MAHI RINGARINGA, a collective name for Maori hand games. The games are played by 2 contenders facing each other, slightly crouching. The game consists of rapid body, arm or hand movements made by the players in response to one another. The starting player makes a call as he makes the first movement. The other player responds with a movement but makes no call. The right to call can be earned in a number of ways, depending on the local var. of the game. In some games a round starts with one of the players issuing a challenge to the other; in other games a round begins when one of the players makes the first call. The responding player must not fall behind or make the wrong movement. If he does so, the opponent earns a point. The player who performs the prescribed hand movements more quickly and precisely wins. The main var. of mahi ringaringa include:
HIPITOI. Players stand facing each other with elbows into the sides with the forearms out from the body parallel to the ground. The starting player begins by calling, 'Hipitoi!' and the responding player answers, 'Ra!', then the starting player makes the first movement. There are 4 basic hipitoi hand movements: hands clenched, both thumbs up, right thumb up, and left thumb up. Every time a player wins a round he starts the new round by calling the number of that round, preceded by the word 'hipitoi':
1 – Hipitoi tahi!
2 – Hipitoi rua!
3 – Hipitoi toru!
4 – Hipitoi wha!
5 – Hipitoi rima!
6 – Hipitoi ono!
7 – Hipitoi whitu!
8 – Hipitoi waru!
9 – Hipitoi iwa!
10 – Hipitoi tekau!
11 – Hipitoi tekau ma tahi!
12 – Hipitoi tekau ma rue!, etc.
A game is usu. 20pts. In some game versions, the winner must be 2 clear rounds ahead of his or her opponent; this method of scoring could have been borrowed from such Eur. games as >TENNIS, >TABLE TENNIS, or >VOLLEYBALL.
MATIMATI. The game is played by 2 contenders facing each other. The players clap their hands rapidly together or slap them on their thighs. All movements must be made in the following sequence:
Matimati – clap clenched fists together;
Tahi matimati – clap open hands together;
Rua matimati – hands open, fingers extended, right thumb struck across left thumb;
Toru matimati – right fist clenched and struck on open palm of left hand;
Wha matimati – 2 open hands brought together, the fingers interlocked;
Rima matimati – thumb of right hand pushed between first and second fingers of left hand, right hand fingers pointing upwards;
Ono matimati – clap clenched fists together;
Whitu matimati – hands open, fingers extended, right thumb struck across left thumb;
Waru matimati – hands open, clap hands but with the heels of the palm only making contact with each other;
Iwa matimati – clap clenched fists together;
Piro matimati – open right hand strikes on the palm of the left hand.
If a player falls behind or makes the wrong movement, the opponent scores a point and the round starts over again; a game consists of 10 rounds; whoever reaches the 10th round first, wins the match. Matimati is widely practiced among the Arawa and Tuhoe tribes which live in the area around Lake Rotorua and Wakaremoana in N.Zealand; var. of the game can be found among other Polynesian tribes as well.
MATE RAWA. The game consists of 7 rounds. A round is won when both players make the same movement at once. The winner is the player who was the caller for that particular movement. The movements are made in the following sequence:
Mate rawa – hands beat on upper legs;
Toro rawa – hands and arms inclined to right, palm of right hand and back of left facing front;
Ngihi ono – reverse of *toro rawa*;
Whitu waru – hands open next to ears;
Te iwa haka – hands on chest.
Mate rawa is an Arawa game but it is played by other tribes as well.
WHAKAROPIROPI. A game known among all Maori tribes under different names. The name *whakaropiropi* is most widely used. The game is extremely fast moving and spectators are often hard put to perceive the individual moves. It consists of 2 different sets of movements: hand movements and wider, arm movements. Some players use only one set in a game while more experienced players make movements of either type. The players crouch opposite each other about 3ft. apart at the start of the game but they move towards each other as the game goes on. The players begin the game by beating their hands on their thighs. Then, the starting player raises his arms bent in elbows, with hands open at ear level. The next movement is extending both arms to one side of the body and then to the other, while hands remain open and below the waist. Finally, the player places both hands on his chest. Experienced players use smaller hand movements with the basic arms movements. They include: 1) both fists closed, elbows into sides; 2) elbows into sides, forearms parallel to the ground and extending straight out from body with hands open; 3) as for 2) but with fingertips touching; 4) right hand open and held over left, resting in the gap between thumb and forefinger. The aim of the game for one player is to catch the other making the same movement simultaneously. When he catches him out, he must call, 'Homai ra!'
E ROPI. Players begin the game with their hands behind their backs. The starting player calls, 'E ropi!' and brings his or her hands out into one of the movements. The responding player tries to bring his or her hands out at the same time and with the same action. If he does, he wins a point. The hand movements are similar to those of *whakaropiropi*. The first player to score 9pts. wins the round (*piro*).
A. Armstrong, *Games and Dancing of the Maori People*, 1986, 33-39.

MAIBAUM, Ger. for 'May tree'; Ger. *maibaum* ceremonies were performed around a bare tree trunk. Apart from dancing, the celebration included a hoax 'auction' of girls, called the *Mailehen* which ended in the coronation of the May queen. Maibaum celebrations were formalized in the early 19th cent. as the *Maiandachten*; they consisted of various games, incl. seeking a boy disguised as a fairy character, e.g. the Leaf Man (*Laubman*), Grasshopper King (*Graskönig*), or – during Whitsunday celebrations – the Whitsun Gnome (*Pfingstbutz*) or Whitsun Simpleton (*Pfingstlümmel*). Maibaum tradition goes back to the early Lombard custom of throwing javelins at a fleece hung on the 'holy tree'. In areas such as Schleswig-Holstein, E Frisian Islands, Holland and even Tirol, Maibaum observances consisted of throwing spears at a ring, wreath or cloth hung on a tree or pole, while riding on horseback; cf. >GAIK MAJOWY, >PALO DE MAYO, >MAYPOLE.

MAIKA, a game consisting of throwing stones or balls at a mark, once practiced in Hawaii; cf. >MAORI BOWLING.

MAIL, Fr. for 'mallet'; a popular, game which originated in medieval France; later its numerous var. became popular in other Eur. countries. Mail survived locally in some areas of France and Walloon Belgium. The rules of the game were only fixed in the 19th cent.; in the early 20th cent. mail was heavily influenced by soccer. The game is played on a field 95x45m, with goal areas at each end, resembling penalty areas in soccer. The aim of the game is to drive a wooden ball, 10-15cm in diameter, into the opposing team's goal area, using special mallets with curved heads. Each team consists of 11 players. In the past, the number of players was not specified. Mail has some historical links to the Eng. game of >PALL-MALL which probably developed in the British Isles as one of its variations. Both games, as their names may suggest, could have been derived from an early It. game of >PALLA MAGLIO.

MAJÓWKA, a countryside pleasure trip combined with all sorts of games and recreational activities, popular in Poland. Ł. Gołębiowski in his work *Gry i zabawy różnych stanów* (*Games and Pastimes of Various Social Classes*, 1831) traces the tradition of Pol. majówka to ancient pagan spring celebrations; see >GAIK MAJOWY.
The earliest forms of majówka bore a resemblance to the Eng. >MAYPOLE or Ger. >MAIBAUM. After the disappearance of old folk celebrations majówka became a simple form of recreation, practiced in municipal schools and social clubs. As Gołębiowski mentions, in the 19th cent. May outings were often combined with sports competitions:

School pupils usually organized trips on the 1st of May. On that day, there were no classes. The pupils and teachers gathered in front of the school building. Each group had their own colors. Next, the entire party went a few miles into the countryside until they reached the village of their destination. They were welcomed and well-treated by the host farmer. In some regions of the country noble landlords made their manors available for the students and teachers on trips. The participants played ball, raced, played on the swings and hide-and-seek. In the evening the whole party came back home singing joyfully.

By the 1850s majówkas were also organized by factory owners as leisure trips for the workers. They featured various sports competitions, such as running, jumping, climbing greasy poles, etc.
Organized May trips survived in Poland until the 1950s. After WWII there were not enough trip sponsors such as factory and manor owners. Labor Day observances in communist Poland gave majówkas a more massive but also ideological character. In the 1960s outings were organized by factory managers who provided trucks which carried the factory workers into the woods. Later, the traffic regulations in Poland prohibited this kind of recreation. Today, May outings in Poland have a mostly individual character with few traces of their past cultural background. See also >PALO DE MAYO.

MALE KAFFEBØNNER, Dan. for 'grinding coffee beans', a type of exercise performed during breaks between classes in Dan. schools. Two contestants clasp their hands high in the air and start rotating – one to the right, the other to the left – trying to not lose the grip. The exercise is mentioned by J. Møller in his lexicon of Dan. sports games (*Gamle idrætslege i Danmark*, 1997, 3, p. 47).

MALKAMBH, a var. of trad. Hindu wrestling.

MALLAKHAMB, (Hindu *malla* – 'gymnast' + *khamb* – 'pole'), a trad. Hindu sport in which complex acrobatic exercises are performed by a group of athletes, who form a pyramid, using a special pole, chains or ropes. Mallakhamb has the following varieties:
MALLAKHAMB FIXED ON THE GROUND. The gymnasts form a 6-story pyramid. The pole stands 225cm above the ground; it has a circumference of 55cm at its lower end, 45cm in the middle, and 30cm at the upper end. The pole is usu. made of teakwood or sheeshum, preferred because of its toughness and smoothness.
HANGING MALLAKHAMB. The gymnasts perform acrobatic figures on a pole suspended with the aid

of hooks and chains. The swinging and revolving motion of the pole renders more dynamic exercises than in other var. of the sport.

ROPE MALLAKHAMB. The gymnasts perform figures on a rope 2.5cm thick, which replaces the wooden pole. The performers strike various yogic poses, without knotting the rope in any way.

REVOLVING BOTTLE MALLAKHAMB. The gymnasts perform exercises on 32 glass bottles placed on a wooden platform.

The sport of mallakhamb has a tendency to introduce new var., employing all sorts of gymnastic apparatus.

History. The origins of mallakhamb go back to the 12th cent. A description of the sport can be found in *Manas Olhas*, an old text from the reign of the Calucya dynasty. Mallakhamb was revived in the first half of the 19th cent. by Balambhatta Dada Deodhar, a courtier of Prince Peshwa Baji Rao II. At present, mallakhamb is practiced in 14 states of India.

The Internet: http://www.meadev.nic.in/sports/tr_games/mallakhamb.html

MALL-STAMBHA, an old form of Hindu wrestling mentioned together with walking and weight lifting (>BHRAMANSHRAM, >BHRASHRAM) by Someshwara in his work *Manas Olhas* (1135 AD). One wrestler stood in the water up to his waist, while his opponent sat on his shoulders. The bout was over if the standing wrestler threw off his opponent.

MAMAU, see >WHATOTO.

MANNED SPACE FLIGHTS. The Ital. *Enciclopedia dello sport* (1965) includes these among sport disciplines characterized by high cognitive values, along with >GEOGRAPHICAL EXPLORATION. There is doubtlessly some sporting element to space flights: for instance, they require exceptional fitness and long-term training. Also, record flight durations are recorded, and there is some competition between nations. However, space flights go beyond sport in their essence, esp. in 1) minimizing the role of fitness in favor of technical equipment – fitness has a negligible influence on the course of the flight itself; 2) no individuality of achievements, which are influenced more by the efforts of thousands of co-workers than by the effort and will of the individual astronaut; 3) the small influence individuals have on the predefined scientific goals of space flights; and 4) no direct 'struggle' against the natural environment. This does not compromise the value of space flights as a non-sporting human activity, reduces their sporting character.

History. The first space flight in history was made by Y. Gagarin in the Vostok 1 spaceship. Before that, animals (dogs and apes) had been sent into outer space. The first 24-hour flight was made by H. Titov (6-7 August 1961, Vostok 2). The first joint flight of 2 spacecraft involved A. Nikolayev and P. Popovich in Vostok 3 and 4, respectively (11-15 August 1962, Vostok 3). The first space walk was made by B. Belayev (18 March 1965, Voskhod 2). V. Tyeryeshkova was the first woman in outer space (June 16-19, 1963, Vostok 6). The first moon landing was made by the Americans N. Armstrong and E. Aldrin (July 16-24, Apollo 11, with M. Collins on the lunar orbit). The first successful flight of a space shuttle (capable of landing safely back on Earth) was made by the Amer. shuttle Columbia (April 12-14, 1981, with J. Young, and R. Crippen on board). After a period of competition between the USA and USSR, the joint flight of Soyuz 19 and Apollo 18 (April 16-24, 1975, a joint flight for 1 day, 19hrs. and 54mins.) was a major symbolic achievement. Later, space flights became routine endeavors, and the competition has been there not so much in the 'conquering' of outer space but in the development of technologies and methods. One manifestation was the construction of the first orbital station. The next challenge will be an interplanetary flight. Many astronauts and cosmonauts have died during space flights. Some of the accidents were concealed by the Soviet government. The first tragedy that saw the light of day was that of Soyuz 11, and was due to a loss of cabin atmosphere during landing (1971). The most disastrous Amer. accidents involved the Challenger space shuttle, which exploded just after launch from Cape Canaveral in 1986, killing all 7 crew members, and the loss of Columbia, which disintegrated upon re-entry, again killing all 7 crew members, on 1 Feb. 2003.

MANNIE ON THE PAVEMENT, a Scot. street game played on the sidewalk near a wall. One of the players, called the 'mannie', is chosen to guard an area marked on the wall; the mannie cannot touch the wall. The remaining players try to outsmart the mannie and touch the wall section without being caught by the mannie; the caught player becomes a new mannie. The game was once popular in Aberdeen. TGESI, II, 443.

MANSEI-KAN, a Jap. martial art, one of the elements of >AIKIDO. The rules of mansei-kan were formulated by Kanshu Sunadomari from Kumamoto (b.1923), a student of Mirohei Ueshiba, the founder of aikido.

MANU TUKUTUKU, a Maori var. of >KITE FLYING.

MAOKIU, also *maoquiu* or *muqiu*, a game similar to >FIELD HOCKEY, played in the Chin. province of Ningsia-Huej. It is modeled on a shepherds' game, which nowadays is played in accordance with formal sports rules. Two teams of 5 players, including the goalkeepers, play with rackets made from a slightly curved plank, 3cm wide at the top and about 10cm wide at the bottom. For safety reasons, players cannot raise the planks above knee level. The game lasts 2 periods of 20min. The goals are similar to those used in handball, with a soft, rope net. In the event of a draw the winner is decided by penalty throws. In international ethnological terminology the game is called *Hui Wood Ball* (after the Huej province).
Mu Fushan et al., 'Maoqiu', TRAMCHIN, 34.

MAORI BOWLING, an ancient Maori game known in N.Zealand before the arrival of Europeans. The game was most likely brought to the islands during the migrations of Polynesian and Hawaii peoples; see >MAIKA. The game became extinct before it could be described by ethnographers. Only some stone bowls, or rather disks (about 5in thick and 3in in diameter), used for the game have survived.

MAORI RACES, see >OMAOMA, >TAUPIRIPIRI.

MARATHON, a common name for a sports competition over a long distance or a long period of time, requiring strenuous physical effort, e.g. >CYCLING

The mud marathon in Schermerhorn, Holland attracts swimmers from over 70 countries.

MARATHON, >DANCE MARATHON, >OLYMPIC MARATHON, >SKATE MARATHON, >LONG DISTANCE SWIMMING, >VERTICAL MARATHON. The name of the competition is derived from Marathon in N-E Greece. It commemorates the legendary feat of a Gk. soldier who, in 490 BC, was supposed to have run from Marathon to Athens in full armor, covering a distance of about 40km, to bring news of the Gk. victory over the Persians. Having delivered this news the messenger died of exhaustion. Historians argue as to the credibility of that event and to the real name of the first marathon runner, which was probably Feidippides (sometimes mistakenly called Filipides). In fact, great feats consisting of running long distances and bringing urgent messages occurred several times in Gk. history.

MARBLES, a family of games played with balls (1-3cm in diameter) made of glass, stone or marble (hence the name). It is usu. played by children. Cornish fishermen used to practice *cherry pits* (see below). The Amer. >ROLLEY HOLE is a professional var. of the game, using bigger marbles and played by adults. Other versions, such as >BRIDGE-BOARD, have developed sophisticated rules and may require extra equipment. J. Strutt in *Glig Gamena Angel Deoth, or the Sports and Pastimes of the People of England* writes that marbles developed as a substitute for bowling (see >LAWN BOWLING). Most sports historians and ethnographers do not regard it as a serious game. Anglo-Saxon studies are an exception. Many types of the game are described in A.B. Gomme's *The Traditional Games of England, Scotland and Ireland* (vol. 1 – 1894, vol. 2- 1898). Some of the simpler Ang.-Sax. var. are:
BONSOR, a London dialect name for marbles (from *bounce*);
BOSS OUT, 'Boss out, or boss and span, also called hit or span, wherein one bowls a marble to any distance that he pleases, which serves as a mark for his antagonist to bowl at, whose business it is to hit the marble first bowled, or lay his own near enough to it for him to span the space between them and touch both the marbles. In either case he wins. If not, his marble remains where it lay, and becomes a mark for the first player, and so alternately until the game be won' [Strutt, 340];
BOUNCER, a London dialect name for marbles (from *bounce*);
BUN-HOLE, 'A hole is scooped out in the ground with the heel in the shape of small dish, and the game consists in throwing a marble as near to this hole as possible. Sometimes, when several holes are made, the game is called holy' [TGESI, I, 51]. The game was esp. popular in Sheffield;
CASTLES, 'Each boy makes a small pyramid of 3

American astronauts John Grunsfeld (left) and Richard Linnehad (right) space-walk the exterior of the space shuttle Columbia on a mission to repair the Hubble telescope.

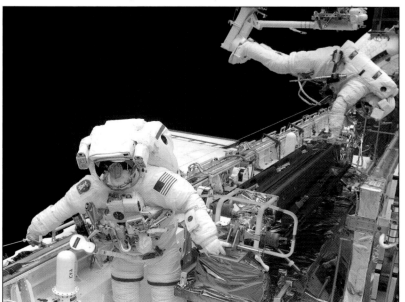

A poster for a French movie The Winner of the Marathon.

David Gilmour Blythe, A Boy Playing Marbles, 1858, oil on canvas.

M
WORLD SPORTS ENCYCLOPEDIA

as a base, and 1 on the top. The players aim at these from a distant stroke with balsers, winning such of the castles as they may in turn knock down. [...]. In London, the marble alluded to as balser was called bonsor or bouncer' [TGESI, I, 60];

CHOCK or chock-hole, 'a game at marbles played by 'chocking' or pitching marbles in a hole made for the purpose, instead of shooting at a ring' [TGESI, I, 67-8];

COB, 'A game at marbles played by 2 or 3 boys bowling a boss marble into holes made in the ground for the purpose, the number of which is generally 4' [TGESI, I, 70];

DAB-AT-THE-HOLE, one of the oldest versions of marbles. The rules are not extant;

DUMPS, 'A game at marbles or taw, played with holes scooped in the ground' and 'leaden counters called dumps' [TGESI, I, 119], chiefly in the Roxburgh area. Other sources mention holes filled with water. Gomme compares the game to >CHERRY PITS.

FOX AND GEESE, 'A game played with marbles or pegs on a board on which are 33 holes, or on the pavement, with holes scraped out of the stones. To play this game there are 17 pieces called Geese, and another one larger or distinguished from the Geese by its color, which is called the Fox. The Fox occupies the center hole, and the Geese occupy 9 holes in front, and 4 on each side of him. The holes behind are for the Geese and Fox to move in. The game is for the Geese to shut up the Fox so that he cannot move. All the pieces can be moved from one spot to another in the direction of the lines, but cannot pass over 2 holes at once. The Geese are not permitted to take the Fox. The Fox's business is to take all, or as many of the Geese as will prevent him from being blockaded. The Fox can take the Geese whenever there is a vacant space behind them, which he passes to, then occupies' [TGESI]. The game was popular in many Eng. schools since medieval times. The oldest mention of it concerns students of the cathedral school in Gloucester, where stone benches were used for the game. Salisbury and Norwich Castle are also mentioned.

HO-GO, 'The first player holds up a number in his closed hand and says, 'Ho-go'; the second says, 'Handful'; the first then says, 'How many?' The other guesses. If he should guess correctly he is entitled to take them all; but otherwise he must give the difference between the number he guessed and the number actually held up [...]. It is also called How many eggs in a basket' [TGESI, I, 218];

HOILAKES, 'The name of a games of marbles which are cast into a hole in the ground' [TGESI, I, 218];

HOLY BANG, 'consists in placing a marble in a hole and making it act as a target for the rest. The marble which can hit it 3 times in succession, and finally be shot into the hole, is the winning ball, and its owner gets all the other marbles which have missed before he played' [TGESI, II, 218-9];

HUNDREDS, 'is carried on until one of the players scores 100 or some other high number agreed upon. Any number can play, but it is best described for 2 players, A. and B. First the players taw up to a hole; if both get in, they repeat the process until one is left out, say B.; then A. counts 10. Should both fail, the nearest goes first. He may now lay his taw about the hole or fire at the other, on hitting which he counts another 10. He now goes for the hole again, and failing, lies where he happens to stop. If he misses, B. from his present position tries to get into the hole, and failing, lies still; but if he reaches the hole, he counts 10, and proceeds as A. had done. The one who first gets the 100 (or other number) now goes in for his 'pizings', which performance takes place thus: The loser, so far, is lying about, and the winner goes back to 'drakes', and again tries to lodge in the hole; and if he succeeds, the game is up. If not, he lies still, and, the loser tries for the hole; if he gets in he counts another 10, or if he should succeed in hitting the winner he scores his adversary's 100 to his own number, and then goes on for his 'pizings' as the other had done. In failure of either securing the game thus, the process is repeated as 'drakes'. When, however, the one who is on for his 'pizings' manages to taw into the hole, the game is concluded' [TGESI, I, 240-1];

HYNNY-PYNNY, 'sometimes called Hyssy-pyssy, played in some parts of Devon and Somerset. A hole of some extent was made in an uneven piece of ground, and the game was to shoot the marbles at some object beyond the hole without letting them tumble into it. The game occasionally commenced by a ceremony of no very delicate description, which sufficed to render the fallen marble still ignominious' [TGESI, 247];

LAB, a var. of marbles played in Antrim, N Ireland;

LAG, 'A number of boys put marbles in a ring, and then they all bowl at the ring. The one who gets nearest has the first shot at the marbles. He has the option of either 'knuckling doon' and shooting at the ring from the prescribed mark, or 'ligging up' (lying up) – that is, putting his taw so near the ring that if the others miss his taw, or miss the marbles in the ring, he has the game all to himself next time. If, however, he is hit by the others, he is said to be 'killed'' [TGESI, I, 324]. The game was played chiefly in Sheffield;

LONG-TAWL, 'Each takes aim at the other in turn, a marble being paid in forfeit to whichever of the players may make a hit' [TGESI, I, 350]. Played chiefly in Berkshire;

PIG-RING, 'A ring is made about 4ft. in diameter, and boys 'shoot' in turn from any point in the circumference, keeping such marbles as they may knock out of the ring, but loosing their own 'taw' if it should stop within [TGESI, II, 40-41];

PITS, 'The favourite recreation with the young fishermen in West Cornwall. Forty years ago 'Pits' and 'Towns' were the common games, but the latter only is now played. Boys who hit their nails are looked on with great contempt, and are said to fire 'Kibby'. When 2 are partners, and one in playing accidentally hits the other's marble, he cries out, 'No custance', meaning that he has a right to put back the marble struck; should he fail to do so, he would be considered 'out' [...] There is description of the method of playing. It may be the same as 'Cherry Pits', played with marbles instead of cherry stones [...]. Mr. Newell, Games and Songs of American Children, p. 187, says 'The pits are thrown over the palm; they must fall so far apart that the fingers can be passed between them. Then with a flip of the thumb the player makes his pit strike the enemy's and wins both' [TGESI, II, 45];

PLUM PUDDING, 'A game [...] of 2 or more boys.

Each puts an equal number of marbles in a row close together, a mark is made at some little distance called a taw; the distance is varied according to the number of marbles in a row. The first boy tosses at the row in such a way as to pitch just on the marbles, and so strike as many as he can out of the line; all that he strikes out he takes; the rest are put close together again, and 2 other players take their turn in the same manner, till all the marbles are struck out of the line, when they all stake afresh and the game begins again.' [TGESI, II, 46]. Played chiefly in Northamptonshire;

PYRAMID, 'A circle of about 2ft. in diameter is made on the ground, in the centre of which a pyramid is formed be several marbles. Nine are placed as the base, then 6, then 4, and then on the top. The keeper of the pyramid then desires the other players to shoot. Each player gives the keeper one marble for leave to shoot at the pyramid, and all that the players can strike out of the circle belong to them' [TGESI, II, 89];

RINGER, a var. of marbles similar to lag.

RING-TAW, 'A rough ring is made on the ground, and the players each place in it an equal share in 'stonies', or alleys. They each bowl to the ring with another marble from a distance. The boy whose marble is nearest has the first chance to taw; if he misses a shot the second boy, whose marble was next nearest to the ring, follows, and if he misses, the next, and so on. If one player knocks out a marble, he is entitled to taw at the rest in the ring until he misses; and if a sure 'tawer' not one of the others may have a chance to taw. Any one's taw staying within the ring after being tawn at the 'shots', is said to be 'fat', and the owner of the taw must then replace any marbles he has knocked out in the ring'. Earls Heaton, Yorks. (Herbert Hardy). Halliwell (Dictionary) describes this game very much as above, except that a fine is imposed on those who leave the taw in the ring. Ross and Stead (Holderness Glossary) give this game as follows: 'Two boys place an equal number of marbles in the form of a circle, which are then shot at alternately, each boy pocketing the marbles he hits. Addy (Sheffield Glossary) says, 'Ring-taw is a marble marked with a red ring used in the game of marbles. This is commonly called 'ring' for short'. Evans (Leicestershire Glossary) describes the game much the same as above, but adds some further details of interest. 'If the game be knuckle-up the player stands and shoots in that position. If the game be knuckle-down he must stoop and shoot with the knuckle of the first finger touching the ground at taw. In both cases, however, the player's toe must be on taw. The line was thus called taw as marking the place for the toe of the player, and the marble a taw as being the one shot from the taw-line, in contradiction to those placed passively in the ring-'line' in the one case, and 'marble' in the other being dropped as superfluous.' Strut (Sports and Pastimes, p. 384) alludes to the game. In Ireland this game is also called 'Ring', and is played with marbles and buttons. A ring is marked out on a level hard place, and every boy puts down a button. The buttons are lightly struck in the center of the ring, and all play their marbles to the buttons. The nearest to them play first. The line from which they play is generally about 8ft. away, and everybody does his best to strike the buttons. Any put out are kept by the boy putting them out, and if a boy strikes a button, or buttons, out, he can play on until he misses. – Waterville, Cos. Kerry and Cork, T.J. Dennachy (through Mrs. B.B. Green of Dublin).' [TGESI, II, 113-114];

RUMPS, a var. of marbles played in Cumberland;

SAGGY, a var. of marbles played in Cumberland;

SHIP SAIL, 'A game usu. played with marbles. One boy puts his hand into his trousers pocket and takes out as many marbles as he feels inclined; he closes his fingers over them, and holds out his hand with the palm down to the opposite player, saying, 'Ship sail, sail fast. How many men on board?' a guess is made by his opponent; if less he has to give as many marbles as will make up the true number; if more, as many as he said over. But should the guess be correct he takes them, and then in his turn says, 'Ship sail,' &c. – Cornwall (Folk-lore Journal, v.59).' [TGESI, II, 191-192];

SHUVVY-HAWLE, 'A boys' game at marbles. A small hole is made in the ground, and marbles are pushed in turn with the side of the first finger; these are won by the player pushing them into the shuvvy-hawle. – Lowsley's Berkshire Glossary.' [TGESI, II, 196];

Morgan Kellman, 13, of Frederick County, Maryland, shoots for the title of Marbles Queen during the annual National Marbles Tournament in Wildwood, N.J. The annual event draws a crowd of young marble players from around the US to compete for the coveted crowns of Marbles King and Queen.

SPANG AND PURLEY, 'A mode resorted to by boys of measuring distances, particularly at the game of marbles. It means a space and something more. – Brockett's *North Country Words*.' [TGESI, II, 210]; SPANGIE, 'A game played by boys with marbles or halfpence. A marble or halfpenny is struck against the wall. If the second player can bring his so near that of his antagonist's as to include both within a *span*, he claims both as his.' – Jamieson. This is the same game as 'Banger', 'Boss Out'. Probably the Old Eng. game of 'Span Counter', or 'Span Farthing', was originally the same. – See Johnson's *Dictionary*.' [TGESI, II, 210]; SPANNIMS, 'A game at marbles played in the eastern parts of England. – Halliwell's *Dictionary*.' [TGESI, II, 211]; SPLINTS, 'A game at marbles, in which they are dropped from the hand in heaps. – Easther's *Almondbury Glossary*.' [TGESI, II, 211]; STROKE, 'A game at marbles, where each player places a certain number on a line and plays in turns from a distance mark called 'scratch', keeping such as he may knock off. – Lowsley's *Berkshire Glossary*.' [TGESI, II, 220]. TEDAMA, Jap. for 'hand marbles', a Jap. var. of a game with 5 stones or marbles. At a certain time it became popular in the USA, esp. in Boston, where it was known as *otadama*.
A.B. Gomme, *The Traditional Games of England, Scotland and Ireland*, vol. 1, 1984.

MARCHÉ, LE, see >FA KOR.

MARCHING, a type of human movement consisting of walking with a firm, regular stride, often exercised by an organized group of people to the accompaniment of musical bands. Technically, marching is similar to >JOG/WALK; the latter, however, emphasizes individual rather than collective achievement. Marching is part of the military tactical training; marching skills are displayed during military parades. Marches are organized as important parts of opening and closing ceremonies of large sports events. The so-called sports marches are based on the military musical even tempo of 4/4, 2/4 or 6/8, but they are often accompanied with lyrics devoted to sports themes. The number of existing sports marches is difficult to estimate. The most popular works include *Olympic Triumphal March* by H. Alexanderson (1908); *Olympic Triumphal March* by R. Barthelemy (gold medal at Olympic music contest 1912); *Triumphal March* (Marcia trionfale) by O. Rivy (silver medal at Olympic music contest 1920); *To the Olympics* (Op ter Olympiade) by J.P. Koppen (the opening march of the Amsterdam OI.G. in 1928). After the October Revolution of 1917 sports marches became immensely popular in the Soviet Union, where they served the purpose of 'raising masses for the common deed'. One of the most renowned marching songs of that time was *Sports March* (music by I. Dunajewski; lyrics by W. Lebiediev):

Keep your body and your spirit young,
Keep them young, keep them young.
Pursue your goal, in the frost and heat,
Temper your body like steel!
Let there be sport!
Defend your goal boldly,
Toughen your arms,
And pick up the weapon and the hammer.

At present, the Olympic opening ceremony is a spontaneous parade rather than a formal march. The legacy of the World Wars and anti-war attitudes of the 1960s young generation caused aversion towards transplantation of military motifs to sport. Nowadays, major sports events are usu. accompanied with mild, melodious songs such as *Hand in Hand* (1988) or *Amigos para siempre* (1992) performed as the athletes walk easily around the stadium during the opening or closing ceremony; see also >MARSZOBIEG and >RACE WALKING.

MARI KOJU, see >KEMARI.

MARI UCHI, also *gitcho*, an ancient Jap. game similar to modern field hockey; originated in the 11th-12th cent.

MARSZOBIEG, Pol. for 'march/run', sports or recreational exercise involving jogging and walking alternately. Marszobiegs were common public forms of recreation in the Eastern Block countries, officially supported by communist authorities. In the 1950s and 1960s they were organized on the occasion of

various important anniversaries, e.g. the October Revolution. Marszobiegs were attended massively by participants of all walks of life, and depending on the participants' physical condition the proportion of marching and jogging varied; see also >JOG/WALK and >RACE WALKING.

MARUA, a Georg. horse bride race involving snatching a bride's scarf held by a fleeing mounted rider in his mouth. Once the scarf is snatched from the rider the winner is allowed to choose the bride as his wife; see other Georg. horse races >MOKNIEWA, >TARCZIA.

MARUMONO, an ancient form of Jap. foot archery, popular at the end of the Heian period (12th cent.) and in the Hojo period. Cf. other Jap. forms of foot archery >BUSHA, >JUMIHAJIME, >KUSAJISI, >MOMOTE; equestrian archery >INUOMONO, >YABASUME, KADAGAKE; and ceremonial archery >JYARAJ, >IBAHAJIME, NORIYUMI, >TANGONO KISHA.

MASANGJAE, a trad. type of Kor. bareback riding.

MASTRO DE COCANHA, a Port. var. of >GREASED POLE.

MÂT DE COCAGNE, LE, a Fr. equivalent of >GREASED POLE, consisting of climbing a greased pole for a reward mounted on top of it; practiced during folk festivals in many countries; see also >WERN, >PALO LUCIO.

MATE RAWA, a Maori hand game; see >MAHI RINGARINGA.

MATIMATI, one of Maori hand games; see >MAHI RINGARINGA.

MAYPOLE, also *maypole dancing*, an Eng. ceremonial folk dance, derived from ancient European pagan spring rites to ensure fertility; see Pol. >GAIK MAJOWY, Ger. >MAIBAUM, Dan >SOMMER I BY. In the popular belief, honoring symbols of fertility such as a blooming tree, ensured the return of spring. In England, maypole observations commenced one day before the dance. Around midnight, village boys, followed by girls, would go to the forest to cut down a tree for the maypole. An Eng. pastor, P. Stubbs (called 'the archenemy of trad. customs' by the US sports historian, B.G. Rader) described the start of the maypole ceremony in the woods in his work *Anatomy of Abuses* (1583), and observed with horror that 'Of forty, three-score, or a hundred maids going to the wood over night there have scarcely the third part of them returned home again undefiled.' After the tree was cut down it was brought triumphantly into the village. Then, among various unspecified rituals, it was cleaned of branches and erected. The crucial part of the maypole erection was attaching long ribbons to the top of the pole. The dancers started moving around the pole and interweaving the ribbons into complex patterns. Maypole celebrations were often accompanied with different local ball games, mentioned in some 19th-cent. ethnographic sources. In Northampton, for example, 'The May garland was suspended by ropes from the school-house to an opposite tree, and the Mayers amused themselves by throwing ball over it' (GOME, I, 14). In the area of Fotheringay, some elderly people recalled that 'The May garland was hung in the centre of the street, on a rope stretched from house to house. Then was made the trial in tossing balls (small white leather ones) through the framework of the garland, to effect which was a triumph (GOME, I, 13-14). The maypole ball games occasionally served fortune-telling purpose, e.g. the number a given player would catch the ball during one game would signify his number of years to live (>BALL DIVINATION).

History. Maypole traditions go back to pagan times. Despite heavy Christian influences maypole celebrations survived through the Middle Ages. Together with many other Eng. folk games and pastimes maypole dancing became the subject of harsh disputes and controversy between the monarchy and the Puritans that were growing in power in the first half of the 17th cent. For the Puritan clergy, games, sports, and dances seemed a threat to public morality. In 1617, King James I asked Bishop Morton of Chester, a renowned religious negotiator between the Catholics and Puritans, whether the maypole dance could be included as a folk pastime in the forthcoming *Declaration of Sports*, also known as the *Book of Sports* (1618). Morton replied that no

games or pastimes can be practiced during religious services but only after them. The congregation is free to choose any sport or game it wishes to play, e.g. archery, running or maypole dancing, after Sunday services and the Puritan clergy must not prohibit these in their parishes. Merton's resolution, was, however, never accepted by the majority of Puritan clergy, which led to a conflict between the Puritans and the king over the *Declaration of Sports*. The king's stance on sports and recreation was clear:

And as for our good Peoples Recreation, our Pleasure likewise is, that after the End of Divine Service, our good People be not disturbed, letted or discouraged from any lawful Recreation; such

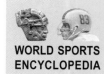

A children's marching band passes a portrait of Sun Yat-sen, the father of modern China, prior to the start of the celebration parade of 500,000 people to mark the People's Republic of China's 50th anniversary at Tiananmen Square in Beijing.

as Dancing, either Men or Women, Archery for Men, Leaping, Vaulting, or any other such harmless Recreation; nor from having of May Games, Withson-Ales, and Morris-Dances, and the setting up of May-Poles, and other sports therewith used, so as the same be had in due and convenient time, without Impediment or Neglect of Divine Service.

But the Puritan clergy refused to read the Declaration to their congregations and maypole dancing was soon under the severe repression of the Puritans and the established Church of England, both in England and the Amer. colonies. Maypole traditions, however, survived Puritan rule in the years 1649-60, and were fully revived during the Restoration and the reign of Charles II. Maypole dances were popular among New England colonists, alongside bowling, billiards and other sports games. Similar dances, known as >PALO DE MAYO, also began to be practiced in Nicaragua, influenced first by the Eng. cultural models, and later modified by the traditions and customs of Ger. settlers, the Bohemian Brethren, Amer. Natives and Afr. slaves.
D. Brailsford, *Sport and Society: Elizabeth to Anne*, 1969; C. Hill, *Society and Puritanism in Pre-Revolutionary England*, 2nd ed. 1967; E.O. James, *Seasonal Feasts and Festivals*, 1961; R. Malcolmson, *Popular Recreations in English Society, 1700-1850*, 1973; W.U. Solberg, *Redeem the Time: The Puritan Sabbath in early America*, 1970; N. Struna, 'Puritans and Sport: The Irretrievable Tide of Change', JSH, 1997, 1.

MAZANDERANI, a var. of wrestling practiced in the north of Iran; similar to *gilaki*.

MAZO, see >ULAMA, ULAMA DE PALO.

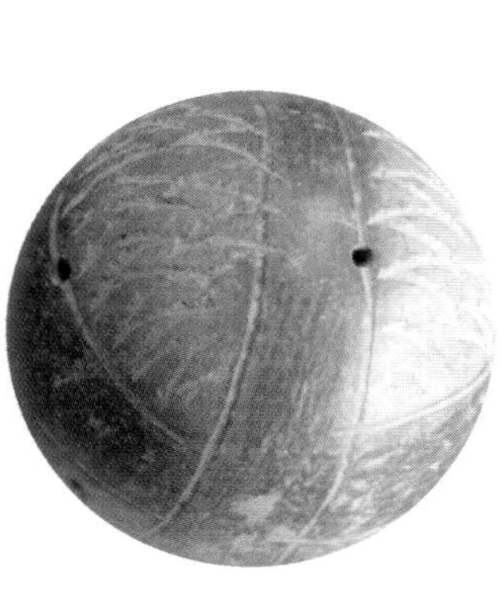

An Olmec ball rattle, pottery, 1000-500 BC, Mexico.

Mesoamerican ball player, pottery, 700-900 AD, Veracruz, Mexico.

Female Huastec ballplayer, pottery, 800-1000 AD, Mexico.

MECRANOTI INDIAN HOCKEY, a game featuring a ball made of hard tropical fruit, similar to >FIELD HOCKEY. Played by the S.Amer. Chaco tribes, mostly by women.

MEGHALAYAN ARCHERY, a trad. form of military archery practiced today as a sport in the Ind. state of Meghalaya. The limbs of a Meghalayan bow are made of bamboo wood, and the bowstring of bamboo fibers. The arrows are made of cane, with iron arrowheads and fletches of four eagle feathers. The bows and arrows are traditionally hand-made by local women. In the modern, sports version of Meghalayan archery, the target is a small oval grass mat; it is 3in. wide and 8-10in. tall. The targets are mounted on wooden poles, 3½ft. above the ground. The poles are notched at a certain height; a shot below the notch does not count. The contenders shoot their arrows from a distance of about 30m. Contests can be held as individual or team events.

MEKEMEKE, a shortened name for Maori pugilism >WHAWHAI MEKEMEKE.

MELANESIAN BALL GAMES, diverse ball games played in the islands of Melanesia, incl. the Bismarck Archipelago, Fiji, Salomon Islands, New Caledonia, and the New Hebrides. The main Melanesian ball games incl. >MELANESIAN FOOTBALL, >MELANESIAN HANDBALL, >MELANESIAN SHINTY, >MELANESIAN BAT AND BALL. Cf. >OCEANIAN BALL GAMES.

MELANESIAN BAT AND BALL, a folk var. of ball and bat game commonly practiced in Melanesia. The ball is usu. a hard fruit of the *kaui kents* tree. The game is played by 2 teams. The players of one team pitch the ball to their opponents who try to hit it with a bat. See also >MELANESIAN BALL GAMES.

MELANESIAN FOOTBALL, a folk var. of a football game practiced in Melanesia, esp. in the New Hebrides, central Papua New Guinea, the Admiralty Islands, Aoba, Wogeo and Manus. In different local traditions, the ball used for the game can be a coconut or breadfruit. The rules of Melanesian football differ in many areas. The uniform rule is that the ball can only be kicked. Melanesian football games are usu. team competitions.

MELANESIAN HANDBALL, a folk var. of handball practiced in the islands of Melanesia, esp. in Papua New Guinea, New Hebrides, the Torres Strait Islands, Matu, and Tanga. The ball can be an inflated pig bladder, a fruit of the *kai* tree, or bundle of screwpine twigs (Lat. *pandanus*). During the game, one player dribbles the ball while others try to intercept it or catch it on the fly. The goal is often a pair of short poles stuck in the ground.

MELANESIAN SHINTY, a popular name given to a folk game known in the region of New Hebrides, the islands of the Torres Strait and the estuary of the Fly River in New Guinea. The game is played with sticks, most often made of bamboo, which are used to drive a wooden ball. Players play on the beach and dunes, where the Fly River flows into the Gulf of Papua. No specific rules apply. The teams, each having a different number of players, compete for possession of the ball. The team, which upon the completion of the 'match', is in possession of the ball, wins. Ethnographers have not observed any attempts to 'score points' by hitting the ball into a goal or making it pass a defined borderline. Cf. >OCEANIAN PEOPLE'S HOCKEY.

MELAT, also *mellat* or *melad*, a violent medieval ball game played with curved sticks. It was a plebeian var. of LA >SOULE, in which a larger ball was used. In Brittany, melat was known as >C'HOARI MELLAD. Due to numerous brawls resulting from the course of play the church and state authorities frequently banned the game, as is evidenced, for instance, in the *Synod Statutes* of Raoul, Bishop of Tréguier, from 1440:

This dangerous and pernicious game must be forbidden due to hatred, malice and hostility it generates in the hearts and souls of many under the disguise of leisurely fun. Our noble citizens often complain that in some parishes in our jurisdiction, people gather to play this destructive game during holidays. The game is played with a large ball, known in the local tongue as the mellat. It has brought upon many a brawl and will bring many more in the future unless we find some measures to stop it. Therefore, we officially ban this outrageous game and shall punish any person who indulges in this game with an excommunication.

Despite the threat of excommunication the bans on melat playing were not effective. A century later a game of melat played near the church in Vauchelles-sur-Authie was mentioned by outraged members of the religious community.

MELLAT, see >MELAT.

MELLEMBOLD, see >TREBOLD.

MESOAMERICAN INDIAN BALL GAMES, ball games practiced by Amer. Indians of C America, whose tradition go back to c.2000 BC. In many regions of C America, e.g. in the village of Xoxo (300km SW of Oaxaca, Mexico) some ancient folk var. of indigenous ball games are still practiced today, which makes them – according to R.L. Humphrey, a researcher of ethnic sports – 'one of the longest-lasting and geographically most widespread games in world history'. Moreover, Humphrey observes that 'The ancient Mesoamerican games also seem to have profoundly influenced 16th-cent. Eur. sports, and these innovations were absorbed, then re-introduced into Mexico along with Eur. elements by the dominant Span. culture, where they mixed differentially with the remaining vestiges of the ancient games.' (*Play as Life: Suggestions for a Cognitive Study of the Mesoamerican Ball Game*, in *Play as Context*, A. Taylor Cheska, TASP, 1980). Mesoamerican Ind. ball games were the first to use rubber balls. Some ancient Aztec drawings, especially those covering the remnants of walls of ancient Teotihuacán near present-day Mexico City, show ball players holding sticks. Most studies of Mesoamerican Ind. ball games before Humphrey were descriptions, while 'little attention has been devoted to the social and cognitive role of the game within the larger framework of the Mesoamerican society' [ibid.].

History. Most likely, the earliest evidence of existence of ball games among indigenous populations of C America is a stone Olmec figure from c.1500 BC, found around the ancient Tenochtitlan (present-day Mexico City), representing a football player. The earliest ball games were, in fact, played by the Olmecs between 1500 and 1200 BC in their main cultural center, situated in the present-day Mexican states of Veracruz and Tabasco, along the Bay of Campeche. The earliest traces of football fields, from c.800 BC, were discovered in the area of San Lorenzo and La Venta. The first fully developed forms of football games were practiced between 800 and 200 BC in the central part of the Mexican Plateau, around Tlatilco, Ticoman and Zacatenco. In later years, similar ball games appeared in the S part of the Plateau and those were extensively documented in numerous pictographs, including a series of 50 stone bas-reliefs constituting the foundation of the pyramid in Dainzu, in the Mexican state of Oaxaca. Similar reliefs were found in Monte Alban. The players represented on these reliefs wore trousers with broad legs, kneepads and gloves. The rules of those games remain unknown.

Mesoamerican Ind. ball games had their heyday between 900 and 1200 AD, i.e. in the Early Post Classic Period. Game courts of that time featured H-shaped courts, most likely referring to the symbol of the 4 cardinal points worn by the God Quezalcoatl. Also the positioning of the courts could suggest an astronomical reference to the positioning of the stars. According to R.L. Humphrey, '...regardless of the precise interpretation placed on the individual court, there seems no question but that the game was based on a kind of cosmic symbolism' (ibid.). A game played by 2 opposing teams was a reflection of natural dualism, e.g. good and evil, day and night, summer and winter. The early game courts varied in size: from large ones, reaching 492ft in length, e.g. Chichen Itza, to small ones, up to 30ft. The larger courts were used by teams, the smaller by individual players. Usually, the larger courts were surrounded with walls, and some of them were situated at the foot of giant pyramids, e.g. Huitzilopochtli and Tlaloca in Tenochtitlan. Regardless of the size and shape the courts were closely linked to religious beliefs or even regarded as temples, Humphrey asserts. Judging from ancient engravings Mesoamerican Ind. ball games were played by teams consisting of 2-11 players. The balls were 8-12in in diameter and weighed about 5-8lbs. each. The aim of the game was probably to keep the ball in continuous motion by hitting it with shoulders, hips, elbows or chest. On some ancient drawings players wear special yokes on their hips and shoulders, made probably of wood, rubber or thick leather. The yokes had various functions. A U-shaped hip yoke (Span. *yugo*) was used to hit the ball with one's hip, control its flight and protect the player. The yugos were often decorated with a representation of the giant toad (Bufo marinus) whose meat is hallucinogenic. According to M. Coe and R.L. Humphrey, 'Representation of the toad on ballgame yokes might tie the game to the ritual and ideology of the religious system and suggests that the game functioned as a vehicle for the dissemination of religious symbolism for the Olmecs' (ibid.).

Smaller ballgame yokes, called *yugoitos*, made of stone, wood or rubber covered with leather, were usu. worn on the shoulders and knees. During ceremonies held before and after the game, the players placed tiny carved figures behind the yugos. The figures, called *palmas*, represented palm trees, jaguars or the quetzal bird. Some players – most likely the team captains who made offerings after the game – also carried kinds of cleavers resembling the players' heads with special helmets, called *hachas*. They probably served as offerings after the game. The helmets were worn for protective rather than ceremonial purposes. As evidenced in numerous sculptures, the ballgame helmets resembled the modern ones used in Amer. football. They were made of flexible materials and strapped to the players' heads. The players also wore special eye protectors, resembling 2 separate monocles. They were made of leather-covered rubber, or big leather patches. The playing glove, called the *manopla* (meaning both gauntlet and whip) by the Spaniards, was a kind of a disk with finger holes. As in most Mesoamerican Ind. ball games hitting the ball with the hand was forbidden, the *manopla* served as a protector against hits by the ball during the game or was used to fend off opponents. In some games, it might have been used for catching and striking the ball.

Points could have been scored in a var. of ways. Once a ball hit the ground a point was won by the opponent. After walled courts with stone hoops were built for the game, points were scored by throwing the ball through them. As the ball in most cases could not be caught by the hand, the players had to display tremendous skill in flicking up the ball with their hips and elbows. Therefore, sending the ball through a ring might have scored more points than if the opponents merely let the ball drop. Mayan courts of the Classic Period did not feature the stone hoops – they appeared later under the influence of the dynamic Aztec civilization – but rather large stones with complex ornamental engravings marking the rules of the game, unknown today. An average court featured 9 such engraved stones. Three stones were usu. fixed in the center of the court, parallel to the longer side; 3 other stones were fixed on one wall and 3 on the opposite wall. The symbolism and the role of those stones has not been discovered. Most probably, once the ball hit any of the stones during the game, the team scored more points, or it contributed in some way to that team's victory. One such stone, found in Copan (Honduras) depicted the Mayan god Macul Xochitla (the Burning Stone), the mythical patron of games and dance. Other stones from Copan featured symbolic representations of the Mayan gods of fire, plants and fertility. In Mayan mythology individual deities often took part in ball games. In the so-called *Codex Borgia*, the God Tlaloc wears a player's uniform. The historical conflict between the head priest of the Toltecs, aiming for a peaceful development of the country, and the caste of warriors was represented in a sculpture found at Tula, the site of the ancient Toltec capital. The sculpture depicts a ball game played by Quetzalcóatl (the Feathered Serpent symbolizing the dawn) against Tezcatlipoca (the god of darkness). In one of the Aztec myths, the god Huitzilopochtli kills his sister Coyoxaugqui on a playing field, which he had built in Tenochtitlan. In the *Book of Popul Buh*, transl. into Span. c.1550, 5 excerpts referring to ball games played by Aztec deities can be found. In one of them, 4 evil gods of famine, poverty, rotting wounds, and bawdiness, envy the 2 positive heroes, Hun-Hunapu and Vucub-Hunapu, their playing equipment. In order to resolve the argument a match is set. This myth is a combination of Mayan culture with later Aztec elements: playing helmets in the shape of crowns, chest and neck protectors, and gloves are typical of the Classic Period of the Mayan civilization; while the playing field is Aztec in character and features the aforementioned stone hoops. The human sacri-

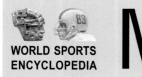
fice which concludes the game is also Aztec in origin. According to some historical sources, ball games constituted part of a young man's initiation and served as a test for newcomers. The latter resembles an ancient Gk. custom mentioned in *The Odyssey*, when Odysseus affirms his noble origin in front of Euryalus, king of the Phaecians, by displaying his discus hurling skills. The Aztec ordeal was known as the 'flower war'; occasionally it consisted of fights; cf. >ZUAR, >OLD RUSSIAN BOXING. One of the codes written by the Spaniards provides a description of a ball match between Axayakatl – the Aztec king-priest, and Xihuiltemoc – the ruler of the Toltec Xochimilco. The barbarian Aztecs envy the Toltects their ancient origins and try to ascribe them to their own nation. The match is arranged in such a way by the Aztecs that the Toltec ruler should lose. Xihuiltemoc, however, wins the match and the Aztec ruler is strangled during a feast, with a wreath he had prepared for his pre-arranged victory. The political and religious dimension of Mesoamerican Ind. ball games can be also illustrated by the legend of the bloody ruler of Coyuacan – Maxtla, the son of Tezozomoc, an Aztec conqueror, who challenged the god of night and darkness to a ball game. After losing the game he relinquished his reign c.1430. A ball game also had some impact on the Span. conquest of C America. During an argument between the Aztec King Montezuma II and the king of Texcoco, the adversaries played a few ball games

before me like a splash of ink,
covering who knows what footsteps
that stirred an ancient dust between
the long walls and the high bleachers.

'It's bigger, than the one I played
at school', an old man said, passing
with an imaginary ball
toward a hoop that was much higher
that he could reach and much smaller
than I had ever imagined.
'Damn,' he said, breathing hard, 'I missed.'
[...]
Somewhere it seemed that voices sang,
though it was only the wind, yes,
and the colliding of bodies
under the sun. 'How could they play,'
he asked between gulps of dry air,
'when the cost of defeat was so
bitter, so utterly final?'
Our shadows were pushed cold against
the carved wall and mingled as one
with those warriors caught by the stone
in their brave gestures of defeat.
'Did you know,' he said, 'those suckers
were allowed only one goal, one
that was the only chance they had?'

For detailed descriptions of ancient Mesoamer. Indian ball games see >TLACHTLI, >TEOTIHUACAN BALL, >POKYAH, >TALADZHI.

the governing body of such Mesoamer. Indian ball games as: >PELOTA MIXTECA, >PELOTA PURHÉPECHA ENCENCIDA, >PELOTA TARASCA, >FIREBALL and ulama.
S.F. and S. de Borhegyi, *The Rubber Ball Game of Ancient America*, 1967; R.L. Humphrey, 'Play as Life. Suggestions for a Cognitive Study of the Mesoamerican Ball Game', *Play as Contest*, ed. A. Taylor Cheska, 1979; *Proceedings of TAASP*, 1980; G. Montoya, 'Games and Sports of Pre-Columbian Origin', OR, Dec. 1995-Jan. 1996; R.C. Piña, *Games and Sport in Old Mexico*, 1969, E.M. Whittington, ed., *The Sport of Life and Death: The Mesoamerican Ballgame*, 2001.

META, also *półmety* or *zbijany*, a ball game popular in Poland in the 18th and the beginning of 19th cent. (Lat. *meta* – 'boundary'). Meta was part of the Old-Pol. family of sports games known as >CHWYTKA. It was described by Gołębiowski in his work *Gry i zabawy różnych stanów* (Games and Pastimes of Various Social Classes, 1831):

Meta was played by two teams of equal number of players. The teams took their positions on two opposite ends of the field and started throwing the ball to each other. Once a ball was thrown, one of the players of the throwing team ran up to the center line and returned to his team, while the receiving team tried to get the runner out by hitting him with the ball.

METAPHORIC FOOTBALL, also *metaphorical football*, a var. of a literary metaphor that employs the

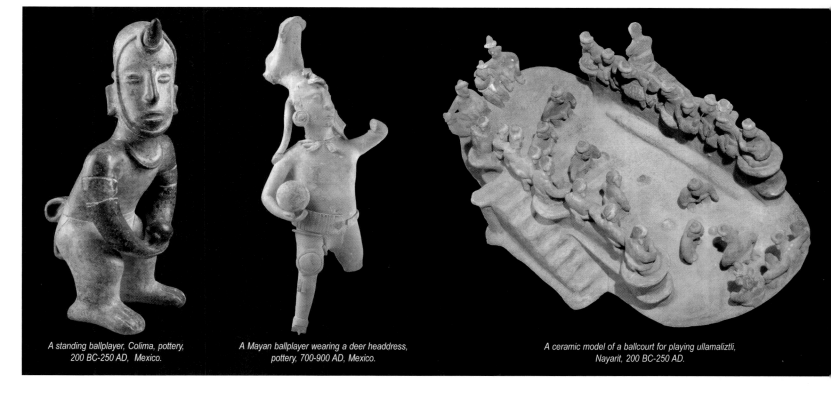

A standing ballplayer, Colima, pottery, 200 BC-250 AD, Mexico.

A Mayan ballplayer wearing a deer headdress, pottery, 700-900 AD, Mexico.

A ceramic model of a ballcourt for playing ullamaliztli, Nayarit, 200 BC-250 AD.

whose score was to determine the winner. Montezuma lost 3 out of 5 games, which undermined the king's credibility among his subjects and might have made it easier for the Spanish to conquer his country. Wagering was common during ball games. Players bet gold, precious stones, women, children, cornfields, prisoners of war, plots of arable land, contentious areas, or even entire kingdoms. Losing a bet sometimes led to enslavement. The serious consequences of ball games were very characteristic of the Mesoamerican understanding of one's honor and social status.
Ball games were likely held on various occasions, e.g. the death of a ruler or nobleman, a holiday of fertility, a solar or lunar eclipse, etc. The elaborate rituals gave a huge prestige to the game and accompanying holiday.
Many ancient Mesoamer. game courts have survived to this today in quite good shape, serving as great tourist attractions, or poetic inspiration, as demonstrated by W. Hollis in his poem *On the Ball Court*, from the collection *Sketches for a Mayan Odyssey* (1982):

As we crossed the field where a ball
had been bounced in a game measured
by life and death, my shadow fell

The ancient Mesoamer. Indian ball games are still practiced by many contemporary Amer. Ind. communities of C America. One such game is >ULAMA, also known as *hulama*, played in the Mexican states of Nayarit and Sinaloa. It has numerous local var., more or less similar to the ancient original. The var. played in the state of Oaxaca resembles the Aztec tlachtli. Many ancient Mesoamer. Indian ball games are gradually giving way to modern games, especially soccer and basketball. The ethnographers, Franz and Truda Bloom working in Chiapas in 1932 were not able to find a single trace of the ancient ball games, which had enjoyed great popularity in the area at the beginning of the 20th cent. Recently, a few C Amer. governments, e.g. Mexico, Guatemala and Honduras, have made some efforts to maintain trad. ball games. A var. of >ULAMA, which declined after 1950, was successfully revived and included in the program of a local folk festival in Culiacán in 1990; today it is also played in many other places. In 1988, the Mexican Federation of Sports and Games of Pre-Spanish Origin was founded in Mexico, which then changed its name to the Mexican Federation of Indigenous and Traditional Sports and Games (Federación Mexicana de Juegos y Deportes Autoctonos y Tradicionales). It is a constituent of the Mexican Sports Confederation and

game of football to express thoughts not related directly with sport. One of the most celebrated examples of metaphoric football in Eng. literature is a poem by E. Waller, devoted to Charles Stuart, the later King of England, *Of the Danger His Majesty Being Prince Escaped in the Road at St. Andere* (c.1624):

With painted oars the youths begin the sweep
Neptune's smooth face, and cleave the yielding deep;
Which soon becomes the seat of sudden war
Between the wind and tide that fiercely jar.
As when a sort of lusty shepherds try
their force at football, care of victory
Makes them salute so rudely breast to breast,
That their encounters seem too rough for jest;
They ply their feet, and still the restless ball,
Tossed to and fro, is urged by them all:
So fares the doubtful barge 'twixt tide and winds,
And like effect of their contention finds.

In his love story *Manaphon* (1589), Elizabethan writer, R. Greene (c.1560-92), employs metaphoric football in the lines of Carmel addressing her beloved, shepherd Doron:

Ah leave my toe, and kisse my lippes, my love,
My lippes and thine, for I have given them thee:

Within thy cap 'tis thou shalt weare my glove,
At football sport, thou shalt my champion be.

Shakespeare uses elements of football as a symbol of ill treatment or ill-mannered behavior. In his *Comedy of Errors* (c.1593, II, 2, 81-85), Adriana flatly rejects Dromio from Ephesus, to which he replies:

I am so round with you as you with me,
That like football you do spurn me thus?
You spurn me hence, and he will spurn me hither,
If I las in this service, you must case me in leather.

Also in *King Lear* (I, 4, 94-95), we have the following dialog between Kent and Oswald:

OSWALD: *I'll not be strucken, my lord.*
KENT: *Nor tripped neither, you base football player.*

Then, Kent, prob. imitating footballers, trips Oswald up so that he falls down.
In W. Rowley's (c.1585-1626) play *All's Lost by Lust* (c.1619), a Span. king Roderigo addresses a soldier named Lothario: 'Dog, hell-hound, thou shalt be my foot-ball, slave.'
In an anonymous play, *The Distracted Emperor* (c.1598; II, 1, 61-64), a knight named Orlando complains about his fate: 'I am the verye foote-ball of the starres.'
In a play titled *The Gamster* (1633; II, 1) by J. Shirley (1596-1666), the main protagonist, Wilding, makes the following comment to his wife, about the presence of an underage relative in their house:

Does she twit thee?
I'll kick her like a foot-ball,
Say but the word.

In T. Randolph's (1605-35) play titled *The Jealous Lovers* (1632), Balio recounts to Techmessie how he illustrated her alleged ugliness to her unknown lover, Pamphilus, in order to probe his feelings towards her:

I said you had no neck: your chin and shoulders
Were so good friends, they would ha' nothing part 'um;
I vow'd your breasts, for colour and proportion
Were like a writheld pair o'reworn footballs.

Austrl. literature is packed with football metaphors that refer to the local >AUSTRALIAN FOOTBALL. J. Harms and I. Jobling – Austrl. sports historians – provide the following explanation concerning the search for the meaning hidden under the football metaphors:

There is something very special, for us true believers, about football. It expresses what seems otherwise impossible to express. It is a consuming passion, of hope and despair, of escape and reality, of religious commitment and frustration. It is an expression of the grand qualities of human endeavour. To some of us

football is the knowing. When Gary Ablett ran around his left foot and goaled from fifty-five metres against Footscray in a 1992 semi-final, word fell short. The goal was the medium. It offered the insight, but how is the moment conveyed? Poets have attempted to put into clever words those esoteric concepts which defy explanation. It seems appropriate then that some poets have tried to capture the qualities of Australian football in their work so that, in combination (the football and the poetry), they might offer some comment on the human condition.

Most of the works devoted to Austrl. football have no real artistic pretensions. There are, however, some that contain deeper remarks and metaphors, demonstrating thus that real poetry does not care so much for the subject as for the ability to notice human problems through the prism of such subjects. Therefore, if people get so deeply involved in football, there must be something very human to it. Consequently, anything that is so deeply human is important enough to be appreciated for its humanistic or artistic value. It can be an exalted depiction of dramatic events taking place on a pitch, or a humorous comment on a still quite dramatic episode, such as in P. Finn's *The Day I Played Football*:

My leg is broken, so I hope
I'll open up a Doctor's shop
All through that game, Futball.

The ruthless character of the game, resulting sometimes in serious injuries or even death, has often provided a motif for existential metaphors, such as the one in the *Elegy On an Australian Schoolboy* (1921) written by Z. Cross after a fatal injury that was witnessed on the pitch:

Brown ball, you should be black. Play is no more;
The fields are desolate
The ghostly goal is kicked; and on death's shore
The awful umpires wait
The skies grow heavy with their blood and tears
The loud exultant cheer
Leaps like a curse along the crying years
Of agony and fear.

An analogy between competitive sports and warfare can also be found in literature. Amer. historian, W.E. Washburn, observed in 1977 that war and football are comparable in that: 'in both war and football, however unjust and immoral they may seem, there is no substitute for victory.'
The events at Heysel stadium in 1985 gave birth to the metaphor of sport as a hazard to the civilization posed by the unrestricted mass culture that destroys the moral achievements of the old world. An example of that would be the poem *Heysel* by D. Masterson, an ex-rugby player, actor, and professor of esthetics at Salford University. The author exploits the

connotations of the word 'field' as the field of combat and of play, referring also to Flanders, where in 1915 a wartime poet, R.C. Brooke, died while fighting for freedom of Europe:

An expeditionary force of fear
Sons of fathers who in yesteryear
Left our shores to fight for freedom's sake
They instead leave mourning in their wake
Surging waves rejoicing in delight
To, on Juventus vent their vicious spite
And with the Stanley knife to make them yield
A corner of a foreign football field.

The wolf knows best to get inside the perm
The inoffensive flock will panic then
And terraces give little chance to hide
On stragglers fast will fall the even' tide
With boot and chain and blade they are cut down
And 'neath the numbing crush their friends will drown
Does this not justify their reputation -
Members of a proud and sporting nation?

Grandsons of men who, carrying the shield
For brothers fell on Flanders poppy field
They, in the name of sport reverse the time
For war they substitute a football game.
They tell us they are 'Champions All' – these Huns,
That our ideals are crap and we're the stupid ones.

J. Harms and I. Jobling, 'Australian Rules Football. Saturday Afternoon Poetry.' *Journal of Australian Studies*, Sept. 1995, 46; W. Lipoński, *Sport, literatura i sztuka*, 1974; W.E. Washburn, 'The Moral Equivalent to Football', *The New Republic*, July 23, 1997.

METTEN, a Hung. bat-and-ball game, similar to >PALANT.

MIACZ, a Ukr. var. of >PALANT; also Ukr. for 'ball'.

MIAO HORSE FIGHTS, fights between unmounted horses popular in the Chin. province of Guangxi, esp. in the region of Rongshui. The horses jump at each other and bite one another. The fight continues until one of the horses escapes. In 1987, in an effort to revive trad. sports, the local Rongshui authorities organized a Miao Horse Fighting Festival, which is now held annually on 26 Nov.
Mu Fushan and others, 'Horse Fight', TRAMCHIN, 106.

MICRONESIAN BALL, a ball game practiced in Micronesia, esp. in the Marshall and Gilbert Islands. The Amer. ethnographer, H.W. Krieger (*Island People of the Western Pacific: Micronesia and Melanesia, 1943*) describes Micronesian balls as plaited rounded cubes made of screw-pine wood. The elastic twigs of screw-pine trees are used to weave mats, nets, baskets and balls. The aim of the game is to flick up the ball with the legs and keep it in the air as long as possible. In some areas, according to Krieger, players try to throw a ball across a designated line. Another ethnographer, J.F. Embree, claims the ball game played in the Marshall Islands does not involve any form of competition. A similar opinion has been expressed by R. Howell: 'If games are a microcosm of society, then the inhabitants of the Marshall Islands lack the competitiveness of their counterparts in Thailand'.
'Traditional Sports. Oceania', EWS, 1996, vol. III, 1083-1093.

MIDDLE-DISTANCE RUNNING, in track and field athletics races that range in distance from 600m to 1 statute mile (i.e. 1609.344m) and include the 600-m, 800-m (and its Ang.-Sax. counterpart of 880yd.), 1,000-yd., 1,000-m, 1,500-m and 1-mi. races.
THE 600-M RACE is never a part of major international competitions. The distance is usu. run for training purposes and at minor competitions.
THE 800-M (880-YD.) RACE originated in England where it was called a half-a-mile run (as it was held over the yard distance). It has been a part of the English championships since 1865 and of the US championships since 1876. R. Webster of Great Britain became the first official world record holder over the yard distance in 1865 (at 2min. 7.5sec.). W. Slade of Great Britain was the first man to run the distance in under 2min. (1min. 59sec. in 1876). The first runner to cover the distance in under 1min. 50sec. was B. Eastman of the US (1min. 49.8sec.) and in under 1min. 45sec. – J. Ryun also of the US (1min. 44.9sec. in 1966). Similarly to other running track-and-field events the metric var. of the distance became popular after the race had been introduced to continental Europe and at the 1896

Otukile Lekote (#116) of Botswana running during the Men's 800m event for the IAAF World Championships at the Commonwealth Stadium in Edmonton, Alberta, Canada.

Colette Liss (#554) of the U.S. runs in the Women's 1,500-m Final Event during the 2000 U.S. Olympic Track & Field Team Trials at the Hornet Stadium in Sacramento, California.

Ol.G. in particular. The first official 800m world record holder was E. Flack of Australia (at 2min. 11sec. in 1896). The first runner to cover the distance in under 2min. was J. Lightbody of the US (1min. 56sec. in 1904), in under 1min. 50sec. – T. Hampson of Great Britain (1min. 49.8sec. in 1932), in under 1min. 45sec. P. Snell of N.Zealand (1min. 44.3sec. in 1962), in under 1min. 44sec. – M. Fiasconaro of Italy (1min. 43.7sec. in 1973), in under 1min. 43sec. and 1min. 42sec. – S. Coe of Great Britain (1min. 42.4sec. in 1979 and 1min. 41.8sec. in 1981, respectively). Since 1976 the times have been also measured electronically and according to this method the first man to cover the distance in under 1min. 44sec. was A. Juantorena (at 1min. 43.50sec in 1976) and to turn in times under 1min. 43sec. and 1 min. 42 sec. – S. Coe (1min. 42.33sec. and 1min. 41.73sec, respectively).
THE 800-M WOMEN'S RACE was included on the Olympic program on a trial basis in 1928 but due to the extreme exhaustion suffered by many runners was declared improper for women and withdrawn from the roster of Ol.G. The race was re-introduced to the Olympics as late as 1960 after as series of practice runs during which women competitors proved that they were much better trained for this distance than during the 1928 trial. After 1960 the results achieved by women began to improve dramatically. The first woman to run 800m in under 2min. and the most outstanding female runner of the 1960s was S. Kum-dan of the Democratic People's Republic of Korea (1min. 59.1sec in 1963 and later 1min. 58sec.). The division of the world into 2 hostile camps at that time and the isolation of North Korea from the rest of the world resulted in the fact that she could not compete in the majority of international competitions and her results were not officially recorded by IAAF. Officially, the first woman to run the distance in under 2min. was, therefore, H. Falck of FRG (1min. 58.5sec. in 1971). The first runner to go under 1min. 55sec. was T. Kazankhina (1min. 54.9sec. in 1976) and under 1min. 54sec. – N. Olizarenko (1min. 53.43sec. in 1980).
THE 1,000-M RACE became particularly popular in 1913 after official world records had begun to be maintained. The first official world record holder was G. Mickler of Germany (at 2min. 32.3sec. in 1913). The first runner to cover the distance in under 2min. 30sec. was A. Bolin of Sweden (2min. 29.1sec. in 1918) and in under 2min. 20sec. – A. Boysen of Norway (2min. 19.5sec. in 1954). The race is not included on the Olympic, W.Ch. or E.Ch. program. It is, on the other hand, often a part of many international competitions, especially those held in Scandinavia, friendly matches and school competitions.
THE 1,500M RACE's success is based on the extreme popularity enjoyed by the 1-mi race in Eng.-speaking countries. It was introduced to the Ol.G. in 1896. World records have been maintained since the same year. The first official world record holder was E. Flack of Australia (at 4min. 32.2sec. in 1896). The first man to run 1,500m in under 4min. was A. Jackson of Great Britain (3min. 56.8sec. in 1912), in under 3min. 50sec. – J. Laudomegue of France (3min. 49.2sec. in 1930), in under 3min. 40sec. – S. Jungwirth of Czechoslovakia (3min. 38.1sec in 1957) and in under 3min. 30sec.- S. Cram of Great Britain (3min. 29.67sec. in 1985).
Women have run 1,500-m races since 1970. The event was introduced to the Ol.G. in 1972. Initially the competition was dominated by runners from the GDR, the USSR and Rumania as well as Italy. After the political changes that took place in the early 1990s Russia and Germany were still holding strong but since the 1980s they have been facing fierce competition from runners representing countries that had never been 'running superpowers' before, i.e. Italy, China and Algeria with the extremely talented H. Bulmerka who not only won many international competitions but also stirred up a social revolution in Arab countries where, up to her times, women were banned from competing in a sports outfit in public, esp. in front of men. The first female runner to cover 1,500m in less than 4min. was T. Kazankhina of the USSR (3min. 56sec. in 1976). She was also the first to equal the result of 3min. 55sec. and to run the distance in under 3min. 55sec. (3min. 52.5sec. in 1980).
THE 1-MILE RACE is the oldest type of middle-distance run held in Eng.-speaking countries. Uniform competition rules were introduced in 1834 in England. C. Lawes became the first official 1mi. record holder in 1864 at 4min. 56sec. The first runner to cover the distance in less than 4min. was R. Bannister (3min. 59.4sec.). The distance is still widely popular in Eng.-speaking countries and constitutes a part of many competitions. It has been a part of All-England Championships since 1864 and the US championship since 1876.

MIDWAM, a sports game practiced in Mecca, briefly mentioned in the dictionary of Arab sports and games *Min al.'abina ash-sha 'biyya* (*Our Folk Games*, 1983) by M. Ibrahim al-Majman.

MIETANNIE KELIEPU, a Ukr. sport of throwing battle axes, once practiced as a competition and combat skill by Cossack troops (Ukr. *mietannie* – 'tossing' + *keliepa* – 'battle axe'). The Cossacks threw the battle axes upwards, at a distance, and at a mark; cf. >CZEKAN THROWING.
B.I. Kowierko, ed., 'Pro sistiemu fizicznogo wdoskonalienija zaporozkich kozakiw', TFKU, 1997.

MILAKIA, a football var. practiced among the female Turk. minority in Greece, part. in the area of Komotini. The game is played by 2 teams, each subdivided into 2 parts, of which the first one, 5-7 players each, face the opponents, at a distance of several meters. The remaining players of both teams stand interspersed between them. The idea is to throw the ball between the 2 subteams so that it is not intercepted by the players in the middle. Interception scores one point, while dropping the ball eliminates the mid-field player. The game is played until one team loses all of its players.
Source: Matina Giorga, University of Thrace, Greece.

MILITARY MULTI-TRIALS, a group of sport events held in a tournament sequence, the purpose of which is to increase military skills. In socialist Poland military multi-trials were held according to the military rank: command multi-trials (pistol shooting, basketball shots, medicine ball target shots, and elements of volleyball); officer's multi-trials (gymnastic exercises, a running-and-power test, 100-m run); officer cadet's multi-trials (pistol shooting, a run-and-skill test, 4-m rope climbing, 100-m swimming, 1-km run); and regular soldiers' multi-trials (a run-and-skill test, 4-m rope climbing, long jump, and 3-km run). Military multi-trials were a predecessor of the modern >PENTATHLON and >BIATHLON. A medieval form of such trials was the chivalric heptathlon.

MILITARY SKI PATROLLING, a predecessor of the winter >BIATHLON. It combined a 25-km ski race with shooting at 3 baloons 35cm in diameter from a distance of 150m. Each missed shot was punished with an extra 1min. added to the final time.The quickest team to cover the whole distance won the race. Teams were comprised of 1 officer, 1 non-commissioned officer, and 2 privates. The equipment included rifles, backpacks, cartridge belts and pouches with 3 rifle shells. The officer had a short pistol instead of a rifle.
History. The tradition derives from Sweden, where in 1521 king Gustavus I Vasa formed military troops on skis. A similar formation developed in other countries, e.g. in Poland during the reign of Stephan Batory, although it did not have any influence upon the development of sport. In the 19th cent. the tradition of military ski patrolling spread into other Scand. countries and the first sport club of milit. ski patrolling enthusiasts was founded in Norway in 1861 (The Ski-Shooting Club in Trysil) with the aim of popularizing the country's defense system through sport. Since 1924 the event was part of the program of the W.Ol.G. and W.Ch. in skiing. After World War II, until 1948, no medals were awarded and later the event was discontinued because of its military nature and the anti-war sentiments within the IOC In 1948 the International Union of Modern Pentathlon and Biathlon (Union Internationale de Pentathlon Moderne et Biathlon, UIPMB) was established and in 1958 it transformed the sport of military ski patrolling into the modern >WINTER BIATHLON.

MINERAL, ANIMAL, VEGETABLE, a simple Eng. game involving calling out the 3 words. One player throws the ball and shouts *mineral*, *animal*, or *vegetable*, and counts to 10. The other player must catch the ball and provide the name of a particular mineral, animal or vegetable before the calling player finishes counting. The names cannot be repeated, which makes the game more difficult as it goes on. A similar game, also played in England, is known as >FIRE, AIR AND WATER.
TGESI, I, 388.

MINIBASKETBALL, a var. of basketball played on a smaller court and using a smaller ball, adapted for children from the age of 8-12. The court, depending on the players' age category, is 14-26m long and 9-12m wide. A basket is suspended from 8ft. 6in. to 10ft. above the floor. A match lasts 1x12 or 4x7min. Minibasketball, initially known as biddy-basketball, was invented by an American, J. Archer, in 1950. It is governed by the International Minibasketball Committee, a constituent of the Fédération Internationale de Basketball Amateur (FIBA). The Minibasketball W.Ch. have been held since 1967.

MINIGOLF, a game based on the rules of >GOLF, but played on a smaller course with artificial obstacles. A minigolf course consists of 9-18 tracks, 6-25m long, made of asphalt or concrete, with a number of obstacles such as curves, bumps and tilts. The aim of the game is to drive a ball with a club into a hole at the end of the track in the fewest strokes possible. Players may not use any golf club other than a putter. A ball is 11.2in. (38mm) in diameter. Minigolf has 4 var.: minigolf proper, miniature golf, cobi-golf, and little golf. They differ in competition rules, shape and length of tracks, and number of obstacles. The rules of the sport were formulated by Swiss P. Bogni in 1953. In 1958 the Fédération Internationale de Minigolf Sportif was founded in Vienna, and in 1960 the Fédération Internationale de Golf Miniature, FIGM, was established. The Minigolf E.Ch. have been held since 1953.

MINITENNIS, one of the names for Amer. >PADDLE TENNIS, sometimes applied to >PADDER TENNIS.

MIXED HOCKEY, a var. of >FIELD HOCKEY, played by mixed teams, usu. of 6 men and 5 women on each team. The idea of mixed hockey competitions was suggested by the Eng. Women's Hockey Association in the 1890s, and under pressure from the women's emancipation movement a few sports clubs

800-M and 1500-M OLYMPIC CHAMPIONS

MEN'S 800-M RUN
1896 Teddy Flack, AUS 2:11.0
1900 Alfred Tysoe, GBR 2:01.2
1904 Jim Lightbody, USA 1:56.0
1906 Paul Pilgrim, USA 2:01.5
1908 Mel Sheppard, USA 1:52.8
1912 Ted Meredith, USA 1:51.9
1920 Albert Hill, GBR 1:53.4
1924 Douglas Lowe, GBR 1:52.4
1928 Douglas Lowe, GBR 1:51.8
1932 Tommy Hampson, GBR 1:49.7
1936 John Woodruff, USA 1:52.9
1948 Mal Whitfield, USA 1:49.2
1952 Mal Whitfield, USA 1:49.2
1956 Tom Courtney, USA 1:47.7
1960 Peter Snell, NZE 1:46.3
1964 Peter Snell, NZE 1:45.1
1968 Ralph Doubell, AUS 1:44.3
1972 Dave Wottle, USA 1:45.9
1976 Alberto Juantorena, CUB 1:43.50
1980 Steve Ovett, GBR 1:45.4
1984 Joaquim Cruz, BRA 1:43.00
1988 Paul Ereng, KEN 1:43.45
1992 William Tanui, KEN 1:43.66
1996 Vebjoern Rodal, NOR 1:42.58
2000 Nils Schumann, GER 1:45.08

WOMEN'S 800-M RUN
1928 Lina Radke, GER 2:16.8
1932-56 Not held
1960 Lyudmila Shevtsova, USSR 2:04.3
1964 Ann Packer, GBR 2:01.1
1968 Madeline Manning, USA 2:00.9
1972 Hildegard Falck, W. Ger 1:58.55
1976 Tatyana Kazankina, USSR 1:54.94
1980 Nadezhda Olizarenko, USSR 1:53.42
1984 Doina Melinte, ROM 1:57.60
1988 Sigrun Wodars, E. Ger 1:56.10
1992 Ellen van Langen, NED 1:55.54
1996 Svetlana Masterkova, RUS 1:57.73
2000 Maria Mutola, MOZ 1:56.15

MEN'S 1,500-M RUN
1896 Teddy Flack, AUS 4:33.2
1900 Charles Bennett, GBR 4:06.2
1904 Jim Lightbody, USA 4:05.4
1906 Jim Lightbody, USA 4:12.0
1908 Mel Sheppard, USA 4:03.4
1912 Arnold Jackson, GBR 3:56.8
1920 Albert Hill, GBR 4:01.8
1924 Paavo Nurmi, FIN 3:53.6
1928 Harry Larva, FIN 3:53.2
1932 Luigi Beccali, ITA 3:51.2
1936 John Lovelock, NZE 3:47.8
1948 Henry Eriksson, SWE 3:49.8
1952 Josy Barthel, LUX 3:45.1
1956 Ron Delany, IRE 3:41.2
1960 Herb Elliott, AUS 3:35.6
1964 Peter Snell, NZE 3:38.1
1968 Kip Keino, KEN 3:34.9
1972 Pekka Vasala, FIN 3:36.3
1976 John Walker, NZE 3:39.17
1980 Sebastian Coe, GBR 3:38.4
1984 Sebastian Coe, GBR 3:32.53
1988 Peter Rono, KEN 3:35.96
1992 Fermin Cacho, SPA 3:40.12
1996 Noureddine Morceli, ALG 3:35.78
2000 Noah Ngeny, KEN 3:32.07

WOMEN'S 1500-M RUN
1972 Lyudmila Bragina, USSR 4:01.4
1976 Tatyana Kazankina, USSR 4:05.48
1980 Tatyana Kazankina, USSR 3:56.6
1984 Gabriella Dorio, ITA 4:03.25
1988 Paula Ivan, ROM 3:53.96
1992 Hassiba Boulmerka, ALG 3:55.30
1996 Svetlana Masterkova, RUS 4:00.83
2000 Nouria Merah-Benida, ALG 4:05.10

M WORLD SPORTS ENCYCLOPEDIA

started to play mixed hockey matches, which soon became a sort of social attraction practiced by representatives of the upper classes. Mixed hockey matches, however, were also the object of derision, reflected in occasional poems:

You came down the field like a shaft from a bow.
The vision remains with me yet.
I hastened to check you: the sequel you know:
You rushed at the ball, whirled your stick like a flail,
And you hit with the vigour of two:
A knight in his armour had surely turned pale,
If he had played hockey with you.

They gathered me up, and they took me to bed;
They called for a doctor a lint.
With ice in a bag they enveloped my head;
My arm they enclosed in a splint.
My ankles are swelled to a terrible size;
My shins are a wonderful blue;
I have lain here a cripple unable to rise,
Since the day I played hockey with you.

Yet still, in the cloud hanging o'er so black,
In silvery lining I spy:
A man who's unhappily laid on his back
Can you have solace? May I?
An angel is woman in moments of pain,
Sang Scott, clever poet he knew;
It may, I perceive, be distinctly a gain
To have fallen at hockey with you.

For if you'll but nurse me (come quickly, come now),
If you'll administer balm,
And press at my bidding my feverish brow
With a cool but affectionate palm;
If you'll sit by my side, it is possible, quite,
That I may be induced to review
With a feeling more nearly akin to delight
That day I played hockey with you.

[*Mr. Punch's Book of Sport*]

In the 1920s and 1930s a woman perceived as behaving in a 'silly' manner during a hockey match, both in a women's and a mixed team, became a symbol of the none-too-bright 'Kewpie doll' and gave rise to the Eng. expression *jolly hockey sticks*. At present, mixed hockey is played in friendly matches only.

MIZO INCHAI, a trad. var. of wrestling practiced in the Ind. state of Manipur. Mizo inchai has been recently regulated by a series of rules. The wrestlers fight on sand; they must not oil their bodies, nor wear any jewelry, particularly rings. Each bout consists of three 3-min. rounds. The bout winner is the wrestler who wins 2 rounds out of 3. Tripping, scratching, fist-fighting, arm locking and foul language during the fight are forbidden. A wrestler can win a round by pinning the opponent down to the ground or lifting him off the ground and holding him up for 5-6 sec.; otherwise points are awarded for each successful action. The bout is officiated by a referee and scoring judges.

MOARI, a Maori aquatic game. The moari is a pole 3-3.5m long, which is erected beside a river or on the edge of a cliff above the sea. It has thick ropes fixed to the top. The players hold on to the ropes and take turns at swinging out above the water and then letting go and falling in feet first.

Ship in a bottle – a model of the six-masted schooner 'Wyoming' crafted by Gil Charbonneau in Topsham, Maine.

MOCK BATTLE, sports imitation of battles or duels, often performed as enactments of historical battle scenes. Typical mock battles are mock castle sieges organized since 1612 as part of the local Chipping Campden 'Olympic Games' in England, on the initiative of R. Dover. A modern form of mock battle in sport is >PAINTBALL. Cf. GIOCO DEL PONTE.

MOCOVITE BOXING, a form of team fist fighting popular in the S.Amer. Native Ind. tribe of Mocovi. Two groups of boxers attack each other and fight with their fists until one of the groups wins. Mocovite boxing is practiced both by men and women.

MODEL BUILDING, making models of automobiles, watercraft and aircraft and using them for stunt or speed sports competitions.
AEROMODELLING, involves various competition classes, with regard to the size and weight of the models. Aeromodelling can be divided into 3 categories: 1) free flight: gliders, rubber powered aircraft, resonant jet, and internal-combustion powered aircraft; 2) control-line: racing, stunt, speed and combat models; and 3) radio control: aerobatic, pylon racing and helicopter models. Model aircraft flown indoors include rubber powered models, magnetic rod models, and control-line models with engine displacement of 2.5, 5, and 10cc. In control-line stunt competitions the models must perform 10 acrobatic figures, while in speed competition the models do 100 laps around the pilot in preliminaries and up to 200 laps in finals. In the combat contest 2 models are flown together in the same circle. The object is to cut the other person's streamer, i.e. a strip of paper towed behind the model, with the propeller. Also very popular are contests involving flying remote-controlled 1/10 scale models of real aircraft.
MODEL ROCKETRY, involving competition in 7 categories and several classes. Rocket models include rockets with an altimeter deploying a drogue parachute, duration rockets, streamer rockets and rocketplanes.
SHIP MODELLING, involving about 30 classes of models, including airscrew-propelled skimming boats, control-line skimming boats, yacht models,

scale boat models, radio-control boats, as well as racing and stunt models. Team competitions (6-20 models) involve racing events, landing operations and other role-playing events such as putting out fire on a model ship. In 1958 the Fédération Europeenne de Modelisme Nautique et de Sport Modelisme Nautique, NAVIG, was established as the governing body of the sport.
AUTOMOBILE MODELLING, involving racing competitions of automobile models in various engine displacement classes on closed circuit courses, usu. over a distance of 500m. The models can be remote controlled or line-controlled, electric or I.C. (internal combustion). Races of scale models based

Models of competition speedboats.

on Formula One races are also held as individual or team events. In 1952 the Fédération Europeenne de Modelismo Automobile, FEMA, was founded.

MODERN PENTATHLON, a sports contest involving 5 events: riding, fencing, shooting and cross-country running (Fr. *pentathlon moderne*; Gk. *pente* – five + *athlon* – competition + Fr. *moderne*). Until 1956, scoring was based on the sum of points equal to the athletes' positions taken in individual events. Theoretically, the lowest, i.e. the best score was 5pts. – 1pt. for each event. Since 1956, the total score has been the sum of points scored in the 5 events. The riding event is a showjumping round over a distance of about 350-450m (since 1988; formerly a 2.5-5km cross-country ride) featuring 12-15 jumps, incl. a double and a triple. The obstacles are 120m high. The horses are selected by lot and each competitor is given 20 min. to practice on the horse. Each competitor begins with 1,100pts. and loses points as penalties are incurred: 30pts. for knocking an

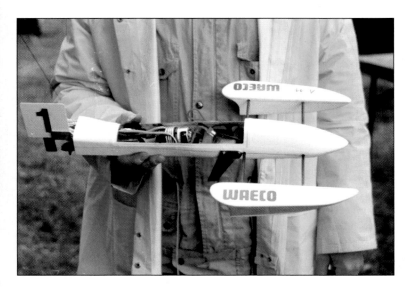

Below left and right: model building.

Model building on a series of stamps issued by the Polish Post.

WORLD SPORTS ENCYCLOPEDIA

M

Modern pentathlon's sequence of events: horse riding, fencing, shooting, swimming, running.

200 max.) equals 1,000pts. Every target point above or below 172 adds or takes 12pts. from the pentathlon score. Each competitor fires 20 shots with a time limit of 40 sec. for each shot. The swimming event is a 300m freestyle race. A time of 3:54.00 equates to 1,000pts. Every half second above or below the prescribed time increases or decreases the total score by 4pts. The swimmers compete in groups selected by lot. The distance of the cross-country event is 4km. The leading competitor sets off first and the intervals between that competitor and those who follow is determined by the point difference between them. The first competitor to cross the line at the end of the run is the pentathlon winner. The modern pentathlon has been held as an individual event since the 1912 Ol.G., and as a team event since 1952. Until 1984, pentathlon events were held over 5 days, and after that over 4 days. At the Atlanta Ol.G. in 1996, for the first time, the modern pentathlon contest was held in a single day. This drastic shortening of the overall time of the contest and the time of particular events was introduced by the IOC because – as Olympic officials put it – the events were too long and failed to attract crowds of viewers, which in turn resulted in shorter television coverage.

History. The origins of the modern pentathlon go back to the early training programs of the Swed. army. As a sport, the modern pentathlon began to be practiced c.1900. The pentathlon as a sport was also an idea of the originator of modern Olympics, P. de Coubertin, who thought that '...the multitrials test the moral strength of man as well as his physical skills and resources and form a complete athlete'. In 1909, the modern pentathlon was approved and included in the Ol.G. The first men's event, called the 'officer's pentathlon', was held in 1912 in Stockholm. Until 1948, only army officers could participate in pentathlon competitions. The sport was initially dominated by the Swedes who won at all Ol.G. until 1956, with the exception of the 1936 Ol.G. From 1952 until the Atlanta Ol.G. in 1996, the modern pentathlon was also held as a team event. Until 1948 the pentathlon was the only event held under the direct auspices of the IOC. In 1948, the Union Internationale Pentathlon Moderne et Biathlon was founded in Lausanne, Switzerland. Since its foundation the Modern Pentathlon W.Ch. have been held every year, apart from Olympic years. The women's W.Ch. have been held since 1978. Leading pentathletes were the Swedes: G. Liliehöök (the first world champion 1912) and L. Hall (world champion 1951, 1952 and Olympic champion 1952 and 1956); I. Novikov from the USSR (4-time world champion 1957-1961), A. Balczo from Hungary (5-time world champion 1963-69 and Olympic champion 1972), and P. Ledniev from the USSR (4-time world champion 1973-75 and 1978). The first women's pentathlon champion was Britain's W. Norman. Other famous female pentathletes included I. Kisielewa (world champion 1986 and 1987) and E. Fjellerup (1990-91).

The modern pentathlon today faces many difficulties. The high costs of practicing make the pentathlon a rather restrictive sport. Television's insistence to hold all the pentathlon events on one day has distorted the noble idea of the modern pentathlon. The team event is no longer part of the Ol.G. The threat of exclusion of the sport from the Olympic program has discouraged many sponsors, in particular national Olympic committees. Moreover, the rapid development of the >TRIATHLON has attracted a great deal of potential pentathletes keen to test themselves in several sports events at once. The survival of the modern pentathlon will depend on the sport's adjustment to the requirements of the medium of television. See also: >FENCING, >RUNNING, >COMPETITIVE SHOOTING, >SWIMMING. E. Woźniak, *Pięciobój nowoczesny* (Modern Pentathlon), 1979.

MOGULS, also *mogul skiing*, one of the 4 events of >FREESTYLE SKIING, incorporated in the FIS program in 1979 and one of its 2 events (the other being >AERIALS) incorporated into Ol.G. in 1992 in Albertville as a demonstration sport. Since the 1994 Ol.G. in Lillehammer it has been a fully admitted Olympic event, held in both the women's and the men's categories. The first Olympic winner was Can. J.L. Brassard.
The FIS regulations describe moguls as a form of skiing down a steep slope thickly covered with moguls, which requires from a skier frequent turns, evolutions, and quick reactions. A slope should be evenly inclined at 24-32° with a run around 18-20m wide, marked with flagpoles between which a skier is supposed to go over a distance of 200-270m. The participants start from a large gate placed at the starting line and they finish after crossing the finish line. The judges' stand, seating 5-7 officials, is located at the foot of the hill, at least 300m from the start line. The final result comprises a score obtained for technique (50% of the total score), jumps (25%), and speed (25%). The dynamics of a run and turns, which have to be made in 2 directions, executed by a skier is scored by 3-5 judges; 2 other judges score the jumps' esthetics and their level of difficulty. The skiers are encouraged to use kneepads in a color different from the rest of the uniform to make it easier for the judges to observe the movements of the knees which play a significant role in scoring. The final score is completed with the speed measurement compared with the model runs executed by the best skiers, referred to as the pacesetters, before the competition. The longer the time, the lower the score. Ski length for men is 190cm and for women – 180cm. During each run a skier has to make a min. of 2 jumps and each such jump has to contain at least 2 or 3 technical elements. The most popular jumps are: the spread eagle – the airborne skier spreads both arms and legs sidewards with his poles and skis pointing outside; the Cossack – both legs are stretched sidewards while the body is tilted forward,

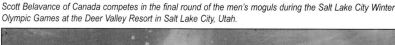

Scott Belavance of Canada competes in the final round of the men's moguls during the Salt Lake City Winter Olympic Games at the Deer Valley Resort in Salt Lake City, Utah.

obstacle; 40pts. if the horse resists the rider; 60pts. for a fall; and 3pts./sec. over the time limit. If the competitor's timing is twice the time limit, the competitor is eliminated from the event. In the fencing event each competitor has a bout against every other competitor using the épée. The bout winner is the first fencer to score a hit. A bout lasts 1min. (3min. before the Atlanta Ol.G. in 1996). If within the prescribed time neither scores a hit, both fencers lose. In the shooting event the competitors shoot at a moving silhouette from a distance of 25m, using a pistol or revolver, or, recently, at a trad. 10-ring target using an air pistol. A target score of 172 (out of

368

M WORLD SPORTS ENCYCLOPEDIA

hands below the stomach and poles hidden under the arms; the twister – the airborne skier spins helping himself with his poles; the daffy – the airborne skier stretches both arms upwards with the poles hidden behind his back while one leg is stretched forward and the other backward with both skis parallel to the body; the helicopter – a 360-720 spin in the air along a vertical axis; the back scratcher – both arms stretched backwards and legs bent backwards at the knees so that skies are nearly parallel to the body. The events are held in singles and doubles (dual mogul competition). In singles, the skiers with best timing qualify for higher rounds, in dual competitions – the winner of a given race.

MOKNIEWA, trad. Georgian horse racing; Cf. >MARUA, >TARCZIA.

MOMOTE, an ancient form of Jap. foot archery, popular at the end of the Heian period (12th cent.) and in the Hojo period; cf. other Jap. forms of foot archery >BUSHA, >JUMIHAJIME, >KUSAJISI, >MARUMOTO; equestrian archery >INUOMONO, >YABUSAME, KADAGAKE; and ceremonial archery >JYARAI, >IBAHAJIME, >NORIYUMI, >TANGONO KISHA.

MONGOL HORSE RACING see >KHURDAAN MOR'.

MONGOLIAN ARCHERY, one of the most sophisticated types of >ORIENTAL ARCHERY. It is traditionally part of the triple event of Mong. warriors called >ERIIN GURVAN NAADAM, but various archery competitions have been practiced among the Mongols as single events. Mong. archery differed from Eur. archery in technique, target types, and bow construction. A Mong. bow was made of larch, elm or pine wood. It was relatively shorter than the Eng. longbow (>ENGLISH ARCHERY). An average Mong. bow, also called the *tatar*, was about 1.5-1.6m tall. The limbs, however, were longer and bent outwards on their ends, which increased the drawing force of the bow. The bowstring was made of silk or the twisted gut of various animals, e.g. of the Siberian tiger. The arrow shafts were made of pine, beech or willow wood, with bone or iron heads. A Mong. arrow was about 1m long. According to a Mong. archery researcher, R. Zorig, the arrow velocity at the moment loosed was about 100m/sec. At present, traditionally hand-made Mong. bows are on the decline and are gradually being replaced with more widely available, manufactured weapons. Manufactured bows are lighter but retain many trad. design characteristics, in which they still differ from their Eur. counterparts.

Mongolian archers.

A typical form of Mong. archery was equestrian archery. The Mongols adopted from the Chinese the construction of a short, flexible bow and the technique of the so-called 'Parthian shot' – shooting the arrows to the rear while riding at full speed, with the rider's body half turned (>PARTHIAN ARCHERY). The most popular form of Mong. equestrian archery consisted of shooting arrows at leather balls mounted on poles, about 1.7m tall, or at a piece of sheep skin spread over wooden stakes. Other targets included: a piece of felt spread between 2 trees; a yellow-painted bull skull; wooden pins, and various circular targets made of thick leather. Some ethnographers, e.g. Y. Sishmarev, mentioned large leather targets spread on a wooden frame, which could only be shot at by archers of noble blood. In the 17th cent. the Mongols used to shoot at an effigy made of 8 sheepskins spread on a tree (the number 8 had a magical meaning in Mong. culture, similar to number 7 in Judeo-Christian culture). The effigy represented the mythical monster Mangas – the embodiment of evil. The Mongols never shot at an effigy representing a human being, which was strictly forbidden in all forms of Mong. archery, even in children's games. Since the beginning of the 20th cent. the main type of Mongolian archery has been the *sur* shooting. A *sur* is a small pouch of tightly coiled straps of camel hides, filled with oak bark or leather; it is 6-8cm tall and 8cm in diameter. Surs were placed in rows or shoulder-high pyramids. In some areas of West Mongolia archers shoot arrows at a row of rolled leather belts, called the *chikh* (Mong. – 'ear'). Chikh shooting enjoyed great popularity among Mong. shepherds, who kept the belts securely in their yurts and believed that they would bring good luck to the herds. Each newly born Mong. boy was given a leather belt to help him gain mastery of archery in the future, and a small figure of the bow and arrow was suspended over his cradle.

During official Mong. archery contests each competitor must wear the trad. outfit consisting of a fur cap with a steel crest, knee-long leather coat tied with a scarf around the archer's waist, and leather boots. The archers stand in a row, sideways towards the targets, behind a shooting line. They cannot use quivers and may only pick up arrows from the ground in front of the shooting line.

The archers shoot their arrows from a distance of 75-80m. Once a sur or chikh is hit it is handed to the lucky archer and hung in his yurt as a talisman symbolizing good fortune, according to the trad. Mong. rule: 'Take the good with you, leave the evil behind'. The Mongols believed each arrow hit killed the evil forces, esp. those affecting health of humans and livestock. The surs or chikhs that were not hit during the competition were buried in the ground in order to prevent the evil forces from spreading out.

After each hit spectators gave a long yell called the *uukhai*, similar to singing. As I. Kabzińska-Stawarz puts it, 'This characteristic hymn is to awaken the Host of Nature, Lus Sabdaga, in case he is still asleep during the contest. He was believed to scare away the evil forces while calling on the good ones, supporting the latter in their struggle against the former. His workings, symbolized by the archery contest, are reinforced with the shouts of the public. [...] besides the shouts given after each hit were to stimulate the archer to fight, weaken his opponents and prevent them from winning.' Mong. shepherds also believed that the evil forces once scared away would not return until the next competition. Still in the early 20th cent. the archer who hit the target approached the grand stand where he was given a handful of dried cheese, and then he shared the gift with the spectators and ghosts of Nature. This custom faded away in the 1980s, and has only survived in a few local archery events. The prizes for victory usu. included domestic animals, e.g. a horse, camel, sheep; or trade goods such as bales of silk or bags of tea. Archery still enjoys great popularity in Mongolia but it exerts less cultural impact than it used to. Since the 1960s it has been gradually replaced with riflery, although political transformations in the country after 1989 have decidedly marked a revival of interest in ancient Mong. art of archery.

The most popular var. of Mong. archery is >SUR KHARVAKH, a rough combination of numerous ancient Mong. traditions. The winner of a sur kharvakh competition must hit the sur 20 times. Depending on the number of hits the competitors are qualified as: *erchimtei mergen* – 'champion of strong shooting'; *galt mergen* – 'champion of rapid shooting'; *tod mergen* – 'champion of accurate shooting'; *tsoo mergen* – 'complete champion'. The name *mergen*, signifying the ideal man and champion, is also applied to Mong. mythical heroes who fought the dangers threatening people, using the bow and arrows. It is also the name for a Mong. wrestling champion (>BÖKHIIN BARILDAAN).

History. The earliest literary reference to Mong. archery is the epic story *Khokh sudar*, written by the old Mong. chronicler and thinker, Injinasshi. In Chapter 12 of Book 4 there is a description of an archery contest among Mong. warriors, which took place in 1194 or 1195. The contenders were four 16-year-old boys: Dzyulgetii from the Dzurgen province, Kuildar from Monguur, Subeedei battar and Togtongo baatar from Djurchid. According to the story, each of them could shoot an arrow at a distance of '500 bows' (1 Mong. bow was about 1m). The distance, however impressive, was not the longest in the history of Mong. archery. In 1225, during one of Genghis Khan's raids, a young archer named Esunge was supposed to have shot an arrow at a distance of 335 *alds*, (approx. 536m). This feat was commemorated by the so-called Stone of Genghis Khan in Nerchinsk. The stone was brought to the Hermitage Museum in Saint Petersburg in 1832. In 1996, the Mong. Ministry of National Heritage ordered that a replica of the stone be placed in the Museum of Natural History in Ulan Bator. The inscription on the stone reads: 'During the tribe council headed by Genghis Khan after the conquest of Startaulu [a town in present-day E Turkmenistan] Esunge shot an arrow at a target 335 alds from where he stood' (an ald is a trad. Mong. measurement unit equal to the width of a man with both arms fully extended – about 160cm). Giovanni da Pian del Carpine, a papal envoy to the Tartar khan in the years 1245-47 mentioned archery and arrow making as major crafts among the Mongols in his Lat. work *History of the Mongols Whom We Call the Tartars*.

Old-Mong. literature abounds in descriptions of feats performed by ancient Mong. archers. They can be found, for instance, in a 17th-cent chronicle *History Decorated with Diamonds* and in numerous epic poems called *ülliger*, in which historical and mythical Mong. heroes fight against the multi-headed monster Manguss, using their bows and arrows.

For many centuries archery was an exclusively male activity with the exception of >BURIAT ARCHERY, where female archers were heroes of the most ancient myths. The trad. social role of the man was that of warrior and hunter, whereas the woman was to care for the household and bring up children. Mong. women could not even assist in manufacturing bows and arrows. One of the few positive changes brought to Mongolia by Communist rule was women's emancipation. In the 1960s Mong. women were allowed to participate in public archery competitions. Still in Mongolia, in the 1980s and 1990s, many of the elderly disapproved of the new archery regulations. Mong. women shoot arrows from a shorter distance, i.e. from about 60m and the number of arrows allotted to each competitor is 20 (40 in the men's event).

C. Lhagvasuren, 'The Stele of Ghengis Khan', OR, Feb-Mar 1997, XXVII-13; I. Kabzińska-Stawarz, 'Competition in liminal situations', part III, EP, 1994, XXXVIII, 1-2.

MONGOLIAN CAMEL RACES, a form of races held over a distance of 5km in Mongolia and some Chin. border provinces. In China a characteristic feature is the participation of women jockeys.

'Camel Racing', TRAMCHIN, 44.

MONGOLIAN FOOTBALL, a game prob. played by some Mong. tribes in ancient times, influenced by other Asian peoples. Most likely, Mong. football remained under the influence of such ancient Chin. ball games as >CUJU and >TSU-KIH (see also >TSU-CHU), while Mong. and Chin. territories were under single rule. No precise information about Mong. football has survived although the sport has played a symbolic role among the Mongols. In contemporary Mong. children's tales a lost ball signifies sickness or misfortune, and a found ball means recovery or good luck. Modern ball games played in Mongolia are not historically linked to the ancient football. Mong. ball games have never reached the level of popularity of the trad. 3-event men's contests of >ERIIN GURVAN NAADAM or >SUR KHARVAKH archery competition. The sport researcher, I. Kabzińska-Stawarz has concluded her studies of Mong. games in the following way: 'I have not met anybody who would list ball games as Mong. national sports, although there may be some of that opinion, especially in the younger generation' (*Games of Mongolian Shepherds*, 1991, 74).

MONGOLIAN POLO, a game once played in ancient Mongolia, prob. influenced by early inhabitants of Tibet and China. Presumably, mounted polo was played by the troops of Genghis Khan (c.1115-1227), but there is no clear confirmation of this. In 1998, on the initiative of J. Edwards (co-founder of the World Elephant Polo Association), his son Kristjan, and a Ger. film-maker C. Giercke, the Chinggis Khaan Polo Club was founded in Ulan Bator, Mongolia. Its aim was to restore the Mong. polo tradition in its natural environment: 'In the UK you're lucky if you have four ponies. Here, the nomadic farmers and herdsmen may have 200. They need no maintenance, they are never fed or groomed, the Mongols' riding skill is second to none and there is enough flat land for 60,000 polo pitches.' The Honorary Chairman of the club became E. Jargalsaikhany, the Mong. Ambassador to the UN. At the same time, the Mongolian Polo Association was formed. Owing to the poverty of the Mongolians and a practically non-existent sports industry, the Edwardses equipped the Mong. polo organizations with balls, mallets, saddles and outfits for a few dozen players. The first Mong. polo tournament, after few-centuries' break, was held in July, 1998 to rules slightly different from those of modern >OUTDOOR POLO. The games were played 5-a-side in 2 chukkas of 10min. The tournament was supervised by Eur. visitors and featured 3 teams: Eternal Sky, Orkhon Eagles, and Windhorse. The tournament showed differences in Asian and Eur. mental attitudes towards sports. For instance, teamwork turned out to be an alien concept to the Mong. players: 'The locals would career after the ball, regardless of which team they were on or position they were supposed to be playing in.' On the other hand, the Mong. players grasped the game very accurately due to well-maintained natural instincts of the riders and horses: 'In international polo, the most dangerous thing is horse collisions, but here they will avoid running into each other [...] they're used to running in huge numbers, and so they stop or swerve by themselves. [...] They caught on rapidly that they had to follow the ball. Sometimes a pony would spot it and turn by itself. They're fast, agile and athletic.' The Mong. players were also surprised on seeing the Europeans care so much about the horses: 'When the foreigners started removing rocks from the stretch of grassland [...] the Mongols threw back their heads with laughter. In Mongolia, horses are respected but there is no sentimentality or cosseting: it's every man – and beast – for himself. 'I was terrified about the rocks and marmot holes, 'says Aimee [one of the foreigners]. 'It's so easy to break a leg. But these horses are so intelligent and sure-footed. Over the centuries they've bred a nation of survivors.'
S. Carpenter, 'Polo in Mongolia', http://www.tigermountain.com/TigerMtn/mongolia98.html

MONSTER TRUCK RACING – An Amer. sport in which specially prepared pickup trucks with huge, oversized wheels cover a short distance and drive over 'crush cars' placed side by side in the middle of the racetrack. Outdoor shows and domes use about 25 cars. Indoor arenas use about 18 cars. The number of cars a truck will jump depends on the length of the track. There are usu. 2 monster trucks competing against each other. The engines are all custom-built and burn up to 2.5 gallons of methanol per run, a length of approx. 250ft. They produce over 1,500hp and generate speeds close to 100mph. Approved motor size differs from one association to another. The tires are 66in. high and 43in. wide. Monster trucks can jump 110-115ft., a distance greater than 14 cars, and up to 20-25ft. in the air. They weigh 10,000-12,000lbs. A monster truck is usu. 11ft. tall and about 12ft. wide. On most of the monster trucks the fiberglass bodies are continuous with a manhole in the passenger side floorboards used for entry. The chassis is also custom-built, there are no 2 alike. The race trucks are built with a center steer seat position and full roll cage. Each vehicle is equipped with a remote ignition interrupter as a safety device. The drivers are required by the regulations to use a 5-point safety harness and wear a helmet, neck collar, gloves and fire suit. There are approximately 300 monster trucks in action in the US. The top trucks compete in 45–50 different cities each year.

History. The origin of monster truck racing is connected with Bob Chandler, a man who built the first monster truck in 1974. He equipped his Ford F-250 pickup with a jacked-up suspension and oversized tires. The resulting creation was dubbed 'Bigfoot'. In 1982 Chandler set a second trend when he decided to drive over a couple of junk cars. Monster trucks soon caught on, but they did not race in the early days. There were typically 1 or 2 such trucks that performed as a half-time act at various motor shows. The first monster truck racing show took place in 1987.
There are numerous monster truck racing associations. The most important are: The Monster Truck Racing Association, The Amer. Monster Truck Association, The United States Hot Rod Association. Among the most famous drivers are: Bob Chandler (truck: 'Bigfoot'), Fred Shafer ('Bear Foot'), Tim Hall ('Executioner'), John Seasock ('Sudden Impact'), Kreg Christensen ('Dragon Slayer' and 'Misbehavin'). The Monster Truck Racing Association produced a video ('Racing to the Finish') in 1989, started printing trading cards in 1990 and producing school supplies in 1992.

MONTENEGRO RACES, held in Montenegro in the Balkan Peninsula on the occasion of various holidays, weddings, etc. Their vast popularity is best exemplified by numerous folk songs:

The brave fellows took off their clothes
And so young Halil undressed.
They left their clothes on the ground,
When five hundred brave fellows started running,
And when they reached level ground
They ran for two whole hours.

[*Hrihjice u Skradinu*]

Similar competitions were related to the Montenegrin military tradition. L. Nenadović described one such competition which was held around 1878 and whose aim was to improve soldiers' endurance:

A guard of a Montenegrin ruler announced the competition by saying: 'Who is a falcon and believes in his wings? Up there, on the peak is a pistol of quality unmatched in the whole of Montenegro. He who reaches it first may put it under his belt for he has won it'. And soon many a fast young man came forward and fell in. And they flew over the rocky rubble like arrows taking steep paths up and down. And after three or four minutes the pistol was under the belt of the one who was first to reach the destination.

[*Pisma sa Cetinja*, 1897]

MOPTI ROWING, a var. of rowing practised on the central part of the river Niger in Africa, in the delta formed with the Niger's tributary, Bani, near the town of Mopti. The regattas are held on local holidays and market days on characteristic fishing pirogues used for fishing and transport. The pirogues are 20-25m in length and are built from long boards forming a flat bottom and slanting side. The stem and stern are pointed upwards above the water level. The sides close to the stem and stern are painted with regular designs. Each pirogue has 2 rows of 15-20 oarsmen. Each group rows on one side of the boat with short oars, dipped into the water almost at a right angle with short, deep and aggressive movements. At both bow and stem is an extra crew member, whose task is to maintain the direction of rowing and keep the rhythm by sounding voice commands.

MORE SACKS TO THE MILL, a brutal game of strength and endurance once popular in the Eng. countryside, particularly in Warwickshire and Staffordshire. A group of players would be 'hunting down' a selected player; once caught he was toppled down and the 'hunters' lay on top of him, one upon another. Shouting *sacks to the mill* or *bags to the mill*, more participants were invited to lie on the player on the ground. The player who endured lying under more bodies became the winner.
TGESI, I, 390.

MORENTREIBEN, a Ger. ball game of medieval origin, similar to Fr. >TRUIE, LA and Pol. >CZOROMAJ. It consisted of driving a ball into holes in the ground using special sticks.
W. Endrei and L. Zolnay, *Fun and Games in Old Europe*, 1986, 112.

MOSCA CIECA, an Ital. var. of >BLIND MAN'S BUFF.

MÖSÖN SHAGAI KHARVAKH, a Mong. game consisting of tossing stones or small ice blocks at a number of targets placed on the frozen surface of a lake or river. The targets can be larger stones, ice cubes, animal bones, or pieces of wood. The game is played by 2 teams of unspecified number of players. The players toss the stones from a distance 50-60m from the target; a tossed stone must fall to the ice in front of the target and slide towards it. Each team has to hit from 8 to 12 targets. The team which manages to hit more targets wins. Scoring is 2pts. for each target hit in the center, and 1pt. for each target hit on the outside. In another version of the game 2 players aim at 4 targets placed on ice – 2 for each player – from a distance 50-60m. The players toss ice blocks or stones. The player who manages to hit one of his targets so that it touches and stays with the other target, splitting the opponent's targets apart, wins the game.

MOTOR SLED, an early name for >SNOWMOBILE.

MOTOR SPORTS, a group of sports involving racing on vehicles propelled by motor engines, e.g. motorcars, motorcycles, motorboats; see collective entries >AUTOCROSS, >AUTO RACING, >DRAG CAR RACING, >MOTORCYCLE SPORTS; and individual entries >DRAG MOTORCYCLE RACING, >GRASSTRACK, >GYMKHANA, ICE SPEEDWAY, >MOTORBOATING, >MOTORCYCLE RALLIES, >MOTORCYCLE ROAD RACING, >MOTORCYCLE TRACK RACING, >MOTORCYCLE STREET RACING, >SAND-TRACK RACING, >SNOWMOBILE, >SPEEDWAY.

MOTOR TOBOGGAN, an early name for >SNOWMOBILE.

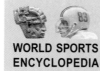

WORLD SPORTS ENCYCLOPEDIA

M

A game of polo, *Persian miniature, 16th cent.*

Driver Dan Runte of the monster truck 'Big Foot' is airborne as he makes his way through the NASCAR Craftsman Truck series monster truck course at Darlington Raceway in Darlington, South Carolina.

M WORLD SPORTS ENCYCLOPEDIA

Motorboating.

Motorcross side car competition.

MOTORBOATING, a sport involving competitive use of powerboats propelled by an internal-combustion engine. Motorboats with electric engines are mostly used for recreation and angling purposes. Piston or ramjet engines can be used. Two types of motorboats can be classified by the way in which the engine is installed. An outboard motorboat has a detachable motor clamped to the stern, e.g. outboard runabouts, cabin cruisers. An inboard motorboat has the engine permanently mounted within the hull. The main types of hulls used on motorboats are: 1) displacement hulls (first built by Amer. constructor D. Bertram) with V-shaped bottoms, sharp bows and narrow sterns, first introduced in 1960 during the Miami-Nassau Race; 2) catamarans with twin V-hulls; and 3) planing hulls with flat bottoms that at higher speeds rise to the surface and skim across the water.

Sports motorboats have a number of classes depending on piston displacement.

International events are held by several organizations, such as the International Union of Motorboating (Union Internationale Motonautique, UIM), the International Jet Sports Boating Association (IJS-BA), and the influential American Power Boat Asso-

Above left and below: motorboating.

ciation (APBA). Racing W.Ch. under the auspices of UIM are held on inland waters, on artificial courses marked by buoys in Formula 1-3, and on an open see in the offshore Class 1-3. Since 1981 the UIM has been holding W.Ch. in Formula 1 according to the rules resembling those of >CAR RACING. They include a series of Grand Prix events (usu. 8-10 in a year), during which the best competitors score points. The races are held on oval courses, the longer run between the turns not exceeding 850m. APBA has been holding US championships in various classes, most of which are not recognized by the UIM. The diversity of boat types used in the races controlled by different organizations is beyond the scope of this entry, so we shall just give a few examples. An UIM Formula 1 boat is 5,8m long and is propelled by a 2-3m³ internal-combustion engine. It must be equipped with protective floaters that are automatically filled in case of an accident. In offshore Class 1 a crew includes a helmsman and a mechanic, who controls the throttles. The boat is propelled by 2-3, either 12-cylinder, 8m³ internal-combustion or 10m³ compression-ignition, engines. An Open Class boat used in APBA races has a turbo- or internal-combustion engine and a large stabilizer in the back part of the hull.

Speed records are held in different categories and classes or over different distances. Apart from the classified motorboats absolute speed records are also held on specially designed hydroplanes. In 1910, the water speed record for a motorboat with an internal combustion engine was 54.07km/h. In 1939 Englishman M. Campbell held the 1-mi. water speed record of 141.74mph (228km/h) with his hydroplane Bluebird II. In 1950 the hydroplane Slo-Mo-Shun IV took the record at 160.323mph (258km/h) in the USA. The 200-mph barrier was broken in 1962 by Miss U.S. with an average speed of 200.52mph (322.53km/h) in Guntersville, Alabama. In 1954 M. Campbell's son, Donald became the first driver to successfully pilot a jet-propelled boat on Lake Mead in Nevada. Campbell reached the speed of 385.4km/h and raised his record in 1959 to 260.35mph (418.90km/h). In 1978, Australian K.P. Warby set a straightaway record of 319.627mph (514.39km/h) with the Spirit of Australia. His water speed record has never been broken.

Outboard motorboats have lagged behind inboard boats in speed. The 100-mph barrier was broken by M. Leto di Priolo from Italy at 100.36mph. In 1960 B. Ross raised the record to 115.547mph.

A var. of motorboating is known as >JET SKI. Powerboats are used also in >AQUAPLANING, >AIR CHAIR, >BAREFOOT WATERSKIING, and >WATER SKIING.

History. The first motorboat with an internal-combustion engine was built in 1865 by J. Lenoire. In the 1880s G. Daimler designed his famous automobile engine, which was later used in boats as well. At the turn of the 19th and 20th cent. The number of existing motorboats was sufficient to set up the first races and regattas. The first motorboat race took place on the Seine during the 1900 Paris World Exhibition. In 1903 a race from Calais to Dover was organized and the Harmsworth Cup was established by the Brit. publisher A. Harmsworth, the first perpetual and most prestigious international event in the sport of motorboat racing. In the same year the Amer. Power Boat Association (APBA) was founded, which vastly contributed to the development of motorboating. In 1907, O. Evinrude constructed the first outboard motor, which made motorboats fairly common means of transportation and recreation. In 1922, on the initiative of the Irishman J. Ward, the Union of International Motorboating (Internationale Motonautique, UIM) was estab. World water speed records have been recorded since 1928; W.Ch. in different motorboat classes have been held since 1938. New engine types and improved hull construction made the sport immensely popular in the inter-war period. The major motorboat manufacturer is the USA. In the 1950s and 1960s the world motorboating clubs' membership increased about 16% every year on the average. Since the 1960s the most successful have been Ger. racers, using König engines, considered the best in the world. The world's top boat racers include the Poles, Swedes, and Russians. Individual motorboat classes have been dominated by Belgians, Dutch, and Italians.

One of the most outstanding motorboat racers is American R. Nordskog who won the largest number of awards in the history of offshore racing, in the 1940s, '50s and '60s. B. Muncey (1928-81) won the premier Gold Cup instituted by the APBA 8 times. Muncey's record was then broken in 1993 by C. Hanauer after he won the prize for the 9th time. Although the sport of motorboat racing has been dominated by men, some women drivers have been fairly successful in different racing competitions, e.g. B. Crook, the 3-time US champion and 2-time world champion in the 1970s and '80s.

The most popular water racing tracks are selected areas of the North Sea, the Eng. Channel, the estuary of the Hudson River, Lake George and the Thousand Islands region in New York, lakes and river mouths around Seattle and the Gulf of Mexico. The longest motorboat events are the races from Florida to the Bahamas, first held in 1959; and from London to Monte Carlo (4,800km), first held in 1972. Poles have been among the best international motorboat racers in history, e.g. W. Marszałek – multitime world and Eur. champion (W.Ch. in 1979, 1980, 1981 and 1983); T. Haręza – the world and Eur. champion and placing 2nd in several classes (W. Ch. In 1993, 1995, 1996, 1997, and 1998); and H. Synoracki – the 1997 Class 0-250 world champion, 1998 runner-up.

T. Adelt, *Śródlądowy jachting motorowy*, 1978; T. Adelt and S. Gajęcki, *Sport motorowodny*, 1954; J. Lee Barrett, *Speed Boat Kings*, 1986; D.W. Fostle, *Speedboat*, 1988); J. Teal, *High-Speed Motor Boats*, 1969.

The Honda British Motorcross Championships at Canada Heights in Swanley, England.

Early days of motorcycle rallying.

MOTORCROSS, among the >MOTORCYCLE SPORTS, a racing event held on a loop, natural surface track, with various irregularities, asperities, or monticles along the entire course. It differs from >SUPERCROSS in that the latter is held on artificially constructed tracks. In both events the winner is the driver who comes to the finish line first. The best 15 drivers in each race score championship points. Races are held in solo and side-car categories. The sport's governing body is the International Motorcycling Federation (FIM), which organizes W.Ch. and various continental and national events. One of the leading drivers is American J. McGrath, the winner of e.g. the famous *Motorcross des Nations* (1996). See also >ENDURANCE RALLY, >OBSERVATION TRIAL, >MOTORCYLE TRACK RACING.

MOTORCYCLE BALL, a game invented in 1928 and practiced first in England, Austria, Germany and Switzerland. The first motorcycles used for the game were of simple construction with no extra accessories such as headlights, fenders, kickstands, etc. In later years, specially designed, lighter and more maneuverable motorcycles with profiled seats and handgrips were introduced. The aim of the game is to shoot the ball into the opposing team's goal. The ball can be kicked or hit with the front wheel of the motorcycle. The game is played by 2 teams of 5 players. Each team consists of 3 forwards, a defender and a goalkeeper. The goalkeeper can touch the ball with his hands. The field is 90-110m long and 50-75m wide; often regular soccer fields are used. A match consists of four 20-min. periods, with three 10-min. breaks in between. The teams change sides at the half-time. The motorcycles weigh 45-90kg and have 250cc engines. After 1945 motorcycle ball became popular in the USSR, East Germany, Bulgaria, England, Belgium, the Netherlands and West Germany. The Motorcycle Ball European Cup has been held since 1970. The sports governing body is the Federation of International Motorcycling in Mies, Switzerland.

MOTORCYCLE RALLIES, long-distance motorcycle racing events in which competitors cover a set course in one or more legs, within a set time limit. The course may include some rough terrain, making it similar to >MOTORCROSS. However, one difference is that motorcycle rallies stress negotiating terrain to a lesser extent. Most rallies use roads but if there are rougher parts, or if the whole rally is set in difficult terrain, the participants may avoid the obstacles by choosing a more suitable course to reach the defined checkpoints. In addition to that, motorcycle rallies use courses much longer than those used in motocross, often several hundred or even thousand km long, and open rather than looped. The participant with the best time and lowest number of penalty points wins. Participants set out in a defined order, like in >AUTOMOBILE RALLIES, at set intervals. Since the 1950s, so-called 'controlled trials' have been developing, involving the participants being controlled by judges not only at checkpoints but also along esp. difficult sections. The Safari Rally, The Paris-Dakar Rally and Americade are among the most famous motorcycle rallies today.

MOTORCYCLE ROAD RACING, competitive motorcycle racing held on public roads. The earliest such event, though 4-wheeled motor cars also took part, was the 1904 Paris-Rouen race over a distance of 126km. The first road-race exclusively for motorcycles was held in 1897 on the Paris--Dieppe route, over a distance of 160km. The first closed-course motorcycle race – the race for the Tourist Trophy – took place on the Isle of Man in 1907. Motorcycle road racing gave rise to many

modern motorcycle track racing events, including Grand Prix W.Ch. estab. in 1949 (>MOTORCYCLE TRACK RACING).

MOTORCYCLE SPORTS, recreational and competitive sports practiced using motorcycles. Motorcycles can be 2- (solos) or 3-wheelers (sidecars). Depending on engine displacement they are divided into several classes, and vary in construction and use for sports events. The main var. of motorcycle sports include: >DRAG MOTORCYCLE RACING, >GRASSTRACK, >GYMKHANA, >ICE SPEEDWAY, >MOTORCROSS, >MOTORCYCLE ROAD RACING, >MOTORCYCLE BALL >MOTORCYCLE TRACK RACING, >MOTORCYCLE STREET RACING, >MOTORCYCLE RALLIES, >MOTOR-PACED CYCLING, >SAND-TRACK RACING, >SPEEDWAY. **History.** The origins of motorcycle sports date back to the construction of the first engine-propelled bicycle by G. Daimler and W. Maybach in 1883. The first motor tricycle was built by an Englishman, E. Butler, in 1885. A German, H. Müller, built the first

motorcycle factory. In 1902, G. Hendee built the first motorcycle in the USA and rode it from New York City to Boston. At the same time, the Davidson Brothers constructed their first machine in their famous factory. It was the Harley-Davidson factory that first began to take advantage of motorcycle races as a testing ground for its constructors. The first documented motorcycle race was held as part of the 1894 Paris-Rouen automobile road race, over a distance of 126km. The first motorcycle race as an independent event was held on the 160-km Paris-Dieppe route in 1897. Before long town-to-town road races gave way to specially designed tracks and racing courses built outside towns. In 1907 the first Tourist Trophy race on a closed course was held on the Isle of Man; in 1913 the annual International Six Days Trial (ISDT) was established, informally known as the 'Motorcycle Olympic Games'. The years 1920-39 saw the heyday of all types of motorcycle road, street and track races as well as rallies, and – esp. in the '20s – speedway racing. Before 1939 the world leading motorcycle manufacturers were BMW, NSU, Zündapp and DKW in Germany; New Imperial, Royal Enfield, BSA and Norton in the UK; Harley Davidson, AJS and Indian in the USA; Velocette and Sarolea in Italy; and Peugeot in France. Most of these companies dominated the motorcycle market until the emergence of Japanese motor companies (Honda, Suzuki, Yamaha) in the 1950s. The latter still dominate the market today together with a few US and Eur. manufacturers.

On the initiative of Great Britain, France and Austro-Hungarian Empire, the Fédération Internation-

South African rider Alfie Cox steers up his KTM motorbike during the third stage of the Granada-Dakar rally between Agadir and Tan-Tan, Morocco.

ale des Clubs Motocyclistes was established in 1904 (renamed the Fédération Internationale Motocycliste, FIM, in 1912) as the governing body of motorcycle road racing, rallies, motocross racing, track racing and motorcycle tourism.

MOTORCYCLE STREET RACING, a competitive racing sport, popular in the early years of motorcycle racing, practiced in large cities on street courses. Motorcycle street racing reached its heyday in the 1930s and '40s. Various forms of motorcycle racing were more popular in Europe than in the USA, where automobile sports enjoyed much higher esteem. Motorcycle street races in W Europe went into decline in the '50s due to the development of special racing tracks outside towns as well as live television coverage of racing events. In E Eur. countries, such as Poland, which faced numerous economic hardships and in which television appeared later, motorcycle races enjoyed public interest well into the '60s as an easily available mass spectacle. A motorcycle street course was usu. polygonal and

A motorcycle desert rally.

M

WORLD SPORTS ENCYCLOPEDIA

comprised a homestretch, backstretch, a tight 'dead man's curve', and a few s-bends. Many cities featured motorcycle courses marked upon existing streets and avenues. In Poznań, Poland the course was marked between Dąbrowskiego and Szamarzewskiego Streets, with a tight bend on the intersection of Szamarzewskiego and Szpitalna Streets, and an s-bend between Szamarzewskiego and Szamotulska Streets. The races attracted a great number of spectators and required numerous measures, such as bales of hay positioned in the most dangerous spots on the course. Motorcycle street racers had their own champions, e.g. U. Masetti in Italy and I. 'Igol' Stefański in Poland.

MOTORCYCLE TRACK RACING, motorcycle competitive racing practiced on specially constructed racing tracks. The racing tracks used to be designated closed-courses, part or all of which were public roads or city streets. Due to the constant increase in motor vehicle traffic on public roads, organizers of motorcycle and automobile races started to hold racing events on specially built courses. Most modern prestigious motorcycle racing events were formerly held on public roads. The W.Ch., consisting of an annual series of Grand Prix races, for example, originated as road races in 1949, but today they are held on different special motorcycle or automobile racing tracks designated by the Fédération Internationale Motocycliste (FIM). The Grand Prix is awarded to the competitor with the highest total of points scored in all constituent races. Each race is held on a course ranging from 70 to 150km. Currently races are held in the following classes: GP-125, GP-250, and su-

Jose Luis Cardoso of Spain puts his Antena 3 Yamaha through its paces during the 500cc Motorcycle Grand Prix at the Bugatti Circuit in Le Mans, France.

E.Ch., but it was changed to 80cc in 1984 and later discontinued altogether. In the years 1977-79 races of 750cc motorcycles were held as well. In 1983 the 350cc class was excluded from the program. Tourist Trophy races have been held since 1997, and endurance races over a distance of 1,000km, for 6-24h, since 1980. In the side-car category only races of 500cc-class machines are held. Italian G. Agostini is considered the greatest motorcycle track racing legend. Between 1965-77 he won 15 W.Ch. titles (8 in the 500cc class and 7 in

Mountain biking – the path not taken.

perbike. The previous 500cc class was replaced with the Moto GP class for motorcycles with 4-stroke engines of a max. capacity of 990cc. It can also be entered by motorcycles with 2-stroke engines and 500cc max. capacity, although the latter are gradually becoming obsolete. The E.Ch. have been held since 1982.
Motorcycle track races are held in solo and side-car categories. The machines are divided into several classes based on engine displacement. In the solo category the classes were first 125, 250, 350 and 500cc. In 1962 the 50cc class was incl. in the

the 350cc class). Among other well known track motorcyclists are Italian V. Rossi (4-times world champion) and M. Biaggi (4-times world champion), and Australian M. Doohan.

MOTOR-PACED CYCLING, a cycling event in which the riders follow a motorcycle. Present in the Ol.G since 1893, it was dropped in 1914, only to be reinstated in 1963. A type of motor-paced cycling called >KEIRIN caught on in Japan and is extremely popular there. Interest in this type of event is spreading from Japan to other countries.

MOUNTAIN BIKE ORIENTEERING, a cycling sport akin to >ORIENTEERING and supervised by the International Orienteering Federation, IOF. The contestants, equipped with a map and compass, try to reach certain control sites in the terrain. The map is attached to the handlebars of the bike (or worn around the neck) and the compass is worn like a wristwatch. Contestants may make necessary repairs to their bikes in their own capacity. For this purpose they carry the necessary tools and a set of spare parts. They may not profit from the help of a third party. The events are held in topographically diverse areas with a network of mountain and woodland paths, which the contestants must keep to. In mountain bike orienteering jargon the sport is referred to as *Bike-O*. This discipline originated in the late 1970s. One of the first races (perhaps the very first) was held in 1977 in Bostock Reservoir near Melbourne, Australia. One

of the pioneers of the sport was Australian K. Haarsma. In 1997 national championships were held in as many as 12 countries.
S. Harvey, M. Nimvik, B. Römvik, *The World of Orienteering,* 1998.

MOUNTAIN BIKING, cycling on bicycles of a special construction, on a mountainous terrain in the form of observed trials. The first attempts to adapt a bicycle to mountainous conditions were made by G. Fisher, who used a Schwinn bike with low-pressure tires for the purpose. Practiced initially in California (since 1966), it shot into popularity in the 1970s. The first open competition was organized in 1976 in Tamalpais, California (20km N of San Francisco), advocated by C. Kelly. The race acquired the name Repack from the constant need to exchange break pads because of the steepness of the hill. In 1977 J. Breeze built a prototype vehicle from which all today's mountain bicycles originate. In 1983 the Specialized company launched the first mountain bike series called Stump-Jumper. One of the top-ranking makes of mountain bikes is Cannondale. Also in 1983 the first US Championships were organized.
The construction of a mountain bike employs the latest technological developments, even achievements of space technology are applied; the frame is made of chromium and molybdenum, aluminum, titanium, and ceramic and composite materials. It has thick knobby tires like cross-country bicycles and straight handlebars which enable faster bend-taking and which can have additional grips. Clips on the pedals and cyclist's shoes quickly secure the feet to pedals to prevent slippage and can just as quickly release the cyclist's feet, a vast improvement on the straps used previously. The bike is equipped with suspension forks which allow for the front wheel to jump by 15cm and the rear wheel by 23cm, and which absorb excess energy that is produced while riding on uneven terrain. A mountain bike also has an advanced variable gear system, which facilitates extremely steep hill-climbs. The following mountain biking events have developed:
MOUNTAIN BIKE CROSS COUNTRY, organized on a circuitous route;
DOWN-HILL, riding on a marked route down a slope, at speeds often exceeding 100km/h,
DUAL SLALOM, a down-hill by pairs following 2 identical slalom routes, the winner of each pair qualifying for further down-hills;
OBSERVED RALLY, a circuitous route with natural obstacles that need to be negotiated, the winner being the competitor with the fewest penalty points for foot-propping;
HILL-CLIMB, an event opposite to down-hill, in which competitors race to the top of a mountain or a slope. The World Cup, also known as the W.Ch., has been held since 1987, and it features 9 cross-country and 6 down-hill (since 1993) events. Men's and women's events are held separately. Under pressure from television broadcasters, the original idea of a route stretched along a longer distance has given way to a number of laps, so that it is more convenient both for the spectators and TV viewers to observe the competition. Competitions are held most often in Laguna Beach, California, and St. Wendel, Germany. The top competitors are: M.

Valentino Rossi of Honda in action leading fellow Italian Max Biaggi of Yamaha during the British Motorcycle Grand Prix at Donington Park, Derbyshire.

Mountain biking.

Nooks, H. Rey, J. Lenosky (USA), L. Karaś (the Czech Republic) – a world champion in 1994; winners of the World Cup in 1996 – C. Dupouey (France) and A. Sydor (Canada). Each event consists of 3 trials. The major organization is the International Mountain Biking Association and the National Off-Road Bicycle Association (the US). Men's and Women's mountain cross-country was first entered into the Ol.G. in Atlanta, 1996 and the first Olympic winners were P. Pezzo (Italy) – women's, and J.B. Brentjens (Holland) – men's.

D. Davies, D. Carter, *Mountain Biking*, 1994; J. Tomlison, 'Mountain Biking', *Encyclopedia of Extreme Sports*, 1996; J. Zarka, *Kolarstwo górskie. Praktyczny podręcznik dla wszystkich miłośników rowerów górskich i terenowych*, 1993.

MOUNTAIN CLIMBING, also *mountaineering*, a sport in which the main objective is to reach inaccessible mountain peaks without the use of advanced technical means (e.g. helicopters). Climbers make use of their skills and relatively simple equipment (hooks, mountain axe, rope, crampons, oxygen bottles, etc.). The essence of mountain climbing is also an idealist approach to nature, as well as testing the physical, volitional and moral abilities of humans in a battle against the forces of nature. Because of its Alpine origin, mountain climbing is sometimes referred to as >ALPINISM, which is understood not only as climbing the Alps, but also a style and group of climbing techniques developed in the Alps, though applied in various equal or higher mountain ranges. In the past mountain climbing was crucial in the learning and exploitation of inaccessible mountain terrains. There are massifs in Asia and the Americas which have not been conquered yet. The future of mountain climbing seems to be locked in the question of how to secure the progress and attractiveness of the sport when all the mountain peaks will have been conquered and all – even the most extreme – paths have been battled.

Similar to other solo sports (>SPELEOLOGY, >SOLO YACHTING, >SCUBA DIVING), mountain climbing offers a rare chance of contact with pristine nature. The difficulties involved in the organization, training, and practice of mountain climbing prevent it from ever becoming a mass sport and so determine its elitist character as demonstrated by various distinctive features incl. clothing, customs, language, and literature.

History. The oldest confirmed event associated with mountain climbing is the ascent of the emperor Hadrian upon Etna (3,263m) in 130 B.C. According to old Scand. chronicles, the Norw. King Olaf Tryggvesson (d. approx. 1000 AD) climbed the rocky peak of Smalserhorn, which he proved by leaving his shield there. In 1336 an Ital. poet F. Petrarch, considered to be the father of alpinism, reached the Alpine peak of Mont Ventoux (1,920m). Up untill 1600 12 high Alpine peaks had been conquered. In 1786 the Frenchman M.G. Paccard with his guide J. Balmont made the first successful attempt to climb the highest Alpine peak – Mont Blanc (4,810m). In the 19th cent. the Alps became the center of mountain climbing, mostly because of their easily accessible location in Europe, the attractiveness of nature, and a large number of inns and hotels which encouraged the development of tourism. The lack of similar facilities delayed the same process in the Pol. Tatra mountains by several decades and by approx. 100 years in the Himalayas and Andes. The sporting nature of mountain climbing was determined in the early stages of Alpine exploration by Brit. tourists. It seems to be the greatest paradox in the history of mountain climbing that its sporting character and moral principles were formed by representatives of a country which lacked any high mountains. A turning point in the history of mountain climbing was the ascent of Mont Blanc in 1855 by 4 Brit. climbers – the Smith brothers, without a guide. In 1857 the Alpine Club

was formed in London and in 1863 it began to publish *The Alpine Journal*. In the years 1859-65 Brit. climbers conquered 68 Alpine peaks. In 1865 E. Whymper climbed with his friends the most difficult of all Alpine peaks – the Matterhorn. Several years after the Brit. Alpine Club was established, similar indigenous clubs were formed in other countries, e.g. Österreicher Alpenverein (1862) and Schweizer Alpen Club (1863), which acknowledged the leading position of Brit. climbers within the Alpine countries. One example is the 1862 appeal by R.T. Simler 'To Swiss climbers and friends of the Alps':

It is a well known fact that Swiss tourists have faced strong competition ever since the establishment of the English Alpine Club. It may soon happen so that in order to learn about the regions of perpetual snow and ice or the possibilities of reaching the glaciers and rocky mountain peaks, the Swiss society will have to refer to the publications of the English club. Such a state of affairs seems to be [...] embarassing.

By 1876 national Alpine associations had been formed in Italy, France and the USA, preceded by several years by various local clubs. In 1932 the International Union of Alpine Associations (Union Internationale des Associations d'Alpinisme, UIAA) was established. By the end of the 19th cent., once all the Alpine peaks had been conquered, the most frequent target of mountain climbing expeditions were the Andes, and at the beginning of the 20th cent. – the Himalayas. There was also a growing interest in other massifs – mostly in Africa and Asia. In 1921 the British began a series of attempts to conquer the highest peak in the world – Mount Everest (8,848m), locally called Chomo-Lungma (Mother Goddess of the Land). In 1922 the first climbers managed to go above 8,000m. It was a Fr. expedition, led by M. Herzog in 1950, however, that for the first time in recorded history climbed a peak whose height exceeded 8,000m – Annapurna. In 1924 the Brit. expedition of G.L. Mallory and A. Irving ended in the mysterious disappearance of both climbers. According to one hypothesis, they reached the peak of Everest and died in a snow storm on the way back (a literary rendering of that hypothesis can be found in J. Kurek's novel *Mount Everest*, 1924). Everest was officially conquered only in 1953 by E.P. Hillary of New Zealand (b. 1919) and Sherpa Tenzing Norgay of Nepal. In 1978 Everest was climbed without the use of oxygen masks (R. Messner and P. Habeler). Climbing the world's highest mountain marked the end of the era of competing for height in mountain climbing. Each subsequent ascent and passage of unconquered massifs has had a smaller dimension and could not rival the achievements of the climbing pioneers. The interest in mountain climbing was sustained for some time by competition for quantity, e.g. climbing all peaks above 8,000m in height or climbing the highest peaks of all continents, etc. That exhausted the further possibilities of development of the sport. The lack of interest in professional mountain climbing is bound to turn the sport into an elitist form of tourism.

Mountain climbing on a Luxembourg postage stamp.

Michael Decker, a 39-year-old Kalamazoo, Michigan, native, celebrates as he nears the summit of Alaska's Danali, the American Indian name for Mount McKinley, in late June, 1997. Diagnosed with non-Hodgkin's lymphoma, Becker climbed Mount McKinley as a fund-raiser for cancer research.

WORLD SPORTS ENCYCLOPEDIA

Women began to enter the sport in the 2nd half of the 19th cent., partly as a result of the women's liberation movement. At first, women participated in men's expeditions, later formed separate teams, and finally began to lead mixed expeditions.
A. Huxley, ed., *Standard Encyclopaedia of the World's Mountains*, 1962; R.L.G. Irving, *La coquète de la montagne*, 1948; M. Kurz, *Chronique himalayenne*, 1959.

MOUNTAIN RESCUE, the activities of organizations and units specializing in mountain rescue operations. Trad. rescue methods include techniques of transportation in the mountains, close to mountaineer-

Mountain climbing is among the most popular summer recreational activities.

ing, but using additional equipment allowing the transport of the injured and bodies recovered. Nowadays, trad. mountain rescue techniques have been enhanced by the use of the helicopter. However, weather conditions often make the use of helicopters perilous or even impossible, and trad. techniques are still indispensable.
Mountain rescue is not a sport in the technical sense. However, any independent and original sport discipline always involves improving one's skills by practicing, and this element is present in mountain rescue. There are specialist national and international competitions.
History. During the first conference in 1863 that initiated actions aimed at establishing the Red Cross Organization, its originator H. Dunant (1828-1910) stressed the need to include in its scope not only soldiers and the infirm but also the victims of various accidents, including those on water and in the mountains. That is why some of the first mountain rescue organizations were established under the auspices of Red Cross societies in Austria, France and Switzerland in the 19th cent.

Mountain rescue.

Mountain rescuers' competition.

MOUNTAINBOARDING, a sport involving downhill riding on a board mounted on 3 or 4 wheels. Like trad. skateboards mountainboards have flexible axles permitting smooth balancing during riding, but they are much bigger.
History. The originators of mountainboarding were 2 snowboarders, P. McConnell and J. Lee. Initially, they used 4-wheel mountainboards as training boards in the summer but soon downhill boarding gained popularity and became a separate sport. McConnell and Lee founded the Mountainboard Company in Colorado Springs, Colorado and soon began to manufacture mountainboards and promote the new sport. A similar board, but with only 3 wheels was invented by the Australian J. Miln. Mountainboarding is still an evolving sport. Two kinds of competitions are organized: freestyle – using short maneuverable boards – consisting of performing evolutions marked by the judges; and downhill – using longer, more stable boards – against the clock. Both, 3-wheelers and 4-wheelers remain in use at present.

MPEEWA, a trad. Afr. girls' game played in Ghana. The girls get in pairs and stand facing each other, with the palm of the right hand facing down, and the palm of the left hand facing up. Next, both players go through the following sequence of action: clapping both hands with the palms making contact with each other; clapping both hands in the air; reversing the initial hand positions and clapping them again with the palms making contact with each other, and so on. The hand clapping gives the game its characteristic rhythm. Mpeewa can also be played using index fingers. A mpeewa var. played by boys is known as *koto-dwe bo nkate*. A similar game called *sang-jao-woni-kilee* is played in Liberia; in Nigeria a similar hand game known as *balibaligun* is played by girls from the Hausa and Gungawa tribes.
A. Taylor Cheska, 'Mpeewa', TGDWAN, 1987, 47; K. Fosu, *African Children's Games with Songsand Illustrations*, 1978; F.A. Salomone, 'Nigerian Children's Games as Ethnic Identity', RSL, 1976, 1.

MUBOLD, Dan. for 'ball against the wall', a Dan. game similar to Pol. >CALLING OUT. The players stand in a row facing a wall. One of them throws the ball against the wall and calls out the name of the player who is to catch the ball next and then throw it again. The ball can also be bounced against the ground. A player who fails to catch the ball is out or earns a penalty point.
J. Møller, 'Krydsbold, Lyrebold, Murbold', GID, 1997.

MUKNA, a form of wrestling practiced in the Ind. state of Manipur and in parts of Nagaland. Mukna enjoys greatest popularity around the towns of Imphal, Thoubal and Bishenpur; and is mainly practiced as part of the Hindu New Year celebration in April. The wrestlers begin their bout facing each other, crouching. They press on each other with their shoulders, placing their heads between the neck and shoulder of the opponent, and holding each other by a special girdle belt called the *ningri*. The aim of a mukna bout is to lift the opponent off by holding him by the belt, and then topple him to the ground. The opponent must be thrown on his back; if not, he must be forced to touch the ground with the whole length of his body. A mukna bout is very fast and resembles a dance performed quickly by two wrestlers. Grabbing the opponent's neck, hair, ears, genitals or legs is not allowed. Usu., mukna bouts are organized outside of a town or village, on a grassy meadow where a few pairs fight at the same time. Customarily, the champions' bouts are fought first, followed by rookies' bouts. There are no formal weight categories but usu. opponents with similar body weight are matched. The winner earns the official title of *yatra*.
According to some historical sources, the tradition of mukna wrestling can be traced back to the 15th

cent. Other historical sources date its origin back to the Hayach period; see also >ASIAN INDIAN WRESTLING.

MULTI-JUMPING, a sports event or a cycle of motions, in which more than one standing or running jump is performed from one leg to the other, on a single leg, or on both legs. Its most popular form is now the athletically recognized >TRIPLE JUMP (RUNNING). At the turn of the 19th cent. the program of international events (also Ol.G.) included a >TRIPLE JUMP (STANDING). Different from the athletic triple jump is the >IRISH TRIPLE JUMP, also deriving from a folk tradition.

MULTI-TRIAL ATHLETICS, versatile tests of psychophysical skills disciplined into a competitive form, the basis of which is a number of athletic events selected in such a way as to reflect the broadest possible scope of abilties. The most common types are: >DECATHLON; Amer. >ALL-AROUND, similar to the decathlon, with minor differences; and >PENTATHLON (also a women's pentathlon, with different events; replaced in 1980 by the women's >HEPTATHLON). A similar competition, though with different events, is held indoors as men's *heptathlon*. Less popular, though also practiced, are forms of athletic octaphlon and the athletic >TRIATHLON. A special multi-trial event has been designed for children as an athletic quadraphlon. Modern athletic events were once part of the ancient pentathlon and later, in the middle ages, of the chivalric heptaphlon (see >CHIVALRIC TOURNAMENTS). The 100m run, shot put, high jump or pole vault had until 1939 been part of >GYMNASTIC ALL-AROUND.

MULTI-TRIALS, a form of sport competition involving more than one event, each of a different nature. The oldest forms of multi-trials were the ancient >PENTATHLON and the medieval chivalric heptathlon. In modern times the most popular multi-trials are > MULTI-TRIAL ATHLETICS and the winter and summer forms of >BIATHLON. In >WEIGHTLIFTING the once popular >OLYMPIC WEIGHTLIFTING TRIATHLON was replaced by *Olympic two-event weightlifting*. Two-trial events are also popular in skiing, the most common forms being the >WINTER BIATHLON and *Alpine combination* (see >ALPINE SKIING). In multi-trial >GYMNASTIC ALL-AROUND an athlete's scores in particular events are added up to form their final score. The multi-trial character is also present in the >TRIATHLON, which consists of running, swimming and cycling.

MUMBLETYPEG, see >HAKKE KNIV MELLEM FINGRENE.

MUNADE VEERETAMINE, Est. for 'rolling eggs'; a trad. game consisting of rolling painted eggs downhill on a natural hillock. The egg rolling downhill must touch another one lying on the ground. If it does, the player can continue playing with both of them. Otherwise, it remains on the spot. The player who has the most eggs after the game is over is the winner.
M. Värv et al., 'Traditional Sports and Games in Estonia', TSNJ, 1996, 33.

MUNDJE VENDCE, an Alb. var. of folk wrestling derived from >PEHLIVAN WRESTLING, introduced in Albania during Turk. occupation.

MUNK MED PRÆDIKEN, see >MUNK.

MUNK, Dan. for 'monk'; a trad. Dan. game whose objective is to knock over a wooden pin placed in the ground, called the munk, by throwing sticks at it. A throwing stick is 40-60cm long; the pin is about 30cm long. The game is played by 8-10 players who stand behind the throwing line, 6m from the munk. One of the players is selected the munk guardian (*Munkevogter*) and takes his position near the munk. The players start throwing their sticks at the munk. If the munk is knocked over the throwing players can cross the throwing line and run to collect their sticks. The Munkevogter's task is to put the munk back in the ground and try to catch the throwing players. The guardian must not catch the players if the munk lies flat on the ground; a throwing player who crosses the throwing line to recover his stick must not return to the throwing line without it. If a throwing player is caught by the Munkevogter, the latter shouts, 'Munkevogter!' and then both race to the standing munk. If the throwing player gets to the munk first he continues the game as a thrower; if the Munkevogter gets to the munk first, the runners change sides and the caught player becomes the munk guardian. If none of the throwing players manages to knock over the munk, the guardian knocks it out himself, picks up one of the sticks from the ground and the owner of this stick must erect the munk and try to catch a participant who tries to get back his throwing stick.

The game of munk has numerous local var. in Denmark. The main ones include:

MUNK MED PRÆDIKEN, (Dan. 'monk with a sermon'). The munk is a wooden pin 65-80cm in length and 4-6cm in diameter. Sometimes the munk has a lump of horse bristle mounted on top. The players try to knock the munk over using wooden logs (*Kloden* – 'celestial body'), 30cm in length and 7-13cm in diameter. The size of the log is not important as the kloden can be matched with the player's skill. In the past the throwers used regular rocks, but for safety reasons, they were later replaced with wooden logs. Each player has one log, with the exception of the munk guardian, called the *Tepmand* (Dan. for 'a lasher'), who is holding a long twig (*Tepkæpen*). The players throw their logs from behind the throwing line, 15-20 steps from the munk. If the munk is knocked over the players can run to recover their logs. After the munk is stuck back in the ground the Tepmand tries to catch the runner by tapping him with the twig. A tapped player races together with the Tepmand toward the munk. If the Tepmand gets first to the munk and knocks it over the tapped player becomes the Tepmand; if the tapped player reaches the munk first he can safely return to the throwing line and play the next round. The game consists of 4 rounds, each named with a different Church term, determining the Tepmand's actions: 1) First Sermon (*første Prædiken*); 2) Closing Prayer (*Messefald*); 3) Seventh Sermon (*Syvprædiken*); 4) Kneeler (*Knæfald*). During the First Sermon the Tepmand can only tap the players before they reach their logs. During the Closing Prayer the players can be tapped right after they cross the throwing line. The Seventh Sermon is similar to the First Sermon but after the last log has been thrown the Tepmand can run after the players and tap them anywhere on the field, even behind the throwing line. If a running player recovers his log and throws it again at the munk he can safely return behind the throwing line. The most complex stage is the Kneeler, during which the players can reach their logs without being tapped but they must pick them up by holding the logs between their knees. A lying log can be helped up with another log but cannot be touched by hand. A player carrying the log between his knees cannot be tapped unless he drops it or touches it with hands.

RISMUNK FRA NORDFYN, (Dan. for 'a monk with a peg'), a var. from North Fyn. The munk is much shorter than in other var. The munk guardian, called the munk raiser (*Munkerejser*), does not catch the players. The player who knocks the munk over runs to recover the stick and bring it back behind the throwing line. If, however, the Munkerejser manages to stand the munk up the running player must stop at once and place his stick on the ground. He can resume running only if another player knocks over the munk. If any player attempts to run with his stick while the munk remains standing the Munkrejser can knock it down and change sides with the runner. If there are no players to throw sticks at the munk the Munkrejser picks up the munk and throws it at one of the sticks lying on the ground. If he succeeds in hitting the stick its owner becomes the Munkrejser.

FOX, also *ræv*, a var. of munk in which players try to knock over a wooden tripod. The name is a borrowing from Ger. or Eng.; near the Ger. border the game is known as *buk* (Dan. for 'buck') and in Germany as *Bock*.

KAV, also *kuk* or *kaud* (Dan. for a pole in the city, to which those who had offended public order, esp. obscene women, were tied and whipped), a var. of munk consisting of knocking out the munk in such a way so that it springs away as far as possible. The player who has thrown his stick at the munk runs to pick the stick up from the ground and returns behind the throwing line dodging the munk guardian. The guardian can only tap the runner after the latter picks up the stick. If the returning player drops the stick and the guardian picks it up from the ground the player is out and becomes the guardian. The player can only be tapped if the pin remains standing; if a player knocks the pin out he shouts, 'Kaud ligger!' (Pin down!) and then the guardian must

promptly run to the munk and put it back. If all the players have thrown their sticks but no one has managed to pick his stick up from the ground and the munk remains standing, the guardian stands above it astride, shouts, 'Paaligge – maaligge!' and knocks it over himself. After that he throws his own stick at the sticks lying about the field; if he hits a player's stick this player becomes the new munk guardian.

Munk is played in many regions of Scandinavia and Germany. It is known under many different names, such as *kampmand* in central Jutland; *kegl* in Nyborg; *at slå kuk* on the island of Samsø; *kagen* on the isle of Als; and also as *munk* in Finland. Some var. of the game are played using throwing stones.

SLÅ KOKKEN AF HØNEN (Dan. for 'knocking the cock off the hen'), The players throw stones at a target made of a small pebble placed atop another larger pebble, situated on a line drawn on the ground. The aim of the game is to knock the smaller pebble off the larger one by throwing stones at it from a throwing line 10-20m from the mark. One of the players is the *kokvogter* – guardian of the 'cock'. If a player throws his stone short of the mark line he can pick it up and start throwing again. If the stone crosses the mark line but fails to hit the cock the throwing player can come to his stone but must wait there until another player knocks the cock off. After that, the kokvogter re-places the cock. After all the players have thrown their stones, the kokvogter runs to the target, jumps over it, and tries to hit one of the lying stones with his own stone. If he succeeds he changes sides with the owner of the stone.

J. Møller, 'Fox; Munk; Munk med prædiken; Munk/ Rismunk fra Nordfyn; Kav/Kuk/Kaud; Slå kokken af hønen', GID, 1997, 1, 106-9.

MUSHTI, a var. of Ind. wrestling.

MUSK OX WRESTLING, a var. of wrestling popular among the Greenland Natives, Can. and Alaskan Inuits, and the Deno of the Yukon Territory. Two wrestlers kneel in an igloo facing each other with their chins touching their own chests. The aim of the bout is to press the opponent with the head and push him to the wall of the igloo. The name of the game has been taken from the characteristic butting action of the musk oxen (Lat. *Ovibos maschatus*) inhabiting Greenland, Spitzbergen, northern Canada and Scandinavia. Musk ox wrestling is one of the 2 types of wrestling practiced by the Inuits and Greenland Natives; the other is >WNA TAG TUG.

W. Baxter, 'Les luttes traditionnelles a traverse le monde', LJP 1998, 75.

MUSTLASEMAADLUS, Est. for 'Gypsy wrestling', a var. of Est. wrestling introduced once into the country by Swed. settlers. Two wrestlers lie on their backs, side by side, with their heads in opposite directions. They raise their inner legs and hook them, trying to turn the opponent over his head. Although mustlasemaadlus is a typical on-the-ground wrestling it bears a resemblance to Swed. >KRAGTAG and Fin. *mustalaspaini*; the latter name also denotes Gypsy wrestling.

M. Värv, et al., 'Traditional Sports and Games in Estonia', TSNJ, 1996, 31.

MUURKAATSEN, Flem. *kaatsen* played against a wall, among the autonomous var. of >KAATSEN. A similar game family played in Great Britain is called *wall-hand-tennis*; the game is also similar to the Eng. >FIVES and Pol. >ŚCIANA. Popular esp. in the French-speaking part of Belgium. In Wallon school competitions are organized. Rules of the game are set by the Royal National Federation of Kaatsen (*Koninklijke Nationale Kaatsbond*). According to tradition, muurkaatsen was described by Erasmus of Rotterdam (1467-1536), a great humanist from the Netherlands. Presently, the game is played in some schools cherishing the oldest traditions, although it is losing its popularity in the face of the development of modern international sports. The game is played with a small, hard ball, which is bounced against a wall with a flat palm (no racket or bat is used). The ball is similar to that used in Amer. >BASEBALL: it is filled with densely packed cloth pieces, covered with 2 longitudinal, ellipsoidal leather pieces, manually sewn, with the stitches on the leather surface. A simple wall with an asphalt or cement surface in front is used to play muurkaatsen. The field, about 5-7m wide, is limited by 2 sidelines (*voslijnen*, sing. *voslijn*). On the field surface, parallel to the wall but 1m from the wall, there is the

'prayer line' (*oremuslijn*) before which the ball must bounce before striking the wall. A ball cannot bounce off the wall at just any height, but only above the line about 1m above the field level (*paslijn*). The throw field is limited on the sides by the lines, which are extensions of the sidelines but are drawn up the wall. There is no top line limiting the throw field; usu. it is the wall edge. A point is awarded to the opponent if a player strikes the ball after it has bounced off the ground twice (instead of once), if the player strikes the ball out of turn, if the player strikes the ball under the bounce line drawn on the wall, or if the ball, struck by the player, bounces outside the field limiting lines.

Though the game can be played by several players at a time, a team version (*kaatsen in ploegen*)

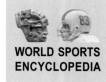

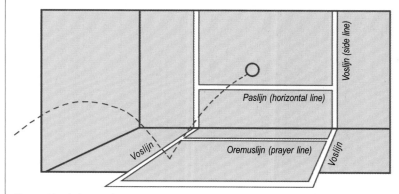

The court for playing muurkaatsen.

is possible and quite popular, in which only 2 players from each team are playing at the same time. The players of each team stand in 2 rows opposite the wall, forming 2 rounds. The first 2 players from each row start the game. The server strikes the ball against the wall above the bounce line so that the ball, bounced off the wall, hits the field. The ball bounced off the field must be returned by hand towards the wall by the first player from the second round of players and when the ball again bounces off the wall and hits the surface, it must be returned by the first server. Depending on the local var. of the game, a player who commits 2 errors, drops out, or goes to the end of his row, and the game is resumed by the 2nd player in the row; when he drops out, the game is resumed by the third player in the row etc.

Another var. of the game is a divided-field kaatsen. In this game the field is divided into 2 zones. Players cannot play on the opponent's zone. Still another var. is kaatsen in the corner (*kaatsen in een hoek*). In this var. the ball is struck not against a straight wall, but against fragments of 2 walls joined by the corners. When the back wall in the arcade with columns in the front is used for the game, the game is called *kaatsen in een zuilengalerij* (literally kaatsen with a gallery of posts, or a colonnade). Individual columns or posts represent an additional obstacle. A number of changes have been introduced to muurkaatsen in Wallon to revive the disappearing game and to make it more attractive. The ball is no longer bounced against the wall but against a 4x5m wooden board off which the ball bounces more dynamically.

E. De Vroede, 'Muurkaatsen', HGVB, 1996, 12-16; E. De Vroede, 'Ball and Bowl Games in the Low Countries. Past and Present', Homo Ludens – Der Spielende Mensch, 1996, vol. VI.

N

Atarashi Naginata (standardized Naginata training)

Atarashi Naginata basics consist of 5 types of movement, 5 different stances (Kamae), and 5 targets that can be attacked for points. The photos above show the basic fighting stances (top to bottom): Jodan-no-kamae, Gedan-no-kamae, Chudan-no-kamae, Waki-no-kamae, Hasso-no-kamae.

NA SAYAR, a trad. Afr. game played in Nigeria and the Fulani region of Niger, usu. by boys aged 6-12, often during school classes. A long piece of rope is used, along with personal belongings as forfeits. The object of the game is to regain possession of the forfeits without being taken captive by the 'guard'. **How the game is played**. The rope is attached to a tree (or held by one of the players), with the 'guard' of the forfeits tied to it at the other end. The players place their forfeits on the other side of the stretched rope. The guard holds in his hands a piece of clothing, e.g. a shirt, which he uses to drive away the players trying to retrieve their possessions. When attempting to do so, the players may not approach the forfeits from outside the field delimited by the length of the rope. The task of the guard is to pat one of the players, who then must replace him, and the game continues.
J.A. Beran, 'Physical education in Nigeria', JPERD; A. Taylor Cheska, 'Na sayar', TGDWAN, 1987, 48.

NAG OG DAG, Dan. for 'night and day'. A Dan. folk game using a disk-shaped object painted white on one side and black on the other. The players are divided into 2 teams – 'day' and 'night'. They stand in 2 rows, about 1.5m apart. The game leader spins the disk. If it lands with the white side up, the 'day' team is supposed to chase the 'night' team, catching the players of the opposite team (a touch is enough) before they have the time to hide in the so-called *frimål* zone. If the disk lands with the black side up, the roles are reversed. Each player caught counts as 1pt.
J. Møller, 'Nag og dag', GID, 1997, 4, 100.

NAGA WRESTLING, a trad. var. of wrestling popular in Nagaland, India, among the Angami, Chakhesang, Mao, Rengma and Zeliang tribes. Naga wrestling is very similar to Greco-Roman wrestling. The fighters stand face-to-face and hold each other around the waist. Holds and grips may be applied anywhere above the waist. A naga wrestling bout consists of 3 rounds. In order to win the bout a fight-

Atarashi Naginata starting position (Shizentai).

Atarashi Naginata attack targets: wrist (Kote, above), thrust-to-throat (Tsuki, below left), and shin (Sune, below right). The remaining two are: body (Do) and head (Men).

er has to win 2 rounds. To win a round he has to throw his opponent to the ground so that he touches it with any part of his body or kneels down on both knees while touching the ground with one hand or, vice versa, touches the ground with both hands while kneeling down on one knee.
The Internet: http://w3.meadev.gov.in/sports/tr_games/naga.htm

NAGINATA JUTSU, a Jap. martial art, primarily practiced by women and dating back to the Middle Ages [Jap. *naginata* – halberd + *jutsu* – a skill, art]. The classical form of naginata, known as *jikishin kegeryu*, uses a halberd (1.98m in length, although some sources report lengths of up to 2.15m) with an oaken handle and a metal blade replaced by a bamboo rod in the modern sporting version. The first participant to succeed in touching with her halberd the head, neck, abdomen, wrist or knee of the opponent is declared the winner. The fighters wear special pleated trousers with the legs narrowing down at the ankles, protective vests, shin protectors and helmets similar to those used in >KENDO. **History.** Naginata dates back to the times of the Nara dynasty (710-794). The *Kojiki*, Japan's oldest chronicle, dating back to those times, mentions the naginata (the halberd itself) as a type of weapon used by monks in the times of Emperor Shotoku. In the Oda and Toyotomi periods, naginata developed further as a martial art of the *bushi* warriors, the predecessors of the samurai. The Edo period (1603-1867) saw the end of feudal wars, and the introduction of Eur. firearms caused the gradual elimination of the naginata as a weapon. In the 17th cent., samurai daughters began to be trained in a self-defense art based on the trad. naginata, or *jikishin kageryu*, which at the same time declined in importance among men. In 1790, the emperor issued a special order which actually obliged samurai daughters to practice naginata. There was even a custom for samurai daughters to take naginatas with gold-plated handles as part of their dowry when they got married. At the same time, the rules of naginata provided inspiration for plebeian martial arts, later known as *tendo ryu* (which used sickles or small scythes and chains). Japan's opening to the outside world in 1868 caused many old traditions, including that of naginata, to deteriorate. Naginata continued to exist on the margins of Japan's social life, decaying together with the social class of the samurai. It was not as fortunate as other martial arts, in having no reformers (such as Jigoro Kano for >JUDO). It was only in 1955 that the All-Japan Naginata Federation was established. The Federation strives to keep the tradition going in Japan, and make it more popular around the world. Today, there are about 200 schools around Japan that have naginata in their curricula, sometimes as a mandatory subject. In 1974, the United States Naginata Federation was founded, and the Fr. federation was estab. in 1977. The Netherlands, Belgium and Sweden followed suit, as did N.Zealand. In 1990, these coun-

tries all formed the International Naginata Federation, which was soon joined by new countries, including Brazil, England and Italy. In Asia outside Japan, naginata is practiced in several countries, e.g. Singapore. The first Naginata W.Ch. was held in Tokyo, Japan in 1995, the second was in Paris in 1999. The third is to take place in San Jose, California in 2003.
K.S. Moorthy, 'Naginata', SS, Oct. 1988; anon., 'Naginata', *Traditional Sports in Japan*, (Program of the) 1st *International Festival of Traditional Sports and Games of the World*, 1992; Consultant: John Prough.

The Naginata is an ancient Jap. pole arm that is essentially a Jap. sword blade mounted on a long handle. The blade varies in length with the average blade being around 50cm long. The length of the pole also varies with the average pole around 170cm. There are 2 types of Naginata used today. A carved hard wood analog of a real Naginata is used in Atarashi Naginata for Kata training and in various Ko-ryu. The other type uses two slats of bamboo to represent the blade. This is the standard type used in Atarashi Naginata. The photo below shows from left to right: Atarashi Naginata, Kata Naginata, a real Naginata, complete with sheath, from c.1600. The middle Naginata is 219cm long.

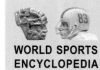

NAKKEDRAG, Dan. for 'dragging by the neck', [Dan. *nakke* – neck + *drage* – to drag]. A Dan. trad. var. of wrestling. Two competitors face each other and put their hands on the opponent's neck. The objective is to bend the opponent's neck without bending oneself.

J. Møller, 'Nakkedrag', GID, 1997, 3, 77.

NAPPE GRYDELÅG, Dan. for 'catching the lid', [Dan. *nappe* – to filch, steal + *grydelåg* – pot lid). An old Dan. folk game. The players sit on chairs arranged in a circle. One of them spins a pot lid and calls the name of another player, who is supposed to run up to the lid before it falls over, spin it again and call the next name.

J. Møller, 'Nappe grydelåg', GID, 1997, 3, 77.

NARREBOLD, Dan. for 'deceptive ball', [Dan. *narre* – to deceive + *bold* – ball]. A ball game for 10 or more people. The players form a row or a semi-circle, with one person, the 'thrower' about 6-7 steps away. Ideally, there should be a fence or wall behind the players' backs as this will keep uncaught balls within the field. The thrower passes the ball to each of the remaining players in turn, but before actually doing so, he marks the throwing motion a number of times. The catchers have to have their arms crossed on their chests or behind their backs until the thrower lets the ball go. If they move their hands too early or if the ball falls to the ground, they are excluded from the game. The catcher who succeeds in catching the ball the agreed number of times without error is declared the winner and takes over as the thrower.

J. Møller, 'Narrebold', GID, 1997, 1, 13.

NAUMACHIA, Gk. 'naval battle' [Gr. *naumachie* – naval battle <Gk. *naus* – ship + *machomai* – to fight]. A type of ancient games in which a mock sea battle was staged. The battles were organized in natural waters, or, if such were lacking, in artificial lakes made e.g. by damming rivers. Stands for the audience were usually built around the water, so that amphitheaters of a kind resulted. A battle would go on until one of the sides actually won, including the killing of opposing sailors. Just like during >GLADIATORIAL FIGHTS, the emperor could pardon the losers, sparing their lives. Gladiators were used in naumachia exhibitions, though more frequently convicts were used. They were divided into 2 groups and clothed in garments typical for the two 'fighting nations', e.g. Athenians and Persians, Romans and Carthaginians, etc.

History. The first recorded naumachia was staged by Julius Caesar in 46 BC. A special lake was dug in Rome's Campus Martius, to be later filled in. Ships and galleys of various types were brought in, with a total of 1,200 of sailors and 2,000 of oarsmen on boards. They were divided into the 'fleets' of Rome and Tyre. The games enjoyed tremendous popularity right from the outset. The Roman historian Svetonius Tranquilus mentioned them in his *De vita Caesarum*:

> *Such a throng flocked to all these shows from every quarter, that many strangers had to lodge in tents pitched in the streets or along the roads, and the press was often such that many were crushed to death, including two senators.*
>
> [Trans. Rolfe Humphries]

Augustus followed in Julius Caesar's footsteps, ordering a Mars Ultor temple to be built in 2 AD. The artificial lake within it was 557x536m (dimensions confirmed by archeological research). An artificial island was built in the middle. The fleets involved were 'Athenians' and 'Persians'. 6,000 gladiators took part in the staged battle, not counting the oarsmen. The show, as Ovid's poetry testifies, was also an opportunity for trysts:

> *When, lately, Caesar, in mock naval battle,*
> *exhibited the Greek and Persian fleets,*
> *surely young men and girls came from either coast,*
> *and all the peoples of the world were in the City?*
> *Who did not find one he might love in that crowd?*
> *Ah, how many were tortured by an alien love!*
>
> [Trans. A.S. Kline]

The most famous ancient naumachia was that staged by Claudius on Fucinus Lacus (today's Lago di Celano in Abruzzia, C Italy). The fleets were 'Sicilian' and 'Rhodesian'. One hundred ships and 19,000 people took part in the show. A silver statue of the god Triton, blowing his horn, emerged from the water to give the starting signal for the staging. Mock naval battles were also staged later on by a number of emperors, including Nero. In 80 AD, Titus celebrated the opening of the Colosseum with gladiatorial games that included a naumachia in Augustus' basin, restored. Titus' brother and successor, Domitian, staged a naval battle in the Colosseum itself, flooding it for the purpose. In 89 AD, he ordered a lake to be dug near the banks of the Tiber River for the next naumachia. Every last participant of Domitian's naumachias died a cruel death. There were also casualties among the spectators, as the cold and rain that accompanied one of the shows caused many to fall ill, while the emperor prohibited the audience from leaving for several days. But the emperor's flatterer Martial praised the marvel:

> *At Augustus' order fleets fought here*
> *And whirled the waters with the sound of battle horns.*
> *But that was just a fraction of what our Caesar prepared.*
> [...]
> *Whatever you can see at a circus or theater,*
> *The generous wave will bring to you, Emperor.*
> *Let us pass in silence over Lake Fucinus and Nero's puddles,*
> *The centuries will remember this naumachia alone.*

Traian, one of Domitian's successors, also staged naumachias, building an artificial lake in Rome known as the Naumachia Vaticana. Emperor Philip the Arab used that for a naumachia to celebrate the 1,000th anniversary of Rome in 248 AD. The area stretching up to St. Peter's Cathedral was known as the 'area of naumachias' up to the Middle Ages.

NAUSICAA BALL, a ball game with unspecified rules mentioned in Book VI of *The Odyssey*. The game was played by the girls from the country of Phaecians, visited by Odysseus:

> *After they had washed them* [i.e. the clothes] *and got them quite clean, they laid them out by the sea side, where the waves had raised a high beach of shingle, and set about washing themselves and anointing themselves with olive oil. Then they got their dinner by the side of the stream* [...] *when they had done dinner they threw off the veils that covered their heads and began to play at ball, while Nausicaa sang for them. As the huntress Diana goes forth upon the mountains* [...] *to hunt wild boars or deer, and the wood-nymphs, daughters of Aegis-bearing Jove, take their sport along with her (then is Leto proud at seeing her daughter stand a full head taller than the others, and eclipse the loveliest amid a whole bevy of beauties), even so did the girl outshine her handmaids.*
>
> [trans. S. Butler]

NEG YO BE, see >KHOMKHOI KHURUU BARIKH.

NETBALL, a var. of basketball played mainly by women and girls. It is one of the most widespread women's sports in Eng.-speaking countries, extremely popular in England, Australia, N.Zealand, S Africa, N Ireland, and Wales. Other nations playing netball include Jamaica, Trinidad, Kenya, Malta, Malaysia, Nigeria, Sierra Leone, Singapore, Sri Lanka, Tanzania, Uganda, Zambia and Iraq. Netball belongs to the family of >BASKETBALL GAMES.

Rules. The main objective of the game is scoring as many points as possible by shooting at a goal. The court is 30.5x15.25m in size. A metal or wooden goalpost, 3.05m high, with a ring attached to it is placed at the mid-point of each goal line. The rings have internal diameters of 380mm and are much like those used in basketball; however, there are no back boards to facilitate shooting. The rings are not mounted on the posts themselves but on special attachments, 150mm long, attached horizontally to the upper part of the posts. This is one difference between netball and >KORBBALL, where the basket is mounted on arch-like supports above the post, or >KORFBALL, where the basket touches the post with its side. The goalposts are located on the goal line, which makes it impossible to play behind the basket (again, differently from korbball or korfball). The ball is 27-28in. (69-71cm) in diameter and 14-16oz. (400-450g) in weight. The surface of the court should be hard – earlier, it was tarmacadam but today, tartan-like materials or natural timber (indoors) are used. In schools, when other surfaces are unavailable, grass or earth courts are used. The court is divided into 3 equal zones ('thirds'), each 10.16m long. The center circle, with a diameter of 90cm, is located in the center third. There are 2 goal circles in front of the goalposts, each with a radius of 490cm. A team consists of 7 players assigned to the thirds which they may not leave (in the past, there were versions of the game with teams of 5 or 9 players). Each team has one *goal shooter* playing in the goal third and goal circle of the opposing team. The *goal attack* player moves in the center and goal thirds. The *wing attack* plays in the center and goal thirds but not in the goal circle. The *center* may move over the whole court but not the goal circles. The *goal defense* may move over the center and her own goal third. The *wing defense* plays in the center third and her own goal third, excluding the goal circle. The *goalkeeper* plays in her own goal third only. If a player exits the area where she is allowed to play, an offside is declared, leading to a free throw being awarded to the opposite team. There is no offside if 2 players of opposing teams are offside simultaneously – e.g. when competing for the ball.

A toss of a coin decides which side begins the match. A player of the beginning team stands in the center circle, and passes the ball to another player of her team at the umpire's whistle (formerly, the match was started by the umpire throwing the ball in the air or bouncing it off the ground, after which 2 players of opposing teams tried to take possession of the ball). The ball may be passed by throwing only; any form of dribbling or running with the ball is prohibited. A player may only run towards the ball; after she intercepts it, she must pass it or shoot for goal. She has 3sec. to throw the ball (formerly, 5sec.), and is allowed to turn around with the ball. Players are also allowed to receive and pass the ball when jumping up or touching the ground with one foot only. There must be at least 2 passes before a shot for goal. Only 2 out of the 3 attack players are entitled to shoot at goal – the goal shooter and goal attack. They may shoot for goal as many times as they like, as long as the opponents allow it. Defense players may defend the goal but they may not touch the ball when it is in the air, or, in particular, change the direction of its flight – this leads to a point being scored by the opposing team. Players are not allowed to snatch the ball from the opponent's hands. Tackles are prohibited, and so is obstructing the play of an opponent (excluding natural movements necessary to keep one's balance). Breaking these rules leads to a so-called *penalty pass* being awarded to the non-offending team. If this happens in the goal circle, the attacking players may choose between a penalty pass and a penalty shot for goal, depending on the tactical situation. When such a pass or shot is performed, the offender must stand out of play alongside the thrower until the ball is released. When the ball lands outside of the court, a player of the opposite team throws it in within 3sec. of the umpire calling, 'Play!' There are 2 umpires (usu. women) who control the game simultaneously, each responsible for a half of the court (from the goal line up to the center circle). The umpires may not rule on what happens in the other half of the court, nor question the decisions of the other umpire. The

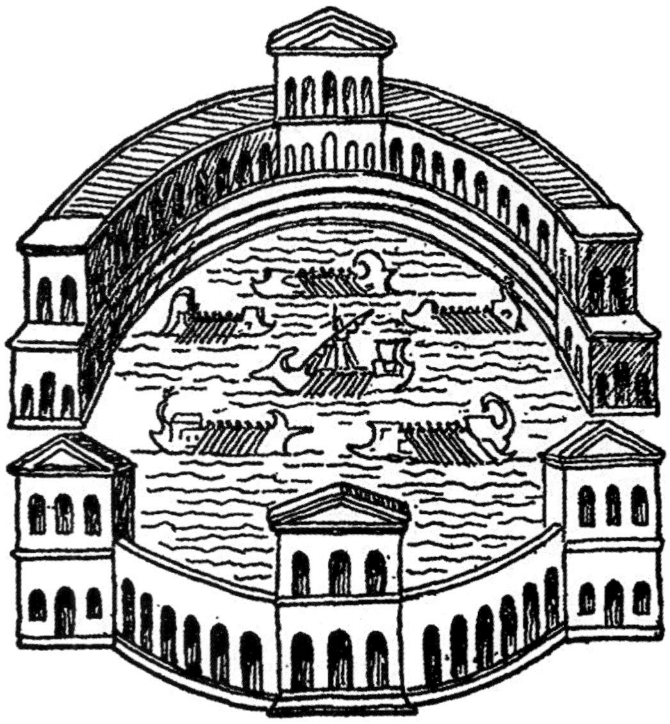

Naumachia, an image from a Roman medal.

N

WORLD SPORTS ENCYCLOPEDIA

umpires' decisions are final. A so-called 'advantage rule' prevents umpires from passing decisions (even if they are justified) that would make worse the tactical position of the non-offending team. Usually, no substitutions are made during a match unless a player is injured. There is no extra time at the end of match, either, unless a penalty shot has been ordered just before the end of the game.

Before these rules were settled, they evolved quickly with considerable changes being introduced

Kathryn Harby of the Adelaide Thunderbirds attempts to keep the ball from her Melbourne Kestrels opponent at the Waverley Netball Centre, Waverley, Australia.

in the process. During the first 2 years of netball, ordinary litter bins were used instead of the rings, and the umpires had to actually climb a ladder to tip the ball out after each basket! The starting throw was soon replaced by a bounce, after which the players competed for the ball. Then, the center line was introduced, to be later dropped again, and replaced by a larger center circle, from which the game was started by a pass, like today. In 1960, the center circle was enlarged to the current dimensions. The time allowed for a pass or shot was cut down from 5 to 3sec., which has made the game more dynamic. Initially, players were not allowed to change their positions after catching the ball but this was liberalized and today they may turn around and lift one foot off the ground. Also, the rule allowing all 3 of the attack players to shoot for goal has been changed.

History. Even though some historians derive the tradition of netball from the ancient games of >TRIGON, > FAININDA and >HARPASTON, the modern rules were established in 1895, after a visit by an American, Dr Toles (first name not recorded), to Madame Osternberg College in Hampstead, London, England. Toles tried to teach the students an indoor version of Amer. >BASKETBALL. The casual rules he presented had not yet even been established in basketball itself, and the imprecise imitation of the game after he left led to the development of netball in England. With time, it became a separate, independent sport.

In 1897, the Hampstead College was moved to Dartford and changed its name to the Physical Training College. An anonymous pioneer of women's American basketball visited the college (at the time, the

women's version of basketball developed side by side with the men's version established by J. Naismith). She advised replacing the ordinary baskets (with bottoms) with metal rings, and dividing the court into the 3 parts known today. Some rules borrowed from Amer. basketball were added. In 1901, the Brit. Ling Association (today, Physical Education Association of Great Britain and Northern Ireland) published 250 copies of the rules under the title *The Game of Netball and How to Play It*. The rules included some further changes borrowed from Amer. basketball, leading to considerable confusion (they seemed too liberal). Among other things, the number of players was to be 5, 7 or 9, which was actually recognizing the extant state of affairs (the game had developed independently throughout the various countries of the Brit. Empire). Various court dimensions were allowed, depending on the number of players (e.g. length of court 100ft. for 5 or 7 players, or 150ft. for 9 players, with the width 75ft. for all the versions). Only later were the court dimensions decreased to what they are today. The number of points scored for a goal was diversified; up to that time, each goal scored 1pt., while according to the new rules a shot from the attack third or a free shot scored 1pt., while a shot from the center third scored 2pts. The circumference of the ball was decreased from 31in. to what it is today, while the goal posts were made higher. At the same time, the original name of 'basketball' was replaced by 'netball' (from the net hanging down from the ring). However, confusion persisted until 1970. Up to that time, the Austrl. and N.Zeal. associations were named All-Australia Women's Basketball Association and New Zealand Basketball Association, vacillating between the Amer. and Eng. rules. In the meantime, the rules of netball crystallized and started to feed back onto the US and Canada where the Eng. version of the game began to be popularized, even though finally this did not prove successful due to the competition form the local, more dynamic sports. The situation in the countries of the Brit. Empire was different, esp. in Australia and N.Zealand, where netball became the leading women's sport.

Before 1920, netball was also taken up in France and Sweden, and attempts at introducing it in Denmark resulted in the development of a local version, known as >KURVBOLD. Netball was mainly played in girls' schools whose graduates began establishing netball clubs which in turn took the sport out of the confines of schools. The first Eng. association was estab. in 1923 under the name of the London and Home Counties Netball Association. As more and more independent netball associations started springing up (in schools, within the Young Women's Christian Association, and in clubs of other sports), a national convention was called, and the All-England Women's Netball Association was established in 1925. After 1926, netball began to develop rapidly, mainly through the establishment of local branches of the new Association in various Eng. counties.

The first championships for Eng. county teams were organized in 1932. *Netball Magazine* started appearing in 1935, and the Association's quarterly, *Netball*, was launched in 1949. Towards the end of WWII, there were local branches in all counties. Things took a surprising turn in the small islands of Jersey and Guernsey (occupied by the Germans for some time), where netball had been slow to catch on before. During the Ger. occupation, the will to demonstrate autonomy showed up mainly in sport, and led to the establishment of strong netball centers, which the Germans allowed to exist to keep peace. The first

international competition was held during 1947's Youth and Students' Festival in Prague, Czechoslovakia, and proved a huge success. There have been official test matches between the Eng., Wel., and Scot. national teams since 1949. In 1951, netball was first included in the program of the Festival of Britain. Close contacts between the UK and the other countries where netball is played date back to the first tour of England by the Austrl. national team (when Eng. rules were used), and to the match between England and S Africa (1956).

The growth of netball in schools was accelerated in the 1970s with the establishing of the Eng. Schools Netball Association. During that decade, the number of clubs in England alone soared to 900, with individual members as well as about 2,000 member school teams. The number of open clubs passed the 1,000 mark in the mid-1970s. In 1984, there were 33,000 netball players in England, while Scotland had 50 adult clubs and 6,000 players in schools. Netball proved even more popular in Australia and N.Zealand, even though they preserved some of the original rules that had been dropped elsewhere. The keys to the explosive growth of netball were the skillful 'exportation' from schools and being able to meet the needs of local communities.

In 1957, the first steps were taken to establish some netball organization at an international level. Under the auspices of the All-England Netball Association, an international tournament was held in London, with teams from England, Australia, N.Zealand, S Africa, N Ireland, USA, and Wales. This led to the organization of a conference in Colombo (1960), where an international association was set up. Its name – the International Federation of Women's Basketball and Netball Associations – reflected the terminological distinctness of Australia and N.Zealand, where the game had been called 'women's basketball'. After Australia and N.Zealand adopted the rules and names used in other countries, the federation changed the name to the International Federation of Netball Associations in 1970. In 1973, there were 23 member countries in the organization, while in 1993, there were 36.

The first W.Ch. were held in 1963, with 12 national teams participating. Since then, W.Ch. have been held every 4 years, in the pre-Olympic year, and a year after the Commonwealth Games. There is also a World Youth Cup. Between 1963 and 1967, the council of the Federation, and its actions, were almost totally monopolized by Australia and N.Zealand, which left the remaining members somewhat disgruntled. In 1967, the rule was adopted to select 7 representatives from the national associations of member states.

Australia. Netball was introduced in Australia shortly after 1901, first under the name of 'women's basket ball', and later 'basketball'. Initially, the game was played in a number of schools. In 1913, Austrl. educational authorities introduced the game to all primary schools, and in 1915 – to secondary schools. Local branches of the Young Women's Christian Association played an important role in popularizing the game. The first open club, Melbourne Girls' Basket Ball Association, was estab. just before WWI. The first inter-state match was played in 1926. The All-Australia Women's Basket Ball Association (AAWBBA) was set up in 1927. It was only in the 1970s that the Austrl. federation adopted the international terminology and the modified rules used in other countries. (N.Zealand stuck with the old name 'women's basketball'). Before that, Aus-

A netball ritual: Liz Ellis of the Swifts claims the net after victory over the Adelaide Thunderbirds during the Commonwealth Bank Trophy Netball Grand Final at the State Sports Centre, Homebush Bay, Sydney.

tralians had used e.g. different court dimensions (90x45ft.). The top netball states were Victoria, Queensland and W Australia, and then New South Wales and S Australia. Tasmania entered national competitions in 1933. The main tournament was the Interstate Carnival, first organized in 1927, and abolished in 1939 due to a polio epidemic. Austrl. interstate championships have been organized since 1928 (suspended 1939-45). The Proud Challenge Cup was organized between 1927 and 1938. The Elix Shield, founded by Madame M. Shield, became the most prestigious event in 1939. After WWII, Australia and N.Zealand played international matches for 7- and 9-player teams. A UK tour by the Austrl. national team, when the matches were played according to international rules, brought the Austrl. version closer to the world standard. The particular Austrl. developments had some influence on the first stage of work of the International Federation of Women's Basket Ball and Netball Federations (1960). The rules were standardized in the 1970s, which led to a change in the name of the international federation to the International Federation of Netball Associations, and that of the Austrl. one to the All-Australia Netball Association. This is how the authors of the *Oxford Companion to Australian Sport* (1994) explain the reasons for the popularity of the game in Australia:

Since its early beginnings [...], netball has become the largest participation sport for girls and women in Australia. Netball is popular because it is simple to play; it can be played on any even surface (grass, bitumen, concrete, or wood) and at any age or skill level; it has a low fee structure and is organised by women for girls and women.

In 1984, netball was played by 317,000 Austrl. girls and women. The number rose to about 400,000 in the '90s. It is estimated that about a half of the Austrl. female population aged 8-40 play netball today. The most famous players include G. Benzie (b.1914), E. Gill (1918-90), A. Sargeant (b.1957) and W. Shakespear (b.1943).

New Zealand. According to some historians, the first community in N.Zealand to play netball was the Otago Girls' High School (c.1902) but the game did not spread from there to other centers. More important was the introduction of the game in Auckland by Reverend J.C. Jamieson, secretary of the Presbyterian Bible Class Union of N.Zealand in 1906. From bible classes, the game spread to other N.Zealand schools, and became one of the most popular girls' school sports. A strong team was formed at the Wellington Technical College in 1914. Just like in the other countries, the YWCA played an instrumental role in popularizing the game. In 1915, the organization expressed the need for the development of netball by explaining that it 'provides girls with healthy open air bodily exercise and promotes interpersonal relations'. In the face of the resistance towards the emancipation of women in sport, netball was a compromise solution, as it was not played by men, and as such was not contested by them. In 1916, W. Lloyd Philips organized N.Zealand's first secondary school team league in Dunedin. In 1929, the *Wangani Herald* described the sport as the 'national women's sport'. As a central organization was lacking, differences between schools persisted for a long time: some played 7-player teams, others – 9-player teams. In 1914, Otago in the South Island used a 7-player system, while the Canterbury Bight area – a 9-player system. In the '20s, the 9-a-side system began to prevail, in contrast to the tendencies observed in other countries, including Australia and the UK. The N.Zealand Basketball Association was estab. in 1924, 'basketball' standing, of course, for netball. In 1938, N.Zealand played the first international match against Australia during the All-Australia Festival. The match was played according to Austrl. rules that preferred 7-a-side teams. The '30s were a period during which women attained administrative positions in the association, prior to which it had mainly been men who controlled this women's sport. The fight led to a full success in the '40s, when most important administrative functions were taken over by women, even though there has always been a small percentage of male officials. After the international federation was estab., the Austrl. and N.Zealand idiosyncrasies concerning the rules were standardized.
The dynamic growth of netball in N.Zealand is best reflected by numbers, even though systematic sta-

tistic data is lacking. In 1924, there were 124 teams in N.Zealand, mostly in schools, churches and open clubs, with the total number of players not exceeding 5,000. WWII hampered the game's further development, but the losses were compensated for in the first few years after the war. In 1951, 35 N.Zealand provinces played netball and the total number of teams reached 2,180. In 1967, the number of teams participating in competitions of various kinds reached 4,232, and in 1992 – 10,928. In 1984, there were about 120,000 players, and in 1988 – 156,600, equivalent to 10% of the total female population of N.Zealand (the percentage was obviously higher in lower age groups). Official data included in the *Life in New Zealand Survey* confirm that 26% of N.Zealand girls aged 15-18 played netball in 1991. Listed together with male sports, netball was the third most popular leisure sport (after aerobic-dance disciplines counted together and joint water sports such as swimming, water polo, surfing etc.). N.Zealand's top players were J. Harnett in the '60s and J. Townsend in the '80s.
Netball has played an important role in integrating the whites and native Maoris in N.Zealand. This process, however, started fairly late. Up to the late '40s, the need for integrating white and Maori players was neglected, even though Maori players had participated in netball games since the '20s, and a Maori, M. Matangi of Auckland, was the captain of the team that played against Australia in 1938. However, these isolated examples did not solve the problem; moreover, there were no Maoris in the national association's authorities. There was a tendency towards segregation and establishing separate associations for the indigenous inhabitants of N.Zealand. In 1950, the problem of including Maoris during the national association was discussed during a special meeting. The Akarana Maori Sports and Athletic Association sent a special delegation to the meeting. Since then, despite some inhibitions, there have been an increasing number of Maoris participating as players, and since the '80s – as officials, too. In 1955, the N.Zealand national team toured Fiji, popularizing the sport among the local population.
Netball has been growing in other Commonwealth countries but it has not been as successful as in the UK, Australia or N.Zealand. In many countries, the role of netball is not reflected in the official statistics, even though their teams are successful during W.Ch. and other international tournaments. IFNA data suggest that there were 7,650 players in Jamaica in 1983. The numbers vary between several hundred and several thousand in other Commonwealth countries. The Singapore Cup and Inter-Club Tournament are quite popular in Singapore. See also >KIWI NETBALL, >NETTA NETBALL.
J. Arlott, 'Netball', OCSG, 1975; Scott A.G., M. Crawford, 'Netball', EWS, 1996, II; I. Jobling and P. Browne, 'Netball', OCAS 1940; J. Nauright and J. Broomhall, 'A Woman's Game. The Development of Netball and a Female Sporting Culture in New Zealand 1906-70', IJHS Dec. 1994; W. Shakespear, *Netball*, 1977; anon. 'Netball – Keeping the Ball in Play', SS, March 1991.

NETIVATUPPAYATU, an ancient Ind. martial art using short sticks. It is one of the 5 basic Ind. fighting techniques collectively known as >ADI MURAI.

NETTA NETBALL, a var. of >NETBALL, developed in Australia under the auspices of the Aussie Sports Programme for kindergartens and lower primary school classes. Netta netball uses smaller courts and lighter balls than netball; also, some rules are simplified.

NEW SQUAT, a neighborhood or schoolyard game in which players form a circle, and put an empty can in the middle. One of the players is the 'guard' of the can, while the others stand outside of the circle. One then enters the circle suddenly and kicks the can outside of the circle, then the remaining players join in, and finally one of them snatches the can and tries to hide it from the guard's view. The guard then tries to find out who snatched the can, and takes one player whom he thinks to be the culprit to the circle as a 'prisoner'. If he is wrong, the actual snatcher runs inside the circle and ostentatiously kicks the can out again. If this occurs after prisoners have been taken, one of the prisoners is freed. The task of the guard is to find and catch all the players with the can. The last one takes over the role of the guard.
TGESI, I, 412-413.

NEW-YORK-BALL, also *New-York game*, one of a group of bat and ball games played in the Brit. colonies in America in the 17th-18th cent. It split from the Eng. >CRICKET, and during the 18th cent. contributed to the development of >BASEBALL, along with other similar games such as >BASTE-BALL, >GOALBALL, >ONE-OLD-CAT, >ROUND BALL, >ROUNDERS, >TOWN-BALL, and >TWO-OLD-CAT.

NIBE STRÅ, in full *at nibe strå*, Dan. for 'nibble the straw'. The players sit in a circle, embracing one another, and at the same time hold onto a piece of rope wrapped around them. The object is to pass a piece of straw from one mouth to another. The thing is made difficult by the players' swaying back and

A Tri Nations Series netball game between Australia and New Zealand played at the State Netball Centre, Melbourne, Australia.

forth and pulling on the rope, so that the moment of the passing of the straw may coincide with a pull on the rope by the swaying partners. A round is completed when the straw makes a full circle.
J. Møller, 'At nibe strå', GID, 1997, 3, 60.

NIGBÉ, an Afr. folk game played in Côte d'Ivoire. Four small objects are needed, usu. cowry shells, but also nuts, large seeds or fruit pits can be used. Objects other than shells are painted on one side so that sides differ noticeably from each other. The min. number of players is 2, but usually 3-4 players participate. The players toss the pieces in front of them and score points depending on how many of the shells land up or down. If all the pieces land with the agreed side down, the player is awarded 10pts. 5pts. are awarded for all the pieces facing up. The player scores no points for 3 pieces landing down and one up, or 3 up and 1 down. 2pts. are awarded if 2 pieces land up and the other 2 land down. A

N

WORLD SPORTS ENCYCLOPEDIA

similar game using cowry shells, known as >IGBA-ITA, is played in Nigeria, while another one in Liberia is called *gbang*.

NIKHII KHARVAKH, Mong. for 'shooting a sheep skin'. A sport of shooting a sheep skin extended on the ground, while galloping on horseback. The shot must be completed without the horse passing a line, before which the rider must turn the horse back. If the horse does pass the line, the rider loses his turn. The winner is the rider who shoots the center part of the skin marked with a circle.

A ninja fighter.

NIN JUTSU, also *nin jitsu*, the art of becoming invisible [Jap. *nin* – invisibility + *jutsu* – skill, art], a Jap. martial art. From the 2nd half of the 13th cent. to the middle of the 17th cent. in the Jap. provinces of Iga (Mie) and Koga (Shiga) there were clans which taught special skills referred to as nin jutsu to warriors who belonged to the class of Bushi, i.e. the samurai. From the early childhood these specialized agents (the Ninja) were trained in all major Jap. schools of martial arts, including *ken jutsu* (sword fighting), *kyu jutsu* (archery), *yari jutsu* (spear fighting), *naginata jutsu* (halberd fighting), *shuriken jutsu* (blade throwing), *kusarigama* (sickle and chain fighting), *baji jutsu* (horse riding), *tai jutsu* (hand-to-hand combat with elements of ac-

Ninja swords.

robatics), as well as in *henso jutsu* (the art of concealment), *shinobi iri* (the skill of remaining invisible and moving quietly), *sui ren* (the skill of swimming quietly), *seshin teki kyoko* (spiritual cleansing). The Ninja fighters were advisors, commanders, spies, and assassins used to settle various conflicts. Their unique strategies and tactics and a very high level of training often gave them advantage over a predominant enemy force. The ninja were divided into 3 categories: *jonin* – commanders, *chunin* – officers, and *genin* – agents. Nin jutsu was also practiced by women called *kunoichi*.

NINE HOLES, an old game, dating back at least to the 16th cent. Nine holes were dug in the ground, at non-defined distances from one another. (Another var. of the game, known as >TRUNKS in Northamptonshire, used a board with 9 goals cut in it instead of the holes.) Players were supposed to hit the holes with a ball. A.B. Gomme writes that the game, also known as *crates*, was 'played by ladies at Buxton for their amusement in wet weather' (TGESI, I, 413). J. Johns depicted the game in his work *The Benefit of the Ancient Bathes of Buckstones* (1572).

NIZA BAZI, an old Afghan form of horseback exercise in which players used spears to pull out a peg embedded in the ground [*niza* – spear + *bazi* – game, competition]. The sport derived from Afghan military exercises, and its original objective was to develop the ability to quickly pull out tent pegs during horseback attacks on enemy camps, causing the tents to collapse and trap the enemies. The game was accompanied by loud drum and pipe music, which intensified as a rider approached the peg (which is similar to some indoor track and field games where the rhythmic music is synchronised with the actions of the contestants).

NÔL TTWIGI, a Kor. folk type of standing seesaw, combined with jumps, played by girls and women. The seesaw itself resembles some Eur. seesaws, such as the Ang.-Sax. teeter-totter, and the Maori *tiemi* (>SWINGS AND SEE-SAWS). A relatively long (about 3m) and thick board is supported on a round tree trunk or a thick sheaf of rice straws. One person stands on each end of the board. Each participant tries to toss the other up by jumping on her own end of the board, using it as a kind of springboard, and landing back on it without losing her balance. The competitor who succeeds in jumping higher than the partner is declared the winner. Experienced players may achieve heights of up to 20m.

NONG-AKNORI, a Kor. type of mock battle fought during some festivals. The fighting was usu. accompanied by music and dancing performed by groups of people standing single file.
Koo-Chul Jung, *Erziehung und Sport in Korea im Kreuzpunkt fremden Kulturen und Mächte*, 1996, 62.
NON-STOP DANCE, see >DANCE MARATHON.

NOR AND SPELL, see >NORTHERN SPELL.

NORDIC SKIING, also *Nordic combination*, a family of skiing events that includes ski jumping and cross-country skiing; see >SKI RUNNING COMPETITIONS and >SKI JUMPING. The name dates back to the period of discussion about seniority in the shaping and development of skiing between Alpine countries (which preferred downhill racing and slaloms; see >ALPINE SKIING) and Scand. countries (which favored Nordic skiing). The most difficult Nordic event is the Nordic combined event (for men

Ski jumping for the Nordic combined event.

only), consisting of a 15-km cross-country race and a 90-m ski jumping competition held on two consecutive days. There is also a team Nordic combined event, where the run is replaced by a 3x10km relay in which all 3 members of each team participate.

NORFOLK STYLE, a wrestling style similar to >CORNWALL AND DEVON. The only difference was that the object was to force the opponent to touch the ground with 2 parts of his body rather than 3. The style is often considered identical with 'Cotswold wrestling'.

Alexei Fadeev of Russia in action during the Men's Nordic Combined Event in the Skiing World Championships in Ramsau, Austria.

W. Baxter, 'Norfolk Style (Cotswold Wrestling)', *Les luttes traditionnelles a traverse le monde*, *LJP*, 1998, 82.

NORIYUMI, an old Jap. form of archery practiced as a form of court ceremonial. Cf. >JYARAI, >IBA-HAJIME, >TANGONO KISHA; see also types of Jap. horseback archery: >KADAGAKE, >INUOMONO, >YABUSAME; and types of foot archery such as >BUSHA, >JUMIHAJIME, >KUSAJISI, >MARUMONO and >MOMOTE.

NORTH AMERICAN INDIAN RACES, a catch-all term for a number of various, local var. of running as practiced by some N.Amer. Ind. tribes living in the Great Plains extending from the lowlands of Canada south to the Big Bend of the Rio Grande. Some events or sports, such as >BALL RACING or >INDIAN COURIER RACES, must have been influenced or shaped by the most advanced tribes of C (mainly the Aztecs) and S America (the Incas). Some were purely indigenous. The best-known N.Amer. Indian races include:
APACHE RACES, practiced by the Apache living over a territory extending from west Arizona and central Texas to west Kansas. The Apache must have borrowed this sport from other tribes living in the same area. The Apache themselves came to the area several centuries before the white colonists, most probably around the 10th century. Before that they lived in what is now Canada together with other Athabascan tribes who, according to what we know now, did not practice the sport of running. Apachee races are held over short running tracks of up to 200m, contrary to the Pimas. The Apache, similar to the Navaho, were often lured by the prizes offered by Eur. settlers.
ARAPAHO RACES, a trad. contest of the Arapaho living in the Great Plains. The oldest mentions of the sport come from the American pioneers who stressed the fact that young Arapaho practiced running regularly in the mornings.
CROW RACES, a running competition popular among the Crow of the Sioux family living E of the Rocky Mountains in the area that is now divided into the states of Wyoming and Montana. The races were organized for young warriors who had to take an endurance test and for adult athletes representing 'warrior clubs' competing with one another. The races were held over a 5-km course whose shape resembled a horseshoe.
HOPI RACES, local folk races held, most frequently, over a distance of some 3mi. (less than 5km). In the 1920s an Amer. scholar W. Myers reportedly met a Hopi runner who was able to cover a distance of 120mi. (approx. 193km) within 15hrs.
MANDAN RACES, popular among the Mandan of the Sioux family living in what is now North Dakota. It was held chiefly among young soon-to-be warriors who had to pass a running test but also among adults who wanted to practice before hunts or battles. The Mandan prepared a special running track, similarly to the Osage (see below). An Amer. expert on N.Amer. running sports, P. Nabokov, quotes an old ethnographic report of 1892 describing Mandan running tracks as 'level prairie ... cleared of every obstruction and kept in condition for racing purposes only'.
NAVAHO RACES, the Navaho are the biggest family of N.Amer. Ind. tribes living in the N-W New Mexico, S-W Utah and N-E Arizona. The Navaho were famous for their division into numerous families who guarded closely their 'clan' identity and the very well-developed systems of 'natural' education where a young Navaho had to confirm that he could be called a member of a given family and that he would not disgrace it. Races were one of the forms of testing young warriors' hunting and military skills. The Navaho, along with the Apache, were known to compete for prizes offered by Eur. settlers. In 1868 a running competition was held among Navaho and Apache runners at Fort Summer in New Mexico. The competition was organized by the US Army and races were held over distances ranging from 100yds. to ½mi. One of the spectators – Major J.C. Cremony – reported that the runners practiced for the whole week preceding the competition.
OSAGE or WASKAZHE RACES, popular among the Osage of the Sioux family who used to live in what is now Missouri and N Arkansas (and have been moved to reservations in N-E Oklahoma). The object of the races was to keep adult warriors fit. They were held over a distance of some 2½mi. (about 4km). Similarly to the Mandan, the Osage 'constructed' a special running track cleared of any obstruction.
PIMA RACES, held by the Pima tribe, and esp. popular among the Sobaipuris Pima, living in the area now divided into the states of Arizona and New Mexico over specially prepared running tracks that were several hundred meters long and 6m wide. Such tracks were discovered near Sacaton Flats and Casa Blanca.
TARAHUMARA RACES, the Tarahumara inhabited and continue to live in what is now north Mexico and the Amer. SW. The races were held over distances of up to several hundred kilometers. The Tarahumara belonged to a family of tribes that had developed a special class of 'professional' runners referred to as *chasqui*. According to linguists who researched the Tarahumara language the term *tarahumara* means 'footrunners'. The footrunners formed a kind of a fraternity whose main role was to carry important messages and small objects (e.g. goods; cf. >INDIAN COURIER RACES). The Tarahumara considered running a sacred activity. According to their beliefs one was not able to win a race thanks only to superior physical ability, one always needed help from the gods. That is why the help of the medicine man was needed in preparing the runner for the race. The shaman assisted the racer by preparing special herb medications to increase his endurance and guarded him against sorcery. W. Myers reported that still at the beginning of the 20th cent. there were Tarahumara runners who, unaided, covered the distance from Batopilas to Chihuahua, Mexico and back, a roundtrip of some 1,000mi. (almost 1,610km) within a week. In 1979, B. Fontana organized a Tarahumara race among girls. The contest was held between 2 pairs of girls wielding trad. staves (in the past they used to signify a given runner's function). The object of the experiment was to test Tarahumara endurance and to make a number of photographs for research purposes.
ZUNI RACES, a trad. form of folk competition popular among the N.Amer. Ind. tribe of Súnyitsi living in present-day New Mexico, esp. in the Valencia reservation and in McKinley County. It appears that the Súnyitsi Zuni are the descendants of the great Indian tribes inhabiting this area in pre-Columbian times. M.C. Stevenson, an Amer. scholar investigating the Zuni culture, observed in 1904 that she 'has never known the Zunis to lose a footrace with other Indians or with the champion runners of the troops at Fort Wingate, who sometimes enter into races with them'. According to Stevenson, Zuni runners practiced from early childhood on so that they were fit later to take part in hunts and battles. Before a race the Zuni covered their bodies with colorful patterns whose central element was the 'emblem' of a given tribe painted across the chest. This made it very similar to the national emblems worn by the modern athletes on their jerseys. Apart from long distance running, the Zuni often engaged in *ball racing*, popular also among other tribes. Ball racers were often accompanied by mounted spectators. In 1891 J.G. Owens, who observed such a race, reported in *Popular Science Monthly* that 'it is not unusual to see a pony drop over dead from exhaustion as they near the village'.
P. Nabokov, *Indian Running*, 1981; J.B. Oxendine, *American Indian Sports Heritage*, 1988; M.C. Stevenson, *The Zuni Indians*, Bureau of American Ethnology, Annual Report, 1904, 23.

NORTHERN SPELL, also *northern-spell* or *northen spell* in a dial. var. A trad. Eng. sport from a larger family of games whose common feature was that a hard ball or short peg was first released into the air by a special lever (trap), and then batted. The family includes many regional games differing in the methods of ball release, materials from which the ball is made, and certain other details. Sometimes the only difference is the name of the game, its pronunciation or spelling. So, the family includes games such as *buckstick*, *dab and stick*, *drab and norr*, *knurr and spell*, *knur and spel*, *knur*, *spel and kibble*, *nurr*, *nur and spell*, *nurspel*, *spell and nur*, *spell and knor*, *spell a'nor*, *spell and ore*, *trevit*, *trivit*, *trippit and coit*, and no doubt others, combining these words in various ways. Folk tradition mixed all the individual techniques, as well as names. One result was that the element *northern* (dialectal *northen*, later shortened to *north* or even *nor*) lost its initial meaning and pronunciation, which made it possible for the form *nor* (pronounced *nur* in some areas) to merge with the word *knurr* or *knor*, used in other var. of the game to refer to the ball. This is where new names for the object of the game originated, such as *nur/nurr* or *nor/norr*, many of them ambiguous. By semantic and phonetic analogy, the term for the ball, which was made of a metal ore, was also incorporated. Cf. also >TRAP, BAT AND BALL.
History and etymology. The tradition of the game dates back to the Middle Ages. The first word of the name, *northern* has been traditionally associated with the conquest of Great Britain by the Vikings, who were then called Norsemen or Northmen. The second word, *spell* or *spel*, was originally derived from the Germanic word meaning 'game' – cf. the modern words for game or play in Norw. (*spill*), Swed. (*spel*), Du. (*spel*), Dan. (*spil*) or Ger. (*Spiele*). However, this meaning of the word was lost during the development of English, perhaps owing to the fact that the word gradually started to be associated exclusively with the special device used to propel the ball used in the game.
Northern spell seems to be the oldest of the many var. of such games. From the second half of the 18th cent. onwards, knur and spell became the most dynamically developing version of the game. One reason may have been that it started to employ more advanced techniques of propelling the ball into the air, and used sophisticated technology to produce the bats and balls.
In the 16th-19th centuries, many var. of bat-and-ball games started to merge in various regions of England, especially in the North. The linguistic merger seemed to help this: the element that referred to the geographical origins of the game in the North became shortened to *nor* and grew more similar to *knurl knurr*, which is a Germanic word for a bat made of a knot in wood used to hit the ball in *knur and spell*. This process gave rise to the intermediate forms of *nur/nurr* in certain cases, which co-occur with *nor* in the names of several of the above mentioned var. of the game, especially in *nur and spell*, *nurspel*, *spel and nur*, *spel and knorr* and *spell a'nor*. J. Strutt gave an extensive description of the game in his *Sports and Pastimes of the People of England*, 1810:

Northen-spell is played with a trap, and the ball is stricken with a bat or bludgeon at the pleasure of the players [...]. The performance of this pastime does not require the attendance of either of the parties in the field to catch or stop the ball, for the contest between them is simply who shall strike it to the greatest distance in a given number of strokes; the length of each stroke is measured before the ball is returned, by the means of a cord made fast at one end near the trap, the other being stretched into the field by a person stationed there for that purpose, who adjusts it to the ball wherever it may lie; the cord is divided into yards, which are properly numbered upon it in succession, so that the person at the bottom of the ground can easily ascertain the distance of each stroke by the number of the yards which he calls to the players, who place it to their account, and the ball is thrown back. This pastime possesses but little variety, and is by no means so amusing to the bystanders as cricket or trap-ball.

[100-101].

NOT, a simple game where a wooden ball is batted with curved sticks. The name derives from the word 'knot' (in wood) which was used to refer to the ball. A.B. Gomme provides some explanation:

The game is called 'not' from the ball being made of a knotty piece of wood.

Two teams take positions at the opposing ends of the field. The players alternately shoot the ball at their opponents. If the ball crosses a designated fragment of the end line, the shooters score a point. Cf. >HAWKEY, >SHINNY, >SHINTY.

NOWOLOTKO, a local var. of >GAIK MAJOWY, practiced in the village of Bukówiec Górny (Wielkopolska, Poland) and in the surrounding areas.

NUMMER STANTO, a var. of the Dan. game whose basic type is known as >BOLD I HUL.

NUR AND SPELL, also *nur and spel*, see >NORTHERN SPELL.

NURSPELL, also *nurspel*, a local Lincolnshire var. of *knur and spell*. Players would bat a raised, straight lever resembling a small swing, called the 'spell', and thus propel a wooden ball placed on the other end of the lever into the air. When the ball was in the air, the player would bat it out using a 'kibble'.

NORDIC COMBINED SKIING OLYMPIC CHAMPIONS

90-K JUMP AND 15-K CROSS-COUNTRY
1924 Thorleif Haug, NOR
1928 Johan Gröttumsbraten, NOR
1932 Johan Gröttumsbraten, NOR
1936 Oddbjorn Hagen, NOR
1948 Heikki Hasu, FIN
1952 Simon Slattvik, NOR
1956 Sverre Stenersen, NOR
1960 Georg Thoma, GER
1964 Tormod Knutsen, NOR
1968 Franz Keller, FRG
1972 Ulrich Wehling, GDR
1976 Ulrich Wehling, GDR
1980 Ulrich Wehling, GDR
1984 Tom Sandberg, NOR
1988 Hippolyt Kempf, SUI
1992 Fabrice Guy, FRA
1994 Fred Borre Lundberg, NOR
1998 Bjarte Engen Vik, NOR
2002 Samppa Lajunen, FIN
TEAM
1988 F.R. Germany
1992 Japan
1994 Japan
1998 Norway
2002 Finland
COMBINED SPRINT
2002 Samppa Lajunen, FIN

NORDIC COMBINED SKIING WORLD CHAMPIONS

90-K JUMP AND 15-K CROSS-COUNTRY
1925 Ottokar Nemecky, CZE
1926 Johan Grottumsbraten, NOR
1927 Rudolf Purkert, CZE
1929 Hans Vinjarengen, NOR
1930 Hans Vinjarengen, NOR
1931 Johan Grottumsbraten, NOR
1933 Sven Selanger (Eriksson), SWE
1934 Oddbjorn Hagen, NOR
1935 Oddbjorn Hagen, NOR
1937 Sigurd Roen, NOR
1938 Olaf Hoffsbakken, NOR
1939 Gustl Berauer, GER
1941 Gustl Berauer, GER
1950 Heikki Hasu, FIN
1954 Sverre Stenersen, NOR
1958 Paavo Korhonen, FIN
1962 Arne Larsen, NOR
1966 Georg Thoma, GER
1970 Ladislav Rygl, TCH
1974 Ulrich Wehling, DDR
1978 Konrad Winkler, DDR
1982 Tom Sandberg, NOR
1985 Herman Weinbuch, GER
1987 Torbjorn Lokken, NOR
1989 Trond Einar Elden, NOR
1991 Fred Borre Lundberg, NOR
1993 Kenji Ogiwara, JAP
1995 Fred Borre Lundberg, NOR
1997 Kenji Ogiwara, JAP
1999 Bjarte Engen Vik, NOR
2001 Bjarte Engen Vik, NOR
2003 Ronny Ackermann, GER
TEAM
1982 German Democratic Republic
1984 Norway
1985 Germany
1987 Germany
1989 Norway Democratic Republic
1991 Austria
1993 Japan
1995 Japan
1997 Norway
1999 Finland
2001 Norway
2003 Austria
COMBINED SPRINT
1999 Bjarte Engen Vik, NOR
2001 Marco Baacke, GER
2003 Johnny Spillane, USA

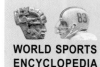

OA, full name *jogo do oa*, a Port. ball game, usu. played by girls. Generally, 2 players participate, each with her own ball. They stand up against a wall, and declare what things they will be doing before throwing the ball. The opponent is supposed to provoke the thrower to break one of the following rules: 1) no moving (*sem mexer*) – the player is forbidden to move out of her place when throwing and catching the ball; 2) no speaking (*sem falar*) – the throw and reception must be performed in silence; 3) no laughing (*sem rir*); 4) stand on one foot (*sem um pé*); 5) stand on the other foot (*com o outro*); 6) throw and catch with the same hand (*com uma mão*); 7) throw and catch with the other hand (*com a outra*); 8) throw and clap hands before the ball is caught (*bate palmas*); 9) wring hands after throwing (*novela*); 10) cross arms on one's chest between the throw and catch (*cruzar*); 11) pat oneself on the thighs between the throw and catch (*cair*). The game goes on until the players reach an agreed number of points. One point is scored for each successful throw and catch. The player who scores the most points is the winner.
M. da Graça Sousa Guedes, 'Jogo do oa', JTP, 1979, 39-40.

Observation trial.

OBSERVATION TRIAL, a type of rally using a motor vehicle, usu. a motorcycle, along a course set in difficult terrain, or along an esp. prepared indoor track with obstacles. The task of a participant is to cover the course without stopping or touching the ground with his feet. The obstacles include stones, felled tree trunks, rock shelves etc. (or artificial obstacles indoors). A 'dab', or touching the ground once, incurs 1 penalty pt.; 'footing', or touching the ground 2 or 3 times incurs 2pts., while touching the ground more than 3 times, or stopping (a 'failure') incurs in 5 penalty pts. In some regional events, 2 individual dabs incur 2 penalty pts. An attempt completed without a single error is known as 'clean'. The starting line is usually also the finish line.
History. Observation trials have been organized in the UK since the early 20th cent., initially as 1-day trials. The courses varied but were usually about 25mi. long. In 1909, a 6-day event was started in Scotland. After WWII, observation trails became increasingly popular in other Eur. countries, esp. Belgium, France and Switzerland. In 1966, the FIM initiated the Henry Groutars Challenge, commemorating a Belgian motor sport official. In 1968, the event was promoted the E.Ch., and in 1975, to W.Ch.

OBUCH, see >CZEKAN THROWING.

OCEANIAN BALL GAMES, folk ball games practiced on the islands of Oceania, i.e. Micronesia, Melanesia (see >MELANESIAN BALL GAMES) and Polynesia. Sometimes Australia and N.Zealand are regarded as part of Oceania. The Oceanian ball games are extremely diverse. A frequent contest is a competition consisting of kicking the ball up as high as possible. The balls are made of various materials incl. marsupial fur and kangaroo scrotum. See >CATCH BALL, >KANGAROO BALL.

OBORONA, a school game recommended for PE classes in the former USSR, and popularized also in the other countries of the Eastern bloc.
A gymnastics club is placed in the middle of a circle, one step in diameter, drawn on the ground. The club defender stands outside the circle, with a ball in his hands (it may be a volley-, foot- or basketball). The remaining players, holding hands, surround the defender, at a distance of an outstretched arm from one another. Then they let go and lower their arms. One of the players receives the ball from the defender, and the players start passing the ball between them, trying to hit the club at a convenient moment. The defender tries to stop the club from being hit by returning the ball in any way he wishes (with the exception of kicking it). The player who succeeds in hitting and overturning the club takes over as the defender. It may so happen that the defender knocks the club over himself; he then gives his place up to the player who was in possession of the ball at that moment. Several clubs can also be placed in the circle, or a tripod with a ball in the fork.
I.N.Chkhannikov, 'Oborona', GIZ, 1953, 9.

OBORONA I NASTUPLYENYE, a Rus. school game using elements of ice hockey, played on a circular rink, 9m in diameter. A concentric circle is drawn in the middle, with a diameter of 3m. The area between the circle and the edge of the rink is divided radially into 8 equal segments. According to Chkhannikov's description, the course of the game is the following:

A club or a wooden block is placed in the smallest circle. Nine players with hockey sticks participate in the game. One of them – the defender – takes his position in the inner circle. The remaining players – the attackers – position themselves in the segments. Their task is to knock the club over using a hockey puck. The defender tries to prevent the club from being hit, and return the puck outside the fields occupied by the attackers. Attackers who allow the puck out of their fields receive one penalty point. If the club is hit by an attacker who has no penalty points, he takes over as the defender. If, in turn, it is knocked down by an attacker who has some penalty points, the defender sets the club back up and stays in his position, while one penalty point is subtracted from the attacker's score. If the defender carelessly knocks the club over himself, he is replaced by one of those attackers who have no penalty points. The attackers may pass the puck from one to another, but neither they nor the defender may exit their respective fields. For breaking this rule, attackers receive one penalty point, and the defender is replaced by another player.

The game is controlled by a referee responsible for counting the points.
I.N. Chkannikov, 'Oborona i nastuplyenye', GIZ, 1953.

OCEANIAN PEOPLES' HOCKEY, a group of games played on various Oceanian islands, sharing the idea of driving a wooden ball with a curved stick. There were no goals and the object of the game was to take possession of the ball and keep it for as long as possible. The game is most popular on the islands of the Torres Strait and in S-W Australia.

OCTOPUSH, see >UNDERWATER HOCKEY.

OGNAZHI-I-I-I, an Afr. folk game played in the Benue region of Nigeria, mainly by children aged 10 and under. Two rows of 4-6 children face each other at a distance of about 2 steps. Each child may break out of the row and run around the opposite row along an oval line, shouting out loudly, 'Ognazhi-i-i-i!' The children in the opposite row try to stop him, forcing the child to run along a broader arch. The most difficult thing is to run the gauntlet between the 2 rows on the way back to one's own row, overcoming the resistance of many pairs of hands. If a child succeeds in doing so, he scores 1pt. The child who scores the most points during a round (there is no time limit) is the winner.
A. Taylor Cheska, 'Ognazhiiii', TGDWAN, 1987, 51.

OHONISTUTS, one of the Native Amer. Indian names applied to a game similar to hockey, and also known as >GUGAHAWAT.

OIBANE, see >HAGOITA.

OINĂ, a Rum. equivalent of Pol. >PALANT [Rum. *oyun* – bat]. Rules are similar to Pol. palant and Ger. >SCHLAGBALL. Oină players are called *oinişti* (sing. *oinist*).

OKINAWA-TE, martial arts practiced in the Ryukyu Is. For centuries, Okinawa was a place strongly involved in trade with China and in 1372 the ruler of the island, Satto, converted it into a Chin. Feudal estate, as a result of which, in 1393, a group of Chin. artisans and artists settled down there. These immigrants may be responsible for the existence of different var. of Chin. >GONGFU on the island. After the kingdoms of Chuzan, Ho-Chuzan, and Nanzan united in 1470, the ruler of Okinawa prohibited his subject to carry let alone use any weapons. Jap. invaders who conquered Okinawa in 1600 later amended the prohibition. It is believed such a ban stimulated the development of all kinds of hand-to-hand fighting techniques. Several great Okinawa-te masters spent long years in China studying gongfu. Another name of Okinawa-te is >KARATE (Chin. *te* – hands). The translation of 'kara-te' as 'empty hands' was popularized in the 1920s by Gihin Funakoshi, provoked by the growing military tendencies and highlighting the distinctiveness of Jap. culture.

OLAHRAGA, a sport var. of >PENCAK SILAT. In Indonesia, olahraga is played during PE lessons.

OLD ENGLISH SKITTLES, the oldest form of >SKITTLES.

OLD RUSSIAN BOXING. In modern times the boxing tradition has existed in at least several Eur. countries. The oldest form of modern Eur. sport is a form of boxing practiced in E Slavic states, particularly in old Russia and the Pol.-Rus. border regions. Pol. medieval chronicler Jan Dugosz described a boxing fight in his *History of Poland* under the date of 997. The fight was between a knight of the Rus. prince Vladimir and a representative of the Połowcy or Pieczyngas tribe (Dugosz makes no distinction between them):

Having set out with his army to meet them, he caught them on the river Trubiesza and – since it was considered dangerous by both armies to engage in battle in such a place – from the Pieczyngas camp emerged a tall knight of great courage, challenging the Russians to select from among them a rival for himself and proposing that the one who lost the fight would have his country open for the enemy to plunder and ravage for three years. One of the Russians, who had stayed at home, was summoned and decided to stand and since his stature did not promise much, the Pieczynga scoffed at him in front of both armies. But when the fight started, the Russian soon knocked down the giant and the Pieczyngas army escaped in panic.

A similar victorious fight with a 'giant Tartar' was fought in 1306 by Borejko, ancestor of the family of the future hetman [commander-in-chief] J.K. Chodkiewicz, who defeated the Swedes at Kircholm (1605). This event was described two and a half centuries later by a poet Osostevicius Stryjkowski, who combined facts from the Slavic history with artificial style borrowed from the fight between Entellus and Dares in Virgil's *Eneid*. (>ANCIENT PUGILISM).

Fist-fighting on the Pol.-Rus. border and in Russia itself was also practiced by peasants. In his *Chronicle of European Sarmatia* (1611) Alexander Gwagnin says: 'This custom has been practiced all over Russia and Moscow every year on certain days. Young boys and certain married men would leave their towns and villages and go to the open fields in the summer or to the ice-bound lakes, ponds and rivers in the winter. (...) There, according to the ancient tradition, they use no other weapon but their fists and they beat their heads, faces, eyes, breasts, necks and other organs so heavily that some come back half-dead, while others are carried away...'

An old Rus. legend telling the story of a fist-fight between merchant Kalasznikow and one of Ivan the Terrible's henchmen was saved from oblivion by a Rus. poet Michail Lermontov, who used it as a basis for his well known poem 'On Tsar Ivan Vasilevich, a young thug and one merchant Kalasznikov'.

OLS DEES TATALTSAKH, Mong. for 'pulling on the rope', a type of game similar to >TUG-OF-WAR. Two teams of participants clutch onto a piece of rope and try to pull it in 2 opposite directions. However, the Mongolian game is more dynamic, performed in short spurts, with 'points' scored. To win, a team must pull the opponents to their side an agreed number of times, e.g. 3, 5, etc. In the event of a tie – and if the participants are exhausted – that team which pulled the other to their side more times in a row is declared the winner.

OLUNCHUN LEATHER SLEDGE GAME, a game popular among the children and youth in the Chin. province of Heilongjiang and the autonomous region of Nei Mongol (Inner Mongolia). Both territories abound in game and thus a tradition of using animal hides for various purposes is firmly established there. Hides are most frequently employed as a construction material when building wooden huts with leather roofs (called *ksjerenahu* or *xierenahu*). In addition, the Olunchun use animal bones to make toys for their children and finally use specially hardened hides to construct a kind of a sled. The hides are shaped in such a way that they look like a shallow bowl with a characteristic protruding bow resembling an animal's head. The game has 2 basic var. – the first involves a race held among a number of sledges, while in the second the sled that travels the longest distance wins.

Mu Fushan et al., 'Olunchun (Oroqen) Leather Sledge Game', TRAMCHIN, 48.

OLYMPIC GYMNASTICS, also *artistic gymnastics* (the latter leading to confusion with *rhythmic gymnastics*, which is also sometimes called so). As a separate sporting discipline it is characterized by competition in exercises on gymnastic equipment. In women's competition these are: the vaulting horse, asymmetric bars, beam and floor. Rhythmic gymnastics is also part of the Ol.G., constituting a historically distinct form of gymnastics and entering the Olympic programme only in 1984, whereas the remaining women's events were introduced earlier, starting with their first inclusion in the 1928 games. The men's competition consists of competitions in the floor exercise, pommel horse, rings, vaulting horse, parallel bars and horizontal bar. The equipment must comply to strict technical specifications concerning their size and construction. In addition there is an overall competition based on the total points scored on all pieces of equipment, both in team and individual events. It is a non-measurable sport, in which the result depends on the subjective evaluation of a jury. 10pts. is the max. score. The highest and lowest scores are discarded in calculating the average. The exercises performed are judged according to a special table in terms of artistic impression, degree of difficulty and execution. Elements such as technical difficulty, precision, amplitude of movement, individual stylistic features and the overall aesthetics of the movement most strongly influence the score.

During competition men wear white vests and long white pants. Women perform in leotards. Leather hand grips may be worn to protect against abrasions and magnesium chalk is used to improve grip.

History. Until the moment when it became recognized as a sport in its own right, the development of Olympic gymnastics has been identical to that of >GYMNASTICS proper, afterwards forming one of its varieties. The transformation of one of the off-shoots of the gymnastic movement into a sporting discipline took place with extreme difficulty, as international gymnastics organizations disassociated themselves with sport for a long time, and particularly with its associated stadium-based spectacles, as a threat to physical culture. In 1897, based on the Eur. Union of Gymnastic Societies (Vereinigung Europischer Turnverbnde, VET) founded earlier in 1881 arose the International Gymnastics Federation (Federation Internationale de Gymnastique, FIG). The first W.Ch. were held in Antwerp in 1903 taking place every 2 years until 1913. After WWI they were reconstituted only in 1922, taking place every 4 years between Olympics. The last games before WWII took place in 1938. They began again

in 1950 and took place every 4 years between Olympics untill 1978, and from 1979 every 2 years. Men's exercises entered the Ol.G. as early as 1896 (without the floor exercises and all-around competition). The men's individual all-around was first competed at an Olympics in 1900, with the first team competition in 1904. Women's competitions, at first only the team competition were included in the Olympic program in Amsterdam (1928). Individual women's competitions started in 1952 (Helsinki). Europeans dominated to start with. Before 1914 the teams of Switzerland, the USA, Sweden, Norway, Great Britain, Hungary, Finland, France, Belgium and, above all, Italy were important. Italy won the men's team gold in 1912, 1920, 1924 and 1932. Yugoslavia and Czechoslovakia also had some impact. The high standard of the Germans wasn't initially reflected in Olympic successes firstly due to the refusal of the Ger. Turnverein to take part in the first games, and later due to the exclusion of Germany from the Games following WWI (in 1920 and 1924). The most famous competitor before 1914 was the Italian A. Braglia Olympic champion in the all-around 1908 and 1912. After 1918 a line of outstanding individuals appeared: Italians G. Zampori and R. Neri, L. Tukelj of Yugoslavia, Swiss G. Miez, Hungarian I. Pelle, and German A. Schwarzman. Immediately after the war, at the 1948 Games, the French dominated, however the situation changed diametrically with the entry of the USSR to Olympic competition. The teams and individuals of this country dominated the gymnastic scene alternately with Japan in the years 1952-1988, in the face of strong competition from E Germany and the People's Republic of China. After 1992 the USSR's gymnastic legacy continued with the Commonwealth of Independent States (CIS) and later Russia and other countries emerging from the framework of the USSR, particularly Ukraine and Belarus, along with the maintenance of the strong positions held by Japan and China. With the change in the political map, as in many other areas of sports, an increase in the importance of certain Western countries could be observed, esp. the USA. This was largely the result of the emigration of leading competitors and trainers, particularly from the USSR and other leading communist countries like Bulgaria, Rumania and the People's Republic of China. During the W.Ch. of 1995 in Japan the new world order was unveiled, as Russia took 4th place in the team competition and for the first time ever took no medals. Greece emerged as a growing power, as the sport had recently undergone an important restructuring there. The most outstanding individuals in Olympic gymnastics, at various times, include the Russians: V. Chukarin (Olympic champion 1952 and 1956, world champion 1954), and N. Andrianov (Olympic champion 1972 and 1976 and world champ.1978), and the Japanese: Olympic champions Y. Endo (1964) and S. Kato (1968 and 1972). Among the best all-around gymnasts of the past few Ol.G. were: Rus. V. Scherbov (1992; also winner of 4 individual events), Chin. Li Xiaoshuang (1996), and Rus. A. Nemov (2000).

Among women the Dutch dominated prior to1939, winning the historic first team Olympic championships in 1928, and also the Italians, British, Hungarians, Germans and Czechoslovakians. Similarly to the men's event, a significant change took place with the entry into international competition of the USSR and E Germany. The Soviet team won all the Olympic gold medals in team competition from 1952-1980. In 1984, due to the boycott of the Los Angeles Olympics the USSR team did not compete and the team

WORLD SPORTS ENCYCLOPEDIA O

Olympic gymnastics – horizontal bar.

Olympic gymnastics – vaulting horse.

Olympic gymnastics – asymmetric bars.

A pommel horse routine demonstration in front of the Capitol Building in Washington, D.C.

Olympic gymnastics – the rings.

WORLD SPORTS ENCYCLOPEDIA

title went to Rumania. In 1988, the USSR competitors regained their supremacy. Following the collapse of the USSR the CIS continued its domination. Since the 1996 Ol.G. the various CIS countries compete individually. During the 1996 Ol.G. in Atlanta the Russian team took 2nd place, and for the first time ever the US team won the gold.

The most outstanding female individuals in Olympic gymnastics are: L. Latynina, Olympic champion 1956 and 1960 and world champion 1958 and 1962; V. Slavska, Olympic champion 1964 and 1968 and world champion in 1966 as well as L. Turisheyeva, Olympic champion 1972 and world champion 1970 and 1974. During the Munich Ol.G. of 1972 a new style of gymnastics based on the introduction of spontaneity and adding elements of natural grace to the mechanistically applied aesthetics of Olympic gymnastics, was instigated by O. Korbut, who nevertheless didn't take the gold medal for the all round, but only in the individual pieces of equipment,

Gezhange Abera of Ethiopia wins the marathon during the 2000 Olympic Games in Sydney, Australia.

the beam and the floor, as well as silver in the asymmetric bars, and silver on the beam in 1976. In the next Ol.G. Rumanian N. Comaneci dominated, taking the all-around title in 1976. Later, the Olympic all-around competition was dominated by E. Davydova of Russia (1980), M.L. Retton of the USA (1984), E. Chouchounova of Russia (1988), T. Goutson of EUN (1992), L. Podkopayeva of Ukraine (1996), and S. Amanar of Romania (2000).

OLYMPIC HANDBALL, the name used in Australia to refer to >TEAM HANDBALL as opposed to the individual version of the game, >HANDBALL. The name was first adopted in Australia during the 1956 Ol.G., when the Australians first encountered team handball.

OLYMPIC MARATHON, the longest race of the track-and-field events of the International Amateur Athletic Federation (IAAF). Initially the Olympic marathon distance was not standardized and varied at individual Ol.G. held between 1896 and 1920, ranging from 42,000m to 42,750m. At the Paris Ol.G. in 1924 the official marathon distance was fixed at 42,195m. This was based on a decision of the British Olympic Committee to start the 1908 Olympic marathon from Windsor Castle and to finish it in front of the royal box in the stadium at London. Modern Ol.G. and track-and-field W.Ch. are commenced with a men's marathon and concluded with a women's marathon race. In the 1970s marathon races began to be held as single, international running events, attended by a large number of participants. The most renowned annual marathons are the Boston and New York Marathons, and the Marine Corps Marathon held in Washington, DC.

History. The idea of the Olympic marathon was conceived by the Fr. philologist M. Breal (1832-1915). He suggested inclusion of the marathon race into the program of modern Ol.G. to P. de Coubertin. The first modern Olympic marathon was won by Gk. S. Louis at the first Ol.G. in Athens in 1896. His victory had a symbolic dimension and helped establish the prestige of modern Ol.G. in general. Until 1912 Olympic marathon races abounded in dramatic events resulting from participants' insufficient training for such a great physical effort. During the 1908 Olympic marathon the judges disqualified Ital. D. Pietri who ran first onto the stadium but weakened a few meters before the finish line. Assisted by a few well-intentioned judges Pietri managed to cross the line but was promptly disqualified. In 1912, a Portuguese Lassaro fainted during the marathon race and died of exhaustion the following day. Instances of cheating were also common in the first decades of the Olympic marathon. At the St. Louis Ol.G. in 1904 American F. Lorz ran first onto the stadium, having covered 20km by bike (or car, in some other sources). He was later disqualified when his deceptive maneuver was disclosed. During the Olympic marathon in Paris a corrupt referee indicated a wrong route to the race leader, E. Fast from Sweden, who, however, managed to win the bronze medal, despite taking a roundabout way and running 8 extra kilometers. Strict regulations introduced in 1912 put an end to the aforementioned sports cheats. El Quafi from Algeria was the first non-Eur. runner to have won a marathon race. The only athlete to win the Olympic marathon twice in a row was

An original form of hitch and kick is practiced in Canada.

Ethiopian B. Abebe (1932-73).

T. Derderian, *Boston Marathon. The First Century of the World's Premier Running Event,* 1996; J. Henderson, *Marathon Training,* 1997; P. Pfitzinger, S. Douglas, *Advanced Marathoning,* 2001; M. Steffny, *Marathoning,* 1979.

OLYMPIC RELAY, see >TRACK AND FIELD RELAY.

OLYMPIC WEIGHTLIFTING TRIATHLON, Olympic competition including 3 events: >SNATCH and >CLEAN-AND-PRESS. It no longer exists, as one of the events, clean-and-press, was banned in 1973 as hazardous to health. The competition has been continued as *Olympic two-event weightlifting*. Cf. >POWERLIFTING.

OMAOMA, a trad. form of Maori running contest practiced before the arrival of Europeans. Distances run by adults reached 75km. The participants ran barefoot, along courses that included all kinds of terrain. The run included a turnaround, just like the modern Olympic Marathon: at the half-way point, there was a tree that the runner had to mark, or a stone that the runner had to pick up and take with him as proof of having covered the whole distance. The run was performed as a trot, with the legs bent slightly at the knees. Cf. >TAUPIRIPIRI.

ON THE HAUL, a simple rowing event, described by the Rus. author I.N. Chkhannikov. Two boats of any shape and size were launched, with any number of rowers on boards. The boats were tied together with a piece of rope so that the distance between them was about 3m. At a signal from the referee, both teams started rowing in opposite directions. The team who succeeded in towing the opponents' boat to the shore was declared the winner. I.N. Chkhannikov, 'On the haul', GIZ, 1953, 81.

ONE FOOT HIGH KICK, a trad. form of >HIGH JUMP, popular among indigeneous peoples of N Canada. A competitor must strike a target with one of his feet, starting with a running or standing approach. The target is a small soft object, usually a piece of stuffed fur, suspended on a piece of rope

Olympic gymnastics – floor exercise.

Olympic gymnastics – beam.

from a horizontal arm mounted on a vertical self-supporting stand. Each competitor has 3 attempts at a given height, after which the target is raised 2in. The time allowed for preparation for an attempt is 3min.; if this is exceeded, a player is charged with an attempt. A player who misses the first attempt must make the second and third attempts in succession. The player who kicks the target at the highest height is declared the winner. In the event of a tie, the target is lowered 1in., and the competitors have 3 attempts at that height. If no winner is determined at the lower level, the winner is determined by counting the total number of kicks of each competitor, with the lowest number of kicks prevailing. Local terminology has one foot high kick among the so-called Arctic sports. The sport is included in the North American Indigenous Games program as a separate event. Cf. >TWO FOOT HIGH-KICK, >ALASKAN HIGH KICK, >HITCH AND KICK.
Source: The Arctic Sports, The Internet: http://www.firstnations.com/naig97/arctic-sports/as-onefoot-highkick.htm

ONE HAND REACH, a trad. form of exercise and competition, popular among indigeneous peoples of N Canada. A player begins by standing on all fours, lifting his feet off the ground and balancing on his hands. Then, the competitor reaches out with one hand, while maintaining balance on the other, and tries to strike the target. The target is usually a piece of fur suspended on a stand. After each successful attempt, it is raised 2in. Local terminology has one hand reach among the so-called Arctic sports. The sport is included in the North American Indigenous Games program as a separate event.
Source: The Arctic Sports, The Internet: http://www.firstnations.com/naig97/arctic-sports/as-onehandreach.htm.

ONE-OLD-CAT, one of a group of bat and ball games played in the Brit. colonies in N.America in the 17th-18th cent. Along with >BASTE-BALL, >GOALBALL, >CRICKET, >NEW-YORK-BALL, >ROUND BALL, >ROUNDERS, >TOWN-BALL and >TWO-OLD-CAT, the game contributed to the development of >BASEBALL. One-old-cat was one of the oldest and simplest rounders-like games, played with one base. Two-old-cat, with two bases, was a higher stage of development of one-old-cat.

ONE-WALL HANDBALL, a var. of >HANDBALL, where the court has only one wall at the end, against which the ball is bounced using the hands. This is different from other var. of handball, where there are 3 (>THREE-WALL HANDBALL) or 4 walls (four-wall handball). The rules are essentially the same as in those other types of handball. See also >IRISH HANDBALL.

ONO-HA ITTO RYU, one of the *budo* schools.

OOMATASHIA, see >GUGAHAWAT.

OOMIAC, also *oomiak*, old spelling forms of >UMIAK.

OPPEKAST, a Dan. game in which players toss a knife so that it lands blade down in sand [Dan. *oppe* – upper + *kast* – throw]. The players form a circle around a sand pit, kneeling on one knee. One of the players places a knife on the upper side of his palm (index and middle fingers), handle towards his body. He sings a counting-out rhyme, and throws the knife. If the knife drives into the sand, he may continue with his throwing (one throw for each word of the rhyme), if not – he passes the knife onto the next player. There are 10 figures that the players have to perform to get through a round. Apart from the initial throw, described above, there are also finger, palm and elbow tosses, where the tip of the knife touches those parts of the player's body, while the other hand is used to toss the knife. Cf. >CIP.
J. Møller, 'Oppekast', GID, 1997, 1, 128.

ORIENTAL ARCHERY, a type of Asian archery, differing in many aspects from archery known in other parts of the world. A characteristic feature of this type of archery is its adoption to human movement on horseback – among the peoples of C Asia, esp. the Mongols – or skis – among the people of Siberia. Geographical expansion of oriental archery took place during migrations of Asian peoples to Europe, esp. during the Hun (4th and 5th cent.) and Mong. (1167-1241) raids. The oriental bow, with numerous varieties, was short, double-bent and flexible, thus excellently fit for horseback riding (see >MONGOLIAN ARCHERY, >ARCHERY). Many

original characteristics were displayed by >CHINESE ARCHERY. A number of archery types and styles developed in Japan (>BUSHA, >IBAHAJIME, >JUMIHAJIME, >JYARAI, >KUSAJISI, >MARU-MONO, >MOMOTE, >NORIYUMI, >RYO, >TANGONO KISHA, >UMA YUMI). Some Jap. var. of archery have been aimed at personality improvement or regarded as pedagogical measures to reach higher values and objectives (>KYUDO, >GOJUKKEN, >HAN-DO, >TOSIYA). In C Asia, such archery forms as >WINESKIN SHOOT and Mong. >SUR KHARVAKH enjoyed great popularity as well. Many less numerous peoples of Asia have also contributed to diversity of oriental archery styles, e.g. >AFGHAN ARCHERY, >BURIAT ARCHERY, CHUKCHEE AND KORIAT ARCHERY, >KALMUCK ARCHERY, >TIBETAN ARCHERY, >PARTHIAN ARCHERY. Some forms of oriental archery were parts of social or religious observations practiced by various cultures; see >BURIAL ARCHERY, >WEDDING ARCHERY.
Significance of archery among the peoples of the Orient can be noticed in the fact that the birth of a boy was welcomed with an archery contest; and a tiny miniature of the bow and arrow was hung over his cradle. Archery was an integral part of boys' education; archery tournaments were held on the occasion of religious holidays, weddings and funerals. Oriental archery traditions have been documented in the mythologies of numerous Asian cultures. In one of the most common myths, the archer fights against drought that descended upon the Earth, by shooting down the suns. In different mythologies the number of the suns varies as well as the archer's actions. In Mong. tradition the archer first misses his target, and ashamed he cuts his thumbs and big toes off and goes into hiding underground. In another Mong. myth the archer does not fight the suns but 12 Pleiades which freeze the earth, and he succeeds in shooting them down to the ground. The Chin. archer named I, who is referred to in the old Chin. text of *Huainan tsy*, had his left arm longer than his right arm. He lived during the tumultuous reign of Emperor Jao (2356-2255 BC), and shot his arrows at evil-doers, bringing peace and happiness to those who suffered. I the Archer was probably a historical character whose heroic and godly feats were embellished in various works of Chin. literature. The motif of the archer saving the common folk from misery and suffering is present also in the literature of ancient India.
One of the characters in Tungus mythology is the archer Main, who retrieves the light stolen by an elk named Heglen. A similar tale is part of the Mong. tradition. In a Kor. folk tale, twin archers shoot down the sun and the sky and hide them away from evil forces. In some cultures of C Asia shooting at the sky is connected with a young man's initiation; in other cultures it is replaced with the wineskin shoot. Ethnologists argue as to possible symbolic links between oriental archery and the sexual act. According to some, shooting arrows can be interpreted as a symbol of fertility, and an arrow can symbolize force, power or energy. Many ethnologists, incl. Rus. N.I. Veselovskij, firmly reject the notion that there are any sexual associations.

ORIENTEERING, an outdoor competitive sport described by its federation (International Orienteering Federation, IOF) as 'navigating one's way round a course with designated control points which are shown on a map' [the word 'orienteering' is a sports neologism, meaning 'positioning (oneself) with reference to the points of the compass', from Lat. *oriens* – rising sun]. Contestants compete in the open air and plot courses, with the help of a topographic map and a special compass, between control points they usu. must visit in sequence. The name of the sport comes from the Swed. *orientering* (orientation) and was coined in 1946 by B. Kjellström. (1910-95). Orienteering is often a generic name for a group of sports including also >SKI ORIENTEERING, >MOUNTAIN BIKE ORIENTEERING and >TRAIL ORIENTEERING.
Fundamentals and equipment. Competitors may reach the destination running or marching, individually or in teams. Orienteering is usu. a competitive sport but may also be practiced for recreational purposes. An orienteering course is usu. from 1 to 15km long. The IOF Map Commission that developed the specific type of map used at present in orienteering was established in the 1960s with the help of H.

Wilbye of Norway. Wilbye was responsible for preparing the first maps based on aerial pictures. He also introduced an internationally recognized set of keys, symbols and 5 colors used in coding orienteering maps. Maps used are of a 1:15,000 scale though maps of a 1:10,000 scale may be used on more difficult routes with a large number of small topographic features. Still more detailed maps are used for training purposes. A special compass used by orienteers was constructed by B. Kjellström. and G. Tillander in the 1930s. The orienteering compass is unique in that the needle is not mounted on a pin but placed in a liquid environment which prevents any mechanical damage to the needle. Another unique feature of such a compass is that it may be easily oriented against the map as its base is made of a transparent material, is extended and equipped with a magnifying glass and a scale. Such a compass is commonly called a *silva compass*.
Competitors set out from the starting point at intervals of 2-5min., employ the map and compass to locate and check in at all the control points along the course and try to cover the distance in the shortest possible time. In the past they used to stamp or punch their cards at each control to prove that they had reached it. Today, the punching systems have been replaced by electronic check-in systems which also record control point times.
There are 2 basic orienteering varieties. In the first type the runners have to check in at controls according to a predefined order. In the *score-O* system the competitors may check in at the controls in any order but have to locate as many of them as possible within a specified period of time. Team competitions may be held according to the ROGAINE

Equipped with map and compass, an orienteering enthusiast hurries to the next control point.

O

WORLD SPORTS ENCYCLOPEDIA

(Rugged Outdoor Group Activity Involving Navigation and Endurance) principles. In the ROGAINE system teams compete over a relatively vast area following an extended system of *score-O* rules and the competition time varies from 6 to 24hrs. A relay-O system is meant for 3-4-member teams whereby each member of a given team reaches controls individually. Younger competitors or people practicing orienteering for recreational purposes usu. follow the so-called *preset course*, whereby a *course setter* (i.e. an umpire plotting the course) marks the route on competitors' maps but does not indicate control points which remain to be found. The *handicapped-O* formula foresees various facilities for the handicapped along the route but does not help them in any way identify controls.

Ostrich races.

Orienteering competitions are held separately for men and women over long distances (also called classic distances) as well as over short distances. There are also orienteering relays. Apart from runners or walkers orienteering may also be practiced by cyclists, skiers and on wheelchairs. An international slang name for the sport is simply O and cyclists and skiers call it *bike-O* and *ski-O*.

History. Running to reach a specified destination has always been popular among various cultures – compare, for example, the New Guinean >CUMN-GO RACES, Old Ir. >FENIAN RUNNING or the >MONTENEGRO RACES, where a prize is placed on top of a mountain. However, the modern principles of orienteering defined as a 'sport combined with conceptual thinking' were first put forward around 1895 in Norway and Sweden. The aim of such orienteering races was to provide physical training to soldiers. The rules of the sport were different from those observed today – a winner was declared on the basis of the time result he achieved, pulse rate taken at the finish line and his ability to provide a coherent account of the route layout. The first purely competitive orienteering race was held in 1896 in Bergen, Norway. The competitive var. of orienteering was introduced to Sweden around 1900 by an engineer S. Stenberg who used to work in the Norw. town of Christiania (Oslo) and observed orienteering competitions held there. The first orienteering

Outdoor polo on a 1967 postage stamp.

Outdoor polo.

competition in Sweden took place in 1902 and involved only 5 runners due to bad weather. A breakthrough came in 1918 when E. Killander (1882-1958) introduced orienteering as a part of the Swed. Scouts' routine. Thanks to him there were as many as 155 competitors who took part in the 1919 Saltsjöbåden race. The course was 12km-long and the winner, O.B. Hansen, completed it in 1hr. 25min. and 39sec. The first international orienteering competition was held between Sweden and Norway. Initially, orienteering was only popular in Scandinavia, but it started spreading throughout Europe in the 1930s. In 1925 R. Henrik organized the first competition in Hungary. The first official competition in Switzerland took place in 1934. In 1946 B. Kjellström introduced orienteering to the US. Orienteering was not particularly popular in America until 1971, when the Amer. Orienteering Federation was established. Orienteering has been known in Canada since 1948. In Czechoslovakia the first competition was held in 1950, in Yugoslavia in 1953, in Bulgaria in 1955, and in the USSR in 1957 (Soviet sources maintain, however, that orienteering first came to the USSR in 1933). Orienteering was introduced to Australia and Israel in 1969. The International Orienteering Federation (IOF) was established in 1961 by representatives of national federations from Sweden, Norway, Finland, Denmark, Switzerland, Hungary, Czechoslovakia, Bulgaria, FRG and GDR. IOF organized the first E.Ch. in 1962 in Løten, Norway; the second was held in Le Brassus in Switzerland (1964). W.Ch. has been held every 2yrs. (except 1978 and 1979 when the championship was held annually) since 1966. Since 1979 the W.Ch. has been organized in odd years. During even years IOF organizes World Cup and Ski Orienteering World Championship. U-21 and veterans (over 35) championships are held every year. The most prestigious orienteering event is the so-called 'Swedish 5-day competition' also known as the *O-Ringen* which usu. attracts around 15,000 participants.

IOF has been recognized by the International Olympic Committee but orienteering has not been introduced to the Ol.G. yet. IOF, quite naturally, supports environmental protection and propagates the principles of ecology. The major magazine read by the orienteering community is *Orienteering World* published by the IOF in English. In 1999 there were, however, as many as 22 various magazines published in the IOF member states, e.g. *The Australian Orienteer*, *Orienteering Canada*, *The Irish Orienteer*, the Rus. *Orienteering Herald*, *Orienteering North America*, *O-Japan*, the Hungarian *Tájfutás*, the Ger. *OL-Information*, the Czech *Orientacni Behu*, the Est. *Orienteeruja*, etc.

The most outstanding orienteers include Ø. Thon of Norway, who won a total of 7 gold medals at W.Ch. and M. Skogum – a female runner from Sweden who took 6 golds at W.Ch. as well as S. Monsparf of Hungary, who in 1972 was the first female runner to overcome the Scand. hegemony. The best Swed. orienteers have formed an elite club called the O-Ringen whose task is to popularize the sport and sponsor an annual open competition. One of the milestones in the history of orienteering was the 1973 Dalarna competition which, for the first time in history, attracted close to 12,000 participants. The competitors, apart from being judged on their performance during the respective competitions, are also classified according to annual rankings. In 1997, when the 100th anniversary of orienteering was celebrated, there were as many as 2,750 men and 1,058 women orienteers classified in the official IOF rankings. B. Valstadt and P. Thoresen (both of Norway) were ranked first and second among men and K. Borg and G. Svärd (both of Sweden) were the best among women.

Orienteering was popularized by famous long-distance runners who were, however, rarely successful in the new sport. One of them was a former 5,000m record holder – G. Pirie of Great Britain who became and active member of the Brit. orienteering federation after 1956 and wrote a book on orienteering. Another famous convert was A. Garderud, the 1972 Olympic steeplechase champion, who, when asked about the future of his career after his 1972 victory he answered: 'I am going to practice steeplechase for one more year or so and then I am going to switch to orienteering. I am going to do it as long as I shall live as orienteering is the kind of sport one may enjoy until he is 60'. It is estimated that towards the end of the '90s there were as many

as 800,000 orienteers in some 50 countries (the IOF had in 1996 41 full and 6 associate members).

S. Andersen, *The Orienteering Book*, 1977; A. Braggins, *Trail Orienteering*, 1993; S. Harvey, M. Nimvik, B. Römvik, *The World of Orienteering*, 1998; P. Palmer, *Pathways to Excellence-Orienteering*, 1994; T. Renfrew, *Orienteering*, 1997.

ORKHON-YENISEY TURKS' WRESTLING, similar to other C Asian wrestling styles but differentiated by a special outfit worn by the fighters. The wrestlers wore trousers, a shirt similar to the trad. Rus. shirt and a long overcoat with a belt fastened tightly around their waists. In addition they put on a cap and high boots. The clothes were usu. red and blue in color, similar to those worn in the Mong. >BÖKHIN BARILDAAN. The object of the game was to floor an opponent and press him to the ground with the whole weight of one's body.

ORTHOPÁLE, also *orthopali*, *orthia pale*, one of the 2 main var. of ancient wrestling collectively known as >PALE (the other was called >STADAIA PALE). One characteristic thing was that the wrestlers took a loose hold on each other, above the waist, by the trunk or shoulders, facing each other (hence the name [Gk. *orthos* – upright]). The objective was to throw the opponent to the ground 3 times. A successful throw was one where the opponent touched the ground with any part of his body apart from his feet. As opposed to many contemporary forms of wrestling, the opponent did not have to be pressed to the ground, which would require wrestling on the ground, and would be against the overall idea of orthopále. If both of the contestants fell to the ground simultaneously, the fight was recommenced from the initial position. The winning contestant was declared the *triakter*. Other var. of ancient wrestling included ground wrestling known as >KATO PALE [Gk. *kata* – down] as well as >ALINDISSIS [Gk. *alindeomai* – to welter] or >KYLISIS [Gk. *kylisis* – to welter in dust]. In those var., the match continued until one of the contestants admitted defeat. See also >WRESTLING; cf. >AKROCHEIRISMOS.

OSSETIAN HORSE RACING, a form of >HORSE RACING popular among the peoples of Ossetia. The most popular var. accompanied burial ceremonies. Similar to the funeral races of the Khevsurs (see >KHEVSUR HORSE RACING), one of the horses represents the deceased and is mounted by a rider selected by his family. The starting ceremony was different, however. The deceased was given a bottle of vodka placed in a sack tied to the horse. One of the elders held a horn or another vessel filled with alcohol and made a farewell speech. Then he spilled a few drops of alcohol over the horse's head and the body of the deceased and broke the vessel against the the right front horseshoe.

I. Kabzińska-Stawarz, 'Competition in Liminal Situations. Comparative Study of Asian Cultures', ETHP, 1994, 18.

OSTOROZHNO, a Rus. school game. A thin, round wooden block is placed on the ground. The players form a circle around it, holding hands, and start whirling around the block, trying to force one another to tip it over. Whoever does so, is excluded. The game stops when there are 3 players in the circle. If there is a larger number of players, the block is not placed in the middle; instead, a circle is drawn on the ground, with a diameter of 2-3 steps, and several blocks are placed on the perimeter, at equal distances. This version of the game is more complicated and interesting. A ball may also be placed next to the block; whoever tips the block over, grabs the ball and tries to hit one of the other players – who start running away in different directions. The person who is finally hit has to jump over the circle without touching the blocks. If he fails, he is excluded from the game.

I. Chkannikov, 'Ostorozhno', GIZ, 1953, 9-10.

OSTRICH RACES (MOUNTED), a form of competition on unharnessed ostriches practiced mainly in S Africa, but gaining some popularity also in the US, mainly California, Kansas and Nebraska. Jockeys sit astride the ostriches or ride small, 2-wheeled sulkies, similar to >HARNESS RACING. Ostriches run at speeds reaching 100km/h.

OTTA, an ancient Indian type of duel where carved sticks are used as weapons, held much like swords, and resembling elephant trunks in shape. Otta is part of the system of martial skills known as >KALARI-PAYAT.

OUTDOOR POLO, (Kashmir Tibetan *pulu* – 'willow root, ball made of willow root'), the most popular game of the >POLO family of games. It is played on horseback between 2 teams of 4 players each. The players in each team are numbered from 1 to 4, according to their positions in the field. Number 1 is the main forward responsible for scoring goals; number 2 is the 'hustler' who scraps for the ball, assisting number 1 and also scoring goals; number 3 is the quarterback and feeds balls to number 1 and number 2; and number 4 is the main defensive player. The aim of the game is to drive a ball with mallets down the field and between the opponent's goal posts. The mallet has a rubber-covered grip with a thong for wrapping around the hand and a long flexible shaft made of bamboo-cane, or recently of fiberglass, with a bamboo head. The mallet measures from 48 to 53in (124.5-134.6m) in length and weighs 17-20oz. (482-567g). The mallet head is made of bamboo or willow root, and the ball is struck with the side of the mallet, not the end. A ball can travel at a speed of 50km/h. Polo is played on an outdoor grass field 300yds. (274.3m) long and 160yds. (146.3m) wide. If the field is boarded on the sides, the height of the boards should be no more than 11in (28cm). An unboarded field can be 200yds. (182.88m) wide. The field is marked at the center with a T and at all boundaries where there are no sideboards and at the edges and center of the 30, 40, and 60yd. lines at each end of the field. The goals are centered at each end line; the goalposts are at least 10ft. high and while they used to be 8yds. apart, at present they are only 8ft. apart. The ball used for polo is made of willow root or plastic 3-3½in. in diameter and weighing approx. 4oz. (113.4g). By convention, the horses used for polo are called ponies. The mount was initially 13.3 hands, i.e. about 136cm; it was elevated later to 148cm. After 1919 restrictions on pony size were removed. Most frequently 3-year-old ponies are used. The pony's legs are bandaged from below the knee to the ankle to prevent injuries. During the game a player may ride off an opponent; there is also the rule of right of way between any 2 players in the proximity of the ball: a player following the ball has right of way over an approaching player. Each player is rated in handicaps from -2 to 10, according to his ability in competition. Goals can be awarded by handicap and their number is determined by finding the difference between the total of the handicaps assigned to the players on one team and the total of the handicaps assigned to the players on the other team. In the early years of development an offside rule was used (abandoned in 1909). A game of polo consists of 6-8 periods of 7½min. each, called chukkers or chukkas (Hindu *chakkar*,

Sanskrit *cakra* 'wheel'). The game is officiated by 2 mounted umpires on the field and a referee on the sidelines. In the case of a disagreement between the umpires, the referee's decision is final. Depending on the foul referees may award free hits to the fouled team from 30, 40 and 60yds. Polo can be also played indoors (>INDOOR POLO), on a smaller field with fewer players on each team. A var. of polo played on snow (>WINTER POLO) was introduced in Switzerland in 1984.

Attire. Players wear protective helmets (since c.1885), special riding boots called chukka boots, and knee pads to prevent injuries while riding off an opponent.

History. The precise origin of the game remains unknown. Some historians make the dubious claim that the sport was already practiced between 4000 and 3000 BC in the Middle and Far East. There are 2 contradictory theories concerning the game's origins. According to one, the earliest forms of polo on horseback were known in ancient China and later they gave rise to the sport called >JIQIU. According to the other theory, backed up by the majority of sports historians, polo may have originated in ancient Persia around 1000 BC and then spread out to other Asian countries with the expansion of Arab civilization and the Ottoman Empire, via Turkistan, India, Tibet, China to Japan (>AL SAWALJAH). One of the arguments in support of the latter theory is the fact that until c.1500 BC horseback riding was unknown. Racing on horseback was introduced into the Ol.G., only in the 7th cent. BC. The ancient Persians were far more advanced in horse breeding than their Mediterranean counterparts, and the game could have originated there, most likely preceded by a similar sport played on foot. The Persian genesis of polo finds its justification in a tale from *The Thousand and One Nights* about king Yunan and the Sage Duban, in which the latter prescribed a special medicine for his king who suffered from leprosy. The physician placed the medicine inside a hollow polo stick. The king was to play polo with the stick and during the game the medicine was absorbed through the king's perspiring hand and healed him. Apart from the legends the earliest references to polo in Persia can be found in an epic poem by Ferdowsi devoted to a game of Persians and a Turkmen tribe, and in one of the works of Al-Jahiz (d. 869 AD). In Isfahan, Iran there is the site of an ancient polo field about 300yds. long with stone goal posts, 8yds. apart. Ancient polo teams consisted of up to 1,000 riders. Some historians trace the beginning of polo to an event from 230 AD described by a great Muslim scholar Tabari (839-923). One of the early Arab rulers, Ardashi I, after he had confirmed the legitimacy of his son (which many of his

subjects doubted), organized a ball game with the use of sticks in the courtyard of his palace. As Tabari makes no clear references to horses many historians associate that event with the beginning of >FIELD HOCKEY. In 1435, a Span. traveler, P. Tafur described a game played in the court of the Sultan of Barsbai (Egypt), Malik al.-Ashraf:

On that day Sultan ate his meal in the field and then he commenced the game. The ball was placed in the middle of the field and about 1,000 mounted riders took their positions on each end of the field, behind a line marked on the ground. Each rider was holding a mallet stick. Suddenly, they all started to charge at the ball trying to drive it behind the opponents' line. Those who accomplished that task first were the winners. During the game some players got into a fierce argument and the Sultan's son drew his sword and attempted to kill one of his opponents. The argument turned into a battle and the Sultan had to intervene and separate the fighting sides.

In medieval Byzantium, a game called >TZYKANIS-TERION was fairly common. It was played on horseback and the riders used long crooked sticks. The game may have been a form of polo, however the shape of sticks could suggest an early version of >FIELD HOCKEY. Modern polo remains under the clear influence of ancient Persian pulu, which once spread to the territory of present-day Pakistan and is still practiced around Hunza and Gilgit. In 1862 a group of riders from Manipur in the N-E of India demonstrated their pulu skills on their visit to Punjab, in front of British officers of the 10th Hussars. The originator of polo as a modern competitive sport was the Brit. Major J.F. Shearer. Initially polo games were played by teams of 5-7 players. In 1859 a polo club was founded in Cachar and in 1862 in Calcutta. Polo clubs in India, although dominated by Brit. officers, enjoyed great popularity among wealthy maharajas. In 1869 the 10th Hussars brought the game to Great Britain. In 1871 a challenge round was held between the 10th Hussars and the 9th Lancers in Hounslow, England. In 1873, the Hurlingham Polo Club was founded. It fixed the rules and regulations of the game, becoming a national governing body of polo. Since that time Brit. troops stationing in India would compete in the Inter-Regiment Polo Cup championships. The most outstanding military polo clubs to win the cup several times were the Durham Light Infantry and the 4th Dragoon Guards. In 1899, the cup was won by the 4th Hussars, represented among others by the young W. Churchill. By that time Churchill had finished his military service in India but, as he puts in his diary, had trained for this match for 3 years. At the end of his military service he decided 'to return to India at the end of November (1898) in order to prepare for the polo tournament

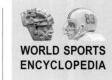

WORLD SPORTS ENCYCLOPEDIA O

A polo game on a 19th cent. lithograph.

A poster advertising a polo tackle company.

George Bellows, Polo at Lakewood, 1910, oil on canvas.

Outdoor polo players, clad in helmets, knee pads, and chukka boots, with mallets at the ready.

O
WORLD SPORTS ENCYCLOPEDIA

in February.' Churchill's team won the match but he sustained an elbow injury. Churchill took part in the final game despite his injury, and he won, scoring 3 out of 4 goals. That dramatic event was later described in his memoirs, *My Early Life* (1944):

The great day arrived. As we had foreseen we met the 4th Dragoon Guards in the Final. The match from the very first moment was severe and even. Up and down the hard, smooth Indian polo ground where the ball was very rarely missed and everyone knew where it should be hit to, we raced and tore. Quite soon we had scored one goal and our opponents two, and there the struggle hung in equipose for some time. I never left the back, and being excellently mounted, kept him very busy. Suddenly in the midst of a confused scrimmage close by the enemy goal, I saw the ball spin towards me [...]. I was able to lift the stick over and bending forward gave it a feeble forward tap. Through the goalposts it rolled. Two all! Apart from the crippled No. 1, we really had a very good team. Our captain, Reginald Hoare, who played No. 3 was not easily to be surpassed in India. Our back, (Reginald) Barnes [...] was a rock, and almost unfailingly sent his strong back-handers to exactly the place where savory was waiting for them with me to clear the way. For three years this contest had been the main preoccupation of our lives, and we had concentrated upon it every resource we possessed. Presently I had another chance. Again the ball came to me close to the hostile goal. This time it was travelling fast, and I had no more to do in one fleeting second than to stretch out my stick and send it rolling between the posts. Three to two! Then our opponents exerting themselves swept us down the ground and scored again. Three all! I must explain that in Indian polo in those days, in order to avoid drawn matches, subsidiary goals could be scored. Half the width of the goalposts was laid off on either side by two small flags, and even if the goals were missed, a ball within these flags counted as subsidiary. No number of subsidiaries equalled one goal, but when goals were equal, subsidiaries decided. Unfortunately our opponents had the best of us in subsidiaries. Unless we could score again we should lose. Once again fortune came to me, and I gave a little feeble hit at the ball among the ponies' hoofs, and for the third time saw it pass through the goal. This brought the 7th chukka to an end.
We lined up for the last period with 4 goals and 3 subsidiaries to our credit, our opponents having 3 goals and 4 subsidiaries. Thus if they got one more goal they would not merely tie, but win the match outright. rarely have I seen such strained faces on both sides. You would not have thought it was a game at all, but a matter of life and death [...]. I do not remember anything of the last chukka except that as we galloped up and down the ground in desperate attack and counter-attack, I kept on thinking, 'Would God that night or Blücher would come'. They came in one of the most welcome sounds I have ever heard: the bell which ended the match, and enabled us to say as we sat streaming and exhausted on our ponies, 'We have won the Inter-Regimental Tournament of 1899'. Prolonged rejoicing, intense inward satisfaction, and nocturnal festivities from which the use of wine was not excluded, celebrated the victory.

George Bellows, Polo Crowd, 1910, oil on canvas.

Churchill's injury sustained during the polo match plagued him for many years to come. In 1876, the Amer. press baron and sportsman, J.G. Bennet (1841-1918) saw polo games played by army officers, while traveling to Britain, and soon after introduced the sport in the US. The most outstanding of early US polo clubs was the Meadow Brook Club in Long Island, NY, formed in 1881. The first international match was played between the USA and England in Newport in 1885, bringing victory to the latter, and establishing the tradition of the annual Westchester Cup played by the 2 countries ever since. The United States Polo Association (USPA) was founded in 1890. Today, it has a membership of about 140 clubs and 1,500 registered players (in 1950 there were some 500 players). Outside Britain and the USA polo is also popular in S Africa, Argentina, Australia, Borneo, Brazil, Chile, Cyprus, Egypt, the Philippines, France, India, Ireland, Jamaica, Canada, Columbia, Malaysia, Malta, Mexico, Nigeria, N.Zealand, Pakistan, Peru, Singapore, Uruguay, Venezuela and Italy. In the 1990s about 40 countries are hosts of international polo competitions. International matches are usually played by teams from Argentina, Mexico, USA, New Zealand and the UK. The most renowned polo clubs in Britain include Hurlingham, Cowdray Park in Sussex (host of the all-England Cowdray Park Gold Cup), Roehampton and Rugby; in the USA – Aiken, Boca Ranton, Meadowbrook, Midwick, Myopia Hunt, Oak Brook, Oklahoma, Old Westbury, Rumson, Santa Barbara; in Argentina – Hurlingham, Coronel Suare, Argentine Jockey Club Polo Team, Mar del Plata, and Tortugas; in S Africa – clubs in Cape Town, Durban, Johannesburg; in Australia – clubs in Adelaide, Perth, Uirindi and Warwick Farm; in N.Zealand – clubs in Christchurch, Fielding, Hamilton, Palmerston North. On the Eur. continent the most famous polo clubs are Deauville (Paris), Bagatelle (Cannes), and clubs from Barcelona, Jerez, Madrid, Soro Grande, Hamburg, Düsseldorf, and Rome. Polo was an Olympic event in 1900, 1908, 1920, 1924 and 1936. The gold medallists of the 1900 Ol.G. polo contest were the Foxhunters, a mixed Brit.-Amer. team; Great Britain I in 1908 (silver medal for Great Britain II); Great Britain in 1920; and Argentina in 1924 and 1938.
The most prestigious polo contest in history was the Hurlingham Champion Cup, established in 1876 and held annually until 1939. The Polo W.Ch. have been held since 1949; the US Open since 1904; the college championships of the Monty Waterburry Memorial since 1922; and the National Intercircuit competition since 1925. Since 1926 the prestigious Cup of the Americas had been held every 4 years until WWII, and then irregularly after 1945. Other renowned polo international competitions include the

Avila Comacho Cup in Mexico, established in 1941 in honor of the famous Mexican president; the Coronation Cup in Great Britain, estab. in 1911 in celebration of the coronation of George V; the Cowdray Park Gold Cup, estab. in 1956 (the original cup was stolen in 1960 and never recovered, at present a replica of the cup is used); the Golden Cup in Australia; the Savile Cup in N.Zealand; and the Argentine Open. Before 1914 the British were supreme in polo, occasionally challenged by US teams. The best Brit. players were J. Watson (1853-1908), L. Cheape 91882-1916) and P. Roark (1895-1939). Many outstanding Brit. polo players perished during WWI, e.g. 2 teammates of W. Churchill. From 1918-39 international polo was dominated by Amer. players such as the Waterbury Brothers, D. Milburn (1885-1942), T.B. Hitchcock (1898-1942), C. Smith (b. 1904) and S. Iglehart (b. 1914). A number of great polo players came also from India, e.g. Maharaja Ratlam, Shah Mirza Beg and Hira Singh. After WWII one of the best known polo players was G. 'Memo' Gracida from Mexico, whose team won the US Open 13 times. Gracida's younger brother Carlos reached a number 10 handicap, and is the only polo player in the world, whose team won US, UK, and Argentine Open championships in one year. The most famous Amer. polo players of the last quarter of the 20th cent. were O. Rinehart and T. Waymann. Since the end of WWI many outstanding polo players have come from Argentina, where the sport was introduced by Brit. settlers c.1875. The first official polo match was played in Estancia Negrete in 1876; amateur games had been played in Cabalito near Buenos Aires since 1875. In the 1970s there were more than 5,000 polo players in Argentina. The leading Argentine players were the Canadian-born L. Lacey (1887-1966), M. Andrad (c.1900 – ?), G. Tanoir (b. 1945) and J.C. Harriott (b. 1936). The player who founded a true 'dynasty' of polo players was A. Heguy (b. 1910), whose sons Horacio (b. 1936) and Alberto (b. 1941) gained huge renown. Heguy's 4 sons have been 10-goal polo players in recent years: Marcos (b. 1969), Bautista (b. 1970), and the twins Horacio Junior and Gonzalo (b. 1964). Alberto Heguy's son, Alberto Jr. (b. 1967) also reached the 10-goal handicap and his brother Ignacio (b. 1973) has been a 9-goal player. One of the best Argentine players of the 1960s and '70s was J.C. Harriot (b. 1939) who led his national team to 2-time victory in the Cup of the Americas, defeating the US team in 1966 and 1969. In Australia, one of the best polo players was R. Skene (b. 1914), who also played in the Brit. national team. The first player to reach the 10-goal handicap was an American, F. Heene (1869-1941).
Polo in art and literature. The sport of polo has been a frequent theme of numerous literary works, such as R. Kipling's *Maltese Cat* or W. Churchill's *My Early Life* (1944). Polo was also depicted in some drawings by M. Liebermann (1847-1935), including *Polo Match in Jenischs Park*. A great Pol. painter W. Kossak (1857-1942) devoted many of his works to the sport of polo as well.
N. Bent, *American Polo*, 1929; J.M. Brown, *Riding in Polo*, 1891, also *Polo*, 1895; F. Ceballos, *El polo en la Argentina*, 1969; G. Cullum, *The Selection and Training of a Polo Pony*, 1934; T.F. Dale, *Polo. Past and Present*, 1895 and *The Game of Polo*, 1897; H. Diston, *Beginning Polo*, 1973; P. Grace, *Polo*, 1991; J. Gosset, 'Le polo', *Jeux et sports*, 1967; P.G. Kendall, *Polo Ponies*, 1933; A.H. Laffaye, *Diccionario de polo*, 1995; P. Meisels, *Polo*, 1992; J.N.P. Watson, *The World of Polo*, 1986.

OUTDOOR TARGET ARCHERY, a sports var. of >ARCHERY, formerly known as *target archery*, a type of archery competition in which contenders shoot arrows along separate tracks, each at least 2.5m wide. In outdoor target archery, competitors shoot a specified number of arrows at set distances at a target. Different regulations and rules concerning the types of bows, arrows, targets and distances were unified under the Fédération Internationale de Tir à l'Arc (FITA) – the governing body of outdoor target archery. Archers shoot arrows from the following distances: 90, 70, 50, and 30m for men; and 70, 60, 50 and 30m for women. The competitors start at the longest distance and finish at the shortest. Two major FITA events are known as the single FITA round and the double FITA round. In the former each archer shoots 12 series, called *ends*, of 3 arrows from each distance – 144 arrows in total; in

A game of polo consists of 6-8 periods of 7½ minutes each.

the latter – 288 arrows in total. Each end of arrows must be shot within the time limit of 2½ min. The final score is the sum of all end scores.

At the 1992 Ol.G. in Barcelona, the FITA Olympic round was introduced in place of the monotonous single FITA round, comprising head-to-head, single-elimination matches. Since the 1996 Ol.G. in Atlanta the following rules of individual archery competition have been used: after the qualification round the top 64 men and top 64 women competitors proceed to the elimination round. From this stage on, the only distance is 70m for both men and women. The archers shoot 3 ends of 6 arrows: 18 arrows in total. The 8 winning archers go on to the final round. Each archer, then, shoots 4 ends of 3 arrows (12 arrows in total) at a separate target. The final matches are shot with the archers alternating their shots. Each archer has up to 40sec. to shoot 1 arrow. In the case of a draw each archer gets 1 extra shot. The archer with the higher score wins.

In Olympic team competition the top 16 teams of 3 archers are selected, using the combined top 3 scores from the individual qualification round. Each team is entitled to 27 arrows which must be shot within 9min.

Shooting distances in Eng.-speaking countries are set in yards, i.e. 100, 80, 60, 50, 40, 30, and 20yds. The number of shots and types of distances on many archery ranges are not standardized. Principal shooting rounds include the Amer. round consisting of 90 arrows, 30 at each of 3 distances (60, 50, and 40yds.); and the York round consisting of 144 arrows – 72 at 100yds., 48 at 80yds., and 24 at 60yds. The outdoor target archers shoot arrows standing astride, sideways, with the head facing the target. Before a shot the archer must judge the wind force and adjust the bowsight and stabilizer.

Equipment. The compound bow used for outdoor target archery consists of 2 limbs, each ending with a wheel holding the bowstring, and a grip in its middle section. The bow is equipped with bowsights, stabilizers, and torque flight compensators (4 max.) used for damping bow vibrations during shooting. Each bow has its drawing force index, i.e. the number of pounds of energy needed to draw back an arrow to the fullest.

Target. The target is made of paper, cardboard or canvas. The following target sizes are used: 122cm in diameter for distances 90m and 70m; 80cm in diameter for distances 50m and 30m; 60cm in diameter for indoor target archery. Each target has 10 concentric rings in 5 colors (2 yellow, 2 red, 2 blue, 2 black, 2 white) scored 10 to 1, outward from the bull's eye. Targets used for recreational purposes usually have 5 scoring rings. A target face is spread on a boss of tightly coiled straw rope mounted on a special stand. In some archery events silhouette targets are also used.

Other equipment carried by the archer includes: a quiver, a glove or finger protector shielding the fingers used to draw the bowstring back, forearm bracer for protection against the released bowstring, chest protector, and field glass for spotting arrows. Each shooting track is numbered. Before shooting the archer awaits his turn on a waiting line in front of his track. Other lines marked on the track include the shooting line, target line and the 3-m safety line.

History. Archery became a separate sport after being replaced by firearms as a weapon skill. In 1673, a group of aristocrats from Yorkshire founded the Ancient Scorton Arrow – an annual archery contest with the aim of promulgating the ancient art of archery. In 1676, Charles II Stuart, a great lover of archery commissioned the Fraternity of Archery to organize annual archery competitions. The winner of each competition was awarded the Marshal of the Fraternity of Archery title and a medal founded by Charles's wife Catherine of Braganza. In 1790, the Royal Toxophilite Society was founded in England; and in 1844 the Grand National Archery Association, which fixed the rules of the sport and held the first Brit. championships in York was established. The first Amer. archery organization was the United Bowmen of Philadelphia, founded in 1828. In 1878, the National Bowmen Association was estab. in Boston. In Australia, the pioneer of sports archery was W.F.E. Liardet, who held the first archery contest in 1840 in Victoria for guests of Brighton Pier Hotel. The first Austrl. open archery championships were held in Melbourne in 1855 at the foot of Emerald Hill. Several Austrl. archery clubs were later set up and in 1948 they merged into the Archery Associa-

Jim O'Connell and Karl Barrio go head to head at the Wellfleet Oyster Festival in Maryland.

tion of Australia. In the first decades of the 20th cent. numerous archery societies began to emerge in Europe and the USA, usu. as sections of firearms shooting associations. In the years 1904-20, several archery W.Ch. were held under the auspices of different organizations. The first archery world champions, in 1904, were the Americans L. Howell and G. Bryant. From 1907 outdoor target archery was represented by the International Sports Shooting Federation, ISSF. During the Archery W.Ch. in 1931, on Poland's initiative, the Federation of International Target Archery (Fédération Internationale de Tir à l'Arc, FITA) was formed in Lvov, as the governing body of the sport. From 1939 until 1959, the Archery W.Ch. were held every year (except for 1951, 1954, 1956); after 1959, every 2 years. Archery was part of the Olympic program in 1900, 1904, 1908, and 1920. Along with tennis it was the first Olympic event in which women were allowed to compete. The sport reappeared in the 1972 Ol.G. in Munich. Shortly after the foundation of FITA, the top men's and women's archers were Polish. Until 1939, the Poles retained their high positions in women's archery; the men's events came to be dominated by the Belgians, Czechs, French, Swedes and Americans. After 1946, the best men's archers came from Sweden, and then from the USA and USSR; and the best women's archers from Poland, the UK, the USA, and USSR. Since the mid-1980s the lead was taken by archers from S Korea and China. The most famous individual archer in Olympic history is American J. Williams (b.1953), 1972 Olympic champion, 4-time world record holder, and 20-time world medallist.

E. Holey Burke, *The History of Archery*, 1957; F. Hadas, *Bogenschiesen – Olympische Disciplin*, 1969; E.G. Heath, *A History of Target Archery*, 1973; Z. Łotocki, *Łucznictwo*, 1934; M. Panuś and M. Golański, *Tenis – łucznictwo*, 1975; R. Renson, 'Archery', *EWS*, 1996, 39-47; I. Werner, *Polska broń – łuk i kusza*, 1974; R. Zawiślański, *Łucznictwo*, 1952; *50 lat sportu łuczniczego w Polsce*, 1989.

OUTRIGGERS, boats equipped with side frameworks and stabilizing pontoons attached to them, characteristic for the southern Pacific Ocean. As with many sports developed on the basis of folk tradition, outrigger races are becoming increasingly popular. The Hawaii Outrigger Canoe Club is the most active promoter of outrigger races as a sport. Outrigger races are organized under the auspices of the International Canoe Federation.

OVER, see >ANTONIUS.

OX-HEAD FIGHTING, a trad. Kor. sport in which 2 teams fight one another with the help of ox heads set on spearshafts.

OYAKAZU, the archery discipline of Jap. martial arts, later also of a sport known as >TOSIYA. Just like in all the tosiya events, the objective was to correctly shoot a short arrow south to north, along the western side of a verandah, about 120m long; the archers would use short bows and shoot from a kneeling position. Each contestant had 24hrs. (starting at 6a.m. on a specified day) to shoot as many arrows as possible. The archer who succeeded in

setting a new record in the number of arrows correctly shot along the verandah, was declared the *So-ichi* or *Tenka-ichi*, which meant 'Japan's best'. The event could also be limited to 12hrs., being then called 'hiyakazu', and held during daytime only.

OYO, see >EGEDE.

OYSTER SHUCKING, a trad. sporting activity in which contestants compete in deftly popping open razor-edged oyster shells with a special knife and detaching the oysters inside. The shuckers must either open 2 dozen oysters in the shortest possible time or open as many as possible within a designated time limit. The largest event is the International Oyster Festival in Ireland, held since 1966 at Moran's Oyster Cottage on an inlet of Galway Bay, which is considered the W.Ch. of oyster shucking. The US national championship takes place in Leonardtown, Maryland and is part of St. Mary's Oyster Festival, which celebrates the opening of the oyster season on the Chesapeake Bay. Other well known events include: the Wellfleet Oyster Festival in Maryland; the North Carolina Oyster Festival in Shallotte; the Mason County Oyster Fest at Shelton, Washington; the Prince Edward Island International Shellfish Festival in Canada; the Oyster Festival at Oyster Bay Harbor in Long Island; and the Urbanna Oyster Festival in Virginia.

Outdoor target archery.

Chris Merl and Shawn Rose compete in oyster shucking at the Wellfleet Oyster Festival in Maryland.

The first International Oyster Shucking Championship at Moran's Cottage in Gallway.

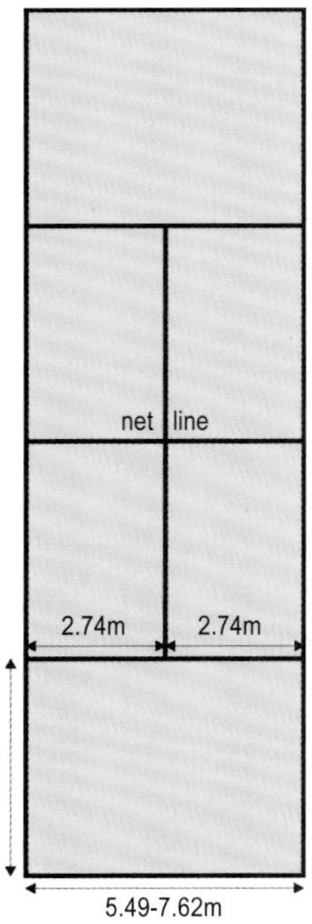

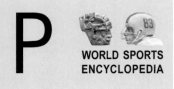

A padder tennis court.

PACK START SKATING, see >SHORT TRACK SPEED SKATING.

PADDER TENNIS, a game similar to >LAWN TENNIS, developed to meet the need for a var. of tennis playable on a smaller area, e.g. in small school gyms, back yards or gardens. Minimum and maximum court dimensions are 39x18ft. (11.89x5.49m) and 55x25ft. (16.77x7.62m), respectively. Padder tennis may be played outdoors or indoors – if there is at least 10ft. (about 305cm) of headroom. The court is different from a trad. tennis court in its dimensions and divisions. Each side is divided into 2 parts by a line parallel to the net, 19ft. 6in. (5.95m) from the net and the baseline. The area on both sides of the net is divided in half by an additional line, perpendicular to the net, 9ft. (2.74m) from the side lines. So, on each side of the net, there are 2 rectangular fields 19ft.½in.x9ft. (5.95x2.74m) in area. The back area is not divided, and forms a rectangle 18x19ft. 6in. (4.49x5.95m) in area. This means that each side is divided into 3 parts (see figure). Standard tennis balls are used, and the short wooden padder bats weighing 8oz. (226g) are meant to shorten the strokes. The height of the net is 2ft. 3in. (68.5cm). The name padder tennis derives from the noun *pad*. Cf. >PADDLE TENNIS.

PADDLE TENNIS, also *mini-tennis*, a var. of >LAWN TENNIS played with a lighter racket. Originally designed for children, it soon grew on adults as well, mainly as a recreational activity. In its early stages, it was played on a regular lawn tennis-size court (39x18ft or 11.9x5.49m). In 1959 the court size was changed to 50ft. (15.24m) in length and 20ft. (6.01m) in width. The net's height was also raised by 1in. to 2ft. 7in. (78.74cm). The ball was originally made from light porous rubber and was slightly bigger than that used in lawn tennis. As it

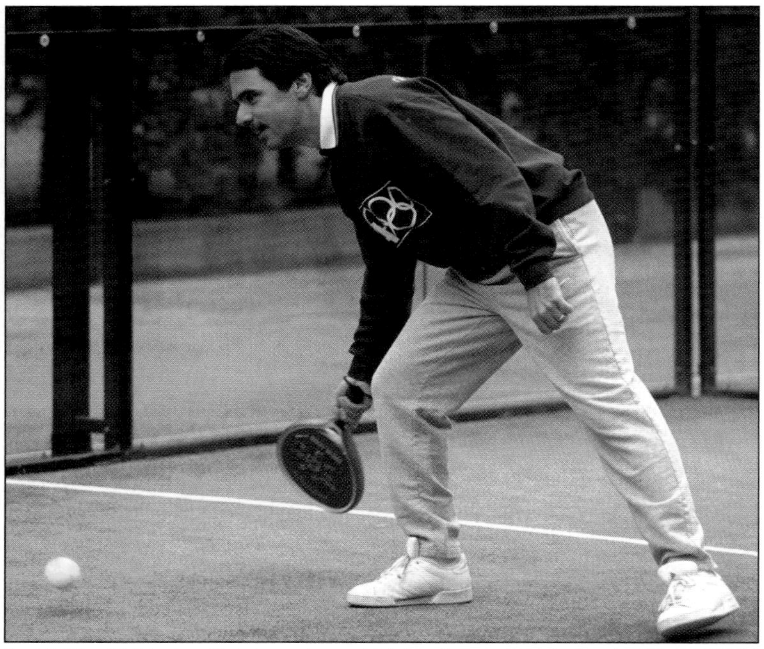
Spain's Prime Minister Jose Maria Aznar plays paddleball on the grounds of the Moncloa Palace in Madrid.

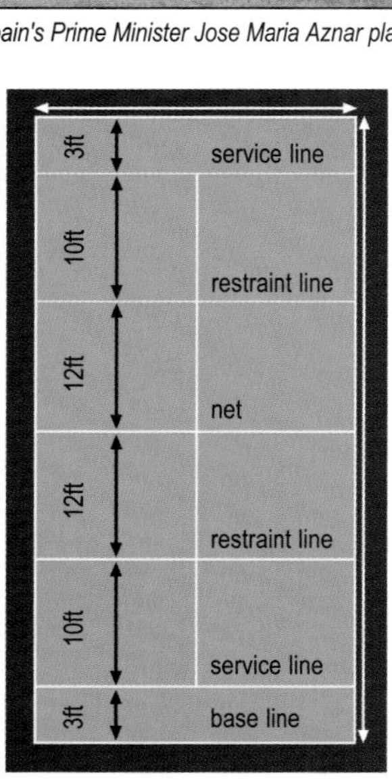

A paddleball court.

quickly became deformed, a decision was made in 1959 to introduce used tennis balls, although rubber balls are still used for recreational games. A wooden or plastic racket is 15-17in. (38-43cm) long, with a short handle and the hitting surface smaller than that of a tennis racket. The rules are similar to lawn tennis, although – while juniors up to 15 years of age can serve overhand – adults can only serve underhand. Except for the serve, the ball must be hit approx. 10ft. above the ground or clearly above the player's head. The service area is 10ft. wide and 12ft. (juniors) or 22ft. (adults) long. The game may be played outdoors or indoors. Paddle tennis courts are often set up on cruise ships.

History. The game was invented in 1897 by an American, F.P. Beal from Albion, Michigan, with the intention to popularize tennis among children, for whom it was otherwise too difficult and too expensive. The new game did not really begin to develop until Beal took over as Episcopal minister of a church in lower Manhattan. In 1915 he managed to convince the city's parks and recreation department to lay out a set of paddle tennis courts around the fountain in Washington Square Park in Greenwhich Village. In the 1930s paddle tennis became one of the most popular children's games in the USA and in 1938 the United States Paddle Tennis Federation was formed, which administers paddle tennis, as well as >PLATFORM TENNIS.The first tournament took place in 1922, while the first Amer. championship was held in 1940.The game's popularity peaked in the 1960s, with over 8,000 courts available throughout the USA. The game was picked up by beach clubs in California, which introduced new rules. In the 1980s the East and West Coast organizations merged.

S. Fessended Blanchard, *Paddle Tennis*, 1944; G. McNickle, 'Paddle tennis', EAI, 1979, 21; J. Townes, 'Tennis, Paddle', EWS, 1996, III; United States Paddle Tennis Association, *Official Rules*, 1961.

PADDLEBALL, a family of Amer. ball games played on 1-, 3-, or 4-wall courts, using small rackets called paddles. Apart from the shape of the courts the 4 kinds of paddleball vary as to the origin and rules of play. The paddle is rimless, made of wood or a composite material, usu. oval in shape. It is about 1ft. 4in. long and 8in. wide. A safety thong is attached to the handle and must be worn around the player's wrist during the game. Formerly, a different ball was used for each paddleball var., e.g. in the 4-wall game a regular tennis ball was used. At present, the ball is $1\frac{7}{8}$in. (4.6cm) in diameter, made of black rubber, with a small pinhole. The bounce should be no more than 3½ft. when dropped from 6ft. In all the game's varieties the same method of serving applies: the ball must be dropped to the floor within the service zone, struck with the paddle on the first bounce, hitting the front wall first and rebounding beyond the short line. Paddleball is most popular in and around New York. The 4-wall var. is least common: in the 1990s it was played by about 10,000 players, while the increasingly popular 1-wall game was played by up to 200,000 people. 4-wall paddleball's popularity is threatened by growing interest in >RACQUETBALL. The 1-wall game is the most accessible var. as it can be played whereever there is a wall. It is esp. popular among Afro-Americans and Hispanics. In all official paddleball games, particularly the 4-wall game, players wear white shirts, shorts, socks and shoes. 1-wall paddleball is derived from >IRISH HANDBALL, introduced to the USA by Ir. immigrants at the turn of the 20th cent. The game became very common in New York, where the ball was hit with a paddle, instead of the hand like in the Brit. variety. In the 1940s about 95% of New York parks featured 1-wall courts. So far, attempts to fix the rules of the game have proved unsuccessful. There are no strict rules concerning the size of the court, which is usu. 34x20ft. The wall should be 16ft. high and cover the width of the court. 16ft. from the front wall runs a short line, and 9ft. from the short line to the back court there are 2 service lines, each 6in. long. The area between the service lines and the short line is called the service zone. The 3-wall game is played on a court with one front wall and 2 side walls reaching down to the short line, no higher than 6ft. tall. The 4-wall game was created at the University of Michigan in Ann Arbor in 1930 by E. Riskey, a PE instructor. During WWII the game was recommended to Amer. troops in the US Armed Forces Conditioning Program. After the war Riskey founded the National Paddleball Association. The US championships were estab. in 1961; they have been held regularly since the 1970s. The 4-wall court is 40ft. long and 20ft. wide with front and side walls 20ft. high and a back wall at least 12ft. high. A line midway between and parallel with the front and back walls divides the court in the center and is called the short line. A line 5ft. in front of the short line and parallel to it is called the service line. The area between the service line and the short line is the service zone. 18in. from the side wall at each end of the service zone is the so-called service box. The game can be played by singles or doubles. The 4-wall game can also be played 'cut throat', i.e. one player against two. Games are to 21pts. The player who wins 2 sets wins the match. Only the serving player can score points, similar to table tennis.

J. Wilkinson, ed., 'Paddleball', *Rules of the Games. The Complete Illustrated Encyclopedia of All the Sports of the World*, 1974; D. Squires, *The Other Racquet Sports*, 1978; A. Trevithick, 'Paddleball', EWS, 1996, II.

PAGANIKA, Lat. *paganica*, originally a rural pastime, then a folk ball game practiced in the Roman Empire, esp. in the legions [Lat. *paganus* – rural, or *pagus* – village]. It entailed striking a small light ball using sticks curved at the lower end. The balls were most likely made of wood or oakum clumps layered with leather. The aim of the game was to shoot the ball into small holes in the ground, often on grassy fields. In some later variations of paganika flight feathers were attached to the balls to increase aiming and hitting accuracy. In the years 43-410 AD the game was brought to Roman Britain where it prob. contributed to the development of Brit. folk games involving hitting balls with curved sticks such as Wel. >KNAPPAN, Scot. >HURLEY, Scand. >BANDY and indirectly Ir. >HURLING. According to some historians, paganika influenced early forms of >GOLF.

PAGSSCHIETEN, also *pagschieten*, a Flem. folk game, known in France as *jeu de billon*. The game is played by 2 teams and consists of tossing special clubs at a tripod made of 3 wooden stakes.

PAINTBALL, a var. of shooting sport using gelatin balls filled with paint. Getting hit with a gelatin ball leaves a splat on a player, which means the player's 'death' and elimination from the game.

Equipment. The basic players' equipment is a special airgun called a 'paintgun' or 'marker' which fires gelatin paintballs. The oldest type of paintgun is the Nel-Spot 007 powered by carbon dioxide. In the 1990s it was challenged by Sheridan guns and full-auto paintguns with 38-round clips. At present, a popular type of paintgun is the semi-automatic Splatmaster Rapide with 20- or 40-round clips. To increase shooting accuracy paintguns may have telescopic sights or barrel extensions. Shooting action is maintained by a compressed air supply tank attached to the gun. The air-tanks are not always allowed on the playing field. The players wear goggles and facemasks similar to those of hockey goalkeepers. Usually the facemask and goggles come in one piece. They protect the eyes and most sensitive parts of the face from splattering paintballs, which – although not lethal – could otherwise damage vision or enter the mouth cavity. Other equipment includes anti-fog spray for goggles, a squeegee used to clean the barrel, and ammo supply.

Attire. The players wear camouflage battle dress in various patterns. The most popular patterns include the desert, the woodland and the tigerstripe. The battle dress should have a number of pockets used for ammo supplies, etc. Usually, there are 6 pockets in the pants and 4 pockets in the jacket. Each player must have a so-called elimination tank top to be put on after the player has been hit to distinguish him or her from the live players in the game. Players have been known to bring along money in order to bribe opponents.

Rules. Paintball matches can be played in 2 categories: single shooting and semi-automatic shooting. Before the game the paintguns' velocity must be checked and adjusted. The international limit on paintball speed is 90m/s and paintgun range is about 20m. Players of the same team wear armbands of the same color.

The object of the game is to capture a flag. Two types of events can be distinguished: 1) the center-flag – both teams capture the same flag; 2) the dual-flag – each team has its own flag in their base and is responsible for protecting it as well as trying to capture the other team's flag. A team wins if it brings the captured flag to their own base and puts it next to their own flag. The game is controlled by 2 referees, one next to each team. The referees communicate with each other on the radio.

Any paintball that hits and breaks on a player counts as a hit. A hit player should yell 'Hit!' or 'I'm out!', or 'I'm dead!'. Depending on the rules applied, a quarter-size splat on the body usu. counts as a hit. Under more advanced rules even a dime-size splat is considered a hit. The body hit areas are subject to convention. On some fields, head hits are not counted, on other fields all body hits are valid hits. If in doubt a player may demand a 'paintcheck.' The hit player then puts on the elimination tank top to avoid being shot at and goes off the field for a check-up. While going off the field the player can only say 'Hit!' or 'Don't shoot!'. After he or she is off the field the game is resumed. The scoring is different under different regulations but usu. each player is assigned a certain number of points at the beginning of the game. If a player is eliminated with a paint-hit his score is added to that of the opponent. The flag may be captured only by a live player. The flag is declared captured if the player has taken the flag without being

hit and manages to take 2 steps carrying it. According to the international scoring system, a 15-player team can score a max. of 145pts. Each player is worth 3pts. Elimination of a whole team gives the opposing team 45pts. Capturing the flag is 20pts., and bringing it to the base is 80pts. The flag-carrier has a special status. After having been hit he has to follow 2 courses of action, depending on game var. In the first var., the flag-carrier becomes a moving flag station. The player shouts 'Hit!', puts on the elimination tank top and returns the flag to its original location; then he or she goes off the field. While returning the flag the flag-carrier must not pass it to his or her teammates or even inform them about his possession of the flag. In the second var., the flag-carrier remains on the spot and passes the flag to any player closest to him or her. If both teams have managed to capture the opponent's flag the game is played until one team places both flags on its base.

Paintball games run from a few hours to 24hrs., depending on the game format. In most capture-the-flag variations, if no team has managed to capture the flag within the prescribed time limit, the game is played until all players of one team are eliminated. The players' actions and maneuvers on the field are signaled with a system of gestures. For instance, an arm extended to the side means 'enemy spotted'; both arms extended to the side mean 'spread out'; straight arm moved to the waist means 'stand up'; arm movement from elbow to the shoulder means 'attack'; arm raised up means 'single file', etc. A team may set its own signals, unrecognizable to the enemy. Paintball techniques are used in the movie industry and military training. The growing popularity of the sport has resulted in the establishment of numerous national and international tournaments. The most effective assault tactic is the *banzai* attack in which the attack of the players is accompanied with a loud cry of 'Banzai!' to distract the enemy (*banzai* – war cry of Jap. soldiers in honor of the emperor).

Game variations. Paintball is a rapidly evolving sport which has given rise to numerous variations. The most popular scenarios include:

Convoy. One team takes a piece of heavy equipment in a convoy from point A to point B. The cargo can be supply containers or old refrigerators. The opposing team attempts to intercept the cargo and eliminate the escorting players.

Relief. One third of Team A is to take designated defensive positions within 10-20min. The group is surrounded and besieged by Team B. The rest of Team A is to break through the siege and evacuate the surrounded teammates. An additional task of the players under siege can be guarding some 'top secret documents', e.g. a special suitcase or notebook.

Delaying action. The game is played by 2 teams with a different number of players each. The smaller team must get to a designated spot whilst incurring casualties less half that of the larger team. Part of the smaller team must 'sacrifice' itself by delaying the enemy's actions.

POWs. The object of the game is to take a defined number of prisoners, e.g. four. The prisoners cannot be 'killed' but 'wounded' being hit in specified parts of the body, e.g. arms or legs. A player is taken prisoner if he or she is 'wounded' with a paintball and touched by the attacker. The team which takes the required number of prisoners first wins the game.

Airborne Landing. The defending team takes defensive positions on the field. The attacking – airborne landing – team is divided into 3 or 4 groups of players. The attacking players are blindfolded and placed by the referees near the positions of the defending team. The airborne landing groups must find one another and capture the opponent's flag station.

Assault Bunker. One or two makeshift bunkers – cardboard or plywood boards – are placed on the field. The boards should be 2.4x1.2m. Each board has loopholes, 45x7.5cm, located about 30cm from the top edge. Ideally, a bunker should be positioned on a hill for better defense. The objective of the attacking team is to capture the bunker by eliminating all the defending players. The defending team wins if it manages to eliminate all the attacking players.

Defend the Fort. One half of the defending team is located in a makeshift fort or camp at one end of the field. The defenders must stay in the fort for the duration of the game. The attacking players take their positions at the opposite end of the field. Before the assault on the fort the attackers designate an evacuation zone to be guarded by a few players. The attacking team tries to capture the fort by inflicting a

predetermined number of casualties on the defenders. After having accomplished the mission the attackers must retreat to the evacuation zone and then to the starting positions. If the defending team has managed to capture the evacuation zone the attackers must retake it before retreating to the starting positions. To complete the mission the attackers may also be required to collect a trophy from the fort.

Water Rats. The game is played along a river or stream. The 'water rats' team must tug a defined number of rafts a specified distance up or down the river. Usually, there is one raft per 10 players. At least 2 players must be in one raft for the duration of the game. Once eliminated, the rafters must be replaced with other live players. This reduces the number of players who tug the raft and makes the mission more difficult. The objective of the opposing team is to eliminate all the 'water rats'.

Evacuation. The defending team is positioned against an obstacle, e.g. a riverbank, cliff edge, or wall, so it cannot retreat. The only way is to break through the attacking team's lines and get to the base at the opposite end of the field. Players hit in the arms or legs are declared 'wounded' and must be carried on stretchers. If the defensive line is situated

against a riverbank the wounded may be evacuated on rafts. 'Wounded' players remain in play but may not use their weapons. The attacking team wins the game if it manages to eliminate all the defenders, suffering no more than 50% casualties. If even a single 'live' defender is evacuated from the base the defending team wins.

The Big Game. A paintball variation with an unlimited number of players. The teams can consist of a few dozen to a thousand players each. The paintball field is much larger, consisting of a few regular fields with natural cover and numerous flag stations. One game can last up to 24hrs. The complex scenarios include 'hostage rescue', 'civil war', etc.

Apart from elaborate role-playing games and scenarios involving hundreds of players, paintball variations also include smaller tactical formats.

Speedball. The game is played on an open field without natural cover. The field is rectangular, 60m long and 40m wide, or circular, 30m in diameter. It has several manmade bunkers which allow the players to take cover while standing upright. The teams consist of 3 to 7 players each. Speedball may be played in both the center-flag and dual-flag variations.

Attack and Defend. One team defends a single flag station on the field. The other team tries to capture the flag and bring it to its own empty flag base. The game is played by teams of up to 10 players with a

10-min. time limit. A game with bigger teams numbering from 10 to 40 players each, can last up to 20min.

American Football. A center-flag game. Both teams try to capture the flag attacking from opposite starting positions. The team which has captured the flag must break through the opposing team's lines and reach its own base. The game is similar to Amer. football in which the objective is to break through the opponent's lines to score the points.

Annihilator. A game played by small teams consisting of a few players each. The object of the game is to eliminate the opposing team. The game is played with a time limit of 5-10min.

Top Gun. The game is played individually, with a time limit of 5-10min. Each player tries to eliminate all opponents. The winner is the top gun.

Fox and Hound. The game is played by 2 teams: the smaller Fox team and the larger Hound team. The Fox team is given few minutes' lead on the field to take positions wherever they wish. Then, the Foxes try to eliminate the Hounds taking advantage of the terrain and avoiding direct contact with the enemy. The Hounds act first in dispersal but once a Fox is spotted they concentrate fire on

A player takes cover during a paintball game at a park near Coral Springs, Florida. Paintball is a growing 'extreme' sport that boasts 8 million players a year.

him or her. The team which eliminates all the opponents wins the game. The game is played with a time limit of 15-20min.

Tagging the Hounds (a variation of Fox and Hound). Each Hound tagged with paint by the Foxes becomes a Fox. This way the Fox team increases in number. If a tagged Hound is hit back by the Hound team he or she is eliminated from play. A Fox can be eliminated only with a double hit. The game ends when all the Hounds become Foxes or all the Foxes are eliminated.

Pink Meanies. The game is played by 2 opposing teams wearing armbands of different colors and 2 individual players who wear pink armbands. The Pinks are given a few minutes' lead on the field and take positions wherever they wish. Their objective is to eliminate the players of both opposing teams and capture one of the teams' flags. The captured flag must be carried to the opposite flag station. Eliminated players leave the field and after having received new pink armbands they re-enter the game as Pinks. Any team can win if it carries its flag to the opponent's base. The original Pinks may re-enter the game only if newly-made Pinks are on the field.

Rambo. The game is played by many teams of up to 7 players each. Each team has its own flag station. The players, however, act individually. The object of the game is to eliminate as many opponents as possible. The players are marked with identifica-

P

WORLD SPORTS ENCYCLOPEDIA

tion numbers indicating the teams and individuals. The team which scores the highest number of hits wins the game. Occasionally, points can be scored by capturing the flags. In another variation each player is to sneak into the opponents' flag stations and receive a special stamp. The team which gets the largest number of stamps wins. The game is usu. played in several rounds. Each round lasts 30min.

Ten Shots. Teams consist of up to 10 players each. Each player gets only 10 paintballs. The game ends once all the players have shot all their paintballs. The team with the largest number of live players wins the game. There is also a variation with 12 paintballs for each player.

Single Shots. A variation similar to Ten Shots or Twelve Shots using only single shot guns. No automatic or semi-automatic paintguns are allowed on the field. Each player has 10 or 12 paintballs.

Reincarnation. A variation in which any eliminated player can re-enter the game after having washed the paint off.

Detention. A variation similar to reincarnation in which the eliminated player is detained off the field for 1-5min. before he or she can re-enter the game.

History. The sport of paintball first came about in the early 1980s in the United States. The originators of paintball were H. Noel and R. Gurnsey who were practicing survival trials and games. Initially, the paintguns were farmer's cattle markers. In 1981, in Henniker, New Hampshire the first paintball championships were played by 12 people. The sport was popularized by *Time* and *People* in numerous articles written on the subject. In the 1980s the association of the National Survival Game was founded in New London, New Hampshire. Shortly after, the New York Open and national championships were played in the USA. Individual play was soon superseded by team competitions. At present, there is an average of 15 players per team, 40 or 50 at bigger events, and during so-called 'weekend wars' the number of players reaches around 500. The latter enjoy immense popularity in California where each 'army' has its own medical, logistic and helicopter transport units. The oldest and the most no-

A Palant Player, *a bronze statute at the Museum of Katowice, Poland.*

table paintball club is the Navarones, consisting of 2 separate teams: the Navarone Armageddon and the Navarone Apocalypse. An important magazine of international renown devoted to paintball is *Action Pursuit Games* published in the USA. Paintball games are sponsored by numerous international companies such as Rockwell International, McDonnell Douglas, Hughes Aircraft and Marriott Corporation. A paintball event called Mickey Mouse's Jihad is organized in Disneyland. Paintball is still most popular in the USA. In California alone there are more than 50 paintball fields and 20 specialist shops selling paintball equipment and accessories. Every weekend paintball is played by about 100,000 to 200,000 people.

B. Barnes and P. Wrenn, *Paintball Strategies & Tactics*, 1996.

PAIP, a simple form of Eng. sports competition consisting of throwing stones and hitting a stack of pebbles placed one upon another; cf. Pol. >SER.

PA-KUA, 1) the Eng. rendering of the Chin. philosophical term for 8 trigrams; 2) the name of a Chin. martial art *baguazhan*, which belongs to the 'internal' styles.

PALA, *pala corta* or *pala larga* see >PELOTA VASCA.

PALAISMA, Gk. wrestling in general; see >PALE.

PALANKARIS, Basq. name for metal rod throwing, also Span. *lanzamiento de barra vasca* (Span. *lanzamiento* – 'throwing', *barra* – 'rod', *vasco* – 'Basque'). A folk sport derived from crowbar throwing competitions among stoneworkers. The iron rods (*palanka*) used in palankaris are known in various Basq. dialects by the names of *balanka, balenga, balenka, palenka, palanga, budrin-palanga, burdinbarra, burdinaga, burdünbarra, bürdünhaga, espeka, zanka, bermazaki, altxaprima, altxakoda,* and *alzapena*. This rich nomenclature reflects the wide scope of var. of palankaris and types of throwing rods. The shortest rods used in the town of Urraul Alto are 60cm in length and 3cm in diameter; the longest ones common in the province of Guipuzcoa reach 180cm in length. Traditionally, the rods weigh from 8 to 25 Basq. *libras* 'pounds' i.e. 4-12kg. The average weight of a *palanka* varies from 10 to 12 libras i.e. around 5-6kg. The rods come in a range of shapes: straight rods, rods with a cone-like thick end (Span. *cono*) and regular thick-ended rods.

The basic throwing techniques of palankaris were incorporated into the national rules of the Span. >LANZAMIENTO DE BARRA ESPAÑOLA drafted in the 1920s. Therefore, the throwing techniques of both sports are almost identical:

THE OVERHAND THROW, Basq. *zuzenkara*, Span. *a pecho*, also *bularrez*; the thrower grabs the palanka near the heavier cone-like end with one hand and swings it backwards below the line of his shoulders. The throwing arm should be kept straight. With one foot forward placed on the throw line the player swings the rod forward and releases it while straightening his arm.

THE HALF-TURN THROW, Basq. *jira erdian*, Span. *a media vuelta, la media vulta*, also *biraka*. The thrower starts by taking a 10-m run-up. On reaching the throw line he takes a half-turn and then releases the rod in a similar way to the overhand throw.

THE UNDERHAND THROW, Basq. *ankabe, zankabe*, Span. *ankape, debajo de las piernas*, also *lanzamiento entepiernas*. The thrower stands approx. 1m from the throw line. Standing astride he holds the rod near its upper end and swings it between his legs back and forth several times. Having gathered momentum he throws the rod forward.

History. The tradition of Basq. rod throwing can be traced back to the Middle Ages or, as some historians suggest, to the Roman occupation of the Iberian Peninsula. Span. historian, N. Azcona says that Basq. stoneworkers working at the construction site of the Escorial (Span. royal palace) in Madrid during the reign of Philip II used to set up rod throwing contests as forms of entertainment. The following centuries witnessed a rapid development of the rod throwing sports. The most famous Basq. rod thrower of the 18th cent. was probably J.B. Mendizábal. J.M. de Elola, living in the 19th cent., is reported to have thrown iron rods a distance of 122.5 pies – 'feet' (around 37.34m). His relative, J.B. de Elola, from the town of Labaka, allegedly beat him by throwing a rod the distance of 140 pies (around 42.68m). The achievements of the best throwers in the first 2 de-

cades of the 20th cent. lagged far behind their 19th cent. counterparts. J.B. de Elola migrated to S America where he contributed to the popularization of palankaris in Buenos Aires and Montevideo. Another 19th cent. palankaris legend was M. Juaristi alias Artazo, frequently exalted in poetry. After various Span. folk sports had begun to fade away due to intensive urbanization and the growing popularity of modern sports after WWI, the well preserved Basq. forms of rod throwing became the basis for the game's revival all over the country. In 1926, on the initiative of the Span. Athletic Federation an exhibition of Basq. palankaris equipment was opened in Berazuri (Span. Tolosa). During the exhibition one type of rod throwing was selected as model equipment for *barra española*, later popularized all over Spain. The person behind the re-birth of the Basq. sport was J. Iguarán, a member of the Span. Olympic Committee and professor of the Central Gymnastic School in Toledo. In the years 1930-58 nationwide palankaris championships were held in Spain. The most outstanding throwers of the 20th cent. were a Basque, F. Errauzquin, lanzamiento de barra española and palankaris champion of Spain in the years 1933, 1945, 1949 and 1950, and J.G. Iguarán, who scored victories in the years 1953-57. The sport of palankaris has been referred to occasionally in poetry in praise of the best performers and is the subject of the poem *Satai edo balanka* (Rod Throwing) included in the collection *Euskaldunak* (We, the Speakers of the Eskuara Language) written by the Span. poet N. Ormaechei, 'Orixe.'

R.A. Franco, 'Palankaris', DRV, 1983, 87-92; the same, 'Palankaris', JYDV, 1978, 333-350; C. Moreno Palos, 'Lanzamiento de barra vasca', JYTE, 1992.

PALANT, a Pol. bat and ball game. The Pol. name *palant* denotes both the bat and the game (Ital. *pallante* – 'ball player', *palla* – 'ball'; also Ital. *pallara* – 'to play ball'). There are dozens of national and regional var. of similar games. See Swed. >KUNGSBOLL, >SÖT OCH SUR, >TRE SLAG OCH RÄNNA; Fin. >KUNINGAS PALLO, >POLTOPALLO; Norw. >LÅNGBOLL; Dan. >LANGBOLD, >LANGBOLD FRA ANHOLT, >TREMANS LANGBOLD; Ger. >SCHLAGBALL; Holstein >TICKBALL; Hung. >METTEN; Czech >VELKA BABORKA; Fr. >PETITE THEQUE; Slovak >DLHA META; Ukrainian >MIACZ; Belarussian >SOLOWIEJ; Rus. >LAPTA; Serb. >LOPTA; Bosnian >TOPUZ; Croatian >KAPUŚ; Bulg. >KULI, >PERKANICA; Rum. >HOIMA (Transylvanian >HENGERLÉ); Gk. >URUM-TOP; Armenian >RUS-TOPI; Georg. >GAKVRA-BUKRTI; Turk. >CHALITA; Hawaiian >KI-NI-HO-LO, >MELANESIAN BAT AND BALL.

Despite numerous differences palant bears a resemblance in play and techniques to such bat and ball games as Amer. >BASEBALL, Eng. >STOOL-BALL and >CRICKET, Fin. >PESÄPALLO, >PITKÉPALLO, and Dan. >PORTBOLD.

Palant had a few regional and technical variations in Poland such as >PALANT BEZ WYKUPNA, >PALANT Z WYKUPNEM, >PALANT Z MATKAMI BEZ GALENIA, >PALANT Z GALENIEM. In some dialects of the Pol. language the game is called *palaj* and *palantern*. The different rules of the once popular varieties of palant were fixed for the purpose of school games and later refined by the Pol. Federation of Palant Ball (Polska Federacja Piłki Palantowej, PZPP), founded in 1957 in Rybnik. The Federation, however, concluded its activities in 1978. According to Federation rules, the game was played on a rectangular field 50-75m long (depending on the players' age) and 20-25m wide. Inside the playing field in the school variation there was a designated area called the home base in the shape of a half-circle 3m in radius, adjacent to the front line of the field. The batter in the home base first tossed the ball up and then batted it out (unlike in Amer. and Fin. bat and ball games in which the ball is first pitched by an opposing player). The field was divided in half by a centerline 25-30m from the home base. The 5-6m long outside base line was 10-15m from the endline of the field. The outside line was usu. marked with flags. The ball was 17-19.5cm in circumference. It had a rubber core layered with yarn and leather. After hitting a fly ball the batter could score a point if he managed to run to the outside line and return to the centerline without being hit with the ball by the opposing players. The outfield players would attempt to catch the ball on the fly and by throwing it back at the running batter put him or her out. A team's captain called the *matka* (Pol. for 'mother'), batted last and was entitled to 3 successive bats. This way, the *matka* made it possible for the runners on the outside base line to finish the run. The *matka* started his run after the third bat. Once the *matka* managed to run the prescribed distance to the centerline the batting team scored 3pts. The game was played by 2 teams of 12 players each and each match lasted 2x30 min. The refined palant rules approved by the Polish Federation of Palant Ball differed slightly from those of the school version. The home base was a rectangular area 5m long and of the same width as the playing field. The outside base line was 6m from the endline. There was no centerline and points could only be scored by hitting a home run.

History. The traditions of palant date back to the Middle Ages. The game was prob. derived from the same family of games that had given rise to Eng. >ROUNDERS, >CRICKET, or Ger. >SCHLAGBALL. According to the earliest sources, initially the ball was not tossed up by the batter but pitched by an opposing player. This was noticed by an Italian called Gaurino who observed the game in Prague in 1610.

The third ball game which I have seen in Bohemia, unknown in Italy, is a game in which a hard leather ball is used. The players of one team spread out over the field standing 70, 80, and 100 steps from one another, prepared to catch the ball in the air. The players of the other team hit the ball in turns with a rounded stick thicker at the barrel end, three feet in length. The ball can be hit with great speed. The ball is pitched underhand to the batter by another player. The batter may hit the ball high and far away. If the ball is caught on the fly by a fielding player the teams change sides. The batters become the catchers, and the catchers the batters. The game is not really a feat of strength or agility. The players must, first of all, be good runners. The game is good for the frailer youths who run back and forth and push the others or trip them up in a friendly way. We quite liked the Prague game and practiced it very often. The most skillful players came from Poland and Silesia that is from the country of the game's origin, I presume.

According to the well-known specialist on old-Pol. culture, A. Brückner, palant was brought to Poland during the reign of Sigismund III Vasa (1587-1632). More likely, however, the game was known in Poland much earlier. A palant bat called a *piłatyk* was listed in the 14th-cent inventories of the Academy of Kraków (Lat. *pilatus* – 'referring to a ball'). The old-Pol. language knew the expression *galić* which meant 'to pitch the ball and bat it'. The verb was derived from the noun *gała* or *gałka* (old-Pol. for 'ball). The early forms of palant were also present in a few old Pol. sayings such as *Jak kto gali, tak mu odbijają* (As you pitch it, so shall they hit you). K.F. Falibogowski, an old Pol. author mentioned the game in his *Diskurs marnotrawstwa i zbytku Korony Polskiej* (A Discourse upon Waste and Excesses in the Kingdom of Poland, 1625): 'When they play ball, one time one bats, and another time he pitches or runs'. The Ital. origin of the game's name suggests that 'palant' replaced the earlier designation at the time of the strongest Ital. cultural influences in Poland, i.e. during the reigns of Sigismund I the Old (1506-48) and Sigismund II Augustus (1548-72). The game of palant may have been a var. of some Bohemian or Ger. game of Ital. origin, long-forgotten in Italy itself. The game was unknown to the aforementioned Gaurino. Later on, 2 main var. of palant were developed: the folk and the school. The latter was described by J. Kitowicz in *Opis obyczajów i zwyczajów za panowania Augusta III* (Description of Customs and Traditions during the Reign of Augustus III, ed. 1840-41):

The ball game was played as a form of recreation. A ball could be thrown high up in the air and run after [...] some tossed the ball lightly and hit it with a bat sidearm so the ball sometimes disappeared out of sight. Other players looked up in the air and holding their arms up desired to catch the ball. Once the ball was spotted they all ran vary fast to catch it on the fly. If the ball hit the ground the game was lost. There was no wagering, no betting, just pure fun. The game was called palant and it was played not only by the students but also by the teachers and headmasters.

[*O zabawach studenckich*, chapter. II, section 6]

Palant's popularity increased in the 19th cent. After 1918, the game became part of physical education classes. Professional games started to be played after 1945 in Silesia. In the years 1945-52 the best clubs were KS Rój Żory, KS Kuźnia Ligocka, and LZS Boguszowice. In 1952 the first unofficial Pol. Championships were held. After its foundation the PZPP set up a professional palant league. The first champion of Poland was KS Silesia Rybnik in 1957. In 1978, on the initiative of B. Przeliorz the PZPP was converted to the Pol. Federation of Baseball and Softball. Palant lost its range and popularity against the invasion of modern team games due to its being somewhat monotonous, the lack of wider interest from sports authorities and organizations, but also the contemptuous attitude of public opinion, which considered palant an 'unserious' sport. This failed to take account of the enormous popularity and status of similar bat and ball games in other countries, e.g. cricket in England, baseball in the USA, or pesäpallo in Finland. The Pol. 'anti-palant' campaign was displayed in a number of ironic statements ridiculing the sport. The legacy of that campaign is the Pol. expression *Ty palancie!* meaning 'You, blockhead!'. Despite the negative public attitude and the disbanding of the Pol. Federation palant traditions have been maintained in the town of Grabów near Łęczyca. The game is played on a pitch with 2 playing areas marked 'niebo' (Pol. 'heaven') and 'piekło' ('hell'). Every year the Palant Day is organized there.

C. Dobrecki, *Gramy w Palanta*, 1960; T. Gradowska, *Palant i kwadrant*, 1951; J. Jasiński, *Palant*, 1938; Z. Paruszewski, *Palant. Przepisy gry*, 1957; *Regulamin i przepisy gry w piłkę palantową*, wyd. Pol. Związek Piłki Palantowej, 1959.

PALANT BEZ WYKUPNA, one of main var. of >PALANT. The game was described in E. Piasecki's *Zabawy i gry ruchowe dzieci i młodzieży* (The Play and Physical Games of Children and Young People, 1916):

The drawing of field positions is made by placing players' hands one upon another on the bat. The winner becomes the first batter and takes the 'kingdom', i.e. the home base, other players take their positions in the outfield. The batter tosses up the ball with his left hand and hits it with the bat held in his right hand. The batter loses the home base if: 1) he fails to hit the ball 3 times in a row or fouls the ball to the ground; 2) the ball is caught on the fly by an outfielder – with both hands by younger players, and one hand by the older players. In the former case, the batter is replaced by a designated outfielder; in the latter the batter is replaced by whoever has caught the ball.

PALANT BRAMKOWY, (Pol. 'wicket palant'), artificial combination of Pol. >PALANT and Eng. >CRICKET, popularized before 1914 by E. Cenar and described in 2 editions of his book *Gry i zabawy ruchowe różnych narodów* (Sports Games of Different Nations, 2nd ed., 1906). The game is played by 2 teams consisting of 3 to 12 players each. The field is 80m long and 50m wide. Approx. 26m from one end of the field is the wicket; at the same distance from the other end of the field is the base marked with a flag. The ball is 5-7cm in diameter. The batter tosses up the ball (the ball is not pitched by an opposing player like in cricket or baseball) and hits it out with a bat called a *palestra*. After hitting the ball the batter runs to the base and remains there until one of the outfielders catches the ball. Only then can he return to the wicket and score a point. If the fielding team fails to catch the ball the batter returns to the wicket without waiting. The fielding team can score a point by hitting the runner or the wicket. Only the 4 infielders who stand closest to the base or the wicket can get the runner out. If the ball is caught by an outfielder it must be thrown back to one of the infielders. After the wicket is hit teams change sides. After a batter is out another player takes his turn at bat. The batting team cannot score points if any players are on the base. A point can be only scored if the runner covers the entire prescribed distance. Palant bramkowy never enjoyed popularity in Pol. schools. In poorer schools the game lost against games that, for instance, did not require the construction of complex wickets. Simpler games, such as the trad. var. of >PALANT, could be arranged without any extra, sophisticated equipment. Palant bramkowy was a typical example of foreign sports borrowings common in Poland at the turn of the 19th and 20th cent. Borrowed sports often lost their original rules and features (palant bramkowy lacked cricket's bowler and 2nd wicket) and such simplified sports games without a cultural context and tradition were not widely accepted in the Pol. environment.

PALANT Z GALENIEM, a var. of >PALANT, regarded by E. Piasecki as more difficult, but more perfect than >PALANT Z MATKAMI BEZ GALENIA. In 1916, E. Piasecki claimed that palant z galeniem 'used to be a popular sport, but it is neglected at present.'

Rules. The general course of the game is similar to palant z matkami bez galenia, the ball is batted after underhand delivery by an opposing player, in which aspect the game resembles, in part, >SOFTBALL. The pitcher stands on the home base area close to the batter and the pitch is delivered upward not forward. The pitching action is called *galenie* in Polish, hence the name of the game (Pol. *palant z galeniem* – 'pitching palant'). *Galenie* was described by E. Piasecki in his work *Zabawy and gry ruchowe dzieci and młodzieży* (Games and Pastimes of Children and Young People, 1916): 'The pitcher stands on the home base close to the batter and tosses the ball up to the height of his head and jumps aside. Pitching can be repeated if the umpire calls it foul'. According to Piasecki, 'the pitcher is one of the best players of the fielding team (the *matka*, or captain). He stands

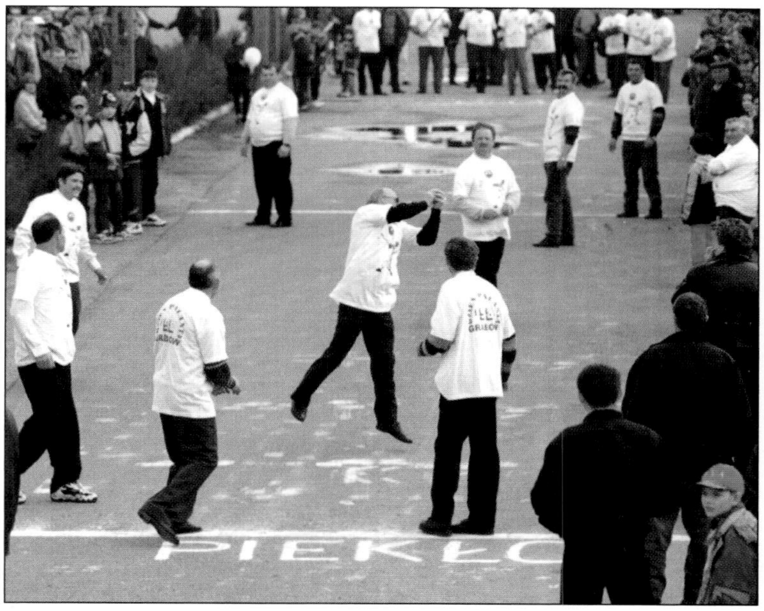

A game of palant in Grabów, Poland.

to the right of the batter, half a step from the home base boundary. First he takes one step forward and holding the ball with a straight arm touches it on the barrel end of the bat. Then, he quickly tosses the ball up and jumps aside to avoid being hit with the bat.' In palant z galeniem the ball may be touched by the body outside the home base area. E. Piasecki defines the game's tactics in the following way:

Batting is more difficult here [...] if, however, the ball is pitched correctly the difference in batting between the two varieties of palant is not that huge. The batter must judge his position from the pitcher carefully as to be sure to hit the ball with the tip of his bat. The runners should remember that they may also be put out by the pitcher. Remaining on the outside base line is often the only possible move. Usually, one infielder should stand directly behind the pitcher and pass the ball to the pitcher after having received it from the outfield. The ball must be passed to the pitcher in a gentle manner.

PALANT Z MATKAMI BEZ GALENIA, one of a few main var. of >PALANT. The rules of the game have been described in E. Piasecki's *Zabawy and gry ruchowe dzieci and młodzieży* (Games and Pastimes of Children and Young People, 1916):

The game is played on a rectangular field 60m long and 25m wide. The area confined by the front line of the field is called the królestwo [Pol. for 'kingdom' – the home zone]. *The home zone extends to the rear without limit. The center base* [Pol. 'półmetek'] *is located in the middle of the centerline parallel to and 25m from the front line of the field. The outside base* [Pol. 'meta'] *is 50m from the front line. The bases are marked with 1.5m-high posts stuck firmly in the ground. Four flags mark the corners of the field; two flags are located on the sidelines 25m from the front line. The wooden bat used for the game is rounded or rectangular with rounded edges, 80-100cm in length, 3.5cm in diameter. The ball is 7cm in diameter and weighs 80g.* [...]. *The teams consist of eleven players each, unless stated otherwise. At the beginning of the game the drawing of team positions is made by placing players' hands one upon another on the bat. A team consists of the captain* [Pol. 'matka' – 'mother'], *the deputy* [Pol. 'wykupnik' – the player who allows the players on bases to run], *and nine regular players called 'kids'* [Pol. 'dzieciaki']. *The batting order is determined by the captain: first, each kid takes his turn at batting, then the depu-*

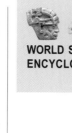

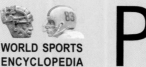

A teenage palant player displaying his bat.

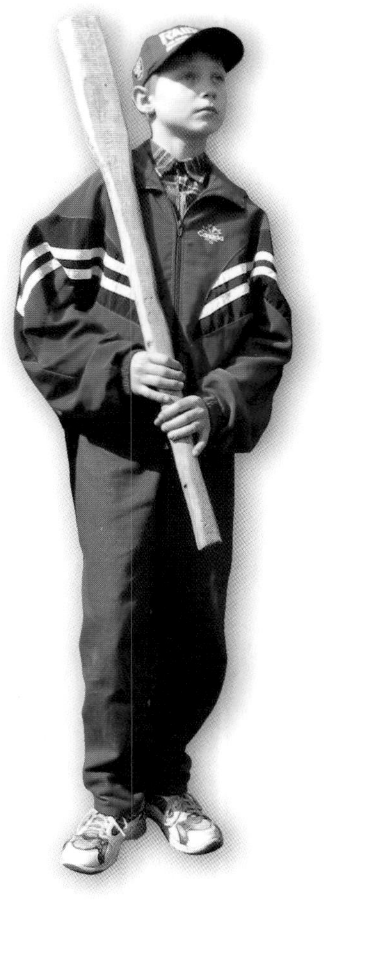

400

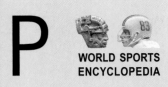

P WORLD SPORTS ENCYCLOPEDIA

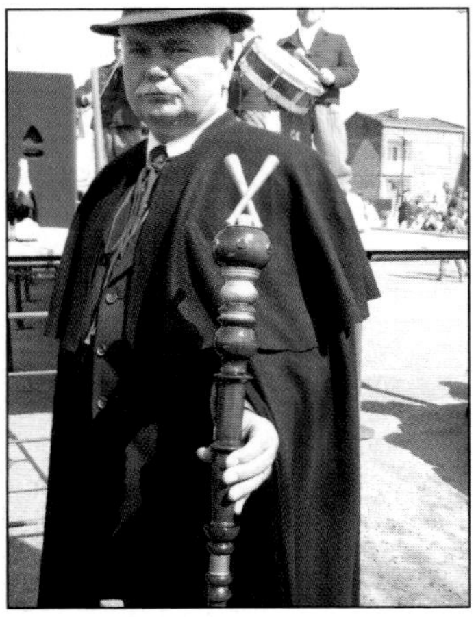

The King of Palant – the master of ceremony during the Palant Day in Grabów, Poland.

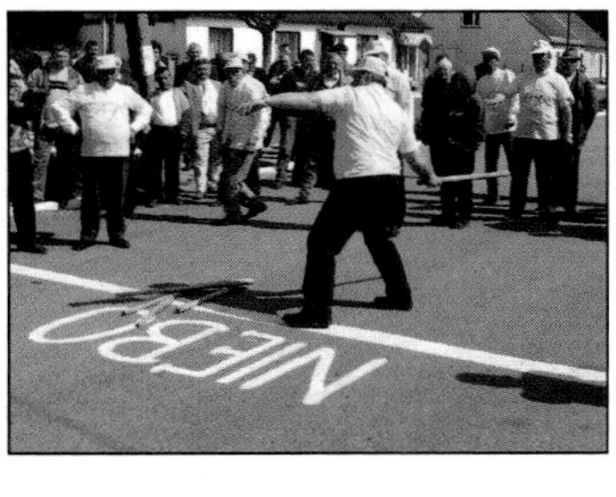

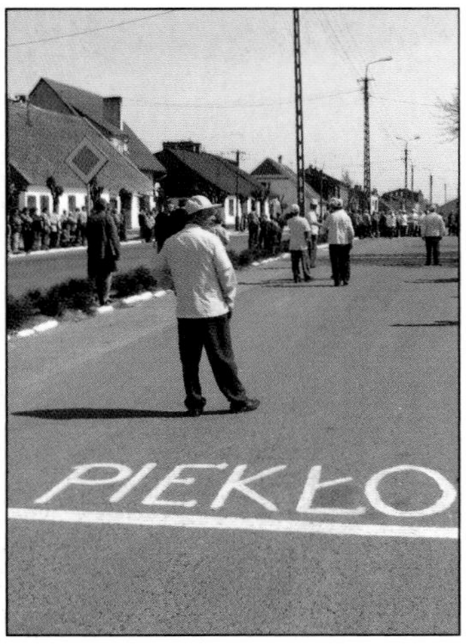

Playing palant in Grabów, Poland: the batter in the 'niebo' (heaven) zone (above) and field players in the 'piekło' (hell) zone (below).

ty bats twice, and finally the captain bats three times. The deputy can bat without waiting for his turn if there are no players entitled to bat in the home zone. After all batting players have been out in the field the fielding team takes the home zone. The batting team may lose the home zone if: a) the batter drops the bat while hitting the ball; b) the batter runs onto the field still holding the bat. After retaking the home zone batting is resumed starting with the player who batted before changing sides. [...] The ball is foul if: a) it is batted out of bounds without hitting the ground or any opposing player; b) it lands on the field before or on the centerline without having hit any opposing player; c) the batter steps out of the home zone while batting. [...] A kid can bat once again (the deputy twice, the captain three times) if he has scored a home run, i.e. has run from the home zone, through the center base, to the outside base and returned to the home zone before his next batting turn. The batter can start running only after hitting a fair ball. The runner can stop at will and return to the home zone or the outside base. The batter cannot score a run if he has been put out or the ball has been lost. Once the ball is lost or returns to the home zone the runner may not continue running but must stop and retreat to the home zone, the first base or the outside base, depending on where he was at the moment the ball was lost or returned to the home zone. To score a run the runner must touch the base post. If the runner crosses the sideline or the backline of the field, the run is foul and should be repeated. However, the runner may be put out while running foul. If the runner has been impeded by a fielder the run is fair and scored. [...] If a runner is out, i.e. hit with the ball by a fielder while he remains outside the home zone or not touching the outside base post, the batting team loses the home zone. A hit is foul if a) before hitting the runner the ball has bounced off any object or the ground; b) the runner was impeded while running; c) the fielder has been running holding the ball in his hand or has held the ball in his hand for more than two seconds; d) if the runner touches the center base post on his way to the outside base. The runner is also out if he touches the ball with any part of his body outside the home zone. [...] If a fielder catches the ball on the fly with one hand it is a 'catch'. After three catches the fielding team takes the home zone. If a fielder is impeded while attempting to catch the ball, it is a catch. [...] A match lasts one hour. If the batting team manages to retain the home zone for half an hour the teams change sides. The team which scores more kreskas (Pol. 'kreska' – 'a mark') *wins the game. The marks can be scored in the following way: a) one mark is scored if all batters have taken their turn at bat and completed a full-run each; b) two marks are scored if all batting players completed full-runs without losing the home zone. The game is controlled by a single umpire who makes decisions on all appeals. If necessary the umpire may be assisted by a home umpire and an outfield umpire.*

Piasecki also provides some additional rules and detailed playing techniques of the game.

The batter stands astride with his left foot near the front line of the field. The ball should be tossed up with the left hand so he can hit it with the tip of the bat. Only then can the ball be hit far out in the field. The ball is hit with a broad swing of the bat held by a straight arm, and with a swift turn of the body to increase the batting force. After batting the batter returns to his starting position. The ball should be hit slightly below its center.

The batter must be careful not to hit a pop-up, i.e. a lob easily caught by the fielders, or a grounder, which is a foul ball. A properly batted ball is one not easily caught and should ideally pass high above the fielders. The ball should also be aimed at those spots on the field which are difficult for fielders to guard by the fielders at a given moment. When receiving the ball being returned from the field to the home zone, the batter must not catch it outside the home zone. In such a case he is out.

The runner should not concentrate only on his speed. He must also watch out for the ball aimed at him. The runner should be always ready to stop, retreat or dodge the ball. The latter requires some skill and agility. If the ball is aimed at the runner's legs or feet he must jump up; if at his head or chest he must bow or squat; or if at the lower part of his trunk he must jump aside or fall to the ground. Sometimes a sharp swerve is enough.

The ball must be caught in one hand after being hit. The catching arm may be gripped by the other hand in support. Ambidexterity is a crucial skill here. A ball passed from another fielder should be caught with both hands in order not to drop it.

A grounder should be stopped with the hand, not the foot. After the ball is picked up it should be passed immediately to a fellow player or returned to the home zone.

He further discusses the game's tactics:

The batting order set by the captain should account for the batting and running skills of individual players. The kids should not hit the ball too lightly and rely exclusively on the batting of the captain and the deputy. The first batter is usually the least skillful. After a worse batter a better one should take his turn at batting and then another more skillful batter. The captain encourages the kids to run only if a run is safe.

The captain and the deputy do not have to use all the bats they are entitled to. If the first bat of the captain or the deputy was far enough so it allowed the runners to return to the home zone, the kids can take their turn at batting.

The runners should proceed along the sidelines of the field to avoid getting out. After a short ball the runner may proceed across the field straight to the center base. In the case of a number of runners being on bases an effective tactic is to run in many directions and along both sidelines in order to confuse the fielders. The runners, however, should avoid running close to one another, in which case they might be easily put out.

The tactics of the fielding team are far more complex. The captain must master the difficult skill of arranging the players' positions on the field. He must take into account the force of an opponent's batting and the overall tactics of the batting team. The fielders should focus on controlling the center base and the outside base. A few worse players should take their positions around the center base so they could easily catch a short ball and put out a runner proceeding to the center base. Better players should be around the outside base (for outs) and the edges and the back of the field (for catches). Standing on their positions the fielders should be careful to not interfere with the runners or intercept the co-players.

Most safely, if trying to get the runner out, the ball should be aimed towards the home zone. If a fielder tries to get out a runner from the sidelines, another fielder should stand on the other side of the runner and be ready to catch a ball which misses the runner. Otherwise the ball could escape the fielders, which would give enough time for the runners to score runs. The fielders can also surround the runner and pass the ball between one another until finding the best moment to get him out. This tactic, however, requires a great deal of coordination and is usually only used by experienced players.

Another tactic may be applied if playing against worse batters. The fielders do not concentrate on catches or outs but return the ball as quickly as possible to the home zone. This way, the fielders make the runners stop, not allowing them to reach the home zone. The batting team may then quickly run out of illegible batters.

PALANT Z WYKUPNEM, a var. of >PALANT. The game resembles >PALANT BEZ WYKUPNA, though it displays some characteristic differences. E. Piasecki in *Zabawy and gry ruchowe dzieci and młodzieży* (The Play and Physical Games of Children and Young People, 1916) describes the game in the following way: 'The outside base, marked with a stone or flag, is twenty steps from the home base. The batter, if he wants to gain the right to 3 extra bats, must hit the ball far enough to be able to reach the outside base and return to the home base without being got out. The runner, who does not drop the bat after hitting the ball, has to touch the outside base with the hand or foot or sometimes hit it 3 times with the bat. The fielders can get the runner out by hitting him with the ball or throwing the ball to the home base before the runner can tag it. In both cases (apart from the other out situations of palant bez wykupna) the home base is taken by the fielder who has got the runner out.'

PALCATY, a. obs. Pol. form of cane fencing (from Hung. *pálca* – 'stick'). The sport of cane fencing as imitation of real fencing was already known in ancient Egypt. Fencing sticks were found in the tomb of King Tutankhamen. In the Middle Ages cane fencing constituted part of knightly education, in some countries, however, a distinction was made between cane fencing as a folk combat art, see e.g. Eng. >QUARTERSTAFF; and the knightly forms of wooden sword fencing and back-sword fencing. As a sports event the various types of fencing were included in the program of the English Cottswold Ol.G. established in 1612 by R. Dover. A similar distinction into plebeian and knightly forms of fencing was known in Japan (>KENDO). In Europe, cane fencing as part of courtly education became immensely popular and widely practiced in Jesuit and Piarist colleges in the 17th and 18th cent. J. Kitowicz (1728-1804) provides descriptions of physical exercises practiced in such 18th cent. colleges:

Besides ball games, another kind of physical exercise practiced by the students was fencing duels using special canes called palcaty. This type of combat training was extremely useful for the young noblemen and followed the tradition of sabre fencing widely practiced by our ancestors. The duels were excellent examples of martial arts mastery. The fencers displayed great mastery of swordsmanship in attack and defense. The defensive techniques had been learnt to a great degree so often an attacker could not easily reach the opponent's face, head or trunk with his cane. Many fencers would become masters who would teach others in the future. Apart from the students, the art of fencing was widely practiced among the professors, both the Jesuits and the Piarists. The students would fight with canes not only during physical exercise classes but also during class breaks. Fearful students who dared not to face opponents in a fencing match were often scolded and ridiculed.

For safety reasons, instead of the wooden palcaty tight straw bundles were used in schools. Ł. Gołębiowski in his work *Gry i zabawy różnych stanów* (Games and Pastimes of Various Social Classes, 1831) wrote that: 'The commonly practiced cane-fencing was often painful for the adversaries and instead of sticks tight straw bundles were used by the fencers.' In course of time, the courtly fencing exercises were taken up by the peasants but the folk variation soon deteriorated. Gołębiowski describes palcaty events set by the servants of Pol. barristers during tribunal sessions in the second half of the 18th cent.

The servants of barristers, solicitors and clients would gather near the town hall after the session had been adjourned. They set up fencing duels in a circle formed by the on-lookers. The canes were made of dogwood or oak. The thinner canes were as thick as a finger; the thicker ones resembled walking sticks. The winner of a series of duels, after artful victory over his opponents was declared the marshal of the circle, the runner-up – the vice-marshal, the third in rank – the instigator and the fourth – the vice-instigator. After the matches all the participants went to the Jews in the market who had to provide gifts for the dignitaries. If any of the Jews refused to donate gifts he would be flogged inside the spectators' circle. The servants then returned to the circle and continued with their competition. Any passers-by of equal rank to the servants or sometimes of higher rank was drawn into the circle and had to fight against an eager adversary. If the newcomer was adequately baptized with a bruise on his face or black eye he was relieved from another fight and became a 'guild journeyman' and joined the circle. If the newcomer was victorious the defeated adversary had to face other opponents until he won or bought himself out. Whoever abstained from fighting was hit with the cane on the head or deprived of his cap or handkerchief unless he bribed himself out. He was freed, therefore, from other duels but was not admitted to the fencing guild and earned an abusive title. If a newcomer challenged the marshal he had to fight first with a few lower rank servants before the match with the champion. Once he defeated the marshal he took his title and was brought to the Jews for free treatment. Sometimes the defeated marshal had to give the winner proper treatment with food and wine, restoring his own honor and reputation. A former marshal could challenge the new winner once again and by winning with the servants first take their positions, gradually rebuilding his lost fame. Occasionally, some professional fencers who happened to be passing by would join the circle and, pretending to be newcomers or cowards beat everybody for the fun of it, including the instigators and the marshal. Onlookers were invited, and reluctant ones forced to fight by the instigators. Serving as seconds the instigators controlled the matches and watched the course of duels carefully to prevent any injuries to the fencers. To avoid any deadly duels outside the circle the cane-fencers had to apologize to one another after the duel. The marshal, and in his absence the vice-marshal, made decisions on all appeals. The custom of cane fencing was also common at sessions of country and burgh courts but the participants had no right of wine and food treatment by the Jews. Palcaty was also practiced in schools and manors.

A few factors contributed to the fall of palcaty in 19th-cent. Poland. First of all, formal military education of young Poles was almost non-existent in the partitioned country. Only in some colleges such as the Krzemieniec College in the years 1805-31 or the Warsaw Cadet Academy until 1830, was palcaty practiced as a form of physical and military training. The Pol. army was disbanded after 1830 in the Rus. sector of partitioned Poland as well as the autonomous Pol. educational institutions. Any continuation of Pol. military tradition was strictly prohibited in the schools of the Prussian sector of Poland undergoing gradual germanization. The policies of Austrian Chancellor Metternich left no room for the Pol. tradition in the Austrian sector either. By the time of liberal politics of Emperor Francis Joseph of Austria the sport of palcaty had already disappeared. Instead, sports fencing was introduced mainly to private colleges run by foreign masters and later practiced in numerous sports and gymnastic societies such as the 'Sokół' Gymnastic Society. Modern regulations preventing injuries sustainable during fencing events and exercises as well as the emergence of blunt blades, masks and protective pads replaced palcaty as a form of fencing practice.

Ł. Gołębiowski, *Gry i zabawy różnych stanów*, 1831; J. Kitowicz, *Opis obyczajów i zwyczajów za panowania Augusta III*, 1840.

PALE, Gk. *pale* – wrestling of ancient Greece (old Gk. *palaiein* – 'to wrestle', 'to fight hand-to-hand'; *palaisima* – 'a wrestling bout'; see Mod. Gk. *pale* – 'wrestling'). Wrestling with no particular reference to any of the two known styles was introduced into the program of the 18th Ol.G. in 708 BC. In different periods of wrestling development the rules and styles may have differed. Weight divisions were not existent and the wrestlers were divided into boys and men on the basis of their physical ability rather than age. All wrestling bouts, including the qualifying rounds and finals, were conducted on the same day in Olympia. A competitor with no opponent in the qualifying round received a bye to the next round. He was called *efedros* – 'the one who rested through the fight'. If he became the winner he kept the sobriquet. Pale wrestling was divided into 2 basic types. In the first one the wrestlers stood upright facing each other and got hold of the opponent's shoulders or trunk above the waist. This type of wrestling was known as *orthia pale* (*orthos* – 'upright'), *orthopale* (*orthios* – 'straight up, raised up') or *stadaia pale* (*stadaios* – 'standing upright'). The fighter who knocked an opponent over 3 times became the winner. A bout was won if any part of the opponent's body apart from the feet touched the ground. A fall was pronounced successful even if a wrestler touched the ground for a very short time. Unlike in modern wrestling, pinning of the opponent was not necessary as it would have required a fighting on the ground and thus contradicted the trad. *orthia pale* principles. If both wrestlers fell to the ground points were not awarded and the fight was resumed from the starting position. The wrestler who obtained a triple take-down was given the name *triakter*. The other wrestling type consisted of performing feints by wrestlers fighting on the ground. It was known as *kato pale* (*kata* – 'downwards'), *alidensis* (*alindeomai* – 'to wallow'), or *kylisis* (*kylisis* – 'to wallow in dirt'). A bout lasted until one of the wrestlers acknowledged defeat. Strangling was allowed in *kato pale*, in which the sport resembled >PANKRATION, however hitting the opponent with hands or fists was forbidden. Both basic types of *pale* were practiced separately in the Olympic palaestra. The name of *palaestra* denoting a gym was derived either from the name of Hermes' daughter Palaistra who had been the legendary inventor of wrestling or from the Gk. term *pale* denoting wrestling in general. Wrestling also constituted part of the >PENTATHLON. Despite its brutality pale was regarded as a fairly ethical competition in the whole history of ancient sport. An anonymous ancient epigram gives the characteristics of a Spartan wrestler: 'Others used stratagems but I won with my strength as all the sons of Sparta did.' Centuries later, the same ancient epigram became the inspiration for the Pol. poet J. Kochanowski (1530-84) who wrote a short poem with reference to Spartan wrestling *Z greckiego* (From the Greek):

Here I am a wrestler not from Messana or Argos,
Praising Sparta, motherland of mine
By the blood of the sons of Lacedaemon
I am strong with the strength of my fortress.

In Gk. mythology wrestling can be traced back to the fight of Heracles with the giant Antaeus, son of Ge and Poseidon. Antaeus was invincible as long as he touched Earth, his mother. Noticing this, Heracles grabbed the giant around the waist and holding him aloft crushed the giant above the ground. The name *pale* was used for the first time by Homer in his description of a wrestling bout between Ajax and Odysseus included in Book XXIII of *The Illiad*. The rules of pale bouts of the ancient games, incl. the Ol.G., were supposedly drawn up by a Sicilian wrestler Orikadmos. Hitting with hands and grabbing the opponent's genitals were forbidden, which is why in some var. of pale the wrestlers wore special protective pouches. Matches were held within a marked area. If a wrestler found himself out of bounds the match was stopped by the referee and resumed in the center of the area from the starting position. Many wrestlers took advantage of the vague rules and made an opponent surrender by inflicting pain on him. For example, Leontiscos of Sicily would crack the knuckles of his opponents, winning once in the Ol.G. and once during the Pythian Games. A wrestling hold that would result in cracking the opponent's knuckles was called *cheirismos*.
Among the characteristic holds practiced in pale the most popular were: *hamma* – lit. 'knot', 'tangle', a kind of lock in a clinch; *anchein* – neck hold;

Wrestlers, a marble group from a Roman portal, Museo Torlonia, Rome.

ankyryzein – hook; *rassein* – a hold resulting in a take-down; *drattein* or *helkein* – dragging the opponent by his arms; *treachelizein* – neck hold; *dialambanein* – waist hold; *perisfingein* – locking opponent's hands; *mesolabe* – waist hold and lift-up; *anabastasai, eis hypsos* – lifting the opponent head down. Before a fight wrestlers oiled their bodies. The purpose of greasing a wrestler's body in oil has not been satisfactorily explained. Most likely the body oil served as a form of sun-screen during the long wait before the fight, a protection against sand or a way to ease the opponent's brutal grips. After the match the sand and oil was taken off the wrestlers' bodies with special scrapers called *stlengis*. One of the best known ancient sculptures presents a wrestler who is scraping oil and sand off his body (Lissipos' *Apoksymenos*).
In both pale varieties the wrestlers were matched by drawing lots. The fights were accompanied by flautists. Living at the turn of the 2nd and 3rd cent., a Gk. writer Philostratus in *Gymnasticus* mentions that a good wrestler should have a proportional body, sensibly long neck, not too short as the head should not look like it is tucked in between the shoulders, broad chest, thick ribs and a flat belly. The ankles should be strong so as to resist the pressure of the opponent.
History. The earliest evidence of highly organized Gk. wrestling dates back to the Cretan-Mycenaean Age (c.3000-1200 BC). *The Iliad* by Homer serves as exceptional literary evidence of ancient wrestling. Book XXIII of *The Iliad*, devoted to the funeral games held in honor of Patroclus who had been killed at Troy, includes a description of wrestling duel between Ajax and Odysseus:

Forthwith up rose great Ajax the son of Telamon, and crafty Ulysses, full of wiles rose also. The two girded themselves and went into the middle of the ring. They gripped each other in their strong hands like the rafters which some master-builder frames for the roof of a high house to keep the wind out. Their backbones cracked as they tugged at one another with their mighty arms and sweat rained from them in torrents. Many a bloody weal sprang up on their sides and shoulders, but they kept on

striving with might and main for victory and to win the tripod*. Ulysses could not throw Ajax, nor Ajax him; Ulysses was too strong for him; but when the Achaeans began to tire of watching them, Ajax said to ulysses, 'Ulysses, noble son of Laertes, you shall either lift me, or I you, and let Jove settle it between us.' He lifted him from the ground as he spoke, but Ulysses did not forget his cunning. He hit Ajax in the hollow at back of his knee, so that he could not keep his feet, but fell on his back with Ulysses lying upon his chest, and all who saw it marvelled. Then Ulysses in turn lifted Ajax and stirred him a little from the ground but could not lift him right off it, his knee sank under him, and the two fell side by side on the ground and were all begrimed with dust. They now sprang towards one another and were for wrestling yet a third time, but Achilles rose and stayed them. 'Put not each other further,' said he, 'to such cruel suffering; the victory is with both alike, take each of you an equal prize, and let the other Achaeans now compete.'

[trans. S. Butler]

* The iron tripod was the prize awarded for victory.

The duel between Ajax and Odysseus may be an indication of an attempt to codify wrestling rules: the wrestlers know the general rules before the fight without any prior arrangements. The legendary codifier of ancient Gk. wrestling c.900 BC was probably Theseus, the son of Aegeus, king of Athens (or Poseidon in other sources) famous for killing the Minotaur in the Labyrinth at Knossos and the crafty use of Ariadne's thread. There are, however, several other Gk. myths that explain the origins of wrestling. Another popular myth traces the origin of wrestling to a duel between Theseus and Cercyon, the son of Poseidon, king of the seas. The duel brought punishment upon Cercyon for piracy and bad treatment of his daughter. The philosopher Polemon (4th cent. BC) credited the invention of wrestling to Theseus' trainer, Forbas of Athens. According to Gk. historiographer Istros of Cyrene (3rd cent. BC) it was Athena who endowed Theseus with superb wrestling skills. Other Gk. historians trace wrestling origins back to the duel between Heracles and the giant Antaeus; the fight of Hermes and Peleus against Atalanta; or the struggle of the river-god Achelous with Triton, son of Poseidon. According to the Gk. writer,

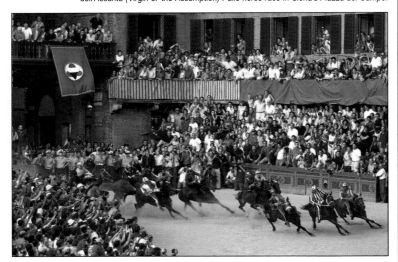

Above: A rider is thrown from his mount during the Palio of Siena horse race in Siena, Tuscany, Italy. Below: Riders push their horses around the St. Martino turn during the Madonna dell'Assunta (Virgin of the Assumption) Palio horse race in Siena's Piazza del Campo.

Palet sur terre

WORLD SPORTS ENCYCLOPEDIA

Philostratus (c.170-249 BC) the originator of wrestling was Palestra (Gk. *Palaistra*), the daughter of Hermes who 'spent her youth in the woods of Arcadia and invented wrestling. The whole land enjoyed the invention as the men discarded the iron weapons of war and they competed with one another naked making the stadiums much sweeter places than military camps.' It is still uncertain whether the name *pale* comes from the goddess *Palestra* or the other way around. A *palestra* was also the place where the

art of wrestling was mastered. (In the literal and figurative meaning *palestra* as a place of competition has been adopted in some Eur. languages to denote the Bar, as a place for lawyers' competition). Initially, the palestra was an outdoor square, then the name was applied to a building in which wrestling was practiced. Later on, the name came to mean any gym. The wrestlers were known as *palestrites*. Philostratus argued for the usefulness of wrestling skills during war and claimed that the battle of Marathon (490 BC) turned out victorious for the Spartans who ferociously attacked the Persians after all the warriors' weapons had been broken and defeated them in hand-to-hand combat. In a similar manner, Plutarch described the victory of the Thebans over the Spar-

tans at Leuctra (371 BC). Pale became part of the Ol.G. in 708 BC during the 18th Olympics as a separate event and part of the >PENTATHLON. In the pentathlon, wrestling was the last and probably most decisive event. Some competitors became wrestling and pentathlon winners during the same Ol.G., e.g. Eutelidas of Sparta who won in the boys' event during the 38th Ol.G. in 628 BC. A remark about a monument erected in honor of Eutelidas, incl. in Pausanias' *Description of Greece* (V, 9, 1 and VI, 15, 8-9), is the earliest example of a sculpture depicting an Olympic champion.

Considerable attention was paid to combat techniques. The master of wrestling skills was Aristodemos of Elis, the wrestling champion of the 98th Ol.G. in 388 BC and the two-time winner of the Isthmian and Nemean Games (mentioned by Pausanias VI, 3, 4). After the victory of Cratinos of Ageira (276 BC) a monument was erected in honor of both the wrestler and his trainer in recognition of his superb wrestling training.

The most famous ancient wrestler was Milon of Croton who won in 6 consecutive Olympics (540-516 BC) as well as in six Pythian, nine Nemean, and ten Isthmian Games. Milon was known for numerous demonstrations of his skills, e.g. he was said to have killed a bull with one punch. As a disciple of Pythagoras Milon participated once in a debate in his master's house during which he knocked down the central support column. He managed to support the roof himself until all the guests left the building safely. Overestimation of his strength was the cause of Milon's death. Once in a forest he found a cracked tree with wedges driven-in and by putting both hands into the crack he tried to split the tree apart. The wedges fell off loose and his hands got stuck in the tree. Defenseless, Milon was eaten by wild beasts. Other outstanding ancient wrestlers included: Timasitheos of Corinth who defeated Milon in his last Olympic fight; Hipposthenes of Sparta who, like Milon, scored 6 consecutive victories in Olymia; his son Etoimokles, the winner of five Ol.G.; Amesinas of Barka, famous for practicing his wrestling skills with bulls; Aristodemos of Elis who was never held at the waist by any opponent; and Isidoros of Alexandria, who, as Flegon of Tralles wrote, 'has never touched the ground.'

Pale wrestling faded away together with other ancient Gk. sports but was still practiced later in Thrace, in the north of Greece and former Gk. colonies under Byzantine rule. The greatest Thracian games with pale as a single event were held in Tomi from the 2nd cent AD and Philippopolis (present-day Plovdiv) in honor of Apollo Kendrissos. E. Sholastikus mentions a certain Marcianus who gained enormous fame after his victories in those games (450-457 AD) and in turn was elected local ruler of Thrace. Games which included pale similar to the Olympic Games were held in the former Gk. colonies in the beginning of the 6th cent. and since 510 AD in Antioch.

Pale wrestling faded out in Thrace after the conquest of the territory by Slavic tribes who introduced a different type of wrestling brought from the Asian steppes. After the fall of Constantinople and the Byzantine Empire the tradition of 'Mediterranean' wrestling was continued by the Turks occupying the Balkan Peninsula. The ensuing conflict of the 2 wrestling types was manifested by a dispute over the oiling of wrestlers' bodies before the bouts. While the Bulgarians disapproved of body oiling the Greeks and Turks maintained the ancient tradition. Pale wrestling was practiced at the court of the Byzantine emperors until the 13th cent. and the conflict between the 'Slavic-steppe' and the 'Greek' wrestling styles continued. In 851, at the Byzantine court a wrestling bout was held between a member of the Bulg. legation and an officer of the Imperial guard, the later Emperor Basil the Macedonian. The Byzantine chronicler, J. Genesius claimed that the Bulg. ruler Boris sent his top wrestler to Constantinople on purpose to show the superiority of his people. Unfortunately, the Gk. style of wrestling failed to suit the Bulg. fighter as he was utterly defeated by Basil.

PALEDOÙ, a Bret. game in which metal discs or quoits are thrown at different targets.

PALET, in full, *le jeu de palet*, a Fr. game consisting of tossing hand-size metal discs or quoits.

PALET D'ILLE-ET-VILAINE; a Bret. game of >QUOITS practiced in the province of Ille-et-Vilaine. The players stand 5m from a wooden board placed

on the ground. They try to toss metal disks or quoits (*palet*), 5cm in diameter and weighing about 130g, at a small quoit called the 'master', (Fr. *Maître*) located on a board. The game is played between single players or teams of 2-4 people.
F. Peru, 'La tradition populaire de jeux de plein air en Bretagne', LJP, 1998. Consultant:: G. Jaouen, FALSAB.

PALET SUR ROUTE, a Fr.-Bret. game of >QUOITS. The players stand 15m from a circle drawn across the road. A small quoit, the 'master', is placed in the middle of the circle. The game consists of tossing quoits weighing about 350g and 6.5cm in diameter into the circle so that they land as close as possible to the master.
F. Peru, 'La tradition populaire de jeux de plein air en Bretagne', LJP, 1998. Consultant: G. Jaouen, FALSAB.

PALET SUR TERRE, LE; a Bret. var. of >QUOITS, in which 2 small earth mounds are built 17m apart. The opposing players toss metal or brass disks, 220g in weight, 6cm in diameter, so that they land on the opponents' mound, as close as possible to a small quoit called the 'master' The team which scores 12pts. first is the winner. The game is played by singles, doubles and by teams of 3 or 4 players each.
F. Peru, 'La tradition populaire de jeux de plein air en Bretagne', LJP, 1998. Consultant: G. Jaouen, FALSAB.

PALET, LE JEU DE, a Fr. game consisting of tossing hand-size metal disks.

PALIN see >CHUECA

PALIO, Ital. *Corsa del Palio*, horse races of medieval origin staged in a few Ital. towns. The earliest mention of palio dates back to 1224. The most famous races have been held continuously in Siena since 1482. The name *palio* denotes the silk painting of the Virgin Mary carried in a procession. The religious service held around the painting commences the race. During the ceremony the horses are blessed. The race is staged on the central square of the city, Il Campo, twice a year; on 2 Jul. and 16 Aug. A few days before each event, i.e. 29 Jun. and 13 Aug. respectively, the horses are classified. The August winners hold their titles until the following year. The horse riders represent 17 city districts, the *contrada*. In earlier times the number of districts was higher. The present-day district boundaries were set in 1729 by the Medici town governess, Duchess Vidante Beatrice di Baviera. In the August race the representatives of 10 best districts can compete. Each district has its own symbol, colors and patterned clothes worn by the participants. The deep-seated tradition of palio accounts for the fact that during the races husbands and wives coming from different districts separate in order to support their teams. The racers must circle the central square 3 times. Sharp bends around the square resulting from its irregular shape, esp. those near the Casato and San Marino streets, are particularly dangerous to the riders. Fatal accidents and severe injuries sustained by riders and horses are not uncommon. Despite increasingly harsh social criticism the course of the competition has not been moderated and the races continue.

PALLA A CACCIA, an old Ital. var. of >PALANT, similar to Ger. >SCHLAGBALL. The purpose of the game was to cover a specified running distance after the ball is batted by a player of the batting team (Ital. *battitori*). The opposing team (Ital. *cacciatori*) would try to prevent the runner from accomplishing his goal by throwing the ball at a target or the batting team players.
Enciclopedia dello sport, 1965, vol. N-Z, 144.

PALLA A DISCO, a var. of >PALLA A SFRATTO, consisting of slinging the ball in a similar manner to a discus throw. The field is 60x30m with two throw lines, each running 10m from one end of the pitch. Other details and differences between palla a disco and palla a sfrato remain unknown.
Enciclopedia dello sport, 1965, vol. N-Z, 144.

PALLA A SFRATTO, a popular Ital. 19th cent. game (Ital. *palla* – 'ball' + *a* – preposition + *sfratto* – 'throwover') still played today on a field 100m long and 25-30m wide. Each team numbers 5 players. A match lasts 2x20 min. (boys' game 2x10 min.) with a 5-min. break in between. Ital. *sfratto* means throwing the ball over the 'put-out line' marked at the end of the field. The game begins from the 'baseline' 15m from the 'put-out' line. The leather-covered ball with a thick 9cm-long strap handle attached is about 1.5kg in weight and 50-56cm in diameter. In the jun-

ior division 1kg balls (50-56cm in diameter) are used and smaller ones in the boys' division. At present the game is practiced by the athletes of the Ital. Gymnastic Federation. The game has different varieties, e.g. *palla vibrata*, >PALLA SPINTA, *palla al Balzo*, and >PALLA A DISCO.
Enciclopedia dello sport, 1965, vol. N-Z, 144.

PALLA AL MURO, the name of 2 games; 1) a game mentioned by Julius Pollux (2nd cent. AD) consisting of hitting a ball against a wall. A player who caught the ball on the fly became the winner and meted out slaps to the losers; 2) poss. Ital. version of >PELOTA (Ital. *palla* – 'ball' + *al* – preposition + *muro* – 'wall').
Enciclopedia dello sport, 1965, vol. N-Z, 144.

PALLA ALLA GABBIA, Ital. women's ball game. The ball is 75cm in diameter and covered in canvass (Ital. *palla* – 'ball' + *alla* – 'to, in' + *gabbia* – 'cage'). The goal is a netted cage 45cm high, 120cm wide and 4m long. The field is 42x30m. The ball can only be pushed or thrown into the cage with the hands. The number of players is not specified and a match may be played by up to 20 people. At the beginning of the match both team captains hold the ball up in the air standing on the end line. The ball must not be carried, it can only be passed or dribbled.
Enciclopedia dello sport, 1965, vol. N-Z, 144.

PALLA CONTESTA, a basketball-like game played without baskets. The teams of 5-10 players each struggle to maintain possession of a large ball for as long as possible (Ital. *palla* – 'ball + *contesta* – 'competition, dispute, quarrel'). The field is 20-40m long and 10-20m wide. The match is played in downs. After the first toss the referee notes for how long the ball remains in possession of one team. The next down starts after the team loses the ball or commits a foul. If the opposing team manages to keep hold of the ball longer than the first team it scores 4pts. The duration of the game is not specified.
Enciclopedia dello sport, 1965, vol. N-Z, 149.

PALLA DI CERCHIO, the name given to an Ital. basketball game by Prof. M. Pastorino from Florence. The game has been modeled after Amer. basketball but it displays several differences (Ital. *palla* – 'ball' + *cerchio* – 'ring, loop'). Pastorino was one of the promoters of the first national palla di cerchio championships held in Venice in 1920. Later the game became identified with basketball as *palla al Canestro* and then *pallacanestro*.
Enciclopedia dello sport, 1965, vol. N-Z, 144.

PALLA MAGLIO, an Ital. game similar to >PALLAPORTA, >U TRUCCU, and Flem. >BEUGELEN. The aim of the game is to drive a ball through an iron wicket stuck in the ground; cf. >PALL-MALL. Poss. the old Pallamaglio Street in Turin derives its name from the game. The name *palla maglio* can also denote other mallet and ball or bat and ball games. This can be confirmed by former application of the Ital. name to >GOLF, >CRICKET or historical associations with >FIELD HOCKEY.

PALLA RIBATTUTA, an Ital. ball game (Ital. *palla* – 'ball' + *ribattuta* – 'bounced, returned'). The game is played by 2 teams of 10 players each on 20x8m court. The ball used for the game is 15cm in diameter. The game was invented by Prof. E. Ferrauto in 1930. The ball is played with the hand after it bounces off the ground and it is returned by the opposing players on their playing area. The aim of the game is to volley the ball to the opposing team and make it touch the opponent's court before it can be returned. Scores are counted as in tennis i.e. 15, 30, 40, and game. A match is won by a team which wins 5 games.
Enciclopedia dello sport, 1965, vol. N-Z, 153.

PALLA RILANCIATA, an Ital. volleyball game invented by Prof. E. Ferrauto c.1930. The teams consist of 9 players each. The leather-covered ball is volleyed over a net spread across the middle of the court (Ital. *palla* – 'ball' + *rilanciata* – 'to return'). Palla rilanciata differs from >VOLLEYBALL as to the way the ball is returned. Unlike in volleyball the ball is first passed to the player in the middle of the court and then it is returned to the opposing team. The court is 21x9m and the net is hung 2.20m above the ground. Each half of the court is divided into nine 3m-wide squares. The net is the dividing line of the 3m-wide central neutral zone.
Enciclopedia dello sport, 1965, vol. N-Z, 153.

PALLA SPINTA, an Ital. push ball game (Ital. *palla* – 'ball' + *spinta* – 'pushed', *spinger* – 'to push'). The game is played with a football-size ball on a field 40x16m by 2 teams of 5 players each. The field is divided into 2 playing areas by the throwing line (Ital. *linee di lancio*) which must not be crossed by the players. Each playing area is divided in half by the depth line (Ital. *linee di fondo*). In order to score a point the ball must be thrown over the opponent's depth line. The teams stand facing each other. The players stand in 2 rows, 3 in the first row and 2 in the second. After the starting signal the first row players throw the ball forward trying to pass it across the opponent's depth line. The ball must be thrown with both hands only and must not be kicked. A player who has caught the ball on the volley is entitled to 3 leaps forward holding both feet together. A team loses the game if its depth line has been crossed by the opposing players 2 times.
Enciclopedia dello sport, 1965, vol. N-Z, 153.

Dosso Dossi, Pallone, c.1515, fresco.

PALLAPORTA, Ital. game similar to Flem. >CLOSH and >BEUGELEN. The game consists of throwing an orange-size ball through a wicket. The game also bears a resemblance to Ital. >U TRUCCO and >PALLA MAGLIO as well as Port. >JOGO DO ARCO. Practiced in the Lipari Islands off the coast of Sicily.

PALLE MAILLE, a Fr. var. of Ital. >PALLA MAGLIO. It most likely influenced the development of Eng. >PALL-MALL.

PALL-MALL, an obsolete Eng. game consisting of driving a wooden ball through 2 iron wickets placed at the opposing ends of the playing field using mallets (Ital. *pallamaglio* <Ital. *palla* – 'ball' + Ital., Lombardian *maglio* – 'crooked stick'). The game bore a resemblance to the later >CROQUET. It enjoyed enormous popularity in 16th and 17th-cent. London in the former Pall-Mall alley (present-day The Mall) near St. James's Park. The abbreviated name was prob. coined by the pall-mall players. Today the area encompasses Pall Mall, Pall Mall End and Pall Mall Plaza. According to S. Pepys, the alley was about 240m long in the 17th cent. The surface of the alley was 'dressed with powdered cockle-shells'. Pall-mall was the favorite game of James II, king of England. An incomplete description of the game can be found in *Sports and Pastimes of the People of England* (1810, II, 96) by J. Strutt. In 1845, during demolition of an old building in The Mall some pall-mall balls 31cm in circumference were found (at present in the Brit. Museum). The game's origins date back to the Ital. cultural influences in Elizabethan England. The name might have been borrowed from Ital. >PALLA MAGLIO or, to some degree, it might have been adopted in England via Fr. >PALLE MAILLE.

PALLONATA SENESE, the old men's ball (Ital. *pallonata* – 'balloon' + *senese* – 'old'). Ital. medieval game played by 2 teams, the 'reds' and the 'whites' consisting of 150 players each. The players try to gain possession of a ball dropped onto the field from

a place called *torre del mangia* 'the grub tower' and carry it to a designated point. The game is mentioned in a chronicle from 1407. In following centuries the game was played during major holidays. The precise details of play remain unknown.
Enciclopedia dello sport, 1965, vol. N-Z, 155-156.

PALLONCINO PIEMONTESE, Piedmont ball, a var. of >PALLONE AL BRACCIALE PIEMONTESE (Ital. *palloncino* – 'small ball' + *piemontese* – 'of Piedmont'). A ball game consisting of hitting a small leather ball, 12cm in diameter, with a wooden handle called a *cacciotino*. Unlike in pallone al bracciale, the handle is prism-shaped and has a plain surface on its upper part.

PALLONE AL BRACCIALE PIEMONTESE, Piedmont fistball similar to >PALLONE ELASTICO. The ball used for the game is 9cm in diameter, 200g in weight. The ball may only be hit with a cogged wooden cylinder (*bracciale*) weighing around 1kg,

inside which there is handle called a pin or peg. A team loses a point if one of the players is hit with the ball. The thrown ball may be caught by the defenders who wear leather knee and shin pads. The first Ital. pallone al braciale piemontese championships were held in 1912 in Vercelli; cf. >PALLONE AL BRACCIALE TOSCANO.
Enciclopedia dello sport, 1965, vol. N-Z, 156.

PALLONE AL BRACIALLE, a ball game played in Italy and S France, similar to Ger. >FAUSTBALL, Fr. >PAUME and Eng. >LAWN TENNIS. It consists of hitting a ball over to the opponent's playing area using a wooden handle, a type of glove (Ital. *bracciale*), worn on the player's forearm. According to Ital. sports historians the tradition of pallone al bracciale stretches back into antiquity. The game was described by the Ital. A Scaino da Sala in his ball-game manual *Trattato del gioucco della palla* (Treatise on Ball Games) and J.W. Goethe in *Italian Journey* (*Italienische Reise*, 1786). At present, the game is played in the Emilia province on the Lombardy-Tuscany border. The name *pallone al bracciale* may also denote football (cf. >CALCIO).

PALLONE AL BRACCIALE TOSCANO, a fistball game popular in Tuscany but also played in other regions of Italy. The air-filled, leather-covered ball is 12cm in diameter and weighs 340g. It is hit with a handle weighing approx. 2kg. The playing field is 90-100m long and 16-18m wide. The ball is hit against an 18-20m-high wall. A match consists of 4 rounds. The winning score in each round is 15pts. Each team consists of 3 players (*terziglia* – 'three'): the batter (Ital. *battitore*), the receiver (Ital. *spalla* – 'arm'), and the defender (Ital. *tercino*). At the beginning of the game the ball is tossed to the batter by the 'mandarin' (*mandarino*) who is not a player of any team. After the ball bounces off the wall it is received by the opposing team's *spalla*. The teams throw the ball alternately. Points are scored depending on the number of return faults made by the opposing team. The

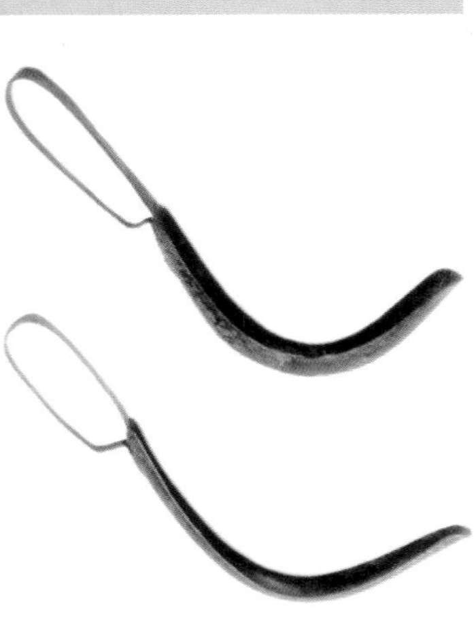

Strigils like these were essential equipment for athletes, who used them to cleanse their bodies of sweat, dust, sand, and oil.

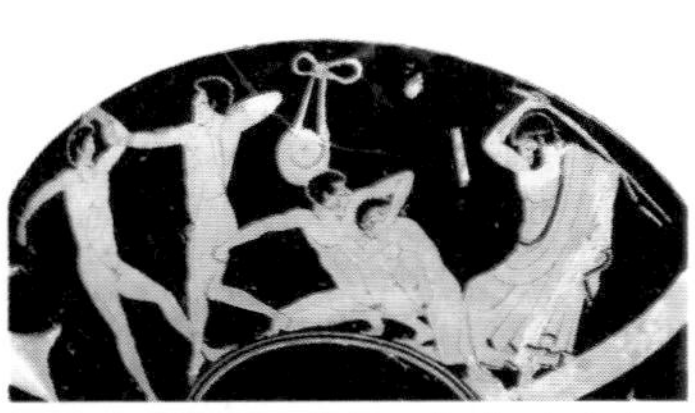

Most of the struggle in pankration took place on the ground. Although the rules were pretty well defined, many athletes tried to avoid them, as portrayed on this Greek drinking cup. The trainer on the right is about to strike one of the athletes with his cleft stick for gouging out the opponent's eye.

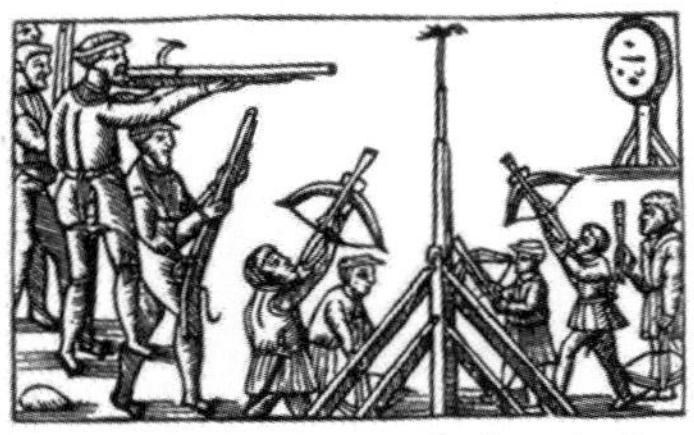

Papingo shooting.

players wear white shirts, pants, and socks with red and blue stripes. In professional matches public betting is made on the field. The first Ital. championships were held in Macerata in 1936.

Enciclopedia dello sport, 1965, vol. N-Z, 156.

PALLONE ELASTICO, a game using a soft, elastic ball, popular in C Italy. Its var. were known in ancient Greece and Rome. The game is also popular in Piedmont. The rectangular, hard-ground field is 96m long and 15m wide (if situated by a wall) or 20m wider (no wall). The rubber ball, 10.5cm in diameter and 180g in weight, is hit with bare or covered hands (fists). The game is played by 2 teams of 4 players each. Each game consists of 11 rounds. Italy's first championships were held in Turin in 1912 (the winner was the team from Mantua). In 1930 the Ital. Federation of Pallone Elastico was formed. The game was mentioned by J.W. Goethe.

Enciclopedia dello sport, 1965, vol. N-Z, 156.

PALMARIS, a term meaning: 1) ancient Roman games held in commemoration of a military success, Lat. *palma* – 'palm sprig' being the symbol of victory, shortened form of *ludi palmaris*; 2) ancient Roman hand ball game, poss. a var. of >LUSUS PILAE CUM PALMA.

PALO DE MAYO, Span. for 'maypole'. A custom brought to some S Amer. and C Amer. countries by Eur. colonists, esp. Germans and Anglo-Saxons, and also to Nicaragua by the Bohemian Brethren. As a result of confrontation with the cultures of the Native Americans and African slaves the Amer. custom of maypole dancing gained its own specificity and became markedly different from its Eur. original. The Eur. tradition of decorating the pole with spiral stripes (Span. *sintas*), dancing around it, and wrapping the pole with the stripes has been sustained. The novelty was the introduction of dancing in pairs (boy-girl) to S Amer. rhythms full of erotic symbolism. By the end of the dance the boy falls to the girl's feet and she dances over him slightly lifting her skirt. Unlike in Europe, the lavish pole decorations are enriched with flowers plaited in wreaths. While in Europe the maypole dancing symbolizes the approaching summer, in C and S America palo de mayo is held during the rainy season, in winter. In the opinion of W. Krämer-Mandeau the Lat. Amer. var. of palo de mayo 'has lost the crucial links with its Eur. archetype and sustains the tradition only partially.' Cf. Pol. >GAIK MAJOWY, Ger. >MAIBAUM, Eng. >MAYPOLE.

W. Krämer-Mandeau, 'Tradition, Transformation and Taboo. European Games and Festivals in Latin America, 1500-1900', IJHS, 1992, 1.

PALO LUCIO, Span. for 'a slippery pole'. A var. of Span. folk sports competition consisting of climbing a greased pole. In genuine Span. varieties it was associated with the cult of individual Christian saints. The sport became widespread among numerous Span. colonies in Lat. America, esp. in Nicaragua and among the Taos Pueblos in Mexico. It was also known in Bolivia where in 1840 it grew to the rank of a folk game sponsored by the Jesuit monastery in Chiquita. The Jesuits funded prizes which were placed on top of the pole such as scissors, spectacles or scarves. The original Span. competition with prizes suspended from a ring placed on top of the pole was known as >CUCAÑA, LA. In the moment a competitor reached the top of the pole trumpet and drum music began to be played by a folk band.

Pankration. A Greek vase.

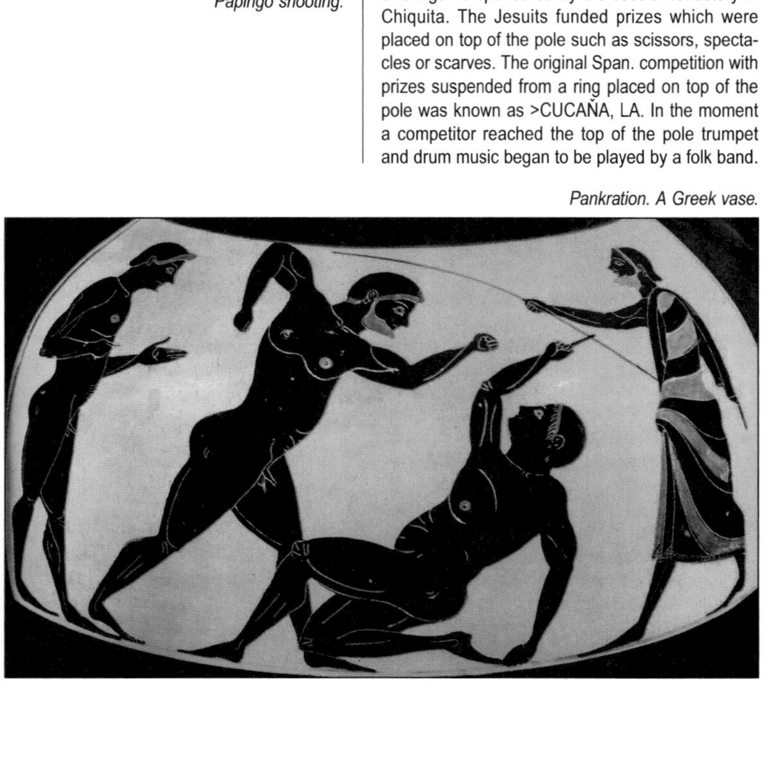

Palo lucio was often part of a more general holiday of >PALO DE MAYO. See also >GREASED POLE, >MÂT DE COCAGNE, >WERN.

PALVANI, Afg. var. of wrestling derived from the Pehlivan tradition. See >PEHLIVAN WRESTLING.

PANGWE WRESTLING, popular in the past in the south of Niger. The Ger. anthropologist G. Tessman described it as follows: 'one can see wrestlers who hold their opponents trying to trip them up. Apart from that they may do anything they want to outsmart their opponent'.

A. Taylor Cheska, 'Wrestling', TGDWAN, 1987, 56; G. Tessman, *Die Pangwe,* 1913.

PANKRATION, (Gk. *Pagkrátion*; *pag* – 'all' + *krateo* – 'to show power'). A sports event of the ancient Ol.G. consisting of a no-holds-barred bout between 2 fighters, similar to modern ultimate fighting events. The fight was waged until the submission of one of the competitors. In 648, pankration was introduced into the XXXIII ancient Ol.G. Initially, the pankratiasts used holds borrowed from wrestling but also such techniques as breaking and twisting arms and legs, eye gouging, nose breaking and biting. The rules of pankration were codified c.440 BC by Leucaros of Acarnania. The code prohibited hair pulling and defined the ceremony of fight initiation and rules of submission. A fighter could surrender by raising his index finger, as in boxing or wrestling, or tapping the opponent on the shoulder. As victory was secured by submission the pankration events were boycotted by the Spartans who considered all forms of surrender disgraceful. The fighters who won in pankration and boxing or wrestling were given the title of *paradoksonikes* i.e. 'miraculously victorious'. The most famous *paradoksonikes*, Teagenes of Thesally was the boxing and pankration champion (twice at the Ol.G. in 480 and 476 BC) and he also won 10 times at the Isthmian Games, 9 times at the Nemean Games, and 3 times at the Delphic Games (mentioned in Pausanias' *Description of Greece*: IV, 6, 5-6; 11, 2-9; 15, 3). Owing to the brutality of fights and their debilitating effects, in the 3rd cent. BC the judges forbade the participation of pankratiasts in other events. If there was only one fighter who came forward to fight he was granted a victory called *akonti* – 'without touching the sand'.

The decline of ancient Games led to the gradual disappearance of pankration, except for some old Gk. colonies, e.g. Corsica, where it has survived until modern times as a form of regional sport called *ghjusta*, practiced during the local votive festival *roumavage*, and Fr. Provance, where it is known as *brancaille*. Since the 1960s, a number of attempts have been undertaken to reinstate pankration by e.g. the International Union of Pankration and Associated Disciplines (Union Internrationale de Pankrace and Disciplines Assimilees) estab. in 1990 by Règis Renault, the World Pankration Federation, and the European Federation of Pankration. New forms of pankration are a much more sublime form of old bouts fought in different weight categories. National federations of various countries, esp. in Europe and the USA, are affiliated with one of the existing international federations. There is a tendency to develop pankration as a form of counteracting the inflow of Asian martial arts. During the 2004 Ol.G. in Athens pankration will be a non-mdeal demonstration sport.

PANUKUNUKU, a type of Maori tobogganing practiced on wet sand, commonly known as >RETI.

PAOQIU, an Old Chin. var. of team handball.

PAPEGAUT, LE, a Fr. var. of >PARROT SHOOTING, an extravagant form of shooting at live parrots, brought to Europe from Africa by returning Crusaders, popular at aristocratic and royal courts of medieval Europe. In some countries, instead of parrots other birds were used as shooting targets; see Pol. >COCK SHOOTING, and Ger. >KÖNIGSSCHIEßEN. The parrots were shot at with bows and arrows, crossbows and firearms. Using live birds as targets soon went out of fashion, however, and the shooters replaced them with metal or wooden parrot figures. Papegaut shooting at inanimate targets was then extensively practiced by various shooting societies. The sport had many varieties in different Eur. countries, e.g. >POPINJAY in England, >PAPINGO SHOOTING in Scotland, >SKYDE PAPEGØJEN, AT in Denmark, and >PAPENGOY in the Netherlands. Until the 1550s, annual papegaut championships were held by independent, local rulers in all large towns of Brittany. The winner won the title of the 'parrot king' and he retained it, enjoying numerous privileges and rewards, until the following championships.

F. Peru, 'La tradition de jeux de plein air en Bretagne', LJP, 1998, 38-39.

PAPENGOY, a Du. var. of >PARROT SHOOTING, popular in the Middle Ages. First, live birds were shot at with bows and arrows and crossbows. Using live bird targets served usu. as a display of wealth and extravagance of the organizer of the shooting contest. With time, the live birds were replaced by wooden or, more rarely, metal figures representing parrots; see also Eng. >POPINJAY, Scot. >PAPINGO SHOOTING, Dan. >SKYDE PAPEGØJEN, AT, and Fr. >PAPEGAUT, LE. In countries where parrots were hardly or not available at all, roosters, pheasants or other brightly feathered birds were used as shooting targets; see Pol. >COCK SHOOTING, and Ger. >KÖNIGSSCHIEßEN.

PAPER CHASE, also *paper chasing* or *hare and hounds*, one of the earliest forms of cross-country running, over a distance of 8-10mi., esp. popular in Brit. public schools of the 18th cent. One of competitors is chosen to be the 'hare', the others are 'hounds' who chase him. The hare sets off first and leaves a trail of paper scraps to be followed by the 'hounds' who start running fifteen minutes after him. The hare can fake the trails by marking diversions over short distances but he must drop the scraps regularly. The hounds try to reach a designated 'home' before the hare. If they fail to do so the hare wins the race. In Wales, a similar game is known as Hunt the Fox. In Cornwall, a paper chase involves the hare performing songs. If he is overtaken by the hounds, the hare must sing the following song:

Uppa, uppa, holye
if you don't speak
my dogs shan't folly

or:

Whoop, whoop, and hollow!
Good dogs won't follow
Without the hare cries, Peewit

or:

Sound your holler,
or my little dog shan't foller.

Paper chases are still held in many Brit. schools. Brit. cross-country runners are, in fact, sometimes called harriers, after the small hound used to chase genuine hares. A var. of Brit. paper chase was introduced in the early 19th cent. to Poland by a great Pol. anglophile Prince A.J. Czartoryski, as part of PE classes in the renowned Krzemieniec College; cf. Pol. >POLOWANIE. In Denmark, a similar cross-country event was known as >RÆVEJAGT.

J. Arlot, 'Paper-Chasing; Hare and Hounds', OCSG, 1975, 467 and 747; A.B. Gomme, 'Hare and Hounds', TGESI, 1894, I, 191.

PAPINGO SHOOTING, a Scot. var. of >PARROT SHOOTING, a medieval form of archery, consisting of shooting at a live bird, and later at a wooden bird figure, with the use of longbows and crossbows; formerly known as *papegault* (from Fr. >PAPEGAUT, LE) or *papejay* (from Eng. >POPINJAY). The tradition of papingo shooting is maintained in the town of Kilwinning, Scotland, where archers positioned near the belfry shoot at a bird figure mounted on the spire of Kilwinning Abbey.

Papingo shooting was a popular, extravagant pastime of the rich nobility of medieval Scotland. King James I (1394-1437) ordered in one of his decrees that every Scotsman should undergo archery training from the age of twelve. In 1457, James II ordered all landlords in Scotland to hold military sports competitions at least 4 times a year. They included archery, fencing and local varieties of papingo shooting. Noblemen who missed shooting contests had to pay two-shilling fines. In 1564, a Scot. archery team challenged 6 Eng. archers and defeated them in 3 events. Archery by that time was so popular in Scotland that it had to be curbed as 'religiously inappropriate'. In 1574, pastors from Edinburgh banned shooting contests during Lent. A great supporter of papingo shooting was R. Hamilton, a pastor from St. Andrews. Another endorser of papingo competitions held after services, and one of the leading Scot. ar-

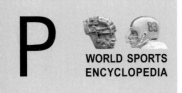

chers, was Pastor Portfield. The records of the city of Ayr mention that in 1595 the Dean of Guild gave five pounds 'for taffatie to the youth for the bend of papingo' (the term 'bend' and later 'benn' signifies a band of cloth worn around the waist or as a sash, which was destinated as the annual prize for papingo shooting in Killwinning). In 1598, the burgh council of Ayr set up a shooting competition for the Silver Hagbut. In 1609, the city records mention again that 6 pounds were given 'in favouris of the archaris and youth of this burgh' to purchase a papingo bend for the competition winner on the condition he would hand the bend to his successor the following year. Similar information can be found in the municipal records from the years 1610-13, 1615, 1616 and 1619-24. The burgh council spent on all sports contests about nine percent of its budget. The competition in Ayr was held in an area of the city called Low Green – a municipal park existing until today. The parrots used for papingo shoting were so common in Scotland that the poet David Lyndsay (c.1486-1555) used the bird as a motif in his famous satire *Testament or Complaynt of Our Soverane Lordis Papyngo* (1530, published in 1538). The poem is a complaint made by a dying royal parrot, which advises the courtiers and criticizes court abuses. Lyndsay's parrot does not die of an arrow but it falls from a tall tree, swept by the wind, as it was too weak to stay on a branch. In the Scots language 'to shoot a parrot' had meant to burst the balloon of conceit and vanity.

One of the largest papingo shooting centers was Edinburgh. 16th and 17th-cent. sources refer only to 3 places in Scotland where papingo shooting was commonly practiced: Irvine, Maybole, and Ayr in Ayrshire. Papingo shooting in Maybole was mentioned by W. Scott in his novel *Old Morality* (1816) in which a fictional Dalserf shooting contest is described. During the Eng. Civil War, also affecting Scotland, papingo shooting went into demise. The sport was revived during the Restoration, first in Irvine in 1655. Papingo shooting was also practiced in other places, e.g. in Kilwinning Abbey in the years 1688-1870, and revived in 1948 under the auspices of the Kilwinning Ancient Society of Archers. Kilwinning became a papingo center thanks to an Edinburgh merchant W. Baillie (1656-1740). In 1688 he bought a plot of land in Monkton and moved to his uncle's manor in Kilwinning. Soon, another great Scot. archer, H. Stevenson, came to live 3mi. from Kilwinning. The presence of those outstanding archers raised the prestige of the town, hitherto known only as a small trade center. Kilwinning was given its city charter in 1889; today it proudly maintains the papingo shooting traditions; see also >PAPENGOY, >SKYDE PAPEGØJEN.

M. Buchanan, *Archery in Scotland. An Elegant and Manly Amusement*, 1979; J. Burnett and R.H.J. Urquhart, *Early Papingo Shooting in Scotland*, Review of Scottish Culture, 1998, 11, 4-12.

PARA WHAWHAI, the Maori name for a school of warrior education which includes exercise of hand-to-hand combat and weapon skills.

PARACHUTING FOR THE DISABLED, a form of >COMPETITIVE PARACHUTING practiced by the disabled accompanied by a fully able instructor.

Paragliders sail towards the Öludeniz laguna, Turkey.

Paragliding at Öludeniz, Turkey, the home of the annual Öludeniz International Games, which bring thousands of devoted paragliders from all over the world to the beautiful Turkish coast.

PARADIS, LE see >FA KOR.

PARAGLIDING, a form of human flight performed with the use of a special flying apparatus called a paraglider, designed for free soaring. The paraglider is a parachute-like canopy without a frame, constructed of rip-stop nylon and steering cords. The sinking speed of a paraglider is about 1.6m/sec.; the wing speed is 35km/h. Paragliding pilots take advantage of thermals (rising air currents) and can remain airborne for hours. The record distances covered by a paraglider reach over 300km.

History. The first flight attempts with the use of apparatuses heavier than air go back to the 19th cent. One of the pioneers of air gliding was a Pole J. Wnęk who flew self-constructed gliders in the village of Odporyszów, near Dąbrowa Tarnowska, in the years 1866-69, i.e. 25yrs. before the experiments of the Ger. engineer and aeronautical pioneer, O. Lilienthal. For take-off J. Wnęk used a specially designed ramp placed on the belfry of the local church. Taking advantage of thermals, he was able to cover a distance of 1.5 to 3km. Wnęk's experiments made many envious and scared. In 1869, before a flight one of his assistants cut the steering cords and Wnęk fell to the ground from a great height and died 3 weeks later. O. Lilienthal flew his glider for the first time in 1891. In the years 1891-96 he made more than 2,000 flights, covering the distance about 500m each time. Using ridge-lifts Lilienthal gained in height over the place of launch. He died in 1896 after his biplane model crashed in flight. Today, it is O. Lielienthal who is considered the father of air gliding, while J. Wnęk who had far more achievements has been completely forgotten. The Lilienthal Medal estab. in honor of the Ger. engineer has been awarded in the sport of hang gliding until the present day.

In the 1960s F. Rogallo of NASA constructed the first modern hang glider, designed as a parachute for spacecraft reentry. Rogallo's project was, however, rejected by NASA, but it was soon put to use in civil aviation. After a number of construction improvements the hang glider became a safe apparatus used for high altitude flights. Along with the development of parachuting sport the problem of precise landing emerged. The ordinary parachutes with round canopies offered little possibility of directional control. The search for more precise steering and landing devices led to the construction of the self-inflatable wing, i.e. the gliding parachute. This type of apparatus was easily maneuverable and could be foot-launched from gentle slopes. The implementation of the gliding parachute was regarded for many years as the birth of the paragliding sport, practiced first in Lake Placid, NY. For the first time the gliding parachute was described in the *Parachutist* magazine in 1968.

According to X. Murillo, a paraglider pilot living in France, the first slope-launched flights were performed in the early 1960s by the American D. Barish, an engineer working for the US Air Force in Dayton and for NASA. In 1955, he constructed the 'Vortex Ring' consisting of 4 flexible, rotating wings. In 1964, Barish designed a NASA parachute to be used for spaceship reentry. Its canopy, called 'Sailwing', had a single rectangular surface divided into 3 sections. The first flight with the use of the new canopy was made in Oct. 1965 in Bel Air Catskills, New York. This date can be seen as the beginning of modern paragliding, although Barish himself admits that similar flying apparatuses could have been used in other countries before. The Sailwing was improved in 1966 by the addition of 2 more sections, large flight stabilizers and much longer connecting lines. Barish made frequent flights on the Sailwing in various US ski centers, including the slopes of Mount Hunter. Low altitude gains (below 30m) and frequent landings on treetops made the Sailwing go into decline in the late 1960s. The 1970s saw rapid improvement of the paraglider's construction. The modifications included a larger number of wind-catching cells, thin profiles, rounded edges of attack and improvements in materials. The wing itself was also lengthened.

Initially, paragliding developed in the Alps where it was distinct from parachuting. The experience of hang-gliding pilots as well as thermal and ridge rising lifts were extensively used by paragliding pilots in order to stay aloft for the longest time possible. A popular var. of the sport is powered paragliding, in which a paraglider is propelled by a special backpack engine, without the assistance of wind or thermals.

The first Paragliding E.Ch. were held in 1988 in France; the Paragliding W.Ch. took place in Kössen, Austria in 1989. Paragliding was one of the constituent events of the World Air Games in Turkey (1997) and Spain (2001). In the former, the first place was taken by H. Miller (UK) on the NOVA Nexon paraglider; the second by R.F. Rodriguez (Spain) on UP Escape; and the third by M. Brunn (Austria)

Paragliding: classical (above) and motor (below).

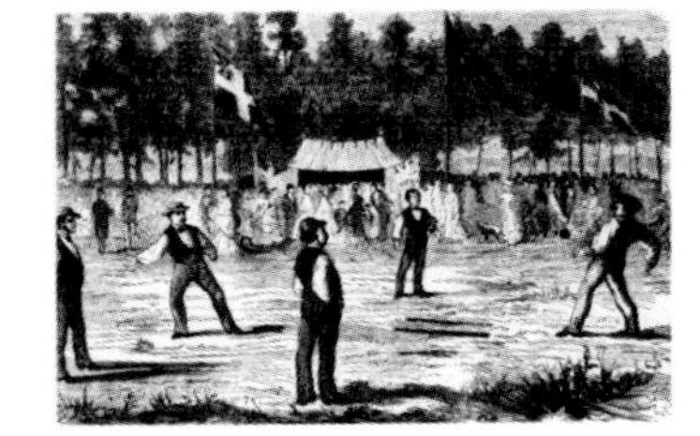

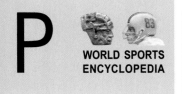

Pärk on a 19th cent. illustration.

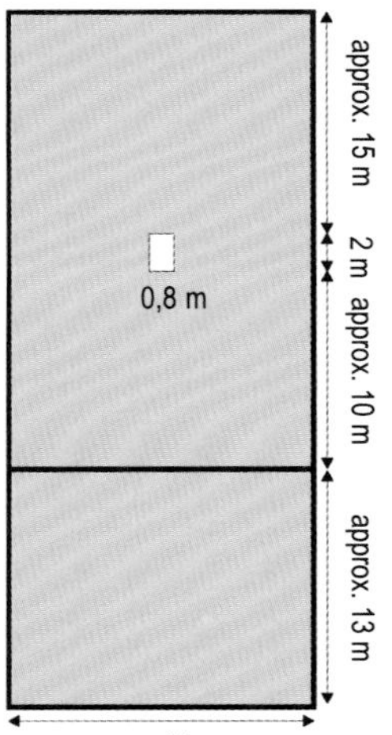
approx. 15 m
2 m
approx. 10 m
approx. 13 m
0,8 m
approx. 15 m

The court for playing pärk.

also on Nexon. In the powered paragliding category the winner was R. Morillas (Spain), followed by J. Moussy (France) and V. Orazi (Italy). In the team event the best was Spain before France and Italy. During the WAG in Spain the first place was taken by L. Donini (Italy) on Gradient Avax; the second by C. Tamegger (Austria) on Gin Boomerang; and the third O. Rosell (Germany) on UP Gambit. The best team was Switzerland, followed by Germany and Italy. In powered paragliding the first was R. Morillas, second C. Moldonado, and third N. Muelas – all from Spain; in the team event the first was Spain before the Czech Republic and Russia. Apart from the World Air Games the most important paragliding event is the Paragliding W.Ch. consisting of a series of events held in various countries. The leading paragliding pilots according to PWC ranking are H. Bollinger, P. Berod, and P. von Kanel from Switzerland; C. Muller from Canada; and B. Goldsmith from the UK. The most outstanding female pilots are L. Crandal from Denmark, N. Nussbaum from Switzerland, P. Krausova from the Czech Republic, and A. Trudel from Germany. The governing body of paragliding is the FAI.

Consultants: Paweł Szukała; Kadri Tuglu (Öludeniz International Games).

PARAWING SAILING, a sport in which competitors plane across a wide water, ice or land surface using various devices or vehicles, being towed by a special wind-catching parachute-like canopy called parawing. The devices include skis, water skis, grass skis, ice skates, roller skates or tricycle buggies. The plane of the parawing is 25-120sq.ft. (0.9-4.7sq.m). The pilot steers the parawing using a special handle attached to the canopy with strings.

History. Parawing sailing was originated by W. Beringer of Germany in the early 1980s. He modified a regular hang glider by the addition of a special steering handle with 3 strings attached to the center and the edges of the canopy. On the initiative of Beringer, nicknamed the king of the parawing, the International Parawing Club was founded. In the early 1990s parawings were used for Antarctic expeditions by R. Messner and A. Fuchs, who thanks to the wind-catching canopies could cover up to 100km a day. The parawing was also taken advantage of by M. Kamiński of Poland, the conqueror of the North and South Poles (1996). In 1992 parawing sailing became immensely popular in the USA, when a kite manufacturer H. Schepker and skier G. Theriault, inspired by W. Beringer, commenced mass production of parawings. Thierault was the first to perform parawing feats on snow and grass in the United States. In 1993 he founded the Amer. Parawing Association and started the publication of the Parawing News bulletin. In 1995, C. Meding took part as the only parawinger in the 15th World Ice and Snow Sailing Championships in Madison, Wisconsin; cf. >ICE BOATING, >ICE SKATE SAILING, >ROLLER SKATE SAILING, >SKI SAILING, >KITEBOARDING.

G. Theriault, 'Sailing, Parawing', EWS, 1996; 'Parawing News', Bulletin of the American Parawing Association.

Goblet, China, Tang dynasty, 8th cent., incised gilded silver. Two horses bolt in a flying gallop, while one of the riders executes a Parthian shot, a technique introduced into China under the Hans (206 BC-220 AD) by nomads from the North-West.

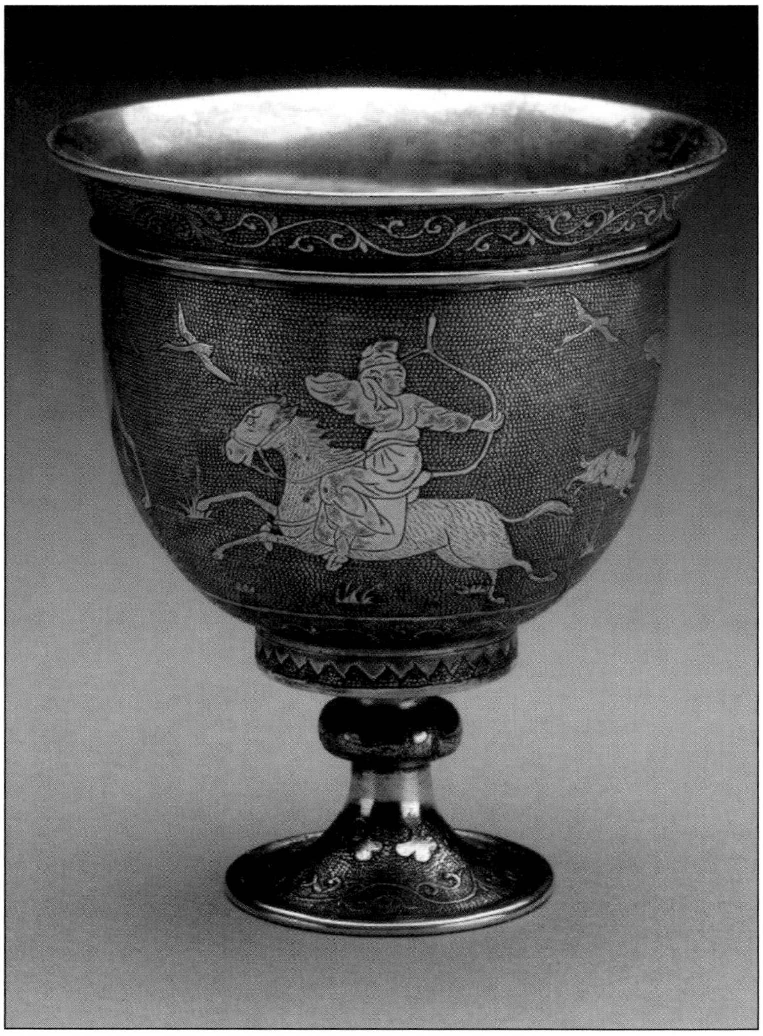

PARDON, LE, a Fr. church festival. In the Fr. and Bret. tradition the day of indulgences was a day of various folk games and competitions. In numerous Catholic parishes the day of the games fell on Saturday but sometimes the games lasted until Tuesday. In Brittany, the long-lasting celebration of indulgences yielded a tradition of folk games held on Monday after the main religious observances. The day of the games was known as *ad Pardon* or simply as *ad* or *had*. The main event of the schedule of the games was >GOUREN and various feats of strength.

F. Peru, 'Le tradition populaire de jeux de plein air en Bretagne', LJP, 1988.

PAREJAS, Span. name for parade and horse-riding shows held every year during the carnival in San Domingo.

PARISH TOP see >TOPS.

PÄRK, also *pärkspel* 'pärk game' [Swed. *pärk*, Lower Ger. *Pferch*, Frisian *perc* – an enclosed space], an old Germanic game ('square-and-border') dating back to at least the Middle Ages, and today mainly played in the island of Gotland in the Baltic Sea as well as in some other regions of Sweden, where it became popular at the turn of the 19th and 20th cent. The game is believed to have originated in the Lower Ger. area but it may also have had links with tennis-like games played on the Walloon-Flemish border in Belgium, and the Frisian game of >KAATSEN. The Ger. sports historian H. Gillmeister claims that such games once spread across much of Europe but the relative isolation of Gotland helped a unique variant develop and settle there. Several facts point to historical relations between various such games, including the use of balls made of 8 straps of leather, and the practice of challenging the opponents by reading a letter calling them to a duel (Swed. *vågbref*). Also, the moment during the game when a team wins ground from the opposing team (see below) is called *kas* in Swedish, while similar games in western Wallonia (the Fr.-speaking part of Belgium) use the term *casse* or *chasse*. Similarly, the line demarcating the area for the next bat is termed the *chase* in the Eng. tradition (>ROYAL TENNIS).

Rules. The game is played on a grass pitch about 40m long and 15m wide. The ball is 10-15cm in diameter and is made of cork or felt (more recently, rubber), covered with leather. An underarm serve is employed, and during the game, the ball may be hit with the open hand or kicked. In older, informal versions of the game, the number of players varied between 4 and 12. Today, there are 7 players in a team. At some distance from one of the shorter sides of the pitch, the actual *pärk* is located. This is a rectangle, 2x0.8m in area. The *pärk* is demarcated by wooden poles with a piece of rope suspended on them. The shorter back side is the so-called *bakstickans linje* (Swed. 'back sticks line'). About 8-10m towards the centre of the pitch from the *pärk*, there is the *stötlinje*, or middle line, dividing the pitch into 2 uneven parts. These are assigned alternately to the 2 teams who take part in the game. The first serve is played by the attacking team from the middle of the *stötlinje*. This team, called the 'outer side' (*utelag*), plays on the part of the pitch without the *pärk*. The team who defend the *pärk* are called the 'inner side' (*innelag*). The attacking team have to serve the ball so that it bounces within the *pärk*. If this happens, the best player of the defending team, called the 'park knight' (*pärkkarl*), who is usu. also the team's captain, is supposed to strike or kick the ball back after the first bounce. The ball may not bounce twice. If he succeeds in doing so, the attacking team have to strike the ball back again after the first bounce and so on. The game is suspended after one of the teams allow the ball to bounce twice. The place where this happens is marked with a line called the *kas*. This stage of the game is termed *spel på kas*. The objective is to win as much ground as possible. The *stötlinje* is then moved within the inner (*inne*) area between the original *stötlinje* and the *bakstickans linje*. A *kas* is won if (1) the inner side fail to intercept the ball after the first bounce in their territory; the line is then moved to the location where the ball was finally intercepted; (2) the inner side succeed in striking the ball back after the first bounce but the stroke is not strong enough; the attacking team then have the right to 'kill' the ball within the inner area. A new *stötlinje* will be drawn at the location where this happens. A rolling ball cannot be hit – it should be stopped with the foot and returned for the next serve. The outer side may choose not to receive the ball after the inner side return the serve. In such a case, the outer side go on to the next serve. This does not influence the score, and the game continues until 7 serves have been played. The attacking team try to hit the ball so as to move the *kas* backwards beyond the *pärk*. When they succeed in doing so, the first stage of the game ends, and the teams swap roles: the defending team attack and vice versa. This second stage is called *spelpåvinst* (Gotlandic dialectal *spelpåvunst*), and starts from the middle of the original *stötlinje*. The new defending team try to defend the line won during the first stage, while the new attacking team attempt to recapture the lost ground within 7 rounds of serves. If they fail, the opponents are granted 10pts., and the first full round (*pärk*) comes to an end. The teams again change sides but the *stötlinje* is kept at the last location achieved during the game. The first team to score 40pts. wins the match.

M. Hellspong, 'Pärk', *Den folkliga idrotten*, 2000.

PAROKOIBA, a kind of horse-fencing practiced in Kazakhstan.

PARROT SHOOTING, a shooting sport practiced in Europe since the Middle Ages, consisting of shooting at a parrot, using bows, crossbows and, later, firearms. Using expensive exotic birds for targets was initially a display of extravagance of wealthy nobility. By the end of the Middle Ages live parrots were replaced with inanimate targets in the form of wooden or metal bird figures. Traditions of parrot shooting are still maintained in some Eur. countries, e.g. Eng. >POPINJAY, Scot. >PAPINGO SHOOTING, Dan. >SKYDE PAPEGØJEN, Fr. >PAPEGAUT, LE, and Du. >PAPENGOY. In some countries parrots were replaced with other birds; see Pol. >COCK SHOOTING; cf. >PIGEON SHOOTING.

PARTHIAN ARCHERY, a type of equestrian archery originated by the Parthians, who lived in the ancient country of Asia, south-east of the Caspian Sea. Freeing themselves from the rule of the Seleucidae, they founded the Parthian empire. At its height, in the 1st cent. BC, this empire extended from the Euphrates across Afghanistan to the Indus and from the Oxus to the Indian Ocean. Having defeated Marcus Licinius Crassus in 53 BC and Marcus Antoninus in 36BC, the Parthians threatened the south-eastern ends of the Roman Empire, until they were conquered by Persia in 226 AD. A warlike people, the Parthians developed and mastered the skill of horseback riding and archery. Their best known contribution to archery was the famous 'Parthian shot', which involved shooting to the rear while riding at full speed, with the rider's body half turned. Over time this became known as a 'parting shot' in Eng., referring to a barbed or pointed comment made while leaving. Adopted by other Asiatic peoples and popularized in China during the reign of the Han dynasty (202 BC -220 AD), this skill was perfected in the Tang era (618-906 AD) and later adopted from China by the Mongols during the reign of Jenghiz Khan (1155-1227). The Parthian shot technique became part of the masterly archery skills demonstrated by the Mongolians and the Tartars during their conquests (12th-14th cent.) The monuments of Asian art, as well as Eur. iconography of the Tartar conquests often portray a galloping Asiatic horseman exercising the Parthian shot.

PASAKA see >PELOTA VASCA.

PASSAGE BALL, a var. of ball game played in the 19th cent. in Eton. The object of the game was to swiftly pass the ball among players to score a point. The game is played occasionally today.

PASSE-BOULES, one of numerous Bret. bowling games [Fr. *passe* – 'passage' + *boules* – 'bowls'], in which a bowl is rolled up a slope with a number of holes. The highest hole is worth the most points. Consultant: G. Jaouen, FALSAB.

PASSING THROUGH RATTAN RINGS, a game of the Chin. Li minority, similar to >CHUNGKE. Players throw long wooden, javelin-like poles called *chuanbial* at rolling rattan rings approx. 70-80cm in diameter. The game is a team competition, in which one team rolls the rings along a line 30m in length, while players of the other team try to target the rings with their poles from a distance of approx. 15m. Each player has 3 attempts and his pole must pass through the center of the ring. After the throwing team members have used all their attempts, teams change roles. The team that scores more hits wins the game. Mu Fushan et al., *Passing through rattan rings*, TRAMCHIN, 82

PAT-BALL, a Scot. var. of >ROUNDERS.

PATIGO, a Gallo dialect name for a Bret. bowling game called >TOUL AR C'HAZH.

PATO, trad. Argentine horse-ball game. It is played by 2 teams of 4 mounted riders each, on a field 200-220m long and 80-90m wide. The objective of the game is to throw a specially made ball through a netted ring, 1m in diameter, mounted on a pole 2.70m above the ground. The ball similar to a regular basketball is placed in a harness of 6 leather straps. The harness makes it possible to grab the ball while riding or pick it up from the ground. While riding, the ball must be carried in straightened arms to make interception by an opponent possible. It must not be put on the saddle or pressed against the trunk. The ball may be picked up from the ground only at full gallop. The players cannot stop to make a pick-up. A match consists of six 8-min. rounds with 5-min. breaks in between. The game is similar to >HORSEBALL. As a rather expensive sport pato is played mainly by wealthy horse breeders and landowners called the *estancieros*.
The players' dress is the trad. attire of the Argentine *gauchos* modified for the game. It consists of a broad-brimmed hat with a flat crown, white baggy pants (*bombachas*), a broad belt (*faia*), high boots (*las botas*) and colored shirt.
History. The game is derived from a trad., 16th-cent. sports competition of Span. *rancheros* who used to compete for a living duck placed in a leather basket. The basket was to be captured and brought to the winner's village (Span. *pato* – 'duck'). The game was brutal and played with no holds barred. It was prohibited by the Catholic church and players might have faced excommunication. In 1822, pato was officially banned by the Argentine government. The game was then practiced illegally and survived into the 20th cent. In 1937, A. del Castillo, a wealthy man and fan of Argentine folklore formulated the modern sports rules of pato, devoid of any brutality. A year later pato was officially approved by Argentine sports authorities and after the Argentine Pato Federation was founded the game became a national sport of the country.
J. Arlot, 'Pato', OCSG, 1975, 752; anon. (Pato), *Enciclopedia dello Sport*, 1965, 482.

PATØK, a Dan. game involving striking wooden pegs into the ground. The pegs are sharpened at one end and must be no longer than knee high and thick enough to hold in one hand. In some regions of Denmark the tip of the peg is hardened in fire or provided with iron or zinc reinforcements. The game is played by 2 or 3 contenders. Each game starts with the command 'Hit it, you crap' (*Hak i Lort*), after which the first player strikes his peg into the ground (peg A). The next player strikes his peg (B) into the ground close to peg A as to knock the latter out. Four possible situations may result from this action: 1) peg B knocks out peg A and remains standing; 2) both pegs remain standing; 3) peg A remains standing and peg B is knocked out; 4) both pegs are knocked out. In the first instance player B pulls out his peg and player A strikes his peg again into the ground. In the second instance player A pulls out his peg and player B leaves his peg in the ground (it is now A's turn to knock B's peg out). In the third instance player A pulls out his or her peg and player B starts out by striking his peg into the ground. In the fourth case player B strikes his peg first. Having knocked the opponent's peg out the player gains a higher 'rank'. He starts as the *Lort* – the crap, then advances to the rank of serf – *bonde*, squire – *herremand*, baron – *Baron*, count – *Greve*, duke – *hertug*, prince – *Prins*, king – *Konge*, emperor – *Kejser*, pope – *Pave*, and then advances to the rank of the tenth pope. Whoever reaches the rank of tenth pope becomes the winner. In some regions of Denmark the game of patøk has been known as *fik-fak*, where the winner of the a match goes one up in rank, while the loser goes one down, e.g. from king to prince. Cf. >KONGEPIND.
J. Møller, 'Fik-fak; Patøk', GID, 1997, 4, 57-59.

PATOLLI, (from Nahuatl *patoloa* – 'to play'). A game played by the Nahuatl of C America. It is played on a large mat on which a cross-shaped or X-shaped figure is drawn. Each arm of the cross is made up of 3 parallel lines. The crossing of the lines constitutes a field comprised of 4 squares. The 4 cross-arm sections outside the middle field comprise twelve squares each. The middle field marked as 'X' is called the *Nahui Ollin* in the Nahuatl language. The entire mat comprises 52 squares, which equal the years of the Mexican calendar cycle. The players sit on small stools, one at each arm of the cross, shake and cast numbered dice or perforated beans. The object and the rules of the game are unknown. See also: >PRECOLUMBIAN GAMES OF THE AMERICAS.
G. Montoya, 'Games and Sports of Pre-Columbian Origin', OR, Dec. 1995/Jan. 1996.

PATRIOTKA, an old Pol. equivalent of the present-day >YO-YO; a small disk hung on a thread. The disk winds and unwinds on the thread if skillfully pulled upwards. The game was described by Ł. Gołębiowski (*Gry i zabawy różnych stanów*, 1831):

> *The patriotka is a wooden disk with a groove around it and a string pulled through the side and the middle. It resembles a flat snuffbox. If pulled up sharply the disk winds towards the holding hand and unwinds downwards. Dexterity, proper application of force and skillful throws were the characteristics of an able player. I do not know what was so patriotic about the game. It might have been invented by some patriot and named after him. It was practiced during the reign of Stanislaw II August and the Four-Year Parliament.*

PAU-FERRO, full name of Port. >JOGO DO PAU-FERRO.

PAUME, an imprecise, general name denoting all varieties of ball games in which the ball is struck with the hand. In some late varieties the ball is hit with a racket (Fr. *paume* – 'palm'). Most paume games date back to the Middle Ages. Former historiographers often confused individual games due to their regional and chronological diversification as well as lack of fixed rules and organizations aimed at the games' standardization. The terminological inconsistency in the use of the noun *paume* in current popular encyclopedias and historical studies accounts for even greater confusion. Even today, sports historians argue as to the proper application of the name *paume* to a var. of games. Cf. >JEU DE COURTE PAUME, >JEU DE LA PAUME, >JEU DE LONGUE PAUME, >JEU DE PAUME.

PCHŁA, an old name for a Pol. folk game practiced in the Kashubia region, also known as >KICZKA or >KLIPA.

PEASANTRY RACES, a form of Pol. country-folk horse racing, which derives from the tradition of free serfs and in the 19th cent. was gradually included into standard horse racing by breeding companies in an attempt to to counter critical claims that they were producing saddle horses, useless for farming. However, peasantry races were never more than a token event in standard horse racing competitions and so they did not contribute to the improvement of farming horses. Poland also failed to develop a form of competition with the use of draught-horses similar to the Span. *arrastre por caballos*.

PECHOÙ, a Bret. game of >QUOITS popular in the Plougastel Daoulas area of W Brittany, consisting of tossing specially made stone quoits weighing around 2.5kg each at a target called the *ar mestr* situated around 10m from the thrower.
F. Peru, 'La tradition populaire de jeux de plein air en Bretagne', LJP, 1998. Consultant: G. Jaouen, FALSAB.

PEDESTRIANISM, predecessor of >RACE WALKING; a sport derived from walking as the basic human motor activity. From ancient times until the emergence of mechanical means of transportation walking was the basic form of movement of troops and large parts of the population who could not afford horses or horse-drawn vehicles. Individual walking feats were recorded very early on. In many cultures a common profession was that of the wandering poet, e.g. the Celtic bards and Germanic Minnsänger, exemplified by the character of Widsith, whose travels all over the Eur. continent were described in an anonymous Old Eng. poem:

> *Thus Widsith spoke, revealing a treasury of words,*
> *he to the greatest degree of the tribes over the Earth,*
> *and its peoples have travelled through;* [...]
> *Thus it is the course of bards to shape and to change into words*
> *the splendour of men through-out the many lands,*
> *profiting from what they say, and speaking words of glory,*
> *travelling South or North they meet*
> *recounting wisdom and giving praise* [...]
>
> [trans. D.B. Killings]

Walking pilgrimages in medieval Europe enjoyed enormous popularity as a result of Christian unification of the continent. Long religious pilgrimages were frequent literary themes, e.g. *The Canterbury Tales* (c.1387) by G. Chaucer. Along with industrial transformations, masses of people moved from the country to the urban centers, often on foot. Before the development of public transportation in the 19th cent. masses of people would cover long distances walking to work in expanding industrial centers. Walking as a competitive sport dates back to the turn of the 18th and 19th cent. Walkers who displayed great skills of endurance, covering long distances in loneliness were highly appraised by the public. The first Eng. walking hero was a London clerk, F. Powell, who covered 10mi. on the way from London to Bath in one hour. In 1773 he went on foot from London to York, over the distance of 200mi. His greatest feat was walking 100mi. in a time of 23hrs. and 25min. At the turn of the 18th and 19th cent. a Scotsman R. Barclay Allardice, known as 'Captain Barclay' (1779-1854) set numerous long-distance walking records. In 1809 he won a bet of one thousand guineas after covering 1,000mi. within 1,000hrs. Barclay's feat attracted huge public interest and thousands of spectators watched him along his walking route. Barclay's other achievement was walking 90mi. in 21hrs. and 30min. He inspired many future professional walkers, and contributed to the development of the race-walking sport by drafting the first rules of walking training. In the 19th cent. Great Britain became a leading center of pedestrianism, visited by professional walking competitors from all over the world. It was also the host of prestigious walking events and races. In 1862, a renowned Amerindian walker, Seneca Deerfoot, took part in one such race. In the USA, a great enthusiast of the sport of walking was the journalist E. Payson Weston (1839-1929). As a young reporter for *The New York Herald*, Weston would de-

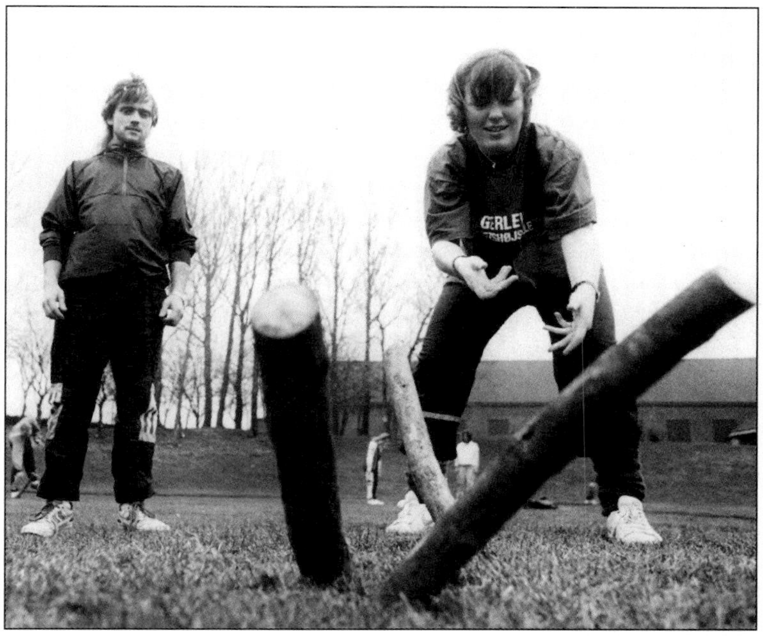

Patøk.

P

liver articles from the editor to a distant printer's and back faster than a special horse-drawn coach, which often got stuck in New York traffic jams. In 1861, celebrating the inauguration of A. Lincoln, he walked 443mi. in 208hrs. Weston began his career as a professional walker in 1867, when he covered the distance of 1326mi., from Portland, Maine to Chicago, Illinois in 26 days. Shortly after, he won a bet after covering 500mi. in 6 days. At the age of 68 in 1907, he set his Portland-Chicago record at 29hrs. less; and two years later he crossed the Amer. continent, from New York to San Francisco (3895mi.) in 104 days and 7hrs. In 1910 Weston covered the same route back, shortened to 3500mi., in 77 days. Pedestrianism as a professional sport reached its heyday in the last quarter of the 19th cent. The first Brit. open event was the first ever London-Brighton Walking Race (53.5mi.), estab. in 1867. The best walker of all time was J. Hocking, a Brit. immigrant to the USA, admitted to the Mark Twain Society at the age of 92 for his outstanding contribution to the development of sports. A famous walking event in Britain is a long race from Land's End in Cornwall to the northernmost cape of Scotland. The 1980s saw the growing popularity of marathon and ultra-marathon competitive and against-the-clock walking events. D. Kunst from the USA was the first person to walk around the world, from 10 Jun. 1970 to 5 Oct. 1974. During an around-the-clock walking marathon in 1985 M. Barnish set the world record by walking 663.17km in 6 days, 10hrs. and 32min.

Pedestrianism was not a sport practiced by women due to social restrictions. In the area of >WALKING, however, women's organizations won their rights to participation in separate women's events much faster. In 1932, the first woman took part in the prestigious London-Brighton Walking Race.

W. Thom, *Pedestrianism*, 1813; A.G. Scott M. Crawford, 'Pedestrianism', EWS, 1996, II.

PEDRINHAS, (Port. for 'stones'; full name *jogo das pedrinhas* – a game of stones). Each player has 5 stones the size of pigeon eggs. The players sit on the ground. According to local traditions, each player kisses his stones before the game. Pedrinhas is played in a series of movements. In the entry movement, called the *entrada*, all stones are thrown up and they drop to the ground. Then, one stone is thrown and before it hits the ground the other stones are scooped up one by one. In the next movement, one stone is thrown and while airborne the other stones are scooped up in twos; then, one stone is thrown, one is picked up, and next the 3 remaining are scooped up together. Other pedrinhas movements include:

pousa – 'landing', the first stone is picked up and thrown and while airborne, the second is scooped up (*pousa uma* – first landing), then the third (*pousa duas*), fourth (*pousa três*), until all 5 stones are thrown and caught.

batata – 'potato', once a stone drops it is pressed into the ground.

velha – 'old lady', all stones are thrown up at the same time and must land on the back of the throwing hand. If any stone slips off the hand, all the remaining stones must be thrown up again and it must be scooped up. Next, all the stones are thrown and once they land they are tapped to the ground. The stones can be caught with both hands.

o beijinho – 'little kiss', one stone is thrown and the others are scooped up and kissed one by one.

o batepeito – 'patting on the chest', a movement similar to *o beijinho*, in which a player pats himself on the chest between throwing one stone and scooping up another.

o cabêço – 'head', 4 stones are held in the hand, the fifth is placed between the tips of two fingers. The single stone is thrown up and before it falls to the ground the player must tap his chest with the 4 stones, place them on the ground and catch the falling stone. Next, the player throws another stone, snatches the four from the ground, taps them against the chest and catches the falling stone.

a capoeira – 'perch', all the stones are placed on the ground. The player places his left hand on the ground forming a scoop and puts one of the stones in. Next, he throws another stone, and while it is in the air, he picks up all the other stones while still holding the first one in his hand.

o burro – 'donkey', a movement similar to *a capoeira* but the stones from the ground are picked up one by one.

M. da Graça Sousa Guedes, 'Jogo das pedrinhas', JTP, 1979, 13-15.

PEG DIVING, a simple swimming exercise recommended by I.N. Chkhannikov under the name of 'diver' in his guide to games and play for school common rooms in the former USSR and so-called socialist countries. 'At a place where the water is shoulder-deep, stick a number of wooden pegs in the sandy bed of the river or lake. The participants take dives in turns, trying to extract the pegs. The person who succeeds in doing so, wins. The pegs should be made of young shoots so that they are visible in the water (one may partially remove the bark), and be placed 5 steps from one another'. 'Diver', GIZ, 1953, 78.

PEG-FICHED, a simple game consisting of throwing sharp-pointed sticks, once popular in the western shires of England. One player strikes his stick firmly into the ground. The other players throw their sticks across trying to dislodge it. Whoever knocks the stick out becomes the winner. The players who miss must run to a prescribed spot and back. TGESI, II, 38.

PEG-IN-THE-RING, a var. of Brit. >TOPS. The object of the game is to set a top spinning such that it spins out of a demarcated area. If the top ceases spinning within the circle it remains in the ring to be smashed into splinters by the other players or it can be redeemed by substituting it with an inferior top called a 'mull'.

PEG-TOP, a var. of >TOPS. One of the players spins his top while the others try to strike the spinning top with the pegs of their own tops as they fling them down to spin. If a player fails to spin his top he has to lay it on the ground for the others to strike at when spinning. The object of each spinner is to split the top which is being aimed at. TGESI, II, 38.

PEHLIVAN WRESTLING, [Serb. *pelivan* <Persian *pehlivan* or *pehlivan* – a plucky fellow, brave young fighter]. A folk wrestling variety originating in Persia that later spread across Turk. Asia Minor and throughout the Balkan Peninsula. Pehlivan wrestling is based on the very old tradition of Iranian wrestling (>VARZESH-E PEHLIVANI). One of the oldest mentions comes from the *Book of Kings* (*Shahnameh*) written in 1010 by the Persian epic poet Ferdowsi (d. around 1020-26). The poem describes the adventures of Rustum who, in recognition of his numerous achievements, receives the title of *jahan pehlivan*, which translates roughly as 'the world champion'. The most outstanding pehlivan fighters in Iran were known as *Pehlivan-e Zoorgar*.

During the Ottoman occupation of the Balkan Peninsula pehlivan wrestling became popular in Serbia, Macedonia and Bulgaria. Despite many regional differences, all the pehlivan wrestling varieties are similar to freestyle wrestling. The wrestlers fight in an open area. The object of the game is to floor one's opponent, bring him down to a bridge or half-bridge

Pehlivan wrestlers.

position or raise him several centimeters above the ground. The fighters wear only leather trousers and cover their bodies with oil. They approach each other from opposite sides of the arena, stroke themselves on their thighs and go around the arena in circles so that they gradually approach its center where the actual fight starts. The bouts are usu. accompanied by drum and *zurla* (a kind of a wind instrument) music. J.S. Jastrebov remarks in his *Stara Serbia i Albania* (*Old Serbia and Albania*, 1904) that 'the music may be unpleasant to the European ear but is thoroughly enjoyed by the local citizens and peasants'. There is no division into weight categories. There are, however, skill categories – in Serbia the highest proficiency category is called *baœe* – uncontested fighters, next come the *baœe alti* – wrestlers who lose only to the *baœe*, followed by *buju korta* – advanced fighters who, however, cannot stand up to the *baœe* and *baœe alti* wrestlers, and finally *kiœei korta* – beginners or veterans who fight only for pleasure.

History. Pehlivan wrestling came to the Balkans during the Ottoman occupation that lasted from the end of the 15th until the 19th century. Pehlivan wrestling tournaments were held at Turk. aghas' or beys' courts to celebrate various religious, national and local holidays. Later, pehlivan wrestling also became popular among less important warlords and in rural areas. The umpires – i.e. the aghas, beys or their representatives – were then replaced by officials elected by local communities usu. from among the former super-champions, i.e. the *pehlivan*. The prizes awarded in the past by rich sponsors were then replaced by smaller amounts donated by the spectators or payments received for performing at wedding parties or other family celebrations. The best *pehlivan* in the Balkans were indigenous Turks and Albanians, especially those from the Prilep and Bitola areas, as well as Macedonians from Berovo. The major bone of contention during the Ottoman occupation was whether the wrestlers should cover their bodies with oil or not. The pehlivan tradition favored such an approach while the Slav nations, especially Bulgarians, had their indigenous wrestling varieties which were then dubbed 'dry'. These indigenous types were more similar to Asian varieties which is further substantiated by the fact that there was a strict ban on greasing a wrestler's body in the Mong. >BUH. The Turks tried to force the Slavic wrestlers to put oil on their bodies. The Slavs, however, thought that in this way Turks wanted to root out their native traditions and opposed any such attempt vehemently. This resulted in numerous conflicts, especially in the 18th and 19th centuries. According to Z. Stoyanov one of the forms of protest against Ottoman rule was to 'publicly challenge a Turk. wrestler to a fight'. To stress their dislike of the Turk. rules the Slavic fighters did not cover their bodies with oil on purpose. The most famous local wrestler of that time was K. Dimo of Terfelia (in the Golyama Detelina district) who defeated many Turks and who often had to pay fines and serve time in prison for failing to observe the 'proper' rules. Some Balkan fighters did, however, recognize the Turk. rules. They were given the derogative name of 'sultans' wrestlers'. The most famous of them were D. Slav and Z. Kokalèuglu both representing the Bulg. town of Sliven. In the second half of the 19th century, after Bulgaria regained its independence, W Eur. wrestling varieties began to dominate in the Balkans. Pehlivan wrestling began to lose popularity since the best wrestlers, to be recognized abroad, started adopting the new fighting styles. However, despite these negative tendencies pehlivan wrestling survived in rural areas. After WWII a number of pehlivan wrestling sections were established throughout Bulgaria and Yugoslavia in regular wrestling clubs.

The collapse of communism in Bulgaria and the disintegration of the Yugoslav Federation in the first half of the 1990s seriously undermined the position of pehlivan wrestling in the region but it, nevertheless, remained a popular folk sport and hopefully it will retain its status in the future. At the same time, and quite unexpectedly for that matter, the older Turk. and Iranian wrestling, involving covering one's body with oil (see >TURKISH WRESTLING, >VARZESH-E PEHLIVANI), has become widely popular in the area.

PÉLA, a Port. ball game (full name *jogo da péla*) played esp. by girls, in which each player has one ball (Port. *péla* – obs. name for 'ball', still used in some regions of Portugal). There are three types of the game: 1) *ao comprido* (alongside), part of the Pentecost observances. Two teams stand on the opposite ends of the field and throw the balls to each other. No points are scored. The game is most likely part of an ancient springtime celebration ritual; 2) *às custas* (advantage). Individual players throw balls up one by one or hit the balls off a wall catching them on the fly; 3) *ao tira* (takeover). The players get in pairs. One of the players throws the ball up in the air and shouts: 'One, two, three, ... pull!' (*Um, dois, tres, tira!*). After the word *'tira'* , i.e. the takeover, the other player takes the ball, throws it up and shouts out the same words. This continues until the ball is dropped to the ground. When all pairs of players have played, the winners of individual bouts carry out a playoff to determine to ultimate winner of the match.
M. da Graca Sousa Guedes, 'Jogo da péla', JTP, 1979.

PELIVANSKI BORBY, a var. of Bulg. wrestling developed during Turk. rule under the influence of >PEHLIVAN WRESTLING. The present rules of the competition were made uniform in 1950. Wrestling bouts are accompanied by music. The most noticeable difference between the Bulg. and Turk. varieties is body oiling practiced in the latter. Under Turk. rule in Bulgaria (before 1875) the refusal of Bulg. wrestlers to oil their bodies was the object of a long-term political conflict.

PELKITUN, Span. *disparar la flecha* (shooting arrows). A combat skill developed by S.Amer. Natives inhabiting the present-day territory of Chile. The bows were made of hard wood and the bowstrings of horsetail bristles. The former chroniclers of the Span. conquest of South America mention the rain of arrows (*lluvias de flechas*) that often fell on the invading Spaniards during skirmishes with S.Amer. Natives. Having proved useless against heavy metal armour, pelkitun as a form of combat graduallydisappeared.
O. Plath, 'Pelkitun', JYDLCH, 1946, 29.

PELOTA, Span. full name *juego de pelota*, also Basq. *pilota*, general name for a number of hand ball or bat and ball games. The name is derived from Lat. *pillata* (dimunitive of Lat. *pila* – 'ball'; cf. Gk. *pilos* – 'a round felt object'). The origins of pelota are ambiguous. It was probably derived from a number of games developed within in the Iberian Peninsula, esp. in the Basq. country, Spain and the French side of the Pyrenees. The games spread all over the peninsula merging with regular variations of ball games in which a ball is hit off a wall, or passed over a net or string similar to tennis. After the Span. conquest of Lat. America some varieties of pelota became popular in the Span. colonies esp. in Mexico, Cuba, and then in California and Florida. Pelota gained huge popularity in Asia, particularly in the Philippines and Indonesia, in northern Africa, Egypt and Morocco. The game is known and practiced to a certain degree in some countries outside the Iberian Peninsula such as Italy, Belgium and Ireland. Generally, pelota games may be divided into: 1) direct, in which the ball is hit between

opponents, usu. over various types of nets (Span. >JUEGOS DIRECTOS, Fr. >JEUX DIRECTS). Most of these games have arisen from the Fr. tradition of >JEU DE LA PAUME; 2) indirect, in which the ball is hit off a wall (Span. >JUEGOS INDIRECTOS, Fr. >JEUX INDIRECTS) derived from or linked to the Basq. tradition of >PELOTA VASCA. Pelota games can be also divided into those played with the hand, both direct and indirect, and those played with bats of different size and material. The most common bat is a long curved basket called *chistera* or *cesta punta*. Pelota varieties may be played singles, doubles or by teams of up to 5 players each. Pelota may be played on a court with a net, the one-walled *plaza libre*, the two- or three-walled *fronton*, and the small, covered three-walled square *trinquet*. The court surfaces (Span. *cancha*, often meaning the court itself) can be dirt, beaten rubble or cement. Many pelota courts are purpose-built although in some smaller towns they may be old building sites, churches, abandoned houses or barns. The ball is served against a wall but also, in some var. of the game, against a special tripod situated on the court. The tripods called *bota harri* or *botillo* differ in size, construction and material depending on local traditions and game variations. The ball hit with a bare hand is called a *mano libre* – 'free hand ball' in the Span. language or *main nue* – 'bare hand' in French. The ball may be hit with simple wooden rackets (*pala larga*), covered with thick leather (*paleta de cuero*) or rubber-covered table tennis-like paddles (*paleta de goma*). In some var. wicker (rattan) or leather curved baskets or scoops with wooden frames are used, such as the short *cesta punta* with a deep leather sack or the *remonte* resembling a boat with elevated bow and stern. In some countries, the local var. of pelota developed their own kinds of rackets such as *paleta argentina* used in Argentina but also in the Fr. part of the Basq. country. In some var. of the game tennis rackets with leather straps are used (*share*). There is also the *pasaka*, a mitt tied to the hand with leather straps that prevent it from sliding off. In many cases the names of the rackets are the names of the games. Due to the numerous var. of courts and equipment pelota cannot be regarded as a single game, but rather a highly diversified family of hand and bat ball games. The diversity of court types and ways of playing the ball accounts for the current mixture of many types of pelota, e.g. the same var. may by played with *chisteras*, *paletas* or bare hands. The tendency to make the game faster and more spectacular has eliminated former rules which, esp. in the chistera types, allowed the players to hold the ball and roll it inside the racket before each return. At present in all pelota var. the ball must be caught and thrown in one continuous motion.

Although the majority of present-day pelota games are of Basq. origin, including the Amer. var. (>JAI ALAI), still some original, non-Basq., regional var. are played today on the Iberian Peninsula. All of them, however, bear a resemblance to the Basq. types. They include:

Francisco José de Goya, Pelota, 1779, oil on cardboard.

PELOTA MANO CANARIO, full name *juego de pelota mano canario*, a Span.-Canarian pelota game in which the ball is struck with the bare hand. The points can be scored by 1) making the opponent miss the ball; or to the opponents by 2) the server fouling the ball out, including hitting it out of bounds or touching the ball with a part of the body other than the hand. The rectangular court called the *cancha* is 30-35m long and is divided into 2 playing areas by a centerline. The game is played by 2 teams of 4-6 players each. The ball is made of rubber covered with goatskin. It is 45-47mm in diameter and weighs 50g. The ball must be served against a special stand called a *bote* placed in the serving zone. The *bote* resembles a 50-60cm high stool. Through the middle of its 'seat' there is a 1m-long adjustable board that can be moved up or down. On the upper end of the board a thick granite plate is mounted with a wooden frame (*loseta de berro*). The plate is 20x30cm and players may adjust the plate's height and slant to obtain the most effective rebound angle.

The game is most likely derived from Fr. >JEU DE LA PAUME, and was popularized in the Canary Islands by the soldiers of the Norman knight, J. de Bethencourt, an aide to King Henry III of Castile. Bethencourt conquered the islands and became King Jean IV of the Canaries. G. Gbass, an Englishman who traveled to the islands in 1764 described the pelota game played by the people of the island of Lanzarote. In the 19th cent., pelota was played in the towns of Corralejo, Vale de Santa, Ines, Llano de San Sebastian, La Antigua and other Lanzarote settlements.

PELOTA VALENCIANA. The object of the game is to strike the ball in such a way so that the opponent fails to return it. Pelota valencianta has 2 basic variations. It is played on an open court such as a street or alley (*la calle*) or on a three-walled court (*trinquete*). Depending on the court, different rules of play are applied in numerous varieties of the game (see below). The court is divided into 2 parts by a centerline (*cuerda central*) or in some varieties, e.g. in *galotxa* by 2 parallel lines. The game can be played by singles or teams. The small hard ball used for the game is made of hand-wound leather. In the trinquet game the ball weighs 30-32g and its diameter is not specified. In the street game the ball is 44mm in diameter and weighs 44g. The ball core is usu. made of Rus. leather or wool-combings. However, the exact construction of each ball as well as the type of leather are often secrets of individual players. The players use protective gloves called *guantes*. The 2 main types of pelota valenciana, i.e. the *trinquete* and *en la calle* are further subdivided.

PELOTA VALENCIANA EN LA CALLE, Span. pelota valenciana played in a street or alley. The game is played between old buildings with balconies, which confines the width of the court to 6-8.5m. The court's length is 60-65m from the dividing galotxa line and 80-85m from the *llargues* line. The scoring is done in sevens i.e.: 7, 14, 21, 28, 35, and 42. Game is 48 points. There are or have been at least seven subvarieties of the game: 1) *Llargues a rattles* (long

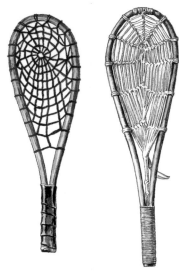

Traditional rackets for playing pelota.

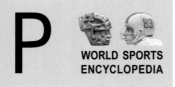

P WORLD SPORTS ENCYCLOPEDIA

410

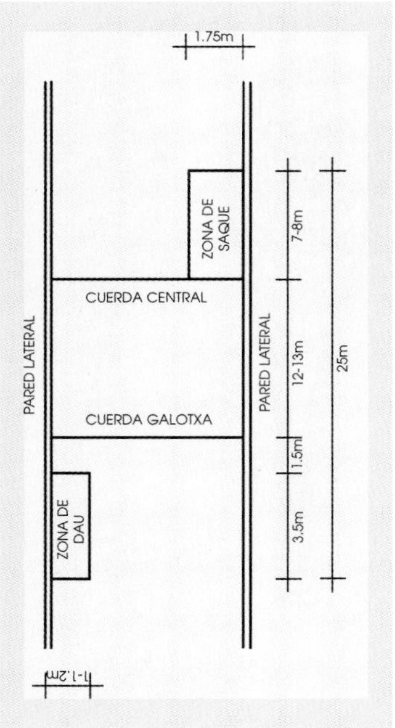

The court for playing pelota valenciana.

lines). The game is played by 2 teams of 3 or 4 players each or by a 3-player team against a 4-player team. The court is 70-75m long and 5-6m wide. It is divided into 2 playing areas by a centerline (*linea central*). On each playing area there is a service line (*rayas de saque*) 30-35m from the centerline. The ball can be hit either on the volley (*al aire*) or on the first bounce (*primer bote*). The game's tempo (*la marcha del juego*) is dictated by the umpire's shouts – the *marchaor*; 2) *Llargues dalt corda* (long over rope). The court is divided into 2 playing areas by a rope suspended 160-175cm above the ground. Each playing area has a parallel service line drawn on the ground 15m from the dividing rope. A serve must pass above the rope and reach the opponent's area as in tennis. The ball is fair if it is promptly returned by the opponent after it has passed above the rope. The opponent may return the serve on the volley or on the first bounce. One of the most common types of llargues dalt corda is a game in which the ball is played with a specially-made stiff glove put on the player's hand called the *bragueta*; 3) *A curtes* (short lines). An unknown var. of the game that became extinct in the 19th cent.; 4) *A contra má* (against the hand). An obsolete game variation from the 19th cent. Detailed rules unknown; 5) *A pertxa*. The game's name comes from a service slat (*pertxa*) mounted on the court wall 2.5-3m above the ground. A serv must bounce off the wall above the slat and land behind a line marked on the court 3m within the end line. The served ball cannot be struck with the hand, but is thrown against the wall (*no golpeándola*); 6) *Galotxa*. Regarded as the most representative of the pelota valenciana varieties. The game is played by 2 teams of 3 players each. A team consists of the *galotxero* (the player standing by the rope called *galotxa*), the *feridor* (pitcher) and the *de bote* (the volley receiver). A particular feature of the galotxa variety is the *galotxa* itself, i.e. a leather belt 1.25m long suspended on a rope across the court, 2.5m above the ground. A 20cm-wide net attached to the galotxa prevents the ball from passing directly below the belt. The galotxa has also small metal clinking bells (*cascabeles*) which sound whenever the ball hits the belt, indicating a loss of service. 12-16m from the galotxa runs the so-called central rope (*cuerda central*). The ball is pitched from the serving zone called *zona de saque* situated on the left side of the court. The *zona de saque* is a rectangular area 3.5m long and 1-1.2m wide. One of the longer sides of the zona forms the sideline of the court and its shorter side runs 1.5m from the galotxa. A pitch must pass above the galoxta without touching it, bounce off the ground in the zone between the galotxa and the cuerda central and reach the receiving zone called *zona de dau*, situated diagonally to the serving zone, where it is received by an opposing player. The *zona de dau* is a rectangular area 7-8m long and 1.75m wide. One of its longer sides forms a section of the court sideline and a shorter side is adjacent to the *cuerda central*. If the serv fails to reach the *dau* zone the serving team loses a point. The ball must not be hit with the hand or fist; 7) *Raspall*. The most free-style var. of pelota valenciana. It is played on a court without a dividing net. The players stand opposite each other and serve and return the ball with the hand or a glove made of hard leather or wood. The game is played until one player scores 20 or 28pts., depending on local traditions.

PELOTA VALENCIANA EN TRINQUETE, a Span. game of pelota played on the *trinquet* i.e. a two-walled rectangular court 45-60m long, most commonly about 57m long, and 8.5-11m wide. Two 3-4m high walls are situated along the shorter sides of the court. Along one of the longer sides of the court and above the walls on the shorter sides are the tiers (*escalera*) which rise in steps of 1.5-1.7m. The ball is struck with the hand. Scoring is in fives i.e. 5, 10, 15, 20 etc. Game is usu. 40 or 50pts. The major varieties of pelota valenciana en trinquete include: 1) *Escalera-cuerda*, a variety common all over Valencia. The ball is served from the center of the court, 50-80cm from the *escalera*. The serv must hit the area above the serving line on the side wall. The serving line is marked 1.5m above the highest stair of the *escalera*. After the ball bounces off the wall it must reach the *dau* zone where an opposing player should rebound it on the volley or on the first bounce. Otherwise the ball is foul and the opposing team serves. The return must hit the wall again passing above the *cuerda central*. During play following the serve the ball can be played outside the *dau* zone, which is used primarily for serving; 2) *Rebote*, full name *rebote sobre cuerda*. A var. of pelota valenciana practiced around Valencia in the neighboring provinces of Castellón and Alicante. The ball is served from the center of the trinquet, one meter from the wall, against a specially-made slanted bench (*banqueta inclinada*). Then, the ball must pass above a rope dividing the court in half which runs 6m from the front wall and 2m before the edge of the *zona de dau*. The ball is hit with a glove called a *suelo* – 'a hoof' or a hand guard (*brazo*). A similar game is played in the Basq. country, where it is regarded as most significant. Span. and Basq. sources provide contradictory information as to the origins of this game; 3) *Raspote*. A var. of pelota valenciana played in the province of Alicante and around Marina de Valencia. This variety does not use the *escelera* or ropes for play. The ball is played against the walls in free ways between the competing teams. The team which fails to return the ball loses a point.

PELOTON, a gradually disappearing folk var. of pelota played in the province of Saragossa. The court is a *trinquete*. The ball, 15cm in diameter, is larger than in other pelota varieties. It is hit with the hand protected by wooden blocks.

History. The traditions of pelota played in the Iberian Peninsula reach back to the Middle Ages. The game was mostly influenced by the Fr. game of >JEU DE LA PAUME. Pelota developed most rapidly in the Basq. country on both sides of the Span.-Fr. border. The first mention of the game, commonly regarded as the ancestor of present-day Valencian pelota, comes from 1392 when by a court regulation included in the official manual of the Town Council of Valencia (*Manual de Coselis*) playing the game on Sundays and holidays was banned, punishable by fine or flogging. The court regulation caused public unrest in the city. When the ban was officially upheld by Juan I, King of Aragon, Catalonia and Valencia riots had to be quelled. In 1412, another regulation was passed which imposed punishments of 'fines, imprisonment, flogging, and driving the culprit seated on an ass in a yellow and red hood around town' on those who refused to obey the law. The punishments and restrictions were ineffective in the long term. In 1539, L. Vives provided a detailed description of pelota in his *Dialogs* (*Dialogos*). The description clearly indicated that the pelota court had been modeled after the Fr. Courts, esp. after those in Paris. A map of the Fr. town of Bayonne from 1610 shows the oldest known pelota court located in the St. André district. The influences of pelota reached beyond the Bay of Biscay and the Basq. country. According to Eng. sources, Henry VII (1457-1509) was said to have awarded a sum of £100 pounds to an unknown 'Biscayman' (a former name for a Basque) for a successful game. In 1528, the Basq. country was visited by a Venetian diplomat, A Navagerro (or Navagierro) who described the game and pelota courts on the Fr. side of the region in the Labourd province: 'The frontyard of their houses consists of a walled square with smooth sanded surface to keep the ground dry. The squares are covered with roofs made of tree branches arranged in a perfect manner. The men can play pelota on these courts all day long.' One of the characters of *Exemplary Novels* (Novelas ejemplares) by the renowned Span. author M. de Cervantes, is a *pilotari* – a pelota player. The game of pelota appears also in the poetry of F. de Quevedo (1580-1645). One of the most significant works of art associated with pelota is *Juego de la pelota a pala* by F. Goya. The popularity of pelota may be reflected in an Span. old saying: *Aun esta la pelota en el tejado* (to jump like a pelota ball bouncing off the roof). The great social impact of pelota has been reflected in tombstones erected in honor of famous pelota players. Instead of angel figures the tombstones depict figures of the players. The second half of the 19th cent. was a crucial period for pelota's development. During that time various types of pelota popular in South America began to exert influence back on the country of game's origin. The process was exemplified by development of the *chistera*, a characteristic wicker basket used for the game. The *chistera*, invented in the Iberian Peninsula in 1857, became popular in the 1860s and was later brought to South America by Span. immigrants. In 1888, an Argentine player, Curuchague designed a larger type of pelota basket known since then as the *grand chistera*. The new curved basket was strapped to player's hand with a special glove.

In some S.American countries, esp. Argentina, Uruguay, and Mexico the rapid development of football has decreased the interest in pelota although the game has not disappeared from public life. Pelota enjoys greatest popularity in countries with a minor interest in football (e.g. in Cuba).

Ethnographic research has shown that in the 1970s pelota was practiced in 1088 Span. towns in 38 provinces. It enjoys greatest popularity in the province of Valencia, where pelota valenciana is played to the present day in 90 towns, Salamanca – 83 towns, Navarra – 78 towns, Soria – 67 towns, and Guadalajara – 62 towns. Pelota is least popular in the provinces of Badajoz, Barcelona, Gerona, and Sevilla, in which it was played in one town of each province.

L.B. Fernandez, *Historia, ciencia y codigo del juego de pelota*, 1946; C. Moreno Palos, 'Juegos y deportes de pelota', JYTE, 1992, 168-187; R. Garcia Serrano, 'Juego de pelota', JDTE, 1974, 207-221.

PELOTA A LA PARED, a Span. name of >PELOTA varieties in which the ball is hit off a wall. It prob. gave rise to its Ital. counterpart >PALLA AL MURO.

PELOTA CONTRA FRONTON, a Span. ball game in which the ball is hit off the wall; also *juego contra frontones*, or simply *fronton* or *frontón*. A S.Amer. var. of the game derived from the Basq. tradition, called >JAÏ ALAÏ was developed by the Spaniards in their former colonies. Local var. of the game are practiced in Chile, Argentina, Bolivia, Mexico, Peru, Venezuela, and Cuba. The most distinctive variety is the Uruguayan >PELOTA EN FRONTONES.

PELOTA EN FRONTONES, a Span ball game in which a ball is thrown against a wall; the Uruguay-

Traditional methods of manufacturing pelota rackets from double- or triple-split twigs.

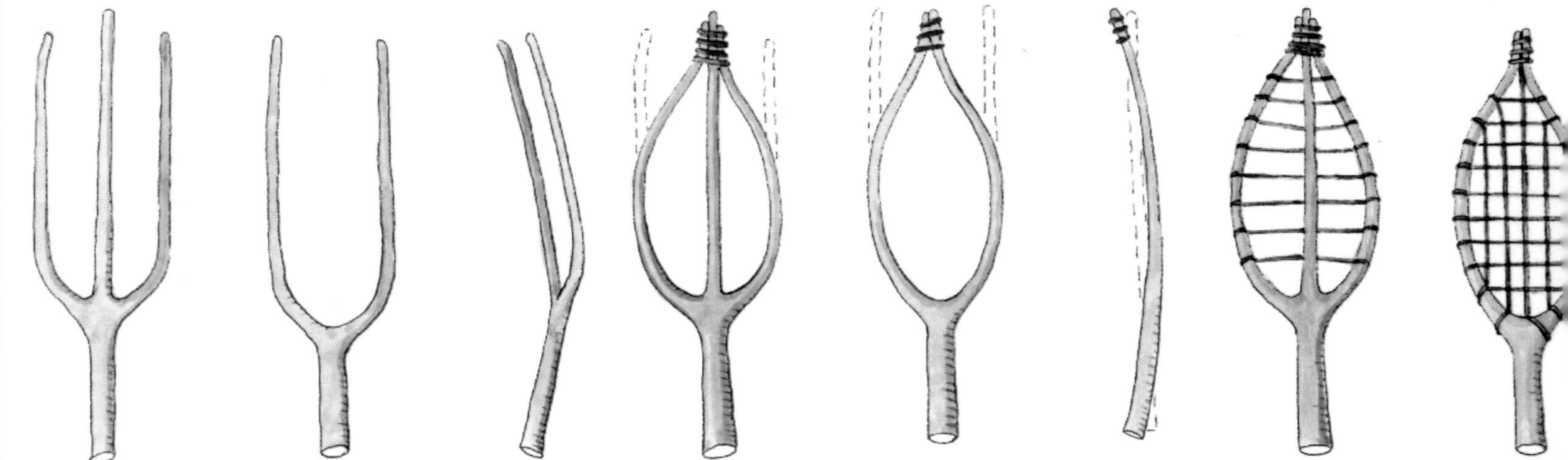

an var. of >PELOTA CONTRA FRONTON, and indirectly >JAÏ ALAÏ; see also >PELOTA.

PELOTA MIXTECA, the name refers to different varieties of a ball game, whose origin can be traced to pre-Columbian C America and the tribes inhabiting it – Mixteca and Zapoteca. The leading organization governing local varieties of pelota mixteca is Federación Mexicana de Juegos y Deportes Autóctonos y Traditionales. Pelota mixteca is played according to different rules and using different kinds of balls. The structure of the ball determines the playing technique and the equipment used to hit the ball it. The varieties of pelota mixteca are:

PELOTA MIXTECA DE HULE, lit. rubber ball of the Mixteca; is a ball that is wholly made of India-rubber, 12cm in diameter and 900g in weight. Because of its considerable weight, the game is played using a special socket as an extension of the hand. The socket, which resembles a large cup, 15-20cm in diameter, is made of stiff, raw leather, and has a thick base that is drawn upon the hand and attached to it by means of leather straps with buckles. The bottom of the cup is directed towards the game. The socket is intended for catching and bouncing the ball. The game has been known and played mainly on the territory of the present Mexican State of Oaxaca and the areas to which the inhabitants of the state migrated, such as Mexico City, the States of Puebla and Cuernavaca, and to a smaller extent the Southwestern USA.

The most common var. of the game involves 2 teams of 5 players. The field is called *cancho, patio de pelota* or *pasajuego*. It is rectangular in shape, 100m long and 8m wide. The game starts with a player tossing the ball so it bounces back from a stone located within the field. The ball should fall down in the field of the opposite team.

The ball used in this var. of pelota mixteca was probably the first known instance of the use of natural rubber in the making of balls. It was probably developed by the Olmecs around the year 300 BC. They manufactured it by driving the needles of a *maguey* cactus through, clippings of birds' or animals' claws through a coil of rubber thread. Such an ensemble was later closely tied with strong thread and dipped in olive oil, before it was steam-boiled. Mod. balls are made using a mould that is heated by electricity.

In one of its earliest, now discontinued forms, the game usu. involved 2 teams of 3 people. The line that divided the field into halves was the location of 2 flat stones. The point of the game was to throw the ball at one of the stones so that it would land on the opponents' territory. A member of the other team would try and bounce the ball back in a similar manner. The game continued until one of the teams allowed the ball to land on its territory, which most probably meant scoring a point. In order to increase the strength of bouncing the players wore leather gloves, covering some of their wrists.

Another form, which is still played today in Danzu, in the Oaxaca Valley, is called in Span. *juego de rayas* (playing for the borderline). The ball is bounced from a wall that is especially erected for this purpose. The court (*cancha*) is limited by a pair of parallel lines (*escaces*). The lines are up to 100m long and are 10-11m apart. Such a rectangular is divided into 2 zones: the throwing one – *zona de saque* – and the receiving one – *zona de resto*, or the rest of the court that the ball must fall within. The latter is 10-11m by 8m. Alongside the receiving zone there is a *botadera,* a flat wall, slightly sloping towards the court. The ball is bounced with a socket weighing 3.5-7kg. The mod. forms of the game involve teams of 6 people. Five of them are *taures*, positioned along the court, and the 6th, *golpeador,* starts the game by tossing the ball at the wall and watches that it never crosses the line ending the throwing zone – *chichi*.

Similar rules apply to a game called *pelota a lo largo* (Span. for 'playing into the distance'), which has only 1 cross line, dividing the 2 zones. The boundaries of the receiving zones are not specified so the ball is allowed to fall in any distance from the bouncing point, as long as it falls between the 2 longitudinal lines or *escaces*. Mod. varieties that are known and played in the S. Amer. countryside do not require the players to wear any special uniforms. The more formalized games, played in larger cities, specify that the participants wear T-shirts with trousers and caps similar to those used in >BASEBALL.

A referee called *chacero,* less often *arbitro,* usu. controls the game. The match consists of 4 rounds, awarded 15, 30, 40 and 50pts.

PELOTA MIXTECA DE FORO, is a game similar to the previous variety, with two differences: the ball is hollow inside and therefore lighter, and the 'cup-like' socket for the hand is replaced by wrapping it with leather straps or insolating tape of the variety used by electricians.

PELOTA MIXTECA DEL VALLE is played according to similar rules as *pelota mixteca de foro* and *pelota mixteca de hulle*. In this case, the player bounces the ball using a straight square plank 20x20cm in size and approx. 3cm thick, which is permanently attached to a glove made of stiff leather with fingers cut off at half length (similar to the gloves used by racing drivers).

A. Caso, T. Gutierez, *El deporte prehispanico,* 3rd ed. 1967; G. Montoya, 'Games and Sports of Pre-Columbian Origin', *OR,* Dec. 1995/Jan. 1996; T. Stern, *The Rubber-Ball Games of the Americas,* 1966.

PELOTA PURHÉPECHA DE TRAPO, full name *pelota purhépecha con pelota de trapo,* also Native Amer. *pisiri-a-kuri.* A ball game played with a rag ball or stone. The game took its name after the Purhépechas living in the Tarascan plateau of central Mexico, in the northeastern part of the State of Michoacán. The main traditions of the game are deep-rooted in the Sierra and around Lake Patzcuaro and Lake Cánada. The game used to be played in two varieties in which the ball was played either with the hand or with long curved sticks. At present pelota purhepecha de trapo is played in the streets of towns and settlements. At each end of the street there is a 6-8m-wide goal. The goal can be marked with a line drawn across the street. The time limit of the game is set by the teams' captains. Sometimes referees are appointed for a game to check players' equipment and control the timing. They also make sure that both teams have the same number of players. The street or the 'field' is 150-200m long. In the stick var. of the game the ball is made of wood and is 15cm in diameter. If touched with a hand or foot the ball is foul and the opposing team takes service. In one of the game's varieties played at night the ball is set on fire for the duration of the match, which makes it a spectacular display. Before a night match the ball remains immersed in oil or gasoline for one or two days. In the past, the ball was layered with the resin of coniferous trees.

PELOTA PURHÉPECHA ENCENDIDA, full name *pelota purhépecha con encendida,* also *uarhukua,* Mex. Ind. burning ball; a game derived from the tradition of the native tribes of Central America, played by the inhabitants of Mexico. The point of the game is to force a burning ball to cross a goal line of the opposing team, pushing it with curved sticks, similar to those used in >FIELD HOCKEY, only thicker, longer and not as processed.

A game of pelota.

One game takes the amount of time agreed upon by the teams' captains, usu. 6hrs., but sometimes a max. number of points is set. There is a short break after each score. The ball is made from naked coral tree (*erythrina americana*). The wood is first cut into blocks and then given the required round shape and the diameter of approx. 15cm. When the balls are ready, they are kept for a few days in a container filled with oil or gasoline. The lighting of the ball (*ceremonia de encendido del fuego*) takes place immediately before the match, usu. as the second element of the event, following the opening. The sticks are made from bent branches of the same tree. The players are dressed in white calico trousers and shirts, leather sandals worn without socks, and red headbands. Men (*hombres*) and women (*mujeres*) play separately.

History. The game is a part of the tradition of Native Central Americans. It used to symbolize a ritual praising the God of the Sun. Performed mostly in the Mexican State of Michoacan, particularly in its capital, Ciudad Mexico, as well as Condesa and Caltontzin. Cf. >FIRE BALL.

A.Z. Bocanegra, 'The Sleep of the Sun', *OR,* April-May, 1999

PELOTA TARASCA, Span.-Mexican name used in many sources to denote a var. of football games of pre-Columbian origin associated with the Tarasco people living around Lake Pátzcuaro. Before the Span. conquest the Tarasco had their own independent kingdom(Span.-Mex. *Reino Tarascó*) with the capital in Tzintzuntzan. Some historical records give evidence of pelota tarasca as a ball game played with a burning ball struck with long curved sticks. The aim of the game was to pass the ball across the opponent's goal line on one end of the playing field. In this version pelota tarasca was played in the state of Michoacán and to some extent in the states of Guerrero, Jalisco, and Nayarit. According to researchers of Central-Amer. cultures that version of the game symbolized the movement of the sun and was part of regional, ancient Native Amer. beliefs. A similar game derived from the same Central-Amer. traditions was practiced among the Purhepecha people (>PELOTA PURHEPECHA DE TRAPO, (>PELOTA PURHEPECHA ENCENDIDA). Both games are most likely derived from or were influenced by the former >TEOTIHUACAN BALL; cf. >FIREBALL.

According to Prof. A.Z. Bocanegra, the Chairman of the Mexican Federation of Native and Trad. Sports and Games (Federación Mexicana de Juegos Y Deportes Autoctonos Y Tradicionales), the name of *pelota tarasca* currently denotes a folk game practiced in the Tierra Caliente, in the states of Michoacán and Guerro. The game is played with a regular rubber ball, although due to the disappearance of the trad. rubber ball it is often replaced with a tennis ball. The ball is hit with the fist clenched around a

WORLD SPORTS ENCYCLOPEDIA

P

Hitting the ball in pelota mixteca de foro.

Hitting the ball in pelota mixteca del valle.

Hitting the ball in pelota mixteca de hule.

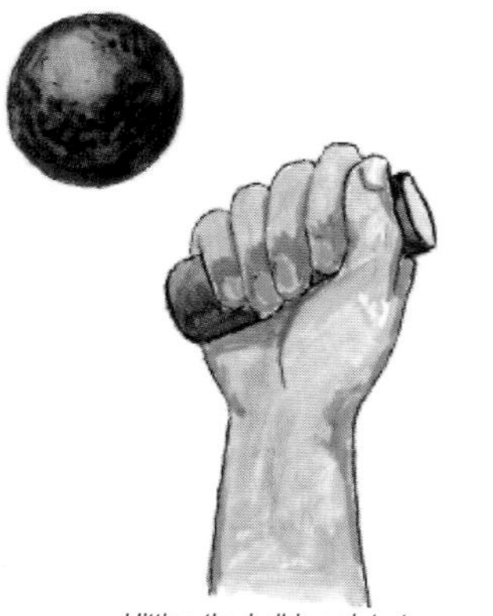

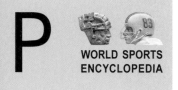

Hitting the ball in pelota tarasca.

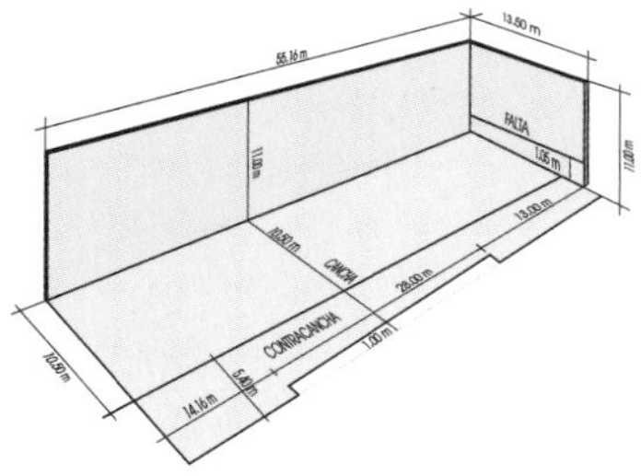

The Euskal-Jai fronton in Pampelona.

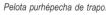

Pelota purhépecha de trapo.

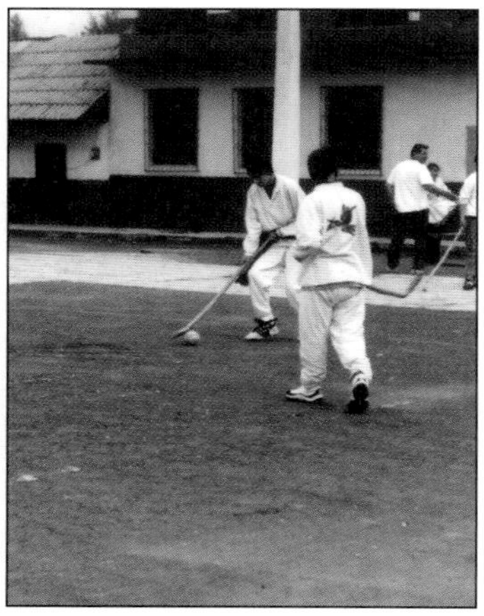

stout, 3cm-long wooden peg. The game is played by 2 teams of 4 players each. Each team consists of a captain (*capitán*), a pitcher (*bolillero*) and 2 wings (*orilleros*). The rectangular field called a *cancha* or *terreno* is 120m long and 11m wide. The object of the game is to push the opposing team towards the end of the field by making them return the ball. If an opposing player fails to make a return and the ball fails to land on the striking team's playing field, the opposing team scores a point. Game score and timing unknown.

Consultant: Prof. A.Z. Bocanegra.

PELOTA VASCA, the most common type of >PELOTA. It is derived from the trad. Basq. folk festival of *jai alai*. The name of the festival is also applied to denote the game of pelota vasca itself. According to Basq. dictionaries and encyclopedias the name *jai alai* functions as the name of the game outside the Basq. country, esp. in Span. speaking countries of South America and the USA. The game became popular in the latter thanks to Cuban and Mexican immigrants as well as Puerto Ricans (>JAI-ALAI). The name *pelota vasca* is applied to a family of various games of similar cultural tradition and the region of origin. In the Basq. tradition individual games were practiced mainly by men, although since the 1920s women have quite often taken up playing. Different types of pelota games have numerous features in common. Some varieties have given rise to other varieties which became separate games and in turn influenced the originals. Therefore, the typology of pelota vasca games is fairly confused and different sports researchers introduce different divisions of the game based on types of courts, equipment, and course of play. The mentioned criteria often seem vague, esp. in the cases where identical types of games are played on different courts with the use of different equipment. In regard to court types and the resulting course of play pelota vasca games can be divided into those played on open courts (*cancha abierta*, the game itself is called *pelota en campo abierto*), walled courts (*cancha cerrada*), or small covered courts called the trinquets (*el trinquete*). The games in which the ball is struck against a long side wall are named depending on the position of the wall on the court. A court with two, 12-14m high walls perpendicular to each other is called a fronton, and the front wall against which the ball is hit is a *frontis*. The wall perpendicular to the *frontis* on the right side of the court is known as *pared de laizquierda* or as the *ble* in players' slang. If the longer side wall is positioned on the right side of the court it is called the *pared de derecha*. In some varieties of the game the side wall is divided into 4m-long sections, called the *cuadros* (Span. *cuatro* – 'four'). The sections are marked on the wall with vertical lines 1.5-2m in height numbered on top. The number of *cuadros* differs depending on regional fronton dimensions. The smallest frontons have 15 cuadros, the largest 18-20. Between the numbered lines there are shorter lines without numbers. The cuadros are used most often for the game called *rebote*. The function of the cuadros is purely informational as they indicate the height of hits and rebounds to the spectators and referees.

The most exemplary fronton is the Euskal-Jai in Pamplona. It is 55.16m long and 13.5m wide. The walls are marked with horizontal foul lines (*falta*) 11m above the ground and the front wall has an additional foul line running 105cm above the ground. The ball is foul if it hits the wall outside the foul lines. Opposite the side wall the court is 5.4m wider at the ends. The service line (*cancha*) parallel to the front wall divides the court in half. The ball must be served from the service zone marked with the service line and a line 10.5m from the side wall. The width of the entire playing area is marked with a line called *contrachancha*. Most frontons differ, however, depending on local conditions. In many cases the courts are old church walls or ruins of public buildings, barns, etc. Many towns have their own purpose-built, modern in-door frontons (the Galaretta fronton in Hernani, Carmela Balda in Donostii, Izarraitz in Azpeitia, Deportivo club fronton in Bilbao, the municipal Artza fronton in Bermeo, Ezkurdi Jai Alai in Durango, municipal frontons in Marquina and Lequeitio, Eder Jai in Benidorm, frontons in Andoain, Oyarzun, Renteria, and – outside the Basq. country – the Principal palacio in Barcelona, etc.). The ball can be struck with the bare hand (*a mano libre*), a flat wooden bat (*pala*), or a curved wicker basket called *chistera* (also spelled *shistera* or *txistera*), or its older version, the *cesta*. (In the Lat. Amer. pelota vasca varieties all types of glove-baskets are called *cesta*, including those named *chistera* on the Iberian Peninsula). Many individual var. of pelota vasca are still practiced in various Basq. towns. The most popular, either historical or present, var. of the game are:

JUEGO LARGO, a game played on an open court, derived most likely from >JEU DE LONGUE PAUME. The court is rectangular with unspecified dimensions. The longest courts reach 100m. Two parallel lines (*escases*) divide the court into 3 parts. The first is the service line (*escas del saque*), the other is the short line (*escas del resto*). In some varieties the lines are replaced with ropes. Scoring is similar to that of tennis. To win a game, a player must win 4 balls. First ball won is called *quince* and is signaled by the scoring referee (*Tanteador*) who shouts *quince nada*; second ball – *trienta* (shouts T*reinta nada*); third ball – *cuarenta* (shouts *Cuarenta nada*). Winning of the fourth ball, which concludes a game, is signaled with a shout *Un juego*. In most varieties of juego largo the ball must be served against a stone, iron or wooden stand (*botillo*) positioned at one end of the court. Once bounced off the botillo the ball must be returned by the opponent. Play stops at an opponent's failure to return the ball.

BOTA LUZEA, also *bote luzea*; some regional varieties of the game are known as *pillota-soro* or *soropil*. In the Zuberoa region and the Fr. provinces of Basse-Navarre and Soule the game is known as *pelota en campo abierto*. Bota luzea is derived from the Fr. >JEU DE LONGUE PAUME. The ball is hit with the hand and served against a tripod called a *botillo* – 'small bottle', from its characteristic shape resembling a bottle turned upside-down. The botillo is positioned near the endline of the court. During play one player must hit the botillo and an opposing player must return the ball. The play stops if a player misses the ball.

Pelota purhépecha con encendida.

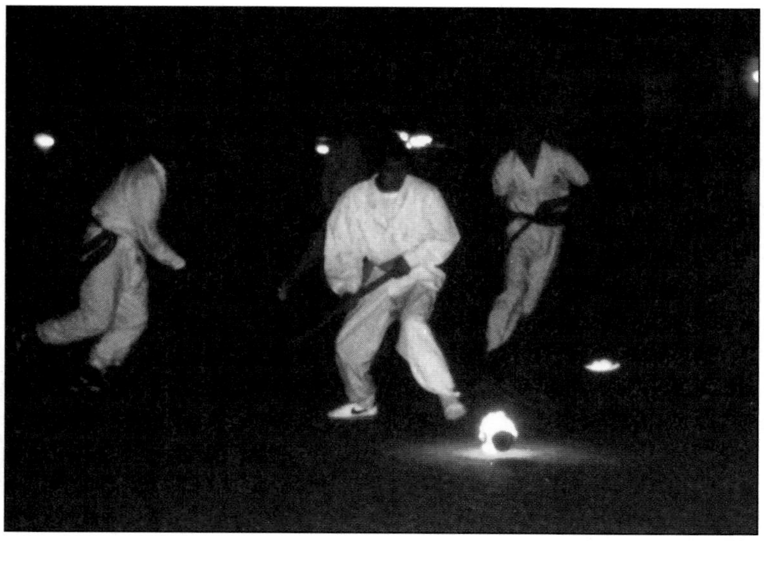

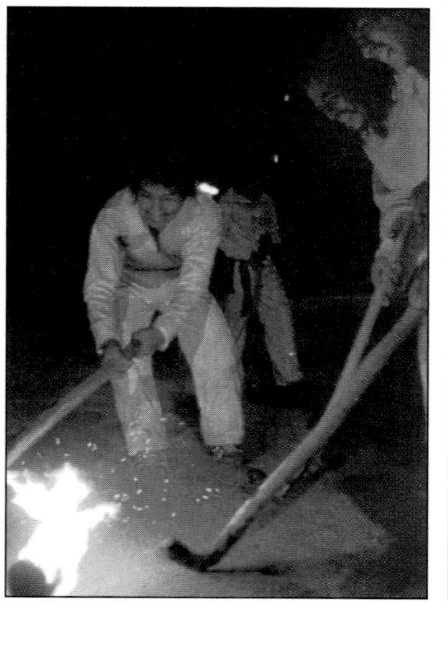

At present bota luzea is played on a 60m-long and 15m-wide open court divided in half by the centerline (Span. *linea central* or *linea divisoria*). The game is played by 2 teams of 5 players each (*jugadores*). A team consists of a pitcher (*sacador*) and 4 receivers (*restadores*). The ball must not be served overhead (Basq. *besagain*) but sidearm (Basq. *beso zehar* or *azpitik*). The serve must cross the centerline. The ball must be returned by the opposing team on the volley or the first bounce.

LAXOA, also spelled *lachoa* or *lushua*. An obsolete var. of pelota vasca known to have been played by the legendary Perkain in the 18th cent. At present, it is played in some Basq. towns on a court 66m long and 12-16m wide by 2 teams of 4 players each. The game is played using specially-made long leather gloves for catching and throwing the ball. The scoring is similar to that of >REAL TENNIS, with the use of the equivalents of the chases and the hazard lines called the *chazas* and *rayas* respectively. According to some sources, the *botillo* is positioned at one end of the court, opposite the shorter side with a wall narrower than the width of the court; other sources indicate the botillo is positioned in the center of the court and serves as an obstacle for play as the ball can be deflected by it and fox the opponent. The shape of the *botillo* resembles a small stone rostrum with 2 separate, square, slanted surfaces. The surfaces are marked in light color against the dark background of the *botillo*. The game is played by 2 teams of 4 players each. The rectangular court is 66m long and 12-16m wide (the courts sizes differ according to regional traditions). Laxoa is played with a small hard ball which is set in motion with long leather gloves (*canal de deslizamiento*). The inside of the glove is waxed before each game as to make the ball slide off easily. After a player strikes the ball against the stone botillo an opposing player must catch the ball with his glove and swing the ball back again against the stone. The team which misses the ball, misses a point.

MAHAI JOKOA, also Span. *juego de la mesa*. A game belonging to the pelota en campo abierto family, but also to >JUEGOS DIRECTOS; influenced by >JEU DE LONGUE PALME. The court is 50-60m long and 15-18m wide. Unlike other games of this family such as laxoa and bote luzea it does not use a stone stand. On the centerline dividing the court in half there is a *botillo* (also known as *mesa*) from which the Span. name of the game is derived. The server stands 5.5m from the mesa. The receiver who returns the ball stands 10m from the mesa in the opposite half of the court.

ESKUZKA, Basq.; also Span. *mano* – 'a hand'; full name *pelota a mano*. A family of games consisting mainly of games called pasaka practiced on the Fr. side of the Basq. territory. It can be classified as direct or indirect (>JUEGOS DIRECTOS, >JUEGOS INDIRECTOS). The game is played in two main variations – *pasaka en trinquette* and *pasaka en arkupe*. In most mano varieties the ball weighs 101-107g, with the proportion of rubber of 30-35g in amateur games and 35-38g in pro games. The minimal court length is 30m and the width 8-10m. The walls are 8-10m high. The most outstanding eskuzka players were L. 'Ciki' from Urruńa and L. Azkoitia in the 19th cent., and J. Apesteguy 'Chiquito de Cambo', J.G. 'Porteno', J.P. Gorostiague and J. Dongaitz in the beginning of the 20th cent.

PASAKA EN TRINQUETTE, the game played on a court resembling >ROYAL TENNIS, and having the same origins. Like in real tennis, the court (*trinquet*) has been modeled on the baileys of old castles, 30-32m long and 9-10m wide. On one side of the court there are shaded arcades. The front wall, known as the main wall (*pared principal*) is 10-11m high; the other walls are 5-6m high. In the corner between the main wall and the right-side wall (*pared derecha*), opposite the left-side arcaded wall (*pared izquierda*), there is a sloping buttress for deflecting the ball. The buttress is called a *frail* (fold) or *tambor* (a similar object in real tennis is called the tambour and is located on a side-wall, not in the corner). The tambor is used mainly during serving. The playing wall surface extends 8m above the ground, below the public gallery. On the wall opposite the main wall, called *pared del fondo* ('in-depth wall'), a net with a tilted roof (*techo*) is mounted 5.7m above the ground. A similar roof runs along the arcaded wall. Two parallel lines divide the back court into 3 equal zones: the net zone, the middle zone, and the back zone. The

A laxoa court.

A botillo for playing laxoa.

front court is divided in half. The whole court is divided by a net (*red*) 115-120cm high. Perpendicular to the net is the centerline (*linea central*) splitting the court in half. The ball is struck with the bare hand or a leather glove. The construction of the glove is not standardized but it usu. resembles a boxing glove, although less padded and without a thumb piece. The glove is held on with 2 broad leather straps. The serve is delivered with the bare hand from the middle zone. The serve must pass over the net and reach the opponent's playing area beyond the dividing line. The server scores a point if the opponent misses a fair ball. The opponent can score a half-point if the server has pitched the ball against the wall above the *techo*, sent it out of bounds, or taken his feet off the ground during service. Two faults by the server give one point to the opponent. The server can score a whole point if the ball hits a small window in the front wall (*ventanillo*). Scoring is similar to that of tennis (15, 30, 40, deuce). If the score is a tie before a deuce it is reset to 30:30 to increase the chance of winning. After each game the players change sides.

PASAKA EN ARKUPE, a game similar to pasaka en trinquette, but played on real courtyards of churches or public buildings, e.g. town halls (Basq. *arkupe* – 'courtyard, a kind of atrium'). Unlike in other variations of the game, there is no tambour or public gallery. Cf. >JEU QUARRÉ.

A MANO LIMPIA EN PLAZA LIBRE, (Fr. *main nue en place libre*; Span. and Fr. lit. 'with bare hand on open court'), a var. of pelota vasca. The game is played by singles or doubles and the ball is struck with the bare hand against a single wall. The court is at least 35m long and 16m wide. The wall is as wide as the court and is 8.5-9m high in the center and 7m high on the sides. The ball, 90-92g in weight, has to hit the wall above a line marked 85cm above the ground. The ball can be returned on the volley or the

Types of botillo used in bota luzea.

The court for playing bota luzea.

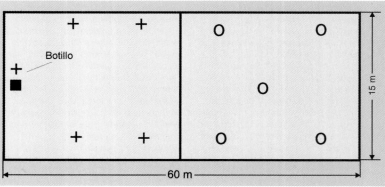

first bounce. Each player or pair has 3 balls at their disposal whose weight must conform to the regulations and be approved by the opponents. The service line runs 15m from the wall. A miss by the opponents is 1pt. for the serving players. The play is controlled by 3 referees. Game is 30pts.

A MANO LIMPIA EN TRINQUET, an equivalent of Fr. *main nue en trinquet* – 'with bare hand on covered court'. The game can be played by singles, doubles or triples. The ball weighs 90g. The length of the court is not specified but it must be at least 16m. The service line is 8.5m from the wall. The ball should be served with enough speed to reach a line 17.5m from the wall, after having bounced off the front wall. Each server is entitled to one more serve if the first one was foul. The game is controlled by a single referee. After service against the front wall the ball may hit any of the other 3 walls. A miss is a point to the opponent. Game is 50pts.

MAIN NUE EN FRONTON MUR À GAUCHE, Fr. for 'with bare hand on fronton with left-side wall'. The game played on a 3-walled court (*fronton*). The service line is 10.5m from the front wall, against which the ball is served. After service the ball must reach the foul line (*falta*) 24m from the front wall. If the ball fails to reach the foul line but has crossed the short line 14m from the front wall the pitcher can repeat the serve. If the ball fails to cross the short line the opponent scores a point. The ball weighs 98g. Each miss is one point to the opponent. Game is 22pts. in singles and 25pts. in doubles.

PALAZ, Basq.; also Span. *pala*, full name *pelota a pala*. A family of pelota vasca games consisting of striking the ball with a flat wooden bat (Basq. *palaz* and Span. *pala* – 'small racket, paddle'). The court is at least 50m long and 9.5-11m wide. The wall is 10-11m high. The pala is 53cm long, 10.5cm wide and weighs 840-880g. It is usu. made of beech or ash wood and has a leather-covered handle. The hard bat makes palaz one of the fastest variations of pelota. The game is spectacular but hard to master. The ball weighs 108-115g with the proportion of rubber of 50-65g in amateur games and 60-75g in pro games. The object of the game is to return the ball served by the opponent and keep it in play as long as possible. Game is usu. 45pts. The match is controlled by one referee and 2 assistant referees, but some varieties may differ. Palaz is played by doubles on long 3-walled frontons with various sizes and sections of the court. The ball served against the front wall must reach the designated falta line, like in *cesta punta*. If it fails to reach the falta the player misses a point. If the ball has reached the area between the falta and the pasa line marked further down the court the player misses a half-point. A serve can be repeated 3 times. Palaz is popular not only in the Basq. country, but also all over Spain and in South America. Its main varieties include:

PALA CORTA, a doubles game. It differs from other varieties of pelota in having a relatively smaller

wall (*fronton espagnol*) against which the ball is struck. The court is at least 30-40m long and 8-10m wide. The front wall is 8-10m high. The ball is struck with a short wooden racket (*pala*) from which the name of the game is derived (Span. *pala* – 'bat, paddle' + *corta* – 'short'). The pala is 49cm long and weighs 600-700g. In both amateur and pro games the ball weighs 85-90g with the proportion of rubber of 34-38g. Service is delivered from behind the service line parallel to and 28m from the front wall. A service is delivered correctly if the ball after having bounced off the wall crosses the *pasa* line marked 17m from the front wall. If the ball has failed to reach the *falta* line it is a miss for the serving team. If it falls to the zone between the *falta* line marked at 10m from the front wall and the *pasa* line the service is repeated. Each team is entitled to 3 repetitions of serve. The object of the game is to keep the ball in play as long as possible. Each miss is a point to the opponent. Each game is 35pts. and is controlled by a single referee.

PALA LARGA, a local var. of pelota vasca played on a one-walled court (Span. *plaza libre*; Fr. *place libre*). The game is played by doubles using long wooden rackets called *pala* (Span. *pala* – 'paddle' + largo – 'long'). Service must be delivered from behind a line 25m from the front wall. A serve must cross a line marked 15m from the wall. A game is 50pts. and is controlled by 3 referees.

PALETA DE CUERO, full name *juego con paleta con pelota de cuero*, Span. game of pelota using a leather ball. Despite gradual replacement of leather-covered balls with rubber balls since the end of the 19th cent. the former still enjoy some popularity. The leather-covered ball used in various kinds of pala is played with a flat wooden bat 49-51cm long and 12cm wide which weighs 580g. The court is at least 30-40m long and 8-10m wide. The walls are 8-10m high.

JUEGO CON PALETA ANCHA CON PELOTA DE GOMA, Span. game played with a wide bat and a rubber ball. The game is derived from Argentine tradition. The bat is 50cm long and 17.8cm wide. The ball weighs 50-52g with the proportion of rubber of 18-20g.

CHISTERA, also spelled *shistera* or *txistera*. The name denotes: 1) a curved leather or wicker basket

A game of pelota vasca.

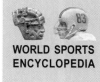

WORLD SPORTS ENCYCLOPEDIA

P

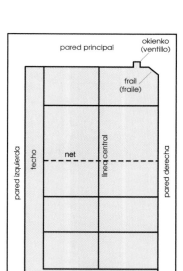

The court for playing pasaka.

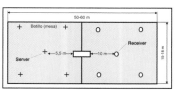

The court for playing mahai jokoa (mahi

P

WORLD SPORTS ENCYCLOPEDIA

strapped to the player's hand with a special glove; 2) a family of games using a big *chistera* (*grand chistera*) or a small one (*petit chistera*). The varieties of chistera games include the *cesta punta*, also *cesta-punta* – 'a pointed basket' [Span. *cesta* – 'basket' + *punta* – 'point, tip], full name *pelota a cesta-punta*. The chistera as a playing bat is known as the *cesta*, esp. in South America. The game is played by doubles, using the grand chistera during the Basq. festival of jai-alai. The ball weighs 115-125g with the proportion of rubber 90-115g. In the *cesta punta corta* variation the ball weighs 105-115g with the proportion of rubber 45-50g. One player stands near the front wall in the so-called front court, the other returning the ball stands in the back court. The court is at least 50m long and 9.5-11m wide with the 10-11m-high wall. In the cesta punta corta variation the court is 30-40m long and 8-10m wide with the front wall 8-10m high. The side-wall is marked with 14 vertical lines called *cuadros* drawn 4m apart (Span. *cuadro* – 'four'). The extension of the fourth line, counting from the front wall, on the court is the *falta* line and the extension of the seventh line on the court is the *pasa* line. A correctly served ball must cross the pasa line. If the ball hits the court within the falta line the server loses a point. If the served ball falls between the lines the server loses a half-point but he can make it up and repeat the serve correctly. The server loses a whole point if he delivers the serve incorrectly for a second time. Service is delivered from behind the tenth *cuadro*, i.e. 40m from the front wall. The *chistera*, measured from the wrist to the tip, is 90-110cm long and 16cm deep. The ball weighs 125g. One game is 35 or 40 points. The match is controlled by one referee and 2 assistant referees.

JOKO GARBI, full name *cesta joko garbi*, also spelled *yoko garbi* or *ioko garbia* (Span. *cesta* – 'basket' + Basq. lit. fair play). The game is played with small *chisteras* by 2 teams of 3 players each. The court is 50m long and 16m wide. The 8.5-9m-high front wall is of the same width as the court. The side-walls are 7m high. The service line is parallel to and 22.5m from the front wall. The object of the game is to make the opponent fail to return the ball. Each miss or ball out of bounds is one point to the opponent. One game is 50pts. The game is controlled by 3 referees. The main tactics are based on effective line-up of players, i.e. one in the front court and two in the back court.

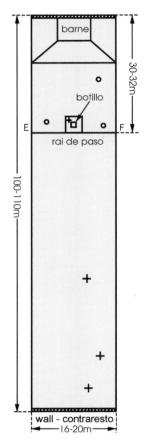

The court for playing pelota vasca el rebote.

Pelota players with chisteras.

El rebote.

In the var. with the use of big *chisteras* the game is also played by 2 teams of 3 players each. The one-walled court is 80m long and 16m wide. The service line is parallel to and 30m from the wall. The chistera is 70cm long from the wrist to the tip. The ball weighs 125g. One game is 50pts., controlled by 5 referees. Low balls are not prohibited, but high balls are better.

EL REBOTE, one of the oldest varieties of pelota vasca, regarded as the most prestigious and often dubbed 'the king of pelota games' (*el rey de los juegos de pelota*). The Fr. equivalent of el rebote is called *rebot* and it is played on the Fr. side of the Basq. country (Span. *rebote* – 'ricochet, rebound'; also old Fr. *reboter* – 'to rebound'). This game is considered the oldest form of pelota derived from >JEU DE LONGUE PAUME, and belongs to the family of direct pelota games (>JUEGOS DIRECTOS). A game of the same name is played in Valencia, where it is considered indigenous. El rebote is played by 2 teams of 5 players each. It is played with the *chistera* (Basq. *txistera*) with a chestnut or ash frame. The *chistera* is strapped to the player's hand with a special leather glove. There are 2 types of *chisteras* – a bigger *chistera grande* (Fr. *grand chistera*) and a smaller *chistera pequeño* (Fr. *petit chistera*). The grand chistera is 70cm long and 16cm deep from the frame to the bottom. The rubber ball weighs 130g. The court is at least 100-110m long and 15-20m wide. The optimal court width is, however, 16-20m. In the past el rebote was played with heavier balls on 80-90m-long courts. The court has 2 walls on its shorter sides. The walls are the same width as the court. The front wall is 10-12m high and the back wall called the *contrarresto* is 7m high. The center part of the wall is usu. 3-4m higher. Adjacent to the front wall on the court is a rectangular area called the *barne* (also *carré, cuadro, arrizabal* in other regions), which is 6.5m long and 5.5m wide. The longer side of the *barne* is the middle section of the front wall. 30-32m from the front wall is a line called the *paso* (also *raie de paso* or *pasamarra*) in the center of which stands the *botillo*, also called the *botarri*. The top bouncing surface of the *botillo* is set at an angle of 45 degrees. The *botillo's* shape depends on regional traditions. Sometimes the *botillo* resembles a short tree trunk, but it may also be an artistically carved tripod resembling a piece of Fr. furniture. A serve must bounce off the *botillo*. The *paso* line divides the court into 2 playing areas. The front court is taken by the receiving team (Span. *campo del resto* and Fr. *defil*); the longer back court is taken by the serving team. The teams change sides in turns. A miss or foul return by one team gives one point to the opponents. Service (*saque*) is delivered by the pitcher called the *sacador* who throws the ball with the bare hand against the botillo. After the ball bounces off the tripod it must hit the wall on the fly or the first bounce off the barna zone. The served ball is received by an opposing player called the *refileur*. The ball is struck with bare hand only on service. During play the ball is caught and hit with the chisteras. If the serving team fails to deliver the service correctly it misses 1pt. If the ball is served correctly the serving team scores 1pt. If the receiving team fails to return the serve or allows

the ball to roll on the ground and cross the *paso* line the referee declares a *chaza*. In such a case a green twig is placed on the ground to mark the spot of foul return. The twig marks a new *paso* line, which makes it more difficult for the serving team to score a point. This way the receiving team gains advantage as the ball must bounce off a reduced zone. In order to restore the original *paso* line the serving team must score 2pts. above the twig line or 1pt., if the game score equals 40pts. Scoring a point above the twig line makes the teams change sides. Scoring is similar to that of tennis (15 – *quince*, 30 – *treinta*, 40 – *cuarenta*, deuce). A game consists of 13 sets (*trece juegos*), and the odd number of sets excludes the possibility of a draw. The players wear long white pants, colored belts and white polo-shirts.

Despite the above differences, in some Basq. sources, rebote and ioko garbia are regarded as the same var. of pelota vasca.

GRAND CHISTERA, Span. *chistera grande*. A game similar to and prob. derived from joko garbi. It is played by doubles or by 2 teams of 3 players each. The serve is played against a wall with a 70cm long chistera from behind the service line. The receiving team can return the ball on the fly or the first bounce. The court is similar to that of *main nue en place libre*, but its length reaches 80m. The service line is 30m from the front wall. There are 2 players in the front court and one in the middle of the court (Fr. *arriére*). The game regulations allow for a change of line-up, but is rarely practiced by the players. Service is delivered by a player on the right side of the forecourt who signals the serve by shouting 'Yo!', meaning 'Hit!' or 'Go' in the Basq. language. The regulations do not prohibit low balls which are hard to return but the players usu. play high balls by convention. The quite balletic high jumps performed by the players constitute one of the most attractive elements of play. The game is a huge tourist attraction of the Basq. country but the Basques themselves more highly praise other varieties of pelota vasca. Once caught in the *chistera* the ball must be stopped, held for a while and then it is swung off against the wall. In Basq. this technique is called *atchiki* – 'stopping'. An average point usu. consists of 20-30 returns. Each miss gives a point to the opponents. The match is controlled by 3 referees. A game is played to 50pts. The originators of the *atchiki* technique were the famous 19th cent. pelota players: Melchior, Antza and Manuael from Spain and Bask Matiu from France (full names unknown).

PALETA, Fr. *palette*, a variation of pelota vasca played on a trinquet with an elongated wooden bat, which gives the game its name (Fr. *palette* – 'bat, paddle'). The bat is 50cm long, 13.5cm wide and 2.5cm thick. The game is played by doubles and the match is controlled by a single referee. A game is played tp 40pts. The leather-covered ball is fairly resilient as it has a rubber core. The court dimensions are those of the *sare* (see below). If a game is played on a *fronton izquierda* (Fr. *mur à gauche*) the *pala* rules apply (see above).

The variation of *paleta con pelota de goma*, Fr. equivalent *palette avec pelote de gomme* (Fr. 'bat and rubber ball') is played by doubles. The ball is struck with an oval paddle which is 55cm long and 13.5cm wide but thinner than the bats used in other varieties, reaching 1cm in thickness. The small rubber ball weighs 45g. The match is controlled by one referee; game is thirty points.

RAQUETA (Span., also Fr. *raquette* – 'racket'). The game is played by doubles with rackets resembling snow-rackets, covered with leather straps. Due to the racket construction the ball is stopped and returned as with a slingshot. A similar type of racket is used in the *sara* var. of pelota vasca. The racket is 50-55cm long. The game is played on a medium-size fronton (Span. *frontones medianos*, Fr. *petit fronton*) which is 30-40m long and 8-10m wide. The fronton has a left-side wall (Span. *pared izquierda*, Fr. *petit fronton mur à gauche*) which is 8-10m high. The ball can be made of rubber or leather depending on regional traditions. The rules of play are similar to those of *pala corta* (see above), but the pasa line is only 50cm from the front wall. According to R. Aquire, a pelota vasca researcher, raqueta is a non-Basq. var. of pelota. This may explain its early and swift adoption in the Basq. country as a women's game.

REMONTE, full name *pelota a remonte*, also *erremontea*. It is played with a long but relatively shallow type of chistera (Span. *remonte* – 'rebound, return'). The size of the ball differs depending on the game category. In the amateur games the ball weighs 105-110g and in pro games 110-117g, with the proportion of rubber 50-60g and 65-80g respectively. The court is at least 50m long and 9.5-11m wide. The wall is 10-11m high. The match is controlled by 3 referees; a game is played to 35pts. The rules of play are similar to cesta punta (see above), but the *chistera* is shallower and made of wicker, which makes the game more dynamic. The game is played not only on the Iberian Peninsula but also in Span. speaking countries of South America, where it is widely used as a medium for gambling. The most famous remonte fronton is Juego Nuevo in Pamplona. Another popular fronton is Frontón Noiz-Bait in Zarauz. At present many modern frontons are built indoors.

SARE, Basq. for 'net', also spelled *share*; Span. *red* – 'net'. The name of the game has been taken from the name of the dividing net spread across the court. Sare is regarded as one of the most trad. and prestigious Basq. games. It is played by doubles on a covered court called a trinquete which is at least 30-40m long and 8-10m wide. The walls are 8-10m high. The racket consists of a chestnut frame and a thick net and is 59cm long and 19cm wide. The frame is 1.2cm thick. The rubber-covered ball weighs 108-115g with the proportion of rubber 24-28g. The match is controlled by a single referee; a game is played to 50pts. Service is delivered from behind the service line 15m from the front wall. The ball is served from the left side of the court and service is correct if the ball after hitting the wall crosses the service line on the right side. If the ball lands on the line or hits the side-wall the server loses a half-point. After a double foul service the serving player loses 1pt. On the Fr. side of the Basq. country the game is known as *raquette Argentine*. The name can be explained by the fact that the original *sare* played on the Fr. side was brought there around 1850 from Argentina, not the Basq. country.

History. The traditions of pelota vasca date back to the Middle Ages. The significance of the game in the Basq. country can be best illustrated by the numerous tombstones erected in honor of the most outstanding pelota players depicting the players themselves. This tradition was already observed in the 17th cent., esp. on the Fr. side. The earliest tombstone of this type dates back to 1629. It commemorates the achievements of Maistre Diriarte from the village of Garris. A similar tombstone was erected to honor a certain Southourrou who died in Banca in 1784.

The earliest, brief mentions of pelota vasca lack any precise descriptions of the sport. In 1755, some more detailed information on the game was included in a letter to a citizen of Bayonne from his Fr. friend. The letter was found by the Fr. historian Ducéré. 'Yesterday, a great game of pelota was played among seven Basques. One of them was Monsieur Hiriart, a doctor from Macayue [...] wearing, like the others, a peasant's shirt and beret. The game attracted many Basques and people from the Spanish frontier [...]. The doctor and his team lost the game but decided to play a return match scheduled for the following Thursday.' In 1761, J. de Ordońez wrote that '... pelota is a traditional pastime in San Sebastian.' The most famous pelota player of the second half of the 18th cent. was Perkain (c.1865-1910, first name unknown) from the mountain village of Les Aldudes on the Fr. side of the Basq. country. He has been credited with giving pelota vasca a high social prestige it had not enjoyed before. Perkain's outstanding peers and successors who enjoyed local fame were Harosteguy, Eskerra, Azantza of Cambo and I. Indart, Simon de Arrayoz, and their later successors: J.R. Indart alias 'Michico' and B. de Arrayoz. A match between Perkain and the left-handed Eserra in 1793 attracted about 10,000 spectators. What made Perkain even more famous was his incident with the Fr. police. Opposing the Fr. National Convention and dodging conscription to the Fr. army Perkain had fled to Spain. In order to play a match against Eskerra he crossed the border back to France running the risk of being arrested. The local constable was to have come for Perkain in the final decisive stage of the game that had been going on for 3hrs. According to the legend, Perkain killed the constable, finished the game, and fled back to Spain. His life provided a literary inspiration for a play in two acts *Perkain. The Drama of Terror.* written by a Basq. playwright, P. Harispe in 1900. At the turn of the 18th and 19th cent. the first female pelota players appeared, e.g. Sister A. Tita. The most famous of the pelotaris was the French Basque J. Erratchun (1817-59) known as El Gaskoina (the Gascon). In 1846, a pelota match was played between a Basq. team led by Erratchun (Eskerra, Domingo of Espelette, and Gamio – a local priest; full name unknown) and a Span. team consisting of Melchior, Tripero and Molinero (the fourth player's name unknown). The match was played in the town of Irun on the Fr.-Span. border and it attracted twelve thousand spectators, with betting sums amounting to 140,000 francs. The interest in the match was so huge that a special pigeon messenger service was set up to inform those who could not attend the game about the result. The match became famous not because of the Gascon's victory, but because of the notorious attempts of the Span. team to defeat the Basques by all means. The Spanish were said to have attempted to buy their victory by offering him 8,000 francs and after they failed, they were said to have placed nails on the court to hurt Erratchun, who played barefoot. The Spaniards were supposed to have bribed one of the Basques to make the Gascon drunk during the game by offering him wine. His strong head and feet, used to jogging on rocky mountain pastures turned out to be too tough. The Gascon drank all the wine and sent for another goatskin. As the prize for the match he won 4,000 francs and 2 oxen. He died of typhoid at the peak of his career.

All famous pelota players were exalted in songs, and the events in which they participated attracted up to 10,000 people, who often traveled to games from distant regions of the country, despite the fact that matches were often held in remote mountain villages and at times of political turmoil such as the French Revolution or the Napoleonic Wars.

The introduction of expensive playing gloves during the reign of such pelota players as Gaskoina, Anza and Maitu made pelota vasca a rather exclusive sport. In the 19th cent., a cheaper, pelota racket, called *matsardia*, became popular, esp. in south-western France, in the Nive valley around Labourd. The new racket resembled a small, wooden hay-fork, tied on top, with string netting. In the Nivelle valley the pelota rackets were modified wooden sieves called *zetabea*. Around 1857 a fourteen-year-old boy Dithurbie from the village of St. Pée on the Fr. side of the Basq. territory used for the first time a long, curved basket to play pelota, the predecessor of the modern chistera. His invention was first ignored, but then it became popular in the 1860s thanks to a pair of unknown players who using the baskets defeated Matiu, a famous pelota player. Popularity of the chistera was influenced by the introduction of the rubber ball (the hard, leather-covered ball used earlier had quickly worn the *chistera* out). One of the early *chistera* players was the Sp. Basque I. Sarasqueta, better known as Chiquito de Eibar (The Child of Eibar, 1860-1928). Sarasqueta made the chistera popular outside his native country, particularly in France and South America, esp. in Argentina (1884), where he would play exhibition matches and won against such local pelota celebrities as P. Zabaleta alias Paysandu from Argentina, and Urgara from Uruguay. Sarasqueta's *chistera* was short and slightly curved. It became longer with the introduction of the backhand technique by El Samperio in 1887. The longer *chistera* made it possible to display effectively the full range of playing skills, not possible with the use of short *chisteras*. Before that time, the ball was played only on the forehand, and in fact, El Sampiero's new technique was the result of an injury sustained after a forehand shot. In 1888, an Argentine player, Curuchaque introduced a larger, 70cm-long *chistera* in Buenos Aires. The new model became to be known as the grand chistera and revolutionized the *chistera* type of pelota vasca games. That significant South American contribution to the development of pelota vasca had a tremendous impact back in Spain where the *grand chistera* caught on in the Span. varieties of pelota. Later on, it became widespread in the Basq. country, first on the Fr. side (c.1895) thanks to A. de Bidart who had seen the new *chistera* in Valencia. Another *chistera*, deeper near the wrist-side, became to be known as *cesta punta*. Due to the apparent similarities, the two types of *chisteras* and, in consequence, the two varieties of pelota have been frequently confused in numerous studies.

The development and social prestige of pelota vasca is closely connected with the tradition of grand families of Basq. players called dynasties (*dinastias*). The members of the multi-generation families have often been known by their first name, the name of their hometown or village, and the succession number. One of the most famous is the Juaristi dynasty whose members have occupied the top positions in the hierarchy of pelota vasca players. The founder of the dynasty was Juan Maria Juaristi alias Atano Lucia (from the village of Atano). His descendants were Juan Maria Juaristi Mendizábal (Atano I), Valentin Atano Mendizábal (Atano II), Luciano Juaristi Mendizábal (Atano III), Eugenio Juaristi Mendizábal (Atano IV), Mariano Juaristi Mendizábal (Atano V), Marcelino Juaristi Mendizábal (Atano VI), and Jose Maria Juaristi Mendizábal (Atano VII). The four sons of Juan Maria: Pedro Juaristi (Atano VIII), Luis Juaristi Alberdi (Atano IX) and Luciano Juaristi Alberdi (Atano X) are the youngest generation of the family. The most famous representative of the Atano dynasty was Atano III who was the top barehand trinquet player in the years 1928-48. Another important family is the Echave dynasty, which contributed nine famous players: Francisco Echave (Echave I – the founder of the family), Estanislao

Manufacturing the chisteras.

P

WORLD SPORTS ENCYCLOPEDIA

(Echave II), Carmelo (Echave III), Juan Arteche (Echave IV), José (Echave V), Romualdo (Echave VI), Estanislao (Echave VIII) and Bibiano (Echave IX). Nothing is known about Echave VII.

Another famous dynasty included pelota players known as the Begoñes. The dynasty was founded by Juan Mata in the beginning of the 19th cent., succeeded then by his son-in-law Antonio Guisasola alias Anton. Juan Mata's sons were Juan Guisasola Bilbao (Begoñes I), Miguel (Begoñes II), Rafael (Begoñes III) and Higinio (Begoñes IV). The dynastic pelota tradition was then maintained by other family members: Jesús Guisasola (Begoñes V), Ignacio (Begoñes VI), and Higinio's son Juan (Begoñes VII), the last of the family. The most outstanding representative of the dynasty was Begoñes I for whom a monument was built by the sculptor Juan Guisasola. Another famous seven-member dynasty was the Guruceaga family founded by Melchor Guruceaga (Guruceaga I).

Other famous pelota players came from less numerous families, e.g. the Abrego dynasty of Navarra founded by Jesús Abrego Narvarte (Abrego I, b. 1910) and represented by Maria Abrego Narvarte (Abrego II) and Julio Abrego Narvarte (Abrego III). The most famous was Abrego I alias El Mago (Wizard), La Maravilla de Arróniz (The Marvel of Arróniz) and El Rey del Remonte (The King of Remonte).

Juan Zabala (Arano I) was the founder of another, three-generational dynasty of pelota players from the town of Arano. His successors were Manuel (Arano II) and Bautista (Arano III).

Players from particular dynasties have usu. been faithful to one var. of pelota vasca although some individual players have represented different pelota variaties. Teams have been composed of players from the same dynasty, sometimes aided by representatives of other dynasties.

At the beginning of the 20th cent. the rapidly developing pelota vasca experienced the numerous problems characteristic of professional sports games. Matches were rigged and the players played for time

A game of pelota.

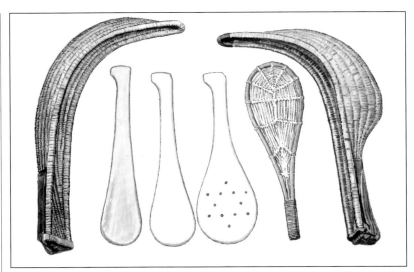

Types of rackets and chisteras for playing pelota.

by keeping the ball in the chisteras before a shot. The spectators often disapproved of such practices. During a game in San Sebastian in 1909 the entire audience left the court in protest against the foul play. In 1912, a Fr.-Basque J. Ibernegaray (1881-1956) came up with the idea of reforming and unifying numerous local varieties of pelota vasca. The implementation of Ibernegaray's idea was interrupted by the outbreak of WWI and the task of unification was accomplished only by the Fr. Federation of Pelota Vasca (Fédération Francaise de Pelote Basque) founded in 1922. In 1929, the International Federation of Pelota Vasca (Federación Internacional de Pelota Vasca, FIVP) was founded in Madrid. The Span. Civil War (1937) slowed down the international development of the game. Only after 1945 did pelota vasca begin to gain international impetus. In 1952 the first Pelota Vasca W.Ch. were held in San Sebastian.

PELOTA MANO, a local Span. game prob. borrowed from the medieval Fr. >JEU DE LA PAUME; see also >COURTE PAUME and the Eng. >ROYAL TENNIS. Practiced mainly in the Las Palmas province in the island of Lanzarote of the Canary Islands.

PENCAK SILAT, also sp. *pentjak silat*, popularly known as *silat*; Indon. and Malay martial art related to some styles of >WU SHU in China and Singapore, and >ARNIS in the Philippines. A variety known as >OLAHRAGA is part of the PE curriculum in Indon. schools. Pencak silat is also popular in Brunei and Celebes. It can be practiced on 3 levels: 1. as a real fight to the death; 2. as military training, combining hand-to-hand combat and bayonet techniques; 3. as a sport without any dangerous combative elements. The women's var. of pencak silat, known as >KESANIAN, incorporates dance elements and resembles ballet. It is also used in scenes of the trad. forms of Asian theater. Pencak silat training is combined with meditation. The most combative forms of pencak silat, generally deprived of sporting elements, are practiced in the Batak region of Sumatra. In the Minangkabau region pencak silat is a highly esthetic dance consisting of rhythmic body movements, full of agility and grace performed to the accompaniment of drums or gongs. **History.** The origins of pencak silat can be traced to the era of animist beliefs in Malaysia. Its genesis is described in ancient tales and legends. According to one legend from the 13th cent., 3 Malay brothers – Burhanmuddin, Shamsuddin, and Aminuddin – were to travel north to study Buddhism. When they emerged out of the jungle in the territory of present-day Thailand the brothers came across their future master's hut. One day, Aminuddin went to a nearby waterfall and found a fragile flower bending under the falling water but firmly resisting its force. The flower led Aminuddin's to reflect on a skillful defensive technique consisting of harmonious body movements similar to the movements of the flower under the pressure of falling water. That event gave rise to the fundamental principle of pencak silat, i.e. subduing the enemy not through applying direct force but through simulating evasive movements and using the inner strength obtained by physical and mental training and constant contact with a guru. The mental training functions regardless of the religious system prevalent in a given area. In Indonesia, for example, the

spiritual system of pencak silat reflects both the tenets of Islam and local Javanese beliefs.

According to another legend, the rules of pencak silat were established by 2 Malay warriors, Hang Tuah and Hang Jebat. In their travels the warriors were supposed to have met a hermit guru living on the Wiwana Mountain who initiated them into his own art of combat. When the warriors returned to the court of Sultan Muzaffar of Malacca and showed him their newly acquired combat skills they were given the sultan's approval to teach the new martial art to others. Despite the numerous legends and fables explaining the birth of this martial art, the real origins of pencak silat remain unknown. The contemporary diversity of pencak silat suggests the sport could be a combination of the different traditions of numerous Indon. and Malay communities which have evolved into their present form. Pencak silat enjoyed a period of enormous popularity in the time of the Majapahit Empire in Java (from the end of the 13th to the beginning of the 16th cent.). The competitors wear black jackets and pants secured by broad sashes, similar to those of >JUDO. Before the more spectacular fights, the competitors pin their hair up in what is known as a *tengkolok*. The most professional forms of pencak silat are practiced in Indonesia, Thailand and Singapore. It is also gaining popularity in some Arabic countries, e.g. Brunei (The Brunei Darussalam Invitation Tournament). The majority of pencak silat masters come from Java and Malaysia. The most outstanding competitors are S. Allaudin and R. Ahmad. The most important pencak silat events include the World Championships held annually since 1984, the South-East Asian Games, and the Thai Open tournament.

Pencak silat is taught in a var. of schools. It is estimated that more than 800 styles of the sport are practiced in Indonesia and 200 in Malaysia. The unifying elements of all the styles and variations are the so-called Four Aspects of pencak silat: 1) combat as artful expression of personal culture; 2) control of the body and spirit; 3) self-defense as the supreme principle; 4) sportsmanship and friendly competition. The Aspects are probably the outcome of the natural Malay philosophy promoting conflict resolution through the *musywarah*, i.e. harmonious dialog leading to *mufakt* – agreement. The most fundamental pencak silat moves are not attack moves, but smooth back and forth movements called the flower dance, which give the opponent a chance to retreat. Pencak silat fighting elements include numerous holds, strikes, kicks, locks, sweeps, take downs as well as weapons such as the *kris* – dagger with serrated edge; *pisau* – short-bladed knife; *tali* – rope; *lawi adam* – knife resembling a tiger jaw; *tongkat* – short wooden club; *tekpi* – thin metal truncheon; *pedang* – sword; *badik* – broad-bladed knife. Holding the opponent by his garment – *chendai*- is allowed as well. The rules of pencak silat were formalized in present-day Malaysia and Singapore and adopted in Indonesia and the Philippines, although all these countries regard the sport as the result of their own traditions. Among the numerous pencak silat styles the most significant in present-day Malaysia include: SILAT CHEKAK. A style based on avoidance of forceful combat in favor of agile movements and light hits with hands and feet.

SILAT JAVA. Despite its name the style does not come from Java but from the south of the Malay Peninsula. The style was formed and in the Malaccan Sultanate. Unlike the flower dance styles, silat java uses quick, strong movements. Basic techniques include the use of the fist as well as combinations of hand and foot movements.
SILAT KEDAH. A style practiced in the northern Malaysian region of Kendah. It is characterized by the upright position of the fighters and the use of various holds, locks, sweeps and kicks. For a long time it was associated with the Royal Siamese Court of Bangkok.
SILAT KELANTAN. A style practiced in the border region of Kelantan between Thailand and Malaysia. It is mainly a defensive style characterized by simple hand strikes, kicks and relatively minimal use of complex locks. Particular emphasis is put on maintaining distance between the opponents.
SILAT LINTAN. A style characterized by strong influences of Chin. martial and self-defense arts, using weapon techniques.
SILAT MEDEN. A style characterized by the extensive use of weapons.
SILAT MINANGKABAU. A style from the Minangkabau region of Sumatra, characterized by groundfighting, quick body movements and low kicks.
SILAT PATANI. A style practiced in the Patani region bordering Thailand. It is characterized by slow, unassertive, defensive movements, with greater emphasis put on handwork rather than footwork. The fighters wait for an attack before moving into action. Silat patani uses holds and locks.
SILAT PENINJUEN. A style characterized by extensive use of jump kicks.
SILAT SENDENG. A style consisting of characteristic jumps which combine both attacking and defensive techniques. The style might have been inspired by characteristic ape movements.
SILAT TERELEK. A style similar to Jap. >KARATE. Emphasis is on put the body's power and use of special breathing techniques.
In the empty-hand styles of pencak silat the combat fundamentals are included in curricula called *langkah sembah* (Malay lit. 'steps of respect'), which play a role similar to that of *kata* in karate or *kuen* in >GONGFU. In Indon. pencak silat emphasis is put on the use of various weapons such as swords, clubs, sticks, *kris* as well as evasive movements, footwork and avoidance of force on force. Among over 150 Indon. styles of pencak silat, the most important are:
SILAT TJIMENDE. A style widely practiced in W Java characterized by cautious body movements, defensive blocking with hands and arms, attempts at predicting the opponent's moves and counterattacking. A silak tjimende fighter aims at the opponent's center of gravity using 4 attack techniques: 1) striking the thigh or calf with the ball of the foot; 2) striking the opponent's knee joint; 3) combination of the two techniques above; 4) striking the opponent with elbow and knee. After the opponent is floored the fight is resumed from the ground position.
SILAT MUSTIKKA KWITANG. A style practiced in Jakarta and western Java. It stresses dynamic attack, bodily contact and sporadic use of evasive moves.
SILAT TJINGRIK. A style based on ape-like body movements using primarily hand-and-arm striking techniques. It is characterized by quick unpredictable moves, and unexpected strikes. One of the objectives is to get hold of the opponent's throat or strike him in the crotch.
SILAT HATI. A style practiced in C Java, based mainly on foot striking techniques. The fighter feints a hand movement and then rapidly attacks with his feet.
PERISAI DIRI. A style from E Java, consisting of rapid arm moves performed in an upright position; very effective in defense.
SILAT HARIMAU. A style known and practiced in C and W Sumatra, known in Indonesia as the 'tiger style'. The fighters stay close to the ground using crouching, lying, sitting and semi-squat positions and employ powerful kicks. The style was developed in swampy areas, hence it relies on the ground fighting position rather than the upright position, in which it is hard to maintain balance.
SILAT KUMANGO. A style developed in sandy areas, using the upright fighting position. It is characterized by advanced hand-striking and kicking techniques, although the former are mainly used to distract the opponent. Silat Kumango makes use of a monotonous rhythm, which is to soften the opponent's senses, and sudden surprising hits and counters.
SILAT PATAI. A style developed in the mountainous regions of Sumatra, particularly in Bukittinggi. It is based on characteristic rhythm and dance movements, suggesting awaiting the opponent's attack. The defensive techniques used in silat patai are more effective if exercised in a position higher than the position assumed by the opponent. Blocks are often used, esp. foot blocks, in case the opponent is armed.
SILAT PAMUR. A style from the island of Madura using a combination of arm and legwork. Emphasis is on evasive and counterattacking forms. Its main techniques include arm and leg holds.
BHAKTI NEGARA. A style common in Bali. It reflects the peaceful nature of the Balinese and stresses evasive and defensive movements. The contenders fight both in the upright and the ground position.
Other popular Indon. styles include: harimau, baru strelak, lintow of Sumatra; setia heti, perisai sahti of central Java; tjikalong, tjendur, mustika kwitang of western Java; tapak suji of E Java; pamur of Madura; and tridherma of Bali.

K.S. Moorthy, 'Silat – A Malay Indigenous Art of Self-Defence', SS, Feb. 1988; anon., 'Pencak Silat. A Traditional Game', OR, Dec. 1995 – Jan. 1996, XXV-6; 'Silat with the Midas Touch', SS, June 1993; anon., 'Silat – A Family Affair', SS, Jun 1993; J. Szymankiewicz, *Sztuki walki Malezji, Indonezji, Filipin, Birmy, Tajlandii*, 1993.

PENDELKEGELN, a Ger. bowling game using pins hung on strings (Ger. *Pendel* – 'something dangling', 'pendulum' + *Kegel* – 'pin, cone'). The game was popularized in other Eur. Countries (e.g. Hungary) by Ger. settlers.

PENNY CAST, also *penny stones*, an obs. Brit. game consisting of tossing round flat stones, 4-6in. in diameter each. The players try to throw their stones onto or close to an opponent's stone. The game's origin suggesting playing with pennies is uncertain. According to some ethnographic sources, the game was not played with coins until 1810. Later on, the stones were tossed at coins placed on pegs, in a similar way to *penny prick*.
TGESI, II, 39.

PENNY PRICK, also Scot. *pennie-pricke*, an obs. Brit. game consisting of casting oblong pieces of iron at a mark, which usu. was a halfpence placed on a peg. The aim of the game was to knock the coin off the peg. Similar to *penny cast*.
TGESI, II, 39.

PENTATHLON, any sports competition consisting of 5 events. The earliest form of the pentathlon was the >PENTATHLON (ANCIENT). In modern times the most common forms have been >ATHLETIC PENTATHLON and >MODERN PENTATHLON. The first, or at least one of the earliest attempts to restore the ancient tradition of pentathlon was its inclusion in the Much Wenlock Games in 1868.

PENTATHLON (ANCIENT), Gk. *pentathlon* – a 5-competition-event (Gk. *pente* – 'five' + *athlon* – 'contest, competition'). In ancient Greece, the pentathlon was an athletic contest entailing: a run (>DROMOS), long jump (>HALMA), discus throw (>DISCOBOLIA), javelin throw (>AKONTISIMA), and wrestling (>PALE). In many Indo-Eur. languages the name *pentathlon* denotes both the ancient athletic event and modern sports competitions consisting of 5 events. Of the 5 ancient pentathlon events only running and wrestling were part of the Ol.G. and they were held separately as single events. The remaining pentathlon events were held as single events only at the other ancient games. Not much is known about the order of events, apart from wrestling, which was always the concluding competition. Most likely, the first event was the long jump followed by the discus, the run, javelin, and wrestling. The winner of the entire contest was probably the winner of the wrestling match between the 2 athletes who had performed best in the previous 4 events, although no precise information is available. According to some researchers, the pentathlon winner had to score victories in at least 3 events including the wrestling match. This may be confirmed by the Gk. term *triakter*, i.e. the winner of 3 events, found in numerous ancient texts. In the contest between Tisamenos of Elis and Hieronymos of Andros the former won in the run and long jump, and the latter in the javelin throw, discus throw, and wrestling. Hieronymos was declared the overall winner.
History. The mythical originator of the pentathlon was Jason. Philostratus, a Gk. writer explains the origins of the pentathlon in the following way: 'In the times of the great voyage of the Argonauts, Telamon was the best discus thrower, Lynceus was the finest javelin thrower, and Boreas' two sons, Zetes and Calais, were undefeated at running and jumping. Peleus was always the runner-up in all these competitions but beat everyone at wrestling. When it came to the prize-giving Jason linked the five events out of a desire to honor his friend Peleus, whom he declared the winner and in this way created the pentathlon.' Initially, the events were held separately and only later did they become combined in an attempt to match the contenders' versatility. This was confirmed by the earlier Gk. sources, e.g. *The Iliad*. In Homer's description of the funeral games held in honor of the late Patroclus, running, the javelin throw, discus throw, and wrestling (similar to >PANKRATION) were single events and there is no mention of treating them collectively by the participating athletes. In *The Odyssey*, the discus throw (in the contest between Odysseus and Euryalus, king of the Phaeacians) is clearly a single event. The pentathlon was a competition for adult men. It was included in the XVIII Ol.G. in 708 BC. An attempt to include the pentathlon as a boys' event in the XXXVIII Ol.G. in 628 BC was unsuccessful. The boys' pentathlon was held, however, during other ancient Gk. games. In the Panathenaean Games, for instance, the pentathlon was held in 3 age categories: men, youths and boys. The pentathlon was also included in the Pythian Games in Delphi, in 586 BC in the men's and boys' categories. In modern times, the first, or at least one of the earliest attempts to restore the ancient tradition, was the inclusion of the pentathlon in the Much Wenlock Games in 1868. The Games themselves, according to their originator W.P. Brookes, were an attempt to revive the ancient Ol.G.. The events, however, differed from their ancient predecessors and included the high jump, long jump, the ½-mile run, rope climb-

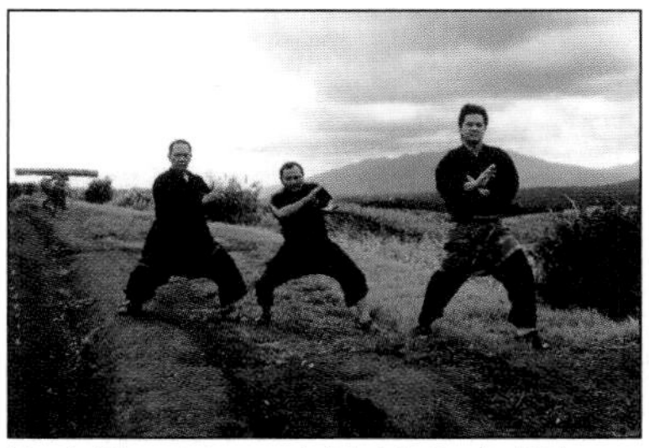

Roedy Wiranatakusumah (R), Ade Supriadi (C), and Robby M.Z.Wiranatakusumah (L) demonstrate the opening position ('pasang') of the 'jurus potong' movement of pencak silat.

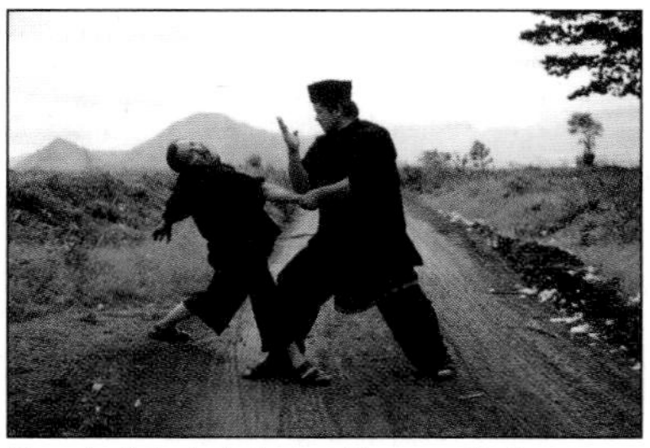

Pencak silat – techniques of jurus application. A wrist breaking technique through the use of elbow from direct attack.

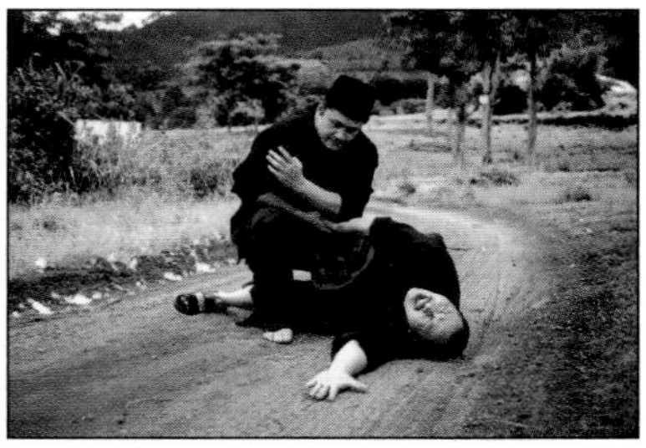

Pencak silat – techniques of jurus application. Completion of a take down technique.

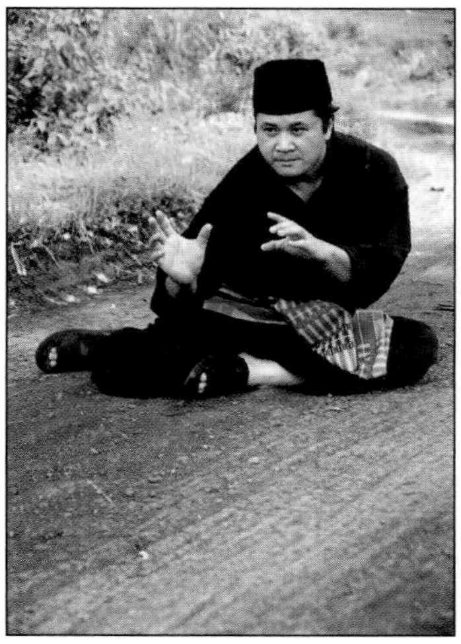

Pencak silat – the lower ground fighting position (Gendong Macan).

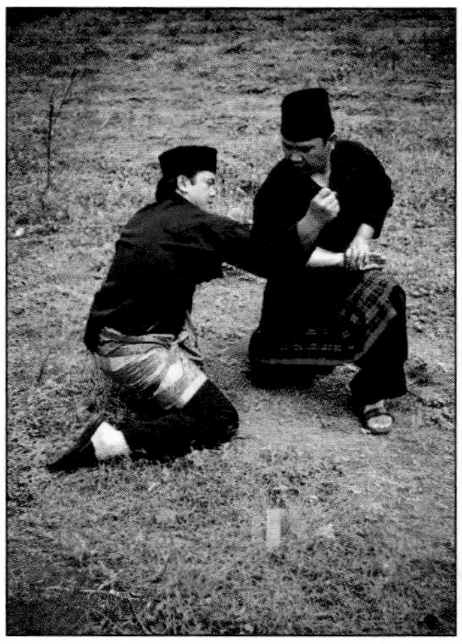

Pencak silat – a take down technique with elbow lock on elbow.

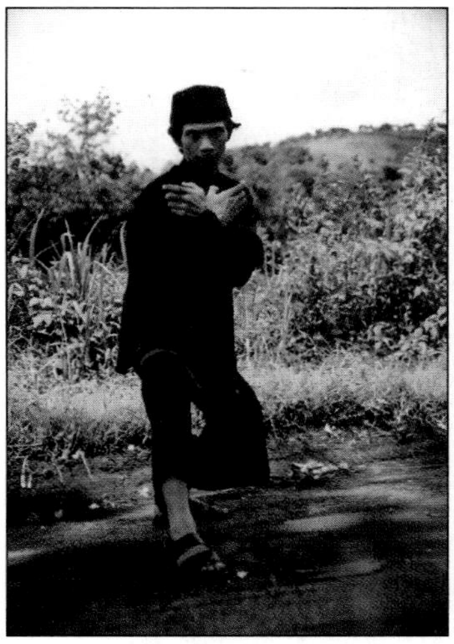

Rosyid Irvan demonstrates the jurus movement's front stance with gunting technique.

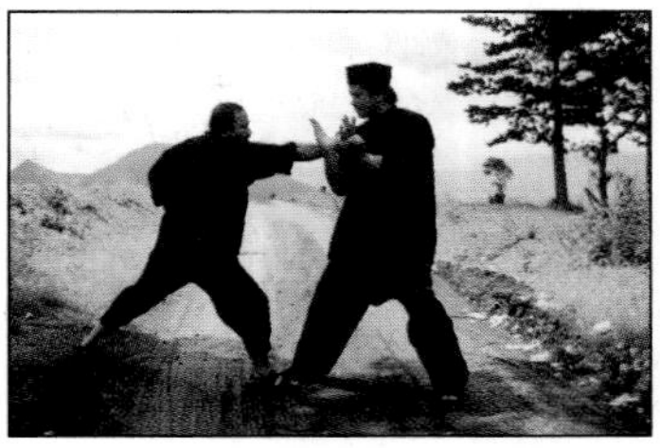

Take down and wrist breaking technique through the use of elbow from direct attack.

WORLD SPORTS ENCYCLOPEDIA

Prof. Lahti Pihkala, the inventor of pesäpallo.

Protective headgear for playing pesäpallo.

The ball for playing pesäpallo.

A monument in honor of Prof. Pihkala.

ing (70ft. in length), and stone throw (32lbs. in weight) executed separately with the right hand and the left hand (the 2 distances were added together). This pentathlon competition was considered the most prestigious event of the Much Wenlock Games and the champions were awarded with the First Class Silver Medal of the Wenlock Olympian Society. Archeological research in the area of ancient Olympia conducted by E. Curtis (1875) aroused interest in the pentathlon among modern sports associations, esp. gymnastic societies. At the turn of the 20th cent. the pentathlon regulations began to more or less reflect their ancient counterparts. The tradition of the ancient pentathlon has given rise to various modern multi-event competitions in present-day athletics such as >MODERN PETATHLON and >ATHLETIC PENTATHLON; cf. also >ALL-AROUND, >ATHLETIC DECATHLON, >HEPTATHLON, >MULTI-TRIAL ATHLETICS, >MULTI-TRIALS, >SUMMER BIATHLON, >TRIATHLON, >WINTER BIATHLON.

Pentathlon in the arts. Ancient coins depicting individual events of the pentathlon were found on the Gk. island of Cos. The most outstanding monument of ancient Gk. art is the *Discus Thrower*, a sculpture by Myron of Eleutherae. The statue was sculpted in the times when the discus was no longer a single Olympic event but part of the pentathlon. Aristotle in his *Rhetoric* expressed the view that '... all-round athletes are the most beautiful, being naturally adapted both for contests of strength and for speed also.' Other ancient authors claimed that the penathletes were those who otherwise had no chance to succeed in various single events. The ancient long jump event (>HALMA) was a frequent motif in vase paintings. Two of Pindar's odes were devoted to pentathlon winners: *Olympic Ode 13* in honor of Xenophon of Corinth, the two-time winner in running and the pentathlon (464 BC); and *Nemean Ode 7* in honor of Sogenes of Aegina, the winner of the boys' event c.487-89 BC. Bacchylides' *Ode 8* was written in honor of Automedes of Phlius, the pentathlon winner in the Nemean Games, sometime after 458 BC. In modern times, individual pentathlon events have been the subject of numerous

the new names coming from various gymnasia and palaestra, [...] was the name of Aristocle-Plato. The Athenians used this name as a secret greeting, others rejected it violently as if in fear of something. The experts knew it. It was not an easy task to defeat the flower of the Hellenes during the games, especially in the pentathlon consisting of the javelin, long jump, running, discus and, after all these hardships, the wrestling bouts. Not many could have gone through it.

The following description of Plato receiving the laurel wreath, written by a 20th-cent. author was inspired by ancient Gk. sculptures, vase paintings, and the poetry of Pindar and Bacchlides. It adequately reflects the significance of the pentathlon in ancient Greece:

Suddenly, [...] the crowd became still. The wreath. Raised up in the air by the priest. The holy laurel wreath [...] more precious to the youths than love and gold. A few fresh sprigs put on the head of the most perfect...

Plato alone walks up the marble stairs.

His face is stern, carved in suffering. One might have said that the glow of innumerable generations of victors had fallen on it, such it is, despite its first flush of youth. He proudly raises his head on its supple neck through which the sap flows up as through a young oak tree. Here comes the victor, his upright harmonious body like a desert palm tree. His body is like the heroon, the hero's chapel. He throws out his chest with pride, like a majestic shield. His shoulders are covered with layers of muscles, his arms alongside the most perfect fibers of statuary bronze. His torso, like the earth, has been sculpted by the sun and the wind. His feet are so nimble as if they had never touched the sand or gravel, like two coils of vibrating strings from the knee down to the steel ankle. Powerful loins underneath, flexible skin, shining like water on rocks, conceal layers of innumerable muscles. Here comes the victor, beautiful as Achilles in the song, beautiful as a god [...].

Thirty three names of ancient pentathlon champions have survived until today. Five of them are partially illegible. Some of the athletes won in more than one Ol.G. They included Philombrotos of Sparta (Olympic winner in 676, 672 and 678 BC), Demetrios of Salamis (Olympic winner in 229 and 233 AD). Gor-

into the central hole, he is assigned a hole and the defending players rush to the holes and try to take one each. Whoever fails to take a hole by placing his or her club into it becomes the new Peter holder.

PERKANICA, a Bulg. game similar to >PALANT; see also >KULI.

PERLALA, the earliest historical name of >PIERBOL.

PERUPERU, a var. of Maori war dance, being a test of warrior's weapon skills; see >HAKA (HAKA PERUPERU).

PESÄPALLO, [Fin. *pes* – nest, a safe place + *pallo* – ball], a Fin. ball game similar to >BASEBALL or >PALANT, which combines the tradition of a Fin. folk game >KUNINGAS PALLO with Amer. influences.
Rules of the game. The game is played between 2 teams of 9 players. To score a point a player, after sending the ball off to the field, must run, like in baseball, around all bases and return to the home base. The stick and ball are lighter than those in Amer. baseball. Other dissimilarities include different rules of hitting the ball, namely from a lob (the ball must be approx. 1m above the batter's head). The batter does not have to hit the ball, however; he may leave the home base, when the ball is released by the pitcher. If he leaves too fast, the pitcher may eliminate him by hitting him with the ball. If the batter avoids the ball, it is considered a bad serve. Two such bad serves give the batter's team the right to claim one base. Each batter is offered 3 serves. The batter is eliminated when: 1) the ball caught by the opposing team reaches the player on the base faster than the player who hit it; 2) when the player running between two bases is touched by a hand holding the ball; 3) when the batter hits the ball out of the field for the third consecutive time.
Teams alternate at hitting and field action, when 3 batters are eliminated or when no players of the batter's team score a point. When the ball is caught by the team in the field, the batter is considered 'injured', though not 'dead' as long as he remains in the base. He may not return to the home-base to hit the ball again, until he is able to score a point after

Pesäpallo.

literary works, although works devoted to the pentathlon itself are rare. The latter include *Parabola Pentatlonista*, a poem by the Rumanian poet, V. Ludu from the collection *Olimpia* (1985). In *Ferenike and Pejsidoros* (1909) a story by the Pol. author L. Rydel, the title character is a pentathlon winner. In *Dysk olimpijski* (*The Olympic Discus*), a novel by the Pol. author J. Parandowski, two characters Sotion and Ikkos train and compete in the pentathlon (the novel was awarded the bronze medal for literature during the Berlin Ol.G. in 1936). The pentathlon victory scored by the young Plato during the Nemean Games is described in *Wiosna grecka* (*Greek Spring*, 1931), a novel by the Pol. author, H. Malewska:

It was a holy day and the Greek put aside his everyday chores. Even the politicking Athenians were indifferent as to the fate of the raving Alcibiades, whether he was still on top or reached the bottom together with his followers. The crowds on their pilgrimage to Delphi, after having pitched their tents around the holy circle, were paying tribute to different gods – the gods of the pentathlon. The names of the champions were pronounced with reverence.
The contenders were many and included outstanding and famous ones as well as others unknown but full of hope [...]. Among

gos of Elis won 4 times in the pentathlon, diaulos and running in armor (the dates of the Games unknown).
G.E. Bean, 'Victory in the Pentathlon', *American Journal of Archeology*, 1956; J. Ebert, *Zum Pentathlon der Antike*, 1963; D.G. Kyle, 'Winning and Watching the Greek Pentathlon', JSH, 1990; S. Parnicki-Pudełko, 'Pięciobój', *Olimpia i olimpiady*, 1964.

PER I GROPEN, Norw. for 'Peter in the hole', also *grop-ball* – 'ball in the hole'; a game identical to Swed. >PER I HÅLA. It is part of a larger Eur. family of games, incl. Pol. >CZOROMAJ, Fr. >TRUIE, LA, Dan. >SO I HUL, and Eng. >CAT I' THE HOLE.

PER I HÅLA, Swed. for 'Peter in the hole', also *peta ball* – 'ball in the hole', a game identical to Norw. >PER I GROPEN. It is similar to Pol. >CZOROMAJ, Fr. >TRUIE, LA, Dan. >SO I HUL, and Eng. >CAT I' THE HOLE. The game is played on a course with holes in the ground. The number of holes is one short of the number of players. The player with no assigned hole tries to strike a ball called the Peter (Per) into a larger hole in the middle of the course. The remaining players attempt to prevent him from doing that. Once the Peter holder succeeds in getting the ball

having run around all bases and providing that any of his team-mates are still in the home-base.
Subsequent bases which must be won do not form, like in American baseball, a square, but rather a zig-zag figure. The distances between them are varied: there is 20m between the home-base and the first base, 30m between the first and second base, 35m between the second and third base, and 45m between the third base and home-base. The position in home-base, from which the ball is hit, called syttlautanen, is a circle 60cm in diameter and is raised 2-5cm. Each base is marked with 2 straight lines and a part of a circle 250cm in diameter. Such large bases are meant to provide a greater capacity to eliminate collisions between players.
Equipment. The bat is 100cm long, weighs 500-700g, and has ashape similar to the American baseball bat. Older bats were wooden and hollow inside, which often made them crack as a result of hits, so now plastic ones are used. The ball has a construction similar to that in baseball and is covered by leather. It has a circumference of 21,5-22,5cm and weighs 155-165g. A leather baseball-like mit makes it easier to catch the ball, though its construction is different – it forms a kind of rim with a leather sack.

History. The originator of pesäpallo was professor Lauri 'Tahko' Pihkala (1887-1979). In 1907 he made a trip to the USA, where he watched baseball, which appeared to him both intriguing in its principles and monotonous in action. Pihkala saw baseball again during the 1912 Olympiad in Stockholm, where American players used it as part of their warm-up routine. In 1912-3 Pihkala went to England and watched the game of cricket. It is there that he got an idea of combining elements of baseball, cricket and kuningas pallo. In one of his lectures to the Fin. National Sports Association he argued in favour of introducing pesäpallo to school sport activities: 'We need a game that could be what cricket is to the English and baseball to the Americans. It would be appropriate to gather the principles of kuningas pallo from the most distant areas of our country and combine them with what is best in cricket and baseball and thus come up with a uniform version of kuningas pallo, so that one school could compete with another, one village with another, one district with another.' However, the principles of pesäpallo had to wait another 10yrs., getting their ultimate, modern form only in 1922.

In 1915 Pihkala publicly demonstrated the first version of his new game of *pitkäpallo* [Fin. for 'long ball']. It met with such an enthusiastic reception by the Fin. education and sport authorities that a 7-member committee was called for to monitor and coordinate further development of the game. One goal of the committee was to liven up the game, which still seemed too static and required too little individual effort. Another was to combine the individual aspect with a sense of responsibility for the team. After Finland gained independence in 1917, the work to develop the game was slowed down by the outbreak of the Civil War and were resumed at full steam in the years 1920-21. Regulations set in 1921 were still not satisfactory to Pihkala, who now turned to baseball and borrowed its system of scoring points after reaching a base and the principle of taking turns at the bat after 3 unsuccessful hits, the duration of the game (9 rounds) and the number of players on a team (9). Pihkala's own contribution was the introduction of a relatively narrow field and penalties for a team whose players were caught by the opponents when running to bases. All the main regulations were finally settled in 1922. The game was first popularized among Fin. reservists. Between the world wars pesäpallo flourished thanks to the period of unprecedented world power of Fin. sport, witnessed by the results of their sports-

A petanque player.

men in athletics and during Ol.G. In the 1930s pesäpallo gained the status of a professional sport, at the same time remaining popular among amateurs and in schools. It is played by men and women alike and, after hockey, is considered – together with skiing and athletics – to be the most important sport in Finland. There are now close to 6000 registered pesäpallo teams in Finland and the main centers of the game are Jyväskylä and Pohjonmaa. Only in S Finland is the popularity of pesäpallo surpassed by that of football. In the 1930s the game became popular in other Baltic states, mainly in Estonia, with which the Fin. national team played official annual international matches. Annexation of Estonia into the USSR stopped the development of the game there, but did not cause its complete extinction. Pesäpallo survives in Estonia until today and efforts are currently under way to revive its previous significance. The game is also popular in countries with a Fin. ethnic minority or migrants, e.g. in Sweden, Norway, Australia and Canada.

The Fin. reformers set forward the following goals: 1) to eliminate the principle of horizontal batting, which causes typical baseball situations, in which the game is mainly played between the pitcher and the batter. Therefore, the principle of the vertical pitch, used in kuningas pallo, was preserved; 2) the Amer. principle of 'no hits no runs' (i.e. if the ball is not hit right, no base can be won) makes the game static, if the ball is not successfully hit for some time. Since the Finns wanted to make the young generation more active, they introduced the possibility of leaving the base without hitting the ball; 3) gradually increasing the distance between particular bases was to imitate war: a growing resistance of circumstances and the 'enemy' as times go by (the necessity to cover longer and longer distances offers more chance to eliminate the player trying to score a point. Experiences were also drawn from other Fin. ball games, particularly >POLTOPALLO and >PITKÉPALLO.

A. Calanoaln, *Suomen kansan leikkejä*, 1904; P. Kärkkäinen, 'Pesäpallo – Finnish Baseball. History and Presentation of the National Game', ISHPES, 1992; E. Laitinen, *Pesäpallo-kansallispeli 60 vuotta*, 1983; T. Okkola, *Suomen kansan kilpaleikit*, 1928; *Pesäpallo rulebook*, 1981.

PETA BALL see >PER I HÁLA.

PÉTANQUE, a Fr. game of the >BOULES family. Like most other games of this type it involves throwing the ball rather than rolling it. The players aim at another, significantly smaller ball, called a *cochon-*

net or piglet. Depending on local tradition this ball is also called *petit bois* – small piece of wood, *ministre* – minister, or, in Provence, as in the local >JEU PROVENÇAL, *gari* or *lé*. Pétangue is played chiefly in France, but it is also popular among Fr. emigrants or people of Fr. descent, especially in Canada (Quebec) and Australia, where it is often called *boule*. The Brit. Pétanque Association prospers despite strong competition from local ball games, though due to a greater number of Austrl. citizens of Ital. descent living in England, its popularity is overshadowed by >BOCCIA.

Equipment and pitch. The balls used for throwing are made of metal, usu. steel, and measure 70.5-80mm in diameter. They may not be weighted with lead or decentered. (Decentering, practiced in similar games, helps curve the ball's track.) The target ball, measuring 25-35mm in diameter, is made of wood and painted white. In popular matches the pitch may be any flat area with a hardened surface, such as a back road, a yard or a town square. More significant events take place on specially prepared tracks, 15m long and 4m wide (in official matches, both domestic and international). In local competitions the track is at least 3m wide.

The course of play. The game is played individually or in teams, two on two or three on three. Every participant has 3 balls (or 2 – in a team of 3). A coin toss determines who begins the round. As in *jeu provençal*, the winner of the toss chooses the starting spot by drawing a circle 35-50cm in diameter. The circle must be at least 1m from the nearest obstacle, such as a tree, a wall, a bench etc. The players throw the balls from a standing position, with at least one leg within the circle. The winner of the toss starts by throwing the piglet, which should fall 6-10m from the perimeter of the circle (for seniors) or 5-9m (for juniors).

The piglet may not fall within 1m from the nearest obstacle. The player throwing the piglet has 3 rounds to do it according to the rules. If he fails, the piglet goes to the next player (in an individual game) or the other team (in a team game). That does not, however, change the order of the players in the actual game. Once the piglet is in place, the pitch may not be altered and participants may not object to any previously unnoticed obstacles, such as uneven ground, which from now on may not be smoothed down (except for defects caused by the throwing of balls).

Again, the players throw from a standing position, now with both legs inside the previously drawn circle, careful not to tread on the line, though people with disabilities may continue to keep one foot outside the circle while throwing, e.g. if it helps them keep their balance. Only when the ball has fallen, may they leave the circle. This requirement of staying inside the circle is a feature distinguishing Pétangue from jeu provençal. The technique and tactics, however, are similar in both games, and the terminology is the same. It involves the following elements: 1) *plomber* (beating down the ground) – a high throw guaranteeing relative precision – the ball hits the ground almost vertically and therefore stops in place; 2) *rouler* (rolling) – the ball is rolled from a low underhand; 3) *pointer* (pinpointing) – the ball is thrown at the ball of the opponent; 4) *boule portée* (accessible ball) – the ball is aimed as close to the piglet as possible. The player bends over slightly, arm outstretched and the hand holding the ball at eye-level; 5) *tir* or *tirer* (shooting) – the ball is aimed at the ball of the opponent closest to the piglet. Thus the opponent's ball is thrown aside and the new ball occupies its position. A precise completion of this (called *carreau*) is the most spectacular element of the game. In team games it is common for each player on a team to specialise in a given type of throw.

Each round is won by the contestant or team whose balls are closest to the piglet. One point is awarded for every ball closer to the piglet than the opponent's nearest ball. In a situation where 1, 2, 3, or even 4 balls are closer to the piglet than any of the opponent's balls, the score is accordingly 1, 2, 3 or 4pts. The match consists of 3 games, each played to 11, 13, 15, 18 or 21pts, depending on local tradition. Official games are conducted by a referee.

History In 1910 in Vallauris – or, according to other sources, Le Ciotat – a group of *jeu provençal* players sought to make the game simpler and less demanding physically. This led to rule changes and finally, to the creation of pétanque, a game of rather static character. However, these simplifications helped pétanque spread far beyond Provence, indeed

WORLD SPORTS ENCYCLOPEDIA P

LA FANNY

This original tradition was started after WWI in the region of Savoy, in southern France, in the local cafè de Grand-Lemps, where a waitress named Fanny used to console the customers who lost the game without scoring a point by allowing them to kiss her on her cheeks. One day the village mayor lost the game and went on to collect his 'prize'. Fanny, who had a grudge against him, wanted to humiliate him and, having stepped up onto a chair, lifted her skirt and presented the mayor with her bare buttocks. The mayor respected the custom and smacked her loudly, thus starting a longstanding tradition.

The players usually do not have a Fanny willing to bare her backside in public and so, instead, the unhappy losers are obliged to kiss a fake in the form of a painting or clay figure, which is always proudly displayed in all places where the game is played. Therefore, what used to be an award has become a form of ultimate punishment.

P
WORLD SPORTS ENCYCLOPEDIA

Théophile Deyrolle, Boules players, 1887, Musée dea Beaux-Arts.

almost throughout the whole of France. In France, winners of pétanque competitions enjoy social prestige comparable to that of champions of professional sports. According to Fr. custom, pétanque players are given humorous nicknames, such as 'The Japanese' (*Le Japonais)*, 'Othello', 'Sardine' etc. In the course of time there began in France championships in single, double and triple games, both in junior and senior categories. Fr. descent is required, except in triple games, where one player may be a foreigner. The transfer of players between clubs is allowed only between January 1 and March 1 of each year. To some extent pétanque is known outside France, esp. in regions of Switzerland and Belgium bordering on France, and also among the Fr. Canadians. Since around 1980 pétanque has been played on a large scale in Singapore. The first Pétanque Open was played in 1987 on the Singapore stadium Toa Payoh. 66 teams took part, among them the Fr. *Union des Assurances de Paris.*

The chief governing body of pétanque (and jeu provençal*)* is the Fédération Internationale de Pétanque et Jeu Provençal on the international level, and the Fédération Française de Pétanque et Jeu Provençal in France.

PETITE THEQUE, a Fr. bat and ball game similar to >PALANT.

PFEILWURFSPIEL, a Ger. folk sports game similar to >DARTS (Ger. *Pfeil* – 'arrow' + *Wurf* – 'throw' + *Spiel* – 'game, play').

PHOENIX-BOAT RACING, a women's var. of >DRAGON-BOAT RACING – a rowing contest derived from the ancient Chin. tradition; nowadays practiced internationally, esp. in Asian countries. Instead of the dragon's head and tail on the bow and stern, the phoenix boat has the head and tail of the phoenix. The boards of the phoenix boats are painted in the pattern of colorful bird feathers. This particular combination of Eg. mythology and Chin. tradition took place in Singapore, a place of intensive contacts between numerous cultures. Phoenix-boat racing exemplifies 20th-cent. eclectic cultural tendencies.

PHYSICAL EDUCATION, the means and methods implemented for the purpose of creating body fitness, hygiene, a sense of discipline and teamwork, and strong will, by developing resistance to fatigue and teaching ethical values, such as respect for an opponent, the ability to accept defeat, and a willingness to win without resort to cheating. Institutionalized physical education serving social purposes was known already in antiquity, where it combined military and sporting education (>EPHEBIA). In the Middle Ages the same function was performed by the

code of chivalry, as well as the formation of defense abilities by the townsmen's guilds. The modern foundations of physical education were established during the eras of the Renaissance and Enlightenment. The Eng. speaking countries developed a system of physical education in schools in the 19th cent., homogeneous with the idea of education through sport, while the Eur. system remained dominated by >GYMNASTICS, clearly distinguished from sport, which deprived physical education of spontaneity and naturalness. Gymnastics was so strongly connected with the development of physical education that both terms have remained interchangeable.

P. Beasbel and J. Taylor, *Physical Education and Sport*, 1996; C.A. Bucher and E.M. Reade, *Physical Education and Health in the Elementary School*, 1964; A. Lumpkin, *Physical Education and Sport. A Contemporary Introduction*, 1994.

PIÃO, formerly *jogo da piam*, a Port. var. of >TOPS. In Portugal, alongside the trad. forms of the game, original varieties, not encountered anywhere else have developed. They include:

Rodinha dos botões, full name *jogo da rodinha dos botões*, Port. for 'a sequence of buttons'. Each player has 1 top (*pião*) and 1 button. A circle, 1m in diameter, with an 80cm line inside it, is marked on the ground. The players determine their turns by spinning their tops towards the inside line. The one whose top stops closest to the line goes first. Then, the players place their buttons within the circle and spin their tops in turns so as to push the buttons out of the circle. The player who succeeds in pushing his button out of the circle first is the winner.

Aparar o pião, Port. for 'lifting up the top'. The players try to lift a spinning top with one hand without stopping its motion. The player on whose hand the top spins for the longest time is the winner. A showy trick is to pass the spinning top from one hand to another or spin the top on one fingernail and pass it from one finger to another. Regional varieties of the top-shows are known as the *cazinha* (a tiny hut) in the Beira province, *cardazola bota-fora* in the Alentejo province and *catazola* in the Azores.

Esgaravelhões, a special 'tricks' top designed to spin for as long as possible.

Jogo do pião as nicas. Each player has one top. A cross is marked on the ground. Individual players attempt to keep their top spinning near the cross – if possible at the center or on one of its arms. The top which spins furthest from the cross is taken off and replaced with another one called the *caranho* or *carcacao*. The replacement is usu. an old, used top called *piorra* or *pião as nicas*, lit. 'a mock top'. The remaining players spin their tops again and try to

push the mock tops off the cross to a designated area. The mock top players try to push their tops back on the cross. In the Azores, a similar game is known as the *aparada*, however it is not played on the cross. One player spits on the ground and the aim of the game is to place the spinning tops as close to the spittle (*cuspidela*) as possible. The mock top is called the *molhado* – 'the wet one'.

The Port. tops (*piorra*) are made of hard, plain laurel or beech wood. The tops come in a var. of forms, in the shape of a cone, pear, balloon with a basket, bowl pierced with a keg, two rings impaled on a pointed stick, etc. Simpler, small top varieties are known as *piorra* and can even be made of slightly baked potato slices pierced with a pointed stick. The piorra are spun by a twist of the hand or by means of a special cord called the *faniqueria*. The cords or whips used in various regions of Portugal are known as the *baraca, capa*, or *guita*.

History. T. Braga, a Port. philologist and one-time president of the country, mentioned in his work *O povo Português nos seus Costumes, Crenças e Tradicóes* (*On the Portuguese Folk, Its Costumes, Beliefs and Traditions*, 1885, I) that pião was played in Portugal as early as in the 15th cent. as exemplified by an epigram found in the *Ordenacóes Alfonsinas*:

And to play spinning tops
Allow me, please.

In the 17th cent., a monk named B. Pereira wrote about a boy from Costa Cascais so skillful at tops he was named *douto do pião* ('Doctor in tops').

In Portugal, the spinning tops playing seasons have traditionally been the spring and the fall. In the Azores pião has been played at Lent with the exception of Holy Week, in which the game was forbidden by the Catholic Church. G. Pitra, a Port. author has written a treatise on pião.

M. da Graca Sousa Guedes, 'Jogo do rodinha dos botões', JTP, 1979, 47-48; ibid. 'Utilizando o Pião', JTP, 1979, 43-47.

PICKA FYR, Swed. for 'to peck fire' (Swed. *picka* – 'to peck' + *fyr* – 'a lantern, fire'), a folk game once practiced in Sweden and Denmark (under the Swed. name). The game was played using a large metal ball and a round metal plate (*blasch*). The ball was stuck slightly into the ground. The aim of the game was to throw the plate so it would land on the ball or close to it. The spot the plate landed on was marked with a coin and then another player took his or her turn. The player whose coin was closest to the ball became the winner (*fyr*), the one whose coin was farthest from the ball was called the sack (*säck*). If the ball was dislodged by the plate the distances between the coins and the ball changed. There is no clear association between the name of the game and course of play. After the game, all the coins were placed tails up (*klöver*), one on top of another. The winner, then, rolled the ball towards the coin pile trying to knock it out and took all the coins which turned heads up (*krone*). The other players rolled the ball after the winner and the game continued until all the coins were turned heads up. J. Møller, 'Picka fyr', GID, 1997, 1, 95.

PICKING UP A GOAT AT A GALLOP, a trad. sport practiced by some ethnic minorities in China, particularly the Kazakhs, Tadzhiks and Kyrgyz. According to Chin. ethnologists, the sport is derived from the shepherd tradition of chasing sheep that went astray from the herd. The mounted shepherds would chase after a running goat, pick it up from the ground and bring it back to the herd. The earliest forms of the game consisted of a group of mounted riders chasing after a running goat and the winner being the rider who managed to catch the goat at a gallop and carry it over his saddle. Later the sport was influenced by >BUZKASHI and the live goat was replaced with a dead one. Today, picking up a goat at a gallop is played as follows: a dead goat weighing about 100 jins (around 50kg.) is placed in the middle of a large open meadow. The game can by played by an unlimited number of mounted riders. The competitors take their positions in a row, far away from the object of the game. At the umpire's signal the riders start racing towards the goat. The first player who manages to pick up the goat must run away from the other chasers who try to snatch the goat from him. Mu Fushan, et al., 'Picking Up a Goat at a Gallop', TRAMCHIN, 6.

PICKLEBALL, a mini-tennis-type game played on a hard surface court the size of which is identical to that of doubles badminton court (20ft.x44ft. for both singles and doubles). The net is suspended 36in. on each end of the net and 34in. in the middle. A non-volley zone extends 7ft. on each side of the net. The game is played with wood or plastic paddle racquets and a plastic, poly baseball with holes.
History. The game was created during the summer of 1965 on Bainbridge Island – a short ferry ride from Seattle, WA. The original purpose of the game was to provide a sport for the entire family, according to co-inventors U.S. Congressman J. Pritchard, W. Bell, and B. McCallum. Pickles was the family dog that would chase after the errant balls and then hide in the bushes, thus Pickle's ball which was later shortened to the namesake of Pickleball. Initially, families played Pickleball in their backyards on a hard surface, on driveways, and on residential dead-end streets. Since the mid-1970's, pickleball has grown and expanded from a family activity game to a paddle court sport with formalized rules. Nowadays the game is played in thousands of school PE programs, parks and recreation centers, correctional facilities, camps, YMCA's and retirement communities. This sport is becoming very popular among active senior adults at community centers.
Rules. The serve must be hit underhand and each team must play their first shot off the bounce. After the ball has bounced once on each side, then both teams can either volley the ball in the air or play it off the bounce. This eliminates the serve and volley advantage and prolongs the rallies.
No volleying is permitted within the 7ft. non-volley zone, preventing players from executing smashes from a position within the 7ft. zone on both sides of the net. This promotes the drop volley or 'dink' shot playing strategies, as pickleball is a game of shot placement and patience, not brute power or strength. Both players on the serving team are allowed to serve, and a team shall score points only when serving. A game is played to 11pts. and a team must win by 2pts. Points are lost by hitting the ball out of bounds, hitting the net, stepping into the non-volley zone and volleying the ball, or by volleying the ball before the ball has bounced once on each side of the net.
http://www.pickleball.com

PI-COW, a game in which one half of the players attack a castle (a hill, ditch, figure drawn on the ground, etc.) defended by the other half. The etymology of the game's name is unclear. It might mean a 'holy war' (*pi* – 'pious' + *cow* – 'subdue'; see Swed. *kuva*, Dan. *kue*).

PIEDRA CANARIA, a folk var. of stone lifting practiced in the Canary Islands (Span. *piedra* – 'stone, boulder' + *canaria* – 'of the Canaries'). The size and weight of the stones is not specified. Usually, each stone is as broad as a man's shoulders and about 2ft. in height and depth. A stone is embraced with both arms and supported with the knees and lifted to chest height.
C. Moreno Palos, 'Piedra canaria', JYTE, 1992, 220.

PIERBOL, half-bowling, lit. 'a half-bowl'. A bowling game practiced in the Flem. part of Belgium and the Du. province of Zeeland. In the Courtai district of West Flanders the game is known as 'mad bowling' (*zottebol*, from one of the pins used for the game).
Equipment. The half-bowl is 25cm in diameter. The game is played with ten or thirteen 35cm-tall thin, wooden pins (the number depends on local regulations). Pierbol is played indoors, usu. on the floors of inns. It has a table var. played with a half-bowl, 19cm in diameter, and 25cm-tall pins. Table pierbol can be played with 9 or 13 pins. In the former var. the pins are arranged in a three-by-three square. In the thirteen-pin var. the pins are arranged in a circle. Two pins: the *negenman* (lit. the nine man) and the *zot* (lit. the fool) are slightly taller. The aim of the game is to roll the half-bowl down so it rolls round the *zot* and knocks down as many pins as possible. Each player is entitled to 2 shots. In the first shot a player must *achterpieren*, i.e. pass the farthest pin round the zot, before he is allowed to knock down any skittle. In the second shot, each player tries to knock down all the remaining outside pins, again after passing round the zot. If the zot is knocked down in the first shot, it is replaced by another pin in the second shot. If all of the outside pins were knocked down in the first shot the zott is replaced with one of the fallen pins. A pin knocked down correctly scores one point for the player. In some varieties of pierbol the pins are numbered and the players try to knock down the pins with the highest numbers first. The game can be played in singles, doubles, triples or by teams of higher number of players.
History. The earliest reference to pierbol was included in the work of A. De Cock and I. Terlick *Kinderspel en Kinderlust in Zuid Nederland* (Children's Games and Plays in the Netherlands) published in eight volumes in the years 1902-1908. This was an ethnographic description of the game, which had been referred to much earlier in Du. drawings and tapestries. The earliest drawing depicting a 9-pin game comes from the 17th cent. The print *Passetemps à la campagne* (Rural pastimes) was etched by C. Stella (1636-97) after a design by J. Stella (1596-1657). Although the drawing depicts a 9-pin game it is uncertain whether the game is pierbol or some other bowling game using specially flattened bowls for curve shots. The game was known in France during the reign of Louis XIV as *le jeu de Siam*. A tapestry by W. Guillaume (1688-1738) after David Teniers the Younger, presenting a game of pier-

Pickleball.

bol played with the typical half-bowl, is in the Museum d'Angers (Lille, Angers). Pierbol became also popular in Spain, where it is played using 10 pins. The Span. names of the game *media bola* or *bolo leones* are the equivalents of the Flem. name. A similar game called >FOOLISH BOWLING once found its way to England but gained almost no popularity and soon faded away. Pierbol enjoyed the greatest popularity in the 18th, 19th, and the first half of the 20th cent. After WWII the game became almost forgotten. In the Du. district of Courtrai, ethnographer B. Dewilde

Pickleball.

recorded 25 pierbol associations in the years 1920-25. In 1981, in the same district there was only one association consisting of 8 players. In 1980, ethnographers found 60 towns and villages in Flanders where pierbol was still known. The locals were able to demonstrate how to play the game but it was not played on a daily basis any more. In Du. Zeeland, once a pierbol center, there is not a single pierbol association today.
A. De Cock, I. Terlick, *Kinderspel en Kinderlust in Zuid Nederland*, vol. III, 1903; B. Dewilde, *Het 'zottebolspel' in Kortrijk en omgeving*, De Leiegouw, 1974, 16; E. De Vroede, 'Ball and Bowl Games in the Low Countries: Past and Present', *Homo Ludens – Der Spielende Mensch*, 1996, V; ibid., 'De zot passeren: pierbol', NVVC, 1989, 9; ibid., *Het Grote Volkssporten Boek*, Leuven, 1996.

PIERLALA, the oldest name of >PIERBOL.

PIERŚCIENIÓWKA, a Pol. ball game being a combination of volleyball, basketball and team handball, invented by W. Robakowski in 1935. The court is 16-20m long and 10m wide. The volleyball-like

A new plastic pickleball racket and ball.

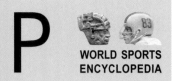

2m-wide net divides the court into 2 playing areas. Within the net there are 3 wooden or aluminum rings. The central ring is 70cm in diameter and the side rings are 50cm in diameter each. The ball is 50cm in circumference. The indoor game is played by 2 teams of 5 players each; the outdoor game by 2 teams of 8 players each (on a larger court). Each game lasts 2x25min. The aim of the game to pass the ball through one of the 3 rings in the net and make the opposing team fail to return it. The ball must not touch the ground and before returning it can only be hit 4 times. At the beginning of the game the ball is served over the net. Pierścieniówka enjoyed some popularity in Pol. schools before 1939 but it gradually faded away after WWII.

W. Robakowski, *Pierścieniówka. Gra sportowa dla młodzieży i starszych*, 1936.

PIĘSTÓWKA, a Pol. var. of Ger. >FAUSTBALL. According to E. Piasecki, the game was introduced to Pol. schools in Galicia c.1885-90, and later popularized by E. Cenar in the beginning of the 20th cent. In some early books of rules, both Pol. and Rus., pięstówka was dubbed *Italian palant*, although it had absolutely nothing to do with the game of >PALANT. Before 1939, pięstówka was immensely popular in the city of Lvov. The players strike the ball with their fists and try to pass it to the opposing team over a string spread across the court. The game is played by 2 teams of 5 players. If a team fails to return the ball the opposing team scores a point. A match lasts 2x15min. The team can hit the ball up to 6 times before returning it. Pięstówka differs from faustball in the court length (40m long instead of 50m), the height of the dividing string (1.8m instead of 2m) and court width, dependant on the players' age and skill categories. Cenar suggested a court 15m wide (instead of 20m) and a string suspended on 3 posts (instead of two). E. Piasecki provides the following description of pięstówka:

The rectangular court is 20x40m. It is divided into two playing areas by a tape, red on one side, white on the other, spread between two posts placed in the middle of the side lines. The game is played by two teams, the reds and the whites, consisting of five to eleven players each. The serving team is selected by drawing lots. The server stands in the middle of his team's area. First, he tosses up the ball to the height of his head and then strikes it with the fist or forearm. The ball must pass over the net to the opponent's side. The receiving team can return the ball on the fly or the first bounce. Before a return the ball may be hit several times but it cannot touch the ground. If the receiving team fails to return the ball, the serving team scores one point. The return is foul if the ball: 1) is caught; 2) is dropped on service; 3) touches any part of player's body but the arm; 4) bounces more than once or rolls on the ground; 5) touches the tape or passes under it; 6) goes out of bounds. After a foul return the receiving team serves. The ball must be passed for service to the opposing team under the string. Whichever team scores more points within the prescribed time of the game (1/2 hr.-1hr.) wins.

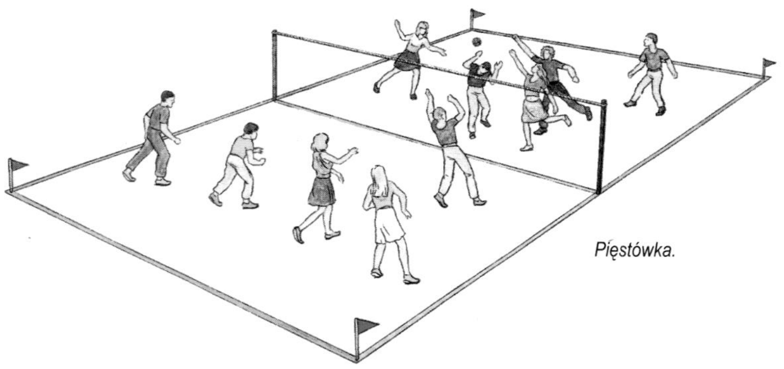

Pięstówka.

A clock used in pigeon racing.

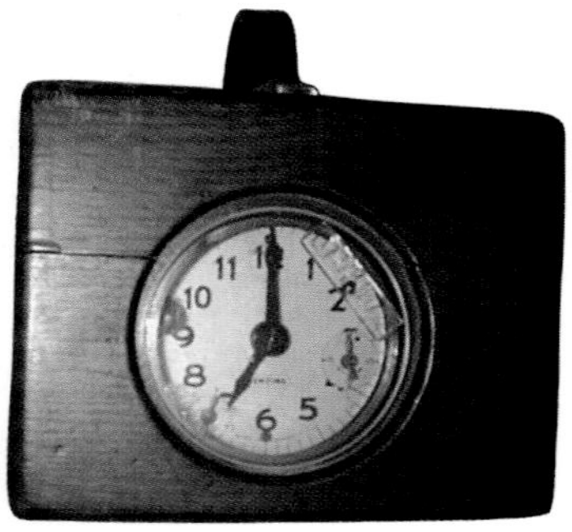

E. Cenar, 'Pięstówka', *Gry i zabawy różnych narodów* (1906); E. Piasecki, 'Pięstówka', *Zabawy i gry ruchowe dzieci i młodzieży* (1916); I.N. Chkhannikov, 'Palant włoski', GIZ, 52-3.

PIGEON RACING, the sport of carrier pigeon breeders in which pigeons fly for the fastest times over various distances. The most important characteristic of pigeons that allows them to be used for carrying messages and for racing is their homing instinct: a pigeon taken from his breeder's loft returns there carrying a message fastened to his legs, neck or tail. In order to reinforce the homing instinct of pigeons breeders use 2 basic methods: widowhood and natural. In the widowhood method, which has several var., such as grass widowhood, semi-widowhood etc., the male and female are separated and the pigeon's sexual drive makes it return home. In the marital triangle method a couple is separated before the race and the male is shown the female in the company of another male The jealous male instinctively returns home to be reunited with his female. In the grass widowhood method the birds' sexual drive is manipulated by periods of temporary separation and reuniting. The Complete widowhood method includes separating a pair, which is then raced independently in the same event. In the natural method the female pigeon is separated from the nest (with either the eggs or the chicken), which increases her desire to return there as quickly as possible. Homing or racing pigeons are divided into 2 categories: old birds and young birds. Old birds are those born prior to December 31st of the previous year and young birds are those born in the current year.

Racing. Shortly after it is born, usu. between 6 and 10 days, a racing pigeon is marked with a plastic (originally metal) ring. Before the competition each pigeon is banded with a rubber 'countermark' – a seamless identification band with a unique identification number placed on the unbanded leg. The numbers are recorded and special racing clocks are set with a universal timer and sealed. Each breeder has his own clock, which can record the flying times of up to 30 pigeons. When a pigeon returns home his countermark is taken off and inserted into the clock box, where it is read and the result is printed out. The printouts are sent to regional breeders' associations for confirmation and are then transferred to the organizing committee, which evaluates the results and pronounces the final ranking. A relatively new method is that of electronic measurement, which is triggered automatically via a short antenna by a transmitter attached to the pigeon, thus allowing the breeder the freedom to be away from the loft when his bird arrives there. Crates with pigeons selected for the competition are shipped to the race point by railway or, more often, by specially modified trucks. A team of pigeons consists of 5, 4 or 3 birds in all classes of events. The birds compete in 4 categories: A – short distances of up to several hundred kilometers with up to 5 birds in one team; B – middle distances below 1,000km with 4 birds per team; C – long distances of 1,000km and more with 3 birds per team; D – the flyer's ranking based on the total score in classes A, B and C. The breeding of pigeons has become a venture resembling training in professional sport – it is backed by scientific research leading to the selection of the best individuals which occur on a scale of 1 in 50,000. The breeder is in fact a trainer who must have specialized knowledge in the area of physiology, genetics and even psychology. Races are held over distances exceeding 1,000km, which the birds cover with an average speed of 65km/h. Depending on their predispositions, racing pigeons can be divided into speed flyers and distance flyers.

Types of pigeons. Modern racing pigeons are considered to be a single breed, defined by their flying abilities, speed and endurance, despite differences in their anatomy, plumage etc. Historically they derive from several species known as Baghdads that come from the Middle East and are one of the most precious species of carriers. One type, known as the Eng. Baghdad, was brought to England at the end of the Crusades. Other popular species include Barbs of Northern Africa, Dragoons (in Spain known as Caballera Española, in Germany – Rittertaube, in England – Horseman Pigeon), Pouters (also called Smytters), Tumblers, Croppers etc. Chin. breeds of carrier pigeons included Tung Koong Paak and Shung Shur Naan. There are dozens of breeds and types of pigeon that can be identified in different cultures, countries and historical periods.

The oldest Eur. names for pigeons are old Gk. *peristera* (modern Gk. *peristeri*) and Lat. *columbus*. Home bred carriers, homing or racing pigeons have different names in various languages, reflecting the birds' characteristics or functions. The Pol. name *gołąb pocztowy* (lit. postal pigeon) refers to its trad. use as a carrier of postal messages (cf. Czech *poštowni holub*, Du. *postduif*, Flemish *postduiv*, Ger. *Brieftaube*, Swed. *brevduve*). In romance languages the name reflects the bird's ability to cover long distances: Fr. *pigeon voyageur*, It. *piccione viaggiatore* – a travelling pigeon. In Span. the name *paloma mensajera* indicates the bird's function as a messenger that brings news. The Eng. name *homing pigeon* focuses on the bird's ability to return home, while the Amer. name *racing pigeon* focuses on the bird's use for sport purposes. The use of pigeons as postal carriers has all but disappeared and so with increasing frequency we come across the simple term *sport pigeon*.

History. Postal pigeons or carriers originated through the domestication of wild pigeons. There are 2 views on the ancestry of the homing pigeon; firstly that it derives from various wild species and the other according to which it derives from one species crossbred several times and in different breeding conditions. The oldest known species of wild pigeon, the rock pigeon, inhabits the mountains and rocky shores of Asia, Northern Africa, the Mediterranean and the Brit. Isles. The use of pigeons for postal services and, later, sporting purposes became possible as soon as man discovered the birds' homing instinct several thousand years ago. The oldest wall paintings presenting pigeons come from around 5,000 years ago and can be found in some Eg. pyramids. Pigeons were used as carriers of postal messages by the ancient Eg. king Djoser (2663-2649 BC), the ruler of the so called Old Kingdom, preceding the era of pharaohs, and later by Ramesses III (1182-1151 BC). According to the Bible, it was a white dove that was sent on the mission of verifying whether the Flood waters had subsided. Having returned, it lands on Noah's hand, which can be viewed as evidence of the tradition of pigeon breeding and their use as carriers of information among the people of the Biblical era:

At the end of forty days Noah opened the window of the ark which he had made, and sent forth a raven; and it went to and fro until the waters were dried up from the earth. Then he sent forth a dove from him, to see if the waters had subsided from the face of the ground; but the dove found no place to set her foot, and she returned to him to the ark, for the waters were still on the face of the whole earth. So he put forth his hand and took her and brought her into the ark with him. He waited another seven days, and again he sent forth the dove out of the ark; and the dove came back to him in the evening, and lo, in her mouth a freshly plucked olive leaf; so Noah knew that the waters had subsided from the earth. Then he waited another seven days, and sent forth the dove; and she did not return to him any more.

[*The Book of Genesis*, 6]

In 637 BC the Persians had a well developed network of carrier pigeon posts and their breeds of oriental pigeons formed the basis of many future species of Eur. carrier pigeons. The use of pigeons for postal services were described by ancient Gk. writers such as Anacreon (570-478). Pliny the Elder (Caius Plinius Secundus) writes in his work *Historia naturalis* that Brutus, besieged in 42 BC at Matina by Mark Anthony, used pigeons to summon relief:

Doves have served for posts and courriers betweene, and been emploied in great affaires: and namely, at the siege of Modenna, Decimus Brutus sent out of the towne letters tyed to their feet, as farre as to the campe where the Consuls lay, and thereby acquainted them with newes, and in what estate they were within.

[trans. by Philemon Holland, 1601]

According to the Koran, King Solomon used pigeons to carry postal messages, and so did the Arabs (then called Saracens) during the crusades, causing much trouble to Richard the Lionheart, who could not understand why all of his ventures were immediately countered. When the Spaniards besieged the cities of Haarlem (1583) and Leiden (1584), the defenders survived thanks to a pigeon post informing them of coming relief. Pigeons were also used to carry information during the siege of Venice by the Aus. army in 1849 and during the siege of Paris at the time of Paris Commune (1870-71), when a total of 363 pigeons were sent out and returned with messages which helped to boost the morale of the defenders. Messages written on thin foil the size of 32x43mm were placed inside duck feathers attached to a pigeon tail. One feather carried up to 3,500 such micro-messages, written and read with the help of a magnifying glass, each containing up to 20 words. Pigeons have been commonly used during many wars. The news of Napoleon's defeat at Waterloo was brought to London by pigeon, which in turn brought a fortune to the Rothschild family, who bought and then sold shares before the news had spread. Pigeons played an important role during the Crimean War (1853-65) and the Amer. Civil War (1861-65). They were still used to carry information during WW I and WW II, whenever modern telegraphic or radio devices could not be used. On 4 June 1916 gen. Henri-Phillipe Petain received the following carrier pigeon message from Fr. forces besieged by the Germans at Fort Vaux (Verdun): 'Still holding out, but we are sustaining a very dangerous gas and smoke attack. Must be relieved soon. Send us visual communication through Fort Souville, which does not answer our appeals. This is our last pigeon.' During WW II the Americans used more than 50,000 pigeons to carry information, while the Brit. air-dropped into Ger.-occupied territories crates with more than 20,000 pigeons, which were used by the resistance to send information back to England. Austrl. breeders donated more than 20,000 pigeons to be used for military purposes. In respect for their merits many of these birds later received a form of 'military pension': they were specially looked after and cared for until their death and some of them were even given military burials, stuffed and placed in museums. The Brit. authorities established the Dicken Medal – an animal distinction equivalent to the Victoria Cross, with which many pigeons were awarded during WW II. Carrier pigeons were still used during the war in Korea (1949-53) and Vietnam (1964-73).

Before the telegraph was invented, pigeons had been used by bankers, stock brokers and early information agencies. The founder of one of them, P.J. von Reuter (1816-99) established in 1849 a permanent carrier pigeon connection between Aachen (Germany) and Verviers (Belgium), complementary to his regular telegraphic network. Pigeons are still used to carry information by insular countries, such as Indonesia or the Philipines. They are also used by the health service to carry blood samples or medicines to and from inaccessible regions.

Carrier pigeons were for the first time used for sporting purposes at the beginning of the 19th cent. by Belgian breeders from Verviers and Antwerp., where the first associations of pigeon breeders were formed. It is Brussels where the International Federation of Pigeon Lovers (Fédération Colombophile International) is located, while Antwerp is known as 'pigeon city'. In 1920 in Antwerp the tradition of releasing doves as part of the Ol.G. opening ceremony was initiated. There are approx. 250,000 pigeon breeders in Belgium today. The most outstanding breeders in history include: K. Wegge (Lier), A. Hansenne, A. Bricoux (Jolimont), G. Stassart (Anderlecht), V. and G. Fabry, J. Commine (Leers Nord). In other countries pigeon breeding and racing became popular in the middle of the 19th cent., esp. in Germany, France and Great Britain. The high quality of Fr. breeding was the work of P. Sion a rich manufacturer of Tourcoing aka 'Textilbaron', who bought the best breeding stock in Belgium and spread it throughout France. In 1892 the Belgian King Leopold presented the young successor to the Brit. throne (later George V) a specially prepared dovecote with young pigeons. Earlier the breeding of pigeons was introduced into several other countries of the Brit. Empire, esp. Australia, where the first Kyneton-Melbourne pigeon race took place in 1875 on the initiative of the Melbourne Pigeon and Canary Society. The most prestigious international event is the biannual Carrier Pigeon Olympics. Australia holds 2 national series of pigeon races: from January to March and from August to November. The sport is becoming more and more commercialized, with winners receiving prizes exceeding $100,000.

Pigeons have been a popular motif in literature and the arts. Besides ancient times, the Sentimentalist era produced the symbol of a pigeon as a bird carrying messages between lovers and formed the image of a pigeon as 'a postman of love' (Fr. *postillon d'amour*). Cooing pigeons became a clichéd symbol of love, ever present in erotic literature, a decorative element found in sculpture, but also on kitchen fabrics and wallpapers. Since 1920 the pigeon has become a symbol of peace, popularized by the famous painting by Picasso. The main hero of *On the Waterfront*, played by M. Brando, is a breeder of sport pigeons, with which he spends most of his spare time.

C. Foy, *Pigeons for Pleasure and Profit*, 1972; M. Hartman, *Das Tauberbuch*, 1986; W. Meischner, *Die Sporttaube*, 1969; W.M. Levi, *Encyclopedia of Pigeon Breeds*, 1965; A. Trevithic, *Pigeon Racing*, EWS, 1996, II; L.F. Whitney, *Basis of Breeding Racing Pigeons*; Consultant: J. Krzyżaniak.

PIG RODEO, a type of folk competition where the participants attempt to ride bareback on pigs for as long as possible. It is known in several countries of various cultural background. The most famous form of pig rodeo is that practiced in the Jap. village of Mikame, where the pigs' weight is limited to 120kg.

PIGEON SHOOTING, one of the oldest varieties of competitive shooting, practiced in the past with the bow and crossbow, and later with firearms; different local varieties; the oldest description in Homer's *The Iliad* – pigeon shooting was one of the competitions at the funeral games organized in memory of Patrokles:

But when Polypoites took the lump in turn, he made it hurtle as far as a herdsman throws a cattle staff, rifling it clear across a herd: so far beyond the ring he hurled it, and the soldiers roared applause. Men of his company carried the royal prize down to the ships. Wrought iron for the archers now – ten axheads double-bladed, ten with single blades – Akhilleus laid in order in the ring. He set a mast up from a black-hulled ship at the sand's edge, and tethered by a crowd around one foot a rockdove. 'Shoot at that!' said he. 'The man who hits the fluttering dove may carry all the double axes home. If someone cuts the cord he'll miss the bird: call it a poor shot! Second prize for him!' At this the kingly archer Teukros rose, followed by Idomeneus' lieutenant, staunch Meriones. And choosing lots they rolled them in a helmet. Teukros' pebble had the luck: he drew and shot his arrow without a pause, also without a vow of rams in hecatomb to Lord Apollo. He missed the bird, begrudged him by Apollo, hitting instead the cord that tethered her. The cutting arrowhead parted the cord, and skyward the bird flew, as the frayed length of cord dangled to earth. All the Akhaians breathed a mighty sigh – but in one motion Meriones whipped the bow out of his hands. He held an arrow ready for his shot and now vowed to Apollo, archer of heaven, to offer first-born lambs in hecatomb. Aloft, dark against cloud, he saw the dove, and as she wheeled he shot her through the body under the wing. His arrow, passing through, plummeted back and stuck before his feet. The wounded rockdove settled on the mast with hanging head and drooping wings, and soon, as life throbbed from her body, she fell down far from the bowman. All the troops looked on and marveled at the shooting. Then Meriones picked up the double blades, Teukros the single, to carry to the ships.

[Homer, *The Iliad*. London: The Everyman's Library. 1992. Trans. Robert Fitzgerald]

Pigeon shooting was criticized in the 19th cent. by animal lovers, particularly after 1832, when the High Hats Club was established in England. Its members shot at live pigeons released from under specially high hats. Due to the criticism club members replaced the pigeons with a special device, the so-called trap. This gave rise to trap-shooting – glass balls filled with feathers were replaced with ceramic discs. In 1860 the trap was used to catapult clay pigeons – brittle platters made from a mixture of limestone and pitch; around 1865 these were in turn replaced with red balloons. In 1910 a form of trap-shooting initially called *round the clock shooting* was developed (>COMPETITIVE SHOOTING). Despite the criticism and all the replacement, live pigeons continued to be shot at. Gradually, they were completely replaced with solid iron pigeons mounted on long metal rods. Pigeon shooting was once featured in the Ol.G. in 1900; the winner was D. Lunden from Belgium. Cf. >PARROT SHOOTING, >COCK SHOOTING.

PILA, Lat. for 'a ball'. A round object made from different materials and used for play by ancient Romans. The most common Roman pila games incl. >FOLLIS PUGILLATORIUS; >HARPASTON, >PAGANICA and >TRIGON; a game borrowed from the Greeks and known in ancient Rome as *harpastum*; cf. >PILA VELOX. The Lat. name pila was applied to various medieval games held under the patronage of the Catholic Church; see >PILA PASCHALIS, >PILA PEDALIS. The pila was covered with hog or deer leather wrapped with strings. It had a core made of thick wool, an inflated pig's bladder, or rolled-up or chopped animal bowels.

PILA PASCHALIS, see >EASTER BALL.

PILA PEDALIS, an unknown type of ball game referred to in some medieval texts as a kind of football (Lat. *pila* – 'ball', pedalis – 'of foot'). J. de Berners in *The Book of Saint Albans*, a description of knightly coats of arms, discusses one of the heraldic devices, providing various ways of understanding of the Lat. term pila in medieval England:

The Latin term pila is often used to mean 'a piece of wood' which is placed under a bridge span [...] sometimes it is understood as a playing device. If it is a device played by hand it is called pila manualis; if played by foot it is called pila pedalis.

The Lat. name was misused as the Lat. past participle *pedalis* meant 'of the shape of foot' not 'moved with a foot'. A ball kicked with a foot ought to have taken the Lat. present participle *pedarius*. The are two possible etymologies of the name: either the name was misapplied to a football game or the ball was not kicked at all but it just had the shape of foot; see etymology of >FOOTBALL.

PILA PEDARIUS, see >PILA PEDALIS, >FOOTBALL.

PILA PRASINA, Lat. lit. 'green ball'. A ball game mentioned by Petronius in *The Satyricon*:

So, forgetting all our troubles, we proceed to make a careful toilette, and bid Giton, who had always hitherto been very ready to act as servant, to attend us at the bath. Meantime in our gala dresses, we began to stroll about, or rather to amuse ourselves by approaching the different groups of ball-players. Amongst these we all of a sudden catch sight of a bald-headed old man in a russet tunic, playing ball amid a troupe of long-haired boys. It was not however so much the boys, though these were well worth looking at, that drew us to the spot, as the master himself, who wore sandals and was playing with green balls (pila prastina). He never stooped for a ball that had once touched ground, but an attendant stood by with a sackful, and supplied the players as they required them. We noticed other novelties too. For two eunuchs were stationed at opposite points of the circle, one holding a silver chamber-pot, while the other counted the balls, not those that were in play and flying from hand to hand, but such as fell on the floor. We were still admiring these refinements of elegance when Menelaus runs up, saying, 'See! that's the gentleman you are to dine with; why! this is really nothing else than a prelude to the entertainment.' He had not finished speaking when Trimalchio snapped his fingers, and at the signal the eunuch held out the chamber-pot for him, without his ever stopping play. After easing his bladder, he called for water, and having dipped his hands momentarily in the bowl, dried them on one of the lads' hair.

[trans. A.R. Allinson]

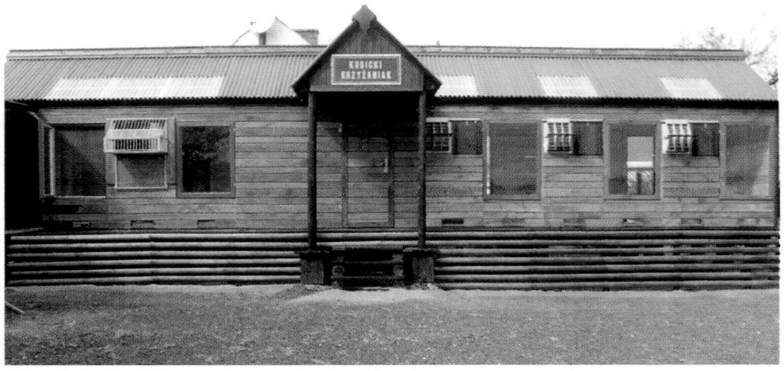

A pigeon loft.

On the basis of the ancient pila prasina the rules of modern >ROMAN BALL have been formulated in the Milwaukee School of Engineering in the USA.

PILA VELOX, a Lat. name of an unspecified ball game, mentioned by Horace in *Satire II* from *Book I*. Horace recommends bodily exercise to whet one's appetite before a sumptuous feast but at the same time he warns against too much 'shoddy food'.

Leporem sectatus equove lassus
ab indomito, vel, si Romana fatigat
militia adsuetum graecari, seu pila velox,
moliter austerum studio fallente laborem,
seu te discus agit, pete cedentem aera disco.

[Chase after a hare, ride a wild horse,
and if you are tired of Roman drills,
being used to Greek exercises, grab the swift ball,
increase your appetites with lively play,
and hurl the discus through the yielding air.]

PILAOUET, also *mouih*, a Bret. game consisting of hitting a pointed stick with a bat; known as *pilouette* or *la Guise*, *le Quinet* in France, similar to such games as Pol. >KLIPA, >SZTEKIEL, Pak. >GULLI DUNDA, Indon. >TAK KADAL, Galician (Spain) *estornela*, Ir. *lug*, Swiss *buemmel*, Scot. >SOW-IN-THE- KIRK.

F. Peru, 'La tradition populaire de jeux de plein air en Bretagne', LJP, 1998.

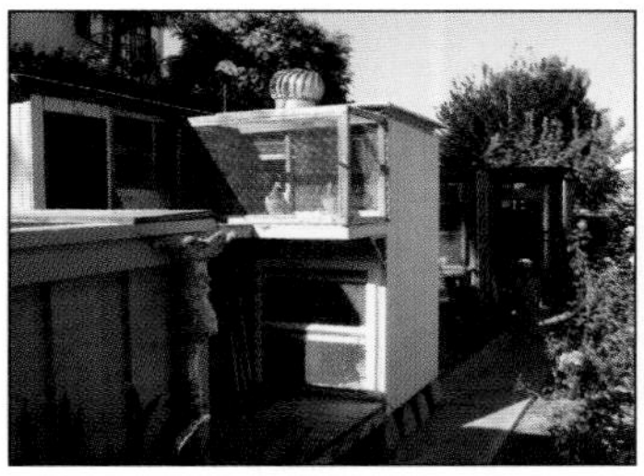

The pigeon loft of Neil Cubbison in San Diego, California.

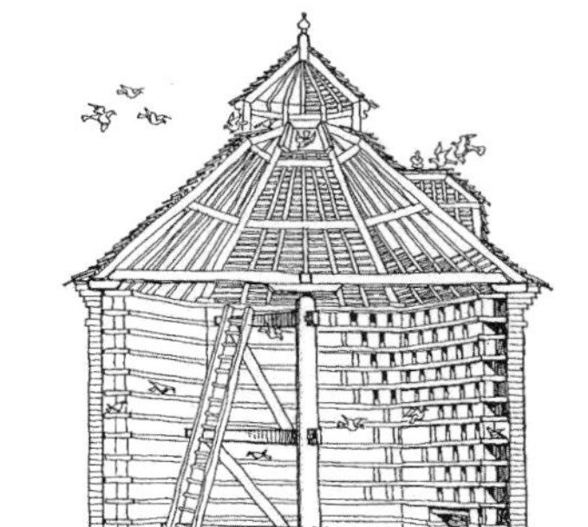

A typical dovecote.

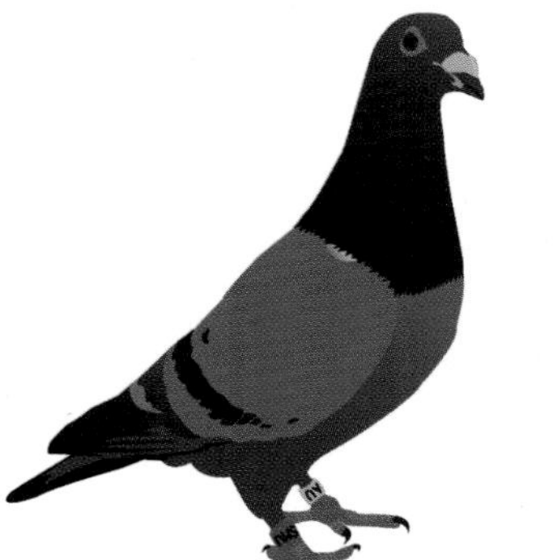

A pigeon.

P

WORLD SPORTS ENCYCLOPEDIA

PILATES, a group of approximately 500 exercises across a wide range of specially designed exercise equipment, used for fitness and rehabilitation, and being a mixture of *yoga*, stretching and physical therapy. Being in essence a way of exercising the muscles through stretching, as well as increasing and releasing muscle tension, the method offers a non-stress approach to better posture and stronger, leaner muscles. Pilates offers an alternative to power exercises, the idea of which is to increase the training load through adding weight or increasing the frequency. The method offers a holistic approach to the body, as opposed to exercising each part of the body separately. Wearing light clothes, pilates practitioners exercise on a blanket or a floor mat and fol-

Pilates.

Pilates – a reformer.

Le pilou.

low 5 fundamental principles, which make the method a fusion of eastern and western philosophies: 1) the use of deep breathing technique, with raising the midriff and stretching the ribs sideways while inhaling; 2) reaching full concentration with complete isolation from the outside world; 3) accurate execution of exercises, where quality prevails over quantity (each exercise is repeated 8-12 times); 4) smooth execution of exercises, eliminating any sudden, quick, uncontrolled movements; 5) self-control and synchronization of all elements.

Equipment. Pilates can be practiced at home with merely the use of a floor mat. However, pilates studios offer a whole range of spring and gravity based resistance equipment such as reformers, circles, Cadillac (trap table), Wunda chair, pedipull, barrels etc. The most popular of them is the reformer – a movable carriage for pushing and pulling, which was invented by J. Pilates in the 1940s.

History. The method was invented by a legendary Ger. physical trainer Joseph Humbertus Pilates at the end of the 1920s. In the 1930s elements of pilates were introduced into the practice routine of New York Ballet dancers. Decades later, in the 1990s, pi-

lates again gained popularity thanks to such celebrities as: Dustin Hoffman, Tom Hanks, Naomi Campbell, Minnie Driver, and others.

Allan Menezes, *The Complete Guide to Joseph H. Pilates' Techniques of Physical Conditioning*, 2000; Brooke Siler, *The Pilates Bod: The Ultimate At-Home Guide to Strengthening, Lengthening, and Toning Your Body – Without Machines*.

PILLE ÆG OP, Dan. for 'picking eggs' (Dan. *pille* – 'to pick' + *æg* – 'eggs' + op – 'up'). A Dan. folk game. Two runners place a few eggs (usu. 6) in line on the ground, a few steps apart, and then pick them all up, trying not to break any. The eggs are kept in a basket to which the competitor must run each time, putting in one egg at a time.

J. Møller, 'Pille æg op', GID, 1997, 4, 102.

PILLMATUN, an aboriginal game of agility played by the Mapuche Indians (Araucanians) in Chile, popular up until the beginning of the 20th century, and not unlike a cross between modern >VOLLEYBALL and >DODGEBALL. An equal-opportunity pastime, it was enjoyed alike by male and female, young and old. The oldest Spanish records mentioning pillmatun date back to 1629 (see Span. >JUEGO DE PELOTA). At the beginning of the 18th century, pillmatun spread to Argentina. A light ball or *pillma*, 7-20cm in diameter and made of rush, straw, dung, sea-weed, feathers, dry leaves, spongy wood, or animal bladder, and covered by cloth or leather, was used. The field – defined by an imaginary line, sticks or rope – was of variable dimensions (circular, square or rectangular) and sizes (usu. about 50ft. long) depending on the number of players. Two teams of 4-30 barefoot players covered only with a breech-clout (Span. *taparrabo*), were arranged according to the shape of the field. Forming a semicircle they stood facing each other. A thrower elected by one of the teams stood in the middle of the circle and began the game by knocking the ball with all his might and speed at any of his opponents, trying to hit one. To achieve this, he would first bounce the ball against the ground, then catch it on the rebound with one hand, raise his right thigh and toss the ball underneath it and up, over his head. As it came down he spiked it with the palm of his hand toward an opponent (*tarjet*) player. This series of actions was performed with the utmost swiftness. One had to perfect 3 skills at top speed in order to excel as a *pillmatufe* (master player): 1) throwing with strength and accuracy against an adversary; 2) cutting and returning the ball with all one's might against an opponent by slamming it only once and with only the palm of one's hand; 3) feinting and dodging in order to avoid being struck by the ball by jumping and throwing oneself down on the ground while remaining in the same spot. Development of these basic pillmatun skills – excellent reflexes to avoid being struck and the ability to return an attempted strike deftly – were considered essential preparation for warriors faced with the mortal blows of Spanish arms. Pillmatun consisted of similar yet distinct varieties. For example, according to the basic var., once struck, a player had to leave the field and the ball was returned to the opposing team. The team with the last player won. Then, in the 19th century, the game was decided by points. The best player was elected by each team and could continue playing even after having been struck. Each team won a point by striking the opponent. If the opponent answered the strike by catching and returning the ball, or if he managed to avoid being hit or the ball went astray, he won a point. He also won a point if the ball went out of bounds. In a >MARATHON var., players were eliminated only by the limits of their own stamina; games went on and on until, one by one, the utterly spent participants all dropped out and there was but one triumphant player left standing on the field. At this point, he was declared the winner while those defeated began a ritual head-dance (*lonkomeo*) moving their heads in honor of the winner, assuming they still had the surplus energy to move at all. Some var. employed 2 balls simultaneously, effectively doubling the game's difficulty and increasing the excitement of the spectators who, when a ball was returned by an opponent, would shout, '*Lai-lai!*' ('Dead! Dead!') in gleeful chorus. Games were usu. played nearby dwellings on any suitably level area, though for important matches there were permanent fields. Such place names as Pillmatun-fields, Pillmahue and Pillmatue provide lasting testimony of this. Not inconsiderable wagers were placed on important games. Players, balls and fields underwent magic rites. The

most magnificent pillmatun practitioners performed incredible acrobatic stunts and dominated the ball, though players frequently suffered injuries, particularly involving deformations of the palms due to the strength of the blows and the demanding acrobatics. Pillmatun and other sporting games of the Mapuche were included in the program of the First National Olympic Games of Santiago, Chile in 1909. See also >AWARKUDEN, >KETCHUKAWE, >LINAO, and >CHUECA, also known as *palin*.

O. Plath, 'Pillmatun', JYDLCH, 1946, 15-16; C. López von Vriessen, 1992, 1994, 1996; the Internet: www.deportesmapuches.cl, www.galeon.com/indiansports

PILOTA, a rarely used name for >PELOTA.

PILOU, LE, a Fr. game that probably begun in 1942, the year of the demonetization of the Fr. coin of 25 centimes. At the end of WWII, the game was well established. It was played in the popular districts of Nice and other towns of S France. The name *pilou* comes from *pile* ('tails'), one of the 2 faces of a coin. It is significant to point out that in the local language of Nice, pilou is written *pilo*, with the 'o' pronounced /ou/ to avoid confusion with a kind of fluffy cotton flannel. How to explain the development of such a game in Nice and in its county at that time? Why the use of a 25 centimes coin perforated? At the beginning of the century, precisely in 1914, a new generation of coins was launched in France, made of nickel. They were bored not to be confused with the traditional silver coins. Indeed pilou requires a stable coin which should not be too heavy to avoid badly making with feet and knees, nor too light not to be carried by the wind. The 25 centimes coin perfectly fills those requirements. This coin was demonetized on February 15, 1942, explaining the rise of this game after this date. Pilou seems to derive from old practices as the different forms of shuttlecock-kicking game played in Asia. A game played with a ball in South America also resembles pilou: the ground is divided in two equal zones and the players must juggle with the ball. The latter should never fall by ground, nor to be caught by the hand. Each team marks a point when the competitive team cannot return the ball or if this one touches the ground. The great vogue of pilou lasted fifteen years in Nice, from 1950 to 1965, with especially local tournaments. In the meantime, the rules of the game were defined and the "four rounds" were developed as the more common practice. In Nice, the game was especially located in the old popular districts. Along the Mediterranean Sea, pilou was mainly practised in ports and old towns. During the Sixties, the game declined and completely disappeared after the May 1968 events for nearly twenty years. It is necessary to wait until 1987 so that the interest for the game re-appeared in Nice, in a climate of nostalgia for local identity. Then the attractiveness for pilou has not ceased growing and, in 1988, the first 'world championship' was organised in Coaraze, with 32 teams engaged.

PILOUETTE, see >PILAOUET.

PIŁKA NOŻNA W KOLE, (Pol. 'circle football'), an obs. form of football game, once played in Pol. schools. The game was described by the pioneer of physical culture in Poland, E. Piasecki:

The game is played with a round, leather-covered, inflated ball, 20cm in diameter. The players stand in a circle, 2-4 steps apart. One player stands in the middle and tries to kick the ball out of the circle and the remaining players in the circle try to prevent him from doing so. If a circle player misses the ball on his right side, he replaces the center player (sometimes a left side rule applies). [...] the players cannot run into the circle; they can only move sideways. The ball can only be touched with the hand if it goes out of bounds.

[Zabawy i gry ruchowe dzieci i młodzieży (Sports and Physical Games of Children and Young People), 1916)]

PIŁKA NOŻNA Z BRAMĄ, (Pol. 'gate football'), an obs. form of football game, one of the archetypes of >FOOTBALL; practiced in Pol. secondary schools bef. 1914. The game was described by E. Piasecki:

The square playing field is 30x30m, divided into half by a centerline, in the middle of which the goal is positioned. The goal is a gate consisting of two posts, seven meters apart, and a crossbar or tape, 2.5m above the ground. The game is played by two teams of 4-6 players who stand in two lines on both sides of the centerline. The first line of players is the attack line consisting of 3-5 players, 6-10m apart. The attack lines of both teams are 11m from the centerline of the field. The remaining player at the back is the short stop whose responsibility is to pass the ball to the attack line players from the outfield. The game is commenced by one team drawn by lot. One of the attack players places the ball on the ground, eleven meters from the goal and tries to kick it into the goal. If a goal is scored the player becomes goalkeeper and his team scores one point. If he misses, the opposing team shoots. With the goalkeeper in goal scoring is more difficult but there is no distance limit from which the ball can be shot. The ball remains in possession of one team if it is in this team's half. The attacking players can dribble and pass the ball to one another before shooting. The game is controlled by a referee. The goalkeeper cannot kick the ball, only catch it or hit it. He cannot catch or hit a ball which is passing outside the goalposts into the opponent's half. While holding the ball the goalkeeper can only take two steps. For any goalkeeping foul the ball is given to the opposing team. A team does not score a point or take the goal if the goalkeeper has purposely missed the shots from his own team. Whichever team gains more points within a specified time wins.

[*Zabawy and gry ruchowe dzieci and młodzieży* (The Sports and Physical Games of Children and Young People), 1916]

PIŁKA NOŻNA Z WIEŻĄ, (Pol. 'tower football'), an obs. football game played in Pol. schools before 1914. The ball was leather-covered, 20cm in diameter. The players' line-up was similar to >PIŁKA NOŻNA W KOLE.

In the middle of the circle stands the tower – a tripod made of 2m-long poles tied on top. The circle players try to topple the tower by hitting it with the ball. The player in the middle guards the tower. He can kick the ball or touch it with his trunk. If the ball goes out of the circle the player over whose head or on whose right side the ball has passed fetches it, places it on the ground and kicks the ball towards the tower. The player who has toppled the tower becomes the new tower guardian.

[E. Piasecki, *Zabawy and gry ruchowe dzieci and młodzieży* (The Sports and Physical Games of Children and Young People), 1916]

PIŁKA Z KOŁA, (Pol. for 'ball outside the circle'), a school sports game popular in the USSR and Poland in the 1950s. 'One player selected by lot stands in the middle of the circle. The other players stand around him with their hands placed on their knees. They roll the ball across the circle while the center player attempts to intercept it and throw it out of the circle. The circle players cannot kick the ball or hold it with their feet. When not rolling the ball they must hold their hands on their knees all the time. A circle player who misses the ball replaces the middle player. If the ball goes ourside the circle, between 2 players, the one on whose right side the ball has passed becomes the center player'.
I.N. Chkhannikov, 'Piłka z koła', GIZ, 1953, 4-5.

PIŁKA Z KONI, (Pol. for 'ball on horses'), and old Pol. ball game played on horses. Only some fragmentary descriptions of the game survived, e.g. in *Gry i zabawy różnych stanów* (Games and Competitions of Different Social Classes, 1831, p. 19) by Ł. Gołębiowski: 'The tossing game of horse ball was played by our forefathers. During the reign of Wladislaw IV (1632-48) the players used to throw the ball at iron or lead bars, or stones placed on long tables trying to knock them off'. No precise information as to the size of the ball and the bars or the rules of play survived.

PIND MED EEN STEN, (Dan. for 'peg and stone'), a Dan. team game consisting of hitting a short, 25cm-long peg, with a longer, 80cm-long stick. The course of play, scoring and eliminating the batters are similar to >PIND, but in the first batting round a single stone or brick is used (Dan. *pind* – 'peg, stick' + *med* – 'with' + *een* – 'one' + *sten* – 'stone'). Batting is performed in three ways. In the so-called long bat (*lang*) the peg is placed on the stone so it sticks out 5cm from the edge of the stone. Then, the peg is hit with the stick on top so it flies up and spins in the air. In the second way, called the elbow (*ron*) the batter holds the peg in one hand and the stick in the other. The peg is hit from above so it flies up and spins in the air. In the third way, called the flutter (*vip*), the batter places the peg in the same way as in the long bat way. Next, the batter hits the peg from underneath and bats it out sidearm.
J. Møller, 'Pind med een sten', GID, 1997, 1, 119.

PIND, [Dan. pind – 'peg'], a Dan. team game consisting of hitting a short peg (*kortpinden*) with a longer stick (*langpinden*). The stick is 80cm and the peg 25cm long; both are 3-4cm in diameter. The playing field has no specified dimensions, although the game is often played on a pitch 15x30m. At one end of the pitch a simple wicket is positioned consisting of 2 stones (*sten*) or bricks 20cm apart. The wicket is called the 'pot' (*gryde*) and serves as a batting base. One of the batting players takes his turn at the pot and hits the peg out with the stick. The fielding team tries to catch the peg and throws it back on the base. The batter remains at the pot until he or she misses the peg or a fielder catches it. The game has two aims: 1) for the fielding team, to get out as many batters as possible, which makes it more difficult for the batting team to score points; 2) for the batting team, to bat the peg out as far as possible, and for the fielding team to reduce the distance from the peg to the base by all means. These two contradictory objectives are crucial as scoring for the batting team is done by counting the stick lengths on the distance between the pot and the spot the peg hit the ground. Batting is performed in 3 successive rounds with increasing difficulty. In the first round, the batter places the peg across the base stones or bricks and strikes it with the stick from underneath. If the fielding team catches the peg on the fly, the batter is out and the next batter takes his turn at the pot. If this time, the batted peg is not caught by the fielding team the batter places the longer stick on the pot. The fielder standing closest to the peg picks it up from the ground and throws it at the pot trying to knock the stick off. In the second round, the batter tosses up the peg and then hits it out with the stick. If a fielder catches the peg on the fly the batter is out. If the peg hits the ground a fielder can pick it up and throw it back at the pot. The batter can return the peg using the stick. If then the peg hits the ground the distance between the pot and the peg is measured and the batting team scores the points. In the third, most difficult round, the batter first flicks up the peg with the stick and then bats it out sidearm. The fielding players cannot catch the peg but hit it on the fly or kick it on the first bounce towards the pot to reduce the scoring distance. The scores from each round are summed up. The game is played until the last batter is out. Then, the teams change over.
J. Møller, 'Pind', GID, 1997, 1, 119.

PINE KALV, (Dan. for 'to torment the calf'), a Dan. form of wrestling contest. Two contenders sit on the ground pressing their backs against each other. One meter in front of each contender a foul line is drawn on the ground. The wrestlers try to push each other across the foul line using only their legs.
J. Møller, 'Pine kalv', GID, 1997, 4, 48.

PIOI see >TUMI.

PIORRA, a var. of >PIĂO.

PIRNANNI U VODU, a Ukrainian form of diving, once practiced by the early Cossacks [Ukr. *pirnuti* – to dive + *u* – *to, in* + voda – water]. The diving competitions were usu. held as public shows of skill. B.I. Kowjerko, a Ukrainian sports historian described diving competitions practiced among the Zaporozhian Cossacks: 'A leader used to throw his pipe into the bay and the young Cossacks would dive and vie with each another to get it. A great feat was picking up the pipe from the sandy bottom with no hands just one's teeth and bringing it back to the surface.'
B.I. Kowjerko, ed., 'Pro sistiemu fizycznogo wdoskonalienija zaporozkich kozakiw', TFKU, 1997, 44-62.

PIRORI, also *porotiti*, a Maori game consisting of bowling hoops made of flexible twigs. Pirori had two varieties. In the first var. two teams of players stand in 2 rows facing each other. The players in one row bowl a hoop forward to the players in the other row who tried to return it. If they miss the hoop the players in the first row win the game. In the second var. a dividing line is marked on the ground between 2 teams standing a few meters apart facing one another. The hoop is thrown by one player so as to strike the ground and rebound across the line. The receiving players try to drive the hoop back by striking it with sticks. The throwing team has to return the hoop and the game continues until one team misses the hoop.
GADOMP, 11.

PISI, a Bulg. folk game consisting of throwing a pointed peg into holes in the ground. The number of players is unspecified, but usu. pisi is played by 6 to 10 players. They stand in a circle. Each player digs a hole in the ground. The first player, chosen by drawing lots, throws a short peg, 10-15cm in length and 3-4cm in diameter, towards another player's hole. If the thrower hits it the player whose hole was hit takes a throw. If the thrower misses the hole he or she must run around the circle of players and return to his or her hole. In the meantime, the player's neighbors stick their pegs into his hole making it wider. The winner is the player whose hole has the smallest diameter by the end of the game.

PITKËPALLO, (Fin. *pitkä* – 'long' + *pallo* – 'ball'), the original name of >PESÄPALLO, coined by the game's inventor, Lauri 'Tahko' Pihkala (1887-1979) in 1915.

PITYLIZEIN, a kind of gymnastic exercise practiced in ancient Greece, consisting of rhythmic, sweeping arm movements imitating rowing movements (Gk. *pitylos* – rowing movements, also *pitylidzo* – 'to move arms fast; *pituleuo* – 'to row or paddle rapidly'). Pitylizein was not a separate sport or gymnastic event but it was used as a supplementary exercise in Gk. gymnasions and paleastras, improving the physical skills required for practicing other sports.

PIU, a Maori var. of >JUMP ROPE.

PIZE BALL, an obs. Eng. sports game (to pize – 'to strike out'). The game was played by 2 teams of an unspecified number of players; usu. 6 per team, on a field with a home base and a field base called the tut. Some ethnographers regard pize ball as a var. of >TUTT-BALL. One team fielded, the opposing, striking team took the positions around the home base. One player of the striking team struck or pized the ball with his hand out in the field and started running to the field base. The fielders tried to catch the ball on the fly and get the runner out by striking him with the ball. Once the runner was hit with the ball he was said to be *burnt* or *out* and the teams changed sides in the field.
TGESI, II, 45.

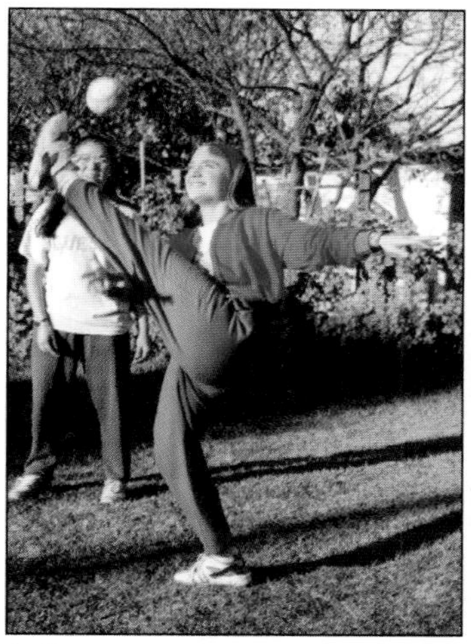

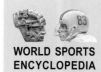

A pillmatun game demonstrated by the students of the Catholic University of Valparaiso.

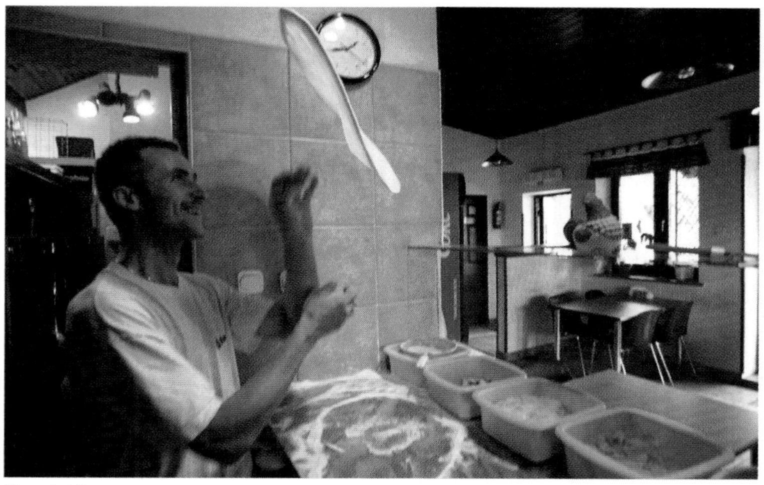

Pizza twirling.

PIZZA TWIRLING, a contest held since 1998 in the Ital. town of Salsomaggiore Terme in the province of Parma; the competition comprises performance of a series of sophisticated twists and turns of a portion of pizza dough held in the hands and kneaded; level of difficulty, sophistication and pace of performance are evaluated.

PLATANISTAS, a Gk. form of brutal physical contest organized in ancient Sparta as part of military upbringing of the youth called the *agoge*. The name of the competition was derived from the plane-trees which grew in a place called Platanistas, situated on the Magula stream in the western part of town. Platanistas was home to one of the two oldest gymnasions in ancient Greece. It was described by Pausanias in *Description of Greece*: 'And there is a place called Platanistas (Plane-tree Grove) from the unbroken ring of tall plane trees growing round it. The place itself, where it is customary for the youths to fight, is surrounded by a moat just like an island in the sea; you enter it by bridges. On each of the two bridges stand images; on one side an image of Heracles, on the other a likeness of Lycurgus' (III, 14, 8). Each platanistas contest was preceded by >BOAR FIGHTING. According to Pausanias, 'A little before the middle of the next day they enter by the bridges into the place I have mentioned. They cast lots during the night to decide by which entrance each band is to go in' (III, 14, 10). At that time Sparta was divided into 5 districts, each of which has its own representation of fighters. The most famous compe-

426

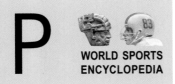

P WORLD SPORTS ENCYCLOPEDIA

tition used to take place between the districts of Lycurgids and Heraclids. Pausanias provided a description of the tournament: 'In fighting they use their hands, kick with their feet, bite, and gouge out the eyes of their opponents. Man to man they fight in the way I have described, but in the melee they charge violently and push one another into the water (III, 14, 10) (trans. W.H.S. Jones and H.A. Ormerod). According to B. Kunicki, a Pol. historian of ancient sports 'Platanistas had, in fact, nothing in common with any sports contest and it allowed fighting techniques prohibited even in >PANKRATION.'

N.B. Crowther, 'Team Sports in Ancient Greece', IJHS, 1995; B.J. Kunicki, 'Platanistas', LAS, 1997.

PLATFORM PADDLE TENNIS, a form of tennis played using plywood paddles and scoring similar to >PADDLE TENNIS. The game is played on a specially constructed wooden platform surrounded by back and side walls of tightly strung wire netting 10ft. (3.7m) high. The court is 44 by 16ft. for singles, and 44 by 20ft. for doubles. The net is 2ft. 10in. high at its center. During the game balls may be taken off the walls after first striking inside the court proper.

PLATFORM TENNIS, or *plat tennis*, a var. of tennis played on a specially constructed wooden platform, which allows the game to be practiced even in wintertime. The sport is also known as platform paddle tennis, as it uses similar paddles to those of >PADDLE TENNIS. The two games are also often confused due to the similar names of their federations. A standard platform is 60 by 30ft. (18.18 by 9.14m); the actual court is 44 by 20ft (13.46 by 6.10m). The sides of the court are hinged, so that snow can be swept off easily. The court is surrounded by walls 12ft. high (3.7m). Balls are made of sponge rubber, 2.5in. in diameter, in orange color; the paddles are made of oval perforated plywood.

The rules are the same as for tennis (same scoring and terminology), except that balls may be hit off the back and side walls after first striking the court proper,

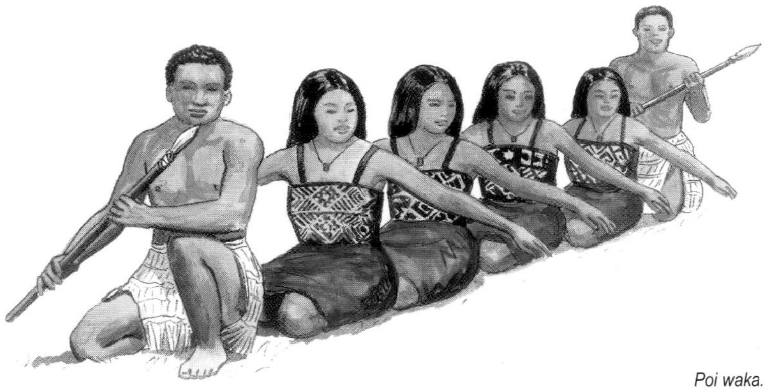

Poi waka.

and only one serve is allowed. In this respect platform tennis bears a resemblance to >ROYAL TENNIS, >SQUASH and >RACQUETBALL. The game is very dynamic, as players can use both long, and faster short balls alternately; it is usu. played by doubles, but singles matches also take place. Platform tennis is often practiced as a recreational sport by many professional tennis players.

History. Platform tennis was devised in the 1930s by the Americans F.S. Blanchard and J.K. Cogswell from Scardale, New York. The first tennis platform was built in 1931 at the Fox Meadow Tennis Club, where the first US platform tennis championships were estab. as well. The playing season is usu. from Oct. to March. Platform tennis enjoys great popularity in northern states, where practicing tennis on open courts in winter is impossible due to heavy snowfalls. Today, there are a few thousand tennis platforms all over the USA. In 1934 the Amer. Paddle Tennis Association was founded, but because of its confusing name it was often associated with a different sport called paddle tennis. In 1950 it was renamed the American Platform Tennis Association, situated in Upper Montclair, New Jersey. The platforms in northern states have special snow screens; in warmer areas the game is played on lower open platforms. In the beginning the game was practiced only in a few exclusive clubs. Along with the development of new materials and cheaper construction of platforms, platform tennis became a popular public sport in many American city parks and resorts in the 1960s and 1970s. The game is also played in Canada, Australia and southern France.

O.H. Durell, ed., *The Official Guide to Platform Tennis*, 1975; R.S. Squires, *How to Play Platform Tennis*, 1978; G. Sullivan, *Paddle. The Beginner's Guide to Platform Tennis*, 1975; J. Townes, 'Tennis, Platform', EWS, 1997.

PLATSCHIEẞEN, [Ger. *Platten* – sheets, plates + *Schießen* – throwing, shooting]. A Swiss game that resembles Ital. >BOCCIA in some respects, even though small toothed metal 'stars' are used instead of balls. The wet clay track is 17m long and 1.5m wide. Swiss championships are organized annually. Plattenschießen is most popular in the cantons of Graubünden (Fr. Grisons) and Bern.

PLATTE BOL, (Flem. for 'flat balls'), a trad. Flem. bowling game, known in the Fr. part of Flanders as *boules flamandes*. The game consists of rolling bowls at a target, which is usu. a feather or a metal blade positioned on end. The name platte bol comes from the shape of balls used for the game. The balls are flattened and weighted on one side to make them do not roll straight.

Playing field and equipment. The platte bol bowling alley is called the *boltra*, and can be found in many Flem. inns and cafeterias. The gutter-shaped alley is 12-20m long, 1.5-3m wide and 5-20cm deep; sometimes 30cm-deep lanes are used. The surface of the lanes is a blend of earth, flour, salt and cow blood; some lanes are lined with asphalt or pressed gravel. The feather or blade is positioned 1.5m from the end of the lane. It is encircled with one or several lines. Each player rolls his or her ball as close to the blade as possible, trying to knock the opponent's balls out. The winner is the player or team whose ball or balls are closer to the target at the end of the game. In this respect, platte bol rules resemble those of Scot. >CURLING. Each wooden ball used for platte bol is 7-10cm in diameter, 18-25cm in circumference and weighs up to 2kg. The one-side flattening of the ball makes it easier to hit an opponent's ball after a curved course. The game can be played by individual players or teams. The team game can be played in two ways: 1) the players of the opposing teams roll the balls alternately; or 2) first, one team's players roll the balls, and then the opposing team's players take their turn.

History. The game's origins go back to the 16th cent. The earliest references to platte bol include vague names, such as *rollen*, *bollen* or *bollebanen*. Platte bol at one time enjoyed once enormous popularity in the border area between East Flanders and Brabant. It was widely practiced during WWII. Today, the platte bol governing body in Belgium is the Platte Bol Federation of West Flanders.

E. de Vroede, 'Ball and Bowl Games in the Low Countries: Past and Present', *Homo Ludens – Der Spielende Mensch*, 1996, vol. VI; E. De Vroede, *Het Grote Volksspelen Boek*, Leuven, 1996.

PLATTENSCHIEẞEN see >PLATSCHIEẞEN.

PLETHRIZEIN, a form of running in ancient Greece, in which one had to run forward and backward alternately, at a shorter distance each time until coming to a stop. The name plethrizein comes from the *plethron*, an ancient unit of length equal one hundred feet. Plethreizein running was practiced on a square field, one-plethron wide, called the *plethrion*. Apart from being a physical exercise, the plethrizein competition served as an qualifying round before the Ol.G. and divided the participants into the boys' and men's skill categories.

PLINIE, also *captivus, król, Rinaldo Rinaldini, á la guerre, alter Bär*; an obs. Pol. school team game. E. Piasecki describes the game in his *Zabawy and gry ruchowe dzieci and młodzieży* (*The Sports and Physical Games of Children and Young People*, 1916): 'The game of plinie used to be common in early Polish schools [...] played until today in some village schools in central Polish Galicia'. The field was 50m long and 25m wide, or smaller for younger children. Ł. Gołębiowski in *Gry i zabawy różnych stanów* (*Games and Pastimes of Various Social Classes*, 1831) describes the game in the following way:

There are two teams of participants. Each team has its own baseline marked with a flag, behind which there is an area designated for captives from the opposing team. Each team comprises the chief and his knights. At a given signal one team sends out one or two challengers to the opposing team's line. They must approach the opponent's line with their arms straightened forward so the opposing players can tag them. Once tagged the challengers run back to their own baseline and can be chased by the opposing players. A player becomes a captive if he or she is tagged outside his or her baseline. If so, such a player is taken behind the opponent's baseline. A captive can be freed if he or she is tagged by a teammate. The chief can free all captives in the opponent's area if he has touched only one of them. A chief can only be tagged and taken captive by the other chief. During the game both teams may agree to exchange captives. The team which first captures the opposing team's chief, half of its knights and the flag wins the game. Plinie was a fun game enjoyed by pupils, class teachers and school headmasters. The game was usually played during spring outings. It had a var. of local names such as plinie, captivity, chasing the prisoners, school captivus, á la guerre from French, Alter Bär – 'old bear' from German, or Rinaldo Rinaldini from Italian.

PLISZKA, one of the names for an obs. Pol. folk game played in central Galicia, otherwise known as >KICZKA or >KLIPA.

PLOWING MATCHES, a sport originated by the end of the 18th cent. at agricultural exhibitions in England; popularized in the 19th cent. in France, Germany, USA and Brit. colonies – particularly in Australia – where the most prestigious plowing contests were held on Werribee Plains. Plowing matches were immensely popular in Britain in the first half of the 19th cent. In 1834, a reporter for the Pol. *Magazyn Powszechny*, described competitions of plowmen in England and Scotland:

The most skillful plowmen gather on the field with their horse-drawn or ox-drawn plows. At a signal they start plowing side by side covering a fixed distance. The English spectators make a great deal of betting. Whichever plowman returns first to the starting point, wins a prize. In Scotland, land tenants also gather for similar purposes. Quite recently a gathering of twenty plowmen took place in the County of Oxford. The audience was huge – there were 110 Englishmen but only 10 Scotsmen. The judges admitted that the English plowmen were excellent but could not match the skill of the Scotsmen. After the prize was awarded all competitors were invited to a feast. In 1813, the owner of a paper shop near Cork organized an unusual country competition: 847 plowmen gathered at his field of almost 1400 acres. The competition began at 10 AM; at 1 PM the entire field was plowed and a feast for the competitors and their families was held. 1200 men, women and children as well as 740 invited guests participated in this huge party.

[*Magazyn Powszechny*, 1834]

Plowing matches were also common in eastern Europe. In Poland, for instance, the first plowing contests were organized in the 1840s by Towarzystwo ku Ulepszaniu Hodowli Koni i Bydła Księstwa Poznańskiego (The Society for the Improvement of Horse and Cattle Breeding in the Grand Duchy of Poznań) as parts of annual agricultural exhibitions.

PLUKKE BJERG-MANDENS ÆRTER, Dan. for 'picking the mountain troll's peas', a Dan. recreational game for small children. One of the players – the 'highlander' – pretends he or she is asleep. The other players walk around the highlander and pick up peas spilled on the ground. Suddenly, the highlander 'wakes up' and tries to catch the other players. A player caught is out of the game, the highlander returns to 'sleep' and the remaining players resume picking up the peas. After all the players are out, the player who was caught first becomes the highlander in the next game.

J. Møller, 'Plukke Bjerg-mmandens ærter', GID, 1997.

PODBIJANKA, (Pol for 'bounced ball'), an obsolete Pol. ball game consisting of tossing a ball and hitting it on the fly. The precise rules of the game remain unknown. Most probably, podbijanka was a simple recreational activity. It was tersely described by Ł. Gołębiowski in *Gry i zabawy różnych stanów* (*Games and Competitions of Different Social Classes*, 1831, p. 18): 'The players stand in a circle. One tosses the ball up and the others try to hit it on the fly, but not catching it.'

PODCHODY, (Pol. for 'stalking the enemy'), a Pol. var. of the hare and hounds team game, practiced by boy and girl scouts or school children at summer camps or in schools. It is played by 2 teams of different number of players. The larger team 'stalks' the smaller team consisting of just a few participants (occasionally, a single participant). The 'stalked' team leaves behind traces, e.g. arrow signs of twigs or branches, hidden objects, etc., and sets up various kinds of ambushes. Podchody is usu. played in the woods. An increased number of child kidnappings in recent years has made camp counselors and instructors abandon the night-time version of the game to avoid potential risk of child abduction.

Podchody is derived from scout training. Horseback scouts were used extensively by the Mongols in their conquests of Asian and Eur. peoples. Stalking the enemy using mounted riders was an integral part of Mong. military maneuvers (>ZEGETEABA). Tracking and stalking of the enemy were skills highly developed among the Native Americans, and were later adopted by trappers of the Wild West. Podchody has been part of the military training of Pol. boy scouts. An original form of podchody is the modern game of >HASHING.

PODEX see >PUDDEX.

PODOLANYE DNYIPROVSKICH POROGIV, Ukrainian for 'crossing the Dnieper rapids', a feat of strength and masculinity performed by the Cossacks, consisting of paddling along some sections of the Dnieper River known for its white water and whirlpools. 'The most important trial for the Cossack youth was to paddle across the cataracts of the Dnieper [...] only then, could they earn the name of real Cossacks.' (Kowjerko). Crossing the rapids was particularly difficult as 'The Dnieper flows through countless rocks and boulders. Some of them remain submerged, some dangerously protrude above the water. Paddling here is very hazardous, especially when the water is low' (Lasjota).

A vivid, literary description of crossing the Dnieper cataracts with the use of swift boats (see >CZAJKI) can be found in *With Fire and Sword*, a novel by H. Sienkiewicz.

The swift boats bearing the knight and his fortunes shot down the current with the speed of swallows. By reason of high water the Cataracts presented no great danger. They passed Surski and Lokhanny; a lucky wave threw them over the Voronoff bar; the boats grated a little on the Knyaji and Streletski, but they were scratched, not broken. At length they beheld in the distance the foaming the whirling of the terrible Nenasytes. There they were obliged to land and drag the boats along the shore, – a tedious and difficult labor, usually occupying an entire day. Fortunately a great many blocks, apparently left by previous travellers, lay along the whole way; these were placed under the boats to ease them over the ground. [...] Only the splash of the waves on the cliff of Nenasytes broke the silence.

While the men were dragging the boats, Skshetuski examined this wonder of Nature. An awful sight met his eyes. Through the entire width of the river extended crosswise seven rocky ridges, jutting out above the water, black, rent by waves which broke through them gaps and passages after their fashion. The river pressed with the whole weight of its waters against those ridges, and was broken on them; then wild and raging, lashed into white foaming pulp, it sought to spring over like an infuriated horse, but, pushed back again before it could sweep through the passage, it seemed to gnaw the rocks with its teeth, making enormous circles in impotent wrath; it leaped up toward the sky, raging like a monster, panting like a wild beast in pain. And then again a roar from it as from a hundred cannon, howls as from whole packs of wolves, wheezing, struggling, and at every ridge the same conflict. Over the abyss were heard screams of birds, as if terrified by the sight. Between the ridges of gloomy shadows of the cliff quivered like spirits of evil. The men, though accustomed to the place, crossed themselves devoutly while dragging the boats, warning the lieutenant not to approach too near the shore; for there were traditions that whoever should gaze too long at Nenasytes would at last see something at which his mind would be disturbed. They asserted, also, that at times there rose from the whirlpool long black hands which caught the unwary who approached too near, and then terrible laughter was heard through the precipices. The Zaporojians did not dare to drag boats along in the night-time. No one could be received into the Brotherhood of the Saitch who had not crossed the Cataracts alone in a boat; but an exception was made of Nenasytes, since its rocks were never under water. Of Bogun alone blind minstrels sang as if he had stolen through Nenasytes; still belief was not given to the song. The transfer of the boats occupied nearly all the day, and the sun had begun to set when the lieutenant resumed his place in the boat. But to make up for this the succeeding Cataracts were crossed with ease, for the rocks were covered entirely, and after that they sailed out into the quiet waters of the lower country.

[Vol. 1, Chapter X; trans. J. Curtin]

E. Ljasota, *Szczczodjennik, Żowtjeń*, 1984, 10; also B.I. Kowjerko, 'Pro sistiemu fizicznogo wdoskonalenija zaporozkich kozakiw', TFKU, 1997, 44-62.

POI, a var. of Maori *haka* dance; see >HAKA, >POI WAKA.

POI WAKA, also known as the *canoe poi*, a trad. Maori dance, being an imitation of the rowing of a canoe (Maori *poi* – a form of dance + *waka* – 'canoe'). The dance is performed by 6 people sitting on the ground in single file, as if in a canoe. The first and the last performers play the role of coxswains, who kneel and hold long ornamented paddles in their hands. The middle 'crew members' are usu. 4 women who imitate rowing by performing rhythmic movements with their arms and bodies, and singing rowing songs, such as the following:

Haul the canoes, ye people,
Row them hard!

Christoph Weiditz, a drawing of Central American ballplayers performing at the court of Charles V, 1528.

Aotea, Tainui, Kurahaupo,
These are the canoes.
Paddle the canoes, ye people
Paddle them with a will!
Mataatua, te Arawa, takitimu,
Tokomaru! Row them hard.

(trans. A. Armstrong)

A. Armstrong, *Games and Dancing of the Maori People*, 1986, 85.

POINT-TO-POINT, an amateur cross-country horse race from one point to another, without a designated route.

POIRIER, see >TOURIG AR PRAD.

POJEZDY, (Rus. for 'trains'), a simple Rus. ice-skating game. Rus. author, I.N. Chkhannikov describes the game in the following way: 'The game is played by two teams of skaters. The teams stand in two lines, parallel to each other behind the start line. Each skater in the line places his or her hands on the shoulders of the player in front of him or her. On a signal, both 'trains' start running to the end line, parallel to and 100m from the start line. The start and end lines should be marked with flags. Once they cross the end line the skaters in lines must turn around and return to the start line [...]. The skaters can be lined up in a var. of ways. Instead of touching each other's shoulder the skaters can hold on to a rope, which would make the race easier. On the racing route there can be a few cones or other obstacles which the skaters should pass around. The end line can be marked with two gates, each consisting of two poles and a crossbar. Each team passes underneath the crossbar, and the last skater in line takes off the crossbar.' I.N. Chkhannikov, 'Poyezdy', GIZ, 1953, 85-86.

POKAUKAU, Maori >KITE FLYING.

POK-TA-POK, see POKYAH.

POKUTA, (Pol. for 'penance'), an obsolete Pol. ball game, derived from ancient >HARPASTON, known in ancient Rome as *harpastum*. The ancient game of harpaston survived well into the Middle Ages and evolved locally into new ball games. In the Poland of the 17th and 18th cent., pokuta was played in schools run by the Church, mostly in Jesuit and Piarist col-

leges. The game consisted of tossing and catching a ball or a wooden bowl (the size varied, depending on a region). Pokuta was played by 3-10 players. A player who missed the ball for the first time continued the game standing on one foot only. Then, on the second miss, he stood on one leg; on the third miss – kneeled on both legs; on the fourth miss – sat on the ground; on the fifth miss – lay down on the ground. The player was out if he missed the ball while lying on the ground; if he managed to catch the ball he could resume the previous position. The player who managed to eliminate all opponents became the winner.

E. Cenar, *Gry i zabawy ruchowe różnych narodów*, 1906.

POKYAH, also *pok-ta-pok* and *pok-tapok*, the holy ball of the Mayas, one of a few varieties of ritual ball game practiced by the peoples of Pre-Columbian C.America; see also >MESOAMERICAN INDIAN BALL GAMES. Pokyah bears a striking resemblance to numerous ancient ball games from the area, played by various tribes, which often conquered one another and exchanged many cultural elements, including designs of playing courts. The origins of Maya pokyah probably go back to 300-900 AD, i.e. to the Classic Period of the Lowland Maya civilization. The game developed greatly between 900 and 1200 AD, i.e. in the early Post-Classic Period. It was played by 2 teams, using a rubber ball. The court was usu. H-shaped but pitches of other shapes were common as well. Some playing fields had stone hoops through which the ball was thrown. Little is known about the rules and course of play, which varied in different areas and historical periods. Ancient drawings represent players hitting the ball with the use of special stone belts worn on their hips and shoulders. Some drawings, like those covering the remnants of walls of ancient Teotihuacán near present-day Mexico City, represent ball players holding sticks.

The knowledge of ancient Mayan culture and customs, including their sports and games, is derived mainly from archeological excavations. Descriptions of a ball game practiced by ancient Quiché Mayas can be found in *Popol Vuh* (The Holy Book), a monumental work of ancient Mayan literature translated into Span. by a Dominican, F. Ximenex. Mayan ball games are also referred to in works written by Span. conquistadors. Those sources, however, are unreliable as the Spanish often misinterpreted the newly encountered reality and disregarded the cultural context of the games. Moreover, the Span. documents were written about 600 years after the heyday of Mayan culture, therefore they refer to games already in decline. The Spanish witnessed only modified var. of pokyah played by the Aztecs (>TLACHTLI) and the natives of the Yucatan Peninsula and highlands on the Guatemalan-Mexican border. After a critical

A pokyah player.

428

P WORLD SPORTS ENCYCLOPEDIA

analysis of facts and details taken from the numerous sources it is after all possible to reconstruct the basic rules and course of play of trad. pokyah.
The H-shaped playing court featured a number of engraved, decorative stones fixed in the floor and the walls. Three stones were usu. positioned in the center of the court, parallel to the longer side; 3 more stones were fixed in one wall and 3 in the opposite wall. The symbolism and the role of those stones has not been revealed. Stone hoops appeared only in the final stage of Mayan civilization, becoming a permanent feature of Aztec ball games. *Popol Vuh* mentions only stone rings held in the hand by the players during the game. The purpose of such hand rings might have been twofold: a player could have thrown the ball through an opponent's ring and scored a point; or used his own ring to intercept a flying ball. According to the American researcher, M.A. Salter, the hoops referred to in *Popol Vuh* might have been stone belts worn by the players during the game, used for hitting the ball. When stone hoops fixed permanently on court walls were introduced in later times the purpose of the game was most likely to throw the ball through them to the opposing team. This type of court was used later by the Aztecs for the game of *tlachtli*.
Little is known about the number of players in each team; most likely a team consisted of 5 players, as seen in the majority of drawings. It is not certain whether the game was open to all Mayan social classes or a particular social caste, e.g. warriors. According to some scientists, the game of pokyah reflected the ancient beliefs of Middle Amer. peoples, particularly the mythical struggle of the sun against the stars or legendary folk heroes. The ritual forms of human sacrifice, so often associated with ancient games of Middle America, were a much later cultural phenomenon and were not practiced by the Lowland Mayas. M.A. Salter states furthermore, in his work devoted to the subject, that 'The Lowland Maya game, unlike those of central Mexico, did not include ritual decapitation.' Human sacrifice was practiced as part of fertility holidays. The blood of the victim was offered to the God as a drink in return for rainfall. Fertility myths and customs of this sort, as evidenced in numerous reliefs and wall drawings, go back to the times of the proto-Olmecs who inhabited the area c.2000 BC. The myths and traditions were later maintained by the Toltecs and other Mesoamerican peoples, including the Maya and Aztecs. The influence of various Maya games reached far into the present-day Southwest of the USA where sites of ancient ball courts were discovered about 25mi. from Phoenix, Arizona. Those courts, however, differed in construction from their Central Amer. counterparts. They were built in the prairies in the form of deep pits, without the use of stone.
The ball games derived from the Mayan pokyah came in numerous distinct varieties and forms, and therefore were a source of various misconceptions included in some historical and ethnological works. Different authors would often mistakenly merge distinctive elements of completely separate Middle Amer. games, played in different periods. As M.A. Salter noticed in 1982:

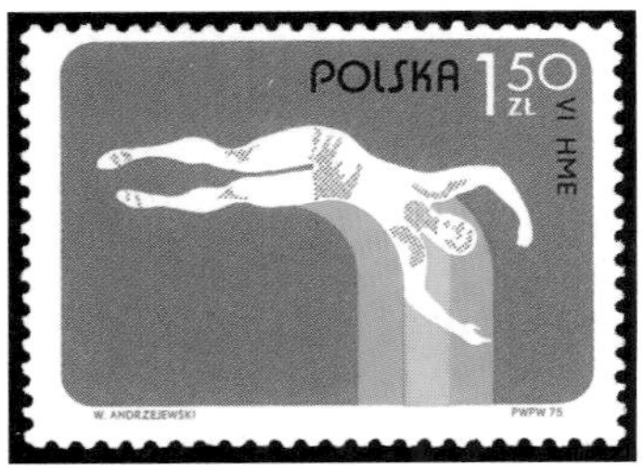

Pole vaulting on a 1975 postage stamp.

Readers are [...] frequently left with the feeling that the structure and function of the game was remarkable similar throughout the breadth and history of Mesoamerica. Unfortunately, such all-embracing conclusions result as authors attempt to 'complete' the picture by clumping together data from a var. of ethnic groups and a range of eras. Writers vividly portray the entry into the stadia of gaily attired young warriors from the nobility, each sporting elaborate headdresses and cumbersome stone game apparel. They attune the reader to the phrenetic behaviour of the spectators as the game progresses, and leave them to shudder as the blood spurs from the severed neck of the ritually decapitated vanquished (victorious?) captain at the contest's conclusion. This scenario has been propagated over the years by those who have tended to study the ball game on a Pan-American basis rather than within the context of a specific society.

'Classic Game, Classic People – Ball Games of the Lowland Maya', in: *The World of Play*, ed. F.E. Manning, TAASP, 1983.

Salter does not exclude the possibility of close relationships between various Mesomerican ball games, whose influences reached far beyond the area of their origin. Games played on H-shaped courts, similar to pokyah, were known not only in the territory of present-day Arizona, but also in many islands of the Caribbean, incl. Cuba, Hispaniola, Puerto Rico and Jamaica. Simplified versions of those games are still played by indigenous peoples of Middle America. Among the Mayas of the so-called Post Classic Period (10th-15th cent.) pokyah games were held together with human sacrifices in honor of the God Kukulcán, a successor of the Toltec god Quetzalcóatl (the Feathered Serpent), worshipped in the ancient Mayan city of Chichen Itza. Pokyah players could only hit the ball with their hips and, quite possibly, knees and elbows, using special thick belts or yokes worn around their waists. The U-shaped hip yokes, called *yugos* in Span. sources, were used to hit the ball with one's hip, control its flight and protect the player from hits. The latter function was very important as an average pokyah ball, made of hard rubber, weighed from 5 to 8lb. and might have caused frequent injuries during play. Scientists argue as to what material the yugos were made of. Prof. N. Helmuth thinks the yokes were made of stone; according to R. de Vries, a researcher of Pre-Columbian cultures, the yokes represented on ancient stone bas-reliefs could have been made of thick leather. First, a hide was wetted and spread upon a stone model. After drying out, the yoke – resembling a life belt – was put around the player's waist. Stone yokes could have served their purpose better than leather belts as they did not lose their shape during the game, but they were definitely less convenient to wear. The leather belts, on the other hand, might have been stuffed with oakum or grass to prevent them from deformation. The yugos were worn on the *palmas*, i.e. special pads covering the player's belly and genitals. Occasionally, flat stone disks called *hachas* were attached to the yugos. Some ancient drawings depict pokyah players holding hachas in their hands. The precise purpose of the hachas remains unknown. They might have been used as extra protectors against being hit by the ball, either attached permanently to the belt or held in the hands during the game. As can be concluded from Mayan drawings and Span. descriptions, hitting the ball with the hachas was not allowed. All parts of pokyah equipment were richly decorated with symbolic and religious figures. Apparently, some hachas featured heraldic devices. The most frequent motifs portrayed on the yugos and hachas included jaguars, snakes, fish and birds, symbolizing respective Mayan gods. Some yugos were often decorated with a representation of the giant toad (*Bufo marinus*) whose meat is hallucinogenic. A number of researchers claim that pokyah players consumed the toad meat before the game in order to fall into a sort of mystic trance. The game culminated in a human sacrifice consisting of decapitation of the vanquished or victorious team captain (for this controversy see >TLACHTLI). The team which first threw the ball through a stone hoop won the game. After the game the victorious team also won the right to confiscate all valuables from the spectators, while the latter fled from the court desperately trying to save their belongings. A Maya epic story *Popol Vuh* speaks of a ritual nature of the game and human sacrifices made of cut off heads.
Court. Several pokyah courts survive until the present day in the ancient Mayan and Toltec cultural center of Chitzen Itza. The best preserved pokyah court is located about 120km east of the town of Mérida in the Yucatan Peninsula. See also >PRECOLUMBIAN GAMES OF THE AMERICAS.
A. Caso, T. Gutierez, *El deporte prehispanico*, 3rd ed., 1967; W.A. Goellner, 'The Court Ball Game of the Aboriginal Mayas', *Research Quarterly*, 1953, 24, 147-168; M.A. Salter, 'Classic Game, Classic People: Ball Games of the Lowland Maya', *The World of Play*, Proceedings of the 7th Annual Meeting of TAASP, ed. F. Manning, 1983, E.M. Whittington, ed., *The Sport of Life and Death: The Mesoamerican Ball Game*, 2001.

The introduction of fiberglass poles has completely revolutionized pole vaulting. Here Tim Lobinger of Germany in action during the men's pole vault final at the 18th European Championships in Athletics at the Olympic Stadium in Munich, Germany.

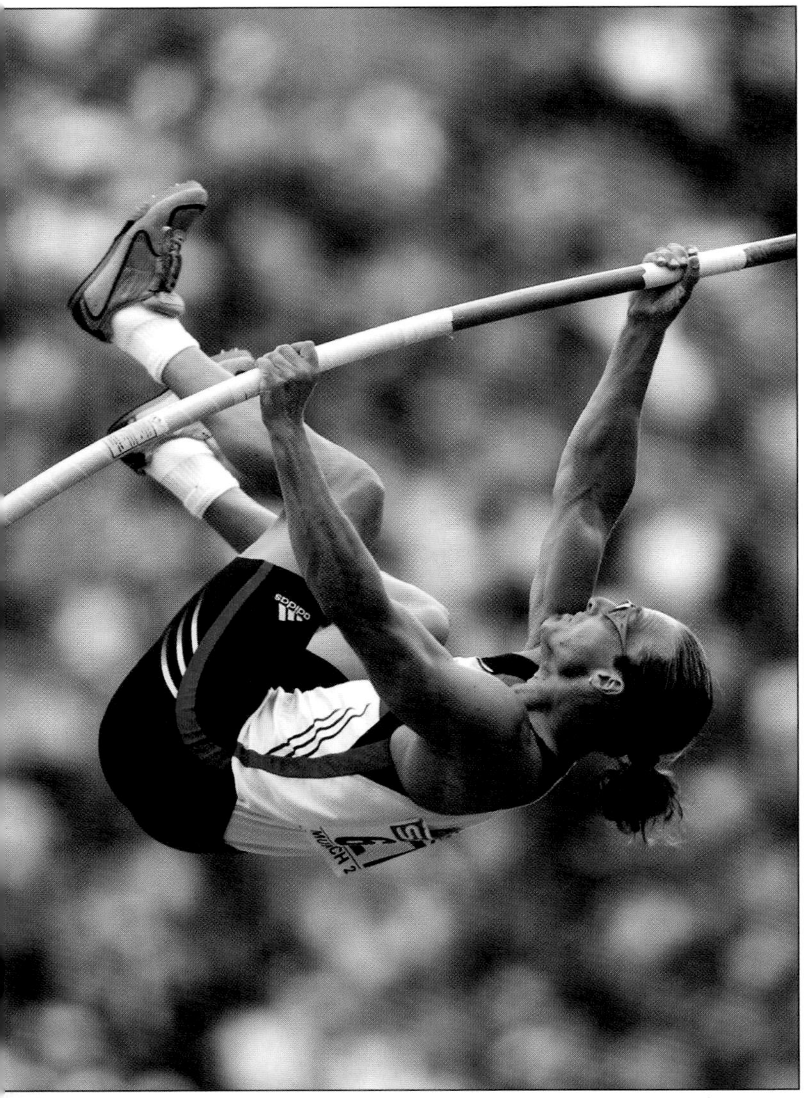

POLE CLIMBING, a form of competition among the Miao people of the Chin. province of Guishu, practiced mainly during a trad. holiday known as 'a mountain of flowers'. The object of the competition is a pole 40-50 chi in length (approx. 13-17m), at the top of which is a bunch of flowers decorated with color ribbons. The sounding of a musical instrument called a *lusheng* starts the competition. The player must climb the pole to reach the flowers and then turn upside down to start climbing down head first. Several *chi* above the ground he jumps off the pole and turns right way up again so that he lands on his feet. The practice is said to date back more than 2000 years.
Mu Fushan et al., 'Pole Climbing', TRAMCHIN.

POLE PROPPING, a folk sport popular in China in which 2 contestants stand opposite each other and one of them tries to twist a pole held in their hands in one direction while the other attempts to twist it in the opposite direction. Depending on the region, the game differs in details, e.g. the length and width of the stick and the way it is held and the visual indication of twist (most often it is a ribbon tied in mid-stick: when the stick is twisted, the ribbon is also twisted, signaling the advantage of one of the contestants). Among the people of Jinuo, a pole 2m long and about 10-12cm in diameter is held in both hands by the ends, by the contestants facing each other. A similar form of competition exists among the people of Yao, who inhabit the province of Guangxi; the pole, however, has different dimensions.
Mu Fushan et al., 'Pole Propping', TRAMCHIN, 102; 'Pole Twisting and Pole Propping', TRAMCHIN, 156.

POLE VAULTING, a track-and-field event consisting of a vault for height over a crossbar with the aid of a long pole. It became a competitive sport in the mid-19th cent. and was included in the first modern Ol.G. In competition, each vaulter is given 3 chances to clear a specific height. The bar is raised progressively until a winner emerges. Initially the pole was made of wood, most often bamboo, then from a metal tube and since 1956 – fiberglass. The vaulter runs with the pole towards the crossbar which rests on two uprights, at the end of the run-up puts the pole into the box, in this way transforming the forward motion into upward, and tries to clear a specific height. The vaulter, who has cleared the highest height or, if the same height has been cleared by 2 or more vaulters, who has cleared a specific height in the smaller number of attempts, is the winner. The pole's elasticity, in the past nearly insignificant (when poles were made of wood or metal), has become very important since fiberglass poles were introduced in 1955. They completely changed the jumping technique and significantly contributed to better

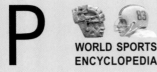

results, from nearly 5m in the case of metal poles to over 6m with fiberglass poles. This change also contributed to partial disappearance of the sporting character of pole vaulting – the vaulter's natural skills, so important in the past, have been substituted by acrobatics with the use of a pole-catapult.

The jump consists of a run-up, box, into which the pole is put, uprights with a crossbar and the landing area, in the past made of a sand heap, presently of thick foam mats with a plastic cover. The run-up must be a min. of 40m long (at international competitions – 45m) and 122-125cm wide. The box must be 1m long, 60m wide from the run-up side, narrowing to 45cm measured at the box bottom. The angle between the box bottom and its back wall is 105° and slopes to a depth of 20cm.

The side walls of the box slope outwards at an angle of 120° with respect to its base; the bottom, covered with sheet metal, is 80cm long, measured from the front edge; the crossbar is made of fiberglass, metal or other material. It is round with flattened ends, which rest on the uprights. The bar is 450cm long, weighs 2.25kg, and has a diameter of 30mm. The uprights can be made of any material and of any design, however they must allow for the adjustment of height and the bar supports. Contestants use their own poles, which, however, they can lend and borrow as they like. Use of somebody else's pole without permission is forbidden. Adhesive tape can be wrapped around the pole to increase the grip strength and, if at the end put into the box, to prevent wear and tear. The landing area should be at least 5x5m, with a characteristic indented square in the front for the box. Mats surround the landing area, thus increasing the safety of vaulters in case of failed jumps.

The order in which vaulters jump is decided by lots. Before the competition the judge announces the initial height and all the successive heights to which the crossbar will be raised until only one contestant remains. However, it must always be raised by at least 5cm. Each contestant can freely position the uprights (up to 40cm in the direction of the run-up and up to 80cm in the direction of the landing area). If during the jump the pole breaks, the contestant can repeat the jump.

History. King Pylos of ancient Greece is said to have been the mythological inventor of a vaulting pole. Attacked by a Caledonian bull during hunting, he was running away and jumping over cracks in the ground using a long, strong spear. A similar tradition was known in Celtic culture – around the 2nd cent. AD the soldiers of Fionn Mac Cumhaill (the so-called

Fenians) used spears or specially prepared poles to cross obstacles in the terrain. From about 550 AD a pole vault was included in the old Ir. games in Tara (Aonach Tailtean). As an element of military art, pole vaulting was used during sieges of castles and strongholds to jump over moats; it was also a useful skill to jump over canals in the Netherlands. It is here that the first attempt to use the pole in sporting competition were made. In the 18th cent. a Ger. J.C.F. Guts-Muths made pole vaulting part of physical exercises in the educational center in Schnepfenthal. Apart from pole vaulting he also promoted >SPRUNG IN DIE TIEFE MIT DEM STABE. His best student vaulters jumped as high as 270cm. An identical event was part of the exercise set used by F.L. Jahn. Modern pole vaulting derives partly from the old Ir. tradition, partly from the Fen Country in England (bordering Lincolnshire, Norfolkshire, Cambridgeshire and Suffolkshire), where poles were used in everyday life to walk over marshes and where folk competitions in pole vaulting were organized. Similar events were included in the program of the competition played during the annual folk festival in Ulverston in the 18th cent. and later in the 19th cent. Since 1829 pole vaulting has been included in the revived Old Ir. Games. Since 1866 it was part of the program of the athletic championships in England and since 1877 part of the US championships. Official world records have been kept since 1867. The first record holder was J. Wheeler (England), with 3.05m. The first to jump 4m was M. Wright (4.02m – 1912), an American. Better results were obtained when the jump technique was changed and new materials for the pole were used. In the 1890s a group of contestants tried to introduce a new technique, namely a very slow run up to the box, putting the pole into the box and keeping it up for some time and then climbing the pole (as if climbing a rope) and, upon reaching the pole's end, jumping over the bar. This technique, immediately banned in the USA, was in use for a very short time, more or less until 1900, in Great Britain. Initially poles were made of ash, cedar or spruce. The first bamboo poles appeared around 1900. Four world records were established with the bamboo pole by K. Hoff (Norway), the only non-Ang.-Sax. contestant before 1962. In 1940-42 an American, C. Warmerdam, established 3 world records, of which the last (4.77m – 1942) was beaten 15 years later, by American R. (Bob) Gutowski, who jumped only 1cm higher. The fact that Warmerdam's record was not beaten for 15 years clearly demonstrated the leveling out of

results due to the inability of the human body to conquer the 'lever border'. Subsequently, the fiberglass pole was introduced, which led not so much to the evolution of pole vaulting as to the development of a new sport. At the 1956 Ol.G. a fiberglass pole was used by the Gk. G. Roubanis. However, it started to be used on a wider scale at the beginning of the 1960s.

Pole vaulting was included in the Ol.G. in 1896. Until 1968 the best pole vaulters were the Americans, who in won all the gold medals in this period and most of the silvers and bronzes. Europeans started to win gold medals in 1972 (1972 – W. Nordwig, GDR; 1976 – T. Ślusarski, Poland; 1980 – W. Kozakiewicz, Poland; 1984 – P. Quinon, France; 1988 – S. Bubka, USSR; 1992 – M. Tarasow, CIS; 1996 – J. Galfione, France).

Women's pole vaulting started to develop in 1988. The first women vaulters came from China. The competition was included in the IAAF program in 1993. The first vaulter to jump 4m was E. George from Australia (4.25m – 1995). In 2000 women's pole vaulting was included in the Ol.G.

POLIKON TETRIPPON, see >TETRIPPON.

POLING, see >BIRLING.

POLO, the name of a number of team games played on horseback or a vehicle, using mallets with long handles to drive a ball between 2 goalposts. The following varieties of polo can be distinguished: >CYCLE POLO, >ELEPHANT POLO, >INDOOR POLO, >OUTDOOR POLO, >POLOCROSSE, >WINTER POLO, and the Asian polo predecessor >PULU. The component *polo* is also found in the names of >WATER POLO or aquatic polo, although these sports are not related to the original mallet game. Regional, folk varieties of polo such as >GUJBOZI, *pulu* and >SOWORIGUJ are still played at the foot of the Himalayas and in the Tien Shan Mountains bordering China, India, Pakistan and Tajikistan.

POLO-CROSSE, also *polo crosse*, a sport being a combination of >OUTDOOR POLO and Can. >LACROSSE, originated in the Brit. National School of Equitation, in the winter of 1938/39. The game is played by 2 teams of 6 players; only 3 players from each team can remain in play at a time. The aim of the game is to shoot a rubber ball into the opponent's goal using a netted stick similar to that of lacrosse. The field is 160x60yds; it has 2 goalposts at each end, 8yds. apart. Shots at goal can only be taken from behind a goal-area line, 30yds. from the goal.

WORLD SPORTS ENCYCLOPEDIA

P

Dean Macey of Great Britain in the pole vault of the Decathlon at the Olympic Stadium during the 2000 Olympic Games in Sydney, Australia.

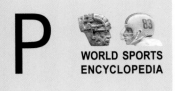

430

P WORLD SPORTS ENCYCLOPEDIA

The ball cannot be carried in the net, only thrown or passed. A game consists of 8 chukkas of 8min. each, with 2-min breaks in between. WWII interrupted the development of the game. After 1945 there were only about 10 polo-crosse clubs, functioning as parts of larger horse-riding clubs. The sport went into sharp decline in the 1960s.

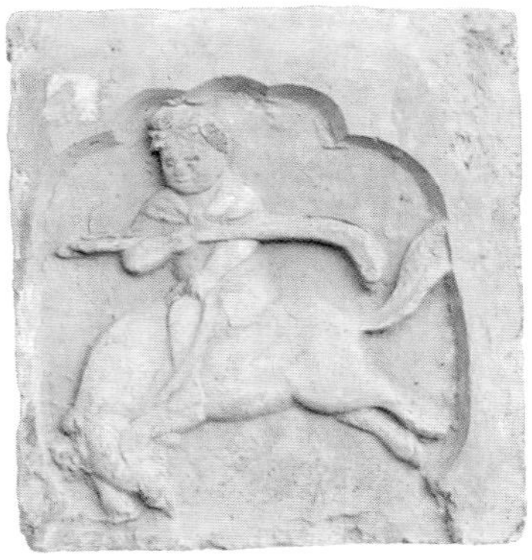

A polo game, engraved brick, unearthed in Luoyang, Henan Province, Song Dynasty (960-1279).

POLOCROSSE, an Austrl. game similar to Brit. >POLO-CROSSE, invented by M. and E. Hirst in 1939. In the Austrl. variety the goals are replaced with baskets mounted on long poles, so that the mounted players can approach them without restraint. The game of polocrosse was first demonstrated by the members of the Horse and Pony Club in Ingleburne, near Sydney, in 1939. Ingleburne was also the site of the first Polocrosse Club presided over by M. Hirst. WWII interrupted the development of the game; the second club – the Bundaroo Polocrosse Club was founded in 1945 near Bowral. In 1946 the two clubs played the first match, which gained huge press coverage. In the late 1940s the game became widespread in Victoria and Queensland, and by the 1950s in other Austrl. states. In the 1970s polocrosse became popular in northern Tasmania. The first interstate championships took place in 1953, with the participation of 4 state teams; the first Austrl. Championships were played in Dubbo in 1968, and have been held every two years ever since. At the beginning of the 1990s Australia featured about 300 polocrosse clubs with a membership of about 5,000 players and 177 professional coaches. The sport is also practiced in New Zealand, Papua New Guinea, Zimbabwe, Canada and Vanuatu. In 1976, on Australia's initiative, the International Polocrosse Council was founded, presided by Australian M. Walters. Polocrosse is not the only mounted game whose object is to toss the ball through a basket, see also >HORSEBALL.

POLON KELES, foal racing practiced in ancient Greece. Polon keles was first included in the Pythian Games in 338 BC and then in the 131st Ol.G. in 256 BC (Gk. *polos* – 'foal' + *keles* – 'a young stud'). The first Pythian foal racing winner was Licormas of Larissa. The first Olympic winner was either Tlepolemos or Hippocrates of Thessaly. The riders raced naked and bareback. The foals were driven with use of simple reins and crops. The last time a polon keles race was held was during the 177th Ol.G. in 72 BC.

Pool billiards.

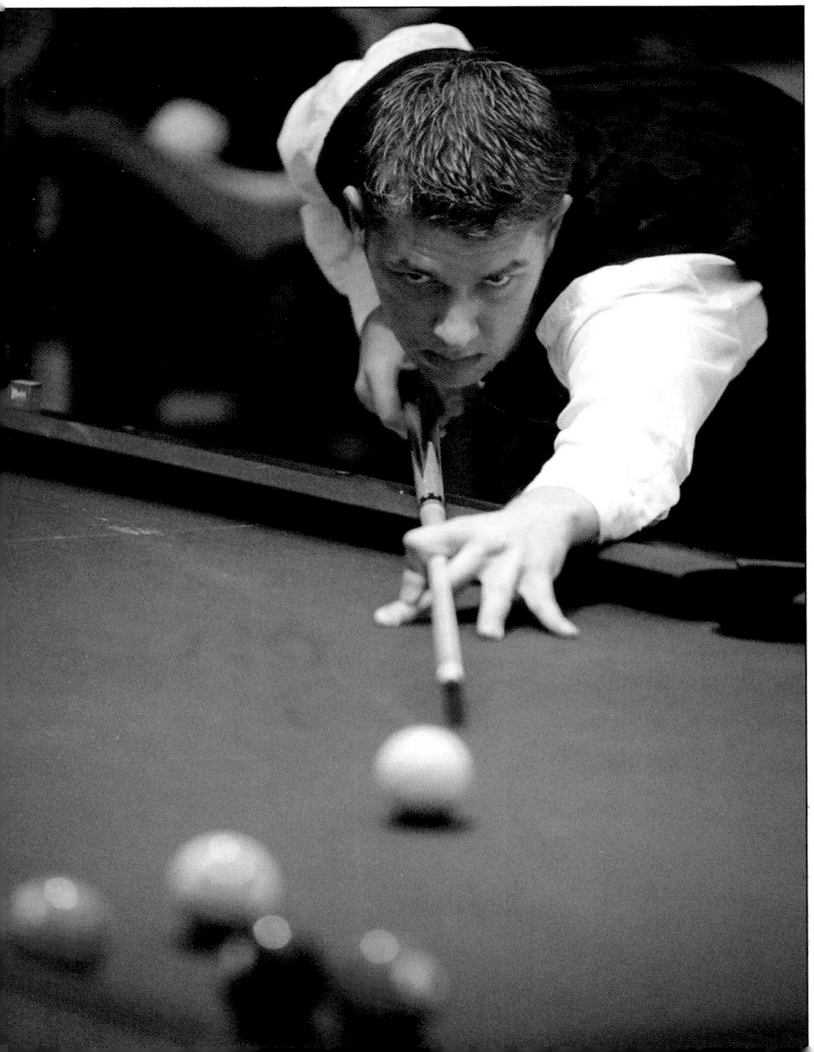

POLON SYNORIS, races of carriages drawn by double-harnessed foals, practiced in ancient Greece; first included in the 131st Ol.G. in 256 BC (Gk. *polos* – 'foal' + *synoris, synoros* – 'twin'). See also >SYNORIS; cf. >HIPPON.

POLOWANIE, (Pol. for 'hunting'), a Pol. var. of cross-country running; an obsolete running game modelled on hunting, practiced by school pupils. Polowanie was mentioned briefly by Ł. Gołębiowski in *Gry i zabawy różnych stanów* (*Games and Competitions of Various Social Classes*, 1831): 'One pretends to be a hare and the others are hounds chasing him.' The sport was clearly influenced by Eng. >PAPER CHASE, >HARE AND HOUNDS; cf. also >CROSS-COUNTRY RUNNING. It was prob. practiced as a cross-country competition in the Krzemieniec College in the beginning of the 19th cent. E. Piasecki in *Zabawy and gry ruchowe dzieci and młodzieży* (*The Sports and Pastimes of Children and Youth*, 1916) regarded the sport as 'appropriate for the male youth.' Due to the physical effort involved in practicing hunting, Piasecki recommended '...medical examination of the participants before the race, as the competition can be very strenuous for the weaker and less fit contenders.'
Two teams of 5 runners each take part in the game. Each team selects one 'hare'. The hares set off first from a base (usu. a cottage serving as a changing room and canteen) leaving a trail of paper scraps, thrown out from belt purses, to be followed by the other players called the 'hounds'. Having covered the route of 5-8km the hares return to the starting point. The hounds start running 15min. after the hares. On their way, the hares can fake the trails by marking diversion over short distances. On returning to the starting point the hounds of both teams are numbered from 1 to 8. The team whose sum of the players' numbers is less wins the game.

POLTOPALLO, a Fin. bat and ball game (Fin. *polto* – 'burnt, burning' + *pallo* – 'ball'), known in Denmark as >RUNDBOLD.

POLYNESIAN BALL, a ball game practiced in the islands of Polynesia. The ball is a bundle of caper wood (Lat. *capparis*) – locally called *kapa* – screw-pine wood (Lat. *pandanus*), or other elastic twigs or plant climbers. The aim of the game is to move the ball across a marked goal line. In some areas of Hawaii the ball has to be stripped from the opponent. In the Society Islands, particularly in Tahiti, Polynesian ball is played more frequently by women than men. (>TAHITIAN BALL).

POLYNESIAN PUGILISM, fist-fighting practiced in all Polynesia, except for a few island groups such as the Society Islands, incl. Tahiti and Moorea. In many aspects, Polynesian pugilism resembles the early stages of Eur. boxing. It has fixed rules and the bouts are officiated by referees. The punchers fight with bare knuckles, although bouts with the use of boxing gloves made of caper wood were reported by ethnographers to be in the Polynesian islands bordering the Hawaii area. A knockout is the most highly valued way to end a bout. The victorious puncher stays in his place and awaits other challengers. The match winner is the puncher who has defeated all challengers.

POOL BILLIARDS, a group of various billiards games that are played on a table with a number of pockets into which balls are struck according to various rules typical of the respective varieties. Points are scored only upon striking the balls into the pockets (as opposed, for instance, to >ENGLISH POCKET BILLIARDS where a player may score points by both striking balls into pockets and shooting caroms). In the US the pool billiards tables are usu. 4.5x9ft. (137x274cm) rectangles. In Germany, according to the local pool billiards association, the tables must be rectangular and from 3.5 to 4.5ft (c.107 to 137cm) wide and from 7 to 9ft. (c.213 to 274cm) long. There are a few major varieties of pool billiards including:
SNOOKER, see separate entry under >SNOOKER.
CHICAGO, also known as *rotation*. The name of the variety comes from the name of the US city where the game was probably born or first developed. The game is also called rotation since after all the balls have been pocketed the game starts anew. The game is played with a cue ball and 15 object balls, numbered 1 through 15. The 15 numbered balls are racked in a triangle (also called a *pyramid*), as in the majority of pool billiards games, the only difference being that balls nos. 1, 2 and 3 must be placed in the respective rack corners. Ball no. 1 is on the foot spot and balls nos. 2 and 3 in the corners alongside the end cushion. The object of the game is to pocket all the object balls following the order in which they are numbered (i.e. a players starts pocketing the balls with ball no. 1 and continues until he has pocketed ball no. 15). For each pocketed ball the player scores a number of points equal to the ball number. The maximum number of points to be scored is, therefore, 120. However, the game is stopped when one of the players has scored 61pts. since then it is impossible for the other player to win.
EIGHT-BALL, usu. spelled 8-ball, is a call shot game played with a white cue ball and 15 object balls, numbered 1 through 15. One player must pocket balls of the group numbered 1 through 7 (solid colors), while the other player has 9 through 15 (stripes). Solid colors have a small white circle with the number of the ball inscribed on it. Stripes are white with a color stripe running around the ball. On the stripe there is, again, a small white circle with the number of the ball. Ball no. 8, which is black, is of key importance for this game, whose name comes from this particular ball. At the beginning of the game the balls are racked in a triangle at the foot of the table with the 8-ball in the center of the triangle, the first ball of the rack (ball no. 1) on the foot spot, a stripe ball in one corner of the rack and a solid ball in the other corner. In order to win the option to break the players engage in the so-called lag or string. Each player receives one ball which is placed on the right- and left-hand side of the table, respectively. Then, they have to strike their respective balls towards the foot cushion so that it bounces off the foot cushion and returns to the front cushion. The player whose ball stops closest to the front cushion wins the option to break. To execute a legal break, the breaker must either pocket a ball (different than the cue ball) or drive at least 4 numbered balls to the rail. Then the players have to pocket all the balls from either group as quickly as possible. The player pocketing either group first wins the right to pocket the 8-ball. When he does so, he wins the game. The order in which the balls are pocketed is not predetermined but a player has to call his shot each time or, in other words, indicate which ball he intends to put into which pocket. If the 8-ball is accidentally and illegally pocketed, the player who did so loses the game. He also loses the game if the 8-ball is put into a pocket other than the declared one or if the 8-ball jumps off the table. Balls are also deemed pocketed illegally when a given player pockets a ball belonging to his opponent without pocketing his own ball. Then, the player does not lose the game but must relinquish his run at the table and the illegally pocketed balls remain pocketed and are scored in favor of the player controlling that specific group of balls. A player must also relinquish his run at the table when the cue ball strikes directly one of his opponent's balls or when he misses his shot.
ONE AND NINE BALL. This game is played with 9 object balls numbered 1 through 9 and a white cue ball. The object balls are racked in a diamond shape, with 3 rows of 3 balls. The 1-ball is put at the top of the diamond and on the foot spot, the 9-ball in the center of the diamond. The 3-ball has to be the closest to the foot cushion, 2- and 4-balls in the remaining corners and the other balls in random order, racked as tightly as possible. The object of the game is to pocket the numbered balls by striking them with the cue ball. In order to win the option to break the players engage in the so-called lag or string. Each player receives one ball which is placed on the right- and left-hand side of the table, respectively. Then, they have to strike their respective balls towards the foot cushion so that it bounces off the foot cushion and returns to the front cushion. The player whose ball stops closest to the front cushion wins the option to break. To execute a legal break, the breaker must strike the 1-ball first and either pocket a ball or drive at least 4 numbered balls to the rail. If he misses or strikes other balls, he commits a foul and is replaced by the other player. The incoming player has 3 options to choose from: 1) he may continue to play the balls as they are; 2) he may break the balls anew; or 3) he may allow the fouling player to repeat his shot. The balls have to be pocketed in numerical order, starting from the lowest and going up to the highest number. Contrary to other pool games, it is not necessary to call one's shots. The player who pockets the 9-ball first is declared the winner. The 9-

Prince Charles plays pool at the headquarters of a British-Romanian foundation that counsels disabled people in the village of Magurele 15km (9 miles) south of Bucharest.

ball should be the last of the balls to be pocketed with one exception – when during an opening break the player legally hits the 1-ball but at the same time pockets the 9-ball. In this case the player wins the game. A player is deemed to have committed a foul and must relinquish his run at the table if: a) he misses the next consecutively numbered ball to be pocketed at a given stage of the game (including the 1-ball upon the opening break); b) he hits an appropriate ball but fails to pocket it; c) he pockets the cue ball; d) the cue ball jumps off the table; e) he shoots his next shot when the balls are still in motion after the previous shot (irrespective of whether it is his own or his opponent's balls); f) he lifts both feet off the ground while taking a shot; g) he touches or moves any of the balls on the table with any part of his body or his clothes (e.g. with the border of his sleeve, his shirt or the lapel of his vest, etc.).

LINE-UP is played with 11 target balls and one white cue ball. At the start of the game the 11 target balls (in colors different than white) are arranged into a line running along the longitudinal axis of the table from the foot cushion to a place called a *foot spot* located at ¼ of the table length from the foot cushion. The object of the game is to put the balls into the pockets as quickly as possible and in any order. The major rule here is that upon each shot at least one ball, except the cue ball, must be pocketed. If a player fails to do so he must relinquish his run at the table. The incoming player must shoot from the position left by the previous player.

FIFTEEN-BALL, also known as 14.1 continuous (fourteen-one continuous). Both names of the game stress the importance of the fifteenth ball, which – after the 14-ball has been pocketed – must remain on the table as an element connecting the current and the next round of the game. The name 'fifteen-ball' stresses the importance of the ball no. 15 for the game, whereas the name '14.1 continuous' is a literal reflection of the game rules whereby 14 balls are pocketed and the 15th remains on the table. When using the latter one should remember not to confuse it with another game called just 14.1 without the adjective 'continuous' and used to refer to one of the balk lines sub-varieties, see >CAROM BILLIARDS.

At the start of the game the 15 numbered object balls are racked in a triangle. The 15 object balls are accompanied by a sixteenth ball – i.e. the cue ball. 14.1 continuous is a nomination game. The player must nominate a ball and a pocket. The player is awarded one point for every correctly nominated and pocketed ball in a legal stroke, and is allowed to continue a turn until he fails to pocket a nominated ball or commits a foul. The player can pocket the first 14 balls, but before continuing a turn by shooting at the 15th (and last remaining) ball on the table, the 14 pocketed balls are racked as before, except with the apex space vacant. The player then attempts to pocket the 15th ball in a manner so that the racked balls are disturbed and he can continue the run. From this moment on the game is continued as previously (i.e. a player has

to pocket the remaining 14 balls). At the end of each round, the 15-ball must remain on the table so that it is possible to open each next round. The balls may be pocketed in any order. When a player pockets a ball different from the one he nominated or fails to pocket a nominated ball he must relinquish his run at the table.

Pool billiards was and continues to be often depicted in literature and film. Billiards scenes often constitute important elements of the plot and are often used as a metaphor of the vicissitudes of life or one's dreams of success, etc. This is best exemplified by one of the episodes in J. Jones's novel *From Here to Eternity* (1951) which was also included in its film version. One of the most famous works devoted entirely to billiards is *The Hustler* by W. Tevis. The novel was later turned into a movie starring the much acclaimed Paul Newman. In 1986 Newman won an Academy Award for his role of an aging pool player in *The Color of Money*. Both movies greatly helped pool billiards regain its popularity as in the 1960s and 1980s the game had almost fallen into oblivion. Since 1990 in the US there have been a number of TV shows devoted to pool billiards where either major international pool games and tournaments are televised or special pool shows are staged. Similar programs are also shown in Europe. See also: >BILLIARD STUNTS.

POONA, a Hindu court game played with a shuttlecock, hit with the hands or flat wooden rackets. The game was brought to Britain by Brit. army officers c.1860 and contributed to the development of >BADMINTON.

POOR MAN'S GOLF see >NORTHERN SPELL.

POPICE, a Rum. bowling game (Rum. *popic* – 'pin' or 'wooden figure'; Serb. *pópica* – 'little priest' – suggesting wooden priest figures used as pins; or *pópić* – 'kinglet' – suggesting wooden kinglet figures used as pins). The game is played with 9 pins of different sizes and a wooden ball. The players roll the balls in a bowling alley called the *popičarie*. For the few last decades popice has been practiced in various regions of Eastern Europe, particularly in Rumania. Under the dictatorial rule of N. Ceausescu the game was officially endorsed by the Rum. Communist Party, as an example of maintenance of folk and national traditions. Two national popice leagues were formed. After the 1990 political transformations in Rumania the game began to decline.

POPINJAY, a medieval Eng. version of >PARROT SHOOTING, a sport consisting of shooting at a figure of a parrot, using the longbow or crossbow, and from the 17th cent. firearms (Middle-Eng. *papejay* or *popingay* < Middle-Fr. *papegay, papingay* <Span. *papagayo* <Arab. *babbagha* – 'parrot'). Parrot shooting was popularized in Western Europe in the early Middle Ages by the Saracens during their occupation of the Iberian Peninsula (>PAPEGAUT, LE). The sport was most likely introduced into England during the reign of Richard the Lionheart (1189-99). It was known in Scotland as >PAPINGO SHOOTING; in Denmark as > SKYDE PAPEGØJEN; and in the Netherlands as >PAPENGOY.

POP-THE-BONNET, an Eng. game for 2 players, each putting down a pin on the crown of a hat or bonnet, alternately pop on the bonnet till one of the pins crosses the other. The player whose pin is on top of the other player's wins (TGESI, II, 64). A similar game played by more than 2 players is called *hattie.*

POROAJOT, (Fin. *poro* – 'reindeer' + *ajo* – 'ride' + *t* – plural ending), Fin. harness racing using reindeer drawing sleighs or skiers; cf. >SKIJÖRING.

POROK-PAMIN SINAM, human imitation of cockfighting; a sport widely practiced in the Ind. state of Arunachal Pradesh. The two contenders fight with each other, standing on one leg and holding the other thigh up with one hand. The other hand is placed across the shoulder. The contenders fight in a circle marked on the ground, trying to knock each other down. A contender can also lose by stepping off the circle or standing on both legs.

The Mosconi Cup between the USA and Europe held at York Hall, in London.

P

WORLD SPORTS ENCYCLOPEDIA

PORT GIGS' REGATTAS, races for rowing boats formerly used in ports. The first regattas of the kind were held in Cornish ports after WWII, when motor boats began replacing rowing boats. Port gigs' regattas are now copied in ports around the world.

PORTBOLD, imitation of Eng. >CRICKET, originated in Denmark in 1801.
J. Møller, 'Portbold', GID, 1997, 1, 72.

POSADIT RYEPU, Rus. for 'plant the turnip', a folk sport, popular in the times of the USSR as a school or social game. Two teams compete in driving a specially prepared stake, called 'a turnip', into the ground. The turnip is a 50cm long cone with a 12cm diameter base. Two holes, 1.5-2cm in diameter, are drilled through the thickest part of the turnip. Two 25cm long wooden pegs are inserted into the holes to make driving the turnip into the ground more difficult. Each team (2-3 players) has its own turnip and a large wooden hammer, most often made of birch or oak. The hammers' heads, with metal edges to protect them against damage, are 15cm in diameter and 25cm long. The handle is 50cm long. As the handle is relatively short, driving the turnip into the ground is no easy task. The game is played on a field with two 1-pace-long squares called 'beds', 8 paces apart. When more teams play, more squares are marked on the ground. The turnip is planted in the beds. 10-30 paces from the beds there is a finish line, where the contestants are lined up. The contestants start the game from circles 3 paces in diameter, marked alongside the finish line, 8 paces apart. Between the finish line and the beds there is another line, the so-called 'fence'. The game is supervised by 2 'guards' – one from each team, elected by the captain who before the game started threw the hammer the farthest. Captains also determine the line-up, i.e. the order in which the contestants play. Rules after I.N. Chkhannikov:

Two players, indicated by the captains, take the hammers and go to the circles on the finish line. Each guard takes one turnip and positions it vertically inside the squares, next to the bed. Next, the guards stand 2-3 steps behind the bed line. One of the captains gives a signal and the first pair starts to run from the finish line to the bed. Each of them tries to hammer their turnip hard, to nail it in as deep as possible. After they have hit the turnip, the captains order another pair of players to go to the circles. The player, who has hit the turnip, throws the hammer to the player in the circle on the finish line, trying to throw it over the fence line, and runs to his team. The player in the circle can leave it and start running towards the bed after the hammer has dropped to the ground. If the hammer has landed between the fence and the bed, the player must pick it up, return to the fence line and then run towards the bed. In this way all players run, pick up the hammer, hit the turnip, throw the hammer and return to their team. Any player, who has run to the bed and returned to the team can be chosen by the captain to run again only after all the other players have run. If a player does not hit the turnip, he cannot repeat the attempt. The first player, who fails to hit the turnip, throws the hammer towards the fence line and substitutes one of the guards. The guard rejoins the team. When the turnip has been nailed in as far as the first transverse peg inserted into the holes in the base, the guard takes hold of the upper peg, pulls the turnip out and again positions it inside the square, as was done at the beginning. The team which first nails in the turnip 5 times wins.
[I.N. Chkhannikov, 'Posadit ryepu', GIZ, 1953, 55-57]

POSTEN GÅR, see >BLIND MAN'S BUFF.

POSTEN KOMMER, (Dan. for 'the mail has come'), a Dan. sports game, played in schools during >PHYSICAL EDUCATION classes. The players stand in a row by a wall; one player becomes the 'mailman'. The 'mail' is a long, thin twig. The mailman comes with the twig to the opposite wall and shouts *Posten kommen!* – 'You've got mail!' The players in the row ask aloud 'Who!', then the mailman shouts a player's name, props the twig against the wall and runs back to his place in the row. The player called is to run to and grab the 'mail', and then catch up with the mailman trying to tap him with the twig. If the player fails , he becomes the next mailman.
J. Møller, 'Posten kommer', GID, 1997, 2, 43.

POT BREAKING, a trad. Ind. sport of forming human pyramids and climbing to their top in order to break large, earthenware pots filled with milk, curds, butter, honey fruits, etc. suspended across the street. The ceremony is part of Janmashtani (Govinda), a festival celebrated in Aug. and Sep. in India, Sri Lanka, Singapore, etc. to commemorate the birth of Lord Krishna. The mischievous young Krishna loved milk and curd, which he used to steal from earthen pots hung by the villagers from the ceilings of their verandas to allow the curd to ferment. In order to do so, young Krishna and his friends would form a pyramid some 10-15ft. high and break the pots in order to gobble up their delectable contents. This tradition is honored each year on the day of Govinda by thousands of young men and children, who go in large groups to form similar human pyramids and break earthen pots suspended usu. 20-40ft., but sometimes as high as 75-100ft. above the ground. To encourage and preserve this tradition local residents collect money, which is either kept in the pots or suspended next to them, and which is given to the group that succeeds in breaking the pot. The practice may be dangerous, particularly for the ones that climb to the top of the pyramid, the more so that enthusiastic spectators splash water over the heads of the contestants, adding to the festivities, but making their task even more difficult.

POTAKA, whip tops once used by the Maori. They came in a number of var., e.g. double-ended and climbing tops. The most characteristic top type used among the Maori was a humming top called *potaka takiri*. It had a shaft rising from the flat upper surface and a flat piece of wood was used to steady the top until it was spun. When spinning the top gave out a humming sound. The whip, called the *ta* or *kare*, consisted of strips of flax tied to a wooden handle. Like in Eur. var. of tops, the flax was wound tightly around the upper portion of the top and then the handle was pulled and the top fell to the ground spinning.
There were 3 kinds of potaka competitions. In the first competition called the *karangi* various obstacles such as small sand mounds, sticks or stones were positioned on the top's path. The players were supposed to spin their tops so they would jump over the obstacles. In the second variety, two lines were drawn on the ground, parallel to each other, which marked the top track. At the end of the track, an end line was marked across it. The players would drive their tops so they would move within the track lines towards the end line. The track was about 100yds. long. If a top came to a stop or crossed the track lines its owner was out of the game. The most interesting was the third var. of potaka, played with specially shaped tops, decorated with the *paua* seashells and ornamental carvings. The top was 3.5in. in diameter and 6in. in height. On the upper part of the top a 3.25in.-long needle with a long string was mounted. The pulling cord was worn around the lower part of the top. The top was hung from a tree branch so it would reach the player's chest. Once the cord was pulled, the twining string pulled up the top towards the branch. The player whose top 'climbed up' higher won the game.
A. Armstrong, *Games and Dancing of the Maori People*, 1986, 11.

POTETEKE, a var. of Maori folk acrobatics, involving tumbling.

POTKUKELKKAILU, Fin. folk var. of tobogganing, using special sleds called the *potkukllkka*. Since 1989, the Potkukelkkailu W.Ch. have been held with the participation of contenders from Finland and countries with Fin. national minorities.

POTS, also *potts*, a simple Eng. ball game, similar to Port. >OA. The game of pots consists of throwing a ball against a wall, letting it bounce and catching it, accompanied by the following movements: 1) three throws; 2) throw, twist hands and catch; 3) clap hands in front, behind, in front; 4) turn around; 5) bounce the ball on the ground 3 times, and catch; 6) again on the ground and catch once at the end of the first 'pot' and twice for the second 'pot'.
TGESI, II, 64-5.

POUTUTEKO, racing on stilts called *puototi* or *puoturu*, practiced by the N.Zealand's Maoris. See also >WALKING ON STILTS.

POWERLIFTING, a type of a weightlifting event which includes 3 disciplines:
THE SQUAT. The lifter stands upright with the barbell resting across the back of his shoulders, then sits or 'squats' down to a required depth and finally attempts to stand up again, returning to the original position.
BENCH PRESS. The lifter lies flat on his back on a bench of a certain height and specification, holding the barbell at arms length above the chest. Then he lowers the bar until it stops on the chest and pushes it or 'presses' it back up again. The event is often held independently.
DEAD LIFT. The lifter grips the barbell, which sits flat on the floor, and attempts to lift the weight until standing upright with his shoulders back.
During powerlifting events, as well as during bench press events, lifters are divided into the following bodyweight categories: women – up to 44, 48, 52, 60, 67.5, 75, 82.5, 90, and above 90kg; men – up to 52, 56, 60, 67.7, 75, 82.5, 90, 100, 125, and above 125kg. Each competitor is allowed 3 attempts at

A group of people form a human pyramid trying to break an earthen pot with a stone in Bombay, India.

People on a terrace look on as Raju Mohite, 12, is drenched with water after breaking an earthen pot with a stone while balancing himself atop a three-tier human pyramid in Bombay, India.

each lift and the best lift in each discipline is added to the total. The final score is multiplied by Wilks' coefficient (R. Wilks was the inventor of powerlifting), which depends on the lifter's sex and bodyweight and drops as the bodyweight increases. E.g. a male lifter weighing 50kg has the coefficient of 1.0232, while one weighing 200kg – 0.5318. Until 1997 Malone's coefficient was used.

History. The origins of powerlifting are connected with the development of various power sports, incl. >WEIGHTLIFTING (despite technical differences between them). The disciplines which now form powerlifting have developed as independent events. Their distinct character can be observed in the fact that in 1957 Aus. regulations of public tournaments listed 120 var. of weightlifting, incl. 6 that resemble the modern dead lift. The 3 events that comprise modern powerlifting were combined together for the first time in England during the 1958 national championships. In the early years of powerlifting the disciplines that comprised it changed several times, until the final arrangement took shape (incl. the replacement of pressing the barbell up with a dead lift). The expansion of powerlifting in the USA provided an impulse for the development of the sport. The first powerlifting event in the USA took place in 1964 and in 1972 the International Powerlifting Federation (IPF) was established there. Several other international and national federations followed, incl. Power Man, which – besides powerlifting – promotes also other power sports. The widespread use of doping in power sports inspired Power Man to begin an original form of battling the plague: instead of testing for illegal drugs the organization offers voluntary declarations of respecting fair rules of sport practice. Every member of the organization merely takes a vow of honesty. Unfortunately, the lack of control over the use of doping within Power Man has led many athletes found guilty of doping by other organizations to find shelter there.

In Europe powerlifting began to grow in popularity in the middle of the 1970s. The tendency culminated in 1977 in Turku (Finland) with the founding of the Eur. Power-Lifting Federation (EPF). The first E.Ch. took place a year later in Birmingham (Gr. Britain). The first event which incl. powerlifters from Eastern Europe took place in 1983 in the Czech city of Most.

The tradition of power sports for women dates back to the 19th century. In 1926 a Frenchwoman Mlle Jane de Vesley lifted 176kg using a technique resembling the modern dead lift. Proper powerlifting events for women were organized sporadically in the 1970s and the first E.Ch. took place in 1983. Since 1995 seperate events for veteran powerlifters have been held.

POWERLIFTING FOR THE DISABLED, a var. of >WEIGHTLIFTING adapted for the disabled. Powerlifting for the disabled as a clean-and-press on the ground was first incl. in the 1964 Paralympic Games as an event for contenders with spine disabilities. At present, the sport has 10 weight categories. Its international governing body is the Powerlifting Committee of the International Paralympics Committee, IPC. The sport is becoming more popular every year. Apart from the Paralympics, separate world, continental, and national powerlifting championships are held. See also >SPORTS FOR THE DISABLED; cf. >POWERLIFTING.
http://www.paralympic.org/sports

POWHIRI, the Maori dance of welcome, in which the dancers perform arm movements similar to those of rhythmic sportive gymnastics; see >HAKA.

PRECOLUMBIAN GAMES OF THE AMERICAS, consisting mostly of a wide range of ball games. Several types of rubber playing balls were known in Central America in ancient times. Balls of natural caoutchouc were common in the times of the Olmec and Toltec civilizations, around the 3rd cent. BC. The most precise, surviving data refers to such ancient games as >TLACHTLI, POKYAH (POK-TA-POK), >TALADZI and their modern descendants such as >ULAMA, >PELOTA TARASCA. See also >MESOAMERICAN INDIAN BALL GAMES.
A. Caso, T. Gutierez, *El deporte prehispanico*, 3rd ed. 1967; J.B. Oxendine, *American Indian Sports Heritage*, 1988; W.A. Goellner, 'The Court Ball Game of the Aboriginal Mayas', *Research Quarterly*, 1953, 24; A.M. Josephy, ed., *The American Heritage Book of Indians*, 1961.

PRELLBALL, an indoor ball game, similar to >FAUSTBALL, in which players hit the ball with their fists. The game is played by 2 teams of 2-4 players each. The court is 16m long and 8m wide, divided in half with a crossbar, 35-40cm above the ground. A match consists of two 10-minute periods. Prellball is very popular in Germany. League and friendly matches are held under the auspices of the Deutscher Gymnastik Bund.

PRISON AND CONCENTRATION CAMP SPORTS, various sports practiced illegally, legally and semi-legally in prisoner-of-war, internee and concentration camps during wars. Until the early 20th cent., no sporting activities were organized in such camps, partly due to the low awareness of the need for physical exercise, and partly due to the lack of legal regulations to guarantee the prisoners a minimum of rights. The American physician S.G. Howe, who in 1832 visited the camps of Pol. internees in Prussia after the unsuccessful uprising of 1830-31, gave this description in a letter to Marquis Lafayette:

I found nearly 4,500 soldiers, separated in different cantonments. Many of them were ill clad – hundreds were without shirts; but all were suffering from anxiety mounting almost to despair. They had been separated from their only friends, officers; they were divided into small bodies, the better to destroy their esprit de corps; they were continually harassed by the Prussians who had them in charge.

[Lafayette Papers, after J.J. Lerski, *A Polish Chapter in Jacksonian America*, 1958]

This situation did not change in the 19th cent. In the early 20th cent., the Eng. allowed sports in their S African concentration camps for the Boers, including cricket, running and jumping. The approach to sport changed with the adoption of the Hague Convention in 1907. The convention set a minimum level of humanitarian treatment in camps. During WWI, some prison camps organized sporting events to alleviate the monotony of prison life and relieve the tensions of captivity. Pol. legionary officers, interned at Szczypiorno near Kalisz, Poland in 1917-18, played team handball matches, actually providing the impulse for the growth of the game, which had not been known in Poland before (the spread of new, cross-cultural sports by prisoners of war from foreign countries was among the very few positive aspects of war). The Geneva Convention entitled *The Treatment of Prisoners of War* called for improvements in camp conditions. During WWII, sport was a frequent pastime of prisoners of war in both Ger. camps for allied soldiers and allied camps for Ger. and Jap. captives. This was true, however, mostly for officers stationed in the so-called 'Offizierlagern'. Privates were only allowed to practice sport in allied camps

for Ger., Ital., and Jap. captives. There were fewer constraints in allied camps, especially those organized by the English and Americans, and captives were not prevented from practicing sports. The situation was different in Ger. camps for allied prisoners, especially in the so-called 'Stalags', i.e. camps for ordinary soldiers, where sport was played only sporadically. As opposed to officers, according to international law, ordinary soldiers could be used as a work force, which meant taxing physical effort. However, irrespective of the camp type, there were always some gymnastic exercises or various ball games, as the memoirs of former prisoners of war attest. The N.Zealand doctor and officer J. Borrie, who was stationed at the Ger. Oflag at Lamsdorf, writes: 'Doctors helped run entertainment, sport and religious services, sustaining camp morale'. (*Despite Captivity. A Doctor's Life as Prisoner of War*, 1975). Sometimes, the guards could be persuaded into allowing prisoners to use ponds on camp premises: 'We persuaded our guard to let us swim in a large dredge hole across the fields'. Other fragments of the diary attest to a peculiar 'hunger for sport': 'Once outside the camp gates, they literally raced along the road [...], guards' lugging rifles and bayonets being left far behind' (ibid.). A classical element of almost any diary, book or film about prisoners of war was a plan to escape through a tunnel. Gymnastic equipment, such as an adapted vaulting horse, was often used to remove the sand and deposit it around the camp. The devices would be left overnight in the room where the entrance to the tunnel was, to be

WORLD SPORTS ENCYCLOPEDIA P

Willie McKinney, of West Virginia, left, gets support from Arnold Schwarzenegger during the bench press competition in the 1999 Special Olympics World Games at Stewart Theater in Raleigh, North Carolina.

An unidentified spotter shouts encouragement as Brent Mikesell strains to lift 487.5kg (1,074lbs.) during the Canadian Powerlifting Championships in Red Deer, Alberta. The 34-year-old lifter from Spokane, Washington, set a new squat division world record with his effort.

Powerlifting: an outdoor bench press competition.

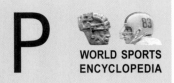

later moved to the camp yard for the exercises. The movements of the players allowed the sand to be deposited unnoticeably across the camp site and traces of fresh earth to be removed. In this way, gymnastics could serve as a smokescreen for the real endeavors of the prisoners. This is what a Brit. prisoner, Captain P.R. Reid, wrote about a camp for captured fugitives, situated in Colditz Castle, on a high, inaccessible rock:

As time went on, the Jerries allowed us a couple of hours' exercise three times a week in a barbed-wire pen in the wooded ground below the castle, but within the external castle walls. Here we played something resembling soccer – the hazards were the trees amongst which the game surged backwards and forwards. Our ball games amused the Jerries.

[P.R. Reid, *Colditz*, 1952]

As Reid writes, also 'the courtyard was the exercise area'. That was where the game known as >STOOL-BALL OF COLDITZ was played, which had little in common with the original >STOOL-BALL, due to the limited space:

I realise that this game was a manifestation of our suppressed desire for freedom. While the game was in action we were free. The surrounding walls were no longer a prison, but the confines of the game we played, and there were no constraining rules to curtail our freedom of action. I always felt much better after a game. Followed by a cold bath it put me on top of the world.

The practice of organizing sports for prisoners was almost non-existent in camps organized by the Jap., who did not adhere to international conventions. The dispute over employing officers in exhausting physical labor in Jap. camps is the starting point of P. Boulle's novel *The Bridge over the River Kwai* (filmed under a slightly changed title by D. Lean). Colonel Yamashita's speech points to what sports enthusiasts could, or perhaps could not, count on in a Jap. camp: 'Reasonable work is the best thing in the world for keeping a man physically fit'. The meaning of this was close to the slogan 'Arbeit macht frei' at the entrance to all Ger. camps. Even though Colonel Nicholson's dramatic protest leads to officers being employed only to supervise ordinary soldiers, the exhausting camp conditions prevent them from being involved in sports. The life of the Pol. officers interned by the Soviet government at Katin, and then murdered at Mednoye, Kozelsk and Ostashkov excluded sport totally. Germans in Soviet captivity as well as Soviet soldiers in Ger. camps were also treated without respect for any international conventions. As J. Borrie writes, in contrast to prisoners from western countries, Soviet captives, 'on 600 calories a day, were dying like flies from famine-oedema and tuberculosis'. Hardly anyone could think of sport in such conditions. However, the Germans allowed restricted forms of sport in their camps for Pol. prisoners of war, as well as in those for other allied soldiers. The situation in Oflag IIC at Dobiegniew (Ger. Woldenberg) was relatively good. The prisoners, having trained since the beginning of their captivity, decided to celebrate the canceled Ol.G. by organizing an international competition. A group of graduates of Warsaw's Central Institute for Physical Education who were among the captives who succeeded in persuading the Germans to agree to a contest that would possibly closely reflect the Olympic program. Several hundred prisoners took part. There were some writers at the camp, including the poet and literary critic S. Flukowski, the organizer of the camp literary group 'Zaułek', who organized an 'Olympic' literary contest to accompany the competition. The first prize was awarded to *The Prayer* by J. Knothe, E. Fischer with *The Song of the Tramp* was second, and the two third prizes went to *The Archer* by W. Milczarek and *The Stadium in the Sunlight* by L. Natanson. However, events like this were faced with grave difficulty in camps for ordinary soldiers where discipline was much stricter, and the captives were occupied by heavy work. Despite all this, underground 'Olympic Games' were held in Stalag XIIIC in Nuremberg-Langwasser, with French, Dutch, Belgian and Pol. participants. The games included frog jumping, stone throwing, archery, high jump over barbed wire, and cycling on a hidden bicycle placed on a podium. The contest was accompanied by recitation of the *Olympic Laurel* by K. Wierzyński, the poetry gold medallist at the 1929 Ol.G. in Amsterdam. Poems written by the prisoners were also read, providing a tragic and piercing document of the time, e.g. the following poem by rifleman Brystek of the 21st Infantry Regiment:

The barbed wire laurel
Nineteen forty... the year of the Olympics
The torch of war is burning, the hordes of the Armada race
Race to victory for the laurel leaf
Sieg heil! Vorwärts! To destruction! To action!
Let every rival know our ability!
Our Führer is with us and Gott mit uns!
The SS relay race to Warsaw,
Where the Icarus of Valhalla will light the bloody torch.
With their accurate throws, the Grenadiers
Turn their house-targets into pitiful stumps.
When there are no more targets in the Sirenian garden,
Jawohl! There is still the shepherd on the road.
The war stadiums have gone quiet in Poland,
The torch of Warsaw has gone out, despite the courage.
The winner is waiting for his russet laurel.
Has he forgotten he is already crowned?
There are laurels on his cap:
Crossbones and skulls.

During these 'Nuremberg Olympics', winners received pennants edged with barbed wire as prizes. A poster by E. Turbaczewski accompanied the games, while a special Olympic stamp was made from a potato (both can be seen at the Museum of Sports and Tourism in Warsaw). Years later, T. Niewiadomski wrote his play *Olimpiada, jakiej nie było* (*The Olympiad that never was*), staged in Łódź in 1973. The games at Stalag XIIIC were also the basis of A. Kotkowski's film *Olimpiada 40*, shot in 1980.
Paradoxically, sport was also practiced in the peculiar conditions of concentration camps, where it took on a particularly tragic and ironic significance. The Nazi management of the Oświęcim (Auschwitz) camp organized sport events for show, thinking of propaganda and Red Cross inspections (the camp orchestra was set up for similar reasons). Such endeavors were aimed at convincing the world of the 'normality' of concentration camp life. Officers organized sport for their own satisfaction, often involving those prisoners who had been professional sportsmen before. The boxer Z. Małecki recalls that, together with him, there were a number of well-known sportsmen in the camp: Pol. champion A. Czortek, the Italian Eufratti, Eur. champion, Third Reich champion Walter, Du. champion Sanders and many more who had fallen into disfavor with the Nazi government. The fights between them had a surreal air under the drastic camp conditions: 'We fought for real, sharply, without faking [...]. The Germans would not allow a soft fight for show. I saw some fighters who would not fight seriously having dogs set at them [...]. A refusal was met with gas chamber' (Z. Małecki, *Sport w Oświęcimiu*, 1945). T. Borowski left a description of the fights in his short story *U nas w Oświęcimiu*:

In the afternoon, I went to the boxing match at the huge barrack of the Waschraum, the place from where the transports for gassing first left. We were let inside with ceremonies even though the room was packed full. The ring was set up in the large waiting room. Light from above, a referee (nota bene a Pol. Olympic referee), world-famous boxers, but only Aryans, because Jews were not allowed to take part. And those same people who would put out teeth by their tens day in day out, many with empty jaws themselves, would get excited over Czortek, Walter of Hamburg and some young boy, who, after having had some training here at the camp, grew to become, as they say, a really classy one. The memory is still there of number 77 who once boxed the Germans as he liked, taking revenge in the ring for what others suffered in the field. The room was full of cigarette smoke, and the boxers pounded at each other as hard as they could. But they did so unprofessionally, even though with much obstinacy. 'This Walter,' Staszek would say, 'Just look at him! At the commando, if he wants, he puts down a Muslim with one punch. And here, just look, three rounds and nothing! And he has got his own face battered. Must be too many spectators, mustn't it?' Still, the audience went into ecstasies, and we in the first row, naturally, tough blokes.

[T. Borowski, *Opowiadania wybrane*, 1971]

Ger. inspiration was not the only factor behind sport in concentration camps. It functioned as a kind of spontaneous psychological counterweight for the camp reality, a way of achieving internal escape and oblivion to the dreary surroundings. When recalling his Christmas Eve at Dachau, the prisoner A. Labenz wrote: 'It was a strange thing, so many extremely important things were going on around the world [...], the whole world was ablaze, while we, the sporting youth, finding ourselves in such tragic conditions, criticized the sportsmen, clubs and sport officials of pre-war Poland with so much zeal, verve and a kind of fury. We argued passionately over the level of football [...], compared athletic results' (A. Labenz, *Wigilia sportowców w Dachau*, 1946). According to a report by K. Małycha, a prisoner of the camp at Mauthausen-Gusen, printed by the Pol. press in 1945, a regular international football league was organized by the prisoners of the camp. 'To keep the footballers on top form, those colleagues who could or who received packets, imposed a tax upon themselves for our footballers, and fed them. Many of them owe their survival to football' (K. Małycha, *Mecz piłkarski Polska-Hiszpania w Mauthausen*, 1945). The final match of this international league, proudly proclaimed the 'World Championships', was played by the Pol. and Span. teams, with Poland winning. In addition to that, boxing and wrestling matches were organized in secret from the camp management in baths and attics. 'Due to the scarcity of space, the events had to be ticketed'. Football was also a tragic antinomy of camp reality in T. Borowski's short story *Ludzie, którzy szli* (1946):

The ball went out of play and rolled up to the barbed wire fence. I ran to fetch it. Picking it up from the ground, I looked at the loading platform. A train had just arrived at the platform. People started getting off the wagons and walking towards the forest [...]. I returned with the ball and kicked it out onto the field. It passed from foot to foot and came back towards the goal in an arc. I cleared it for a corner. It rolled into high grass. And when I was picking it up form the ground, I came to a halt: the platform was empty [...]. I came back with the ball and passed it for the corner kick. Between the first and second corner kick, three thousand people were gassed behind my back.

J. Hen's short story *Bokser i śmierć* (*The Boxer and Death*, 1952) is among the most famous literary pieces describing matches played at concentration camps. In a camp commanded by the ex-world champion Kraft (a character clearly modeled on M. Schmeling), the Pol. boxer Kominek is one of the prisoners. Kraft wishes to win back his title after the war, and uses Kominek as his sparring partner to maintain his form. It soon turns out that Kominek surpasses him in his boxing skills but he is afraid to disclose it as the partner could order him to be gassed. However, when one of Kominek's friends is killed by the Germans, he lets loose and knocks Kraft out during their next sparring. In revenge, Kraft sentences him to death but under the pressure of other people, and in the name of fair play, lets him go. S. Dygat's short story *Faul* (*Foul Play*) has a similar thread. An SS-officer, Pfirsterer, who lost a match against the Pole Mielczarski before the war, can now take revenge on him, as Mielczarski is a prisoner at his camp. When liberation comes, however, the Pole fights a match against the German, and gives him an object lesson in boxing. The literature demonstrates the social importance of the problem, mainly in those countries whose citizens spent a large part of the 20th cent. in Ger. or Soviet camps.
The games organized both in prisoner-of-war camps and in concentration camps, irrespective of where and when they took place, and of how they were presented in literature, have been among the more optimistic points in the history of modern sport. Despite their limited scope, which failed to go beyond the confines of the individual camps, they were a symbol of the peaceful message that sport carries with it, and which proved stronger than the evil of war.
A. Labenz, *Wigilia sportowców w Dachau*, 'Kurier Sportowy', 1946, 66; Z. Małecki, *Sport w Oświęcimiu*, 'Kurier Sportowy', August 16, 1945; K. Małycha, *Mecz piłkarski Polska-Hiszpania w Mauthausen*, 'Kurier Sportowy', 1945, 1; F.J.G. van der Merwe, 'Sport as Means to Secure Sanity and Health in Prisoner-of-War Camps During the Anglo-Boer War 1899-1902', T. Terret, ed., *Sport et santé dans l'histoire*, 1999; T. Niewiadomski, *Olimpiada, której nie było*, 1973; R. Siuda, 'Olimpijski konkurs poezji w obozie jenieckim II C w Woldenbergu', KF, 1965.

PRISONER'S BASE, or *prisoner's bars*; also known in some regions of England as *country base* or *Billy-base*; the Eng. equivalent of a Fr. medieval street game called >AUX BARES. First called *à barres*, it is mentioned in a document issued during the reign of Edward III (1327-77), forbidding its playing around the Houses of Parliament in Westminster, due to the noisy conduct of play. In Scotland, the game was known as *bar*, and it was also forbidden in a decree issued by James IV in 1491. The game of prisoner's base was used by W. Shakespeare in *Cymbeline* (V,

435

U.S. Border agents Tom Castloo, in back, and Bob Zambramo sail down the Rio Grande using an airboat near Del Rio, Texas.

WORLD SPORTS
ENCYCLOPEDIA

P

3) as a metaphor for heroic struggle of an anonymous old man for his country against the Romans:

...athwart the lane
He, with two striplings, lad more like to run
The country base than to commit such slaughter,
Make good the passage...

J. Strutt describes prisoner's base like this:

The performance of this pastime requires two parties of equal number, each of them having a base or home, as it is usually called, to themselves, at the distance of about twenty or thirty yards. The players then on either side taking hold of hands, extend themselves in length, and opposite to each other, as far as they conveniently can, always remembering that one of them must touch the base; when any one of them quits the hand of his fellow and runs into the field, which is called giving the chase, he is immediately followed by one of his opponents; he again is followed by a second from the former side, and he by a second opponent; and so on alternately, until as many are out as choose to run, every one pursuing the man he first followed, and no other; and if he overtake him near enough to touch him, his party claims one toward their game and both return home. [It is to be observed, that every person on either side who touches another during the chase, claims one for his party, and where many are out, it frequently happens that many are touched]. They then run forth again and again in like manner, until the number is completed that decided the victory; this number is optional, and I am told rarely exceeds twenty. About thirty years back, I saw a grand match at base played in the fields behind Montague house [Now better known by the name of the British Museum], by the twelve gentlemen of Cheshire against twelve of Derbyshire, for a considerable sum of money, which afforded much entertainment to the spectators. In Essex they play this game with the addition of two prisons, which are stakes driven into the ground, parallel with the home boundaries, and about thirty yards from them; and every person who is touched on either side in the chase, is sent to one or other of these prisons, where he must remain till the conclusion of the game, if not delivered previously by one of his associates, and this can only be accomplished by touching him, which is difficult task, requiring the performance of the most skilful players, because the prison belonging to either party is always much nearer to the base of their opponents than to their own; and if the person sent to relieve his confederate be touched by an antagonist before he reaches him, he also becomes a prisoner, and stands in equal need of deliverance. The addition of the prisons occasions a considerable degree of variety in the pastime, and is frequently productive of much pleasantry.

Sports and Pastimes of the People of England, 1810 , p. 72.

PROBAR A JUNTAR, a folk var. of wrestling practiced in the Balearic Islands. It consists of taking an opponent down so that he would fall on his back (Span. for 'clinch test'; *probar* – 'to test' + *juntar* – 'contact, clinch'). The sport is currently on the de-

cline; details unavailable.
C. Moreno Palos, 'Otras luchas rituales', JYTE, 1992.

PROPELLER SPEEDBOAT RACES, initially such speedboats (also called airboats) were used by the rangers of the Amer. national parks, particularly in the Everglades (vast freshwater marshes) in Florida and Bayous in Louisiana. In the 1980s spontaneous forms of competitions turned into a competitive sport. Presently, competitions are held in 11 categories, depending on the engine cubic capacity. The most popular is the standard class, using the compressor engine. The boats are driven on nitrogen suboxide. The speed reached by top class boats is 180km/h. The race starts with a green light signal. In the most prestigious competitions the prizes amount to $12-15,000. Cf. >SWAMP BUGGY.

PRYLIS, see >PYRRHICHE.

PRZERYWANE WOJSKO, (Pol. for 'breaking a line of troops'), a running and wrestling game played by 2 teams. The game was described by R. Trześniowski: 'The teams stand in two rows opposite each other, 15-20 steps apart. The players hold one another by the hand very tight. [...] The captain of one team shouts 'Captain! A soldier for you!', while the captain of the opposite team replies 'Ready!' After this exchange, one player from the 'challenging team' runs forward and tries to break through the opponent's line in some section. If the charging 'soldier' succeeds all the players of the opposing team to the left of the breaking point join the challenging team. If the charging soldier fails to break through he is taken prisoner and joins the defending team. The teams charge at each other alternately, each time changing the number of players on the teams. The team with more soldiers after a designated time wins the game. The captains can charge the opposing team 3 times in a row without being taken prisoner'. Similar games are known in Eng.-speaking countries, e.g. >RAX, >RED ROVER.
R. Trześniowski, 'Przerywane wojsko', ZIGR, 1995.

PUA, a sport consisting of throwing wooden balls at a target, once practiced among the inhabitants of the Cook Islands.

PUAVANYE S'RAPORTOM, Rus. for 'swimming with a report', a swimming game popular in the former USSR and its satellite countries aimed at providing swimming training necessary for soldiers who had to clear various water obstacles. According to I.N. Chkhannikov: 'two or three players form a row standing in neck-deep water, each of them holding a sheet of paper. Some 30-50 steps away from them there is the umpire. At his signal the competitors start swimming towards him while trying to keep the sheet of

paper above water level. The first swimmer to reach him and to hand him a dry sheet is declared the winner'.
'Puavanye s'raportom', GIZ, 1953, 79.

PUCK SHOOTING, Rus. skating game featuring elements of >HOCKEY; the aim is to shoot a puck against a special numbered board 5m long and 0.5m high, on which short planks are mounted at the ends to hold it upright on the ice. The central part of the board is divided into 8 fields numbered symmetrically 5, 5, 3, 1, 1, 3, 5, 5; in order to score the required amount of points one must shoot the highest scoring field. The game is played by 6-7 players equipped with hockey sticks; one of them is the goalkeeper, others fight for scores either individually or divided into 2 symmetrical teams. The old Rus. sports handbook advises that, lacking appropriate equipment, players may form a snow embankment at the end of the playing rink and hollow out the appropriate number of holes in it to play the role of a numbered board; scores ascribed to a particular hole varied complying with the local conditions and invention of the players; anything resembling a puck, e.g. a piece of ice, could play its role, whereas a straight branch or a pole from a fence could easily be used as a substitute stick.
I.N. Chkhannikov, 'Shayba v tselu', GIC, 1953, 97.

PUDDEX, also *puddocks* or *podex*, a var. of >CRICKET invented by A. Lang in the 19th cent. in Great Britain, played in the Loretto Public School. The game was originally played with the ball used in the early var. of tennis called >ROYAL TENNIS. The ball was hit with a thick wooden bat. Puddex had two varieties: the house (played by teams of up to 4 players each) and the bedroom (played by teams of more than 4 players each). The wickets were 12in. wide and positioned 42ft. apart. The etymology of the game's name is unknown. Possibly, the name was coined at some school or social meetings, after the Lat. *podex* – 'buttocks'; *putus* – 'boy, clear or simple'; *pudens* – 'modest, decent' (with reference to the nature of the game, developing the required character features of a good schoolboy); Gk. *poderes* – 'stuck in the ground' (with reference to the positioning of wickets). Borrowings from Lat. and Gk. were very popular in jargons of local public schools in 19th-cent. England. Many headmasters of the public schools were classic philologists who would frequently introduce elements of the classic cultures into the sports and everyday life of their schools.

PUDEBAK, a Flem. game played in local taverns; an equivalent of the Fr. *jeu de grenouille*, Span. >RANA, LA, Port. >JOGO DO SAPO, and Eng. >TOAD IN THE HOLE.

P

PUERITA, a Lat. name denoting boyhood and all types of boys' games and competitions.

PUFF-DARTS, a var. of >DARTS, played in England in the 19th cent. The darts were blown at a target board from special tubular blowguns. The dart was about 1in. long; the tube about 3ft. long. The board was 7-8in. in diameter, divided into twenty radial sec-

Tourists take a cross-country ride in Muonio, Finland. Such reindeer-drawn sleighs are used in the Lap folk sledding sport called pulka.

tors, resembling the boards used in the modern games of darts.

PUGILISM, fighting with the fists known in numerous cultures of various ages. The term pugilism is understood here as fist-fighting before the appearance of >BOXING, independent of the Brit. sport. The term boxing applies to the modern forms of Amer. and Western Eur. forms of pugilism, and it is not associated with other cultures or historical periods. See also >POLYNESIAN PUGILISM, >ANCIENT PUGILISM, >OLD RUSSIAN BOXING, >AKROTERI PUNCHING; cf. >THAI BOXING, >KICKBOXING.

PUKSIVARVLIMAADLEMINE, one of three var. of Est. >MAADLEMINE wrestling.

PULKA, the name of a Lap folk sledding sport, using special reindeer-drawn sleighs made of reindeer leather. The sleigh resembles a small canoe with an elevated bow. (Lap *pulkhe* or *pulkke*; Fin. *pulkka*). A sport using a similar type of sleigh, known as ski pulk, is practiced by the Alaskan and Can. Inuit. Ski pulk consists of skiing behind a pulk sleigh pulled by sled dogs. The sport is represented by the North Amer. Skijoring and Ski Pulk Association.

PULLING SHOULDER-POLE, a sports competition practiced by the Yao people in China, consisting of pulling a rope by 2 teams of players, similar to >TUG-OF-WAR, using the handles of long garden tools, e.g. forks. Pulling shoulder-pole is practiced by men or women, in singles, doubles or teams of 3 people. The sport is a common recreational activity during harvest.
Mu Fushan, et al., 'Pulling Shoulder-Pole', TRAMCHIN.

PULLING THE TORTOISE, a game known and practiced on the Chin. island of Hainan. Among the local people of Li it forms a popular pastime, as an element of local holidays. In international ethnological terminology it is known as *pulling the tortoise*. A playing field is marked with 2 parallel lines signifying riverbanks. One player takes a position at each 'bank' and one of them ties a rope around his waist and then gets down on all fours in a tortoise position. The rope has to be long enough, usu. a few meters, so that the player on the other bank is able to reach it. The center point of the rope is marked with a piece of red silk, precisely over the middle of the riverbed. At the referee's command two participants start wrestling: the 'tortoise' attempts to run away from the river as far from its bank as possible, whereas the opponent is trying to pull the tortoise into the river. The position of the red scarf indicates the winner: the winning party is the one who manages to pull the rope far enough to have the silk scarf over their bank.
Mu Fushan, et al., 'Pulling the Tortoise', TRAMCHIN.

PULU, (Kashmir Tibetan *pulu* – 'a soft willow root or ball made of it), the original name of >POLO.

PUNGRYO-DO, an ancient Kor. martial art, derived from medieval tradition. Pungryo-do was an impor-

tant element of the great Kor. tradition of noble military training called the hwarang-do. In later years, pungryo-do became so significant that its name was used to denote the entire hwarang-do. Before it was incorporated into the hwarang-do system, pungryo-do was probably a local or temporary var. of ancient Korean martial arts, together with >KUKSUN-DO and >PUNGWAL-DO.

PUNGWAL-DO, one of a few medieval Kor. martial arts. Together with >KUKSUN-DO and >PUNGRYO-DO it constituted the *hwarang-do*, the noble military training system of ancient Korea.

PUNTING, an Eng. leisure activity of going along a river in a punt, i.e. a shallow, square-ended, flat-bottomed boat, usu. 21ft. (6m) long and 3ft. (1m) wide, propelled by thrusting a 16ft. (5m) pole on the riverbed. The pole is also used to steer the boat. Punting is esp. popular in Cambridge, where it is practiced by the students of the University of Cambridge on the river Cam. The English Punting Championships have been held since 1876; amateur championships since 1886.

PUSHBALL, a team game played on foot, horseback or in the water with a huge inflated ball, up to 6ft. in diameter, covered with real or artificial leather. The ball is pushed by players, or horses in the equestrian version.
PUSHBALL ON FOOT, played on a field 140yds long and 50yds wide or a modified soccer or rugby field. The goals consist of 2 upright posts 18ft. high and 20ft. apart with a crossbar 7ft. from the ground. The ball is 6ft. in diameter and weighs 50lbs. Each team consists of 11 players, 5 forwards, 2 left-wings, 2 right-wings, and 2 goal-keepers. The object of the game is to drive the ball to the opponent's side and score points by way of pushing the ball under the bar, throwing it over the bar, or a touchdown behind goal for safety. A game lasts 2x30min. with an intermission.
PUSHBALL ON HORSEBACK, played by 2 teams of 5 riders – one goalkeeper and 4 fielders.
WATER PUSHBALL, played in lakes or pools without goals.
Pushball has numerous local varieties, with different rules and regulations. Teams may number from 10 to 25 players, the goals can be even 10m wide. In some recreational forms it is enough to score a point

Scudamore's punting in Cambridge, Great Britain.

WORLD SPORTS
ENCYCLOPEDIA

P

Puszta ötös.

by pushing the ball behind the opponent's end line. Pushball fields vary in size, and games may last 4x8 or 4x10min. Generally, a ball less than 1.5m in diameter is not considered a pushball. The game is practiced in the USA, Canada and the countries of the former Soviet Union. Pushball was already mentioned in eastern Europe in the early 20th cent.:

The recent Anglo-American game of football is being slowly superceded by a similar game called push-ball. A ball more than a man's height in diameter and weighing about 50 pounds is pushed, rolled or lifted by two opposing parties of players, who try to drive it into the opponent's area. The game is attractive entertainment for the spectators, but the players have to sweat a lot.

['Nowa amerykańska gra w piłkę: Push-Ball', *Tygodnik Ilustrowany*, 1903, 36]

PUSZTA ÖTÖS, Hungarian for 'the Puszta five', a show of horsemanship popular among local herdsmen. The rider (*csikós*) stands on the backs of 2 horses, one foot on each. Three more horses run abreast in front of him. The *csikós* holds the reins connecting all 5 horses (hence the name of the sport). He is elegantly dressed in high boots, black trousers, a richly embroidered waistcoat, a white, wide-sleeved shirt and a high, small-brimmed hat with a colourful ribbon tied around it.

PUTANO, a Kenyan game resembling >MARBLES.

PUTKA, an obsolete folk game, once practiced in Pol. inns. Putka is briefly mentioned by Ł. Gołębiowski in *Gry i zabawy różnych stanów* (*Games and Pastimes of Various Social Classes*, 1831).

PYEONGRYEOK, also *pyeonryeok*, a Kor. form of pilgrimage perceived as spiritual and physical exercise, constituting a part of the Kor. military training system called the hwarang-do. Pyeongryeok consisted of a lonely stay in the mountains during which the candidates for the hwarang warriors practiced their will and meditation. In *The Chronicle of the Three Kingdoms* (*Samguk Sagi*) written by the sage Dae-mun Kima, living in the Songdok period (702--37), the future ruler of the Shilla Kingdom – Kim You-sin – went on a pilgrimage in the mountains ridden by a plague of worms. By overcoming numerous obstacles Kim You-sin was supposed to have practiced moderation and self-restraint. During the pyeongryeok pilgrimages the prospective hwaranga warriors improved their sensitivity to nature as well as practiced singing, poetry writing and weapon skills. The most famous pilgrimage destinations included Gyoungpo-dae, Hanson-jung, and Kunran-gul in present-day Kangwon province; Posuk-jung in the northern province of Kyongsang; Sasun-bong and Samil-po on the Kor. east coast in the Kangwon province; Kyongpodae in the Kangwon province; the city and lake Kangnung and several places in Wolsong county. A description of a pyeongryeok is found in a great work of ancient Kor. literature – *Haedong Konsun*

chon (The Notes of Famous Korean Monks). The pilgrimage was made by 4 'immortal' hwarang warrior-sages of the Silla kingdom: Namsokhaeng (Namnang), Sullang, Yongnang and An sang. As the chronicler puts it, '...among the beautiful places they visited the most renowned was Samilp'o, exalted in numerous Korean poems [...]. Lake Yongyang and Arangp'o in the west were also frequently visited by those immortals.'

Visiting the mountains was an important tradition of the early pre-Buddhist shamanism in Korea. The mountains were the mythical seat of gods, called the Sinsun, and the place in which the gods contacted the earth. The name Sinsun was also applied to denote the most renowned hwarang warriors. According to the earliest Korean mythology, during the creation of Korea, Taeback Hwanung, the son of the god of heaven descended upon a mountain summit. His son, Dangun, was the alleged founder of the first Kor. kingdom.

PYERYESMYESHNIK, (Rus. for 'mocker'), a simple Rus. game described by I.N. Chkhannikov: 'The game of mocker is played in a dense forest so the players can hide easily. The players select a captain and a mocker from among themselves. The captain and the mocker have whistles, each sounding a different pitch. The mocker sets off first and hides himself in the woods; after five minutes he blows his whistle signaling the start of the game. The captain and the remaining players follow the mocker. The captain blows his whistle from time to time, and the mocker responds with his own. The players try to stalk and catch the mocker following the signals of his whistle. Whoever catches the mocker becomes the new captain and the former captain becomes the new mocker.'

'Przedrzeźniacz', GIZ, 1953, 71-2.

PYGME, also *pygmachos*, a form of pugilism in ancient Greece, introduced into the XXIII ancient Ol.G. in 688 BC, but widely known and practiced long before. The Old-Gk. word *pygme* denoted both the fist and the fight. Pygme was also included in other Gk. games, such as the Pythian Games in Delphi, whose patron was Apollo the Pyktes (the Pugilist). Later on, Apollo also became the pygme patron outside Delphi. See also >ANCIENT PUGILISM, >AKROTERI PUNCHING.

PYKS ATREMIZEIN, a test of endurance practiced in ancient Greece. The competitors would stand upright with both arms extended upwards or sideways. Whoever managed to stand longer in such a position won.

PYONG HWA DO, an eclectic form of self-defense based on a few Asian styles of martial arts (Kor. *pyong* – 'peaceful' + *hwa* – 'system' + *do* – 'way, principle'). Such elements of pyong hwa do as predicting an enemy's movements, blocking moves and arousing the fighting will were taken from the Okinawan

tomari te >KARATE. The Korean >HAPKIDO was the contributor of the following elements: relaxation skills, holding the opponent in clinch, feints, take-downs and counterattack. Finally, Chin. >GONGFU provided pyong hwa do with meditation techniques and smooth movements. The sport enjoys increasing popularity in the USA. One of the Amer. pyong hwa do pioneers is Sigung A.F. Walker. The most popular pyong hwa do centers in the USA are in Austin and Houston, Texas and Boise, Idaho.

PYRRHICHE, also *pyrrhiche orchesis*, a kind of war dance in full armor; a kind of mime show performed to the accompaniment of music (Gk. *orchesis* – 'dance' + *pyre* – 'funeral pyre, funeral pyre dance'). In Cretan mythology, the first pyrrhiche performers were the Curetes – demons who guarded the infant Zeus in Crete, by clashing their spears on their shields so that his cries would not be heard by his father, the bloodthirsty Cronos. One of the demons, Pyrrychos gave pyrrhiche its name. The custom of clashing spears on the shields, performed with some additional gestures and body movements, was later adopted and practiced by the Dorians after their conquest of Crete. Achilles performed a pyrrhiche dance during Patroclus' funeral. As a funeral pyre dance, pyrrhiche was adopted by the Athenians around the 6th cent. BC. Later on, pyrrhiche became a contest with prizes.

In Cyprus, pyrrhiche was known as *prylis*. At funerals of the Cypriot rulers, the soldiers participating in the funeral procession performed dances in full armor. Stasinos of Cyprus (7th cent. BC) mentions in his epic poem *Cypria* that the Cyprist warriors went into combat dancing to the music.

C. Constantinou-Hadjistephanou, *Athletics in Ancient Cyprus and the Greek Tradition from 15th/14th Century BC-AD 330*, 1991.

Punting in Cambridge, Great Britain.

QIGONG, [Chin. *qi* – energy of life + *gong* – work, effort, skill], a Chin. school of controlling the self and perfecting human life through breathing control (breathing is seen here as a basic vital activity). *Qi* is one of the fundaments of harmony between the form, the spirit that gives life to the form, will and vitality, as well as a unity of opposites such as hardness and softness, motion and stillness, the inside and the outside. In this light, qigong is one of the ways of realizing the qi. Qigong includes breathing exercises that are supposed to boost fitness and prevent disease, thus lengthening the practitioner's lifespan. A basic assumption of qigong is perfecting or improving the *xinqi*, or the flow of energy within a human being, which is identified with the volatility of the air. It stands for the totality of the vital energy achieved through repeated exercise, giving a human being the ability to live more intensively. Under the control of the human mind, or *yi*, the energy so construed flows through the body and is deposited in the limbs. This approach is, then, well known in contemporary sport training, even though it may be explained differently in the Eur. tradition, where physiological accumulation is considered to be fundamental, along with the so-called training effect that includes all the post-effort building processes in the human body and the associated psychosomatic phenomena. In both approaches, an improved state of the body and mind is achieved through effort. Qigong differs from the Eur. approach in its kind of intensity, where less emphasis is placed on physical effort, and more on spiritual effort. The ultimate goal is not professional performance but overall control over one's body and, as a consequence, over one's existence.

History. According to Chin. tradition, qigong first appeared about 4,700yrs. ago, in the Huang Di period, but there are no records to confirm this. One thing that makes it more difficult to establish the facts is that, in those times, qigong was not referred to by this name, and the individual exercises were included in other systems such as *chiki*, *fuqi*, *tuna*, *xinqi*, and, above all, *daoyin*. However, it is certain that exercises which historians of physical culture and medicine consider the basis of qigong

A Chinese monk from the Shaolin Temple shows off his qigong or breathing exercise gongfu by being lifted up on five spears, which leaves only white marks on his body, during a show in Beijing.

Members of the Falun Gong perform breathing exercises in Beijing's Ritan Park. The group borrows heavily from Buddhist and Taoist philosophies and styles itself as a school of qigong, a traditional Chinese practice using meditation and martial arts exercises to channel unseen forces and improve health.

were known as early as in the 5th or 6th cent. BC. In the times of the sage Lao Zi, the fundamental principles were written down in the *Dao-De-Jing* book. In the book, Guang Chenzi explains to the Chin. emperor how to exercise to keep in good health and improve one's fitness. That was the basis for what became qigong later: 'As soon as you achieve a peaceful state of mind, your body will be ordered in a natural way. Keep your body upright, and your mind calm. Do not think of anything else, do not overburden your body and do not waste its energy. You will then come to live a long life'. In the Warring States period (475-221 BC), qigong was already well known. The Tianjin museum has in its collection a sword on which 45 ancient Chin. signs are engraved, explaining the flow and storing of qi in the human body. In that period, the principles functioned as *Huangdi Neijing – The Yellow Emperor's Inner Classic*. They are also expressed in the text of the *Jade Inscription on the Xingqi Yuming Breathing Technique*:

Breathe, breathe deeply to reap the effect,
Reaping, to transcend, transcending, to exist,
Existing, to strengthen, strengthening, to sprout,
Sprouting until the advent of heavenly spring
That completes the earthly spring.
Such regular motion lengthens the life
For lack of regularity makes life shorter.

Texts written in the Han period (206 BC-220 AD) contain many references to qingong being practiced by the Chinese. For example, Zhang Liang, the dignitary who helped Emperor Liu Bang take over the power and set up the Han dynasty, gave up his high ranks to study qigong under the guidance of the famous philosopher Chi Songzi, and then lived a hermit's life. In 1973, a map dating back to the so-called western Han dynasty was found in a tomb near the town of Chansha in the Hunan province. On it, there are pictures of 44 figures practicing qigong. Later, qigong developed along an uneven path, sometimes increasing in importance, and decreasing at other times. In the Taoist era, especially in the 3rd cent. BC-4th cent. AD, qigong became a means of enriching meditation and striving for longevity. Books written in the period of the eastern Han dynasty (23-220 AD), such as *Zou Yi Kan Tong* and *Taiping Jin*, give a detailed theory of qigong for the first time, along with a range of practical exercises. At the end of the Han period, qigong was augmented with *yindaoshu* ('a way of preserving good health') exercises. In the 3rd cent. BC, Hua Tuo, a physician and philosopher considered to have been one of the fathers of Chinese medicine, enriched the concept of *yindaoshu* by producing the *wuqinxi*, a list and description of exercises used to physically and mentally improve the human being. He took his inspiration from the surrounding nature, especially the movements of animals: the tiger, deer, bear, monkey and crane. Hua Tuo's *Wuqinxi* included a wide range of quick and gentle movements that formed a kind of a system engaging the mind and the whole of the body. At the turn of the 5th and 6th cent. AD, Tao Jinghong, a Taoist philosopher and physician, wrote the book *Be Healthy and*

Lengthen Your Life, where he collected all of the then current Chin. knowledge of methods aimed at conserving and improving the mental and physical state of human beings. In the book, he also included *daoyin* exercises, which were for the most part identified with qingong. About 6th cent. AD, Buddhism and Yoga began to become popular in China, and as a result *daoyin*, including the principles of qingong, was enriched philosophically and technically (as far as the execution of specific exercises was concerned). Descriptions of self-contained system of exercises first appeared in the times of the Sui (581-618) and T'ang (618-906) dynasties. The system was recommended by consecutive rulers and their court philosophers as a means of assuring longer and healthier lives for their subjects, and obviously of preventing disease. The *General Treatise on the Causes and Symptoms of Disease*, written in 610, contained within *daoyin* the basic assumptions of qigong and descriptions of qigong exercises, next to strictly medical recipes and advice. The book recommended *daoyin* exercises as a method of preventing 40 diseases. Another set that appeared was that of *baduanjin* – containing 8 exercises of the respiratory system that engaged all the body parts. *Baduanjin* was perfected in the Song period (960-1279). However, the interest in qigong as a medical method declined during this period. This led to qigong's 'independence' as a system of bodily exercises aimed at improving the performance of the body. The book *Exercises for Each of the Twelve Months of the Year* by Chen Xiyi introduced the notion of *jingluo* referring to the main channels in the human body through which vital fluids flow. The notion was also associated with the location of places where the flow of energy could be influenced through acupuncture. During the Ming (1368-1644) and Qing (1644-1911) dynasties, the concept of >TAIJIQUAN (>TAI CHI) started emerging, mainly on the basis of qigong. In the 1st half of the 20th cent., as a result of the stormy transformation that took place in China, the importance of qigong dwindled. First, the strong westernization of Chin. culture between 1912 and 1937 led to the demise of many oriental traditions of physical exercise and medicine. During the Cultural Revolution qigong was declared an antidemocratic relic of feudalism, and formally banned. The introduction of communism in 1949 consolidated this approach to qigong. Qigong survived in small Taoist monk communities, where, along with other Chin. traditions banned by the communists, it was taught to small groups of younger people. 1979 brought a change in the attitude towards qigong, and the treasury of Chin. traditions was opened once again. With the new approach, qigong at first developed without considerable restrictions as an effective method of promoting fitness and health, and a manifestation of homogeneity of the Chin. nation at the same time. A drastic change in the Chin. authorities' approach to qigong occurred in 1999. It became apparent that master Li Hongzhi used the wide appeal of qigong to organize a broader democratic movement called *Falun Gong*. In July, 1999, the police made many arrests, declaring qigong practitioners an opposition movement. Between 40,000 and 60,000 practitioners of breathing exercises, performed in the parks and squares of Chin. cities and towns, were jailed within a short time. As the Pol. weekly *Polityka* wrote:

For the first time in the history of the People's Republic of China, there has appeared an organization – albeit an informal one – that is just as, or more, numerous than the Communist Party of China (58 million members), and is aware of that. It has an extremely effective system of operation and a dynamic structure, including the latest communication technologies. Despite all that, it remains in the shade, without stirring too much fuss around itself. So, it is not a handful of dissidents who are just beginning to co-ordinate their actions, staying in constant touch with international media, and thus exposing themselves from the very outset to the accusation of co-operating with foreign powers. This is a resilient organization that also includes, or has included, party members.

It turned out, at the same time, that using the self-discipline – qigong within it – that the Orient has been developing for thousands of years, and has been so famous for, one can achieve not only personal but also social and political goals. Chin. authorities are at a crossroads – should they write off the experience of their own civilization, or should they respect the tradition and accelerate their own downfall?

QUADRIGA RACES, in ancient Gk. and Roman athletic contests, races of 2-wheel chariots pulled by 4 horses [Lat. *quattuor* – four; *quadr-* four-, in compounds]. A Roman var. of the Gk. >TETRIPPON, held in specially built stadiums with oval racecourses based on the Gk. *hippodrome*. Among Roman amphitheaters the following had such racecourses: Circus Maximus (built in the 4th cent. BC, 600m long, able to hold 150,000 spectators), Circus Flaminius (built on the Campus Martius) and Circus Neronianus (built in the gardens of Agrippina). Starting spans, each in a separate box (of which the Circus Maximus had 6), were shut off from the track by a richly decorated crate. The referee raised and lowered the crate with a special lever and a rope. The starting points took into account the different lengths of the lanes so at the start of the race the contestant on the outside lane seemed to be first. Above the starters' boxes (situated along the longer side of the track) rose the *oppidum*, a construction holding among others the box of the official presiding over the event. It had 2 towers which enabled the supervision of the race. Along the longer sides of the inside lane there was a low wall, the *spina*, which stopped the charioteers maneuvering their spans off the lane, thus shortening the way. On the *spina* there were 2 porticoes signaling the number of laps left. One portico held 7 oval balls, the other 7 stat-

and has a metal spike at each end, narrower than the shaft. In the past, the sticks did not have any spikes but were sharpened and charred at the ends. No blades are used in the sporting variety. The fight itself resembles >FENCING and >PALCATY, and bears some similarity to certain Asian self-defense techniques, notably >KENDO. The name is associated with the Eng. length measure of 'rod', which is about 5m; hence the hypothesis that originally the staff was shorter, about 1.25m in length (a 'quarter of a rod'), and was lengthened with time and as the fighting techniques developed. A basic technique was the 2-hand grip, with the fighter using the bottom hand to spin the staff which made it possible to deliver swift attacking blows at unexpected moments. Other folk fighting techniques developed on the basis of quarterstaff, such as >SINGLE-STICK and >CUDGEL.

History. Quarterstaff has been known from 'time immemorial' but the oldest records date back to the Middle Ages. The quarterstaff was mainly a peasant weapon used in real fights but it was also employed in duels, which with time developed into a folk sport. In the Eng. tradition, it was the main weapon of Robin Hood, the legendary defender of the Anglo-Saxons after the Norman conquest. Almost all the preserved versions of the legend contain quarterstaff duel scenes. One of the ballads men-

Berlin's Brandenburg Gate quadriga on a poster announcing the 1936 Olympic Games.

Apollo's quadriga, a sculpture designed in 1825 to embellish the facade of the Grand Opera in Warsaw, was elevated to its destination in May 2002.

A. Burckhardt, 'Nauka oddychania', *Polityka*, 1999, 32; J.-P. Desroches, 'The Human Body and Its Metamorphoses. Acrobatics (in China)', YOSICH, 1999, 20-23; *Le qigong*, in: *Les sports traditionelles en Chine. Chine – Aperçu général*, anon., 1991, 5-7; Zhenliang He, '5000 Years of Sport in China: Art and Tradition', OR, June-July 1999, 75-76; S. Qinglong, 'The History of Sport in China since Antiquity', YOSICH, 1999, 15-18.

QIN NA, (also *Chin na*), an element of Chin. martial arts [*qin* – to catch, block + *na* – to control, hold]. Being the ability to overpower the opponent, it forms a part of any trad. >GONGFU style, together with the techniques of throwing and flooring (*schuei*), kicks (*ti*), and strikes (*da*). Besides grappling, qin na includes the techniques of pressing and immobilizing the opponent, which may lead to the loss of consciousness and even death. Specific techniques may be divided into: *fen gin* – dividing or grabbing the muscles and tendons; *tsuoh guu* – displacing the bones; *bich chi* – sealing the breath; *duam mie* – pressing the veins; *tien hsueh* – cavity press; and *dim mak* – pressing the meridians. According to tradition, qin na techniques were brought to Japan by a monk Chen Yuan Ping at the beginning of the 17th cent. and – together with >SHUAI JIAO (techniques of overpowering, throwing, and grappling) – gave birth to >JU JUTSU, which later formed the basis for >JUDO and >AIKIDO.

ues of dolphins. One dolphin and one ball were lowered after each lap. See also >CHARIOT RACING.

QUAGGA RACES, a type of races popular in Africa at the turn of the 19th and 20th cent., in which the competing riders mount animals which are a cross between a donkey and a zebra. The name *kuaga* comes from the Afrikaans *quagga*, modern *kwagga*, where it was adopted from the language of the Bantu people of the equatorial and S regions of Africa. The upper part of the kuaga's body has red stripes, while the lower part was dark grey. Their hair was longer than that of the donkey and zebra. The South Afr. artist W. Battiss painted *The Quagga Races*, for which he won an award during an Olympic Art Competition in London in 1948.

QUAIL FIGHTS, a form of bird fights similar to cock fights, commonly practiced in India, mainly by women.

QUANFA, also *quanshu*, a hand-to-hand combat without the use of weapons, often identified with the Chin. martial art >GONGFU, of which it formed a part. It involves the following techniques: *Ti* – kicks, *Da* – strikes, *Shuai* – wrestling, *Na* – grappling. In Western countries it is commonly referred to as gongfu, while in Japan – as >KENPO (or *Kempo*).

QUARTERSTAFF, colloquially also shortened to 'staff', a type of stick and the Eng. fighting system using such sticks. Usually, the staff is 1.8-2.4m long,

tions a duel with Arthur-a-Blind, lasting more than 2hrs. The contestants supposedly used sticks 8½ ft. long, and the force of the blows was such that the 'forest thundered after each blow'. In the 12th cent., there were informal quarterstaff schools in Eng. cities. Towards the end of the Middle Ages, quarterstaff was promoted to a weapon worthy of people of nobler birth. Representatives of different social classes could compete against one another (as opposed to e.g. fencing, reserved for the knighthood). In 1540, Henry VIII granted a society known as the Maisters of the Noble Science of Defence a charter to organize their own schools. The program of the society included training in fighting with a 'plainge with the two hande sworde, the Pike, the bastard sword, the dagger, the backe sworde, the sworde and buckeler, and the staffe and all the other manor of weapons appertayinge to the same science'. The Maisters also organized public shows that considerably contributed to the growing popularity of fencing and quarterstaffing. In 1578, the subsequently famous Elizabethan writer R. Greene (1558-92) passed a test in quarterstaff at the Chelmsford school to receive a prize for outstanding achievements. In 1579, cadet Blinkinsop, when passing his final examination at the Leadenhall Artillery School had to fight against 6 masters of the backsword and 2-handed sword, as well as fighting sword-and-buckler and quarterstaff duels. In 1625, R. Peecke (also

Quadrigas on postage stamps issued for the Olympic Games in Athens (1896) and Antwerp (1928).

A quagga.

Q

known as Peeke or Peake) fought a famous fight against 3 Spaniards armed with rapiers, beating them in the presence of the Royal Council of War. Peacke described the event in a book with an exceptionally long title: *Three to One – Being an English-Spanish Combat Performed by a Western gentleman of Tavystock in Devonshire with an English Quarterstaff against Three rapiers and pommerds at Sherries in Spain in the Presence of the Dukes, Condes, marquises and Other Great Dons of Spain being the Council of War* (1626). It is impossible to recount all the literary sources describing quarterstaff fights. J. Dryden (1631-1700) was one of the most famous Brit. writers to recall quarterstaff duels. A quarterstaff fight was also described by W. Scott (*Ivanhoe*, XI, 1820).

Quarterstaffing declined in the 18th cent. but was revived as a sport in the mid-19th cent. In 1883, the first handbook appeared – T.A. McCarthy's *Quarterstaff. A Practical Manual with 23 Figures of Position*. Quarterstaff fights are still organized today during Eng. regional festivals.

QUBB, Arab. for 'ankle', a game whose rules we know little about, mentioned without a description in M. Ibrahim al-Majman's dictionary of Arab games and sports *Min al'abina ash-sha 'bbiya* (1983). It may be similar to >K'ABA in using die, with the outcome depending on the position in which the die landed on the ground.

QUERTERMILIK, a family of folk games from Greenland, where 2 sticks, about 10cm long and connected with a piece of strong rope (about 5cm long), are used in wrestling-like competitions. One of the participants lies down on the ground on his right side,

Quilles du poher.

embraces his left leg, bent at the knee, and grasps one of the sticks so that the rope comes out of his fist between the index and middle fingers. The other contestant stands astride above him, seizes the other stick with his right hand and tries to lift him off the ground. The one who lets go loses.

QUEŠTO, an Arab var. of >JUMP ROPE, esp. popular in Syria. Participants jump over a piece of rope revolved by 2 people.

QUIANG POLE PUSHING, a Chin. competition consisting of pushing an 8cm-thick and 3m-long pole between 2 contenders. It is practiced by the Qiang people of the Sichuan province. One contender is the attacker and the other is the defender. The defender sits on the ground and holds the pole in both hands between his legs. At the referee's signal the attacker starts pushing the pole. He wins if he manages to push the defender off the marked area within 5min. The pole must remain in its original position and it cannot be moved sidewise. If the defender is unusually strong 2 contenders are allowed to attack him. The game consists of men's and women's events. In the oral tradition the game is said to have been invented after the successful defense of a Qiang village during which the defenders pushed the attackers off the defensive embankment with spears. The villagers then got into an argument trying to resolve the question of who had pushed the attackers off most successfully. In order to settle the ensuing dispute the village leader set up a pole pushing competition between the arguing defenders.
Mu Fushan, et al., 'Qiang Pole Pushing', TRAMCHIN.

Quilles de loudeac.

Quilles an allez a dro.

QUILLES AN ALLEZ A DRO, a Bret. game of >SKITTLES, in which 9 wooden skittles are knocked down indirectly with a bowl which is 23cm in diameter and has a mortice to improve the grip. The bowl is thrown into a wooden semi-circle, from which it bounces back out at the skittles, each worth 1pt.

QUILLES DE LOUDEAC, a Bret. game of >SKITTLES, in which 6 wooden skittles worth 1pt each are arranged in 2 rows with a 7th skittle placed in front of both rows. The player throws the bowl at the 7th skittle, which should knock down one row of skittles, while the other row of skittles is knocked down by the bowl itself. If either the bowl or the 7th skittle knocks down pins in both rows, the throw does not count.
Consultant: G. Jaouen, FALSAB.

QUILLES DE MUEL, a Bret. game of >SKITTLES, in which a player takes 9 throws from a distance of 6m at 9 wooden skittles of various sizes using a 10-12cm bowl which is not round. If knocked down individually, the skittles are worth 1-9pts.
Consultant: G. Jaouen, FALSAB.

QUILLES DE POMEULEUC, a Bret. game of >SKITTLES, in which a player uses a 16-18cm bowl which is not round to knock down 9 wooden skittles of a different point value from a distance of 7m. The object of the game is to score exactly 36pts., exceeding which takes the player back to the score of 27pts. The bowl is not allowed to touch the ground before striking the skittle. If only 1 skittle is knocked down, the player scores that skittle's point value. If the skittle is knocked outside of the playing area, the point value doubles. The two major var. of the game are *quilles de Pont Ruellan* and *quilles de Marsac*.
Consultant: G. Jaouen, FALSAB.

QUILLES DU CAP, a Bret. game of >SKITTLES, in which 9 wooden skittles arranged in a square are knocked down with 5 stone bowls from a dstance of 7m. The skittle in the center is worth 9pts., the corner skittles – 5pts., and the remaining 4 – 1pt. each. To get the highest score, all the remaining skittles must stand intact. The goal is to obtain 36pts., exceeding which a player's score is taken back to 18pts. Cf. >KILHOÜ-KOZH.
Consultant: G. Jaouen, FALSAB.

QUILLES DU POHER, a Bret. game of >SKITTLES, in which 3 bowls (23cm in diameter and with a mortice) are thrown from a distance of 9m at 9 wooden skittles worth 1pt. each and arranged in a square. Each player has 3 shots.
Consultant: G. Jaouen, FALSAB.

QUILLES DE PAYS GLAZIK, a Bret. game of >SKITTLES, in which 3 bowls (22cm in diameter and with a mortice) are thrown from a distance of 8m at 9 wooden skittles worth 1pt. each and arranged in a lozenge. If all 9 skittles are knocked down in 1 shot, the player gets an extra turn.
Consultant: G. Jaouen, FALSAB.

QUINET, see>BATE.

QUINTAIN, full name *combating at the quinatin*, (Ital. *quintana*, Fr. *quintaine*, Dan. *quintanridninger* or *kvintløb*), part of an ancient military drill, also a separate competition in medieval >CHIVALRIC TOURNAMENTS [Lat. *quintana* or *quintanus* – a

Combating at the quintain at the Schloss Kaltenberg, Geltendorf, Germany.

path in an ancient Roman military camp, separating the tents of the 5th division from those of the 6th; Lat. *quintus* – fifth]. According to J. Strutt the creator of the quintain was an obscure Roman soldier called Quinctus or Quintas, hence the name. Mounted contestants tilted at a rotating shield resembling a knight on foot. In one hand this 'knight' held a small shield (the target for the contestant) and in the other – a metal ball hanging by a short chain; in milder versions, esp. for young squires, sand-filled bags were used instead. After hitting the shield the contestant had to slip through a narrow path near the quintain to avoid being hit by the metal ball as it swung round. This resembles passing between soldiers of different divisions in a Roman military camp, hence the name. The quintain figure was often made to look like a Saracen – with Arab features and a turban.

History. Wooden rotating figures that hit sluggish soldiers were known as early as Roman times. In times of peace this exercise was to be performed in the legions twice a day – in the morning and in the evening, before retiring for the night. Similar exercises were known in the courts of Byzantine emperors. A famous description of the quintain can be found in an anonymous 14th century Fr. text *The Establishment of Chivalry (Les etablissmentz des chevalerie).* The author writes about the need for practicing military skill with the aid of the *post-quintain.* He recommends that all competing be armed as in battle. An anonymous Eng. author in the poem *Knighthood and Battle (Knyghtode and Batayle)* refers to the exercise: 'Therewith a bacheler, or a yong knyght shal first be taught to stonde and lerne to fight'. The quintain also served as a target for spear throwing. Combating at the quintain was described among others by the medieval Eng. chronicler, M. Paris, in his monumental work *Historia Anglorum*: in the times of Henry III young Londoners practiced the sport; the king himself attended the event. The prize was a peacock. The quintain was practiced in the summer as well as in winter, yet Christmas was the most special occasion. Whoever missed the shield was jeered at. Anyone who hit the shield correctly but failed to get away quickly enough would get hit with a bag full of sand. In modern times annual quintain competitions are held in such places as the Ital. town of Foligno.

Bartolomeo Pinelli's illustration showing a folk pastime in Lazio in the 19th century, clearly modelled after the chivalric quintain.

QUOITS, [old Eng. *coyte* – throwing ring], an Eng. game wherein metal (mostly iron) rings are thrown onto short pins embedded in the ground (sometimes rope rings are used). The cast-iron ring used in quoits may weigh up to 9lbs. (4.082kg) and is usually flat. Most popular rings weigh 6lbs. (2.72kg) and have a special hollow for one of the fingers. The ring may not be wider than 2¼in. (57.2mm); the min. outer and inner diameters are, respectively, 8½in. (21.6cm) and 3½in. (8.9cm); the max. outer and inner diameters are 9in. (22.86cm) and 4in. (10.16cm). The pitch is 18yds. (16.5m) long. A metal hob is embedded at each end of the pitch, in the center of a circular area of hard clay with a diameter of 3ft. (91.4cm). The hob protrudes about 1in. (2.54cm) over the surface of the clay. The players stand on a line 54-60in. (137-152cm) from the hob. Quoits may be played individually or in teams, usually in pairs. 3pts. are awarded if the quoit lands on the pin, and this is called a *ringer* or *hobber*, just like in >HORSESHOE PITCHING. Placing one's quoit on top of the opponent's quoit ('a cover') scores 6pts. If 2 rings cover the opponent's quoits, the player is awarded 7pts. Two *hobbers* won by opposing players cancel each other out. If none of the players succeeds in placing their ring on the hob, the one with his/her ring nearer to the pin scores 1pt. The game is won by the first player to reach the agreed number of points, usu. 21. Much like in >LAWN BOWLING, each player may flip the opponent's quoit out of play, as what counts is the final positions of the rings; cf. >DECK GAMES.

History. Though some historians date quoits back to ancient times, the earliest preserved records date back to the times of Edward III (1327-77). Quoits were esp. popular in the Eng. Midlands, Lancashire and Scotland in Tudor times but declined in the second half of the 17th and in the 18th cent., becoming a folk sport. However, some people still played quoits in the Midlands, Lancashire and Scotland in the 1930s. Some regions still play quoits today.

A ring used for playing quoits.

Quoits Players, from London Illustrated News, *19th century.*

Playing at Quintain, c.1500, French Colorless glass, silver stain, and vitreous paint; The Cloisters Collection.
Balance quintain was a variation of the original knightly quintain to amuse those of a lower station: a seated player held up one leg, placing a foot against the foot of a standing player; one person then tried to upend the other. By the 15th cent., balance quintain was often played as a courting game, as is depicted here. In the later Middle Ages, stained-glass roundels often decorated the windows of affluent burghers' houses in cities of northwestern Europe.

MEN

20KM WALK OLYMPIC CHAMPIONS

1956 Leonid Spirin, URS 1:31:28
1960 Vladimir Golubnichiy, URS 1:34:08
1964 Ken Matthews, GBR 1:29:34
1968 Vladimir Golubnichiy, URS 1:33:59
1972 Peter Frenkel, GDR 1:26:43
1976 Daniel Bautista, MEX 1:24:41
1980 Maurizio Damilano, ITA 1:23:36
1984 Ernesto Canto, MEX 1:23:13
1988 Jozef Pribilinec, TCH 1:19:57
1992 Daniel Plaza, ESP 1:21:45
1996 Jefferson Pérez, ECU 1:20:07
2000 Robert Korzeniowski, POL 1:18:59

50KM WALK OLYMPIC CHAMPIONS

1932 Tommy Green, GBR 4:50:10
1936 Harold Whitlock, GBR 4:30:42
1948 John Ljunggren, SWE 4:41:52
1952 Giuseppe Dordoni, ITA 4:28:08
1956 Norman Read, NZL 4:30:43
1960 Don Thompson, GBR 4:25:30
1964 Abdon Pamich, ITA 4:11:13
1968 Christoph Höhne, GDR 4:20:14
1972 Bernd Kannenberg, FRG 3:56:12
1976 Not held
1980 Hartwig Gauder, GDR 3:49:24
1984 Raúl González, MEX 3:47:26
1988 Vyacheslav Ivanenko, URS 3:38:29
1992 Andrey Perlov, EUN 3:50:13
1996 Robert Korzeniowski, POL 3:43:30
2000 Robert Korzeniowski, POL 3:42:22

WOMEN

10KM WALK OLYMPIC CHAMPIONS

1992 Chen Yueling, CHN 44:32
1996 Yelena Nikolayeva, RUS 41:49
discontinued

20KM WALK OLYMPIC CHAMPIONS

2000 Liping Wang, CHN 1:29:05

RACE FOR A POUND OF TEA, a humorous event practiced in England, usu. between older ladies. It used to be an event of the Much Wenlock Games, sometimes called 'Olympic', held since 1850 in England. According to the local newspaper, a very exciting race took place:

[...] between old women, who acquitted themselves remarkably well, considering the disadvantage under which they laboured of not being provided with the 'Blomert Costume' attired in which they would have run capitally. A Mrs. Mary Speake bore off triumphantly the prize-woman's much beloved herb – amid the laud plaudits of her neighbours.

RACE WALKING, a track and field event in which competitors cover a determined distance on foot. The event originates from >PEDESTRIANISM – a competition in walking during a predetermined time or at a predetermined distance. The essence of race walking, as opposed to running, is – in accordance with the International Association of Athletic Federations' (IAAF) regulations – 'a progression of steps so taken that the walker makes contact with the ground, so that no visible (to the human eye) loss of contact occurs. The advancing leg shall be straightened (i.e. not bent at the knee) from the moment of first contact with the ground until the vertical upright position' (Rule 230, item 1, http://www.iaaf.org/InsideIAAF/index.asp). Prior to this update, the regulation had a slightly different wording: 'at each step, the advancing foot of the walker must make contact with the ground before the rear foot leaves the ground.' This wording lead to a series of conflicts, esp. since the moment race walking attained so high a level that even without running the dynamics of pushing the foot against the ground and retreating it resulted in a brief flying phase, which was against the IAAF's regulations. The only difference was that with some walkers the phase was so brief it was still not visible to the human eye, whereas with others it was discernible, at least to the judges, whose human eyes were the only ones to decide whether the progression was correct or not. A classic and recurring example of such disqualifications were performances of a Pol. walker R. Korzeniowski, e.g. during 1992 Ol.G. he was disqualified a few hundreds yards from the finish, although his position was clearly a medallist one. The fragment referring in the definition to the phase 'visible to the human eye', though still leaving room for interpretation, in practice substantially reduces conflicts between judges and walkers. However, as of this writing, judges are still barred from using any electronic gear to monitor the correctness of race walking events; point b of item 2, Rule 230 specifies clearly that 'All the Judges shall act in an individual capacity and their judgments shall be based on observations made by the human eye,' (http://www.iaaf.org/InsideIAAF/index.asp).

Along the road course there should be a min. of 6 and a max. of 9 judges, including the Chief Judge. At the Ol.G. and W.Ch., as well as World Cup competitions, all judges are members of the IAAF Panel of International Race Walking Judges. The first violation of race walking rules by a walker results in a caution from a judge but any subsequent violation leads to a proposal for disqualification being passed to the Chief Judge, whose decision is final. A competitor receiving a caution is shown a white sign with the symbol of an offence on each side. A walker disqualified during the race is informed by means of a red sign. Disqualified competitors are obliged to take off their starting numbers and leave the course immediately. During a competition, esp. of higher international rank, the course should be closed for any vehicle traffic. Refreshment points along a course up to 10km are located depending on the weather and at the organizer's discretion. In the case of races of more than 10km, the first refreshment point should be located at a distance of 5km from the start and then every 5km. If the race is held along the course forming a closed circuit, for a walk of up to 10km a single lap should not exceed 1.5km, for a walk of up to 20km – 2.5km, and in the case of longer walks, one lap should be about 2.5km. If held on an 'out-and-back' course, the distance out should not be longer than 5km.

Besides purely technical disputes, race walking has been a subject of debates concerning its practical usefulness and socio-locomotive essence. Critics of the sport claim the human's natural locomotive behavior, when intending to cover a given distance in the shortest possible time, is to break into a trot passing on to a full-fledged run. Therefore, any attempt at perfecting the skill of walking, where an artificial barrier on efficiency is placed by consciously withholding from running, is pointless and – moreover – deprives race walking of one of the objectives attributed to sport: perfection of the human body in adjusting to certain conditions. This point of view deems race walking an unproductive perfection of skills that can easily be exchanged for ones more effective and natural. However, arguments in favor of this discipline take root in the economics and ergonomics of human movement in the modern conditions of the civilized world. In a number of situations where a sustained and exhausting motion is inevitable, running turns out to be uneconomical or even impossible, e.g. during long army marches, sports trekking, pilgrimage trips, etc.; this is where the perfection of walking technique is most justified. Race walking can be used as an experimental laboratory, just like swimming where professional experience can serve as a basis for improving swimming skills generally. In addition, the urban environment, such as a crowded sidewalk, often precludes running but facilitates quick walking. Consequently, the patterns of ergonomic movement developed in race walking can prove beneficial in the modern world, provided such patterns are put to use in everyday life. In Eng.-speaking countries recreational race walking is referred to as >HIKING; often it is identified with tourism as opposed to competition.

History. The ability of efficient movement on foot has been of great importance for humans since time immemorial. At any given moment, the human capacity of quick mobility was decisive in the course of history. It applied to migrations of primitive tribes, then more and more developed groups and nations, war marches, religious pilgrimages, etc. The homeland of modern race walking is Great Britain where, in the 17th and 18th cent., competitions in long marches with prizes and financial bonuses, which has come to be known as pedestrianism, grew increasingly popular. Substantial influence on the evolving basics of future race walking was exerted by Englishman R.B. Allardicea, christened Captain Barclay (1779-1854), who set the first records in long-distance walking at the beginning of the 19th cent.

Race walking became an Olympic discipline in 1908 and was performed on the distance of 3.5km and 10mi. Later on, the distances of Olympic race walking were modified: in 1912-24 and 1948-52 it was 10km. A 50-km walk has been present at the Ol.G. since 1932 to this day (with the exception of the 1976 Ol.G. in Montreal); the 20-km distance has been regularly held since 1956 in men's competition.

The most outstanding figure in race walking before 1939 was Ital. U. Frigerio, a gold medallist at the 1920 Ol.G. in a 10-km walk and a 3-km walk, which has since been abandoned, and at the 1924 Ol.G. in a 10-km walk. During WWII the discipline was practiced in neutral countries. In 1943 a Swed. female walker A. Bengtsson Johansson set the world record, being the first to walk 5km in less than 25min. After 1945, the most spectacular achievements belonged to a USSR representative W. Golubnitchy, the winner of 2 gold medals in a 20-km walk during the 1960 and 1968 Ol.G., and a bronze medallist during the 1964 Ol.G. and the 1974 E.Ch.

The major organization guiding the development of race walking is the IAAF, whose former name the International Amateur Athletic Federation was changed in 2001 to the International Association of Athletic Federations. The sport's high rank among Olympic disciplines was for the most part achieved thanks to activists from the USSR, a judge, Froktovov, and a coach, Polyakov, who, as J. Arlott – a Brit. journalist and author of *The Oxford Companion to Sports and Games* – indicates, played an important role in maintaining high standards achieved in this sport. The Rus. school of race walking was present only during Ol.G., continental championships, and international matches, whereas they refrained from taking part in friendly meetings. It was also characterized by its focus on psychophysical resilience and strength with little regard for esthetic elements of style, which were indicative of Ang.-Sax. and Scand. schools. In the majority of countries the development of the discipline is administered by special committees within national track and field associations. There are, however, several independent race walking organizations, esp. of professional character, the largest being the World's Professional Walking Association. Since 1961 the Lugano Cup competition has been organized, which evolved into the race walking W.Ch. with both individual and team competitions, where 4-walker teams can compete. In the case of a team competition for 20 or 50km, times of all the members are added up and the 3 best teams are winners. Also in Great Britain there is an independent Race Walking Association.

Women have practiced race walking since the beginning of the 20th cent. In 1923, a women's race was included in the Eng. Championships, first at a distance of 880yds. and then other ones (since the beginning of the '70s, 2.5km among others). In 1956, a women's 5-km race walk was incorporated into the Scand. Championships. A frequent form of women's race walking competition was a correspondence tournament – because the discipline was missing from the program of many international competitions. The most outstanding female walkers were: Swed. Bengtsson (the most eminent achievements in 1943-46) and Nilsson (1957-68), and Brit. Farr (1962-70). Only at the 1992 Ol.G. was women's race walking, for the distance of 10km, finally inaugurated.

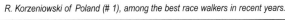

R. Korzeniowski of Poland (# 1), among the best race walkers in recent years.

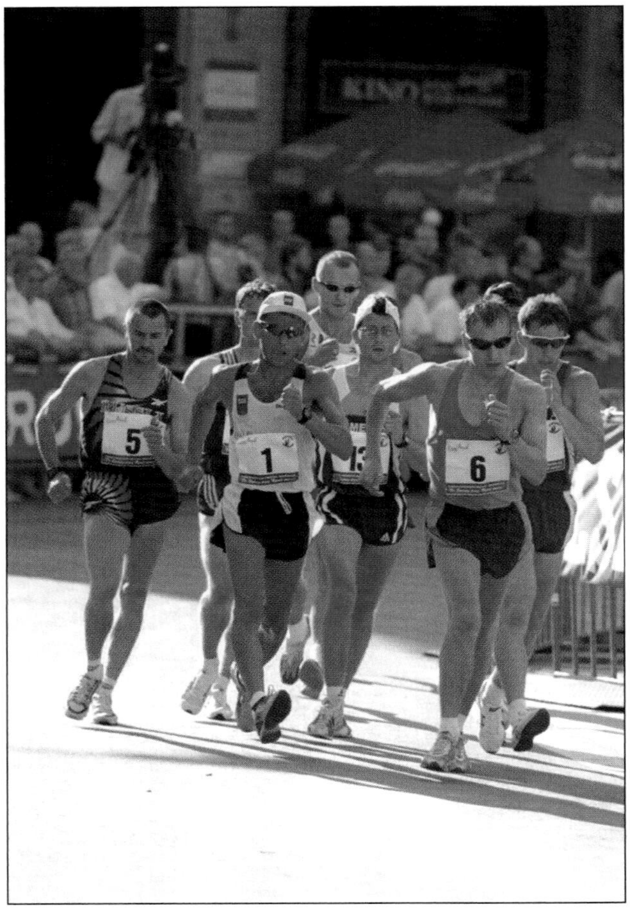

RACES ON TOILET HOPPERS, a form of competition initiated in 1999 by a N.Zealand restaurant owner R. Kirkland. The toilet hoppers have small wheels and handle-bars, and are propelled by pushing the feet against the ground. Races are held in restaurants, on tracks marked around the tables, and are an indication of the fun-loving nature of modern sport.

RACING WHILE PUTTING ON COLORFUL BLOUSES AND SKIRTS, a trad. Chin. running game of the Miao minority from the Zhaotong region in the province of Yunnan, played exclusively by girls and women. Each contestant brings with her a skirt and a blouse of any color. The master of the game places the blouses on the starting line and the skirts at the half-distance line. Depending on the local tradition the running distance is 50-100m. The contestants line up on the starting line and at a signal grab their blouses and put them on, while running towards the skirts. A contestant that reaches the half-distance line and has failed to put on and button her blouse must stop and do so, before she is allowed to pick up her skirt and continue the race. At the last stage the contestants run while putting on their skirts, which they must do before reaching the finish line. The fastest one wins the race.

Mu Fushan et al., 'Racing While Putting On Colorful Blouses and Skirts', TRAMCHIN, 112.

RACING WITH JARS ON THE HEAD, a form of competition popular in Korea and among the Kor. minority in China. Little girls begin to practice walking with small jars on their heads to acquire the skill of running with large jars filled with water. At the age of 10 they enter the competition usu. held during various Kor. festivals. There are 2 main types of events: walking and running with a jar filled with water on the head and participants are divided into age categories: young girls, younger and older married women, and older women. On the start line the jars are placed in front of the contestants on the ground. At a signal each girl must place the jar on her head without spilling any water and begin the race, during which she may not support the jar with her hands. Spilling the water or dropping the jar disqualifies the contestant. The racing distance varies, usu. 60-100m for running races and larger distances for walking races.
Mu Fushan et al., 'Racing with Jars on the Head', TRAMCHIN, 70.

RACKETS, see >RACQUETS.

RACQUETBALL, a racket game played mainly indoors, individually or in pairs, combining the elements of >HANDBALL as known is Eng.-speaking countries (bouncing the ball off a wall without a racket) and >SQUASH. Racquetball is played on a standard court, 40x20ft. (12.2x6.1m), with front and side walls 20ft. (6.1m) high, and a back wall at least 12ft. (3.6m) high. The ball has a diameter of 5.71cm and weighs 39.7g. The racket, max. 55.88cm long and 25cm wide, is fixed to the player's hands using a special leather strap loop and has a gut or synthetic string. Players must wear protective goggles. The game developed very quickly in the 1950s, and peaked in the '60s and '70s. In 1968, the International Racquetball Federation was established, which is recognized by the International Olympic Committee. So far, racquetball has not been included in the program of the Ol.G., but – since 1995 – it has been an event of the PanAmerican Games. The game is popular in at least 70 countries, with the number of players exceeding 17 million.

RACQUETS, also *rackets* [from Ital. *racchetta*, diminutive *retichetta* – net, or from Fr. *raquette*], a game using rackets and a ball bounced off one or many walls. The surface of the court may be granite, asphalt or concrete. The hardness and smoothness of the walls and the ball make the game the fastest and most dangerous racket game. The court was originally 80ft. (24-38m) long and 10yds. (9.14m) wide; today, the length has been set to 60ft. (18.28m). The face and side walls are 30ft. (9.14m) or even 40ft. (12.19m) high, while the back wall is 15ft. (4.57m) high. Formerly, courts were usually outdoors but today indoor courts predominate, with outdoor courts only used in warmer climates. The ball has to be bounced off the face wall above special lines drawn on it. There are usu. 2 lines. The so-called service line (or cut line) at a height of 9ft. 7½in. (2.94m) in Brit. racquets, or 8ft. (243.84cm) in Amer. racquets (and, with increasing frequency, the international standard today), which the ball has to hit the wall above after the serve and the play line at a height of 2ft. 2in. (66cm) which the ball should hit the wall above during play. About 1895 the so-called telltale, a wooden board, was introduced in the USA on the front wall, covering it up to that height, or, according to some sources (e.g. P. Cummings's *Dictionary of Sports* and *Encyclopaedia Britannica*), up to the height of 27in. (68.58cm). The board makes a dull sound after the ball hits it, indicating an invalid ball under the play line. The back line, 36ft. (10.97m) from the front wall, divides the court into 2 parts, the front and back. The ball, after rebounding off the front wall, must land between that line and the back wall. The back part of the court is divided by the so-called middle line (or error line), dividing the back part into 2 service boxes (or service courts), each 24ft15in. (731.52x457.2cm). After a serve, the ball must land in the service court opposite to that from which it was served. In the Brit. var., there are 2 boxes in the corners by the back line, 7ft. 6in. square, used as the actual service courts. (In the Amer. var., there was initially just one square, 2ft. 8in., on the right hand side). The entrance onto the court is in the middle of the back wall, which is cov-

ered with felt. There is a spectator gallery behind the back wall, where the 'marker' who counts the points sits, too. The game starts by drawing lots, usu. by a spin of the racket: depending on which side the racket lands on, the winning player chooses a side of the court. Then, the other player servers for the first 'rally' or 'bully'.
The gut-strung racket has a round head with a diameter of 17.8-20.3cm, and a handle 76.2cm long. The diameter of the ball used to vary up to 4in. (10.2cm) but the ball used today is 1in. (2.48cm) in diameter, and weighs 1oz. (28.35g). Formerly, the ball was made of packed wool covered with goat skin, but today it has a plastic core covered with thread and a polyethylene coat, taped for better grip. Formerly, 50-100 balls were allowed during a match; today, 10-20 balls are sufficient. The players play side by side, positioned near the back wall, and alternately striking the ball against the front or side walls. Striking the ball against the ceiling or the back wall gallery is prohibited. The ball, after being hit by

one player, must be received by the other before the second bounce. One may not hit the ball after the second bounce, or twice in succession. However, volley strikes – that is after a rebound off the wall but before the ball touches the ground – are permitted. A point (called an 'ace') is scored if a valid ball is not received by the opponent, or if he strikes it into one of the prohibited areas. One of the best moves is sending the ball near the corner between the front and side wall, where it is most difficult for the opponent to strike it back. The first side to reach 15pts. wins. However, if both sides (singles or doubles) reach 13pts., an advantage of 3-5 aces is required to win. The number of advantage points is at the receiver's discretion. At 14-14, however, the number of advantage points required to win is 3, and the game goes on until one of the sides reaches 17 aces without the other scoring. The scoring rules are similar to those of >VOLLEYBALL in that only a 'hand-in' player (the one who serves for the rally) may score points, while if the 'hand-out' side (those who do not serve) win the rally, they first become hand-in and are allowed to score only in the next rally. In doubles, the players of one side serve alternately, with the exception of the first rallies of the match – the same player serves until the first rally is lost. The serve is made from the service square, with the player at least 1ft. (30.5cm) from each of the sides. A serve is invalid if 1) the ball strikes the wall under the service line; 2) the ball, after rebounding off the front wall, hits the court before the short line; 3) the ball bounces beyond the

short line but on the wrong side. However, if the opponent decides to receive such a bad ball, the game continues. If he refuses the ball, the serve must be repeated. If a serve hits the telltale board or the ground, a double error occurs and the serve passes to the opponent without a right to repeat it. In the USA and Canada, serves may not be repeated at all. The last player to serve in a given game is the first to serve in the next. There are 3-5 sets in a match, or even up to 7 in the USA. There is an informal rule that singles matches are 5 sets long, while doubles matches are 7 sets long. The side to win the most sets wins the match. During play, the player who has just hit the ball should make room for the other player as quickly as possible. However, the tempo of the game does not always allow that. If an umpire controls the game, one can appeal any decision apart from stepping on the line at serve. Individual clubs also have their own rules, that sometimes differ in particulars and have to be agreed upon immediately before the

game. A simpler and less expensive var. of racquets has evolved from the Amer. variant. It uses a court almost 4 times smaller than in the original racquets and is known as >SQUASH RACKETS.
History. The game dates back to the Middle Ages, and the earliest forms were played in Italy and France. From there, it traveled to England in the 12th-14th cent. It is considered the predecessor of many modern raquet games. In the 18th cent., the game spread throughout England, and was also played in courts with only one wall. The Eng. writer W. Hazlitt (1778-1830), besides a eulogy of the >FIVES player Cavanagh, d.1819, also mentions a whole group of famous racquets players in his essay *The Indian Jugglers*:

The only person who seems to have excelled as much in another way as Cavanagh did in his, was the late John Davies, the racket-player. It was remarked of him that he did not seem to follow the ball, but the ball seemed to follow him. The four best racket-players of that day were Jack Spines, Jem Harding, Armitage, and Church. Davies could give any one of these two hands a time, that is, half the game and each of these, at their best, could give the best player now in London the same odds.

Racquets developed most rapidly among the inmates of London's Debtor's Prison in Fleet Street. A prison yard, surrounded by walls, thus became the prototype of the racquets court. C. Dickens (1812-72) mentioned the game in one of the chapters of *The Pickwick Papers*. When Pickwick arrived at Debtor's Prison, he noticed that:

A game dating back to the Middle Ages, racquets was finally codified about 180 years ago by a prisoner of London's Fleet Street Gaol.

R

WORLD SPORTS ENCYCLOPEDIA

The area formed by the wall in that part of the Fleet in which Mr. Pickwick stood was just wide enough to make a good racket court; one side being formed, of course, by the wall itself and the other by that portion of the prison which looked (or rather would have looked, but for the wall) towards St. Paul's Cathedral ... Lolling from the windows which commanded a view of this promenade were a number of persons [...] looking on at the racket-players, or watching the boys as they cried the game.

In the earliest stages of the game's history on the continent, the ball was hit with the hand, much like in >FIVES. Later, special bats with flat ends came to be used. The use of rackets was probably due to the fact that some upper class prisoners were also detained at the prison, having had contact with games such as >ROYAL TENNIS, which used similar rackets at that stage in its development. In 1875 *The Book of Racquets* was published in the USA, where the author suggested that racquets had derived from the same old game as royal tennis: 'both games have so much in common that it is impossi-

and a doubles event was first held in 1890. Strict written rules were first published the same year, written by the tennis historian J. Marshall together with a racquets specialist Major Spens. Until the turn of the 19th and 20th cent., the Brit. and Amer. versions of the game developed in loose contact, which led to a number of differences. In 1928, a Brit. national team visited the USA, inaugurating the International Racquets Cup. The tour opened a period of renewed contacts between the 2 var. of the game, and they started to become increasingly similar again after 1945. However, minor differences still persist. In 1949, P. Cummings claimed that they were mainly of a social character: 'nowadays, it is a rather exclusive game, limited to the rich and well-off in a few clubs in the United States but played on a much wider scale in England [...]. We have 10 or 12 clubs in the USA today, most of them relatively expensive and elitist. This makes the game expensive, and is added to by the hardness of the ball: many nets and racket heads are broken by it' (CUM, 338).

stick or how exactly it is used. Players of both teams try to hit their opponents with the ball. The team who receives the ball become 'rotten', while the other team – 'fresh'. As a result, each team tries to get rid of the ball as quickly as possible. The game starts when one of the players of the team in possession of the ball tries to hit one of the players of the opposite team with the ball, while the rest of the players of that team run away in all directions. If a player is hit, his team have to make up for the loss by hitting one of the opponents. If a player catches the ball to avoid being hit, he cannot further move with it but has to throw from wherever he caught the ball (a step forward with one foot is allowed). Players may avoid being hit in other ways, too, e.g. by running or jumping away, dodging, crouching, hiding behind an opponent etc. If the ball falls outside of the pitch, the responsible player must bring it back. Cf. >DODGEBALL.
J. Møller, 'Radden-fersk', GID, 1997, 1, 28.

RADIO-ORIENTEERING, formerly *amateur radio direction finding* (ARDF) or *fox hunting*, a sport using radio receivers and transmitters, combining elements of >ORIENTEERING and amateur short-wave radio. According to official rules:

A competitor uses a specialist radio receiver with a directional antenna, a map of the competition area and a compass to find a number (3-5) of low power transmitters ('foxes') concealed in a forest. As the transmitters use the same frequency (or very similar frequencies), they may not transmit continuously. A five-minute transmitting cycle is used. During the first minute of the cycle, 'fox 1' transmits, and the remaining transmitters are off. After the first minute is over, 'fox 1' turns off to be replaced by 'fox 2' and so on up to 'fox 5', after which the cycle begins again. [...] The organizers place the transmitters so that consecutive numbers do not neighbor on each other [...].

Each transmitter has an attached stamp that the competitors use to confirm that they have reached all the targets. Competitors set out in groups, usu. 3 persons each, in 5-min. intervals. They enter the transmitters on a special card, and they decide themselves in what sequence they wish to localize the transmitters. Usually, competitors run the sections of the course between the transmitters. After a competitor has located all the transmitters, he has to run to the finish line. The overall length of the course on which the transmitters are placed is 4km for juniors and up to 10km for adults. There are both individual and team competitions in 2 bandwidths, 3.5MHz short wave and 144MHz ultra short wave according to the rules of the International Amateur Radio Union (IARU). There have also been attempts at using 28MHz transmitters. The competitor or team who takes the shortest time to locate the transmitters and arrive at the finish line is declared the winner.
History. It is an object of dispute whether radio-orienteering was invented in western or eastern Europe. It seems that it began evolving at more or less the same time in both parts of the continent. However, it was a 'private' amateur sport in the west (under the auspices of the IARU), while in eastern Europe it was quickly covered by the patronage of the armies of the Warsaw Pact, and was developed with the view to augment military training. W.Ch. and E.Ch. are organized under the auspices of the IARU. Radio-orienteering techniques have changed with the rapid advances in microelectronics. Authors who can remember the beginnings of the discipline recall how even 15 years ago each 'fox' had to be controlled by a referee looking at his stopwatch and monotonously repeating 'this is fox 1, this is fox 1...' or using a Morse key to send signals. Today, automatic transmitters are used, programmed before the competition starts, and the referee's role is limited to monitoring the competitors, or perhaps turning on a reserve transmitter should such need arise, and, of course, assuring that the transmitters do not 'walk off'. In the past, competitors would participate in pairs, one of them carrying an RBM1 radio (weighing about 15kg) on his back and a directional antenna mounted on a broom stick. The other carried a container with batteries and the map and compass. As the RBM had to be connected to batteries, one could hardly speak of such a tandem 'running'. Later, individual radio locators appeared (lighter, smaller and more sensitive), and today competitors mainly use small devices weighing about 0.5kg that they can use to locate the foxes literally on the run. Ordinary topographic maps were used in the past,

Once the favorite pastime of the inmates of London's Debtor's Prison in Fleet Street, racquets developed into both a popularly enjoyed discipline in England, and a rather elitist sport in the United States.

ble to separate them historically'. The game became really popular about 1820, thanks to the activities of R. Mackey, formerly a prisoner of London's Fleet Street Gaol. Mackey formulated the first relatively stable rules. In 1824, he organized the first larger public tournament. However, sporadic events turned into regular W.Ch. only a few decades later. In the meantime, the game was adopted by Harrow College students in 1822, where a 4-wall court was used, and the ball was at first allowed to rebound off all of them. The exclusive Rackets Club was estab. at Woolwich in 1840 by the officers and cadets of the Royal Artillery; the first indoor court was built there. In 1853, the game was adopted by the tennis-and-cricket Prince's Club, where the architecture of the court underwent noticeable changes, and the game became a prestige social skill practiced at bourgeois clubs, among officers of the British Army, and students. It blossomed in England in the 1860s and 1870s. Then, it spread to a number of countries outside England: Argentina, India, Canada, the USA, and Malta. It arrived in the USA via Canada c.1849. Initially, it functioned in its original Brit. form but then some alterations were introduced. It had been called 'rackets' earlier, but then the American spelling of 'racquets' caught on. In 1850, the first permanent club and court, the Broadway Racquets Club, was estab. The foundation of the New York Racquets Club in 1875 added considerably to the popularity of the game. The London Queen's Club (estab. 1887) became the Brit. center of the sport. In 1888, amateur Eng. singles championships were started,

The main racquets events are open for both professionals and amateurs.
The first World Singles Championships were held in 1862. The amateur Sir W. Hart-Dyke was the winner. The best player of the late 19th and early 20th cent. was the Eng. professional P. Latham, multiple world champion between 1887 and 1902; Latham was also an outstanding royal tennis player. W.Ch. have been organized annually since 1951. The years 1954-70 were the era of G. Atkins, who is considered to have been the best player of all time. However, best players have not always been professionals, e.g. during the 1937 W.Ch., the Eng. amateur champion D.S. Milford beat the Amer. professional N. Setzler. In addition to the W.Ch., there are national championships in individual countries. The international Tuxedo Gold Racquet is a prestige event. The game made a single appearance during the 1908 Ol.G.s in London (the Brit. var.). Brit. players won all the medals: E. Noel won the gold, H. Leaf – silver and J. Astor – bronze.
C.N. Bruce, *First Steps to Rackets*, 1926; A. Danzig, *The Racquet Game*, 1930; S. Kittleson, *Teaching Racquetball. Steps to Success*, 1993; E.O. Pleydell-Bouverie, *Rackets*, 1890; E. Turner & W. Clouse, *Winning Racquetball. Skills, Drills and Strategies*, 1996.

RADDEN-FERSK, Dan. for 'rotten-fresh', a Dan. ball-and-stick game where 8-20 players participate, divided in 2 teams. The stick is used to defend oneself from being hit by the ball. Sources do not provide any information on the dimensions of the

but they have been replaced by special orienteering maps, which represent the terrain much more faithfully, esp. with respect to the so-called 'passability', or the possibility of running between trees or bushes. The events themselves have changed, too. Stationary radio location, where the competitors located a target from 2 or more spots, and their marking it on the map was compared against the actual location of the transmitter, has been completely given up. The short wave (3.5MHz) and ultra short wave (144MHz) running events have survived, and new events have appeared, such as the 'marathon', where the competitors run to the mid-way point with one receiver, change it there and run back to the finish line with another. Other new events include chasing a mobile fox, relays etc.

'Co to jest radioorientacja sportowa', *Informator Polskiego Związku Radioorientacji Sportowej*, 1999, 2.

RADKI, [Ger. *Rad* – wheel or *Rädchen* – small wheel + Pol. ending *–ka*]. A type of >SCOOTERS competition. Radki scooters are referred to by the same name [Sing. *radka*]. The sport was once popular among children and teenagers of western Pol. and Ger. cities. The sport first became popular at the beginning of the 1920s, when 2 elements of the modern industrial civilization became commonplace – steel bearings and asphalt. The main element in which a radka was different from an ordinary scooter was steel bearings used instead of the wheels. Radki were usu. assembled on a DIY basis, using second-hand bearings from machines, vehicles and farming equipment, which were good enough for riding the scooter on asphalt surfaces, much like in some older roller skates. In most radka types, the handlebar and footboard were made of simple wooden boards, connected with nuts and bolts that had small rings instead of heads. Some of the bolts, usu. 10-12, were screwed into the handlebar board and the transverse ending of the footboard so that one could put a long nail through them and connect the 2 parts of the radka. Instead of wheels, 1 large bearing was mounted in special cuttings in the handlebar board, and 1 or 2 bearings were mounted in the footboard. Since about the mid-19th cent., the Pol. city of Poznań had had a large number of factories where such bearings were used or produced. Before WWII, Poznań also had Poland's most ex-

Radki.

tensive network of asphalt streets (other Polish cities had mostly cobble stone streets where radki riding was impossible). As a result, many spontaneous competitions were organized in Poznań. The riders liked to imitate the famous Poznań motorcycle racers of the 1930s, '40s and early '50s, such as J. Mieloch and I. 'Igol' Stefański, mounting pieces of cardboard with their numbers on the handlebars. Mieloch's number 4 was the most popular one. Radka owners often showed contempt towards the owners of regular factory-made scooters, with rubber-rimmed wheels. Such ordinary scooters moved quietly which prevented the users from imitating their favorite motor cyclists. In contrast, radki made quite a lot of noise, esp. that the riders usu. moved in packs of 4-10 which accumulated the rattle of the bearings against the hard surface, making it not unlike the passing of a bulldozer. The conflict between radka riders and scooter riders was also one between the poorer and more affluent children. The richer could afford a real scooter, while the poorer built their own with the help of their fathers. As a radka was relatively easy to build, children would make them as early as at an age of about 10-12. One could see 'expert panels' in the street, discussing new 'technologies', or even making small repairs or improvements. Boys traded bearings obtained from various sources. Usu. children aged 14 or older did not ride radki any more. Girls did not use them, either, apart from exceptional situations. There were also official radka competitions included in the programs of children's games organized by newspapers. The era of radki came to an end when the growing numbers of cars made it impossible to ride freely along streets. Riding on sidewalks was out of the question, as the flagstones, esp. when uneven, made it impossible to ride vehicles that used small bearings instead of wheels. Also, relatively cheap bicycles appeared after WWII. The last radka was seen on Poznań's streets in the mid-1960s.

RADLEY GAME, a ball game played until 1882 at Radley Public School, England. The rules were partially borrowed from >HARROW FOOTBALL. Two teams with 15 players each (including the goalkeeper) participated. The pitch was 100yds. by 60yds. (91.4x54.86m). The goal was 3yds. (2.75m) wide, and had 2 posts but no crossbar. A point was scored

after the ball was shot between the posts at any height, even above the posts (as long as the ball passed between the imaginary extensions of the posts upwards). The ball had to be kicked so that it bounced off the ground before passing between the posts, and the goalkeeper was not allowed to catch the ball before the bounce. The teams changed ends after each goal. The ball could be caught by hand and carried for a distance of 3yds. (2.75m) but only after receiving it by air from another player – one was not allowed to pick the ball up from the ground using his hands.

RÆV OG ULV, [Dan. *ræv* – fox + *og* – and + *ulv* – wolf]. A Dan. game where 2 participants, the 'fox' and the 'wolf', marked with scarves of different colors, are supposed to catch the other players, who try to run away. When they catch a player, they give him the scarf. To protect themselves from being

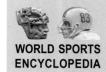

Rafting.

caught by the fox or wolf, the players may form pairs or threes, respectively. The victory of the 'fox' or 'wolf' depends on the number of players they have caught.
J. Møller, 'Ræv og ulv', GID, 1997, 2, 66.

RÆVEJAGT, Dan. for 'fox hunt', [Dan. *ræv* – fox + *jagt* – hunt]. Two players are chosen as 'foxes', while the remaining ones are 'dogs'. The foxes run away, sprinkling confetti as they go. After a few of minutes, the dogs are unleashed and begin chasing the foxes following the trail of confetti, which may, of course, be misleading. Cf. >PAPER CHASE.
J. Møller, 'Rævejagt', GID, 1997, 2.

RAFFBALL, [Ger. *raffen* – to reap + *Ball* – ball], a game much like handball, with a number of var., 3 of them the most widespread ones. The first uses a pitch 200x25m, without goals. A point is scored after the ball is carried outside the pitch over the opposing team's end line. The second var. uses a 60x20m pitch with goals 2.5m in width, delimited by flagpoles 2m high. In front of the goals, across the whole width of the pitch, there is the goal box, about 5m long. Attacking players may not enter the box. The third var. is played on a 80x20m field, with the goals, 2.5m wide, marked in chalk on the goal lines. In front of each goal, there is a semicircular field with a radius of 8m; again, attacking players may not enter the field. In all these var., a match lasts 2x15 min. Running with the ball is forbidden. A stationary or walking player may not hold the ball for more than 3sec. Players may only run without the ball. It is forbidden to snatch the ball from an opponent's hands, or tackle him.

History. According to the tradition, raffball is believed to descend from the ancient game of >HARPASTON. Modern raffball was invented by the Ger. K. Koch, who suggested introducing it in Brunswick schools in 1891. The rules and regulations were written down in 1897. Raffball was played in many Ger. workers sport associations between 1900 and 1933.

RAFTING, a mountain sport involving rafting down dangerous rivers in broad pontoons looking much like rafts. Rivers are rated into 6 classes: I – easy, without major obstacles; II – moderate, with relatively weak currents and not too difficult to navigate; III – difficult, with many rocks and changing currents, requiring huge physical strength for ma-

A variety of rafting practiced on snowy slopes.

Rafting.

neuvering but with relatively stable banks; IV – difficult, with large numbers of obstacles and rapids, capsizing of the raft possible, with sparse chances of helping the rafters; V – extremely difficult, with violent currents and sharp, usually rocky, inaccessible banks; VI – theoretically unrunnable rivers, with steep descents, narrower than the pontoon at some places, with rapids and waterfalls. All the same, the most difficult class VI rivers attract the best rafters and are sometimes passed. Rafting on rivers of the higher classes is sometimes called 'white water rafting', from the white foam on the water. There is also a marine var. of rafting, where the participants set out on the open sea to face all dangers, including storms.

History. Rafting is a manifestation of man's penchant for negotiating difficult waters. The first Amer. trappers had experiences still available to modern rafters, transporting animal hides along difficult mountain rivers. They borrowed some techniques from the Amer. Indians, who used their leather canoes and wooden dug-outs to navigate difficult rivers. During the conquest of the Amer. Wild West, so-called flat-boats were a distant prototype of modern rafts, carrying settlers' possessions up the Mississippi and Missouri Rivers. Though those facts have not had a direct technical influence on modern rafting, they have given rise to a kind of 'spiritual' approach to negotiating difficult rivers in the USA. This became truly possible only after the appearance of modern technologies. Rafting became

Ram fights.

a real sport as late as the 1960s, when nylon and neoprene came to be used in the construction of pontoons instead of the vulnerable rubber. The sport gradually gained popularity in the 1970s, and by the '80s and '90s had grown to be an extremely popular pastime. It is also popular in Asia, esp. in India, where it is practiced on some Himalayan rivers, including the upper course of the Indus and its tributaries in the Ladakh region of the state of Himachal Pradesh, on the Sutley in Garhwal, Uttar Pradesh, and on the Tista in Western Bengal. Rafting is a sport for people seeking adventure and the rush of adrenaline and has some connections with ecological philosophies. An extreme form of rafting is *power rafting*, also called *jet-boot*, in which the rafters swim down dangerous mountain rivers at high speeds in power hydrorafts.

L.D. Armstead, *Whitewater Rafting in Western North America*, 1990; S. Curtis, E. Perry and N. Strung, *Whitewater*, 1976; J. Tomlinson, 'Dangerous rivers', *Encyclopedia of Extreme Sports*, 1996.

RAID GAULOISES, a comprehensive performance test initiated by the Fr. journalist G. Fusil. The object of the rally is to reach the finish line using all means needed to negotiate the natural hazards encountered, such as swamps, mountains, rivers etc. The rally is a 10-day team event, with 5 participants in each team. The course is about 400mi. long. Each year, the rally is organized in some other location with demanding terrain, such as Madagascar, Borneo, Patagonia etc.

RAIOLA, see >JOGO DA RAIOLA.

RALLY AND PRECISION FLYING, a discipline of sport aviation where individual pilots or 2-person teams (pilot plus navigator) compete in various fields of flying. There are day and night events, precision events, fly-ins and flights for punctuality, landing precision, regularity in covering the course stages, often combined with finding terrain marks based on a map or photographs. Rally and precision flying W.Ch. have been organized since 1976, while rally flying championships – since 1980.

RALLY, a form of sport competition or a tourist event where the participants are supposed to cover a set cross-country course within a defined time, passing through a number of control points (defined in regulations binding for all the participants). Depending on how the course is covered, there are foot rallies and rallies using mechanical vehicles: bicycles, canoes, motorcycles, cars or airplanes. Depending on the organization and character of the course, there are also such types of rallies as AUTOMOBILE RALLIES, >ENDURANCE RALLY, >MOTORCYCLE RALLIES, >OBSERVATION TRIAL, >STAR RALLY,. Cf. >RADIO-ORIENTEERING.

RAM FIGHTS, a type of animal competition, in which trained rams take a short running start, butt heads and lockhorns with one another. The sport is cultivated in many world cultures. It has a long tradition in e.g. India, where women are allowed to participate, both as spectators and animal teasers. Ram fights are also popular in some regions of C Asia, where they are often held as part of the New Year's celebrations. In the cities of Chiwa and Buchara in Uzbekhistan they were organized during the Red Flower festival. In Europe they are still popular among the Basques, where they are called >AARI TALKA (also spelled *ahari talka*, Span. name *lucha de cameros*). They have been known here since ancient times and are held on village or city squares, while more important events take place in the corrida arenas and are watched by thousands. Fights are administered by judges and accompanied by betting. The local community is known for specialist breeding of fighting rams and among the best known breeders were G. Aguirre from Icíar, A. Pagaizabal from Irun and J. Albisu from Tolosa. A popular ram fighting center is Azpeitia, 'the mecca of ram fighting', while high class breeds of rams come from the villages of Arrona, Errezil, Urrestilla, Azkoitia, Elgoibar and Asteasu. Cf. Mong. >RAM RACES (MOUNTED). R. Aguirre Franco, *Aari talka*, DRV (2nd ed., 1978, 68-71); C. Moreno Palos, *Lucha de cameros*, JYTE (1992, 270-2); J. Velasco, 'Nacidos para combatir cameros de pelea' in *El Diario Vasco*, 3 Oct. 1999.

RAM RACES (MOUNTED), a trad. sport of the Uigurians, Kazakhs and Tajiks of C Asia, both within the countries of the former Soviet Union and in China, esp. on the wide plains of Xinjiang. Races on rams are most often held during the Chin. New Year. Before the start the rams are held down to facilitate mounting. At a signal the rams jump off with the riders on their backs and run along rows of spectators towards the finish line. The rider of the fastest ram wins an award.

'Le course au mouton dans le Xinjiang', *Les sports traditionnels en Chine*, Beijing, 1991, 14.

RANA, LA, a Span. game mainly played in local inns. It has equivalents in the Fr. game of *jeu de grenouille*, Port. *jogo de sapo*, Flem. >PUDEBAK, and Eng. >TOAD IN THE HOLE.

RANGE THE BUS, an Eng. children's game. The field is divided into 2 halves by a row of caps. Each of the 2 teams participating tries to 'abduct' as many opponents as possible, and put the hats on their heads. The team who thus 'crown' more of the opposing team's players, and have at least one or more players without hats, is declared the winning team.

RANGELN, an Aus. var. of folk wrestling. The wrestlers may take grips on the opponent's clothes and

All 375lbs. of Mr. Joe Pike sail through the air to an appreciative audience during the mudpit belly flop at the 2nd annual Summer Redneck Games in East Dublin, Georgia.

body. They wear special outfits with short leather trousers as a main component. The fight starts in an upright position but is continued on the ground. The wrestler who succeeds in forcing a touch-fall is declared the winner.

RAPTIM LUDERE, in ancient times and the Middle Ages, any ball game where the players fight for the ball, i.e. there are moments where the ball is seized, snatched or knocked out of the hands of the opponents [Lat. *raptim* – steal, abduct + *ludere* – play]; cf. >DATIM LUDERE and >EXPULSIM LUDERE. In certain local situations, e.g. in the language of Lat. documents (e.g. bans on games), the name was applied to the local var. of such games known in the specific area.

RASHES, an Eng. children's game, deriving from an old custom associated with the harvesting of rush for wicker products [*rashes* – Derbyshire dialectal form of 'rush', the plant]. Children would compete in carrying green rush from the shores of nearby lakes or ponds to their villages. After the rush was transported, it was put into one large pile, and the children would compete in weaving simple products which they would then hang in their homes until the next spring or Christmas cleaning. The weaving was preceded or accompanied by dances, during which tufts of the rush were thrown up into the air, forming a 'rain' one had to escape. The ritual was accompanied by trad. songs, e.g.:

Mary Green and Bessy Bell,
They were two bonny lasses;
They built a house in yonder hill.
And covered it with rashes.
Rashes, rashes, rashes.

A.B. Gomme, 'Rashes', TGESI, 1898, II, 452-453.

RASKOLNITSY HORSE RACING, a form of >HORSE RACING held before the holiday of *maslenitsa* as a way of stimulating nature, land fertility and animal reproductiveness.

RATSEPAEKSAM, Est. for 'sailor's examination'. A game requiring agility and co-ordination, where a participant (usu. female) sits on a round log or bottle lying on the ground, places the heel of one foot on the toes of the other and tries to thread a needle in this position. According to folk tradition, if a girl succeeds in performing the feat, she will get married soon.
M. Värv et al., 'Traditional Sports and Games in Estonia', TSNJ, 1996, 32.

RAU'S PLAYGROUNDS, a type of playgrounds for children and teenagers initially inspired by the idea of >FRÖBEL'S PLAYGROUNDS, and then evolving independently under the auspices of the Playground Fund estab. by the Warsaw banker, industrialist and philantropist, W.E. Rau (1825-99). Cf. >JORDAN'S PLAYGROUNDS.

RAX, [Scot. Eng. *rax* – drag], also *raxie-boxie* [approximately 'drag-boxing'] and *King of Scotland*. A Scot. game where 2 teams participate, standing on lines at opposing ends of the field. When all players are ready, one of the players at the edge of a row shouts, 'Cock!' or 'Caron!'. At the referee's signal, the players run towards the opponents. In the passing area, each of the participants tries to catch and hold on to an opponent, and drag him as a prisoner. The team who, after a number of rounds, thus eliminate all of the opposing players, is declared the winning team. In the island of Tiree in the Hebrides, a similar game is called *Dyke King* or *Dyke Queen* (for girls), and the start signal is 'King!' or 'Queen!'. In the US and some other Eng.-speaking countries, a similar, but not identical game is called >RED ROVER (TGESI, II, 106-7). In Poland, a similar game is known as >PRZERYWANE WOJSKO.

REAL TENNIS, see >ROYAL TENNIS.

REBASE PÜÜDIME, Est. for 'catching the fox', a trad. folk game. 'Three players participate: two catchers and one fox. The catchers have a piece of rope, 3-4m long, which they use to make a loop large enough to catch the fox. They put the loop on the floor, and the fox tries to pass through it. When he is inside it, the catchers quickly tighten the rope to catch the fox'.
M. Värv et al., 'Traditional Sports and Games in Estonia', TSNJ, 1996, 31.

RECOGIDA DE MAZORKAS, see >LOKOTX EDO SOKOR APOSTUA.

RED ROVER, a children's game, esp. popular in the USA. A part of a field or lawn is divided into 2 parts. A group of players form a line in one of them, holding hands. They encourage the other group, standing about 30ft. away, to break this 'chain' and get to the other side by chanting the following rhyme:

Red Rover, Red Rover,
Come over!

The group who succeed in breaking the other chain wins. The game, together with the rhyme, has many different variants. In one of them, individual players are called one after the other, to try to break the chain and get to the finish line. This was reflected by the rhyme:

Red Rover, Red Rover,
Let Tommy (Johnny, etc.) come over!

The game is similar to Ind. >KABADDI but it never gained comparable social status. In India, the variant is played not only by children but also by adults, and is actually one of the most popular sports, while it has remained a children's game in the USA. However, it was most popular in 19th-cent. Liverpool, from where it spread to other regions of the UK and other Eng.-speaking countries. A similar, albeit not identical, game, known exclusively in some of the Hebrides, was called >RAX, 'raxie-boxie' or 'King of Scotland'. In Poland, a similar game is known as >PRZERYWANE WOJSKO.

REDNECK GAMES, an event that started as a parody of the 1996 Atlanta Olympics. Each year thousands of people come to East Dublin, Georgia, a former Olympic wrestling training camp to celebrate the Redneck Games. L-Bow, the self-proclaimed 'King of the Rednecks' and the official mascot for the Redneck Games sets it off with a ceremonial lighting of Bubba's barbeque grill using a propane torch constructed from beer cans.
Initially christened 'Bubbalympics' the games attract folks with rather unique disciplines like Hubcap Hurl, Mudpit Belly Flopping, Spitting Melon Pips, Tractor Pulling. The most interesting ones seem to be Bobbin' for Pig's Trotters and Armpit Serenade. In the former, contestants have their heads down in a bowl of fetid water and try to retrieve as many pig's feet as possible in 2min. Still undefeated is M. Davis. Armpit Serenade champion J. Upshaw won the title playing a faux-flatulent rendition of 'Dixie' with his hand under his armpit. Each winner receives a large trophy topped off with a squashed, empty beer can.

REGATA STORICA, the most important and spectacular of all rowing events held in Venice annually, on the 1st Sunday of Sept., the others being Regata di Caorle, Regata di Burano and Regata di Sant'-

Regata storica in Venice.

Making a splash at the Redneck Games in East Dublin, Georgia.

R

Sailing regattas.

Above and below: regata storica on Canal Grande in Venice.

Regata storica in Venice.

Erasmo. The first information of regata storica dates back to the 2nd half of the 13th cent., although the origins of the event must reach further in history, for at that time it was already a popular form of competition in Venice, which – being a sea-inclined city – needed experienced oarsmen, whose training involved taking part in rowing races. The etymology of the word *regatta* is uncertain: some derive it from *riga* (line), others from *aurigare* (to race), other yet from *ramigium* (the act of rowing). The Venetian term *regata* entered most European languages to designate a boat competition.

In the Reneissance *regattas* were mainly organized by associations of young patricians (*Compagnie della Calza*), which in the 16th century was entrusted to noblemen selected by the government, known as regatta directors. For centuries *regattas* were part of spectacular celebrations accompanying the arrivals of Doges, Dogaressas, St Mark's procurators into Palazzo Ducale, as well as visits of distinguished guests of the Republic.

R.s. begins with the Historical Procession, a parade of Venetians dressed in XVIth century costumes, that commemorates the arrival in Venice of Caterina Cornar, the Queen of Cyprus. It is followed by a cortege of the *bissioni* (8-oared gondolas), the *balotine* (6-oared gondolas), the splendid ceremonial gondolas, and the multi-oared boats representing various rowing clubs.

The *regattas* are held in Canal Grande, which has several reference points: *spagheto* – a rope stretched across the starting point (in front of the Castello public gardens), *paleto* – a pole placed in the centre of Canal Grande in front of the church of Sant'Andrea de la Zirada, around which the boats must turn for their return course, and *machina* – a wooden, richly decorated construction which marks the finish line, on which VIPs sit and on which the prize winning ceremonies are held. There is a separate competition for the young (Regata dei Giovanissimi), for women (Regata delle Donne), for boats called *caorline* (Regata delle Caorline) and – the most enthralling event – for 2-oared gondolas, which are numbered and differently colored. All that is witnessed by a cheering crowd of passionate and excited Venetians mixed with tourists. After the *regat-*

Rejse sig med to på ryggen.

tas are over, the canals come to life with myriads of boats, while the streets and squares swarm with crowds, watching numerous artistic displays.

REGATTAS, from the name of the event organized by Venetian gondoliers [Venetian Ital. *regatta*]; see >REGATA STORICA. All types of competitive events using vessels (yachts, canoes, rowing boats, windsurfing boards; see >COMPETITIVE ROWING, >KAYAKING, >ROWING AND PADDLING SPORTS, >SAILING, >WINDSURFING, >YACHTING). The term is used universally, also to refer to boat races that have nothing to do with the Eur. sailing or rowing traditions, such as >DRAGON BOAT RACING; cf. also >REGATTAS OF OYSTER DREDGERS. All the same, it is dubious whether the term may be applied to sailing competitions held on land or ice, such as >ICE BOATING, >ROLLER SKATE SAILING, SAND YACHTING, >SKI SAILING.

REGATTAS OF OYSTER DREDGERS, regattas organized at the mouth of the Truro River, near Falmouth, Cornwall. The old tradition, dating back to the Middle Ages, is continued today by the Falmouth Working Boat Association.

REJSE DEN ARME VÆDDER, Dan. for 'raising the poor ram'. An old Dan. game. The participant sits on the ground with a stick under his knees. He puts his hands under the stick, between his knees, and bows his head so that he can touch his forehead with his fingers. In this position, he begins to roll so as to get up on his feet.
J. Møller, 'Rejse den arme vædder', GID, 1997, 3, 31.

REJSE EN VÆDDER, in full *at rejse en vædder*, Dan. for 'raising the ram', [Dan. *rejse* – raise + *vædder* – ram], a form of acrobatic show, performed individually. The acrobat sits cross-legged on the ground, with his left foot over the right one. Then, he grabs the toes of his right foot with his right hand, and his right ear with the left hand, and tries to stand up. The show may be arranged as a timed competition.
J. Møller, 'At rejse en vædder', GID, 1997, 3, 19.

REJSE MAST, Dan. for 'raising a pole' or 'mast'. A simple weight lifting event. One competitor lies down on his back, the other crouches on the upper sides of his feet, pressing them to the ground, and takes a grip on the upper parts of the lying one's legs – usu. at above the knees or somewhat further up – and then tries to lift him off the ground into an upright position. The lying competitor has to tense up by placing his hands on his neck or stretching them above his head to make the task more difficult.
J. Møller, 'Rejse mast', GID, 1997, 3, 15.

REJSE SIG MED ET HALMSTRÅ OVER SKULDEREN, Dan. for 'standing up with a blade of grass on one's shoulders', [Dan. *rejse* – raise + *sig* – oneself + *med* – with + *et* – a + *halmstrå* – grass blade + *over* – over, on + *skulderen* < *skulder* – shoulders]. A Dan. exercise where the competitor kneels down, throws a piece of rope, folded in half, over his shoulder, and puts his left foot into the loop. By pulling on the rope, he lifts the foot off the ground. The task is to stand up from the kneeling position without letting go of the rope or touching the ground with the left foot. In Finland and Sweden, a participant of a similar exercise would wind the rope around his left leg and pull it up towards the body.

J. Møller, 'Rejse sig med et halmstrå over skulderen', GID, 1997, 3, 39.

REJSE SIG MED ET LÆSSERTRÆ, Dan. for 'standing up with a pole', [Dan. *rejse* – rise = *sig* – oneself + *med* – with + *et* – a + *læssertræ* – wooden pole]. A Dan. folk game. The competitor lies down on his back, while one end of a 4-m wooden pole is placed on his chest so that it touches his chin. Another participant presses the pole down to the ground at the other end. The task is to stand up with the pole by gradually moving under it towards the other person.
J. Møller, 'Rejse sig med et læssertræ', GID, 1997, 3, 104.

REJSE SIG MED MAND PÅ RYGGEN, Dan. for 'rising with somebody on one's back', [Dan. *rejse* – rise + *sig* – oneself + *med* – with + *mand* – man + *på* – on + *ryggen* – the back]. A basic weight lifting exercise. One of the participants gets down on all fours, while the other sits down on his shoulders. The task is, for the crouching one, to rise, and for the one sitting on his shoulders, to stand up on his shoulders.
J. Møller, 'Rejse sig med mand på ryggen', GID, 1997, 3, 91.

REJSE SIG MED TO PÅ RYGGEN, Dan. for 'standing up with two [people] on one's back', [Dan. *rejse* – raise + *sig* – oneself + *med* – with + *to* – two + *på* – on + *ryggen* – the back]. A basic form of weight lifting. One participant lies down on his stomach, while the remaining 2 lie down transversely atop him facing opposite directions. They clutch each other's feet (almost at their chins). The task for the first participant is to stand up. First, he gets up on all fours, and then grabs the other 2 participants with 1 hand and stands upright. After doing so, he makes a number of spins and lets the other 2 go, so that they fall to the ground on either side of him.
J. Møller, 'Rejse sig med to på ryggen', GID, 1997, 3, 88.

REJSE TIL JERUSALEM, Dan. for 'traveling to Jerusalem'. A Dan. game where one participant bends down, with the next bending down behind him and taking a hold on his hips, and so on. After a file is formed, a 'rider' mounts on each of the participants' necks, and so they all set out on a ride in a circle. This leads to a gallop, during which most of the participants fall over or fall off their mounts.
J. Møller, 'Rejse til Jerusalem', GID, 1997, 3, 58.

RELAY WITH BALLS, a school game for 2 teams. The teams choose their captains. Two parallel lines are drawn on the field, about 10 spaces apart. The teams line up in rows about 5 spaces apart behind the first line. The captains stand behind the second finishing line. At the referee's signal the captains throw the balls to the first players of their teams, who catch the ball and throw it back to their captains and then go to the end of the row. The captain throws the ball to the next player, then the third until all the members of one team have gone, thereby winning. The game can be played without captains. The players run with the ball from the start line to the finish line from where they throw the ball back to the next player and go to the end of their row. When more players participate, they are divided into 4 teams. A square is drawn on the pitch – its size depends on the number of players; usu. it is about 1m

per player. Inside the square a circle, about 1.5m in diameter, is drawn. The players of each team stand along one side of the square, facing the center. One player from each team stands in the circle, facing his team holding a ball. At the referee's signal they throw the ball to the player on the right end and run to the left end. The catcher runs to the circle and from there throws the ball to the next player on the right and so on. The rules forbid the players from stepping across the lines that form the square without the ball. Bad throws must be repeated.
I.N. Chkhannikov, 'Sztafeta z piłkami', GIZ, 1953.

RELAY WITH CLUBS, a school racing game. The contestants form 2 rows, one behind the other, 3-4 paces apart. In front of each row a start line is drawn. Circles, each about 1 pace in diameter, are drawn a few to several paces from the start line; clubs are put in their centers. Clubs are also given to the first runners. At the referee's signal the runners start to run towards the circles, when in the circles they change the clubs, return to the row, pass the club to the next player etc. The team which first completes the runs wins.
I.N. Chkhannikov, 'Sztafeta z maczugami', GIZ, 1953, I, 19-20.

RELAY WITH HOOPS, also relay with obstacles. A school game with 2 teams of any number of players competing. The pitch is divided by 2 parallel lines, about 30 paces apart; one is the start and finish line and the other – the halfway line. Between the start line and the halfway line there is a hoop, about 1m in diameter, stood vertically, through which the contestants must pass; at the halfway point there is another hoop, about 60cm in diameter, which each contestant must put over his head and let fall to his feet; when the hoop has touched the ground he can start running back to the finish line. The players wait at the start line, lined up, the teams being about 4 paces apart. The player returning to the start line touches the next player in the row who starts to run towards the hoop; the first player joins the row end. The team whose players have all formed the row as it was at the beginning wins the game.
I.N. Chkhannikov, 'Relay with hoops', GIZ, 1953.

RELAYS, 1) a sports event in which a defined distance is covered by a few contestants, each running a different section or leg of the main distance, e.g. an athletic 4x100m relay race. Most often a relay is a 4-man event. The most typical relay races include: >TRACK AND FIELD RELAY, >SKI RELAY, and >SWIMMING RELAY; there are also >TORCH RELAYS and a number of relay races organized on different holidays or anniversaries etc.; 2) a type of running contest whose aim is to carry an object, usu. a wooden or plastic baton passed from one relay member to another relay member, to a finish line in the shortest possible time.

History. Various types of relay races have been known since ancient times. In ancient Greece one of the most popular relay events was a torch relay (>LAMPADEDROMIA). Some cultures have developed modern forms of relays, e.g. the Swed. >WÄDE-DELÖB, one var. of which involved a contest of a single competitor against a team of females. Here a large key was employed instead of a baton. The S.Amer. >LOG RUNNING is also a relay event esp. popular among indigenous tribes (see also >GE INDIAN RELAY).

RETI, an old Maori form of sledding down a sandy slope which was generously sprinkled with water so that slippery mud formed. The sleds used were simple structures made of a wooden block with a wide runner, much like that of a snowboard. Other var. of Maori sand sledding were called *horua*, *panukunuku*, *torehorere*.
Source: R. Love, *Sport among the Maori People*, 'Te Ao Hou', Winter 1952.

RHYTHMIC GYMNASTICS, known in some countries as *artistic gymnastics*. This leads to the understanding that it is a sporting discipline whose main foundation is the perfection of not only physical abilities but also the rhythm and aesthetics of the movements of the body. Rhythmic gymnastics is based mainly on competition in performing exercises in time to music with various pieces of equipment, such as a skipping rope, hoop, ball, club or ribbon. Important international competitions comprise 4 individual events, selected by the Fédération Internationale

de Gimnastique (FIG), as well as the individual all-around and team competition. In individual competition a competitor performs a series of routines using the different pieces of equipment. The points total gained in the 4 events forms the end result of the competition. The nature of the movements performed is at the competitor's discretion but must come within the scope of the FIG's general rules, defining the content and degree of difficulty of particular sequences. The exercises are judged twice by a 5 person jury, once for technical merit, once for artistic impression. 10pts. is the max. mark. The final total is the average of both sets of marks. The 8 best competitors then take part in the final, performing their routines once more. The final total is composed of the marks from both rounds. Teams of 6 with 2 reserves take part in competitions. Each team performs 2 different routines judged by 2 juries – one of which marks technical merit, the other artistic impression. As in individual competition the average of the 2 marks gives the end result. Again, as in individual competition, the top 8 teams go through to the final, in which each team performs only its best routine. The final total is composed of the marks from both rounds. In Olympic competition the team qualifying round is held before the games and only the final takes place during them.

The individual exercises are performed on a soft surface (usu. a carpet) or sometimes a harder one, measuring 12x12m with a 1m protective border. Competitors perform in leotards with bare feet of gym slippers.

History. The origins of rhythmic gymnastics can be traced back to the ancient >GYMNASIA, which entailed public displays by the ephebans in time to music and singing. Its modern beginnings, however, go back to the end of the 19th cent., when a Swiss educator, musician, and composer, E. Jaques-Dalcroze (1865-1950), laid the foundations. Its basic principle was 'uniting the conscious and unconscious, linking intellectual, emotional, neural and muscular functions through the help of music, so as, in this way, to create a feeling of order, balance and clarity in the human organism'. His system gained widespread publicity and became included in many Eur.

WORLD SPORTS ENCYCLOPEDIA

R

Alina Kabaeva of Russia performs her ribbon routine during the Women's Rhythmic Gymnastics Final of the Sydney 2000 Olympic Games in Sydney, Australia.

Passing the baton in an Olympic relay.

R

**WORLD SPORTS
ENCYCLOPEDIA**

and Amer. schools of gymnastics. At the same time, during the first years of the 20th cent. there was a fashion for restoring the human body's natural beauty through aesthetic movement, at one time termed natural gymnastics. A large role in this aestheticizing of sporting and gymnastic movement was played by borrowings from Classical times, such as famous actors and Hellenophile intellectuals posing as ancient Gk. statues, such as Myron's *Discus Thrower*. These efforts, in spite of their naive character, gained wide publication in the press and contributed to an increase in the significance of the aesthetics of the human body by referring to an epoch in which physical beauty was less threatened than in the course of the later development of civilization, and was at the same time very highly valued by ancient Gk. society. In 1928 was published F.E. Bjoerksten's *Women's Gymnastics* (*Kvinnogymnastik*, 1929), which pointed to the particular importance of female bodily aesthetics and methods of shaping it. This book was one of the main impulses behind the process of rhythmic gymnastics developing as a separate field. It developed as a competitive discipline aimed exclusively at women and young girls after WWII, in large part thanks to the interest shown in it by the sporting authorities of the USSR. In 1948 the first large scale competitions took place. The first W.Ch. were held in 1963. To start with competitors from the USSR and Bulgaria dominated. The development of rhythmic gymnastics is controlled by the Female Technical Committee of the FIG. In 1983 a world cup was held the first time, continuing to the present day. It was included in the Ol.G. in Los Angeles (1984), initially as an individual competition and since 1996 in Atlanta as a team event. Individual Olympic champions include: L. Fung (Canada, 1984); M. Lobatch (USSR, 1988), A. Timoshenko (EUN, 1992), E. Serebryanskaya (Ukraine, 1996), and Y. Barsoukova (Russia, 2000). The team Olympic champions include Spain (1996) and Russia (2000).

RIDE PICK-A-BACK, also *ride piggy-back*, a family of spontaneous games, where one partner carries the other on his back. The pairs can compete in a race or fight, as well as in ball games, e.g. >OURANIA, a game known in ancient Greece. The riders ('kings') competed with the carriers ('donkeys') – when a 'donkey' caught the ball, he could change places with his 'king'. Pick-a-back riding has rarely been considered a sport in its own right. Ang.-Sax. countries are an exception, noting the following var. of the game:

KNIGHTS, 'two big boys take two smaller ones on their shoulders. The big boys act like horses, while the younger ones seated on their shoulders try to pull each other over. The 'horses' may push and strike each other with their shoulders, but must not kick or trip each other up with their feet, or use their hands or elbows. The game is usu. won by the horse and knight who throw their opponent twice out of three times.' J. Strutt about the knights: 'A sport of this kind was in practice with us at the commencement of the fourteenth century.'

SHIVER THE GOOSE, a boys' game. Two persons are trussed somewhat like fowls; they then hop about on their 'hunkers', each trying to upset the other – Patterson's *Antrim and Down Glossary*.

A.B. Gomme, 'Knapsack, Knights, Shiver the Goose', TGESI, 1894, I, 311-312; 1898, II, 192.

RIDE, Dan. for 'to ride'; the Dan. equivalent of >RIDE PICK-A-BACK.

RIDING, (Ger. *Reitsport*, Fr. *l'hippisme*, Ital. *equazione*, Span. *caballeria*, Du. *paardensport*, Port. *equitaçao*), a family of sports, where contestants are mounted on animals able to support a man's weight, esp. horses (>EQUESTRIAN EVENTS), camels (>CAMEL RACES (MOUNTED)) and elephants (>ELEPHANT RACES (MOUNTED)). It includes such exotic sports as >QUAGGA RACES, as well as humorous disciplines, e.g. >RAM RACES

(MOUNTED). Riding was a characteristic feature of many cultures and even those who did not know it initially (e.g. Native Amer. Indians, who did not have animals large enough for this task), achieved great skill, once horses were introduced (>INDIAN HORSEBACK RIDING). Many cultures evolved forms of equestrian acrobatics, such as the Hung. >PUSZTA ÖTÖS or >DZHIGITOVKA, popular among Cossacks and peoples of the Caucasus. Some forms of equestrian archery are included in this classification, e.g. >ORIENTAL ARCHERY, >YABUSAME, >MONGOLIAN ARCHERY, >PARTHIAN ARCHERY. Most disciplines of >CHIVALRIC TOURNAMENTS were of equestrian character. Many sports games are mounted, e.g. the old Chin. >JIQIU, the Jap. >DAKYU, the Persian-Arab >AL SAWALJAH, >OUTDOOR POLO, >POLOCROSSE, >BUZKASHI. Such disciplines as >KYS KATCHAR, >SAIS and >ELEPHANT POLO are closely linked to riding. Attempts are made to popularize >HORSE RIDING FOR THE DISABLED.

RINALDO RINALDINI, a running game, see >PLINIE.

RING BOWLS, an Austrl. game similar to >LAWN BOWLS but using wooden rings instead of bowls, with their centers of gravity deliberately displaced. The rules are the same as in lawn bowls. The game uses a lawn track, 15m long. The object is to place the rings as close as possible to a heavy disk called the 'kitty'. The player or team (2-4 people) who succeed in placing their disks closer to the kitty are declared winners. The only place in Australia where ring bowls are played is Holdfast Ring Bowls Club in Adelaide.

RING RIDING, see >RINGRIDING. Cf. >ALKA, >QUINTAIN, >RUNNING AT THE RING.

RING TOSS, also called *the rings at the goal*, a simple tossing game, popular in the 1940s and '50s in the USSR and other socialist countries. It was

Elena Vitrichenko of Ukraine performs her routine with the ball at the World Rhythmic Gymnastics event at Bercy, Paris.

Gymnast Audrey Valero of France performs in the rope exercise discipline of the women's rhythmic gymnastics competition in Great Britain.

Christiane Klump of Germany performs her routine with the hoop during the rhythmic all-around competition at the 1992 Barcelona Olympics.

Italy perform their routine with the clubs during Rhythmic Gymnastics at the 2000 Olympic Games in Sydney, Australia.

practiced as a supplementary sport during PE classes and as a recreational sport. Ring toss resembles Eng. >QUOITS. The rings used for the game were made of plywood, 5-6mm thick, 23cm in outer diameter and 16cm in inner diameter. The peg was 50cm high, 3cm thick at the bottom and 1.5cm thick at the top. It was placed on a cross-stand with arms 50cm in length. The peg was stuck into the ground on a cross-stand in such a way that it swayed after a toss. In simpler var. the pegs were stuck directly into the ground. The rings were tossed onto 3 pegs arranged perpendicularly to the throwing line, 5m from one another. The closest peg was situated 6m from the throwing line. In another var. of ring toss 9 pegss were used. They were arranged in 3 rows of 4, 3, and 2 pegs respectively, on a wooden, portable board 150x100cm. The board was placed on 2 legs, 60cm above the ground. Rings which missed the pegs fell into a net attached beneath the board. Each player was entitled to a number of throws, set at the beginning of the game. A ring on a peg scored 1pt. for the thrower. A standard playing set consisted of 15 rings.
I.N. Chkhannikov, 'Rzucanie kółek do celu', GIZ, 1953, 60-61.

RINGBOLD, a Dan. rounders-like game. The pitch is divided into 2 parts of non-defined dimensions but large enough to accommodate a max. of 20 players, 10 in each team. More than 10 circles (usu. 14) are drawn on the ground, each with a diameter of 1m. They are arranged in a square whose diagonal coincides with the middle line of the pitch, so that half of the circles (usu. 7) are in one half of the pitch. The circles, on the perimeter of the square, are 6 steps away from one another. The distance between the circles close to the middle line is 3 steps. The exact number of the circles depends on the number of the players. Those players for whom there are not enough circles may play the role of 'buccaneers' or 'pirates' (fribyttere). The first team, usu. called the 'whites', place one player in each of the circles on one side of the middle line, with the rest of the team taking positions in front of the circles on the other side. The other team, called the 'blacks', take equivalent positions: where the 'whites' are inside the circles, they take positions in front of them, and vice versa. In each of the teams, the player positioned in the circle that is most distant from the middle line is called the 'king' (konge). The players positioned inside the circles are called 'insiders' (indespilerne, Sing. indespiler), while those outside the circles are called 'outsiders' (udespillerne). The object of the game is to pass the ball between the insiders and outsiders in one team so as to prevent the players of the opposite team from intercepting it. If they succeed in doing so, they pass it between them in the opposite direction. So, the 'outsiders' perform the double task of alternately blocking the ball from the 'insiders' of the opposite team, or attacking them to intercept the ball. The 'outsiders', while trying to intercept the ball, may not enter the circles, while the 'insiders' may not leave them to catch the ball more easily. Points are scored when outsiders succeed in passing the ball to their 'king'. Successful passes to the remaining players are important tactically but do not score. If the rules are broken, the referee may grant the non-offending team an additional pass, or a point without a pass.
J. Møller, 'Ringbold', GID, 1997, 1, 39.

RINGETTE, a sport similar to >ICE HOCKEY but played with sticks without blades. It was meant to be a winter sport, an alternative of hockey for women, but it quickly developed new variants played on in-line skates both in- and outdoors (>IN-LINE RINGETTE).
An ice ringette match starts with a free pass in the middle of the rink, much like in football. After the referee's whistle, the player starting the game has 5sec. to pass the hollow rubber ring (used instead of a puck) to a team mate. One player may not carry the ring the full length of the rink. No more than 3 players of a team may be within one zone of the rink at any given time. The object is to score goals on the net of the opponents.
History. The game was invented by S. Jacks of North Bay, Ontario, Canada in 1963. This is how his wife Agnes recalls the endeavors of her husband, who died in 1975:

For a long time Sam had seen a need for a sport for females, a team sport, on ice using skates [...]. It was approximately in 1963 when he experimented with the basic rules on outdoor rinks [...]. The equipment was a conglomeration of used figure skates, broken hockey sticks, deck tennis rings or any kind of rubber rings available. Pieces of coloured cloth were tied around the players arms to identify positions. As time went by Sam had many little teams in West Ferris and surrounding areas playing on outdoor rinks and using boys' skates. He never doubted for a moment that his game would flourish. He'd drive his friends crazy promoting it.

[Ringette Review, Jan. 1994]

In 1963, Jacks presented his idea to the Northern Ontario Directors of Municipal Recreation Association. The association ordered R. MacCarthy, Recreation Director for Espanola, Ontario (near the northern shore of Lake Huron) to organize a trial game. The first match was played during the winter of 1963-64. Teams from an Espanola girls' high school participated. The rules were finally codified by Jack's friend H. Lindner in 1966. The first club was founded in Sudbury in 1967. In 1969, the Ontario Ringette Association was established. In 1971, the first open tournament was organized at Oshawa, Ontario. The Manitoba Ringette Association was estab. in 1972, and the Quebec Association – in 1973. Alberta followed in 1974, and then all the remaining Canadian provinces. The growth of ringette was sometimes accompanied by tension resulting from separatist tendencies in Quebec – the local association withdrew from the national federation in 1978 to rejoin it in 1981. To avoid this kind of conflict in the future, a bilingual Eng. and Fr. standard was introduced in ringette organizations at the all-Canadian level, and the bilingual principle has been rigorously followed ever since. The all-Can. association, Ringette Canada, was estab. in 1974. The first all-Can. tournament was held in Halifax, Nova Scotia, in 1976. In 1975, a ringette match was televised for the first time in history; the discipline had kindled public interest. In 1977, the Ringette Hall of Fame was founded. In 1985, the number of players exceeded 20,000. After 1985, ringette saw some international expansion as well. That year, the game was introduced into the USSR (after a visit by the St. James Ringette Association of Winnipeg, Manitoba), and Japan (thanks to B. Mattern). In 1986, the game caught on in Finland and the Finnair International Ringette Tournament was held. The same year, the sport reached Australia and N.Zealand as a result of a tour by the Maples Ringette team. Can. championships have been organized since 1979, and a world cup has been held every second year since 1990. The following teams have been world champions: Gloucester (Ontario, Canada, 1990), Helsinki (Finland, 1992), St. Paul (Minnesota, USA, 1994), Stockholm (Sweden, 1996), Moncton (New Brunswick, Canada, 2000).
Ontario is the strongest center of ringette, with about 120 clubs and 10,763 players (but only 500 men) in 1999. It is estimated that a further 5,000 play the sport for recreation outside organized clubs. In all, there are about 35,000 players and 1,200 coaches in Canada. About 60 large national and international tournaments are played each year.
There are 9 unusual age categories in the game (not encountered in any other sport): the 'bunnies' (7 and under); 'novice' (9 and under), 'petite' (11 and under), 'tween' (13 and under), 'junior' (15 and under), 'belle' (18 and under), 'deb' (23 and under), 'intermediate' (21 and over) and 'masters' (30 and over).

RINGO, a game similar to deck tennis (see >DECK GAMES). It was invented independently from deck tennis by the Pol. sports official and social worker W. Strzyżewski. The rubber ring used (the 'ringo' itself) is thicker than in deck tennis (section diameter 2.5-3cm; total diameter 17cm, weight 160--165g), with a hole in the middle. A volleyball court is used, divided into halves by a tape (rather than a net, like in deck tennis) at least 1cm wide, with ribbons (25cm long) suspended from it every 20cm. A standard volleyball net may be used instead of the tape. The height of the tape depends on the ages and skills of the players: 200cm for players aged 10 and younger, 224cm for players aged 11-13, and 243cm for players aged 14 and older. The dimensions of the court also depend on the ages of the players: 6x12m for players aged 13 and younger, 8x16m for players aged 14-18, and 8x18m for players aged 19 and older. Women aged 30 and older,

and men aged 35 and older use the 18 and under dimensions. The formats of the game are singles, doubles or triples; men, women or mixed. Matches are supervised by an umpire and 2 linesmen. The game starts with a drawing to decide the ends; serves are played from behind the back line. Violating the back line during the serve scores a point for the opponent. The serve is played at the umpire's commands 'ready' and 'go'. Singles matches use 1 ringo, while doubles and triples – 2 ringos. If 1 of the 2 ringos falls to the ground in doubles or triples, the exchange is continued with the remaining 1 until a point is scored. Players may catch the ringo with any hand, but they have to use the same hand to return it. After catching the ringo, a player may take 4 steps to decelerate but he may not take a run up for a throw. Drops, somersaults, jumps and dodges are allowed. The time elapsed before the ringo is returned is not limited but if a player holds the ringo for too long, the referee may impose a 5-sec. limitation. A match lasts until one of the sides scores 15pts. (a 1pt.-advantage is sufficient). After one of the sides reaches 8pts., the players change ends. A point is scored when: 1) the ringo, after being correctly passed to the opponent's side of the court, is not intercepted before it falls to the ground; 2) the ringo lands outside the boundaries of the court; 3) a player touches the tape or net with the ringo held in his hand; 4) the ringo hits the tape or net twice in succession; 5) the flight of the ringo is incorrect (there is uneven 'pulsation' or 'somersaulting'; horizontal revolution around the vertical axis is correct).
History. The rules of ringo were first laid out by W. Strzyżewski in 1959. In 1973, the first Open Warsaw Championships took place; later, regular Pol. Championships began to be organized. In 1974, some matches were played during the 2nd Polonia Sport Games in Cracow (for expatriate Poles). Later, Czech citizens of Pol. descent who had taken part in the Games organized a Beskid Cup in what was then Czechoslovakia. In 1990, the 1st World Ringo Tournament was organized in Warsaw, under the auspices of the Pol. Committee for

WORLD SPORTS ENCYCLOPEDIA

R

William Merritt Chase, Ring Toss, 1896, oil on canvas.

Ringo.

Ringtennis.

Physical Culture and Tourism, the Warsaw Metropolitan Curia and the St. Michael Congregation (with congratulatory letters from Pope John Paul II and the UN Secretary General J.P. de Cuellar). This produced the momentum for subsequent tournaments. Ringo has even reached the campus of Boston University at Agassiz, Maine, USA, where Professor J. Cagigal has been trying to popularize it (albeit with but moderate success). The first ringo association outside the borders of Poland was estab. under the auspices of the Youth Institute in Moscow, Russia in 1991.

W. Strzyżewski, *Ringo – przepisy gry*, 1975; W. Strzyżewski, *Ringo. A Sport for You*, 1991.

RINGRIDING, Dan. for 'riding at the ring', an equivalent of >RUNNING AT THE RING. In Denmark, this sport, derived from knightly traditions, has been preserved as a local festival at Søndoborg, county Sønderjylland, south Jutland.
The participants, mounted on horseback, hold short lances. Under the vault of the city gate, or under a structure similar to a football goal (but narrower and higher, without the net at the back), a ring is suspended on a piece of rope, which the riders try to stick on their lances. The rider who succeeds in achieving this more times than the others in a set number of trials is declared the winner. Several scores of competitors may take part in a modern event. Cf. >ALKA, >QUINTAIN.

J. Møller, 'Ringriding', GID, 1997, 4, 81.

RINGSCHIESSEN, Ger. for 'shooting at the ring' [Ger. *Ring* – ring + *schiessen* – shoot]. A winter sport from the curling family, where special weights are slid down a rink (in the Ger. tradition, such sports are referred to collectively as >EISSCHIEßEN). The weight used in ringschiessen is similar to those used in other var. of eisschiessen; it is made of wood, has an iron 'foot' (Ger. *Fuss*), and is shaped like an irregular cone with a base diameter of 27-30cm, and a weight of 4-6kg. From the top of the cone, a handle protrudes, narrow at the base and widening towards the tip. Such weights are slid down a special rink known as the *Eisshiessbahn*, 4m wide and 42m long. The center part of the rink (*Mittelfeld*) is 21m long. Other sources say the game uses rinks 28m long and 3m wide, and weights with base diameters of 30-38cm. The starting positions (*Standritze*) are placed at opposite ends of the rink, shaped like rectangles 4m wide and 2.5m long. At each end of the rink, there is a 6-8m sliding (run-up) zone. The weights may be slid both ways. In each of the run-up zones, there is the target (*Daubenkranz*, from Ger. *Dauben* – block, stave + *kranz* – wreath) used for shoots coming in from the other end. The target consists of concentrically arranged circles. The smallest circle has a diameter of 10cm, and the larger ones are, respectively, 40, 70, 100 and 130cm in diameter. At the center of the target, there is a cross of 2 short lines, called the *Daubenkreuz*, where the *Zieldaube* (or *Daube* for short) is placed – a simple block of soft wood, 10cm high. The object of the game (usu. played individually) is to place a weight as close as possible to the center of the target without actually jostling the *Daube*. Points scored depend on the final locations of the weights. The game may also be played by two 4-a-side teams (*Moarschaften*). Cf. >EISKEGELN, >KALUDDERSCHIEßEN, >WEITSCHIEßEN, >ZIELSCHIEßEN.

Road bowling.

'Eisschießen', *Kleine Enzyklopädie Körperkultur und Sport*, 1965, 283-285; *Encyclopedia Britannica (Micropedia)*, 1991, vol. 4, 407-408.

RINGSPIL MED STOK, a Dan. var. of >SERSO.

RINGSPIL TIL NI PÆLE, a Dan. game where rings are thrown onto poles. Between 2 and 10 players may participate. Nine metal rings are needed (with a diameter of 8-9cm each), and 9 metal or wooden poles. The latter are set in the ground in 3 rows of 3 (forming a square), so that they protrude 10cm above it. The poles are numbered 1-9 (this corresponds to points), with the poles in the nearest row numbered 1-3, those in the middle row – 4-6, and those in the furthest row – 7-9. The players attempt to throw the rings onto the poles, starting with pole num. 1. The player who scores the most points wins. The game has a folk tradition and uses simple equipment; however, today, plastic sets are manufactured in Denmark and sold in sports and toy shops.

J. Møller, 'Ringspil til ni pæle', GID, 1997, 1, 103.

RINGSTAFET, Dan. for 'circular relay'. A Dan. game where a number of teams (usu. 5 during physical education lessons) take positions around a circle with a diameter of 10m, forming a 'star': the first competitor of each team faces the circle, while the remaining players form a file behind him, with their backs turned towards him. The batons are in the middle of the circle. The first competitor runs for the baton, then the next takes over and runs around the circle, and so on. The team whose last runner is the first to place the baton back in the middle of the circle wins.

J. Møller, 'Ringstafet', GID, 1997, 4.

RINGSTEKEN TE PAARD, a Flem. folk sport deriving from old knightly tournaments, an equivalent of Eng. >RUNNING AT THE RING, and Croatian >ALKA. The objective is to aim one's lance at a ring from the saddle while riding a horse. See also Dan. >RINGRIDING.

RINGTENNIS, a game where the players pass a rubber ring over a net. The formats are men's and women's singles, doubles and mixed doubles. The court (*Spielfeld*) for singles is 12.2x3.7m, and for doubles – 12.2x5.5m. It is divided into 2 halves by the blocking zone (*Sperraum*), 1.8m long. The blocking zone extends 1m beyond the side lines. The side lines are called *Seitelinien*, and the back lines are *Grundlinien*. All the lines are drawn with chalk or marked in some other way, e.g. using thin strips of wood buried in the ground or stones. The lines are parts of the court. Around the court, there should be a safety zone about 3m wide. Across the middle of the court, the net (*Netz*) is suspended on 2 poles, with a height of 152m at the sides and 145cm in the center. The length of the net is 4.2m for singles, and 6m for doubles, so that it extends 25cm beyond the side lines in each event. The net is 40cm wide so that there is a clearance of more than 1m between it and the ground. It has a white tape, 2cm wide, along the top edge. The rubber ring is made of spongy rubber covered with a harder material, and has a thickness of 3cm; the hole in the middle has a diameter of 11.8cm. Its weight is about 225g. Each player (or pair) uses 2 rings – one is used for playing, and the other as reserve. The ends and right to serve first are decided by a drawing so that the player who chooses the court automatically surrenders the first serve to the other player. A match consists of halves (2x15min. for men's singles, men's doubles, women's doubles and mixed doubles, and 2x8min. for women's singles, juniors' singles and doubles). Time lost during play is compensated for by adding extra time at the end. In the event of a tie in the regular time, 2x3mins. are added, after a new drawing. If the score is inconclusive after this extra time, an additional 2x3mins. are added. If this gives no result, the match must be replayed at another time. When passing the ring, the player must have at least 1 foot on the ground. He may not step on the outside lines or the lines demarcating the blocking zone. In doubles, the partners may change at the serve at will. A player commits an error if he: 1) touches the ground with the ring in his own court; 2) is the last to touch the ring landing in the blocking zone or outside the court; 3) touches the blocking zone or its side extensions; 4) touches or grabs the net when returning the ring; 5) has made an error while catching or throwing the ring.

The ring, after being passed by the opponent, must be caught with one hand and returned with the same hand, from the location at which it has been intercepted (even if this is outside the boundaries of the court). The following maneuvers are allowed when intercepting the ring: 1) the player may adjust his grip on the ring with the same hand; 2) he may use the trunk of his body to help catch the ring (e.g. the ring may bounce off his trunk); 3) in doubles, the players may both catch the ring simultaneously or in succession if this is done using one hand each only. One player may not catch the ring with both hands, either simultaneously or in succession. If a player falls on the ring when catching it, he may continue after a while but must return the ring to the opponent using a lob throw. Before lowering one's arm after a throw, the ring must have travelled at least 15cm. The ring must cover the whole flight distance in the same way (it may e.g. turn somersaults if this continues throughout the flight). Feints are forbidden (such as slowly taking aim for a pass and then throwing the ring quickly and unexpectedly, or making a quick throwing motion and stopping).
Each game is supervised by an umpire (*Schiedsrichter*) accompanied by 2 linesmen (*Linienrichter*). The umpire's position is 1-2m from the net pole. The linesmen are positioned at the opposite ends of the side lines.
History. The game was developed during the winter 1927-28 by H. Schneider of Karlsruhe, Germany. Before WWII, ring tennis was very popular on board Ger. passenger ships. Cf. the Pol. game of >RINGO, sharing several characteristics.

W. Braungardt, *Ringtennis*, in: *Turnspiele. Lehrbuch für Spieler, Spielwarte und Schiedsrichter*, 1949, 60-65.

RINTAPAINI, a trad. Fin. var. of wrestling where the opponents bend down slightly and take a grip on each other's back somewhat below the shoulders, 'chest to chest' [Fin. *rinta* – chest + *paini* – press]. The Dan. and Swed. equivalents of rintapaini are known by the name of >LIVTAG, while a similar Scot. sport is called >BACKHOLD.

RISMUNK FRA NORDFYN, see >MUNK.

RIVE HØNS NED, Dan. for 'knocking hens down' [Dan. *rive* – sweep + *høns* – hens + *ned* – down]. A trad. country folk game. A sturdy beam is placed on 2 chairs facing each other, with 2 milk cans suspended on the back of each chair. The participant sits on the beam, with a stick in his hand, and tries to knock the cans over without losing his balance.

J. Møller, 'Rive høns ned', GID, 1997, 3.

ROAD BOWLING, a game for 2 players who roll balls, once made of stone and nowadays of iron, along an unfrequented road over a pre-specified distance. A similar game has been known for centuries in Holland under the name of >KLOOTSCHIEN.
Equipment. The balls are made of cast iron and weigh approx. 790g. In the players' jargon they are referred to as 'bullets'.
Rules. The players roll their balls along the road over a pre-arranged distance. The game may be played by 2 players or by 2-player-teams. In the latter case the second player picks the ball from the place where it stopped having been tossed by his team mate. The winner is the player or team that covers the distance in the fewer number of tosses. If a player wins by one toss it is called 'a bowl of odds'. The main problem in long distance games is to cover the bends. This obstacle is overcome by applying a special wide arm sweep. Sending the ball off the road limits entails penalties, chiefly by disallowing the specific toss.
History. Some claim the game has existed since ancient times, despite the fact that the game could scarcely have existed as we have come to know it without a well developed road system. The peak of its popularity came in the 19th cent., when roads, though modern, were still not overburdened by heavy traffic. In the 20th cent. there were many accidents involving players and automobiles, but the game was not banned; it was rather moved away from main thoroughfares. In 1954 The Bowl Playing Association [Ir. Gaelic An Bol Cumann] was estab., with more than 100 local associations, mainly from the counties of Cork, West Waterford, Armagh, and Limerick. The Association organizes Irish championships and also international events with the participation of the representatives of Du. and Ger. *klootschien*.

ROAD CYCLING, one of major var. of single- or multi-stage cyling races held on public roads. See >CYCLING.

ROAD RACES, also *road racing* or *road running*. A form of running competition held outside city limits, usu. along highways or public roads. The modern form of road races was preceded by >LONG DISTANCE RUNNING competitions held on off-city roads, which, however, were discontinued as soon as stadiums with elliptical running tracks appeared. A specific example of a road race is the >OLYMPIC MARATHON, as well as supermarathon. The Guinness Road Race, originated in 1984 in Singapore at a distance of 25km, has been held annually ever since at a distance of 10km in men's, women's and junior's categories. It has been co-organized by the Singapore Amateur Athletic Association.

ROCHWIST, an old type of folk horseback race as practiced mainly by farm-hands and stablemen in S-W Poland. The race was still organized in the village of Lastkowice near Wrocław as late as the early 19th cent. The tradition probably goes back to the old horseback contests of the Lusatian Slavs who borrowed it from the Celtic peoples. The object was to race to a pole planted in the ground on the top of a hill, or, less frequently, at the end of a ravine or gorge. Below is Ł. Gołębiowski's description of rochwist in the early 19th cent.:

One and a half miles from Wrocław, in Lastkowice and other Polish villages, there is a custom that farm-hands who graze horses set out on races at dawn on the first day of Pentecost. The finish line is at a pole planted on a hill. The race starts from Lake Próchnik; the first rider to reach the pole is the winner; the last is declared Rochwist. The youth return home led by their king, with Rochwist as his jester; he is carried in a decorated two-wheeled cart to all the inns in the village, asking for small gifts for the evening's supper. Rochwist plays all kinds of tricks, getting out of his cart, rolling in the backyards, turning somersaults, and diving in puddles to make the king, his company, and the host, laugh. Sorbs in Lusatia have had races of this kind since their pagan times.

[*Games and Pastimes of Various Social Classes*, 1831, 276]

The fact that the neighboring Ger. communities organized similar races may be explained by the joint influence of the Celtic tradition on both Germanic and Slavonic peoples. Gołębiowski also suggests that the Slavonic custom of settling disputes by racing to a pole on horseback might be somehow related to rochwist. One description of such a 'duel' was given by the Pol. medieval chronicle writer W. Kadłubek, to be later repeated by another medieval historian, J. Długosz:

After Przemysł [a Pol. prince] died, many were tempted by power, and the Pol. people agreed to resolve the matter in a horseback race to a pole: the first rider to reach it was to be elected king. Leszek secretly scattered spikes on the road along which the race was to be run, and gave his own horse iron horse shoes; so when the horses of the other riders became crippled on the way and limped, he reached the finish line first and was declared king. But another youth reached the pole by foot, passing by another route, and revealed the ruse of the former, and the traitor was killed, and the latter was declared king under the name of Leszko.

[*Dziejów Polski ksiąg dwanaście*, trans. from Latin K. Mecherzyński, 1861, I, 65]

RODE HEE FOOTBALL, a local var. of >SHROVE TUESDAY FOOTBALL, played in Chester, Cheshire, England. The oldest record dates back to 1533 but presents the game as an old custom, well planted in the local tradition, so a longer history may be inferred. Subsequent documents, as well as the local dialect, also call it the 'Roodeye Game', which derives from the local term for marshy meadows where rode hee football was played. The first part of the name also surfaces in various local documents as 'Rodehee', 'Rood Hee', 'Roodee' etc. In 1540, King Henry VIII issued a special edict ordering the locals to give up the game, which used a leather football and was played under the Rod Dee cross, as it was said to be played for the pleasure of ill-disposed people.

RODEO, [from Span. *rodear* – to drive cattle, and *rodeo* – cattle-yard in which horses are broken in], an Amer. show of skill popular among horse- and cattle-breeders, which usu. takes place in a *corral*. Forms akin to Amer. rodeo are also practiced in other countries, e.g. in Canada, where the biggest event

of the sort is the annual Calgary Stampede. Similar competitions are held in Mexico, Australia, N.Zealand and Argentina. The Jap. version stems from Asian tradition. See also >CHILEAN RODEO. Elements similar to rodeo can be found in the sports of Mong. herdsmen, who use an original lasso (see >LASSOING, >LAZU) called >URGA (Turk. >ARKAN THROWING). Yet it is Amer. rodeo that has developed the most spectacular and consistent forms. The program includes the following competitions (each played for time, which is the decisive factor):

Garrett Nokes, of McCook, Nebraska, wrestles a steer to the ground during the first day of rodeo action at the Calgary Stampede.

BAREBACK RIDING – staying bare-back on an unbroken horse for at least 10sec.;
SADDLE-BRONCO RIDING (BUSTING) – remaining in the saddle of an unbroken horse with the help of 1 hand and 1 rein for at least 10sec.;
BULL RIDING – riding bare-back on a bull, holding a rope tied around the animal's thorax. Again, the rope may only be held with 1 hand;
CALF ROPING – catching a running calf on a lasso from horseback; after dismounting the contestant knocks the calf down and ties its legs together;
STEER ROPING – catching a young ox on a lasso;
PAIR LAZOOING – catching a calf by 2 contestants; the first throws the lasso around the animal's neck, the other performs the exceptionally difficult trick of throwing the lasso around its hind legs with an upward throw while the calf is making a leap;
STEER WRESTLING – knocking down a young bull by grabbing its horns and forcing its head and neck downwards;
CATCHING A GREASED PIG – catching a piglet smeared with grease (a competition known in many folk games other than rodeo; see also >CATCHING THE GREASED PIG).
Women also take part in rodeo, but in different competitions: usu. riding a galloping horse in figure eights around 2 barrels. As a consequence of the feminist movement, women have started taking part in many sports traditionally considered masculine, such as >ASSOCIATION FOOTBALL, >POWERLIFTING, >WEIGHTLIFTING, >POLE-VAULTING, etc. Yet in rodeo this process is slower on account of the conservative character of the Amer. Southwest, where most rodeo events take place. The biggest event in women's rodeo is the Miss Rodeo Pageant, a beauty contest sponsored by the International Rodeo Association, while a children's version of rodeo is known as Kiddie Rodeo.
History. Rodeo competitions are derived from the

daily activities of Mexican herdsmen, *charros*. The first recorded rodeo events took place in the first decades of the 19th cent. in what is now the S-W US, during annual cattle round-ups. Between 1870-1885 rodeo forms evolved during great round-ups from the South to the cities of the North. The major centers were: Cheyenne, Wyoming; Deertail, Colorado; Point of Rocks, Arizona; Santa Fe, New Mexico. In the second half of the 19th cent. the various spontaneously created forms of rodeo became standardized. Influential in the process was the first circus specializing in cowboy shows (1883-1916), organized by Buffalo Bill (real name W. F. Cody; 1846-1917). The performances, known as Wild West Shows, commercialized the sport and popularized many of its elements, among them the costumes which are now considered characteristic of rodeo The first ticketed rodeo performance took place in 1888 in Prescott, Arizona.
In 1936 the Rodeo Cowboys' Association (formerly Cowboys' Turtle Association) came into being. Nowadays the biggest rodeo organization is the Professional Cowboy Association, under whose auspices the annual US national championships are held. An estimated 3,000 local rodeo events with 40-50 million spectators take place each year. A special form of rodeo developed in the 19th and

Bull riding at a rodeo contest.

R

WORLD SPORTS ENCYCLOPEDIA

the first half of the 20th cent. in Amer. prisons, many of whose inmates were rowdy cowboys. Horse-breeding, riding and saddlery became consciously applied methods of social rehabilitation. In the pioneering Texas State Prison the rehabilitation programme was carried out between 1931-1986. It was in this prison that the well-known movie *Stir Crazy* (1981) was shot (directed by S. Poitier, starring G. Wilder and R. Pryor). The 1971 *Wild Free-*

Junior Bonner, C. Robertson's *J.W. Coop*, S. Millar's *When Legends Die* and S. Ihnat's *The Honkers* (1972). One of the most famous literary works featuring rodeo is *A Connecticut Yankee in King Arthur's Court* by Mark Twain. It is a novel in which a contemporary New Englander is transported into the Middle Ages. Besides impressing his host with electricity and gunpowder, he takes Merlin on with various tricks of rodeo origin. Among modern realistic

the people present call: 'Roduś! Roduś!' What does the word mean, and what is the reason behind the game? Even the village elders cannot explain'. (*Games and Pastimes of Various Social Classes*)

ROLLER HOCKEY, a game similar to >BANDY, played on a field with a hard surface, usu. wooden or asphalt. The game is played with curved sticks and a little, hard ball. The field is 40m long, 20m

Bareback riding during a rodeo contest.

Roaming Horse and Burro Act allowed the keeping of horses on prison grounds. Some prisons initiated programs known as *Prison Rodeos* whose purpose was to fight off demoralizing idleness, and occasionally also to train the inmates to be professional rodeo-riders. Among those institutions is the Colorado State Prison, where a special *Wild Horse Inmate Program* was established in 1988.

Rodeo is a popular subject of film and literature. The most widely-known picture is *The Misfits* (1961), directed by J. Houston, starring M. Clifton. Among many others are: B. Toeticher's *Bronco Buster* (1952), N. Ray's *Lusty Men* (1952), S. Peckinpah's

Roller skate sailing.

novels dedicated to rodeo are: *The Bronco Rider* by W. Crawford (1965), *Goldenrod* by H. Harker (1972), *Cowboy* by A. Fletcher (1977) and *Omar, Fats and Trixie* by J. Reese, the story of a rodeo-rider who became a detective. Competition with current rodeo events resulted in a TV series about rodeo being taken off the air. Such was the fate of *Stoney Burke* (ABC) and *Wide Country* (NBC) in 1962 and V. McEveety's *The Busters* (CBS) in 1978.

RODINHA DOS BOTÕES, a Port. var. of >TOPS, where the objective is to use the spinning top to displace a button from a circle drawn on the ground. See >PIÃO.

RØDT LYN – STOP, Dan. for 'red lightning – stop', [Dan. *rødt* – red + *lyn* – lightning + stop]. A Dan. game. One of the participants stands facing a wall. The others make a row about 30m away. Their task is to creep up on him and touch him or the wall. The player facing the wall may turn round at any moment and shout out the name of the game. Any player who moves after that has to return to their initial position. Whoever is the first to touch the player facing the wall takes over from him in the next round. J. Møller, 'Rødt lyn: stop', GID, 1997, 2, 4.

RODUŚ, an old folk race behind an ox as practiced in the Podlaskie region of E Poland (esp. in the vicinity of the town of Siedlce). On the second day of Pentecost, an ox was driven through the village, with a straw figure of a farmer mounted on its back. Ł. Gołębiowski gave a description of the event: 'there is an ancient custom that a pack of boys drive an ox through the village, with a straw man on its back, wearing a peasant coat, cap and boots. The ox walks through the village, and all

wide; the goal is 4ft. (1.23m) wide and 3ft. (0.92m) high. The team consists of 5 players, including the goalkeeper. There are 2 halves, 25min. each. Players move on box skates with 4 wheels.

History. Roller hockey was created in the beginning of the 20th cent. as a mixture of hockey and roller-skating, popular in England, esp. in London, since the 18th cent. (>ROLLER SKATING). The game spread later to other Eur. countries, with the most dynamic development in the Netherlands and Belgium. Popular also in Great Britain, Germany, Switzerland, Portugal and Spain. It is supervised by the Roller Hockey Commission of the Roller-Skating Federation (Fédération Internationale de Roller Sports, before 1999 known as Fédération Internationale de Roller-Skating; both abbreviated to FIRS). Played as a demonstration sport during the Ol.G. in Barcelona in 1992, it has been revolutionized by the introduction of in-line skates (see >IN-LINE ROLLER HOCKEY). W.Ch. have been held since 1995.

ROLLER SKATE SAILING, a hybrid of >ROLLER SKATING and >SAILING, in which the roller skater or inline skater is propelled by a sail or parawing held in his hands.

The parawing consists of 2 surfaces: the back surface, resembling a trad. triangular sail, and the front surface, transparent, held at eye level, and controlling the sailing direction. Both are stretched over a construction resembling that of a kite, with an additional frame running along the entire circumference. The triangular rear part of the parawing is connected with the semicircular front part. The frame of the front part is made of an aluminum pipe and forms an arch to stretch the sail in the transparent section

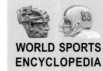

Roller skiing combines roller skating with skiing technique.

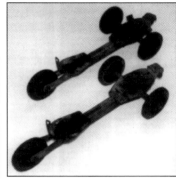

Early 3-wheel roller skates.

Early 4-wheel roller skates.

which is called a window. The sail surface is 21-61sq. ft (2.0-5.7m²). This type of construction allows for speeds of up to 45mph (approx. 72km/h). Roller skate sailing often uses a Hopatcong type of sail, which is also used in >ICE SKATE SAILING. The most popular sails are simple and triangular in shape, with a surface of 35-40sq. ft. (3-4m²). An important piece of equipment is a helmet and other types of protective gear like knee-pads, elbow pads, or wrist bands. The course must be thoroughly checked for irregularities, small obstacles, stones or branches.

History. The first attempts to roller skate with sails were made in the USA in the 1930s. The hard sands of the Mohave Desert spreading N of San Bernardino and Los Angeles provided the best environment for practicing the sport, along with deserted runways, uninhabited side roads with an asphalt or concrete surface, and large parking areas empty at night. Roller skate sailing enjoys great popularity in California and Colorado. Originally the sport was practiced on trad. roller skates, which were later substituted with in-line roller skates.

ROLLER SKATING, a sport event including various forms of competition on roller skates, i.e. small platforms fastened to the shoes or being a part of them, with wheels attached to the bottom either as 2 pairs (one in the front and one in the rear) or in one central line (the so-called *in-line skates*, developed at the end of the 1970s). Similar to >FIGURE SKATING, traditional roller skating events include >SPEED ROLLER SKATING, individual and team >FIGURE ROLLER SKATING, and dancing. The construction of in-line skates resulted in the emergence of new events called stunts, performed on skateboarding tracks. Other sports on roller skates include >ROLLER HOCKEY, >IN-LINE ROLLER HOCKEY, and >ROLLER SKATE SAILING.

History. Roller skates were invented in England in 1720 and until the end of the 19th cent. the sport developed mainly there. In 1849 a Frenchman L. Legrange used roller skates to imitate ice skating during a theatre performance of *La Prophete.* In the 2nd half of the 19th cent. the invention underwent many improvements, of which the most significant was the introduction in 1863 by an American J. Plimpton of a new construction enabling a change in the riding direction by exerting pressure on the wheels on one side. Plimpton was also the first to build, in the USA and Europe, commercial roller skating rinks, which popularized roller skating among the upper classes. When Plimpton's patent expired, roller skating's exclusivity disappeared, while the cheaper production of roller skates opened roller skating to the middle classes. In the 2nd half of the 19th cent. the sport became popular in the USA,

where it was promoted by the Chicago Skate Company, and in Canada. The sport was codified at the turn of the 20th cent. In 1924 the International Roller Skating Federation (Fédération Internationale de Patinage ê Roulettes, FIPR) was estab., later transformed into Fédération Internationale de Roller Skating, under the auspices of which E.Ch. have been held since 1937 and W.Ch. since 1947. Until 1947 the countries affiliated in the FIPR did not include the USA, which had its own national structure and it was only in 1955 that the USA took part for the first time in the W.Ch. held by the FIPR. In 1976 the Eur. Confederation of Roller Skating (Confédération Européenne de Roller Skating, CERS) was formed. A turning point in the development of the sport was the construction in 1979 of in-line skates by S. and B. Olsen from Minnesota (see >IN-LINE ROLLER SKATING). Their skates were called *Rollerblades* and were modelled after the equipment used by the Chicago Skate Company for the purpose of ice hockey training in summer. The Olsens have improved the old construction by adding new materials, e.g. polyurethane wheels, and extending foot mountings. They established a specialized production plant – the Rollerblade Company, which in 1983 they unexpectedly sold to Robert Jr. Thanks to a successful marketing strategy, Rollerblades have become a byword for in-line skates. In 1989 annual sales exceeded 3 million pairs. According to the National Sporting Goods Association, in 1994 the number of in-line skaters in the USA alone reached 12 million. Among other athletes who use in-line skates for off-season practice are skiers, while the third largest community of in-line skate users includes various aerobic and fitness groups. The sport was originally practiced without any safety equipment and resulted in frequent injuries, which led to the development of various kinds of protective gear, such as knee-pads, elbow pads and helmets. In-line skating is currently practiced in 2 main styles: street style and vert. The first style involves roaming the streets in search of anything that can be skated over, or jumped at or above, which brought about the necessity to strengthen the bottom platform, now made of titanium. The vert style involves figure and stunt skating practiced in skateboarding half-pipes, which led to open conflicts between the representatives of both sports. A rich spectrum of in-line stunts has been developed, demonstrated by such outstanding in-line skaters as T. Fry (Australia), who invented the most difficult vert in-line stunts.

The development of the sport led to the formation of characteristic terminology and jargon, much resembling that of skateboarders, but including various unique elements:

Anti-rockered – an inline skate construction in which the 2 middle wheels are smaller than the front and

back wheels to allow for grinds and curbsides;
Rockering –the configuration of wheels on an inline skate aimed at simulating the curve of an ice skate blade to enhance maneuverability by shortening the turning radius. As opposed to anti-rockering, all the wheels are the same size, but placed differently in the frame;
Spacer – plastic or aluminum hub that separates bearing casings;
Cheese grater asphalt – poor quality surface;
Slam tan – a body tan with paler spots in places where protective gear is worn.

ROLLER SKIING, formerly also >GRASS SKIING (the first attempts were made on grassy slopes). A type of skiing where the skiers travel across snowless ground on skis equipped with rollers. Roller skiing was developed to enable trad. skiers to practice in summer but with time it has turned into a separate discipline.

ROLLER SOCCER, see >IN-LINE FOOTBALL.

ROLLEY HOLE, also 'rolley hole marbles'; an Amer. var. of >MARBLES, where the object is to place the marbles in holes in the ground. The playing area is 7.5x12m, with a surface of packed sand or clay. Along the longitudinal axis of the field, there are 3 holes, positioned every 2.5m, with diameters slightly larger than those of the marbles, additionally marked with chalk circles 25-30cm in diameter. The object of the game is to place both of a player's marbles in the holes 2 or 3 times. The marbles are set into motion by a flick of the thumb. Moving the marble into a more convenient position is allowed if

Max Klinger, A Roller Skating Rink, *engraving.*

Roller skating.

R

**WORLD SPORTS
ENCYCLOPEDIA**

that is no further from the final position of the marble than the distance of a spread hand. As opposed to similar children's games played in many countries around the world, it is adults who play rolley hole in the USA. The game is esp. popular in county Clay, Tennessee. On average, 30 teams participate in the Amer. championships that are held every year. The game is played in an individual or pair format. The marbles used in rolley hole are not factory-made glass or plastic balls, as they may be elsewhere; they are made on a DIY basis from polished flint. Top players of the 1990s included the 4-time US champion R. Roberts and W. Rhoten.

ROLY-POLY, see >HALF-BALL.

The base of a marble relief of a funerary statue in Athens (c. 510BC) shows six athletes, of whom one (far left) is a ball player.

ROMAN BALL, a game based on a Roman model described by Petronius in *Satiricon*. Revived at the Milwaukee School of Engineering (USA) to be played during a Roman Ball Tournament in 2000. The playing area has 2 circles convergent to one another, the smaller being approx. 5ft. and the larger 20ft. in diameter. At least 3 players take any position outside the larger circle. The ball thrown by one of the players must bounce in the inside circle before it is caught outside the larger circle by another player. The player throwing the ball must remain stationary. If the ball fails to bounce outside the larger circle, the throw must be repeated by the same or another player. The thrower scores if a correctly bounced ball is not caught by any player. If the ball is caught, the catcher becomes the thrower. The first player to score 21pts. wins the game, which is mon-

Rope climbing at the 1912 Stockholm Olympic Games.

itored by a referee. Any ball can be used (rubber covered are the best). The game can be played on any surface, though grass is preferred, as catching a flying ball frequently ends in falls.

RONDERS, a game similar to Eng. >ROUNDERS, popularized in Poland in the early 20th cent. by E. Cenar's book *Gry i zabawy różnych narodów* (2nd ed., 1906). Each team had 3-8 players. The dimensions of the pitch were not fixed, but were similar to those of a football pitch, with a central area demarcated much like in >BASEBALL. The rules, in turn, resembled those of rounders, with the following modifications: the central area was an octagon with a diameter of 13-18m; the batter 'served' the ball for his own bat rather than hitting it after a pitch from a player of the opposing team; the last player of the offensive (batting) team, called the 'mother', could 'buy out' with successful bats those players of his own team who had made invalid bats or had not managed to run around the octagon and were 'trapped' at different points within it; the ball could be caught not only on the volley but also after a bounce. The teams swapped positions when the defensive team (catchers) intercepted an agreed number of balls or when the offensive team, including the 'mother', missed all their bats, or when none of their players completed a run around the octagon. Each player was allowed to bat 5 times. A round was completed after all the players of both teams had used all their bats.

ROODEYE GAME, see >RODE HEE FOOTBALL.

ROPE CLIMBING, in some Asian cultures was the skill of heroes, while in modern times it is a form of ludic competition or even a gymnastic event.
During the 1924 Ol.G. in Paris it was part of the official gymnastic program and athletes competed for time. The gold medalist was B. Supcik (Czechoslovakia, 7.2sec.), the silver medal went to A. Seguin (France, 7.4sec.), and the bronze – to L. Vacha (Czechoslovakia, 7.8sec.). The sport is an important event in many competitions for military personnel, fire fighters, etc.
I. Kabzińska-Stawarz, 'Competition in Liminal Situations. Comparative Study of Asian Cultures', ETHP, 1994, 18.

ROPE PULLING, a simple, trad. game of speed, strength, and balance, introduced into the programs of physical education in some countries of the former socialist bloc. Two contestants stand back to back, at a distance of 1 pace from one another with their legs spread, and put a 1m long rope between their legs so that its ends are exactly between their feet. They raise their arms and wait for the starting signal, upon which they bend down, snatch the rope and try to pull it to their side. The first one to do so, wins the game.
I.N. Chkhannikov, GIZ, 1953, 7.

ROPE SKIPPING, see >JUMP ROPE.

ROQUE, a professional game derived from >CROQUET, introduced around 1894-95 in an attempt to counteract the decreasing popularity of croquet, displaced by newer games such as >TENNIS and >BADMINTON gaining considerable popularity among the social elite. Roque is one of several var. of Brit. croquet played according to the rules set out by E. Routledge, differing in the number of wickets (10 instead of 9), and in the dimensions of the field: 60x30ft. (about 18.3x9.1m), surrounded by side boards. The corners of the field are cut so that the field has 8 sides. The course has 2 pegs. The rules

are the same as those of croquet but the actual game is different in its techniques and speed, which was influenced by the introduction in 1899 of clay field surfaces, speeding the game up considerably. The more springy balls and mallets (with endings made of hard rubber or special packed cement instead of wood) also make the game faster. The wickets, embedded in concrete in the field surface, are half the size of those used in trad. croquet, which makes the game more demanding. The partners use 2 balls each. During the 1904 Ol.G. in St. Louis, roque made its sole Olympic appearance. Four Amer. players took part in the tournament; C. Jacobus won the gold medal (score 5-1), S.O. Streeter – the silver (4-2), and C. Brown – the bronze (3-3). The Amer. Roque League was estab. in 1916. Amer. championships are organized jointly with those for the 9-wicket version of croquet. The name 'roque' was coined by dropping the letters 'c' and 't' from the word 'croquet', which was supposed to stress the connection to trad. croquet as well as indicating the new shape of the game.
F.G. Menke, 'Roque and Croquet', EOS, 1969, 793-794.

RØRE MELGRØD, Dan. for 'semolina stirring', [Dan. *røre* – to stir + *melgrød* – fine groats], a Dan. game played by children aged 5-8. The children sit in a circle, and each starts making circles in the air with his or her finger as if stirring semolina. One of the children is selected the *Fatter* ('father'), who sits in the center and has the task of patting the other players on the hands. The players may avoid this by getting up quickly, as the fatter may only hit them while they are seated. If a player does not succeed in getting up quickly enough, he takes over as the fatter.
J. Møller, 'Røre melgrød', GID, 1997, 2, 66.

RØRE PINDSO, Dan. for 'moving the hedgehog', [Dan. *røre* – to move + *pindso, pindsvin* – hedgehog]. Two players sat back to back, with their ankles and wrists joined. Sticks were placed under their knees and over their elbows. The object of the game was unclear: most probably, the participants were supposed to stand up from the initial position, which they could only achieve by helping each other. The difficulty was that each one had to stand up but, at the same time, prevent the other player from doing so. The connection with hedgehogs is not clear – possibly the double bent position of the participants resembled with the animal.
J. Møller, 'Røre pindso', GID, 1997, 4, 50.

ROSCA, LA, a trad. Span. loaf of bread shaped like a large pretzel. Also, an old Span. folk running competition where a loaf of such bread was the prize for the winner. Span. ethnographers claim that the last rosca games were held as late as 1974 and 1984. The competitors ran in pairs, the number of series corresponding to the number of participants. Two runners from 2 different localities were selected for the first pair, usu. bachelors, sometimes rivals courting the same young woman. According to tradition, the distance was chosen by a native of the locality where the run was organized. The winning runner defined the distance to be run by the next pair, where he competed against the next participant, and so on. Using the right to decide the distance, participants selected such distances as not to exhaust themselves prematurely. The final winner was selected after a number of races. For the last race, a loaf of rosca was suspended on a ribbon on the finish line. The winner had the honor of breaking the loaf into pieces and distributing them among all the contestants, who in turn offered the bread to the girls they were courting.
C. Moreno Palos, 'La rosca', JYTE, 1992, 37.

ROUND BALL, among the bat-and-ball games played in the Brit. colonies in N.America in the 17th-18th cent. Round ball contributed to the growth of >BASEBALL along with other similar games, such as >BASTE-BALL, >GOAL-BALL, >CRICKET, >NEW-YORK-BALL, >ONE-OLD-CAT, >ROUNDERS, >TOWN-BALL, and >TWO-OLD-CAT.

ROUNDERS, a bat-and-ball game played in England since the 16th cent., and then in the Brit. colonies in N.America in the 17th-18th cent. Rounders contributed to the growth of >BASEBALL along with other similar games, such as >BASTE-BALL, >GOAL-BALL, >CRICKET, >NEW-YORK-BALL, >ONE-OLD-CAT, >STICKBALL, >TOWN-BALL, and >TWO-OLD-CAT. See also >PALANT.

The rules. The game is played on a pitch similar in size to a football pitch. In the middle of it, an inside area is marked, shaped like a pentagon with the length of each side roughly 39½ft. (about 12m). In each corner of the pentagon, there is a post, 4ft. (about 1.2m) high. The distance between the first and fifth post is a little shorter due to the irregular layout of the pentagon. Earlier versions of rounders (played until more or less the end of the 19th cent.) used pentagons with sides measuring 15-20m. The ball weighs between 2½oz. and 3oz. (70-80g), with a circumference of 7½in. (about 19cm). It is solid, covered with light-colored leather. The bat is circular in cross-section, 18in. (about 46cm) long, with a circumference of 6¾in. (about 17cm) in the thickest part, and a weight of 13oz. (about 0.37kg). Two teams participate: the batting team bat the ball, and the fielding team try to intercept it. The general objective of the game is for the batting team to bat the ball and run around all the posts while the ball is in the air, scoring points in the process. The task for the fielding team is to prevent this. The course of the game is as follows. A player of the fielding team, called the 'feeder', takes his position in the middle of the pentagon. He throws the ball towards a player of the opposing team, called the 'striker', who is positioned in one of the corners of the pentagon (the 'castle'), and is supposed to hit the ball. Increasingly often, this old terminology has been replaced, under the influence of >CRICKET, by a newer one, where the throwing player is called the 'bowler', and the batting one – the 'batsman'. The ball must be served using a smooth underarm action, at a height between the batsman's head and knees. If the batsman is not satisfied with the quality of the delivery, he may demand the bowler to be replaced by another player. After hitting the ball, the batsman runs around the pentagon, scoring a 'rounder' for his team on completing the run. The run does not have to be completed in one attempt, which anyway only happens quite rarely. A player running around the field may wait at poles for long periods allowing them to safely complete the rounder. One batsman may only run one rounder after successfully batting the ball. Instead of scoring a point, he may also 'free' a player who was earlier put out of the game after being hit with the ball. The batsman is out if he steps on or over the lines of the batting square before hitting the ball. After all the players have batted, the round ('innings') comes to an end, and the teams change ends. Two umpires control the game – the 'bowler's umpire' and the 'batsman's umpire'. A match consists of 2 innings. A clean catch from the air leads to the end of an inning. If the ball is caught in some other way, it may be used to hit a batsman during his run to put him out of play. The batsman is also out if the ball he has batted is intercepted after the first bounce. A batsman may strike 3 balls. After a third unsuccessful attempt, irrespectively of the quality of the bat, he must try to complete a rounder, becoming an easy target. Players running may not be put out of play when they are at one of the corners of the field, called 'sanctuaries'. Players of the opposing team may not impede running players or try to stop them in any way. Depending on the var., there may be between 10 and 30 players in a team. **History**. The earliest record of rounders dates back

to J. Newberry's 1744 *A Little Pretty Pocket-Book* (one of the first children's books in history) which included an engraving depicting the game. The book had 11 editions until 1790, and contributed considerably to the popularization of the game, which was called 'baseball' in those times. In 1829, W. Clarke published the rules of rounders in *The Boy's Own Book*. In 1839, the direction of the run was reversed – before that, players ran clockwise. In his *Ball, Bat and Bishop. The Origin of Ball Games* (1947), the ball game researcher R.W. Henderson suggested that rounders contributed in a meaningful way to the development of Amer. >BASEBALL. The first organizations, clubs and associations were formed in Liverpool and Scotland c.1889. However, the Brit. National Rounders Association was only estab. in 1943. Today, the game has almost vanished from the international arena, and is played mainly in England, where there are local leagues. In 1995, a group of Amer. actors and workers of the Renaissance Pleasure Faire in northern California made an attempt at reviving the game. See also >RONDERS. J. Arlott, 'Rounders', OCSG, 1975, 850-851; A.B. Gomme, 'Rounders', TGESI, 1898, II, 145-146; R.W. Henderson, 'Baseball. Infancy', *Ball, Bat and Bishop. The Origin of Ball Games*, 1947, 132-137.

RØVE DET GYLDNE SKIND, Dan. for 'stealing the golden skin', [Dan. *røve* – to steal + *gylden* – golden + *skind* – skin/fleece]. Two teams stand facing each other at some distance. An object, e.g. a large handkerchief, is placed between them. At a signal, one player of each team runs towards the handkerchief. Whoever reaches it first, grabs it and runs back to his own team, while the opposing player is supposed to catch him. If the first player manages to escape, the 'catcher' has to join his team. If not, the first player has to change sides.
J. Møller, 'Røve den gyldne skind', GID, 1997, 2, 41.

RØVER, Dan. for 'robber'. A Dan. game usu. played by small children in a forest. The robber first hides, and then gives a signal, upon which the remaining participants start singing: *Det er slet ingen Røver i den grønne skov* ('there is no robber in the green forest'). The player who succeeds in finding the robber, shouts out loud, 'Robber! Robber!', upon which all the remaining players try to run quickly towards a target to avoid being caught by the robber. Those he succeeds in catching are supposed to help him capture the remaining participants.
J. Møller, 'Røver', GID, 1997, 2, 38.

ROVING ARCHERY, also *rovers*, a var. of open country archery, where natural targets, such as felled tree trunks, hills or stones are used instead of artificial targets imitating animal figures. The first target is indicated to all the archers. The archer who succeeds in hitting it with the greatest accuracy is allowed to select the next target. In this way, the archers continue from one target to another across open terrain which thus becomes a natural shooting field.

ROWING, moving in vessels propelled by oars. Since ancient times rowing has been used not only for transport, commerce and war, but also for sporting competition. Almost every culture has developed its own rowing var. and tradition. The most popular

modern international rowing sports are: >COMPETITIVE ROWING and >DRAGON BOAT RACING. See also >ROWING AND PADDLING SPORTS, which – apart from trad. rowing sports – include also >KAYAKING, usu. not defined as rowing since paddles are used instead of oars and paddlers face forward. In modern terminology the word 'rowing' refers to boats that use pairs of single-bladed oars, in which the rowers sit facing opposite to the direction

WORLD SPORTS ENCYCLOPEDIA

R

Basque rowing regatta.

they are moving, though there are methods of rowing facing forward or even standing.
History. Oar-propelled boats and ships are among the oldest means of transport, the origins of which can hardly be determined. Sport historians believe that the roots of rowing must be searched for in ancient China, India and Egypt, where evidence for the existence of rowing boats of various types has been found, without, however, any traces of sporting competition. A detailed study of Eg. rowing, published by A.D. Touny and S. Wenig in their work *Sport in Ancient Egypt* (1969), indicated that there were no grounds for a claim that rowing existed in Egypt in any other form than common people's ordinary travels or tourist trips taken by the ruling class. Numerous rowing boats and galleys were used in the Nile delta and upstream regions, but there is only one inscription on the stele of Amenophis II which mentions the ruler's greater proficiency in rowing skills than that of his subjects. That alone cannot be taken as evidence that the ruler demonstrated his skills in any river rowing competition. Rather, the demonstration of the ruler's skills was coincidental and occurred during a trip along the Nile, when his suite lagged behind, unable to keep up with him. Rowing galleys, richly decorated with garlands, were paraded in ancient Acroteri on the island of Santorin before 1500 BC and on Crete during the Minoan era (c.2500-1200 BC), but the surviving paintings do not indicate that it was done in the form of a regatta. Occasional duels of rowing galleys took place in continental Greece, Carthage, Phoenicia and Rome – all known for their splendid fleets – but this was a result of the ambition of their commanding officers or owners rather than a mark of a regulated form of competition. An event of this sort was described by Virgil in Book 5 of his *Aeneid*:

Now came the day desir'd.
The skies were bright
With rosy luster of the rising light:
The bord'ring people, rous'd by sounding fame
Of Trojan feasts and great Acestes name,
The crowded shore with acclamations fill,
Part to behold, and part to prove their skill.
And first the gifts in public view they place,
Green laurel wreaths, and palm, the victors' grace:
Within the circle, arms and tripods lie,
Ingots of gold and silver, heap'd on high,

An ancient rowing boat.

Thomas Eakins, The Pair-Oared Scull, *1872, oil on canvas.*

John Ekenaes, Catching Fish On A River, *1892, oil on canvas.*

A replica of a 54-ft. Viking ship floats amidst a flotilla of curious onlookers during the launching cermony at Hermit Island in Phippsburg, Maine. The re-creation of a 1,000-year-old adventure, the voyage of Viking explorer Leif Ericsson, was organized by author W. Hodding Carter.

R

WORLD SPORTS ENCYCLOPEDIA

And vests embroider'd, of the Tyrian dye.
The trumpet's clangor then the feast proclaims,
And all prepare for their appointed games.
Four galleys first, which equal rowers bear,
Advancing, in the wat'ry lists appear.
The speedy Dolphin, that outstrips the wind,
Bore Mnestheus, author of the Memmian kind:
Gyas the vast Chimaera's bulk commands,
Which rising, like a tow'ring city stands;
Three Trojans tug at ev'ry lab'ring oar;
Three banks in three degrees the sailors bore;
Beneath their sturdy strokes the billows roar.
Sergesthus, who began the Sergian race,
In the great Centaur took the leading place;
Cloanthus on the sea-green Scylla stood,
From whom Cluentius draws his Trojan blood.
Far in the sea, against the foaming shore,
There stands a rock [...]
On this the hero fix'd an oak in sight,
The mark to guide the mariners aright.
To bear with this, the seamen stretch their oars;
Then round the rock they steer, and seek the former shores.
The lots decide their place. Above the rest,
Each leader shining in his Tyrian vest;
The common crew with wreaths of poplar boughs
Their temples crown, and shade their sweaty brows:
Besmear'd with oil, their naked shoulders shine.
All take their seats, and wait the sounding sign:
They gripe their oars; and ev'ry panting breast
Is rais'd by turns with hope, by turns with fear depress'd.
The clangor of the trumpet gives the sign;
At once they start, advancing in a line:
With shouts the sailors rend the starry skies;
Lash'd with their oars, the smoky billows rise;
Sparkles the briny main, and the vex'd ocean fries.
Exact in time, with equal strokes they row:
At once the brushing oars and brazen prow
Dash up the sandy waves, and ope the depths below.
Not fiery coursers, in a chariot race
Invade the field with half so swift a pace;
Not the fierce driver with more fury lends
The sounding lash, and, ere the stroke descends,
Low to the wheels his pliant body bends.
The partial crowd their hopes and fears divide,
And aid with eager shouts the favor'd side.
Cries, murmurs, clamors, with a mixing sound,
From woods to woods, from hills to hills rebound.
Amidst the loud applauses of the shore,
Gyas outstripp'd the rest, and sprung before:
Cloanthus, better mann'd, pursued him fast,
But his o'er-masted galley check'd his haste.
The Centaur and the Dolphin brush the brine
With equal oars, advancing in a line;
And now the mighty Centaur seems to lead,
And now the speedy Dolphin gets ahead;
Now board to board the rival vessels row,

Thomas Eakins, John Biglin In A Single Scull, 1874, oil on canvas.

Rowing enthusiasts participate in a dragon boat race near Hong Kong's Aberdeen Island as part of celebrations marking the Chinese Dragon Boat Festival, held throughout Hong Kong.

The billows lave the skies, and ocean groans below.
They reach'd the mark. Proud Gyas and his train
In triumph rode, the victors of the main;
But, steering round, he charg'd his pilot stand
More close to shore, and skim along the sand
'Let others bear to sea!' Menoetes heard;
But secret shelves too cautiously he fear'd,
And, fearing, sought the deep; and still aloof he steer'd.
With louder cries the captain call'd again:
'Bear to the rocky shore, and shun the main.'
He spoke, and, speaking, at his stern he saw
The bold Cloanthus near the shelvings draw.
Betwixt the mark and him the Scylla stood,
And in a closer compass plow'd the flood.
He pass'd the mark; and, wheeling, got before:
Gyas blasphem'd the gods, devoutly swore,
Cried out for anger, and his hair he tore.
Mindless of others' lives (so high was grown
His rising rage) and careless of his own,
The trembling dotard to the deck he drew;
Then hoisted up, and overboard he threw:
This done, he seiz'd the helm; his fellows cheer'd,
Turn'd short upon the shelfs, and madly steer'd.
Hardly his head the plunging pilot rears,
Clogg'd with his clothes, and cumber'd with his years:
Now dropping wet, he climbs the cliff with pain.
The crowd, that saw him fall and float again,
Shout from the distant shore; and loudly laugh'd,
To see his heaving breast disgorge the briny draught.

The following Centaur, and the Dolphin's crew,
Their vanish'd hopes of victory renew;
While Gyas lags, they kindle in the race,
To reach the mark. Sergesthus takes the place;
Mnestheus pursues; and while around they wind,
Comes up, not half his galley's length behind;
Then, on the deck, amidst his mates appear'd,
And thus their drooping courage he cheer'd:
'My friends, and Hector's followers heretofore,
Exert your vigor; tug the lab'ring oar;
Stretch to your strokes, my still unconquer'd crew,
Whom from the flaming walls of Troy I drew.
In this, our common int'rest, let me find
That strength of hand, that courage of the mind,
As when you stemm'd the strong Malean flood,
And o'er the Syrtes 'broken billows row'd.
I seek not now the foremost palm to gain;
Tho' yet'mdash; but, ah! that haughty wish is vain!
Let those enjoy it whom the gods ordain.
But to be last, the lags of all the race!
Redeem yourselves and me from that disgrace.'
Now, one and all, they tug amain; they row
At the full stretch, and shake the brazen prow.
The sea beneath 'em sinks; their lab'ring sides
Are swell'd, and sweat runs gutt'ring down in tides.
Chance aids their daring with unhop'd success;
Sergesthus, eager with his beak to press
Betwixt the rival galley and the rock,
Shuts up th' unwieldly Centaur in the lock.
The vessel struck; and, with the dreadful shock,
Her oars she shiver'd, and her head she broke.
The trembling rowers from their banks arise,
And, anxious for themselves, renounce the prize.
With iron poles they heave her off the shores,
And gather from the sea their floating oars.
The crew of Mnestheus, with elated minds,
Urge their success, and call the willing winds;
Then ply their oars, and cut their liquid way
In larger compass on the roomy sea.
As, when the dove her rocky hold forsakes,
Rous'd in a fright, her sounding wings she shakes;
The cavern rings with clatt'ring; out she flies,
And leaves her callow care, and cleaves the skies:
At first she flutters; but at length she springs
To smoother flight, and shoots upon her wings:
So Mnestheus in the Dolphin cuts the sea;
And, flying with a force, that force assists his way.
Sergesthus in the Centaur soon he pass'd,
Wedg'd in the rocky shoals, and sticking fast.
In vain the victor he with cries implores,
And practices to row with shatter'd oars.
Then Mnestheus bears with Gyas, and outflies:
The ship, without a pilot, yields the prize.
Unvanquish'd Scylla now alone remains;
Her he pursues, and all his vigor strains.
Shouts from the fav'ring multitude arise;
Applauding Echo to the shouts replies;
Shouts, wishes, and applause run rattling thro' the skies.
These clamors with disdain the Scylla heard,
Much grudg'd the praise, but more the robb'd reward:
Resolv'd to hold their own, they mend their pace,
All obstinate to die, or gain the race.
Rais'd with success, the Dolphin swiftly ran;
For they can conquer, who believe they can.
Both urge their oars, and fortune both supplies,

Scott Gault, left foreground and Ante Kusurin, right, in the University of Washington men's freshmen boat, race the junior varsity, center, and varsity boats during practice on Lake Washington in Seattle.

462

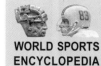

And both perhaps had shar'd an equal prize;
When to the seas Cloanthus holds his hands,
And succor from the wat'ry pow'rs demands:
'Gods of the liquid realms, on which I row!
If, giv'n by you, the laurel bind my brow,
Assist to make me guilty of my vow!
A snow-white bull shall on your shore be slain;
His offer'd entrails cast into the main,
And ruddy wine, from golden goblets thrown,
Your grateful gift and my return shall own.'
The choir of nymphs, and Phorcus, from below,
With virgin Panopea, heard his vow;
And old Portunus, with his breadth of hand,
Push'd on, and sped the galley to the land.
Swift as a shaft, or winged wind, she flies,
And, darting to the port, obtains the prize.
The herald summons all, and then proclaims
Cloanthus conqu'ror of the naval games.
The prince with laurel crowns the victor's head,
And three fat steers are to his vessel led,
The ship's reward; with gen'rous wine beside,
And sums of silver, which the crew divide.
The leaders are distinguish'd from the rest;
The victor honor'd with a nobler vest,
Where gold and purple strive in equal rows,
And needlework its happy cost bestows. [...]
Mnestheus the second victor was declar'd;
And, summon'd there, the second prize he shard.
A coat of mail [...]
The third, succeeding to the last reward,
Two goodly bowls of massy silver shar'd,
With figures prominent, and richly wrought,
And two brass caldrons from Dodona brought.

Men's competitive rowing crew of eight with a coxwain.

Thus all, rewarded by the hero's hands,
Their conqu'ring temples bound with purple bands;
And now Sergesthus, clearing from the rock,
Brought back his galley shatter'd with the shock.
Forlorn she look'd, without an aiding oar,
And, houted by the vulgar, made to shore.
As when a snake, surpris'd upon the road,
Is crush'd athwart her body by the load
Of heavy wheels; or with a mortal wound
Her belly bruis'd, and trodden to the ground:
In vain, with loosen'd curls, she crawls along;
Yet, fierce above, she brandishes her tongue;
Glares with her eyes, and bristles with her scales;
But, groveling in the dust, her parts unsound she trails:
So slowly to the port the Centaur tends,
But, what she wants in oars, with sails amends.
Yet, for his galley sav'd, the grateful prince
Is pleas'd th' unhappy chief to recompense.
Pholoe, the Cretan slave, rewards his care,
Beauteous herself, with lovely twins as fair. [...]

[trans. J. Dryden]

There are no surviving ancient sources that would prove the use of any rowing boat or ship specifically for sporting purposes or that any regattas, following the style of other ancient Gk. or Roman games, were organized. There is ample evidence, however, that rowing as a sport originated in the Middle Ages. The art of rowing on large water basins was perfected by the Vikings, whose boats were propelled by oars until about the 7th cent., and even the subsequent use of sails did not eliminate the oars, e.g. while travelling against the wind or on windless days. The Vikings were also the first to build a hydrodynamically-shaped boat, the construction of which was a departure from the large, heavy ships of their contemporaries, even on into the next era. Their style of shipbuilding did not, however, have any direct influence on the construction of rowing boats in continental Europe, where heavy galleys remained an alternative means of transport on coastline waters to lighter sail boats until the appearance of steamships. Venetian gondolas, used for transport because of the unusual nature of Venice, gave in the 14th cent. an impulse to the development of competitive rowing (>REGATA STORICA). Another impulse appeared at the other end of Europe, in England, which since Roman times developed on its rivers and its rich network of canals a system of water transport.

ROWING AND PADDLING SPORTS, a group of sports the essence of which is competing in water vessels propelled by oars of various types. A vessel's construction and type of oars or paddles determine the nature of a given var., e.g. >ROWING, >KAYAKING, >CANOEING. There is also an undetermined number of trad. rowing sports, among which the best known ones are: >CORACLES, >REGATA STORICA, >PUNTING, >BOAT RACE, >DRAGON BOAT RACING, and >JAPANESE FISHERMEN'S REGATTAS.

ROYAL TENNIS, also *court tennis*, *real tennis*; a game deriving from the medieval tradition of Fr. >JEU DE LA PAUME, a var. which is now called >JEU DE LONGUE PAUME. Modern royal tennis is referred to in Fr. as >JEU DE COURTE PAUME.

A royal tennis court in Paris.

Introduced into England, royal tennis became a predecessor of modern >LAWN TENNIS. Different names of the game come from the Eng. *court*, old Fr. *cohort*, Lat. *cohors*; Eng. *tennis*, Fr. *tennez* (to keep); Eng. and Fr. *royal*, Lat. *regalis*; Eng. *real*, Lat. *realis*. See also >TENNIS.

The rules and scoring system are similar to modern tennis, the basic difference being the possibility of playing the ball against the walls and ceiling of the court (see below).

Court design. The size of the court, the penthouse and galleries are not precisely defined and average at 96ft. (29.26m) in length, 32ft. (9.75m) in width, and approx. 30ft. (9.14m) in height. The roof is usu. partly glass for lighting purposes. The ball can bounced off the side walls up to a height of 24ft. (7.32m). The court is divided into 2 equal halves separated by a net 5ft. (152.4cm) high at the sides and 3ft. (91.44cm) high in the center.

The net divides the court into a *hazard side* and a *service side*. On the service side the court is further divided across by 18 lines called *chases*. A similar, though not identical, line arrangement can be found on the hazard side, where the dividing lines are called *hazards*. Chases and hazards allow the players to locate the spot where the ball has bounced, which influences the scoring of the double bounces on the same side, when a player has failed to volley the ball or return it after the first bounce (see below). The chases cover the entire service side, while the hazards cover only part of the hazard side adjacent to the net, the remaining part being empty. The 2 parts are separated by a service line running across the court parallel to the net at a distance of 8.3m from the

net and 6.4m from the end line. The hazard lines are closer to one another, which makes it more difficult to play the ball within their limits. The part of the hazard side between the service line and the end line is the service area.

The walls as a playing area. On the hazard side the *main wall* has a sloping buttress called a *tambour*, which narrows the court by 1ft. 6in. (approx. 0.5m) over the length of 14ft. (approx. 4.3m). Its role is to allow the player on the service court to change the direction of a ball bouncing off it. Except for the tambour, the main wall is empty and may be used for bouncing the ball up to a height of 5.34m. The same holds for the remaining walls above the penthouse galleries. All walls are built from rough bricks. Wall play involves 2 basic techniques: cut and twist.

Galleries. On the wall opposite to the main wall there are 8 galleries, 4 on each side of the net. These are, counting from the net: the *first gallery*, the *door*, the *second gallery*, and the *last gallery* (also called the *winning gallery*). The poles separating the galleries and supporting their roof are located in line with the chases, so that a point won within the bounds of a chase is attributed to the name of the corresponding gallery. At the back of the court, on the hazard side there is a single gallery, the width of which is marked with a pass-line. It holds an opening called a *grille* or *grill* which gives the name to the end wall called the *grille wall* (or *grill wall*). On the service side, under the penthouse, there is an opening in the end wall called the *dedans*, where provision is made for the spectators, who are protected by a net. The sloping roof which tops all galleries and the penthouse is – similar to the walls – used for bouncing the ball off.

Rules of play. At first, royal tennis was played in a palace courtyard surrounded by penthouse galleries, while modern courts are built indoors and imitate the original setting. The principles of serving and returning the ball are similar to modern tennis, with the additional element of playing the ball against the walls and the roof of the penthouse. The tambour and solid nets placed in the corners of the court allow for a rapid change in the direction of the flying ball. In the Eng. var. there are 6 games in a set, while in the Fr. var. – 8 games. The number of sets can be agreed amongst the players or the management of a tournament. In W.Ch. there are 13 sets played over 3 days.

Similar to modern tennis, the idea is to play the ball over the net in a way that makes it difficult for the opponent to return it. The ball can be played directly over the net or by rebounding it against one of the side walls, mainly the penthouse, or the tambour. The number of times the ball can be rebounded against the walls in 1 exchange is not limited, providing the ball is not played above the play line. A ball served by player 'A' and not returned by player 'B' before it bounces twice on his side of the court is considered *dead*. This does not mean losing a point by player 'B', who still has a chance to reverse the loss and even score a point in additional play. In this situation player 'A' does not win the point, which is 'suspended' until the next exchange is completed. Winning a point is dependent upon one of the players meeting certain requirements. Players change sides: player 'B'

A royal tennis court in Oxford, Great Britain.

Jacob van der Heyden, Strasbourg Students Playing Tennis in the Ball House, *1618, copperplate.*

begins to serve, while player 'A' must return the ball so that it bounces further from the net than the previous double bounce. If the ball bounces closer to the net, 'B' scores a point. If the player returning the ball hits the net, he loses a point. However, if he fails to return the ball altogether, the service is repeated. Other rules are similar to modern tennis, i.e. if the ball is not correctly returned, not returned at all, or played out of the court, one player loses a point, while the other gains it. The scoring system is also similar: 15-30-40-game. A score of 40:40 is a deuce and to win the game, one needs to win 2 consecutive exchanges. In fact, the scoring of modern tennis follows that of royal tennis. That mysterious scoring system is mentioned in a poem about the Battle of Agincourt written in 1415. Originally, the scoring may have been in fifteens, going 15:30:45, but over time, instead of saying 'forty-five', people started to say 'forty' for short. The origin of the increments of 15 is also Fr. and may come from the fact that 60 was in medieval France what 100 is today (the Fr. words for seventy, eighty, and ninety are all based on sixty, e.g. seventy is 'soixante-dix' or 'sixty and ten', etc.). Tennis was played for money and matches were accompanied by betting. There were laws in nearby Germany in the 13th and 14th cent. that forbade stakes greater than 60 *deniers*, and one of the coins in circulation, called *gros denier tournois*, was worth 15 *deniers*. A possibility is that the public were playing for one *gros denier tournois* per point up to the max. stake of 60 deniers for a game. Players use asymmetric rackets with handles bent in relation to the netted surface. There are 3 types of balls in use: Eng. balls are hard and enable fast play, while Fr. and Amer. balls are soft and enable slower, more subtle play. The ball is approx. 2½in. (64mm) in diameter and weighs approx. 2½-2¹/₄oz. (71-78g). Called in Fr. *l'esteuf*, they used to be made of sheep's wool or pressed animal hair covered with goat's skin. Modern balls are made of stringed layers of cotton and cloth covered with Melton cloth.

History. The game derives from Fr. >JEU DE PAUME. According to a legend the game was introduced to the Fr. Royal Court in the 10th cent. by a wandering minstrel. By the 11th cent. early tennis was being played in Fr. monasteries. The monks usu. stretched a rope across the cloistered central quadrangles in the monastery or sometimes played immediately adjacent to a castle. In the 14th cent. the game was played in the courtyards of inns and gambling dens called tripots, later specially adjusted to the playing requirements. Soon the court design began to resemble that used in modern times. The game was frequently banned in France and England as an entertainment which distracted townspeople from more serious military exercises and religious duties, but numerous episcopal and

Britain's Prince Edward plays an exhibition match at the Real Tennis Club at Maquarie University in Sydney.

royal edicts were unsuccessful. The most famous court in the early period of royal tennis history was built at the beginning of the 15th cent. at rue Grenier Saint Lazare in Paris and was known as *Le Petit Temple*. Here in 1427 a woman named Margot allegedly went undefeated against all male challengers. In the 16th cent., approx. from the reign of Francis I, a great fan of all sports (1515-47), royal tennis gradually gained prestige and turned from a popular entertainment into a courtly game. Henry II (1547-59) played it himself, thus sanctioning its high social status. The sport also became popular in Italy, promoted by such writings as *Trattato del giucco della palla* by A. Scaino (1555). In 1657 there were 114 courts in Paris alone. In England the game was episodically mentioned in J. Gower's *In Praise of Peace* (1400), then in the anonymous *Promptorium parvulorum* (1440) and a medieval mystery play *Tercius Pastor* by Towneley. It enjoyed great popularity during the times of Henry VIII (1509-47), who loved the game and ordered a royal tennis court to be built at his palace at Hampton Court. Shakespeare mentions tennis in several plays: *Hamlet* (II), *Henry IV* (p. 2, II), *Henry V* (I), *Henry VIII* (I), *Much Ado About Nothing* (III), *Pericles* (II). In 1615 there were 15 royal tennis courts in London, and the game was also played in other buildings. In 1970 during preservation works at Westminster Hall in London workers found in the roof beams several old royal ten-

nis balls, prob. stuck there after mishit serves. The popularity of the game began to fade in the 18th cent. In Italy, Germany and Spain it disappeared altogether. In France there were only 6 courts in the 19th cent., half of which survived until the beginning of the 20th cent. In England the game was preserved owing to the first Eur. sport clubs, such as Marylebone Cricket Club, Queen's Club, and Prince's Club, as well as the universities at Oxford and Cambridge which still cultivate the tradition. A total of 12 courts survived in Great Britain until modern times. A significant factor contributing to the drop in interest in royal tennis was the emergence in 1873 of >LAWN TENNIS. Nevertheless, royal tennis was still practiced and even moderately developed. In 1876 the first royal tennis court was built in the USA, followed by others – in Boston, New York, and Philadelphia. During the 1908 Ol.G. in London royal tennis was a one-off event under the name of jeu de paume. A report written for the IOC after the Games stated that royal tennis is 'too expensive and complicated to become popular and, therefore, it is limited only to France, the United Kingdom and America'. As a result of that report the game was removed from the Olympic program. At the beginning of the 21st cent. there were 9 active royal tennis courts in Great Britain, 7 in the USA, 2 in France, and 2 in Australia. These centers hold various social, as well as championship events, the most prestigious ones being the open championships of the USA and the UK (both for amateurs and professionals), French Open Championships, The Burthust Cup played since 1922 in London and Paris, the annual Oxford-Cambridge match (since 1859), Van Alen Trophy played since 1956 between the academic teams of Great Britain and the USA, Coupe de Paris (since 1910), Coupe de Bordeaux (since 1919). Other tournaments include: Raquette d'Argent, a tournament played alternately in Paris and Bordeaux since 1899; Golden Rackets, a tournament in Australia; and events organized by Hobart Tennis Club incl. H.J. Hill Cup in singles, Captain James Johnson Cup in men's doubles, and Bendena Cup for women. Irregular W.Ch. are held in the country that currently holds the title. From 1928-55 the title was held by a Frenchman P. Eychebaster. Outstanding players of the 1980s and 1990s include the world champions W. Davis and R. Fahey (Australia). There is international cooperation based on agreements between national organizations. No international federation exists. In 1993 the number of clubs was as follows: Great Britain – 11; Australia – 3; France – 3; USA – 9. The sport is regulated by various national organizations: the Tennis and Rackets Association (Great Britain), the Austrl. Royal Tennis Association, the Canadian Real Tennis Association, Comité Française de Tennis, the United States Court Tennis Association; Dutch Real Tennis Association.

L.St.J. and P.J. Wordie, eds, *The Royal Game*, 1989; M. Garnett, *A History of Royal Tennis in Australia*, 1963; V. Mursell, *An Introduction to Royal Tennis*, 1986; http://www.tradgames.org.uk/games/Tennis.htm

Gabriele Bella, A Game of Tennis, *18th cent., oil on canvas.*

RUBBER-BAND DUCKPINS, also 'small-pin bowling', a bowling game, where the pins have rubber bands around them, making the action more dynamic after the ball hits them. See >BOWLING, >EUROPEAN BOWLING.

RUGBY FIVES, a var. of the Eng. game of >FIVES, developed at the well-known Eng. public school in Rugby, also famous for the game of the same name (>RUGBY). The object of Rugby fives is to bounce a ball against a wall using one's hand. As opposed to >ETON FIVES, which is only played by doubles, there are both singles and doubles in Rugby fives.
The construction and dimensions of the court. Rugby fives is played on a rectangular court with 4 walls, unlike Eton fives but similar to >WINCHESTER FIVES. The length of the court is 18ft. (5.5m). The ball may be bounced off the side walls only up to the height demarcated by the lines painted on them: these adjoin the head wall at a height of 15ft. (4.6m), continue at that height inwards for 12ft. (3.7m), and drop to 6ft. (1.8m) at the back wall. There is a board in the lower part of the head wall, up to a height of 2½ft. (0.76m). These dimensions were codified in 1931; however, not all courts adhere to them, as some had been built earlier and could not follow the model. The high costs prevent many schools from converting the courts, esp. as the game seems to be losing popularity among pupils. The walls are painted black so that it contrasts sharply with the small white ball, while the floor is usu. red.
Equipment. Until the 1950s, the ball was made from cork covered by straps of fabric sewn together with a dense thread, which provided additional bounce. The surface of the ball was made of leather but nowadays the coat is usu. plastic. Players wear lightweight leather padded gloves.
How the game is played. Before the actual match, a preliminary rally is played, whose winner is 'up', i.e. he becomes the receiver, which is a privileged position in Rugby fives. The loser is 'down', i.e. the first to serve. The server throws the ball at the wall and may receive it himself after the first bounce, which he usu. does. He can also call the other player to receive the ball but this is done much less frequently. The serve should first bounce off a side wall, and only then off the other walls or the ground. It is not forbidden to serve off the front wall but the opponent does not have to receive such a serve; if he, after all, does decide to receive it, he must call his intention to do so by shouting 'blackguard'. When receiving the serve, the ball may not be bounced off the ceiling or the ground. Further during the game, the ball may be bounced off all 4 walls, and off the ground if receiving a ball aimed at the back wall. The ball may only be hit with the hand or forearm. Points may be scored, after winning a rally, only by the receiver. In doubles games, the players of one team usu. position themselves on the same side of the court, and warn their partners when they intend to intercept the ball by calling 'mine'. A match consists of 3 games. A game is completed when one of the sides scores 15pts. with at least a 2-pt. advantage. This means that in a situation called 'game-ball all' (14:14) one has to reach 16pts. (unless the opponent scores his 15th point in the meantime, where the winning score must be 17:15, and so on). The first side to win 2 games wins the whole match. In team matches (e.g. matches between schools), games are not counted but all the game points are added up – it may so happen that a team that has won more games lose the whole match as they have fewer 'small points'. This system is intended to motivate the players until the last moments of a match. A match team consists of 2 doubles pairs, but apart from the doubles matches, each player of each team plays individually against all players of the opposing team. When longer games might disrupt the plan of a match, they are shortened to 11pts. Umpires only appear on Rugby fives courts very rarely. The school tradition of the game means that most players are under 30, and one can usu. meet older players only at alumni meetings.
History. Until specific rules developed in Rugby, the history of Rugby fives was the same as the general history of >FIVES. The game started taking shape in Rugby in the first half of the 19th cent. An important period in its growth was the time when T. Arnold was the headmaster of the Rugby school – even though he was not a sportsman himself, Arnold

thought that sport was extremely important in education. The status of fives in Rugby had a strong influence on its position in other Eng. schools. However, the actual formalization of the game started elsewhere, which led to the development of a number of competing var., the most important of those being Eton fives and Winchester fives. The Rugby Fives Association was finally established in 1927. It later succeeded in reaching a compromise regarding the rules between a number of schools. The RFA upholds the high educational tradition initiated by Arnold, offering help and assistance to pupils even after they graduate. This manifests itself in special tournaments organized to celebrate those pupil-players who achieved high social status in the UK, and so provided a good example for future generations. The Jester's Cup, considered to be the Brit. singles championship, has been organized since 1932. The prestige of the Rugby school championships rose in 1934 with the inauguration of the Cyriax Cup, commemorating the former Rugby pupil and outstanding player Dr. E. Cyriax. Since 1930, a national championship for Eng. and Scot. schools has been held under the auspices of the RFA. For many years, Oundle School dominated the doubles in those championships, and so did St. Paul's School, albeit to a lesser extent. None of the schools was able to dominate the singles competition, though, and so representatives of 7 different schools won the championship before WWII. After 1945, Oundle School came to dominate both the singles and doubles, even though teams from other schools were also successful, incl. Denston College, Alleyn's School, St. Dunstan's College, Merchiston Castle School, Clifton School and Bedford School. YMCA Manchester, too, joined the championships. Today, there are separate championships in N and W England, and Scotland. Oxford is the leading team in university tournaments, with many more titles than Cambridge University, 2nd in the ranking. However, Rugby fives is almost totally unknown outside of the Brit. Isles, apart from a number of isolated courts built in some Commonwealth countries by Rugby graduates.

RUGBY UNION, a ball game using an oval ball, played by 2 teams of 15 players each in the amateur version, and 2 teams of 13 players each in the professional version. The pitch is 100x69m (formerly, it was defined in the Imperial standard as 110x75yds., or 105.4x68.55m). The goals consist of posts 3.4m high, with a crossbar at a height of 3.05m. The inflated oval ball is covered with leather or plastic, and has a length of 280-300mm, and a max. circumference of 760-790mm, and weighs 400-440g. The object of the game is to move the ball by carrying, passing or kicking it, into the opponents'

scoring zone at the far end of the pitch. Points are scored in the following situations (professional scoring in parentheses): grounding the ball in the opponents' scoring zone (the so-called 'try' or 'touch down') scores 5pts., formerly 4; a successful conversion, or shooting the ball by place kick or drop kick over the crossbar is worth 2pts.; a penalty kick scores 3pts.; and a drop kick in general play is also worth 3pts. The ball may be passed by hand only backwards, but it can be kicked in any direction. A match consists of two 40-min. halves with a 5-min. interval. Due to the frequent injuries, protective helmets were introduced in the 1990s, but they are recommended rather than obligatory. Players sent off for offences or eliminated due to injuries may not be substituted for. As a result, the game shapes the ability to make up for unexpected losses of players by testing the effectiveness of a reduced team. For that reason, it promotes those features of team work that are closer to real life than e.g. the tactics of substitution in football, basketball or ice hockey. See also >WHEELCHAIR RUGBY.
History. It is traditionally believed that rugby originated during a football game played at Rugby School on 7 April 1823, when one of the pupils, W.W. Ellis, after an unsuccessful effort, grabbed the ball, ran to the goal, and scored, which was obviously not recognized as a valid goal by the referee. The incident became well known in England as an example of breaking the rules of fair play but did not lead to any changes in the rules of football. However, in 1839, the Cambridge student A. Pell, a member of the university's football team, suggested that they should

A ball used in rugby union.

England captain Lawrence Dallaglio breaks from the scrum during the Five Nations match against France at Twickenham in London.

Rugby on a Polish postage stamp issued in 1990.

A rugby match on a 19th-century watercolor.

R

WORLD SPORTS ENCYCLOPEDIA

copy the famous incident of Rugby. The experiment succeeded, leading to the development of a new game which came to be known as 'rugby football' in Cambridge. However, in contrast to what many sport historians believe, W.W. Ellis's exploit was not an innovation but rather a conscious breach of the rules of one game to unexpectedly introduce those of another, known as >WINCHESTER COLLEGE FOOTBALL. The name 'rugby football' was to be later truncated to 'rugby'. From about the half of the 19th cent., the game caught on at Eng. public schools and universities, which led to the estab. of an inter-university committee who introduced codified rules. In 1866, Amer. journalist H. Chadwick started popularizing rugby in the USA, along with football and cricket, initially with poor results. The first Amer. rugby club was founded in 1875 but the game was later absorbed by >AMERICAN FOOTBALL, which actually borrowed many elements from it. In 1871, a general meeting of Eng. rugby clubs was held, and the Eng. Rugby Union (today Rugby Football) was established. Similar national organizations were set up in Scotland (1873), Ireland (1874) and Wales (1881). They were all amateur associations. In 1887-88, a team consisting of players of a number of Eng. clubs traveled to Australia and N.Zealand. The game turned out to be esp. suited to the physical and mental predispositions of the Maoris, who took the N.Zealand rugby team to many successes in the following decades. In 1895, 22 Eng. clubs broke away from the RFU and formed the Rugby Football League (RFL), whose professional character has been maintained to this day. (The RFU remained amateur.) In 1934, the Fédération Internationale de Rugby Amateur (FIRA) was established. Rugby is a mass sport mainly in the United Kingdom, with about 2,500 clubs and about 120,000 players. The most important international tournaments include the so-called Five Nations tournament (England, Wales, Ireland, Scotland, and France) and the Triple Crown tournament. In N.America, amateurs participate in the International Rugby Union Pacific Coast Series. Although the name suggests participation by a large number of teams from all over the world, or at least the Pacific Coast, in actuality only 2 teams participate – Berkeley University (USA) and University of Brit. Columbia (Canada). Amateur rugby was on the Olympic program in 1900, 1908, 1920 and 1924 but was not too successful – sometimes there were fewer teams than medals to be given away. A general fight between the players occurred during the 1924 final match between the USA and France, eventually sealing the game's fate; the suggestion to drop it from the program had already been made as it was an unpopular event that burdened the national teams with large numbers of players. The Olympic gold went to France (1900), Australasia (1908), and the USA (1920 and 1924).

After WWII, the game became popular in socialist countries. It developed esp. well in Czechoslovakia and Rumania (the latter team had won an Olympic medal in 1924). Today, the main events under the auspices of the FIRA are the FIRA Cup, and the W.Ch. and E.Ch. Top international teams include France, England, Wales, Scotland, Ireland, N.Zealand, Australia, S.Africa and the USA. Rugby played with 7 players in a team has been increasingly popular. A World Cup was first organized in 1998 for both men and women. 91 teams participate in international >SEVEN-A-SIDE RUGBY events (1999).

Professional rugby. During the 1893 meeting of Eng. clubs, most delegates supported a purely amateur status of the game. Delegates supporting professionalism formed the separatist Northern Union (1895), initially combining amateur and professional rugby. After 1898, the Union became an exclusively professional organization. In 1906, the rules were changed, cutting the number of players from 15 to 13, while the name was changed to Rugby League in 1922. Under the auspices of the League, there are local leagues at the level of counties. In the second half of the season, the best 16 local teams take part in a cup-system championship with a final match which has traditionally been held at Wembley Stadium, London. There is a clause in the rules of professional rugby preventing players from social degradation after they end their careers (as opposed to many other professional sports, such as football or boxing). The clause requires the players to have a permanent profession in addition to the sport. Failing this requirement is punished with severe financial penalties that make playing unprofitable. There are also regulatory limitations of the fees paid for playing rugby. The salary is higher for a victory than for a loss and, on the average, is comparable to salaries in other professions, making profiteering on players more difficult. However, these rules are often evaded by offering the players well-paid jobs outside rugby. The World Cup is the main international event. International matches also enjoy high prestige. Tendencies towards cooperation between amateur and

Rookie Charlie Hodgson of England scores a penalty kick during the Rugby Union International match against Romania played at Twickenham in London.

professional rugby organizations are increasingly visible, resulting from the globalization of the sport and the influence of the mass media.

Rugby in literature and art. Rugby has never been an obsession in literature and art but it has been included in some outstanding works. The history of literature associated with Rugby College, where the game originated, was started by T. Hughes's famous novel *Tom Brown's School Days* (1857). It includes a chapter entitled *The Last Match*, devoted to rugby. The atmosphere of an Eng. public school, in rugby's pioneering days is depicted, together with unique rugby terminology. In 1963, one of the most famous novels of the 'angry young men' trend, *This Sporting Life* (1960), became the basis for a screenplay of the equally famous film under the same title, directed by L. Anderson. The film was awarded the FIPRESCI prize at the Cannes Festival in 1963, and R. Harris received the prize for the best male actor. Another well-known film associated with rugby is the French *Allez, France!* (1964, directed by R. Dhéry, real name R. Foulley). The film is a comedy that at the same time points to the serious and growing problem of nationalism in sport, and the behavior of rugby fans.

The painting *Rugby* by A. Lhotte (1917) is among the classics of Eur. cubism. Another painting under the same title, by the Luxembourg artist L. Jacoby was awarded the Watercolor prize during the Olympic Art Contest in Amsterdam (1928).

R.O. Bause, *Hrajte rugby*, 1947; M. Bondarowicz, J. Grochowski, *Rugby – rys historyczny, podstawy techniki i taktyki oraz przepisy gry*, 1976; J. Pignon, *Langue du rugby*, 1952; R. Poulain, *Rugby – jeu et entrainement*, 1964; J. Macrory, *Running with the Ball. The Birth of Rugby Football*, 1991; *Rugby Union. Know the Game*, anon. 1994; personal contact: M. Gise.

RUILHAL AR BROC'H, a Bret. game whose equivalents are Fr. *rouler le blaireau* and Eng. *roll the badger*.

L. Peru, 'La tradition populaire de jeux de plein air en Bretagne', LJP, 1998.

RUINNUTSIMAADLUS, one of the 3 var. of Est. folk wrestling (>MAADLEMINE).

RUN SHEEP, RUN, a children's game popular in the USA. The participants form 2 groups, each selecting a leader. The leader hides his players around and comes back to the other group, which is a signal for them to start looking for the other team. The leader of the hidden team may use agreed signals to tell the searchers whether they are closing onto the 'targets' or not. Usually, color terms are used for that purpose, e.g. 'yellow, yellow' would mean that the searchers are moving away from the targets. When a hidden player is found, he tries to run to the base without getting caught.

RUNDBOLD, a Dan. bat-and-ball game where the ball is batted and points are scored by runners when the ball is in the air, [Dan. *rund* – round + *bold* – ball; the game is also called *brandbold* – bullet, lit. 'burn-ball', from *brænde* – to burn, shoot + *bold* – ball; this also refers to players put out of the game after being hit (burnt) with the ball]. Rundbold did not originate in Denmark and most likely

is a borrowing from Eng. >ROUNDERS. The borrowing must have occurred in the 19th cent., the first period of expansion of Brit. sports in Europe. The game is similar to Amer. and Wel. >BASE-BALL, Ir. rounders and >TUTT-BALL. Two teams with 10 players each participate in a game of rundbold. The pitch is a rectangle about 50x30m, divided unevenly into 2 smaller rectangles. In the corners of the larger field, there is a square about 20x20m with 4 'bases'. As opposed to Amer. baseball, the position of the batter – the *slagmål* (which was often marked by a *stor brændeknude*, or 'large log') – is not at the last, 'fourth base' (home plate), but half way between the first and fourth bases, often away from the line connecting the two. This means that the infield has the shape of a pentagon, like in rounders. The first team takes up positions in the infield, while the other – in the outfield. The outfielders choose from among them the best catchers (*gribere*) and one bowler (*opgiver*). The bowler pitches the ball at a height of about 1m so that the batter (*slære*) can hit it with his bat (*boldtræ*) or with his arm (straightened at the elbow). Each batter has 3 attempts. If he does not succeed in hitting the ball, he loses his right to any further hits and moves onto the first base. After a successful hit, he runs to the first base, at the same time trying to assess whether he will manage to get to any of the further bases before the ball is intercepted by the players of the other team and passed back to the catcher. At the same time, all the other players who had started their runs before but could not complete an entire circuit may proceed to the next base or bases. Each player of the batting team who completes a whole run, making it to the fourth base, scores a point for the team. The players must stop as soon as the catcher receives the ball from his team mates and touches the batting line with it (he cannot throw the ball but must touch the line with the ball in his hand). Players who have not completed their runs are considered 'dead' and put out of play. If the defensive (catching) team intercepts the ball in the infield, all the players of the offensive team currently at bases are considered 'dead' even if they have reached them before the ball was intercepted. The current batter is also declared 'dead'. However, if he completes a full run before the ball returns to the batting line, he is considered a 'freer' and may at his own discretion 'free' one of the 'dead' infielders (*indespiller*). If none of the infielders currently at bases may be freed at that time, the right to do so is postponed until such an opportunity arises. Similar games are known as *brännboll* in Sweden and >POLTOPALLO in Finland.

RUNGKUN, a type of folk acrobatic show performed by the Araucanians or Mapuche Indians of Chile (the Span. equivalent is known as *saltos*). Today it is no longer practiced. Chilean Indians saw rungkun as both a form of military exercise and competition. They were excellent jumpers referred to as *saltadores* in Span. sources. They could make high jumps without a run-up, and jump over wide gorges in the mountains. One of the most famous Chilean strongmen of the time was Caupolican. Among other things, he was awarded the title of Toqui General for supporting a huge tree trunk on his shoulders for a longer time than his competitors. But he was

also an excellent *saltador*. His feats were described by the Span. poet Alonso de Ercilla y Zuñiga:

The Sun had set when he thrust
the enormous burden off his back.
He jumped up high, twisting his body,
And showing that he had even more strength.
The village people around said in one voice:
We can lay our heavy burdens
On shoulders so firm.

M. Manquilef, 'Comentarios del Pueblo Araucano II. La Gimnasia Nacional', *Revista de Folklore Chileno*, 1914, 129; O. Plath, 'Rungkun', JYDLCH, 1946, 24.

RUNNING, a natural form of fast human movement, a type of competition and the pivotal element of many sports. From a purely motor point of view the running movement, or running step, consists of resistance and flight stages. The flight stage, i.e. the instant when both feet are off the ground, differentiates running from >RACE WALKING. This rule applies, of course, to running proper and not to cross-country skiing and speed skating.

Running girls, *an image from a Greek vase.*

S. Petkiewicz, a runner and one of the rivals of J. Kusociński, described the cultural nature of running in his manual *Biegi lekkoatletyczne* (*Light Athletic Running*, 1936) in the following way:

If when discussing running we want to substantiate its development, then we have to go back in time to a very distant past, that is to the very beginning of human existence on the Earth [...]. In order to survive man had to overcome major obstacles, had to hunt, had to run fast and far when fleeing a stronger enemy and in this way, due to natural causes and everyday circumstances, man developed this ability. If we approach running from this particular perspective we will understand how fundamental it was for humans. It was a forced and, most likely, the only way to survive, it became part and parcel of human existence and although modern man does not have to rely on it to the extent that prehistoric man had to, he still feels instinctively attracted to it. When, due to civilizational advancement, humankind significantly departed from the way it originally led its existence and the threat of physical degradation loomed, various types of physical exercise [...] whose task was to maintain the necessary balance between the spirit and the flesh were developed. [...] running is the most natural and the most suitable type of physical exercise for human development.

It is no surprise that the oldest preserved writings treat running as a vital ability. In the Biblical Psalms David thanks God for endowing him with the ability to run fast:

Who made my feet swift as those of hinds
and set me secure on the heights

[18, 34]

Running was developed in the sports sense in ancient Greece where it was a regular event first during burial games and then during the Ol.G. and all of the most important Hellenic games (>DIAULOS, >DOLICHOS, >DROMOS, >HOPLITODROMO, >STADIODROMOS). In ancient Celtic culture running played a crucial role as it constituted a test of fitness and usefulness of a warrior in battle (>FENIAN RUNNING). In the Middle Ages and Renaissance various forms of running constituted parts of local, usu. city or town, competitions and esp. of races 'on foot and naked' during Roman games (*ludi romani*). A Pol. traveler, M. Rywocki, saw and described such races in his *Księgi peregrynackie* (*Books of Peregrination*, 1586): 'There is this cus-

Runners on a 1906 Greek postage stamp.

A *Running Girl, statuette in bronze from the Temple of Zeus at Dodone, c.550 BC.*
Events for young girls were held every 4 years in the stadium at Olympia during the festivities held in honor of the goddess Hera. The participants were divided into different categories according to age: children, adolescents and young women. They wore a short chiton leaving the shoulder uncovered down to the breast and ran the distance of 32.28m – less than the length of the stadium.

A running competition in New York, from London Illustrated News, *19th century.*

*A runner on a stamp issued for the 1920
Olympic Games in Antwerp.*

A 3,000-m steeplechase run.

with more accurate stopwatches (in the second
half of the 19th cent.). >ORIENTEERING has
been borrowed from the modern Scand. running
tradition. The modern >JOGGING is a recreational
and health-oriented var. of running.

The most noteworthy folk var. of running include
the >MONTENEGRO RACES, CHUKCHEE RAC-
ES, >ROAD RACES, >INDIAN COURIER RAC-
ES, >YAKUTE RACES, >KALMUCK RACES,
>KIRGHIZ RACES, >KUKINI RACES, >BURIAT
LAMA RACES, >CHUKCHEE CIRCLE RUN, >SA-
MOAN RACES, >TAHITIAN RACES, >TAPIRAPI
RACES, >TURKMEN RACES, >TIBETAN RAC-
ES, >WEDDING RACES, >HAIR CLIPPING RAC-
ES, >BALL RACING, >FETTER-CUTTING RACE,
>LAMJEI, >OMAOMA, >TAUPIRIPIRI; cf. also
>SKI ORIENTEERING, >MARATHON, >VERTI-
CAL MARATHON, >LOG RUNNING, >WIFE
PICK-A-BACK RACES.

J. Fixx, *Second Book of Running,* 1980; B. Glover &
J. Shepherd, *Runner's Handbook,* 1978; J. Lynch,
Running Within, 1999; G. Sheenhan, *This Running
Life,* 1980; J. Ullyot, *Women's Running,* 1978; *The
Running Times Guide to Breakthrough Running,* 2000.

RUNNING AT THE RING, also *tilting at the ring* or
ring riding, Ital. *la punta della lancia,* Dan. >RIN-
GRIDING, Ger. *Ringrennen* or *Ringreiten,* Flem.
>RINGSTEKEN TE PAARD or Croatian >ALKA. An
old form of chivalric contest, the object of which was
to target the lance at the inside of a small metal ring
suspended above the ground. The size of the ring,
as well as the height at which it was suspended varied
according to local trad. Many written sources indicate that the ring was level with the mounted knight's
head. The run-up could have been as much as 80-
100 paces or, according to other sources, not more
than 20-30 paces. J. Strutt records the following:

*The excellency of the pastime was to ride at full speed, and
thrust the point of the lance through the ring, which [...] might*

tom in Rome whereby people take part in races
naked. On this day (16 Feb. 1586) 8 young men
competed naked for a bolt of red damask; an hour
later 7 old men competed naked for a bolt of green

Development of modern running was largely influenced by the introduction of timing – first with
the imprecise timepieces used solely in long-distance races (as early as the 18th cent.) and later

Runners, a mesolythic rock painting, Pays des Basuto, South Africa.

Running at the ring during an international chivalric tournament at the Golub-Dobrzyń castle in Poland.

damask; and an hour after that 9 boys ran naked for
a bolt of red cloth' (manuscript in the Pol. Academy
of Sciences (PAN) Library in Cracow, no. 1760). Similar competitions may be deemed the archetype of
modern >STREET RUNNING. Modern forms of running, and the track and field events in particular, were
largely molded by the running competitions held in
18th- and 19th-cent. England (>ATHLETIC RUN-
NING, >TEAM RUNNING, >LONG DISTANCE RUN-
NING, >FLAT RACES, >CROSS-COUNTRY RUN-
NING, >HURDLING, >RELAYS, >MIDDLE-DIS-
TANCE RUNNING, >STEEPLECHASE, >OLYMPIC
MARATHON, >SPRINT, >ATHLETIC SPRINT). In
the past running was an exclusively male sport in
almost all cultures with few exceptions whereby separate running competitions were held for women,
as in the case of the Hera games held in Olympia.
At the turn of the 19th cent. female athletes, taking
full advantage of tendencies toward women's emancipation, started to overcome, similarly to other
sports, the trad. barriers that had prevented them
from taking part in running events. Amer. (since
1903) and Fin. women (since 1913) were the first to
officially participate in competitions at the national
level and whose results were maintained as official
national and international records. In the majority of
countries (including the US and Poland) the first
women's track and field championships were organized in 1923. During the Ol.G. female runners competed in a few selected events for the first time in
1928 in Amsterdam.

Johann Christoph Neyffer, Ring-jousting at the Knights' Academy, Tübingen, *1606-1608, copperplate.*

be readily drawn out by the force of the stroke, and remain upon the top of the lance. [...] At the commencement of the seventeenth century, the pastime of running at the ring was reduced to a science; the length of the course was measured, and marked out according to the properties of the horses that were to run; for one of the swiftest kind [...] one hundred paces from the starting place to the ring, and thirty paces beyond it, to stop him, were deemed necessary; but such horses as had been trained to the exercise, and were more regular in their movements, eighty paces to the ring, and twenty beyond it, were thought to be sufficient. The ring [...] ought to be placed with much precision, somewhat higher than the left eyebrow of the practitioner, when sitting upon his horse; because it was necessary for him to stoop a little running towards it. In tilting at the ring, three courses were allowed to each candidate; and he who thrust the point of his lance through it the oftenest, or in case no such thing was done, struck it the most frequently, was the victor; but if so happened, that none of them did either the one or the other, or that they were equally successful, the courses were to be repeated until such time as the superiority of one put an end to the contest.

[Strutt, 1801, 113]

As chivalric knighthood collapsed, the event gradually disappeared. At present, the oldest Eur. tournament where running at the ring has been annually played since medieval times, is the Croatian >ALKA. The first attempts to revive running at the ring coincided with the growing interest in medieval matters during Romanticism. In 1858 the event was introduced into the program of the Much Wenlock Ol.G., which were originated in England in 1850 by W.P. Brookes. Riders competing at running at the ring were dressed in medieval costumes and followed rules modeled after the description offered by J. Strutt in *The Sports and Pastimes of the People of England* (1801). Running at the ring contests were often diversified by setting up a >QUINTAIN, which punished a rider who slowed down to take a more accurate aim.

RUQUM, [Arab *ruqum* – numbering, counting], a game played in Mecca, Saudi Arabia. The rules are unclear. The game is mentioned, without a description, in M. Ibrahim al-Majman's dictionary of Arab sports and games *Min al'abina ash-sha 'biyya* (1983).

RUS-TOPI, an Armenian bat-and-ball game similar to Pol. >PALANT. It was introduced into Armenia via Rus. >LAPTA, hence the name, meaning the 'Russian ball' [Armenian *rus* – 'Russian' + *topi* – 'ball'].

RUTZEN, a Swiss folk wrestling style. The fight is fought in an upright position. Wrestlers can take holds on all parts of the opponent's body. Touching the ground with any part of the body other than the legs means losing the fight. Wrestlers wear characteristic leather shorts.

RYGGETAK, also *ryggjekneppa*, the Norw. equivalent of Swed. >RYGGTAG folk wrestling style.

RYGGTAG, a Swed. folk wrestling style, also called *ryggkast* in some areas, and >RYGGETAK in Norway. The Swed. ethnologist M. Hellspong thinks it is a var. of a more general folk wrestling style known as >LIVTAG. According to the wrestling historian W. Baxter, it is cultivated in Gotland even today and features as the final event of the local sports festival. Baxter asserts that ryggtag belongs to the same group of simple wrestling contests as Icel. >HRYGGSPENNA, Scot. >BACKHOLD, and Fin. >RYSSÄNKASTI.

RYKKE ARMENE FRA HINANDEN, Dan. for 'pulling arms apart', [Dan. *at rykke* – to pull apart + *armene* – arms + *fra* – from + *hinanden* – one another]. A trad. Dan. strength test. One of the participants stands with his arms crossed, pressings his palms against his chest. The other participant grabs him by the elbows and tries to force his arms apart with a strong yank.

J. Møller, 'At rykke armene fra hinanden', GID, 1997, 4.

RYKKE FINGRENE FRA HINANDEN, in full *at rykke fingrene fra hinanden*, Dan. for 'pulling fingers apart', [Dan. *at rykke* – to pull apart + *fingrene* – the fingers + *fra* – from + *hinanden* – one another]. A trad. Dan. strength test. One participant presses the fingertips of one hand against those of the other at chest height, forming a figure much like the bow of a boat, with the palms facing towards his chest. The other participant grabs him by the wrists and tries to pull his hands apart.

J. Møller, 'At rykke fingrene fra hinanden', GID, 1997, 4, 16.

RYKKE KALVEN FRA KOEN, Dan. for 'pulling the calf out from the cow'. A trad. daily game of Dan. farm-hands. Two farm-hands lie down on the ground next to each other, on their stomachs, with heads pointing in the same direction, thus imitating a 'cow'. A third farm-hand lies in between them, but with his head in the opposite direction, pretending to be the 'calf'. They all lock their arms and legs. A further 2 participants, pretending to be attending the 'delivery', try to pull the calf out from the cow by tugging on the intertwined limbs. The cow imitators keep their legs and arms crossed for as long as they can, making the delivery of the calf more difficult and more similar to giving birth to a real calf. According to old descriptions, they are also supposed to accompany this with 'bovine sounds'.

J. Møller, 'At rykke kalven fra koen', GID, 1997, 4, 34.

RYO, Jap. for 'shooting', included a number of var. or archery in ancient Japan, e.g. horseback archery which encompassed >INUOMONO, >KASA-GAKE, >YABUSAME, and >KYUDO.

RYSSÄNKASTI, a Fin. folk wrestling style where the objective is to throw the opponent to the ground and press him to it with one's body. Even though the name means 'Russian trick', it really derives from Swed. *rysskast* (literally 'Russian grip'). According to W. Baxter, the Swed. equivalent of ryssänkasti is >RYGGTAG, while the Swed. sport ethnologist M. Hellspong suggests that one of the grips of >KRAGTAG is the counterpart.

W. Baxter, 'Les luttes traditionelles a traverse le monde', LJP, 1998, 83; M. Hellspong, 'Kragtag, Brottning som folkling leg', RIG, 1991, 4.

RZUCANIE KULKI, Pol. for 'throwing a ball', a Pol. children's sporting game from the village of Bukówiec Górny (Wielkopolska, Poland). The idea is to toss and hit a ball made of tow and linen. The game is described by a local ethnographer, A. Kowol-Marcinek:

[...] It was a unique skill game in which some 10 different movements were involved. It was played by hitting the ball against a wall, fence or gate, while constantly changing positions. Hits were forehand, backhand, with both hands, with the elbow, head, or bended knee, by throwing the ball from behind the back etc. The important thing was not to let the ball fall to the ground. The game was usually a competition between several girls, but could also be played individually for practice and as a form of pastime. The player that scored the largest number of hits would be the winner.

A. Kowol-Marcinek, 'Rzucanie kulki', *Dawne gry i zabawy dziecięce w Bukówcu Górnym*, Dom Kultury, Leszno, 1999, p. 17.

RZUCANKA, a simple Pol. ball game played in schools. According to the Pol. game theorist R. Trześniowski, the course of the game is as follows:

One player stands apart from the others. He begins by throwing the ball in a high lob so that it lands between the other players, who try to catch it in any way they like. Whoever catches the ball, takes over from the thrower. However, if the ball lands on the ground, it must be returned to the thrower, who repeats the throw.

[Zabawy i gry ruchowe, 1995, 268]

Chrispyn de Passe the Younger, Ring Tournament, *1626, copperplate.*

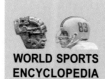

WORLD SPORTS ENCYCLOPEDIA

R

S

S'ISTRUMPA, a type of folk wrestling, known and presently practiced in the mountainous northern regions of Sardinia; a technical sport, similar to Scot. >BACKHOLD and Swed. >LIVTAG; it nearly disappeared at the beginning of the 1880s; in 1985 a local association was established with the aim of restoring the tradition of s'istrumpa; the sport was codified, weight divisions were introduced for the first time; soon after the Federazione S'istrumpa was established, since 1995 a member of the International Federation of Celtic Wrestling.
W. Baxter, 'S'Istrumpa', 'Les luttes tradtionnelles a traverse le monde', LJP, 1998, 77.

SABRE, see >FENCING.

SABT SBUT, Arab. for. 'Saturday of Saturdays', a regional var. of the Arab folk game generally known as >ŠRIH EŠŠARH.

SACK RACING, (Span. *carreras de sacos*, Dan. *sækkeløb* also *sækkevæddeløb* or *spandevæddeløb*, Ger. *Sackhüpfen* or *Sacklaufen*), a folk sport popular in many countries and involving a race in which each contestant has legs enclosed in a sack, usu. reaching up to the waist, and moves forward by running, or rather jumping, towards the finish line. In Spain the distance to be covered is usu. 30-60m, while it is 20-30m in Denmark. The contestants have to hold the sacks up with the hands to prevent them from sliding down. Since the sacks seriously restrain freedom of movement the contestants often fall to the ground which, of course, is very amusing for the spectators. Sack races take place between individual contestants or pairs using one sack (a *sack race for two*). Genuine folk sack-racing competitions (in contrast to popular or commercial, mass-media-inspired contests) are still widely popular in Arenas (Malaga province), Hornachuelos (Cordoba), Vilamartin (Cadiz), Provedilla (Albacete) and Villarino de los Aires (Salamanca).
J. Møller, 'Sækkeløb', GID, 1997, 98-9; C. Moreno Palos, 'Carreras de sacos', JYTE, 1992, 40; R. Garcia Serrano, 'Carreras de sacos', JDTE, 1974, 54.

SADDLE BRONC-RIDING, see >RODEO.

SADDLE THE NAG, a game of skill and acrobatics with 2 teams participating. The teams elect their chiefs. One of them stands erect next to a wall, and the rest of the team, bending over, form a line behind the chief. The first player of the opposite team jumps onto the last player in the line and tries to 'crawl' to the chief on the contestants' backs. Having reached the chief, the player taps his head. The bending players try to shrug off the player on their backs, before he reaches the chief. Once shrugged off, a player is eliminated and must await the next round. A player who manages to tap the chief scores one point. If in a given round none of the players manage to score a point, the teams change sides. A game usually consists of 6 rounds. The team with the most points wins the game. Cf. >BUNG THE BUCKET, >SHIP.
A.B. Gomme, 'Saddle the Nag', TGESI, 1898, II, 147.

SÆKKELØB, see >SACK RACING.

SÆLHUNDEFANGST, Dan. for 'seal catching, seal hunting', [Dan. *sælhunde* – seal + *fange* – fish,

Sack racing.

catch]. A Dan. children's game. Two players sit facing each other with their legs straight so that their feet touch. Then they hold hands and start to 'row', i.e. one of them leans backwards and the other forwards etc. The other players are 'seals', who walk around. When a 'seal' gets too close to the rowers, the rowers stop rowing and immediately throw themselves at the 'seal'. If a 'seal' is caught, the rowers put it to one side and when they catch another 'seal', they change sides with the caught 'seals'.
J. Møller, 'Sælhundefangst', GID, 1997, 2, 47.

SAFARI, a tourist journey or rally across a stretch of land, relating to the old Arab hunting expeditions, trade or war caravans organized usually in E Africa (Arab. *safar* – trip). There are different types of safari, organized for adventure-seeking tourists, the main ones including:
AUTOMOBILE SAFARI, most often practiced in Afr. countries, where the extensive savannah is suitable for traveling in off-road vehicles and getting close to exotic animals. Kenya, with its natural parks and game reserves, is the most frequent destination of automobile safari lovers.
HORSEBACK SAFARI, organized in a few Afr. and Asiatic countries. The best developed forms are in India and Kenya. They include camping in wildlife areas, bonfires at night, arranged 'adventures' and the like.
CAMEL SAFARI, organized in some Arab countries, but its most highly developed forms are practiced in India in the Thar desert (the regions of Jodhpur, Jaisalmer and Bikaner). The region of Shekhawati is another popular area. Safari on camels is usually modeled on the old merchant caravans with arranged 'adventures'. It visits settlements untouched or little touched by civilization. It is usually either a single day trip or a 2-week expedition.
ELEPHANT TREKKING, a more gentle form of safari or a trip with staged adventures for tourists, organized in some of the better developed countries of Asia and Africa. The most highly developed elephant trekking, also based on a sophisticated program promoting ecology, is offered by India and Thailand. For example, in Thailand it is organized under the auspices of the Elephant Conservation Center in Lampang. The main elephant breeding and, at the same time, tourist centers are located in Kanchanaburi, Chiang Mai and Chiang Rai. Elephant trekking is held in the jungle and is accompanied by simple and ecological forms of camping, riding over hills and mountains on elephants etc. The elephants are tamed and led by trainers (drivers or keepers) called mahouts.

SAFARI TRIATHLON, a sport originated at the beginning of the 1990s in the Ocala National Forest in N-C Florida (USA) and sponsored by Warn, Superlift, BFGoodrich, and Detroit Locker. It combines different skills: driving 300-400mi. through mud, water, and desert, canoeing, trap shooting, navigation and special tasks, and tests the participants' strength, intelligence, endurance, and resistance to fatigue through a 3-day trial that includes various events. Teams consisting of a driver and co-driver score points by completing each event and the team with the most points at the end wins the competition. Teams remain self-sufficient from start to fin-

Safari triathlon.

ish. No outside assistance of any sort including supplies, labor, or technical advice is permitted and each team must carry all necessary food, fuel, equipment (incl. a canoe), and supplies. It is, however, permitted to borrow equipment, spare parts, or supplies from other teams, which develops a deep sense of camaraderie. Participants must either be of legal age or have the notarized consent of a parent or guardian. In order to qualify for a winning position participants must attempt all stages of the event, though full completion of each stage is not required. Points are awarded in the following way: 1) rally stages – 150pts. minus 1pt. for every minute late or early; a delay of over 60min. scores 0pts.; 2) special stages – canoe, obstacle, and skeet are each worth 300pts. awarded to the winner, with a deduction of 15pts. for each subsequent place (lower than 20th place, 0pts.); 3) special events – each special event is worth 100pts. awarded to the winner, with a deduction of 5pts. for each subsequent place. The competition is spread over 3 days in the following way: 1) day 1 – a special event in the form of a timed canoe race in which the driver paddles across a lake, while the co-driver runs around the shore, then enters the canoe and both paddle back across the lake to the finish line; a navigational event ending with the special task of hand-winching a vehicle 20ft. while being timed; a TSD (time-speed-distance) rally, a daylight navigational event, and a night navigational event; 2) day 2 – a special task canoe sprint; a navigational event ending at a boat landing; a 10-mile canoe race; a sand bowl test (incl. a timed Hi Lift Jack winching competition, a sand drag race, a tire change competition, a sand obstacle course); a TSD rally; 3) day 3 – a skeet shooting competition at 3 stations; a navigational event; mud bog and obstacle course competitions.
Equipment and supplies. Every team must have a 4x4 vehicle, which is street legal, carries a current license plate and insurance. Because of the extremely difficult conditions teams should waterproof ignitions and air intakes, and vehicles should feature aggressive and locking axles. The vehicle's fuel mileage is crucial, as teams must carry all the fuel necessary for the 3 days. Winches are mandatory. Other equipment includes: a very accurate odometer or rally computer, good compass and plotting tools, pull straps-tree saver, tire changing equipment, a canoe, 2 single-blade paddles, life preservers, a fire extinguisher, two 12, 16 or 20 gauge shot guns, steal shot ammunition, a first aid kit, eye and ear protection, front and rear vehicle hook points, two helmets, roll bars for open vehicles, camping gear, seat belts, secured battery, GPS, flash lights, good interior lighting, a polaroid camera to photograph navigational checkpoints, and a calculator. Maps are provided by the organizers.
Source: http://safaritriathlon.com/rules_description.htm; www.truckworld.com/Travel-Adventure/00-safari/safari.htm

SAGOL KANGJEI, old Ind. form of a game played on horseback using long-handled mallets and a wooden ball, considered to be one of the predecessors of >POLO, practiced today in Manipur [Manipur *sagol* – pony + *kang* – ball + *jej* – stick]. Unlike many Asian games, which were played by aristocrats,

President Bill Clinton and his wife ride a jeep during a safari at the Chobe National Park in Botswana.

sagol kangjei was played by ordinary people. In Manipur, sagol kangjei and >KHONG KANGJEI are considered to be the same game, although one is played on horseback and the other on foot (cf. players' names and the name *kangjei*, which, without the word *sagol*, denotes a ball game using a stick, played on foot). The team consists of 7 players on horseback. They have the following positions: first defender (*pun-ngak*), second defender (*pun-ngak-chun*), left and right wings (*pulluk*), middle forward (*langiel*), left and right forwards (*pun jen*) and (*pun-jen-chun*). No goals are used. A goal is scored when the ball passes the field's backline on the opponent's side. The white ball is made of bamboo root. Balls are from 3 to 3½ inches (7.62-8.89cm) in diameter and approx. 14in. (35.6cm) in circumference. The stick (*kang-hu*) is made of thick cane or wood. Its average length ranges from 4 to 4½ft. (approx. 122-137cm). The part that hits the ball is curved at an angle and made of hard wood. The players wear a loincloth (*khadangchet*) and a turban. Knee guards (*khongyom*) protect the knees against the opponent's sticks or horse. The game is played in two styles: the original Manipur style (*pana*) and the modern style, very similar to >OUTDOOR POLO.

History. The tradition of sagol kangjei goes back to 3100 BC. According to different sources, it was first

etc. The original meaning of the word sailing referred to the use of sails, but there is a tendency to use the word with reference to ships without sails (e.g. in the sense of 'steam sailing'). Therefore the word sailing often embraces motor ships, both sport yachts and large sailing boats and passenger liners, including cruise boats.

There are 3 general categories of sailing competitions: regattas on Olympic-type courses, ocean races and match, or head-to-head, races.

There are 9 classes of boats in the Olympics, and the races take place on a triangular Olympic course, the length of which is determined by the stretch of water used, the prevailing wind direction, weather conditions and the number of sailboats racing. The course is marked by buoys that must be passed in a specific order so that the team, usually composed of a helmsman who steers the boat and a crew, sails clause hauled, in a reach, and in a run. The distance between the buoys varies according to the type of boat in the competition.

In ocean racing the competing vessels must be navigated over extensive stretches of open sea. Notable ocean races include the Sydney to Hobart Yacht Race that is held in December each year, the Newport to Bermuda race, and the Fastnet Race.

Inshore races are generally held on lakes or inshore

Santorini depicting boats competing in a sailing festival comes from the times prior to the destruction of the islanders' civilization by the erupting volcano in 1500 BC. Sailing was also developed by the Greeks and Romans. The oldest works of Gk. and Lat. literature, to a large extent, are sailing epics. Odysseus's adventures are described in Homer's *Odyssey*, one of the oldest literary masterpieces describing man's attempts to conquer the seas. A great voyage undertaken by Pytheas in about 325 BC was described in his book, *On the Ocean*. Pytheas set off from his native Massalia (present-day Marseille, then a Gk. colony) and sailed round the coast of Spain and through the Straits of Gibraltar, and continuing north along the coasts of Portugal, Spain, and France, he crossed the Eng. Channel to Land's End, Cornwall. Virgil's Aeneid describes river and sea regattas in Roman times, although these were generally dominated by oar galleys. In addition to the sail, oars were the main means of propulsion of ships. Sailing was obviously vital to Mediterranean culture, and even developed a special literary genre, the poetic description of a sea voyage. The oldest of them is an anonymous piece in Gk. written in the 6th cent. BC. The original, unfortunately, has not survived, but fragments translated into Lat. were included by the Roman poet R. Festus Avienus in his poem *Ora*

e: the Polish yacht 'Pogoria' sails by the Statue of Liberty in New York during 'Operation Sail 2000'. Right: sailing as a motif on post stamps from various countries.

played around 2000-1500 BC. It was first mentioned in *Kangjeiron Purana*, written in 34 AD. The game was very popular at the times of Ind. rulers: Kyamba and Khagemba (1597-1672) and Chandra Kirti (1850-86). The latter made it very popular among Brit. soldiers stationed in India. The game is played from Manipur *mera* (Sept./Oct.) to *ingen* (June/July). The Internet: http://www.w3.meadev.gov.in/sports/tr_games/sagol.htm

SAILING, propulsion of a boat or other vessel by means of the driving force of the wind through the use of sails. The art of sailing is also used in competitive sports using vehicles equipped with sails or some other basic source of energy necessary to move about the water, ice or land; in the sporting sense the best known form of sailing is using sailing boats (see also >YACHTING; >ARAB SAILING; >SAILING FOR THE DISABLED; >SPEED SAILING). However, there are myriad other sports using the sail in competition, including competition on water, such as e.g. >WINDSURFING; >TRIFOILING; on ice, e.g. >ICE BOATING, and off water, e.g. >ICE SKATE SAILING, >PARAWING SAILING, >ROLLER SKATE SAILING, SAND YACHTING, >SKI SAILING,

waters over a multi-leg course from about 5 to 24km (3 to 15mi.) long. The boats are generally smaller.

History. The beginnings of moving on water using wind power go back to around 3300 BC. An engraving from that time featuring a boat with a sail was found in Wadi Hamma-Mat in the valley of the Nile. In the 4th cent. BC the Egyptians used the power of the wind to push their papyrus rafts on the Nile, and the Polynesians used outriggers to make their dugout canoes with sails – the ancestors of today's multihull boats – go faster. In 2000-1500 BC the sailing technique was greatly improved by the Egyptians, Cretans as well as the inhabitants of Tortosa, a city-state established just past the Strait of Gibraltar, on the Atlantic side of the Iberian Peninsula. Tortosans were the main link in the tin trade, the tin being delivered by their boats from Cornwall to the Mediterranean Sea. Routinely sailing distances of over 1,000km they greatly contributed to the improvement of boat and sail design. In 1580-1200 BC the development of sailing owes much to the Phoenicians and later to the strongest Phoenician town – Carthage. Information about the oldest forms of competitive sailing comes from the Mediterranean islands of Santorini and Crete. A drawing found on

maritime (*Sailing along the coast*). The Mediterranean Sea continued to be the heart of sailing development through the early Middle Ages. Occasional forms of competition in sailing, although not codified, can be encountered in the following centuries in many cultures. In the 6th cent. BC, when Norse culture became prominent, a sailing culture comparable to that of the Mediterranean Sea appeared in northern Europe. Vikings made a number of geographical discoveries and during the occupation of England (Danelaw) they formed a commercial union of towns, the first in the history of Europe, which contributed considerably to the development of trade and sailing. Likewise, the Cinque Ports, chronologically the 2nd confederation of channel ports, was formed shortly before the Ger. Hanseatic League. Therefore, many inventions that revolutionized sailing technique were made in the region of the North Sea. Some of them included new types of hull, sails, and, above all, the rudder, unknown in ancient times, where its role was played by a side oar, with a wider blade. The advancement of navigational knowledge considerably influenced the development of sailing. From time immemorial, sailors steered by the stars. Early sailing culture no doubt inspired and influenced the development of astronomy. Among the most important technical inventions is the compass. The name of its inventor is not known, but it was mentioned for the first time in a treaty on science by the Eng. monk A. Neckam (1157-1217). The invention of the log (1574), as well as the improvement of techniques of map drawing were equally important. Progress in navigational technique helped to make many >GEOGRAPHICAL EXPLORATION, which were also an important stimulator in the development of sailing technique, like the colonial expansion and the sea wars between such powers as France, Holland, Spain, and Great Britain. Rapid developments in trade relations stemming from sailing progress also contributed to the development of buccaneering and piracy. The period between the 15th and 18th cent. is an exceptionally important and at the same time colorful period of sailing development. New forms of sailing practiced in Holland and England, where the foundations of >YACHTING were established, had a decisive influence on the development of the sporting varieties of sailing. In the 18th and 19th cent. the development of the more effective steam sailing diminished the importance and the romanticism of sailing, depicted in the literary works of J. Conrad, a Pole, who was elevated to the rank of captain. He juxtaposed the natural beauty of sails and wind with the smoky hulls of steamers, particularly in The Mirror of the Sea:

Farr 40-class boats hoist their spinnakers after rounding an upwind marker buoy during the final match of the eight-race Yachting Key West Race Week sailing regatta off the Florida Keys.

Olympic sailing regatta.

Gigantic fans provide the wind for boats racing in an indoor sailing competition.

For machinery it is, doing its work in perfect silence and with a motionless grace, that seems to hide a capricious and not always governable power, taking nothing away from the material stores of the earth. Not for it the unerring precision of steel moved by white steam and living by red fire and fed with black coal. The other seems to draw its strength from the very soul of the world, its formidable ally, held to obedience by the frailest bonds, like a fierce ghost captured in a snare of something even finer than spun silk.

Conrad's literature became a tribute to the art of trad. sailing, which, in his opinion:

... like all fine arts, [...] must be based upon a broad, solid sincerity, which, like a law of Nature, rules an infinity of different phenomena. Your endeavor must be single-minded. You would talk differently to a coal-heaver and to a professor. But is this duplicity? I deny it. The truth consists in the genuineness of the feeling, in the genuine recognition of the two men, so similar and so different, as your two partners in the hazard of life. Obviously, a humbug, thinking only of winning his little race, would stand a chance of profiting by his artifices. Men, professors or coal-heavers, are easily deceived; they even have an extraordinary knack of lending themselves to deception, a sort of curious and inexplicable propensity to allow themselves to be led by the nose with their eyes open. But a ship is a creature which we have brought into the world, as it were on purpose to keep us up to the mark. In her handling a ship will not put up with a mere pretender, as, for instance, the public will do with Mr. X, the popular statesman, Mr. Y, the popular scientist, or Mr. Z, the popular – what shall we say? – anything from a teacher of high morality to a bagman.

Conrad's works deny mechanical sailing some values which were created in trad. sailing, based on the power of wind:

The taking of a modern steamship about the world (though one would not minimize its responsibilities) has not the same quality of intimacy with nature, which, after all, is an indispensable condition to the building up of an art. It is less personal and a more exact calling; less arduous, but also less gratifying in the lack of close communion between the artist and the medium of his art. It is, in short, less a matter of love. Its effects are measured exactly in time and space as no effect of an art can be. It is an occupation which a man not desperately subject to sea-sickness can be imagined to follow with content, without enthusiasm, with industry, without affection. Punctuality is its watchword. The incertitude which attends closely every artistic endeavor is absent from its regulated enterprise. It has no great moments of self-confidence, or moments not less great of doubt and heart-searching. It is an industry which, like other industries, has its romance, its honor [...], its bitter anxieties [...]. But such sea-going has not the artistic quality. [A] modern ship [...] makes her passages on other principles than yielding to the weather and humoring the sea. She receives smashing blows, but she advances; it is a slogging fight, and not a scientific campaign. The machinery, the steel, the fire, the steam, have stepped in between the man and the sea. A modern fleet of ships does not so much make use of the sea as exploit a highway. The modern ship is not the sport of the waves. Let us say that each of her voyages is a triumphant progress; and yet it is a question whether it is not a more subtle and more human triumph to be the sport of the waves and yet survive, achieving your end.

The development of motor sailing, as well as equipment such as the radio, radar, satellite navigation, have to some extent deprived sailing of the value of ultimate struggle between man and nature, although in many cases nature has remained dangerous. At the same time it accelerated the development of competitive sailing as a form of contact with nature, uncontaminated by the development of industrial civilization. This sporting character was also observed by Conrad. In his opinion the sailing traditions of the nations leading the development of this field of human activity made seamen and sailors '[strive] for victory that has elevated the sailing of pleasure craft to the dignity of a fine art.' (J. Conrad, *The Mirror of the Sea*). Probably Conrad meant here the forms of speed competitions between transport sailing boats and passenger ships. Competition between the two developed in the mid 19th cent. In the following years yachting competitions were more frequent, the first of them being the America's Cup commenced in 1851 (see >YACHTING). Sailing regattas, today the basic form of sporting varieties of sailing, held in inshore waters and on oceans, developed mainly when separate international and national events were staged, and particularly when races of sailing boats were included in the program of the Ol.G. The first sailing regattas were to be held at the 1896 Olympics, but they were abandoned due to bad weather. And so the first yacht regattas were held during the 1900 Ol.G. in Paris. The 1904 Ol.G. in St. Louis did not feature any sailing events, but since 1908 yachting has been a permanent feature of the Ol.G., although the boat class has changed frequently. Until 2000 there was a total of 37 yacht classes in the Ol.G., some of them non-existent today, e.g. 6 classes with a displacement of 0.5 to 20 tons, several classed according to the sail size (from 5.5 to 40sq. m. Some other classes were abandoned during the more recent Ol.G., among them the 5.5m (1968), the Swallow (1972), the Dragon (1976), the Tempest (1976) and the Flying Dutchman (1992). At the Ol.G. in Atlanta yachting regattas were held in the following classes: the 470, the Finn, the Soling, the Star, the Laser, and the Tornado; during the 2000 Ol.G. in Sydney – the 470, the Finn, the Soling, the Laser, the Tornado, the Star, the 49er (separately for men and women). The winner of 4 consecutive Ol.G. (1948-60), the Dane P. Elvström became an Olympic yachting legend. The first W.Ch. were held in 1922 in Star class sailboats (first winners – Inslee-Nelson from the USA) and since 1956 in the Finn (first winner – A. Nelis from Belgium) and the Flying Dutchman (won by a crew from the Federal Republic of Germany, Mulka-von Bredow). In all the sailboat classes held at the Ol.G. and in W.Ch. the best crews came from Denmark, France, Holland, Canada, Germany, Sweden, the USA, Great Britain and, until 1990, from the USSR. Sailing competitions are run and governed by the International Sailing Federation (ISF), established in 1907 and formerly known as the International Yacht Racing Union, IYRU).

A. Aleksandrowicz, *Sport żeglarski*, 1930; Michael Bond, *The Handbook of Sailing*, 1980; W. Głowacki, *Wspaniały świat żeglarstwa*, 1970; Michael Richey, *The Sailing Encyclopaedia*, 1980.

SAILBOARDING, see >WINDSURFING.

SAILING FOR THE DISABLED, a var. of >SAILING adapted to the needs of the physically impaired. Introduced to the program of the Paralympics in 1996 in Atlanta as a demonstration sport, it was recognized as a 'medal' sport in Sydney 2000. Contestants are classified according to 5 criteria: stability, hand function, maneuverability, visability and hearing impairment. All yachts used in sailing for the disabled must be equipped with a keel to facilitate stability. Sailboats have open decks to make moving easier. The yachts start at the same time, and the points scored are the same as the place taken in the regattas; the contestant with the lowest number of points is the winner. The sport is governed by the International Federation for Disabled Sailors (IFDS), which in 1999 affiliated 28 national federations. In 1991 it was recognized and affiliated by the International Sailing Federation (IDF), then called the International Yachting Regatta Union (IYRU).

SAIS, according to other sources also *audaryspak*, a form of wrestling on horseback practiced by Kazakhs in the past to celebrate changes of seasons or the autumn feast of abundance (in honor of the god Kurman). The contest started with the riders on horseback. When one of the wrestlers was brought down, the struggle continued on the ground. The contest was usually followed by a few days of feasting and koumiss drinking. Sais wrestlers used both hands, distinguishing this sport from similar Kyr. wrestling >KYS KATCHAR, in which wrestlers used only one hand.

SAIWEIHU, a trad. sport of the Chin. Man minority, practiced during folk holidays in the middle of the 7th lunar month. A team competition in which the contestants run, imitating a boat. The 'crews' usually consist of 5 persons. The 'rowers' form a row – one of them acts as helmsman and faces the other four. Crews maintain a straight line with the help of 2 long horizontal bars, held by the 'rowers' on both sides. The bars represent the port and starboard of the boat. At least 2 crews take part in the competition. At the starter's signal the crews start to race to the finish line, usu. approx. 80m away. The 'helmsman' must run backwards. If the pace is too fast, the helmsman may lose his balance and keel over, thus his 'crew' has less chance of winning.
The tradition of saiweihu derives from the former greatness of the Man people, who, in the past, settled on the banks of rivers, where the people developed different forms of competition involving fishing boats. In the course of historical migration and resettlement, the Man people were scattered all over China and their settlements are presently in areas without any rivers or other bodies of water. Saiweihu is an attempt to uphold their old tradition.

Mu Fushan et al., 'Saiweihu', TRAMCHIN, 58.

SALDU, a trad. var. of team wresting, similar to >KABADDI, practiced in the Nicobar Islands, an archipelago in the Bay of Bengal. Players wrestle on a pitch divided into 2 parts by a line. One team can have as many as 20 wrestlers. The teams line up along the central line, facing each other. The team, which won the right to begin, selects its first wrestler whose task is to cross the line and while on the opposing team's side, tap a wrestler from the opposing team. If he succeeds, he scores a point for his team. A tapped wrestler is eliminated. Now another wrestler tries to do the same. When all the wrestlers have managed to complete the task or when one of them fails to tap an opponent, the teams change sides. The defending wrestlers try to oppose the 'invasion' or try to prevent a wrestler from returning to his side of the pitch. This is when wrestling proper between individual wrestlers begins. A wrestler who is successfully prevented from returning to his side is eliminated and the defending team scores a point. Wrestlers can also compete against the clock; the team which scores the most points within an agreed time or the team which has eliminated all the opposing team's wrestlers wins the match. The sport is practiced by both men and women, some of them over 40yrs. old.

SALMON JUMP, a jump over a wall or a palisade, practiced by the ancient Celts. It used to be a military skill exercised during sieges of forts surrounded with pales, or during battles, in which the warriors jumped over their enemies in order to attack them from behind. The master of salmon jumping was Diarmaid, the mythical originator of >POLE-VAULTING who performed the jumps using his magic spear. Salmon jumping was an integral part of military training of a Celtic warrior and jumping competitions among Celtic troops were frequently organized.

SALPINGTON AGON, an Olympic trumpeters contest held on the first day of the Ol.G.. Its aim was to select the best (loudest) trumpeter (Gr. *salpistes*) who later had the honor to give *salpings*, a special short signal (*salpingos endosimos*) that preceded the verbal announcements by *keryks* (a herald), particularly the announcement of the winners in sports events (>KERYKON AGON). Salpinga was a simple, metal (usu. bronze) horn with a mouthpiece. The trumpeters contest was held on the same day as that of kerykon agon or just before it. Trumpeters played on an altar in front of the entrance to the stadium. Scant information on Olympic winners in salpington agon contests has been preserved. At the 96th Ol.G. in 396 BC the contest was won by Timaios of Elida. The most famous salpistes was Herodoros (other sources have Herodotos of Megara), who won ten times at ten Ol.G., starting at the 113th Games in 328 BC and the last time at the 122nd Games in 292 BC. Demostenes of Milet won 3 times (the 189th Games in 24 BC, the 190th Games in 20 BC and the 191st Games in 16 BC). Diogenes of Efez won 5 times (at the 212th Games in 69 BC, the 213th Games in 73 BC, the 214th Games in 77 BC, the 215th Games in 81 BC, and the 216th Games in 85 BC. At the 249th Games in 217 BC the contest was won by Publius Aelius Aurelius Seraption of Efez.
Information on 10 victories by Markus Aurelius Silvanus of Hermopolis is uncertain; no dates of his victories have been preserved.

SALT WEIGHING, a sporting exercise known in many countries, e.g. in Denmark as *veje salt* [Dan. *veje* – to weigh + *salt* – salt]. Players stand with their backs to one another and interweave their arms. Then they take turns bending forwards and lifting the partner. A more acrobatic form of the exercise is called *rulle sæk* (rolling a sack), in which the players stand with their backs to one another, grab each other's hands and one partner lifts the other, who attempts to roll over his back and stand in front of him.
J Møller, 'Veje salt', GID, 1997, 3.

SALTARIS, Span. jumps, a folk var. of different jumps, held for competition in Spain, particularly in the Basq. country, where the following varieties are practiced:
salto con impulso y carrera, a running long jump;
salto con los pies juntos, a jump with the feet joined together;
salto con makilla haciendo apoyo, a long jump from a pole;
salto con pértiga, a jump with a pole;
orpo-junto, also dialectally *opajuntu*, a type of decajump with both feet, with the legs held together;
salto del pastor, Span. lit. 'a jump with a shepherd's stick', a folk sport known and practiced in the Canary Islands, on the slopes of the hills and from the rocks;
salto guanche con bastón, a type of folk jump jusing a shepherd's crook, practiced in the mountains of the Canary Islands, particularly in Tenerife, on the slopes of the Teide mountains. Jumpers were supposed to jump over different fissures, ravines, and faults, using the staff;
salto pasiego, Span. jump from the Pas valley in Santander province, a type of jump with a shepherd's staff, approx. 2m long and 6cm in diameter. There

are two types of this jump: *brincar* and *arastrar*. In *brincar* jumps (Span. drag, tow) both legs are wrapped around the stick, the stick is held with both hands and the chin rests on its top. Using his legs, the jumper quickly raises the stick from the ground and takes small jumps forward. The winner is the jumper who covers a predetermined distance with the fewest jumps. In the *arrastrar* var. (Span. to leap) the jumper digs the stick into the ground (like in the pole vault) and tries to cover a predetermined distance with the fewest number of leaps.
Saltaris has been practiced for at least several hundred years in the farming areas and the tradition of the sport is attributed mainly to shepherds. In the 19th cent. a form of folk competition developed, during which bets were taken. The development of jumps as field events and the adoption of modern types of jumps by sports clubs and schools contributed to the decline of the folk variety, which practically disappeared after WWII.
The most skilled jumpers were: J. Mendizabal of Zumárraga, J.J. Eguiguren of Azpeitia and B. Ascasibar of Villareal. A. Irastorza became a legend – although he had his leg amputated after a snake bite when he was a child he was able to jump up to 31ft. (approx. 9.41m) with a stick, and his best double jumps were 58ft. (approx. 17.69m) long. F. Aizpuru of Beizama's best jump (standing, take off with both feet) was 2.62m long. However, had he competed at the Ol.G. in 1900-1912, he would not have won a gold medal – an American, R. Ewry won with jumps over 3m long.
R. Aguirre Franco, 'Salataris', JYDV, 1978, 455-456; C. Moreno Palos, 'Saltaris', JYTE, 1992; ibid. 'Salto guanche con bastón', JYTE, 1992, 43; ibid. 'Salto pasiego', JYTE, 1992.

SALTO DEL COLACHO, or *jumping over babies*, a medieval ritual still practiced in Castrillo de Murcia near Burgos (N Spain) during the Corpus Christi octave. Masked and dressed in bright-colored trousers, El Colacho – who represents the devil – carries a horse's tail, which he uses to whip the people of the village during the 'corridas' (runs); cf. >BULL RUNNING, >CORRIDA. On the Sunday after Corpus Christi, the village is decked out, placing altars along the procession route, before which they lay down the children born in Castrillo that year. The Colacho jumps over the babies and in this way symbolically takes the evil from them.

SALTO DELLA CORDA, an Ital. name of >JUMP ROPE, also see >HOP-SCOTCH.

SAMBO, a Rus. wrestling sport, also known in Eng. speaking countries as *sombo*.
Etymology. The name *sambo* is a compilation of Rus. words *sam(ozashchita)* + abbr. *b(ez)* + *o(ruzhia)* = self defence without weapons.
History. Sambo originated in the former Soviet Union (USSR). It is considered to have been born on 16 Nov. 1938, the date it was officially accepted as a sport by the National Committee of Physical Culture of the USSR. The roots of sambo go back to ancient times, however, with techniques drawn from the many folk styles of wrestling that existed in the fifteen republics of the former Soviet Union. Sambo was further developed by the Soviet military and extensively taught as a form of hand to hand combat for soldiers.
The International Amateur Wrestling Federation (FILA) first recognized sambo as a sport of world stature in 1966 at the FILA Congress in Toledo, Ohio (USA) and adopted it alongside freestyle and Greco-Roman wrestling as the third international wrestling discipline. The first Sambo W.Ch. were held in

Carlos Esteban Estebanez jumps over six babies during El Salto del Colacho, The Jump of the Colacho, in the village of Castrillo de Murcia, Spain.

Teheran (Iran) in 1973, in conjunction with the FILA World Freestyle and Greco-Roman Wrestling Championships. Subsequent W.Ch. were held in 1974 and 1975, then annually beginning in 1979. World Cup Team championships began in 1977 and have taken place periodically to date.
In 1984 sambo separated from FILA and the International Amateur Sambo Federation (FIAS) was formed. At the organizational Congress in Bilbao (Spain) Fernando Compte of Spain was elected the first president. Josh Henson of the United States was elected Vice-President and later became the 2nd president of FIAS. In 1985 FIAS was accepted into the General Association of International Sports Federations (GAISF), and sambo was included in the World Games for the first time in London (Great Britain) 1985.
In 1991, a rival international sambo federation was formed by Etienne Labrousse, former Secretary General of FIAS, called Federation Mondiale de Sambo (FMS). FMS consisted primarily of various soviet republics which could not be recognized by FIAS, which recognized the Soviet Union. FMS held separate W.Ch. each year until it finally disbanded in 1997.

Sambo.

S

WORLD SPORTS ENCYCLOPEDIA

President Compte retired in 1991 and Mr. Henson assumed the presidency until the next elections in 1992, at which time he was elected as Compte's successor. In 1991, the Soviet Union dissolved and the FIAS recognized Russia as the successor to the Soviet Union. Other Soviet republics that had been part of the FMS were invited to join. In 1993, the FMS asked for recognition by the GAISF in place of the FIAS and was denied. Later in 1993, a third international sambo federation was formed, consisting largely of former Soviet States that had not previously been members of the FIAS. That group also chose to use the name the FIAS and claimed to be the controlling international federation, but that claim was rejected by the presidents of the FMS and FIAS alike. Former FIAS Secretary General Tomoyuki Horimai of Japan was elected president of the new group (FIAS East). In 1994, the FMS signed an accord to unite the original FIAS (FIAS West, under Josh Henson of the USA) and the two held joint championships for 3 years. In 1997, the FMS was dissolved and some of the former FMS countries broke away to join the alternative FIAS (FIAS East). Thus in 1999, the split in sambo continued in a different way, with two organizations claiming the same name. Discussion to unify the two FIAS groups began in 1999.

Uniform. A sambo wrestling competition uniform consists of 1) shoes, 2) a red outfit (red jacket, red belt and red shorts or singlet), and 3) a blue outfit (blue jacket, blue belt and blue shorts or singlet). Each competitor must have one complete red and one complete blue uniform. Jacket, shorts and belt must be worn with matching colors (all red or all blue, but not mixed). The jacket (called 'kurtka' in Russian) should be made of canvas or other heavy material. Sleeves must be long enough to extend to the wrists and wide enough at the end to fit the wrist and 4 fingers (held side by side). The jacket should be tight fitting around the torso and extend no more than 8in. below the belt (roughly equal to the bottom of the sleeve). The belt must be wrapped snugly around the body and knotted at the front. It must pass through at least 3 belt loops on the jacket. Only national patches may be attached to the left side of the chest area (club patches may be worn on the right side). The jacket must have cuffs or epaulets sewn onto the shoulder of the jacket. A judo jacket is not acceptable at official competitions. Shorts should be tight fitting and cover at least one-third of the leg above the knee. Wrestling singlets (red or blue) may be used, although strapless trunks are preferred. Shoes should made of soft leather or other pliable material and should have a soft leather sole with seams inside. Rubber soled wrestling shoes are acceptable, but soft soled shoes are preferred.

Rules. A sambo wrestling match can be won in one of three ways: 1) by Total Victory (a perfect throw or

submission hold), which ends the match immediately, 2) by technical superiority (12pt. difference in score), which ends the match immediately, or 3) by point difference at the end of the match. Tied matches are decided by a 1-min. overtime period. If there is no winner at the end of overtime, the match is decided by majority decision of the officials. A sambo competition match is one period of 6min. in length for seniors, 5min. for espoirs and juniors and 4min. for masters, schoolboys/girls and cadets. The bout can be stopped by the officials at any time and athletes returned to the center of the mat for a standing start, if: 1) athletes are out of bounds; 2) a time out is called for injury or adjusting the uniforms; 3) there is no activity by the athletes while on the ground; 4) an athlete is cautioned for an illegal hold; 5) Total Victory is earned by a perfect throw or submission hold. Unlike in freestyle or Greco-Roman wrestling, there is no parterre or down starting position in sambo.

Points are scored by the successful application of 3 types of technical moves:

HOLD DOWN (immobilization): similar to a judo hold down or a prolonged wrestling 'predicament' or 'near fall'. In order to score, one athlete must hold the back of the other athlete towards the mat in a danger position (less than 90 degrees), with the chest, side or back of the attacker in unbroken contact with the chest of the opponent. A hold down is 'broken' when 1) contact between the athletes is interrupted because space is created between the two, or 2) the defending athlete turns over to the stomach or the side with an angle greater than 90 degrees. A hold down may only be scored once in a match and will earn either 2pts. for a 10-sec. hold down or 4pts. for a 20-sec. hold down. Once a hold down is scored, an athlete cannot attempt another. A hold down does not end the match (it only scores points).

SUBMISSION HOLD: a pressure hold (key or lock), applied to the arm or leg of the opponent which makes the opponent surrender or submit by calling out or tapping the mat at least twice (not permitted in youth age categories). Submission holds cannot be applied in the standing position. A submission hold ends the match by Total Victory.

THROW: a throw is scored anytime one athlete takes another to the mat in a single, continuous and uninterrupted action. A sambo throw is more than a simple wrestling takedown, however. Like a Judo or Greco-Roman wrestling throw, 1) it must start with both athletes on their feet, 2) one athlete must unbalance the other, and 3) the attacker must take the opponent directly to the mat with one action without stopping. A throw must knock the defender off their feet either by lifting or tripping them, not merely dragging them down. A throw is scored based on two factors: 1) how the thrown athlete lands (on the back, on the side or on the chest/buttocks) and 2) whether

the thrower remains standing (the throw scores twice as much if the thrower stays up). A throw results in Total Victory and stops the match if it is a 'perfect throw' (the attacker throws the defender to the back and remains standing). Other throws will score 4pts., 2pts., or 1pt.

Holds not permitted in sambo wrestling include: 1) bending arms behind the back (hammerlock or chicken wing), 2) submission hold on shoulder, wrist, neck, fingers or toes, 3) holding the mat, 4) gripping the jacket of the opponent below the belt or inside the sleeve, 5) twisting or squeezing the opponent's head, 6) pressure to the face, 7) twisting arms, legs, fingers, toes or ankles, 8) punching or slapping, 9) driving the opponent's head in the mat, 10) standing or throwing submission holds, 11) gouging, 12) strangling or choke holds.

SAMOAN RACES, type of a folk running competition popular among the native inhabitants of Samoa in the S Pacific.

SAMPAN, a small skiff, widely used in the Orient, that is propelled by oars or a scull. Since 1984 used in the Singapore River Regatta. The first winner of the regatta was A.B. Aton, who, as he himself said, used to organize unofficial contests between sampan users 20yrs. earlier.

SAMPSEL, see >VÅG.

SAMSØKEGLER, bowling from Samsø island, a game similar to >KEGLER MED OPHÆNGT KUGLE. Eight pins are piled around a central, larger one, called *kukken*. A letter-T shaped object, resembling a carpenter's hammer, is thrown at the pins. The first player's task is to knock down the pile. After each throw the pins are set up at the place where they fell and the other players throw at the pins thus randomly placed in the field, which makes hitting several pins at the same time much more difficult. The winner is the player who knocks down a predetermined number of pins, e.g. 20 pins and 5 *kuks*.
J. Möller, 'Samsøkegler', GID, 1997, 1, 102-3.

SAN DA, also *san shou* [Chin. for a freestyle fight], a form of full contact bout in >GONGFU and >WUSHU, somehow resembling >THAI BOXING, but also incl. throwing techniques.

SANAMA BOJO NE, lit. my name is Bojo; a folk game played by girls in Hausa and Yauri (Nigeria). Games are accompanied by drum beating. 10-15 girls take part – they form a semicircle, with one girl inside. Girls take turns to take the central position, their height being the determining factor. The girls in the semicircle hold hands and, singing to the beat of the drums, start moving counterclockwise. The girl in the middle claps her hands and pretends to dance. She starts to sing the first verses of a song about 3 boys in love, and the other girls complete the song. At some point the girl in the middle turns around and tries to join the semicircle. The final step must be a leap, with both feet in the air. The girls in the semicircle must catch her while she is up. If they manage, another girl takes the first girl's place. A similar game, known as 'three boys', is known in the Nigerian region of Dungawa – the boys form a full circle, the pace is faster and there is more dancing. Songs include elements of story telling – boys mime the plot.
A. Taylor Cheska, 'Sanama bojo ne', TGDWAN, 1987.

SAND TRACK RACING, also *beach racing*, a motorcycle racing sport held on sand tracks, usu. on large beaches. The inside track circumference markings should not exceed 365m. Races are held on 2- or 3-wheel motorcycles (in the latter category a passenger assists the rider). All machines must have at least one efficient brake and be fitted with a lanyard style engine cut-out switch. Road tires are not permitted. The contestants must wear protective outer clothing, made of leather or a substitute, with substantially padded shoulders, elbows, hips and knees, as well as knee-length boots, leather gloves, and helmets. Races are held in the following age group categories: cadet, junior, intermediate, and senior. The sport has enjoyed a great popularity in Great Britain, USA, and Australia since the 1940s. W.Ch. have been held irregularly since 1971.

SAND YACHTING, sailing of land yachts on sandy beaches and other areas of land (disused airfield runways, dry lake beds, tracts of desert, and open prairie). In its simplest form it requires only a small sailing dinghy mounted on a basic chassis with 3 or

Quad dirt bikers participate in the Thunder On The Sand Motorcross races on the beach in Wildwood, New Jersey.

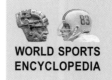

Adriaen van de Venne, Sailing and Cruising in
Scheveningen, *gouache.*

Sand yachting may be considered purely ecological in that speeds of up to 240km/h are reached without burning any fuel or polluting the air.

Sand yachting.

4 car wheels. Instead of a rudder or tiller the craft has a steering wheel and/or pedals. Modern Eur. designs have streamlined fiberglass fuselages which may be as long as 7.3m (24ft.), with a wheelbase of 5.5m (18ft.), and tires 61cm (2ft.) in diameter. One sail is used but this may be as much as 37m² (400 sq. ft.). Yachts carry a crew of up to three. Amer. designs tend to be smaller and lighter, the body often an open chassis 3m (10ft.) long, with a sail area of 4m² (45sq. ft.), and room only for the pilot in a bucket seat a few inches above the ground. Aside from the tracks left in the soil by a land-yacht's tires, which may scar certain landscapes or lead to soil erosion, this sport may be considered purely ecological in that speeds of up to 240km/h are reached without burning any fuel or polluting the air, thus offering 'clean' contact with nature. See also >SAILING and >YACHTING.

History. Vehicles were probably adapted for wind propulsion in the ancient civilizations of China and Egypt. Around 600 BC the Chinese developed wind-propelled war chariots capable of carrying up to 30 warriors. Sails were also used in ancient China to assist plowing. In the 16th cent. the Chinese organized the first recorded races, with members of the royal family participating. The Dutch, who were pioneers of yachting, also had land yachts on wooden wheels in the 16th cent., which they used to transport their army across sandy beaches. In about 1600 in Flanders, S. Stevin designed a land vehicle with 2 masts, capable of carrying 28 passengers and moving with the speed of about 30km/h between Scheveningen and Petter. This model was later copied by many in the construction of similar vehicles. In 1834 a Fr. land yacht, L'Eolienne, was demonstrated near Paris. It had 4 wheels, 2 masts, 6 sails, and carried 15-20 passengers. However, narrow roads stymied the development of this form of public transport. The development of the railroad effectively put an end to further initiatives, although there were attempts to equip wheeled vehicles with a sail, which provided additional propulsion, thus making the journey shorter. This was witnessed, for example, during the gold rush in California in 1849. Some prospectors added canvas or leather sails to the Conestoga wagons, waiting for favorable back winds. The 'Windwagon' Smith became particularly famous. The serious development of land yachts began in the US in 1902 in Muroc, California. Attempts were made to use the sail in rail transport. A 'sail wagon' was demonstrated to the ambassador of Russia, who ordered a similar one for his monarch. In 1937 two Amer. journalists conceived and built the DN Utility Land Sailor (convertible for ice yachting) whose basic design remains one of the most popular. The beginnings of sand yachting as a sport go back to 1898 when in Belgium the Domunt brothers from De Panne in West Flanders started work on a sporting var. of a sand yacht. The design attracted the attention of L. Bleriot, an airman famous for the first flight over the Eng. Channel. About 1912 land

yachts were a frequent feature here. They usu. had 4 wheels on pneumatic tires, fixed to a bicycle-like frame. In 1913 the sand yachting competitions held in Hardelot attracted 43 contestants. The outbreak of WWI halted the development of this sport. After the war, in the 1920s sand yachting became popular on the Brit. beaches, where speed of over 60km/h were easily achieved. Sand yachts also returned to the beaches of Belgium and their use spread in France. The development of the automotive industry helped to solve one of the most difficult problems of sand yachting – bicycle wheels were not strong enough to resist side winds. The sport gained in popularity after WWII, particularly in the US. It is also popular in France, near Bordeaux, where the broad expanses of sand in the Les Landes country are ideal. In Britain experiments were made with a number of designs, the most interesting of them being the crabber, a vehicle with a rigid sail fixed to each of 3 independently controlled wheels so that the helmsman could respond to side winds with his body. The movements were similar to those of a crab, and hence the name of the vehicle. In order to increase the speed, larger vehicles were built to accommodate a larger sail. However, increased sail surface required alterations to the dinghy to maintain balance, which, in turn, upset the ratio of sail size to vehicle weight. In 1963 the Dutch adapted the Amer. DN Utility Land Sailor design, and built a vehicle with 3 wheels – 1 controllable in the front and two fixed in the back. As the design was very light, the speed and maneuverability of the craft were increased, although the sail was relatively small – 5.5m². The craft could also be used in weak winds. Sand yachting as a sport also developed in the USSR, on the Kara Kum desert. After the collapse of the USSR (1991), the sport disappeared there. Internationally, the development of sand yachting is governed by the International Federation of Sand and Land Yachting (Fédération Internationale de Sand et Land Yachting, FISLY), established in 1961 by representatives of France, Germany, Belgium and Great Britain. The first official E.Ch. were held in 1963 in only one class. In 1965 land yachts were divided into 3 classes depending on the sail size. In the 2nd half of the '60s class I, the largest sails, was discontinued, whereas class III, the smallest sails, developed rapidly. At that time yachts were given the streamlined body and parachute-like sails typical of the Flying Dutchman class in sailing (aerofoil). Another revolution came about in 1975, when the windstake design was introduced. The length of the craft was 1.75yds. (1.6m), the span of side wheel 1.5yds. (1.37m) and the sail's surface was 4.8sq. yds. (4m²). This was the so-called class IV. As the regulators had neglected to limit yacht size, modifications soon followed and the wheel span and sail size were increased. This led to some confusion, resulting in the origin of class V, with sail surface limited to 6sq. yds. (5m²). As the advantages of the large design of class IV were adapted by yachts of

class III, class IV began to disappear. Presently, with class I gone, class II is particularly popular in extensive areas, such as the oceanic beaches in the US and Canada. Most of international events are presently held in the most popular classes III and V. The best land yachts can reach speeds 3-4 times greater than wind speed. The record in the open class, set in 1991 by the Frenchman B. Lambert, is 94.55mph (152.13km/h) at a wind speed of 31mph (48km/h). It was not long before crafts began attaining speeds of over 100mph (160km/h). This is possible as the crafts are mostly made of plastics and light metals, reduced resistance of the wheel, and special tire designs. In a yacht of class III the span of its side wheels must be 3.8yds. (3.5m), and the craft itself must be 4.15yds. (3.8m) long. The minimum weight is 220lbs. (100kg). On a wing mast there is a 7.35m² sail. The cigar-like body is usu. made of fiberglass, with a flexible wooden axle, at the end of which the front wheel is fixed. The yacht can achieve speeds up to 85mph (137km/h). A contestant assumes a prone position, like in ice yachting, and wears a crash helmet and sun goggles. In Europe competitions are usu. held in autumn and winter when there are strong winds and the beaches are empty. In addition to helmet and goggles, the contestants wear gloves, a diver's wetsuit and Wellington boots.

A class V yacht should meet the following requirements: the longitudinal length between the wheels 2.7yds. (2.5m), the width of the side wheels 2.2yds. (2.0m). The sail, fixed to a tubular straight mast, cannot be greater than 6sq. yds. (5m²). The min. weight is 110lbs. (50kg). Class V yachts reach the maximum speeds of about 70mph (113km/h).

According to the rules contestants start from a stopped position. Yachts can be aligned in 2 or 3 rows. It is permitted to push the yacht forward at start to gain momentum and find its proper position with respect to the wind. A race is held on a course marked by two markers about 2 mi. (about 3.2km) apart. The race is held clockwise. The contestant, who covers the longest distance within a fixed time, usu. 30min., is the winner. Information about the lapse of time and end of the race is given by a referee, who, like in car races, waves a checkered flag. As the yachts do not have any brakes, turns are made at top speed on 2 wheels, which is possible owing to the vehicle's low center of gravity. Rally races, e.g. on the Nevada desert in the USA and on the Sahara in Africa, are held irregularly. In the United States sand yachting is practiced by about 1,000 contestants, whereas in Great Britain as many about 150,000. In countries with a highly developed sand yachting tradition the sport can be practiced with a permit only, as a precautionary measure to provide for the safety of people using public beaches.

A.R. Parr, *Sand yachting. A History of the Sport and its Development in Britain,* 1991; ibid, 'Sand yachting', *Encyclopaedia of World Sports,* eds. D. Levinson and K. Christensen, 1996, vol. III.

S

SANDBOARDING, a sport of riding on a board down sand dunes, modelled after >SNOWBOARDING.
History. The first obscure reports of using flat objects to ride down sand dunes come from ancient times. The objects could have been sand shoes, similar to snow shoes used in northern countries. During WWII soldiers on both sides sought relief from fighting in the sands of N Africa by riding on pieces of metal from the destroyed machinery or pieces of cardboard, which was documented in photographs. In the 1970s Americans J. Smith and G. Fluitt began to popularize sandboarding in the Amer. media, at first with very little success. In 1973 L. Beal watched a friend practicing sand rides in the Mojave Desert and soon supported the pioneers of the sport by publishing 'Sandboard Magazine'.
At first sandboarding was neither impressive nor easy. The spread of snowboarding, however, resulted in introducing a number of technical innovations, which were applied to sandboarding. Those concerned mostly the shape of boards, but the key problem still remained: that of the base surface, which was excellent for snow rides, but proved disappointing on sand. The solution came from a ceramic material known by its brand name – 'formica', the sliding characteristics of which were improved by special waxes, allowing for much greater speeds (up to 60mph) on steep slopes, but also making it possible to glide down smoother sand dunes. The average rides are short – 30-45sec. The new base surface also made it possible to perform air evolutions, as well as to introduce a new var. of sandboarding called >SANDSURFING, practiced on sand dunes in a way similar to surfing waves.
The spread of sandboarding was hindered by a lack of media interest. The big break came with the development of the Internet, which allowed for easy contacts between sandboarders in different regions of the world. The sandboarding elite now comes from many countries: the USA, Australia, N.Zealand, Namibia, Egypt, Peru, Chile, Argentina, Urugway, Brazil, France, Italy, Germany, Hungary, Holland, Belgium, England, and some Arab countries (e.g. El-Faouar in Tunisia). The number of sandboarders around the world is estimated at 4,000 and is led by an American, P. Pilcic, and a Peruvian, M. Malaga Mullerl. The governing body for the sport is Dune Riders International. W.Ch. have been held annually since 1995 (the 4th W.Ch. in Monte Kaolino (Germany) was watched by 50,000 spectators). One of the best known sandboarding shows is Sand Master Jam in Dumont Dunes (California). South Africa has an important center in Cape Town, as well as the first sandboarding school.

SANDSURFING, a var. of >SANDBOARDING. A sport involving riding on a board down sand dunes and performing special evolutions. The main centers of sandboarding are located in South Africa and Namibia.

SANECZKI Z DŹGACZEM, Pol. for 'poke sledding', a folk type of luge practiced in many villages of Wielkopolska (Poland), in which one rides a sled by using a spear called a *dźgacz* or *dzigacz* to push off [from Pol. *dźgać* – to jab or poke]. The region of Wielkopolska lies in the lowlands, where the lack of hills inspired children to invent ways of propelling the sled. Poke sledding races usu. took place on snowy fields or frozen lakes. According to a local

Sandboarding.

Sandboarding.

ethnographer, A. Kowol-Marcinek, sleds were usu. homemade:

[…] They would make them with four slats, of which two were thick and would serve as runners. The boys put wire around them, so that they would skid better. For pushing off and turning the sled they would use a spear made from a pole with a headless nail driven into the bottom of one end.

Antoni Kowol-Marcinek, 'Saneczkarze', *Dawne gry i zabawy dziecięce w Bukówcu Górnym*, Dom Kultury, Leszno, 1999, pp. 33-34.

SANG-JAO-WONI-KILEE, see >MPEEWA.

SANNA, in old Pol. culture leisure sledding in horse-drawn sleds, taking the form of >KULIG. In the 19th cent. Pol. sanna also denoted sledding by children.

SAPARAGA, also *sapparaga*, a Malaysian folk game with a leather ball or a ball made from sappanwood that yields a characteristic red dye.
W.W. Skeat, *Malay Magic*, London 1900.

SAPATHIN' DOLEGAD, an Afr. running game played on Fogo and Sao Antão islands (Cape Verde Isles). There are 6 to 10 contestants, who form a circle. One of them runs around the circle on the outside, singing aloud: '*Sapatinh' Dolegad samusé, samusé*', which means, more or less, 'too small shoes…' followed by meaningless words. The runner has a piece of cloth in his hand, which he drops behind the back of a player of his choice. After he has dropped the cloth, the runner must run the full circle, while the player behind whose back the cloth was dropped tries to catch him. If he manages, he takes a place outside the circle and the player who was caught goes inside the circle where, blindfolded, he awaits to be freed. He is freed when another player running around the circle is caught. The freed player takes a place in the circle. A game similar to an Amer. game >DROP HANDKERCHIEF, and not unlike 'duck, duck, goose'.
A. Taylor Cheska, 'Sapatinh' dolegad', TGDWAN, 1987.

SARBACANE, Fr. for 'blowpipe', a form of archery that appeared in Saint-Etienne (Loire department) towards the end of the 18th cent. It takes as a starting point the development of archery going up in the Middle Ages when the kings of France encouraged the training of local militias equipped with bows. In the 19th cent. archery and blowpipe were exclusively practiced by the authorized craftsmen of the city (weapons, ribbon, and velvet). They were under the rules of the existing brotherhoods of the Middle Ages. Known and used as an arm by certain people throughout the world, sarbacane profited in Saint-Etienne of the old and famous munitions factory, where many tubes launching darts were built. In 1843, 49 companies (*sociétés*) of 'slobberys' (name given to the players because they spit somewhat in the tube) were listed in and around Saint-Etienne. The rules of admission and behaviour were very closed to those of the brotherhoods, even of Freemasonry. It was necessary to be co-opted by the elder ones to be allowed as *chevalier* (mem-

ber). The president was called *capitaine* and the winner of the annual contest became 'king' for the year. Members were plain between them by a strong solidarity. The sociétés (local name of the clubs) regularly collected money which was used as mutual relief fund for sick members. This sporting game belongs to the Saint-Etienne's inheritance since the middle of the 19th cent. and is now the only area – with North of France – where the play still exists.
Contributed by: Jean-Yves Guillain, University of Lyon.

SARCH'H, see >GWINTRAN AR SARC'H.

SARGENT'S JUMP, an exercise named after its inventor, an Amer. educator D.A. Sargent (1849-1924), also a method of measurement and a test of jumping abilities. The person under examination raises his arm and makes a mark on a special board or on the wall, after which he jumps up and makes another mark. The examiner measures the difference between the two marks.

SARI, Arab. for 'walking', a game observed in Jidda and Nejd (Najd or Nedjed) by M. Ibrahim al-Majman and described in his dictionary of Arab sports. The main var. is played usu. during winter nights in the light of the moon. According to Nejd a similar game is called *'adim sair* (large sari) or *'adim lah* (large throw) and is held on summer nights. The game requires agility, speed and physical strength and it is mainly played by boys. A game similar to sari is called *raksa*, which, in turn, is close to >ŠUQQ EL-QAN. Al-Majman provides the following description:

The players are divided into 2 teams of an equal number of 10-20 persons. A large circle (da'ira) is drawn on the playing area – it is the home of the defending team. The circle is about 50m from the outer line of the playing area – this area is called 'madd'. The attackers try to touch the defenders anywhere on the body between the wrist and the shoulder. If anybody succeeds, the attacking player calls, 'Sari', which is a signal to start running after the defenders. The attackers can chase the defenders anywhere within the playing area, as long as they catch at least one of them. When they fail to catch anybody, the defenders score a point. On the other hand, if any of the defenders is caught (that player is referred to as 'mayyit' – dead), the attackers score a point. The caught player is dropped to the ground and cannot rise until he says, 'Ala [lit. I have been lain on the ground].
[Our folk games, 1983, 57-58]

SARIT-SARAK, old-Ind. art of combat without weapons against an armed or unarmed person. Its features include avoidance of the attacker's blows and surprise attacks aimed at putting the attacker out of action. Often includes elements of >THANG-TA, a combat with a spear and a sword.

SASIYA, an alternative name of old Jap. archery, also known as >TOSIYA.

SAUBALL, a Swiss game originating in the Middle Ages, similar to Fr. LA >TRUIE and Pol. >CZORO-MAJ. Its aim was to tap a ball into holes in the ground, using a stick [Ger. *Sau* – swine + *ball*].
W. Endrei and L. Zolnay, *Fun and Games in Old Europe*, 1986, 112.

Scad diving.

SAUT DU CANAL É LA PERCHE, also *saute du canal à la perche*, Fr. name of long pole jump over water obstacles, [Fr. *saut* – jump + *perche* – pole]; the Du.-speaking nations refer to it as >FIERLJEP-PEN. See also >LONG-POLE JUMPING, POLE VAULTING.

SAVAGE CAMP, see >CAMP.

SAVATE, a folk var. of fighting, with foot kicks dominating and with simultaneous use of fists [Fr. *savate* – an old shoe]. Historically, and in its modern version, savate is similar to >THAI BOXING and modern >KICKBOXING.

History. Some sport historians derive savate from the Celtic past of present-day France, where there was a form of fighting in which the competitors kicked each other (cf. Brit. >SHIN-KICKING). Savate developed during numerous fights in the narrow streets of Fr. towns, particularly Paris and Marseille. The first attempts at informal codification of savate were made in the 18th cent. when in many Eur. wars and the seven year war, fought in S.America between the colonists and the Eng. and Fr. armies, many Fr. soldiers were taken prisoners of war by the English. The latter were looking for something that could occupy their prisoners and allowed them to fight. Fighting developed particularly on ships which served as floating prisoner-of-war camps. It is quite possible that at that time savate made its first borrowings from Eng. >BOXING. In the mid 18th cent. the best savate fighter was a dancer by the name of Batist or Batiste. He is considered the inventor of a fighting technique in which kicks above the waistline were inflicted. Some other last names have been retained since that time, spelled with no respect for the grammar of the Fr. language, which indicate their plebeian origin: Fanfan, Fransua, Champan, Karp, Minion, Rauchero, Sabatier. The very number of these names is indicative of the great popularity of savate in the 18th cent., unfortunately also among criminals, who treated savate as a skill very useful in their profession. A different var. of fighting was developing at the same time in France, namely >CHAUSSON. At the turn of the 18th cent. both types started to mix and it is difficult to separate the two in historical records, particularly as authors describing them used the two names interchangeably. In the old original formula savate developed until 1824, when M. Casseux (born 1794) published the first systematic manual of street fighting and self-defence, with an extensive section on savate. In 1825 Casseux opened the first official savate school. One of his students was Charles Lecour, who in 1830 opened his own school, attended by townspeople, industrialists, journalists and even artists. After a fight lost to a Brit. boxer Owen Swift in 1830 Lecour started studies on boxing in England. Upon his return to France he introduced elements of Eng. boxing into savate, calling the new var. French boxing (boxe française). Soon Fr. boxing dominated other varieties of fighting. Because of the obvious links to the tradition of savate it was often called Fr. boxing savate (savate boxe française). At the turn of the 19th cent. systematic regional and Fr. championships were held, continued until 1939, where the last Fr. championships in savate were held. In the 1960s attempts were made to restore the old rank to Fr. boxing, and also to savate. In 1965 P. Baruzi organized the National Committee of French Boxing in France, which soon had 30 affiliated clubs. In 1976 the Committee transformed into the National Federation of Fr. Boxing and when the original traditions of savate were adopted and the federation became more active in other countries, in 1985 it changed its name to the International Federation of Fr. Boxing Savate. The most dynamically developing savate organizations include, e.g. the Californian Association of Savate in the USA. Savate is practiced by both men and women.

B. Tegner, *Savate. French Foot Fighting*; P. Reed and R. Muggeridge, *Savate. Martial Art of France* (1998).

SAVLAJAN, old Persian ball game with curved sticks. The genesis of >POLO is attributed to savlajan.

SBOURA, a var. of >TOPS played in modern Greece; cf. O.Gk. var. of this game: >STROMBS and >STROBILOS.

SCAD-DIVING, an extreme sport, jumping from a basket or a platform fastened to a tall crane or hoist into a net similar to a springboard hung below [Engl. *scad* – probably short from <*scaddle* – wild + *diving*]. Scad-diving gained limited popularity in the early 1990s.

SCALING, an extreme, mostly illegal sport, which emerged in the 1970s and was popularized in the 1990s by a Frenchman A. Robert. Scaling means climbing tall structures without any protective gear or an assistant. The only form of help is talcum powder which scalers carry to rub their hands for a better grip. When climbing a building the scaler makes use of any construction elements on which he can rest his feet or get a grip. According to A. Robert the sport involves a number of elements: practice, studying the construction design, defying inevitable objections from the structure management and law enforcement services, the climbing itself, and escaping arrest. Proper reconnaisance is crucial in learning about the constructional elements that are the climber's main ally. Regularity of design, characteristic of most scyscrapers, allows the scaler to focus on several lower floors and climb the upper ones fairly fast. To deceive the police and security services scalers often have doubles who draw the attention of spectators by faking climbing attempts, while the scaler undertakes the proper attempt in a completely different spot. In rare cases scalers are granted the permission of the local authorities. In all cases their attempts usu. gather crowds of spectators, along with rescue services, police and security forces, and the mass media. In some cases photographers climb the lower floors together with the scaler to get a better picture, which was the case during A. Robert's unsuccessful attempt at climbing the Warsaw Mariott Hotel (he was stopped by security). Reactions to the sport vary. Mountain climbers generally agree that from the technical point of view, scaling and >MOUNTAIN CLIMBING have much in common, although they stress that scaling, contrary to mountain climbing, offers no esthetic break from the civilized world. Some believe that the difference between mountain climbing and scaling can be compared to that between indoor swimming and ocean swimming. According to a psychologist E. Krzemiński, the skills necessary for scaling are not related to man's evolutionary adjustment to performing life functions. Practiced by few, the sport is a form of experiencing extreme, almost ecstatic pleasure. Doctors believe that scaling is possible because some of man's organic systems are autonomous, independent of our will. If they were not, the tremendous stress that the sport generates would not allow a man to undertake such ventures.

By 1998 A. Robert had climbed approx. 70 skyscrapers around the world, incl. the ones he views as the most difficult – the Red Cross building in Philadelphia and the Deutsche Bank in Frankfurt. To climb a building 150m tall, of an average level of construction complexity, he usu. takes approx. 15-20min.

SCAT, a simple game using a blunt knife (to open letters) or a stick of a similar length, which is put on the open palm of one of the players, slightly extended forward. The other player tries to grab the knife/stick and tap the opponent's hand with it before he draws it back. The player with the most taps wins. TGESI, II, 182.

SCHAGGUN, a medieval Ger. game in which players hit a ball with curved sticks or hammers, probably a loan from Persian >CHUGAN. Although banned, it was played in some monasteries. Monks, who gave in to the temptations of schaggun and disobeyed the ban, had to say several 'Hail Marys' as penance. W. Endrei and L. Zolnay, *Fun and Games in Old Europe*, 1986, 110.

SCHLAGBALL, a Ger. var. of >PALANT, a game between 2 teams competing for the right to bat (*Schlagrecht*), the batting team (*Schlagpartei*) defends this right, the team catching the ball in the field (*Fangpartei*) tries to get this right; the game is played on a pitch divided into the following segments:
The batting zone (*Schlagmal*) is located on the so-called top side, in front of the running field. The line, from which the ball must be batted, is defined as the batting line (*Schlagmallinie*). The ball can be batted from any place on the line. In the batting zone a blocking border is marked, parallel to the line of the batting zone, 5m away from it. The blocking zone (*Sperraum*), which is between the blocking line and the batting zone line, is occupied by the batting players who have acquired the right to run having batted the ball. The other batters should avoid the blocking zone before they have batted the ball and after they have completed their run.

'Savate is exactly the same thing as Boxing, except that it's all the opposite.'
Alexandre Dumas c.1830s.

Alain Robert scaling the Warsaw Marriott Hotel.

Behind the batting and blocking zone, towards the inside of the pitch, there is the running field (*Lauffeld*) with a half-way point (*Laufmale*). The running field is a 25m wide and 70m long rectangle for men and boys and a 25m wide and 50m long rectangle for women and girls. The half-way point is 10m from the end of the running field and 60m from the batting zone side. It is marked with 2 poles nailed into the ground, 4m apart, and 150cm above the ground. Behind the running field there is the so-called diagonal zone (*Schrägraum*). It is formed by the diagonals of the rectangular part of the pitch, extended up to 140m. All the border lines belong to the pitch and must be clearly marked. The corners of the running field and the centers of the longitudinal sides are marked with bordering poles, min. 150cm high. 10m from the side lines of the running field and the lines bordering the diagonal zone there is a line that separates the pitch from the spectators (*Zuschauergrenze*), 10m away from the batting zone. The pitch must be 140m long and 45m wide.
The game is played with a ball (*Lederball*) and a bat (*Schlagholz*). The leather ball is filled with oakum. Its weight, measured before the game, must be 70--85g and its circumference – 19-21cm. The leather should not be too shiny in sunlight. The bat should be made of solid wood. Its length and thickness on the batting side are not standardized, whereas the diameter of the thinner grip end should not exceed 3cm. The handle can be fitted with a knob and a loop, which help to hold the bat. The batting end cannot be artificially loaded. It is forbidden to wrap it in leather, wire, or metal. Each player may use his own bat, provided it meets the above standards, but should also make it available to other players.
A team is composed of 12 players. A match can also be played by a 9-man team. If a minimum of 9 players cannot be assembled, a team can add players during the game. A team, which is complete, does not have to reduce the number of players. In the course of the game players cannot be substituted.
A game begins with a toss to decide the right to bat. After the toss the batting team takes their positions in the batting zone and the catchers take the field. Players bat in a predetermined order, which cannot be changed during the game. The ball is in play once it has been hit by the bat. From that moment on, the right to play the ball rests with the catchers and the batters cannot touch the ball with any part of their bodies or with the bat, on purpose or unintentionally. If batting is prevented by any of the catchers or any player from the batting team, the referee orders a repeat batting. Each player can bat the ball only once in any round. A bat can be held and the ball batted with one or both hands. First the ball is tossed up in the air and then batted (unlike in >BASEBALL and Pol. >PALANT Z GALENIEM, where the ball is thrown by another player). A ball has been batted properly if it drops to the ground in the running field or in the diagonal zone or is touched by a catcher with both feet in the running field or in the diagonal zone. A ball has been batted improperly if both the batter's feet are not in the batting zone or if the bat falls from his hands or the bat breaks during batting. If the bat breaks, a player can repeat the batting with another bat.
When the ball has been batted, the players of the batting team drop their bats to the ground and try to reach the half-way point, indicated with running marks (*Laufmale*), which are at the end of the running zone (*Lauffeld*). When they have reached the half-way point and touched either of the 2 poles, the runners must return to the batting zone. A complete run scores one point for the player's team. If a runner fails to leave his bat in the batting zone, the run is invalid and must be repeated without the bat. No runs are allowed if the bat was invalid. A player who decided to run before a bat was called invalid, must (when the invalidity has been explained by the referee) return to the starting point. The invalidity of a bat is announced by the referee or linesman with a long whistle. In case of an invalid bat the ball belongs to the catchers only – until it is caught or until it has touched the ground – then it is considered to be dead (*der tote Ball*). Then the ball must be brought to the batting zone as quickly as possible or given to the batting team. A point is also awarded for a so-called long bat (*Weitschlag*), i.e. a bat, after which the ball crosses the back border of the running zone and, not having been caught by the players of the catching team, lands in the diagonal zone, in which case the batter scores a point. The catching team take positions in the running field and the diagonal zone and score points when 1) they catch the ball in the air, 2) they hit a player of the batting team with the ball or outrun the player running to the blocking zone (*Sperraum*). Skilful ball catching in the air, passing the ball and quick throwing to the batting zone may prevent the players from returning to their positions. This is called 'starving the opponent' (*Ausgehungert*). If the batter, while running, intentionally prevents the catcher from throwing the ball, a penalty substitution takes place (*Strafwechsel*); the batters forfeit the batting zone and take to the field while the catchers become the batters. Catching (*das Fangen*) means that each ball, be the bat valid or invalid, both in the field or outside the field, can be caught validly. Each catch scores 1pt. A catch is valid if it is made with one hand and only when the ball, before it is caught, has not touched the ground, any part of the body or any other object. When a runner or batter prevents the catcher from catching the ball, the ball is considered to be caught. The team with more points wins the game. In tournaments a win is worth 2pts., a tie – 1pt., and 0pts. are awarded for a lost game. In game reports its elements are described as follows: correct run 'I'; valid long bat 'V'; valid hit 'X' and valid catch 'O'. The game is supervised by judges (*Spielrichters*): 1 referee (*Schiedrichter*) and 3 linesmen (*Linienrichter*), (who cannot be members of any team). The referee has his position on the field, inside the batting zone. He calls the points, which are recorded by scorers and supervises the records as well as makes final decisions in case the linesmen disagree. His decisions are final and cannot be appealed. The first linesman stands opposite the referee, by the batting zone. The other two walk by the pitch borders, next to the running zone and the back line. During batting they take positions by the corner flags. They decide if the line has been crossed, whether a bat was valid, if a bat was long, if a hit was made, the positions of the runners and off-sides. The first linesman also keeps record of the batters and supervises the order of batting and validity of runs. Each team appoints one score judge (*Anschreiber*). One of them records the points and the other supervises him. The game is played for 60min. and extended by any injury time. In case of a tie, after a 10-min. break the game is continued for another 20min. The team, who played as catchers, start the extra time as batters. No substitutions are allowed, the order of batting cannot be changed either. Each player can bat only once. If there is a tie after extra time, the game is resumed and the team who scores the first point wins. All players of one team must wear the shirts and shorts in same color, which must distinctly differ from that of the other team. Each player must have a clearly visible number. Shoes with spikes are forbidden as they could lead to injury.
History. The game derives from medieval tradition. About 30 players took part in the game. The game is similar to Ital. varieties of palant games, referred to as >PALLA A CACCIA. In the 18th cent. a pioneer of physical educiation, J.C.F. Guts-Muths (1759-1839) called this game *das deutsche Ballspiel*. Later, the game became a national sport (*Art Nationalspiel*). Its popularity continued right up through the beginnings of the 20th cent. It never gained the status of a national game, as was the case with similar batting games, e.g. Eng. >CRICKET or Amer. >BASEBALL. This was prevented by the development of other sports, particularly football. Schlagball gradually became a school sport, where it was very popular for some time, particularly after WWII. Americanization of West-Ger. sports after WWII was another obstacle to preserving the popularity of schlagball, particularly preference given to basketball and volleyball, which did not require such large areas to play.
W. Braungardt, 'Schlagball', *Turnspiele. Lehrbuch für Spieler, Spielwarte und Schiedsrichter*, 1949; 'Schlagball', *Kleine Enzyklopädie. Körperkultur und Sport*, ed. G. Erbach, 1965, 592-594.

SCHLEUDERBALL, [Ger. *Schleuder* – leather band, sling, band + *Ball*]; a var. of a ball game, in which 2 teams in a narrow field compete in throwing a ball with a loop (ear) from one place to another; the ear, made of a leather band, 28cm long and 1.5cm wide, is sewn into a leather case; the case can be made of canvas; in a men's game the ball is 65-70cm in circumference, it has a weight of 1.5kg and the leather band is 2.5cm wide; players aged 12-15yrs. use a 1kg ball, younger ones – an 800g ball, 55-60cm in circumference.
The rectangular field is 80-110m long (most often 100m) and 15m wide. Children play on a field 70-90m long and 12m wide. The field is divided across with zone lines (*Mallinien*) into 5 parts. The central part is 40m long, the two adjacent zones – 30m long each. 20m from the field's center (10m when children play), on both sides, there is a throw line (*Abwurflinie*), which forms the central zone of the field, the so-called neutral zone, which can only be occupied by the team which at a given moment has the right to throw the ball. Along the side lines there are 8m wide spectator free zones, so called protection zones. There are also such zones at either end of the field. The field's length with the protection zones is 160m and its width – 31m. The field's corners feature border poles with flags, at least 150cm high. The playing time is 2x20min. with a 5-10min. break for older boys and 2x15min. with a 5-10min. break for younger boys. If tied, the game is continued for 2x5min. extra time, after a 5min. break. Teams change sides after each 5min. If the winner is still not decided, after another 5min. break the game continues until one of the teams wins. The teams consist of 5-8 players; each team takes its place. The team winning the toss selects which end they want to play from. Teams change ends after the break. The players should be identified by clearly visible, 8x10cm numbers from 1 to 8. No substitutions are permitted during the game.
The game starts with a throw from the throw line. The objective is to throw the ball as far as the back part of the opposing team's half. There are two types of throws: standing and running. A ball can be thrown back only from where it was caught with one or both hands, but it must touch the ground before it is caught. A good throw means a zone capture, i.e. it scores a point. A zone is captured when the ball flies over or rolls over the opposing team's zone line. The team, which captures more zones, wins the game. When the balls goes out of play, it is thrown back to the opposing team's half from the place where it crossed the out line. A player who manages to catch the ball in the air, wins the right to take 3 steps or 3 jumps of any length in the direction of the opposing team's half. The ball must be thrown from inside or on the sideline. When a player of the opposing team catches the ball before it touches the ground he throws it back immediately. If the ball is caught again – the catcher throws it back. If the opponent then catches the ball for a third time – the throw is invalid. The game is resumed with a throw from the place where the ball has stopped. A player catching the ball, throwing the ball or running cannot be interfered with. The minimum distance between the thrower and an opponent is 3m. The penalty in case the players intentionally delay the play is a throw from the place in which the error was made. From the tactical point of view the teams are usu. divided into 3 back players and 3 forward players. Between the two trios there are 2 midfield players, who defend their half against shorter throws. However, this division is flexible and can change, depending on what is needed at a given time.
The match is supervised by a referee (*Schiedrichter*) and 2 linesmen (*Linienrichter*). They are assisted by one scoring judge (*Anschreiber*).
History. The game became popular in the 2nd half of the 19th cent., when the ball, earlier used in exercises practiced for general physical development, started to be used in medicine and gymnastics. In the first half of the 20th cent. it was very popular in north Germany, particularly on the Baltic coast, where locally, although more and more sporadically, it has been practiced till today. Played according to formally recognized rules, it was part of the program of Ger. gymnastic organizations and also part of various training programs. A nearly identical game, having the same roots, is known in Denmark as >SLYNGBOLD. Presently, like many other old sports, it is disappearing.
W. Braungardt, 'Schleuderball', *Turnspiele*, 1949; anonymous, 'Schleuderball', *Kleine Enzyklopädie. Körperkultur und Sport*, ed. G. Erbach, 1965, 594-595.

SCHOONER RACE, full name *The Great Chesapeake Bay Schooner Race*, an event held on the 3rd weekend in Oct. to attract vessels making their seasonal migration south and the potential for hurricane-season weather always adds excitement to the outcome, sometimes requiring a shortened

American Nathan Holdener, left, of Washington D.C., challenges Switzerland's Richard Arnold during the Swiss Wrestling and Alpine Games Festival in Nyon, Switzerland.

course. The event kicks off on Wednesday, with a parade through Baltimore's Inner Harbor followed by a friendly gathering for sponsors and participants in Fells Point, and safety meetings for the captains. On Thursday the fleet musters for the start just south of the Bay Bridge off Annapolis. By Saturday the fleet is moored all around Nauticus, Norfolk's National Maritime Museum, where participants, volunteers and sponsors celebrate with a pig and oyster roast and the awards ceremony. Dockside and on-board festivities continue on into the night as crews gather for the traditional 'Sailors Evening' to gam and sing sea chanties. On Sunday sponsors join the crews for a hearty farewell breakfast.

History. The genesis of this event reaches back 200 years, to the era when cargo between Baltimore and Norfolk moved under sail, generating a fierce rivalry between these historic ports. Swift schooners vied for prime markets for bay-area oysters, watermelon, peanuts and other crops. The schooner reaching port soonest got the best prices and first choice among return cargoes, and such lucrative trade inspired development of fast, beautiful, weatherly fore-and-aft-rigged designs, of which the *Pride of Baltimore II* is one example.

In modern times, schooners carry young cadets, paying passengers or yachtsmen rather than oysters. Capt. Lane Briggs' schooner *Norfolk Rebel* (59ft.) is a working tug. Briggs challenged the *Pride of Baltimore II* (170ft.) to a down-the-bay race, winner to buy the beer at the finish, and in 1990 seven schooners battled their way down the bay. Every fall since then, a steadily increasing number of schooners large and small from all over the world have gathered at Fells Point to revive this ancient spirit of competition, tempered by a new mood of cooperation between the bay's largest ports to promote a cleaner Chesapeake. About 40 schooners register for the event.
The Internet: http://www.schoonerrace.org/index.htm

SCHUIFTAFEL, Flem. for 'slippery table', a Flem. competitive game practiced mainly in the west of Flanders, the Bachten de Kupe region and Pajottenland in the province of Flemish-Brabant. Similar games are known in the Fr. speaking part of Belgium as >JEU DE FER.

Equipment and rules. The game is played on a table, 2.1m long and 45m wide and less than 1m high. The object of the game is to slide metal pieces (discs). Each player or team gets 5 discs, marked with the same letter on the bottom: 'V' and 'X'. If during the play there is any doubt who a given disc belongs to, it is turned up and then replaced. The discs are 0.7cm thick and 4cm in diameter. Depending on the prevailing local tradition, they can be made of iron, copper or lead. The players move the discs on the table, using cues, in the past similar to those used in billiards, presently actual billiard cues. The cues are traditionally slightly burnt at a length of about 20cm from the top and, unlike billiard cues, they do not have the felt tip (*pomerancy*). At the back of the table pieces (sometimes figures similar in shape to the king used in chess), are arranged. They are about 20-25cm high. Depending on the prevailing local tradition, 5-7 such figures are arranged on the table. The object of the game is to scatter the discs on the table in such a way that they are as close as possible to the farthest figures. An important element of strategy is to move one's own discs so that they not only are as close as possible to the farthest figures but at the same time push away the opponent's pieces. The disc closest to a given figure scores a point. The game continues until 12pts. are scored. Before the game fine sand is poured on the table to help the metal discs move. Along the back and side edges there is a 10cm wide groove. Any discs which fall into the groove during the game score no points. The game can be played according to two systems: 1) players or teams take turns to slide their discs, 2) the first player or first team slides all the discs, one after another, and then the other player or team takes over.
E. de Vroede, 'Ball and Bowl Games in the Low Countries: Past and Present', *Homo Ludens – Der Spielende Mensch*, 1996, vol. VI; ibid, *Het Grote Volkssporten Boek*, Leuven 1996; ibid, *Schuiftafel*, NVVC, 1989,9.

SCHWINGEN, Swiss folk wrestling in which the wrestlers hold on to the opponent's clothes [Ger. *schwingen* – rock in convulsive movements]. The opponent is gripped by trad., reinforced, knee high trousers specially sewn with a small cut at the back under the belt (Ger. *Schwinghosen*). The contes-

tants are matched by the referee, who takes into account their weight and talent – there is no official division into weights. A round lasts 5 min. and the objective is to put the opponent on his back. The contestants put on their trousers, tighten the belt and roll up the trouser legs. The bout is held in the open air on a ring 30ft. in diameter, on saw dust. The ring is called the 'Platz'. The starting position grips are taken in the following order: first each wrestler places his right hand on the small of the back of his opponent: only the thumb, index finger and middle finger may hold on to the material of the trad. clothing, however the entire hand has to be in the rear of the opponent's belt. Next, the left hand grips the bottom of the rolled up left pant leg. The thumb may not be 'rolled up' into the material to help with gripping, but as mentioned before the fabric must be held with the fingers throught the bout. The body weight must be evenly spread on both legs. The opponents must allow each other to take the starting position grips and only then does the referee signal the beginning of the bout. The bout ends when one of the contestants is pushed out of the Platz or when he breaks the grip.
History. The Easter Monday Schwingfest in Berg, known until today, was first held around 1750. The best wrestlers from Emmenthal, Oberland, Entlebuch and central Switzerland (Innerschweiz) came regularly. In 1864 the first manual on the principles and techniques of schwingen was published. Schwingen is practiced during holidays and folk festivals in the vicinity of Bern, Lucerne and Emental; see and cf. >GLÍMA, >HOSENLUPF, >CORNWALL AND DEVON.

ŚCIANA, Pol. for 'wall', also *gra w ścianę, łapa*, an old Pol. folk game, especially popular in schools in the 18th, 19th and the beginning of the 20th cent. Ł. Gołębiowski in his *Gry i zabawy różnych stanów* (1831) refers to the game as *łapa* (paw), whereas E. Piasecki in his *Gry i zabawy ruchowe dzieci i młodzieży* (1916) prefers the name *ściana*. The game was also described by E. Cenar (*Gry i za-*

Ships participating in a Parade of Sail pass through Baltimore's Inner Harbor prior to sailing to the Bay Bridge for the start of the Great Chesapeake Bay Schooner Race.

bawy ruchowe różnych narodów, 2nd ed. 1906). It was part of a larger family of ball games in which the ball was caught, in old Pol. called >CHWYTKA. The game, now forgotten, is described by Gołębiowski as follows:

A large group of volunteers gather, and stand by the wall or pay their footing to join. Next each of them takes turn at throwing the ball at the wall and catching it. Whoever fails to catch the ball or the last to throw, if all of them catch it, becomes the first thrower [in the game proper]; he throws with his right hand. Has he hit anybody or not? as soon as he got hold of the ball he has the right to throw again; whoever has dropped the ball, must go to the wall and a ball will be thrown at his palm first by the player who was the łapa before him and then by anybody who catches the ball. And so they change their roles all the time until they are tired and stop. A hit at the arm, not at the palm, called the krawiec (tailor), is punished – whoever hits the arm becomes the łapa.

ŚCIEŻKA ZDROWIA, Pol. for 'health trail', a configuration of outdoor trails with stops en route where there is simple, rusticated exercise equpment.

A table for playing schuiftafel.

S

WORLD SPORTS ENCYCLOPEDIA

Ścieżka zdrowia is an excellent opportunity to exercise in the open. The distances between the stops, the length of which depends on personal health, skill and strength, should be covered by running, trotting, marching or a combination of marching and running. At the stops there are bars, benches, and other exercise equipment like ladders. Depending on the designers, ścieżka zdrowia can feature any equipment lending itself to different exercises, and sets of instructions geared to age categories and the sex, indicating the minimum or maximum number of exercises.

SCOOTERS, Ger. *Roller*, Hung. *Robogo*, Du. *autoped*, Ital. *monopattino*. The name refers both to the equipment and the sport, usu. for children. The competition features a 2-wheel vehicle, more rarely with 3 wheels (with 2 small parallel wheels at the back). The person riding the scooter stands with one foot placed on the board that links the rear wheel with the front wheel and the steering unit. The handle is situated at waist level or slightly higher. The scooter may be equipped with a rear break or a cog-gear mechanism that powers the rear wheel. Typically, the vehicle is moved by shoving off with the other foot. There are many different constructions of scooters. The oldest and the simplest, coming from the 2nd half of the 19th cent, had wooden wheels and no steering unit. The end of the 19th cent. saw the introduction of the steering device and solid rubber tires. In the 1920s, scooters with pneumatic tires were popular among the rich. However, they were bigger and heavier. To make them easier to ride, the constructors equipped them with a mechanism that powered the rear wheel (or 2 rear wheels) by pressing a small pedal. Wooden scooters were popular among the less affluent members of most Eur. societies. They had full wooden wheels that were carved and painted black, imitating tires. Another inexpensive vehicle was >RADKI, known after the 1920s. In 2000-2001, a new type of scooter, called *holly top* or >KICK-BOARD became extremely popular. See also >SKATEBOARDING.

Top and above: scooter riding.

Senegalese traditional wrestlers fight during an inter-village match in Hathioune, Senegal.

SCOTS STYLE WRESTLING, a general name for wrestling practiced in Scotland, comprising >BACKHOLD and >DINNIE STYLE; the tradition and original character of Scot. wrestling, irrespective of the style, is attested by the support given to this sport by the ruler of Hebrides, Domhnuil Gruamach; about 1400 he ordered a special building, Tigh Sunndas (House of Joy) to be built for his soldiers, who practiced wrestling, on the North Uist island, in an area designated for practicing sword fighting (Pairc na Claidhaimh, lit. Garden of Swords); the building is considered to be the first building erected in Scotland for sports purposes. W. Baxter, 'Scots Style (Dinnie Style)', 'Les lutes traditionnelles a traverse le monde', LJP, 1998, 85.

SCOUTING, a youth movement, started by Lord R. Stephenson Baden-Powell (1857-1941), an officer in the Brit. army, who recognized the need for better physical and moral preparation of young soldiers, particularly officers. In 1907 he formed the Boy Scouts. The main assumptions of scouting include improvement of physical skills and morality and culture of youth through contact with nature. As such, scouting was a pioneer organization in the formation of environmentally friendly attitudes among the young, despite the existence of the international ecological movement. Character building through physical effort is the element linking scouting with sport. Cf. >HARCERSTWO.

SCUBA DIVING, a name denoting a var. of underwater swimming, deriving from *scuba* (*self-contained underwater breathing apparatus*). In Eng.-speaking countries, particularly in the USA, scuba diving is basically identical to >SCUBA DIVING.
J.D. Craig, M. Clint Degn, *Invitation to Skin and Scuba Diving*, 1965; B.E. Empleton, *The New Science of Skin and Scuba Diving*, 1974; D.K. Graver, *Scuba Diving*, 1993.

SEER SHAAKH, Mong. for 'striking the bone'. A group of contestants sit in a circle; a piece of a cow's or bull's vertebra (*seer*) is passed between them. The contestants take turns in trying to break the bone with one blow of the fist. Contests of this type usu. accompany the Mong. feast of slaughter – *nair*. A contestant who fails to break the bone must drink a bowlful of koumiss. In some Mong. regions a silver coin had to be paid by contestants who failed to break the bone. Usually a few contestants had to pay, before the bone was broken. The silver coins then became the prize collected by the successful contestant. Sometimes it happened that none of the contestants managed to break the bone. When this happened, the contestants rode on horseback to the neighboring settlement to find somebody able to break the bone. During contests marrow from the bone with which the men played was eaten. It was supposed to give the necessary strength to the contestants. Mongolians believed that the bone which they attempted to break had magic properties and, if burnt together with other bones, it would help the spirit of the killed animal to be reborn. In some regions of Cent. Asia, particularly among the inhabitants of Altai, the shoulder-blade of a 2-yr.-old bull was broken, instead of the spine bone. The contestants told legends of their predecessors who were able to break the shoulder-blade with one blow of the index finger. The shoulder-blade was also used in some throwing competitions (>ANIMAL SHOULDER-BLADE THROW).

SEESAWING, see >TEETER-TOTTERING, >SWINGS AND SEESAWS, >SKAKANIE NA DESKACH, and >NÓL TTWIGI.

SEGALARIAK, Basq. competition in grass mowing, also Span. *segalaris*, *sega apostua* or *sega apustua*, officially *concursos de siega* – competitions in mowing, [Span. dial. *sega*, standard Span. *siega* – mowing + *apostua*, dialectally *apustua* – competition, *apostar* – to compete; *concursos* – contest, competition]. A folk sport deriving from the tradition of work in the field, particularly popular in the Basq. country and the Navarre province. Contestants cut long grass using a scythe (*guadaña*) with a very long blade. Blades (*cuchilla*) in scythes made specially for Basq. competition are 118-124cm long (blades in ordinary scythes are about 75cm long in the Navarre province and 90-95cm in Gui); its width at the base is 15-18cm. In the top part the blade has a thick rib (*lomo*), which gives the edge (*corte*) its rigidity. The wooden shank (*mango kidera*) is made

of beech, and has a small handle in the middle (*manija inferios*) and an additional lateral handle at the end (*manija superior*). Women compete with sickles – these competitions are called *corte de hierba con hoz* – lit. 'grass mowing with a sickle', [Span. *corte* – cut + *hierba* – grass + *con* – z + *hoz* – sickle). Contests are held on a meadow (*pradera*), where a plot to be mowed is designated (Basque *balardia*; Span. *campa* or *herbazal*). Mowing starts from the edge of the plot and proceeds inwards, towards the center which is marked with a 5m tall pole. There are areas particularly famous for segalariak contests, such as Trincha-Leku or Ari-Barrutia in the vicinity of the Iturrioz hermitages or Etxea-Atzea in the Guipúzcoa province. Traditionally, the contests are held over an agreed time, usu. 60, 90 or 120min. and the contestants try to mow as much grass as possible. The grass is then collected and weighed on a special scales, made up of a 2m tall gate. In the middle of the gate's top beam there is a hook, on which scales are hung. Grass is put in layers on the scales, and the weight of each layer is added up. If the contest lasts 60min. the mower has the right to change 3 scythes; if 90min. – 4 scythes; if 120min. – 5 scythes. Contestants compete individually (if they are famous) or in teams (in case of regular championships) – depending on the meadow size, teams usu. have 4, or less frequently 6 contestants. Beginning with the championships of the Basq. country in 1969, regular grass mowing championships against the clock have been held, usu. on a 900-1200sq. m meadow. Each mower is accompanied by a partner, who collects the grass (he can use a rake or a specially prepared stick to move the swath away).

History. The tradition of segalariak goes back to the Middle Ages. The sport was practiced in the 18th and 19th cent. in the form typical of modern day competitions,. One of the most famous was an hour long contest between P. Mendizábal, nicknamed 'Lokata', against J. Arrieta, nicknamed 'Prantxesa'. It was held in 1925 with 6,000 spectators watching and the bets were as high as 150,000 pesetas. The contest was won by Mendizábal, who mowed 4292kg of grass (Arrietta mowed 3957kg). In 1957 J.Ch. Vitoria, in a 2-hr. contest beat an equally famous mower M. Irazusta 'Polipasao', mowing 8,955kg of grows against 8,098kg. The second best 2-hour result was made in 1964 by M.M. Zulaika 'Pascualsoro', who beat J. Aburuza with 8,744.5kg to 8732.5kg, winning also a 50,000 pesetas bet. The contest attracted 16,000 spectators. The best 90-minute contest was held in Jauregua, in which E. Tapia beat 'Polipasao' (5,693.5kg to 5,519kg). The best sickle contestants include M.A. Arceo Exquerra, who also competed against men, usu. with an agreed handicap. The most famous contest was held in 1967 in which Exquerra was beaten by A. Larraza (2,325kg to 1,896kg). Official championships of the Basque country have been held since 1965. In 1969 grass weighing was replaced with contests against the clock in which grass from a designated plot had to be mowed. The first champion of the Basque country was B. Irastorza (1969), who mowed two plots of total area 1,143.17sq. m in 35min. 7sec. Presently, segalariak is regulated by the Federación de Juegos y Deportes Vascos (Federation of Basque Games and Sports). R. Aguirre, 'Sega apustua', GHJD, 1989, 9-36; C. Moreno Palos, 'Sega apostua', JYTE, 1992.

SEN-CHA, an event of the Jap. art of archery >TOSIYA. The archer's main task was to shoot an arrow so that it went northwards along the narrow western passage of the Sanju-Sangen-Do temple in Kyo, presently in Kyoto. The arrow was not allowed to hit the temple wall or eaves. Arrows were shot from up to 120m away. An archer who wanted to test his accuracy had the right to shoot 1000 times at any time. The number of shots made in accordance with the Sanji-Sange-Do rules decided the result. *Hjaku-sha* was a shorter var. of sen-cha; only 100 arrows were shot.

SENEGALESE WRESTLING, a folk wrestling var. allowing not only typical wrestling holds but also hitting one's opponent with the open hand or fist. Older and more brutal varieties have been replaced by a milder style based on the Eur. rules of wrestling where, for example, fist blows are banned. The competitors wear trunks or a hip band. The wrestlers (and their managers) rank among the most affluent athletes in Senegal. National championships con-

A sepak takraw game.

sist of a series of matches. The Senegalese Champion receives 1 million Senegalese francs and a national flag. One of the most ardent fans of Senegalese wrestling was the President of the Republic of Senegal – L. Sédar Senghor who, being at the same time a poet, praised the sport as a 'source of beauty, poetry and emotion'.
S. Aly Cisse, 'Senegalese Wrestling. Deep-Rooted and Open Minded', OR, Dec. 1995/Jan. 1996.

SEPAK TAKRAW, an Asiatic game, in Thailand called *takraw* or *takro*, in the Phillipines *sipak*, in Malaysia *sepak raga*. The name sepak takraw was determined during the South Asian Games in 1965, by combining the Malaysian word *sepak* (strike, kick) and Thai *takraw* (rattan ball).
Sepak takraw is played on a court with an area like a badminton court, with a spherical ball woven from rattan leaves and fibers, 40cm in circumference (16in.) and weighing 298g (10½oz.). The net is 155cm (5ft. 1in.) at the posts. The court is 44ft. long and 22ft. wide (13.41x6.71 m). The game is played between two 'Regu's' consisting of 3 players on each side. One of the players, called the *tekong*, takes position in the semicircle by the base line. The second player is called the *apit kiri* or striker and the third – the feeder. The rules are a combination of the rules of >BADMINTON and >VOLLEYBALL. The ball is served with a kick and can be hit over the net with the head (*balas tandok*). In the course of the game the ball cannot be touched with the arm, from the shoulders down. The ball must not touch the court's surface or a point is lost. Each team can hit the ball three times in their court and the next hit must be directed at the opponents' side. The ball is served like in volleyball, but the game ends when 15pts. have been scored. 2 sets out of 3 must be won to win the game.
History. The genesis of sepak takraw is not known. For decades Thailand, the Philippines and Malaya, and even Burma, where a similar game was known, have been in dispute about the game's beginnings. The oldest legends and tales suggest Malay genesis of sepak takraw. It was a game played at the courts of Malay rulers. The mythical hero Hang Tuah is associated with the old forms of the games and depicted in legends and drawings. In the old var. of the game the players formed a circle and the team that managed to keep the ball in the air the longest time won. Contests between 2 players were also held. The colonization of S-E Asia by the British contributed to the decline of the game as a court game. It was preserved in Malay villages – *kampongs*. The diaries of Brit. governors and officers confirm that the game was a favorite pastime of their servants and drivers; in its oldest forms the game was played only by men, presently it is also played by women.

Since 1982 it has been an event in the Asiatic Games. The first W.Ch. were held in 1993 in Kheon Khaen (Thailand). Sepak takraw is played mainly in S-E Asia: Burma, the Philippines, Cambodia, Laos, Malaysia, Singapore, Sri Lanka, Thailand and Vietnam. However, it is also popular in Europe (Finland, France, Germany, the Netherlands, Switzerland, United Kingdom), North and South America, and Australia. In Malaysia and Singapore, where it is considered a national sport, it is also part of physical education classes at schools. The most important events in Singapore include the Pesta Sukan Championships, first division championships and the Singaporean President's Cup. Winning all three contests constitutes a Grand Slam. In 1993 the Grand Slam was won by the Sri Kallang club, with N. Adam as its captain, one of the best sepak takraw players in history, who played as a *tekong*. In Thailand the most important event is the Thai King's Cup. The best trainers are S. Mor Diti (Singapore) and H. Abdul Rahman (Malaysia). The governing body is the International Sepaktakraw Federation (ISTAF).

SER, Pol. for 'cheese', a simple urban game, played on empty yards by youths till the middle of the 1950s, when it almost completely disappeared. In Poznań (Poland), in the local var. of the Pol. language, the game was referred to as 'syr', also as 'gra w syra'. An identical game is known in England as *cocklyjock* or *cogs*. Before the game started a few (usu. 4-5) stones or brick fragments were arranged vertically, one upon another . They were piled on a natural or man-made mound or often on low walls around domestic gardens, squares, foundations of fences etc., which resulted in never-ending quarrels between the players and the owners or even the police or administrators as the walls were often damaged as a result of the game. The object of the game was to knock down the stone or brick structure with a large stone, about 5-10cm in diameter, thrown from a distance of about 10-20m, depending on the players' age, strength and skill. Scoring was not formalized and in local varieties of the game 1pt. was awarded for knocking down all the stones in the pile or 1pt. was awarded for each stone knocked off. The last stone, which was most difficult to be knocked off, the 'ser', scored from 2-5pts. The game was played from the end of the 19th cent., usu. by poor boys and girls, who had no access to sports clubs and equipment. When such equipment became more easily accessible (following sports popularization campaigns in Poland after 1945), ser started to decline. It disappeared completely in the middle of the 1960s.

SERSO, a game involving throwing rings made of wicker, wire or plastic, about 30-60cm in diameter. Rings are placed on an 80-100cm long stick which

is twirled and then the spinning ring is released. A partner, standing opposite the thrower, usu. several meters away, tries to catch the ring in the air, with his own stick. A Dan. var. of serso is called *Ringspil med stok*. The Pol. var. is played by teams of 3-6 standing 10-15m apart: 'a player standing in front of the row throws the ring to the first player in the row who tries to catch it with his stick. If he manages, this scores 2pts. He throws the ring back to the first player, passes the stick to the next player in the row who in turn tries to catch the ring. In this way the players take turns and score points. The winner is the player who scores the most points in the agreed number of throws (e.g. 5, 10). If 2 players have scored the same number of points, an extra game of 3-5 throws is played between them'.
J. Møller, 'Ringspil med stok', GID, 1997, 1, 126; R. Trześniowski, 'Serso', ZIGR, 1995, 291-291.

SEVEL AR BERCHENN, also *gwernian ar berchernn*, Fr. *le lever de la perche*, Eng. *lifting the pole*; Bret. display of physical strength in which contestants lift a long pole with a handle at its base and try to stand it vertically, in this way overcoming the resistance of the leverage and the pole's weight. The pole is made of the hewed trunk of a young tree, about 6m long. It is held by the thinner end, the thick end providing a counterweight during lifting. The thinner end of the pole is rammed into the ground and at the same time the pole is lifted. Each contestant has 3 attempts. Two techniques are used: *krog pertchenn*, in which the contestant stands sideways with the pole and holds it with both hands, and *krog sac'h*, in which the contestants stand astride the pole. If the pole proves to be too long and heavy for all the contestants, the organizers cut pieces off the trunk until at least one of the contestants manages to lift it vertically. In some regions instead of cutting off sections of the pole balance weights are used, which are moved along the trunk, which helps to more accurately measure the contestants' abilities. However, in this way the game loses somewhat its

A sepak takraw ball.

A sepak takraw match played at Santa Monica, California.

S WORLD SPORTS ENCYCLOPEDIA

natural character and becomes less spectacular. F. Peru, 'La tradition populaire de jeux de plein air en Bretagne', LJP, 1998.

SEVEN-A-SIDE RUGBY, also *rugby sevens* or *sevens rugby*, a var. of >RUGBY UNION for teams of 7 players, invented in a Scot. town of Melrose in 1883 by a local butcher's apprentice and Melrose 20-a-side rugby club's quarterback, Ned Haig, as part of an effort to raise funds at the end of the rugby season. As running a tournament for 20-a-side teams was considered unworkable, it was agreed that the participating teams would have a number of players reduced to 1 full back, 2 quarterbacks, and 4 forwards. Later, the forwards were reduced to 3 and an extra half-back was introduced. The game combines speed, dummy movements, and step-work, and is much quicker and less brutal than rugby union. The original Melrose tournament was played with the time of each match limited to 15min. and was an instant hit, with approx. 1,600 tickets sold each day. It also established another rule, according to which the first team to score in extra time is the winner of the match. Since then, the popularity of seven-a-side rugby has continued to grow and the game spread to other countries, including Great Britain, Australia, N.Zealand, South Africa, Argentina, the USA, Samoa, Fiji, Tonga, France, Canada, Georgia, Uruguay, Morocco, Papua New Guinea, Spain, Japan, and others. The governing body for rugby sevens is the International Rugby Board es-

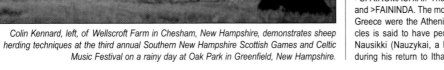

Colin Kennard, left, of Wellscroft Farm in Chesham, New Hampshire, demonstrates sheep herding techniques at the third annual Southern New Hampshire Scottish Games and Celtic Music Festival on a rainy day at Oak Park in Greenfield, New Hampshire.

USA's Olo Fifita holds on to the ball as he's held down by Wales' David Weatherly, left, during the Plate final event of the Rugby Sevens tournament.

tab. in Ireland in 1886, which organizes the World Sevens Series.

SEX AS SPORT, although a surprising parallel, it is in the history of mankind one of the more frequent recreational contests between two people, the aim of which is not to defeat the partner but, quite opposite – give both partners satisfaction and pleasure from the 'duel' (except for some religious doctrines, which exclude this). In this sense it meets the criterion of sport and in this meaning it functions in the Eng. language, where the word 'sport' also means sexual satisfaction/fulfillment. This way it is used by W. Shakespeare in *Othello*, act II, scene 1:

Her eye must be fed; and what delight shall she have to look on the devil? When the blood is made dull with the act of sport, there should be – again to inflame it, and to give satiety a fresh appetite – loveliness in favor, sympathy in years, manners, and beauties; all which the Moor is defective in.

Sex as sport was practiced by G.G. Casanova (1725-98), the famous seducer. He described his many conquests in his memoirs *Histoire de ma vie* (the story of Casanova's life till 1744), which became one of the greatest erotic bestsellers of all times. Some cultures developed competitive sports of a sexual character, directly or symbolically. An example of the former is the Mongolian game of camel untying >TÖÖ CHECHMEY. Erotic symbolism plays an important role in the Flem. bowling sport >TROU-MADAME.

SFAIRA, also from O.Gk. *sphaira* [O.Gk. *sfaira*], a game played in ancient Greece, similar to and probably the prototype of the Roman >FOLLIS. The field was called *sfairisterion* (Latinized form: *sphairisterium*). It was part of the gymnasion, but could also be a separate building. The relation of sfaira to >EPISKYROS is not known; see also >SFAIRISEIS.

SFAIRISEIS, also *sphairiseis*, ball games [Gk. *sfairisis* – ball game, O.Gk. *sfaira* – ball]; a group of ball games played in ancient Greece for recreation. They never became part of the ancient games. A special subgroup of sfairiseis were *sfairomachiaj*, i.e. brutal games involving fighting for the ball. In Greece sfairiseis included: >APORRHAXIS, >URANIA, >SFAIRA, >EPISKYROS, >KERETIZEIN. The brutal ball games were in ancient Greece called >SFAIROMACHIAI. They included >HARPASTON and >FAININDA. The most ardent players in ancient Greece were the Athenians and Spartans. Sophocles is said to have personally played the part of Nausikki (Nauzykai, a heroine met by Odysseus during his return to Ithaca) in one of his plays, in

which a ball game is an element of the plot; the scene is said to have been applauded by the spectators (>NAUSICAA BALL). The monument to Isocrates, a famous orator from Athens, in Acropol, depicted him playing *keretizein*. Some ancient authors considered the Spartans the inventors of the ball. In the Spartan educational system ball games played an important role; the older group of ephebes, aged 9-10yrs., was called *sphaireis*, after the game played by them. >SFAIROMACHIAI played by the Spartans became famous for their brutality, which was intentional as it was meant to make the ephebes resistant to the perils of life.

SFAIROMACHIAI, also *sphairomachiaj*, pl. noun [O.Gk. sg. *sfairomachia* – a ball game, but also a fist fight in gloves, resembling balls, O.Gk. *sfaira* – ball]. In ancient Greece a type of game combined with brutal fighting for the ball. Sfairomachiai include >HARPASTON and >FAININDA; see also >SFAIRISEIS.

SHAFT JUMP, also *mowing the grass*, a Rus. running and jumping game described by I.N. Chkhannikov.

Two teams of the same number of players stand in 2 rows opposite each other, 5m apart. The players on each team stand next to one another 2 shoulders-width apart. Two players from each team come forward and take a 1m-long shaft. On a signal, the two players with the shafts lean forward and start running along the rows holding the shaft low, just slightly above the ground. Each player in the row must jump over the shaft. On reaching the end of the row one runner joins the row while the other runs back with the shaft on the outside to the beginning of his row. Then, the first player on the row gets hold of the shaft and they run forward together forcing the players in the row to jump over the shaft again. The game is over after each player has completed 2 runs with the shaft. The team which first manages to complete all the runs and jumps wins.

[I.N. Chkhanikov, 'Shaft jump', GIZ, 1953, 27]

SHAFT PROPPING, a school wrestling game, popular in the former USSR and eastern Eur. socialist countries. Two contenders stand inside a circle, 6 steps in diameter. Each contender holds one end of a thick, 2-m shaft. The wrestlers try to push each other out of the circle by pressing on the shaft. A wrestler, who like in >SUMO, manages to push his opponent out of the circle and remain inside is the winner. A wrestler can also lose if he drops the shaft during the bout. The wrestlers are not allowed to press on the shaft with their bellies or grab it in front of the designated end. I.N. Chkhannikov, GIZ, 2nd ed. 1953, 9.

SHAHARDI. The trad. acrobatic show of the Uygurs, a Chin. minority, held on a structure that resembles a merry-go-round. It is made of a vertical pole, ab. 10-12m tall, held vertically with the help of guy-ropes. At the top of the pole a round platform is fixed, to which 2 seats for the acrobats are in turn fixed. Each seat consists of a piece of rope, both ends of which are fixed to the top platform, and its loose middle, about 8-10m long (always slightly less than the pole length over the ground), forms an elongated letter 'U'. The bottom part of the 'U', when in the resting position, touches a ramp, about 1m high, which the acrobats climb to get to the rounded bottom of the rope, at the same time holding the upper parts of the rope with their hands. Next the platform is set in rotation, with the centrifugal force thus generated making the acrobats spin round a few meters above the ground. During the rotating movement they perform complicated acrobatic exercises, which are the essence of the display. Mu Fushan et al., 'Shahardi', TRAMCHIN, 4.

SHEAF TOSSING, see >HAY TOSSING.

SHEEP HERDING, an event held during the Scottish Highland Games. Contestants herd a group of four or five sheep around the field with the help of the famous border collie sheep dogs. Tricks include separating an individual sheep from the group and getting the sheep back in the pen.

SHEEP SHEARING, an Austrl. sport that originated from cattle raising activities and wool production. The tradition of sheep shearing dates back to the point of importing sheep into Australia in 1797. During the 19th cent. the sport spread to N.Zealand, where similar forms of sheep shearing came into existence. The number of sheep in both countries: approx. 158 million in Australia and approx. 50 million in N.Zealand, as well as the annual fleece production – respectively, approx. 1,6 billion and 600 million, defines the role both countries perform in the development, as well as the economic and sport status of sheep shearing.

Technique. At first shearing was carried out with the use of straight scissors with long blades called simply blades or sheares. In 1868 J.A.B. Higham introduced a mechanical device called a shearing machine, similar to a barber's shaving machine, though larger and – powered by a steam engine. This technology was not used extensively, because – on the one hand – the technique of manual shearing had been perfected to such a degree that it was actually faster than the machine, while – on the other hand – the new device was expensive, often broke down and had other liabilities which hindered effective competition. The extraordinary manual capabilities of clippers can be illustrated by fact that the daily record in shearing – 321 sheep – set in 1892 by Howe (first name unknown), was broken only with the use of an electric machine at the beginning of the 1950s by a clipper named Riech from S Australia. In 1885 the shearing machine was improved by introducing electric power and demonstrated by Wolsey from Dunlop Station on the river Darling. In 1886 a sheep shearing competition held on a Queensland farm was for the first time won by a team using the new device. Since 1915 the majority of Austrl. farms have been using electric shearing machines, which in Australia are called electric cutters, while in the USA – electric clippers.

Organization. Before the introduction of mechanical devices sheep shearing teams averaged approx. 60 clippers. Technological progress made it possible to reduce that number, because at the beginning of the 20th cent. the same amount of work could be done by only 20 clippers. In the early days sheep shearing was a work competition initiated by the grazier in order to obtain better economic results. Not only the speed but also the quality of shearing was evaluated. At the same time, spontaneously formed teams competed with one another for employment by better paying graziers. The form of sheep shearing closest to sport and practiced as a separate discipline during folk festivals, country shows, etc. was speed shearing, first initiated around 1890. The daily record in the number of sheep was set in 1964 by Colin Bosher of N.Zealand, who managed to shear 565 sheep in 8hrs and 53min. Separate records are registered for merino sheep, which are more difficult to clip because of their thick fleece. The record set in 1965 by an Austrl. Kevin Sarre is 346 sheep in 7hrs and 48min. Merino sheep form 75% of sheep population in Australia and only 5% in N.Zealand. The leading breed among them is half-breed, while only 4% is the most noble breed of the merino – comebacks. Other breeds of sheep include the Eng. breed of romney and the cross-breeds, which are the merino crossbred with other breeds. Competition usu. takes place between two teams of one grazier. Both speed and the quality of shearing are evaluated. Besides ordinary clippers a typical team of shed hands includes the main, fastest shearing clipper called the gun shearer, selected on the basis of previous results and setting the tempo. Another member of the team – the board boy – collects the fleece from the clipper and delivers it to be inspected as to its quality. The team also includes a cook, who does not take part in the competition. The competition begins with letting the first group of sheep into a small catching pen, which makes it easier to catch individual sheep for shearing and to deliver them to each shearing stand. It also allows for a visual comparison of the actual shearing speed of each team. Ideally the entire fleece of one sheep should be taken in one piece. If a sheep is injured by shearing a tar boy is summoned and he treats the wound. As competition continues new sheep are constantly let into the catching pen. The end of shearing is signalled by the clipper with a cry of 'wool away'. Fleece is then taken by the board boy and placed on a special table, where wool-rollers skirt it, i.e. extract from it dirty or bad hair. Refined fleece, known as skirting, is rolled and presented for inspection. Then piece-pickers sort the delivered fleece and the accompanying wool-classer determines its brand and class. Raw fleece [Austrl. greasy fleece; Amer. raw wool] is divided into two basic classes – the superior apparels-class wool and, inferior to it, carpet-class wool. After the early inspection the fleece passes on to a wool presser, who packs it into bails

ready for transport and sale. The sheared sheep are driven to another pen – the counting-out pen – where they are counted and branded.
Sheep shearing is also practiced by the inhabitants of the Pol. Tatra mountains.

SHINEI-TAIDO, Jap. marital arts, deriving from and belonging to the tradition of >AIKIDO, created by N. Inoue (1902-94), the disciple of the creator of aikido, M. Ueshiba. Like proper aikido, it is based on the Shintoist philosophy of *omoto-kyo*.

SHIN-KICKING, Brit. folk sport, standing wrestling; the partners hold each other by their extended hands and try to bring the opponent down by kicking him on the ankles and shins so that he loses his balance or is no longer able to stand the pain. Shin-kicking is best known in the borderland between England and Wales, in the vicinity of Chipping Campden. It probably derives from the old Celtic traditions. In different varieties it was practiced in some regions of western Europe. Presently it is part of the Cotswold Ol.G., sports competitions started in England by R. Dover at the beginning of the 17th cent. Shin-kicking was one of the first Eur. attempts to revive the Ol.G. before P. de Coubertin. The com-

petitions, held annually, have been continued as a folklore event in England till the present.

SHINNEY, see >SHINNY.

SHINNY, also shinney, a game played in different regions of England, similar to Scot. >SHINTY. The name was coined in Derbyshire. In other regions of England the game was also referred to as shin-nop. In Lincolnshire it was called cabsow, which was probably a borrowing from a game known elsewhere as crabsowl. It is not known whether the game was borrowed by the English from the Scots or whether the two (shinny and shinty) developed independently. At the time different games with similar rules developed on the Brit. Isles, e.g. Ir. >IOMÁINT, >CAMÁNACHT, >HURLING and Welsh >KNAPPAN. All of them follow the same principle in which the ball is hit with a curved stick into a goal, which makes them similar to >FIELD HOCKEY. *Blackwood's Magazine* (1821) carried the following description of the game:

The boys attempt to drive with curved sticks a bal, or what is more common, part of the vertebral bone of a sheep, in opposite directions. When the object driven along reaches the appointed place in either termination, they cry of hail! stops the

play till it is knowcked off anew by the boy who was fortunate as to drive it past the gog.

Ethnographers use the names of shinny and hockey to refer to all the games of the peoples outside Europe the object of which is to drive a ball with a stick, particularly a curved one. Some games of N.Amer. Indians are called Ind. Shinny in accounts written by white settlers and ethnographers (>GUGAHAWAT, >TS'IITS'QWEL'O'OL; see also >MECRANOTI INDIAN HOCKEY, >CHACO INDIAN HOCKEY, >INDIAN SPORTS AND GAMES; cf. also >OCEANIAN PEOPLES' HOCKEY).

SHINTY, also shintie, a bat and ball game played in Scotland. The stick (*caman*) is curved at the top; in Fifeshire it is known as a *carrick*. According to some ethnographers the name derives from the Eng. word *shin* 'the shins or under parts of the legs are in danger during the game of being struck, hence the name from *shin*' (*Mactaggart's Gallovidian Encyclopaedia*). In England it was known as >SHINNY. The ball is called a *shintie*. The game derives from the Celtic tradition and comprises a few similar games, among them the old Ir. >IOMÁINT, >CAMÁNACHT, >HURLING and Wel. >KNAPPAN and >CAMOGIE, created

A sheep shearing contest in the Polish Tatra Mountains.

later for women. Probably all of them are related to a game known in France as >SOULE, particularly its var. *a la crosse*. The game resembles >FIELD HOCKEY, although there are some basic differences (e.g. the ball can be carried on the stick, in a special hollow). According to A.B. Gomme, the oldest forms of shinty and field hockey are different: 'in the latter two goals are erected, each being formed by a piece of stick with both ends stuck in the ground. The players divide into two parties; to each of these the care of one of the goals belongs. The game consists in endeavouring to drive the ball through the goal of the opposite party [...]. But in Shinty there are also two goals, called *hails*; the object of each party being to drive the ball beyond their own *hail*, but there is no hole through which it must be driven' (GOM, II, 190-191). In Perthshire the game was played with sticks similar to those used in >GOLF, probably under its influence, then becoming very popular in Scotland. Shinty is a fast game and more brutal than any of the games it is related to, as there are not many strict rules to be observed. In Great Britain competitions are held under the auspices of the Camanachd Association. The largest event is the Camanachd Association Cup. In the 1980s and 1990s, with increasing interest in Scot. traditions,

S

WORLD SPORTS ENCYCLOPEDIA

interest in the game grew. As a result, on the initiative of A. McMillan, the *First Shinty* project was launched in schools to get more children interested in the game.

Rules. Irrespective of the trad. and regional varieties, the contemporary game is played by 2 teams, each consisting of not more than 12 players, one of whom is the goal-keeper (*hail-keeper*). Both teams compete in a manner similar to *camánacht* and partly to >FIELD HOCKEY, but with shorter sticks (*caman*, old regional names *golley*, *nag*). The *caman* or stick is curved at the top and is similar to the Ir. >HURLING stick, but the head (*bas*) is narrower and wedge-shaped; the shaft (*cas*) is cylindrical. The head must be able to pass through a ring 2.5in. (6.3cm) in diameter. The ball is made of cork and worsted and has a leather covering. It weighs between 2.5-3oz. (70-85g). A shinty pitch is 70-100yds. (64-82m) in width and 140-200yds. (128-182m) in length. The half-circle around each set of hail posts marks the area in which the hailkeeper (goalkeeper) may handle the ball. A goal (*hail*) is scored when the whole of the ball crosses the goal-line and under the cross-bar. The goals are 12ft. wide (about 3.7m) and 10ft. high (about 3.05m). Unlike the old varieties, the modern *hail* has a cross-bar. 10yds. in front of the *hail* (about 9.1m) there is the penalty area, which cannot be entered by a player before the ball. The penalty spot is 20yds. in front of the *hail* (about 18.3m). A penalty hit is awarded when a defender has fouled an attacker within the penalty area. The game is played 2x45min. and is supervised by a referee, who is assisted by linesmen and goal judges. When a defender puts the ball over the bye-line, either in the air or on the ground, a corner-hit is taken. Historically, shinty has been played by men only. The *First Shinty* program is co-educational.

History. Historians derive shinty from the old Ir.-Celt. game, which in Ireland gave rise to >HURLING. At the beginning of the 6th cent., the Irish, referred to as Scots, started to migrate to present-day Scotland (which was not called Scotland in those days, as it was inhabited by Picts). As N Britain was gradually conquered by the Scots, their culture and games, including shinty, became very popular. Owing to the common Gaelic heritage, in the oldest sources the game is referred to first as *camánacht* and the name shinty appeared later. Up till the end of the 19th cent. and even at the beginning of the 20th cent. both names, in different written variants, appeared together. In the Middle Ages and during periods of conflict between Catholics and Protestants the game was banned by the clergy as it was most often played on Saturdays and Sundays, i.e. against the commandment 'thou shalt honor the Holy Day'. Yet, it did not disappear. T. Pennant, an antique dealer, traveling in Scotland in the 18th cent., wrote that 'the shinty, or the striking of a ball of wood or hair [is played here]. This game is played between two parties, furnished with clubs, in a large plain. Whichever side strikes it first to the goal wins the match' (*Tour of Scotland*, 1769). In *Clans of the Scottish Highlands* a Maclan described shinty in the following way: 'Two opposing parties endeavour by means of the camac or club to drive the ball to a certain spot on either side, and the distance is sometimes so great that a whole day's exertion is needed to play out the game [...]. When there is a numerous meeting, the field has much the appearance of a battle scene. There are banners, bagpipes playing, and a keen mêlée around the ball']. In January 1821 the 'Edinburgh Evening Courier' described 'the most spirited camack matches in Badenoch'. The game was also played between representatives of Scot. clans, which was testified by a report on the match played in Calgary Sands between the Campbell and MacLean clans, published in 'Highland Home Journal': 'The contest grew fast and furious. Hail after hail was scored by the Macleans until the Campbells were compelled to give in and leave the field, vanquished and crestfallen'. In 1841 a match of shinty was organized in London by the Scots who lived there. In the middle of the 19th cent. the popularity of the game started to wane. It continued to be played in the most remote regions of Scotland, particularly in the vicinity of Badenoch, Lochaber and Strathglass. In 1880 Captain Chisholm (first name unknown) of Glassburn decided to revive the game. He managed to organize a few matches played according to the rules he himself had defined. In 1887 a match was played in Inverness between two teams of 15 players each, representing the towns of Strath-

glass and Glen Urquhart. The match was won 2:0 by the team from Glen Urquhart. A year later a return match was played, also won by Glen Urquhart. Irregularities observed during the match resulted in the first revision of Chisholm's rules. At the same time other rules were formulated in Glasgow by the officials of the Celtic Club. This made playing matches between teams from different regions, in which other rules prevailed, more difficult. In 1893 representatives of the different systems of rules met in Kingussie and established the Camanachd Association. In 1895 the Challenge Trophy was awarded for the Scot. championships in shinty. The first winners were the team from Kingussie, who beat Glasgow Cowal (1896). In 1918 another trophy was awarded, the Southerland Cup, for juniors. Despite the development of more popular sports, shinty retained its position as the national sport of Scotland. Occasionally, matches were played against an Ir. hurling team, according to provisional rules defined for the purpose.

J.N. MacDonald, *Shinty. A Short History of the Ancient Highland Game*, 1932; A. McMillan, 'First Shinty – On the High Road', *GAA Coaching News*, 1994, 3, 2.

SHIP, also *ships and sailors coming on*. A game of strength and skill played by boys, individually or in teams. In the individual var. one of the boys faces the wall and bends over. Another jumps onto his back, shouting 'Ships!' or 'Ships are coming on!'. If the jump is made without this shout, the players swap roles. If the first player manages to shrug off the jumper at the moment of the jump, again, they swap. If the jumper manages to stay on the back, a sort of endurance test is performed: a player can stay on his opponent's back as long as he wants to, provided that he keeps silent; he is not allowed to utter a single word or laugh. The first one to fail – fail to keep a player on the back or fail to keep silent, loses the game.

In the team var. the test is similar; a few boys stand in front of the wall and the same number of boys jump on their backs, following the same rules as in the individual variety. Before the game the toss of a coin decides which team first faces the wall. Cf.

>BUNG THE BUCKET, >SADDLE THE NAG.
A.B. Gomme, 'Ship', TGESI, 1898, II, 191.

SHIRDEG TATAKH, Mong. felt pulling; 2 players compete in pulling a felt rag, 50-60cm long. The object of the game is to pull the opponent over to one's side. If the competitors are of equal strength, the winner is the one who has stretched the felt more. Felt had special value in the Mong. culture. A bride would sit on a felt mat, in front of the groom's yurt (a Mong. tent). During felt production certain phenomena were considered important and treated as omens, e.g. if after the felt was rolled upright hairs could be seen, the sheep flock would be plentiful. When the hairs were upright when the felt was unrolled, a new baby would be born. I. Kabzińska-Stawarz quotes

Wim de Deyne (#307) of Belgium competes in the men's 500-m short track during the Salt Lake City Winter Olympic G...

an ending to a folk tale about felt: 'Tsevondordj lived in the Uvs aimag. One day he found a small piece of felt, which he took to his yurt. From then on he was very prosperous. He became rich'.

SHOOTING, a Brit. var. of wrestling called >CATCH-AS-CATCH-CAN; victory is declared when the enemy has surrendered because of exhaustion or injury; a type of fighting continued today illegally in secret gambling clubs – hence any precise information on shooting is practically unavailable; a more civilized var. has been recently popularized on Sky TV. W. Baxter, 'Shooting', 'Les lutes traditionnelles a traverse le monde', LJP, 1998, 82.

SHOOTING, an art of shooting different types of weapons. The oldest type of shooting, going back with its beginnings to prehistoric times, is >ARCHERY. In the Middle Ages archery was perfected by making the bow and the string stronger and using a cranking mechanism, which resulted in the invention of >CROSSBOW SHOOTING. Once gunpowder was invented, initially used in cannons, firearms developed, which became the basic of different var. of >COMPETITIVE SHOOTING. In Europe all the forms of shooting, from the bow to firearms, were practiced by shooting brotherhoods, organized in towns (>COCK SHOOTING). In the 19th cent. air shooting joined the trad. types of shooting, and at the end of the 1980s shooting using guns that fire gelatin capsules filled with water-soluble marking dye, became popular (>PAINTBALL); see also >SHOOTING FOR THE DISABLED.

SHOOTING BETEL NUTS INTO A BASKET CAR-RIED ON A GIRL'S BACK, a courtship game played by young girls and boys of the Guoshan people in China. Participants are divided into 2 teams, each including a girl who carries a decorative bamboo basket on her back. The girls begin the game by running away. They are chased by the boys from the opposite team, who try to throw into her basket red betel nuts of the pinang tree (also called areta nuts, *arecca catechu*), which in the regional tradition symbolize happiness and love. In another var. of the game the nuts are substituted with small bags.

Each nut or bag placed inside the basket scores a point, providing the throwing distance is kept at a min. of 3m. The team that scores the most points, wins the game. The game is presently a care-free pastime, though its tradition derives from the times when young courtiers hid behind trees on pinang plantations, trying to place as many betel nuts in the basket of their beloved as possible. If the girl reciprocated the boy's feelings, she would slow down and turn her back (with the basket) at him, making the task easier. If she did not like the boy, she could turn in such a way as to make it difficult for him or even remove 'his' betel nuts from the basket, a sign that the boy should choose another girl. Mu Fushan et al., 'Shooting Betel Nut into a Basket Carried on a Girl's Back', TRAMCHIN, 78.

SHOOTING FOR THE DISABLED, a var. of >COM-PETITIVE SHOOTING, adapted to the needs of the disabled, including the wheelchair bound. The final results take into account the differences in disability and, using conversion tables, allow for the joint classification of competitors with different degrees of disability. The development of shooting for the disabled is coordinated by the Shooting Committee for the Disabled). See also >DISABLED SPORTS.

SHORT MAT GAME, a mini version of the indoor var. of >LAWN BOWLING played on a shorter track covered with artificial grass.

SHORT-TENNIS, one of many var. of tennis, played with a racket with a much shorter arm [for etymology of 'tennis' see >TENNIS]. Depending on the age and the players' skills the game is played on different size courts of >MINITENNIS, >PLATFORM TENNIS and >FIELD TENNIS, with a standard tennis ball.

SHORT TRACK SPEED SKATING, also pack start skating, held on trad. ice hockey or figure skating rinks. The track's circumference, marked with special signs, is 111.12m, the longest straight section is only 28.85m. Contestants move in groups of 4 (formerly 6). In eliminations usu. the first 2 contestants qualify for the next round. All the contestants start simultaneously. A contestant who has been lapped must leave the track. Finals 'A' and 'B' are held to decide the contestants who qualify for the 8-man finals. In relay races changes are made by touching the partner's body with the hand. Changes can be made at any time; there is no division of the distance into equal segments. However, no changes can be made during the last 2 laps. Short track speed skating is much more dynamic than trad. speed skating. The clothes and equipment are similar to those used in speed skating, with the addition of a helmet protecting against head injuries.
History. Short track speed skating was introduced into the 1988 Ol.G. in Calgary as a display sport. During the 1992 Ol.G. in Albertville only 4 events were held: 1,000m for men, 5,000-m relay for men, 500m for women and 3,000-m relay for men. In Lillehamer two additional events were held – 1,000m for women and 500m for men. In Salt Lake City seven events were held: women: 500m, 1,500m and 3,000-m relay, and men: 500m, 1,000m, 1,500m and 5,000-m relay.
From the very beginning the events were dominated by contestants from South Korea, the USA, Russia, China, Holland, Japan, Canada, Great Britain and Italy. The best contestants include the Korean K. Ki-hoon, who won the 1,000m at the Ol.G. in 1992 and 1994 and the Canadian C. Turner, who won 500m and 1,000m. In the 1970s C. Turner was a top skater on the trad. track. After a break she made a spectacular comeback.

SHOT PUT, an athletic field event where the object is to use one hand to throw ('put') a heavy metal ball ('shot') as far as possible. The 'put' is performed from a throwing circle (213.5cm in diameter) towards a landing sector marked with lines at an angle of '60s. Stepping outside the throwing circle or landing the shot outside the landing sector means a bad put. The shot has a weight of 7.25kg for men and 4kg for women. Shots weighing between 3.0 and 6.25kg are also used in various junior age groups.
History. The shot put undeniably descends from heavy stone throwing, which was practiced in all primitive civilizations. Varieties closer to the modern form of the shot put were known in medieval Europe. The modern sporting var. developed in the UK where stones were replaced by cannonballs with the advent of artillery. In the 18th-cent., the Brit. army mainly used 16-lb. cannonballs, and that weight was later used as a standard for sports shots. The throwing area was initially square (this persisted in England until 1914) but a circle was introduced in the USA in 1876. The first unofficial record holder was the American J.M. Mann (9.44m – 1876), while the Canadian G. Gray (14.32m – 1893) was the first in the official tables. The American W. Coe was the first to pass the 15m mark (15.09m – 1905), while the German E.I. Hirschfeld was the first to put the shot over 16m (16.00m and 16.04m – 1928). J. Torrance (USA) was the first to break the 17m barrier (17.40m – 1934), and the distance of 18m was exceeded by P. O'Brien (USA; 18.00 and 18.04 – 1953). O'Brien was also the first contestant to pass the 19m mark (19.06m – 1956). W. (Bill) Nieder (USA) reached 20m (20.06m – 1960). The 21m barrier was broken by R. Matson (USA; 21.05m – 1965), that of 22m – by A. Baryshnikov (USSR; 22.00m – 1976), and then U. Beyer (GDR; 22.15m – 1978), and finally U. Timmermann of the GDR passed the 23m mark in 1988 (23.06m).
A both-hands contest was held only once, during the 1912 OG in Stockholm. The contestants put the shot using both hands alternately, and the best results for each hand were then added. The American R. Rose was the winner with an aggregate of 27.70m (15.23m+12.47m).
Women's shot put. The event was regarded as unsuitable for women for a long time, as it was said to 'deform the body' and be generally 'un-womanly'. Women's world records have been documented since 1920, and the first record holder was the Czech M. Meizliková (8.32m). The Frenchwoman V. Gourard was the first to pass the 9m mark (9.42m – 1922). The 10m barrier was broken by E. Haux (Germany; 10.27m – 1925), 11m – by F. Grase (Germany; 11.04 – 1926), 12m – by G. Herrmann (Germany; 12.26m – 1928), 13m – by G. Heublein (Germany; 13.70m – 1931), 14m – by G. Mayermayer (14.38 – 1934), 15m – by A. Andreyeva (USSR; 15.02m – 1950), 16m – by G. Zybina (USSR; 16.00m – 1952, 16.10m – 1953), 17m – by R. Garisch (GDR; 17.18m – 1961), 18m – by N. Chizhova (USSR; 18.67m – 1968), 19m – by M. Gummel (GDR; 19.07m – 1968), 20m – by N. Chizhova (USSR; 20.09m – 1969), 21m – by N. Chizhova (USSR; 21.03m – 1972), 22m – by H. Fibengerová (Czechoslovakia; 22.32m – 1977).
Women's shot put was only included in the Olympic program in 1948 but the event had been organized during the 1922 Women's World Games and 1938 E.Ch.
The most outstanding personalities of women's shot put include: G. Zybina (USSR), the 1952 Olympic champion and 14-time world record holder; T. Press (USSR), 2-time Olympic champion (1960 and 1964); N. Chizhova (USSR), 9-time world record holder, Olympic champion of 1972 and silver medallist of 1976; M. Gummel-Helmboldt (GDR), the 1968 Olympic champion and silver medallist of 1972; M. Adam (GDR) with 3 world records in 1975-76; I. Slupianek (GDR) with 2 world records in 1980; and N. Lisovskaya (USSR) with 3 world records between 1984 and 1987. However, those latter results were probably due to the use of prohibited substances. After the fall of the USSR and GDR, and the introduction of stricter anti-doping measures by the IOC, the results achieved by top putters fell by about 2m. In Atlanta in 1996, the winner was the German A. Kumbernuss with 20.56m; none of the other contestants passed the 20m mark.
The Book of Rules, Athletics. Shot put, 1998. Polish Athletic Federation, Przepisy zawodów w lekkoatletyce. Pchnięcie kulą, 1996.

WORLD SPORTS ENCYCLOPEDIA

S

SHOT PUT OLYMPIC CHAMPIONS
MEN
1896 Robert Garrett, USA 11.22
1900 Richard Sheldon, USA 14.10
1904 Ralph Rose, USA 14.81
1906 Martin Sheridan, USA 12.325
1908 Ralph Rose, USA 14.21
1912 Patrick McDonald, USA 15.34
1920 Ville Pörhölä, FIN 14.81
1924 Clarence 'Bud' Houser, USA 14.995
1928 John Kuck, USA 15.87
1932 Leo Sexton, USA 16.005
1936 Hans Woellke, GER 16.20
1948 Wilbur Thompson, USA 17.12
1952 Parry O'Brien, USA 17.41
1956 Parry O'Brien, USA 18.57
1960 Bill Nieder, USA 19.68
1964 Dallas Long, USA 20.33
1968 Randy Matson, USA 20.54
1972 Wladyslaw Komar, POL 21.18
1976 Udo Beyer, GDR 21.05
1980 Vladimir Kiselyov, URS 21.35
1984 Alessandro Andrei, ITA 21.26
1988 Ulf Timmermann, GDR 22.47
1992 Mike Stulce, USA 21.70
1996 Randy Barnes, USA 21.62
2000 Arsi Harju, FIN 21.29
WOMEN
1948 Micheline Ostermeyer, FRA 13.75
1952 Galina Zybina, URS 15.28
1956 Tamara Tyshkevich, URS 16.59
1960 Tamara Press, URS 17.32
1964 Tamara Press, URS 18.14
1968 Margitta Gummel, GDR 19.61
1972 Nadyezhda Chizhova, URS 21.03
1976 Ivanka Khristova, BUL 21.16
1980 Ilona Slupianek, GDR 22.41
1984 Claudia Losch, FRG 20.48
1988 Natalya Lisovskaya, URS 22.24
1992 Svetlana Krivelyova, EUN 21.06
1996 Astrid Kumbernuss, GER 20.56
2000 Yanina Korolchik, BLR 20.56

Shot put on a stamp issued for the 1928 Olympic Games in Amsterdam.

488
S WORLD SPORTS ENCYCLOPEDIA

SHOULDER POLE STRIKING, a game that forms a demonstration of one's physical agility, known and practiced by the people of Zhuang in the region of Duan and Mashan in the Chin. province of Guangxi. A group of players, whose number varies from 2 to as many as 100, stand in front of small benches, holding wooden poles, usu. hammer or ax handles. The object of the game is to perform, as fast as possible, a series of complex juggling tricks that imitate various field and manual work or even a var. of fencing with a partner. In the course of the demonstration the participants form a kind of team in which all the parties try to copy any new elements introduced by the most inventive participants. Throughout the display the tempo of movement increases and the least skilful drop out one after another, and only those who are able to imitate new movements and to keep up with the growing speed are able to finish the game.

Mu Fushan, 'Shoulder-Pole Striking', TRAMCHIN, 92.

SHROVE TUESDAY FOOTBALL, a ritual game related to the *Dies Mercuri*, a festival adopted by the Christians of pagan Rome and continued in France as Mardi Gras, which then gave birth to a Fr. game *la balle de mardi grass*. In some other parts of Europe, Shrove Tuesday celebrations were accompanied by folk sports events other than football (cf. >WÄDELÖB). A number of old forms of the game have survived in the Brit. Isles, esp. in England and Scotland, where it was known also under other names, such as 'fat Tuesday football', 'shrovetide football', 'Goodish-Tuesday football', 'gooddit footbale' (in early documents), 'goteddes-day foutbale' (in Henry VII's edict prohibiting the game), 'fastenseen game' (Scot.), or 'balliomair' (Scot. Gaelic). Brit. Shrove Tuesday football is a combination of customs brought by Ang.-Sax. tribes with the pre-existing Celtic rites. The game is played on Shrove Tuesday in a number of Eur. countries, esp. in Germany, the Netherlands, Italy, Spain, England, and Scotland where this tradition seems to be strongest. In many places, Shrove Tuesday matches are followed by >ASH WEDNESDAY FOOTBALL. References to the tradition of Shrove Tuesday football appear in a number of early sources, including pictures, such as famous Pieter Brueghel the Elder's *Strijd Tussen Vasten En Vastenavond* (*Fight Between Carnival and Lent*, 1559). As far as Britain is concerned, it is believed the game originates from the times of either Roman or Scand. occupation. According to a legend, Shrove Tuesday football stems from the tradition of decapitating a defeated enemy's chieftain and then kicking the head around (see >FOOTBALL WITH A SEVERED HEAD).

The earliest historical record concerning Shrove Tuesday football dates back to 1533 and comes from Chester where there is an old and well-established tradition of >RODE HEE FOOTBALL (the first part of the name originates from the term for fields on which the game was played, also known as Roodeye, Rodehee, Rood Hee, Roodee, etc.), but there are no indications of its relationship with the Roman or Norse occupation of Britain. We can read in these old records that, in the presence of the local mayor, Henry Gee, on Shrove Tuesday, 'offering of Ball and footballs were put down, and the silver bell offered.' The signal for starting the game was the so-called pancake bell, usu. the bell of a local church, whose toll called everybody to stop working and to start preparing pancakes, and finally to begin the match. The festival was so overwhelmed by the game that in some Brit. towns, e.g. Nuneaton or Kirby Grindalythe, Shrove Tuesday came to be called Ball Day. From time to time, the game was prohibited by either royal or church edicts, as was the case in 1540 during Henry VIII's reign. Despite all that, the tradition was continued in a number of Brit. towns and villages, which seems to be confirmed by a lengthy list made by F.P. Magoun in 1938 (the date quoted is the year of the earliest historical record):

Alnwick – 1788; Asbourne – 1683; Atherstone – 1923; Beverley – 1825; Botriphnie, Banffshire – 1880; Bristol – 1660; Bromfield – 1770; Bushey Park – 1815; Chester – 1533; Chester-le-Street – 1887; Corfe Castle – 1551; Derby – 1746; Dorking – 1857; Duns – 1724; Epsom – 1862; Glasgow – 1573; Hampton Wick – 1815; Ilderton – 1889; Inveresk – 1795; Jedburgh – 1704; Kingston-upon-Thames – 1790; Kirby Grindalythe – c.1900; Kirkmichael – 1795; London – 1642; Melrose, Roxburgshire – 1866; Nuneaton -1881; Oxford – 1622; Rothbury – 1867; Scarborough – 1870; Seascales – c.1770; Sedgefield – 1827; Shrewsbury – 1601; Skipton – about 1800; Stonyhurst – 1904; Teddington – 1815; Twickenham – 1815; Whitby – 1876; Wooler – 1889; Workington – 1889; Yetholm – 1932.

The list does not, however, include the names of places where the custom had disappeared before it was noticed by folklore researchers. In some places, festival football matches were held not only on Shrove Tuesday, such as in Stonyhurst where football was played also on the last Sat., Sun., and Mon. of the carnival (>STONYHURST FOOTBALL). In Mediterranean countries and in Devon, there was also a custom of playing >GOOD FRIDAY FOOTBALL and in a number of Eur. countries trad. >EASTER BALL or >EASTER TUESDAY GAME matches were known. In some Brit. towns, typical Shrove Tuesday football matches were sometimes played on other days in order to prolong a local festival or make an event more interesting or raise its importance. For example, in Botriphnie (formerly Fumack Kirk), the game was moved to a day on which the annual fair is held, consequently changing its trad. name. Many localities where Shrove Tuesday matches were recorded in the 20th cent., actually continue an old tradition which, needless to say, had been there for years but had never been recorded.

In 1551, shortly after Henry VIII's prohibition was imposed, old privileges of the royal stone guild on Purbeck Island were confirmed in Corfe castle. Shrove Tuesday football formed a regular event during the celebration of the guild's festival, held on Shrove Tuesday. We learn that, 'the last married man [is] to bring a foot-ball according to the Custome of our Company.' As a reward, he was exempt from a payment for leaving his unmarried status which was normally imposed by the guild. If none of the guild members had married during a given year, players used the ball that had been brought the year before. The custom continued for centuries and in 1887 it was recorded by historians in a form which was nearly identical to the one employed in 1551. The municipal records of Glasgow indicate that in 1578-79 Shrove Tuesday balls were made by a John Andro. In 1589-90, while trying to buy his way to municipal privileges, Johnne Neill agreed to provide every year, 'during his lyftime, sufficient fut ballis.' The municipal records of Shrewsbury, covering the period 1601-3, contain a petition from John Gyttyns, in which he pleads that he should be released from prison in which he found himself for having struck sergeant Harding with a ball during a Shrove Tuesday match. From a political satire written by P. Hausted in 1642 against puritan Separatists who wanted to ban all types of entertainment, theater and sports activities, it appears that London apprentices played Shrove Tuesday football on the Finnisbury Fields. In the 17th cent., Shrove Tuesday football was so popular that local notables had an official proclamation announced every single year, according to which the game was prohibited. In 1660, the crowd, outraged at such a proclamation, ended up rioting in the streets for reinstating the game. In 1638, a Shrove Tuesday match was played between 2 towns: Ashbourne vs. Compton (today forming the single city of Ashbourne). The event became a theme in a poetic burlesque by C. Cotton:

Two towns, that long that war had waged,
Being at football now engaged,
For honour, as both sides pretended,
Left the brave trial to be ended
Till the next thaw, for they were frozen
On either part at least a dozen.

138 years later, an annual meeting of the 2 towns became a motif of a song performed on 21 Feb., 1821, by an actor named Fawcett in the Ashbourne Theater:

Shrove Tuesday, you know, is always the day
When pancake's the prelude and Football's the play;
Where upwards and downwards men ready for fun,
Like the French at the Battle of Waterloo run.
If they get to the Park, the upwards men shout
And think all the downwards men put to the rout;
But a right about face they soon have to learn,
And the upwards men shout and huzza in their turn.
Then into Shaw Croft, where the bold and the brave,
Get a ducking in trying the foot-Ball to save;
For 'tis well known they fear not a watery grave,
In defence of the Foot-Ball at Ashbourne.

In 1858, curate J. Errington attempted to move the game from the downtown streets to the meadows surrounding the city, but the tradition was too deeply rooted and his attempts failed. In 1860, pursuant to paragraph 72 of the Highways Act, a number of players were sentenced for causing public unrest. In 1862, the game was back on the streets of Ashbourne, and this time detained players signed a contract with the municipal authorities according to which they agreed to play in the suburbs in the future. Since then, Shrove Tuesday football began to acquire a certain prestige and in 1928 a new custom was initiated according to which the game is started by the toss of a coin executed by the Duke of Winsdor or the Prince of Wales.

The city of Derby claims to be the birthplace of Eng. Shrove Tuesday football but the earliest document indicating the presence of the game in the city dates back to 1746. It is an announcement made by the mayor, H. Booth, published by the *Derby Mercury*:

It having been represented to the magistrates of this Borough that on Shrove Tuesday which will be Tuesday the third day of March next there will be a public football playing in the said Borough and that such has been lately Notyfied and proclaimed in Towns and Counties adjacent to the Borough aforesaid by some person or persons disposed to be at the head of Tumults and Disorders. These (advertisements) are to give notice that Mr Mayor and others of His Majesty's Justices of the Peace for the said Borough do direct and order that there be no Riotous and Tumultuous meeting of any Persons (and more particularly of Foreigners at this unhappy time of Contagion among horned cattle)... do appear at the time and for the Purpose aforesaid in the said Borough on Pain of being Rigorously Prosecuted for the same as well as for the consequences of breaking of Windows and doing other mischiefs to the Persons and Properties of the Inhabitants of this Borough.

In 1762, a silver watch in a china casing was lost during the Shrove Tuesday match, which did nothing to make the game more popular among the city dwellers. W. Hutton observed in 1790 that:

There is also one amusement of the amphibious kind, which, if not peculiar to Derby, is pursued with an avidity I have not observed elsewhere, football, I have seen this coarse sport carried to the barbarous height of an election-contest; nay, I have known a foot-ball hero chaired through the streets like a successful Member (of the Parliament), although his utmost elevation of character was no more than that of a butcher's apprentice. Black eyes, bruised arms, and broken shins, are equally the marks of victory and defeat. I need not say that this is the delight of the lower ranks, and is attained at an early period: the very infant learns to kick, and then to walk. The professors of this athletic art think themselves bound to follow the ball wherever it flies; and as Derby is fenced in with rivers, it seldom flies far without flying into the water; and I have seen these amphibious practitioners of foot-ball-kicking jump into the river upon a Shrove-Tuesday when the ground was covered with snow. Whether the benefits arising from exercise pay for the bloody nose is doubtful; whether this rough pastime improves the mind, I leave to the decision of its votaries; and whether the wounds in youth produce the pains in age, I leave to threescore.

The game 'of the amphibious kind' was sometimes dangerous, because although we can read about fearless jumps into water, occasionally jumpers drowned as *Derby Mercury* reported in 1796:

Yesterday was observed here by playing at football according to the annual custom and John Snape of Darby attempting to cross the Der went with the ball near the boat house in the Holmes was unfortunately drowned in the presence of a great number of people who could not render any assistance. His body was found this afternoon.

The accident was, of course, used as an argument against the football game and a special committee appointed to investigate the causes of Snape's death presented a petition addressed to the mayor, R. Leaper, and 2 justices of the peace, W. Edwards and T. Mather, whichreads:

John Snape lost his life, an unfortunate victim to the custom of Playing at Football at Shrove Tide; a custom which has no better recommendation than its antiquity for its further continuance, is disgraceful to humanity and civilization, subversive of good order and Government and destructive to the Morals, Properties, and very Lives of our Inhabitants. Impelled by a sense of our duty as members of Society we have presumed humbly to represent these our sentiments to you and to solicit, thus ardently, that you will be pleased to exert those powers with which the law has invested you, as Guardians of the Public Peace, for the future Prevention of those evils of which we complain and of which we have now so shocking an example before us.

The response was immediate:

Having taken the subject of this address into our most serious consideration and being full satisfied that many public and private evils have been occasioned by the custom of playing at football in this Borough on Shrove Tuesday, We have unanimously resolved that such customs shall from henceforth be discontinued.

Apparently, this prohibition was not terribly compelling, as already in 1829 Stephen Glover observed that Shrove Tuesday football was flourishing not only in Derby but also in many other towns.

Football continues to be played at in many parts of England on Shrove Tuesday and Ash Wednesday, but the mode of playing this game at Asbourne and Derby, differs very much from the usual practice of this sport. In the town of Derby the contest lies between the parishes of St. Peter and All Saints, and the goals to which the ball is to be taken are, Nun's mill for the latter, and the Callow's balk on the Normanton road for the former. None of the other parishes of the borough take any direct part in the contest, but the inhabitants of all join in the sport, together with persons from all parts of the adjacent country.

In 1847, attempts were made to discontinue the tradition of Shrove Tuesday football on the basis of a parliamentary Act on public unrests. In Derby, the enforcement of the act required 2 regiments of regular army. In 1866, the game was prohibited in Kingston as a result of dramatic events and numerous injuries that had taken place there the previous year.
C.S. Burne, ed., 'Shropshire Folk-Lore' in *Collections of Georgina F. Jackson*, London, 1883; F.P. Magoun, 'Shrove Tuesday in England and Scotland' a chapter in *History of Football from the Beginnings to 1871*, 1938, 99-138.

SHROVE TUESDAY LUGE, a trad. competition held in Estonia. On Shrove Tuesday in Estonia, unlike in many other Eur. countries, dances are forbidden. They were replaced with different games and plays, among which shrove Tuesday luge was very popular. Its one aim was to forecast the crop yield in the coming summer. Different sleds were used for the rides. It was believed that the rider who rode the longest distance would have the best harvest of flax. If there was a frozen pond or lake nearby, a carousel with sleds was built. A hole was made in the ice in which a pillar with a wheel on its top was put. A large pole was put on the wheel and the sled was tied to the pole's ends. When the turnstile was moved, the carousel effect was obtained.
M. Vär et al., 'Traditional Sports and Games in Estonia', TSNJ, 1996, 32.

SHUAI JIAO, a Chin. system of fast wrestling, which requires skill, dexterity, precision, and quick action enabling the execution a range of throws and trips. The tradition of shuai jiao also allowed for punches and kicks, which – however – are excluded in the modern wrestling variety. The bout is held on a square mat and resembles the Eur. style of wrestling. Shuai jiao techniques form part of all Chin. styles of >GONGFU.

SHUFFLEBOARD, see DECK GAMES.

SHUI HORSE RACING, a form of >HORSE RACING practiced among the Chin. Shui minority during the Duakije holiday. The number of riders usu. reaches several hundred and the route, going over several hills, is planned in such a way that the spectators located between the hills can follow the entire race (cf. Pol. >ROCHWIST). The origin of the races is explained by a local legend, according to which the chief of a local village was so lazy that he refused to leave his house and became sluggish. When he intended to take part in a local equestrian event, he needed help to mount his horse, which earned him laughs from the villagers. In an attempt to prove his fitness he decided to ride his horse to the top of a hill and – with great difficulty and completely exhausted – he succeeded. On the subsequent Duakije holiday he climbed 2 hills, then 3, etc. To commemorate his determination the competitors ride along all the hilltops which he once covered.
Mu Fushan et al., 'Shui Horse Race', TRAMCHIN.

SHUR-SHIDEH, also *sur sirdeg*, a folk var. of a ball game played by Mongols and Tuvans. The ball was made of compacted wool.

SHUTTLE RELAY, a skating race in which members of competing teams shuttle back and forth along a single stretch of track. 2 start lines are marked on the ice rink about 50 steps apart. The teams split in

two, one group at each end of the track. Each team receives a puck which must be pushed along the course with a hockey stick by each team member in turn. Every team member may have a stick or it can be played with only one stick per team, which makes passing the puck at each changeover more difficult and time consuming.
I.N. Tchkannikov, 'Sztafeta wahadłowa', GIZ, 1953, 89.

SHUTTLEBALL, a game similar to >BADMINTON but played with a shuttle in which instead of a small, flexible end, there is a relatively large ball, usu. two-colored, with one half white and the other dark, most often red. The rackets made of a plastic mass look like table-tennis bats, but are much thicker and densely perforated to reduce their weight. The game originated in the 1980s in the United States. It has been gaining popularity in some countries of Latin America, particularly in Mexico, where it is known as *volante gigante*.

SHUTTLECOCK GAMES, games using shuttlecocks and rackets, known in many cultures around the world, such as Chin. >TEBEG, Mong. >TEBEG OSHIGLOOKH, Kor. >CHEGI CHAGI, S.Amer. >INDIACA, Stóólo (N.Amer. Ind.) >TS'ÉQWELA, and Eur. >VOLANT and >BADMINTON.

SHUTTLECOCK KICKING, the Eng. name of an international game, called in Pol. >ZOŚKA, in the Kor. tradition >CHEGI CHAGI, Chin. >TEBEG, Mong. >TEBEG ÖSHIGLÖÖKH.

SIBERIAN BOAT RACING, a sporting event deriving from hunting traditions and religious rituals. Among the Siberian tribes of Nanaytse, Gleenyaks, and Ulche the white bear religious holiday provided an opportunity for holding boat races. At the end of the 19th cent. on Sachalin, a place of exile for many opponents of the Rus. tsars, rowing boat races took place at the end of the seal hunting season. The stretch of water was a mediator between humans and the world of the gods, who determined the wealth or indigence of animals as the basic means of subsistence of the local tribes. Therefore, such races often symbolized man's efforts to draw on the goods provided by the deities, but only to the extent to which man has been able to gain their favours. In the Soviet Union these holidays were abolished and replaced with a state-promoted Fisherman's Holiday. In the 1960s trad. rowing boat races began to be gradually replaced with motorboat races.

SIBERIAN SLEDGE RACING, a form of winter competition practiced in northern Siberia among the Nanaya, Nivche and Ulche tribes. It is usu. of a religious nature, connected with funeral ceremonies and the symbolic concept of a sledge as a carrier to the underworld. A similar symbolic nature is attributed to the dogs, which are believed to guide humans to the world of the departed (cf. the symbolism of boats in Asian cultures, e.g. in >SIBERIAN BOAT RACING and >DRAGON BOAT RACING with Eur. cultures, e.g. the myth of Charon who conveyed the shades of the departed across the river Styx to Hades). Among the Oroche tribe on the island of Sakhalin races of dog-driven sledges were held on the Holiday of the White Bear accompanied by rowing boat races. Very similar dog-driven sledge races were held by the Oroche as part of the funeral ceremonies for a departed twin. This was a result of the Oroche belief that twins and white bears have similar characters. Races of sledges pulled by reindeer are held on stretches of straight land or around a looping track with the start and finish in the same spot. Teams of up to 5 reindeer are controlled with a pair of reins, while the sledges have adequately long shafts. Ethnographers studying these regions claim that the art of driving teams of reindeer is mastered by children as young as 10.

SIDDENDE HANEKAMP, Dan. for 'a fight of sitting roosters', [Dan. *sidde* – to sit + *hane* – rooster + *kamp* – fight]. Two contestants squat down facing each other, put a stick into their knee bends, wrap their arms around under the stick and clasp hands in front of the knees. In this position they jump towards each other, trying to knock each other over.
J. Möller, 'Siddende hanekamp', GID, 1997, 4.

SIDEHOLD WRESTLING, one of many varieties of wrestling, popular in the 19th cent. and at the beginning of the 20th cent. in Europe and the USA; players wrestle in the standing position trying to hold the opponent by a special type of harness worn by

the contestants, which had to be held on the sides, at the hips (hence the name); the contestant who made his opponent touch the ground with 3 parts of the body above the legs won.
W. Baxter, 'Sidehold Wrestling, in: Les lutes traditioinnelles a traverse le monde', LJP, 1998, 82.

SIDESADDLE RIDING, also Fr. *d'amazone or de dame*, Ger. *Damensattel*, a form of horse riding using saddles which can be mounted sidewise and not traditionally astride, mainly for women, presently also practiced by men. This is possible to a specially designed sidesaddle, which prevents sliding off the horse owing to a special bail at the height of the right thigh.
History. This is one of the older horse riding techniques known to man. The art of side horse riding was known to the Afr. tribes of the Berber people in S.Africa; it was adopted by the Arabs about the 7th cent. A Byzantine monk and metropolitan of Ephe-

Jean Baptiste Chardin, A Girl With A Shuttlecock, oil on canvas, 1741.

sus, Niketas (1118-1205) criticized Persian women for 'immodest astride riding, instead of, as becomes women, on a sidesaddle'. The crusaders fighting with the Arabs for the Holy Land, although they did not practice side riding, adopted the technique and introduced it to their ladies. Initially side saddles for women sitting behind the men on the same horse were used. Soon, however, women, particularly from the aristocracy, started to use side saddles on their own. The first side saddles were relatively simple and equipped with footrests in the form of a rigid step, called in Fr. a *planchette*, which was fixed below the seat. Queen Catherine de Médicis (1519-89) was a great reformer of the saddle for women. As a young daughter-in-law of Francis I, the king of France (1515-47), she accompanied her father-in-law during his hunting expeditions. She eliminated the planchette and ordered the mounting of a type of bar which prevented her from sliding off the saddle. Court rumor had it that she did this not to increase riding safety but to show both her legs, as they were very slender. In England the side saddle was introduced about 1550 by a young princess, from 1558 Queen Elizabeth I. About 1800 the design of the side saddle was improved – a special belt was added to help maintain balance during riding. Other improvements included additional lining of the seat and in the balls restricting the rider from moving sideways. The balls were moved closer to each other so that there was not much space between the rider's hips and horse mount-

Nicolas Arnoult, Featherball (Le Jeu de Volant), 1698, copperplate.

S

WORLD SPORTS ENCYCLOPEDIA

ing was more stable. In order to protect expensive clothes against tearing or dust, specially mounted saddle cloths or imitations of outer skirts were used, buckled during riding. In 1830 the Frenchman C. Pellier designed a leaping strap, which revolutionized sidesaddle riding, as it helped to maintain balance at high speeds and during jumps and remove the elevated edges of the saddle, which prevented sliding sideways and backwards. Sidesaddle became truly popular in the first decade of the 20th cent. After WWI its popularity rapidly declined though, which historians of horse riding attribute to the increased emancipation of women, including female horse riders, who tried to adopt manly patterns of behavior, also in horse riding. On the other hand, the sidesaddle required assistance during the mounting and more wealthy female horse riders rather ostentatiously used the help of their servants, which additionally stressed their privileged social position. When horse riding became relatively democratized and joined by representatives of less wealthy classes, the significance of sidesaddle further declined. This does not mean that sidesaddle completely disappeared from horse riding. There continued to be defenders of the female horse riding traditions, among them I. Maddison, who in 1923 published a manual of astride horse riding, but who added a chapter in which she did not condemn sidesaddle riding:

While people predicted that the side saddle will go out entirely and be looked upon as an odd contrivance of the past, I believe they are wrong, for although it is considered less safe for jumping, the greater security and superior appearance which it affords, should enable it to always hold its own. The fact that the side saddle offers a stronger seat is to my mind its greatest asset. The build of many girls and women handicap them in gaining a secure seat astride. A fat person is particularly at a disadvantage in regard to grip on a cross saddle and when her horse gives an awkward move, her legs are apt to fly out, and her hands to catch hold of her horse's mouth for support. In a side saddle however, such a rider often acquires a firm seat, for there is something definite for her to hold on to, and the leaping head (lower pommel) comes down over her left leg, keeping it in its proper place.

[*Riding Astride for Girls*, 1923]

The revival of sidesaddle riding came first in the USA, where the bicentennial celebrations in 1976 increased the demand for historical forms of horse riding, included by women, useful in parades and costume performances imitating the old customs.

Skateboards.

Old saddles became the model for new ones, and the latter proved attractive not only for women but also for recreational riders or riders who had not had any riding training, necessary in trad. astride riding. A sidesaddle almost automatically keeps even the poorest rider in the proper position. This was one of the reasons for the rapid interest in recreational riding, but also therapeutic riding (a disabled rider could easily maintain balance). Interest in sidesaddle riding also grew in competitive riding, where it became a separate, attractive event. This first happened in the western riding organizations, where sidesaddle riding was introduced in competitions and shows involving different horse breeds, such as Arabians and Appaloosa (>WESTERN HORSEBACK RIDING). Competitions in which the apparel of the riders was particularly evaluated became very popular. Sidesaddle riding was soon adopted by some feminist organizations, which, contrary to the emancipated women of the 1920s and 1930s started to ostentatiously avoid imitating men, including the men's style of horseback riding and opted for everything that was different. The sidesaddle riding style was considered to have been created by women and for women and thus worthy of development in order to emphasize female identity. In 1980 the World Sidesaddle Federation, WSFI was established in Bucyrus, Ohio, USA, at the initiative of L.A. Bowlby. Soon other federations were established, usu. satellite ones and affiliated to the WSFI. In 1995 chapters of the WSFI existed in all the US states and in seven other countries. The federation promotes sidesaddle riding on horses, ponies and mules. It also sponsors publication of manuals, brochures and video films promoting sidesaddle riding, and cooperates with many riding organizations, among them the Amer. Horse Shows Association and the Amer. Donkey and Mule Society, the National Saddle Mule Association, and others.

B. Beach, *Riding for Women*, 1912; E. Christy, *Modern Side Saddle Riding*, 1907; M. Friddle and L.A. Bowlby,

Skateboards on display in a sport shop.

The Sidesaddle Legacy, 1994; J. Macdonald, *Teaching Side-saddle*, 1993.

SIDT-TIK, Dan. for 'touching, striking a sitting opponent'. A game in which one or a few running players try to catch other players. Players can avoid being caught by sitting down with their legs crossed. Each player can sit twice; on the third attempt to sit he can be caught. Then he becomes the catcher. J. Möller, 'Sidt-tik', GID, 1997, 2.

SILAMBAM, old Tamil var. of stick fencing. Four basic stick types were developed. The design of the first produces a whistling sound due to the grooves and holes cut into it; another one has spherical end-

Buster Halterman grabs the lip of his board during the men's skateboard vert competition.

ings wrapped with cloth, called *torch silambam*; another is a short, heavy stick, used in defense rather than attack. Silambam uses a range of techniques: rapid dashing movements that create a large space around the fighter, in which the opponent cannot freely operate; fighting with two hands; strengthening and underlining hits by means of additional movements with the head, shoulders, hips and legs; a technique of circular blows; a technique based on anticipation of the opponent's intentions and movements and dodging them. The old techniques also included feints against stones thrown by a hostile crowd. Called 'monkey', 'snake', or 'twisting' movements, they referred to leg movements and the balancing movements of the sticks.

Silambam contests are held as follows: fighting until a stick or sticks are dislodged from the opponent's hands; forcing the opponent to release a sack of coins held between the legs; a fight for the largest number of touches on the opponent's body. In the last var. the winner is the contestant who manages to leave a mark on the opponent's forehead. To make it possible, the stick ends are covered with special sticky powder, which leaves a clear mark. If none of the players manage to touch the opponent's forehead, touching any other part of the body scores 1pt. In some areas a mark on the opponent's body above the waist scores 2pts. In some places a rule prevails according to which the winner is the player who first 'marks' the opponent 3 times.

The fight begins with the competitors paying respect

to the gods, the spectators and the instructor. Silambam is played in a ring of ab. 20-25ft. (ab. 6.1-7.6m) in diameter, marked on a hard even surface. A contest consists of 4 rounds ranging from 6 to 10min. each, with 1min. breaks after the first and the third rounds and a 3min. break after the 2nd round. The attire of the contestants consists of a round-necked full-sleeved vest or a jersey, shorts (*langots*), stockings, turbans, canvas shoes, chest protection, hand gloves and a shield.

History. The tradition of silambam fencing goes back to the oldest Tamil mythological tales, in which the god Muruga conquered his enemies in stick fights. It is generally believed that silambam was created by Agasthya, a mythological wise man and co-author of a collection of hymns, *Rygwedy*. Presently, the art of silambam is continued in the Tamilnad state (Tamil Nadu).

J. Raj, D. Manuel, *Silambam Technique and Evaluaation*, 1971; *Silambam Fencing from India*, 1975; The Internet: http://w3.meadev.gov.in/sports/mr_arts/silambam.htm

SILAT, see >PENCAK SILAT.

SINGLE-STICK, the name of a folk sport, and at the same time a type of a stick used in the fight and self-defense in England. Single-stick was held in one hand, unlike the longer >QUARTERSTAFF, which had to be handled with both hands. The contestants' left hands were tied behind their back. The aim of the game was to 'let the first blood' from the opponent's head. Cf. also >CUDGEL.

SINHALESIAN TUG-OF-WAR, an athletic contest organized by the Sinhalese of Sri Lanka, as part of the New Year's celebration. The rope was pulled by two teams, one representing Goddess Pattini – the protector against natural disasters- and the other representing her evil husband. The contest was set as a form of oracle. If the Pattini team won, the land would be protected against outbreaks of plagues, particularly against black smallpox fairly common in Sri Lanka. The victory of the evil husband's team meant the possibility of a plague outbreak. See >TUG-OF-WAR.

SIPAK, see >SEPAK TAKRAW.

SIPASIPA, see >FOOTBAG.

SITKO, also *gra w sitko*, a little known peasant game practiced in 16th and 17th cent. Poland. Information given after M. Bielski by Ł. Gołębiowski in *Gry i zabawy różnych stanów*, 1831, 63.

SIUM LAM PAI, also in Cantonese *Shaolin shu*, a Chin. style of >WUSHU martial arts from the Shaolin temple. It was split into a southern and northern variety, and formed a direct basis for many separate styles, such as *hung kuen, hun gar, choy gar, hop gar, choy lee fut*, etc.

Union of Sjoelbak), established in 1977, and in Belgium the Belgische Sjoelfederatie Vlaamse Vleugel (Belgium-Flemish Sjoelbak Federation), estab. in 1978. The Du. federation includes about 100 clubs, scattered evenly all over the country, whereas the Belgian one only about 10 clubs, mainly from the vicinity of Antwerp. In both countries the game is played also for recreation at home and in many local pubs.
E. De Vroede, 'Ball and Bowl Games in the Low Countries: Past and Present', *Homo Ludens – Der Spielende Mensch*, 1996, vol. VI; ibid, *Het Grote Volkssporten Boek*, Leuven 1996.

SKATE SCOOTER, see >KICK-BOARD.

SKATEBOARDING, also *skateboard* or simply *boarding* [Eng. *skate + board*]; a common graffito is *SK8*. A sports discipline practiced in a number of var. and competitions with the use of a board resembling a miniature surf board (>SURFING) in shape, equipped with small wheels or rollers that can be turned by pressing either side of the board. The front end of the board is referred to as the 'tip', the rear end is the 'tail', and the sides are called 'rails'. The rail supporting the toes is the 'front rail' and the one supporting the heels is the 'back rail'. The wheels (or rollers) are fixed on small, turning frames – 'trucks'. The rollers are made of different materials and they have different diameters and widths. They are selected depending on the user's preferences or the skating technique. If made of hard and resistant material, they cause less friction allowing greater speed, but poorer traction.
There are 2 major types of skateboards: 'stunt boards' mostly employed on a ramp to do tricks; and 'cruiser boards' for covering longer distances. They are used for 2 principal var. of skating: 'ramp' and 'street'. The ramp boards have larger wheels than the street ones. Among the stunt boards two major types can be distinguished, namely the 'old school' and the 'new school'. The former have broad boards with tails longer than tips, whereas the latter have narrower boards with tips only a little longer than tails. Their trucks also differ – the old school's are wider. Cruiser boards are substantially longer and their trucks are wider than in stunt models.
The technique of standing on a board can be divided into 2 major types: a 'regular foot' – with the left foot resting on the front part; and a 'goofy foot' – with the right foot placed in front.
The original var. of skateboarding is referred to as 'vert skating' [from Eng. *vertical*, which originates from the track that changes from a vertical wall into a horizontal plane and then opposite vertical again]. The track is a special ramp made for skating. Examples of such ramps are half-pipes, pools, basins, quarter pipes, 2.5m-high banks, funboxes (large jumping pads of trapezoid shape), transfers (pyramid-shaped obstacles), lump ramps, and grindboxes (cubes 30cm tall and 2.5m long). A half-pipe is 32ft. (about 9.75m) wide, 10ft. (3.05m) tall, with vertical edges 12-18in. (30.5-45.7cm) high and the horizontal plane 16ft. (about 4.88m) long. The top of the vertical edges is welded with a pipe called the 'coping', about $2^5/_{16}$in. (6.35cm) in diameter. It protrudes

skaters (11,000 participants in 1997). For some years now, due to mild winters in Holland, the Elfstedentnocht race has been held together with other skating races in other places, e.g. on Lake Weissensee in Austria (2000) or on Lake Akan on the Jap. island of Hokkaido. Most popular Eur. skate marathons include races on Lake Kallevesi in Finland and Lake Vikingarännet in Sweden. Very spectacular are the US Marathon Championships under the auspices of the N.Amer. Marathon Skating Association. The most prestigious Can. skate marathons are the races held in Ottawa and Lac Beauport, Quebec. The world top marathon skaters are A. Schreuder, K. Lankhaar, B. Van Hest; and among women, G. Smit, B. Duursma and V. Vergeer.

X-GAMES SKATEBOARDING CHAMPIONS

VERT SINGLES
1995 Tony Hawk
1996 Andy Macdonald
1997 Tony Hawk
1998 Andy Macdonald
1999 Bucky Lasek
2000 Bucky Lasek
2001 Bob Burnquist
VERT DOUBLES
1997 Tony Hawk and Andy Macdonald
1998 Tony Hawk and Andy Macdonald
1999 Tony Hawk and Andy Macdonald
2000 Tony Hawk and Andy Macdonald
2001 Tony Hawk and Andy Macdonald
STREET/PARK
1995 Chris Senn
1996 Rodil de Araujo Jr.
1997 Chris Senn
1998 Rodil de Araujo Jr.
1999 Chris Senn
2000 Eric Koston
2001 Kerry Getz
BEST TRICK
2000 Bob Burnquist
2001 Matt Dove

Philippe Cridelauze is towed by a motorcycle during his record breaking skateboarding feat at La Garenne airport runway in Agen, France. He was able to reach the speed of 168km/h.

Skateboarding motif on a 1999 postage stamp.

SJIPPE OVER EGET BEN, Dan. jump over one's leg – jump over one's toes [Dan. *sjippe* – jump + *over* – over + *eget* – own + *ben* – leg (among others)]. A Dan. form of physical competition. The contestant, standing, holds the toe of the left foot with his right hand. Jumping on one leg he tries to jump over the other leg. In the same way attempts can be made to 'jump backwards'.
J. Möller, 'Sjipe over eget ben', GID, 1997, 3, 15.

SJOELBAK, a Flem. folk game. It is played on a wooden board (*sjoelbak*), about 2m long and about 40cm wide. At the back of the board there are 4 arched goals with equal clearances but different point values. A player has 30 discs, which he slides so that they go through the goal and score points. When all the 30 discs have been used up, the player starts his 2nd round, in which he can only throw the discs that in the first round did not go through any of the goals. The game is over after 3 rounds and the winner is the player who scores most points.
History. The oldest, somewhat imprecise information about sjoelbak comes from the 16th cent. In a water color painted by R. Savery (1576-1639), entitled *May Celebration* (held by the Hermitage in Sankt Petersburg), a game of sjoelbak can be seen. A copy made after Savery's watercolor, probably by Pieter Brueghel III, is held by the Albertina Museum in Vienna.
The main organization for sjoelbak in Holland is the Algemene Nederlandse Sjoelbond (General Du.

SKÆRE FLÆSK NED, Dan. for 'bacon slicing', [Dan. *skære* – slice + *flæsk* – bacon, pork + *ned* – down]; a game of skill. A double rope is thrown across a horizontal beam, forming a loop. An object is placed on the beam. The contestant puts one leg into the loop and holds the ends of the rope with his hands. Then he pulls himself up so he is hanging in mid-air. His task is to knock the object on the beam off with his leg.
J. Möller, 'Skære flæsk ned', GID, 1997, 3, 43.

SKAKANIE NA DESKACH, Pol. for 'jumping on boards', a Pol. trad. game. A pair of girls alternatingly jumped on both sides of a board under which there was a wooden log. Ł. Gołębiowski provides rather surprising information about the game: 'in Lithuania playing the game was permitted from Easter until the time when flax was sown, then it was forbidden in the belief that this might be harmful to its growth' (*Games and pastimes of various social states*, 1831, 63). Cf. >NÓL TTWIGI, >TEETER-TOTTERING, >SWINGS AND SEESAWS.

SKATE MARATHON, an ice-skating race held over long distances, usu. about 200km. It is derived from trad. skating races held on frozen canals of Holland. The most famous skate marathon is the so-called Marathon of Eleven Cities (Elfstedentnocht or De Friesche Elf Steden) organized irregularly – depending on winter conditions – by the Frisian Skating Association. The race starts in Leeuwarden, the Netherlands, and is attended by a few thousand

A skating marathon in Holland.

S

0.6-1.0cm above the edges of vertical walls, informing the skaters about crossing the edge. In addition, the coping provides a skater with better control over the board when airborne; it directs the tip of the board towards the user and facilitates catching the board when the track's edge has been crossed. If the coping is too high, which makes such acrobatics easier, the ramp is considered uninteresting, whereas too little coping makes skating too difficult. The most popular tricks are as follows: 'CAB' – during a jump the skater spins 360° mid-air without catching the board, the name of the trick originates

Biker Sherlock, right, manipulates a corner in front of Dane von Bommel, center, and Emanuel Antuna, left, during the final run of the Gravity Games' downhill skateboard competition in Providence, R.I.

from the first 3 letters of the trick's inventor S. Caballero; 'half CAB' – during a jump the skater pivots 180° without catching the board; 'slow half' – half turn; 'shuvit' – the skater presses against the tip so that the tail wheels are not touching the floor and then he kicks the board's side hard enough to have it do a 1-80; '540 trick' – a 540° spin while airborne; 'frontside trick' – a turn on a board during which the skater is bent backwards so much that he cannot see his feet; 'backside trick' – a jump accompanied by a turn and bending forward; 'backside hip flip' – a jump accompanied by a turn-around with thighs raised to the level of hips and arms stretched out; 'kick flip' – the board is kicked with the toes of the front foot so that it flips around on its axis, the figure is usu. specified with more detail by giving the degree of a flip, e.g. 360°; 'heel flip' – the board is kicked with the heel of the front foot so that it flips around on its longitudinal axis; 'nose grab' – when airborne a skater grabs the tip; 'tail grab' – when an airborne skater grabs the tail; 'frontside air' – a jump accompanied by bending backward and grabbing the back rail on the back side of the board; 'slob' – a jump accompanied by grabbing the front rail on the

Dany Locati of Italy practices for the women's skeleton event during the Salt Lake City Winter Olympic Games at the Peaks Ice Arena in Provo, Utah.

front side of the board; 'stale fish' – a skater jumps like in a frontside trick, grabbing the back rail; 'lean air' – a skater jumps like in a frontside trick grabbing the back rail on the front side; 'backside air' – a skater jumps backwards and grabs the back rail on the front side; 'mute' – a jump backwards accompanied by grabbing the front rail with the front hand; 'indy air' – a jump backwards accompanied by grabbing the front rail with the back hand.
In street skateboarding skaters attempt to jump over or skate through any possible obstacles encountered in urban areas, such as benches, stairs, fountains, monuments, and subways.

History. Skateboarding developed from the children's game *pushcooter* that was popular in the 1950s, in which a board with wheels taken from roller skates was used. In the '70s new technical elements led to rapid popularization of skateboarding, the pioneers in this field being Americans T. Alva, J. Nelson, and S. Caballero. Parks in Western countries, later on in other parts of the world, were equipped with special constructions intended for skating, e.g. concrete tracks and half pipes.
In the course of the next years the sport's popularity dwindled because of high fees charged for entering skateboarding grounds, many of which went bankrupt at that time. Then the street era began, during which the skaters practiced their favorite sport in the streets, as well as on amateur constructions they made themselves. To some extent they became an urban pest; chased away from one square to another they were persistently improving their skills. On the international scale, their leader was S. Caballero, followed later on by T. Hawk. The search for new skating techniques and new technological solutions in the board's construction brought independent disciplines such as >WAKEBOARDING and >STREET LUGE. Developing skating technique substantially influenced other disciplines, such as >SURFING, >SNOWBOARDING, and >IN-LINE ROLLER SKATING. All these sports were also affected in the cultural sense, which consisted of establishing a specific youth subculture marked by a sense of autonomy and nonconformity with the order of civilization. The most conspicuous, although not the most important, sign of the group has become a baseball cap worn with its bill turned backwards, which, in time, was adopted by youth culture in the broad sense. Cf. KICK-BOARD, >RADKI, and >SCOOTERS.
B. Bral. *Disqualifying the Official. An Exploration of Social Resistance through the Subculture of Skateboarding*, SSJ, 1995, 12; J.A. Davidson, *Sport and Modern Technology. The Rise of Skateboarding 1963-1978*, JPC, 1985, 18, 4; A. Mountfield, *Skateboarding*, 1979.

SKATING, see >ICE SKATING, >FIGURE SKATING, >IN-LINE ROLLER SKATING, >ROLLER SKATING, >SHORT TRACK SPEED SKATING, >SKATE MARATHON, >SKATEBOARDING, >SKATING FOR THE DISABLED, >SKATING ON ONE FOOT, >SKATING OBSTACLE RACE, >SPEED SKATING.

SKATING FOR THE DISABLED, a var. of ice skating, known as sledge racing, adapted for the disabled. Instead of regular ice skates the racers use two-blade sledges, propelled and steered with two sticks with spoke-ends. The competitors race over distances of 100, 500, 700, 1,000, and 1,500m, in both men's and women's categories.
The Internet: http://www.paralympic.org/sports/sections/sledge-racing/general.html

SKATING OBSTACLE RACE, a Rus. skating race with obstacles. The racers compete on a U-shaped track. Formerly, skating steeplechase was practiced on frozen ponds and lakes; at present races are held on regular speed-skating tracks. The sport was described by the Rus. author, I.N. Chkhannikov: 'The racing track is divided into sections with obstacles. The first obstacle consists of 5 pylons set along the track, 20m from the start. 5m from the first pylon an ice-hockey stick and a puck are placed on the ice. A skater has to pick up the stick and steer the puck in between the pylons. The second obstacle is an ice-hockey board, 10m ahead of the furthest pylon. Having crossed the pylons, the skater has to hit the puck over the board. The third obstacle is a wicket, similar to that in >WYBIJANKA, 10m in front of the board. The skater has to knock the wicket over with the puck. The fourth obstacle is a goal marked with 2 flags, 8m ahead of the wicket. The skater should strike the puck in between the flags, pass by the

goal and leave the stick in the goal. The next obstacle consists of 3 consecutive uprights, 4m apart, each with a movable crossbar. The skater must squat and pass below the first two crossbars without knocking down either of them, and take the third one off the upright. After that, the skater can straighten up and, holding the crossbar in his right hand, cover the last 10m to the finish line.' The length of the steeplechase skating track is not precisely defined; it can be lengthened or shortened by changing the distances between the obstacles or adding other obstacles, for example: racing with a table tennis ball held on a spoon, over a distance of 10m; throwing wooden blocks into a box placed along the track; slaloming using a route made of twenty blocks; or tossing wicker quoits onto wooden pegs.
I.N. Chkhannikov, 'Bieg z przeszkodami (łyżwiarski)', GIZ, 1953, 92-96.

SKATING ON ONE FOOT, a type of folk skating practiced in the Wielkopolska region of Poland. According to A. Kowol-Marcinek, scholar of regional culture: 'children skated on one foot only, although by then they already knew that bi-footed skating was possible. They preferred to use one foot, as this was easier and offered more stability. The skate was secured to one (usu. the right) boot, while the other foot was used as a propeller that made it possible to skate around a lake or from one end to the other. They even tried their skills at races to find out who could skate faster. While skating, after several strong thrusts, the skater would raise the skate-free leg and glide as if he were riding on a bike without pedalling'.
Antoni Kowol-Marcinek, 'Na łyżwie', *Old children's games and pastimes in Bukówiec Górny*, Dom Kultury, Leszno, Poland, 1999, 33.

SKÂTSJES-ZEILEN, Flem. for 'scow sailing' (sailing on scows), a var. of folk fishing competition using sailing boats.

SKELETON, a var. of luge, practiced on sleds made of steel or fiberglass, with a trolley moving on rails like a rower's seat, on which the slider lies face down. The bottom of the sled is a flat pan. The skeleton sled itself measures 3ft. in length and 16in. in width, weighing from 70-115lbs. depending on the slider's body weight, which helps reach speeds of up to 120km/h. The slider wears a helmet with a chin guard as the face is a mere 2in. off the ice. A skin tight rubber suit is used to increase aerodynamics and sprinters spikes are worn to achieve the quick 50m start in a bent over position while pushing the sled along a curved ice track, Once up to speed the competitor jumps onto the sled as smoothly as possible. At speeds of 70 to 80mph, the athlete negotiates the curved track using subtle shifts in body weight and positioning. The sled was built for the first time in 1884 by an Englishman called Shild in St. Moritz, Switzerland. Skeleton appeared in the 1928 and 1948 Olympic Games at St. Moritz, where an American won the Gold medal. The sport faded from popularity until the late 1970s when a resurgence in Europe started to bring the sport back into the public eye. A World Cup series of races began in 1985, with the USA team sliding in Europe since 1984. It was also featured in the 2002 OI.G. in Salt Lake City – the gold medal again went to the Americans Jim Shea Jr. (men) and Tristan Gale (women). World championships in skeleton gather teams from approx. 20 countries, including – since 1996 – women.
The Internet: www.usabobsledandskeleton.org

SKI AERIALS, one of the 4 major events in > FREESTYLE SKIING, see >AERIALS. For the etymology of the phrase 'acrobatic feat(s)' see >ACROBATICS.

SKI FLYING, a variant of ski jumping using ski jumps with longer runways. The most famous jumps of this type are in Oberstdorf (Germany) and Planica (Slovenia). Record distances have been documented since 1923, when the Norwegian T. Hemmestveit reached 23m on the Huseby jump. The 100m barrier was first broken by the Austrian J. Bradl (101.5m, 1936, Planica). The Norwegian L. Grini was the first to jump 150m (1967, Oberstdorf), while the Austrian R. Bachler was the first to jump over that distance (154m, 1967, Vikersund). In the 1970s and 1980s, jumpers slowly approached the barrier of 200m. The Austrian A. Kogler was the first to jump 180m (1981, Oberstdorf), and the Czechoslovak P. Ploc reached 181m (1983, Harrachov). M. Nykkänen (Finland) broke the 190m barrier (191m, 1985, Planica), while his compatriot T. Nieminen was the first

Catherine Sauer leads fellow Special Olympic athlete Courtney Steinmetz toward the finish line of their race at an ice skating competition in Des Moines, Iowa.

Adam Malysz of Poland competes in the Team K120 Ski Jumping event at the Utah Olympic Park in Park City during the Salt Lake City Winter Olympic Games.

SKI JUMPING OLYMPIC CHAMPIONS

NORMAL HILL
1964 Veikko Kankkonen, FIN 229.9
1968 Jiri Raska, CZE 216.5
1972 Yukio Kasaya, JPN 244.2
1976 Hans-Georg Aschenbach, E. Ger 252.0
1980 Anton Innauer, AUT 266.3
1984 Jens Weissflog, E. Ger 215.2
1988 Matti Nykänen, FIN 229.1
1992 Ernst Vettori, AUT 222.8
1994 Espen Bredesen, NOR 282.0
1998 Jani Soininen, FIN 234.5
2002 Simon Amman, SWI, 269
LARGE HILL
1924 Jacob Tullin Thams, NOR 18.960
1928 Alf Andersen, NOR 19.208
1932 Birger Ruud, NOR 228.1
1936 Birger Ruud, NOR 232.0
1948 Petter Hugsted, NOR 228.1
1952 Arnfinn Bergmann, NOR 226.0
1956 Antti Hyvärinen, FIN 227.0
1960 Helmut Recknagel, GER 227.2
1964 Toralf Engan, NOR 230.7
1968 Vladimir Beloussov, USSR 231.3
1972 Wojciech Fortuna, POL 219.9
1976 Karl Schäabl, AUT 234.8
1980 Jouko Törmänen, FIN 271.0
1984 Matti Nykänen, FIN 231.2
1988 Matti Nykänen, FIN 224.0
1992 Toni Nieminen, FIN 239.5
1994 Jens Weissflog, GER 274.5
1998 Kazuyoshi Funaki, JPN 272.3
2002 Simon Ammann, SWI, 281,4

to finally jump over 200m (203m, 1993, Planica). Today, many top jumpers reach distances over 200m. In 2003, the Finn M. Hautamäki became the record holder with 231m.

SKI FOOTBALL, also *Kennedy game*, a combination of downhill skiing and a ball game, in which the ball is passed between skiers during a downhill run, according to the rules of >FLYING DISC. Two teams (18 players in all) begin at the top of the hill. The ball is usu. made of plastic and is approx. 10cm in diameter (a plastic bottle filled with snow may be used). The team winning a draw begins the downhill ride. The other team runs along without interfering. While running down skiers pass the ball between one another and the player who catches the ball must stop for a moment and pass the ball on to another player within 10sec. Failure to maintain the 10sec. limit results in losing the ball in favor of the rival team. The aim of the game is to score points by bringing the ball down and placing it inside a goal in a way similar to >AMERICAN FOOTBALL. The goals are placed along the slope and may be formed by two slalom posts. After a goal is scored, the game continues.

History. Ski football was conceived and developed by the Kennedy family in the 1970s. Members of the family, who are enthusiastic skiers, practiced it on the slopes of the Aspen Mountain in Colorado, beginning at the top of the mountain known as Sundeck Lounge and skiing down the Copper Bowl Trail. In the 1990s the game caught on among skiers and around 1996-8 gained the status of a snobbish, extreme hobby. Its popularity was at a peak when Michael Kennedy (the 4th son of Robert Kennedy, brother of John Kennedy, the assassinated president of the USA) was killed on the slope in Aspen, having hit a tree during a fast run in hostile weather conditions, with poor visibility and on frozen ice. The accident sparked widespread media criticism of the risk involved in this sport and reinforced the popular belief regarding the 'Kennedy curse' – the tragic fate of the Kennedy clan, several members of which died as a result of dramatic events.

In another var. a football is rolled down the slope. Both teams ski down the mountain trying to get possession of the ball. When the person with the ball is touched with 2 hands, the team loses possession and the other team gets to play it. If the ball is passed forward and is dropped, it is a turn over. If a player tries a hand-off or a pitch and the ball is dropped, it is a fumble and anyone can grab it. The team with the ball at the bottom of the mountain scores a touchdown. The first team with 3 touchdowns wins.

SKI JUMPING, an event of >NORDIC SKIING, in which skiers compete to make the longest jump from a high ramp overhanging a slope. In competition on both smaller and larger hills, each competitor takes 2 official jumps, which are scored for distance and style. The scores for each jump are added together and the competitor with the highest total after the two rounds is declared the winner. The distance the jumper leaps is measured along the curve of the landing hill from the takeoff point to the point between the jumper's two feet as he first touches the hill. Video cameras record the distance of each jump. Once the distance has been measured, that meter figure is then translated into distance points.

In the small hill competition, a jump to the K point (critical or construction point) is worth 60pts. Each meter over or under that distance is reflected by an increase or decrease of 2pts. Style points for each jump are evaluated on a scale of 0 to 20 by five International Ski Federation-appointed judges. The highest and lowest style scores are eliminated; thus, a competitor can only earn up to 60 style points per jump. Style is determined by the power, boldness, precision, fluidity and control of the jump, as derived from the takeoff, the flight, the landing and the out-run. Standing jumps are scored from 11 to 20 style points, while falls bring scores in the range of 0 to 10 style points. Each judge may award up to 20pts. per jump. Judges deduct points for each type of error. For the individual competitions, the jumpers are divided into 4 groups. Each nation is allowed to enter one jumper in each group, and teams generally place their best jumpers in the final two groups. This is because the hill tends to speed up as the competition goes on, often leading to longer jumps. For the first round of jumping, the 4 groups simply go one after the other, with the start order within each group determined by chance. The start order for the 2nd round is the reverse order of finish from the 1st round. Thus, the leader after the first round will jump last in the second round. Unlike World Cup events, all jumpers who compete in the first round are allowed to compete in the 2nd round.

Jumpers adopt a natural and relaxed aerodynamic position. In this crouch, the jumper is coiled, prepared to thrust himself forward at takeoff. The jumper has a 15-sec. window in which he must start; jumpers may strategically wait the full 15sec. or jump immediately depending on wind conditions. The jumper may not use ski poles or similar aids to increase his speed, nor may he be pushed off by another person. These infractions would result in disqualification. The takeoff is solely initiated by the legs. The skier takes off with a rhythmic, aggressive and quick straightening of the knees and stretching of the body. The skier's ankles are locked so that, in the air, the tips of his skis come up. With the V-technique, the jumper must spread out his skis quickly in a symmetrical fashion. Timing is extremely important in the takeoff, because an early or late take-

off will greatly reduce distance. Every jumper is judged on the same criteria for the landing. A proper landing should be accomplished with steadiness, elasticity and 'skis together,' meaning that the distance between both skis shall not be more than the width of one ski. The landing impact should be absorbed by a telemark landing, which allows the jumper to absorb most of the force on his front leg at impact and then distribute his weight evenly on both legs to stabilize himself for the out-run. The out-run is an area at the bottom of the hill, usu. sloping upwards, where skiers decelerate and stop. The jumper should hold the telemark landing for a mini-

The K116, right, and K90 ski jumping hills in Lahti, Finland.

Before the introduction of the V-style, ski jumpers used a completely different technique based on keeping the skis parallel.

The famous ski flying hill in Planica on a 1972 postage stamp.

Ski marathon on a 1993 postage stamp.

mum of 15m. If a jumper is unsteady after the landing because he has made a mistake in flight or at landing, he will be monitored by the judges until he passes the fall line. If a jumper falls on the out-run prior to the fall line because he has not recovered his balance lost on landing, the jump counts as a fall. The fall line is located 20m past the end of the landing transition (R-2 transition curve). If a jumper falls after he has passed this line, he will not lose any style points. The jump is over as soon as the jumper has reached this line, making the subjective portion of the competition the distance from the edge of takeoff to the fall line.

History. The oldest information about ski jumping comes from a book by the Dutchman J. Scheffers, *Lapponia* (Amsterdam, 1682), in which he described folk ski jumping practiced by the Lapps. In 1792 an award was founded in Norway for ski jumps and runs, given until 1825. In 1800 R. Berge from Telemark composed a song with the following lyrics:

And in winter they ski down the steepest slopes.
The hill is so high and the field so steep;
They fly through the air as if on wings.
With jumps some six yards;
That is how they while away their hours.
And as they hover in the air;
The spectators gaze in amazement.

In 1809 O. Rye, a lieutenant in the Norw. army jumped 9.5m. This jump is considered to be the first measured jump in the history of skiing. In 1860 a Norw. carpenter and ski producers from Morgedal, S. Auverson Nordheim (1825-97), jumped 'without poles and straightened up' to a distance of 30m, thus setting an unofficial record which was not beaten for 33yrs. In 1897 the Christiania Ski Club, estab. 2yrs. earlier, organized in Oslo (then Christiania) the first official ski jumping competition, which was watched by thousands of spectators. The competition was held on the Huseby Bakken hill, and the winner, T.T. Hemmestveidt (1861-1930) jumped to a distance of 23m, which was considered the first official world record. F. Huitfeld provided the following description of Hemmestveidt's jump:

Off he went like a meteor amidst the crowd of astounded onlookers who stood there as if rooted to the spot [...]. The telemark people were invited and came to the race in Christiania. The shouts of joy rose heavenward, rending the air and causing the old trees on the Huseby-hill to tremble and shake.

F. Nansen, a well-known explorer, in his book *Paa Ski over Gronland*, 1890, devoted a short text to ski jumping:

To see how an expert ski jumper executes a jump is one of the most sublime sights the earth can offer us.

The first competition in continental Europe was organized by the Skiing Association of Steiermark in 1893 in Mürzzuschalg am Semmering (Austria). It was won by a guest from Norway, a baker's assistant, W. Bismarck Samson, who jumped to a distance of 6m. Jumps were made from a ramp of compacted snow, whereas in Norway wooden ramps were already being used. The first competition in Germany was held one year later, in Tauberberg, near Munich, where the Norwegian Wium (first name unknown) jumped to a distance of 14.5m. The first European to jump to a distance of 20m was A. Walter from Germany in 1904.

A ski marathon.

Modern ski jumping was started in 1861 in Telemark in Norway. It was initiated by S. Norheim, who designed bindings with a loose foot, which permitted a forwards inclination during the flight. The first competition was held in 1892, when ski jumping was made part of ski running, thus forming >NORDIC SKIING. The first ramps were made from compacted snow on naturally sloping hills or mountains. In 1892 in Oslo the first ski jump was built in the place of the present day famous Holmenkollen jump. Ski jumping was included into the Ol.G. program in 1924. In the same year the first permanent ski jump was built in Oslo. In the first decades of ski jumping the best jumpers came from Scand. countries, particularly Norway and Finland. Before 1939 the best jumpers were the Ruud brothers (Sigmund 1907-94; Birger, born in 1911 and Asbjörn, born in 1920), who in the interwar period together won 5 W.Ch., 2 gold medals at Ol.G. and 5 other medals in W.Ch. and Ol.G.. After WWII jumpers from Czechoslovakia and the GDR and, although to a lesser extent, from the USSR, ranked among the best jumpers. The best jumpers of the years from 1945 through 1989 include: T. Engan (world champion on the small hill in 1962 and Olympic champion on the large hill in 1964) and B. Wirkola (world champion on normal and large hills in 1966) from Norway, a representative of East Germany H. Recknagel (Olympic champion on the small hill in 1960 and world champion on the large hill in 1962), Y. Kasaya from Japan (Olympic champion in 1972). In the beginnings of the 1980s jumpers from Austria (A. Kögler, world champion on the small hill, 1982) ranked among the best jumpers. After 1945 most titles were won by, J. Weissflog of E. Germany, an Olympic champion in 1984 and twice world champion (1985 and 1989) on the small hill and the winner of many international cups, among them the Four Hills Competition (Oberstdorf, Garmisch-Partenkirchen-Innsbruck and Bischofshofen). A Finn, M. Nykänen was twice champion of the Ol.G. (small hill, 1988 and large hill, 1988) and world champion on the small hill in 1982. After the collapse of the German Democratic Republic the former GDR representatives retained their high positions (J. Weisslog). During the 1992 and 1994 Ol.G. Jap. jumpers came again to the forefront; at the 1998 Ol.G. in Nagano they dominated. At the end of the 1990s a new group of jumpers began to dominate the Ski Jumping World Cup. It included M. Schmitt and S. Hannavald (Germany), A. Małysz (Poland, the winner of 3 world cups (2001-2003) and a double world champion in 2003), S. Amman (Switzerland, winner of 2 Olympic gold medals in 2002).

In a search for originality, a var. of ski jumping on Alpine equipment, known as >GALONDEE JUMPING, has started to gain popularity in recent years.

Anonymous, 'A Short History of Ski Jumping', OR, Febr. 1994, 315, 41-42; M. Kozdruń, *Skoki narciarskie*, 1953; Z. Ryn et al., *Skoczkowie narciarscy. Studium psychologiczne*, 1990.

SKI MARATHON, a skiing race over a distance of 50km. The name *ski marathon* is also applied to the longest ski running event held at the Ol.G. and world championships (>NORDIC SKIING). In Europe, the best known ski marathons are the Swiss Engadin Ski Marathon in southern Tirol; Ger.-Ital. Pustertaler Ski Marathon (since 1976); and the Troll Ski Marathon in Lillehamer, Norway. The leading Eur. marathon skiers are the Swiss B.A. Loretan and German P. Schlieckenrieder, the winners of the 33rd Engadin Marathon in 2001. In the United States, marathon ski races are organized in the form of the Amer. Ski Marathon Series consisting of twelve events, e.g. the Tour of Anchorage, Yellowstone National Park Lodges Rendezvous, First Security Boulder Mountain Tour and Royal Gorge's California Gold Rush. In Canada, the most renowned events are the Can. Ski Marathon (Fr. Marathon Canadien de Ski).

SKI ORIENTEERING, a type of a competitive sport drawing upon the tradition of >ORIENTEERING and supervised by the International Orienteering Federation (IOF). Ski orienteering competitions are held during winter months on skis and are known in the contestants' jargon as 'Ski-O's' [Eng., Scandinavian *ski + orienteering*]. Similarly to orienteering, the object of the race is to identify isolated control points which must be reached on skis. Ski orienteering competitions involve both men's and women's long- and short-distance events. Long-distance W.Ch. have been held since 1975 and short-distance ones since 1988. Ski orienteers use the same equipment as that employed in >SKI RUNNING COMPETITIONS and trad. orienteering competitions with a map case and a compass attached to it hanging loosely around a competitor's chest due to the fact that he has to hold the poles in his hands. The card that has to be punched, stamped or otherwise marked at the respective control points is fastened to a skier's sleeve.

History. Ski orienteering began in the 1890s when the first skiing competitions involving the identification of various topographic features were held in Sweden. Ski orienteering developed parallel to orienteering proper. Long-distance W.Ch. have been held since 1975 and short-distance ones since 1988 and have involved both men and women. The World Cup is held every year. The most outstanding woman ski orienteer of the 2nd half of the 1980s and the beginning of the '90s was the 4-time world champion R. Bratberg of Norway (1988, 1990 – short-distance champion and 1986 and 1990 – long-distance winner). A. Hanus of Sweden was one of her major rivals winning the long-distance W.Ch. in 1982 and the short-distance W.Ch. in 1992. Among men the most outstanding orienteers of the same period were A. Juutilainen of Finland (short-distance world champion in 1990 and long-distance world champion in 1984 and 1988) and V. Benjaminsen of Norway (long- and short-distance world champion in 1992 and a silver long- and short-distance medallist at the 1996 W.Ch.). The leading ski orienteers of the 2nd half of the 1990s were the following women's and men's world champions. Women: P. Milutsheva of Bulgaria (long-distance world champion in 1994), A. Nuolioja of Finland (short-distance world champion in 1996), A. Zell (long-distance world champion in 1992 and 1996, short-distance world champion in 1998 and a silver long-distance medallist in 1998) and L. Antilla of Finland (long-distance world champion in 1998). Men: N. Corradini of Italy (long- and short-distance world champion in 1994, long-distance world champion in 1996), B. Lans of Sweden (short-distance world champion in 1996) and V. Kortshagin of Russia (long-distance world champion in 1998). As far as women's relays are concerned the 1990s competitions were dominated by Sweden, Finland, Norway and Russia. The Swedish women's team won in 1992, 1994 and 1996 and the Finns in 1990 and 1998. The situation was exactly the same with regard to men's relays with the Swed. team winning the golds in 1990 and 1996, the Finnish in 1992, the Norwegians in 1994 and the Russians in 1998. Other major ski orienteering competitors include – men: K. Junnikalla, A. Lilja and M. Keskinarkus of Finland as well as P.-O. Berquist of Sweden; women: A. Nuolioja of Finland, O. Isavnina of Russia and A.C. Carlsson of Sweden. IOF aims to have ski orienteering included in the Winter Ol.G. U-21 and veterans W.Ch. are held annually.

S. Harvey, M. Nimvik, B. Römvik, *The World of Orienteering*, 1998.

SKI RELAY, ski races run by 4 (formerly 3) skiers over different distances. The program of the Ol.G. features 4x10km (men) and 4x5km (women) (until 1972 – 3x5km) relays. Women's relays were first featured in the W.Ch. in 1954 and in the Ol.G. in 1956. Up till 1972 women's relays were run over 3x5km, later 4x5km. Men's 4x10km relays first featured in the program of the W.Ch. in 1933 and in the Ol.G. in 1936. Initially Scandinavian teams dominated, after WWII those from the USSR (later CIS and Russia) and, occasionally, from the GDR and Italy; see >NORDIC SKIING.

SKI ROLLERS, the equipment used in >ROLLER SKIING. Basically, these are skis with rollers that make it possible to ski on surfaces other than snow. See also >GRASS SKIING.

SKI RUNNING COMPETITIONS, a group of skiing events where the competitors run on skis. Most ski running competitions are considered to be >NORDIC SKIING events (also called *cross-country skiing*), where the skiers have to run a set course as fast as possible. Special varieties of ski running include >SKI ORIENTEERING as well as those comprising the >WINTER BIATHLON and >SKI-ARCHERY. Typical Nordic distances are: 15, 30 and 50km and the 4x10-km relay for men; 5, 10 and 20km and the 4x5-km relay for ladies; 10 and 15km and

Emmanuel Jonnier of France tags off on teammate Stephane Passeron in the Men's Cross-Country 4x10km Relay of the FIS Ski World Cup event in Davos, Switzerland.

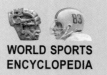

the 3x10-km relay for men under 21; and 5 and 10 km and the 3x5-km relay for ladies under 20. Apart from these, there is the special 'pursuit' event, consisting of two runs on two days, where the starting order on the 2nd day (freestyle) is decided on the basis of the results of the first day (classic) – the competitors do not start at equal intervals, as usual, but at intervals equal to the differences after the first day. There are also trad. events using atypical distances, such as the Swed. *Vasaloppet* (Vasa Run) between the towns of Sälen and Mora, which is 85.5km long (this was the distance covered in 1520 by king Gustav Vasa of Sweden, who, according to legend, ran the route before starting an uprising against the Dan. ruler Christian II). The oldest cross-country event is the Norw. Holmenkollen race (first held in 1892).

During classic style events, the skiers start every 30 sec. in an order decided by a drawing before the race. If a skier is to be overtaken by a competitor who had been chasing him or her, they have to give way after being signaled to do so. In relay events, the competitors all start simultaneously from a line that is an arc of a circle with a diameter of 100m. During the run, a skier may replace one ski and both poles. Two main techniques are used today: the 'classic' step (the only one used before 1985) and the 'skating' step, which makes it possible to run 5-10 per cent faster. The latter technique was initially the object of much discussion but was finally allowed in 1985 for events designated as 'freestyle'. After 1988, a division was introduced where men's 10 and 30km events, and ladies' 5 and 15km events use the classic technique, while the remaining distances (men's 50km and 15km pursuit, and ladies' 30km and 10km pursuit) use the skating step technique.

The equipment for classic runs is different from that used in the skating step technique. The length of classic skis should be, in principle, equal to the distance from the ground to the fingertips of the skier's raised hand (but not more than 230cm). The boots should be lightweight and flexible, with the toes only attached to the bindings of the skis. The skis themselves are much narrower than alpine or jumping skis, with a more noticeable upward arch in the middle part, and the tip curved upwards more sharply. The poles should not be longer than from the ground to the skier's armpit.

The skating step technique requires rigid boots that are more similar to alpine boots, even though they are attached to the binding at the front only rather than along the whole length. The rigidity is supposed to make the side push easier, at the same time protecting the ankles from too much pressure and twisting. The skis and bindings are the same as in the classic technique. The poles are usu. longer but their length may not be greater than the skier's height.

Among the most famous cross-country skiers in history are: the Finn V. Hakulinen (b. 1925), winner of 10 individual and 4 relay W.Ch. and Ol.G. medals; and the Swede S. Jernberg (b. 1929), considered to be the cross-country skier of all time, winner of 10 individual and 5 relay W.Ch. and Ol.G. medals, and twice winner of the *Vasaloppet*. Among ladies, the Russian A. Kolchina (b. 1931) holds a similar position, with 7 individual and 6 relay W.Ch. and Ol.G. medals.

SKI SAILING, a var. of skiing practiced since the early 20th cent. It involves using the force of the wind to move on skis by holding onto a sail. The earliest types of sails were kite-like, and the solution is continued today by the Amer. Hopatcong structure, used on the leeward side. Average sails of this type are 55-65sq. ft. (5-6m²) in area. There are also other types of sail: the Fin. 2-walled Skimbat and the Ger. structure resembling an inflatable parawing. The boots and skis used in ski sailing are of the downhill type, as their metal edges make decelerating easier, without which the ski-sailor would be helpless in the face of the force of the wind. The min. thickness of snow for ski sailing is about 2in. (5cm). For fastest racing, snow with an iced surface is best, allowing speeds of up to 50mph (80 km/h). Damp, loose snow is much worse. Ski sailing competitions are organized on frozen lakes, golf courses, or even ordinary arable fields. Due to the casual rules, the type of event largely depends on agreement among the participants. In the USA, ski sailing is made more varied by jumps from specially built platforms resembling small ski-jumping hills, and allowing jumps of about 6m without stopping.

History. Ski sailing first appeared in Europe, and then in N.America c.1917. It mainly developed in Scandinavia (chiefly Finland and Sweden), the USA and Canada. >PARAWING SAILING derives from ski sailing, even though some researchers consider it a separate discipline due to the structure of the parawing, which is different from the sails used in ski sailing. Cf.: >WINDSKATING, >ROLLER SKATE SAILING.
R. Friary, 'Ski Sailing', EWS, 1996, vol. III.

SKI SLALOM, an event of >ALPINE SKIING, the object of which is to race downhill, over a winding course marked by artificial obstacles. There are 4 varieties of ski slalom:

SPECIAL SLALOM, in which the contestants ski down a course with the height difference up to 220m (during the 1998 Ol.G. in Nagano the height difference was 200m for women and 220m for men). The final result depends on two runs on different courses. The course is marked with gates, 55-75 for men and 45-60 for women (flags on 180cm tall poles). The gates are alternately marked blue and red. The event has been featured in the Women's W.Ch. since 1931 and Men's W.Ch. since 1932. Special slalom was included in the Ol.G. in 1936.

GIANT SLALOM – two runs down a course with a height difference, which during the 1998 Ol.G. in Nagano was 439m for men and 393m for women. The course is marked with banner-like gates up to 8m wide, with alternating colors red and blue. The distance between the gates cannot be less than 10m. Included into W.Ch. in 1950 and into Ol.G. in 1952.

SUPER GIANT SLALOM, also called *Super-G*, included in international competitions in 1983, W.Ch. in 1987 and Ol.G. in 1988. During the 1998 Ol.G. in Nagano the height difference was 650m for men and 587m for women. The minimum number of banner-like gates is 35 for men and 30 for women. The final result is decided after 2 runs.

PARALLEL SLALOM, in which 2 (exceptionally more) contestants race alongside parallel courses. On each course there is a start gate, 20-30 direction flags and a finish gate. The height difference must be 80-100m. Each gate consists of 2 poles, vertically positioned in the ground, with a 30cm wide piece of cloth strung between them. On the left hand side of the course the flags are red, on the right side – blue. Parallel slalom is, as yet, not part of the Ol.G. For history of ski slalom, see the history of >ALPINE SKIING.

SKIAMACHIA, [Gk. *skia* – shadow + *mache* – combat], in ancient Greece a var. of a shadow fighting, used as boxing practice. A contestant taking part in skiamachia was called a *skiamachos*. In the 2nd cent. AD the satirist Lukian of Samosat ridiculed one of the contestants, who 'practices before the contest, flings up his heels in the air or strikes a blow into the vacuum so as to hit a non-existent opponent' (*Hermotimos*, 33). Another type of shadow fighting was >CHEIRONOMIA. The probable difference between skiamachia and cheironomia was that skiamachia denoted shadow fighting and cheironomia a fight in which a real partner skillfully feigned hits and it looked as if his opponent were fighting with a shadow, being unable to hit him.

SKI-ARCHERY, a sports discipline having the character of the >WINTER BIATHLON, combining, as the name indicates, a ski run and archery; it is also called *ski-arc*. A counterpart of ski-archery but without skis is >ARCATHLON. Ski-archery was started in the 1990s. Presently, it is developing dynamically, particularly in the USA and the Alpine countries. The

Ski slalom on a stamp issued for the 1968 Winter Olympic Games in Grenoble.

Mikhail Botvinov (#31) of Austria leads Andrus Veerpalu (#30) of Estonia and Anders Aukland (#28) of Norway in the men's 50-km cross-country event during the Salt Lake City Winter Olympic Games at Soldier's Hollow in Heber City, Utah.

S

WORLD SPORTS ENCYCLOPEDIA

Ski-archery.

Scott McNeice competes in the 15K sitski event during the Salt Lake 2002 Paralympics at Soldier Hollow in Heber, Utah.

The postage stamp issued for the 2001 winter Universiada in Zakopane.

Fredy Wolf and Viva Commo, left, and Jakob Broger with Volta are seen racing during the skijøring event of the White Turf Horse Race on the frozen lake in St. Moritz, Switzerland.

rules given below are recognized by the US Olympic Committee, but soon they will most probably be modified as ski-archery develops. The contest is held similarly to >WINTER BIATHLON. The course is 12km for men and 8km for women and juniors and consists of 4km laps. Every 4km, that is after the completion of each lap, a contestant, kneeling or standing, makes 4 shots to 4 targets, from a distance of 18m. One arrow is shot at each target. The targets depend on the bow type: if a trad. curved bow is used, the target is black, 16cm in diameter, with a 4cm diameter bull's eye. If composite bows are used, the target is also black, but has a diameter of 10cm with a 3cm diameter bull's eye. The targets are at a height of 1m and can be made of paper, which must be shot through, or from log-like circles, which must be knocked off a special type of ramp. The shooting range cannot be farther than 500m from the end of a lap, forming at the same time the start/finish line in the stadium. The course must cover terrain varying in height from between 25m to 90m. For juniors and contestants practicing ski-archery for fun the course is 4km long with 2 shooting stations. There are also relay races over a distance of 3x4 km, in which each contestant completest a single lap and shoots 4 arrows. Patrol races are held over an identical distance but the rules are different: contestants run together as a team, but after each lap a different contestant does the shooting. The targets are 16cm in diameter. After each miss a contestant must complete a penalty lap, 350m long.

The Internet: United States Olympic Committee – USOC Olympic Online http://www.usoc.org/sports_az/ar/az_rules.html

SKIBOBBING, also skibob racing. A winter sport in which players travel over snow using a vehicle similar to bicycle that has skis instead of wheels. The first skibobs included a frame with 2 runners – the back one fixed and the front one maneuverable, with the rider maintaining balance using the legs and short skis. The recreational version of the skibob has 2 back runners fixed to the frame, which helps to maintain balance, and the third steering runner. In Eng.-speaking countries skibobs are 6-7½ft. long (1.9-2.29m), and courses are 3-5km long. Contestants have two attempts at either a downhill, slalom, giant slalom or parallel slalom (as in Alpine skiing). In professional skibobbing the course must be a minimum of 1,200ft. (about 365m) for women and 2,000ft. (about 600m) for men. In slalom the slope is less steep. In giant slalom contestants must pass through 31 gates. The special slalom has 50-60 gates for men and 30-40 for women. The minimum distance between the slalom gate poles is 4m, in giant slalom – min. 5 and 6m and in downhill – 8 and 10m. Skibobbers reach speeds of up to 160kmh; in recreational skibobbing speeds range from 40 to 65km/h.

History. The first structure with runners and toothed wheels to help it travel over a snow or ice surface was made by an Englishman J.C. Stevens (1892). He called it an ice velocipede. Structures similar to the skibob were used by mountain postmen in Switzerland (about 1902). In 1948 the German G. Gefäller made a prototype skibob, calling it after his name Gefäller Ei (Gefäller's egg). After a series of improvements the structure was patented in 1952.

It was used for the first time in competition in 1951. In 1961 the Fédération Internationale de Skibob, FISB, was established. E.Ch. have been held since 1963 and W.Ch. since 1967.

'Skibobbing', *Encyclopaedia Britannica, Micropaedia*, 1992, vol. 10, 863.

SKI-DOO, see >JET SKI.

SKIING, a family of sport disciplines, including many variants and events. The common feature of all of them is using skis (or a single ski) to move across snow, water, or dry land (grass or roads). The main varieties of >SNOW SKIING are >ALPINE SKIING, >NORDIC SKIING, >FREESTYLE SKIING,>SPEED SKIING and >SKI SAILING.

>SNOWBOARDING uses one ski to move across the surface of snow. Recently, there have been attempts to organize ball games on skis (>SKI FOOTBALL). Folk variants of skiing, different from the Eur. tradition, have survived in some areas of Siberia. There are also various forms of ski racing where the skiers are drawn by animals, e.g. horses or, in Scand. countries, reindeer (*skijoering*). Ski running is also part of >WINTER BIATHLON, with its archery variant (>SKI-ARCHERY).

>WATERSKIING and >BAREFOOT WATERSKIING use techniques similar to those employed in snow skiing but as the names imply, they involve moving across water behind a motor boat.

In >GRASS SKIING and ROLLER SKIING, roller skis are used to move across land on surfaces other than snow.

SKIING FOR THE DISABLED is a var. of skiing technically tailored to the needs of disabled skiers. The 2 main types are cross-country skiing and alpine skiing. Cross-country distances vary between 2.5km and 20km. Skiers with lower limb impairments use so-called seat-skis or chair-skis. Visually impaired skiers are accompanied by guides. Since 1998, there have been international events (including Paralympic Games) for mentally handicapped skiers.

All classical alpine events are practiced by disabled skiers, including the downhill race, slalom, giant slalom and super-giant. Depending on the type of disability, the skiers use single skis or seat-skis. There are also events for visually handicapped skiers, using guides. See also >SPORTS FOR THE DISABLED.

The Internet: http://www.paralympic.org. sports/sections/ask/general.htm

SKIJØRING, a Norw. folk sport, skiing behind an animal [Norw. *ski* + *kjør* – go or *kjoerie* – drive, giving a ride]. The original forms of skijøring comprised skiing behind a reindeer or a horse, presently dogs; the strongest skijøring centers are in northern US states and in Canada. Races are held over a distance of 3-10mi., but there are also *enduro* races over a distance of 20-50mi. A skier is usu. towed by 1-3 dogs. Use of more dogs is not recommended but not forbidden, either.

The equipment consists of shoes and skis (any type, although skis without metal fittings are recommended), ski poles, a harness belt, 3-4in. (7.5-10cm) wide at the back and narrowing towards the front. The dog must have a safety clasp which will release the belt in any danger, e.g. a fall, dogs bolting, entering an area where proper skiing is not possible etc.

Chris Devlin-Young of the USA skis to a gold-medal in the Men's Super-G, class LW-12 sit-ski, during the Salt Lake City Winter Paralympic Games at the Snowbasin Resort in Ogden, Utah.

There are 2 types of belt: with and without braces. The harness cords are 8-15ft. (about 243-457cm) long, and consist of a shock-cord, made of rubber. Two types of harness are used, with the cords forming an 'X' or an 'H'.

History. The tradition of skijøring derives from the use of reindeer to quickly cover long stretches of snow-covered land in countries in the north, particularly in Scandinavia, Finland and northern Russia. As a sport, skijøring developed in the 19th cent. in Norway and northern Sweden, initially as a folk sport. At the beginning of the 20th cent. attempts were made to promote it on the international arena, e.g. in the region of Pol. Podhale, particularly Bukowina Tatrzańska and Zakopane, annual competitions are

Summer skijøring.

Skijøring in the Polish Tatra Mountains.

held. The lack of reindeer in regions other than northern countries and replacement of the horse by mechanical vehicles started vehicle towed skiing, including motor sled towed skiing. In N.America the sport was adopted at the beginning of the 20th cent. and initially was practiced with horses. In time, however, dogs started to be used. Up to the middle of the 1980s skiing behind dogs was considered a training technique for sled dog racing. In 1985 the Alaska Dog Mushers' Association added skijøring to its championships as a separate event. In 1986 the Alaska Skijoring and Pulk Association (ASPA) was established, cf. >PULKA. Next to ASP, the most dynamic organization presently is the N.Amer. Skijoring and Ski Pulk Association, under the auspices of which N.Amer. Championships are held. The sport is practiced mainly in the states of Maine, New England, Minnesota and in Alaska.

B. Hannahs, 'Distance Skijoring', *Tugline*, October 1995; M. Hoe-Raitto and C. Kaynor, *Skijoring. An Introduction to the Sport*, 1988; The Internet: http://www.sleddog-central.com/skijoring.htm

SKINDTRÆKNING, Dan. for 'skin tug-of-war'; a trad. form of wrestling. It consists in pulling a piece of animal skin with both hands; the object is to pull the skin out of the opponent's hands. A var. of this sport is *skinndráttur* [Icel. *skinn* – skin + *dráttur* – pulling], an old Icel. form of competition in which the contestants, sitting on the ground and digging their feet into the ground, held an animal skin by its edges and tried to pull the opponent towards their side or take possession of the largest possible part of the skin and pull it out from the opponent's hands. Cf. >TUG-OF-WAR.

J. Möller, 'Skindtrækning', GID, 1997, 4, 23.

SKIPPING THE FIRE ROPE, a form of competition practiced by the Yi people (about 6.5 mln), one of the 55 ethnic minorities of the People's Republic of China. The Yi live in the southern Chin. provinces of Kwangsi, Kweichow, Sichuan and Yunnan. The competition is part of the annual Flaming Torches Holiday (Huoba Jie) celebrations. Outside a village a 30-50m-long racetrack is marked. The contenders race along the track, each skipping a single fire rope. A contender can be disqualified if he or she starts walking or running. In the course of the competition the runners sometimes burn themselves accidentally. See also other sports and games of the Yi people: >YI COCK FIGHTS, >YI HORSE RACING, >YI PEOPLE JUMPING, >YI PEOPLE SWIMMING, >YI WRESTLING.

Mu Fushan, et al., 'Skipping the Fire Rope', TRAMCHIN.

SKITTLE BOARD, see >DECK GAMES.

SKITTLES, [Dan. *skyttel* – shuttle], one of the oldest bowling games in Europe, known in many countries in different varieties. The oldest manuscripts describe skittles played by Germanic tribes in the first centuries of the modern age. According to L. Kessler, a historian of skittles, skittles was played in the first medieval monasteries in Germany. The game was played with a kegel which was a club carried for self defence. In the game, the kegel represented a sin or temptation and the monks would throw stones at it until they knocked it over. In France, probably owing to Germanic Francs, the oldest manuscripts describe a game called *kayles*, which gave rise to a few types of bowling games. The name of the game in Fr., *quilles*, is today the generic name for bowling. The object of skittles is to knock over nine pins standing in a rhombus or square with a thick oval-ended hardwood log looking like a cheese roll. In many varieties of skittles known in continental Europe, and in some counties of central and western England the log is replaced with balls, which makes the game similar to other varieties of bowling. There are table varieties of skittles, known in Belgian Flanders as >TAFELKEGELSPEL, in England >TABLE SKITTLES or >DEVIL AMONG THE TAILORS, and >BIRINIC in Brittany. Despite all the differences, the table skittles games are similar in that the wooden ball is tied to the pole with a light rope so that it does not fall off the table during the throws. The ball is thrown at the skittles so as to knock them over.

In England, depending on the local tradition, the game is also called >CLOSH, also *cloddy* – something heavy, the name probably comes from the heavy, cigar-like shape of the pins, or >HALF-BALL and *rolly-poly* or *dutch bowls* (the name perhaps comes from a Du. var. of the game brought to England during the reign of the Orange dynasty in the 2nd half of the 17th cent.). The game is played with 9 pins – skittles, shaped like a thick cigar. The skittles (pins) are 1ft. high and weigh 7-9lbs. The 'cheese' (projectile) weighs 12-14lbs. The pins are positioned a minimum of 21ft. from the place from which the 'cheese' is thrown in an effort to knock them down. The alley's width is 3ft. Scoring varies depending on the local tradition. Most frequently, 3pts. are awarded for knocking over all the pins in one throw; 2pts. are awarded if all the pins are knocked over with 2 throws and 1pt. is awarded if all the pins are knocked over with 3 throws. If the player does not knock over all the pins in 3 throws, no points are awarded. According to a different system 1pt. is awarded for each skittle knocked over, which gives a maximum score of 27pts. if all 9 skittles are knocked over three times in 3 attempts. Very often a player who has knocked over all the skittles in the first 3 throws gets 3 additional throws.

Different varieties of skittles are known in Flanders and the Netherlands. Depending on the alley, there are 2 continental varieties of skittles, played in alleys or on large tables with an even, horizontal surface (*glijbaan*) or on slanting or sloping tables (*hellende baan*). The best known var. of skittles played on a flat alley is >VLUGBAAN, also called *vluchtbaan*, played in the vicinity of Belgian Limburg.

SKRABNÆSE, Dan. for 'nose scratching', [Dan. *skrabe* – scratch + *næse* – nose]; a game of skill. Contestants get one stick or a thin bone each. The stick (or bone) has a small hook. The game also needs 50 or more sticks (figures) with different forms, endings, and textures. The sticks are scattered on the table and the object is to pull with the hooked stick the greatest number of sticks, one after another, without causing the other sticks to move. The name derives from the fact that the winner had the right to scratch the loser's nose with a stick most resembling a saw.

J. Möller, 'Skrabnæse', GID, 1997, 3, 74-75.

SKRIDSKO, Dan. for 'skating on bones'; the name is used to refer to a historical form of >SKATING.

SKRUTBOLD, see >STANTO.

SKUBBEKAMP MED HÆNDERNE, Dan. for 'pushing with hands', [Dan. *skubbe* – push + *kamp* – fight + *med* – with + *hænder* – hands, *hånd* – hand]. Two contestants stand facing each other 60cm apart with their own feet forming a straight line heel-to-toe. In this position they push each other with open hands or hit each other with twisted shawls. The contestant who loses balance first loses the contest.

J. Möller, 'Skubbekamp med hænderne', GID, 1997, 47.

SKŰTSJES-ZEILEN, Flem. for 'barge sailing', a trad. var. of a competition between fishing sailboats.

SKŰTSJESILEN, a Frisian type of sailing, developed when the old form of sea fishing started to disappear; its origin was enabled by local traditions, which in the past included competitions on the sea, including regatta-type ones, between fisher's families. Around 1955 the fishers from the ports in Earnewâld, Sneek and Grou started a movement to save the old tradition and organized local committees which bought the aging sailing ships, repairing and restoring them to their former beauty. Regattas between representatives of different towns became one of the forms of their revival; soon the Sintrale Kommisje Skűtsjesilen (SKS) was established, which coordinated these activities in Frisia; it managed to turn formerly arduous sailing skills to sport. In regattas organized by SKS the object is not so much to win but to maintain the ship's class and demonstrate sailing skills. A sort of competition originated in which, in addition to sporting aspects, the ability to preserve tradition was also evaluated. The best skűtsjesilen regatta sailor on record is T. Brouwer of Heerenvin; A. van Akker of Leeuwarden is considered an eminent custodian of the tradition.

Variations in displacement and sail area were among the most difficult elements of standardization; it was agreed that the crew should consist of 14 persons; an average sized fishing boat taking part in the regattas should be about 60ft. long (approx. 18.3m) with a displacement of 35-50 tons. With the old skippers dying out, the young had to learn the old skills. By the 1970s, skűtsjesilen was a full-fledged sport, extremely popular, spectacular and elitist, hence its restriction to family regattas. Wealthier advocates of skűtsjesilen, who wished to practice this sport, but who, for lack of family traditions or connections with the local fishing communities, could not do so, purchased and refurbished a few sailing boats and in the 2nd half of the 1970s started to take part in such open trad. regattas as the Harlingen-Terschelling or the one from Workum in Flandria to the coasts of Holland; they soon grew bored, however, with this restricted access to closed communities and in 1981 they estab. the Lepen Fryske Kampioenskippen Skűtsjesilen whereas the SKS remained restricted to Frisia; this new society was active throughout Holland, comprising the province of Groningen and even engaged in a campaign against the SKS, accusing it of extreme conservatism and elitism. After conflicts lasting a few years, an agreement was reached during the 1989 regatta. Presently skűtsjesilen continues to develop; in Europe it has become a model example of the resuscitation of old sea traditions to create an original sport preserving cultural heritage, as is the case in Cornwall >CORNISH LUGGERS' REGATTAS, >PORT GIGS' REGATTAS.

SKY SURFING, a sport involving jumping from a plane and gliding through the air using a surfboard attached to one's feet. The fall speed, which is usu. about 200km/h, given an initial altitude of about 4,000m, leaves a competitor with about 50sec. to perform his feats. The minimum opening altitude is, according to Amer. standards, 4,000ft. (1,312m). In experimental jumps the admissible minimum opening altitude is 3,500-2,500ft. (1,150-820m). The most spectacular sky surfing figures include the *cartwheel motion* – a cartwheel with right and left turns and the *helicopter* – an evolution consisting of falling headfirst while spinning. The evolutions are judged for 1) technical merit and 2) artistic impression, marks are awarded after the judges have watched a recording made with a helmet-camera carried by another jumper falling parallel to the competitor. Given the fact that both the jumper and the cameraman may lose consciousness during the fall both parachutes are equipped with automatic opening devices so that they open at a safe altitude. This automatic device also helps those jumpers who lose control of their board. Despite all these safety measures there have been a number of fatal accidents reported. J. Jennings died in California when his parachute did not open fully. The most publicized fatal sky surfing accident took place in 1995, when R. Harris died while shooting a TV commercial featuring sky surfing sturds.

History. Sky surfing as sport dates back to the early 1980s and was developed in California. Initially jumpers used ordinary surfboards lying on them as if on a sledge. A Fr. jumper, J. Cruciani, was the first to make a jump in the standing position using a sea surfboard with snowboard bindings. His jump is shown in a movie called *Hibernator*. In 1988 another Fr. jumper, L. Boquet, started jumping with broader boards, similar to those used in skateboarding, and attached permanently to his feet. Yet another Frenchman, P. de Gayardon, developed a unique system of bindings allowing for immediate board release in case of danger or when opening the parachute (called a soft binding and cutaway system). This system was used by the stuntman who played the Silver Surfer in T. Donard's *Pushing the Limits 2.* The main character of this movie was an inspiration for many jumpers and the sport took off immediately after. The first World Freestyle Federation Championship was held in 1990 in Texas and it included some sky surfing events. The WFF chairman P. McKeeman suggested that a camera should be used to record and evaluate jumpers' evolutions. This, in turn, enabled the use of sky surfing sequences on TV which enhanced the popularity of the sport even further. In 1992 the Fr. Parachuting Federation (Federation Française de Parachutisme) was the first in the world to officially recognize sky surf-

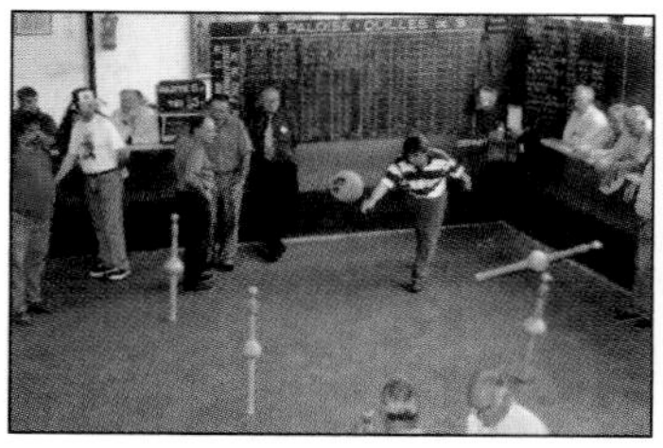

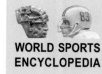

French 9-pin skittles.

Jan Steen, Skittle Players Outside an Inn, *1660-65, oil on canvas.*

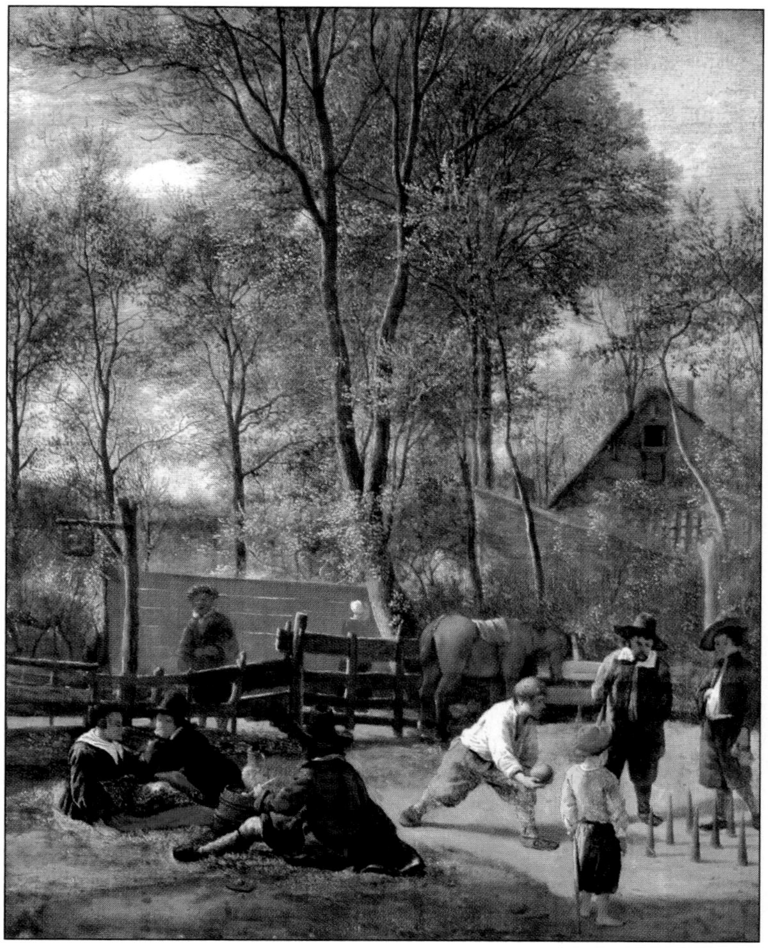

S

WORLD SPORTS ENCYCLOPEDIA

ing as an autonomous sport. In the same year an American, J. Loftis, established the Surflite company which was the first company ever to manufacture sky surfing equipment. The first independent sky surfing world championship took place in 1993 and the first gold medal in team evolutions was awarded to an Amer. team called Gus Wings with de Gayardon as one of its members. The number of competitions held locally in the US (especially in California and Illinois), as well as in Germany and France, was growing quickly. In 1994 a

Skysurfing.

4-member sky surfing team performed during the opening ceremony of the Winter Ol.G. in Albertville. Later Belgium became one of the most active countries in propagating this sport. In the same year women started competing in sky surfing. An Amer. jumper, A. Baylie-Haass, was one of the first women to take up sky surfing. 10 sky surfing teams competed in the 1995 Extreme Sports Games. Today, the major international sky surfing organization is Skysportif International after it replaced the World Freestyle Federation. National, continental and world records are not recognized and maintained yet but work is in progress on developing appropriate standards. Several sky surfing couples got married in the air, e.g. A. Baylie-Haass and G. Haass. The sport, although it does not enjoy fully international popularity, still attracts a lot of spectators due to its particularly spectacular character and is still developing.

J. Tomlison, 'Skysurfing', *The Ultimate Encyclopedia of Extreme Sports*, 1996.

SKYDE KRAGE, Dan. for 'shooting the crow', [Dan. *skyde* – shoot + *krage* – crow]. A game of strength and skill. One contestant lies on his back with his hands stretched out; the other contestant stands on his hands. The lying contestant raises his legs and the standing contestant leans down so as to support his chest against the lying contestant's soles and holds him by the ankles. The lying contestant must then throw the other contestant forward. The relation between the name and the exercise is not clear; the sport is known not only in Denmark but it seems that only in Denmark has it been granted its status and a name.

J. Möller, 'Skyde krage', GID, 1997, 3, 93.

SKYDE PAPEGØJEN, Dan. for 'shooting the parrot', a var. of shooting developed in Denmark, as well as in other countries (LE >PAPEGAUT, >PAP-

Slå trilla on a 19th cent. illustration.

INGO SHOOTING, >POPINJAY, >COCK SHOOTING). The tradition of skyde papegøjen in Denmark goes back to the 14th cent. First a bow was used and later, once gunpowder had been discovered, firearms became popular. The sport is also known as *fugleskydning* (bird shooting). Initially the bird was positioned sideways to the shooter and the object was to shoot it down with one shot. When rifles were introduced, the bird was placed on an 8-10m high pole, facing the shooter, who was about 30m away from the target. The shooters were awarded bonus points for shooting off individual parts of the bird, to which special copper plates were fastened. These parts were the tail, wings, neck, crown on the bird's head, ring in the beak, an 'armor' wrapped around the bird's body and apples or 'eggs', i.e. copper balls attached to the bird's wings or feet.

J. Möller, 'Fugleskydning', GID, 1997, 4, 74.

SKYDE SOLDATER, Dan. for 'shooting the soldiers', [Dan. *skyde* – shoot + *soldater* – soldiers, *soldat* – soldier]. Two teams compete, facing each other in rows a few steps apart and taking turns aiming at each other with a ball. The players' positions are decided by the captain; usu. with the best players at the top and the poorest at the end. The player at whom the ball is thrown can neither escape nor duck. When hit, he joins the opponents' team, and is positioned at the very end of the row. The game ends when all the players are in one row.

J. Möller, 'Skyde soldater', GID, 1997, 1, 24.

SKYDE UGLER, Dan. for 'shooting the owls', [Dan. *skyde* – shoot + *ugler* – owls, *ugle* – owl, eagle owl]. A target is drawn on the wall and attempts are made to hit it with a cane. Ten steps from the target a player touches one end of a cane to the ground, holding it with his hand; the other end touches his forehead. Then he runs around the cane, all the time keeping one end on the ground. After ten spins the player starts a dizzy run towards the target with the cane still held against the forehead.

J. Möller, 'Skyde ugler', GID.

SKYGGEFANGER, Dan. for 'a shadow catcher', [Dan. *skygge* – shadow + *fanger* – catcher, *fanger* – catch]; a game of skill, the object of which is to catch one's opponent's shadow, which can hide where the shadow disappears.

J. Möller, 'Skyde ugler', GID, 1997, 2.

SKYROS, a present-day Gk. urban game. Two teams, of usu. 10-15 children, form 2 rows about 75ft. apart from one another. In the middle there is a ball. At a whistle, the players all start running towards the ball. The player who gets there first tries to pass it to his partners so that they can take it beyond the opposing team's line. If successful, they score a point. The game is not unlike the ancient >EPISKYROS.

SLÅ EN ANDENS HÆNDER FRA HINANDEN, Dan. for 'to break up the other's hands', [Dan. *slå* – strike, break + *andens* – other, another + *hænder* – hands, *hånd* – hand + *fra* – from + *hinanden* – one another]. A folk form of hand wrestling. One contestant extends his hands forward, with the fists held together, thumbs up. The other player's task is to separate the fists, using the index fingers.

J. Möller, 'Slå andens hænder fra hinanden', GID, 1997, 4, 46.

SLÅ HINANDEN AF PINDEN, Dan. for 'knocking off the stick', [Dan. *slå* – strike, break up + *hinanden* – one another + *af* – off + *pinden, pind* – pole, stick]. Two players, each holding a sack of hay, sit astride a thick pole, at least 1m above the ground, and try to knock each other off the pole, using the sacks. Only the body or the legs can be struck. In principle only one back is used, the other is held behind the back. It is important that the pole is suspended over a soft surface, so that the players are not injured when falling down.

J. Möller, 'Slå hinanden af pinden', 1997, 4, 49.

SLÅ KATTEN AF TØNDEN, Dan. for 'knocking a cat off the barrel', also known as *katten af tønden* or *tøndeslagning*, [Dan. *slå* – strike, break up + *katten* <*kat* – cat + *af* – off + *tønden, tønde* – barrel, keg]. A Dan. folk sport connected with the last day of the carnival. A barrel is hung on a rope over the street. In the past (more or less until the end of the 18th cent.) the barrel contained a live cat or 2 cats tied together. This was later replaced with a dead animal or a cat puppet. In the 20th cent. the game trans-

formed into a children's game and the barrel contained oranges, apples and candy. The object was to break up the barrel with a club. The player who managed to do this was elected the Cat King of the Year (*Kattekonge*). The king elected the Cat Queen (*Kattedronning*), with whom he went to a grand reception, being admitted for free whereas the other participants had to pay.

J. Möller, 'Slå katten af tønden', GID, 1997, 4.

SLÅ KATTEN UR TUNNAN, Swed. for 'knocking the cat off the barrel', a folk game. There were a few varieties: in one the cat was placed in a barrel, the barrel was closed with a heavy top; players threw stones at the barrel or hit it with clubs. When the panic-stricken animal tried to jump out of the barrel and escape this torment, it merely hit its head against the lid. This game, like others in which an animal was hurt, was considered unbecoming a moral Christian in Protestant Sweden and disappeared in the 18th cent., together with other similar or even more brutal games, such as >DRA HUVUDET AV GÅSEN. When at the beginning of the 19th cent. an owner of an inn in Malmö tried to offer slå katten ur tunnan to his guests, he was forcibly persuaded to abandon the idea under the indignant pressure of public opinion. M. Helspong, a historian of Swed. sport, wrote: 'Swedish rural sport in the eighteenth and nineteenth centuries reveals relative lack of violence. In a Eur. context this is somewhat exceptional [...]. We can sense a Lutheran attitude towards tormenting animals as a popular amusement behind this state of affairs'. 'A Timeless Excitement, Swedish Agrarian Society and Sport in the Pre-Industrial Era', IJHS, Dec. 1997, p. 20.

SLÅ KNO, Dan. for 'hitting the bones', [Dan. *slå* – strike, break up + *kno, knogle* – bone]. The players take turns hitting their opponent's fist with their own fist. The game ends when either of the contestants withdraws. Blows can be inflicted from the top, from any side and directed at the opponent's bones or metacarpus.

J. Möller, 'Slå kno', GID, 1997, 4, 52.

SLÅ KOKKEN AF HØNEN, see >MUNK.

SLÅ POTTER I STYKKER, Dan. for 'breaking up pots', [Dan. *slå* – strike, break up + *potter* – pots, flower pots, sg. *potte* + *i* – into + *stykker* – pieces, sg. *stykke*]. A folk game, connected with the celebrations of the last Monday before Lent. A pot or a large clay flower pot or bowl is put at a certain distance from the contestant, who is blindfolded. A stick is put into his hand. He is turned round, like in >BLIND-MAN'S BUFF, and his task is to strike the vessel with the stick. He has only 3 attempts; if unsuccessful, the game is continued by another player. The player, who completely breaks up the vessel, is the winner.

J. Möller, 'Slå potter i stykker', GID, 1997, 4, 88.

SLÅ EN SKRÆDDER AF BÆNKEN, Dan. for 'throwing the tailor off the bench', [Dan. *slå* – strike, break up + *en* – one + *skrædder* – tailor + *af* – off + *bænken, bænk* – bench]. A folk form of an old Dan. game. Two players sit opposite each other on a bench, legs crossed, each of them covering his left ear with his left hand. The players then take turns striking the hands covering the ear until one of them falls off the bench.

J. Möller, 'Slå en skrædder af bænken', GID, 1997, 4, 49-50.

SLÅ SMUT, a Dan. var. of >DUCKS AND DRAKES, [Dan. *slå* – strike + *smut, smutte* – to speed].

SLÅ TRILLA, a Swed. folk game between 2 teams of 3-4 persons. The contestants are lined up on a long, narrow pitch with a hard, even surface. The object is to strike a hard wooden disc using sticks with curved or flattened ends.

Equipment. The *trilla* or *trissa* is made of wood; most often it is an 8-in. thick circle cut off a trunk. The curved stick used to strike the *trilla* looks like a hockey stick, although in some varieties the stick is not curved but flattened and looks more like a long oar. In games played among rural populations, fence pales were used.

Pitch. In the old var. the game was played on dirt roads and village streets. In this original version the pitch dimensions were defined by natural obstacles, e.g. the road width or its length, along which the rolling *trilla* could reach the place where the opponent was standing.

Rules of play. As rules were local and varied considerably from place to place, it is difficult to refer to any real standard. More often than not, however, the game was played according to the following rules: the game begins with the players of one team throwing the *trilla* towards the players of the opposing team, all lined up. They try to stop the rolling *trilla* with their sticks; if the first player fails to stop the disc, the next players, standing at a certain distance from the preceding players, try to stop the disc. When the disc is finally stopped or when it comes to rest on its own, the team receiving the *trilla* strikes it back from that spot. The object of the game is to strike the *trilla* so hard towards the opponents that they find it very difficult to stop; as the distance grows, returning the disc becomes increasingly difficult. There is no time limit; in Swed. villages the game was often played for hours on end, to be stopped only by the setting sun. Many comic elements were connected with slå trilla.

History. The oldest information about slå trilla comes from the middle of the 18th cent.. The game was very popular mainly in southern and central Sweden, but it had its counterparts in Finland (then under the influence of Sweden), in Denmark (see >SLÅGTRILLE) and northern Germany, where it was known as *trudespiel* and *verdriewen*. At the end of the 19th cent. V. Balck, an officer in the Swed. army, attempted to popularize many sports in Sweden and in his *Illustrated book of sports* (*Illustrerad idrottsbok*, 1886) he advocated the adaptation of Swed. folk games to modern sports; he proposed many modifications of the folk var. of slå trilla, e.g. backlines were introduced and the teams changed sides after half time. The sticks were to be made from especially bent wooden rods, so that they did not break during the game and the disc – *trilla* – was to be specially reinforced. The rules were not generally adopted, however. Today slå trilla is disappearing, although in many places attempts are made by local folk and ethnographic societies to revive it.

M. Hellspong, *Slå trilla. En lek på gränsen mellan folklig och modern idrott, Rig. Tidskrift Utgiven av Föreningen för Svensk Kulturhistoria i Samarbete med Nordiska Museet och Folklivsarkivet i Lund*, årgång 73, 1990, 1.

SLÅGTRILLE, a Dan. street game, [Dan. *slag* – strike, blow + *trille* – roll, also a piece of a cylindrically shaped trunk]. The game is played by 2-12 players, divided into 2 teams. A relatively heavy circle or a hoop, 3cm thick and 10-20cm in diameter is used (an ordinary wheel can be used). Each player gets a thick stick, at least 1m long (e.g. like a hockey stick). The teams line up facing each other. The server takes hold of the hoop and starts to roll it towards the opponents. Their task is to stop the hoop, using their sticks, legs or hands. From the place where it was stopped it is rolled back (a 3-step run up is allowed). The hoop cannot be thrown. Sometimes it can be pushed with a stick, particularly if it gets stuck. Cf. >SLÅ TRILLA.

J. Möller, 'Slagtrille', GID, 1997, 1.

SLALOM RUNNING, a type of running event that has its origins in ski slalom and during which runners run along a grassy course where they have to pass specially arranged poles. The most popular slalom running distances are 100 and 400m (the latter called the grand slalom). The sport requires excellent motor coordination and a good sense of balance. The races are most frequently pair events (similarly to ski parallel slalom) and the poles are spaced at 2-3m intervals.

SLALOM, a method of moving downhill over a winding course marked by artificial obstacles [Norw. *slad* – sloping + *lom* – path]. It is the basis of many obstacle races, among them >SKI SLALOMS (see >ALPINE SKIING) or >WHITE WATER KAYAKING AND CANOEING. A slalom race is also an element of competition in contests of skill, car and motorcycle races, e.g. the best policeman of the year contest or in popular car and motorcycle rallies.

SLANGEBØSSE, a Dan. var. of sling; see >SLING-SHOOTING.

SLÄNGTAJ, a Swed. var. of folk wrestling, in which the contestants hold each other by the collars or lapels of the jacket; during the game the opponents face each other, [Swed. *slänga* – throw, throw back + *taj, tag* – hold, grip]. A form of wrestling practiced under this name in Småland is, in principle, a regular var. of wrestling, better known in Sweden as >KRAGTAG. In Norway a similar form of wrestling is called >SLENGJETAK. In other parts of Sweden a similar form of wrestling is practiced under the names of: >ARMKAST, >ARMTAG, >KRAVETAG, >SLÅNGTAJ. Cf. other var. of Scand. wrestling, in which contestants hold their opponents by the collar, e.g. the Icel. >LAUSA GLÍMA; see also >CLOTHES HOLD (BELT HOLD) WRESTLING.

SLAVENHANDEL, Dan. for 'slave trade', [Dan. *slave* – slave + *handel* – trade]. A hide-and-seek type game played in Dan. school yards or playgrounds. The players include a 'slave trader', a 'grower' and 4 'overseers', of whom 2 belong to the 'grower' and 2 to the 'trader'. The rest are 'slaves'. The 'grower' buys a few 'slaves' and gives them to the overseers to be looked after. Then he returns to buy new slaves. At this point the ones bought earlier attempt to escape. The 'overseers' try to catch them – they must touch them and shout 'One!'. The 'slave' must then go back to the overseer. The 'grower' returns and asks how many 'slaves' have escaped and then goes to the 'trader' for help. If the trader still has 'slaves', they are given to the 'overseers' whereas the 'grower' and the 'trader' start looking for the escapees. Obviously, the 'slaves', who are being looked after by the 'overseers', try to escape. The game ends when all the 'slaves' have been caught.

J. Möller, 'Slavehandel', GID, 1997, 2.

SLED DOG RACING, a sport in which sleds or carriages hauled by pure breed dogs compete with one another. The sport in its original form was a race of dog-drawn sleds and for a century the sport was limited to polar zones. In the 1970s the sport grew in popularity, first among foreign competitors coming to the region, then in several remote countries in the south. The racing tracks range anywhere from a dozen km in length for one-day races up to several hundred km in longer races. Short races are held 3 times on the same course, all three results adding up to a competitor's final score. During the W.Ch. in 1978 a course of 17.5mi. (28km) was covered 3 times (52.5mi. = 84km in total) by the winner within 3hrs. 13min. 4sec. Minimal differences in time results are characteristic of even long races, e.g. during the 15-day Iditarod race in 1978 the winner beat the runner-up by only 1sec.

Wheel carriage dog races are held not only as the summer var. of the sport but in some countries also as an option to sled races in the case of insufficient snow fall.

Dogs. The main breeds of sled dogs are the Siberian husky and the Alaskan malamute. Both are extremely resistant to cold and strain and can sleep in temps. as low as –40°F (-72°C) by burrowing into the snow. In summer they normally burn about 800 calories a day, while in winter during competitions their daily need is roughly 10,000cal. The number of dogs per sled is not universally determined and it is usu. 7-9. In some prestigious races the number of dogs can reach up to 16. Their usual speed during a race is up to 7mph (11km/h).

Equipment. In winter the main piece of equipment is a tapered sled, capable of storing enough personal equipment and food for several days of racing. Occasionally, an injured or ill dog is transported on a sled. In the summer sleds are replaced with 3-wheel carriages open at the back, so as to allow the driver to mount and dismount easily.

History. Sled dog racing is an ancient sport known in regions inhabited by Eskimos and in Scandinavia since at least the 18th cent. It was popularized in N.Amer., esp. Canada and Alaska in the 19th cent., when races took place to areas where gold had just been discovered. Such races and the way trappers used dog sleds for traveling were described by the Amer. writer J. London (1876-1916), who took part himself in those travels, in such novels as *The Call of the Wild* (1903), and *White Fang* (1906). The topic was also reflected in the writings of many other Amer. and Can. authors, e.g. *Baree, Son of Kazan* (1917) and *The Gold Hunters* (1910), both among the works of J.O. Curwood (1878-1927). Even after the gold fever let up, sled dogs continued to be a popular means of transportation in winter in areas where there was but one alternative: to go on foot. Dog sleds were used by R. Amundsen (1872-1928) during his travels to polar regions and in 1911 dog sleds let him win the race to the South Pole against the Englishman R. F. Scott. In 1908 the first proper sports race, the *All-Alaskan Sweepstake*, had sled teams racing from Candle to Nome and back, 408mi (656km). In 1916 the first race called the Hudson Bay Derby took place, and in 1923 the Banff Alberta Dog Derby was held. When in 1925 in the Alaskan town of Nome a diphtheria epidemic broke out, in the severe winter the only possible contact with the sick town inhabitants was by means of dog sleds. The dramatic transport of vaccines had broad coverage in the press and added to the popularity of dog sleds, esp. in Canada and Northern New England, USA. In 1936 the Laconia Sled Dog club from New Hampshire organized a W.Ch. Derby. In 1966 the International Sled Dog Racing Association was established. In Europe, outside Scandinavia, sled dog racing became popular only around 1992. Among the most important international events are, apart from the W.Ch., also Iditarod and Yukon Quest (in 1998 sponsored by the Ger. company Fulda). Now, worldwide over 200 races are held each year. The most outstanding racers before 1939 were considered to be the Canadian E. St. Goddard and Alaskan L. Spala; after 1945, in the 1970s G. 'Muhammad' Attla, an Indian from the Athabaskan tribe, and D. Macky and R. Swenson were impressive performers.

Women had already made their mark in sled dog racing before 1928, when in one of the races in Alaska, 123mi (198km) long, a woman known as E.P. Ricker's wife took part (female names related to sport were not published in the press, in order 'not to violate the good of the household'). *The New York Times* described her as 'the only woman who ever had courage or skill to enter this race against the best men drivers of the continent'. However, Ms Ricker failed to finish the race because two of her dogs were exhausted and she decided to spare them. In

Sled dog racing.

Three-time Iditarod Trail Sled Dog Race champion Jeff King, from Denali Park, Alaska, with rider Angelo Grelli of San Francisco, drives his dog team up 4th Avenue in Anchorage, Alaska during the ceremonial start of the Anchorage to Nome sled dog race in March 2003.

S

WORLD SPORTS ENCYCLOPEDIA

the 1980s and '90s several women became internationally successful, also in the Iditarod race. The most famous of them is S. Butcher. Cf. > SKIJØRING. S.A.G.M. Crawford, 'Sled Dog Racing', EWS, 1996, III.

SLEDGE HOCKEY, a var. of >ICE HOCKEY for the disabled, played by contestants sitting on sleds with runners similar to skates. The sport was developed for amputees or patients with leg injuries preventing skating. The game is played on a standard ice rink between two teams of 6 players each, including the goal keeper. Three periods of 15min. each are played. The basic equipment includes flat sleds with metal skates, a seat and a backrest. The players have 2 short ice hockey sticks, which they use to strike the puck and push themselves against the ice in order to move around the rink; on one end of the stick there is a metal tip used to push back and on the other – blades used to strike the puck. The clothing includes protectors against puck and stick hits and a helmet with a wired face mask. The game originated in the 1980s. As it became very popular, particularly in the Scand. countries, Canada and Great Britain, it also attracted able-bodied contestants. Sledge hockey teams have participated in winter Paralympics since 1994. Contestants also compete in the world cup. See also >SPORTS FOR THE DISABLED.
The Internet: Slege-Hockey Games, http://www.lboro.ac.uk/research/paad/wheelpower/shgame.htm; http://www.paralympic.org/sports/sections.sledge-hockey/general.htm

Slyngbold.

SLENGJETAK, also >ARMESLOENGJA, a form of Norw. folk wrestling, in which the contestants pull by one another the collar; similar to the Swed. >SLÄNGTAJ and Icelandic >LAUSA GLÍMA.

SLIDING, a term denoting any ice sliding, on shoe soles or using small wooden blocks to extend the slide, and also using skates (>SKATING). These simple forms of sliding, so popular in the past, are gradually disappearing as skating equipment is becoming more and more easily available. Preparation of the slides was an art and its tradition was passed from generation to generation. When the slide could not be 'naturally' made on a pond, lake, river, stream or simple ditch, then the snow was first trampled, then leveled with a piece of cloth (sometimes a coat or jacket), and finally made slippery with the shoes until a glassy, icy surface was obtained. When made, it lent itself to excellent slides, the length of which varied from a few to a few dozen meters. Weather and topography permitting, ice paths were prepared on hill slopes. Wealthier boys and girls had skates, but the poorer ones used the soles of their shoes. Ł. Gołębiowski provided the following description of the game:

A frozen surface tempts one to slide, the young learn to slide and then slide on a small stream, or a ditch. And the adults enjoy sliding. Later skates began to be used – made of bones or steel. They were tied to the shoes and soon the skilled runner, keeping his balance, slides, makes turns and seems to be more agile than a bird, he is faster than a horse, your eye can hardly see him, soon he covers the longest distances, he will bring you a loaf of bread, still warm, from a few miles afar; but brave sailor, in your swallow-like flight beware of the holes in the frozen sur-

face, before your eye can see, you will be thrust into it, soon you will be under the ice and your beloved one, your friend, your parents will wait in vain for your return.
[Games and Pastimes of Various Social Classes, 1831, 21]

SLING SHOOTING, one of the oldest forms of projectile fighting in many ancient cultures. Mentioned in the *Bible*, where David with the help of a sling defeats Goliath, a Philistine giant, whom nobody else has dared oppose:

When the Philistine drew nearer to meet David, David ran quickly toward the battle line in the direction of the Philistine. David put his hand in his bag, took out a stone, slung it, and struck the Philistine on his forehead; the stone embedded itself in his brow, and he fell prostrate on the ground. Thus David prevailed over the Philistine with a sling and a stone; he dealt the Philistine a mortal blow, and there was no sword in David's hand.
[1 Samuel, 17, 48]

The sling was used by Assyrian, Persian and Gk. armies. In ancient Rome it was known as the *funda*. The sling was used effectively in battle until the Middle Ages. Kon, an Icelandic hero, was described in the *Poetic Edda*, as one who liked to use the sling for fun:

A young Kon was riding in a young forest
He shot his sling, he lured the birds;
a crow, sitting on the branch, spoke to him:
"Why, my young king, do you lure the birds?
It becomes you to bridle a horse
[...] and conquer armies [...]'.
[*Rightula*, trans. from Polish after A. Załuska-Strömberg]

The sling is still used today among the tribes of Oceania, Indonesia and South America. It was a popular recreational activity in primitive cultures. Among the Ind. tribes living in the southeast of USA, sling shooting competitions at which bets were placed were referred to as >CHENCO.
The oldest types of sling consisted of 2 cords attached to a piece of leather on which the missile was placed. The thrower, in military tradition referred to as the slinger (in ancient Rome Lat. *fundibalarius* or *fundibalator*, Ger. *Schleuderer*, and later *Wurfschütze*) whirled the weapon above his head, imparting centrifugal force to it, before releasing one of the 2 cords discharging the missile at the target. The basic concept of the sling was present in early catapults, but the technical design was different. It usu. consisted of a single arm or 2 arms of wooden logs, the ends of which were platforms hollowed out in the shape of a big spoon, on which the missile (usu. a large stone) was placed. The arms of the *ballista* were tensioned by ropes and a connecting rod, and then the tension was rapidly released, which resulted in the stone being propelled over a distance of a few dozen meters, sufficient to hurl stones at the castle under siege. In ancient Rome this piece of military equipment was dubbed the catapult, a word that survives to this day and one which gave rise to many similar names in most Eur. languages (Fr. *catapulte*, Ger. *Katapult* etc.). In time, such slings (catapults) were used to hurl not only stones, but also spears. Its much smaller version was called a crossbow. After the invention of elastic the trad. sling, in time withdrawn from the military use and more often used by boys in various competitions, was

gradually replaced by another device, which in most languages retained the name of sling or its derivates (Eng. *slingshot*, Ger. *Steinschleuder*, Rus. *rogatka*), although its principle was slightly different. It was made of a 'Y' shaped twig or metal, with two pieces of elastic stretched between the two top points of the Y, into which a stone 1-2cm in diameter was put. The stone was hurled when tension was applied to both pieces of elastic and then simultaneously and suddenly released at a target. The trad. homemade slingshot has evolved into a modern rendition called a 'wrist rocket'.

SLINGER, a var. of >SKITTLES, with elements of >CRICKET, practiced in Great Britain. The object of the game is to knock off 6 figures using a ball, which is not rolled but thrown. The ball must not only knock off the figures but also hit a stone target, similar to the wicket in cricket.

SLINGING THE MONKEY, see >DECK GAMES.

SLOPE RUNNING, also known as mountain, hill, etc. running. A type of running competition in which the contestants have to run up a slope, hill or a mountain to reach the finish line. This sport is or was known in many cultures (see >MONTENEGRO RACES, the Eng. >FELL RUNNING, or the Scot. >HILL RUNNING). Certain elements of slope running were present in the trad. Native Amer. Indian races although running up a slope was not their main objective (>NORTH AMERICAN INDIAN RACES).

SLYNGBOLD, Dan. for 'a ball with a loop', [Dan. *slynge* – loop + *bold* – ball]. A strength sport, fairly static. Its object is to seize the largest possible part of the field by throwing a light medicine ball with a loop; the ball's weight depends on the players' age – the younger the players, the lighter the ball. The game is played on a rectangular field, about 150m long and about 15-20m wide. The center field, about 40m long, is marked in its middle; on both sides of the center field there are side fields, each about 30m long; behind the end fields there are 2 retreat fields, each about 30m long. The game is played by 2 teams of 5-10 players. The game begins with a player taking a running start and throwing the ball towards the opponents, who try to catch the ball and throw it right back. If none of the players manages to catch the ball, it is picked up from where it has fallen by the player who is closest to it. If a player manages to catch the ball in flight, he can run up to 3 steps towards the opponents' field before throwing the ball back. If the ball thrown in this way is caught by the opponents, the team throwing the ball does not score any points unless the receiver succeeds in reaching the end line, within his 3 allotted steps. If he does not manage to do this or if he fails to catch the ball, the throwing team scores a point and the team losing the points resumes the game from the throw line. If the throw is poor and drops to the ground, without reaching the opponents' field, it can be repeated. If a thrown ball drops behind the side lines, it is thrown in perpendicularly to the side line and the game is continued from this spot.
A similar game called >SCHLEUDERBALL, is practiced in northern Germany, where the sport was very common in gymnastic organizations. Presently, it is

Sling shooting.

Billy Bridges of Canada is tackeled by Marcus Holm of Sweden during the Canada and Sweden Bronze Medal Sledge Hockey match during the Salt Lake City Winter Paralympic Games.

almost completely forgotten; the Ger. slyngbold was different from the Dan. var.: instead of the 3 steps rule the so-called *Shockstoss*, a surprise throw, was used, made with one hand or both hands without any loop and without swinging the arm. In the Dan. var. throws using this hook shot can be made with the body turning around the vertical axis (*drejekast*) or by the Frisian throw technique (*frisisk kast*), in which the ball is whirled around the loop.
J. Möller, 'Slyngbold', GID, 1997, 1, 39.

SLYNGE, see >WIUCHA.

SMÆKKE FLEUR, Dan.for 'to swat flies' or 'fly-swatter'. The contestants sit on the chairs in a circle and put their hand palms up on their knees. One contestant walks around and tries to strike the sitting players' hands. If a player does not want to be struck, he must take his hands back, but only when the striker has taken a swing.
J. Möller, 'Smække fluer', Gid, 1997, 3.

SMOKE-FREE WALK, a var. of recreational walk instituted by the Singaporean Ministry of Health with the cooperation of the Sports Council. The first Smoke-Free Walk took place in Singapore in 1987 under the slogan 'Towards a Non-Smoking Nation' – there were 1,600 participants. The objective of the event is not merely the popularization of anti-nicotine slogans, but also affording smokers an opportunity to go a few hours without a cigarette in the midst of a supportive community. In addition, the event is intended as a psychological synchronization of physical training and the mustering of will power. The ultimate aim is to apply this exercise in self-control in everyday life.

SNAIL RACING, a form of competition in which snails race across a distance of 50cm or more, popular in France (World Mollusc Racing Championships in Marseilles) and Great Britain (Snail Racing World Championships). The fastest snails cover the distance of 50cm in less than 3min.

SNAKES, a simple skating game in which a team of skaters has to slalom around various obstacles on ice, while driving a puck with a hockey stick. The game may be played on a frozen pond and the hockey stick may be substituted with a branch. Obstacles can be formed by poles, slalom gates, clubs driven into wooden bases, etc. Participants form two teams. The leading players of each team hold hockey sticks and pucks and, at a signal, begin to slalom between the obstacles. Having completed the slalom track, they return to the starting point and pass the stick and the puck on to the next player and so on. If a skater knocks down an obstacle, he can continue only after he has lifted it up and placed it back in its original position. The team which successfully completes the track first, wins the game.
I.N. Chkhannikov, 'Snakes', GIZ, 1953, 90.

SNEBOLDKAMP, Dan. for 'snow battle, snowball fight', [Dan. *sne* – snow, *bold* – ball + *kamp* – battle, fight]. A snow castle was built, which was defended by one group while the other group attempted to seize it. The tradition of a battle for a snow castle in Denmark and Sweden goes back to the Middle Ages. *The Description of Northern Countries* by O. Magnus (1490-1557) contains information about sneboldkamp and a drawing featuring a grand bastion built of snow, which was conquered in various ways, not only by throwing snowballs but also by digging tunnels under it.
J. Møller, 'Sneboldkamp', GID, 1997, 4.

SNOB, see >CRICKET.

SNOOKER, considered to be a different game than pool because of the different number of balls on the table, see *Rules of the Games* (1974) and *The Concise Columbia Encyclopedia* (1984). However, as snooker is very similar to pool games, in many specialist publications and rules it is considered one of the pool games, see e.g. M. Bach and K.W. Kühn, *Pool Billiards. Equipment, rules, strategy* (1991). Other publications either avoid any distinctions into the trad. pool billiards and snooker (e.g. *The Cambridge Encyclopedia*, ed. D. Crystal, 1990) or distinguish between pocket billiards (a table with pockets) and carom billiards (a table without pockets) (e.g. *Encyclopedia Americana International*, 1979); in the latter case snooker belongs to the same group as other pool games and Eng. billiards.
Rules. Snooker is played upon a billiards table. Different balls are used – 1 white cue ball is used by

both players together with 15 red balls worth 1pt. each and 6 colored balls worth differing points: yellow – 2pts., green – 3pts., brown – 4pts., blue – 5pts., pink – 6pts., black – 7pts.
The 15 red balls are set in a triangle (using a special triangular frame, in the US called the rack) between the pink and the black balls so that the triangle points towards baulk with the red at the tip touching the pink ball.
The object is to score more points than the opponent by potting (i.e. sinking) balls and, less commonly, by playing snookers that will force the opponent to make a foul stroke and thus give points away. Players flip a coin to decide who goes first. To prepare for the first shot, the player concerned sets the cue ball anywhere within the D so that it can be aimed at a red ball.
Each turn is called a 'break' and consists of a series of strikes of the cue ball that come to an end when a player makes a non-scoring strike or a foul stroke. While there are reds on the table, a break must always start by potting a red. When a red has been potted the player must next pot a nominated colored ball (if it is not obvious which color is being aimed at, the player is required to orally make this clear). A colored ball that has been potted after a red is immediately returned to the table on its home spot. After a colored ball, another red ball must be potted followed by a color and so on until there are no red balls left. After the final red ball and its accompanying color have been potted, the balls must be potted in order starting with yellow and finishing with black.
In all cases, the next ball to be potted or color nominated to be potted must be the first ball struck by the cue-ball or a foul shot is declared. So when a player has next to pot a red ball, if a ball other than a red ball is struck first, it is a foul stroke.
As soon as the break comes to an end the other player has a chance to make a break which must always start with a red ball if there are any left, regardless of how the last break ended. The cue ball must be played from where it finished after the previous shot unless it went in-off. Points are scored according to the value of each ball potted.
Snooker is not all about potting balls – very often it is more advantageous to play safe by putting the cue ball into a position such that the opponent will find the next shot very difficult to play or to score from. Whenever a player is not able to directly play the ball to be struck with a straight shot, that player is said to be 'snookered' on that ball. In this case the opponent is required either to swerve the white ball around another ball or to bounce the cue ball off one or more cushions in order to hit the target ball. With either type of shot, it is difficult to judge the outcome and so the player who engineered the snooker has a good chance either of winning points because the opponent plays a foul shot or at least benefiting from a good position for the next turn.
A foul shot is declared in any of the following scenarios: a) The cue-ball first strikes a ball other than the next ball to be potted or the color nominated to be potted, b) whenever the cue ball goes in-off (into a pocket) or leaves the table, c) whenever an incorrect ball is potted.
The player who committed a foul stroke receives no points for that stroke even if a legitimate ball was potted and the break is over. However, any points made in the break prior to the foul shot are kept.
Whenever a foul stroke is committed, the opponent receives some penalty points: if the ball being played is the black or the foul occurred because the black ball was struck first incorrectly or potted incorrectly, then 7pts. are forfeited; if the ball being played is the pink or the foul occurred because the pink ball was struck first incorrectly or potted incorrectly, then 6pts. are forfeited; if the ball being played is the blue or the foul occurred because the blue ball was struck first incorrectly or potted incorrectly, then 5pts. are forfeited, otherwise 4pts. are forfeited.
Where more than one foul occurs in one stroke, only one penalty applies but it is always the largest applicable penalty. So if a red is being played and the player misses hits the yellow first, pots the green and goes in-off, only 4pts. are awarded to the opponent. However, if the brown is being played and the player hits it first but accidentally knocks it onto the pink ball which falls into a pocket, 6pts. are awarded to the opponent.
Eventually all balls except the black have been potted. At this stage, if the difference in score is more

than 7pts., the game ends since it is only sporting to assume that a player will not miss a direct shot and so there is no way for the losing player to win. Otherwise, the last ball is potted in the usual way.
If the game is drawn, then the black is re-spotted and the cue ball is moved to and played from anywhere within the D. The players flip a coin to decide who plays first and play continues. The player who pots the black wins the game.
At any point during the game a player can concede the game. A player would normally concede when

WORLD SPORTS ENCYCLOPEDIA

S

Snail races.

Matthew Stevens plays an awkward shot during his game against Jimmy White during the Embassy World Snooker match at the Crucible in Sheffield.

S

**WORLD SPORTS
ENCYCLOPEDIA**

the score is such that even with all the balls and 2 or 3 snookers he would not overtake the other player. Points are kept with a special device with 2 lines in its center, one divided into 0-20pts. and the other, above, 0-200. On each line there are 2 short markers (1 for each player), which are moved along the line. The name derives from the combination of old Celtic *snotadh* and old Scandinavian *snoca*, from which an old Eng. word *snaca* and modern Eng. *snook* evolved. The rules were formulated in England, and then in the USA in the 19th cent.

Snow shoes.

The modern, dynamic character of snooker was achieved in the 1930s, largely owing to J. Davis, who after 30yrs. of studying the tactical and mathematical aspects of the game developed in 1960 600 basic techniques leading to the scoring of over 100pts. Davis was the first player to score 146pts. Other great players include Steve Davis and Ray Reardon – both of them won six champion titles. In recent years, the best player of snooker has been Stephen Hendry, the winner of 8 champion titles.

SNØRE VIBE, Dan. for 'tying a lapwing', [Dan. *snøre* – to lace, tie + *vibe* – lapwing]. A strength-testing contest, in which a rope, 6m long and 1-1.5cm thick is used. Two contestants stand opposite each other, a few steps apart. Then each of them 'gets tangled' in a rope – it is first tied around the right hand of one of the players, then around his right foot, then it goes to the right foot of the other player and is also tied around it, then to his right hand, then to his left hand, his left foot and back across to the left foot of the first player, round it and on to his left hand. The object of the game is to make the opponent tumble down by pulling hard on the rope.

J. Møller, 'Snøre vibe', GID, 1997, 4, 32.

SNOW RAFTING, see >RAFTING.

SNOW SHOES, equipment used to move across the surface of snow; also, a type of sport ('snowshoeing'). Snow shoes make it possible to walk in soft snow. They consist of lightweight, elongated, oval wooden frames on which leather thongs are strung. The decking is usu. divided into 3 parts, and has an elaborate weave. The middle part of a snow shoe,

Snow shoes.

where the user's foot is, has denser decking, additionally strengthened with two cross bars to bear the body weight of the user. The remaining parts have thinner decking that allows loose snow to pour through it but 'floats' on more packed snow. Snow shoes are fastened to one's feet using special leather bindings that allow the heel – much like in cross-country skis – to 'detach' from the shoe, with the toes attached permanently. When running, one has to lift the front part of the shoe off the snow first, and then drag the rear part along the surface. One may reach speeds of up to 5mph (8km/h). Snow shoes have no standard sizes; usu., they are about 3ft. (1m) long, and 1½ft. (0.5m) wide.

History. Snow shoes as we know them today descend from those used by Native Amer. Indians and the Inuit. When Europeans arrived in N.America, snow shoes became part of the standard gear of trappers, lumberjacks, farmers and sportsmen. In Canada, snow shoe races became quite popular. Since c.1840, a group of people from Montreal under the leadership of N. 'Evergreen' Hughes went on excursions using snow shoes. In 1843, the same people established the Montreal Snow Shoe Club that initiated systematic trips, combining those with cultural activities. During an outing – a 'tramp' – the participants would stop at an inn at the half-way point to have a meal, sing and recite poetry. The Montreal club also organized the first competitions along 2-mile courses, with obstacles such as tree trunks or fences 4ft. (1.2m) high. In the 1860s, there were more snow shoe clubs set up in Canada, in such places as Montreal, Ottawa or Quebec, which was essential in establishing the interdisciplinary Montreal Amateur Sport Association, which in turn was instrumental for the development of Can. sport in general. In the 1890s, snowshoeing became Canada's most popular winter sport. The international Tecumseh Cup competition was organized, and the equipment was improved (among other things, the weight of the shoes fell from 4lb. (1.81km) to 1.5lb. (0.68kg)). Between 1883 and 1889, the Montreal Amateur Sport Association organized the Mardi Gras carnival, which was a week of games and sports. The growth of skiing and Eur. winter sports diminished the interest in snowshoeing at the turn of the 19th and 20th cent. However, the Can. Snowshoe Union was established in 1907, responsible for the co-ordination and development of snowshoeing in that country. Outside of Canada, the largest association for snow shoe users and fans is the Amer. Snowshoe Union of Lewiston, Minnesota. Snow shoes have been less popular in the Eur. tradition, even though they can be encountered in the northern countries. In the Carpathian mountains of Eastern Europe, another type of the snow shoe, known as >KARPLE, was used in the past.

W.E. Osgood & L.E. Hurley, *Snowshoe Book*, 1971; 'Snowshoeing', *The Canadian Encyclopedia*, 1985, vol. 3, PAT-Z, 1712.

SNOW SKIING, a var. of >SKIING where the skis are used in running, jumping, slaloming, downhill racing and ski sailing events to move across the surface of snow. The most popular snow skiing disciplines are >NORDIC SKIING with its variants, such as >SKI RUNNING COMPETITIONS and >SKI JUMPING, and >ALPINE SKIING, incl. 2 combined events (described in that entry) in addition to >DOWNHILL SKIING and >SKI SLALOM. Newer varieties of snow skiing include >FREESTYLE SKIING, which in turn includes >ACROSKI, >MOGULS and >AERIALS. In the shade of the new, fashionable varieties of snow skiing, the various forms of >LEISURE SKIING still exist. >SKI MARATHON and >STEEP SKIING have been growing in importance, too. >SNOWBOARDING must also be included under the heading of 'skiing', as it uses a single ski, or 'snowboard', to move across the surface of the snow. There are also some varieties of skiing which, though less popular, are all the same present on the international arena, such as >SKI SAILING, and >PARAWING SAILING.

History. Until the 1890s, Scandinavia was thought to have been the birthplace of snow skiing. However, that was disproved by F. Nasen's research undertaken in connection with his 1888 ski crossing of Greenland. According to Nansen, whose findings are still accepted today, skiing originated in the region of Lake Baikal and the Altai Mountains in Asia. From there, nomadic tribes carried it westwards, and cultural borrowing by the nations they encountered

Snow skiing.

helped the process, so that skiing eventually reached Europe after some time. The Swed. researcher A. Zelfersten, and the Ger. scientist C.J. Luther thought that there was once dry land in the area of what is today the Baltic Sea, and that was where the 'path' of skiing split into the northern (Scand.) and southern branches (the latter taking skiing into continental Europe). Another theory the two scientists proposed was that skiing equipment reached Europe along two paths that separated already in Asia, the northern reaching Scandinavia, and the southern – what is today Poland, Germany and Denmark. Further research added new details to our knowledge of the 'path' of skiing, and moved skiing's 'date of birth' from 200 AD to several thousand years ago. In 1926, the Rus. researcher A.M. Linevski discovered near Lake Onega a rock painting depicting a group of skiers, thought to be about 5,000 years old. The same year, a series of paintings with similar motifs was found on the Norw. island of Rödöy. In 1936, V.Y. Ravdonikas discovered in the village of Zalavrug a stone-age painting depicting 15 skiers, with 12 among them using poles with discs in addition to their skis. However, it has not been possible to give even an approximate date of the invention of the first skis. According to one theory, proposed in 1930 by C.J. Luther, skis were invented just after the end of the ice age. In his writings for the *På Skidor* yearly (1925-36), the Swed. researcher B.J. Wiklund equated the impact of the invention of skis and sledges for northern peoples with that of the invention of the wheel in other parts of the world. The Pol. sports historian G. Młodzikowski hypothesized that skis appeared in the North at the same time as hunting weapons, seeing that hunting without skis is practically impossible in those areas. Archeological findings in Scandinavian peat bogs have provided convincing evidence that skis, invented in Asia, developed variants only in Europe, reaching a high level of technical sophistication. For example, the skis found in Arnäs, Sweden, dating back to about 2000-800 BC, are narrower in the front and rear parts, and are equipped with wooden clamps, foot holes and additional edges on the bases. The Gk. historian and geographer Strabon (1st cent. BC-1st cent. AD) wrote about skis covered with animal fur, making it possible to climb hills. Allegedly, they were used by tribes north and east of the Carpathian Mts. As time passed, skis were mentioned with increasing frequency in written sources. Scandinavian legends and sagas, included in the Edda and scald songs, are an especially rich source of evidence. A mention of a skier 'racing like the wind' dates back to the times of King Harald Fairhair, along with a record suggesting that the king used ski couriers. The *Heimskringla* (*Chronicle of the Kings*) by the medieval chronicle writer S. Sturluson exalts the skiing skills of Einar, 'the fastest runner of all men', and mentions the contemporary equipment (1015-30). A description of downhill skiing dates back to the reign of Harald Hardrada (1046-66), along with a dialogue, in which Eystein reprimands Sigurd for his poor skills: 'I could run upon snow-skates so well that nobody could beat me, and you could no more do it than an ox'. In the Edda, there is a mention of Ull, who was 'such a good archer and ski-runner that no one [could] rival him'. About 1200, the Dan. chronicler Saxo Grammaticus observed in his *Gesta Danorum* that skiing was a vital element of life in Scandinavia. Another description of skiing dates back to 1250 and E. Gunnarsson's *Konungs skuggsja* (*The King's Mirror*), an important work of Old Norw. literature. A legend, based on facts, and dating back to 1522, describes how King Gustav Vasa of Sweden returned to his country to incite an uprising and dethrone the despotic King Christian II. When the people refused to support him at the beginning, the king skied back to Norway but the inhabitants of the village of Mora sent two skiers to catch up with him and convince him to return, contributing to an important turn in Swed. history. A mass cross-country event, known as the Vasaloppet, has been organized since 1922 along the route used by the two skiers chasing Gustav Vasa. The first mentions of ski post in Norway appeared in 1525-35. Apart from Scandinavia, snow skiing also developed in Russia. In 1444, Vasil IV's troops, equipped with skis, fought back a Tartar invasion near Ryazan. In 1483, Knyaz Ivan Vasilevich organized a war expedition on skis. Similar references appear in larger numbers in the 16th-17th cent. In 1578, the Pol. historic writer of Maciej Osostevicius Stryjkowski wrote

Snowboarding.

the *Historia sarmacji* (later plagiarized by the Italian Alessandro Guagnini, then travelling around Poland, as his own work under the title of *Sarmatiae Europae Descriptio*, *Description of Eur. Sarmatia*, 1578; he applied the name *Sarmatia* to East-Eur. Slavic countries, mainly Poland and Russia). The Pol. translation by M. Paszkowski appeared soon after that (1603), with a description of Russian troops moving on skis:

Strange is running on skis. Pedestrians on skis (as the custom has been preserved in many places in the Russian countries) run across the surface of the snow very fast indeed. The skis are made of wood, elongated, covered with iron on the bottom, about two or three ells long, and they put these on their feet instead of shoes, and support themselves with longish sticks, sharpened at the ends, and they run very fast so that even a very swift horse cannot catch up with them, as the thickness of the snow, hills and other snowdrifts are obstacles for a running horse. But those who run on their skis can jump over logs and pits easily and so are perfectly suited for catching and shooting animals of all sorts [...] And those skis are used by almost all northern peoples in Muscovy, Russia and other extreme countries.

The Pol. King Stefan Batory had similar ski troops. The following excerpt comes from W. Dyamentowski's *Diariusz* (1608) and concerns a military action against an 'excursion' from a besieged Moscow: 'On one day, some men exited the city [of Moscow], against whom several hundred people set out from the camp on skis, causing great damage to the city dwellers'. The diminishing cultural status of Russia in the following period – due to the feudal character of the countryside, where folk sports, incl. snow skiing, blossomed – prevented the Rus. var. of skiing from influencing the remaining Eur. countries. The assignment of peasants to their land, preventing them from free movement and the ban on hunting on the landlords' grounds caused many elements of the culture of old Russia to collapse. The political fall of Poland, which lost independence and was partitioned between Prussia, Austria and Russia in 1795, meant skiing had little chance of developing in that part of Europe, in spite of the promising beginnings in the 15th and 16th cent., as described above. As a result, the sporting influence in the discipline mainly originated in the northern and western parts of the continent. The first mention of alpine snow skiing dates back to 1574 and comes from J. Simmler's *De Alpibus commentarius*. In 1728, the first plan of entering the interior of Greenland on skis was developed in Denmark. In 1746, the brochure *Information of Ireland, Greenland and Davies Strait* was published in Hamburg, including a mention of a sailor who tried exploring Iceland 'on long wooden boards'. One of the most crucial factors increasing the popularity of skiing in western and central Europe was the adaptation of skis as training equipment by the pedagogues and theorists of physical education in the 18th-19th cent. G.U.A. Vieth's *Enzyklopädie der Leibesübungen* (*Encyclopedia of Bodily Exercise*), published in 1794, contained a long description of snow skiing as practiced in Scandinavia, along with a suggestion that it should be practiced likewise in Germany and Switzerland. 'So many fashions have we taken over from the southern countries, partly unsuitable in our climate, why should we not adopt the Lappish people's and Ostiaks' fash-

ion should it prove useful?' In 1804, J.C. Guts-Muths included snow skiing as a sport shaping the balance and general fitness in his *Gimnastik für die Jugend* (*Gymnastics for the Youth*). He added some remarks on the methodical teaching of skiing, technical descriptions of the equipment and a justification of skiing's usefulness:

Even though we do not live in such a cold country as the Norwegians do, we often have so much snow that transportation is difficult or even discontinued. For such cases, the introduction of skiing would be very useful. However, regardless of that, it is doubtlessly a useful exercise for any youth, to fill his hours of idleness and make his body more agile and stronger.

Guts-Muths' remarks pass as Europe's first ever snow skiing handbook. In the 19th cent., snow skiing took on a fully sporting character in Scandinavia, and spread to other mountainous areas of the continent. The gradual disappearance of the original utilitarian uses of skiing (such as hunting, which was among the chief forms of maintenance even in the Middle Ages but was pushed to the background with the growth of animal breeding and farming; or the development of transportation, especially of railways, meant long-distance transportation was no more supported by skiers etc.) contributed to the development of the discipline as a sport. In 1843, the first known public skiing competition took place in Tromsø, Norway, along a 5-km course. Between 1860 and 1880, the foundations of all the basic variants of Nordic skiing were laid. Many names in Eur. skiing terminology derive from the names of the areas where skiing techniques were particularly frequent (Christiania, Telemark), along with other Norw. words. In 1875, the first modern skiing club was founded in Christiania, while the Norw. Society for the Promotion of Skiing was established in 1892. The first skiing organization outside of Scandinavia was the skiing section of the Skating Club in Prague (1887). In 1891, the first two Ger. clubs were set up in Munich and Todtnau (Schwarzwald), while more than a dozen alpine clubs were founded in

Austria, Germany and Switzerland in 1892-93. In 1894, the Kruzhok Lyznikov was established at the Cyclist Club in Moscow, while the independent skiing club Polyarnaya Zvezda was established in St. Petersburg in 1897. The first skiing association was the Czech one (1903), then Swiss and Amer. (1904), Austria and Germany (1905), and only then, surprisingly late, those of Norway, Sweden and Finland (1908). In 1910, the first International Skiing Congress was held. During the congress, a long-standing dispute about the main direction of the development of skiing became apparent for the first time. The alpine countries preferred downhill racing, while the Scand. nations opted for Nordic skiing. The dispute was not resolved during the next five congresses (1911-23) but only after the foundation of the Fédération Internationale de Ski (FIS) during the winter sports week in Chamonix (1924). The event was later recognized as the first Olympic Winter Games, and the first W.Ch. (but only after a decision by FIS in 1965!). Since 1901, the Nordic Skiing Championships were held, which were the largest Eur. event before the introduction of the Winter Ol.G. and W.Ch. Today, FIS considers the Winter Ol.G. to be W.Ch. but organizes special events of the type in non-Olympic years.

SNOW SNAKE, the Eng. name of an Amer. Indian sport, in which contestants aim a short spear at a line marked in the snow, the object being to throw the spear so that it lands exactly on the line.

SNOW-BALLS, also *snow-ball throwing*, a game known all over the world where there is snow. Ł. Gołębiowski described it as follows:

winter has come, the young hide the balls away, they prefer to make snow balls and throw them at one another or at a person made of snow (snowman) or at a castle and they conquer the castle proving their skill, stamina and courage; their hands are red and their young faces are red and their bodies hot but this movement and resistance to cold teach them how to play at this time of the year, not giving in to the cold and knowing how to protect themselves against the blowing winds.

[Games and Pastimes of Various Social Classes, 1831, 20]

SNOWBOARDING, or *snowboard*, a sport practiced on snow in which contestants slide down snowy slopes using a board, standing laterally to the direction of slide. The board is usu. 140-180cm long and 26-32cm wide. A board used in international competition cannot be narrower than 18cm. Foot bindings are set at an angle to the board's longitudinal line and cannot be released during a fall, lest they should cause a hazard to spectators. Unlike downhill skiing, snowboarding contestants don't use sticks. There are 2 competition types – Alpine competitions and freestyle. The former include:
PARALLEL SLALOM – held on a wide, steep slope, with a drop ranging from 80 to 150m. Two parallel courses of similar technical difficulty are marked on the slope. Each course features 20-30 slalom gates on flexible poles with flags. The gates are 7-12m apart. The winner is decided in 2 qualification runs and one final run.
GIANT SLALOM – held on a slope with a drop of 150-300m. The contestant must maneuver through 20 gates, made up of 2 flexible poles connected with

SNOWBOARD OLYMPIC CHAMPIONS
MEN'S SLALOM
1998 Ross Rebagliati, CAN 2:03.96
2002 Philipp Schoch SWI
WOMEN'S SLALOM
1998 Karine Ruby, FRA 2:17.34
2002 Isabelle Blanc FRA
MEN'S HALFPIPE
1998 Gian Simmen, SWI 85.2
2002 Ross Powers, USA 46.1
WOMEN'S HALFPIPE
1998 Nicola Thost, GER 74.6
2002 Kelly Clark, USA 47.9

Kenny Meadows, Snow balls, Illustrated London Times, 1844.

Snow skiing old style.

Snow skiing in the Polish Tatra Mountains.

Snowboarders take air during snowboard cross competition at Whistler in British Columbia.

S

WORLD SPORTS ENCYCLOPEDIA

Snowboarding.

a kind of a banner of the shape of an elongated triangle. Contestants compete against time. The winner is decided in two runs – the qualification run, upon the completion of which the 16 contestants with the best times compete in the final run. The times in the first run are important as they decide the order in which the contestants compete in the final run – the slowest contestants go first. The contestant with the fastest combined time for the 2 runs is the winner.

SUPER GIANT SLALOM – held on a slope with a drop of 300-500m. Contestants go down a course marked with direction gates – their number is not fixed and depends on course conditions. Contestants must wear protective helmets because of the steep drop.

BOARDCROSS. 6 contestants compete in each race at the same time. They must cover a course with many turns and bumps (like in motocross). Women and men compete together. A knockout system applies during competitions, which means that only the best 3 contestants qualify for the next round. The first contests were held in 1995. Boardcross originated in the United States, but it soon started to develop very dynamically in Alpine countries, particularly in Germany, Switzerland and France. In 2002 boardcross was featured in the program of the winter Olympics in Salt Lake City.

Freestyle snowboarding features the following events:

HALFPIPE – the name derives from the course shape, which looks like the bottom half of a pipe. The object is to slide onto the pipe's edges and perform tricks, which are evaluated by the judges. The most characteristic evolutions involve sliding up to the halfpipe edge, taking off and performing a var. of spins before landing safely in order to continue the run.

JUMPS include straight airs (take off, half turn and front landing), spin tricks (turns of more than 180° with front or back landing (fakie) and flips (somersaults in air after take off from snow surface). In addition to these basic evolutions contestants can also perform any other attractive acrobatic movements in air. The performance is evaluated by 4 referees – the amplitude referee, who evaluates the height of the jumps, the rotation referee, who evaluates the turns, their difficulty and body position, transition referee, who evaluates run ups, take offs and landings (including any falls and touches on the ground) and the movement referee, who evaluates the runs along the edge and bottom of the halfpipe and the general features of the downhill run. Each referee can award from 1-10pts. A contestant can score a maximum of 40pts.; the contestant with the most points wins.

History. The beginnings of snowboarding go back to 1929 when an American, J. Burtchett, attempted to slide down a hill on a longitudinal piece of board with feet bindings. For a few dozen years his experiments were not widely known and were not imitated. In 1965 another American, S. Poppen, used a

surfing board to slide down a snow hill. This is how the name of the snowboarding equipment, snurfer (snow + surfer) came into being. When at the end of the 1960s and 1970s youth subculture took to snowboarding, it became truly popular and soon was one of the most important manifestations of being a member of some youth subcultures, particularly the grunge style of life, which opposed the excessive consumption and competitiveness of capitalist societies and was based on a simple philosophy combining elements of hedonism, unbounded freedom and opposition to industrial civilization. Representatives of this trend wear a couture range of ragged 'grunge' clothing and associate in informal groups looking for satisfaction in life away from the ideal of urban culture. They often take drugs. The rapid development of snowboarding was considered a threat to the skiing community and also a purely technical threat to other skiers on the slopes. For this reason in the initial phases of its development it was banned in many winter sports centers, thus gaining the attractiveness of forbidden fruit, which paradoxically contributed to the increase of its popularity among young rebels. In the 1970s the development of snowboarding was affected by >SKATEBOARDING, which was felt in the improved design of the board. At the beginning of the 1980s some skiing centers officially agreed to allow snowboarding on their slopes. Snowboarding developed very rapidly in the early 1990s, and was soon recognized by the International Skiing Federation FIS, where a special committee was founded. However, an independent International Snowboarding Federation, ISF, was established as an expression of opposition to the activity of the FIS. Initially the IOC wanted to recognize the ISF, but it changed its mind and only allowed snowboarding in the OI.G. in Nagano in 1998 under the auspices of the FIS committee. The first historic Olympic snowboarding contests were won by N. Thost from Germany (halfpipe – women) and G. Simmen from Switzerland (halfpipe) and R. Rebagliati from Canada (giant slalom), both representing men.

Apart from the OI.G., snowboarding is presently featured in the ISF World Tour, where prizes amount to $50,000 on average. However, most competitors, who ignore the formal structures of modern civilization so typical of the snowboarding community, take no account of there being two snowboarding federations and take part in competitions organized under the auspices of both.

The leading snowboarders include an American S. Palmer, K. Jeffrey from Canada, T. Bruserud (Norway), Austrian I. Ploetzl, G. Raitmeier and B. Denervaud from Switzerland. Cf. also >KITE SNOWBOARDING.

G. Daniells, *The Powder and the Glory. The Ultimate Guide to Snowboarding*, 1997; R. Reichenfeld & A. Bruechert, *Snowboarding*, 1995; Ch. Weiss, *Snowboarding know-how*, 1995; D. Werner, *Snowboarder's Start-Up*, 1993.

SNOWMOBILE, also *motor sled, motor toboggan, snow buggy*. A sport practiced using a small open motor vehicle for traveling on snow, steered by 2 skis at the front and driven by a caterpillar track underneath. These vehicles are used in professional sport, recreation, by rescuers, forest rangers and also to deliver letters in areas with considerable snowfall and without regular roads. Speeds can be as high as 130km/h on race courses, whereas typically snowmobiles go at speeds of 50-65km/h.

History. Although vehicles similar in design to snowmobiles were probably built at the beginning of the 20th cent., C.J. Eliason from Sayner (Wisconsin, USA) is considered the first designer. In 1927 he built a vehicle, which was initially called a *motor toboggan*. The design used a combustion engine and barrel staves as runners. Considerable improvements were introduced in 1930 by J. Armand-Bombardier from Quebec (Canada). The vehicles looked like sleds, were very heavy and difficult to maneuver. In 1958 a company established by Bombardier built the first vehicle similar to the present-day snowmobile, with a light engine, wide runners and aluminum cockpit. In the 1960s the first clubs of snowmobile users and lovers were established in USA and Canada. Most of them are part of the US Snowmobile Association). The association is considered the main authority defining the sports rules of snowmobile events. In the 1970s there were over 2 million snowmobiles in N.America alone. Every year about 300 different snowmobile contests are held in America. The best known is the 626mi. (1007.4km) race started in Winnipeg (Canada), through Manitoba to Minneapolis (Minnesota, USA). A Grand Prix is held annually in Lancaster (New Hampshire).

The relatively large weight of the mobile and considerable speeds, combined with the deceptive ease of maneuvering have led to serious accidents and injuries. Their number grew proportionally to the growing number of vehicles, despite preventive measures such as: minimum age, obligatory crash helmet, safety belts, etc. In medicine special terminology is used to refer to snowmobile induced injuries, e.g. *snowmobiler's back*. Snowmobile rides have also been heavily criticized by ecological organizations, which object not only to the pollution of the natural environment with exhaust fumes, but also to the noise generated by snowmobile engines, which scares away animals and birds.

J.J. Tuite, 'Snowmobile', EAI, 1979, 25; The Internet: http://republika.pl/piotrwojt/snow/snowmobil.htm

SNURR, a Swed. var. of >TOPS.

SNURREBASS, a Norw. var. of >TOPS.

SO I HUL, Dan. for 'a sow in the hole', [Dan. *so* – sow + *i* – in + *hul* – hole]. A folk ball game, practiced in central Jutland in the vicinity of Sorø, Ringsted and Roskilde, similar and probably belonging to the same tradition as Pol. >CZOROMAJ, Fr. LA >TRUIE, Eng. >CAT I' THE HOLE, Swed. >PER I HÅLA, Norw. >PER I GROPEN and Ger. >TREIBBALL. The game is played by 5-6 players, who, prior to the competition, dig out a central hole in an open space, referred to, depending on the local tradition, as the pot (*gryden*), the sow's hole (*sohullet*) or the mud hole (*sutten*). The hole is 6-7cm deep and 9-10cm wide. About 3-4m from the 'pot' smaller holes are dug out – one less than the number of players. Each of them is called the farm yard (*gård*). Each player has a stick, about 1m long, most often curved at the end. A player claims ownership of the hole by putting his stick into it. The game is played with a ball called a sow (*so*). A player, who has not got his own hole, called, depending on the local tradition, swine-herd (*sodriveren*), or the mudman from Krøjerup or Løng (*suttemanden i Krøjerup*), starts the game and tries to get the ball-sow into the 'pot'. The other players prevent him from doing this with their sticks. If the shepherd manages to put the ball into the 'pot', he can select a hole and 'take possession' of it by putting his stick into it. This is also a signal for the other players to start running and claim title to the hole by putting a stick into it. As there is one hole less than the players, one player will become the sowherd. J. Møller, 'So i hul', GID, 1997, 1, 76.

SO I HUL (UDEN MIDTERHUL), Dan. for 'a sow in the hole' (without the central hole), a game similar to >SO I HUL, but played on a pitch without any holes for the ball. Instead of holes there are circles, into which a ball should be propelled using a curved

Keith Dierkes of the USA leads D.J. Eckstrom during the snowmobile Hillcross competition at the Winter X Games in Aspen, Colorado.

So i hul.

stick; there is no central circle. There is one circle less than there are players. Each circle is guarded by a player with a curved stick. The ball is similar to a cricket ball and is called a 'pig' or lit. a sow – *so*. A player without a circle is called a swine-herd (*søt-drive*). He tries to break into one of the circles by propelling a ball into it with his stick. The player, who guards his circle tries to prevent this, which he can do only by using his own stick with which he tries to repel the ball as far as possible. He does not have to stand inside his circle all the time; he can stand to one side, but then the stick must be in the circle, which is a sign that the circle belongs to the player. When the circle is attacked, its defender can run around the circle and drive the ball out from the outside. The player whose circle was seized (the ball landed in it) becomes the swine-herd and from now on his task is identical to that of his predecessor. The ball can be set in motion only with the stick; when kicked, a circle is automatically lost to the then swine-herd. Cf. Pol. >CZOROMAJ.

J. Møller, 'So i hul (uden midterhul)', GID, 1997, 1, 81.

SOAP BOX, a type of race down a mountain or steep hill, in which gravity is the only driving force. The vehicles start rolling without pushing and must pick up momentum on their own. The course is ¹/₅mi., i.e. 321.9m long. Three vehicles race at the same time. If the course is not wide enough, racers compete in pairs; the cup system is used. In order to take part in the races, a contestant must build a vehicle himself for less than $100. When entering a competition, the contestant must prove that he has built the vehicle himself. The total weight of the vehicle with the driver cannot exceed 250lb. (113.4kg), max. length – 80in. (203cm) and max. width – 34in., i.e. 89cm. The height cannot exceed 28in. (71cm). A decent brake is also required. The vehicle's front cannot be pointed. The sport originated in the 1930s in the United States. The vehicle, which is only slightly bigger than a pram, consists of the body and 4 wheels, of which the 2 front ones can be steered. As the sport developed, the vehicle became more streamlined. Today an average soap box looks like a race car from the 1950s. Timber, of which the body was made in the past, has been replaced with fiberglass. The sport is practiced mainly by children aged 11-15yrs. The largest international event is the Soap Box Derby, also called the World's Gravity Grand Prix, sponsored by Chevrolet (a branch of General Motors Corporation, GMC). Every year, eliminations to the race attract about 50,000 children and are held in about 300 US cities. The finals are held every year in Akron (Ohio, USA). Prizes for the winners include scholarships.
In Europe the sport became popular later than in the USA. It developed most dynamically in the Federal Republic of Germany, where it was made popular by Amer. soldiers, who came there with their families. Today one of the largest soap box centers in Germany is Berlin.

SOCCER, see >ASSOCIATION FOOTBALL.

SOFT TENNIS. The game is played according to the same rules and on an identical court as >LAWN TENNIS, but the ball is made of rubber, inflated with a needle pump. The game is played in pairs only – the ball is so unpredictable that one player is unable to control it on his own. Soft tennis games are not played on lawn courts. The strings in the racket are not so tight as in the tennis racket. Players use the so-called 'western grip', i.e. the racket is held by the base end and therefore they use only one side of the racket in the forehand and backhand.
History. Soft tennis was 'invented' in Japan at the end of the 19th cent. and made popular outside Japan, first in occupied Korea and then in Taiwan and China. In 1987, following a series of show tournaments organized by the Jap. Soft Tennis Association, JSTA), it appeared in Singapore, where it became extremely popular owing to the Kallang Tennis Center and the management board of the Bayshore Park. The first Asian soft tennis championships were held in Nagoya (Japan) in 1988, organized by the Asian Soft Tennis Federation). The first president of the federation was the then prime minister of Japan, T. Kaifu, a great lover of the game, which testifies to the importance and prestige of soft tennis in Japan and Asia.
In 1990 soft tennis was included in the program of the 9th Asian Games in Beijing as a show sport and 4yrs. later as a regular event. In Asia the dynamic development of soft tennis owes a lot to the work of the Asian Soft Tennis Federation and many national federations, of which the most active are the Jap. and Singaporean federations.
A.T.C. Koh, 'Soft Tennis Anyone?', SS, Nov., Dec., 1989.

SOFTBALL, a game derived from Amer. >BASEBALL, originally called *soft-baseball*. The rules are much less strict than in baseball; likewise, the pitch is smaller. The distance between the bases is 18.29m for fast-pitch and 19.81m for slow-pitch (27.45m in baseball), and teams have 9 players. The distance between the pitcher and home base is 14.17m for men and 12.19m for women at fast-pitch and 15.24m for men and 14.02m for women at slow-pitch. The match lasts 7 rounds. The ball is 8.25cm in diameter and weighs 180-200g. Softball was introduced for the first time at the Farragut Boat Club in Chicago (1883) and then in the 1880s in Chicago schools. In 1895 L. Rober, a fireman from Minneapolis, adapted softball to indoor conditions. For decades softball had the status of a school sport and developed mainly under the auspices of the National Recreation Association and also the Young Men's Christian Association (YMCA) and the Young Women's Christian Association (YWCA). Until 1933 there were various rules of the game, differently interpreted, the common elements of which included the smaller size of the pitch and the larger ball, making batting easier. In 1933 the International Softball Committee was established, which started to standardize the rules. In 1952 the International Softball Federation, ISF, was established. Women's softball, including professional softball, developed very dynamically in the 1970s and 1980s. Softball was included in the program of the PanAmer. Games; W.Ch. started to be organized (for women in 1965, Melbourne, Australia, and for men in 1966, Mexico City). In 1991 the World Olympic Committee agreed to introduce softball into the program of the Ol.G.. In 1995 in Columbus (Georgia, USA), Superball Classic, a great pre-Olympic tournament, was held, won by USA, and with the People's Republic of China and Australia coming in second and third. During the 1996 Ol.G. in Atlanta softball was a demonstration sport and 4 years later it was included in the official program of the Ol.G. in Sydney. The gold medal was won by the USA.
P. Dickson, *The Worth Book of Softball, A Celebration of America's First National Pastime*, 1994; J. Garman, *Softball Skills and Drills*, 2001; R.G. Meyer, *The Complete Book of Softball*, 1984; D. Potter & G.A. Brockmeyer, *Softball. Steps to Success*, 1989.

SOGDCHON, a folk contest in stone throwing, held in Korea in the meadows surrounding a village as a defence exercise. Until the end of the 16th cent. sogdchon was a type of eliminator, in which the best rural pitchers were recruited by the army for the time of war. According to T.K. Kim, a Kor. scholar, sogdchon contests were accompanied by other sports, such as a fight with clubs or wrestling in the river.
K.-C. Jung, *Erziehung und Sport in Korea im Kreuzpunkt fremder Kulturen und Mächte*, 1996, 61.

WORLD SPORTS ENCYCLOPEDIA

S

NCAA SOFTBALL CHAMPIONSHIPS

DIVISION ONE RESULTS

1982 UCLA 2, Fresno St. 0
1983 Texas A&M 2, Cal St.-Fullerton 0
1984 UCLA 1, Texas A&M 0
1985 UCLA 2, Nebraska 1
1986 Cal St. Fullerton 3, Texas A&M 0
1987 Texas A&M 4, UCLA 1
1988 UCLA 3, Fresno St. 0
1989 UCLA 1, Fresno St. 0
1990 UCLA 2, Fresno St. 0
1991 Arizona 5, UCLA 1
1992 UCLA 2, Arizona 0
1993 Arizona 1, UCLA 0
1994 Arizona 4, Cal. St.-Northridge 0
1995 UCLA 4, Arizona 2
1996 Arizona 6, Washington 4
1997 Arizona 10, UCAL 2
1998 Fresno State 1, Arizona 0
1999 UCLA 3, Washington 2
2000 Oklahoma 3, UCLA 1
2001 Arizona 1, UCLA 0
2002 California 6, Arizona 0

Terry French tries to tag out Greg Peters (bottom) as he slides through the snow and into 2nd base during their Anchorage Fur Rendezvous Snowshoe Softball game in Anchorage, Alaska.

Des Moines Lincoln's Erin Breese, right, slides past Muscatine catcher Aubrey Martin, left, during the 5th inning of their Class 3A at the girls state softball tournament in Fort Dodge, Iowa.

S

SOL OG MÅNE, Dan. for 'sun and moon'. A Dan. game, similar to Pol. >KLASY. Two circles (sun and moon), connected with a straight line, are drawn on the ground. The players must complete 8 rounds as follows: 1) a jump from the sun to the moon with the line joining both figures between the legs; halfway the player turns round and jumps the remainder of the course backwards; 2) jumps with joined legs, alternately on either side of the line; halfway the player turns round and jumps the remainder of the course backwards; 3) jumps as in (1), but in each jump the legs are joined; 4) jumps on the right leg, as in (2); 5) jumps as in (4), but on the left leg; 6) jumps on crossed legs; 7) jumps as in (1), but after each jump the player turns round on one leg; 8) jumps as in (7) but after each jump a full turn is jumped. In all jumps when the player is halfway he turns round and completes the jumps backwards.

J. Møller, 'Sol og måne', GID, 1997, 4, 104.

SOLLEN, 1) a var. of a game known in medieval France as >SOULE, played in Flanders. 2) a simple Flem. var. of football, played in the Netherlands, the Flem. part of Belgium, and in northern France inhabited by people of Flem. origin.

SOLO BASTON, a type of fencing using one stick, known in the Philippines, a combination of the local tradition of a stick fight (>KALI) and modern Eur. fencing, the rules of which were brought to the motherland in the 19th cent. by natives studying in Spain [Span. *solo* – singly + *baston* – cane, stick]; cf. >DOBLE BASTON.

resilience, ability to overcome extreme obstacles unassisted, and a high level of intellectual and moral standards that facilitate practical application of a philosophy defining the ethical attitude of man towards nature. The social value of solo yachting consists of providing cultural and moral models that can be followed on a smaller scale, for instance in recreational sailing, or on a larger, more philosophical plane as lessons in living. Solo yachtsmen find self-fulfillment and an opportunity to overcome the social anonymity; anonymity and alienation that have become epidemic in modern civilization. Therefore, the sports disciplines practiced individually, such as mountain climbing or solo yachting, play an important role in preserving the natural and trad. human need to assert an exceptional identity, a pursuit that seems to be on the wane in today's world.

History. Vessels that would allow a single person to navigate unaided were unknown in ancient times. The forces of nature had definite and insurmountable advantage over man, which made humans try to tame it and extend the space known to civilization in the form of >GEOGRAPHICAL EXPLORATIONS. Thus, antiquity was familiar with individuals that found themselves unaided in their efforts to handle situations that simply resulted from circumstances allotted to them (Odysseus, Aeneas), rather than individuals intentionally undertaking certain actions. However, beginning with Pytheas who navigated through the Pillars of Hercules (the Strait of Gibraltar) in the 4th cent. BC and then explored the N coasts of Europe, premeditated attempts started to take place. The first fully planned venture to cross

(1899) contributed considerably to disseminating the idea of solo yachting. In 1897, H. Blackburn navigated from Gloucester, along the east coast of S.America up to San Francisco, circumnavigating thus South America. Impressed by Slocum's book, Blackburn navigated in 1899 from America to Europe and then repeated this achievement in 1901. The number of solo yacht trips continued to grow. The most spectacular events are believed to include: American H. Pidgeon's circumnavigation of the globe in 1921-25 in *Islander*; the first single-handed trip from Europe to America in 1923 by Frenchman A. Gerbault in *Firecrest*; the 1936-38 circumnavigation of the globe by the Frenchman L. Bernicot in *Anahita*. A. Gerbault's (1893-1941) achievement was particularly publicized because the sailor had had no previous sailing experience. This memorable trip was described by the Fr. hero and tennis champion in his book *The Fight of the Firecrest*, and was taken up as the subject of a number of literary works, such as A. Słonimski's *Ode To Alain Gerbault*.

The technical developments in navigation, such as radars, short-wave transmitters, and course-keeping devices, as well as improved weather forecasts and life-saving capacities, most of which was introduced on yachts after WWII, on the one hand substantially undermined the heroism of single-handed navigators, but on the other contributed to enlarging their number. In 1955, the Slocum Society was founded in order to sponsor solo yachting events. 1960 saw the first attempts to institutionalize solo yachting in the form of so-called Solo Regattas. Since the '90s, the presence of TV crews in aircraft accompanying lone navigators has to a large extent deprived the sport of its very essence: a sailor's solitude at sea.

A. Davidson of England became the first woman to cross the Atlantic alone in *Felicity Ann* (1952-53). The first woman to solo circumnavigate the globe was K. Choynowska-Liskiewicz (b. 1936) from Poland in 1976-78. Englishman R. Knox-Johnston, for the first time in history, circumnavigated the globe without calling at a single port in 1969. In the '60s, the philosophy behind solo yachting changed. Instead of humankind's endeavor to tame the forces of nature, solo yachting came to be seen as a way to recover values lost by modern civilization: Conrad's romantic and fair duel free from any immoral deals, contact with a wholly intact natural environment, return to old seamen's traditions, self-realization of an individual who intentionally separates himself from the destructive modern world, etc. The first representative of such a new intellectual formula of yachting was a Brit. sportsman, boxer, pilot, and yachtsman, F. Chichester (1901-72) who sailed alone around the globe in *Gipsy Moth IV* (1966-67) calling only at one port. The commercial genre in solo yachting was born during the Golden Globe Challenge regatta in which the participation of sponsoring companies was heavily manifested and the application of expensive up-to-date technological solutions (carbon fiber, electronically controlled water balance system, autopilots, etc.) introduced. Another prestigious event for solo yachtsmen is the Vendée Globe, a regatta initiated in 1989 and held on a 25,000-mi. course starting and finishing in Sables d'Olonne, France. This regatta is exceptional in the sense that participants must not employ any advanced modern navigation gear, taking their position only from the stars or the sun; neither is any external assistance in the case of a breakdown allowed. This is solo yachting in its purest form.

K. Baranowski, *Polonezem dookoła świata*, 1973; F. Chichester, *Gipsy Moth Circles the World*, 1967; L. Teliga, *Opty of Gdyni do Fidżi*, 1970; L. Teliga, *Opty of Fidżi do Casablanki*, 1970; L. Teliga, *Samotny Rejs Opty*, 1976; A. Urbańczyk, *Samotne rejsy*, 1972.

SOLOWIEJ, a Byelorussian var. of >PALANT.

SOMBO, see >SAMBO.

French skipper Yvan Bourgnon, on Rexona, sails shortly after the start of multihull boats in the prestigious Route du Rhum trans-Atlantic solo race, off Saint Malo, Brittany

SOLO YACHTING, a var. of >SAILING (see also >YACHTING) whose object is to cover long distances at sea alone. Solo yachting may also include inland or ice yachting if the sailor navigates over a long distance unaccompanied.

The most characteristic feature of solo yachting is the confrontation of man with the forces of nature in which the navigator attempts to face the overwhelming power of nature unaided and with minimal technical support in order to prove his determination and strength. In today's high-tech world, except perhaps as training for the event of a power loss or the complete failure of the modern sailor's many electronic gadgets, solo yachting would seem to have little practical value, similarly to >MOUNTAIN CLIMBING or >BALLOONING. What is of supreme importance here is mankind's direct contact with nature in extreme conditions, far from any creature comforts. It is a highly exclusive sport, unavailable to most people, not only due to the expense of equipment but first and foremost because of the features of character required of navigators: physical and mental

a certain sea region and unaided is thought to be Dutchman H. de Voogt's journey from the Netherlands to London, which took place in 1601 in a small open boat. No records confirming the successful completion of the undertaking have survived. In the 19th cent. the idea of open-water cruising in small yachts developed in England thanks to such pioneers as R.T. McMullen (1830-91). In 1887, a Brit. lawyer and journalist, E.F. Knight, navigated alone from the Thames estuary to the Baltic Sea in a lifeboat converted into a 19ft. (9m) sailboat. In 1876, American A. Johnson navigated in a double-deck fishing boat with extra ballast across the Atlantic as a commemoration of the 100th anniversary of constituting the USA. Solo yachting was later popularized by J. Slocum (1844-1909), an Amer. sailing ship captain who lost his job because of steaming boats taking over the market. After a barge he commanded, *Aquidneck*, sank in 1887, he devoted himself to building a yacht he named *Spray* which then in 1895 served him for the first solo circumnavigation of the globe. His book *Sailing Alone Around the World*

SOMMER I BY, Dan. for 'summer in town', a Dan. var. of a holiday known in Poland as >GAIK MAJOWY, in Germany as >MAIBAUM, and in England as >MAYPOLE; cf. also >PALO DE MAYO. In Denmark sommer i by was celebrated on May 1st, as the holiday of the approaching summer. In more recent times the tradition was connected with Labor Day, celebrated mainly in towns and hence the name of the holiday. Earlier, like in other Eur. countries, the holiday was called after the name of a decorated pole (Dan. *Majstang*). A Maypole was erected and

decorated with wreaths by girls. In the morning horse riders on beautifully decorated horses gathered round the pole and the procession, carrying a small Maypole, started a tour of the city. In the evening the riders gathered round the pole again. Each of them held a long stick. The riders rode round the pole and the girls threw wreaths up in the air, which the riders tried to skewer with their lances. The rider who caught the wreath, became the May king (*Majkonge*), and ruled until the next summer. The May king elected a May queen (*Majdronning*); to do this he got close to one of the girls and dropped a wreath on her head down the lance.
J. Møller, 'Sommer i by', GID, 1997, 4.

SOO BAHK KI, see >HAPKIDO.

SOO BAHK-DO, see >TANG SOO DO.

SOOBAK, a medieval var. of Kor. hand-to-hand combat, known at the Time of Three Kingdoms or the co-existence of alternately dominating states: Koryo, Paekche and Shilla; 37 BC-668 AD, with Shilla dominating between 668-918); most probably one of the most important predecessors and at the same time elements of modern >TAE-KWON-DO.

SÖT OCH SUR, Swed. for 'sweet and sour', a folk ball game, practiced in old Sweden, similar to >PALANT. The name derives from 2 parts of the field and corresponds, roughly, to the concepts of 'heaven' and 'hell' in similar games played on the continent.

SOULE À LA CROSSE, a var. of medieval game known as >SOULE, LA. Unlike soule, it was played not with a ball thrown with hands or kicked, but passed using curved sticks that resembled a bishop's crozier, hence its name [Fr. *crosse – inter alia* crozier, a rod bent at the top]. Historians point to the relationship between soule à la crosse and the Wel. >KNAPPAN, Ir. >HURLING, Scot. >HURLEY; there may also be a link between the continental >KOLVEN and Scot. >GOLF. As regards the relationship between soule à la crosse and the Celtic var., particularly knappan, it is not known which game var. was played first. Soule à la crosse probably derives from the territory of Celtic Brettany; the local inhabitants were Briton emigrants, who fled there in the 6th-7th cent. before the invasion of Britain by Anglo-Saxons. So it is probable that some primary form of the game, deriving from Celtic Brettany, developed into soule à la crosse popular on the continent, which would explain the similarities between the Wel. and Bret.-Fr. var. of the game. Perhaps from France the game spread to the Iberian Peninsula, where in Portugal it developed as >CHOCA and in the Span.-speaking countries as >CHUECA.

SOULE, LA, old spelling *choule*, a medieval ball game, popular in present-day France in a few varieties. In a variety, in which the ball is played with curved sticks, it was known as >SOULE À LA CROSSE. In some areas a more brutal var. of the game, namely >MELAT, was played. In Avranches or on the Mont-Saint Michel island a var. called >CROSSERIE developed. In Flanders >SOLLEN was played, in England – >CAMP-BALL. A game played without the sticks, in which the ball was kicked, was called >SOULE LA PIED. Historians and ethnographers once thought that soule is an old Celtic game. P. Pezron in his *Antiquities of different nations, particularly the Celts* (1706) was quite convinced: 'I have no doubts that the round ball, which we call *la soule*, was invented by the ancient Celts to honor the Sun and for this reason it was thrown up'. At the beginning of the 20th cent. this opinion was challenged by L. Gougaud: 'Today, for lack of other evidence, one cannot say with certainty that the beginnings of *la soule* are as remote as the Celts. It seems that all we can say about the oldness of this game, if we can trust the evidence from the 2nd half of the 12th cent., is that at that time it had been played for a long time in many countries'. R.W. Henderson, an Amer. historian, thinks that soule was a continuation of a game known earlier in France as >CHUGAN and the latter in turn was adopted from the Muslims, through the Arabs, who for a few centuries occupied the Iberian Peninsula that bordered France and, for some time, a large territory of present-day France. In Henderson's opinion '*La soule* is closely related to the old Muslim customs: the same division of players into sides, sometimes divided with respect to the region, sometimes with respect to their marital status. The game started in the pitch center, sticks, large, small, curved or with a basket-like net at the end were used. And the game was also associated with the spring of a given year [...]'. A Fr. philologist and diplomat, J.J. Jusserand (1855-1932), following detailed studies, came to the conclusion that '*La soule*, although played between nobles and church dignitaries, and even monarchs, became a folk game. A parish would play against a parish, bachelors would play against husbands. These small tournaments stirred up the entire community. The evenings were a time of drinking and dancing and generally merriment as the entire village would make up the teams. Those were the happy days which everybody was looking forward to and which broke up the monotony of labor in the workshop or toil in the field. The day chosen for the game was usu. Shrove Tuesday, but often it was a day celebrated in memory of the patron of a given parish, Easter or Christmas. Very rarely was the day chosen arbitrarily'.
Soule was so popular in the 12th cent. that players were granted different local privileges and even special legacies of wealthy people. In 1147 de Trincavel, when confirming the privileges of the church in Beaumont in the province of Rouergue (district of Averyron and Tarn et Garrone), retained those granted by his predecessor, among them the right to get 7 large soule balls. In many regions of medieval France feudal levies included a soule ball or a certain number of soule balls that were given to the local lord. Often the latter was privileged to start the game by striking the ball with a wooden stick. The ball was often given to him by one of his subjects, esp. one who had married last in the previous year, which was sometimes related to the tradition of >BRIDEBALL. In the Josselin district of Morbihan, which was ruled by the Lusignan family, the ball was symbolically given to the lord at midday on Shrove Tuesday, in front of a cross known as Croix de Martray, together with 2 loaves of bread and 2 pitchers of wine. In Gué-de-Isle and in Langest a levy consisting of a soule ball was placed in the lord's pew right after the mass. In Chatelain de Mareuil, in the historical province of Berry, each newly wed man, after the 2nd night spent with his wife, was obliged to give his lord a stick and 2 new soule balls. The balls were usu. made of oakum, hay or rags, covered in leather. In Normandy, in La Pemmeraie, the local liege was given a leather ball as annual levy. Many historians think that the rights of the feudal lord connected with soule were a form of exercising control and keeping order in the course of the game, which attracted many players and spectators and led to many rows. For this reason official bans were constantly being issued. In 1369 Charles V banned soule, however without much effect since in 1440 the bishop of Trevir threatened excommunication upon anyone who dared play soule in his diocese. In some regions of France the lords tried to keep order during the game by taking part in it.
J.J. Jusserand, *Les sports et jeux d'exercise dans l'ancienne France*, 1901; R.W. Henderson, *Ball, Bat and Bishop. The Origin of Ball Games*, chapter: *La Soule*, 1947; L. Gougaud, 'La Soule en Bretagne', *Annales de Bretagne*, 1911, 27.

SOULE LA PIED, Fr. foot soul, a var. of >SOULE, LA, in which the ball was kicked by the players.

SOUND ARROW, a type of Tibetan archery. The tradition goes back to legendary times, when prince Gesar and his warriors fought with the dragon that oppressed his people. The dragon was invincible as he was too swift to be hit by spears and arrows. Then Gesar 'invented' arrows that produced a whistling sound. The frightened dragon could not move and soon was conquered. In memory of this event archery competitions are held in which arrows with short pipes attached to their heads are used. When the air flows through the pipes, a whistling sound is produced. The targets are square mats, about 30cm in diameter, with the bull's eye marked in red and the other circles in white, black and yellow. Before the contest the contestants sing the song of the Tibetan archers, composed specially for this occasion. Then they come to the line from which the shots are made. The contestant who first hits the bull's eye with two consecutive arrows wins.
Mu Fushan et al., 'Sound Arrow', TRAMCHIN, 22.

SOW-IN-THE-KIRK, an old Scot. game, in Fifeshire known as *church and mice*. A large hole (*kirk*) is dug in a field. Smaller holes, the number of which depends on the number of players, are dug around the central hole. Each player has a curved stick, which they put into their holes, to prevent a wooden peg or an animal backbone ('sow') being driven into the hole. A swine-herd is elected by lots. The swine-herd can drive the 'sows' into the large hole or to the smaller holes, when the players have taken their sticks out of them to prevent him from driving the 'sow' into the large hole. If the swine-herd succeeds, his role is taken over by the player into whose hole the 'sow' was driven into. Cf. >SO I HUL.
A.B. Gomme, 'Sow-in-the-Kirk', TGESI, 1898, II, 209-10.

SOWORIGUJ, one of 2 var. of Tajik folk horseback game, practiced in the Pamirs. Soworiguj is similar to contemporary >POLO. A regional var. of soworiguj is called >GUJ-BOZI. Because of the vicinity from which polo derives, close to the borders between Tibet, India, Pakistan and Tajikistan and the Himalayas and the Tian Mountains, the origin of soworiguj is very likely the same as that of >PULU, from which polo derives. The goal is made of two sticks put into the ground. Leather embroidered trousers are an original element of the players' dress.

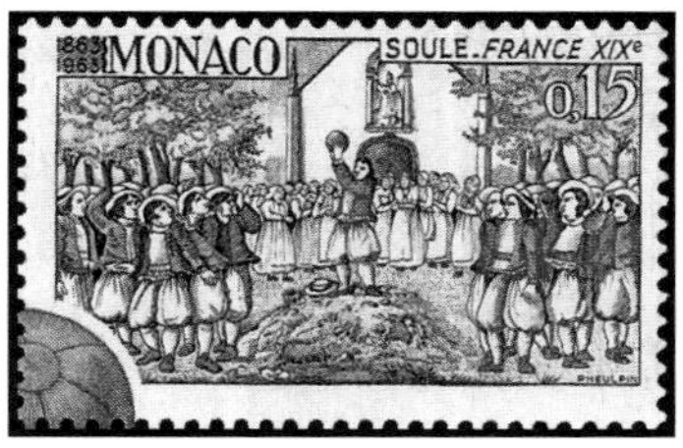

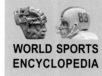

La soule on a postage stamp.

SPACE BALL, a sports competition combining volleyball, basketball and gymnastics. The game is played on a 4.5mx3m trampoline, the shorter sides of which are guarded by protective trampolines, slightly inclined, with a net sprung on a frame. Two players (singles) or 4 players (doubles) are separated by a double net structure, in which at a height of about 2.75m there is a ring with a basket, through which the players try to hit the ball so that it lands on the opposite side. The receiving player scores a point if the opponent fails to hit the ball and it touches the trampoline or the back guard. A point can also be scored from the service, if the ball bounces off the back guard of the opponent's side and touches the centrally placed partition, unless the defender manages to take possession of the rebound. A set consists of two games and seven points are needed to win a game. The tactics are to make the opponent lose the rhythm, feign the service and make feints to mislead the opponent.

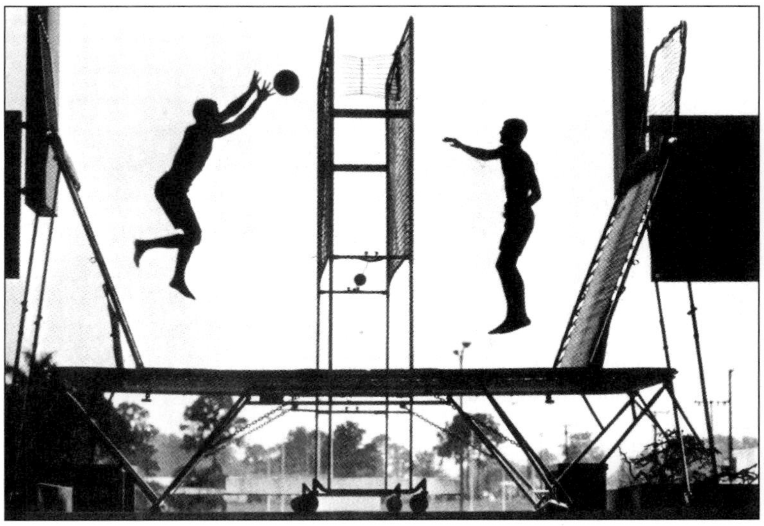
Space ball.

SPÆNDE FINGRE, Dan. for 'to squeeze fingers', [Dan. *spænde* – to tighten + *finger* – fingers, sg. *finger*]. Two contestants shake hands and then try to squeeze the opponent's fingers so that he is forced to kneel.
J. Møller, 'Spænde fingre', GID, 1997, 4.

SPÆNDE MUSKEL, Dan. for 'to tense the muscle', [Dan. *spænde* – tense + *muskel* – muscle]. Hand muscle tensing is known all over the world, but only in J. Møller's lexicon was it featured as a sports competition. In it the strength of the biceps is tested – when flexed it cannot be loosened even if pricked with a knife tip.
J. Mølller, 'Spænde muskel', GID, 1997, 4, 72-73.

SPARZAK, also *sparzony*, regional names of a Pol. game known popularly as >ZBIJAK.

SPEED CLIMBING, see >INDOOR CLIMBING.

SPEED HILL CLIMBING, a fast controlled ascent of a pre-arranged course by means of an automobile. The sport originated in France and the first event was held at Chanteloup in Nov. 1898. In 1899 the

S

WORLD SPORTS ENCYCLOPEDIA

first Brit. event was organized by the Automobile Club of Great Britain and Northern Ireland at Richmond-on-Thames, with 40 competitors climbing a 325yd. Petersham Hill. The winner was a Barriere tricycle, which infringed the speed limit law (12mph) with an average speed of 14mph. The next event was held at Mucklow Hill, Halesowen, and the winner covered the snowy 1mi. course in 9min. 2.4sec. By 1903 there were 26 hillclimb courses on Britain's

Argentine's Andrea Gonzalez leads Colombia's Erika Rueda and Berenice Moreno during 1000-m speed roller skating at Gran Park High School track in Winnipeg, Manitoba,Canada.

Butch Hardman of Golden, Colorado, guides his sprint car through the turn on the way victory in the Championship division of the 80th annual Pikes Peak International Hill Climb near Cascade, Colorado.

Speed skating.

public roads. On 12 Aug. 1905 the first event ever was held on a special motorsporting venue, a 1000yds. course created by leasing a private drive for sporting purposes. The event was won by E. Instone, who climbed the hill in his 35ph Daimler in 77.6sec. The main centers of Brit. motor racing in the pre-WWI era were Brooklands, Shelsley Walsh, and Aston Hill. In the 1930s new hillclimb courses were created at Prescott near Cheltenham and Tregwainton in Cornwall. The sport came into an abrupt end in 1925, which resulted from a growing number of accidents involving members of the public. The only hillclimb to continue was Shelsley Walsh. After WWII hillclimbing became the first motor sport to be reactivated, with 18 events held in 1946. In 1947 the National Hillclimb Championship was originated. The 1950s saw the complete domination of Brit. speed hillclimbing by the 1,000cc and 1,100cc Cooper-JAP racing cars. In the following years new events at Wiscombe Park, Oddicombe, Longleat, Gurston Down, Tregrehan, Werrington, Crocket St. Thomas, and Finlake Park were added to the calendar.

The administration of the rules and regulations of the sport in Great Britain is carried out by the RAC Motor Sports Association and clubs affiliated with it organize local events. Each driver is entitled to 2 practice and 2 competition runs and the competing cars are divided into several classes: road cars (both saloon and sports), modified saloons and sports, sports racing cars, and single seater racing cars, each class additionally split by engine cubic capacity. Sport hillclimbing is also popular in several other countries, the major events including: Pikes Peak International Hill Climb held in the Rocky Mountains in Colorado, Virginia City Hill Climb held in Nevada, New England Hillclimb Association events (USA); Queenstown Goldrush International Auto Hillclimb (N.Zealand); Mt. Cotton Hillclimb organized by MG Car Club of Queensland (Australia); Homburg ADAC Hillclimb (Germany), or a cycle of FIA-sponsored E.Ch. in Hillclimbing events throughout Europe.

A sport similar to speed hillclimbing is *hillclimbing*, or *trialling*, which simply involves driving a car or motorcycle up a steep muddy track.

The Internet: www.patjennings.com/hillclimb.html.

SPEED ROLLER SKATING, a var. of >ROLLER SKATING in which the objective is to cover a specified distance in the shortest time or to cover the longest distance in a specified time (1hr., 24hrs., etc). Races take place on flat courses a min. 5m in width and 124-400m in length (usu. between 200 and 400m), banked courses 168m in length, or roads. They may be held indoors or outdoors, on asphalt courses or on streets or roads with a 250-1000m loop. One of the best known courses is the 7-Eleven Velodrome in Colorado Springs (USA). Speed roller skating developed at the beginning of the 20th cent. in Great Britain. The first Brit. champion was H. Bert. In 1910 M. Borda covered a distance of 476,033km in 24hrs. In 1924 in Antwerp J. Carey set a world record in a 1hr. race, during which he covered a distance of 28,830km. The first W.Ch. took place in 1937 on a road in Manzy in France over distances of 500, 1000, 10,000, and 20,000m The first W.Ch. held on a course took place in 1938 and was then continued irregularly. Regular annual W.Ch. began in 1960 (road races) and 1978 (course races). The sport enjoys the greatest popularity in the USA, Japan, N.Zealand, Italy, Belgium, France, and Portugal. It is governed by the International Federation of Roller Skating (Fédération Internationale de Patinage ê Roulettes).

Women have participated in the W.Ch. since 1953 (road races) and 1954 (course races).

Inline skating. The construction of inline skates caused confusion within the tradition of speed roller skating, as they allow for greater speeds than the trad. pair-wheeled skates. They are also associated with an autonomous youth subculture, which makes them difficult to be recognized by some organizations of trad. speed roller skating. As a result of pressures exerted by the US Amateur Confederation of Roller Skating, which was the first organization to recognize the revolutionary changes in roller skating offered by inline skates, inline speed skating was introduced into the program of the W.Ch. in 1992. Both events may still find a compromise solution or, as in the case of >IN-LINE ROLLER HOCKEY, inline speed skating may well develop into a fully autonomous sport governed by a separate organization.

SPEED SAILING, a var. of sailing with the object being to reach top speeds over a specific distance, the course being flat and straight. Record setting on natural bodies of water is as old as boats and clocks, however, speed sailing is known for record setting on man-made reservoirs, where the only objective is to sail at top speed. The construction of a boat known as a trifoiler was the turning point in speed sailing. It consists of 2 front and 1 back foil, connected with a light frame made of 2 crossed pipes forming 3 arms with floaters at the ends. At the crossing of the pipes there is a mast with a single-flap, rigidly strung sail. A craft of this type was demonstrated for the first time in 1992 during the Fr. Trench regattas held in Saintes Maries de la Mer near Calais. It reached a speed of 50.02 knots (92.64km/h). This place is known for strong winds, but due to features of the coastline there are almost no waves along the narrow water course. The trifoiler was designed by an American, G. Ketterman. This design was soon followed by more perfected trifoilers, e.g. the Austrl. Yellow Pages, which has very small floaters, which decrease water resistance. Experience with large trifoilers led to the designing of smaller crafts, used in the regattas (>TRIFOILING).

The influence that J. Verne's book *In Eighty Days Around the World* (1873) had on the development of speed sailing found its expression in attempts to circumnavigate the globe in less than 80 days, which was not done until 1993 by the commodore Explorer catamaran with a 6-man crew skippered by a Frenchman B. Peyron (a competing yacht from N.Zealand suffered damage and never finished the race). Peyron's crew sailed round the world in 79 days 6hrs. 16min. and 56sec., covering a distance of 27,327 nautical miles (50,609.61km). This record was broken a year later by the same crew from N.Zealand which in 1993 was eliminated from the race after crashing into a rock below the surface. This time, the crew skippered by P. Blake and R. Knox-Johnson sailed round the world in 72 days 22hrs. 17mins. and 22sec., covering a distance roughly 1,000mi. shorter than that covered in 1993.

SPEED SKATING, a var. of >ICE SKATING consisting of racing on ice skates against the clock for the fastest time. Speed skaters race two at a time on a double track course measuring from 333.33m to 400m with 2 straight sides and curved ends. Each lane is 4-5m wide. The advantage of the inner curve is given alternately, and a space is left open between the tracks at one point for the skaters to switch tracks. At the W.Ch., E.Ch. and Ol.G. the official racing distances are 500, 1,500, 5,000 and 10,000m for men; and 500, 1,000, 1,500 and 3,000m for women. At the world and E.Ch. medals are given for the fastest total times of all events; at the Winter Ol.G. each event is scored separately. The most recent var. of speed skating is >SHORT TRACK SPEED SKATING. There are also many local var. of speed skating over long distances, sometimes exceeding 100km (>SKATE MARATHON).

History. The oldest forms of speed skating are connected with the origins of ice skating in general. The early invention of skates in ancient times must have involved some simple form of skate racing. The earliest written evidence of a clearly sporting competition on skates comes from Scotland, from the records of the Skating Club of Edinburgh (1642). Speed skating championships were organized by several Brit. skating clubs in the 18th cent. The earliest record of skating championships between the teams of Brit. towns and counties comes from 1763. After the end of the 18th cent. speed skating underwent rapid development in the Netherlands. The origins of speed skating on the Eur. continent date back to 1801, when the first women's championships were held in Groningen. Men's skating competitions became regular sports events in the 2nd half of the 19th cent. The first speed skating celebrities were the Englishmen W. 'Turkey' Smart and T. Watkinson, between 1854 and 1864; and, after 1870, the brothers J. and G. Smart. The renowned skaters of that time were professionals practicing exhibition skating and competing in betting races. In the years 1860-70 a number of amateur skating clubs were founded which provided regular training facilities for their members and filled the gap in ability between professional and amateur skaters. In 1887, G.G. Tebbutt from Bluntishon, England won the then most prestigious speed skating championships – the International Amateur Race in Leeuwarden – using

Speedway.

Speedway.

Speed skiing.

A postage stamp commemorating the speleological expedition to Cuba in 1961.

A rescue worker descends into the Berger cave, among of Europe's deepest, near Autrans at the foot of the French Alps in an effort to bring to the surface 4 surviving spelunkers trapped by flash flooding.

special speed skates of his own design. The construction of Tebbutt's skate was a combination of the Eng. fen skate (used in winter on frozen bogs in the Fens in England) and the Norw. skate. The new skate was very light and had a hollow ridge which greatly improved its speed and effectiveness. Tebbutt's skates were later refined and successfully used by 2 world top speed skaters, American J.T. Donoghue and Russian A. Panszyn, in the years 1888-92. The first Eur. speed skating championships were held in Hamburg (1891) and Vienna (1892) under the auspices of the German and Aus. national skating unions respectively.

The first speed skating W.Ch. were held in 1893 in Amsterdam, one year after the foundation of the official governing body of the sport – the International Skating Union (ISU); the first world champion was the legendary Du. skater J. Eden (1873-1925). Eden won also in 1895 and 1896 and set 5 official world records; he also became the world cycling champion in 1894 and 1895. Until the 1930s speed skating championships included only men's events. The first official women's W.Ch. were held in Stockholm in 1936. Men's speed skating was included in the first Winter Ol.G. in Chamonix in 1924; women's speed skating only in 1960 in Squaw Valley, although women's events were held as an exhibition sport in 1932. Before WWII the best male speed skaters came from the USA, Netherlands, Scandinavia and Russia (until 1914); after 1945 Soviet skaters took the lead. After 1990 former Soviet skaters represented the Commonwealth of Independent States; and after 1994 Russia, Belarus, and Ukraine respectively. For some periods of time the top skating class included competitors from Canada and Hungary; and after 1960 Japan and East Germany. The most outstanding speed skaters in history are J. Eden, Holland (world champion 1893-96); O. Mathiesen, Norway (world champion 1908, 1912-14); C. Thunberg, Finland (world champion 1923, 1925, 1928-9, 1931, 14-time champion at individual distances, Olympic champion 1924 and at 1500 and 5000m, and Olympic champion 1928); A. Schenk, Holland (world champion 1970-72, nine-time champion at individual distances, Olympic champion 1972 at 1500, 5000 and 10,000m); E. Heiden, USA (Olympic champion 1980 at 500, 1000, 1500, 5000 and 10,000m, world champion 1977-80, and ten-time world champion at individual distances).

Women's speed skating was dominated until 1947 by competitors from the USA, Scandinavia, and later from the USSR and Netherlands. After the inclusion of women's events in the Olympic program the top skaters represented East Germany. Up till the unification of Germany in 1990 East German women's speed skaters won seven Olympic gold medals. The best female skaters in history are L. Skoblikova, USSR, b.1939 (6-time Olympic gold medallist 1960-68, twice world champion and 3-

time world-record holder); K. Enke, East Germany, b.1961 (world-record holder, 3-time Olympic champion 1980-84, and 3-time world champion 1980-84); Y. van Gennip, Holland (3-time Olympic champion 1988); and B. Blair, USA (4-time Olympic champion 1988-94).

Z. Osiński, W. Starosta, *Łyżwiarstwo szybkie i fugurowe*, 1977; B. Publow, *Speed on Skates*, 1999; M.P. Sokołów, *Speed skating* (in Russian), 1959.

SPEED SKIING, a var. of >DOWNHILL SKIING where the objective is to break speed records. Speed skiers wear special suits providing excellent aerodynamics and protecting from burns that can result from friction against the snow at speeds exceeding 200km/h. Speed skiing events are esp. popular in Europe and the USA. The Ital. town of Cervina is considered the main center of speed skiing, while others include: La Plagne (France), Timberline (USA), Blackcomb, Whistler and Sun Peaks (Canada). Official world records have been registered by the International Skiing Federation (FIS) since 1931, when Italian L. Gasperi reached 136.6km/h during a downhill run. The current record holder is the Australian Harry Egger, who reached a speed of 248.1km/h in Les Arcs, France, in 1999.

SPEEDWAY, dirt-track racing on lightweight motorcycles. The track has a solid base, its surface is a loose mixture of shale or granite or a mixture of both. Many tracks are in greyhound racing stadia, or in football grounds. A track comprises 2 straights joined by 2 sweeping bends. The shape may vary a good deal; the length also varies from about 275m (300yds.) to 430m (470yds.). Width is dictated by the size of the venue. It is a highly professional sport in which 4 riders, as a rule, race against each other over 4 laps. Riders most often compete on motorcycles, although motorcycles with sidecars have sometimes also been used. Single cylinder, four stroke engines are allowed. The width of the back tire cannot exceed 10cm or a cubic capacity of 500ccm. The scoring system is as follows: 1st place – 3pts., 2nd place – 2pts., 3rd place – 1pt. and 4th place – 0pts. The tracks are licensed by national federations (local competitions) and the International Motorcycle Federation (W.Ch., E.Ch., international competitions).

History. Dirt-track racing on motorcycles dates back to about 1902 in the United States, and the first races in England were held in 1904 at Ipswich. In the 1920s-30s races were held in the Austrl. towns of Adelaide, Brisbane and Trebarton, from where the sport was exported to other Eng.-speaking countries. The first meeting on a cinder track took place at High Beech, Essex, in 1928. The first unofficial W.Ch. were held in 1929 on the initiative of *The Star*. Modern speedway derives from short-track racing staged at the West Maitland Agricultural Show in New South Wales, Australia, in 1923. The organizer

of that meeting, Johnnie Hoskins, exported the sport to Britain. W.Ch. for individual riders were first held at Wembley, London, in 1936. Initially standard motorcycles were used in dirt-track racing. Around 1930 a specialized motorcycle evolved. It is light, with a small fuel tank, sufficient for 4 laps, with an engine capable of reaching large short accelerations and maximum power over short track sections, light front wheel and heavy back wheel. In 1937 leg trailing was allowed, initially with the knee protected with a metal sheet, later with the foot forward. In 1930-35 speedway became popular in Czechoslovakia, Denmark, Yugoslavia, Germany and Poland. In Sweden speedway was banned until 1936. Official W.Ch. have been held since 1936, usu. annually. A team competition was introduced in 1960 and a Pairs competition in 1970. The Long Track Championship was inaugurated in 1971. Initially W.Ch. were held on Wembley in London, later they were moved to other countries, e.g. Sweden and Poland, and occasionally to the USSR and Denmark. The best speedway riders are B. Briggs, R. Moore, I. Mauger (N.Zealand) and O. Fundin (Sweden). Presently, speedway seems to be losing its popularity, mainly in countries of Western Europe, while retaining it in some countries of Eastern Europe, including Poland. LONGTRACK (also called *Sandbahn*) is a var. of speedway which takes place on 1000m tracks and, consequently, involves higher speeds. A longtrack bike is slightly larger and has a 2-speed gearbox. A total of 6 or sometimes even 8 riders compete in a race. The sport is popular mainly in Germany, but also in the Czech Republic, Finland, and Norway. Events in the USA and Australia take place around converted horse trotting arenas.

A. Martynkin, *Czarny sport*, 1972; B. Koperski, *Żużel, żużlowcy*, 1975; D. Lanning, *Speedway and Short Track Racing*, 1974.

SPELEOLOGY, the scientific study of caves and their exploration. Cave explorers are commonly known as 'cavers' or 'potholers'. Cavers explore holes in the ground, including lava caves, sandstone rifts, sea caves, and even man-made mines and sewers, but most interest is in natural limestone caves. From the technical point of view speleology combines elements of >MOUNTAIN CLIMBING and >SCUBA DIVING. The essential equipment includes protective clothing, boots with rubber molded soles, helmets, and lighting (formerly carbide lamps, today with long life batteries). Each caver must have 3 independent sources of light. For vertical descents ropes, harnesses, ascenders, descenders, karabiners, and ladders are required. Spare lighting, food, a whistle, and first-aid and survival equipment are essential, and survey equipment, cameras, and flashguns may also be carried. Neoprene wetsuits are the only suitable clothing for deep-water sections. A principle of 'take back what you brought'

S

**WORLD SPORTS
ENCYCLOPEDIA**

A postage stamp issued for the European Championship in Latin American dances in Berlin, 1983.

applies – no objects can be left in the caves, be it food packaging or broken equipment etc.

History. Scientific study of caves was started in the late 17th cent. Modern speleology derives from the mid 19th cent. The first national speleological society was the Fr. Société de Spéléologie de France, established in 1895 by E.A. Martel (1859-1938). The theoretical foundations of speleology were advanced by an Aus. G. Kyrle in *Grundriss des Theorischen Speläologie* (An outline of theoretical speleology, 1923). Speleology developed rapidly after WWII. In 1953 the 1st International Speleological Congress was held in Paris. The congresses, held every few years, are the main forum of international exchange. The most famous 'objects of study' includes the Fr. grotto in Lascaux, which has famous primitive rock drawings.

SPELL A'NOR, see >NORTHERN SPELL.

SPELL AND KNOR, see >NORTHERN SPELL.

SPELL AND NUR, a var. of a game from the >NORTHERN SPELL family, but featuring a few distinct differences. According to old ethnographic descriptions the game was played using a wooden ball and a stick with the club-shaped end on the batting side.

The *spell*, or the lever used to lift the ball, was made of a straight piece of wood, about 1in. thick (approx. 2.54cm) and a few inches long. The ball is put on the spell's end and the player knocks it up by hitting the other end, producing a see-saw effect. This operation is performed with one hand, while the other holds a piece of wood with which the player attempts to hit the ball once it has been launched. Each player has 2 attempts to drive the ball into the field. The object is to drive the ball the farthest distance. Points are awarded for segments of the distance covered. The winner is the player with the most points. Each player has the same number of hits and there is usu. only one round played.

A.B. Gomme, 'Nur and Spel', TGESI, 1894, I, 421-423.

SPELL AND ORE, see >NORTHERN SPELL.

SPIDSROD, see >STANTO.

SPIL MED BOLDTRÆ, Dan. for 'games with a stick to drive the ball away', a group of different games played in Denmark which, despite similarities to the games played in other countries, differ with respect to many elements characteristic of Denmark only. Among these elements are the bats, richly decorated and sculpted, which is not a feature of such games as Ger. >SCHLAGBALL, Pol. >PALANT, Eng. >CRICKET, Am. >BASEBALL, or Fin. >PESÄPALLO in which the bats, while differently shaped, are not ornamented. The Dan. bats feature carved ornaments of the highest artistic quality, on the handle and on the flat end, with which the ball is batted. This is not to say that every bat used in folk games is similarly ornamented.

Another characteristic feature of spil med boldtræ is using the sticks to decide the sides or the player (team) to begin the game. According to J. Møller, a Dan. historian of trad. and folk sports, 'one player, representing the team, throws the stick to another player, who must catch it with one hand. In this way, he grasps the stick at any part of its length. Now the first player, also with one hand, takes hold of the stick right over his opponent's hand so that his little finger touches the opponent's thumb. Then the 2nd player does the same, etc. The player, who last manages to hold the stick so that it can be whirled over the head three times and does not fall from the hand or thrown to a predetermined distance, wins the right to choose the pitch side. Team players can be chosen in the same way: those who manage to hold the stick in a specific way, become players of one team, the others become players of the other team'. These activities are accompanied (or rather were accompanied, as such trad. games are disappearing) by different short poems, rhymes etc. In the village of Ronne players recited the following words: *Tjyckan ejls smartan, kryss ejls tvarss, altinj* – thick or thin, cross or beam, all.

Ball batting games appeared in Denmark relatively late, in the 18th cent., under the Ger. influence, which is evidenced by such names as >TYSKBOLD, lit. 'German ball'. Spil med boldtræ also features more individual games than team ones, the mixing of elements of local games and Ger. and Eng. ones as Denmark had cultural, economic and political as well as sports relations with these countries.

J. Møller, 'Spil med boldtræ', GID, 1997, 1.

SPILLE HESTESKO, a Dan. game with a horseshoe. An old game played on a field with two very large metal stakes or pins (*Pind*), 1-2cm in diameter, about 25cm high and about 6-7m apart. The contestants take turns in throwing the horseshoe from the opposite sides so that they ring the pins or at least land very close to them. 2pts. are awarded if the horseshoe touches the pin with its side, 4pts. if it rings the pin and 8pts. if the horseshoe rings the pin and covers the opponent's horseshoe; when this happens, the opponent loses the 4pts. scored earlier. The game is usu. played until 20-30pts. are scored. Locally a different scoring system of 1, 3, and 5pts. is used. The game is similar to the Ang.-Sax. >HORSESHOE PITCHING also called, simply, horseshoes.

J. Møller, 'Spille hestesko', GID, 1997, 1, 98.

SPILLE RAADEN, full name *at spille raaden*, see >HALVRAADDEN.

SPILLE STAK, a Dan. var. of a knife game, similar to Pol. >CIP, [Dan. *spile* – play + *stak* – stack]. The game consists of 17 rounds: 1) the knife is thrown once from the inner side of the palm; 2) from the outer side of the palm, once; 3) from the left wrist,

once; 4) from the left elbow, once; 5) from the left arm, once; 6) from the forehead or a cap's visor, twice; 7) from the left thumb, 5 times; 8)-11) from the index, middle etc. fingers, once from each; 12)-15) the knife rests on the thumb and is pressed with the index finger, then the middle finger, ring and little fingers, once each; 16) the knife is put on the clasped hand, with the blade outwards and then flung into the ground; 17) the knife's blade is supported against either knee and from this position flung into the ground. The round is won by the player who completes it without any faults. A fault, e.g. if the knife simply falls to the ground instead of being stuck in it, results in the round being forfeited to the opponent. If a player manages to drive the knife in the ground so that the blade points upwards, he wins the round. A contestant, who drives the knife in the ground at an angle, may skip 3 subsequent throws.

J. Møller, 'Spille stak', GID, 1997, 1, 129.

SPIRAL BALL, a game popular in the former USSR, practiced in schools and summer resorts. The game was played in a circle, 6m in diameter, with a 4-5m-high pole placed in the middle. The ball was mounted on a string attached to the top of the pole. Spiral ball was played by two players standing on both sides of the diameter line, who hit the ball in order to wind it around the pole from one side or the other. The aim of the game was to prevent the ball from winding around and touching the pole. Players were not allowed to cross the dividing diameter line.

I.N. Chkhannikov, 'Piłka na spirali', GIZ, 1953, 63-64.

SPORT DANCING, any form of dancing viewed as a human activity characterized by rhythmic body movements to the accompaniment of music having the nature of an aesthetic competition. Each form of sport dancing has elements that relate it to the development of physical education. Therefore, dancing, esp. trad. and party dances, is usu. part of teaching programs and research at universities of physical education and sport academies. Modern forms of sports dance are practiced in 2 basic categories: standard dances, incl. Eng. waltz, Viennese waltz, tango, slow foxtrot, quickstep; and Lat. Amer. dances, incl. cha-cha-cha, rumba, samba, paso doble, and jive. These dances form the core of the program of international tournaments. At the same time there are numerous tournaments of other dances, usu. administered by separate organizations. These dances are sometimes incorporated into the programs of standard tournaments, without any direct consequence for the dancer's score or ranking. The status of tournament dances has in recent years been undergoing various modifications, and the resulting new class systems can scarcely be predicted. The multitude of professional dance organizations further obscures the picture of this dynamically developing branch of sport.

Elements evaluated by the umpires include: general movements and choreography, harmony, expression, figure variations and originality. The dancers are assessed by 5-7 judges, depending on the tournament rank. Not more than 6 couples are allowed in the finals. The scoring reflects the final position. The couple with the lowest grades is the winner.

Dress. Until 1999 there were no precise requirements as to the dress style of dancers, except for certain fixed criteria. Some specific rules, different for various dance classes, have traditionally been observed, however. For standard dances they included a long, trailing dress for a woman and a black or dark blue suit for a man. In Lat. Amer. dances, which require more dynamic body movements, the dress style of women began to evolve towards more nudity and eroticism, achieved by wearing split dresses showing the thighs and panty area, deep décolletage, see-through fabrics showing the entire body, etc. This tendency was countered by the new, more rigorous regulations of the International Dance Sport Federation (IDSF), according to which the area between the hip line and the panty line, plus the breast area must be covered completely. No see-through materials can be used and excessively scanty underwear is prohibited so that 'the panties show as little as possible during dancing'. If a two-piece suit is used for Lat. Amer. dances, 'then the top must not be a bra'. In standard dances deep décolletage both in the front and the back of the dress is prohibited, just as eccentric hairstyles and excessive make-up are. Jewelry is allowed, but only if it does not present a danger to the dancer or other competitors. Men

Spille hestesko.

Sport dancing.

should wear 'tail suit, black or midnight blue, with all the accessories (dress shirt, bow tie, studs etc.)' for standard dances, while for Latin dances they should wear black or midnight blue trousers and black, midnight blue, or white shirt or top with long sleeves. Any other colour of the man's top is allowed, only if it matches the material or colour of the lady's dress. Short hairstyle is preferred for men. The use of religious symbols as decoration or jewelry is not allowed. There have never been any serious restrictions as to the type of shoes allowed, but it is customary that the shoes match the rest of the dress.

History. The history of civilization has witnessed the development of many different forms of dancing, which has been present in all world cultures. Its most popular forms and traditions are connected with religious rituals. The oldest forms of ritual dances were connected with the Mediterranean culture, evidence of which can be found in the pyramids of Egypt. The oldest Gk. forms of ritual dances were part of the Minoan culture, on the island of Crete and in Akroteri on the island of Santorini. The best known of them was the ritual dance honoring Dionysus (or Bacchus). Modern ethnological research indicates that forms of ritual dancing, preserved among the peoples of the Americas, Africa, and Oceania, derive from the beginning of mankind. One of the earliest is the >SUN DANCE, still practiced among the Great Plains Indians of N.America, part of which were tests of skill and endurance. Others, preserved until modern times and closely connected with forms of sport competition or testing various skills, include e.g. the Maori >HAKA, Afr. >GLE GBEE, >ISKPA, >KAO GLE, >SANAMA BOJO NE, a dance known under the Eng. name of >FALSE LION, etc. Relics of old pagan ritual dancing forms have survived the longest in the Eur. varieties of >GAIK MAJOWY, which are present in several cultures, e.g. in Germany as >MAIBAUM, in Denmark as >SOMMER I BY, in Britain as >MAYPOLE, and in South America as >PALO DE MAYO. In medieval Europe the most popular religious dance, connected with the Christian tradition, was the dance of death.

Civilizational progress caused dancing to break off from its strictly ritual forms and evolve into more popular and recreational varieties. On the other hand, the development of centers of royal authority promoted the development of court dancing. The patronage of royal courts led to the evolution of artistic forms, such as ballet and pantomime. As democratization of society progressed, court dancing yielded to a new form – party dancing. The court predecessors of party dancing were such dances as: *contredanse* (Ital. *contradanza*), Pol. *polonez* (Fr. *polonaise*), quadrille and others. A turning point in the democratization of dancing was the adaptation of the trad. waltz, in which the partners faced one another, to the purposes of court dancing. More and more types of dances, such as galop (or galope) or tango – brought from Argentina and popularized in Europe and later also in the US – made their way to the aristocratic salons. 19th cent. balls, esp. cotillions, were often accompanied by various types of dancing competitions, e.g. selecting the best dancing couple of the evening. On the other hand, direct competition was always present in trad. dances, such as the Eng. *country dance*, and particularly the Amer. *square dance*. In fact, square dancers winning dancing competitions during local festivals acquired a high social status as early as the 19th century. At the beginning of the 20th cent. new forms of competition appeared in party dancing, at that time referred to as salon dancing. The first decades of the 20th cent. saw the emergence of numerous new dances, which – along with the Viennese waltz and tango – formed the program of official dancing balls and parties. They included the foxtrot (with its slow var. of *slowfox* and quicker var. of *quick-step*) and the Eng. waltz, which later began to be called standard. A clearly competitive form that was popular in the USA in the 1920s and 1930s was the >DANCE MARATHON, in which the longest surviving couple were the winners. The first dance based on Lat. Amer. rhythms was the Cuban rumba, popularized by D. Azpiazu's performances in New York in 1929 and his triumphal Eur. tour in 1930. In the 1930s the rumba was followed by the paso doble and in 1945 – by samba, then jive and cha-cha-cha. In the 1930s and 1940s great popularity was enjoyed by such dances deriving from the jazz tradition as swing or boogie-woogie, and in the 1950s – rock'n'roll. The 1960s became dominated by the madison and the twist, the latter popularized by Chubby Checker, while the Lat. Amer. group gained another favourite – the bossa nova. Dance associations have long resisted any attempts to formalize the regulations regarding dance competitions, but the rapid development of that form of competition in the 1960s was clearly that of a sport, irrespective of the terminology associated with it, just as in the case of >FIGURE SKATING. In 1963 the International Council of Dancing Teachers came up with a World Dance Program, which formed a basis for modern tournament dancing in the classes of standard and Lat. Amer. dances. This program does not include new, dynamically evolving dances, e.g. dances based on the jazz tradition, rock'n'roll or disco. At the same time new ephemeral forms are emerging, such as the erotic lambada or kung-fu, imitating Eastern martial arts. Not all of them deserve our attention, but even those that fail to remain in the permanent dancing repertoire of modern societies introduce new elements which silently enter the style of performing other dances and remain present in the general approach to dancing. It seems quite reasonable that the list of tournament dances should soon be extended over several new categories or classes, which would reflect much better the structure of competitive dancing worldwide. This has not yet been undertaken by the International Dance Sport Federation (IDSF) established in the mid-1960s and based on the split that occurred in 1963. In the meantime, the non-standard dances keep developing dynamically and form their own regional, specialized associations and clubs, of which only few maintain any relations with the IDSF. An impulse to integrate the international dance associations came in 1997, when the IDSF was recognized by the IOC, which may result in including sport dancing in the 2008 Olympic program. Among the international associations that co-operate with IDSF are World Dance and the Dance Sport Council. There are also independent international and regional associations of specific, usu. non-standard, dances, e.g. the World Rock'n'Roll Confederation. The result of consultations between the IDSF and these organizations was an agreement reached in 1999, intended to eliminate the division into professional and amateur dancers. Among the most prominent activists within the IDSF is its co-founder and president for many years (1965-1997) D. Hegemann (b. 1917), who was succeeded in 1998 by R. Baumann of Switzerland. The IDSF currently affiliates the national organizations of 74 countries (2000) and has over 9 million dancers registered worldwide, who compete in tournaments of various kinds. The most important event organized by IDSF is the annual W.Ch., held in the general and specific categories. Among the best dancers in the 1990s were – in the standard class – W. Pino and A. Buciarelli (Italy), W.Ch. gold medalists in 1998 and silver medalists in 1997; Allan and Donna Shingler (Great Britain); M. Bonsignori and M. Baldosseroni (Italy) and – in the Lat. Amer. class – B. Watson and Carmen (Germany), Nicolle and Matthew Cutler (W.Ch. gold medal in 1999); J. Leunis and S. Kryklyvy (Belgium); A. Bezikova and D. Timochin (Russia); K. Venturini and A. Skufca (Slovenia). Besides W.Ch. and E.Ch., the most prestigious tournaments of specific dances or the 10 combined dances are the Dance Festival in Blackpool, the Dans tournament in Slagharen, the Elsa Wells International Championships, the Kopenhagen tournament, the Munich tournament, and the International Championships of Great Britain (the British are considered to be the best teachers of dancing). The rank list in rock and roll was topped in 1999-2000 by K. Fialova and R. Vercak (Czech Republic), G. Masinova and R. Kolb (Czech Republic), M. Ventura and J. Tomero (Spain), Claudia and Christian Rüssel (Germany). One of the most dynamically developing forms of tournament dancing is >WHEELCHAIR DANCE for the disabled.

SPORTS ACROBATICS, is different from >RHYTHMIC GYMNASTICS and >OLYMPIC GYMNASTICS in that it places different emphasis on the same motor elements. Whereas in gymnastics the aim is to achieve movement and esthetic perfection, sports acrobatics is more focused on defeating the existing preconceptions of the motor limitations of the human body. What counts here is the extent to which an acrobat can push back such limitations rather than the esthetic perfection (though it also counts).

Fundamentals. There are a number of women's and men's events including: tumbling, trampolining as well as pair and group events. Each event involves 3 passes judged on a 10-pt. scale (10 being the highest score from which deductions are made for each mistake or error detected).

TUMBLING involves 3 series of acrobatic jumps performed on a sprung floor that is 25m long, 1.5m wide and has a run-up track of 10m. The first of the 3 passes – the straight – comprises a series of round-offs, whips, flips, straight jumps, pike back somersaults, kick outs, side somersaults and straight back somersaults. The second run, the twisting, utilizes single and double somersaults combined with flips and 180°, 360°, 720° and even 900° twists. The third pass, the combined, involves a combination of somersaults and twists.

TRAMPOLINING is broken down into 1) individual men's and women's routines and 2) synchronized trampoline routine performed by 2 competitors (both men and women) on 2 separate trampolines. A competitor performs 1 compulsory routine and 2 voluntary ones. Each routine consists of 10 pre-set skills.

GROUP EXERCISE comprises team exercises performed by 3-member teams (women) and teams of 4 (men). The exercises are choreographed to music and are performed on the so-called Reuther field (named after its inventor) which is a large board introduced to sports acrobatics in 1974. Both men and women perform 3 routines: 1) static, without the flights characteristic of the dynamic pass, whereby the competitors form various pyramids and have to keep their balance for a specified period of time. The structure so formed is called a 'picture'. A women's 'picture' is composed of the 3 competitors dubbed the 'base', the 'middle' and the 'top'. In men's events the competitors are referred to as the 'base', the 'first middle', the 'second middle' and the 'top', respectively. Each 'picture' has to correspond to a description submitted by the team before the competition. In a 1-picture pyramid the competitors have to keep their balance for 4sec. each time and in the so-called 2-picture pyramid the time is set at 2sec.; 2) a dynamic routine has to incorporate flight elements such as tossing and acrobatic jumps as well as body flexing (only in women's routines); 3) a combined pass is a combination of various static, dynamic, individual and choreographic elements.

History. Displays of sports acrobatics date back to ancient times (although the term sports acrobatics had not been coined). This is best exemplified by the various paintings and drawings which have been preserved in many cultures. The most famous instance of sports acrobatics were the Cretan tauromachias practiced until c.1500 BC on Crete and Santorin. An athlete approached a bull from the front, grabbed him by the horns and, in a manner similar to gymnasts performing on parallel bars, he performed an acrobatic tumble to get onto the bull's back (>TAUROMACHY). While on the bull's back he tried to execute as many evolutions as possible and stay there as long as he could. The winner was determined on the basis of the total number of evolutions performed and time he managed to stay on the bull's back. There are ancient Eg. prints from the 12th cent. BC which also depict acrobatic feats. Circus acrobatics and street acrobatics appeared as soon as ancient cities were established. 'Living architecture' contests were organized during the Renaissance in which the acrobatic constructions were sometimes as high as 9m. Span. acrobats and their >CASTELLS were particularly popular on the Iberian Peninsula but also known in the Span. colonies in Cent. America and Mexico.

The dynamic development of display acrobatics during the Renaissance provoked severe criticism by intellectuals and the Royal. There was a movement to propagate the importance of physical fitness, which had been much ignored during the Middle Ages and there was a learned debate on which forms of bodily exercise should be accepted and which rejected. Since acrobatics was deemed to be of common, folk origin, it was dismissed as a method of body training for the upper classes. B. Castiglione's *Il Cortegiano* (*The Courtier*, 1528) contained the harshest critique of sports acrobatics.

Acrobatics developed independently in Asia, and especially in China within the tradition of 'the feasts of one hundred pleasures' called >BAXI (see also Chin. acrobatics varieties such as >LIAN ACROBAT-

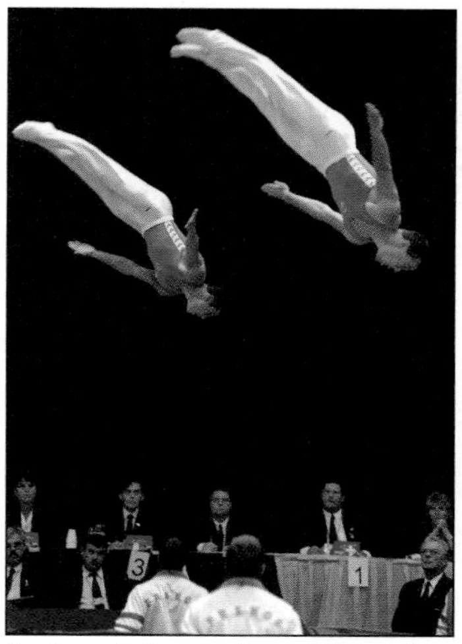

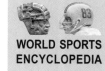

Sports acrobatics – men's parallel trampoline.

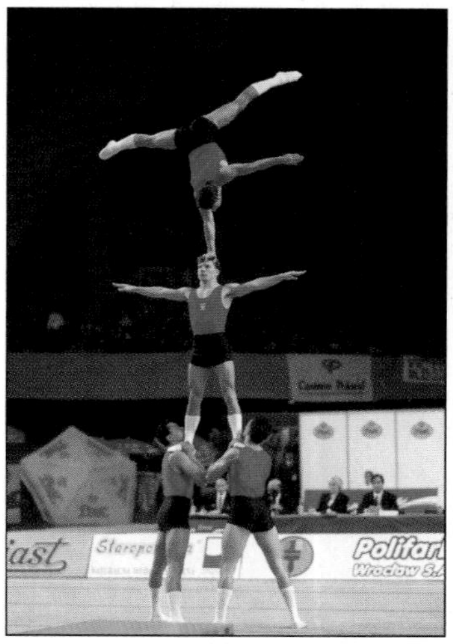

Sports acrobatics – men's team exercise.

Sports acrobatics – women's team exercise.

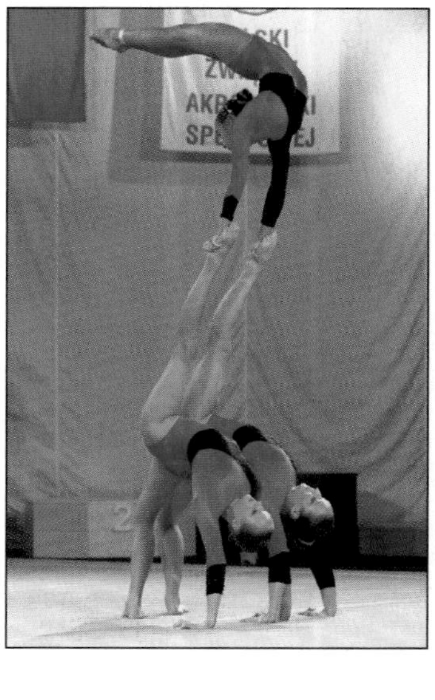

S
WORLD SPORTS ENCYCLOPEDIA

Joey Johnson of Canada takes an off-balance shot during the Netherlands vs. Canada Men's Wheelchair Basketball match as part of the 2000 Sydney Paralympic Games.

Brad Dubberley of Australia (right) takes on Michael Roethlisberger of Switzerland as Australia defeat Switzerland 42-32 in the Pool, A Rugby Wheelchair game in The Dome during the Sydney 2000 Paralympics.

Jeff Adams celebrates after winning Gold in the Men's 800-m T54 Final at Olympic Park during the Sydney 2000 Paralympics.

A shot put competition at the Paralympic Games.

ICS or >ACROBATICS ON A POLE). The great reformer of circus art P. Astley (1742-1814) brought about the rapid development of the circus and its arts, including acrobatics, after he introduced the covered circus arena. The next stage was the travelling circus, after the Americans N. Howe and A. Turner developed the large marquee circus (1826). During that period the common-origin reputation of acrobatics was further strengthened and acrobatics was deemed unworthy of any serious interest. In 1860 the Pol. 'Tygodnik Ilustrowany' ('The Illustrated Weekly') criticized sports acrobatics severely: 'Leaving aside the physical danger, we hasten to add that mastering arts of such provenance has a significant influence on lowering one's moral standards, on turning a person into an animal or beast, to put it in a nutshell. [...] That is why we are delighted that there are not so many Polish names on the list of those [...] buffoons'. The intellectual elites found it particularly annoying that while theaters were empty, circuses often attracted full houses. In 1873 'Kurier Poznański' ('Poznań Herald') wrote the following about circus acrobatics shows: 'Maybe it is nice and funny when people arrive in droves [...] but I do not find it amusing. I do not appreciate all those crude arts in a city that pays so little attention to the fine ones'. Despite all the criticism, street acrobatics still enjoyed popularity in various Eur. countries until the beginning of the 20th century when more modern forms of sports shows evolved and the rapid development of mass media resulted in waning interest in trad. folk performances including street acrobatics. In Poland the last acrobatics troupes, usu. associated with strongmen's feats (bar bending, weightlifting, wrestling), operated until the 1960s. At the turn of the 19th cent. certain acrobatic feats became more prestigious due to the fact that they became part of public shows organized by open gymnastics associations whose aim was to prove the need of physical exercise to develop a spirit of patriotism and nationalism. Such shows were particularly popular among the members of the Ger. Turnvereins ('unions to practice gymnastics', since about 1840) and then the Czech 'Sokol' and Pol. 'Sokół' ('Falcon') (since 1861 and 1867, respectively). Thanks to the fact that acrobatic exercises were included in the programs of such societies, acrobatics could develop as a separate sport and was demonstrated, on a one-off basis, during the 1932 Ol.G. in Los Angeles. The foundations of sports acrobatics as a fully autonomous sport were developed in 1939 in the USSR followed by the all-Union championship that took place in the same year. After 1945 sports acrobatics developed rapidly, especially in Czechoslovakia, Bulgaria and the German Democratic Republic, i.e. in the countries that remained under Soviet influence. When the USSR was reunited with the international sports community (in 1952), sports acrobatics became popular in the Federal Republic of Germany, the US and Great Britain as well. The International Federation of Sports Acrobatics (IFSA) was founded in 1973. W.Ch. have been held since 1974 and E.Ch. since 1978. The International Trampoline Federation (FIT) was established around the same time. In the mid-1990s they both decided to strengthen their links with the International Gymnastics Federation (FIG) and the three federations were united under the name of FIG in Jan. 2000. Trampolining was included in the gymnastics during the 2000 Ol.G. in Sydney.

SPORTS AERONAUTICS, a group of sports comprising many separate events that consist in moving through the air with 1) lighter-than-air equipment (>BALLOONING) and 2) heavier-than-air equipment (>SKY SURFING, >HANG GLIDING, >AEROPLANE SPORTS, >COMPETITIVE PARACHUTING, >B.A.S.E. JUMPING, >GLIDING).

SPORTS FOR THE DISABLED, every sport practiced by physically or mentally impaired; the impairment resulting from the amputation of hands or legs, paralysis or other reasons, which clearly restrict physical ability, such as dwarfism, blindness, arthritis, osteogenesis imperfecta, multiple sclerosis, mental retardation etc. Disabled sports are divided into 2 main types: 1) athletic and sporting events and games for the disabled and partially disabled (e.g., the blind and visually impaired, amputees, and those suffering cerebral palsy, and learning difficulties), the events being called Paralympics; and 2) sports training and athletic competitions for people with mental retardation, called Special Olympics.

Paraplegic Games are organized for the paraplegics. Development of sports for the disabled has become a permanent feature in highly civilized countries, while in many Third World communities any type of disability is still a common cause of discrimination and elimination from social life. Likewise, in societies, where social movement for disabled sports has made considerable progress, the tendency to discriminate against the disabled can still be observed. C. Sherill, the author and editor of countless scientific articles and books on disabled sports,

Monte Meier of the USA competes in the Men's Giant Slalom, class LW2, during the Salt Lake City Winter Paralympic

responding to such tendencies, offers the following definition of the ultimate athlete, not in the sense of complete physical ability but in the sense of aspirations and desire to achieve the objectives:

The ultimate athlete can be anyone, disabled or able-bodied, who demonstrates the capacity to dream, the unwavering intent to be the best, and the willingness to pay the price of long, hard and strenuous training.

'Disability' is today a pejorative generic term, which avoids defining the type of disability. University graduate, M. Kaziów, a blind Pol. writer without both hands, wrote the following words:

A word denoting some degree of disability, e.g. 'deaf', 'blind', 'hump-backed', 'paralytic', 'cripple' is a shameful thing for some. All these names irritate disabled persons and trigger unfounded feelings of shame. But it is not the extent of disability that determines our humanity but our attitude, attitude to our self, ability, skills. Disability of any kind is a problem and must be accepted. To help us accept it we have different types of adaptation or, as we say, rehabilitation. A rehabilitated invalid, despite the disfunction of some organ, hand or leg, is professionally able. It is this ability that contributed to the coining of a notion that replaces the word 'invalid' with the word, or rather a rhetorical figure of speech, namely 'disability'. This figure of speech has been accepted by society, is understood, everybody knows what it entails.

M. Kaziów is against the use of euphemisms since they obscure the picture of complete ability. One such euphemism is the term 'differently able':

Creation [...] of different euphemisms is not always useful. Sometimes it obscures the true meaning of the word. This is the case when we are ashamed of something and we do not want to call something its true name. Then we use a substitute word, sometimes even a figure of speech [...]. Some 'mindful' person came up [...] with a figure of speech, intended to integrate the invalid with society, completely conceal the disability from the eyes of

'healthy' society. I am referring to the euphemistic term of 'differently able'. The sound of it is interesting, I admit, and the mass media or even the magazines dealing with disability have started to use this term. I have a feeling that it is very misleading. What does 'able' mean? We know. So if we put this word before the word 'differently' we must come to the conclusion that somebody is e.g. able but differently, healthy but differently, intelligent but differently – but how? Disability relates to something – movement, hearing, speaking, seeing, whereas ability relates to everything since an able person is simply able. And nothing else. This way of reasoning can be understood differently than intended. If somebody is able, s/he does not need any assistance, and the fact that s/he is able differently is his/her problem. Let us help the disabled not with euphemisms but with a proper attitude to their effort, their lot, their actual state. Let us simply help them in the human way, not differently!

History. The idea of disabled sports was born in 1924, when the first world games for the deaf were organized in Paris. During the games the International Deaf Sports Committee (Comité International des Sports des Sourds) was established. Every four years the committee organized summer games for the deaf. In 1949 winter games for the deaf were organized for the first time. Initiatives not connected with the mainstream of disabled sports sometimes determined the development of sports events adapted to the needs of the disabled. This was the

case of >PÉTANQUE, a var. of >BOULES, adapted to the needs of the disabled by E. Pitiot, who wanted to help his friend J. Le Noire, injured in an accident, to play the game. Development of disabled sports picked up speed after WWII, which left a record number of amputees and paralytics. The development of mass rehabilitation forced in this way attracted the attention of medical personnel to the role of sport in the process of physical and psychological rehabilitation of the disabled and their integration with the healthy part of society. This tendency was strengthened along with the intensification of civilizational processes that led to illnesses and different types of disability resulting from the increasing number of road accidents, use of chemistry in nutrition, side effects of medicines (increased number of congenital diseases). As early as 1944 the National Spinal Injuries Centre of the Stoke Mandeville Hospital in Aylesbury in Great Britain was established, where the rehabilitation process included competition between wheelchair-bound disabled patients. In 1948 L. Guttmann started the first games on the lawn in front of the hospital, in which 16 patients took part. The games proved effective not only in the process of motorial rehabilitation but also considerably contributed to the improvement of their psychological state, boosting their confidence and decreasing the feeling of social isolation. Soon other events, among them archery, bowling, fencing, table tennis, and athletic events were included in the games. The first international games for paralysed patients with about 130 contestants participating were held in 1952 in Stoke Mandeville; subsequently they were organized every year. In the 1950s the idea of competition between wheelchair bound patients was transferred to the United States by B.H. Lipton, who introduced it to the Joseph Bulova School of Watchmaking. Thanks to Lipton's activity, the First National Wheelchair Games in the United States were organized in 1958. During the event the National Wheelchair Association, later renamed Wheelchair Sport USA, was established. The association does not embrace wheelchair basketball, which in the United States is supervised by the National Wheelchair Basketball Association, established in 1949. Soon other events were included in the Stoke Mandeville games, such as weight lifting, fencing and swimming. The International Stoke Mandeville Games Federation was also established. In 1960 the games were organized for the first time not in Stoke Mandeville, but in Rome, to coincide with the OI.G. held there. The games attracted 400 contestants from 23 countries. The contestants were received at an audience by Pope John XXIII, who said in his powerful speech 'You are the Coubertins for the paralyzed'. In this way the tradition soon termed 'Olympic Games for the Disabled' was started. It was planned that the games be held every 4 years in the town hosting the OI.G.; for different reasons this was not always possible. In 1964 the OI.G. for the Disabled were held in Tokyo. In 1968, instead of Mexico City, the OI.G. for the Disabled were held in Ramat Gan near Tel Aviv in Israel; they attracted 29 national teams and 750 contestants. The wheelchair basketball finals between the US and Israel attracted about 5,000 spectators. The trophy was presented to the winner, the Israeli team, by Gen. M. Dayan. In the same year E. Kennedy Shriver started the Special Games. The event was an extension of previous events organized on a smaller scale, started in Rockville, Maryland (USA) in 1963. It comprised 23 summer, winter and spectator sports for ages 8 and up. The First Wheelchair Pan Amer. Games were held In 1967 in Winnipeg, in the Can. province of Manitoba.

Meanwhile, in 1972 the OI.G. for the Disabled were held in Heidelberg, to parallel the OI.G. held in Munich. At the same time the social movement for disabled sports made considerable inroads in Canada. In 1973 E. Reimer, the wheelchair world champion, was named the best sportsman of Canada. The OI.G. for the Disabled of Canada were held in Edmonton in 1975. They were supplemented by other events, organized on a state scale, e.g. the games of the Ontario province, started in 1975 and continued until 1985, initially held annually and later biannually. In this way Canada prepared the ground for the further development of the OI.G. for the Disabled. The experience of this country bore fruit during the International Games for the Disabled held in Montreal in 1976, soon after the OI.G. Among the participants were 38 national teams and the events attracted 100,000 spectators. For the first time in history, apart from the paralyzed the blind and amputees were invited to take part in the OI.G. for the Disabled. In 1980 the OI.G. for the Disabled were not held in Moscow, as planned, but in Arnhem in Holland, with 2,000 contestants representing 42 countries participating. For the first time multiple sclerosis patients were invited. 1981 was declared by the UN the Year for Disabled Persons. Paradoxically, in 1981 the International Olympic Committee protested against the use of the word 'Olympiad' or 'OI.G.' in the names denoting games for the disabled. As a result, the name 'OI.G. for the Disabled' was replaced with 'Paralympics'. The Special Olympics International, the organization responsible for the mentally retarded, however, retained its name.

During the OI.G. in Los Angeles (1984) two disabled sports were included as spectator sports in the main program: the women's wheelchair 800m race, which was won by an American, S.R. Hedrick (2:15,50), and men's wheelchair 1,500m race, won by P. Van Winkle from Belgium (3:58,50). The events were watched by approx. 90,000 spectators and approx. 1.5 billion TV viewers. The organizers of the Paralympics did not manage to hold them in Los Angeles; it was held on Long Island in New York. The event attracted approx. 3,000 disabled sportsmen and sportswomen from 45 countries. In Seoul in 1988 as many as 370 world records and over 600 Paraympic records were set.

The International Paralympic Committee (IPC) was established in 1989. Different organizations specialized in the sports of different disabilities were established, among them the International Deaf Sports Committee, existing since 1924, the Cerebral Palsy International Sports and Recreation Association (CPISRA), the International Blind Sports Association, the International Sports Organization of the Disabled (ISOD). The Stoke Mandeville center continued its activity, also outside the United States through the International Stoke Mandeville Wheelchair Sports Federation.

The 1992 Paralympics were held in Barcelona in the main Olympic stadium, right after the OI.G.. The opening ceremony was attended by 70,000 spectators and the games attracted about 4,000 contestants from 60 countries. The basketball finals were watched by 12,000 spectators. The torch was lit with an arrow by A. Rebollo, a disabled archer, who had done the same during the regular OI.G. held in Barcelona. The Paralympics in Barcelona were held under the auspices of the Span. queen, Sophia, with the motto 'Sport without Limits'. The Barcelona Paralympics had their first mascot, Petra, a smiling girl, full of energy, without arms, created by J. Mariscal. The Paralympics organized after the 1996 OI.G. in Atlanta attracted 4,000 contestants from over 100 countries. Contests were held in 19 sports, including 14 Olympic ones, e.g. athletic events, basketball, judo, cycling, swimming, horseriding, fencing, table tennis, archery, football, boccia, weight lifting (lying), goalball, lawn bowling and tennis. The new sports included wheelchair racquetball. The motto of the Paralympics was *The Triumph of the Human Spirit*.

The first Winter Paralympic Games were held in Sweden in 1976. They were not organized by any non-Eur. country until 1998 when they were organized after the Winter OI.G. in Nagano with the motto *Paralympics! Catch the Excitement!*. The games included 34 competitions in 5 different sports: ice sledge racing, sledge hockey, Alpine skiing, cross-country skiing and biathlon.

The Special Olympics movement was developing concurrently; in 1988 it was recognized by the International Olympic Committee. Today the program of Special Olympics comprises 140 national programs in 18 summer and 6 winter events.

Bin Houl of China in action in the Men's High Jump Final F42 at Olympic Park during the Sydney 2000 Paralympic Games.

A marathon competition for the disabled.

Dean Thomas of Great Britain in action during his match against Stacey Roche of New Zealand at boccia during the Sydney 2000 Paralympic Games.

Martin Evans (right) and Scott Robertson of Great Britain in action during their table tennis doubles match against Jan-Krister Gustavsson and Ernst Bollden of Sweden during the Sydney 2000 Paralympic Games.

In 1995 the Special Olympics were held in New Haven, USA, with approx. 7,000 contestants from 140 countries participating. The Olympic torch was lit in Greece and the event was opened by then US President, Bill Clinton. For the first time the program included a marathon and a wide range of other sports, e.g. badminton, equestrian sports, volleyball, rollerskating and softball. Coverage of the event was provided by ABC in cooperation with other Amer. broadcasting corporations. Networks of other countries showed little interest in the event, making only scant references to it in the news.
The latest tendency in sports for the mentally impaired is mainstreaming with fully abled sportsmen, particularly during training. In order to accelerate the process, the Special Olympics Unified Sports program was started in 1991, during the Special Olympics held in Minneapolis (USA). The program aims to include positive joint activity of young contestants carrying developmental incentives. In the US such contests are casually called Games of Inclusion. In 1991 the program comprised only 100 contestants, whereas in 1995 it embraced as many as 1,000.
International federations are attempting with increasing frequency to adapt their sports to the needs of the disabled. The leader in this respect is the International Orienteering Federation (>TRAIL ORIENTEERING). Attempts are being made to enable the disabled to practice such challenging sports as mountaineering. Next to trad. disabled sports such as wheelchair races, new ones have appeared, particularly fit for specific groups of the disabled, for example >GOALBALL. Adapting sports to accommodate the needs of the blind is more difficult. In running this was solved by introducing a parallel race by a seeing contestant; in cycling – in 1986, when tandem bikes were used for the first time, with one seeing cyclist, followed by tricycle bikes (see >CYCLING FOR THE DISABLED). In ball games, in which the ball is rolled towards the opponents' goal, special sound signals are used to facilitate orientation; see also >ARCHERY FOR THE DISABLED, >BOCCIA FOR THE DISABLED, >HORSE RIDING FOR THE DISABLED, >JUDO FOR THE DISABLED, >FOOTBALL FOR THE DISABLED, >POWERLIFTING FOR THE DISABLED, >SHOOTING FOR THE DISABLED, >SKIING FOR THE DISABLED, >SLEDGE HOCKEY, >SWIMMING FOR THE DISABLED, >VOLLEYBALL FOR THE DISABLED, >WHEELCHAIR BASKETBALL, >WHEELCHAIR FENCING, >WHEELCHAIR RUGBY, >WHEELCHAIR TABLE TENNIS, >WHEELCHAIR TENNIS, >SAILING FOR THE DISABLED.
Disabled sports in film and literature. Although not connected with sport, such films as The Phantom of the Opera, 1925, with C. Laughton, and The Hunchback of Notre Dame, 1939, with L. Chaney, increased public awareness of and sensitivity to the disabled and prepared the ground for the emancipation of the disabled in sport. A similar role with respect to the mentally impaired was played by the novel *One Flew Over the Cuckoo's Nest*, written in 1962 by K. Kesey, and adapted to film by D. Wasserman in 1974 with an excellent performance by J. Nicholson. The disabled were depicted in film much earlier, although not necessarily in connection with sport. *Freaks* released in 1932, directed by T. Browning, featured dwarfs and cripples employed in the circus. In 1975 and 1977 a two-part film *The Other Side of the Mountain* depicted the true story behind attempts to regain complete motorial functionality by an Amer. skier J. Kilmont, paralyzed after an accident during competitions. *The Eleanor and Lou Gehrig Story*, released in 1978, was a story of a baseball player fighting amyothropic lateral sclerosis. *The Terry Fox Story* (1983) told the true story of the title hero, a Canadian, who, despite amputation, made the famous Marathon of Hope over a distance of 300 miles (over 4,800km). Champions (1984) was about the life of the jockey B. Champion (played by J. Hurt), who struggled to maintain high standards in steeplechase despite debilitating cancer. *My Left Foot*, released in 1989, is the story of C. Brown (played by D. Day Lewis), who became a well-known artist despite advanced multiple sclerosis. The film is not about sport; however, in one of the first scenes little Chris, standing in goal, plays with his peers. He bounces the ball awkwardly, but effectively with his head, which his peers find amusing. Despite this, he proves to be a great goalkeeper.

R.C. Adams, J.A. McCubbine, *Games, Sports and Exercises for the Physically Disabled*, 1991; A. Allen, *Sports for the Handicapped*; 1981; W. Duński, *Ucieczka w życie*, 1996; G. Frazer, ed. *Ontario Cerbral Palsy Sports Association's Coaches Manual*, 1991; M. Kaziów, 'Sprawni inaczej – czyli jak?', *Serce i Troska*, 1995; M.E. Ridgway, 'Disabled Sport', EWS, 1996, I; C. Sherill, ed., *Sports and Disabled Athletes*, 1986; J.U. Sein, 'New Vistas in Competitive Sports for Athletes with Handicapping Conditions', *Exceptional Educational Quarterly*, May, 1982.

Peter Nicol of England plays a shot during his match against Anthony Ricketts of Australia in Men's Singles Squash at the 2002 Commonwealth Games, Manchester, England.

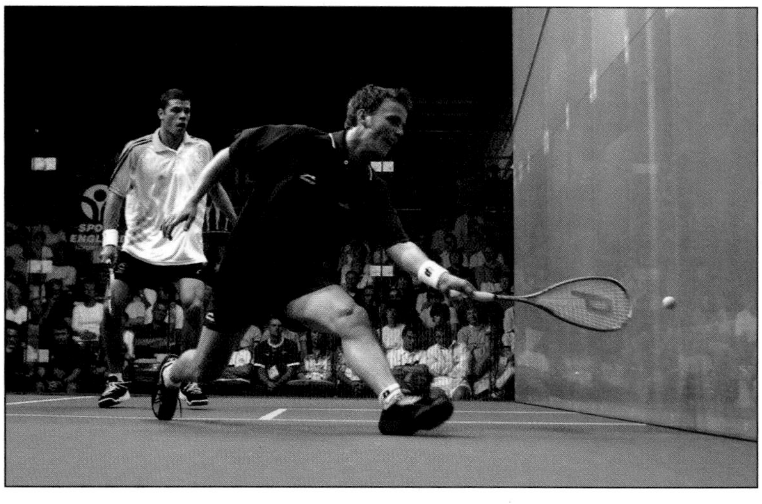

SPORTS JUMP, a var. of jump as one of the 4 main motor abilities of man, next to >RUNNING, walking and throwing, made for competition. From the motor point of view sports jump is a quick movement of the body, consisting of a take off from 1 or 2 feet followed by flight.
Each jump, irrespective of its specific features, consists of 3 phases: take off, flight and landing. Depending on the type of sport, a jump can be made from a standing position or after a run up. In athletics there are the following jumps: >POLE- VAULTING, >LONG JUMP (RUNNING), >HIGH JUMP (RUNNING); and formerly >LONG JUMP (STANDING), >HIGH JUMP (STANDING); vaulting horse in >OLYMPIC GYMNASTICS, >HITCH AND KICK; see also >GYMNASTICS; in >ACROBATICS – jumps on a track, jumps on a catapult; in >DIVING there are dives from the highboard and springboard; in >SKI JUMPING there are jumps from large, medium and small hills and giant hill. In >COMPETITIVE PARACHUTING there are different ways of making landing accuracy jumps, group jumps etc. (cf. >B.A.S.E. JUMPING). In >FIGURE SKATING there is a wide range of jumps evaluated for the difficulty level and style, such as axel, euler, lutz, salchov, flip (somersault) etc.; the same is true of >FIGURE ROLLER SKATING. A starting jump (dive) is an element of >SWIMMING. There are also many competitions not included in major sporting events, but practiced for fun, e.g. roller skating jumps, skate jumps over barrels. In the tradition of different world cultures there are folk varieties of jumps, such as >HIGH JUMP OVER A STONE, >JUMPS ON SKIN, >SALTO DEL COLACHO, >JUMP FOR A SHAWL, >JUMPING OVER FIRE, >JUMPING OVER SLEDGES.

SPORTS-DO, a method of achieving psychological and physical ability through sport in the militarized Jap. system of education known as >TAIREN-KA. Cf. >ISHITEKI-TAIIKU, >TAIIKU-DO.

SPRANGGAAILBOLLEN, a Flem. folk game, a var. of >GAAIBOLLEN. The object of the game, like in gaibollen, is to knock blocks off a ramp, which are called 'birds' [Flem. *gaai* – bird]. The basic difference is that the blocks, which imitate the birds, are cylindrical in shape and are fastened to the ramp with a metal skewer. The blocks used to knock the 'birds' off are small, 2cm in diameter, and have a metal foot.

SPRIETBOLLING, a var. of a folk game known in Belgium as >TROU-MADAME.

SPRINGE BUK, see >LEAPFROG.

SPRINGE KONGE, see >KING'S JUMP.

SPRINGE OVER ET HALMSTRÅ, full name at springe over et halmstrå, Dan. for 'to jump over straw', [Dan. *at* – lit. in order to + *springe* – jump + *over* – over + *et* – one (numeral) + *halmstrå* – stalk of corn]. A contestant holds his toes and tries to jump over the straw, which is placed right before his feet. A more complicated form of the game is held on a plank, put on a roller made of a peg. Jumping over the straw results in upsetting the balance of the contestant on the plank, as when he attempts to take off and jump over the straw, the plank slides away.
J. Møller, 'At springe over et halmstrå', GID, 1997, 3.25.

SPRINGSTOK, Dan. pole vault. Before the pole vault was introduced as a regular athletic event, in some countries, including Denmark, folk varieties of pole vault were developed. Vikings used poles to jump over the stockades of the castles they sought to conquer. Probably a folk var. of pole vaulting encountered in the past in Scand. countries, particularly in Iceland, where many old forms of the Viking culture have been preserved, can also be attributed to the Viking tradition. See also >POLE-VAULTING, >LONG-POLE JUMPING, >SPRUNG IN DIE TIEFE MIT DEM STABE, DER.
J. Møller, 'Springstok', GID, 1997, 4.

SPRINT, a short race run or cycled at a very high speed, e.g. >ATHLETIC SPRINT, cycling, swimming.

SPRUNG IN DIE TIEFE MIT DEM STABE, a jump in which the contestants cover spaces using a pole or a stick. It was promoted by the Ger. educator, J.Ch.F. Guts-Muths (1759-1839) in his book *Gymnastik für die Jugend* (1804, 256-257). He assumed that jumps must serve practical exercising of human skills, particularly to cover difficult terrain. He believed that equally important as the ability to jump a wall (e.g. by firemen rescuing people from buildings on fire) is the ability to jump down from a high floor using a pole, e.g. during a fire.
J.C.F. Guts-Muths, 'Der Sprung mit dem Stabe', *Gymnastik für die Jugend*, 1804, 241-156.

SPRUNG IN DIE TIEFE, DER, jumping down from a height or deep into sth, promoted as an exercise by Ger. educator J.Ch.F. Guts-Muths (1759-1839) in his book *Gymnastic für die Jugend* (1804, 217-219). The author assumed that such jumps must be useful in human life and jumping down, e.g. during fire, is equally important as climbing a wall, e.g. during an army's assault of a town.

SPYT, see >TYSKBOLD.

SQUARE HOLD WRESTLING see >COLLAR AND ELBOW WRESTLING.

SQUASH, the name comprises 2 similar but not identical games. The first is >SQUASH RACKETS, popularly called squash, the other >SQUASH TENNIS. Both games are played according to identical rules and on the same court but differ in the equipment used: in squash rackets players use lightweight rackets, similar to those used in badminton, whereas in squash tennis players use tennis rackets (hence the name). Also, the balls are different: in squash rackets the ball is made of hard rubber, hollow inside, 4.5cm in diameter, and squash tennis players use a standard tennis ball, which allows for a more dynamic game.

SQUASH RACKETS, also *squash racquets* or *squash*, a racket-and-ball court game for 2 or 4 players. The overall length of the racket may not exceed 68.5cm (27in.) and the round head must not exceed 21.5cm (8.5in.) in length or 18.4cm (7.25in.) in width. The racket weighs 150g. The ball, usu. rubber or butyl, is black with a diameter of 39.5 to 45mm. Its weight should be between 23.3 and 24.6g (ab. 1oz.). Though not mandatory, the use of protective goggles is strongly recommended. The court is an enclosed, 4-walled area with smooth walls which are painted white or off-white. The floor is of hardwood planks laid parallel to the side walls. The game begins with service from a service box into the opposite half-court and is made on the volley. Thereafter the aim is to hit the ball on the volley or on the first bounce so that it rebounds off the front wall, above the tell-tale or tin, either directly into the court or off another wall in such a way that the opponent is unable to return it correctly. Each player hits the ball alternately, and it must reach the front wall, directly or off another wall, without first touching the floor or going out of court. Under the rules of the International Squash Rackets Federation only the server may win points, the receiver having to win a rally to gain service. Games are to nine points, and matches the best of five games. In the United States, points

55

The famous Fleet Street Prison in London described by Dickens in Pickwick Papers. *Prisoners on the left are playing squash rackets – a game they invented.*

may be won by the receiver as well as the server, and both singles and doubles games go to 15pts.
History. The game was 'invented' by boys at Harrow School, Greater London, about between 1820 to 1840. Rackets (which derived from real tennis) was already an established game. Playing impromptu games outside the rackets court, the boys found they needed a slower and softer ball, one that could be squeezed (squashed) in the hand. Early courts were built at private houses, schools, and social clubs. By the mid-1880s the game was becoming popular in Eng. public schools, at universities and in social clubs. From around 1890 it was promoted in England by the Queen's Club and Marylebone Cricket Club. At the time enthusiasts of the game included the Prince of Wales and king Edward VIII. In around 1870 the game was taken to Canada and in 1880 to the USA by J.P. Conover. In time it became recognized as a school game in St. Paul's School in Concord, New Hampshire. Around 1882 students of that school replaced the rubber ball with a standard tennis ball, which gave rise to >SQUASH TENNIS, a game with almost identical rules but with different techniques and tactics. In 1922 the Tennis and Rackets Association produced an acceptable code of rules and in 1928 the Squash Rackets Association was founded. The Women's Squash Rackets Association was created in 1934. Later, the armed services, especially the Royal Air Force and the army, were to do much to popularize the game round the world. The International Squash Rackets Federation was founded in 1967 and in 1992 was reconstituted as the World Squash Federation. Brit. Open Championships were first held in 1922 for women and in 1930 for men. This was regarded as the unofficial W.Ch. until the creation of the World Amateur Championship in 1967. The Brit. Amateur Championship was also instituted in 1922. When the amateur/professional distinction disappeared in 1979 the tournament came to an end. World Open Championships were begun in 1976 and are now held annually for men and women. The US Open was inaugurated in 1986, as the US Professional (Softball) Championship. The N.Amer. Open was first held in 1953 after the amalgamation of the US and Can. Open Championships. Outside Britain and the United States the game is popular internationally, particularly in Pakistan (which has provided a succession of brilliant players), Australia (also a country of notable players), N.Zealand, Egypt, India, Malaysia, Indonesia, and Japan. Among the best players of the recent decades were: among women – M. Martin (Australia, 3-times world champion in 1993-95 and 6-times winner of the British Open) and among men – I. Khan (Pakistan, world champion in 1982-88), who won 500 games in a row and won one world championship title without losing a single set. The game is often confused with its predecessor, i.e. >RACQUETS.
H. Khan and R. Randall, *Squash Rackets. The Khan Game*, 1967; *U.S. Squash Rackets Association Year Book* (annual edition).

SQUASH TENNIS, a var. of >SQUASH RACKETS (>RACQUETS), played with a ball 'borrowed' from >LAWN TENNIS, which requires a different technique and tactics of play. The court, equipment and rules are identical to those of squash rackets. Squash tennis was started around 1882 by the students of St. Paul's College in Concord (USA), who wanted to make the game faster and used a tennis ball. The game is not governed by any federation, it is usu. a section of other associations, mainly tennis ones. It is most popular in the USA, where annual national championships are held.
D.P. Kingley, 'Squash tennis', EAI (1979, 25).

ŠRIH EŠŠARH, an Arab game of skill in which contestants jump over a kneeling player. The winner is decided on the basis of the number of successful jumps. The following description comes from the dictionary of Arab games and sports by M. Ibrahim al-Majman:
A joyful game with ancient origin, which in the past was played by the youth and today by the older generation. It is based on muscular strength and motor agility, as in the course of the game many jumps are made. It gives a lot of pleasure to both the spectators and the players, everybody has a very good time, jumping and singing. It can be played by one or more persons. It is most attractive when seven players take part, i.e. the number corresponding to the days of the week. For this reason in Qsim it is called sabt sbut [the Saturday of Saturdays].
First the player over whom other players will be jumping is chosen. To that end the player acting as the captain conceals a
small stone, the size of a pea, under one of his fingers. The other players take turns guessing under which finger the stone is hidden. The player who guessed correctly becomes the 'object' of jumps. He kneels, while other players take turns in jumping over him to the tune of a song sung by both the kneeling and jumping players. The captain of the jumping players is usually the referee. The game is best played on a sandy field, as some players may fall during the jumps.
The players are lined up at a run up distance of about 10m from the kneeling player. The first to jump is the captain. Supporting his hands against the kneeling player's back, before the actual jump, in a deep, sonorous voice he sings: šrih essarh [something like O-ho-ho!]. The kneeling player responds with: 'Ydibb el-farh!' [lit. I bring a nestling]. Then another player runs up to the kneeling player. When preparing for the jump, he sings: 'Dagagitna!' [our hen], to which the kneeling player responds: 'Erreq iyye!' [with colorful feathers]. Then the third player prepares for the jump. While jumping, he sings: 'Abu Qdida' [father Qdida], and the kneeling player responds with: 'Laqa wli-da' [found his child]. The fourth player adds: 'That elt'dida' [under 'dida'; the word dida is meaningless and is added only as a rhyme, it can be translated as 'under something'] etc. The referee should have a strong personality, be just and of strong body build. It is important that people like him and obey him. The captain is not always the referee; it happens that the captain nominates the referee from among the spectators.
The game can have a different character, when the players form two opposing teams. Then each team tries to choose the tallest players from among themselves, over which players of the opposite team will be jumping. The following rules are observed: during the jump players are allowed to touch only the hands of the kneeling players; during the jump the legs must be astride [to avoid kicking the kneeling player]; it is also forbidden to hit the kneeling player with the hands.
In order to be able to effectively play the sabt sbut variety, popular in the Qsim region, names of the days of the week must be known. It is important because the names are part of the song sung by the leader and repeated by the players he leads. Sometimes the leader asks the players about the name of the day. A player who gives an incorrect answer must kneel. The leader can also make the player, who gave an improper jump or who cheated, replace the kneeling player.
In conclusion it must be added that people play this game at daytime or during bright summer nights (in the middle of the month). No time limits are set; the game continues until dusk or until the players get tired. The author thinks that the game has not disappeared and is still played in elementary schools where children jump over a wooden donkey during their physical education classes.
[*Min al.'abina ash-sha 'biyya – Our folk games*, 1983, 22-25]

SSIRŮM, or *ssireum*, a Kor. var. of folk wrestling with a tradition of 1,500 (possibly even 1,700-1,800) years. This is suggested by the paintings on ancient tomb walls from the 2nd half of the existence of the kingdom of Koguryo (37 BC-668 AD). It is practiced during folk festivals. The trad. prize for the winner has been a healthy bull. The sport is administered by the Kor. Association of Ssirům; cf. also >WRESTLING.

South Korea's LG Ssirum Team wrestler Yeom Won-jun, left, fights with Shin Bong-min of the Hyundai Ssirům Team during the final event of the 2001 Lunar New Year Hercules Competition at the Changchoong Gymnasium in Seoul.

S

WORLD SPORTS ENCYCLOPEDIA

ST. CUTHBERT'S BALL, a ball game mentioned in the anon. text *Life of St. Cuthbert*, devoted to the Brit. missionary living in the 7th cent. According to the text, the saint in his youth '...pleyde atte ball with the children that his fellowes were'. The work was written many centuries after the saint's death and may lack historical credibility; the author may have included some fictional information just to make the saint a more down-to-earth human being. It is beyond all doubt, however, that the saint liked physical games. Another biography of St. Cuthbert *Life and Miracles of St. Cuthbert, the Bishop of Lindisfarne*, written by the Venerable Bede includes excerpts referring to the saint's sporting interests:

He [...] as was natural at his age, rejoiced to attach himself to the company of other boys, and to share in their sports: and because he was agile by nature, and of a quick mind, he often prevailed over them in their boyish contests, and frequently, when the rest were tired, he alone would hold out, and look triumphantly around to see if any remained to contend with him for victory. For in jumping, running, wrestling (sive enim saltu, sive cursu, sive luctatu), or any other bodily exercise, he boasted that he could surpass all those who were of the same age, and even some that were older than himself.

[trans. A. Holder]

STAABOLD see >BOLD I HUL.

STÁÁY, canoe races of the Stóólo tribe living on the western coast of N.America, in areas bordering Canada, among others on Vancouver Island, in Fraser valley and around Washington state (stá:y in the spelling of the Stóólo-Stó:lo tribe). Contestants compete individually or in teams. The best known races are held annually on Lake Cultus in the first weekend of June. In their present form the races were started in the 1950s, as part of the celebrations of Amer. Indian culture. Both women and men can participate. In a period of training lasting the few weeks preceding the races no alcohol or drugs can be taken and on the competition day contestants can only consume herbs, which, in Amer. Indian beliefs, boost physical and spiritual strength. One of the training methods includes increasing water resistance by lowering the boat's stem, tying a trawl-net to the stern or attaching a bunch of branches to the stern – thanks to which rowing during the actual regatta requires less effort. The preparation, open to everybody interested in taking part in the regatta, also serves as an eliminator. Only 10 contestants are admitted to the actual regatta. The races are held in singles, doubles, 6- and 11-person crew categories. The longest canoe is 52ft. (about 15.6m) but weighs only about 35lbs. (15.75kg). The canoe is hollowed out of a trunk of the cedar tree; the oars

In a new steep skiing extravaganza called heliskiing, a helicopter airlifts the skier or snowboarder into untracked terrain, where powder runs in pristine wilderness offer an unforgettable experience.

are also made of cedar. Originally, the oars were narrow, with the flat ends 4in. wide; presently the flat ends are 8in. wide. Contestants race over a distance of 3-4mi., turning at a buoy that marks the halfway point. The boat is commanded by a skipper, who has a caller in the front (to control the strength of rowing and boat's balance. The bowman sits at the bow; he keeps the pace of the boat. Turning around the buoy, the most difficult element of the regatta, is accomplished by a special technique: 2 contestants sitting in the front stop rowing and keep their oars motionless in the water, while the others row very rapidly, in this way making the boat pivot almost on the spot. In the past obstructing the turn was permitted, today it is forbidden. Three contestants are responsible for bailing water out of the canoe, which the boat takes on turning and during intensive rowing. Races start at a shot from a gun.

STADAIA PALE, [Gk. *stadaios* – straight, upright, erect], a type of ancient wrestling in which the contestants stand facing each other; see >PALE.

STADIODROMOS, also stadion, an ancient race of one stadium [Gk. *stadion* – a free space forming and surrounding *dromos* – the track]. The name derives from the measure of length, slightly less than 200m, which was the length of the track in ancient games. The name denoting both the track and the spectators' stands was derived from the architectural structure that formed a 1 stadium long straight track. The word 'stadion' appeared for the first time in written Gk. texts in the 5th cent. BC – in the hymns by Pindar, Bacchylides and Symonides. The length of 1 stadium varied from place to place: in Olympia it was 192.27m; at the Pythian Games in Delphi – about 165m; at the Panathenian Games in Athens – 177.55m; at the games in Epidauros – 181.08m. The contestants, like in other races, started from the balbis, a stone board with lateral grooves for the feet. The start was facilitated by the hyspleks, a device similar to that used nowadays at horse races. Its most important element was a gate with a bar, separate for each runner. Until the start, the bar was raised and kept in the horizontal position by means of a rope or leather strap. The ends of long ropes from each bar, well greased to allow easy sliding at places of bending, were held in the hands by the starting judge – afetes, who was seated centrally right behind the runners. At the start signal, with a quick jerk, the afetes released the ropes from all the bars at the same time, and the runners started the race. On the other side of the track was the finish line, called terma or gramme (the word gramme also denoted the start line equivalent to the edge of the balbis). In the oldest times the finish

Steep skiing.

line was marked with a line drawn in the sand, later with wooden poles, and finally with stone poles.

History. Stadiodromos is believed to be the first historically confirmed Olympic event. Its first winner at the games of the 1st Olympiad in 776 BC was Koroibos of Els. The last – Dyonizos of Alexandria at the 264th Olympiad in 277 BC. Chionis of Sparta won this race in the 3 consecutive Olympiads, i.e. in 664, 660 and 656 BC (he also won the diaulos at all these Olympiads, thus winning 6 olive wreaths). Leonidas of Rhodos won 4 times (164, 160, 156 and 152 BC). Atenodoros of Ekion and Demetrios of Salamina won 3 times each (respectively, 49, 53 and 61 BC and 229, 233 and 237 BC). As many as 17 contestants won stadiodromos at Olympiads twice. The fastest runner in ancient times was Ladas of Aigion, although he won only once, at the 125th Olympiad in 280 BC. The last identified historical winner of stadidromos was Dyonizos of Alexandria (269 BC). However, it is possible that among the Olympic winners, whose names were preserved without dates, there is one from a later period.

STAFF STANDING, a game of strength and co-ordination in which one stands up from a kneeling position with the help of a pole 1m in height, driven vertically into the ground. The pole must be held in both hands and does not have to be fastened solidly in the ground. It is enough to place it in a small hole, which prevents any sideways movement.
I.N. Chkhannikov, GIZ, 1953, 22.

STAGGING, an Eng. var. of folk wrestling, in which the contestants' legs are tied at the ankles and their wrists are tied behind their backs. Despite this, their task is to do all they can to overturn their opponent. This form of fighting was relatively popular in Antrimshire in Northern Ireland.
TGESI, 1898, II, 215.

STÅNGASPELEN, [Swed. *stånga* – throwing + *spleen* – games], throwing competitions on the island of Gotland, mockingly called 'the Ol.G. of Gotland'. Stångaspelen was initiated in 1924 by a teacher who, while in Gotland, came across a living museum of old Scand. sports, that had resisted the invasion of Ang.-Sax. sports; in other parts of Sweden in the 2nd half of the 19th cent. and at the beginning of the 20th cent. many games disappeared. Stångaspelen games are organized annually in July in Visby, the only town and, thus, by default, the capital of Gotland. The secret behind the preservation of the old folk sports is explained by M. Hellspong as follows: 'When modern international sports were introduced on the island of Gotland, trad. sports were of course seriously threatened. But at the same time strong forces were activated, especially in the folklore movement and within different associations in Visby, the only town on the island, which wanted to preserve the old sports of Gotland and transfer them into the twentieth century. And they succeeded [...] because trad. sports were so well integrated in the local farming society and because regular competitions have been arranged in trad. sports on Gotland for centuries'.
The folk varieties of stångaspelen include: >VARPA, a stone throw at a pole driven into the ground, >PÄRK, a ball throwing game, >STÖRTA STÄNG, a trunk throw, >DRA HANK – tug of war between 2 contestants.
A typical form of competition in Gotland is also >VÅG, lit. a bet, a competition between individual parishes.
M. Hellspong, *Organized, Traditional Sports on the Island of Gotland in the Eighteenth and Nineteenth Centuries*, 1996.

STANGE BUH, Dan. for 'horning, butting', [Dan. *stange* – to horn, butt]. Two contestants, down on all fours, with their heads facing each other, attempt to force each other to give up by pushing foreheads. This game has its unpleasant equivalent in fights, which are called *nikke skaller*, i.e. lit. butting.
J. Møller, 'Stange buh', GID, 1997, 4, 52-53.

STÅNGSTÖRTNING, a Swed. folk sport of throwing a trunk over a distance; similar to the Scot. >TOSSING THE CABER.

STANTO, a Dan. ball game deriving from the trad. monastery school. The name is probably a distorted Lat. word [Lat. *station* – a stopping place, or *statuo* – to put, to stop]. The first player throws a ball up and calls out a name of the player who should catch it. If the player named catches the ball, he repeats

the activity. However, if he does not catch the ball in flight, he has to run after it while the other players run away; when finally the ball is picked up, the player calls out: 'Stanto!' – the other players must stop and the player with the ball tries to throw it at any of the other players; depending on the distance to the players the task is more or less difficult. A player hit with the ball gets a negative point; if the player who picked up the ball does not hit any other player, he gets a negative point. The minus is defined as 'becoming one year old' (*at blive eet Aar*) or players say that somebody 'has 5 years left until death' (*at have fem Aar til Døden*). Any player with 3 minus points is 'sentenced to death' and 'stoned' and is thus eliminated from the game. Stoning is a ritual allowing the sentenced to escape an elected 'executioner' with 3 steps and a 'clot of spittle', after which the executioner has 3 attempts to hit (stone) the unfortunate with the ball. Locally, in Sjørslev, Jutland – the game was called 'running the gautlet' (*løbe spidsrod*); in Jyderup on Zeeland – *skrutbold* [reg. Zeelandian *skrut* – body or bent back + *bold* – ball]; apart from less important details the main difference in the varieties was the call stopping the players (*spidsrod* or *skrut*). In some areas stanto was also known in more recent times as *jeg melder krig mod* – to declare war on somebody.
J. Møller, 'Stanto', GID, 1997, 1, 29.

STAR RALLY, a var. of a rally where the participants follow different routes to one target, practiced, especially formerly, in Eastern Bloc countries. Star rallies are often organized to commemorate important cultural, political or historical events, as they usu. end in large festivals or demonstrations, stressing participation by people from all parts of the country or region (or even the whole world). For that reason, totalitarian systems eagerly used star rallies for political reasons, e.g. the anniversary of the outbreak of the October Revolution was commemorated by star rallies, and so were the birthdays or anniversaries of deaths of famous communist leaders, such as Lenin.

STEEP SKIING, formerly alpine skiing, a sport performed by moving across difficult mountainous terrain on skis, with no trails prepared in advance. It entails climbing a hill, traversing across mountain slopes, and sliding or jumping down difficult mountain slopes, incl. glacial ones. Skiers often use climbing equipment, such as ice axes, ropes, and drogue chutes specially designed to control the rate of descent. To facilitate the goal of the sport, which is to ski down an exceptionally attractive and dangerous slope, skiers are sometimes transported with snowmobiles or even helicopters to their starting point.
History. The beginnings of steep skiing date back to the 19th cent., when it was practiced in the Alps, and hence the original name 'alpine skiing'. In the first decades of the 20th cent. the sport began to be practiced also in other countries outside the Alps: in the Caucasus, the Andes, the Rocky Mts., and the Himalayas. In 1943, during WWII the Norw. J. Baalsrudd was dropped by parachute together with 12 companions. He was then surrounded by Germans and managed to escape on his own, part of the way on skis, through the inaccessible areas of the Kjřlen Mts. at the Norw.-Swed. border. This feat was later described by the Eng. writer D. Howarth in his book *We die alone*, 1955. The most outstanding representatives of steep skiing are: Jap. Yuichiro Miura, who became famous when he skied down Fujiyama, and later from the southern pass of Mount Everest at an altitude of 8,000m. An account of this achievement was included in Miura's book written together with the Amer. journalist E. Perlman, *The Man Who Skied Down Everest* (1978).
The pioneers of dangerous steep skiing were, among others: Frenchman S. Saudan, and German K. Jeschke, and his compatriot, H. Holzer, who died when he was skiing down the Piz Rozeg wall in the Rhaetian Alps (1977).
The filmmakers W. Miller and G. Stump, whose films won international recognition due to their emotional and esthetic values, popularized steep skiing. The most attractive places for steep skiing are: Trush Chutes in Whiteater in Brit. Columbia and a number of places in the Alps, Andes, and Sothern Alps in N.Zealand.

STEEPLECHASE, in track-and-field athletics a group of long-distance races (>LONG DISTANCE RUNNING) over an obstacle course incl. water

ditches, open ditches and fences. Steeplechase races are held over a specially prepared 400-m running track. One lap includes 4 fences and one water ditch. All the fences (including the water jump) are 91.4cm-high and must be at least 3.66m wide (across the 3 inside lanes). It is recommended that the first fence after the starting line be at least 500cm wide given the still large group of competitors running together. The water jump is 3.66x3.66m square and may be up to 70cm deep. A single fence should weigh from 80 to 100kg and the base should be from 120 to 140cm wide. The

Switzerland's Christian Belz, top, Greece's Georgios Giannelis, upper left, Stathis Stasi, of Cyprus, 2nd from upper right, and Anthony Cosey of the USA, upper right, compete in a heat of the men's 3000-m steeplechase at the Summer Olympics.

crossbar is 5in. or 12.7cm square. The first lap does not have any obstacles. The standardized men's Olympic, continental and W.Ch. distance is 3,000m. Its Ang.-Sax. counterpart used to be a 2mi. steeplechase. Younger runners sometimes compete over a distance of 1,500m.
History. The beginnings of steeplechase, similar to >CROSS-COUNTRY RUNNING, are closely linked to the Eng. open field races and the founding of the Crick Run at Rugby School in 1837 and a similar run held annually since 1838 the Birmingham College. Both race types, i.e. cross-country and steeplechase, became separate events in the 19th cent. In 1843 a flat cross-country and a steeplechase were first held at Eton College in England. Due to a lack of clear-cut distinctions cross-country running and steeplechase, although informally treated as two separate events, were deemed one sport until the turn of the 19th cent. (compare *Encyclopaedia of Sports*, vol. 1, pp. 49-58). Cross-country steeplechase competitions are still held in the Eng.-speaking countries and France. As an Olympic track event it was run in the 1900 Games and it was held over various distances until 1920 when it was standardized at 3,000m. In Paris the distances were 2,500 and 4,000m, during the St. Louis Games the distance was 2,590m and the London 1908 Ol.G. steeplechase was 3,200m-long. No steeplechase was held in Stockholm and the distance was finally standardized, as mentioned above, in 1920 in Antwerp. During the next few decades the distance remained the same, however, the rules on the number and spacing of the obstacles have changed several times. During the Los Angeles 1932 Games the referees made a mistake and told the competitors to run an extra lap, which – given the fact that the water ditch was located along the longest, outside lane and the fact that the starts were staggered improperly – resulted in the runners covering a distance of 3460m. The rules finally established in 1954 have remained largely unchanged until the present day. Official world records have been maintained since that time. The best pre-WWI runners came mostly from Great Britain and the US, after 1920 it was the Finns and the British who dominated the compe-

tition. The greatest runners of the 1920-39 period were the Finns – V. Ritola and the 2-time Olympic champion V. Iso-Hollo (1932, 1936). The Swedes won all the steeplechase medals at the 1948 Olympics. In the 1950s and 60s the competition was dominated by runners from Great Britain, the USSR, Poland, Belgium as well as Norway, the US and Hungary. The greatest runners of that time were the first official world record holder S. Rozsnyói of Hungary, Z. Krzyszkowiak of Poland and G. Roelants of Belgium (a 2-time world record holder and the 1964 Olympic Cham-

pion). Since 1968 the competition has been dominated by Afr., especially Kenyan, runners such as K. Keino, B. Jipcho, H. Rono (towards the end of the 1970s) and J. Kariuki (in the 1980s). Their supremacy was overcome for a short period of time by A. Gärderud of Sweden and B. Malinowski of Poland. The Kenyan team swept the 3,000-m steeplechase at the 1992 Ol.G. in Barcelona by winning all the medals. The Kenyans also won the Olympic golds and silvers at the 1988 and 1996 Games. Steeplechase records have been maintained since 1910. The first world record holder was P. Styfert of Germany (at 10min. 27.4sec. in 1910). The first man to run a steeplechase in less than 10min. was J. Ternström of Sweden (9min. 49.8sec. in 1914), in less than 9min. – E. Elmsäter (8min. 59.6sec. in 1944), in less than 8min. 30sec. – G. Roelants (8min. 29.6sec. in 1963) and in less than 8min. – G. Kiptanui (7min. 59.18sec. in 1995).

STEEPLECHASE HORSE RACING, a form of >HORSE RACING which combines >FLAT HORSE RACING with tackling various natural or man-made obstacles. The type of obstacles determines the type of race: 1) *hurdling* – a race with jumping over low barriers or hedges; 2) *steeplechase proper* – a race with jumping over walls or fences with water ditches or basins; 3) *point-to-point* – a cross-country race to a pre-selected location tackling

Steeplechase horse racing.

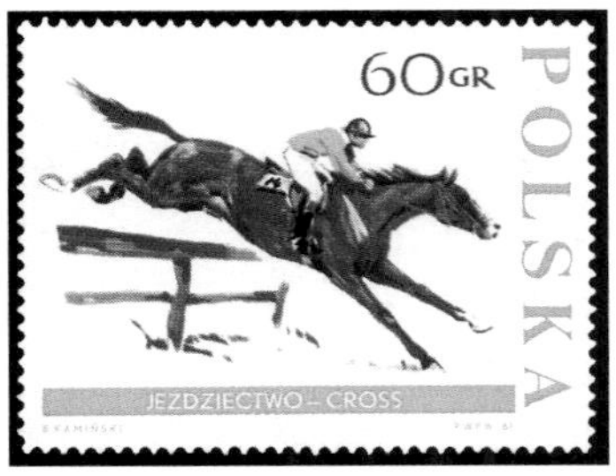

Steeplechase horse racing on a 1967 Polish postage stamp.

natural obstacles. Steeple-chase racing originated in England together with flat horse racing, though while the latter were a consciously planned event, the former derived from cross-country races and hunts organized spontaneously by the aristocracy. At the turn of the 18th and 19th cent. they became part of regular horse racing events, but later evolved into a separate sporting discipline. The most important international steeple-chase events are: The Grand National held at the Aintree track in Liverpool, England; the Foxcatcher National Cup at Fair Hill, Maryland (USA); The Great Pardubice Race in the Czech Republic. Most steeple-chase races are professional events. During the 1920 Ol.G. cross-country steeple-chase races were held over distances of 20km and 50km. They were later discontinued and are now part of the Olympic *three day event* (see >EQUESTRIAN EVENTS), while point-to-point races are a professional var. of >FOX HUNTING, a popular literary theme. Steeplechasing has inspired literature less frequently than other equestrian sports, but was often depicted in other arts, esp. painting, which was fascinated with the dramatic nature of jumping over obstacles, equal to that of a horse at full gallop. The theme was tackled by numerous artists, e.g the Ger. painter A. Janke (*Amazon*, 1933), the Pol. painters S. Gorazdowski and W. Kossak, the Fr. painters E.Degas, E. Manet, T. Géricault and others. **The horse in the cinema.** The most famous feature movie on the subject of steeplechasing was *National Velvet*, the story of a girl who enters the male-dominated race (1944). Years later B. Forbes made a sequel called *International Velvet* (1978), starring T. O'Neal and C. Plummer.

STEHALLEE, see >BOLD I HUL.

STEHT ALLEE, also *Lochball*, Ger. for 'a sow's ball', a Ger. var. of a ball game, in which the ball is thrown into holes dug out in the ground, with the rules similar to those of the Dan. >BOLD I HUL.

STEHVENIE, a trad. horse race in Slovenia [Slov. *stehvenje* – competitions in iron pole hitting, Slov. *stehvan* – a tapered steel pole with a ball]. The object of the game is to gallop around a 2.9m tall pole, with a barrel about 0.5m long and about 35-40cm in diameter on its top. The referee sees to it that the barrel is rotating continuously. The riders try to knock out the largest number of staves using the *stehvan*, which is about 0.7m long. The most remarkable feat is not only to knock out a stave but to pierce it with the stehvan. The winner receives a wreath on a special plate presented by an unmarried girl.

STELTS, Du. stilts; see >WALKING ON STILTS.

STELZE, Ger. stilts; see >WALKING ON STILTS.

STENKEGLER, Dan. for 'stone skittles', [Dan. *sten* – stone + *kegler* – skittles, sg. *kegle*]. The game is played with 3 flat stones of different sizes. They are buried in the ground to form a straight line, so close to each other that a stone once thrown cannot get lodged between them. The throwing stone should weigh 1-1.5kg. 10pts. are awarded for hitting the largest stone, 20 – for hitting a smaller stone and 30 – for hitting the smallest stone; if the stone thrown by the player lands at least 1ft. behind the target, the player scores an additional 50pts. The player continues to throw until he misses, which is called the *bos*. The game is played until one player has scored 120pts. If in the first round a player scores more than 120pts., e.g. 130pts., he starts the next round with the number of points in excess of 120. On the island of Mors the game is called *slå til kile* (wedging); The stones are placed in front of each other, the largest one in front..

J. Møller, 'Stenkegler', GID, 1997, 1, 100.

Steve Plerqui, of the 111th Street Bad Boys, connects on a pitch during the 29th annual 111th 'Old Timers' stickball game in New York.

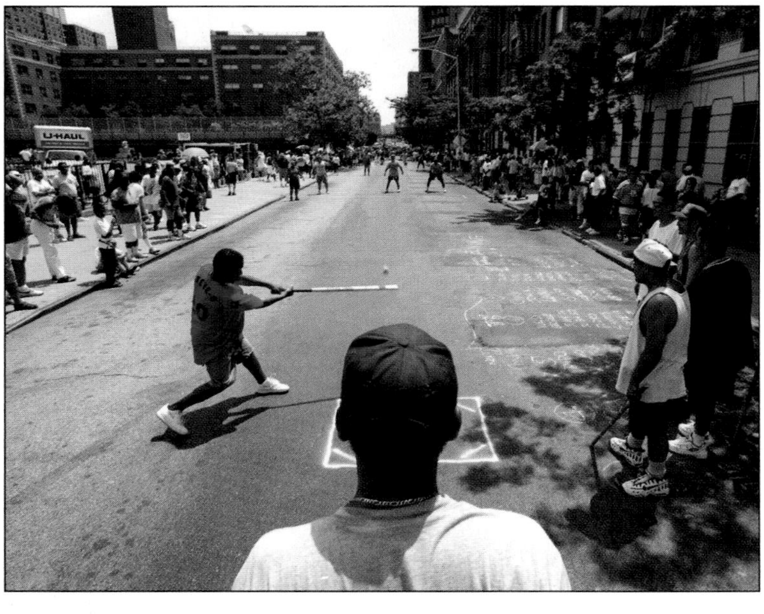

STENLØFTNING, also ÄFT STEN, a Dan. folk sport of stone lifting; see also and cf. Swed. >LYFTESTEN, >DRÄNGALØFTEN, >DRÄNGASTENAR, >KAMPASTEN, >LYFTESTENAR, Basq. >ARRISJASOKETA; see also names of stones, at the same time denoting the local types of stone lifting competitions: >GGET, KÖLNÅKERN, >KUNGSSTEN, >KUNGSSTENARNA, >STORA OCH LILLA DAGSVERKARN, >TYFTEHÖNAN.

J. Møller, *Gamle idracatslege i Danmark*, 1997, 3, 105-106.

STICKBALL, a ball game in which the ball is knocked with a stick. One of the names of the game known as >ROUNDBALL or a simpler competition played before roundball.

STICKY-STACK, a folk competition, known in northern Britain, in which a stack of hay is 'attacked' with a stick, the object being to take as much hay as possible and toss it up.

STIK'N SNAEL, see >TIP-CAT.

STIKEBOLD, see >TREBOLD.

STIKKE PALLES ØJE UD, Dan. for 'to poke out Palle's eye', [Dan. *stikke ud* – stick out + *øje* – eye + *Palle* – proper name]; a Dan. game of motion; its name is actually not related to the type of activity involved; perhaps the old var. of the game featured an activity which justified its name. 2 contestants stand with their backs to each other. Between their legs there is a 1.5-2m long stick. Using the stick, each contestant tries to pull the opponent to his side. In front of each contestant there is a lit candle (Palles øje), which they try to blow out or knock over. The closer they get to the candle, the greater chance they have to blow it out. However, each contestant is prevented by his opponent, who is pulling the stick in the opposite direction.

J. Møller, 'Stikke palles øje ud', GID, 1997, 4, 33.

STIKKE SVANER, Dan. for 'aiming at the swans', a ball game, [Dan. *stikke* – pierce + *svaner* – swans, sg. *svane*]. The contestants, called swans, line up in one row, at least one large step apart, in the middle of the field. On both sides of the field there are 'shooters', who aim at the 'swans' with a ball. To avoid being hit, a player can move only one step sideways, backwards or forwards. Ducking is not allowed. A 'swan' hit by the 'shooter' may assist him in shooting, but only if the 'shooter' agrees to this, in a convenient moment or situation. When all the 'swans' have been 'shot', the 'shooters' start counting their trophies; the winner is the player who 'shot' the most 'swans'. In old Denmark the game was played with a hand-sewn rag ball, usu. beautifully embroidered. The varieties of the game, with only minor differences between them, were called *i skyde immelem* (shooting at the center – the vicinity of Spentrup), *i stikke i midten* (aiming at the center – Ålborgegnen), *i stikkebold* (ball at the target – Væggeläse, Sydfalster): *i svie bold* (a scorching ball game – Vedsted).

J. Møller, 'Stikke svaner', GID, 1997, 1, 22.

STJÆLE ÆG, Dan. for 'to steal eggs', [Dan. *stjæle* – steal + *æg* – egg, also pl. eggs]. Each team stands on its side of a demarcation line indicating a home field for each; a nest (*rede*) with 'eggs' (pebbles) is behind each team. The contestants try to steal the eggs from the opponents' nest, put them into their nest while trying to avoid being touched by the opponents in the enemy field. If a player is touched, he must take the egg back to the opponents' nest, return to his side and reattempt the steal. Cf. >STJÆLE STAV.

J. Møller, 'Stjæle æg', GID, 1997, 2.

STJÆLE SMØR, Dan. for 'to steal the butter', [Dan. *stjæle* – steal + *smør* – butter]. A Dan. game of motion, often organized on the beach. It is played in a complex maze, which is drawn on the wet sand. Inside the maze there is a 'butter hole' (*smørhul*). Around it there is a path, along which the players can get to the hole from all sides. Other paths are drawn radially from the one closest to the hole, which are connected with the paths on the outer ring and which are also connected with arcs. Outside this maze each 'thief' has his hole, marked with a number. One player guards the butter (i.e. wet sand) and the others try to steal it. The guarding player can chase a player but only when he has got the sand from the 'butter hole' in his hands. If he manages to catch him, the two trade places. If the thief goes beyond the paths, he becomes the guard, and if the guard happens to go beyond the paths, he must stop the chase.

J. Møller, 'Stjæle smør', GID, 1997, 2, 44.

STJÆLE STAV, Dan. for 'to steal the stick', [Dan. *stj1>le* – steal + *stav* – stick]. A game similar to >STJÆLE ÆG; instead of the stones that imitate the eggs players try to 'steal' sticks from the opponents' field. Each of the 2 teams has 24 sticks in their 'nest'. If a player was touched while in the opponents' field, he must stop. If all the players of one team were caught in this way, they must surrender 3 sticks in order to continue play. The team, which after a few rounds has no sticks left, loses.

J. Møller, 'Stjæle stav', GID, 1997, 2, 59.

STOBALL, see >STOOL-BALL.

STOCKSCHIEßEN, Ger. sliding weights, a sport practiced in a few Ger.-speaking countries, the object of which is to slide special weights [Ger. *Stock* – e.g. log + *Schießen* – sliding, lit. shooting]; stockschießen belongs to the game family called in Ger. >EISSCHIEßEN; the object being to hit a stone propelled on ice with another stone, called *Zielstocke*; the game is played on a track (*Eisschießbahn*) 42m long and 4m wide; according to *Encyclopedia Britannica (Micropedia*, 1991, vol. 4, 407-408) the game is played on tracks 28m long and 3m wide with a stone (weight) 30-38cm of base diameter; the central part of the track (*Mittelfeld*), where the stones are propelled, is 21m long; the track is symmetrical – thanks to this the game can be played from both ends, where the run-up zones are located (*Standritze*); each forms a 4x2.5cm rectangle; the shorter sides overlap the side line of the entire track and the others are lines marked across the track; on each side of the track there is an 8m long sliding zone (according to *Encyclopedia Britannica* – 6m); the stones are placed in circles; in the first attempt the stones must be slid towards the central stone so that they hit it from the front on the left side, in the second – from the front on the right side, in the third – in the back edge on the left side and in the fourth – in the back on the right side; in the fifth slide the stone should be hit from the back; after each round (*Kehre*) the teams change sides; the game is played individually or in teams; a team is composed of 4 players who form the *Moarschaften*; the game is played by both men and women.

'Eischießen', *Kleine Enzyklopädie Körperkultur und Sport*, 1965, 283-285.

STØDE PEBER, Dan. for 'grinding pepper', [Dan. *støde* – strike, hit + *peber* – pepper]. A bullying game with 3 aggressors and a victim. One player gets down on all fours with his buttocks protruding, two others hold the victim by his hands and legs and swing him, eventually slamming his backside against the buttocks of the player on all fours; the player on all fours tries to prevent being knocked over when struck by the swinging player.

J. Møller, 'Støde peber', GID, 1997, 3, 66.

STONE DIVING, an old test of physical skill and strength, which combined diving with lifting rocks from the bottom of a sea or lake. According to a scandinavian saga, a skald called E. Skallagrimson was looking for a large stone for his blacksmith's practice. He took a boat into the open sea, dived into the water and brought up a huge stone, which he took home and placed in front of his forge. Legend has it that the stone could not be lifted by 4 warriors. In many cultures various other objects are dived for and lifted up. A Cossack masculinity test included diving for a pipe that belonged to one of the Elders (>PIRNANNI U WODU).

STONE FIGHTING, known since ancient times, it functioned in the cultures of the Middle East; e.g. stoning appears in the Bible as a form of punishment. Various forms of cruel competition existed between groups distinguished by their social status or place of living (>BATTLES BETWEEN CITY DISTRICTS; >BATTLES BETWEEN VILLAGES, >GIOCO DEL PONTE). One example, immediately following New Year's Day, is that of the inhabitants of medieval Fergan, who fought one another in teams representing the local ruler and his commanders. The participants were supported by the spectators, who threw stones and bricks until one of the participants was killed. Hindu ascetics fought fiercely in the name of local gods, seeking to be wounded or killed, by which they followed the fundamental principle of Hindu asceticism expressed by Krishna in chapter 18 of the *Bhagavad Gita*: 'He who tortures his body and soul, touches me, who lives in them'. During the annual Hindu festival of Holi 2 teams of young men participated in stone fights, in an effort to recreate the mythical saga of the evil demon Hiranyakasipu and his son Prahlad, whose pious deeds so irritated his father that he decided to destroy him. The father's efforts were futile, however, and he turned for help to his witch-sister. All this proved fruitless, because the youth and noble character of the boy were stronger than the anger of the father and the witch-sister. The fights commemorating this duel between good and evil resulted in many people being wounded or killed and so it was moderated in time by means of replacing the stones with sand, powder and in some regions even... cookies. Stone fights were praticed in many cultures of the Far East, incl. early medieval Korea as >SUCKJUN.

STONE THROW, a folk sport, known, in many regional varieties, in most of the world's cultures. Throwing smaller stones derives from hunting and warring activities. Throwing or pushing larger stones or boulders evolved from strongman shows at folk festivals. In the Swed. island of Gotland, there is a tradition of throwing flat stones at a pole dug into the ground (>VARPA).
In modern times, there have been attempts at formalizing some var. of stone or boulder throws using rule systems typical for modern sports. One of these var. is the stone throw using a 6.4kg stone with a 15-m run-up. The event was incl. in the program of the so-called Intercalated Ol.G. held in Greece in 1906. The Greek N. Georgantas won the tournament with a result of 19.925m. The event then became popular in Germany, where it was officially practiced until 1956. Cf. >WEIGHT THROW and >SHOT PUT.

M. Hellspong, 'Organized, Traditional Sports on the Island of Gotland in the Eighteenth and Nineteenth Centuries', SSSS, 1996.

STONYHURST FOOTBALL, a var. of SHROVE TUESDAY FOOTBALL, practiced annually in the English town of Stonyhurst (hence the name). It is also played on Shrove Thursday and on the last Monday of the carnival. The local tradition was continued for the longest time in Stonyhurst College. A description of the game, made in 1904, comes from that college:

At Stonyhurst College, Lancashire, the Shrove-tide 'Grand Matches' were until recently, one of the red-letter events of the year. These matches were played on the Thursday preceding Quinquagesima Sunday, and on the Monday and Tuesday following. Technically, the game was known as 'Stonyhurst Football', a species of football that allowed some sixty or seventy to play in one match. The opposing sides were known as 'English' and 'French'; during the match great enthusiasm always prevailed; flags were flying and cannons firing. At the 'Lemonade' on Shrove Monday or Tuesday, extra pancakes were provided for such of the players as had especially distinguished themselves. 'Stonyhurst football' is now, alas! being superseded by the more up-to-date 'Association rules', and the 'Grand matches' at Stonyhurst are a thing of the past'

[*Notes and Querries*, ser. 10, vol. 1, 1904]

STOOLBALL OF COLDITZ, a ball game organized by Brit. prisoners of war in the Ger. camp in Colditz castle 1940-45. Its resemblance to the Eng. game known as >STOOL-BALL is only superficial. It featured bouncing, borrowed from >BASKETBALL. P.R. Reid, one of the prisoners, provided the following description of the game in his diary:

The Colditz variety, which we called 'stoolball' was played, of course, in the granite cobbled courtyard. It is the roughest game, I ever played, putting games like rugby football in the shade. The rules were simple. Two sides, consisting of any number of players and often as many as thirty a side, fought for possession of the football by any means. A player having the ball could run with it but could not hold it indefinitely; he had to bounce it occasionally while on the move. When tackled, he could do whatever he liked with it. A 'goalie' at each end of the yard sat on a stool – hence the name – and a goal was scored by touching the opponent's stool with the ball. Goal defense was by any means, including strangulation of the ball-holder, if necessary. There was a half-time when everybody was too tired to continue. There was no referee and there were, of course, no touch-lines. The game proceeded as a series of lighting dashes, appalling crashes, deafening shouts, formidable scrums – generally involving the whole side – rapid passing movements, as in rugby three-quarter line, and with a cheering knot of spectators at every window. Nobody was ever seriously hurt, in spite of the fury and the pace at which the game was played. Clothing was ripped to pieces, while mass wrestling and throwing of bodies was the order of the day. To extract an opponent from a scrum it was recommendable to grab him by the scalp and one leg. I never saw any 'ripping'. This was probably due to instinctive reaction of players to long schooling in our various ball games where tripping is forbidden.

Representatives of other nationalities most often restricted themselves to observing the game played by the British:

The Poles, and later the French, when they arrived, were always interested spectators. Although we had no monopoly of the courtyard, they naturally took to their rooms and watched the game from windows.

Obviously, there were matches played between the British and the Poles or the French. However, their character was different:

They eventually put up sides against the British and games were played against them, but these were not a success. Tempers were lost and the score became a matter of importance, which it never did in an 'all-British' game.

P.R. Reid, *Colditz*, 1962.

STOOL-BALL, formerly also *stobal, stobbal*, an Eng. team game. The team consists of 11 players, The object of the game is to throw the ball at a target fixed on a stool, which is defended by a player of the opposite team holding a bat similar to that used in >CRICKET; in the old varieties of the game the stool was defended with a wicker rod or the hand. One of the elements of stool-ball, namely the throwing of the ball at a target defended by a player of the opposite team directly contributed to the development of cricket. In simple folk varieties stool-ball was also played in Sussex where it was known as bittle-battle.
Field and equipment. The pitch is 16yds. (14.63m) long; formerly, from 13yds. (12.75m). One stool with a target is put on both opposite ends. The stool with the target is 4ft. 8in. (1.4m; formerly from 4ft. – 1.22m). The old targets were of any shape, presently they are most often square with sides 1ft. (30.48m) long fixed atop the stool. The stool, up to 1ft long, painted black, is on the end line of the pitch, which is referred to as the running line. 10yds. (9.14m) in front of each stool with the target there is a throw line. The pitch is symmetrical in shape and the game can be played in both directions.
The ball cannot be bigger than 7½in. (19.1cm) in diameter and is solid and made of goat's skin. The bat is short with a flattened end, similar to a solid wood racket.
Clothes. Women wear loose skirts, men loose slacks, all – loose shirts or vests. Plimsolls are required. The players who defend the stools wear gloves and leg protection.
Rules of game. Before the game the sides of the pitch and the right to start the game are decided by drawing lots. Throws are made in series of 8 valid balls (invalid or 'wide' balls – see below, are not counted), after which the teams change (formerly after 5 throws). If the target is hit by the bat, the defender is eliminated and replaced with another player from the same team. Once the ball has been batted into the field, the batsman drops the bat and runs to the opposite stool. At the same time another batsman from the same team starts to run from the opposite side to the stool and back to the line from which the ball was batted. The number of runs they make depends on the length and way in which the ball has been batted and is identical with the number of points scored. In the case of an uneven number of runs, when the other batsman is closer to the ball batting line, he continues the game and not the first batsman. The bowler stands behind the throw line, which he cannot cross during the throw. The throw line at each end of the pitch is 10yds. (1.14m) from the opposite target. The ball is bowled 'underarm'. The ball is considered bad if it bounces off the ground before it hits the target or the stool or if it hits the black-painted part of the stool. A ball bowled beyond the reach of the defender is considered wide and is valid only when the defender decides to bat it. If the defender does not bat the ball, the bowler does not score any points but the batsman gets the right to a single run in order to score. The batsman is eliminated when 1) the ball hits the target or 2) when the ball is batted into the field and is caught 'clean' by the bowler's team; a clean catch means that the ball has not touched any part of the catcher above the wrist, 3) the batsman covers the target with any part of his body except for the hand with the bat, 4) the team defending the stool, instead of waiting for the throw, throw the ball themselves at the opponent's stool. The defender is not eliminated when he is hit by an invalid ball. The game is officiated by 2 referees, 1 by each stool. In case of any doubt the referees may consult. Breaks between rounds last 10min.
History. The tradition of the game goes back to the times of Queen Elizabeth I. The Earl of Leicester, together with his guest and the local peasants 'went to Wotton Hill, where he played a game of stoball'. However, old written sources do not carry any description of the game. R. Herrick (1591-1674) mentions stool-ball in a collection of poems by Hesperida (1648). Information about stool-ball is also given in B. Franklin's (1706-1790) *Poor Richard's Almanack*, a few editions between 1733 and 1758). In 1671 J. Aubrey (1626-97) in the *Natural History of Wiltshire* described one of the regional var. of the game:

It is peculiar to North Wiltshire, North Gloucestershire, and a little part of Somerset near Bath. They smite a ball stuffed very hard with quills and covered with soale leather, with a staffe commonly made of withy, about three and a half feet long [...]. A stobball ball is about four inches in diameter and as hard as a stone.

There is, however, information about stool-ball played in other areas of Great Britain, e.g. Wales, Lancashire and, particularly, Sussex, where it is still played today. T. D'Urfey (1653-1723), a Huguenot exiled from France and living on the Eng. court, mentions stool-ball in the dramatized version of Cervantes' *Don Kichot* which he wrote c.1694-96:

Down in a vale on a summer's day
All the lads and lasses met to be merry;

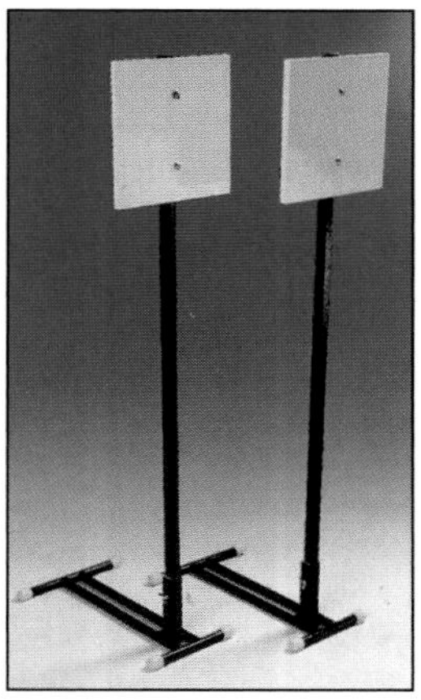

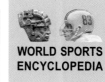

Stool-ball posts.

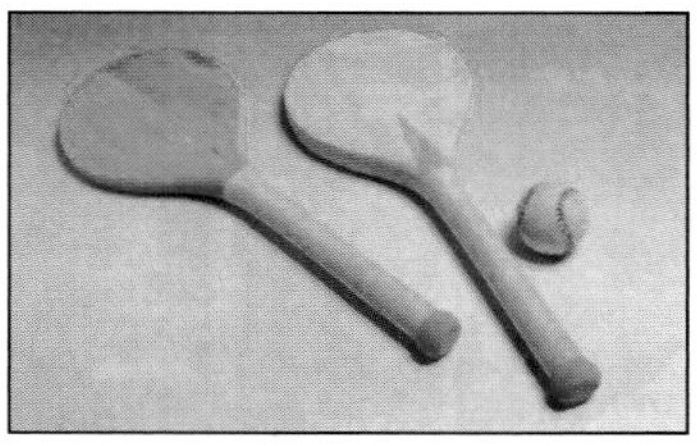

Stool-ball bats.

Stoolball of Colditz, illustration by John Watton.

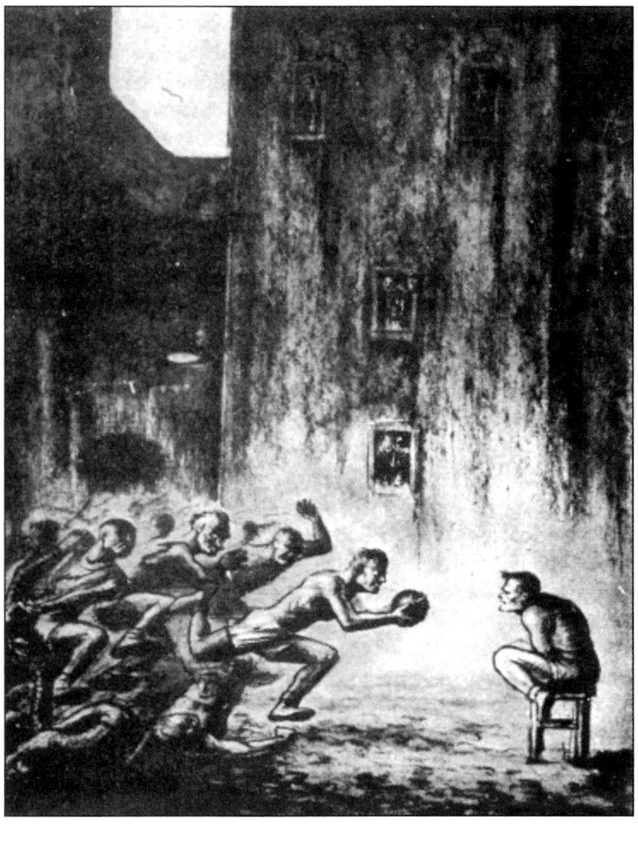

S

WORLD SPORTS ENCYCLOPEDIA

A match for kisses at stool-ball to play,
And for cakes, and ale, and sider, and perry.

It follows from this text that stool-ball has been played by both sexes ever since it was invented. The choir, imitating those of antiquity, would sing 'Come all, great small, short tall, away to stool-ball'. S. Johnson's (1709-84) Eng. language dictionary says that stool-ball is a game in which a ball is thrown from a stool to a stool. In the old var. a point was not scored by the batsman's runs but when the players

Street luge.

Street luge.

changed positions when the batted ball was up in the air. A point was also scored after each good bat into the field.

In J. Strutt's times (around 1800), stool-ball was played in northern England. Strutt left the first relatively complete description of the game and some of its local varieties:

a pastime called stool-ball [...] consists in simply setting a stool upon the ground, and one of the players takes his place before it, while his antagonist, standing at a distance, tosses a ball with the intention of striking the stool; and this it isthe business of the former to prevent by beating it away with the hand, reckoning one to the game for every stroke of the ball; if, on the contrary, it should be missed by the hand and touch the stool, the players change places (I believe the same also happens if the person who threw the ball can catch and retain it when driven back, before it reaches the ground); the conqueror at this game is he who strikes the ball most times before it touches the stool. Again, in other parts of the country a certain number of stools are set up in a circular form, and at a distance from each other, and every one of them is occupied by a single player; when the ball is truck, which is done as before with the hand, they are every one of them obliged to alter his situation, running in succession from stool to stool, and if he who threw the ball can regain it in time to strike any one of the players, before he reaches the stool to which he is running, he takes his place, and the preson touched must throw the ball, until he can in like manner return to the circle.

[J. Strutt, *Sports and Pastimes of the People of England*, 1810]

Presently stool-ball is played mainly in schools in Sussex, where a local association of this game organizes a league. In the past a game played by men only, today it is becoming more and more popular among girls.

W.W. Grantham, *Stoolball*, 1919; W.W. Grantham, *Stoolball and How to Play It*, 2nd ed. London, 1931; J. Lowerson, 'Stoolbal. Conflicting Values in the revivals of a Traditional Sussex Game', *Sussex Archeological Collections*, 1995, 133.

STORA OCH LILLA DAGSVERKARN, Swed. for 'Great and Small Hireling'; this name denotes the local var. of the stone lifting competition. See also: >LYFTESTEN, Dan. >STENLØFTING, Basq. >ARRISJASOKETA, cf. >DRÄNGASTENAR, >DRÄNGALÖFTEN, >KAMPASTEN, >KØLNÅKERN, >KUNGSSTEN, >KUNGSSTENARNA, >LYFTESTEN, >TYFTEHÖNAN.

M. Hellspong, 'Lifting Stones. The Existence of Lifting Stones in Sweden', ST, 1993-94, XIX-XX.

STÖRTA STÄNG, Dan for 'throwing the trunk', one of the folk sports which is part of >STÅNGASPELEN, similar to Scot. >TOSSING THE CABER.

STOW-BALL, a var. of a ball game in old England, in which the ball is propelled with a curved stick into holes in the ground. J. Strutt's *Glig Gamena Angel*

Deoth, or the Sports and Pastimes of the People of England published in 1810, describes stow-ball as one of the varieties of early >GOLF, referred to as >GOFF: 'A pastime called stow-ball is frequently mentioned by the writers of the sixteenth and seventeenth centuries, which, I presume, was a species of goff, at least it appears to have been played with the same kind of ball' (Strutt, 95-96).

STÓJKA, an old folk game played in Galicia (in the former Austro-Hungarian Empire), particularly in the former counties of Tarnobrzeg and Niskie. It was made popular thanks to the description and recommendations of E. Piasecki as the standard school game played during physical education classes in elementary schools. Its rules given by E. Piasecki in *Zabawy i gry ruchowe dzieci i młodzieży* (1916) are as follows:

The children form a circle, with the leader inside. The leader throws the ball up. At that time all the other players start running in any direction. However, when 'Stop!' is called out by the leader (provided he has caught the ball), they must stop. Then the leader aims the ball at the player closest to him. When he hits him, the player who was hit takes the ball (or stops it) and again everybody runs in any direction to stop when 'Stop!' is called out (the ball must land in the hit player's hands). Failing to hit anybody, the player with the ball must continue throwing the ball up until he has hit somebody.

STREET CYCLING, a type of cycling competition held in towns and cities, popular in the first half of the 20th cent. in places where no cycling tracks were available. Its advantage was improved spectating opportunities in comparison with road races. Even though the course and the finishing line in the case of road races were packed full, the spectators stood little chance of observing the competition, since the riders would pass them only once and that at full speed. Street races resembled cross-country observed trials in that the riders would do numerous laps on a street course, ranging from 2-10km, depending on the type of race and the city itself. The popularity of this type of racing came to an abrupt end with the advent of television coverage which enabled the spectators to watch the competition over the entire course uninterruptedly. Advanced television technology, allowing numerous cameras to follow the riders closely from a var. of angles, including cameras mounted on bumpers and even inside cars for the drivers' perspective, brought about the complete downfall of street racing, a fate shared by motor events of a similar character, esp. >MOTORCYCLE STREET RACING. >STREET RUNNING, however, was not affected, and new forms developed, e.g. >STREET LUGE.

STREET LUGE, a sport in which the contestants ride along steep streets on a trolley looking like a skateboard but much bigger to accommodate a competitor lying on his back, usu. in a special hollowed place in the middle; the front wheels can be steered, they are mounted on a longitudinal deck far in the front. The soles of the shoes serve as brakes. Before 1996 no standard dimensions or standard design had been determined. The deck is approx. 2.5m long. About ²/₃ of the way from the front there is a seat with short boards at hip height. The best street luge contestants include B. Pereyro, S. Wagner and J. Lewis. In recent times youths have treated street

luge as a cult sport. They wear black leather clothes, black gloves and black helmets with a visor covering the face and laced shoes with reinforced soles, resistant to friction. Street luge is developing particularly dynamically in the towns of California, mainly in San Francisco, which has specially designated street luge courses down its picturesque hills of ideal steepness.

J. Tomlinson, 'Street Luge', *Ultimate Encyclopedia of Extreme Sports*, 1996.

STREET RACES, races held within town limits. In the pre-television era races held within the limits of urban centers provided for the spectators gathered on pavements and special podiums built along the streets a multiple viewing opportunity, which was impossible in the case of cycling road races or road marathons. A polygonal track set up within the town limits made it possible for the viewers to witness live the on-going race. Street races were usu. held in towns which did not have stadiums or specialized cycling, motorcycling or automobile tracks. Many different sports made use of this form of competition: see >AUTO STREET RACING, >MOTORCYCLE STREET RACING, >RADKI, >SCOOTERS, >STREET CYCLING, >STREET RUNNING.

STREET RUNNING, races taking place in towns and cities along a course following the streets. Contrary to other types of running they are not strictly regulated and are not treated as a separate sport by the IAAF. Street running has its origins in the displays of running skills by traveling runners who visited different towns to cover a specific route within a specified period of time and claim prize money for their achievements (see >LONG-DISTANCE RUNNING). At the turn of the 19th cent. street running became the most popular type of running throughout continental Europe where the tradition of cross country running was not so established. In addition, town races have always attracted large crowds of spectators. That is why many social and political organizations tried to use the sport, and the media covering such events, to popularize their ideas and attract more supporters for their causes. Street races are often held to commemorate certain anniversaries. A unique form of street running are marathon races held in big cities such as Boston, New York or London.

STREET SOCCER, a street var. of >ASSOCIATION FOOTBALL. See also >FUTSAL.

STREET SURFING, a var. of >WIND SURFING practiced on land.

STRITKLEMME, a Dan. form of competition in stone throwing using a catapult made of a simple stick. The stick is 50cm long with one end split a little and a stone inserted into the slit. Then the player, holding the stick by the other end, takes a swing as if wanting to lash somebody with a whip and lets the stone loose. This 'weapon' was used to hunt small birds.

J. Møller, 'Stritklemme', GID, 1997, 4, 69.

STROBILOS, also *strombs*, in ancient Greece a type of >TOPS set spinning on a hard base using a whip made of a stick and string. Similar to Roman >BUXUS. It seems that strobilos came to Greece from the Far East, thanks to the expeditions of Alex-

Street soccer.

ander the Great. From Greece it came to Rome, where it soon became popular as *turbo* or >BUX-US. In Greece strobilos was also called >TROCHOS, but the latter name also referred to a game of rolling a rim. The modern var. of strobilos is called in Greece *sboura*; see >TOPS.

STROKE BIAS, the old form of folk team races, popular in Kent and described in 1700 by James Brome:

The Kentish men have a peculiar exercise, especially in the eastern parts, which is nowhere else used in any other country, I believe, but their own: it is called 'Stroke Bias' and the manner is thus. In the summer time one or two parishes convening make choice of twenty, and sometimes more, of the best runners which they can cull out of their precincts, who send a challenge to an equal number of racers within the liberties of two other parishes, to meet them at a set day upon some neighboring plain; which challenge, if accepted, they repair to the place appointed, whither also the country resort in great numbers to behold the match, when having stripped themselves at the goal to their shirts and drawers, they begin the course, every one bearing in his eye a particular man at which he aims; but after several traverses and courses on both sides, that side, whose legs are the nimblest to gain the first seven strokes from their antagonists, carry the day and win the prize. Nor is this game only appropriated to the men, but in some places the maids have their set matches too, and are as vigorous and active to obtain a victory.

[James Brome, *Travels over England*, 264].

A.B. Gomme, 'Stroke Bias', TGESI, 1898, II, 220-221.

STROMBS, also >STROBILOS, in ancient Greece a var. of >TOPS.

STRUIFVOGELSPEL, Flem. for 'a game of launching a bird', a Flem. folk sport, similar to Aus. *taubenschießen*.

STRZELANIE DO CZAPKI, Pol. for 'shooting at a cap', a type of competition practiced in old Poland, until the bow and crossbow were replaced with firearms; for some time both weapons were used on the same scale. It was probably borrowed from the Mong. tradition of >SUR KHARVAKH, owing to the many military encounters with the Tartars in the 13th-17th cent.; it helped to train specific military skills, but it also developed into purely sports competitions, played in military camps, during different holidays and celebrations; its peak came in the 2nd half of the 16th cent. and in the 17th cent. The most valuable literary descriptions of strzelanie do czapki come from this time. The most extensive description comes from M. Borzymowski's rhymed diary-poem entitled *Morska nawigacyja do Lubeka* (*A Sea Voyage to Lübecka*), written around 1651. The competitions were organized in rather unusual circumstances: in 1651 a group of Poles headed by J. Zawadzki, a *starosta* (mayor) from Puck, travelled to Lubeca. Due to unfavorable winds, they stopped in Rostock, where, during the local holiday, the Poles competed in shooting at a cap against the Germans. According to Borzymowski's description, the competition went something like this:

And the Poles, when they have drunk
Some liquor, they did not want to idle away
Their humor, but having mounted their horses
They rode to the wide common
Having taken the bows, others stayed
In the inn to make the guests
More willing to follow. However, great
Crowds and almost all the families
Went from the town after those
Who were going to the field
And who started to shoot the cap.
First Gołecki – having drawn an arrow
From the quiver said: 'My arrow
Full of feathers, you were with me
In battle and in peace, always
Gentle, now, when I have a target
In front of my eye, show what
Mars can do with you! May foreign
Countries say that they know here
A Pole with a bow, who is sure
To hit the target. And the arrow
Is going straight at it now! – And
The shooter will let it go and will
Hit the target made of cap, so hard
That the cap jumps up in the air
Several times in front of the spectators'
Eyes. He hit well – everybody's praising
Him; the Germans alike for they
Know not such a rifle in their country.

Yet, they were rejoicing and
Everybody was gazing at us.
And now Krotoszyński – with colors
On his cheeks – willingly takes the bow
Into his hands and, as if boasting of
His Fortune summons its assistance:
'My Fortune, my Fortune, you gave
Me such strength and you have always
Known me, do not forget me now but
Show your ship to the people's eyes!
May they not call you thoughtless and
Shy but a staid lady and queen!'
Having said this he shot, and the arrow
Flew over the target and did not hit
The cap's colors. However, when it
Flew over the target, the shooters said
It was a good shot, worthy of a prize.
Chudziński was third, stirring courage in
Himself and luring his heart with such words:
'Oh, heart! You know who has always
Been your friend? Do you know who
Always made you happy? Who set the
Fires of love in your depth?
If these fires yet burn
And they still have your refinement
If there is a ship, if love is not
Lost in affections, – Oh! She, who
Rules the arrow of love, when I pull
My bow, may Venus help me to aim!'
And he fired the arrow. Alas, somehow
Poorly let loose – it ended its flight
Before it reached the target
Which made the crowd laugh.
Krzysztof Brant was fourth, having
Polished the arrow with his hands
And having tested the string
Said 'I was told by my parents
When I was born – There is no
Better aim in the world but
Death, it will take everybody.
We give you the life, so live in virtue
Son, and may you hit the target!
So if my parents were right then
I, to confirm their words, will right now
Hit the target! – So saying he aimed
At the cap and hit it dead on.

STRZELEC, Pol. for 'shooter', an old Pol. game played by boys, particularly in the Cracow province. The rules of the game, given by E. Piasecki in his *Zabawy i gry ruchowe dzieci i młodzieży* (1916) are as follows:

The children are lined up in a single row and they get names of different birds from the leader [host]. Now a player, who has been on the side, comes in and a bargain begins. – Knock, knock! Who's there? – It's me, a devil with a burnt pot. – What do you need? – Birds. – What birds do you want? Golden oriole (jay, stork etc.). – Not here (if he has not guessed). Moreover, if he pointed to the wrong boy, the latter aims a ball at him. If the devil guessed right, he throws the ball at the bird. When he hits, he takes it; when he misses, a ball is thrown at him. The bird, which missed, becomes the devil's prisoner. The game ends when all the birds have been taken captive.

SUCKJUN, in early medieval Korea a var. of fight between 2 warrior candidates or 2 teams, which hurled stones at each other (>STONE FIGHTING) in a demonstration of courage by the young contestants, who sought to become soldiers and defenders of the country (*hwaranga*) in the Kor. system of military education (*hwarang-do*). Resistance to the blows of stones hurled by the partner was adequate proof of the uncompromising attitude that would later be conferred upon the *hwaranga* by gods in actual fighting (cf. YANOMAMO DUELS). A pilgrimage, particularly >PYEONGRYEOK, to the mountains was another element of this type of military upbringing.

SUICIDE HORSE RACE, a race held by the descendants of the Nez Percez Indians of Washington state (USA) along a course formed by: a steep slope, crossing the river Okanogon, rushing towards the finish line at the Ind. settlement, where the winner receives a prize. Races last 2 days and the contestant with best rankings in 4 consecutive races is proclaimed the winner.

SULKY, see >HARNESS RACING.

SULTISMAADLEMINE, see >MAADLEMINE.

SUMERIAN WRESTLING, popular among Sumerians, the inhabitants of Mesopotamia during the 4th and 3rd cent. BC. The existence of Sumerian wres-

tling was proved beyond any doubt by an Amer. scholar S.A. Speiser, who discovered an ancient statuette depicting two fighting wrestlers during his archeological works in the Khafajah Temple near Baghdad. The statuette is said to be a typical example of Sumerian sculpture and its age is estimated at 5-7,000 years. The wrestling style depicted in the statuette consisted in holding one's opponent above his hips and later became popular in the Mediterranean and, after a series of substantial modifications, gave rise to contemporary >GRECO-ROMAN WRESTLING.

SUMMER BIATHLON, a combination of a cross country race and competitive shooting, modelled after >WINTER BIATHLON. Events include: 10-km individual race, 6-km sprint, 8-km pursuit, 4x6-km relay (for men), and 8-km individual race, 4-km sprint, 6-km pursuit, 4x4-km relay (for women).

SUMO, [Jap. *sumo* – protect, secure oneself], trad. Jap. wrestling in which each contestant tries to force the other outside a circle or to touch the ground with any body part other than the soles of his feet. The effectiveness of forcing an opponent outside the circle depends largely on one's height and body mass. The *sumatori* (sumo competitors) are gargantuan men, who seldom weigh less than 130kg (285lbs.). Often they are much heavier and may be 200kg (440lbs.) and more. However, the tallest and heaviest competitors are not always guaranteed a win. One sumo trainer observes, 'The fact that a smaller and lighter competitor can win is one of the most exciting elements of sumo.' E.g. in the 1990s a competitor by the name of Tomonohala defeated his opponent, Kinishiki, who weighed over 200kg. The wrestlers fight barefoot and naked to the waist. They wear a fringed loin covering (*mae-tate-mitsu*) and a thick silk belt (*mawashi*). The trad. topknot hairstyle is ancient and called *o-icho-mage* or *chonmage* according to the category of the *sumotori*. A fight takes place in a circular ring which has a diameter of about 3.66m (12ft), which is covered with a roof shaped like that of a Shinto sanctuary, called a

WORLD SPORTS ENCYCLOPEDIA **S**

Street surfing.

Below: Wearing specially-designed belt over leotard, Naoko Sekine, left, and Yuko Adachi stare at each other following instructions by a referee, center, in a ring made of styrene foam in preparation for their middleweight bout in the 1st All-Japan New Sumo Tournament by female amateur sumo wrestlers in Osaka. Above: a traditional sumo bout.

S

WORLD SPORTS ENCYCLOPEDIA

dojo. The floor is covered with smooth earth. A fight is supervised by a referee called a *gyoji* who wears a silk kimono and a special court hat. He traditionally bears a fan as a symbol of authority, and a dagger, said to have been originally supplied so that a referee might disembowel himself if he gave a miscall. There is also a panel of 5 judges – often *yokozuna* (ex-grand champions). Sumo is accompanied by much hallowed ritual. Before the competitors enter the ring (*dojo*) they water their lips using a special scoop. In the old ritual this meant that the competitor saturated himself with courage. Once this has been accomplished the competitors enter the ring and, after some stretching and flexing of muscles, scatter handfuls of salt in a shinto purification ritual, which symbolizes the intention to fight a clean fight, without any tricks. They then crouch, pound the floor with their fists (to put the underground evil spirits at ease) and have an 'eye battle'. This ritual is known as *shikiri-naoshi* and is allowed to go on for up to 4min. The preliminary display also includes minatory marching to and fro. The fight does not begin at the referee's signal but by the competitor who first decides to charge. Sumo wrestlers are trained in sumo stables or schools (*sumo beya*)

called *makuuchi* (the division containing the top five ranks in sumo: *yokozuna, ozeki, sekiwake, komusubi* and *maegashira*). The following ranks are below the master class: *juryo, makushita, sandanme, jonidan* and *jonokuchi*. *Juryo* is a transitional class. Once attained, it means a radical change of the *sumori* status – the competitor starts to receive a salary, has the right to a single room in the corporation, the right to select the color of *mawashi* – the silk belt worn by the *rikishi*, to the *sekitori* title, the privilege to wear the topknot hairstyle, similar to the leaf of the *gingko* tree and to be served by lower rank wrestlers. There are not many sumo wrestlers in Japan: in 1996 the 2 master ranks numbered 66 wrestlers and about 800 wrestlers in 5 junior categories. The wrestlers from the *makushita* rank and below it do not receive any salary. In sumo there is no division into weight categories. The time between tournaments is spent on training and test fights with wrestlers belonging to another corporation. *Sumotori* training starts at dawn. The day's first meal is eaten after an exhausting training session. Older rank wrestlers are served by younger rank ones. There is a principle of absolute respect for better and higher rank wres-

the opponent out of the arena; 2) *ketaguri*, where the opponent's legs are pulled from beneath him as he makes a rush; 3) *ashi-tori*, where the opponent's leg is seized and held on to until he loses his balance and falls over. In grappling techniques the basic maneuver is to seize the opponent's belt. Using this as a hold and lever the wrestler tries to march his opponent out of the ring. This is called *yori-kiri*. A variant is *yori-taoshi* in which both wrestlers go crashing out of the ring together with the winner on top. Sometimes a wrestler literally hoists his opponent out of the ring. Another variant is *uttchari*. This happens when a wrestler, on the very point of being toppled out, hoists his rival over his stomach and throws him out, at the same time following his opponent to land on top of him.

The ring is made of specially compacted clay. It is a sort of elevated platform, which is entered from a special step, framed with a straw net. Traditionally, its borders are marked by a plaiting made of rice straw. Sumo wrestlers from outside Japan, who want to participate in the main tournaments, must first adopt Jap. citizenship. In 1993 the Hawaiian-born Akebono became the first foreign-born *rikishi* (wrestler) to be promoted to the top rank of sumo wrestler, that of yokozuna. In the 1990s high sumo ranks were also acquired by an American called Musashimaru (holder of the *ozeki* rank) and another American, Konishiki (*makuuchi* rank), a Mongolian, and a Brazilian of Jap. origin. Sumo is becoming popular outside Japan. W.Ch. in sumo were first organized in 1992. In the E.Ch., first organized in 1997, the first bronze medal was won by a Pole – S. Luto. Sumo tournaments are very popular in Hawaii, where many inhabitants are of Jap. origin. The tournaments organized there also attract representatives of many other ethnic groups and are exclusively for competitors of Jap. origin. The growing number of foreigners attaining master classes disturbed the Jap. Sumo Association so much that it recommended to the heads of the school to restrict admission by foreigners. Organizers of sumo matches outside Japan, and particularly in Europe and USA, admit also women wrestlers.

History. The beginnings of sumo date back to legendary times. A legend about sumo tells a story about a fight between Mikazuchi-no-Mikoto, who represented the ruler of Japan and Take Minakanushi-no-Mikoto, who represented the province of Izumo (today the prefectures of Tottori and Shimane). The bout was for the province of Izumo, until that time independent of Jap. rule. Legend has it that Mikazuchi-no-Mikoto won the fight, and the province became the property of his monarch. Another legend carries a description of a match between Nomino Sukune and Taima-no-Kehaya. The reason for the fight was the desire to punish Taima, who was 'insubordinate, badly brought up, and also nasty to the peasants'. The emperor ordered Nomino Sukune to challenge Taima and teach him a lesson. The oldest history of sumo is connected with religious rituals and prayers for good harvest. Sumo fights also played a role similar to the Eur. wager of battle – the gods were to decide which of the competitors was right and who should be awarded the victory. Sumo also became an important element of *Shinto* ritual, stressing reverence for the forces of nature and spirits of the ancestors, particularly outstanding characters and heroes. In time sumo became a form of entertainment at the imperial court, the first symptoms of which could be observed in the Nara period (7th cent. AD), when sumo bouts were called *sumo-sechi* – the sumo holiday. In the Kamakura period (1180-1333) sumo bouts became a form of sport practiced by knights and became an element of court etiquette. In the Muro-machi period (1333-1573) a new format of tournament appeared, featuring competitions (fights) between sumo wrestlers specially invited by the emperor, aristocratic houses as well as municipal boards and rural communities to give splendor to various celebrations. In the 17th cent. in the so-called Edo period, rules similar to the present-day rules started to crystallize: round-shaped rings and wrestler ranking based on results. In 1790 sumo assumed a national character and started to be held under the auspices of the emperor or his local administrators and governors. Despite the Europeanization of Jap. sports after 1868, sumo has retained the status of one of the most popular and most prestigious sports of Japan.

Junior champion Kaio, left, hurls grand champion Takanohana down with an arm throw during the 15-day New Year Grand Sumo Tournament in Tokyo.

which are run by retired champions (*oyakata*) who direct and control all wrestlers, who become apprenticed at the age of 15. The training is rigorous and the discipline strict.

Presently in Japan there are two branches of sumo. The most important is the professional variety, managed by the Jap. Sumo Association, which organizes numerous tournaments, including 6 grand tournaments or *basho* each year: 3 in Tokyo, the others in Osaka, Nagoya, and Fukuoka. Each lasts 15 days, during which every wrestler faces a different opponent each time. Results made at these tournaments determine the competitors' classification.

The highest rank in sumo is *yokozuna* – the grand master. In the entire history of sumo this rank has been attained by only 65 wrestlers. Presently two *rikishi* (sumo wrestlers) hold this rank, from which one cannot be demoted. The second rank from the top, below *yokozuna* is *ozeki* – master, followed by *sekiwake* – younger master, *komusubi* – lower rank younger master, one of the two *sanyaku* ranks, 4th from the top. The lowest master class is *maegashira* – a higher rank wrestler, ranking below *komusubi* and above *juryo*; the lowest of the *makuuchi* division. In each class, the rank can be held by only two competitors. All the master class competitors, from the rank of *yokozuma* to that of *maegashira* wrestle in higher class tournaments,

tlers. An *okayata*, who ran one of the sumo schools in Tokyo, observed that 'today many forget to respect those who are successful. The order in sumo society is a reminder of values resulting from human effort and achievement'.

The basic food of the *sumotori* is a high-protein stew called *chanko nabe*. Apart from the professional class, there is also the amateur class.

Only the highest rank *sumatori*, *yokozuna*, has the right to perform the complete ritual in the main tournaments. A *yokozuna* wrestler enters the ring. In front of each yokozuna walks his *tsuyuharai* (personal attendant or herald) behind whom him comes his *tachimochi* (sword bearer). The *yokozuna* takes the central part of the ring and performs a number of religious rituals, followed by the actual fight. There are 48 movements in sumo wrestling: 12 throws, 12 twists, 12 lifts, and 12 throws across the back. Each has its name. They come under the comprehensive heading of *kimarite*. Most bouts last less than half a minute. Some are concluded in a few seconds. A basic maneuver and method of attack is slapping. This is called *tsuppari*. A series of hard slaps (sledgehammer blows to ordinary mortals) delivered very rapidly can force the opponent out of the ring. There are also shoving, snatching, and grabbing techniques. Three basic ones are: 1) *hataki-komi*, which involves stepping aside and pushing

The importance attached to sumo by Jap. society is exemplified by the fact that Y. Akebono was asked to welcome Emperor Akichito to the opening ceremony of the 1998 Ol.G. in Nagano. Accompanied by his 2 lower rank attendants, unclad despite the low temperature and wearing only the trad. silk belt, he staged a ceremony, which is performed when entering the ring. Also at this opening ceremony the national teams were led by a *sumotori*, dressed in >KENDO apparel (owing to the extended time spent at low temperatures). Each *sumotori* was accompanied by a child, carrying on its back a structure resembling an angel's wing with the team's name inscribed on it.

Women's sumo. Most works on sumo mistakenly report that the sport is the exclusive domain of men. Historical accounts belie this assumption. The oldest accounts about female sumo fighters come from the 8th cent. (the *Nihon-syoki* chronicle). Emperor Yuuryaku is said to have ordered his female courtiers (*uneme*) to undress and fight while he had his meal. Numerous literary texts (*Ukiyoo zoushi i jyoururi*) from the Edo dynasty period (also referred to as Tokugawa, 1603-1867) contained descriptions of women sumo wrestlers. The most famous historical fights were held in 1744 and 1769. Information from the 2nd half of the 18th cent. and the first half of the 19th cent. has been preserved, according to which women sumo wrestlers fought with blind *sumotori* men. During the reign of the Meiji dynasty (1868-1912) women's sumo was banned (1873). Despite this, a few years later, women's sumo was revived in Jap. villages and towns. The first press account of such fights comes from 1890: it says that women sumo wrestlers staged fights in Tokyo in the district of Ryouguku-Kaikouin, next to the temple, with rules identical to those applied to men's fights. They were preceded with displays of strength – for example, 3 bales of rice, their weight totaling 245kg, were put on the wrestler's abdomen, while another wrestler climbed atop the bales. The tournament attracted 17 wrestlers. The same year marked the appearance of S. Saito, a manager of female sumo wrestlers, who organized women's sumo tournaments in Tokyo, in the prefectures of Akita, Aomori and on Hokkaido. Women's sumo became most popular on Hokkaido island. As women's sumo was still banned, in many areas organizers had to oppose the police, as a result of which many tournaments featured only displays of strength. However, the demand for fights was stronger than any bans. In 1901 a large tournament was held in Meiji. Also in 1901 a tournament called *Takatama-ichiza* was organized in Osaka, with sumo wrestlers brought from the village of Takatama (presently the town of Tendou in the Yamagata prefecture) competing. In 1923 a tournament was organized in Kyoto, with 34 women wrestlers competing. At a tournament held the same year in Tokyo a man was allowed to wrestle against women, which resulted in the termination of the tournament. In 1925 Tiomezou Tsukamoto (1878-1968) managed to organize a large tournament, combining it with Shinto festival celebrations in honor of the god Amano. In this way he could freely organize tournaments in different parts of the country, in which he presented approx. 30 women wrestlers. In 1930 women sumo wrestlers appeared for the first time outside Japan. A team called Ishiyama went on a six-month tour of the Hawaiian islands. During WWII, despite a strict ban on organizing sumo tournaments, one was held in Uji (1941). In 1951 the Ishiyama team was revived. Apart from fights its tournaments featured also displays of strength, e.g. a wrestler entered the ring carrying 5 other wrestlers, or a bale of rice straw weighing approx. 100kg, or bales of rice straw weighing 675kg were put on the abdomen of one wrestler while 2 women on the top thrashed rice in a large pestle, using wooden maces. In many provinces, particularly in Akita (the towns of Himai, Kazuno, Dokko, Tashiro and Nishi-senboku) and also in the province of Saga (Kiyama) women's sumo were staged to propitiate the god of rain. Fights were usu. staged in July or August. Eiko Kaneda describes them as follows: '[...] all parties involved visited the Ougida shrine and the priest recited a Shinto prayer for rainfall. Then a women's sumo bout took place. The results of the bouts were unimportant as the main intention was to arouse the god's anger to bring rainfall. Therefore, the women took deliberate falls. Next two snakes made from rice straw were dedicated to the god of the Yatsugashira-gingen shrine and there was a prayer for

rainfall. The snakes were two metres in length and measured about 20 centimeters in girth. Finally, the decorative cords and the snakes were floated down the Yobashiro River to remove impurities' (IJHS, 1993, 3). The westernization of Japan after WWII halted the development of women's sumo and in many areas the tradition of women's sumo disappeared. It started to revive when the Jap. economy stabilized and the need to organize sophisticated entertainment for the hordes of tourists flocking to Japan appeared. Presently, women's sumo matches are organized in Tokyo, Najoya, Sen-nichi, Ryougoku, Hakata, Nijyou and even in locations with no tradition of women's sumo, e.g. in Kawayu (1972) and Fukushima on the island of Honsiu (1991). In many areas of Japan women's sumo is used as an element of different local celebrations, not necessarily connected with religion, particularly in the province of Saga (towns of Imari, Takeo, Ohmachi, Kouhoku, Shiota), the province of Nagasaki (Goto, Mie), Kunamoto (Kusomoto, Gazu, Senkoyu, Yatushiro). Nijyou boasts of the tradition of women's sumo, in which the wrestlers' eyes are blindfolded. Despite the interest, in many areas of Japan women's sumo fights are disappearing. For example, in Hatatsu the fights disappeared when the local fish processing factory was liquidated and the local community disintegrated. The new community did not take up the tradition.

In keeping with the trad. view that women are unclean, and thus can corrupt holy places, women's sumo fights are not held on men's rings, built by the temples, but are built separately. The only exception is the rain-making ritual, when women are allowed to enter the temples in order to anger the gods into making it rain. Eiko Kaneda describes this as follows:

People marched in procession to the Obadake shrine, which was usually closed to women, and spread Miso (soya bean paste) on the large stone front of the shrine to give it a dirty appearance, so arousing the god's anger. To this end, men and women also drank alcohol and wrestled, so that they would fall over in the Dainichi shrine.

[IJHS, 1999, 3]

Women sumo wrestlers are divided into groups, according to their skill: *maegashira, komusubui, sekiwake* and the top category – *ohzeki*. In any category they are divided into 2 opposing groups *hihashikata* and *nishikata*. Judges wear the so-called *hakama*. Women's dress is similar to that worn by men, except that women wear underwear under the loin covering, and a kind of vest covering the breasts. A women's sumo fight starts with the *sumo-jinku* songs, sung during the ceremony preceding the actual fights, in stanzas of 7-7-7-5 verses. Presently, there

are 15 var. of *sumo-jinku*. After the songs the wrestlers take 3 steps forward and 3 steps backwards, following which they begin to charge each other. The revival of the old tradition of women's sumo has stirred the attention of the mass media, owing to which tournaments of women's sumo have become popular in the USA, particularly in the Hawaiian islands, where a considerable percentage of the population is of Jap. origin. At the beginning of the 1990s the first great star of women's sumo was H. Yamada, who earlier practiced judo (under the name of Sasaki she won the demonstration fight during the 1988 Ol.G. in Seoul). In 1999 tournaments of women's sumo were opened to wrestlers from outside Japan. The first wrestler to have taken this opportunity was M. Madill from Canada, a teacher of English employed in Japan.

P.L. Kuyler, *Sumo. From Rite to Sport*, 1979; A. Kamiya, 'Sumo in Japan', OR Dec. 1995/Jan. 1996; K. Kahaulua, *Takamiyama*, 1973.

SUN DANCE, despite its name, not a form of dance in its proper meaning, but rather a ritual of initiation to a warrior among various Amer. Ind. tribes of the Great Plains, connected with a test of physical endurance and resistance to pain. During the ceremony a young man was tied with leather straps to a centrally located pole. At the end of the straps were sharpened pieces of wood or bone which were skewered into the dancer's skin in the breast area or, in the tradition of some tribes, in the shoulder blade area. The dancer's task was to tug and pull until the skin broke free. Despite sustaining great pain, the dancer was expected not to show any sign of physical weakness. During the entire ordeal he would make dance-like feet movements and, in order not to yield a cry, he would bite on a kind of whistle or small pipe made of eagle's feather bone, which produced a penetrating sound with each breath. When the test was over, the entire tribe would celebrate a feast accompanied by demonstrations of various military skills like bow shooting or tomahawk throwing. The scars inflicted by the dancer remained a token of his pride.

SUOPUNGIN HEITTO, see >LASSOING, >RODEO.

SUPER G, see >ALPINE SKIING.

SUPERCROSS, a type of motorcycle race deriving from the Eur. tradition of >MOTORCROSS but evolving into an autonomous motorcycle discipline, in which the most important are the spectacular character of the sport and catering for the needs of TV broadcasts. What differentiates the two sports is the venue – supercross is usu. held in great sports arenas or indoors on a man-made track, whereas motorcross is held outdoors and on a much larger track,

Sun Dance on a painting by George Catlin (above) and a photograph by Lummis (1888).

Michael Craig takes his 250cc Honda motorbike wide during the 250cc race at the Supercross Australian Masters at the Rod Laver Arena, Melbourne, Australia.

S
WORLD SPORTS ENCYCLOPEDIA

Craig Anderson takes his 250cc KTM motorbike over the triple jumps during 250cc race at the Supercross Australian Masters at the Rod Laver Arena, Melbourne, Australia.

without the large run-ups so typical of supercross. The father of supercross is Gary Bailey, who organized the first professional supercross competitions in the Coliseum in Los Angeles (1972). The motorcross riders of the time were not used to very high jumps, in fact they were afraid of them, so when designing his first track in Daytona Bailey thought of the so-called 'coward's path', i.e. a detour of a large run-up, which forced the riders to make the jump. The first great supercross star was Bob 'Hurricane' Hannah, who won the AMA supercross championship title 3 times in a row in 1977-79. His career ended after an accident while water skiing. The most champion titles ever (7) were won by J. McGrath.

In recent years supercross has become one of the most spectacular 'television' sports. Competitions are held in two classes: 125 and 250ccm. The start is identical to that in motorcross. The start line must be at least 24m long. A straight section of the track right after the start line, of a min. length of 36m, narrows down rapidly to 6m, which forces the riders to quickly find their place in the group before the first turn. This is a test of the ability to find one's way in the motorcycle crowd. Supercross lends itself to the most accidents, often multiple crashes. The obstacles appearing on the track require the riders to make long and high flights. Large mounds, in turn, force the riders to make the following jumps:

A SINGLE JUMP – 6-18m long, with landing on a flat segment of the track;

A DOUBLE JUMP – after the first jump the rider drops down to the run-up of the second jump and after a short run-up makes the other jump; each jump is 6-20m on average;

A TRIPLE JUMP – the rider rides over 3 mounds, which act as a trampoline; it is also possible to go over them in 2 or 1 long jump. A jump over 3 mounds requires the rider to jump to a height of up to 8m and cover the distance of up to 20m;

WHOOP – a short, steep obstacle, in series of more

hell clicker – an airborne motorcyclist clicks his feet over the handlebars, an evolution made up and introduced by K. Windham; bar hop – an airborne rider puts his feet on the steering wheel just prior to landing; superman air – the rider takes the feet off the footrests, jerks his body upwards and flies with the motorcycle held by the handlebars, the position resembles the flight of batman or superman, hence the name. This evolution was made for the first time by J. McGrath. Supercross is governed by the Amer. Motorcyclist Association Pro Racing, AMA.

The Internet: www.pacesupercross.com and www.supercross.com

ŠUQQ EL-QAN, Arab for 'to cut the ditch', a game described in M. Ibrahim Al-Majman's dictionary of Arab sports and games:

The game differs from other old folk games in that it is played only at night, to preserve the anonymity of the players. It is played mainly by boys, especially strong ones, who are divided into two teams, five to each team. However, the more players take part, the more beautiful and effective the game is and the more lively rivalry. In order to play the game, a spacious field is needed, called braha or hiala.

The rules of the game are as follows: two parallel straight lines, about 3m apart, are marked on the field. Players line up alongside each line, facing the opponents. The first line is about 40m from the finish. So the players of the first team, say (A), face the finish line, while the players of the opposite team (B) – stand with their backs to it. A toss decides which team begins the game. The game is started by team B with an order-like opening: 'Šuqq el-qan!' [jump over the ditch]. Team A responds with: 'Lakom el-'n!' [lit. you will carry this burden]. This verbal exchange is finished by team B: 'Min 'enkom!' [off your eyes], to which team A responds with: ''Il'en 'ana. 'Illéaqċh…' [I am the eye. Chase him…]. Then a player from team A jumps out and tries to force himself through the players of team B, past whom the finish line is located. In order to help the player to escape and mislead the opponents, the other members of his team try to run very close to him and perform different maneuvers during the run. The ob-

very short or very long. For this reason sandy fields lend themselves best to the game. The game is particularly charming on spring nights, when the moon shines. It is liked very much by the Bedouins, in a slightly modified form of a verbal polemic. After the words 'Šuqq el-qan' a question is asked: 'Munu el 'an?' [who carries the burden?]. Then a provocative answer is heard: 'Šehkim' [your sheik], to which a reply is shouted: "Ana eš-šeh!' [I am the sheik]. Another innovation introduced by the Bedouins is that the escaping 'sheik' is surrounded by his colleagues to guard him from being hit by the aggressive players of the opposite team. Each 'sheik' anticipates that a player will get through to him and then he can touch one of the players who defend access to him and make him the 'sheik'. Only the arms and the back can be touched.

The game is similar to >SARI. The author praises the game because it embodies healthy rivalry and sports competition. It also creates opportunities for excellent cooperation. However, it requires agility, strength and stamina.

[*Min al'abina ash-sha 'biyya, (Our Folk Games), 1983, 16-19]*

SUR KHARVAKH, Mong. shooting at leather bundles, formerly at leather caps [Mong. *sur* – a narrow leather bundle]. The target was made of 50-100 leather bundles, which formed a kind of pyramid, usu. 13 layers high. One leather bundle was about 6-9cm in diameter and 8cm wide. Most often it was made of plaited strips of camel skin and filled with oak bark or leather. Presently, sur kharvakh is a competition for a team of 8-12 men. Each competitor can shoot 4 times from a distance of 75-80m. In order to qualify for the next round, a team must hit 33 *sur* using a maximum of 48 shots. Then it gets the right to shoot at 15 scattered *surs*. The team that hits 15 *surs*, scores 45pts. (3 for each *sur*). A team can shoot at *surs*, which are being shot at by the opposing team, and has the right to make 5 such shots, each of which scores 5pts. Sur kharvakh can also be played individually over a distance of 100m. Each competitor has 30 arrows. The target is made of 1,000 leather caps piled up to form a pyramid. The winner is the competitor who hits the most caps with 20 arrows; see also >ARCHERY.

After each good shot the spectators produce a characteristic lengthy shout, similar to singing – *uukhai*, stand up and raise their arms towards the sky. In the past it was believed that the shout scared evil forces away from the next competition. Any *surs* hit by the competitors are taken by them to their tents as a talisman, in accordance with the Mong. principle that 'everyone should take what is good and leave behind what is bad'. The Mongolians believed that evil powers, especially those which reside in human and animal diseases, that often decimated the Mong. herds, can be killed with an arrow. If any of the many *sur* was not hit in the course of the competition, it was buried in the ground in order to prevent evil powers from spreading.

Sur kharvakh as practiced by the Tartars, who often invaded the eastern territories of Poland, and who later were allies of the Polish Republic, probably contributed to the development in the 13th-17th cent. of the old Pol. form of archery known as >STRZELANIE DO CZAPKI.

I. Kabzińska-Stawarz, *Games of Mongolian Shepherds*, 1991.

SURFING, a water sport of riding waves with the aid of a board or other floating object, or sometimes with the body alone. The surfer usu. stands on a tapered, hollow board and rides down the face of a breaking wave, steering the board by shifting the weight of the body. The modern surfboard measures 2.7-3.0m (9-10ft.) in length, 56-58cm (22-23in.) in width, and 7.6-10.2cm (3-4in.) in thickness. Its weight ranges from 11-26kg, depending on the surfer's body weight and the purposes for which it is used. The board's front and back are slightly bent upwards; from the 1970s there has been a tail fin looking like the centerboard of a sailing boat at the back of the board, and from the 1980s there have been as many as 3 tail fins. Although it is possible to surf on waves only 0.3m (1ft.) high, steeper waves provide a faster, more exciting ride. Southern California, with more than 40 surfing beaches, has become a major United States center for small-wave riding. The best surf is found in Hawaii, where waves may peak at 9m (30ft.). Many Austrl. beaches, such as Bondi, also provide ideal conditions. Small seas, like the Baltic, do not lend themselves to surfing and the sport is much less popular there or even non-existent. From the technical point of view the surfer starts to surf kneeling on the board or lying on it on his front

1999 Association of Surfing Professionals (ASP) world champion Mark Occilupo during the Rio Surf International at Arpoador, Rio.

An indoor surfing competition.

than one; it jerks the rider up in different directions. Supercross developed in the 2nd part of the 1980s, when television 'discovered' its spectacular nature. The pressure to make supercross more attractive led to the addition of special evolutions, such as whip it – swaying the motorcycle during the flight, pancake – positioning the airborne motorcycle parallel to the track surface, cancan – when airborne the rider moves one leg over the motorcycle to the other side and back; nac nac – when airborne the rider takes one leg off the footrest, sways the motorcycle to the side and ostentatiously observes what is happening under the motorcycle (probably from Eng. slang *nac* – a flyer of a sea patrolling plane, usu. ship based, whose task is to observe water surface), an evolution made up and introduced by J. McGrath;

ject is to mislead team A as to who is the 'en [the eye]. If the escapee manages to get to the finish line, his team (B) wins the round. He scores a point and restarts the game. If he is caught, then team B loses a point, the teams change sides and the initiative rests with team A. Team A will start the game. It must be pointed out that the escapee ('en) can avoid being caught. When he feels that he is being touched by the hand of a player from the chasing team, then during the escape he can touch the shoulder of any of his mates, which means that the teammate he has touched becomes the 'en [the eye]. It may turn out that the chosen 'en is faster and more agile and can reach the finish line without any problems. Then he will be chased. But he also has the right to designate another 'en even right before the finish line, e.g. if he feels that he stands no chance of reaching the finish line [...]. The game is rather brutal, the players run full tilt, obstruct each other, try to tackle the 'en, etc. A round may be

and paddling with the arms towards the oncoming wave. At the same time he distributes his body weight so that the board's tip is raised over the water. Once in contact with the wave, the surfer chases it and, continuing to paddle with the arms, tries to gain the speed of the wave so as to keep balance in a standing position. When the proper speed has been achieved, the surfer stands up and with the help of the hands steers the board crosswise to the direction of the wave and parallel to the coastline. He uses the wave's energy until the wave gets so close to the coastline that continued surfing is not possible. Surfing is made more attractive by the different evolutions performed on the wave, e.g. breaking the wave with the board's tip, jumps into the air and airborne evolutions. During surfing competitions judges evaluate the following elements: the degree of difficulty of a given evolution or maneuver, the degree of commitment and the risk involved, evaluated not with respect to the body movements but rather the board movements, radical controlled maneuvers; the place where the maneuver is performed on the wave, particularly the ability to move close to its ridge called the pocket by surfers, and the length of ride. The quality of the evolutions depends on the choice of an appropriate wave and flexible adjustment to its type. Presently judges pay less attention to the wave size and the maneuvers performed as was the case in the earlier times of surfing. However, it is obvious that a larger wave, if properly used, offers more opportunities to show one's skills. Refereeing in surfing has for years been a controversial and disputable issue, particularly between Austrl. and Hawaiian contestants. Presently, the refereeing system used at professional championships seems to be the most objective. Eliminations are held in groups of 3 contestants – the winner qualifies for the next round and meets the winner of another 3-man group. Each group has 20min. to surf in, although the judges can extend the time up to 40min., depending on the conditions. Over this time surfers try to make the most rides, usu. up to 10, and the 4 best are scored. A single ride is evaluated on a 10-pt. scale by 5 judges. The best and the worst scores are dropped and the remaining ones are used to calculate the average score. During W.Ch. four events are held: classical surfing (standing), bodyboarding, kneeboarding and long boarding.
In addition to classical surfing there are also the following var.: skimboarding, which is a sport similar to surfing which takes place near the shore. The skimboarder stands about twenty feet from the ocean with skimboard in hand and waits for a wave. When they see a wave they run towards it with their skimboard still in hand. Upon reaching the wet sand they drop the board and jump onto it as quickly as possible. Once on the board, the skimmer must remain as stable as possible and prepare to make the transition to the ocean. The skimmer then (hopefully) glides out into the ocean toward the oncoming wave, banks off of it, and rides it back into shore. Modern skimboards are made out of fiberglass or carbon fiber and high density foam to serve as a core. Skimboards vaguely resemble surfboards, they are about half the length, half the thickness, and slightly wider. Unlike surfboards, skimboards have no *skegs* (fins on the bottom of the board used for controlling direction). They are much less stable and require a lot of practice to be able to control. The other var. is called bodysurfing – riding the waves without a board, where the surfer makes his body a type of a 'rigid board'. Both types are recognized by the International Surfing Association, but so far they have not been included in the official program of W.Ch.
Surfing terminology is identical in all countries where surfing is practiced. Most typically Eng. terms are used; some terms include: *bottom turn* – a turn at the wave base, which starts the ride proper when the surfer meets the wave front and turns the board tip towards the coastline to gain speed; *cutback* – when the surfer suddenly cuts into the wave and turns the board (after a short period of surfing in the wave direction to gain speed); *down-the-line* – the ride's direction is identical with the wave direction before the surfer cuts into the wave (see cutback); *floater* – keeping close to the wave's ridge; *glassy* – the smooth surface of the water during windless weather; *offshore* – wind direction into the ocean that creates the best surfing conditions; *onshore* – wind direction towards the coast, eliminating the waves and not lending itself to good surfing conditions; *off-the-lip* – when the surfboard bounces off the wave towards its front (other names: off-the-tops or snaps); *peak* – wave peak, the place where the ride starts and where it starts to move forward and the wave breaks, 'flowing over itself'; *re-entry* – a change of the board's direction with the surfer approaching the oncoming wave; *section* – the place where the wave ends its flow and breaks into a few segments and where the surfer must decide whether to jump over the decreasing wave to the next or to end the ride; *swell* – a long wave made by a storm or hurricane, distant from the place where the competition is held; *take-off* – a start to the ride proper, when the surfer stands up after surfing in the kneeling or lying position; *tube ride* – surfing under a wave breaking over the surfer.

Etymology and history. The Eng. name derivers from the word *surf*, which denotes the lines of foamy waves that break on a seashore. However, the Hawaiian terminology, passed over verbally from generation to generation, dating back to the arrival of the white man to the islands, surfing is termed he'enalu, which roughly means 'to swim' or 'to move on the wave'. In fact, the words have many meanings. He'e means 'to swim' but also 'to change into a liquid matter', so it suggests the element of man's association with water or man's transformation into water. Nalu means 'movement' or 'wave splashing'. In the language of the Hawaiian aborigines ocean terms are exceptionally numerous. The rapid movements of the ocean are believed to be the driving force of the world. Gentle movements are termed kai malie, rapid and angry ones as kai pupule. Surfing, in the Hawaiian tradition called alaia, was believed to calm the sea and for this reason in the old tradition wave taming in the ikuwa period (roughly in November) was very important. This is how K. Keauokalani, a 19th cent. ethnographer, described the ceremony of wave taming:

This is a period of rough ocean and high waves, which attracts men to the shoreline. Experienced surfers stop all the work, and withdraw into the mainland [...], pick the leaves of banana trees, ti and imbiru trees, put them round their necks and face the sea holding sugar canes in their hands. Then they run towards their homes, take their boards and come back to the shoreline. They stop thinking about any work; only surfing is on their minds. At that time the wife can go hungry and so can the children and the rest of the family; the man does not care. He gives himself whole to this sport, which becomes his food. All the day long, he does nothing else but surfs.

Surfing originated in Oceania and was highly developed in the Hawaiian Islands by the time the Eng. explorer Captain J. Cook reached them in 1778. Christian missionaries, who arrived in the Hawaiian islands around 1820, shocked by the shameless nudity of the aborigines, did all they could to ban surfing, which they largely managed to do. But the sport did not die completely. Practiced in hiding by the aborigines, surfing was revived at the turn of the 19th cent. thanks to Amer. tourists who spent their holidays in Hawaii. Among those who promoted surfing were G. Freeth (1883-1919) and A.H. Ford who in 1908 founded the famous Canoe Club in Honolulu, where he promoted not only sailing the local outriggers but also surfing. Other promoters of surfing include D. Kahanamoku (1890-1968; a Hawaiian swimmer and water jumper, 3 times world champion and 3 times gold medal winner in freestyle swimming at the Ol.G. in 1912 and 1920). He made a surfing promotional tour and visited Los Angeles, Sydney, Wellington and Christchurch. Demand for new forms of recreation, being born then in the western world, and particularly in the US, created the proper climate for the spread of surfing. Since Gaugin's times holidaying in the South Seas has become the prototypical representation of 'paradise on earth' and as such influenced the image of ideal recreation and vacation, with their freedom, not obstructed by Eur. clothes, replaced with skirts of long grass, flower bracelets (leis) and dancing full of bodily expression (hula) in the company of naturally sensual women (wahines). Surfing became an important element of the Hedonist philosophy of relaxation and first took in the Pacific countries, particularly Hawaii, the western coast of the US, Australia and N.Zealand. Cheap flights intensified this form of recreation, which, after WWII became a type of fad and lifestyle, characterized by the desire for pleasure, and even a sociological phenomenon, defined as surfing subculture. The development of professional surfing was held up for a long time by the imperfect board. The trad. board was not stable, and practically did not allow surfing against the waves and the surfer was very much dependent on accidental movements. In the 1920s T. Blake, an American from California, introduced a board with a single fin, thus increasing its maneuverability. By the 1930s, solid planks had been replaced by plywood and balsa boards with fins for steering. As a professional sport, surfing was initiated by B. Simmons and J. Quigg from California at the turn of the 1940s, who introduced considerable improvements in board

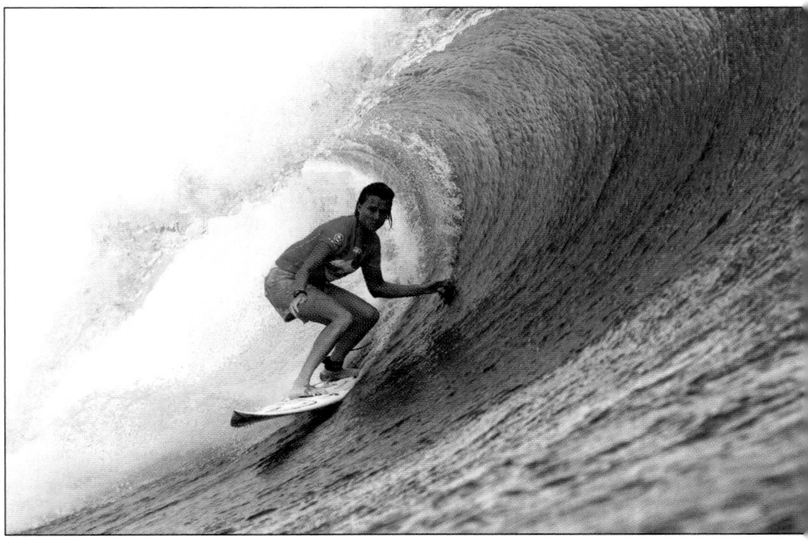

2000 Teahupoo event champion Keala Kennelly (HAW) rides the tube during the Billabong Pro at Teahupoo, Tahiti.

design. The trad. boards of that time were long hardwood slabs weighing 68kg (150lb) or more; so only the strongest athletes could handle them. Simmons shortened the board to about 3m and introduced modern materials such as Styrofoam, which reduced its weight. When Simmons died in 1953, his work was continued by Quigg, who used fiberglass to further reduce the board's weight (up to 11-13kg). This was the birth of the Malibu board, from the name of the Californian coastline. Another revolution came in 1958 when H. Alter, D. Sweet and G. Clark introduced polyurethane instead of wooden elements. At the beginning of the 1970s T. Hoye added a twin-fin to the board, with which the surfer could maneuver on the wave front. The twin-fin, however, reduced the board's speed and stability. Around 1980 S. Anderson from Australia introduced a thruster board, with a set of 3 fins. This design eliminated the drawbacks of the twin-fin board, while retaining the latter's advantages. The first international championships were organized by the Waikiki Surfer Club in 1954 in Hawaii. The first great surfers came to light, e.g. B. Pile from Australia. The first W.Ch. were staged in 1964, the year of the establishment of the International Surfing Federation (ISF). The W.Ch. have continued ever since, every 2 years. The first historical world champion was B. Farrelly from Australia, known as Midget (born 1944). In 1976 the ISF changed to the International Surfing Association, ISA), which today is the main governing surfing organization. Every 2 years it organizes the World Amateur Surfing Championships and junior W.Ch.. In 1988 the Women's Surfing Committee was estab. within the ISA, headed by an American S. Powers. There is also the Association of Surfing Professionals, ASP, which organizes the W.Ch. Tour of Surfing. In 1995 the ISA was provisionally recognized by the IOC, to be fully recognized in 1977, as a result of which surfing may become an Olympic sport. In 1999 the ISA had 38 national associations, incl. some from countries with no access to the sea or ocean, such as Switzerland, whose surfers practice surfing outside the country. The best developed national associations are in the USA (divided into 3 independent regional associations – of the E and W coasts and of Hawaii), in S.Africa, N.Zealand, Brazil, Mexico and in Europe in France, Spain, Holland, Germany, Portugal and Great Britain.

SVINGFIGUR, Dan. for 'a spinning figurine'. A game for small children, known in Denmark and elsewhere. One child spins another and then lets go; the one who stops in the funniest pose becomes the spinner in the next round.

J. Møller, 'Svingfigur', GID, 1997, 3, 58.

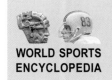

SWAMP BUGGY RACES – WINNERS OF MAIN EVENTS

1949 Johnny Jones
1951 George Espenlaub/Bubba Frank (ex equo)
1952 R.L.Walker
1953 R.L.Walker
1954 H.W. McCurry
1955 Sippy Morris
1956 Arnold Walker
1957 H.W. McCurry
1958 H.W. McCurry
1959 H.W. McCurry
1960 Chester Bryant
1961 Chester Bryant
1962 Jack Hatcher
1963 Tony Carmo
1964 Benny Collins
1965 Jack Hatcher
1966 Daniel Phypers
1967 Jack Hatcher
1968 Lee Hancock
1969 Jack Hatcher
1970 Leonard Chesser
1971 Leonard Chesser
1972 Leonard Chesser
1973 Leonard Chesser
1974 Leonard Chesser
1975 (May event) Leonard Chesser
1975 (Oct. event) Roger McCandless
1976 (May event) David Sims
1976 (Oct. event) David Sims
1977 (Feb. event) Leonard Chesser
1977 (Oct. event) Leonard Chesser
1978 (Feb. event) Leonard Chesser
1978 (Oct. event) Leonard Chesser
1979 (Feb. event) Leonard Chesser
1979 (Oct. event) Lee Hancock
1980 (Feb. event) David Sims
1980 (Oct. event) Terry Langford
1981 (Feb. event) Lonnie Chesser
1981 (Oct. event) David Sims
1982 (Feb. event) Lonnie Chesser
1982 (Oct. event) Terry Langford
1983 (by class)
Roger McCandless (Feb. event)
Lonnie Chesser (Oct. event)
David Sims (Feb. event)
Leonard Chesser (Oct. event)
Terry Langford (Feb. event)
Terry Langford (Oct. event)
Leonard Chesser (Nov. event)
David Sims (Mar. event)
1984 Lonnie Chesser (Oct. event)
David Sims (Feb. event)
Leonard Chesser (Oct. event)
1985
Terry Langford (Feb. event)
Terry Langford (Oct. event)
1986 Leonard Chesser (Nov. event)
1987
David Sims (Mar. event)
Lonnie Chesser (Oct. event)
1988
David Sims (Feb. event)
Tommy Turner (Oct. event)
1989
Terry Langford (Feb. event)
Terry Lanford (Oct. event)
1990
David Sims (Feb. event)
Wayne Cochran (Oct. event)
1991
Lenny Dunn (May event)
David Simms (Oct. event)
1992
David Sims (Mar. event)
Eddie Chesser (May event)
Terry Langford (Oct. event)
1993
David Sims (Mar. event)
Don Jolly (May event)

A swamp buggy.

SVIPTINGAR, a form of Icelandic folk wrestling in which the contestants hold the sleeves of the opponent's jacket and pull them hard so as to make the opponent fall to the ground.
W. Baxter, 'Les lutes tradtionnelles a traverse le monde', LJP, 1998, 84.

SVØMME OVER DET RØDE HAV, Dan. for 'to swim across the Red Sea', [Dan. *svømme* – to swim + *over* – across, over + *det* – definite article + *Røde Hav* – the Red Sea]. A game of social contact. The participants divide into 2 groups: the 'swimmers' and the 'sea'. Non-swimmers form 2 rows, facing each other and make a bridge with their hands. The contestant or contestants who are going to swim, lie on their hands and are then thrown forward. The pair, which the contestants 'swam over', leave the line and run to the front, where they make another link. In this way the game can be played ad infinitum.
J. Møller, 'Svømme over det Røde Hav', GID, 1997, 3.

SWAMP BUGGY RACES, races of special wheeled vehicles held on the shallow waters of Florida's Everglades and the swamps of Louisiana and Alabama (USA). Vehicles are of different types: from jeeps to special constructions resembling anything from a boat to a 1930s race car. Their bodies must be waterproof in order to keep the vehicle afloat in deeper water. The vehicles ride on 4 wheels attached to the sides in a way resembling that of old steamboats with narrow tires threaded with scoops. During the race the vehicles seem to be riding on the water.
Once held in one unspecified class, the races are now divided into the following classes:
JEEP: for vehicles which must have a construction based on a 4-cylinder Amer. Jeep;
AIR COOLED: for vehicles which must be air cooled and, usually, powered by motorcycle or Volkswagen engines;
FOUR CYLINDER: for vehicles with 4-cylinder engines;
SIX CYLINDER: for vehicles with 6-cylinder engines;
V8 STOCK: for vehicles with stock V8 engines;
MODIFIED 4WD: for vehicles driven by all 4 wheels and engines of driver's choice;
PRO MODIFIED: for vehicles similar as in Modified 4WD class, but driven by 2 wheels and having engines producing up to 1,000-hp.
Races are held on a mile-long, figure 8 track set up in a swamp area with an off-track pit similar to that of typical automobile races.
Crowding is banned and vehicles must keep a safe distance from one another. It is allowed to cross the track's side line with 2 wheels only, while running outside the track's limits with more than 1 wheel – called *running the banks* or *running out of bounds* – disqualifies the race. Drinking alcohol during the race or even having alcohol inside the vehicles within the track's limits, including the pit stop, is banned.
Safety helmets and 5-point safety belts are obligatory. Safety regulations also call for each vehicle to be equipped with a *kill switch* that turns off all fuel and electric drive systems. Only standard or race fuel with no additives is allowed. Refueling under pressure is banned, just as are turbo engines. To become a participant, a racer must be at least 18

A swamp buggy.

years of age. Each racer is allowed a number of test rides on a given track before the actual race. The best 3 racers of each competition score championship points. The racer with the highest number of championship points scored within one year becomes the world champion.
Ethymology. The earliest swamp buggy vehicles of the 1930s were called *dirt dobbers*. Later the name *tumblebug* was coined, while in the 1940s the present name came into existence, at first to denominate just the vehicle type and later also the competition itself. Other names that were used over the years include *wood buggy* and *hunting buggy*.
History. The earliest races of modern swamp buggy prototypes were held in the 1930s in Collier County in south-eastern Florida (USA), where local farmers, having to move around the swamp areas of the Everglades, equipped their tractors and cars with disproportionally large wheels that kept the vehicles above the water surface. Technical progress limited that role of wheels in favor of the waterproof body, which in turn led to the use of smaller tires. The swamp buggy sporting tradition was at first connected with the beginning of the hunting season at the end of Oct. or beginning of Nov. The swamp hunts were competitive in nature and the participating farmers made many improvements to their vehicles, such as waterproofing the engine, camouflaging the body, or adaptations to combat the swamp environment. The earliest – local and spontaneously arranged – swamp hunting competitions took place in 1943. By the end of the 1940s approx. 30-40 swamp buggy competitions were held in Collier County, with the racing center in Naples. The greatest prestige is attributed to the *Swamp Buggy Races*, which took place for the first time on 1 Nov. 1949 as part of *Swamp Buggy Days*, with 50 participants, of whom one J. Jones made his way into the history of the event by winning the first race. The races were a great success and became an annual event, governed by a board of directors. The races were usu. organized on off-days and were accompanied by parades and festivals. Participation was at first purely for fun, but as soon as the event's fame spread, sponsors soon began offering prize money for the winners. In the 1950s the races aroused the interest of ABC Television Network. The popularity of the event reached its peak with the participation as drivers of Gary Cooper among other Hollywood movie stars. Since 1991 the driver that scores the highest number of winning points within a given year becomes the World Champion and receives the Budweiser Cup. The Florida Sports Park Track registers world records in each class. The one mile track all-class record holder is B. Langford, who covered the track on his 'Rubber Duck' (pro-modified) in 2000 within 48.75sec.
The growing popularity of the races gave birth to new attractions that became a tradition. The best know is the Swamp Buggy Queen's Annual Mudbath, which originated in 1957, when the winner, H.W. McCurry, grabbed a young girl selected as a Swamp Buggy Queen and dipped her in the muddy track known as Mile O' Mud. The races also have a mascot in the form of *Swampy* – an unspecified, fish-headed species.
Swamp Buggy Races 50th Anniversary Commemorative Program, Oct. 1999; Inform. The Internet.: http://www.swampbuggy.com/rules9.htm

SWEDISH GYMNASTICS, general term for a number of systems created in Sweden, esp. during the 19th cent. The main creators were P. Ling (1776--1839) and his son Hjalmar (1820-86). At the roots of the technical theory underpinning Swed. gymnastics lay the conviction that systematic physical education must be supported by scientific principles, which to this day constitutes an everpresent element of all physical education systems. The characteristic feature of Swed. gymnastics was the linking of exercising movements with the possibilities and requirements of man's bodily structure and then their separation into simple elements practiced in isolation. After its discovery this system was very quickly turned into schematic routines and in the long run lost out to more attractive forms of physical educa-

Swimming, an illustration for Frederick II's (1212-1250) hunting book Dete venandi cum avibus.

tion, especially sporting ones. In this way the further development of gymnastics was mainly featured by the gradual withdrawal from Swed. gymnastics as the dominant 19th cent. form involving a system of artificially calculated movements towards movements more associated with everyday life and sport.

SWELE'I, a pole throw at a rolling ring, practiced among the Stóólo Indians, who inhabit the western coast of N.America, the area bordering Canada, near Coast Salish. An Amer. Ind. sport, defined in Amer. ethnography as >HOOP-AND-POLE, it has its counterparts in other Ind. cultures, e.g. >CHUNGKE among the Choctows living in the estuary of the Mississippi river, Arapaho and Cheyennes, who live in present-day Oklahoma. The pole looks like a primitive spear; it is made of hazel or spruce, sharpened at one end, usu. 4-6ft. (about 1.2-1.8m) long. The ring, which is the moving target, is of plaited cane or supple wicker twigs and is about 1ft. (30cm) in diameter.
Rules of the game. The contestants form 2 rows, facing each other. Players from one row take turns in throwing their rings down the rows, each player throwing two rings. The players of the opposite team take turns in throwing the poles so as to hit inside the rolling ring and stop it moving, thereby scoring a point. The players agree how many hits are needed to win, usu. it is 10; in the past the game was used to practice spear throwing for warring and hunting purposes. With the disappearance of the old Amer. Ind. tradition, it has become a recreational sport.
The Internet: *http://web20.mindlink.net/stolo/games.htm*

SWIMMING, in sports, the propulsion of the body through water by body motions without assistance of any mechanical devices, against other competitors or the clock. The majority of swimming events take place now in indoor swimming pools, e.g. races over fixed distances; swimming areas in natural bodies of water are currently on decline. Other swimming competitions include long distance swimming events held on inland or sea waters (cf. >TRIATHLON). The object of these swimming events is to cover specific open-water distances, e.g. crossing sea straits, channels, lakes, or rivers (competitions on the decline due to environmental pollution); see >LONG DISTANCE SWIMMING. The oldest, most natural swimming strokes are the frog kick and the sidestroke. The former is an imperfect breaststroke – a recreational style using asymmetrical leg kicks with the head above the water. The frog kick is used extensively in early swimming practice, without any professional swimming instruction. The latter is a swimming technique used in >WATER POLO and >WATER RESCUE.
In competitive swimming the following techniques can be distinguished: the crawl, the back crawl, the frog kick and the dolphin kick. These techniques are used in the following swimming strokes: 1) freestyle, in which the swimmer may swim any style except that in medley swimming events; 2) backstroke; 3) breaststroke; 4) butterfly stroke; 5) medley swimming, i.e. a combination of 4 swimming styles in a designated order.
BREASTSTROKE consists of a wide pull of the arms combined with a symmetrical action of the legs. According to the FINA rules, 'The swimmer's body shall be kept on the breast. [...] All movements of the arms shall be simultaneous and in the same horizontal plane without alternating movements. [...] The hands

shall be pushed forward together from the breast on, under, or over the water. The elbows shall be under water except for the final stroke before the turn, during the turn and for the final stroke at the finish. The hands shall be brought back on or under the surface of the water. The hands shall not be brought back beyond the hip line, except during the first stroke after the start and each turn. All movements of the legs shall be simultaneous and in the same horizontal plane without alternating movement. The feet must be turned outwards during the propulsive part of the kick. A scissors, flutter or downward dolphin kick is not permitted. Breaking the surface of the water with the feet is allowed unless followed by a downward dolphin kick'.
FREESTYLE, according to the FINA rules, means 'any style other than backstroke, breaststroke or butterfly'. The freestyle rule is open to inclusion of any prospective swimming techniques. In practice, however, the most universal stroke used in competitive freestyle swimming is the crawl. The crawl consists of alternate arm movements above the water and alternate, fluttering up-and-down, leg movements under the water.
BACKSTROKE, in practice, consists of the back-crawl technique. As defined by the FINA rules, 'The swimmer shall [...] swim upon his back throughout the race except when executing a turn. Some part of the swimmer must break the surface of the water throughout the race, It shall be permissible for the swimmer to be completely submerged during the turn, at the finish and for a distance of not more than 15m after the start and each turn.' The 15m restriction is set to eliminate the widespread tendency to swim underwater.
BUTTERFLY, according to the FINA rules, 'The swimmer's body shall be kept on the breast. It is not permitted to roll onto the back at any time. Both arms shall be brought forward together over the water and brought backward simultaneously throughout the race. All up and down movements of the legs must be simultaneous. The position of the legs or the feet need not be on the same level, but they shall not alternate in relation to each other. A breaststroke kicking movement is not permitted. At each turn and at the finish of the race, the touch shall be made with both hands simultaneously, at, above or below the water surface. At the start and at turns, a swimmer is permitted one or more leg kicks and one arm pull under the water, which must bring him to the surface.' As the swimmer's legs and feet are put together, they make a fishtail-like movement.
MEDLEY SWIMMING, is a combination of the four strokes. As defined by the FINA rules, 'In individual medley events, the swimmer covers the four swimming styles in the following order: butterfly, backstroke, breaststroke and freestyle. In medley relay events, swimmers will cover the four swimming styles in the following order: backstroke, breaststroke, butterfly and freestyle. Each section must be finished in accordance with the rule applicable to the style concerned.'
Beside the above strokes, there is also the sidestroke, supplanted in the competitive swimming by the crawl. The swimmer's body stays on its side and the arms propel alternately. The leg motion is called the scissors kick, in which the legs open slowly, under leg backward, upper leg forward. A kind of sidestroke with movement of one arm only was used in army's swimming competitions, in which the swim-

mers swam with one hand above the water holding a hand grenade. This type of swimming was part of military training in the Pol. Army in the years 1946-55. A modified sidestroke is currently used in water polo and lifesaving.
World records, according to FINA rules, are recognized in 50m and 25m courses. For world records in 50m courses, the following distances and styles for both sexes are recognized: freestyle – 50, 100, 200, 400, 800 and 1,500m; backstroke – 50, 100 and 200m; breaststroke – 50, 100 and 200m; butterfly – 50, 100 and 200m; individual medley – 200 and 400m; freestyle relays – 4x100 and 4x200m; medley relay – 4x100m.
For world records in 25m courses, the following distances and styles for both sexes are recognized: freestyle – 50, 100, 200, 400, 800 and 1,500m; backstroke – 50, 100 and 200m; breaststroke – 50, 100 and 200m; butterfly – 50, 100 and 200m; butterfly – 50, 100 and 200m; individual medley – 100, 200 and 400m; freestyle relays – 4x100 and 4x200m; medley relay – 4x100m. Members of relay teams must be of the same nationality.
Different swimming events have been included in or excluded from the program of Ol.G.. Today, for Olympic records, the following distances and styles are recognized: women's freestyle – 50, 100, 200, 400, 800 and 4x100m; women's backstroke – 100 and 200m; women's breaststroke – 100 and 200m; women's butterfly – 100 and 200m; women's individual medley – 200, 400 and 4x100m; men's freestyle – 50, 100, 200, 400, 1,500, 4x100 and 4x200m; men's backstroke – 100 and 200m; men's breaststroke – 100 and 200m; men's butterfly – 100 and 200m; men's individual medley – 200, 400 and 4x100m.
In open-water swimming the most distinct competition is >LONG DISTANCE SWIMMING. Other swimming events governed by the FINA include >DIVING, >WATER POLO, >SYNCHRONIZED SWIMMING; see also >SWIMMING FOR THE DISABLED.
Swimming pools. Swimming pools can be divided into competitive courses, i.e. for sports swimming events; recreational pools for training purposes, incl. paddling pools; rehabilitation pools; and, most often, multi-purpose pools. The 1980s and 1990s saw the construction of huge swimming pool complexes called aquaparks, which are becoming more and more popular.
In competitive swimming, 50- and 25m courses are used. They must comply with FINA regulations. The depth of swimming pools used in sport depends on the kind of swimming event. Pools of different depth and other technical parameters are used for swimming races, synchronized swimming, water polo or diving. FINA also regulates the construction of swimming pool facilities such as cloakrooms, showers, etc.
History. Swimming skills have been known to people since the earliest times, the beginnings of competitive swimming, however, remain unknown. The earliest surviving written evidence referring to swimming is an Eg. epitaph dated back to the Middle Kingdom (22nd-17th cent. BC), which reads: 'Prince Sintu was encouraged to take swimming lessons with the royal children.' Some forms of competitive swimming were already practiced by Eg. sailors in the years 2470-2320 BC. From the period of the New Kingdom (17th-11th cent. BC) come numerous reliefs depicting swimming girls. In some surviving papyruses, whose age is impossible to determine, a fragmentary poem was deciphered, which refers to the act of swimming: 'I will jump into water to swim with you, and with my love to you I shall catch the red

Swimming on an old Japanese drawing.

WORLD RECORDS BY CLASS (CLASS, TIME, RACER, VEHICLE, YEAR):
modified 4WD, 52.51sec., Eddie Chesser, 'Outlaw', 1996
pro-modified, 48.75sec., Brian Langford, 'Rubber Duck', 2000
V8 stock, 58.32sec., Eddie Barnhill, 'Reel Thing', 2000
6 cylinder, 53.75sec., Kenny Langford, 'Seminole Win', 1997
4 cylinder, 1min. 08sec., Ray Thornton, 'Cold Duck', 1998
air cooled, 2min. 14.34sec., John Parks, 'Sidewinner', 1999
jeep, 2min. 28.65sec., Thomas Blanton, 'Catfish II', 1999

Thomas Eakins, Bather's refuge, 1884-85, oil on canvas.

S

fish.' One of the hieroglyphs is, in fact, an ideogram representing a swimmer using a crawl-like stroke. This may be evidence of the popularity swimming enjoyed in ancient Egypt. The art of swimming was a frequent theme in classic literature, for example in *The Odyssey*. Having lost his companions, Ulysses (Odysseus), floating on a raft is caught by a storm. He falls into the water and has to swim to shore:

Neptune sent a terrible great wave that seemed to rear itself above his head till it broke right over the raft, which then went to pieces ... Ulysses got astride of one plank and rode upon it as if he were on horseback; he then took off the clothes [...] and

POPULAR SWIMMING STYLES

Breaststroke

Butterfly

Freestyle

Backstroke

plunged into the sea meaning to swim on shore. King Neptune watched him as he did so, and wagged his head, muttering to himself and saying, 'There now, swim up and down as you best can till you fall in with well-to-do people'. [...] Thereon he floated about for two nights and two days in the water, with a heavy swell on the sea and death staring him in the face; but when the third day broke, the wind fell and there was a dead calm without so much as a breath of air stirring. As he rose on the swell he looked eagerly ahead, and could see land quite near. Then, as children rejoice when their dear father begins to get better after having for a long time borne sore affliction sent him by some angry spirit, but the gods deliver him from evil, so was Ulysses thankful when he again saw land and trees, and swam on with all his strength that he might once more set foot upon dry ground.
[*The Odyssey*, Book V, trans. S. Butler]

In ancient times swimming was not, however, part of any of the four great games, i.e. Olympic, Nemean, Pythian or Isthmian. It was a leisure activity during holidays as well as part of military training. Within each Gr. gymnasion there was a swimming pool called the kolymbethra. In the 3rd cent. BC, the Greeks, and later the Romans, built swimming pools as integral parts of larger public >BATHS. The open pool in the Olympian palaestra was 4.19m long, 3.02 wide and 1.38m deep. It was used for swimming training and ablutions. A larger swimming pool existed near the river Kladeos; it was 24m long, 16m wide and 1.6m deep. The swimming pool in the Gk. colony of Poseidonia (Lat. *Paestum*; present-day Italy) had a 2.6m-tall diving tower with a protruding diving platform. An impression of that tower is depicted on an ancient fresco in the museum in Pesto. Some ancient Gk. swimmers were reported to dive and sink enemy ships, e.g. before the battle off Cape Artemision against the Persians. A Gk. boxer, Tisandros of Naxos used to swim in the sea off the coast of Sicily. Swimmers from the towns of Sphacteria and Syracuse were known to break the siege of their towns by swimming under the enemy ships and bringing relief. According to Herodotus, during the battle of Salamis the Persians drowned in larger number than the Greeks as the latter could swim. The Spartans practiced swimming in the Eurotas river. Old Gk. paintings portray the Spartans using a crawl-like stroke. Also, one painting in Louvre depicts a Gk. female swimmer using the crawl stroke. Many ancient texts refer to swimmers as those who 'paddle with their hands'.

Swimming skills were also documented in ancient Germanic texts. In the old-Eng. Beowulf, the main character dives deep in the sea to kill a monster (>SCUBA DIVING) and '...swims over ocean [...] lonely and sorrowful'. The following dialog referring to swimming can be found in an Icel. saga describing a quarrel between Sigurd and King Eystein (c.1046-66):

Sigurd
Can you not remember
The conclusion of our swimming races?
Whenever I wanted to I always
Defeated you in the water.
Eystein
I swam at distances
Shorter than yours
But I dived better.

Swimming became part of a nobleman's upbringing in the Middle Ages. A Pol. knight, Ścibór Ostoja was supposed to have swum across the Danube in full armor. The first treatises on swimming appeared in the Renaissance, e.g. *The Swimmer. A Dialogue Easy and Pleasant to Read* (*Colymbetes, sive de arte natandi dialogus et festivus et iucundus lectu*, 1538) by the German N. Wynmann or *The Art of Swimming* (1588) by an Eng. humanist, E. Digby. The first swimming schools were founded in 1777 in Germany, 1781 in Austria, and 1787 in France. The originator of an innovative swimming methodology was the Italian O. de Bernardi, the author of the manual *The Swimming Man or the Rational Art of Swimming* (*L'uomo gallegiante o sia l'arte ragionata del puoto scoperta fisica*, 1794). In 1798, on the basis of Bernardi's theories and methods, J.C.F. Guths-Muths (1759-1839) wrote *A Concise Swimming Handbook with Exercises* (*Ein kleines Lehrbuch der Schwimmkunst zum Selbstunterricht*). Guths-Muths' methods, then, were refined and expanded by German, E. von Pfül, promoter of swimming practice in the army and originator of military swimming schools. Von Pfül's first school was founded in Prague (1810), and the second in Berlin (1817).

He also invented a special swimming belt with a rope mounted on a long pole. Using the pole the trainer could easily guide a beginner while walking on the side of the pool. An originator of natural swimming techniques without the use of any mechanical devices was Austrian, K. Weissner, author of *The Natural Method of Swimming*. Together with the development of training methods evolved the sport of swimming. In 1515, a swimming race was held alongside a gondola race in Venice. Modern forms of competitive swimming were developed in England at the turn of the 18th and 19th cent. In 1837, London had six public swimming pools, in one of which the first swimming contest was held under the auspices of the National Swimming Association of Great Britain. In 1844, on the Association's initiative a group of Native Americans was brought to London to participate in the swimming contest for the Silver Medal of the Association. The Native Americans demonstrated a new, crawl-like stroke, hitherto unknown in Europe. The winner was Flying Gull who swam a 130ft-long pool in the 1930s. The Native Amer. stroke was, however, regarded as too primitive in the face of the dominant breaststroke practiced widely all over the Brit. Isles and the Eur. continent. In 1837, the Association of Swimming Friends was formed in Berlin. The first indoor swimming pools were built in Vienna and Liverpool in 1842. In 1862, a few clubs took part in a swimming event in London under the auspices of the Associated Swimming Club, which ultimately became the Amateur Swimming Association of Great Britain in 1869, comprising about 300 clubs. The first Brit. Championships were held in 1877. In 1878, an Englishman, F. Cavill began to popularize swimming in Australia. Swimming became part of the Ol.G. in 1896, although events changed many times. At the Ol.G. in 1896, a swimming freestyle event was held in the sea, attended by 28 participants. At the 1900 Ol.G., 100 swimmers took place in the swimming competition, consisting of freestyle and backstroke races. Other swimming events included underwater swimming and a 200m obstacle race (floating barrels, rings and rafts). The breaststroke was included in the 1908 Ol.G. In the same year, the International Amateur Swimming Federation (Fédération Internationale de Natation Amateur, FINA) was founded. The first Olympic women's swimming events took place in Stockholm in 1912.

Alongside the development of swimming organizations swimming techniques evolved. In 1873, Eng. J. Trudgen demonstrated a stroke which included some elements of the later crawl: alternate arm movement above the water and a fluttering up-and-down leg action performed once for each arm stroke. The new style was called the *trudgen* stroke. Trudgen's successors tried to combine alternate arm movements with the frog kick of the breaststroke. Their stroke was used by the Hung. A. Hajós, the first Olympic champion in 1896. In 1902, Australian R. Cavill (Frederick's son, see above) demonstrated the crawl stroke for the first time. The crawl was later refined by a Hawaian-American, D.P. Kahanamoku (1890-1968). Another great contributor to swimming as an international sport was J. Weissmuller (1904-84), a 6-time world record holder and 4-time Olympic champion in 1924 and 1928. His Hollywood career, most notably his role as Tarzan, elevated swimming to a high popular level, previously unknown. The first E.Ch. were held in 1926. An important event in the history of swimming was the first participation of the Jap. national team. At the 1932 Ol.G., the Japanese won 5 out of 6 gold medals in the men's events. The Japanese represented a new training school based on wider arm and leg movement and extensive practice. In 1934, the Amer. swimmers refined the breaststroke by bringing both arms forward above the water. The new butterfly stroke was recognized as a distinct competitive stroke, as FINA declared it did not conform to the rules of breaststroke as then defined. Around 1937, the Amer. J. Sieg used the dolphin kick in the butterfly. In the early 1950s the Austrl. trainers, F. Galagher, F. Carlisle and the Dutch I. Stender began swimming training experiments with a few-year-old children, which then resulted in a series of world records set by 14-16-year-old swimmers. The new training methods have been successful although they bring about a negative consequence: despite inclusion of a var. of physical exercises and supplementary sports to the training program, the focused and intensive physical efforts have negative impact on the physical development of children. The enormous mental pressure on children practicing sports professionally exert a destructive impact on the developing child's personality (a similar tendency can be observed in >GYMNASTICS). Training children as professional athletes in their early years is an example of the dehumanization of modern sports. On the other hand, intensive training has been recognized as an effective method of rehabilitation, owing to an experiment carried out on two Austrl. siblings, John and Ilsa Konrads (b.1942 and 1944). John suffered from polio and underwent rehabilitation by training together with his healthy sister. After years of intensive and systematic training not only did he manage to get over the disease but in the years 1958-60, together with his sister, set 37 world records and won 4 Olympic medals. Another outstanding Austrl. swimmer of the time was M. Rose (b. 1939), who became famous for her races with the Jap. T. Yamanaka (b. 1939). Since the 1960 Ol.G., the Australians began losing their world leading positions in favor of the Americans. In the USA swimming became part of PE classes in primary schools in the 1960s. This had a tremendous impact on the level of Amer. swimming in general. At the 1964 Ol.G. D. Scholander from the USA won 4 gold medals. His record was broken by M. Spitz, who won seven Olympic medals for the USA in 1972. W.Ch. in swimming have been held since 1973. In the 1970s, East Ger. swimmers joined the world's best. Swimming successes in East Germany were regarded as part of the ideological prestige of the communist regime. After the unification of Germany in 1990, many former East Ger. swimmers and coaches admitted having taken steroids and using various forms of doping, incl. such outrageous methods as blood doping inserting special inflated bubbles in the anus in order to increase body buoyancy. During their short Olympic presence, the East Germans won 92 medals, incl. 38 golds (6 in men's events and 32 in women's events). After the fall of East Germany and the USSR, the 1990s' top swimming teams included Russia, the USA, Australia, Canada, Spain, Hungary in men's events; and China, Hungary and Japan in women's events. Some countries joined the world leaders thanks to individual swimmers, e.g. P. Heyns from South Africa and M. Smith from Ireland (both 2-time Olympic champions at the 1996 Ol.G. in Atlanta).

Breaking swimming world records has been most spectacular in the freestyle, nevertheless record setters in the other swimming strokes have been famous as well.

The first to break the 1-min. barrier in the 100-m freestyle was J. Weismuller, USA (59.0 in 1924), and the 50-sec. barrier, J. Montgomery (49.99 in 1976). The first world record below 2min. in the 200-m freestyle was set by D. Schollander (1:58.6 – 1963), and below 1min. 50sec. by S. Kopyliakow from the USSR (1:49.83 – 1979). In the 400-m freestyle, the 5-min. barrier was broken by J. Weismuller (4.52 – 1927), and the 4-min. barrier by R.Demont, USA (3:58.18 – 1973). In the 1,500-m freestyle, A. Borg, Sweden was the first to cover the race distance below 20min. (19:07.2 – 1927). Subsequent record breakers included T. Amano, Japan below 19min. (18:58.8 – 1938), M. Rose, Australia below 18min. (17:59.5 – 1956), R. Saari, USA below 17min. (16:58.7 – 1964), J. Kinsella, USA below 16min. (15:57), and W. Salnikov, USSR below 15min. (14:58.27 – 1980).

The first female swimmer to break the 1-min. barrier in the 100-m freestyle was D. Fraser, Australia (59.9 – 1962), and the 55-sec. barrier was first crossed by B. Krazuse, GDR (1:59.78 – 1976). In the 400-m freestyle, G. Ederle, USA was the first below 6min. (5:53.2 – 1922) and L. Crapp, Australia below 5min. (4:52.4 – 1956). The first woman to cover the 800-m freestyle distance below 10min. was J. Cederquist, Sweden (9:55.6 – 1960), below 9min. – A. Simmons, USA (8:59.4 – 1971).

The first man to swim below 3min. in the 200-m breaststroke was R. Skelton, USA (2:56 – 1924), below 2min. 30sec. – C. Jastremski, USA (2:29.6 – 1961).

In the women's 100-m breaststroke, the 1-min. barrier has yet to be broken. I. Schmidt, Germany was the first to swim below 3 min. in the 200-m breaststroke (2:59.9 – 1942) and L. Kaczuszite, USSR below 2min. 30sec. (2:28.36 – 1979).

The first swimmer below 1min. in the 100-m butterfly was L. Larson, USA (59.9 – 1958); and the first one below 2min. in the 200-m butterfly was R. Pyttel, GDR (1:59.63 – 1976).

In the women's 100-m butterfly the first swimmer to break the 1-min. barrier was C. Kacke, GDR (59:78 – 1977); below 3min. in the 200-m butterfly – G. Peter, USA (2:58.3 – 1953); and below 2min. 30sec. – S. Pit, USA (2:29.1 – 1963).

In the 100-m backstroke, the first swimmer below 1min. was T. Mann, USA (59:6 – 1964); in the 200-m backstroke, below 2min. – J. Naber, USA (1:59.19 – 1976).

In the 200-m individual medley, the first to swim below 2min. was T. Darnyi, Hungary (1:59.36 – 1991); in the 400-m medley, below 5min – T. Stickles, USA (4:55.6 – 1961); below 4min. 30sec. – A. Hargitay, Hungary (4:28.89 – 1974).

In the women's 200-m medley, no record has gone below 2min. since 1959. The first 200-m swimmer below 2min. 30sec. was D. de Varona, USA (2:29.9 – 1964). In the 400-m medley, the first below 6min. was S. Mann, USA (5:52.5 – 1956); below 5min. – G. Wegner, GDR (4:57.51 – 1973).

In the relays, famous record breakers included: USA below 4min., in the men's 4x100-m medley (3:59.2 – 1936); USA below 8min. in the men's 2x200-m freestyle (7:52.1 – 1964); USA below 4min. in the women's 4x100-m freestyle (3:58.1 – 1972); Hungary below 5min. in the women's 4x100-m medley (4:57.8 – 1955); USA below 8min. in the women's 4x200-m freestyle (7:59.87 – 1996).

E. Bartkowiak, *Pływanie*, 1974; M. Goldstein, D. Tanner, *Swimming Past 50*, 1999; D. Hannula, N. Thornton, *The Swim Coaching Bible*, 2001; A. Sinclair, *Swimming*, 1894; K.H. Stichert, *Sport Schwimmen*, 1975; M. Thevenot, *The Art of Swimming*, 1699; D.G. Thomas, *Swimming*, 1996; G. Werner, ed., *FINA. Constitution and Rules*, 1997-98; Consultant – E. Rostkowska, AWF Poznań.

SWIMMING FOR THE DISABLED, a var. of >SWIMMING adapted for the disabled, based on rehabilitation swimming methods and techniques. At international events and the Paralympic Games the swimmers are grouped according to their disabilities. The disabled swimmers compete using trad. swimming strokes at regular (50, 100, 200, 400m) or special (150-m medley) distances. Swimming events, numbering 100, are the largest group of the Paralympic events. See also >SPORTS FOR THE DISABLED.

The Internet: http://www.paralympic.org/sports/sections/swimming/general.html

SWIMMING RELAY, a type of swimming race in which teams usu. consisting of 4 swimmers (3 or 5 in the past) race in turn; their aggregate time determines the winner. Swimming relay races originated in English-speaking countries. Initially, they were swum over yard distances. For the first time they were featured in the Ol.G. in 1900 in Paris – the 5x40-m race was won by a Ger. team. At the 1904 Olympics in St. Louis a swimming relay race over the distance of 4x50yds. was won by the US team. The history of swimming relay races was started at the 1908 Olympics, when men raced freestyle over a distance of 4x200m. Women joined the event for the first time at the 1912 Olympics in Stockholm (4x100m freestyle). Presently, at international meets held under the auspices of the Fédération Internationale de Natation Amateur, the following relay races are held (both for women and men): 4x100m and 4x200m freestyle and 4x100m medley race. The Olympic program features 4x100m freestyle, 4x100m medley and 4x200m freestyle (the latter race in women's events was introduced as late as 1996).

THE 4X100-M MEDLEY FOR WOMEN was introduced into the Olympic program in 1960. The first winners were the Americans; they have also won all the other Ol.G.. The first result below 5min. was recorded by the Hungarians (4min. 57.8sec. – 1955); below 4min. 30sec. – the Americans (1968 – 4min. 28.3sec.); below 4min. 10sec. – swimmers from the GDR (1976 – 4min. 7.95sec.); below 4min. 5sec. – also swimmers from the GDR (1984 – 4min. 3.69sec.).

THE 4X100-M FREESTYLE FOR WOMEN. Internationally first held at the E.Ch. in 1927, it has been in the Olympic program since 1928. W.Ch. have been held since 1973. It was won most often by the US, Du. and Austrl. teams, and also, between 1970

and 1988, by swimmers from the GDR. The first to swim the distance below 5min. were the Americans (1924 – 4min. 58.6sec.); below 4min. – also the Americans (1972 – 3min. 58.1sec.).

THE 4X200-M FREESTYLE FOR WOMEN was first featured in the W.Ch. in the 1990s, in the Ol.G. at the 1996 Olympics in Atlanta. The first winners were the Americans who beat the Germans and the Australians (7min. 59.87sec.).

The start of the men's 50-m freestyle 'B' final during the U.S. Open Swimming Championships at the University of Minnesota Aquatic Center in Minneapolis, Minnesota.

THE 4X100-M MEDLEY FOR MEN was made an Olympic event in 1960, first featured in the E.Ch. in 1958, and in the W.Ch. in 1973. The Olympic gold was won 9 times by the Americans, once by the Austrl. team (1980); the first result below 4 min. was recorded by the Americans (1964 – 3min. 58.4sec.); below 3min. 40sec. – also by the Americans (1984 – 3min. 39.30sec.).

THE MEN'S 4X100-M FREESTYLE was made an Olympic event in 1964, first featured in the E.Ch. in 1962, and in the W.Ch. in 1973. All the Olympic gold medals have been won by the Americans. The first result below 4min. was made by the Americans (1938 – 3min. 59.2sec.); below 3 min. 30sec. – a team representing the University of California (1970 – 3min. 28.8sec.); below 3min. 20sec. – the US team (1978 – 3min. 19.74sec.).

THE MEN'S 4X200-M FREESTYLE was introduced into the Olympic program in 1908, to the E.Ch. in 1926, to the W.Ch. in 1975. The Olympic gold has been won 13 times by the US team, twice by the Japanese (1932 and 1936), twice by the Australians (1912, with some swimmers from N.Zealand and in 1956 only Austrl. swimmers), twice by the Russians (representing the USSR in 1980 and the CIS in 1992); Great Britain won once (1908). The first result below 10min. was recorded by the Americans

Robert Tait McKenzie's sculpture Swimmer on a stamp issued for the Olympics in Montreal.

A swimming relay.

S

WORLD SPORTS ENCYCLOPEDIA

(1924 – 9min. 59.4sec.); below 8min. – also by the Americans (1964 – 7min. 51.1sec.); below 7min. 30sec. – also by the Americans (1976 – 7min. 23.22sec.).

Apart from metric distances, equally popular were swimming relay races over yard distances, particularly in Eng.-speaking countries: the 4x110-yd. relay and 4x220-yd. relay). In the United States 3-man relay races were very popular, e.g. 3x110yds., held at the US championships since 1924 (men), initially in indoor and then outdoor pools. Women swam 3x110-yd. races in indoor pools since 1927 and in outdoor pools since 1934 (USA). The 3-man relay races at US championships were discontinued in 1954.

SWINGS AND SEESAWS, popular pastimes known in a few principal varieties and a number of sub-varieties both in technical, recreational, and socio-cultural sense.

Suspended swings have a seat – made of a board or a piece of leather, sailcloth, rubber, plastic, etc. – suspended on 2 ropes, chains, or metal rods. The swing is either pushed by persons standing beside it or 'propelled' by the user by swaying or rocking, or by pumping the legs and pulling the ropes. There are many types of such swings: simple ones that are hung on tree branches; colorful swings resembling boats, animals, or spacecrafts that can be found in amusement parks; and children's home swings fixed to a doorframe.

A seesaw resembles a lever in which a horizontal plank or beam, usu. with a seat at each end, is supported in the center by a hinge or – in simpler models – by a cylindrical block on a fulcrum. See also >TEE-TER-TOTTERING, >SKAKANIE NA DESKACH.

History. Swings and seesaws appear in the oldest folk tales and legends of various peoples. In the *Vedas* they played a part of a ship headed for heaven. Ethnologists J. Auboyer suggests the swing was for Hindus a harbinger of the annual rebirth of the Mother Nature. They believed the higher the swing rocks the better the harvest will be. Auboyer also asserts the swing could symbolize rain and sometimes it was associated with a rainbow, as a link between the earth and the sky. A number of researchers of Far Eastern culture believe the swing was a symbol of fertility and a sexual intercourse. A Pol. researcher of Asian games, I. Kabzińska-Stawarz, explains the symbolism of the swing in the following manner: 'Movement itself, being a natural feature of a competition, has fundamental influence on the revival and stimulation of nature. It is also a visible and symbolic opposite of stillness, deadly tranquility.' In Kor. traditions, the swing had more practical functions: it was used to cool oneself and to get rid of mosquitoes. A form of acrobatics on a type of a seesaw called >NÔL TTWIGI (Kor. for 'standing seesaw') was developed in Korea. In China, swings are quite popular during various folk festivals and they sometimes form a part of the cultural heritage of minorities, e.g >TU SWING.

The earliest references to the swing in Eur. cultures can be found in Homer's *Iliad*. Greeks called a suspended swing *eukustinda*, whereas ancient Romans – *oscillum*. The same Lat. name was used in the Middle Ages. In J.A. Comenius's *Orbis Sensualium Pictus* (1658), the swing is mentioned as a kind of a game: *oscillum est genus ludi*. It also appears in G. Chaucer's works. In Ang.-Sax. culture, the swing and seesaw acquired numerous forms, which was reflected in the rich vocabulary applied to them: *teeter-totter, teter-cum-tawter, titti cum totter, meritot, merry-totter, titty cum tawtay, coup-the-ladle, weight, Jack-a-daw, sack-a-day, coggle-te-carry*, and *hightte*. In Ireland, it was known as shuggy-shoo, copple-thurrish, or horse and pig, depending on the type. In some var. of seesaw except for two participants sitting at both ends there is one more person standing in the middle of a plank and balancing from one side to the other in order to keep it rocking. Swings and seesaws are currently known in all the Eur. cultures as a form of a recreational pastime, which is validated by their country-specific names: Fr. *balançoire*, Ital. *altalena*, Port. *balanço or gongorra*, Span. *columpio*, Ger. *Schaukel*, Aus. *Hutsche*, Du. *schomme or wip*, Dan. *gynge or vippe*, Pol. *huśtawka*, Swed. *gunga*, Norw. *dumphuske or vippebret*, Wel. *siglenydd*, and Hung. *hinta*.

In the past, the swing was not only a children's pastime, but also a courtly one. It was popular during

Jean-Honoré Fragonard, The Swing, *1766, oil on canvas.*

town festivals and school games and has become an indispensable element on children's playgrounds. Swing plays were often accompanied by simple songs and rhymes, such as *Titty cum Tawtay, The Duck in the Water, See-saw Margery Draw*, etc. In arts, the swing appears in the paintings of, for example, Frenchmen J.A. Watteau (1684-1721) and J.H. Fragonard (1732-1806), as well as in literary works, such as J. Gay's poem:

On two near elms the slacken'd cord I hung,
Now high, now low, my Blouzalinda swung.

The swing is employed as a symbol by Amer. playwright W. Gibson, in his *Two for the Seesaw* (1958). One of the countries where different types of swings and seesaws flourished is Poland, where they have been known since time immemorial. An extensive comment on the subject can be found in Ł. Gołębiowski's *Gry i zabawy różnych stanów* (*Games and Pastimes of Various Social Classes*, 1839) in which the author derives the swing's history from antiquity:

The swing was known by the Greeks. During the Bacchus festival people swung on ropes tied to tree branches. Wherever they spot a plank supported by another object in the middle, the children sit on its ends and ride up and down pressing harder and pushing on the ground alternatingly. However this type of movement, once started, acquires velocity and becomes dangerous as the plank may slide down from its support at any time and both players can suffer from such an accident. Therefore, the play was improved by making the swings and seesaws more comfortable and safer, with 4 seats equipped with rails spun by those running around the cross fixed to a cylinder, or swung if the seats are fixed to a rope, gathering speed. Nevertheless, let the speed be moderate, especially if the spun one is a young lady who sat there being ignorant and apprehensive at the same time. She may become dizzy and even faint, so listen to her voice and slow down, because if she falls down the result can be tragic. Even more anxiety is caused by a high swing in which a person flies up along the end of a circle's radius. When in the uppermost position, she suddenly turns and then, laughing, falls down into a precipice. Wind plays with her hair but you are concerned about her life! Free and self-confident she soothes your fears with her charming smile.

Ł. Gołębiowski's *Gry i zabawy różnych stanów*, 1839, 21-22; A.B. Gomme, 'See-Saw', TGESI, II, 185-186; I. Kabzińska-Stawarz, 'Competition in Liminal Situations', EP, 1994, XXXVIII, 1-2.

ŚWINKA, see >CZOROMAJ.

SWISS-STYLE WRESTLING, a wrestling style popular in circus wrestling in the 19th and beginning of the 20th cent. It derived from different var. of folk wrestling in which wrestlers held their opponents by the clothes, mainly by the belt and trousers, such as Swiss >HOSENLUPF, >SCHWINGEN, >KRAGENRINGEN, >LEIBRINGEN, >RUTZEN or Fr. *la lutte de caleçon*. In Swiss-style wrestling the contestants stood and used only their hands and legs. It was forbidden to fight on the floor. The contestants wore characteristic stocking-like ankle-high trousers, which were usu. black, and wide belts. Most important was the belt grip. The winner was the wrestler who brought his opponent to the ground or made him touch the ground with any part of his body, except the feet. Cf. >CORNWALL AND DEVON, >GLÍMA.

SYNCHRONIZED SWIMMING, also called *water ballet*, swimming competition practiced by women, and, informally, by men. The swimmers execute movements, called figures, described in the rules of the International Amateur Swimming Federation (FINA), in solos, duets, and teams of 4-10 persons. The figures are synchronized with musical accompaniment. The executive body of synchronized swimming is the Technical Synchronized Swimming Committee of the FINA. The competitions consist of 2 parts: compulsory (senior technical routine and junior figures) and free routine. At the FINA World Cups each of the swimmers exercises all 3 programs.

Figures. Each competitor performs 4 figures from the FINA official list. The figures for different age groups are selected by the TSSC every 4 years. All judgements are made from the standpoint of perfection. The movements should be precise and controlled, with each section of the figure clearly defined and in uniform motion. A 2-pt. penalty is deducted if a swimmer performs the announced figure incorrectly or stops voluntarily, even if the swimmer does the figure correctly again. The number of judges is 5-7; the competitor can score from 0 to 10pts. The highest and the lowest awards are cancelled and the result is multiplied by the degree of difficulty of a given program. Correct execution of the figures is the basis of the free routines.

Technical routine consists of solo, duet and team events. Technical routine is a combination of ten selected required elements, performed in a designated order. There are no restrictions as to choice

of music or choreography. The time limits for technical routines range from 2min. for solos to 2min. 50sec. for teams, with an allowance of 15sec. plus or minus the allotted time. The routine in the water can begin with a 10-sec. introduction, called deckwork, performed on the deck of the pool.
Free routine is executed in solo, duet and team events. It consists of any listed figures, strokes and parts thereof to music. The time limits for free routines range from 3min. 30sec. for solos to 5min. for teams, with an allowance of 15sec. plus or minus the allotted time. The routines may start on the deck and continue there for no longer than 10sec., but they must finish in the water. The competition is evaluated by 2 panels of 5-7 judges. In the routines the competitor can obtain from 0-10pts. with a 0.1 accuracy. One panel awards scores for technical merit (degree of difficulty, execution, synchronization with the other and with the music), the other awards scores for artistic impression (creativity, choreography, music interpretation, manner of presentation).
The officials. Synchronized swimming competitions are officiated by a team of 5-7 judges, placed on opposite sides of the pool. The judging team is headed by the referee. Other judges include 2 timers, an announcer, a clerk of course, 2 recorders and the sound center manager. The judges can deduct a 2-pt. penalty if 1) a swimmer has made a deliberate use of the bottom of the pool; 2) a swimmer has made deliberate use of the bottom of the pool to assist another swimmer; 3) a routine is interrupted by a competitor during the deck movements. A 1-pt. penalty can be deducted if 1) the time limit of 10sec. for deck movements is exceeded; 2) there is a deviation from the specified routine time limit allowance (less or more) for a routine. A half point penalty can be deducted from the score for each part of a required element or action omitted, or for each team member less than specified. Similar to the figures scoring, the highest and the lowest awards are cancelled. The technical merit score is the average result multiplied by 6; the artistic impression score is the average result multiplied by 4. The final result is determined by adding the results of the different performed sessions. In free routines the choice of music, content or choreography is not restricted.
Pool and equipment. The swimming pool must be at least 12x12m and 2.5m deep. In addition to speakers mounted outside the pool for spectators, a pool must be equipped with underwater speakers so that swimmers can hear the music the entire time they are performing. The competitors are required to wear swimsuits in dark colors and caps.
History. The first synchronized swimming shows, called ornamental swimming, took place in England in 1892. In the 1920s, synchronized swimming became popular in Germany and the USA, where it was refined by K. Curtis. Due to moral restrictions in the Ang.-Sax. countries, the sport was initially practiced mainly by men. At the 1934 World Exposition in Chicago, a group of girls demonstrated swimming synchronized with a musical accompaniment. During the radio coverage of the show the Amer. broadcasters used the name *synchronized swimming* for the first time. In 1955, the sport became part of the Panamerican Games. FINA recognized synchronized swimming as a single event in 1956; it was a display event at the Ol.G. in 1976. Synchronized swimming was admitted as Olympic competition at the 1984 Ol.G. in Los Angeles (won by Americans, T. Ruiz in solo and T. Ruiz and Costie in duet). The solo and duet events were dropped at the 1996 Ol.G. in Atlanta in favor of a single team event.
The most outstanding competitors in the history of synchronized swimming have been T. Ruiz, world champion 1982 and Olympic gold medallist 1984 (solo and in duet with C. Costie); C. Waldo, Olympic silver medallist 1984, world champion 1986 and 2-time Olympic gold medallist 1988 (solo and in duet with M. Cameron). The most dramatic career was that of Can. S. Frechette. She won the gold medal at the Commonwealth Games in 1986 and became the world champion in 1991. At the 1992 Olympics in Barcelona Frechette was deprived of the medal as a result of a judge's error, although, in the opinion of the public she had won without the slightest doubt. After appeal, the IOC awarded her the gold medal 16 months later. In 1991, at the World Aquatic Games in Australia, Frechette set the absolute world record by scoring 10pts. in each of the seven figures sessions. As part of the Can. national team she won the silver medal at the 1996 Ol.G. in Atlanta. The first world champions in duet were Anderson and Johnson from the USA. Other top duet competitors came from Great Britain, USA, Canada, France and the USSR (later the CIS). The first duet Olympic champions were Amer. C. Costie and T. Ruiz. The last duet winners, before the event was dropped from the Ol.G., were Karen and Sarah Josephson from the USA (1992).
In the team event, the first world champions were the Americans. Like in duets, the best synchronized swimming teams come from the UK, USA, Canada, France, the USSR (later the CIS). The first Olympic champion team was the US before Canada and Japan.

J. Ciereszko, *Pływanie synchroniczne*, 1990; B.O. Gundling and J.E. White, *Creative Synchronized Swimming*, 1988; 'Synchronized Swimming', *FINA Handbook*, 1996-1998; Consultants: M. Habiera and P. Kluj.

SYNORIS, horse races in which 2 horses pull a 2-wheeled cart [*synoris, synoros* – twin]. At the Ol.G. carts were pulled by 2 adult horses, the sport being called *hippon synoris* [Gr. *hippos* – horse + *synoris*, see above]. Later, the program of the Ol.G. also included cart races pulled by 2 colts, known as >POLON SYNORIS, and 2 mules, called >APENE or *synoris hemionon*. In ancient Rome a cart pulled by 2 animals including draft animals called *biiuga* and later *biga*, although the plural form *bigae* was more frequent. The 2-horse cart was supposed to have been invented by the Gk. goddess Thebe. The first drivers to use a 2-horse team in competition were Adrastos, the mythical king of Argos and the initiator of the Pythian games, and Enyalios, the mythical son of Poseidon, the god of the sea. According to Pausanias' *Travels in Hellas*, 2-horse team races were introduced for the first time to the Ol.G. in 408 BC (V, 8, 10). This was probably a result of the impoverishment of the Greeks after the Peloponnesian Wars, and also the progress of democracy, which led to greater access of free Greeks to the games, who had been blocked until then by the 4-horse team races (>TETRIPPON). The first winner of synoris at the Olympic Games was Euagoras of Elida. The latest piece of information about this competition comes from 60 BC, which Mededemos of Elida is said to have won. Synoris was introduced to the Pythian games in 398 BC.

SZEWC, see >CIP.

SZLICHTADA, a var. of >KULIG. Originally kulig had Lith. and old Pol. features whereas szlichtada developed under Ger. influence, as shown by the etymology of the word, which derives from *Schlittage* or *Schlittade*, which means sledding or a sledding cavalcade. Cf. Ger. *Schlitten* – sled and *Schlittsport* – sled sports. The object of szlichtada was to pay 'sled' visits to neighbors of an estate, who were almost exclusively representatives of the gentry. The host, having treated their guests to some drinks and food, joined the cavalcade and together the group paid another visit to the next neighbor. The host of the last estate visited organized a feast for the guests, with singing and dancing. The joining of the cavalcade by new neighbors and the overall feast at the last mansion are two features that differentiate szlichtada from kulig where a party of friends simply visited neighbors who did not join the cavalcade. In time, however, the two became so mixed that by the 18th cent. both names were used interchangeably.

SZTEKIEL, a trad. Eur. game known in Poland and Germany, and corresponding to the Eng. >TIP-CAT, Pak. >GULLI DUNDA, Bret. *mouilh*, Fr. *pilouette*. Practiced most often by poor youths in western Poland and eastern Germany. Almost identical to >KLIPA, in the past it was played like *klipa* but after the partitions of Poland in the territory annexed by Russia it developed differently to the game subjected to Ger. influence. The object of the game was to knock off a short stick into a box using a longer stick. As the game had a folk character it is difficult to define any precise dimensions of the equipment. Most often, however, the shorter stick (sztekiel) was 10-15cm long, 2cm in diameter. It was sharpened at both ends, like a pencil. The longer stick was usu. 60-70cm long and 2-3cm in diameter. In the ground a hole was dug out, shaped like a trough, perpendicular to the direction of the game, about 7cm wide and 20cm long and 2-5cm deep. The sztekiel was put on the ground so that one of its pointed ends was suspended over the trough (about 3-4cm) and the other, longer part, was resting on the flat surface around the trough. The player who won the toss struck the sharpened end of the sztekiel with a stick so that it flipped up and then to hit it again, on the volley, towards the finish. The finish was marked with a circle about 1.5m in diameter drawn on the ground, into which the player hitting the sztekiel with his both feet. He was not allowed to touch the ground outside the circle as a round could be forfeited in this way (not always and not on every ground where the game was played). Usually 2 misses were allowed before the sztekiel was driven into the field. The third miss eliminated the player from a given round (but not from the game, in which usu. 3 substitutions were made) and a new player started to play. Each player had to hit the sztekiel past the line drawn at different distances from the finish. Depending on the age, strength and skill of the players, the line was about 5-10m from the finish. The games consisted of a different number of rounds, in the course of which each player hit 3-5 sztekiel. When he hit the sztekiel farther than his opponent, he scored a point. The winner was the player who scored most points in the game with an agreed number of rounds or who first scored the agreed number of points, e.g. 10, 20 etc. There were dozens of sztekiel varieties, with different scoring systems. Sztekiel, as a sport of the poor, who had no access to sports equipment, started to disappear when after 1918 and later after 1945 sport was popularized in Poland. It disappeared completely in towns at the end of the 1940s and in the countryside by the end of the 1950s.

SZUHALEJA, a type of rowing boat in old Lithuania, used for transport, but also in local contests between rowers. Ł. Gołębiowski described szuhaleja in 1831 as 'a type of wider boat, holding up to 30 persons, used in Lithuania, and more precisely in the Pińczów county' (*Gry i zabawy różnych stanów*, 330). Local legend connects the unique name of the boat with an unusual event: 'The gutter press of 1818 in an amusing way explains the origin of the name and relates it to Shah Ali, who traveled from the Black Sea to the Pińczów lagoon by ship. Its anchors were uncovered during the reign of King Stanislav August. In a very funny way they describe how an assessor, used to having a bell when traveling on land so as to make walkers give way to him, takes the bell to the szuhaleje when he travels by sea so that it is heard from afar and all other boats give way to him. Smoking a pipe, he rings the bell himself or makes [others] do so' (ibid., 303).

SZWEDKI, a type of two-person sledge with one seat for a passenger and the runners extending a long way back so that the person pushing the sledge could stand on them having got the sledge moving. The sledge was known in the vicinity of Krynica (Poland) as Scand. sledge before 1939; after 1945 it disappeared. It was reintroduced in some holiday resorts in the Bieszczady Mountains (S-E Poland) in winter 1997.

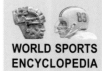

SYNCHRONIZED SWIMMING OLYMPIC CHAMPIONS

DUET
1984 Candy Costie
& Tracie Ruiz, USA 195.584
1988 Michelle Cameron
& Carolyn Waldo, CAN 197.317
1992 Sarah Josephson
& Karen Josephson, USA 192.715
1996 Not held
2000 Olga Brusnikina
& Mariya Kisyelyeva, RUS 99.580
TEAM
1996 United States 99.720
2000 Russia 99.146
SOLO
1984 Tracie Ruiz, USA 198.467
1988 Carolyn Waldo, CAN 200.150
1992 Kristen Babb-Sprague, USA 191.848
Sylvie Fréchette, CAN 191.717

Spending the Eid Holiday relaxing, Bibi Haji, 9, left, and her friend Sabna, 10, soar on a homemade swing in Kabul, Afghanistan.

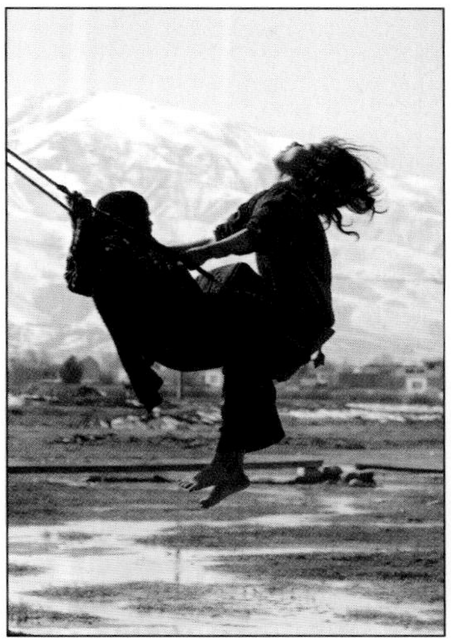

The Japan Team on their way to silver in the Synchronized Swimming Team Free Routine Final at the World Swimming Championships in Fukuoka, Japan.

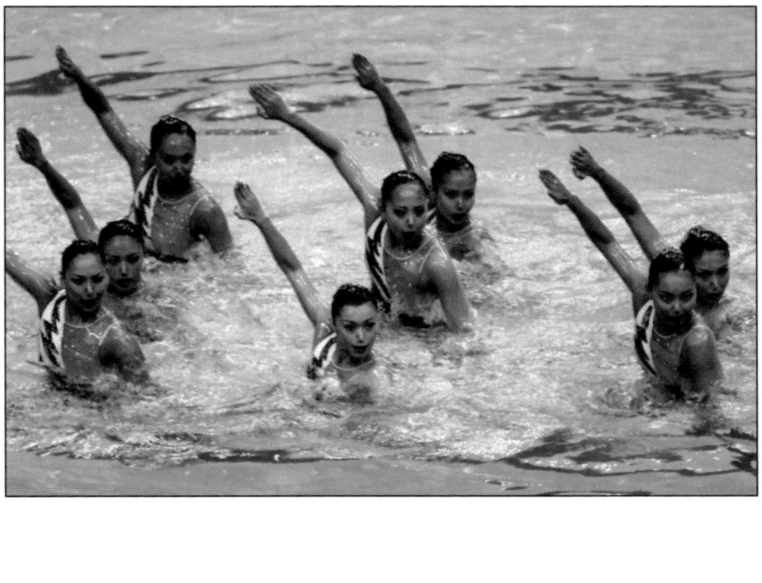

**WORLD SPORTS
ENCYCLOPEDIA**

TA RÖCK, a Swed. var. of trad. wrestling practiced in the area of Närke [Swed. dial. *ta* – take, catch + *röck* – collar, lapel]. The essential element of this wrestling style is that the opponents may grab each other's jacket collars or lapels. It is a regular var. of a wrestling style known as >KRAGTAG, similar to other styles, like >ARMKAST, >ARMTAG, >KRAVE-TAG, >SLÄNGTAJ.

TABLE SKITTLES, see >SKITTLES

TABLE TENNIS, also the popular trade name *Ping-Pong*, a ball game played on a flat table 274cm long and 152.5cm wide, divided into 2 equal courts by a fixed net with its upper edge 15cm above the playing surface. The hollow celluloid ball used for the game is 37.2-38.2mm in diameter. The paddles or rackets are flat and rigid, covered with rubber, not thicker than 4mm. The object of the game is to hit the ball over the net so it bounces on the opponent's half in such a way that the opponent cannot return it correctly. A point is scored when the server fails to make a good service or when either player fails to make a good return. The ball can bounce only once on each half of the table. A match consists of the best of 3 or 5 games, each game being won by the player who first reaches 21pts., though he must win by at least 2pts., i.e. 21:19, 22:20, 23:21, etc.

which gave the game a specific rhythm and charm. Taking advantage of the popularity of Gibb's invention, Parker Brothers, a US company from Salem, began to manufacture table tennis equipment and advertise it in the USA and Europe, in Great Britain in particular. In 1902, another Englishman, E.C. Gould introduced paddles covered with pimpled rubber. Initially, table tennis was an exclusive game played in Eng. clubs. In 1898, the first public games took place in the Queen's Hall in London. In 1902, the Eng. Table-Tennis Association was founded. Later, the sport gained popularity in Germany, first as a social attraction available in clubs and dining halls. The first Table-Tennis E.Ch. were held in 1907. The game underwent rapid development after WWI. In 1925, the Deutscher Tisch-Tennis Verband was founded in Germany, which included 38 clubs. Its president, G. Lehmann contributed to the foundation of the International Table Tennis Federation (ITTF) in 1926. The first ITTF President was Englishman, I. Montagu, awarded later with the Lenin Prize for proliferation of international friendship. One year after the ITTF foundation the first table tennis W.Ch. were held in London. In the W.Ch. individual prizes are awarded in particular events: St. Bride Vase in men's singles; G. Geist Prize in women's singles; W.J. Pope Trophy in women's doubles; Zdenek Hey-

players from Asia emerged. The new wave made their outstanding appearance at the W.Ch. in 1980 when the PRC team swept all the titles, wining altogether 15 out of 26 medals. Asian table-tennis domination was briefly arrested by the Swedes, J.O. Waldner (world champion 1989, 1992) and J. Persson (1991). In the 1980s and 1990s, Asian-Eur. competition continued with alternate success. In the women's events, however, all W.Ch. victories since 1955 were scored by Jap., Chin. and N.Kor. players. The most outstanding male table-tennis players of the 1980s include Swede J.O. Waldner, who apart from his numerous W.Ch. titles, reached the Olympic championship in 1992; Chinese J. Jialang, (world champion 1985, 1987); and L. Guoliang, a 2-time Olympic champion (singles and doubles with K. Linghui, 1996). The best female players include Chinese D. Yaping, the singles world champion in 1991 and 1992, doubles world champion in 1989 and 1992, 2-time Olympic champion in singles in 1992 and 1996, and in doubles in 1992 and 1996 (together with H. Qiao). Today, table tennis uses the Grand Prix ranking similar to that of >LAWN TENNIS. The sports clubs are associated in national leagues and the World League. The sport is extensively sponsored and regarded as ideal for televised broadcast. The number of international table tennis tournaments increases year by year. Cf. >WHEELCHAIR TABLE TENNIS.

L. Hodges, *Table Tennis. Steps to Success*, 1930; D. Seemiller & M. Holowchak, *Winning Table Tennis. Skills, Drills and Strategies*, 1997.

TABLE TOP GAMES, a group of games characterized by tossing or moving coins or metal (usu. brass or copper) tokens on a table surface with the use of hands, fingers, specially prepared wooden cleats or combs.

TADZHIK WRESTLING is similar to many other C Asian wrestling var. (e.g. >BÖKHIIN BARILDAAN or >KALMUCK WRESTLING). A match would always start with one wrestler challenging the other to come out and fight. To do so, he would sing the following song as recorded by W. Godlewski, a Pol. wrestling historian:

I am an outstanding billy-goat,
I have two horns and two nostrils.
Who ate my son?
Who ate my daughter?
Who has a bow and arrows?
Who wants to fight with me?

Then, after an opponent came forward, the fight began.

TAE-KWON-DO, also *taekwondo, tae kwon-do*, a Kor. martial art of striking the opponent with the hands and feet [Kor. *tae* – to kick or jump and strike + *kwon* – a fist or to strike with a fist + *do* – art or method of ethical conduct]. Being also a philosophy of life, it allows for externalizing aggression through codified sport activity. The ultimate goal is to counter the opponent's attack with a well-timed and perfected action of quick, linear movements (similar to >KARATE) or wide, circular hand strikes (like in >WUSHU or TAIJIQUAN), as well as various techniques of striking with the feet. The use of the feet makes tae-kwon-do a defense sport very appropriate for children, whose hip-bones and legs are much more flexible than those in adults, for whom other Asian martial arts – focusing more on upper body movements – are better suited. The most important elements in mastering tae-kwon-do are: rhythm, timing, sense of balance, breath control and continuity of movements. The basic mental training involves practicing readiness to receive an attack from any direction with the use of hands, legs, and the abilities of the entire body. Actions taken in practice and in combat fall into 4 categories: kicks, strikes, body positioning, and blocks. Kicks are powerful thrusts of the legs aimed at hitting the opponent or keeping him at a distance, while strikes – though similar in goal – are more frequent. The sport is practiced by more than 20 million people in more than 140 countries under the auspices of several competing federations.

Practice and combat rules. Tae-kwon-do is divided into practice forms (*poomse*) and combat forms (*kyurugi*). *Poomse* is a presentation of individual techniques in a mock combat similar to *kata* in karate. There are 9 basic *poomse*, which lead to obtaining different degrees of mastership called *dan*.

A match between Any Feng and Jun Gao at the US Table Tennis Championships at the Convention Center in Las Vegas, Nevada.

Etymology. The alternative name Ping-Pong seems to corroborate one of the game's many origin theories, that it hails from the Far East; it is most likely an onomatopoeia derived from the echoic sound made by the ball bouncing from paddle to table. The name was prob. coined by the Hemley brothers. 'Ping' was to signify the sound of the ball struck with a paddle; 'Pong' was the sound of the ball bouncing off the table. The official and more staid name table tennis, is associated with the full-sized court game of >TENNIS, played in miniature, with increased dynamics, on a table top. In earlier times, the name *indoor tennis* was used as well.

History. There are several hypotheses explaining the origin of table tennis, none of which has been satisfactorily confirmed. The game was to have originated 1) in China or India and later brought to Europe by Brit. merchants or soldiers in the second half of the 18th or in the 19th cent.; 2) in 19th-cent. England; 3) in New England by the end of the 19th cent.; 4) in S.Afr. by Brit. soldiers stationing in barracks during the Boer Wars. The first indoor tennis sets, incl. a rubber ball, were sold in London in the 1880s. They enjoyed, however, moderate popularity. Only when the celluloid ball had been invented by the Englishman, J. Gibb in the 1890s did the game generate more interest. The decisive factor was prob. the characteristic sound made by the ball

dusek Prize in mixed competition; Lady Swaythling Cup in men's team competition; and Marcel Corbillon Cup in women's team competition. Before 1939, the most outstanding table tennis player was the Hungarian and later naturalized Brit. citizen, V. Gyözö Barna (1912-72), a multiple singles, doubles, mixed and team world champion. After a few years, the game became dominated by players from Czechoslovakia, England and Austria. During the W.Ch. in Bombay, 1953, Jap. players appeared whose supremacy over the others proved absolute due to the introduction of a new, dynamic style of play. The Japanese were unseated 5yrs. later by players from the People's Republic of China. All titles in the years 1961-65 were won by the Chinese, C. Tse Tung. Only in the women's events could the Jap. players compete successfully with their Chin. counterparts. During the Cultural Revolution the Chin. players withdrew from international competitions and were replaced in the game's elite first by the Japanese, and then by the Europeans who had taken almost 2 decades to recover from the shock. In 1971, the world champion title was won by the Swede, S. Bengtsson and in 1975 by the Hungarian, I. Joyner. Eur. table-tennis had finally begun to approach the Asian level. During the W.Ch. in 1973, the Europeans won the men's team event for the first time after 20 years. In the early 1980s another class of top

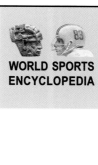

Jang Soon-ho of South Korea kicks Qu Enqiang of China during the men's 80-kg class Tae-kwon-do first round match at the 3rd East Asian Games in Osaka, western Japan.

There are also 8 *poomse* for pupil's degrees, which are called *kup*. Direct combat, *kyurugi*, involves 2 opponents and lasts 3 rounds of 3min. each at the W.Ch. semi-finals or finals level or 3 rounds of 2min. each at lower level competitions, incl. qualifying events for W.Ch. Men and women fight separately in the following weight categories: below 48, 52, 56, 60, 64, 68, 73, 78, 84 and above 84kg (men) and below 40, 44, 48, 52, 57, 62, 67 and above 67kg (women).

Attire. The main element is a white uniform called the *dobuk*. The front part of the body is protected with special guards called *hogoo*.

Philosophy. The history of tae-kwon-do is strongly related to Eastern philosophies. The last segment of the name, *do*, indicates – following other Asian sports – that it is not only a martial art or a system of self-defense, but also a concept of conduct and a way of life. The oldest forms, *soobak* and *tae kyon*, formed a Kor. educational system called *hwarang-do*, which incl. religious elements of old Kor. shamanism, and was later influenced by Confucianism and buddhist philosophy. Ultimately, tae-kwon-do incorporated certain elements of Chin. Taoism and Zen-Buddhism. Its modern formula is mostly associated with urban areas, esp. academic centers, representing different religions and systems of beliefs, which focus more on etiquette and spiritual rules resulting from carnal experience, than the realization of Far Eastern religious principles. The nature of meditation preceding practice and combat is not defined by the requirements which are a limitation for other beliefs. Therefore, communities in different countries practicing tae-kwon-do according to the same general principles have a different approach to their cultural and spritual justification. For example, in Korea the sport is included in the system of general and military education, where it follows a principle of unquestioning obedience towards superiors, while in the West it is taught mostly in independent clubs and private schools (*do jang*), where strict obedience is not required, particularly not of those who consider the sport more as a form of self-defense against crime and violence, than as a means of spiritual development. Nevertheless, even there, the practice is accompanied by the learning of the history and culture of the Far East, esp. Korea. Each practice session, as well as each competition opens with the following oath:
1. I shall observe the tenets of Tae-Kwon-Do.
2. I shall respect the instructor and seniors.
3. I shall never misuse Tae-Kwon-Do.
4. I shall be a champion of freedom and justice.
5. I shall build a more peaceful world.
The basic tenets of tae-kwon-do are: courtesy, integrity, honesty, perseverance, self-control, indomitable spirit, love, community service. There are 10 separate rules for children, which take into account their age and mentality:
1. Must show respect to their parents and family members at all times.
2. Shall greet their parents when they enter the house and say goodbye to them when they leave.
3. Will be truthful at all times.
4. Will maintain a good relationship with their brothers and sisters.
5. Must help with household chores.
6. Will keep their own rooms neat and clean.
7. Must keep their body, hair, and teeth clean at all times, every day.
8. Will not interrupt adult conversations.
9. Will study their schoolwork at school and at home.
10. Must show respect for teachers and peers at all times.

History. There are 3 theories regarding the origins of tae-kwon-do. According to the most complete and most justified one, its beginnings derive from the period of formation of the original Kor. martial art called >SOOBAK (or *subak*), which took place in the Middle Ages, in the period of the so-called Three Kingdoms (Silla, Paekche and Koguryo), i.e. 57 BC--935. The second theory claims that the basic elements of the sport formed under the influence of Chin. martial arts, esp. the principles formulated in the monastery of Shaolin in c.520 by the legendary monk and philosopher Bodhidharma (Bhodidharma). The third theory is supported by researchers, who consider tae-kwon-do as a form of Jap. karate, part. the Okanawa var. called >OKINAWA-TE. They claim that in the course of its development the combat turned into an original sport, independent of karate, which is witnessed by many similarities between the 2 events. It seems, however, that all 3 theories can be reconciled. The oldest forms of tae-kwon-do derive from the trad. Kor. martial art *soobak*, which was part of *hwarang-do*, sometimes referred to as >TAE-KYON (Kor. for 'foot-hand'), which in turn forms the basis of the modern name. Strong cultural, religious, and philosophical ties enriched the oldest forms of Kor. soobak/tae-kyon with elements worked out in the Shaolin monastery, which reached Korea in a way similar to the influences of Buddhism or Confusianism. Finally, the equally important relations with the culture of Japan, even though very often imposed by Jap. milit. and economic superiority, are responsible for tae-kwon-do's similarity with karate. During their direct occupation of Korea (1905-45), the Japanese banned the orig. trad. forms of *soobak/ tae kyon*, which produced a countereffect: the declining art became a symbol of resistance against Jap. occupation and started to be even more intensely practiced in societies called *kwan*. During the Kor. war (1949-53) S.Kor. soldiers implemented their tae-kyon skills in their combat activities and introduced them to their Amer. allies, who began to transplant the principles of tae-kyon onto Amer. soil in the same way as the interest in >JUDO or karate was recognized and brought to America by the soldiers occupying Japan after 1945. The growing interest in tae-kyon encouraged the Kor. specialists in the sport to organize a conference in 1955, during which they formulated the principles of the sport and – for the first time ever – called it *tae kwon do*. The conference designated Gen. Choi Hong-Hi to introduce the new sport into the social structure, beginning with the Kor. army. During his studies in Japan, Gen. Choi Hong-Hi (1918-2002) practiced Shotokan karate with its creator Gihin Funakoshi and received the 2nd dan. Having returned to Korea he graduated from the Military Academy and began to train soldiers within a system that combined the hand techniques of Shotokan karate and the leg techniques of tae kyon. The training uplifted the soldiers' morale and was adopted as a standard practice routine within the army and soon began to enjoy an international career. Gen. Choi Honh-Hi has put together a team, with which he travelled around the world promoting the new sport. In 1966 he formed the International Taekwondo Federation (ITF) based in Toronto, which is still active, although its headquarters have moved to Vienna. ITF Taekwondo fights take place according to a formula of light contact, with the contestants wearing boxing gloves and foot protectors. Simple striking techniques targeting the head are allowed, along with almost all leg techniques above the waist. Gen. Choi Hong-Hi also became an outstanding theoretician of the sport and the author of a unique, 15-vol. encyclopedia of taekwondo. His promotional efforts contributed to the founding, in 1973, of the World Tae-Kwon-Do Federation (WTF). In 1980 the WTF was recognized by the IOC. Since the beginning of the 1960s tae-kwon-do has been practiced in some Far Eastern countries, e.g. in Singapore (since 1963, although Singapore's national federation was not formed until 1974). In the middle of the decade the sport spread to Europe, first to Switzerland, Austria and West Germany. W.Ch. have been held since 1975. A turning point in the international career of the sport was the third W.Ch. in Chicago, where the number of national teams reached 47. The introduction of the event into the program of the OI.G. in Sydney in 2000, preceded by its earlier demonstration in Seoul in 1988, contributed to a fast growth of interest in tae-kwon-do around the world. In 1997 the number of athletes practicing the sport in approx. 140 countries was estimated at over 20 million. A factor which hinders the development of the event is the multitude of federations claiming their 'national' and 'international' status, esp. in the USA. Another barrier is an increasingly muddled reception of tae-kwon-do as compared with other Asian martial arts, some of which – like >HAPKIDO – try to elevate their level of attractiveness by adopting certain elements of tae-kwon-do, which often obscures the differences between these 2 basically different sports. Korea hosts an annual event called Kor. Masters Taekwondo Demo and the leading masters of the sport are: Chang Myung Sam, a Kor. world champion in 1982, Olympic champion in 1988 and Asian champion in 1984 and 1988.

Hong-Hi Choi, *Taekwondo.The Korean Art Of Self-Defense* (3rd ed., 15 vols., 1993); L. Frederic, *A Dictionary of the Martial Arts* (1991); J. Hee Park and J. Liebowitz, *Taekwondo For Children. The Ultimate Reference Guide For Children Interested In the World's Most Popular Martial Art* (1993); by the same, *Fighting Back, Taekwondo For Women* (1993); Yeon Hwan Park, T. Seabourne, *Taekwondo Techniques and Tactics*, 1997.

TABLE TENNIS OLYMPIC CHAMPIONS
MEN'S SINGLES
1988 Yoo Nam-Kyu, KOR
1992 Jan-Ove Waldner, SWE
1996 Liu Guoliang, CHN
2000 Kong Linghui, CHN
WOMEN'S SINGLES
1988 Chen Jing, CHN
1992 Deng Yaping, CHN
1996 Deng Yaping, CHN
2000 Wang Nan, CHN
MEN'S DOUBLES
1988 Chen Longcan/Wei Qingguang, CHN
1992 Lu Lin/Wang Tao, CHN
1996 Kong Linghui/Liu Guoliang, CHN
2000 Wang Liqin/Yan Sen, CHN
WOMEN'S DOUBLES
1988 Hyun Jung-Hwa/Yang Young-Ja, KOR
1992 Deng Yaping/Qiao Hong, CHN
1996 Deng Yaping/Qiao Hong, CHN
2000 Li Ju/Wang Nan, CHN

Rep. Nick Smith, left, and Rep. Jessie Jackson Jr. warm-up before taking part in the congressional Tae-Kwon-Do Black Belt examination presented by Grand Master Jhoon Rhee on Capitol Hill in Washington.

TAE-KYON, Kor. for 'to push away the attacker', an old Kor. martial art, a predecessor of >TANG SOO DO and >TAE-KWON-DO. Its origins can be found in the royal tombs of Mu Yong Chong and Gag Jeo Chong at Tongku in Manchuria (the Chin. province of Jilin), once the site of the ancient Kor. state of Koguryo. A ceiling fresco in one of the tombs depicts standing men, who may be practicing tae kyon or >SOOBAK. Nowadays tae kyon is practiced in villages on various holidays. The contenders, wearing white baggy pants and shirts, stand facing one another and move rhythmically, balancing their body, raising and lowering their arms, placing their feet to the right and left, forward and backward. At different moments during the fluent motions various techniques are executed. The bouts are graceful and elegant, characterized by circular, harmonious motions that follow the natural body rhythm. There are many ducking motions and leg techniques and the attack with the hands is often camouflaged by a leg trick. Light and medium contact is allowed, including leg hooking techniques and throws. The targeted areas include the solar plexus, forehead, shins, inside thighs, lower ribs, and shoulders. The advanced level allows for targeting the eyes and nose. Similar to >TAIJIQUAN, the competitors focus on the center of gravity (*dan tien*), in which they try to accumulate the vital energy (*Ki*). The energy is emitted with a light outcry. Three types of training include: individual training (*honja ikhigi*), technical training with a partner (*maju megigi*), and sparring (*gyeon jugi*). The bout is often accompanied by the sound of trad. Kor. drums or a bamboo flute. Tae-kyon is practiced by both men and women, irrespective of age.

TAFELBEUGELEN, also *jensen*, a Du. game – a table var. of >BEUGELEN. The playing area is reduced to the size of the table, usu. a billiards table with a small ring, through which typical billiards balls are rolled. Instead of the racket characteristic of beugelen, a billiard cue is used to strike the balls. Other rules are identical. The game was invented in Limburg, the center of beugelen activity, on the Du./Belgian border. After WWII it gradually began to disappear. It is still practiced in Brabant in a rudimentary form known as *jensen*.

TAFELKEGELEN, a Flem. var. of bowling; cf. >PIERBOL.

TAFELKEGELSPEL, Flem. for 'table skittles', a table var. of >SKITTLES practiced in W Limburg and N Brabant. Cf. >BIRINIC, >DEVIL AMONG THE TAILORS, >TABLE SKITTLES. A box, 80x50cm, placed on a table, holds figures to be knocked over by a ball tied to a short line.

Tafelkegelspel.

TAGBOLD, Dan. for 'roof ball', [Danish *tag* – roof + *bold* – ball], a game for 2-5 persons, usu. children or teenagers. The game requires a house with a steep roof and a wooden stick 1½-2ft. long, with a flat end for striking the ball and a round handle. Players take turns at throwing the ball or striking it against the roof and try to catch it when it comes down. The player who does not take part in the competition (*opgiveren*) throws the ball into the air, which is called *lovde* (to lob), and one of the participants strikes it up onto the roof. Under the roof are 2 players, one of whom catches the falling ball, the other striking it back up onto the roof. In 1989 the students of Gerlev Sports School formed new rules of the game, according to which players take turns at striking the ball onto the roof using only the striking techniques of modern volleyball.
J. Möller, 'Tagbold', GID, 1997, 1, 66.

The sword technique of taijiquan Yang style.

TAGE EN TING OP MED MUNDEN, Dan. for 'to pick up sth. with one's mouth', [Dan. *tage* – to take + *en* – one + *ting* – a thing + *op* – up + *med* – with + *munden* <*mund* – mouth], a trad. game in which a player sits on a chair. A small object is placed on the ground behind the back of the chair. The player is to pick the object up with his mouth by stretching around the back of the chair, while trying to keep balance with his legs. The task may be performed at a high or low level of difficulty. In the former version, the player may not touch the ground, while in the latter, he may use one hand to support himself. Having reached the object, the player should keep his balance and return to the starting position.
J. Möller, 'Tage en ting op med munden', GID, 1997.

TAGE FIRSTAGE, a Dan. game, [Dan. *tage* – take + *fir* – four]. Four bases are placed in a square and function as protective zones. One player stands inside the square and tries to catch anybody moving from one base to another. Upon succeeding, he should strike the captured player 3 times and say a counting rhyme (*a be'er mi Faalaaw*).
J. Möller, 'Tage firstage', GID, 1997, 2, 63.

TAGE FLASKE OP FRA GULVET, lifting bottles from the ground, a Dan. game of skill [Dan. *tage* – to take + *flaske* – a bottle + *op* – up + *fra* – from + *gulvet* <*gulv* – floor]. The player stands with his legs straight and his forehead against the wall. In this position he must lift a bottle from the floor.
J. Möller, 'Tage flaske op fra gulvet', GID, 1997, 3, 40.

TAGE NÆSE OG ØRE, Dan. for 'to grab a nose and ear', [Dan. *tage* - to take + *næse* – nose + *og* – and + *øre* – ear]. A simple game of coordination of movements. A player grabs his nose with his left hand and his left ear with his right hand. Now he quickly changes the arrangement and grabs the nose with his right hand and the right ear with his left hand. The quicker the changes, the better.
J. Möller, 'Tage næse of øre', GID, 1997, 3, 79.

TAGU, the name of 2 trad. Chin. games, also known in Korea, where one of them was modified and in a new form returned to China. The first game was similar to modern >GOLF, while the other derived from a folk var. of >POLO played without horses. A common feature of both of them was the use of sticks to strike the ball. That, along with a rather obscure hist. documentation, makes the distinction between them unclear and is subject to much speculation. Tagu seems to derive from a Chin. game known in China as >CHÚI WAN and in Korea as >BONGHI. Both names were used at the same time. During the reign of the Kor. Konyo dynasty the game gained significantly in popularity. According to one source, it was played in 1320 by Emperor Tchungsug. Later, during the reign of the first 3 rulers from the Choson dynasty (estab. 1392), the game was in decline and the lower classes began to imitate another game similar to modern polo, known in China and Korea as >GYÔGGU. The imitation was not very precise, mostly because of the lack of horses and the high cost of equipment (esp. saddles). For that reason plebeian *gyôggu* resembled the old, abandoned *tagu*. According to the *Encyclopedia of Korean History* by Hong Ryul Ryu (1989), during the rule of Sechong the Great (1418-50) the name *tagu* came to mean a form of foot polo derived from *tagu*. Moreover, *tagu* also functioned under the Kor. name *chang-tchigi*. It was a team sport, in which a ball was played with a curved stick on a grass field, which made the game more similar to >FIELD HOCKEY than to polo. Each team had 10 field players and a goalkeeper, the sticks were made from mulberry wood, and points were scored by driving the ball into the opponent's goal. The ball was a wooden sphere covered with leather. A rectangular pitch had the size of 100x50 footsteps. In the center of the end line was the goal in the form of 2 bamboo poles separated by 5 footsteps, without a crossbar. The game was controlled by a referee – in China this was usu. a court officer. The ball could be touched only with a stick. Hooking the opponent's stick, hitting the opponent with a stick or striking the ball out of the playing area were banned.
Koo-Chul Jung, *Erziehung und Sport in Korea im Kreuzpunkt fremder Kulturen und Mächte*, 1996, 65.

TAGUMINE PAAR, Est. for 'last pair', a trad. form of a running competition. Players, teamed in pairs, queue up in a column. A single player stands at the front and gives a signal to start the game. The last pair starts running, separately, along each side of the column of players, trying to make their way to the front of the column and join hands. The player at the front tries to prevent them from doing so by catching one of the running players before they join hands. If he succeeds, he and the caught player form a new pair, while the remaining player stays at the top of the column. If unsuccessful, he has to wait for a chance to separate the next pair.
M. Värv and others, 'Traditional Sports and Games in Estonia', TSNJ, 1996, 33-34.

TAHITIAN BALL, one of numerous var. of >POLYNESIAN BALL, practiced in some of the Society Is., particularly in Tahiti. The game is played more frequently by women than men.

TAHITIAN BANDY, a game popular on the Polynesian isle of Tahiti and resembling the Eur. >BANDY since it employs similar sticks and ball. Obviously, given the geographical location of the island it has never been played on ice there. The ball is made of tightly pressed pieces of fabric and the sticks are 0.9-1.2m-long. It is not played according to any specific rules. The size of the field has not been defined, either.

TAHITIAN RACES, held by the indigenous Polynesian inhabitants of Tahiti. The natives' interest in the human body and beauty of movement is well documented in the paintings of P. Gaugin (1848-1903) who lived in Tahiti from 1891 until his death in 1903.

TAI CHI, see >TAIJIQUAN.

TAIDO, a Jap. martial art formed and adjusted to the needs of industrial societies, based on 'three-dimensional movements' universally implementing the abilities of the human body in all its aspects. Taido combines the elements of physical control and hand-to-hand combat with breathing techniques, the awareness of one's body and harmony with man's environment. It also involves subjecting oneself to the principles of yin and yang, which in Chin. philosophy denominate the phases of stability and changeability of the world.
History. Taido was created by S. Shukumine, who designed it – in his own words – as 'the martial art of the 21st century'. At the end of WWII Japan was desperately seeking ways and means to carry on its struggle against the pressing Amer. army. Shukumine, then a *saiko shihan* i.e. the Supreme Instructor of sport and military training at the Gensei school, was given the secret task of designing a system of combat that could be implemented by special forces in their attacks on Amer. ships. The system was to account for unique conditions of ship boarding, such as a small area of action, condensation of objects and persons, rapid translocation of people in combat, the possibility of observing and carrying out the combat from ever-changing angles. Shukumine's solution was a method of combat based on rapid, spatial movements in 3 dimensions. He failed to complete the method by the end of the war and continued his efforts after 1945. In 1946 in the village of Meiji, at the Oita prefecture, he concluded his work on the techniques of moving (*ungi*), changing (*hengi*), and tumbling (*tengi*). In 1948 he moved to an uninhabited island near Okinawa, where he perfected the techniques, and in 1949 he arranged for its first public demonstration in Ito City in the Shizuoka prefecture. For the next 10 years he worked on the final elements of his system – spiraling (*sengi*) and twisting (*nengi*), as well as on theoretical and spiritual aspects of the new martial art, which he called taido – the way of body and the mind. The method, originally aimed at preparing a person to fight in the cramped environment of sea combat, proved very successful in the densely populated urban areas of modern Jap. civilization. The 3-dimensional style of fighting was to protect a person from any undesired interference, as well as offer him a contemplational approach leading him to the self-evident truth. He was to achieve it through combining the principles of body control (*doko*) with body awareness (*hokei*), principles of combat (*seigyo*), principles of breathing (*taiki*), and the harmonization of yin and yang (*keiraku*). All these elements were fully discovered and correlated in 1965, 20 years after Shukumine started his work. Taikido is currently practiced in 12 countries outside of Japan, incl. in Europe, the United States and Australia.

TAIIKU-DO, the method of acquiring psychophysical fitness through physical training in the militarized Jap. system of education known as >TAIREN-KA. Cf. >ISHITEKI-TAIIKU, >SPORTS-DO.

TAIJIQUAN, (Eng. *Tai Chi Chuan*), abbrev. to *taiji* (Eng. *Tai Chi*), the ultimate martial art [*taiji* – great extremity, the ultimate + *quan* – a fist, martial art]. Based on the philosophical principles of Taoism, esp. its meditational and medical tradition, it is the internal (*neija*) style of >GONGFU, and – together with *baguazhang* and >XINGYIQUAN – forms the 3 best known systems of martial arts. Taijiquan involves fighting at short range and countering physical strength with perfect technique. A student of taijiquan is first taught self-awareness and how to develop stability and balance. All movements begin at the *dantian*, an anatomical center of gravity located slightly below the navel. They must be performed without any muscle tension, but with max. physical efficiency, the sense of balance, deep serenity, main-

Taijiquan Yang style.

taining buoyant readiness to explode at any time. The sense of energy passing from the legs to the feet and from the arms to the hands triggers the tension of flexible backbone arches and the hip belt, so that – even though physical strength is not used – the body is ready for a tremendous effort. The feet should imitate a cat's walk, while the mind must remain cautious, so that the body – ostensibly relaxed – is ready to violently emit a tremendous force (*fa jing*). The movement is like that of the water in a river – it has no beginning and no end. All body parts are like beads on a string, which move one after another. When the entire body structure is formed, the student of taijiquan develops the awareness of the partner's *dantian*. He learns to feel the opponent's balance in order to be able to 'thrust the weight of thousands of pounds with the force of 4 ounces'. The fundamental principle is 'not to counter force with force'. Each contact with the opponent should be 'soft like cotton', only to become 'firm as steel' or explode with untamed energy targeted at the unconcealed vital parts of the opponent's body. The first contact with the opponent (*nien*) brings neutralization (*hua*) and violating his stability, followed by the execution of one of 4 groups of techniques: kicks (*ti*), strikes (*da*), throws (*shuei*), and lever or pressing (*qinna*). The early stage of defence is like 'unwinding a thread of a silk cocoon'; the mind is like a 'charging eagle', while the spirit – like 'a cat on the look-out for a mouse'. Although it is generally believed (esp. in the Western Hemisphere) that taijiquan is a soft and subtle art of self-defence, its techniques may easily lead to a heavy knock-out and even death of the opponent. Experienced masters, however, have a considerable range of control, which allows them to hold ultimate force safely in check. The weapons used in taijiquan include a sword, a saber, and a stick. The ability to control the opponent in taijiquan is developed by practicing *tui shou* (Chin. for 'pushing hands'), which means throwing the opponent off his balance without the use of strikes, kicks or holds. During taijiquan competitions *tui shou* events are held in different weight categories.

History. According to a legend, the principles of taijiquan were formulated by a Taoist monk Zhang San Feng during the rule of the Yuan dynasty (1271--1368). Taijiquan is divided into 5 basic styles: *chen*, *yang*, *wu*, *wu*, *sun*. Chen Wangtin, the commander of the military garrison at the end of the rule of the Ming dynasty (1368-1644), created a system practiced until this day in the Chen family. This style involves jumps, sudden outbursts of energy (*fa jing*), and dynamic techniques. It includes forms (sequences of harmonious movements connected together) that are executed slowly and very rapidly.

The principles of taijiquan were observed in Chenjiagou and formally defined for the first time by Yang Luchan (1799-1872). Having learnt taijiquan, he challenged the masters of other schools in Beijing, defeating them without causing any injury. This won him the title of 'Undefeated Yang' and made him the emperor's master of the art of self-defense. Instead of various old techniques, Luchan practiced his own version of them and preferred only one long form consisting of 108 movements. At first, he called his art *hua quan* – the art of neutralization, and soon adopted the philosophical term *taiji*, later also taken over by the Chen family. Yang's style had a reputation of 'the most effective martial art'. It is characterized by gentle, natural, and relatively slow movements of a broad amplitude, which can be learnt even by older – also weak and ill – people. Yang's grandson, Yang Chen Fu, has made this style very popular. In the 1950s, a simplified version of the long 108-step form of Yang's style was put together by compiling 24 easily assimilable movements. Called 'the Beijing form', it forms the most popular modern taijiquan sequence in the world. Wa Quanyu (1834--1902) and his son Wu Jianquan (1870-1942) used Yang's style to come up with their own style called *wu*. Wu Yuxiang (1812-1880) combined the styles of Chen and Yang to form another *wu* style, which focused on coordination and the so-called opening and closing movements executed with a straight upper body position and light footwork. The last of the 5 styles of taijiquan, *sun*, takes its name after Sun Lutang (1861-1932) and is characterized by buoyant and flexible movements executed in long, drawn-out sequences and with dynamic footwork. At the end of China's imperial era the popularity of taijiquan was so great that its demonstrations accompanied the performances of Chin. opera. Its development was hindered during the Cultural Revolution in China in the 1960s. Taijiquan was charged with being a relic of the past, incompatible with the revolutionary mission of the people. Yet, after the Cultural Revolution the Chin. authorities recognized the exceptional role of taijiquan in the country's history. Currently there is a section of taijiquan in the National Wushu Institute. In his outline of the history of sport in China, Shao Quinlong, director of the Museum of Internal Mongolia, called taijiquan 'China's original contribution to the heritage of humanity'. An outstanding 20th cent. master of taijiquan was Sha Guozheng of China (b. 1905), the author of textbooks entitled *Taijiquan training* and *Xing-Yi Quan*. His work has been continued by Sha Junjie. In re-

cent years taijiquan spread beyond China. In Japan there is an annual taijiquan competition known as the Japan Taijiquan Tournament. Among the best taijiquan athletes are: Li Cheng Xiang, Wang Er Ping, Gao Jia Min (China) and Ayako Nakamura (Japan). A National T'ai chi Competition has been organized annually in Singapore since 1987, gathering thousands of practitioners and enthusiasts. In 1981 Singapore also introduced a plan of universal health exercises based on taijiquan, introduced as a pay service in 15 centers. In 1992 the number of people actively practicing taijiquan exceeded 100,000. A special, simplified 36-step version of the sport for children was designed and 2 primary schools included taijiquan in their mandatory curriculum, while several high schools in Singapore offer it among their extra-curricular activities. Taijiquan is becoming more popular also in Western countries, both among those who practice it and in medical circles. The sport is widely used in various forms of psychotherapy. It has a very positive influence on the nervous system and blood circulation. Practicing taijiquan increases the inflow of blood to heart vessels, intensifies the heart muscle contractions, improves hemodynamic processes, strengthens the muscles, tendons and bones, which effectively battles osteoporosis. Taijiquan seems to be a perfect remedy for various civilizational deseases. It combines the benefit of aerobic and anarobic exercises and stimulates the hormonal system, which produces a rejuvenating effect and offers a perfect frame of mind at every age.

C. Man-Ching, *Tai Chi Chuan. A Simplified Method of Calisthenics for Health and Self Defence*, 1956; *Le taijiquan*, in: *Les sports traditionnels en Chine. Chine – Aperçu général*, 1991, 3-5; S. Quinglong, *The History of Sport in China since Antiquity*, YOSICH, 1999, 15-18; N. Sutton, *Applied Tai Chi Chuan*, 1991.

TAIREN-KA, Jap. for 'physical discipline', a Jap. gymnastic system based on the extreme subordination of physical training to military purposes, introduced into Jap. schools in 1941 by the Decree on National School Order in an attempt to educate a 'nation of emperors' (*Kokokumin*). It replaced an earlier and less militarized system of school gymnastics known as >TAISO-KA and included various methods aimed at reaching the desired goal: the trad. physical education >TAIIKU-DO, the practice of >SPORTS-DO, and a combination of physical education and the shaping of will power in the extreme conditions of >ISHITEKI-TAIIKU. All of them were characterized by the desire to reject the Eur. and Amer. models of physical education and replace them with a domestic, adequately modernized model based upon Jap. philosophy and the samurai ethical code. Additional efforts included the eradication from the Jap. language of Eur. and Amer. names of sports and exercises, as well as their terminology.

TAISO-KA, a Jap. system of school gymnastics shaped under the influence of Amer. and Eur. pedagogy, replaced in 1941 with a rigid, militarized system of >TAIREN-KA.

TAJAK-DZHUGURTU, a trad. Kazakh form of competition. 'It is a running throw with a shepherd's staff. When the cattle strays from the trail, the shepherd throws his *tajak*, which whistles through the air and lands in front of the animals, making them go back.' When Kazakhstan was a Soviet republic, efforts were undertaken to adjust the event to the requirements of modern Eur. sport, incl. the registration of world records. According to the sources from that time the best throw at the end of the 1940s was approx. 80m.

'Regional sport', *Sport in the USSR*, Polish ed., 1948, 215.

TAK KADAL, lit. 'lizard's game', a trad. Indon. sport, in which a small stick is placed upon a stone, with one end protruding beyond it. The player bats it with a larger bamboo stick, while his opponent tries to catch it. If successful, the batter is eliminated. If not, he has to pick the stick up and throw it back at the stone. If the stick hits the stone or lands at a distance from it smaller than the length of the batting stick, the batter is eliminated. However, the batter may defend the stone with his bat and volley the stick back into the air. The game resembles the Pak. and Indon. sport of >GULLI DUNDA; Pol. >KLIPA and >SZTEKIEL; Fr. *pilouette*; Breton *mouilh*.

The Internet: http://www.users.bigopond.com/cougar74/indosports.htm

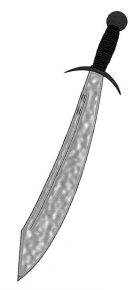

Chinese short saber (Duan Dao).

Li Fai, women's taijiquan form silver medalist in the Busan Asian Games, demonstrates a stance in Hong Kong.

T

TAKARO OMAOMA, a form of trad. running competition among the Maori people of N.Zealand.

TAKARO TUPEKE, a form of trad. jumping competition among the Maori people of N.Zealand.

TAKENOUCHI, a Jap. school of self-defense from the >JU JUTSU family.

TAKEUMA, a Jap. var. of >WALKING ON STILTS, practiced mainly by children. The walker uses 2 bamboo sticks with crossbar foot supports, sometimes with 2 leather straps allowing for an imitation of horse riding – hence the name [Jap. *take* – bamboo + *uma* – horse]. Currently the game is in decline, practiced only in a few schools as an element of cultivating the domestic tradition of physical education.

TAKOAGE, a Jap. var. of >KITE FLYING.

TAKRAW, see >SEPAK TAKRAW.

TAKRO, also *takraw*, Thai varieties of a rattan ball game >SEPAK TAKRAW, which incl. playing a rattan ball over the net, inside a circle and with a small goal.

TAL, one of 2 var. of a Mong. game of skill >ADUU KHUMIKH.

TALADZHI, a holy ball game of the Zapotecs, which derives from a religious game similar to Aztec >TLACHTLI and Mayan >POKYAH. It probably developed at the same time as pokyah and prior to

by 2 opponents.The catchers may become runners only after they catch at least 2 runners. To confirm their success they strike the caught runner 10 times in the back. The runners move between the protective zones at randomly selected moments, but if they fail to take the risk before the catchers are able to count to 10, they must either all start running immediately, or face being caught in their protective zones. Cf. >DØDNING, >GÅ OVER ELVEN, >ISBJØRN OG LANDSBJØRN, >KLIM-KLEM, >TULLEHUT, >TYRHOLDE; see also similar running events over one zone, such as >KREDSTROLD.
J. Møller, 'Tamanj', GID, 1997, 2, 54.

TAMBURINO, an Ital. ball game (known in France as *jeu du tambourin*) that takes its name from the sort of bat used to hit the ball, which resembles a tambourine. It is played on a court measuring 80x20m (the indoor version may be played on a basketball court), with no net, but a line (*cordino*) dividing it into 2 halves called the *baltuta* and the *rimessa*. Two teams consist of 5 players each: 2 backcourt players, 1 mid-court player, 1 returner, and 1 server. The ball is made of rubber, weighs 78g, has a diameter of 61mm, and moves with a speed of up to 250km/h (for the indoor game a softer ball is used). The tamburello is a round wooden frame, upon which a cover of horse-hide is stretched tightly. Two types of *tamburello* are used to bat the ball: the oval kind, used for serving, and the round kind, which

ing; 3) the ball is returned with any part of the body excluding the forearm of the arm holding the tamburello; 4) the ball is touched by 2 players of the same team consecutively; 5) a player invades the other team's side of the field; 6) the server, in the act of serving, touches the back line.
Tamburello is a modification of the ancient game of >PALLONE and has many var. (e.g. in Piedmont it is called *tabasso*). The main organization that governs the sport in Italy is Federazione Italiana Palla Tamburello, FIPT, located in Rome, while an international federation was formed in Mantova in 1988.

TAMIS, also Fr. *jeu de tamis*, *balle au tamis*. A Belgian game played on a pitch formed by 2 adjacent geometric figures: a rectangle 30mx6m and a trapezoid with a base of 15m and a height of 20m, the shorter side of which adjoins one of the shorter sides of the rectangle. In the middle of the trapeze there is a stand with a metal drum strapped with a net. The ball is 3cm in diameter and made of clay or hard plastic covered with white chamois. Two teams of 5 players each select their playing area by drawing. One player of the team inside the trapeze bumps the ball against the drum's net so that it falls within the other team's rectangular area. The rectangle team tries to strike the ball back outside of the trapeze with a special glove that has a leather indent 14cm in length, 10cm in width and 6cm in depth. Each fault by any of the players equals the loss of

Tamburello.

tlachtli, although the traditions of all these games interlocked, thanks to the complicated history of the pre-Columbian peoples of S.America. Declining civilizations were replaced by new ones, which to an extensive degree adopted the cultural elements of the losers. Taladzhi appears to have been a game, the tradition of which enriched both *tlachtli* and *pokyah*, although in the process it became so similar to them that in modern times all 3 are perceived as 1 sport with different names attributed to it by various ethnic groups. Many elements of trad. taladzhi survive until today.

TAMANJ, the origin of the name is obscure. A Dan. running game, in which a player must run from one protective zone to another and escape being caught

is 28cm in diameter. Tamburello is a team sport, which requires agility, a sharp eye, intelligence, and confidence. Matches are played to the best of 13 games for major leagues. Each game consists of a series of 'points' counted with the following sequence: 15:30:40:50 (game). The first team to score '50' wins the game. If the score is 40:40, the game is awarded to the first team which gains a 2pt. advantage. After every 3 games (called a 'trampoline') the teams change ends. When served or returned, the ball must pass the dividing line and can be hit back while still in the air or after bouncing off the ground within the court's limits just once. A point is lost if: 1) a team fails to return the ball, 2) the ball – when returned – does not pass the center line before bouncing, or goes out of court before bounc-

1pt. When all players of one team have completed their tosses against the drum's net, the teams change playing areas. The game is part of the program of the Belgian Festes Nationales held annually in Brussels. The name *tamis* is an abbrev. form of the full name *jeu de tamis* [Fr. *jeu* – a game + *tamis* – a net or a strainer].

TANG SOO DO, Kor. for 'the way of the worthy hand', a martial art that uses a large number of leg techniques often combined with jumps. It includes the learning of forms (*hyungs*) both with and without the weapons, as well as the techniques of self-defence. Similar to other Asian martial arts, it is not centered around physical abilities, but rather spiritual and moral values. A rigorous routine focuses on developing self-awareness and the respect for others and the cultural tradition. It also guards the purity and elegance of the language used by its followers, not only during the practice and competition, but also in the course of daily life. It is a coeducational sport, the principles of which are promoted through presentations and school programs. Tang soo do officials actively participate in the preparations for various paralympics. Tang soo do was created by a Korean named Hwang Kee, who was educated in China and spent many years there. After 1945 he returned to Korea and became a tang soo do promotor, combining his Chin. experience (esp. the northern >GONGFU styles) with the Kor. martial art of >TAE-KYON. The Moodukkwan association, which affiliated the followers of tang soo do, soon split into the faction that supported the newly formed >TAE-KWON-DO and those faithful to master Hwang Kee who opposed sport competition. The group of instructors who did not join the Tae-kwondo movement emigrated and began to establish schools of tang soo do abroad. The World Tang Soo Do Association, stationed at Philadelphia, is headed by grand master Jae C. Shina and tries to preserve the sport's heritage and its value as a trad. way of life. One of the pioneers of tang soo do in the USA was Cheezic, who mastered the principles of this martial art during his military service in Korea. In 1960 he received the highest, black belt from Hang Kee and founded a school (*dojang*) in Terbury, Connecticut. The school later developed into Cheezic Tang Soo Do Federation, which has its clubs in 50 locations in 12 Amer. states, with more than 20,000 students, of whom 775 had black belts in 1999. The World Tang Soo Do Association has grown to a membership of over 100,000 in 36 countries.

TANGONO KISHA, an ancient Jap. form of archery being part of the courtly ritual. Cf. >JYA-RAI, >IBAHAJIME, >NORIYUMI. See also forms of Jap. equestrian archery >KADAGAKE, >IN-UOMONO, >YABUSAME; cf. forms of foot archery >BUSHA, >JUMIHAJIME, >KUSAJISI, >MARU-MONO, >MOMOTE.

TAPARAHI, a var. of Maori haka dancing, which has the nature of a skill competition. See >HAKA.

TAPDORI, Kor. for 'circling a tower' (a buddhist temple), a form of physical show being a combination of trad. Kor. games and a Buddhist ritual. According to the old Kor. work *Samgunk-Yusa*,

a porter named Jikui fell in love with Queen Son-dog (632-647) but, his love unreciprocated, he grew seriously ill. When this news reached the queen, she felt mercy for the poor man and – in order to offer him a chance to meet her – she decided to visit the temple of Ryongchos. There Jikui waited for her performing the ritual of tapdori, hoping his dreams might come true. Alas, when the queen arrived, he was so tired that he fell asleep under the tower, so the queen rode away leaving a ring in his hands. When Jikui woke up, he knew that his only chance to meet the queen was lost. He fell into shock and lost consciousness. Then his pain-stricken heart yielded a spark, which set the tower ablaze.

Koo-Chul Jung, *Erziehung und Sport in Korea im Kreuzpunkt fremder Kulturen und Mächte*, 1996, 62.

TAPIRAPI RACES, a type of competition popular among the Tapirapi Indians of S.America. The races involve running contests held between representatives of the same tribe which, for this purpose, is then divided into 2 groups (*moiety*).

TARCZIA, a local Georg. var. of horse racing; cf. >MARUA, >MOKNIEWA.

TARERE, see >TUMI.

TARGET DARTS, a game similar to >DARTS but using 5 small round targets with 4 concentric rings each, scoring 20, 15, 10 and 5pts. (counting from the center). The target, made of soft pine wood, should be 4cm thick and have a diameter of 25cm. The 5 targets are attached to a main board (80cm in height and 100cm in width, with 2 legs buried in the ground), arranged 4 in the corners and 1 in the center. A dart consists of 3 parts. The 'handle' is barrel-shaped, with a length of 6cm, and a width of 3cm in the central part and 1.5cm at the endings. A metal 'head' is embedded in one of the endings, protruding 2cm. A feather flight is placed at the other end of the dart, about 18-20cm long. Each player has 5 attempts separately for each target, from a distance of 4m. The player with the highest total number of points is the winner. The game was rec-

Francesco del Cossa, Allegory of April: Triumph of Venus *(detail), 1476-84, fresco, Palazzo Schifanoia, Ferrara.*

ommended by handbooks for holiday center workers and school common rooms in the former Soviet Union and the so-called socialist countries.
I.N. Chkhannikov, 'Target darts', GIZ, 1953, 62-63.

TÅRNBOLD, Dan. for 'tower ball', [Dan. *tårn* – tower + *bold* – ball]. The object of the game is for players in a circle to shoot a ball against a tower defended by 1 player. The tower may be symbolically represented by 3 sticks 1m in length, with their tops joined to form a tripod, similar to a stand used by soldiers to lean their rifles against. 10-15 players form a circle around the tower, standing at a distance of 4-5m from it. They begin to pass the ball among themselves to fake out the randomly selected defender (*tårnvogler*) until one of them suddenly tries to knock the tower down with the ball. If successful, he takes the defender's position. The balls used for playing the game may be of a different kind, e.g. a volleyball.
J. Møller, 'Tårnbold', GID, 1997, 1, 38.

TATAR KÜRES, a form of wrestling practiced by the Tartars of Crimea, in which the opponents grab each other by the hips and try to knock each other down. Tripping is allowed.

TATAU MANAWA, a Maori competition in holding one's breath. Participants recited simple poems without inhaling air. The one who recited the longest poem, won the game. Cf. >TIANG-KAI-SII, >KAN-KA BILO.

TAUPIRIPIRI, also *taupiupiu*, a Maori form of running competition practiced prior to the Eur. discovery of N.Zealand. The competition is between pairs of runners holding each other's necks.

TAUROMACHY, an ancient form of acrobatics performed on the back of a bull, deriving prob. from the earliest, esp. zoomorphic, pastoral cultures, in which fighting and controlling animals gained a ritual form, later passed on to the centers of power, where it ultimately evolved into a courtly show. The earliest court var. of tauromachy come prob. from Egypt, where one of the chief gods, Ptah, had an earthly representation as a bull named Apis. The bull cult developed within the Minoan predecessor of Gk. culture, as indicated by numerous myths that include a bull figure, e.g. Zeus assumed the figure of a bull in order to kidnap the Tyrian king's daughter, Europe, to Crete. Having done so, the white bull flew into the skies, where it can still be seen today in the form of the constellation Taurus. Meanwhile, on Crete, Europe became the mother of Minos, the legendary king of Crete, whom the god of the sea Poseidon gave an extraordinary bull to be offered to the gods. Minos, however, kept the bull for himself, which brought unto him a misfortune in the form of Minotaur [Gk. for 'Minos' bull'], a half-man half-bull, also called Asterios, born of Minos' wife Pasiphaë and his bull. The Minotaur is the hero of other myths, of which the best known speaks of his confinement in a labyrinth, where every year he was fed with the flesh of 7 boys and 7 girls from Athens, retribution for the death of Minos' only son Androgeios, killed

by a bull while a guest of King Aegeus. He was finally killed by Aegeus' son Theseus with the help of Ariadne. The Cretan bull has also been fought by Heracles. The Cretan bull cult found its representation through tauromachy, the essence of which was a peculiar form of competition between the bull and the athlete. Surviving iconographic sources indicate that the athlete approached the bull from the front, caught it by the horns and, utilizing its powerful efforts to shake him off, somersaulted over the bull's head and onto its back. The number of acrobatic stunts he was able to perform before he fell off most probably determined the quality of his act and the final result in relation to other athletes. Various iconographic sources indicate that during their stunts athletes were guarded by a person standing on the arena and ready to help them land. Similar acrobatic displays enjoyed great popularity within the Minoan culture in the 2nd millenium BC. Bull's horns were, in fact, the main religious symbol of this civilization. The oldest pictorial representations of tauromachy can be found in the series of frescos discovered in the royal palace at Knossos (Crete). With a varied intensity and in different circumstances the tradition of tauromachy spread over other territories within the Gk. civilization. The mythical hero Entellus is said to have killed a bull with a single blow of his fist. Teocritus speaks of an ancient glutton Aigion, who could eat 80 loaves of bread at a time and walked a bull down from the hills holding it by the leg. Milon of Croton displayed his strength by carrying a 4-year-old bull on his back. Polydamas (or Pulydamas) of Skotoussa was able to stop a charging bull by catching its rear hooves. In his work *Oneirokritika* (*Interpretation of Dreams*) a 2nd cent. Gk. writer Artemidorus of Daldis says that 'boys from Ionian Ephesus voluntarily take part in bull fighting, Athenian youngsters display similar skills every year in front of the goddesses at Eleusis, the citizens of Thessalian Larisa risk their lives in a similar way, while in other lands such fights are undertaken only by the condemned'. The patriarch of Constantinople Focius, living in the times of the Byzantine Empire, compiled the writings of old Gk. authors and in his work mentioned the famous pankratiast Theagenes of Thasos, who was able 'to subdue a bull bravely to the great joy of the spectators'. In ancient Rome bull fights were part of >BESTIARIA. In his *De Vita Caesarum* a Roman biographer Suetonius (c.69-after 122) writes that Claudius displayed 'Thessalian horsemen, who drive fierce bulls round the circus, leap upon their backs when they have exhausted their fury, and drag them by the horns to the ground' (*The Lives of the Twelve Caesars*, C. Tranquillus Suetonius, The Translation of Alexander Thomson, R. Worthington, New York, 1883). Similar descriptions can be found in Cassius Dion's *Roman History* and Heliodor's *A History of Ethiopia*.
The bull has also a significant role in the Bible, where – disguised as a golden calf made by Aaron in the absence of Moses – it became a symbol of valuing material things over faith in God. When Moses returns from Sinai, it is destroyed.

WORLD SPORTS ENCYCLOPEDIA

T

Tauromachy or bull-leaping motif on a bronze finger ring from Asine, 15-14th cent. BC.

Bull rhyton from Koumasa, clay, 2500-1900 BC.

T
WORLD SPORTS ENCYCLOPEDIA

Team handball on a 1978 Danish stamp (top) and a Polish stamp issued for the 1984 Olympic Games in Los Angeles.

In the Persian tradition the god of war and victory Verethragna has assumed many times the figure of a bull in order to defeat his enemies. The bull is also a frequently encountered element of Hindu mythology. A monstrous ghost of a bull is defeated by a son of Shiva called Scanda, a 6-headed, multi-handed, and multi-legged god of war and thieves. The bull Nandin was said to be the first author of a well known Hindu poem *Kamasutra*. The thundering god Indra helps a bull called Dasadju fight his enemies. Bloodless bullfights were popular among the Hindu herdsmen, who – unarmed – displayed various tricks threatening the animal, but never coming near to killing or injuring it. Duels of this type can already be found in ancient Tamil literature.

The bull cult was also widespread within Celtic culture. A fight over a herd of bulls forms the basis of the most important epic poem of ancient Ireland *Táin Bó Cuailnge* (*The Cattle Raid of Cooley*). The essential scene portrays a fight between 2 bulls – The Whitehorned Bull (Finnbhennach) and the Brown Bull of Cuailnge (Donn), during which Cormac, the son of the king of Ulster, helps the Whitehorned bull by treacherously delivering 3 blows to the Brown Bull with his spearshaft. In spite of this the Brown Bull is victorious, but after the fight his heart breaks. His name survives today in many Irish placenames. Irish pagan rulers were elected during the bull festival in Ireland, while a soup made from a white bull was thought to stimulate the ability to foretell the future. Other Celtic countries practiced the cult of a 3-horned bull: the inhabitants of Gaul worshipped a bull called Donnotaurus.

The old Icel. epic poem *Edda* introduces the figure of Hymir, who plans to hunt for a sea dragon and sends a brave youngster Wëur to the forest to fetch him bait in the form of a bull's head.

Swift to the wood the hero went,
Till before him an ox all black he found;
From the beast the slayer of giants broke
The fortress high of his double horns.

[trans. by Henry Adams Bellows, 1936]

The general idea of bullfights, in the Gk. tradition always referred to as tauromachy, irrespective of the type and culture, has been an important concept within the Indo-Eur. civilization, and the element of human skill displayed through it unquestionably relate it to sport. Bullfights have also been known, however, within the Far Eastern tradition, e.g. in China, where a popular form of competition was called >BULL WRESTLING. See also >BULL RUNNING, >CORRIDA, >ANIMAL BAITING, >BUFFALO FIGHTS.
J.R. Conrad, *Le Culte du taureau*, 1961; T. Mihailovici, 'Der Kult und kretische...', *Das Altertum*, 1974, 20, 4; J. Sakellarakis, *Athletics in Crete and Mycenae*, OGIAG, 1976.

TCHIDAOBA, also *tchdaobe*, forms of international spelling of Georg. wrestling; see >KARTULI CHIDAOBA.

TCHOS AGADJI, an Azerbaijani folk sport which used to be popular in that country in the past; resembling >FIELD HOCKEY to some extent.

Above and below: tchoukball games held under the auspices of the International Tchoukball Federation.

TCHOUKBALL, a team football game, in which the object is to score a point by shooting the ball at one of 2 peculiar goals placed on opposite sides of the pitch. The goal, resembling a small gymnastic trampoline, is in fact a square, metal frame (90cm²) with a rebound net made of synthetic fiber elastically suspended from it. There are no goalkeepers and each team may score at either frame. A player scores a point if a ball rebounding from the frame: 1) touches the playing area before an opponent can catch it; 2) touches an opponent who fails to control it by dropping it to the floor, or knocking it out of play; 3) touches a defender below the waist. A given team may score only 3 consecutive points at one frame. The recommended playing area is a rectangle 40x20m. In front of each frame is a 'forbidden' zone, semicircular in shape, with a 3-m radius measured from the center of each base line. The semicircle is not regular and resembles the shape of the letter 'D' – in fact, it is often called a 'dee' in the players' jargon. Only the players of the attacking team may remain within the forbidden zone. The game is started (and re-started after a point is scored) by throwing the ball at either frame, so that when it rebounds, it must land outside of the forbidden zone, but within the playing area. The opposite team must try to gain possession of the ball and throw it at either frame to score a point. Each team consists of 12 players, of whom 9 may be within the playing area, while the remaining 3 act as substitutes. At least 6 players must be present at the start of the game and additional players may join the team only after a point has been scored. Substitutions are made without stopping the game. Body contact is prohibited. Each player may assume any position, though players tend to specialize as attackers (shooters), midfielders (pivots), and defenders (end pivots or inners). The ball has a circumference of 58-60cm and weighs 425-475g in men's matches and, respectively, 54-56cm, 325-400g in women's and juniors' matches. Before the match the home team must produce a choice of balls, of which the referees select the match ball, which may not be replaced during the game, except when it is damaged or lost. The length of the match is 3 periods of 15min. for men and 3 periods of 12min. for women and juniors, with a max. interval of 5min. between periods. The ball may be played with any part of the body, but the legs. It may be caught, thrown, hit or impelled, but one player may not hold it longer than 3sec. and may not make more than 3 contacts with his feet and the ground. If a player drops the ball, the team loses possession. The game is controlled by 3 referees, of whom one is responsible for scoring and time-keeping, while the others have 'leading and trailing' responsibilities according to the direction of play. A player committing an offense may be dismissed from the playing area and may not be substituted by another player. If a team loses 4 players, it is unable to comply with the min. requirement of 6 players on the playing area, which automatically ends the game. The final score is the number of points scored until that moment.
History. The game was invented by a Swiss biologist Dr. H. Brandt, whose intention was to test some of his experiments in the motory characteristics of the human body, which provided the subject for his book *From Physical Education to Sport Through Biology*. Brandt had also observed the developing routine nature of the existing games and decided to offer an alternative to them. In 1970 during a conference at the University of Lisbon he presented a speech entitled 'Scientific criticism of team sports', which brought him the Thulin Prize for science. Brandt died in 1972, but the game he had initiated caught on fairly well in Switzerland, France and S England. Tchoukball has also gained popularity in other Eur. countries, such as Belgium, the Czech Republic, Finland, Malta, Germany, Slovakia, Norway, Sweden and Italy, in both Americas – in Argentina, Brazil, Canada, Mexico and the USA, as well as in Australia, Saudi Arabia, Hong Kong, Japan, South Korea and Taiwan. The governing body for the sport is the Fédération Internationale de Tchoukball (FITB). W.Ch. are held every three years.
The Internet: http://www.tchoukball.org

TCHUNG-KEE, see >CHUNGKE.

TE'XWETS SA'KWELA'X, a type of archery practiced by the Stóólo (or Stó:lo) tribe. The bow (*te'xwets*) is held horizontally with 3 fingers, where the thumb and little finger are on the archer's side. The arms of the bow extend over 3-4ft. (90-120cm) and the construction is made of white cedar roots or yew wood. The length of arrow shafts (*sa'kwela'a*), usu. made of red cedar, depends on the archer's height and is equal to the distance between the hand that strings the bow in the ultimate backward position and the fingertips of the hand that holds the bow. The arrowheads are made of hardened wood, bones, or stone. The arrows have rare feather flips. Targets are made of bulrush formed into a ball the size of a large potato and are placed on the ground or suspended from trees for practice. The competition is usu. between 4-5 archers, each having 2 arrows. The archer that succeeds in placing both arrows in the target, which is extremely difficult, wins the competition. If more than one archer is successful, another round is called for and shooting continues until the winner can be determined. The shooting distance is not specified and depends on the rank of the competition and the archers' skills.
The Internet: http//web20.mindlink.net/stolo/games.htm

TEAM HANDBALL, 1) a game played between 2 teams consisting of throwing or hitting the ball into a goal using hands only (only the goalkeeper may kick the ball). Historically, the game has had different forms and varieties. The most popular version is indoor team handball played by 2 teams of 7 players each. The playing field is 40m long and 20m wide; the goal cage is 3m wide and 2m high; the ball is 58-60cm in diameter (men's) and 54-56cm (women's). In front of each goal cage there is a semicircular goal area, 7m from the center of the goal. Only the goalkeeper is allowed within the goal area. All shots at the goal must be taken from behind the goal-area line. 3m from the goal-line area runs another arc-shaped line called the free-throw line. The earlier 11-player outdoor version of team handball was played on an >ASSOCIATION FOOTBALL field, 90-110m long and 55-65m wide. The goal cage was 732cm wide and 244cm high. Team handball or Olympic handball is unrelated to var. of 2- or 4-

Kjersti Grini (#3) of Norway shoots as goalkeeper Aniko Meksz (#1) of Hungary jumps to block the shot during the Hungary vs. Norway team handball match at the 1996 Centennial Olympic Games in Atlanta, Georgia.

player games, often called *court handball* games.
History. Like many other ball games, team handball derived from numerous, ancient and medieval folk games. The rules of those trad. games did not distinguish between hitting the ball with the hands or kicking it. The first historical attempt to ban the use of feet in ball playing was the Scot. >BALL OF SCONE. Contemporary team handball took its shape thanks to the Dane, H. Nielsen (1859-1924). In 1898, he introduced a 7-player team handball game to Ollerup secondary school called *handbold*. In 1911, the game became part of the PE curriculum in all Dan. schools. At the same time a number of handball games were developing in other Eur. countries. A Czech teacher, A. Kristof formulated the rules of >HAZENA, and c.1897, a Ger. PE teacher from Brunswick, K. Koch developed an 11-player team handball. Until 1920, Koch's handball game was played on a field which was 80m long and 40m wide; the goal was 5m wide and 2.1m high. Initially, the Ger. var. gained more popularity in Europe than Nielsen's game. In 1928, the International Amateur Handball Federation was founded. 11-player team handball was included in the Ol.G. only once, in 1936. The 7-player men's game became part of the Ol.G. in 1972, and the wom-

BALL, >IRISH HANDBALL. In Australia the game is known as >OLYMPIC HANDBALL.
R.C. Clanton & M.P. Dwight, *Team Handball*. Steps to Success, 1997.

TEAM RUNNING, a type of running event where the final result is an aggregate of individual runners' results. Long-distance team running events were held during the 1912 Ol.G. in Stockholm, the 1920 Ol.G. in Antwerp and the 1924 Ol.G. in Paris (3,000-m race), during the 1908 Ol.G. in London (3-mi. or 4,828.02-m race), during the 1900 Ol.G. in Paris (5,000-m race), during the 1904 Ol.G. in St. Louis (4-mi. or 6,437.32-m race), during the 1912 Ol.G. in Stockholm (8,000-m cross-country race) and during the 1920 Ol.G. in Antwerp as well as the 1924 Ol.G. in Paris (10-km cross-country race). Finland and the US both won the most gold medals (3 each) at various Ol.G. and over various distances. P. Nurmi of Finland greatly contributed to Finland's successes by winning the 3,000-m race in 1924 and the 10-km races in 1920 and 1924. The British won 2 gold Olympic medals and the French one.
>RELAYS are a separate var. of team running, while *patrol races* were often held as team events in the modern times. Team races were also popular among other cultures. They were practiced by Native Amer. Indians, particularly by the Timbira and Krahow in central Brazil, where they aimed at developing teamwork skills (>LOG RUNNING). The Siberian Chukchees and Yakuts also held their races as team events (>CHUKCHEE RACES, >YAKUTEE RACES). The Maori >TAUPIRIPIRI is a very special var. of team running whereby pairs of runners compete with one another.

TEAM WRESTLING, a var. of wrestling involving usu. 2 teams of 5-10 members. The team who managed to defeat all the players from the opposing team was declared the winner. Team wrestling used to be one of the events during the Cotswold Games (1670-1853).

TEBEG, a Chin. game similar to Pol. >ZOŚKA, known in the Kor. tradition as >CHEGI CHAGI, in the Eng. tradition as >SHUTTLECOCK KICKING, and in the Mong. tradition as >TEBEG ÖSHI-GLÖÖKH. The idea is to kick up a ball made of feathers, animal hair, or wool tied to a stone or metal weight. The inventor is said to have been Ti Jian Zi, who lived in the 1st cent. In the old Chin. tradition the ball could be kicked, hit with one's hand or struck with a wooden stick. The game spread around Asia, Japan, Siam, and among many tribes of Middle Asia, where it was probably popularized by the Mongo-

lians living in N-W China. From there it travelled through the Middle East to Europe, where it arrived at the decline of antiquity or at the beginning of the Middle Ages. The tradition of tebeg and its Asian var. gave birth to the Eng. game of >BATTLEDORE SHUTTLECOCK.

TEBEG ÖSHIGLÖÖKH, Mong. for 'to toss up a wisp many times'; a game similar to Pol. >ZOŚKA, Eng. SHUTTLECOCK KICKING, Kor. >CHEGI CHAGI, and Chin. >TEBEG. The tebeg is made of a wisp of camel hair, horse hair, or a piece of goat's fur and a piece of metal. In modern times the metal piece was often an empty gun shell. The game is described in one of the Mong. tales, in which the hero kicks the *tebeg* so strongly that it hits the mother-in-law of an evil spirit and deters her from any evil doing in the second part of the tale. *Tebeg* is also part of the ritual of *oboo takhikh* performed around the holy pile of rocks called *oboo* in honor of the ancestors' spirits. That part of the ritual has been known only among the Mongolians living in the Chin. province of Quinghai, as ethnographers have not discovered any traces of it in Mongolia proper. The essence of it is that one of the armed men circles round the *oboo* 10 times following the direction of the sun, while another man kicks up the *tebeg*, also circling round the *oboo* in the opposite direction.
I. Kabzińska-Stawarz, 'Tebeg öshiglöökh', GOMS, 1991, 135.

TEDAMA, see >MARBLES.

TEETER-TOTTERING, see >SWINGS AND SEE-SAWS, >NÔL TTWIGI.

TEK MEK FRISTED, a Dan. game, [Dan. *tek* – a word uttered upon touching a chased rival + *med* – with + *fristed* – shelter]. A part of the playing area is marked as *fristed* (shelter) and one of the players is designated as a catcher. The remaining players scatter around the playing area and are chased by the catcher, who must touch one of them and say *tek*. The runners may escape being caught by finding shelter in the fristed.
J. Møller, 'Tek mek fristed', GID, 1997, 2, 62.

TEKA, a game of the Maori of N.Zealand similar to >DARTS. In its oldest forms the darts were large leaves of pampas grass, called *toetoe*, or short wooden arrows called *karo*. The length of the arrows varied depending on the local tradition; the longest ones were approx. 90cm. The object was to throw the arrows at a partner standing at a distance of approx. 15m. Both partners had an equal number of arrows and whoever had more successful hits, won the game. Another var. involved throwing for

Cristian Bajan of Australia attempts to stop a shot from Rolando Urios of Cuba during the men's handball match at the 2000 Olympic Games in Sydney, Australia.

en's game in 1976. The first men's W.Ch. were held in 1936 and then revived in 1956. Until 1970, the Team Handball W.Ch. were held every 3 years and after 1970 every 4 years. Team handball was brought to N.America by Ger. POWs who played the game in Camp Borden in Ontario, Canada. It made its way to the USA in 1959 along with Eur. immigrants. In 1937, team handball became a women's event in Norway. The first women's team handball W.Ch. were held in 1957; since 1971 they have been held every 2 years. After WWII, the best national teams were the USSR, Yugoslavia, East Germany, Rumania, Czechoslovakia, Korea, Sweden, West Germany, and France. In the 1980s and 1990s the team handball traditions were maintained by Russia and Croatia (1996 Olympic champion). The best women's national teams after WWII included the teams of the USSR, East Germany, Yugoslavia, Hungary, Rumania, and since 1988 South Korea (2-time Olympic champions 1988, 1992, and placing second 1996). The traditions of the USSR team were for a while maintained by the CIS team but after further splits the Rus. national team failed to qualify for the Atlanta Ol.G. in 1996. At present, the leading teams incl. Denmark (1996 Olympic champion), Norway, China, and Germany. 2) an Eng. name for >HANDBALL played as a team sport, as opposed to a group of games of a similar name, but played as individual or pair events. See >HAND-

TEAM HANDBALL WORLD CHAMPIONS

MEN
1938 Germany
1954 Sweden
1958 Sweden
1961 Romania
1964 Romania
1967 Czechoslovakia
1970 Romania
1974 Romania
1978 West Germany
1982 Soviet Union
1986 Yugoslavia
1990 Sweden
1993 Russia
1995 France
1997 Russia
1999 Sweden
2001 France
2003 Croatia
WOMEN
1957 Czechoslovakia
1962 Romania
1965 Hungary
1971 East Germany
1973 Yugoslavia
1975 East Germany
1978 East Germany
1982 Soviet Union
1986 Soviet Union
1990 Soviet Union
1993 Germany
1995 South Korea
1997 Denmark
1999 Norway
2001 Russia

OLYMPIC CHAMPIONS
MEN
1936 Germany
1948-68 Not held
1972 Yugoslavia
1976 Soviet Union
1980 German D.R.
1984 Yugoslavia
1988 Soviet Union
1992 Unified Team
1996 Croatia
2000 Russia
WOMEN
1976 Soviet Union
1980 Soviet Union
1984 Yugoslavia
1988 Republic of Korea
1992 Republic of Korea
1996 Denmark
2000 Denmark

T

distance and yet another raising a small mound, at which the arrows were thrown from a short run and from a distance of 8-10m. The player who drove his arrow deeper into the ground won the game. The game was played in a way similar to the Eur. sport competition, although its main objective was to develop a skill used in battle.

A. Armstrong, *Games and Dancing of the Maori People*, 1986, 7-8.

TENCHIN SHIN'YO, a Jap. school of martial arts which are part of the family of >JU JUTSU.

TENDO-RYU, a Jap. martial art deriving from the tradition of >AIKIDO, created by K. Shimuzu (b. 1940), a student of M. Ueshiba (the creator of aikido) in the later period of his activity.

A children's kick boxing bout at a boxing stadium in the outskirts of Bangkok, Thailand.

Tennis on two 19th-century lithographs.

TENNIS, a type of game originating in France, the main idea of which is to return a ball between partners over a net with bare hands, later gloves, short bats and, finally, rackets. The game spread and evolved into many varieties. Such games appeared in the Middle Ages, in France, as >JEU DE LA PAUME and in England as >ROYAL TENNIS. They were the starting point for modern tennis, first known as >LAWN TENNIS. Today, the term 'tennis' unaccompanied by any adjective usu. refers to the lawn variety. There are several var. of tennis other than the lawn one, such as >PADDLE TENNIS, PADDER >TENNIS, etc.

Ethymology. The name 'tennis' comes from Latin and – through O.Fr. – entered Eng. in the Middle Ages to assume the final form [Middle-Eng. *tenetz*, Old Fr. *tennez*, Lat. *tenere* – to rule, reign; cf. modern Fr. *tenir* – to keep, catch]. In Middle-Eng., similar to O.Fr., it meant, 'Take it!' or 'Play!', an exclamation informing the partner of beginning the game with a serve. In 1400 J. Gower in his *In Praise of Peace* used the phrase 'of the tenetz to winne', meaning 'to win in tennis'. An anonymous work *Promptorium parvulorum* written around 1400 contains an Eng.-Lat. translation of the idea of the game: 'teneys, play teniludus, manupilatus tenisia' – 'tennis, a game of tennis, a manual game of tenisia'. A Lat. court verdict from Pershore, Worcester, contains a ban on the game because it caused public unrest and distracted the players from more useful sports like archery: 'Nullus eorum [...] frequentabit ludum qui vocatur the tenyse playng in communi via domini Regis nec in aliquo loco privato ibidem' – 'None of them [...] shall take part in the game called tennis, either on the public roads of His Majesty the King or in any private place'. In Towneley's *Mystery Plays* (XIII, Tercius Pastor) written in 1460 we find the following passage:

I bryng the bot a ball
haue and play the with all,
And go to the tenys.

Shakespeare uses the word tennis 6 times in 3 different meanings: as *tennis game* (*Hamlet*, II, 1, 59; *Henry VIII*, I, 3, 30; as *tennis ball* (*Much Ado About Nothing*, III, 2, 47; *Henry V*, I, 2, 258); and as *tennis court* (*Pericles*, II, 1, 64; *Henry IV*, p.2, II, 2, 21). The modern spelling of the word *tenis* as 'tennis' originated in Shakespeare's times and under his influence.

TEN-PIN BOWLING, also *tenpins*, a var. of bowling popular esp. in the USA. See >AMERICAN BOWLING, >BOWLING, >EUROPEAN BOWLING.

TEOMEHE EKSAM, Est. for 'the testing of serfs'; a trad. game. A wooden yoke of a horse, used in carriages, is placed on the ground. Players must go under it without knocking it down or touching the ground with their buttocks.

TSNJ, 1996, 31.

TEOTIHUACAN BALL, a ball game practiced in pre-Columbian C Amerca. The rules of the game remain unknown. The game is known only from the El Tlalocan frieze from the Tapentila palace, discovered in the town of Teotihuacan in C Mexico. The frieze depicts players striking at a flaming ball with sticks. Researchers suggest that a flying fireball developed a fire trail which symbolized the movement of the sun. The game bears a resemblance to a folk ball game practiced today by the Purhepecha people, called >PELOTA PURHÉPECHA ENCENCIDA, which very likely descended from Teotihuacan ball; cf. >FIREBALL.

TERRIN AR C'HOZH, a Bret. game of skill similar to Fr. *le casse-pot* and Eng. *break the pots*. It is usu. an element of church patron's festivals (Le >PARDON) and is played a week after Easter Sunday (Fr. *Quasimodo*). A horizontal beam is suspended above an average man's height, with a dozen or so pots hanging from it. The pots conceal various surprises – from handkerchiefs to live pigeons. A participant is blindfolded and is given a wooden stick. To make him lose his orientation he is turned around several times, after which he may start aiming for the pots. If he succeeds in breaking one, he is awarded the surprise it contains.

F. Peru, 'La tradition populaire de jeux de plein air en Bretagne', LJP, 1998.

TESTULAM MARINAM IACERE, Lat. for throwing sea shells, [Lat. *testula* – a shell + *marina* – sea +

iacere – to throw, cast]; also *testula marina* – a sea shell, or *iaculatio testarum*, [Lat. *iaculatio* – to throw + *testa* – shell]. In ancient Rome a game similar to modern >DUCKS AND DRAKES, but executed with large shells of Mediterranean shellfish. Its Gk. equivalent was >EPOSTRAKSIMOS. A description of the game was left by Minutius Felix:

We can see the boys jumping and competing in throwing shells at the sea [testarum in mare iaculationibus ludere]. The idea is to search the shore for shells that had been smoothed down by sea waves, hold a shell with one's fingers, lean down, and throw it at a wave so that it gently slides over the top of the wave or bounces off the highest wave. The winner is the one whose shell reaches the farthest distance and with the largest number of bounces.

TETHER-BALL, see >DECK GAMES.

TE-TO-TUM, an alternative name of Eng. >TOPS, played with hands, rather than with the use of a whip.

TETRIPPON POLIKON, see >TETRIPPON.

TETRIPPON, Gk. *tethrippon* or *tethrippon harma*, lit. 'a quadruple carriage', in ancient Greece a 2-wheeled carriage drawn by 4 horses, as well as a type of races on such vehicles [Gk. *tetripon* – a team of 4 animals + *tetra* – quadruple + *harma* – a carriage]. A race of carriages drawn by teams of 4 animals, called *hippon tetrippon*, was included in the program of the Ol.G. in 680 BC. Another race, for carriages drawn by teams of ponies, was called *tetrippon polikon* [Gk. polikos – a pony] and was introduced into the Ol.G. in 344 BC. Each horse or pony performed a different function. The 2 middle ones were draft horses, which was secured by the construction of the harness (*epomidion*). The harness of the outside horses was constructed in such a way that their primary role was to maneuver, rather than draw the carriage, which proved crucial for overtaking or making turns. The driver was called *terippos*. Actual participation in the races was restricted for men, although women could put the carriages they owned up for racing. A 2-time winner of *tetrippon* was a noblewoman from Athens named Kynisca (396 and 392 BC), although it remains a puzzle how she was presented with the wreath, for women were not allowed into Olympia during the games. There were several other women, besides Kynisca, who put their carriages up for racing, not only during the Ol.G., and won. One of the most renowned winners was the Macedonian king, Phillip II (353 BC). Driving a *tetrippon* was much more difficult than driving a 2-horse carriage (>SYNORIS), mostly because the carriage was much broader and the risk of collision much greater. The Greeks viewed *tetrippon* as the most noble form of Olympic racing. See also >CHARIOT RACING.

TEWAARATHON, a ball game of the Mohawk Ind. tribe played with a racket, which was a bent stick ended with a net. Along with other Ind. games, such as >BAGATAWAY and >TOLI, it was a predecessor of the Can. summer sport of >LACROSSE. In the 1960s a Montreal dentist G. Beers, who played tewaarathon in Kahnawake on the St. Lawrence river, came up with a uniform set of rules for lacrosse.

B. Kidd, *The Struggle for Canadian Sport*, 1996, 15.

THAI BOXING, Thai *muay thai*, a national sport of Thailand in which blows can be delivered not only with the fists but also with the feet, shinbones, knees, and elbows. Boxers are barefoot, wearing only loose shorts and boxing gloves. Points are scored solely for kicks; hands and arms are only employed to prepare hits executed with the legs and feet. The division into weight categories is similar to that in >BOXING. The bout is preceded by performing 2 rituals: *wai kru*, consisting of a sequence of bows which express respect for the master and the school, and *ram muay*, a form of meditative dance, the nature of which indicates the affiliation with a given school. Both rituals are at the same time a form of warming up and preparing for the bout. The bout itself is accompanied by music performed on a drum, dulcimer and Javanese pipe, which is coordinated with the rhythm of the fighting boxers.

History. Thais emigrated from China in the 13th cent. when they were dislodged by Mongolian invaders. For centuries they fought against the neighboring Khmers and Vietnamese. Thai martial arts stem from Chin. >GONGFU but evolved in the course of incessant wars, acquiring a specific character. Originally, martial arts with the use of weapons (today >KRABI-KRABONG) and hand-to-hand techniques were practiced together. The earliest historical record concerning Muay Thai dates back to 1560 and describes a fight between Thai Naresuen and a Burmese pretender to the throne. The fight lasted for a couple of hours and terminated with the death of the Burmese contender. Naresuen then started to organize Muai Thai tournaments, which contributed substantially to the popularization of this discipline. The golden age of Thai boxing was the reign of Pra-Choo-Sua, called the Tiger King. He traveled across the country in disguise, taking part in various local tournaments and winning them one after another. Since that time, Thai boxing has been an element of military training in all Thai schools. In the 1930s the principles of trad. Thai boxing were re-modelled after boxing (e.g. the introduction boxing gloves), which made the sport safer. Currently, Thai boxing is gaining on popularity around the world.

THAI BULL RACING, a trad. sport practiced for many generations in W Thailand, in the locations of Kanchanaburi, Suphan Buri, Petchburi, Nakhon Pathom, Prachuap Khiri Khan, Ratchaburi. The races are part of the harvest festivals taking place between Jan. and May and are a test of speed and endurance for the animals, which are normally used on farms. They are held in the evening so that the animals may get some rest after a day's work. Farmers bring their bulls to a lighted arena, line them up and tie the first one to a centrally located post. The number of bulls depends on the size of the arena and is usu. 20-40. Each race is between the last 2 bulls, who circle the post counterclockwise 3 or 4 times. The bull that gets ahead in each race is the winner. Bull owners take special care of their animals and crown them at the end of the races with colored decorations. The idea of the races follows the behavior of the bulls which run around the vast rice fields and separate rice seeds from the plant. In another form of the races bulls are harnessed to 2-wheeled carts ridden by jockeys.

THANG-TA, a Hindu martial art and school of self-defense that teaches fighting techniques between opponents of whom one has a sword and the other a spear [Hindu *hang* – sword + *ta* – spear, lance]. It is often used for combat in which one person is armed (with a spear or sword) and the other relies on unarmed >SARIT-SARAK. Thang-ta occurs in 3 forms: one has the nature of a ritual connected with Tantric practices (Tantricism being a Hindu movement in which one identifies himself with the highest being by developing one's self), the second one is a display of dancing with arms, the third one is a sport competition.
History. Thang-ta refers to mythological stories, in which the dragon god Lainingthou Pakhangba ordered King (or Prince) Mungyamba to kill Moydana, the demon of Khaga, with his spear and sword. In another Hindu myth, God began to create the Earth by constructing a sword and spear. These weapons were also to be used by the God and ruler Nongda Lairel Pakhangba. The school of thang-ta began to emerge in the 17th cent. and was developed in the times of the independent kingdom of Manipur. Under Brit. rule, the old fighting techniques were banned. When India regained independence in 1947, and particularly during the 1950s, the policy of Nehru's government supported the revival of old traditions, incl. thang-ta.

THERMAE, Lat. *thermae*, in ancient Rome a complex of public buildings and sanitary devices used for maintaining health and for sport purposes; also a var. of hygienic and recreational treatments incl. baths, massages, and cultural activities. The best known thermae were constructed in the Roman Empire after 31 AD and were named after their founders: Agrippa, Diocletian, Domitian, Caracalla, Constantine, Trajan, and Titus. Many of them have survived to this day and are tourist attractions. For history and architecture see >BATHS. Cf. >BALANEIA.

THETHKW'OOTEL, a trad. sport of Stóólo Indians (orig. spelled thethkw'o:tel, Eng. equivalent – 'push-of-war'), in which 2 teams hold a wooden rod approx. 4.2m long horizontally in both hands. Each team consists of 12-14 players, who are placed one behind another, which makes the game the opposite of tug-of-war. (Cf. >GIOCO DEL PONTE). The competition is controlled by referees. The objective is to push the other team behind a line marked on

the ground. The game may also be played individually. Competitors sit with their feet against each other. The rod's length is approx. 3ft. (90cm). In order to win one must lift the opponent up, which usu. results in the winner's landing on his back. In another var. both competitors stand against each other and try to push the opponent behind a marked line. In all var. the rod must not touch the ground and must remain in a horizontal position. The use of gloves is allowed.
The Internet: http//:web20.mindlink.net/stolo/games.htm

THODA, a var. of ancient archery practiced as a team sport in the Hindu state of Himachal Pradesh. The wooden arms of the bows are 1.5-2m in length and, along with the arrows, are adjusted to the height of the archers. The name refers to a round piece of wood fastened to the arrowhead in order to prevent injuries. The object is to strike the opponent in the leg below the knee.
History. The sport derives from tribal wars between the Pandawas and Kaurawas of the Kulu valley in India. The competition was accompanied by an interesting ritual. A group of inhabitants of one village would go at the sunrise to the neighboring village, drop 3 leaves on the square among the huts and hide in the bushes. When the leaves, a symbol of challenge, were discovered, the villagers would call for their neighbors in hiding to stand to battle. These days the annual sport event takes place on 13 and 14 April on the trad. Hindu holiday of Baisakhi, during which people pray to Maskoo and Durga nicknamed 'Angry', 'Furious', 'Terrifying', 'Cheating' etc., to propitiate the deities and acquire their favors. The festivities are accompanied by a duel of archers. The local rural festival gathers several hundred villagers, most of whom take part in ritual dancing which provides an artistic setting for the archery event. Archers are divided into 2 opposing teams called Saathi and Pashi. Although old tribal disagreements no longer exist, it is assumed for the occasion of the festival that both teams are inheritors of old quarrels manifested through a sport competition. Both teams go the village square, where there is ritual dancing, singing, and sword swinging. One of the teams assumes the role of defenders, the other – that of attackers (*chakravyuh*). Archers aim at the rivals' legs below the knee from a distance of approx. 10m. The defenders try to avoid being hit by dodging and jumping up. The team that eliminates the opponents wins the competition.

THREE HOLES, an Eng. game of shooting balls at 3 holes in the ground. It belongs to the family of >MARBLES, mostly because of a similar construction of balls, which – however – are larger in three holes than in other marbles games (e.g. >KULKI) and resemble more the balls used in >RACQUETS. The balls are called *bouncers* or *bucks*. The ground holes are in one line and are approx. 2-3ft. (60-90cm) from one another. They should only be slightly larg-

er than the balls. The idea is to conclude a round called *firsts* (the player shoots in a sequence of holes 1-2-3), then *seconds* (2-1) and *thirds* (2-3). If a player successfully hits all 3 holes 3 times, he takes a game. If a player's ball stops short of the hole, the game is resumed by the next player, who is allowed to aim at consecutive holes, but also can make use of the opponent's ball, by hitting it away from the hole. However, if he misses or the opponent's ball which he hit reaches the hole, the opponent resumes his play and may continue aiming at the holes or hitting his opponent's ball which is now left on the ground.
A.B. Gomme, *Three Holes*, TGESI, 1898, II, 256.

Thai villagers watch as racing bulls, tied up abreast, run during a race around an arena in Ban Lard district in Pethcaburi province, 65 miles southwest of Bangkok, Thailand.

THREE-WALL HANDBALL, a var. of >HANDBALL in which the court is surrounded by 3 walls: the front wall and 2 side walls – the left-hand wall and the right-hand wall. The ball may rebound off any wall. All remaining rules are quite similar to other var. of handball, in which the ball rebounds off 1 wall (>ONE-WALL HANDBALL) or 4 walls (>FOUR-WALL HANDBALL).

THUMB WRESTLING, a folk var. of wrestling popular in the past in Hawaii involving throwing one's opponent off balance by pressing one's thumb against his thumb.

TI RAKAU, a common name for several var. of a stick game practiced by the Maori of N.Zealand. The name derives from a tree called *ti*, which according to local mythology wandered from place to place. Encountering it brought misfortunes and the game of *ti* was meant to symbolically defy evil. Stick games are accompanied by music and in the past were a ritual form of preparing for battle carried out to the beating of war drums. Modern var., laicized as a result of a decline of ancient beliefs, are commonly referred to as >TITI TOREA.

 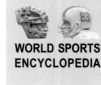
A man guides racing bulls with his bamboo pole topped with a sharp nail during racing at an arena in Ban Lard district in Petchaburi province, Thailand. For generations farmers would bring their bulls to run en masse through each other's rice fields to thresh the crop during the harvest season. Nowadays, mechanization makes such use of bulls unnecessary. But tradition lives on in the local form of bull racing, a tribute to the good old days as well as a popular and prestigious sport.

T

WORLD SPORTS ENCYCLOPEDIA

TIANG-KAI-SII, an Afr. endurance game practiced by the Kpelle people in Liberia, similar to Ghanaian >KANKA BILO. Prior to starting the game the players line up 10-25 stones at approx. 1-pace intervals. One after another the players breathe in, hold their breath, and start walking along the row of stones. They must touch each stone and say loudly: *tiang-kai-sii*, adding a consecutive numeral (*taang* – one, *verre* – two, etc.). Missing a stone or making a mistake in counting means losing a turn. The player who touched the largest number of stones in one breath, wins the game. If a player gets to the end of the row, he may continue backwards. Cf. >TATAU MANAWA. A. Taylor Cheska, 'Kanka-bilo (Millipede)', TGDWAN, 1987, 38; D.F. Lancy, 'The Play Behaviour of Kpelle Children during Rapid Cultural Change', *The Study of Play. Problems and Prospects*. eds. D.F. Lancy and B.A. Tindall, 1977.

TIBETAN ARCHERY, archery contests practiced in Tibet, during which the competitors drank beer to '...stop their hands from shaking', as stated in an old Tibetan song.

TIBETAN HORSE RACING, a form of equestrian competition practiced among the Tibetan people of Zhang on the Qinghai heights. Of the 2 events, the first is judged according to the smoothness and sta-

Armed Chinese military policemen relax as Tibetans race their horses on the opening day of the Qiangtang Qiaqing Horse Racing Festival at Nagqu, Tibet.

bility of the gallop, while in the other horsemen compete in a trad. race. Competitions are held in the summer months of June and July.
Mu Fushan et al., 'Tibetan Horse Race', TRAMCHIN, 16.

TIBETAN RACES, held to celebrate the most important religious holidays, esp. the Tibetan New Year. Each competitor carried a clay jug in his hands. The object of the race was to reach a spring or well and bring some 'water of happiness' back. The participants held that they would ensure good luck for themselves to the extent to which they surpassed others during the competition. Tibetan races were often held along with >UNMOUNTED HORSE RACING after the horses had departed from the place where the people had gathered.
I. Kabzińska-Stawarz, 'Competition in Liminal Situations', part II, EP, 1993, XXXVII, 1.

TIBETAN WRESTLING formed a part of the festival held on the 25th day of each New Year. The fighters were almost naked and wore only hip bands. Tibetan wrestling was esp. popular among the Derbet tribe. One of the most distinctive features of this wrestling var. was that the fighters drank beer before each match. This differentiated it from >KIRGHIZ WRESTLING where beer was banned.

TIBOLD, a Dan. 10-round ball game, [Dan. *ti* – ten + *bold* – ball]. The name refers to 10 rounds of play, during which the number of times the ball must be played increases consistently. In the 1st round the ball must be bounced off the floor and caught in the hand with the inner side up. In the 2nd round the ball must be rolled twice on the shoulders from one arm to another. In the 3rd round the ball must be thrown straight up and caught 3 times with both hands. In the 4th round the ball must be bounced off the wall 4 times and caught in both hands. In the 5th round the ball must be bounced off the floor 5 times and caught on the upper side of 1 hand. In the 6th round the ball must be bounced off the wall 6 times and caught only after it rebounds off the floor. In the 7th round the ball must be bounced off the ceiling so hard that it rebounds off the floor, hits the ceiling again and drops to the floor, after which it must be smashed against the floor with 1 hand and caught (the entire cycle is repeated 7 times). In the 8th round the ball must be bounced off the ceiling and after it drops to the floor, it must be struck with 1 hand agaist the ceiling and – after it bounces off the floor again – it must be caught (8 repetitions). In the 9th round the ball must be bounced off the floor twice and caught in the air in 1 hand, after which the hand with the ball must be returned down (9

repetitions). In the 10th round the ball is bounced off the floor 10 times, after which it must be caught in 1 hand. In some regions of Denmark the elements are played in a different order and with a different style of bouncing. In one var. called *oldermortrip* (grandma's trip) the number of rounds is not fixed. In 1895 the game was observed at Alminde in the area of Kolding.
J. Møller, 'Tibold', GID, 1997, 1, 10.

TICKBALL, a var. of a trad. game played at Holstein (Germany), similar to the Ger. >SCHLAGBALL and Pol. >PALANT.

TIDI TOURETA, also *titi toureta*, see >TI RAKAU.

TILTING ON SKATES, a type of violent ice-skating competition practiced in the 12th cent. in London. It was described together with other London folk sports and customs by W. Fitz-Stephen in the preface to his work *Vita Sancti Thomae*. Tilting on skates was a mock battle between 2 skaters who charged each other with leveled lances. It was the cause of numerous accidents and serious physical injuries, although Fitz-Stephen claimed it trained courage and perseverance. The sport was mainly practiced on moor fields near London (present-day Moorfields).

R.J. Mitchell and M.D.R. Leys, *A History of London Life*, 1958; F.M. Stenton, *Norman London*, 1934.

TILTING-AT-THE-RING, also *tilting*, see >RUNNING AT THE RING; cf. >ALKA, >QUINTAIN.

TIMBER SPORTS, a general name for a var. of woodcutter's sport events, such as competitive woodcutting, sawing, rafting, as well as other events connected with trad. festivals and holidays. A group of sports in which wood is worked up with axes is called competitive woodchopping. Connected with the tradition of wood rafting by Amer. and Can. raftsmen, it shows distinctive marks of a separate group of sports, although some of its events are held along with typical woodcutter's events. See also >DRWALI ZAWODY, >BIRLING; cf. >AIZKOLARIS, >TRONZOLARIS.

History. The oldest traces of timber sports can be found in the Brit. Isles, where the ancient woodcutting profession began to disappear at the end of the Middle Ages, because of a constantly shrinking number of forest areas. Some old traditions were preserved through various sports, e.g. Scot. >TOSSING THE CABER, in which wooden logs are tossed for distance – a successor of old competitions in which strong men cast logs into the water for rafting or onto carriages for road transport. The tradition of timber sports has also survived in N.America and Australia, where 2 main events were known in the mid-19th cent.: tree-felling and splitting of timber.
In 1874 the first competition was held in Ulverstone on Tasmania. The finals were played between J. Smith of Tasmania and J. Biggs from the state of Victoria (Australia). Their competition was immortalized in a monument depicting a stump with a cut out wedge erected by the Australasian Axemen's Association founded around 1900. In 1891 in Latrobe (Tasmania) the first Austrl. W.Ch. were held, since then an annual event. Currently the most important event in Australia is a tournament called The Sydney Royal Easter Show. The most outstanding Austrl. athletes were M. McCarthy, who practiced the sport for 58 years until 1980, when he turned 78, and J. O'Toole, who won the W.Ch. 24 times.
Rapid deforestation in Australia led to the necessity of economizing on the quantity of wood required for sport tournaments. One method was to use trunks which were cut at different lengths, another was to use one trunk to which a new top was added for each event. The same trunk could be used up to 3 times. Australia has also invented a method of cutting a trunk at a certain level with the help of a wedged foot support called a springboard, on which the cutter stood. The method was soon adopted by other countries, e.g. Canada and the USA, where it is now a standard tournament method. The first tournaments in Canada and the USA took place at the end of the 19th cent. The first event observed by an audience was held in 1888, while 10yrs. later the Lumbersmen's Association of America initiated the first national championships, which also included some >BIRLING events. Grandiloquently called W.Ch., they were held in Omaha, Nebraska during the Trans-Mississippi Exhibition. In the course of preparations for the event basic rules of the sport were worked out, which survive until today, with later modifications accounting for the development of mechanical devices (mainly chainsaws) and the emergence of new events.
The beginning of the 1970s brought the integration of different var. of timber sports. The number of Australians and N.Zealanders taking part in tournaments in the USA, as well as Americans competing in Australia and Tasmania, kept growing. An important step forward in the development of these contacts was a tournament (called the Centenary of Wood Chopping) held on Tasmania in 1974 to commemorate the 100th anniversary of the sport. The event gathered, besides the native teams, also representatives from Canada and the USA. Soon afterwards international tournaments in timber sports began to gather also representatives of Japan. Another important step to popularize the sport was a tournament held in Washington, D.C. in 1976 to commemorate the bicentennial of American independence.
In 1970 a group of old and current choppers, incl. D. Geer, A. Cogar, B. Waibel, M. Lents, S. Johnson, E. Rosemeyer, E. Marcellus, and manager D. Drushella, a rich real estate agent, organized an all-Amer. event called the Timber Carnival in Albany (1970). Their integrating influence resulted in the

In the 1970s among the best known contestants, both in the chopping and the power sawing events, were: Americans J. Miller, M. Lentz, B. Waibel, E. Rosemeyer, R. Booth, and an Australian C. Stewart, while in the 1990s – N.Zealanders J. Wynyard, M. Bush, and D. Jewett.

American Lumberjack Association Sanctioned Events, http//:www.riverdale.k12.or.us; K. Moore, 'Woodchopping', OCAS, 1994, 463.

TIP-CAT, an Eng. game also known as *cat*, in which a stick sharpened at both ends is batted into the field. The game was played between 2 individuals or 2 teams of several players each. The idea of the game and the equipment necessary to play it were described by J. Strutt in *Sports and Pastimes of the People of England* (1810 edition):

Tip-cat, or perhaps more properly, the game of cat, is a rustic pastime well known in many parts of the kingdom. Its denomination is derived from a piece of wood called a cat, with which it is played; the cat is about six inches in length and an inch and a half or two inches in diameter, and diminished from the middle to both the ends in the shape of a double cone; by his curious contrivance the places of the trap and of the ball are at once supplied, for when the cat is laid upon the ground the player with his cudgel strikes it smartly, it matters not at which end, and it will rise with a rotatory motion, high enough for him to beat it away as it falls, in the same manner as he would a ball.

Strutt continues to describe 2 of many possible var. of the game:

There are various methods of playing the game of cat, but I shall only notice the two that follow. The first is exceedingly simple, and consists in making a large ring upon the ground, in the middle of which the striker takes his station; his business is to beat the cat over the ring. If he fails in so doing he is out, and another player takes his place; if he is successful he judges with his eye the distance the cat is driven from the centre of the ring, and calls for a number at pleasure to be scored towards his game: if the number demanded be found upon measurement to exceed the same number of lengths of the bludgeon, he is out; on the contrary, if it does not, he obtains his call.
The second method is to make four, six or eight holes in the ground in a circular direction, and as nearly as possible at equal distances from each other, and at every hole is placed a player with his bludgeon: one of the opposite party who stands in the field, tosses the cat to the batsman who is nearest him, and every time the cat is struck the players are obliged to change their situations, and run once from one hole to another in succession; if the cat be driven to any great distance they continue to run in the same order, and claim a score towards their game every time they quit one hole and run to another; but if the cat

---

Bob Bruce of Dartmouth University grimaces as he saws through a log during the Lumberjack competition at McGill University near Montreal, Canada.

Amanda Breneman of Paul Smith's College in upstate New York goes all out to chop her log during the Lumberjack competition at McGill University near Montreal.

estab. of the Northwest Association of Logging Sports (NWALS). A year earlier an association of Canadian choppers was formed, later known as Can-Log. Those were the first associations stressing the sporting nature of woodchopping events. A pioneer and 1st president of NWALS was D. Nelson, succeeded by another ex-chopper D. Coop. Since 1976 NWALS has regularly organized an event called the Grand Finals.

Timber sport events are held under the auspices of several institutions, which independently organize their own competitions. According to the most widely used standards of the Amer. Lumberjack Association, the following timber sport events are among the most popular:

Springboard – the contestant climbs a 9ft. spar pole using only his axe and springboards (hardwood planks about 5ft. long, 2in. thick and 8in. across), which are wedged into the pole, and chops the block. The leading specialists are N.Zealanders R. Hartill and B. Herlihy and an American B. Waibel.

Speed climbing – climbing a 65ft. spar with the use of a safety rope of at least $^7/_8$in. in diameter with a steel core rope and spurred boots. Climbers start with 1 foot on the ground and, when reaching the top, must ring a bell. Among the fastest climbers in the 1970s were L. Downing and D. Carpenter of Castle Rock.

Vertical chop – the contestant must cut at least halfway through 1 side of a 12in. log, shift positions and finish the cut from the other side. The chopping log is generally secured by clamps set on a 26in. high chopping stand. The leading specialist in this event is B. Bosworth (USA).

Underhand chopping (also called *horizontal chopping*) – the contestant stands on a turned log 12-14in. in diameter and chops halfway through one side then turns around and cuts through the other

side until the log breaks in half. The axe weighs 6lb (2.72kg). The leading specialist in this event in the 1990s was B. Miller.

Single bucking – the contestant makes a starting cut within 1½in. of an assigned mark and then must saw in half a log 6ft. (1.82m) long. using a 2-handled saw. He is not allowed any help from any 'second' or 'manager', except to have the saw oiled and put in wedges. A separate event is held for women. The best specialists are: among women – B. Boyko, among men – M. Forrester.

Obstacle pole bucking - the contestant begins by racing up a 36ft. (10.97m) pole with one end on the ground and one end suspended 5ft. (1.52m) from the ground. Having reached the end of the pole he starts a power saw, saws through an 8-in. block and races back down the pole to a designated line. The leading specialist is B. Waibel.

Hot saw – using a power saw, the contestant must cut 3 slabs off a log 24in. in diameter with 3 movements of the saw – downwards, upwards, and downwards again.

Choker setting – contestants race across a track of several dozen yards with various obstacles, e.g. running along a tree trunk which turns on hinges, jumping over a water ditch, etc.

Axe throwing – the contestant tries to hit the bull's eye of a target 20ft. (6m) away with an axe held in one hand, in both hands, with an underhand throw or an overhead throw. The target is 36in. in diameter with 5 scoring areas: A 4-in. bull's eye, and then four 4-in. rings for the center and outer areas.

Double bucking (also called *two jack bucking*) – 2 teams saw a log 20-30in. in diameter. The log is placed on a chopping stand. Among women the best specialists are J. Bradley and H. Cramsey.

Chain saw carving – carving various figures out of a log with a power saw.

546
T WORLD SPORTS ENCYCLOPEDIA

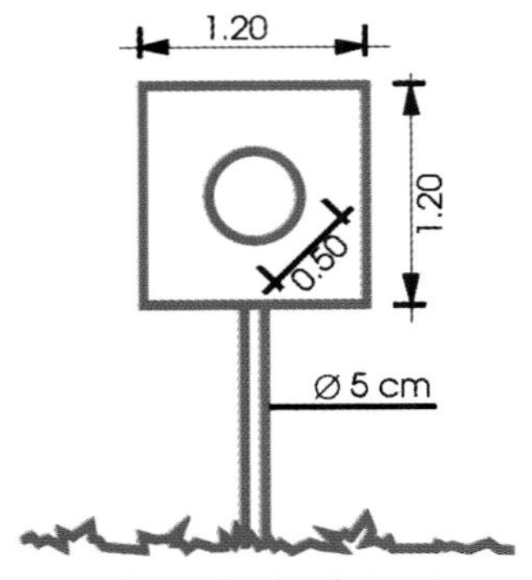

Tiro con honda – the target.

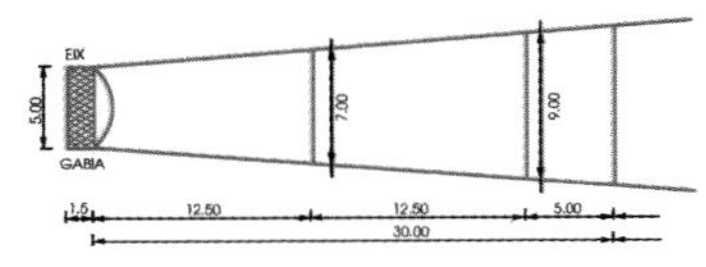
Tiro con honda – throwing area.

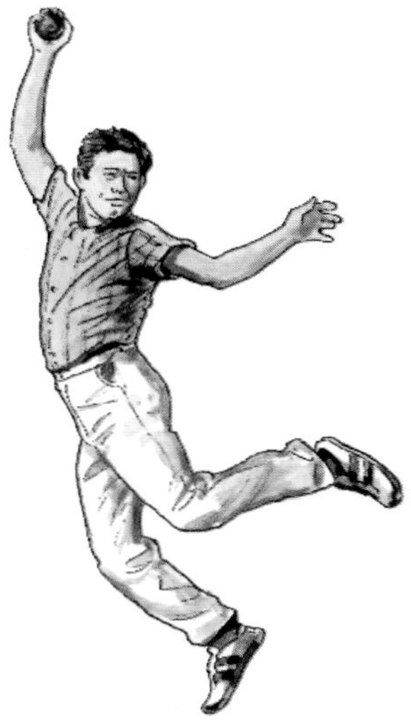
A tiro de bola player.

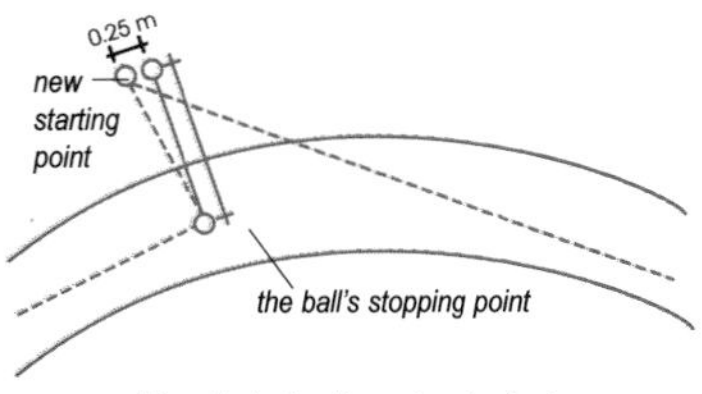

Tiro de bola: throwing technique.

Tiro de bola: throwing phase.
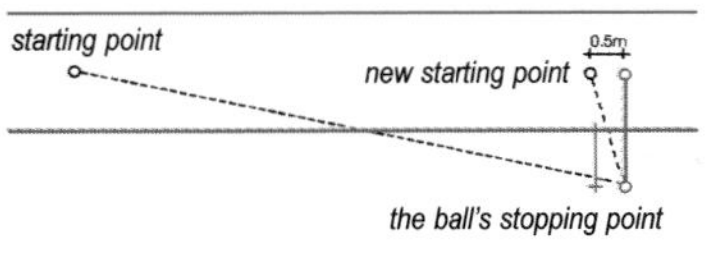

be stopped by their opponents and thrown across between any two of the holes before the player who has quitted one of them can reach the other, he is out.

[Strut, 1810, 101-102]

A Brit. scholar in trad. and children's games, A.B. Gomme, claims after her source, Kinahan, that

there is among old Irish games one sometimes called cat, played with three or more players on each side, two stones or holes as stations, and a lobber, but the regular cat is played with a stick four inches long, bevelled at each end, called the cat. This bevelled stick is laid on the ground, and one end hit with a stick to make it rise in the air, when it is hit by the player, who runs to a mark and back to his station. The game is made by a number of runs; while the hitter is out if he fails three times to hit the cat, or if he is hit by the cat while running.

In the Dorset var. of tip-cat the tapered peg was called a *kitten*, while the longer stick used for batting was called a *cat*, and the whole game was referred to as *cat-and-kitten*. In Somerset the same game was called *stik'n snael*, or – in modern Eng. spelling – *stick and snell*. In Britain's northern shires the game was also known as *trippit and coit* and *trippit and rack*.
History. The game was probably introduced in England in the 14th cent. and reached its greatest popularity in the 18th cent. and the first half of the 19th cent. It was most commonly played in the streets and squares of large cities, but increasing traffic soon hindered its development and it was officially banned in London at the end of the 19th cent. It survived longer in the provinces, but even there it had to make way for more attractive forms of modern sports. The main advantage of games similar to tip-cat was that they could be easily arranged and the equipment to play them could be obtained at almost no cost, which proved important for youngsters of limited means. The 1835 Parliamentary Bill on Municipal Reform gave the local authorities the right to provide for public recreation grounds. Although executed slowly and with some reluctance, it ultimately resulted in establishing a significant number of public grounds and playing areas, which – however – were not fit for tip-cat. At the same time increasingly cheaper sport equipment, esp. for football, almost completely eliminated the game. See also similar games of other nations: Arab >AL-BA' 'A; Indon. >TAK KADAL; Pak. and Ind. >GULLI DUNDA; Pol. >KLIPA, >SZTEKIEL, >KICZKA; Chin. >FLYING CUDGELS.

TIRO CON HONDA, throwing with a *honda*, i.e. a sling, [Span. *tiro* – to throw, cast + *con* – with + *honda* – an elastic strap or string device resembling a sling or Pol. >WIUCHA]. A Span. trad. sport of casting stones at a target with the help of a string or leather strap loop, practiced mainly on the Balear Islands. According to the rules the material for the loop must be of plant or animal origin; no synthetics are allowed. The loop is formed by a double bending of the string at the length of approx. 100cm. The caster places a stone at the bend, grasps both ends of the string, and begins to swing it. One end of the string has a small loop for the index finger, while the other end has a knot and is held in the hand. Both the loop and the knot prevent the string from slipping out of the hand. The rotation of the string produces a centrifugal force, which – when the knotted end of the string is let free – shoots the stone towards the target. The stones used for casting are natural stones of an unspecified size. The casting area is protected by a netted goal called the *gabia*, which is 5m wide, 2.5m high, and 1.5m deep. The casting track is V-shaped, with its base the width of the goal, then expanding to the width of 7m at a distance of 12.5m from the goal and ultimately to 9m at 25m from the goal. The target is a square (120x120cm), made of boards 2cm thick, and is placed 50cm above the ground on a pole 100cm high, 3cm in diameter (when round) or 5x5cm. In the middle of it is a *diana* – a circle made of tin 1mm thick and 50cm in diameter. Hitting the *diana* scores more points than hitting the outside square (called *cuadro*). Casting is for distance measured in footsteps (*pasos*), where one *paso* is equal to 65cm. Three tournament distances are used: 30, 60, and 90 pasos. Before the standardization of regulations in 1986 all distances were measured in *brazas* (one *braza* = 167cm). Each caster is allowed 3 test shots for each distance. The caster with the largest total score wins the game. Points scored for particular distances are presented below:

Distance	Hitting the cuadro	Hitting the diana
30 footsteps	1pt.	2pts.
60 footsteps	2pts.	4pts.
90 footsteps	3pts	6pts.

The casting is usu. done in a combination of 2 distances: 30 and 60 or 30 and 90 pasos. In another type casting is complete (*hondero completo*), i.e. all

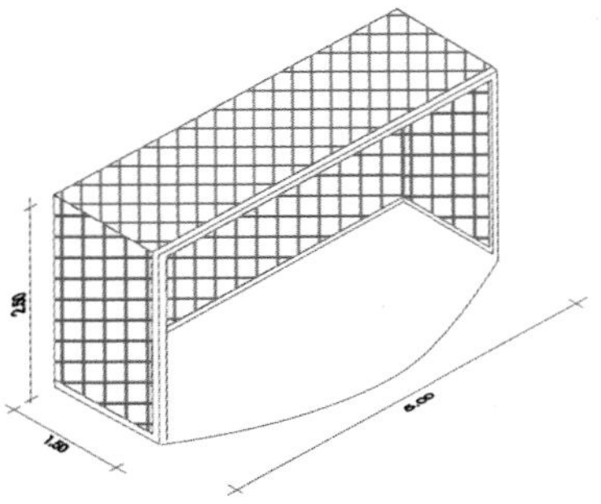
Tiro con honda – gabia.

competitors cast consecutively for all 3 distances. The type of hit is recognized by an assistant referee (*juez-árbitro*), who remains inside a protective cage placed along the target line. Final decisions, however, are made by the main referee (*juez principal*). Hits and misses are signalled by waving flags: a miss – red flag in a vertical position; incorrect hit (e.g. at the target edge) red flag in a horizontal position; hitting the *cuadro* – white flag in a horizontal position; hitting the *diana* – white flag in a vertical position. The accuracy is recognized by the judges both optically and acoustically; a stone hitting the *diana* produces a sound distinct from that of a stone striking the *cuadro*.
Competitors must wear protective head gear. Casting techniques include rotating the honda horizontally (*volteo horizontal*), vertically (*volteo vertical*), and diagonally (*volteo oblicuo*).
Besides casting for accuracy, competitions may also include casting for distance. The competitor with the longest cast is the winner and casting is usu. executed along the same track used for target casting. The stone must not fall outside of the track limits.
History. Span. historians derive the tradition of the game from the times of Phoenician migrations, which began on the island of Iviça in 654 BC. A Gk. historian Diodor of Sicily (b. c.80 BC) and a Roman chronicler Titus Livius (b. 59 BC) note a similar type of stone casting. The honda was used in the Span. army for military purposes until the end of the Renaissance. It survived even longer among the shepherds, who used it for casting stones at the cattle going astray from the desired direction. Currently the sport is governed by regulations issued in 1986 by the Balearic Tiro con Honda Federation (Federacion Balear de Tiro con Honda). Cf. >SLING SHOOTING.
C. Moreno Palos, 'Tiro con honda', JYTE, 1992, 65-8.

TIRO DE BARROT, a Span. sport of casting a metal bar for distance, [Span. *tiro* – to cast + *barrot* – a bar]. The bar is 6cm in diameter, 60-70cm long, and weighs at least 15kg. It is held in the middle, perpendicular to the ground, and with one hand only. To gain momentum competitors are allowed to take 3 swings, while their legs remain inside special footholes separated by a distance of 25-30cm. The competitor must not remove his feet from the footholes until he has completed his cast. In order for the cast to be legal, the bar must touch the ground vertically, which is acknowledged with a cry of 'Tiro!' The distance is measured from the center of the line between the caster's feet to the bar's landing spot. Each competitor has 3 attempts and if none succeeds in obtaining a *tiro*, the longest cast determines the winner. The game is best known in the area of Valencia. In the town of Tipica en Calles it is part of the local festival in honor of St. Anthony del Porket. It is often one of the events in the competitions between the married and unmarried men.

TIRO DE BOLA, a trad. Span. (Aragonian) sport of casting for distance a light metal ball along a road, [Span. *tiro* – to cast + *bola* – a ball]. The object of the game is to cover a marked section of the road (*camina*) with a min. number of casts. Similar games are known in Great Britain (>ROAD BOWLING), the Netherlands (>KLOOTSCHIEN), and Germany (>KLOOTSCHIEßEN, >BOSSELN) and were once practiced according to local rules with balls of different weights. Currently tiro de bola is played according to a uniform set of rules fixed by the Federation of Aragon Sports (Reglamento de Tiro de Bola). The ball weighs 1,679g and has a diameter of 77mm for competitors over 18 years of age. In junior categories the ball measurements are, respectively, 1,634g and 60mm (15-17yrs.), 1,000g and 45mm (12-14yrs.), 680g and 30mm (8-11yrs.). The cast is made after a run of 15-20 footsteps. At the end of the run the caster takes a swing from behind the head and shoots the ball overhead in the air. If the road is winding the subsequent casts can be made from the shoulder, which – however – is punished by subtracting 0.25m from the distance the caster has reached thus far. In such a case a line is drawn from the ball's landing spot (*punto de parada*), perpendicular to the direction of casting. The caster then selects a spot on that line and must move 0.25m back from that spot. If the road is straight but the ball strays from its limits, the competitor may return to the road to take his next cast, but is he punished by having to move 0.5m backwards. The new casting spot (*nuevo punto de tiro*) is determined by drawing a line from the ball's landing spot, perpendicular to the direction of casting, and subtracting 0.5m from the crossing of that line with the center of the road.
History. According to Span. historians the tradition of tiro de bola derives from ancient Greece. It is probably the later version of the game that is mentioned by Oribas of Perhamo (c.300 BC), who writes about casting the balls in gymnasiums for practice, but does not mention any official form of competition. The sport was continued by Roman legionnaires occupying Iberia (modern Spain), who introduced the tradition to the region. A clearly documented practice of the game in Spain comes from the 17th and 18th cent., when it enjoyed great popularity in the provinces of Valencia, Alicante, Cuenca, Albacete and Ciudad Real. Before the practice of forging metal balls became quite common in the 19th cent., players usu. used stone balls, sometimes also cannon balls. In the 20th cent., after the Civil War, tiro de bola was recognized as a folk sport, gained governmental support and developed dynamically in the years 1940-48. By the 1970s the sport was in retreat, but in the middle of the decade the local Aragon authorities (Diputación de Aragón) initiated efforts aimed at reviving the tradition. In 1983 the Aragon Sport Federation standardized the existing rules of the game and put them into Reglamento de Tiro de Bola. There is a regular league for senior and junior players, culminating in the Aragon championships, as well as various types of local events.
C.M. Palos, 'El tiro de bola', JYTE, 1992, 62-64.

TIRO DE REJA, Span. for 'casting a plowshare', [Span. *tiro* – to cast + *reja* – a plowshare]. A trad. sport once popular in the province of Albacete, in Montiel, and the province of Ciudad Real, also practiced in La Mancha (Castile) and in N Andalucia. In the area of Fiñana in the province of Almeria, Span. tiro de reja was similar to a sport practiced by Basq. miners, who also cultivated the land. The blade used for casting came from what was called in Spain a Roman plow (*arado romano*). The weight of the plowshare averages 1-15kg. The most popular style of casting is called *a pecho*, when the caster faces forward (*posición frente*), feet parallel, close to the line of casting, which must not be crossed. The caster usu. holds the upper part of the plowshare, takes a swing, turns his body to the back (*giro de tronco*), and finally thrusts it forward, shooting the plowshare parabolically off into the air. The caster must not raise either foot off the ground although he is allowed to move them. The longest cast determines the winner.
C. Moreno Palos, 'Tiro de reja', JYTE, 1992, 65; R. Garcia Serrano, 'Tiro de reja', JDTE, 1974, 64.

TISSY BALL, a simple Eng. children's ball game, in which a ball is thrown into the air and must be caught. The number of times it is caught determines the length of one's life. In some areas it was simply called 'ball'. See also >BALL DIVINATION.
TGESI, 1894, I, 13.

TITI TOREA, a game of skill played with wooden sticks by the Maori population of N.Zealand. The name is an abbr. of *titi to ure* – a Maori curse, also spelled *tidi toureta*. It is also referred to as *e papa waiari* – sighing and grieving, from the opening words of a love song that accompanies the con-

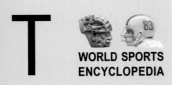

test. One can imagine a boy courting a girl showing off for her, playing with the sticks or war clubs, while serenading her with this song. Today, when the sport is practiced mainly to maintain the tradition or as a tourist attraction, the song has little relation to the game:

Sighing and grieving,
This is what I do,
This is what I do.
These are my tears of adversity.
(chorus) Alas!
Alas! The pain is killing me!
Oh maiden, come back to me.
I will count your footsteps,
(chorus) O yes!
O yes, I will count them,
O yes, I will count them
(chorus) Forever!
Forever will I direct my thoughts, my love,
To you, to you, to you.
Yet not a thought is spared
for me, my beloved.
E papa waiari
Taku nei mahi,
Taku nei mahi
He tuku roimata
E aue!
E aue! Ka mate au!
E hine! Hoki iho ra,
Maku e!
Maku e! kaute o hikoitanga
Maku et! kaute o hikoitanga

The game. There are 4 wooden sticks, 16-20in. (40-50cm) long, 1-1¼in. in diameter, 2 for each player. The contestants sit facing each other, at a distance of about 1m. Players play in pairs or all players play together, when there are many pairs (sometimes up to 40) sitting opposite one another. But each player plays against the one sitting opposite him, never against the pairs sitting next to him. At the beginning of the game the sticks are held separately, one in each hand and touching the ground. The 'conductor', sitting on the side, utters a command: 'Kia rite!' (Ready!). A sequence of movements with the sticks are made in time with the song. First the players hold the sticks vertically on the ground, then they twist them like screws. They lightly strike their sticks against those of the partner, cross their sticks with the partner's sticks, and finally both partners begin to throw their sticks back and forth. The throws are made simultaneously, always with the left hand. The opponent's stick must also be caught with the left hand. The sticks pass in mid-flight so the players must be careful to throw them so that they do not collide in mid-air; the players usu. agree beforehand to throw slightly to the right. The object is not to knock the opponent's sticks over but to wait for the moment when the opponent is unable to catch the stick thrown to him.
In the next phase the game is played with the sticks joined along their axis and held by both hands. After the 'Ready!' command the players take turns putting their sticks together and then touching the ground with them, on both sides of the opponent. Next the players throw their sticks lightly up and catch them in the air by their ends, alternating the ends at each throw.
In the final phase, signaled by the shout 'Hurihuri!', which symbolizes the counting of the beloved's steps, the tempo picks up and catching the sticks becomes increasingly difficult. The movements are made in the following fixed sequence: the opponents make twisting movements with single sticks on the right; hit the sticks against each other; touch the ground with their ends, and twist them like screws, first separately and then while holding them together, each player rotating his right stick opposite the right stick of his opponent. The sequence is then repeated on the left side. When the second series of movements is completed, a third , also repeated twice, begins: each player taps his sticks, then drills them into the ground – first separately, then jointly. In the final sequence the players are tapping with both sticks joined together against the ground – the resulting sound signals the end of the game.
In a 2-pair game the players form a square, in which the partners face each other diagonally so that the sticks' trajectories cross. To avoid collision, a 'shift displacement' technique is used, e.g. when one pair screws the sticks into the ground with single turns, the other does the same with double turns. In this

way stick exchanges in the air are synchronized and take place in turn, rather than simultaneously.
In all var. of titi torea the common feature is an airborne exchange of objects between the participants. In the oldest var. long sticks resembling spears were thrown. Men, standing in 2 rows, would throw a vertically-held spear. A player who failed to catch the spear dropped out. The last player to remain in the game was the winner. Presently, instead of the spear, players throw a rugby ball.
A. Armstrong, *Games and Dancing of the Maori People*, 1986, 27-32.

TLACHTLI, also *hachtli*, a type of ball game practiced by the Aztecs. The name comes from the Aztec dialect of Nahuatl and means 'ballcourt'. Tlachtli is one of many var. of ritual ball games of the precolumbian peoples of C America. The Aztecs, who conquered the territories between Mexico City, Guatemala and the Yucatán, probably took the game over from the native peoples who occupied the lands before them. At the time of the Span. conquest in the 16th cent. the aztecs were a dominating people in C America and it is their descriptions of tlachtli that were preserved in sources written by Span. conquistadors and monks, thanks to which our knowledge of tlachtli is greater than that of other ball games of the region. Tlachtli seems to have incorporated many elements of games that were played there earlier, such as >POKYAH or the Zapotec >TALADZHI (see also >MESOAMERICAN INDIAN BALL GAMES). All of these games have much in common, were played on similar or identical fields, taken over, developed, or redesigned by subsequent peoples that dominated the region. Another common feature of those sports was their religious nature: they were ritual games, described in various Eur., esp. Span., sources as 'holy ball games'. They may have been, according to some scholars of C Amer. culture, a reflection of the myth of the battle between the sun and the stars or the conflict between particular local deities and the sun. Their relation with the cult of the sun is observed quite clearly in the modern games which follow the old traditions, esp. different var. of >FIREBALL, such as >PELOTA PURHEPÉCHA ENCENDIDA (see >PELOTA PURHEPÉCHA). They were also connected with human sacrifices offered to the deities, esp. sacrifices of blood or the heart torn out of a live man. Within the Aztec culture sacrifices were offered at the end of a game to a God named Huitzilopochtli.
The object of the game was a solid ball made from natural caoutchouk. The pitches that survive are surrounded by stone walls and, from a bird's eye view, are H-shaped with a 'double hyphen'. In the middle of both lines of the 'double hyphen', suspended

vertically several meters above the ground, were 2-stone, netless rims. Such pitches were built not only in C but also in N.America, which is indicated by archeological discoveries in Arizona and New Mexico (USA). The idea of the game was to shoot the ball through the opponent's rim. The ball could be hit only by the hips, driven close to the ground in a unique squat jump, although some researchers believe that players could also use elbows and knees. Catching the ball or throwing it with the hands was forbidden. Descriptions made by Span. colonists and reliefs on the walls of Aztec buildings allow for at least a partial reconstruction of the ritual connected with the game of tlachtli. The game could be played only by spiritually pure warriors, who on the eve of the game kept guard around the pitch, fumigated their uniforms and the ball, and performed other purifying actions. On the day of the game spectators took their seats on the walls surrounding the pitch, while the player-warriors, divided into 2 teams, gathered at the farthermost opposite ends of the pitch. As seen in the reliefs or drawings, the points scored by the teams were announced by displaying grass leaves – natural green for one team and dyed black for the oppo-

WORLD SPORTS ENCYCLOPEDIA

T

Titi torea.

nents. We do not know the exact rules, whether the game was played until a 'big' point was scored by shooting the ball through the rim, until a designated number of points were scored, or until a designated time passed. Points could be scored when the opponents hit the ball outside of the pitch, but we do not know the significance of points scored by hitting the ball through the rim, which was much more difficult than scoring through the opponent's error. The game must have been long and exhausting, for some sources mention the death of players from physical waste. The game often ended with a human sacrifice offered in a special religious ceremony. According to Mexican scholars, it was the captain of the winning – not losing – team who was sacrificed. They claim that the Aztec tradition considered 'decapitation after the game as the apotheosis of human sacrifice. Although some speculate that the captain of the winning team was given the honor to sacrifice the captain of the losers, such idea of sacrifice as punishment seems to be a product of Western thinking and disagrees with recent studies.' (A. Caso, T. Gutierez, *El deporte prehispanico*, 3rd ed., 1967, p. 29). Another scholar, E. Matos Moctezuma, is more cautious:

During an annual festival known as panquetzaliztli, four captives were sacrificed in the Teotlachco, or ballcourt. Two were sacrificed in honor of Amapam, and the other two were sacrificed in honor of the god Oappatzan.

['The Ballcourt in Tenochtitlan', E.M. Whittington, ed., *The Sport of Life and Death: The Mesoamerican Ballgame*, 2001, p.91]

T WORLD SPORTS ENCYCLOPEDIA

J.B. Osendine, *American Indian Sports Heritage*, 1988; R.L. Humphrey, *Play as Life – Suggestions for a Cognitive Study of Mesoamerican Ball Game, Play as Context*, ed. A. Taylor Cheska, TAASP, 1980.

TO MAND FREM FOR ENKE, Dan. for 'two boys step forward for a widow', [Dan. *to* – two + *mand* – man + *frem* – forward + *for* – for + *enke* – widow]. A Dan. game in which pairs of runners line up one after another. In front of them, facing forwards, stands a 'widow', whose task is to catch the runners. The widow claps his/her hands and utters the phrase which gives the game its name. Upon this the last pair separates and runs along each side of the line in an effort to take a place in front of the widow. The widow, being passed, tries to catch one of the runners to be her 'husband', before they can join hands again. If the widow succeeds, she teams up with the runner she has caught, while the other runner becomes the widow. Otherwise, she tries her luck with the next pair, etc.

J. Møller, 'To mand frem for enke', GID, 1997, 2, 65.

Toad in the hole.

TOAD IN THE HOLE, an Eng. pub game of casting a heavy brass ring at a hole in a box placed on 4 legs, similar to Fr. *jeu de grenouilee*, Span. LA >RANA, Port. *jogo do sapo*, and Flem. >PUDEBAK.

Description. The table for toad in the hole is about 15in. across and 24in. long. The playing surface slopes towards the players who stand behind a line 8ft. from the front of the board. In the center of the table is a hole of about 2in. in diameter through which the toads can fall. Each of the 4 toads is about 1in. in diameter and is traditionally made from brass although other materials such as hardwood or rubber can be used. In some versions, players simply throw coins at the board. Scoring can be recorded in any fashion but the use of a cribbage board is recommended since cribbage boards are both trad. and practical.

The Play. A coin is tossed to decide who throws first. Each player then takes it in turns to throw all four toads at the board, scoring 1pt. for each toad lying completely flat on the surface of the table and 3pts. for each toad in the hole. Good players tend to land the toad flat just in front of the hole so that it slides in rather than aiming directly for the target. Should any player manage to throw all 4 toads in the hole in one turn, he is immediately the outright winner of the game. Otherwise, the winner is the first player to score exactly 31pts. However, if a player should exceed 31pts. in a turn, then the points for that turn, instead of being added, are deducted from that player's score.

The Internet: Masters Games: www.mastersgames.com

TOBOGGANING, riding on a tobbogan [Eng. *toboggan* <Fr. Can. *tabagane* <Fr. Indian *tabagun* <Ind. *mikmak odobaggan* – a type of winter sled]. In its sport form tobogganing includes races of dog teams [>SLED DOG RACING] or reindeer teams pulling tobbogans, or downhill races on a >SKELETON. Separate events are held for mountain rescue

Joe Appel, front, Sara Needleman, center, and Lynn Sullivan, all of Portland, Maine, speed down the chute at the National American Toboggan Championships

squads, in which the practical use of a toboggan for transporting the injured is tested.

History. The oldest form of tobogganing involves races of husky or reindeer teams, driven by single riders and held among the Innuits and Algonquins. Similar forms of cempetition were also known among the Siberian Yakute and Samoyeds [>SIBERIAN SLEDGE RACING]. However, the use of a toboggan for sport purposes has yet to develop on a large scale. Toboggan races were popular among the pioneers during the Alaskan gold rush of 1880-98, and throughout tobogganing history, races have often been held locally. Recently races of dog teams (both in a winter and summer var.) have gained more international interest, though only once did they find their way into the olympic program: toboggan races for teams of 7 dogs were a regular event during the 1932 games in Lake Placid. The gold medal for the quickest run over an 81-km track went to S. Goddard of Canada.

Ever since an Englishman named Shild constructed a skeleton in 1894, skeleton downhill races, similar to sledge races, though characterized by greater speeds obtained on ice tracks by much heavier skeletons, have gained increasing popularity. Skel-

eton races were an Olympic event in 1928-48. Stricter requirements for skeleton tracks are the reason why most Eur. events are held in St. Morritz, which is also the home of the International Toboggan Club functioning under the auspices of the International Federation of Bobsled and Tobogganing (Fédération Internationale de Bobsleigh et de Tobogganing, FIBT) founded in 1923.

TODORICA, see >KUSHIYA.

TOLI, also *kapucha toli* (stickball), a N.Amer. Ind. game, called 'little brother of war' by many tribes. It derives from the same family of games as >BAGATAWAY and >TEWAARATHON, which – in one way or another – were archetypes of the Can. national summer sport >LACROSSE. Similar games are played under various names among the Creek and Cherokee (see below), but the most popular var. is Choctaw toli. The game is played by 2 teams of 30-40 players, each having 2 sticks called *kapucha*. The field is 100yds. (91.14m) long. The duration of the game is divided over four 15-min. periods, which is probably the influence of >AMERICAN FOOTBALL. The ball, called *towa*, is a small stone or a round, grounded piece of rock covered with soft material and seamed with leather. A *kapucha* is 0.75-1m long and made of hickory. On one end it has a handle wrapped in a leather strap for a better grip, while on the other – a rounded frame slightly bigger than the ball. The frame is made from the same stick whittled to a smaller diameter and dipped in hot oil to make it flexible for bending. It has 2 leather straps running across and slightly concave to stop the caught ball. The object of the game is to move the ball into the opponent's goal. The goal is 13ft. (3.96m) high with poles 9in. (22.86cm) in diameter and no crossbar. The distance between the posts varies according to different regions. Points can be scored by throwing the ball into the goal with the sticks or by touching either goalpost with the sticks while holding the ball in them. Touching the ball with one's hands is forbidden. At the begining of each period and after each goal the game starts in the middle of the field. The rules are basic: there are no out-of-bounds, time-outs, fouls, free kicks, off-sides, or extra point kicks. One may only tackle the person who has possession of the ball and body checks are legal. Besides Choctaw toli, there are other var., which have slightly different rules:

Cherokee toli is played with 1 stick instead of 2. One may catch and carry the ball with one's hands. The goal's inside diameter is about 2m. To score a point the player holding the ball in his hands or in his stick must run through the goal and return through it to the field. The latter poses extra difficulty, as the de-

Tim Cook of Kennebunkport, Maine, braces himself as his team's toboggan starts to flip at the end of a run at the National American Toboggan Championships.

fenders chasing the scorer are usu. crowded inside the goal. Body checks are legal, as is stopping the attacker by catching him. Cherokee toli is not as well developed and organized as Choctaw toli. It is usu. played once a year by a few teams from various Cherokee tribes and reserves.

Creek toli is played by the Creek Indians. Its distinctness is featured by much stricter rules on tackling. Instead of a 2-pole goal there is 1 pole 5-10m high placed in the middle of the field. To score a point a player must strike the ball against the upper part of the pole (the top 60cm), which is painted blue and has an animal skull on the top. Hitting the skull also scores a point. The game lasts until one team has scored 4pts. The ball is slightly smaller than in other var. of toli. The game may also be played by women, who do not use sticks, however.

History. The game has been played for at least 400yrs. It had once been used to settle disputes between different tribes and often involved hundreds of players per team. Such games were played on fields several miles long and often lasted from dawn to dusk. After it lost its significance in the 2nd half the 19th cent., it was revived in the 20th cent. as a sport competition. Once a year, in mid-July a large tournament is held, in which teams from almost all Choctaw reserves compete, and which is witnessed by thousands of spectators.

The Internet: http//www.uga.edu/~toli/

TOLVBOLD, Dan. for 'a ball of twelve', [Dan. *tolv* – twelve + *bold* – a ball]. A form of children's street game, in which 1 player stands in the middle of a square, throws a rubber ball into the air and strikes it with a round stick flat at one end. The remaining players try to catch the ball and throw it back to the batter. Catching the ball from the air scores 12pts. and allows the catcher to take the batter's position. If a ball bounces off a roof, a wall or any other object and is caught, the catcher scores 6pts. If the ball bounces off the ground or is picked up from the ground before it stops, the catcher scores 1pt. The catching players may interfere with one another. Points are awarded only after the catcher throws the ball back to the batter. If, however, the ball is intercepted by another player before it reaches the batter, that player is allowed to throw it towards the batter, for which he scores 1pt. The batter is also allowed to catch the ball and the points he scores can be used by him after he becomes a catcher. If the ball is batted out of bounds, all players may chase it and the player who gets to it first has the right to bat it from the center as if he has scored 12pts. All points he has scored so far, however, are cancelled and may not be stored for next rounds.

J. Møller, 'Tolvbold', GID, 1997, 1, 67.

TOMANDSBOLD, see >TYSKBOLD.

TOMIKI, a Jap. martial art which derives from the school of >AIKIDO with an additional element of combat with the use of a knife. It was named after its creator K. Tomiki (1900-79), a student of M. Ueshiba since 1926, from whom he received 8th dan, the highest distinction available. The great multitude and dispersion of various schools of aikido, which rendered the contacts between representatives of different styles virtually impossible, inspired Tomiki to form the basis of *randori* – a test match modelled after other Far Eastern martial arts, e.g. >JUDO or >KENDO. For that purpose he founded in 1960 the Japan Aikido Association.The introduction of controversial techniques, incl. the use of knives, unleashed a fierce discussion on the limits of the trad. understanding of aikido. Tomiki has had a pioneering role in popularizing aikido in the USA, where it was introduced during Ueshiba's tour of 15 Amer. states in 1952.

TØNDEBÅND, Dan. for 'a barrel rim'. A Dan. var. of a simple game of driving a wheel or rim with the use of a short stick (see >DRIVING A WHEEL). While driving the rim the player performed various artistic figures (e.g. a slalom around the rim, passing through the rim etc.).

J. Møller, 'Tøndebånd', GID, 1997, 4.

TÖÖ CHECHMEY, also spelled *töö čečmej*, a Mong. form of sexually-oriented competition in which a naked woman tries to ustrap a camel loaded down with prizes, while a man interferes with her efforts by trying to possess her. The competition has also been known among the Kazakhs and the Kirghiz.

The main figure [...] *of the competition was* [...] *a married woman with children (therefore, able to prove her ability to give life), almost naked. Her task was to unstrap a great number of fine knots with which a camel was tied to a pole driven into the ground. On the animal's back was a load of precious commodities, such as carpets, clothing, jewelry etc. The woman, in a squatting position, was striving to untie the knots, which usu. took her about 15-40min. If she succeeded, she could take the camel with her to her yurt, where she could put on her clothes. In another form of the competition the woman, called 'a mare', was accompanied by a naked man, called 'a colt'. The woman's task was to untie a rope, while a man tried to interfere with her efforts and imitated the colt's sexual acitivity. The woman defended herself with her legs, imitating the movements of a mare. If her defense was successful and she managed to unstrap the camel, she took the camel – with all the goods – as a prize. Otherwise, the camel went to the man. If the outcome was undecided, the woman took the camel and the man went away with its load. From time to time the woman would turn towards the spectators and – pointing towards her abdomen – she explained that her nudity is nothing to be ashamed of, because that part of her body gave life to all the people on Earth, incl. such heroes as Manas, Almambet, Shabdan, and others.*

The game probably originated in the times of Genghis Khan, when women captured in the territories conquered by the Mongols were given a chance to regain freedom.

I. Kabzinska-Stawarz, 'Competition in Liminal Situations', p. II-III, EP, 1993, XXXVII, 1; 1994, XXXVIII, 1-2.

TOPS, a form of entertainment popular in many countries and in various cultures, the main idea of which is to spin a wooden, inversely conical or ring-like, pointed object. The top is kept spinning with a small, leather whip or piece of string employed to touch it up. In the process the string coils around the upper part of the top. When the string (or whip) is pulled back it makes the top spin faster depending on the force applied. There are also other var. of tops. In N.Zealand, there is a Maori type of top which is spun in the air on 2 pieces of string permanently attached to the top's surface (>POTAKA). On Torres Islands, located between New Guinea and the Austrl. Cape York Peninsula, large tops resembling huge grave candles in bowls are spun with a thin stick inserted in the middle of the top surface of such a top. Tops come in various shapes, most frequently, however, they resemble an inverse cone with convex sides. The upper part of a top is usu. most diversified and sometimes it looks like a spire and sometimes is the widest part of the top with special grooves to make it easier for a piece of string to coil around it. The sizes of tops are also different. Tops are from a few to a several dozen centimeters high and despite being generally conically-shaped, they look like either thin, regular cones or like swollen cones or simply like rings with a pointed bottom and a peg attached to the top used to spin it. In the past tops were made of wood or several layers of cardboard glued together and more recently of plastic. There are also playing tops that emit sound when spinning. The sound is made by the air flowing through openwork elements. They are also used as children's toys that are put in motion by a special handle with a long screw or screw-like metal band which spins the top when pressed or pumped. Some such tops even feature a hollow chamber beneath transparent colored plastic, in which sparks are emitted as the top spins.

History. Some historians date tops back to ancient China where they are still immensely popular, esp. among the Yao people. Major tops competitions are held on Chin. holidays, simpler street competitions that were very popular until recently are being replaced by other, chiefly western, sports. Tops has been also well-liked in Japan where it has evolved into a particular kind of art (>KOMA). Tops is a major sport and an art in many Asian countries (e.g. Malaysia, Singapore). A Singaporean, Chiang Leng Un, is one of the most outstanding tops players in the world. There were numerous types of tops in Africa such as *umusongwa* and *irehe*, as reported by various ethnographers. Until recently, the tradition of tops was cultivated with extreme care in Rwanda.

Tops have been known in Europe since ancient times as the Gk. >STROBILOS or >STROMBS or the Latin *turbo* or >BUXUS. There are numerous mentionings of the ancient Gk. and Roman var. of tops in the works of authors such as Plato, Virgil and Ovid. The Jews have played tops during the Hannukah since the biblical times. The tradition is still alive among Jewish children as >DREIDEL GAME. In continental and N Europe tops have been known since the Middle Ages when they enjoyed extreme popularity and appeared in various forms in Romance, Germanic and Slavic countries. This is best exemplified by the tops terminology preserved in many Eur. languages including, among others, the Fr. *toupie*, Port. >PIÃO, Ital. *trompo*, Span. *trompo* (particularly popular in Andalusia), and also Span. *repión* (more typical of the W parts of Spain such as Estremadura), Du. *drijftol*, Ger. *Kreisel*, Dan. >TOPSPIL, modern Gk. *sboura*, Norw. *snurrebass*, Swed. *snurr*, Hung. *csiga* or *búgócsiga*, etc. According to an Eng. writer W. Hone, who traveled in France, there was an old medieval Easter custom in Paris in which choir boys drove a spinning top across a church. Driving a top through the medieval streets of Rome was a popular custom observed towards the end of the Carnival on Shrove Tuesday and introduced during the reign of Pope Paul II (1464-71). According to Brady's *Clavis Calendaria*, a similar Shrove Tuesday custom was allegedly observed but discontinued in England.

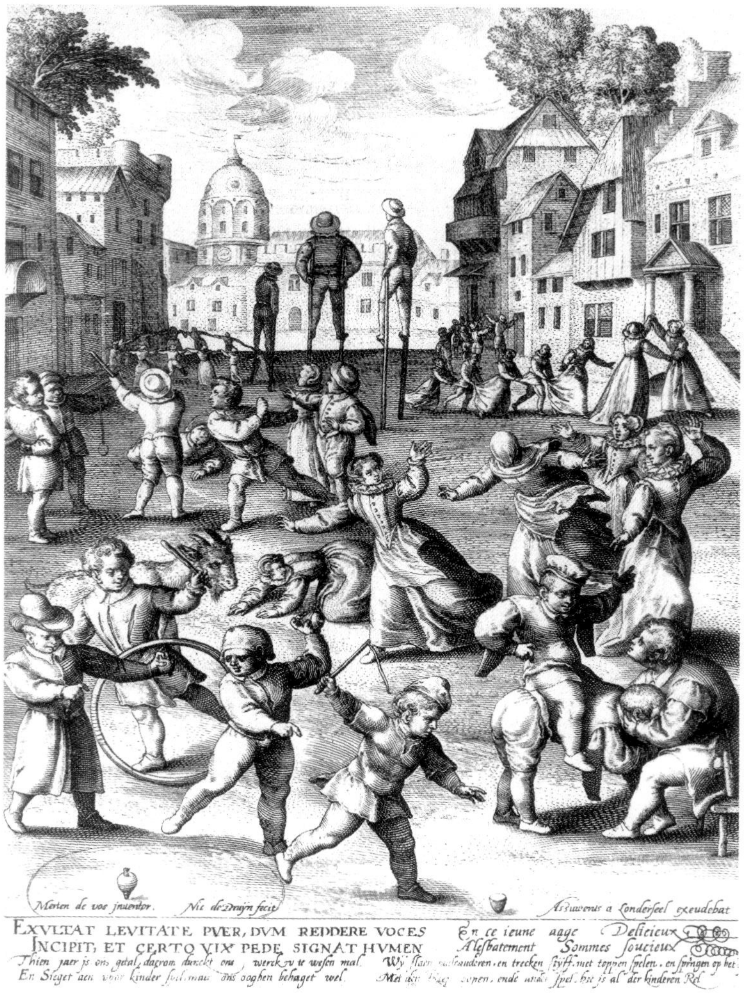
EXVLTAT LEVITATE PVER, DVM REDDERE VOCES
INCIPIT, ET CERTO VIX PEDE SIGNAT HVMEN
Nicolas de Bruyn & Assuerus van Londerseel, after Martin van de Vios, Xjaer, *from a* Period of Life, *c.1600, copperplate.*

Tops require a smooth and even surface and therefore were originally practiced indoors on the floor. The game reached the peak of its popularity when street surfaces began to be covered with asphalt which constituted an ideal surface for spinning a top. Then, tops became more of a street rather than an indoor game. At some point in time there were special carpenter's shops which specialized in the manufacture of tops. Increased vehicle traffic drove the players out of the streets which, coupled with a rapid development of other forms of entertainment for the young, esp. computer games, resulted in the fact that tops rapidly lost their popularity and appeal, though this process began as early as the mid-1960s.

Tops in English culture. Many var. of tops were popular in Ang.-Sax. culture. The most popular were: the peg top – a standard spinning top propelled with a whip; the string-wound top – resembling an upside-down pear with a sharp tip, set in motion with the use of a thin string wound around the lower part, usu. along special shallow grooves cut in the surface; and the whistling top – a large one with wholes in its upper part which produced a characteristic

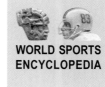

T

WORLD SPORTS ENCYCLOPEDIA

whistle while the top was in motion. This last type was improved in modern times, acquiring metal construction and a spiral handle driven inside the center of the top.

One of the oldest var. of tops, often mentioned in literary works, is parish top. In Shakespeare's *Twelfth Night*, Sir Toby Belch refers to his niece's suitor as 'a coward and a coystril that will not drink to my niece till his brains turn o'the toe like a parish-top' (I, 3). Other references to parish top can be

David Schleuen after Daniel Chodowiecki, Six Boys With Tires, Top, Marbels and Kites, *copperplates from* Elementarwerk für die Jugend und ihre Lehrer und Freunde gesitteter Stände, *1770.*

found in *New Inn* (staged in 1629, published in 1631) by B. Jonson (around 1572-1637): 'A merry Greek, and cants in Latin comely, spins like the parish-top' (II, 5), and in a play *Thierry and Theodoret* written in 1621 by F. Beaumont, P. Massinge, and J. Fletcher:

My life upon it, that a boy of twelve,
Should scourge him hither like a parish top
And make him dance before you.

[II, 2]

Tops were sometimes called town top, as can be observed in *Night Walker* by the same authors: 'And dances like a town top, and reels and hobbles' (I, 1), as well as in R. Dodsley 18th-cent. *Grim the Collier of Croydon*: 'Every night I dream I am a town-top, and that I am whipt up and down with the scourage stick of love' (XI, 206).

According to A.B. Gomme, the names town top and parish top, 'seem to refer to a custom of keeping tops by a township or parish' (TGESI, II, 301). Perhaps the intention was to provide the parishioners or townspeople with some entertainment. Indeed, G. Steevens (1736-1800), a researcher of Shakespeare's works, seems to corroborate such a theory, suggesting that: 'this is one of the customs now laid aside: a large top was formerly kept in every village,

to be whipt in frosty weather, that the peasants might be kept warm by exercise, and out of mischief, while they could not work.' However, an equally plausible theory claims that the names 'town' or 'parish' could refer to a zone, usu. circular, outside of which the top could not be whipped. A similar usage of the word 'parish' is found in >CURLING, where it indicates a circular field within which stones shifted on ice are supposed to come to rest. The fact that tops should be spun within a limited area is also substantiated in a rhyme quoted by an Eng. writer and satirist, W. Hone (1780-1842), in his *Every day Book*:

Tops are in, spin 'em agin;
Tops are out, smuggin' about.

The hierarchy of street games in 19th-cent. England was succinctly articulated by an adolescent Londoner, quoted by A.B. Gomme: 'Marble furst, then comes tops, then comes kites and hoops' (TGESI, II, 302). A special var. of tops was 'the totum' also known as 'tee-to-tum', or hand-spun top. 'It is made of a square piece of wood or bone, the four sides being each marked with a letter, and the peg is put through a hole in the centre. Sometimes the totum is shaped to a point on the under side, and a pin fixed in the upper part, by which it is twirled round.' It was used in all kinds of lottery games, having various inscriptions on its sides. The word or a letter placed on the side which was uppermost after the top came to rest decided about the prize. The following system of letters was frequently applied: T – take it all; N – 'nikil' [from Lat. *nihil*], nothing; H – half content; P – put (you have to put in what you have taken), etc. If the upper side revealed T, the game was started from the beginning, as the winner was cleaning out the kitty. 'We played the game with children, usually at Christmas time. The players sat around the table. A pool was made, each player putting in the same amount of stakes, either pins, counters, nuts or money. One player collected the pool and then spun the tee-totum by his fingers. Whichever letter was uppermost when it stopped, the player had to obey.' [TGESI, II, 303].

The earliest mention concerning such a top can be found in *Schir As It Remembir as of Befoir* by a Scot. poet, W. Dunbar: 'He playis with totum, and I with nichell' (I, 74). There was also a little children's var. of tops known as 'scop-peril' or 'scoperel', a little top made of a horn button which was set in motion by placing a small wooden needle through its hole and spun with fingers.

A.B. Gomme, 'Tops', TGESI, 1898, II, 299-303; A.B. Gomme, 'The Totum, or Tee-to-tum', TGESI, 1898, II, 303-304, A.B. Gomme, 'Scop-Peril, or Scoperel', TGESI, 1898, II, 182; M. da Graça Sousa Guedes, 'Pião', *Jogos tradicionais de portuguese*, 1979, 43-7; J. Møller, 'Topspil', GID, 1997, 3.

TOPSPIL, a Dan. var. of >TOPS. A typical Dan. top resembles a small skittle 5-6cm high and 4-5cm in diameter. The lower, thicker part has 3 grooves for the string to set the top in motion. When tops of this kind are hit with a string, they bounce and turn around their axis, and when they stop rotating, they may be set in motion again with the string. Other tops shaped like an upside-down pear are set in motion by being wound with a string and then thrown down with the end of the string held in the hand.
J. Møller, 'Topspil', GID, 1997, 4, 111-113.

TOPUZ, a Bosnian trad. sport similar to >PALANT.

TORAN, an old Ind. type of spear excavated in the area of Harappa and Mohenjodaro, popular during the period of the Indus Valley Civilization (2500-1550 BC). It was used mainly for military purposes, but also for sport competition in casting.

TORCH FIGHTING, a trad. Kor. sport in which 2 teams face each other and cast burning torches at the opposing team, trying to force their rivals to withdraw.

TORCH RELAYS, a type of relay race, the aim of which is to carry the torch to a place where it has a symbolic function, formerly connected with religious purposes and presently mainly sporting purposes. The tradition of torch relays derives from the ancient custom of carrying a message about a victory and ceremonies of lighting a sacrificial or funeral pyre. When because of war or other disaster the holy fire of Hestia, burning in all Gk. cities, died out, fast runners were sent to bring 'new, pure' fire to the nearest temple. In time these races became ritual races to the altar with fire. The winner acquired the right to light the fire in honor of the god which was the patron of the given games: Zeus in Olympia, Apollo in Delphi etc. In Greece torch carrying was called >LAMPADEDROMIA, lit. a race with a torch; also *lampadeforia*, lit. 'torch carrying'; from the name of the torch – *lampter* or *lampas* (smaller – *lampadion*). The runner who carried the torch was called *lampadeforos* or *lampadouchos*. The runner's coach and, at the same time, judge at the races with torches, was called *lampadarchai*.

The most important *lampadeforii* included races held in Athens in honor of the goddess Pallas Athena. The race was held over the distance from the city walls to the Achedemos Grove, to the altar of Prometheus. Five teams of 40 participated. The runners ran in 5 lanes. Exchanges were made every 25m. The entire race was divided into 39 sections. The prize went to the team who first passed the torch to the priests at the steps of Prometheus's altar. Apart from Athens, similar races were held in other cities, depending on its size and local tradition, with teams of 48, 40 and 10 men participating. In Olympia *lampadedromie* were held from the first games in 776 – described by Philostratos (about 179-249 AD) in his *On gymnastics* (*Perí gymnastikes*). The race was run by the youngest pilgrims attending the games over a distance of 1 stadion. The winner acquired the right to light the torch at the altar of Zeus, which was the symbolic beginning of the games. The torch was lit in the god's temple. According to other sources the boys raced without the torch and the winner received the torch on the altar steps from the priest. Similar races were held at the Delphi games, where young runners ran over a distance of about 1.5km (from the gymnasium to Apollo's altar) and in Epidaurus a distance of about 800m (from Asclepius' altar to Apollo's altar). In ancient times, in addition to torch races there were horse races with torches, called *apipolampas* or *hippolampas*. It is not known what distances were covered. In modern times 2 scientists, I. Ketseas from Greece and C. Diem from Germany suggested that the torch should be lit by the rays of the Sun and brought from Greece to the main stadium of the games. They presented their idea at the IOC session in Athens in 1934. It was modeled on the ancient text on Numa Pompilius in Plutarch's *Parallel Lives*. Olympic torches, although not brought to the Olympic city by

The Sydney Olympics torch relay on an Australian highway (below) and under water (left).

relay runners, were lit at the Ol.G. in 1912 and then in 1928. Once the idea had been accepted by the IOC, the first torch was lit on 21 July 1936 in ancient Olympia. Then 3,075 runners covered the distance of 3,075km in 11 days and 12 nights, crossing the borders of 7 countries. The torch reached Berlin on 1 September 1936. The last runner was E. Schilgen. From that time on this ceremony has accompanied all the Ol.G. It should be emphasized that this symbol of peace was introduced to the Olympic tradition by Diem, a Nazi sports activist, during the games which historians perceive as an event at which the Olympic idea was abused to serve the purposes of Nazi propaganda.

Many cities hosting the Ol.G. tried to introduce new ideas to the torch tradition. In Tokyo the torch was lit by Y. Sakai, the last relay runner, who was born when the first atomic bomb was dropped on Hiroshima. In Mexico City the torch was lit for the first time by a woman – E. Basilo (1968). In Montreal – by a pair, a boy and a girl (1976). In Seoul, the runner with the torch climbed a platform which, as a lift, took him up to the torch bowl (1988). In Barcelona the torch was lit by A. Rebollo, a disabled wheelchair-bound sportsman, who shot a burning arrow at the bowl.

At the W.Ol.G. the torch relay appeared for the first time in Oslo (1952). The Norwegians thought their country was the home of winter sports as Greece is home of summer games. They ignored the Gk. flame and the torch lighting ceremony was arranged in the village of Morgedal in Telemark, the birthplace of S. Nordheim (1825-97), the pioneer of skiing. The torch was not lit in Olympia for the relay team going to the winter games in Squaw Valley (1960), as the Americans approached the Greeks too late to organize a trad. relay race in Greece. The Greek Olympic Committee did not agree to transporting the torch from Olympia to Athens on a vehicle. The torch was again lit in Norway and, when brought over to the Olympic stadium in Los Angeles, it was taken over by a relay team composed of 600 high school students. Near Squaw Valley the torch was taken by helicopter, and then by A. Mead-Lawrence, who won 2 Olympic golds at the 1952 games. With the torch in her hand she skied down a hill to the Olympic stadium where the torch was taken over by K. Henry, a skater, who first made a lap of the ice track and then lit the torch in the bowl on the stadium.

During the Ol.G. in Nagano the torch was lit by C. Moon from Great Britain, a member of the international peace mission who lost his right arm and a part of his right leg when disarming a mine in Mozambique. Moon entered the stadium surrounded by the children whom he had protected against the explosive mines.

TOREHORERE, a form of luge practiced by the Maori of N.Zealand on muddy slopes. See also >RETI.

TOSIYA, also called *sasiya*, one of the various schools of archery in feudal Japan, which evolved into a form that is close to the Eur. idea of archery, incl. registering records. The oldest sources speak of teaching tosiya in the Edo period (c.1600-1867) in a Buddhist temple of Sanju-Sangen-Do in Kyo (modern Kyoto). The school's growing popularity resulted in building a similar temple at Edo (modern Tokyo), surrounded by a veranda, which had a significant function in archery. The archer's task was to shoot his arrow from the southern end towards the northern end so that it travelled along the narrow western side of the veranda approx. 120m in length without touching the wall of the temple or the roof of the veranda. The shot was performed from a kneeling position. Bows were short and had a powerful draw. Arrows were also short. Many traces of arrows in the veranda's roof provide ample evidence that completing the task was quite difficult. There were several var. of tosiya, of which the most prestigious was >OYAKAZU, in which the archer must perform as many correct shots as possible within 24hrs. 12-hr. shooting was called *hiyakazu*. There were also other var., in which shooting was limited not by time, but by the number of arrows. In >SEN-CHA the archer had to shoot 1,000 arrows during one session, of which only the correct shots formed the final score. In a shorter var. called *hyaku sha* the archer had to shoot 100 arrows. For younger archers the distance was shortened to 90m and that var. was called >GO-JUKKEN. In a 'junior' var., called >HAN-DO, the distance was half of that in oyakazu, i.e. 60m.

The shooting was controlled by 2 judges. The first of them, *domi* (master of bow and arrows), checked whether the arrow travelled correctly along the wall of the veranda. If that was the case, he would wave a baton called *sirusibata*, one end of which was very richly ornamented. In order to become a *domi* one had to graduate from a 6-level school of archery called Heki. The second judge, called *kemi*, kept records of the shots rendered as correct by the *domi*. The 2 main judges were accompanied by several assistants, who controlled the correct way of kneeling, the arrow's landing spot, etc. Each of them had a *sirusibata*, with which they singalled their verdict, additionally confirmed by crying out an appropriate command. Each archer that participated in the test aimed at setting a new record. If successful, he was allowed to hang a special tablet in the temple of Sanju-Sangen-Do, which commemorated his achievement. So far there have been 3 such tablets, of which the first one commemorates a record in *oyakazu* set in 1669 by K. Hosino of the Owari family, who shot 10,542 arrows in 24hrs, of which 8,000 were rendered as correct. His record was broken in 1686 by D. Wasa, who shot 13,053 shots, of which 8,133 were successful. His record survives to this day. The third tablet commemorates a record set by some youngster in han-do. Despite its physical relation with the temple tosiya has never had the nature of a religious ritual. The sport was practiced almost exclusively by the samurai. Lower classes were limited by the costs one had to spend on the supply of arrows. However, a young man who scored a good result stood a decent chance of reaching the status of a samurai.

H. Isioka, *Kyudo-si* (in:) Y. Imamura and others, *Nikon Budo taikei*, vol. 10 *Budo no Rekisi*, 1982; S. Homma, 'Archery as Contest. The Development of Japanese Archery', PISHPES, 1991 (1993).

TOSSED BALL, an Eng. name applied to a few folk var. of a ball game known among numerous N.Amer. Natives. Some var. of tossed ball resembled Eur. children's ball games. The game consisted of passing a ball between 2 players while others tried to intercept the ball in the air. Other var. consisted of tossing up the ball and keeping it in the air as long as possible. A player was out if he missed the ball. Ball games in which the ball was caught with hands were very rare among Native Americans. G. Cartwright, who observed games played by the indigenous peoples of Labrador in 1792, judged the players as 'very bad catchers'. He stressed, however, that the natives enjoyed '...tossing the ball at pleasure from one another, each striving who should get it' (*A Journal of Transactions and Events During a Residency of Nearly Sixteen Years on the Coast of Labrador*; quot. after J.B. Oxendine, *American Indian Sports Heritage*, 1988, 63). According to early Eur. records of tossed ball, the usual size of the ball was 6-8in. in diameter.

TOSSING THE CABER, also *cabertossing*, one of the most popular trad. sports in Scotland, also practiced throughout the Commonwealth and in countries with a significant Scot. community [Scot.-Gaelic *cabar* – a pole, trunk]. The objective is to carry and toss a several-meter-long pole over the longest distance. Tossing is now the most popular form of the sport, although other var. were popular in the past, incl. carrying a pole around 'St. Catherine's circle'. The one who picked up the caber from the center of the circle, carried it around the cirle the greatest number of times, and put it back at the starting point, was proclaimed the winner.

Technique of tossing. The caber is usu. about 16-18ft. (5-5.5m) long and weighs 100-120lbs. (45-55kg). The tosser grabs it at the bottom, where its diameter is smaller, with hands clasped to form a bridge, and carries it vertically, supported with one arm, several feet to gain momentum, after which the caber is released horizontally in such a way that its top is in the front, while its bottom at the back. It's flight should be flat, which is called 'a twelve o'clock toss'. Each tosser has usu. 3 attempts. The longest toss determines the winner.

Rules of competition. All tossers use the same caber. There are no limits of the run distance or the spot from which the caber must be released. The result is measured from the front heel to the thinner end of the caber. The same caber is used for the same tournament over many years. If it needs to be replaced, its length and weight may be diminished.

History. The sport may be derived from the tradi-

tion of Scot. Highland woodcutters. Probably around the mid-18th cent. they developed a custom of individually loading the cleared tree trunks on carriages, and this soon turned into a sport competition. In the 2nd half of the 19th cent. the rapid exploitation of forests in Scotland led to a smaller demand for woodcutters and the game became a relic of a dying profession. It is currently part of the program of Highland Games and Gatherings held in many parts of Scotland, as well as among the Scottish communi-

WORLD SPORTS ENCYCLOPEDIA

T

Wayne Pogany of Lebanon, Connecticut, prepares to toss the caber, in this case, a 14-foot, 75-pound log, to qualify in the Masters Heavy Athletic Division during the 3rd Annual Southern New Hampshire Scottish Games and Celtic Music Festival held at Oak Park in Greenfield, New Hampshire.

ties in the USA and Canada. It is also a separate event of police games held in some N.Amer. states and Can. provinces.

Trad. sports modelled after tossing the caber can also be found e.g. in Portugal (*jogo do panco*) and Sweden (>STÄNGSTÖRTNING).

TOTUM, also spelled *tee-to-tum*; see >TOPS.

TOUHU, old Chin. art of casting arrows by hand into a special vase. Touhu vases were made of various materials, most often porcelain or bronze, and had a different number of apertures which had to be aimed at. The most beautifully preserved porcelain vase comes from the Kangxi period (1662-1722) during the reign of the Manchurian dynasty of Cing (1644-1911). It has only one central aperture, the upper and lower parts are ornamented with butterflies, and the neck with a dragon. The preserved bronze vases usu. have 3-9 apertures. A 3-aperture vase has 1 central and 2 side apertures, with short pipes attached to the neck. Vases with more apertures have a similar construction and each aperture had a different point or symbolic value, which is indicated by appropriate inscriptions.

History. The oldest mentions and illustrations of touhu come from the so-called Period of Spring and Fall (740-476 BC). One of the most extensive descriptions of the sport is incl. in a text entitled *Touhu Xin'ge* written in 1072 by Sim Guang. It speaks of 2

Touhu arrow vase, China, Jiangxi, Ch'ing dynasty, Kangxi period (1662-1722), white porcelain with 'famille verte' and gold highlights.

T

competitors sitting opposite one another on a floor mat and separated by a vase to which they cast their arrows. Each had an equal number of arrows and the one who placed all of his arrows in the vase won the game. The player who missed an arrow had to drink a cup of alcoholic beverage. During the Ming dynasty (1368-1644) Wang Ti (1490-1530) introduced new regulations, which included side pipes attached to the neck that could also be aimed at. In one round each player cast 12 arrows. For 2 centuries touhu enjoyed the status of a court game and was immensely popular, but since then it has been on the decline. See also >CHINESE ARCHERY.

G. André, 'Arrow Games. Hunting, Contests and War.' YOSICH, 1999, 38-41; I. Lee, 'Touhu. The Chinese Archery and Game of Pitch-Pot', *Transactions of the Oriental Ceramic Society*, 1992, 56.

TOUL AR C'HAZH, Bret. for 'cat hole', a var. of bowls, [Bret. *toul* – hole + *ar* – article + *hazh* – cat], an equivalent of Fr. *la chatière*. The essence of the game is to roll the bowl towards a hole in the track.

TOUPIE, a Fr. var. of >TOPS.

TOURIG AR PRAD, also *plantan peul er prad*, a Bret. equivalent of Fr. *poirier* (lit. 'pear' – probably from placing a pear in an upright position), a form of trad. competition in standing on one's head.

TOURISM, an active way of spending free time in the form of trips made on foot, on skis, or with the help of various vehicles, such as kayaks, canoes, rowboats, sailboats, motor boats, ships, bicycles, motorbikes, cars, etc. In order to be viewed as tourism the activity must combine elements of physical endevor (often of sports nature) and hiking and must not be job-oriented (e.g. a distinction between the participants and organizers should be apparent). A form of extreme tourism involves reaching otherwise inaccessible topographic areas. A unique form of tourism is Austrl. >BUSHWALKING.

History. The origins of organized tourism reach the Middle Ages and –according to historians – include pilgrimages to various holy places and even – to some degree – the elements of the Crusades. Modern forms of tourism were shaped in the 19th cent. and were enabled by the development of means of transportation, mostly steam propelled, such as the railroad or steam ships, which led tourist agencies to organize tourist expeditions on a large scale. The process was pioneered by T. Cook (1802-92), the founder of the first Eur. tourist agency, who in 1841 organized the first ever commercial expedition. Until around 1865 Cook's tourist offices could be found in most Eur. countries. An original form of modern tourism was >CYCLISM, originated in the latter half of the 19th cent., which later developed into bicycle tourism. The invention of an internal combustion engine at the end of the 19th cent. superseded steam engine to revolutionize individual tourism by introducing the car and the motorbike and leading to various specialized forms of motorized tourism using campers and trailers.

TOUSEG, a Bret. abbr. of *an touseg* – a toad; a var. of >VAZH A BENN, in Fr. known as *le crapaud*. A game in which 2 teams of 3 persons each try to snatch from one another a toad-shaped board (hence the name) with 2 handles. In each team 2 players join hands to form a bridge on which the 3rd

Jim Green, Official Town Crier of the Town of West Lincoln, Ontario (Canada), performing at the Unionville Festival.

Tourist cyclers pause off-road in Nova Scotia to study a map.

Tom MacMillan, Official Town Crier of Colburg, Ontario (Canada) performing at the Unionville Festival.

player lies down with his hands and legs above the ground. Both teams approach one another so that the carried players – facing each other – can grab the board by its handles and try to snatch it away from the opponent. The partners who carry them try to help by keeping them balanced. If the carried player loses his balance and touches the ground with any part of his body, the game is lost. The team that snatches the 'toad' from its rival wins the game. A Bret. scholar of trad. games, F. Peru, has put forward a claim that a real toad once used to be the object of competition, but that this practice was discontinued either for humanitarian reasons or for a lack of toads. That old tradition seems to be confirmed by the names of older var. of the game, such as >DÉCAISSER LA GRENOUILLE or *écaisser la grenouille*, which may be rendered as tearing apart toad's legs.

L. Esquieu, *Les jeux populaires de l'enfance à Rennes*; F. Peru, 'La tradition populaire de jeux de plein air en Bretagne', LJP, 1998.

TOWN CRIERS' COMPETITION, a trad. event for town criers, who are judged in 5 categories (regulations of the Ontario Guild of Town Criers): attention device (effectiveness to attract, suitability to the occasion, originality of style and device, appropriateness of device to crier, the ability to use device – max. 10pts.), deportment (confidence, appearance, appropriate movement, overall image – max. 15pts.), sustained volume (max. 20pts.), call content (adherence to required subject, effective use of appropriate language, continuity and flow, overall literary effectiveness, comprehension – max. 30pts.), clarity (enunciation, diction and phrasing, loss of voice or hoarsness – max. 25pts.).

History. The origins of the institution of town crying are not clear. Messengers of the early Gk. Empire, such as the famous Spartan runners, who ran from town to town announcing news and proclamations, are believed to have been the first town criers in history. The Romans picked up the fastest runners and used them as messengers to communicate between army commanders and battling troops. The Roman word for 'runner' is pronounced 'crier', while

the Eng. adjective 'stentorian' is derived from the Gk. herald Stentor, mentioned in the Iliad as having a voice equal to that of 50 men. The Romans have also used heralds to pronounce various news and proclamations to their citizens. In many Ital. cities today one can still find town stones or pedestals located usu. in the squares, which were once used by Roman town criers, as well as for other purposes. As the Roman Empire spread, so did the institution of town crying. According to historical documents soldiers of the 20th Roman Legion assembled in the hall of the Principia (now the Forum Arcade) in Chester, England, for a daily ear-bashing from their commanding officer. The Cross, where the 4 main streets of the Roman fortress still intersect, has been the site of public proclamations since medieval times, and remains so today. However, it was not until the era of William the Conqueror (1066-87) that a more formal system of town criers was introduced. In medieval England town criers were appointed by the civil authorities, often the Mayor, to inform the citizens of various matters – from important state business e.g. royal events, wars, executions, taxes, etc. to such trivialities as lost dogs or misdemeanors. To distinguish them from the common folk, town criers were lavishly dressed and protected by law. Any harm done to a town crier was considered an offence against the king. Apart from the loud voice, other tools of the trade include a bell and a scroll.

The coat of arms of Britain's Ancient & Honourable Guild of Town Criers.

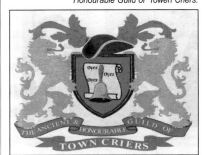

The bell was used to draw the attention of the crowd (town criers used also to be called Bellmen), although occasionally it was substituted with a drum or horn. The scroll was a convenient way of reading straight along the lines of text and after the proclamation it was often nailed to a post (hence the expression 'to post a notice'). The famous town criers' call of 'Oyez! Oyez! Oyez!' comes from Old Fr. and meant 'Listen!' or 'Hear Ye!'. The trad. conclusion of a town crier's proclamation is 'God Save the Queen! (or King)'. Today the institution is still alive, with about 200 town criers active in Great Britain alone and more in various countries such as Australia, the USA, Canada, Japan, Belgium, etc. Modern town criers are affiliated with guilds (e.g. the Amer. Guild of Town Criers, the Ancient and Honorable Guild of Town Criers, AHGTC, in Great Britain, etc.), who organize various events. The most important of them are the World Town Criers Championships held in odd numbered years, the European Town Criers Championships held in even numbered years, and the Guild Championships held annually and open only to members of the AHGTC.

TOWN-BALL, a bat and ball game played in Brit. colonies in N.America in the 17th-18th cent. Together with >BASTE-BALL, >GOALBALL, >CRICKET, >NEW-YORK-BALL, >ONE-OLD-CAT, >ROUND BALL, >ROUNDERS, >TWO-OLD-CAT, it contributed to the development of Amer. >BASEBALL. Played with 4 bases, it was a logical continuation of its predecessors, namely one-old-cat, played with one base, then two-old-cat, played with 2 bases. Town-ball was popular among the Amer. soldiers fighting for independence (1775-1783). A match played in the Valley Forge soldiers' camp on 7 April 1778 is mentioned in G. Ewing's diary. In 1787 a game of town-ball was played at Princeton university.

TRACK AND FIELD ATHLETICS, a sporting discipline including many events that are themselves separate sports. They have a common basis: the natural motions of the human body such as running, jumping, throwing and walking. The character of the individual events has changed over the centuries (see below). Until the mid-19th cent., the events that make up track and field athletics today were not a separate group of sports. When athletics started to be isolated, the modern repertoire of track and field events was not estab. all at once. In various periods and areas, sports were included that still match the spirit of athletics today but have been dropped since for various reasons, such as not being dynamic or spectacular enough, poor audience interest or low developmental usefulness etc. Today, athletics comprises track and field events. The track events (races) included are the following (with all their internal divisions into various metric and imperial distances): >ATHLETIC RUNNING with the subtypes of >SPRINT, >MIDDLE-DISTANCE RUNNING, >LONG DISTANCE RUNNING, >CROSS-COUNTRY RUNNING, >HURDLING, >RELAYS, hurdle relays, >STEEPLECHASE, and >MARATHON. The following disciplines are also athletic races despite their taking place beyond the confines of the stadium: >ROAD RACES, >JOGGING, and >SLOPE RUNNING. >ORIENTEERING events are controlled by a separate federation and are not considered to belong to the 'classical' inventory of races, as opposed to >PEDESTRIANISM, which does so, even though it is controlled by an independent professional federation. The following jumps are athletic events: >LONG JUMP, >POLE VAULTING, >HIGH JUMP, and >TRIPLE JUMP, as well as the following throws: >DISCUS THROW, >SHOT PUT, >JAVELIN THROW, and >HAMMER THROW. Multiple events are a separate category of athletics: >ALL-AROUND, >PENTATHLON, >ATHLETIC DECATHLON, and >HEPTATHLON.

History. The forms of competition that are today collectively called 'athletics' have existed since the earliest times in human history. Prehistoric cave paintings are evidence that as early as in the Lower Paleolithic (60,000-50,000 BC), Mesolithic and Neolithic periods, there were some forms of rivalry in running and throwing. However, it was only the first Mediterranean civilizations that developed more advanced forms of the would-be athletic events. The stele of Amenhotep II's (1438-1412 BC) tomb in Egypt contains the world's oldest reference to how useful the skill of running is. The Egyptians organized soldiers' races similar to the Gk. hoplite races (>HOPLITODROMO). In the Minoan culture in Crete

A javelin thrower with a trainer, a detail from a Greek vase.

and Santorin (before 1500-1400 BC), running was practiced as well as throwing the discus and javelin. The Minoan culture in Santorin was destroyed at its high point by the eruption of the volcano c.1500 BC, and the cultural heritage of the island was lost as a result. However, the athletic events survived the Achaean invasion of Crete, and we have descriptions of them in both the *Iliad* and *Odyssey*. The ancient Gk. Olympiads initially consisted mostly of running events, and the race once round the stadium marked the beginning of the development of the games (776 BC). Other sports today considered to be athletic events were parts of the >PENTATHLON (ANCIENT) in the ancient Olympics (even though, according to Homer, they were also organized independently). The pentathlon was introduced during the 18th Ol.G. in 708 BC, and included running, throwing the discus and javelin, and wrestling. When the ancient Olympics were discontinued, organized forms of athletic events in Europe died out. However, there were games organized in Ireland even earlier than that (since c.1800 BC), including events unknown to the Greeks, or not practiced by them: the pole vault, hammer throw, triple jump and a var. of the cross-country race (held independently) which was part of the fitness test of an Irish warrior. The Irish games reached their peak about the 3rd cent. BC-4th cent. AD. The typically Irish forms of competition were then transferred to N Great Britain by an Irish tribe (the Scots) who migrated to the area in the 4th cent. AD. Their sports, in spite of the nation mixing with the Picts who had inhabited the area earlier, have survived in the folk forms of the Highland Games and Gatherings. Since about the 11th cent., historical sources attest to simple types of running events in England. These were so popular in London that a suburban green was set aside for the purpose in 1154. In 1130, some sporting events, incl. races and jumps (as well as ball games) were banned by King Edward III as they pulled youths away from practicing archery. The ineffectiveness of the ban was confirmed by another edict, issued in 1414. Finally, Henry VIII allowed races to be run in London in 1510. Earlier, Pope Paul II (1464-71) allowed an annual carnival to be organized in Rome, including various types of races. These included races where the participants ran naked, in an imitation of the ancient Gk. tradition. Such contests became a lasting element of the carnival for the next 2 centuries. They may have been the first systematically organized athletic competitions of modern times (they were, after all, held every year). In 1586, the Pol. traveler M. Rywocki observed the races, and gave a description in his *Księgi peregrynackie*:

> *There is a custom in Rome that people run naked in a race. On this day, first, there were 8 naked youths running for a piece of red damask, then 7 old people ran for a piece of green damask, and an hour later 9 boys, all naked, ran for a piece of red cloth.*

At the same time Renaissance England saw numerous borrowings from Ital. culture, incl. the influence of ancient games on sport, which was well visible in the first half of the 17th cent. In 1618, King James I tried to promote taking part in sporting events after Sunday mass, issuing the famous *Book of Sports* (reissued as the *Declaration of Sports* by his son Charles I in 1633). The document mentioned 'leaping', and even though the author does not refer to other athletic events such as races or throws, we may suspect that, being the most natural forms of rivalry, they were included in the text as 'other such harmless recreation [...] and other sports therewith used'. Before the war against the Puritans was lost, R. Dover supported the King with the idea of the Ol.G., explicitly modeled on the ancient games, and organized in Chipping Campden in the Cotswolds. The games included races, the javelin throw, hammer throw and jumps. Towards the end of the 17th cent., travelling professional runners appeared in England, running set distances for time, and competing against local opponents. In 1817, the first Eng. athletic club – the Necton Guild – was estab. in Necton, Suffolk. In 1825, a competitive race was organized in Newmarket Road, Uxbridge near London, and then a similar event was held in Lord's Cricket Ground. In 1829, a tournament modeled on the old Celtic games was started in Tara, Ireland. It had a profound influence on the setting of the modern inventory of athletic events, as it included the triple jump, hammer throw and pole vault. In 1837, Eton College started organizing a 100-yd. hurdles. Sprints and steeple chases were begun there in 1843. In 1849, the Royal Military Academy started organizing a multi-event meeting at Woolwich. Since 1850, the winner of the most events in the meeting was awarded the prize of Captain E. Wilmot's Silver Bugle. This may have been the first challenge prize in the history of athletics. The meeting at Oxford's Exeter College was also initiated in 1850, including flat races with distances of 100, 330, 440yds., and 1mi., as well as a 140-yd. hurdles. In 1853, a systematic multi-event tournament was held at Cheltenham. Tournaments like these were instrumental in the setting of the modern repertoire of athletic events. Two years later, the first Eng. handbook of running training was published. In 1856, the Exeter College meeting was extended to include the whole of Oxford University. In 1857, similar tournaments were also started in Cambridge and Dublin. In 1860, Oxford initiated an athletic contest open for the students of all Brit. universities. The first match between Oxford and Cambridge took place in 1864. In 1866, the Amateur Athletic Club was estab., which in its early years functioned as an all-Eng. athletics federation. However, it excluded people who were not gentlemen, or, according to the AAC's definition, 'mechanics, artisans or labourers'. As a result of the growing interest in athletics of other social classes, the Amateur Athletic Association was set up to wipe the class division away. In 1883, the AAA already included Scotland, Wales and Ireland (in 1922, the Republic of Ireland gained independence, and a branch of the AAA was established that was separate from that for Northern Ireland).

At the same time, athletics saw rapid growth in the USA, where the Olympic Club was estab. in San Francisco in 1860. In 1868, the New York Athletic Club was set up, stressing the role of the amateur movement without class barriers. In 1896, the club organized the first indoor meeting in history. In 1876, the Intercollegiate Athletic Association was formed, organizing the first official Amer. championships. Modern Eng. athletic programs were copied in Germany (1874), where they were made popular by a group of Eng. students in Dresden.

In the 1890s, the basic repertoire of athletic events

Various track and field athletes portrayed on Greek vases.

Olympic athletes, a Greek amphora.

The ancient Olympic stadium in Athens rebuilt for the first modern Games in 1896.

T

was set. In 1892, electric time measurement for races was first introduced in England, while the concept of relay races appeared in America. The first international match between Yale University and Oxford University was held in London in 1894. The inclusion of athletics into the Olympic program in 1896 meant further stabilization of the individual events. Whether or not they were 'spectator-friendly' was the main selection criterion.

During the first modern Ol.G. in 1896, the following athletic events were held: the 100-, 400-, 800-, and 1500-m races, marathon, 110-m hurdles, high jump, long jump, triple jump, pole vault, shot put and discus throw. With time, the more static events were dropped from the program, such as the standing high and long jumps. Their fate was shared by those events where it was impossible to assess

TRACK AND FIELD EVENTS

the result at once, such as both-hands throws (where the throwers used both hands alternately, and the results were added up), as competition was not clearly visible in them. Such events were later replaced by more spectacular ones such as new flat and hurdle races. These grew in importance due to the development of new training methods and equipment, such as special running shoes (with spikes), the low start from holes in the ground and then starting blocks in sprints, improvements in the 'speed' of the track etc.

Initially, only men participated in the Olympic athletic events. In the early 20th cent., separate women's games were organized under the auspices of the Young Women's Christian Association (YWCA). In 1921, the International Federation of Women's Sport was founded, which organized the first women's Olympics the same year, including athletic events (despite the name, these games were unaffiliated with the International Olympic Committee).

The growth of international athletics accelerated with the formation in 1912 of the International Association of Athletic Federations (IAAF), which was the successor of the Eur. Athletic Federation (EAF). In 1934, the first E.Ch. were held in Turin, to be then organized regularly every 4 years in the second year after the Olympics. Between the late 1920s and early 1970s, international matches were among the most popular forms of competition. Before 1939, their role was amplified by nationalist tensions. Just like in other sports (e.g. boxing), matches between rival nations, such as Germany and France or Czechoslovakia and Poland, were used to prove the 'superiority' of one nation over the other, with frequent chauvinism (this is not to suggest, however, that all such matches were held in an atmosphere of 'warring nationalism'). After 1945, athletic matches took on a new meaning – that of ideological confrontation typical of the cold war period. Sport played a double role: it was used to propagandize one system's superiority over the other, but at the same time it served as a surrogate for international relations, which were politically hostile, and drastically limited or non-existent in such areas as economics, tourism or cultural exchange. For Eastern Bloc countries, the matches provided an opportunity to manifest in the international arena their sovereignty, which was drastically constrained in politics. This was esp. visible in matches between the USSR and USA, which enjoyed huge interest of the mass media, going far beyond the purely sportive element. The appearance of TV, especially international television organizations, with their interest in the globalization of sport, killed the tradition of matches as they did not guarantee broader international appeal. Eurovision was estab. in 1954, and Intervision (Eurovision's Eastern Bloc equivalent) was founded in 1961. The 2 organizations competed in some areas, and sport was one of the most important of them. In response to TV's demand for a tournament that would attract a majority of Eur. viewers, the Europa Cup was initiated, where 8 national teams participated in the final, with one contestant in each event. The first final of the Europa Cup was held in Stuttgart, Germany, in 1965. Eng.-speaking countries played a leading role in the development of athletics, the UK at the outset, and the US since the turn of the 20th cent. Finland achieved considerable success between 1906 and 1939, esp. in long-distance running and the javelin throw. Just prior to WWII, Germany approached the Amer. level. From the early 1950s, the Soviets could match the Americans in most events. In the early 1960s, athletics started developing rapidly in East Germany, where sport was used more than in the other communist countries to break the political isolation and demonstrate the superiority of the political system. Athletics and boxing play a similar role in Cuba even today, the only difference being that the economic resources of the USSR and GDR guaranteed a high level in the full range of disciplines, while the less-capable Cuba developed athletics gradually, first achieving good results in the sprints (A. Juantorena), and then jumping (J. Sotomayor). The proliferation of modern training methods coupled with the natural dispositions of sportsmen from various countries led to considerable changes in the 'distribution of power' in the late 1960s. Some 'Third World' countries have achieved success in certain disciplines, e.g. Kenya, Ethiopia or the Caribbean nations. This trend has been intensified by the fact that talented sportsmen from less developed countries have studied in industrialized countries (e.g. the Namibian sprinter F. Fredericks studied in the USA). Another noticeable factor has been the migration of sportsmen to Western countries where the training and living conditions are much more favorable (Caribbean sportsmen have emigrated e.g. to Canada, while some Africans – to Europe; one example is the multiple middle-distance record breaker W. Kipketer, a Kenyan by birth, who has been a Dan. citizen since 1996). However, developing nations have achieved high levels only in some disciplines, mainly running, where a complex and costly infrastructure is not so crucial (at least at the initial stage). Athletes from those countries have made less impact in field events.

Under the leadership of Briton Marquis Exeter (Lord David G.B.C. Burghley, 1905-81 before knighting), and then Dutchman A. Paulen, IAAF presidents in 1946-76 and 1976-81, respectively, the organization defended the amateur formula. With the taking over of the post by Italian P. Nebiolo, the adjective 'amateur' was adjudged fictional (even though it was preserved in the name of the federation), and international athletics was announced a professional sport. Towards the end of 1990, Nebiolo started the organization of the international athletic 'circus', which, after several re-namings, took the name of the Golden League in 1998. In 1998-99, it included 8 important meetings. The winners (and other participants) receive prizes for individual appearances, as well as points to be included in the yearly standings. The winners of all the meetings in a season are awarded a prize of $1million.

G.A. Carr, *Fundamentals of Track and Field*, 1999; G. Lawson, *World Record Breakers in Track and Field Athletics*, 1997; R.L. Quercetani, *The World History of Track and Field Athletics*, 1964; H. Schifeelbein, M. Seifert, *Leichathletik – Krone Olympios*, 1974; J. Vives, *L'Athletisme*, 1963; *USA Track and Field Coaching Manual*, 2000; M.F. Watman, *The Encyclopedia of Athletics*, 1967.

TRACK AND FIELD RELAY, race events in which the distance is divided into several sections or legs, run by different players, who pass a relay round; the baton must be passed within the passing zone extending for 20m, of which the first 10m are in the preceding section of the race and the second 10m are the first meters of the next section. The race can be completed in case the baton has been dropped on condition that this happens within the passing zone and the baton is picked up by the player who dropped it. In the quarter finals, semi finals and finals the composition of the team must be the same; a player can be substituted only with the referee's consent (due to injury or illness). A runner can race only once (formerly 1 runner could race 2 sections, if the number of runners was not sufficient, particularly over longer distances, e.g. 4x400m); the runner can mark on the track the points helping him to start but only with his spikes (or chalk in the case of a synthetic compound track). The baton is a rigid hollow tube, made of wood, light metal (aluminum) or plastic, 280-300mm long, and not lighter than 50g. It has a vibrant color because it must be visible during the race. The main relay races are as follows: THE 4x100-M RELAY – 4 runners race round the track, divided into 4 sections. There are 3 passing zones, 20m long (10m within each section). The longer circumference of the outer tracks is compensated for by the stagger. The IAAF rules do not specify any handicap for individual tracks; the length is measured separately for each track, 30cm from the inner line of each track. Track and field relays were introduced to the Ol.G. in 1912 (men) in Stockholm. The first winners were Great Britain (42.4sec.). The US relay team won the Olympics in 1920-56, then in 1964-76 and in 1984 and 1992. In 1960 the race was won by the Germans (A. Hary completed his section in 10sec.); in 1980 – the USSR (the USA boycotted the Ol.G.); 1988 – the USSR and in 1996 – Canada, with D. Bailey, the Olympic champion. In W.Ch. the 4x100-m relay was raced from the very beginning. The first result below 40sec. was recorded by the US team during the 1936 Olympics in Berlin (39.8sec. with J. Owens); the first result below 39sec. was made by a Jamaican team (38.6sec. – 1968); below 38sec. – USA (37.86sec. – 1983). THE WOMEN'S TRACK AND FIELD RELAY (4x100m) was introduced to the Olympics during the 1928 Olympics in Amsterdam. The first winners were Canada. Up to 1996 the US team won 9

Robert Tait McKenzie, A Relay Runner, bronze.

Greek stamps depicting running Olympians.

Christian Arrue leads the USA men's Olympic sprint team at the Dunc Gray Velodrome during the track cycling event of the Sydney 2000 Olympic Games in Sydney, Australia.

An indoor track and field relay race.

times (1932, 1936, 1952, 1960, 1968, 1984-96). German athletes from the GDR won twice (1976 and 1980) and from the FRG – once (1972); Holland won once (1948 – with the famous F. Blankers-Koen), Australia (1956) and Poland (1964) also won once. Polish sprinters also won bronze medals at the 1960 Ol.G. in Rome and during the E.Ch. in 1974 and 1986. The first result below 50sec. was made by Brit. sprinters (1926 – 49.8sec.); below 45sec. – Australia (1956 – 44.9sec.); below 42sec. – GDR sprinters (1980 – 41.85sec.).

THE 4x400-M RELAY is part of major international events, such as the Ol.G. or continental championships. Sprinters complete 4 laps of a typical 400-m track (a total of 1,600m). The athletes run the first 600m in lanes at which point the stagger unwinds and they break to the inside of the track. It was initially raced by men only. In Eng.-speaking countries it is referred to as the mile relay (1609.3m). At the US championships in 1918-31 and 1958-62 distances were run in yards. It was first practiced at a university in Pennsylvania, where it was raced over a distance of 1 mile divided into sections of 4x440yds. in 1893. In 1911 it was included in the program of the US championships. Officially recognized as an Olympic event by the IAAF in 1912, it was included in the Olympic games in Stockholm. As in the case of the 4x100-m relay, the USA dominated the event initially. This dominance was broken by the British in 1920, the Jamaicans in 1952 and the Kenyans in 1972. In 1980 in Moscow the US relay team did not participate, boycotting the Olympics. The race was won by the Soviet team. The US team has won at all the other Olympics. The 4x400m relay has been a world championship event since their inception. The first result below 3min. was recorded by the US team (1966 – 2min 59.6sec.). Women raced the 4x400m relay first in 1909. However, the event became an Olympic sport as late as 1972. The first race was won by a team from the GDR, which also won in 1976. Rus. sprinters representing the USSR won in 1980 and 1988 and those representing the Community of Independent States in 1992. Amer. sprinters won in 1984 and 1996.

The first result below 4min. was made by the British (3min. 49.9sec. – 1958); below 3min. 30sec. – Germans from the GDR (1971 – 3min. 29.3sec.); below 3min. 20sec. – also a team from the GDR (1976 – 3min. 19.2sec.).

In THE OLYMPIC RELAY 4 sprinters run over a distance of 1,500m, divided into 4 sections,

100+200+400+ +800m or 800+400+200+100m. In some Eur. countries, particularly Germany, the name 'Olympic relay' also refers to relays of 400+200+200+800m or 800+200+200+400m; it was run once at the 1908 Ol.G. in London.

In the SWEDISH RELAY 4 sprinters run 4 sections, each 100m longer or shorter than the previous one (100+200+300+400m or 400+300+200+100m).

In Eng.-speaking countries, particularly in the USA, Relay Holidays are organized during which hurdle relays or other less typical relay races are organized, e.g. 10x100m, 10x400m, 20x100m, 20x400m etc. The best known Relay Holiday is organized annually by Pennsylvania State University in University Park. Every year the International Student Olympic Academy in ancient Olympia organizes the trad. relay of 10x the length of a football pitch (about 90m), in which 10-15 teams participate.

TRACK BALLET, a sport similar to figure skating involving 6-member teams running along a track. During one lap the competitors perform a number of complex and interrelated figures to music judged by a panel of referees on their style, technical difficulty, choreography and creativity. As a type of running, track ballet is related to the tradition of ancient games where reaching the finish line first did not always equal victory since the style, rhythm and grace (judged by referees) of a competitor's movement was equally important.

TRACK CYCLING, cycling on oval tracks, most often in velodromes with bleachers for the spectators. The tracks are made of wood, concrete or asphalt. The number and character of track cycling events had gone through a number of changes before the current competition format set in – e.g. starting from the 1976 Ol.G. tandem races were dropped. At the Ol.G. and the W.Ch. the following events are held: 1,000-m time trial from a standing start, sprint race (depending on the track length they are either 2 or 3 laps, the event held mostly during championships like the W.Ch. and Ol.G. where only the last 200m are timed), 4,000-m individual or team pursuit. Since 1984 a points race has been one of the Olympic events, in which every 8th lap is a sprint race, and the top 4 cyclists receive points; the rider with the highest total at the end of the entire race wins. This event had been popular mainly in Japan and recently was introduced into the Ol.G. In trad. track cycling at low-key championships the Austrl. race (in which the last rider after each lap drops out); Amer. race

(in 2-man teams, at any given moment only 1 cyclist is on the track, and once he wears out the other rider of the team takes over) and distance track races are held. Women's track cycling incl. sprint, 3,000-m pursuit, and points race. >MOTOR-PACED CYCLING and Jap. >KEIRIN are specific types of track cycling. To read about the history of track cycling see >CYCLING.

TRÆD AN TIL FLÆSK, a Dan. var. of >BOLD I HUL.

TRÆDE EN SYNÅL, Dan. for 'threading a needle'. A player sits on a thick solid beam, places his feet on the beam and tries to thread a needle without falling off the unstable beam. In another var. – called *tænde et* (lighting up a candle) – a player balances on the beam with one candle placed on each side. One of the candles is lighted. The player must pick up both candles, light one from the other, and put both of them back without falling off the beam.
J. Møller, 'Træde en synål', GID, 1997, 3, 26.

556

T WORLD SPORTS ENCYCLOPEDIA

TRÆKKE BRØD AF OVNEN, Dan. for 'pulling bread from the oven' [Dan. *trække* – pull + *brød* – bread + *af* – out of, from + *ovnen* < *ovn* – oven]. A simple game of strength, in which several players sit astride a bench and each holds the next by the waist. Two other players stand in front of the first player on the bench and take hold of his hands. Their task is to pull him so that he is separated from the other players on the bench.
J. Møller, 'Trække brød af ovnen', GID, 1997, 3, 82.

TRÆKKE DÅSE, Dan. for 'pulling a can' [Dan. *trække* – pull + *dåse* – a can]. A Dan. trad. sport in which 2 players wrestle with one another by means of holding the opposite ends of a can with one hand. Players frequently use a tobacco tin, which they hold between the thumb and index finger or between the index and middle fingers. The other hand should rest on the hip. The object of the game is to pull the tin towards oneself (twisting or wringing is prohibited). The player who loses his grip or is drawn to the opponent's side, loses the game.
J. Møller, 'Trække dåse', GID, 1997, 4, 15.

Trække okse.

TRÆKKE EN FINGER FRA NÆSEN, (*at trække en finger fra næsen*) Dan. for 'separating the finger from the nose' [Dan. *at* – in order to + *trække* – pull, separate + *en* – one + *finger* – finger + *fra* – from + *næsen* – nose]. A Dan. trad. wrestling game, in which one of the competitors places a clenched fist next to his nose with the thumb touching its tip, while he grabs the wrist with his other hand. The other competitor grabs his opponent's wrist with one hand and places the other hand on his chest. He must now separate his opponent's thumb from his nose, which is no easy task.
J. Møller, 'At trække en finger fra næsen', GID, 1997.

TRÆKKE FINGERKROG, Dan. for 'pulling a crooked finger' [Dan. *trække* – pull + *finger* – finger + *krog* – crook, bending]. A Dan. trad. game in which 2 players hold each other's right hands, cross the crooked index or ring fingers of their left hands, and begin to pull. The pulling is usu. done in a standing position and the person who releases his finger or is drawn to the opponent's side loses the game.
J. Møller, 'Trække fingerkrog', GID, 1997, 4, 14.

TRÆKKE KAT (*at trække kat*), Dan. for 'pulling a cat' [Dan. *at* – in order to + *trække* – pull + *kat* – cat]. A trad. wrestling game in which 2 opponents in a squatting position have their backs facing each other and are connected with a rope that runs around their necks, under their stomachs and between each player's legs. At the starting signal each begins to edge forward trying to pull the opponent to his side. Such bouts were often held by a stream, with both opponents starting on 2 opposite banks. In such a location the victory was easily 'documented' by the loser's landing in the water. In another var. of the game, called *heste hunde*, the rope connecting the wrestlers runs only around their necks.
J. Møller, 'At trække kat', GID, 1997, 4, 18.

TRÆKKE OKSE (*at trække okse*), Dan. for 'pulling the oxen' [Dan. *at* – in order to + *trække* – pull + *okse* – ox]. A Dan. game of strength, once popular among peasants, in which the competition is between 2 pairs of participants, 2 of which take a squatting position facing in opposite directions, while the other 2 lie on their partners' backs and grab a stick or rod 3-4cm thick and 50cm long with both hands – one hand from the top and the other hand from the bottom. At the starting signal each pair tries to pull the opponents to their side. In order to win a pair must be successful in 2 of 3 attempts.
J. Møller, 'At trække okse', GID, 1997, 4, 20.

TRÆKKE SKO (*at trække sko*), Dan. for 'pulling a horseshoe' [Dan. *at* – in order to + *trække* – pull + *sko* – horseshoe, also a shoe]. An old Dan. trad. form of competition in which 2 opponents wrestle over a horseshoe lying on a table, each trying to pull the opponent to his side.
J. Møller, 'At trække sko', GID, 1997, 4, 24.

TRÆKKE SØMANDSHANDSKE, Dan. for 'pulling a sailor's glove' [Dan. *trække* – pull + *sømandshandske* – a sailor's glove]. A Dan. trad. wrestling game, in which 2 people sit on the ground so that the soles of their shoes are against each other and their knees are bent. At the starting signal each player grabs the opponent's hands and tries to either knock him down or pull him to his side. Despite the name, no sailor's glove is used.
J. Møller, 'Trække sømandshandske', GID, 1997.

TRÆKKE STAVKROG, Dan. for 'pulling a pole' [Dan. *trække* – pull + *stav* – a pole + *krog* – a curve]. A trad. form of physical competition, in which the participants (usu. 6-10) sit on the ground, alternately facing opposite directions. All players facing the same direction form a team. All players sit with knees bent, under which a long pole is placed. Both teams grab the pole with both hands and each tries to pull it to one side. The team which succeeds wins the game.
J. Møller, 'Trække stavkrog', GID, 1997, 4, 26.

TRÆKKE STOK, Dan. for 'pulling a stick' [Dan. *trække* – pull + *stok* – *a* stick]. A trad. competition in which 2 players sit on the ground facing one another with their feet joined together. They reach out and grab a stick 50cm in length and 3-4cm thick which is kept horizontally above their feet and across the feet's axis. The task is to pull the stick and make the opponent stand up. It is prohibited to straighten the legs, but both opponents may change their grip. Three bouts are fought and to win the game it is necessary to win 2 bouts.
J. Møller, 'Trække stok', GID, 1997, 4, 21.

TRÆKKE TIL VEJRS, Dan. for 'pulling up or into the air' [Dan. *trække* – pull + *till* – towards + *vejrs* <*vejr* – the air, also something high in the air]. A trad. form of physical competition, in which 2 opponents or pairs of opponents engage in a tug-of-war over a rope thrown over a beam or a pulley fastened approx. 3m above the ground. The players grab the ends of the rope and pull it towards themselves in an effort to lift the opponent off the ground.
J. Møller, 'Trække til vejrs', GID, 1997, 4, 27.

TRÆKKE TOMMELSTIK, Dan. for 'pulling a thumb plug' [Dan. *trække* – pull + *tommel* – thumb + *stik* – plug]. A trad. form of wrestling in which 2 players cross their thumbs and place a small stick between them. At the starting signal they begin to pull the stick with their thumbs. Whoever lets the stick go, loses the game.
J. Møller, 'Trække tommelstik', GID, 1997, 4, 15.

TRÆKKE TOV, Dan. for 'pulling a rope' [Dan. *trække* – pull + *tov* – a rope]. A Dan. var. of >TUG-OF-WAR. The rope should be 20-30m long and 8-12cm in diameter. The center of the rope is marked and additional markers are placed 2m from center on both sides. The marks on the ground should correspond to those on the rope. Teams consist of 6-10 persons. The competition begins with both teams holding the rope in such a way that the marks on the rope are synchronized with those on the ground. No player may stand within or touch in any way the area within the markers. The rope may not be wrapped around the hands or legs. At the starting signal both teams begin to pull the rope and continue until any of the side markers on the rope moves beyond the ground marker of the opposite team.
J. Møller, 'Trække tov', GID, 4.

TRAIL ORIENTEERING, (Swed. *præcisions-orienteering*) a form of orienteering meant for contestants on wheelchairs. It originated from the tradition of >ORIENTEERING and is supervised by the same International Orienteering Federation, IOF. Participants do not reach control sites – which would be impossible in view of terrain irregularities – but places from which the control sites can be seen. Their task is to find the control site using a map and then point to it. Time measurements are taken from the moment contestants receive the information they need to the moment they are able to identify the point in question. There are no time restrictions as to the whole route. Participants may use electric or mechanical wheelchairs. Persons using crutches or needing the help of a third party are also allowed in the competition. Most trail orienteering competitions (including Swed. national championships) are of an open character, i.e. can be entered into by non-disabled persons. Trail orienteering is an integral part of the biggest orienteering event, the O-Ringen. E.Ch. have been held since 1994. The first World Cup was organized during the 1999 orienteering W.Ch. Every national team has the right to enter 3 competitors. The first competition involving wheelchairs powered with manual pedals – connected to the wheels with bicycle chains – was held during the same event (as a show discipline). The most outstanding trail orienteering competitor is the Swede J. Åkeson.
S. Harvey, M. Nimvik, B. Römvik, *The World of Orieteering*, 1998.

TRAMPOLI, an Ital. var. of >WALKING ON STILTS.

TRAMPOLINING, see >SPORTS ACROBATICS.

TRANSPORTE DE TXINGAS, see >TXINGAK.

TRAP, BAT AND BALL, also in a simplified form *trap-ball*, a trad. Eng. game popular in the 16th-19th cent. According to A.B. Gomme,

the trap is of wood made like a slipper, with a hollow at the heel end for the ball, and a kind of wooden spoon moving on a pivot, in the bowl of which the ball is placed. Two sides play – one side bats, the other fields. One of the batsmen strikes the end or handle of the spoon, the ball then rises into the air, and the art of the game is for the batsman to strike it as far as possible with the bat before it reaches the ground. The other side who are 'fielding', try either to catch the ball before it falls to the ground, or to bowl it from where it falls to hit the trap. If they succeded in catching the ball all the 'inns' are out, and their side goes in to strike the ball, and the previous batsmen to field; if the trap is hit the batsman is out and another player of his side takes his place. The batsman is also aout if he allows the ball to touch the trap when in the act of hitting it.

A game with a trap on a hinged lever was typical of cities, while in the countryside, with limited possibilities of constructing a complex trap, boys would bat a ball with their hands from a substitute springboard placed at an angle, so that the ball thrown at it from the side bounced up and was batted out into the field by another player. The springboard was a simple slat driven obliquely into the ground and used for bouncing the ball against it, or an old shoe with its top fitted into the ground and its sole raised upwards so that the heel could function as a small target, which – hit by the ball – sprang from the rest of the sole. Such substitute traps – a slat, bone, or shoe – could easily be turned into a cricket goal or wicket, which led Strutt to the conclusion that cricket could have originated from the country-folk var. of trap, bat and ball: 'Trap-ball is anterior to cricket' (p. 99). The question is whether the simplified version can still be considered the same game and so, whether we should rather not speak of a simple folk game which derived from trap, bat and ball (though it was already a separate game) and influenced the development of cricket. The classical trap, bat and ball made use of a hinged wooden lever since the Middle Ages, which is indicated by old drawings. Strutt clearly distinguishes the 2 var.:

Trap ball, when compared with cricket, is but a childish pastime; but I have seen it played by the rustics in Essex in a manner differing materially from that now practised in the vicinity of the metropolis, and which required much more dexterity in the performance, for instead of a broad bat with a flatted face, they used a round cudgel about one inch and a half in diameter and three feet in length, and those who had acquired the habit of striking the ball with this instrument rarely miss their blow, but frequently drive it to an astonishing distance; the ball being stopped by one of the opponent party, the striker forms his judgment of the ability of the person who is to throw it back, and calls in consequence for any number of scores towards his game that he thinks proper; it is then returned, and if it appears to his antagonist to rest at a sufficient distance to justify the striker's call, he obtains his number; but when a contrary opinion is held, a measurement takes place, and if the scores demanded exceed in number the lengths of the cudgel from the trap to the ball, he loses the whole, and is out; while on the other hand, if the lengths of the bat are more than the scores called for, the matter terminates in the striker's favour, and they are set up to his account.

[J. Strutt, *Sports and Pastimes of the People of England*, 1810, 100]

The trap and ball game had different names, such as *trap ball*, *trap-ball*, or *trapball*. They must have, in fact, been one game, named differently in various regions, although there may have been some insignificant technical differences between re-

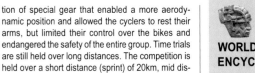

Triathlon's first event: swimming.

gions. In most ethnographic works these var. are used interchangeably. In *The Traditional Games of England, Scotland and Ireland* (1898, II, 306-7) A.B. Gomme explains the principles of trap, bat and ball, but she uses the name trap ball and later presents another var. of this game called trap and ball played in Bury St. Edmund on Shrove Tuesday, Easter Monday and Whitsuntide. She also claims that trap, bat and ball formed the basis for many other games, such as >NORTHERN SPELL. She believes that trap, bat and ball was a predecessor of these games and was played with less sophisticated equipment, and so she calls knur and spell 'a superior form of Trap ball' (TGESI, II, 307). In later editions of *The Oxford Companion to Sports* J. Arlott prefers the name trapball, relating it to >ROUNDERS, and even >BASEBALL (1975, 1051). This shows the rather haphazard approach to the history of trap, bat and ball, of various authors, who easily lump together all games in which a ball, sphere, or even a sharpened peg is batted. Irrespective of the degree of deformation of the oldest, 'classical' var. of trap, bat and ball, the game could have been played between 2 partners or teams of several players each. Strutt believes that the history of the game dates to the 14th cent. and the number of players averaged 6-8.

TRAP, see >SHOOTING.

TRE SLAG OCH RÄNNA, Swed. for 'three bats and a run' (a Dan. var. is called *tre slag och renna*), a bat and ball game played in Scandinavia, similar to >PALANT.

TREBOLD, Dan. for 'triangle' or 'triple ball game'. 3-4 players stand at a distance of 6-10m from one another, with 1 of them in the center and the other 3 forming a triangle around him (hence the name). The player in the center attacks the player who has possession of the ball, who in turn may throw the ball to one of the partners to avoid the attack or throw the ball at the attacker. The attacker must avoid being hit by dodging the ball or jumping, but he may not run away to either side. If the attacker is hit, he changes places with the player who hit him. The player with the best record of successful dodges wins the game. In another var., called *stikbold*, the attacker can be hit only in the head, hands or legs. In yet another var., called *mellembold*, popular in the town of Hillerslev in the area of Thistedegnen, the rules are similar to *stikbold*, but with more players in the center.
J. Møller, 'Trebold', GID, 1997, 1, 21.

TREIBBALL, Ger. for 'pushball', a trad. game in which a ball is struck with a stick in order to be placed in a hole. It belongs to a family of Eur. games with rules similar to Pol. >CZOROMAJ, Fr. LA >TRUIE, Eng. >CAT I' THE HOLE, Swed. >PER I HÅLA, and Norw. >PER I GROPEN.

TREMANS LANGBOLD, a var. of Dan. >LANGBOLD for 3 players. Despite the name the game may be played by 3-10 persons.
J. Møller, 'Tremans langbold', GID, 1997, 1, 64.

TRENSELEN, see >BOLD I HUL.

TREVIT, see >NORTHERN SPELL.

TRIAL BY SACK WITH WATER, a competition accompanying wedding celebrations, popular among some Mong. peoples. The trial by sack with water was the third and most important event of the >WEDDING SPORT EVENTS. The trial consisted of crossing the threshold of the bride's parents' yurt by the groom. The groom was supposed to step on a goatskin filled with water, placed on the threshold; if he

Triathlon's second event: cycling.

lost his balance the bride's parents could withdraw their consent for him to marry the bride and another candidate could step on the sack and take the bride if successful.

TRIATHLON, a 3-event sport for both men and women which tests the physical versatility of athletes, called triathlonists or triathletes. The 3 events are: swimming, cycling and running [*triathlon* <Gk. *tria* – three + *athlon* – competition]. The competition is held over classical, short distances, but also mid and long distances.
Swimming. Irrespective of the distance, all competitors start simultaneously by jumping into the water or standing in the water and waiting for the signal. Swimming distances are: 750m, 1.5km and 2-4km.
Cycling. Originally cycling races took place according to time trial regulations, i.e. each athlete competed individually with drafting rules prohibiting cycling closer than 10m to another competitor or any moving vehicle. Notorious protests, disqualifications, the necessity to engage a great number of judges, lack of attraction for the spectators, and TV coverage requirements resulted in a change of regulations. In short and mid distances competitors start and race simultaneously, which led to the elimina-

tion of special gear that enabled a more aerodynamic position and allowed the cyclers to rest their arms, but limited their control over the bikes and endangered the safety of the entire group. Time trials are still held over long distances. The competition is held over a short distance (sprint) of 20km, mid distance of 40km and long distance of 50-180km. The drafting zone is defined as a rectangular area 7m long and 2m wide surrounding each bicycle.
Running immediately follows cycling and follows the rules of street running competitions. The running race is held, depending on the type of event, over a distance of 5, 10 or 15-42km.
A less popular var. – winter triathlon – includes a 15-km skiing race, a 50-km cycling race and a 50-km skating race. Similar to summer triathlon, the final result is the combined times of all 3 events. A separate form of triathlon is held indoors. Another similar sport affiliated in the same international federation is >DUATHLON.
History. The idea was born in the USA in the 1970s. The first documented triathlon took place in San Diego, California, in 1974 and included a 600-yd. swimming race, a 5-mi. cycling race and a 6-mi. running race. The first international event, called Hawaiian Ironman Triathlon, was staged in Kailua Kona and continues to be held. It combined the trad. Waikiki swimming race over a distance of 3.9km, a 180-km cycling race around Oahu, and a Honolulu marathon (42.195km). The first event was won by an American, G. Haller. The Hawaiian triathlon now hosts approx. 2,000 athletes from approx. 45 countries, who must qualify by taking part in various triathlon competitions around the world. Among the first winners of the Hawaian triathlon were D. Scott (5-time winner), M. Allen (6-time winner), L. van Lier-

Triathlon's third event: running.

T

WORLD SPORTS ENCYCLOPEDIA

A lesson in trigon, from the baths of Titus.

de (men's event) and P. Newby-Frazer (women's event). In 1989 the International Triathlon Union was formed, which currently affilitaes more than 100 countries. In the same year the 1st official W.Ch. took place in Avignon (France), won by M. Allen (unofficial W.Ch. had been held since 1978). Along W.Ch. the main annual triathlon events include The Triathlon World Cup and Lifeforce Nike Triathlon (held in Singapore). In 1984 the European Triathlon Union was formed and a year later the first E.Ch. were held in Almere (Holland) over long distances of 3.8km (swimming), 180km (cycling) and 42.195km (running), in Rodekro (Denmark) over mid distances of, respectively, 2, 80, and 20km, and in Immenstadt (Germany) over short distances of 1.5, 40, and 10km, a division meant to popularize triathlon and increase its attractivenss. The first Olympic triathlon was held at Sidney in 2000 and the first gold medalists were Simon Whitfield (Canada, men's competition) and Brigitte McMahon (Switzerland, women's competition).
G.P. Town, *Science of Triathlon Training and Competition*, 1985; *International Triathlon Union Manual*, 1997; J. Mora, *Triathlon 101*, 1999; M. Pigg, *Triathlon Bundle Pack*, 1997.

TRIB AND KNURR, a type of ball game, similar to >NORTHERN SPELL, in which the ball is levered up and batted into the field. Precise regulations are

Britain's triple jump champion Jonathan Edwards.

French yachtsman Michel Desjoyeaux steers his trimaran 'Geant' during training for the Route du Rhum trans-Atlantic solo sailing race.

not known, but the nature of the game can be deducted from its name. The *knurr* is a wooden ball batted into the field, while *trib* comes from Eng. *trib*, most prob. an abbr. for *tribet* or *trippet*. These, in turn, had a number of spelling var. and meanings used randomly in different locations and in reference to different sports. An additional complication comes from the word *trevit* (or *trivit*), which occurred in similar contexts. The meaning of *trib* as an object batted into the field in the game of *trib and knurr* cannot stand, as that was clearly the role of *knurr*. Thus *trib* could have meant either the lever with which the ball was thrown up before being batted, or the bat itself. Most Eng. dictionaries do not record the word *trib*, or *tribit* meaning a stick or a bat. Yet, a local Yorkshire ethnographer and linguist mentions the following expressions in reference to this family of games: *tribit stick*, *tribbit stick*, and *trivit stick*, which A.B. Gomme, following another ethnographer, distinguishes from the name of the trap, defined as *trevit* (TGESI, I, 423). It is then quite probable that the word *stick* was eliminated, while *tribit* was shortened to *trib*, which occurs as the first element of the name of the game. However, the exact meaning of it can hardly be determined.

TRIBET, a children's var. of a trad. Eng. game once popular in Lancashire, prob. a var. of >TRAP, BAT AND BALL. The game is played with a short lever, about 1ft. (30.48cm) in length and approx. 2in. (5.1cm) in diameter, called *pum*, which is used to strike a small wooden block called *tribet*. Games of this type played in other locations have similar names, e.g. *trippets* (Newcastle). The word *tribet* and its regional var., e.g. *trippit*, *trippet* etc., had several meanings and – besides the wooden block – it could have denominated a type of small lever. Thus it could have meant both the wooden block and the lever, which was the case in another game called *trippit and coit*, derived by J. Arlott in his *The Oxford Companion to Sports and Games* (1975, 1052) from *trippets*. Arlott also believes that other varieties of tribet incl. >DAB-AND-TRICKER, >DRAB AND NORR and >LUKING.

TRIERA (Gk. *trieres*, Lat. *triremis*, lit. having 3 rows, a trireme), an ancient (orig. Gk., later also Roman) galley with 3 ranks of oars, one above another. The name also denominated a type of rowing competition held on such ships. Triera galleys had been constructed before the Persian wars and were manned by 200 oarsmen and 18 soldiers. Triera races were part of the ancient Gk. (incl. Isthmian and Panathenaic) games.
Well estab. triera races were also held in Salamine (Salamis, Cyprus, not to be confused with historical Salamine on Peloponneus). Repeatedly invaded by the Persians, the island sought to maintain the effectiveness of its fleet by organizing competitions between war galleys. The earliest information about such an event comes from Isocrates' *To Nicocles* and refers to 374 BC, when the hero Nicocles, the son of the prince of Salamine, patronized the triera regatta held in honor of his father Evagoras.
C. Constantinou-Hajdistephanou, *Athletics in Ancient Cyprus and the Greek Tradition from 15th-14th Century BC-AD 330*, 1991.

TRIFOILING, a type of ocean sailing on trifoilers, i.e. ships with 3 floats – 1 on each side and 1 in the back. The floats are connected with a pipe construction or a triangular panel resembling the wing of an airplane. Directly above the back float is a cockpit for 1 or 2 sailors. Trifoilers have 1 central sail located at the junction of the ship's arms that hold the floats or 2 side sails directly above the floats. The floats usu. have a complex construction: the upper part supports the ship at halt and during sailing at slow speeds; at greater speeds the trifoiler rises up and the lower, smaller and much narrower part of the float touches the surface of the water. This distinguishes a trifoiler from a >TRIMARAN, which has identical side floats, maintaining the ship's draft and contact with water on the same level. The last element of the trifoiler's rigging is a light and rigid hydrofoil sail. A race trifoiler follows the constructions used in >SPEED SAILING, also called trifoilers and built by G. Ketterman. Race trifoilers offer much better steering capabilities, are able to travel faster – up to 80km/h, and are smaller than speed boats. They have an open cockpit, as opposed to the built in one used on speed trifoilers in order to reduce air resistance. Great speeds and a constantly improv-

ing maneuverability of trifoilers are bound to increase the attractiveness of the sport, both on the professional and amateur level.
J. Tomlison, 'Speed sailing', 'Trifoiling', *The Ultimate Encyclopedia of Extreme Sports*, 1996.

TRIGON [Lat. <Gk. *trigonon* – triangle], an ancient, prob. Gk., ball game, also known in Rome, played by 3 players who formed a triangle and threw or hit the ball with their hands, or – as some sources claim – with a racket or stick. The name also referred to the ball itself. Marcialis wrote about a player who 'caught the trigon lightly thrown from the left or right'. Among the well known trigon players was the Roman poet Horace, who wrote in one of his satires: 'Fatigued with the heat, I practice, then go to the bath, leaving the Fields of Mars and the game of trigon' (Satire I, 6, 126).
The rules of the game are unclear and only the general nature can be reconstructed. Players passed the ball among themselves and, probably, it was valued more to rebound the ball in the air than simply to throw it to one of the partners. A dropped ball earned a point for the partner who had passed it. The players loudly counted the points themselves, as indicated by Seneca, who writes ironically about a palestra located within the baths compound close to his house, from where he heard the cries of the players, which vexed him: 'whenever a player begins to count his passes, I have to put everything to rest'. The games that were played for bets were judged by referees, as indicated by an epigram by Marcialis: 'Let the referee honor your victory at trigon with a splendid wreathe' (*Epigrammata*, 7, 72, 9). The presence of referees may also indicate that the game and scoring system were quite complex. Some scholars believe that a winning pass with the right hand earned 1pt., with the left hand – 2pts., a winning rebound – 3pts. One famous player, Ursus, is said to have played with a glass ball. Faking the receivers out was not only tolerated, but apparently feinting was all part of the game, as indicated by Plautus: 'the player who has the ball pretends that he wants to throw it at one person, but actually throws it at another'. Even criminals sentenced to death are known to have played trigon in the amphitheatres. The winners were spared, while the losers were duly executed. Cf. >PILA PRASINA.
N.B. Crowther, 'Team Sports in Ancient Greece', IJHS, 1995.

TRIGONO, or *trigonon*, a popular, modern Gk. game described by M.Z. Kontou in the following way: 'a large triangle is drawn on the ground. Approx. 3-5m behind each of its sides stands 1 player. The triangle is subdivided into zones that have different point values. The players throw a small ball or stone and earn points according to the zone where it landed'. Cf. ancient >TRIGON.
Source: M.Z. Kontou, Aristotle University, Thesalonica, Greece.

TRILLE ÆG, Dan. for 'rolling an egg', [Dan. *trille* – to roll + *æg* – an egg(s)], a Dan. trad. game, in which hard-boiled eggs were rolled down a plank propped against a stone or a wall. The goal was to roll the egg as close to the opponent's egg as possible and – ideally – to touch it. The game was played in the area of Sorøkanten until the 1950s.

TRILLEBØRSLØB, a var. of >WHEELBARROW RACES.

TRIMARAN, a type of boat and a technique of sailing, also for sport purposes. The construction is based on 3 hulls or floats, propelled by sails or a motor engine. The Eng. name is a combination of a Lat. numeral *tri* (triple) and the ending borrowed from the name of a 2-hulled sail-boat called a >KATAMARAN. Cf. also >TRIFOILING.

TRÎNTA, a Rom. trad. form of wrestling, in which the opponents fight in a standing position, embracing one another with their arms throughout the duration of the bout. According to wrestling expert W. Baxter, trînta is similar to Scottish >BACKHOLD.
'Les luttes traditionnelles a traverse le monde', LJP, 1998, 77.

TRIPLE JUMP, an athletic event in which contestants compete for distance by performing a sequence of 3 jumps, respectively the hop, step and jump. According to IAAF rules:

the hop shall be made so that the competitor lands first upon the same foot as that from which he has taken off; in the step he shall land on the other foot, from which subsequently the jump is performed. If the competitor while jumping touches the ground with the 'sleeping' leg it shall be considered as a failure [...]. The runway shall have a minimum width of 1.22 metres. The length of the runway is unlimited. The minimum length provided for the runway shall be of 40 metres. [...] The take-off shall be marked by a board sunk level with the runway and the surface of the landing area and placed at least 13 metres from the landing area. [...] Immediately beyond the take-off line there shall be placed a board of plasticine or other suitable material for recording the athlete's footprints when he has foot-faulted.

The result is determined by the distance 'measured from the nearest break in the landing area made by any part of the body or limbs to the take-off line, or take-off line extended. The measurement must be taken perpendicular to the take-off line or its extension.'

Until recently the triple jump was exclusively a men's event. It is now part of the program of all international athletic events, incl. the Ol.G. At the turn of the 19th and 20th cent. a certain popularity was enjoyed by the >TRIPLE JUMP (STANDING).

History. The tradition of the triple jump may reach back as far as ancient Greece. According to some scholars the ancient Gk. long jump (>HALMA) may have, in fact, been a triple jump. Even so, the modern triple jump bears no relation to its predecessor. It derives from Ireland, where it used to be an event of competitions among the Celtic people. In the 19th cent. it was adopted by the English and incorporated into the structure of athletic events, which were taking shape at that time. It was introduced into Brit. athletic championships in 1884 under the name *hop, step and jump*, and in 1893 it reached the USA. The Celtic origin and tradition of triple jump resulted in the domination of Irish jumpers in the early years of the event. The first world record holder was the Irishman J. Purcell (13.06m – 1984). The 15-m barrier was crossed for the first time by the American, D. Ahearn (15.52m – 1909), 16m – by a Japanese, N. Tadjima (16.00m – 1936), 17m – a Pole, J. Szmidt (17.03m – 1965), 18m – a Brit. athlete, J. Edwards (18.16 and 18.29 – 1995).

The years 1928-39 were dominated by Jap. jumpers, who won gold medals at Ol.G. in 1928 (Mikio Oda), 1932 (Chuhei Nambu), and 1936 (Naota Tajima). 1950-56 was the era of A. Ferreira da Silva, who broke the world record 5 times and was twice the Olympic champion (1952, 1956). By the end of Ferreira's domination there was a strong competition between Rus. and Poli. jumpers. When the Pol. school of triple jump collapsed, Rus. jumpers began to dominate the event, from around 1968 on. W. Saneyew was the first athlete to win 3 Olympic gold medals (1968, 1972, 1976). During the 1975 Panamerican Games a Brazilian athlete, J.C. de Oliveira, jumped an unbelievable 17.89m.

Women's triple jump is a relatively new event, introduced into the Ol.G. only in 1996. The first Olympic champion was the Ukrainian I. Kravec (15.33m).

TRIPLE JUMP (STANDING), a discontinued athletic event in which 3 jumps in a sequence were performed from a standing position. It was part of the Olympic program in 1900 (Paris) and 1904 (St. Louis) – both events were won by an American, R. Ewry, a specialist also in other, similar events, such as >LONG JUMP (STANDING) and >HIGH JUMP (STANDING).

TRIPLE TRIAL OF MONGOLIAN WARRIORS, see >ERIIN GURVAN NAADAM.

TRIPPIT AND COIT, see >NORTHERN SPELL.

TRIP-TROUT, a game that enjoyed short-lived popularity in Scotland at the end of the 19th cent., in which – similar to >SHUTTLECOCK – a small ball is used instead of a shuttle.
TGESI, II, 308.

TRISSE TØRV AF, Dan. for 'jumping over a peat bog', lit. 'roving round a peat bog', [Dan. *trisse* – to rove around + *tørv* – peat + *af* – from]. A trad. running game popular in N Jutland (Nordøstjylland). The first 2 lines are marked across the running track at a distance of 30cm from one another, while the subsequent lines are marked at intervals increasing 30 times with each line. The runners must place their feet on the lines and whoever reaches the furthest one, wins the race.
J. Møller, 'Trisse tørv af', GID, 1997, 4, 104.

TRIVIT, see >NORTHERN SPELL.

TROCHOS, in ancient Greece the name of 2 different children's games, the common feature of which was the action of rotating. In one of them a hoop or rim was pushed with one's hand or a stick, often in a speed contest; the other game was spinning a top (see >TOPs), also called >STROBILOS.

TROCHUS, in ancient Rome a boy's game, either in the form of performing various stunts with a wooden or metal hoop or rim or a speed contest in rolling the hoop or rim (Lat. *trochus*) with one's hand or a stick (*clavis*). A 19th cent. classical scholar, F. Bobrowski, described trochus as 'a metal wheel which children rolled for speed with a metal handle called a key' (*Lexicon latino-polonicum*, 1844, vol. II, p. 833). Roman trochus was most certainly modelled after the Gk. >TROCHOS. Some believe that the name may have additionally referred to >TOPS, which was known in ancient Rome also as >BUXUS and *turbo*.

TROCCO, also *lawn billiards*, an Eng. game and a crossover between >BILLIARDS and >LAWN BOWLS, in which small balls were pushed with metal-ended sticks resembling those used in billiards [Ital. *trucco* – a trick, a game with tricks]. The object of the game was to shoot the ball through metal gates resembling those used in crocket. Cf. >TRUCKS.

TROLDEHOVED, Dan. for 'troll's head', a form of physical competition. A circle (troll's head) is marked on the floor, the size of which must allow the players to jump over it. Players form another circle, hold one another by the hand, and start running around pulling one another and trying to force one another to step onto the troll's head. A player may avoid this by jumping over the troll's head, but if he touches the inside of the marked circle even with 1 foot, he is eliminated. Any player that loses his grip is likewise eliminated. Instead of a marked circle, it is possible to use a pin to serve as the troll's head.
J. Møller, 'Troldehoved', GID, 1997, 2, 28.

TROMPO, a Span. var. of >TOPS, popular esp. in Andalucia, also popular in Chile.

TRONZADORA, a Span. form of competition within >TIMBER SPORTS, an equivalent of the Basque >TRONZOLARIS. Pairs compete in hand sawing 15-cm thick slabs off a log approx. 130cm in diameter. The log is placed on a stand, approx. 40cm above the ground. The number of slabs which must be sawn off varies from 10-20, depending on the region. The blade of the saw is 190-210cm long, while the handles are approx. 30cm long.
C.M. Palos, 'Tronzadora', JYTE (1992, 283).

TRONZOLARIS, Basq. for 'cutting wood', a trad. sport in which a log is cut with a hand saw manned by 2 contestants. Events include cutting logs of 2 diameters: 54 and 60 *pulgadas*, i.e. 137 and 152cm. The length of logs are 45-50cm. The contestants must cut off a 5-7cm thick slab. As opposed to similar Amer. or Can. sports, the slab is not fastened, but has a wedge which is fitted onto a stand. During the contest an assistant holds it on the stand.

History. Contrary to >AIZKOLARIS (cutting wood with an axe), this sport has a relatively short tradition in the Basq. culture. Basque woodcutters began to use the saw only around the mid-19th cent. and the first competitions were held in the years 1926-33, pioneered by, among others, J. Medizábal. Basq. championships (Campeonato de Eskuadi de Tronzalaris) became a regular event in the 1970s, promoted by Centro de Atracción y Turismo as a tourist attraction. Contests are held on city and town squares (e.g. Plaza de la Trinidad in San Sebastian) and corrida stadiums (e.g. in Eibar) under the auspices of the Guipuzcoana Federation of Traditional Basque Sports (Federación Guipuzoana de Herri Kirolak). Among the leading pairs of contestants in the 1980s and 1990s were: M. Errandonea/ A. Leitza, J. Bergara/J.I. Orbegozo, and J.M. Galarraga/J.M. Etxeberria.
R. Aguirre, 'Tronzalaris', GHJD, vol. 1-3, 1989, 209-214.

TROODE MADAMME, the oldest name of a Flem. game >TROU-MADAME, found in the 1567 inventory of a Flem. burgher, J. Vander Noot.

TROTTOLA, an Ital. var. of >TOPS.

TROULE IN MADAME, a Eng. var. of a Flem. game >TROU-MADAME, similar to >NINE HOLES. It prob.

Troldehoved.

A tronzolaris competition.

contributed to the development of the var. in which 11 arches are cut out in the playing board, through which various balls had to pass. The oldest mention of the game comes from J. Jones' *Benefits of the Auncient Bathes of Buckstones* dated 1572:

The ladyes, gentle woomen, wyves, and maydes, maye in one of the galleries walke; and if the weather bee not aggreeable too theire expectacion, they may haue in the ende of a benche eleuen holes made, intoo the which to trowle pummetes, or bowles of leade, bigge, little, or meane, or also of copper, tynne, woode, eyther vyolent or softe, after their owne discretion; the pastyme troule-in-madame *is termed.*

(TGESI, II, 309)

TROU-MADAME, Fr. for 'lady's hole', [Fr. *trou* – hole + *madame* – lady], a Fr. equivalent of a Belgian trad. game, also known as *troode madamme*, Flem. *door den uil bollen*, also *bakbolling* and *ladderbolling*, Eng. *troule in madame*. The game is played mainly in eastern Flanders, but also in Brabant, mostly on holidays and during local festivals. The idea is to roll a bowl along a wooden platform so that it passes through a hole or, in some var., an arch or a gate. The term 'bowl' is purely conventional: in fact, players use round slabs the shape of which resembles a wheel of cheese. Each hole or arch has a different point value and each player has 5 'bowls' which average 10-12cm in diameter. Most var. have 9 arches, which are shaped like miniature aqueducts. The balls are rolled from a distance of approx. 6m, though this is not a universal principle. Particular var. may differ in the length of track, the type of obstacles and the shape of arches. Among the best known var. are *hoepelbolling*, *sprietbolling*, and *tuinbolling*. In Perenchies (French Flanders, France) the gates are formed by vertically placed rails which form a fence-like structure with clearances large enough to let the ball pass through. 20-25cm above the ground level is a board with point values attributed to particular gates in an irregular sequence, counting from right to left: 9, 3, 6, 1, 8, 2, 4, 5, 7, 10. At the beginning of the 17th cent. a table-top var. of trou-madame was developed, with smaller balls averaging 2-3cm in diameter and rolled on the table through miniature arches. The oldest drawing showing a table-top var. of trou-madame comes from a hand-colored album printed in Leuven in 1606 entitled *Album Amicorum, habitibus mulierum omnium nationum Europae, tum tabulis ac scutisvacuis in aes incisis adomatum, ut quisque et symbola et in(s)ignia sua gentilitia inijs depingi commode cuare possit.* The drawing depicts 2 women and 1 man playing, which indicates that the game was not sex-discriminate.
The earliest mention of trou-madame comes from a 1567 inventory of Flemish townsman J. van der Noot. J. Strutt writes about 'the pastyme Troule in Madame' on the basis of a work dated 1572, in which it is described as rolling 'large, small and medium-size balls of lead, tin, copper and wood' to 11 holes. Among the players Strutt mentions 'ladies, noble women, widows and girls'. The game enjoyed such a tremendous popularity in the 16th cent. that even erotically scented poems were written about it, an example of which comes from the 1626 volume of poetry entitled *Minneplicht*:

In the game of Trou-Madame [...]
everyone tries to stick his balls into the hole
and not stop before it

The erotic context of the game had already been displayed earlier. A modern Fr. dictionary by Huguet (1967) offers the following quotation from 1594:

He slept with two nice Flemish girls, who gave him syphylis for the seventh time, for which reason he was named the master of Trou-Madame.

Considering the above, one can hardly be surprised by the instructions offered in *Scriptoris Nova Poemata* (unknown author, 1624):

To play with skill and luck you must push through the center of the hole, which they call Trou-Madame, or else you lose. The inside of the hole is your object and a point of honor. To place your tool there is not enough, however, as you must do it energetically, all the way through, as soon as you are allowed in.

As time passed, the game began to gain popularity also among the common folk, mainly women. Today women constitute the majority of players.
K. Bostoen, De Van der Noots en hun 'troode madamme', *Meta*, 1978, 12 (5); E. de Vroede, Ball and Bowl Games in the Low Countries: Past and Present, (in:) *Homo Ludens – Der Spielende Mensch*, 1996, vol. VI; E. de Vroede, *Het Grote Volkssporten Boek*, Leuven, 1996; E. de Vroede, 'Het spel van trou-madame', *Nieuwsbrief van de Vlaamse Volkssport Centrale*, 1988, 8.

Truck racing.

TROUNCE-HOLE, a trad. Eng. game resembling >TIP-CAT, as well as *trippit and coit*. A piece of wooden slat or bone was placed with one end above a groove in the ground. The game began with hitting that end, sending the slat into the air and hitting it again with a stick, which started a sequence that varied from region to region, but which was similar to that of many other games of this type found in different countries, e.g. Pol. >SZTEKIEL, >KLIPA; >AL-BA'A; >GULLI DUNDA; >PILAOUET, *mouilh*; etc.

TRUCK RACING, a form of >CAR RACING practiced with trucks used for transporting heavy loads. Trucks race without trailers and the competition is part of >FOUR BY FOUR. Races are held on tracks similar to those of Formula 1 and enjoy the greatest popularity in Europe. Among the leading producers involved in sport racing are MAN and Mercedes Benz. Trucks reach speeds of up to 160km/h and compete in 2 basic classes: super race truck and race truck. The Eur. governing body for the sport is the Fédération Internationale de l'Automobile.

TRUCKS, a game that derives from >TROCCO. Instead of large lawn bowls smaller balls on a board placed on a table are used. Sticks are similar to those used in >BILLIARDS, but smaller. The object of the game is to drive the balls into goals called *trucks*, hence the name of the game [Eng. *trucks*, <Lat. *trochus*, Gk. *trocho* – a metal ring].

TRUDELN, see >BOLD I HUL.

TRUDELN, a Ger. var. of a game in which a ball is thrown into a number of holes in the ground. The rules are similar to those of Dan. >BOLD I HUL.

TRUIE, LA, a Fr. trad. game resembling Pol. >CZOROMAJ. The objecti was to send a wooden ball into several holes in the ground with the use of a stick. The 2 games differed in the shape of holes, which in la truie were not round, but shaped like a horseshoe. Also, a czoromaj player threw the ball into the hole with his hands, while only the remaining players used sticks to prevent him from doing so.

TRUNKS, an old Eng. game in which a flat, rounded stone is driven into one of 9 holes in the ground with the use of long (or sometimes short) bent sticks. It is sometimes referred to as >NINE HOLES or >BRIDGEBOARD, although it differs from both in that a bowl (instead of a stone) is propelled using a stick (instead of throwing with the hands). In front of each hole is a small, wooden gate numbered from 1-9, which denots the number of points a player may score by driving the bowl through it. The sequence of playing the holes is fixed: 7, 5, 3, 1, 9, 2, 4, 6, 8. Each player has 2 flat, puck-shaped stones. The player who reaches 45pts. wins the game. An Eng. ethnographer, J.T. Mickletwaithe, has found a description of the game carved on a stone bench in a church in Ardeley, Hertfordshire. He has also witnessed the game being played in London.

TRUNSELEN, a Ger. game in which a ball is thrown into a number of holes in the ground, similar to Dan. >BOLD I HUL.

TRYNTE-KUPEDIKE, a Moldavian form of hand-to-hand combat; See Rom. >TRÎNTA and Scot. >BACKHOLD.

TS'ÉQWELA, an Native Amer. shuttlecock game practiced by the Stóólo (or Stó:lo) tribe inhabiting the Pacific coast of the USA and Canada, Vancouver Island, Fraser Valley, and the N-W edges of the state of Washington. Different types of shuttlecocks are used, e.g. a small, round stone with cedar twigs tied to it, or a piece of cedar wood ½-1in. (1.3-2.5cm) in diameter, with 3 feathers with charred ends stuck in it. The racket is made of a cedar board, about 10in. (approx. 24cm) long, with a short handle. The game is played individually and the final score is the number of times the shuttlecock is struck without falling to the ground.
The Internet: http://web20.mindlink.net/stolo/games.htm

TS'IITS'QWEL'O'OL, also spelled *ts'i:ts'qve'o:l*, the name of 2 different ball games of the Native Amer. Stóólo (or Stó:lo) tribe of the N-W part of Washington state, Vancouver Island, and Fraser Valley.

Game 1 resembles >FIELD HOCKEY or >SHINNY and is sometimes referred to as Indian shinny. Originally, the number of players was unspecified, while the modern, more formalized version is played by 2 teams of 11 players each. Curved sticks are used to play a ball in such a way that it reaches the side occupied by the opposing team. Instead of setting up goals, natural objects were trad. aimed at, such as trees or protruding rocks. The field is not limited in size. Sticks are approx. 4ft. (122cm) long and have flat blades. Hooking the opponent's legs is permitted. The ball is a sphere the size of a tennis ball and used to be made of maple wood. Nowadays grass hockey equipment is standard and the game is played on a football or lacrosse field, with goals similar to those in lacrosse, but smaller (2x2m). There is no goalie and players wear ankle and shin protectors. Teams group in rows and the game begins with a hockey-like face-off: the ball is thrown between the rows and 2 designated players battle over it to get possession. Goals may be scored by any player on the field and the game is played until one team scores a fixed number of points, usu. 21. After each goal a mid-field face-off is used to resume the game.
Game 2 belongs to a family of games known in Eng. ethnography as >DOUBLE BALL, in all of which a double ball is used, originally in the form of 2 leather sacks coupled by straps or strings, later replaced by 2 tennis balls. The ball is played and passed between players with sticks ending in pegs used for hooking the straps. The game is now played on football or lacrosse fields by 2 teams of 11 players each. Teams line up on their goal lines and the ball is placed in the center. When the referee gives a signal, both teams rush towards the center to get possession of the ball. The ball may not be touched with the hands. Points are scored by wrapping the strap coupling the balls around the goal post, which is the most advanced technical skill. After each goal the game is resumed from the center and is continued until either team scores 21pts. There is no designated goalie and each player may score goals.
The Internet: http://web20.mindlink.net/stolo/games.htm

TSAGAAN MOD, Mong. for 'white tree'; also *tsagaan mod khaiakh* and, in E Mongolia, *tsüü khajakh* (splinter throwing). A game of throwing wooden pegs with unstripped bark, approx. 10-16cm in length, for distance. The pegs are called *khuwkhai mod* – dead tree. The game is played by young men, usu. 16-33yrs. old, divided into 2 teams of 9-15 players each. A selected player throws a peg into the steppe, while standing on an imaginary line dividing 'this world' and 'the other world', which is probably the borderline between the land considered to belong to a given tribe and the open steppe. The remaining players turn their backs on the caster to avoid seeing the peg's landing place, called a 'nest'. Once the peg has landed in the grass, the remaining players rush off to find it. The first player to locate it carries it to the winning spot (often arbitrary and unspecified, or sometimes marked with a small circle called the *gal* – fire), which earns a point. While running, he can pass the peg on to another player, like a relay baton. The team that scores more points, wins the game. Traditionally, the game was played during the summer pastures in Mongolia, in a precisely specified time – from the 1st or 2nd day of mid-summer to the 16th or 17th day of the 2nd month of fall. This is a period in which, according to Mong. beliefs, the Earth is visited by the deity personifying the Host of the Earth, to whom the game is dedicated. The game was usu. played before another one, called >TSAGAAN TEMEE and was to prevent weed poisoning of the cattle and the spreading of pox among the people. It was also viewed as a symbolic rejection of misfortunes and bringing happiness, welfare, rain, etc. upon the tribe, as well as a symbol of good harvest and fertility. The winning spot, to which the peg is carried, is often marked with a pile of clothing and furs, usu. prepared by the local community to demonstrate their skills. The entire game is accompanied by loud cries, laughing and hand clapping, which the locals explain in the following way: 'You must cry and laugh during the game to wake up Nature. The Earth rejoices when it hears the voices of its children. And when the Earth is satisfied, it provides man with all of its riches.' The game often ended in sexual contact between the players and the young women who watched them, which ethnographers interpret as coinciding with the event's fertility rites. Among the Mongolians only wooden pegs could be used, for 'a tree is live and grows, while a stone does not'. However, other peoples of C and E Asia played a var. of the game in which they used stone balls or earth clods covered with lose animal hair (>TSAGAAN MONDA). The game enjoyed a certain popularity also among e.g. Kalmucks and Turk. tribes. The Uzumcs used longer pegs (*cho*), while the Zakhchins had a similar game called >GUI KHEE.

I. Kabzińska-Stawarz, 'Tsagaan mod', GOMS, 1991, 135 and 69-70.

TSAGAAN MONDA, Mong. for 'white, round thing'; a Kalmuck var. of Mong. >TSAGAAN MOD, in which various objects are thrown onto the steppe. Similar to *tsagaan mod* the purpose of the game was to throw away evil and secure success and well being for the players. The game often ended in sexual contact between the male players and female spectators. The game was conducted on moonlit nights and the objects were thrown in the direction of the moon. Contrary to the Mongolians, who played exclusively with pieces of wood, the Kalmucks used various objects, depending on the season of the year. In the fall they used pieces of wood, while in the spring – earth clods or stones covered with lose animal hair. In the 20th cent. these var. began to merge in some regions and players used e.g. pieces of wood covered with animal hair.

TSAGAAN TEMEE, also *tsagaan temeetsekh*, Mong. for 'white camel', a game in which one of the participants plays the role of a white camel – different from all others – while the remaining players defend him against a figure which – depending on local traditions – personifies an ordinary camel, a pauper with a sick camel, an old woman, a camel thief, etc. The defenders of the white camel form a circle around him or group in 2 rows and place him inside, trying to protect him agaist being stolen or kidnapped. If the attacker breaks the circle or gets inside the rows of defenders, he wins, upon which players change roles and the game continues. The sport is connected with Mong. beliefs, according to which a white camel was an object of worship as a creature sent by the heavens, where he is ridden by the mythological hero Burkhanabagsha. White camels, along with white horses, had traditionally been highly valued as gifts for Tartar Khans. A white camel was believed to bring good luck and affluence and so the game was played during all holidays connected with welcoming the seasons of the year or harvest festivals, although it usu. came after >TSAGAAN MOD. Cf. >TSAGAAN MONDA.

TSOUMAKA, a contemporary Gk. game played with short (approx. 15cm), finger-thick sticks called *tsiliki*, which are batted with longer sticks towards the opponents. It belongs to the same family of games as Pol. >SZTEKIEL, KLIPA; Pak. >GULLI DUNDA; Eng. >TIP-CAT, and Bret. *mouilh*.

TSU-CHU, in the tradition of Chin. culture a general name for a ball played with the feet [Chin. *tsu-chu* – a leather ball]. In modern Chin. it refers to Eur. >FOOTBALL. Older var. of tsu-chu included kicking the ball between several players so that it does not fall to the ground (similar to >KEMARI, which may have originated in China). The idea of playing a ball with one's feet is attributed to the legendary ruler Hung-Ti, who reigned around 2697 BC. Different names of old Chin. balls, such as >TSU-KIH, >CUJU or *cuqiu*, are related to the earliest Chin. ball games, some of which later developed separately. There is a clear distinction between ball games played on the ground and a Chin.var. of polo, >JIQIU. The father of the originator of the Han dynasty (206 or 202 BC-220 AD) was a great fan of football. The oldest surviving image of tsu-chu comes from 1697 BC.

TSU-KIH, also spelled *tsu küh*, an old Chin. var. of ball game played by soldiers during the reign of the Shang dynasty (approx. 16th-17th cent.). No details are known, but the name may be a var. of >CUJU or *cuqiu*. See also >TSU-CHU.

TU SWING, a var. of trapeze acrobatics practiced by the Tu minority, living in the Datong and Qinghai provinces in China. The swing is made of a rope both ends of which are tied to tree branches at a height of around 20m. At the bottom of a U-shaped loop, about 10m above the ground, stands an acrobat or a pair of acrobats. In order to get to the loop, the acrobats climb up a special ladder fixed to the central part of the rope. The object is to execute a var. of acrobatic figures while swinging. Smaller swings are used by less skillful acrobats, children, and even the elderly. The Tu people believed that swinging helped to throw evil spirits out of one's body. See >SWINGS AND SEESAWS and >CIRCUS ACROBATICS.

Mu Fushan, et al., 'Tu Swing', TRAMCHIN, 29-30.

TUB RACING, a humorous form of sporting competition known in many countries. One of the most popular international var. is a rowing race called *two-in-a-tub*. The tubs used in Singapore are 1.2m in diameter and 70cm deep. The contestants use short, single-bladed oars, each rowing on one side to maintain a straight course.

TUDABARAI, see >BUZKASHI.

TUG-OF-WAR, also *tug o' war*, an athletic competition between 2 teams – or occasionally 2 single players – at opposite ends of a rope (though some var. feature tributary ropes branching off from the main one), each team trying to drag the other across a center line, which frequently takes the form of a ditch of water or mud. Injuries are not infrequent. Apart from Europe, tug-of-war contests are also known in some Asian cultures, e.g. in Mongolia; see >OLS DEES TATALTSAKH; or among the Sinhalese, where it serves ritual and religious purposes: one team represents the protective Goddess Pattini and the opposing team the goddess's evil husband (>SINHALESIAN TUG-OF-WAR). An original form of the sport is the Swedish >DRA HANK.

Tug of war was an Olympic event in the years 1900-1920, but it enjoyed limited interest, being played only by 2 or 3 teams. At some Ol.G. medals were not awarded due to the participation of barely 2 teams. Except for the 1920 Ol.G., teams from the host countries usu. dominated the tug-of-war contests. The largest number of teams (5) took part in the 1920 tug-of-war Olympic event. C.J.P Lucas, the author of *The Olympic Games 1904*, criticized the tug-of-war participants for their violation of the rules of Olympic amateur participation and advocated exclusion of the sport from the Olympic program. During the 1908 Ol.G. in London a heated controversy arose concerning the design of shoes worn by the Brit. team, strongly objected to by the Americans. They were heavier than the shoes of other teams and had specially enlarged soles. The Amer. objection was overruled on the grounds that the Brit. players' shoes were the casual shoes worn by the Brit. police. As a result of the debate, a regulation was passed that no tug-of-war player should wear any customized shoes having any spikes, studs, or other protruding parts. The Olympic tug-of-war was exclusively a men's event. In the years 1900-08 it was part of the track and field program; and in 1920 it became a single event. A joint Dan.-Swed. team won the Olympic gold medal in 1900, the US in 1904, Sweden in 1912, and the UK in 1920. The Tug-of-War W.Ch. have been held every year since 1975 (every 2 years in the years 1978-

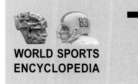

WORLD SPORTS ENCYCLOPEDIA

T

Marie Riegner keeps her eyes on the road ahead as she is pushed by co-worker Ronnie Sterling during the annual Bath Tub Races in Berlin, Germany, as part of the Annual Berlin Village Fair.

Brazilian indians belonging to the Enawene Nawe tribe participate in a tug-of-war competition as fellow tribesmen cheer them on during the 5th edition of the Games of the Indian Peoples in Marapanim, state of Para, northern Brazil.

T
WORLD SPORTS ENCYCLOPEDIA

84 and 1986-88) under the auspices of the Tug-of-War International Federation (TWIF). Men's contests were initially held in 2 team weight categories: up to 720 and 640kg; in 1982 3 more categories were added: up to 560, 600 and 680kg. Women's competitions are held in 480-, 520-, and 560-kg team weight categories. The championship has most often been won by the Eng. team. Other leading national teams include Ireland, Wales and Switzerland. Indoor tug-of-war W.Ch. have been held since 1994, as well as continental championships. Cf. >SHAFT PROPPING, Mong. >SHIRDEG TATAKH, and Kor. >KOSSAUM.

A Basque tug-of-war contest.

TUHO, a trad. Kor. sport resembling >DARTS.

TUINBOLLING, a var. of a trad. game known in Belgium as >TROU-MADAME.

TULLEHUT, Dan. for 'wander around'. A running game, in which players move between 2 safety zones trying to avoid being caught by one designated player who remains between the 2 zones. The catcher must stop a running player, hold him until he counts to 3, and cry, '*Tullehut!*'. The victim then becomes the catcher (*tekkemand*). If nobody dares to leave his safety zone, the catcher counts to 10 and cries, '*Tullehut!*'. All players that still remain in the safety zones are then considered caught and the last of them becomes the catcher in the next game. Cf. >DØDNING, >GÅ OVER ELVEN, >KÆDETIK, >KLIM-KLEM, >TAMANJ, >ISBJØRN OG LANDSBJØRN, >TYRHOLDE. See similar games with 1 safety zone, e.g. >KREDSTROLD.
J. Møller, 'Tullehut', GID, 1997, 2.

TULLIUT, a Dan. run-and-catch game, in which the catcher holds the head of the person he caught and counts to 10, lightly striking his victim's head with each count. Finally he cries 'Tulliut!'. If the victim moves his head, the counting starts anew, after which both become catchers.
J. Møller, 'Tulliut', GID, 1997, 2, 12.

TUMBLING, see >SPORTS GYMNASTICS.

TUMI, also *tarere, pioi,* a Maori form of acrobatic display while hanging from a tree branch or a slender tree bent towards the ground.

F.A. Weinzheimer, Tug-of-war, detail.

Tug-of-war is one of the most universal sporting competitions, known among numerous nations and ethnic communities.

TURBO, a Lat. name for >TOPS. See also >BUXUS.

TURKISH WRESTLING, a number of wrestling styles practiced by Turk. peoples and originating from various regions of Turkey itself and other countries of the former Ottoman Empire. The most influential wrestling var. shaping the development of Turk. styles were >ABA GÜREŞI, the Turkmen >KUSAK GÜREŞI, certain Persian styles (>VARZESH-E PEHLIVANI, >PEHLIVAN WRESTLING), and indigenous var. mixed with ancient wrestling types involving covering one's body with oil as in >YAGLI GÜREŞ. Some Turk. var. are based on the wrestling styles popular among nomadic Mong. tribes, esp. the Huns.

There are different combat styles and clothing across Turk. wrestling var. In *yagli güreş* wrestlers wear leather trousers, in *salvar güresi* – various types of trad., baggy Turk. pants. Umpires usu. wear a trad. tunic-like shirt called a *gomlek*, which is made of thick linen or white batiste and is usu. knee-length, though is sometimes much shorter. In most cases a bout is preceded by a challenge during which a fighter walks around the arena or mat looking for the right opponent. This action is called *dolanma*. After he has found a match for himself, the fighter dresses in his wrestling outfit and returns to the arena. The pre-bout ritual and the bout itself are held to trad. music performed by a drum and pipe duet called a *davul-zurna* (Turk. *duval* – drum + *zurna* – pipe, whistle, flute). *Zurnas* are similar to Eur. flutes but are wider towards the end and thus resemble trumpets. The broad part is made of wood or metal. Additionally, the *zurna* is adorned with a few metal chains, often made of silver, with beads. The arena in which bouts are held is called a *çukur* or *güreş alani*. It may be any village square, a place where cereal crops are threshed, a grassy meadow or even a freshly plowed field. The place is selected in such a way that it is appropriate for the given occasion that is being celebrated. If the arena is messy it is covered with hay and all slippery spots, stones and sharp objects are removed and the soil is softened. During the bout the spectators form a ring. Nowadays, the trad., natural çukurs has been replaced by wrestling a mat similar to those used in official wrestling sports.

Due to the fact that Turk. wrestling tradition is so rich and varied, Turk. wrestlers easily adapted to the officially recognized rules of Greco-Roman or freestyle wrestling and since the second half of the 19th cent. have played a major role in the E.Ch. and W.Ch. as well as Olympic arenas. The following Turk. wrestlers won the Olympic freestyle titles: H. Gemici (1952), A. Bilek (1960) – at 52kg; N. Akar (1948; also the world champion in 1951), M. Dagistanli (1956; also the Olympic champion at 62kg in 1960, world champion at 57kg in 1954, and world champion at 62kg in 1959) – at 57kg; G. Bilge (1948), Bayram Şit (1952) – at 62kg; C. Atik (1948; also the world champion at 74kg in 1951), Y. Dogu (1948), I. Ogan (1964), M. Atalay (1968) – at 74kg; H. Güngör (1960) – at 82kg; I. Atli (1960), A. Ayik (1968; also the world champion in 1965 and 1967) – at 90kg; H. Kaplan (1956) and D. Mahmut (1996) – at 100kg (later renamed to up to 130kg category). Other freestyle Turk. world champions included: H. Akbas (1954; also the world champion at 57kg in 1959 and 1962), M. Kartal (1957), C. Yanilmaz (1963), A. Riozan Alan (1970) – at 52kg; N. Zafer (1951) – at 62kg; M. Atalay – at 74kg; H. Zafer (1951) – at 82kg; and Y. Dogu (1951) – at 90kg.

The following Turk. wrestlers won the Olympic Greco-Roman golds: Y. Erkan (1936), M. Oktav (1948), M. Sille (1960) and A. Prim (1992) – at 62kg; K. Ayvaz (1964; also the world champion in 1962 and the world champion at 74kg in 1958) – at 68kg; Mithat Bayrak (1956 and 1960) – at 74kg; Y. Hamza (1996, also the Olympic champion at 85kg in 2000) – at 82kg; T. Kis (1960; also the world champion in 1962-63) - at 90kg; A. Kireçci – at over 100kg. M. Candas won the W.Ch. at 90kg in 1950.

Turkish wrestling in literature. The fact that the Turks placed great emphasis on physical training and revered the human body is well reflected in certain epic poems based on Persian tradition such as *Gilgamesh, Ergenekon, Manas* and *Oghuz Khan*. They often describe combat skills as the major indicator of manliness. Wrestling was treated as a type of military training for heroes who later fought in wars. *Oghuz Khan*, the oldest preserved

Turk. epic poem, ends with the following lines praising military craft:

Listen boys! I have gone through a lot.
I have seen many wars.
I have shot many arrows.
I have fought a great deal.
I made my foes cry.
I made my friends happy.

Abdulkerim, a Turk. scholar who lived in Tashkent, wrote in one of his works that 'in order to prepare young Turks to fight in a war, body tossing (wrestling) is obligatory'. J. Emre, a Turk. poet, describes wrestling as a source of ecstatic feelings:

I fell in love, the arena is mine today.
The strongman is mine, mine is the arena.
No one can take away my weapons from my arena.
Today the arena, weapons, tshegwan [a polo mallet] are mine.

One Turk. prince, famous for his strength and agility, was described in *Desturname*, another Turk. epic poem, as:

This pasha, on his way to Karaburun,
He was called Hazir Bey – a pehlivan plucky fellow.

Said, a *shahid* (lit. 'witness' – the Islamic equivalent of 'martyr') and a pehlivan wrestler, sacrificed his life in the Alasehir war:

There was a pehlivan called Said
He went up the stairs [...]
He was also followed by Ilias Bey and Dundar Bey
And on that day Said became a shahid
He took his path leading to faith and he became a follower.

The oldest Turk. epic poem *Oghuz Khan* describes the adventures of Oghuz Khan who wanted to rule the whole world and be the master of Nature. To do so, he declared a war on the forces of nature, animals, and humans. The only things he was interested in were hunting, mountain climbing, horse riding, archery, wrestling and other ancient sports. Oghuz was also described as a person who did various bodily exercises to imitate strong animals and the stronger he became, the more elevated the status he achieved. Similar legends are also related in *The Book of Dede Korkut*.

Turk. nomads and warriors could not be weak. So their epic poems praised strongmen who, after successful hunts and victorious battles, returned home to play and compete in archery, horse riding and wrestling. In this sense, the fact that wrestling matches were thought to be an amusement rather than anything else, similarly to other folk sports and competitions, corresponds to the universal trend observed across all cultures.
H. Murat Sahin, *Turk Spor Kulturunde Aga Güreşi*, 1999.

TURKMEN HIGH JUMP, a folk var. of high jump for a prize. 'At a certain place prizes are hung, the most valuable one hangs of the highest point. The best jumper takes the prize. The order and sequence of jumps are supervised by the judges'. >JUMP FOR A SHAWL is a specific var. of this type of jump among Turkmen.
'Sport regionalny', *Sport w ZSRR*, trans. from Russian, 1948, 217.

TURKMEN RACES, held to celebrate various religious holidays and family occasions such as the birth of a child or circumcision of a son. The race was usu. held among young men from a given village or tribe.

TURKMEN WRESTLING, a type of folk wrestling, popular among Iranian Turkmen, esp. in the N, mountainous part of the country.
W. Baxter, 'Les luttes traditionnelles à travers le monde', LJP, 1998, 77.

TURNEN, a Ger. social and gymnastic movement which culminated in the 19th cent. [Ger. *Turnen* – gymnastics, meaning a social movement, as opposed to Ger. *Gimnastik*, meaning the type of exercise and a sport discipline]. The idea of Turnen is attributed to F.L. Jahn who – in his work entitled *Deutsches Volkstum* (1810) – suggested a plan to raise the level of fitness and sense of patriotic duty among all Ger. peoples by forming associations and practicing gymnastics. Jahn's idea was successfully introduced in the 19th cent. by establishing gymnastic societies which spontaneously organized, mainly in cities, mass exercises, walking trips, parades and displays. However, such activities were soon taken over by nationalist and mili-

tary movements. Estab. in 1868, the Turnen movement in Germany was headed by Deutsche Turnschaft, which began to set up the centers of modern sport gymnastics. The organization was soon incorporated into the Nazi Deutsche Reichsbund für Leibensübungen, which brought an end to the functioning of Turnen as an independent social movement, although there still existed in Germany several other Turnen organizations, incl. the antisemitic and pro-Nazi Deutsche Turnerbund, and a shortlived (1848-49), progressive Democratische Turnerbund Deutschlands, initiated by A. Scharttner in Hanau and after the collapse of the Spring of Nations continued by various socialist and revolutionary organizations, all of which were ephemeral, impugned by the Ger. nationalist and military organizations. At the end of the 19th cent. Turnen became part of the program of Ger. labor organizations. In other German-speaking countries, such as Austria and Switzerland, it never reached the level of ideological coherence achieved in Germany. Irrespective of its ideological character, Turnen did manage to give shape to many modern forms of organizational, publishing, and sports activity.

TUTANKHAMEN'S ARCHERY, a form of archery practiced in Egypt c.1358 BC, during the 18th dynasty, reconstructed on the basis of finds from the tomb of Tutankhamen, King Tut, discovered by a Brit. archeologist, H. Carter, in 1922. Three bows were found in the tomb; they were made of wood, horns, tree bark and textiles. The Eg. bows had either limbs made of a single rod or 2 separate limbs connected with a grip; they were 27-49in. in length. The shortest bow was probably used by Tutankhamen, often referred to as 'the boy king', when he was a small child. The arrows for that bow were only about 6in. long. Carter also found 278 arrows, 36in. in length. The bowstrings were made of animal sinew. The longest bow found by Carter was named the Bow of Honor. Its limbs were covered with scales of gold and incrusted with precious stones. Finds from the tomb point to the fact that Tutankhamen was a true aficionado of archery. Several wall paintings from the tomb depict Tutankhamen bowhunting jackasses, ostriches, hyenas, antelopes and cows on his own; or hunting fish and fowl together with his wife. A wall-painting from the temple in Karnak also represents King Tutankhamen hunting with a bow, bearing an inscription: 'He went on hunting, running fast across the valley.'
H. Carter, *The Tomb of Tutankhamen*, 1972; Z. Habashi, 'King Tutankhamen – Sportsman in Antiquity', HEDS-GDC, HISPA, 1975; W. McLeod, *Composite Bows from the Tomb of Tut'Ankhamum*, 1970.

TUTT-BALL, a Brit. bat-and-ball game, in which the ball is batted with the hand and points are earned by running along a marked line. The game was popular in England in the 18th and first half of the 19th cent. In the area of Holderness it was a popular Ash Wednesday entertainment. Coeducational at first, it was later played only by girls, esp. the girls' school at Shiffnal. The pitch had 3 regular bases called 'tuts' and 1 home plate called the 'den', from which the ball was batted. The player of one team threw the ball at the player of the other team located at the den, who batted it with her hand. While the ball was in the air the batter attempted to run along a line connecting the 3 tuts, equally distanced from one another and marked with bricks or stones. Touching all 3 bases earned 1pt. If the batter could not complete all 3 bases at one time, another batter of the same team took her place at the den and the procedure was repeated until one of the batters failed to return the ball within the specified number of trials (which varied according to region). The players of the opposing team were trying to intercept the ball and throw it at the running batter in order to eliminate her. If the flying ball was caught in the air or picked up and thrown at the running batter, teams changed places. Cf. >BASTE-BALL, >CRICKET, >NEW-YORK-BALL, >PALANT, >ROUND BALL, >ROUNDERS, SCHLAGBALL, >TYSKBOLD.
A.B. Gomme, 'Tutt-ball', TGESI, 1898, II, 314.

TUVIN WRESTLING, identical to Mong. >BÖKHIIN BARILDAAN, but for the clothing worn by the wrestlers. Tuvin fighters wore special trousers made of ram leather. Their torsos remained bare.

TWIN SWORDS WITH BELLS, a form of a fencing duel, derived from >WUSHU tradition, practiced by the Li people of China. One of the fighters attacks the opponent with 2 swords and the latter defends himself using special bells called *quiangling*, made of strings of several coins. The duel is accompanied with the characteristic clinking of the bells being hit with the swords. Twin swords with bells is primarily a feat of agility. The contenders wear richly decorated tunics and jewelry, incl. earrings, and headdresses resembling turbans.
Mu Fushan, et al., 'Li Twin Swords with Bells', TRAMCHIN, 80.

TWO FOOT HIGH KICK, an Eng. name of a trad. form of >HIGH JUMP popular among Native Alaskans and Indians of Canada's northern provinces. The jumps are executed after a run of unspecified length. The jumper must take-off and touch with both feet an object suspended on a rope from a jib fastened to a wooden stand and must then land on both feet at the same time. The object to touch is soft, usu. a piece of animal skin. The knees should not be bent during the jump. Each jumper has 3 trials at every height. If a jumper fails at a given height, he is given 2 more trials in which he must succeed at 2 subsequent heights. After the full series of jumps, the height is raised by 2in. (5cm). The jumper that reaches the greatest height wins the competition. If two or more jumpers remain with the same result after the last series, the height is lowered by 1in. and each jumper has 3 trials. The number of successful trails determines the winner. If there is still a tie, the jumper with the lowest total of failures wins the competition. In local terminology the event belongs to arctic sports and, as a separate competition, is part of the N.Amer. Indigenous Games. Cf. >ONE FOOT HIGH KICK, >ALASKAN HIGH KICK, >HITCH AND KICK.
The Internet: The Arctic Sports, http://www.firstnations.com/naig97/arctic-sports/as-twofoothighkick.htm

TWO-OLD-CAT, a bat-and-ball game practiced in the Brit. colonies in N.America in the 17th-18th cent. Along with >BASTE-BALL, >GOALBALL, >CRICKET, >NEW-YORK-BALL, >ROUND BALL, >ROUNDERS, it contributed to the development of Amer. >BASEBALL. The game was centered around 2 bases adopted from an earlier game >ONE-OLD-CAT. A more sophisticated var., with 4 bases, was known as >TOWN-BALL.

TXINGAK, a Basq. trad. competition in carrying heavy objects, an equivalent of Span. *txingas*. Contestants must carry 2 solid metal weights of 50kg each over a distance of 28m. The shape of the weights differs according to local tradition. Most often the weights are rectangular and resemble fuel containers with handles in the upper part or are shaped like vertical cylinders with triangular handles. Competitions are usu. held in public squares of villages or small towns, or on corrida arenas.
R. Aguirre, 'Txingak-Txingas', GHJD, 1989, III, 92-95; C. Moreno-Palos, 'Transporte de txingas', JYTE, 1992.

TXOKO, a Basq. trad. sport deriving from the Middle Ages. It is related in a linguistically viable way to the Span. >CHUECA and Port. >CHOCA.

TYFTEHÖNAN, a rock used in displays of strength and a trad. sport in which villagers in the Naverstad parish in the area of Bohuslän in Sweden compete in rock lifting. The name comes from a farm called Tyft, on which the event was originally held. In the middle of the 19th cent. the Tyft rock was stolen and was later found on the Stengrimseröd farm. See also >LYFTESTEN; cf. >DRÄNGASTENAR, >DRÄNGA-LÖFTEN, >KAMPASTEN; Dan. >STENLØFTNING; Basq. >ARRIJASOKETA, >KØLNÄKERN, >KUNGSSTEN, >KUNGSSTENARNA, >LYFTES-TEN, >STORA OCH LILLA DAGSVERKARN.
G. Drougge, *Ortnammen i Bullarens härad* (local names in the Bullaren shire), 1938, p. 235; M. Hellspong, 'Lifting Stones. The Existence of Lifting-Stones in Sweden', ST, 1993-94, XIX-XX.

TYNTEDRAPTE, a Moldavian form of hand-to-hand combat. Cf. Rom. >TRÎNTA, Scot. >BACKHOLD.

TYNZJAN, a var. of >LASSOING with a thick rope lasso, practiced by the Nency, a tribe belonging to Siberian Samoyeds inhabiting the region of Krasnoyarsk. Contestants throw the lasso with both their hands and legs onto different objects, both standing and mobile. The longest recorded throw is 54m. Cf. >ARKAN THROWING, >LAZU, >URGA.

TYRHOLDE, Dan. for 'holding a bull', [Dan. *tyr* – bull + *holde* – to hold]. A running game in which the players move between safety zones trying to avoid being caught by the catcher. It is more violent than other similar games, because the caught player is forced to become a catcher by being 'tortured', which includes pulling the victim's hair, ears and nose. Cf. >DØDNING, >GÅ OVER ELVEN, > ISBJØRN OG LANDSBJØRN, >KÆDIK, >KLIM-KLEM, >TAMANJ, >TULLEHUT; see also similar races with 1 safety zone, e.g. >KREDSTROLD.
J. Møller, 'Tyrholde', GID, 1997, 2, 57.

TYSKBOLD, Dan. for 'German ball', [Dan. *Tysk* – German + *bold* – a ball]. The name probably indicates the influence of Ger. bat and ball games, such as >SCHLAGBALL or >PALANT. The game is also called *tomansbold* – lit. 'two players' ball' [Dan. *to* – two + *mand* – a man + *bold* – a ball] or *spyt* – 'spit', [Dan. *spyt* – saliva, to spit, probably from spitting in the hands before taking the bat and hitting the ball]. The game is played by 2 players on a narrow field divided into the home base (*Hovedmaalet*), from which the ball is batted, and the back base (*Bagmaalet*). The first batter has 3 attempts to strike the ball. If he bats it into the field, he runs towards the back base and, having touched it, returns to the home base. If he completes the task without being hit by the ball thrown by his opponent, he may continue the game. Otherwise, the players change roles. Tyskbold is very similar to palant, with the exception that, unlike in the latter, there are only 2 players. The strategy of the game is defined in terms difficult to translate because of their additional meanings. The word *leg*, meaning a game in general, also indicates a constructive activity aimed at achieving something. It is countered by *ulleg* – the outfielder's strategy of interfering with his opponent's efforts. The name *tyskbold* is also applied to a game played in the town of Aakirby according to identical rules, but without a bat. In that var. one player throws the ball and begins to run. He may be stopped if his opponent throws the ball back and strikes him with it. The terminology is also different: the division is not into the home base and back base, but into infield (*inde*) and outfield (*ude*).
J. Møller, 'Tyskbold', GID, 1997, 1, 62.

TYVELEG, Dan. for 'thieves' game', [Dan. *tyve* – a thief + *leg* – a game]. The players are grouped in 2 rows separated by a distance of at least 3m from the gym's wall. The first player from the first row runs to the second row, makes funny gestures, and strikes every player 3 times on their raised hand. When he completes his task, he begins to run away, being chased by the last player he struck. The runner must reach the row of his teammates, who catch him so that he does not fall into the wall. If he is not caught, the next player from the second row runs towards the players in the first row and the routine is continued.
J. Møller, 'Tyveleg', GID, 1997, 2, 39.

TZYKANISTERION, in Latinized Gk. *tsicanisterium*, a medieval Byzantine ball game played on horseback, not unlike modern >POLO and – because of the netted bat – Can. >LACROSSE. The term also denominates the field on which the game was played. A Byzantine writer, J. Kinnamos, offers the following description of the sport:

A group of youngsters is divided into 2 teams, who pass amongst themselves an apple-sized leather ball on a flat ground which is measured in such a way that its center is at an equal distance from each team. As soon as the ball is in the center, both teams run full steam at each other, carrying in their right hands long sticks bent, split, and widened at the end, with dried gut strings formed into a net attached in the middle. The aim of the game is to move the ball towards the target zone of the opponents with the bats. The team that succeeds, wins the game. The game is risky and dangerous, because every player must lean forwards, backwards and from side to side, and turn his horse back and move it in every direction, executing all kinds of moves required by the position of the ball.

According to Kinnamos, the game was played only by players who belonged to a higher social class, which is confirmed by another Byzantine writer, K. Porfirogenitus: 'by an old custom the ball on horses was played by kings and sons of the nobility'. According to a French philologist and historian, S. Du Cange (1610-88), tzykanisterion was transferred by the crusaders to France, where it gave birth to another game called *chicane*. Cf. the Persian >CHUGAN.

WORLD SPORTS ENCYCLOPEDIA

U KOSTI, a trad. var. of Croatian wrestling [serbo-croatian *u kosti* – to teach sb. a good lesson], based on classical style of wrestling. Popular among some nations of former Yugoslavia, it offers them a common cultural basis, despite historical conflicts and political differences, such as the conflict between Serbia and Croatia during the early 1990s. Wrestling bouts often accompany country festivals or family gatherings like weddings, baptismal parties, etc. Currently in decline. Cf. >U POJAS; see also >WRESTLING.

The bout. Contenders face each other and, sometimes, place one or both feet against a metal bar driven into the ground. It is allowed to catch the opponent over the shoulders and under the arms or – in some regions – just under the arms. The aim is to knock the opponent to the ground by a side throw or back throw.

Ulama de cadera.

U POJAS, a form of trad. wrestling practised in some countries of former Yugoslavia, mainly in Serbia. The starting position is unspecified. Pushing and tripping up are allowed. Depending on local tradition, the goal is to knock the opponent down on his back once, twice or 3 times. Wrestling bouts are usu. held during local village festivals or family gatherings. Currently in decline. Cf. >U KOSTI, see also >WRESTLING.

U TRUCCU, a game similar to >PALLAPORTA, >PALLA MAGLIO, and Flem. >BEUGELEN. The idea is to roll a ball through a ring placed vertically on the ground.

UIST WRESTLING, Eng. name for Scot. folk wrestling >CARACHD UIBHIST.

An ulama de cadera player.

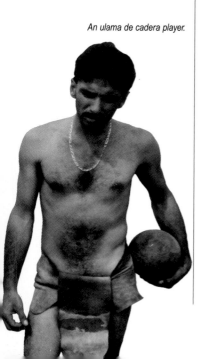

ULAMA, also *hulama*, a type of ball game practiced among C Amer. Indians. The name *ulama* comes from the Aztec *ullamaliztli*, a combination of two words: *ullama* – a ball game and *ulli* – rubber. Many elements relate it to pre-Columbian >MIDDLE AMERICAN INDIAN BALL GAMES. According to Amer. ethnographer Robert L. Humphrey, the original pre-Columbian Indian games adopted by the Spaniards in the 16th cent. influenced first the ball games of Europe and later were reintroduced through the Spanish into Mexico, where they became part of a complex mixed heritage of ancient games (*Play as Life: Suggestions for a Cognitive Study of the Mesoamerican Ball Game*, in: *Play as Context*, A. Taylor Cheska, TASP, 1980). The following var. of ulama are still practiced in C America and Mexico (esp. in the province of Sinaloa):
ULAMA DE ANTEBRAZO, also *ulama de brazo* – played by using one's forearm [Span. *antebrazo* – forearm]. The game is played between 2 teams of

Underwater cycling.

3 persons each, on a field 100m in length and 1.5m in width, with lines feet-marked on the ground. The name of the field – *taste* – is probably a distortion of an ancient Aztec game >TLACHTLI. The game can be played with low balls, hit just above the field surface [cf. *abajo* – downwards] or with high balls [cf. *arriba* – upwards]. Players wear knee guards (*rodillera*), protecting them against scratches resulting from frequent contact with the ground. The forearm hitting the ball is wrapped with a cotton bandage (*faja*), usu. 3m in length and 3cm in width. The ball is several centimeters in diameter and weighs 500g. The aim of the game is to keep the ball in the air. Letting the ball fall causes the loss of a point. The game is controlled by a referee (*veedor* – lit. 'the one who sees'). The game is esp. popular in N Sinaloa between its capital Culiacán and the Guamuchil river.

ULAMA DE CADERA – played by using one's hip [Span. *cadera* – hip]. The rules are similar to *ulama de antebrazo*, except that the ball is hit with a hip. The field, called *taste*, 65m long and 4m wide, is divided into 2 halves by the middle line (*analco*). The game is controlled by a referee (*veedor*). Hip protectors (*fajado*) consist of a goat or deer leather band (*gamuza de venado*), supported by a cotton cloth (*faja de algodón*). To keep the buttocks squeezed together, which guarantees adequate hitting of low balls, players wear leather belts (*chimali* or, in Nahuatl, *chimalli*). Both high balls and low balls are permitted. The game is practiced in S Sinaloa and south of the city of Mazatlán.
ULAMA DE PALO – played with a stick, also *ulama de mazo* – cudgel ulama. A game similar to the other 2 var. of ulama, except for the use of bats with a flat ending resembling a tennis racket [Span. *palo*

Ulama de palo.

– stick]. *Palo* weighs 5-7kg, while *taste* is 120m long and 2m wide. The ball weighs 500-600g. The game can be played as singles, doubles, or by teams of 3 players. It became extinct in the 1950s, but was revived in 1990 during a cultural festival in Culiacán, Mexico. Since then it has been promoted by the Mexican government. See also >PRECOLUMBIAN GAMES OF THE AMERICAS.

G. Burnand, *Ulama. The Pre-Columbian Ballgame*, 'Olympic Magazine', June 1997; *Ulama. Ballgame from the Olmecs to the Aztecs*, 1997; T.J.J. Leyenaar, 'The Modern Ballgames of Sinaloa: A Survival of the Aztec Ullamaliztli', *The Sport of Life and Death: The Mezoamerican Ballgame*, ed. E.M. Whittington, 2001.

ULE PORANDAPRAO HUPPAMINE, Est. for 'jumping over a crack in the floor'; a game in which each player bends down, grabs his feet and tries to jump over a crack in the floor. Popular particularly between New Year's Eve and the Twelfth Night, the game is connected with a custom of sealing floor cracks with hay.

Marge Värv and others, 'Traditional Sports and Games in Estonia', TSNJ, 1996, 32.

UMA YUMI, Jap. forms of mounted archery practiced throughout the ages, which include: >ARCHERY, >ORIENTAL ARCHERY, >INUOMONO, >YABUSAME, >KASA-GAKE.

UMIAK, also *umiac, oomiac, umiaq*; a type of large Innuit vessel, constructed on a wooden, leather-clad framework with crosswise benches for the rowers and passengers. It is used for transporting persons and goods, and – during local religious festivals – for competition, esp. between women and young girls. The name, deriving from the language of Greenland natives, denotes a boat for women. The umiak was described for the first time by and Eng. sailor M. Frobischer (c.1535-1594), who travelled into what is now Baffin Bay, where he encountered a group of Innuits rowing in their boats and forced them onto the deck of his ship. Most of them died before the expedition returned to England.

In 1982 Dan. Queen Margrethe visited Greenland, where she was offered a sea ride in an umiak (called *konebåd* in Dan.), esp. reconstructed for the occasion by 7 elder Innuit men and women.

UNDERWATER CYCLING, a bizarre sporting extravaganza, in which the participants dressed in diving suits and equipped with aqualungs race on bicycles at the bottom of water basins.

UNDERWATER CROSSBOW SHOOTING, a var. of an aquatic sport consisting of target shooting while diving, most often with a snorkel. The equipment consists of a neoprene wetsuit, weighted belt, flippers, a special type of underwater crossbow (usu. 1.5-1.8m long), and stainless steel arrows (about 1.8m long). The end of the crossbow is specially stabilized so that the skin diver can operate more easily. Underwater crossbow shooting is used for hunting of big fish weighing 30-300kg, like bluefin and yellowfin tuna, black marlin, Span. mackerel, etc. The aim of the hunt is to kill the fish with one shot, because a long struggle with the fish under water is dangerous. There have been cases when the fish drew the diver into deep water, which resulted in the death of the diver. Thus, underwater crossbow shooting can be a brutal confrontation between man and nature, not unlike other fights with animals, e.g. >CORRIDA. In the South Seas the technique of underwater crossbow shooting has to take into account numerous perils like the sudden appearance of sharks. The advanced technique of underwater crossbow hunting in seas distant from the equator takes advantage of seals for driving fish.

UNDERWATER FOOTBALL, an underwater team game. It is played with a non-buoyant ball which is usu. a rubber-covered brick, 1ft. long and 4in. high and wide. Quite frequently an NFL football filled with corn syrup is used, weighing about 8-9lbs. The game is played by 2 teams consisting of no more than 13 players each. Only 5 players of one team can be in the playing area at any one time. Substitutions may be made at any natural break in play, i.e. when a goal is scored or at half time. The match consists of two 10-min. periods with a 3-min. break at half time. Each player wears fins, a facemask, and snorkel. The playing area is a swimming pool 60ft. long, 40ft.

Underwater football.

wide, and 15-20ft. deep. The object of the game is to move the football underwater and deposit it within the opponent's goal area. The goal is marked with lines, 6ft. apart. The goal lines should be a min. of 1m inside of the sideline. The game is commenced from the center of the pool. In order to score the ball must be placed in the goal area in such a manner that it comes momentarily to rest on the pool deck with the scorer's hand still grasping the ball. The player in control of the ball may be tackled but the tackler cannot butt the ball carrier with the head, use wrestling holds, or grab the opponent's facemask. All team members wear colored tape on their wrists, each team displaying a different color. The game is controlled by 5 officials: the chief referee conducting his duties from a position on the pool side; 2 water referees, each responsible for one half of the pool and conducting their duties from the water; the lines persons equipped with red flags and whistles, who are positioned on the sides of the pool and signal the scoring of goals; and a timekeeper.

History. The game was originated in 1989 by S.D. Ennis from Manitoba. Underwater football is a rel-

atively unknown sport. Until 1999, it was played by a few Can. teams from Winnipeg, Manitoba and Calgary, Alberta. The governing body of underwater football is the Manitoba Underwater Council in Winnipeg.

S.D. Ennis, *Underwater football*, http://www.gfi.uib.no/%7Eaven/boblen/uvfootball.html; Manitoba Underwater Council, *Underwater Football Rules and Regulations*, 1999.

UNDERWATER HOCKEY, a game played on the bottom of a swimming pool by 2 teams of players. The puck is pushed with a short stick and the objective is to place it in the opponent's goal.

Court and rules. The pool is 2-3.65m deep, and the court area itself is 20-25 by 10-15m. There are 12 players in the pool at any one time (6 players per team) with 4 subs each waiting at the side. Two substitutions per match are allowed. At the start of play, after the sides have been chosen by tossing a coin, both teams line up at their goal and the puck is placed in the middle of the court. The water referees are

located at the center line. The chief referee announces the start of play 30sec. in advance. Then he or she hits a gong or siren to start play. The puck is played by the team whose attackers reach it first. The goals are 120mm away from the back of the court; they are 3m wide and 1.8m high.

Underwater hockey is a non-contact sport so it is forbidden to push away other players with the free hand. The only thing that can touch the puck is the stick. The game lasts 30min. with a 3-min. break at half time. During the break the teams change ends which is especially important in pools with a sloping bottom. In the case of a draw, an extra period of 2x5min. is given. If necessary, the game is continued until one side scores, which is known as a sudden-death overtime.

The referee team consists of the chief referee, who conducts the game from the side of the pool, 2 water referees, who supervise the game from inside the pool, the timekeeper and the scorekeeper. The beginning and end of the game is signaled by underwater and outside sirens, sounded by the chief referee. Inside the pool, the referees use gestures. The most common penalties are elimination from the game for 1 or 2min. (signaled with 1 or 2 fingers raised, respectively). It is also possible to be ejected for the rest of the game. A foul in the penalty area, marked by the 3-m radius from the goal, results in a penalty stroke, also executed from the 3-m mark.

Equipment needed to play the game is a mask, snorkel, flippers, padded glove, or something similar to protect the hand that holds the stick. Head caps with firm polyethylene or rubber ear protectors must be worn. The puck is weighted, usually made of lead with a plastic coating to protect the pool bottom. It weighs 1.3kg and has a diameter of 80mm and a thickness of 30mm. The players may also wear protective knee and elbow pads, provided they are constructed of soft materials. All members of each team wear identical bathing suits with respect to design and color, which are of a light shade if the team is using white sticks (all team members have identical sticks) or of a dark shade if the team is using black sticks. All players of each team wear identification caps, either black (or dark

blue) or white, to match the color of the sticks the team is using. The caps of each team's players in each division must have 12 different numbers for the identification of players i.e. any number may be used, but no player can use the same number as another player from any team in the same division. The stick is made of wood, plywood, or other homogenous material that floats horizontally in water. It may be of any shape or design within the min. and max. dimensions (length: 25-35cm, width: no more than 10cm). It may not protrude from the heel of the hand (or gloved hand) by more than 25mm.

History. The game was created in 1954 in England and given the name *octopush*. In the '50s and '60s, it spread across the Commonwealth, especially Australia, N.Zealand, Canada, and Zimbabwe; and in the '70s and '80s also in the USA, Japan, S.Africa, Colombia, Belgium, the Netherlands and France. The first W.Ch. in both men's and women's categories were held in 1988. Today, other categories in W.Ch. cover masters (over 35) and juniors (under 17). In order to participate in the W.Ch., a country must have

WORLD SPORTS ENCYCLOPEDIA

U

Top and above: underwater rugby.

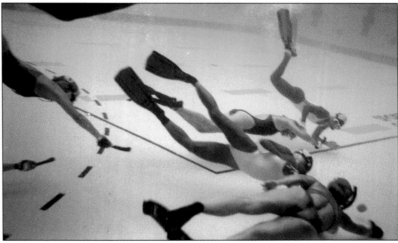

Canada's women's underwater hockey team, in red, competes against the Colombian national team during the underwater hockey world championships in San Jose, California.

at least 5 men's teams or 3 teams in other categories. On the international scale, the game is supervised by the Underwater Hockey Commission at the World Confederation of Underwater Activities (Confédération Mondiale des Activités Subaquatiques, CMAS). Although the official language of CMAS is French, within the Underwater Hockey Commission the official language is English, so is the basic version of the rules of the game. Each member country has the right to suggest amendments to the rules and the Commission's statute.

UNDERWATER RUGBY, a game played under water, in a pool (12-18m long, 8-12m wide and 3.5-5m

deep) by 2 teams of 11-15 players each (6 participating in the game with the remainder waiting on the surface as substitutes; any number of substitutions may be made at any time). Each player is equipped with a snorkel and a mask, a special helmet with ear protectors and flippers with a max. length of 60cm. The objective of the game is to score points by placing the ball in the basket of the opposing team. Each of the metal baskets, located at the opposite ends of the pool, is 450mm high and 390-400mm in diameter, with a rubber top edge. The rubber ball is 490-510mm in diameter for women, and 520-540mm for men. It is filled with a solution of sugar and salt so that it sinks at a speed of 0.75-1.0m/s (this means dissolving approx. 1kg of both salt and sugar in 10 liters of water). To make it more visible, the ball is red or has 'TV patterns' painted on it. At least 3 umpires control the game: 2 under water, 1 in each pool half, and 1 on the surface, watching from the side. Tackles on the swimming suit, mask, helmet or fins are prohibited, as are kicking opponents, tackles without the ball, grabbing the basket or moving it. For breaking these rules, players are ejected from the game for 2mins. **History**. The basics of the game were laid out in 1961 by L. von Bersuda, a member of the Ger. Underwater Club in Cologne. The physician F.J. Grimmeisen was another pioneer, thanks to whom the Duisburg underwater club came into contact with a similar club in Müllheim. As a result of that, the first underwater rugby tournament was played in Müllheim in 1965, with 6 clubs from Müllheim, Düsseldorf, Bochum, Duisburg and Essen. At the time, underwater rugby was played with 8 players in each team, but it was decided later that 6 was a more suitable number. The Müllheim tournament has been held annually ever since. E.Ch. have been organized since 1978, and W.Ch. – since 1980. The sport has become popular in Austria, the Czech Republic, Denmark, Finland, Germany, Slovakia, and outside Europe – in Colombia. Norway is the leading underwater rugby nation, with 40 teams active in 1999 (500-600 members each). Norw. national championships and about 10 other events are organized every year. Show tournaments were begun in Denmark in 1973, and in Finland and Czechoslovakia – in 1975. In 1978, underwater rugby was recognized by the Confédération Mondiale des Activités Subaquatiques (CMAS). The first E.Ch. were held that same year. Germany has organized academic championships since 1986. Cf. >UNDERWATER FOOTBALL, >UNDERWATER HOCKEY.
R. Wiesner, *Entwicklung des UW-Rugbys*, 'Sporttaucher', 1994, 4; *What is UW-Rugby?*, The Internet: http://www.gfi.uib.no/%7Eeven/boblen/eng_what.html

UNICYCLE HOCKEY, Ger. *Einradhockey*. A game played by unicycle riders using hockey sticks. The object of the game is to force the ball into the opponent's goal. The pitch is 35-45m long, 20-25m wide, divided in the middle by a center line with a center mark, from which the referee starts the game by throwing the ball between 2 players from opposing teams. The pitch is surrounded by barriers, which limit the field of play. The posts are 2.5m in from the ends of the pitch (ground lines), ensuring that the players can go behind them. The goal mouths are 1.2m high and 1.8m wide. The goals must not have sharp, pointed or protruding parts. A team consists of 5 players and can be co-educational. There are no designated goalkeepers. Penalties are taken from the 6.5-m mark.
All times mentioned refer to actual playing time. Time is stopped during interruptions in play. There are two 15min. halves, separated by a 5-min. break. The teams change sides during the break. If the game ends in a draw and a decision is necessary, play is continued for 10 more min.: two 5-min. periods after a 5-min. break. If the match is still unresolved, each of the 5 current players from each team shoots from the 6.5-m mark. If it is still a draw, each team continues shooting until there is a result. A player falling off the unicycle remains in play until touching the ground. This is crucial in the case of a shot at the goal, when it has to be estab. if the ball was shot before or after contact was made. Right of way is also important. No player may endanger another player by forcing him to give way. A player who is idling must be evaded. During one-on-one confrontations right of way goes to the player who, however minimally, is in front of the other.
Blocking a player with the stick is not allowed and is punished with a free shot or a penalty shot if committed in the penalty area. Intentional fouls are considered unsporting behavior. The player responsible is sent off the field for at least 2min. The lower end of the stick must always be below the players' hips. Each player must take care not to hit an opponent with his or her stick, esp. after a shot. Only goals shot with the stick are allowed. A goal is disallowed, if 1) scored with arms or hands; 2) the ball was shot from one's own half and was not touched by anyone afterwards; 3) the ball entered the goal through the net from the side or the back, e.g., through a hole in the net. If the ball gets stuck in the wheel of a unicycle after a shot, the opposing team gets a free shot.
For international competitions, max. wheel size is 24in. Unicycles must not have sharp or protruding parts that might cause injuries. This refers esp. to quick-release levers and bolts. The pedals must be plastic or rubber. A small saddle is mounted directly on the fork of the wheel and

Unicycle hockey.

Sam Whittingham of Victoria, British Columbia, puts in an unofficial world record speed of 73.34mph in his aerodynamic shelled bicycle during the 22nd Annual World Human Powered Vehicle Speed Competition 200-meter land sprints hosted by the U.S. Department of Energy at the Test Site in Mercury, Nevada.

A unicycle.

The fastest bicycles in the world

Barracuda

Bearacuda

Mango

Mephisto

cle Association (unrestricted meaning not limited by anything, incl. regulations). Among the members of the IHPVA are: Australia, Belgium, Denmark, Finland, France, Germany, Great Britain, the Netherlands, the USA, Sweden, and Switzerland. A number of solutions noticeably transgress the rules and standards of the UCI (*Union Cycliste Internationale* – the International Cycling Union). The most crucial issues in alternative bicycle construction are reducing rolling friction and improving aerodynamics – as a result of these quests, recumbent and panel-streamlined bicycles have been introduced. These bicycle types outclass trad. bicycles in terms of their speeds, the absolute speed record in flat cycling being 80.552mph set by Sam Whittingham in Varna Diablo in 2001. The official 200m flying start world speed record was set at 72.75mph (117.07km/h) by Sam Whittingham (vehicle Varna Mephisto) in 2000. The 1-hr. trial record was set at 50.42mi. (81.158km) by Lars Teutenberg (vehicle White Hawk) in 1999, and the record in the 24-hr. trial is 634.64mi. (1021.36km), set by Axel Fehlau in 1995.
E.R. Burke, *High-Tech Cycling*, 1996; E.R. Burke, *Serious Cycling*, 1995; www.ihpva.org/

UPOKO TITI, a Maori children's skill game of interlocking the fingers of hands placed one upon another by as many participants as possible. A similar game is played by aborigine children in the Austrl. state of Queensland.

URAL WRESTLING is distinguished by the fact that the competitors never fight on the ground but always is a standing position. The major technique employed is holding an opponent by a special band worn around the waist. Ural wrestling matches are usu. accompanied by musical performances.
W. Baxter, 'Les luttes traditionnelles à travers le monde', LJP, 1998, 79.

URANIA [Gk. *ourania* – a name related to the old-Gk. *ouranios* – subcelestial, reaching to the sky, or possibly *ouranizo*], a ball game played in Ancient Greece. One player threw the ball up and the other attempted to catch it. In its oldest form it was connected with dance; not only the physical skill of players was evaluated, but also their personal charm, as indicated by a short description included in Book VIII of Homer's *Odyssey*, in which the Faecians Laodamas and Halios are amusing themselves during the feat in honor of Odysseus (Ulysses):

Then Alcinous told Laodamas and Halius to dance alone, for there was no one to compete with them. So they took a red ball which Polybus had made for them, and one of them bent himself backwards and threw it up towards the clouds, while the other jumped from off the ground and caught it with ease before it came down again. When they had done throwing the ball straight up into the air they began to dance, and at the same time kept on throwing it backwards and forwards to one another, while all the young men in the ring applauded and made a great stamping with their feet.

[trans. Samuel Butler]

Later urania players started throwing the ball at each other. Whoever failed to catch the ball was called 'an ass' and would carry the winner, called 'the king', on his shoulders in front of the spectators. The scene of parading 3 'kings' by 3 'asses' is depicted on a black-figure vase (*lekythos*) dated at the end of the 6th cent. BC. The number of players indicates that the scene portrays a training session. The trainer (*paidotribes*), sitting in front of the parading figures, is holding an ornamental ball that fits in his hands. The players reach for it, as if awaiting the throw to start the game. In the course of the game, both the 'asses' and the 'kings' tried to catch the ball – if the 'ass' caught it, he became the 'king'. The game has survived until today in various forms as a children's game (see e.g. >RIDE PICK-A-BACK).

URGA, a Mong. type of a lasso used for catching cattle or horses. One end of the lasso is driven into a handle, which makes it easier for the rider to keep the rope rigid while throwing. Mong. herdsmen use it in their occasional competitions in catching cattle. It never reached the level of Amer. >RODEO. Cf. >ARKAN THROWING, >LASSOING, >LAZU, >TYNZJAN.

URUM-TOP, a Gk. var. of >PALANT.

UTYUG, a Rus. ice game, in which specially shaped stones are propelled on ice towards a target made up of wooden blocks; the name derives from the shape of the stone, which looks like an

iron. The object of the game is to knock a wooden block out of a circle drawn on ice. The wooden stone is 25cm in diameter and about 6cm thick, with a thick metal sheet protecting it against friction on the ice; in its top part there is a simple handle about 30cm long, which is at an angle of 30° to the stone's surface. Usu. 3 stones are used in the game, the object being to hit the 'iron' against the wooden blocks, usu. round, about 7-

Urania on a Greek vase.

8cm in diameter, and about 10cm in height. A rectangular course, called the field, is usu. 15 paces long and 4 paces wide; the back line is both the starting and finish line. On the opposite side of the field there is a circle, 1 step in diameter. There are 2 tracks next to each other, in which the stones are propelled in opposite directions (unlike in >CURLING and >ZIELSCHIEßEN, where the stones can be propelled in both directions on the same track after changing sides). The game is played individually or by teams of 2-5 men. The rules of the game are as follows: the team starting the game has 3 stones and 3 blocks, the other team has the remaining 3 blocks. A player aims the stone at the block in the center of the circle. If the block is hit and pushed out of the circle, the player scores a point and an opponent puts another block in the circle. If the block is hit but remains in the circle, the player loses a point. The game continues until all the blocks of one team have been used. The players (or teams) change sides and the game is resumed. Cf. >EISKEGELN, >EISSCHIEßEN, >ICE BOWLING, >KALLUDER-SCHIEßEN, >KNATTLEIKR, >KINGSSCHIEßEN, >MÖSÖN SHAGAI KHARVAKH, >RINGSSCHIEßEN, >STOCKSCHIEßEN, >WEITSCHIEßEN.
I.N. Chkhannikov, 'Utyug', GIZ, 1953, 102-103.

UUL, one of 2 var. of a Mong. game of skills called >ADUU KHUMIKH.

Utyug

---

its height can be adjusted. All sticks legal for playing ice-hockey (apart from those for the goalkeeper) can be used. Cracked or splintered sticks must be taped or repaired before play. An upper end made of rubber is recommended. The type of ball used depends on the region. In some areas a 'dead' tennis ball that reaches 30 to 50% of its original height after bouncing onto concrete is used. In other areas street hockey balls are used. For international competitions, the choice is made by the hosting organization if the opposing teams do not agree on which ball to use. The chosen type of ball must be announced well in advance of the competition, and must be obtainable in all participating countries. Shoes must be worn. Players wear cycling shorts or tracksuit bottoms, kneepads, gloves, helmets and gumshields.
History. The game originated in the 1970s. The W.Ch. are held every 2 years, with 24 teams participating. The leading teams are from Germany: Bochum, LaHiMo of Lagensfeld and SKV Mörfelden. Other important teams include the US national team and Verein für Einradhockey. There is also a unicycle league in Germany.

UNMOUNTED HORSE RACING, known among the peoples of C Asia, esp. in Tibet, where they are part of New Year's celebrations. In his book *The People of Tibet* (1968) C. Bell described an event in which unmounted horses set off from the starting line and were followed by riders driving them in the desired direction. Unmounted horse races took place at the same time and over the same distance as running events. In some cases horses would come to the finish line together with the best runners.

UNRESTRICTED BICYCLES, a type of cycling done by constructors experimenting with new mechanical and aerodynamic solutions in bicycles under the auspices of the International Human Powered Vehi-

WORLD SPORTS ENCYCLOPEDIA

VÆDDER PÅ FINGRENE, Dan. for 'finger ram', (Dan. *vædder* – ram + *på* – for + *fingrene* – fingers]. An old game in which each of the 2 players places his middle finger on his forefinger, and his little finger on his ring finger. Then he strikes the opponent's fist with his own, trying to maintain his fingers in their original position. The player whose fingers slip off, loses the game.
J. Møller, 'Vædder på fingrene', GID, 1997, 4.

VÆLTE TÆNDSTIKÆSKE MED NÆSEN, Dan. for 'knocking down a matchbox with one's nose', [Dan. *vælte* – knock down + *tændstikæske* –matchbox + *med* – with + *næsen* – nose]. A game of skill, in which a matchbox is placed between kneeling competitors at a forearm's distance from each of them. The aim of the game is to knock the matchbox down with one's nose, while keeping one's hands behind one's back.
J. Møller, 'Vælte tændstikæske med næsen', GID, 1997.

VÆVERLEGEN, Dan. for 'weaving game', [Dan. *væver* – weaver < *væve* – to weave + *lege* < *leg* – a game]. A game of skill, in which a bench is placed in the middle of the room. The 'weaver' stands in a straddling position over the bench and performs a ritual of hitting it 3 times, after which he grabs the bench and strikes it 3 times against the floor. Then he grabs the edges of the bench and jumps from one side of it to the other, making a full turn at the same time, so that he faces the opposite side. The action is repeated until the entire bench has been 'woven'.
J. Møller, 'Væverlegen', GID, 1997, 3, 26.

VÅG, a form of folk competition in Gothland, in which parishes compete against one another in 3 different sports events. 'Våg' lit. means 'a bet' and has a sense identical to the Eng. 'wager'. The competition begins with the captain of one parish sending a letter of challenge (vågbrev) to the captain of another parish. The letter includes the time, place and size of the wager, which usu. amounts to $^2/_3$ of the cost of preparing the event, which is paid by the losers, while the winners cover the remaining $^1/_3$ of the cost. The letter also defines the 3 events in which the parishes will compete. One of them is called *sampsel* – lit. 'a mutually selected game', the other 2 are called *frispel* – lit. 'a game of choice', in which each parish decides what

Vallamkali.

Vande svaner.

the event is going to be and keeps it secret until the competition is about to start. Then each parish selects its players. If a given team believes that it will not succeed in the mutually selected *sampsel*, the captain may designate the best players to compete in one of the *frispel* events. That decision is made on the basis of who has been designated for a given event by the other teams. For that reason the privilege to designate team players for particular events after other teams have already made their selection is a very important element. The team that excels in 2 of the 3 events, wins the competition. The first 2 events are *frispels*, which often makes the neutral *sampsel* a decisive one. For a *sampsel* teams often select a game of >PÄRK, while for *frispels* they often select >DRA HANK, a form of running event popular in Gothland, >STÖRTA STÅNG, a local form of tug-of-war, or a local var. of high jump. Våg is usu. held in August, at the end of the harvest season, and ends in a feast in which everybody participates. Teams competing in particular events usu. consist of 5-9 players. Players may participate in only 1 of the 3 events, and so each parish's team must have approx. 15-27 players. Team affiliation follows the administrative structure of Gothland, which has no villages, but is divided into loosely scattered settlements and parishes. The oldest mention of this trad. event, without yet using the name våg, comes from *Cronica Guthilandorum* written in 1633 by H.N. Strelow, which quotes the local bishop's report on the competition between various settlements.
M. Hellspong, 'A Timeless Excitement. Swedish Agrarian Society and Sport in the Pre-Industrial Era', IJHS, Dec. 1997.

VAGIKAIKA VEDAMINE, Est. for 'pulling the stick', a trad. folk game, in which 2 players sit on the floor facing each other, with legs straightened and feet pressed against each other's feet. They hold the opposite ends of a stick with both hands. The player that succeeds in pulling the opponent to his side, wins the game.
M. Värv and others, 'Traditional Sports and Games in Estonia', TSNJ, 1996, 31.

VALLAMKALI, a form of rowing races held in India on long, multi-oar boats called *chundan vallams* or 'snake boats', similar to >DRAGON BOAT RACING. One boat holds up to 100 oarsmen, dressed in white *dhotis* and *turbans*, who row to the rhythm of drums and cymbals located at the stern of each boat and sing chanteys. The boats are decorated with characteristic silk umbrellas ornamented with golden coins and pendants, which represent the material status of families that put the boats up for racing. The races are held at various locations in India during the Onam harvest festival in the province of Kerala. The most colorful and splendid races are held in Aranmula, Champakulam and Kottayam.

VANDE SVANER, Dan. for 'watering the swans', [Dan. *vande* – to water + *svaner* – swans], a folk game of skill, in which 2 ropes with loops at the end are tied to a horizontal branch. The player places his feet in the loops and keeps his hands on the ground. Then he grabs the ropes with both hands and tries to reach with his head for an object (e.g. a matchbox) placed on the ground.
J. Møller, 'Vande svaner', GID, 1997, 3, 42.

VANDREBOLD, Dan. for 'wanderball', [Dan. *vandre* – wander + *bold* – ball], a game for 10--15 participants, in which all but 2 form a ring (*kreds*), standing at a distance of approx. 3m from one another and facing its center. The 2 midfield players (*midtelspiler*) stand in the center at the point where a small circle (*mærke*) is marked, from which a ball is thrown to resume any interrupted game. The ring players throw the ball across the ring without changing their positions, while the midfield players try to intercept the ball or at least strike it so that it falls to the ground, which they must do before the ring players make 25 successful passes, otherwise they are punished by having to execute a series of gymnastic exercises. If a midfielder intercepts the ball, he changes places with the player who threw it.
J. Møller, 'Vandrebold', GID, 1997, 1, 38.

VARMA ADI, a Hindu martial art technique of recognizing and striking the vital points of the opponent's body.

VARPA, throwing rocks 2-3 kg in weight at a pole driven into the ground. One of various trad. sporting games practiced in Gothland, which are part of the

local competition called >STÅNGASPELEN, once also popular in other parts of Scandinavia, mostly in Sweden. The rocks are usu. flat and round, though their size and weight is not specified. The participants throw them at a stick or pole approx. 20cm in height, driven into the ground at a distance of 10-20m from the throwing line, with the aim of placing them as close to the pole as possible. The rock must be thrown in such a way that when it hits the ground, it does not keep rolling. The game may be played individually or as a team event. Along with >VÅG and >PÄRK, it is one of the few Swed. trad. sports that has survived an invasion of other modern sports and games, even though only locally – on a small area, isolated from the main centers of such sports. The sport has been adapted to contemporary requirements through a league play-off system.
M. Hellspong, 'A Timeless Excitement. Swedish Agrarian Society and Sport in the Pre-Industrial Era', IJHS, Dec. 1997; by the same author, 'Organized, Traditional Sports on the Island of Gothland in the Eighteenth and Nineteenth Centuries', SSSS, 1996.

VARZESH-E PEHLIVANI, a trad. type of Persian wrestling, originating in the kingdom of Parthia (modern Iran), which flourished between 238 BC-225 AD. The word *pelivan* derives from the Parthian *pahlav*, meaning lit. a plucky youth and later also an athlete, who – by demonstrating his strength – was not only the best wrestler, but a folk hero as well. (Cf. >PEHLIVAN WRESTLING) Pelivan is trad. associated with such characteristics as: philanthropy, courage, standing against injustice and a sense of brotherhood with other people. During the rule of the Qajar dynasty (19th cent.) M. Sadegh Bolourforoosh (who became a rich merchant of gold and crystal after ending his wrestling career) once a month fed the poor of Teheran. *Pelivani* were also guardsmen of moral values and principles similar to the modern-day concept of fair play.
The wrestlers, wearing tight-fitting, richly decorated matador trousers with knee guards, oiled the upper parts of their bodies before the fight. Victory could be secured by knocking the opponent down on to his back. The wrestler with the highest number of successful bouts won the tournament. Every bout was trad. preceded by an opening song called *Ey Vatan*. The most outstanding *pelivani* in Iran were called *Pehlivan-e Zoorgar*.
The popularity of *pelivan* fights climaxed during the rule of the Safavid dynasty (1500-1737), when a tradition of wrestling schools called *zoorkhaneh* (lit. the house of strength) was originated. These institutions honored the memory of the achievements of Mahomet Imam Ali's son-in-law and companion, who had been an outstanding wrestler.
Another upsurge of popularity of Iranian pelivan wrestling took place in the 19th cent., during the reign of shah Qajar Naser-e-din (1848-96). Thanks to his influence representatives of Iran's most noble families took up wrestling. One of the best pehlivani, Prince (Shahzadech) Amir Azam, was a kinsman to the shah. The most respected pelivani from other noble families of the 2nd half of the 19th cent. and beginning of the 20th cent. were Bozorg Razaz of Yazd, Sarhang Khan, Shahzadech Seyful Mulk, Aseful Doleh, Malekul-Tojar Khorosani, and Mirza Hadayatullah Vazir Daftar. The official tournament which determined the title of Iran's best pelivan was an annual event held on the first day of the local New Year, *Nawruz*, i.e. 21 March, honored by the presence of the shah himself, who presented the champion with a sash of victory (*bazoo*). The turn of the cent. witnessed the spread of wrestling schools (*zoorkhaneh*) in Teheran, one of which was built by shah Naser-e-din in his palace of Golestan. Their original architecture followed the style of Mithraic temples: they were round, with an entry placed under the surface of the ground and an elevation in the middle, where practice sessions and wrestling bouts took place. Later this architecture influenced the construction of Eur. circus arenas, which in the 19th cent. specialized in wrestling shows. Great pelivani were affiliated with their schools, where they not only fought, but also trained their students. Famous pelivani such as Yazdi Bozorg and Abolkasem Qumi were affiliated with Noroz Khan Zoorkhaneh, while Bozorg Razazm – with Sarcheshmeh Zoorkhaneh. Following the example of Far-Eastern masters of martial arts and self-defense, some of them founded their own schools, e.g. Aga Seyyed Mohammadali Masjedhovzi – the founder of zoorkhaneh in Shamsul-Emareh.

After 1925, during the reign of the Pahlavi dynasty, the interest in varzesh-e pehlivani declined significantly. Shahanshah (King of Kings) Reza Pahlavi considered wrestling bouts a relic of the past and directed his interest towards introducing western institutions, building roads and popularizing western sports. His son, Mohammed Reza Pahlavi, enthroned in 1941, at first tried to revive the old wrestling traditions. However, from approx. 1953 his policy of modernizing Iran in the western style accelerated the development of western style wrestling, while the trad. one was again neglected. That policy was executed by the Chairman of the Federation of Traditional Athletics, Shaban Jafari, a key figure in the coup d'etat aimed at overthrowing Prime Minister Mahammad Mossadegh, who defied the shah and sought to put Iran back on a track of development consistent with its traditions and national interests. Jafari's uncompromising management of the federation led to a significant weakening of the position of trad. wrestling. In an effort to deprive it of its still-strong social backing, hearsay was spread that the zoorkhaneh schools were centers for homosexual practices, where young boys were seduced. The trad. style of wrestling gave way to modern western wrestling forms, which made it possible for Iranian wrestlers to participate in olympic and other international tournaments as early as 1948.

The political change that followed Ayatollah Khomeini's coup d'etat in 1979 improved the situation of trad. wrestling once again. The old zoorkhanehs were reinstated, like the school in the province of Khorasan, which has the largest territorial scope and is considered to be the oldest in Iran, with branch divisions in Meshed, Sabzevar, Kopuchan, Bojnourd, Shiravan and Neyshabour. It enjoys

Verti bike.

great popularity, although the national wrestling federation still prefers to support olympic wrestling.

VAZH A BENN, in full, *ar vazh a benn*, also *ar bazh a benn*, Fr. equivalent *le bâton par le bout*. A trad. Bret. game, in which each participant tries to snatch a stick from the other three. The one who succeeds wins the game.

VAZH YOD, in full, *ar vazh yod*, also called *bazh yod*; a trad. Bret. competition, in which 2 participants sit on the ground, facing each other, with their feet against a wooden beam, and hold a stick, trying to pull it towards themselves. To win the game one must either tug the opponent over the beam or snatch the stick from his hands.

VDARIVANYE SPISA, Ukr. for 'driving the lance', a military skill of Cossack troops. For exercise purposes the lance was thrown at tree trunks. The Cossack lance, called *ratishche*, was made from light wood, had a length of 3.5m and was tipped with a metal head (*zaliznij nakonyechnik*). At the other end was a hole, through which a leather loop was threaded, meant for hooking the lance against the leg while riding a horse to keep it ready for use. The lance enjoyed tremendous prestige: the Cossack elders used it as a mark of their dignity. It was also the subject of numerous myths and stories: a famous Cossack hetman M. Doroshenko allegedly used it in the Battle of White Church with such force that he could not pull it out from the enemy's body. According to an old proverb, a Cossack without his lance is like a girl without her coral beads.
B.I. Kowierko, 'Pro sistiemu fizichnogo vdoskonalyeny-ja zaporozhkih kozakiv', TFKU (1997, 44-62).

VEJE GRISE, Dan. for 'piggy weigh', [Dan. *veje* – to weigh + *grise* – a piggy]. A trad. Dan. game, in which 2 participants grab one another's hands and form a cradle on which another person lies. Then they begin to swing the cradle and recite a casual poem. Finally, they ask the 'piggy' what he would like to eat and, irrespective of his answer, flip him over by tossing him up into the air.
J. Møller, 'Veje grise', GID, 1997, 3, 57.

VELAT, a trad. Bret. var. of ball game.

VELKA BABORKA, a Czech var. of >PALANT.

VELL, in full, *ar vell*, Bret. for 'a ball', a Bret. equivalent to the Fr. LA >SOULE. In lower Brittany the game is called >C'HOARI MELLAD (cf. Fr. >MELAT). The rules of the game were loosely defined and not uniform. The general principle is to group the players into 2 teams – usu. representing villages or parishes. The game is basically a team sport, although the last player to carry the ball to a designated spot or line was recognized as an individual winner. Historians of the game noted that in 1899 it was played on the turbaries of *Lanneier Gallhouarn*, separating the districts of Côtes d'Armor and Morbihan, between the 3 parishes of Locuon, Mellionec and Plouray. The ball was carried to a designated spot by a Locuon player and his team was the winner. The game usu. started with throwing the ball up into the air over a small chapel on the borderland between the 3 parishes. The terrain had many natural obstacles, which – according to the criteria of enthusiasts – made the game more attractive. Any action was allowed to steal the ball, which was carried through swamps, rivers and lakes, over the hills. The chronicles mention a dramatic event during a game held in the area of Pont l'Abbe, when 50 participants drowned in spring floods. This brought about restrictions on the game. The famous edict issued in 1365 by the Fr. king Charles V, banning the game of *la soule*, was still strongly supported in 1440 by the rulers and clergy in Brittany, then an independent Fr. duchy. In many areas of Brittany local feudal lords treated the game with forbearance, and sometimes openly supported it. In some cases a ball or a number of balls to play vell were presented to the local lord by the villagers in fulfillment of their feudal obligation, which indicates the lord must have been playing the game himself. The lord also enjoyed the exclusive right to initiate the game on certain days defined by local tradition. In Josselin (district of Morbihan), ruled by the family of Lusignan, the ball was symbolically handed over to the local lord on midday of Fat Thursday in front of a cross known as *Croix de Martray*, along with 2 other tributes in the form of 2 loaves of bread and 2 jars of wine. It was often done by a serf who had recently married, which related *vell* with the trad. of >BRIDEBALL.
F. Peru, 'La tradition populaire de jeux de plein air en Bretagne', LJP, 1998.

VENDE PANDEKAGE, Dan. for 'pancake flip', [Dan. *vende* – to turn over + *pandekage* – a pancake]. A skill exercise often required of children by fathers or teachers. Two participants – an adult and a child – face each other standing with their legs spread. The child bends down forwards and puts his/her hands between his/her legs. The adult grabs the child's hands and pulls them up, letting the child perform a somersault.
J. Møller, 'Vende pandekage', GID, 1997, 3, 56.

VENDE SIG I EN HALFTØNDE, Dan. for 'barrel somersault', [Dan. *vende* - to turn over + *sig* – oneself + *i* – in + *en* – this + *half* – half + *tønde* – barrel]. In this exercise one person grabs the sides of a barrel, places his head inside it, and flips forward. The trick is to land securely on one's feet on the other side without knocking the barrel over. Cf. Chin. >LIAN ACROBATICS.
J. Møller, 'Vende sig i en halftønde', 1997, 3, 45.

Vazh yod.

VENDE STEG, Dan. for 'turning a steak', [Dan. *vende* – to turn over + *steg* – a steak]. Two persons face each other and one grabs the other by the waist, lifts him up and turns him head down, while the other one also grabs his partner by the waist. The first one bends backwards, so that his partner may land on his feet. Now he lifts his partner and bends backwards, etc.
J. Møller, 'Vende steg', GID, 1997, 3, 53.

VERBOVAJA DOSHKA, Ukr. for 'willow board', a game of skill usu. played after Sunday services. It has been described by Ł. Gołębiowski as:

a game and tradition in Russia that most probably derives from ancient times, though it is still in practice. Youths and beautiful girls would form a large circle in front of the church, while a carefully selected boy, guarded by both sides so that he does not fall, would run on their backs around the circle. If he made it, it would be viewed as a good sign, so after the trial he was kissed and hugged and thanked and offered gifts by everyone.
[Games and Pastimes of Various Social Classes, 1831, 67]

VERTI BIKE, a recent extreme extravaganza, in which the bicycle rider moves while being suspended on a rope high above the ground.

VERTICAL MARATHON, a running competition in which the contestants climb the staircases of tall structures, such as skyscrapers. The first such event took place in 1987 and involved climbing the stairs of Singapore's Westin Stamford Hotel, at that time considered the tallest building in the world. The winner, K. Keng, climbed 1336 stairs to the 73rd floor in 7min. 20sec. His record was broken in 1989,

Vazh yod.

Australian Paul Crake (#25), center, and other entrants start the Empire State Building run-up in the lobby of the New York skyscraper. Crake came in first, completing the race up 86 flights of stairs in 9 minutes 48 seconds.

V

WORLD SPORTS ENCYCLOPEDIA

when B. Singh covered the same distance in 6min. 55sec. The first record holder among women was H. Gilbey (8min. 46sec.). In 1990 the Korean Vertical Marathon was originated at the World Trade Center in Seoul. A similar event is also held in New York City, where runners compete in the annual Empire State Building Run-Up.

VIGEBOLD, a Dan. var. of >DODGEBALL, [Dan. *vige* – to dodge + *bold* – a ball]. A game for 16 players, 12 of whom form a ring, standing at an arm's distance from one another. The remaining 4 players stand inside the ring. The ring players try to oust the inside players by striking any part of their body with a ball. The player who successfully dodges the ball and is the last to remain in the game wins the title of 'king' (*Konge*). The game is played in 4 rounds and each time a new king is nominated. A fifth and final round is played between the 4 kings, of whom the best becomes a 'cesar' (*Kejser*). J. Møller, 'Vigebold', GID, 1997, 1, 25.

VIGORO, an Austrl. sport similar to >CRICKET, invented by an Englishman J.G. Grant and brought by him to Australia around 1908. The first unsuccessful attempt to popularize the game was its demonstration at the Carlton Cricket Ground. Ten years later Grant made another, more successful attempt and the game caught on in the final grades of girls' schools. In 1919 the first vigoro federation was formed in New South Wales and in 1932 – the All Australian Association of Vigoro (AAAV) came into being. The rules of the game are copyrighted. After Grant's death the rights were transferred to Mrs R.E. Dodge, the first President of the AAAV, and after her death in 1973 – to her daughter. Outside of New South Wales the game is popular also in Queensland and Tasmania and is mainly school sport

The Duke of Kent driving his vintage car during a London-Brighton race.

Vintage cars during the London-Brighton race.

Maurice Denis, The Game of Volant, 1900, oil on canvas, detail.

for girls up to the age of 18. The most important annual event is the Dodge Junior Cup, held since 1980. The AAAV also sponsors vigoro veterans tournaments, which are gaining popularity.
Rules of the game. The playing area is similar to cricket, with 2 goals in the center, each formed with 3 stumps. Teams of 12 players each are equipped with special bats, similar to the paddles used in >CANOEING. Two players, one from each team, take turns at throwing differently colored balls at one goal, while 2 other players take turns at defending the goal and striking the ball back into the field. Both teams play simultaneously and, unlike in cricket, do not have to wait for switching their roles from fielding to batting, which makes the game more dynamic than cricket. Once a ball is struck outside of the crease (goal area), the player must circle the crease in order to score a point; cf. >CRICKO. Players wear white, thigh-length and short-sleeved tunics, soft, white shoes, and white socks.

VINTAGE AUTO RACING, a sport, in which the competition is between old models of cars, incl. racing cars. Participants are usu. collectors and restorers of vintage cars, which they combine with the spirit of competition. Races are held between cars of all classes and types, incl. old F-1 models. An important condition of qualifying for vintage auto racing is that any modification to the original construction must be from the same historic period as the auto itself. It is recommended that alterations or repairs be done with the use of original parts. A very popular form of vintage auto competition is various kinds of rallies. The first attempts to organize races between vintage cars date back to the 1920s. The collecting of vintage cars developed rapidly after WWII, which led to a greater number of specialized race events. In the USA alone more than 100 competitions are held every year. In Germany the Vintage Auto Grand Prix held annually by the Automobil Club von Deutschland at the Nürburgringen track attracts approx. 600 cars and more than 100,000 spectators. The sport involves not only restoring the cars, but also the clothing and style of a given epoch. Some associations which sponsor the races and rallies of vintage cars go even further and restore the original tracks. E.g. the Mille Maglia mountain track closed in 1956 has not only been re-opened, but also copied in the mountainous regions of California.
J. Townes, 'Vintage Auto Racing', EWS, 1996, III..

VIPPE STOL, Dan. for 'chair swing', [Dan. *vippe* – to swing + *stol* – a chair, stool]. A trad. show of skills, in which a player lies down on 3 chairs, with his head supported by one chair, his buttocks by another and his feet by the third chair. The player's task is to grab the middle chair, carry it over his body to the other side and place it back in its original place.
J. Møller, 'Vippe stol', GID, 1997, 3, 100.

VLOERBOL, a trad. Flem. game similar to >KRULBOL, but played with smaller bowls 12.7cm in diameter and 5.4cm thick. Popular in bars and inns, where it is played directly on the floor, hence its name [Dutch *vloer* – floor + *bol* – a bowl]. The players must roll the rings in such a way that they stop closest to the target. The game is usu. played by 3 people, each having 4 rings. The target is drawn on the floor. Each ring that stops closer to the center than that of the opponent scores a point. One round lasts until any of the players scores 11pts. The game, now in decline, is still played in E Flandria.
E. de Vroede, 'Vloerbol', HGVB, 1996, 27-28.

VLUCHTBAAN, see >VLUGBAAN.

VLUGBAAN, also *vluchtbaan*, a Flem. type of >SKITTLES, which has many regional var. difficult to categorize. A common feature of all of them is that the ball is thrown down on a wooden track which starts approx. 2m before various arrangements of skittles. It is required that the ball, after reaching the track, rolls for some time towards the skittles in order to hit them. The skittles are approx. 70cm high and are placed at a distance of 75cm from one another. The balls have finger indentations to facilitate throwing.

VOETBAL, a Du. and Flem. equivalent of Eng. >ASSOCIATION FOOTBALL; cf. Dan. >FODBALL; Ger. >FUSSBALL; Swed. >FOTBOLL.

VOGELPIK, a Flem. trad. sport.

Atop a 100-ft. wooden pole, four Totonaco Indians fling themselves upside down as another plays a flute and drum to the sky and cresent moon at the Rankokus Indian reservation near Rancocos, New Jersey. Traveling from their home in Papantua, near Veracruz, Mexico, the troupe participated in the 14th Annual Juried American Indian arts festival on the reservation with their voladeros show.

VOLADEROS, LOS, also in sing. *el volador*, Span. for 'flying', a name given by the Spaniards to Indian shows, as well as athletes performing during public holidays. A group of well-trained men, dressed as birds, climbed a high pole driven into the ground in the central square and danced on a small platform. Then, to the accompaniment of flutes, they were tied with ropes to the top of the pole, where they imitated flying birds by turning around the pole on special jibs. The flight lasted until the rope was unwound and the athletes reached the ground. According to a written report by a Span. monk it usu. lasted approx. 13 swings around the pole. The tradition had its roots in the skills of the pre-Columbian peoples of C America, of which we are just vaguely aware today. According to the researchers of pre-Columbian Mexico A. Caso and T. Gutierrez:

Demonstrations of strength and balance had a great significance in the early Mexican cultures. Acrobats, trained to walk on the tight-rope, jump, fist fight, perform somersaults, or roll unbelievably heavy tree trunks, surprised and enchanted the Spaniards. One of these acrobatic groups was even sent to Rome and exhibited in front of the papal court, which was most certainly the first international performance of Mexican athletes.
[El deporte prehispanico, Mexico, 1967, 28]

VOLANT, a Eur. game that has several equivalents, e.g. >INDIACA, >TS'ÉQWELA, >HAGOITA, and also modern >BADMINTON [Fr. *voler* – to fly]. The word also denominates the subject of the game, i.e. a weight with feathers played with a racket similar in shape to a tennis or badminton racket, but smaller in size. The game's popularity peaked in Europe in the 18th cent. According to B. Linde's *Dictionary of the Polish Language* it was 'a feathery ball played with a net' (vol. VI, 1814). Another dictionary, by J. Karłowicz, A. Kryński, and W. Niedźwiecki, specifies ivory, wood or cork as the materials for constructing *volants*. A tuft of feathers was fastened into a ball made of one of these materials (vol. VII, 1919). Z. Gloger's *Encyclopedia of Old Poland* defines volant as 'a party game, an equivalent to what a ball game is for children. Volant, which is used to play it, was made of cork shaped [...] as an egg cut lengthwise, covered with chamois-leather, braided and full of feathers like a bird so that it could fly better. To play it, one used hazel or bird-cherry rackets netted with gut'. The game itself was described by Ł. Gołębiowski:

Once hit, the volant flies and returns a thousand times, each time more forcefully. What a sight when a beautiful girl plays with her beloved, when her merry eyes follow the flight of this feathery arrow, and yet she still has time to gaze with happiness at her lover. She jumps to the side, moves forward and back, turns towards her partner to strike the volant and not let it fall. How graceful is her figure and her moves, how happy is her face and her smile. She will not utter a word, breathes heavily and has rosy cheeks. At times two volants meeting in air will indicate a yet greater skill of the players. At other times four people pass it amongst themselves, trying to keep it in the air as long as possible and counting the number of 'shells'. Or, what is even more difficult, they catch it in a wine glass, throw it up into the air, and strike it with the glass bottom. Skillful strikes display the elegance of the players in the same way as

the mishits display poor expertness.
[Games and Pastimes of Various Social Classes, 1831, 36]

VOLANTE GIGANTE, see >SHUTTLEBALL.

VOLATA, a sport invented in the summer of 1928 in Italy by A. Turati, Chairman of the Fascist National Party and President of the Ital. Olympic Committee (after Mussolini, the second most important political figure in Italy), who wanted to replace >ASSOCIATION FOOTBALL (soccer) with a sport that would have national character. The game was soon called 'the most fascist of all sports' (*sport fascistissimo*). After a wave of criticism accusing football of corrupting the morality of Italians and the lack of success of Ital. athletes during the 1928 Ol.G. in Amsterdam, a Sports Charter (*Carta dello Sport*) was issued in January 1929, defining new dimensions of fascist sport. The recognition of volata as a game supported by the fascist regime was announced during a meeting of the Opera Nazionale Dopolavoro, a fascist labor organization. In his speech Turati outlined the mission of the new sport in the following way:

We intend to reeducate the athletes in order for them to breathe some fresh air, to teach them to compete for pleasure. Football is an English sport [...] incomplete [...] full of verminous mercenaries. Volata is a truly Italian sport. It allows harmony in the development of the human body. It offers no money. By creating volata we revive the spirit of calcio, which had emigrated to the north and later returned under the exotic name of football. Volata is a superfascist sport for the Italians of tomorrow.

The first volata game was played on 6 Jan. 1929 on the fascist Party Stadium in Rome (Stadio del Partito di Roma). Under pressure from the fascist party more than 1,000 teams were formed. In 1930 the Federation of Volata (Federazione di Volata) was founded, which supervised the organization of the Ital. Championships. The finals of the event were always attended by Mussolini himself. Despite strong political support, the game did not develop as well as football and in 1936 was given up altogether.
Rules of the game. Volata was an eclectic combination of football, rugby and basketball. The game was played by 2 teams of 8 players each: a goalkeeper, 2 defenders, 3 midfielders and 2 offensive players. The ball could be played with both hands and legs, but a player could not hold it for more than 3sec. The ball could be snatched from a player by grabbing him above the waist. The game lasted 60min., played in 3 periods of 20min. each. The goals were 5m wide and 2.44m high. Corner 'kicks' were executed with the hands. The goalkeeper and the defenders could not cross the halfway line. Similar to modern >HANDBALL, a goal was scored only if a shot was made from outside of the goal area. After each goal the game was started from the center of the pitch by a hand throw. The procedure was identical for starting the game and resuming it during each of the 3 periods. The pitch was similar to a football pitch and was approx. 60-90m in length and 40-60m in width.
M. Impiglia, 'The Volata Game. When Fascism Forbade Italians to Play Football', *La comune eredita dello sport in Europa*, ed. A. Krüger & A. Teja, 1997.

VOLLEYBALL FOR THE DISABLED, a ball game with rules based on >VOLLEYBALL, but adapted to the needs of the disabled. There are 2 basic var. of volleyball for the disabled: for those who can play in a standing position (e.g. with the aid of prostheses) and for those unable to stand, in which case the court is smaller in size and the net is at a height similar to that in tennis. The game is played in sitting or kneeling positions. See also >SPORTS FOR THE DISABLED.

VOLLEYBALL, the object of the game is for each team of 6 players to send the ball repeatedly over the net to ground it on the opponent's court, and to prevent the ball from being grounded on its own court. The ball is put into play by the right-hand back-row player who serves the ball by hitting it over the net to the opponent's court. A team is allowed to hit the ball 3 times (in addition to the block contact) before returning it to the opponent's court. A player is not allowed to hit the ball twice consecutively, except when attempting a block. The playing court measures 18x9m, and is divided into 2 halves by a net 91.4m wide, the top border of which much be at a height of 243cm for men and 224cm for women. The mesh is 10cm². The ball can only be played with the hands, however, it cannot be caught and held. A set is won by the first team to

score a determined number of points, with a 2-pt. advantage; 3 or 5 sets are played. Points are scored when 1) the ball touches the floor; 2) the ball goes 'out' or the opponents commit a fault (e.g. touch the net during play).
For the first hundred years from the origin of the game teams had to score 15pts. to win a set. At the meeting of the International Volleyball Federation in autumn 1998 it was decided that in a 5-set match each of the first 4 sets will be played until one team scores 25pts. and the 5th set will be played to 15pts. The principle of the 2-pt. advantage (e.g. 25:23 or 15:13) needed to win a set has been retained. At the same meeting the principle, according to which only the team serving could score, was replaced with the principle by which points can be scored by both the serving and receiving teams in any successful rally. These regulations were implemented by national volleyball federations in Jan. 1999 and govern also the Men's World Volleyball League, Women's Grand Prix, W.Ch. and championships of individual continents. The new regulations were implemented internationally beginning with the Ol.G. in Sydney 2000. See also >BEACH VOLLEYBALL.
History. The game originated in the US. Its creator was W.G. Morgan (c.1865-1942), an American sports instructor. Studying in Springfield, he observed the activities of J.A. Naismith, the originator of basketball. When in 1895 he became principal of a school in Holyoke, Mass., he created the foundations of a game, which he originally called *minonette*. In 1896 the principles of the game were presented to the Physical Education Committee of the Young Men's Christian Association (YMCA) and were adopted. After a demonstration game played in the same year it was incorporated into the sports curriculum of the YMCA, which was the beginning of the rapid development of the game. By 1913 the game had become popular in the USA, Canada, the Philippines, Cuba, Puerto Rico and Uruguay, and after 1913 also in China and Japan. The first US Championships were held under the auspices of the YMCA in 1922 and in 1928 the U.S. Volleyball Association was estab., which contributed to the popularization of the game, particularly when open national championships, treated as unofficial W.Ch., started to be organized. In 1947 the Fédération Internationale de Volleyball, FIVB) was estab. Prior to the FIVB, there was the Volleyball Technical Committee estab. in 1936 at the initiative of Poland, which was affiliated with the International Amateur Handball Federation, IAHF. The first proposal to include volleyball into the Olympics was made by YMCA officials to the International Olympic Committee in 1922. However, volleyball only became an Olympic sport as late as 1961 and the first Olympic tournament was played in Tokyo in 1964. Since 1948 men's E.Ch. have been held, initially at non-regular intervals, and since 1976 every 2yrs. Official men's W.Ch. have been held since 1949 and women's W.Ch. – since 1952. Before 1939 the best teams came from the USA, Czechoslovakia, France, Germany and since the 1930s also Poland. After 1949, for a very long time the best teams came from the USSR and, at different periods, teams from Czechoslovakia, Romania, the GDR, Bulgaria and Japan. Since the 1992 Olympics the Brazilian team and since the 1996 Olympics the Du. team have ranked among the best. Strong teams have also come from Italy, Cuba, Brazil, the USA, and Yugoslavia. Since the middle of the 1970s the Pol. team has been a leading team.
Women's volleyball was initially much less popular. Officially recognized rules of women's volleyball in the USA were introduced as late as 1949. After WWII the best women's volleyball teams came from the USSR (later Community of Independent States and Russia), Romania, Czechoslovakia and Poland, and since the 1960s also Japan and South Korea. Since the 1988-92 Olympics teams from Cuba, Brazil, Russia, the USA, and China have been ranked among the best.
C. McGown, ed., *Science of Coaching Volleyball*, 1994; S.D. Fraser, *Strategies to Competitive Volleyball*, 1988; R. Gassignol, *Le volley-ball*, 1961; B. Viera & B.J. Ferguson, *Volleyball. Steps to Success*, 1996.

VRASJA E ARIUT, Alb. for 'killing a bear', [Alb. *vrasja* – killing + *ariut* – bear], a folk game for 3 persons, of whom the strongest performs the role of the bear, while the other 2 are trying to wrestle him to the ground. Players make gestures encouraging the 'bear' to fight and perform a ritual dance around

him. Any method of toppling the bear can be used, although the bear should touch the ground with his back or at least 1 arm.
Source: Arben Kaçurri, Alb. National Committee; by the same *Heritage – System of Values and Device of Education*, a paper presented during XI Seminar for Post-Graduate Students at International Olympic Academy, Ancient Olympia, 2001.

A World Cup volleyball match between Poland and Brazil.

VRIDE KAPUL, Dan. for 'twisting a rod', [Dan. *vride* – to turn, twist + *kapul* – a stick, rod]. Two players grab with both hands a rod 2-3cm thick and approx. 50cm long. Each player tries to twist the rod from his opponent's hands.
J. Møller, 'Vride kapul', GID, 1997, 4.

VRIKKE MAND NED, Dan. for 'flicking a man off', [Dan. *vrikke* – to flick + *mand* – a man + *ned* – downwards]. A trad. form of competition for 2 players. One of them lies down on his stomach, the other climbs on to his buttocks. The lying player is to move in such a way that the other one loses his balance and is 'flicked off'.
J. Møller, 'Vrikke mand ned', GID, 1997, 3, 20.

VYÖPAINI, a Fin. trad. form of wrestling. A bout is held in a sitting position and the task is to overpower one's opponent by grabbing his trousers and hooking him with one's legs [Fin. *vyö* – a belt + *paini* – wrestling]. This var. of wrestling is also known under the Swed. names of >BOLTEKAST and >BYXKAST; it belongs to a larger family of wrestling sports called >CLOTHES HOLD (BELT HOLD) WRESTLING.

Volleyball for the disabled.

VOLLEYBALL OLYMPIC CHAMPIONS
MEN
1964 USSR
1968 USSR
1972 Japan
1976 Poland
1980 USSR
1984 United States
1988 United States
1992 Brazil
1996 Netherlands
2000 Yugoslavia
WOMEN
1964 Japan
1968 USSR
1972 Japan
1976 Japan
1980 USSR
1984 China
1988 USSR
1992 Cuba
1996 Cuba
2000 Cuba

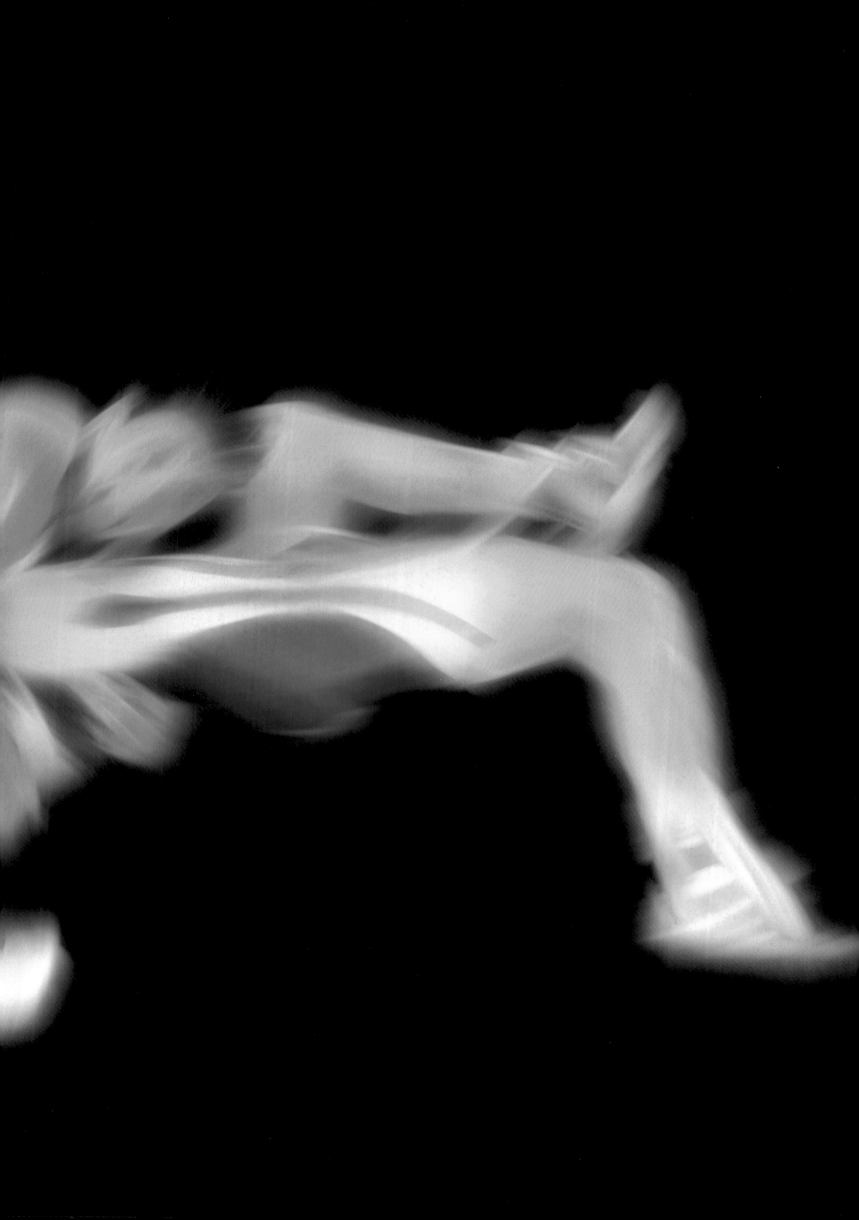

W

WAKEBOARDING X_GAMES CHAMPIONS

MEN
1996 Parks Bonifay
1997 Jeremy Kovak
1998 Darin Shapiro
1999 Parks Bonifay
2000 Darin Shapiro
2001 Danny Harf
WOMEN
1997 Tara Hamilton
1998 Andrea Gaytan
1999 Meaghan Major
2000 Tara Hamilton
2001 Dallas Friday

WABUJIZE, also *dundou*, Chin. for 'bent-kneed fight' or, in international ethnological terminology, *squatting fight*. A form of competition among the Yi people of the Sichuan province. Two opponents assume a crouching position and begin to fight by jumping at one another and executing violent strikes with their upper arms. Hands may not be used and are kept on the breast throughout the fight. The fight is carried on individually or in pairs and is accompanied by the music of pipes similar to Eur. flutes. Knocking the opponent down or making him touch the ground with his hand brings victory.
Mu Fushan et al., 'Squatting Fight', TRAMCHIN, 136.

WÄDELÖB, a local name of a Swed. race held on Shrove Tuesday among young men or, with the imposition of a handicap, between a man and a relay of girls. A large key was used as the relay baton. One such 19th cent. event in the area of Falsterbonäset in Scone (S Sweden) is given by N. Loven (alias Nicolovius) in his book *Folklivet I Skytts härad I Skåne I början av 1800-talet* (1957):

On Shrove Tuesday young people enjoyed various pleasurable activities. All the villages organized wädelöb races, in which either two men competed with each other or one man with a dozen girls. In the latter form the route was set at about 1/8 of a mile from the village. The girls were dispersed at equal intervals. The one who started the race carried a key, which she passed to the next one etc. When everything was ready and the girls, holding their skirts up to their knees, waited on their positions, a pistol shot gave the signal to start the wädelöb. The runners were accompanied by horse riders and musicians

Dean Lavelle of Lake Alfred, Florida, performs during the wakeboarding semi-finals of the Gravity Games in Providence, Rhode Island.

Nate Moyer of Saco, Maine, loses hold of the tow rope in mid flight while knee-boarding on Ossipee Lake in Waterboro, Maine.

[...]. The first girl and the man begin to run together, holding each other's hands. Then the girl lets the man go and he tries to gain an advantage. If the girl despairs and slows down [...], the man is sure to win. However, if she is determined and keeps up the speed to pass the key on to the next one quickly, and that other one does not despair that the man is in front of her, they have a chance of catching up with him, because new girls begin running fresh while the man is getting tired. Most often the man does win, because there is always such a one among the girls, who is less interested in a group effort, but is rather too affected or passes on the key in a clumsy way, thus losing time to the man who runs on.

Wädelöb is one of few trad. Swed. sports in which women participate. Holding hands at the beginning of the race was probably meant to guarantee an equal start, which is indicated by other Swed. running races. For example, in Gothland pairs of runners competing to reach a pole to snatch a scarf placed on it hold a stick, which they throw away upon a start signal. That form of a running race is described by P.A. Säva in his book *Pastimes of Gothland* (*Gotlandska lekar*, 1948).
M. Hellspong, 'A Timeless Excitement. Swedish Agrarian Society and Sport in the Pre-Industrial Era', IJHS, Dec. 1997.

WAGGLES, an old Eng. game, in which a wooden block (a feeder) is struck with a bat. The game is played by four players forming two pairs, each occupying a position close to a large rock. The players take turns at throwing the feeders towards the batters. Once the feeder is struck into the play-ing field, the batter runs towards the opposite rock to score a point. If the batter fails to hit the feeder, the pairs change roles. A similar game, played in London, was known as whacks.
TGESI, II, 329.

WAI DAN GONG, (*wai* – external + *dan* – elixir + *gong* – a skill). Psychophysical exercise Qigong in which energy produced in the limbs in order to redirect it back into the body can be divided in wai dan gong into static and moving ones. Master Shang Schi Tong describes wai dan gong as energy that flows through your body making you feel as if you were rocking to and fro. Once the body is overcome by a feeling of comfort and internal organs are strengthened, one is healthy and will live a long life. Some of the wai dan gong exercises have been known and practiced in China for 2,000yrs. Typical combinations include *wedan da mo qigong, baduanjin, zhangzhuan, wuji qigong*.

WAIKITUN, Span. *pelea con lanza*, a type of combat with the use of a spear or gig practiced by the Araucanian Indians of Chile and the Argentine pampas. Originally the spears were single pieces of wood with burnt and sharpened ends. After the ar-rival of Europeans metal heads were strapped to them. Such spears were also used in sport events, such as a form of javelin or spear snatching. Among the best javelin throwers, described in *La Araucana* by 16th-cent. Span. writer Alonso de Ercilla y Zuñiga, were Orompello, Lepomande, Crino, Pillolco, Guambo and Mareande.
Today waikitun is practiced during religious ceremonies called Nguillatun. Two teams of 20-40 men face each other with *colihue* sticks (*Chuming coleu*), similating fencing attack and defense techniques by moving forwards and backwards to the accompaniment of loud cries. Then they vigorously beat the sticks against the ground near the sacred tree (*rewe*) as a form of reminiscence of the war and to scare away bad spirits interfering with the festivities.
C. López von Vriessen, 'Some recreational and social sporting activities of the Mapuche Indians in the South of Chile', *Sport and International Understanding* (M. Illmarinen ed.), 1984, 339-44; O. Plath, 'Waikitun', JYDLCH, 1946, 25-6.

WAIST PULLING WRESTLING, a wrestling var. popular among the Hani people living in the Qinnghai province in China. The object of the game is to lift one's opponent up by holding him above the hips, around the waist or by the legs. The loser leaves the arena and the winner – after a few moments' rest – takes on another opponent. The player to win the last match in a given tournament is declared the winner. The matches are accompanied by songs sung by the spectators.
Mu Fushan et al., 'Waist Pulling Wrestling', TRAMCHIN.

WAKA HOEHOE, Maori rowing races of characteristic long boats. The importance of boat transportation among the Maori reflects their social structure: the highest organized class was *waka* – a boat which indicated the number of warriors that could fit into a large boat (together with their families). *Waka* was even larger than *iwi* – a tribe, and was divided into large families – *hapu*, and small families – *whanau*.

WAKA RAU, Maori races of small toy boats made of wood or leaves, sometimes decorated with feathers.

WAKEBOARDING, a hybrid of >SURFING and >WATERSKIING, in which a person standing on a special board is hauled by a speedboat and executes a var. of aerial tricks. The name of the sport is derived from the track left on the water's surface by a boat.
History. The sport was created in 1985 by surfer T. Finn, who combined the principles of waterskiing with surfing on a board, which he called a *skurfer*. Finn's skurfer was narrower than a regular surfboard and had additional foot straps. After several years gaining experience in wakeboarding, J. Redmond designed a new type of board, redesigned in 1990 by H. O'Brien, who called his board a *Hyperlite*. His model had better floating characteristics, a narrower profile and sharp edges allowing for more precise turns and evolutions, which proved very useful esp. in the slalom. Surfboarding figures were copied to make it easier for the rider to launch off into the air and perform aerial tricks, as well as land on the water. Some aerial tricks were borrowed from >SKATEBOARDING and >SNOWBOARDING. Wakeboarding is to waterskiing what snowboarding is to >ALPINE SKIING. The sport is developing rapidly. In 1989 the World Wakeboard Association was formed to introduce people to the sport of wakeboarding worldwide and provide consistent standards of competition. Since 1992 the WWA has organized an event called Wakeboard Worlds. The 2001 W.Ch. took place in Lake Elsinore, California. Wakeboarding events include: slalom and aerials which are evaluated by judges according to their intensity and composition, and jumps similar to those in waterskiing. The sport is esp. popular in the USA, Canada, Japan, Australia, Great Britain, Sweden and Mexico.
J. Tomlinson, *The Ultimate Encyclopedia of Extreme Sports*, 1976.

WAKES, in the N Eng. tradition – the feast days of local saints, celebrated also in the West Country as 'revels'. The term referred to the medieval custom of keeping vigil in the local parish church on the eve of a saint's feast day. After the Reformation this changed into a festival of social events and fairs. Activities included dancing and competing in various sports and games. The main annual festival traditionally took place in November. It began on a Sunday and lasted several days.

579

WALKA NARODÓW, see >WOKATUS.

WALKASHOW, see >DANCE MARATHON.

WALKING, see >RACE WALKING.

WALKING HORSE, a var. of horse racing stemming from Mong. tradition, held in Chin. regions bordering on Mongolia. The distance to cover in a competition is 25-30km and the central square of a village or settlement constitutes the finishing line. Characteristically for this discipline the riders' bodies re-

Performers on stilts march in a parade to open Guatemala City's cultural festival. In the background: Goya, *Walking on Stilts, 1791-92, oil on canvas.*

main as close as possible to the horse's back and neck. Apart from this contiguity of riders and horses, another feature of the race is noteworthy: riders are not measured for time they need to complete the route. At the end of the race those who have reached the finish line are introduced to the public, the best get prizes. The best horses, interestingly, are awarded a poem recited in their honor.
Mu Fushan et al., 'Horse Race (Walking Horse)', TRAMCHIN, 38

WALKING ON STILTS, a method of walking on long sticks equipped with supports for feet, used for taking large steps. Stilts are used on various occasions: circus shows, sports events, open-air theater performances, etc. With respect to the technique of fixing the feet and walking 2 basic types of stilts are distinguished: 1) those where the feet are placed on supports with no additional binding and the balance is maintained by holding the upper part of the stilts with the hands; 2) those equipped with bindings and straps for calves which fasten the feet securely to the stilts, leaving the hands free. The tradition of walking on stilts goes back to ancient times and has been known among peoples of various cultural circles. It was practiced for example by Indians of pre-Columbian America, esp. N and C. According to Amer. ethnographer J.C. McCaskill, stilts were popular on the entire N.Amer. continent long before the arrival of Europeans, esp. among the Zuni, Hopi, and Shoshone tribes, and to the present day, walking on stilts is practiced by Native American Indians inhabiting SW states of the USA and in Mexico. In Mexico and some other countries of C America the tradition goes back to the Mayan culture, where stilts were employed during a ceremony in honor of a god embodied as a holy bird. That tradition can still be seen in today's popular Mexican holidays. Nowadays numerous forms of walking on stilts are preserved in the cultures of India, esp. in the state of Madhya Pradesh where stilts are used for some trad. dances and races. In N.Zeal., stilts referred to as *poutogi* are employed in various popular shows such as races or runs across brooks (>POUTUTEKO), as well as in a trad. form of >WRESTLING ON STILTS, also known in Hawaiian and other cultures. In Japan, a children's var. of stilts is known as >TAKEUMA. In Europe, shepherds from the dept. of Les Landes, France, used stilts (Fr. *échasses*) in marshy meadows where some forms of popular competitions could be encountered. In S Eur. stilts are sometimes used for picking fruit from trees and such regions usu. celebrate the end of the fruit-picking season with various shows using stilts. In Portugal the art of walking on stilts is called >ANDAS, in Spain >ZANCOS, in Denmark and Norway *stylter*, in Intaly *trampoli*, in Germany *Stelze*, in The

Netherlands *stelts*, in Russia *chodyli*, etc. The simplest stilts were made from branches where the supports for feet were formed of boughs cut at appropriate lengths. More sophisticated ones were equipped with comfortable supports attached with pins or leather straps. Maori stilts are made of light wood and the supports are complete with a rope that functions as stirrups securing the feet. Modern stilts are generally mass-produced in factories, for the most part from light metals (e.g. aluminum), and feature adjustable foot supports. Stilts are used not only for entertainment but also for various jobs that involve smaller heights, such as: hanging posters, simple tasks on construction sites, laying wallpaper or painting higher walls.
M. da Graça Sousa Guedes, 'Jogo das andas', JTP, 1979, 61; J. Møller, 'Stylter', GID, 1997, 4, 108-109; C. Moreno Palos, 'Pruebas de zancos', JYTE, 1992, 45-46; 'Stilts', EAI, 1879, 25, 716.

WALLEYBALL, a var. of >VOLLEYBALL played on a much smaller indoor court. The name indicates the main difference between the two: with the possibility existing of striking the ball against the walls and ceiling.

WALL-GAME, see >ETON WALL GAME.

WAR CANOE, an Amer. boating sport. The vessel, approx. 25-30ft. long, holds up to 20 paddlers with single-bladed paddles and is modelled after an Indian canoe or dug-out. Races are held over different distances, depending on local tradition. A humorous var. of war canoe involves paddling with the hands instead of paddles.

WATER AEROBICS, see >AEROBICS.

WATER BALLET, one of the original names attributed in the 1940s to a pioneer sport which later developed into >SYNCHRONIZED SWIMMING.

WATER BUFFALO RACES (MOUNTED), Thai name *makepung*, a trad. sport of Thai farmers. Having a tradition of over 130 years, the races are held annually in October, at the end of the Buddhist Lent, in various cities of Thailand (e.g. in the province of Chonburi, less than one hundred kilometers from Bangkok) and Bali, as well as in the Phillipines, where they are held in the province of Nueva Ecija as part of the celebrations of St. Isidore's Holiday in May. In Thailand the water buffalo is one of the mainstays in the life of local farmers, used as a beast of burden for working the rice fields. Water buffalo races receive a strong backing of the government, which supports them as a way of preserving the animal, now an endangered species. Races begin with a whistle and are held on a 100-m track, which the buffalos, weighing up to several hundred kilograms each, cover in a dozen or so seconds.

WATER POLO, a sport played in a swimming pool by 2 teams. The aim of the game is to score a goal by playing the ball into the opponents' goal. Each team consists of 7 players, incl. the goalkeeper. The pool is 30x20m wide max. for men, and 25mx17m wide max. for women. The minimum depth of the pool is 1m, and 1.8m for international matches. For men's games the ball should be 68-71cm in circumference and its pressure should be 90-97 kilo Pas-

cals. For the women's game the ball is 65-67 cm in circumference with pressure of 83-97 kilo Pascals. The duration of the game is 4 periods, each of 5min. actual play with 2-min. intervals. The width between goalposts is 3m, the crossbar being 0.9m above the surface of the water. If the pool depth is less than 150cm the crossbar is 240cm from the bottom of the pool. The ball cannot be touched with both hands at the same time; this rule does not apply to the goalkeeper. The teams wear caps of different colors. The goalkeepers wear red caps. During play the caps cannot be taken off. For the Ol.G. and W.Ch. all players must wear caps with protective ear guards. All caps have plainly visible numbers, 10cm in height. The caps of each team are numbered from 2 through 13. For international games the caps must contain a 3-letter country code placed on the front. The letters are 6cm in height. The players' swimming suits must not be transparent; if so the players must wear underwear. Before the start of the game the teams choose the pool ends by tossing a coin. At the beginning of the game the players take positions on their respective goal lines, about 1m apart. The referee then throws the ball into play on the half-distance line and the players swim towards the line to gain possession of the ball. The game is controlled by one referee assisted by 2 goal judges, 1 or 2 timekeepers, and 1 or 2 secretaries. The officials exercise their duties by means of specified whistle signals. The goal judges are provided with a supply of balls. When the original ball has gone outside the field of play a goal judge immediately throws a new ball to the nearest player of the attacking team. During play, goal, corner, free and neutral throws may be awarded. The latter are awarded when, at the start of a period, the referee is of the opinion that the ball has fallen in a position to one team's advantage. The major fouls include: 1) advancing beyond the goal line at the start of a period, before the referee's starting signal; 2) taking active part in the game when standing on the floor of the pool (not applicable to the goalkeeper); 3) taking or holding the entire ball under the water; 4) striking at the ball with a clenched fist (not applicable to the goalkeeper); 5) playing the ball with both hands at the same time (not applicable to the goalkeeper); 6) impeding the free movement of an opponent who is not holding the ball; 7) staying within 2m of the opponents' goal except when behind the line of the ball; 8) interfering with the taking of a free, goal or corner throw; 9) intentionally splashing water in the face of an opponent; 10) sinking an opponent; 11) using foul lan-

WORLD SPORTS ENCYCLOPEDIA W

WATERPOLO OLYMPIC CHAMPIONS

MEN
1900 Great Britain
1904 United States
1906 NOT HELD
1908 Great Britain
1912 Great Britain
1920 Great Britain/Ireland
1924 France
1928 Germany
1932 Hungary
1936 Hungary
1948 Italy
1952 Hungary
1956 Hungary
1960 Italy
1964 Hungary
1968 Yugoslavia
1972 Soviet Union
1976 Hungary
1980 Soviet Union
1984 Yugoslavia
1988 Yugoslavia
1992 Italy
1996 Spain
2000 Hungary

WOMEN
2000 Australia

A Thai jockey races in the 131st annual traditional water buffalo race in Chonburi province, 70 kilometers (44 miles) south of Bangkok.

W

A waterpolo game.

Waterpolo on German and Luxembourg postage stamps.

WATER POLO WORLD CHAMPIONS

MEN

1973 Hungary
1975 Soviet Union
1978 Italy
1982 Soviet Union
1986 Yugoslavia
1991 Yugoslavia
1994 Italy
1998 Spain
2001 Spain

WOMEN

1986 Australia
1991 Netherlands
1994 Hungary
1998 Italy
2001 Italy

guage during play; 12) brutality or disrespect. The fouls are punished by the award of a free or penalty throw to the opposing team, or by exclusion of the fouling player for the amount of time indicated by the referee, no shorter, however, than 20sec.

History. An early var. of water polo was known in ancient Rome. The game was played in public baths by Roman legionnaires. Different kinds of balls were used in >BATHS. Most likely, the game was brought by the legions to such towns of Roman Britain as Verulamium and Bath. The game of water polo has evolved over the centuries. In the 19th cent., water polo was adopted by sports organizations as a recreational game. The first water polo games, according to rules close to the modern ones, were played by the members of the London Bournemouth Rowing Club in 1869. The first fixed rules of the game were formulated by the London Swimming Club in 1870. The first modern rules were estab. c.1876. The first inter-club match took place in the London Crystal Palace in 1874. The first international water-polo match was played between England and Scotland in 1885. Soon, Scotland developed its own distinct water-polo var. known as *aquatic football*, remaining popular until today. The most outstanding Brit. clubs in the early period of water-polo development were the Burton-on-Trent Club (first Champion of England, 1888), Nautilus London, Tunbridge Wells, and Manchester Osborne. In 1884,

A women's waterpolo match between Australia and the Netherlands at Ryde Aquatic Center in Sydney, Australia during the 2000 Sydney Olympics.

the Amateur Swimming Association of Great Britain became the governing body of water polo in the country. The Eng. Water-Polo Championships were held since 1888. At the same time the sport was being developed in Ireland, Scotland and Wales. In 1897, the Knickerbocker Athletic Club formulated its own water-polo rules in the USA. In 1906, the governing body of Amer. water polo became the Amateur Athletic Union (AAU). Until 1939, the leading US clubs were the New York Athletic Club and the Illinois Athletic Club from Chicago. The Amer. var. of water polo, called *softball* (not to be confused with >SOFTBALL), used a semi-inflated ball. It emphasized a rugged, body-contact style of play, allowing one, for instance, to sink and hold an opponent. The more prevalent Eur. style was played using a fully-inflated ball. The Amer. 'softball' was, nevertheless, practiced until the 1930s. Since 1911, water polo games have been played under the auspices of the International Amateur Swimming Federation (Féderation Internationale de Natation Amateur, FINA) through its International Water Polo Committee. The sport was included in the Ol.G. in 1900. Until 1920, the international water-polo leader was the Brit. team. In the inter-war period the best water-polo teams were those of France, Belgium, Sweden, Hungary and Germany. After WWII, Britain fell behind and the teams of the USSR, Yugoslavia and Italy took over. The Water Polo E.Ch. have been held every 2yrs. since 1926. Since 1973 The Men's Water Polo W.Ch. have been held in even years; the Women's Water Polo W.Ch. have been held since 1986; and since 1979, every 2yrs. the Water Polo World Cup has been held. The leading national water-polo team in the history of the Ol.G. has been Hungary, which has won 6 gold, 3 silver and 3 bronze medals. The most dramatic event in the history of Hung. water polo took place at the Melbourne Ol.G. in 1956. The Austrl. Ol.G. coincided with the Rus. invasion of Hungary and bloody crushing of the Budapest uprising by the Red Army. The Hung. water polo team played a dramatic match against the Soviet team in the semi-finals. The match turned to a savage brawl between the 2 teams and was stopped at 4:0 to Hungary. The New York Times reported on the match as full of flying blows and blood letting. The worst impression was made by a Rus. player, W. Prokopov, who went round the pool kicking, punching and head-butting opponents. Magazines around the world published a photograph of the bleeding face of the Hung. player, E. Zádor. In spite of the horrific incident the Hung. team made its way through the finals and won the gold medal, after defeating Yugoslavia 4:0. The Hung. goalkeeper was D. Gyarmati, acclaimed the

most valuable water polo player in the world. Despite the difficult political situation he returned to Hungary in 1958. Gyarmati participated in 5 Ol.G. in the years 1948-64 and together with his team won a medal at each of them (3 gold, 1 silver, 1 bronze). Indirectly, he also managed to win a 6th medal at the Montreal Ol.G. in 1976 as the coach of the champion team.

The most prestigious magazine devoted to water polo is *Scoreboard* published in the United States.

The trad. water polo leader has been Hungary, a multiple Olympic and world champion. Other leading teams have included Yugoslavia, Russia and, in the 1990s, Croatia.

The women's version of water-polo developed in the mid-1970s. The top women's national teams are the Netherlands, Italy, Hungary, Australia and the USA. D. Barr, *A Guide to Water Polo*, 1964; G. Brown, ed., *New York Times Encyclopedia of Water Sports*, 1979; P.J. Cutino, *[Water] Polo. Manual for Coach and Player*, 1976; C. Hines, *How to Play and Teach Water Polo*, 1967; K. Juba, *Water Polo*, 1978; B. Pawełko, *Piłka wodna*, 1981-83, Part 1-2; R. Smith-James, *The World Encyclopedia of Water Polo*, 1989; S. Strumph-Wojtkiewicz, *Agent Nr 1*, 1959.

WATER QUINTAIN, also *water butt*, a folk version and sometimes a parody of the chivalric >QUINTAIN, still practiced in the 19th cent. in villages of the Ital. province Lazio. The target was a ring attached to the bottom of a large round water container made of wooden staves, 1.5m in diameter and almost 1m high. The container hung in a gate festooned with garlands, a little above the rider's head. Riding through this gate, the rider tilted at the ring. If he missed or was too slow to run away, he would get drenched with the water from the container – sometimes the spout would be powerful enough to knock the rider off his horse, to the great amusement of the spectators. A similar competition is featured in the drawing *Giostra rusticana in un paese del Lazio* by B. Pinelli, an Ital. illustrator, famous for drawings depicting many folk games. Another version of the water quintain played by young Londoners in the 12th cent. is described by the Anglo-Norman author W. Fitstephen in *Vita Sancti Thomae* (c.1190). A pole with a rotating shield was placed in the middle of the Thames. The contestant neared it, standing in his boat and holding a lance. The water quintain required a blow strong enough to break the lance, otherwise it would get stuck in the shield – this, combined with the inertia of the boat, would push the contestant into the water. If this happened, other competitors, waiting for their turn in their boats, were obliged to perform a >WATER RESCUE.

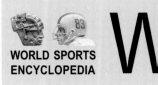

Above: a competition for water rescue squads; below right: water rescuers in action.

WATER RESCUE, all the organized activities associated with drowning prevention, together with the practice activities, also in the form of sporting events aimed at the improvement of the effectiveness of lifesaving. There are specialized lifesaving and lifeguarding networks in most developed countries, with trained staff and specialist equipment. They are usu. parts of various organizations, usu. the police and various medical and sporting organizations, or the Red Cross in the USA, but some of them are independent units, such as the Brit. Royal Life Saving Society, Ger. Deutsche Lebens-Rettungs-Gesellschaft and Pol. Wodne Ochotnicze Pogotowie Ratunkowe.

The main techniques used in various drowning situations (e.g. drowning under ice, in a swamp, whirlpool or getting entangled in seaweed) include rescue from dry land (e.g. by throwing a lifebelt), from a boat, or directly from the water. Lifesaving methods also include hauling the drowning person. Lifeguards are also trained in first aid techniques, including circulatory and respiratory resuscitation, assessment of the person's status after injuries in water (head, spine injuries etc.), as well as techniques not directly related to drowning, such as first aid after sunstroke, sunburns, exhaustion, hypothermia, and animal and insect bites. Rescuers use a variety of equipment, from the simplest masks, to flippers and snorkels, life-belts, ropes, boat hooks, and ordinary row boats, to advanced technical equipment such as motor boats and aqualungs. The technical equipment at a bathing beach with a lifeguard stand usu. also includes loudspeakers enabling the lifeguard to make announcements to the bathers, information boards with details of the weather and state of the water, as well as a flag mast used to hoist flags indicating whether swimming is allowed (white) or not (red, formerly black).

History. The ancient Chinese and Egyptians had methods of removing water from the bodies of drowned people. The Egyptians would achieve this by hanging the person by their heels and pressing on their chest. The Chinese and then Japanese would put the person on the back of an ox: the ox would jump to shake the 'burden' off and in doing so saved many a life. The Bible includes 2 descriptions of rescuing dying people by stimulating the heart or artificial respiration. In the 1st Book of Kings (17:17-22), prophet Elijah resuscitates the son of a widow in Zarephath of Sidon by stretching himself out upon the boy 3 times; in the 2nd Book of Kings (4:34-35), the prophet Elisha ressurects the son of a hospitable Shunammite woman: 'And he went up, and lay upon the child: and put his mouth upon his mouth, and his eyes upon his eyes, and his hands upon his hands. As Elisha stretched himself upon him, and the child's flesh grew warm. [...A]nd the child gasped seven times and opened his eyes'. In the 2nd cent. BC, the Greek Asclepiades recommended tracheotomy. In the 14th cent., the Fr. surgeon G. de Chauliac inserted a pipe into a drowned person's trachea, and pumped air into their lungs. S.Amer. Indians rescued drowned people by pumping tobacco smoke into their lungs, causing them to choke and trigger a resuscitation reflex. The method was then adopted by the Brit. Royal Navy, and was used until better methods were introduced in 1812. In E Europe, the need for lifesaving was first recognized in Poland, where its beginnings date back to 1602, when H. Gostomski (d.1609) founded a cloister and Jesuit hospital in Sandomierz, entrusting them the task of rescuing drowning people from the nearby river Vistula. In 1767, A. Cakoen established the first known lifeguard organization in Amsterdam – the Maatschapij tot Redding van Drenkelingen (Association for the Rescue of Drowning People). A similar organization was founded in Hamburg the next year (Anstalt für im Wasser Verunglückter Menschen), and then in Paris (1773), London (1774) and Copenhagen (1792). In 1774, J. Curry (d.1780) wrote about rescuing drowning men in *Some Thoughts on the Nature of Fevers, on the Causes of their Becoming Mortal and on the Means to Prevent It*. In 1788, C. Kite (?-1780) took on the same topic in *An Essay on the Recovery of the Apparently Dead*. In the 19th cent., the Deutsche Gesellschaft zur Rettung Schiffbrüchige (Ger. Association for the Rescue of Ship Castaways, estab. 1866) had outstanding achievements in the field. The first national lifeguard organization was estab. in the UK in 1874. The rather breathtaking name Royal Human Society for the Recovery of Persons Apparently Dead by Drowning was changed to the more succinct Royal Life Saving Society in 1904. Soon after that, the Russian Imperial Association for Life Saving was founded. In 1898, on the initiative of the journalist J. Radwan, a similar organization was estab. in the Pol. city of Kalisz, then under Rus. rule. In 1902, the organization commissioned Pol. physician L. Wernic to write the handbook *How to rescue drowned people*, one of the best such publications in Europe in those days. Ger. institutions played a very important role in the development of modern methods of lifesaving, developing effective organizational structures. These included the Deutsche Schwimm-Verband (Ger. Swimming Union, estab. 1886), the Gesellschaft der Wassersportvereine von Berlin und Umgebung (Society of Water Sports of Berlin and Vicinities, estab. 1899), and the Zentralstelle für das Rettungswesen und Binnen-und Küstenwässer (Central Administration for Rescue Operations and Inland and Coastal Waters, estab. 1906). In 1913, the specialized Deutsche Lebens-Rettungs-Gesellschaft (DLRG) was estab. Its activities were curtailed by WWI but revived in 1922, when sporting organizations, such as the Deutsche Turnerschaft, became involved (see >TURNEN). In 1922, on the initiative of the DLRG, the first Water Rescue Congress took place in Bonn, Germany. The DLRG was backed by military circles as the organization was considered to be useful in military training. Until 1941, it provided lifeguard training to about 1 million people. In 1944, a specialist lifeguard school, controlled by the DLRG, was estab. in Stuttgart. After WWII, the organization continued in W Germany, to become an all-German organization again after 1989. (The Wasserrettung Dienst, established in 1952, was responsible for lifeguarding in E Germany, and later the responsibilities were taken over by the Ger. Red Cross). In 1910, the international water rescue organization, after a number of transformations, finally settled under the name of the International Life Saving Federation (ILS). In 2000, the ILS had more than 13 million members in 131 countries, with many national lifesaving organizations. The aim of the organization is the improvement of life-saving equipment and techniques. In the initial period, the most active members of the ILS included the Brit. Royal Life Saving Society, Du. Koninklijke Nederlandsche Bond tot Het Redden van Drenkelingen, Fr. Fédération Française de Sauvetage et de Secourisme, Ital. Federazione Italiana Nuoto Secione Salvamento, Swed. Svenska Livräddningssallskapet-Simfrämjandet, Dan. Dansk Livrednings-Forbund, and later also the Algerian Fédération Algerienne de Sauvetage et de Secourisme, Argentine Asociacion Santafesina de Guardavidas, Gk. Fédération Panhellenique de Sauvetage (Hellena Nauagososte), Ir. Water Safety Association, Luxembourg Fédération Luxembourgeoise de Natation et de Sauvetage, Moroccan Fédération Royale Marocaine de Sauvetage, Aus. Österreichische Wasserrettung, Port. Instituto de Socorros a Naufragos, Senegalese Fédération Senegalaise de Sauvetage et de Premier Secours, Span. Federacion Española de Salvamento y Socorrismo, S.African Life Saving Society, Turk. Can Kurtarma Cemiyeti, and Tunisian Fédération Tinisienne de Natation. Life saving was almost totally neglected in E Europe under Soviet influence. Poland was the only country where the situation was somewhat better, even approaching western standards. Poland and Bulgaria were the only communist countries in those times that were members of the ILS, and Poland was the only one represented by an independent, specialist organization. W.Ch., held every 2yrs. under the name of the Rescue Series, and continental championships are among the methods of improving and testing life guards' skills. Selected rescue events were demonstration sports during the 2000 Ol.G. in Sydney (which was also the host of the W.Ch. that same year). How popular life saving is may be attested to by the fact that the number of W.Ch. participants must be limited to 5,000, and international qualifying rounds are organized at lower levels (continental championships, including E.Ch., are held during those qualifiers).

WATERSKIING, a sport where single or double skis are used to move across the surface of water while being hauled by a motor boat. There are 4 waterskiing events: the trick race (2 runs, single or double skis 102-112cm in length, unlimited boat speed); the slalom (along a more or less sinusoid line, usu. on a single ski, 160-180cm in length, with sharp edges and rounded tips narrowing towards the back, unlimited boat speed); the long jump using a ramp with a length of 6.2m and height of 1.82m (men) or 1.52m (women), where the deciding factor is the distance or duration of the jump with max. boat speeds of 57km/h for men and 51km/h for women; jumps are executed on 2 skis 172-238cm in length made from Kevlar or aluminum. The 3 former disciplines together form the combined event. A separate event is >WAKEBOARDING. There are also attempts at breaking records in jump lengths and absolute speeds. See also >KITEBOARDING.

History. Waterskiing first appeared in c.1920 among a group of wealthy Fr. eccentrics in the Fr. Riviera. Initially, trad. snow skis were used. In 1922, an American, R.W. Samuelson, developed special waterskis whose shape resembled that of modern ones. That same year, Samuelson gave the first shows in Lake City, Minnesota, and an anonymous waterskier appeared in Michigan and Miami Beach. In 1925, Samuelson gave the first shows of jumps from a ramp. The first major competition took place in Massapegua, USA, as a special addition to an air show. The first waterski federations were estab. in Italy, France and the US in the 1930s. And it was those countries that led the growth of waterskiing before WWII. In 1939, Donald Hain, a waterskier and official of the Amer. waterski federation, laid out the rules of the combined event which are still used today. The World Waterski Federation was estab. in the USA in 1942 (however, it did not include Eur. countries). In turn, the Fédération Mondiale de Ski Nautique, estab. in Italy in 1946, did not include the US. The 2 federations functioned independently until 1954, when they merged to form the Union Mondiale de Ski Nautique. Since 1956, W.Ch. and E.Ch. have been held, as well as a Europe Cup. However, leisure waterskiing is more important today, as the sport provides excellent relaxation and is a pleasure to watch. Its popularity has been growing with the democratization of leisure activities and growing availability of equipment.

WEDDING ARCHERY, archery competitions held during weddings, popular among different peoples of C Asia; esp. in Afghanistan, and among the Chukchee and Koriak; see >AFGHAN ARCHERY, >CHUKCHEE AND KORIAK ARCHERY.

WEDDING RACES, popular among certain peoples of C Asia, esp. the Bayat. The races constituted one of the 10 or 12 events of various competitions accompanying wedding ceremonies. A starting line was usu. located by the yurt in which a 'hair joining' ceremony, also known as the 'life joining' ceremony, (i.e. the wedding ceremony) had taken place just before the race. The finish line was drawn by the new yurt to which the newlyweds were to move. The race was held among the couple and 2 bridesmaids who took the caps that belonged to the bride and the groom. Then, they swapped the caps which symbolized confusion and change taking place in the couple's life resulting from them being excluded from the up-to-date social structure of the local community. The maids threw the caps into the new yurt, then went inside picked them up and ran back to the couple to hand the caps back to the bride and the groom. The throwing of the caps into the yurt symbolized the entering of a new stage in the couple's life and returning the caps to the couple was a visual sign of this. Bridesmaids represented the respective families giving up their children during the marriage ceremony and the race was in fact between the 2 bridesmaids. A victory of one of the maids meant a victory of one of the families. After the race the 2 families took the 'finish-line' yurt down together and brought it, along with the bride's dowry, to the groom's parents' abode.

I. Kabzińska-Stawarz, 'Competition in Liminal Situations', part II, EP, 1993, XXXVII, 1.

WEDDING SPORTS EVENTS, trad. sporting events practiced among certain peoples of C Asia, esp. among the Bayats, and involving 10-12 events accompanying the wedding ceremony. The first and most important event was the >FIGHT FOR A NEW YURT, the second – >FIGHT FOR A CARPET, and the third – >TRIAL BY SACK WITH WATER. The number of other forms of competition varied and often incl.: >WEDDING RACES and >COMPETING FOR A BRIDE. In order to avoid being discredited, the bridegroom could designate somebody else, usu. the most skillful and physically able member of his tribe, to participate in some events. See also >FIGHT FOR A BRIDE.

WEIGH THE BUTTER, a spontaneous form of wrestling, practiced as a warm-up exercise before many other sports games. Two contenders stand back to back, with their arms locked. One stoops as low as he or she can and supports the other on his or her back, and says, 'Weigh the butter'; he or she rises, and the other contender stoops in turn saying, 'Weigh the cheese'. The first responds, 'Weigh the old woman', which the second completes with, 'Down to her knees'. Then, the 2 go on bending and rising, lifting each other alternately, and repeating:

Weigh butter, weigh cheese,
Weigh a pun [pound] o' can'le grease.

In some regions of England the game was played to other rhymes. Weigh the butter was also played in the Ulster counties of Antrim and Down.
TGESI, 362.

WEIGHT THROW, an athletic event derived from folk competitions in stone throwing. The old, locally varied forms are still practiced during folk festivals in Scotland, Scandinavia and the Swiss Alps. Weight throwing using a 56-lb. (about 25.4-kg) weight was an unofficial sport during the 1904 Ol.G. in St. Louis, and an official one, just once, during the 1920 Games in Antwerp, where American P. McDonald was the winner with a distance of 11.265m.
In the USA, weights of 35lbs. (15.88kg) are also used. One var. of the event is part of the Amer. >ALL-AROUND. There are no differences as far as the technique is concerned, even though weights may differ in their shapes, weights and handles. The 35-lb. weight has a triangular steel handle with a diameter of ½in. (1.27cm). The handle is connected to the weight by a chain link, 3/8in. (0.95cm) in diameter. The weight may not be longer than 16in. (40.64cm). The throw is made with a spin over the thrower's head, from a throwing circle, 7ft. (213cm) in diameter. The thrower may not step outside the circle. The 56-lb. weight has a similar structure. The longest distances for 35-lb. weights are over 20m, and over 13m for 56-lb. weights. There are no official world records. Between 1876 and 1965, throws using 56-lb. weights were included in Amer. athletic championships. Today, they are organized during competitions sponsored by the Amateur Athletic Union. Events with 35-lb. weights are mainly organized indoors, esp. in the eastern cities.

Waterskiing.

Waterskiing on postage stamps issued in France and the Bahamas.

Carl Braun, of Fredricksburg, Va., throws a 56-lb weight, during competition at the 47th Annual Grandfather Mountain Highland Games and Gathering of Scottish Clans, held at MacRae Meadows, near Linville, N.C.

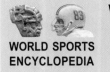

WEIGHTLIFTING, a competitive sport consisting of lifting weights. Until the beginning of the 20th cent numerous kinds of metal weights of different shapes were used for the sport. The weight used in modern weightlifting is a barbell consisting of a steel bar to which cast-iron or steel disk weights (formerly balls) are attached at each end, secured with collars. The max. length of the bar is 220cm; the distance between the inside collars 131cm. The bar is 28mm in diameter and weighs 25kg. The disks weigh from 0.25 to 50kg. At international events the range of weights added is 25, 20, 15, 10, 5, 2.5, and 1.25kg. The progression after the first successful lift attempt is 5kg; after further successful attempts 2.5kg. Each competitor is assigned 3 attempts and can enter the competition at any weight level. Skipping 1 or 2 lighter weights is possible if a competitor successfully lifts a heavier weight. Three unsuccessful attempts eliminate the lifter from the contest and his highest lift is recorded. In world record setting events a competitor can be given 4 attempts. One minute is allowed to each competitor between the calling of his or her name and the beginning of the attempt on the platform. After 30sec., a warning signal is heard. World, continental and national records are recorded in all lifters' weight categories.

In the modern weightlifting 2 lifts are recognized: the *snatch*, and the *clean and jerk*. According to the Olympic rules,

In the snatch a lifter must place the bar horizontally on the floor, lift it with two hands starting with the palms downwards to the full extent of his arms above his head in one movement, while splitting or bending his legs. Then he must bring his feet back in line with one another and hold the weight motionless until the referee signals him to put it back down. If he drops the bar after this signal from any height above his waist the lift is disallowed. For the clean and jerk the lifter starts in the same position but hoists the bar to rest against the chest or clavicles before performing the jerk during which the bar is lifted to the full stretch of the arms above the head. Once again the lifter must finish by holding the bar motionless with his feet in a line parallel to the plane of his trunk.

[*Official Olympic Companion*, International Olympic Committee, 1996]

Until 1972, there was another international lift called the *press*. First, the barbell was brought to the lifter's shoulders without any restrictions on leg movements, and then the lifter had to stand erect until the referee signaled for the completion of the lift, which was achieved by pressing the barbell upward in a steady continuous movement to arm's length overhead but without any assistance by moving the legs. The press was abandoned by the International Weightlifting Federation at Poland's initiative, as it had been a cause of numerous spine injuries.

The total score is the sum of scores achieved in all individual weightlifting events. If 2 competitors reach the same score, the one with the lighter body weight wins. The competition is officiated by a panel of 3 referees, who signal the attempts using an electronic light system or flags. A white light or flag indicates a successful attempt; a red light or flag a failed attempt. A majority decision is required. Before the contest the lifters are weighed and assigned to appropriate weight categories, which often vary at different events. At the Sydney Ol.G. in 2000 there were 8 men's body-weight categories: up to 56, up to 62, up to 69, up to 77, up to 85, up to 94, up to 105 and over 150kg; and seven women's weight categories: up to 48, up to 53, up to 58, up to 63, up to 69, up to 75 and over 75kg.

Until the 1980s weightlifting was only practiced by men; women sporadically competed in the sport in the 1940s. Today women's weightlifting is becoming more and more popular; see also >POWERLIFTING, >POWERLIFTING FOR THE DISABLED.

History. The origins of weightlifting go back to various forms of stone lifting practiced by ancient cultures. Weightlifting may have stemmed from one of 2 geographical areas: the Middle East and Europe. The tomb of the Eg. Prince Baqti in Beni Hassa features a drawing representing 3 men competing in lifting large pear-like objects, prob. made of stone or iron (>EGYPTIAN WEIGHTLIFTING). Numerous forms of weightlifting have been common among various peoples of the Middle East. This legacy can still be observed in today's huge popularity of the sport in the region and the international achievements of lifters from such countries as Turkey, Iran, Iraq, and, since the 1940s, Egypt. The Eur. origin of weightlifting dates back to various folk traditions and the 17th and 18th-cent. performances of wandering strong men during town fairs. In the 18th cent. the first barbell consisting of an iron rod with 2 metal balls came into use. In the second half of the 18th cent. W. Curtis of England was declared the best lifter in the world. At the same time the Attila School for training circus strong men was estab. in London. The 19th cent. model of the strong man was promoted in society thanks to circus athletic programs, including both wrestling and weightlifting, watched by low-class spectators. As a rather typical circus entertainment, weightlifting faced numerous difficulties on its way to being taken seriously as sport. 19th cent. Eng. encyclopedias of sport either ignored weightlifting altogether or slighted it as an 'ungentlemanly' activity. The social barriers were finally broken in Germany, where the first weightlifting association was founded in 1880, followed by many other weightlifting clubs in Hamburg, Cologne, Duisburg, Frankfurt and Leipzig. In 1881 these clubs formed the Deutscher Athleten Bund, encompassing wrestlers and weight lifters. In 1885, on the initiative of the Pole W. Krajewski the Kružok Liubitielej Atletikie was estab. in St. Petersburg. The first athletic meeting of circus strong men and amateur lifters took place in 1887 in London. The first weightlifting E.Ch., regardless of body weight categories, were held in Rotterdam in 1896. The athletes competed in a sort of weightlifting decathlon, each having 10 attempts to lift various weights (not only barbells). The winner was an Austrian, W. Turk. Due to its folk and circus background weightlifting became an attractive sport practiced by the working class. Before long weightlifting as well as >WRESTLING were incorporated into workers' sports associations, becoming the favorite working class sports, later superceded only by >FOOTBALL. The first international conference aimed at fixing the rules and regulations of the sport took place in 1913. In 1920 the International Weightlifting Federation (Fédération Halterophile Internationale, FHI) was founded with the aim to supervise international competitions; in the years 1949-68 it was also the governing body of international >BODY BUILDING. The Ol.G. of 1896 and 1904 included 1- and 2-hand weightlifting events. Weightlifting was not included in the 1900, 1908, and 1912 Ol.G. Until 1939 the sport was dominated by lifters from Austria, France and Egypt, and to a lesser extent, from Italy, the USA and Estonia. The most outstanding lifters of that time were Olympic champions: Egyptians E.S. Nosseir (1928 – body weight category 82.5kg), M.A. Mesbah (1936 – 67.5), and K. El Touni (1936 – 75.0); Austrians F. Andrysek (1928 – 60.0), and H. Haas (1928 – 67.5); Frenchmen E. Decotignies (1924 – 67.5), R. Duverger (1932), L. Hostin (1932, 1936), R. François 91928), and R. Suvigny (1932 – 60.0); Italians P. Gabetti (1924 – 60.0, silver medallist 1928), and C. Galimberti (1924, silver medallist 1928 and 1932); American A. Therlazzo (1936 – 60.0, bronze medallist 1932); and Estonian A. Neuland (1920 – 67.5). Eg. lifters dominated the sport of weightlifting until the 1948 Ol.G. but later they began to give way to others. Briefly after WWII the lead was taken by Americans, to be followed by the Soviets, Poles, Bulgarians, and E Germans. A few weightlifting celebrities came from Norway, Rumania and W Germany. In the 1980s the weightlifting leadership took a completely different shape. After the migration of Bulgarian N. Suleimanogliu to Turkey, interest in weightlifting was hugely revived in Asia Minor. Top lifters also represented Greece and China. At the 1996 Ol.G. in Atlanta 2 gold medals were won by Greece (D. Pyrros up to 83kg and A. Kakiasvilis up to 99kg) and China (Tang Ninngsheng up to 59kg and Zhuan Xugang up to 70kg). The 1980s also saw the departure of the Poles who won only a few occasional silver and gold medals. During the Sydney Ol.G. in 2000 the contestants were divided into 8 (instead of 10) body weight categories. The gold medal ranking was the following: 2 medals for Greece (D. Pyrros 85kg and A. Kakiasvilis 94kg), 2 medals for Iran (H. Tavakoli up to 105kg and H. Rezazadeh over 105kg), 1 medal for Turkey (H. Mutlu up to 56kg), 1 medal for Croatia (N. Pechalov up to 62kg), 1 medal for Bulgaria (G. Boevsky up to 69kg), and 1 medal for China (Zhuan Xugang up to 77kg). The Weightlifting W.Ch. have been held since 1920.

Record setting has been a very important part of the sport of weightlifting, esp. with regard to the superheavyweight category. The first to break the 200-kg barrier in the snatch was American D. Ashman (201.0kg – 1960); in the clean and jerk, the barrier was first reached by Bulgarian C. Placzkov (200.0kg – 1976) and crossed by S. Rachmanov from the USSR (200.5 – 1978). In the clean and press the 200kg barrier was broken by L. Żabotyński from the USSR (201.5kg – 1967). In the >OLYMPIC WEIGHTLIFTING TRIATHLON (replaced by >WEIGHTLIFTING DECATHLON in 1971) the psychological barrier of 400kg was first reached by the Egyptian S. Nossir (1931) and broken by the German J. Manger (402.5kg – 1935); the 500kg barrier was broken by the Amer. P. Anderson (517.5kg – 1955) and the 600kg barrier, was both reached and broken by W. Aleksyeyev from the USSR in the same year (602.5kg – 1970). In the weightlifting biathlon, the first world record was set by W. Aleksyeyev (415.0kg – 1971); in 1982 the barrier of 450kg was reached and then broken by A. Pisarenko (455.0kg). One of the most outstanding weightlifters in history was the Pole W. Baszanowski (2-time Olympic champion, up to 67.5kg in 1964 and 1968; 5-time world champion in different weight categories in the years 1961, 1964, 1965, 1968, 1969). Until the 1940s weightlifting enjoyed little popularity among women. Except for a few 19th cent. circus shows performed by women, the first women's weightlifting contest took place in the USA in 1947. Unlike many other 'unwomanly' sports that have lately become part of the Olympic program (soccer, pole jump, triple jump), women's weightlifting remained out of the Ol.G. for a long time. It was during the Olympic Festival in St. Louis before the 1996 Atlanta Ol.G. that the first women's weightlifting competition was held. Accusations of the supposedly detrimental effects of weightlifting upon feminine beauty

Olympic weightlifting.

Russia's Aleksei Petrov lifts 187.5kg in the snatch for a new world and Olympic weightlifting record in the 91kg weight class at the Centennial Summer Games in Atlanta, 1996.

Poland's super heavyweight silver medallist from the 2000 Sydney Games, Agata Wróbel.

W

WORLD SPORTS ENCYCLOPEDIA

were promptly belied by the attractively well-muscled Amer. female lifter C. Clark. At present women's weightlifting is practiced mainly in the USA, Canada, UK, Hungary and China. At the 2000 Ol.G. in Sydney the sport was dominated by the Chinese who won 4 gold medals out of 7 (Yang Xia up to 53kg; Chen Xiaomin 63kg; Lin Weinintg 69kg; Ding Meiyuan 75kg). The other 3 gold medals were won by T. Nott, USA (up to 48kg), S.J. Mendivil, Mexico (up to 58kg), and M.I. Urrutia, Columbia (75kg). Women's Weightlifting W.Ch. have been held since 1986.

R.V. Fodor, *Competitive Weightlifting*, 1979; J. Lear, *Weight Training and Lifting*, 1989; T. Dodd, *Inside Powerlifting*, 1978.

WEIGHTLIFTING DECATHLON, a set of 10 contests in lifting various types of weights, with 1 or 2 hands, initiated during the 1st E.Ch. in 1896 in Rotterdam. The first winner was W. Turk from Austria.

WEIGHTLIFTING PENTATHLON, a >WEIGHTLIFTING event practiced until 1934. It consisted of 1-hand snatch, 1-hand clean-and-press, and 2-hand lifts of *snatch*, *clean-and-jerk*, and >CLEAN-AND-PRESS. The weightlifting pentathlon was included in the W.Ch. and Ol.G. in 1924, and the E.Ch. in 1924 and 1933.

WEITSCHIEßEN, Ger. for 'sliding (shooting) on ice', [Ger. *Weit* – distance + *Schießen* – to shoot], a game that belongs to the family of winter sports referred to in the Ger. tradition as >EISSCHIEßEN, in which specially constructed weights are slid on ice. The weight (called *Eisstock*) is made of wood and has a metal base (*Fuß*). Its shape resembles a flattened cone with a base of 27-30cm and a weight of 4-6kg. From the top of the cone protrudes a handle with a thicker outward end. The weight is slid along an ice track, which at the starting point (*Schutzkreis*) is 2m wide and ends in a half-circle, while its width ultimately reaches 8m. The length of the track is 300m and may be extended, if necessary. Cf. >EISKEGELN; >KALLUDERSCHIEßEN; >RINGSCHIEßEN; >ZIELSCHIEßEN; cf. also other games of a similar kind like >CURLING or >UTYUG.

'Eisschießen', *Kleine Enzyklopädie Köroperkultur und Sport*, 1965, 283-285.

WERN, a Bret. var. of >GREASED POLE.

WESTERN HORSEBACK RIDING, an art of riding which comprises elements from Eur. and Native Amer. Ind. traditions (see >INDIAN HORSEBACK RIDING). The following circumstances contributed to its formation: detachment from the Eur. continent, new riding conditions (difficult terrain), the supplanting of chivalric elitism with a more common, robust form of heroism and the natural riding style of Native Amer. Indians. Eur. chivalry and aristocracy, as well as soldiers, were seated in such a way as to keep their knees close to the horse's side and their thighs diagonally forward. This helped them accommodate to the rise and fall of the horse's steps by lifting their buttocks off the saddle (weight resting on knees) and then lowering them softly and flexibly back into the saddle. Western riders, however, relinquish the up-and-down movement in the saddle in favor of sitting in it firmly, with the trunk reclining slightly. This is

Frederic Remington, The Bronco Buster, *1888, bronze.*

Charles Schreyvogel, Saving Their Lieutenant.

Jerzy Kossak, Cowboys with a Herd of Horses on a Prairie, *1939.*

Charles Schreyvogel, A Skirmish.

connected to a type of saddle different from the one used in Europe. The *Western saddle* (or *stock saddle*) can be traced back to the high saddle of the Span. conquistadors. This saddle had a characteristic pommel with a high horn. The Western saddle differs from it by a wider and deeper seat with a high cantle. The seat is moved backward as regards the saddle's center of gravity. This caused the stirrups to be fastened in the middle of the saddle's length. The stirrups are also longer than the Eur. ones and support a larger area of the feet, enabling a firmer seating. The rider holds the reins in one hand (in trad. Eur. riding – in both hands), which leaves him the other hand to reach for the gun or use a lasso. In this type of reining the rider steers the horse not through the bit, but through the strap on the horse's neck, which means that when the rider pulls the left strap, the horse turns right and vice versa. The most conspicuous element is the rider's outfit: wide leather trousers, loose shirts, bandanas tied around the neck, wide-brimmed hats protecting from the sun (influenced by the Mexican sombrero) and high-heeled boots with pointed toe-caps, preventing feet slipping in the stirrups. Horse breeding in the Wild West brought forth breeds which could not only run fast, but also withstand changing weather conditions and rough terrain. Their agility made them suitable for herding cattle. The most famous breeds are the Amer. Quarter Horse, Appaloosa, Buckskin, Mustang, Paint, Pinto, Palomino and Span. Barb.

History. The art of Western horseback riding is strictly connected to the conquest of the Wild West. This process was begun by the Span. ranchers (*vaqueros*), who came from the direction of the Gulf of Mexico. Later Ang.-Sax. farmers and cattle-breeders joined them, moving in from the Atlantic Coast. In the states which were for a long time a matter of dispute between the US and Mexico (i.e. California, Colorado, New Mexico and esp. Texas), Span. and Ang.-Sax. riding traditions merged. This manifests itself in horse riding terminology: Eng. *ranchers, lasso* and Span. *rancheros, lazzo*. From the immigrant's point of view the conquest of the Wild West was risky

yet fascinating, giving him the chance to test himself and gain control of a whole new environment (see >GEOGRAPHICAL EXPLORATION). The horse had a major role to play in this process, serving as a main form of transport until the building of a substantial number of railroad lines. The crowning achievement of communication based on horse riding was the Pony Express, a postal service between the westernmost villages connected to the railway network and settlements on the Pacific coast. It consisted of relay teams of about 200 riders and 500 horses altogether. The Pony Express was initiated in 1860 by W.H. Russel and his partners A. Majors and W.B. Wadell. It went out of business after both coasts were connected by telegraph lines (Oct. 1861) and railway tracks (1866). From the Native Amer. Indians' point of view the Europeans were intruders. The Indians, having quickly mastered the skill of horseback riding, were often able to successfully defend themselves. To fight them, the settlers hired professional riders, called posse. This theme is present in countless westerns, both books and movies. Small colonial communities had been organizing horseback riding events since the very beginning. They were used to give color to cattle round-ups, celebrate holidays and even settle accounts between neighbors. The first thoroughbred race horse, the stallion Bullee Rock, was brought to Virginia in 1730. The first jockey association, the Maryland Jockey Club, was created in 1743. Since then racing events, although in large cities dominated by major associations and stadiums (e.g. the Union Race Course in New York), have developed independently in the country, creating >RODEO. Riding contests held under the auspices of the Amer. Horse Shows Association (AHSA) greatly differ from Eur. competitions, on account of the dissimilar riding technique. In the *Stock Seat* competition mounting the horse and the correct seating is judged. In the *Western Pleasure* the horse, not the rider, is evaluated. In the *Reining* competition riders must perform several figures. In *Freestyle Reining* rider and horse perform their own program set to music. A separate category is the working cow horse division, where evolutions necessary for cattle round-ups are performed. Other competitions include *cutting* and *trail horse*.

The horse in the art and literature of the Wild West. Most literary works devoted to the Wild West devotes some attention to the horse and the art of horseback riding. Countless novels and movies are concerned first and foremost with horses. The most celebrated painters of the theme were: C.M. Russell (1864-1926) and F. Remington (1861-1909). In all works of this type the horse is an attribute of modern chivalry, associated with western riders in the 19th cent. The culmination of this was the novel *Knights of the Range* (1936) by Z. Grey. Many cowboys have also become authors themselves, e.g. S.O. Barker (1894-1985), who wrote *Some Horses I Have Rode*.

M. Conti, 'Horseback Riding. Western', EWS, 1996, II, 474-477; D. Dary, *Cowboy Culture*, 1981; P. Durham and W.L. Jones, *The Negro Cowboys*, 1983; J.B. Frantz and J.E. Choate, *The American Cowboy. The Myth and the Reality*, 1955; E. Hough, *The Story of the Cowboy*, 1898; T. Jordan, *Women of the American West*, 1982; T. Kirksmith, *Ride Western Style. A guide for Young Riders*, 1991; W.W. Savage Jr., *The Cowboy Hero. His Image in American History and Culture*, 1979; C. Strickland, *Western Riding*, 1995.

WHACKS, an old Eng. game in which a wooden block is batted with sticks. See also >WAGGLES.

WHAI, a Maori art of forming geometric string combinations through manipulating the fingers of both hands. During a competition the moderator calls out the name of the combination and the first to complete it, scores a point.

WHAKAHEKE-NGARU, a trad. var. of >SURFING practiced by the Maori of N.Zealand.

WHAKAHORO TARATAHI, a Maori var. of >KITE FLYING.

WHAKAROPIROPI, a var. of Maori hand skill games; cf. >MAHI RINGARINGA.

WHATOTO, also *whatotoa* or *mamau*, a var. of Maori wrestling known before the arrival of Europeans in N.Zealand. The object of the bout was to knock one's opponent down. At the beginning of the bout each wrestler grabbed the waist of his opponent. The bout was accompanied by rythmic singing and the chanting of incantations which were believed to bring about success. Some bouts were held with the active involvement of women, in which case 1 man would wrestle against 2 women.

WHAWHAI MEKEMEKE, also *mekemeke*, a Maori form of hand-to-hand combat similar to Eur. >BOXING. One style of fighting involved striking the opponent with a clenched fist with knuckles aimed forward, the other – striking with the side of the clenched fist. Such fights were often used as a means of solving minor social conflicts or to enhance the fighter's prestige within the community. Cf. >PUGILISM. See also >YANOMAMO DUELS.

WHEEL-AND-POLE, see >HOOP-AND-POLE.

WHEELBARROW, also *riding a wheelbarrow*, *wheelbarrow race*, etc. A simple competition between 2-player teams. One player, the 'wheelbarrow', puts his hands on the ground, while the other grabs his feet and raises them up. To ride the wheelbarrow, both partners must move forwards at a speed which the hands of the 'wheelbarrow' can handle. The team that covers a specified distance first, wins the race. An alternative form of competition offers victory for covering the longest distance. The game is a popular exercise in all Eur. systems of physical education. In Denmark it is referred to as >TRILLEBØRSLØB.

J. Møller, 'Køre trillebør', GID, 1997, 3, 19.

WHEELBARROW RACES, a form of trad. competition in which participants race over a fixed distance, while rolling in front of them wheel-barrows filled with various types of cargo: from bricks or other heavy objects to fellow participants. Trivial and humorous in nature, it was rarely recorded in historical sources and usu. formed an event that accompanied festivals or country fairs since the late Middle Ages. A Dan. var. of the competition is mentioned by J. Möller in his dictionary *Sports Games in Denmark* (*Game idrætslege i Danmark*, 1997, vol. 4, p.100). An original form of wheel-barrow races developed

in Great Britain, where elements of >BLIND MAN'S BUFF were added to form *blindfolded wheel-barrow races*, a form of trad. competition held during festivals and country-folk fairs in England throughout the 19th cent. and at the beginning of the 20th cent. It was a one-time event during the so-called Ol.G. at Much Wenlock in 1855, of which the local *Eddowes' Salopian Journal* said that they 'afforded much amusement owing to the tortous circuit by which many of the blindfolded competitors approached goal. The winner was John Skeat who completed his performance by a somersault into the hedge at the end of the field'.

WHEELCHAIR BASKETBALL, sport for the disabled, applying the rules for >BASKETBALL, but played on wheelchairs. It has been developed best in the US, however, it does not belong to Wheelchair Sport USA, as do other >SPORTS FOR THE DISABLED, but constitutes a separate organization called the National Wheelchair Basketball Association. Founded in 1948 as the first national wheelchair basketball organization, it is still the biggest wheelchair basketball organization in the world. At present, it comprises 181 clubs. Wheelchair basketball is also well developed in Germany, Great Britain, France, Australia and many other countries characterized by dynamic development. World Wheelchair Basketball Championships are held, and wheelchair basketball is included in the Paralympic Games program. The top paralympic teams come from Spain, Russia, Poland, Portugal, Brazil and Australia.

WHEELCHAIR DANCE, a form of tournament dancing with the participation of disabled persons in wheelchairs. The formal requirement is that a dance couple must be comprised of a male and female partner and one of them must be a wheelchair user with a permanent impairment in the lower part of the body of such a degree that it is obvious and easily recognizable and makes walking, and consequently dancing, impossible. The minimum disabilities, as defined by the regulations, include: amputation through the ankle, loss of 10 muscle strength points in both legs, ankylosis (fusion) of ankle joint extension defect of at least 30 degrees or ankylosis of knee joint, spasticity/discoordination corresponding to CP class 7, or leg shortening by least 7cm. The upper part of the body should not be impaired in any way. The sport is internationally governed by the Wheelchair Dance Committee initiated by G. Kromholz of Germany. Independent at first, in 2000 the Committee became part of the International Paraolympics Committee (IPC). In 2002 wheelchair dancing became a demonstration sport during the Winter Paraolympic Games. The most important events are W.Ch., E.Ch. and the World Cup. Similar to ordinary sport dancing, the following elements are evaluated: time and rhythm, technique and character, harmony and expression, choreography and originality. The rules governing wheelchair dancing must be in accordance with the regulations of the International Dance Sport Federation. The trad. division into standard dances (Eng. waltz, Viennese waltz, tango, slow fox-trot, quickstep) and Lat.-Amer. dances (samba, cha-cha, rumba, paso doble, jive) is preserved. The man's dress must be black or dark blue; the woman's dress must cover her buttocks at all times and tangas are not allowed. The floor is a rectangle with a total surface of at least 200m², of which neither side is shorter than 10m. Not more than 6 couples are allowed on the floor at one time. The IPC Wheelchair Dance Committee registers a rank list of the best international couples.

IPC Wheelchair Dance Committee web page; IDSF web page; personal inform. from Iwona Ciok.

WHEELCHAIR FENCING, a var. of >FENCING practiced by paraplegics. Bouts are conducted on specially prepared strips, which help to stabilize the wheelchairs in a strictly defined position and distance. The following weapons are competed in: sabre, foil, épée; the latter two by both women and men, the first as a men's event only. Additionally, special bouts between quadriplegic contestants are held in foil and épée.

History. Fencing was one of the first sports introduced to rehabilitation programs of the disabled in the National Spinal Injuries Center in Stoke Mandeville in England in 1953. Later, in 1960, the sport was included in the program of Paralympics.

WHEELCHAIR RUGBY, a ball game for disabled players using wheelchairs. It is said to derive from >RUGBY but actually combines elements of rugby, >BASKETBALL, >FOOTBALL and >ICE HOCKEY. The game is usu. played in a basketball court. The players are assigned between 0.5 and 3.5pts. depending on their disability. A 4-person team may not be assigned a combined total of more than 8pts. on the scale. A volleyball is used, which may be passed between players in any way apart from being kicked. The ball may not be held by a player for more than 10sec. A match consists of four 8-min. periods. The idea of the game was born in Canada in 1977 but it has spread considerably since that time. See also >SPORTS FOR THE DISABLED.

Internet: Wheelchair Rugby: http://www.paralympic. org.sports/sections/w_rugby/general.htm

WORLD SPORTS ENCYCLOPEDIA

W

Joey Johnson (#8) of Canada prepares to rebound during the Men's Gold Medal Wheelchair Basketball Match between Canada and the Netherlands at the Superdome, Sydney, Australia.

Wheelchair dancing.

European Championships in wheelchair fencing in Warsaw, Poland.

W

WORLD SPORTS ENCYCLOPEDIA

WHEELCHAIR TABLE TENNIS, a var. of >TABLE TENNIS adapted to the needs of disabled persons based on the regulations of the International Table Tennis Federation (ITTF). There are 2 basic forms of wheelchair table tennis depending on the player's level of disability: wheelchair tennis and standing tennis, and players participate and compete in 1 of 10 disability classes. All matches are played best of 3 games to 21pts. The sport is included in the official program of the Paralympic Games, the Pan Amer. Games, the Pan Afr. Games, and the Far East Games. In addition to these events W.Ch. are staged every 4 years, as well as various annual, top-class tournaments. It is a truly international sport, played in over 50 countries worldwide in all classes. See also >SPORTS FOR THE DISABLED.

WHEELCHAIR TENNIS, a game based on the rules of >LAWN TENNIS, but adapted to the needs of disabled persons in wheelchairs. The main difference is that players of wheelchair tennis are allowed to return the ball after it has bounced twice and the second bounce may even be outside the court. Players move on special light, easily manageable wheelchairs with an additional small balancing wheel at the front.

History. The game was created at the beginning of the 1970s in the USA. In 1978 an American, B. Parks, drew up the regulations. In 1988 during the Seoul Paralympic Games wheelchair tennis was a special event and 4yrs. later it was included in the official Olympic program in Barcelona. The sport is governed by the International Tennis Federation (ITF), which registers a ranking of the best players. The highest ranked player becomes the world champion (separately for men and women). The sport is played in approx. 100 countries. See also >SPORTS FOR THE DISABLED.

WHIPPING TOMS, an Eng. var. of a game with the use of a small wooden ball and a stick, also called *hockey* or *shinney*. Its uniqueness lies in the fact that it was not played on a pitch, but within the streets of Newark in Nottinghamshire on Fat Tuesday. Two teams of an unspecified number of players were to drive a ball from one end of the town to the other. The name of the game refers to 3 men disguised in monk's frocks carrying long whips, who appeared after the game was over. They were accompanied by 3 other men in disguise holding bells and symbolically driving the players out of Newark, which was to commemorate the expulsion of its Viking conquerors. As the beating occasionally turned violent, the town council banned the tradition in 1847. TGESI, I, 217-218.

WHITE WATER KAYAKING AND CANOEING, a form of kayaking and canoeing competitions contested on courses of swift, turbulent water with natural and artificial hazards (natural water reservoirs or artificial facilities). In order to complete the race competitors must negotiate the distance passing a series of 20-30 gates constructed of 2 rods suspended vertically over the water. The winner's title goes to the competitor with the best time after 2 correctly completed passages.

History. The origins of whitewater kayaking may be traced back to tourist excursions encompassing shooting through the rapids. The first competition in wild water kayaking was held even before 1939 in Germany. After 1945 white water kayaking enjoyed increasing popularity. In 1949 a World Cup was initiated and the first winners in women's slalom races in K-1 were H. Pillwein and O. Eiterer (both Austrians), and in C1 slalom race for men the Frenchman P. d'Alençon. In 1955 the Can. slalom race C2 was included in the programme of W.Ch. (the first winner was Fr. team Neuveul/Paris). In 1959 C1 and C2 categories were added to the W.Ch. agenda (M. Schubert (DDR) – first winner in C1; Fr. Team Dransart/Turlier won in C2). Various non-fixed disciplines, which are no longer practiced, were included in the first W.Ch.. P. Sodomka from Czechoslovakia was the leading competitor of those times; he scored 16 medals (including 8 gold). White water kayaking entered the Ol.G. for the first time in 1972. A. Bachman was a winner for K-1 for women and S. Horn among men (both from the DDR). In the exclusively male C1 gold went to L. Pollert from Czechoslovakia and in C2 to the DDR team of R.D. Armend and W. Hofmann. This discipline was withdrawn in the course of the following Olympics and reintroduced in 1992 when the winner of the gold medal in K-1 for women was E. Miheler (Germany) and in C1 P.Ferrazzi (Italy), whereas in C-2 the team from the USA – J. Jacobi and S. Strasbaugh. In 1996 in K-1 the winners were: for men O. Fix (Germany) and for women S. Hilgertova (Czech Republic). In C1 which is still a discipline contested exclusively among men, the winner was M. Martikan (Slovakia), and in C2 the Fr. Team of F. Addison and W. Forgues.

K. Ford, *Kayaking*, 1995; R. Rowe, *White Water Kayaking*, 1988; P.D. Whitney, *White Water Sport*, 1960

WHITE WATER RAFTING, see >RAFTING.

WHO JUMPS HIGHER, a simple game played in water, in which a thin rope with a ball attached to it is tied to one end of a long pole. The pole is then placed in the water and the players jump up trying to reach the ball and hit it. The judge, who holds the pole, raises it up after each round until there is only one contestant left– the winner – who is able to reach the ball. The game was described by a Russian ethnographer I. Chkhannikov (GIZ, 1953, 81-82).

WIEKO, an old trad. Pol. game practiced by boys in the region of Rzeszów. According to E. Piasecki's *Games and sports of children and youth* (1916), it was played as follows:

The game was played with a 'palerka', or a kind of bat, a wooden plank driven diagonally into the ground, and a small piece of wood, which the batter had to knock off the plank. They competed in pairs: one player batting and the other trying to catch the little piece of wood. If he succeeds, he goes to the 'winning place'. If he fails, he has to throw the piece of wood towards the plank so that it lands as close to it as possible. However, the batter tries to strike it in the air. Then he measures the distance from the spot where the piece of wood landed to the plank, scoring 10 points for each length of his bat. If the piece of wood landed close to the plank, he goes to the 'losing place'.

WIFE PICK-A-BACK RACES, a running event over a distance of approx. 200m, in which runners carrying their wives (or a 'significant other') on their backs must tackle 3 obstacles in the form of fences or hurdles, similar to those used in the athletic 3-km steeplechase race, and one water basin approx. 10m in length and 70cm deep. The race ends on a small sand dune. In 1997 the 1st W.Ch. were held in Kiantajärvi, Finland.

WILD BOAR, in full *shoeing the wild boar*, an old form of rural show and competition, practiced in a shed or barn, where a short girder was suspended from its tie-beam on 2 ropes. The player would sit on the girder with both legs on the same side and a whip-like withe in his hand, making movements imitating the whipping of a horse's side and trying to keep his balance. The player who made the most whipping movements before he fell off the girder

General action during the Men's Wheelchair Rugby Gold Medal Match between the USA and Australia during the 2000 Paralympic Games at the Dome, Homebush Bay, Sydney, Australia.

E. Vergeer of the Netherlands in action against her compatriot opponent S. Walraven during the 2002 Australian Wheelchair Tennis Open women's final at Melbourne park in Melbourne, Australia.

White water kayaking.

A wife pick-a-back race.

was the winner. The name of the game bears no obvious relation to the idea behind it, so the game could have once been part of a different tradition which gradually disappeared.
TGESI, II, 383.

WINCHESTER COLLEGE FOOTBALL, also the *Winchester game*, a local var. of an Eng. football game practiced since around 1550 at Winchester College (Great Britain) on a goalless field 73.2m in length and 22.9m in width. Points are scored by carrying the ball across the end line. Dribbling and passing the ball forward are prohibited. The game's length is 60min.

WINCHESTER FIVES, a var. of an Eng. game of >FIVES, developed separately at Winchester College (Great Britain). It is played mainly as doubles, similar to >ETON FIVES, but different from >RUGBY FIVES, played also as a single game. The priority of doubles in Winchester fives results from the nature of the court, which is surrounded by 4 walls. **Court and equipment.** The court is asymmetric, its longer axis being 28ft. (8.53m) in length. The court's width at its front wall is 18ft. (5.49m) and remains so to a depth of 9ft. 10in. (3m) from the front wall. At this point the left wall has a slant (*butress*) at an angle of 135°, which is 9in. (24.8cm) long and tapers toward the back of the court. This butress – used for deflecting the ball – is crucial for the game's tactics and presents one of the main differences between Winchester fives and other var. of fives. This irregularity makes the single game difficult, if not impossible, because the player is unable to control both parts of the court – in front of and to the back of the buttress. Staying at the back of the court, the player is rarely able to reach the ball, which – deflected by the butress – abruptly changes its direction, and even if he is successfull, the deflection usu. makes his play at the front of the court ineffective. On the other hand, the court's irregularity is usu. successfully dealt with by a team, in which one player stays at the front and the other at the back of the court. The butress, which offers an additional advantage to left-handed players, who can make better use of it, could have been modelled after the court structure in >ROYAL TENNIS. The Winchester fives court structure has been adopted by several other Eng. schools, where the game of fives was practiced. New courts of this kind are no longer built and Winchester fives remains popular only in Winchester, while in other schools which once followed the Winchester fives tradition it is gradually disappearing. Some of them – contrary to their tradition – now belong to the Rugby Fives Association.

WIND SKIING, a var. of >WINDSURFING practiced on snow, in which contestants move on skis propelled by a sail.

WINDSKATING, a var. of windsurfing practiced on land (>WINDSURFING). Contestants use rectangular boards, never longer than 1m, fixed to 4 large rollers or rather wheels with rubber rims, about 12-15cm in diameter. The board is propelled by a sail, borrowed from windsurfing. The board is maneuvered like in trad. >SKATEBOARDING, i.e. by exerting pressure on one side of the board, which makes the wheeled axis turn, and properly positioning the sail. Owing to relatively larger rollers, competitions can be held on sandy surfaces, particularly on beaches.

WINDSURFING, also *sailboarding*, *boardsailing*, a watersport, combining the trad. >SURFING with evolutions using the sail fixed to the board. The sailor and board are propelled across the water by wind and waves. The first board was created by Brit. inventor Peter Chilvers in the mid 1960s – it was a large and relatively heavy board, 375cm long. However, it was not until Hoyle Schweitzer from California produced a commercial design 10 years later that the sport became popular. In the 1990s the so-called 'short board' was invented, which incorporated the best features of its 2 predecessors. At the same time the latest materials were used to design the sail, including the Rotating Aerodynamic Foil (RAF). Sails are usu. constructed from transparent monofilm material, with between 4 and 8 full-length fiberglass-carbon battens, to hold the rig shape as rigid as possible for maximum aerodynamic efficiency. The flexible mast is made of fiberglass and carbon. A sailboard consists of 2 components: the board and the rig – the latter consists of the

sail, the mast, and the boom (the horizontal bar that is used to steer the board). The board has a foam core, and either a blow-molded polypropylene skin, or a thermoformed epoxy-fiberglass skin (which is lighter but more fragile and slightly more expensive), often including carbon, Kevlar, or a mixture of both for increased strength. Boards over 3m (10ft.) in length have a retractable daggerboard for increased stability in light winds and better performance when sailing into the wind. The daggerboard projects beneath the board and can be retracted into the hull. Boards under 3m (10ft.) in length are for use in strong winds only, and are fitted with footstraps to hold the sailor to the board when traveling at speed or in the air.

Windsurfing is a compact form of sailing, and the craft's small size, weight, and low drag make it the fastest sail-powered watercraft available. The stronger the wind, the faster sailboards can go, and speeds of more than 80km/h (50mph) are regularly recorded by experienced windsurfers. Windsurfers stand sideways on the board and face the direction in which they are traveling. The board is then steered by the sailor manipulating the sail, mast, and boom to take best advantage of any wind, and by shifting his or her body weight on the board to guide it. Beginners start on large, high-volume boards in light winds. They can then progress to faster and smaller slalom boards, and learn how to make fast banked turns in stronger winds. The most advanced form of windsurfing is wave sailing, where board, sail, and sailor leap off the tops of waves to heights of more than 10m (30ft.), performing full 360° or 720° loops while airborne, then riding the waves as in surfing back to the beach.

There are a few var. of windsurfing. One of the most popular contests include regattas where the object is to take the best place in sailing competitions similar to those in yachting. The boards are divided into 2 classes – I (with a flat bottom) and II (with a rounded bottom). Apart from class category, there is also a type classification, such as Winglider, Mistral Lechner. The longest race is a marathon. Other contests include a slalom and free windsurfing, during which evolutions are made, e.g. jumps in the air. The latest form of windsurfing is practiced indoors, in a pool, with wind generated by special blowers. Occasionally, boards for 2 or even 3 sailors are seen (tandems and tridems).

History. Initially windsurfing was an amateur and anonymous sport, practiced by a group of enthusiasts on the Californian coastline. Windsurfing became popular after the publication of an article by S. Newman Darby entitled 'Sailboarding: New Exciting Water Sport' in the *Popular Science Monthly* (1965). Newman was right on the mark in declaring that 'this sport, so new that less than 10 people know what its

rules are, will be a cheap sailing entertainment for many'. It is widely believed that windsurfing was 'invented' by H. Schweitzer, a businessman from California, and J. Drake, an aeronautics engineer. Drake said later that he had had first discussions on the new sport with F. Payne back in 1961. When the first windsurfing board, called the Baja Board, was built, Drake patented its design and estab. the Windsurfer company (no longer in existence) that manufactured windsurfing equipment. In 1970 Schwitzer bought Drake's company and started to popularize his equipment and windsurfing all over the world. As the name Windsurfing was copyrighted, other manufacturers of similar equipment call the sport *boardsailing* or *sailboarding*. However, patent rights did not extend to all countries, incl. France. The confusion caused by 3 different names for the same sport helped skirt the original patent. This led to a slew of lawsuits in which many asserted that they had made a similar design much earlier than the Americans. Among such early 'inventors' of the windsurfing board was P. Chilvers, an Englishman, who claimed that he had done this in 1958, whereas R. Eastaugh from Australia maintained that he had built a board with a sail right after WWII. Among companies that had secured the legal right to manufacture windsurfing equipment on an Amer. license was the Ten Cate company, which significantly contributed to making the sport as popular in Europe as it is today; between 1973-78 the company sold about 150,000 boards. In 1977 L. Stanley from Hawaii introduced footstraps. In 1981-82 a Frenchman C. Marty sailboarded across the Atlantic from Dakar in Senegal to Cayenne in the Fr. Guyana, sailing 8hrs. every day. The food was provided

WINDSURFING

....*on snow*

....*sand*

... *and sea.*

W

WORLD SPORTS ENCYCLOPEDIA

from a yacht that accompanied him. He never left his board, although he did fix a floating collar to the board so as to keep equilibrium in the water. He covered the route in 37 days 16hrs. and 14min.

Windsurfing became an Olympic sport for men in 1984 (Los Angeles) and for women in 1992 (Barcelona). The gold medallists were: in 1984, S. van den Berg (Netherlands); in 1988, B. Kendall (N.Zealand); and in 1992, F. David (France), and B. Kendall (N.Zealand). Four years later the title was won by Shan Lee Lai from Hong Kong.

W.Ch. and E.Ch. have been held since 1990. The first world champion was P. Way (Great Britain) and among men – M. Quintin (France). The best windsurfers in the 1990s included: among men – R. Naish (USA), R. Bachschuster (Germany) and P. Belbeoch (France), and among women – N. le Liévre and M. Herbert (France), J. Horgen (Norway). The first championships were held with *lechner* boards and at the 1996 Ol.G. *mistral* boards were used. Apart from the Ol.G., the best known regattas include those held in Hookipa on Maui island (Hawaii), the estuary of the Columbia River in Oregon, where the upstream wind blows with the speed of nearly 100km/h, Canary Islands, the vicinity of Nice in France, Caribbean Islands, the vicinity of Perth in Australia, Garda Lake in Italy, the N-E coast of Sardinia, and the coasts of Spain. Windsurfing is also popular in Germany and Holland, and in Great Britain on the coasts of Cornwall.

J. Evans, *Complete Guide to Windsurfing*, 1983; S. Turner, *Windsurfing*, 1986; K. Winner and R. Jones, *Windsurfing with Kenn Winner*, 1980.

WINESKIN SHOOT, Pol. *strzelanie do bukłaka*, shooting arrows, usu. while sitting on a horse, at a wineskin hung on a pole. Ethnologists derive this custom from many myths of C Asia, the heroes of which fought with evil forces that took the day or yield from the earth by shooting at the sun to prevent drought or restore stolen daylight (see >ORIENTAL ARCHERY). In some cultures the wineskin was replaced with a panache bearing a ball or a horse-tail ensign, in modern times – with a rubber ball stuck on a mast. The panache was a symbol of power and that is why the new ruler or military commander was put to the test of shooting at it. The wineskin shoot was known in the E borderland territories of Poland, where it was made popular by the peoples that invaded these lands, and later by the Tartars who settled there, as well as among the peoples of the Caucasus. In Georgia it was known as >KABACHI.

WINGCHUN, also *vingtsun*, a >GONGFU style classified in the weija group (external styles). It was developed mostly in Guang-cho, Oshana, Nankai, and Hong-Kong. Unlike the 'classic' styles, which take several or even several dozen years to master, wingchun is intended to be learned in a relatively short time. From a technical point of view, it bears a certain resemblance to Shi-We (white crane style) although blows are far shorter – sometimes only 1in. (around 2.5cm) – and they are delivered in quick series, tangling and blocking the opponent's arms at the same time. Like Shi-We, wingchun was developed by a woman and presupposes that the opponent is stronger. The style encompasses 3 hand-to-hand techniques and 2 with the use of weapons. The fundamental exercise is *Chi sau*

(sticky hands) whose object is to feel the direction of the opponent's blow by touching his forearm. Because tactile receptors' reaction time is shorter than that of eyesight, the counteraction of an adept practitioner of wingchun is much quicker than that of persons depending solely on their eyesight. Fighters often use wooden dummies to practice combinations of blocks, blows, and kicks. A classic reaction is a vertical hit at the opponent's chin while simultaneously diverting his attacking hand.

WINTER BIATHLON, the sport involving both cross-country skiing and the use of firearms, also simply known as >BIATHLON [Lat. *bi* – double + Gr. *athlon* – competition, prize]. Running events in this discipline include 10 and 20-km runs in men's senior, 10 and 7.5km in women's, and 10 and 15km in juniors', as well as 4x7.5-km relays both in men's and women's categories and 3x7.5km in juniors'. Each run is accompanied by target shooting using a 5.6-mm small-caliber rifle at a distance of 50m. The targets – 40-45mm for shooting prone and 110-115mm from a standing position – have no bull's-eye. Seniors and juniors running 10km take 2 series – one prone, one standing – of 5 shots each; whereas on a 20-km course seniors take 4 series (alternating prone and standing) of 5 shots. Juniors running 15km take 3 series – prone, standing, and prone again – of 5 shots each, whereas relays involve 2 series – again one prone, one standing – of 5 shots each using up to 8 bullets. In relays and 10-km runs a penalty round is imposed for each missed target, whereas in 15 and 20-km courses a penalty minute is added to a competitor's final result in the same situation. There are 3 types of targets: mechanical, electronic, and those that shatter upon being struck. All targets in a given competition must be of the same type and are arranged in rows or in a square with one target in the center. The course is a loop, conforming to the FIS (Fédération International de Ski) regulations.

History. Evidence suggests that winter biathlon goes back to prehistoric times. Stone carvings discovered in Norway, dating back to 2000 BC, show spear-wielding hunters on skis shooting arrows with bows, combined activities not unlike today's winter biathlon. A similar union of skiing and shooting, this time performed by a Scand. winter hero, Ultra, who was worshipped as a remarkable skier and bow shooter, has also been mirrored in a number of later human activities, such as Norw. and Rus. army maneuvers from the Middle Ages up to the 17th cent. At the end of the 16th cent. the Pol. king, Stefan Batory, established an elite corps of skiing sharpshooters to combat their Rus. counterparts, which is illustrated in a woodcut of skiers at the ready included in the work of A. Gwagnin *Sarmatiae Europae Descriptio* (1578). The new-era prototypes of winter biathlon include army patrol runs held in Norway and Sweden up to the 18th cent. The first recorded military ski runs combined with shooting, dating back to 1767, involved border guards on both sides of the Nor.-Swed. frontier. Between 1792 and

1818 these drills led to regular events from which formal codification evolved. The first winter biathlon sports club was estab. in Trysil, Norway, in 1861. The 1924 OG in Chamonix were the first during which ski runs formed one of the events, although up to 1948 no medals were awarded in this discipline. After that, the event was cancelled because of its military character and the antiwar sentiments reigning in the Comité International Olympique (CIO) after WWII. In 1948 the Union Internationale de Pentathlon Moderne et Biathlon (UIPMB) was founded and until 1999, when International Biathlon Union (IBU) was estab., winter biathlon remained under its auspices. The first winter biathlon W.Ch., which are continued up to this day, were organized in 1958 in Saalfelden (Austria). At the beginning, only 20-km seniors' runs were held in which each country could put up 4 runners and a team's final score was the total of the 3 best individual scores. In 1957, in the wake of the Swedish initiative, the CIO decided to include winter biathlon in the program of the 1960 OG in Squaw Valley during which skiers ran a 20-km course shooting with 7.62 caliber rifles at distances of 250, 200, and 150m prone, and 100m standing. In the 1966 W.Ch. in Garmisch-Partenkirchen the team scoring system used so far was replaced by 4x7.5-km relay, shooting at a distance of 150m only. The W.Ch. held in 1974 in Minsk were the first to witness a 10-km run, later included in the OG program during the 1980 games in Lake Placid. In addition, a 150-m penalty loop was introduced. Since 1978 only 5.6mm caliber rifles have been allowed. In 1980, the first mechanical targets were employed and in 1981 2-min. penalty breaks were eliminated. An important influence on the skier's performance was the development of the skating technique introduced in 1985 which pushed the results to a higher level and necessitated certain modifications in the equipment, such as shorter skis and longer poles. The development of TV technology contributed in the 1990s to establishing a World Cup.

Among men, the best winter biathlon teams come from Germany, Norway, Russia, Byelorussia, and Austria. The most outstanding individuals include: W. Melanin from the USSR who won the gold medal in the 20km category during the 1964 Ol.G. and was the world champion in 1959, 1962, and 1963; F.P. Roetsch from Germany, the gold medallist in 20km during the 1988 Ol.G. and 1987 W.Ch., as well as in 10km at the 1988 Ol.G. and 1985 and 1987 W.Ch.; and M. Kirchner also from Germany, the Olympic winner in 10km in 1992 and the world champion in the same distance category in 1990 and 1993.

Women's winter biathlon started around 1978 and the women's events were first included in the W.Ch. in 1984 (initially in 5 and 10-km runs and then in 7.5 and 15-km ones), whereas in the Ol.G. program they were incl. in 1992 in Albertville (7.5 and 15-km runs and the 3x7.5-km relay; since the 1994 Ol.G. in Lillehammer the 3x7.5-km relay was replaced by the 4x7.5-km one). In the '90s the women's winter biathlon was dominated by Germany, Russia, Swe-

Argentina's M. Magrini (R) is pursued by D. Alberdi (2nd from R) and J.W. Manconi (2nd from L) of Canada, during a polo match on snow in St. Moritz, Switzerland, as part of the 15th Polo World Cup on Snow.

Ole Einar Bjoerndalen – winner of 3 gold medals in winter biathlon at the Salt Lake City Olympics.

den, Canada, and Norway. The most celebrated individuals include: Canadian M. Bedard, double gold medallist during the 1994 Ol.G. and the 1993 W.Ch.; German P. Schaaf, the world champion in 15km in 1989, 1991, and 1993, as well as in 10km in 1988; and Norwegian A. Elvebank, the world champion in 15km (1988) and 7.5km (1989 and 1990).

The development of TV technology led to significant modifications of the discipline aimed at making it more spectacular, e.g. introducing the so-called pursuit events in which men compete along a 12.5-km course and women – a 10-km one. Also the World Cup is held, in which, since 1997, all the skiers start simultaneously and the run is accompanied by 2 shooting series.

Since the 1990s a variety of winter biathlon in which bows, instead of rifles, are used has been growing in popularity (>SKI-ARCHERY). Still under the auspices of the UIPMB, >SUMMER BIATHLON is organized.

Consultant: R. Nowakowski.

WINTER POLO, or *polo on the snow,* a var. of >POLO played on snowy surfaces, rather than on grassland. The ponies have special hoof-spikes that prevent them from skidding and hoof-pads that prevent them from hurting other horses. The sport originated in Switzerland c.1984 and then it was brought to the USA. The most popular winter polo clubs are located in Aspen and Denver in Colorado.

WIUCHA, a Pol. name for a stone throwing device that consisted of a long leather strap folded in half. The strap was quickly rotated above the head and by letting one of its ends loose freed a stone which was shot forward. In Great Britain it was known as a *sling,* in Germany – *Schleuder,* in Russian – *rogatka,* in Dan. – *Slynge.* There were only minor construction differences between all of them, e.g. the Dan. *slynge* had a leather piece with 2 straps attached independently on both sides. There was also a hole in the leather piece, large enough to hold the stone better, but small enough not to let the stone pass through. The caster would hold the straps, rotate the *Slynge* 2-3 times above the head and let one of the straps loose to shoot off the stone. See also >SLING SHOOTING, >TIRO CON HONDA.
J. Møller, 'Slynge', GID, 1997, 4.

WŁÓCZKI FIGHTS, an unspecified form of competition connected with timber rafting. The Włóczki were raftsman from Cracow (Poland), who enjoyed the royal patronage of King Władysław IV in 1633 and several of his successors. Their job was to transport the wood from royal forests by water, which was often accompanied by various types of entertainment, incl. >JUMPING OVER FIRE and a form of fencing with long rafting poles which often resulted in falling into the water. No detailed descriptions of the game survives although their water duels must have resembled similar events popular in France and Germany known as >BOAT JOUSTING. Their services during the defence of Cracow against the Turks in the 13th cent. earned them the privilege of celebrating a holiday by displaying a >LAJKONIK.

WNA TAG TUG, a power competition, which – along with *musk-deer propping* – was another form of wrestling practiced among the aboriginal tribes of Greenland, in which a bout is held in a sitting position. In order to win the bout the competitor must lift his opponent so that both of his feet are above the ground.
W. Baxter, 'Les luttes traditionnelles a traverse le monde', in LJP, 1998, 75.

WOJNA NARODÓW, see >WOKATUS.

WOKATUS, also *a ball in the hole* or *the war of nations,* an old school game, popular esp. in secondary schools within the former Congress Kingdom of Poland before 1914 [Lat. *vocatus* – being called; *vocatur* – being named]. E. Piasecki gives the following description of the game:

The children stand in a circle. Inside the circle is a hole in the ground, in which the ball is rested. Each child assumes the name of a nationality (Polish, German, French, English etc.). On the side stands an umpire, who calls one nationality by crying: 'Vocatur! – French'. Then the 'Frenchman' runs quickly towards the ball, takes it and shoots it at his companions, who try to run away. The one who is hit, is marked in the umpire's notebook, if the ball misses, the mark goes to the thrower. Then the game starts anew and is continued until an agreed number of marks (e.g. 10) have been reached.

Whoever reaches that number first, is 'crowned' or 'executed', i.e. every player can strike the loser with the ball the number of times equal to his number of marks below '10'.
[*Games and pastimes of children,* 1916]

WOODBALL, a game in which a wooden ball is hit with a mallet to different targets. This general principle makes it similar to >GOLF, with 2 basic differences: 1) the ball is not placed in holes, but must pass through small gates located at the end of subsequent areas; 2) the ball is heavy and the mallet can only make it roll on the ground, instead of letting it fly in the air.

The equipment includes a wooden ball, a mallet and gates. The ball is 9.5cm in diameter and weighs 350g (with a tolerance of 60g). The mallet is T-shaped, with a handle 90cm in length and a bottle-shaped head 21.5cm in length and 6.6cm in diameter at the widest spot. It is this so-called 'bottom of the bottle' part of the mallet – protected with a rubber cap – that hits the ball. Hitting the ball with the side of the mallet's head is not allowed. The gate is constructed of 2 wooden blocks – also bottle-shaped – each driven into the ground with metal pins 15cm in length, fastened to the bottom of each block. The neck parts of the blocks are cross-connected with a metal rod, in the middle of which a wooden wineglass-shaped cup, 15-15.5cm in length is inversely suspended. The bottom of the cup hangs 5cm above the ground level, so that the ball passing through the gate can hit it and make it turn around the metal rod, thus signalling a properly scored point. A standard playing area is 500m in length and is divided into 12 fairways, each of which must be played separately. Each fairway is 20-100m in length, depending on the shape and level of difficulty of the terrain. Four fairways must be curved – 2 left curving and 2 right curving; 2 are short distance fairways, no less than 20m in length, while 2 are long distance fairways. At the end of each fairway is a circular gate area 5m in diameter, separated with a 1-m buffer zone from the end of the fairway.

At each fairway the game – played individually or in teams – begins with hitting the ball from the starting area 2m in width and 3m in length. In order to win, a player or team must cover all fairways by passing the ball through the gates with a fewer number of hits than the opponents. In team play a player hits the ball once and is followed by his teammates until all have had a go, after which the first player starts hitting again. During the play all other players must stand at least 3m aside or to the back of the hitter. Holding a mallet between feet is banned and violating that principle is punished by adding an extra hit to the score. Hitting the ball outside of the fairway results in starting the play again from the center of the fairway and adding an extra hit to the score. The first hit on long distance fairways cannot exceed 30m. A team consists of 4-8 players, of whom only 4-6 may play at a time. The team score is made by the results of the best 4 players. The are no specific rules regarding attire, except that it should be indentical for all team members.
History. The game was invented in 1990 by 2 Taiwanese: Ming Hui-Weng and Kuang-Chu Young. The first playing field was built in Nei Shuang His in the area of Taipei. In 1993 the Chin. Teipei Woodball Association was founded. In 1994-98 woodball slowly spread to other Asian countries,

Wrestlers, a wooden sculpture in the townhall in Wrocław, Poland.

mainly Japan and China, but also to N.America, Australia and Europe. In 1998 a tournament was held in Shenyang, China, now recognized as the first unofficial Asian Championships. The first official Asian Championships were held in 1999 in Lanjut in Malasia. In 1999 the International Woodball Federation was estab. and in 2001 it assembled 19 national federations. In 1999 the first International Woodball Invitation Championships were held and the first Eur. Woodball Championships in Budapest the following year.
International Woodball Federation, *Rules of Woodball* (2001); *The 1st European Woodball Conference Program Book* (2001).

WOODCHOPPING, see >TIMBER SPORTS.

WRESTLE ROYAL, an Amer. var. of wrestling, in which more than 2 wrestlers fight simultaneously on a specially adjusted ring, trying to pin the opponent's shoulders to the ground. Whoever survives last, wins the bout. Cf. a similar boxing event >BATTLE ROYAL.

WRESTLING, a generic name of a number of combat styles as practiced in various countries and cultures. The common, distinguishing feature of all wrestling styles is that the sport involves a hand-to-hand struggle without dealing any blows to one's opponent. There are, however, a great number of local styles and rules which demand that an opponent be floored with one or both shoulder blades touching the ground, with any part of his body touching the ground, etc. The most popular modern Olympic var. involve pinning both shoulder blades to the mat and holding an opponent in such a position for about 1sec. The 2 main styles included in the Olympic and W.Ch. program are the classical (>GRECO-ROMAN WRESTLING) and free style (>FREESTYLE WRESTLING). Until 1970 there were 8 weight categories observed for both styles and then – 10 and again 8 (since 1997). Apart from these 2 main and officially recognized styles, there are numerous folk wrestling var. in almost every country in the world. The most popular wrestling types are >A BRACCIUTA, >A BRAZZOS, >ARMTAG, >ASIAN INDIAN WRESTLING, >ATHABASCAN WRESTLING, >BACKHOLD, >BÖKHIIN BARILDAAN, >BOSNIAN WRESTLING, >BROERA-

A Wrestler, *an Olmec sculpture in stone.*

Romeyn De Hooghe, Wrestlers.

Gustave Courbet, Wrestlers, *oil on canvas.*

W

WORLD SPORTS ENCYCLOPEDIA

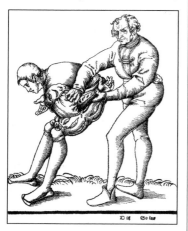

Thomas Eakins, The Wrestlers, *1899, oil on canvas, Columbus Museum of Art.*

Lucas Cranach the Elder, A Pair of Wrestlers, *woodcuts.*

A wushu presentation during the Chinese Championships in Macao.

TOK, >BRÓKATÖK, >BUKSETAG, >BUKSETAK, >BUXNATÖK, >BYXTAG, >CARACHD BHAR-RAIDH, >CARACHD UIBHIST, >CATCH-AS-CATCH-CAN, >CATCHHOLD, >CLOTHES HOLD (BELT HOLD) WRESTLING, >COLLAR AND EL-BOW WRESTLING, >COTSWOLD WRESTLING, >CUMBERLAND AND WESTMORELAND, >DIN-NIE STYLE, >ERHIM-BUHUDBUR, >FAMNKAST, >FREESTYLE WRESTLING, >GALHOFA, >GLÍ-MA, >GOUREN, >GRECO-ROMAN WRESTLING, >HICKLING, >HOSENLUPF, >HRYGSPENNA, >IRANIAN WRESTLING, >IRISH WRESTLING, >JUNTA, >JUPPENRINGEN, >KABADDI, >KARAYA WRESTLING, >KÄRNTENRINGEN, >KOKH, >KRAGENRINGEN, >KRAGTAG, >KOSH-TI CHOUKHEH, >LAUSATOK, >LIVTAG, >LOITA, LA, >LUCHA DE BANDERA, LA, >LUCHA DE RON-CAL, >MUNDJE VENDCE, >NORFOLK STYLE, >ORTHOPÁLE, >PALE, >PEHLIVAN WRESTLING, >RINTAPAINI, >RYGGTAG, >RYSSÄNKASTI, >SAMBO, >SCHWINGEN, >SENEGALESE WRES-TLING, >S'ISTRUMPA, >SHOOTING, >SIDEHOLD WRESTLING, >SSIRÙM, >SUMERIAN WRES-TLING, >SUMO, >SVIPTINGAR, >SWISS-STYLE WRESTLING, >TEAM WRESTLING, >TRÎNTA, >TURKISH WRESTLING, >URAL WRESTLING, >VARZESH-E PEHLIVANI, >VYÖPAINI, >WNA TAG TUG, >YAGLI GÜREŞ, >YAKUTI WRESTLIN, YI WRESTLING, and >ZORAN BAZI.

History. Hand-to-hand struggle, often described by sports sociologists as an 'instinct-based competition' must have been known across all civilizations and cultures as the simplest and most direct way to gain recognition and to stress one's physical dominance over others. However, only a few wrestling styles were widely popularized. The oldest proof of the existence of wrestling as a sport in its own right is the ancient statuette discovered in 1938 by an Amer. archeologist S.A. Speiser in the Khafajah Temple near Baghdad. The statuette is said to be a typical example of Sumerian sculpture and its age is estimated at 5,000-7,000 years. The wrestling style depicted in the statuette consisted of holding one's opponent above his hips which is very similar to the ancient Gk. style which was probably

modeled on the Middle Eastern styles. One of the oldest depictions of the sport is a mural found in Egypt in the tomb of Ptahhotep – one of the 5th Dynasty (2470-2320 BC) rulers. The mural shows 6 pairs of wrestlers competing simultaneously during a court ceremony. Numerous drawings and statuettes depicting Eg. wrestlers were made in Aswan, Thebes, Deir El Bersheh, Meine and Beni Hassan during the so-called Middle Kingdom (22nd-17th cent. BC). The number of wrestling pairs fighting simultaneously was a direct reflection of a given ruler's or ceremony's status. The Amenemhet tomb mural shows 59 fighting pairs while the Baqti III tomb painting depicts as many as 219 pairs. The paintings found in the Neher tomb in Deir El Bersheh are the first to depict referees. A tomb mural discovered in Medinet Habu shows a referee giving a warning to a fighter failing to observe the rules of fair play. The best wrestling pictures in terms of their artistic quality are those found in Ramses III's (1190-1158 BC) tomb which may indicate that during his reign Eg. wrestling was at the peak of its popularity. After the end of the so-called New Kingdom (17th-11th cent. BC), wrestling murals were no longer painted in tombs, which may suggest that the sport died out around that time.

In Europe, the oldest mentions of wrestling date back to the Cretan-Mycenaean period (c.3000-1200 BC). The oldest literary reference to wrestling comes from Homer's *Iliad*, or more precisely from Book XXXIII which contains a description of a wrestling bout held between Ajax and Odysseus during the funeral games after Patroclus's death (>PALE).

The legend has it that wrestling rules as we know them from ancient Gk. descriptions were standardized by Theseus, the son of Aegeus (c.900 BC). There are, however, a few conflicting records of who actually did this. The most advanced form of ancient wrestling was called *pale*. Wrestling was introduced to the Olympic program during the 18th Games in 708 BC simultaneously as a separate event and as part of the >PENTATHLON.

Different wrestling styles have been known since ancient times throughout Asia – esp. in China but also in Japan, Korea, Mongolia and India. Wrestling was also popular among certain N. and S.Amer. Indian tribes. In the Middle Ages wrestling was already known in almost all Eur. countries. It was one of the 7 knightly skills to be employed during the last stage of a sword or axe duel when, after knocking the weapon out of one's opponent's hand, the knight had to floor him and kill him with a misericord. Numerous drawings from the 16th cent., including A. Dürer's (1471-1528) *Fechthandschrift* (1512) and various sketches by L. Cranach the Elder (1472-1553), depict the then combat styles and holding techniques. In 1539 F. von Auerswalde published his *Ringerkunst* devoted to the arts of wrestling. Numerous wrestling styles developed in England in the Middle Ages and the Renaissance. Henry VIII was a keen wrestling supporter and his Cornish strongmen (>CORNWALL AND DEVON) fought in a series of tournaments against wrestlers representing Francis I of France. This series of matches may be considered the first ever international wrestling competition. Since the English team won, Francis I challenged Henry VIII to a direct match to make up for the tarnished reputation of his country. The bout was, however, prevented by high-ranking court officials from both countries. *Wurstle Kunst* – a treatise on wrestling accompanied by 71 drawings by R. de Hooge, an outstanding painter and drawer – was published in 1674 in the Netherlands.

Wrestling as we know it today developed in the 19th cent. as one of the arts performed at traveling circuses that greatly contributed to popularizing the sport in the various countries they visited. Circus directors employed strongmen from different countries, very often from Asia and Africa. That is why circus arenas became a melting pot of various national and regional wrestling traditions which had to be standardized to provide all fighters with equal chances. It was, therefore, circus managers who played the leading role in standardizing wrestling rules. Circus wrestling began to flourish around 1840. Between 1840 and 1860 a number of major circuses estab. very strong wrestling troupes (in Berlin, Vienna, Warsaw and Saint Petersburg). The most famous of them was, however, based in Paris (the Cirque d'Hiver). Paris is also claimed to have

been the host of the first Greco-Roman Wrestling Championship Tournament. Proper wrestling schools were estab. in the above cities around the 1870s and '80s. One of the first internationally recognized wrestling schools was founded in St. Petersburg in 1885 by a Pole, W. Krajewski. It had numerous branches throughout Russia thus contributing to turning that country into one of the wrestling superpowers. Another famous wrestling training establishment was the Viennese *Bodenkultur Schule*. In Great Britain, the home of many wrestling styles, the development of this sport was seriously hampered by the fact that boxing was far more popular. 'In Great Britain, wrestling, although much practiced in days gone by [...] cannot in any sense be considered a national pastime, or one that is cultivated so generally throughout the land as the sister science, boxing.' (*Encyclopaedia of Sport,* 1898, vol. 2). After a period in which numerous, unofficial W.Ch. were often held in parallel by many wrestling organizations and centers, the first official W.Ch. and E.Ch. took place in 1898. Until 1914 the driving force behind wrestling development were the lower classes. It was precisely the working class audiences that largely shaped the nature of this sport. (Later, a similar process could be observed in the case of soccer). This popular interest was skillfully exploited by circus managers who began deriving enormous profits from staging wrestling matches. The 1890-1914 period was the heyday of Eur. professional wrestling. The most popular wrestlers of that time were I. Poddubnyi, a Don Cossack, G. Hackenschmidt of Estonia, O. de Bouillon of Belgium, Y. Mahmoud of Turkey as well as W. Pytlasiński and Z. Cyganiewicz of Poland. After 1918 professional wrestling lost its popularity to more dynamic and spectacular sports such as boxing and soccer. Irregular professional tournaments were replaced by continental championships and Olympic tournaments (held every 4yrs.). National wrestling federations vehemently opposed all the 'freak' wrestling var. as practiced in circuses and called for severe restrictions to be imposed on them. In extreme cases these federations managed to introduce official legislation banning professional matches. In Switzerland, for example, in addition to imposing a ban on professional wrestling, the authorities prohibited any publications on the subject. 'The professional wrestling once had wide appeal but it gradually degenerated until today it is classified as an exhibition, to be viewed much as a farce or comedy' (F. Menke, *Encyclopedia of Sport,* 1969). The tradition of professional circus wrestling was revived in the 1960s in the US where a specific wrestling var. called *American wrestling* was born. Amer. wrestling combines elements of theater-like, farcical performance with extreme brutality. This var. is becoming increasingly popular among women.

W. Armstrong, *Wrestling,* 1893; D. Gable, *Coaching Wrestling Successfully,* 1999; A. Mysnyk, B. Davis, B. Simpson, *Winning Wrestling Moves,* 1994; P. Godlewski, *Sport zapaśniczy w Polsce w latach 1890-1939,* 1994; G. Morton, *Wrestling to Rasslin. Ancient Sport to American Spectacle,* 1985; M.B. Poliakoff, *Combat Sport in the Ancient World. Competition, Violence, and Culture,* 1987.

WRESTLING ON STILTS, a unique folk wrestling var. popular among the Maori in N.Zealand. The stilts used during a match are called *poutogi*, whose foot supports are made of rope and thus similar to stirrups. This makes it easy for a competitor to keep his balance.

WUSHU, also *wu-shu* [Chin. *wu* – related to war + *shu* – art], kung fu, >GONGFU, *Kuo Shu (Guoshu).* An old Chin. term denoting martial arts, incl. the strategy, fortification, horse riding, and armed combat – i.e. all skills required to conduct a war. Before WWII the term Kuo Shu (Guoshu) was used meaning the national martial art. In 1928 the Kuo Shu Nankin Institute was formed with the aim of preserving the tradition of Chin. martial arts and searching for outstanding masters, who could propagate the national spirit and develop physical fitness of the society, as well as the skills and morale of the army. The Wushu movement, on the other hand, tended towards achieving sporting goals and so it promoted wushu as a sporting event (performing forms), with a system of evaluation and scoring similar to that in >OLYMPIC GYMNASTICS. It tried to exert control over the masters of martial arts and sometimes even stood against them, displaying the state's inclination towards monopolizing an area of life which – for centuries – remained outside of government control. Traditional forms have been modified, simplified, and standardized – e.g. by shortening the performance from 5min. to 1min. 20 sec. – while new forms were subjected to non-traditional goals. The trainer was often accompanied by a choreographer, who designed the sequence of movements to fit the overall dramatic expression of the show. The elements which the performers had to consider as most important included the elegance and beauty of movement, dynamics, and display of physical fitness – all following the means of expression characteristic of rhythmic gymnastics. Older forms were modified by adding acrobatic elements, which drew the attention of the spectators and which – in some forms – accounted for as much as 90% of the technical quality. Traditional sequences – which required an aggressive and powerful execution – were instead performed with grace and dignity. The communist party permitted the masters to teach only such forms as could be used at sporting events, while teaching of any combat forms, tactics, or strategy – anything that developed actual fighting abilities – was strictly prohibited. To become skillful in one traditional style, a student had to learn from one master for many years, while the so-called Wushu Institutes at Chin. Physical Education Academies began teaching numerous forms from various styles, often in their modified, sport versions. As the biomechanical principles of one style are often in opposition to those of another, practicing all at the same time leads to a superficial knowledge of merely the sequences of movements. During the Cultural Revolution many masters of martial arts were prosecuted, exiled to camps, and even murdered. Many followers of trad. styles were deprived of an opportunity to practice and develop their art, which resulted in various styles sinking into complete oblivion, so that their reconstruction is an extremely difficult task.

A positive element that stemmed from the Wushu movement was the popularization of sport on a mass scale. The old masters may have become trainers, but – under the umbrella of sport - they still functioned and developed their art. Many sport events were attended by real experts in the field, who initially competed only in displaying the forms, but – beginning in 1982 – were allowed to stage fights called San Shou [Chin. *San* – free + *Shou* – a fight] or >SAN DA [Chin. *San* – free + *da* – strike], performed in the following weight categories: 52, 56, 60, 70, 75, and 80kg. Bouts are held on an 8x8m platform called *lei tai*, elevated approx. 6m and surrounded by rubber walls. Contestants may use both hands and feet. The latter are considered more important, which is reflected in the old principle of teaching gongfu: 'The two fists are gates through which the feet may attack'. The rules, still far from being uniform, prohibit targeting the head with a series of blows, i.e. after dealing the first blow at the head, another part of the body must be targeted, which is in total contradiction with e.g. the rules of boxing. Striking with elbows and knees is banned and the contestants must wear protective gloves and helmets similar to those used in Eur. boxing. The following events are distinguished: 1) Changquan (the northern style of 'long fist'); 2) nanchuan (southern style); 3) trad. forms; 4) trad. forms with long weapons (e.g. a spear); 5) trad. forms with short weapons (e.g. a sword); 6) Yang Taijiquan; 7) Chen Taijiquan; 8) other Taijiquan styles (Wu, W'u, Sun, etc.); 9)other internal styles (e.g. Xingyi, Baguazhan, etc.); 10) broadsword; 11) sword; 12) spear; 13) club or cudgel; 14) other weapons (e.g. dagger, hooking sword, halberd, flail, axe, etc.); 15) open category; 16) double set sparring forms; 17) san shou/san da (freestyle); 18) tui shou (pushing hands) standing; 19) tui shou moving. Among outstanding wushu athletes was a multiple gold medallist in many forms Li Lianjie, later featured in the movie *The Temple of Shaolin*, together with his trainer, master Wu Bin. In 1985 the 1st International Wushu Tournament was held in Xian. In 1987 the 1st wushu W.Ch. was held in Yokohama, while a year later the 1st sanda tournament took place in Shengzou. Wushu enjoys the greatest popularity in Japan, Malaysia, the Philippines, Singapore, Russia, Belgium, Gabon, Mexico, Switzerland, Sweden, Great Britain, Italy, the USA, Canada, and other countries. It is included in the program of South East Asia Games. Since 1991 an International Shaolin Wushu Festival has been held in Zhengzou and in 2008 wushu will become an Olympic event. Wushu may be divided into modern sport wushu (yundong wushu) and trad. wushu (chuantong wushu or trad. gongfu). One may hope that the development the wushu as a sport will not bring the decline of the old trad. fighting style, which gave birth to almost all Asian martial arts.

G. André, 'Wushu', *Strategy and Weapons. Martial Arts*, YOSICH, 1999, 100-101; B. Liu, 'Free Sparring on Its Start', SS, Jan. 1989; no author, 'Le Wushu', *Les sports traditionnels en Chine. Chine – Aperçu général*, 1991, 1-2; Z. Wei and T. Xiujun, 'Wushu', *Handbook of Chinese Popular Culture*, eds. W. Dingbo and P. Murphy, 1994, 155-168.

WYBIJANKA, the name of 2 different sport games: 1) a school game promoted in Poland in the 1920s by F. Gilewski, played on a field (30-50m, depending on the number of players) with a regular soccer ball. At the start one player has the ball and throws it at any other player in the field, who must run away and avoid being hit. A player who is hit is either eliminated from the game or joins the attacking team. The last player to survive being hit wins the game; 2) Pol. equivalent of Rus. >GORODKI, in which sticks are thrown at various compositions of wooden blocks.

WYSADZANIE CHLEBA, Pol. for 'removing the bread', a folk game of strength practiced in the village of Bukówiec Górny in the region of Wielkopolska, described by a local ethnographer, A. Kowol-Marcinek:

The game referred to the action of removing bread from a bread oven. It was played by two persons, the stronger of which would lie on his back with his hands above his head and legs raised up and towards the back. The other person would then stand on the lying man's hands and grab his feet. At that point the lying man would straighten his hands, thus raising his partner up, and thrust him forwards. The flying partner looked as if he were making a sommersault, similar to that of certain gymnastic exercises.

A. Kowol-Marcinek, 'Wysadzanie chleba', *Dawne gry i zabawy dziecięce w Bukówcu Górnym*, Dom Kultury, Leszno, 1999, p. 25.

WYŚCIGI Z KLEKOTAMI, Pol. for 'clapper racing', sometimes abbr. to *klekoty*, a var. of trad. clapper races held in the village of Bukówiec Górny in the Wielkopolska region of Poland during the last 3 days of the Holy Week. They take place 3 times a day, at 6 a.m., 12 noon, and 6 p.m., to remind Catholics to say their prayers. Some time ago it also used to be held before early morning mass on Easter Sunday (called Resurrection Mass). In the Catholic tradition clappers replace in the last days of the Holy Week the regular altar bells, which may not be used as this time commemorates Christ's crucifiction and death. The local term *lotanie* (or *latanie*) means running, while the noun *klekot* indicates in the local dialect a type of 'clapping wheelbarrow' coupled with 2 large clappers. The wheelbarrow's axis had large wooden gear racks with wooden folds that produced a characteristic clapping sound (thus the alternative name for the wheelbarrow – *rechotka*).

The Bukówiec Górny tradition of clapper races was once popular in many other regions of Wielkopolska, e.g. in the villages of the Trzcianka region. The organization of every race followed a longheld tradition: first, 2 groups of boys gathered around the local church – one from what was known as the Small End of the village, the other from the Greater End. This division was a result of the earlier existence of in fact 2 settlements – Bukówiec Górny and Bukówiec Dolny, now forming one village, approx. 2km in length. Each group had its own clapping wheelbarrow, called, respectively, 'male' and 'female'. Both constructions used currently were built around 1920 and, according to their owners, will remain in use for another 10-20 years. The clapping wheelbarrow runners are accompanied by numerous small boys holding little wooden clappers, which may be constructed in the following 3 ways: 1) a board with a small wooden hammer hinged in the middle and producing the clapping sound by hitting the opposing ends of the board; 2) a similar construction with 2 hammers hinged in the middle of the board; 3) three boards parallel to one another loosely connected with ribbons or lines, of which the middle one produces the sound by hitting the other two. In the 1990s and into the 21st cent. they were produced by a local sculptor Jerzy Sowijak, though some clappers are homemade. Races are held in the following order: starting at an arbitrary signal the clapping wheelbarrow runners begin the 3-part relay around the church. Runners change after a full circle and after completing the 3rd circle the entire Small End team follows its leader to their end of the village, while the Greater End team runs towards theirs. When teams reach the road shrines located at the village limits, they circle them 3 times and return to the church. The teams must be complete at the finish line and the one that returns first, wins the race. Earlier they used to finish the race by circling the church 3 times, while now they just cross the finish line located at the church gate. As the distance each team has to cover is different, it is compensated by a number of times they have to circle the shrines, or at least the areas where the shrines once stood. Until 1945 there were 19 road shrines in Bukówiec Górny, all of which were destroyed by the withdrawing Ger. army. They were not rebuilt, but the villagers put two large crucifixes at each end of the village, which the clapping wheelbarrow runners now circle. Other spots, where the shrines once stood, function as reference points – contemporary runners circle them following the tradition, but are generally unaware of their historical significance. The sound of the clapping wheelbarrows and the cries of runners form a unique atmosphere of the race.

After WWII, when the Stalinist government tried to discourage the local community from holding the races, as a practice too closely related with religion, the tradition – already on the wane – was suddenly and enthusiastically revived by the local church organ player Józef Maćkowiak. Thanks to him Bukówiec Górny can still boast of this interesting trad. sporting activity, which in other villages of Wielkopolska has long been extinct.

A. Kowol-Marcinek, 'Jak chłopcy z klekotem lotali', *Dawne gry i zabawy dziecięce w Bukówcu Górnym*, Dom Kultury, Leszno, 1999, pp. 11-13; personal inform. from Zofia Dragan, a regionalist from Bukówiec Górny.

Children in Bukówiec Górny, Poland preparing for a 'clapper race', a local Holy Week tradition.

Wrestling on a Polish postage stamp issued for the 1985 world championships in Norway and a Greek stamp issued for the 10th anniversary of the 1st modern Olympics in Athens.

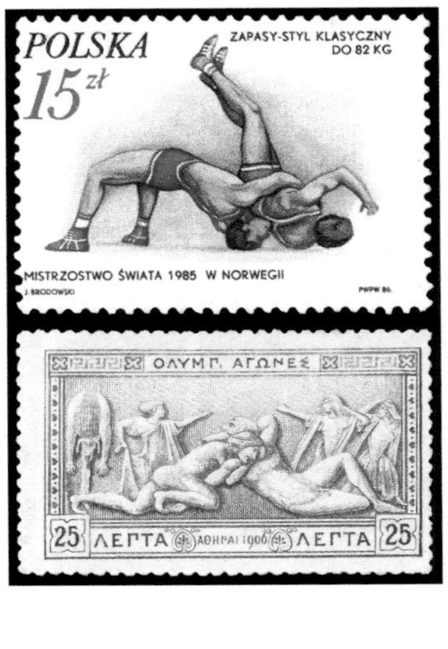

POZNAŃ —

Port Lotniczy
POZNAŃ-ŁAWICA Sp. z o.o.

POZNAŃ
WARSZAWA

ŁAWICA AIRPORT

x: (61) 847-49-09 Informacja: (61) 84-92-343 www.airport-poznan.com.pl airport@man.poznan.pl

X

WORLD SPORTS ENCYCLOPEDIA

XINGYIQUAN, a style of form and will [*Xing* – shape, form + *Yi* – mind, will + *Quan* – fist, style]. Together with >TAIJIQUAN *baguazhan*, it is one of the three most famous internal systems of Chin. >GONGFU (>WUSHU) and the only one that is battlefield proven. Its is said to have been created by the famous marshal of the southern Song dynasty, Yue Fei (1103-1142), a Chin. national hero who fought against the Jin dynasty. An outstanding strategist and talented commander, he joined the Song army at the age of 19 to defend the country against the barbaric invasions. Within 6 years he was promoted to the rank of a general and several years later became the commander-in-chief. To prepare his soldiers for strenuous, long-lasting battles, Yue Fei designed a system of Baduaqin exercises (the famous Eight Pieces of Brocade), which remain an extremely popular form of >QIGONG and Xingyiquan. Fei is also traditionally believed to have created an external system of >YING YI (Eagle Claw). The systematic practice of Baduaqin and Xingyiquan helped the soldiers to survive through even the longest battles, which allowed Yue Fei to conduct numerous successful military campaigns. Opposed to peaceful negotiations, Fei was hated by the emperor Gao Zong's military commander Qin Kuei, who insigated his followers to trump up a charge a charge against Fei's subordinate Zhang Xian and his son son Yue Yun for plotting treason. With hearsay evidence and unwarranted charges Yue Fei was dismissed, imprisoned, and treacherously murdered.

Chi Lung Feng was the first master of Xingyiquan, followed by such famous masters as Li Nen Jang, Kuo Yum Shen (nicknamed 'Demon's Hand'), and Sun Lu Tang.

On the battlefield, Fei's soldiers formed a line standing close to one another. For that reason Xingyiquan prefers forward steps, with an occasional change of direction aimed at dodging the line of attack and charging the enemy diagonally. The transitions be-

Xingiquan.

Keeping balance on a galloping horse, a mounted archer aims an arrow at a target during a Yabusame, or mounted archery, performance at Anahachiman Shinto Shrine in Tokyo.

tween various techniques are short and abrupt. Xingyiquan followers fight at a short range, applying strong, dynamic techniques executed with explosive power. The strength of each movement has its source in Dan Tien, a spot located ab. 3in. below the navel. Each technique is initially soft, but soon becomes hard as a strike of a rattan stick. Althoug Xingyiquan is an internal system, which makes use of a precisely positioned and relaxed body, deep breathing techniques, and the flow of internal energy (Qi or Chi), it is still predominantly offensive in nature. Xingyiquan positions are designed to be executed by an armoured soldier, whose body assumes six styles: Trunk of a Dragon; Hands of an Eagle; Legs of a Chicken; Shoulders of a Bear; Poise of a Tiger; and Thunder and Roaring. The techniques are designed in such a way that they can be executed with or without the use of weapons. Leg techniques are executed at hip height, the most famous being a smashing kick with a diagonally placed foot. The basis of a Xingyiquan drill is learning the San Ti Shi posture, which allows the students to develop stability and the circulation of internal energy Qi.

The principles of emitting internal strength in Xingyiquan are based on the Taoist theory of 5 elements (Wu Xing), according to which there are 5 types of energy exlosion: Pi – metal, Tzuann – water, Beng – wood, Pau – fire, and Hern – earth. These elements are combined in a creation cycle (metal creates water, water creates wood, wood creates fire, fire creates earth, earth creates metal) and a destruction cycle (metal cuts the wood, the wood cuts through the earth, the earth contains water, water cools the fire, the fire melts the metal). Therefore, a *beng* charge must be countered with a *pi* technique, a *pi* charge – with a *pau* technique, a *pau* charge – with a *tzuann* technique, etc. The *pi* technique (splitting) is like cutting with an axe, *beng* (crushing) is a powerful fist blow that lashes the face like a springing tree branch, *pau* (pounding) is a blow that explodes like a cannon rifling in a spiral, while *hern* (crossing) is a deceptive blow with a change of direction targeting the lower body parts. To generate power from each of the 5 elements, one must make use of the difference of potentials between Ying and Yang (or between relaxation and tension). Each technique initially deflects or avoids the opponent's blows, only to finally explode at the target.

YABUSAME, an old Jap. archery contest involving shooting at 3 targets while riding a horse. Competitors use a special bow that is over 2m high and characteristic whistling arrows – *kaburaya*. They wear trad. Jap. costumes with some elements of ancient military uniforms. Yabusame was originally associated with a special religious ceremony. The ritual was, however, a secret one and that is why it was never described or depicted. The oldest mentions of yabusame date back to the 14th cent. Today, the sport has a number of var. the most popular of which is called *takeda*. The run-up track for the horses is 218m long. This distance was determined centuries ago when competitors rode the relatively slow Jap. horses. It is often extended nowadays as the riders prefer horses of Eur. or Arab descent which pass the targets at a higher speed. This makes it impossible for the archer to draw the bow and aim 3 times within a very short period of time. The 3 targets are placed along the track. They are 54cm^2 boards made of Jap. cypress. They are covered with a sheet of paper marked with concentric circles in 5 colors. Additionally, a bunch of flowers is placed behind each target. The object of the game is to hit either the target or the flowers. The competition is accompanied by an elaborate ritual. The contest is supervised by a senior umpire, starting line umpire, target umpire (scorer), and a special official responsible for handing out 'sacred gifts' for the most esthetically pleasing attempts. In contrast to other Jap. var. of horseback archery such as >INUOMONO, >KADAGAKE, yabusame contests lack the competitive aspect and are held mainly as displays of agility and have an aesthetic character. Other officials assisting the contestants include an arrow collector, flag bearer and a drummer setting the pace during a competitor's approach to the targets. The sport is governed by the Jap. Equestrian Archery Association with its official seat in Kamakura. See other var. of Jap. archery on foot: >BUSHA, >JUMIHAJIME, >KUSAJISI, >MARUMONO, and >MOMOTE, as well as ceremonial archery var. such as >JYARAI, >IBAHAJIME, >NORIYUMI and >TANGONO KISHA.

W.R.B. Acker, *Japanese Archery*, 1965; E. Herrigel, *Zen in der Kunst des Bogenschiessens*, 1948; A. Sollier & Z. Gyobiro, *Japanese Archery. Zen in Action*, 1969.

YACHTING, the sport or practice of navigating a yacht – i.e. a vessel propelled by sail, sometimes also power, less frequently power only – for sports, tourist or recreational purposes. As such, the term yachting functions as a synonym to >SAILING. Although there is no clear-cut delimitation of a yacht's size, in order to distinguish it from small inland sailing boats and motorboats, the term is usu. applied to vessels larger than those used inland that carry only up to 4 people. This practically means that any such vessel navigating across the seas or large inland waters, such as the Great Lakes, can be referred to as a yacht. Yachting is sometimes used as a short form for >SAND YACHTING, also called sandyachting, and >ICE BOATING, also known as iceyachting.

Etymology. The term yacht is related to Indo-Eur. *yati* (Sanskrit *yahu*), which means 'to move' or 'to follow sth.', also in the sense of hunting, and a noun *Jagd* – the chase, the hunt. The Eng. 'yacht' originates from Old Du. *yaght, yaghte* – a small sailing vessel used for both commerce and piracy. The name, accompanied by a number of other borrowings from Du., arrived in England at the end of the 17th cent. during the reign of William of Orange and his wife Mary II. Before it acquired its final form, the word appeared in Eng. in a var. of spellings which can be found in historical documents: *yeagh, yoath, yaugh, yuagh, yought, yaucht, jacht, yach, yat, yott, yatch, yatcht, yatchs, yatches*, etc. One of the first references approaching the original Eng. term 'yacht', and hence 'yachting', appears in R. Hakluyt's (around 1552-1616) *Principal Navigations, Voyages and Discoveries of the English Nation* (1589): 'three or foure Norway yeaghes.' One of the first uses of 'yacht' in its sportive meaning in Eng. can be found in R. Ferreira's *Journal in Camden* (1678): 'A fair small River which ey King has there cut to take his pleasure on, there being several yots.' For a long time, however, the term could be applied to any sailing vessel, particularly a military or a shipping one. Only after such periodicals as *The Sporting Magazine* (later *The New Sporting Magazine*) and the *Royal Yacht Club Gazette* started to employ the terms 'yacht' and 'yachting' in sports contexts, did the semantic scope of the terms settle. The 1898 *Encyclopaedia of Sports*, vol. II, claims that the military and mercantile references of the word 'yacht' belong to the remote past.

History. The beginnings of yachting are closely related to the development of sailing. Yachting, in the sense of recreational or sports sailing, first appeared in the Netherlands in the 16th-17th cent. and then developed into a more refined activity in Great Britain at the end of the 17th cent. In 1601, a Dutchman, H. de Voogt, was given an official passport allowing him to travel from the Netherlands to London on a small, open boat, assisted only by Providence, i.e. alone. This episode is generally believed to be the birth of both sports yachting and solo yachting. The sportive character of yachting was ultimately profiled among the Brit. aristocracy. In 1640, a yacht was being built for the man who would soon become Charles II. The first yachting race in history was held as a result of a bet staking 100 guineas, on 1 Oct. 1661, on the Thames, between Charles II's *Anna* and the Duke of York's yacht, on the Greenwich-Gravesand route and back. The King's yacht was the winner. In 1715, the Cumberland Cup was estab., the oldest regatta cup which is still held in the center of Cowes on the Isle of Wight, in the English Channel. In the same year the Duke of Cumberland formed the first yachting organization, known later as the Cumberland Fleet and then transformed in 1823 into the Royal Thames Yacht Club. In 1720, the Cork Harbour Water Club was set up in Ireland, which later operated under the name the Royal Cork Yacht Club. Since 1796, the Bristol Channel has been witness to regattas organized by the Bristol Sailing Society. The description of this regatta, published the same year in *The Sporting Magazine* (21 July 1796) is thought to be the earliest press coverage on yacht racing. The Yacht Squadron, the club most prominent in 19th cent. Eng. sports yachting, was estab. in 1812. It was renamed the Royal Yacht Squadron in 1820, and went on to disqualify the yacht *Menai* from the 1827 regattas for using both sail and steam engine. As it turned out later, such a solution was inevitable in order to maintain the sportive character of sail yachting.

The first yacht was brought to N.America by settlers to the New Netherlands, a Du. colony estab. in 1625 (today's New York was once New Amsterdam) and then incorporated in 1664 into the Brit. dominion. Until the mid 19th cent., this area had the best developed yachting traditions in N.America. The 1st yacht constructed in America by Anglo-Saxons was prob. *Fancy* (1717). During the Fr.-Ind. war (1754-63) and shortly afterwards, colonist used yachts and cutters for smuggling. Soon after independence, from around 1801, Salem, Massachusetts, grew into a powerful shipbuilding center. In 1801, the famous *Jefferson* was assembled there. In about 1809, J. & J.C. Stevens's yacht shipyard commenced its operation in New York and that same year a yacht named *Diver* was launched. The first Amer. yacht club, the Knickerbocker Boat Club, was opened in 1811 only to be closed the following year. The New York Yacht Club, estab. in 1844, managed to operate a little longer. Among the first clubs on continental Europe were the Kungelinga Svenska Segel Sällskapet (1830) in Sweden and the Sociéte des Régates du Hâvre (1838) in France. Significant input into the development of Fr. yachting was delivered by the Cercle de la Voile de Paris (1858) and the Yacht Club de France (1861). In Russia, Tsar Nicholas I gave his permission in 1846 to found the the Tsar's Saint Petersburg Yacht Club which organized a series of regattas in the Gulf of Finland. The most active sailing society in pre-1917 Russia was, however, the Saint Petersburg River Yacht Club estab. in 1860. The first Ger. yacht club was set up in Königsberg in 1855; Dan. – in Copenhagen (1866); Ital. – in Gemi (1879); and Fin. – in Helsinki (1883).

Brit. primacy in international yachting was severely undermined in 1851 when the Amer. schooner *America* won the regatta around the Isle of Wight. The cup that was won on that occasion evolved into the America's Cup, which for the first century of its existence was held rather irregularly – only if there was a crew challenging the Americans who held the cup incessantly until the 1983 race between Amer. *Liberty* and Austrl. *Australia II*. In 1987, Amer. *Stars and Stripes* regained the US leadership, winning also the 1988 regatta, but the myth of Amer. invincibility had been dispelled. As the number of challengers grew, elimination races were introduced. In 1992, *America III* beat Ital. *Il Moro di Venezia* but then, in 1995, *Black Magic* from N.Zealand took the prize, repeating its success in 2000.

Beginning from the last decades of the 19th cent., a >SOLO YACHTING branch was flourishing, achieving the form of a regular rivalry in 1969 under the name the Golden Globe Race. In 1973, the Whitbread Race for double or larger crews was estab. and is still held to this day. The first regattas were amateur in character but in the course of time sponsors, such as Reebok, started to offer considerable prizes. Average skipper's remuneration for participation in the Whitbread Race amounted in the 1990s to around $150,000.

Among the other most celebrated international regattas are an exceptionally demanding Sydney-Hobarth race and Brit. Admiral's Cup, comprising 6 races held in the Irish Sea, the Eng. Channel, and along the SW coast of England; 2 of them Olympictype regattas, 2 coastal, and 2 off-shore.

When comparably small and powerful combustion engines appeared on the market, they became standard equipment on larger sailing yachts. Also motor yachting developed. Until the 19th cent. possessing a yacht was viewed as a symbol of high social prestige. Most of the royal and duke's families, as well as numerous affluent businessmen – or their multinational firms – are still yacht owners and race sponsors. The yacht has also long been a subject of artistic paintings, photographs, and literary works, esp. adventure or detective ones, where a yacht scene highlights the exclusiveness of the context. One of the first examples was *Duncan* in J. Verne's *The Children of Captain Grant*. While Western societies grew wealthier, smaller yachts became increasingly popular with the middle class. Sometimes they are transported on special trailers from areas quite distant from water regions. It is now standard for the shores of large lakes and sea bays to host special

marinas, i.e. docking facilities and ramps to accommodate yachts and other pleasure boats.

W. Głowacki, *Dzieje jachtingu światowego*, 1983; R. Knox Johnston, *History of Yachting*, 1990.

YAGLI GÜREŞ, Turk. for 'oil wrestling'. Many characteristic features distinguish it from other types of wrestling. It shows strong relations with the tradition of >PEHLIVAN WRESTLING, which is manifested through the use of oil on the body before the fight and by wearing hand-made leather breeches (*kispet*). The wrestlers' bodies remain uncovered from the waist up. It is believed that oil makes for an even match between competitors, who must show not only strength, but also dexterity. Before the fight wrestlers wipe their bodies in the grass and perform a ritual dance, which includes a prayer. The fighting begins with the official's invocation: 'May God guide him of the truest heart to victory'. When a wrestler is turned over so that 'his stomach sees the moon and the sun', or if he is lifted off the ground and carried 3 paces, he loses the bout.

History. The oldest tradition of hand-to-hand combat in Turkey comes from the culture of the Seldjuks, who migrated to Turkey in the 10th cent. and a century later conquered Persia, where they came into contact with the local wrestling tradition [>VARZESH-E PEHLIVANI]. Wrestling fights – at first considered as a way of whipping troops into shape for raids in C Europe – became established as a sport during a campaign launched by the Ottoman sultan Orhan Gazi to capture Rumelia (a hist. region in the Balkans). Having captured forts in the region, which is now located at the Gk./Turk./Bulg. border, the sultan's brother, Sleyman Pasha, and his 40 soldiers were celebrating victory and started wrestling fights for the purpose of entertainment. One of the fights went on for several hours without a definite settlement. Sleyman then decided to continue the fight during the annual Spring festival on 6 May held at Ahirky and promised the winner a pair of leather breeches. However, that fight also was undecided, as both wrestlers died of exhaustion. Their burial place (today inside Greece) was later revered by the soldiers, who named it Kirkpinar (Forty Springs). From 1360 an annual wrestling competition was held there, which later moved to Adrianopol, the capital of Turkey in the years 1361-1453 (now Edirne in the Eur. part of Turkey). To commemorate the original place the tournament was named Edirne Kirkpinar. The city soon became a mekka for the best wrestlers from Turkey and also fighters from the conquered Balkan countries, who used wrestling fights with Turks as a means of manifesting their independence, e.g. by refusing to fight with wrestlers who oiled their bodies. Events are held on a picturesque island of Sarayii and include an elaborate ritual, a parade of wres-

tlers marching to trad. Turk. music and dancing. Kirkpinar is probably the oldest sport tournament in the world held uninterruptedly (643 consecutive annual tournaments have been held so far). Among the best known wrestlers are: Cengiz Elbeye, Mehmed Ali Susuz, Hsein Akar.

Since the 19th century winners of Kirkpinar tournaments have received a champion's belt (*altin kemer*) and significant money prizes. A revival of yagli güreş took place in the 1980s thanks to the Turk.

A luxurious yacht sails by the Sydney Opera House.

immigrants in Germany and the Netherlands. The 1996 agreement between the Turk. Wrestling Federation officials and the President of Mokum TV Amsterdam provided for promoting Turkish oil wrestling in Holland and throughout Europe. Since then Amsterdam's Westerpark has had an annual tournament, resembling the Edirne Kirkpinar. E.Ch. have been held since 1997, broadcast by CNN and the BBC, while smaller events are organized in Germany and Switzerland.

YAK RACES, a Tibetan folk sport, where contestants are mounted on yaks. Yaks are bred in mountain regions of C Asia for milk, meat and fur. They are also rideable beasts of burden. Racing yaks wear artistic harnesses and their heads are adorned with red flowers. The races are accompanied by music and dancing. The first rider past the post wins.

'Le cours de yacks', *Les sports traditionnels en Chine*, 1991, 15.

YAKUTE HORSE RACING, a form of >HORSE RACING which accompanied burial ceremonies. Following the path of the sun, the Yakute circled the body of the deceased 3 times. The symbolic meaning of

A yagli güreş match in Kirklareli, Turkey.

596

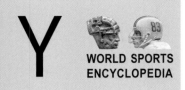

Y WORLD SPORTS ENCYCLOPEDIA

Under the influence of various hallucinogens, such as ebene, a jungle vine extract (above) the Yanomamo people of the Brazilian/Venezuelan frontier (map below) engage in violent duels.

Yezda na barabanye.

the sport followed the tradition of similar equestrian events practiced by other peoples of C Asia (>KHURDAAN MOR', >KIRGHIZ HORSE RACING, >KHEVSUR HORSE RACING).

YAKUTE MULTI-JUMP, a form of trad. competition among the Yakute peoples of Siberia, in which 3 series of jumps are performed, each being a multi-jump. The first series is a running jump performed on a single leg, the second series – a similar jump on the other leg, the third series – a standing jump on both legs with feet joined. The winner was determined by the total score of all 3 series. The competition was part of the Yakute holiday of >YSYECH and offered a symbolic presentation of a mythical bird's flight, frequently referred to in trad. Yakute literature. It also expressed man's longing for super human abilities, so typical of Eur. and other cultures.

YAKUTE WRESTLING, a wrestling var. whose object was to make one's opponent touch the ground with 3 points of his body including his leg. The wrestlers followed a strict diet and observed special rules of conduct. W. Sieroszewski (1858-1945), a renowned scholar of Yakute culture, reported that before a match the wrestlers were examined by the most senior members of a given family – the so-called *sasani* – who 'before the games [...] examined the wrestlers and judging by the look in their eyes, their faces, and the strength of their muscles determined who was not fit to fight, who had sinned with a woman just before the competition and who did not observe the prescribed diet and decided to disqualify him so that he would not be a disgrace to his people'.

W. Sieroszewski, 'Dwanaście lat w kraju Jakutów', *Dzieła zebrane*, vol. I-II, 1935.

YAKUTEE NEW YEAR TRIATHLON, an event that consisted of wrestling, running and horse racing contests, described by I. Kabzińska-Stawarz: 'At the beginning of the year two youngsters, one wearing the skin of a white pony and considered to be the embodiment of the spirit of New Year's host, the other wearing the skin of a black or red pony, competed in wrestling, running and horse racing events. The victory of that representing New Year's host was a promise of prosperity. The other contestant often consented to be the loser.

YAKUTEE RACES, organized by the Yakuts to celebrate the advent of summer. During the first stage of the race a whole body of runners ran together holding one another by the hands. Later, the runners separated and everyone competed individually which is something of an ethnological mystery. I. Kabzińska-Stawarz, a Pol. scientist researching the games of Asian peoples, has put forward a hypothesis that 'perhaps [...] this change in behavior during a race had a symbolic meaning whereby it represented a transition from the original, indivisible single being into a number of various beings – a notion which was rather typical of those peoples'.

I. Kabzińska-Stawarz, 'Competition in Liminal Situations', part II, EP, 1993, XXXVII, 1.

Yagli güreş, Turkish oil wrestling.

YANOMAMO DUELS, trad. chest-pounding/head-clubbing contests practiced by the Yanomamo people, a group of S.Amer. Indians numbering about 10,000. Napoleon Chagnon, an ethnographer from Penn State who lived among the warring clans of Yanomamoland along the Brazilian/Venezuelan frontier, has dubbed them 'the fierce people'. The duels involve pairs of men representing different, allied tribes trading blows – each striving to outlast the damage inflicted by the other – thus testing both themselves and their ally. The duels also take place between warriors within a given tribe or even family to settle disputes, usu. over women, of whom the Yanomamo are notorious for their mistreatment. Under the influence of such hallucinogens as *ebene*, a jungle vine extract with analgesic properties, warriors of a visiting guest tribe and warriors of the hosting home tribe face off for a controlled exchange of blows. Yanomamo duels not only test masculinity but also offer a powerful display to dispel any doubts about one's tribe's willingness and ability to suffer abuse as well as dish it out. Although the duels are performed in a ritualistic fashion and the opponents are in fact friends rather than enemies, the intense punishment being meted out is very real indeed. In his *Cows, Pigs, Wars and Witches; The Riddles of Culture*, Columbia University anthropologist Marvin Harris offers the following description after Professor Chagnon's eyewitness account:

Picture a shouting, milling crowd of men, bodies painted in red and black designs, white feathers glued to their hair, and exposed penises tied with string upright against their bellies. They brandish bows and arrows, axes, clubs, and machetes, rattling and clacking them as they threaten each other. The men, divided into hosts and guests have assembled in the main clearing of a Yanomamo village, anxiously watched by their women and children, who stay back under the eaves of the large circular communal dwelling. The hosts accuse the guests of stealing from the gardens. The guests shout that the hosts are stingy and that they are keeping the best food for themselves. The guests have already been given their farewell gifts, so why haven't they gone home? Now, to get rid of them, the hosts challenge them to a chest-pounding duel.

A warrior from the host village pushes into the center of the clearing. He spreads his legs apart, puts his hands behind his back, and thrusts his chest toward the opposite group. A second man pushes forward from among the guests and enters the arena. He looks his adversary over calmly and gets him to change his stance. He crooks the target's left arm so that it rests on his head, assesses the new stance, and makes a final adjustment. With his opponent properly situated, the guest puts himself at correct arm's length, firming and deepening his toe-hold on the hard-packed earth, feinting forward repeatedly to test the distance and check his balance. Then, leaning back like a baseball pitcher, he puts his entire strength and weight behind his clenched fist as it thuds against the target's chest between nipple and shoulder. The struck man staggers, knees buckling, head shaking, but silent and expressionless. His supporters yell and scream, 'Another one!' The scene is repeated. The first man, a huge welt already rising on his pectoral muscle, puts himself back into position. His adversary lines him up, tests for distance, leans back, and delivers a second blow to the same spot. The recipient's knees buckle and he sinks to the ground. The attacker waves his arms victoriously over his head and dances around the victim, making fierce growling noises and moving his feet so fast that they are a blur lost in the dust, while his screaming supporters clack their wooden weapons together and bounce up and down from a squatting position. The fallen man's comrades again urge him to absorb more punishment. For every blow that he receives, he will be able to return one. The more he takes, the more he can give in return and the more likely it is that he will be able to cripple his adversary or make him give up. After taking two more blows, the first man's left chest is swollen and red. Amid the delirious howling of his supporters, he now signals that he has had enough, demanding that the adversary stand still to receive his due.

Sometimes the blows described above are delivered by a fist clutching a rock, leaving the combatant spitting up blood. Nevertheless, numb to the excruciating pain of such repeated battering (thanks to the hallucinogenic drugs he has inhaled) and egged on by his side's encouraging shouts, a true warrior will continue to allow his opponent to strike him to just within the limits of what he can withstand. Other var. of duels include side-slapping, wherein a well-placed whack with an open hand, delivered just below the ribcage results in paralysis of the diaphragm and loss of consciousness. Contestants may also smack each other with the flat of their machete blades. While these exchanges generally take place in a relaxed, if festive, ceremonial atmosphere, such duels sometimes escalate into full-blown brawls. In another time-honored form of duel, a Yanomamo bearing a grudge against another, bows his head patiently and invites his rival to crack him over the skull with a 10-ft. pole resembling a pool cue. He then, of course, returns the favor. The two take turns at this until one cries uncle, whereupon the dispute is settled. The numerous jagged scars these and other forms of Yanomamo entertainment leave on the head and body are worn proudly. A lack of scars on a man is interpreted as a sign of cowardice, while, according to Dr. Judith Shapiro of the University of Chicago, the absence of scars and bruises on a woman indicates that her husband doesn't care enough about her.

M. Harris, 'The Savage Male', *Cows, Pigs, Wars and Witches*, 1974.

YARIHAGO, see >HAGOITA.

YAURIAN WRESTLING, a var. of folk wrestling popular in the Yauri region in Nigeria.

'Gungawa Wrestling as an Ethnic Boundary Marker', SSB, 1974, 3.

YAWALA, an old name of >HAPKIDO.

YEZDA NA BARABANYE, Rus. for 'drum riding', an agility game recommended in the former USSR and the Soviet bloc, played in community centers and holiday resorts. Square frames were made from 4-5cm thick boards. Specially trimmed round boards were attached to the frames. The 2 wheels were joined with crosswise boards, forming a drum, 140cm in diameter and 85cm wide. The contestants had to jump onto the drum and move their feet to make the drum roll, taking care not to lose their balance and fall. Var. of the game are known, where 2 players ride on one drum, or each on their own (drum racing).

I.N. Chkhannikov, GIZ, 1953.

YI COCK FIGHTS, practiced among the Chin. ethnic minority of Yi with a population of approx. 6.5 million people. The Yi people inhabit the area of 4 southern provinces: Guangxi, Guishou, Sichuan and Yunnan. Four fighters squat, facing each other, interlocking their hands, and raising their heads. There are 2 ways of fighting: 1) fighters jump at each other and the one who knocks all the opponents down wins the bout, 2) competitors keep jumping in the squatting position and the one who endures the longest wins the bout. See also other competitions of the Yi people: >SKIPPING THE FIRE ROPE, >YI SWIMMING, >YI STONE THROW, YI JUMPING, >YI HORSE RACING, >YI WRESTLING.

YI HORSE RACING, a form of >HORSE RACING practiced among the Yi people, one of 55 official ehtnic minorities of China. The races continue the oldest hunting and military tradition of the Yi people. Their origin is a subject of various legends and tales, speaking of man-eating horses tamed by a local hero Zhigealong, who hiked in the area and encountered a herd of wild horses, which came to the conclusion that one man was not able to appease their hunger and so they questioned him as to where his fellow-humans lived. Zhigealong claimed he was too tired to get there on foot, so the beasts offered to carry him on their backs. He complained, however, that a horse's back is too hard and got their permission to make a saddle. Once he mounted the first horse, he drew the rein and used his whip to bring all the beasts into obedience, and they have served humans ever after.

Later the Yi people developed original methods of breeding race horses. The races are held in Dec. during the Small Year Holiday (Xiaonian Jie), along a route usu. 300-400m in length, marked in a field outside a village. On the racing day ceremonially dressed riders appear on their horses with richly decorated saddles and harnesses. Races are held in 2 categories – Eur.-like trotting and gallop. In order to win, the competitor must ride smoothly and come first to the finish line. Smooth riding while trotting is verified by a vessel filled with water which every rider must carry. It is, therefore, not enough to come first, but also vital not to spill the water. On the other hand, during the galloping race riders perform various acrobatic stunts. A separate form of racing is held in a very rich setting during the Holiday of Paying Tribute to the Ancestors. Such races are extremely costly and even the most wealthy members of the Yi people cannot afford to take part in

them more than once in a lifetime. According to the tradition, the participants must receive their relatives and friends, the number of whom often reaches several thousand.

YI JUMPING, practiced by the Yi people of China. Yi jumping competitions are organized often and unlike other competitions they are not related to any holidays. These are: jumps over fire, jumps over a horse or, if a horse is lacking, over a wall and jumps over a rope. Sometimes contestants jump over streams and small pond bays and even puddles. The most interesting are the jumps over a rope. One contestant lies on the ground and spins a long rope with a bundle of straw tied to its far end.

YI SWIMMING, swimming practiced by the Yi people of China. The Yi live in the southern Chin. provinces of Kwangsi, Kweichow, Sichuan and Yunnan. The Yi take part in swimming competitions usually on the occasion of sheep-shearing. Before the competitions begin, the sheep are driven into the river to have their fleece washed. The most popular Yi swimming event is diving. The divers either try to remain submerged as long as possible or to pick up stones from the bottom. Other swimming competitions include catching fish with bare hands and white-water swimming.

YI STONE THROW, a stone throw event practiced by the nation of Yi in China. Competitions are organized without special occasions. There are 2 types of Yi stone throw – for distance and for accuracy. The size of the stones is not strictly defined but usu. the stones selected have masses sufficient for giving the throw the necessary momentum but not too so so that good distances cannot be achieved. Hand throws may yield distances of over 100m, while stones shot from slingshots may reach distances of over 300m.

YI WRESTLING, popular among the Yi people of China. Yi wrestling bouts are held in the fields, town squares or special arenas. The fighters are divided into a number of categories depending on their weight and height. Tournaments are held to celebrate local holidays such as the Big Year Festival (Danian Jie), the Small Year Festival (Ksiaonian Jie), the Burning Torches Festival (Huoba Jie), national holidays and weddings. In the case of the latter the groom sends a group of his friends to the bride's house where they fight with her relatives to win her for the groom. The competition continues throughout the wedding party. During the party, the bouts are started by the party hosts wearing colorful bands around their hips. In the Liangshan area the wrestlers wear white bands around their hips and additional bands around their legs to help their opponents grab them. The Stone Forest wrestlers from the Yünnan province usu. wear short trunks and fight with their torsos naked. They start the bout in a squatting position, similar to that in >SUMO, waiting for the opponent to appear. The spectators drink large quantities of alcohol, as do the wrestlers themselves. The best and most ceremonious Yi wrestling matches are held on the occasion of the Burning Torches Festival. The contests take place in towns and cities and attract many people from the countryside. The oldest Yi wrestler is selected to be the host of the competition. There are no umpires and the bouts are as if officiated by the spectators. Tournament rules are simple – the loser is eliminated whereas the winner fights on. The wrestler who wins the last bout is declared the winner of the whole tournament. Before the fight the opponents bow and exchange a special greeting. Even during the fiercest fights the wrestlers compliment each other on their performance and wish each other victory.
Technically speaking, there are 2 major Yi wrestling types. The first involves embracing and flooring one's opponent. In the second type, the attacker has to throw his opponent off balance so that he falls to the ground.
There are many legends associated with Yi wrestling. One of the most interesting is about Haierbyi, a strongman, who could not find an appropriate opponent among humans and so, instead, he fought with bears, wolves and tigers. Another legend has it that when one Sirabi was defeated and killed by Atilaba, the gods, who liked Sirabi very much, decided to punish his killer's tribe by sending a plague of locusts upon them. Atilaba led his people against the insects and destroyed them with fire. That is how the Burning Torches Festival tradition was born. See also other Yi games such as >SKIPPING THE FIRE ROPE, >YI SWIMMING, >YI JUMPING, >YI COCK FIGHTS and >YI HORSE RACING.
Mu Fushan et al., 'Yi Wrestling', TRAMCHIN, 132.

YING YI, an old Chin. martial art developed in the 10th century by Ngok Fei.

YÖNNALIGI, a Kor. var. of >KITE FLYING.

YOSEI-KAN, a Jap. martial art and one of the subvar. of >AIKIDO. Yosei-kan was developed by M. Mochizuki (b. 1907) who was a disciple of M. Ueshiba – the father of modern aikido and J. Kano – the creator of >JUDO. While teaching in Shizuoka, Mochizuki developed yosei-kan by incorporating various techniques from judo and >KARATE into his style. In 1951-53 he popularized his art in France which has been one of the leading yosei-kan centers worldwide ever since. According to the *Aiki Journal* in 1993 there were some 2,500 aikido schools in France, most of them specializing in yosei-kan. They are governed by the Fr. Judo Federation that has managed to win government support to promote the sport.

YOSHIN-KAN, a Jap. martial art and one of the subvar. of >AIKIDO. Yoshin-kan was developed by G. Shioda (1915-94) who was a disciple of M. Ueshiba – the father of modern aikido. Shioda started developing his style in 1932 while working at his master's old school called Kobu-kan but later moved to Tokyo where he founded his own yoshin-kan school. Shioda became one of the most active promoters of aikido after WWII.
L. Frederic, *A Dictionary of the Martial Arts,* 1991; D. Mitchell, *The New Official Martial* Arts Handbook, 1989.

YO-YO, a spool-like toy that is spun out and reeled in by an attached string that loops around a player's finger. The term is also used as a name for yo-yo competitions. The toy consists of 2 rings of usu. about 5cm (2in.) in diameter joined with a short spool-like shaft so that the gap between the rings is only 0.5cm. Yo-yos are also made of a single wooden ring with a deep groove carved in the middle. The string is attached to the shaft or looped around the groove. While spinning the toy out and reeling it in a player tries to perform various tricks sometimes involving 2 or more yo-yos, such as *walk the dog*, *cat's cradle*, and *around the world*.
History. Not much is known about the origins of the game. The most probable hypothesis is, however, that it was conceived in ancient China. In the 18th century a similar toy was known in England as the *Prince of Wales' toy.* In France, in turn, it was called a *bandalore*, which might point to an Ind. origin. It may be the case that the toy was brought from India before the English replaced Fr. and Port. colonists. A similar toy made of ivory was called an *émigrette* since it was popular among the Fr. aristocrats driven out of Paris during the Fr. Revolution. In N.Zealand the toy is known as the Maori *poi* used in the >HAKA dances. Yo-yo flourished in the US and Europe in the 1930s when it was popularized by the mass media. In 1957 there were unsuccessful attempts to revive the game. Yo-yo did remain, however, a popular toy, used in various agility exercises, esp. those practiced in kindergartens, elementary schools, and by jugglers.

YSYECH, also *ysyach*, a Mong. festival of koumiss involving fermented mare's milk drinking contests popular not only in Mongolia but also among peoples related to the Mongols. The festival is often accompanied by a number of sports competitions such as the >YAKUTE MULTI JUMP. The Yakuts also held koumiss-drinking contests between fathers of soon-to-be-married couples. The father who drank more koumiss could expect to be luckier in the future. Ysyech was held twice a year. In spring the festival was limited to one family and their friends. In summer, however, it often extended over a whole village or even a number of villages. Unfortunately, according to Sieroszewski, the custom began to die out as early as the 1930's:

In the past people liked to have fun, they were merrier [...] they ate, drank, wrestled and danced. [...] Now ysyechs are no longer so popular. The Yakuts do not milk their mares that often, they do not make so much koumiss and fail to observe their ancient customs. Their wealth has been dissipated, the herds are smaller and everybody has become greedier. There are very few who want to feed so many and even they do not have enough milk and koumiss. There are not so many eager fencers, wrestlers and jumpers any more. All the brave, wealthy and generous people observing ancient traditions are gone.

I. Kabzińska-Stawarz, 'Competition in Liminal Situations', II, EP, 1993, XXXVII, 1; W. Sieroszewski, 'Dwanaście lat w kraju Jakutów', *Dzieła zebrane,* 1935, vol. 2, 66-7.

YU KWAN SOOL, one of the names of >HAPKIDO.

YU KWON SUL, also *yu kwan sool, yu kwan sool hap ki do,* an old name of >HAPKIDO.

YU SOOL, also spelled *yusul*, an old name of >HAPKIDO.

YUBBEE LAKPEE, or 'coconut snatch', a trad. ball game played by men in Manipur, India [Manipur *yubee* – coconut + *lakpee* – snatch]. It is akin to rugby. The object of the game is to carry the coconut into the box area on the opposing team's side of the pitch. The box area is 4.5x3m, and is located on the field, with the central portion of the goal line forming one of its sides. A point is scored after a player succeeds in entering the box area and carrying the coconut beyond the goal line. The player may only enter the box area from the front – if he does so from the side, no points are awarded. In formal matches, the teams each consist of 7 players, but up to 24 players may participate in spontaneously organized games. The pitch is 50x20yds. (45.72x18.29m) in area. The coconut is greased in order to make it more difficult to catch. The players oil their bodies, too, to make challenges more demanding. The *ningri* waist belt is a characteristic garment, similar to the one used in >MUKNA wrestling.
How the game is played. At the beginning of the game, the coconut is placed in the center of the pitch. It may also be thrown in by the referee so that it bounces in the center of the field. The referee starts the game by shouting, 'Swa!' and the players of both teams race towards the coconut, trying to seize it. The coconut is carried at chest height, and the players are not allowed to kick it. Just beyond the goal line sits the judge who decides whether points are scored in the correct manner. Those players who get carried away in the heat of the game, most usu. in team action, are often doused with water.
The oldest forms of the game were associated with the rituals at the Bijoy Govinda temple during the *pichakari* festival. In the past, the place of the judge beyond the goal line was occupied by the local king, or *ningthou*. After a player crossed the goal line, he dedicated the coconut to the ruler. It may be inferred from this that in those times the game ended after a single point was scored.

YUMIHADJIME, see >JUMIHAJIME.

A variety of yo-yos.

Yi tribesmen, dressed as spirits of fire, dance before a bonfire at the You Zha Di village in Yunnan Province, China, during Lunar New Year festivities. The Yi are the fourth-largest of China's 55 officially recognized ethnic minority groups.

Z

**WORLD SPORTS
ENCYCLOPEDIA**

ZAKLYATYI KRUG, an East Eur. school game played on a field on which a circle of 4-5 steps in diameter is drawn. One of the players called the 'guard' or 'janitor' stands in the middle of the circle and tries to prevent the other players from entering it. He pursues everyone who enters the circle (*krug*) and the one who is caught receives a light pat on his shoulder thus becoming the guard's helper. The number of helpers increases as the game progresses. The last player's task is to enter the krug 3 times without being caught. If he manages to do so, he becomes the guard in the next round. In one of the zaklyatyi krug var. a smaller, 1m circle is drawn within the large one. The small circle is a place where all the players, except the guard, deposit their forfeits such as boxes, handkerchiefs, pencil cases, etc. During the game the players try to 'steal their belongings back' while the guard stands outside the circle and tries to prevent them from doing so. The first player to be caught by the guard swaps places with him.
I. Chkhannikov, 'Zaklyatyi krug', GIZ, 10-1.

ZANCOS, also known as *pruebas de zancos*, a Span. var. of >WALKING ON STILTS [Span. *zanco* – stilt] involving various feats of agility. Usu. zancos is quite similar to other var. of walking on stilts; there exists,

however, a special var. of zancos, also known as *los zancos anguiano*, practiced chiefly on the feast day of St. Mary Magdalene, in which the performers dance to castanet music. The dancers, wearing colorful costumes, approach a town from the mountains and they proceed to the central square, usu. situated in front of a church, where the festival continues. Zancos is particularly popular in the Rioja region (Logroño province) and near Anguia.
C. Moreno Palos, 'Pruebas de zancos', JYTE, 1992.

ZASHUA, Chin. for 'various amusements'. A type of athletic, acrobatic and juggling show popular in ancient China during the Ch'ing Dynasty (1644-1911). The shows drew upon the ancient tradition of >BAXI.

ZAXI, a type of athletic, acrobatic and juggling show popular in ancient China during the Tang Dynasty (618-907). The shows drew upon the ancient tradition of >BAXI.

ZBIJAK, (Pol. for 'batter') also called >SPARZAK or *sparzony żydek* (cf. also >ŻYDEK which is also the name of a different game, >CHWYTKA). A Pol. trad. game described by E. Piasecki in his *Zabawy i gry ruchowe dzieci i młodzieży* (*Sports and Games of Children and Youth*, 1916):

One of the players stands by a wall as the one who was sparzony (i.e. scalded, burnt) - also called a żydek (i.e. a little Jew) – while the other players stand at various distances from the wall. The one by the wall throws a ball against it so that it bounces off and travels as far as possible. Then, he turns towards the other players. If no one catches the ball, it is returned to the sparzony one. However, if one of the players catches it, he throws it back at the sparzony from where he caught it. If a ball that has bounced off the wall hits one of the players on the back such a player becomes the sparzony. If a player catches the ball with both hands he has one throw at the sparzony, if with the right hand, he has 2 throws and if with the left hand, 3 throws.

ZCHENBURTI, a Georg. equestrian game involving a ball with sticks and thus similar to >POLO. Today, a game of zchenburti is played by 2 teams of 6. The ball is 12-15cm in diameter and is hit with a triangular racket attached to a long stick. The game consists of 2 halves of 15min. each.

ZEGETEABA, a Mong. form of military exercise [lit. 'great hunt'], initiated by the founder of the Mong. Empire, Genghis Khan (c.1155-1227). It consisted in performing an operation typical for Mong. conquest in the form of a military exercise on a large scale. The tradition declined with the demise of the Mong. Empire, and then of the individual khanates. The last recorded zegeteaba took place around the middle of the 18th cent.

ZHALANGPAO, a form of competition of the Chin. minority Nu. Contestants jump over a bowed shaft of soft bamboo, the ends of which, initially widely spaced out, are dug into the ground. When all the contestants have cleared a given height, the bamboo ends are dug into the ground with less space between them, which results in the raising of the 'bar', i.e. the top edge of the bow. A long bamboo stick is ideal as the 'bar' can be raised to a considerable height. The contestant who clears the greatest height is the winner.
Mu Fushan et al. 'Skipping Bamboo Bow', TRAMCHIN.

ZHAMBY ATU, a var. of Turkmen archery.
H. Eichberg, 'A Revolution of Body Culture? Traditional Games on the Way from Modernization to Postmodernity', LJP, 1988, 198.

ZHMURKI, see >BLINDMAN'S BUFF.

ZHONGHEQUAN, an ancient Chin. system of mind and body exercises.

ZHUANG SILK BALL, a sport practiced for 800-900 years by China's Zhuan people in the region of Guiyang. Zhuang silk ball was originally a trad. part of boys' advances to girls. At present, it is a popular game separated from the ancient match-making custom. The game is played on a field of unspecified size, in the middle of which stands an 8-9m post with a vertical target board mounted on top. The board consists of 2 hoops and is covered with red silk. The inner hoop is 60cm in diameter; the outer is 1m in diameter. In the center of the board runs a long slit. In the space between the hoops 10 shorter slits are cut around the board.
The balls are made of silk hanks and weigh 150-200g. Each ball has a strap handle used for swinging before hurling. The silk balls can be round, cu-

bic, or in the shape of flower, bird, fish, insect, or crescent. The game is played in pairs and the players throw the balls to each other, through the central slit in the board or, which happens rarely, through 1 of the 10 short slits outside the inner hoop. Whichever partner manages to throw the ball through any slit first wins. Before releasing the ball, a player swings it around a few times. The winner gets a prize from his or her opponent. It was customary for the winning boy to be given a pair of shoes or other souvenirs made by the girl, and for the winning girl various souvenirs, depending on the boy's preferences, e.g. hair combs, brooches, etc.
Mu Fushan, et al., 'Zhuang Throwing Silk Balls', TRAMCHIN.

ZIELSCHIEßEN, Ger. for 'target shooting', [*Ziel* – target + *Schießen* – shooting], a winter sport in which special weights, equipped with handles, are slid on ice towards a target. The weight (*Eisstock*) resembles a flattened cone with an irregular outline, with a base diameter of 27-30cm and weight of 4-6kg. The stone is made of wood and has a cast-iron base (*Fuß*). The handle protrudes from the top of the cone, is bent towards one side, thinner at the root and thicker at the end. The 2 basic var. of zielschießen are >RINGSCHIEßEN, where the weights are slid towards a target with a wooden block in the middle, and >STOCKSCHIEßEN, where the object is to hit another weight. The game belongs to the family of games where weights or stones are slid on ice, which is known in Germany by the collective name of >EISSCHIEßEN. The main family is >ICE BOWLING, which also includes >CURLING and >UTYUG. See also >EISKEGELN; >KALLUDERSCHIEßEN; >WEITSCHIEßEN.

ZORAN BAZI, Kurdish folk wrestling, which, due to the fact that most of Kurdistan is a part of Turkey today, is very similar to the Turk. >KARAKUCAK GÜREŞI.
W. Baxter, 'Les luttes traditionnelles ŕ travers le monde', LJP, 1998, 81.

ZORBING, a type of sporting activity and extreme competition sport practiced inside a large, transparent, plastic sphere, approx. 3m in diameter and inflated with approx. 13m³ of air, inside which is a smaller, round chamber. The chamber is entered through a special sleeve by a zorbonaut, who is strapped inside it in a harness that maintains him in a star position. The zorbonaut is protected by an air cushion formed by the approx. 70cm air space between the riding chamber and the outside sphere. The sphere hustling down a slope reaches speeds of up to 50km/h. In some spheres no harness is used, which allows the zorbonaut to balance his body to speed up the sphere, to use the centrifugal force to maintain his position on the inside wall, and to decelerate the zorb at the end of the ride, all of which require considerable experience. The zorb may be run down a grass or snowy slope or raced on water, where it utilizes the windpower. The idea of zorbing was invented by two New Zealanders, Dwane van der Sluis and Andrew Akers, who – inspired by Leonardo da Vinci's famous drawing of human figures inscribed in a sphere – constructed a prototype zorb. Currently zorbing is winning enthusiasts in many countries, where special zorbing arenas are built.

ZOŚKA, a Pol. game in which the 'zośka', a woolen ball with a small weight fitted inside it is kicked repeatedly into the air. One var. consists of kicking the ball with any part of the foot as many times as possible without letting the ball touch the ground. Another var. is played on a rectangular field of unspecified size (usu. 4-6m long and 1.5-2.5m wide) and divided into 2 halves. Players take turns at kicking the *zośka* into the opponent's half, while the opponent tries to return it before it touches the ground. Each player may kick the *zośka* a limited number of times, usu. 3, before returning it. A similar game in the Eng. tradition is called >SHUTTLECOCK KICKING, in the Kor. tradition – >CHEGI CHAGI, in the Chin. tradition – >TEBEG, in the Mong. tradition – >TEBEG OSHIGLOOKH. See also >FOOTBAG.

ZOTTEBOL, see >PIERBOL.

ZOTTEGEM, see >PIERBOL.

ZUAR, a trad. sport of the Afr. tribe of Kau. The fight is bloody in nature and sometimes ends in death. The idea is to hit the opponent with special double-

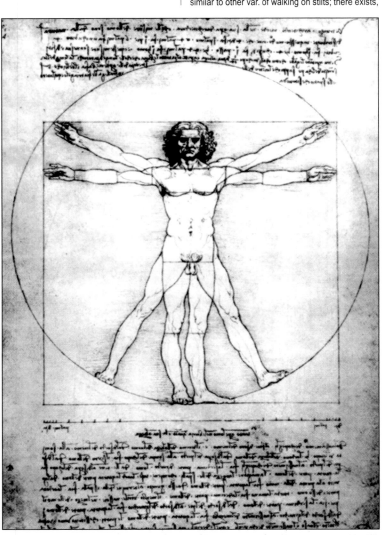

Leonardo da Vinci, Scheme of the proportions of the Human Body, *c.1485-1490*.

A zorbing sphere.

A zorbing arena.

edge bracelets worn around the wrist. The bout resembles a boxing fight, except that wrists, instead of fists, are used. The fight is regulated by 2 judges, who do their best to prevent overtly fierce blows and inflicting heavy injuries, which – in the heat of the battle – is not always possible. To separate the overtly hot-headed opponents each judge has 2 sticks. The fights are held between representatives of neighboring tribes or off-shots of one tribe of Kau. Since the times registered by ethnography the Kau tribes have not been at war and vent their agression in annual zuar tournaments. A zuar fight is also the final stage of the adolescent Kau males obtaining the status of adults – *kadundor*.

ZULLI, an Afr. game played by the Yauri people of Nigeria and on the Côte d'Ivoire. Each of several players (usu. 3-5) builds a sand ramp leading to a hole in the ground approx. 5in. (12.7cm) in depth. Then each player takes a turn rolling two *yangdid-da* nuts at a time down the ramp towards the hole. The object of the game is to place one's own nuts on top of those belonging to the opponents, which is called a *sarki*. The game continues until each player scores a *sarki* at least once and is won by the player with the largest number of *sarkis*. A similar game called >IDO is popular in the Yoruba region of Nigeria.
A. Taylor Cheska, 'Ido', TGDWAN, 1987, 35-36.

ŻURAWKA, a mysterious game or form of competition mentioned by Ł. Górnicki in his *Dworzanin polski* [*A Polish Courtier*]. The game was described by Ł. Gołębiowski in the first decades of the 19th cent. as an unknown game 'the rules of which we are no longer able to explain' (*Games and Pastimes of Various Social Classes*, 1881, 63). What we do know, however, is that the name of the game derived from Pol. 'żuraw' – crane.

ŻYDEK, (Pol. for 'little Jew'), a var. of a ball game, practiced in old Poland, also known as *kowal*. It was one of the hand-catching ball games, commonly known as >CHWYTKA, most popular in the 17th and 18th cent. A fairly accurate description is found in Ł. Gołębiowski's *Gry i zabawy różnych stanów* (1831):

This was a game of great accuracy, which could prove the skills of the players and convince the spectators what the players could do with their body and the ball. The game consists of different tricks: the first six were mandatory and a kind of elimination. Whoever failed to perform the first six tricks accurately, had to repeat them; having gone through the first six tricks, the player, even if unsuccessful in any of the following tricks, had to repeat only those tricks which he failed to perform well. 1) First the player had to bounce the ball off the ground so that it hit the wall, bounced off it and only then was the player allowed to catch it; 2) The ball had to bounce off the ground, under the thigh of the player's raised leg and then it was caught; 3) The player leaned against the wall, bounced the ball off the bottom part of the wall and when it bounced off the wall he would run after it to catch it; 4) a trick called 'fat letting' – the player leaned, his back bent, head against the wall, threw the ball over his head so that it bounced off the wall and had to catch it before it fell to the ground; 5) As in 4), but the ball, having bounced off the wall, had to bounce off the ground and then was caught; 6) a trick called the 'stamp', in which the palm with the index finger and the thumb forming a ring was put on the wall; the player had to throw the ball so as to hit the ring, then quickly remove the hand and catch the rebounding ball with the same hand. All these tricks had to be repeated three times; when done once, the player might just be lucky, but when done three times, the player exhibited his great skill. Whoever failed to do the tricks three times, had to let another player have a go at them, while he would go to the end of the players' row to await his turn. When his turn came, he would resume play from where he had failed. Whoever performed the six mandatory tricks well, waited for other players to do the same. Only then did the players begin the game proper, i.e. the following tricks: 7) the player bounced the ball off the ground and caught it when on the up; 8) the player bounced the ball off the ground and caught it while falling; 9) a trick called a 'loaf of bread' – the ball was thrown with one hand so that it bounced off the clasped fist of the other hand and when it bounced off, it had to be caught; 10) a trick called the 'dish' – like in the 'loaf of bread' but the ball was thrown with one hand against the open palm of the other hand and then caught; both these tricks, i.e. the 'loaf of bread' and the 'dish' had to be repeated with the fist or palm out or in; 11) the ball thrown upwards had to land and rest on the palm with outstretched fingers; this trick is called the 'soup bowl'; 12) the ball was tossed up so that it landed on the tip of the finger and stayed there for a

while in balance; 13) the 'fork' – the same, but the ball had to land on the tips of two fingers, then as the 'triple' – where the ball had to land on the tips of three fingers, the 'four' – the ball landed on the tips of four fingers; 14) a trick called 'counting one hand's fingers' – the ball was tossed up and caught and supported with the individual fingers; 15) 'Blood letting' – the ball rolled down the forearm of one hand and had to be caught before it fell to the ground; 16) the same, but the ball was first bounced off the ground and had to land on the hand from where it rolled along the forearm; 17) the ball had to be bounced off the wall 24 times; it was bounced off the wall with the hand, like with a racket; 18) the ball had to be tossed up 48 times, before it hit the ground it had to be tossed back up with the inner part of the palm; the same had to be repeated with the back of the hand; 19) during a series of successive tosses of the ball up in the air, the player pretended he was getting up and dressing, after each of such activities he had to catch the ball and then again toss it up and imitate another dressing activity (one activity per toss up). The successive tricks were called 'washing', 'putting on trousers', 'putting on shoes', 'putting on the vest', 'putting on the tuxedo', 'combing'; each of these tricks had to be repeated 3 times; 20) 'Water flushing' – performed once or twice up to six times; the ball was thrown at the wall above the rebounding line at an angle so that it first bounced off the wall and then off the ground whereupon it had to be caught; 21) 'Hand clapping' – tossing the ball up, when the ball is airborne, the player had to clap his hands 3 times facing the ball, 3 times standing with his back to the ball and again 3 times facing the ball; 22) 'Top turning' and 'bottom turning', tricks in which the player had to throw the ball at the wall, while it was airborne, he had to turn round his axis and catch the ball, the ball being either close to the ground or up in the air; 23) 'Hand' – the ball was thrown between the legs against the wall, with the player standing with his back to the wall and then the ball had to be caught; 24) the ball was thrown against the wall so that it landed on the player's head and when it bounced off the head, it had to be caught. Whoever managed to do all these tricks was called the king. During the crowning ceremony all the other players tried to hit the king's open hand with the ball; whoever failed, was hit three times by the royal hand. Hardly was there a player who became king as this required the utmost skills and even the most skilled one found it very difficult to do all the tricks without any fault.

The name 'żydek' also denoted another game, more often known as *sparzony* or >SPARZAK.

PHOTO CREDITS

Gregg Aamot, Henry Ray Abrams, Agence Zoom, Toni Albir, Charles Rex Arbogast, Kuba Atys, Auto Imagery, Inc., Sayyid Azim, Shirley Bahadur, Brian Bahr, Eduardo di Baia, Amshid Bairami, Greg Baker, Edward Baldys, Arno Balzarini, Scott Barbour, Steve Bardens, Pete Barnes, Simon Barnett, Dominic Baumann, Michael Becker, Jacek Bednarczyk, Al Bello, Oliver Berg, Nathan Bilow, Torsten Blackwood, Hamish Blair, Alida Zurita Bocanegra, Robert Boesch, Stephen J. Boitano, Roberto Borea, Gregorio Borgia, Shaun Botterill, Tim Boyd, Tim Brakemeier, Gary Brown, Clive Brunskill, Brunswick Corp., Simon Bruty, Jamie Budge, Robert F. Bukaty, Louisa Buller, Chuck Burton, Dan Burton, David Cannon, Pornvilai Carr, Francesca Castelli, Dave Caulkin, Derrick Ceyrac, Graham Chadwick, Mary Ann Chastain, Lusa Lim Choi, Stanley Chou, Chien-min Chung, Robert Cianflone, Lionel Cironneau, Pietro Cinotti, Thomas Coex, Chris Cole, Paul Connors, Sherwin Crasto, Roberto Cubeddu (www.horseclub.co.uk), Darron Cummings, Roy Dabner, Paweł Dajnowicz, Barbara K. Deans, Arne Dedert, Jack Dempsey, Hans Deryk, Fernando Diaz, Jon Dimis, Sergey Dolzhenko, Denis Doyle, Tony Duffy, Jim Edds, Ron Edmonds, Joe Ellis, Don Emmert, Dieter Endlisher, Douglas Engle, J.M. Espinosa, Michel Euler, Bruno Fablet, Joan C. Fahrenthold, Fred Faulk, Jerome Favre, Eric Feferberg, Ric Feld, Jonathan Ferrey, Mohamde el-Fers, Randy Fiedler, Andre Forget, Stu Forster, Stuart Franklin, Herbert Frei, Greg Garay, Patrick Gardin, Sean Garnsworthy, Andy Gatt, Louisa Gauerke, Eric Gay, Vadim Ghirda, Anat Givon, Mary Godleski, Adam Golec, Przemysław Graf, Michael S. Green, Otto Greule Jnr, Rob Griffith, Laurence Griffiths, Dennis Griggs, Al Grillo, Mike Grueter, Marco Grundt, Andrzej Grzyb, Jerzy Gumowski, Grant L. Gursky, David Guttenfelder, Ng Han Guan, Tomasz Gzell, Bill Haber, Kevin Hagarty, Jeffrey Hage, Mat Hage, Mateusz Halawa, Scott Halleran, Stuart Hannigan, Nati Harnik, John Harrell, Cheryl Hatch, Adam Hawałej, Douglas Healey, Jacob Henifin, Patrick Hertzog, Mike Hewitt, Eugene Hoshiko, Tomas van Houtryve, Jaume Ignes, Itsuo Inouye, Jed Jacobsohn, Kim Jaehwan, Stephen Jaffe, Maciej Janczy, Piotr Janowski, Yun Jay-hyoung, Roman Jocher, Shizuo Kambayashi, Mieczysław Kamiński, Sławomir Kamiński, Tomasz Kamiński, John S. Kennedy, Michael Kennedy, Rusty Kennedy, Thomas Kienzle, Andy King, Naomi Koppel, Roman Koszowski, Robert Kowalewski, Jeff Kowalsky, Adam Kozak, Damian Kramski, Stefan Kraszewski, Charles Krupa, Robert Krzanowski, Jarosław Kubalski, Małgorzata Kujawka, Robert Laberge, Nick Laham, Sakchai Lalit, Keith Larrett, Marco di Lauro, Christoph Leib, Zdzisław Lenkiewicz, Eric S. Lesser, Ken Levine, Dean Lewins, Tony Lewis, Wojciech Lipoński, Pat Little, Alex Livesey, Dan Loh, Wolfgang Luif, Efrem Lukatsky, Vince Lupo, Andy Lyons, Marcin Łobaczewski, M. Machnikowski, Mariusz Makowski, Kimmo Mantyl, Bogdan Marciniak, Jacek Marczewski, Maxim Marmur, Alan Marler, Lee Marriner, Enric Marti, Clive Mason, Kimimasa Mayama, Piotr Mazur, Jamie McDonald, Chris McLennan, Jeff McIntosh, Darren McNamara, Russell McPhedran, Robert Mecea, Andrew Medichini, Melbourne Age, Toby Melville, Andrea Merola, Dimitri Messinis, MGM, Stuart Midgley, Doug Mills, Stew Milne, Donald Miralle, Piotr Molęcki, Beata Momot, Grzegorz Momot, Martinez Monsivais, Don Montague, Oliver Morin, Gray Mortimore, J.S. Moses, Tomas Munita, Tauseef Mustafa, Michal Mutor, Fabio Muzzi, Amr Nabil, Andy Newman, Niels Nyholm, Robby Naish, Charlie Neibergall, Kazuhiro Nogi, Team O'Neall, Nick Oza, Alessia Paradisi, Doug Pensinger, Eraldo Peres, Christian Perret, Radosław Pietruszka, Lefteris Pitarakis, Douglas C. Pizac, Susan Plunkett, Piotr Polak, Lisa Poole, Denis Poroy, Mike Powell, Adam Pretty, Franck Prevel, Karel Prinsloo, Gary M. Prior, Fernando Projetti, Jaime Puebla, Kenika Pukalani, Ben Radford, Joe Raedle, Piotr Rayski-Pawlik, Josh Reynolds, Janusz Romaniszyn, Pascal Rondeau, Rossa Camogie Club, Don Ryan, Andrzej Rybczyński, Rick Rycroft, Paul Sacuma, Paul Sancya, Martina Sandkühler, Paulo Santos, Krzysztof Sawala, Richard Schabl, Steffen Schmidt, Arkadiusz Scichocki, Wahyu Setiadi, Murad Sezer, Aman Sharma, Erza Shaw, Tom Shaw, Remigiusz Sikora, Piotr Skornicki, Grzegorz Skowronek, Waldemar Sosnowski, Jamie Squire, Donald Stampfli, Chris Stanford, Michael Steele, Rick Stewart, Matthew Stockman, Chuck Stoody, Kai Stuht, Erico Sugita, Wojciech Surdziel, Manish Swarup, Barry Sweet, Andrzej Szozda, Grzegorz Szymański, Toby Talbot, Tomasz Talarczyk, Sandra Teddy, Mark J. Terrill, Beata Tomaszewska, Pierre Tostee, Sion Touhig, Mirosław Trembecki, Dean Treml, Alessandro Trovati, Jacek Turczyk, Matt Turner, Pedro Ugarte, Paweł Ulatowski, Jerzy Undro, Sanu Vajracharya, Drago Vejnovic, Kristiane Vey, Thierry-Daniel Vidal, Rui Vieirab, Bozidar Vikicevic, Richard Vogel, Eric de Vroede, Ingo Wagner, Orlin Wagner, Ralph Wagner, Carl D. Walsh, Susan Walsh, Barbara Walton, Emile Wamsteker, Apichart Weerawong, Pat Wellenbach, William West, Douglas van Wolde, Przemysław Wierzchowski, Nick Wilson, Damon Winter, Andrzej Wojciak, Greg Wood, Leszek Wróblewski, Toru Yamanaka, Masahiro Yokoto, Matt York, Ahn Young-joon, Vincent Yu, Muchtar Zakaria, David Zalubowski, Andrzej Zarzeczny, Roman Zawistowski, Anna Zbierska-Sawala, Luca Zennaro, Maciej Zienkiewicz, Tomasz Żurek

The publisher has made every effort to include the names of all photographers whose works appear in this publication. Unfortunately, in some cases this proved impossible. We wish to apologize to all those whose names have been inadvertently ommitted and ask them kindly to contact the publisher's office at the address below:

Oficyna Wydawnicza Atena
Wawrzyniaka 39
60-502 Poznań, Poland
e-mail: atena@mtl.pl